Sports Illustrated 2007 Almanac

By the Editors of Sports Illustrated

Sports Illustrated

2007

Almanac

First Edition
ISBN10: 1-933405-46-5
ISBN 13: 978-1-933405-46-9

SPORTS ILLUSTRATED Executive Editor: Rob Fleder
SPORTS ILLUSTRATED Director, New Product Development: Bruce Kaufman

SPORTS ILLUSTRATED 2007 Almanac was prepared by
TPG Sports, Bishop Publishing, of White Plains, N.Y.

Editorial Director: Morin Bishop	Art Director: Barbara Chilenskas
Managing Editor: Reed Richardson	Photo Editor: John Blackmar
Associate Editor: Chris Freeburn	Editorial Intern: Stephen Santulli

Proofreaders: George Henn, Bill Price, Lisa Ann Smith

Cover photography credits:
Ben Roethlisberger: David Bergman
Albert Pujols: John W. McDonough
Tiger Woods: Robert Beck/Sports Illustrated
Dwyane Wade: Greg Nelson/Sports Illustrated

Back cover photography credits:
Vince Young: Darren Carroll
Shaun White: Al Tielemans
Rod Brind'Amour: David E. Klutho/Sports Illustrated

Spine photography credit: Maria Sharapova: Bob Martin/Sports Illustrated

Title page photography credit: Thomas E. Witte/Getty Images

TIME INC. HOME ENTERTAINMENT

Publisher .... Richard Fraiman
Executive Director, Marketing Services .... Carol Pittard
Director, Retail & Special Sales .... Tom Mifsud
Marketing Director, Branded Businesses .... Swati Rao
Director, New Product Development .... Peter Harper
Financial Director .... Steven Sandonato
Assistant General Counsel .... Dasha Smith Dwin
Book Production Manager .... Jonathan Polsky
Brand Manager .... Danielle Radano
Design & Prepress Manager .... Anne-Michelle Gallero

Special thanks: Bozena Bannett, Alexandra Bliss, Glenn Buonocore, Suzanne Janso, Robert Marasco,
Brooke McGuire, Chavaughn Raines, Mary Sarro-Waite, Ilene Schreider, Adriana Tierno

We welcome your comments and suggestions about Sports Illustrated Books. Please write to us
at: Sports Illustrated Books, Attention: Book Editors, PO Box 11016, Des Moines, IA 50336-1016
If you would like to order any of our hardcover Collector's Edition books, please call us at
1-800-327-6388. (Monday through Friday, 7:00 a.m.- 8:00 p.m. or Saturday, 7:00 a.m.- 6:00 p.m.
Central Time)

CONTENTS

In compiling the Sports Illustrated 2007 Almanac, the editors would like to extend their gratitude to the media relations offices of the following organizations for their help in providing information and materials relating to their sports: Major League Baseball; the Canadian Football League; the National Football League, Arena Football League; the National Collegiate Athletic Association; the National Basketball Association; the National Hockey League; the Association of Tennis Professionals; the Women's Tennis Association; the U.S. Tennis Association; the U.S. Golf Association; the Ladies Professional Golf Association; the Professional Golfers Association; National Thoroughbred Racing Association; the U.S. Trotting Association; the Breeders' Cup; Churchill Downs; the New York Racing Association, Inc.; the Jockey's Guild, Inc.; the Champ Car Auto Racing circuit; the National Hot Rod Association; the International Motor Sports Association; the National Association for Stock Car Auto Racing; the Professional Bowlers Association; the United Soccer Leagues; Major League Soccer; the Fédération Internationale de Futbol Association; the U.S. Soccer Federation; the U.S. Olympic Committee; USA Track & Field; U.S. Swimming; U.S. Diving; U.S. Skiing; U.S. Figure Skating Association; the U.S. Chess Federation; U.S. Curling; the Iditarod Trail Committee; the International Game Fish Association; USA Gymnastics; U.S. Handball Association; the Lacrosse Foundation; the American Power Boat Association; the Unlimited Hydroplane Racing Association; the Professional Rodeo Cowboys Association; U.S. Rowing; the American Amateur Softball Association; U.S. Speed Skating ; U.S. Rugby Football Union; USA Triathlon; the National Archery Association; USA Wrestling; the U.S. Squash Racquets Association; the U.S. Polo Association; ABC Sports; and the U.S. Volleyball Association.

The following sources were consulted in gathering information:

Baseball mlb.com, worldseries.com, baseballhalloffame.org, baseball-almanac.com, Associated Press

Pro Football nfl.com, superbowl.com, nfleurope.com arenafootball.com, arenabowl.com, profootballhof.com

College Football ncaasports.com, *Official 2006 NCAA Division I-A and I-AA Football Records Book, Official 2006 Division II and III Football Records Book*

Pro Basketball nba.com, hoophall.com

College Basketball ncaasports.com, *Official 2007 NCAA Division I Men's Basketball Records Book, Official 2007 NCAA Division I Women's Basketball Records Book, Official 2007 NCAA Division II and III Men's Basketball Records Book*

Hockey nhl.com, hhof.com, ushockeyhall.com

Tennis atptennis.com, sonyericssonwtatour.com, usopen.org, australianopen.com, wimbledon.org, rolandgarros.com, masters-cup.com, daviscup.com, fedcup.com, tennisfame.com

Golf pgatour.com, masters.org, usopen.org, usga.org, opengolf.com, pga.com, randa.org, lpga.com, knc.com, ussenioropen.com, usamateur.org, rydercup.com, walkercup.org, curtiscup.org, pinggolf.com

Boxing wbaonline.com, wbcboxing.com, ibf-usba-boxing.com, ibhof.com, thering-online.com, usaboxing.org, olympic.org

Horse Racing ntra.com, ustrotting.com, equibase.com, bloodhorse.com, kentuckyderby.com, belmontstakes.nyra.com, preakness.com

Motor Sports nascar.com, formula1.com, indycar.com, americanlemans.com, nhra.com, champcarworldseries.com, lemans.org, indy500.com, daytona24hr.com

Soccer fifa.com, fifaworldcup.yahoo.com, mlsnet.com, ussoccer.com, uefa.com, rsssf.com, premierleague.com, uslsoccer.com

NCAA Sports ncaasports.com

Olympics torino2006.org, olympic.org, en.beijing2008.com, usoc.org

Track and Field iaaf.org, usatf.org, chicagomarathon.com, parismarathon.com, usoc.org, bostonmarathon.org, nycmarathon.org, maratonadiroma.it, london-marathon.co.uk, fortismarathonrotterdam.nl, asahi.com/tokyo-marathon, *Track and Field News*

Swimming fina.org, usaswimming.org, ishof.org, panpacs2006.com, usoc.org

Skiing fis-ski.com, torino2006.org, skiworldcup.org, usskiteam.com

Figure Skating isu.org, torino2006.org, usfsa.org, usoc.org

Miscellaneous Sports letour.fr, usarchery.org, fide.com, uschesschampionship.com, worldcurling.org, usacurl.org, usacycling.org, uci.ch, iditarod.com, igfa.org, fig-gymnastics.com, usa-gymnastics.org, ushandball.org, uscla.org, nll.com, littleleague.org, abrahydroplanes.com, us-polo.org, prorodeo.com, usrowing.org, usarugby.org, rugbyworld cup.com, amnrl.com, ussailing.org, americascup.com, issf-shooting.org, asasoftball.com, isu.org, us-squash.org, ironmanlive.com, usatriathlon.org, fivb.org, usavolleyball.org, themat.com

Sports Illustrated

BARRY BONDS
at Giants training camp
FEBRUARY 22

THE TRUTH
BARRY BONDS AND STEROIDS

by MARK FAINARU-WADA
AND LANCE WILLIAMS

• • •
Exclusive Book Excerpt

MARCH 13, 2006 www.SI.com
AOL Keyword: Sports Illustrated

In 2006, cheating
scandals rocked one
sport after another

The Year
In Sports

Pretenders To The Throne

While some athletes further heightened their legacies in 2006, many others were laid low by boorish behavior, bad luck, poor timing and questions about cheating

BY MARK BECHTEL

They shared that rarest of sensations: invincibility. True, Tiger Woods had faded at the U.S. Open at Winged Foot; grieving after the death of his father, Earl, nine weeks earlier, he failed to make the cut at a major for the first time in his professional career. But after that Woods regained his predatory focus and went on a roll that included two major championships—the PGA and the British Open, running his total to 12—six straight Tour victories and repeated genuflections from even his staunchest rivals.

In the midst of that scorching streak he took time to turn his golf cap backwards, sit courtside and observe the closest thing he had on the planet to an athletic peer. At the finals of tennis's U.S. Open in Flushing, Queens, Woods watched with an awe normally reserved for those who watch Woods, as Roger Federer filleted Andy Roddick. With Federer roaring through the clinching fourth set 6-1, Woods stopped cheering long enough to say, "He's just gone to another level."

Federer reached unprecedented heights in 2006, becoming the first player ever to win Wimbledon and the U.S. Open three years running. The elegant 25-year-old from Switzerland also became the first man since Rod Laver in 1969 to reach all four Grand Slam finals in a calendar year, and he claimed his ninth major title, ranking him sixth on the alltime list. But the highlight of his season came after his defeat of Roddick, when he and his new friend Tiger shared beers and discussed that fourth set, when Federer's unmatched arsenal and unparalleled calm proved decisive. "I felt I was not going to miss a shot anymore, and everything Andy tried I knew I had an answer for," Federer recalled. "And Tiger knew exactly what I was talking about. It was a very strong moment for me."

In fact, these now bosom buddies of butt-kicking—already Federer was planning to track Woods at one of *his* major tournaments—could have spent the year watching a parade of aspirants come up short. Let us count the ways they did.

JAW-DROPPINGLY. On the one hand there was the ascent of Woods and Federer; on the other, the descent into madness of soccer star Zinedine Zidane. After announcing that he would play the last match of his career at the World Cup in Germany, "Zizou" had taken France on an improbable run to the final. The 34-year-old midfield maestro even gave *Les Bleus* the early lead on a penalty kick, scoring the first goal by an Italian opponent in seven tournament games. But with 10 minutes remaining in

Zidane's head-butt near the end of the World Cup's final match added a sour note to an otherwise successful tournament.

MIKE HEWITT/GETTY IMAGES

the second overtime, Zidane, reacting to a snide remark about his sister by defender Marco Materazzi, drove his close-cropped noggin into the head of the Italian defender. Materazzi fell, Zidane received a red card and France bowed in penalty kicks, 5–3. Instead of taking a final bow on the world's largest stage, Zidane exited to ignominy.

HEARTBREAKINGLY. At the Kentucky Derby, the dark bay Barbaro so thoroughly trampled the field in a 6½-length victory that an end to the 28-year-old Triple Crown drought seemed in sight. But a fortnight later, a mere 15 seconds into Barbaro's run for the Preakness, talk of matching Affirmed was replaced by collectively held breath. "I was right behind him," said jockey Alex Solis, riding Brother Derek. "I heard a crack. I knew [his leg] was broken." An uneven hoof plant had caused the colt's right hind leg to land off-center, shattering the cannon bone. He ran another 100 yards, breaking a sesamoid near the ankle and splintering the long pastern below that joint. And while fans along the rail at Pimlico shrieked and cried as ambulance attendants raced to the fallen horse, Barbaro's fate could have been worse: Although his racing career was over, his life would be saved by veterinary surgeons at the University of Pennsylvania who inserted 27 screws and a titanium plate to fuse his leg bones together.

RULE-BENDINGLY. Floyd Landis had lost the Tour de France. Early in the climb of an Alp called La Toussuire, the 30-year-old in the yellow jersey simply cracked, his face a mask of suffering, his breathing tortured. He ended the 16th stage in 11th place, eight minutes and eight seconds behind the leader. With only one mountain stage remaining to make up lost ground, he was seemingly out of contention. But the Phonak captain from Farmersville, Pa., who had raced four years with a degenerative hip condition, knew he could respond. He decided to attack on the first of five climbs in the 17th stage, at the base of Col des Saisies, an approach that

would consume so much energy it would almost certainly be doomed to failure.

Only this time it didn't fail. "He was taking great, huge chunks of time out of us," said Australian rider Stuart O'Grady. "I've done 10 Tours de France, and I've never seen anything like it." None of the other teams could pull Landis back; with his solo attack over 80 miles and three mountain passes he won the stage and made up his entire deficit. *"INCROYABLE"* and *"GRAND"* and *"MONUMENTAL"* read the next day's headlines in France. And when he rode triumphant into Paris in Stage 20, the prerace doping scandal that had led to the expulsion of favorites Ivan Basso and Jan Ullrich, among others—including two Phonak team members—had been erased from memory by Landis's ride for the ages.

At least, that is, until the urine sample he submitted after Stage 17 tested positive for abnormal levels of testosterone. Landis had

CHRISTIAN PETERSEN/GETTY IMAGES

gone 13-8 with a 1.87 ERA for the Houston Astros. Before leaving, he did promise to play for the U.S. in March for the 16-team World Baseball Classic, an MLB-sponsored event designed to spread the gospel of baseball from Australia to South Africa to the Netherlands over a 17-day stretch in March.

Clemens took the mound in a must-win second-round game and pitched well, allowing Mexico two runs over 4⅓ innings. But not well enough: After the Americans bowed 2–1, the Rocket took off. "For me, right now, it's goodbye," he said. In June, however, the Astros' offer of a $12.6 million contract for the balance of the season persuaded him to return once more. Although he went 7-6 with a 2.30 ERA, Houston failed to catch the St. Louis Cardinals and missed the playoffs.

UNASHAMEDLY. "Measuring success with medal counts is pretty f----- up," said U.S. skier Bode Miller before the Winter Olympics in Turin. So, too, is achieving a high profile in your sport and availing yourself of all the resources your nation's federation has to offer only to squander your opportunities when it matters most. In 2005, Miller won world championships in the downhill and Super G while taking the World Cup overall title. Flush with endorsements, he was the brash, iconoclastic poster boy for the most promising men's ski team in U.S. history.

Once in Italy, though, the 28-year-old Miller seemed to measure his success by cocktail counts; he frequently went out drinking at night and finished no higher than fifth in his five races. Twice he was disqualified for straddling a gate, the second time in the Super G; with his left leg thrown behind him, he still glided down the rest of the course on just one ski. "He has maybe the most talent of any skier in history," said former World Cup skier Luc Alphand of France. "He goes out at night, maybe every night, and that works sometimes, but maybe it doesn't work so much for Bode anymore."

indeed lost the Tour de France: Race officials announced that they would no longer consider him the winner.

In plunging his already tainted sport into further disrepute, Landis joined 42-year-old San Francisco Giants slugger Barry Bonds, whose serial use of performance-enhancing drugs was documented in the book *Game of Shadows*. Undaunted and unapologetic, Bonds passed Babe Ruth for second place on the alltime home run list in May, and at season's end had belted 26, moving him 21 behind Hank Aaron's record of 755.

UNFAIRLY. The assignment—to anchor the national team in the debut of a much-hyped global baseball tournament—would have ordinarily gone to a pitcher young enough to be his son. But age has never been a consideration when it comes to Roger Clemens. In 2005, during what he said (again) would be his last major-league season, the 42-year-old Clemens had merely

WHILE THE YEAR HAD NO SUCCESS STORIES perhaps more unsurprising that those of Woods and Federer, the course of hoops history did take a strange migratory turn: Thanks to a couple of dynamic performers, both major titles wound up in the Sunshine State. Joakim Noah was ranked No. 68 in his high school recruiting class when he entered Florida from Lawrenceville (N.J.) Prep in 2004. The son of a Swedish-born mother (Cecilia, a former Miss Universe finalist) and a French-Cameroonian father (Yannick, a tennis Hall of Famer), the 6'11", 227-pound sophomore improved game by game, and the Gators, unranked in the preseason, improved with him. In a 73–57 demolition of UCLA in Indianapolis, Noah had 16 points, nine rebounds and a championship-game record six blocks. "This is better than sex!" the ponytailed Noah shouted afterward. "And trust me, I'm doing it right."

Dwyane Wade wasn't a high shool hot shot in Oak Lawn, Ill., either: Only three Division I schools recruited him. Drafted by the Miami Heat out of Marquette in 2003, he was overshadowed by the top pick, LeBron James. But in the 2006 Finals, the 6'4" Wade commanded the spotlight, even upstaging teammate Shaquille O'Neal. After Miami dropped the first two games to the Dallas Mavericks, Wade scored 42, 36, 43 and 46 points in the four ensuing Heat wins, and averaged 34.7 points, 7.8 rebounds and 3.8 assists for the series. Down two points with 9.1 seconds left in a pivotal Game 5, Wade dribbled through four Mavericks, got fouled and nailed both free throws for a 101-100 victory. "Besides Dwyane," Miami's Hall of Fame coach, Pat Riley, said, "we did not have a second option."

"You send this script to Hollywood, they'd say, 'This is too fake,'" Pittsburgh Steelers' fullback Jerome (the Bus) Bettis posited, though he could have used a number of other words. Like corny. Or saccharine. Or perfect. Bettis's NFL playing days began so long ago (1993) that he played for a team in Los Angeles, and in 13 seasons he rushed for 13,622 yards (fifth alltime) on 3,479 carries (fourth). With his team owning a decidedly mediocre 7–5 record and on the brink of postseason elimination, it seemed one of the league's most beloved players would end his career with a whimper.

But the Steelers closed out the season with four wins to grab the AFC's No. 6 seed and then reeled off three playoff road victories. That put them in Super Bowl XL, which happened to be in Detroit, which happened to be Bettis's hometown. A 21–10 victory over the Seatle Seahawks—aided by some of Bettis's signature, clock-eating runs—gave Pittsburgh its record-tying fifth championship and sent the Bus, key to the city in hand, rolling happily on to his post-NFL life.

While the Steelers came out of nowhere to win a title, the St. Louis Cardinals came back from near-rigor mortis. They ended the season with nine losses in 12 games and were within a whisper of the worst late-season collapse in major-league history. But thanks to an improbable two-run homer by .216-hitting catcher Yadier Molina they squeezed by the New York Mets 3–1 in Game 7 of the National League Championship Series, then drew the Detroit Tigers, who had done a Lazarus act of their own in 2006 under new manager Jim Leyland and gone 7-1 against the New York Yankees and Oakland A's in the AL playoffs.

But in five World Series games the Tigers' lineup delivered a mere 11 runs, and while their pitchers found the plate, they had trouble locating fielders: In 14 fielding attempts they erred five times, a World Series record. That the Cards capitalized on most of those miscues was no surprise; this was a team of opportunists. Righthander Jeff Weaver, discarded during the season by the Los Angeles Angels, went eight brilliant innings to win the clinching game 4–2. Middle reliever Adam Wainwright, thrust into the closer's role after an injury to Jason Isringhausen, won Game 4 and saved Game 5. And 5'7" shortstop David Eckstein, unwanted by the Angels after the '04 season, drove in four runs in the final two games to be named Series MVP.

Yes, St. Louis had the worst regular season winning percentage (.516) of any of the 102 World Series winners, but no matter. "It's not the best team that wins," said St. Louis manager Tony La Russa. "It's the team that plays the best baseball." In the end, that team can truly feel—yes—invincible.

Late October - November 2005

BILL FRAKES / SPORTS ILLUSTRATED

NOV 7, 2005
Garret Gomez celebrates the second anniversary of his sobriety by riding Stevie Wonderboy to victory in the Breeders' Cup Juvenile.

THEY SAID IT

Bill Walton, broadcaster and former NBA star, on the league's dress code: "I have spent all summer sewing collars on my tie-dyed t-shirts."

GO FIGURE

31 consecutive games, an NFL record, in which Shane Lechler has had a punt of at least 50 yards.

54 Career touchdowns by Brown running back Nick Hartigan, an Ivy League record; the Bears clinched their first outright Ivy Championship with a win over Columbia.

191 Percentage increase in sales of Bengals merchandise from $9.3 million in 2004 to $27.1 million in 2005.

.357 Combined winning percentage of the 14 teams the Dolphins beat during their undefeated 1972 season.

DAVID E. KLUTHO

NOV 21, 2005 Chicago's Nathan Vasher makes the longest play in NFL history, returning a 49ers' field gold attempt 108 yards for a touchdown.

THIS MONTH'S SIGN OF THE
APOCALYPSE

The NCAA took Division III Carthage College off its list of schools with banned Native American nicknames after the school changed its nickname from Redmen to Red Men.

December 2005

DEC 10 2005 Reggie Bush wins the Heisman trophy, becoming the seventh USC Trojan to win the trophy and the third in the last four years.

STEPHEN CHERNIN/GETTY IMAGES

GO FIGURE

0 Number of American-born players on the NAIA men's soccer All-America first team.

1,183 Receiving yards by Tulsa's Garrett Mills this season, an NCAA record for a tight end.

-3 The Packer's scoring differential during their 2-10 start; Green Bay had been outscored 242-239 at that point.

-157 the 49ers' scoring differential during their 2-10 start (they had been outscored 340-183).

THEY SAID IT

Bob McNair, Houton Texans owner, on his 1-11 team: "I'm not going to drive off any cliffs. There aren't any around here anyway. I know because I've been looking."

EZRA SHAW/GETTY IMAGES

DEC 20 Johnny Damon ditches the Red Sox for a four-year deal with Boston's arch-rivals, the New York Yankees, resulting in the inevitable shearing of his famed long hair, as per George Steinbrenner's club rules.

January 2006

ROBERT BECK

JAN 9 Vince Young racks up 467 yards to lead the Longhorns to a 41-38 victory over the Trojans at the Rose Bowl, Texas's first national title in 35 years.

JAN 24 Hockey Hall of Famer Mario Lemieux announces his second retirement from the NHL at the age of 40, the result of a heart condition.

JAN 30 Kobe Bryant scores the second highest point total in NBA history with 81 points against the Toronto Raptors in the Lakers 122-104 win.

GO FIGURE

90 Years the Florida basketball team went without a triple double before guard Corey Brewer achieved one against Jacksonville.

$300 Stipend that 275 Rutgers students will receive to finance trips to watch the school play in the Insight Bowl in Phoenix; the money is from alumni donations and a state grant.

$10,305 Winning bid in an auction for a Peyton Manning-themed Indiana license plate inscribed QB 18; the state is selling specialty vehicle tags to raise money for a new Colts stadium.

4 Consecutive NAIA football titles won by Carroll College in Montana; Div. III Augustana (1983-86) is the only other college to win four straight national football championships.

February 2006

FEB 13 Pittsburgh QB Ben Roethlisberger leads the Steelers to a 21-10 victory over Detroit in Superbowl XL.

FEB 25 Duke's J.J. Redick breaks Dickie Hemric's 1955 ACC career scoring record after racking up 11 points against Temple, boosting his career total to 2,590 points, three more than Hemric.

GO FIGURE

$3 million
Appearance fee Tiger Woods received for playing in the Dubai Desert Classic.

$2.4 million Total purse for the event, of which Woods pocketed another $400,000 by winning.

3 Rank of Yao Ming on the list of best-selling NBA jerseys in China; his Rockets teammate Tracey McGrady's jersey is the most popular and Allen Iverson's ranks second.

11 Games over .500 that the NBA's L.A. Clippers were after a win over the Toronto Raptors in mid-January, the best mark in team history.

March 2006

MARCH 12 Duke sweeps past Boston College to win its seventh ACC conference title in eight years.

GO FIGURE

1,001 Career victories for Gene Bess of The Rivers Community College in Popular Bluff, MO; he's the first college basketball coach at any level to win 1,000 games.

3-13 The Saints' record last season, the second worst in the NFL.

.539 Combined 2005 winning percentage of the 13 opponents New Orleans will face next season, tied for the second toughest schedule in the league.

7.8 Increase in Kobe Bryant's scoring average from 2005 (27.6) to 2006 (35.4); among players who averaged 25 points, only Wilt Chamberlain (in 1961-62) and Rick Barry (1966-67) had bigger jumps in consecutive seasons, according STATS Inc.

BOB ROSATO/SPORTS ILLUSTRATED

MARCH 15 Jeff King wins the XXXIV Iditarod, becoming the fifth four-time race champion and oldest winner, at 50.

THIS MONTH'S SIGN OF THE
APOCALYPSE

A Romanian soccer player retired after he found out he had been traded for 33 pounds of meat.

THEY SAID IT

Curt Schilling, Red Sox pitcher, on being named to *GQ*'s list of the 10 most hated athletes: "I was actually talking to my wife about that because I thought maybe she had some input."

April 2006

APR 2 White Sox infielder Jim Thome high-fives A.J. Pierzynski as the World Champion Sox open their season with a 10-4 win over the Cleveland Indians.

APR 3 Final Four MOP Joakim Noah and Al Horford of Florida celebrate after defeating UCLA 73-57 to win the NCAA Men's Div. I Basketball Tournament.

APR 9 With Tiger Woods looking on, Phil Mickelson dons the Green Jacket after winning his second Masters in three years.

May 2006

MAY 15 Ridden by Edgar Prado, Barbaro, a 6-to-1 shot, breaks from the pack at Churchill Downs to handily win the 132nd Kentucky Derby. Barbaro's shot at the Triple Crown was foiled after suffering multiple leg fractures in the Preakness a few weeks later.

GO FIGURE

15 Consecutive victories by the Devils, tying the NHL record for longest winning streak spanning the regular season and playoffs.

24 Games it took for the Cardinals' Albert Pujols to hit 14 home runs, the fewest ever by a major leaguer.

40 Pick with which Nebraska safety Daniel Bullocks was taken by the Lions in the 2006 NFL draft.

40 Pick with which Nebraska safety Josh Bullocks, Daniel's twin, was taken by the Saints in the 2005 NFL draft.

MAY 20 Under a cloud of steroid accusations, Barry Bonds hits his 714th career home run to tie Babe Ruth for second place on the alltime home runs list.

ROBERT BECK/SPORTS ILLUSTRATED

MAY 15 Returning from a 20-month layoff from boxing, Oscar De La Hoya regains his championship form by battering Ricardo Mayorga to win the super welterweight title in Las Vegas.

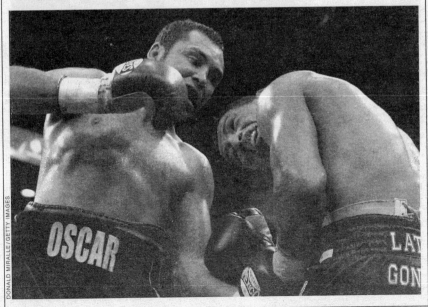

DONALD MIRALLE/GETTY IMAGES

June 2006

FRED VUICH

JUN 5 Sam Hornish Jr. overtakes Marco Andretti on the final lap to win the Indianapolis 500 by 0.0635 seconds, the second closest margin in the race's history. Andretti's father, Michael, finished third.

THIS MONTH'S SIGN OF THE
APOCALYPSE

A pin position at the rain-delayed PGA Memorial tournament had to be changed because someone had defecated in the cup during the night.

GO FIGURE

3 Percentage of the NHL's revenue derived from its television contract.

66 Percentage of the NFL's revenue derivved from its television contract.

481 Consecutive games bowled by Dave Wilson, 40, of Mason, Ohio; his 102-hour marathon for charity was two hours longer than the world record.

961 At bats between home runs for A's catcher Jason Kendall, who ended the major's longest current dinger drought on May 31 with a shot off Joel Peralta of the Royals.

$1.9 million Amount given to David Beckham to write an autobiography—the 31-year-old's third in the last five years.

JUNE 9 After losing the first set, Rafael Nadal pummels his way past Roger Federer to win his second straight French Open in Paris, becoming the first player to beat Federer in a Grand Slam final match.

June 2006

HEINZ KLUETMEIER/SPORTS ILLUSTRATED

THEY SAID IT

Pepe Reina, Spanish national team goalkeeper, on joining the team a week after getting married: "Now I'm going to have to spend my honeymoon with 22 other blokes."

JUNE 18 Phil Mickelson suffers a meltdown on the 18th hole of the U.S. Open. Geoff Ogilvy goes on to win the event, becoming the first Australian to win a men's major tournament since 1995. Mickelson had led Ogilvy by a stroke, but double-bogeyed the final hole. Ogilvy's five-over-par total was the highest for the tournament since 1974.

JOHN W. McDONOUGH/SPORTS ILLUSTRATED

JUNE 20 A jubilant Pat Riley helps his Miami Heat hoist the Larry O'Brien trophy in the air after the team defeated the Dallas Mavericks 95-92 in the sixth game of the series. The win marked the first NBA title in Miami's franchise history.

July 2006

BOB MARTIN/SPORTS ILLUSTRATED

JULY 7 Amelie Mauresmo defeats Justine Henin-Hardenne to win her first Wimbledon title and her second major championship of the year.

THIS MONTH'S SIGN OF THE
APOCALYPSE

Police in Berlin arrested two men for causing serious physical injury by placing cement-filled soccer balls around the city with signs that said CAN U KICK IT?

JULY 9 Responding to a verbal jab, France's soccer hero Zinedine Zidane head-butts Italian player Marco Materazzi, prompting his ejection from the game and stunning French fans. Italy went on defeat France to win its fourth World Cup title.

AFP PHOTO/FILES/JOHN MACDOUGALL

JULY 21 Tiger Woods finishes with a par to win the British Open and became the Open's first repeat champion since Tom Watson in 1983.

AFP PHOTO/JACK GUEZ

GO FIGURE

August 2006

AUGUST 5 Just weeks after winning the Tour de France, Floyd Landis is accused of doping after a test of his urine drawn during the Tour shows highly elevated levels of testosterone. After a second round of tests produces similar results, Landis is fired by his racing team, which then dissolves, and Tour officials say they no longer consider him the winner of the race.

THEY SAID IT

LeBron James, Cavaliers' 21-year-old swingman, when asked on *The Best Damn Sports Show* when he last looked at a price tag: "A long time ago."

GO FIGURE

2 NFL owners who have teams in the English Premier League: Malcom Glazer, who owns the Buccaneers and Manchester United; and Browns owner Randy Lerner, who agreed to buy Aston Villa for $118.8 million.

3.8 Average number of hours per week that fantasy sports players spend managing their teams, according to a University of Mississippi study.

100 Length in hours of a soccer game—believed to be the longest ever in the U.S.—played in Bell Gardens, Calif., to celebrate the centennial of Mexican team Chivas; more than 2,000 players participated in the game.

AUGUST 20 The world of international cricket erupts in scandal after Pakistani bowlers are accused of ball tampering during a match with England. Protesting a decision to award England five additional runs as penalty, Pakistan refuses to return to the field. When Pakistan finally does, the umpires declare the match forfeited to England—the first match forfeited in Test cricket history. The scandal intensifies later in the month, when emails released by the International Cricket Council (ICC) reveal that the lead umpire of the disputed match, Darrel Hair, said he would retire in exchange for a payment of $500,000 from the ICC.

August 2006 (Cont.)

AUG 21 After trailing his opponent on two out of three scorecards in the ninth round, Oleg Maskaev rebounds to drop Hasim Rahman twice in the twelfth round, forcing the referee to stop the bout and making Maskaev the new WBC heavyweight champion.

ETHAN MILLER/GETTY IMAGES

DAMIAN STROHMEYER

GO FIGURE

0 NFL tight ends who make more than 49ers rookie Vernon Davis, who became the highest paid before playing a down when he signed for five years and $23 million.

4 Times in his career that the Cardinals' Albert Pujols has swung at and missed three pitches in the same at bat, according to STATS Inc.

8 Birdies by Corey Pavin in the first nine holes of the first round of the U.S. Bank Championship; Pavin set a PGA nine-hole record by shooting a 26 on the front nine.

AUGUST 28 Columbus, Georgia, defeats Saitama, Japan, 2-1, to claim the championship at the Little League World Series.

September 2006

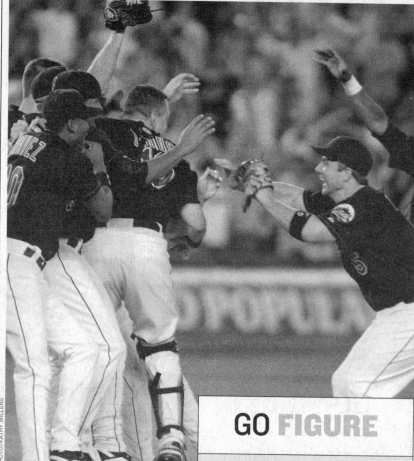

AP PHOTO/KATHY WILLENS

SEPT 18 The New York Mets clinch the National League East title for the first time since 1988, defeating the Florida Marlins 4-0, in front of a crowd of 49,726 at Shea Stadium. The Mets become the first team other than than Atlanta Braves to claim the NL East title since 1991.

GO FIGURE

50 Career TD catches by New Hampshire senior David Ball, tying the Division I-AA record set by Jerry Rice at Mississippi Valley State.

41 Doubles by the Nationals' Alfonso Soriano, the first player ever with 40 home runs, steals and doubles in a season.

734 Home runs by Barry Bonds, who broke Hank Aaron's career NL record with a homer in a agame against the Brewers.

ROSS KINNAIRD/GETTY IMAGES

SEPT 24 Tiger Woods tries to hide under his cap as Europe crushes the U.S., 18½ to 9½ to claim its third straight Ryder Cup. Not only did Europe retain the cup, but it won by the same margin as it did when it handily beat the U.S. in 2004.

THIS MONTH'S SIGN OF THE
APOCALYPSE

The father of a Pennsylvania high school football player posed as a college scout to videotape an opponent's practice.

October 2006

LOU CAPOZZOLA

GO FIGURE

1 NFL players who have had multiple interception returns of at least 100 yards: the Eagles' Lito Sheppard, who had a 102-yard return in 2006 and a 101-yard return in '04.

3 Consecutive games in which Arizona has rushed for negative yardage; the Wildcats had a combined total of -36 yards in losses to USC, Washington and UCLA.

OCT 4 The Buffalo Sabres win a shootout to beat the Carolina Hurricanes 3-2 in their season opener and go on to win their first 10 games, tying the NHL record.

THEY SAID IT

Torii Hunter, Twins outfielder, on why Oakland DH Frank Thomas is called the Big Hurt: "He'll hurt you. And he's big, too."

OCT 11 Yankees pitcher Cory Lidle and his flight instructor are killed when their small private plane slams into the side of an Upper East Side residential tower.

Late October 2006

OCT 15 A sidelines-clearing brawl erupts at a football game between the University of Miami (Fla.) and Florida International University, leading to the suspensions of 31 players from both teams and the firing of Lamar Thomas, a former Hurricanes player and color analyst for Comcast Sports SouthEast, who praised the players for taking part in the meelee.

OCT 22 Kenny Rogers pitches the Tigers to a Game 2 World Series victory , but it is the noticeable smudge on his throwing hand during the first inning—pine tar or dirt?—that draws fans' attention.

Baseball

BELLI 7

The World Series champion St. Louis Cardinals

Upset? It's In The Cards

After stumbling into the playoffs with an 83-win season, the underdog Cardinals started overachieving, beating the highly favored Mets and Tigers on their way to the title

BY MARK BECHTEL

IT WAS ONE OF THE MORE unlikely World Series matchups in history. A team three years removed from a 43-win season against a team that won 83 regular season games. Predictably, they played one of the stranger Fall Classics in recent memory.

In the opener, Anthony Reyes of the Cardinals, a pitcher who had five wins in the regular season (the lowest ever for a Series Game 1 starter), humbled dart-thrower Justin Verlander in the first ever Game 1 matchup of rookies, won 7–2 by St. Louis. The second game featured a bizarre non-argument. Television cameras picked up a noticeable smudge on the throwing hand of Detroit starter Kenny Rogers, who was riding a 15-inning postseason scoreless streak. Instead of asking the umpires to inspect Rogers, which presumably would have led to his ejection, Cards manager Tony LaRussa let it slide. Rogers washed his hands after the inning and proceeded to shut out St. Louis over eight innings. After the game, which the Cardinals lost 3–1, LaRussa refused to explain his decision, saying, "It's not important to talk about." A couple of his players weren't buying that. They thought he was taking it easy on Detroit manager Jim Leyland, an old friend.

At that point, it looked as if the Tigers were sitting pretty. After dropping the first game of the division series against the Yankees, they took the next three. In the ALCS they swept the A's. And it looked like they once again had the momentum on their side. And then they imploded. The Cardinals ripped off three wins in a row, thanks largely to the inability of Detroit pitchers to make simple throws. They made five errors in the series, including throwing errors on routine sacrifices in each of the last three games. And David Eckstein, who was 0 for 11 in the first three games, had six hits in the final two, driving in four runs and walking away with the World Series MVP award. "Whenever David is playing, there is absolutely no doubt that our club responds to how hard he plays," La Russa said. "He is a wonderful leader."

The Tigers were left scratching their heads. After Game 5, Verlander tried to explain his crucial error. "I picked it up and said, Don't throw it away, instead of just throwing it," he said. "I got tentative. We kind of cut our own throats." Had you told Verlander in mid-April that six months later he'd be answering questions about his World Series performance, he probably would have given you quite the sideways look. The regular season began the same way pretty much every season has begun for

the past decade: with the Tigers in turmoil. After a 5-0 start, Detroit, which had lost 91 games in 2005 and 119 in 2003, dropped six of eight. The final loss was a 10-2 shellacking at the hands of Cleveland in the finale of a four-game series. The Tigers could have taken three of four with a win, but, according to Leyland, the players were more concerned with their impending road trip to the West Coast. And Leyland, back in the dugout after a six-year hiatus, let his players know he didn't appreciate their effort. "It's been going on here before, and it's not going to happen here. I'm not talking about anybody in particular, I'm talking about the team. Myself, the coaches, and everybody. It's my responsibility to have the team ready to play today. They weren't ready to play. They were ready to get on a plane and go to Oakland. If they won it was OK, if we lost it was OK, and that's not good enough."

The entire rip job lasted less than a minute, but the players got the message. Detroit won 28 of its next 37, stretching its record to 35-15 and inspiring some heady behavior by fans. After an 8-3 win over the Indians in May, a

Twins lefthander Santana became the first AL pitcher since Pedro Martinez in 1999 to lead (or tie for the lead) in single-season wins (19), strikeouts (245) and ERA (2.77).

fan in Comerica Park waved a sign reading "WHEN DO PLAYOFF TICKETS GO ON SALE?" Leyland's take: "My cigarettes have filters on them. I'm not sure that guy's cigarettes have filters on them."

It turned out to be a relevant question. Detroit stayed atop the Central standings throughout the summer, thanks to a slew of hard-throwing young pitchers. The best was Justin Verlander, the second player taken in the 2004 draft. Despite having just 20 minor league starts under his belt, Verlander was a fixture in the Tigers rotation, going 17-9 with a 3.63 ERA. And he did it in style, flashing a fastball that topped out at 101 mph. "I don't know where it comes from," reliever Joel Zumaya said of his lanky teammate. "His body is ... rubbery."

"KitKats," was Verlander's response. (He was eating one of the candy bars at the time.) "That's how I do it."

As well as they played, the Tigers couldn't hold off the surging Twins, who won the division on the final day of the season, relegating Detroit to the wild card. Minnesota got back in the race thanks to a rookie pitcher of its own. On May 19, the Twins were 17-24. That day Francisco Liriano was promoted into the starting rotation. Thanks to the lefty, whose resemblance to Johan Santana went farther than their uniforms, the Twins' rotation stabilized and the team went on a tear. Relying on his fastball and a changeup almost as nasty as Santana's, Liriano went 12-3 before arm troubles shelved him.

Verlander and Liriano were just two of a slew of young pitchers who comprise what is arguably the most talented class of arms the game has seen. (Rookies won more games in 2006 than in any season.) Jeremy Sowers was given a spot in the Indians' rotation in the middle of the summer and won six of his last seven decisions (including back-to-back shutouts) before being shut down in late September. John Maine went 6-5 with a 3.60 ERA for the Mets and started their first playoff game. The Marlins had four rookie pitchers with 10 or more wins, among them Anibal Sanchez, a late call-up who threw a no-hitter in early September. And Boston's Jonathan Papelbon proved to be one of the game's top closers—despite the fact that he hadn't relieved since college.

Papelbon's stellar work—he gave up only three earned runs in his first 55 innings—turned out to be for naught. The Red Sox led the Yankees throughout the early summer, but ultimately injuries to virtually every regular doomed them. (At one point late in the season, the Sox fielded only two starters who were with the team last year.) Most notably, perpetually disgruntled outfielder Manny Ramirez had a bum knee, and DH David Ortiz suffered from an irregular heartbeat. Not even manager Terry Francona was immune. In September, Francona spit up blood at a press conference in Seattle. "Of course it's been hard," Francona said. "But regardless of how I feel, when I come through that [clubhouse] door, those guys can't see me dragging my tail. I won't let them see me that way. If they do, I'm not doing my job."

Francona went about his business, but he could do little except watch the Yankees run away with the AL East. The Bombers did it despite a subpar season from Alex Rodriguez, who learned a thing or two about the levels of scrutiny one must endure in New York. After a string of five errors in five games—manager Joe Torre moved him to DH for a night—he was renamed E-Rod by the tabloids. One scribe opined "It's no secret that Alex Rodriguez has sunk to the bottom of a cesspool filled by self-doubt." Said teammate Mariano Rivera, in his 12th season in the Bronx, "I haven't seen anything like it since I've been here."

During an 80-game stretch from June 1 until the end of August—essentially half a season—A-Rod hit .257, struck out 81 times and made 13 errors. Things got so bad that his teammates intervened. First baseman Jason Giambi went to Torre and said, "Skip, it's time to stop coddling him." Torre took Giambi's words to heart, calling his slugger in for a meeting. It was clear somebody had to do something, not only to get Rodriguez to get his game in order, but to get him to see that he had a problem. Giambi had tried—and he didn't coddle him. After a 13-5 win in Boston on Aug. 19, Giambi approached Rodriguez, who had left four runners on base in the first three innings. "We're all rooting for you and we're behind you 100 percent," Giambi told *Sports Illustrated*, recounting a conversation he had with Rodriguez, "but you've got to get the big hit."

Giambi said Rodriguez's response was, "What do you mean? I've had five hits in Boston."

"You f------ call those hits?" Giambi said. "You had two f------ dinkers to rightfield and a ball that bounced over the third baseman! Look at how many pitches you missed!"

Giambi had a theory about A-Rod's problem: "He's guessing, and he's doing a bad job of it, which is inevitable when you guess as often as he guesses. He's squeezing the f------ sawdust out of the bat."

Other teammates weighed in. "I think he ought to get his eyes checked," one told *SI*.

In 2006, Howard's slugging prowess down the stretch—he finished with 58 HRs and 149 RBIs on the year—earned him 31 intentional walks after the All-Star break.

"I'm not kidding. I don't think he's seeing the ball."

Another said: "I honestly think he might be afraid of the ball."

Despite their star's struggles and the shocking amount of candor his teammates showed in discussing them, the Yankees had little to worry about. Their ride was almost as smooth as their neighbors'. The Mets ran away with the NL East, ending Atlanta's run of 14 straight division titles.

They did it by bringing in a handful of vets who produced—and kept things loose. Catcher Paul Lo Duca called the team's clubhouse "Rip City"—in a good way. "Look at the personalities they brought in here,"

closer Billy Wagner said. "We're all extroverts. Me, Lo Duca, [Carlos] Delgado, Pedro [Martinez]....It's not like guys came here and were afraid to say something. I think that's why we clicked right away. This is the best clubhouse I've ever been involved in. And the secret is that guys can say anything they want to anyone at any time."

The Mets won the East by 12 games over the Phillies, who rode second-year slugger Ryan Howard to the brink of the postseason. "Without him, we wouldn't be close to making the playoffs," said Phillies second baseman Chase Utley. "Ryan was so dominant in the second half—he carried us. He got the Barry Bonds treatment [at the plate]."

He didn't get the Bonds treatment from the fans or the media, though. Howard made a run at 60 homers and although he came up short—he hit 58—he did it under a

hit four in a row. (Ironically, the Dodgers, who were last in the NL in home runs, hadn't hit more than three in a game all year.)

San Diego answered with a run in the top of the tenth, but Los Angeles won it on yet another long ball, a two-run shot from Nomar Garciaparra, who proved to be a fantastic pickup, hitting .303 with 20 homers. "That's one, if you TiVo-ed it, you're going to watch it over and over again to the end. I was glad to be a part of it," Garciaparra said.

As the Padres and Dodgers separated themselves from the pack, one team was heading back to it at an alarming rate. The Cardinals led the Astros by 8½ games on Sept. 20—then proceeded to go into a wretched funk, losing eight of nine. The Astros, meanwhile, ripped off nine wins in a row. Houston would have passed the Cards were it not for the late-inning heroics of Albert Pujols and Scott Spiezio. Each provided a game-winning, eighth inning three-run hit in the final week. (Pujols's was a homer, Spiezio's a bases-clearing triple), and St. Louis barely held on to win the NL Central.

They didn't look like much of a threat heading into October. But after beating the Padres in four games in the NLDS and taking a thrilling seventh game from the Mets in the NLCS, they put themselves in position to become the most improbable world champs the game had seen. "It's not the best team that wins," La Russa said after the Series. "It's the team that plays the best baseball."

much stricter steroid testing program than had previously been in effect. In the minds of many, he was the first player not tainted by suspicion to make a run at Roger Maris's mark of 61 homers. Even Maris's family endorsed Howard: "In my mind, I feel Ryan Howard's clean," Rich Maris, Roger's son, told Yahoo.com.

Eventually the Phillies fell out of wild card contention, as the Dodgers and Padres pulled away. But before they were both safely in the playoffs, they provided one of the most dramatic finishes in years. Locked in a battle for first, the teams met in L.A. on Sept. 18. San Diego took a 9-5 lead into the bottom of the ninth, sending many of the 55,831 on hand to an early exit. But in the bottom of the ninth, the Dodgers hit four consecutive solo homers to tie the game— just the fourth time in history a team had

Final Standings

National League

EASTERN DIVISION

Team	Won	Lost	Pct	GB	Home	Away
NY Mets	97	65	.599	--	50-31	47-34
Philadelphia	85	77	.525	12	41-40	44-37
Atlanta	79	83	.488	18	40-41	39-42
Florida	78	84	.512	19	45-36	38-43
Washington	71	91	.438	26	41-40	30-51

CENTRAL DIVISION

Team	Won	Lost	Pct	GB	Home	Away
St. Louis	83	78	.516	--	49-31	34-47
Houston	82	80	.506	1½	44-37	38-43
Cincinnati	80	82	.494	3½	42-39	38-43
Milwaukee	75	87	.463	8½	48-33	27-54
Pittsburgh	67	95	.414	16½	43-38	24-57
Chi. Cubs	66	96	.407	17½	36-45	30-51

WESTERN DIVISION

Team	Won	Lost	Pct	GB	Home	Away
San Diego	88	74	.543	--	43-38	45-36
†LA Dodgers	88	74	.543	--	49-32	39-42
San Francisco	76	85	.472	11½	43-38	33-47
Arizona	76	86	.469	12	39-42	37-44
Colorado	76	86	.469	12	44-37	32-49

American League

EASTERN DIVISION

Team	Won	Lost	Pct	GB	Home	Away
NY Yankees	97	65	.599	--	50-31	47-34
Toronto	87	75	.537	10	50-31	37-44
Boston	86	76	.531	11	48-33	38-43
Baltimore	70	92	.432	27	40-41	30-51
Tampa Bay	61	101	.377	36	41-40	20-61

CENTRAL DIVISION

Team	Won	Lost	Pct	GB	Home	Away
Minnesota	96	66	.593	--	54-27	42-39
†Detroit	95	67	.586	1	46-35	49-32
Chi. White Sox	90	72	.556	6	49-32	41-40
Cleveland	78	84	.481	18	44-37	34-47
Kansas City	62	100	.383	34	34-47	28-53

WESTERN DIVISION

Team	Won	Lost	Pct	GB	Home	Away
Oakland	93	69	.574	--	49-32	44-37
LA Angels	89	73	.549	4	45-36	44-37
Texas	80	82	.494	13	39-42	41-40
Seattle	78	84	.481	15	44-37	34-47

†Wild-card team.

2006 Playoffs

National League Division Playoffs

Oct 3	St. Louis 5 at San Diego 1
Oct 5	St. Louis 2 at San Diego 0
Oct 7	San Diego 3 at St. Louis 1
Oct 8	San Diego 2 at St. Louis 6

(St. Louis won series 3–1)

Oct 4	LA Dodgers 5 at NY Mets 6
Oct 5	LA Dodgers 1 at NY Mets 4
Oct 7	NY Mets 9 at LA Dodgers 5

(NY Mets won the series 3–0)

National League Championship Series

Oct 12	St. Louis 0 at NY Mets 2
Oct 13	St. Louis 9 at NY Mets 6
Oct 14	NY Mets 0 at St. Louis 5
Oct 15	NY Mets 12 at St. Louis 5
Oct 17	NY Mets 2 at St. Louis 4
Oct 18	St. Louis 2 at NY Mets 4
Oct 19	St. Louis 3 at NY Mets 1

(St. Louis won series 4–3)

GAME 1

St. Louis	0	0	0	0	0	0	0	0	0	**0**	**4**	**0**
NY Mets	0	0	0	0	0	2	0	0	x	**2**	**6**	**0**

W—NYM: Glavine. **L**—StL: Weaver. **SV**—Wagner. **LOB**—NYM: 7; StL: 6. **2B**—NYM: Delgado 2. **HR**—NYM: Beltran. **SB**—NYM: Green. **IBB**—NYM: Wright. **T**—2:52. **A**—56,311.

Recap: After Mets starter Tom Glavine danced around several Cardinals' threats early in the game, Carlos Beltran took advantage of the only mistake that Jeff Weaver made all night and turned it into the home run that was the difference in a 2-0 win. Glavine was helped by excellent defense from Endy Chavez, David Wright and Beltran, who became the first Mets outfielder with a home run and an assist in the same postseason game. The Mets' bullpen took care of the last two innings in the same fashion it has all season, and Albert Pujols, at least for one day, turned out to be a non-factor.

GAME 2

St. Louis	0	2	2	0	0	0	2	0	3	**9**	**10**	**1**
NY Mets	3	1	0	0	1	1	0	0	0	**6**	**9**	**2**

W—Kinney. **L**—Wagner. **LOB**—StL: 8; NYM: 9. **2B**—StL: Molina, Pujols, Spiezio; NYM: Reyes, Chavez, Lo Duca. **3B**—StL: Spiezio. **HR**—StL: Edmonds, Taguchi; NYM: Delgado 2. **SB**—StL: Eckstein. **GIDP**—NYM: Valentin, Beltran. **HBP**—NYM: Tucker. **E**—StL: Belliard; NYM: Delgado. **T**—3:58. **A**—56,349.

Recap: Scott Spiezio started in place of injured Scott Rolen and ended up as the Cardinals' hitting standout, driving in three runs with a two-run triple in the seventh and an RBI double in the ninth. Mets closer Billy Wagner entered the game in the top of the ninth, trying to preserve a 6–6 tie. Instead, Taguchi hit a tiebreaking homer and the Cardinals added two more runs on a pair of doubles and a single, making the score 9–6 by the time Wagner was removed from the game.

National League Championship Series *(Cont.)*

GAME 3

NY Mets	0 0 0	0 0 0	0 0 0	**0**	**3**	**0**
St. Louis	2 3 0	0 0 0	0 0 X	**5**	**8**	**0**

W—Suppan. **L**—Trachsel. **LOB**—NYM 3; StL: 8.
3B—NYM: Reyes; StL: Spiezio. **HR**—StL: Suppan.
SB—NYM: Beltran.
T—2:53. **A**—47,053

Recap: Cards' starter Jeff Suppan pitched brilliantly, allowing the Mets just three harmless hits over eight innings of work as the two runs produced by Scott Spiezio's two-out triple in the first inning proved to be all the offense the Cards would need. Mets starter Steve Trachsel, on the other hand, had a miserable night, walking five and allowing five earned runs in less than two innings. The Mets bullpen, Darren Oliver in particular, pitched well, blanking St. Louis the rest of the way, but Suppan never let the Mets back in the game and even helped his own cause with a solo home run in the second inning to extend the Cardinal lead.

GAME 4

NY Mets	0 0 2	0 3 6	1 0 0	**12**	**14**	**1**
St. Louis	0 1 1	0 1 2	0 0 0	**5**	**11**	**1**

W—NYM: Perez. **L**—StL: Thompson. **LOB**—NYM: 8; StL: 5. **2B**— NYM: Delgado, Valentin. **3B**—StL: Encarnacion. **HR**—NYM: Beltran 2, Wright, Delgado; StL: Eckstein, Edmonds, Molina. **SB**—StL: Belliard. **GIDP**—StL: Encarnacion, Spiezio, Rodriguez. **HBP**—StL: Eckstein. **E**—StL: Belliard; NYM: Delgado. **T**—3:31. **A**—46,600.

Recap: The mighty Mets offense finally made an appearance as New York bashed four home runs, including a pair from Carlos Beltran, to even the series and ensure a Game 6 in Shea Stadium. Oliver Perez pitched just well enough to keep the Mets in it until the offense exploded in the fifth and sixth innings to put the game out of reach. Cardinals' righthander Brad Thompson relieved Anthony Reyes to start the fifth inning, but offered no relief at all, lasting just one-third of an inning and allowing three runs (two earned) on a Carlos Delgado home run that put the Mets in front 5–2. They never looked back after that.

GAME 5

NY Mets	0 0 0	2 0 0	0 0 0	**2**	**8**	**0**
St. Louis	0 0 0	2 1 1	0 0 X	**4**	**10**	**0**

W—StL: Weaver. **L**—NYM: Glavine. **SV**—Wainwright. **LOB**—StL: 10; NYM: 8. **2B**—StL: Wilson; NYM: Chavez, Green, Valentin, Wright. **3B**—StL: Miles: **HR**—StL: Pujols, Duncan. **SB**—StL: Eckstein. **IBB**—StL: Pujols, Edmonds. **T**—3:26. **A**—46,496.

Recap: With the score tied 2–2, St. Louis shortstop David Eckstein led off the fifth inning with a single, then scored the go-ahead run on a double by Preston Wilson. Mets starter Tom Glavine, who had been brilliant in his previous two playoff starts, was outpitched by the Cards' Jeff Weaver, who combined with the St. Louis bullpen to limit the Mets' vaunted offense to just two runs. Albert Pujols, held in check for most of the series, hit a solo home run to get the Cardinals offense started in the fourth inning.

GAME 6

St. Louis	0 0 0	0 0 0	0 0 2	**2**	**7**	**1**
NY Mets	1 0 0	1 0 0	2 0 x	**4**	**10**	**0**

W—NYM: Maine. **L**—StL: Carpenter. **LOB**—StL: 8; NYM: 7. **2B**—StL: Rolen, Taguchi. **HR**—NYM: Reyes. **GIDP**—StL: Rolen, Duncan; NYM: Valentin. **SB**—StL: Eckstein; NYM: Reyes 2, Tucker. **HBP**—StL: Encarnacion; NYM: Green. **IBB**—StL: Pujols. **E**—StL: Rolen. **T**—2:56. **A**—56,334.

Recap: Right-hander John Maine tossed 5⅓ shutout innings for the Mets, allowing just two hits, both of them in the first inning when he faced his only real trouble, escaping a bases-loaded jam without allowing a run. Jose Reyes then led off the bottom of the inning with a solo homer off St. Louis ace Chris Carpenter to get the Mets offense on track. Shawn Green singled in a run in the fourth inning and Paul LoDuca put the game out of reach by driving in two with a single in the seventh.

GAME 7

St. Louis	0 1 0	0 0 0	0 0 2	**3**	**6**	**1**
NY Mets	1 0 0	0 0 0	0 0 0	**1**	**4**	**1**

W—StL: Flores **L**—NYM: Heilman. **SV**—Wainwright. **LOB**—NYM: 11; StL: 6. **2B**—StL: Eckstein; NYM: Beltran. **HR**—StL: Molina. **GIDP**—StL: Encarnacion. **HBP**—NYM: Valentin; StL: Eckstein. **IBB**—StL: Pujols 2; NYM: Green. **E**—StL: Rolen; NYM: Delgado. **T**—3:23. **A**—56,357.

Recap: Cardinals' righthander Jeff Suppan reprised his brilliant performance in Game 3, allowing one run on a David Wright single in the first inning before settling down and holding the Mets hitless until he was removed after walking the leadoff hitter in the eighth inning. Closer Adam Wainwright entered the game in the ninth and allowed a pair of hits and a walk to load the bases but struck out Carlos Beltran looking to end the game and deliver the Cardinals the National League pennant and a trip to the World Series. The Mets' Oliver Perez pitched almost as well as Suppan, allowing the Cardinals just a single run in six innings of work, but Aaron Heilman, pitching his second inning in relief, allowed a two-run homer by St. Louis catcher Yadier Molina in the top of the ninth for the winning margin of victory. In recognition of his two brilliant outings, Suppan was named the NLCS MVP.

American League Division Playoffs

Oct 3 ....Oakland 3 at Minnesota 2
Oct 4 ....Oakland 5 at Minnesota 2

Oct 6 ....Minnesota 3 at Oakland 8

(Oakland won series 3–0)

Oct 3 ....Detroit 4 at NY Yankees 8
Oct 5 ....Detroit 4 at NY Yankees 3

Oct 6 ....NY Yankees 0 at Detroit 6
Oct 7 ....NY Yankees 3 at Detroit 8

(Detroit won series 3–1)

American League Championship Series

Oct 10 ....Detroit 5 at Oakland 1
Oct 11 ....Detroit 8 at Oakland 5

Oct 13 ....Oakland 0 at Detroit 3
Oct 14 ....Oakland 3 at Detroit 6

(Detroit won series 4–0)

GAME 1

Detroit	0	0	2	3	0	0	0	0	0	**5**	**11**	**1**
Oakland	0	0	0	0	0	0	0	1	0	**1**	**8**	**1**

W—Robertson. **L**—Zito. **LOB**—Det 11, Oak 9.
2B—Oak: Payton 2, Bradley; Det: Granderson, Inge.
HR—Det: Inge, Rodriguez. **GIDP**—Oak: Scutaro,
Bradley, Kotsay 2. **E**—StL: Jimenez; Det: Guillen.
T—3:20. **A**—35,655.

Recap: Detroit third baseman Brandon Inge, batting
ninth, went three-for-three, driving in two runs on a
solo home run in the third inning and a double in the
fourth as the Detroit Tigers overwhelmed the
Oakland A's 5–1 in the opening game of the ALCS.
Catcher Ivan Rodriguez also homered for the Tigers,
who got strong pitching from starter Nate Robertson
and their talented bullpen, which combined to hold
the A's to a single run on an eighth-inning double by
Oakland leftfielder Jay Payton. A's ace Barry Zito
wasn't sharp, allowing five runs on seven hits in just
3⅔ innings.

GAME 2

Detroit	0	1	0	4	0	2	0	0	1	**8**	**11**	**0**
Oakland	1	0	2	0	0	1	1	0	0	**5**	**11**	**1**

W—Verlander. **L**—Loaiza. **SV**—Jones. **LOB**—Det: 5;
Oak: 8. **2B**—Det: Guillen, Monroe; Oak: Kotsay 2.
HR—Det: Gomez, Granderson. Oak: Bradley 2,
Chavez. **GIDP**—Det: Ordonez. **SAC**—Det: Monroe,
Inge. **IBB**—Det: Polanco. **E**—Oak: Jimenez.
T—3:06. **A**—36,168.

Recap: Tigers second baseman Placido Polanco
ignited the Detroit offense, sparking a four-run fourth
inning with a single and a run. He finished three-for-
four, reached base four times and, up to that point,
was hittiing .440 (11 for 25) in the postseason.
Estaban Loaiza, the A's starter was unable to tame
the Tigers. Despite being staked to leads in the first
and third innings, Loaiza gave back all of the runs
(and then some) in the second and fourth frames to
put the A's in the hole. He allowed seven runs on
nine hits over six innings. In the top of the fourth,
after falling behind 3-1, the Tigers roared back and
scored four runs on four hits, one walk and a sac fly.
They never trailed again.

GAME 3

Oakland	0	0	0	0	0	0	0	0	0	**0**	**2**	**0**
Detroit	2	0	0	0	1	0	0	0	X	**3**	**6**	**0**

W—Rogers. **L**—Harden. **SV**—Jones. **LOB**—Oak: 3;
Det: 9. **2B**—Det: Polanco. **HR**—Det: Monroe.
GIDP—Oak: Jimenez, Kielty; Det: Guillen. **HBP**—Oak: Thomas. **SB**—Det: Granderson, Infante.
T—2:57. **A**—41,669.

Recap: The Tigers leadoff batter Curtis Granderson
walked three times, including in the first inning,
when he eventually came around to score the first
run of the game. The middle of the A's batting
order—Milton Bradley, Frank Thomas, Jay Payton
and Eric Chavez—went a combined 0-for-12 in the
game. A's starter Rich Harden struggled with his
control early as he walked Granderson on four
pitches. Harden then proceeded to allow back-to-
back singles to Craig Monroe and Placido Polanco,
who knocked in Granderson. Monroe scored the
second run of the game on a fielder's choice
grounder by Magglio Ordonez. The A's never
seriously threatened the Tigers' lead thereafter.

GAME 4

Oakland	2	0	0	1	0	0	0	0	0	**3**	**8**	**1**
Detroit	0	0	0	0	2	1	0	0	3	**6**	**11**	**0**

W—Ledezma. **L**—Street. **LOB**—Oak: 9; Det: 8.
2B—Det: Bradley, Chavez; Det: Granderson,
Monroe. **HR**—Oak: Payton; Det: Ordonez. **GIDP**—
Oak: Thomas; Det: Guillen. **IBB**—Det: Inge.
E—Oak: Chavez.
T—3.23. **A**—42,967.

Recap: Placido Polanco, the Tigers no. 3 hitter, had
three hits, including a single in the ninth inning that
preceded Magglio Ordonez's game-winning, three-
run home run. Polanco batted .529 in the Tigers'
four-game ALCS sweep, and was named MVP of
the series. Frank Thomas went 0-for-3 in this game,
stranding three baserunners in the process, and
finished 0-for-13 in the series. At the bottom of the
fifth, with the A's holding a 3-0 lead, the Tigers
suddenly got back into the game thanks to back to
back doubles by Curtis Granderson and Craig
Moore, which drove in two runs. The Tigers
advanced to the World Series for the first time
since 1984.

Oct 21 ....St. Louis 7 at Detroit 2
Oct 22 ....St. Louis 1 at Detroit 3

Oct 24 ....Detroit 0 at St. Louis 5
Oct 26 ....Detroit 4 at St. Louis 5
Oct 27 ....Detroit 2 at St. Louis 4

(St. Louis won series 4–1)

GAME 1

St. Louis	0	1	3	0	0	3	0	0	0	**7**	**8**	**2**
Detroit	1	0	0	0	0	0	0	0	1	**2**	**4**	**3**

W—A. Reyes. **L**—Verlander. **LOB**—StL: 4, Det: 4. **2B**—StL: Duncan, Rolen; Det: Monroe. **HR**—StL: Pujols, Rolen; Det: Monroe. **E**—StL: Encarnacion, Rolen; Det: Inge 2, Verlander. **T**—2:54. **A**—42,479.

Recap: Rest can be overrated. The St. Louis Cardinals managed just fine in Game 1 of the World Series without much. Rookie Anthony Reyes easily outpitched Detroit rookie Justin Verlander, lasting into the ninth inning. Albert Pujols made Detroit pay for pitching to him, and Scott Rolen also homered to help St. Louis cruise past the ragged Tigers 7-2 in the World Series opener. First base was open and Chris Duncan was on second when Pujols stepped to the plate with two outs in the third inning and St. Louis ahead 2-1. Verlander challenged him right away with a 93 mph fastball that the slugger drove over the right-field fence for a 4-1 lead. The three-run cushion was more than enough for Reyes, who retired 17 consecutive batters before Carlos Guillen's seventh-inning single. The right-hander was finally lifted after Craig Monroe's homer on the first pitch of the ninth and Braden Looper was brought in to finish the game.

GAME 2

St. Louis	0	0	0	0	0	0	0	0	1	**1**	**4**	**1**
Detroit	2	0	0	0	1	0	0	0	X	**3**	**10**	**1**

W—Rogers. **L**—Weaver. **SV**—Jones. **LOB**—StL: 7; Det: 10. **2B**—StL: Edmonds; Det: Guillen. **3B**—Det: Guillen. **HR**—Det: Monroe. **SAC**—Det: Santiago. **GIDP**—StL: Eckstein; Det: Granderson, Rodriguez. **HBP**—StL: Wilson; Det: Casey, Polanco. **E**—StL: Pujols; Det: Jones. **T**—2:55. **A**—42,533.

Recap: An embarrassing error by Detroit closer Todd Jones helped St. Louis get within two runs Sunday night, and the Cardinals loaded the bases with two outs in the ninth inning for Yadier Molina. But Jones got Molina to hit an easy grounder to shortstop, preserving a 3-1 victory that tied the World Series at a game apiece. Craig Monroe hit a solo shot in the first and Carlos Guillen, Detroit's quiet star, who went three-for-three with a walk in the game, doubled in what ended up being the winning run in the same innning. But it was Kenny Rogers' smudged throwing hand that drew all the attention. After Cardinals' manager LaRussa made mention of it to the home plate umpire during the first inning and Rogers was discreetly warned to clean off whatever it was, his hand looked noticeably cleaner for the rest of the game. Still, his breaking balls befuddled the big bats in the Cardinals' lineup all night long, and he gave up only three hits over eight-plus innings to earn the victory.

GAME 3

Detroit	0	0	0	0	0	0	0	0	0	**0**	**3**	**1**
St. Louis	0	0	0	2	0	0	2	1	X	**5**	**7**	**0**

W—Carpenter. **L**—Robertson. **LOB**—StL: 11; Det: 2. **2B**—StL: Pujols, Edmonds, Molina. **GIDP**—Det: Rolen; Det: Inge. **IBB**—StL: Molina, Edmonds. **HBP**—StL: Pujols. **E**—Det: Zumaya. **T**—3:03. **A**—46,513.

Recap: Chris Carpenter was every bit the ace the St. Louis Cardinals expected and only Brandon Inge made it as far as third base when he reached with a single and then advanced on a sacrifice and a wild pitch in the third inning. Edmonds started the Cardinals scoring in the fourth, rifling a double down the right-field line with the bases loaded. St Louis then put the game away for good in the seventh, scoring two more runs on a throwing error from Detroit reliever Joel Zumaya, who had come in with one out and one on in the sixth.

GAME 4

Detroit	0	1	2	0	0	0	0	1	0	**4**	**10**	**1**
St. Louis	0	0	1	0	0	1	2	1	X	**5**	**9**	**0**

W—Wainwright. **L**—Zumaya. **LOB**—StL: 9; Det: 9. **2B**—StL: Eckstein, Molina, Rolen 2; Det: Granderson, Rodriguez, Inge. **HR**—Det: Casey. **GIDP**—StL: Duncan. **SB**—StL: Miles; Det: Guillen. **IBB**—StL: Miles, Pujols; Det: Inge. **E**—Det: Rodney. **T**—3:35. **A**—46,470.

Recap: Fernando Rodney's error in the pivotal seventh inning was the fourth by a Detroit pitcher in the World Series—breaking a record—and the St. Louis Cardinals went on to win 5-4 and take a 3-1 series lead. Rodney fielded a sacrifice bunt cleanly in front of the mound, turned and threw to first base, but the toss went far over 5'10" second baseman Placido Polanco's head. David Eckstein scored on the error to tie it at 3. Eckstein, Game 4's undisputed hero, went 4-for-5 with two RBIs, including the game-winner, a two-out double in the eighth inning. Detroit's listless bats had reawakened in Game 4 and they had tied the game at four apiece in the top of the eighth on a RBI double by Inge, one of four extra-base hits by the Tigers on the night. However, Detroit's stumbling defense cost them once again, as two miscues in the Busch Stadium outfield, one by Monroe, one by Granderson, fueled a seventh-inning Cardinals rally that gave St. Louis its first lead of the night.

GAME 5

```
Detroit      000  200  000   2  5  2
St. Louis    010  200  10X   4  8  1
```

W—StL: Weaver. **L**—Det: Verlander. **SV**—StL: Wainwright. **LOB**—StL: 8; Det: 6. **HR**—Det: Casey. **2B**—Det: Casey 2, Inge. **E**—StL: Duncan; Det: Inge, Verlander.
T—2:56. **A**—46,638.

Recap: "I think we shocked the world," Cardinals center fielder Jim Edmonds said, only moments after closer Adam Wainwright struck out Brandon Inge for the final out, sealing the Cardinals' Game 5 victory and the franchise's tenth World Series title. "No one believed in us, but we believed in ourselves," added David Eckstein, the 5'7"shortstop who was selected as Series MVP after batting .364. St. Louis had gone ahead on Eckstein's infield single in the second, with Inge making a diving stop over the bag but throwing the ball low and wide to first.

Tigers starter Verlander also continued the Tigers' fielding woes, throwing away a routine force out at third during the bottom of the fourth that eventually led to a 3–2 lead for St. Louis. That error raised the Tigers' World Series total to eight and their eight unearned runs in the Series were the most allowed by a team in forty years. Detroit had gone ahead 2–1 in the top of the fourth when Casey, who batted a Series-high .529, while his team hit a combined .199, homered for the second straight night. Rolen, who led Cardinals' batters at .421, added a big run with a two-out RBI single in the seventh off reliever Fernando Rodney, extending his postseason hitting streak to 10 games.

2006 World Series Composite Box Score

DETROIT

BATTING	AB	R	H	HR	RBI	Avg
Granderson	21	1	2	0	0	.095
Monroe	20	3	3	2	2	.150
Ordonez	19	2	2	0	0	.105
Rodriguez	19	1	3	0	1	.158
Casey	17	2	9	2	5	.529
Guillen	17	2	6	0	2	.353
Inge	17	0	6	0	1	.353
Polanco	17	0	0	0	0	.000
Santiago	5	0	1	0	0	.200
Gomez	3	0	0	0	0	.000
Infante	1	0	0	0	0	.000
Thames	1	0	0	0	0	.000
Pitchers	4	0	0	0	0	.000
Totals	**161**	**11**	**32**	**4**	**19**	**.199**

PITCHING	G	IP	H	BB	SO	ERA
Verlander	2	11	12	5	12	5.73
Rogers	1	8	2	3	5	0.00
Bonderman	1	5.1	6	4	4	3.38
Robertson	1	5	5	3	3	3.60
Rodney	4	4	5	4	5	4.50
Zumaya	3	3	1	3	3	3.00
Grilli	2	1.2	0	1	0	0.00
Jones	2	1.2	3	0	0	0.00
Ledezma	2	1.1	2	0	1	0.00
Miner	1	0.2	0	0	0	0.00
Walker	1	0.1	0	0	1	0.00
Totals	**5**	**42**	**36**	**23**	**34**	**3.00**

ST.LOUIS

BATTING	AB	R	H	HR	RBI	Avg
Eckstein	22	3	8	0	4	.364
Rolen	19	5	8	1	2	.421
Edmonds	17	1	4	0	4	.235
Molina	17	3	7	0	1	.412
Pujols	15	3	3	1	2	.200
Belliard	12	0	0	0	0	.000
Taguchi	11	3	2	0	0	.182
Wilson	10	1	2	0	1	.200
Duncan	8	1	1	0	1	.125
Encarnacion	8	0	0	0	1	.000
Miles	6	2	1	0	0	.167
Spiezio	4	0	0	0	0	.000
Pitchers	9	0	0	0	0	.000
Totals	**158**	**22**	**36**	**2**	**16**	**.228**

PITCHING	G	IP	H	BB	SO	ERA
Weaver	2	13	13	2	14	2.77
Carpenter	1	8	3	0	6	0.00
Reyes	1	8	4	1	4	2.25
Suppan	1	6	8	2	4	4.50
Wainwright	3	3	2	1	5	0.00
Looper	3	2.1	1	0	1	3.86
Flores	1	1	1	0	0	0.00
Johnson	2	1	0	0	1	0.00
Kinney	2	1	0	2	1	0.00
Thompson	1	0.2	0	0	1	0.00
Totals	**5**	**44**	**32**	**8**	**37**	**2.05**

National League Batting

BATTING AVERAGE

Freddy Sanchez, Pit .... .344
Miguel Cabrera, Fla.............. .339
Albert Pujols, StL .... .331
Garrett Atkins, Col .... .329
Matt Holliday, Col .... .326
Paul Lo Duca, NYM .... .318
Lance Berkman, Hou .... .315
Ryan Howard, Phil................ .313
David Wright, NYM.............. .311
Chase Utley, Phi .... .309

HITS

Juan Pierre, Chi 204
Chase Utley, Phi....................203
Freddy Sanchez, Pit..............200
Garrett Atkins, Col.................198
Rafael Furcal, LAD................196
Matt Holliday, Col..................196
Miguel Cabrera, Fla 195
Jose Reyes, NYM 194
Jimmy Rollins, Phi 191
Hanley Ramirez, Fla...............185

DOUBLES

Freddy Sanchez, Pit.................53
Luis Gonzalez, Ari....................52
Miguel Cabrera, Fla 50
Garrett Atkins, Col....................48
Scott Rolen, StL 48
Ryan Zimmerman 47

TRIPLES

Jose Reyes, NYM 17
Juan Pierre, Chi 13
Dave Roberts, SD 13
Steve Finley, SF........................12
Kenny Lofton, LAD....................12
Hanley Ramirez, Fla..................11

HOME RUNS

Ryan Howard, Phil 58
Albert Pujols, StL 49
Alfonso Soriano, Was................46
Lance Berkman, Hou.................45
Carlos Beltran, NYM 41
Andruw Jones, Atl.....................41
Adam Dunn, Cin 40
Carlos Delgado, NYM...............38
Aramis Ramirez, Chi 38
Jason Bay, Pit 35

RUNS SCORED

Chase Utley, Phi.....................131
Carlos Beltran, NYM 127
Jimmy Rollins, Phi 127
Jose Reyes, NYM 122
Matt Holliday, Col....................119
Albert Pujols, Stl.....................119
Hanley Ramirez, Fla................119
Alfonso Soriano, Was...............119
Garrett Atkins, Col...................117
Rafael Furcal, LAD..................113
Miguel Cabrera, Fla 112

STOLEN BASES

Jose Reyes, NYM 64
Juan Pierre, Chi 58
Hanley Ramirez, Fla.................51
Dave Roberts, SD 49
Felipe Lopez, Was 44

RUNS BATTED IN

Ryan Howard, Phil 149
Albert Pujols, StL 137
Lance Berkman, Hou................136
Andruw Jones, Atl....................129
Garrett Atkins, Col...................120
Aramis Ramirez, Chi 119
Carlos Beltran, NYM 116
David Wright, NYM...................116
Miguel Cabrera, Fla 114
Carlos Delgado, NYM...............114

SLUGGING PERCENTAGE

Albert Pujols, StL .... .671
Ryan Howard, Phi .... .659
Lance Berkman, Hou................ .621
Carlos Beltran, NYM .... .594
Matt Holliday, Col.................... .586

ON-BASE PERCENTAGE

Albert Pujols, StL .... .431
Miguel Cabrera, Fla .... .430
Nick Johnson, Was .... .428
Ryan Howard, Phi .... .425
Lance Berkman, Hou .... .420

BASES ON BALLS

Barry Bonds, SF.......................115
Adam Dunn, Cin 112
Nick Johnson, Was 110
Ryan Howard, Phi 108
Brian Giles, SD 104

National League Pitching

EARNED RUN AVERAGE

Roy Oswalt, Hou 2.98
Chris Carpenter, StL 3.09
Brandon Webb, Ari 3.10
Bronson Arroyo, Cin................3.29
Carlos Zambrano, Chi 3.41
Chris Young, SD.....................3.46
John Smoltz, Atl 3.49
Jason Schmidt, SF..................3.59
Derek Lowe, LAD...................3.63
Clay Hensley, SD 3.71

SAVES

Trevor Hoffman, SD..................46
Billy Wagner, Phi 40
Joe Borowski, FLA 36
Tom Gordon, Phi 34
Jason Isringhausen, StL 33
Brad Lidge, Hou 32
Brian Fuentes, Col 31
Chad Cordero, Was 29
Ryan Dempster, Chi.................24

WINS

Aaron Harang, Cin 16
Derek Lowe, LAD......................16
Brad Penny, LAD......................16
John Smoltz, Atl........................16
Brandon Webb, Ari 16
Carlos Zambrano, Chi 16

Five tied with 15.

GAMES PITCHED

Salomón Torres, Pit 94
Matt Capps, Pit 85
Jon Rauch, Was........................85
Bob Howry, Chi 84
Mike Stanton, SF......................82

INNINGS PITCHED

Bronson Arroyo, Cin.............240.2
Brandon Webb, Ari 235.0
Aaron Harang, Cin................234.1
John Smoltz, Atl 232.0
Dontrelle Willis, Fla...............223.1

STRIKEOUTS

Aaron Harang, Cin....................216
Jake Peavy, SD 215
John Smoltz, Atl 211
Carlos Zambrano, Chi 210
Brett Myers, Phi........................189
Bronson Arroyo, Cin..................184
Chris Carpenter, StL 184
Jason Schmidt, SF....................180
Matt Cain, SF 179

COMPLETE GAMES

Aaron Harang, Cin.......................6
Chris Carpenter, StL 5
Brandon Webb, Ari 5
Dontrelle Willis, Fla.....................4
Bronson Arroyo, Cin....................3

SHUTOUTS

Chris Carpenter. StL 3
Brandon Webb, Ari 3
Dave Bush, Mil...........................2

American League Batting

BATTING AVERAGE
Joe Mauer, Min 347
Derek Jeter, NYY 343
Robinson Cano, NYY 342
Miguel Tejada, Bal 330
Vladimir Guerrero, LAA........329
Ichiro Suzuki, Sea.................322
Justin Morneau, Min .321
Manny Ramírez, Bos 321
Carlos Guillen, Det 320
Reed Johnson, Tor..............319

HITS
Ichiro Suzuki, Sea.................224
Michael Young, Tex..............217
Derek Jeter, NYY 214
Miguel Tejada, Bal 214
Vladimir Guerrero, LAA........200
Gary Matthews, Tex..............194
Justin Morneau, Min 190
Grady Sizemore, Cle 190
Vernon Wells, Tor 185
Carl Crawford, TB.................183

DOUBLES
Grady Sizemore, Cle 53
Michael Young, Tex...............52
Mike Lowell, Bos...................47
Lyle Overbay, Tor 46
Orlando Cabrera, LAA............45
Mark Teixeira, Tex 45

TRIPLES
Carl Crawford, TB.................16
Grady Sizemore, Cle 11
Curtis Granderson, Det 9
Ichiro Suzuki, Sea...................9
Chone Figgins, LAA 8

HOME RUNS
David Ortiz, Bos 54
Jermaine Dye, Chi.................44
Travis Hafner, Cle 42
Jim Thome, Chi.....................42
Frank Thomas, Oak 42
Troy Glaus, Tor 39
Jason Giambi, NYY 37
Paul Konerko, Chi 35
Manny Ramírez, Bos.............35
Alex Rodríguez, NYY 35

RUNS SCORED
Grady Sizemore, Cle 134
Derek Jeter, NYY 118
Johnny Damon, Bos 115
David Ortiz, Bos 115
Alex Rodríguez, NYY 113
Ichiro Suzuki, Sea.................110
Jim Thome, Chi.....................108
Nick Swisher, Oak.................106
Troy Glaus, Tor 105
Jermaine Dye, Chi 103

STOLEN BASES
Carl Crawford, TB 58
Chone Figgins, LAA 52
Corey Patterson 45
Ichiro Suzuki, Sea..................45
Scott Podsednik.....................33

RUNS BATTED IN
David Ortiz, Bos 137
Justin Morneau, Min 130
Raul Ibanez, Sea 123
Alex Rodríguez, NYY 121
Jermaine Dye, Chi.................120
Travis Hafner, Cle 117
Vladimir Guerrero, LAA..........116
Frank Thomas, Oak 114
Jason Giambi, NYY 113
Paul Konerko, Chi 113

SLUGGING PERCENTAGE
Travis Hafner, Cle 659
David Ortiz, Bos 636
Jermaine Dye, Chi 622
Manny Ramírez, Bos 619
Jim Thome, Chi......................598

ON-BASE PERCENTAGE
Travis Hafner, Cle 439
Manny Ramírez, Bos..............439
Joe Mauer, Min 429
Derek Jeter, NYY 417
Jim Thome, Chi......................416

BASES ON BALLS
David Ortiz, Bos 119
Jason Giambi, NYY 110
Jim Thome, Chi......................107
Travis Hafner, Cle 100
Manny Ramírez, Bos..............100

American League Pitching

EARNED RUN AVERAGE
Johan Santana, Min...............2.77
Roy Halladay, Tor 3.19
C.C. Sabathia, Cle.................3.22
Mike Mussina, NYY...............3.51
John Lackey, LAA..................3.56
Kelvim Escobar, LAA.............3.61
Justin Verlander, Det.............3.63
Chien-Ming Wang, NYY........3.63
Erik Bedard, Bal....................3.76
Barry Zito, Oak 3.83

SAVES
Francisco Rodríguez, LAA 47
Bobby Jenks, Chi 41
B.J. Ryan, Tor 38
Todd Jones, Det 37
Huston Street, Oak 37
Joe Nathan, Mln 36
J.J. Putz, Sea........................36
Jonathan Papelbon, Bos 35
Mariano Rivera, NYY 34
Chris Ray, Bal 33

WINS
Johan Santana, Min................19
Chien-Ming Wang, NYY...........19
Jon Garland, Chi 18
Freddy Garcia, Chi 17
Randy Johnson, NYY..............17
Kenny Rogers, Det 17
Justin Verlander, Det..............17

Six tied with 16.

GAMES PITCHED
Scott Proctor, NYY 83
Shawn Camp, TB....................75
Juan Rincon, Minn..................75
Scot Shields, LAA...................74
Kyle Farnsworth, NYY.............72
J.J. Putz, Sea.........................72

INNINGS PITCHED
Johan Santana, Min...............233.2
Danny Haren, Oak..................223.2
Barry Zito, Oak 221.0
Roy Halladay, Tor...................220.0

SHUTOUTS
John Lackey, LAA.........................2
C.C. Sabathia, Cle........................2
Jeremy Sowers, Cle......................2
Jake Westbrook, Cle.....................2

COMPLETE GAMES
C.C. Sabathia, Cle........................6
Roy Halladay, Tor.........................4
Kris Benson, Bal..........................3

Three tied with 3.

STRIKEOUTS
Johan Santana, Min............... 245
Jeremy Bonderman 202
John Lackey, LAA...................190
Javier Vazquez, Chi................184
Curt Schilling, Bos 183
Danny Haren, Oak...................176
Felix Hernandez, Sea 176
Randy Johnson, NYY.............. 172
Mike Mussina, NYY.................172
C.C. Sabathia, Cle..................172

National League

TEAM BATTING	G	AB	R	H	2B	3B	HR	TB	RBI	BA	OBP	SLG	OPS
Los Angeles Dodgers..	162	5628	820	1552	307	58	153	2434	787	.276	.348	.432	.780
Colorado Rockies......	162	5562	813	1504	325	54	157	2408	761	.270	.341	.433	.774
Atlanta Braves..........	162	5583	849	1510	312	26	222	2540	818	.270	.337	.455	.792
St. Louis Cardinals	161	5522	781	1484	292	27	184	2382	745	.269	.337	.431	.768
Chicago Cubs	162	5587	716	1496	271	46	166	2357	677	.268	.319	.422	.741
Arizona Diamondbacks..	162	5645	773	1506	331	38	160	2393	743	.267	.331	.424	.755
Philadelphia Phillies ..	162	5687	865	1518	294	41	216	2542	823	.267	.347	.447	.794
New York Mets	162	5558	834	1469	323	41	200	2474	800	.264	.334	.445	.779
Florida Marlins..........	162	5502	758	1454	309	42	182	2393	713	.264	.331	.435	.766
Pittsburgh Pirates......	162	5558	691	1462	286	17	141	2205	656	.263	.327	.397	.724
San Diego Padres	162	5576	731	1465	298	38	161	2322	698	.263	.332	.416	.748
Washington Nationals..	162	5495	746	1437	322	22	164	2295	695	.262	.338	.418	.756
San Francisco Giants..	161	5472	746	1418	297	52	163	2308	711	.259	.324	.422	.746
Milwaukee Brewers ...	162	5433	730	1400	301	20	180	2281	695	.258	.327	.420	.747
Cincinnati Reds.........	162	5515	749	1419	291	12	217	2385	718	.257	.336	.432	.768
Houston Astros..........	162	5521	735	1407	275	27	174	2258	708	.255	.332	.409	.741

TEAM PITCHING	GP	W	L	SV	SVO	CG	SHO	R	ERA	IP	Ks	BB
San Diego Padres	162	88	74	50	71	4	11	629	3.87	1463.2	1097	468
Houston Astros..........	162	82	80	42	60	5	12	666	4.08	1468.2	1160	480
New York Mets	162	97	65	43	58	5	12	673	4.14	1461.1	1161	527
Los Angeles Dodgers..	162	88	74	40	61	1	10	686	4.23	1460.1	1068	492
Florida Marlins...........	162	78	84	41	68	6	6	696	4.37	1433.1	1088	622
Arizona Diamondbacks..162	162	76	86	34	54	8	9	727	4.48	1459.2	1115	536
Cincinnati Reds.........	162	80	82	36	60	9	10	725	4.51	1445.2	1053	464
Pittsburgh Pirates......	162	67	95	39	60	2	10	720	4.52	1435.0	1060	620
St. Louis Cardinals	161	83	78	38	57	6	9	721	4.54	1429.2	970	504
Philadelphia Phillies ..	162	85	77	42	64	4	6	747	4.60	1460.1	1138	512
Atlanta Braves..........	162	79	83	38	67	6	6	736	4.60	1441.1	1049	572
San Francisco Giants..	161	76	85	37	59	7	9	735	4.63	1429.2	992	584
Colorado Rockies......	162	76	86	34	58	5	8	749	4.66	1447.1	952	553
Chicago Cubs	162	66	96	29	46	2	7	758	4.74	1439.0	1250	687
Milwaukee Brewers ...	162	75	87	43	67	7	8	763	4.82	1425.2	1145	514
Washington Nationals..	162	71	91	32	55	1	3	803	5.03	1436.1	960	584

American League

TEAM BATTING	G	AB	R	H	2B	3B	HR	TB	RBI	BA	OBP	SLG	OPS
Minnesota Twins	162	5602	801	1608	275	34	143	2380	754	.287	.347	.425	.772
New York Yankees	162	5651	930	1608	327	21	210	2607	902	.285	.363	.461	.824
Toronto Blue Jays	162	5596	809	1591	348	27	199	2590	778	.284	.348	.463	.811
Cleveland Indians	162	5619	870	1576	351	27	196	2569	839	.280	.349	.457	.806
Chicago White Sox	162	5657	868	1586	291	20	236	2625	839	.280	.342	.464	.806
Texas Rangers	162	5659	835	1571	357	23	183	2523	799	.278	.338	.446	.784
Baltimore Orioles	162	5610	768	1556	288	20	164	2376	727	.277	.339	.424	.763
Los Angeles Angels	162	5609	766	1539	309	29	159	2383	737	.274	.334	.425	.759
Detroit Tigers	162	5642	822	1548	294	40	203	2531	785	.274	.329	.449	.778
Seattle Mariners	162	5670	756	1540	266	42	172	2406	703	.272	.325	.424	.749
Kansas City Royals	162	5589	757	1515	335	37	124	2296	718	.271	.332	.411	.743
Boston Red Sox	162	5619	820	1510	327	16	192	2445	777	.269	.351	.435	.786
Oakland Athletics	162	5500	771	1429	266	22	175	2264	735	.260	.340	.412	.752
Tampa Bay Devil Rays	162	5474	689	1395	267	33	190	2298	650	.255	.314	.420	.734

TEAM PITCHING	GP	W	L	SV	SVO	CG	SHO	R	ERA	IP	Ks	BB
Detroit Tigers	162	95	67	46	62	3	16	675	3.84	1448.0	1003	489
Minnesota Twins	162	96	66	40	50	1	6	683	3.95	1439.1	1164	356
Los Angeles Angels	162	89	73	50	63	5	12	732	4.04	1452.2	1164	471
Oakland Athletics	162	93	69	54	74	5	11	727	4.21	1451.2	1003	529
Toronto Blue Jays	162	87	75	42	62	6	8	754	4.37	1428.1	1076	504
Cleveland Indians	162	78	84	24	47	13	13	782	4.41	1423.1	948	429
New York Yankees	162	97	65	43	60	5	8	767	4.41	1443.2	1019	496
Seattle Mariners	162	78	84	47	67	6	6	792	4.60	1446.2	1067	560
Texas Rangers	162	80	82	42	65	3	8	784	4.60	1431.1	972	496
Chicago White Sox	162	90	72	46	63	5	11	794	4.61	1449.0	1012	433
Boston Red Sox	162	86	76	46	69	3	6	825	4.83	1441.1	1070	509
Tampa Bay Devil Rays	162	61	101	33	54	3	7	856	4.96	1420.1	979	606
Baltimore Orioles	162	70	92	35	56	5	9	899	5.35	1419.0	1016	613
Kansas City Royals	162	62	100	35	66	3	5	971	5.65	1426.1	904	637

Chicago Cubs

BATTING	G	AB	R	H	2B	3B	HR	RBI	TB	BB	SO	SB	OBP	SLG	BA
Juan Pierre	162	699	87	204	32	13	3	40	271	32	38	58	.330	.338	.292
Aramis Ramirez	157	594	93	173	38	4	38	119	333	50	63	2	.352	.561	.291
Ronny Cedeno	151	534	51	131	18	7	6	41	181	17	109	8	.271	.339	.245
Jacque Jones	149	533	73	152	31	1	27	81	266	35	116	9	.334	.499	.285
Matt Murton	144	455	70	135	22	3	13	62	202	45	62	5	.365	.444	.297
Michael Barrett	107	375	54	115	25	3	16	53	194	33	41	0	.368	.517	.307
Henry Bianco	74	241	23	64	15	2	6	37	101	14	38	0	.304	.419	.266
Neifi Perez	87	236	27	60	13	1	2	24	81	5	21	0	.266	.343	.254
John Mabry	107	210	16	43	8	1	5	25	68	23	57	0	.283	.324	.205
Cesar Izturis	54	192	14	47	9	1	1	18	61	12	14	1	.295	.318	.245
Phil Nevin	67	179	26	49	4	0	12	33	89	17	52	0	.335	.497	.274

PITCHING	GP	GS	W–L	SV	SHO	R	ERA	IP	Ks	BB
Carlos Zambrano	33	33	16-7	0	0	91	3.41	214.0	210	115
Sean Marshall	24	24	6-9	0	0	85	5.59	125.2	77	59
Rich Hill	17	16	6-7	0	1	51	4.17	99.1	90	39
Carlos Marmol	19	13	5-7	0	0	54	6.08	77.0	59	59
Bob Howry	84	0	4-5	5	0	28	3.17	76.2	71	17
Roberto Novoa	66	0	2-1	0	0	47	4.26	76.0	53	32
Ryan Dempster	74	0	1-9	24	0	47	4.80	75.0	67	36
Glendon Rusch	25	9	3-8	0	0	57	7.46	66.1	59	33
Will Ohman	78	0	1-1	0	0	30	4.13	65.1	74	34
Scott Eyre	74	0	1-3	0	0	25	3.38	61.1	73	30
Angel Guzman	15	10	0-6	0	0	48	7.39	56.0	60	37

Cincinnati Reds

BATTING	G	AB	R	H	2B	3B	HR	RBI	TB	BB	SO	SB	OBP	SLG	BA
Adam Dunn	160	561	99	131	24	0	40	92	275	112	194	7	.365	.490	.234
Brandon Phillips	149	536	65	148	28	1	17	75	229	35	88	25	.324	.427	.276
Scott Hatteberg	141	456	62	132	28	0	13	51	199	74	41	2	.389	.436	.289
Royce Clayton	137	454	49	117	30	1	2	40	155	30	85	14	.307	.341	.258
Ryan Freel	132	454	67	123	30	2	8	27	181	57	98	37	.363	.399	.271
Rich Aurilia	122	440	61	132	25	1	23	70	228	34	51	3	.349	.518	.300
Ken Griffey	109	428	62	108	19	0	27	72	208	39	78	0	.316	.486	.252
Edwin Encarnacion	117	406	60	112	33	1	15	72	192	41	78	6	.359	.473	.276
David Ross	90	247	37	63	15	1	21	52	143	37	75	0	.353	.579	.255
Jason LaRue	72	191	22	37	5	0	8	21	66	27	51	1	.317	.346	.194
Javier Valentin	92	186	24	50	6	1	8	27	82	13	29	0	.313	.441	.269
Chris Denorfia	49	106	14	30	6	0	1	7	39	11	21	1	.356	.368	.283
Juan Castro	54	95	8	27	5	1	2	14	40	5	13	0	.320	.421	.284

PITCHING	GP	GS	W–L	SV	SHO	R	ERA	IP	Ks	BB
Bronson Arroyo	35	35	14-11	0	1	98	3.29	240.2	184	64
Aaron Harang	36	35	16-11	0	2	109	3.76	234.1	216	56
Eric Milton	26	26	8-8	0	0	94	5.19	152.2	90	42
Elizardo Ramirez	21	19	4-9	0	0	70	5.37	104.0	69	29
Todd Coffey	81	0	6-7	8	0	34	3.58	78.0	60	27
Ryan Franklin	66	0	6-7	0	0	42	4.54	77.1	43	33
Brandon Claussen	14	14	3-8	0	0	56	6.19	77.0	57	28
David Weathers	67	0	4-4	12	0	31	3.54	73.2	50	34
Gary Majewski	65	0	4-4	0	0	38	4.61	70.1	43	29
Kyle Lohse	12	11	3-5	0	0	33	4.57	63.0	51	19
Bill Bray	48	0	3-2	2	0	27	4.09	50.2	39	18

Colorado Rockies

BATTING	G	AB	R	H	2B	3B	HR	RBI	TB	BB	SO	SB	OBP	SLG	BA
Garrett Atkins	157	602	117	198	48	1	29	120	335	79	76	4	.409	.556	.329
Mattt Holliday	155	602	119	196	45	5	34	114	353	47	110	10	.387	.584	.326
Todd Helton	145	546	94	165	40	5	15	81	260	91	64	3	.404	.476	.302
Brad Hawpe	150	499	67	146	33	6	22	84	257	74	123	5	.383	.515	.293
Clint Barmes	131	478	57	105	26	4	7	56	160	22	72	5	.264	.335	.220
Jamey Carroll	136	463	84	139	23	5	5	36	187	56	66	10	.377	.404	.300
Cory Sullivan	126	386	47	103	26	10	2	30	155	32	100	10	.321	.402	.267
Vinny Castilla	87	275	26	63	10	0	5	27	88	9	49	0	.258	.320	.229
Kazuo Matsui	70	243	32	65	12	3	3	26	92	16	46	10	.310	.379	.267
Yorvit Torrealba	65	223	23	55	16	3	7	43	98	11	49	4	.293	.439	.247
Choo Freeman	88	173	24	41	6	3	2	18	59	14	42	5	.298	.341	.237
Ryan Spilborghs	67	167	26	48	6	3	4	21	72	14	30	5	.337	.431	.287
Luis Gonzalez	61	149	7	36	9	1	2	14	53	4	27	1	.269	.356	.242
Danny Ardoin	35	109	12	21	5	1	0	2	28	8	27	0	.261	.257	.193
Jason Smith	49	99	9	26	1	0	5	13	42	7	29	3	.324	.424	.263

PITCHING	GP	GS	W-L	SV	SHO	R	ERA	IP	Ks	BB
Aaron Cook	32	32	9-15	0	0	107	4.23	212.2	92	55
Jason Jennings	32	32	9-13	0	2	94	3.78	212.0	.142	85
Jeff Francis	32	32	13-11	0	1	101	4.16	199.0	117	69
Josh Fogg	31	31	11-9	0	1	115	5.49	172.0	93	60
Byung-Hyun Kim	27	27	8-12	0	0	103	5.57	155.0	129	61
Jose Mesa	79	0	1-5	1	0	32	3.86	72.1	39	36
Ramon Ramirez	61	0	4-3	0	0	28	3.46	67.2	61	27
Brian Fuentes	66	0	3-4	30	0	25	3.44	65.1	73	26
Tom Martin	68	0	2-0	0	0	37	5.07	60.1	46	25
Ray King	67	5	1-4	1	0	26	4.43	44.2	23	20
Manny Corpas	35	0	1-2	0	0	13	3.62	32.1	27	8
David Cortes	30	0	3-1	0	0	14	4.30	29.1	14	6
Jeremy Affeldt	27	0	4-2	1	0	23	6.91	27.1	20	13

Florida Marlins

BATTING	G	AB	R	H	2B	3B	HR	RBI	TB	BB	SO	SB	OBP	SLG	BA
Hanley Ramirez	158	633	119	185	46	11	17	59	304	56	128	51	.353	.480	.292
Dan Uggla	154	611	105	172	26	7	27	90	293	48	123	6	.339	.480	.282
Miguel Cabrera	158	576	112	195	50	2	26	114	327	86	108	9	.430	.568	.339
Josh Willingham	142	502	62	139	28	2	26	74	249	54	109	2	.356	.496	.227
Mike Jacobs	136	469	54	123	37	1	20	77	222	45	105	3	.325	.473	.262
Miguel Olivo	127	430	52	113	22	3	16	58	189	9	103	2	.287	.440	.263
Alfredo Amezaga	132	334	42	87	9	3	3	19	111	33	46	20	.332	.332	.260
Jeremy Hermida	99	307	37	77	19	1	5	28	113	33	70	4	.332	.368	.251
Cody Ross	101	269	34	61	12	2	13	46	116	22	65	1	.293	.431	.227
Reggie Abercrombie	111	255	39	54	12	2	5	24	85	18	78	6	.271	.333	.212
Wes Helms	140	240	30	79	19	5	10	47	138	21	55	0	.390	.575	.329
Joe Borchard	108	230	30	53	7	1	10	28	92	28	66	0	.322	.400	.230
Matt Treanor	67	157	12	36	6	1	2	14	50	19	34	0	.328	.318	.229
Chris Aguila	47	95	5	22	8	1	0	7	32	9	26	2	.298	.337	.232

PITCHING	GP	GS	W-L	SV	SHO	R	ERA	IP	Ks	BB
Dontrelle Willis	34	34	12-12	0	1	106	3.87	223.1	160	83
Scott Olsen	31	31	12-10	0	0	94	4.04	180.2	166	75
Josh Johnson	31	24	12-7	0	0	63	3.10	157.0	133	68
Ricky Nolasco	35	22	11-11	0	0	86	4.82	140.0	99	41
Brian Moehler	29	21	7-11	0	0	95	6.57	122.0	58	38
Anibal Sanchez	18	17	10-3	0	1	39	2.83	114.1	72	46
Matt Herges	66	0	2-3	0	0	42	4.31	71.0	36	28
Joe Borowski	72	0	3-3	36	0	31	3.75	69.2	64	33
Randy Messenger	59	0	2-7	0	0	42	5.67	60.1	45	24
Jason Vargas	12	5	1-2	0	0	39	7.33	43.1	25	30

Houston Astros

BATTING	G	AB	R	H	2B	3B	HR	RBI	TB	BB	SO	SB	OBP	SLG	BA
Craig Biggio	145	548	79	172	33	0	21	62	231	40	84	3	.306	.422	.246
Lance Berkman	152	536	95	156	29	0	45	136	333	98	106	3	.420	.621	.315
Willy Taveras	149	529	83	136	19	5	1	30	179	34	88	33	.333	.338	.278
Adam Everett	150	514	52	149	28	6	6	59	181	34	71	9	.290	.352	.239
Brad Ausmus	139	439	37	138	16	1	2	39	125	45	71	3	.308	.285	.230
Morgan Ensberg	127	387	67	137	17	1	23	58	179	101	96	1	.396	.463	.235
Mike Lamb	126	381	70	100	22	3	12	45	181	35	55	2	.361	.475	.307
Chris Burke	123	366	58	76	23	1	9	40	153	27	77	11	.347	.418	.276
Jason Lane	112	288	44	79	10	0	15	45	113	49	75	1	.318	.392	.201
Aubrey Huff	68	224	31	58	10	1	13	38	107	26	39	0	.341	.478	.250
Luke Scott	65	214	31	46	19	6	10	37	133	30	43	2	.426	.621	.336
Eric Munson	53	141	10	24	6	0	5	19	49	11	32	0	.269	.348	.199
Eric Bruntlett	73	119	11	25	8	0	0	10	41	13	21	3	.351	.345	.277
Orlando Palmeiro	103	119	2	17	6	1	0	17	38	6	17	1	.294	.319	.252

PITCHING	GP	GS	W–L	SV	SHO	R	ERA	IP	Ks	BB
Roy Oswalt	33	32	15-8	0	0	76	2.98	220.2	166	38
Andy Pettite	36	35	14-13	0	1	114	4.20	214.1	178	70
Wandy Rodriguez	30	24	9-10	0	0	96	5.64	135.2	98	63
Roger Clemens	19	19	7-6	0	0	34	2.30	113.1	102	29
Taylor Buchholz	22	19	6-10	0	1	80	5.89	113.0	77	34
Fernando Nieve	40	11	3-3	0	0	46	4.20	96.1	70	41
Chad Qualls	81	0	7-3	0	0	38	3.76	88.2	56	28
Brad Lidge	78	0	1-5	32	0	47	5.28	75.0	104	36
Dan Wheeler	75	0	3-5	9	0	22	2.52	71.1	68	24
Dave Borkowski	40	0	3-2	0	0	38	4.69	71.0	52	23

Los Angeles Dodgers

BATTING	G	AB	R	H	2B	3B	HR	RBI	TB	BB	SO	SB	OBP	SLG	BA
Rafael Furcal	159	654	113	196	32	9	15	63	291	73	98	37	.369	.445	.300
J.D. Drew	146	494	84	140	34	6	20	100	246	89	106	2	.393	.498	.283
Nomar Garciaparra	122	469	82	142	31	2	20	93	237	42	30	3	.367	.505	.303
Kenny Lofton	129	469	79	141	15	12	3	41	189	45	42	32	.360	.403	.301
Russell Martin	121	415	65	117	26	4	10	65	181	45	57	10	.355	.436	.282
Jeff Kent	115	407	61	119	27	3	14	68	194	55	69	1	.385	.477	.292
Andre Ethier	126	396	50	122	20	7	11	55	189	34	77	5	.365	.477	.308
Wilson Betemit	143	373	49	98	23	0	18	53	175	36	102	3	.326	.469	.263
Marlon Anderson	134	279	43	83	16	4	12	38	143	25	49	4	.354	.513	.297
Jose Cruz	86	223	34	52	16	1	5	17	85	43	54	5	.353	.381	.233
Olmedo Saenz	103	179	30	53	15	0	11	48	101	14	47	0	.363	.564	.296
Ramon Martinez	82	176	20	49	7	1	2	24	64	15	20	0	.339	.364	.278
Matt Kemp	52	154	30	39	7	1	7	23	69	9	53	6	.289	.448	.253
Julio Lugo	49	146	16	32	5	1	0	10	39	12	29	6	.278	.267	.219
Jason Repko	69	130	21	33	5	1	3	16	49	15	24	10	.345	.377	.254
Bill Mueller	32	107	12	27	7	0	3	15	43	17	9	1	.357	.402	.252

PITCHING	GP	GS	W–L	SV	SHO	R	ERA	IP	Ks	BB
Derek Lowe	35	34	16-8	0	0	97	3.63	218.0	123	55
Greg Maddux	34	34	15-14	0	0	109	4.20	210.0	117	37
Brad Penny	34	33	16-9	0	0	94	4.33	189.0	148	54
Brett Tomko	44	15	8-7	0	0	67	4.73	112.1	76	29
Aaron Sele	28	15	8-6	0	0	57	4.53	103.1	57	30
Chad Billingsley	18	16	7-4	0	0	43	3.80	90.0	59	58
Takashi Saito	72	0	6-2	24	0	19	2.07	78.1	107	23
Jonathan Broxton	68	0	4-1	3	0	25	2.59	76.1	97	33
Mark Hendrickson	18	12	2-7	0	0	45	4.68	75.0	48	28
Joe Beimel	62	0	2-1	2	0	26	2.96	70.0	30	21
Jae Seo	19	10	2-4	0	0	45	5..78	67.0	49	25

Milwaukee Brewers

BATTING	G	AB	R	H	2B	3B	HR	RBI	TB	BB	SO	SB	OBP	SLG	BA
Prince Fielder	157	569	82	154	35	1	28	81	275	59	125	7	.347	.483	.271
Bill Hall	148	537	101	145	39	4	35	85	297	63	162	8	.345	.553	.270
David Bell	145	504	60	136	27	4	10	63	201	50	68	3	.337	.399	.270
Geoff Jenkins	147	484	62	131	26	1	17	70	210	56	129	4	.357	.434	.271
Brady Clark	138	415	51	109	14	2	4	29	139	43	60	3	.348	.335	.263
Carlos Lee	102	388	60	111	18	0	28	81	213	38	39	12	.347	.549	.286
Rickie Weeks	95	359	73	100	15	3	8	34	145	30	92	19	.363	.404	.279
Damian Miller	101	331	34	83	28	0	6	38	129	33	86	0	.322	.390	.251
Jeff Cirillo	112	263	33	84	16	0	3	23	109	21	33	1	.369	.414	.319
Corey Koskie	76	257	29	67	23	0	12	33	126	29	58	1	.343	.490	.261
Corey Hart	87	237	32	67	13	2	9	33	111	17	58	5	.328	.468	.283
Tony Graffanino	60	236	34	66	17	3	2	27	95	20	37	2	.345	.403	.280
Gabe Gross	117	208	42	57	15	0	9	38	99	36	60	1	.382	.476	.274

PITCHING	GP	GS	W-L	SV	SHO	R	ERA	IP	Ks	BB
Chris Capuano	34	34	11-12	0	2	108	4.03	221.1	174	47
Dave Bush	34	32	12-11	0	2	111	4.41	210.0	166	38
Doug Davis	34	34	11-11	0	1	118	4.91	203.1	159	102
Ben Sheets	17	17	6-7	0	0	47	3.82	106.0	116	11
Tomo Ohka	18	18	4-5	0	0	58	4.82	97.0	50	35
Jose Capellan	61	0	4-2	0	0	37	4.40	71.2	58	31
Derrick Turnbow	64	0	4-9	24	0	51	6.87	56.1	69	39
Geremi Gonzalez	24	4	4-2	0	0	43	5.79	56.0	44	23
Carlos Villanueva	10	6	2-2	0	0	22	3.69	53.2	39	11
Dan Kolb	53	0	2-2	1	0	28	4.84	48.1	26	20
Matt Wise	40	0	5-6	0	0	24	3.86	44.1	27	14
Zach Jackson	8	7	2-2	0	0	26	5.40	38.1	22	14
Ricky Helling	20	2	0-2	0	0	17	4.11	35.0	32	15

New York Mets

BATTING	G	AB	R	H	2B	3B	HR	RBI	TB	BB	SO	SB	OBP	SLG	BA
Jose Reyes	153	647	122	194	30	17	19	81	315	53	81	64	.354	.487	.300
David Wright	154	582	96	181	40	5	26	116	309	66	113	20	.381	.531	.311
Shawn Green	149	530	73	147	31	3	15	66	229	45	82	4	.344	.432	.277
Carlos Delgado	144	524	89	139	30	2	38	114	287	74	120	0	.361	.548	.265
Paul Lo Duca	124	512	80	163	39	1	5	49	219	24	38	3	.355	.428	.318
Carlos Beltran	140	510	127	140	38	1	41	116	303	95	99	18	.388	.594	.275
Jose Valentin	137	384	56	104	24	3	18	62	188	37	71	6	.330	.490	.271
Endy Chavez	133	353	48	108	22	5	4	42	152	24	44	12	.348	.431	.306
Cliff Floyd	97	332	45	81	19	1	11	44	135	29	58	6	.324	.407	.244
Chris Woodward	83	222	25	48	10	1	3	25	69	23	55	1	.289	.311	.216
Lastings Milledge	56	166	14	40	7	2	4	22	63	12	39	1	.310	.380	.241
Julio Franco	95	165	14	45	10	0	2	26	61	13	49	6	.330	.370	.273
Ramon Castro	40	126	13	30	7	0	4	12	49	15	40	0	.322	.389	.238
Eli Marrero	55	93	11	19	4	0	6	15	41	15	31	5	.324	.441	.204
Ricky Ledee	70	85	8	16	6	0	2	9	28	6	16	1	.242	.329	.188

PITCHING	GP	GS	W-L	SV	SHO	R	ERA	IP	Ks	BB
Tom Glavine	32	32	15-7	0	0	94	3.82	198.0	131	62
Steve Trachsel	30	30	15-8	0	0	94	4.97	164.2	79	78
Orlando Hernandez	29	29	11-11	0	0	90	4.66	162.1	164	61
Pedro Martinez	23	23	9-8	0	0	72	4.48	132.2	137	39
Oliver Perez	22	22	3-13	0	1	90	6.55	112.2	102	68
John Maine	16	16	6-5	0	1	40	3.60	90.0	71	33
Aaron Heilman	74	74	4-5	0	0	37	3.62	87.0	73	28
Darren Oliver	45	45	4-1	0	0	33	3.44	81.0	60	21
Billy Wagner	70	0	3-2	40	0	22	2.24	72.1	94	21
Dave Williams	14	13	5-4	0	0	52	6.52	69.0	32	20
Roberto Hernandez	68	0	0-3	2	0	32	3.11	63.2	48	32
Chad Bradford	70	6	4-2	2	0	22	2.90	62.0	45	13
Pedro Feliciano	64	0	7-2	0	0	15	2.09	60.1	54	20
Duaner Sanchez	49	0	5-1	0	0	19	2.60	55.1	44	24
Alay Soler	8	8	2-3	0	1	33	6.00	45.0	23	21
Brian Bannister	8	6	2-1	0	0	18	4.26	38.0	19	22

Philadelphia Phillies

BATTING	G	AB	R	H	2B	3B	HR	RBI	TB	BB	SO	SB	OBP	SLG	BA
Jimmy Rollins	158	689	127	191	45	9	25	83	329	57	80	36	.334	.478	.277
Chase Utley	160	658	131	203	40	4	32	102	347	63	132	15	.379	.527	.309
Ryan Howard	159	581	104	182	25	1	58	149	383	108	181	0	.425	.659	.313
Pat Burrell	144	462	80	119	24	1	29	95	232	98	131	0	.388	.502	.258
Shane Victorino	153	415	70	119	19	8	6	46	172	24	54	4	.346	.414	.287
Aaron Rowand	109	405	59	106	24	3	12	47	172	18	76	10	.321	.425	.262
Bobby Abreu	98	339	61	94	25	2	8	65	147	91	86	20	.427	.434	.277
Abraham Nunez	123	322	42	68	10	2	2	32	88	41	58	1	.303	.273	.211
David Dellucci	132	264	41	77	14	5	13	39	140	28	62	1	.369	.530	.292
Mike Lieberthal	67	209	22	57	14	0	9	36	98	8	19	0	.316	.469	.273
Chris Coste	65	198	25	65	14	0	7	32	100	10	31	0	.376	.505	.328
Jose Hernandez	85	152	12	40	4	1	3	19	55	12	40	0	.317	.362	.263
Sal Fasano	50	140	9	34	8	0	4	10	54	5	47	0	.284	.386	.243
Jeff Conine	28	100	11	28	6	1	1	17	39	5	12	0	.327	.390	.280
Carlos Ruiz	27	69	5	18	1	1	3	10	30	5	8	0	.316	.435	.261

PITCHING	GP	GS	W–L	SV	SHO	R	ERA	IP	Ks	BB
Brett Myers	31	31	12-7	0	0	93	3.91	198.0	189	63
Jon Lieber	27	27	9-11	0	1	100	4.93	168.0	100	24
Ryan Madson	50	17	11-9	2	0	92	5.69	134.1	99	50
Cole Hamels	23	23	9-8	0	0	66	4.08	132.1	145	48
Cory Lidle	21	21	8-7	0	0	74	4.74	125.1	98	39
Geoff Geary	81	0	7-1	1	0	34	2.96	91.1	60	20
Aaron Fultz	66	1	3-1	0	0	39	4.54	71.1	62	28
Rick White	64	0	4-1	1	0	44	5.15	64.2	40	20
Tom Gordon	59	0	3-4	34	0	23	3.34	59.1	68	22
Randy Wolf	12	12	4-0	0	0	37	5.56	56.2	44	33
Gavin Floyd	11	11	4-3	0	1	48	7.29	54.1	34	32
Jamie Moyer	8	8	5-2	0	0	25	4.03	51.1	26	7

Pittsburgh Pirates

BATTING	G	AB	R	H	2B	3B	HR	RBI	TB	BB	SO	SB	OBP	SLG	BA
Freddy Sanchez	157	582	85	200	53	6	6	85	275	31	52	3	.378	.473	.344
Jason Bay	159	570	101	163	29	3	35	109	303	102	156	11	.396	.532	.286
Jack Wilson	142	543	70	148	27	1	8	35	201	33	65	4	.316	.370	.273
Jose Castillo	148	518	54	131	25	0	14	65	198	32	98	6	.299	.382	.253
Xavier Nady	130	468	57	131	28	1	17	63	212	30	85	3	.337	.453	.280
Ronny Paulino	129	442	37	137	19	0	6	55	174	34	79	0	.360	.394	.310
Jose Bautista	117	400	58	94	20	3	16	51	168	46	110	2	.335	.420	.235
Chris Duffy	84	314	46	80	14	3	2	18	106	19	71	26	.317	.338	.255
Jeromy Burnitz	111	313	35	72	12	0	16	49	132	22	74	1	.289	.422	.230
Nate McLouth	106	270	50	63	16	2	7	16	104	18	59	10	.293	.385	.233
Craig Wilson	85	255	38	68	11	2	13	41	122	24	88	1	.339	.478	.267
Sean Casey	59	213	30	63	15	0	3	29	87	23	22	0	.377	.408	.296
Joe Randa	89	206	23	55	13	0	4	28	80	16	26	0	.316	.388	.267
Ryan Doumit	61	149	15	31	9	0	6	17	58	15	42	0	.322	.389	.208

PITCHING	GP	GS	W–L	SV	SHO	R	ERA	IP	Ks	BB
Zach Duke	34	34	10-15	0	1	116	4.47	215.1	117	68
Ian Snell	32	32	14-11	0	0	104	4.74	186.0	169	74
Paul Maholm	30	30	8-10	0	0	98	4.76	176.0	117	81
Victor Santos	25	19	5-9	0	0	80	5.70	115.1	81	42
Salomon Torres	94	0	3-6	12	0	42	3.28	93.1	72	38
Matt Capps	85	0	9-1	1	0	37	3.79	80.2	56	12
John Grabow	72	0	4-2	0	0	34	4.13	69.2	66	30
Tom Gorzelanny	11	11	2-5	0	0	29	3.79	61.2	40	31
Damaso Marte	75	0	1-7	0	0	30	3.70	58.1	63	31
Mike Gonzalez	54	0	3-4	24	0	13	2.17	54.0	64	31
Shawn Chacon	9	9	2-3	0	0	32	5.48	46.0	27	27

St. Louis Cardinals

BATTING	G	AB	R	H	2B	3B	HR	RBI	TB	BB	SO	SB	OBP	SLG	BA
Juan Encarnacion	153	557	74	155	25	5	19	79	247	30	86	6	.317	.443	.278
Albert Pujols	143	535	119	177	33	1	49	137	359	92	50	7	.431	.671	.331
Scott Rolen	142	521	94	154	48	1	22	95	270	56	69	7	.369	.518	.296
Preston Wilson	135	501	58	132	25	2	17	72	212	29	121	12	.307	423	.263
David Eckstein	123	500	68	146	18	1	2	23	172	31	41	7	.350	.344	.292
Aaron Miles	135	426	48	112	20	5	2	30	148	38	42	2	.324	.347	.263
Yadier Molina	129	417	29	90	26	0	6	49	134	26	41	1	.274	.321	.216
Jim Edmonds	110	350	52	90	18	0	19	70	165	53	101	4	.350	.471	.257
So Taguchi	134	316	46	84	19	1	2	31	111	32	48	11	.335	.351	.266
Chris Duncan	90	280	60	82	11	3	22	43	165	30	69	0	.363	.589	.293
Scott Spiezio	119	276	44	75	15	4	13	52	137	37	66	1	.366	.496	.272
Hector Luna	76	223	27	65	14	1	4	21	93	21	34	5	.355	.417	.291
Ronnie Belliard	54	194	20	46	9	1	5	23	72	15	36	0	.295	.371	.237
John Rodriguez	102	183	31	55	12	3	2	19	79	21	45	0	.374	.432	.301
Gary Bennett	60	157	13	35	5	0	4	22	52	11	30	0	.274	.331	.223

PITCHING	GP	GS	W-L	SV	SHO	R	ERA	IP	Ks	BB
Chris Carpenter	32	32	15-8	0	3	82	3.09	221.2	184	43
Jason Marquis	33	33	14-16	0	0	110	6.02	194.1	96	75
Jeff Suppan	32	32	12-7	0	0	90	4.12	190.0	104	69
Jorge Sosa	45	13	3-11	4	0	93	5.42	118.0	75	40
Mark Mulder	17	17	6-7	0	0	101	7.14	93.1	50	35
Anthony Reyes	17	17	5-8	0	0	28	5.06	85.1	72	34
Jeff Weaver	15	15	5-4	0	0	15	5.18	83.1	45	26
Josh Hancock	62	0	3-3	1	0	14	4.09	77.0	50	23
Adam Wainwright	61	0	2-1	3	0	22	3.12	75.0	72	22
Braden Looper	69	0	9-3	0	0	22	3.56	73.1	41	20
Sidney Ponson	14	13	4-4	0	0	17	5.24	68.2	33	29
Jason Isringhausen	59	0	4-8	33	0	25	3.55	58.1	52	38

San Diego Padres

BATTING	G	AB	R	H	2B	3B	HR	RBI	TB	BB	SO	SB	OBP	SLG	BA
Brian Giles	158	604	87	159	37	1	14	83	240	104	60	9	.374	.397	.263
Adrian Gonzalez	156	570	83	173	38	1	24	82	285	52	113	0	.362	.500	.304
Mike Cameron	141	552	88	148	34	9	22	83	266	71	142	25	.355	.482	.268
Josh Barfield	150	539	72	151	32	3	13	58	228	30	81	21	.318	.423	.280
Dave Roberts	129	499	80	146	18	13	2	44	196	51	61	49	.360	.393	.293
Todd Walker	138	442	56	123	22	2	9	53	176	55	38	2	.356	.398	.278
Khalil Greene	121	412	56	101	26	2	15	55	176	39	87	5	.320	.427	.245
Mike Piazza	126	339	39	113	19	1	22	68	200	34	66	0	.342	.501	.283
Geoff Blum	109	276	27	70	17	1	4	34	101	17	51	0	.293	.336	.254
Mark Bellhorn	115	253	26	48	11	2	8	27	87	32	90	0	.285	.344	.190
Josh Bard	93	231	28	78	19	0	9	40	124	27	39	1	.406	.537	.338
Eric Young	56	128	19	26	5	0	3	13	40	13	16	8	.281	.313	.203
Ben Johnson	58	120	19	30	5	2	4	12	51	14	36	3	.333	.425	.250
Rob Bowen	94	94	22	23	5	0	3	13	37	13	26	0	.339	.394	.245

PITCHING	GP	GS	W-L	SV	SHO	R	ERA	IP	Ks	BB
Jake Peavy	32	32	11-14	0	0	93	4.09	202.1	215	62
Clay Hensley	37	29	11-12	0	1	82	3.71	187.0	122	76
Chris Young	31	31	11-5	0	0	72	3.46	179.1	164	69
Woody Williams	25	24	12-5	0	0	68	3.65	145.1	72	35
Chan Ho Park	24	21	7-7	0	0	81	4.81	136.2	96	44
Mike Thompson	19	16	4-5	0	0	56	4.99	92.0	35	30
Scott Linebrink	73	0	7-4	2	0	31	3.57	75.2	68	22
Trevor Hoffman	65	0	0-2	46	0	16	2.14	63.0	50	13
Brian Sweeney	37	0	2-0	2	0	22	3.20	56.1	23	16
Jon Adkins	55	0	2-1	0	0	26	3.98	54.1	30	20
Alan Embree	73	0	4-3	0	0	21	3.27	52.1	53	15
Cla Meredith	45	0	5-1	0	0	6	1.07	50.2	37	6

San Francisco Giants

BATTING	G	AB	R	H	2B	3B	HR	RBI	TB	BB	SO	SB	OBP	SLG	BA
Pedro Feliz	160	603	75	147	30	5	22	98	258	33	112	1	.281	.428	.244
Omar Vizquel	153	579	88	171	28	10	4	58	225	56	51	24	.361	.389	.295
Randy Winn	149	573	82	150	33	5	11	56	227	48	63	10	.324	.396	.262
Ray Durham	137	498	79	146	34	7	26	93	268	51	61	7	.360	.538	.293
Steve Finley	139	426	66	105	21	12	6	40	168	46	55	7	.320	.394	.246
Barry Bonds	130	367	74	99	17	0	26	77	200	115	51	3	.454	.545	.270
Moises Alou	98	345	52	104	17	1	22	74	197	28	31	2	.352	.571	.301
Eliezer Alfonzo	87	286	27	76	18	2	12	39	133	9	74	1	.302	.465	.266
Mark Sweeney	114	259	32	65	16	2	5	37	99	28	50	0	.330	.382	.251
Shea Hillenbrand	60	234	33	58	22	0	9	29	97	7	40	0	.275	.415	.248
Lance Niekro	66	199	27	49	8	2	5	31	77	11	32	0	.286	.387	.246
Mike Matheny	47	160	10	37	4	0	3	18	54	9	30	0	.276	.338	.231

PITCHING	GP	GS	W-L	SV	SHO	R	ERA	IP	Ks	BB
Jason Schmidt	32	32	11-9	0	1	94	3.59	213.1	180	80
Matt Morris	33	33	10-15	0	0	123	4.98	207.2	117	63
Matt Cain	32	31	13-12	0	1	93	4.15	190.2	179	87
Noah Lowry	27	27	7-10	0	1	89	4.74	159.1	84	56
Jamey Wright	34	21	6-10	0	0	95	5.19	156.0	79	64
Brad Hennessey	34	12	5-6	1	0	53	4.26	99.1	42	42
Kevin Correia	48	0	2-0	0	0	27	3.49	69.2	57	22
Mike Stanton	82	0	7-7	8	0	30	3.99	67.2	48	27
Steve Kline	72	0	4-3	1	0	24	3.66	51.2	33	26
Jeremy Accardo	38	0	1-3	3	0	23	4.91	40.1	40	11
Jonathan Sanchez	27	4	3-1	0	0	26	4.95	40.0	33	23
Armando Benitez	41	0	4-2	17	0	15	3.52	38.1	31	21

Washington Nationals

BATTING	G	AB	R	H	2B	3B	HR	RBI	TB	BB	SO	SB	OBP	SLG	BA
Alfonso Soriano	159	647	119	179	41	2	46	95	362	67	147	41	.351	.560	.277
Felipe Lopez	156	617	98	169	27	3	11	52	235	81	102	44	.358	.381	.274
Ryan Zimmerman	157	614	84	176	47	3	20	110	289	61	148	11	.351	.471	.287
Austin Kearns	150	537	86	142	33	2	24	86	251	76	82	9	.363	.467	.264
Nick Johnson	147	500	100	145	46	0	23	77	260	110	76	10	.428	.520	.290
Jose Vidro	126	463	52	134	26	1	7	47	183	41	87	1	.348	.395	.289
Brian Schneider	124	410	30	105	18	0	4	55	135	38	48	2	.320	.329	.256
Jose Guillen	69	241	28	52	15	1	9	40	96	15	30	1	.276	.398	.216
Marlon Byrd	78	197	28	44	8	1	5	18	69	22	55	3	.317	.350	.223
Ryan Church	71	196	22	54	17	1	10	35	103	26	70	6	.366	.526	.276
Robert Fick	60	128	14	34	4	0	2	9	44	10	34	1	.324	.344	.266
Damian Jackson	67	116	16	23	6	1	4	10	43	12	83	1	.295	.371	.198
Bernie Castro	42	110	18	25	1	3	0	10	32	9	50	7	.286	.291	.227
Nook Logan	27	90	13	27	3	1	1	8	35	6	37	2	.337	.389	.300
Alex Escobar	33	87	14	31	3	2	4	18	50	8	17	2	.394	.575	.356

PITCHING	GP	GS	W-L	SV	SHO	R	ERA	IP	Ks	BB
Ramon Ortiz	33	33	11-16	0	0	127	5.57	190.2	104	64
Tony Armas	30	30	9-12	0	0	96	5.03	154.0	97	64
Livan Hernandez	24	24	9-8	0	0	94	5.34	146.0	89	52
Michael O'Conner	21	20	3-8	0	0	61	4.80	105.0	59	45
Jon Rauch	85	0	4-5	2	0	37	3.35	91.1	86	36
Pedro Astacio	17	17	5-5	0	1	64	5.98	90.1	42	31
Chad Cordero	68	0	7-4	29	0	27	3.19	73.1	69	22
Jason Bergmann	29	6	0-2	0	0	49	6.68	64.2	54	27
Saul Rivera	54	0	3-0	1	0	28	3.43	60.1	41	32
Gary Majewski	46	0	3-2	0	0	24	3.58	55.1	34	25
Mike Stanton	56	0	3-5	0	0	22	4.47	44.1	30	21
Billy Traber	15	8	4-3	0	0	33	6.44	43.1	25	14

Baltimore Orioles

BATTING	G	AB	R	H	2B	3B	HR	RBI	TB	BB	SO	SB	OBP	SLG	BA
Miguel Tejada	162	648	99	214	37	0	24	100	323	46	83	6	.379	.498	.330
Melvin Mora	155	624	96	171	25	0	16	83	244	54	112	11	.342	.391	.274
Brian Roberts	138	563	85	161	34	3	10	55	231	55	83	36	.347	.410	.286
Ramon Hernandez	144	501	66	138	29	2	23	91	240	43	56	1	.343	.479	.275
Nick Markakis	147	491	72	143	25	2	16	62	220	43	68	2	.351	.448	.291
Corey Patterson	135	463	75	128	19	5	16	53	205	21	58	45	.314	.443	.276
Kevin Millar	132	430	64	117	26	0	15	64	188	59	84	1	.374	.437	.272
Jeff Connie	114	389	43	103	20	3	9	49	156	35	43	3	.325	.401	.265
Jay Gibbons	90	343	34	95	23	0	13	46	157	32	60	0	.341	.458	.277
Brandon Fahey	91	251	36	59	8	2	2	23	77	23	32	3	.307	.307	.235
Chris Gomez	55	132	14	45	7	0	2	17	58	7	17	1	.387	.439	.341
David Newhan	39	131	14	33	4	0	4	18	49	7	45	4	.294	.374	.252
Luis Matos	55	121	14	25	7	1	2	5	40	10	49	7	.278	.331	.207
Chris Widger	36	93	6	16	3	0	1	9	22	11	41	0	.255	.237	.172
Fernando Tatis	28	56	7	14	6	1	2	8	28	6	38	0	.313	.500	.250
Luis Terrero	27	40	4	8	1	0	1	6	12	1	23	0	.238	.300	.200

PITCHING	GP	GS	W–L	SV	SHO	R	ERA	IP	Ks	BB
Erik Bedard	33	33	15-11	0	0	92	3.76	196.1	171	69
Rodrigo Lopez	36	29	9-18	0	0	129	5.90	189.0	136	59
Kris Benson	30	30	11-12	0	0	105	4.82	183.0	88	58
Daniel Cabrera	26	26	9-10	0	1	82	4.74	148.0	157	104
Adam Loewen	22	19	6-6	0	0	72	5.37	112.1	98	62
Bruce Chen	40	12	0-7	0	0	81	6.93	98.2	70	35
Chris Ray	61	0	4-4	33	0	22	2.73	66.0	51	27
LaTroy Hawkins	60	0	3-2	0	0	30	4.48	60.1	27	15
Todd Williams	62	0	2-4	1	0	36	4.74	57.0	24	19
Chris Britton	52	0	0-2	1	0	22	3.35	53.2	41	17
Sendy Rleal	42	0	1-1	0	0	25	4.44	46.2	19	23
Russ Ortiz	20	5	0-3	0	0	39	8.48	40.1	23	18
Kurt Birkins	35	0	5-2	0	0	19	4.94	31.0	27	16
John Halama	17	1	3-1	0	0	20	6.14	29.1	12	13
Julio Manon	22	0	0-1	0	0	13	5.40	20.0	22	16

Boston Red Sox

BATTING	G	AB	R	H	2B	3B	HR	RBI	TB	BB	SO	SB	OBP	SLG	BA
Mark Loretta	155	635	75	181	33	0	5	59	229	49	63	4	.345	.361	.285
Mike Lowell	153	573	79	163	47	1	20	80	272	47	61	2	.339	.475	.284
Kevin Youkilis	147	569	100	159	42	2	13	72	244	91	120	5	.381	.429	.279
David Ortiz	151	558	115	160	29	2	54	137	355	119	117	1	.413	.636	.287
Manny Ramirez	130	449	79	144	27	1	35	102	278	100	102	0	.439	.619	.321
Coco Crisp	105	413	58	109	22	2	8	36	159	31	67	22	.317	.385	.264
Alex Gonzalez	111	388	48	99	24	2	9	50	154	22	67	1	.299	.397	.255
Trot Nixon	114	381	59	102	24	0	8	52	150	60	56	0	.373	.394	.268
Jason Varitek	103	365	46	87	19	2	12	55	146	46	87	1	.325	.400	.238
Javier Lopez	94	342	36	86	20	1	8	35	132	20	76	0	.297	.386	.251
Eric Hinske	109	277	43	75	17	2	13	34	135	35	79	2	.353	.487	.271
Wily Mo Pena	84	276	36	83	15	2	11	42	135	20	90	0	.349	.489	.301
Alex Cora	96	235	31	56	7	2	1	18	70	19	29	6	.312	.298	.238
Doug Mirabelli	59	161	12	31	6	0	6	25	55	11	54	0	.261	.342	.193
Gabe Kapler	72	130	21	33	7	0	2	12	46	14	15	1	.340	.354	.254
Dustin Pedroia	31	89	5	17	4	0	2	7	27	7	7	0	.258	.303	.191

PITCHING	GP	GS	W–L	SV	SHO	R	ERA	IP	Ks	BB
Josh Beckett	33	33	16-11	0	0	120	5.01	204.2	158	74
Curt Schilling	31	31	15-7	0	0	90	3.97	204.0	183	28
Tim Wakefield	23	23	7-11	0	0	80	4.63	140.0	90	51
Jason Johnson	20	20	3-12	0	0	81	6.35	106.1	50	35
Julian Tavarez	58	6	5-4	1	0	54	4.47	98.2	56	44
Jon Lester	15	15	7-2	0	0	43	4.76	81.1	60	43
Jonathan Papelbon	59	0	4-2	35	0	8	0.92	68.1	75	13
Matt Clement	12	12	5-5	0	0	50	6.61	65.1	43	38
Mike Timlin	68	0	6-6	9	0	51	4.36	64.0	30	16
Kyle Snyder	17	11	4-5	0	0	51	6.56	60.1	57	20
Manny Delcarmen	50	0	2-0	0	0	32	5.06	53.1	45	17
Keith Foulke	44	0	3-1	0	0	24	4.35	49.2	36	7
David Wells	8	8	2-3	0	0	30	4.98	47.0	24	8
Rudy Seanez	41	0	2-1	0	0	28	4.82	46.2	48	26

Chicago White Sox

BATTING	G	AB	R	H	2B	3B	HR	RBI	TB	BB	SO	SB	OBP	SLG	BA
Paul Konerko	152	566	97	177	30	0	35	113	312	60	104	1	.381	.551	.313
Tadahito Iguchi	138	555	97	156	24	0	18	67	234	59	110	11	.352	.422	.281
Joe Crede	150	544	76	154	31	0	30	94	275	28	58	0	.323	.506	.283
Jermaine Dye	146	539	103	170	27	3	44	120	335	59	118	7	.385	.622	.315
Scott Podsednik	139	524	86	137	27	6	3	45	185	54	96	40	.330	.353	.261
A. J. Pierzynski	140	509	65	150	24	0	16	64	222	22	72	1	.333	.436	.295
Jim Thome	143	490	108	141	26	0	42	109	293	107	147	0	.416	.598	.288
Juan Uribe	132	463	53	109	28	2	21	71	204	13	55	1	.257	.441	.235
Brian Anderson	134	365	46	82	23	1	8	33	131	30	90	4	.290	.359	.225
Alex Clinton	91	288	35	82	10	3	5	41	113	10	35	10	.310	.392	.285
Rob Mackowiak	112	255	31	74	12	1	5	23	103	28	59	5	.365	.404	.290
Pablo Ozuna	79	189	25	62	12	2	2	17	84	7	16	6	.365	.444	.328
Ross Gload	77	156	22	51	8	2	3	18	72	6	15	6	.354	.462	.327
Sandy Alomar	19	46	5	10	3	0	1	8	16	3	7	0	.255	.348	.217
Ryan Sweeney	18	35	1	8	0	0	0	5	8	0	7	0	.229	.229	.229

PITCHING	GP	GS	W–L	SV	SHO	R	ERA	IP	Ks	BB
Freddy Garcia	33	33	17-9	0	0	116	4.53	216.1	135	48
Jon Garland	33	32	18-7	0	1	112	4.51	211.1	112	41
Mark Buehrle	32	32	12-13	0	0	124	4.99	204.0	98	48
Javier Vazquez	33	32	11-12	0	0	116	4.84	202.2	184	56
Jose Contreras	30	30	13-9	0	1	101	4.27	196.0	134	55
Brandon McCarthy	53	2	4-7	0	0	44	4.68	84.2	69	33
Bobby Jenks	67	0	3-4	41	0	32	4.00	69.2	80	31
Neal Cotts	70	0	1-2	1	0	33	5.17	54.0	43	24
Matt Thornton	63	0	5-3	2	0	20	3.33	54.0	49	21
David Riske	41	0	1-2	0	0	20	3.89	44.0	28	17
Cliff Politte	30	0	2-2	0	0	30	8.70	30.0	15	15
Mike MacDougal	29	0	1-1	1	0	5	1.55	29.0	21	6
Charlie Haeger	7	1	1-1	1	0	10	·3.44	18.1	19	13

Cleveland Indians

BATTING	G	AB	R	H	2B	3B	HR	RBI	TB	BB	SO	SB	OBP	SLG	BA
Grady Sizemore	162	655	134	190	53	11	28	76	349	78	153	22	.375	.533	.290
Victor Martinez	153	572	82	181	37	0	16	93	266	71	78	0	.391	.465	.316
Jhonny Peralta	149	569	84	146	28	3	13	68	219	56	152	0	.323	.385	.257
Jason Michaels	123	494	77	132	32	1	9	55	193	43	101	9	.326	.391	.267
Travis Hafner	129	454	100	140	31	1	42	117	299	100	111	0	.439	.659	308
Casey Blake	109	401	63	113	20	1	19	68	192	45	93	6	.356	.479	.282
Aaron Boone	104	354	50	89	19	1	7	46	131	27	62	5	.314	.370	.251
Ronnie Belliard	93	350	43	102	21	0	8	44	147	21	45	2	.337	.420	.291
Joe Inglett	64	201	26	57	8	3	2	21	77	14	39	5	.332	.383	.284
Ryan Garko	50	185	28	54	12	0	7	45	87	14	37	0	.359	.470	.292
Andy Marte	50	164	20	37	15	1	5	23	69	13	38	0	.287	.421	.226
Shin-shi Choo	49	157	23	44	12	3	3	22	71	18	50	5	.360	452	.280
Todd Hollandsworth	56	156	21	37	12	1	6	27	69	4	33	0	.253	.454	.237

PITCHING	GP	GS	W–L	SV	SHO	R	ERA	IP	Ks	BB
Jake Westbrook	32	32	15-10	0	2	106	4.17	211.1	109	55
Cliff Lee	33	33	14-11	0	0	114	4.40	200.2	129	58
C.C. Sabathia	28	28	12-11	0	2	83	3.22	192.2	172	44
Paul Byrd	31	31	10-9	0	0	120	4.88	179.0	88	38
Jeremy Sowers	14	14	7-4	0	2	36	3.57	88.1	35	20
Jason Johnson	14	14	3-8	0	0	55	5.96	77.0	32	22
Fausto Carmona	38	7	1-10	0	0	46	5.42	74.2	58	31
Fernando Cabrera	51	0	3-3	0	0	36	5.19	60.2	71	32
Rafael Betancourt	50	0	3-4	3	0	25	3.81	56.2	48	11
Jason Davis	39	0	3-2	1	0	28	3.74	55.1	37	14
Guillermo Mota	34	0	1-3	0	0	27	6.21	37.2	27	19
Bob Wickman	29	0	1-4	15	0	15	4.18	28.0	17	11
Brian Sikorski	17	0	2-1	0	0	10	4.58	19.2	24	4
Jeremy Guthrie	9	1	0-0	0	0	15	6.98	19.1	14	15
Edward Mujica	10	0	0-1	0	0	6	2.95	18.1	12	0

Detroit Tigers

BATTING	G	AB	R	H	2B	3B	HR	RBI	TB	BB	SO	SB	OBP	SLG	BA
Curtis Granderson	159	596	90	155	31	9	19	68	261	66	174	8	.335	.438	.260
Magglio Ordonez	155	593	82	177	32	1	24	104	283	45	87	1	.350	.477	.298
Ivan Rodriguez	136	547	74	164	28	4	13	69	239	26	86	8	.332	.437	.300
Carlos Guillen	153	543	100	174	41	5	19	85	282	71	87	20	.400	.519	.320
Brandon Inge	159	542	83	137	29	2	27	83	251	43	128	7	.313	.463	.253
Craig Monroe	147	541	89	138	35	2	28	92	261	37	126	2	.301	.482	.255
Placido Polanco	110	461	58	136	18	1	4	52	168	17	27	1	.329	.364	.295
Chris Shelton	115	373	50	102	16	4	16	47	174	34	107	1	.340	.466	.273
Matt Stairs	117	348	42	86	21	0	13	51	146	40	86	0	.328	.420	.247
Marcus Thames	110	348	61	89	20	2	26	60	191	37	92	1	.333	.549	.256
Omar Infante	78	224	35	62	11	4	4	25	93	14	45	3	.325	.415	.277
Sean Casey	53	184	17	45	7	0	5	30	67	10	21	0	.286	.364	.245
Dmitri Young	48	172	19	43	4	1	7	23	70	11	39	1	.293	.407	.250
Vance Wilson	56	152	18	43	9	0	5	18	67	2	33	0	.304	.441	.283
Alexis Gomez	62	103	17	28	5	2	1	6	40	6	21	4	.318	.388	.272
Ramon Santiago	43	80	9	18	1	1	0	3	21	1	14	2	.244	.263	.225

PITCHING	GP	GS	W–L	SV	SHO	R	ERA	IP	Ks	BB
Jeremy Bonderman	34	34	14-8	0	0	104	4.08	214.0	202	64
Nate Robertson	32	32	13-13	0	0	98	3.84	208.2	137	67
Kenny Rogers	34	33	17-8	0	0	97	3.84	204.0	99	62
Justin Verlander	30	30	17-9	0	1	78	3.63	186.0	124	60
Zach Miner	27	16	7-6	0	0	53	4.84	93.0	59	32
Joel Zumaya	62	0	6-3	1	0	20	1.94	83.1	97	42
Fernando Rodney	63	0	7-4	7	0	36	3.52	71.2	65	34
Todd Jones	62	0	2-6	37	0	31	3.94	64.0	28	11
Jason Grilli	51	0	2-3	0	0	31	4.21	62.0	31	25
Wilfredo Ledezma	24	7	3-3	0	0	28	3.58	60.1	39	23
Mike Maroth	13	9	5-2	0	0	26	4.19	53.2	24	16
Jamie Walker	56	0	0-1	0	0	15	2.81	48.0	37	8
Roman Colon	20	1	2-0	1	0	21	4.89	38.2	25	14
Bobby Seay	14	0	0-0	0	0	11	6.46	15.1	12	9
Jordan Tata	8	0	0-0	0	0	11	6.14	14.2	6	7

Kansas City Royals

BATTING	G	AB	R	H	2B	3B	HR	RBI	TB	BB	SO	SB	OBP	SLG	BA
Mark Grudzielanek	134	548	85	163	32	4	7	52	224	28	69	7	.331	.409	.297
Emil Brown	147	527	77	151	41	2	15	81	241	59	95	10	.358	.457	.287
David DeJesus	119	491	83	145	36	7	8	56	219	43	70	3	.364	.446	.295
Angel Berroa	132	474	45	111	18	1	9	54	158	14	88	5	.259	.333	.234
Mark Teahen	109	393	70	114	21	7	18	69	203	40	85	3	.357	.517	.290
Joey Gathright	134	383	59	91	12	3	1	41	112	42	75	7	.321	.292	.238
John Buck	114	371	37	91	21	1	11	50	147	26	84	2	.306	.396	.245
Reggie Sanders	88	325	45	80	23	1	11	49	138	28	86	1	.304	.425	.246
Doug Mientkiewicz	91	314	37	89	24	2	4	43	129	35	50	2	.359	.411	.283
Esteban German	106	279	44	91	18	5	3	34	128	40	49	4	.422	.459	.326
Shane Costa	72	237	23	65	20	1	3	23	96	6	29	3	.304	.405	.274
Tony Graffanino	69	220	34	59	16	0	5	32	90	25	31	1	.346	.409	.268
Mike Sweeney	60	217	23	56	15	0	8	33	95	28	48	0	.349	.438	.258
Ryan Shealy	51	193	29	54	10	1	7	36	87	15	50	0	.338	.451	.280

PITCHING	GP	GS	W–L	SV	SHO	R	ERA	IP	Ks	BB
Mark Redman	29	29	11-10	0	1	110	5.71	167.0	76	63
Scott Elarton	20	20	4-9	0	0	73	5.34	114.2	49	52
Runelvys Hernandez	21	21	6-10	0	1	87	6.48	109.2	50	48
Luke Hudson	26	15	7-6	0	0	62	5.12	102.0	64	38
Jimmy Gobble	60	6	4-6	2	0	51	5.14	84.0	80	29
Joel Peralta	64	0	1-3	1	0	37	4.40	73.2	57	17
Ambiorix Burgos	68	1	4-5	18	0	49	5.52	73.1	72	37
Jeremy Affeldt	27	9	4-6	0	0	51	5.91	70.0	28	42
Odalis Perez	12	12	2-4	0	0	44	5.64	67.0	48	18
Mike Wood	23	7	3-3	0	0	51	5.71	64.2	29	23
Andrew Sisco	65	0	1-3	1	0	47	7.10	58.1	52	40
Todd Wellemeyer	28	0	1-2	1	0	25	3.63	57.0	37	37

Los Angeles Angels of Anaheim

BATTING	G	AB	R	H	2B	3B	HR	RBI	TB	BB	SO	SB	OBP	SLG	BA
Orlando Cabrera	153	607	95	171	45	1	9	72	245	55	101	27	.335	.404	.282
Vladimir Guerrero	156	607	92	200	34	1	33	116	335	50	108	15	.382	.552	.329
Chone Figgins	155	604	93	161	23	8	9	62	227	65	84	52	.336	.376	.267
Garret Anderson	141	543	63	152	28	2	17	85	235	38	50	1	.323	.433	.280
Adam Kennedy	139	451	50	123	26	6	4	55	173	39	48	16	.334	.384	.273
Juan Rivera	124	448	65	139	27	0	23	85	235	33	64	0	.362	.525	.310
Maicer Izturis	104	352	64	103	21	3	5	44	145	38	41	14	.365	.412	.293
Mike Napoli	99	268	47	61	13	0	16	42	122	51	71	2	.360	.455	.228
Howie Kendrick	72	267	25	76	21	1	4	30	111	9	44	6	.314	.416	.285
Robb Quinlan	86	234	28	75	11	1	9	32	115	7	44	2	.344	.491	.321
Jose Molina	78	225	18	54	17	0	4	22	83	9	64	1	.273	.369	.240
Tim Salmon	76	211	30	56	8	2	9	27	95	29	21	0	.361	.450	.265
Kendry Morales	57	197	21	46	10	1	5	22	73	17	41	1	.293	.371	.285
Dallas McPherson	40	115	16	30	4	0	7	13	54	6	26	1	.298	.478	.321
Darin Erstad	40	95	8	21	8	1	0	5	31	6	18	1	.279	.326	.221

PITCHING	GP	GS	W–L	SV	SHO	R	ERA	IP	Ks	BB
John Lackey	33	33	13-11	0	0	98	3.56	217.2	190	72
Ervin Santana	33	33	16-8	0	0	106	4.28	204.0	141	70
Kelvim Escobar	30	30	11-14	0	0	93	3.61	189.1	147	50
Jered Weaver	19	19	11-2	0	0	36	2.56	123.0	105	33
Hector Carrasco	56	3	7-3	1	0	42	3.41	100.1	72	27
Jeff Weaver	16	16	3-10	0	0	68	6.29	88.2	62	21
Scot Shields	74	0	7-7	2	0	30	2.87	87.2	84	24
Kevin Gregg	32	3	3-4	0	0	41	4.14	78.1	71	21
Francisco Rodriguez	69	0	2-3	47	0	16	1.73	73.0	98	28
Joe Saunders	13	13	7-3	0	0	42	4.71	70.2	51	29
Brendan Donnelly	62	0	6-0	0	0	32	3.94	64.0	53	28
Bartolo Colon	10	10	1-5	0	0	39	5.11	56.1	31	11

Minnesota Twins

BATTING	G	AB	R	H	2B	3B	HR	RBI	TB	BB	SO	SB	OBP	SLG	BA
Justin Morneau	157	592	97	190	37	1	34	130	331	53	93	3	.375	.559	.321
Luis Castillo	142	584	84	173	22	6	3	49	216	56	53	25	.358	.370	.296
Michael Cuddyer	150	557	102	158	41	5	24	109	281	62	130	6	.362	.504	.284
Torii Hunter	147	557	86	155	21	2	31	98	273	45	108	12	.336	.490	.278
Joe Mauer	140	521	86	181	36	4	13	84	264	79	54	8	.429	.507	.347
Nick Punto	135	459	73	133	21	7	1	45	171	47	68	17	.352	.373	.290
Rondell White	99	337	32	83	17	1	7	38	123	11	54	1	.276	.365	.246
Jason Bartlett	99	333	44	103	18	2	2	32	131	22	46	10	.367	.393	.309
Lew Ford	104	234	40	53	6	1	4	18	73	16	43	9	.287	.312	.226
Jason Kubel	73	220	23	53	8	0	8	26	85	12	45	2	.279	.386	.241
Phil Nevin	62	218	28	46	9	0	10	35	85	31	54	0	.313	.390	.211
Jason Tyner	62	218	29	68	5	2	0	18	77	11	18	4	.345	.353	.312
Mike Redmond	47	179	20	61	13	0	0	23	74	4	18	0	.365	.413	.341
Tony Batista	50	178	24	42	12	0	5	21	69	15	27	0	.303	.388	.236
Shannon Stewart	44	174	21	51	5	1	2	21	64	14	19	3	.347	.368	.293
Juan Castro	50	156	10	36	5	2	1	14	48	6	23	1	.258	.308	.231
Luis Rodriguez	59	115	11	27	4	0	2	6	37	14	16	0	.315	.322	.235

PITCHING	GP	GS	W–L	SV	SHO	R	ERA	IP	Ks	BB
Johan Santana	34	34	19-6	0	0	79	2.77	233.2	245	47
Carlos Silva	36	31	11-15	0	0	130	5.94	180.1	70	32
Brad Radke	28	28	12-9	0	0	87	4.32	162.1	83	32
Francisco Liriano	28	16	12-3	1	0	31	2.16	121.0	144	32
Boof Bonser	18	18	7-6	0	0	50	4.22	100.1	84	24
Scott Baker	16	16	5-8	0	0	63	6.37	83.1	62	16
J.D. Crain	68	0	4-5	1	0	31	3.52	76.2	60	18
Juan Rincon	75	0	3-1	1	0	30	2.91	74.1	65	24
Matt Guerrier	39	1	7-0	0	0	29	3.36	69.2	37	21
Joe Nathan	64	0	7-0	36	0	12	1.58	68.1	95	16
Kyle Lohse	22	8	2-5	0	0	50	7.07	63.2	46	25
Willie Eyre	42	0	1-0	0	0	36	5.31	59.1	26	22

New York Yankees

BATTING	G	AB	R	H	2B	3B	HR	RBI	TB	BB	SO	SB	OBP	SLG	BA
Derek Jeter	154	623	118	214	39	3	14	97	301	69	102	34	.417	.483	.343
Johnny Damon	149	593	115	169	35	5	24	80	286	67	85	25	.359	.482	.285
Alex Rodriguez	154	572	113	166	26	1	35	121	299	90	139	15	.392	.523	.290
Robinson Cano	122	482	62	165	41	1	15	78	253	18	54	5	.365	.525	.342
Jorge Pasada	143	465	65	129	27	2	23	93	229	64	97	3	.374	.492	.277
Melky Cabrera	130	460	75	129	26	2	7	50	180	56	59	12	.360	.391	.280
Jason Giambi	139	446	92	113	25	0	37	113	249	110	106	2	.413	.558	.253
Bernie Williams	131	420	65	118	29	0	12	61	183	33	53	2	.332	.436	.281
Andy Phillips	110	246	30	59	11	3	7	29	97	15	56	3	.281	.394	.240
Miguel Cairo	81	222	28	53	12	3	0	30	71	13	31	13	.280	.320	.239
Bobby Abreu	58	309	37	69	16	0	7	42	106	33	52	10	.419	.507	.330
Hideki Matsui	51	172	32	52	9	0	8	29	85	27	23	1	.393	.494	.302
Gary Sheffield	39	151	22	45	5	0	6	25	68	13	16	5	.355	.450	.298
Aaron Guiel	63	132	25	32	6	0	7	18	59	14	31	2	.338	.447	.242

PITCHING	GP	GS	W-L	SV	SHO	R	ERA	IP	Ks	BB
Chien-Ming Wang	34	33	19-6	1	1	92	3.63	218.0	76	52
Randy Johnson	33	33	17-11	0	0	125	5.00	205.0	172	60
Mike Mussina	32	32	15-7	0	0	88	3.51	197.1	172	35
Jaret Wright	30	27	11-7	0	0	76	4.49	140.1	84	57
Scott Proctor	83	0	6-4	1	0	41	3.52	102.1	89	33
Ron Villone	70	0	3-3	0	0	48	5.04	80.1	72	51
Mariano Rivera	63	0	5-5	34	0	16	1.80	75.0	55	11
Kyle Farnsworth	72	0	3-6	6	0	34	4.36	66.0	75	28
Shawn Chacon	17	11	5-3	0	0	55	7.00	63.0	35	36
Cory Lidle	10	9	4-3	0	0	26	5.16	45.1	32	19
Jeff Karstens	8	6	2-1	0	0	20	3.80	42.2	16	11
Mike Myers	62	0	1-2	0	0	14	3.23	30.2	22	10
Aaron Small	11	3	0-3	0	0	29	8.46	27.2	12	12
Brian Bruney	19	0	1-1	0	0	2	0.87	20.2	25	15
Darrell Rasner	6	3	3-1	0	0	10	4.43	20.1	11	5

Oakland Athletics

BATTING	G	AB	R	H	2B	3B	HR	RBI	TB	BB	SO	SB	OBP	SLG	BA
Jay Payton	142	557	78	168	32	3	10	59	233	22	52	8	.325	.418	.296
Nick Swisher	157	556	106	141	24	2	35	95	274	97	152	1	.372	.493	.254
Jason Kendall	143	552	76	163	23	0	1	50	189	53	54	11	.367	.342	.295
Mark Kotsay	129	502	57	138	29	3	7	59	194	44	55	6	.332	.386	.275
Eric Chavez	137	485	74	117	24	2	22	72	211	84	100	3	.351	.435	.241
Frank Thomas	137	466	77	126	11	0	39	114	254	81	81	0	.381	.545	.270
Mark Ellis	124	441	64	110	25	1	11	52	170	40	76	4	.319	.385	.249
Marco Scutaro	117	365	52	97	21	6	5	41	145	50	66	5	.350	.397	.266
Bobby Crosby	96	358	42	82	12	0	9	40	121	36	76	8	.298	.338	.229
Milton Bradley	96	351	53	97	14	2	14	52	157	51	65	10	.370	.447	.276
Dan Johnson	91	286	30	67	13	1	9	37	109	40	45	0	.323	.381	.234
Bobby Kielty	81	270	35	73	20	1	8	36	119	22	49	2	.329	.441	.270
Adam Melhuse	49	128	10	28	8	0	4	18	48	9	34	0	.278	.375	.219
Antonio Perez	57	98	10	10	5	1	1	8	20	10	44	0	.185	.204	.102
D'Angelo Jimenez	28	71	8	13	3	0	1	8	19	16	13	0	.333	.268	.183

PITCHING	GP	GS	W-L	SV	SHO	R	ERA	IP	Ks	BB
Darren Haren	34	34	14-13	0	0	109	4.12	223.0	176	45
Barry Zito	34	34	16-10	0	0	99	3.83	221.0	151	99
Joe Blanton	32	31	16-12	0	1	111	4.82	194.1	107	58
Esteban Loaiza	26	26	11-9	0	1	92	4.89	154.2	97	40
Kirk Saarloos	35	16	7-7	2	0	70	4.75	121.1	52	53
Brad Halsey	52	7	5-4	0	0	53	4.67	94.1	53	46
Huston Street	69	0	4-4	37	0	28	3.31	70.2	67	13
Chad Gaudin	55	0	4-2	2	0	24	3.09	64.0	36	42
Kiko Calero	70	0	3-2	2	0	22	3.41	58.0	67	24
Justin Duchscherer	53	0	2-1	9	0	18	2.91	55.2	51	9
Rich Harden	9	9	4-0	0	0	22	4.24	46.2	49	26
Joe Kennedy	39	0	4-1	1	0	10	2.31	35.0	29	13

Seattle Mariners

BATTING	G	AB	R	H	2B	3B	HR	RBI	TB	BB	SO	SB	OBP	SLG	BA
Ichiro Suzuki	161	695	110	224	20	9	9	49	289	49	71	45	.370	.416	.322
Raul Ibanez	159	626	103	181	33	5	33	123	323	65	115	2	.353	.516	.289
Adrian Beltre	156	620	88	166	39	4	25	89	288	47	118	11	.328	.465	.268
Jose Lopez	151	603	78	170	28	8	10	79	244	26	80	5	.319	.405	.282
Richie Sexson	158	591	75	156	40	4	34	107	298	64	154	1	.338	.504	.264
Yuniesky Betancourt	157	558	68	161	28	6	8	47	225	17	54	11	.310	.403	.289
Kenji Johjima	144	506	61	147	25	1	18	76	228	20	46	3	.332	.451	.291
Ben Broussard	144	432	61	125	21	0	21	63	209	26	103	2	.331	.484	.289
Carl Everett	92	308	37	70	8	0	11	33	111	29	57	1	.297	.360	.227
Willie Bloomquist	102	251	36	62	6	2	1	15	75	24	40	16	.320	.299	.247
Jeremy Read	67	212	27	46	6	5	6	17	80	11	31	2	.260	.377	.217
Eduardo Perez	80	186	22	47	10	0	9	33	84	18	33	0	.324	.452	.253
Rene Rivera	35	99	8	15	4	0	2	4	25	3	29	1	.184	.253	.152
Chris Snelling	36	96	14	24	6	1	3	8	41	13	38	2	.360	.457	.250
Adam Jones	32	74	6	16	4	0	1	8	23	2	22	3	.237	.311	.216

PITCHING	GP	GS	W–L	SV	SHO	R	ERA	IP	Ks	BB
Felix Hernandez	31	31	12-14	0	1	105	4.52	191.0	176	60
Jarrod Washburn	31	31	8-14	0	0	103	4.67	187.0	103	55
Gil Meche	32	32	11-8	0	0	106	4.48	186.2	156	84
Joel Pineiro	40	25	8-13	1	0	123	6.36	165.2	87	64
Jamie Moyer	25	25	6-12	0	1	85	4.39	160.0	82	44
Jake Woods	37	8	7-4	1	0	51	4.20	105.0	66	53
J.J. Putz	72	0	4-1	36	0	20	2.30	78.1	104	13
Rafael Soriano	53	0	1-2	2	0	15	2.25	60.0	65	21
Julio Mateo	48	0	9-4	0	0	27	4.19	53.2	31	22
George Sherrill	72	0	2-4	1	0	19	4.28	40.0	42	27
Emiliano Fruto	23	0	2-2	1	0	24	5.50	36.0	34	24
Cha Seung Baek	6	6	4-1	0	0	15	3.67	34.1	23	13
Sean Green	24	0	0-0	0	0	16	4.50	32.0	15	13
Eddie Guardado	28	0	1-3	5	0	14	5.48	23.0	22	11

Tampa Bay Devil Rays

BATTING	G	AB	R	H	2B	3B	HR	RBI	TB	BB	SO	SB	OBP	SLG	BA
Carl Crawford	151	600	89	183	20	16	18	77	289	37	85	58	.348	.482	.305
Ty Wigginton	122	444	55	122	25	1	24	79	221	32	97	4	.330	.498	.275
Jorge Cantu	107	413	40	103	18	2	14	62	167	26	91	1	.295	.404	.249
Jonny Gomes	117	385	53	83	21	1	20	59	166	61	116	4	.325	.431	.216
Rocco Baldelli	92	364	59	110	24	6	16	57	194	14	70	10	.339	.533	.302
Travis Lee	114	343	35	77	11	2	11	31	125	42	73	5	.312	.364	.224
Damon Hollins	121	333	37	76	20	0	15	33	141	19	64	3	.269	.423	.228
Greg Norton	98	294	47	87	15	0	17	45	153	35	69	1	.374	.520	.296
Julio Lugo	73	289	53	89	17	1	12	27	144	27	47	18	.373	.498	.308
Tomas Perez	99	241	31	51	12	0	2	16	69	5	44	1	.224	.286	.212
Aubrey Huff	63	230	26	65	15	1	8	28	106	24	25	0	.348	.461	.283
Toby Hall	64	221	15	51	13	0	8	23	88	8	17	0	.261	.398	.231
Dioner Navarro	56	193	23	47	7	0	4	20	66	20	33	1	.316	.342	.244
Ben Zobrist	52	183	10	41	6	2	2	18	57	10	26	2	.260	.311	.224

PITCHING	GP	GS	W–L	SV	SHO	R	ERA	IP	Ks	BB
Scott Kazmir	24	24	10-8	0	1	59	3.24	144.2	163	52
Casey Fossum	25	25	6-6	0	0	89	5.33	130.0	88	63
James Shields	21	21	6-8	0	0	69	4.84	124.2	104	38
Seth McClung	39	15	6-12	6	0	77	6.29	103.0	59	68
Tim Corcoran	21	16	5-9	0	0	48	4.38	90.1	59	48
Jae Seo	17	16	1-8	0	0	56	5.00	90.0	39	31
Mark Hendrickson	13	13	4-8	0	1	42	3.81	89.2	51	34
Ruddy Lugo	64	0	2-4	4	0	39	3.81	85.0	48	37
Shamp Camp	75	0	7-4	8	0	43	4.68	75.0	53	19
Brian Meadows	53	0	3-6	0	0	43	5.17	69.2	35	15
Doug Waechter	11	10	1-4	0	0	40	6.62	53.0	25	19
Jason Hammel	9	9	0-6	0	0	38	7.77	44.0	32	21
J.P. Howell	8	8	1-3	0	0	25	5.10	42.1	33	14

American League Team-by-Team Statistical Leaders (Cont.)

Texas Rangers

BATTING	G	AB	R	H	2B	3B	HR	RBI	TB	BB	SO	SB	OBP	SLG	BA
Michael Young	162	691	93	217	52	3	14	103	317	48	96	7	.356	.459	.314
Mark Teixeira	162	628	99	177	45	1	33	110	323	89	128	2	.371	.514	.282
Gary Matthews	147	620	102	194	44	6	19	79	307	58	99	10	.371	.495	.313
Hank Blalock	152	591	76	157	26	3	16	89	237	51	98	1	.325	.401	.266
Mark DeRosa	136	520	78	154	40	2	13	74	237	44	102	4	.357	.456	.296
Ian Kinsler	120	423	65	121	27	1	14	55	192	40	64	11	.347	.454	.286
Rod Barajas	97	344	49	88	20	0	11	41	141	17	51	0	.298	.410	.256
Kevin Mench	87	320	36	91	18	1	12	50	147	23	42	1	.338	.459	.284
Brad Wilkerson	95	320	56	71	15	2	15	44	135	37	116	3	.306	.422	.222
Gerald Laird	78	243	46	72	20	1	7	22	115	12	54	3	.332	.473	.296
Carlos Lee	59	236	42	76	19	1	9	35	124	20	26	7	.369	.525	.322
Nelson Cruz	41	140	15	29	3	0	6	22	50	7	32	1	.261	.385	.223
Jerry Hairston	63	88	17	18	3	1	0	6	23	9	20	2	.286	.261	.205
Jason Botts	20	50	8	11	4	0	1	6	18	9	18	0	.317	.360	.220

PITCHING	GP	GS	W–L	SV	SHO	R	ERA	IP	Ks	BB
Kevin Millwood	34	34	16-12	0	0	114	4.52	215.0	157	53
Vincente Padilla	33	33	15-10	0	0	108	4.50	200.0	156	70
John Koronka	23	23	7-7	0	0	80	5.69	125.0	61	47
Joaquin Benoit	56	0	1-1	0	0	49	4.86	79.2	85	38
Kameron Loe	15	15	3-6	0	1	54	5.86	78.1	34	22
Robinson Tejeda	14	14	5-5	0	0	40	4.28	73.2	40	32
Rick Bauer	58	1	3-1	2	0	31	3.55	71.0	35	25
John Rheinecker	21	13	4-6	0	0	46	5.86	70.2	28	19
Adam Eaton	13	13	7-4	0	0	38	5.12	65.0	43	24
Mike Wood	23	7	3-3	0	0	51	5.71	64.2	29	23
Akinori Otsuka	63	0	2-4	32	0	17	2.11	59.2	47	11
Ron Mahay	62	0	1-3	0	0	30	3.95	57.0	56	28
Francisco Cordero	49	0	7-4	6	0	27	4.81	48.2	54	16
C.J. Wilson	44	0	2-4	1	0	23	4.06	44.1	43	18
Scott Feldman	36	0	0-2	0	0	19	3.92	41.1	30	10
Wes Littleton	33	0	2-1	1	0	7	1.73	36.1	17	13

Toronto Blue Jays

BATTING	G	AB	R	H	2B	3B	HR	RBI	TB	BB	SO	SB	OBP	SLG	BA
Vernon Wells	154	611	91	185	40	5	32	106	331	54	90	17	.357	.542	.303
Lyle Overbay	157	581	82	181	46	1	22	92	295	55	96	5	.372	.508	.312
Aaron Hill	155	546	70	159	28	3	6	50	211	42	66	5	.349	.386	.291
Troy Glaus	153	540	105	136	27	0	38	104	277	86	134	3	.355	.513	.252
Reed Johnson	134	461	86	147	34	2	12	49	221	33	81	8	.390	.479	.319
Alex Rios	128	450	68	136	33	6	17	82	232	35	89	15	.349	.516	.302
Frank Catalanotto	128	437	56	131	36	2	7	56	192	52	37	1	.376	.439	.300
Bengie Molina	117	433	44	123	20	1	19	57	202	19	47	1	.319	.467	.284
Shea Hillenbrand	81	296	40	89	15	1	12	39	142	14	40	1	.342	.480	.301
Gregg Zaun	99	290	39	79	19	0	12	40	134	41	42	0	.363	.462	.272
John McDonald	104	260	35	58	7	3	3	23	80	16	41	7	.271	.308	.223
Russ Adams	90	251	31	55	14	1	3	28	80	22	41	1	.282	.319	.219
Edgardo Alfonzo	30	87	5	11	2	0	0	5	13	7	4	0	.200	.149	.126
Adam Lind	18	60	8	22	8	0	2	8	36	5	12	0	.415	.600	.367

PITCHING	GP	GS	W–L	SV	SHO	R	ERA	IP	Ks	BB
Roy Halladay	32	32	16-5	0	0	82	3.19	220.0	132	34
Ted Lilly	32	32	15-13	0	0	98	4.31	181.2	160	81
A.J. Burnett	21	21	10-8	0	1	67	3.98	135.2	118	39
Casey Janssen	19	17	6-10	0	0	58	5.07	94.0	44	21
Gustavo Chacin	17	17	9-4	0	0	51	5.05	87.1	47	38
Shaun Marcum	21	14	3-4	0	0	44	5.06	78.1	65	38
Scott Downs	59	5	6-2	1	0	38	4.09	77.0	61	30
B.J. Ryan	65	0	2-2	38	0	12	1.37	72.1	86	20
Josh Towers	15	12	2-10	0	0	62	8.42	62.0	35	17
Brian Tallet	44	1	3-0	0	0	24	3.81	54.1	37	31
Justin Speier	58	0	2-0	0	0	18	2.98	51.1	55	21
Jason Frasor	51	0	3-2	0	0	24	4.32	50.0	51	17
Brandon League	33	0	1-2	1	0	17	2.53	42.2	29	9

FOR THE RECORD • Year by Year

The World Series

Results

1903..............Boston (A) 5, Pittsburgh (N) 3	1955..............Brooklyn (N) 4, New York (A) 3
1904..............No series	1956..............New York (A) 4, Brooklyn (N) 3
1905..............New York (N) 4, Philadelphia (A) 1	1957..............Milwaukee (N) 4, New York (A) 3
1906..............Chicago (A) 4, Chicago (N) 2	1958..............New York (A) 4, Milwaukee (N) 3
1907..............Chicago (N) 4, Detroit (A) 0; 1 tie	1959..............Los Angeles (N) 4, Chicago (A) 2
1908..............Chicago (N) 4, Detroit (A) 1	1960..............Pittsburgh (N) 4, New York (A) 3
1909..............Pittsburgh (N) 4, Detroit (A) 3	1961..............New York (A) 4, Cincinnati (N) 1
1910..............Philadelphia (A) 4, Chicago (N) 1	1962..............New York (A) 4, San Francisco (N) 3
1911..............Philadelphia (A) 4, New York (N) 2	1963..............Los Angeles (N) 4, New York (A) 0
1912..............Boston (A) 4, New York (N) 3; 1 tie	1964..............St. Louis (N) 4, New York (A) 3
1913..............Philadelphia (A) 4, New York (N) 1	1965..............Los Angeles (N) 4, Minnesota (A) 3
1914..............Boston (N) 4, Philadelphia (A) 0	1966..............Baltimore (A) 4, Los Angeles (N) 0
1915..............Boston (A) 4, Philadelphia (N) 1	1967..............St. Louis (N) 4, Boston (A) 3
1916..............Boston (A) 4, Brooklyn (N) 1	1968..............Detroit (A) 4, St. Louis (N) 3
1917..............Chicago (A) 4, New York (N) 2	1969..............New York (N) 4, Baltimore (A) 1
1918..............Boston (A) 4, Chicago (N) 2	1970..............Baltimore (A) 4, Cincinnati (N) 1
1919..............Cincinnati (N) 5, Chicago (A) 3	1971..............Pittsburgh (N) 4, Baltimore (A) 3
1920..............Cleveland (A) 5, Brooklyn (N) 2	1972..............Oakland (A) 4, Cincinnati (N) 3
1921..............New York (N) 5, New York (A) 3	1973..............Oakland (A) 4, New York (N) 3
1922..............New York (N) 4, New York (A) 0; 1 tie	1974..............Oakland (A) 4, Los Angeles (N) 1
1923..............New York (A) 4, New York (N) 2	1975..............Cincinnati (N) 4, Boston (A) 3
1924..............Washington (A) 4, New York (N) 3	1976..............Cincinnati (N) 4, New York (A) 0
1925..............Pittsburgh (N) 4, Washington (A) 3	1977..............New York (A) 4, Los Angeles (N) 2
1926..............St. Louis (N) 4, New York (A) 3	1978..............New York (A) 4, Los Angeles (N) 2
1927..............New York (A) 4, Pittsburgh (N) 0	1979..............Pittsburgh (N) 4, Baltimore (A) 3
1928..............New York (A) 4, St. Louis (N) 0	1980..............Philadelphia (N) 4, Kansas City (A) 2
1929..............Philadelphia (A) 4, Chicago (N) 1	1981..............Los Angeles (N) 4, New York (A) 2
1930..............Philadelphia (A) 4, St. Louis (N) 2	1982..............St. Louis (N) 4, Milwaukee (A) 3
1931..............St. Louis (N) 4, Philadelphia (A) 3	1983..............Baltimore (A) 4, Philadelphia (N) 1
1932..............New York (A) 4, Chicago (N) 0	1984..............Detroit (A) 4, San Diego (N) 1
1933..............New York (N) 4, Washington (A) 1	1985..............Kansas City (A) 4, St. Louis (N) 3
1934..............St. Louis (N) 4, Detroit (A) 3	1986..............New York (N) 4, Boston (A) 3
1935..............Detroit (A) 4, Chicago (N) 2	1987..............Minnesota (A) 4, St. Louis (N) 3
1936..............New York (A) 4, New York (N) 2	1988..............Los Angeles (N) 4, Oakland (A) 1
1937..............New York (A) 4, New York (N) 1	1989..............Oakland (A) 4, San Francisco (N) 0
1938..............New York (A) 4, Chicago (N) 0	1990..............Cincinnati (N) 4, Oakland (A) 0
1939..............New York (A) 4, Cincinnati (N) 0	1991..............Minnesota (A) 4, Atlanta (N) 3
1940..............Cincinnati (N) 4, Detroit (A) 3	1992..............Toronto (A) 4, Atlanta (N) 2
1941..............New York (A) 4, Brooklyn (N) 1	1993..............Toronto (A) 4, Philadelphia (N) 2
1942..............St. Louis (N) 4, New York (A) 1	1994..............Series canceled due to players' strike.
1943..............New York (A) 4, St. Louis (N) 1	1995..............Atlanta (N) 4, Cleveland (A) 2
1944..............St. Louis (N) 4, St. Louis (A) 2	1996..............New York (A) 4, Atlanta (N) 2
1945..............Detroit (A) 4, Chicago (N) 3	1997..............Florida (N) 4, Cleveland (A) 3
1946..............St. Louis (N) 4, Boston (A) 3	1998..............New York (A) 4, San Diego (N) 0
1947..............New York (A) 4, Brooklyn (N) 3	1999..............New York (A) 4, Atlanta (N) 0
1948..............Cleveland (A) 4, Boston (N) 2	2000..............New York (A) 4 , New York (N) 1
1949..............New York (A) 4, Brooklyn (N) 1	2001..............Arizona (N) 4, New York (A) 3
1950..............New York (A) 4, Philadelphia (N) 0	2002..............Anaheim (A) 4, San Francisco (N) 3
1951..............New York (A) 4, New York (N) 2	2003..............Florida (N) 4, New York (A) 2
1952..............New York (A) 4, Brooklyn (N) 3	2004..............Boston (A) 4, St. Louis (N) 0
1953..............New York (A) 4, Brooklyn (N) 2	2005..............Chicago (A) 4, Houston (N)
1954..............New York (N) 4, Cleveland (A) 0	2006..............St. Louis (N) 4, Detroit (A) 1

Most Valuable Players

1955	Johnny Podres, Bklyn
1956	Don Larsen, NY (A)
1957	Lew Burdette, Mil
1958	Bob Turley, NY (A)
1959	Larry Sherry, LA
1960	Bobby Richardson, NY (A)
1961	Whitey Ford, NY (A)
1962	Ralph Terry, NY (A)
1963	Sandy Koufax, LA
1964	Bob Gibson, StL
1965	Sandy Koufax, LA
1966	Frank Robinson, Balt
1967	Bob Gibson, StL
1968	Mickey Lolich, Det
1969	Donn Clendenon, NY (N)
1970	Brooks Robinson, Balt
1971	Roberto Clemente, Pitt
1972	Gene Tenace, Oak
1973	Reggie Jackson, Oak
1974	Rollie Fingers, Oak
1975	Pete Rose, Cin
1976	Johnny Bench, Cin
1977	Reggie Jackson, NY (A)
1978	Bucky Dent, NY (A)
1979	Willie Stargell, Pitt
1980	Mike Schmidt, Phil
1981	Ron Cey, LA; Steve Yeager, LA; Pedro Guerrero, LA
1982	Darrell Porter, StL
1983	Rick Dempsey, Balt
1984	Alan Trammell, Det
1985	Bret Saberhagen, KC
1986	Ray Knight, NY (N)
1987	Frank Viola, Minn
1988	Orel Hershiser, LA
1989	Dave Stewart, Oak
1990	Jose Rijo, Cin
1991	Jack Morris, Minn
1992	Pat Borders, Tor
1993	Paul Molitor, Tor
1994	Series canceled due to strike.
1995	Tom Glavine, Atl
1996	John Wetteland, NY (A)
1997	Livan Hernandez, Fla
1998	Scott Brosius, NY (A)
1999	Mariano Rivera, NY (A)
2000	Derek Jeter, NY (A)
2001	Randy Johnson, Ariz Curt Schilling, Ariz
2002	Troy Glaus, Ana
2003	Josh Beckett, Fla
2004	Manny Ramirez, Bos
2005	Jermaine Dye, Chi (A)
2006	David Eckstein, StL

Career Batting Leaders (Minimum 40 at bats)

GAMES

Yogi Berra	75
Mickey Mantle	65
Elston Howard	54
Hank Bauer	53
Gil McDougald	53
Phil Rizzuto	52
Joe DiMaggio	51
Frankie Frisch	50
Pee Wee Reese	44
Roger Maris	41
Babe Ruth	41

AT BATS

Yogi Berra	259
Mickey Mantle	230
Joe DiMaggio	199
Frankie Frisch	197
Gil McDougald	190
Hank Bauer	188
Phil Rizzuto	183
Elston Howard	171
Pee Wee Reese	169
Roger Maris	152

HITS

Yogi Berra	71
Mickey Mantle	59
Frankie Frisch	58
Joe DiMaggio	54
Pee Wee Reese	46
Hank Bauer	46
Phil Rizzuto	45
Gil McDougald	45
Lou Gehrig	43
Eddie Collins	42
Babe Ruth	42
Elston Howard	42

BATTING AVERAGE

Bobby Brown	.439
Paul Molitor	.418
Pepper Martin	.418
Hal McRae	.400
Lou Brock	.391
Marquis Grissom	.390
Thurman Munson	.373
George Brett	.373
Pat Borders	.372
Hank Aaron	.364

HOME RUNS

Mickey Mantle	18
Babe Ruth	15
Yogi Berra	12
Duke Snider	11
Reggie Jackson	10
Lou Gehrig	10
Frank Robinson	8
Bill Skowron	8
Joe DiMaggio	8
Goose Goslin	7
Hank Bauer	7
Gil McDougald	7

RUNS BATTED IN

Mickey Mantle	40
Yogi Berra	39
Lou Gehrig	35
Babe Ruth	33
Joe DiMaggio	30
Bill Skowron	29
Duke Snider	26
Reggie Jackson	24
Bill Dickey	24
Hank Bauer	24
Gil McDougald	24

RUNS

Mickey Mantle	42
Yogi Berra	41
Babe Ruth	37
Lou Gehrig	30
Joe DiMaggio	27
Derek Jeter	27
Roger Maris	26
Elston Howard	25
Gil McDougald	23
Jackie Robinson	22

STOLEN BASES

Lou Brock	14
Eddie Collins	14
Frank Chance	10
Davey Lopes	10
Phil Rizzuto	10
Honus Wagner	9
Frankie Frisch	9
Kenny Lofton	9
Johnny Evers	8
Roberto Alomar	7
Joe Tinker	7
Pepper Martin	7
Joe Morgan	7
Rickey Henderson	7

Career Batting Leaders (Cont.)

TOTAL BASES

Mickey Mantle	123
Yogi Berra	117
Babe Ruth	96
Lou Gehrig	87
Joe DiMaggio	84
Duke Snider	79
Hank Bauer	75
Reggie Jackson	74
Frankie Frisch	74
Gil McDougald	72

SLUGGING AVERAGE

Reggie Jackson	.755
Babe Ruth	.744
Lou Gehrig	.731
Bobby Brown	.707
Lenny Dykstra	.700
Al Simmons	.658
Lou Brock	.655
Pepper Martin	.636
Paul Molitor	.636
Joe Harris	.625

STRIKEOUTS

Mickey Mantle	54
Elston Howard	37
Duke Snider	33
Derek Jeter	33
Babe Ruth	30
David Justice	30
Gil McDougald	29
Bill Skowron	26
Bernie Williams	26
Hank Bauer	25

Career Pitching Leaders

GAMES

Whitey Ford	22
Mariano Rivera	20
Mike Stanton	19
Jeff Nelson	16
Rollie Fingers	16
Allie Reynolds	15
Bob Turley	15
Clay Carroll	14
Clem Labine	13
Mark Wohlers	13

INNINGS PITCHED

Whitey Ford	146
Christy Mathewson	101⅔
Red Ruffing	85⅝
Chief Bender	85
Waite Hoyt	83⅔
Bob Gibson	81
Art Nehf	79
Allie Reynolds	77
Jim Palmer	65
Catfish Hunter	63

WINS

Whitey Ford	10
Bob Gibson	7
Red Ruffing	7
Allie Reynolds	7
Lefty Gomez	6
Chief Bender	6
Waite Hoyt	6
Jack Coombs	5
Three Finger Brown	5
Herb Pennock	5
Christy Mathewson	5
Vic Raschi	5
Catfish Hunter	5

LOSSES

Whitey Ford	8
Eddie Plank	5
Schoolboy Rowe	5
Joe Bush	5
Rube Marquard	5
Christy Mathewson	5
Andy Pettite	5

SAVES

Mariano Rivera	9
Rollie Fingers	6
Allie Reynolds	4
Johnny Murphy	4
John Wetteland	4
Robb Nen	4

*EARNED RUN AVERAGE

Jack Billingham	0.36
Harry Brecheen	0.83
Babe Ruth	0.87
Sherry Smith	0.89
Sandy Koufax	0.95
Hippo Vaughn	1.00
Monte Pearson	1.01
Christy Mathewson	1.06
Mariano Rivera	1.16
Babe Adams	1.29

SHUTOUTS

Christy Mathewson	4
Three Finger Brown	3
Whitey Ford	3
Bill Hallahan	2
Lew Burdette	2
Bill Dinneen	2
Sandy Koufax	2
Allie Reynolds	2
Art Nehf	2
Bob Gibson	2

*Minimum 25 innings pitched.

COMPLETE GAMES

Christy Mathewson	10
Chief Bender	9
Bob Gibson	8
Red Ruffing	7
Whitey Ford	7
George Mullin	6
Eddie Plank	6
Art Nehf	6
Waite Hoyt	6

STRIKEOUTS

Whitey Ford	94
Bob Gibson	92
Allie Reynolds	62
Sandy Koufax	61
Red Ruffing	61
Chief Bender	59
George Earnshaw	56
John Smoltz	52
Waite Hoyt	49
Roger Clemens	49
Christy Mathewson	48

BASES ON BALLS

Whitey Ford	34
Allie Reynolds	32
Art Nehf	32
Jim Palmer	31
Bob Turley	29
Paul Derringer	27
Red Ruffing	27
Don Gullett	26
Burleigh Grimes	26
Vic Raschi	25

Alltime Team Rankings (by championships)

Team	W	L	Appearances	Pct.	Most Recent	Last Championship
New York Yankees	26	13	39	.666	2003	2000
St. Louis Cardinals	10	7	17	.588	2006	2006
Phil/KC/Oakland Athletics	9	5	14	.643	1990	1989
Brooklyn/LA Dodgers	6	12	18	.333	1988	1988
Boston Red Sox	6	4	10	.600	2004	2004
Pittsburgh Pirates	5	2	7	.714	1979	1979
Cincinnati Reds	5	4	9	.556	1990	1990
New York/San Francisco Giants	5	12	17	.294	2002	1954
Detroit Tigers	4	6	10	.400	2006	1984
Washington/Minnesota Twins	3	3	6	.500	1991	1991

Alltime Team Rankings (by championships)

Team	W	L	Appearances	Pct.	Most Recent	Last Championship
St. Louis/Baltimore Orioles	3	4	7	.429	1983	1983
Boston/Milwaukee/Atlanta Braves	3	6	9	.333	1999	1995
Florida Marlins	2	0	2	1.000	2003	2003
Toronto Blue Jays	2	0	2	1.000	1993	1993
New York Mets	2	2	4	.500	2000	1986
Chicago White Sox	3	2	5	.600	2005	2005
Cleveland Indians	2	3	5	.400	1997	1948
Chicago Cubs	2	8	10	.200	1945	1908
Anaheim Angels	1	0	1	1.000	2002	2002
Arizona Diamondbacks	1	0	1	1.000	2001	2001
Kansas City Royals	1	1	2	.500	1985	1985
Philadelphia Phillies	1	4	5	.200	1993	1980
Houston Astros	0	1	1	.000	2005	—
San Diego Padres	0	2	2	.000	1998	—
Seattle/Milwaukee Brewers	0	1	1	.000	1982	—

League Pennant Winners

National League

Year	Team	Manager	W	L	Pct	GA
1900	Brooklyn	Ned Hanlon	82	54	.603	4½
1901	Pittsburgh	Fred Clarke	90	49	.647	7½
1902	Pittsburgh	Fred Clarke	103	36	.741	27½
1903	Pittsburgh	Fred Clarke	91	49	.650	6½
1904	New York	John McGraw	106	47	.693	13
1905	New York	John McGraw	105	48	.686	9
1906	Chicago	Frank Chance	116	36	.763	20
1907	Chicago	Frank Chance	107	45	.704	17
1908	Chicago	Frank Chance	99	55	.643	1
1909	Pittsburgh	Fred Clarke	110	42	.724	6½
1910	Chicago	Frank Chance	104	50	.675	13
1911	New York	John McGraw	99	54	.647	7½
1912	New York	John McGraw	103	48	.682	10
1913	New York	John McGraw	101	51	.664	12½
1914	Boston	George Stallings	94	59	.614	10½
1915	Philadelphia	Pat Moran	90	62	.592	7
1916	Brooklyn	Wilbert Robinson	94	60	.610	2½
1917	New York	John McGraw	98	56	.636	10
1918	Chicago	Fred Mitchell	84	45	.651	10½
1919	Cincinnati	Pat Moran	96	44	.686	9
1920	Brooklyn	Wilbert Robinson	93	61	.604	7
1921	New York	John McGraw	94	59	.614	4
1922	New York	John McGraw	93	61	.604	7
1923	New York	John McGraw	95	58	.621	4½
1924	New York	John McGraw	93	60	.608	1½
1925	Pittsburgh	Bill McKechnie	95	58	.621	8½
1926	St. Louis	Rogers Hornsby	89	65	.578	2
1927	Pittsburgh	Donie Bush	94	60	.610	1½
1928	St. Louis	Bill McKechnie	95	59	.617	2
1929	Chicago	Joe McCarthy	98	54	.645	10½
1930	St. Louis	Gabby Street	92	62	.597	2
1931	St. Louis	Gabby Street	101	53	.656	13
1932	Chicago	Charlie Grimm	90	64	.584	4
1933	New York	Bill Terry	91	61	.599	5
1934	St. Louis	Frankie Frisch	95	58	.621	2
1935	Chicago	Charlie Grimm	100	54	.649	4
1936	New York	Bill Terry	92	62	.597	5
1937	New York	Bill Terry	95	57	.625	3
1938	Chicago	Gabby Hartnett	89	63	.586	2
1939	Cincinnati	Bill McKechnie	97	57	.630	4½
1940	Cincinnati	Bill McKechnie	100	53	.654	12
1941	Brooklyn	Leo Durocher	100	54	.649	2½
1942	St. Louis	Billy Southworth	106	48	.688	2
1943	St. Louis	Billy Southworth	105	49	.682	18
1944	St. Louis	Billy Southworth	105	49	.682	14½

National League *(Cont.)*

Year	Team	Manager	W	L	Pct	GA
1945	Chicago	Charlie Grimm	98	56	.636	3
1946	St. Louis*	Eddie Dyer	98	58	.628	2
1947	Brooklyn	Burt Shotton	94	60	.610	5
1948	Boston	Billy Southworth	91	62	.595	6½
1949	Brooklyn	Burt Shotton	97	57	.630	1
1950	Philadelphia	Eddie Sawyer	91	63	.591	2
1951	New York†	Leo Durocher	98	59	.624	1
1952	Brooklyn	Chuck Dressen	96	57	.627	4½
1953	Brooklyn	Chuck Dressen	105	49	.682	13
1954	New York	Leo Durocher	97	57	.630	5
1955	Brooklyn	Walter Alston	98	55	.641	13½
1956	Brooklyn	Walter Alston	93	61	.604	1
1957	Milwaukee	Fred Haney	95	59	.617	8
1958	Milwaukee	Fred Haney	92	62	.597	8
1959	Los Angeles‡	Walter Alston	88	68	.564	2
1960	Pittsburgh	Danny Murtaugh	95	59	.617	7
1961	Cincinnati	Fred Hutchinson	93	61	.604	4
1962	San Francisco#	Al Dark	103	62	.624	1
1963	Los Angeles	Walter Alston	99	63	.611	6
1964	St. Louis	Johnny Keane	93	69	.574	1
1965	Los Angeles	Walter Alston	97	65	.599	2
1966	Los Angeles	Walter Alston	95	67	.586	1½
1967	St. Louis	Red Schoendienst	101	60	.627	10½
1968	St. Louis	Red Schoendienst	97	65	.599	9
1969	New York (E)††	Gil Hodges	100	62	.617	8
1970	Cincinnati (W)††	Sparky Anderson	102	60	.630	14½
1971	Pittsburgh (E)††	Danny Murtaugh	97	65	.599	7
1972	Cincinnati (W)††	Sparky Anderson	95	59	.617	10½
1973	New York (E)††	Yogi Berra	82	79	.509	1½
1974	Los Angeles (W)††	Walter Alston	102	60	.630	4
1975	Cincinnati (W)††	Sparky Anderson	108	54	.667	20
1976	Cincinnati (W)††	Sparky Anderson	102	60	.630	10
1977	Los Angeles (W)††	Tommy Lasorda	98	64	.605	10
1978	Los Angeles (W)††	Tommy Lasorda	95	67	.586	2½
1979	Pittsburgh (E)††	Chuck Tanner	98	64	.605	2
1980	Philadelphia (E)††	Dallas Green	91	71	.562	1
1981	Los Angeles (W)††	Tommy Lasorda	63	47	.573	**
1982	St. Louis (E)††	Whitey Herzog	92	70	.568	3
1983	Philadelphia (E)††	Pat Corrales/ Paul Owens	90	72	.556	6
1984	San Diego (W)††	Dick Williams	92	70	.568	12
1985	St. Louis (E)††	Whitey Herzog	101	61	.623	3
1986	New York (E)††	Davey Johnson	108	54	.667	21½
1987	St. Louis (E)††	Whitey Herzog	95	67	.586	3
1988	Los Angeles (W)††	Tommy Lasorda	94	67	.584	7
1989	San Francisco (W)††	Roger Craig	92	70	.568	3
1990	Cincinnati (W)††	Lou Piniella	91	71	.562	5
1991	Atlanta (W)††	Bobby Cox	94	68	.580	1
1992	Atlanta (W)††	Bobby Cox	98	64	.605	8
1993	Philadelphia (E)††	Jim Fregosi	97	65	.599	3
1994	Season ended Aug. 11 due to players' strike.					
1995	Atlanta (E)††	Bobby Cox	90	54	.625	21
1996	Atlanta (E)††	Bobby Cox	96	66	.593	8
1997	Florida (wc)††	Jim Leyland	92	70	.568	-9
1998	San Diego (W)††	Bruce Bochy	98	64	.605	9½
1999	Atlanta (E)††	Bobby Cox	103	59	.636	6½
2000	New York (wc)††	Bobby Valentine	94	68	.580	-6½
2001	Arizona (W)††	Bob Brenly	92	70	.568	2
2002	San Francisco (wc)††	Dusty Baker	95	66	.590	-2½
2003	Florida (wc)††	Jack McKeon	91	71	.562	-10
2004	St. Louis (C)††	Tony La Russa	105	57	.648	13
2005	Houston (wc)††	Phil Garner	89	73	.549	-11
2006	St. Louis (C)††	Tony La Russa	83	78	.516	1½

*Defeated Brooklyn, two games to none, in playoff for pennant. †Defeated Brooklyn, two games to one, in playoff for pennant. ‡Defeated Milwaukee, two games to none, in playoff for pennant. #Defeated Los Angeles, two games to one, in playoff for pennant. ††Won Championship Series. **First half 36–21; second half 27–26, in season split by strike; defeated Houston in playoff for Western Division title.

American League

Year	Team	Manager	W	L	Pct	GA
1901	Chicago	Clark Griffith	83	53	.610	4
1902	Philadelphia	Connie Mack	83	53	.610	5
1903	Boston	Jimmy Collins	91	47	.659	14½
1904	Boston	Jimmy Collins	95	59	.617	1½
1905	Philadelphia	Connie Mack	92	56	.622	2
1906	Chicago	Fielder Jones	93	58	.616	3
1907	Detroit	Hughie Jennings	92	58	.613	1½
1908	Detroit	Hughie Jennings	90	63	.588	½
1909	Detroit	Hughie Jennings	98	54	.645	3½
1910	Philadelphia	Connie Mack	102	48	.680	14½
1911	Philadelphia	Connie Mack	101	50	.669	13½
1912	Boston	Jake Stahl	105	47	.691	14
1913	Philadelphia	Connie Mack	96	57	.627	6½
1914	Philadelphia	Connie Mack	99	53	.651	8½
1915	Boston	Bill Carrigan	101	50	.669	2½
1916	Boston	Bill Carrigan	91	63	.591	2
1917	Chicago	Pants Rowland	100	54	.649	9
1918	Boston	Ed Barrow	75	51	.595	2½
1919	Chicago	Kid Gleason	88	52	.629	3½
1920	Cleveland	Tris Speaker	98	56	.636	2
1921	New York	Miller Huggins	98	55	.641	4½
1922	New York	Miller Huggins	94	60	.610	1
1923	New York	Miller Huggins	98	54	.645	16
1924	Washington	Bucky Harris	92	62	.597	2
1925	Washington	Bucky Harris	96	55	.636	8½
1926	New York	Miller Huggins	91	63	.591	3
1927	New York	Miller Huggins	110	44	.714	19
1928	New York	Miller Huggins	101	53	.656	2½
1929	Philadelphia	Connie Mack	104	46	.693	18
1930	Philadelphia	Connie Mack	102	52	.662	8
1931	Philadelphia	Connie Mack	107	45	.704	13½
1932	New York	Joe McCarthy	107	47	.695	13
1933	Washington	Joe Cronin	99	53	.651	7
1934	Detroit	Mickey Cochrane	101	53	.656	7
1935	Detroit	Mickey Cochrane	93	58	.616	3
1936	New York	Joe McCarthy	102	51	.667	19½
1937	New York	Joe McCarthy	102	52	.662	13
1938	New York	Joe McCarthy	99	53	.651	9½
1939	New York	Joe McCarthy	106	45	.702	17
1940	Detroit	Del Baker	90	64	.584	1
1941	New York	Joe McCarthy	101	53	.656	17
1942	New York	Joe McCarthy	103	51	.669	9
1943	New York	Joe McCarthy	98	56	.636	13½
1944	St. Louis	Luke Sewell	89	65	.578	1
1945	Detroit	Steve O'Neill	88	65	.575	1½
1946	Boston	Joe Cronin	104	50	.675	12
1947	New York	Bucky Harris	97	57	.630	12
1948	Cleveland†	Lou Boudreau	97	58	.626	1
1949	New York	Casey Stengel	97	57	.630	1
1950	New York	Casey Stengel	98	56	.636	3
1951	New York	Casey Stengel	98	56	.636	5
1952	New York	Casey Stengel	95	59	.617	2
1953	New York	Casey Stengel	99	52	.656	8½
1954	Cleveland	Al Lopez	111	43	.721	8
1955	New York	Casey Stengel	96	58	.623	3
1956	New York	Casey Stengel	97	57	.630	9
1957	New York	Casey Stengel	98	56	.636	8
1958	New York	Casey Stengel	92	62	.597	10
1959	Chicago	Al Lopez	94	60	.610	5
1960	New York	Casey Stengel	97	57	.630	8
1961	New York	Ralph Houk	109	53	.673	8
1962	New York	Ralph Houk	96	66	.593	5
1963	New York	Ralph Houk	104	57	.646	10½
1964	New York	Yogi Berra	99	63	.611	1
1965	Minnesota	Sam Mele	102	60	.630	7
1966	Baltimore	Hank Bauer	97	63	.606	9
1967	Boston	Dick Williams	92	70	.568	1

Arizona Diamondbacks

BATTING	G	AB	R	H	2B	3B	HR	RBI	TB	BB	SO	SB	OBP	SLG	BA
Chad Tracy	154	597	91	168	41	0	20	80	269	54	129	5	.343	.451	.281
Luis Gonzalez	153	586	93	159	52	2	15	73	260	69	58	0	.352	.444	.271
Orlando Hudson	157	579	87	166	34	9	15	67	263	61	78	9	.354	.454	.287
Eric Byrnes	143	562	82	150	37	3	26	79	271	34	88	25	.313	.482	.267
Conor Jackson	140	485	75	141	26	1	15	79	214	54	73	1	.368	.441	.291
Johnny Estrada	115	414	43	125	26	0	11	71	184	13	40	0	.328	.444	.302
Craig Counsell	105	372	56	95	14	4	4	30	129	31	47	15	.327	.347	.255
Jeff DaVanon	87	221	38	64	12	4	5	35	99	31	42	10	.371	.448	.290
Stephen Drew	59	209	27	66	13	7	5	23	108	14	50	2	.357	.517	.316
Damion Easley	90	189	24	44	6	1	9	28	79	21	30	1	.323	.418	.233
Chris Snyder	61	184	19	51	9	0	6	32	78	22	39	0	.349	.424	.277
Carlos Quentin	57	166	23	42	13	3	9	32	88	15	34	1	.342	.530	.253
Tony Clark	79	132	13	26	4	0	6	16	48	13	40	0	.279	.364	.197
Andy Green	73	86	15	16	4	0	1	6	23	13	20	1	.293	.267	.186

PITCHING	GP	GS	W-L	SV	SHO	R	ERA	IP	Ks	BB
Brandon Webb	33	33	16-8	0	3	91	3.10	235.0	178	50
Livan Hernandez	34	34	13-13	0	0	125	4.83	216.0	128	78
Miguel Baptista	34	33	11-8	0	1	116	4.58	206.1	110	84
Claudio Vargas	31	30	12-10	0	0	101	4.83	167.2	123	52
Enrique Gonzalez	22	18	3-7	0	0	71	5.67	106.1	66	34
Juan Cruz	31	15	5-6	0	0	45	4.18	94.2	88	47
Brandon Medders	60	0	5-3	0	0	37	3.64	71.2	47	28
Brandon Lyon	68	0	2-4	0	0	32	3.89	69.1	46	22
Jorge Julio	62	0	2-4	16	0	35	4.23	66.0	88	35
Luis Vizcaino	70	0	4-6	0	0	26	3.58	65.1	72	29
Jose Valverde	44	0	2-3	18	0	32	5.84	49.1	69	22
Greg Aquino	42	0	2-0	0	0	27	4.47	48.1	51	24
Edgar Gonzalez	11	5	3-4	0	0	20	4.22	42.2	28	9
Tony Pena	25	0	3-4	1	0	21	5.58	30.2	21	8
Jason Grimsley	19	0	1-2	0	0	15	4.88	27.2	10	8

Atlanta Braves

BATTING	G	AB	R	H	2B	3B	HR	RBI	TB	BB	SO	SB	OBP	SLG	BA
Jeff Francoeur	162	651	83	169	24	6	29	103	292	23	132	1	.293	.449	.260
Edgar Renteria	149	598	100	175	40	2	14	70	261	62	89	17	.361	.436	.293
Andruw Jones	156	565	107	148	29	0	41	129	300	82	127	4	.363	.531	.262
Marcus Giles	141	550	87	144	32	2	11	60	213	62	105	10	.341	.387	.262
Adam LaRoche	149	492	89	140	38	1	32	90	276	55	128	0	.354	.561	.285
Brian McCann	130	442	61	147	34	0	24	93	253	41	54	2	.388	.572	.333
Chipper Jones	110	411	87	133	28	3	26	86	245	61	73	6	.409	.596	.324
Ryan Langerhans	131	315	46	76	16	3	7	28	119	50	91	1	.350	.378	.241
Matt Diaz	124	297	37	97	15	4	7	32	141	11	49	5	.364	.475	.327
Willy Aybar	79	243	32	68	18	0	4	30	98	28	36	1	.364	.403	.280
Pete Orr	102	154	22	39	3	4	1	8	53	5	30	2	.277	.344	.253
Todd Pratt	62	135	14	28	6	0	4	19	46	12	43	1	.272	.341	.207
Daryle Ward	98	130	17	40	10	0	7	26	71	15	27	0	.380	.546	.308
Scott Thorman	55	128	13	30	11	0	5	14	56	5	21	1	.263	.438	.234
Brian Jordan	48	91	11	21	2	0	3	10	32	7	23	0	.287	.352	.231
John Smoltz	33	64	5	8	3	0	0	4	11	4	27	0	.176	.172	.125

PITCHING	GP	GS	W-L	SV	SHO	R	ERA	IP	Ks	BB
John Smoltz	35	35	16-9	0	1	93	3.49	232.0	211	55
Tim Hudson	35	35	13-12	0	1	129	4.86	218.1	141	79
Chuck James	25	18	11-4	0	0	54	3.78	119.0	91	47
Oscar Villarreal	58	4	9-1	0	0	41	3.61	92.1	55	27
John Thomson	18	15	2-7	0	0	55	4.82	80.1	46	32
Horacio Ramirez	14	14	5-5	0	0	42	4.48	76.1	37	31
Lance Cormier	29	9	4-5	0	0	44	4.89	73.2	43	39
Ken Ray	69	0	1-1	5	0	36	4.52	67.2	50	38
Kyle Davies	14	14	3-7	0	0	60	8.38	63.1	51	33
Danys Baez	57	0	5-6	9	0	35	4.53	59.2	39	17
Macay McBride	71	0	4-1	1	0	28	3.65	56.2	46	32
Chad Paronto	65	0	2-3	0	0	23	3.18	56.2	41	19
Tyler Yates	56	0	2-5	1	0	23	3.96	50.0	46	31
Chris Reitsma	27	0	1-2	8	0	27	8.68	28.0	13	8
Bob Wickman	28	0	0-2	18	0	7	1.04	26.0	25	2

American League *(Cont.)*

Year	Team	Manager	W	L	Pct	GA
1968	Detroit	Mayo Smith	103	59	.636	12
1969	Baltimore (E)‡	Earl Weaver	109	53	.673	19
1970	Baltimore (E)‡	Earl Weaver	108	54	.667	15
1971	Baltimore (E)‡	Earl Weaver	101	57	.639	12
1972	Oakland (W)‡	Dick Williams	93	62	.600	5½
1973	Oakland (W)‡	Dick Williams	94	68	.580	6
1974	Oakland (W)‡	Al Dark	90	72	.556	5
1975	Boston (E)‡	Darrell Johnson	95	65	.594	4½
1976	New York (E)‡	Billy Martin	97	62	.610	10½
1977	New York (E)‡	Billy Martin	100	62	.617	2½
1978	New York (E)†‡	Billy Martin, Bob Lemon	100	63	.613	1
1979	Baltimore (E)‡	Earl Weaver	102	57	.642	8
1980	Kansas City (W)‡	Jim Frey	97	65	.599	14
1981	New York (E)‡	Gene Michael/Bob Lemon	59	48	.551	#
1982	Milwaukee (E)‡	Buck Rodgers, Harvey Kuenn	95	67	.586	1
1983	Baltimore (E)‡	Joe Altobelli	98	64	.605	6
1984	Detroit (E)‡	Sparky Anderson	104	58	.642	15
1985	Kansas City (W)‡	Dick Howser	91	71	.562	1
1986	Boston (E)‡	John McNamara	95	66	.590	5½
1987	Minnesota (W)‡	Tom Kelly	85	77	.525	2
1988	Oakland (W)‡	Tony La Russa	104	58	.642	13
1989	Oakland (W)‡	Tony La Russa	99	63	.611	7
1990	Oakland (W)‡	Tony La Russa	103	59	.636	9
1991	Minnesota (W)‡	Tom Kelly	95	67	.586	8
1992	Toronto‡	Cito Gaston	96	66	.593	4
1993	Toronto‡	Cito Gaston	95	67	.586	7
1994	Season ended Aug. 11 due to players' strike.					
1995	Cleveland (C)‡	Mike Hargrove	100	44	.694	30
1996	New York (E)‡	Joe Torre	92	70	.568	4
1997	Cleveland (C)‡	Mike Hargrove	86	75	.534	6
1998	New York (E)‡	Joe Torre	114	48	.704	22
1999	New York (E)‡	Joe Torre	98	64	.605	4
2000	New York (E)‡	Joe Torre	87	74	.540	2½
2001	New York (E)‡	Joe Torre	95	65	.594	13½
2002	Anaheim (wc)‡	Mike Scioscia	99	63	.611	-4
2003	New York (E)‡	Joe Torre	101	61	.623	6
2004	Boston (wc)‡	Terry Francona	98	64	.605	-3
2005	Chicago (C)‡	Ozzie Guillen	99	63	.611	6
2006	Detroit (wc)‡	Jim Leyland	95	67	.586	-1

†Defeated Boston in one-game playoff. ‡Won championship series.
#First half 34–22; second half 25–26, in season split by strike; defeated Milwaukee in playoff for Eastern Divison title.

League Championship Series

National League

1969	New York (E) 3, Atlanta (W) 0
1970	Cincinnati (W) 3, Pittsburgh (E) 0
1971	Pittsburgh (E) 3, San Francisco (W) 1
1972	Cincinnati (W) 3, Pittsburgh (E) 2
1973	New York (E) 3, Cincinnati (W) 2
1974	Los Angeles (W) 3, Pittsburgh (E) 1
1975	Cincinnati (W) 3, Pittsburgh (E) 0
1976	Cincinnati (W) 3, Philadelphia (E) 0
1977	Los Angeles (W) 3, Philadelphia (E) 1
1978	Los Angeles (W) 3, Philadelphia (E) 1
1979	Pittsburgh (E) 3, Cincinnati (W) 0
1980	Philadelphia (E) 3, Houston (W) 2
1981	Los Angeles (W) 3, Montreal (E) 2
1982	St. Louis (E) 3, Atlanta (W) 0
1983	Philadelphia (E) 3, Los Angeles (W) 1
1984	San Diego (W) 3, Chicago (E) 2
1985	St. Louis (E) 4, Los Angeles (W) 2
1986	New York (E) 4, Houston (W) 2
1987	St. Louis (E) 4, San Francisco (W) 3
1988	Los Angeles (W) 4, New York (E) 3
1989	San Francisco (W) 4, Chicago (E) 1
1990	Cincinnati (W) 4, Pittsburgh (E) 2
1991	Atlanta (W) 4, Pittsburgh (E) 3
1992	Atlanta (W) 4, Pitsburgh (E) 3
1993	Philadelphia (E) 4, Atlanta (W) 2
1994	Playoffs canceled due to players' strike.
1995	Atlanta (E) 4, Cincinnati (C) 0
1996	Atlanta (E) 4, St. Louis (C) 3
1997	Florida (wc) 4, Atlanta (E) 2
1998	San Diego (W) 4, Atlanta (E) 2
1999	Atlanta (E) 4, New York (wc) 2
2000	New York (wc) 4, St. Louis (C) 1
2001	Arizona (W) 4, Atlanta (E) 1
2002	San Francisco (wc) 4, St. Louis (C) 1
2003	Florida (wc) 4, Chicago (C) 3
2004	St. Louis (C) 4, Houston (wc) 3
2005	Houston (wc) 4, St. Louis (C) 2
2006	St. Louis (C) 4, New York (E) 3

American League

1969	Baltimore (E) 3, Minnesota (W) 0
1970	Baltimore (E) 3, Minnesota (W) 0
1971	Baltimore (E) 3, Oakland (W) 0
1972	Oakland (W) 3, Detroit (E) 2
1973	Oakland (W) 3, Baltimore (E) 2
1974	Oakland (W) 3, Baltimore (E) 1
1975	Boston (E) 3, Oakland (W) 0
1976	New York (E) 3, Kansas City (W) 2
1977	New York (E) 3, Kansas City (W) 2
1978	New York (E) 3, Kansas City (W) 1
1979	Baltimore (E) 3, California (W) 1
1980	Kansas City (W) 3, New York (E) 0
1981	New York (E) 3, Oakland (W) 0
1982	Milwaukee (E) 3, California (W) 2
1983	Baltimore (E) 3, Chicago (W) 1
1984	Detroit (E) 3, Kansas City (W) 0
1985	Kansas City (W) 4, Toronto (E) 3
1986	Boston (E) 4, California (W) 3
1987	Minnesota (W) 4, Detroit (E) 1
1988	Oakland (W) 4, Boston (E) 0
1989	Oakland (W) 4, Toronto (E) 1
1990	Oakland (W) 4, Boston (E) 0
1991	Minnesota (W) 4, Toronto (E) 1
1992	Toronto (E) 4, Oakland (W) 2
1993	Toronto (E) 4, Chicago (W) 2
1994	Playoffs canceled due to players' strike.
1995	Cleveland (C) 4, Seattle (W) 2
1996	New York (E) 4, Baltimore (wc) 1
1997	Cleveland (C) 4, Baltimore (E) 2
1998	New York (E) 4, Cleveland (C) 2
1999	New York (E) 4, Boston (wc) 1
2000	New York (E) 4, Seattle (wc) 2
2001	New York (E) 4, Seattle (W) 1
2002	Anaheim (wc) 4, Minnesota (C) 1
2003	New York (E) 4, Boston (wc) 3
2004	Boston (wc) 4, New York (E) 3
2005	Chicago (C) 4, Los Angeles (W) 1
2006	Detroit (wc) 4, Oakland (W) 0

NLCS Most Valuable Player

1977	Dusty Baker, LA	
1978	Steve Garvey, LA	
1979	Willie Stargell, Pitt	
1980	Manny Trillo, Phil	
1981	Burt Hooton, LA	
1982	Darrell Porter, StL	
1983	Gary Matthews, Phil	
1984	Steve Garvey, SD	
1985	Ozzie Smith, StL	
1986	Mike Scott, Hou	
1987	Jeffrey Leonard, SF	
1988	Orel Hershiser, LA	
1989	Will Clark, SF	
1990	R. Myers/R. Dibble, Cin	
1991	Steve Avery, Atl	
1992	John Smoltz, Atl	
1993	Curt Schilling, Phil	
1994	Playoffs canceled	
1995	Mike Devereaux, Atl	
1996	Javier Lopez, Atl	
1997	Livan Hernandez, Fla	
1998	Sterling Hitchcock, SD	
1999	Eddie Perez, Atl	
2000	Mike Hampton, NY	
2001	Craig Counsell, Ariz	
2002	Benito Santiago, SF	
2003	Ivan Rodriguez, Fla	
2004	Albert Pujols, StL	
2005	Roy Oswalt, Hou	
2006	Jeff Suppan, StL	

ALCS Most Valuable Player

1980	Frank White, KC	
1981	Graig Nettles, NY	
1982	Fred Lynn, Calif	
1983	Mike Boddicker, Balt	
1984	Kirk Gibson, Det	
1985	George Brett, KC	
1986	Marty Barrett, Bos	
1987	Gary Gaetti, Minn	
1988	Dennis Eckersley, Oak	
1989	Rickey Henderson, Oak	
1990	Dave Stewart, Oak	
1991	Kirby Puckett, Minn	
1992	Roberto Alomar, Tor	
1993	Dave Stewart, Tor	
1994	Playoffs canceled	
1995	Orel Hershiser, Clev	
1996	Bernie Williams, NY	
1997	Marquis Grissom, Clev	
1998	David Wells, NY	
1999	Orlando Hernandez, NY	
2000	David Justice, NY	
2001	Andy Pettitte, NY	
2002	Adam Kennedy, Ana	
2003	Mariano Rivera, NY	
2004	David Ortiz, Bos	
2005	Paul Konerko, Chi	
2006	Placido Polanco, Det	

Divisional Playoffs

National League

1995	Atlanta (E) 3, Colorado (wc) 1
	Cincinnati (C) 3, Los Angeles (W) 0
1996	St. Louis (C) 3, San Diego (W) 0
	Atlanta (E) 3, Los Angeles (wc) 0
1997	Atlanta (E) 3, Houston (C) 0
	Florida (wc) 3, San Francisco (W) 0
1998	San Diego (W) 3, Houston (C) 1
	Atlanta (E) 3, Chicago (wc) 0
1999	Atlanta (E) 3, Houston (C) 1
	New York (wc) 3, Arizona (W) 1
2000	St. Louis (C) 3, Atlanta (E) 0
	New York (wc) 3, San Francisco (W) 1
2001	Atlanta (E) 3, Houston (C) 0
	Arizona (W) 3, St. Louis (wc) 2
2002	St. Louis (C) 3, Arizona (W) 0
	San Francisco (wc) 3, Atlanta (E) 2
2003	Chicago (C) 3, Atlanta (E) 2
	Florida (wc) 3, San Francisco (W) 1
2004	St. Louis (C) 3, Los Angeles (W) 1
	Houston (wc) 3, Atlanta (E) 2
2005	Houston (wc) 3, Atlanta (E) 1
	St. Louis (wc) 3, San Diego (W) 1
2006	St. Louis (C) 3, San Diego (W) 1
	NY Mets (E) 3, Los Angeles (wc) 0

American League

1995	Cleveland (C) 3, Boston (E) 0
	Seattle (W) 3, New York (wc) 2
1996	Baltimore (wc) 3, Cleveland (C) 1
	New York (E) 3, Texas (W) 1
1997	Baltimore (E) 3, Seattle (W) 1
	Cleveland (C) 3, New York (wc) 2
1998	New York (E) 3, Texas (W) 0
	Cleveland (C) 3, Boston (wc) 1
1999	New York (E) 3, Texas (W) 1
	Boston (wc) 3, Cleveland (C) 2
2000	New York (E) 3, Oakland (W) 2
	Seattle (W) 3, Chicago (C) 0
2001	Seattle (W) 3, Cleveland (wc) 2
	New York (E) 3, Oakland (wc) 2
2002	Minnesota (C) 3, Oakland (W) 2
	Anaheim (wc) 3, New York (E) 1
2003	New York (E) 3, Minnesota (C) 1
	Boston (wc) 3, Oakland (W) 2
2004	New York (E) 3, Minnesota (C) 1
	Boston (wc) 3 Anaheim (W) 0
2005	Los Angeles (W) 3, New York (E) 2
	Chicago (C) 3, Boston (wc) 0
2006	Oakland (W) 3, Minnesota (C) 0
	Detroit (wc) 3, NY Yankees (E) 1

The All-Star Game

Results

Date	Winner	Score	Site	Date	Winner	Score	Site
7-6-33	American	4–2	Comiskey Park, Chi	7-23-69	National	9–3	R.F.K. Stadium, Wash.
7-10-34	American	9–7	Polo Grounds, NY	7-14-70	National	5–4	Riverfront Stadium, Cin
7-8-35	American	4–1	Municipal Stadium, Clev	7-13-71	American	6–4	Tiger Stadium, Det
7-7-36	National	4–3	Braves Field, Bos	7-25-72	National	4–3	Atlanta Stadium, Atl
7-7-37	American	8–3	Griffith Stadium, Wash	7-24-73	National	7–1	Royals Stadium, KC
7-6-38	National	4–1	Crosley Field, Cin	7-23-74	National	7–2	Three Rivers Stadium, Pitt
7-11-39	American	3–1	Yankee Stadium, NY	7-15-75	National	6–3	County Stadium, Mil
7-10-40	National	4–0	Sportsman's Park, StL	7-13-76	National	7–1	Veterans Stadium, Phil
7-8-41	American	7–5	Briggs Stadium, Det	7-19-77	National	7–5	Yankee Stadium, NY
7-6-42	American	3–1	Polo Grounds, NY	7-11-78	National	7–3	Jack Murphy Stadium, SD
7-13-43	American	5–3	Shibe Park, Phil	7-17-79	National	7–6	Kingdome, Sea
7-11-44	National	7–1	Forbes Field, Pitt	7-8-80	National	4–2	Dodger Stadium, LA
1945	No game due to wartime travel restrictions.			8-9-81	National	5–4	Municipal Stadium, Clev
7-9-46	American	12–0	Fenway Park, Bos	7-13-82	National	4–1	Olympic Stadium, Mtl
7-8-47	American	2–1	Wrigley Field, Chi	7-6-83	American	13–3	Comiskey Park, Chi
7-13-48	American	5–2	Sportsman's Park, StL	7-10-84	National	3–1	Candlestick Park, SF
7-12-49	American	11–7	Ebbets Field, Bklyn	7-16-85	National	6–1	Metrodome, Minn
7-11-50	National	4–3	Comiskey Park, Chi	7-15-86	American	3–2	Astrodome, Hou
7-10-51	National	8–3	Briggs Stadium, Det	7-14-87	National	2–0	Oakland Coliseum, Oak
7-8-52	National	3–2	Shibe Park, Phil	7-12-88	American	2–1	Riverfront Stadium, Cin
7-14-53	National	5–1	Crosley Field, Cin	7-11-89	American	5–3	Anaheim Stadium, Cal
7-13-54	American	11–9	Municipal Stadium, Clev	7-10-90	American	2–0	Wrigley Field, Chi
7-12-55	National	6–5	County Stadium, Mil	7-9-91	American	4–2	SkyDome, Tor
7-10-56	National	7–3	Griffith Stadium, Wash	7-14-92	American	13–6	Jack Murphy Stadium, SD
7-9-57	American	6–5	Busch Stadium, StL	7-13-93	American	9–3	Camden Yards, Balt
7-8-58	American	4–3	Memorial Stadium, Balt	7-12-94	National	8–7	Three Rivers Stadium, Pitt
7-7-59	National	5–4	Forbes Field, Pitt	7-11-95	National	3–2	The Ballpark in
8-3-59	American	5–3	Memorial Coliseum, LA				Arlington, Tex
7-11-60	National	5–3	Municipal Stadium, KC	7-9-96	National	6–0	Veterans Stadium, Phil
7-13-60	National	6–0	Yankee Stadium, NY	7-8-97	American	3–1	Jacobs Field, Clev
7-11-61	National	5–4	Candlestick Park, SF	7-7-98	American	13–8	Coors Field, Col
7-31-61	Tie*	1–1	Fenway Park, Bos	7-13-99	American	4–1	Fenway Field, Bos
7-10-62	National	3–1	D.C. Stadium, Wash	7-11-00	American	6–3	Turner Field, Atl
7-30-62	American	9–4	Wrigley Field, Chi	7-10-01	American	4–1	Safeco Field, Sea
7-9-63	National	5–3	Municipal Stadium, Clev	7-9-02	Tie (11 inn)	7–7	Miller Park, Milwaukee
7-7-64	National	7–4	Shea Stadium, NY	7-15-03	American	7–6	Comiskey Park, Chicago
7-13-65	National	6–5	Metro. Stadium, Minn	7-13-04	American	9–4	Minute Maid Park, Hou
7-12-66	National	2–1	Busch Stadium, StL	7-12-05	American	7–5	Comerica Park, Det
7-11-67	National	2–1	Anaheim Stadium, Cal	7-11-06	American	3-2	PNC Park, Pittsburgh
7-9-68	National	1–0	Astrodome, Hou				

*Game called because of rain after nine innings.

Most Valuable Players

1962...Maury Wills, LA NL	1976...George Foster, Cin NL	1992...Ken Griffey Jr., Sea AL
Leon Wagner, LA AL	1977...Don Sutton, LA NL	1993...Kirby Puckett, Minn AL
1963...Willie Mays, SF NL	1978...Steve Garvey, LA NL	1994...Fred McGriff, Atl NL
1964...Johnny Callison, Phil NL	1979...Dave Parker, Pitt NL	1995...Jeff Conine, Fla NL
1965...Juan Marichal, SF NL	1980...Ken Griffey, Cin NL	1996...Mike Piazza, LA NL
1966...Brooks Robinson, Balt AL	1981...Gary Carter, Mtl NL	1997...Sandy Alomar, Clev AL
1967...Tony Perez, Cin NL	1982...Dave Concepcion, Cin NL	1998...Roberto Alomar, Balt AL
1968...Willie Mays, SF NL	1983...Fred Lynn, Calif AL	1999...Pedro Martinez, Bos AL
1969...Willie McCovey, SF NL	1984...Gary Carter, Mtl NL	2000...Derek Jeter, NY AL
1970...Carl Yastrzemski, Bos AL	1985...LaMarr Hoyt, SD NL	2001...Cal Ripken Jr., Balt AL
1971...Frank Robinson, Balt AL	1986...Roger Clemens, Bos AL	2002...None selected
1972...Joe Morgan, Cin NL	1987...Tim Raines, Mtl NL	2003...Garret Anderson, Ana AL
1973...Bobby Bonds, SF NL	1988...Terry Steinbach, Oak AL	2004...Alfonso Soriano, Tex AL
1974...Steve Garvey, LA NL	1989...Bo Jackson, KC AL	2005...Miguel Tejada, Balt AL
1975...Bill Madlock, Chi NL	1990...Julio Franco, Tex AL	2006...Michael Young, Tex AL
Jon Matlack, NY NL	1991...Cal Ripken Jr., Balt AL	

The Regular Season

Most Valuable Players
NATIONAL LEAGUE

Year	Name and Team	Position	Noteworthy
1911	Wildfire Schulte, Chi	Outfield	21 HR†, 121 RBI†, .300
1912	*Larry Doyle, NY	Second base	10 HR, 90 RBI, .330
1913	Jake Daubert, Bklyn	First base	52 RBI, .350†
1914	*Johnny Evers, Bos	Second base	FA .976†, .279
1915–23	No selection		
1924	Dazzy Vance, Bklyn	Pitcher	28†–6, 2.16 ERA†, 262 K†
1925	Rogers Hornsby, StL	Second base, Manager	39 HR†, 143 RBI†, .403†
1926	*Bob O'Farrell, StL	Catcher	7 HR, 68 RBI, .293
1927	*Paul Waner, Pitt	Outfield	237 hits†, 131 RBI†, .380†
1928	*Jim Bottomley, StL	First base	31 HR†, 136 RBI†, .325
1929	*Rogers Hornsby, Chi	Second base	39 HR, 149 RBI, 156 runs†, .380
1930	No selection		
1931	*Frankie Frisch, StL	Second base	4 HR, 82 RBI, 28 SB†, .311
1932	Chuck Klein, Phil	Outfield	38 HR†, 137 RBI, 226 hits†, .348
1933	*Carl Hubbell, NY	Pitcher	23†–12, 1.66 ERA†, 10 SO†
1934	*Dizzy Dean, StL	Pitcher	30†–7, 2.66 ERA, 195 K†
1935	*Gabby Hartnett, Chi	Catcher	13 HR, 91 RBI, .344
1936	*Carl Hubbell, NY	Pitcher	26†–6, 2.31 ERA†
1937	Joe Medwick, StL	Outfield	31 HR‡, 154 RBI†, 111 runs†, .374†
1938	Ernie Lombardi, Cin	Catcher	19 HR, 95 RBI, .342†
1939	*Bucky Walters, Cin	Pitcher	27†–11, 2.29 ERA†, 137 K‡
1940	*Frank McCormick, Cin	First base	19 HR, 127 RBI, 191 hits†, .309
1941	*Dolph Camilli, Bklyn	First base	34 HR†, 120 RBI†, .285
1942	*Mort Cooper, StL	Pitcher	22†–7, 1.78 ERA†, 10 SO†
1943	*Stan Musial, StL	Outfield	13 HR, 81 RBI, 220 hits†, .357†
1944	*Marty Marion, StL	Shortstop	FA .972†, 63 RBI
1945	*Phil Cavarretta, Chi	First base	6 HR, 97 RBI, .355†
1946	*Stan Musial, StL	First base, Outfield	103 RBI, 124 runs†, 228 hits†, .365†
1947	Bob Elliott, Bos	Third base	22 HR, 113 RBI, .317
1948	Stan Musial, StL	Outfield	39 HR, 131 RBI, .376†
1949	*Jackie Robinson, Bklyn	Second base	16 HR, 124 RBI, 37 SB†, .342†
1950	*Jim Konstanty, Phil	Pitcher	16–7, 22 saves†, 2.66 ERA
1951	Roy Campanella, Bklyn	Catcher	33 HR, 108 RBI, .325
1952	Hank Sauer, Chi	Outfield	37 HR‡, 121 RBI†, .270
1953	*Roy Campanella, Bklyn	Catcher	41 HR, 142 RBI†, .312
1954	*Willie Mays, NY	Outfield	41 HR, 110 RBI, 13 3B†, .345†
1955	*Roy Campanella, Bklyn	Catcher	32 HR, 107 RBI, .318
1956	*Don Newcombe, Bklyn	Pitcher	27†–7, 3.06 ERA
1957	*Hank Aaron, Mil	Outfield	44 HR†, 132 RBI†, .322
1958	Ernie Banks, Chi	Shortstop	47 HR†, 129 RBI†, .313
1959	Ernie Banks, Chi	Shortstop	45 HR, 143 RBI†, .304
1960	*Dick Groat, Pitt	Shortstop	2 HR, 50 RBI, .325†

*Played for pennant or, after 1968, division winner. †Led league. ‡Tied for league lead.

Most Valuable Players (Cont.)
NATIONAL LEAGUE (Cont.)

Year	Name and Team	Position	Noteworthy
1961	*Frank Robinson, Cin	Outfield	37 HR, 124 RBI, .323
1962	Maury Wills, LA	Shortstop	104 SB†, 208 hits, .299, GG
1963	*Sandy Koufax, LA	Pitcher	25‡–5, 1.88 ERA†, 306 K†
1964	*Ken Boyer, StL	Third Base	24 HR, 119 RBI†, .295
1965	Willie Mays, SF	Outfield	52 HR†, 112 RBI, .317, GG
1966	Roberto Clemente, Pitt	Outfield	29 HR, 119 RBI, 202 hits, .317, GG
1967	*Orlando Cepeda, StL	First base	25 HR, 111 RBI†, .325
1968	*Bob Gibson, StL	Pitcher	22–9, 1.12 ERA†, 268 K†, 13 SO†, GG
1969	Willie McCovey, SF	First base	45 HR†, 126 RBI†, .320
1970	*Johnny Bench, Cin	Catcher	45 HR†, 148 RBI†, .293, GG
1971	Joe Torre, StL	Third base	24 HR, 137 RBI†, .363†
1972	*Johnny Bench, Cin	Catcher	40 HR†, 125 RBI†, .270, GG
1973	*Pete Rose, Cin	Outfield	5 HR, 64 RBI, .338†, 230 hits†
1974	*Steve Garvey, LA	First base	21 HR, 111 RBI, 200 hits, .312, GG
1975	*Joe Morgan, Cin	Second base	17 HR, 94 RBI, 67 SB, .327, GG
1976	*Joe Morgan, Cin	Second base	27 HR, 111 RBI, 60 SB, .320, GG
1977	George Foster, Cin	Outfield	52 HR†, 149 RBI†, .320
1978	Dave Parker, Pitt	Outfield	30 HR, 117 RBI, .334†, GG
1979	Keith Hernandez, StL	First base	11 HR, 105 RBI, 210 hits, .344†, GG
	*Willie Stargell, Pitt	First base	32 HR, 82 RBI, .281
1980	*Mike Schmidt, Phil	Third base	48 HR†, 121 RBI†, .286, GG
1981	Mike Schmidt, Phil	Third base	31 HR†, 91 RBI†, 78 runs†, .316, GG
1982	*Dale Murphy, Atl	Outfield	36 HR, 109 RBI‡, .281, GG
1983	Dale Murphy, Atl	Outfield	36 HR, 121 RBI†, .302, GG
1984	*Ryne Sandberg, Chi	Second base	19 HR, 84 RBI, 114 runs†, .314, GG
1985	*Willie McGee, StL	Outfield	10 HR, 82 RBI, 18 3B†, .353†, GG
1986	Mike Schmidt, Phil	Third base	37 HR†, 119 RBI†, .290, GG
1987	Andre Dawson, Chi	Outfield	49 HR†, 137 RBI†, .287, GG
1988	*Kirk Gibson, LA	Outfield	25 HR, 76 RBI, 106 runs, .290
1989	*Kevin Mitchell, SF	Outfield	47 HR†, 125 RBI†, .291
1990	*Barry Bonds, Pitt	Outfield	33 HR, 114 RBI, .301
1991	*Terry Pendleton, Atl	Third base	23 HR, 86 RBI, .319†
1992	Barry Bonds, Pitt	Outfield	34 HR, 103 RBI, .311
1993	Barry Bonds, SF	Outfield	46 HR†, 123 RBI†, .336
1994	Jeff Bagwell, Hou	First base	39 HR, 116 RBI†, .368
1995	*Barry Larkin, Cin	Shortstop	15 HR, 66 RBI, 51 SB, .319
1996	*Ken Caminiti, SD	Third base	40 HR, 130 RBI, .326
1997	Larry Walker, Col	Outfield	49 HR†, 130 RBI, .452 OBA†, .366, GG
1998	Sammy Sosa, Chi	Outfield	66 HR, 158 RBI†, 134 runs†, 416 TB†, .308
1999	*Chipper Jones, Atl	Third Base	45 HR, 110 RBI, 116 runs, .319
2000	*Jeff Kent, SF	Second Base	33 HR, 125 RBI, 114 runs, .334
2001	Barry Bonds, SF	Outfield	73 HR†, 137 RBI. 177 BB†, .328, .863 SLG†
2002	Barry Bonds, SF	Outfield	46 HR, 110 RBI, .582 OBP, 198 BB† .370
2003	Barry Bonds, SF	Outfield	45 HR, .341, .529 OBP†, .749 SLG†
2004	Barry Bonds, SF	Outfield	45HR, 101 RBI, .609 OBP, .812 SLG
2005	Albert Pujols, StL	First Base	41 HR, 117 RBI, .330, .430 OBP†, .609 SLG†

*Played for pennant or, after 1968, division winner. †Led league. ‡Tied for league lead.

Most Valuable Players *(Cont.)*

AMERICAN LEAGUE

Year	Name and Team	Position	Noteworthy
1911	Ty Cobb, Det	Outfield	8 HR, 144 RBI†, 24 3B†, .420†
1912	*Tris Speaker, Bos	Outfield	10 HR‡, 98 RBI, 53 2B†, .383
1913	Walter Johnson, Wash	Pitcher	36†–7, 1.09 ERA†, 11 SO†, 243 K†
1914	*Eddie Collins, Phil	Second base	2 HR, 85 RBI, 122 runs†, .344
1915–21	No selection		
1922	George Sisler, StL	First base	8 HR, 105 RBI, 246 hits†, .420†
1923	*Babe Ruth, NY	Outfield	41 HR†, 131 RBI†, .393
1924	*Walter Johnson, Wash	Pitcher	23†–7, 2.72 ERA†, 158 K†
1925	*Roger Peckinpaugh, Wash	Shortstop	4 HR, 64 RBI, .294
1926	George Burns, Clev	First base	114 RBI, 216 hits‡, 64 2B†, .358
1927	*Lou Gehrig, NY	First base	47 HR, 175 RBI†, 52 2B†, .373
1928	Mickey Cochrane, Phil	Catcher	10 HR, 57 RBI, .293
1929	No selection		
1930	No selection		
1931	*Lefty Grove, Phil	Pitcher	31†–4, 2.06 ERA†, 175 K†
1932	Jimmie Foxx, Phil	First base	58 HR†, 169 RBI†, 151 runs†, .364
1933	Jimmie Foxx, Phil	First base	48 HR†, 163 RBI†, .356†
1934	*Mickey Cochrane, Det	Catcher	2 HR, 76 RBI, .320
1935	*Hank Greenberg, Det	First base	36 HR‡, 170 RBI†, 203 hits, .328
1936	*Lou Gehrig, NY	First base	49 HR†, 152 RBI, 167 runs†, .354
1937	Charlie Gehringer, Det	Second base	14 HR, 96 RBI, 133 runs, .371†
1938	Jimmie Foxx, Bos	First base	50 HR, 175 RBI†, .349†
1939	*Joe DiMaggio, NY	Outfield	30 HR, 126 RBI, .381†
1940	*Hank Greenberg, Det	Outfield	41 HR†, 150 RBI†, 50 2B†, .340
1941	*Joe DiMaggio, NY	Outfield	30 HR, 125 RBI†, .357
1942	*Joe Gordon, NY	Second base	18 HR, 103 RBI, .322
1943	*Spud Chandler, NY	Pitcher	20†–4, 1.64 ERA†, 5 SO‡
1944	Hal Newhouser, Det	Pitcher	29†–9, 2.22 ERA†, 187 K†
1945	*Hal Newhouser, Det	Pitcher	25†–9, 1.81 ERA†, 8 SO†, 212 K†
1946	*Ted Williams, Bos	Outfield	38 HR, 123 RBI, 142 runs†, .342
1947	*Joe DiMaggio, NY	Outfield	20 HR, 97 RBI, .315
1948	*Lou Boudreau, Clev	Shortstop	18 HR, 106 RBI, .355
1949	Ted Williams, Bos	Outfield	43 HR†, 159 RBI‡, 150 runs†, .343
1950	*Phil Rizzuto, NY	Shortstop	125 runs, 200 hits, .324
1951	*Yogi Berra, NY	Catcher	27 HR, 88 RBI, .294
1952	Bobby Shantz, Phil	Pitcher	24†–7, 2.48 ERA
1953	Al Rosen, Clev	Third base	43 HR†, 145 RBI†, 115 runs†, .336
1954	Yogi Berra, NY	Catcher	22 HR, 125 RBI, .307
1955	*Yogi Berra, NY	Catcher	27 HR, 108 RBI, .272
1956	*Mickey Mantle, NY	Outfield	52 HR†, 130 RBI†, 132 runs†, .353†
1957	*Mickey Mantle, NY	Outfield	34 HR, 94 RBI, 121 runs†, .365
1958	Jackie Jensen, Bos	Outfield	35 HR, 122 RBI†, .286
1959	*Nellie Fox, Chi	Second base	2 HR, 70 RBI, .306, GG
1960	*Roger Maris, NY	Outfield	39 HR, 112 RBI†, .283, GG
1961	*Roger Maris, NY	Outfield	61 HR†, 142 RBI†, .269
1962	*Mickey Mantle, NY	Outfield	30 HR, 89 RBI, .321, GG
1963	*Elston Howard, NY	Catcher	28 HR, 85 RBI, .287, GG
1964	Brooks Robinson, Balt	Third base	28 HR, 118 RBI†, .317, GG
1965	*Zoilo Versalles, Minn	Shortstop	126 runs†, 45 2B†, 12 3B‡, .273
1966	*Frank Robinson, Balt	Outfield	49 HR†, 122 RBI†, 122 runs†, .316†
1967	*Carl Yastrzemski, Bos	Outfield	44 HR‡, 121 RBI†, 112 runs†, .326†, GG
1968	*Denny McLain, Det	Pitcher	31†–6, 1.96 ERA, 280 K
1969	*Harmon Killebrew, Minn	Third base, First base	49 HR†, 140 RBI†, .276
1970	*Boog Powell, Balt	First base	35 HR, 114 RBI, .297
1971	*Vida Blue, Oak	Pitcher	24–8, 1.82 ERA†, 8 SO†, 301 K
1972	Dick Allen, Chi	First base	37 HR†, 113 RBI†, .308
1973	*Reggie Jackson, Oak	Outfield	32 HR†, 117 RBI†, 99 runs†, .293
1974	Jeff Burroughs, Tex	Outfield	25 HR, 118 RBI†, .301
1975	*Fred Lynn, Bos	Outfield	21 HR, 105 RBI, 103 runs†, .331, GG
1976	*Thurman Munson, NY	Catcher	17 HR, 105 RBI, .302
1977	Rod Carew, Minn	First base	100 RBI, 128 runs†, 239 hits†, .388†
1978	Jim Rice, Bos	Outfield, DH	46 HR†, 139 RBI†, 213 hits†, .315
1979	*Don Baylor, Calif	Outfield, DH	36 HR, 139 RBI†, 120 runs†, .296
1980	*George Brett, KC	Third base	24 HR, 118 RBI, .390†
1981	*Rollie Fingers, Mil	Pitcher	6–3, 28 saves†, 1.04 ERA

Most Valuable Players *(Cont.)*
AMERICAN LEAGUE *(Cont.)*

Year	Name and Team	Position	Noteworthy
1982	*Robin Yount, Mil	Shortstop	29 HR, 114 RBI, 210 hits†, .331, GG
1983	*Cal Ripken Jr., Balt	Shortstop	27 HR, 102 RBI, 121 runs†, 211 hits†, .318
1984	*Willie Hernandez, Det	Pitcher	9–3, 32 saves, 1.92 ERA
1985	Don Mattingly, NY	First base	35 HR, 145 RBI†, 48 2B†, .324, GG
1986	*Roger Clemens, Bos	Pitcher	24†–4, 2.48 ERA†, 238 K
1987	George Bell, Tor	Outfield	47 HR, 134 RBI†, .308
1988	*Jose Canseco, Oak	Outfield	42 HR†, 124 RBI†, 40 SB, .307
1989	Robin Yount, Mil	Outfield	21 HR, 103 RBI, 101 runs, .318
1990	*Rickey Henderson, Oak	Outfield	28 HR, 119 runs†, 65 SB†, .325
1991	Cal Ripken Jr., Balt	Shortstop	34 HR, 114 RBI, .323
1992	Dennis Eckersley, Oak	Pitcher	7–1, 1.91 ERA, 51 saves
1993	Frank Thomas, Chi	First base	41 HR, 128 RBI, .317
1994	Frank Thomas, Chi	First base	38 HR, 101 RBI, .353
1995	*Mo Vaughn, Bos	First base	39 HR, 126 RBI, .300
1996	*Juan Gonzalez, Tex	Outfield	47 HR, 144 RBI, .314
1997	*Ken Griffey Jr., Sea	Outfield	56 HR†, 125 runs†, 393 TB†, 147 RBI†, .304
1998	*Juan Gonzalez, Tex	Outfield	45 HR, 157 RBI†, 50 2B†, .318
1999	*Ivan Rodriguez, Tex	Catcher	35 HR, 113 RBI, 116 runs, .332, GG
2000	*Jason Giambi, Oak	First Base	43 HR, 137 RBI, .333
2001	*Ichiro Suzuki, Sea	Outfield	.350†, 242 H†, 127 R, 56 SB†
2002	*Miguel Tejada, Oak	Shortstop	34 HR, 131 RBI, .308
2003	Alex Rodriguez, Tex	Shortstop	47 HR†, 118 RBI, .600 SLG†
2004	*Vladimir Guerrero, Ana	Outfield	39 HR, 126 RBI, .598 SLG
2005	*Alex Rodriguez, NYY	Third Base	48 HR†, 130 RBI, .610 SLG†

*Played for pennant or, after 1968, division winner. †Led league. ‡Tied for league lead.
Notes: 2B=doubles; 3B=triples; FA=fielding average; GG=won Gold Glove, award begun in 1957;
K=strikeouts; O=shutouts; SB=stolen bases; TB=total bases.

Rookies of the Year

NATIONAL LEAGUE		AMERICAN LEAGUE	
1947*	Jackie Robinson, Bklyn (1B)	1949	Roy Sievers, StL (OF)
1948*	Alvin Dark, Bos (SS)	1950	Walt Dropo, Bos (1B)
1949	Don Newcombe, Bklyn (P)	1951	Gil McDougald, NY (3B)
1950	Sam Jethroe, Bos (OF)	1952	Harry Byrd, Phil (P)
1951	Willie Mays, NY (OF)	1953	Harvey Kuenn, Det (SS)
1952	Joe Black, Bklyn (P)	1954	Bob Grim, NY (P)
1953	Junior Gilliam, Bklyn (2B)	1955	Herb Score, Clev (P)
1954	Wally Moon, StL (OF)	1956	Luis Aparicio, Chi (SS)
1955	Bill Virdon, StL (OF)	1957	Tony Kubek, NY (OF, SS)
1956	Frank Robinson, Cin (OF)	1958	Albie Pearson, Wash (OF)
1957	Jack Sanford, Phil (P)	1959	Bob Allison, Wash (OF)
1958	Orlando Cepeda, SF (1B)	1960	Ron Hansen, Balt (SS)
1959	Willie McCovey, SF (1B)	1961	Don Schwall, Bos (P)
1960	Frank Howard, LA (OF)	1962	Tom Tresh, NY (SS)
1961	Billy Williams, Chi (OF)	1963	Gary Peters, Chi (P)
1962	Ken Hubbs, Chi (2B)	1964	Tony Oliva, Minn (OF)
1963	Pete Rose, Cin (2B)	1965	Curt Blefary, Balt (OF)
1964	Dick Allen, Phil (3B)	1966	Tommie Agee, Chi (OF)
1965	Jim Lefebvre, LA (2B)	1967	Rod Carew, Minn (2B)
1966	Tommy Helms, Cin (2B)	1968	Stan Bahnsen, NY (P)
1967	Tom Seaver, NY (P)	1969	Lou Piniella, KC (OF)
1968	Johnny Bench, Cin (C)	1970	Thurman Munson, NY (C)
1969	Ted Sizemore, LA (2B)	1971	Chris Chambliss, Clev (1B)
1970	Carl Morton, Mtl(P)	1972	Carlton Fisk, Bos (C)
1971	Earl Williams, Atl (C)	1973	Al Bumbry, Balt (OF)
1972	Jon Matlack, NY (P)	1974	Mike Hargrove, Tex (1B)
1973	Gary Matthews, SF (OF)	1975	Fred Lynn, Bos (OF)
1974	Bake McBride, StL (OF)	1976	Mark Fidrych, Det (P)
1975	John Montefusco, SF (P)	1977	Eddie Murray, Balt (DH)
1976	Pat Zachry, Cin (P)	1978	Lou Whitaker, Det (2B)
	Butch Metzger, SD (P)	1979	Alfredo Griffin, Tor (SS)
1977	Andre Dawson, Mtl (OF)		John Castino, Minn (3B)
1978	Bob Horner, Atl (3B)	1980	Joe Charboneau, Clev (OF)
1979	Rick Sutcliffe, LA (P)	1981	Dave Righetti, NY (P)
1980	Steve Howe, LA (P)	1982	Cal Ripken Jr., Balt (SS)

*Just one selection for both leagues.

Rookies of the Year *(Cont.)*

NATIONAL LEAGUE *(Cont.)*	AMERICAN LEAGUE *(Cont.)*
1981 ....Fernando Valenzuela, LA (P)	1983 ....Ron Kittle, Chi (OF)
1982 ....Steve Sax, LA (2B)	1984 ....Alvin Davis, Sea (1B)
1983 ....Darryl Strawberry, NY (OF)	1985 ....Ozzie Guillen, Chi (SS)
1984 ....Dwight Gooden, NY (P)	1986 ....Jose Canseco, Oak (OF)
1985 ....Vince Coleman, StL (OF)	1987 ....Mark McGwire, Oak (1B)
1986 ....Todd Worrell, StL (P)	1988 ....Walt Weiss, Oak (SS)
1987 ....Benito Santiago, SD (C)	1989 ....Gregg Olson, Balt (P)
1988 ....Chris Sabo, Cin (3B)	1990 ....Sandy Alomar Jr, Clev (C)
1989 ....Jerome Walton, Chi (OF)	1991 ....Chuck Knoblauch, Minn (2B)
1990 ....Dave Justice, Atl (OF)	1992 ....Pat Listach, Mil (SS)
1991 ....Jeff Bagwell, Hou (3B)	1993 ....Tim Salmon, Calif (OF)
1992 ....Eric Karros, LA (1B)	1994 ....Bob Hamelin, KC (DH)
1993 ....Mike Piazza, LA (C)	1995 ....Marty Cordova, Minn (OF)
1994 ....Raul Mondesi, LA (OF)	1996 ....Derek Jeter, NY (SS)
1995 ....Hideo Nomo, LA (P)	1997 ....Nomar Garciaparra, Bos (SS)
1996 ....Todd Hollandsworth, LA (OF)	1998 ....Ben Grieve, Oak (OF)
1997 ....Scott Rolen, Phil (3B)	1999 ....Carlos Beltran, KC (OF)
1998 ....Kerry Wood, Chi (P)	2000 ....Kazuhiro Sasaki, Sea (P)
1999 ....Scott Williamson, Cin (P)	2001 ....Ichiro Suzuki, Sea (OF)
2000 ....Rafael Furcal, Atl (SS)	2002 ....Eric Hinske, Tor (3B)
2001 ....Albert Pujols, StL (OF)	2003 ....Angel Berroa, KC (SS)
2002 ....Jason Jennings, Col (P)	2004 ....Bobby Crosby, Oak (SS)
2003 ....Dontrelle Willis, Fla (P)	2005 ....Huston Street, Oak (P)
2004 ....Jason Bay, Pit (OF)	
2005 ....Ryan Howard, Phi (1B)	

Cy Young Award

Year	W–L	Sv	ERA	Year	W–L	Sv	ERA
1956....*Don Newcombe, Bklyn (NL)	27–7	0	3.06	1962....Don Drysdale, LA (NL)	25–9	1	2.83
1957....Warren Spahn, Mil (NL)	21–11	3	2.69	1963....*Sandy Koufax, LA (NL)	25–5	0	1.88
1958....Bob Turley, NY (AL)	21–7	1	2.97	1964....Dean Chance, LA (AL)	20–9	4	1.65
1959....Early Wynn, Chi (AL)	22–10	0	3.17	1965....Sandy Koufax, LA (NL)	26–8	2	2.04
1960....Vernon Law, Pitt (NL)	20–9	0	3.08	1966....Sandy Koufax, LA (NL)	27–9	0	1.73
1961....Whitey Ford, NY (AL)	25–4	0	3.21				

NATIONAL LEAGUE				AMERICAN LEAGUE			
Year	W–L	Sv	ERA	Year	W–L	Sv	ERA
1967....Mike McCormick, SF	22–10	0	2.85	1967.....Jim Lonborg, Bos	22–9	0	3.16
1968.....*Bob Gibson, StL	22–9	0	1.12	1968.....*Denny McLain, Det	31–6	0	1.96
1969....Tom Seaver, NY	25–7	0	2.21	1969....Denny McLain, Det	24–9	0	2.80
1970....Bob Gibson, StL	23–7	0	3.12	.............Mike Cuellar, Balt	23–11	0	2.38
1971....Ferguson Jenkins, Chi	24–13	0	2.77	1970....Jim Perry, Minn	24–12	0	3.03
1972....Steve Carlton, Phil	27–10	0	1.97	1971.....*Vida Blue, Oak	24–8	0	1.82
1973....Tom Seaver, NY	19–10	0	2.08	1972....Gaylord Perry, Clev	24–16	1	1.92
1974....Mike Marshall, LA	15–12	21	2.42	1973....Jim Palmer, Balt	22–9	1	2.40
1975....Tom Seaver, NY	22–9	0	2.38	1974....Catfish Hunter, Oak	25–12	0	2.49
1976....Randy Jones, SD	22–14	0	2.74	1975....Jim Palmer, Balt	23–11	1	2.09
1977....Steve Carlton, Phil	23–10	0	2.64	1976....Jim Palmer, Balt	22–13	0	2.51
1978....Gaylord Perry, SD	21–6	0	2.72	1977....Sparky Lyle, NY	13–5	26	2.17
1979....Bruce Sutter, Chi	6–6	37	2.23	1978....Ron Guidry, NY	25–3	0	1.74
1980....Steve Carlton, Phil	24–9	0	2.34	1979....Mike Flanagan, Balt	23–9	0	3.08
1981....Fernando Valenzuela, LA	13–7	0	2.48	1980....Steve Stone, Balt	25–7	0	3.23
1982....Steve Carlton, Phil	23–11	0	3.10	1981....*Rollie Fingers, Mil	6–3	28	1.04
1983....John Denny, Phil	19–6	0	2.37	1982....Pete Vuckovich, Mil	18–6	0	3.34
1984.....†Rick Sutcliffe, Chi	16–1	0	2.69	1983....LaMarr Hoyt, Chi	24–10	0	3.66
1985....Dwight Gooden, NY	24–4	0	1.53	1984....*Willie Hernandez, Det	9–3	32	1.92
1986....Mike Scott, Hou	18–10	0	2.22	1985....Bret Saberhagen, KC	20–6	0	2.87
1987....Steve Bedrosian, Phil	5–3	40	2.83	1986....*Roger Clemens, Bos	24–4	0	2.48
1988....Orel Hershiser, LA	23–8	1	2.26	1987....Roger Clemens, Bos	20–9	0	2.97
1989....Mark Davis, SD	4–3	44	1.85	1988....Frank Viola, Minn	24–7	0	2.64
1990....Doug Drabek, Pitt	22–6	0	2.76	1989....Bret Saberhagen, KC	23–6	0	2.16
1991....Tom Glavine, Atl	20–11	0	2.55	1990....Bob Welch, Oak	27–6	0	2.95
1992....Greg Maddux, Chi	20–11	0	2.18	1991....Roger Clemens, Bos	18–10	0	2.62
1993....Greg Maddux, Atl	20–10	0	2.36	1992....*Dennis Eckersley, Oak	7–1	51	1.91
1994....Greg Maddux, Atl	16–6	0	1.56	1993....Jack McDowell, Chi	22–10	0	3.37

Cy Young Award

NATIONAL LEAGUE				AMERICAN LEAGUE			
Year	W–L	Sv	ERA	Year	W–L	Sv	ERA
1995.....Greg Maddux, Atl	19–2	0	1.63	1994.....David Cone, KC	16–4	0	2.94
1996.....John Smoltz, Atl	24–8	0	2.94	1995.....Randy Johnson, Sea	18–2	0	2.48
1997.....Pedro Martinez, Mtl	17–8	0	1.90	1996.....Pat Hentgen, Tor	20–10	0	3.22
1998.....Tom Glavine, Atl	20–6	0	2.47	1997.....Roger Clemens, Tor	21–7	0	2.05
1999.....Randy Johnson, Ariz	17–9	0	2.48	1998.....Roger Clemens, Tor	20–6	0	2.65
2000.....Randy Johnson, Ariz	19–7	0	2.64	1999.....Pedro Martinez, Bos	23–4	0	1.55
2001.....Randy Johnson, Ariz	21–6	0	2.49	2000.....Pedro Martinez, Bos	18–6	0	1.74
2002.....Randy Johnson, Ariz	24–5	0	2.32	2001.....Roger Clemens, NY	20–3	0	3.51
2003.....Eric Gagne, LA	2–3	55	1.20	2002.....Barry Zito, Oak	23–5	0	2.75
2004.....Roger Clemens, Hou	18–4	0	2.98	2003.....Roy Halladay, Tor	22–7	0	3.25
2005.....Chris Carpenter, StL	21-5	0	2.83	2004.....Johan Santana, Min	20-6	0	2.61
				2005.....Bartolo Colon, LAA	21-8	0	3.48

*Won the MVP and Cy Young awards in the same season.
†NL games only. Sutcliffe pitched 15 games with Cleveland before being traded to the Cubs.

Career Individual Batting

GAMES

Pete Rose	3562
Carl Yastrzemski	3308
Hank Aaron	3298
Rickey Henderson	3081
Ty Cobb	3034
Eddie Murray	3026
Stan Musial	3026
Cal Ripken Jr.	3001
Willie Mays	2992
Dave Winfield	2973
Rusty Staub	2951
Brooks Robinson	2896
*Barry Bonds	2860
Robin Yount	2856
Al Kaline	2834
Rafael Palmeiro	2831
Harold Baines	2830
Eddie Collins	2826
Reggie Jackson	2820
Frank Robinson	2808

AT BATS

Pete Rose	14053
Hank Aaron	12364
Carl Yastrzemski	11988
Cal Ripken Jr.	11551
Ty Cobb	11429
Eddie Murray	11336
Robin Yount	11008
Dave Winfield	11003
Stan Musial	10972
Rickey Henderson	10961
Willie Mays	10881
Paul Molitor	10835
Brooks Robinson	10654
Rafael Palmeiro	10472
Honus Wagner	10430
*Craig Biggio	10359
George Brett	10349
Lou Brock	10332
Cap Anson	10278
Luis Aparicio	10230

HOME RUNS

Hank Aaron	755
*Barry Bonds	734
Babe Ruth	714
Willie Mays	660
Sammy Sosa	588
Frank Robinson	586
Mark McGwire	583
Harmon Killebrew	573
Rafael Palmeiro	569
*Ken Griffey Jr.	563
Reggie Jackson	563
Mike Schmidt	548
Mickey Mantle	536
Jimmie Foxx	534
Willie McCovey	521
Ted Williams	521
Ernie Banks	512
Eddie Mathews	512
Mel Ott	511
Eddie Murray	504

HITS

Pete Rose	4256
Ty Cobb	4189
Hank Aaron	3771
Stan Musial	3630
Tris Speaker	3515
Carl Yastrzemski	3419
Cap Anson	3418
Honus Wagner	3415
Paul Molitor	3319
Eddie Collins	3313
Willie Mays	3283
Eddie Murray	3255
Nap Lajoie	3251
Cal Ripken Jr.	3184
George Brett	3154
Paul Waner	3152
Robin Yount	3142
Tony Gwynn	3141
Dave Winfield	3110
Rickey Henderson	3055

BATTING AVERAGE (5,000 AB)

Ty Cobb	.367
Rogers Hornsby	.358
Ed Delahanty	.346
Tris Speaker	.345
Billy Hamilton	.344
Ted Williams	.344
Dan Brouthers	.342
Harry Heilmann	.342
Babe Ruth	.342
Willie Keeler	.341
Bill Terry	.341
Lou Gehrig	.340
George Sisler	.340
Jesse Burkett	.338
Tony Gwynn	.338
Nap Lajoie	.338
Al Simmons	.334
Cap Anson	.333
Eddie Collins	.333
*Todd Helton	.333

RUNS

Rickey Henderson	2295
Ty Cobb	2246
Hank Aaron	2174
Babe Ruth	2174
Pete Rose	2165
*Barry Bonds	2152
Willie Mays	2062
Cap Anson	1996
Stan Musial	1949
Lou Gehrig	1888
Tris Speaker	1882
Mel Ott	1859
Frank Robinson	1829
Eddie Collins	1821
Carl Yastrzemski	1816
Ted Williams	1798
Paul Molitor	1782
*Craig Biggio	1776
Charlie Gehringer	1774
Jimmie Foxx	1751

* Active in 2006.

Career Individual Batting (Cont.)

DOUBLES

Tris Speaker	792
Pete Rose	746
Stan Musial	725
Ty Cobb	724
George Brett	665
Nap Lajoie	657
Carl Yastrzemski	646
Honus Wagner	640
*Craig Biggio	637
Hank Aaron	624
Paul Molitor	605
Paul Waner	605
Cal Ripken Jr.	603
*Barry Bonds	587
Rafael Palmeiro	585
Robin Yount	583
Cap Anson	581
Wade Boggs	578
Charlie Gehringer	574
Eddie Murray	560

TRIPLES

Sam Crawford	309
Ty Cobb	295
Honus Wagner	252
Jake Beckley	243
Roger Connor	233
Tris Speaker	222
Fred Clarke	220
Dan Brouthers	205
Joe Kelley	194
Paul Waner	191
Bid McPhee	188
Eddie Collins	187
Ed Delahanty	185
Sam Rice	184
Jesse Burkett	182
Ed Konetchy	182
Edd Roush	182
Buck Ewing	178
Rabbit Maranville	177
Stan Musial	177

BASES ON BALLS

*Barry Bonds	2426
Rickey Henderson	2190
Babe Ruth	2062
Ted Williams	2021
Joe Morgan	1865
Carl Yastrzemski	1845
Mickey Mantle	1733
Mel Ott	1708
Eddie Yost	1614
Darrell Evans	1605
Stan Musial	1599
Pete Rose	1566
Harmon Killebrew	1559
*Frank Thomas	1547
Lou Gehrig	1508
Mike Schmidt	1507
Eddie Collins	1499
Willie Mays	1464
Jimmie Foxx	1452
Eddie Mathews	1444

RUNS BATTED IN

Hank Aaron	2297
Babe Ruth	2213
Cap Anson	2076
Lou Gehrig	1995
Stan Musial	1951
Ty Cobb	1937
*Barry Bonds	1930
Jimmie Foxx	1922
Eddie Murray	1917
Willie Mays	1903
Mel Ott	1860
Carl Yastrzemski	1844
Ted Williams	1839
Rafael Palmeiro	1835
Dave Winfield	1833
Al Simmons	1827
Frank Robinson	1812
Honus Wagner	1732
Reggie Jackson	1702
Cal Ripken Jr.	1695

SLUGGING AVERAGE (5,000 AB)

Babe Ruth	.690
Ted Williams	.634
Lou Gehrig	.632
Jimmie Foxx	.609
*Barry Bonds	.608
Hank Greenberg	.605
*Manny Ramirez	.600
*Todd Helton	.593
Mark McGwire	.588
*Vladimir Guerrero	.583
Joe Dimaggio	.579
Rogers Hornsby	.577
*Alex Rodriguez	.573
*Frank Thomas	.566
*Jim Thome	.565
Larry Walker	.565
Albert Belle	.564
Johnny Mize	.562
Juan Gonzalez	.561
Stan Musial	.559

STOLEN BASES

Rickey Henderson	1406
Lou Brock	938
Billy Hamilton	912
Ty Cobb	892
Tim Raines	808
Vince Coleman	752
Eddie Collins	745
Max Carey	738
Honus Wagner	722
Joe Morgan	689
Willie Wilson	668
Bert Campaneris	649
Otis Nixon	620
George Davis	616
Tom Brown	615
*Kenny Lofton	599
Dummy Hoy	594
Maury Wills	586
George Van Haltren	583
Ozzie Smith	580

ON-BASE PERCENTAGE (5,000 AB)

Ted Williams	.482
Babe Ruth	.469
*Barry Bonds	.443
Lou Gehrig	.442
*Todd Helton	.430
Jimmie Fox	.425
Ty Cobb	.424
Rogers Hornsby	.424
*Frank Thomas	.424
Mickey Mantle	.422
Edgar Martinez	.418
Stan Musial	.417
Tris Speaker	.417
Wade Boggs	.415
*Jason Giambi	.413
*Bobby Abreu	.412
*Manny Ramirez	.411
Mel Ott	.410
Mickey Cochrane	.409
Hank Greenberg	.409

TOTAL BASES

Hank Aaron	6856
Stan Musial	6134
Willie Mays	6066
Ty Cobb	5859
Babe Ruth	5793
*Barry Bonds	5784
Pete Rose	5752
Carl Yastrzemski	5539
Eddie Murray	5397
Rafael Palmeiro	5388
Frank Robinson	5373
Dave Winfield	5221
Cal Ripken Jr.	5168
Tris Speaker	5101
Lou Gehrig	5060
George Brett	5044
Mel Ott	5041
Jimmie Foxx	4956
Ted Williams	4884
Honus Wagner	4862

STRIKEOUTS

Reggie Jackson	2597
Sammy Sosa	2194
Andres Galarraga	2003
Jose Canseco	1942
Willie Stargell	1936
*Jim Thome	1909
Mike Schmidt	1883
Fred McGriff	1882
Tony Perez	1867
Dave Kingman	1816
Bobby Bonds	1757
Dale Murphy	1748
Lou Brock	1730
Mickey Mantle	1710
Harmon Killebrew	1699
Chili Davis	1698
Dwight Evans	1697
Rickey Henderson	1694
Dave Winfield	1686
*Craig Biggio	1641

The 30–30 Club (30 HR, 30 SB in single season)

Year	HR	SB	Year	HR	SB
1922......Kenny Williams, StL	39	37	1995......Sammy Sosa, ChiC	36	34
1956......Willie Mays, NYG	36	40	1996......Barry Bonds, SF	42	40
1957......Willie Mays, NYG	35	38	1996......Ellis Burks, Col	40	32
1963......Hank Aaron, Mil	44	31	1996......Barry Larkin, Cin	33	36
1969......Bobby Bonds, SF	32	45	1996......Dante Bichette, Col	31	31
1970......Tommy Harper, Mil	31	38	1997......Larry Walker, Col	49	33
1973......Bobby Bonds, SF	39	43	1997......Jeff Bagwell, Hou	43	31
1975......Bobby Bonds, NYY	32	30	1997......Raul Mondesi, LA	30	32
1977......Bobby Bonds, Cal	37	41	1997......Barry Bonds, SF	40	37
1978......Bobby Bonds, Chi/Tex	31	43	1998......Alex Rodriguez, Sea	42	46
1983......Dale Murphy, Atl	36	30	1998......Shawn Green, Tor	35	35
1987......Joe Carter, Clev	32	31	1999......Jeff Bagwell, Hou	42	30
1987......Eric Davis, Cin	37	50	1999......Raul Mondesi, LA	33	36
1987......Darryl Strawberry, NYM	39	36	2000......Preston Wilson, Fla	31	36
1987......Howard Johnson, NYM	36	32	2001......Vladimir Guerrero, Mtl	34	37
1988......Jose Canseco, Oak	42	40	2001......Jose Cruz Jr., Tor	34	32
1989......Howard Johnson, NYM	36	41	2001......Bobby Abreu, Phil	31	36
1990......Ron Gant, Atl	32	33	2002......Alfonso Soriano, NYY	39	41
1990......Barry Bonds, Pitt	33	52	2002......Vladimir Guerrero, Mtl	39	40
1991......Ron Gant, Atl	32	34	2003......Alfonso Soriano, NYY	38	35
1991......Howard Johnson, NYM	38	30	2004......Carlos Beltran, KC/Hou	38	42
1992......Barry Bonds, Pitt	34	39	2004......Bobby Abreu, Phil	30	40
1993......Sammy Sosa, ChiC	33	36	2005......Alfonso Soriano, Tex	36	30
1995......Barry Bonds, SF	33	31	2006......Alfonso Soriano, Wash	46	41

Career Individual Pitching

GAMES		INNINGS PITCHED		WINS	
Jesse Orosco	1251	Cy Young	7356.0	Cy Young	511
John Franco	1119	Pud Galvin	6003.1	Walter Johnson	417
*Mike Stanton	1109	Walter Johnson	5914.1	Grover Alexander	373
Dennis Eckersley	1071	Phil Niekro	5404.1	Christy Mathewson	373
Hoyt Wilhelm	1070	Nolan Ryan	5386.0	Pud Galvin	365
Dan Plesac	1064	Gaylord Perry	5350.1	Warren Spahn	363
Kent Tekulve	1050	Don Sutton	5282.1	Kid Nichols	361
Lee Smith	1022	Warren Spahn	5243.1	*Roger Clemens	348
Mike Jackson	1005	Steve Carlton	5217.1	Tim Keefe	342
Goose Gossage	1002	Grover Alexander	5190.0	*Greg Maddux	333
Lindy McDaniel	987	Kid Nichols	5056.1	Steve Carlton	329
*Jose Mesa	966	Tim Keefe	5049.2	John Clarkson	328
*Mike Timlin	961	Bert Blyleven	4970.0	Eddie Plank	326
*Roberto Hernandez	960	Bobby Mathews	4956.0	Nolan Ryan	324
Rollie Fingers	944	*Roger Clemens	4817.2	Don Sutton	324
Gene Garber	931	Mickey Welch	4802.0	Phil Niekro	318
Cy Young	906	Tom Seaver	4782.2	Gaylord Perry	314
Sparky Lyle	899	Christy Mathewson	4780.2	Tom Seaver	311
Jim Kaat	898	Tommy John	4710.1	Charley Radbourn	309
Paul Assenmacher	884	Robin Roberts	4688.2	Mickey Welch	307

* Active in 2006.   ** Minumum 100 victories.

Career Individual Pitching (Cont.)

LOSSES

Cy Young	316
Pud Galvin	310
Nolan Ryan	292
Walter Johnson	279
Phil Niekro	274
Gaylord Perry	265
Don Sutton	256
Jack Powell	254
Eppa Rixey	251
Bert Blyleven	250
Bobby Mathews	248
Robin Roberts	245
Warren Spahn	245
Steve Carlton	244
Early Wynn	244
Jim Kaat	237
Frank Tanana	236
Gus Weyhing	232
Tommy John	231
Bob Friend	230
Ted Lyons	230

SAVES

*Trevor Hoffman	482
Lee Smith	478
John Franco	424
*Mariano Rivera	413
Dennis Eckersley	390
Jeff Reardon	367
Randy Myers	347
Rollie Fingers	341
John Wetteland	330
*Roberto Hernandez	326
*Troy Percival	324
*Billy Wagner	324
*Jose Mesa	320
Rick Aguilera	318
Robb Nen	314
Tom Henke	311
Goose Gossage	310
Jeff Montgomery	304
Doug Jones	303
Bruce Sutter	300

SHUTOUTS

Walter Johnson	110
Grover Alexander	90
Christy Mathewson	79
Cy Young	76
Eddie Plank	69
Warren Spahn	63
Nolan Ryan	61
Tom Seaver	61
Bert Blyleven	60
Don Sutton	58
Pud Galvin	57
Ed Walsh	57
Bob Gibson	56
Three Finger Brown	55
Steve Carlton	55
Jim Palmer	53
Gaylord Perry	53
Juan Marichal	52
Rube Waddell	50
Vic Willis	50

WINNING PERCENTAGE**

Al Spalding	.795
Spud Chandler	.717
*Pedro Martinez	.691
Whitey Ford	.690
Dave Foutz	.690
Bob Caruthers	.688
Don Gullett	.686
Lefty Grove	.680
Joe Wood	.672
Vic Raschi	.667
*Roger Clemens	.667
Larry Corcoran	.665
*Tim Hudson	.665
Christy Mathewson	.665
Sam Leever	.660
Sal Maglie	.657
*Randy Johnson	.656
Dick McBride	.656
Sandy Koufax	.655
Johnny Allen	.654

EARNED RUN AVERAGE (2,000 IP)

Ed Walsh	1.82
Addie Joss	1.89
Al Spalding	2.04
Three Finger Brown	2.06
John Ward	2.10
Christy Mathewson	2.13
Tommy Bond	2.14
Rube Waddell	2.16
Walter Johnson	2.17
Ed Reulbach	2.28
Will White	2.28
Eddie Plank	2.35
Larry Corcoran	2.36
Eddie Cicotte	2.38
Candy Cummings	2.39
Doc White	2.39
Nap Rucker	2.42
George Bradley	2.43
Jim McCormick	2.43
Chief Bender	2.46

COMPLETE GAMES

Cy Young	749
Pud Galvin	639
Tim Keefe	554
Walter Johnson	531
Kid Nichols	531
Mickey Welch	525
Bobby Mathews	525
Charley Radbourn	489
John Clarkson	485
Tony Mullane	468
Jim McCormick	466
Gus Weyhing	448
Grover Alexander	437
Christy Mathewson	434
Jack Powell	422
Eddie Plank	410
Will White	394
Amos Rusie	392
Vic Willis	388
Tommy Bond	386

STRIKEOUTS

Nolan Ryan	5714
*Roger Clemens	4604
*Randy Johnson	4544
Steve Carlton	4136
Bert Blyleven	3701
Tom Seaver	3640
Don Sutton	3574
Gaylord Perry	3534
Walter Johnson	3509
Phil Niekro	3342
Ferguson Jenkins	3192
*Greg Maddux	3169
Bob Gibson	3117
*Curt Schilling	3015
*Pedro Martinez	2998
Jim Bunning	2855
Mickey Lolich	2832
Cy Young	2803
*John Smoltz	2778
Frank Tanana	2773

BASES ON BALLS

Nolan Ryan	2795
Steve Carlton	1833
Phil Niekro	1809
Early Wynn	1775
Bob Feller	1764
Bobo Newsom	1732
Amos Rusie	1707
Charlie Hough	1665
Gus Weyhing	1566
*Roger Clemens	1549
Red Ruffing	1541
Bump Hadley	1442
Warren Spahn	1434
Earl Whitehill	1431
*Randy Johnson	1409
Tony Mullane	1408
*Tom Glavine	1399
Sad Sam Jones	1396
Jack Morris	1390
Tom Seaver	1390

* Active in 2006.   ** Minumum 100 victories.

Alltime Winningest Managers

CAREER

	W	L	Pct	Yrs		W	L	Pct	Yrs
Connie Mack	3755	3967	.486	53	Gene Mauch	1907	2044	.483	26
John McGraw	2810	1987	.586	33	Bill McKechnie	1904	1737	.523	25
Sparky Anderson	2238	1855	.547	26	*Joe Torre	1882	1681	.532	24
*Tony LaRussa	2221	1896	.536	27	Ralph Houk	1627	1539	.514	20
Bucky Harris	2168	2228	.493	29	Fred Clarke	1609	1189	.575	19
Joe McCarthy	2155	1346	.616	24	Dick Williams	1592	1474	.519	21
Walter Alston	2063	1634	.558	23	Tommy Lasorda	1589	1434	.526	20
Leo Durocher	2015	1717	.540	24	Earl Weaver	1506	1080	.582	17
*Bobby Cox	2004	1534	.566	23	Clark Griffith	1491	1367	.522	20
Casey Stengel	1942	1868	.510	25	Lou Pinella	1540	1441	.523	19

REGULAR SEASON

	W	L	Pct	Yrs		W	L	Pct	Yrs
Connie Mack	3731	3948	.486	53	Gene Mauch	1902	2037	.483	26
John McGraw	2784	1959	.587	33	Bill McKechnie	1896	1723	.524	25
*Tony La Russa	2214	1908	.534	27	*Joe Torre	1876	1637	.532	24
Sparky Anderson	2194	1834	.545	26	Ralph Houk	1619	1531	.514	20
Bucky Harris	2157	2218	.493	29	Fred Clarke	1602	1181	.576	19
Joe McCarthy	2125	1333	.615	24	Dick Williams	1571	1451	.520	21
*Bobby Cox	2092	1603	.567	24	Tommy Lasorda	1558	1404	.526	20
Walter Alston	2040	1613	.558	23	Lou Piniella	1519	1420	.523	19
Leo Durocher	2008	1709	.540	24	Clark Griffith	1491	1367	.522	20
Casey Stengel	1905	1842	.508	25	Earl Weaver	1480	1060	.583	17

WORLD SERIES

	W	L	T	Pct	App	WS		W	L	T	Pct	App	WS
Casey Stengel	37	26	0	.587	10	7	Billy Southworth	11	11	0	.500	4	2
Joe McCarthy	30	13	0	.698	9	7	Earl Weaver	11	13	0	.458	4	1
John McGraw	26	28	2	.482	9	2	*Bobby Cox	11	18	0	.379	5	1
Connie Mack	24	19	0	.558	8	5	Whitey Herzog	10	11	0	.476	3	1
*Joe Torre	21	11	0	.657	6	4	*Tony La Russa	9	13	0	.409	5	2
Walter Alston	20	20	0	.500	7	4	Bill Carrigan	8	2	0	.800	2	2
Miller Huggins	18	15	1	.544	6	3	Cito Gaston	8	4	0	.667	2	2
Sparky Anderson	16	12	0	.571	5	3	Danny Murtaugh	8	6	0	.571	2	2
Tommy Lasorda	12	11	0	.522	4	2	Tom Kelly	8	6	0	.571	2	2
Dick Williams	12	14	0	.462	4	2	Ralph Houk	8	8	0	.500	3	2
Frank Chance	11	9	1	.548	4	2	Bill McKechnie	8	14	0	.364	4	2
Bucky Harris	11	10	0	.524	3	2							

* Active in 2006.

Individual Batting (Single Season)

HITS

Ichiro Suzuki, 2004	262
George Sisler, 1920	257
Lefty O'Doul, 1929	254
Bill Terry, 1930	254
Al Simmons, 1925	253
Rogers Hornsby, 1922	250
Chuck Klein, 1930	250
Ty Cobb, 1911	248
George Sisler, 1922	246
Ichiro Suzuki, 2001	242

BATTING AVERAGE

Levi Meyerle, 1871	.492
Hugh Duffy, 1894	.440
Tip O'Neill, 1887	.435
Ross Barnes, 1872	.432
Cal McVey, 1871	.431
Ross Barnes, 1876	.429
Nap Lajoie, 1901	.426
Ross Barnes, 1873	.425
Willie Keeler, 1897	.424
Rogers Hornsby, 1924	.424

DOUBLES

Earl Webb, 1931	67
George Burns, 1926	64
Joe Medwick, 1936	64
Hank Greenberg, 1934	63
Paul Waner, 1932	62
Charlie Gehringer, 1936	60
Tris Speaker, 1923	59
Chuck Klein, 1930	59
Todd Helton, 2000	59
Billy Herman, 1936	57
Billy Herman, 1935	57
Carlos Delgado, 2000	57

TOTAL BASES

Babe Ruth, 1921	457
Rogers Hornsby, 1922	450
Lou Gehrig, 1927	447
Chuck Klein, 1930	445
Jimmie Foxx, 1932	438
Stan Musial, 1948	429
Sammy Sosa, 2001	425
Hack Wilson, 1930	423
Chuck Klein, 1932	420
Luis Gonzalez, 2001	419
Lou Gehrig, 1930	419

TRIPLES

Chief Wilson, 1912	36
Dave Orr, 1886	31
Heinie Reitz, 1894	31
Perry Werden, 1893	29
Harry Davis, 1897	28
George Davis, 1893	27
Sam Thompson, 1894	27
Jimmy Williams, 1899	27
Sam Crawford, 1914	26
Kiki Cuyler, 1925	26
Joe Jackson, 1912	26
John Reilly, 1890	26
George Treadway	26

HOME RUNS

Barry Bonds, 2001	73
Mark McGwire, 1998	70
Sammy Sosa, 1998	66
Mark McGwire, 1999	65
Sammy Sosa, 2001	64
Sammy Sosa, 1999	63
Roger Maris, 1961	61
Babe Ruth, 1927	60
Babe Ruth, 1921	59
Jimmie Foxx, 1932	58
Hank Greenberg, 1938	58
Mark McGwire, 1997	58
Ryan Howard, 2006	58

RUNS BATTED IN

Hack Wilson, 1930	190
Lou Gehrig, 1931	184
Hank Greenberg, 1937	183
Lou Gehrig, 1927	175
Jimmie Foxx, 1938	175
Lou Gehrig, 1930	174
Babe Ruth, 1921	171
Chuck Klein, 1930	170
Hank Greenberg, 1935	170
Jimmie Foxx, 1932	169

STRIKEOUTS

Adam Dunn, 2004	195
Bobby Bonds, 1970	189
Jose Hernandez, 2002	188
Bobby Bonds, 1969	187
Preston Wilson, 2000	187
Rob Deer, 1987	186
Jose Hernandez, 2001	185
Pete Incaviglia, 1986	185
Jim Thome, 2003	185
Cecil Fielder, 1990	182
Jim Thome, 2003	182

RUNS

Billy Hamilton, 1894	192
Tom Brown, 1891	177
Babe Ruth, 1921	177
Lou Gehrig, 1936	167
Tip O'Neill, 1887	167
Billy Hamilton, 1895	166
Willie Keeler, 1894	165
Joe Kelley, 1894	165
Lou Gehrig, 1931	163
Arlie Latham, 1887	163
Babe Ruth, 1928	163

STOLEN BASES

Hugh Nicol, 1887	138
Rickey Henderson, 1982	130
Arlie Latham, 1887	129
Lou Brock, 1974	118
Charlie Comiskey, 1887	117
Billy Hamilton, 1891	111
Billy Hamilton, 1889	111
John Ward, 1887	111
Vince Coleman, 1985	110
Vince Coleman, 1987	109
Arlie Latham, 1888	109

BASES ON BALLS

Barry Bonds, 2004	232
Barry Bonds, 2002	198
Barry Bonds, 2001	177
Babe Ruth, 1923	170
Ted Williams, 1947	162
Ted Williams, 1949	162
Mark McGwire, 1998	162
Ted Williams, 1946	156
Barry Bonds, 1996	151
Eddie Yost, 1956	151
Babe Ruth, 1920	150

SLUGGING AVERAGE

Barry Bonds, 2001	.863
Babe Ruth, 1920	.847
Babe Ruth, 1921	.846
Barry Bonds, 2004	.812
Barry Bonds, 2002	.799
Babe Ruth, 1927	.772
Lou Gehrig, 1927	.765
Babe Ruth, 1923	.764
Rogers Hornsby, 1925	.756
Mark McGwire, 1998	.752

Individual Pitching (Single Season)

GAME APPEARANCES

Mike Marshall, 1974 106
Kent Tekulve, 1979 94
Salomon Torres, 2006..........94
Mike Marshall, 1973 92
Kent Tekulve, 1978 91
Wayne Granger, 1969...........90
Mike Marshall, 1979 90
Kent Tekulve, 1987 90
Steve Kline, 2001..................89
Jim Brower, 2004..................89
Mark Eichhorn, 1987 89
Steve Kline, 2001..................89

GAMES STARTED

Will White, 1879....................75
Pud Galvin, 1883...................75
Jim McCormick, 1880 74
Charley Radbourn, 1884 73
Guy Hecker, 1884..................73
Jim Galvin, 1884...................72
John Clarkson, 1889..............72
Bill Hutchison, 1892..............71
John Clarkson, 1885..............70
Bobby Mathews, 1875...........70

INNINGS PITCHED

Will White, 1878................680.0
Charley Radbourn, 1884 ...678.2
Guy Hecker, 1884..............670.2
Jim McCormick, 1880 .....657.2
Jim Galvin, 1883...............656.1
Jim Galvin, 1884...............636.1
Charley Radbourn, 1883 ...632.1
Bill Hutchison, 1892..........627.0
Bobby Mathews, 1875........626.2
John Clarkson, 1885.........623.0

WINS

Charley Radbourn, 1884 59
Al Spalding, 1875..................55
John Clarkson, 1885..............53
Guy Hecker, 1884..................52
Al Spalding, 1874..................52
John Clarkson, 1889..............49
Charlie Buffinton, 1884 48
Charley Radbourn, 1883 48
Al Spalding, 1876..................47
John Ward, 1879 47
Matt Kilroy, 1887..................46

LOSSES

John Coleman, 1883 48
Will White, 1880....................42
Larry McKeon, 1884..............41
George Bradley, 1879 40
Jim McCormick, 1879 40
Bobby Mathews, 1875..........38
Kid Carsey, 1891 37
George Cobb, 1892 37
Henry Porter, 1888................37

WINNING PERCENTAGE

Roy Face, 1959 947
Johnny Allen, 1937.............938
Greg Maddux, 1995 905
Randy Johnson, 1995 900
Ron Guidry, 1978 893
Freddie Fitzsimmons, 1940...889
Lefty Grove, 1931...............886
Bob Stanley, 1978 882
Preacher Roe, 1951............880
Fred Goldsmith, 1880........875
Tom Seaver, 1981 875

SAVES

Bobby Thigpen, 1990...........57
Eric Gagne, 2003 55
John Smoltz, 2002...............55
Mariano Rivera, 2004 53
Randy Myers, 1993 53
Trevor Hoffman, 1998 53
Eric Gagne, 2002 52
Rod Beck, 1998....................51
Dennis Eckersley, 1992 51
Mariano Rivera, 2001 50
Francisco Cordero, 2004.......49

EARNED RUN AVERAGE

Tim Keefe, 1880 ....0.86
Dutch Leonard, 1914..........0.96
Three Finger Brown, 1906 ...1.04
Bob Gibson, 1968 ....1.12
Christy Mathewson, 1909...1.14
Walter Johnson, 1913........1.15
Jack Pfiester, 1907 ....1.15
Addie Joss, 1908................1.16
Carl Lundgren, 1907 ....1.17
Denny Driscoll, 1882........1.21

SHUTOUTS

Grover Alexander, 1916.........16
George Bradley, 1876 16
Jack Coombs, 1910 13
Bob Gibson, 1968 13
Grover Alexander, 1915.........12
Jim Galvin, 1884...................12
Ed Morris, 1886 12
Tommy Bond, 1879...............11
Dean Chance, 1964 11
Dave Foutz, 1886 11
Walter Johnson, 1913............11
Sandy Koufax, 1963 11
Christy Mathewson, 1908......11
Charles Radbourn, 1884.......11
Ed Walsh, 1908 11

COMPLETE GAMES

Will White, 1879....................75
Charley Radbourn, 1884 73
Pud Galvin, 1883...................72
Guy Hecker, 1884..................72
Jim McCormick, 1880...........72
Pud Galvin, 1884...................71
Bobby Mathews, 1875...........69
John Clarkson, 1885..............68
John Clarkson, 1889..............68

STRIKEOUTS

Matt Kilroy, 1886..................513
Toad Ramsey, 1886 499
Hugh Daily, 1884..................483
Dupee Shaw, 1884 451
Charley Radbourn, 1884 441
Charlie Buffinton, 1884.........417
Guy Hecker, 1884..................385
Nolan Ryan, 1973.................383
Sandy Koufax, 1965 382

BASES ON BALLS

Amos Rusie, 1890 289
Mark Baldwin, 1889...............274
Amos Rusie, 1892 267
Amos Rusie, 1891 262
Mark Baldwin, 1890...............249
Jack Stivetts, 1891 232
Mark Baldwin, 1891...............227
Phil Knell, 1891....................226
Bob Barr, 1890 219

Manager of the Year

	NATIONAL LEAGUE		AMERICAN LEAGUE
1983	Tommy Lasorda, LA	1983	Tony La Russa, Chi
1984	Jim Frey, Chi	1984	Sparky Anderson, Det
1985	Whitey Herzog, StL	1985	Bobby Cox, Tor
1986	Hal Lanier, Hou	1986	John McNamara, Bos
1987	Buck Rodgers, Mtl	1987	Sparky Anderson, Det
1988	Tommy Lasorda, LA	1988	Tony La Russa, Oak
1989	Don Zimmer, Chi	1989	Frank Robinson, Balt
1990	Jim Leyland, Pitt	1990	Jeff Torborg, Chi
1991	Bobby Cox, Atl	1991	Tom Kelly, Minn
1992	Jim Leyland, Pitt	1992	Tony La Russa, Oak
1993	Dusty Baker, SF	1993	Gene Lamont, Chi
1994	Felipe Alou, Mtl	1994	Buck Showalter, NY
1995	Don Baylor, Col	1995	Lou Piniella, Sea
1996	Bruce Bochy, SD	1996	Joe Torre, NY/Johnny Oates, Tex
1997	Dusty Baker, SF	1997	Davey Johnson, Balt
1998	Larry Dierker, Hou	1998	Joe Torre, NY

Manager of the Year *(Cont.)*

NATIONAL LEAGUE

1999	Jack McKeon, Cin
2000	Dusty Baker, SF
2001	Larry Bowa, Phil
2002	Tony La Russa, StL
2003	Jack McKeon, Fla
2004	Bobby Cox, Atl
2005	Bobby Cox, Atl

AMERICAN LEAGUE

1999	Jimy Williams, Bos
2000	Jerry Manuel, Chi
2001	Lou Piniella, Sea
2002	Mike Scioscia, Ana
2003	Tony Pena, KC
2004	Buck Showalter, Tex
2005	Ozzie Guillen, Chi

Individual Batting (Single Game)

MOST RUNS

7 ....Guy Hecker, Lou — Aug 15, 1886

MOST HITS

7 ....Wilbert Robinson, Balt — June 10, 1892
Rennie Stennett, Pitt — Sept 16, 1975

MOST HOME RUNS

4 ....Bobby Lowe, Bos (N) — May 30, 1894
Ed Delahanty, Phil — July 13, 1896
Lou Gehrig, NY (A) — June 3, 1932
Gil Hodges, Bklyn — Aug 31, 1950
Joe Adcock, Mil (N) — July 31, 1954
Rocky Colavito, Clev — June 10, 1959
Willie Mays, SF — April 30, 1961
Mike Schmidt, Phil — April 17, 1976
Bob Horner, Atl — July 6, 1986
Mark Whiten, StL — Sept 7, 1993
Mike Cameron, Sea — May 2, 2002
Shawn Green, LA — May 23, 2002
Carlos Delgado, Tor — Sept 25, 2003

MOST GRAND SLAMS

2 ....Tony Lazzeri, NY (A) — May 24, 1936
Jim Tabor, Bos (A) — July 4, 1939
Rudy York, Bos (A) — July 27, 1946
Jim Gentile, Balt — May 9, 1961
Tony Cloninger, Atl — July 3, 1966
Jim Northrup, Det — June 24, 1968
Frank Robinson, Balt — June 26, 1970
Robin Ventura, Chi (A) — Sept 4, 1995
Chris Hoiles, Balt — Aug 14, 1998
Fernando Tatis, StL — Apr 23, 1999
N. Garciaparra, Bos — May 10, 1999
Bill Mueller, Bos — July 29, 2003

MOST RBIs

12 .....Jim Bottomley, StL — Sept 16, 1924
Mark Whiten, StL — Sept 7, 1993

Note: All single-game hitting records for a nine-inning game.

Individual Batting (Single Inning)

MOST RUNS

3 ....Tommy Burns, Chi (N) Sept 6, 1883, 7th inning
Ned Williamson, Chi (N) Sept 6, 1883, 7th inning
Sammy White, Bos (A) June 18, 1953, 7th inning

MOST HITS

3 ....Tommy Burns, Chi (N) Sept 6, 1883, 7th inning
Fred Pfeiffer, Chi (N) Sept 6, 1883, 7th inning
Ned Williamson, Chi (N) Sept 6, 1883, 7th inning
Gene Stephens, Bos (A) June 18, 1953, 7th inning

MOST RBIs

8 ....Fernando Tatis, StL — Apr 23, 1999, 3rd inning

Individual Pitching (Single Game)

MOST INNINGS PITCHED

26 .....Leon Cadore, Bklyn — May 1, 1920, tie 1–1
Joe Oeschger, Bos (N) — May 1, 1920, tie 1–1

MOST RUNS ALLOWED

24 .....Al Travers, Det — May 18, 1912

MOST HITS ALLOWED

36 .....Jack Wadsworth, Lou — Aug 17, 1894

MOST STRIKEOUTS

20 .....Roger Clemens, Bos — April 29, 1986
20 .....Roger Clemens, Bos — Sept 18, 1996
20 .....Kerry Wood, Chi (N) — May 6, 1998
20 .....Randy Johnson, Ariz — May 8, 2001

MOST WALKS ALLOWED

16 .....Bill George, NY (N) — May 30, 1887
George Van Haltren, Chi (N) — June 27, 1887
Henry Gruber, Clev — Apr 19, 1890
Bruno Haas, Phil (A) — June 2, 1915

MOST WILD PITCHES

6 .......J.R. Richard, Hou — April 10, 1979
Phil Niekro, Atl — Aug 14, 1979
Bill Gullickson, Mtl — April 10, 1982

Individual Pitching (Single Inning)

MOST RUNS ALLOWED		MOST WILD PITCHES	
13 .....Lefty O'Doul, Bos (A)	July 7, 1923	4 ....Walter Johnson, Wash	Sept 21, 1914
		Phil Niekro, Atl	Aug 14, 1979
MOST WALKS ALLOWED		Kevin Gregg, Ana	July 25, 2004
8 ....Dolly Gray, Wash	Aug 28, 1909		

Miscellaneous

LONGEST GAME, BY INNINGS		LONGEST NINE-INNING GAME, BY TIME
26 .....Brooklyn 1, Boston 1	May 1, 1920	4:27...Los Angeles 11, San Francisco 10 Oct 5, 2001

Baseball Hall of Fame

Players

	Position	Career	Selected		Position	Career	Selected
Hank Aaron	OF	1954–76	1982	Andrew Cooper*	P	1920–41	2006
Grover Alexander	P	1911–30	1938	Stan Coveleski	P	1912–28	1969
Cap Anson	1B	1876–97	1939	Sam Crawford	OF	1899–1917	1957
Luis Aparicio	SS	1956–73	1984	Joe Cronin	SS	1926–45	1956
Luke Appling	SS	1930–50	1964	Candy Cummings	P	1872–77	1939
Richie Ashburn	OF	1948–62	1995	Kiki Cuyler	OF	1921–38	1968
Earl Averill	OF	1929–41	1975	Ray Dandridge*	3B		1987
Jose Mendez Baez*	P	1908–26	2006	George Davis	SS	1890–1909	1998
Frank Baker	3B	1908–22	1955	Leon Day*	P		1995
Dave Bancroft	SS	1915–30	1971	Dizzy Dean	P	1930–47	1953
Ernie Banks	SS-1B	1953–71	1977	Ed Delahanty	OF	1888–1903	1945
Jake Beckley	1B	1888–1907	1971	Bill Dickey	C	1928–46	1954
Cool Papa Bell*	OF		1974	Martin Dihigo*	P-OF		1977
Johnny Bench	C	1967–83	1989	Joe DiMaggio	OF	1936–51	1955
Chief Bender	P	1903–25	1953	Larry Doby	OF	1947–59	1998
Yogi Berra	C	1946–65	1972	Bobby Doerr	2B	1937–51	1986
Wade Boggs	3B	1982-99	2005	Don Drysdale	P	1956–69	1984
Jim Bottomley	1B	1922–37	1974	Hugh Duffy	OF	1888–1906	1945
Lou Boudreau	SS	1938-52	1970	Dennis Eckersley	P	1975–98	2004
Roger Bresnahan	C	1897–1915	1945	Johnny Evers	2B	1902–29	1939
George Brett	3B	1973–93	1999	Buck Ewing	C	1880–97	1946
Lou Brock	OF	1961–79	1985	Red Faber	P	1914–33	1964
Dan Brouthers	1B	1879–1904	1945	Bob Feller	P	1936–56	1962
Ray Brown*	P	1930–48	2006	Rick Ferrell	C	1929–47	1984
Three Finger Brown	P	1903–16	1949	Rollie Fingers	P	1968–85	1992
Willard Jesse Brown*	OF	1935–58	2006	Carlton Fisk	C	1969–93	2000
Jim Bunning	P	1955–71	1996	Elmer Flick	OF	1898–1910	1963
Jesse Burkett	OF	1890–1905	1946	Whitey Ford	P	1950–67	1974
Roy Campanella	C	1948–57	1969	Bill Foster*	P		1996
Rod Carew	1B-2B	1967–85	1991	Nellie Fox	2B	1947–65	1997
Max Carey	OF	1910–29	1961	Jimmie Foxx	1B	1925–45	1951
Steve Carlton	P	1965–88	1994	Frankie Frisch	2B	1919–37	1947
Gary Carter	C	1974–92	2003	Pud Galvin	P	1879–92	1965
Orlando Cepeda	1B	1958–74	1999	Lou Gehrig	1B	1923–39	1939
Frank Chance	1B	1898–1914	1946	Charlie Gehringer	2B	1924–42	1949
Oscar Charleston*	OF		1976	Bob Gibson	P	1959–75	1981
Jack Chesbro	P	1899–1909	1946	Josh Gibson*	C		1972
Fred Clarke	OF	1894–1915	1945	Lefty Gomez	P	1930–43	1972
John Clarkson	P	1882–94	1963	Goose Goslin	OF	1921–38	1968
Roberto Clemente	OF	1955–72	1973	Ulysses F. Grant*	2B	1886–1903	2006
Ty Cobb	OF	1905–28	1936	Hank Greenberg	1B	1930–47	1956
Mickey Cochrane	C	1925–37	1947	Burleigh Grimes	P	1916–34	1964
Eddie Collins	2B	1906–30	1939	Lefty Grove	P	1925–41	1947
Jimmy Collins	3B	1895–1908	1945	Chick Hafey	OF	1924–37	1971
Earle Combs	OF	1924–35	1970	Jesse Haines	P	1918–37	1970
Roger Connor	1B	1880–97	1976	Billy Hamilton	OF	1888–1901	1961

Note: Career dates indicate first and last appearances in the majors.
*Elected on the basis of their career in the Negro leagues.

Players *(Cont.)*

Name	Position	Career	Selected
Gabby Hartnett	C	1922–41	1955
Harry Heilmann	OF	1914–32	1952
Billy Herman	2B	1931–47	1975
Jospeh Hill*	OF	1899–1925	2006
Harry Hooper	OF	1909–25	1971
Rogers Hornsby	2B	1915–37	1942
Waite Hoyt	P	1918–38	1969
Carl Hubbell	P	1928–43	1947
Catfish Hunter	P	1965–79	1987
Monte Irvin*	OF	1949–56	1973
Reggie Jackson	OF	1967–87	1993
Travis Jackson	SS	1922–36	1982
Ferguson Jenkins	P	1965–83	1991
Hugh Jennings	SS	1891–1918	1945
Judy Johnson*	3B		1975
Walter Johnson	P	1907–27	1936
Addie Joss	P	1902–10	1978
Al Kaline	OF	1953–74	1980
Tim Keefe	P	1880–93	1964
Willie Keeler	OF	1892–1910	1939
George Kell	3B	1943–57	1983
Joe Kelley	OF	1891–1908	1971
George Kelly	1B	1915–32	1973
King Kelly	C	1878–93	1945
Harmon Killebrew	1B-3B	1954–75	1984
Ralph Kiner	OF	1946–55	1975
Chuck Klein	OF	1928–44	1980
Sandy Koufax	P	1955–66	1972
Nap Lajoie	2B	1896–1916	1937
Tony Lazzeri	2B	1926–39	1991
Bob Lemon	P	1941–58	1976
Buck Leonard*	1B		1977
Fred Lindstrom	3B	1924–36	1976
Pop Lloyd*	SS-1B		1977
Ernie Lombardi	C	1931–47	1986
Ted Lyons	P	1923–46	1955
James Mackey*	C	1920–47	2006
Mickey Mantle	OF	1951–68	1974
Heinie Manush	OF	1923–39	1964
Rabbit Maranville	SS-2B	1912–35	1954
Juan Marichal	P	1960–75	1983
Rube Marquard	P	1908–25	1971
Eddie Mathews	3B	1952–68	1978
Christy Mathewson	P	1900–16	1936
Willie Mays	OF	1951–73	1979
Bill Mazeroski	2B	1956–72	2001
Tommy McCarthy	OF	1884–96	1946
Willie McCovey	1B	1959–80	1986
Joe McGinnity	P	1899–1908	1946
Bid McPhee	2B	1882–99	2000
Joe Medwick	OF	1932–48	1968
Johnny Mize	1B	1936–53	1981
Paul Molitor	3B	1978–98	2004
Joe Morgan	2B	1963–84	1990
Eddie Murray	1B	1977–97	2003
Stan Musial	OF-1B	1941–63	1969
Hal Newhouser	P	1939–55	1992
Kid Nichols	P	1890–1906	1949
Phil Niekro	P	1964–87	1997
Jim O'Rourke	OF	1876–1904	1945
Mel Ott	OF	1926–47	1951
Satchel Paige*	P	1948–65	1971
Jim Palmer	P	1965–84	1990
Herb Pennock	P	1912–34	1948
Tony Perez	1B	1964–86	2000
Gaylord Perry	P	1962–83	1991
Eddie Plank	P	1901–17	1946
Kirby Puckett	OF	1984–95	2001
Charley Radbourn	P	1880–91	1939
Pee Wee Reese	SS	1940–58	1984
Sam Rice	OF	1915–35	1963
Eppa Rixey	P	1912–33	1963
Phil Rizzuto	SS	1941–56	1994
Robin Roberts	P	1948–66	1976
Brooks Robinson	3B	1955–77	1983
Frank Robinson	OF	1956–76	1982
Jackie Robinson	2B	1947–56	1962
Joe (Bullet) Rogan*	P		1998
Edd Roush	OF	1913–31	1962
Red Ruffing	P	1924–47	1967
Amos Rusie	P	1889–1901	1977
Babe Ruth	OF	1914–35	1936
Nolan Ryan	P	1966–93	1999
Ryne Sandberg	2B	1981-97	2005
Louis Santop*	C	1909–26	2006
Ray Schalk	C	1912–29	1955
Mike Schmidt	3B	1972–89	1995
Red Schoendienst	2B	1945–63	1989
Tom Seaver	P	1967–86	1992
Joe Sewell	SS	1920–33	1977
Al Simmons	OF	1924–44	1953
George Sisler	1B	1915–30	1939
Enos Slaughter	OF	1938–59	1985
Hilton Smith*	P		2001
Ozzie Smith	SS	1978–96	2002
Duke Snider	OF	1947–64	1980
Warren Spahn	P	1942–65	1973
Al Spalding	P	1871–78	1939
Tris Speaker	OF	1907–28	1937
Willie Stargell	OF-1B	1962–82	1988
Turkey Stearns*	CF		2000
Don Sutton	P	1966–88	1998
Bruce Sutter	P	1976–88	2006
George Suttles*	C	1923–44	2006
Benjamin Harrison Taylor*	P-1B	1908–29	2006
Bill Terry	1B	1923–36	1954
Sam Thompson	OF	1885–1906	1974
Joe Tinker	SS	1902–16	1946
Cristóbal Torriente*	OF	1913–32	2006
Pie Traynor	3B	1920–37	1948
Dazzy Vance	P	1915–35	1955
Arky Vaughan	SS	1932–48	1985
Rube Waddell	P	1897–1910	1946
Honus Wagner	SS	1897–1917	1936
Bobby Wallace	SS	1894–1918	1953
Ed Walsh	P	1904–17	1946
Lloyd Waner	OF	1927–45	1967
Paul Waner	OF	1926–45	1952
John Ward	2B-P	1878–94	1964
Mickey Welch	P	1880–92	1973
Willie Wells*	SS	1924–49	1997
Zach Wheat	OF	1909–27	1959
Hoyt Wilhelm	P	1952–72	1985
Billy Williams	OF	1959–76	1987
Ted Williams	OF	1939–60	1966
Vic Willis	P	1898–1910	1995
Ernest Judson Wilson*	3B	1922–45	2006
Hack Wilson	OF	1923–34	1979
Dave Winfield	OF	1973–95	2001
Early Wynn	P	1939–63	1972
Carl Yastrzemski	OF	1961–83	1989
Cy Young	P	1890–1911	1937
Ross Youngs	OF	1917–26	1972
Robin Yount	SS	1974–93	1999

*Elected on the basis of their career in the Negro leagues.

Pioneers/Executives

	Selected
Ed Barrow (manager-executive)	1953
Morgan Bulkeley (executive)	1937
Alexander Cartwright (executive)	1938
Henry Chadwick (writer-executive)	1938
Happy Chandler (commissioner)	1982
Charles Comiskey (manager-executive)	1939
Rube Foster (player-manager-executive)	1981
Ford Frick (commissioner-executive)	1970
Warren Giles (executive)	1979
Will Harridge (executive)	1972
William Hulbert (executive)	1995
Ban Johnson (executive)	1937
Kenesaw M. Landis (commissioner)	1944
Larry MacPhail (executive)	1978
Lee MacPhail Jr. (executive)	1998
Effa Manley (owner)	2006
Alex Pompez (owner-executive)	2006
Cum Posey (player-manager-owner)	2006
Branch Rickey (manager-executive)	1967
Al Spalding (player-executive)	1939
Bill Veeck (owner)	1991
George Weiss (executive)	1971
Sol White (player-manager)	2006
J.L. Wilkinson (owner)	2006
George Wright (player-manager)	1937
Harry Wright (player-manager-executive)	1953
Tom Yawkey (executive)	1980

Managers

	Managed	Selected
Walter Alston	1954–76	1983
Sparky Anderson	1970–94	2000
Leo Durocher	1939–73	1994
Clark Griffith	1901–20	1946
Bucky Harris	1924–56	1975
Ned Hanlon	1899–1907	1996
Miller Huggins	1913–29	1964
Tommy Lasorda	1977–96	1997
Al Lopez	1951–69	1977
Connie Mack	1894–1950	1937
Joe McCarthy	1926–50	1957
John McGraw	1899–1932	1937
Bill McKechnie	1915–46	1962
Wilbert Robinson	1902–31	1945
Frank Selee	1890–1905	1999
Casey Stengel	1934–65	1966
Earl Weaver	1968–82, 85–86	1996

Umpires

	Selected
Al Barlick	1989
Nestor Chylak	1999
Jocko Conlan	1974
Tom Connolly	1953
Billy Evans	1973
Cal Hubbard	1976
Bill Klem	1953
Bill McGowan	1992

Notable Achievements

No-Hit Games, Nine Innings or More
NATIONAL LEAGUE

Date	Pitcher and Game
1876......July 15	George Bradley, StL vs Hart 2–0
1880......June 12	John Richmond, Wor vs Clev 1–0 (perfect game)
June 17	Monte Ward, Prov vs Buff 5–0 (perfect game)
Aug 19	Larry Corcoran, Chi vs Bos 6–0
Aug 20	Pud Galvin, Buff vs Wor 1–0
1882......Sept 20	Larry Corcoran, Chi vs Wor 5–0
Sept 22	Tim Lovett, Bklyn vs NY 4–0
1883......July 25	Hoss Radbourn, Prov vs Clev 8–0
Sept 13	Hugh Daily, Clev vs Phil 1–0
1884......June 27	Larry Corcoran, Chi vs Prov 6–0
Aug 4	Pud Galvin, Buff vs Det 18–0
1885......July 27	John Clarkson, Chi vs Prov 4–0
Aug 29	Charles Ferguson, Phil vs Prov 1–0
1891......July 31	Amos Rusie, NY vs Bklyn 6–0
June 22	Tom Lovett, Bklyn vs NY 4–0
1892......Aug 6	Jack Stivetts, Bos vs Bklyn 11–0
Aug 22	Alex Sanders, Lou vs Balt 6–2
1892......Oct 15	Bumpus Jones, Cin vs Pitt 7–1 (first major league game)
1893......Aug 16	Bill Hawke, Balt vs Wash 5–0
1897......Sept 18	Cy Young, Clev vs Cin 6–0
1898......Apr 22	Ted Breitenstein, Cin vs Pitt 11–0
Apr 22	Jim Hughes, Balt vs Bos 8–0
July 8	Frank Donahue, Phil vs Bos 5–0
Aug 21	Walter Thornton, Chi vs Bklyn 2–0

Date	Pitcher and Game
1899......May 25	Deacon Phillippe, Lou vs NY 7–0
Aug 7	Vic Willis, Bos vs Wash 7–1
1900......July 12	Noodles Hahn, Cin vs Phil 4–0
1901......July 15	Christy Mathewson, NY vs StL 5–0
1903......Sept 18	Chick Fraser, Phil vs Chi 10–0
1904......June 11	Bob Wicker, Chi at NY 1–0 (hit in 10th; won in 12th)
1905......June 13	Christy Mathewson, NY vs Chi 1–0
1906......May 1	John Lush, Phil vs Bklyn 6–0
July 20	Mal Eason, Bklyn vs StL 2–0
1906......Aug 1	Harry McIntire, Bklyn vs Pitt 0–1 (hit in 11th; lost in 13th)
1907......May 8	Frank Pfeffer, Bos vs Cin 6–0
Sept 20	Nick Maddox, Pitt vs Bklyn 2–1
1908......July 4	George Wiltse, NY vs Phil 1–0 (10 innings)
Sept 5	Nap Rucker, Bklyn vs Bos 6–0
1909......Apr 15	Leon Ames, NY vs Bklyn 0–3 (hit in 10th; lost in 13th)
1912......Sept 6	Jeff Tesreau, NY vs Phil 3–0
1914......Sept 9	George Davis, Bos vs Phil 7–0
1915......Apr 15	Rube Marquard, NY vs Bklyn 2–0
Aug 31	Jimmy Lavender, Chi vs NY 2–0
1916......June 16	Tom Hughes, Bos vs Pitt 2–0
1917......May 2	Jim Vaughn, Chi vs Cin 0–1 (hit in 10th; lost in 10th)
May 2	Fred Toney, Cin vs Chi 1–0 (10 innings)

No-Hit Games, Nine Innings or More *(Cont.)*

NATIONAL LEAGUE *(Cont.)*

1919......May 11	Hod Eller, Cin vs StL 6–0	
1922......May 7	Jesse Barnes, NY vs Phil 6–0	
1924......July 17	Jesse Haines, StL vs Bos 5–0	
1925......Sept 13	Dazzy Vance, Bklyn vs Phil 10–1	
1929......May 8	Carl Hubbell, NY vs Pitt 11–0	
1934......Sept 21	Paul Dean, StL vs Bklyn 3–0	
1938......June 11	Johnny Vander Meer, Cin vs Bos 3–0	
June 15	Johnny Vander Meer, Cin vs Bklyn 6–0	
1940......Apr 30	Tex Carleton, Bklyn vs Cin, 3–0	
1941......Aug 30	Lon Warneke, StL vs Cin 2–0	
1944......Apr 27	Jim Tobin, Bos vs Bklyn 2–0	
May 15	Clyde Shoun, Cin vs Bos 1–0	
1946......Apr 23	Ed Head, Bklyn vs Bos 5–0	
1947......June 18	Ewell Blackwell, Cin vs Bos 6–0	
1948......Sept 9	Rex Barney, Bklyn vs NY 2–0	
1950......Aug 11	Vern Bickford, Bos vs Bklyn 7–0	
1951......May 6	Cliff Chambers, Pitt vs Bos 3–0	
1952......June 19	Carl Erskine, Bklyn vs Chi 5–0	
1954......June 12	Jim Wilson, Mil vs Phil 2–0	
1955......May 12	Sam Jones, Chi vs Pitt 4–0	
1956......May 12	Carl Erskine, Bklyn vs NY 3–0	
Sept 25	Sal Maglie, Bklyn vs Phil 5–0	
1959......May 26	Harvey Haddix, Pitt vs Mil 0–1	
	(hit in 13th; lost in 13th)	
1960......May 15	Don Cardwell, Chi vs StL 4–0	
Aug 18	Lew Burdette, Mil vs Phil 1–0	
Sept 16	Warren Spahn, Mil vs Phil 4–0	
1961......Apr 28	Warren Spahn, Mil vs SF 1–0	
1962......June 30	Sandy Koufax, LA vs NY 5–0	
1963......May 11	Sandy Koufax, LA vs SF 8–0	
May 17	Don Nottebart, Hou vs Phil 4–1	
June 15	Juan Marichal, SF vs Hou 1–0	
1964......Apr 23	Ken Johnson, Hou vs Cin 0–1	
June 4	Sandy Koufax, LA vs Phil 3–0	
June 21	Jim Bunning, Phil vs NY 6–0	
	(perfect game)	
1965......June 14	Jim Maloney, Cin vs NY 0–1	
	(hit in 11th; lost in 11th)	
Aug 19	Jim Maloney, Cin vs Chi 1–0	
	(10 innings)	
Sept 9	Sandy Koufax, LA vs Chi 1–0	
	(perfect game)	
1967......June 18	Don Wilson, Hou vs Atl 2–0	
1968......July 29	George Culver, Cin vs Phil 6–1	
Sept 17	Gaylord Perry, SF vs StL 1–0	
Sept 18	Ray Washburn, StL vs SF 2–0	
1969......Apr 17	Bill Stoneman, Mtl vs Phil 7–0	
Apr 30	Jim Maloney, Cin vs Hou 10–0	
May 1	Don Wilson, Hou vs Cin 4–0	
Aug 19	Ken Holtzman, Chi vs Atl 3–0	
Sept 20	Bob Moose, Pitt vs NY 4–0	
1970......June 12	Dock Ellis, Pitt vs SD 2–0	
July 20	Bill Singer, LA vs Phil 5–0	
1971......June 3	Ken Holtzman, Chi vs Cin 1–0	
June 23	Rick Wise, Phil vs Cin 4–0	
Aug 14	Bob Gibson, StL vs Pitt 11–0	
1972......Apr 16	Burt Hooton, Chi vs Phil 4–0	
Sept 2	Milt Pappas, Chi vs SD 8–0	
Oct 2	Bill Stoneman, Mtl vs NY 7–0	
1973......Aug 5	Phil Niekro, Atl vs SD 9–0	
1975......Aug 24	Ed Halicki, SF vs NY 6–0	
1976......July 9	Larry Dierker, Hou vs Mtl 6–0	
Aug 9	John Candelaria, Pitt vs LA 2–0	
Sept 29	John Montefusco, SF vs Atl 9–0	
1978......Apr 16	Bob Forsch, StL vs Phil 5–0	
June 16	Tom Seaver, Cin vs StL 4–0	
1979......Apr 7	Ken Forsch, Hou vs Atl 6–0	
1980......June 27	Jerry Reuss, LA vs SF 8–0	
1981......May 10	Charlie Lea, Mtl vs SF 4–0	
Sept 26	Nolan Ryan, Hou vs LA 5–0	
1983......Sept 26	Bob Forsch, StL vs Mtl 3–0	
1986......Sept 25	Mike Scott, Hou vs SF 2–0	
1988......Sept 16	Tom Browning, Cin vs LA 1–0	
	(perfect game)	
1990......June 29	Fernando Valenzuela, LA vs StL 6–0	
1990......Aug 15	Terry Mulholland, Phil vs SF 6–0	
1991......May 23	Tommy Greene, Phil vs Mtl 2–0	
July 26	Mark Gardner, Mtl vs LA 0–1	
	(hit in 10th, lost in 10th)	
July 28	Dennis Martinez, Mtl vs LA 2–0	
	(perfect game)	
Sept 11	Kent Mercker (6), Mark Wohlers (2), and Alejandro Pena (1), Atl vs SD 1–0	
1992......Aug 17	Kevin Gross, LA vs SF 2–0	
1993......Sept 8	Darryl Kile, Hou vs NY 7–1	
1994......Apr 8	Kent Mercker, Atl vs LA 6–0	
1995......June 3	Pedro Martinez, Mtl vs SD 1–0	
	(perfect through nine, hit in 10th)	
July 14	Ramon Martinez, LA vs Fla 7–0	
1996......May 11	Al Leiter, Fla vs Col 11–0	
Sept 17	Hideo Nomo, LA vs Col 9–0	
1997......June 10	Kevin Brown, Fla vs SF 9–0	
July 12	Francisco Cordova (9) and Ricardo Rincon (1), Pitt vs Col 3–0	
1999......June 25	Jose Jimenez, StL vs Ariz 1–0	
2001......May 12	A.J. Burnett, Fla vs SD 3–0	
Sept 3	Bud Smith, StL vs SD 4–0	
2003......June 11	R. Oswalt (1), P. Munro (2.2), K. Saarloos (1.1), B. Lidge (2), O. Dotel (1), B. Wagner (1), Hou vs NYY 8–0	
April 27	Kevin Millwood, Phil vs SF 1–0	
2004......May 18	Randy Johnson, Ariz vs Atl 2–0	
	(perfect game)	
2006......Sept 6	Anibal Sanchez, Fla vs Ariz 2–0	

Note: Includes the games struck from the official record book on Sept. 4, 1991, when baseball's committee on statistical accuracy voted to define no-hitters as games of nine innings or more that end with a team getting no hits.

No-Hit Games, Nine Innings or More *(Cont.)*

AMERICAN LEAGUE

Date	Pitcher and Game
1901......May 9	Earl Moore, Clev vs Chi 2–4 (hit in 10th; lost in 10th)
1902......Sept 20	Jimmy Callahan, Chi vs Det 3–0
1904......May 5	Cy Young, Bos vs Phil 3–0 (perfect game)
Aug 17	Jesse Tannehill, Bos vs Chi 6–0
1905......July 22	Weldon Henley, Phil vs StL 6–0
Sept 6	Frank Smith, Chi vs Det 15–0
Sept 27	Bill Dinneen, Bos vs Chi 2–0
1908......June 30	Cy Young, Bos vs NY 8–0
Sept 18	Bob Rhoades, Clev vs Bos 2–1
Sept 20	Frank Smith, Chi vs Phil 1–0
1908......Oct 2	Addie Joss, Clev vs Chi 1–0 (perfect game)
1910......Apr 20	Addie Joss, Clev vs Chi 1–0
May 12	Chief Bender, Phil vs Clev 4–0
Aug 30	Tom Hughes, NY vs Clev 0–5 (hit in 10th; lost in 11th)
1911......July 29	Joe Wood, Bos vs StL 5–0
Aug 27	Ed Walsh, Chi vs Bos 5–0
1912......July 4	George Mullin, Det vs StL 7–0
Aug 30	Earl Hamilton, StL vs Det 5–1
1914......May 14	Jim Scott, Chi vs Wash 0–1 (hit in 10th; lost in 10th)
May 31	Joe Benz, Chi vs Clev 6–1
1916......June 21	George Foster, Bos vs NY 2–0
Aug 26	Joe Bush, Phil vs Clev 5–0
Aug 30	Dutch Leonard, Bos vs StL 4–0
1917......Apr 14	Ed Cicotte, Chi vs StL 11–0
Apr 24	George Mogridge, NY vs Bos 2–1
May 5	Ernie Koob, StL vs Chi 1–0
May 6	Bob Groom, StL vs Chi 3–0
June 23	Ernie Shore, Bos vs Wash 4–0 (perfect game)
1918......June 3	Dutch Leonard, Bos vs Det 5–0
1919......Sept 10	Ray Caldwell, Clev vs NY 3–0
1920......July 1	Walter Johnson, Wash vs Bos 1–0
1922......Apr 30	Charlie Robertson, Chi vs Det 2–0 (perfect game)
1923......Sept 4	Sam Jones, NY vs Phil 2–0
Sept 7	Howard Ehmke, Bos vs Phil 4–0
1926......Aug 21	Ted Lyons, Chi vs Bos 6–0
1931......Apr 29	Wes Ferrell, Clev vs StL 9–0
Aug 8	Bob Burke, Wash vs Bos 5–0
1934......Sept 18	Bobo Newsom, StL vs Bos 1–2 (hit in 10th; lost in 10th)
1935......Aug 31	Vern Kennedy, Chi vs Clev 5–0
1937......June 1	Bill Dietrich, Chi vs StL 8–0
1938......Aug 27	Mtle Pearson, NY vs Clev 13–0
1940......Apr 16	Bob Feller, Clev vs Chi 1–0 (opening day)
1945......Sept 9	Dick Fowler, Phil vs StL 1–0
1946......Apr 30	Bob Feller, Clev vs NY 1–0
1947......July 10	Don Black, Clev vs Phil 3–0
Sep 3	Bill McCahan, Phil vs Wash 3–0
1948......June 30	Bob Lemon, Clev vs Det 2–0
1951......July 1	Bob Feller, Clev vs Det 2–1
July 12	Allie Reynolds, NY vs Clev 1–0
Sept 28	Allie Reynolds, NY vs Bos 8–0
1952......May 15	Virgil Trucks, Det vs Wash 1–0
Aug 25	Virgil Trucks, Det vs NY 1–0
1953......May 6	Bobo Holloman, StL vs Phil 6–0 (first major league start)
1956......July 14	Mel Parnell, Bos vs Chi 4–0

Date	Pitcher and Game
1966......Oct 8	Don Larsen, NY (A) vs Bklyn (N) 2–0 (World Series) (perfect game)
1957......Aug 20	Bob Keegan, Chi vs Wash 6–0
1958......July 20	Jim Bunning, Det vs Bos 3–0
Sept 20	Hoyt Wilhelm, Balt vs NY 1–0
1962......May 5	Bo Belinsky, LA vs Balt 2–0
June 26	Earl Wilson, Bos vs LA 2–0
Aug 1	Bill Monbouquette, Bos vs Chi 1–0
Aug 26	Jack Kralick, Minn vs KC 1–0
1965......Sept 16	Dave Morehead, Bos vs Clev 2–0
1966......June 10	Sonny Siebert, Clev vs Wash 2–0
1967......Apr 30	Steve Barber (8⅔) and Stu Miller (⅓), Balt vs Det 1–2
Aug 25	Dean Chance, Minn vs Clev 2–1
Sept 10	Joel Horlen, Chi vs Det 6–0
1968......Apr 27	Tom Phoebus, Balt vs Bos 6–0
May 8	Catfish Hunter, Oak vs Minn 4–0 (perfect game)
1969......Aug 13	Jim Palmer, Balt vs Oak 8–0
1970......July 3	Clyde Wright, Cal vs Oak 4–0
Sept 21	Vida Blue, Oak vs Minn 6–0
1973......Apr 27	Steve Busby, KC vs Det 3–0
May 15	Nolan Ryan, Cal vs KC 3–0
July 15	Nolan Ryan, Cal vs Det 6–0
July 30	Jim Bibby, Tex vs Oak 6–0
1974......June 19	Steve Busby, KC vs Mil 2–0
July 19	Dick Bosman, Clev vs Oak 4–0
Sept 28	Nolan Ryan, Cal vs Minn 4–0
1975......June 1	Nolan Ryan, Cal vs Balt 1–0
Sept 28	Vida Blue (5), Glenn Abbott and Paul Lindblad (1), Rollie Fingers (2), Oak vs Cal 5–0
1976......July 28	John Odom (5) and Francisco Barrios (4), Chi vs Oak 2–1
1977......May 14	Jim Colborn, KC vs Tex 6–0
May 30	Dennis Eckersley, Clev vs Cal 1–0
Sept 22	Bert Blyleven, Tex vs Cal 6–0
1981......May 15	Len Barker, Clev vs Tor 3–0 (perfect game)
1983......July 4	Dave Righetti, NY vs Bos 4–0
Sept 29	Mike Warren, Oak vs Chi 3–0
1984......Apr 7	Jack Morris, Det vs Chi 4–0
Sept 30	Mike Witt, Cal vs Tex 1–0 (perfect game)
1986......Sept 19	Joe Cowley, Chi vs Cal 7–1
1987......Apr 15	Juan Nieves, Mil vs Balt 7–0
1990......Apr 11	Mark Langston (7), Mike Witt (2), Cal vs Sea 1–0
June 2	Randy Johnson, Sea vs Det 2–0
June 11	Nolan Ryan, Tex vs Oak 5–0
June 29	Dave Stewart, Oak vs Tor 5–0
1990......July 1	Andy Hawkins, NY vs Chi 0–4 (pitched eight of nine-innning game)
Sept 2	Dave Stieb, Tor vs Clev 3–0
1991......May 1	Nolan Ryan, Tex vs Tor 3–0
July 13	Bob Milacki (6), Mike Flanagan (1), Mark Williamson (1), and Gregg Olson (1), Balt vs Oak 2–0
Aug 11	Wilson Alvarez, Chi vs Balt 7–0
Aug 26	Bret Saberhagen, KC vs Chi 7–0
1993......Apr 22	Chris Bosio, Sea vs Bos 7–0

No-Hit Games, Nine Innings or More *(Cont.)*

AMERICAN LEAGUE *(Cont.)*

1993......Apr 22	Chris Bosio, Sea vs Bos 7–0	
Sept 4	Jim Abbott, NY vs Clev 4–0	
1994......Apr 27	Scott Erickson, Minn vs Mil 6–0	
July 28	Kenny Rogers, Texas vs Cal 4–0 (perfect game)	
1996......May 14	Dwight Gooden, NY vs Sea 2–0	
1998......May 17	David Wells, NY vs Minn 4–0 (perfect game)	
1999......July 18	David Cone, NY vs Mtl 6–0 (perfect game)	
Sept 11	Eric Milton, Minn vs Ana 7–0	
2001......Apr 4	Hideo Nomo, Bos vs Balt 3–0	
2002......Apr 27	Derek Lowe, Bos vs TB 10–0	

Longest Hitting Streaks

NATIONAL LEAGUE

Player and Team	Year	G
Willie Keeler, Balt	1897	44
Pete Rose, Cin	1978	44
Bill Dahlen, Chi	1894	42
Tommy Holmes, Bos	1945	37
Billy Hamilton, Phil	1894	36
Jimmy Rollins, Phil	2005–06	36
Luis Castillo, Fla	2002	35
Fred Clarke, Lou	1895	35
Chase Utley, Phil	2006	35
Benito Santiago, SD	1987	34
George Davis, NY	1893	33
Rogers Hornsby, StL	1922	33

AMERICAN LEAGUE

Player and Team	Year	G
Joe DiMaggio, NY	1941	56
George Sisler, StL	1922	41
Ty Cobb, Det	1911	40
Paul Molitor, Mil	1987	39
Ty Cobb, Det	1917	35
Ty Cobb, Det	1912	34
George Sisler, StL	1925	34
John Stone, Det	1930	34
George McQuinn, StL	1938	34
Dom DiMaggio, Bos	1949	34
Hal Chase, NY	1907	33
Heinie Menush, Wash	1933	33

Triple Crown Hitters

NATIONAL LEAGUE

Player and Team	Year	HR	RBI	BA
Paul Hines, Prov	1878	4	50	.358
Hugh Duffy, Bos	1894	18	145	.438
Heinie Zimmerman*, Chi	1912	14	103	.372
Rogers Hornsby, StL	1922	42	152	.401
	1925	39	143	.403
Chuck Klein, Phil	1933	28	120	.368
Joe Medwick, StL	1937	31	154	.374

*Zimmerman ranked first in RBIs as calculated by Ernie Lanigan, but only third as calculated by Information Concepts Inc.

AMERICAN LEAGUE

Player and Team	Year	HR	RBI	BA
Nap Lajoie, Phil	1901	14	125	.422
Ty Cobb, Det	1909	9	115	.377
Jimmie Foxx, Phil	1933	48	163	.356
Lou Gehrig, NY	1934	49	165	.363
Ted Williams, Bos	1942	36	137	.356
	1947	32	114	.343
Mickey Mantle, NY	1956	52	130	.353
Frank Robinson, Balt	1966	49	122	.316
Carl Yastrzemski, Bos	1967	44	121	.326

Triple Crown Pitchers

NATIONAL LEAGUE						AMERICAN LEAGUE					
Player and Team	Year	W	L	SO	ERA	Player and Team	Year	W	L	SO	ERA
Tommy Bond, Bos............1877		40	17	170	2.11	Cy Young, Bos 1901		33	10	158	1.62
Hoss Radbourn, Prov 1884		60	12	441	1.38	Rube Waddell, Phil 1905		26	11	287	1.48
Tim Keefe, NY.................1888		35	12	333	1.74	Walter Johnson, Wash 1913		36	7	303	1.09
John Clarkson, Bos..........1889		49	19	284	2.73		1918	23	13	162	1.27
Amos Rusie, NY...............1894		36	13	195	2.78		1924	23	7	158	2.72
Christy Mathewson, NY ...1905		31	8	206	1.27	Lefty Grove, Phil 1930		28	5	209	2.54
	1908	37	11	259	1.43		1931	31	4	175	2.06
Grover Alexander, Phil 1915		31	10	241	1.22	Lefty Gomez, NY..............1934		26	5	158	2.33
	1916	33	12	167	1.55		1937	21	11	194	2.33
	1917	30	13	201	1.86	Hal Newhouser, Det.........1945		25	9	212	1.81
Hippo Vaughn, Chi 1918		22	10	148	1.74	Roger Clemens, Tor 1997		21	7	292	2.05
Grover Alexander, Chi 1920		27	14	173	1.91		1998	20	6	271	2.64
Dazzy Vance, Bklyn 1924		28	6	262	2.16	Pedro Martinez, Bos 1999		23	4	313	2.07
Bucky Walters, Cin...........1939		27	11	137	2.29	*Johan Santana, Min........2006		19	6	245	2.77
Sandy Koufax, LA 1963		25	5	306	1.88						
	1965	26	8	382	2.04						
	1966	27	9	317	1.73						
Steve Carlton, Phil 1972		27	10	310	1.97						
Dwight Gooden, NY 1985		24	4	268	1.53						
Randy Johnson, Ariz........2002		24	5	334	2.32	*Tied with another pitcher for wins					

Consecutive Games Played, 500 or More Games

Cal Ripken Jr. 2,632		Frank McCormick 652	
Lou Gehrig..........................2,130		Sandy Alomar Sr. 648	
Everett Scott 1,307		Eddie Brown 618	
Steve Garvey 1,207		Miguel Tejada 599	
Billy Williams......................1,117		Roy McMillan 585	
Joe Sewell 1,103		George Pinckney.................577	
Miguel Tejada 1,069		Steve Brodie 574	
Stan Musial 895		Aaron Ward...........................565	
Eddie Yost 829		Alex Rodriguez 546	
Gus Suhr 822		Candy LaChance 540	
Nellie Fox...............................798		Buck Freeman 535	
Pete Rose 745		Fred Luderus 533	
Dale Murphy 740		Clyde Milan...........................511	
Richie Ashburn 730		Charlie Gehringer 511	
Ernie Banks 717		Vada Pinson.........................508	
Pete Rose 678		Tony Cuccinello 504	
Earl Averill..............................673		Charlie Gehringer 504	

Unassisted Triple Plays

Player and Team	Date	Pos	Opp	Opp Batter
Neal Ball, Clev 7-19-09		SS	Bos	Amby McConnell
Bill Wambsganss, Clev 10-10-20		2B	Bklyn	Clarence Mitchell
George Burns, Bos 9-14-23		1B	Clev	Frank Brower
Ernie Padgett, Bos...........10-6-23		SS	Phil	Walter Holke
Glenn Wright, Pitt.............5-7-25		SS	StL	Jim Bottomley
Jimmy Cooney, Chi 5-30-27		SS	Pitt	Paul Waner
Johnny Neun, Det 5-31-27		1B	Clev	Homer Summa
Ron Hansen, Wash 7-30-68		SS	Clev	Joe Azcue
Mickey Morandini, Phil.....9-20-92		2B	Pitt	Jeff King
John Valentin, Bos 7-15-94		SS	Minn	Marc Newfield
Randy Velarde, Oak.........5-29-00		2B	NYY	Shane Spencer
Rafael Furcal, Atl..............8-10-03		SS	StL	Woody Williams

Leading Batsmen

Year	Player and Team	BA	Year	Player and Team	BA
1900	Honus Wagner, Pitt	.381	1954	Willie Mays, NY	.345
1901	Jesse Burkett, StL	.382	1955	Richie Ashburn, Phil	.338
1902	Ginger Beaumtl, Pitt	.357	1956	Hank Aaron, Mil	.328
1903	Honus Wagner, Pitt	.355	1957	Stan Musial, StL	.351
1904	Honus Wagner, Pitt	.349	1958	Richie Ashburn, Phil	.350
1905	Cy Seymour, Cin	.377	1959	Hank Aaron, Mil	.355
1906	Honus Wagner, Pitt	.339	1960	Dick Groat, Pitt	.325
1907	Honus Wagner, Pitt	.350	1961	Roberto Clemente, Pitt	.351
1908	Honus Wagner, Pitt	.354	1962	Tommy Davis, LA	.346
1909	Honus Wagner, Pitt	.339	1963	Tommy Davis, LA	.326
1910	Sherry Magee, Phil	.331	1964	Roberto Clemente, Pitt	.339
1911	Honus Wagner, Pitt	.334	1965	Roberto Clemente, Pitt	.329
1912	Heinie Zimmerman, Chi	.372	1966	Matty Alou, Pitt	.342
1913	Jake Daubert, Bklyn	.350	1967	Roberto Clemente, Pitt	.357
1914	Jake Daubert, Bklyn	.329	1968	Pete Rose, Cin	.335
1915	Larry Doyle, NY	.320	1969	Pete Rose, Cin	.348
1916	Hal Chase, Cin	.339	1970	Rico Carty, Atl	.366
1917	Edd Roush, Cin	.341	1971	Joe Torre, StL	.363
1918	Zach Wheat, Bklyn	.335	1972	Billy Williams, Chi	.333
1919	Edd Roush, Cin	.321	1973	Pete Rose, Cin	.338
1920	Rogers Hornsby, StL	.370	1974	Ralph Garr, Atl	.353
1921	Rogers Hornsby, StL	.397	1975	Bill Madlock, Chi	.354
1922	Rogers Hornsby, StL	.401	1976	Bill Madlock, Chi	.339
1923	Rogers Hornsby, StL	.384	1977	Dave Parker, Pitt	.338
1924	Rogers Hornsby, StL	.424	1978	Dave Parker, Pitt	.334
1925	Rogers Hornsby, StL	.403	1979	Keith Hernandez, StL	.344
1926	Bubbles Hargrave, Cin	.353	1980	Bill Buckner, Chi	.324
1927	Paul Waner, Pitt	.380	1981	Bill Madlock, Pitt	.341
1928	Rogers Hornsby, Bos	.387	1982	Al Oliver, Mtl	.331
1929	Lefty O'Doul, Phil	.398	1983	Bill Madlock, Pitt	.323
1930	Bill Terry, NY	.401	1984	Tony Gwynn, SD	.351
1931	Chick Hafey, StL	.349	1985	Willie McGee, StL	.353
1932	Lefty O'Doul, Bklyn	.368	1986	Tim Raines, Mtl	.334
1933	Chuck Klein, Phil	.368	1987	Tony Gwynn, SD	.370
1934	Paul Waner, Pitt	.362	1988	Tony Gwynn, SD	.313
1935	Arky Vaughan, Pitt	.385	1989	Tony Gwynn, SD	.336
1936	Paul Waner, Pitt	.373	1990	Willie McGee, StL	.335
1937	Joe Medwick, StL	.374	1991	Terry Pendleton, Atl	.319
1938	Ernie Lombardi, Cin	.342	1992	Gary Sheffield, SD	.330
1939	Johnny Mize, StL	.349	1993	Andres Galarraga, Col	.370
1940	Debs Garms, Pitt	.355	1994	Tony Gwynn, SD	.394
1941	Pete Reiser, Bklyn	.343	1995	Tony Gwynn, SD	.368
1942	Ernie Lombardi, Bos	.330	1996	Tony Gwynn, SD	.353
1943	Stan Musial, StL	.357	1997	Tony Gwynn, SD	.372
1944	Dixie Walker, Bklyn	.357	1998	Larry Walker, Col	.363
1945	Phil Cavarretta, Chi	.355	1999	Larry Walker, Col	.379
1946	Stan Musial, StL	.365	2000	Todd Helton, Col	.372
1947	Harry Walker, StL-Phil	.363	2001	Larry Walker, Col	.350
1948	Stan Musial, StL	.376	2002	Barry Bonds, SF	.370
1949	Jackie Robinson, Bklyn	.342	2003	Albert Pujols, StL	.359
1950	Stan Musial, StL	.346	2004	Barry Bonds, SF	.362
1951	Stan Musial, StL	.355	2005	Derrek Lee, Chi	.335
1952	Stan Musial, StL	.336	2006	Freddy Sanchez, Pitt	.334
1953	Carl Furillo, Bklyn	.344			

Leaders in Runs Scored

Year	Player and Team	Runs	Year	Player and Team	Runs
1900	Roy Thomas, Phil	131	1953	Duke Snider, Bklyn	132
1901	Jesse Burkett, StL	139	1954	Stan Musial, StL	120
1902	Honus Wagner, Pitt	105		Duke Snider, Bklyn	120
1903	Ginger Beaumont, Pitt	137	1955	Duke Snider, Bklyn	126
1904	George Browne, NY	99	1956	Frank Robinson, Cin	122
1905	Mike Donlin, NY	124	1957	Hank Aaron, Mil	118
1906	Honus Wagner, Pitt	103	1958	Willie Mays, SF	121
	Frank Chance, Chi	103	1959	Vada Pinson, Cin	131
1907	Spike Shannon, NY	104	1960	Bill Bruton, Mil	112
1908	Fred Tenney, NY	101	1961	Willie Mays, SF	129
1909	Tommy Leach, Pitt	126	1962	Frank Robinson, Cin	134
1910	Sherry Magee, Phil	110	1963	Hank Aaron, Mil	121
1911	Jimmy Sheckard, Chi	121	1964	Dick Allen, Phil	125
1912	Bob Bescher, Cin	120	1965	Tommy Harper, Cin	126
1913	Tommy Leach, Chi	99	1966	Felipe Alou, Atl	122
	Max Carey, Pitt	99	1967	Hank Aaron, Atl	113
1914	George Burns, NY	100		Lou Brock, StL	113
1915	Gavvy Cravath, Phil	89	1968	Glenn Beckert, Chi	98
1916	George Burns, NY	105	1969	Bobby Bonds, SF	120
1917	George Burns, NY	103		Pete Rose, Cin	120
1918	Heinie Groh, Cin	88	1970	Billy Williams, Chi	137
1919	George Burns, NY	86	1971	Lou Brock, StL	126
1920	George Burns, NY	115	1972	Joe Morgan, Cin	122
1921	Rogers Hornsby, StL	131	1973	Bobby Bonds, SF	131
1922	Rogers Hornsby, StL	141	1974	Pete Rose, Cin	110
1923	Ross Youngs, NY	121	1975	Pete Rose, Cin	112
1924	Frankie Frisch, NY	121	1976	Pete Rose, Cin	130
	Rogers Hornsby, StL	121	1977	George Foster, Cin	124
1925	Kiki Cuyler, Pitt	144	1978	Ivan DeJesus, Chi	104
1926	Kiki Cuyler, Pitt	113	1979	Keith Hernandez, StL	116
1927	Lloyd Waner, Pitt	133	1980	Keith Hernandez, StL	111
	Rogers Hornsby, NY	133	1981	Mike Schmidt, Phil	78
1928	Paul Waner, Pitt	142	1982	Lonnie Smith, StL	120
1929	Rogers Hornsby, Chi	156	1983	Tim Raines, Mtl	133
1930	Chuck Klein, Phil	158	1984	Ryne Sandberg, Chi	114
1931	Bill Terry, NY	121	1985	Dale Murphy, Atl	118
	Chuck Klein, Phil	121	1986	Von Hayes, Phil	107
1932	Chuck Klein, Phil	152		Tony Gwynn, SD	107
1933	Pepper Martin, StL	122	1987	Tim Raines, Mtl	123
1934	Paul Waner, Pitt	122	1988	Brett Butler, SF	109
1935	Augie Galan, Chi	133	1989	Howard Johnson, NY	104
1936	Arky Vaughan, Pitt	122		Will Clark, SF	104
1937	Joe Medwick, StL	111		Ryne Sandberg, Chi	104
1938	Mel Ott, NY	116	1990	Ryne Sandberg, Chi	116
1939	Billy Werber, Cin	115	1991	Brett Butler, LA	112
1940	Arky Vaughan, Pitt	113	1992	Barry Bonds, Pitt	109
1941	Pete Reiser, Bklyn	117	1993	Lenny Dykstra, Phil	143
1942	Mel Ott, NY	118	1994	Jeff Bagwell, Hou	104
1943	Arky Vaughan, Bklyn	112	1995	Craig Biggio, Hou	123
1944	Bill Nicholson, Chi	116	1996	Ellis Burks, Col	142
1945	Eddie Stanky, Bklyn	128	1997	Craig Biggio, Hou	146
1946	Stan Musial, StL	124	1998	Sammy Sosa, Chi	134
1947	Johnny Mize, NY	137	1999	Jeff Bagwell, Hou	143
1948	Stan Musial, StL	135	2000	Jeff Bagwell, Hou	152
1949	Pee Wee Reese, Bklyn	132	2001	Sammy Sosa, Chi	146
1950	Earl Torgeson, Bos	120	2002	Sammy Sosa, Chi	122
1951	Stan Musial, StL	124	2003	Albert Pujols, StL	137
	Ralph Kiner, Pitt	124	2004	Albert Pujols, StL	133
1952	Stan Musial, StL	105	2005	Albert Pujols, StL	129
	Solly Hemus, StL	105	2006	Chase Utley, Phil	131

Leaders in Hits

Year	Player and Team	Hits	Year	Player and Team	Hits
1900	Willie Keeler, Bklyn	208	1956	Hank Aaron, Mil	200
1901	Jesse Burkett, StL	228	1957	Red Schoendienst, NY-Mil	200
1902	Ginger Beaumont, Pitt	194	1958	Richie Ashburn, Phil	215
1903	Ginger Beaumont, Pitt	209	1959	Hank Aaron, Mil	223
1904	Ginger Beaumont, Pitt	185	1960	Willie Mays, SF	190
1905	Cy Seymour, Cin	219	1961	Vada Pinson, Cin	208
1906	Harry Steinfeldt, Chi	176	1962	Tommy Davis, LA	230
1907	Ginger Beaumont, Bos	187	1963	Vada Pinson, Cin	204
1908	Honus Wagner, Pitt	201	1964	Roberto Clemente, Pitt	211
1909	Larry Doyle, NY	172		Curt Flood, StL	211
1910	Honus Wagner, Pitt	178	1965	Pete Rose, Cin	209
	Bobby Byrne, Pitt	178	1966	Felipe Alou, Atl	218
1911	Doc Miller, Bos	192	1967	Roberto Clemente, Pitt	209
1912	Heinie Zimmerman, Chi	207	1968	Felipe Alou, Atl	210
1913	Gavvy Cravath, Phil	179		Pete Rose, Cin	210
1914	Sherry Magee, Phil	171	1969	Matty Alou, Pitt	231
1915	Larry Doyle, NY	189	1970	Pete Rose, Cin	205
1916	Hal Chase, Cin	184		Billy Williams, Chi	205
1917	Heinie Groh, Cin	182	1971	Joe Torre, StL	230
1918	Charlie Hollocher, Chi	161	1972	Pete Rose, Cin	198
1919	Ivy Olson, Bklyn	164	1973	Pete Rose, Cin	230
1920	Rogers Hornsby, StL	218	1974	Ralph Garr, Atl	214
1921	Rogers Hornsby, StL	235	1975	Dave Cash, Phil	213
1922	Rogers Hornsby, StL	250	1976	Pete Rose, Cin	215
1923	Frankie Frisch, NY	223	1977	Dave Parker, Pitt	215
1924	Rogers Hornsby, StL	227	1978	Steve Garvey, LA	202
1925	Jim Bottomley, StL	227	1979	Garry Templeton, StL	211
1926	Eddie Brown, Bos	201	1980	Steve Garvey, LA	200
1927	Paul Waner, Pitt	237	1981	Pete Rose, Phil	140
1928	Freddy Lindstrom, NY	231	1982	Al Oliver, Mtl	204
1929	Lefty O'Doul, Phil	254	1983	Jose Cruz, Hou	189
1930	Bill Terry, NY	254		Andre Dawson, Mtl	189
1931	Lloyd Waner, Pitt	214	1984	Tony Gwynn, SD	213
1932	Chuck Klein, Phil	226	1985	Willie McGee, StL	216
1933	Chuck Klein, Phil	223	1986	Tony Gwynn, SD	211
1934	Paul Waner, Pitt	217	1987	Tony Gwynn, SD	218
1935	Billy Herman, Chi	227	1988	Andres Galarraga, Mtl	184
1936	Joe Medwick, StL	223	1989	Tony Gwynn, SD	203
1937	Joe Medwick, StL	237	1990	Brett Butler, SF	192
1938	Frank McCormick, Cin	209		Lenny Dykstra, Phil	192
1939	Frank McCormick, Cin	209	1991	Terry Pendleton, Atl	187
1940	Stan Hack, Chi	191	1992	Terry Pendleton, Atl	199
	Frank McCormick, Cin	191		Andy Van Slyke, Pitt	199
1941	Stan Hack, Chi	186	1993	Lenny Dykstra, Phil	194
1942	Enos Slaughter, StL	188	1994	Tony Gwynn, SD	165
1943	Stan Musial, StL	220	1995	Dante Bichette, Col	197
1944	Stan Musial, StL	197		Tony Gwynn, SD	197
	Phil Cavarretta, Chi	197	1996	Lance Johnson, NY	227
1945	Tommy Holmes, Bos	224	1997	Tony Gwynn, SD	220
1946	Stan Musial, StL	228	1998	Dante Bichette, Col	219
1947	Tommy Holmes, Bos	191	1999	Luis Gonzalez, Ariz	206
1948	Stan Musial, StL	230	2000	Todd Helton, Col	216
1949	Stan Musial, StL	207	2001	Rich Aurilia, SF	206
1950	Duke Snider, Bklyn	199	2002	Vladimir Guerrero	206
1951	Richie Ashburn, Phil	221	2003	Albert Pujols, StL	212
1952	Stan Musial, StL	194	2004	Juan Pierre, Fla	221
1953	Richie Ashburn, Phil	205	2005	Derrek Lee, Chi	199
1954	Don Mueller, NY	212	2006	Juan Pierre, Chi	204
1955	Ted Kluszewski, Cin	192			

Home Run Leaders

Year	Player and Team	HR	Year	Player and Team	HR
1900	Herman Long, Bos	12	1950	Ralph Kiner, Pitt	47
1901	Sam Crawford, Cin	16	1951	Ralph Kiner, Pitt	42
1902	Tommy Leach, Pitt	6	1952	Ralph Kiner, Pitt	37
1903	Jimmy Sheckard, Bklyn	9		Hank Sauer, Chi	37
1904	Harry Lumley, Bklyn	9	1953	Eddie Mathews, Mil	47
1905	Fred Odwell, Cin	9	1954	Ted Kluszewski, Cin	49
1906	Tim Jordan, Bklyn	12	1955	Willie Mays, NY	51
1907	Dave Brain, Bos	10	1956	Duke Snider, Bklyn	43
1908	Tim Jordan, Bklyn	12	1957	Hank Aaron, Mil	44
1909	Red Murray, NY	7	1958	Ernie Banks, Chi	47
1910	Fred Beck, Bos	10	1959	Eddie Mathews, Mil	46
	Wildfire Schulte, Chi	10	1960	Ernie Banks, Chi	41
1911	Wildfire Schulte, Chi	21	1961	Orlando Cepeda, SF	46
1912	Heinie Zimmerman, Chi	14	1962	Willie Mays, SF	49
1913	Gavvy Cravath, Phil	19	1963	Hank Aaron, Mil	44
1914	Gavvy Cravath, Phil	19		Willie McCovey, SF	44
1915	Gavvy Cravath, Phil	24	1964	Willie Mays, SF	47
1916	Dave Robertson, NY	12	1965	Willie Mays, SF	52
	Cy Williams, Chi	12	1966	Hank Aaron, Atl	44
1917	Dave Robertson, NY	12	1967	Hank Aaron, Atl	39
	Gavvy Cravath, Phil	12	1968	Willie McCovey, SF	36
1918	Gavvy Cravath, Phil	8	1969	Willie McCovey, SF	45
1919	Gavvy Cravath, Phil	12	1970	Johnny Bench, Cin	45
1920	Cy Williams, Phil	15	1971	Willie Stargell, Pitt	48
1921	George Kelly, NY	23	1972	Johnny Bench, Cin	40
1922	Rogers Hornsby, StL	42	1973	Willie Stargell, Pitt	44
1923	Cy Williams, Phil	41	1974	Mike Schmidt, Phil	36
1924	Jack Fournier, Bklyn	27	1975	Mike Schmidt, Phil	38
1925	Rogers Hornsby, StL	39	1976	Mike Schmidt, Phil	38
1926	Hack Wilson, Chi	21	1977	George Foster, Cin	52
1927	Hack Wilson, Chi	30	1978	George Foster, Cin	40
	Cy Williams, Phil	30	1979	Dave Kingman, Chi	48
1928	Hack Wilson, Chi	31	1980	Mike Schmidt, Phil	48
	Jim Bottomley, StL	31	1981	Mike Schmidt, Phil	31
1929	Chuck Klein, Phil	43	1982	Dave Kingman, NY	37
1930	Hack Wilson, Chi	56	1983	Mike Schmidt, Phil	40
1931	Chuck Klein, Phil	31	1984	Dale Murphy, Atl	36
1932	Chuck Klein, Phil	38		Mike Schmidt, Phil	36
	Mel Ott, NY	38	1985	Dale Murphy, Atl	37
1933	Chuck Klein, Phil	28	1986	Mike Schmidt, Phil	37
1934	Ripper Collins, StL	35	1987	Andre Dawson, Chi	49
	Mel Ott, NY	35	1988	Darryl Strawberry, NY	39
1935	Wally Berger, Bos	34	1989	Kevin Mitchell, SF	47
1936	Mel Ott, NY	33	1990	Ryne Sandberg, Chi	40
1937	Mel Ott, NY	31	1991	Howard Johnson, NY	38
	Joe Medwick, StL	31	1992	Fred McGriff, SD	35
1938	Mel Ott, NY	36	1993	Barry Bonds, SF	46
1939	Johnny Mize, StL	28	1994	Matt Williams, SF	43
1940	Johnny Mize, StL	43	1995	Dante Bichette, Col	40
1941	Dolph Camilli, Bklyn	34	1996	Andres Galarraga, Col	47
1942	Mel Ott, NY	30	1997	Larry Walker, Col	49
1943	Bill Nicholson, Chi	29	1998	Mark McGwire, StL	70
1944	Bill Nicholson, Chi	33	1999	Mark McGwire, StL	65
1945	Tommy Holmes, Bos	28	2000	Sammy Sosa, Chi	50
1946	Ralph Kiner, Pitt	23	2001	Barry Bonds, SF	73
1947	Ralph Kiner, Pitt	51	2002	Sammy Sosa, Chi	49
	Johnny Mize, NY	51	2003	Jim Thome, Phil	47
1948	Ralph Kiner, Pitt	40	2004	Adrian Beltre, LA	48
	Johnny Mize, NY	40	2005	Andruw Jones, Atl	51
1949	Ralph Kiner, Pitt	54	2006	Ryan Howard, Phil	58

Runs Batted In Leaders

Year	Player and Team	RBI	Year	Player and Team	RBI
1900	Elmer Flick, Phil	110	1955	Duke Snider, Bklyn	136
1901	Honus Wagner, Pitt	126	1956	Stan Musial, StL	109
1902	Honus Wagner, Pitt	91	1957	Hank Aaron, Mil	132
1903	Sam Mertes, NY	104	1958	Ernie Banks, Chi	129
1904	Bill Dahlen, NY	80	1959	Ernie Banks, Chi	143
1905	Cy Seymour, Cin	121	1960	Hank Aaron, Mil	126
1906	Jim Nealon, Pitt	83	1961	Orlando Cepeda, SF	142
	Harry Steinfeldt, Chi	83	1962	Tommy Davis, LA	153
1907	Sherry Magee, Phil	85	1963	Hank Aaron, Mil	130
1908	Honus Wagner, Pitt	109	1964	Ken Boyer, StL	119
1909	Honus Wagner, Pitt	100	1965	Deron Johnson, Cin	130
1910	Sherry Magee, Phil	123	1966	Hank Aaron, Atl	127
1911	Wildfire Schulte, Chi	121	1967	Orlando Cepeda, StL	111
1912	Heinie Zimmerman, Chi	103	1968	Willie McCovey, SF	105
1913	Gavvy Cravath, Phil	128	1969	Willie McCovey, SF	126
1914	Sherry Magee, Phil	103	1970	Johnny Bench, Cin	148
1915	Gavvy Cravath, Phil	115	1971	Joe Torre, StL	137
1916	Heinie Zimmerman, Chi-NY	83	1972	Johnny Bench, Cin	125
1917	Heinie Zimmerman, NY	102	1973	Willie Stargell, Pitt	119
1918	Sherry Magee, Phil	76	1974	Johnny Bench, Cin	129
1919	Hi Myers, Bklyn	73	1975	Greg Luzinski, Phil	120
1920	George Kelly, NY	94	1976	George Foster, Cin	121
	Rogers Hornsby, StL	94	1977	George Foster, Cin	149
1921	Rogers Hornsby, StL	126	1978	George Foster, Cin	120
1922	Rogers Hornsby, StL	152	1979	Dave Winfield, SD	118
1923	Irish Meusel, NY	125	1980	Mike Schmidt, Phil	121
1924	George Kelly, NY	136	1981	Mike Schmidt, Phil	91
1925	Rogers Hornsby, StL	143	1982	Dale Murphy, Atl	109
1926	Jim Bottomley, StL	120		Al Oliver, Mtl	109
1927	Paul Waner, Pitt	131	1983	Dale Murphy, Atl	121
1928	Jim Bottomley, StL	136	1984	Gary Carter, Mtl	106
1929	Hack Wilson, Chi	159		Mike Schmidt, Phil	106
1930	Hack Wilson, Chi	190	1985	Dave Parker, Cin	125
1931	Chuck Klein, Phil	121	1986	Mike Schmidt, Phil	119
1932	Don Hurst, Phil	143	1987	Andre Dawson, Chi	137
1933	Chuck Klein, Phil	120	1988	Will Clark, SF	109
1934	Mel Ott, NY	135	1989	Kevin Mitchell, SF	125
1935	Wally Berger, Bos	130	1990	Matt Williams, SF	122
1936	Joe Medwick, StL	138	1991	Howard Johnson, NY	117
1937	Joe Medwick, StL	154	1992	Darren Daulton, Phil	109
1938	Joe Medwick, StL	122	1993	Barry Bonds, SF	123
1939	Frank McCormick, Cin	128	1994	Jeff Bagwell, Hou	116
1940	Johnny Mize, StL	137	1995	Dante Bichette, Col	128
1941	Dolph Camilli, Bklyn	120	1996	Andres Galarraga, Col	150
1942	Johnny Mize, NY	110	1997	Andres Galarraga, Col	140
1943	Bill Nicholson, Chi	128	1998	Sammy Sosa, Chi	158
1944	Bill Nicholson, Chi	122	1999	Mark McGwire, StL	147
1945	Dixie Walker, Bklyn	124	2000	Todd Helton, Col	147
1946	Enos Slaughter, StL	130	2001	Sammy Sosa, Chi	160
1947	Johnny Mize, NY	138	2002	Lance Berkman, Hou	128
1948	Stan Musial, StL	131	2003	Preston Wilson, Col	141
1949	Ralph Kiner, Pitt	127	2004	Vinny Castilla, Col	131
1950	Del Ennis, Phil	126	2005	Andruw Jones, Atl	128
1951	Monte Irvin, NY	121	2006	Ryan Howard, Phil	149
1952	Hank Sauer, Chi	121			
1953	Roy Campanella, Bklyn	142			
1954	Ted Kluszewski, Cin	141			

Leading Base Stealers

Year	Player and Team	SB	Year	Player and Team	SB
1900	George Van Haltren, NY	45	1953	Bill Bruton, Mil	26
	Patsy Donovan, StL	45	1954	Bill Bruton, Mil	34
1901	Honus Wagner, Pitt	48	1955	Bill Bruton, Mil	35
1902	Honus Wagner, Pitt	43	1956	Willie Mays, NY	40
1903	Jimmy Sheckard, Bklyn	67	1957	Willie Mays, NY	38
	Frank Chance, Chi	67	1958	Willie Mays, SF	31
1904	Honus Wagner, Pitt	53	1959	Willie Mays, SF	27
1905	Billy Maloney, Chi	59	1960	Maury Wills, LA	50
	Art Devlin, NY	59	1961	Maury Wills, LA	35
1906	Frank Chance, Chi	57	1962	Maury Wills, LA	104
1907	Honus Wagner, Pitt	61	1963	Maury Wills, LA	40
1908	Honus Wagner, Pitt	53	1964	Maury Wills, LA	53
1909	Bob Bescher, Cin	54	1965	Maury Wills, LA	94
1910	Bob Bescher, Cin	70	1966	Lou Brock, StL	74
1911	Bob Bescher, Cin	80	1967	Lou Brock, StL	52
1912	Bob Bescher, Cin	67	1968	Lou Brock, StL	62
1913	Max Carey, Pitt	61	1969	Lou Brock, StL	53
1914	George Burns, NY	62	1970	Bobby Tolan, Cin	57
1915	Max Carey, Pitt	36	1971	Lou Brock, StL	64
1916	Max Carey, Pitt	63	1972	Lou Brock, StL	63
1917	Max Carey, Pitt	46	1973	Lou Brock, StL	70
1918	Max Carey, Pitt	58	1974	Lou Brock, StL	118
1919	George Burns, NY	40	1975	Davey Lopes, LA	77
1920	Max Carey, Pitt	52	1976	Davey Lopes, LA	63
1921	Frankie Frisch, NY	49	1977	Frank Taveras, Pitt	70
1922	Max Carey, Pitt	51	1978	Omar Moreno, Pitt	71
1923	Max Carey, Pitt	51	1979	Omar Moreno, Pitt	77
1924	Max Carey, Pitt	49	1980	Ron LeFlore, Mtl	97
1925	Max Carey, Pitt	46	1981	Tim Raines, Mtl	71
1926	Kiki Cuyler, Pitt	35	1982	Tim Raines, Mtl	78
1927	Frankie Frisch, StL	48	1983	Tim Raines, Mtl	90
1928	Kiki Cuyler, Chi	37	1984	Tim Raines, Mtl	75
1929	Kiki Cuyler, Chi	43	1985	Vince Coleman, StL	110
1930	Kiki Cuyler, Chi	37	1986	Vince Coleman, StL	107
1931	Frankie Frisch, StL	28	1987	Vince Coleman, StL	109
1932	Chuck Klein, Phil	20	1988	Vince Coleman, StL	81
1933	Pepper Martin, StL	26	1989	Vince Coleman, StL	65
1934	Pepper Martin, StL	23	1990	Vince Coleman, StL	77
1935	Augie Galan, Chi	22	1991	Marquis Grissom, Mtl	76
1936	Pepper Martin, StL	23	1992	Marquis Grissom, Mtl	78
1937	Augie Galan, Chi	23	1993	Chuck Carr, Fla	58
1938	Stan Hack, Chi	16	1994	Craig Biggio, Hou	39
1939	Stan Hack, Chi	17	1995	Quilvio Veras, Fla	56
	Lee Handley, Pitt	17	1996	Eric Young, Col	53
1940	Lonny Frey, Cin	22	1997	Tony Womack, Pitt	60
1941	Danny Murtaugh, Phil	18	1998	Tony Womack, Pitt	58
1942	Pete Reiser, Bklyn	20	1999	Tony Womack, Ariz	72
1943	Arky Vaughan, Bklyn	20	2000	Luis Castillo, Fla	62
1944	Johnny Barrett, Pitt	28	2001	Juan Pierre, Col	46
1945	Red Schoendienst, StL	26	2002	Luis Castillo, Fla	48
1946	Pete Reiser, Bklyn	34	2003	Juan Pierre, Fla	65
1947	Jackie Robinson, Bklyn	29	2004	Scott Podsednik, Mil	70
1948	Richie Ashburn, Phil	32	2005	Jose Reyes, NY	60
1949	Jackie Robinson, Bklyn	37	2006	Jose Reyes, NY	64
1950	Sam Jethroe, Bos	35			
1951	Sam Jethroe, Bos	35			
1952	Pee Wee Reese, Bklyn	30			

Leading Pitchers—Winning Percentage

Year	Pitcher and Team	W	L	Pct	Year	Pitcher and Team	W	L	Pct
1900	Jesse Tannehill, Pitt	20	6	.769	1955	Don Newcombe, Bklyn	20	5	.800
1901	Jack Chesbro, Pitt	21	10	.677	1956	Don Newcombe, Bklyn	27	7	.794
1902	Jack Chesbro, Pitt	28	6	.824	1957	Bob Buhl, Mil	18	7	.720
1903	Sam Leever, Pitt	25	7	.781	1958	Warren Spahn, Mil	22	11	.667
1904	Joe McGinnity, NY	35	8	.814		Lew Burdette, Mil	20	10	.667
1905	Sam Leever, Pitt	20	5	.800	1959	Roy Face, Pitt	18	1	.947
1906	Ed Reulbach, Chi	19	4	.826	1960	Ernie Broglio, StL	21	9	.700
1907	Ed Reulbach, Chi	17	4	.810	1961	Johnny Podres, LA	18	5	.783
1908	Ed Reulbach, Chi	24	7	.774	1962	Bob Purkey, Cin	23	5	.821
1909	Christy Mathewson, NY	25	6	.806	1963	Ron Perranoski, LA	16	3	.842
	Howie Camnitz, Pitt	25	6	.806	1964	Sandy Koufax, LA	19	5	.792
1910	King Cole, Chi	20	4	.833	1965	Sandy Koufax, LA	26	8	.765
1911	Rube Marquard, NY	24	7	.774	1966	Juan Marichal, SF	25	6	.806
1912	Claude Hendrix, Pitt	24	9	.727	1967	Dick Hughes, StL	16	6	.727
1913	Bert Humphries, Chi	16	4	.800	1968	Steve Blass, Pitt	18	6	.750
1914	Bill James, Bos	26	7	.788	1969	Tom Seaver, NY	25	7	.781
1915	Grover Alexander, Phil	31	10	.756	1970	Bob Gibson, StL	23	7	.767
1916	Tom Hughes, Bos	16	3	.842	1971	Don Gullett, Cin	16	6	.727
1917	Ferdie Schupp, NY	21	7	.750	1972	Gary Nolan, Cin	15	5	.750
1918	Claude Hendrix, Chi	19	7	.731	1973	Tommy John, LA	16	7	.696
1919	Dutch Ruether, Cin	19	6	.760	1974	Andy Messersmith, LA	20	6	.769
1920	Burleigh Grimes, Bklyn	23	11	.676	1975	Don Gullett, Cin	15	4	.789
1921	Bill Doak, StL	15	6	.714	1976	Steve Carlton, Phil	20	7	.741
1922	Pete Donohue, Cin	18	9	.667	1977	John Candelaria, Pitt	20	5	.800
1923	Dolf Luque, Cin	27	8	.771	1978	Gaylord Perry, SD	21	6	.778
1924	Emil Yde, Pitt	16	3	.842	1979	Tom Seaver, Cin	16	6	.727
1925	Bill Sherdel, StL	15	6	.714	1980	Jim Bibby, Pitt	19	6	.760
1926	Ray Kremer, Pitt	20	6	.769	1981*	Tom Seaver, Cin	14	2	.875
1927	Larry Benton, Bos-NY	17	7	.708	1982	Phil Niekro, Atl	17	4	.810
1928	Larry Benton, NY	25	9	.735	1983	John Denny, Phil	19	6	.760
1929	Charlie Root, Chi	19	6	.760	1984	Rick Sutcliffe, Chi	16	1	.941
1930	Freddie Fitzsimmons, NY	19	7	.731	1985	Orel Hershiser, LA	19	3	.864
1931	Paul Derringer, StL	18	8	.692	1986	Bob Ojeda, NY	18	5	.783
1932	Lon Warneke, Chi	22	6	.786	1987	Dwight Gooden, NY	15	7	.682
1933	Ben Cantwell, Bos	20	10	.667	1988	David Cone, NY	20	3	.870
1934	Dizzy Dean, StL	30	7	.811	1989	Mike Bielecki, Chi	18	7	.720
1935	Bill Lee, Chi	20	6	.769	1990	Doug Drabeck, Pitt	22	6	.786
1936	Carl Hubbell, NY	26	6	.813	1991	John Smiley, Pitt	20	8	.714
1937	Carl Hubbell, NY	22	8	.733		Jose Rijo, Cin	15	6	.714
1938	Bill Lee, Chi	22	9	.710	1992	Bob Tewksbury, StL	16	5	.762
1939	Paul Derringer, Cin	25	7	.781	1993	Tom Glavine, Atl	22	6	.786
1940	Freddie Fitzsimmons, Bklyn	16	2	.889	1994	Ken Hill, Mtl	16	5	.762
1941	Elmer Riddle, Cin	19	4	.826	1995	Greg Maddux, Atl	19	2	.905
1942	Larry French, Bklyn	15	4	.789	1996	John Smoltz, Atl	24	8	.750
1943	Mort Cooper, StL	21	8	.724	1997	Denny Neagle, Atl	20	5	.800
1944	Ted Wilks, StL	17	4	.810	1998	John Smoltz, Atl	17	3	.850
1945	Harry Brecheen, StL	15	4	.789	1999	Mike Hampton, Hou	22	4	.846
1946	Murray Dickson, StL	15	6	.714	2000	Randy Johnson, Ariz	19	7	.730
1947	Larry Jansen, NY	21	5	.808	2001	Curt Schilling, Ariz	22	6	.786
1948	Harry Brecheen, StL	20	7	.741	2002	Randy Johnson, Ariz	24	5	.828
1949	Preacher Roe, Bklyn	15	6	.714	2003	Jason Schmidt, SF	17	5	.773
1950	Sal Maglie, NY	18	4	.818	2004	Roger Clemens, Hou	18	4	.818
1951	Preacher Roe, Bklyn	22	3	.880	2005	Chris Carpenter, StL	21	5	.808
1952	Hoyt Wilhelm, NY	15	3	.833	2006	Carlos Zambrano, Chi	16	7	.695
1953	Carl Erskine, Bklyn	20	6	.769					
1954	Johnny Antonelli, NY	21	7	.750					

*1981 percentages based on 10 or more victories. Note: Percentages based on 15 or more victories in all other years.

Leading Pitchers—Earned Run Average

Year	Player and Team	ERA	Year	Player and Team	ERA
1900	Rube Waddell, Pitt	2.37	1954	Johnny Antonelli, NY	2.29
1901	Jesse Tannehill, Pitt	2.18	1955	Bob Friend, Pitt	2.84
1902	Jack Taylor, Chi	1.33	1956	Lew Burdette, Mil	2.71
1903	Sam Leever, Pitt	2.06	1957	Johnny Podres, Bklyn	2.66
1904	Joe McGinnity, NY	1.61	1958	Stu Miller, SF	2.47
1905	Christy Mathewson, NY	1.27	1959	Sam Jones, SF	2.82
1906	Three Finger Brown, Chi	1.04	1960	Mike McCormick, SF	2.70
1907	Jack Pfiester, Chi	1.15	1961	Warren Spahn, Mil	3.01
1908	Christy Mathewson, NY	1.43	1962	Sandy Koufax, LA	2.54
1909	Christy Mathewson, NY	1.14	1963	Sandy Koufax, LA	1.88
1910	George McQuillan, Phil	1.60	1964	Sandy Koufax, LA	1.74
1911	Christy Mathewson, NY	1.99	1965	Sandy Koufax, LA	2.04
1912	Jeff Tesreau, NY	1.96	1966	Sandy Koufax, LA	1.73
1913	Christy Mathewson, NY	2.06	1967	Phil Niekro, Atl	1.87
1914	Bill Doak, StL	1.72	1968	Bob Gibson, StL	1.12
1915	Grover Alexander, Phil	1.22	1969	Juan Marichal, SF	2.10
1916	Grover Alexander, Phil	1.55	1970	Tom Seaver, NY	2.81
1917	Grover Alexander, Phil	1.83	1971	Tom Seaver, NY	1.76
1918	Hippo Vaughn, Chi	1.74	1972	Steve Carlton, Phil	1.98
1919	Grover Alexander, Chi	1.72	1973	Tom Seaver, NY	2.08
1920	Grover Alexander, Chi	1.91	1974	Buzz Capra, Atl	2.28
1921	Bill Doak, StL	2.58	1975	Randy Jones, SD	2.24
1922	Rosy Ryan, NY	3.00	1976	John Denny, StL	2.52
1923	Dolf Luque, Cin	1.93	1977	John Candelaria, Pitt	2.34
1924	Dazzy Vance, Bklyn	2.16	1978	Craig Swan, NY	2.43
1925	Dolf Luque, Cin	2.63	1979	J.R. Richard, Hou	2.71
1926	Ray Kremer, Pitt	2.61	1980	Don Sutton, LA	2.21
1927	Ray Kremer, Pitt	2.47	1981	Nolan Ryan, Hou	1.69
1928	Dazzy Vance, Bklyn	2.09	1982	Steve Rogers, Mtl	2.40
1929	Bill Walker, NY	3.08	1983	Atlee Hammaker, SF	2.25
1930	Dazzy Vance, Bklyn	2.61	1984	Alejandro Pena, LA	2.48
1931	Bill Walker, NY	2.26	1985	Dwight Gooden, NY	1.53
1932	Lon Warneke, Chi	2.37	1986	Mike Scott, Hou	2.22
1933	Carl Hubbell, NY	1.66	1987	Nolan Ryan, Hou	2.76
1934	Carl Hubbell, NY	2.30	1988	Joe Magrane, StL	2.18
1935	Cy Blanton, Pitt	2.59	1989	Scott Garrelts, SF	2.28
1936	Carl Hubbell, NY	2.31	1990	Danny Darwin, Hou	2.21
1937	Jim Turner, Bos	2.38	1991	Dennis Martinez, Mtl	2.39
1938	Bill Lee, Chi	2.66	1992	Bill Swift, SF	2.08
1939	Bucky Walters, Cin	2.29	1993	Greg Maddux, Atl	2.36
1940	Bucky Walters, Cin	2.48	1994	Greg Maddux, Atl	1.56
1941	Elmer Riddle, Cin	2.24	1995	Greg Maddux, Atl	1.63
1942	Mort Cooper, StL	1.77	1996	Kevin Brown, Fla	1.89
1943	Howie Pollet, StL	1.75	1997	Pedro Martinez, Mtl	1.90
1944	Ed Heusser, Cin	2.38	1998	Greg Maddux, Atl	1.98
1945	Hank Borowy, Chi	2.14	1999	Randy Johnson, Ariz	2.48
1946	Howie Pollet, StL	2.10	2000	Kevin Brown, LA	2.58
1947	Warren Spahn, Bos	2.33	2001	Randy Johnson, Ariz	2.49
1948	Harry Brecheen, StL	2.24	2002	Randy Johnson, Ariz	2.32
1949	Dave Koslo, NY	2.50	2003	Jason Schmidt, SF	2.34
1950	Jim Hearn, StL-NY	2.49	2004	Jake Peavy, SD	2.27
1951	Chet Nichols, Bos	2.88	2005	Roger Clemens, Hou	1.87
1952	Hoyt Wilhelm, NY	2.43	2006	Roy Oswalt, Hou	2.98
1953	Warren Spahn, Mil	2.10			

Note: Based on 10 complete games through 1950, then 154 innings until National League expanded in 1962, when it became 162 innings. In strike-shortened 1981, one inning per game required.

Leading Pitchers—Strikeouts

Year	Player and Team	SO	Year	Player and Team	SO
1900	Rube Waddell, Pitt	133	1953	Robin Roberts, Phil	198
1901	Noodles Hahn, Cin	233	1954	Robin Roberts, Phil	185
1902	Vic Willis, Bos	226	1955	Sam Jones, Chi	198
1903	Christy Mathewson, NY	267	1956	Sam Jones, Chi	176
1904	Christy Mathewson, NY	212	1957	Jack Sanford, Phil	188
1905	Christy Mathewson, NY	206	1958	Sam Jones, StL	225
1906	Fred Beebe, Chi-StL	171	1959	Don Drysdale, LA	242
1907	Christy Mathewson, NY	178	1960	Don Drysdale, LA	246
1908	Christy Mathewson, NY	259	1961	Sandy Koufax, LA	269
1909	Orval Overall, Chi	205	1962	Don Drysdale, LA	232
1910	Christy Mathewson, NY	190	1963	Sandy Koufax, LA	306
1911	Rube Marquard, NY	237	1964	Bob Veale, Pitt	250
1912	Grover Alexander, Phil	195	1965	Sandy Koufax, LA	382
1913	Tom Seaton, Phil	168	1966	Sandy Koufax, LA	317
1914	Grover Alexander, Phil	214	1967	Jim Bunning, Phil	253
1915	Grover Alexander, Phil	241	1968	Bob Gibson, StL	268
1916	Grover Alexander, Phil	167	1969	Ferguson Jenkins, Chi	273
1917	Grover Alexander, Phil	200	1970	Tom Seaver, NY	283
1918	Hippo Vaughn, Chi	148	1971	Tom Seaver, NY	289
1919	Hippo Vaughn, Chi	141	1972	Steve Carlton, Phil	310
1920	Grover Alexander, Chi	173	1973	Tom Seaver, NY	251
1921	Burleigh Grimes, Bklyn	136	1974	Steve Carlton, Phil	240
1922	Dazzy Vance, Bklyn	134	1975	Tom Seaver, NY	243
1923	Dazzy Vance, Bklyn	197	1976	Tom Seaver, NY	235
1924	Dazzy Vance, Bklyn	262	1977	Phil Niekro, Atl	262
1925	Dazzy Vance, Bklyn	221	1978	J.R. Richard, Hou	303
1926	Dazzy Vance, Bklyn	140	1979	J.R. Richard, Hou	313
1927	Dazzy Vance, Bklyn	184	1980	Steve Carlton, Phil	286
1928	Dazzy Vance, Bklyn	200	1981	Fernando Valenzuela, LA	180
1929	Pat Malone, Chi	166	1982	Steve Carlton, Phil	286
1930	Bill Hallahan, StL	177	1983	Steve Carlton, Phil	275
1931	Bill Hallahan, StL	159	1984	Dwight Gooden, NY	276
1932	Dizzy Dean, StL	191	1985	Dwight Gooden, NY	268
1933	Dizzy Dean, StL	199	1986	Mike Scott, Hou	306
1934	Dizzy Dean, StL	195	1987	Nolan Ryan, Hou	270
1935	Dizzy Dean, StL	182	1988	Nolan Ryan, Hou	228
1936	Van Lingle Mungo, Bklyn	238	1989	Jose DeLeon, StL	201
1937	Carl Hubbell, NY	159	1990	David Cone, NY	233
1938	Clay Bryant, Chi	135	1991	David Cone, NY	241
1939	Claude Passeau, Phil-Chi	137	1992	John Smoltz, Atl	215
	Bucky Walters, Cin	137	1993	Jose Rijo, Cin	227
1940	Kirby Higbe, Phil	137	1994	Andy Benes, SD	189
1941	Johnny Vander Meer, Cin	202	1995	Hideo Nomo, LA	236
1942	Johnny Vander Meer, Cin	186	1996	John Smoltz, Atl	276
1943	Johnny Vander Meer, Cin	174	1997	Curt Schilling, Phil	319
1944	Bill Voiselle, NY	161	1998	Curt Schilling, Phil	300
1945	Preacher Roe, Pitt	148	1999	Randy Johnson, Ariz	364
1946	Johnny Schmitz, Chi	135	2000	Randy Johnson, Ariz	347
1947	Ewell Blackwell, Cin	193	2001	Randy Johnson, Ariz	372
1948	Harry Brecheen, StL	149	2002	Randy Johnson, Ariz	334
1949	Warren Spahn, Bos	151	2003	Kerry Wood, Chi	266
1950	Warren Spahn, Bos	191	2004	Randy Johnson, Ariz	290
1951	Warren Spahn, Bos	164	2005	Jake Peavy, SD	216
	Don Newcombe, Bklyn	164	2006	Aaron Harang, Cin	216
1952	Warren Spahn, Bos	183			

Leading Pitchers—Saves

Year	Player and Team	SV	Year	Player and Team	SV
1947	Hugh Casey, Bklyn	18	1977	Rollie Fingers, SD	35
1948	Harry Gumpert, Cin	17	1978	Rollie Fingers, SD	37
1949	Ted Wilks, StL	9	1979	Bruce Sutter, Chi	37
1950	Jim Konstanty, Phil	22	1980	Bruce Sutter, Chi	28
1951	Ted Wilks, StL, Pitt	13	1981	Bruce Sutter, StL	25
1952	Al Brazle, StL	16	1982	Bruce Sutter, StL	36
1953	Al Brazle, StL	18	1983	Lee Smith, Chi	29
1954	Jim Hughes, Bklyn	24	1984	Bruce Sutter, StL	45
1955	Jack Meyer, Phil	16	1985	Jeff Reardon, Mtl	41
1956	Clem Labine, Bklyn	19	1986	Todd Worrell, StL	36
1957	Clem Labine, Bklyn	17	1987	Steve Bedrosian, Phil	40
1958	Roy Face, Pitt	20	1988	John Franco, Cin	39
1959	Lindy McDaniel, StL	15	1989	Mark Davis, SD	44
	Don McMahon, Mil	15	1990	John Franco, NY	33
1960	Lindy McDaniel, StL	26	1991	Lee Smith, StL	47
1961	Stu Miller, SF	17	1992	Lee Smith, StL	42
	Roy Face, Pitt	17	1993	Randy Myers, Chi	53
1962	Roy Face, Pitt	28	1994	John Franco, NY	30
1963	Lindy McDaniel, Chi	22	1995	Randy Myers, Chi	38
1964	Hal Woodeshick, Hou	23	1996	Jeff Brantley, Cin	44
1965	Ted Abernathy, Chi	31		Todd Worrell, LA	44
1966	Phil Regan, LA	21	1997	Jeff Shaw, Cin	42
1967	Ted Abernathy, Cin	28	1998	Trevor Hoffman, SD	53
1968	Phil Regan, Chi, LA	25	1999	Ugueth Urbina, Mtl	41
1969	Fred Gladding, Hou	29	2000	Antonio Alfonseca, Fla	45
1970	Wayne Granger, Cin	35	2001	Robb Nen, SF	45
1971	Dave Giusti, Pitt	30	2002	John Smoltz, Atl	55
1972	Clay Carroll, Cin	37	2003	Eric Gagne, LA	55
1973	Mike Marshall, Mtl	13	2004	Armando Benitez, Fla	47
1974	Mike Marshall, LA	21		Jason Isringhausen, StL	47
1975	Al Hrabosky, StL	22	2005	Chad Cordero, Wash	47
	Rawly Eastwick, Cin	22	2006	Trevor Hoffman, SD	46
1976	Rawly Eastwick, Cin	26			

Leading Batsmen

Year	Player and Team	BA	Year	Player and Team	BA
1901	Nap Lajoie, Phil	.422	1954	Bobby Avila, Clev	.341
1902	Ed Delahanty, Wash	.376	1955	Al Kaline, Det	.340
1903	Nap Lajoie, Clev	.355	1956	Mickey Mantle, NY	.353
1904	Nap Lajoie, Clev	.381	1957	Ted Williams, Bos	.388
1905	Elmer Flick, Clev	.306	1958	Ted Williams, Bos	.328
1906	George Stone, StL	.358	1959	Harvey Kuenn, Det	.353
1907	Ty Cobb, Det	.350	1960	Pete Runnels, Bos	.320
1908	Ty Cobb, Det	.324	1961	Norm Cash, Det	.361
1909	Ty Cobb, Det	.377	1962	Pete Runnels, Bos	.326
1910	Nap Lajoie, Clev*	.383	1963	Carl Yastrzemski, Bos	.321
1911	Ty Cobb, Det	.420	1964	Tony Oliva, Minn	.323
1912	Ty Cobb, Det	.410	1965	Tony Oliva, Minn	.321
1913	Ty Cobb, Det	.390	1966	Frank Robinson, Balt	.316
1914	Ty Cobb, Det	.368	1967	Carl Yastrzemski, Bos	.326
1915	Ty Cobb, Det	.369	1968	Carl Yastrzemski, Bos	.301
1916	Tris Speaker, Clev	.386	1969	Rod Carew, Minn	.332
1917	Ty Cobb, Det	.383	1970	Alex Johnson, Cal	.329
1918	Ty Cobb, Det	.382	1971	Tony Oliva, Minn	.337
1919	Ty Cobb, Det	.384	1972	Rod Carew, Minn	.318
1920	George Sisler, StL	.407	1973	Rod Carew, Minn	.350
1921	Harry Heilmann, Det	.394	1974	Rod Carew, Minn	.364
1922	George Sisler, StL	.420	1975	Rod Carew, Minn	.359
1923	Harry Heilmann, Det	.403	1976	George Brett, KC	.333
1924	Babe Ruth, NY	.378	1977	Rod Carew, Minn	.388
1925	Harry Heilmann, Det	.393	1978	Rod Carew, Minn	.333
1926	Heinie Manush, Det	.378	1979	Fred Lynn, Bos	.333
1927	Harry Heilmann, Det	.398	1980	George Brett, KC	.390
1928	Goose Goslin, Wash	.379	1981	Carney Lansford, Bos	.336
1929	Lew Fonseca, Clev	.369	1982	Willie Wilson, KC	.332
1930	Al Simmons, Phil	.381	1983	Wade Boggs, Bos	.361
1931	Al Simmons, Phil	.390	1984	Don Mattingly, NY	.343
1932	Dale Alexander, Det-Bos	.367	1985	Wade Boggs, Bos	.368
1933	Jimmie Foxx, Phil	.356	1986	Wade Boggs, Bos	.357
1934	Lou Gehrig, NY	.363	1987	Wade Boggs, Bos	.363
1935	Buddy Myer, Wash	.349	1988	Wade Boggs, Bos	.366
1936	Luke Appling, Chi	.388	1989	Kirby Puckett, Minn	.339
1937	Charlie Gehringer, Det	.371	1990	George Brett, KC	.329
1938	Jimmie Foxx, Bos	.349	1991	Julio Franco, Tex	.341
1939	Joe DiMaggio, NY	.381	1992	Edgar Martinez, Sea	.343
1940	Joe DiMaggio, NY	.352	1993	John Olerud, Tor	.363
1941	Ted Williams, Bos	.406	1994	Paul O'Neill, NY	.359
1942	Ted Williams, Bos	.356	1995	Edgar Martinez, Sea	.356
1943	Luke Appling, Chi	.328	1996	Alex Rodriguez, Sea	.358
1944	Lou Boudreau, Clev	.327	1997	Frank Thomas, Chi	.347
1945	Snuffy Stirnweiss, NY	.309	1998	Bernie Williams, NY	.339
1946	Mickey Vernon, Wash	.353	1999	Nomar Garciaparra, Bos	.357
1947	Ted Williams, Bos	.343	2000	Nomar Garciaparra, Bos	.372
1948	Ted Williams, Bos	.369	2001	Ichiro Suzuki, Sea	.350
1949	George Kell, Det	.343	2002	Manny Ramirez, Bos	.349
1950	Billy Goodman, Bos	.354	2003	Bill Mueller, Bos	.326
1951	Ferris Fain, Phil	.344	2004	Ichiro Suzuki, Sea	.372
1952	Ferris Fain, Phil	.327	2005	Michael Young, Tex	.331
1953	Mickey Vernon, Wash	.337	2006	Joe Mauer, Minn	.347

*League president Ban Johnson declared Ty Cobb batting champion with a .385 average, beating Lajoie's .384. However, subsequent research has led to the revision of Lajoie's average to .383 and Cobb's to .382.

Leaders in Runs Scored

Year	Player and Team	Runs	Year	Player and Team	Runs
1901	Nap Lajoie, Phil	145	1956	Mickey Mantle, NY	132
1902	Dave Fultz, Phil	110	1957	Mickey Mantle, NY	121
1903	Patsy Dougherty, Bos	108	1958	Mickey Mantle, NY	127
1904	Patsy Dougherty, Bos-NY	113	1959	Eddie Yost, Det	115
1905	Harry Davis, Phil	92	1960	Mickey Mantle, NY	119
1906	Elmer Flick, Clev	98	1961	Mickey Mantle, NY	132
1907	Sam Crawford, Det	102		Roger Maris, NY	132
1908	Matty McIntyre, Det	105	1962	Albie Pearson, LA	115
1909	Ty Cobb, Det	116	1963	Bob Allison, Minn	99
1910	Ty Cobb, Det	106	1964	Tony Oliva, Minn	109
1911	Ty Cobb, Det	147	1965	Zoilo Versalles, Minn	126
1912	Eddie Collins, Phil	137	1966	Frank Robinson, Balt	122
1913	Eddie Collins, Phil	125	1967	Carl Yastrzemski, Bos	112
1914	Eddie Collins, Phil	122	1968	Dick McAuliffe, Det	95
1915	Ty Cobb, Det	144	1969	Reggie Jackson, Oak	123
1916	Ty Cobb, Det	113	1970	Carl Yastrzemski, Bos	125
1917	Donie Bush, Det	112	1971	Don Buford, Balt	99
1918	Ray Chapman, Clev	84	1972	Bobby Murcer, NY	102
1919	Babe Ruth, Bos	103	1973	Reggie Jackson, Oak	99
1920	Babe Ruth, NY	158	1974	Carl Yastrzemski, Bos	93
1921	Babe Ruth, NY	177	1975	Fred Lynn, Bos	103
1922	George Sisler, StL	134	1976	Roy White, NY	104
1923	Babe Ruth, NY	151	1977	Rod Carew, Minn	128
1924	Babe Ruth, NY	143	1978	Ron LeFlore, Det	126
1925	Johnny Mostil, Chi	135	1979	Don Baylor, Cal	120
1926	Babe Ruth, NY	139	1980	Willie Wilson, KC	133
1927	Babe Ruth, NY	158	1981	Rickey Henderson, Oak	89
1928	Babe Ruth, NY	163	1982	Paul Molitor, Mil	136
1929	Charlie Gehringer, Det	131	1983	Cal Ripken, Balt	121
1930	Al Simmons, Phil	152	1984	Dwight Evans, Bos	121
1931	Lou Gehrig, NY	163	1985	Rickey Henderson, NY	146
1932	Jimmie Foxx, Phil	151	1986	Rickey Henderson, NY	130
1933	Lou Gehrig, NY	138	1987	Paul Molitor, Mil	114
1934	Charlie Gehringer, Det	134	1988	Wade Boggs, Bos	128
1935	Lou Gehrig, NY	125	1989	Rickey Henderson, NY-Oak	113
1936	Lou Gehrig, NY	167		Wade Boggs, Bos	113
1937	Joe DiMaggio, NY	151	1990	Rickey Henderson, Oak	119
1938	Hank Greenberg, Det	144	1991	Paul Molitor, Mil	133
1939	Red Rolfe, NY	139	1992	Tony Phillips, Det	114
1940	Ted Williams, Bos	134	1993	Rafael Palmeiro, Tex	124
1941	Ted Williams, Bos	135	1994	Frank Thomas, Chi	106
1942	Ted Williams, Bos	141	1995	Albert Belle, Clev	121
1943	George Case, Wash	102		Edgar Martinez, Sea	121
1944	Snuffy Stirnweiss, NY	125	1996	Alex Rodriguez, Sea	141
1945	Snuffy Stirnweiss, NY	107	1997	Ken Griffey Jr., Sea	125
1946	Ted Williams, Bos	142	1998	Derek Jeter, NY	127
1947	Ted Williams, Bos	125	1999	Roberto Alomar, Clev	138
1948	Tommy Henrich, NY	138	2000	Johnny Damon, KC	136
1949	Ted Williams, Bos	150	2001	Alex Rodriguez, Tex	133
1950	Dom DiMaggio, Bos	131	2002	Alfonso Soriano, NY	128
1951	Dom DiMaggio, Bos	113	2003	Alex Rodriguez, Tex	124
1952	Larry Doby, Clev	104	2004	Vladimir Guerrero, Ana	124
1953	Al Rosen, Clev	115	2005	Alex Rodriguez, NY	124
1954	Mickey Mantle, NY	129	2006	Grady Sizemore, Clev	134
1955	Al Smith, Clev	123			

Leaders in Hits

Year	Player and Team	Hits	Year	Player and Team	Hits
1901	Nap Lajoie, Phil	229	1954	Nellie Fox, Chi	201
1902	Piano Legs Hickman, Bos-Clev	194		Harvey Kuenn, Det	201
1903	Patsy Dougherty, Bos	195	1955	Al Kaline, Det	200
1904	Nap Lajoie, Clev	211	1956	Harvey Kuenn, Det	196
1905	George Stone, StL	187	1957	Nellie Fox, Chi	196
1906	Nap Lajoie, Clev	214	1958	Nellie Fox, Chi	187
1907	Ty Cobb, Det	212	1959	Harvey Kuenn, Det	198
1908	Ty Cobb, Det	188	1960	Minnie Minoso, Chi	184
1909	Ty Cobb, Det	216	1961	Norm Cash, Det	193
1910	Nap Lajoie, Clev	227	1962	Bobby Richardson, NY	209
1911	Ty Cobb, Det	248	1963	Carl Yastrzemski, Bos	183
1912	Ty Cobb, Det	227	1964	Tony Oliva, Minn	217
1913	Joe Jackson, Clev	197	1965	Tony Oliva, Minn	185
1914	Tris Speaker, Bos	193	1966	Tony Oliva, Minn	191
1915	Ty Cobb, Det	208	1967	Carl Yastrzemski, Bos	189
1916	Tris Speaker, Clev	211	1968	Bert Campaneris, Oak	177
1917	Ty Cobb, Det	225	1969	Tony Oliva, Minn	197
1918	George Burns, Phil	178	1970	Tony Oliva, Minn	204
1919	Ty Cobb, Det	191	1971	Cesar Tovar, Minn	204
	Bobby Veach, Det	191	1972	Joe Rudi, Oak	181
1920	George Sisler, StL	257	1973	Rod Carew, Minn	203
1921	Harry Heilmann, Det	237	1974	Rod Carew, Minn	218
1922	George Sisler, StL	246	1975	George Brett, KC	195
1923	Charlie Jamieson, Clev	222	1976	George Brett, KC	215
1924	Sam Rice, Wash	216	1977	Rod Carew, Minn	239
1925	Al Simmons, Phil	253	1978	Jim Rice, Bos	213
1926	George Burns, Clev	216	1979	George Brett, KC	212
	Sam Rice, Wash	216	1980	Willie Wilson, KC	230
1927	Earle Combs, NY	231	1981	Rickey Henderson, Oak	135
1928	Heinie Manush, StL	241	1982	Robin Yount, Mil	210
1929	Dale Alexander, Det	215	1983	Cal Ripken Jr., Balt	211
	Charlie Gehringer, Det	215	1984	Don Mattingly, NY	207
1930	Johnny Hodapp, Clev	225	1985	Wade Boggs, Bos	240
1931	Lou Gehrig, NY	211	1986	Don Mattingly, NY	238
1932	Al Simmons, Phil	216	1987	Kirby Puckett, Minn	207
1933	Heinie Manush, Wash	221		Kevin Seitzer, KC	207
1934	Charlie Gehringer, Det	214	1988	Kirby Puckett, Minn	234
1935	Joe Vosmik, Clev	216	1989	Kirby Puckett, Minn	215
1936	Earl Averill, Clev	232	1990	Rafael Palmeiro, Tex	191
1937	Beau Bell, StL	218	1991	Paul Molitor, Mil	216
1938	Joe Vosmik, Bos	201	1992	Kirby Puckett, Minn	210
1939	Red Rolfe, NY	213	1993	Paul Molitor, Tor	211
1940	Rip Radcliff, StL	200	1994	Kenny Lofton, Clev	160
	Barney McCosky, Det	200	1995	Lance Johnson, Chi	186
	Doc Cramer, Bos	200	1996	Paul Molitor, Minn	225
1941	Cecil Travis, Wash	218	1997	Nomar Garciaparra, Bos	209
1942	Johnny Pesky, Bos	205	1998	Alex Rodriguez, Sea	213
1943	Dick Wakefield, Det	200	1999	Derek Jeter, NY	219
1944	Snuffy Stirnweiss, NY	205	2000	Darin Erstad, Ana	240
1945	Snuffy Stirnweiss, NY	195	2001	Ichiro Suzuki, Sea	242
1946	Johnny Pesky, Bos	208	2002	Alfonso Soriano, NY	209
1947	Johnny Pesky, Bos	207	2003	Vernon Wells, Tor	215
1948	Bob Dillinger, StL	207	2004	Ichiro Suzuki, Sea	262
1949	Dale Mitchell, Clev	203	2005	Michael Young, Tex	221
1950	George Kell, Det	218	2006	Ichiro Suzuki, Sea	224
1951	George Kell, Det	191			
1952	Nellie Fox, Chi	192			
1953	Harvey Kuenn, Det	209			

Home Run Leaders

Year	Player and Team	HR	Year	Player and Team	HR
1901	Nap Lajoie, Phil	13	1959	Rocky Colavito, Clev	42
1902	Socks Seybold, Phil	16		Harmon Killebrew, Wash	42
1903	Buck Freeman, Bos	13	1960	Mickey Mantle, NY	40
1904	Harry Davis, Phil	10	1961	Roger Maris, NY	61
1905	Harry Davis, Phil	8	1962	Harmon Killebrew, Minn	48
1906	Harry Davis, Phil	12	1963	Harmon Killebrew, Minn	45
1907	Harry Davis, Phil	8	1964	Harmon Killebrew, Minn	49
1908	Sam Crawford, Det	7	1965	Tony Conigliaro, Bos	32
1909	Ty Cobb, Det	9	1966	Frank Robinson, Balt	49
1910	Jake Stahl, Bos	10	1967	Harmon Killebrew, Minn	44
1911	Frank Baker, Phil	9		Carl Yastrzemski, Bos	44
1912	Frank Baker, Phil	10	1968	Frank Howard, Wash	44
	Tris Speaker, Bos	10	1969	Harmon Killebrew, Minn	49
1913	Frank Baker, Phil	13	1970	Frank Howard, Wash	44
1914	Frank Baker, Phil	9	1971	Bill Melton, Chi	33
1915	Braggo Roth, Chi-Clev	7	1972	Dick Allen, Chi	37
1916	Wally Pipp, NY	12	1973	Reggie Jackson, Oak	32
1917	Wally Pipp, NY	9	1974	Dick Allen, Chi	32
1918	Babe Ruth, Bos	11	1975	Reggie Jackson, Oak	36
	Tilly Walker, Phil	11		George Scott, Mil	36
1919	Babe Ruth, Bos	29	1976	Graig Nettles, NY	32
1920	Babe Ruth, NY	54	1977	Jim Rice, Bos	39
1921	Babe Ruth, NY	59	1978	Jim Rice, Bos	46
1922	Ken Williams, StL	39	1979	Gorman Thomas, Mil	45
1923	Babe Ruth, NY	41	1980	Reggie Jackson, NY	41
1924	Babe Ruth, NY	46		Ben Oglivie, Mil	41
1925	Bob Meusel, NY	33	1981	Tony Armas, Oak	22
1926	Babe Ruth, NY	47	1981	Dwight Evans, Bos	22
1927	Babe Ruth, NY	60		Bobby Grich, Cal	22
1928	Babe Ruth, NY	54		Eddie Murray, Balt	22
1929	Babe Ruth, NY	46	1982	Reggie Jackson, Cal	39
1930	Babe Ruth, NY	49		Gorman Thomas, Mil	39
1931	Babe Ruth/ Lou Gehrig NY	46	1983	Jim Rice, Bos	39
1932	Jimmie Foxx, Phil	58	1984	Tony Armas, Bos	43
1933	Jimmie Foxx, Phil	48	1985	Darrell Evans, Det	40
1934	Lou Gehrig, NY	49	1986	Jesse Barfield, Tor	40
1935	Jimmie Foxx, Phil	36	1987	Mark McGwire, Oak	49
	Hank Greenberg, Det	36	1988	Jose Canseco, Oak	42
1936	Lou Gehrig, NY	49	1989	Fred McGriff, Tor	36
1937	Joe DiMaggio, NY	46	1990	Cecil Fielder, Det	51
1938	Hank Greenberg, Det	58	1991	Jose Canseco, Oak	44
1939	Jimmie Foxx, Bos	35		Cecil Fielder, Det	44
1940	Hank Greenberg, Det	41	1992	Juan Gonzalez, Tex	43
1941	Ted Williams, Bos	37	1993	Juan Gonzalez, Tex	46
1942	Ted Williams, Bos	36	1994	Ken Griffey Jr., Sea	40
1943	Rudy York, Det	34	1995	Albert Belle, Clev	50
1944	Nick Etten, NY	22	1996	Mark McGwire, Oak	52
1945	Vern Stephens, StL	24	1997	Ken Griffey Jr., Sea	56
1946	Hank Greenberg, Det	44	1998	Ken Griffey Jr., Sea	56
1947	Ted Williams, Bos	32	1999	Ken Griffey Jr., Sea	48
1948	Joe DiMaggio, NY	39	2000	Troy Glaus, Ana	47
1949	Ted Williams, Bos	43	2001	Alex Rodriguez, Tex	52
1950	Al Rosen, Clev	37	2002	Alex Rodriguez, Tex	57
1951	Gus Zernial, Chi-Phil	33	2003	Alex Rodriguez, Tex	47
1952	Larry Doby, Clev	32	2004	Manny Ramirez, Bos	43
1953	Al Rosen, Clev	43	2005	Alex Rodriguez, NY	48
1954	Larry Doby, Clev	32	2006	David Ortiz, Bos	54
1955	Mickey Mantle, NY	37			
1956	Mickey Mantle, NY	52			
1957	Roy Sievers, Wash	42			
1958	Mickey Mantle, NY	42			

Runs Batted In Leaders

Year	Player and Team	RBI	Year	Player and Team	RBI
1907	Ty Cobb, Det	116	1956	Mickey Mantle, NY	130
1908	Ty Cobb, Det	108	1957	Roy Sievers, Wash	114
1909	Ty Cobb, Det	107	1958	Jackie Jensen, Bos	122
1910	Sam Crawford, Det	120	1959	Jackie Jensen, Bos	112
1911	Ty Cobb, Det	144	1960	Roger Maris, NY	112
1912	Frank Baker, Phil	133	1961	Roger Maris, NY	142
1913	Frank Baker, Phil	126	1962	Harmon Killebrew, Minn	126
1914	Sam Crawford, Det	104	1963	Dick Stuart, Bos	118
1915	Sam Crawford, Det	112	1964	Brooks Robinson, Balt	118
	Bobby Veach, Det	112	1965	Rocky Colavito, Clev	108
1916	Del Pratt, StL	103	1966	Frank Robinson, Balt	122
1917	Bobby Veach, Det	103	1967	Carl Yastrzemski, Bos	121
1918	Bobby Veach, Det	78	1968	Ken Harrelson, Bos	109
1919	Babe Ruth, Bos	114	1969	Harmon Killebrew, Minn	140
1920	Babe Ruth, NY	137	1970	Frank Howard, Wash	126
1921	Babe Ruth, NY	171	1971	Harmon Killebrew, Minn	119
1922	Ken Williams, StL	155	1972	Dick Allen, Chi	113
1923	Babe Ruth, NY	131	1973	Reggie Jackson, Oak	117
1924	Goose Goslin, Wash	129	1974	Jeff Burroughs, Tex	118
1925	Bob Meusel, NY	138	1975	George Scott, Mil	109
1926	Babe Ruth, NY	145	1976	Lee May, Balt	109
1927	Lou Gehrig, NY	175	1977	Larry Hisle, Minn	119
1928	Babe Ruth/ Lou Gehrig, NY	142	1978	Jim Rice, Bos	139
1929	Al Simmons, Phil	157	1979	Don Baylor, Cal	139
1930	Lou Gehrig, NY	174	1980	Cecil Cooper, Mil	122
1931	Lou Gehrig, NY	184	1981	Eddie Murray, Balt	78
1932	Jimmie Foxx, Phil	169	1982	Hal McRae, KC	133
1933	Jimmie Foxx, Phil	163	1983	Cecil Cooper, Mil	126
1934	Lou Gehrig, NY	165		Jim Rice, Bos	126
1935	Hank Greenberg, Det	170	1984	Tony Armas, Bos	123
1936	Hal Trosky, Clev	162	1985	Don Mattingly, NY	145
1937	Hank Greenberg, Det	183	1986	Joe Carter, Clev	121
1938	Jimmie Foxx, Bos	175	1987	George Bell, Tor	134
1939	Ted Williams, Bos	145	1988	Jose Canseco, Oak	124
1940	Hank Greenberg, Det	150	1989	Ruben Sierra, Tex	119
1941	Joe DiMaggio, NY	125	1990	Cecil Fielder, Det	132
1942	Ted Williams, Bos	137	1991	Cecil Fielder, Det	133
1943	Rudy York, Det	118	1992	Cecil Fielder, Det	124
1944	Vern Stephens, StL	109	1993	Albert Belle, Clev	129
1945	Nick Etten, NY	111	1994	Kirby Puckett, Minn	112
1946	Hank Greenberg, Det	127	1995	Albert Belle, Clev	126
1947	Ted Williams, Bos	114		Mo Vaughn, Bos	126
1948	Joe DiMaggio, NY	155	1996	Albert Belle, Clev	148
1949	Ted Williams, Bos	159	1997	Ken Griffey Jr., Sea	147
	Vern Stephens, Bos	159	1998	Juan Gonzales, Tex	157
1950	Walt Dropo, Bos	144	1999	Manny Ramirez, Clev	165
	Vern Stephens, Bos	144	2000	Edgar Martinez, Sea	145
1951	Gus Zernial, Chi-Phil	129	2001	Bret Boone, Sea	141
1952	Al Rosen, Clev	105	2002	Alex Rodriguez, Tex	142
1953	Al Rosen, Clev	145	2003	Carlos Delgado, Tor	145
1954	Larry Doby, Clev	126	2004	Miguel Tejada, Balt	150
1955	Ray Boone, Det	116	2005	David Ortiz, Bos	148
	Jackie Jensen, Bos	116	2006	David Ortiz, Bos	137

Leading Base Stealers

Year	Player and Team	SB	Year	Player and Team	SB
1901	Frank Isbell, Chi	48	1909	Ty Cobb, Det	76
1902	Topsy Hartsel, Phil	54	1910	Eddie Collins, Phil	81
1903	Harry Bay, Clev	46	1911	Ty Cobb, Det	83
1904	Elmer Flick, Clev	42	1912	Clyde Milan, Wash	88
	Harry Bay, Clev	42	1913	Clyde Milan, Wash	75
1905	Danny Hoffman, Phil	46	1914	Fritz Maisel, NY	74
1906	Elmer Flick, Clev	39	1915	Ty Cobb, Det	96
	John Anderson, Wash	39	1916	Ty Cobb, Det	68
1907	Ty Cobb, Det	49	1917	Ty Cobb, Det	55
1908	Patsy Dougherty, Chi	47	1918	George Sisler, StL	45

Note: Runs Batted In not compiled before 1907; officially adopted in 1920.

Leading Base Stealers *(Cont.)*

Year	Player and Team	SB	Year	Player and Team	SB
1919	Eddie Collins, Chi	33	1963	Luis Aparicio, Balt	40
1920	Sam Rice, Wash	63	1964	Luis Aparicio, Balt	57
1921	George Sisler, StL	35	1965	Bert Campaneris, KC	51
1922	George Sisler, StL	51	1966	Bert Campaneris, KC	52
1923	Eddie Collins, Chi	49	1967	Bert Campaneris, KC	55
1924	Eddie Collins, Chi	42	1968	Bert Campaneris, Oak	62
1925	John Mostil, Chi	43	1969	Tommy Harper, Sea	73
1926	John Mostil, Chi	35	1970	Bert Campaneris, Oak	42
1927	George Sisler, StL	27	1971	Amos Otis, KC	52
1928	Buddy Myer, Bos	30	1972	Bert Campaneris, Oak	52
1929	Charlie Gehringer, Det	27	1973	Tommy Harper, Bos	54
1930	Marty McManus, Det	23	1974	Bill North, Oak	54
1931	Ben Chapman, NY	61	1975	Mickey Rivers, Cal	70
1932	Ben Chapman, NY	38	1976	Bill North, Oak	75
1933	Ben Chapman, NY	27	1977	Freddie Patek, KC	53
1934	Bill Werber, Bos	40	1978	Ron LeFlore, Det	68
1935	Bill Werber, Bos	29	1979	Willie Wilson, KC	83
1936	Lyn Lary, StL	37	1980	Rickey Henderson, Oak	100
1937	Bill Werber, Phil	35	1981	Rickey Henderson, Oak	56
	Ben Chapman, Wash-Bos	35	1982	Rickey Henderson, Oak	130
1938	Frank Crosetti, NY	27	1983	Rickey Henderson, Oak	108
1939	George Case, Wash	51	1984	Rickey Henderson, Oak	66
1940	George Case, Wash	35	1985	Rickey Henderson, NY	80
1941	George Case, Wash	33	1986	Rickey Henderson, NY	87
1942	George Case, Wash	44	1987	Harold Reynolds, Sea	60
1943	George Case, Wash	61	1988	Rickey Henderson, NY	93
1944	Snuffy Stirnweiss, NY	55	1989	Rickey Henderson, NY-Oak	77
1945	Snuffy Stirnweiss, NY	33	1990	Rickey Henderson, Oak	65
1946	George Case, Clev	28	1991	Rickey Henderson, Oak	58
1947	Bob Dillinger, StL	34	1992	Kenny Lofton, Clev	66
1948	Bob Dillinger, StL	28	1993	Kenny Lofton, Clev	70
1949	Bob Dillinger, StL	20	1994	Kenny Lofton, Clev	60
1950	Dom DiMaggio, Bos	15	1995	Kenny Lofton, Clev	54
1951	Minnie Minoso, Clev-Chi	31	1996	Kenny Lofton, Clev	75
1952	Minnie Minoso, Chi	22	1997	Brian Hunter, Det	74
1953	Minnie Minoso, Chi	25	1998	Rickey Henderson, Oak	66
1954	Jackie Jensen, Bos	22	1999	Brian Hunter, Sea	44
1955	Jim Rivera, Chi	25	2000	Johnny Damon, KC	46
1956	Luis Aparicio, Chi	21	2001	Ichiro Suzuki, Sea	56
1957	Luis Aparicio, Chi	28	2002	Alfonso Soriano, NY	41
1958	Luis Aparicio, Chi	29	2003	Carl Crawford, TB	55
1959	Luis Aparicio, Chi	56	2004	Carl Crawford, TB	59
1960	Luis Aparicio, Chi	51	2005	Chone Figgins, LA	62
1961	Luis Aparicio, Chi	53	2006	Carl Crawford, TB	58
1962	Luis Aparicio, Chi	31			

Leading Pitchers—Winning Percentage

Year	Pitcher and Team	W	L	Pct	Year	Pitcher and Team	W	L	Pct
1901	Clark Griffith, Chi	24	7	.774	1920	Jim Bagby, Clev	31	12	.721
1902	Bill Bernhard, Phil-Clev	18	5	.783	1921	Carl Mays, NY	27	9	.750
1903	Earl Moore, Clev	22	7	.759	1922	Joe Bush, NY	26	7	.788
1904	Jack Chesbro, NY	41	12	.774	1923	Herb Pennock, NY	19	6	.760
1905	Jess Tannehill, Bos	22	9	.710	1924	Walter Johnson, Wash	23	7	.767
1906	Eddie Plank, Phil	19	6	.760	1925	Stan Coveleski, Wash	20	5	.800
1907	Wild Bill Donovan, Det	25	4	.862	1926	George Uhle, Clev	27	11	.711
1908	Ed Walsh, Chi	40	15	.727	1927	Waite Hoyt, NY	22	7	.759
1909	George Mullin, Det	29	8	.784	1928	General Crowder, StL	21	5	.808
1910	Chief Bender, Phil	23	5	.821	1929	Lefty Grove, Phil	20	6	.769
1911	Chief Bender, Phil	17	5	.773	1930	Lefty Grove, Phil	28	5	.848
1912	Smoky Joe Wood, Bos	34	5	.872	1931	Lefty Grove, Phil	31	4	.886
1913	Walter Johnson, Wash	36	7	.837	1932	Johnny Allen, NY	17	4	.810
1914	Chief Bender, Phil	17	3	.850	1933	Lefty Grove, Phil	24	8	.750
1915	Smoky Joe Wood, Bos	15	5	.750	1934	Lefty Gomez, NY	26	5	.839
1916	Eddie Cicotte, Chi	15	7	.682	1935	Eldon Auker, Det	18	7	.720
1917	Reb Russell, Chi	15	5	.750	1936	Monte Pearson, NY	19	7	.731
1918	Sad Sam Jones, Bos	16	5	.762	1937	Johnny Allen, Clev	15	1	.938
1919	Eddie Cicotte, Chi	29	7	.806	1938	Red Ruffing, NY	21	7	.750

Leading Pitchers—Winning Percentage *(Cont.)*

Year	Pitcher and Team	W	L	Pct	Year	Pitcher and Team	W	L	Pct
1939	Lefty Grove, Bos	15	4	.789	1973	Catfish Hunter, Oak	21	5	.808
1940	Schoolboy Rowe, Det	16	3	.842	1974	Mike Cuellar, Balt	22	10	.688
1941	Lefty Gomez, NY	15	5	.750	1975	Mike Torrez, Balt	20	9	.690
1942	Ernie Bonham, NY	21	5	.808	1976	Bill Campbell, Minn	17	5	.773
1943	Spud Chandler, NY	20	4	.833	1977	Paul Splittorff, KC	16	6	.727
1944	Tex Hughson, Bos	18	5	.783	1978	Ron Guidry, NY	25	3	.893
1945	Hal Newhouser, Det	25	9	.735	1979	Mike Caldwell, Mil	16	6	.727
1946	Boo Ferriss, Bos	25	6	.806	1980	Steve Stone, Balt	25	7	.781
1947	Allie Reynolds, NY	19	8	.704	1981*	Pete Vuckovich, Mil	14	4	.778
1948	Jack Kramer, Bos	18	5	.783	1982	Pete Vuckovich, Mil	18	6	.750
1949	Ellis Kinder, Bos	23	6	.793		Jim Palmer, Balt	15	5	.750
1950	Vic Raschi, NY	21	8	.724	1983	Richard Dotson, Chi	22	7	.759
1951	Bob Feller, Clev	22	8	.733	1984	Doyle Alexander, Tor	17	6	.739
1952	Bobby Shantz, Phil	24	7	.774	1985	Ron Guidry, NY	22	6	.786
1953	Ed Lopat, NY	16	4	.800	1986	Roger Clemens, Bos	24	4	.857
1954	Sandy Consuegra, Chi	16	3	.842	1987	Roger Clemens, Bos	20	9	.690
1955	Tommy Byrne, NY	16	5	.762	1988	Frank Viola, Minn	24	7	.774
1956	Whitey Ford, NY	19	6	.760	1989	Bret Saberhagen, KC	23	6	.793
1957	Dick Donovan, Chi	16	6	.727	1990	Bob Welch, Oak	27	6	.818
	Tom Sturdivant, NY	16	6	.727	1991	Scott Erickson, Minn	20	8	.714
1958	Bob Turley, NY	21	7	.750	1992	Mike Mussina, Balt	18	5	.783
1959	Bob Shaw, Chi	18	6	.750	1993	Jimmy Key, NY	18	6	.750
1960	Jim Perry, Clev	18	10	.643	1994	Jimmy Key, NY	17	4	.810
1961	Whitey Ford, NY	25	4	.862	1995	Randy Johnson, Sea	18	2	.900
1962	Ray Herbert, Chi	20	9	.690	1996	Charles Nagy, Clev	17	5	.773
1963	Whitey Ford, NY	24	7	.774	1997	Randy Johnson, Sea	20	4	.833
1964	Wally Bunker, Balt	19	5	.792	1998	David Wells, NY	18	4	.818
1965	Mudcat Grant, Minn	21	7	.750	1999	Pedro Martinez, Bos	23	4	.852
1966	Sonny Siebert, Clev	16	8	.667	2000	Tim Hudson, Oak	20	6	.769
1967	Joel Horlen, Chi	19	7	.731	2001	Roger Clemens, NY	20	3	.870
1968	Denny McLain, Det	31	6	.838	2002	Pedro Martinez, Bos	20	4	.833
1969	Jim Palmer, Balt	16	4	.800	2003	Roy Halladay, Tor	22	7	.759
1970	Mike Cuellar, Balt	24	8	.750	2004	Curt Schilling, Bos	21	6	.778
1971	Dave McNally, Balt	21	5	.808	2005	Cliff Lee, Cle	18	5	.783
1972	Catfish Hunter, Oak	21	7	.750	2006	Roy Halladay, Tor	16	5	.762

*1981 percentages based on 10 or more victories. Note: Percentages based on 15 or more victories in all other years.

Leading Pitchers—Earned Run Average

Year	Player and Team	ERA	Year	Player and Team	ERA
1913	Walter Johnson, Wash	1.14	1940	Bob Feller, Clev†	2.62
1914	Dutch Leonard, Bos	1.01	1941	Thornton Lee, Chi	2.37
1915	Smoky Joe Wood, Bos	1.49	1942	Ted Lyons, Chi	2.10
1916	Babe Ruth, Bos	1.75	1943	Spud Chandler, NY	1.64
1917	Eddie Cicotte, Chi	1.53	1944	Dizzy Trout, Det	2.12
1918	Walter Johnson, Wash	1.27	1945	Hal Newhouser, Det	1.81
1919	Walter Johnson, Wash	1.49	1946	Hal Newhouser, Det	1.94
1920	Bob Shawkey, NY	2.46	1947	Spud Chandler, NY	2.46
1921	Red Faber, Chi	2.47	1948	Gene Bearden, Clev	2.43
1922	Red Faber, Chi	2.80	1949	Mel Parnell, Bos	2.78
1923	Stan Coveleski, Clev	2.76	1950	Early Wynn, Clev	3.20
1924	Walter Johnson, Wash	2.72	1951	Saul Rogovin, Det-Chi	2.78
1925	Stan Coveleski, Wash	2.84	1952	Allie Reynolds, NY	2.07
1926	Lefty Grove, Phil	2.51	1953	Ed Lopat, NY	2.43
1927	Wilcy Moore, NY#	2.28	1954	Mike Garcia, Clev	2.64
1928	Garland Braxton, Wash	2.52	1955	Billy Pierce, Chi	1.97
1929	Lefty Grove, Phil	2.81	1956	Whitey Ford, NY	2.47
1930	Lefty Grove, Phil	2.54	1957	Bobby Shantz, NY	2.45
1931	Lefty Grove, Phil	2.06	1958	Whitey aFord, NY	2.01
1932	Lefty Grove, Phil	2.84	1959	Hoyt Wilhelm, Balt	2.19
1933	Monte Pearson, Clev	2.33	1960	Frank Baumann, Chi	2.68
1934	Lefty Gomez, NY	2.33	1961	Dick Donovan, Wash	2.40
1935	Lefty Grove, Bos	2.70	1962	Hank Aguirre, Det	2.21
1936	Lefty Grove, Bos	2.81	1963	Gary Peters, Chi	2.33
1937	Lefty Gomez, NY	2.33	1964	Dean Chance, LA	1.65
1938	Lefty Grove, Bos	3.07	1965	Sam McDowell, Clev	2.18
1939	Lefty Grove, Bos	2.54	1966	Gary Peters, Chi	1.98

Leading Pitchers—Earned Run Average *(Cont.)*

Year	Player and Team	ERA	Year	Player and Team	ERA
1967	Joe Horlen, Chi	2.06	1987	Jimmy Key, Tor	2.76
1968	Luis Tiant, Clev	1.60	1988	Allan Anderson, Minn	2.45
1969	Dick Bosman, Wash	2.19	1989	Bret Saberhagen, KC	2.16
1970	Diego Segui, Oak	2.56	1990	Roger Clemens, Bos	1.93
1971	Vida Blue, Oak	1.82	1991	Roger Clemens, Bos	2.62
1972	Luis Tiant, Bos	1.91	1992	Roger Clemens, Bos	2.41
1973	Jim Palmer, Balt	2.40	1993	Kevin Appier, KC	2.56
1974	Catfish Hunter, Oak	2.49	1994	Steve Ontiveros, Oak	2.65
1975	Jim Palmer, Balt	2.09	1995	Randy Johnson, Sea	2.48
1976	Mark Fidrych, Det	2.34	1996	Juan Guzman, Tor	2.93
1977	Frank Tanana, Cal	2.54	1997	Roger Clemens, Tor	2.05
1978	Ron Guidry, NY	1.74	1998	Roger Clemens, Tor	2.64
1979	Ron Guidry, NY	2.78	1999	Pedro Martinez, Bos	2.07
1980	Rudy May, NY	2.47	2000	Pedro Martinez, Bos	1.74
1981	Steve McCatty, Oak	2.32	2001	Freddy Garcia, Sea	3.05
1982	Rick Sutcliffe, Clev	2.96	2002	Pedro Martinez, Bos	2.26
1983	Rick Honeycutt, Tex	2.42	2003	Pedro Martinez, Bos	2.22
1984	Mike Boddicker, Balt	2.79	2004	Johan Santana, Minn	2.61
1985	Dave Stieb, Tor	2.48	2005	Kevin Millwood, Cle	2.86
1986	Roger Clemens, Bos	2.48	2006	Johan Santana, Minn	2.77

Note: Based on 10 complete games through 1950, then 154 innings until the American League expanded in 1961, when it became 162 innings. In strike-shortened 1981, one inning per game required. Earned runs not tabulated in American League prior to 1913.

#Wilcy Moore pitched only six complete games—he started 12—in 1927 but was recognized as leader because of 213 innings pitched. †Ernie Bonham, New York, had 1.91 ERA and 10 complete games in 1940 but appeared in only 12 games and 99 innings, and Bob Feller was recognized as leader.

Leading Pitchers—Strikeouts

Year	Player and Team	SO	Year	Player and Team	SO
1901	Cy Young, Bos	159	1939	Bob Feller, Clev	246
1902	Rube Waddell, Phil	210	1940	Bob Feller, Clev	261
1903	Rube Waddell, Phil	301	1941	Bob Feller, Clev	260
1904	Rube Waddell, Phil	349	1942	Bobo Newsom, Wash	
1905	Rube Waddell, Phil	286		Tex Hughson, Bos	113
1906	Rube Waddell, Phil	203	1943	Allie Reynolds, Clev	151
1907	Rube Waddell, Phil	226	1944	Hal Newhouser, Det	187
1908	Ed Walsh, Chi	269	1945	Hal Newhouser, Det	212
1909	Frank Smith, Chi	177	1946	Bob Feller, Clev	348
1910	Walter Johnson, Wash	313	1947	Bob Feller, Clev	196
1911	Ed Walsh, Chi	255	1948	Bob Feller, Clev	164
1912	Walter Johnson, Wash	303	1949	Virgil Trucks, Det	153
1913	Walter Johnson, Wash	243	1950	Bob Lemon, Clev	170
1914	Walter Johnson, Wash	225	1951	Vic Raschi, NY	164
1915	Allie Reynolds, Clev	203	1952	Allie Reynolds, NY	160
1916	Walter Johnson, Wash	228	1953	Billy Pierce, Chi	186
1917	Walter Johnson, Wash	188	1954	Bob Turley, Balt	185
1918	Walter Johnson, Wash	162	1955	Herb Score, Clev	245
1919	Walter Johnson, Wash	147	1956	Herb Score, Clev	263
1920	Stan Coveleski, Clev	133	1957	Early Wynn, Clev	184
1921	Walter Johnson, Wash	143	1958	Early Wynn, Chi	179
1922	Urban Shocker, StL	149	1959	Jim Bunning, Det	201
1923	Walter Johnson, Wash	130	1960	Jim Bunning, Det	201
1924	Walter Johnson, Wash	158	1961	Camilo Pascual, Minn	221
1925	Lefty Grove, Phil	116	1962	Camilo Pascual, Minn	206
1926	Lefty Grove, Phil	194	1963	Camilo Pascual, Minn	202
1927	Lefty Grove, Phil	174	1964	Al Downing, NY	217
1928	Lefty Grove, Phil	183	1965	Sam McDowell, Clev	325
1929	Lefty Grove, Phil	170	1966	Sam McDowell, Clev	225
1930	Lefty Grove, Phil	209	1967	Jim Lonborg, Bos	246
1931	Lefty Grove, Phil	175	1968	Sam McDowell, Clev	283
1932	Red Ruffing, NY	190	1969	Sam McDowell, Clev	279
1933	Lefty Gomez, NY	163	1970	Sam McDowell, Clev	304
1934	Lefty Gomez, NY	158	1971	Mickey Lolich, Det	308
1935	Tommy Bridges, Det	163	1972	Nolan Ryan, Cal	329
1936	Tommy Bridges, Det	175	1973	Nolan Ryan, Cal	383
1937	Lefty Gomez, NY	194	1974	Nolan Ryan, Cal	367
1938	Bob Feller, Clev	240	1975	Frank Tanana, Cal	269

Leading Pitchers—Strikeouts *(Cont.)*

Year	Player and Team	SO	Year	Player and Team	SO
1976	Nolan Ryan, Cal	327	1992	Randy Johnson, Sea	241
1977	Nolan Ryan, Cal	341	1993	Randy Johnson, Sea	308
1978	Nolan Ryan, Cal	260	1994	Randy Johnson, Sea	204
1979	Nolan Ryan, Cal	223	1995	Randy Johnson, Sea	294
1980	Len Barker, Clev	187	1996	Roger Clemens, Bos	257
1981	Len Barker, Clev	127	1997	Roger Clemens, Tor	292
1982	Floyd Bannister, Sea	209	1998	Roger Clemens, Tor	271
1983	Jack Morris, Det	232	1999	Pedro Martinez, Bos	313
1984	Mark Langston, Sea	204	2000	Pedro Martinez, Bos	284
1985	Bert Blyleven, Clev-Minn	206	2001	Hideo Nomo, Bos	220
1986	Mark Langston, Sea	245	2002	Pedro Martinez, Bos	239
1987	Mark Langston, Sea	262	2003	Esteban Loaiza, Chi	207
1988	Roger Clemens, Bos	291	2004	Johan Santana, Minn	265
1989	Nolan Ryan, Tex	301	2005	Johan Santana, Minn	238
1990	Nolan Ryan, Tex	232	2006	Johan Santana, Minn	245
1991	Roger Clemens, Bos	241			

Leading Pitchers—Saves

FYear	Player and Team	SV	Year	Player and Team	SV
1947	Joe Page, NY	17	1978	Goose Gossage, NY	27
1948	Russ Christopher, Clev	17	1979	Mike Marshall, Minn	32
1949	Joe Page, NY	29	1980	Dan Quisenberry, KC	33
1950	Mickey Harris, Wash	15	1981	Rollie Fingers, Mil	28
1951	Ellis Kinder, Bos	14	1982	Dan Quisenberry, KC	35
1952	Harry Dorish, Chi	11	1983	Dan Quisenberry, KC	35
1953	Ellis Kinder, Bos	27	1984	Dan Quisenberry, KC	44
1954	Johnny Sain, NY	22	1985	Dan Quisenberry, KC	37
1955	Ray Narleski, Clev	19	1986	Dave Righetti, NY	46
1956	George Zuverink, Bal	16	1987	Tom Henke, Tor	34
1957	Bob Grim, NY	19	1988	Dennis Eckersley, Oak	45
1958	Ryne Duren, NY	20	1989	Jeff Russell, Tex	38
1959	Turk Lown, Chi	15	1990	Bobby Thigpen, Chi	57
1960	Mike Fornieles, Bos	14	1991	Bryan Harvey, Cal	46
	Johnny Klippstein, Clev	14	1992	Dennis Eckersley, Oak	51
1961	Luis Arroyo, NY	29	1993	Jeff Montgomery, KC	45
1962	Dick Radatz, Bos	24		Duane Ward, Tor	45
1963	Stu Miller, Bal	27	1994	Lee Smith, Bal	33
1964	Dick Radatz, Bos	29	1995	Jose Mesa, Clev	46
1965	Ron Kline, Wash	29	1996	John Wetteland, NY	43
1966	Jack Aker, KC	32	1997	Randy Myers, Balt	45
1967	Minnie Rojas, Cal	27	1998	Tom Gordon, Bos	46
1968	Al Worthington, Minn	18	1999	Mariano Rivera, NY	45
1969	Ron Perranoski, Minn	31	2000	Todd Jones, Det	42
1970	Ron Perranoski, Minn	34	2001	Mariano Rivera, NY	50
1971	Ken Sanders, Mil	31	2002	Eddie Guardado, Minn	45
1972	Sparky Lyle, NY	35	2003	Keith Foulke, Oak	43
1973	John Hiller, Det	38	2004	Mariano Rivera, NY	53
1974	Terry Forster, Chi	24	2005	Francisco Rodríguez, LA	45
1975	Goose Gossage, Chi	26		Bob Wickman, Cle	45
1976	Sparky Lyle, NY	23	2006	Francisco Rodriguez, LA	47
1977	Bill Campbell, Bos	31			

The Commissioners of Baseball

Kenesaw Mountain Landis	Elected Nov. 12, 1920. Served until his death on Nov. 25, 1944.
Happy Chandler	Elected April 24, 1945. Served until July 15, 1951.
Ford Frick	Elected Sept. 20, 1951. Served until Nov. 16, 1965.
William Eckert	Elected Nov. 17, 1965. Served until Dec. 20, 1968.
Bowie Kuhn	Elected Feb. 8, 1969. Served until Sept. 30, 1984.
Peter Ueberroth	Elected March 3, 1984. Took office Oct. 1, 1984. Served through March 31, 1989.
A. Bartlett Giamatti	Elected Sept. 8, 1988. Took office April 1, 1989. Served until his death on Sept. 1, 1989.
Francis Vincent Jr.	Appointed Acting Commissioner Sept. 2, 1989. Elected Commissioner Sept. 13, 1989. Served through Sept. 7, 1992.
Allan H. (Bud) Selig	Elected chairman of the executive council and given the powers of interim commissioner on Sept. 9, 1992. Unanimously elected Commissioner July 9, 1998.

HARRY HOW/GETTY IMAGES

Pro Football

Jerome Bettis of the
Super Bowl champion
Pittsburgh Steelers

On the Road to Victory

After sneaking into the playoffs, the wild-card Steelers rode "The Bus" to the franchise's fifth Super Bowl title

BY HANK HERSCH

I
T SEEMS TOO SHORT, DOESN'T IT? How can so much happen in a regular season that lasts a mere 16 games, followed by four weekends' worth of playoffs? The arc of a 162-game baseball season stretches like a long bridge across the summer, starting in spring and ending in fall. The NBA and NHL grind on and on for months—and that's just their postseasons. The NFL campaign almost seems like a Cliff Notes edition by comparison, yet because it's so brief, the significance of every moment is amplified; events take place at a neck-snapping pace. Take 2005: A pivotal partnership in Philadelphia sparks and flickers and dies out in a week; a juggernaut in Indianapolis loses its sure footing for an instant and plummets into the abyss; a scandal-scarred team in Minnesota rallies around a lame-duck coach and a backup quarterback to make an improbable postseason push.

It seems an eternity, doesn't it? Thirteen years and 3,479 carries by an NFL running back, and not as some sprightly speedster who outran the pursuit either, but as a 5'11", 255-pound blunderbuss who welcomed the contact as much as his tacklers did. He had taken the blows and plowed on (first as a battering *Ram* in Los Angeles, for goodness' sake), hoping that

when he finally chose a less debilitating lifestyle he would have a championship ring to flash. And so, just as the Steelers were on the verge of playoff extinction, they staged the greatest, most unexpected and, for star back Jerome (the Bus) Bettis, most heartwarming turnaround the league has ever seen.

Things change: Pittsburgh's 2005 season did a 180 from despair to delight; the New Orleans Saints went from low to high to low again. When Hurricane Katrina devastated their city and turned their lives upside down in late August, the players decamped to San Antonio and tried to focus on football. "Everybody on this team is on the same page now—to do everything we can to help the survivors, and to play for each other," said star receiver Joe Horn. No single game may have been as stirring as the Saints' opener at Charlotte, when they were greeted by a standing ovation and an F-16 flyover. The Panthers rallied from a 10-point deficit to tie it up at 20-all, but in the final minute Horn's lunging catch set up John Carney's winning 47-yard field goal and a dose of inspiration. "If we can show people that hope is real," said New Orleans running back Fred McAfee, "we'll be doing our part."

It seemed that the Saints were destined to be America's Team—until they began their tumble to a 3–13 finish, and America

REOPENING 9-24-2006
GO SAINTS

DAVID WALBERG

looked elsewhere for amusement. And what more diverting drama could there be than *As TO Turns*? After threatening to stay out of Eagles' training camp because he was unhappy with the seven-year, $49-million deal he'd signed a year earlier, star wideout Terrell Owens made a symbolic gesture in support of Philadelphia quarterback Donovan McNabb, whom he had trashed for tiring in Super Bowl XXXIX and branded a "hypocrite." In Philly's home opener the pair hooked up for two long touchdowns, and by the end of the 42–3 victory over the San Francisco 49ers they were yukking it up along the sidelines. "Whatever happened in the past, hopefully, is in the past," McNabb said.

Emphasis on *hopefully*. Just six weeks later, after a loss to the Denver Broncos, Owens got into a scuffle with retired Eagles defensive end Hugh Douglas, blasted the organization for failing to publicly acknowledge his 100th TD catch and said the team would be better off with Brett Favre at QB. Coach Andy Reid demanded that TO apologize to the organization, to the team and to

Hurricane Katrina ravaged New Orleans' Superdome in late summer, forcing the Saints to play games in San Antonio, Texas.

its All-Pro quarterback, but Owens's contrition rate was just .667—he refused to say he was sorry to McNabb. The Eagles suspended Owens without pay for the rest of their season (which concluded with a 6–10 record, their worst since Reid's first year, in 1999) and released him afterward. Next stop on the TO Bonhomie Tour: the Dallas Cowboys, who signed him after the season to a three-year deal.

The Vikings also provided a sordid diversion: An Oct. 6 "rookie party" cruise on Lake Minnetonka attended by players and dozens of female companions drew the attention of police investigators for the allegedly lewd conduct of some revelers, including graphic sex acts. That was only the latest in a string of public embarrassments for Team Turmoil in '05, from coach Mike Tice's admission to scalping 12 Super Bowl tickets to running back Onterrio Smith's year-long suspension after being caught with a fake penis and bladder that is used to beat drug tests (a.k.a., the Original Whizzinator). Yet after bottoming out at 1–4 and losing Daunte Culpepper to a knee injury, the Vikes somehow rallied behind Tice and backup QB Brad Johnson to win eight of 11 and fall just short of making the playoffs.

Winning, after all, quells controversy. Few peeps of discontent were heard in Seattle, for instance, as the Seahawks roared to a 13–3 finish. The previous year, running back Shaun Alexander had sounded off about coach Mike Holmgren's last-game play-calling after falling one yard short of the NFL rushing crown. In 2005, however, the 28-year-old Alexander roared to the title with 1,880 yards and set the season record with 28 touchdowns—though for an MVP winner, he flew well below most fans' radars. "People on the East Coast think we're in Siberia," said Holmgren. Added quarterback Matt Hasselbeck, "If it weren't for fantasy football, I don't know if anybody would know who Shaun was."

Indianapolis, likewise, plowed placidly along behind their old reliables: the arm of Peyton Manning and the legs of Edgerrin James. What enabled the Colts to win their first 13 games was something new in blue: a lockdown defense. Keyed by pass rushing ends Robert Mathis (11.5 sacks) and Dwight Freeney (11), the league's 11th-ranked D seemed strong enough to carry Indy to its first Super Bowl. "They have a little swagger to them," said Manning of his defensive mates. "I like that they're getting attention. It's about time."

Turnaround teams were in abundance in 2005. After failing to make the playoffs since 1990, the Bengals surged to the AFC North title behind third-year quarterback Carson Palmer, who finished second to Manning in passer rating, and wide receiver Chad Johnson, whose creative touchdown celebrations (from Riverdance jigs to using an end-zone marker like a golf putter to tap the football) led the Sunday night highlights. In his second season with the Redskins after an 11-year retirement, Hall of Fame coach Joe Gibbs recalled his days of glory with a rugged, disciplined team that won its final five games to make the playoffs. Another long-forlorn franchise, the Chicago Bears, won the NFC North thanks to a defense built around middle linebacker Brian Urlacher, the Defensive Player of the Year, that evoked both the Monsters of the Midway and a Magic Johnson fast break. "The job of the defense isn't to just stop the offense," coach Lovie Smith said. "It's to score points."

No one did a sharper U-turn than the Steelers. On Dec. 4 they were 7–5, having lost their third straight game, 38–31 to Cincinnati. His team reeling, coach Bill Cowher used two motivational ploys. On a board that charts the players' weekly performance, he removed all reference to the first dozen games and left up only the next opponent, the suddenly ferocious Bears. Cowher also gave his troops an assignment: Each player was to grade himself against the Bengals based on technique, effort and how well he handled his assignment. The idea was to heighten the players' sense of accountability. Said Bettis, "It drove home the message: Before you start to point fingers, you've got to look at yourself first."

Thus began a run so hair-raising it might have even stood Troy Polamalu's locks on end. The third-year Samoan safety, who hadn't visited a barber since 2002, helped pick up the Steelers' pace, playing at a feverish pitch and disrupting offenses from myriad angles. Pittsburgh toppled Chicago 21–9, then beat the Vikings, Browns and Lions in successive weeks to squeeze into the playoffs as the lowest seed; all the Steelers' games would be on the road. Their first opponent, Cincinnati, effectively lost on its second snap, when defensive end Kimo von Oelhoffen, attempting a sack, tore Palmer's left ACL. Final score: 31–17.

Pittsburgh embraced its long-shot status entering Indianapolis, where it had lost 26–7 in Week 12. "If you asked our families, even they probably didn't think we could get this far," said quarterback Ben Roethlisberger. "But the best thing about being an underdog is that it forces us to depend on

Thanks to hard-charging defensive ends like Dwight Freeney (93), the Colts' defense was much improved in 2005.

each other." The Colts were closing ranks as well. On Dec. 22, coach Tony Dungy's 18-year-old son, James, committed suicide at his apartment near Tampa, Fla., casting a dark cloud over what had been a glorious season. Instead of relying on Bettis and his power running game, Cowher came out throwing; Roethlisberger passed for 147 yards in the first 12 minutes to seize a 14–0 lead. Indianapolis rallied from a 21–3 deficit, but Roethlisberger's game-saving tackle on Nick Harper's interception return and a bad miss by Indy kicker Mike Vanderjagt—the most accurate field-goal kicker in history—from 46 yards out sealed the Steelers' 21–18 upset.

Next trip: Denver. A week earlier, the Broncos had knocked off the defending champion Patriots 41–27 at Invesco Field at Mile High behind a rebuilt defense that forced normally unflappable QB Tom Brady into mistakes—the worst being an interception that cornerback Champ Bailey returned

100 yards to the New England one-yard line. The night before the AFC title show-down, Bettis addressed his teammates at a suburban Denver hotel. He asked them to give everything they had on the field and to reach Super Bowl XL, which would be played at Ford Field, six miles from his parents' house in Detroit. "The last thing I'll ever ask you is, 'Take me home,'" he said.

Reflecting on Bettis's appeal, the 23-year-old Roethlisberger said, "All I was thinking was, 'Hey, Bussie, go sit down. You're going to make me cry.'"

In Denver, the Steelers stuck to their familiar formula: They took an early lead, let their running game eat up the clock and forced the Broncos to play catch-up—and cough-up—against an aggressive defense. After going up 24–3 at halftime behind the

JOHN BIEVER

Seattle's Shaun Alexander led all rushers in the NFL with 1,880 yards and 27 rushing TDs in 2005.

rushing and two TDs, and Hasselbeck's near-flawless play (20 of 28 for 219 yards), Seattle dominated Carolina 34–14.

Super Bowl XL was not a thing of beauty, but its outcome validated Cowher's pregame speech. "It's not going to take a super effort from any one individual," he told his players. "You play as a team, and you're going to walk away as champions." While the Seahawks kept Bettis out of the end zone, speedy Willie Parker raced 75 yards to score on the second play of the second half to put Pittsburgh up 14–3. While the Steelers' D had a number of lapses, cornerback Ike Taylor atoned for his by snagging an interception at the Steelers' five-yard line with 10:46 to play and his team clinging to a 14–10 advantage. And while Roethlisberger struggled mightily (nine of 21 for 123 yards), wide receiver Antwaan Randel El provided air support, delivering a 43-yard TD pass to Hines Ward on a double reverse (Zero Strong Z Short Fake Toss 39 X Reverse Pass) that delivered the final margin of victory, 21–10.

As Ward walked away with the game's MVP award, the 49-year-old Cowher received validation after 13 titleless seasons in Pittsburgh and the Rooney family earned its fifth Super Bowl victory. For the Bus, though, Super Bowl XL was the perfect coda to a Hall of Fame career. "I am the luckiest football player ever to play the game," said Bettis, whose 13,662 yards rushing ranks fifth on the all-time list. "I've been waiting for this day for 13 years, and for it to come in my hometown, with the team I love, in front of so many of the fans I love.... You send this script to Hollywood, they'd say, 'This is too fake.'"

Not really. Just another improbable twist in another eventful NFL season.

maturing Roethlisberger, who finished with 21 completions in 29 attempts for 275 yards, the Steelers coasted to a 34–17 victory. Bettis led all rushers with 39 yards on 15 carries and Pittsburgh became the first No. 6 seed to reach the Super Bowl. "We took the scenic route," said linebacker Joey Porter. "And now we're in the biggest game in sports."

The Seahawks arrived at Ford Field on no less of a roll. The NFC's top seed first bumped off Washington 20–10, then took on the surging Panthers in the NFC championship game. Known for having the league's top offense, anchored by left tackle Walter Jones, Seattle had developed one of its more formidable defenses as well, spearheaded by rookie linebacker Lofa Tatupu. In the first quarter Tatupu set the tone: He stepped in front of All-Pro receiver Steve Smith to make an interception, then he leveled running back Nick Goings in a head-on collision. With Alexander's 132 yards

2005 NFL Final Standings

American Football Conference

EAST DIVISION

	W	L	T	Pct	Pts	OP
New England	10	6	0	.625	379	338
Miami	9	7	0	.563	318	317
Buffalo	5	11	0	.313	271	367
NY Jets	4	12	0	.250	240	355

NORTH DIVISION

	W	L	T	Pct	Pts	OP
Cincinnati	11	5	0	.688	421	350
†Pittsburgh	11	5	0	.688	389	258
Baltimore	6	10	0	.375	265	299
Cleveland	6	10	0	.375	232	301

SOUTH DIVISION

	W	L	T	Pct	Pts	OP
Indianapolis	14	2	0	.875	439	247
†Jacksonville	12	4	0	.750	361	269
Tennessee	4	12	0	.250	299	421
Houston	2	14	0	.125	260	431

WEST DIVISION

	W	L	T	Pct	Pts	OP
Denver	13	3	0	.813	395	258
Kansas City	10	6	0	.625	403	325
San Diego	9	7	0	.563	418	312
Oakland	4	12	0	.250	290	383

† Wild-card team.

National Football Conference

EAST DIVISION

	W	L	T	Pct	Pts	OP
NY Giants	11	5	0	.688	422	314
†Washington	10	6	0	.625	359	293
Dallas	9	7	0	.563	325	308
Philadelphia	6	10	0	.375	310	388

NORTH DIVISION

	W	L	T	Pct	Pts	OP
Chicago	11	5	0	.688	260	202
Minnesota	9	7	0	.563	306	344
Detroit	5	11	0	.313	254	345
Green Bay	4	12	0	.250	298	344

SOUTH DIVISION

	W	L	T	Pct	Pts	OP
Tampa Bay	11	5	0	.688	300	274
†Carolina	11	5	0	.688	339	259
Atlanta	8	8	0	.500	351	341
New Orleans	3	13	0	.188	235	398

WEST DIVISION

	W	L	T	Pct	Pts	OP
Seattle	13	3	0	.813	452	271
St. Louis	6	10	0	.375	363	429
Arizona	5	11	0	.313	311	387
San Francisco	4	12	0	.250	239	428

† Wild-card team.

2005–06 NFL Playoffs

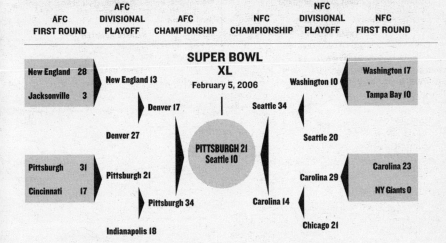

AFC FIRST ROUND	AFC DIVISIONAL PLAYOFF	AFC CHAMPIONSHIP		NFC CHAMPIONSHIP	NFC DIVISIONAL PLAYOFF	NFC FIRST ROUND

SUPER BOWL XL
February 5, 2006

New England 28 / Jacksonville 3

New England 13
Denver 17

Denver 27

Pittsburgh 31 / Cincinnati 17

Pittsburgh 21

Pittsburgh 34

Indianapolis 18

PITTSBURGH 21 / Seattle 10

Seattle 34

Seattle 20

Carolina 29

Carolina 14

Chicago 21

Washington 10

Washington 17 / Tampa Bay 10

Carolina 23 / NY Giants 0

NFL Playoff Recaps

AFC Wild-card Games

Pittsburgh	0	14	14	3—31
Cincinnati	10	7	0	0—17

FIRST QUARTER
Cincinnati: FG Graham 23, 6:54.
Cincinnati: Johnson 20 (Graham kick), 1:09.

SECOND QUARTER
Pittsburgh: Parker 19 pass from Roethlisberger (Reed kick), 13:11.
Cincinnati: Houshmandzadeh 7 pass from Kitna (Graham kick), 6:13.
Pittsburgh: Ward 5 pass from Roethlisberger (Reed kick), 3:48.

THIRD QUARTER
Pittsburgh: Bettis 5 run (Reed kick), 5:12.
Pittsburgh: Wilson 43 pass from Roethlisberger (Reed kick), 1:13.

FOURTH QUARTER
Pittsburgh: FG Reed 21, 10:29.

A: 65,820; 3:03.

Jacksonville	0	3	0	0—3
New England	0	7	14	7—28

SECOND QUARTER
New England: Brown 11 pass from Brady (Vinatieri kick), 12:08.
Jacksonville: FG Scobee 36, 1:05.

THIRD QUARTER
New England: Givens 3 pass from Brady (Vinatieri kick), 7:13.
New England: Watson 63 pass from Brady (Vinatieri kick), 3:03.

FOURTH QUARTER
New England: Samuel 73 interception return (Vinatieri kick), 14:46.

A: 68,726; 2:55.

NFC Wild-card Games

Carolina	0	10	7	6—23
New York	0	0	0	0—0

SECOND QUARTER
Carolina: Smith 22 pass from Delhomme (Kasay kick), 9:41.
Carolina: FG Kasay 31, 0:30.

THIRD QUARTER
Carolina: Smith 12 run (Kasay kick), 6:57.

FOURTH QUARTER
Carolina: FG Kasay 45, 13:33.
Carolina: FG Kasay 18, 2:40.

A: 79,378; 2:39.

Washington	14	3	0	0—17
Tampa Bay	0	3	7	0—10

FIRST QUARTER
Washington: Portis 6 run (Hall kick), 8:40.
Washington: Taylor 51 fumble return (Hall kick), 4:15.

SECOND QUARTER
Tampa Bay: FG Bryant 43, 10:02.
Washington: FG Hall 47, 5:34.

THIRD QUARTER
Tampa Bay: Simms 2 run (Bryant kick), 9:40.

A: 65,514; 3:01.

AFC Divisional Games

New England	0	3	3	7—13
Denver	0	10	7	10—27

SECOND QUARTER
New England: FG Vinatieri 40, 3:48.
Denver: Anderson 1 run (Elam kick), 1:42.
Denver: FG Elam 50, 0:43.

THIRD QUARTER
New England: FG Vinatieri 32, 7:49.
Denver: Anderson 1 run (Elam kick), 0:43.

FOURTH QUARTER
Denver: Smith 4 pass from Plummer (Elam kick), 8:38.
New England: Givens 4 pass from Brady (Vinatieri kick), 8:05.
Denver: FG Elam 34, 3:20.

A: 76,328; 3:15.

Pittsburgh	14	0	7	0—21
Indianapolis	0	3	0	15—18

FIRST QUARTER
Pittsburgh: Randle El 6 pass from Roethlisberger (Reed kick), 9:25.
Pittsburgh: Miller 7 pass from Roethlisberger (Reed kick), 3:12.

SECOND QUARTER
Indianapolis: FG Vanderjagt 20, 1:20.

THIRD QUARTER
Pittsburgh: Bettis 1 run (Reed kick), 1:26.

FOURTH QUARTER
Indianapolis: Clark 50 pass from Manning (Vanderjagt kick), 14:09.
Indianapolis: James 3 run (Manning pass to Wayne for 2 pt. conversion), 4:24.

A: 57,449; 3:18.

NFC Divisional Games

Washington	0	3	0	7—10
Seattle	0	7	7	6—20

SECOND QUARTER
Washington: FG Hall 26, 8:59.
Seattle: Jackson 29 pass from Hasselbeck (Brown kick), 3:22.

THIRD QUARTER
Seattle: Hasselbeck 6 run (Brown kick), 9:35.

FOURTH QUARTER
Seattle: FG Brown 33 14:16.
Washington: Moss 20 pass from Brunell (Hall kick), 11:59.
Seattle: FG Brown 31, 2:54.

A: 67,551; 3:01.

Carolina	7	9	7	6—29
Chicago	0	7	7	7—21

FIRST QUARTER
Carolina: Smith 58 pass from Delhomme (Kasay kick), 14:05.

SECOND QUARTER
Carolina: FG Kasay 20, 14:57.
Carolina: FG Kasay 38, 6:26.
Chicago: Peterson 1 run (Gould kick), 1:57.
Carolina: FG Kasay 37, 0:00.

THIRD QUARTER
Chicago: Clark 1 pass from Grossman (Gould kick), 11:21.
Carolina: Smith 39 pass from Delhomme (Kasay kick), 2:07.

FOURTH QUARTER
Chicago: McKie 3 run (Gould kick), 12:23.
Carolina: Mangum 1 pass from Delhomme (Kasay kick failed), 8:04.

A: 62,209; 3:23.

AFC Championship

Pittsburgh	3	21	0	10—34
Denver	0	3	7	7—17

FIRST QUARTER
Pittsburgh: FG Reed 47, 4:11.

SECOND QUARTER
Pittsburgh: Wilson 12 pass from Roethlisberger (Reed kick), 14:54.
Denver: FG Elam 23, 9:23.
Pittsburgh: Bettis 3 run (Reed kick), 1:55.
Pittsburgh: Ward 17 pass from Roethlisberger (Reed kick), 0:07.

THIRD QUARTER
Denver: Lelie 30 pass from Plummer (Elam kick), 3:36.

FOURTH QUARTER
Pittsburgh: FG Reed 42, 13:38.
Denver: Anderson 3 run (Elam kick) 7:52.
Pittsburgh: Roethlisberger 4 run (Reed kick) 2:59.

A: 76,775; T: 3:03.

NFC Championship

Carolina	0	7	0	7—14
Seattle	10	10	7	7—34

FIRST QUARTER
Seattle: Stevens 17 pass from Hasselbeck (Brown kick), 5:31.
Seattle: FG Brown 24, 2:23.

SECOND QUARTER
Seattle: Alexander 1 run (Brown kick), 14:53.
Carolina: Smith 59 punt return (Kasay kick), 9:05.
Seattle: FG Brown 39, 4:03.

THIRD QUARTER
Seattle: Jackson 20 pass from Hasselbeck (Brown kick), 11:09.

FOURTH QUARTER
Seattle: Alexander 1 run (Brown kick), 6:00.
Carolina: Carter 47 pass from Delhomme (Kasay kick), 5:09.

A: 67,837; T: 3:09.

Super Bowl XL Recap

Seattle	3	0	7	0—10
Pittsburgh	0	7	7	7—21

FIRST QUARTER
Seattle: FG Brown 47, 0:22.
Seattle 3–0.

SECOND QUARTER
Pittsburgh: Roethlisberger 1 run (Reed kick), 1:55.
Pittsburgh 7–3.

THIRD QUARTER
Pittsburgh: Parker 75 run (Reed kick), 14:38.
Pittsburgh 14–3.
Seattle: Stevens 16 pass from Hasselbeck (Brown kick), 6:45.
Pittsburgh 14-10.

FOURTH QUARTER
Pittsburgh: Ward 43 pass from Randle El (Reed kick). 6:04.
Pittsburgh 21-10.

A: 68,206; T: 3:36.

Team Statistics

	Seattle	Pittsburgh
FIRST DOWNS	20	14
Rushing	5	6
Passing	15	8
Penalty	0	0
THIRD DOWN EFF	5-17	8-15
FOURTH DOWN EFF	1-2	0-0
TOTAL NET YARDS	396	339
Total plays	77	56
Avg gain	5.1	6.1
NET YARDS RUSHING	137	181
Rushes	25	33
Avg per rush	5.5	5.5
NET YARDS PASSING	259	158
Completed–Att.	26-49	10-22
Yards per pass	5.0	6.9
Sacked–yards lost	3-14	1-8
Had intercepted	1	2
PUNTS–Avg	6-50.2	6-48.7
PENALTIES–Yds	7-70	3-20
FUMBLES–Lost	0-0	0-0

Passing

SEATTLE

	Comp	Att	Yds	Int	TD
Hasselbeck	26	49	273	1	1

PITTSBURGH

	Comp	Att	Yds	Int	TD
Roethlisberger	9	21	123	2	0
Randle El	1	1	43	0	1

Rushing

SEATTLE

	No.	Yds	Lg	TD
Alexander	20	95	21	0
Hasselbeck	3	35	18	0
Strong	2	7	7	0

PITTSBURGH

	No.	Yds	Lg	TD
Parker	10	93	75	1
Bettis	14	43	12	0
Roethlisberger	7	25	10	1
Ward	1	18	18	0
Haynes	1	2	2	0

Receiving

SEATTLE

	No.	Yds	Lg	TD
Jurevicius	5	93	35	0
Engram	6	70	21	0
Jackson	5	50	20	0
Stevens	3	25	16	1
Strong	2	15	13	0
Hannam	2	12	9	0
Morris	1	6	6	0
Alexander	2	2	4	0

PITTSBURGH

	No.	Yds	Lg	TD
Ward	5	123	43	1
Randle El	3	22	8	0
Wilson	1	20	20	0
Parker	1	1	1	0

Defense

SEATTLE

	Tck	Ast	Int	Sack
Hill	7	1	0	0
Tatupu	6	3	0	0
Pruitt	4	0	0	0
Babineaux	3	0	0	0
Trufant	3	0	0	0
Bernard	2	0	0	0
Boulware	2	3	1	0
Koutouvides	2	0	0	0
Lewis	2	2	0	0
Tubbs	2	0	0	0
Wistrom	1	0	0	1
Darby	1	0	0	0
Hasselbeck	1	0	0	0
Kacyvenski	1	0	0	0
Manuel	1	0	0	0
Herndon	0	1	1	0

PITTSBURGH

	Tck	Ast	Int	Sack
Taylor	6	1	1	0
Haggans	5	0	0	1
Townsend	5	1	0	1
Farrior	4	2	0	0
Foote	4	1	0	0
Hampton	4	0	0	1
Polamalu	4	1	0	0
Keisel	3	0	0	0
Porter	3	0	0	0
Smith	3	1	0	0
Carter	2	1	0	0
Harrison	2	1	0	0
McFadden	2	0	0	0
Randel El	2	0	0	0
von Oelhoffen	2	0	0	0
Colclough	1	0	0	0
Hoke	1	0	0	0
Hope	1	2	0	0
Iwuoma	1	0	0	0
Kriewaldt	1	1	0	0

2005 Associated Press All-Pro Team

OFFENSE

Peyton Manning, Indianapolis	Quarterback
Shaun Alexander, Seattle	Running Back
Tiki Barber, NY Giants	Running Back
Mack Strong, Seattle	Fullback
Antonio Gates, San Diego	Tight End
Steve Smith, Carolina	Wide Receiver
Chad Johnson, Cincinnati	Wide Receiver
Walter Jones, Seattle	Tackle
Willie Anderson, Cincinnati	Tackle
Steve Hutchinson, Seattle	Guard
Alan Faneca, Pittsburgh	Guard
Brian Waters, Kansas City	Guard
Jeff Saturday, Indianapolis	Center

DEFENSE

Dwight Freeney, Indianapolis	Defensive End
Osi Umenyiora, NY Giants	Defensive End
Jamal Williams, San Diego	Defensive Tackle
Richard Seymour, New England	Defensive Tackle
Lance Briggs, Chicago	Linebacker
Derrick Brooks, Tampa Bay	Linebacker
Brian Urlacher, Chicago	Linebacker
Al Wilson, Denver	Linebacker
Ronde Barber, Tampa Bay	Cornerback
Champ Bailey, Denver	Cornerback
Troy Polamalu, Pittsburgh	Safety
Bob Sanders, Indianapolis	Safety

SPECIALISTS

Neil Rackers, Arizona	Kicker
Jerome Mathis, Houston	Kick Returner
Brian Moorman, Buffalo	Punter

2005 AFC Team-by-Team Results

BALTIMORE RAVENS (6-10)

7	INDIANAPOLIS	24
10	at Tennessee	25
13	NY JETS	3
17	at Detroit	35
16	CLEVELAND	13
6	at Chicago	10
19	at Pittsburgh	20
9	CINCINNATI	21
3	at Jacksonville	30
16	HOUSTON	15
29	at Cincinnati	42
16	HOUSTON	15
10	at Denver	12
48	GREEN BAY	3
30	MINNESOTA	23
16	at Cleveland	20
265		299

BUFFALO BILLS (5-11)

22	HOUSTON	7
3	at Tampa Bay	19
16	ATLANTA	24
7	at New Orleans	19
20	MIAMI	14
27	NY JETS	17
17	at Oakland	38
16	at New England	21
14	KANSAS CITY	3
10	at San Diego	48
9	CAROLINA	13
23	at Miami	24
7	NEW ENGLAND	35
17	DENVER	28
37	at Cincinnati	27
26	at NY Jets	30
271		367

CINCINNATI BENGALS (11-5)

27	at Cleveland	13
37	MINNESOTA	8
24	at Chicago	7
16	HOUSTON	10
20	at Jacksonville	23
31	at Tennessee	23
13	PITTSBURGH	27
21	GREEN BAY	14
21	at Baltimore	9
37	INDIANAPOLIS	45
42	BALTIMORE	29
38	at Pittsburgh	31
23	CLEVELAND	20
41	at Detroit	17
27	BUFFALO	37
31	at Kansas City	37
421		350

CLEVELAND BROWNS (6-10)

13	CINCINNATI	27		21	at Pittsburgh	34
26	at Green Bay	24		22	MIAMI	0
6	at Indianapolis	13		12	at Minnesota	24
20	CHICAGO	10		14	JACKSONVILLE	20
3	at Baltimore	16		20	at Cincinnati	23
10	DETROIT	13		9	at Oakland	7
16	at Houston	19		0	PITTSBURGH	41
20	TENNESSEE	14		232		301

DENVER BRONCOS (13-3)

10	at Miami	34
20	SAN DIEGO	17
30	KANSAS CITY	10
20	at Jacksonville	7
21	WASHINGTON	19
28	NEW ENGLAND	20
23	at NY Giants	24
49	PHILADELPHIA	21
31	at Oakland	17
27	NY JETS	0
24	at Dallas	21 (OT)
27	at Kansas City	31
12	BALTIMORE	10
28	at Buffalo	17
22	OAKLAND	3
23	at San Diego	7
395		**258**

HOUSTON TEXANS (2-14)

7	at Buffalo	22
7	PITTSBURGH	27
10	at Cincinnati	16
20	TENNESSEE	34
10	at Seattle	42
20	INDIANAPOLIS	38
19	CLEVELAND	16
14	at Jacksonville	21
17	at Indianapolis	31
17	KANSAS CITY	45
27	ST. LOUIS	33 (OT)
15	at Baltimore	16
10	at Tennessee	13
30	ARIZONA	19
20	JACKSONVILLE	38
17	at San Francisco	20 (OT)
260		**431**

INDIANAPOLIS COLTS (14-2)

24	at Baltimore	7
10	JACKSONVILLE	3
13	CLEVELAND	6
31	at Tennessee	10
28	at San Francisco	3
45	ST. LOUIS	28
38	at Houston	20
40	at New England	21
31	HOUSTON	17
45	at Cincinnati	37
26	PITTSBURGH	7
35	TENNESSEE	3
26	at Jacksonville	18
17	SAN DIEGO	26
13	at Seattle	28
17	ARIZONA	13
439		**247**

JACKSONVILLE JAGUARS (12-4)

26	SEATTLE	14
3	at Indianapolis	10
26	at NY Jets	20 (OT)
7	DENVER	20
23	CINCINNATI	20
23	at Pittsburgh	17 (OT)
21	at St. Louis	24
21	HOUSTON	14
30	BALTIMORE	3
31	at Tennessee	28
24	at Arizona	17
20	at Cleveland	14
18	INDIANAPOLIS	26
10	SAN FRANCISCO	9
38	at Houston	20
40	TENNESSEE	13
361		**269**

KANSAS CITY CHIEFS (10-6)

27	NY JETS	7
23	at Oakland	17
10	at Denver	30
31	PHILADELPHIA	37
28	WASHINGTON	21
30	at Miami	20
20	at San Diego	28
27	OAKLAND	23
3	at Buffalo	14
45	at Houston	17
26	NEW ENGLAND	16
31	DENVER	27
28	at Dallas	31
17	at NY Giants	27
20	SAN DIEGO	7
37	CINCINNATI	3
403		**325**

MIAMI DOLPHINS (9-7)

34	DENVER	10
7	at NY Jets	17
27	CAROLINA	24
14	at Buffalo	20
13	at Tampa Bay	27
20	KANSAS CITY	30
21	at New Orleans	6
10	ATLANTA	17
16	NEW ENGLAND	23
0	at Cleveland	22
33	at Oakland	21
24	BUFFALO	23
23	at San Diego	21
24	NY JETS	20
24	TENNESSEE	10
28	at New England	26
318		**317**

NEW ENGLAND PATRIOTS (10-6)

30	OAKLAND	20
17	at Carolina	27
23	at Pittsburgh	20
17	SAN DIEGO	41
31	at Atlanta	28
20	at Denver	28
21	BUFFALO	16
21	INDIANAPOLIS	40
23	at Miami	16
24	NEW ORLEANS	17
16	at Kansas City	26
16	NY JETS	3
35	at Buffalo	7
28	TAMPA BAY	0
31	at NY Jets	21
26	MIAMI	28
379		**338**

NEW YORK JETS (4-12)

7	at Kansas City	27
17	MIAMI	7
20	JACKSONVILLE	26 (OT)
3	at Baltimore	13
14	TAMPA BAY	12
17	at Buffalo	27
14	at Atlanta	27
26	SAN DIEGO	31
3	at Carolina	30
0	at Denver	27
19	NEW ORLEANS	21
3	at New England	16
26	OAKLAND	10
20	at Miami	24
21	NEW ENGLAND	31
30	BUFFALO	26
240		**355**

OAKLAND RAIDERS (4-12)

20	at New England	30
17	KANSAS CITY	23
20	at Philadelphia	23
19	DALLAS	13
14	SAN DIEGO	27
38	BUFFALO	17
34	at Tennessee	25
23	at Kansas City	27
17	DENVER	31
16	at Washington	13
21	MIAMI	33
10	at San Diego	34
10	at NY Jets	26
7	CLEVELAND	9
3	at Denver	22
21	NY GIANTS	30
290		**383**

PITTSBURGH STEELERS (11-5)

34	TENNESSEE	7
27	at Houston	7
20	NEW ENGLAND	23
24	at San Diego	22
17	JACKSONVILLE	23 (OT)
27	at Cincinnati	13
20	BALTIMORE	19
20	at Green Bay	10
34	CLEVELAND	21
13	at Baltimore	16 (OT)
7	at Indianapolis	26
31	CINCINNATI	38
21	CHICAGO	9
18	at Minnesota	3
41	at Cleveland	0
35	DETROIT	21
389		258

SAN DIEGO CHARGERS (9-7)

24	DALLAS	28
17	at Denver	20
45	NY GIANTS	23
41	at New England	17
22	PITTSBURGH	24
27	at Oakland	14
17	at Philadelphia	20
28	KANSAS CITY	20
31	at NY Jets	26
48	BUFFALO	10
23	at Washington	17 (OT)
34	OAKLAND	10
21	MIAMI	23
26	at Indianapolis	17
7	at Kansas City	20
7	DENVER	23
418		312

TENNESSEE TITANS (4-12)

7	at Pittsburgh	34
25	BALTIMORE	10
27	at St. Louis	31
10	INDIANAPOLIS	31
34	at Houston	20
23	CINCINNATI	31
10	at Arizona	20
25	OAKLAND	34
14	at Cleveland	20
28	JACKSONVILLE	31
33	SAN FRANCISCO	22
3	at Indianapolis	35
13	HOUSTON	10
24	SEATTLE	28
10	at Miami	24
13	at Jacksonville	40
299		421

2005 NFC Team-by-Team Results

ARIZONA CARDINALS (6-10)

19	at NY Giants	42
12	ST. LOUIS	17
12	at Seattle	37
31	SAN FRANCISCO	14
20	CAROLINA	24
20	TENNESSEE	10
13	at Dallas	34
19	SEATTLE	33
21	at Detroit	29
38	at St. Louis	28
17	JACKSONVILLE	24
17	at San Francisco	10
13	WASHINGTON	17
19	at Houston	30
27	PHILADELPHIA	21
13	at Indianapolis	17
311		387

ATLANTA FALCONS (8-8)

14	PHILADELPHIA	10
18	at Seattle	21
24	at Buffalo	16
30	MINNESOTA	10
28	NEW ENGLAND	31
34	at New Orleans	31
27	NY JETS	14
17	at Miami	10
25	GREEN BAY	33
27	TAMPA BAY	30
27	at Detroit	7
6	at Carolina	24
36	NEW ORLEANS	17
3	at Chicago	16
24	at Tampa Bay	27 (OT)
11	CAROLINA	44
351		341

CAROLINA PANTHERS (11-5)

20	NEW ORLEANS	23
27	NEW ENGLAND	17
24	at Miami	27
32	GREEN BAY	29
24	at Arizona	20
21	at Detroit	20
38	MINNESOTA	13
34	at Tampa Bay	14
30	NY JETS	3
3	at Chicago	13
13	at Buffalo	9
24	ATLANTA	6
10	TAMPA BAY	20
27	at New Orleans	10
20	DALLAS	24
44	at Atlanta	11
391		259

CHICAGO BEARS (11-5)

7	at Washington	9
38	DETROIT	6
7	CINCINNATI	24
10	at Cleveland	20
28	MINNESOTA	3
10	at Cleveland	20
19	at Detroit	13 (OT)
20	at New Orleans	17
17	SAN FRANCISCO	9
13	CAROLINA	3
13	at Tampa Bay	10
19	GREEN BAY	7
9	at Pittsburgh	21
16	ATLANTA	3
24	at Green Bay	17
10	at Minnesota	34
260		202

DALLAS COWBOYS (9-7)

28	at San Diego	24
13	WASHINGTON	14
34	at San Francisco	31
13	at Oakland	19
33	PHILADELPHIA	10
16	NY GIANTS	13 (OT)
10	at Seattle	13
34	ARIZONA	13
21	at Philadelphia	20
20	DETROIT	7
21	DENVER	24 (OT)
10	at NY Giants	17
31	KANSAS CITY	28
7	at Washington	35
24	at Carolina	20
10	ST. LOUIS	20
325		308

DETROIT LIONS (5-11)

17	GREEN BAY	3
6	at Chicago	38
13	at Tampa Bay	17
35	BALTIMORE	17
20	CAROLINA	21
13	at Cleveland	10
13	CHICAGO	19 (OT)
14	at Minnesota	27
29	ARIZONA	21
7	at Dallas	20
7	ATLANTA	27
16	MINNESOTA	21
13	at Green Bay	16 (OT)
17	CINCINNATI	41
13	at New Orleans	12
21	at Pittsburgh	35
254		345

GREEN BAY PACKERS (4-12)

3	at Detroit	17
24	CLEVELAND	26
16	TAMPA BAY	17
29	at Carolina	32
52	NEW ORLEANS	3
20	at Minnesota	23
14	at Cincinnati	21
10	PITTSBURGH	20
33	at Atlanta	25
17	MINNESOTA	20
14	at Philadelphia	19
7	at Chicago	19
16	DETROIT	13 (OT)
3	at Baltimore	48
17	CHICAGO	24
23	SEATTLE	17
298		344

MINNESOTA VIKINGS (9-7)

13	TAMPA BAY	24
8	at Cincinnati	37
33	NEW ORLEANS	16
10	at Atlanta	30
3	at Chicago	28
23	GREEN BAY	20
13	at Carolina	38
27	DETROIT	14
24	at NY Giants	21
20	at Green Bay	17
24	CLEVELAND	12
21	at Detroit	16
27	ST. LOUIS	13
3	PITTSBURGH	18
23	at Baltimore	30
34	CHICAGO	10
306		344

NEW ORLEANS SAINTS (3-13)

23	at Carolina	20
10	at NY Giants	27
16	at Minnesota	33
19	BUFFALO	7
3	at Green Bay	52
31	ATLANTA	34
17	at St. Louis	28
6	MIAMI	21
17	CHICAGO	20
17	at New England	24
21	at NY Jets	19
3	TAMPA BAY	10
17	at Atlanta	36
10	CAROLINA	27
12	DETROIT	13
13	at Tampa Bay	27
235		398

NEW YORK GIANTS (11-5)

42	ARIZONA	19
27	NEW ORLEANS	10
23	at San Diego	45
44	ST. LOUIS	24
13	at Dallas	16 (OT)
24	DENVER	23
36	WASHINGTON	0
24	at San Francisco	6
21	MINNESOTA	24
27	PHILADELPHIA	17
21	at Seattle	24 (OT)
17	DALLAS	10
26	at Philadelphia	23 (OT)
27	KANSAS CITY	17
20	at Washington	35
30	at Oakland	21
422		314

PHILADELPHIA EAGLES (6-10)

10	at Atlanta	14
42	SAN FRANCISCO	3
23	OAKLAND	20
37	at Kansas City	31
10	at Dallas	33
20	SAN DIEGO	17
21	at Denver	49
10	at Washington	17
20	DALLAS	33
17	at NY Giants	27
19	GREEN BAY	14
0	SEATTLE	42
23	NY GIANTS	26 (OT)
17	at St. Louis	16
21	at Arizona	27
20	WASHINGTON	31
310		388

ST. LOUIS RAMS (6-10)

25	at San Francisco	28
17	at Arizona	12
31	TENNESSEE	27
24	at NY Giants	44
31	SEATTLE	37
28	at Indianapolis	45
28	NEW ORLEANS	17
24	JACKSONVILLE	21
16	at Seattle	31
28	ARIZONA	38
33	at Houston	27 (OT)
9	WASHINGTON	24
13	at Minnesota	27
16	PHILADELPHIA	17
20	SAN FRANCISCO	24
20	at Dallas	10
363		429

SAN FRANCISCO 49ERS (4-12)

28	ST. LOUIS	25
3	at Philadelphia	42
31	DALLAS	34
14	at Arizona	31
3	INDIANAPOLIS	28
17	at Washington	52
15	TAMPA BAY	10
6	NY GIANTS	24
9	at Chicago	17
25	SEATTLE	27
22	at Tennessee	33
10	ARIZONA	17
3	at Seattle	41
9	at Jacksonville	10
24	at St. Louis	20
20	HOUSTON	17 (OT)
239		428

SEATTLE SEAHAWKS (13-3)

14	at Jacksonville	26
21	ATLANTA	18
37	ARIZONA	12
17	at Washington	20 (OT)
37	at St. Louis	31
42	HOUSTON	10
13	DALLAS	10
33	at Arizona	19
31	ST. LOUIS	16
27	at San Francisco	25
24	NY GIANTS	21 (OT)
42	at Philadelphia	0
41	SAN FRANCISCO	3
28	at Tennessee	24
28	INDIANAPOLIS	13
17	at Green Bay	23
452		271

TAMPA BAY BUCCANEERS (11-5)

24	at Minnesota	13
19	BUFFALO	3
17	at Green Bay	16
17	DETROIT	13
12	at NY Jets	14
27	MIAMI	13
10	at San Francisco	15
14	CAROLINA	34
36	WASHINGTON	35
30	at Atlanta	27
10	CHICAGO	13
10	at New Orleans	3
20	at Carolina	10
0	at New England	28
27	ATLANTA	24 (OT)
27	NEW ORLEANS	13
300		274

WASHINGTON REDSKINS (10-6)

9	CHICAGO	7	13	OAKLAND	16
14	at Dallas	13	17	SAN DIEGO	23 (OT)
20	SEATTLE	17(OT)	24	at St. Louis	9
19	at Denver	20	17	at Arizona	13
21	at Kansas City	28	35	DALLAS	7
52	SAN FRANCISCO	17	35	NY GIANTS	20
0	at NY Giants	36	31	at Philadelphia	20
17	PHILADELPHIA	10	359		293
35	at Tampa Bay	36			

American Football Conference

Scoring

TOUCHDOWNS	TD	Rush	Rec	Ret	2PT	Pts		KICKING	PAT	FG	Pts
L. Johnson, Kan	21	20	1	0	0	126		Graham, Cin	47	28	131
Tomlinson, SD	20	18	2	0	0	120		Tynes, Kan	44	27	125
James, Ind	14	13	1	0	0	84		Vanderjagt, Ind	52	23	121
Dillon, NE	13	12	1	0	0	78		Reed, Pitt	45	24	117
Anderson, Den	13	12	1	0	0	78		Elam, Den	43	24	115
Harrison, Ind	12	0	12	0	0	72		Stover, Balt	23	30	113
R. Johnson, Cin	12	12	0	0	0	72		Lindell, Buff	26	29	113
Jordan, Oak	11	9	2	0	1	68		Kaeding, SD	49	21	112
Ward, Pitt	11	0	11	0	0	66		Mare, Mia	33	25	108
Chambers, Mia	11	0	11	0	0	66		Scobee, Jac	38	23	107

Passing

	Att	Comp	Yds	TD	Int	Lg	Rating Pts
Manning, Ind	453	305	3747	28	10	80	104.1
Palmer, Cin	509	345	3836	32	12	70	101.1
Roethlisberger, Pitt	268	168	2385	17	9	85	98.6
Brady, NE	530	334	4110	26	14	71	92.3
Plummer, Den	456	277	3366	18	7	72	90.2
Green, Kan	507	317	4014	17	10	60	90.1
Leftwich, Jac	302	175	2123	15	5	45	89.3
Brees, SD	500	323	3576	24	15	54	89.2
Holcomb, Buff	230	155	1509	10	8	65	85.6
McNair, Tenn	476	292	3161	16	11	57	82.4

Pass Receiving

RECEPTIONS	No.	Yds	Avg	Lg	TD		YARDS	Yds	No.	Avg	Lg	TD
C. Johnson, Cin	97	1432	14.8	70	9		C. Johnson, Cin	1432	97	14.8	70	9
Gates, SD	89	1101	12.4	38	10		Harrison, Ind	1146	82	14.0	80	12
Mason, Balt	86	1073	12.5	39	3		Chambers, Mia	1118	82	13.6	77	11
R. Smith, Den	85	1105	13.0	72	6		R. Smith, Den	1105	85	13.0	72	6
Wayne, Ind	83	1055	12.7	66	5		Gates, SD	1101	89	12.4	38	10
Harrison, Ind	82	1146	14.0	80	12		Mason, Balt	1073	86	12.5	39	3
Chambers, Mia	82	1118	13.6	77	11		Wayne, Ind	1055	83	12.7	66	5
Moulds, Buff	81	816	10.0	55	4		Branch, NE	998	78	12.8	51	5
Branch, NE	78	998	12.8	51	5		Houshmandzadeh, Cin	956	78	12.3	43	7
Houshmandzadeh, Cin	78	956	12.3	43	7		Gonzalez, Kan	905	78	11.6	39	2
Gonzalez, Kan	78	905	11.6	39	2		Moulds, Buff	816	78	10.0	55	4

Rushing

	Att	Yds	Avg	Lg	TD
Johnson, Kan	336	1750	5.2	49	20
James, Ind	360	1506	4.2	33	13
Tomlinson, SD	339	1462	4.3	62	18
R. Johnson, Cin	337	1458	4.3	33	12
McGahee, Buff	325	1247	3.8	27	5
Droughns, Cle	309	1232	4.0	75	2
Parker, Pitt	255	1202	4.7	80	4
Jordan, Oak	272	1025	3.8	26	9
Anderson, Den	239	1014	4.2	44	12
Davis, Hou	230	976	4.2	44	2

Interceptions

	No.	Yds	Lg	TD
Law, NYJ	10	195	74	1
O'Neal, Cin	10	103	37	0
Bailey, Den	8	139	65	2
Wesley, Kan	6	106	51	0
June, Ind	5	115	36	2

Sacks

Burgess, Oak	16.0
Vanden Bosch, Tenn	12.5
Taylor, Mia	12.0
Schobel, Buff	12.0
Mathis, Ind	11.5

American Football Conference *(Cont.)*

Punting

	No.	Yds	Avg	Net Avg	TB	In 20	Lg	Blk	Ret	Ret Avg
Moorman, Buff	71	3242	45.7	41.6	9	22	68	0	42	6.8
Lechler, Oak	82	3744	45.7	40.0	9	26	64	0	39	11.8
Miller, NE	76	3431	45.1	39.8	4	22	59	1	42	9.6
Smith, Ind	52	2301	44.3	39.0	5	23	58	0	25	10.9
Sauerbrun, Den	72	3157	43.8	40.2	6	24	66	1	36	7.4

Punt Returns

	No.	Yds	Avg	Lg	TD
Sams, Balt	33	401	12.2	51	0
Northcutt, Cle	35	368	10.5	62	1
Randle El, Pitt	44	448	10.2	81	2
Jones, Tenn	29	272	9.4	52	1
Welker, Mia	43	390	9.1	47	0

Kickoff Returns

	No.	Yds	Avg	Lg	TD
McGee, Buff	46	1391	30.1	99	1
Mathis, Hou	54	1542	28.6	99	2
Miller, NYJ	60	1577	26.3	95	1
Jones, Tenn	43	1127	26.2	85	0
Morgan, Pitt	23	583	25.3	74	0

National Football Conference

Scoring

TOUCHDOWNS	TD	Rush	Rec	Ret	2PT	Pts
Alexander, Sea	28	27	1	0	0	168
S. Smith, Car	13	1	12	0	0	78
Davis, Car	12	12	0	0	0	72
Barber, NYG	11	9	2	0	1	68
Portis, Wash	11	11	0	0	1	68
Galloway, TB	10	0	10	0	0	60
Jurevicius, Sea	10	0	10	0	0	60
Fitzgerald, Ariz	10	0	10	0	0	60
S. Jackson, StL	10	8	2	0	0	60
Holt, StL	9	0	9	0	0	54

KICKING	PAT	FG	Pts
Feely, NYG	43	35	148
Rackers, Ariz	20	40	140
Kasay, Car	43	26	121
Wilkins, StL	36	27	117
Brown, Sea	56	18	110
Edinger, Minn	31	25	106
Peterson, Atl	35	23	104
Carney, NO	22	25	97
Nedney, SF	19	26	97
Bryant, TB	31	21	94

Passing

	Att	Comp	Yds	TD	Int	Lg	Rating Pts
Hasselbeck, Sea	449	294	3459	24	9	56	98.2
Bulger, StL	287	192	2297	14	9	57	94.4
B. Johnson, Minn	294	184	1885	12	4	80	88.9
Delhomme, Car	435	262	3421	24	16	80	88.1
Brunell, Wash	454	262	3050	23	10	78	85.9
Warner, Ariz	375	242	2713	11	9	63	85.8
McNabb, Phil	357	211	2507	16	9	91	85.0
Bledsoe, Dal	499	300	3639	23	17	71	83.7
Simms, TB	313	191	2035	10	7	78	81.4
Manning, NYG	557	294	3762	24	17	78	75.9

Pass Receiving

RECEPTIONS	No.	Yds	Avg	Lg	TD
Smith, Car	103	1563	15.2	80	12
Fitzgerald, Ariz	103	1409	13.7	47	10
Boldin, Ariz	102	1402	13.7	54	7
Holt, StL	102	1331	13.0	44	9
Driver, GB	86	1221	14.2	59	5
Moss, Wash	84	1483	17.7	78	9
Galloway, TB	83	1287	15.5	80	10
Burress, NYG	76	1214	16.0	78	7
Johnson, Dal	71	839	11.8	34	6
Cooley, Wash	71	774	10.9	32	7

YARDS	Yds	No.	Avg	Lg	TD
Smith, Car	1563	103	15.2	80	12
Moss, Wash	1483	84	17.7	78	9
Fitzgerald, Ariz	1409	103	13.7	47	10
Boldin, Ariz	1402	102	13.7	54	7
Holt, StL	1331	102	13.0	44	9
Galloway, TB	1287	83	15.5	80	10
Driver, GB	1221	86	14.2	59	5
Burress, NYG	1214	76	16.0	78	7
Johnson, Dal	839	71	11.8	34	6
Cooley, Wash	774	71	10.9	32	7

National Football Conference *(Cont.)*

Rushing

	Att	Yds	Avg	Lg	TD
Alexander, Sea	370	1880	5.1	88	27
Barber, NYG	357	1860	5.2	95	9
Portis, Wash	352	1516	4.3	47	11
Dunn, Atl	280	1416	5.1	65	3
Jones, Chi	314	1335	4.3	42	9
Williams, TB	290	1178	4.1	71	6
S. Jackson, StL	254	1046	4.1	51	8
J. Jones, Dal	257	993	3.9	51	5
Foster, Car	205	876	4.3	70	2
K. Jones, Det	186	664	3.6	40	5

Interceptions

	No.	Yds	Lg	TD
Sharper, Minn	9	276	92	2
Vasher, Chi	8	145	46	1
Gamble, Car	7	157	61	1
Hall, Atl	6	177	65	0
Lucas, Car	6	70	32	0
Bly, Det	6	54	28	0

Sacks

Umenyiora, NYG	14.5
Rice, TB	14.0
Strahan, NYG	11.5
Peppers, Car	10.5
Coleman, Atl	10.5

Punting

	No.	Yds	Avg	Net Avg	TB	In 20	Lg	Blk	Ret	Ret Avg
Bidwell, TB	90	4101	45.6	40.4	13	24	61	0	49	9.5
Kluwe, Minn	71	3130	44.1	37.5	6	17	62	0	41	11.5
Player, Ariz	73	3206	43.9	39.4	7	18	60	1	39	8.4
Harris, Det	84	3656	43.5	37.3	2	34	60	0	50	10.4
Baker, Car	72	3118	43.3	40.0	4	23	59	0	36	6.5

Punt Returns

	No.	Yds	Avg	Lg	TD
Mahe, Phil	21	269	12.8	44	0
Moore, Minn	21	245	11.7	71	1
Smith, Car	27	286	10.6	44	0
Jones, TB	51	492	9.6	31	0
Morton, NYG	47	453	9.6	58	1
Wade, Chi	33	317	9.6	73	1

Kickoff Returns

	No.	Yds	Avg	Lg	TD
Robinson, Minn	47	1221	26.0	86	1
Betts, Wash	24	621	25.9	94	1
Ponder, NYG	35	905	25.9	95	1
Thompson, Dal	57	1399	24.5	49	0
Hood, Phil	38	900	23.7	53	0

2005 NFL Team Leaders

AFC Total Offense

	Total Plays	Yds/ Game	Yds/ Play	F Dwns/ Game	Time of Poss
Kansas City	1059	387.0	5.8	21.7	32:09
Indianapolis	1000	362.4	5.8	22.7	30:22
Denver	1030	360.4	5.6	20.6	32:37
Cincinnati	1018	358.1	5.6	21.4	30:52
New England	1031	352.0	5.5	20.9	30:19
San Diego	1022	347.9	5.4	21.1	31:34
Miami	1026	324.9	5.1	17.1	27:25
Jacksonville	1021	321.8	5.0	18.8	31:33
Pittsburgh	960	321.8	5.4	18.6	31:16
Tennessee	1022	320.1	5.0	17.4	31:13
Oakland	997	309.4	5.0	18.4	28:07
Baltimore	1056	293.3	4.4	17.9	30:22
Cleveland	938	284.8	4.9	15.1	28:00
Buffalo	930	257.6	4.4	16.2	29:04
Houston	954	253.3	4.2	15.2	28:10
NY Jets	907	248.1	4.4	15.7	26:37

AFC Total Defense

	Opp Total Plays	Opp Yds/ Game	Opp Yds/ Play	Opp T of Poss
Pittsburgh	998	284.0	4.6	28:44
Baltimore	998	284.7	4.6	29:38
Jacksonville	963	290.9	4.8	28:27
Indianapolis	953	307.1	5.2	29:38
NY Jets	1047	308.8	4.7	33:23
San Diego	999	309.2	5.0	28:26
Denver	985	312.9	5.1	27:23
Cleveland	1021	316.8	5.0	32:00
Miami	1078	317.4	4.7	32:35
Tennessee	960	319.4	5.3	28:47
Kansas City	971	328.1	5.4	27:51
New England	997	330.2	5.3	29:41
Oakland	1029	330.8	5.1	31:53
Cincinnati	976	338.7	5.6	29:09
Buffalo	1030	343.5	5.3	30:56
Houston	1012	364.0	5.8	31:50

NFC Total Offense

	Total Plays	Yds/ Game	Yds/ Play	F Dwns/ Game	Time of Poss
Seattle	1020	369.7	5.8	22.6	29:17
NY Giants	1055	361.7	5.5	19.5	30:26
Arizona	1075	348.4	5.2	19.0	31:20
St. Louis	1025	348.2	5.4	19.6	30:14
Washington	1037	330.6	5.1	18.8	31:33
Atlanta	1021	326.6	5.1	19.6	29:58
Dallas	1071	325.1	4.9	19.9	32:24
Green Bay	1051	319.9	4.9	19.9	30:48
Philadelphia	1027	319.3	5.0	17.6	28:22
New Orleans	1017	314.4	4.9	19.5	30:32
Carolina	964	309.4	5.1	17.4	30:48
Tampa Bay	985	294.8	4.8	16.8	30:45
Minnesota	945	288.3	4.9	17.8	28:46
Detroit	955	269.9	4.5	16.1	29:13
Chicago	937	256.3	4.4	14.6	28:41
San Francisco	865	224.2	4.1	11.9	27:18

NFC Total Defense

	Opp Total Plays	Opp Yds/ Game	Opp Yds/ Play	Opp T of Poss
Tampa Bay	950	277.8	4.7	29:15
Chicago	1034	281.8	4.4	31:19
Carolina	981	282.6	4.6	29:12
Green Bay	969	293.1	4.8	29:12
Arizona	936	295.6	5.1	28:40
Washington	981	297.9	4.9	28:27
Dallas	946	300.9	5.1	27:36
New Orleans	946	312.1	5.3	29:28
Seattle	1041	316.8	4.9	30:43
Detroit	1006	322.4	5.1	30:47
Minnesota	1029	323.3	5.0	31:14
Atlanta	1001	325.0	5.2	30:02
Philadelphia	1038	325.4	5.0	31:38
NY Giants	1049	327.5	5.0	29:34
St. Louis	1007	350.1	5.6	29:46
San Francisco	1090	391.2	5.7	32:42

Takeaways/Giveaways

American Football Conference

	Takeaways			Giveaways			Net
	Int	Fum	Total	Int	Fum	Total	Diff
Cincinnati	31	13	44	14	6	20	24
Denver	20	16	36	7	9	16	20
Indianapolis	18	13	31	11	8	19	12
Jacksonville	19	9	28	6	11	17	11
Kansas City	16	15	31	10	13	23	8
Pittsburgh	15	15	30	14	9	23	7
Buffalo	17	13	30	16	10	26	4
Miami	14	17	31	16	14	30	1
Oakland	5	14	19	14	9	23	-4
New England	10	8	18	15	9	24	-6
NY Jets	21	7	28	15	19	34	-6
Tennessee	9	11	20	14	12	26	-6
Cleveland	15	8	23	18	12	30	-7
San Diego	10	10	20	16	12	28	-8
Houston	7	9	16	13	11	24	-8
Baltimore	12	14	26	21	15	36	-10

National Football Conference

	Takeaways			Giveaways			Net
	Int	Fum	Total	Int	Fum	Total	Diff
Carolina	23	19	42	16	10	26	16
NY Giants	17	19	36	17	8	25	11
Seattle	16	11	27	10	7	17	10
Tampa Bay	17	13	30	14	9	23	7
Chicago	24	10	34	15	13	28	6
Minnesota	24	11	35	16	14	30	5
Washington	16	12	28	11	16	27	1
Detroit	19	12	31	18	12	30	1
Atlanta	16	13	29	13	16	29	0
Dallas	15	11	26	17	14	31	-5
Philadelphia	17	10	27	20	14	34	-7
San Francisco	16	10	26	21	14	35	-9
St. Louis	13	14	27	24	13	37	-10
Arizona	15	11	26	21	16	37	-11
Green Bay	10	11	21	30	15	45	-24
New Orleans	10	9	19	24	19	43	-24

Baltimore Ravens

SCORING

	TD Rush	Rec	Ret	PAT	FG	S	Pts
Stover	0	0	0	23/23	30/34	0	113
Heap	0	7	0	0	0	0	42
Lewis	3	1	0	0	0	0	24
Mason	0	3	0	0	0	0	18
Thomas	0	0	3	0	0	0	18
Clayton	3	1	2	0	0	0	18

RUSHING

	No.	Yds	Avg	Lg	TD
Lewis	269	906	3.4	25	3
Taylor	117	487	4.2	52	0

PASSING

	Att	Comp	Pct Comp	Yds	Avg Gain	TD	Int	Rating Pts
Boller	293	171	58.4	1799	6.14	11	12	71.7
Wright	266	164	61.7	1582	5.95	6	9	71.7

RECEIVING

	No.	Yds	Avg	Lg	TD
Mason	86	1073	12.5	39	3
Heap	75	855	11.4	48	7
Clayton	44	471	10.7	47	2
Taylor	41	292	7.1	20	1
Lewis	32	191	6.0	15	1
Wilcox	20	154	7.7	17	1

INTERCEPTIONS: Thomas, Suggs, 2

PUNTING

	No.	Yds	Avg	Net Avg	TB	In 20	Lg	Blk
Zastudil	84	3653	43.5	37.8	7	11	60	0

SACKS: Thomas, 9

Buffalo Bills

SCORING

	TD Rush	Rec	Ret	PAT	FG	S	Pts
Lindell	0	0	0	26/26	29/35	0	113
Evans	0	7	0	0	0	0	42
McGahee	5	0	0	0	0	0	30
Moulds	0	4	0	0	0	0	24
Reed	0	2	0	0	0	0	12
McGee	0	0	2	0	0	0	12

RUSHING

	No.	Yds	Avg	Lg	TD
McGahee	325	1247	3.8	27	5
Williams	45	161	3.6	28	0

PASSING

	Att	Comp	Pct Comp	Yds	Avg Gain	TD	Int	Rating Pts
Holcomb	230	155	67.4	1509	6.56	10	8	85.6
Losman	228	113	49.6	1340	5.88	8	8	64.9

RECEIVING

	No.	Yds	Avg	Lg	TD
Moulds	81	816	10.1	55	4
Evans	48	743	15.5	65	7
Reed	32	449	14.0	51	2
McGahee	28	178	6.4	19	0
Parris	15	148	9.9	28	1

INTERCEPTIONS: McGee, Vincent, 4

PUNTING

	No.	Yds	Avg	Net Avg	TB	In 20	Lg	Blk
Moorman	71	3242	45.7	41.6	9	22	68	0

SACKS: Schobel, 12

Cincinnati Bengals

SCORING

	TD Rush	Rec	Ret	PAT	FG	S	Pts
Graham	0	0	0	47/47	28/32	0	131
R. Johnson	12	0	0	0	0	0	72
C. Johnson	0	9	0	0	0	0	54
Houshmandzadeh	1	7	0	0	0	0	48
Henry	0	6	0	0	0	0	36
J. Johnson	0	3	0	0	0	0	18

RUSHING

	No.	Yds	Avg	Lg	TD
R. Johnson	337	1458	4.3	33	12
Perry	61	279	4.6	30	0

PASSING

	Att	Comp	Pct Comp	Yds	Avg Gain	TD	Int	Rating Pts
Palmer	509	345	67.8	3836	7.54	32	12	101.1

RECEIVING

	No.	Yds	Avg	Lg	TD
C. Johnson	97	1432	14.8	70	9
Houshmandzadeh	78	956	12.3	43	7
Perry	51	328	6.4	28	2
Henry	31	422	13.6	47	6
Walter	19	211	11.1	33	1
Schobel	18	193	10.7	28	1

INTERCEPTIONS: O'Neal, 10

PUNTING

	No.	Yds	Avg	Net Avg	TB	In 20	Lg	Blk
Larson	60	2591	43.2	38.9	8	13	75	0

SACKS: Smith, 6

Cleveland Browns

SCORING

	TD Rush	Rec	Ret	PAT	FG	S	Pts
Dawson	0	0	0	19/21	27/29	0	100
Bryant	0	4	0	0	0	0	24
Heiden	0	3	0	0	0	0	18
Northcutt	0	2	1	0	0	0	18
Edwards	0	3	0	0	0	0	18
Droughns	2	0	0	0	0	0	12

RUSHING

	No.	Yds	Avg	Lg	TD
Droughns	309	1232	4.0	75	2

PASSING

	Att	Comp	Pct Comp	Yds	Avg Gain	TD	Int	Rating Pts
Dilfer	333	199	59.8	2321	6.97	11	12	76.9
Frye	165	98	59.4	1002	6.07	4	6	69.8

RECEIVING

	No.	Yds	Avg	Lg	TD
Bryant	69	1009	14.6	54	4
Heiden	43	401	9.3	62	3
Northcutt	42	441	10.5	58	2
Droughns	39	369	9.5	51	0
Edwards	32	512	16.0	80	3
Jackson	24	287	12.0	68	1
Shea	18	153	8.5	27	1

INTERCEPTIONS: Russell, Bodden, 3

PUNTING

	No.	Yds	Avg	Net Avg	TB	In 20	Lg	Blk
Richardson	78	3181	40.8	36.3	9	22	61	0

SACKS: Thompson, McKinley, 5

Denver Broncos

SCORING	Rush	TD Rec	Ret	PAT	FG	S	Pts
Elam	0	0	0	43/44	24/32	0	115
Anderson	12	1	0	0	0	0	78
Bell	8	0	0	0	0	0	48
Smith	0	6	0	0	0	0	36
Johnson	1	5	0	0	0	0	36

RUSHING	No.	Yds	Avg	Lg	TD
Anderson	239	1014	4.2	44	12
Bell	173	921	5.3	68	8
Dayne	53	270	5.1	55	1

PASSING	Att	Comp	Pct Comp	Yds	Avg Gain	TD	Int	Rating Pts
Plummer	456	277	60.7	3366	7.38	18	7	90.2

RECEIVING	No.	Yds	Avg	Lg	TD
Smith	85	1105	13.0	72	6
Lelie	42	770	18.3	56	1
Putzier	37	481	13.0	32	0
Adams	21	203	9.7	21	0
Alexander	21	170	8.1	15	1
Anderson	18	212	11.8	66	1

INTERCEPTIONS: Bailey, 8

PUNTING	No.	Yds	Avg	Net Avg	TB	In 20	Lg	Blk
Sauerbrun	72	3157	43.8	40.2	6	24	66	0

SACKS: Lynch, Pryce, Ekuban, 4

Indianapolis Colts

SCORING	Rush	TD Rec	Ret	PAT	FG	S	Pts
Vanderjagt	0	0	0	52/52	23/25	0	121
James	13	1	0	0	0	0	84
Harrison	0	12	0	0	0	0	72
Wayne	0	5	0	0	0	0	30
Rhodes	4	0	0	0	0	0	24
Clark	0	4	0	0	0	0	24

RUSHING	No.	Yds	Avg	Lg	TD
James	360	1506	4.2	33	2
Rhodes	40	118	3.0	24	4

PASSING	Att	Comp	Pct Comp	Yds	Avg Gain	TD	Int	Rating Pts
Manning	453	305	67.3	3747	8.27	28	10	104.1

RECEIVING	No.	Yds	Avg	Lg	TD
Wayne	83	1055	12.7	66	5
Harrison	82	1146	14.0	80	12
James	44	337	7.7	20	1
Stokley	41	543	13.2	45	1
Clark	37	488	13.2	56	4
Fletcher	18	202	11.2	23	3

INTERCEPTIONS: June, 5

PUNTING	No.	Yds	Avg	Net Avg	TB	In 20	Lg	Blk
Smith	52	2301	44.3	39	5	23	58	0

SACKS: Mathis, 11.5

Houston Texans

SCORING	Rush	TD Rec	Ret	PAT	FG	S	Pts
Brown	0	0	0	24/24	26/34	0	102
Davis	2	4	0	0	0	0	36
Bradford	0	5	0	0	0	1	32
Wells	4	0	0	0	0	0	24
Mathis	0	1	2	0	0	0	18

RUSHING	No.	Yds	Avg	Lg	TD
Davis	230	976	4.2	44	2
Wells	90	325	3.6	14	4

PASSING	Att	Comp	Pct Comp	Yds	Avg Gain	TD	Int	Rating Pts
Carr	423	256	60.5	2488	5.88	14	11	77.2

RECEIVING	No.	Yds	Avg	Lg	TD
Johnson	63	688	10.9	53	2
Gaffney	55	492	8.9	29	2
Davis	39	337	8.6	33	4
Bradford	34	436	12.8	50	5
Rivers	24	168	7.0	20	0
Wells	22	179	8.1	20	0

INTERCEPTIONS: Earl, 2

PUNTING	No.	Yds	Avg	Net Avg	TB	In 20	Lg	Blk
Stanley	77	2990	38.8	36	1	29	61	0

SACKS: Orr, 7

Jacksonville Jaguars

SCORING	Rush	TD Rec	Ret	PAT	FG	S	Pts
Scobee	0	0	0	38/39	23/30	0	107
Wilford	0	7	0	0	0	0	42
Smith	0	6	0	0	0	0	36
Jones	0	5	0	0	0	0	30
Toefield	4	0	0	0	0	0	24
Jones	4	0	0	0	0	0	24

RUSHING	No.	Yds	Avg	Lg	TD
Taylor	194	787	4.1	71	3
Jones	151	575	3.8	27	4

PASSING	Att	Comp	Pct Comp	Yds	Avg Gain	TD	Int	Rating Pts
Leftwich	302	175	57.9	2123	7.03	15	5	89.3
Garrard	168	98	58.3	1117	6.65	4	1	83.9

RECEIVING	No.	Yds	Avg	Lg	TD
Smith	70	1023	14.6	45	6
Wilford	41	681	16.6	39	7
Jones	36	432	12.0	42	5
Williams	35	445	12.7	41	0
Pearman	32	240	7.5	19	0

INTERCEPTIONS: Mathis, 5

PUNTING	No.	Yds	Avg	Net Avg	TB	In 20	Lg	Blk
Hanson	82	3517	42.9	40	11	33	74	0

SACKS: Hayward, 8.5

Kansas City Chiefs

SCORING	Rush	TD Rec	Ret	PAT	FG	S	Pts
L. Johnson	20	1	0	0	0	0	126
Tynes	0	0	0	44/45	27/33	0	125
Holmes	6	1	0	0	0	0	42
Kennison	0	5	0	0	0	0	30
Hall	0	3	1	0	0	0	24
Parker	0	3	0	0	0	0	18

RUSHING	No.	Yds	Avg	Lg	TD
L. Johnson	336	1750	5.2	49	20
Holmes	119	451	3.8	35	6

PASSING	Att	Comp	Pct Comp	Yds	Avg Gain	TD	Int	Rating Pts
Green	507	317	62.5	4014	7.92	17	10	90.1

RECEIVING	No.	Yds	Avg	Lg	TD
Gonzalez	78	905	11.6	39	2
Kennison	68	1102	16.2	55	5
Parker	36	533	14.8	49	3
Hall	34	436	12.8	52	3
L. Johnson	33	343	10.4	36	1
Holmes	21	197	9.4	60	1

INTERCEPTIONS: Wesley, 6

PUNTING	No.	Yds	Avg	Net Avg	TB	In 20	Lg	Blk
Colquitt	65	2564	39.4	36.7	5	27	62	0

SACKS: Allen, 11

New England Patriots

SCORING	Rush	TD Rec	Ret	PAT	FG	S	Pts
Vinatieri	0	0	0	40/41	20/25	0	100
Dillon	12	1	0	0	0	0	78
Branch	0	5	0	0	0	0	30
Vrabel	0	3	1	0	0	0	24
Watson	0	4	0	0	0	0	24

RUSHING	No.	Yds	Avg	Lg	TD
Dillon	209	733	3.5	29	12
Pass	54	245	4.5	31	3

PASSING	Att	Comp	Pct Comp	Yds	Avg Gain	TD	Int	Rating Pts
Brady	530	344	63.0	4110	7.76	26	14	92.3

RECEIVING	No.	Yds	Avg	Lg	TD
Branch	78	998	12.8	51	5
Givens	59	738	12.5	40	2
Brown	39	466	11.9	71	2
Watson	29	441	15.2	35	4
Faulk	29	260	9.0	23	0
Dwight	19	332	17.5	59	3

INTERCEPTIONS: Samuel, Hobbs, 3

PUNTING	No.	Yds	Avg	Net Avg	TB	In 20	Lg	Blk
Miller	76	3431	45.1	39.8	4	22	59	0

SACKS: Colvin, 7

Miami Dolphins

SCORING	Rush	TD Rec	Ret	PAT	FG	S	Pts
Mare	0	0	0	33/33	25/30	0	108
Chambers	0	11	0	0	0	0	66
Williams	6	0	0	0	0	0	36
McMichael	0	5	0	0	0	0	30
Brown	4	1	0	0	0	0	30
Booker	0	3	0	0	0	0	18

RUSHING	No.	Yds	Avg	Lg	TD
Brown	207	907	4.4	65	4
Williams	168	743	4.4	35	6

PASSING	Att	Comp	Pct Comp	Yds	Avg Gain	TD	Int	Rating Pts
Frerotte	494	257	52.0	2996	6.07	18	13	71.9
Rosenfels	61	34	55.7	462	7.57	4	3	81.5

RECEIVING	No.	Yds	Avg	Lg	TD
Chambers	82	1118	13.6	77	11
McMichael	60	582	9.7	30	5
Booker	39	686	17.6	60	3
Brown	32	232	7.3	38	1
Welker	29	434	15.0	47	0

INTERCEPTIONS: Schulters, 4

PUNTING	No.	Yds	Avg	Net Avg	TB	In 20	Lg	Blk
Jones	88	3827	43.5	40.9	7	31	63	0

SACKS: Taylor, 12

New York Jets

SCORING	Rush	TD Rec	Ret	PAT	FG	S	Pts
Nugent	0	0	0	24/24	22/28	0	90
Martin	5	0	0	0	0	0	30
Coles	0	5	0	0	0	0	30
Sowell	1	2	0	0	0	0	18
Testaverde	2	0	0	0	0	0	12
McCareins	0	2	0	0	0	0	12
Houston	2	0	0	0	0	0	12

RUSHING	No.	Yds	Avg	Lg	TD
Martin	220	735	3.3	49	5
Houston	81	302	3.7	17	2

PASSING	Att	Comp	Pct Comp	Yds	Avg Gain	TD	Int	Rating Pts
Bollinger	266	150	56.4	1558	5.86	7	6	72.9
Pennington	83	49	59.0	530	59.0	2	3	70.9
Testaverde	106	60	56.6	777	7.33	1	6	59.4

RECEIVING	No.	Yds	Avg	Lg	TD
Coles	73	845	11.6	43	5
McCareins	43	713	16.6	45	2
Jolley	29	324	11.2	60	1
Sowell	28	155	5.5	28	2
Martin	24	118	4.9	14	0

INTERCEPTIONS: Law, 10

PUNTING	No.	Yds	Avg	Net Avg	TB	In 20	Lg	Blk
Graham	74	3233	43.7	39.6	6	18	6	0

SACKS: Abraham, 10.5

Oakland Raiders

SCORING	Rush	Rec	Ret	PAT	FG	S	Pts
Janikowski	0	0	0	30/30	20/30	0	90
Jordan	9	2	0	0	0	1	68
Moss	0	8	0	0	0	0	48
Porter	0	5	0	0	0	0	30
Gabriel	0	3	0	0	0	0	18
Anderson	0	3	0	0	0	0	18

RUSHING	No.	Yds	Avg	Lg	TD
Jordan	272	1025	3.8	34	9
Crockett	60	208	3.5	24	1

PASSING	Att	Comp	Pct Comp	Yds	Avg Gain	TD	Int	Rating Pts
Collins	565	302	53.5	3759	6.65	20	12	77.3

RECEIVING	No.	Yds	Avg	Lg	TD
Porter	76	942	12.4	49	5
Jordan	70	563	8.0	28	2
Moss	60	1005	16.8	79	8
Gabriel	37	554	15.0	38	3
Anderson	24	303	12.6	36	3

INTERCEPTIONS: Schweigert, 2

PUNTING	No.	Yds	Avg	Net Avg	TB	In 20	Lg	Blk
Lechler	82	3744	45.7	40	9	26	64	0

SACKS: Burgess, 16

Pittsburgh Steelers

SCORING	Rush	Rec	Ret	PAT	FG	S	Pts
Reed	0	0	0	45/45	24/29	0	117
Ward	0	11	0	0	0	0	66
Bettis	9	0	0	0	0	0	54
Miller	0	6	0	0	0	0	36
Parker	4	1	0	0	0	0	30

RUSHING	No.	Yds	Avg	Lg	TD
Parker	255	1202	4.7	80	4
Bettis	110	368	3.3	39	9
Haynes	74	274	3.7	20	3

PASSING	Att	Comp	Pct Comp	Yds	Avg Gain	TD	Int	Rating Pts
Roethlisberger	268	168	62.7	2385	8.9	17	9	98.6
Batch	36	23	63.9	246	6.83	1	1	81.5
Maddox	71	34	47.9	406	5.74	2	4	51.7

RECEIVING	No.	Yds	Avg	Lg	TD
Ward	69	975	14.1	85	11
Miller	39	459	11.8	50	6
Randle El	35	558	15.9	63	1
Wilson	26	451	17.3	46	0
Parker	18	218	12.1	48	1

INTERCEPTIONS: Hope, 3

PUNTING	No.	Yds	Avg	Net Avg	TB	In 20	Lg	Blk
Gardockl	67	2803	41.8	36.8	7	22	65	0

SACKS: Porter 10.5

San Diego Chargers

SCORING	Rush	Rec	Ret	PAT	FG	S	Pts
Tomlinson	18	2	0	0	0	0	120
Kaeding	0	0	0	49/49	21/24	0	112
Gates	0	10	0	0	0	0	60
McCardell	0	9	0	0	0	0	54
Parker	0	3	0	0	0	0	18
Turner	3	0	0	0	0	0	18

RUSHING	No.	Yds	Avg	Lg	TD
Tomlinson	339	1462	4.3	62	18
Turner	57	335	5.9	83	3

PASSING	Att	Comp	Pct Comp	Yds	Avg Gain	TD	Int	Rating Pts
Brees	500	323	64.6	3576	7.15	24	15	89.2

RECEIVING	No.	Yds	Avg	Lg	TD
Gates	89	1101	12.4	38	10
McCardell	70	917	13.1	54	9
Parker	57	725	12.7	49	3
Tomlinson	51	370	7.3	41	2
Caldwell	28	352	12.6	43	1
Neal	24	145	6.0	21	1

INTERCEPTIONS: Jue, 3

PUNTING	No.	Yds	Avg	Net Avg	TB	In 20	Lg	Blk
Scifres	71	3104	43.7	40.3	8	25	71	0

SACKS: Merriman, 10

Tennessee Titans

SCORING	Rush	Rec	Ret	PAT	FG	S	Pts
Bironas	0	0	0	30/32	23/29	0	99
Brown	5	2	0	0	0	0	42
Bennett	0	4	0	0	0	0	24
Troupe	0	4	0	0	0	0	24

RUSHING	No.	Yds	Avg	Lg	TD
Brown	224	851	3.8	38	5
Henry	88	335	3.8	29	0

PASSING	Att	Comp	Pct Comp	Yds	Avg Gain	TD	Int	Rating Pts
McNair	476	292	61.3	3161	6.64	16	11	82.4

RECEIVING	No.	Yds	Avg	Lg	TD
Bennett	58	738	12.7	55	4
Kinney	55	543	9.9	27	2
Troupe	55	530	9.6	35	4
Scaife	37	273	7.4	19	2
Brown	25	327	13.1	57	2
Jones	23	299	13.0	38	2
Calico	22	191	8.7	18	0
Williams	21	299	14.2	50	2
Roby	21	289	13.8	32	1

INTERCEPTIONS: Hill, 3

PUNTING	No.	Yds	Avg	Net Avg	TB	In 20	Lg	Blk
Hentrich	78	3371	43.2	41.4	14	21	59	0

SACKS: Vanden Bosch, 12.5

Arizona Cardinals

SCORING	Rush	TD Rec	Ret	PAT	FG	S	Pts
Rackers	0	0	0	20/20	40/42	0	140
Fitzgerald	0	10	0	0	0	0	60
Boldin	0	7	0	0	0	1	44
Dansby	0	0	2	0	0	0	12
Arrington	2	0	0	0	0	0	12

RUSHING	No.	Yds	Avg	Lg	TD
Shipp	157	451	2.9	19	0
Arrington	112	370	3.3	32	2

PASSING	Att	Comp	Pct Comp	Yds	Avg Gain	TD	Int	Rating Pts
Warner	375	242	64.5	2713	7.24	11	9	85.8
McCown	270	163	60.4	1836	6.8	9	11	74.9

RECEIVING	No.	Yds	Avg	Lg	TD
Fitzgerald	103	1409	13.7	47	10
Boldin	102	1402	13.7	54	7
Johnson	40	432	10.8	41	1
Shipp	35	255	7.3	28	0
Avanbadelo	34	231	6.8	18	0
Bergen	28	270	9.6	32	1

INTERCEPTIONS: Dansby, 3

PUNTING	No.	Yds	Avg	Net Avg	TB	In 20	Lg	Blk
Player	73	3206	43.9	39.4	7	18	60	0

SACKS: Wilson, 8

Atlanta Falcons

SCORING	Rush	TD Rec	Ret	PAT	FG	S	Pts
Peterson	0	0	0	35/35	23/25	0	104
Duckett	8	0	0	0	0	0	48
Vick	6	0	0	0	0	1	36
Crumpler	0	5	0	0	0	1	32
Dunn	3	1	0	0	0	0	24

RUSHING	No.	Yds	Avg	Lg	TD
Dunn	280	1416	5.1	65	3
Vick	102	597	5.9	32	6
Duckett	121	380	3.1	25	8

PASSING	Att	Comp	Pct Comp	Yds	Avg Gain	TD	Int	Rating Pts
Vick	387	214	55.3	2412	6.23	15	13	73.1
Schaub	64	33	51.6	495	7.73	4	0	98.1

RECEIVING	No.	Yds	Avg	Lg	TD
Crumpler	65	877	13.5	48	5
Finneran	50	611	12.2	53	2
Jenkins	36	508	14.1	58	3
White	29	446	15.4	54	3
Dunn	29	220	7.6	24	1
Griffith	21	111	5.3	17	3

INTERCEPTIONS: Hall, 6

PUNTING	No.	Yds	Avg	Net Avg	TB	In 20	Lg	Blk
Koenen	78	3300	42.3	39.3	9	23	67	0

SACKS: Coleman, 10.5

Carolina Panthers

SCORING	Rush	TD Rec	Ret	PAT	FG	S	Pts
Kasay	0	0	0	43/44	26/34	0	121
Smith	1	12	0	0	0	0	78
Davis	12	0	0	0	0	0	72
Proehl	0	4	0	0	0	0	24
Foster	2	1	0	0	0	0	18

RUSHING	No.	Yds	Avg	Lg	TD
Foster	205	879	4.3	70	2
Davis	180	549	3.1	39	12
Goings	37	133	3.6	17	0

PASSING	Att	Comp	Pct Comp	Yds	Avg Gain	TD	Int	Rating Pts
Delhomme	435	262	60.2	3421	7.86	24	16	88.1

RECEIVING	No.	Yds	Avg	Lg	TD
Smith	103	1563	15.2	80	12
Foster	34	372	10.9	47	1
Proehl	25	441	17.6	69	4
Colbert	25	282	11.3	42	2
Mangum	23	202	8.8	24	2

INTERCEPTIONS: Gamble, 7

PUNTING	No.	Yds	Avg	Net Avg	TB	In 20	Lg	Blk
Baker	72	3118	43.3	40	4	23	59	0

SACKS: Peppers, 10.5

Chicago Bears

SCORING	Rush	TD Rec	Ret	PAT	FG	S	Pts
Gould	0	0	0	19/20	21/27	0	82
Jones	9	0	0	0	0	0	54
Muhammad	0	4	0	0	0	0	24

Five tied with 12.

RUSHING	No.	Yds	Avg	Lg	TD
Jones	314	1335	4.3	42	9
Peterson	76	391	5.1	36	2
Benson	67	272	4.1	36	0

PASSING	Att	Comp	Pct Comp	Yds	Avg Gain	TD	Int	Rating Pts
Orton	368	190	51.6	1869	5.08	9	13	59.7
Grossman	39	20	51.3	259	6.64	1	2	59.7

RECEIVING	No.	Yds	Avg	Lg	TD
Muhammad	64	750	11.7	33	4
Gage	31	346	11.2	25	2
Jones	26	143	5.5	41	0
Clark	24	229	9.5	31	2
Bradley	18	230	12.8	54	0
Berrian	13	246	18.9	54	0

INTERCEPTIONS: Vasher, 8

PUNTING	No.	Yds	Avg	Net Avg	TB	In 20	Lg	Blk
Maynard	96	3937	41	38	11	24	11	0

SACKS: Ogunleye, 10

Dallas Cowboys

SCORING	Rush	TD Rec	Ret	PAT	FG	S	Pts
Cortez	0	0	0	13/14	12/16	0	49
Glenn	1	7	0	0	0	0	48
K. Johnson	0	6	0	0	0	1	38
Witten	0	6	0	0	0	0	36
J. Jones	5	0	0	0	0	0	30
Barber	5	0	0	0	0	0	30
Cundiff	0	0	0	14/14	5/8	0	29

RUSHING	No.	Yds	Avg	Lg	TD
Jones	257	993	3.9	51	5
Barber	138	538	3.9	28	5

PASSING	Att	Comp	Pct Comp	Yds	Avg Gain	TD	Int	Rating Pts
Bledsoe	499	300	60.1	3639	7.29	23	17	83.7

RECEIVING	No.	Yds	Avg	Lg	TD
Johnson	71	839	11.8	34	6
Witten	66	757	11.5	34	6
Glenn	62	1136	18.3	71	7
Jones	35	218	6.2	26	0
Crayton	22	341	15.5	63	2

INTERCEPTIONS: Glenn, 4

PUNTING	No.	Yds	Avg	Net Avg	TB	In 20	Lg	Blk
McBriar	81	3439	42.5	39.4	9	28	63	0

SACKS: Ware, Ellis, 8

Green Bay Packers

SCORING	Rush	TD Rec	Ret	PAT	FG	S	Pts
Longwell	0	0	0	30/31	20/27	0	90
Gado	6	1	0	0	0	0	42
Driver	0	5	0	0	0	0	30
Chatman	0	4	1	0	0	0	30
Ferguson	0	3	0	0	0	1	20
Martin	0	3	0	0	0	1	20

RUSHING	No.	Yds	Avg	Lg	TD
Gado	143	582	4.1	64	6
Green	77	255	3.3	13	0

PASSING	Att	Comp	Pct Comp	Yds	Avg Gain	TD	Int	Rating Pts
Favre	607	372	61.3	3881	6.39	20	29	70.9

RECEIVING	No.	Yds	Avg	Lg	TD
Driver	86	1221	14.2	59	5
Chatman	49	549	11.2	25	4
Fisher	48	347	7.2	15	1
Lee	33	294	8.9	27	2
Henderson	30	264	8.8	32	0
Ferguson	27	366	13.6	51	3

INTERCEPTIONS: Harris, 3

PUNTING	No.	Yds	Avg	Net Avg	TB	In 20	Lg	Blk
Sander	64	2508	39.2	34.5	2	11	53	0

SACKS: Gbaja-Biamila, 8

Detroit Lions

SCORING	Rush	TD Rec	Ret	PAT	FG	S	Pts
Hanson	0	0	0	27/27	19/24	0	84
R. Williams	0	8	0	0	0	0	48
Jones	5	0	0	0	0	0	30
Pollard	0	3	0	0	0	0	18
Pinner	3	0	0	0	0	0	18

RUSHING	No.	Yds	Avg	Lg	TD
Jones	186	664	3.6	40	5
Pinner	106	349	3.3	19	3
Bryson	64	306	4.8	77	1

PASSING	Att	Comp	Pct Comp	Yds	Avg Gain	TD	Int	Rating Pts
Harrington	330	188	57.0	2021	6.12	12	12	72.0
Garcia	173	102	59.0	937	5.42	3	6	65.1

RECEIVING	No.	Yds	Avg	Lg	TD
Pollard	46	516	11.2	86	3
R. Williams	45	687	15.3	51	8
Vines	40	417	10.4	40	0
Bryson	37	284	7.7	63	0
M. Williams	29	350	12.1	49	1

INTERCEPTIONS: Bly, 6

PUNTING	No.	Yds	Avg	Net Avg	TB	In 20	Lg	Blk
Harris	84	3656	43.5	37.3	2	34	60	0

SACKS: Edwards, 7

Minnesota Vikings

SCORING	Rush	TD Rec	Ret	PAT	FG	S	Pts
Edinger	0	0	0	31/31	25/34	0	106
M. Robinson	0	5	0	0	0	1	32
Bennett	3	2	0	0	0	0	30
Taylor	0	4	0	0	0	0	24
Moore	1	2	1	0	0	0	24
Fason	4	0	0	0	0	0	24

RUSHING	No.	Yds	Avg	Lg	TD
Moore	155	662	4.3	33	1
Bennett	126	473	3.8	61	3

PASSING	Att	Comp	Pct Comp	Yds	Avg Gain	TD	Int	Rating Pts
Johnson	294	184	62.6	1885	6.41	12	4	88.9
Culpepper	216	139	64.4	1564	7.24	6	12	72.0

RECEIVING	No.	Yds	Avg	Lg	TD
Wiggins	69	568	8.2	24	1
Taylor	50	604	12.1	31	4
Moore	37	339	9.2	29	2
M. Robinson	31	515	16.6	68	5
Burleson	30	328	10.9	20	1
Williamson	24	372	15.5	56	2
K. Robinson	22	347	15.8	80	1

INTERCEPTIONS: Sharper, 9

PUNTING	No.	Yds	Avg	Net Avg	TB	In 20	Lg	Blk
Kluwe	71	3130	44.1	37.5	6	17	62	0

SACKS: Johnstone, 7.5

New Orleans Saints

SCORING	Rush	Rec	Ret	PAT	FG	S	Pts
Carney	0	0	0	22/22	25/32	0	97
Stallworth	0	7	0	0	0	0	42
A. Smith	3	0	0	0	0	0	18
McAllister	3	0	0	0	0	0	18
Henderson	0	3	0	0	0	0	18

RUSHING	No.	Yds	Avg	Lg	TD
A. Smith	166	659	4.0	42	3
Stecker	95	363	3.8	32	0
McAllister	93	335	3.6	26	3

PASSING	Att	Comp	Pct Comp	Yds	Avg Gain	TD	Int	Rating Pts
Brooke	431	240	55.7	2882	6.69	13	17	70.0
Bouman	122	68	55.7	722	5.92	2	7	54.7

RECEIVING	No.	Yds	Avg	Lg	TD
Stallworth	70	945	13.5	43	7
Horn	49	654	13.3	30	1
Hilton	35	396	11.3	29	1
Stecker	35	281	8.0	41	0
Kakim	34	489	14.4	42	2
Henderson	22	343	15.6	66	3

INTERCEPTIONS: Craft, 3

PUNTING	No.	Yds	Avg	Net Avg	TB	In 20	Lg	Blk
Berger	71	3006	43.2	39.5	3	28	69	0

SACKS: Smith, 8.5

Philadelphia Eagles

SCORING	Rush	Rec	Ret	PAT	FG	S	Pts
Akers	0	0	0	23/23	16/22	0	71
Westbrook	3	4	0	0	0	1	44
Owens	0	6	0	0	0	0	36
Brown	0	4	0	0	0	0	24
France	0	0	0	5/5	6/7	0	23

RUSHING	No.	Yds	Avg	Lg	TD
Westbrook	156	617	4.0	31	3
Moats	55	278	5.1	59	3

PASSING	Att	Comp	Pct Comp	Yds	Avg Gain	TD	Int	Rating Pts
McNabb	357	211	59.1	2507	7.02	16	9	85.0
McMahon	207	94	45.4	1158	5.59	5	8	55.2

RECEIVING	No.	Yds	Avg	Lg	TD
L. Smith	61	682	11.2	48	3
Westbrook	61	616	10.1	62	4
Lewis	48	561	11.7	34	1
Owens	47	763	16.2	94	6
Brown	43	571	13.3	56	4

INTERCEPTIONS: Brown, 4

PUNTING	No.	Yds	Avg	Net Avg	TB	In 20	Lg	Blk
Landeta	34	1483	43.6	39.4	2	7	56	0
Johnson	39	1615	41.4	38.4	0	11	59	0
Hodges	22	836	38	32	1	3	55	0

SACKS: Kearse, 7.5

New York Giants

SCORING	Rush	Rec	Ret	PAT	FG	S	Pts
Feely	0	0	0	43/43	35/42	0	148
Barber	9	2	0	0	0	1	68
Shockey	0	7	0	0	0	1	44
Toomer	0	7	0	0	0	0	42
Burress	0	7	0	0	0	0	42
Jacobs	7	0	0	0	0	0	42

RUSHING	No.	Yds	Avg	Lg	TD
Barber	357	1860	5.2	95	9
Ward	35	123	3.5	12	0
Jacobs	38	99	2.6	21	7

PASSING	Att	Comp	Pct Comp	Yds	Avg Gain	TD	Int	Rating Pts
Manning	557	294	52.8	3762	6.75	24	17	75.9

RECEIVING	No.	Yds	Avg	Lg	TD
Burress	76	1214	16.0	78	7
Shockey	65	891	13.7	59	7
Toomer	60	684	11.4	37	7
Barber	54	530	9.8	48	2

INTERCEPTIONS: Alexander, 4

PUNTING	No.	Yds	Avg	Net Avg	TB	In 20	Lg	Blk
Feagles	73	3070	42.1	37.8	3	26	56	0

SACKS: Umenyiora, 14.5

St. Louis Rams

SCORING	Rush	Rec	Ret	PAT	FG	S	Pts
Wilkins	0	0	0	36/36	27/31	0	117
Jackson	8	2	0	0	0	0	60
Holt	0	9	0	0	0	0	54
Curtis	1	6	0	0	0	0	42
Bruce	0	3	0	0	0	0	18

RUSHING	No.	Yds	Avg	Lg	TD
Jackson	254	1046	4.1	51	8
Faulk	65	292	4.5	20	0

PASSING	Att	Comp	Pct Comp	Yds	Avg Gain	TD	Int	Rating Pts
Bulger	287	192	66.9	2297	8.00	14	9	94.4
Martin	177	124	70.1	1277	7.22	5	7	83.5
Fitzpatrick	135	76	56.3	777	5.76	4	8	58.2

RECEIVING	No.	Yds	Avg	Lg	TD
Holt	102	1331	13.0	44	9
Curtis	60	801	13.4	83	6
McDonald	46	523	11.4	31	0
Faulk	44	291	6.6	18	1
Jackson	43	320	7.4	27	2
Bruce	36	525	14.6	46	3

INTERCEPTIONS: Furrey, 4

PUNTING	No.	Yds	Avg	Net Avg	TB	In 20	Lg	Blk
Barker	50	2137	42.7	37.2	4	13	63	0
Hodges	22	836	38	32	1	3	55	0

SACKS: Little, 8.5

San Francisco 49ers

SCORING

SCORING	Rush	TD Rec	Ret	PAT	FG	S	Pts
Nedney	0	0	0	19/19	26/28	0	97
Lloyd	0	5	0	0	0	0	30
Barlow	3	0	0	0	0	0	18
Battle	0	3	0	0	0	0	18
Hicks	3	0	0	0	0	0	18
Gore	3	0	0	0	0	0	18

RUSHING	No.	Yds	Avg	Lg	TD
Gore	127	608	4.8	72	3
Barlow	176	581	3.3	29	3
Hicks	59	308	5.2	73	3

PASSING	Att	Comp	Pct Comp	Yds	Avg Gain	TD	Int	Rating Pts
Rattay	97	56	57.7	667	6.88	5	6	70.3
Dorsey	90	48	53.3	481	5.34	2	2	66.9
Smith	165	84	50.9	875	5.3	1	11	40.8

RECEIVING	No.	Yds	Avg	Lg	TD
Lloyd	48	733	15.3	89	5
Battle	32	363	11.3	39	3
Barlow	31	241	7.8	24	0
Morton	21	288	13.7	30	1

INTERCEPTIONS: Spencer, Adams, 4

PUNTING	No.	Yds	Avg	Net Avg	TB	In 20	Lg	Blk
Lee	107	4447	41.6	37.2	3	15	58	0

SACKS: Young, 8

Tampa Bay Buccaneers

SCORING	Rush	TD Rec	Ret	PAT	FG	S	Pts
Bryant	0	0	0	31/31	21/25	0	94
Galloway	0	10	0	0	0	0	60
Alstott	6	1	0	0	0	1	44
Williams	6	0	0	0	0	0	36
Pittman	1	1	0	0	0	0	12
Smith	0	2	0	0	0	0	12

RUSHING	No.	Yds	Avg	Lg	TD
Williams	290	1178	4.1	71	6
Pittman	70	436	6.2	64	1

PASSING	Att	Comp	Pct Comp	Yds	Avg Gain	TD	Int	Rating Pts
Simms	313	191	61.0	2035	6.5	10	7	81.4
Griese	174	112	64.4	1136	6.53	7	7	79.6

RECEIVING	No.	Yds	Avg	Lg	TD
Galloway	83	1287	15.5	80	10
Smith	41	367	9.0	24	2
Pittman	36	300	8.3	41	1
Hilliard	35	282	8.1	22	1
Clayton	32	372	11.6	41	0
Alstott	25	222	8.9	24	1

INTERCEPTIONS: Barber, 5

PUNTING	No.	Yds	Avg	Net Avg	TB	In 20	Lg	Blk
Bidwell	90		41.1	45.6	40.4	13	24	61 0

SACKS: Rice, 14

Seattle Seahawks

SCORING	Rush	TD Rec	Ret	PAT	FG	S	Pts
Alexander	27	1	0	0	0	0	168
Brown	0	0	0	56/57	18/25	0	110
Jurevicius	0	10	0	0	0	0	60
Stevens	0	5	0	0	0	0	30
Engram	0	3	0	0	0	0	18
Jackson	0	3	0	0	0	0	18

RUSHING	No.	Yds	Avg	Lg	TD
Alexander	370	1880	5.1	88	27
Morris	71	288	4.1	49	1

PASSING	Att	Comp	Pct Comp	Yds	Avg Gain	TD	Int	Rating Pts
Hasselbeck	449	294	65.5	3459	7.7	24	9	98.2

RECEIVING	No.	Yds	Avg	Lg	TD
Engram	67	778	11.6	56	3
Jurevicius	55	694	12.6	52	10
Stevens	45	554	12.3	35	5
Jackson	38	482	12.7	48	3
Hackett	28	400	14.3	47	2
Strong	22	166	7.5	27	0

INTERCEPTIONS: Boulware, 4

PUNTING	No.	Yds	Avg	Net Avg	TB	In 20	Lg	Blk
Rouen	61	2539	41.6	37.3	7	20	62	0

SACKS: Fisher, 9

Washington Redskins

SCORING	Rush	TD Rec	Ret	PAT	FG	S	Pts
Portis	11	0	0	0	0	1	68
Hall	0	0	0	27/27	12/14	0	63
Moss	0	9	0	0	0	0	54
Sellers	1	7	0	0	0	0	48
Cooley	0	7	0	0	0	0	42
Novak	0	0	0	0	5	15	30

RUSHING	No.	Yds	Avg	Lg	TD
Portis	352	1516	4.3	47	11
Betts	89	338	3.8	22	1
Cartwright	27	199	7.4	52	2
Brunell	42	111	2.6	25	0

PASSING	Att	Comp	Pct Comp	Yds	Avg Gain	TD	Int	Rating Pts
Brunell	454	262	57.7	3050	6.72	23	10	85.9
Ramsey	25	15	60.0	279	11.16	1	1	95.3

RECEIVING	No.	Yds	Avg	Lg	TD
Moss	84	1483	17.7	78	9
Cooley	71	774	10.9	32	7
Portis	30	216	7.2	23	0
Patten	22	217	9.9	32	1

INTERCEPTIONS: Marshall, 4

PUNTING	No.	Yds	Avg	Net Avg	TB	In 20	Lg	Blk
Frost	76	3074	40.4	38.3	6	23	55	0

SACKS: Washington, 7.5

First two rounds of the 70th annual NFL Draft, held April 29–30, 2006 in New York City.

First Round

Team	Selection	Position
1. Houston	Mario Williams, North Carolina State	DE
2. New Orleans	Reggie Bush, USC	RB
3. Tennessee	Vince Young, Texas	QB
4. NY Jets	D'Brickashaw Ferguson, Virginia	OT
5. Green Bay	A.J. Hawk, Ohio State	LB
6. San Francisco	Vernon Davis, Maryland	TE
7. Oakland	Michael Huff, Texas	DB
8. Buffalo	Donte Whitner, Ohio State	S
9. Detroit	Ernie Sims, Florida State	LB
10. Arizona	Matt Leinart, USC	QB
11. Denver	Jay Cutler, Vanderbilt	QB
12. Baltimore (from Cleveland)	Haloti Ngata, Oregon	DT
13. Cleveland (from Baltimore)	Kamerion Wimbley, Florida State	OLB
14. Philadelphia	Broderick Bunkley, Florida State	DT
15. St. Louis (from Atlanta through Denver)	Tye Hill, Clemson	CB
16. Miami	Jason Allen, Tennessee	WR
17. Minnesota	Chad Greenway, Iowa	LB
18. Dallas	Bobby Carpenter, Ohio State	LB
19. San Diego	Antonio Cromartie, Florida State	CB
20. Kansas City	Tamba Hali, Penn State	DE
21. New England	Laurence Maroney, Minnesota	RB
22. San Francisco (from Washington through Denver)	Manny Lawson, NC State	DE
23. Tampa Bay	Davin Joseph, Oklahoma	G
24. Cincinnati	Johnathan Joseph, South Carolina	CB
25. Pittsburgh (from NY Giants)	Santonio Holmes, Ohio State	WR
26. Buffalo (from Chicago)	John Mc Cargo, North Carolina State	DT
27. Carolina	DeAngelo Williams, Memphis	RB
28. Jacksonville	Marcedes Lewis, UCLA	TE
29. NY Jets (from Denver through Atlanta)	Nick Mangold, Ohio State	C
30. Indianapolis	Joseph Addai, LSU	RB
31. Seattle	Kelly Jennings, Miami (FL)	CB
32. NY Giants (from Pittsburgh)	Mathias Kiwanuka, Boston College	DE

Second Round

Team	Selection	Position
33. Houston	DeMeco Ryans, Alabama	DE
34. Cleveland	D'Qwell Jackson, Maryland	LB
35. Washington (from NY Jets)	Rocky McIntosh, Miami (FL)	LB
36. New England (from GreenBay)	Chad Jackson, Florida	WR
37. Atlanta (from S.F. through Denver through Green Bay)	Jimmy Williams, Virg. Tech	CB
38. Oakland	Thomas Howard, UTEP	OLB
39. Philadelphia (from Tennessee)	Winston Justice, USC	OT
40. Detroit	Daniel Bullocks, Nebraska	S
41. Arizona	Deuce Lutui, USC	OG
42. Chicago (from Buffalo)	Danieal Manning, Abilene Christian	DB
43. New Orleans (from Cleveland)	Roman Harper, Alabama	S
44. NY Giants (from Baltimore)	Sinorice Moss, Miami (FL)	WR
45. Tennessee (from Philadelphia)	LenDale White, USC	RB
46. St. Louis	Joe Klopfenstein, Colorado	TE
47. Green Bay (from Atlanta)	Daryn Colledge, Boise State	OT
48. Minnesota	Cedric Griffin, Texas	CB
49. NY Jets (from Dallas)	Kellen Clemens, Oregon	QB
50. San Diego	Marcus McNeil, Auburn	OT
51. Minnesota (from Miami)	Ryan Cook, New Mexico	C
52. Green Bay (from New England)	Greg Jenning, Western Michigan	WR
53. Dallas (from Washington through NY Jets)	Anthony Fasano, Notre Dame	TE
54. Kansas City	Bernard Pollard, Purdue	S
55. Cincinnati	Andrew Whitworth, LSU	OT
56. Baltimore (from NY Giants)	Chris Chester, Oklahoma	C/G
57. Chicago	Devin Hester, Miami (FL)	WR
58. Carolina	Richard Marshall, Fresno State	CB
59. Tampa Bay	Jeremy Trueblood, Boston College	OT
60. Jacksonville	Maurice Drew, UCLA	RB
61. Denver	Tony Schieffer, Western Michigan	TE
62. Indianapolis	Tim Jennings, Georgia	CB
63. Seattle	Darryl Tapp, Virginia Tech	DE
64. Minnesota (from Pittsburgh)	Tarvarius Jackson, Alabama State	QB

Final Standings

	W	L	T	Pct	Pts	OP
Amsterdam	7	2	0	.777	238	200
Frankfurt	6	3	0	.666	158	147
Rhein	5	4	0	.555	186	155
Cologne	4	5	0	.444	141	149
Hamburg	2	6	0	.222	160	172
Berlin	2	6	0	.222	167	227

2006 World Bowl

May 27, 2006, in Düsseldorf, Germany

Frankfurt Galaxy	2	0	10	10—22
Amsterdam Admirals	0	7	0	0—7

FIRST QUARTER

Frankfurt: J. Nichols safety 1:55.
Frankfurt 2–0.

SECOND QUARTER

Amsterdam: L. Croom 12 run (R. Killeen kick), 7:32.
Amsterdam 7–0.

THIRD QUARTER

Frankfurt: B. Wallace 4 run (D. Kimball kick) 4:35
Frankfurt 9–7.
Frankfurt: FG D. Kimball 29, 2:08.
Frankfurt 12–7.

FOURTH QUARTER

Frankfurt: FG D. Kimball 37, 8:42.
Frankfurt 15–7.
Frankfurt: J. Niklos 12 run (D. Kimball kick) 0:40.
Frankfurt 22–7.

A: 35,134. T: 3:59.

NFL Europe Individual Leaders

PASSING

	Att	Comp	Pct Comp	Yds	Avg Gain	TD	Pct TD	Int	Pct Int	Lg	Rating Pts
G. Hamdan, Ams	162	102	63.0%	1,629	10.06	12	7.4%	3	1.9	65t	113.4
D. Henson, Rhe	203	109	53.7%	1,321	6.51	10	4.9%	3	1.5	56	84.2
C. Ochs, Fra	142	84	59.2%	1,019	7.18	6	4.2%	4	2.8	49t	83.6
L. Campbell Ber	204	116	56.9%	1,264	6.20	10	4.9%	4	2.0	68	83.5
B. Berlin, Ham	181	99	54.7%	1,041	5.75	7	3.9%	7	3.9	52t	68.4

RECEIVING

RECEPTIONS	No.	Yds	Avg	Lg	TD
S. Fulton, Ams	53	992	18.7	65t	7
S. McCready, Ham	41	486	11.9	35	2
A. Hosack, Fra	36	473	13.1	49t	4
C. Samp, Rhe	32	370	12.5	30t	5
W. Young, Fra	31	395	11.9	34	3

YARDS	Yds	No.	Avg	Lg	TD
S. Fulton, Ams	992	53	18.7	65t	7
S. McCready, Ham	486	41	11.9	35	2
A. Hosack, Fra	473	36	13.1	49t	4
C. Lucas, Ams	440	27	16.3	50t	8
C. Samp, Rhe	400	32	12.5	30t	5

RUSHING

	Att	Yds	Avg	Lg	TD
R. Robinson, Fra	214	1,087	5.1	66t	4
F. Jackson, Rhe	157	731	4.7	80t	2
F. Russell, Col	150	522	3.5	32	3
L. Croom, Ams	106	427	4.0	50	6
M. Johnson, Ber	101	422	4.2	18	2

Other Statistical Leaders

Points (TDs)	C. Lucas, Ams	48
Points (Kicking)	R. Killeen, Ams	71
Yards from Scrimmage	R. Robinson, Fra	1,200
Interceptions	B. Haw, Fra	5
Sacks	J. Nichols, Fra	7
Net Punting Avg	G. Pakulak, Ams	33.6
Punt Return Avg	J. Broussard, Col	9.9
Kickoff Return Avg	N. Curry, Ham	27.9

2005 Canadian Football League

EASTERN DIVISION

	W	L	T	Pts	PF	PA
†Toronto	11	7	0	22	486	387
*Montreal	10	8	0	20	592	519
Ottawa	7	11	0	14	458	578
Hamilton	5	13	0	10	383	583

WESTERN DIVISION

	W	L	T	Pts	PF	PA
†*British Columbia	12	6	0	24	550	444
*Calgary	11	7	0	22	529	443
*Edmonton	11	7	0	22	453	421
*Saskatchewan	9	9	0	18	441	433
Winnipeg	5	13	0	10	474	558

†Clinched division title.

*Clinched playoff berth.

2005 Playoff Results

FIRST ROUND

MONTREAL 30, Saskatchewan 14
Edmonton 33, CALGARY 26

SEMI-FINALS

Montreal 33, TORONTO 17,
Edmonton 28, BRITISH COLUMBIA 23

Home team in caps.

2005 Grey Cup Championship

Nov. 27, 2005, at Vancouver

Edmonton Eskimos	3	7	10	8	10—38
Montreal Alouettes	1	0	17	10	7—35

A: 59,157.

2006 Arena Football League

AMERICAN CENTRAL DIVISION

	W	L	T	PF	PA
†Colorado	11	5	0	903	833
*Nashville	8	8	0	818	799
*Chicago	7	9	0	825	834
Grand Rapids	5	11	0	722	875

AMERICAN WESTERN DIVISION

	W	L	T	PF	PA
†*San Jose	10	6	0	884	849
*Arizona	8	8	0	774	756
*Utah	7	9	0	871	904
Los Angeles	5	11	0	809	906
Las Vegas	5	11	0	769	895

NATIONAL EASTERN DIVISION

	W	L	T	PF	PA
†Dallas	13	3	0	929	710
*New York	10	6	0	848	887
Philadelphia	9	7	0	777	747
Columbus	8	8	0	724	717

NATIONAL SOUTHERN DIVISION

	W	L	T	PF	PA
†*Orlando	10	6	0	816	760
*Austin	10	9	0	816	757
*Georgia	8	8	0	855	735
Tampa Bay	7	9	0	810	862
Kansas City	3	13	0	704	842

†Clinched division title.

*Clinched playoff berth.

2006 AFL Playoff Results

DIVISIONAL ROUND

SAN JOSE 62, Arizona 48
DALLAS 62, Georgia 27
ORLANDO 31, Philadelphia 27
Chicago 63, COLORADO 46

CONFERENCE CHAMPIONSHIPS

Chicago 59, SAN JOSE 56
Orlando 45, DALLAS 28

Home team in caps.

Arena Bowl XX

June 11, 2006 at Las Vegas

Chicago Rush	0	28	6	27—69
Orlando Predators	10	24	14	21—61

FIRST QUARTER

Chi: D'Orazio 1 run (Frantz kick), 12:03 **Chicago 7-0.**
Chi: FG Frantz 23, 1:49. **Chicago 10-0.**

SECOND QUARTER

Orl: Dudley 4 pass from Hamilton (Taylor kick), 14:22. **Chicago 10-7.**
Orl: Dudley 7 pass from Hamilton (Taylor kick), 11:56 **Orlando 14-10.**
Chi: Molden 24 pass from D'Orazio (Frantz kick), 10:38 **Chicago 17-14.**
Orl: Carter 36 run (Taylor kick), 8:39 **Orlando 21-14.**
Chi: Sippio 3 pass from D'Orazio (Frantz kick), 4:39 **Chicago 24-21.**
Orl: Rubin 30 pass from Hamilton (Taylor kick), 14:22. **Orlando 28-24.**
Chi: Sippio 8 pass from D'Orazio (Frantz kick), 0:06 **Chicago 31-28.**
Chi: FG Frantz 51, 0:00. **Chicago 34-28.**

THIRD QUARTER

Chi: D'Orazio 5 run (Frantz kick), 14:31 **Chicago 41-28.**
Chi: Robinson 44 Int return (Frantz kick), 9:07 **Chicago 48-28.**
Orl: Dudley 45 pass from Hamilton (kick failed), 7:58 **Chicago 48-34.**

FOURTH QUARTER

Chi: Sippio 31 pass from D'Orazio (Frantz kick), 13:09 **Chicago 55-34.**
Orl: Fryzel 11 pass from Eaton (Taylor kick), 9:00 **Chicago 55-41.**
Orl: Hamilton 5 run (kick failed), 4:04 **Chicago 55-47.**
Chi: Molden 2 pass from D'Orazio (Frantz kick), 1:58 **Chicago 62-47.**
Orl: Dudley 1 pass from Hamilton (Taylor kick), 0:33. **Chicago 62-54.**
Chi: Alfonzo 15 pass from D'Orazio (Frantz kick), 0:27. **Chicago 69-54.**
Orl: Davidson 29 pass from Hamilton (Taylor kick), 0:13. **Chicago 69-61.**
A: 13,476.

Season-by-Season NFL Final Standings

1920

	W	L	T	Pct	Pts	OP
Akron Pros	6	0	3	.667	95	7
Decatur Staleys	5	1	2	.625	67	14
Buffalo All-Americans	4	1	1	.667	74	19
Rock Island Independents	4	2	1	.571	98	35
Dayton Triangles	4	2	2	.500	127	47
Chicago Cardinals	3	2	1	.500	34	26
Canton Bulldogs	4	3	1	.500	72	44
Cleveland Tigers	1	5	1	.143	22	63
Detroit Heralds	1	3	0	.250	6	61
Chicago Tigers	1	5	1	.143	22	63
Muncie Flyers	0	1	0	.000	0	45
Columbus Panhandles	0	5	0	.000	7	107
Hammond Pros	0	3	0	.000	7	98
Rochester Jeffersons	0	1	0	.000	6	17

1921

	W	L	T	Pct	Pts	OP
Chicago Staleys	9	1	1	.818	128	53
Buffalo All-Americans	9	1	2	.750	211	29
Akron Pros	8	3	1	.667	148	31
Canton Bulldogs	5	2	3	.500	106	55
Rock Island Independents	4	2	1	.571	65	30
Evansville Crimson Giants	3	2	0	.600	89	46
Green Bay Packers	3	2	1	.500	70	55
Chicago Cardinals	3	3	2	.35	54	53
Dayton Triangles	4	4	1	.444	96	67
Rochester Jeffersons	2	3	0	.400	85	76
Cleveland Tigers	3	5	0	.375	95	58
Washington Senators	1	2	0	.333	21	43
Hammond Pros	1	3	1	.200	17	45
Cincinnati Celts	1	3	0	.250	14	117
Minneapolis Marines	1	3	0	.250	37	41
Detroit Tigers	1	5	1	.143	19	109
Columbus Panhandles	1	8	0	.111	47	222
Muncie Flyers	0	2	0	.000	0	28
Louisville Brecks	0	2	0	.000	0	27
Tonawanda Kardex	0	1	0	.000	0	45
New York Giants	0	2	0	.000	0	72

1922

	W	L	T	Pct	Pts	OP
Canton Bulldogs	10	0	2	.833	184	15
Chicago Bears	9	3	0	.750	123	44
Chicago Cardinals	8	3	0	.727	96	50
Toledo Maroons	5	2	2	.556	94	59
Rock Island Independents	4	2	1	.571	154	27
Racine Legion	6	4	1	.545	122	56
Dayton Triangles	4	3	1	.500	80	62
Buffalo All-Americans	5	4	1	.500	87	41
Green Bay Packers	4	3	3	.400	70	54
Akron Pros	3	5	2	.300	146	95
Milwaukee Badgers	2	4	3	.222	51	71
Oorang Indians	3	6	0	.333	69	190
Louisville Brecks	1	3	0	.250	13	140
Minneapolis Marines	1	3	0	.250	19	40
Rochester Jeffersons	0	4	1	.000	13	76
Hammond Pros	0	5	1	.000	0	69
Columbus Panhandles	0	8	0	.000	24	174
Evansville Crimson Giants	0	3	0	.000	6	88

1923

	W	L	T	Pct	Pts	OP
Canton Bulldogs	11	0	1	.917	246	19
Chicago Bears	9	2	1	.750	123	35
Green Bay Packers	7	2	1	.700	85	34
Milwaukee Badgers	7	2	3	.583	100	49
Cleveland Indians	3	1	3	.429	52	49
Chicago Cardinals	7	4	0	.636	139	37
Duluth Kelleys	4	3	0	.571	35	33
Columbus Tigers	5	4	1	.500	119	35
Buffalo All-Americans	5	4	3	.417	94	43
Racine Legion	4	4	2	.400	86	76
Toledo Maroons	3	3	2	.375	35	66
Minneapolis Marines	3	5	1	.333	48	80
Rock Island Independents	2	4	2	.250	83	62
St. Louis All-Stars	1	4	2	.143	14	32
Hammond Pros	1	5	1	.143	14	59
Dayton Triangles	1	6	1	.125	16	95
Akron Pros	1	6	0	.143	25	74
Oorang Indians	1	9	0	.100	24	235
Rochester Jeffersons	0	4	0	.000	6	141
Louisville Brecks	0	3	0	.000	0	90

1924

	W	L	T	Pct	Pts	OP
Duluth Kelleys	5	1	0	.833	56	16
Cleveland Bulldogs	7	1	1	.778	229	60
Frankfort Yellow Jackets	11	2	1	.786	326	109
Rock Island Independents	5	1	2	.625	81	15
Chicago Bears	6	1	4	.545	136	55
Green Bay Packers	7	4	0	.636	108	38
Racine Legion	4	3	3	.400	69	47
Chicago Cardinals	5	4	1	.500	90	67
Buffalo Bisons	6	5	0	.545	120	140
Hammond Pros	2	2	1	.400	18	45
Columbus Tigers	4	4	0	.500	91	68
Milwaukee Badgers	5	8	0	.385	142	188
Akron Pros	2	6	0	.250	59	132
Dayton Triangles	2	6	0	.250	45	148
Kansas City Blues	2	7	0	.222	46	124
Kenosha Maroons	0	4	1	.000	12	117
Canton Bulldogs	0	0	0	.000	0	0
Rochester Jeffersons	0	8	0	.000	14	179
Minneapolis Marines	0	6	0	.000	14	108

1925

	W	L	T	Pct	Pts	OP
Pottsville Maroons	10	2	0	.833	280	45
Chicago Cardinals	11	2	1	.786	230	65
Detroit Panthers	8	2	2	.667	118	42
New York Giants	8	4	0	.667	122	67
Akron Pros	4	2	2	.500	65	51
Frankfort Yellow Jackets	13	8	0	.619	196	189
Chicago Bears	9	5	3	.529	158	96
Green Bay Packers	8	5	0	.615	151	120
Rock Island Independents	5	3	3	.455	99	58
Providence Steam Roller	7	5	1	.538	131	108
Canton Bulldogs	4	4	0	.500	50	73
Cleveland Bulldogs	5	8	1	.357	75	134
Kansas City Cowboys	2	6	1	.222	68	106

1925 (Cont.)

	W	L	T	Pct	Pts	OP
Buffalo Bisons	1	6	2	.111	33	113
Hammond Pros	1	4	0	.200	23	87
Rochester Jeffersons	0	5	1	.000	26	91
Dayton Triangles	0	7	1	.000	3	84
Milwaukee Badgers	0	6	0	.000	7	191
Duluth Kelleys	0	3	0	.000	6	25
Columbus Tigers	0	9	0	.000	28	124

1926

	W	L	T	Pct	Pts	OP
Chicago Bears	12	1	3	.750	216	63
Frankfort Yellow Jackets	13	2	2	.765	223	43
Pottsville Maroons	10	2	2	.714	155	29
Kansas City Cowboys	8	3	0	.727	76	54
Los Angeles Buccaneers	6	3	1	.600	67	57
NY Giants	7	4	1	.583	140	45
Detroit Panthers	6	4	2	.500	115	52
Green Bay Packers	6	4	3	.462	144	68
Duluth Eskimos	6	5	3	.429	114	81
Buffalo Rangers	4	4	2	.400	53	62
Chicago Cardinals	5	6	1	.417	67	86
Providence Steam Roller	5	6	1	.417	94	96
Akron Indians	1	4	3	.125	23	89
Hartford Blues	3	7	0	.300	57	99
Brooklyn Lions	3	8	0	.273	60	150
Dayton Triangles	1	4	1	.167	15	82
Milwaukee Badgers	2	7	0	.222	41	66
Racine Tornadoes	1	4	0	.200	8	92
Canton Bulldogs	1	9	3	.077	46	172
Columbus Tigers	1	6	0	.143	26	93
Louisville Colonels	0	4	0	.000	0	108
Hammond Pros	0	4	0	.000	3	56

1927

	W	L	T	Pct	Pts	OP
NY Giants	11	1	1	.846	197	20
Green Bay Packers	7	2	1	.700	113	43
Chicago Bears	9	3	2	.643	149	98
Cleveland Bulldogs	8	4	1	.615	209	107
Providence Steam Roller	8	5	1	.571	105	88
New York Yankees	7	8	1	.438	142	174
Frankfort Yellow Jackets	6	9	3	.333	152	166
Pottsville Maroons	5	8	0	.385	80	163
Chicago Cardinals	3	7	1	.273	69	134
Dayton Triangles	1	6	1	.125	15	57
Duluth Eskimos	1	8	0	.111	68	134
Buffalo Bisons	0	5	0	.000	8	123

1928

	W	L	T	Pct	Pts	OP
Providence Steam Roller	9	1	1	.818	128	36
Detroit Wolverines	7	2	1	.700	189	76
Frankfort Yellow Jackets	11	4	1	.688	169	84
Green Bay	6	4	3	.462	120	92
Chicago Bears	7	5	1	.538	182	85
NY Giants	4	7	2	.308	79	137
NY Yankees	4	8	1	.308	104	179
Pottsville Maroons	2	8	0	.200	74	134
Chicago Cardinals	1	5	0	.167	7	107
Dayton Triangles	0	7	0	.000	9	131

1929

	W	L	T	Pct	Pts	OP
Green Bay Packers	12	0	1	.923	198	22
NY Giants	13	1	1	.867	312	86
Frankfort Yellow Jackets	10	4	5	.526	139	128
Chicago Cardinals	6	6	1	.462	154	83
Boston Bulldogs	4	4	0	.500	98	73
Staten Island Stapletons	3	3	4	.300	89	62
Providence Steam Roller	4	6	2	.333	107	117
Orange Tornadoes	2	5	5	.167	32	90
Chicago Bears	4	9	2	.267	119	227
Buffalo Bisons	1	7	1	.111	48	142
Minneapolis Red Jackets	1	9	0	.100	48	185
Dayton Triangles	0	6	0	.000	7	136

1930

	W	L	T	Pct	Pts	OP
NY Giants	13	4	0	.765	308	98
Green Bay Packers	10	3	1	.714	234	111
Chicago Bears	9	4	1	.643	169	71
Brooklyn Dodgers	7	4	1	.583	154	59
Providence Steam Roller	6	4	1	.545	90	125
Staten Island Stapletons	5	5	2	.417	95	112
Portsmouth Spartans	5	6	3	.357	176	161
Chicago Cardinals	5	6	2	.385	128	132
Frankfort Yellow Jackets	4	13	1	.222	113	321
Minneapolis Red Jackets	1	7	1	.111	27	165
Newark Tornadoes	1	10	1	.083	51	190

1931

	W	L	T	Pct	Pts	OP
Green Bay Packers	13	2	0	.867	318	94
Portsmouth Spartans	10	3	0	.769	161	77
Chicago Bears	8	5	0	.615	145	92
Chicago Cardinals	5	4	0	.556	120	128
NY Giants	7	7	1	.467	161	127
Providence Steam Roller	4	4	3	.364	78	127
Staten Island Stapletons	4	6	1	.364	79	118
Frankfort Yellow Jackets	1	5	1	.143	13	85
Cleveland Indians	2	8	0	.200	45	137
Brooklyn Dodgers	2	12	0	.143	64	199

1932

	W	L	T	Pct	Pts	OP
Green Bay Packers	10	3	1	.714	152	63
Chicago Bears	7	1	6	.500	160	44
Portsmouth Spartans	6	2	4	.500	116	71
Boston Braves	4	4	2	.400	55	79
NY Giants	4	6	2	.333	93	113
Chiago Cardinals	2	6	2	.200	72	114
Staten Island Stapletons	2	7	3	.167	77	173
Brooklyn Dodgers	3	9	0	.250	63	131

1933

EAST

	W	L	T	Pct	Pts	OP
NY Giants	11	3	0	.786	244	101
Brooklyn Dodgers	5	4	1	.500	93	54
Boston Redskins	5	5	2	.417	103	97
Philadelphia Eagles	3	5	1	.333	77	158
Pittsburgh Pirates	3	6	2	.273	67	208

1933 (Cont.)

WEST

	W	L	T	Pct	Pts	OP
Chicago Bears	10	2	1	.769	133	82
Portsmouth Spartans	6	5	0	.545	128	87
Green Bay Packers	5	7	1	.385	170	107
Cincinnati Reds	3	6	1	.300	38	110
Chicago Cardinals	1	9	1	.091	52	101

1934

EAST

	W	L	T	Pct	Pts	OP
NY Giants	8	5	0	.615	147	107
Boston Redskins	6	6	0	.500	107	94
Brooklyn Dodgers	4	7	0	.364	60	153
Philadelphia Eagles	4	7	0	.364	127	85
Pittsburgh Pirates	2	10	0	.167	51	206

WEST

	W	L	T	Pct	Pts	OP
Chicago Bears	13	0	0	1.000	286	86
Detroit Lions	10	3	0	.769	238	59
Green Bay Packers	7	6	0	.538	156	112
Chicago Cardinals	5	6	0	.455	80	84
St. Louis Gunners	1	2	0	.333	27	61
Cincinnati Reds	0	8	0	.000	10	243

1935

EAST

	W	L	T	Pct	Pts	OP
NY Giants	9	3	0	.750	180	96
Brooklyn Dodgers	5	6	1	.417	90	141
Pittsburgh Pirates	4	8	0	.333	99	209
Boston Redskins	2	8	1	.182	65	122
Philadelphia Eagles	2	9	0	.182	60	179

WEST

	W	L	T	Pct	Pts	OP
Green Bay Packers	8	4	0	.667	181	96
Detroit Lions	7	3	2	.583	191	111
Chicago Cardinals	6	4	2	.500	99	97
Chicago Bears	6	4	2	.500	192	106

1936

EAST

	W	L	T	Pct	Pts	OP
Boston Redskins	7	5	0	.583	149	110
Pittsburgh Pirates	6	6	0	.500	98	187
NY Giants	5	6	1	.417	115	163
Brooklyn Dodgers	3	8	1	.250	92	161
Philadelphia Eagles	1	11	0	.083	51	206

WEST

	W	L	T	Pct	Pts	OP
Green Bay	10	1	1	.833	248	118
Chicago Bears	9	3	0	.750	222	94
Detroit Lions	8	4	0	.667	235	102
Chicago Cardinals	3	8	1	.250	74	143

1937

EAST

	W	L	T	Pct	Pts	OP
Washington Redskins	8	3	0	.727	195	120
NY Giants	6	3	2	.545	128	109
Pittsburgh Pirates	4	7	0	.364	122	145
Brooklyn Dodgers	3	7	1	.273	82	174
Philadelphia Eagles	2	8	1	.182	86	177

WEST

	W	L	T	Pct	Pts	OP
Chicago Bears	9	1	1	.818	201	100
Green Bay Packers	7	4	0	.636	220	122
Detroit Lions	7	4	0	.636	180	105
Chicago Cardinals	5	5	1	.455	135	165
Cleveland Rams	1	10	0	.091	75	207

1938

EAST

	W	L	T	Pct	Pts	OP
NY Giants	8	2	1	.727	194	79
Washington Redskins	6	3	2	.545	148	154
Brooklyn Dodgers	4	4	3	.364	131	161
Philadelphia Eagles	5	6	0	.455	154	164
Pittsburgh Pirates	2	9	0	.182	79	169

WEST

	W	L	T	Pct	Pts	OP
Green Bay Packers	8	3	0	.727	223	118
Detroit Lions	7	4	0	.636	119	108
Chicago Bears	6	5	0	.545	194	148
Cleveland Rams	4	7	0	.364	131	215
Chicago Cardinals	2	9	0	.182	111	168

1939

EAST

	W	L	T	Pct	Pts	OP
NY Giants	9	1	1	.818	168	85
Washington Redskins	8	2	1	.727	242	94
Brooklyn Dodgers	4	6	1	.364	108	219
Philadelphia Eagles	1	9	1	.091	105	200
Pittsburgh Pirates	1	9	1	.091	114	216

WEST

	W	L	T	Pct	Pts	OP
Green Bay Packers	9	2	0	.818	233	153
Chicago Bears	8	3	0	.727	298	157
Detroit Lions	6	5	0	.545	145	150
Cleveland Rams	5	5	1	.455	195	164
Chicago Cardinals	1	10	0	.091	84	254

1940

EAST

	W	L	T	Pct	Pts	OP
Washington Redskins	9	2	0	.818	245	142
Brooklyn Dodgers	8	2	0	.800	179	110
NY Giants	6	4	1	.545	131	133
Pittsburgh Pirates	2	7	2	.182	67	174
Philadelphia Eagles	1	10	0	.091	121	200

1940 (Cont.)

WEST

	W	L	T	Pct	Pts	OP
Chicago Bears	8	3	0	.727	238	152
Green Bay	6	4	1	.545	238	155
Detroit	5	5	1	.455	120	177
Cleveland Rams	4	6	1	.364	181	191
Chicago Cardinals	2	7	2	.182	139	222

1941

EAST

	W	L	T	Pct	Pts	OP
NY Giants	8	3	0	.727	238	114
Brooklyn Dodgers	7	4	0	.636	158	127
Washington	6	5	0	.545	176	174
Philadelphia	2	8	1	.182	119	218
Pittsburgh Steelers	1	9	1	.091	103	276

WEST

	W	L	T	Pct	Pts	OP
Green Bay	10	1	0	.909	258	120
Chicago Bears	10	1	0	.909	396	147
Detroit	4	6	1	.364	121	195
Chicago Cardinals	3	7	1	.273	127	197
Cleveland Rams	2	9	0	.182	116	244

1942

EAST

	W	L	T	Pct	Pts	OP
Washington	10	1	0	.909	227	102
Pittsburgh Steelers	7	4	0	.636	167	119
NY Giants	5	5	1	.455	155	139
Brooklyn Dodgers	3	8	0	.273	100	168
Philadelphia	2	9	0	.182	134	239

WEST

	W	L	T	Pct	Pts	OP
Chicago Bears	11	0	0	1.000	376	84
Green Bay	8	2	1	.727	300	215
Cleveland Rams	5	6	0	.455	150	207
Chicago Cardinals	3	8	0	.273	98	209
Detroit	0	11	0	.000	38	263

1943

EAST

	W	L	T	Pct	Pts	OP
Washington	6	3	1	.600	229	137
NY Giants	6	3	1	.600	197	170
Phi/Pitt Eagles/Steelers	5	4	1	.500	225	230
Brooklyn Dodgers	2	8	0	.200	65	234

WEST

	W	L	T	Pct	Pts	OP
Chicago Bears	8	1	1	.800	303	157
Green Bay	7	2	1	.700	264	172
Detroit	3	6	1	.300	178	218
Chicago Cardinals	0	10	0	.000	95	238

1944

EAST

	W	L	T	Pct	Pts	OP
NY Giants	8	1	1	.800	206	75
Philadelphia	7	1	2	.700	267	131
Washington	6	3	1	.600	169	180
Boston Yanks	2	8	0	.200	82	233
Brooklyn Tigers	0	10	0	.000	69	166

WEST

	W	L	T	Pct	Pts	OP
Green Bay	8	2	0	.800	238	141
Chicago Bears	6	3	1	.600	258	172
Detroit	6	3	1	.600	216	151
Cleveland Rams	4	6	0	.400	188	224
Chi/Pitt Cards/Steelers	0	10	0	.000	116	336

1945

EAST

	W	L	T	Pct	Pts	OP
Washington	8	2	0	.800	209	121
Philadelphia	7	3	0	.700	272	133
NY Giants	3	6	1	.300	179	198
Bos/Bkn Yanks/Tigers	3	6	1	.300	123	211
Pittsburgh	2	8	0	.200	79	220

WEST

	W	L	T	Pct	Pts	OP
Cleveland Rams	9	1	0	.900	244	136
Detroit	7	3	0	.700	195	194
Green Bay	6	4	0	.600	258	173
Chicago Bears	3	7	0	.300	192	235
Chicago Cardinals	1	9	0	.100	98	228

1946

EAST

	W	L	T	Pct	Pts	OP
NY Giants	7	3	1	.636	236	162
Philadelphia	6	5	0	.545	231	220
Washington	5	5	1	.455	171	191
Pittsburgh	5	5	1	.455	136	117
Boston Yanks	2	8	1	.182	189	273

WEST

	W	L	T	Pct	Pts	OP
Chicago Bears	8	2	1	.727	289	193
Los Angeles Rams	6	4	1	.545	277	257
Chicago Cardinals	6	5	0	.545	260	198
Green Bay	6	5	0	.545	148	158
Detroit	1	10	0	.091	142	310

1947

EAST

	W	L	T	Pct	Pts	OP
Pittsburgh	8	4	0	.667	240	259
Philadelphia	8	4	0	.667	308	242
Boston Yanks	4	7	1	.333	168	256
Washington	4	8	0	.333	295	367
NY Giants	2	8	2	.167	190	309

1947 (Cont.)

WEST

	W	L	T	Pct	Pts	OP
Chicago Cardinals	9	3	0	.750	306	231
Chicago Bears	8	4	0	.667	363	241
Green Bay	6	5	1	.500	274	210
LA Rams	6	6	0	.500	259	214
Detroit Lions	3	9	0	.250	231	305

1948

EAST

	W	L	T	Pct	Pts	OP
Philadelphia	9	2	1	.750	376	156
Washington	7	5	0	.583	291	287
Pittsburgh	4	8	0	.333	200	243
NY Giants	4	8	0	.333	297	388
Boston Yanks	3	9	0	.250	174	372

WEST

	W	L	T	Pct	Pts	OP
Chicago Cardinals	11	1	0	.917	395	226
Chicago Bears	10	2	0	.833	375	151
LA Rams	6	5	1	.500	327	269
Green Bay	3	9	0	.250	154	290
Detroit Lions	2	10	0	.167	200	407

1949

EAST

	W	L	T	Pct	Pts	OP
Philadelphia	11	1	0	.917	364	134
Pittsburgh	6	5	1	.500	224	214
NY Giants	6	6	0	.500	287	298
Washington	4	7	1	.333	268	339
New York Bulldogs	1	10	1	.083	153	368

WEST

	W	L	T	Pct	Pts	OP
LA Rams	8	2	2	.667	360	239
Chicago Bears	9	3	0	.750	332	218
Chicago Cardinals	6	5	1	.500	360	301
Detroit Lions	4	8	0	.333	237	259
Green Bay	2	10	0	.167	114	329

1950

EAST

	W	L	T	Pct	Pts	OP
Cleveland Browns	10	2	0	.833	310	144
NY Giants	10	2	0	.8333	268	150
Philadelphia	6	6	0	.500	254	141
Pittsburgh	6	6	0	.500	180	195
Chicago Cardinals	5	7	0	.417	233	287
Washington	3	9	0	.250	232	326

WEST

	W	L	T	Pct	Pts	OP
Chicago Bears	9	3	0	.750	279	207
LA Rams	9	3	0	.750	466	309
New York Yanks	7	5	0	.583	366	367
Detroit	6	6	0	.500	321	285
San Francisco 49ers	3	9	0	.250	213	300
Green Bay	3	9	0	.250	244	406
Baltimore Colts	1	11	0	.067	213	462

1951

AMERICAN

	W	L	T	Pct	Pts	OP
Cleveland	11	1	0	.917	331	152
NY Giants	9	2	1	.750	254	161
Washington	5	7	0	.417	183	296
Pittsburgh	4	7	1	.333	183	235
Philadelphia	4	8	0	.333	234	264
Chicago Cardinals	3	9	0	.250	210	287

NATIONAL

	W	L	T	Pct	Pts	OP
LA Rams	8	4	0	.667	392	261
Detroit Lions	7	4	1	.583	336	259
San Francisco 49ers	7	4	1	.583	255	205
Chicago Bears	7	5	0	.583	286	282
Green Bay	3	9	0	.250	254	375
New York Yanks	1	9	2	.083	241	382

1952

AMERICAN

	W	L	T	Pct	Pts	OP
Cleveland	8	4	0	.667	310	213
Philadelphia	7	5	0	.583	252	271
NY Giants	7	5	0	.583	234	231
Pittsburgh	5	7	0	.417	300	273
Washington	4	8	0	.333	240	287
Chicago Cardinals	4	8	0	.333	172	221

NATIONAL

	W	L	T	Pct	Pts	OP
Detroit	9	3	0	.750	344	192
LA Rams	9	3	0	.750	349	234
San Francisco	7	5	0	.583	285	221
Green Bay	6	6	0	.500	295	312
Chicago Bears	5	7	0	.417	245	326
Dallas Texans	1	11	0	.083	182	427

1953

EAST

	W	L	T	Pct	Pts	OP
Cleveland	11	1	0	.917	348	162
Philadelphia	7	4	1	.583	352	215
Washington	6	5	1	.500	208	215
Pittsburgh	5	7	0	.417	211	272
NY Giants	4	8	0	.333	188	277
Chicago Cardinals	1	10	1	.083	190	337

WEST

	W	L	T	Pct	Pts	OP
Detroit	10	2	0	.833	271	205
San Francisco	9	3	0	.750	372	237
LA Rams	8	3	1	.667	366	236
Chicago Bears	3	8	1	.250	218	262
Baltimore Colts	3	9	0	.250	182	350
Green Bay	2	9	1	.167	200	338

1954

EAST

	W	L	T	Pct	Pts	OP
Cleveland	9	3	0	.750	336	162
Philadelphia	7	4	1	.583	284	230
NY Giants	7	5	0	.583	293	184
Pittsburgh	5	7	0	.417	219	263
Washington	3	9	0	.250	207	432
Chicago Cardinals	2	10	0	.167	183	347

WEST

	W	L	T	Pct	Pts	OP
Detroit	9	2	1	.750	337	189
Chicago Bears	8	4	0	.667	301	279
San Francisco	7	4	1	.583	313	251
LA Rams	6	5	1	.500	314	285
Green Bay	4	8	0	.333	234	251
Baltimore	3	9	0	.250	131	279

1955

EAST

	W	L	T	Pct	Pts	OP
Cleveland	9	2	1	.750	349	218
Washington	8	4	0	.667	246	222
NY Giants	6	5	1	.500	267	223
Philadelphia	4	7	1	.333	248	231
Chicago Cardinals	4	7	1	.333	224	252
Pittsburgh	4	8	0	.333	195	285

WEST

	W	L	T	Pct	Pts	OP
LA Rams	8	3	1	.667	260	231
Chicago Bears	8	4	0	.667	294	251
Green Bay	6	6	0	.500	258	276
Baltimore	5	6	1	.417	214	239
San Francisco	4	8	0	.333	216	298
Detroit	3	9	0	.250	230	275

1956

EAST

	W	L	T	Pct	Pts	OP
NY Giants	8	3	1	.667	264	197
Chicago Cardinals	7	5	0	.583	240	182
Washington	6	6	0	.500	183	225
Pittsburgh	5	7	0	.417	217	250
Cleveland	5	7	0	.417	167	177
Philadelphia	3	8	1	.250	143	215

WEST

	W	L	T	Pct	Pts	OP
Chicago Bears	9	2	1	.750	269	169
Detroit	9	3	0	.750	300	188
San Francisco	5	6	1	.417	233	284
Baltimore	5	7	0	.417	270	322
Green Bay	4	8	0	.333	264	342
LA Rams	4	8	0	.333	291	307

1957

EAST

	W	L	T	Pct	Pts	OP
Cleveland	9	2	1	.750	269	169
NY Giants	7	5	0	.583	251	211
Pittsburgh	6	6	0	.500	155	178
Washington	5	6	1	.417	251	230
Philadelphia	4	8	0	.333	173	224
Chicago Cardinals	3	9	0	.250	200	299

WEST

	W	L	T	Pct	Pts	OP
San Francisco	8	4	0	.667	260	264
Detroit	8	4	0	.667	251	231
Baltimore	7	5	0	.583	303	235
LA Rams	6	6	0	.500	307	278
Chicago Bears	5	7	0	.417	203	211
Green Bay	3	9	0	.250	218	311

1958

EAST

	W	L	T	Pct	Pts	OP
Cleveland	9	3	0	.750	302	217
NY Giants	9	3	0	.750	246	183
Pittsburgh	7	4	1	.583	261	230
Washington	4	7	1	.333	214	268
Chicago Cardinals	2	9	1	.167	261	356
Philadelphia	2	9	1	.167	235	306

WEST

	W	L	T	Pct	Pts	OP
Baltimore	9	3	0	.750	381	203
LA Rams	8	4	0	.667	344	278
Chicago Bears	8	4	0	.667	298	230
San Francisco	6	6	0	.500	257	324
Detroit	4	7	1	.333	261	276
Green Bay	1	10	1	.083	193	382

1959

EAST

	W	L	T	Pct	Pts	OP
NY Giants	10	2	0	.833	284	167
Philadelphia	7	5	0	.583	268	278
Cleveland	7	5	0	.583	270	214
Pittsburgh	6	5	1	.500	257	216
Washington	3	9	0	.250	185	350
Chicago Cardinals	2	10	0	.167	231	324

WEST

	W	L	T	Pct	Pts	OP
Baltimore	9	3	0	.750	374	251
Chicago Bears	8	4	0	.667	246	196
Green Bay	7	5	0	.583	248	240
San Francisco	7	5	0	.583	255	237
Detroit	3	8	1	.250	203	275
LA Rams	2	10	0	.167	242	315

1960

NFL EAST

	W	L	T	Pct	Pts	OP
Philadelphia	10	2	0	.833	321	246
Cleveland	8	3	1	.667	362	217
NY Giants	6	4	2	.500	271	261
St. Louis Cardinals	6	5	1	.500	288	230
Pittsburgh	5	6	1	.417	240	275
Washington	1	9	2	.083	178	309

NFL WEST

	W	L	T	Pct	Pts	OP
Green Bay	8	4	0	.667	332	209
Detroit	7	5	0	.583	239	212
San Francisco	7	5	0	.583	208	205
Baltimore	6	6	0	.500	288	234
Chicago Bears	5	6	1	.417	194	299
LA Rams	4	7	1	.333	265	297
Dallas Cowboys	0	11	1	.000	177	369

AFL EAST

	W	L	T	Pct	Pts	OP
Houston Oilers	10	4	0	.714	379	285
NY Titans	7	7	0	.500	382	399
Buffalo Bills	5	8	1	.357	296	303
Boston Patriots	5	9	0	.357	286	349

AFL WEST

	W	L	T	Pct	Pts	OP
Los Angeles Chargers	10	4	0	.714	373	336
Dallas Texans	8	6	0	.571	361	253
Oakland Raiders	6	8	0	.429	319	388
Denver Broncos	4	9	1	.286	309	393

1961

NFL EAST

	W	L	T	Pct	Pts	OP
NY Giants	10	3	1	.714	368	220
Philadelphia	10	4	0	.714	361	297
Cleveland	8	5	1	.571	319	270
St. Louis Cardinals	7	7	0	.500	279	267
Pittsburgh	6	8	0	.429	295	287
Dallas Cowboys	4	9	1	.286	236	380
Washington	1	12	1	.071	174	392

NFL WEST

	W	L	T	Pct	Pts	OP
Green Bay	11	3	0	.786	391	223
Detroit	8	5	1	.571	270	258
Baltimore	8	6	0	.571	302	307
Chicago	8	6	0	.571	326	302
San Francisco	7	6	1	.500	346	272
LA Rams	4	10	0	.286	263	407
Minnesota Vikings	3	11	0	.214	285	407

AFL EAST

	W	L	T	Pct	Pts	OP
Houston Oilers	10	3	1	.714	513	242
Boston Patriots	9	4	1	.643	413	313
New York Titans	7	7	0	.500	301	390
Buffalo Bills	6	8	0	.429	294	342

1961 (Cont.)

AFL WEST

	W	L	T	Pct	Pts	OP
San Diego Chargers	12	2	0	.857	396	219
Dallas Texans	6	8	0	.429	334	343
Denver	3	11	0	.214	251	432
Oakland	2	12	0	.143	237	458

1962

NFL EAST

	W	L	T	Pct	Pts	OP
NY Giants	12	2	0	.857	398	283
Pittsburgh	9	5	0	.642	312	363
Cleveland	7	6	1	.500	291	257
Washington	5	7	2	.357	305	376
Dallas Cowboys	5	8	1	.357	398	402
St. Louis Cardinals	4	9	1	.286	287	361
Philadelphia	3	10	1	.214	282	356

NFL WEST

	W	L	T	Pct	Pts	OP
Green Bay	13	1	0	.929	415	148
Detroit	11	3	0	.786	315	177
Chicago	9	5	0	.643	321	287
Baltimore	7	7	0	.500	293	288
San Francisco	6	8	0	.429	282	331
Minnesota	2	11	1	.143	254	410
LA Rams	1	12	1	.071	220	334

AFL EAST

	W	L	T	Pct	Pts	OP
Houston	11	3	0	.786	387	270
Boston	9	4	1	.643	346	295
Buffalo	7	6	1	.500	309	272
NY Titans	5	9	0	.357	278	423

AFL WEST

	W	L	T	Pct	Pts	OP
Dallas Texans	11	3	0	.786	389	233
Denver	6	7	0	.462	323	313
San Diego	4	9	0	.308	293	362
Oakland	1	13	0	.071	213	370

1963

NFL EAST

	W	L	T	Pct	Pts	OP
NY Giants	11	3	0	.786	448	280
Cleveland	10	4	0	.714	343	262
St. Louis	9	5	0	.643	341	283
Pittsburgh	7	4	3	.500	321	295
Dallas Cowboys	4	10	0	.286	305	378
Philadelphia	2	10	2	.143	242	381
Washington	3	11	0	.214	279	398

NFL WEST

	W	L	T	Pct	Pts	OP
Chicago	11	1	2	.786	301	144
Green Bay	11	2	1	.786	369	206
Baltimore	8	6	0	.571	316	285
Minnesota	5	8	1	.357	309	390
Detroit	5	8	1	.357	32	265
LA Rams	5	9	0	.357	210	350
San Francisco	2	12	0	.143	198	391

1963 (Cont.)

AFL EAST

	W	L	T	Pct	Pts	OP
Buffalo	7	6	1	.500	304	291
Boston	7	6	1	.500	327	257
Houston	6	8	0	.429	302	372
NY Jets	5	8	1	.357	249	399

AFL WEST

	W	L	T	Pct	Pts	OP
San Diego	11	3	0	.786	399	255
Oakland	10	4	0	.714	363	282
Kansas City Chiefs	5	7	2	.357	347	263
Denver	2	11	1	.143	301	473

1964

NFL EAST

	W	L	T	Pct	Pts	OP
Cleveland	10	3	1	.786	415	293
St. Louis	9	3	2	.643	357	331
Philadelphia	6	8	0	.429	312	313
Washington	6	8	0	.429	307	305
Dallas	5	8	1	.357	250	289
Pittsburgh	5	9	0	.357	253	315
NY Giants	2	10	2	.143	241	399

NFL WEST

	W	L	T	Pct	Pts	OP
Baltimore	12	2	0	.857	428	225
Minnesota	8	5	1	.571	355	296
Green Bay	8	5	1	.571	342	245
Detroit	7	5	2	.500	280	260
LA Rams	5	7	2	.357	283	339
Chicago	5	9	0	.357	260	379
San Francisco	4	10	0	.286	236	330

AFL EAST

	W	L	T	Pct	Pts	OP
Buffalo	12	2	0	.857	400	242
Boston	10	3	1	.714	365	297
NY Jets	5	8	1	.357	278	315
Houston	4	10	0	.286	310	355

AFL WEST

	W	L	T	Pct	Pts	OP
San Diego	8	5	1	.571	341	300
Kansas City Chiefs	7	7	0	.500	366	306
Oakland	5	7	2	.357	303	350
Denver	2	11	1	.143	240	438

1965

NFL EAST

	W	L	T	Pct	Pts	OP
Cleveland	11	3	0	.786	363	325
NY Giants	7	7	0	.500	270	338
Dallas	7	7	0	.500	325	280
Washington	6	8	0	.429	257	301
St. Louis	5	9	0	.357	296	309
Philadelphia	5	9	0	.357	363	359
Pittsburgh	2	12	0	.143	202	397

1965 (Cont.)

NFL WEST

	W	L	T	Pct	Pts	OP
Green Bay	10	3	1	.714	316	224
Baltimore	9	3	1	.692	348	263
Chicago	9	5	0	.643	409	275
Minnesota	7	6	0	.538	362	362
San Francisco	7	6	1	.500	421	402
Detroit	6	7	1	.429	257	295
LA Rams	4	10	0	.286	269	328

AFL EAST

	W	L	T	Pct	Pts	OP
Buffalo	10	3	1	.714	313	226
NY Jets	5	8	1	.357	285	303
Boston	4	8	2	.286	244	302
Houston	4	10	0	.286	298	429

AFL WEST

	W	L	T	Pct	Pts	OP
San Diego	9	2	3	.643	340	227
Oakland	8	5	1	.571	298	239
Kansas City	7	5	2	.500	322	285
Denver	4	10	0	.286	303	392

1966

NFL EAST

	W	L	T	Pct	Pts	OP
Dallas	10	3	1	.714	445	239
Cleveland	9	5	0	.643	403	259
Philadelphia	9	5	0	.643	326	340
St. Louis	8	5	1	.571	264	265
Washington	7	7	0	.500	351	355
Pittsburgh	5	8	1	.357	316	347
Atlanta Falcons	3	11	0	.214	204	437
NY Giants	1	12	1	.071	263	501

NFL WEST

	W	L	T	Pct	Pts	OP
Green Bay	12	2	0	.857	335	163
Baltimore	9	5	0	.643	314	226
LA Rams	8	6	0	.571	289	212
San Francisco	6	6	2	.429	320	325
Chicago	5	7	2	.357	234	272
Detroit	4	9	1	.286	206	317
Minnesota	4	9	1	.286	292	304

AFL EAST

	W	L	T	Pct	Pts	OP
Buffalo	9	4	1	.643	358	255
Boston	8	4	2	.571	315	283
NY Jets	6	6	2	.429	322	312
Houston	3	11	0	.214	335	396
Miami Dolphins	3	11	0	.214	213	362

AFL WEST

	W	L	T	Pct	Pts	OP
Kansas City	11	2	1	.786	448	276
Oakland	8	5	1	.571	315	288
San Diego	7	6	1	.500	335	284
Denver	4	10	0	.286	196	381

1967

NFL CENTURY

	W	L	T	Pct	Pts	OP
Cleveland	9	5	0	.643	334	297
NY Giants	7	7	0	.500	369	379
St. Louis	6	7	1	.429	333	356
Pittsburgh	4	9	1	.283	281	320

NFL COASTAL

	W	L	T	Pct	Pts	OP
LA Rams	11	1	2	.786	398	196
Baltimore	11	1	2	.786	394	198
San Francisco	7	7	0	.500	273	337
Atlanta	1	12	1	.071	175	422

NFL CAPITAL

	W	L	T	Pct	Pts	OP
Dallas	9	5	0	.643	342	268
Philadelphia	6	7	1	.429	351	409
Washington	5	6	3	.359	347	353
New Orleans Saints	3	11	0	.214	233	379

NFL CENTRAL

	W	L	T	Pct	Pts	OP
Green Bay	9	4	1	.643	332	209
Chicago	7	6	1	.500	239	218
Detroit	5	7	2	.357	260	259
Minnesota	3	8	3	.214	233	294

AFL EAST

	W	L	T	Pct	Pts	OP
Houston	9	4	1	.643	258	199
NY Jets	8	5	1	.571	371	329
Buffalo	4	10	0	.286	237	285
Miami	4	10	0	.286	219	407
Boston	3	10	1	.214	280	389

AFL WEST

	W	L	T	Pct	Pts	OP
Oakland	13	1	0	.929	468	233
Kansas City	9	5	0	.643	408	254
San Diego	8	5	1	.571	360	352
Denver	3	11	0	.214	256	409

1968

NFL CENTURY

	W	L	T	Pct	Pts	OP
Cleveland	10	4	0	.714	394	273
St. Louis	9	4	1	.643	325	289
New Orleans	4	9	1	.286	246	327
Pittsburgh	2	11	1	.143	244	397

NFL COASTAL

	W	L	T	Pct	Pts	OP
Baltimore	13	1	0	.929	402	144
LA Rams	10	3	1	.714	312	200
San Francisco	7	6	1	.500	303	310
Atlanta	2	12	0	.143	202	351

1968 (Cont.)

NFL CAPITAL

	W	L	T	Pct	Pts	OP
Dallas	12	2	0	.857	431	186
NY Giants	7	7	0	.500	294	325
Washington	5	9	0	.357	249	358
Philadelphia	2	12	0	.143	202	351

NFL CENTRAL

	W	L	T	Pct	Pts	OP
Minnesota	8	6	0	.571	282	242
Chicago	7	7	0	.500	250	333
Green Bay	6	7	1	.429	281	227
Detroit	4	8	2	.286	207	241

AFL EAST

	W	L	T	Pct	Pts	OP
NY Jets	11	3	0	.786	419	280
Houston	7	7	0	.500	303	248
Miami	5	8	1	.357	276	355
Boston	4	10	0	.286	229	406
Buffalo	1	12	1	.071	199	367

AFL WEST

	W	L	T	Pct	Pts	OP
Oakland	12	2	0	.857	453	233
Kansas City	12	2	0	.857	371	170
San Diego	9	5	0	.643	382	310
Denver	5	9	0	.357	255	404
Cincinnati Bengals	3	11	0	.214	215	329

1969

NFL CENTURY

	W	L	T	Pct	Pts	OP
Cleveland	10	3	1	.714	351	300
NY Giants	6	8	0	.429	264	298
St. Louis	4	9	1	.286	314	389
Pittsburgh	1	13	0	.071	218	404

NFL COASTAL

	W	L	T	Pct	Pts	OP
LA Rams	11	3	0	.786	320	243
Baltimore	7	5	2	.500	307	319
Atlanta	6	8	0	.429	276	268
San Francisco	4	8	2	.286	277	319

NFL CAPITAL

	W	L	T	Pct	Pts	OP
Dallas	11	2	1	.786	369	223
Washington	7	5	2	.500	307	319
New Orleans	5	9	0	.357	311	393
Philadelphia	4	9	1	.286	279	377

NFL CENTRAL

	W	L	T	Pct	Pts	OP
Minnesota	12	2	0	.857	379	133
Detroit	9	4	1	.643	259	188
Green Bay	8	6	0	.571	269	221
Chicago	1	13	0	.071	210	339

1969 (Cont.)

AFL EAST

	W	L	T	Pct	Pts	OP
NY Jets	10	4	0	.714	353	269
Houston	6	6	2	.429	278	279
Buffalo	4	10	0	.286	230	359
Boston	4	10	0	.286	266	316
Miami	3	10	1	.214	233	332

AFL WEST

	W	L	T	Pct	Pts	OP
Oakland	12	1	1	.857	377	242
Kansas City	11	3	0	.786	359	177
San Diego	8	6	0	.571	288	276
Denver	5	8	1	.357	297	344
Cincinnati	4	9	1	.286	280	367

1970

AFC EAST

	W	L	T	Pct	Pts	OP
Baltimore	11	2	1	.786	321	234
Miami	10	4	0	.714	297	228
NY Jets	4	10	0	.286	255	286
Buffalo	3	10	1	.214	204	337
Boston	2	12	0	.143	149	361

AFC CENTRAL

	W	L	T	Pct	Pts	OP
Cincinnati	8	6	0	.571	312	255
Cleveland	7	7	0	.500	286	265
Pittsburgh	5	9	0	.357	210	272
Houston	3	10	1	.214	217	352

AFC WEST

	W	L	T	Pct	Pts	OP
Oakland	8	4	2	.571	300	293
Kansas City	7	5	2	.500	272	244
San Diego	5	6	3	.357	282	278
Denver	5	8	1	.357	253	264

NFC EAST

	W	L	T	Pct	Pts	OP
Dallas	10	4	0	.714	299	221
NY Giants	9	5	0	.643	301	270
St. Louis	8	5	1	.571	325	228
Washington	6	8	0	.429	297	314
Philadelphia	3	10	1	.214	241	332

NFC CENTRAL

	W	L	T	Pct	Pts	OP
Minnesota	12	2	0	.857	335	143
Detroit	10	4	0	.714	347	202
Green Bay	6	8	0	.429	196	293
Chicago	6	8	0	.429	256	261

NFC WEST

	W	L	T	Pct	Pts	OP
San Francisco	10	3	1	.714	352	267
LA Rams	9	4	1	.643	325	202
Atlanta	4	8	2	.286	206	261
New Orleans	2	11	1	.143	172	347

1971

AFC EAST

	W	L	T	Pct	Pts	OP
Miami	10	3	1	.714	315	174
Baltimore	10	4	0	.714	313	140
New England Patriots	6	8	0	.429	238	325
NY Jets	6	8	0	.429	212	299
Buffalo	1	13	0	.071	184	394

AFC CENTRAL

	W	L	T	Pct	Pts	OP
Cleveland	9	5	0	.643	285	273
Pittsburgh	6	8	0	.429	246	292
Houston	4	9	1	.286	251	330
Cincinnati	4	10	0	.286	284	265

AFC WEST

	W	L	T	Pct	Pts	OP
Kansas City	10	3	1	.714	302	208
Oakland	8	4	2	.571	344	278
San Diego	6	8	0	.429	311	341
Denver	4	9	1	.286	203	275

NFC EAST

	W	L	T	Pct	Pts	OP
Dallas	11	3	0	.786	406	222
Washington	9	4	1	.643	276	190
Philadelphia	6	7	1	.429	221	302
St. Louis	4	9	1	.286	231	279
NY Giants	4	10	0	.286	228	362

NFC CENTRAL

	W	L	T	Pct	Pts	OP
Minnesota	11	3	0	.786	245	139
Detroit	7	6	1	.500	341	286
Chicago	6	8	0	.429	185	276
Green Bay	4	8	2	.286	274	298

NFC WEST

	W	L	T	Pct	Pts	OP
San Francisco	9	5	0	.643	300	216
LA Rams	8	5	1	.571	313	260
Atlanta	7	6	1	.500	274	277
New Orleans	4	8	2	.286	266	347

1972

AFC EAST

	W	L	T	Pct	Pts	OP
Miami	14	0	0	1.00	385	171
NY Jets	7	7	0	.500	367	324
Baltimore	5	9	0	.357	235	252
Buffalo	4	9	1	.286	257	377
New England	3	11	0	.214	192	446

AFC CENTRAL

	W	L	T	Pct	Pts	OP
Pittsburgh	11	3	0	.786	343	175
Cleveland	10	4	0	.714	268	249
Cincinnati	8	6	0	.571	299	229
Houston	1	13	0	.071	164	380

1972 (Cont.)

AFC WEST

	W	L	T	Pct	Pts	OP
Oakland	10	3	1	.714	365	248
Kansas City	8	6	0	.571	287	254
Denver	5	9	0	.357	325	350
San Diego	4	9	1	.286	264	344

NFC EAST

	W	L	T	Pct	Pts	OP
Washington	11	3	0	.786	336	218
Dallas	10	4	0	.286	319	240
NY Giants	8	6	0	.571	331	247
St. Louis	4	9	1	.286	193	303
Philadelphia	2	11	1	.143	145	352

NFC CENTRAL

	W	L	T	Pct	Pts	OP
Green Bay	10	4	0	.714	304	226
Detroit	8	5	1	.571	339	290
Minnesota	7	7	0	.500	301	252
Chicago	4	9	1	.286	225	275

NFC WEST

	W	L	T	Pct	Pts	OP
San Francisco	8	5	1	.571	353	249
Atlanta	7	7	0	.500	269	274
LA Rams	6	7	1	.429	291	286
New Orleans	2	11	1	.143	215	361

1973

AFC EAST

	W	L	T	Pct	Pts	OP
Miami	12	2	0	.857	343	150
Buffalo	9	5	0	.643	259	230
New England	5	9	0	.357	258	300
Baltimore	4	10	0	.286	226	341
NY Jets	4	10	0	.286	240	306

AFC CENTRAL

	W	L	T	Pct	Pts	OP
Pittsburgh	10	4	0	.714	347	210
Cincinnati	10	4	0	.714	286	231
Cleveland	7	5	2	.500	234	255
Houston	1	13	0	.071	199	447

AFC WEST

	W	L	T	Pct	Pts	OP
Oakland	9	4	1	.643	292	175
Kansas City	7	5	2	.500	231	192
Denver	7	5	2	.500	354	296
San Diego	2	11	1	.143	188	386

NFC EAST

	W	L	T	Pct	Pts	OP
Washington	10	4	0	.714	325	198
Dallas	10	4	0	.714	325	198
Philadelphia	5	8	1	.357	310	393
St. Louis	4	9	1	.286	286	365
NY Giants	2	11	1	.143	226	362

1973 (Cont.)

NFC CENTRAL

	W	L	T	Pct	Pts	OP
Minnesota	12	2	0	.857	296	168
Detroit	6	7	1	.429	271	247
Green Bay	5	7	2	.143	202	259
Chicago	3	11	0	.214	195	334

NFC WEST

	W	L	T	Pct	Pts	OP
LA Rams	12	2	0	.857	388	178
Atlanta	9	5	0	.643	318	224
New Orleans	5	9	0	.357	163	312
San Francisco	5	9	0	.357	262	319

1974

AFC EAST

	W	L	T	Pct	Pts	OP
Miami	11	3	0	.786	327	216
Buffalo	9	5	0	.643	264	244
NY Jets	7	7	0	.500	279	300
New England	7	7	0	.500	348	289
Baltimore	2	12	0	.143	190	329

AFC CENTRAL

	W	L	T	Pct	Pts	OP
Pittsburgh	10	3	1	.714	305	189
Houston	7	7	0	.500	236	282
Cincinnati	7	7	0	.500	283	259
Cleveland	4	10	0	.283	251	344

AFC WEST

	W	L	T	Pct	Pts	OP
Oakland	12	2	0	.857	355	228
Denver	7	6	1	.500	302	294
Kansas City	5	9	0	.357	233	293
San Diego	5	9	0	.357	212	285

NFC EAST

	W	L	T	Pct	Pts	OP
Washington	10	4	0	.714	320	196
St. Louis	10	4	0	.714	285	218
Dallas	8	6	0	.571	297	235
Philadelphia	7	7	0	.500	242	217
NY Giants	2	12	0	.143	195	299

NFC CENTRAL

	W	L	T	Pct	Pts	OP
Minnesota	10	4	0	.714	310	195
Detroit	7	7	0	.500	256	270
Green Bay	6	8	0	.429	210	206
Chicago	4	10	0	.286	152	279

NFC WEST

	W	L	T	Pct	Pts	OP
LA Rams	10	4	0	.714	263	181
San Francisco	6	8	0	.429	226	236
New Orleans	5	9	0	.357	166	263
Atlanta	3	11	0	.214	111	271

1975

AFC EAST

	W	L	T	Pct	Pts	OP
Miami	10	4	0	.714	357	222
Baltimore	10	4	0	.714	395	269
Buffalo	8	6	0	.571	420	355
NY Jets	3	11	0	.214	258	433
New England	3	11	0	.214	258	358

AFC CENTRAL

	W	L	T	Pct	Pts	OP
Pittsburgh	12	2	0	.857	373	162
Cincinnati	11	3	0	.786	340	246
Houston	10	4	0	.714	293	226
Cleveland	3	11	0	.214	218	372

AFC WEST

	W	L	T	Pct	Pts	OP
Oakland	11	3	0	.786	375	255
Denver	6	8	0	.429	254	307
Kansas City	5	9	0	.357	282	341
San Diego	2	12	0	.143	189	345

NFC EAST

	W	L	T	Pct	Pts	OP
St. Louis	11	3	0	.786	356	276
Dallas	10	4	0	.714	350	268
Washington	8	6	0	.571	325	276
NY Giants	5	9	0	.357	216	306
Philadelphia	4	10	0	.286	225	302

NFC CENTRAL

	W	L	T	Pct	Pts	OP
Minnesota	12	2	0	.857	377	180
Detroit	7	7	0	.500	245	262
Green Bay	4	10	0	.286	226	285
Chicago	4	10	0	.286	191	379

NFC WEST

	W	L	T	Pct	Pts	OP
LA Rams	12	2	0	.857	312	135
San Francisco	5	9	0	.357	255	286
Atlanta	4	10	0	.286	240	289
New Orleans	2	12	0	.143	165	360

1976

AFC EAST

	W	L	T	Pct	Pts	OP
Baltimore	11	3	0	.786	417	246
New England	11	3	0	.786	376	236
Miami	6	8	0	.429	263	264
NY Jets	3	11	0	.214	169	383
Buffalo	2	12	0	.143	246	363

AFC CENTRAL

	W	L	T	Pct	Pts	OP
Cincinnati	10	4	0	.714	335	210
Pittsburgh	10	4	0	.714	342	138
Cleveland	9	5	0	.643	267	287
Houston	5	9	0	.357	222	273

1976 (Cont.)

AFC WEST

	W	L	T	Pct	Pts	OP
Oakland	13	1	0	.929	350	237
Denver	9	5	0	.643	315	206
San Diego	6	8	0	.429	248	285
Kansas City	5	9	0	.357	290	376
Tampa Bay Buccaneers	0	14	0	.000	125	412

NFC EAST

	W	L	T	Pct	Pts	OP
Dallas	11	3	0	.786	296	194
Washington	10	4	0	.714	291	217
St. Louis	10	4	0	.714	309	267
Philadelphia	4	10	0	.286	165	286
NY Giants	3	11	0	.214	170	250

NFC CENTRAL

	W	L	T	Pct	Pts	OP
Minnesota	11	2	1	.786	305	176
Chicago	7	7	0	.500	253	216
Detroit	6	8	0	.429	218	299
Green Bay	5	9	0	.357	218	299

NFC WEST

	W	L	T	Pct	Pts	OP
LA Rams	10	3	1	.714	351	190
San Francisco	8	6	0	.571	270	190
Atlanta	4	10	0	.286	172	312
New Orleans	4	10	0	.286	253	346
Seattle Seahawks	2	12	0	.143	229	429

1977

AFC EAST

	W	L	T	Pct	Pts	OP
Miami	10	4	0	.714	313	197
Baltimore	10	4	0	.714	295	221
New England	9	5	0	.643	278	217
Buffalo	3	11	0	.214	160	313
NY Jets	3	11	0	.214	191	313

AFC CENTRAL

	W	L	T	Pct	Pts	OP
Pittsburgh	9	5	0	.643	283	243
Houston	8	6	0	.571	299	230
Cincinnati	8	6	0	.571	238	235
Cleveland	6	8	0	.429	269	267

AFC WEST

	W	L	T	Pct	Pts	OP
Denver	12	2	0	.857	274	148
Oakland	11	3	0	.786	351	230
San Diego	7	7	0	.500	222	205
Seattle	5	9	0	.357	282	373
Kansas City	2	12	0	.143	225	349

NFC EAST

	W	L	T	Pct	Pts	OP
Dallas	12	2	0	.857	345	212
Washington	9	5	0	.643	196	189
St. Louis	7	7	0	.500	272	287
NY Giants	5	9	0	.357	181	265
Philadelphia	5	9	0	.357	220	207

1977 (Cont.)

NFC CENTRAL

	W	L	T	Pct	Pts	OP
Chicago	9	5	0	.643	255	253
Minnesota	9	5	0	.643	231	227
Detroit	6	8	0	.429	183	252
Green Bay	4	10	0	.286	134	219
Tampa Bay	2	12	0	.143	103	223

NFC WEST

	W	L	T	Pct	Pts	OP
LA Rams	10	4	0	.714	302	146
Atlanta	7	7	0	.500	179	129
San Francisco	5	9	0	.357	220	260
New Orleans	3	11	0	.214	232	336

1978

AFC EAST

	W	L	T	Pct	Pts	OP
New England	11	5	0	.688	358	286
Miami	11	5	0	.688	372	254
NY Jets	8	8	0	.500	359	364
Buffalo	5	11	0	.313	302	354
Baltimore	5	11	0	.313	239	421

AFC CENTRAL

	W	L	T	Pct	Pts	OP
Pittsburgh	14	2	0	.875	356	195
Houston	10	6	0	.625	283	298
Cleveland	8	8	0	.500	334	356
Cincinnati	4	12	0	.250	252	284

AFC WEST

	W	L	T	Pct	Pts	OP
Denver	10	6	0	.625	282	198
Seattle	9	7	0	.563	345	358
Oakland	9	7	0	.563	311	283
San Diego	9	7	0	.563	355	309
Kansas City	4	12	0	.250	243	327

NFC EAST

	W	L	T	Pct	Pts	OP
Dallas	12	4	0	.750	384	208
Philadelphia	9	7	0	.563	270	250
Washington	8	8	0	.500	273	283
St. Louis	6	10	0	.375	248	296
NY Giants	6	10	0	.375	264	298

NFC CENTRAL

	W	L	T	Pct	Pts	OP
Green Bay	8	7	1	.500	249	269
Minnesota	8	7	1	.500	294	306
Detroit	7	9	0	.438	290	300
Chicago	7	9	0	.438	253	274
Tampa Bay	5	11	0	.313	241	259

NFC WEST

	W	L	T	Pct	Pts	OP
LA Rams	12	4	0	.750	316	245
Atlanta	9	7	0	.563	240	290
New Orleans	7	9	0	.438	281	298
San Francisco	2	14	0	.125	219	350

1979

AFC EAST

	W	L	T	Pct	Pts	OP
Miami	10	6	0	.625	341	257
New England	9	7	0	.563	411	326
NY Jets	8	8	0	.500	337	383
Buffalo	7	9	0	.438	268	279
Baltimore	5	11	0	.313	271	351

AFC CENTRAL

	W	L	T	Pct	Pts	OP
Pittsburgh	12	4	0	.750	416	262
Houston	11	5	0	.688	362	331
Cleveland	9	7	0	.563	359	352
Cincinnati	4	12	0	.250	337	421

AFC WEST

	W	L	T	Pct	Pts	OP
San Diego	12	4	0	.750	411	246
Denver	10	6	0	.625	289	262
Seattle	9	7	0	.563	378	372
Oakland	9	7	0	.563	365	337
Kansas City	7	9	0	.438	238	262

NFC EAST

	W	L	T	Pct	Pts	OP
Dallas	11	5	0	.688	371	313
Philadelphia	11	5	0	.688	339	282
Washington	10	6	0	.625	348	295
NY Giants	6	10	0	.375	237	323
St. Louis	5	11	0	.313	307	358

NFC CENTRAL

	W	L	T	Pct	Pts	OP
Chicago	10	6	0	.625	306	249
Tampa Bay	10	6	0	.625	273	237
Minnesota	7	9	0	.438	259	337
Green Bay	5	11	0	.313	246	316
Detroit	2	14	0	.125	219	365

NFC WEST

	W	L	T	Pct	Pts	OP
LA Rams	9	7	0	.563	323	309
New Orleans	8	8	0	.500	370	360
Atlanta	6	10	0	.375	300	388
San Francisco	2	14	0	.125	308	416

1980

AFC EAST

	W	L	T	Pct	Pts	OP
Buffalo	11	5	0	.688	320	260
New England	10	6	0	.625	441	325
Miami	8	8	0	.500	266	305
Baltimore	7	9	0	.438	355	387
NY Jets	4	12	0	.250	302	395

AFC CENTRAL

	W	L	T	Pct	Pts	OP
Cleveland	11	5	0	.688	357	310
Houston	11	5	0	.688	295	251
Pittsburgh	9	7	0	.563	352	313
Cincinnati	6	10	0	.375	244	312

1980 (Cont.)

AFC WEST

	W	L	T	Pct	Pts	OP
San Diego	11	5	0	.688	418	327
Oakland	11	5	0	.688	364	306
Denver	8	8	0	.500	310	323
Kansas City	8	8	0	.500	319	336
Seattle	4	12	0	.250	291	408

NFC EAST

	W	L	T	Pct	Pts	OP
Dallas	12	4	0	.750	454	311
Philadelphia	12	4	0	.750	384	222
Washington	6	10	0	.375	261	293
St. Louis	5	11	0	.313	299	350
NY Giants	4	12	0	.250	249	425

NFC CENTRAL

	W	L	T	Pct	Pts	OP
Detroit	9	7	0	.563	334	272
Minnesota	9	7	0	.563	317	308
Chicago	7	9	0	.438	304	264
Tampa Bay	5	10	1	.313	271	341
Green Bay	5	10	1	.313	231	371

NFC WEST

	W	L	T	Pct	Pts	OP
Atlanta	12	4	0	.750	405	272
LA Rams	11	5	0	.688	424	289
San Francisco	6	10	0	.375	320	415
New Orleans	1	15	0	.063	291	487

1981

AFC EAST

	W	L	T	Pct	Pts	OP
Miami	11	4	1	.688	345	275
NY Jets	10	5	1	.625	355	287
Buffalo	10	6	0	.625	311	276
Baltimore	2	14	0	.125	259	533
New England	2	14	0	.125	322	370

AFC CENTRAL

	W	L	T	Pct	Pts	OP
Cincinnati	12	4	0	.750	421	304
Pittsburgh	8	8	0	.500	356	297
Houston	7	9	0	.438	281	355
Cleveland	5	11	0	.313	276	375

AFC WEST

	W	L	T	Pct	Pts	OP
Denver	10	6	0	.625	321	289
San Diego	10	6	0	.625	478	390
Kansas City	9	7	0	.563	343	290
Oakland	7	9	0	.438	273	343
Seattle	6	10	0	.375	322	388

NFC EAST

	W	L	T	Pct	Pts	OP
Dallas	12	4	0	.750	367	277
Philadelphia	10	6	0	.625	368	221
NY Giants	9	7	0	.563	295	257
Washington	8	8	0	.500	347	349
St. Louis	7	9	0	.438	315	407

1981 (Cont.)

NFC CENTRAL

	W	L	T	Pct	Pts	OP
Tampa Bay	9	7	0	.563	315	268
Detroit	8	8	0	.500	397	322
Green Bay	8	8	0	.500	324	361
Minnesota	7	9	0	.438	325	369
Chicago	6	10	0	.375	253	324

NFC WEST

	W	L	T	Pct	Pts	OP
San Francisco	13	3	0	.813	357	250
Atlanta	7	9	0	.438	426	355
LA Rams	6	10	0	.375	303	351
New Orleans	4	12	0	.250	207	378

1982

AFC EAST

	W	L	T	Pct	Pts	OP
Miami	7	2	0	.778	198	131
NY Jets	6	3	0	.667	245	166
New England	5	4	0	.556	143	157
Buffalo	4	5	0	.444	150	154
Baltimore	0	8	1	.000	113	236

AFC CENTRAL

	W	L	T	Pct	Pts	OP
Cincinnati	7	2	0	.778	232	177
Pittsburgh	6	3	0	.667	204	146
Cleveland	4	5	0	.444	140	182
Houston	1	8	0	.111	136	245

AFC WEST

	W	L	T	Pct	Pts	OP
Los Angeles Raiders	8	1	0	.889	260	200
San Diego	6	3	0	.667	288	221
Seattle	4	5	0	.444	127	147
Kansas City	3	6	0	.333	176	184
Denver	2	7	0	.222	148	226

NFC EAST

	W	L	T	Pct	Pts	OP
Washington	8	1	0	.889	190	128
Dallas	6	3	0	.667	226	145
St. Louis	5	4	0	.556	135	170
NY Giants	4	5	0	.444	164	160
Philadelphia	3	6	0	.333	191	195

NFC CENTRAL

	W	L	T	Pct	Pts	OP
Green Bay	5	3	1	.556	226	169
Tampa Bay	5	4	0	.556	158	178
Minnesota	5	4	0	.556	187	198
Detroit	4	5	0	.444	181	176
Chicago	3	6	0	.333	141	174

NFC WEST

	W	L	T	Pct	Pts	OP
Atlanta	5	4	0	.556	183	199
New Orleans	4	5	0	.444	129	160
San Francisco	3	6	0	.333	209	206
Los Angeles Rams	2	7	0	.222	200	250

1983

AFC EAST

	W	L	T	Pct	Pts	OP
Miami	12	4	0	.750	389	250
Buffalo	8	8	0	.500	283	351
New England	8	8	0	.500	274	289
Baltimore	7	9	0	.438	264	354
NY Jets	7	9	0	.438	313	331

AFC CENTRAL

	W	L	T	Pct	Pts	OP
Pittsburgh	10	6	0	.625	355	303
Cleveland	9	7	0	.563	356	342
Cincinnati	7	9	0	.438	346	302
Houston	2	14	0	.125	288	460

AFC WEST

	W	L	T	Pct	Pts	OP
LA Raiders	12	4	0	.750	442	338
Seattle	9	7	0	.563	403	397
Denver	9	7	0	.563	302	327
San Diego	6	10	0	.375	358	462
Kansas City	6	10	0	.375	386	367

NFC EAST

	W	L	T	Pct	Pts	OP
Washington	14	2	0	.875	541	332
Dallas	12	4	0	.750	479	360
St. Louis	8	7	1	.500	374	428
Philadelphia	5	11	0	.313	233	322
NY Giants	3	12	1	.188	267	347

NFC CENTRAL

	W	L	T	Pct	Pts	OP
Detroit	9	7	0	.563	47	286
Minnesota	8	8	0	.500	316	348
Chicago	8	8	0	.500	311	301
Green Bay	8	8	0	.500	429	439
Tampa Bay	2	14	0	.125	241	380

NFC WEST

	W	L	T	Pct	Pts	OP
San Francisco	10	6	0	.625	432	293
LA Rams	9	7	0	.563	361	344
New Orleans	8	8	0	.500	319	337
Atlanta	7	9	0	.438	370	389

1984

AFC EAST

	W	L	T	Pct	Pts	OP
Miami	14	2	0	.875	513	298
New England	9	7	0	.563	362	352
NY Jets	7	9	0	.438	332	364
Indianapolis Colts	4	12	0	.250	239	414
Buffalo	2	14	0	.125	250	454

AFC CENTRAL

	W	L	T	Pct	Pts	OP
Pittsburgh	9	7	0	.563	387	310
Cincinnati	8	8	0	.500	339	339
Cleveland	5	11	0	.313	250	297
Houston	3	13	0	.188	240	437

1984 (Cont.)

AFC WEST

	W	L	T	Pct	Pts	OP
Denver	13	3	0	.813	353	241
Seattle	12	4	0	.750	418	282
LA Raiders	11	5	0	.313	368	278
Kansas City	8	8	0	.500	314	324
San Diego	7	9	0	.438	394	413

NFC EAST

	W	L	T	Pct	Pts	OP
Washington	11	5	0	.688	426	310
NY Giants	9	7	0	.563	299	301
Dallas	9	7	0	.563	308	308
St. Louis	9	7	0	.563	423	345
Philadelphia	6	9	1	.375	278	320

NFC CENTRAL

	W	L	T	Pct	Pts	OP
Chicago	10	6	0	.625	325	248
Green Bay	8	8	0	.500	390	309
Tampa Bay	6	10	0	.375	335	380
Detroit	4	11	1	.250	283	408
Minnesota	3	13	0	.188	276	484

NFC WEST

	W	L	T	Pct	Pts	OP
San Francisco	15	1	0	.938	475	227
LA Rams	10	6	0	.625	346	316
New Orleans	7	9	0	.438	298	361
Atlanta	4	12	0	.20	281	382

1985

AFC EAST

	W	L	T	Pct	Pts	OP
Miami	12	4	0	.750	428	320
New England	11	5	0	.688	362	290
NY Jets	11	5	0	.688	393	264
Indianapolis	5	11	0	.313	320	386
Buffalo	2	14	0	.125	200	381

AFC CENTRAL

	W	L	T	Pct	Pts	OP
Cleveland	8	8	0	.500	287	294
Cincinnati	7	9	0	.438	441	437
Pittsburgh	7	9	0	.438	379	355
Houston	5	11	0	.313	284	412

AFC WEST

	W	L	T	Pct	Pts	OP
LA Raiders	12	4	0	.750	354	308
Denver	11	5	0	.688	380	329
Seattle	8	8	0	.500	349	303
San Diego	8	8	0	.500	467	435
Kansas City	6	10	0	.375	317	360

NFC EAST

	W	L	T	Pct	Pts	OP
Washington	10	6	0	.625	297	312
NY Giants	10	6	0	.625	399	283
Dallas	10	6	0	.625	357	333
Philadelphia	7	9	0	.438	286	310
St. Louis	5	11	0	.313	278	414

1985 (Cont.)

NFC CENTRAL

	W	L	T	Pct	Pts	OP
Chicago	15	1	0	.938	456	198
Green Bay	8	8	0	.500	337	355
Detroit	7	9	0	.438	307	366
Minnesota	7	9	0	.438	346	359
Tampa Bay	2	14	0	.125	294	448

NFC WEST

	W	L	T	Pct	Pts	OP
LA Rams	11	5	0	.688	340	277
San Francisco	10	6	0	.625	411	263
New Orleans	5	11	0	.313	294	401
Atlanta	4	12	0	.250	282	452

1986

AFC EAST

	W	L	T	Pct	Pts	OP
New England	11	5	0	.688	412	307
NY Jets	10	6	0	.625	364	386
Miami	8	8	0	.500	430	405
Buffalo	4	12	0	.250	287	348
Indianapolis	3	13	0	.188	299	400

AFC CENTRAL

	W	L	T	Pct	Pts	OP
Cleveland	12	4	0	.750	391	310
Cincinnati	10	6	0	.625	409	394
Pittsburgh	6	10	0	.375	307	336
Houston	5	11	0	.313	274	329

AFC WEST

	W	L	T	Pct	Pts	OP
Denver	11	5	0	.688	378	327
Kansas City	10	6	0	.625	358	326
Seattle	10	6	0	.625	366	293
LA Raiders	8	8	0	.500	323	346
San Diego	4	12	0	.250	335	396

NFC EAST

	W	L	T	Pct	Pts	OP
NY Giants	14	2	0	.875	371	236
Washington	12	4	0	.750	368	296
Dallas	7	9	0	.438	346	337
Philadelphia	5	10	1	.313	256	312
St. Louis	4	11	1	.250	518	351

NFC CENTRAL

	W	L	T	Pct	Pts	OP
Chicago	14	2	0	.875	352	187
Minnesota	9	7	0	.563	398	271
Detroit	5	11	0	.313	277	326
Green Bay	4	12	0	.250	254	418
Tampa Bay	2	14	0	.125	239	473

NFC WEST

	W	L	T	Pct	Pts	OP
San Francisco	10	5	1	.625	374	247
LA Rams	10	6	0	.625	309	267
Atlanta	7	8	1	.438	280	280
New Orleans	7	9	0	.438	288	287

1987

AFC EAST

	W	L	T	Pct	Pts	OP
Indianapolis	9	6	0	.643	300	238
Miami	8	7	0	.533	362	335
New England	8	7	0	.533	320	293
Buffalo	7	8	0	.467	320	293
NY Jets	6	9	0	.400	334	360

AFC CENTRAL

	W	L	T	Pct	Pts	OP
Cleveland	10	5	0	.667	390	239
Houston	9	6	0	.600	345	349
Pittsburgh	8	7	0	.533	285	299
Cincinnati	4	11	0	.267	285	370

AFC WEST

	W	L	T	Pct	Pts	OP
Denver	10	4	1	.667	379	288
Seattle	9	6	0	.600	371	314
San Diego	8	7	0	.563	253	317
LA Raiders	5	10	0	.333	301	289
Kansas City	4	11	0	.267	276	388

NFC EAST

	W	L	T	Pct	Pts	OP
Washington	11	4	0	.733	379	285
Dallas	7	8	0	.467	340	348
St. Louis	7	8	0	.467	362	368
Philadelphia	7	8	0	.467	337	380
NY Giants	6	9	0	.400	280	312

NFC CENTRAL

	W	L	T	Pct	Pts	OP
Chicago	11	4	0	.733	356	282
Minnesota	8	7	0	.533	336	335
Green Bay	5	9	1	.333	255	300
Tampa Bay	4	11	0	.267	286	360
Detroit	4	11	0	.267	269	384

NFC WEST

	W	L	T	Pct	Pts	OP
San Francisco	13	2	0	.867	459	253
New Orleans	12	3	0	.800	422	283
LA Rams	6	9	0	.400	317	361
Atlanta	3	12	0	.200	205	436

1988

AFC EAST

	W	L	T	Pct	Pts	OP
Buffalo	12	4	0	.750	329	237
New England	9	7	0	.563	250	284
Indianapolis	9	7	0	.563	354	315
NY Jets	8	7	1	.500	372	354
Miami	6	10	0	.375	319	380

AFC CENTRAL

	W	L	T	Pct	Pts	OP
Cincinnati	12	4	0	.750	448	329
Cleveland	10	6	0	.625	304	288
Houston	10	6	0	.625	424	365
Pittsburgh	5	1	0	.313	336	421

1988 (Cont.)

AFC WEST

	W	L	T	Pct	Pts	OP
Seattle	9	7	0	.563	339	329
Denver	8	8	0	.500	327	352
LA Raiders	7	9	0	.438	325	369
San Diego	6	10	0	.375	231	332
Kansas City	4	11	1	.250	254	320

NFC EAST

	W	L	T	Pct	Pts	OP
NY Giants	10	6	0	.625	359	304
Philadelphia	10	6	0	.625	379	319
Phoenix Cardinals	7	9	0	.438	344	398
Washington	7	9	0	.438	345	387
Dallas	3	13	0	.188	265	381

NFC CENTRAL

	W	L	T	Pct	Pts	OP
Chicago	12	4	0	.750	312	215
Minnesota	11	5	0	.688	406	233
Tampa Bay	5	11	0	.313	261	350
Detroit	4	12	0	.250	220	313
Green Bay	4	12	0	.250	240	315

NFC WEST

	W	L	T	Pct	Pts	OP
New Orleans	10	6	0	.625	312	283
San Francisco	10	6	0	.625	369	294
LA Rams	10	6	0	.625	407	293
Atlanta	5	11	0	.313	244	315

1989

AFC EAST

	W	L	T	Pct	Pts	OP
Buffalo	9	7	0	.563	407	317
Miami	8	8	0	.500	331	379
Indianapolis	8	8	0	.500	298	301
New England	5	11	0	.313	297	391
NY Jets	4	12	0	.250	253	411

AFC CENTRAL

	W	L	T	Pct	Pts	OP
Cleveland	9	6	1	.563	334	254
Houston	9	7	0	.563	365	412
Pittsburgh	9	7	0	.563	265	326
Cincinnati	8	8	0	.500	404	285

AFC WEST

	W	L	T	Pct	Pts	OP
Denver	11	5	0	.688	362	226
Kansas City	8	7	1	.500	318	286
LA Raiders	8	8	0	.500	315	297
Seattle	7	9	0	.438	241	327
San Diego	6	10	0	.375	266	290

NFC EAST

	W	L	T	Pct	Pts	OP
NY Giants	12	4	0	.750	348	252
Philadelphia	11	5	0	.688	342	274
Washington	10	6	0	.625	386	308
Phoenix	5	11	0	.313	258	377
Dallas	1	15	0	.063	204	393

1989 (Cont.)

NFC CENTRAL

	W	L	T	Pct	Pts	OP
Green Bay	10	6	0	.625	362	356
Minnesota	10	6	0	.625	351	275
Detroit	7	9	0	.438	312	364
Chicago	6	10	0	.375	358	377
Tampa Bay	5	11	0	.313	320	419

NFC WEST

	W	L	T	Pct	Pts	OP
San Francisco	14	2	0	.875	442	253
LA Rams	11	5	0	.688	426	344
New Orleans	9	7	0	.563	386	301
Atlanta	3	13	0	.188	279	437

1990

AFC EAST

	W	L	T	Pct	Pts	OP
Buffalo	13	3	0	.813	428	263
Miami	12	4	0	.750	336	242
Indianapolis	7	9	0	.438	281	353
NY Jets	6	10	0	.375	295	345
New England	1	15	0	.063	181	446

AFC CENTRAL

	W	L	T	Pct	Pts	OP
Pittsburgh	9	7	0	.563	292	240
Cincinnati	9	7	0	.563	360	352
Houston	9	7	0	.563	405	307
Cleveland	3	13	0	.188	228	462

AFC WEST

	W	L	T	Pct	Pts	OP
LA Raiders	12	4	0	.750	337	268
Kansas City	11	5	0	.688	369	257
Seattle	9	7	0	.563	306	286
San Diego	6	10	0	.375	315	281
Denver	5	11	0	.313	331	374

NFC EAST

	W	L	T	Pct	Pts	OP
NY Giants	13	3	0	.813	335	211
Washington	10	6	0	.625	381	301
Philadelphia	10	6	0	.625	396	299
Dallas	7	9	0	.438	244	308
Phoenix	5	11	0	.313	268	396

NFC CENTRAL

	W	L	T	Pct	Pts	OP
Chicago	11	5	0	.688	348	280
Green Bay	6	10	0	.375	271	347
Minnesota	6	10	0	.375	351	326
Detroit	6	10	0	.375	373	413
Tampa Bay	6	10	0	.375	264	367

NFC WEST

	W	L	T	Pct	Pts	OP
San Francisco	14	2	0	.875	353	239
New Orleans	8	8	0	.500	274	275
LA Rams	5	11	0	.313	345	412
Atlanta	5	11	0	.313	348	365

1991

AFC EAST

	W	L	T	Pct	Pts	OP
Buffalo	13	3	0	.813	458	318
Miami	8	8	0	.500	343	349
NY Jets	8	8	0	.500	314	293
New England	6	10	0	.375	211	305
Indianapolis	1	15	0	.063	143	381

AFC CENTRAL

	W	L	T	Pct	Pts	OP
Houston	11	5	0	.688	386	251
Pittsburgh	7	9	0	.438	292	344
Cleveland	6	10	0	.375	293	298
Cincinnati	3	13	0	.188	263	435

AFC WEST

	W	L	T	Pct	Pts	OP
Denver	12	4	0	.750	304	235
Kansas City	10	6	0	.625	322	252
LA Raiders	9	7	0	.563	298	297
Seattle	7	9	0	.438	276	261
San Diego	4	12	0	.250	274	342

NFC EAST

	W	L	T	Pct	Pts	OP
Washington	14	2	0	.875	485	224
Dallas	11	5	0	.688	342	310
Philadelphia	10	6	0	.625	285	244
NY Giants	8	8	0	.500	281	297
Phoenix	4	12	0	.250	196	344

NFC CENTRAL

	W	L	T	Pct	Pts	OP
Detroit	12	4	0	.750	339	295
Chicago	11	5	0	.688	299	269
Minnesota	8	8	0	.500	301	306
Green Bay	4	12	0	.250	273	313
Tampa Bay	3	13	0	.188	199	365

NFC WEST

	W	L	T	Pct	Pts	OP
New Orleans	11	5	0	.688	341	211
Atlanta	10	6	0	.625	361	338
San Francisco	10	6	0	.625	393	239
LA Rams	3	13	0	.188	234	390

1992

AFC EAST

	W	L	T	Pct	Pts	OP
Buffalo	11	5	0	.688	381	283
Miami	11	5	0	.688	340	281
Indianapolis	9	7	0	.563	216	302
NY Jets	4	12	0	.250	220	315
New England	2	14	0	.125	205	363

AFC CENTRAL

	W	L	T	Pct	Pts	OP
Pittsburgh	11	5	0	.688	299	225
Houston	10	6	0	.625	352	258
Cleveland	7	9	0	.438	272	275
Cincinnati	5	11	0	.313	274	364

1992 (Cont.)

AFC WEST

	W	L	T	Pct	Pts	OP
San Diego	11	5	0	.688	335	241
Kansas City	10	6	0	.625	348	282
Denver	8	8	0	.500	262	329
LA Raiders	7	9	0	.438	249	281
Seattle	2	14	0	.125	140	312

NFC EAST

	W	L	T	Pct	Pts	OP
Dallas	13	3	0	.813	409	243
Philadelphia	11	5	0	.688	354	245
Washington	9	7	0	.563	300	255
NY Giants	6	10	0	.375	306	367
Phoenix	4	12	0	.250	243	332

NFC CENTRAL

	W	L	T	Pct	Pts	OP
Minnesota	11	5	0	.688	374	249
Green Bay	9	7	0	.563	276	296
Tampa Bay	5	11	0	.313	267	365
Detroit	5	11	0	.313	273	332
Chicago	5	11	0	.313	295	361

NFC WEST

	W	L	T	Pct	Pts	OP
San Francisco	14	2	0	.875	431	236
New Orleans	12	4	0	.750	330	202
Atlanta	6	10	0	.375	327	414
LA Rams	6	10	0	.375	313	383

1993

AFC EAST

	W	L	T	Pct	Pts	OP
Buffalo	12	4	0	.750	329	242
Miami	9	7	0	.563	349	351
NY Jets	8	8	0	.500	270	247
New England	5	11	0	.313	238	286
Indianapolis	4	12	0	.250	189	378

AFC CENTRAL

	W	L	T	Pct	Pts	OP
Houston	12	4	0	.750	368	238
Pittsburgh	9	7	0	.563	308	281
Cleveland	7	9	0	.438	304	307
Cincinnati	3	13	0	.188	187	319

AFC WEST

	W	L	T	Pct	Pts	OP
Kansas City	11	5	0	.688	328	291
LA Raiders	10	6	0	.625	306	326
Denver	9	7	0	.563	373	284
San Diego	8	8	0	.500	322	290
Seattle	6	10	0	.375	280	314

NFC EAST

	W	L	T	Pct	Pts	OP
Dallas	12	4	0	.750	376	229
NY Giants	11	5	0	.688	288	205
Philadelphia	8	8	0	.500	293	315
Phoenix	7	9	0	.438	326	269
Washington	4	12	0	.250	230	345

1993 (Cont.)

NFC CENTRAL

	W	L	T	Pct	Pts	OP
Detroit	10	6	0	.625	298	292
Green Bay	9	7	0	.563	340	282
Minnesota	9	7	0	.563	277	290
Chicago	7	9	0	.438	234	230
Tampa Bay	5	11	0	.313	237	375

NFC WEST

	W	L	T	Pct	Pts	OP
San Francisco	10	6	0	.625	473	295
New Orleans	8	8	0	.500	317	343
Atlanta	6	10	0	.375	316	385
LA Rams	5	11	0	.313	221	367

1994

AFC EAST

	W	L	T	Pct	Pts	OP
Miami	10	6	0	.625	389	327
New England	10	6	0	.625	351	312
Indianapolis	8	8	0	.500	307	320
Buffalo	7	9	0	.438	340	356
NY Jets	6	10	0	.375	264	320

AFC CENTRAL

	W	L	T	Pct	Pts	OP
Pittsburgh	12	4	0	.750	316	234
Cleveland	11	5	0	.688	340	204
Cincinnati	3	13	0	.188	276	406
Houston	2	14	0	.125	226	352

AFC WEST

	W	L	T	Pct	Pts	OP
San Diego	11	5	0	.688	384	306
LA Raiders	9	7	0	.563	303	327
Kansas City	9	7	0	.563	319	298
Denver	7	9	0	.438	347	396
Seattle	6	10	0	.375	287	323

NFC EAST

	W	L	T	Pct	Pts	OP
Dallas	12	4	0	.750	414	248
NY Giants	9	7	0	.563	279	305
Arizona Cardinals	8	8	0	.500	235	267
Philadelphia	7	9	0	.438	308	308
Washington	3	13	0	.188	320	412

NFC CENTRAL

	W	L	T	Pct	Pts	OP
Minnesota	10	6	0	.625	356	314
Green Bay	9	7	0	.563	382	287
Detroit	9	7	0	.563	357	342
Chicago	9	7	0	.563	271	307
Tampa Bay	6	10	0	.375	251	351

NFC WEST

	W	L	T	Pct	Pts	OP
San Francisco	13	3	0	.813	505	296
New Orleans	7	9	0	.438	348	407
Atlanta	7	9	0	.438	317	385
LA Rams	4	12	0	.250	286	365

1995

AFC EAST

	W	L	T	Pct	Pts	OP
Buffalo	10	6	0	.625	350	335
Miami	9	7	0	.563	398	332
Indianapolis	9	7	0	.563	331	316
New England	6	10	0	.375	294	377
NY Jets	3	13	0	.188	233	384

AFC CENTRAL

	W	L	T	Pct	Pts	OP
Pittsburgh	11	5	0	.688	407	327
Houston	7	9	0	.438	348	324
Cincinnati	7	9	0	.438	349	374
Cleveland	5	11	0	.313	289	356
Jacksonville Jaguars	4	12	0	.250	275	404

AFC WEST

	W	L	T	Pct	Pts	OP
Kansas City	13	3	0	.813	358	241
San Diego	9	7	0	.563	321	323
Oakland Raiders	8	8	0	.500	348	332
Denver	8	8	0	.500	388	345
Seattle	8	8	0	.500	363	366

NFC EAST

	W	L	T	Pct	Pts	OP
Dallas	12	4	0	.750	435	291
Philadelphia	10	6	0	.625	318	338
Washington	6	10	0	.375	326	359
NY Giants	5	11	0	.313	290	340
Arizona	4	12	0	.250	275	422

NFC CENTRAL

	W	L	T	Pct	Pts	OP
Green Bay	11	5	0	.688	404	314
Detroit	10	6	0	.625	436	336
Chicago	9	7	0	.563	392	360
Minnesota	8	8	0	.500	412	385
Tampa Bay	7	9	0	.438	238	335

NFC WEST

	W	L	T	Pct	Pts	OP
San Francisco	11	5	0	.688	457	258
Atlanta	9	7	0	.563	362	349
St. Louis Rams	7	9	0	.438	309	418
Carolina Panthers	7	9	0	.438	289	325
New Orleans	7	9	0	.438	319	348

1996

AFC EAST

	W	L	T	Pct	Pts	OP
New England	11	5	0	.688	418	313
Buffalo	10	6	0	.625	319	266
Indianapolis	9	7	0	.563	317	334
Miami	8	8	0	.500	339	325
NY Jets	1	15	0	.063	279	454

1996 (Cont.)

AFC CENTRAL

	W	L	T	Pct	Pts	OP
Pittsburgh	10	6	0	.625	344	257
Jacksonville	9	7	0	.563	325	334
Houston	8	8	0	.500	345	319
Cincinnati	8	8	0	.500	372	369
Baltimore Ravens	4	12	0	.250	371	441

AFC WEST

	W	L	T	Pct	Pts	OP
Denver	13	3	0	.813	391	275
Kansas City	9	7	0	.563	297	300
San Diego	8	8	0	.500	310	376
Seattle	7	9	0	.438	317	375
Oakland	7	9	0	.438	340	293

NFC EAST

	W	L	T	Pct	Pts	OP
Dallas	10	6	0	.625	286	250
Philadelphia	10	6	0	.625	363	341
Washington	9	7	0	.563	364	312
Arizona	7	9	0	.438	300	397
NY Giants	6	10	0	.375	242	297

NFC CENTRAL

	W	L	T	Pct	Pts	OP
Green Bay	13	3	0	.813	456	210
Minnesota	9	7	0	.563	298	315
Chicago	7	9	0	.438	283	305
Tampa Bay	6	10	0	.375	221	293
Detroit	5	11	0	.313	302	368

NFC WEST

	W	L	T	Pct	Pts	OP
San Francisco	12	4	0	.750	398	257
Carolina	12	4	0	.750	367	218
St. Louis	6	10	0	.375	303	409
New Orleans	3	13	0	.188	229	339
Atlanta	3	13	0	.188	309	461

1997

AFC EAST

	W	L	T	Pct	Pts	OP
New England	10	6	0	.625	369	289
Miami	9	7	0	.563	339	327
NY Jets	9	7	0	.563	348	287
Buffalo	6	10	0	.375	255	367
Indianapolis	3	13	0	.188	313	401

AFC CENTRAL

	W	L	T	Pct	Pts	OP
Jacksonville	11	5	0	.688	394	318
Pittsburgh	11	5	0	.688	372	307
Tennessee Oilers	8	8	0	.500	333	310
Cincinnati	7	9	0	.438	355	405
Baltimore	6	9	1	.375	326	345

1997 (Cont.)

AFC WEST

	W	L	T	Pct	Pts	OP
Kansas City	13	3	0	.813	375	232
Denver	12	4	0	.750	472	287
Seattle	8	8	0	.500	365	362
Oakland	4	12	0	.250	324	419
San Diego	4	12	0	.250	266	425

NFC EAST

	W	L	T	Pct	Pts	OP
NY Giants	10	5	1	.625	307	265
Washington	8	7	1	.500	327	289
Philadelphia	6	9	1	.375	317	372
Dallas	6	10	0	.375	304	314
Arizona	4	12	0	.250	283	379

NFC CENTRAL

	W	L	T	Pct	Pts	OP
Green Bay	13	3	0	.813	422	282
Tampa Bay	10	6	0	.625	299	263
Detroit	9	7	0	.563	379	306
Minnesota	9	7	0	.563	354	359
Chicago	4	12	0	.250	263	421

NFC WEST

	W	L	T	Pct	Pts	OP
San Francisco	13	3	0	.813	375	265
Carolina	7	9	0	.438	265	314
Atlanta	7	9	0	.438	320	361
New Orleans	6	10	0	.375	237	327
St. Louis	5	11	0	.313	299	359

1998

AFC EAST

	W	L	T	Pct	Pts	OP
NY Jets	12	4	0	.750	416	266
Miami	10	6	0	.625	321	265
Buffalo	10	6	0	.625	400	333
New England	9	7	0	.563	337	329
Indianapolis	3	13	0	.188	310	444

AFC CENTRAL

	W	L	T	Pct	Pts	OP
Jacksonville	11	5	0	.688	392	338
Tennessee	8	8	0	.500	330	320
Pittsburgh	7	9	0	.438	263	303
Baltimore	6	10	0	.375	269	335
Cincinnati	3	13	0	.188	268	452

AFC WEST

	W	L	T	Pct	Pts	OP
Denver	14	2	0	.875	501	309
Oakland	8	8	0	.500	288	356
Seattle	8	8	0	.500	372	310
Kansas City	7	9	0	.438	327	363
San Diego	5	11	0	.313	241	342

1998 (Cont.)

NFC EAST

	W	L	T	Pct	Pts	OP
Dallas	10	6	0	.625	381	275
Arizona	9	7	0	.563	325	378
NY Giants	8	8	0	.500	287	309
Washington	6	10	0	.375	319	421
Philadelphia	3	13	0	.188	161	344

NFC CENTRAL

	W	L	T	Pct	Pts	OP
Minnesota	15	1	0	.938	556	296
Green Bay	11	5	0	.688	408	319
Tampa Bay	8	8	0	.500	314	295
Detroit	5	11	0	.313	306	378
Chicago	4	12	0	.250	276	368

NFC WEST

	W	L	T	Pct	Pts	OP
Atlanta	14	2	0	.875	442	289
San Francisco	12	4	0	.750	479	328
New Orleans	6	10	0	.375	305	359
Carolina	4	12	0	.250	336	413
St. Louis	4	12	0	.250	285	378

1999

AFC EAST

	W	L	T	Pct	Pts	OP
Indianapolis	13	3	0	.813	423	333
Buffalo	11	5	0	.688	320	229
Miami	9	7	0	.563	326	336
NY Jets	8	8	0	.500	309	309
New England	8	8	0	.500	299	284

AFC CENTRAL

	W	L	T	Pct	Pts	OP
Jacksonville	14	2	0	.875	396	217
Tennessee Titans	13	3	0	.813	392	324
Baltimore	8	8	0	.500	324	277
Pittsburgh	6	10	0	.375	317	320
Cincinnati	4	12	0	.250	283	460
Cleveland Browns	2	14	0	.125	217	437

AFC WEST

	W	L	T	Pct	Pts	OP
Seattle	9	7	0	.563	338	298
Kansas City	9	7	0	.563	390	322
Oakland	8	8	0	.500	390	329
San Diego	8	8	0	.500	269	316
Denver	6	10	0	.375	314	318

NFC EAST

	W	L	T	Pct	Pts	OP
Washington	10	6	0	.625	443	377
Dallas	8	8	0	.500	352	276
NY Giants	7	9	0	.438	299	358
Arizona	6	10	0	.375	245	382
Philadelphia	5	11	0	.313	272	357

1999 (Cont.)

NFC CENTRAL

	W	L	T	Pct	Pts	OP
Tampa Bay	11	5	0	.688	270	235
Minnesota	10	6	0	.625	399	335
Green Bay	8	8	0	.500	357	341
Detroit	8	8	0	.500	322	323
Chicago	6	10	0	.375	272	341

NFC WEST

	W	L	T	Pct	Pts	OP
St. Louis	13	3	0	.813	526	242
Carolina	8	8	0	.500	421	381
Atlanta	5	11	0	.313	285	380
San Francisco	4	12	0	.250	295	453
New Orleans	3	13	0	.188	260	434

2000

AFC EAST

	W	L	T	Pct	Pts	OP
Miami	11	5	0	.688	323	226
Indianapolis	10	6	0	.625	429	326
NY Jets	9	7	0	.563	321	321
Buffalo	8	8	0	.500	315	350
New England	5	11	0	.313	276	338

AFC CENTRAL

	W	L	T	Pct	Pts	OP
Tennessee	13	3	0	.813	346	191
Baltimore	12	4	0	.750	333	165
Pittsburgh	9	7	0	.563	321	255
Jacksonville	7	9	0	.438	367	327
Cincinnati	4	12	0	.250	185	359
Cleveland	3	13	0	.188	161	419

AFC WEST

	W	L	T	Pct	Pts	OP
Oakland	12	4	0	.750	479	299
Denver	11	5	0	.688	485	369
Kansas City	7	9	0	.438	355	354
Seattle	6	10	0	.375	320	405
San Diego	1	15	0	.063	269	440

NFC EAST

	W	L	T	Pct	Pts	OP
NY Giants	12	4	0	.750	328	246
Philadelphia	11	5	0	.688	351	245
Washington	8	8	0	.500	281	269
Dallas	5	11	0	.313	294	361
Arizona	3	13	0	.188	210	443

NFC CENTRAL

	W	L	T	Pct	Pts	OP
Minnesota	11	5	0	.688	397	371
Tampa Bay	10	6	0	.625	388	269
Green Bay	9	7	0	.563	353	323
Detroit	9	7	0	.563	307	307
Chicago	5	11	0	.313	216	355

2000 (Cont.)

NFC WEST

	W	L	T	Pct	Pts	OP
New Orleans	10	6	0	.625	354	306
St. Louis	10	6	0	.625	540	471
Carolina	7	9	0	.438	310	310
San Francisco	6	10	0	.375	388	422
Atlanta	4	12	0	.250	252	413

2001

AFC EAST

	W	L	T	Pct	Pts	OP
New England	11	5	0	.688	371	272
Miami	11	5	0	.688	344	290
NY Jets	10	6	0	.625	413	486
Indianapolis	6	10	0	.375	413	486
Buffalo	3	13	0	.188	265	420

AFC CENTRAL

	W	L	T	Pct	Pts	OP
Pittsburgh	13	3	0	.813	352	212
Baltimore	10	6	0	.625	303	265
Cleveland	7	9	0	.438	285	319
Tennessee	7	9	0	.438	336	388
Jacksonville	6	10	0	.375	294	286
Cincinnati	6	10	0	.375	226	309

AFC WEST

	W	L	T	Pct	Pts	OP
Oakland	10	6	0	.625	399	327
Seattle	9	7	0	.563	301	324
Denver	8	8	0	.500	340	339
Kansas City	6	10	0	.375	320	344
San Diego	5	11	0	.313	332	321

NFC EAST

	W	L	T	Pct	Pts	OP
Philadelphia	11	5	0	.688	343	208
Washington	8	8	0	.500	256	303
NY Giants	7	9	0	.438	294	321
Arizona	7	9	0	.438	295	343
Dallas	5	11	0	.313	246	338

NFC CENTRAL

	W	L	T	Pct	Pts	OP
Chicago	13	3	0	.813	338	203
Green Bay	12	4	0	.750	390	266
Tampa Bay	9	7	0	.563	324	280
Minnesota	5	11	0	.313	290	390
Detroit	2	14	0	.125	270	424

NFC WEST

	W	L	T	Pct	Pts	OP
St. Louis	14	2	0	.875	503	273
San Francisco	12	4	0	.750	409	282
Atlanta	7	9	0	.438	291	377
New Orleans	7	9	0	.438	333	409
Carolina	1	15	0	.938	253	410

2002

AFC EAST

	W	L	T	Pct	Pts	OP
New England	9	7	0	.563	384	346
Miami	9	7	0	.563	378	301
NY Jets	9	7	0	.563	359	336
Buffalo	8	8	0	.500	379	397

AFC NORTH

	W	L	T	Pct	Pts	OP
Pittsburgh	10	5	1	.625	390	345
Cleveland	9	7	0	.563	344	320
Baltimore	7	9	0	.438	316	354
Cincinnati	2	14	0	.125	279	456

AFC SOUTH

	W	L	T	Pct	Pts	OP
Tennessee	11	5	0	.688	367	324
Indianapolis	10	6	0	.625	349	313
Jacksonville	6	10	0	.375	328	315
Houston Texans	4	12	0	.250	213	356

AFC WEST

	W	L	T	Pct	Pts	OP
Oakland	11	5	0	.688	450	304
Denver	9	7	0	.563	392	344
Kansas City	8	8	0	.500	467	399
San Diego	8	8	0	.500	333	367

NFC EAST

	W	L	T	Pct	Pts	OP
Philadelphia	12	4	0	.750	415	241
NY Giants	10	6	0	.625	320	279
Washington	7	9	0	.438	307	365
Dallas	5	11	0	.313	217	329

NFC NORTH

	W	L	T	Pct	Pts	OP
Green Bay	12	4	0	.750	398	328
Minnesota	6	10	0	.375	390	442
Chicago	4	12	0	.250	281	379
Detroit	3	13	0	.188	306	451

NFC SOUTH

	W	L	T	Pct	Pts	OP
Tampa Bay	12	4	0	.750	346	196
Atlanta	9	6	1	.563	402	314
New Orleans	9	7	0	.563	432	388
Carolina	7	9	0	.438	258	302

NFC WEST

	W	L	T	Pct	Pts	OP
San Francisco	10	6	0	.625	367	351
St. Louis	7	9	0	.438	316	367
Seattle	7	9	0	.438	355	369
Arizona	5	11	0	.313	262	417

2003

AFC EAST

	W	L	T	Pct	Pts	OP
New England	14	2	0	.875	348	238
Miami	10	6	0	.625	311	261
Buffalo	6	10	0	.375	243	279
NY Jets	6	10	0	.375	283	299

AFC NORTH

	W	L	T	Pct	Pts	OP
Baltimore	10	6	0	.625	391	281
Cincinnati	8	8	0	.500	346	384
Pittsburgh	6	10	0	.375	300	327
Cleveland	5	11	0	.313	254	322

AFC SOUTH

	W	L	T	Pct	Pts	OP
Indianapolis	12	4	0	.750	447	336
Tennessee	12	4	0	.750	435	324
Houston	5	11	0	.313	255	380
Jacksonville	5	11	0	.313	276	331

AFC WEST

	W	L	T	Pct	Pts	OP
Kansas City	13	3	0	.813	484	332
Denver	10	6	0	.625	381	301
Oakland	4	12	0	.250	270	379
San Diego	4	12	0	.250	313	441

NFC EAST

	W	L	T	Pct	Pts	OP
Philadelphia	12	4	0	.750	374	287
Dallas	10	6	0	.625	289	260
Washington	5	11	0	.313	287	372
NY Giants	4	12	0	.250	243	387

NFC NORTH

	W	L	T	Pct	Pts	OP
Green Bay	10	6	0	.625	442	307
Minnesota	9	7	0	.563	416	353
Chicago	7	9	0	.438	283	346
Detroit	5	11	0	.313	270	379

NFC SOUTH

	W	L	T	Pct	Pts	OP
Carolina	11	5	0	.688	325	304
New Orleans	8	8	0	.500	340	326
Tampa Bay	7	9	0	.438	301	264
Atlanta	5	11	0	.313	299	422

NFC WEST

	W	L	T	Pct	Pts	OP
St. Louis	12	4	0	.750	447	328
Seattle	10	6	0	.625	404	327
San Francisco	7	9	0	.438	384	337
Arizona	4	12	0	.250	225	452

2004

AFC EAST

	W	L	T	Pct	Pts	OP
New England	14	2	0	.875	437	260
NY Jets	10	6	0	.625	333	261
Buffalo	9	7	0	.562	395	284
Miami	4	12	0	.250	275	354

AFC NORTH

	W	L	T	Pct	Pts	OP
Pittsburgh	15	1	0	.938	372	251
Baltimore	9	7	0	.562	317	268
Cincinnati	8	8	0	.500	374	372
Cleveland	4	12	0	.250	275	354

AFC SOUTH

	W	L	T	Pct	Pts	OP
Indianapolis	12	4	0	.750	522	351
Jacksonville	9	7	0	.562	261	280
Houston	7	9	0	.438	309	339
Tennessee	5	11	0	.312	344	439

AFC WEST

	W	L	T	Pct	Pts	OP
San Diego	12	4	0	.750	446	313
Denver	10	6	0	.625	381	304
Kansas City	7	9	0	.438	483	435
Oakland	5	11	0	.312	320	442

NFC EAST

	W	L	T	Pct	Pts	OP
Philadelphia	13	3	0	.812	386	260
NY Giants	6	10	0	.375	303	347
Dallas	6	10	0	.375	293	405
Washington	6	10	0	.375	240	265

NFC NORTH

	W	L	T	Pct	Pts	OP
Green Bay	10	6	0	.625	424	380
Minnesota	8	8	0	.500	405	395
Detroit	6	10	0	.375	296	350
Chicago	5	11	0	.312	231	331

NFC SOUTH

	W	L	T	Pct	Pts	OP
Atlanta	11	5	0	.688	340	337
New Orleans	8	8	0	.500	348	405
Carolina	7	9	0	.438	355	339
Tampa Bay	5	11	0	.312	301	304

NFC WEST

	W	L	T	Pct	Pts	OP
Seattle	9	7	0	.562	371	373
St. Louis	8	8	0	.500	319	392
Arizona	6	10	0	.375	284	322
San Francisco	2	14	0	.125	259	452

Results

	Date	Winner (Share)	Loser (Share)	Score	Site (Attendance)
I	1-15-67	Green Bay ($15,000)	Kansas City ($7,500)	35–10	Los Angeles (61,946)
II	1-14-68	Green Bay ($15,000)	Oakland ($7,500)	33–14	Miami (75,546)
III	1-12-69	NY Jets ($15,000)	Baltimore ($7,500)	16–7	Miami (75,389)
IV	1-11-70	Kansas City ($15,000)	Minnesota ($7,500)	23–7	New Orleans (80,562)
V	1-17-71	Baltimore ($15,000)	Dallas ($7,500)	16–13	Miami (79,204)
VI	1-16-72	Dallas ($15,000)	Miami ($7,500)	24–3	New Orleans (81,023)
VII	1-14-73	Miami ($15,000)	Washington ($7,500)	14–7	Los Angeles (90,182)
VIII	1-13-74	Miami ($15,000)	Minnesota ($7,500)	24–7	Houston (71,882)
IX	1-12-75	Pittsburgh ($15,000)	Minnesota ($7,500)	16–6	New Orleans (80,997)
X	1-18-76	Pittsburgh ($15,000)	Dallas ($7,500)	21–17	Miami (80,187)
XI	1-9-77	Oakland ($15,000)	Minnesota ($7,500)	32–14	Pasadena (103,438)
XII	1-15-78	Dallas ($18,000)	Denver ($9,000)	27–10	New Orleans (75,583)
XIII	1-21-79	Pittsburgh ($18,000)	Dallas ($9,000)	35–31	Miami (79,484)
XIV	1-20-80	Pittsburgh ($18,000)	Los Angeles ($9,000)	31–19	Pasadena (103,985)
XV	1-25-81	Oakland ($18,000)	Philadelphia ($9,000)	27–10	New Orleans (76,135)
XVI	1-24-82	San Francisco ($18,000)	Cincinnati ($9,000)	26–21	Pontiac, MI (81,270)
XVII	1-30-83	Washington ($36,000)	Miami ($18,000)	27–17	Pasadena (103,667)
XVIII	1-22-84	LA Raiders ($36,000)	Washington ($18,000)	38–9	Tampa (72,920)
XIX	1-20-85	San Francisco ($36,000)	Miami ($18,000)	38–16	Stanford (84,059)
XX	1-26-86	Chicago ($36,000)	New England ($18,000)	46–10	New Orleans (73,818)
XXI	1-25-87	NY Giants ($36,000)	Denver ($18,000)	39–20	Pasadena (101,063)
XXII	1-31-88	Washington ($36,000)	Denver ($18,000)	42–10	San Diego (73,302)
XXIII	1-22-89	San Francisco ($36,000)	Cincinnati ($18,000)	20–16	Miami (75,129)
XXIV	1-28-90	San Francisco ($36,000)	Denver ($18,000)	55–10	New Orleans (72,919)
XXV	1-27-91	NY Giants ($36,000)	Buffalo ($18,000)	20–19	Tampa (73,813)
XXVI	1-26-92	Washington ($36,000)	Buffalo ($18,000)	37–24	Minneapolis (63,130)
XXVII	1-31-93	Dallas ($36,000)	Buffalo ($18,000)	52–17	Pasadena (98,374)
XXVIII	1-30-94	Dallas ($38,000)	Buffalo ($23,500)	30–13	Atlanta (72,817)
XXIX	1-29-95	San Francisco ($42,000)	San Diego ($26,000)	49–26	Miami (74,107)
XXX	1-28-96	Dallas ($42,000)	Pittsburgh ($27,000)	27–17	Tempe, AZ (76,347)
XXXI	1-26-97	Green Bay ($48,000)	New England ($29,000)	35–21	New Orleans (72,301)
XXXII	1-25-98	Denver ($48,000)	Green Bay ($27,500)	31–24	San Diego (68,912)
XXXIII	1-31-99	Denver ($53,000)	Atlanta ($32,500)	34–19	Miami (74,803)
XXXIV	1-30-00	St. Louis ($58,000)	Tennessee ($33,000)	23–16	Atlanta (72,625)
XXXV	1-28-01	Baltimore ($58,000)	NY Giants ($34,500)	34–7	Tampa (71,921)
XXXVI	2-3-02	New England ($63,000)	St. Louis ($34,500)	20–17	New Orleans (72,922)
XXXVII	1-26-03	Tampa Bay ($64,000)	Oakland ($35,000)	48–21	San Diego (67,603)
XXXVIII	2-1-04	New England ($64,000)	Carolina ($35,000)	32–29	Houston (71,525)
XXXIX	2-6-05	New England ($68,000)	Philadelphia ($36,500)	24–21	Jacksonville (78,125)
XL	2-5-06	Pittsburgh ($73,000)	Seattle ($38,000)	21–10	Detroit (68,206)

Most Valuable Players

Super Bowl	Player/ Team	Position	Super Bowl	Player/ Team	Position
I	Bart Starr, GB	QB	XXI	Phil Simms, NYG	QB
II	Bart Starr, GB	QB	XXII	Doug Williams, Wash	QB
III	Joe Namath, NYJ	QB	XXIII	Jerry Rice, SF	WR
IV	Len Dawson, KC	QB	XXIV	Joe Montana, SF	QB
V	Chuck Howley, Dall	LB	XXV	Ottis Anderson, NYG	RB
VI	Roger Staubach, Dall	QB	XXVI	Mark Rypien, Wash	QB
VII	Jake Scott, Mia	S	XXVII	Troy Aikman, Dall	QB
VIII	Larry Csonka, Mia	RB	XXVIII	Emmitt Smith, Dall	RB
IX	Franco Harris, Pitt	RB	XXIX	Steve Young, SF	QB
X	Lynn Swann, Pitt	WR	XXX	Larry Brown, Dall	DB
XI	Fred Biletnikoff, Oak	WR	XXXI	Desmond Howard, GB	KR
XII	Randy White, Dall	DT	XXXII	Terrell Davis, Den	RB
	Harvey Martin, Dall	DE	XXXIII	John Elway, Den	QB
XIII	Terry Bradshaw, Pitt	QB	XXXIV	Kurt Warner, StL	QB
XIV	Terry Bradshaw, Pitt	QB	XXXV	Ray Lewis, Balt	LB
XV	Jim Plunkett, Oak	QB	XXXVI	Tom Brady, NE	QB
XVI	Joe Montana, SF	QB	XXXVII	Dexter Jackson, TB	S
XVII	John Riggins, Wash	RB	XXXVIII	Tom Brady, NE	QB
XVIII	Marcus Allen, Rai	RB	XXXIX	Deion Branch, NE	WR
XIX	Joe Montana, SF	QB	XL	Hines Ward, Pitt	WR
XX	Richard Dent, Chi	DE			

Composite Standings

	W	L	Pct	Pts	Opp Pts
San Francisco 49ers	5	0	1.000	188	89
Baltimore Ravens	1	0	1.000	34	7
Chicago Bears	1	0	1.000	46	10
New York Jets	1	0	1.000	16	7
Tampa Bay Buccaneers	1	0	1.000	48	21
Pittsburgh Steelers	5	1	.833	141	110
Green Bay Packers	3	1	.750	127	76
Oakland/LA Raiders	3	2	.600	132	114
New York Giants	2	1	.667	66	73
Dallas Cowboys	5	3	.625	221	132
Washington Redskins	3	2	.600	122	103
New England Patriots	3	2	.600	107	148
Baltimore Colts	1	1	.500	23	29
Kansas City Chiefs	1	1	.500	33	42
Miami Dolphins	2	3	.400	74	103
Denver Broncos	2	4	.333	115	206
Los Angeles/St. Louis Rams	1	2	.333	59	67
Carolina Panthers	0	1	.000	29	32
San Diego Chargers	0	1	.000	26	49
Atlanta Falcons	0	1	.000	19	34
Tennessee Titans	0	1	.000	16	23
Seattle Seahawks	0	1	.000	10	21
Philadelphia Eagles	0	2	.000	31	51
Cincinnati Bengals	0	2	.000	37	46
Buffalo Bills	0	4	.000	73	139
Minnesota Vikings	0	4	.000	34	95

Career Leaders

Passing

	GP	Att	Comp	Pct Comp	Yds	Avg Gain	TD	Pct TD	Int	Pct Int	Lg	Rating Pts
Joe Montana, SF	4	122	83	68.0	1142	9.36	11	9.0	0	0.0	44	127.8
Jim Plunkett, Rai	2	46	29	63.0	433	9.41	4	8.7	0	0.0	t80	122.8
Terry Bradshaw, Pitt	4	84	49	58.3	932	11.10	9	10.7	4	4.8	t75	112.8
Troy Aikman, Dall	3	80	56	70.0	689	8.61	5	6.3	1	1.3	t56	111.9
Bart Starr, GB	2	47	29	61.7	452	9.62	3	6.4	1	2.1	t62	106.0
Tom Brady, NE	3	108	71	65.7	735	6.81	6	5.5	1	0.9	52	99.9
Brett Favre, GB	2	69	39	56.5	502	7.28	5	7.2	1	1.4	t81	97.7
Roger Staubach, Dall	4	98	61	62.2	734	7.49	8	8.2	4	4.1	t45	95.4
Kurt Warner, StL	2	89	52	58.4	779	8.75	3	3.4	1	1.1	t73	93.8
Len Dawson, KC	2	44	28	63.6	353	8.02	2	4.5	2	4.5	t46	84.8

Note: Minimum 40 attempts.

Rushing

	GP	Yds	Att	Avg	Lg	TD
Franco Harris, Pitt	4	354	101	3.5	25	4
Larry Csonka, Mia	3	297	57	5.2	9	2
Emmitt Smith, Dall	3	289	70	4.1	38	5
Terrell Davis, Den	2	259	75	4.1	15	3
John Riggins, Wash	2	230	64	3.6	43	2
Timmy Smith, Wash	1	204	22	9.3	58	2
Thurman Thomas, Buff	4	204	52	3.9	31	4
Roger Craig, SF	3	198	52	3.8	18	2
Marcus Allen, Rai	1	191	20	9.6	t74	2
Antowain Smith, NE	2	175	44	4.0	17	2

Receiving

	GP	No.	Yds	Avg	Lg	TD
Jerry Rice, SF	4	33	589	17.9	t48	8
Andre Reed, Buff	4	27	323	11.9	40	0
Deion Branch, NE	2	21	286	13.1	52	1
Roger Craig, SF	3	20	212	10.6	40	2
Thurman Thomas, Buff	4	20	144	7.2	24	0
Jay Novacek, Dall	3	17	178	10.5	23	2
Lynn Swann, Pitt	4	16	364	22.8	t64	3
Michael Irvin, Dall	3	16	256	16.0	25	2
Troy Brown, NE	3	16	182	11.4	23	0
Chuck Foreman, Minn	3	15	139	9.3	26	0

Single-Game Leaders

Scoring

	Pts
Roger Craig: XIX, San Francisco vs Miami (1 R, 2 P)	18
Jerry Rice: XXIV, San Francisco vs Denver (3 P); XXIX, SF vs San Diego (3 P)	18
Ricky Watters: XXIX, San Francisco vs San Diego (1 R, 2 P)	18
Terrell Davis: XXXII, Denver vs Green Bay (3 R)	18

Rushing Yards

	Yds
Timmy Smith: XXII, Washington vs Denver	204
Marcus Allen: XVIII, LA Raiders vs Washington	191
John Riggins: XVII, Washington vs Miami	166
Franco Harris: IX, Pittsburgh vs Minnesota	158
Terrell Davis: XXXII, Denver vs Green Bay	157
Larry Csonka: VIII, Miami vs Minnesota	145
Clarence Davis: XI, Oakland vs Minnesota	137
Thurman Thomas: XXV, Buffalo vs NY Giants	135
Emmitt Smith: XXVIII, Dallas vs Buffalo	132
Michael Pittman: XXXVII, Tampa Bay vs Oakland	124

Receptions

	No.
Dan Ross: XVI, Cincinnati vs San Francisco	11
Jerry Rice: XXIII, San Francisco vs Cincinnati	11
Deion Branch: XXXIX, New England vs Phila.	11
Tony Nathan: XIX, Miami vs San Francisco	10
Jerry Rice: XXIX, San Francisco vs San Diego	10
Andre Hastings: XXX, Pittsburgh vs Dallas	10
Deion Branch: XXXVIII, New England vs Carolina	10
Ricky Sanders: XXII, Washington vs Denver	9
Antonio Freeman: XXXII, Green Bay vs Denver	9
Seven tied with eight.	

Touchdown Passes

	No.
Steve Young: XXIX, San Francisco vs San Diego	6
Joe Montana: XXIV, San Francisco vs Denver	5
Terry Bradshaw: XIII, Pittsburgh vs Dallas	4
Doug Williams: XXII, Washington vs Denver	4
Troy Aikman: XXVII, Dallas vs Buffalo	4
Seven tied with three.	

Passing Yards

	Yds
Kurt Warner: XXXIV, St. Louis vs Tennessee	414
Kurt Warner: XXXVI, St. Louis vs New England	365
Joe Montana: XXIII, San Francisco vs Cincinnati	357
Donovan McNabb, XXXIX, Phila vs. New England	357
Tom Brady: XXXVIII, New England vs. Carolina	354
Doug Williams: XXII, Washington vs Denver	340
John Elway: XXXIII, Denver vs Atlanta	336
Joe Montana: XIX, San Francisco vs Miami	331
Steve Young: XXIX, San Francisco vs San Diego	325
Jake Delhomme: XXXVIII Carolina vs New England	323
Terry Bradshaw: XIII, Pittsburgh vs Dallas	318
Dan Marino: XIX, Miami vs San Francisco	318

Receiving Yards

	Yds
Jerry Rice: XXIII, San Francisco vs Cincinnati	215
Ricky Sanders: XXII, Washington vs Denver	193
Isaac Bruce: XXXIV, St. Louis vs Tennessee	162
Lynn Swann: X, Pittsburgh vs Dallas	161
Andre Reed: XXVII, Buffalo vs Dallas	152
Rod Smith: XXXIII, Denver vs Atlanta	152
Jerry Rice: XXIX, San Francisco vs San Diego	149
Jerry Rice: XXIV, San Francisco vs Denver	148
Deion Branch: XXXVIII, New England vs Carolina	143

I - 1967

Green Bay	7	7	14	7—35
Kansas City	0	10	0	0—10

FIRST QUARTER
GB: McGee 37 pass from Starr (Chandler kick), 8:56. **Green Bay 7–0.**

SECOND QUARTER
KC: McClinton 17 pass from Dawson (Mercer kick), 4:20. **7–7.**
GB: Taylor 14 run (Chandler kick), 10:23. **Green Bay 14–7.**
KC: FG Mercer 31, 14:06. **Green Bay 14–10.**

THIRD QUARTER
GB: Pitts 5 run (Chandler kick), 2:27. **Green Bay 21–10.**
GB: McGee 13 pass from Starr (Chandler kick), 14:09. **Green Bay 28–10.**

FOURTH QUARTER
GB: Pitts 1 run (Chandler kick), 8:25. **Green Bay 35–10.**
A: 61,946

II - 1968

Green Bay	3	13	10	7—33
Oakland	0	7	0	7—14

FIRST QUARTER
GB: FG Chandler 39 5:07. **Green Bay 3–0.**

SECOND QUARTER
GB: FG Chandler, 20, 3:08. **Green Bay 6–0.**
GB: Dowler 62 pass from Starr (Chandler kick), 4:10. **Green Bay 13–0.**
Oak: Miller 23 pass from Lamonica (Blanda kick), 8:45. **Green Bay 13–7.**
GB: FG Chandler 43, 14:59. **Green Bay 16–7.**

THIRD QUARTER
GB: Anderson 2 run (Chandler kick), 9:06. **Green Bay 23–7.**
GB: FG Chandler 31, 14:58. **Green Bay 26–7.**

FOURTH QUARTER
GB: Adderley 60 int return (Chandler kick), 3:57. **Green Bay 33–7.**
Oak: Miller 23 pass from Lamonica (Blanda kick), 5:47. **Green Bay 33–14.**
A: 75,546

III - 1969

NY Jets	0	7	6	3—16
Baltimore	0	0	0	7—7

SECOND QUARTER
Jets: Snell 4 rush (Turner kick), 5:57. **Jets: 7–0.**

THIRD QUARTER
Jets: FG Turner 32, 4:52. **Jets: 10–0.**
Jets: FG Turner 30, 11:02. **Jets: 13–0.**

FOURTH QUARTER
Jets: FG Turner 9, 1:34. **Jets: 16–0.**
Balt: Hill 1 run (Michaels kick), 11:41. **Jets: 16–7.**
A: 75,389

IV - 1970

Kansas City	3	13	7	0—23
Minnesota	0	0	7	0—7

FIRST QUARTER
KC: FG Stenerud 48, 8:08. **Kansas City 3–0.**

SECOND QUARTER
KC: FG Stenerud 32, 1:40. **Kansas City 6–0.**
KC: FG Stenerud 25, 7:08. **Kansas City 9–0.**
KC: Garrett 5 run (Stenerud kick), 9:26. **Kansas City 16–0.**

THIRD QUARTER
Minn: Osborn 4 run (Cox kick), 10:28. **Kansas City 16–7.**
KC: Taylor 46 pass from Dawson (Stenerud kick), 13:38. **Kansas City 23–7.**
A: 80,562

V - 1971

Baltimore	0	6	0	10—16
Dallas	3	10	0	0—13

FIRST QUARTER
Dal (9:28): FG Clark 14, 9:28. **Dallas 3–0.**

SECOND QUARTER
Dal: FG Clark 30, 0:08. **Dallas 6–0.**
Balt: Mackey 75 pass from Unitas (kick blocked). 0:50. **6–6.**
Dal: Thomas 7 pass from Morton (Clark kick), 7:07. **Dallas 13–6.**

FOURTH QUARTER
Balt: Nowatzke 2 run (O'Brien kick), 7:25. **13–13.**
Balt: FG O'Brien 32, 14:55. **Baltimore 16–13.**
A: 79,204

VI - 1972

Dallas	3	7	7	7—24
Miami	0	3	0	0—3

FIRST QUARTER
Dal: FG Clark 9, 13:37. **Dallas 3–0.**

SECOND QUARTER
Dal: Alworth 7 pass from Staubach (Clark kick), 13:45. **Dallas 10–0.**
Mia: FG Yepremian, 31, 14:56. **Dallas 10–3.**

THIRD QUARTER
Dal: D. Thomas 3 run (Clark kick), 5:17. **Dallas 17–3.**

FOURTH QUARTER
Dal: Ditka 7 pass from Staubach (Clark kick), 3:18. **Dallas 24–3.**
A: 81,023

---

*-From 1967 to 1999, Super Bowl scoring times indicate the time elapsed in each quarter. Starting in 2000, times listed give the time remaining in each quarter.

VII - 1973

Miami	7	7	0	0—14
Washington	0	0	0	7—7

FIRST QUARTER

Mia: Twilley 28 pass from Griese (Yepremian kick), 14:59. **Miami 7-0.**

SECOND QUARTER

Mia: Kiick 1 run (Yepremian kick), 14:42. **Miami 14-0.**

FOURTH QUARTER

Wash: Bass 49 fumble recovery return (Knight kick), 12:53. **Miami 14-7.**
A: 90,182

VIII - 1974

Miami	14	3	7	0—24
Minnesota	0	0	0	7—7

FIRST QUARTER

Mia: Csonka 5 run (Yepremian kick), 9:33. **Miami 7-0.**
Mia: Kiick 1 run (Yepremian kick), 13:38. **Miami 14-0.**

SECOND QUARTER

Mia: FG Yepremian 28, 8:58. **Miami 17-0.**

THIRD QUARTER

Mia: Csonka 2 run (Yepremian kick), 6:16. **Miami 24-0.**

FOURTH QUARTER

Minn: Tarkenton 4 run (Cox kick), 1:35. **Miami 24-7.**
A: 71,882

IX - 1975

Pittsburgh	0	2	7	7—16
Minnesota	0	0	0	6—6

SECOND QUARTER

Pit: White tackled Tarkenton for safety, 7:49.
Pittsburgh 2-0.

THIRD QUARTER

Pit: Harris 9 run (Gerela kick), 1:35. **Pittsburgh 9-0.**

FOURTH QUARTER

Minn: T. Brown recovered blocked punt in end zone (kick failed), 4:27. **Pittsburgh 9-6.**
Pit: L. Brown 4 pass from Bradshaw (Gerela kick), 11:29. **Pittsburgh 16-6.**
A: 80,997

X - 1976

Pittsburgh	7	0	0	14—21
Dallas	7	3	0	7—17

FIRST QUARTER

Dal: D. Pearson 29 pass from Staubach (Fritsch kick), 4:36. **Dallas 7-0.**
Pit: Grossman 7 pass from Bradshaw (Gerela kick), 9:03. **7-7.**

SECOND QUARTER

Dal: FG Fritsch 36, 0:15. **Dallas 10-7.**

FOURTH QUARTER

Pit: Harrison blocked Hoopes's punt for safety, 3:32. **Dallas 10-9.**
Pit: FG Gerela 36, 6:19. **Pittsburgh 12-10.**
Pit: FG Gerela 18, 8:32. **Pittsburgh 15-10.**
Pit: Swann 64 pass from Bradshaw (kick failed), 11:58. **Pittsburgh 21-10.**
Dal: P. Howard 34 pass from Staubach (Fritsch kick), 13:12. **Pittsburgh 21-17.**
A: 80,187

XI - 1977

Oakland	0	16	3	13—32
Minnesota	0	0	7	7—14

SECOND QUARTER

Oak: FG Mann, 24, 0:48. **Oakland 3-0.**
Oak: Casper 1 pass from Stabler (Mann kick), 7:50. **Oakland 10-0.**
Oak: Banaszak 1 run (kick failed), 11:27. **Oakland 16-0.**

THIRD QUARTER

Oak: FG Mann, 40, 9:44. **Oakland 19-0.**
Min: S. White 8 pass from Tarkenton (Cox kick), 14:13. **Oakland 19-7.**

FOURTH QUARTER

Oak: Banaszak 2 run (Mann kick), 7:21. **Oakland 26-7.**
Oak: Brown 75 int return (kick failed), 9:17. **Oakland 32-7.**
Min: Voigt 13 pass from Lee (Cox kick), 14:35. **Oakland 32-14.**
A: 103,438

XII - 1978

Dallas	10	3	7	7—27
Denver	0	0	10	0—10

FIRST QUARTER

Dal: Dorsett 3 run (Herrera kick), 10:31. **Dallas 7-0.**
Dal: FG Herrera 35, 13:29. **Dallas 10-0.**

SECOND QUARTER

Dal: FG Herrera 43, 3:44. **Dallas 13-0.**

THIRD QUARTER

Den: FG Turner 47, 2:28. **Dallas 13-3.**
Dal: Johnson 45 pass from Staubach (Herrera kick), 8:01. **Dallas 20-3.**
Den: Lytle 1 run (Turner kick), 9:21. **Dallas 20-10.**

FOURTH QUARTER

Dal: Richards 29 pass from Newhouse (Herrera kick), 7:56. **Dallas 27-10.**
A: 76,400

XIII - 1979

Pittsburgh	7	14	0	14—35
Dallas	7	7	3	14—31

FIRST QUARTER

Pit: Stallworth 28 pass from Bradshaw (Gerela kick), 5:13. **Pittsburgh 7-0.**

Dal: Hill 39 pass from Staubach (Septien kick), 15:00. **7-7.**

SECOND QUARTER

Dal: Hegman 37 fumble recovery return (Septien kick), 2:52. **Dallas 14-7.**

Pit: Stallworth 75 pass from Bradshaw (Gerela kick), 4:35. **14-14.**

Pit: Bleier 7 pass from Bradshaw (Gerela kick), 14:34. **Pittsburgh 21-14.**

THIRD QUARTER

Dal: FG Septien 27, 12:24. **Pittsburgh 21-17.**

FOURTH QUARTER

Pit: Harris 22 run (Gerela kick), 7:50. **Pittsburgh 28-17.**

Pit: Swann 18 pass from Bradshaw (Gerela kick), 8:09. **Pittsburgh 35-17.**

Dal: DuPree 7 pass from Staubach (Septien kick), 12:37. **Pittsburgh 35-24.**

Dal: B. Johnson 4 pass from Staubach (Septien kick), 14:38. **Pittsburgh 35-31.**

A: 79,484

XIV - 1980

Pittsburgh	3	7	7	14—31
LA Rams	7	6	6	0—19

FIRST QUARTER

Pit: FG Bahr, 41, 7:29. **Pittsburgh 3-0.**

LA: Bryant 1 run (Corral kick), 12:16. **LA Rams 7-3.**

SECOND QUARTER

Pit: Harris 1 run (Bahr kick), 2:08. **Pittsburgh 10-7.**

LA: FG Corral 31, 7:39. **10-10.**

LA: FG Corral 45, 14:46. **LA Rams 13-10.**

THIRD QUARTER

Pit: Swann 47 pass from Bradshaw (Bahr kick), 2:48. **Pittsburgh 17-13.**

LA: Smith 24 pass from McCutcheon (kick failed), 4:45. **LA Rams 19-17.**

FOURTH QUARTER

Pit: Stallworth 73 pass from Bradshaw (Bahr kick), 2:56. **Pittsburgh 24-19.**

Pit: Harris 1 run (Bahr kick), 13:11. **Pittsburgh 31-19.**

A: 103,985

XV - 1981

Oakland	14	0	10	3—27
Philadelphia	0	3	0	7—10

FIRST QUARTER

Oak: Branch 2 pass from Plunkett (Bahr kick), 6:04. **Oakland 7-0.**

Oak: King 80 pass from Plunkett (Bahr kick), 14:51. **Oakland 14-0.**

SECOND QUARTER

Phi: FG Franklin 30, 4:32. **Oakland 14-3.**

THIRD QUARTER

Oak: Branch 29 pass from Plunkett (Bahr kick), 2:36. **Oakland 21-3.**

Oak: FG Bahr 46, 10:25. **Oakland 24-3.**

FOURTH QUARTER

Phi: Krepfle 8 pass from Jaworski (Franklin kick), 1:01. **Oakland 24-10.**

Oak: FG Bahr, 35, 6:31. **Oakland 3-0.**

A: 76,135

XVI - 1982

San Francisco	7	13	0	6—26
Cincinnati	0	0	7	14—21

FIRST QUARTER

SF: Montana 1 run (Wersching kick), 9:08. **San Francisco 7-0.**

SECOND QUARTER

SF: E. Cooper 11 pass from Montana (Wersching kick), 8:07. **San Francisco 14-0.**

SF: FG Wersching 22, 14:45. **San Francisco 17-0.**

SF: FG Wersching 26, 14:58. **San Francisco 20-0.**

THIRD QUARTER

Cin: Anderson 5 run (Breech kick), 3:35. **San Francisco 20-7.**

FOURTH QUARTER

Cin: Ross 4 pass from Anderson (Breech kick), 4:54. **San Francisco 20-14.**

SF: FG Wersching 40, 9:35. **San Francisco 23-14.**

SF: FG Wersching 23, 13:03. **San Francisco 26-14.**

Cin: Ross 3 pass from Anderson (Breech kick), 14:44. **San Francisco 26-21.**

A: 81,270

XVII - 1983

Washington	0	10	3	14—27
Miami	7	10	0	0—17

FIRST QUARTER
Mia: Cefalo 76 pass from Woodley (Von Schamann kick), 6:49. **Miami 7-0.**

SECOND QUARTER
Wash: FG Moseley 31, 0:21. **Miami 7-3.**
Mia: FG Von Schamann 20, 9:00. **Miami 10-3.**
Wash: Garrett 4 pass from Theismann (Moseley kick), 13:09. **10-10.**
Mia: Walker 98 kick return (von Schamann kick), 13:22. **Miami 17-10.**

THIRD QUARTER
Wash: FG Moseley 20, 6:51. **Miami 17-13.**

FOURTH QUARTER
Wash: Riggins 43 run (Moseley kick), 4:59.
Washington 20-17.
Wash: Brown 6 pass from Theismann (Moseley kick), 13:05. **Washington 27-17.**
A: 103,667

XVIII - 1984

LA Raiders	7	14	14	3—38
Washington	0	3	6	0—9

FIRST QUARTER
LA: Jensen 0 blocked punt return (Bahr kick), 4:52.
LA Raiders 7-0.

SECOND QUARTER
LA: Branch 12 pass from Plunkett (Bahr kick), 5:46.
LA Raiders 14-0.
Wash: FG Moseley 24, 11:55. **LA Raiders 14-3.**
LA: Squirek 5 int return (Bahr kick), 14:53.
LA Raiders 21-3.

THIRD QUARTER
Wash: Riggins 1 run (kick blocked), 4:08.
LA Raiders 21-9.
LA: Allen 5 run (Bahr kick), 7:54. **LA Raiders 28-9.**
LA: Allen 74 run (Bahr kick), 15:00. **LA Raiders 35-9.**

FOURTH QUARTER
LA: FG Bahr 21, 12:36. **LA Raiders 38-9.**
A: 72,920

XIX - 1985

San Francisco	7	21	10	0—38
Miami	10	6	0	0—16

FIRST QUARTER
Mia: FG Von Schamann 37, 7:36. **Miami 3-0.**
SF: Monroe 33 pass from Montana (Wersching kick), 11:48. **San Francisco 7-3.**
Mia: D. Johnson 2 pass from Marino (Von Schamann kick), 14:15. **Miami 10-7.**

SECOND QUARTER
SF: Craig 8 pass from Montana (Wersching kick), 3:26. **San Francisco 14-10.**
SF: Montana 6 run (Wersching kick), 8:02.
San Francisco 21-10.
SF: Craig 2 run (Wersching kick), 12:55.
San Francisco 28-10.
Mia: FG Von Schamann 31, 14:48.
San Francisco 28-13.
Mia: FG Von Schamann 30, 15:00.
San Francisco 28-16.

THIRD QUARTER
SF: FG Wersching 27, 4:48. **San Francisco 31-16.**
SF: Craig 16 pass from Montana (Wershing kick), 8:42. **San Francisco 38-16.**
A: 84,059

XX - 1986

Chicago	13	10	21	2—46
New England	3	0	0	7—10

FIRST QUARTER
NE: FG Franklin 36, 1:19. **New England 3-0.**
Chi: FG Butler 28, 5:40. **3-3.**
Chi: FG Butler 24, 13:34. **Chicago 6-3.**
Chi: Suhey 11 run (Butler kick), 14:37. **Chicago 13-3.**

SECOND QUARTER
Chi: McMahon 2 run (Butler kick), 7:36. **Chicago 20-3.**
Chi: FG Butler 24, 15:00. **Chicago 23-3.**

THIRD QUARTER
Chi: McMahon 1 run (Butler kick), 7:38. **Chicago 30-3.**
Chi: Phillips 28 int return (Butler kick), 8:44. **Chicago 37-3.**
Chi: Perry 1 run (Butler kick), 11:38. **Chicago 44-3.**

FOURTH QUARTER
NE: Fryar 8 pass from Grogan (Franklin kick), 1:46.
Chicago 44-10.
Chi: Waechter safety 0, 9:24. **Chicago 46-10.**
A: 73,818

XXI - 1987

NY Giants	7	2	17	13—39
Denver	10	0	0	10—20

FIRST QUARTER
Den: FG Karlis 48, 4:09. **Denver 3-0.**
NYG: Mowatt 6 pass from Simms (Allegre kick), 9:33. **NY Giants 7-3.**
Den: Elway 4 run (Karlis kick), 12:54. **Denver 10-7.**

SECOND QUARTER
NYG: Martin safety, 12:14. **Denver 10-9.**

THIRD QUARTER
NYG: Bavaro 13 pass from Simms (Allegre kick), 4:52. **NY Giants 16-10.**
NYG: FG Allegre 21, 11:06. **NY Giants 19-10.**
NYG: Morris 1 run (Allegre kick), 14:36. **NY Giants 26-10.**

FOURTH QUARTER
NYG: McConkey 6 pass from Simms (Allegre kick), 4:04. **NY Giants 33-10.**
Den: FG Karlis 28, 8:59. **NY Giants 33-13.**
NYG: Anderson 2 run (kick failed), 11:42. **NY Giants 39-13.**
Den: Johnson 47 pass from Elway (Karlis kick), 12:54. **NY Giants 39-20.**
A: 101,063

XXII - 1988

Washington	0	35	0	7—42
Denver	10	0	0	0—10

FIRST QUARTER
Den: Nattiel 56 pass from Elway (Karlis kick), 1:57. **Denver 7--0.**
Den: FG Karlis 24, 5:51. **Denver 10-0.**

SECOND QUARTER
Wash: Sanders 80 pass from D. Williams (Haji-Sheikh kick), 0:53. **Denver 10-7.**
Wash: Clark 27 pass from D. Williams (Haji-Sheikh kick), 4:45. **Washington 14-10.**
Wash: Smith 58 run (Haji-Sheikh kick), 8:33. **Washington 21-10.**
Wash: Sanders 50 pass from D. Williams (Haji-Sheikh kick), 11:18. **Washington 28-10.**
Wash: Didier 8 pass from D. Williams (Haji-Sheikh kick), 13:56. **Washington 35-10.**

FOURTH QUARTER
Wash: Smith 4 run (Haji-Sheikh kick), 1:51. **Washington 42-10.**
A: 73,302

XXIII - 1989

San Francisco	3	0	3	14—20
Cincinnati	0	3	10	3—16

FIRST QUARTER
SF: FG Cofer 41, 11:46. **San Francisco 3-0.**

SECOND QUARTER
Cin: FG Breech 34, 13:41. **3-3.**

THIRD QUARTER
Cin: FG Breech 43, 9:15. **Cincinnati 6-3.**
SF: FG Cofer 32, 14:10. **6-6.**
Cin: Jennings 93 kick return (Breech kick), 14:26. **Cincinnati 13-6.**

FOURTH QUARTER
SF: Rice 14 pass from Montana (Cofer kick), 0:57. **13-13.**
Cin: FG Breech 40, 11:40. **Cincinnati 16-13.**
SF: Taylor 10 pass from Montana (Cofer kick), 14:26. **San Francisco 20-16.**
A: 75,129

XXIV - 1990

San Francisco	13	14	14	14—55
Denver	3	0	7	0—10

FIRST QUARTER
SF: Rice 20 pass from Montana (Cofer kick), 4:54. **San Francisco 7-0.**
Den: FG Treadwell 42, 8:13. **San Francisco 7-3.**
SF: Jones 7 pass from Montana (kick failed), 14:57. **San Francisco 13-3.**

SECOND QUARTER
SF: Rathman 1 run (Cofer kick), 7:45. **San Francisco 20-3.**
SF: Rice 38 pass from Montana (Cofer kick), 14:26. **San Francisco 27-3.**

THIRD QUARTER
SF: Rice 28 pass from Montana (Cofer kick), 2:12. **San Francisco 34-3.**
SF: Taylor 35 pass from Montana (Cofer kick), 5:16. **San Francisco 41-3.**
Den: Elway 3 run (Treadwell kick), 8:07. **San Francisco 41-10.**

FOURTH QUARTER
SF: Rathman 3 run (Cofer kick), 0:03. **San Francisco 48-10.**
SF: Craig 1 run (Cofer kick), 1:13. **San Francisco 55-10.**
A: 72,919

XXV - 1991

NY Giants	3	7	7	3—20
Buffalo	3	9	0	7—19

FIRST QUARTER

NYG: FG Bahr 28, 7:46. **NY Giants 3-0.**
Buff: FG Norwood 23, 9:09. **3-3.**

SECOND QUARTER

Buff: D. Smith 1 run (Norwood kick), 2:30. **Buffalo 10-3.**
Buff: B. Smith safety 0, 6:33. **Buffalo 12-3.**
NYG: Baker 14 pass from Hostetler (Bahr kick), 14:35. **Buffalo 12-10.**

THIRD QUARTER

NYG: Anderson 1 run (Bahr kick), 9:29. **NY Giants 17-12.**

FOURTH QUARTER

Buff: Thomas 31 run (Norwood kick), 0:08. **Buffalo 19-17.**
NYG: FG Bahr 21, 7:40. **NY Giants 20-19.**
A: 73,813

XXVI - 1992

Washington	0	17	14	6—37
Buffalo	0	0	10	14—24

SECOND QUARTER

Wash: FG Lohmiller 34, 1:58. **Washington 3-0.**
Wash: Byner 10 pass from Rypien (Lohmiller kick), 5:06. **Washington 10-0.**
Wash: Riggs 1 run (Lohiller kick), 7:43. **Washington 17-0.**

THIRD QUARTER

Wash: Riggs 2 run (Lohmiller kick), 0:16. **Washington 24-0.**
Buff: FG Norwood 21, 3:01. **Washington 24-3.**
Buff: Thomas 1 run (Norwood kick), 9:02. **Washington 24-10.**
Wash: Clark 30 pass from Rypien (Lohmiller kick), 13:36. **Washington 31-10.**

FOURTH QUARTER

Wash: FG Lohmiller 25, 0:06. **Washington 34-10.**
Wash: FG Lohmiller 39, 3:24. **Washington 37-10.**
Buff: Metzelaars 2 pass from Kelly (Norwood kick), 9:01. **Washington 37-17.**
Buff: Beebe 4 pass from Kelly (Norwood kick), 11:05. **Washington 37-24.**
A: 63,130.

XXVII - 1993

Dallas	14	14	3	21—52
Buffalo	7	3	7	0—17

FIRST QUARTER

Buff: Thomas 2 run (Christie kick), 5:00. **Buffalo 7-0.**
Dal: Novacek 23 pass from Aikman (Elliott kick), 13:24. **7-7.**
Dal: J.Jones 2 fumble return (Elliott kick), 13:39. **Dallas 14-7.**

SECOND QUARTER

Buff: FG Christie 21, 11:36. **Dallas 14-10.**
Dal: Irvin 19 pass from Aikman (Elliott kick)13:08. **Dallas 21-10.**
Dal: Irvin 18 pass from Aikman (Elliott kick), 13:24. **Dallas 28-10.**

THIRD QUARTER

Dal: FG Elliott 20, 6:39. **Dallas 31-10.**
Buff: Beebe 40 pass from Reich (Christie kick), 15:00. **Dallas 31-17.**

FOURTH QUARTER

Dal: Harper 45 pass from Aikman (Elliott kick), 4:56. **Dallas 38-17.**
Dal: E. Smith 10 run (Elliot kick), 8:12. **Dallas 45-17.**
Dal: Norton 9 fumble return (Elliott kick), 7:29. **Dallas 52-17.**
A: 98,374

XXVIII - 1994

Dallas	6	0	14	10—30
Buffalo	3	10	0	0—13

FIRST QUARTER

Dal: FG Murray 41, 2:19. **Dallas 3-0.**
Buff: FG Christie 54: 4:41. **3-3.**
Dal: FG Murray 24, 11:05. **Dallas 6-3.**

SECOND QUARTER

Buff: Thomas 4 run (Christie kick), 2:34. **Buffalo 10-6.**
Buff: FG Christie 28, 15:00. **Buffalo 13-6.**

THIRD QUARTER

Dal: Washington fumble return (Murray kick), 0:55. **13-13.**
Dal: Smith16 run (Murray kick), 0:55. **Dallas 20-13.**

FOURTH QUARTER

Dal: Smith1 run (Murray kick), 5:10. **Dallas 27-13.**
Dal: FG Murray 20, 12:10. **Dallas 30-13.**
A: 72,817

XXIX - 1995

San Francisco	14	14	14	7—49
San Diego	7	3	8	8—26

FIRST QUARTER

SF: Rice 44 pass from Young (Brien kick), 1:24.
San Francisco 7-0.
SF: Watters 51 pass from Young (Brien kick), 4:55.
San Francisco 14-0.
SD: Means 1 run (Carney kick), 12:16.
San Francisco 14-7.

SECOND QUARTER

SF: Floyd 5 pass from Young (Brien kick), 1:58.
San Francisco 21-7.
SF: Watters 8 pass from Young (Brien kick), 10:16.
San Francisco 28-7.
SD: FG Carney 31, 13:16. **San Francisco 28-10.**

THIRD QUARTER

SF: Watters 9 run (Brien kick), 5:25. **San Francisco 35-10.**
SF: Rice 15 pass from Young (Brien kick), 11:42.
San Francisco 42-10.
SD: Coleman 98 kickoff return (Humphries pass to Seay), 11:59. **San Francisco 42-18.**

FOURTH QUARTER

SF: Rice 7 pass from Young (Brien kick), 1:11.
San Francisco 49-17.
SD: Martin 30 pass from Humphries (Humphries pass to Pupunu), 12:35. **San Francisco 49-26.**
A: 74,107.

XXX - 1996

Dallas	10	3	7	7—27
Pittsburgh	0	7	0	10—17

FIRST QUARTER

Dal: FG Boniol 42, 2:55. **Dallas 3-0.**
Dal: Novacek 3 pass from Aikman (Boniol kick), 9:37.
Dallas 10-0.

SECOND QUARTER

Dal: FG Boniol 35, 8:57. **Dallas 13-0.**
Pitt: Thigpen 6 pass from O'Donnell (N. Johnson kick), 14:47. **Dallas 13-7.**

THIRD QUARTER

Dal: E. Smith 1 run (Boniol kick), 8:18. **Dallas 20-7.**

FOURTH QUARTER

Pitt: FG N. Johnson 46, 3:40. **Dallas 20-10.**
Pitt: Morris 1 run (N. Johnson kick), 8:24. **Dallas 20-17.**
Dal: E. Smith 4 run (Boniol kick), 11:17. **Dallas 27-17.**
A: 76,347.

XXXI - 1997

Green Bay	10	17	8	0—35
New England	14	0	7	0—21

FIRST QUARTER

GB: Rison 54 pass from Favre (Jacke kick), 3:32.
Green Bay 7-0.
GB: FG Jacke 37, 6:18. **Green Bay 10-0.**
NE: Byars 1 pass from Bledsoe (Vinatieri kick), 8:25.
Green Bay 10-7.
NE: Coates 4 pass from Bledsoe (Vinatieri kick), 12:27. **New England 14-10.**

SECOND QUARTER

GB: Freeman 81 pass from Favre (Jacke kick), 0:56.
Green Bay 17-14.
GB: FG Jacke 31, 6:45. **Green Bay 20-14.**
GB: Favre 2 run (Jacke kick), 13:49. **Green Bay 27-14.**

THIRD QUARTER

NE: Martin 18 run (Vinatieri kick), 11:33. **Green Bay 27-21.**
GB: Howard 99 kickoff return (Chmura pass from Favre for two-pt. conversion), 11:50. **Green Bay 35-21.**
A: 72,301.

XXXII - 1998

Denver	7	10	7	7—31
Green Bay	7	7	3	7—24

FIRST QUARTER

GB: Freeman 22 pass from Favre (Longwell kick), 4:02. **Green Bay 7-0.**
Den: Davis 1 run (Elam kick), 9:21. **7-7.**

SECOND QUARTER

Den: Elway 1 run (Elam kick), 0:05. **Denver 14-7.**
Den: FG Elam 51, 2:39. **Denver 17-7.**
GB: Chmura 6 pass from Favre (Longwell kick), 14:48. **Denver 17-14.**

THIRD QUARTER

GB: FG Longwell 27, 3:01. **17-17.**
Den: Davis 1 run (Elam kick), 14:26. **Denver 24-17.**

FOURTH QUARTER

GB: Freeman 13 pass from Favre (Longwell kick), 1:28. **24-24.**
Den: Davis 1 run (Elam kick), 13:15. **Denver 31-24.**
A: 68,912

XXXIII - 1999

Denver	7	10	0	17—34
Atlanta	3	3	0	13—19

FIRST QUARTER

Atl: FG Andersen 32, 5:25. **Atlanta 3–0.**
Den: Griffith 1 run (Elam kick), 11:05. **Denver 7–3.**

SECOND QUARTER

Den: FG Elam 26, 5:43. **Denver 10–3.**
Den: Smith 80 pass from Elway (Elam kick), 10:06. **Denver 17–3.**
Atl: FG Andersen 28, 12:35. **Denver 17–6.**

FOURTH QUARTER

Den: Griffith 1 run (Elam kick), 0:04. **Denver 24–6.**
Den: Elway 3 run (Elam kick), 3:40. **Denver 31–6.**
Atl: Dwight 94 kickoff return (Andersen kick), 3:59. **Denver 31–13.**
Den: FG Elam 35, 7:52. **Denver 34–13.**
Atl: Mathis 3 pass from Chandler (two-point conversion failed), 12:56. **Denver 34–19.**
A: 64,060

XXXIV - 2000

St. Louis	3	6	7	7—23
Tennessee	0	0	6	10—16

FIRST QUARTER

StL: FG Wilkins 27, 3:00. **St. Louis 3–0.**

SECOND QUARTER

StL: FG Wilkins 29, 4:16. **St. Louis 6–0.**
StL: FG Wilkins 28, 0:15. **St. Louis 9–0.**

THIRD QUARTER

StL: Holt 9 pass from Warner (Wilkins kick), 7:20. **St. Louis 16–0.**
Tenn: George 1 run (two-point conversion failed), 0:14. **St. Louis 16–6.**

FOURTH QUARTER

Tenn: George 2 run (Del Greco kick), 7:21. **St. Louis 16–13.**
Tenn: FG Del Greco 43, 2:12. **16–16.**
StL: : Bruce 73 pass from Warner, 1:54. **St. Louis 23–16.**
A: 74,803

XXXV - 2001

Baltimore	7	3	14	10—34
NY Giants	0	0	7	0—7

FIRST QUARTER

Balt: Stokely 38 pass from Difer (Stover kick), 6:50. **Baltimore 7–0.**

SECOND QUARTER

Balt: FG Stover 47, 1:41. **Baltimore 10–0.**

THIRD QUARTER

Balt: Starks 49 int return (Stover kick), 3:49. **Baltimore 17–0.**
NYG: Dixon 97 kickoff return (Daluiso kick), 3:31. **Baltimore 17–7.**
Balt: Je Lewis 84 kickoff return (Stover kick), 3:13. **Baltimore 24–7.**

FOURTH QUARTER

Balt: Ja. Lewis 3 run (Stover kick), 8:45. **Baltimore 31–7.**
Balt FG Stove 34, 5:28. **Baltimore 34–7.**
A: 71,921

XXXVI - 2002

New England	0	14	3	3—20
St. Louis	3	0	0	14—17

FIRST QUARTER

StL: FG Wilkins 50, 3:50. **St. Louis 3–0.**

SECOND QUARTER

NE: Law 47 int return (Vinatieri kick), 8:49. **New England 7–3.**
NE: Patten 8 pass from Brady (Vinatieri kick), 0:31. **New England 14–3.**

THIRD QUARTER

NE: FG Vinatieri 37, 1:18. **New England 17–3.**

FOURTH QUARTER

StL: Warner 2 run (Wilkins kick), 9:31. **New England 17–10.**
StL: Proehl 26 pass from Warner (Wilkins kick), 1:30. **17–17.**
NE: FG Vinarieri 48, 0:00. **New England 20-17.**
A: 72,922

XXXVII - 2003

Tampa Bay	3	17	14	14—48
Oakland	3	0	6	12—21

FIRST QUARTER

Oak: FG Janikowski 40, 10:20. **Oakland 3–0.**
TB: FG Gramatica 31, 7:51. **3–3.**

SECOND QUARTER

TB: FG Gramatica 43, 11:16. **Tampa Bay 6–3.**
TB: Alstott 2 run (Gramatica kick), 6:24.
Tampa Bay 13–3.
TB: McCardell 5 pass from B. Johnson (Gramatica kick), 0:30. **Tampa Bay 20–3.**

THIRD QUARTER

TB: McCardell 8 pass from B. Johnson (Gramatica kick), 5:30. **Tampa Bay 27–3.**
TB: Smith 44 int. return (Gramatica kick), 4:47.
Tampa Bay 34–3.
Oak: Porter 39 pass from Gannon (two-pt. conversion failed), 2:14. **Tampa Bay 34–9.**

FOURTH QUARTER

Oak: Johnson 13 return of blocked punt (two-pt. conversion failed), 14:16. **Tampa Bay 34–15.**
Oak: Rice 48 pass from Gannon (two-pt. conversion failed), 6:06. **Tampa Bay 34–21.**
TB: Brooks 44 int. return (Gramatica kick), 1:18.
Tampa Bay 41–21.
TB: Smith 50 int. return (Gramatica kick), 0:02.
Tampa Bay 48–21.
A: 67,603

XXXVIII - 2004

New England	0	14	0	18—32
Carolina	0	10	0	19—29

SECOND QUARTER

NE: Branch 5 pass from Brady (Vinatieri kick), 3:11.
New England 7–0.
Car: Smith 39 pass from Delhomme (Kasay kick), 1:14. **7–7.**
NE: Givens 5 pass from Brady (Vinatieri kick), 0:23.
New England 14–7.
Car: FG Kasay 50, 0:05. **New England 14–10.**

FOURTH QUARTER

NE: Smith 2 run (Vinatieri kick), 14:55.
New England 21–10.
Car: Foster 33 run (two-pt. conversion failed), 12:48.
New England 21–16.
Car: Muhammad 85 pass from Delhomme (two-pt. conversion failed), 7:12. **Carolina 22–21.**
NE: Vrabel 1 pass from Brady (Faulk ran for two-pt. conversion), 2:58. **New England 29–22.**
Car: Proehl 12 pass from Delhomme (Kasay kick), 1:16. **29–29.**
NE: FG Vinatieri 41, 0:09. **New England 32–29.**
A: 71,323

XXXIX - 2005

New England	0	7	7	10—24
Philadelphia	0	7	7	7—21

SECOND QUARTER

Phil: Smith 6 pass from McNabb (Akers kick), 10:02.
Philadelphia 7–0.
NE: Givens 4 pass from Brady (Vinatieri kick), 1:24. **7–7.**

THIRD QUARTER

NE: Vrabel 2 pass from Brady (Vinatieri kick), 11:05.
New England 14–7.
Phil: Westbrook 10 pass from McNabb (Akers kick), 3:44. **14–14.**

FOURTH QUARTER

NE: Dillon 2 run (Vinatieri kick), 13:52. **New England 21–14.**
NE: FG Vinatieri 22, 9:21. **New England 24–14.**
Phil: Lewis 30 pass from McNabb (Akers kick), 13:12.
New England 24–21.
A: 78,125

1933
NFL championship Chicago Bears 23, NY Giants 21

1934
NFL championship NY Giants 30, Chicago Bears 13

1935
NFL championship Detroit 26, NY Giants 7

1936
NFL championship Green Bay 21, Boston 6

1937
NFL championship Washington 28, Chicago Bears 21

1938
NFL championship NY Giants 23, Green Bay 17

1939
NFL championship Green Bay 27, NY Giants 0

1940
NFL championship Chicago Bears 73, Washington 0

1941
W. div. playoff Chicago Bears 33, Green Bay 14
NFL championship Chicago Bears 37, NY Giants 9

1942
NFL championship Washington 14, Chicago Bears 6

1943
E. div. playoff Washington 28, NY Giants 0
NFL championship Chicago Bears 41, Washington 21

1944
NFL championship Green Bay 14, NY Giants 7

1945
NFL championship Cleveland 15, Washington 14

1946
NFL championship Chicago Bears 24, NY Giants 14

1947
E. div. playoff Philadelphia 21, Pittsburgh 0
NFL championship Chi Cardinals 28, Philadelphia 21

1948
NFL championship Philadelphia 7, Chi Cardinals 0

1949
NFL championship Philadelphia 14, Los Angeles 0

1950
Am. Conf. playoff Cleveland 8, NY Giants 3
Nat. Conf. playoff Los Angeles 24, Chicago Bears 14
NFL championship Cleveland 30, Los Angeles 28

1951
NFL championship Los Angeles 24, Cleveland 17

1952
Nat. Conf. playoff Detroit 31, Los Angeles 21
NFL championship Detroit 17, Cleveland 7

1953
NFL championship Detroit 17, Cleveland 16

1954
NFL championship Cleveland 56, Detroit 10

1955
NFL championship Cleveland 38, Los Angeles 14

1956
NFL championship NY Giants 47, Chicago Bears 7

1957
W. Conf. playoff Detroit 31, San Francisco 27
NFL championship Detroit 59, Cleveland 14

1958
E. Conf. playoff NY Giants 10, Cleveland 0
NFL championship Baltimore 23, NY Giants 17

1959
NFL championship Baltimore 31, NY Giants 16

1960
NFL championship Philadelphia 17, Green Bay 13
AFL championship Houston 24, LA Chargers 16

1961
NFL championship Green Bay 37, NY Giants 0
AFL championship Houston 10, San Diego 3

1962
NFL championship Green Bay 16, NY Giants 7
AFL championship Dallas Texans 20, Houston 17

1963
NFL championship Chicago 14, NY Giants 10
AFL E. div. playoff Boston 26, Buffalo 8
AFL championship San Diego 51, Boston 10

1964
NFL championship Cleveland 27, Baltimore 0
AFL championship Buffalo 20, San Diego 7

1965
NFL W. Conf. playoff Green Bay 13, Baltimore 10
NFL championship Green Bay 23, Cleveland 12
AFL championship Buffalo 23, San Diego 0

1966
NFL championship Green Bay 34, Dallas 27
AFL championship Kansas City 31, Buffalo 7

1967
NFL E. Conf. championship Dallas 52, Cleveland 14
NFL W. Conf. championship Green Bay 28, Los Angeles 7
NFL championship Green Bay 21, Dallas 17
AFL championship Oakland 40, Houston 7

1968
NFL E. Conf. championship Cleveland 31, Dallas 20
NFL W. Conf. championship Baltimore 24, Minnesota 14
NFL championship Baltimore 34, Cleveland 0
AFL W. div. playoff Oakland 41, Kansas City 6
AFL championship NY Jets 27, Oakland 23

1969
NFL E. Conf. championship Cleveland 38, Dallas 14
NFL W. Conf. championship Minnesota 23, Los Angeles 20
NFL championship Minnesota 27, Cleveland 7
AFL div. playoffs Kansas City 13, NY Jets 6
Oakland 56, Houston 7
AFL championship Kansas City 17, Oakland 7

1970
AFC div. playoffs Baltimore 17, Cincinnati 0
Oakland 21, Miami 14
AFC championship Baltimore 27, Oakland 17
NFC div. playoffs Dallas 5, Detroit 0
San Francisco 17, Minnesota 14
NFC championship Dallas 17, San Francisco 10

1971

AFC div. playoffs	Miami 27, Kansas City 24
	Baltimore 20, Cleveland 3
AFC championship	Miami 21, Baltimore 0
NFC div. playoffs	Dallas 20, Minnesota 12
	San Francisco 24, Washington 20
NFC championship	Dallas 14, San Francisco 3

1972

AFC div. playoffs	Pittsburgh 13, Oakland 7
	Miami 20, Cleveland 14
AFC championship	Miami 21, Pittsburgh 17
NFC div. playoffs	Dallas 30, San Francisco 28
	Washington 16, Green Bay 3
NFC championship	Washington 26, Dallas 3

1973

AFC div. playoffs	Oakland 33, Pittsburgh 14
	Miami 34, Cincinnati 16
AFC championship	Miami 27, Oakland 10
NFC div. playoffs	Minnesota 27, Washington 20
	Dallas 27, Los Angeles 16
NFC championship	Minnesota 27, Dallas 10

1974

AFC div. playoffs	Oakland 28, Miami 26
	Pittsburgh 32, Buffalo 14
AFC championship	Pittsburgh 24, Oakland 13
NFC div. playoffs	Minnesota 30, St Louis 14
	Los Angeles 19, Washington 10
NFC championship	Minnesota 14, Los Angeles 10

1975

AFC div. playoffs	Pittsburgh 28, Baltimore 10
	Oakland 31, Cincinnati 28
AFC championship	Pittsburgh 16, Oakland 10
NFC div. playoffs	Los Angeles 35, St Louis 23
	Dallas 17, Minnesota 14
NFC championship	Dallas 37, Los Angeles 7

1976

AFC div. playoffs	Oakland 24, New England 21
	Pittsburgh 40, Baltimore 14
AFC championship	Oakland 24, Pittsburgh 7
NFC div. playoffs	Minnesota 35, Washington 20
	Los Angeles 14, Dallas 12
NFC championship	Minnesota 24, Los Angeles 13

1977

AFC div. playoffs	Denver 34, Pittsburgh 21
	Oakland 37, Baltimore 31
AFC championship	Denver 20, Oakland 17
NFC div. playoffs	Dallas 37, Chicago 7
	Minnesota 14, Los Angeles 7
NFC championship	Dallas 23, Minnesota 6

1978

AFC 1st-rd. playoff	Houston 17, Miami 9
AFC div. playoffs	Houston 31, New England 14
	Pittsburgh 33, Denver 10
AFC championship	Pittsburgh 34, Houston 5
NFC 1st-rd. playoff	Atlanta 14, Philadelphia 13
NFC div. playoffs	Dallas 27, Atlanta 20
	Los Angeles 34, Minnesota 10
NFC championship	Dallas 28, Los Angeles 0

1979

AFC 1st-rd. playoff	Houston 13, Denver 7
AFC div. playoffs	Houston 17, San Diego 14
	Pittsburgh 34, Miami 14
AFC championship	Pittsburgh 27, Houston 13
NFC 1st-rd. playoff	Philadelphia 27, Chicago 17
NFC div. playoffs	Tampa Bay 24, Philadelphia 17
	Los Angeles 21, Dallas 19
NFC championship	Los Angeles 9, Tampa Bay 0

1980

AFC 1st-rd. playoff	Oakland 27, Houston 7
AFC div. playoffs	San Diego 20, Buffalo 14
	Oakland 14, Cleveland 12
AFC championship	Oakland 34, San Diego 27
NFC 1st-rd. playoff	Dallas 34, Los Angeles 13
NFC div. playoffs	Philadelphia 31, Minnesota 16
	Dallas 30, Atlanta 27
NFC championship	Philadelphia 20, Dallas 7

1981

AFC 1st-rd. playoff	Buffalo 31, NY Jets 27
AFC div. playoffs	San Diego 41, Miami 38
	Cincinnati 28, Buffalo 21
AFC championship	Cincinnati 27, San Diego 7
NFC 1st-rd. playoff	NY Giants 27, Philadelphia 21
NFC div. playoffs	Dallas 38, Tampa Bay 0
	San Francisco 38, NY Giants 24
NFC championship	San Francisco 28, Dallas 27

1982

AFC 1st-rd. playoffs	Miami 28, New England 13
	LA Raiders 27, Cleveland 10
	NY Jets 44, Cincinnati 17
	San Diego 31, Pittsburgh 28
AFC div. playoffs	NY Jets 17, LA Raiders 14
	Miami 34, San Diego 13
AFC championship	Miami 14, NY Jets 0
NFC 1st-rd. playoffs	Washington 31, Detroit 7
	Green Bay 41, St Louis 16
	Minnesota 30, Atlanta 24
	Dallas 30, Tampa Bay 17
NFC div. playoffs	Washington 21, Minnesota 7
	Dallas 37, Green Bay 26
NFC championship	Washington 31, Dallas 17

1983

AFC 1st-rd. playoff	Seattle 31, Denver 7
AFC div. playoffs	Seattle 27, Miami 20
	LA Raiders 38, Pittsburgh 10
AFC championship	LA Raiders 30, Seattle 14
NFC 1st-rd. playoff	LA Rams 24, Dallas 17
NFC div. playoffs	San Francisco 24, Detroit 23
	Washington 51, LA Rams 7
NFC championship	Washington 24, San Francisco 21

1984

AFC 1st-rd. playoff	Seattle 13, LA Raiders 7
AFC div. playoffs	Miami 31, Seattle 10
	Pittsburgh 24, Denver 17
AFC championship	Miami 45, Pittsburgh 28
NFC 1st-rd. playoff	NY Giants 16, LA Rams 13
NFC div. playoffs	San Francisco 21, NY Giants 10
	Chicago 23, Washington 19
NFC championship	San Francisco 23, Chicago 0

1985

AFC 1st-rd. playoff	New England 26, NY Jets 14
AFC div. playoffs	Miami 24, Cleveland 21
	New England 27, LA Raiders 20
AFC championship	New England 31, Miami 14
NFC 1st-rd. playoff	NY Giants 17, San Francisco 3
NFC div. playoffs	LA Rams 20, Dallas 0
	Chicago 21, NY Giants 0
NFC championship	Chicago 24, LA Rams 0

1986

AFC 1st-rd. playoff	NY Jets 35, Kansas City 15
AFC div. playoffs	Cleveland 23, NY Jets 20
	Denver 22, New England 17
AFC championship	Denver 23, Cleveland 20
NFC 1st-rd. playoff	Washington 19, LA Rams 7
NFC div playoffs	Washington 27, Chicago 13
	NY Giants 49, San Francisco 3
NFC championship	NY Giants 17, Washington 0

1987

AFC 1st-rd. playoff	Houston 23, Seattle 20
AFC div. playoffs	Cleveland 38, Indianapolis 21
	Denver 34, Houston 10
AFC championship	Denver 38, Cleveland 33
NFC 1st-rd. playoff	Minnesota 44, New Orleans 10
NFC div playoffs	Minnesota 36, San Francisco 24
	Washington 21, Chicago 17
NFC championship	Washington 17, Minnesota 10

1988

AFC 1st-rd. playoff	Houston 24, Cleveland 23
AFC div. playoffs	Cincinnati 21, Seattle 13
	Buffalo 17, Houston 10
AFC championship	Cincinnati 21, Buffalo 10 NFC
1st-rd. playoff	Minnesota 28, LA Rams 17
NFC div. playoffs	Chicago 20, Philadelphia 12
	San Francisco 34, Minnesota 9
NFC championship	San Francisco 28, Chicago 3

1989

AFC 1st-rd. playoff	Pittsburgh 26, Houston 23
AFC div. playoffs	Cleveland 34, Buffalo 30
	Denver 24, Pittsburgh 23
AFC championship	Denver 37, Cleveland 21
NFC 1st-rd. playoff	LA Rams 21, Philadelphia 7
NFC div. playoffs	LA Rams 19, NY Giants 13
	San Francisco 41, Minnesota 13
NFC championship	San Francisco 30, LA Rams 3

1990

AFC 1st-rd. playoffs	Miami 17, Kansas City 16
	Cincinnati 41, Houston 14
AFC div. playoffs	Buffalo 44, Miami 34
	LA Raiders 20, Cincinnati 10
AFC championship	Buffalo 51, LA Raiders 3
NFC 1st-rd. playoffs	Chicago 16, New Orleans 6
NFC 1st-rd playoffs	Washington 20, Philadelphia 6
NFC div. playoffs	San Francisco 28, Washington 10
	NY Giants 31, Chicago 3
NFC championship	NY Giants 15, San Francisco 13

1991

AFC 1st-rd. playoffs	Houston 17, NY Jets 10
	Kansas City 10, LA Raiders 6
AFC div. playoffs	Denver 26, Houston 24
	Buffalo 37, Kansas City 14
AFC championship	Buffalo 10, Denver 7
NFC 1st-rd. playoffs	Atlanta 27, New Orleans 20
	Dallas 17, Chicago 13
NFC div. playoffs	Washington 24, Atlanta 7
	Detroit 38, Dallas 6
NFC championship	Washington 41, Detroit 10

1992

AFC 1st-rd. playoffs	San Diego 17, Kansas City 0
	Buffalo 41, Houston 38 (OT)
AFC div. playoffs	Buffalo 24, Pittsburgh 3
	Miami 31, San Diego 0
AFC championship	Buffalo 29, Miami 10
NFC 1st-rd. playoffs	Washington 24, Minnesota 7
	Philadelphia 36, New Orleans 20
NFC div. playoffs	San Francisco 20, Washington 13
	Dallas 34, Philadelphia 10
NFC championship	Dallas 30, San Francisco 20

1993

AFC 1st-rd. playoffs	LA Raiders 42, Denver 24
	Kansas City 27, Pittsburgh 24 (OT)
AFC div. playoffs	Buffalo 29, LA Raiders 23
	Kansas City 28, Houston 20
AFC championship	Buffalo 30, Kansas City 13
NFC 1st-rd. playoffs	NY Giants 17, Minnesota 10
	Green Bay 28, Detroit 24
NFC div. playoffs	San Francisco 44, NY Giants 3
	Dallas 27, Green Bay 17
NFC championship	Dallas 38, San Francisco 21

1994

AFC 1st-rd. playoffs	Miami 27, Kansas City 17
	Cleveland 20, New England 13
AFC div. playoffs	San Diego 22, Miami 21
	Pittsburgh 29, Cleveland 9
AFC championship	San Diego 17, Pittsburgh 13
NFC 1st-rd. playoffs	Green Bay 16, Detroit 12
	Chicago 35, Minnesota 18
NFC div. playoffs	Dallas 35, Green Bay 9
	San Francisco 44, Chicago 15
NFC championship	San Francisco 38, Dallas 28

1995

AFC 1st-rd. playoffs	Buffalo 37, Miami 22
	Indianapolis 35, San Diego 20
AFC div. playoffs	Pittsburgh 40, Buffalo 21
	Indianapolis 10, Kansas City 7
AFC championship	Pittsburgh 20, Indianapolis 16
NFC 1st-rd. playoffs	Philadelphia 58, Detroit 37
	Green Bay 37, Atlanta 20
NFC div. playoffs	Dallas 30, Philadelphia 11
	Green Bay 27, San Francisco 17
NFC championship	Dallas 38, Green Bay 27

1996

AFC 1st-rd. playoffs	Jacksonville 30, Buffalo 27
	Pittsburgh 42, Indianapolis 14
AFC div. playoffs	Jacksonville 30, Denver 27
	New England 28, Pittsburgh 3
AFC championship	New England 20, Jacksonville 6
NFC 1st-rd. playoffs	Dallas 40, Minnesota 15
	San Francisco 14, Philadelphia 0
NFC div. playoffs	Green Bay 35, San Francisco 14
	Carolina 26, Dallas 17
NFC championship	Green Bay 30, Carolina 13

1997

AFC 1st-rd. playoffs	Denver 42, Jacksonville 17
	New England 17, Miami 3
AFC div. playoffs	Denver 14, Kansas City 0
	Pittsburgh 7, New England 6
AFC championship	Denver 24, Pittsburgh 21
NFC 1st-rd. playoffs	Minnesota 23, NY Giants 22
	Tampa Bay 20, Detroit 10
NFC div. playoffs	Green Bay 21, Tampa Bay 7
	San Francisco 38, Minnesota 22
NFC championship	Green Bay 23, San Francisco 10

1998

AFC 1st-rd. playoffs	Miami 24, Buffalo 17
	Jacksonville 25, New England 10
AFC div. playoffs	Denver 38, Miami 3
	NY Jets 34, Jacksonville 24
AFC championship	Denver 23, NY Jets 10
NFC 1st-rd. playoffs	Arizona 20, Dallas 7
	San Francisco 30, Green Bay 27
NFC div. playoffs	Atlanta 20, San Francisco 18
	Minnesota 41, Arizona 21
NFC championship	Atlanta 30, Minnesota 27 (ot)

1999

AFC 1st-rd. playoffs	Tennessee 22, Buffalo 16
	Miami 20, Seattle 17
AFC div. playoffs	Jacksonville 62, Miami 7
	Tennessee 19, Indianapolis 16
AFC championship	Tennessee 33, Jacksonville 14
NFC 1st-rd. playoffs	Washington 27, Detroit 13
	Minnesota 27, Dallas 10
NFC div. playoffs	Tampa Bay 14, Washington 13
	St Louis 49, Minnesota 37
NFC championship	St Louis 11, Tampa Bay 6

2000

AFC 1st-rd. playoffs	Baltimore 21, Denver 3
	Miami 23, Indianapolis 17 (ot)
AFC div. playoffs	Baltimore 24, Tennessee 10
	Oakland 27, Miami 0
AFC championship	Baltimore 16, Oakland 3
NFC 1st-rd. playoffs	New Orleans 31, St. Louis 28
	Philadelphia 21, Tampa Bay 3
NFC div. playoffs	NY Giants 20, Philadelphia 10
	Minnesota 34, New Orleans 16
NFC championship	NY Giants 41, Minnesota 0

2001

AFC 1st-rd. playoffs	Oakland 38, NY Jets 24
	Baltimore 20, Miami 3
AFC div. playoffs	New England 16, Oakland 13(ot)
	Pittsburgh 27, Baltimore 10
AFC championship	New England 24, Pittsburgh 17
NFC 1st-rd. playoffs	Philadelphia 31, Tampa Bay 9
	Green Bay 25, San Francisco 15
NFC div. playoffs	Philadelphia 33, Chicago 19
	St. Louis 45, Green Bay 17
NFC championship	St. Louis 29, Philadelphia 24

2002

AFC 1st-rd. playoffs	NY Jets 41, Indianapolis 0
	Pittsburgh 36, Cleveland 33
AFC div. playoffs	Tennessee 34, Pittsburgh 31 (ot)
	Oakland 30, NY Jets 10
AFC championship	Oakland 41, Tennessee 24
NFC 1st-rd. playoffs	Atlanta 27, Green Bay 7
	San Francisco 39, NY Giants 38
NFC div. playoffs	Philadelphia 20, Atlanta 6
	Tampa Bay 31, San Francisco 6
NFC championship	Tampa Bay 27, Philadelphia 10

2003

AFC 1st-rd. playoffs	Tennessee 20, Baltimore 17
	Indianapolis 41, Denver 10
AFC div. playoffs	New England 17, Tennessee 14
	Indianapolis 38, Kansas City 31
AFC championship	New England 24, Indianapolis 14
NFC 1st-rd. playoffs	Carolina 29, Dallas 10
	Green Bay 33, Seattle 27 (ot)
NFC div. playoffs	Carolina 29, St. Louis 23
	Philadelphia 20, Green Bay 17 (ot)
NFC championship	Carolina 14, Philadelphia 3

2004

AFC 1st-rd. playoffs	Denver 24, Indianapolis 49
	NY Jets 20, San Diego 17
AFC div. playoffs	New England 20, Indianapolis 3
	Pittsburgh 20, NY Jets 17
AFC championship	New England 41, Pittsburgh 27
NFC 1st-rd. playoffs	Minnesota 31, Green Bay 17
	St. Louis 27, Seattle 20
NFC div. playoffs	Atlanta 47, St. Louis 17
	Philadelphia 27, Minnesota 14
NFC championship	Philadelphia 27, Atlanta 10

2005

AFC 1st-rd. playoffs	Pittsburgh 31, Cincinnati 17
	New England 28, Jacksonville 3
AFC div. playoffs	Pittsburgh 21, Indianapolis 18
	Denver 27, New England 13
AFC championship	Pittsburgh 34, Denver 17
NFC 1st-rd. playoffs	Washington 17, Tampa Bay 10
	Carolina 23, NY Giants 0
NFC div. playoffs	Seattle 20, Washington 10
	Carolina 29, Chicago 21
NFC championship	Seattle 34, Carolina 14

Alltime NFL Individual Statistical Leaders

Career Leaders

Scoring

	Yrs	TD	FG	PAT	Pts
Gary Anderson	23	0	538	820	2,434
Morten Andersen	23	0	520	798	2,358
George Blanda	26	9	335	943	2,002
Norm Johnson	18	0	366	638	1,736
Nick Lowery	18	0	383	562	1,711
Jan Stenerud	19	0	373	580	1,699
†John Carney	17	0	390	464	1,634
Eddie Murray	19	0	352	539	1,594
Al Del Greco	17	0	347	543	1,584
†Matt Stover	15	0	376	453	1,581
†Jason Elam	13	0	343	537	1,566
Steve Christie	15	0	336	468	1,476
Pat Leahy	18	0	304	558	1,470
Jim Turner	16	1	304	521	1,439
Matt Bahr	17	0	300	522	1,422

Rushing

	Yrs	Att	Yds	Avg	Lg	TD
Emmitt Smith	15	4,409	18,355	4.2	75	164
Walter Payton	13	3,838	16,726	4.4	76	110
Barry Sanders	10	3,062	15,269	5.0	85	99
†Curtis Martin	11	3,518	14,101	4.0	70	90
†Jerome Bettis	13	3,479	13,662	3.9	71	91
Eric Dickerson	11	2,996	13,259	4.4	85	90
Tony Dorsett	12	2,936	12,739	4.3	99	77
Jim Brown	9	2,359	12,312	5.2	80	106
†Marshall Faulk	12	2,836	12,279	4.3	71	100
Marcus Allen	16	3,022	12,243	4.1	61	123
Franco Harris	13	2,949	12,120	4.1	75	91
Thurman Thomas	13	2,877	12,074	4.2	80	66
John Riggins	14	2,916	11,352	3.9	66	104
O.J. Simpson	11	2,404	11,236	4.7	94	61
†Corey Dillon	9	2,419	10,429	4.3	96	69

Touchdowns

	Yrs	Rush	Rec	Ret	Total TD
Jerry Rice	20	10	197	1	208
Emmitt Smith	15	164	11	0	175
Marcus Allen	16	123	21	1	145
†Marshall Faulk	12	100	36	0	136
Cris Carter	15	0	130	1	131
Jim Brown	9	106	20	0	126
Walter Payton	13	110	15	0	125
John Riggins	14	104	12	0	116
Lenny Moore	12	63	48	2	113

	Yrs	Rush	Rec	Ret	Total TD
†Marvin Harrison	10	0	110	0	110
Barry Sanders	10	99	10	0	109
Tim Brown	17	1	100	4	105
Don Hutson	11	3	99	3	105
†Terrell Owens	10	2	101	0	103
Steve Largent	14	1	100	0	101
†Shaun Alexander	6	89	11	0	100
Franco Harris	13	91	9	0	100

†-active player in 2005–06.

Career Leaders (Cont.)
Combined Yards Gained

	Yrs	Total	Rush	Rec	Int Ret	Punt Ret	Kickoff Ret	Fum Ret
Jerry Rice	20	23,546	645	22,895	0	0	6	0
Brian Mitchell	14	23,330	1,967	2,336	0	4,999	14,014	14
Walter Payton	13	21,803	16,726	4,538	0	0	539	0
Emmitt Smith	15	21,564	18,355	3,224	0	15	0	-15
Tim Brown	17	19,682	190	14,734	0	3,320	1,235	3
†Marshall Faulk	12	19,154	12,279	6,875	0	0	18	18
Barry Sanders	10	18,308	15,269	2,921	0	0	118	0
Herschel Walker	12	18,168	8,225	4,859	0	0	5,084	0
Marcus Allen	16	17,648	13,366	5,411	0	0	0	-6
†Curtis Martin	11	17,430	14,101	3,329	0	0	0	-9
Eric Metcalf	13	17,230	2,392	5,572	0	3,453	5,813	0
Thurman Thomas	13	16,532	12,074	4,458	0	0	0	0
Tony Dorsett	12	16,326	12,739	3,554	0	0	0	33

Passing
PASSING EFFICIENCY*

	Yrs	Att	Comp	Pct Comp	Yds	Avg Gain	TD	Pct TD	Int	Pct Int	Rating Pts
Steve Young	15	4,149	2,667	64.3	33,124	7.9	232	5.6	107	2.6	96.8
†Kurt Warner	8	2,340	1,537	65.7	19,214	8.2	119	5.1	78	3.3	94.1
†Peyton Manning	9	4,333	2,769	63.9	33,189	7.7	244	5.6	140	3.2	93.5
Joe Montana	15	5,391	3,409	63.2	40,551	7.5	273	5.2	139	2.6	92.3
†Daunte Culpepper	7	2,607	1,678	64.4	20,162	7.7	135	5.3	86	3.3	91.5
†Marc Bulger	5	1,518	987	65.0	11,932	7.9	71	4.7	51	3.4	90.6
†Tom Brady	6	2,548	1,577	61.9	18,035	7.1	123	4.8	66	2.6	88.5
†Trent Green	12	3,329	2,022	60.7	25,621	7.7	150	4.5	92	2.8	88.3
†Brett Favre	15	7,116	4,379	61.5	50,472	7.1	381	5.4	233	3.3	87.1
†Matt Hasselbeck	7	2,205	1,342	60.9	15,925	7.2	96	4.4	57	2.6	86.6
Dan Marino	17	8,358	4,967	59.4	61,361	7.3	420	5.0	252	3.0	86.4
†Jeff Garcia	7	2,785	1,695	60.9	19,076	6.8	126	4.5	71	2.5	85.8
†Drew Brees	5	1,809	1,125	62.2	12,348	6.8	80	4.4	53	2.9	84.9
†Brian Griese	8	2,318	1,463	63.1	16,344	7.1	103	4.4	78	3.4	84.8
Rich Gannon	18	4,206	2,533	60.2	28,743	6.8	180	4.3	104	2.3	84.7
†Jake Delhomme	7	1,503	888	59.1	11,160	7.4	75	5.0	52	3.5	84.5
†Brad Johnson	14	3,798	2,350	61.9	25,798	6.8	155	4.1	102	2.7	84.4
Jim Kelly	11	4,779	2,874	60.1	35,467	7.4	237	5.0	175	3.7	84.4
†Mark Brunell	13	4,334	2,576	59.4	30,037	6.9	174	4.0	102	2.4	84.1
†Donovan McNabb	7	2,943	1,718	58.4	19,433	6.6	134	4.6	66	2.2	84.1
Roger Staubach	11	2,958	1,685	57.0	22,700	7.7	153	5.2	109	3.7	83.4
†Steve McNair	11	3,871	2,305	59.5	27,141	7.0	156	4.0	103	2.7	83.3

*1,500 or more attempts. The passer ratings are based on performance standards established for completion percentage, interception percentage, touchdown percentage and average gain. Passers are allocated points according to how their marks compare with those standards.

YARDS

	Yrs	Att	Comp	Pct Comp	Yds		Yrs	Att	Comp	Pct Comp	Yds
Dan Marino	17	8,358	4,967	59.4	61,361	Boomer Esiason	14	5,205	2,969	57.0	37,920
†Brett Favre	15	7,612	4,678	61.5	53,615	Jim Kelly	11	4,779	2,874	60.1	35,467
John Elway	16	7,250	4,123	56.9	51,475	Jim Everett	12	4,923	2,841	57.7	34,837
Warren Moon	17	6,823	3,988	58.5	49,325	Jim Hart	19	5,076	2,593	51.1	34,665
Fran Tarkenton	18	6,467	3,686	57.0	47,003	Steve DeBerg	17	4,746	2,924	61.6	34,241
†Vinny Testaverde	19	6,526	3,691	56.6	45,262	†Kerry Collins	11	5,062	2,826	56.6	33,637
†Drew Bledsoe	13	6,548	3,749	57.3	43,447	John Hadl	16	4,687	2,363	50.4	33,503
Dan Fouts	15	5,604	3,297	58.8	43,040	Phil Simms	14	4,647	2,576	55.4	33,462
Joe Montana	15	5,391	3,409	63.2	40,551	†Peyton Manning	9	4,333	2,769	63.9	33,189
Johnny Unitas	18	5,186	2,830	54.6	40,239	Steve Young	15	4,149	2,667	64.3	33,124
Dave Krieg	19	5,311	3,105	58.5	38,147	Troy Aikman	12	4,715	2,898	61.5	32,942

† Active in 2005–06.

Career Leaders *(Cont.)*

TOUCHDOWNS

	No.		No.		No.
Dan Marino	420	Dan Fouts	254	Terry Bradshaw	212
†Brett Favre	396	Boomer Esiason	247	Y.A. Tittle	212
Fran Tarkenton	342	†Drew Bledsoe	244	Jim Hart	209
John Elway	300	John Hadl	244	Randall Cunningham	207
Warren Moon	291	†Peyton Manning	244	Jim Everett	203
Johnny Unitas	290	Len Dawson	239	Phil Simms	199
Joe Montana	273	Jim Kelly	237	Ken Anderson	197
†Vinny Testaverde	269	George Blanda	236	Joe Ferguson	196
Dave Krieg	261	Steve Young	232	Bobby Layne	196
Sonny Jurgensen	255	John Brodie	214	Norm Snead	196

† Active in 2005–06.

Receiving
RECEPTIONS

	Yrs	No.	Yds	Avg	Lg	TD		Yrs	No.	Yds	Avg	Lg	TD
Jerry Rice	20	1,549	22,895	14.8	96	197	Henry Ellard	16	814	13,777	16.9	81	65
Cris Carter	16	1,101	13,899	12.6	80	130	†Isaac Bruce	12	813	12,278	15.1	80	77
Tim Brown	17	1,094	14,934	13.7	80	100	†Rod Smith	11	797	10,877	13.6	85	65
Andre Reed	16	951	13,198	13.9	83	87	James Lofton	16	764	14,004	18.3	80	75
Art Monk	16	940	12,721	13.5	79	68	Michael Irvin	12	750	11,904	15.9	87	65
†Marvin Harrison	10	927	12,331	13.3	80	110	Charlie Joiner	18	750	12,146	16.2	87	65
†Jimmy Smith	13	862	12,287	14.3	75	67	†Keyshawn Johnson	10	744	9,756	13.1	76	60
Irving Fryar	17	851	12,785	15.0	80	84	Andre Rison	12	743	10,205	13.7	80	84
Larry Centers	14	827	6,797	8.2	54	28	Marshall Faulk	11	729	6,627	9.1	85	36
†Keenan McCardell	14	825	10,680	12.9	76	62	Gary Clark	11	699	10,856	15.5	84	65
Steve Largent	14	819	13,089	16.0	74	100	Terance Mathis	13	689	8,809	12.8	81	63
Shannon Sharpe	15	815	10,060	12.3	82	62	†Eric Moulds	10	675	9,096	13.5	84	48

YARDS

Jerry Rice	22,895	Irving Fryar	12,785	Don Maynard	11,834
Tim Brown	14,934	Art Monk	12,721	Gary Clark	10,856
James Lofton	14,004	†Marvin Harrison	12,331	†Rod Smith	10,877
Cris Carter	13,899	†Jimmy Smith	12,287	Stanley Morgan	10,716
Henry Ellard	13,777	†Isaac Bruce	12,278	†Keenan McCardell	10,680
Andre Reed	13,198	Charlie Joiner	12,146	Harold Jackson	10,372
Steve Largent	13,089	Michael Irvin	11,904	Lance Alworth	10,266

SACKS

Bruce Smith	200.0	Chris Doleman	150.5
Reggie White	198.0	John Randle	137.5
Kevin Greene	160.0	Richard Dent	137.5

Note: Officially compiled since 1982.

Interceptions

	Yrs	No.	Yds	Avg	Lg	TD
Paul Krause	16	81	1185	14.6	81	3
Emlen Tunnell	14	79	1282	16.2	55	4
Rod Woodson	17	71	1483	20.9	98	17
Dick (Night Train) Lane	14	68	1207	17.8	80	5
Ken Riley	15	65	596	9.2	66	5

Punting

	Yrs	No.	Yds	Avg	Lg	Blk
†Shane Lechler	6	442	20,266	45.9	73	0
Sammy Baugh	16	338	15,245	45.1	85	9
Tommy Davis	11	511	22,833	44.7	82	2
Yale Lary	11	503	22,279	44.3	74	4
†Todd Sauerbrun	11	832	36,600	44.0	73	0

Note: 250 or more punts.

Punt Returns

	Yrs	No.	Yds	Avg	Lg	TD
George McAfee	8	112	1431	12.8	74	2
Jack Christiansen	8	85	1084	12.8	89	8
Claude Gibson	5	110	1381	12.6	85	3
Bill Dudley	9	124	1515	12.2	96	3
Rick Upchurch	9	248	3008	12.1	92	8
Desmond Howard	11	244	2895	11.9	95	8

Note: 75 or more returns.

Kickoff Returns

	Yrs	No.	Yds	Avg.	Lg	TD
Gale Sayers	7	91	2781	30.6	103	6
Lynn Chandnois	7	92	2720	29.6	93	3
Abe Woodson	9	193	5538	28.7	105	5
Claude (Buddy) Young	6	90	2514	27.9	104	2
Travis Williams	5	102	2801	27.5	105	6

Note: 75 or more returns.

† Active in 2005–06.

Single-Season Leaders
Scoring

POINTS

	Year	TD	PAT	FG	Pts
Paul Hornung, GB	1960	15	41	15	176
†Shaun Alexander, Sea	2005	28	0	0	168
Gary Anderson, Minn	1998	0	59	35	164
†Jeff Wilkins, StL	2003	0	46	39	163
†Priest Holmes, KC	2003	27	0	0	162
Mark Moseley, Wash	1983	0	62	33	161
†Mike Vanderjagt, Ind	2003	0	46	37	157
†Marshall Faulk, StL	2000	26	0	0	156
Gino Cappelletti, Bos	1964	7	38	25	155
Emmitt Smith, Dall	1995	25	0	0	150
Chip Lohmiller, Wash	1991	0	56	31	149
†Jay Feely, NYG	2005	0	43	35	148

Note: Cappelletti's total includes a two-point conversion.

TOUCHDOWNS

	Year	Rush	Rec	Ret	Total
†Shaun Alexander, Sea	2005	27	1	0	28
†Priest Holmes, KC	2003	27	0	0	27
†Marshall Faulk, StL	2000	18	8	0	26
Emmitt Smith, Dall	1995	25	0	0	25
John Riggins, Wash	1983	24	0	0	24
†Priest Holmes, KC	2002	21	3	0	24
O.J. Simpson, Buff	1975	16	7	0	23
Jerry Rice, SF	1987	1	22	0	23
†Terrell Davis, Den	1998	21	2	0	23

FIELD GOALS

	Year	Att	No.
†Neil Rackers, Ari	2005	42	40
†Olindo Mare, Mia	1999	46	39
†Jeff Wilkins, StL	2003	42	39
†John Kasay, Car	1996	45	37
†Mike Vanderjagt, Ind	2003	37	37
Cary Blanchard, Ind	1996	40	36
Al Del Greco, Tenn	1998	39	36

Rushing

YARDS GAINED

	Year	Att	Yds	Avg
Eric Dickerson, LA Rams	1984	379	2105	5.6
†Jamal Lewis, Balt	2003	387	2066	5.3
Barry Sanders, Det	1997	335	2053	6.1
†Terrell Davis, Den	1998	392	2008	5.1
O.J. Simpson, Buff	1973	332	2003	6.0
Earl Campbell, Hou	1980	373	1934	5.2
Jim Brown, Clev	1963	291	1883	6.4
†Ahman Green, GB	2003	355	1883	5.3
Barry Sanders, Det	1994	331	1883	5.7
†Shaun Alexander, Sea	2005	370	1880	5.1
Tiki Barber, NYG	2005	357	1860	5.2
Ricky Williams, Mia	2002	383	1853	4.8

AVERAGE GAIN

	Year	Avg
Beattie Feathers, Chi	1934	8.44
Randall Cunningham, Phil	1990	7.98
†Michael Vick, Atl	2002	6.88
Bobby Douglass, Chi	1972	6.87

Minimum 100 attempts.

TOUCHDOWNS

	Year	No.
†Shaun Alexander	2005	27
†Priest Holmes, KC	2003	27
Emmitt Smith, Dall	1995	25
John Riggins, Wash	1983	24
†Priest Holmes, KC	2002	24
Emmitt Smith, Dall	1994	21
Joe Morris, NYG	1985	21
Terry Allen, Wash	1996	21
†Terrell Davis, Den	1998	21

Passing

YARDS GAINED

	Year	Att	Comp	Pct	Yds
Dan Marino, Mia	1984	564	362	64.2	5084
†Kurt Warner, StL	2001	546	375	68.7	4830
Dan Fouts, SD	1981	609	360	59.1	4802
Dan Marino, Mia	1986	623	378	60.7	4746
†Daunte Culpepper	2004	548	379	69.2	4717
Dan Fouts, SD	1980	589	348	59.1	4715
Warren Moon, Hou	1991	655	404	61.7	4690
Warren Moon, Hou	1990	584	362	62.0	4689
Rich Gannon, Oak	2002	618	418	67.6	4689
Neil Lomax, StL Cards	1984	560	345	61.6	4614
†Peyton Manning, Ind.	2004	497	336	67.6	4557
†Drew Bledsoe, NE	1994	691	400	57.9	4555

PASSER RATING

	Year	Rat.
Steve Young, SF	1994	112.8
Joe Montana, SF	1989	112.4
†Daunte Culpepper, Minn	2004	110.9
Milt Plum, Clev	1960	110.4
Sammy Baugh, Wash	1945	109.9
†Kurt Warner, Rams	1999	109.2

TOUCHDOWNS

	Year	No.
†Peyton Manning, Ind	2004	49
Dan Marino, Mia	1984	48
Dan Marino, Mia	1986	44
†Kurt Warner, StL	1999	41
†Daunte Culpepper, Minn	2004	39
†Brett Favre, GB	1995	38

Four tied with 36.

† Active in 2005–06.

Single-Season Leaders *(Cont.)*
Receiving

RECEPTIONS

	Year	No.	Yds
†Marvin Harrison, Ind	2002	143	1722
Herman Moore, Det	1995	123	1686
Cris Carter, Minn	1994	122	1256
Jerry Rice, SF	1995	122	1848
Cris Carter, Minn	1995	122	1371
†Isaac Bruce, Rams	1995	119	1781
†Torry Holt, StL	2003	117	1696
†Jimmy Smith, Jac	1999	116	1636
†Marvin Harrison, Ind	1999	115	1663
†Rod Smith, Den	2001	113	1343

YARDS GAINED

	Year	Yds
Jerry Rice, SF	1995	1848
†Isaac Bruce, Rams	1995	1781
Charley Hennigan, Hou	1961	1746
†Marvin Harrison, Ind	2002	1722
†Torry Holt, StL	2003	1696

TOUCHDOWNS

	Year	No.
Jerry Rice, SF	1987	22
Mark Clayton, Mia	1984	18
Sterling Sharpe, GB	1994	18
Seven tied with 17.		

All-Purpose Yards

	Year	Run	Rec	Ret	Total
Michael Lewis, NO	2002	15	200	2432	2647
Lionel James, SD	1985	516	1027	992	2535
Terry Metcalf, StL Cards	1975	816	378	1268	2462
Mack Herron, NE	1974	824	474	1146	2444
Gale Sayers, Chi	1966	1231	447	762	2440
†Marshall Faulk, Rams	1999	1381	1048	0	2429
Timmy Brown, Phil	1963	841	487	1100	2428
†Tiki Barber, NYG	2005	1860	530	0	2390
Barry Sanders, Det	1997	2053	305	0	2358
Tim Brown, LA Rai	1988	50	725	1542	2317
Marcus Allen, LA Rai	1985	1759	555	–6	2308
Timmy Brown, Phil	1962	545	849	912	2306

Punting

	Year	No.	Yds	Avg
Sammy Baugh, Wash	1940	35	1799	51.4
Yale Lary, Det	1963	35	1713	48.9
Sammy Baugh, Wash	1941	30	1462	48.7
Yale Lary, Det	1961	52	2516	48.4
Sammy Baugh, Wash	1942	37	1783	48.2

Sacks

	Year	No.
†Michael Strahan, NYG	2001	22.5
Mark Gastineau, NYJ	1984	22
Reggie White, Phil	1987	21
Chris Doleman, Minn	1989	21
Lawrence Taylor, NYG	1986	20.5

Interceptions

	Year	No.
Dick (Night Train) Lane, LA Rams	1952	14
Dan Sandifer, Wash	1948	13
Spec Sanders, NY Yanks	1950	13
Lester Hayes, Oak	1980	13
Nine tied with 12.		

Kickoff Returns

	Year	Avg
Travis Williams, GB	1967	41.1
Gale Sayers, Chi	1967	37.7
Ollie Matson, Chi Cards	1958	35.5
Jim Duncan, Balt Colts	1970	35.4
Lynn Chandnois, Pitt	1952	35.2

Punt Returns

	Year	Avg
Herb Rich, Balt Colts	1950	23.0
Jack Christiansen, Det	1952	21.5
Dick Christy, NY Titans	1961	21.3
Bob Hayes, Dall	1968	20.8

Single-Game Leaders
Scoring

POINTS

	Date	Pts
Ernie Nevers, Chi Cards vs Chi	11-28-29	40
Dub Jones, Clev vs Chi	11-25-51	36
Gale Sayers, Chi vs SF	12-12-65	36
Paul Hornung, GB vs Balt Colts	10-8-61	33

On Thanksgiving Day, 1929, Nevers scored all the Cardinals' points on six rushing TDs and four PATs. The Cards defeated Red Grange and the Bears, 40–6. Jones and Sayers each rushed for four touchdowns and scored two more on returns in their teams' victories. Hornung scored four touchdowns and kicked 6 PATs and a field goal in a 45-7 win over the Colts.

† Active in 2005–06.

FIELD GOALS

	Date	No.
Jim Bakken, StL Cards vs Pitt	9-24-67	7
Rich Karlis, Minn vs Rams	11-5-89	7
Chris Boniol, Dall vs GB	11-18-96	7
†Billy Cundiff, Dall vs NYG	9-15-03	7

Bakken was 7 for 9; Cundiff was 7 for 8; and Karlis and Boniol 7 for 7.

Single-Game Leaders *(Cont.)*

Scoring *(Cont.)*

TOUCHDOWNS

	Date	No.
Ernie Nevers, Chi Cards vs Chi	11-28-29	6
Dub Jones, Clev vs Chi	11-25-51	6
Gale Sayers, Chi vs SF	12-12-65	6
Bob Shaw, Chi Cards vs Balt Colts	10-2-50	5
Jim Brown, Clev vs Balt Colts	11-1-59	5
Abner Haynes, Dall Texans vs Oak	11-26-61	5
Billy Cannon, Hou vs NY Titans	12-10-61	5
Cookie Gilchrist, Buff vs NYJ	12-8-63	5
Paul Hornung, GB vs Balt Colts	12-12-65	5
Kellen Winslow, SD vs Oak	11-22-81	5
Jerry Rice, SF vs Atl	10-14-90	5
James Stewart, Jax vs Phil	10-12-97	5
†Shaun Alexander, Sea vs Minn	9-29-02	5

Rushing

YARDS GAINED

	Date	Yds
†Jamal Lewis, Balt vs Clev	9-14-03	295
†Corey Dillon, Cin vs Den	10-22-00	278
Walter Payton, Chi vs Minn	11-20-77	275
O.J. Simpson, Buff vs Det	11-25-76	273
†Shaun Alexander, Sea vs Oak	11-11-01	266

TOUCHDOWNS

	Date	No.
Ernie Nevers, Chi Cards vs Chi	11-28-29	6
Jim Brown, Clev vs Balt Colts	11-1-59	5
Cookie Gilchrist, Buff vs NYJ	12-8-63	5
James Stewart, Jac vs Phil	10-12-97	5
Clinton Portis, Den vs KC	12-7-03	5

CARRIES

	Date	No.
Jamie Morris, Wash vs Cin	12-17-88	45
Butch Woolfolk, NYG vs Phil	11-20-83	43
James Wilder, TB vs GB	9-30-84	43
†Rudi Johnson, Cin vs Hou	11-9-03	43
James Wilder, TB vs Pitt	10-30-83	42
†Terrell Davis, Den vs Buff	10-26-97	42
†Ricky Williams, Mia vs Buff	9-21-03	42

Passing

YARDS GAINED

	Date	Yds
N. Van Brocklin, Rams vs NY Yanks	9-28-51	554
Warren Moon, Hou vs KC	12-16-90	527
Boomer Esiason, Ariz vs Wash	11-10-96	522
Dan Marino, Mia vs NYJ	10-23-88	521
Phil Simms, NYG vs Cin	10-13-85	513

TOUCHDOWNS

	Date	No.
Sid Luckman, Chi vs NYG	11-14-43	7
Adrian Burk, Phil vs Wash	10-17-54	7
George Blanda, Hou vs NY Titans	11-19-61	7
Y. A. Tittle, NYG vs Wash	10-28-62	7
Joe Kapp, Minn vs Balt Colts	9-28-69	7

COMPLETIONS

	Date	No.
†Drew Bledsoe, NE vs Minn	11-13-94	45
Rich Gannon, Oak vs Pitt	9-15-02	43
Richard Todd, NYJ vs SF	9-21-80	42
†Vinny Testaverde, NYJ vs Sea	12-6-98	42
Warren Moon, Hou vs Dall	11-10-91	41
Ken Anderson, Cin vs SD	12-20-82	40
Phil Simms, NYG vs Cin	10-13-85	40
†Brad Johnson, TB vs Chi	11-18-01	40
†Marc Bulger, StL Rams vs. NYG	10-02-05	40

Receiving

YARDS GAINED

	Date	Yds
Flipper Anderson, Rams vs NO	11-26-89	336
Stephone Paige, KC vs SD	12-22-85	309
Jim Benton, Clev vs Det	11-22-45	303
Cloyce Box, Det vs Balt Colts	12-3-50	302
†Jimmy Smith, Jax vs Balt Ravens	9-10-00	291

RECEPTIONS

	Date	No.
†Terrell Owens, SF vs Chi	12-17-00	20
Tom Fears, Rams vs GB	12-3-50	18
Clark Gaines, NYJ vs SF	9-21-80	17
Sonny Randle, StL Cards vs NYG	11-4-62	16
Jerry Rice, SF vs Rams	11-20-94	16
†Keenan McCardell, Jax vs Rams	10-20-96	16
†Troy Brown, NE vs KC	9-22-02	16

Six tied with 15.

† Active in 2005–06.

Single-Game Leaders *(Cont.)*

Receiving *(Cont.)*
TOUCHDOWNS

	Date	No.
Bob Shaw, Chi Cards vs Balt Colts	10-2-50	5
Kellen Winslow, SD vs Oak	11-22-81	5
Jerry Rice, SF vs Atl	10-14-90	5

All-Purpose Yards

	Date	Yds
Glyn Milburn, Den vs Sea	12-10-95	404
Billy Cannon, Hou vs NY Titans	12-10-61	373
Tyrone Hughes, NO vs LA Rams	10-23-94	347
Lionel James, SD vs LA Rai	11-10-85	345
Timmy Brown, Phil vs StL Cards	12-16-62	341

Longest Plays

RUSHING	Opponent	Year	Yds
Tony Dorsett, Dall	Minn	1983	99
†Ahman Green, GB	Den	2003	98
Andy Uram, GB	Chi Cards	1939	97
Bob Gage, Pitt.	Chi	1949	97
Jim Spavital, Balt Colts	GB	1950	96
Bob Hoernschemeyer, Det	NY Yanks	1950	96
Garrison Hearst, SF	NYJ	1998	96
†Corey Dillon, Cin	Det	2001	96

PASSING	Opponent	Year	Yds
Frank Filchock to Andy Farkas, Wash	Pitt	1939	99
George Izo to Bobby Mitchell, Wash	Clev	1963	99
Karl Sweetan to Pat Studstill, Det	Balt Colts	1966	99
Sonny Jurgensen to Gerry Allen, Wash	Chi	1968	99
Jim Plunkett to Cliff Branch, LA Rai	Wash	1983	99
Ron Jaworski to Mike Quick, Phil	Atl	1985	99
Stan Humphries to Tony Martin, SD	Sea	1994	99
Brett Favre to Robert Brooks, GB	Chi	1995	99
Trent Green to Marc Boerigter, KC	SD	2002	99
Jeff Garcia to Andre Davis, Cle	Cin	2004	99

FIELD GOALS	Opponent	Year	Yds
Tom Dempsey, NO	Det	1970	63
†Jason Elam, Den	Jax	1998	63
Steve Cox, Clev	Cin	1984	60
Morten Andersen, NO	Chi	1991	60

PUNTS	Opponent	Year	Yds
Steve O'Neal, NYJ	Den	1969	98
Joe Lintzenich, Chi	NYG	1931	94
Shawn McCarthy, NE	Buff	1991	93
Randall Cunningham, Phil	NYG	1989	91

INTERCEPTION RETURNS	Opponent	Year	Yds
Ed Reed, Balt	Clev	2004	106
Vencie Glenn, SD	Den	1987	103
Louis Oliver, Mia	Buff	1992	103
Seven players tied at 102.			

KICKOFF RETURNS	Opponent	Year	Yds
Al Carmichael, GB	Chi	1956	106
Noland Smith, KC	Den	1967	106
Roy Green, StL Cards	Dall	1979	106

PUNT RETURNS	Opponent	Year	Yds
Robert Bailey, LA Rams	NO	1994	103
Gil LeFebvre, Cin	Brooklyn	1933	98
Charlie West, Minn	Wash	1968	98
Dennis Morgan, Dall	StL Cards	1974	98
Terance Mathis, NYJ	Dall	1990	98

MISSED FIELD GOAL RETURNS	Opponent	Year	Yds
†Nathan Vasher, Chi	SF	2005	108
†Chris McAllister, Balt	Den	2002	107
Aaron Glenn, NYJ	Ind	1998	104

Rushing

Year	Player, Team	Att	Yards	Avg	TD
1932	Cliff Battles, Bos	148	576	3.9	3
1933	Jim Musick, Bos	173	809	4.7	5
1934	Beattie Feathers, Chi	101	1004	9.9	8
1935	Doug Russell, Chi Cards	140	499	3.6	0
1936	Alphonse Leemans, NY	206	830	4.0	2
1937	Cliff Battles, Wash	216	874	4.0	5
1938	Byron White, Pitt	152	567	3.7	4
1939	Bill Osmanski, Chi	121	699	5.8	7
1940	Byron White, Det	146	514	3.5	5
1941	Clarence Manders, Bklyn	111	486	4.4	5
1942	Bill Dudley, Pitt	162	696	4.3	5
1943	Bill Paschal, NY	147	572	3.9	10
1944	Bill Paschal, NY	196	737	3.8	9
1945	Steve Van Buren, Phil	143	832	5.8	15
1946	Bill Dudley, Pitt	146	604	4.1	3
1947	Steve Van Buren, Phil	217	1008	4.6	13
1948	Steve Van Buren, Phil	201	945	4.7	10
1949	Steve Van Buren, Phil	263	1146	4.4	11
1950	Marion Motley, Clev	140	810	5.8	3
1951	Eddie Price, NY	271	971	3.6	7
1952	Dan Towler, LA	156	894	5.7	10
1953	Joe Perry, SF	192	1018	5.3	10
1954	Joe Perry, SF	173	1049	6.1	8
1955	Alan Ameche, Balt	213	961	4.5	9
1956	Rick Casares, Chi	234	1126	4.8	12
1957	Jim Brown, Clev	202	942	4.7	9
1958	Jim Brown, Clev	257	1527	5.9	17
1959	Jim Brown, Clev	290	1329	4.6	14
1960	Jim Brown, Clev, NFL	215	1257	5.8	9
	Abner Haynes, Dall Texans, AFL	156	875	5.6	9
1961	Jim Brown, Clev, NFL	305	1408	4.6	8
	Billy Cannon, Hou, AFL	200	948	4.7	6
1962	Jim Taylor, GB, NFL	272	1474	5.4	19
	Cookie Gilchrist, Buff, AFL	214	1096	5.1	13
1963	Jim Brown, Clev, NFL	291	1863	6.4	12
	Clem Daniels, Oak, AFL	215	1099	5.1	3
1964	Jim Brown, Clev, NFL	280	1446	5.2	7
	Cookie Gilchrist, Buff, AFL	230	981	4.3	6
1965	Jim Brown, Clev, NFL	289	1544	5.3	17
	Paul Lowe, SD, AFL	222	1121	5.0	7
1966	Jim Nance, Bos, AFL	299	1458	4.9	11
	Gale Sayers, Chi, NFL	229	1231	5.4	8
1967	Jim Nance, Bos, AFL	269	1216	4.5	7
	Leroy Kelly, Clev, NFL	235	1205	5.1	11
1968	Leroy Kelly, Clev, NFL	248	1239	5.0	16
	Paul Robinson, Cin, AFL	238	1023	4.3	8
1969	Gale Sayers, Chi, NFL	236	1032	4.4	8
	Dickie Post, SD, AFL	182	873	4.8	6
1970	Larry Brown, Wash, NFC	237	1125	4.7	5
	Floyd Little, Den, AFC	209	901	4.3	3
1971	Floyd Little, Den, AFC	284	1133	4.0	6
	John Brockington, GB, NFC	216	1105	5.1	4
1972	O.J. Simpson, Buff, AFC	292	1251	4.3	6
	Larry Brown, Wash, NFC	285	1216	4.3	8
1973	O.J. Simpson, Buff, AFC	332	2003	6.0	12
	John Brockington, GB, NFC	265	1144	4.3	3
1974	Otis Armstrong, Den, AFC	263	1407	5.3	9
	Lawrence McCutcheon, LA, NFC	236	1109	4.7	3
1975	O.J. Simpson, Buff, AFC	329	1817	5.5	16
	Jim Otis, StL, NFC	269	1076	4.0	5
1976	O.J. Simpson, Buff, AFC	290	1503	5.2	8
	Walter Payton, Chi, NFC	311	1390	4.5	13
1977	Walter Payton, Chi, NFC	339	1852	5.5	14
	Mark van Eeghen, Oak, AFC	324	1273	3.9	7
1978	Earl Campbell, Hou, AFC	302	1450	4.8	13
	Walter Payton, Chi, NFC	333	1395	4.2	11
1979	Earl Campbell, Hou, AFC	368	1697	4.6	19
	Walter Payton, Chi, NFC	369	1610	4.4	14
1980	Earl Campbell, Hou, AFC	373	1934	5.2	13
	Walter Payton, Chi, NFC	317	1460	4.6	6
1981	George Rogers, NO, NFC	378	1674	4.4	13
	Earl Campbell, Hou, AFC	361	1376	3.8	10
1982	Freeman McNeil, NY Jets, AFC	151	786	5.2	6
	Tony Dorsett, Dall, NFC	177	745	4.2	5
1983	Eric Dickerson, LA Rams, NFC	390	1808	4.6	18
	Curt Warner, Sea, AFC	335	1449	4.3	13
1984	Eric Dickerson, LA Rams, NFC	379	2105	5.6	14
	Earnest Jackson, SD, AFC	296	1179	4.0	8
1985	Marcus Allen, LA Raiders, AFC	380	1759	4.6	11
	Gerald Riggs, Atl, NFC	397	1719	4.3	10
1986	Eric Dickerson, LA Rams, NFC	404	1821	4.5	11
	Curt Warner, Sea, AFC	319	1481	4.6	13
1987	Charles White, LA Rams, NFC	324	1374	4.2	11
	Eric Dickerson, Ind, AFC	223	1011	4.5	5
1988	Eric Dickerson, Ind, AFC	388	1659	4.3	14
	Herschel Walker, Dall, NFC	361	1514	4.2	5
1989	Christian Okoye, KC, AFC	370	1480	4.0	12
	Barry Sanders, Det, NFC	280	1470	5.3	14
1990	Barry Sanders, Det, NFC	255	1304	5.1	13
	Thurman Thomas, Buff, AFC	271	1297	4.8	11
1991	Emmitt Smith, Dall, NFC	365	1563	4.3	12
	Thurman Thomas, Buff, AFC	288	1407	4.9	7
1992	Emmitt Smith, Dall, NFC	373	1713	4.6	18
	Barry Foster, Pitt, AFC	390	1690	4.3	11
1993	Emmitt Smith, Dall, NFC	283	1486	5.3	9
	T. Thomas, Buff, AFC	355	1315	3.7	6
1994	Barry Sanders, Det, NFC	331	1883	5.7	7
	Chris Warren, Sea, AFC	333	1545	4.6	9

Rushing *(Cont.)*

Year	Player, Team	Att	Yards	Avg	TD
1995	Emmitt Smith, Dall, NFC	377	1773	4.7	25
	Curtis Martin, NE, AFC	368	1487	4.0	14
1996	Barry Sanders, Det, NFC	307	1553	5.1	11
	Terrell Davis, Den, AFC	345	1538	4.5	13
1997	Barry Sanders, Det, NFC	335	2053	6.1	11
	Terrell Davis, Den, AFC	369	1730	4.7	15
1998	Terrell Davis, Den, AFC	392	2008	5.1	21
	Jamal Anderson, Atl, NFC	410	1846	4.5	14
1999	Edgerrin James, Ind, AFC	369	1553	4.2	13
	Stephen Davis, Wash, NFC	290	1405	4.8	17
2000	Edgerrin James, Ind, AFC	387	1709	4.4	13
	Robert Smith, Minn, NFC	295	1521	5.2	7
2001	Priest Holmes, Kan, AFC	327	1555	4.8	8
	Stephen Davis, Wash, NFC	356	1432	4.0	5
2002	Ricky Williams, Mia, AFC	383	1853	4.8	16
	Deuce McAllister, NO, NFC	325	1388	4.3	13
2003	Jamal Lewis, Balt, AFC	387	2066	5.3	14
	Ahman Green, GB, NFC	355	1883	5.3	15
2004	Curtis Martin, NY Jets, AFC	371	1697	4.6	12
	Shaun Alexander, Seattle, NFC	353	1696	4.8	16
2005	Shaun Alexander, Seattle, NFC	370	1880	5.1	27
	Larry Johnson, KC, AFC	336	1750	5.2	20

Passing*

Year	Player, Team	Att	Comp	Yards	TD	Int
1932	Arnie Herber, GB	101	37	639	9	9
1933	Harry Newman, NY	136	53	973	11	17
1934	Arnie Herber, GB	115	42	799	8	12
1935	Ed Danowski, NY	113	57	794	10	9
1936	Arnie Herber, GB	173	77	1239	11	13
1937	Sammy Baugh, Wash	171	81	1127	8	14
1938	Ed Danowski, NY	129	70	848	7	8
1939	Parker Hall, Clev	208	106	1227	9	13
1940	Sammy Baugh, Wash	177	111	1367	12	10
1941	Cecil Isbell, GB	206	117	1479	15	11
1942	Cecil Isbell, GB	268	146	2021	24	14
1943	Sammy Baugh, Wash	239	133	1754	23	19
1944	Frank Filchock, Wash	147	84	1139	13	9
1945	Sammy Baugh, Wash	182	128	1669	11	4
	Sid Luckman, Chi	217	117	1725	14	10
1946	Bob Waterfield, LA	251	127	1747	18	17
1947	Sammy Baugh, Wash	354	210	2938	25	15
1948	Tommy Thompson, Phil	246	141	1965	25	11
1949	Sammy Baugh, Wash	255	145	1903	18	14
1950	Norm Van Brocklin, LA	233	127	2061	18	14
1951	Bob Waterfield, LA	176	88	1566	13	10
1952	Norm Van Brocklin, LA	205	113	1736	14	17
1953	Otto Graham, Clev	258	167	2722	11	9
1954	Norm Van Brocklin, LA	260	139	2637	13	21
1955	Otto Graham, Clev	185	98	1721	15	8
1956	Ed Brown, Chi	168	96	1667	11	12
1957	Tommy O'Connell, Clev	110	63	1229	9	8
1958	Eddie LeBaron, Wash	145	79	1365	11	10
1959	Charlie Conerly, NY	194	113	1706	14	4
1960	Milt Plum, Clev, NFL	250	151	2297	21	5
	Jack Kemp, LA, AFL	406	211	3018	20	25
1961	George Blanda, Hou, AFL	362	187	3330	36	22
	Milt Plum, Clev, NFL	302	177	2416	18	10
1962	Norm Snead, Wash, NFL	310	189	2759	29	17
	Bart Starr, GB, NFL	285	178	2438	12	9
1963	Y.A. Tittle, NY, NFL	367	221	3145	36	14
	Tobin Rote, SD, AFL	286	170	2510	20	17
1964	Len Dawson, KC, AFL	354	199	2879	30	18
	Bart Starr, GB, NFL	272	163	2144	15	4
1965	Rudy Bukich, Chi, NFL	312	176	2641	20	9
	John Hadl, SD, AFL	348	174	2798	20	21
1966	Bart Starr, GB, NFL	251	156	2257	14	3
	Len Dawson, KC, AFL	284	159	2527	26	10
1967	Sonny Jurgensen, Wash, NFL	508	288	3747	31	16
	Daryle Lamonica, Oakland, AFL	425	220	3228	30	20
1968	Len Dawson, KC, AFL	224	131	2109	17	9
	Earl Morrall, Balt, NFL	317	182	2909	26	17
1969	S. Jurgensen, Wash, NFL	442	274	3102	22	15
	Greg Cook, Cin, AFL	197	106	1854	15	11
1970	John Brodie, SF, NFC	378	223	2941	24	10
	Daryle Lamonica, Oak, AFC	356	179	2516	22	15
1971	Roger Staubach, Dall, NFC	211	126	1882	15	4
	Bob Griese, Mia, AFC	263	145	2089	19	9
1972	Norm Snead, NY, NFC	325	196	2307	17	12
	Earl Morrall, Mia, AFC	150	83	1360	11	7
1973	Roger Staubach, Dall, NFC	286	179	2428	23	15
	Ken Stabler, Oak, AFC	260	163	1997	14	10
1974	Ken Anderson, Cin, AFC	328	213	2667	18	10
	Sonny Jurgensen, Wash, NFC	167	107	1185	11	5
1975	Ken Anderson, Cin, AFC	377	228	3169	21	11
	Fran Tarkenton, Minn, NFC	425	273	2994	25	13
1976	Ken Stabler, Oak, AFC	291	194	2737	27	17
	James Harris, LA, NFC	158	91	1460	8	6
1977	Bob Griese, Mia, AFC	307	180	2252	22	13
	Roger Staubach, Dall, NFC	361	210	2620	18	9
1978	Roger Staubach, Dall, NFC	413	231	3190	25	16
	Terry Bradshaw, Pitt, AFC	368	207	2915	28	20
1979	Roger Staubach, Dall, NFC	461	267	3586	27	11
	Dan Fouts, SD, AFC	530	332	4082	24	24
1980	Brian Sipe, Clev, AFC	554	337	4132	30	14
	Ron Jaworski, Phi, NFC	451	257	3529	27	12
1981	Ken Anderson, Cin, AFC	479	300	3754	29	10
	Joe Montana, SF, NFC	488	311	3565	19	12
1982	Ken Anderson, Cin, AFC	309	218	2495	12	9
	Joe Theismann, Wash, NFC	252	161	2033	13	9
1983	Steve Bartkowski, Atl, NFC	432	274	3167	22	5
	Dan Marino, Mia AFC	296	173	2210	20	6

Passing (Cont.)

Year	Player, Team	Att	Comp	Yards	TD	Int
1984	Dan Marino, Mia, AFC	564	362	5084	48	17
	Joe Montana, SF, NFC	432	279	3630	28	10
1985	Ken O'Brien, NY, AFC	488	297	3888	25	8
	Joe Montana, SF, NFC	494	303	3653	27	13
1986	Tommy Kramer, Minn, NFC	372	208	3000	24	10
	Dan Marino, Mia, AFC	623	378	4746	44	23
1987	Joe Montana, SF, NFC	398	266	3054	31	13
	Bernie Kosar, Clev, AFC	389	241	3033	22	9
1988	Boomer Esiason, Cin, AFC	388	223	3572	28	14
	Wade Wilson, Minn, NFC	332	204	2746	15	9
1989	Joe Montana, SF, NFC	386	271	3521	26	8
	Boomer Esiason, Cin, AFC	455	258	3525	28	11
1990	Jim Kelly, Buffalo, AFC	346	219	2829	24	9
	Phil Simms, NY, NFC	311	184	2284	15	4
1991	Steve Young, SF, NFC	279	180	2517	17	8
	Jim Kelly, Buff, AFC	474	304	3844	33	17
1992	Steve Young, SF, NFC	402	268	3465	25	7
	Warren Moon, Hou, AFC	346	224	2521	18	12
1993	Steve Young, SF, NFC	462	314	4023	29	16
	John Elway, Den, AFC	551	348	4030	25	10
1994	Steve Young, SF, NFC	461	324	3969	35	10
	Dan Marino, Mia, AFC	615	385	4453	30	17
1995	Brett Favre, GB, NFC	570	359	4413	38	13
	Jeff Blake, Cin, AFC	567	326	3822	28	17
1996	Vinny Testaverde, Balt, AFC	549	325	4177	33	19
	Brett Favre, GB, NFC	543	325	3899	39	13
1997	Steve Young, SF, NFC	356	241	3029	19	6
	Mark Brunell, Jax, AFC	435	264	3281	18	7
1998	Randall Cunningham, Minn, NFC	425	259	3704	34	10
	Vinny Testaverde, NYJ, AFC	421	259	3256	29	7
1999	Kurt Warner, StL, NFC	499	325	4353	41	13
	Peyton Manning, Ind, AFC	533	331	4135	26	15
2000	Trent Green, StL, NFC	240	145	2063	16	5
	Brian Griese, Den, AFC	336	216	2688	19	4
2001	Kurt Warner, StL, NFC	546	375	4830	36	22
	Rich Gannon, Oak, AFC	549	361	3828	27	9
2002	Brad Johnson, TB, NFC	451	281	3049	22	6
	Chad Pennington, NYJ, AFC	399	275	3120	22	6
2003	Steve McNair, Tenn, AFC	400	250	3215	24	7
	Daunte Culpepper, Minn, NFC	454	295	3479	25	11
2004	Peyton Manning, Ind, AFC	497	336	4557	49	10
	Daunte Culpepper, Minn, NFC	548	379	4717	39	11
2005	Tom Brady, NE, AFC	530	334	4110	26	14
	Brett Favre, GB, NFC	607	372	3881	20	29

*Since 1973, the annual passing leaders have been determined by a passer rating system that compares individual performances to a fixed performance standard.

Pass Receiving*

Year	Player, Team	No.	Yds	Avg	TD
1932	Ray Flaherty, NY	21	350	16.7	3
1933	John Kelly, Brooklyn	22	246	11.2	3
1934	Joe Carter, Phil	16	238	14.9	4
	Morris Badgro, NY	16	206	12.9	1
1935	Tod Goodwin, NY	26	432	16.6	4
1936	Don Hutson, GB	34	536	15.8	8
1937	Don Hutson, GB	41	552	13.5	7
1938	Gaynell Tinsley, Chi Cards	41	516	12.6	1
1939	Don Hutson, GB	34	846	24.9	6
1940	Don Looney, Phil	58	707	12.2	4
1941	Don Hutson, GB	58	738	12.7	10
1942	Don Hutson, GB	74	1211	16.4	17
1943	Don Hutson, GB	47	776	16.5	11
1944	Don Hutson, GB	58	866	14.9	9
1945	Don Hutson, GB	47	834	17.7	9
1946	Jim Benton, LA	63	981	15.6	6
1947	Jim Keane, Chi	64	910	14.2	10
1948	Tom Fears, LA	51	698	13.7	4
1949	Tom Fears, LA	77	1013	13.2	9
1950	Tom Fears, LA	84	1116	13.3	7
1951	Elroy Hirsch, LA	66	1495	22.7	17
1952	Mac Speedie, Clev	62	911	14.7	5
1953	Pete Pihos, Phil	63	1049	16.7	10
1954	Pete Pihos, Phil	60	872	14.5	10
	Billy Wilson, SF	60	830	13.8	5
1955	Pete Pihos, Phil	62	864	13.9	7
1956	Billy Wilson, SF	60	889	14.8	5
1957	Billy Wilson, SF	52	757	14.6	6
1958	Raymond Berry, Balt	56	794	14.2	9
	Pete Retzlaff, Phil	56	766	13.7	2
1959	Raymond Berry, Balt	66	959	14.5	14
1960	Lionel Taylor, Den, AFL	92	1235	13.4	12
	Raymond Berry, Balt, NFL	74	1298	17.5	10
1961	Lionel Taylor, Den, AFL	100	1176	11.8	4
	Jim Phillips, LA, NFL	78	1092	14.0	5
1962	Lionel Taylor, Den, AFL	77	908	11.8	4
	Bobby Mitchell, Wash, NFL	72	1384	19.2	11
1963	Lionel Taylor, Den, AFL	78	1101	14.1	10
	Bobby Joe Conrad, St. Louis, NFL	73	967	13.2	10
1964	Charley Hennigan, Houston, AFL	101	1546	15.3	8
	Johnny Morris, Chi, NFL	93	1200	12.9	10
1965	Lionel Taylor, Den, AFL	85	1131	13.3	6
	Dave Parks, SF, NFL	80	1344	16.8	12
1966	Lance Alworth, SD, AFL	73	1383	18.9	13
	Charley Taylor, Wash, NFL	72	1119	15.5	12
1967	George Sauer, NY, AFL	75	1189	15.9	6
	Charley Taylor, Wash, NFL	70	990	14.1	9
1968	Clifton McNeil, SF, NFL	71	994	14.0	7
	Lance Alworth, SD, AFL	68	1312	19.3	10
1969	Dan Abramowicz, NO, NFL	73	1015	13.9	7
	Lance Alworth, SD, AFL	64	1003	15.7	4
1970	Dick Gordon, Chi, NFC	71	1026	14.5	13
	Marlin Briscoe, Buff, AFC	57	1036	18.2	8

*Most catches.

Pass Receiving *(Cont.)*

Year	Player, Team	No.	Yds	Avg	TD
1971	Fred Biletnikoff, Oak, AFC	61	929	15.2	9
	Bob Tucker, NY, NFC	59	791	13.4	4
1972	Harold Jackson,				
	Phil, NFC	62	1048	16.9	4
	Fred Biletnikoff, Oak, AFC	58	802	13.8	7
1973	Harold Carmichael,				
	Phil, NFC	67	1116	16.7	9
	Fred Willis, Hou, AFC	57	371	6.5	1
1974	Lydell Mitchell, Balt, AFC	72	544	7.6	2
	Charles Young,				
	Phil, NFC	63	696	11.0	3
1975	Chuck Foreman,				
	Minn, NFC	73	691	9.5	9
	Reggie Rucker,				
	Clev, AFC	60	770	12.8	3
	Lydell Mitchell, Balt, AFC	60	544	9.1	4
1976	MacArthur Lane,				
	KC, AFC	66	686	10.4	1
	Drew Pearson, Dall, NFC	58	806	13.9	6
1977	Lydell Mitchell, Balt, AFC	71	620	8.7	4
	Ahmad Rashad,				
	Minn, NFC	51	681	13.4	2
1978	Rickey Young, Minn, NFC	88	704	8.0	5
	Steve Largent, Sea, AFC	71	1168	16.5	8
1979	Joe Washington,				
	Balt, AFC	82	750	9.1	3
	Ahmad Rashad,				
	Minn, NFC	80	1156	14.5	9
1980	Kellen Winslow, SD, AFC	89	1290	14.5	9
	Earl Cooper, SF, NFC	83	567	6.8	4
1981	Kellen Winslow, SD, AFC	88	1075	12.2	10
	Dwight Clark, SF, NFC	85	1105	13.0	4
1982	Dwight Clark, SF, NFC	60	913	15.2	5
	Kellen Winslow, SD, AFC	54	721	13.4	6
1983	Todd Christensen,				
	LA, AFC	92	1247	13.6	12
	Roy Green, StL, NFC	78	1227	15.7	14
	Charlie Brown, Wash, NFC	78	1225	15.7	8
	Earnest Gray, NY, NFC	78	1139	14.6	5
1984	Art Monk, Wash, NFC	106	1372	12.9	7
	Ozzie Newsome,				
	Clev, AFC	89	1001	11.2	5
1985	Roger Craig, SF, NFC	92	1016	11.0	6
	Lionel James, SD, AFC	86	1027	11.9	6
1986	Todd Christensen,				
	LA Rai, AFC	95	1153	12.1	8
	Jerry Rice, SF, NFC	86	1570	18.3	15
1987	J.T. Smith, StL Card, NFC	91	1117	12.3	8
	Al Toon, NY, AFC	68	976	14.4	5
1988	Al Toon, NY, AFC	93	1067	11.5	5
	Henry Ellard,				
	LA Rams, NFC	86	1414	16.4	10
1989	Sterling Sharpe, GB, NFC	90	1423	15.8	12
	Andre Reed, Buff, AFC	88	1312	14.9	9
1990	Jerry Rice, SF, NFC	100	1502	15.0	13
	Haywood Jeffires,				
	Hou, AFC	74	1048	14.2	8
	Drew Hill, Hou, AFC	74	1019	13.8	5
1991	Haywood Jeffires,				
	Hou, AFC	100	1181	11.8	7
	Michael Irvin, Dall, NFC	93	1523	16.4	8
1992	Sterling Sharpe,				
	GB, NFC	108	1461	13.5	13
	Haywood Jeffires,				
	Hou, AFC	90	913	10.1	9
1993	Sterling Sharpe,				
	GB, NFC	112	1274	11.4	11
	Reggie Langhorne,				
	Ind, AFC	85	1038	12.2	3
1994	Cris Carter, Minn, NFC	122	1256	10.3	7
	Ben Coates, NE, AFC	96	1174	12.2	7
1995	Herman Moore,				
	Det, NFC	123	1686	13.7	14
	Carl Pickens, Cin, AFC	99	1234	12.5	17
1996	Jerry Rice, SF, NFC	108	1254	11.6	8
	Carl Pickens, Cin, AFC	100	1180	11.8	12
1997	Herman Moore, Det, NFC	104	1293	12.4	8
	Tim Brown, Oak, AFC	104	1408	13.5	5
1998	Frank Sanders,				
	Ariz, NFC	89	1145	12.9	3
	O.J. McDuffie, Mia, AFC	90	1050	11.7	7
1999	Muhsin Muhammad,				
	Car, NFC	96	1253	13.1	8
	Jimmy Smith, Jax, AFC	116	1636	14.1	6
2000	Mushin Muhammad,				
	Car, NFC	102	1183	11.6	6
	Marvin Harrison, Ind, AFC	102	1413	13.9	14
2001	Rod Smith, Den, AFC	113	1343	11.9	11
	Keyshawn Johnson,				
	TB, NFC	106	1266	11.9	1
2002	Marvin Harrison, Ind, AFC	143	1722	12.0	11
	Randy Moss, Minn, NFC	106	1347	12.7	7
2003	LaDainian Tomlinson,				
	SD, AFC	100	725	7.3	4
	Torry Holt, StL, NFC	117	1696	14.5	12
2004	Tony Gonzalez, KC, AFC	102	1258	12.3	7
	Joe Horn, NO, NFC	94	1399	14.9	11
2005	Chad Johnson, Cin, AFC	97	1432	14.8	9
	Steve Smith, Car, NFC	103	1563	15.2	12

Scoring

Year	Player, Team	TD	FG	PAT	TP
1932	Earl Clark, Portsmouth	6	3	10	55
1933	Ken Strong, NY	6	5	13	64
	Glenn Presnell, Ports	6	6	10	64
1934	Jack Manders, Chi	3	10	31	79
1935	Earl Clark, Det	6	1	16	55
1936	Earl Clark, Det	7	4	19	73
1937	Jack Manders, Chi	5	18	15	69
1938	Clarke Hinkle, GB	7	3	7	58
1939	Andy Farkas, Wash	11	0	2	68
1940	Don Hutson, GB	7	0	15	57
1941	Don Hutson, GB	12	1	20	95
1942	Don Hutson, GB	17	1	33	138
1943	Don Hutson, GB	12	3	36	117
1944	Don Hutson, GB	9	0	31	85
1945	Steve Van Buren, Phil	18	0	2	110
1946	Ted Fritsch, GB	10	9	13	100
1947	Pat Harder, Chicago Cards	7	7	39	102
1948	Pat Harder, Chicago Cards	6	7	53	110
1949	Pat Harder, Chicago Cards	8	3	45	102
	Gene Roberts, NY	17	0	0	102
1950	Doak Walker, Det	11	8	38	128
1951	Elroy Hirsch, LA	17	0	0	102
1952	Gordy Soltau, SF	7	6	34	94
1953	Gordy Soltau, SF	6	10	48	114

Scoring *(Cont.)*

Year	Player, Team	TD	FG	PAT	TP
1954	Bobby Walston, Phil	11	4	36	114
1955	Doak Walker, Det	7	9	27	96
1956	Bobby Layne, Det	5	12	33	99
1957	Sam Baker, Wash	1	14	29	77
	Lou Groza, Clev	0	15	32	77
1958	Jim Brown, Clev	18	0	0	108
1959	Paul Hornung, GB	7	7	31	94
1960	Paul Hornung, GB, NFL	15	15	41	176
	Gene Mingo, Den, AFL	6	18	33	123
1961	Gino Cappelletti, Bos, AFL	8	17	48	147
	Paul Hornung, GB, NFL	10	15	41	146
1962	Gene Mingo, Den, AFL	4	27	32	137
	Jim Taylor, GB, NFL	19	0	0	114
1963	Gino Cappelletti, Bos, AFL	2	22	35	113
	Don Chandler, NY, NFL	0	18	52	106
1964	Gino Cappelletti, Bos, AFL	7	25	36	155
	Lenny Moore, Balt, NFL	20	0	0	120
1965	Gale Sayers, Chi, NFL	22	0	0	132
	Gino Cappelletti, Bos, AFL	9	17	27	132
1966	Gino Cappelletti, Bos, AFL	6	16	35	119
	Bruce Gossett, LA, NFL	0	28	29	113
1967	Jim Bakken, StL, NFL	0	27	36	117
	George Blanda, Oak, AFL	0	20	56	116
1968	Jim Turner, NY, AFL	0	34	43	145
	Leroy Kelly, Clev, NFL	20	0	0	120
1969	Jim Turner, NY, AFL	0	32	33	129
	Fred Cox, Minn, NFL	0	26	43	121
1970	Fred Cox, Minn, NFC	0	30	35	125
	Jan Stenerud, KC, AFC	0	30	26	116
1971	Garo Yepremian, Mia, AFC	0	28	33	117
	Curt Knight, Wash, NFC	0	29	27	114
1972	Chester Marcol, GB, NFC	0	33	29	128
	Bobby Howfield, NY AFC	0	27	40	121
1973	David Ray, LA, NFC	0	30	40	130
	Roy Gerela, Pitt, AFC	0	29	36	123
1974	Chester Marcol, GB, NFC	0	25	19	94
	Roy Gerela, Pitt, AFC	0	20	33	93
1975	O.J. Simpson, Buff, AFC	23	0	0	138
	Chuck Foreman, Minn, NFC	22	0	0	132
1976	Toni Linhart, Balt, AFC	0	20	49	109
	Mark Moseley, Wash, NFC	0	22	31	97
1977	Errol Mann, Oak, AFC	0	20	39	99
	Walter Payton, Chi, NFC	16	0	0	96
1978	Frank Corral, LA, NFC	0	29	31	118
	Pat Leahy, NY, AFC	0	22	41	107
1979	John Smith, NE, AFC	0	23	46	115
	Mark Moseley, Wash, NFC	0	25	39	114
1980	John Smith, NE, AFC	0	26	51	129
	Ed Murray, Det, NFC	0	27	35	116
1981	Ed Murray, Det, NFC	0	25	46	121
	Rafael Septien, Dall, NFC	0	27	40	121
	Jim Breech, Cin, AFC	0	22	49	115
	Nick Lowery, KC, AFC	0	26	37	115

Year	Player, Team	TD	FG	PAT	TP
1982	Marcus Allen, LA, AFC	14	0	0	84
	Wendell Tyler, LA, NFC	13	0	0	78
1983	Mark Moseley, Wash, NFC	0	33	62	161
	Gary Anderson, Pitt, AFC	0	27	38	119
1984	Ray Wersching, SF, NFC	0	25	56	131
	Gary Anderson, Pitt, AFC	0	24	45	117
1985	Kevin Butler, Chi, NFC	0	31	51	144
	Gary Anderson, Pitt, AFC	0	33	40	139
1986	Tony Franklin, NE, AFC	0	32	44	140
	Kevin Butler, Chi, NFC	0	28	36	120
1987	Jerry Rice, SF, NFC	23	0	0	138
	Jim Breech, Cin, AFC	0	24	25	97
1988	Scott Norwood, Buff, AFC	0	32	33	129
	Mike Cofer, SF, NFC	0	27	40	121
1989	Mike Cofer, SF, NFC	0	29	49	136
	David Treadwell, Den, AFC	0	27	39	120
1990	Nick Lowery, KC, AFC	0	34	37	139
	Chip Lohmiller, Wash, NFC	0	30	41	131
1991	Chip Lohmiller, Wash, NFC	0	31	56	149
	Pete Stoyanovich, Mia, AFC	0	31	28	121
1992	Pete Stoyanovich, Mia, AFC	0	30	34	124
	Morten Anderson, NO, NFC	0	29	33	120
	Chip Lohmiller, Wash, NFC	0	30	30	120
1993	Jeff Jaeger, Rai, AFC	0	35	27	132
	Jason Hanson, Det, NFC	0	34	28	130
1994	John Carney, SD, AFC	0	34	33	135
	Fuad Reveiz, Minn, NFC	0	34	30	132
	Emmitt Smith, Dall, NFC	22	0	0	132
1995	Emmitt Smith, Dall, NFC	25	0	0	150
	Norm Johnson, Pitt, AFC	0	34	39	141
1996	John Kasay, Car, NFC	0	37	34	145
	Cary Blanchard, Ind, AFC	0	36	27	135
1997	Richie Cunningham, Dall, NFC	0	34	24	126
	Mike Hollis, Jax, AFC	0	41	31	134
1998	Gary Anderson, Minn, NFC	0	35	59	164
	Steve Christie, Buff, AFC	0	33	41	140
1999	Jeff Wilkins, StL, NFC	0	20	28	124
	Mike Vanderjagt, Ind, AFC	0	34	38	145
2000	Marshall Faulk, StL, NFC	26	0	0	156
	Matt Stover, Balt, AFC	0	35	30	135
2001	Marshall Faulk, StL, NFC	21	0	0	128
	Mike Vanderjagt, Ind, AFC	0	28	41	125
2002	Jay Feely, Atl, NFC	0	32	43	138
	Priest Holmes, KC, AFC	24	0	0	144
2003	Jeff Wilkins StL, NFC	0	39	46	163
	Priest Holmes, KC, AFC	27	0	0	162
2004	Adam Vinatieri, NE, AFC	0	31	48	141
	David Akers, Phil, NFC	0	27	41	122
2005	Shayne Graham, Cin, AFC	0	28	47	131
	Shaun Alexander, Sea, NFC	28	0	0	168

Interceptions

Year	Player, Team	Int	Yds
1940	Clarence Parker, Brooklyn	6	146
	Kent Ryan, Det	6	65
	Don Hutson, GB	6	24
1941	Marshall Goldberg, Chicago Card	7	54
	Art Jones, Pitt	7	35
1942	Clyde Turner, Chicago Bears	8	96
1943	Sammy Baugh, Wash	11	112
1944	Howard Livingston, NYG	9	172
1945	Ray Zimmerman, Phil	7	90
1946	Bill Dudley, Pittsburgh	10	242

Year	Player, Team	Int	Yds
1947	Frank Reagan, NYG	10	203
	Frank Seno, Bos	10	100
1948	Dan Sandifier, Wash	13	258
1949	Bob Nussbaumer, Chicago Car	12	157
1950	Orban Sanders, NY Yanks	13	199
1951	Otto Schnellbacher, NYG	11	194
1952	Dick Lane, LA	14	298
1953	Jack Christiansen, Det	12	238
1954	Dick Lane, Chicago Card	10	181
1955	Will Sherman, LA	11	101

Interceptions *(Cont.)*

Year	Player, Team	Int	Yds
1956	Lindon Crow, Chicago Card	11	170
1957	Milt Davis, Balt	10	219
	Jack Christiansen, Det	10	137
	Jack Butler, Pitt	10	85
1958	Jim Patton, NYG	11	183
1959	Dean Derby, Pitt	7	127
	Milt Davis, Balt	7	119
	Don Shinnick, Balt	7	70
1960	Goose Gonsoulin, Den, AFL	11	98
	Dave Baker, SF, NFL	10	96
	Jerry Norton, StL, NFL	10	96
1961	Billy Atkins, Buff, AFL	10	158
	Dick Lynch, NYG, NFL	9	60
1962	Lee Riley, NY Titans, AFL	11	122
	Willie Wood, GB, NFL	9	132
1963	Fred Glick, Hous, AFL	12	180
	Dick Lynch, NYG, NFL	9	251
	Roosevelt Taylor, Chi, NFL	9	172
1964	Dainard Paulson, NYJ, AFL	12	157
	Paul Krause, Wash, NFL	12	140
1965	W. K. Hicks, Hous, AFL	9	156
	Bobby Boyd, Balt, NFL	9	78
1966	Larry Wilson, StL, NFL	10	180
	Johnny Robinson, KC, AFL	10	113
	Bobby Hunt, KC, AFL	10	113
1967	Miller Farr, Hous, AFL	10	264
	Tom Janik, Buff, AFL	10	222
	Dick Westmoreland, Mia, AFL	10	127
	Lem Barney, Det, NFL	10	232
	Dave Whitsell, NO, NFL	10	178
1968	Dave Grayson, Oak, AFL	10	195
	Willie Williams, NYG, NFL	10	103
1969	Mel Renfro, Dall, NFL	10	118
	Emmitt Thomas, KC, AFL	9	146
1970	Johnny Robinson, KC, AFC	10	155
	Dick LeBeau, Det, NFC	9	96
1971	Bill Bradley, Phil, NFC	11	248
	Ken Hou, Hou, AFC	9	220
1972	Bill Bradley, Phil, NFC	9	73
	Mike Sensibaugh, KC, AFC	8	65
1973	Dick Anderson, Mia, AFC	8	163
	Mike Wagner, Pitt, AFC	8	134
	Bobby Bryant, Minn, NFC	7	105
1974	Emmitt Thomas, KC, AFC	12	214
	Ray Brown, Atl, NFC	8	164
1975	Mel Blount, Pitt, AFC	11	121
	Paul Krause, Minn, NFC	10	201
1976	Monte Jackson, LA, NFC	10	173
	Ken Riley, Cin, AFC	9	141
1977	Lyle Blackwood, Balt, AFC	10	163
	Rolland Lawrence, Atl, NFC	7	138
1978	Thom Darden, Clev, AFC	10	200
	Ken Stone, StL, NFC	9	139
	Willie Buchanon, GB, NFC	9	93
1979	Mike Reinfeldt, Hou, AFC	12	205
	Lemar Parrish, Wash, NFC	9	65
1980	Lester Hayes, Oak, AFC	13	273
	Nolan Cromwell, LA, NFC	8	140
1981	Everson Walls, Dal, NFC	11	133
	John Harris, Sea, AFC	10	155
1982	Everson Walls, Dal, NFC	7	61
	Ken Riley, Cin, AFC	5	88
	Bobby Jackson, NYJ, AFC	5	84
	Dwayne Woodruff, Pitt, AFC	5	53
	Donnie Shell, Pitt, AFC	5	27
1983	Mark Murphy, Wash, NFC	9	127
	Ken Riley, Cin, AFC	8	89
	Vann McElroy, LA Raiders, AFC	8	68
1984	Ken Easley, Sea, AFC	10	126
	Tom Flynn, GB, NFC	9	106
1985	Everson Walls, Dal, NFC	9	31
	Albert Lewis, KC, AFC	8	59
	Eugene Daniel, Ind, AFC	8	53
1986	Ronnie Lott, SF, NFC	10	134
	Deron Cherry, KC, AFC	9	150
1987	Barry Wilburn, Wash, NFC	9	135
	Mike Prior, Ind, AFC	6	57
	Mark Kelso, Buff, AFC	6	25
	Keith Bostic, Hou, AFC	6	-14
1988	Scott Case, Atl, NFC	10	47
	Erik McMillan, NYJ, AFC	8	168
1989	Felix Wright, Clev, AFC	9	91
	Eric Allen, Phil, NFC	8	38
1990	Mark Carrier, Chi, NFC	10	39
	Richard Johnson, Hou, AFC	8	100
1991	Ronnie Lott, LA Raiders, AFC	8	52
	Ray Crockett, Det, NFC	6	141
	Deion Sanders, Atl, NFC	6	119
	Aeneas Williams, Phoenix, NFC	6	60
	Tim McKyer, Atl, NFC	6	24
1992	Henry Jones, Buff, AFC	8	263
	Audray McMillian, Minn, NFC	8	157
1993	Eugene Robinson, Sea, AFC	9	80
	Nate Odomes, Buff, AFC	9	65
	Deion Sanders, Atl, NFC	7	91
1994	Eric Turner, Clev, AFC	9	199
	Aeneas Williams, Ariz, NFC	9	89
1995	Orlando Thomas, Minn, NFC	9	108
	Willie Williams, Pitt, AFC	7	122
1996	Tyrone Braxton, Den, AFC	9	128
	Keith Lyle, StL, NFC	9	152
1997	Ryan McNeil, StL, NFC	9	127
	Mark McMillian, KC, AFC	8	274
	Darryl Williams, Sea, AFC	8	172
1998	Ty Law, NE, AFC	9	133
	Kwamie Lassiter, Ariz, NFC	8	80
1999	Rod Woodson, Balt, AFC	7	195
	Sam Madison, Mia, AFC	7	164
	James Hasty, KC, AFC	7	98
	Donnie Abraham, TB, NFC	7	115
	Troy Vincent, Phil, NFC	7	91
2000	Darren Sharper, GB, NFC	9	109
	Samari Rolle, Tenn, AFC	7	140
	Brian Walker, Mia, AFC	7	80
2001	Ronde Barber, TB, NFC	10	86
	Anthony Henry, Clev, AFC	10	177
2002	Rod Woodson, Oak, AFC	8	225
	Brian Kelly, TB, NFC	8	68
2003	Brian Russell, Minn, NFC	9	185
	Tony Parrish, SFo, NFC	9	202
	Patrick Surtain, Mia, AFC	7	59
	Ed Reed, Balt, AFC	7	132
	Marcus Coleman, Hou, AFC	7	95
2004	Ed Reed, Balt, AFC	9	358
	Chris Gamble, Car, NFC	6	15
	Ken Lucas, Sea, NFC	6	46
2005	Ty Law, NYJ, AFC	10	195
	Deltha O'Neal, Cin, AFC	10	103
	Darren Sharper, Minn, NFC	9	276

Sacks*

Year	Player, Team	Sacks
1982	Doug Martin, Minn, NFC	11.5
	Jesse Baker, Hou, AFC	7.5
1983	Mark Gastineau, NYJ, AFC	19.0
	Fred Dean, SF, NFC	17.5
1984	Mark Gastineau, NYJ, AFC	22.0
	Richard Dent, Chi, NFC	17.5
1985	Richard Dent, Chi, NFC	17.0
	Andre Tippett, NE, AFC	16.5
1986	Lawrence Taylor, NYG, NFC	20.5
	Sean Jones, LA, AFC	15.5
1987	Reggie White, Phil, NFC	21.0
	Andre Tippett, NE, AFC	12.5
1988	Reggie White, Phil, NFC	18.0
	G. Townsend, LA, AFC	11.5
1989	Chris Doleman, Minn, NFC	21.0
	Lee Williams, SD, AFC	14.0
1990	Derrick Thomas, KC, AFC	20.0
	Charles Haley, SF, NFC	16.0
1991	Pat Swilling, NO, NFC	17.0
	William Fuller, Hou, AFC	15.0
1992	Clyde Simmons, Phil, NFC	19.0
	Leslie O'Neal, SD, AFC	17.0
1993	Neil Smith, KC, AFC	15.0
	Renaldo Turnbull, NO, NFC	13.0
	Reggie White, GB, NFC	13.0

Year	Player, Team	Int	Yds
1994	Kevin Greene, Pitt, AFC		14.0
	Ken Harvey, Wash, NFC		13.5
	John Randle, Minn, NFC		13.5
1995	Bryce Paup, Buff, AFC		17.5
	William Fuller, Phil, NFC		13.0
	Wayne Martin, NO, NFC		13.0
1996	Kevin Greene, Car, NFC		14.5
	Michael McCrary, Sea, AFC		13.5
	Bruce Smith, Buff, AFC		13.5
1997	John Randle, Minn, NFC		15.5
	Bruce Smith, Buff, AFC		14.0
1998	Michael Sinclair, Sea, AFC		16.5
	Reggie White, GB, NFC		16.0
1999	Kevin Carter, StL, NFC		17.0
	Jevon Kearse, Tenn, AFC		14.5
2000	La'Roi Glover, NO, NFC		17.0
	Trace Armstrong, Mia, AFC		16.5
2001	Michael Strahan, NYG, NFC		22.5
	Peter Boulware, Balt, AFC		15.0
2002	Jason Taylor, Mia, AFC		18.5
	Simeon Rice, TB, NFC		15.5
2003	Michael Strahan, NYG, NFC		18.5
	Adewale Ogunleye, Mia, AFC		15.0
2004	Dwight Freeney, Ind, AFC		16.0
	Bertrand Berry, Ariz, NFC		14.5
2005	Derrick Burgess, Oak, AFC		16.0
	Osi Umenyiora, NYG, NFC		14.5

*Sacks were not kept as official NFL statistics until 1982.

Pro Bowl Alltime Results

Date	Result
1-15-39	NY Giants 13, Pro All-Stars 10
1-14-40	Green Bay 16, NFL All-Stars 7
12-29-40	Chi Bears 28, NFL All-Stars 14
1-4-42	Chi Bears 35, NFL All-Stars 24
12-27-42	NFL All-Stars 17, Washington 14
1-14-51	A. Conf. 28, N. Conf. 27
1-12-52	N. Conf. 30, A. Conf. 13
1-10-53	N. Conf. 27, A. Conf. 7
1-17-54	East 20, West 9
1-16-55	West 26, East 19
1-15-56	East 31, West 30
1-13-57	West 19, East 10
1-12-58	West 26, East 7
1-11-59	East 28, West 21
1-17-60	West 38, East 21
1-15-61	West 35, East 31
1-7-62	AFL West 47, East 27
1-14-62	NFL West 31, East 30
1-13-63	AFL West 21, East 14
1-13-63	NFL East 30, West 20
1-12-64	NFL West 31, East 17

Date	Result
1-19-64	AFL West 27, East 24
1-10-65	NFL West 34, East 14
1-16-65	AFL West 38, East 14
1-15-66	AFL All-Stars 30, Buffalo 19
1-15-66	NFL East 36, West 7
1-21-67	AFL East 30, West 23
1-22-67	NFL East 20, West 10
1-21-68	AFL East 25, West 24
1-21-68	NFL West 38, East 20
1-19-69	AFL West 38, East 25
1-19-69	NFL West 10, East 7
1-17-70	AFL West 26, East 3
1-18-70	NFL West 16, East 13
1-24-71	NFC 27, AFC 6
1-23-72	AFC 26, NFC 13
1-21-73	AFC 33, NFC 28
1-20-74	AFC 15, NFC 13
1-20-75	NFC 17, AFC 10
1-26-76	NFC 23, AFC 20
1-17-77	AFC 24, NFC 14
1-23-78	NFC 14, AFC 13
1-29-79	NFC 13, AFC 7
1-27-80	NFC 37, AFC 27
2-1-81	NFC 21, AFC 7
1-31-82	AFC 16, NFC 13

Date	Result
2-6-83	NFC 20, AFC 19
1-29-84	NFC 45, AFC 3
1-27-85	AFC 22, NFC 14
2-2-86	NFC 28, AFC 24
2-1-87	AFC 10, NFC 6
2-7-88	AFC 15, NFC 6
1-29-89	NFC 34, AFC 3
2-4-90	NFC 27, AFC 21
2-3-91	AFC 23, NFC 21
2-2-92	NFC 21, AFC 15
2-7-93	AFC 23, NFC 20
2-6-94	NFC 17, AFC 3
2-5-95	AFC 41, NFC 13
2-4-96	NFC 20, AFC 13
2-2-97	AFC 26, NFC 23
2-1-98	AFC 29, NFC 24
2-7-99	AFC 23, NFC 10
2-6-00	NFC 51, AFC 31
2-4-01	AFC 38, NFC 17
2-9-02	AFC 38, NFC 30
2-2-03	AFC 45, NFC 20
2-8-04	NFC 55, AFC 52
2-13-05	AFC 38, NFC 27
2-12-06	NFC 23, AFC 17

Chicago All-Star Game* Results

Date	Result (Attendance)
8-31-34	Chi Bears 0 (79,432)
8-29-35	Chi Bears 5, All-Stars 0 (77,450)
9-3-36	All-Stars 7, Detroit 7 (76,000)
9-1-37	All-Stars 6, Green Bay 0 (84,560)
8-31-38	All-Stars 28, Washington 16 (74,250)
8-30-39	NY Giants 9, All-Stars 0 (81,456)
8-29-40	Green Bay 45, All-Stars 28 (84,567)
8-28-41	Chi Bears 37, All-Stars 13 (98,203)
8-28-42	Chi Bears 21, All-Stars 0 (101,100)
8-25-43	All-Stars 27, Washington 7 (48,471)
8-30-44	Chi Bears 24, All-Stars 21 (48,769)
8-30-45	Green Bay 19, All-Stars 7 (92,753)
8-23-46	All-Stars 16, Los Angeles 0 (97,380)
8-22-47	All-Stars 16, Chi Bears 0 (105,840)
8-20-48	Chi Cardinals 28, All-Stars 0 (101,220)
8-12-49	Philadelphia 38, All-Stars 0 (93,780)
8-11-50	All-Stars 17, Philadelphia 7 (88,885)
8-17-51	Cleveland 33, All-Stars 0 (92,180)
8-15-52	Los Angeles 10, All-Stars 7 (88,316)
8-14-53	Detroit 24, All-Stars 10 (93,818)
8-13-54	Detroit 31, All-Stars 6 (93,470)
8-12-55	All-Stars 30, Cleveland 27 (75,000)

Date	Result (Attendance)
8-10-56	Cleveland 26, All-Stars 0 (75,000)
8-9-57	NY Giants 22, All-Stars 12 (75,000)
8-15-58	All-Stars 35, Detroit 19 (70,000)
8-14-59	Baltimore 29, All-Stars 0 (70,000)
8-12-60	Baltimore 32, All-Stars 7 (70,000)
8-4-61	Philadelphia 28, All-Stars 14 (66,000)
8-3-62	Green Bay 42, All-Stars 20 (65,000)
8-2-63	All-Stars 20, Green Bay 17 (65,000)
8-7-64	Chicago 28, All-Stars 17 (65,000)
8-6-65	Cleveland 24, All-Stars 16 (68,000)
8-5-66	Green Bay 38, All-Stars 0 (72,000)
8-4-67	Green Bay 27, All-Stars 0 (70,934)
8-2-68	Green Bay 34, All-Stars 17 (69,917)
8-1-69	NY Jets 26, All-Stars 24 (74,208)
7-31-70	Kansas City 24, All-Stars 3 (69,940)
7-30-71	Baltimore 24, All-Stars 17 (52,289)
7-28-72	Dallas 20, All-Stars 7 (54,162)
7-27-73	Miami 14, All-Stars 3 (54,103)
1974	No game
8-1-75	Pittsburgh 21, All-Stars 14 (54,103)
7-23-76	Pittsburgh 24, All-Stars 0 (52,895)

*Discontinued.

Alltime Winningest NFL Coaches

Most Career Wins

Coach	Yrs	Teams	Regular Season				Career			
			W	L	T	Pct	W	L	T	Pct
Don Shula	33	Colts, Dolphins	328	156	6	.676	347	173	6	.665
George Halas	40	Bears	318	148	31	.671	324	151	31	.671
Tom Landry	29	Cowboys	250	162	6	.605	270	178	6	.601
Curly Lambeau	33	Packers, Cardinals, Redskins	226	132	22	.624	229	134	22	.623
Paul Brown	25	Browns, Bengals	213	104	9	.667	222	112	9	.660
Chuck Noll	23	Steelers	193	148	1	.566	209	156	1	.572
Dan Reeves	23	Broncos, Giants, Falcons	190	165	2	.535	201	174	2	.536
Chuck Knox	22	Rams, Bills, Seahawks	186	147	1	.558	193	158	1	.550
†M. Schottenheimer	20	Browns, Chiefs, Redskins, Chargers	186	124	1	.606	191	136	1	.582
†Bill Parcells	18	Giants, Patriots, Jets, Cowboys	163	123	1	.568	174	130	1	.570
Bud Grant	18	Vikings	158	96	5	.620	168	108	5	.607
†Joe Gibbs	14	Redskins	140	76	0	.648	157	82	0	.657
Marv Levy	17	Chiefs, Bills	143	112	0	.561	154	120	0	.562
Steve Owen	23	Giants	151	100	17	.595	153	108	17	.581
†Bill Cowher	14	Steelers	141	82	1	.629	153	91	1	.624
†Mike Holmgren	14	Packers, Seahawks	138	86	0	.616	149	95	0	.611
Hank Stram	17	Chiefs, Saints	131	97	10	.571	136	100	10	.573
Weeb Ewbank	20	Colts, Jets	130	129	7	.502	134	130	7	.507
Jim Mora	15	Saints, Colts	125	106	0	.541	125	112	0	.527
Mike Ditka	14	Bears, Saints	121	95	0	.560	127	101	0	.557

Top Winning Percentages

	W	L	T	Pct		W	L	T	Pct
Vince Lombardi	105	35	6	.750	Paul Brown	222	112	9	.660
John Madden	112	39	7	.731	†Joe Gibbs	157	82	0	.657
George Allen	118	54	5	.681	George Seifert	124	67	0	.649
George Halas	324	151	31	.671	†Bill Cowher	153	91	1	.624
Don Shula	347	173	6	.665	Curly Lambeau	229	134	22	.623

Note: Minimum 100 victories.

†Active in 2005–06.

Pro Football Most Valuable Players

Year	Player/Team	Position
1938	Mel Hein, NYG (NFL)	C
1939	Parker Hall, Clev (NFL)	HB
1940	Ace Parker, Brooklyn (NFL)	QB
1941	Don Hutson, GB (NFL)	E
1942	Don Hutson, GB (NFL)	E
1943	Sid Luckman, Chi Bears (NFL)	QB
1944	Frank Sinkwich, Det (NFL)	HB
1945	Bob Waterfield, Clev (NFL)	QB
1946	Bill Dudley, Pitt (NFL)	HB
	Glenn Dobbs, Brooklyn (AAFC)	HB
1947	No Selection (NFL)	
	Otto Graham, Clev (AAFC)	QB
1948	No Selection (NFL)	
	Otto Graham, Clev (AAFC-tie)	QB
	Frankie Albert, SF (AAFC-tie)	QB
1949	No Selection (NFL)	
1950	No Selection (NFL)	
1951	Otto Graham, Clev (UP)	QB
1952	No Selection (NFL)	
1953	Otto Graham, Clev (UP)	QB
1954	Joe Perry, SF (UP)	FB
	Lou Groza, Clev (TSN)	OT/K
1955	Otto Graham, Clev (UP, TSN)	QB
	Harlon Hill, Chi Bears (NEA)	E
1956	Frank Gifford, NYG (UP, NEA, TSN)	HB
1957	Y.A. Tittle, SF (UP)	QB
	Jim Brown, Clev (AP, TSN)	FB
	John Unitas, Balt (NEA)	QB
1958	Jim Brown, Clev (UP, AP, NEA, TSN)	FB
1959	John Unitas, Balt (UP, MCP, TSN)	QB
	Charley Conerly, NYG (AP, NEA)	QB
1960	Norm Van Brocklin, Phil, NFL (UP, AP, NEA, TSN, MCP)	QB
	Joe Schmidt, Det, NFL (UP- tie)	LB
	Abner Haynes, Dal Texans, AFL (UP, TSN)	HB
1961	Paul Hornung, GB, NFL (UP, AP, TSN, MCP)	HB
	Y.A. Tittle, NYG, NFL (NEA)	QB
	George Blanda, Hous, AFL (UP, TSN)	QB
1962	Y.A. Tittle, NYG, NFL (UP, TSN)	QB
	Jim Taylor, GB, NFL (AP, NEA)	FB
	Andy Robustelli, NYG, NFL (MCP)	DE
	Cookie Gilchrist, Buff, AFL (UP)	FB
	Len Dawson, Dal Texans, AFL (TSN)	QB
1963	Jim Brown, Clev, NFL (UP, NEA tie), MCP)	FB
	Y.A. Tittle, NYG, NFL (AP, NEA tie), TSN)	QB
	Lance Alworth, SD, AFL (UP)	WR
	Clem Daniels, Oak, AFL (TSN)	HB
1964	Johnny Unitas, Balt, NFL (UP, AP, TSN, MCP)	QB
	Lenny Moore, Balt, NFL (NEA)	HB
	Gino Cappelletti, Boston, AFL (UP, TSN)	WR
1965	Jim Brown, Clev, NFL (UP, AP, TSN, NEA)	FB
	Pete Retzlaff, Phil, NFL (MCP)	TE
	Jack Kemp, Buff, AFL (UP)	QB
	Paul Lowe, SD, AFL (TSN)	RB
1966	Bart Starr, GB, NFL (UP, AP, NEA, TSN)	QB
	Don Meredith, Dal, NFL (MCP)	QB
	Jim Nance, Boston, AFL (UP, AP, TSN)	FB
1967	Johnny Unitas, Balt, NFL (UP, AP, NEA, TSN, MCP)	QB
	Daryle Lamonica, Oak, AFL (UP, AP, TSN)	QB
1968	Earl Morrall, Balt, NFL (UP, AP, NEA, TSN, PFW)	QB
	Leroy Kelly, Clev, AFL (MCP)	HB
	Joe Namath, NY Jets, AFL (UP, TSN, PFW)	QB
1969	Roman Gabriel, LA Rams, NFL (UP, AP, NEA, MCP, TSN, PFW)	QB
	Daryle Lamonica, Oak, AFL (UP, TSN, PFW)	QB
	Joe Namath, NY Jets, AFL (AP)	QB
1970	John Brodie, SF (AP, NEA)	QB
	George Blanda, Oak (MCP)	QB/K
1971	Alan Page, Minn (AP)	DT
	Bob Griese, Miami (NEA)	QB
	Roger Staubach, Dal (MCP)	QB
1972	Larry Brown, Washington (AP, NEA, MCP)	RB
1973	O.J. Simpson, Buff (AP, NEA, MCP)	RB
1974	Ken Stabler, Oak (AP, NEA)	QB
	Merlin Olsen, LA Rams (MCP)	DT
1975	Fran Tarkenton, Minn (PFWA, AP, NEA, MCP)	QB
1976	Bert Jones, Balt (PFWA, AP, NEA)	QB
	Ken Stabler, Oak (MCP)	QB
1977	Walter Payton, Chi (PFWA, AP, NEA)	RB
	Bob Griese, Miami (MCP)	QB
1978	Earl Campbell, Hous (PFWA, NEA)	RB
	Terry Bradshaw, Pitt (AP, MCP)	QB
1979	Earl Campbell, Hous (PFWA, AP, NEA, MCP)	RB
1980	Brian Sipe, Clev (PFWA, AP, TSN)	QB
	Earl Campbell, Hous (NEA)	RB
	Ron Jaworski, Phil (MCP)	QB
1981	Ken Anderson, Cin (PFWA, AP, NEA, TSN, MCP)	QB
1982	Dan Fouts, SD (PFWA, NEA)	QB
	Mark Moseley, Washington (AP, TSN)	K
	Joe Theismann, Washington (MCP)	QB
1983	Joe Theismann, Washington (PFWAA, AP, NEA)	QB
	Eric Dickerson, LA Rams (TSN)	RB
	John Riggins, Washington (MCP)	RB
1984	Dan Marino, Miami (PFWAA, AP, NEA, MCP, TSN)	QB
1985	Marcus Allen, LA Raiders (PFWAA, AP, TSN)	RB
	Walter Payton, Chi Bears (NEA, MCP)	RB
1986	Lawrence Taylor, NYG (PFWAA, AP, MCP, TSN)	LB
	Phil Simms, NYG (NEA)	QB
1987	Jerry Rice, SF (PFWAA, NEA, MCP, TSN)	WR
	John Elway, Den (AP)	QB
1988	Boomer Esiason, Cin (PFWAA, AP, TSN)	QB
	Roger Craig, SF (NEA)	RB
	Randall Cunningham, Phil (MCP)	QB
1989	Joe Montana, SF (PFWAA, AP, NEA, MCP, TSN)	QB
1990	Randall Cunningham, Phil (PFWAA)	QB
	Joe Montana, SF (AP)	QB
	Jerry Rice, SF (TSN)	WR
1991	Thurman Thomas, Buff (PFWAA, AP, TSN)	RB
	Barry Sanders, Det (MCP)	RB
1992	Steve Young, SF (PFWAA, AP, MCP, TSN)	QB
1993	Emmitt Smith, Dal (PFWAA, AP, MCP, TSN)	RB
1994	Steve Young, SF (PFWAA, AP, MCP, TSN)	QB
1995	Brett Favre, GB (PFWAA, AP, MCP, TSN)	QB
1996	Brett Favre, GB (PFWAA, AP, MCP, TSN)	QB
1997	Brett Favre, GB (AP – tie)	QB
	Barry Sanders, Det (PFWAA, AP (tie), MCP, TSN)	RB
1998	Terrell Davis, Den (PFWAA, AP, TSN)	RB
	Randall Cunningham, Minn (MCP)	QB

Year	Player/ Team	Position	Year	Player/ Team	Position
1999	Kurt Warner, StL (AP, PFWAA, MCP)	QB	2002	Rich Gannon, Oak (AP)	QB
2000	Marshall Faulk, StL (AP, PFWAA)	RB	2003	Peyton Manning, Ind (AP - tie)	QB
	Rich Gannon, Oak (MCP)	QB		Steve McNair, Tenn (AP - tie)	QB
2001	Kurt Warner, StL (AP)	QB	2004	Peyton Manning, Ind (AP)	QB
	Marshall Faulk, StL (PFWAA, MCP, TSN)	RB	2005	Shaun Alexander, Sea (AP)	RB

NOTE: AP-Associated Press, UP-United Press, PFW-*Pro Football Weekly*, TSN-*The Sporting News*, PFWAA-Pro Football Writers Association of America, PFWA-Pro Football Writers of America, MCP-Maxwell Club of Philadelphia, NEA-Newspaper Enterprise Association.
The NFL began awarding its MVP award, the Joe F. Carr Trophy (Carr was league president from 1921-39), in 1938, and continued to do so until 1946. Since that time, the NFL's Most Valuable Players and Players of the Year have been named by a variety of sources, among them, the United Press, the Associated Press, the Maxwell Club of Philadelphia, and the Pro Football Writers Association of America as well as magazines such as *Pro Football Weekly* and *The Sporting News*.

Pro Football Rookies of the Year

Year	Player/ Team	Position	Year	Player/ Team	Position
1955	Alan Ameche, Balt (UP, TSN)	FB	1971	Jim Plunkett NE (UP-AFC)	QB
1956	Lenny Moore, Balt (UP)	HB		John Brockington GB (AP-Off, UP-NFC)	RB
	J.C. Caroline, Chi Bears (TSN)	DB		Isiah Robertson, SF (AP-Def)	LB
1957	Jim Brown, Clev (UP, AP, TSN)	FB	1972	Franco Harris, Pitt (AP-Off, PFW, UP-AFC)	RB
1958	Jimmy Orr, Pitt (UP, AP)	OE		Chester Marcol, GB (UP-NFC)	PK
	Bobby Mitchell, Cleveland (TSN)	HB		Willie Buchanan, GB (AP-Def)	CB
1959	Nick Pietrosante, Det (AP, TSN)	FB	1973	Chuck Foreman, Minn (AP-Off, PFW)	RB
	Boyd Dowler, GB (UP)	OE		Wally Chambers, Chi (AP-Def)	DT
1960	Gail Cogdill, Det, NFL (AP, UP, TSN)	OE		Bobbie Clark, Cin (UP-AFC)	RB
	Abner Haynes, Dal Texans, AFL (UP, TSN)	HB		Charle Young Phil (UP-NFC)	TE
1961	Mike Ditka, Chi Bears, NFL (AP, UP, TSN)	OE	1974	Don Woods, SD (AP-Off, PFW, UP-AFC)	RB
	Earl Faison, SD, AFL (UP, TSN)	DE		John Hicks, NYG (UP-NFC)	G
1962	Ronnie Bull, Chi Bears, NFL (AP, UP, TSN)	HB		Jack Lambert, Pitt (AP-Def)	LB
	Curtis McClinton, Dal, AFL (UP, TSN)	FB	1975	Steve Bartkowski, Atl (PFW)	QB
1963	Paul Flatley, Minn, NFL (AP, UP, TSN)	OE		Robert Brazile, Hous (AP-Def, UP-AFC)	LB
	Billy Joe, Den, AFL (UP, TSN)	FB		Mike Thomas, Wash (AP-Off, UP-NFC)	RB
1964	Charley Taylor, Wash,	HB	1976	Mike Haynes, DB NE (AP-Def, UP-AFC)	DB
	NFL (AP, UP, TSN, NEA)			Sammy White, Minn (AP-Off, UP-NFC)	WR
	Matt Snell, NYJ, AFL (UP, TSN)	FB	1977	Tony Dorsett, Dal (NEA, AP-Off, UP-NFC)	RB
1965	Gale Sayers, Chi, NFL (AP, UP, TSN, NEA)	HB		A.J. Duhe, Mia (AP-Def, UP-AFC)	DE
	Joe Namath, NYJ, AFL (UP, TSN)	QB	1978	Earl Campbell, Hous Oilers	RB
1966	Johnny Roland, StL, NFL (UP)	HB		(NEA, PFWA, AP-Off, UP-AFC)	
	Tommy Nobis, Atl, NFL (AP, TSN, NEA)	LB		Al "Bubba" Baker, Det (AP-Def, UP-NFC)	DE
	Bobby Burnett, Buff, AFL (UP, TSN)	HB	1979	Ottis Anderson, StL Card	RB
1967	Mel Farr, Det, NFL (AP-Off, UP, TSN, NEA)	HB		(NEA, PFWA, AP-Off, UP-NFC)	
	Lem Barney, Det NFL (AP-Def)	CB		Jerry Butler, Buff (UP-AFC)	WR
	George Webster, Hous, AFL (UP)	LB		Jim Haslett, Buff (AP-Def	LB
	Dickie Post, SD, AFL (TSN)	HB	1980	Billy Sims, Det	RB
1968	Earl McCullouch, Det, NFL	OE		(NEA, TSN, PFWA, AP-Off, UP-NFC)	
	(AP-Off, UP, TSN, NEA)			Joe Cribbs Buff (UP-AFC)	RB
	Claude Humphrey NFL (AP-Def)	DE		Buddy Curry, Atl (AP-Def tie)	LB
	Paul Robinson, Cin, AFL (UP, TSN)	HB		Al Richardson, Atl (AP-Def tie)	LB
1969	Calvin Hill, Dal, NFL	HB	1981	Lawrence Taylor, NYG (NEA, AP-Def)	LB
	(AP-Off, UP, TSN, NEA)			George Rogers, NO	RB
	Joe Greene NFL (AP-Def)	DT		(TSN, PFWA, AP-Off, UP-NFC)	
	Greg Cook, Cin, AFL (UP)	QB		Joe Delaney, KC (UP-AFC)	RB
	Carl Garrett, Boston, AFL (TSN)	HB	1982	Marcus Allen, LA Raiders	RB
1970	Raymond Chester, Oak (NEA)	TE		(NEA, TSN, PFWA, AP-Off, UP-AFC)	
	Dennis Shaw Buff (AP-Off, UP-AFC)	QB		Jim McMahon, Chi (UP-NFC)	QB
	Bruce Taylor, DB SF (AP-Def, UP-NFC)	DB		Chip Banks, Cle (AP-Def)	LB

Year	Player/ Team	Position	Year	Player/ Team	Position
1983	Eric Dickerson, LA Rams (NEA, PFWA, AP-Off, UP-NFC)	RB	1993	Jerome Bettis, LA Rams (PFWA, TSN, AP-Off, UP-NFC)	RB
	Dan Marino, Mia (TSN)	QB		Rick Mirer, Sea (UP-AFC)	QB
	Curt Warner, Sea (UP-AFC)	RB		Dana Stubblefield, SF (AP-Def)	DT
	Vernon Maxwell, Balt (AP-Def)	LB	1994	Marshall Faulk, Ind (PFWA, TSN, AP-Off, UP-AFC)	RB
1984	Louis Lipps, Pitt (NEA, TSN, PFWA, AP-Off, UP-AFC)	WR		Bryant Young, SF (UP-NFC)	DT
	Paul McFadden, Phil (UP-NFC)	PK		Tim Bowens, Mia (AP-Def)	DT
	Bill Maas, KC (AP-Def)	DT	1995	Curtis Martin, NE (PFWA, TSN, AP-Off, UP-AFC)	RB
1985	Eddie Brown, Cin (NEA, TSN, AP-Off, PFWA)	WR		Rashaan Salaam Chi (UP-NFC)	RB
	Kevin Mack, Clev (UP-AFC)	RB		Hugh Douglas, NYJ (AP-Def)	DE
	Jerry Rice, SF (UP-NFC)	WR	1996	Eddie George, Tenn (AP, PFWA, AP-Off, TSN)	RB
	Duane Bickett, Ind (AP-Def)	LB		Terry Glenn, NE (UP-AFC)	WR
1986	Reuben Mayes, NO (NEA, TSN, PFWA, AP-Off, UP-NFC)	RB		Simeon Rice, Ariz (AP-Def, UP-NFC)	DE
	Leslie O'Neal, SD (AP-Def, UP-AFC)	DE	1997	Warrick Dunn, TB (PFWA, AP-Off, TSN)	RB
1987	Shane Conlan, Buff (PFWA, AP-Def, UP-AFC)	LB		Peter Boulware, Balt (AP-Def)	LB
	Bo Jackson, LA Raiders (NEA)	RB	1998	Randy Moss, Minn (PFWA, AP-Off, TSN)	WR
	Robert Awalt, StL Card (TSN, UP-NFC)	TE		Charles Woodson LA Raiders (AP-Def)	CB
	Troy Stradford, Mia (AP-Off)	RB	1999	Edgerrin James, Ind (AP-Off, TSN)	RB
1988	John Stephens, NE (NEA, AP-Off, PFWA)	RB		Jevon Kearse, Tenn (AP-Def)	DE
	Keith Jackson, Phil (TSN, UP-NFC)	TE	2000	Mike Anderson, Den (AP-Off, TSN)	RB
	Eric McMillan, NYJ (AP-Def)	S		Brian Urlacher, Chi (AP-Def)	LB
1989	Barry Sanders, Det (NEA, TSN, PFWA, AP-Off, UP-NFC)	RB	2001	Anthony Thomas, Chi (AP-Off)	RB
	Derrick Thomas KC (AP-Def, UP-AFC)	LB		Kendrell Bell, Pitt (AP-Def)	LB
1990	Mark Carrier, Chi (PFWA, UP-NFC, AP-Def)	S	2002	Clinton Ports, Den (AP-Off)	RB
	Emmitt Smith, Dal (AP-Off)	RB		Julius Peppers, Car (AP-Def)	DE
	Richmond Webb, Mia (TSN, UP-AFC)	OT	2003	Anquan Boldin, Ariz (AP-Off)	WR
1991	Mike Croel, Den (PFWA, TSN, AP-Def, UP-AFC)	LB		Terrell Suggs, Bal (AP-Def)	LB
	Lawrence Dawsey TB (UP-NFC)	WR	2004	Ben Roethlisberger, Pitt (AP-Off)	QB
	Leonard Russell, NE (AP-Off)	RB		Jonathan Vilma, NYJ (AP-Def)	LB
1992	Dale Carter, KC (PFWA, AP-Def, UP-AFC)	CB	2005	Carnell Williams, TB (AP-Off)	RB
	Carl Pickens, Cin (AP-Off)	WR		Shawne Merriman, SD (AP-Def)	LB
	Santana Dotson, TB (TSN)	DE			
	Robert Jones, Dal (UP-NFC)	LB			

NOTE: AP-Associated Press, UP-United Press, PFW-*Pro Football Weekly*, TSN-*The Sporting News*, PFWAA-Pro Football Writers Association of America, PFWA-Pro Football Writers of America, MCP-Maxwell Club of Philadelphia, NEA-Newspaper Enterprise Association
Starting in1960, the United Press annually awarded two Rookie of the Year awards, one to an AFL player and one to a NFL player. After the AFL-NFL merger, the UP kept the two-award format for the AFC and NFC. The UP stopped awarding RoY awards after the 1996 season.
Starting in 1967, the Associated Press began announcing two annual Rookie of the Year awards, as well. One went to the best offensive rookie in the NFL, the other to the best defensive rookie.

Alltime Number-One Draft Choices

Year	Team	Selection	Position
1936	Philadelphia	Jay Berwanger, Chicago	HB
1937	Philadelphia	Sam Francis, Nebraska	FB
1938	Cleveland	Corbett Davis, Indiana	FB
1939	Chicago Cardinals	Ki Aldrich, Texas Christian	C
1940	Chicago Cardinals	George Cafego, Tennessee	HB
1941	Chicago Bears	Tom Harmon, Michigan	HB
1942	Pittsburgh	Bill Dudley, Virginia	HB
1943	Detroit	Frank Sinkwich, Georgia	HB
1944	Boston	Angelo Bertelli, Notre Dame	QB
1945	Chicago Cardinals	Charley Trippi, Georgia	HB
1946	Boston	Frank Dancewicz, Notre Dame	QB
1947	Chicago Bears	Bob Fenimore, Oklahoma A&M	HB

Year	Team	Selection	Position
1948	Washington	Harry Gilmer, Alabama	QB
1949	Philadelphia	Chuck Bednarik, Pennsylvania	C
1950	Detroit	Leon Hart, Notre Dame	E
1951	New York Giants	Kyle Rote, SMU	HB
1952	Los Angeles	Bill Wade, Vanderbilt	QB
1953	San Francisco	Harry Babcock, Georgia	E
1954	Cleveland	Bobby Garrett, Stanford	QB
1955	Baltimore	George Shaw, Oregon	QB
1956	Pittsburgh	Gary Glick, Colorado A&M	DB
1957	Green Bay	Paul Hornung, Notre Dame	HB
1958	Chicago Cardinals	King Hill, Rice	QB
1959	Green Bay	Randy Duncan, Iowa	QB
1960	Los Angeles	Billy Cannon, LSU	RB
1961	Minnesota	Tommy Mason, Tulane	RB
	Buffalo (AFL)	Ken Rice, Auburn	G
1962	Washington	Ernie Davis, Syracuse	RB
	Oakland (AFL)	Roman Gabriel, North Carolina St	QB
1963	LA Rams	Terry Baker, Oregon St	QB
	Kansas City (AFL)	Buck Buchanan, Grambling	DT
1964	San Francisco	Dave Parks, Texas Tech	E
	Boston (AFL)	Jack Concannon, Boston College	QB
1965	NY Giants	Tucker Frederickson, Auburn	RB
	Houston (AFL)	Lawrence Elkins, Baylor	E
1966	Atlanta	Tommy Nobis, Texas	LB
	Miami (AFL)	Jim Grabowski, Illinois	RB
1967	Baltimore	Bubba Smith, Michigan St	DT
1968	Minnesota	Ron Yary, Southern California	T
1969	Buffalo (AFL)	O.J. Simpson, USC	RB
1970	Pittsburgh	Terry Bradshaw, Louisiana Tech	QB
1971	New England	Jim Plunkett, Stanford	QB
1972	Buffalo	Walt Patulski, Notre Dame	DE
1973	Houston	John Matuszak, Tampa	DE
1974	Dallas	Ed Jones, Tennessee St	DE
1975	Atlanta	Steve Bartkowski, California	QB
1976	Tampa Bay	Lee Roy Selmon, Oklahoma	DE
1977	Tampa Bay	Ricky Bell, Southern California	RB
1978	Houston	Earl Campbell, Texas	RB
1979	Buffalo	Tom Cousineau, Ohio St	LB
1980	Detroit	Billy Sims, Oklahoma	RB
1981	New Orleans	George Rogers, South Carolina	RB
1982	New England	Kenneth Sims, Texas	DT
1983	Baltimore	John Elway, Stanford	QB
1984	New England	Irving Fryar, Nebraska	WR
1985	Buffalo	Bruce Smith, Virginia Tech	DE
1986	Tampa Bay	Bo Jackson, Auburn	RB
1987	Tampa Bay	Vinny Testaverde, Miami (Fla.)	QB
1988	Atlanta	Aundray Bruce, Auburn	LB
1989	Dallas	Troy Aikman, UCLA	QB
1990	Indianapolis	Jeff George, Illinois	QB
1991	Dallas	Russell Maryland, Miami (Fla.)	DT
1992	Indianapolis	Steve Emtman, Washington	DT
1993	New England	Drew Bledsoe, Washington St	QB
1994	Cincinnati	Dan Wilkinson, Ohio St	DT
1995	Cincinnati	Ki-Jana Carter, Penn St	RB
1996	New York Jets	Keyshawn Johnson, USC	WR
1997	St Louis	Orlando Pace, Ohio St	OT
1998	Indianapolis	Peyton Manning, Tennessee	QB
1999	Cleveland	Tim Couch, Kentucky	QB
2000	Cleveland	Courtney Brown, Penn St	DE
2001	Atlanta	Michael Vick, Virginia Tech	QB
2002	Houston	David Carr, Fresno St	QB
2003	Cincinnati	Carson Palmer, USC	QB
2004	San Diego	Eli Manning, Mississippi	QB
2005	San Francisco	Alex Smith, Utah	QB
2006	Houston	Mario Williams, North Carolina St	DE

From 1947 through 1958, the first selection in the draft was a bonus pick, awarded to the winner of a random draw. That club, in turn, forfeited its last-round draft choice. The winner of the bonus choice was eliminated from future draws. The system was abolished after 1958, by which time all clubs had received a bonus choice.

Members of the Pro Football Hall of Fame

Herb Adderley
Troy Aikman
George Allen
Marcus Allen
Lance Alworth
Doug Atkins
Morris (Red) Badgro
Lem Barney
Cliff Battles
Sammy Baugh
Chuck Bednarik
Bert Bell
Bobby Bell
Raymond Berry
Elvin Bethea
Charles W. Bidwill Sr.
Fred Biletnikoff
George Blanda
Mel Blount
Terry Bradshaw
Bob (the Boomer) Brown
Jim Brown
Paul Brown
Roosevelt Brown
Willie Brown
Buck Buchanan
Nick Buoniconti
Dick Butkus
Earl Campbell
Tony Canadeo
Joe Carr
Harry Carson
Dave Casper
Guy Chamberlin
Jack Christiansen
Earl (Dutch) Clark
George Connor
Jimmy Conzelman
Lou Creekmur
Larry Csonka
Al Davis
Willie Davis
Len Dawson
Joe DeLamielleure
Eric Dickerson
Dan Dierdorf
Mike Ditka
Art Donovan
Tony Dorsett
John (Paddy) Driscoll
Bill Dudley
Albert Glen (Turk) Edwards
Carl Eller
John Elway
Weeb Ewbank
Tom Fears
Jim Finks
Ray Flaherty
Len Ford
Dan Fortmann
Dan Fouts
Benny Friedman
Frank Gatski
Bill George
Joe Gibbs

Frank Gifford
Sid Gillman
Otto Graham
Harold (Red) Grange
Bud Grant
Joe Greene
Forrest Gregg
Bob Griese
Lou Groza
Joe Guyon
George Halas
Jack Ham
Dan Hampton
John Hannah
Franco Harris
Mike Haynes
Ed Healey
Mel Hein
Ted Hendricks
Wilbur (Pete) Henry
Arnie Herber
Bill Hewitt
Clarke Hinkle
Elroy (Crazylegs) Hirsch
Paul Hornung
Ken Houston
Cal Hubbard
Sam Huff
Lamar Hunt
Don Hutson
Jimmy Johnson
John Henry Johnson
Charlie Joiner
David (Deacon) Jones
Stan Jones
Henry Jordan
Sonny Jurgensen
Jim Kelly
Leroy Kelly
Walt Kiesling
Frank (Bruiser) Kinard
Paul Krause
Earl (Curly) Lambeau
Jack Lambert
Tom Landry
Dick (Night Train) Lane
Jim Langer
Willie Lanier
Steve Largent
Yale Lary
Dante Lavelli
Bobby Layne
Alphonse (Tuffy) Leemans
Marv Levy
Bob Lilly
Larry Little
James Lofton
Vince Lombardi
Howie Long
Ronnie Lott
Sid Luckman
William Roy (Link) Lyman
Tom Mack
John Mackey
John Madden

Tim Mara
Wellington Mara
Gino Marchetti
Dan Marino
George Preston Marshall
Ollie Matson
Don Maynard
George McAfee
Mike McCormack
Tommy McDonald
Hugh McElhenny
Johnny (Blood) McNally
Mike Michalske
Wayne Millner
Bobby Mitchell
Ron Mix
Joe Montana
Warren Moon
Lenny Moore
Marion Motley
Mike Munchak
Anthony Munoz
George Musso
Bronko Nagurski
Joe Namath
Earle (Greasy) Neale
Ernie Nevers
Ozzie Newsome
Ray Nitschke
Chuck Noll
Leo Nomellini
Merlin Olsen
Jim Otto
Steve Owen
Alan Page
Clarence (Ace) Parker
Jim Parker
Walter Payton
Joe Perry
Pete Pihos
Fritz Pollard
Hugh (Shorty) Ray
Dan Reeves
Mel Renfro
John Riggins
Jim Ringo
Andy Robustelli
Art Rooney
Dan Rooney
Pete Rozelle
Bob St. Clair
Barry Sanders
Gale Sayers
Joe Schmidt
Tex Schramm
Lee Roy Selmon
Billy Shaw
Art Shell
Don Shula
O.J. Simpson
Mike Singletary
Jackie Slater
Jackie Smith
John Stallworth
Bart Starr

Members of the Pro Football Hall of Fame (Cont.)

Roger Staubach
Ernie Stautner
Jan Stenerud
Dwight Stephenson
Hank Stram
Ken Strong
Joe Stydahar
Lynn Swann
Fran Tarkenton
Charley Taylor
Jim Taylor
Lawrence Taylor
Jim Thorpe
Y.A. Tittle

George Trafton
Charley Trippi
Emlen Tunnell
Clyde (Bulldog) Turner
Johnny Unitas
Gene Upshaw
Norm Van Brocklin
Steve Van Buren
Doak Walker
Bill Walsh
Paul Warfield
Bob Waterfield
Mike Webster
Arnie Weinmeister

Randy White
Reggie White
Dave Wilcox
Bill Willis
Larry Wilson
Kellen Winslow
Alex Wojciechowicz
Willie Wood
Rayfield Wright
Ron Yary
Steve Young
Jack Youngblood

Champions of Other Leagues

Canadian Football League Grey Cup

Year	Results	Site	Attendance
1909	U of Toronto 26, Parkdale 6	Toronto	3,807
1910	U of Toronto 16, Hamilton Tigers 7	Hamilton	12,000
1911	U of Toronto 14, Toronto 7	Toronto	13,687
1912	Hamilton Alerts 11, Toronto 4	Hamilton	5,337
1913	Hamilton Tigers 44, Parkdale 2	Hamilton	2,100
1914	Toronto 14, U of Toronto 2	Toronto	10,500
1915	Hamilton Tigers 13, Toronto RAA 7	Toronto	2,808
1916–19	No game	—	—
1920	U of Toronto 16, Toronto 3	Toronto	10,088
1921	Toronto 23, Edmonton 0	Toronto	9,558
1922	Queen's U 13, Edmonton 1	Kingston	4,700
1923	Queen's U 54, Regina 0	Toronto	8,629
1924	Queen's U 11, Balmy Beach 3	Toronto	5,978
1925	Ottawa Senators 24, Winnipeg 1	Ottawa	6,900
1926	Ottawa Senators 10, Toronto U 7	Toronto	8,276
1927	Balmy Beach 9, Hamilton Tigers 6	Toronto	13,676
1928	Hamilton Tigers 30, Regina 0	Hamilton	4,767
1929	Hamilton Tigers 14, Regina 3	Hamilton	1,906
1930	Balmy Beach 11, Regina 6	Toronto	3,914
1931	Montreal AAA 22, Regina 0	Montreal	5,112
1932	Hamilton Tigers 25, Regina 6	Hamilton	4,806
1933	Toronto 4, Sarnia 3	Sarnia	2,751
1934	Sarnia 20, Regina 12	Toronto	8,900
1935	Winnipeg 18, Hamilton Tigers 12	Hamilton	6,405
1936	Sarnia 26, Ottawa RR 20	Toronto	5,883
1937	Toronto 4, Winnipeg 3	Toronto	11,522
1938	Toronto 30, Winnipeg 7	Toronto	18,778
1939	Winnipeg 8, Ottawa 7	Ottawa	11,738
1940	Ottawa 12, Balmy Beach 5	Ottawa	1,700
1940	Ottawa 8, Balmy Beach 2	Toronto	4,998
1941	Winnipeg 18, Ottawa 16	Toronto	19,065
1942	Toronto RCAF 8, Winnipeg RCAF 5	Toronto	12,455
1943	Hamilton F Wild 23, Winnipeg RCAF 14	Toronto	16,423
1944	Montreal St H-D Navy 7, Hamilton F Wild 6	Hamilton	3,871
1945	Toronto 35, Winnipeg 0	Toronto	18,660
1946	Toronto 28, Winnipeg 6	Toronto	18,960
1947	Toronto 10, Winnipeg 9	Toronto	18,885
1948	Calgary 12, Ottawa 7	Toronto	20,013
1949	Montreal Als 28, Calgary 15	Toronto	20,087
1950	Toronto 13, Winnipeg 0	Toronto	27,101
1951	Ottawa 21, Saskatchewan 14	Toronto	27,341
1952	Toronto 21, Edmonton 11	Toronto	27,391
1953	Hamilton Ticats 12, Winnipeg 6	Toronto	27,313
1954	Edmonton 26, Montreal 25	Toronto	27,321
1955	Edmonton 34, Montreal 19	Vancouver	39,417
1956	Edmonton 50, Montreal 27	Toronto	27,425
1957	Hamilton 32, Winnipeg 7	Toronto	27,051

Canadian Football League Grey Cup

Year	Results	Site	Attendance
1958	Winnipeg 35, Hamilton 28	Vancouver	36,567
1959	Winnipeg 21, Hamilton 7	Toronto	33,133
1960	Ottawa 16, Edmonton 6	Vancouver	38,102
1961	Winnipeg 21, Hamilton 14	Toronto	32,651
1962	Winnipeg 28, Hamilton 27	Toronto	32,655
1963	Hamilton 21, British Columbia 10	Vancouver	36,545
1964	British Columbia 34, Hamilton 24	Toronto	32,655
1965	Hamilton 22, Winnipeg 16	Toronto	32,655
1966	Saskatchewan 29, Ottawa 14	Vancouver	36,553
1967	Hamilton 24, Saskatchewan 1	Ottawa	31,358
1968	Ottawa 24, Calgary 21	Toronto	32,655
1969	Ottawa 29, Saskatchewan 11	Montreal	33,172
1970	Montreal 23, Calgary 10	Toronto	32,669
1971	Calgary 14, Toronto 11	Vancouver	34,484
1972	Hamilton 13, Saskatchewan 10	Hamilton	33,993
1973	Ottawa 22, Edmonton 18	Toronto	36,653
1974	Montreal 20, Edmonton 7	Vancouver	34,450
1975	Edmonton 9, Montreal 8	Calgary	32,454
1976	Ottawa 23, Saskatchewan 20	Toronto	53,467
1977	Montreal 41, Edmonton 6	Montreal	68,318
1978	Edmonton 20, Montreal 13	Toronto	54,695
1979	Edmonton 17, Montreal 9	Montreal	65,113
1980	Edmonton 48, Hamilton 10	Toronto	54,661
1981	Edmonton 26, Ottawa 23	Montreal	52,478
1982	Edmonton 32, Toronto 16	Toronto	54,741
1983	Toronto 18, British Columbia 17	Vancouver	59,345
1984	Winnipeg 47, Hamilton 17	Edmonton	60,081
1985	British Columbia 37, Hamilton 24	Montreal	56,723
1986	Hamilton 39, Edmonton 15	Vancouver	59,621
1987	Edmonton 38, Toronto 36	Vancouver	59,478
1988	Winnipeg 22, British Columbia 21	Ottawa	50,604
1989	Saskatchewan 43, Hamilton 40	Toronto	54,088
1990	Winnipeg 50, Edmonton 11	Vancouver	46,968
1991	Toronto 36, Calgary 21	Winnipeg	51,985
1992	Calgary 24, Winnipeg 10	Toronto	45,863
1993	Edmonton 33, Winnipeg 23	Calgary	50,035
1994	British Columbia 26, Baltimore 23	Vancouver	55,097
1995	Baltimore 37, Calgary 20	Regina, Saskatchewan	52,564
1996	Toronto 43, Edmonton 37	Hamilton, Ontario	38,595
1997	Toronto 47, Saskatchewan 23	Edmonton	60,431
1998	Calgary 26, Hamilton 24	Winnipeg	34,157
1999	Hamilton 32, Calgary 21	Vancouver	45,118
2000	British Columbia 28, Montreal 26	Calgary	43,822
2001	Calgary 27, Winnipeg 19	Montreal	65,255
2002	Montreal 25, Edmonton 16	Edmonton	62,531
2003	Edmonton 34, Montreal 22	Regina, Saskatchewan	50,909
2004	Toronto 27, British Columbia 19	Ottawa	51,242
2005	Edmonton 38, Montreal 35 (OT)	Vancouver	59,157

In 1909, Earl Grey, the Governor-General of Canada, donated a trophy for the Rugby Football Championship of Canada. The trophy, which subsequently became known as the Grey Cup, was originally open only to teams registered with the Canada Rugby Union. Since 1954, it has been awarded to the winner of the Canadian Football League's championship game.

AMERICAN FOOTBALL LEAGUE I

Year	Champion	Record
1926	Philadelphia Quakers	7-2

AMERICAN FOOTBALL LEAGUE II

Year	Champion	Record
1936	Boston Shamrocks	8-3
1937	LA Bulldogs	8-0

AMERICAN FOOTBALL LEAGUE III

Year	Champion	Record
1940	Columbus Bullies	8-1-1
1941	Columbus Bullies	5-1-2

ALL-AMERICAN FOOTBALL CONFERENCE

Year	Championship Game
1946	Cleveland 14, NY Yankees 9
1947	Cleveland 14, NY Yankees 3
1948	Cleveland 49, Buffalo 7
1949	Cleveland 21, San Francisco 7

WORLD FOOTBALL LEAGUE

Year	World Bowl Championship
1974	Birmingham 22, Florida 21
1975	Disbanded midseason

UNITED STATES FOOTBALL LEAGUE

Year	Championship Game
1983	Michigan 24, Philadelphia 22
1984	Philadelphia 23, Arizona 3
1985	Baltimore 28, Oakland 24

X FOOTBALL LEAGUE

Year	Championship Game
2001	Los Angeles 38, San Francisco 6

NFL EUROPE

Year Record	Champion	
1991	London	9-1-0
1992	Sacramento	8-2-0
1995	Frankfurt	6-4-0
1996	Scotland	7-3-0
1997	Barcelona	5-5-0
1998	Rhein	7-3-0
1999	Frankfurt	6-4-0
2000	Rhein	7-3-0
2001	Berlin	6-4-0
2002	Berlin	6-4-0
2003	Frankfurt	6-4-0
2004	Berlin	9-1-0
2005	Amsterdam	6-4-0
2006	Frankfurt	6-3-0

Known as World League of American Football until 1998.

Arena Bowl Results

Results

	Date	Winner	Loser	Score	Site (Attendance)
I	8-1-87	Denver	Pittsburgh	45–16	Pittsburgh (13,232)
II	7-30-88	Detroit	Chicago	24–13	Chicago (15,018)
III	8-18-89	Detroit	Pittsburgh	39–26	Detroit (19,875)
IV	8-11-90	Detroit	Dallas	51–27	Detroit (19,875)
V	8-17-91	Tampa Bay	Detroit	48–42	Detroit(20,357)
VI	8-22-92	Detroit	Orlando	56–38	Orlando (13,680)
VII	8-21-93	Tampa Bay	Detroit	51–31	Detroit (12,989)
VIII	9-2-94	Arizona	Orlando	36–31	Orlando (14,368)
IX	9-1-95	Tampa Bay	Orlando	48–35	St. Petersburg (25,087)
X	8-26-96	Tampa Bay	Iowa	42–38	Des Moines (11,411)
XI	8-25-97	Arizona	Iowa	55–33	Phoenix (17,436)
XII	8-23-98	Orlando	Tampa Bay	62–31	Tampa (17,222)
XIII	8-21-99	Albany	Orlando	59–48	Albany, N.Y. (13,652)
XIV	8-20-00	Orlando	Nashville	41–38	Orlando (15,989)
XV	8-19-01	Grand Rapids	Nashville	64–42	Grand Rapids (11,217)
XVI	8-18-02	San Jose	Arizona	52–14	San Jose (16,942)
XVII	6-22-03	Tampa Bay	Arizona	43–29	Tampa (20,469)
XVIII	6-27-04	San Jose	Arizona	69–62	Phoenix (17,391)
XIX	6-12-05	Colorado	Georgia	51–48	Las Vegas (10,822)
XX	6-11-06	Chicago	Orlando	69–61	Las Vegas (13,476)

Arena Bowl Recaps*

I - 1987

Denver Dynamite	12	6	14	13—45
Pittsburgh Gladiators	0	0	0	16—16

FIRST QUARTER
Den: Forte fumble recovery (Morales kick), 8:27. **Denver 6-0.**
Den: Prather 2 run (pass failed), 9:37. **Denver 12-0.**

SECOND QUARTER
Den: Mullen 26 pass from W. Taylor (pass failed), 4:38. **Denver 18-0.**

THIRD QUARTER
Den: Rodgers 32 pass from W. Taylor (Morales kick), 9:48. **Denver 25-0.**
Den: Trimble 47 int return (Morales kick), 15:00. **Denver 32-0.**

FOURTH QUARTER
Pitt: Hairston 11 pass from Hohensee (two-point conversion), 3:43. **Denver 32-8.**
Den: Mullen 5 pass from W. Taylor (Morales kick), 6:13. **Denver 39-8.**
Den: Mullen 19 pass from W. Taylor (kick blocked), 11:49. **Denver 45-8.**
Pitt: Richmond 14 pass from Folmar (two-point conversion), 14:28. **Denver 45-16.**
A: 13,232

II - 1988

Detroit Drive	7	14	0	3—24
Chicago Bruisers	7	0	0	6—13

FIRST QUARTER
Det: Ingold 1 run (Bojovic kick), 3:36. **Detroit 7-0.**
Chi: McDade 3 pass from Bennett (Morales kick), 9:31. **7-7.**

SECOND QUARTER
Det: Holman 8 pass from Bojovic kick), 0:05. **Detroit 14-7.**
Det: Browne 2 run (Bojovic kick), 14:19. **Detroit 21-7.**

FOURTH QUARTER
Chi: Stone 10 run (kick failed), 2:42. **Detroit 21-13.**
Det: FG Bojovic 17, 14:04. **Detroit 24-13.**
A: 15,018

III - 1989

Detroit Drive	16	10	13	0—39
Pittsburgh Gladiators	3	9	14	0—26

FIRST QUARTER
Det: Safety, fumble through endzone, 1:07. **Detroit 2-0.**
Det: Burris 1 run (Bojovic kick), 7:35. **Detroit 9-0.**
Pitt: FG Fricke 55, 9:58. **Detroit 9-3.**
Det: Bradford 17 run (Bojovic kick), 13:29. **Detroit 16-3.**

SECOND QUARTER
Det: FG Bojovic 50, 3:09. **Detroit 19-3.**
Pitt: FG Fricke 30, 5:41. **Detroit 19-6.**
Det: Bradford 2 run (Bojovic kick), 12:53. **Detroit 26-6.**
Pitt: Powell 2 run (pass failed), 14:50. **Detroit 26-12.**

THIRD QUARTER
Pitt: Ross 23 fumble return (Fricke kick), 0:42. **Detroit 26-19.**
Det: LaFrance 32 pass from Burris (kick failed), 7:05. **Detroit 32-19.**
Det: Mullen 12 pass from Burris (Bojovic kick), 8:53. **Detroit 39-19.**
Pitt: Gardner 19 pass from Totten (Fricke kick), 13:56. **Detroit 39-26.**
A: 19,875

IV - 1990

Detroit Drive	14	17	13	7—51
Dallas Texans	0	14	0	13—27

FIRST QUARTER
Det: Schlichter 2 run (Bojovic kick), 5:52. **Detroit 7-0.**
Det: Schlichter 5 run (Bojovic kick), 7:00. **Detroit 14-0.**

SECOND QUARTER
Det: Rettig 1 run (Bojovic kick), 3:04. **Detroit 21-0.**
Det: Rettig 11 pass from Schlichter (Bojovic kick), 5:24. **Detroit 28-0.**
Dal: Ward 1 run (Morales kick), 10:00. **Detroit 28-7.**
Dal: Kenney 6 pass from Bennett (Morales kick), 14:49. **Detroit 28-14.**
Det: FG Bojovic 42, 15:00. **Detroit 31-14.**

THIRD QUARTER
Det: Schlichter 1 run (Bojovic kick), 2:20. **Detroit 38-14.**
Det: Mullen 37 pass from Schlichter (kick failed), 8:58. **Detroit 44-14.**

FOURTH QUARTER
Dal: Ward 1 run (Morales kick), 2:13. **Detroit 44-21.**
Dal: Blackmon 3 run (pass failed), 12:19. **Detroit 44-27.**
Det: Schlichter 2 run (Bojovic kick), 14:25. **Detroit 51-27.**
A: 19,875

V - 1991

Tampa Bay Storm	7	21	14	6—48
Detroit Drive	14	7	9	12—42

FIRST QUARTER
TB: Gruden 1 run (Hickert kick), 5:15. **Tampa Bay 7-0.**
Det: Mullen 10 pass from Schlichter (Bojovic kick), 7:42. **7-7.**
Det: LaFrance 32 pass from Schlichter (Bojovic kick), 14:38. **Detroit 14-7.**

SECOND QUARTER
TB: Thomas 13 pass from Gruden (Hickert kick), 4:53. **14-14.**
Det: Rettig 2 run (Bojovic kick), 8:10. **Detroit 21-14.**
TB: Bradford 3 run (Hickert kick), 14:20. **21-21.**
TB: Thomas 42 pass from Gruden (Hickert kick), 15:00. **Tampa Bay 28-21.**

THIRD QUARTER
Det: McClay 13 pass from Schlichter (kick failed), 3:14. **Tampa Bay 28-27.**
TB: Willis 37 pass from Gruden (Hickert kick), 5:58. **Tampa Bay 35-27.**
Det: FG Bojovic 46, 9:30. **Tampa Bay 35-30.**
TB: Thomas 17 pass from Gruden (Hickert kick), 14:08. **Tampa Bay 42-30.**

FOURTH QUARTER
Det: Mullen 23 pass from Schlichter (kick failed), 0:50. **Tampa Bay 42-36.**
Det: Anderson 1 run (pass failed), 13:40. **42-42.**
TB: Thomas 35 pass from Gruden (kick failed), 14:21. **Tampa Bay 48-42.**
A: 20,357

*-From 1987 to 1992, scoring times listed indicate time elapsed in each quarter. After 1992, scoring times listed indicate time remaining.

VI - 1992

Detroit Drive	7	21	14	14—56
Orlando Predators	6	17	0	15—38

FIRST QUARTER
Orl: FG Cimadevilla 48, 8:41. **Orlando 3-0.**
Det: Sargent 1 run (Langeloh kick), 5:14. **Detroit 7-3.**
Orl: FG Cimadevilla 36, 1:44. **Detroit 7-6.**

SECOND QUARTER
Orl: FG Cimadevilla 26, 5:50. **Orlando 9-7.**
Det: Langley 6 pass from Renfroe (Langeloh kick), 3:28. **Detroit 14-9.**
Det: McSwain fumble recovery (Langeloh kick), 3:03. **Detroit 21-9.**
Orl: Drakes 8 pass from Bennett (Cimadevilla kick), 0:51. **Detroit 21-16.**
Det: LaFrance 57 kickoff return (Langeloh kick), 0:45. **Detroit 28-16.**
Orl: Aikens 8 pass from Bennett (Cimadevilla kick), 0:15. **Detroit 28-23.**

THIRD QUARTER
Det: Fleming 1 run (Langeloh kick), 10:25. **Detroit 35-23.**
Det: LaFrance 24 pass from Renfroe (Langeloh kick), 4:12. **Detroit 42-23.**

FOURTH QUARTER
Orl: FG Cimadevilla 31, 14:51. **Detroit 42-26.**
Det: Langley 15 pass from Renfroe (Langeloh kick), 11:08. **Detroit 49-26.**
Orl: Walls 20 pass from Bennett (kick failed), 6:38. **Detroit 49-32.**
Det: Mullen 17 pass from Renfroe (Langeloh kick), 4:02. **Detroit 56-32.**
Orl: Moore 7 pass from Bennett (conversion failed), 1:00. **Detroit 56-38.**
A: 13,680; T:

VII - 1993

Tampa Bay Storm	10	20	7	14—51
Detroit Drive	0	17	7	7—31

FIRST QUARTER
TB: FG Czyzewski 24, 8:25. **Tampa Bay 3-0.**
TB: Thomas 15 pass from Gruden (Czyzewski kick), 10:56. **Tampa Bay 10-0.**

SECOND QUARTER
Det: FG Langeloh 21, 0:46. **Tampa Bay 10-3.**
TB: FG Czyzewski 47, 3:55. **Tampa Bay 13-3.**
TB: Browner fumble recovery (Czyzewski kick), 5:49. **Tampa Bay 20-3.**
Det: LaFrance 27 pass from Renfroe (Langeloh kick), 7:38. **Tampa Bay 20-10.**
TB: Field 18 pass from Gruden (Czyzewski kick), 12:38. **Tampa Bay 27-10.**
Det: Goode 2 pass from Renfroe (Langeloh kick), 14:03. **Tampa Bay 27-17.**
TB: FG Czyzewski 26, 14:56. **Tampa Bay 30-17.**

THIRD QUARTER
TB: Browner 9 pass from Byrd (Czyzewski kick), 8:55. **Tampa Bay 37-17.**
Det: Bell 34 pass from Renfroe (Langeloh kick), 10:25. **Tampa Bay 37-24.**

FOURTH QUARTER
TB: Brown 7 pass from Gruden (Czyzewski kick), 1:29. **Tampa Bay 44-24.**
Det: Burse 1 run (Langeloh kick), 5:24. **Tampa Bay 44-31.**
TB: Barley 4 run (Czyzewski kick), 11:12. **Tampa Bay 51-31.**
A: 12,989

VIII - 1994

Arizona Rattlers	7	13	7	9—36
Orlando Predators	10	7	7	7—31

FIRST QUARTER
Orl: Shell 5 pass from Bennett (Cimadevilla kick), 10:51. **Orlando 7-0.**
Ariz: Tillman 33 pass from Bonner (Zendejas kick), 7:54. **7-7.**
Orl: FG Cimadevilla 24, 3:41. **Orlando 10-7.**

SECOND QUARTER
Ariz: Schexnaer 6 pass from Bonner (Zendejas kick), 11:25. **Arizona 14-10.**
Orl: Shell 42 pass from Bennett (Cimadevilla kick), 9:53. **Orlando 17-14.**
Ariz: FG Zendejas 23, 0:53. **17-17.**
Ariz: FG Zendejas 40, 0:00. **Arizona 20-17.**

THIRD QUARTER
Ariz: Vaughn 2 pass from Bonner (Zendejas kick), 2:45. **Arizona 27-17.**
Orl: Walls 38 pass from Bennett (Cimadevilla kick), 0:47. **Arizona 27-24.**

FOURTH QUARTER
Ariz: FG Zendejas 21, 11:49. **Arizona 30-24.**
Orl: Wagner 3 run (Cimadevilla kick), 6:55. **Orlando 31-30.**
Ariz: Schexnaer 24 pass from Bonner (dropkick failed), 0:31. **Arizona 36-31.**
A: 14,368

IX - 1995

Tampa Bay Storm	15	14	6	13—48
Orlando Predators	15	0	7	13—35

FIRST QUARTER
Orl: Wagner 2 run (two-point conversion), 13:14. **Orlando 8-0.**
TB: Thomas 10 pass from Gruden (two-point conversion), 8:39. **8-8.**
Orl: Shell 4 pass from O'Hara (Bennett kick), 3:23. **Orlando 15-8.**
TB: LaFrance 57 kickoff return (Cimadevilla kick), 2:23. **15-15.**

SECOND QUARTER
TB: LaFrance 3 pass from Gruden (Cimadevilla kick), 9:03. **Tampa Bay 22-15.**
TB: LaFrance 1 pass from Gruden (Cimadevilla kick), 0:03. **Tampa Bay 29-15.**

THIRD QUARTER
Orl: Wagner 3 MFG return (Bennett kick), 9:42. **Tampa Bay 29-22.**
TB: Thomas 35 pass from Gruden (kick failed), 7:43. **Tampa Bay 35-22.**

FOURTH QUARTER
Orl: Fleming 14 run (Bennett kick), 11:16. **Tampa Bay 35-29.**
TB: Gruden 1 run (pass failed), 6:30. **Tampa Bay 41-29.**
TB: Sanders 47 int return (Cimadevilla kick), 2:15. **Tampa Bay 48-29.**
Orl: Wagner 3 pass from O'Hara (pass failed), 1:00. **Tampa Bay 48-35.**
A: 25,087

X - 1996

Tampa Bay Storm	13	15	7	7—42
Iowa Barnstormers	14	14	3	7—38

FIRST QUARTER

TB: Rowland 12 pass from Gruden (Cimadevilla kick), 9:32. **Tampa Bay 7–0.**
Iowa: Spencer 16 pass from Warner (Black kick), 6:48. **7–7.**
Iowa: Cooper 30 pass from Warner (Black kick), 2:02. **Iowa 14–7.**
TB: LaFrance 30 pass from Gruden (kick failed), 0:00. **Iowa 14–13.**

SECOND QUARTER

Iowa: Jacox 9 pass from Warner (Black kick), 10:46. **Iowa 21–13.**
TB: Thomas 35 pass from Gruden (two-point conversion), 0:59. **21–21.**
TB: Thomas 9 int return (Cimadevilla kick), 0:36. **Tampa Bay 28–21.**
Iowa: Moran 1 run (Black kick), 0:09. **28–28.**

THIRD QUARTER

TB: Caesar 21 pass from Gruden (Cimadevilla kick), 5:46. **Tampa Bay 35–28.**
Iowa: FG Black 32, 0:03. **Tampa Bay 35–31.**

FOURTH QUARTER

TB: Thomas 7 pass from Gruden (Cimadevilla kick), 11:55. **Tampa Bay 42–31.**
Iowa: Spencer 4 pass from Warner (Black kick), 8:22. **Tampa Bay 42–38.**
A: 11,411

XI - 1997

Arizona Rattlers	3	21	21	10—55
Iowa Barnstormers	7	6	7	13—33

FIRST QUARTER

Ariz: FG Brenner 19, 6:19. **Arizona 3–0.**
Iowa: L. Cooper 30 pass from Warner (Black kick), 4:59. **Iowa 7–3.**

SECOND QUARTER

Ariz: McMillen 1 run (Brenner kick), 14:57. **Arizona 10–7.**
Iowa: FG Black 25, 9:44. **10–10.**
Ariz: H. Cooper 4 run from Davis (Brenner kick), 4:33. **Arizona 17–10.**
Iowa: FG Black 20, 0:28. **Arizona 17–13.**
Ariz: H. Cooper 56 kickoff return (Brenner kick), 0:21. **Arizona 24–13.**

THIRD QUARTER

Ariz: Davis 1 run (Brenner kick), 9:09. **Arizona 31–13.**
Ariz: H. Cooper 30 int return (Brenner kick), 7:22. **Arizona 38–13.**
Iowa: L. Cooper 30 pass from Warner (Black kick), 4:33. **Arizona 38–20.**
Ariz: Schexnaer 49 pass from Davis (Brenner kick), 3:47. **Arizona 45–20.**

FOURTH QUARTER

Iowa: Jacox 1 run (Black kick), 14:56. **Arizona 45–27.**
Ariz: Schexnaer 28 pass from Davis (Brenner kick), 9:01. **Arizona 52–27.**
Ariz: FG Brenner 44, 3:43. **Arizona 55–27.**
Iowa: Conley 9 pass from Warner (conversion failed), 0:21. **Arizona 55–33.**
A: 17,436

XII - 1998

Orlando Predators	10	14	26	12—62
Tampa Bay Storm	14	3	8	6—31

FIRST QUARTER

Orl : FG Cool 23, 10:52. **Orlando 3–0.**
TB: LaFrance 12 pass from Willis (Nittmo kick), 7:34. **Tampa Bay 7–3.**
Orl : Gordon 23 pass from O'Hara (Cool kick), 4:16. **Orlando 10–7.**
TB: LaFrance 9 pass from Willis (Nittmo kick), 0:31. **Tampa Bay 14–10.**

SECOND QUARTER

Orl: Maynor 3 run (Cool kick), 7:47. **Orlando 17–14.**
TB: FG Nittmo 44, 4:34. **17–17.**
Orl: Hamilton 36 run (Cool kick), 2:31. **Orlando 24–17.**

THIRD QUARTER

Orl: Hamilton 5 run (Cool kick), 14:03. **Orlando 31–17.**
Orl: Burnett safety, 13:12. **Orlando 33–17.**
Orl: Hamilton 10 run (Cool kick), 10:02. **Orlando 40–17.**
Orl: Wagner 48 MFG return (Cool kick), 5:25. **Orlando 47–17.**
TB: LaFrance 7 pass from Willis (two-point conversion), 4:01. **Orlando 47–25.**
Orl: FG Cool 20, 0:24. **Orlando 50–25.**

FOURTH QUARTER

Orl: Mason 22 int return (kick failed), 14:22. **Orlando 56–25.**
TB: Thomas 8 pass from Willis (pass failed), 11:34. **Orlando 56–31.**
Orl: Gordon 8 kickoff return (kick failed), 10:46. **Orlando 62–31.**
A: 17,222

XIII - 1999

Albany Firebirds	21	17	0	21—59
Orlando Predators	14	7	13	14—48

FIRST QUARTER

Alb: Brown 12 pass from Pawlawski (Silvestri kick), 13:18. **Albany 7–0.**
Orl: Wagner 22 pass from Maynor (Cool kick), 11:38. **7–7.**
Alb: Krick 1 run (Silvestri kick), 8:50. **Albany 14–7.**
Orl: Law 37 pass from Maynor (Cool kick), 7:09. **14–14.**
Alb: Johnson 2 pass from Pawlawski (Silvestri kick), 2:14. **Albany 21–14.**

SECOND QUARTER

Orl: Wagner 22 pass from Maynor (Cool kick), 13:21. **21–21.**
Alb: Hopkins 6 pass from Pawlawski (Silvestri kick), 10:34. **Albany 28–21.**
Alb: Brown 29 pass from Pawlawski (Silvestri kick), 3:59. **Albany 35–21.**
Alb: FG Silvestri 18, 0:00. **Albany 38–21.**

THIRD QUARTER

Orl: Jackson 33 pass from Maynor (Cool kick), 7:24. **Albany 38–28.**
Orl: Jackson 34 pass from Maynor (kick failed), 2:00. **Albany 38–34.**

FOURTH QUARTER

Alb: Brown 14 pass from Pawlawski (Silvestri kick), 12:35. **Albany 45–34.**
Orl: Dorsey 4 run (two-point conversion), 4:35. **Albany 45–42.**
Alb: Brown 5 pass from Pawlawski (Silvestri kick), 0:54. **Albany 52–42.**
Orl: Jackson 39 pass from Maynor (kick failed), 0:26. **Albany 52–48.**
Alb: Krick 6 pass from Pawlawski (Silvestri kick), 0:10. **Albany 59–48.**
A: 13,652

XIV - 2000

Orlando Predators	15	14	3	9—41
Nashville Kats	7	16	7	8—38

FIRST QUARTER
Orl: Allen safety, 14:01. **Orlando 2–0.**
Orl: Dell 16 pass from Maynor (Cool kick), 10:13. **Orlando 9–0.**
Orl: Douglass 3 run (kick failed), 4:08. **Orlando 15–0.**
Nash: Russell 33 pass from Kelly (McLaughlin kick), 1:40. **Orlando 15–7.**

SECOND QUARTER
Orl: Hamilton 18 pass from Maynor (Cool kick), 14:04. **Orlando 22–7.**
Orl: Douglass 5 pass from Maynor (Cool kick), 10:45. **Orlando 29–7.**
Nash: Gaines safety, 2:50. **Orlando 29–9.**
Nash: Fleming 1 pass from Kelly (McLaughlin kick), 0:39. **Orlando 29–16.**
Nash: Hammond 5 pass from Kelly (McLaughlin kick), 0:00. **Orlando 29–23.**

THIRD QUARTER
Nash: Baron 28 pass from Kelly (McLaughlin kick), 9:43. **Nashville 30–29.**
Orl: FG Cool 38, 3:20. **Orlando 32–30.**

FOURTH QUARTER
Orl: Cool 15 pass from Maynor (McLaughlin miss), 12:23. **Orlando 39–30.**
Nash: Hammond 45 pass from Brown (Fleming pass), 6:26. **Orlando 39–38.**
Orl: FG Cool 19, 0:00. **Orlando 41–38.**
A: 15,989

XV -2001

Grand Rapids Rampage	14	23	14	13—64
Nashville Kats.................	14	7	14	7—42

FIRST QUARTER
GR: Shaw 6 pass from Dolezel (Gowins kick), 10:08. **Grand Rapids 7–0.**
Nash: Jones 17 pass from Kelly (McLaughlin kick), 7:10. **7–7.**
GR: Shaw 6 pass from Dolezel (Gowins kick), 2:21. **Grand Rapids 14–7.**
Nash: Grant 1 run (McLaughlin kick), 0:00. **14–14.**

SECOND QUARTER
GR: Shaw 41 pass from Dolezel (Gowins kick), 13:34. **Grand Rapids 21–14.**
GR: Odems 14 pass from Dolezel (kick failed), 9:23. **Grand Rapids 27–14.**
Nash: Jones 34 pass from Kelly (McLaughlin kick), 4:54. **Grand Rapids 27–21.**
GR: Avery 1 run (Gowins kick), 1:00. **Grand Rapids 34–21.**
GR: FG Gowins 36, 0:03. **Grand Rapids 37–21.**

THIRD QUARTER
Nash: Reece 1 run (McLaughlin kick), 11:45. **Grand Rapids 37–28.**
GR: Shaw 31 pass from Dolezel (Gowins kick), 9:33. **Grand Rapids 44–28.**
Nash: Hillery 33 pass from Kelly (McLaughlin kick), 6:33. **Grand Rapids 44–35.**
GR: H. Shaw 1 run (Gowins kick), 0:41. **Grand Rapids 51–35.**

XV -2001 *(Cont.)*

FOURTH QUARTER
Nash: Baron 28 pass from Fleming (McLaughlin kick), 14:24. **Grand Rapids 51–42.**
GR: Shaw 15 pass from Dolezel (Gowins kick), 8:11. **Grand Rapids 58–42.**
GR: Odems 17 pass from Dolezel (kick failed), 2:05. **Grand Rapids 64–42.**
A: 11,217

XVI - 2002

San Jose SaberCats	7	17	14	14—52
Arizona Rattlers	0	0	0	14—14

FIRST QUARTER
SJ: Hundon 28 pass from Dutton (Alcorn kick), 9:17. **San Jose 7–0.**

SECOND QUARTER
SJ: Hundon 2 pass from Dutton (Alcorn kick), 14:18. **San Jose 14–0.**
SJ: FG Alcorn 31, 0:50. **San Jose 17–0.**
SJ: Wagner 2 run (Alcorn kick), 0:11. **San Jose 24–0.**

THIRD QUARTER
SJ: Roe 12 pass from Dutton (Alcorn kick), 12:38. **San Jose 31–0.**
SJ: Reese 32 pass from Dutton (Alcorn kick), 6:55. **San Jose 38–0.**

FOURTH QUARTER
SJ: McMillen 1 run (Alcorn kick), 12:05. **San Jose 45–0.**
Ariz: M. Bryant 30 pass from Bonner (Cooper pass), 9:24. **San Jose 45–8.**
SJ: Hundon 2 pass from Dutton (Alcorn kick), 6:01. **San Jose 52–8.**
Ariz: Kelly 3 run (Cooper pass failed), 2:30. **San Jose 52–14.**
A: 16,942

XVII - 2003

Tampa Bay Storm	14	9	7	13—43
Arizona Rattlers	10	6	6	7—29

FIRST QUARTER
Ariz: FG Garner 36 , 11:02. **Arizona 3–0.**
TB: Samuels 33 pass from Kaleo (Stucker kick failed), 7:43. **Tampa Bay 7–3.**
Ariz: Bonner 1 run (Garner kick), 5:07. **Arizona 10–7.**
TB: Proctor 1 run (Dell pass), 1:24. **Tampa Bay 14–10.**

SECOND QUARTER
TB: Kinney 26 fumble recovery (Stucker kick failed), 12:52. **Tampa Bay 20–10.**
Ariz: Kelly 8 run (Garner kick failed), 7:53. **Tampa Bay 20–16.**
TB: FG Stucker 23, 0:04. **Tampa Bay 23–16.**

THIRD QUARTER
TB: Samuels 9 pass from O'Hara (Stucker kick), 7:26. **Tampa Bay 30–16.**
Ariz: Bryant 3 pass from Bonner (Garner kick failed), 2:38. **Tampa Bay 30–22.**

FOURTH QUARTER
TB: Samuels 43 pass from O'Hara (Stucker kick), 14:54. **Tampa Bay 37–22.**
TB: O'Hara 3 run (Stucker kick failed), 10:39. **Tampa Bay 43–22.**
Ariz: Gatewood 3 pass from Bonner (Garner kick), 8:02. **Tampa Bay 43–29.**
A: 20,469

XVIII - 2004

San Jose SaberCats	14	21	7	27—69
Arizona Rattlers	14	14	14	20—62

FIRST QUARTER

Ariz: Burley 29 pass from Bonner (Garner kick), 10:13. **Arizona 7-0.**

SJ: Roe 8 pass from Grieb (Frantz kick), 6:59. **7-7.**

Ariz: Bryant 33 pass from Bonner (Garner kick), 5:18. **Arizona 14-7.**

SJ: Coleman 22 pass from Grieb (Frantz kick), 1:27. **14-14.**

SECOND QUARTER

SJ: Roe 11 pass from Grieb (Frantz kick), 8:34. **San Jose 21-14.**

Ariz: Burley 26 pass from Bonner (Garner kick), 4:33. **21-21.**

SJ: Roe 3 pass from Grieb (Frantz kick), 0:52. **San Jose 28-21.**

Ariz: Cooper 4 run (Garner kick), 0:07. **28-28.**

SJ: Roe 38 pass from Grieb (Frantz kick), 0:00. **San Jose 35-28.**

THIRD QUARTER

Ariz: Kelly 6 run (Garner kick), 11:35. **35-35.**

SJ: Roe 31 pass from Grieb (Frantz kick), 8:42. **San Jose 42-35.**

Ariz: Bryant 21 pass from Bonner (Garner kick), 3:51. **San Jose 42-42.**

FOURTH QUARTER

SJ: Wagner 1 run (Frantz kick), 14:50. **San Jose 49-42.**

Ariz: Bryant 7 pass from Bonner (Garner kick), 11:31. **49-49.**

SJ: Hundon 33 pass from Grieb (Frantz kick), 8:36. **San Jose 56-42.**

Ariz: Burley 5 pass from Bonner (Garner kick), 6:03. **56-56.**

SJ: Coleman 2 pass from Grieb (Frantz kick), 3:44. **San Jose 63-56.**

Ariz: Burley 9 from Bonner (Bonner pass failed), 0:31. **San Jose 63-62.**

SJ: Reed 7 kickoff return (Frantz kick failed), 0:30. **San Jose 69-62.**

A: 17,391

XIX - 2005

Colorado Crush	10	14	7	20—51
Georgia Force	7	13	7	21—48

FIRST QUARTER

Col: Marshall 1 run (Rush kick), 12:18. **Colorado 7-0.**

Col: FG Rush 20, 4:42. **Colorado 10-0.**

Geo: Nagy 1 run (Garner kick), 0:42. **Colorado 10-7.**

SECOND QUARTER

Col: Marshall 4 run (Rush kick), 11:56. **Colorado 17-7.**

Geo: Aldridge 27 run (Garner kick failed), 5:42. **Colorado 17-13.**

Col: Marshall 3 run (Rush kick), 0:52. **Colorado 24-13.**

Geo: Thomas 2 run (Garner kick), 0:29. **Colorado 24-20.**

THIRD QUARTER

Col: Harrell 12 pass from Dutton (Rush kick), 7:53. **Colorado 31-20.**

Geo: Lee 2 pass from Nagy (Garner kick), 3:01. **Colorado 31-27.**

FOURTH QUARTER

Col: FG Rush 26, 12:03. **Colorado 34-27.**

Geo: Lee 34 pass from Nagy (Garner kick), 9:19. **34-34.**

Col: Marshall 45 pass from Dutton (Rush kick), 7:57. **Colorado 41-34.**

Geo: Lee 27 pass from Nagy (Garner kick), 4:47. **41-41.**

Col: Harrell 30 pass from Dutton (Rush kick), 3:36. **Colorado 48-41.**

Geo: Jackson 20 pass from Nagy (Garner kick), 0:18. **48-48.**

Col: FG Rush 20, 0:00. **Colorado 51-48.**

A: 10,822

College Football

QB Vince Young led
the Texas Longhorns to the
national championship

The Fall of Troy

Texas head coach Mack Brown let Vince be Vince and his dynamic young QB ended USC's reign, hooking the 'Horns their first title in 35 years

BY B.J. SCHECTER

SOMETIMES WHEN THE PLANETS align, fate cooperates and dreams coincide with reality, we witness unforgettable moments. It rarely happens in sports and the events we build up for months and months usually come tumbling down faster than a Shaquille O'Neal slam dunk. But every so often we have games (and individuals) that actually live up to the hype. And even when everything works out the way we hope and we get our dream matchups and otherworldly performances, we sometimes see things that blow our minds. It's moments like these that leave us shaking our heads, turning to our buddies, mouths agape, and saying: "Can you believe (insert name) did that?"

The 2005 college football season featured two such moments and perhaps the greatest individual performance with the national championship on the line. They say when the bright lights go on and the stakes are the highest, the stars come out. And while the statement has been proven to be true over the years, historians may have to come up with something new for Vince Young. Young not only carried Texas to its first national championship since 1970 with a dramatic 41–38 victory over USC in the Rose Bowl, he also did so against a team which had won 34 straight games and the

last two titles. What's more, with the game on the line, USC knew exactly what he was going to do (as did millions of people watching around the world) and he still was able to do it and make it look so effortless you would think Young was playing a pickup game in the park.

Ever since the September night in Columbus, Ohio, when Young led Texas to a dramatic win over Ohio State, college football fans were clamoring for a Texas-USC matchup. Sure, both teams overcame scares during the season, but Longhorns-Trojans for the national title was the game everyone wanted to see. Even when it became a reality, however, some were skeptical that it would live up to the billing because a year earlier USC-Oklahoma was billed as the Game of the Century and the Trojans blew the Sooners off the field before halftime. USC featured an offense for the ages in 2005, but Young had been waiting for this moment his whole life. He had predicted it after leading Texas to a come-from-behind victory over Michigan on the same field in 2005 and was further motivated after finishing a distant second to USC's Reggie Bush for the Heisman Trophy.

In a remarkable game that featured 79 points, 1,130 yards of offense and was everything college football fans hoped it would be,

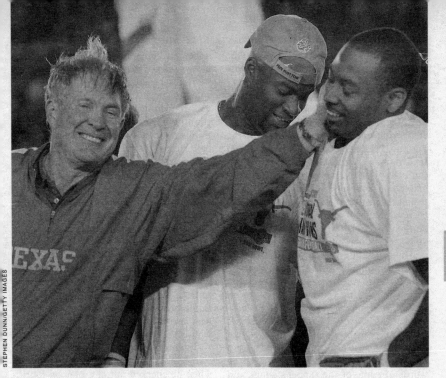

STEPHEN DUNN/GETTY IMAGES

Young left no doubt that he was the best player on the field that night and literally took the game away from the two-time defending champs. Young didn't panic when Dwayne Jarrett caught a 22-yard touchdown pass from Matt Leinart to put USC up 38–26 with 6:42 remaining. And neither did his teammates. Said Texas tackle Justin Blalock, "We kept our poise, put the ball in Vince's hands and let the man do what he does."

What Young did was march Texas down the field twice and scored a pair of touchdowns, one more awe-inspiring than the next. After Jarrett's TD reception, Young completed five of six passes and then cut the deficit to 38–33 with a 17-yard touchdown run. USC tried to run out the clock, and facing a fourth-and-two at midfield, Trojans coach Pete Carroll decided to go for it. A first down meant that for all intents and purposes the game was over. LenDale White, who had run through the Texas defense all night long, got the ball and was immediately stopped in his tracks. He was two inches short of the first down and the Longhorns were still alive.

Thanks to QB Vince Young (c.) and DB Michael Huff (r.), Mack Brown's 2005 Texas Longhorns went undefeated.

In nine plays, Young brought Texas to the USC 8-yard-line. Then, on fourth-and-five with less than 30 seconds left, Young scrambled, took off downfield, and after making at least three defenders miss, beat everyone to the corner of the end zone, making. Touchdown. Young's two-point conversion run made it 41-38, and after USC was unable to move in position for a game-tying field goal Texas was the national champion.

When the clock struck 0:00, a nation marveled at Young's performance—he had completed 30 of 40 passes for 267 yards and rushed for 200 yards and three touchdowns—but nobody more so than USC's Carroll. "That's the best single-game performance I've ever had against me," he said. "[It was] a night for champions. The question you ask is, 'Who's going to get it?' They took it."

Young took the game from the last two Heisman winners (Leinart and Bush) and afterward the quarterback still displayed the chip on his shoulder that helped motivate him to victory. "We didn't get no respect," said Young, "but nobody gave us 12-0."

Nobody gave Texas coach Mack Brown anything over the years either, except constant criticism for not being able to win the big one. Personable and charming, Brown landed top recruiting class after top recruiting class, but five straight losses to rival Oklahoma knocked the Longhorns out of the national title picture. Some fans were even calling for Brown's job, an absurd suggestion for a coach who had won more than 70 percent of his games.

The constant criticism forced Brown to look deep inside himself and what he found was that he was taking things too seriously, putting too much pressure on himself, and in turn his players. So he loosened up, tried to understand his players more and even developed a liking for some of their musical tastes. Mack Brown a 50 Cent fan? You bet. The coach knew the words of some of the rapper's songs and that helped him connect to his players on a different level. Brown allowed Young to be himself on and off the field and earned the respect of his team. The coach was understandably emotional after beating USC, but even he didn't expect to be speechless in the postgame locker room.

"I told them I've been planning this talk for 33 years, and now I don't know what to say," said Brown. "Winning a national championship is really special for our school and our state. It's unbelievable."

Unbelievable was a word often used to describe USC's Bush and Leinart. After winning the 2004 Heisman Trophy Leinart was almost guaranteed to be a top-three pick (and could have even been No. 1) in the NFL draft, but decided to return to school for his senior year because he loved being a college student (as the BMOC at USC, who could blame him?) and wanted to lead the Trojans to an unprecedented third straight national title. With Leinart at the controls, USC's offense was more dominant than ever, averaging 580 yards and 50 points per game, and even though the Trojans' defense appeared breakable at times, the offense always seemed to bail the team out.

That's because whenever USC needed some magic Bush provided it. Whether it was returning punts, catching passes or running out of the backfield, Bush made things happen every time he touched the ball. He could take what looked like a five-yard loss and turn it into a zigzagging, criss-cross-the-field-five-times 60-yard touchdown. USC would need both Bush and Leinart to survive a heart-stopping trip to South Bend in mid-October.

After getting drilled by USC in each of the previous two seasons, Notre Dame was a different team under former New England Patriots offensive coordinator Charlie Weis, who put the Fightin' back into the Irish. And as the sun came down over Notre Dame Stadium, the Irish had the Trojans beat and it appeared as if USC's 27-game winning streak would come to an end.

Trailing 31-28, the Trojans had one last chance and Leinart displayed some moxie when he checked out of a play on fourth-and-nine at the USC 26 with 1:32 remaining and completed a pinpoint strike to Jarrett for a 61-yard gain. "We had the perfect defense [called]," said Weis. "They threw a fade route into our Two Tampa [scheme]. It's complete by an inch. I mean, you don't throw fade routes into Two Tampa, but this guy did."

USC caught another break when Leinart was tackled and fumbled out of bounds at the Notre Dame one-yard line. The Trojans didn't have any timeouts left and if he was tackled anywhere else on the field or didn't fumble, the game would have been over. But with one final play, Carroll gave Leinart a choice: spike the ball so USC could kick the game-tying field goal or try and sneak it into the end zone.

"You going to go for it?" Bush asked Leinart.

"You think I should?" Leinart responded.

"Man, just do it!" Bush said.

With that added assurance, Leinart went for it, but an initial surge by the Notre Dame defensive line left Leinart short...until Bush pushed the quarterback into the end zone

Matt Leinart's (11) last-second TD against Notre Dame kept alive the Trojans's hopes for a third-straight national championship.

for the decisive touchdown. "It happened so quick," said Bush. "I'll never know if it really helped or it didn't. I definitely gave him a good enough push, though."

Notre Dame may have lost the game, but Weis helped push the Irish onto the cusp of the elite much sooner than expected. Having mentored Tom Brady and helped the Patriots win three Super Bowls, Weis had immediate credibility, but after the first practice in South Bend he knew he had his work cut out for him. The Irish were far from a championship team. "In the beginning," says Weis, "I beat them down, physically and psychologically. Things had to hit rock bottom before they got better." They did.

Said Brady, "He would ride you and ride you and ride you. He'd take you to the point where you thought, Man, I just want to go to

sleep. I just want it to be tomorrow."

After surviving Weis' training camp, the Irish were a different team and showed confidence and fire they had lacked. Notre Dame finished the regular season 9–2 and earned a berth in the Fiesta Bowl. And even though the Irish lost to Ohio State 34–20, Weis' troops made quite a statement in 2005: Notre Dame is back.

New Florida coach Urban Meyer hoped to make a similar statement in Gainesville. The Gators got off to a good start, but it proved to be fool's gold as Florida went to Alabama on Oct. 1 with a 4–0 record and got drilled, 31–3. It was an up-and-down season for the Gators—wins over rivals Florida State and Georgia; losses to LSU and the Gators' former coach at South Carolina—and though Florida ended on a high note with a win over Iowa in the Outback Bowl, one question persisted: what the heck was wrong with Chris Leak?

Many expected Leak to flourish in

"Joe Pa" (r.) coached a resurgent Nittany Lions team that lost only once and finished the season with an Orange Bowl victory.

Meyer's innovative spread option offense, but the junior quarterback struggled and the Gators were forced to largely scrap the option, a move that pained Meyer. "Why didn't we run the option very well? Because we didn't block very well," said Meyer. "Not to break your hearts, but we're not a great team." Still, a 9–3 finish is nothing to cry about and after landing the No. 1 recruiting class in the nation, Gators fans took solace in the fact that the program is in good hands.

Much-maligned Penn State coach Joe Paterno proved the Nittany Lions were still in good hands after a miraculous 11–1 season, which culminated with a victory over Florida State in the Orange Bowl. Penn State was one second from an undefeated

season as it lost to Michigan in Ann Arbor on the final play. For all the criticism Joe Pa endured recently, it was sweet vindication, but he refused to gloat. Instead, he focused on the program and said he was the same coach he had always been. That may be debatable given how much he opened up the offense and how he finally allowed freshmen to come in and play right away, but what's not is the fact that Penn State's future looks bright again.

So does Mack Brown's. While the pressure to win at Texas will always be immense, he will no longer be saddled with the reputation of a coach who isn't able to win the big one. Young had a lot to say about that, and as he accepted the Rose Bowl MVP award, he marveled at his—and the Longhorns'—accomplishment. "It's so beautiful," Young said of the trophy. "And it's coming all the way home to Austin, Texas."

Final Polls

Associated Press

	Record	Pts	Head Coach	SI Preseason Rank
1. Texas (65)	13-0	1625	Mack Brown	2
2. USC	12-1	1560	Pete Carroll	1
3. Penn St	11-1	1484	Joe Paterno	30
4. Ohio St	10-2	1428	Jim Tressel	8
5. West Virginia	11-1	1325	Rich Rodriguez	42
6. LSU	11-2	1314	Les Miles	13
7. Virginia Tech	11-2	1197	Frank Beamer	9
8. Alabama	10-2	1081	Mike Shula	41
9. Notre Dame	9-3	1019	Charlie Weis	44
10. Georgia	10-3	994	Mark Richt	10
11. TCU	11-1	937	Gary Patterson	62
12. Florida	9-3	817	Urban Meyer	3
12. Oregon	10-2	817	Mike Bellotti	43
14. Auburn	9-3	799	Tommy Tuberville	18
15. Wisconsin	10-3	786	Barry Alvarez	40
16. UCLA	10-2	778	Karl Dorrell	34
17. Miami (Fla.)	9-3	589	Larry Coker	6
18. Boston College	9-3	545	Tom O'Brien	37
19. Louisville	9-3	410	Bobby Petrino	11
20. Texas Tech	9-3	359	Mike Leach	29
21. Clemson	8-4	339	Tommy Bowden	52
22. Oklahoma	8-4	329	Bob Stoops	7
23. Florida St	8-5	232	Bobby Bowden	15
24. Nebraska	8-4	128	Bill Callahan	56
25. California	8-4	45	Jeff Tedford	17

Note: As voted by a panel of 65 sportswriters and broadcasters following bowl games (1st place votes in parentheses).

USA Today/ESPN

	Pts	SI Preseason Rank		Pts	SI Preseason Rank
1. Texas (62)	1550	2	13. UCLA	774	34
2. USC	1483	1	14. Auburn	760	18
3. Penn St	1421	30	15. Wisconsin	739	40
4. Ohio St	1357	8	16. Florida	718	3
5. LSU	1281	13	17. Boston College	584	37
6. West Virginia	1176	42	18. Miami (Fla.)	558	6
7. Virginia Tech	1176	9	19. Texas Tech	422	29
8. Alabama	1066	41	20. Louisville	342	11
9. TCU	914	62	21. Clemson	310	52
10. Georgia	900	10	22. Oklahoma	274	7
11. Notre Dame	866	44	23. Florida St	209	15
12. Oregon	837	43	24. Nebraska	109	56
			25. California	68	17

Note: Voted by a panel of 62 Div. I-A head coaches; 25 points for 1st, 24 for 2nd, etc. (First place votes in parentheses).

Bowls and Playoffs

NCAA Division I-A Bowl Results

Date	Bowl	Result	Payout/Team ($)	Attendance
12-20-05	New Orleans	Southern Miss. 31, Arkansas 19	750,000	18,388
12-21-05	GMAC	Toledo 45, UTEP 13	750,000	35,422
12-22-05	Las Vegas	California 35, Brigham Young 28	750,000	40,053
12-22-05	Poinsettia	Navy 51, Colorado St 30	750,000	36,842
12-23-05	Fort Worth	Kansas 42, Houston 13	750,000	33,505
12-24-05	Hawaii	Nevada 49, Central Florida 48	750,000	16,134
12-26-05	Motor City	Memphis 38, Akron 31	750,000	50,616
12-27-05	Champs Sports	Clemson 19, Colorado 10	862,500	31,470
12-27-05	Insight	Arizona St 45, Rutgers 40	750,000	43,536
12-28-05	MPC Computers	Boston College 27, Boise St 21	750,000	30,493

NCAA Division I-A Bowl Results *(Cont.)*

Date	Bowl	Result	Payout/Team ($)	Attendance
12-28-05	Alamo	Nebraska 32, Michigan 28	1.65 million	62,000
12-29-05	Emerald	Utah 38, Georgia Tech 10	750,000	25,742
12-29-05	Holiday	Oklahoma 17, Oregon 14	2 million	65,416
12-30-05	Music City	Virginia 34, Minnesota 31	780,000	40,519
12-30-05	Sun	UCLA 50, Northwestern 38	1.575 million	50,426
12-30-05	Independence	Missouri 38, South Carolina 31	1.2 million	41,332
12-30-05	Peach	LSU 40, Miami (Fla.) 3	2.4 million	65,620
12-31-05	Meineke	North Carolina 14, South Florida 0	750,000	57,937
12-31-05	Liberty	Tulsa 31, Fresno St 24	1.5 million	54,894
12-31-05	Houston	TCU 27, Iowa St 24	1.2 million	37,286
01-02-06	Outback	Florida 31, Iowa 24	2.85 million	65,881
01-02-06	Cotton	Alabama 13, Texas Tech 10	2.5 million	74,222
01-02-06	Gator	Virginia Tech 35, Louisville 24	1.6 million	63,780
01-02-06	Capital One	Wisconsin 24, Auburn 10	5.312 million	57,221
01-02-06	Fiesta	Ohio St 34, Notre Dame 20	14.9 million	76,196
01-02-06	Sugar	West Virginia 38, Georgia 35	14.9 million	74,458
01-03-06	Orange	Penn St 26, Florida St 23 (3 OT)	14.9 million	77,773
01-04-06	Rose	Texas 41, USC 38	14.9 million	93,986

NCAA Division I-AA Championship Box Score

Northern Iowa	6	10	0	0 —16
Appalachian State	0	7	7	7 —21

FIRST QUARTER
Northern Iowa: FG Wingert 50, 11:36.
Northern Iowa: FG Wingert 26, 9:45.

SECOND QUARTER
Appalachian St: Richardson 5 run (Rauch kick) 13:18.
Northern Iowa: Horne 2 run (Wingert kick), 8:20.
Northern Iowa: FG Wingert 31, 1:09

THIRD QUARTER
Appalachian St: Richardson 1 run (Rauch kick), 6:05.

FOURTH QUARTER
Appalachian St: Hunter 15 fumble return (Rauch kick), 9:14.

	NORTHERN IOWA	APPALACHIAN ST
First downs	21	18
Rushes–yards	47-102	28-46
Passing yards	181	252
Comp/Att/Int	17-31-0	19-42-1
Punts	9-341	7-293
Fumbles-lost	3-1	2-2
Penalties-yards	5-45	4-40
Time of possession	36:26	23:34

12-16-05, Chattanooga, Tennessee; Att: 20,236.

Small College Championship Summaries

NCAA DIVISION II

First round: Central Arkansas 28, Albany St., Ga. 20; N. Alabama 40, Valdosta St., Ga. 13; Pittsburg St., Kan. 49, Nebraska-Kearney, 20; NW Missouri St. 45, Angelo St, Tex. 14; C.W. Post, N.Y. 24, West Chester, Pa. 20; East Stroudsburg, Pa. 55, South. Conn. St. 33; N. Dakota 23, Minn-Duluth 12; Saginaw Valley St., Mich. 31, Northwood, 16

Second Round: Central Arkansas 52, Presbyterian, S.C. 28; N Alabama 24, North Car. Central 21; NW Missouri St. 42, Washburn, Kan. 32; Pittsburg St., Kan. 41, West Texas A&M 3; C.W. Post, N.Y. 28, Shepherd, W.V. 21; East Stroudsburg, Pa. 52, Bloomsburg, Pa. 39; Grand Valley St., Mich. 17, N Dakota 3; Saginaw Valley St 24, Neb-Omaha 21

Quarterfinals: N Alabama 41, Central Arkansas 38; NW Missouri St. 38, Pittsburg St., Kan. 10; East Stroudsburg, Pa. 55, C.W. Post, N.Y. 28; Grand Valley St., Mich. 24, Saginaw Valley St., Mich. 17

Semifinals: NW Missouri St. 25, N Alabama 24; Grand Valley St., Mich. 55, East Stroudsburg, Pa. 20

Championship: 12-10-05, Florence, Alabama

NW Missouri St.	7	7	0	3—17
Grand Valley St., Mich.	7	0	7	7—21

NCAA DIVISION III

First round: Linfield 63, Occidental 21; Concordia-Moorhead 27, Coe 14; St. John's 62, Monmouth 3; Central 14, UW-Whitewater 34; Trinity 6, Mary Hardin-Baylor 35; Ferrum 14, Wesley 59; Bridgewater, Va. 30, Wash. and Jeff. 21; Johns Hopkins 3, Thiel 28; Wabash 38, Albion 20; Capital 21, North Central 19; Augustana 49, Lakeland 22; Mt. St. Joseph 6, Mt Union 49; Del Valley 37, Curry 22; Cortland St. 22, Hobart 23; Rowan 42, Wilkes 3; Ithaca 41, Union 55

Second Round: Linfield 28, Concordia-Moorhead 14; St. John's 7, UW-Whitewater 34; Mary Hardin-Baylor 36, Wesley 46; Bridgewater, Va 24, Thiel 7; Wabash 11, Capital 14; Augustana 7, Mt Union 44; Del Valley 21, Hobart 14; Union 24, Rowan 28

Quarterfinals: Linfield 41, UW-Whitewater 44; Wesley 46, Bridgewater, Va 7; Capital 31, Mt Union 34; Del Valley 21, Rowan 27

Semifinals: UW-Whitewater 58, Wesley 6; Mt Union 19, Rowan 7

Championship: 12-17-05, Salem, Virginia

Mt. Union	7	7	14	7—35
UW-Whitewater	7	0	0	21—28

NAIA CHAMPIONSHIP

12-17-05, Savannah, Tennessee

St. Francis, Ind.	3	0	7	0—10
Carroll Coll. Mont.	7	10	7	3—27

Heisman Memorial Trophy

Player, School	Class	Pos	1st	2nd	3rd	Total
Reggie Bush, USC	Jr.	RB	784	89	11	2541
Vince Young, Texas	Jr.	QB	79	613	145	1608
Matt Leinart, USC	Sr.	QB	18	147	449	797
Brady Quinn, Notre Dame	Jr.	QB	7	21	128	191
Michael Robinson, Penn St	Sr.	QB	2	7	29	49

Note: Former Heisman winners and the media vote, with ballots allowing for three names (3 points for 1st, 2 for 2nd, 1 for 3rd).

Other Awards

Maxwell Award (Player)	Vince Young, Texas, QB
Sporting News Player of the Year	Reggie Bush, USC, RB
Walter Camp Player of the Year	Reggie Bush, USC, RB
Chuck Bednarik Award (Defense)	Paul Posluszny, Penn St, LB
Vince Lombardi/Rotary Award (Lineman/LB)	A.J. Hawk, Ohio St,LB
Outland Trophy (Interior Lineman)	Greg Eslinger, Minnesota, C
Davey O'Brien Award (QB)	Vince Young, Texas, QB
Unitas Golden Arm Award (Senior QB)	Matt Leinart, USC, QB
Doak Walker Award (RB)	Reggie Bush, USC, RB
Biletnikoff Award (WR)	Mike Hass, Oregon St,WR
Butkus Award (Linebacker)	Paul Posluszny, Penn St, LB
Jim Thorpe Award (Defensive Back)	Michael Huff, Texas, DB
Associated Press Player of the Year	Reggie Bush, USC, RB
Walter Payton Award (Div I-AA Player)	Erik Meyer, Eastern Washington, QB
Harlon Hill Trophy (Div II Player)	Jimmy Terwilliger. East Stroudsburg,QB
Gagliardi Trophy (Div III Player)	Brett Elliott, Linfield,QB

Coaches' Awards

Walter Camp Award	Joe Paterno, Penn St
Eddie Robinson Award (Div I-AA)	Sean McDonnell, New Hamp.
Bobby Dodd Award	Joe Paterno, Penn St
Bear Bryant Award	Mack Brown, Texas

AFCA COACHES OF THE YEAR

Division I-A	Joe Paterno, Penn St
Division I-AA	Jerry Moore, Appalachian St
Division II	Chuck Martin, Grand Valley St
Division III	Bob Berezowitz, UW-Whitewater

Football Writers Association of America All-America Team

OFFENSE

QB	Vince Young, Texas, Jr.
RB	Reggie Bush, USC, Jr.
RB	Jerome Harrison, Washington St, Sr.
WR	Dwayne Jarrett, USC, So.
WR	Jeff Samardzija, Notre Dame, Jr.
TE	Marcedes Lewis, UCLA, Sr.
OL	Taitusi Lutui, USC, Sr.
OL	Marcus McNeill, Auburn, Sr.
OL	Jonathan Scott, Texas, Sr.
OL	Zach Strief, Northwestern, Sr.
C	Greg Eslinger, Minnesota, Sr.
K	Mason Crosby, Colorado, Jr.
KR	Maurice Drew, UCLA, Jr.

DEFENSE

DL	Brodrick Bunkley, Florida St, Sr.
DL	Elvis Durnervil, Louisville, Sr.
DL	Haloti Ngata, Oregon, Jr.
LB	A. J. Hawk, Ohio St, Sr.
LB	Paul Posluszny, Penn St, Jr.
LB	DeMeco Ryans, Alabama, Sr.
DB	Michael Huff, Texas, Sr.
DB	Brandon Meriweather, Miami (Fla.), Jr.
DB	Ko Simpson, S. Carolina, So.
DB	Jimmy Williams, Virginia Tech, Sr.
P	Ryan Plackemeier, Wake Forest, Sr.

Division I-A

ATLANTIC COAST CONFERENCE

| | Conference | | Full Season | | |
	W	L	W	L	Pct
Virginia Tech	7	1	11	2	.846
Miami (Fla.)	6	2	9	3	.750
Boston College	5	3	9	3	.750
Clemson	4	4	8	4	.667
Florida St	5	3	8	5	.615
North Carolina St	3	5	7	5	.583
Georgia Tech	5	3	7	5	.583
Virginia	3	5	7	5	.583
Maryland	3	5	5	6	.455
North Carolina	4	4	5	6	.455
Wake Forest	3	5	4	7	.364
Duke	0	8	1	10	.091

BIG EAST CONFERENCE

| | Conference | | Full Season | | |
	W	L	W	L	Pct
West Virginia	7	0	11	1	.917
Louisville	5	2	9	3	.750
Rutgers	4	3	7	5	.583
South Florida	4	3	6	6	.500
Pittsburgh	4	3	5	6	.455
Connecticut	2	5	5	6	.455
Cincinnati	2	5	4	7	.364
Syracuse	0	7	1	10	.091

BIG TEN CONFERENCE

| | Conference | | Full Season | | |
	W	L	W	L	Pct
Penn St	7	1	11	1	.917
Ohio St	7	1	10	2	.833
Wisconsin	5	3	10	3	.769
Iowa	5	3	7	5	.583
Michigan	5	3	7	5	.583
Northwestern	5	3	7	5	.583
Minnesota	4	4	7	5	.583
Purdue	3	5	5	6	.455
Michigan St	2	6	5	6	.455
Indiana	1	7	4	7	.364
Illinois	0	8	2	9	.182

BIG 12 CONFERENCE

| | Conference | | Full Season | | |
	W	L	W	L	Pct
NORTH					
Nebraska	4	4	8	4	.667
Iowa St	4	4	7	5	.583
Missouri	4	4	7	5	.583
Kansas	3	5	7	5	.583
Colorado	5	3	7	6	.538
Kansas St	2	6	5	6	.455
SOUTH					
Texas	8	0	13	0	1.00
Texas Tech	6	2	9	3	.750
Oklahoma	6	2	8	4	.667
Texas A&M	3	5	5	6	.455
Baylor	2	6	5	6	.455
Oklahoma St	1	7	4	7	.364

Division I-A (Cont.)

CONFERENCE USA

| | Conference | | Full Season | | |
	W	L	W	L	Pct
Tulsa	6	2	9	4	.692
UTEP	5	3	8	4	.667
Central Florida	7	1	8	5	.615
Memphis	5	3	7	5	.583
Southern Miss	5	3	7	5	.583
Houston	4	4	6	6	.500
East Carolina	4	4	5	6	.455
SMU	4	4	5	6	.455
Ala.-Birmingham	3	5	5	6	.455
Marshall	3	5	4	7	.364
Tulane	1	7	2	9	.182
Rice	1	7	1	10	.091

MID-AMERICAN ATHLETIC CONFERENCE

| | Conference | | Full Season | | |
	W	L	W	L	Pct
EAST					
Miami (Ohio)	5	3	7	4	.636
Bowling Green	5	3	6	5	.545
Akron	5	3	7	6	.538
Ohio U	3	5	4	7	.364
Buffalo	1	7	1	10	.091
Kent St	0	8	1	10	.091
WEST					
Toledo	6	2	9	3	.750
Western Michigan	5	3	7	4	.636
Northern Illinois	6	2	7	5	.583
Central Michigan	5	3	6	5	.545
Ball St	4	4	4	7	.364
Eastern Michigan	3	5	4	7	.364

MOUNTAIN WEST CONFERENCE

| | Conference | | Full Season | | |
	W	L	W	L	Pct
TCU	8	0	11	1	.917
Utah	4	4	7	5	.583
New Mexico	4	4	6	5	.545
BYU	5	3	6	6	.500
Colorado St	5	3	6	6	.500
San Diego St	4	4	5	7	.417
Air Force	3	5	4	7	.364
Wyoming	2	6	4	7	.364
UNLV	1	7	2	9	.182

PACIFIC 10 CONFERENCE

| | Conference | | Full Season | | |
	W	L	W	L	Pct
USC	8	0	12	1	.923
Oregon	7	1	10	2	.833
UCLA	6	2	10	2	.833
California	4	4	8	4	.667
Arizona St	4	4	7	5	.583
Stanford	4	4	5	6	.455
Oregon St	3	5	5	6	.455
Arizona	2	6	3	8	.273
Washington St	1	7	4	7	.364
Washington	1	7	2	9	.182

Division I-A *(Cont.)*

SOUTHEASTERN CONFERENCE

EAST	Conference		Full Season		
	W	L	W	L	Pct
Georgia	6	2	10	3	.769
Florida	5	3	9	3	.750
South Carolina	5	3	7	5	.583
Tennessee	3	5	5	6	.455
Vanderbilt	3	5	5	6	.455
Kentucky	2	6	3	8	.273
WEST					
LSU	7	1	11	2	.846
Alabama	6	2	10	2	.833
Auburn	7	1	9	3	.750
Arkansas	2	6	4	7	.364
Mississippi St	1	7	3	8	.273
Old Miss	1	7	3	8	.273

SUN BELT CONFERENCE

	Conference		Full Season		
	W	L	W	L	Pct
La.-Lafayette	5	2	6	5	.545
Arkansas St	5	2	6	6	.500
La.-Monroe	5	2	5	6	.455
Florida Int'l	3	4	5	6	.455
Middle Tennessee St	3	4	4	7	.364
Troy	3	4	4	7	.364
Florida Atlantic	2	5	2	9	.182
North Texas	2	5	2	9	.182

WESTERN ATHLETIC CONFERENCE

	Conference		Full Season		
	W	L	W	L	Pct
Nevada	7	1	9	3	.750
Boise St	7	1	9	4	.692
Louisiana Tech	6	2	7	4	.636
Fresno St	6	2	8	5	.615
Hawaii	4	4	5	7	.417
San Jose St	2	6	3	8	.273
Utah St	2	6	3	8	.273
Idaho	2	6	2	9	.182
New Mexico St	0	8	0	12	.000

INDEPENDENTS

	Full Season		
	W	L	Pct
Notre Dame	9	3	.750
Navy	8	4	.666

Division I-AA

ATLANTIC 10 CONFERENCE

	Conference		Full Season		
	W	L	W	L	Pct
New Hampshire	7	1	11	2	.846
Richmond	7	1	9	4	.692
James Madison	5	3	7	4	.636
Massachusetts	6	2	7	4	.636
Hofstra	5	3	7	4	.636
Delaware	3	5	6	5	.545
Towson	3	5	6	5	.545
Maine	3	5	5	6	.455
William and Mary	3	5	5	6	.455
Rhode Island	2	6	4	7	.364
Villanova	2	6	4	7	.364
Northeastern	2	6	2	9	.182

BIG SKY CONFERENCE

	Conference		Full Season		
	W	L	W	L	Pct
Montana	5	2	8	4	.667
Montana St	5	2	7	4	.636
Eastern Washington	5	2	7	5	.583
Portland St	4	3	6	5	.545
Weber St	4	3	6	5	.545
Idaho St	3	4	5	6	.455
N. Arizona	1	6	3	8	.273
Sacramento St	1	6	2	9	.182

BIG SOUTH CONFERENCE

	Conference		Full Season		
	W	L	W	L	Pct
Coastal Carolina	3	1	9	2	.818
Charleston Southern	3	1	7	4	.636
Gardner-Webb	2	2	5	6	.455
Va Military Inst	2	2	3	8	.273
Liberty	0	4	1	10	.091

GATEWAY COLLEGIATE ATHLETIC CONFERENCE

	Conference		Full Season		
	W	L	W	L	Pct
Northern Iowa	5	2	11	4	.733
Youngstown St	5	2	8	3	.727
Southern Illinois	5	2	9	4	.692
Illinois St	4	3	7	4	.636
Western Kentucky	4	3	6	5	.545
Western Illinois	3	4	5	6	.455
Missouri St	2	5	4	6	.400
Indiana St	0	7	0	11	.000

IVY LEAGUE

	Conference		Full Season		
	W	L	W	L	Pct
Brown	6	1	9	1	.900
Harvard	5	2	7	3	.700
Princeton	5	2	7	3	.700
Cornell	4	3	6	4	.600
Penn	3	4	5	5	.500
Yale	4	3	4	6	.400
Dartmouth	1	6	2	8	.200
Columbia	0	7	2	8	.200

METRO ATLANTIC ATHLETIC CONFERENCE

	Conference		Full Season		
	W	L	W	L	Pct
Duquesne	4	0	7	3	.700
Marist	3	1	7	4	.636
La Salle	2	2	4	7	.364
Iona	1	3	3	7	.300
St. Peters	0	4	1	9	.100

Division I-AA *(Cont.)*

MID-EASTERN ATHLETIC CONFERENCE

	Conference		Full Season		
	W	L	W	L	Pct
Hampton	8	0	11	1	.917
South Carolina St	7	1	9	2	.818
Delaware St	6	2	7	4	.636
Bethune-Cookman	4	4	7	4	.636
Norfolk St	2	6	7	4	.636
Florida A&M	6	3	6	5	.545
North Carolina A&T	2	6	4	7	.364
Howard	1	7	4	7	.364
Morgan St	1	7	2	9	.182

NORTHEAST CONFERENCE

	Conference		Full Season		
	W	L	W	L	Pct
Central Connecticut St	5	2	7	4	.636
Monmouth (N.J.)	4	3	6	4	.600
Stony Brook	5	2	6	5	.545
Wagner	3	4	6	5	.545
Albany	4	3	5	6	.455
Sacred Heart	3	4	4	6	.400
St. Francis (Pa.)	3	4	3	8	.273
Robert Morris	1	6	2	8	.200

OHIO VALLEY CONFERENCE

	Conference		Full Season		
	W	L	W	L	Pct
Eastern Kentucky	7	1	7	4	.636
Jacksonville St	6	2	6	5	.545
Tenn.-Martin	4	4	6	5	.545
Samford	4	4	5	6	.455
Tennessee Tech	3	5	4	7	.364
Tennessee St	1	7	2	9	.182
Murray St	0	7	2	9	.182

PATRIOT LEAGUE

	Conference		Full Season		
	W	L	W	L	Pct
Lehigh	4	2	8	3	.727
Colgate	5	1	8	4	.667
Lafayette	5	1	8	4	.667
Holy Cross	3	3	6	5	.545
Georgetown	2	4	4	7	.364
Fordham	2	4	2	9	.182
Bucknell	0	6	1	10	.091

PIONEER LEAGUE

	Conference		Full Season		
	W	L	W	L	Pct
NORTH					
San Diego	4	0	11	1	.917
Dayton	3	1	9	1	.900
Drake	2	2	6	4	.600
Valparaiso	1	3	3	8	.273
Butler	0	4	0	11	.000
SOUTH					
Morehead St	3	0	8	4	.667
Jacksonville	2	1	4	4	.500
Davidson	1	2	4	6	.400
Austin Peay	0	3	2	9	.182

Division I-AA *(Cont.)*

SOUTHERN CONFERENCE

	Conference		Full Season		
	W	L	W	L	Pct
Appalachian St	6	1	12	3	.800
Furman	4	2	11	3	.786
Georgia Southern	5	2	8	4	.667
Western Carolina	4	3	5	4	.556
Wofford	3	3	6	5	.545
Chattanooga	3	4	6	5	.545
Citadel	2	5	4	7	.364
Elon	0	7	3	8	.273

SOUTHLAND CONFERENCE

	Conference		Full Season		
	W	L	W	L	Pct
Texas St	5	1	11	3	.786
Nicholls St	5	1	6	4	.600
McNeese St	3	3	5	4	.556
Northwestern St	3	3	5	5	.500
Stephen F. Austin	1	5	5	6	.455
SE Louisiana	2	4	4	6	.400
Sam Houston St	2	4	3	7	.300

SOUTHWESTERN ATHLETIC CONFERENCE

	Conference		Full Season		
EASTERN	W	L	W	L	Pct
Alabama A&M	7	2	9	3	.750
Alabama St	6	3	6	5	.545
Alcorn St	5	4	6	5	.545
Mississippi Valley St	5	4	6	5	.545
Jackson St	2	7	2	9	.182
WESTERN					
Grambling St	9	0	11	1	.917
Prairie View	3	6	5	6	.455
Southern Univ.	4	5	4	5	.444
Ark.-Pine Bluff	3	6	3	8	.273
Texas Southern	1	8	1	10	.091

INDEPENDENTS

	Full Season		
	W	L	Pct
Cal Poly–SLO	9	4	.692
North Dakota St	7	4	.636
UC-Davis	6	5	.545
South Dakota St	6	5	.545
Northern Colorado	4	7	.364
Southern Utah	1	9	.100

Division I-A

SCORING

	Class	GP	TD	XP	FG	Pts	Pts/Game
Michael Bush, Louisville	Jr	10	24	0	0	144	14.40
LenDale White, USC	Jr	13	26	0	0	156	12.00
Steve Slaton, West Virginia	Fr	10	19	0	0	114	11.40
Garrett Wolfe, Northern Illinois	Jr	9	17	0	0	102	11.30
Brian Calhoun, Wisconsin	Jr	13	24	0	0	144	11.08
Taurean Henderson, Texas Tech	Sr	12	22	0	0	132	11.00
DeAngelo Williams, Memphis	Sr	11	19	0	0	114	10.36
Maurice Drew, UCLA	Jr.	12	20	0	0	120	10.00
Gary Russell, Minnesota	So	12	19	0	0	116	9.67
DonTrell Moore, New Mexico	Sr	11	17	0	0	104	9.45

FIELD GOALS

	Class	GP	FGA	FG	Pct	FG/Game
Paul Martinez, Oregon	Jr	9	24	19	.792	2.11
Alexis Serna, Oregon St.	So	11	28	23	.821	2.09
Jad Dean, Clemson	Jr	12	31	24	.774	2.00
Darren McCaleb, Southern Miss	Jr	12	28	23	.821	1.92
Josh Huston, Ohio St.	Sr	12	28	22	.786	1.83

TOTAL OFFENSE

			Rushing		Passing			Total Offense	
	Class	GP	Car	Net	Att	Yds	Yds	Yds/Play	Yds/Game
Colt Brennan, Hawaii	So	12	99	154	515	4301	4455	7.26	371.3
Cody Hodges, Texas Tech	Sr	12	109	191	531	4238	4429	6.92	369.1
Brett Basanez, Northwestern	Sr	12	113	423	497	3622	4045	6.63	337.1
Brian Johnson, Utah	So	10	152	478	330	2892	3370	6.99	337.0
Brady Quinn, Notre Dame	Jr	12	70	90	450	3919	4009	7.71	334.1
Vince Young, Texas	Jr	13	155	1050	325	3036	4086	8.51	314.3
John Beck, Brigham Young	Jr	12	73	61	512	3709	3770	6.43	314.2
Drew Stanton, Michigan St.	Jr	11	121	338	354	3077	3415	7.19	310.5
Brad Smith, Missouri	Sr	12	229	1301	399	2304	3605	5.74	300.4
Jay Cutler, Vanderbilt	Sr	11	106	215	462	3073	3288	5.79	298.9

RUSHING

	Class	GP	Car	Yds	TD	Avg	Yds/Game
DeAngelo Williams, Memphis	Sr	11	310	1964	18	6.34	178.55
Garrett Wolfe, Northern Illinois.	Jr	9	242	1580	16	6.53	175.56
Jerome Harrison, Washington St.	Sr	11	308	1900	16	6.17	172.73
Reggie Bush, USC	Jr	13	200	1740	16	8.70	133.85
Laurence Maroney, Minnesota	Jr	11	281	1464	10	5.21	133.09
Brian Calhoun, Wisconsin	Jr	13	348	1636	22	4.70	125.85
Marshawn Lynch, California	So	10	196	1246	10	6.36	124.60
Tyrell Sutton, Northwestern	Fr	12	250	1474	16	5.90	122.83
Yvenson Bernard, Oregon St.	So	11	299	1321	13	4.42	120.09
DonTrell Moore, New Mexico	Sr	11	275	1298	14	4.72	118.00

PASSING EFFICIENCY

	Class	GP	Att	Comp	Pct Comp	Yds	Yds/Att	TD	Int	Rating Pts
Rudy Carpenter, Arizona St.	Fr	9	228	156	68.42	2273	9.97	17	2	175.0
Brian Broham, Louisville	So	10	301	207	68.77	2883	9.58	19	5	166.7
Vince Young, Texas	Jr	13	325	212	65..23	3036	9.34	26	10	163.9
Troy Smith, Ohio St.	Sr	11	237	149	62.87	2282	9.63	16	4	162.7
Drew Olson, UCLA	Sr	12	378	242	64.02	3198	8.46	34	6	161.6
Phil Horvath, Northern Illinois	Jr	9	238	168	70.59	2001	8.41	18	8	159.4
Brady Quinn, Notre Dame	Jr	12	450	292	64.89	3919	8.71	32	7	158.4
Matt Leinart, USC	Sr	13	431	283	65.66	3815	8.85	28	8	157.7
Colt Brennan, Hawaii	So	12	515	351	67.96	4301	8.35	35	13	155.5
Drew Stanton, Michigan St.	Jr	11	354	236	66.67	3077	8.69	22	12	153.4

Note: Minimum 15 attempts per game.

Division I-A *(Cont.)*

RECEPTIONS PER GAME

	Class	GP	No.	Yds	TD	R/Game
Greg Jennings, Western Michigan	Sr	11	98	1259	14	8.91
Mike Hass, Oregon St.	Sr	11	90	1532	6	8.18
Jeffery Webb, San Diego St.	Sr	12	92	1109	10	7.67
Aundrae Allison, East Carolina	Sr	11	83	1024	7	7.55
Davone Bess, Hawaii	Fr	12	89	1124	14	7.42

RECEIVING YARDS PER GAME

	Class	GP	No.	Yds	TD	Yds/Game
Mike Hass, Oregon St.	Sr	11	90	1532	6	139.27
Greg Jennings, Western Michigan	Sr	11	98	1259	14	114.45
Jason Hill, Washington St.	Jr	10	62	1097	13	109.70
Jeff Samardzija, Notre Dame	Jr	12	27	1249	15	104.08
Sidney Rice, South Carolina	Fr	11	70	1143	13	103.91

ALL-PURPOSE RUNNERS

	Class	GP	Rush	Rec	PR	KOR	Yds	Yds/Game
Reggie Bush, USC	Jr	13	1740	478	179	493	2890	222.31
Garrett Wolfe, Northern Illinois	Jr	9	1580	222	0	0	1802	200.22
Jerome Harrison, Washington St.	Sr	11	1900	206	0	7	2113	192.09
DeAngelo Williams, Memphis	Sr	11	1964	78	0	33	2075	188.64
Rafael Little, Kentucky	So	11	1045	449	355	133	1982	180.18

INTERCEPTIONS

	Class	GP	No.	Int/Game
Aaron Gipson, Oregon	Sr	12	7	.58
Anthony Smith, Syracuse	Sr	11	6	.55
Dion Byrum, Ohio	Sr	11	6	.55
Jelani Jordan, Bowling Green	Sr	11	6	.55
Chaz Williams, La.-Monroe	So	10	5	.50

PUNTING

	Class	No.	Avg
R.Plackemeier, Wake Forest	Sr	67	47.24
Sam Koch, Nebraska	Sr	71	46.51
Daniel Sepulveda, Baylor	Jr	62	46.18
Jim Kaylor, Colorado St.	So	53	45.28
John Torp, Colorado	Sr	80	45.16

Note: Minimum of 3.6 per game.

PUNT RETURNS

	Class	No.	Yds	TD	Avg
Maurice Drew, UCLA	Jr	15	427	3	28.47
Quinton Jones, Boise St.	Jr	22	459	3	20.86
Terrence Nunn, Nebraska	So	16	293	0	18.31
Willie Reid, Florida St.	Sr	31	541	3	17.45
Rafael Little, Kentucky	So	21	355	0	16.90

Note: Minimum 1.2 per game.

KICKOFF RETURNS

	Class	No.	Yds	TD	Avg
Jonathan Stewart, Oregon	Fr	12	404	2	33.67
Felix Jones, Arkansas	Fr	17	543	1	31.94
Cory Rodgers, TCU	Jr	17	515	2	30.29
Ted Ginn, Ohio St.	So	18	532	1	29.56
Tony Pennyman, Utah	Jr	23	675	2	29.35

Note: Minimum 1.2 per game.

Division I-A Team Single-Game Highs

RUSHING AND PASSING

Rushing and passing yards: 604—Cody Hodges, Texas Tech, QB, Oct. 15, 2005 (vs. Kansas)
Rushing and passing plays: 84—Brad Smith, Missouri, QB, Sept. 10, 2005 (vs. New Mexico)
Rushing plays: 46—Laurence Maroney, Minnesota, RB, Sept. 24, 2005 (vs Purdue)
Net rushing yards: 294—Reggie Bush USC, RB, Nov. 19, 2005 (vs Fresno St)
Passes attempted: 70—Kent Smith, Central Michigan, QB, Nov. 12, 2005 (vs Western Michigan)
Passes completed: 46—Kent Smith, Central Michigan, QB, Nov. 12, 2005 (vs Western Michigan)
Passing yards: 643—Cody Hodges, Texas Tech, QB, Oct. 15, 2005 (vs Kansas)

RECEIVING AND RETURNS

Passes caught: Five tied with 11.
Receiving yards: 269—Daniel Smith, Idaho, WR, Oct. 29, 2005 (vs New Mexico St.)
Punt return Yards: 189—Clifton Smith, Fresno St. Sept. 10, 2005 (vs Weber St)
Kickoff return yards: 219—Jovon Bouknight, Wyoming, Nov. 5, 2005 (vs Utah)

Division I-AA

SCORING

	Class	GP	TD	XP	FG	Pts	Pts/Game
Nick Hartigan, Brown	Sr	10	21	0	0	126	12.60
David Bell, New Hampshire	Jr	13	24	0	0	144	11.08
Jayson Foster, Georgia Southern	So	12	21	0	0	126	10.50
Henry Tolbert, Grambling	Sr	12	20	0	0	120	10.00
Omar Cuff, Delaware	So	11	18	0	0	108	9.82

FIELD GOALS

	Class	GP	FGA	FG	Pct	FG/Game
Steve Morgan, Brown	So	10	23	18	.783	1.80
Blake Bercegeay, McNeese St.	Fr	9	19	16	.842	1.78
Andrew Paterini, Hampton	Jr	12	30	20	.667	1.67
Derek Javarone, Princeton	Sr	10	18	16	.889	1.60
Peter Gaertner, Delaware St.	Jr	10	21	16	.762	1.60

TOTAL OFFENSE

			Rushing		Passing		Total Offense		
	Class	GP	Car	Net	Att	Yds	Yds	Yds/Play	Yds/Game
Bruce Eugene, Grambling	Sr	12	80	157	456	4360	4517	8.43	376.4
Erik Meyer, Eastern Washington	Sr	12	92	221	410	4003	4224	8.41	352.0
Ricky Santos, New Hampshire	So	13	119	499	429	3797	4296	7.84	330.5
Trey Willie, SE Louisiana	Sr	10	133	449	404	2777	3226	6.01	322.6
Josh Johnson, San Diego	So	12	86	379	371	3256	3635	7.95	302.9

RUSHING

	Class	GP	Car	Yds	Avg	TD	Yds/Game
Nick Hartigan, Brown	Sr	10	314	1727	5.50	20	172.70
Scott Phaydavong, Drake	So	10	204	1550	7.60	8	155.00
Joe Rubin, Portland St.	Sr	11	345	1702	4.93	17	154.73
James Noble, Cal Poly-SLO	Fr	11	223	1578	7.08	16	143.45
Jermaine Austin, Georgia Southern	Sr	12	233	1546	6.64	14	128.83

PASSING EFFICIENCY

					Pct					Rating
	Class	GP	Att	Comp	Comp	Yds	Yds/Att	TD	Int	Pts
Bruce Eugene, Grambling	Sr	12	456	254	55.70	4360	9.56	56	6	173.9
Josh Johnson, San Diego	So	12	371	260	70.08	3256	8.78	36	8	171.5
Ricky Santos, New Hampshire	So	13	429	301	70.16	3797	8.85	39	9	170.3
Erik Meyer, Eastern Washington.	Sr	12	410	269	65.61	4003	9.76	30	5	169.3
Eric Sanders, Northern Iowa	So	13	312	213	68.27	2929	9.39	23	5	168.2

Note: Minimum 15 attempts per game.

RECEPTIONS PER GAME

	Class	GP	No.	Yds	TD	R/G
Michael Cupto, St. Francis (Pa.)	Jr	11	92	1433	12	8.36
Laurent Robinson, Illinois St	Jr	11	86	1465	12	7.82
Luke Palko, St. Francis (Pa.)	Jr	11	85	812	7	7.73
J.J. Outlaw, Villanova	Sr	11	83	878	7	7.55
Eric Kimble, Eastern Washington	Sr	12	87	1419	12	7.25

RECEIVING YARDS PER GAME

	Class	GP	No.	Yds	TD	Yds/G
Laurent Robinson, Illinois St.	Jr	11	86	1465	12	133.18
Michael Caputo, St. Francis (Pa.)	Jr	11	92	1433	12	130.27
Miles Austin, Monmouth	Sr	8	49	1004	11	125.50
David Ball, New Hampshire	Jr	13	87	1551	24	119.31
Eric Kimble, Eastern Washington	Sr	12	87	1419	12	118.25

INTERCEPTIONS

	Class	GP	No.	Yds	TD	Int/G
Jay McCareins, Princeton	Sr	10	9	236	2	.90
James Gasparella, Brown	Sr	10	7	42	0	.70
Bobbie Williams, Bethune	So	10	6	80	0	.60
Casey Klaus, Dayton	Jr	10	6	146	1	.60
Brian Ford, Wofford	So	11	6	5	0	.55

PUNTING

	Class	No.	Avg
Wesley Taylor, Florida A&M	So	59	45.88
Erik Contos, Delaware St.	Sr	65	44.25
Christian Koegel, Massachusetts	Jr	49	43.02
Rhlan Madrid, Northern Arizona	Jr	61	43.00
David Simonhoff, SE Missouri St	Jr	63	42.84

Division I-AA (Cont)
ALL-PURPOSE RUNNERS

	Class	GP	Rush	Rec	PR	KOR	Yds	Yds/Game
Steve Silva, Holy Cross	Sr.	10	912	364	395	462	2133	213.30
Clay Green, Jacksonville St.	Jr.	11	1352	134	0	562	2048	186.18
Nick Hartigan, Brown	Sr.	10	1727	74	0	0	1801	180.10
Arkee Whitlock, Southern Illinois.	Jr.	12	1457	190	0	408	2055	171.25
Tyluan Massey, Robert Morris	Sr.	10	51	899	133	615	1698	169.80

Division II
SCORING

	Class	GP	TD	XP	FG	Pts	Pts/Game
Jamar Brittingham, Bloomsburg	So.	12	34	0	0	204	17.0
Germaine Race, Pittsburg St.	Jr.	13	33	0	0	198	15.2
Antoine Bagwell, California (Pa.)	Sr.	10	25	0	0	152	15.2
Dervon Wallace, Shepherd	So.	12	27	0	0	162	13.5
Danny Woodhead, Chadron St.	So.	10	21	0	0	126	12.6

FIELD GOALS

	Class	GP	FGA	FG	Pct	FG/Game
Jeff Glas, North Dakota.	Sr.	13	36	30	.833	2.3
Paul Williams, Tarleton St	Jr.	8	15	15	1.00	1.9
Michael Green, Valdostra St	Sr.	12	26	19	.731	1.6
Jamie Reder, Shippensburg	So.	11	18	17	.944	1.5
Rush Rollins, Catawba	Sr.	11	18	15	.833	1.4

TOTAL OFFENSE

	Class	GP	Yds	Yds/Game
Jimmy Terwilliger, East Stroudsburg	Jr.	14	4960	354.3
Joey Conrad, Glenville St.	Sr.	11	3868	351.6
Dalton Bell, West. Texas A&M	Jr.	11	3841	349.2
Matt Gutierrez, Fort Lewis	Jr.	10	3205	320.5
Wesley Beschorner, South Dakota	Sr.	11	3500	318.2

RUSHING

	Class	GP	Car	Yds	TD	Yds/Game
Jamar Brittingham, Bloomsburg	So.	12	316	2260	32	188.3
Danny Woodhead, Chadron St.	So.	10	278	1769	21	176.9
Derrick Ross, Tarleton St.	Sr.	9	236	1512	13	168.0
Stefan Logan, South Dakota	Jr.	11	217	1751	11	159.2

PASSING EFFICIENCY

	Class	GP	Att	Comp	TD	Int	Rating Pts
Wesley Beschorner, South Dakota	Sr.	11	255	172	39	4	215.2
Jimmy Terwilliger, East Stroudsburg	Jr.	14	424	262	50	11	186.1
Toby Korrodi, Central Missouri St	Jr.	10	240	179	23	2	176.9
Matt Gutierrez, Fort Lewis	Jr..	10	277	174	27	6	171.6
Nathan Brown, Central Ark.	Fr.	14	273	189	25	10	166.3

RECEPTIONS PER GAME

	Class	GP	No.	Yds	TD	R/G
Justin Gallas, Colorado Mines	Sr.	11	91	1199	8	8.3
Wade Ginsbach, Northern St.	Jr.	10	74	803	8	7.4
Brian Potucek, Central Washington	Sr.	10	73	894	9	7.3
Richie Ross, Neb.-Kearney	Sr.	12	87	1360	19	7.3
Vincent Matfield, Northern Michigan	Sr.	10	69	898	6	6.9

RECEIVING YARDS PER GAME

	Class	GP	No.	Yds	TD	Yds/G
Brian Hynes, Winona St.	Sr.	11	68	1420	17	129.1
Evan Prall, East Stroudsburg	Jr.	14	88	1766	23	126.1
James Lukowiak, Southern Connecticut St.	Sr.	11	63	1311	17	119.2
Richie Ross, Neb.-Kearney	Sr.	12	87	1360	19	113.3
Drew Bohannan, Mesa St.	So.	11	65	1236	11	112.4

Division II (*Cont.*)

INTERCEPTIONS

	Class	GP	No.	Yds	Int/Game
Dan Peters, Shepherd	Jr.	12	12	171	1.0
Kashif Easley, Glenville St.	Jr.	11	9	93	0.8
Randy Kush, Neb.-Omaha	So.	11	9	99	0.8
Andrew Knight, SE Oklahoma	Jr.	10	8	2	0.8
Keon Gaither, West Tex A&M	Jr.	12	9	134	0.8

PUNTING

	Class	No.	Avg
Jeff Williams, Adams St.	Sr.	49	45.7
Richard Hammond, Tex A&M-Kngsvl	Sr.	42	43.5
Jeff Carpenter, West Georgia	Sr.	63	42.4
Jason Davis, Western St.	So.	66	42.3
Craig McFarlin, Ouachita Baptist	So.	62	41.7

Note: Minimum 3.6 per game.

Division III

SCORING

	Class	GP	TD	XP	FG	Pts	Pts/Game
Matt Willis, Hartwick	Sr.	10	22	0	0	132	13.2
Brenden Kavey, Bridgewater St.	Sr.	10	21	0	0	128	12.8
Casey Allen, Linfield	Sr.	11	22	0	0	132	12.0
R.J. Meadows, Ohio Northern	Fr.	10	20	0	0	120	12.0
Javon Williams, N.C. Wesleyan	So.	8	16	0	0	96	12.0

FIELD GOALS

	Class	GP	FGA	FG	Pct	FG/Game
Geoff Troy, Merchant Marine	Fr.	10	21	18	.857	1.8
Sean Conway, Redlands	Fr.	9	17	12	.706	1.3
James Spencer, Adrian	Jr.	10	15	13	.867	1.3
Matt Spitz, Capital	So.	11	16	14	.875	1.3
Matt Denny, Carthage	So.	10	18	12	.667	1.2

TOTAL OFFENSE

	Class	GP	Yds	Yds/Game
Wesley Cooper, Louisiana Col.	Sr	9	3415	379.4
J.D. Ricca, Hampden-Sydney	Sr	10	3748	374.8
Brett Elliot, Linfield	Sr	11	4088	371.6
Josh Vogelbach, Guilford	Fr	10	3638	363.8
Josh Breham, Alma	Jr	10	3589	358.9

RUSHING

	Class	GP	Car	Yds	TD	Yds/Game
Justin Beaver, UW-Whitewater	Jr.	14	428	2420	24	172.9
Don Thibodeau, Maine Maritime	Sr.	9	251	1531	15	170.1
Denny Kimmel, Anderson (Ind.)	Jr.	8	189	1308	10	163.5
Tom Arcidiacono, Union (N.Y.)	Jr.	12	350	1954	20	162.8
Phil Porta, Bethel (Minn.)	Jr.	10	262	1559	10	155.9

PASSING EFFICIENCY

	Class	GP	Att	Comp	Pct Comp	Yds	TD	Int	Rating Pts
Brett Elliott, Linfield	Sr.	11	396	277	.669	4019	49	9	191.5
Mitch Tanney, Monmouth (Ill.)	Sr.	11	292	215	.736	2587	33	3	183.3
Joel Clark, Whitworth	Jr.	8	235	150	.638	2234	29	7	178.4
J.D. Ricca, Hampden-Sydney	Sr.	10	391	262	.670	3731	42	13	176.0
Michael Jorris, Mount Union	Jr.	15	378	253	.669	3736	35	11	174.7

Note: Minimum 15 attempts per game.

RECEPTIONS PER GAME

	Class	GP	No.	Yds	TD	Rec/Game
Chris Barnette, Guilford	Jr.	10	101	1369	15	10.1
Nick Bublavi, Catholic	Sr.	10	101	1797	15	10.1
Mike Russell, Hanover	Sr.	10	89	1044	8	8.9
Kyle Pearson, Luther	Jr.	10	87	981	7	8.7
Steve Angeletta, Union (N.Y.)	Jr.	12	99	1612	11	8.3

RECEIVING YARDS PER GAME

	Class	GP	No.	Yds	TD	Yds/Game
Nick Bublavi, Catholic	Sr.	10	101	1797	15	179.7
Chris Barnette, Guilford	Jr.	10	101	1369	15	136.9
Jack Martin, Wash. & Lee	So.	10	70	1353	15	135.3
Steve Angeletta, Union (N.Y.)	Jr.	12	99	1612	11	134.3
Drew Smith, Hampden-Sydney	So.	10	79	1284	13	128.4

Division III *(Cont.)*

INTERCEPTIONS

	Class	GP	No.	Yds	Int/G
Colin Carrier, Chicago	Sr	9	10	85	1.1
Tom Anthony, Augustana (Ill.)	Sr	12	13	169	1.1
Rusty Midlam, Ohio Northern	Sr	10	9	97	0.9
Rick Hutchins, Concordia (Wis)	So	9	8	138	0.9
Four tied with eight.					

PUNTING

	Class	No.	Avg
Hunter Hamrick, Mary Hardin-Baylor	Jr	42	43.3
Brendon Fulmer, Williams	Jr	33	42.7
Jonathan Russelll, Mississippi Coll	Jr	57	42.5
Brandon Stevens, Howard Payne	So	53	42.5
Clint Rushing, Austin	Jr	51	42.3

Note: Minimum 3.6 per game.

2005 NCAA Division I-A Team Leaders

Offense

SCORING

	GP	Pts	Avg
Texas	13	652	50.15
USC	13	638	49.08
Louisville	12	521	43.42
Texas Tech	12	473	39.42
UCLA	12	469	39.08
Fresno St.	13	491	37.77
Arizona St.	12	442	36.83
Notre Dame	12	440	36.67
Boise St.	13	469	36.08
Minnesota	12	429	35.75

RUSHING

	GP	Car	Yds	Avg	TD	Yds/Game
Navy	12	671	3824	5.70	45	318.67
Texas	13	605	3574	5.91	55	274.92
Minnesota	12	610	3277	5.37	34	273.08
West Virginia	12	625	3269	5.23	34	272.42
Memphis	12	597	3215	5.39	28	267.92
USC	13	525	3380	6.44	51	260.00
La.-Lafayette	11	531	2797	5.27	34	254.27
Air Force	11	588	2712	4.61	28	246.55
California	12	483	2823	5.84	27	235.25
Texas A&M	11	452	2584	5.72	24	234.91

TOTAL OFFENSE

	GP	Plays	Yds	Avg	TD	Yds/Game
USC	13	1006	7537	7.49	87	579.77
Arizona St	12	940	6229	6.63	59	519.08
Texas	13	941	6657	7.07	68	512.08
Northwestern	12	974	6004	6.16	51	500.33
Michigan St.	11	834	5470	6.56	50	497.27
Texas Tech	12	896	5950	6.64	62	495.83
Minnesota	12	933	5937	6.36	56	494.75
Washington St.	11	821	5382	6.56	47	489.27
Louisville	12	848	5785	6.82	69	482.08
Notre Dame	12	945	5728	6.06	58	477.33

PASSING

	GP	Att	Comp	Int	Pct Comp	Yds	Yds/Gm	TD
Texas Tech	12	588	391	12	66.50	4666	388.8	34
Hawaii	12	578	379	15	65.57	4611	384.3	37
Arizona St.	12	493	312	11	63.29	4481	373.4	38
Notre Dame	12	454	294	8	64.76	3963	330.3	32
USC	13	481	312	10	64.86	4157	319.8	32
Brigham Young	12	516	332	13	64.34	3721	310.1	27
Northwestern	12	512	320	9	62.50	3681	306.8	22
Oregon	12	482	303	10	62.86	3654	304.5	25
UTEP	12	458	268	20	58.52	3607	300.6	29
Oregon St.	11	459	267	23	58.17	3261	296.5	13

Single-Game Highs

Points Scored: 80—Texas Tech, Sept 17, 2005 (vs Sam Houston St).
Net Rushing Yards: 490—Navy, Dec 3, 2005 (vs Army)
Passing Yards: 699—Texas Tech, Oct 15, 2005 (vs Kansas St.)
Rushing and Passing Yards: 773—Arizona St., Sept 17, 2005 (vs Northwestern)
Fewest Rushing and Passing Yards Allowed: 35—Virginia Tech, Sept 10, 2005 (vs. Duke)

Defense

SCORING

	GP	Pts	Avg
Alabama	12	128	10.7
Virginia Tech	13	168	12.9
LSU	13	185	14.2
Miami (Fla.)	12	171	14.3
Ohio St.	12	183	15.3
Auburn	12	186	15.5
Boston College	12	191	15.9
Georgia	13	213	16.4
Texas	13	213	16.4
Penn St.	12	204	17.0

TOTAL DEFENSE

	GP	Plays	Yds	Avg Y/Play	Avg Y/G
Virginia Tech	13	789	3219	4.08	247.62
Alabama	12	713	3061	4.29	255.08
LSU	13	833	3469	4.16	266.85
Miami (Fla.)	12	828	3241	3.91	270.08
Ohio St.	12	780	3376	4.33	281.33
Connecticut	11	732	3269	4.47	297.18
Tennessee	11	720	3280	4.56	298.18
North Carolina St.	12	841	3584	4.26	298.67
Florida	12	748	3598	4.81	299.83
Texas	13	897	3938	4.39	302.92

RUSHING

	GP	Car	Yds	Avg	TD	Yds/Game
Ohio St.	12	375	881	2.35	12	73.4
Tennessee	11	356	907	2.55	8	82.5
Kansas	12	414	999	2.41	8	83.3
Oklahoma	12	392	1087	2.77	11	90.6
Boston College	12	420	1090	2.60	6	90.8
LSU	13	402	1190	2.96	8	91.5
Penn St.	12	442	1116	2.52	12	93.0
Virginia Tech	13	402	1214	3.02	6	93.4
Alabama	12	361	1132	3.14	5	94.3
Florida	12	373	1139	3.05	14	94.9

TURNOVER MARGIN

		Turnovers Gained			Turnovers Lost			
	GP	Fum	Int	Total	Fum	Int	Total	Mar/Gm
TCU	12	14	26	40	8	11	19	1.75
USC	13	16	22	38	7	10	17	1.62
Florida	12	15	16	31	6	7	13	1.50
Tulsa	13	14	22	36	10	8	18	1.38
Louisiana Tech	11	15	16	31	8	10	18	1.18
Miami (Ohio)	11	15	20	35	8	14	22	1.18
Iowa St.	12	13	22	35	11	10	21	1.17
Southern Miss.	12	19	15	34	7	13	20	1.17
West Virginia	12	14	17	31	10	7	17	1.17
Oregon	12	9	23	32	9	10	19	1.08

PASSING EFFICIENCY

	GP	Att	Comp	Pct Comp	Int	Pct Int	Yds	Yds/Att	TD	Pct TD	Rating Pts
Texas	13	336	218	64.88	11	3.27	3083	9.18	26	7.74	160.96
Arizona St.	12	493	312	63.29	11	2.23	4481	9.09	38	7.71	160.62
Louisville	12	376	246	65.43	10	2.66	3523	9.37	24	6.38	159.85
UCLA	12	389	247	63.50	6	1.54	3244	8.34	34	8.74	159.31
Notre Dame	12	454	294	64.76	8	1.76	3963	8.73	32	7.05	157.86
Northern Ill.	12	337	229	67.95	10	2.95	2849	8.45	24	7.12	156.58
Ohio St.	12	302	196	64.90	5	1.66	2708	8.97	18	5.96	156.58
USC	13	481	312	64.86	10	2.08	4157	8.64	32	6.65	155.29
Michigan St	11	381	252	66.14	13	3.41	3250	8.53	24	6.30	151.77
Utah	12	415	258	62.17	10	2.41	3534	8.52	26	6.27	149.59

National Champions

Year	Champion	Record	Bowl Game	Head Coach
1883	Yale	8-0-0	No bowl	Ray Tompkins (Captain)
1884	Yale	9-0-0	No bowl	Eugene L. Richards (Captain)
1885	Princeton	9-0-0	No bowl	Charles DeCamp (Captain)
1886	Yale	9-0-1	No bowl	Robert N. Corwin (Captain)
1887	Yale	9-0-0	No bowl	Harry W. Beecher (Captain)
1888	Yale	13-0-0	No bowl	Walter Camp
1889	Princeton	10-0-0	No bowl	Edgar Poe (Captain)
1890	Harvard	11-0-0	No bowl	George A. Stewart/George C. Adams
1891	Yale	13-0-0	No bowl	Walter Camp
1892	Yale	13-0-0	No bowl	Walter Camp
1893	Princeton	11-0-0	No bowl	Tom Trenchard (Captain)
1894	Yale	16-0-0	No bowl	William C. Rhodes
1895	Pennsylvania	14-0-0	No bowl	George Woodruff
1896	Princeton	10-0-1	No bowl	Garrett Cochran
1897	Pennsylvania	15-0-0	No bowl	George Woodruff
1898	Harvard	11-0-0	No bowl	W. Cameron Forbes
1899	Harvard	10-0-1	No bowl	Benjamin H. Dibblee
1900	Yale	12-0-0	No bowl	Malcolm McBride
1901	Michigan	11-0-0	Won Rose	Fielding Yost
1902	Michigan	11-0-0	No bowl	Fielding Yost
1903	Princeton	11-0-0	No bowl	Art Hillebrand
1904	Pennsylvania	12-0-0	No bowl	Carl Williams
1905	Chicago	11-0-0	No bowl	Amos Alonzo Stagg
1906	Princeton	9-0-1	No bowl	Bill Roper
1907	Yale	9-0-1	No bowl	Bill Knox
1908	Pennsylvania	11-0-1	No bowl	Sol Metzger
1909	Yale	10-0-0	No bowl	Howard Jones
1910	Harvard	8-0-1	No bowl	Percy Houghton
1911	Princeton	8-0-2	No bowl	Bill Roper
1912	Harvard	9-0-0	No bowl	Percy Houghton
1913	Harvard	9-0-0	No bowl	Percy Houghton
1914	Army	9-0-0	No bowl	Charley Daly
1915	Cornell	9-0-0	No bowl	Al Sharpe
1916	Pittsburgh	8-0-0	No bowl	Pop Warner
1917	Georgia Tech	9-0-0	No bowl	John Heisman
1918	Pittsburgh	4-1-0	No bowl	Pop Warner
1919	Harvard	9-0-1	Won Rose	Bob Fisher
1920	California	9-0-0	Won Rose	Andy Smith
1921	Cornell	8-0-0	No bowl	Gil Dobie
1922	Cornell	8-0-0	No bowl	Gil Dobie
1923	Illinois	8-0-0	No bowl	Bob Zuppke
1924	Notre Dame	10-0-0	Won Rose	Knute Rockne
1925	Alabama (H)	10-0-0	Won Rose	Wallace Wade
	Dartmouth (D)	8-0-0	No bowl	Jesse Hawley
1926	Alabama (H)	9-0-1	Tied Rose	Wallace Wade
	Stanford (D)(H)	10-0-1	Tied Rose	Pop Warner
1927	Illinois	7-0-1	No bowl	Bob Zuppke
1928	Georgia Tech (H)	10-0-0	Won Rose	Bill Alexander
	Southern Cal (D)	9-0-1	No bowl	Howard Jones
1929	Notre Dame	9-0-0	No bowl	Knute Rockne
1930	Notre Dame	10-0-0	No bowl	Knute Rockne
1931	Southern Cal	10-1-0	Won Rose	Howard Jones
1932	Southern Cal (H)	10-0-0	Won Rose	Howard Jones
	Michigan (D)	8-0-0	No bowl	Harry Kipke
1933	Michigan	7-0-1	No bowl	Harry Kipke
1934	Minnesota	8-0-0	No bowl	Bernie Bierman
1935	Minnesota (H)	8-0-0	No bowl	Bernie Bierman
	Southern Methodist (D)	12-1-0	Lost Rose	Matty Bell
1936	Minnesota	7-1-0	No bowl	Bernie Bierman
1937	Pittsburgh	9-0-1	No bowl	Jock Sutherland
1938	Texas Christian (AP)	11-0-0	Won Sugar	Dutch Meyer
	Notre Dame (D)	8-1-0	No bowl	Elmer Layden
1939	Southern Cal (D)	8-0-2	Won Rose	Howard Jones
	Texas A&M (AP)	11-0-0	Won Sugar	Homer Norton

Year	Champion	Record	Bowl Game	Head Coach
1940	Minnesota	8-0-0	No bowl	Bernie Bierman
1941	Minnesota	8-0-0	No bowl	Bernie Bierman
1942	Ohio St	9-1-0	No bowl	Paul Brown
1943	Notre Dame	9-1-0	No bowl	Frank Leahy
1944	Army	9-0-0	No bowl	Red Blaik
1945	Army	9-0-0	No bowl	Red Blaik
1946	Notre Dame	8-0-1	No bowl	Frank Leahy
1947	Notre Dame	9-0-0	No bowl	Frank Leahy
	Michigan*	10-0-0	Won Rose	Fritz Crisler
1948	Michigan	9-0-0	No bowl	Bennie Oosterbaan
1949	Notre Dame	10-0-0	No bowl	Frank Leahy
1950	Oklahoma	10-1-0	Lost Sugar	Bud Wilkinson
1951	Tennessee	10-1-0	Lost Sugar	Bob Neyland
1952	Michigan St	9-0-0	No bowl	Biggie Munn
1953	Maryland	10-1-0	Lost Orange	Jim Tatum
1954	Ohio St	10-0-0	Won Rose	Woody Hayes
	UCLA (UPI)	9-0-0	No bowl	Red Sanders
1955	Oklahoma	11-0-0	Won Orange	Bud Wilkinson
1956	Oklahoma	10-0-0	No bowl	Bud Wilkinson
1957	Auburn	10-0-0	No bowl	Shug Jordan
	Ohio St (UPI)	9-1-0	Won Rose	Woody Hayes
1958	Louisiana St	11-0-0	Won Sugar	Paul Dietzel
1959	Syracuse	11-0-0	Won Cotton	Ben Schwartzwalder
1960	Minnesota	8-2-0	Lost Rose	Murray Warmath
1961	Alabama	11-0-0	Won Sugar	Bear Bryant
1962	Southern Cal	11-0-0	Won Rose	John McKay
1963	Texas	11-0-0	Won Cotton	Darrell Royal
1964	Alabama	10-1-0	Lost Orange	Bear Bryant
1965	Alabama	9-1-1	Won Orange	Bear Bryant
	Michigan St (UPI)	10-1-0	Lost Rose	Duffy Daugherty
1966	Notre Dame	9-0-1	No bowl	Ara Parseghian
1967	Southern Cal	10-1-0	Won Rose	John McKay
1968	Ohio St	10-0-0	Won Rose	Woody Hayes
1969	Texas	11-0-0	Won Cotton	Darrell Royal
1970	Nebraska	11-0-1	Won Orange	Bob Devaney
	Texas (UPI)	10-1-0	Lost Cotton	Darrell Royal
1971	Nebraska	13-0-0	Won Orange	Bob Devaney
1972	Southern Cal	12-0-0	Won Rose	John McKay
1973	Notre Dame	11-0-0	Won Sugar	Ara Parseghian
	Alabama (UPI)	11-1-0	Lost Sugar	Bear Bryant
1974	Oklahoma	11-0-0	No bowl	Barry Switzer
	Southern Cal (UPI)	10-1-1	Won Rose	John McKay
1975	Oklahoma	11-1-0	Won Orange	Barry Switzer
1976	Pittsburgh	12-0-0	Won Sugar	Johnny Majors
1977	Notre Dame	11-1-0	Won Cotton	Dan Devine
1978	Alabama	11-1-0	Won Sugar	Bear Bryant
	Southern Cal (UPI)	12-1-0	Won Rose	John Robinson
1979	Alabama	12-0-0	Won Sugar	Bear Bryant
1980	Georgia	12-0-0	Won Sugar	Vince Dooley
1981	Clemson	12-0-0	Won Orange	Danny Ford
1982	Penn St	11-1-0	Won Sugar	Joe Paterno
1983	Miami (Fla.)	11-1-0	Won Orange	Howard Schnellenberger
1984	Brigham Young	13-0-0	Won Holiday	LaVell Edwards
1985	Oklahoma	11-1-0	Won Orange	Barry Switzer
1986	Penn St	12-0-0	Won Fiesta	Joe Paterno
1987	Miami (Fla.)	12-0-0	Won Orange	Jimmy Johnson
1988	Notre Dame	12-0-0	Won Fiesta	Lou Holtz
1989	Miami (Fla.)	11-1-0	Won Sugar	Dennis Erickson
1990	Colorado	11-1-1	Won Orange	Bill McCartney
	Georgia Tech (UPI)	11-0-1	Won Citrus	Bobby Ross
1991	Miami (Fla.)	12-0-0	Won Orange	Dennis Erickson
	Washington (CNN)	12-0-0	Won Rose	Don James
1992	Alabama	13-0-0	Won Sugar	Gene Stallings
1993	Florida St	12-1-0	Won Orange	Bobby Bowden
1994	Nebraska	13-0-0	Won Orange	Tom Osborne
1995	Nebraska	12-0-0	Won Fiesta	Tom Osborne
†1996	Florida	12–1	Won Sugar	Steve Spurrier
1997	Michigan	12–0	Won Rose	Lloyd Carr
	Nebraska (ESPN)	13–0	Won Orange	Tom Osborne

Year	Champion	Record	Bowl Game	Head Coach
1998	Tennessee	13–0	Won Fiesta	Phillip Fulmer
1999	Florida St	12–0	Won Sugar	Bobby Bowden
2000	Oklahoma	13–0	Won Orange	Bob Stoops
2001	Miami (Fla.)	12–0	Won Rose	Larry Coker
2002	Ohio St	14–0	Won Fiesta	Jim Tressel
2003	Louisiana St	13–1	Won Sugar	Nick Saban
	Southern California	12–1	Won Rose	Pete Carroll
2004	Southern California	13–0	Won Orange	Pete Carroll
2005	Texas	13–0	Won Rose	Mack Brown

*The AP, which had voted Notre Dame No. 1, took a second vote, giving the national title to Michigan after its 49–0 win over Southern Cal in the Rose Bowl.   Note: Selectors: Helms Athletic Foundation (H) 1883–1935, The Dickinson System (D) 1924–40, The Associated Press (AP) 1936–present, United Press International (UPI) 1958–90, *USA Today*/CNN (CNN) 1991–96, and *USA Today*/ESPN (ESPN) 1997–present. †In 1996 the NCAA introduced overtime to break ties.

Results of Major Bowl Games

Rose Bowl

1-1-02 ....Michigan 49, Stanford 0	1-1-53 ....USC 7, Wisconsin 0
1-1-16 ....Washington St 14, Brown 0	1-1-54 ....Michigan St 28, UCLA 20
1-1-17 ....Oregon 14, Pennsylvania 0	1-1-55 ....Ohio St 20, Southern Cal 7
1-1-18 ....Mare Island 19, Camp Lewis 7	1-2-56 ....Michigan St 17, UCLA 14
1-1-19 ....Great Lakes 17, Mare Island 0	1-1-57 ....Iowa 35, Oregon St 19
1-1-20 ....Harvard 7, Oregon 6	1-1-58 ....Ohio St 10, Oregon 7
1-1-21 ....California 28, Ohio St 0	1-1-59 ....Iowa 38, California 12
1-2-22 ....Washington & Jefferson 0, California 0	1-1-60 ....Washington 44, Wisconsin 8
1-1-23 ....USC 14, Penn St 3	1-2-61 ....Washington 17, Minnesota 7
1-1-24 ....Navy 14, Washington 14	1-1-62 ....Minnesota 21, UCLA 3
1-1-25 ....Notre Dame 27, Stanford 10	1-1-63 ....USC 42, Wisconsin 37
1-1-26 ....Alabama 20, Washington 19	1-1-64 ....Illinois 17, Washington 7
1-1-27 ....Alabama 7, Stanford 7	1-1-65 ....Michigan 34, Oregon St 7
1-2-28 ....Stanford 7, Pittsburgh 6	1-1-66 ....UCLA 14, Michigan St 12
1-1-29 ....Georgia Tech 8, California 7	1-2-67 ....Purdue 14, USC 13
1-1-30 ....USC47, Pittsburgh 14	1-1-68 ....USC 14, Indiana 3
1-1-31 ....Alabama 24, Washington St 0	1-1-69 ....Ohio St 27, USC16
1-1-32 ....USC 21, Tulane 12	1-1-70 ....USC 10, Michigan 3
1-2-33 ....USC 35, Pittsburgh 0	1-1-71 ....Stanford 27, Ohio St 17
1-1-34 ....Columbia 7, Stanford 0	1-1-72 ....Stanford 13, Michigan 12
1-1-35 ....Alabama 29, Stanford 13	1-1-73 ....USC 42, Ohio St 17
1-1-36 ....Stanford 7, Southern Methodist 0	1-1-74 ....Ohio St 42, USC 21
1-1-37 ....Pittsburgh 21, Washington 0	1-1-75 ....USC 18, Ohio St 17
1-1-38 ....California 13, Alabama 0	1-1-76 ....UCLA 23, Ohio St 10
1-2-39 ....USC 7, Duke 3	1-1-77 ....USC 14, Michigan 6
1-1-40 ....USC 14, Tennessee 0	1-2-78 ....Washington 27, Michigan 20
1-1-41 ....Stanford 21, Nebraska 13	1-1-79 ....USC 17, Michigan 10
1-1-42 ....Oregon St 20, Duke 16	1-1-80 ....USC 17, Ohio St 16
1-1-43 ....Georgia 9, UCLA 0	1-1-81 ....Michigan 23, Washington 6
1-1-44 ....USC 29, Washington 0	1-1-82 ....Washington 28, Iowa 0
1-1-45 ....USC 25, Tennessee 0	1-1-83 ....UCLA 24, Michigan 14
1-1-46 ....Alabama 34, USC 14	1-2-84 ....UCLA 45, Illinois 9
1-1-47 ....Illinois 45, UCLA 14	1-1-85 ....USC 20, Ohio St 17
1-1-48 ....Michigan 49, USC 0	1-1-86 ....UCLA 45, Iowa 28
1-1-49 ....Northwestern 20, California 14	1-1-87 ....Arizona St 22, Michigan 15
1-2-50 ....Ohio St 17, California 14	1-1-88 ....Michigan St 20, USC 17
1-1-51 ....Michigan 14, California 6	1-2-89 ....Michigan 22, USC 14
1-1-52 ....Illinois 40, Stanford 7	1-1-90 ....USC 17, Michigan 10

Note: The Fiesta, Orange, Rose and Sugar Bowls constitute the Bowl Alliance, formed in 1995 and running through the 2009 regular season and 2010 bowl season. Starting in January 2007, it will include a separate BCS National Championship game as well. The four other BCS Bowls will host the following conference champions with consideration for the following conference tie-ins: the ACC or Big East champion in the FedEx Orange Bowl, the SEC champion in the Allstate Sugar Bowl, the Big Ten and the Pac-10 champions in the Rose Bowl and the Big 12 champion in the Tostitos Fiesta Bowl. rankings. There are also four at-large positions in the BCS that are open to any Division I-A team. This allows any Division I-A school in the nation the opportunity to play in a BCS bowl game.

Rose Bowl *(Cont.)*

1-1-91 ....Washington 46, Iowa 34
1-1-92 ....Washington 34, Michigan 14
1-1-93 ....Michigan 38, Washington 31
1-1-94 ....Wisconsin 21, UCLA 16
1-2-95 ....Penn St 38, Oregon 20
1-1-96 ....USC 41, Northwestern 32
1-1-97 ....Ohio St 20, Arizona St 17
1-1-98 ....Michigan 21, Washington St 16
1-1-99 ....Wisconsin 38, UCLA 31
1-1-2000 ....Wisconsin 17, Stanford 9
1-1-2001 ....Washington 34, Purdue 24
1-3-2002 ....Miami 37, Nebraska 14
1-1-2003 ....Oklahoma 34, Washington St 14
1-1-2004 ....USC 28, Michigan 14
1-1-2005 ....Texas 38, Michigan 37
1-4-2006 ....Texas 41, USC 38

City: Pasadena. Stadium: Rose Bowl, capacity 96,576.
Playing Sites: Tournament Park (1902, 1916–22), Rose Bowl
(1923–41, since 1943), Duke Stadium, Durham, NC (1942).

Orange Bowl

1-1-35 ....Bucknell 26, Miami (Fla.) 0
1-1-36 ....Catholic 20, Mississippi 19
1-1-37 ....Duquesne 13, Mississippi St 12
1-1-38 ....Auburn 6, Michigan St 0
1-2-39 ....Tennessee 17, Oklahoma 0
1-1-40 ....Georgia Tech 21, Missouri 7
1-1-41 ....Mississippi St 14, Georgetown 7
1-1-42 ....Georgia 40, Texas Christian 26
1-1-43 ....Alabama 37, Boston College 21
1-1-44 ....Louisiana St 19, Texas A&M 14
1-1-45 ....Tulsa 26, Georgia Tech 12
1-1-46 ....Miami (Fla.) 13, Holy Cross 6
1-1-47 ....Rice 8, Tennessee 0
1-1-48 ....Georgia Tech 20, Kansas 14
1-1-49 ....Texas 41, Georgia 28
1-2-50 ....Santa Clara 21, Kentucky 13
1-1-51 ....Clemson 15, Miami (Fla.) 14
1-1-52 ....Georgia Tech 17, Baylor 14
1-1-53 ....Alabama 61, Syracuse 6
1-1-54 ....Oklahoma 7, Maryland 0
1-1-55 ....Duke 34, Nebraska 7
1-2-56 ....Oklahoma 20, Maryland 6
1-1-57 ....Colorado 27, Clemson 21
1-1-58 ....Oklahoma 48, Duke 21
1-1-59 ....Oklahoma 21, Syracuse 6
1-1-60 ....Georgia 14, Missouri 0
1-2-61 ....Missouri 21, Navy 14
1-1-62 ....Louisiana St 25, Colorado 7
1-1-63 ....Alabama 17, Oklahoma 0
1-1-64 ....Nebraska 13, Auburn 7
1-1-65 ....Texas 21, Alabama 17
1-1-66 ....Alabama 39, Nebraska 28
1-2-67 ....Florida 27, Georgia Tech 12
1-1-68 ....Oklahoma 26, Tennessee 24
1-1-69 ....Penn St 15, Kansas 14
1-1-70 ....Penn St 10, Missouri 3
1-1-71 ....Nebraska 17, Louisiana St 12
1-1-72 ....Nebraska 38, Alabama 6
1-1-73 ....Nebraska 40, Notre Dame 6
1-1-74 ....Penn St 16, Louisiana St 9
1-1-75 ....Notre Dame 13, Alabama 11
1-1-76 ....Oklahoma 14, Michigan 6
1-1-77 ....Ohio St 27, Colorado 10
1-2-78 ....Arkansas 31, Oklahoma 6

Orange Bowl

1-1-79 ....Oklahoma 31, Nebraska 24
1-1-80 ....Oklahoma 24, Florida St 7
1-1-81 ....Oklahoma 18, Florida St 17
1-1-82 ....Clemson 22, Nebraska 15
1-1-83 ....Nebraska 21, Louisiana St 20
1-2-84 ....Miami (Fla.) 31, Nebraska 30
1-1-85 ....Washington 28, Oklahoma 17
1-1-86 ....Oklahoma 25, Penn St 10
1-1-87 ....Oklahoma 42, Arkansas 8
1-1-88 ....Miami (Fla.) 20, Oklahoma 14
1-2-89 ....Miami (Fla.) 23, Nebraska 3
1-1-90 ....Notre Dame 21, Colorado 6
1-1-91 ....Colorado 10, Notre Dame 9
1-1-92 ....Miami (Fla.) 22, Nebraska 0
1-1-93 ....Florida St 27, Nebraska 14
1-1-94 ....Florida St 18, Nebraska 16
1-1-95 ....Nebraska 24, Miami (Fla.) 17
1-1-96 ....Florida St 31, Notre Dame 26
12-31-96 ....Nebraska 41, Virginia Tech 21
1-2-98 ....Nebraska 42, Tennessee 17
1-2-99 ....Florida 31, Syracuse 10
1-1-00 ....Michigan 35, Alabama 34 (ot)
1-3-01 ....Oklahoma 13, Florida St 2
1-2-02 ....Florida 56, Maryland 23
1-2-03 ....Southern Cal 38, Iowa 17
1-1-04 ....Miami (Fla.) 16, Florida St 15
1-4-05 ....Southern Cal 55, Oklahoma 19
1-3-06 ....Penn State 26, Florida State 23 (3OT)

City: Miami. Stadium: Pro Player Stadium, capacity
75,192. Playing Sites: Orange Bowl (1935–96), Pro
Player Stadium (since 1996).

Sugar Bowl

1-1-35 ....Tulane 20, Temple 14
1-1-36 ....Texas Christian 3, Louisiana St 2
1-1-37 ....Santa Clara 21, Louisiana St 14
1-1-38 ....Santa Clara 6, Louisiana St 0
1-2-39 ....Texas Christian 15, Carnegie Tech 7
1-1-40 ....Texas A&M 14, Tulane 13
1-1-41 ....Boston Col 19, Tennessee 13
1-1-42 ....Fordham 2, Missouri 0
1-1-43 ....Tennessee 14, Tulsa 7
1-1-44 ....Georgia Tech 20, Tulsa 18
1-1-45 ....Duke 29, Alabama 26
1-1-46 ....Oklahoma St 33, St. Mary's (Ca.) 13
1-1-47 ....Georgia 20, N Carolina 10
1-1-48 ....Texas 27, Alabama 7
1-1-49 ....Oklahoma 14, N Carolina 6
1-2-50 ....Oklahoma 35, Louisiana St 0
1-1-51 ....Kentucky 13, Oklahoma 7
1-1-52 ....Maryland 28, Tennessee 13
1-1-53 ....Georgia Tech 24, Mississippi 7
1-1-54 ....Georgia Tech 42, W Virginia 19
1-1-55 ....Navy 21, Mississippi 0
1-2-56 ....Georgia Tech 7, Pittsburgh 0
1-1-57 ....Baylor 13, Tennessee 7
1-1-58 ....Mississippi 39, Texas 7
1-1-59 ....Louisiana St 7, Clemson 0
1-1-60 ....Mississippi 21, Louisiana St 0
1-2-61 ....Mississippi 14, Rice 6
1-1-62 ....Alabama 10, Arkansas 3
1-1-63 ....Mississippi 17, Arkansas 13
1-1-64 ....Alabama 12, Mississippi 7
1-1-65 ....Louisiana St 13, Syracuse 10
1-1-66 ....Missouri 20, Florida 18

Sugar Bowl *(Cont.)*

1-2-67	Alabama 34, Nebraska 7
1-1-68	Louisiana St 20, Wyoming 13
1-1-69	Arkansas 16, Georgia 2
1-1-70	Mississippi 27, Arkansas 22
1-1-71	Tennessee 34, Air Force 13
1-1-72	Oklahoma 40, Auburn 22
12-31-72	Oklahoma 14, Penn St 0
12-31-73	Notre Dame 24, Alabama 23
12-31-74	Nebraska 13, Florida 10
12-31-75	Alabama 13, Penn St 6
1-1-77	Pittsburgh 27, Georgia 3
1-2-78	Alabama 35, Ohio St 6
1-1-79	Alabama 14, Penn St 7
1-1-80	Alabama 24, Arkansas 9
1-1-81	Georgia 17, Notre Dame 10
1-1-82	Pittsburgh 24, Georgia 20
1-1-83	Penn St 27, Georgia 23
1-2-84	Auburn 9, Michigan 7
1-1-85	Nebraska 28, Louisiana St 10
1-1-86	Tennessee 35, Miami (Fla.) 7
1-1-87	Nebraska 30, Louisiana St 15
1-1-88	Syracuse 16, Auburn 16
1-2-89	Florida St 13, Auburn 7
1-1-90	Miami (Fla.) 33, Alabama 25
1-1-91	Tennessee 23, Virginia 22
1-1-92	Notre Dame 39, Florida 28
1-1-93	Alabama 34, Miami (Fla.) 13
1-1-94	Florida 41, West Virginia 7
1-2-95	Florida St 23, Florida 17
12-31-95	Virginia Tech 28, Texas 10
1-2-97	Florida 52, Florida St 20
1-1-98	Florida St 31, Ohio St 14
1-1-99	Ohio St 24, Texas A&M 14
1-4-00	Florida St 46, Virginia Tech 29
1-2-01	Miami (Fla.) 37, Florida 20
1-1-02	Louisiana St 47, Illinois 34
1-1-03	Georgia 26, Florida St 13
1-4-04	Louisiana St 21, Oklahoma 14
1-3-05	Auburn 16, Virginia Tech 13
1-1-06	West Virginia 38, Georgia 35

City: New Orleans. Stadium: Louisiana Superdome, capacity 76,791. Playing Sites: Tulane Stadium (1935–74), Louisiana Superdome (since 1975). Due to Hurricane Katrina, 2006 Sugar Bowl played at Atlanta's Georgia Dome.

Cotton Bowl

1-1-37	Texas Christian 16, Marquette 6
1-1-38	Rice 28, Colorado 14
1-2-39	St. Mary's (Ca.) 20, Texas Tech 13
1-1-40	Clemson 6, Boston Col 3
1-1-41	Texas A&M 13, Fordham 12
1-1-42	Alabama 29, Texas A&M 21
1-1-43	Texas 14, Georgia Tech 7
1-1-44	Texas 7, Randolph Field 7
1-1-45	Oklahoma St 34, Texas Christian 0
1-1-46	Texas 40, Missouri 27
1-1-47	Arkansas 0, Louisiana St 0
1-1-48	Southern Methodist 13, Penn St 13
1-1-49	Southern Methodist 21, Oregon 13
1-2-50	Rice 27, N Carolina 13
1-1-51	Tennessee 20, Texas 14
1-1-52	Kentucky 20, Texas Christian 7
1-1-53	Texas 16, Tennessee 0
1-1-54	Rice 28, Alabama 6

Cotton Bowl *(Cont.)*

1-1-55	Georgia Tech 14, Arkansas 6
1-2-56	Mississippi 14, Texas Christian 13
1-1-57	Texas Christian 28, Syracuse 27
1-1-58	Navy 20, Rice 7
1-1-59	Texas Christian 0, Air Force 0
1-1-60	Syracuse 23, Texas 14
1-2-61	Duke 7, Arkansas 6
1-1-62	Texas 12, Mississippi 7
1-1-63	Louisiana St 13, Texas 0
1-1-64	Texas 28, Navy 6
1-1-65	Arkansas 10, Nebraska 7
1-1-66	Louisiana St 14, Arkansas 7
12-31-66	Georgia 24, Southern Methodist 9
1-1-68	Texas A&M 20, Alabama 16
1-1-69	Texas 36, Tennessee 13
1-1-70	Texas 21, Notre Dame 17
1-1-71	Notre Dame 24, Texas 11
1-1-72	Penn St 30, Texas 6
1-1-73	Texas 17, Alabama 13
1-1-74	Nebraska 19, Texas 3
1-1-75	Penn St 41, Baylor 20
1-1-76	Arkansas 31, Georgia 10
1-1-77	Houston 30, Maryland 21
1-2-78	Notre Dame 38, Texas 10
1-1-79	Notre Dame 35, Houston 34
1-1-80	Houston 17, Nebraska 14
1-1-81	Alabama 30, Baylor 2
1-1-82	Texas 14, Alabama 12
1-1-83	SMU 7, Pittsburgh 3
1-2-84	Georgia 10, Texas 9
1-1-85	Boston Col 45, Houston 28
1-1-86	Texas A&M 36, Auburn 16
1-1-87	Ohio St 28, Texas A&M 12
1-1-88	Texas A&M 35, Notre Dame 10
1-2-89	UCLA 17, Arkansas 3
1-1-90	Tennessee 31, Arkansas 27
1-1-91	Miami (Fla.) 46, Texas 3
1-1-92	Florida St 10, Texas A&M 2
1-1-93	Notre Dame 28, Texas A&M 3
1-1-94	Notre Dame 24, Texas A&M 21
1-2-95	Southern Cal 55, Texas Tech 14
1-1-96	Colorado 38, Oregon 6
1-1-97	Brigham Young 19, Kansas St 15
1-1-98	UCLA 29, Texas A&M 23
1-1-99	Texas 38, Mississippi St 11
1-1-00	Arkansas 27, Texas 6
1-1-01	Kansas St 35, Tennessee 21
1-1-02	Oklahoma 10, Arkansas 3
1-1-03	Texas 35, Louisiana St 20
1-2-04	Mississippi 31, Oklahoma St 28
1-1-05	Tennessee 38, Texas A&M 7
1-2-06	Alabama 13, Texas Tech 10

City: Dallas. Stadium: Cotton Bowl, capacity 68,252.

Sun Bowl

1-1-36	Hardin-Simmons 14, New Mexico St 14
1-1-37	Hardin-Simmons 34, UTEP 6
1-1-38	W Virginia 7, Texas Tech 6
1-2-39	Utah 26, New Mexico 0
1-1-40	Catholic 0, Arizona St 0
1-1-41	Case Reserve 26, Arizona St 13
1-1-42	Tulsa 6, Texas Tech 0
1-1-43	2nd Air Force 13, Hardin-Simmons 7
1-1-44	Southwestern (Tex.) 7, New Mexico 0
1-1-45	Southwestern (Tex.) 35, New Mexico 0
1-1-46	New Mexico 34, Denver 24
1-1-47	Cincinnati 18, Virginia Tech 6
1-1-48	Miami (OH) 13, Texas Tech 12
1-1-49	W Virginia 21, UTEP 12
1-2-50	UTEP 33, Georgetown 20
1-1-51	W Texas St 14, Cincinnati 13
1-1-52	Texas Tech 25, Pacific 14
1-1-53	Pacific 26, Southern Miss 7
1-1-54	UTEP 37, Southern Miss 14
1-1-55	UTEP 47, Florida St 20
1-2-56	Wyoming 21, Texas Tech 14
1-1-57	George Washington 13, UTEP 0
1-1-58	Louisville 34, Drake 20
12-31-58	Wyoming 14, Hardin-Simmons 6
12-31-59	New Mexico St 28, N Texas 8
12-31-60	New Mexico St 20, Utah St 13
12-30-61	Villanova 17, Wichita St 9
12-31-62	W Texas St 15, Ohio 14
12-31-63	Oregon 21, Southern Methodist 14
12-26-64	Georgia 7, Texas Tech 0
12-31-65	UTEP 13, Texas Christian 12
12-24-66	Wyoming 28, Florida St 20
12-30-67	UTEP 14, Mississippi 7
12-28-68	Auburn 34, Arizona 10
12-20-69	Nebraska 45, Georgia 6
12-19-70	Georgia Tech 17, Texas Tech 9
12-18-71	Louisiana St 33, Iowa St 15
12-30-72	N Carolina 32, Texas Tech 28
12-29-73	Missouri 34, Auburn 17
12-28-74	Mississippi St 26, N Carolina 24
12-26-75	Pittsburgh 33, Kansas 19
1-2-77	Texas A&M 37, Florida 14
12-31-77	Stanford 24, Louisiana St 14
12-23-78	Texas 42, Maryland 0
12-22-79	Washington 14, Texas 7
12-27-80	Nebraska 31, Mississippi St 17
12-26-81	Oklahoma 40, Houston 14
12-25-82	N Carolina 26, Texas 10
12-24-83	Alabama 28, Southern Methodist 7
12-22-84	Maryland 28, Tennessee 27
12-28-85	Georgia 13, Arizona 13
12-25-86	Alabama 28, Washington 6
12-25-87	Oklahoma St 35, W Virginia 33
12-24-88	Alabama 29, Army 28
12-30-89	Pittsburgh 31, Texas A&M 28
12-31-90	Michigan St 17, Southern Cal 16
12-31-91	UCLA 6, Illinois 3
12-31-92	Baylor 20, Arizona 15
12-24-93	Oklahoma 41, Texas Tech 10
12-30-94	Texas 35, N Carolina 31
12-29-95	Iowa 38, Washington 18
12-31-96	Stanford 38, Michigan St 0
12-31-97	Arizona 17, Iowa 7
12-31-98	Texas Christian 28, Southern Cal 19
12-31-99	Oregon 24, Minnesota 20
12-29-00	Wisconsin 21, UCLA 20

Sun Bowl

12-31-01	Washington St 33, Purdue 27
12-31-02	Purdue 34, Washington 24
12-31-03	Minnesota 31, Oregon 30
12-31-04	Arizona State 27, Purdue 23
12-30-05	UCLA 50, Northwestern 39

City: El Paso. Stadium: Sun Bowl, capacity 51,270.
Name Changes: Sun Bowl (1936–86; 94–), John Hancock
Sun Bowl (1987–88), John Hancock Bowl (1989–93).
Playing Sites: Kidd Field (1936–62), Sun Bowl (since
1963).

Gator Bowl

1-1-46	Wake Forest 26, S Carolina 14
1-1-47	Oklahoma 34, N Carolina St 13
1-1-48	Maryland 20, Georgia 20
1-1-49	Clemson 24, Missouri 23
1-2-50	Maryland 20, Missouri 7
1-1-51	Wyoming 20, Washington & Lee 7
1-1-52	Miami (Fla.) 14, Clemson 0
1-1-53	Florida 14, Tulsa 13
1-1-54	Texas Tech 35, Auburn 13
12-31-54	Auburn 33, Baylor 13
12-31-55	Vanderbilt 25, Auburn 13
12-29-56	Georgia Tech 21, Pittsburgh 14
12-28-57	Tennessee 3, Texas A&M 0
12-27-58	Mississippi 7, Florida 3
1-2-60	Arkansas 14, Georgia Tech 7
12-31-60	Florida 13, Baylor 12
12-30-61	Penn St 30, Georgia Tech 15
12-29-62	Florida 17, Penn St 7
12-28-63	N Carolina 35, Air Force 0
1-2-65	Florida St 36, Oklahoma 19
12-31-65	Georgia Tech 31, Texas Tech 21
12-31-66	Tennessee 18, Syracuse 12
12-30-67	Penn St 17, Florida St 17
12-28-68	Missouri 35, Alabama 10
12-27-69	Florida 14, Tennessee 13
1-2-71	Auburn 35, Mississippi 28
12-31-71	Georgia 7, N Carolina 3
12-30-72	Auburn 24, Colorado 3
12-29-73	Texas Tech 28, Tennessee 19
12-30-74	Auburn 27, Texas 3
12-29-75	Maryland 13, Florida 0
12-27-76	Notre Dame 20, Penn St 9
12-30-77	Pittsburgh 34, Clemson 3
12-29-78	Clemson 17, Ohio St 15
12-28-79	N Carolina 17, Michigan 15
12-29-80	Pittsburgh 37, S Carolina 9
12-28-81	N Carolina 31, Arkansas 27
12-30-82	Florida St 31, W Virginia 12
12-30-83	Florida 14, Iowa 6
12-28-84	Oklahoma St 21, S Carolina 14
12-30-85	Florida St 34, Oklahoma St 23
12-27-86	Clemson 27, Stanford 21
12-31-87	Louisiana St 30, S Carolina 13
1-1-89	Georgia 34, Michigan St 27
12-30-89	Clemson 27, W Virginia 7
1-1-91	Michigan 35, Mississippi 3
12-29-91	Oklahoma 48, Virginia 14
12-31-92	Florida 27, N Carolina St 10
12-31-93	Alabama 24, North Carolina 10
12-30-94	Tennessee 45, Virginia Tech 23
1-1-96	Syracuse 41, Clemson 0
1-1-97	N Carolina 20, W Virginia 13

Gator Bowl *(Cont.)*

1-1-98 ....N Carolina 42, Viginia Tech 13
1-1-99 ....Georgia Tech 35, Notre Dame 28
1-1-00 ....Miami 27, Georgia Tech 13
1-1-01 ....Virginia Tech 41, Clemson 20
1-1-02 ....Florida St 30, Virginia Tech 17
1-1-03 ....N Carolina St 28, Notre Dame 6
1-1-04 ....Maryland 41, W Virginia 7
1-1-05 ....Florida State 30, West Virginia 18
1-2-06 ....Virginia Tech 35, Louisville 24

City: Jacksonville, FL. Stadium: Alltel Stadium, capacity 76,976.

Florida Citrus Bowl

1-1-47 ....Catawba 31, Maryville (Tenn.) 6
1-1-48 ....Catawba 7, Marshall 0
1-1-49 ....Murray St 21, Sul Ross St 21
1-2-50 ....St. Vincent 7, Emory & Henry 6
1-1-51 ....Morris Harvey 35, Emory & Henry 14
1-1-52 ....Stetson 35, Arkansas St 20
1-1-53 ....E Texas St 33, Tennessee Tech 0
1-1-54 ....E Texas St 7, Arkansas St 7
1-1-55 ....NE-Omaha 7, Eastern Kentucky 6
1-2-56 ....Juniata 6, Missouri Valley 6
1-1-57 ....W Texas St 20, Southern Miss 13
1-1-58 ....E Texas St 10, Southern Miss 9
12-27-58 ....E Texas St 26, Missouri Valley 7
1-1-60 ....Middle Tennessee St 21, Presbyterian 12
12-30-60 ....Citadel 27, Tennessee Tech 0
12-29-61 ....Lamar 21, Middle Tennessee St 14
12-22-62 ....Houston 49, Miami (Ohio) 21
12-28-63 ....Western Kentucky 27, Coast Guard 0
12-12-64 ....E Carolina 14, Massachusetts 13
12-11-65 ....E Carolina 31, Maine 0
12-10-66 ....Morgan St 14, W Chester 6
12-16-67 ....TN-Martin 25, W Chester 8
12-27-68 ....Richmond 49, Ohio 42
12-26-69 ....Toledo 56, Davidson 33
12-28-70 ....Toledo 40, William & Mary 12
12-28-71 ....Toledo 28, Richmond 3
12-29-72 ....Tampa 21, Kent St 18
12-22-73 ....Miami (Ohio) 16, Florida 7
12-21-74 ....Miami (Ohio) 21, Georgia 10
12-20-75 ....Miami (Ohio) 20, S Carolina 7
12-18-76 ....Oklahoma St 49, Brigham Young 21
12-23-77 ....Florida St 40, Texas Tech 17
12-23-78 ....N Carolina St 30, Pittsburgh 17
12-22-79 ....Louisiana St 34, Wake Forest 10
12-20-80 ....Florida 35, Maryland 20
12-19-81 ....Missouri 19, Southern Miss 17
12-18-82 ....Auburn 33, Boston Col 26
12-17-83 ....Tennessee 30, Maryland 23
12-22-84 ....Georgia 17, Florida St 17
12-28-85 ....Ohio St 10, Brigham Young 7
1-1-87 ....Auburn 16, USC 7
1-1-88 ....Clemson 35, Penn St 10
1-2-89 ....Clemson 13, Oklahoma 6
1-1-90 ....Illinois 31, Virginia 21
1-1-91 ....Georgia Tech 45, Nebraska 21
1-1-92 ....California 37, Clemson 13
1-1-93 ....Georgia 21, Ohio State 14
1-1-94 ....Penn State 31, Tennessee 13
1-2-95 ....Alabama 24, Ohio St 17
1-1-96 ....Tennessee 20, Ohio St 14
1-1-97 ....Tennessee 48, Northwestern 28
1-1-98 ....Florida 21, Penn St 6

Florida Citrus Bowl *(Cont.)*

1-1-99 ....Michigan 45, Arkansas 31
1-1-00 ....Michigan St 37, Florida 34
1-1-01 ....Michigan 31, Auburn 28
1-1-02 ....Tennessee 45, Michigan 17
1-1-03 ....Auburn 13, Penn St 9
1-1-04 ....Georgia 34, Purdue 27 (OT)
1-1-05 ....Iowa 30, LSU 25
1-2-06 ....Wisconsin 24, Auburn 10

City: Orlando, FL. Stadium: Florida Citrus Bowl, capacity 70,000. Name Change: Tangerine Bowl (1947–82). Playing Sites: Tangerine Bowl (1947–72, 1974–82); Florida Field, Gainesville (1973); Orlando Stadium/Florida Citrus Bowl-Orlando (since 1983).

Liberty Bowl

12-19-59 ....Penn St 7, Alabama 0
12-17-60 ....Penn St 41, Oregon 12
12-16-61 ....Syracuse 15, Miami (Fla.) 14
12-15-62 ....Oregon St 6, Villanova 0
12-21-63 ....Mississippi St 16, N Carolina St 12
12-19-64 ....Utah 32, W Virginia 6
12-18-65 ....Mississippi 13, Auburn 7
12-10-66 ....Miami (Fla.) 14, Virginia Tech 7
12-16-67 ....N Carolina St 14, Georgia 7
12-14-68 ....Mississippi 34, Virginia Tech 17
12-13-69 ....Colorado 47, Alabama 33
12-12-70 ....Tulane 17, Colorado 3
12-20-71 ....Tennessee 14, Arkansas 13
12-18-72 ....Georgia Tech 31, Iowa St 30
12-17-73 ....N Carolina St 31, Kansas 18
12-16-74 ....Tennessee 7, Maryland 3
12-22-75 ....Southern Cal 20, Texas A&M 0
12-20-76 ....Alabama 36, UCLA 6
12-19-77 ....Nebraska 21, N Carolina 17
12-23-78 ....Missouri 20, Louisiana St 15
12-22-79 ....Penn St 9, Tulane 6
12-27-80 ....Purdue 28, Missouri 25
12-30-81 ....Ohio St 31, Navy 28
12-29-82 ....Alabama 21, Illinois 15
12-29-83 ....Notre Dame 19, Boston Col 18
12-27-84 ....Auburn 21, Arkansas 15
12-27-85 ....Baylor 21, Louisiana St 7
12-29-86 ....Tennessee 21, Minnesota 14
12-29-87 ....Georgia 20, Arkansas 17
12-28-88 ....Indiana 34, S Carolina 10
12-28-89 ....Mississippi 42, Air Force 29
12-27-90 ....Air Force 23, Ohio St 11
12-29-91 ....Air Force 38, Mississippi St 15
12-31-92 ....Mississippi 13, Air Force 0
12-28-93 ....Louisville 18, Michigan St 7
12-31-94 ....Illinois 30, E Carolina 0
12-30-95 ....East Carolina 19, Stanford 13
12-27-96 ....Syracuse 30, Houston 17
12-31-97 ....Southern Miss 41, Pittsburgh 7
12-31-98 ....Tulane 41, Brigham Young 27
12-31-99 ....Southern Miss 23, Colorado St 17
12-29-01 ....Colorado St 22, Louisville 17
12-31-01 ....Louisville 28, Brigham Young 10
12-31-02 ....Texas Christian 17, Colorado St 3
12-31-03 ....Utah 17, Southern Mississippi 0
12-31-04 ....Louisville 44, Boise State 40
12-31-05 ....Tulsa 31, Fresno State 24

City: Memphis (since 1965). Stadium: Liberty Bowl Memorial Stadium, capacity 62,921.
Playing Sites: Philadelphia (Municipal Stadium, 1959–63), Atlantic City (Convention Center, 1964).

Bluebonnet Bowl

12-19-59 ....Clemson 23, Texas Christian 7
12-17-60 ....Texas 3, Alabama 3
12-16-61 ....Kansas 33, Rice 7
12-22-62 ....Missouri 14, Georgia Tech 10
12-21-63 ....Baylor 14, LSU 7
12-19-64 ....Tulsa 14, Mississippi 7
12-18-65 ....Tennessee 27, Tulsa 6
12-17-66 ....Texas 19, Mississippi 0
12-23-67 ....Colorado 31, Miami (Fla.) 21
12-31-68 ....Southern Methodist 28, Oklahoma 27
12-31-69 ....Houston 36, Auburn 7
12-31-70 ....Alabama 24, Oklahoma 24
12-31-71 ....Colorado 29, Houston 17
12-30-72 ....Tennessee 24, Louisiana St 17
12-29-73 ....Houston 47, Tulane 7
12-23-74 ....N Carolina St 31, Houston 31
12-27-75 ....Texas 38, Colorado 21
12-31-76 ....Nebraska 27, Texas Tech 24
12-31-77 ....Southern Cal 47, Texas A&M 28
12-31-78 ....Stanford 25, Georgia 22
12-31-79 ....Purdue 27, Tennessee 22
12-31-80 ....N Carolina 16, Texas 7
12-31-81 ....Michigan 33, UCLA 14
12-31-82 ....Arkansas 28, Florida 24
12-31-83 ....Oklahoma St 24, Baylor 14
12-31-84 ....W Virginia 31, Texas Christian 14
12-31-85 ....Air Force 24, Texas 16
12-31-86 ....Baylor 21, Colorado 9
12-31-87 ....Texas 32, Pittsburgh 27

City: Houston. Playing sites: Rice Stadium (1959–67;
1985–86), Astrodome (1968–84, 1987).
Name change: Astro-Bluebonnet Bowl (1968–76). Bowl
was discontinued after 1987.

Peach Bowl

12-30-68 ....Louisiana St 31, Florida St 27
12-30-69 ....W Virginia 14, S Carolina 3
12-30-70 ....Arizona St 48, N Carolina 26
12-30-71 ....Mississippi 41, Georgia Tech 18
12-29-72 ....N Carolina St 49, W Virginia 13
12-28-73 ....Georgia 17, Maryland 16
12-28-74 ....Vanderbilt 6, Texas Tech 6
12-31-75 ....W Virginia 13, N Carolina St 10
12-31-76 ....Kentucky 21, N Carolina 0
12-31-77 ....N Carolina St 24, Iowa St 14
12-25-78 ....Purdue 41, Georgia Tech 21
12-31-79 ....Baylor 24, Clemson 18
1-2-81 ....Miami (Fla.) 20, Virginia Tech 10
12-31-81 ....W Virginia 26, Florida 6
12-31-82 ....Iowa 28, Tennessee 22
12-30-83 ....Florida St 28, N Carolina 3
12-31-84 ....Virginia 27, Purdue 24
12-31-85 ....Army 31, Illinois 29
12-31-86 ....Virginia Tech 25, N Carolina St 24
1-2-88 ....Tennessee 27, Indiana 22
12-31-88 ....N Carolina St 28, Iowa 23
12-30-89 ....Syracuse 19, Georgia 18
12-29-90 ....Auburn 27, Indiana 23
1-1-92 ....E Carolina 37, N Carolina St 34
1-2-93 ....N Carolina 21, Mississippi St 17
12-31-93 ....Clemson 14, Kentucky 13

Peach Bowl *(Cont.)*

1-1-95 ....N Carolina St 28, Mississippi St 24
12-30-95 ....Virginia 34, Georgia 27
12-28-96 ....Louisiana St 10, Clemson 7
1-2-98 ....Auburn 21, Clemson 17
12-31-98 ....Georgia 35, Virginia 33
12-30-99 ....Mississippi St 17, Clemson 7
12-29-00 ....Louisiana St 28, Georgia Tech 14
12-31-01 ....N Carolina 16, Auburn 10
12-31-02 ....Maryland 30, Tennessee 3
1-2-04 ....Clemson 27, Tennessee 14
12-31-04 ....Miami (Fla.) 27, Florida 10
12-30-05 ....LSU 40, MIami (Fla.) 3

City: Atlanta. Stadium: Georgia Dome, capacity 71,500.
Playing Sites: Grant Field (1968–70), Atlanta–Fulton
County Stadium (1971–92), Georgia Dome (since 1993).

Fiesta Bowl

12-27-71 ....Arizona St 45, Florida St 38
12-23-72 ....Arizona St 49, Missouri 35
12-21-73 ....Arizona St 28, Pittsburgh 7
12-28-74 ....Oklahoma St 16, Brigham Young 6
12-26-75 ....Arizona St 17, Nebraska 14
12-25-76 ....Oklahoma 41, Wyoming 7
12-25-77 ....Penn St 42, Arizona St 30
12-25-78 ....Arkansas 10, UCLA 10
12-25-79 ....Pittsburgh 16, Arizona 10
12-26-80 ....Penn St 31, Ohio St 19
1-1-82 ....Penn St 26, USC 10
1-1-83 ....Arizona St 32, Oklahoma 21
1-2-84 ....Ohio St 28, Pittsburgh 23
1-1-85 ....UCLA 39, Miami (Fla.) 37
1-1-86 ....Michigan 27, Nebraska 23
1-1-87 ....Penn St 14, Miami (Fla.) 10
1-1-88 ....Florida St 31, Nebraska 28
1-2-89 ....Notre Dame 34, W Virginia 21
1-1-90 ....Florida St 41, Nebraska 17
1-1-91 ....Louisville 34, Alabama 7
1-1-92 ....Penn St 42, Tennessee 17
1-1-93 ....Syracuse 26, Colorado 22
1-1-94 ....Arizona 29, Miami (Fla.) 0
1-2-95 ....Colorado 41, Notre Dame 24
1-1-96 ....Nebraska 62, Florida 24
1-1-97 ....Penn St 38, Texas 15
12-31-97 ....Kansas St 35, Syracuse 18
1-4-99 ....Tennessee 23, Florida St 16
1-2-00 ....Nebraska 31, Tennessee 21
1-1-01 ....Oregon St 41, Notre Dame 9
1-1-02 ....Oregon 38, Colorado 16
1-3-03 ....Ohio St 31, Miami (Fla.) 24 [2 OT]
1-2-04 ....Ohio St 35, Kansas St 28
1-1-05 ....Utah 35, Pittsburgh 7
1-2-06 ....Ohio State 34, Notre Dame 20

City: Tempe, AZ. Stadium: Sun Devil Stadium,
capacity 73,471.

Independence Bowl

12-13-76 ....McNeese St 20, Tulsa 16
12-17-77 ....Louisiana Tech 24, Louisville 14
12-16-78 ....E Carolina 35, Louisiana Tech 13
12-15-79 ....Syracuse 31, McNeese St 7
12-13-80 ....Southern Miss 16, McNeese St 14
12-12-81 ....Texas A&M 33, Oklahoma St 16
12-11-82 ....Wisconsin 14, Kansas St 3
12-10-83 ....Air Force 9, Mississippi 3
12-15-84 ....Air Force 23, Virginia Tech 7
12-21-85 ....Minnesota 20, Clemson 13
12-20-86 ....Mississippi 20, Texas Tech 17
12-19-87 ....Washington 24, Tulane 12
12-23-88 ....Southern Miss 38, UTEP 18
12-16-89 ....Oregon 27, Tulsa 24
12-15-90 ....Louisiana Tech 34, Maryland 34
12-29-91 ....Georgia 24, Arkansas 15
12-31-92 ....Wake Forest 39, Oregon 35
12-31-93 ....Virginia Tech 45, Indiana 20
12-28-94 ....Virginia 20, Texas Christian 10
12-29-95 ....Louisiana 45, Michigan St 26
12-31-96 ....Auburn 32, Army 29
12-28-97 ....Louisiana St 27, Notre Dame 9
12-31-98 ....Mississippi 35, Texas Tech 18
12-31-99 ....Mississippi 27, Oklahoma 25
12-31-00 ....Mississippi St 43, Texas A&M 41
12-27-01 ....Alabama 14, Iowa St 13
12-27-02 ....Mississippi 27, Nebraska 23
12-31-03 ....Arkansas 27, Missouri 14
12-28-04 ....Iowa State 17, Miami (Ohio) 13
12-30-05 ....Missouri 38, South Carolina 31

City: Shreveport, LA. Stadium: Independence Stadium,
capacity 50,459.

All-American Bowl

12-22-77 ....Maryland 17, Minnesota 7
12-20-78 ....Texas A&M 28, Iowa St 12
12-29-79 ....Missouri 24, S Carolina 14
12-27-80 ....Arkansas 34, Tulane 15
12-31-81 ....Mississippi St 10, Kansas 0
12-31-82 ....Air Force 36, Vanderbilt 28
12-22-83 ....W Virginia 20, Kentucky 16
12-29-84 ....Kentucky 20, Wisconsin 19
12-31-85 ....Georgia Tech 17, Michigan St 14
12-31-86 ....Florida St 27, Indiana 13
12-22-87 ....Virginia 22, Brigham Young 16
12-29-88 ....Florida 14, Illinois 10
12-28-89 ....Texas Tech 49, Duke 21
12-28-90 ....N Carolina St 31, Southern Miss. 27

City: Birmingham, AL. Stadium: Legion Field.
Name Change: Hall of Fame Classic (1977–84). Bowl
was discontinued after 1990.

Holiday Bowl

12-22-78 ....Navy 23, Brigham Young 16
12-21-79 ....Indiana 38, Brigham Young 37
12-19-80 ....Brigham Young 46, SMU45
12-18-81 ....Brigham Young 38, Washington St 36
12-17-82 ....Ohio St 47, Brigham Young 17
12-23-83 ....Brigham Young 21, Missouri 17
12-21-84 ....Brigham Young 24, Michigan 17
12-22-85 ....Arkansas 18, Arizona St 17
12-30-86 ....Iowa 39, San Diego St 38
12-30-87 ....Iowa 20, Wyoming 19
12-30-88 ....Oklahoma St 62, Wyoming 14
12-29-89 ....Penn St 50, Brigham Young 39
12-29-90 ....Texas A&M 65, Brigham Young 14
12-30-91 ....Iowa 13, Brigham Young 13
12-30-92 ....Hawaii 27, Illinois 17
12-30-93 ....Ohio St 28, Brigham Young 21
12-30-94 ....Michigan 24, Colorado St 14
12-29-95 ....Kansas St 54, Colorado St 21
12-30-96 ....Colorado 33, Washington 21
12-29-97 ....Colorado St 35, Missouri 24
12-30-98 ....Arizona 23, Nebraska 20
12-29-99 ....Kansas St 24, Washington 20
12-29-00 ....Oregon 35, Texas 30
12-28-01 ....Texas 47, Washington 43
12-27-02 ....Kansas St 34, Arizona St 27
12-30-03 ....Washington St 28, Texas 20
12-30-04 ....Texas Tech 45, California 31
12-29-05 ....Oklahoma 17, Oregon 14

City: San Diego. Stadium: Qualcomm Stadium,
capacity 70,000.

Las Vegas Bowl

12-19-81 ....Toledo 27, San Jose St 25
12-18-82 ....Fresno St 29, Bowling Green 28
12-17-83   Northern Illinois 20,
                 Cal St–Fullerton 13
12-15-84 ....UNLV 30, Toledo 13*
12-14-85 ....Fresno St 51, Bowling Green 7
12-13-86 ....San Jose St 37, Miami (Ohio) 7
12-12-87 ....Eastern Michigan 30, San Jose St 27
12-10-88 ....Fresno St 35, Western Michigan 30
12-9-89 ....Fresno St 27, Ball St 6
12-8-90 ....San Jose St 48, Central Michigan 24
12-14-91 ....Bowling Green 28, Fresno St 21
12-18-92 ....Bowling Green 35, Nevada 34
12-17-93 ....Utah St 42, Ball St 33
12-15-94 ....UNLV 52, Central Michigan 24
12-14-95 ....Toledo 40, Nevada 37
12-19-96 ....Nevada 18, Ball St 15
12-19-97 ....Oregon 41, Air Force 13
12-19-98 ....N Carolina 20, San Diego St 13
12-18-99 ....Utah 17, Fresno St 16
12-21-00 ....UNLV 31, Arkansas 14
12-25-01 ....Utah 10, USC 6
12-25-02 ....UCLA 27, New Mexico 13
12-24-03 ....Oregon St 55, New Mexico 14
12-23-04 ....Wyoming 24, UCLA, 21
12-22-05 ....California 35, BYU 28

* Toledo won later by forfeit. City: Las Vegas (since
1992). Stadium: Sam Boyd Silver Bowl Stadium,
capacity 40,000. Name change: California Bowl
(1981–91).
Playing sites: Fresno, CA (Bulldog Stadium, 1981–91),
Las Vegas.

Aloha Bowl

12-25-82 ....Washington 21, Maryland 20
12-26-83 ....Penn St 13, Washington 10
12-29-84 ....Southern Methodist 27, Notre Dame 20
12-28-85 ....Alabama 24, USC 3
12-27-86 ....Arizona 30, N Carolina 21
12-25-87 ....UCLA 20, Florida 16
12-25-88 ....Washington St 24, Houston 22
12-25-89 ....Michigan St 33, Hawaii 13
12-25-90 ....Syracuse 28, Arizona 0
12-25-91 ....Georgia Tech 18, Stanford 17
12-25-92 ....Kansas 23, Brigham Young 20
12-25-93 ....Colorado 41, Fresno St 30
12-25-94 ....Boston College 12, Kansas St 7
12-25-95 ....Kansas 51, UCLA 30
12-25-96 ....Navy 42, California 38
12-25-97 ....Washington 51, Michigan St 23
12-25-98 ....Colorado 51, Oregon 43
12-25-99 ....Wake Forest 23, Arizona St 3
12-25-00 ....Boston College 31, Arizona St 17

City: Honolulu. Stadium: Aloha Stadium. Bowl was discontinued after 2000.

Freedom Bowl

12-16-84 ....Iowa 55, Texas 17
12-30-85 ....Washington 20, Colorado 17
12-30-86 ....UCLA 31, Brigham Young 10
12-30-87 ....Arizona St 33, Air Force 28
12-29-88 ....Brigham Young 20, Colorado 17
12-30-89 ....Washington 34, Florida 7
12-29-90 ....Colorado St 32, Oregon 31
12-30-91 ....Tulsa 28, San Diego St 17
12-29-92 ....Fresno St 24, USC 7
12-30-93 ....USC 28, Utah 21
12-29-94 ....Utah 16, Arizona 13

City: Anaheim. Stadium: Anaheim Stadium. Bowl was discontinued after 1994.

Outback Bowl

12-23-86 ....Boston College 27, Georgia 24
1-2-88 ....Michigan 28, Alabama 24
1-2-89 ....Syracuse 23, Louisiana St 10
1-1-90 ....Auburn 31, Ohio St 14
1-1-91 ....Clemson 30, Illinois 0
1-1-92 ....Syracuse 24, Ohio St 17
1-1-93 ....Tennessee 38, Boston College 23
1-1-94 ....Michigan 42, N Carolina St 7
1-2-95 ....Wisconsin 34, Duke 20
1-1-96 ....Penn St 43, Auburn 14
1-1-97 ....Alabama 17, Michigan 14
1-1-98 ....Georgia 33, Wisconsin 6
1-1-99 ....Penn St 26, Kentucky 14
1-1-00 ....Georgia 28, Purdue 25
1-1-01 ....S Carolina 24, Ohio St 7
1-1-02 ....S Carolina 31, Ohio St 28
1-1-03 ....Michigan 38, Florida 30
1-1-04 ....Iowa 37, Florida 17
1-1-05 ....Georgia 24, Wisconsin 21
1-2-06 ....Florida 31, Iowa 24

City: Tampa. Stadium: Raymond James Stadium, capacity 75,000. Name change: Hall of Fame Bowl (1986–95).

Insight.com Bowl

12-31-89 ....Arizona 17, N Carolina St 10
12-31-90 ....California 17, Wyoming 15
12-31-91 ....Indiana 24, Baylor 0
12-29-92 ....Washington St 31, Utah 28
12-29-93 ....Kansas St 52, Wyoming 17
12-29-94 ....Brigham Young 31, Oklahoma 6
12-27-95 ....Texas Tech 55, Air Force 41
12-27-96 ....Wisconsin 38, Utah 10
12-27-97 ....Arizona 20, New Mexico 14
12-26-98 ....Missouri 34, W Virginia 31
12-31-99 ....Colorado 62, Boston College 28
12-28-00 ....Iowa St 37, Pittsburgh 29
12-29-01 ....Syracuse 26, Kansas St 3
12-26-02 ....Pittsburgh 38, Oregon St 13
12-26-03 ....California 52, Virginia Tech 49
12-28-04 ....Oregon State 38, Notre Dame 21
12-27-05 ....Arizona State 45, Rutgers 40

City: Tucson. Stadium: Arizona Stadium, capacity 55,883. Name change: Copper Bowl 1989–97.

Tangerine Bowl

12-28-90 ....Florida St 24, Penn St 17
12-28-91 ....Alabama 30, Colorado 25
1-1-93 ....Stanford 24, Penn St 3
1-1-94 ....Boston College 31, Virginia 13
1-2-95 ....S Carolina 24, W Virginia 21
12-30-95 ....N Carolina 20, Arkansas 10
12-27-96 ....Miami (Fla.) 31, Virginia 21
12-29-97 ....Georgia Tech 35, W Virginia 30
12-29-98 ....Miami (Fla.) 46, N Carolina St 23
12-30-99 ....Illinois 62, Virginia 21
12-28-00 ....N Carolina St 38, Minnesota 30
12-20-01 ....Pittsburgh 34, N Carolina St 19
12-23-02 ....Texas Tech 55, Clemson 15
12-22-03 ....N Carolina St 56, Kansas 26

City: Miami. Stadium: Pro Player Stadium, capacity 75,192. Name change: Blockbuster Bowl (1990–93), Carquest Bowl (1994–97), Micron PC Bowl (1998–01). Discontinued after 2003.

Alamo Bowl

12-31-93 ....California 37, Iowa 3
12-31-94 ....Washington St 10, Baylor 3
12-28-95 ....Texas A&M 22, Michigan 20
12-29-96 ....Iowa 27, Texas Tech 0
12-30-97 ....Purdue 33, Oklahoma St 20
12-29-98 ....Purdue 37, Kansas St 34
12-28-99 ....Penn St 24, Texas A&M 0
12-30-00 ....Nebraska 66, Northwestern 17
12-29-01 ....Iowa 16, Texas Tech 13
12-28-02 ....Wisconsin 31, Colorado 28 (OT)
12-29-03 ....Nebraska 17, Michigan St 3
12-29-04 ....Ohio State 33, Oklahoma State 7
12-28-05 ....Nebraska 32, Michigan 28

City: San Antonio, TX. Stadium: Alamodome, capaciity 67,000.

1936

		Record	Coach
1.	Minnesota	7-1-0	Bernie Bierman
2.	Louisiana St	9-0-1	Bernie Moore
3.	Pittsburgh	7-1-1	Jack Sutherland
4.	Alabama	8-0-1	Frank Thomas
5.	Washington	7-1-1	Jimmy Phelan
6.	Santa Clara	7-1-0	Buck Shaw
7.	Northwestern	7-1-0	Pappy Waldorf
8.	Notre Dame	6-2-1	Elmer Layden
9.	Nebraska	7-2-0	Dana X. Bible
10.	Pennsylvania	7-1-0	Harvey Harman
11.	Duke	9-1-0	Wallace Wade
12.	Yale	7-1-0	Ducky Pond
13.	Dartmouth	7-1-1	Red Blaik
14.	Duquesne	7-2-0	John Smith
15.	Fordham	5-1-2	Jim Crowley
16.	Texas Christian	8-2-2	Dutch Meyer
17.	Tennessee	6-2-2	Bob Neyland
18.	Arkansas	7-3-0	Fred Thomsen
19.	Navy	6-3-0	Tom Hamilton
20.	Marquette	7-1-0	Frank Murray

1937

		Record	Coach
1.	Pittsburgh	9-0-1	Jack Sutherland
2.	California	9-0-1	Stub Allison
3.	Fordham	7-0-1	Jim Crowley
4.	Alabama	9-0-0	Frank Thomas
5.	Minnesota	6-2-0	Bernie Bierman
6.	Villanova	8-0-1	Clipper Smith
7.	Dartmouth	7-0-2	Red Blaik
8.	Louisiana St	9-1-0	Bernie Moore
9.	Notre Dame	6-2-1	Elmer Layden
	Santa Clara	8-0-0	Buck Shaw
11.	Nebraska	6-1-2	Biff Jones
12.	Yale	6-1-1	Ducky Pond
13.	Ohio St	6-2-0	Francis Schmidt
14.	Holy Cross	8-0-2	Eddie Anderson
	Arkansas	6-2-2	Fred Thomsen
16.	Texas Christian	4-2-2	Dutch Meyer
17.	Colorado	8-0-0	Bunnie Oakes
18.	Rice	5-3-2	Jimmy Kitts
19.	N Carolina	7-1-1	Ray Wolf
20.	Duke	7-2-1	Wallace Wade

1938

		Record	Coach
1.	Texas Christian	10-0-0	Dutch Meyer
2.	Tennessee	10-0-0	Bob Neyland
3.	Duke	9-0-0	Wallace Wade
4.	Oklahoma	10-0-0	Tom Stidham
5.	#Notre Dame	8-1-0	Elmer Layden
6.	Carnegie Tech	7-1-0	Bill Kern
7.	USC	8-2-0	Howard Jones
8.	Pittsburgh	8-2-0	Jack Sutherland
9.	Holy Cross	8-1-0	Eddie Anderson
10.	Minnesota	6-2-0	Bernie Bierman
11.	Texas Tech	10-0-0	Pete Cawthon
12.	Cornell	5-1-1	Carl Snavely
13.	Alabama	7-1-1	Frank Thomas
14.	California	10-1-0	Stub Allison
15.	Fordham	6-1-2	Jim Crowley
16.	Michigan	6-1-1	Fritz Crisler
17.	Northwestern	4-2-2	Pappy Waldorf

1938 *(Cont.)*

		Record	Coach
18.	Villanova	8-0-1	Clipper Smith
19.	Tulane	7-2-1	Red Dawson
20.	Dartmouth	7-2-0	Red Blaik

#Selected No. 1 by the Dickinson System.

1939

		Record	Coach
1.	Texas A&M	10-0-0	Homer Norton
2.	Tennessee	10-0-0	Bob Neyland
3.	#USC	7-0-2	Howard Jones
4.	Cornell	8-0-0	Carl Snavely
5.	Tulane	8-0-1	Red Dawson
6.	Missouri	8-1-0	Don Faurot
7.	UCLA	6-0-4	Babe Horrell
8.	Duke	8-1-0	Wallace Wade
9.	Iowa	6-1-1	Eddie Anderson
10.	Duquesne	8-0-1	Buff Donelli
11.	Boston College	9-1-0	Frank Leahy
12.	Clemson	8-1-0	Jess Neely
13.	Notre Dame	7-2-0	Elmer Layden
14.	Santa Clara	5-1-3	Buck Shaw
15.	Ohio St	6-2-0	Francis Schmidt
16.	Georgia Tech	7-2-0	Bill Alexander
17.	Fordham	6-2-0	Jim Crowley
18.	Nebraska	7-1-1	Biff Jones
19.	Oklahoma	6-2-1	Tom Stidham
20.	Michigan	6-2-0	Fritz Crisler

#Selected No. 1 by the Dickinson System.

1940

		Record	Coach
1.	Minnesota	8-0-0	Bernie Bierman
2.	Stanford	9-0-0	C. Shaughnessy
3.	Michigan	7-1-0	Fritz Crisler
4.	Tennessee	10-0-0	Bob Neyland
5.	Boston College	10-0-0	Frank Leahy
6.	Texas A&M	8-1-0	Homer Norton
7.	Nebraska	8-1-0	Biff Jones
8.	Northwestern	6-2-0	Pappy Waldorf
9.	Mississippi St	9-0-1	Allyn McKeen
10.	Washington	7-2-0	Jimmy Phelan
11.	Santa Clara	6-1-1	Buck Shaw
12.	Fordham	7-1-0	Jim Crowley
13.	Georgetown	8-1-0	Jack Hagerty
14.	Pennsylvania	6-1-1	George Munger
15.	Cornell	6-2-0	Carl Snavely
16.	SMU	8-1-1	Matty Bell
17.	Hard.-Simmons	9-0-0	Abe Woodson
18.	Duke	7-2-0	Wallace Wade
19.	Lafayette	9-0-0	Hooks Mylin
20.	—		

Only 19 teams selected.

1941

		Record	Coach
1.	Minnesota	8-0-0	Bernie Bierman
2.	Duke	9-0-0	Wallace Wade
3.	Notre Dame	8-0-1	Frank Leahy
4.	Texas	8-1-1	Dana X. Bible
5.	Michigan	6-1-1	Fritz Crisler

Note: Except where indicated with an asterisk, the polls from 1936 through 1964 were taken before the bowl games and those from 1965 through the present were taken after the bowl games.

1941 *(Cont.)*

		Record	Coach
6.	Fordham	7-1-0	Jim Crowley
7.	Missouri	8-1-0	Don Faurot
8.	Duquesne	8-0-0	Buff Donelli
9.	Texas A&M	9-1-0	Homer Norton
10.	Navy	7-1-1	Swede Larson
11.	Northwestern	5-3-0	Pappy Waldorf
12.	Oregon St	7-2-0	Lon Stiner
13.	Ohio St	6-1-1	Paul Brown
14.	Georgia	8-1-1	Wally Butts
15.	Pennsylvania	7-1-1	George Munger
16.	Mississippi St	8-1-1	Allyn McKeen
17.	Mississippi	6-2-1	Harry Mehre
18.	Tennessee	8-2-0	John Barnhill
19.	Washington St	6-4-0	Babe Hollingbery
20.	Alabama	8-2-0	Frank Thomas

1942

		Record	Coach
1.	Ohio St	9-1-0	Paul Brown
2.	Georgia	10-1-0	Wally Butts
3.	Wisconsin	8-1-1	H. Stuhldreher
4.	Tulsa	10-0-0	Henry Frnka
5.	Georgia Tech	9-1-0	Bill Alexander
6.	Notre Dame	7-2-2	Frank Leahy
7.	Tennessee	8-1-1	John Barnhill
8.	Boston College	8-1-0	Denny Myers
9.	Michigan	7-3-0	Fritz Crisler
10.	Alabama	7-3-0	Frank Thomas
11.	Texas	8-2-0	Dana X. Bible
12.	Stanford	6-4-0	Marchie Schwartz
13.	UCLA	7-3-0	Babe Horrell
14.	William & Mary	9-1-1	Carl Voyles
15.	Santa Clara	7-2-0	Buck Shaw
16.	Auburn	6-4-1	Jack Meagher
17.	Washington St	6-2-2	Babe Hollingbery
18.	Mississippi St	8-2-0	Allyn McKeen
19.	Minnesota	5-4-0	George Hauser
	Holy Cross	5-4-1	Ank Scanlon
	Penn St	6-1-1	Bob Higgins

1943

		Record	Coach
1.	Notre Dame	9-1-0	Frank Leahy
2.	Iowa Pre-Flight	9-1-0	Don Faurot
3.	Michigan	8-1-0	Fritz Crisler
4.	Navy	8-1-0	Billick Whelchel
5.	Purdue	9-0-0	Elmer Burnham
6.	Great Lakes	10-2-0	Tony Hinkle
7.	Duke	8-1-0	Eddie Cameron
8.	Del Monte P-F	7-1-0	Bill Kern
9.	Northwestern	6-2-0	Pappy Waldorf
10.	March Field	9-1-0	Paul Schissler
11.	Army	7-2-1	Red Blaik
12.	Washington	4-0-0	Ralph Welch
13.	Georgia Tech	7-3-0	Bill Alexander
14.	Texas	7-1-0	Dana X. Bible
15.	Tulsa	6-0-1	Henry Frnka
16.	Dartmouth	6-1-0	Earl Brown
17.	Bainbridge NTS	7-0-0	Joe Maniaci
18.	Colorado College	7-0-0	Hal White
19.	Pacific	7-2-0	Amos A. Stagg
20.	Pennsylvania	6-2-1	George Munger

1944

		Record	Coach
1.	Army	9-0-0	Red Blaik
2.	Ohio St	9-0-0	Carroll Widdoes
3.	Randolph Field	11-0-0	Frank Tritico
4.	Navy	6-3-0	Oscar Hagberg
5.	Bainbridge NTS	9-0-0	Joe Maniaci
6.	Iowa Pre-Flight	10-1-0	Jack Meagher
7.	USC	7-0-2	Jeff Cravath
8.	Michigan	8-2-0	Fritz Crisler
9.	Notre Dame	8-2-0	Ed McKeever
10.	March Field	7-1-2	Paul Schissler
11.	Duke	5-4-0	Eddie Cameron
12.	Tennessee	8-0-1	John Barnhill
13.	Georgia Tech	8-1-0	Bill Alexander
	Norman P-F	6-0-0	John Gregg
15.	Illinois	5-4-1	Ray Eliot
16.	El Toro Marines	8-1-0	Dick Hanley
17.	Great Lakes	9-2-1	Paul Brown
18.	Fort Pierce	9-0-0	Hamp Pool
19.	St. Mary's P-F	4-4-0	Jules Sikes
20.	2nd Air Force	7-2-1	Bill Reese

1945

		Record	Coach
1.	Army	9-0-0	Red Blaik
2.	Alabama	9-0-0	Frank Thomas
3.	Navy	7-1-1	Oscar Hagberg
4.	Indiana	9-0-1	Bo McMillan
5.	Oklahoma A&M	8-0-0	Jim Lookabaugh
6.	Michigan	7-3-0	Fritz Crisler
7.	St. Mary's (CA)	7-1-0	Jimmy Phelan
8.	Pennsylvania	6-2-0	George Munger
9.	Notre Dame	7-2-1	Hugh Devore
10.	Texas	9-1-0	Dana X. Bible
11.	USC	7-3-0	Jeff Cravath
12.	Ohio St	7-2-0	Carroll Widdoes
13.	Duke	6-2-0	Eddie Cameron
14.	Tennessee	8-1-0	John Barnhill
15.	Louisiana St	7-2-0	Bernie Moore
16.	Holy Cross	8-1-0	John DeGrosa
17.	Tulsa	8-2-0	Henry Frnka
18.	Georgia	8-2-0	Wally Butts
19.	Wake Forest	4-3-1	Peahead Walker
20.	Columbia	8-1-0	Lou Little

1946

		Record	Coach
1.	Notre Dame	8-0-1	Frank Leahy
2.	Army	9-0-1	Red Blaik
3.	Georgia	10-0-0	Wally Butts
4.	UCLA	10-0-0	B. LaBrucherie
5.	Illinois	7-2-0	Ray Eliot
6.	Michigan	6-2-1	Fritz Crisler
7.	Tennessee	9-1-0	Bob Neyland
8.	Louisiana St	9-1-0	Bernie Moore
9.	N Carolina	8-1-1	Carl Snavely
10.	Rice	8-2-0	Jess Neely
11.	Georgia Tech	8-2-0	Bobby Dodd
12.	Yale	7-1-1	Howard Odell
13.	Pennsylvania	6-2-0	George Munger
14.	Oklahoma	7-3-0	Jim Tatum
15.	Texas	8-2-0	Dana X. Bible
16.	Arkansas	6-3-1	John Barnhill
17.	Tulsa	9-1-0	J.O. Brothers
18.	N Carolina St	8-2-0	Beattie Feathers
19.	Delaware	9-0-0	Bill Murray
20.	Indiana	6-3-0	Bo McMillan

1947

		Record	Coach
1.	Notre Dame	9-0-0	Frank Leahy
2.	#Michigan	9-0-0	Fritz Crisler
3.	SMU	9-0-1	Matty Bell
4.	Penn St	9-0-0	Bob Higgins
5.	Texas	9-1-0	Blair Cherry
6.	Alabama	8-2-0	Red Drew
7.	Pennsylvania	7-0-1	George Munger
8.	USC	7-1-1	Jeff Cravath
9.	N Carolina	8-2-0	Carl Snavely
10.	Georgia Tech	9-1-0	Bobby Dodd
11.	Army	5-2-2	Red Blaik
12.	Kansas	8-0-2	George Sauer
13.	Mississippi	8-2-0	Johnny Vaught
14.	William & Mary	9-1-0	Rube McCray
15.	California	9-1-0	Pappy Waldorf
16.	Oklahoma	7-2-1	Bud Wilkinson
17.	N Carolina St	5-3-1	Beattie Feathers
18.	Rice	6-3-1	Jess Neely
19.	Duke	4-3-2	Wallace Wade
20.	Columbia	7-2-0	Lou Little

#The AP, which had voted Notre Dame No. 1 before the bowl games, took a second vote, giving the title to Michigan after its 49–0 win over Southern Cal in the Rose Bowl.

1948

		Record	Coach
1.	Michigan	9-0-0	Bennie Oosterbaan
2.	Notre Dame	9-0-1	Frank Leahy
3.	N Carolina	9-0-1	Carl Snavely
4.	California	10-0-0	Pappy Waldorf
5.	Oklahoma	9-1-0	Bud Wilkinson
6.	Army	8-0-1	Red Blaik
7.	Northwestern	7-2-0	Bob Voigts
8.	Georgia	9-1-0	Wally Butts
9.	Oregon	9-1-0	Jim Aiken
10.	SMU	8-1-1	Matty Bell
11.	Clemson	10-0-0	Frank Howard
12.	Vanderbilt	8-2-1	Red Sanders
13.	Tulane	9-1-0	Henry Frnka
14.	Michigan St	6-2-2	Biggie Munn
15.	Mississippi	8-1-0	Johnny Vaught
16.	Minnesota	7-2-0	Bernie Bierman
17.	William & Mary	6-2-2	Rube McCray
18.	Penn St	7-1-1	Bob Higgins
19.	Cornell	8-1-0	Lefty James
20.	Wake Forest	6-3-0	Peahead Walker

1949

		Record	Coach
1.	Notre Dame	10-0-0	Frank Leahy
2.	Oklahoma	10-0-0	Bud Wilkinson
3.	California	10-0-0	Pappy Waldorf
4.	Army	9-0-0	Red Blaik
5.	Rice	9-1-0	Jess Neely
6.	Ohio St	6-1-2	Wes Fesler
7.	Michigan	6-2-1	Bennie Oosterbaan
8.	Minnesota	7-2-0	Bernie Bierman
9.	Louisiana St	8-2-0	Gaynell Tinsley
10.	Pacific	11-0-0	Larry Siemering
11.	Kentucky	9-2-0	Bear Bryant
12.	Cornell	8-1-0	Lefty James
13.	Villanova	8-1-0	Jim Leonard
14.	Maryland	8-1-0	Jim Tatum

1949 *(Cont.)*

		Record	Coach
15.	Santa Clara	7-2-1	Len Casanova
16.	N Carolina	7-3-0	Carl Snavely
17.	Tennessee	7-2-1	Bob Neyland
18.	Princeton	6-3-0	Charlie Caldwell
19.	Michigan St	6-3-0	Biggie Munn
20.	Missouri	7-3-0	Don Faurot
	Baylor	8-2-0	Bob Woodruff

1950

		Record	Coach
1.	Oklahoma	10-0-0	Bud Wilkinson
2.	Army	8-1-0	Red Blaik
3.	Texas	9-1-0	Blair Cherry
4.	Tennessee	10-1-0	Bob Neyland
5.	California	9-0-1	Pappy Waldorf
6.	Princeton	9-0-0	Charlie Caldwell
7.	Kentucky	10-1-0	Bear Bryant
8.	Michigan St	8-1-0	Biggie Munn
9.	Michigan	5-3-1	Bennie Oosterhaan
10.	Clemson	8-0-1	Frank Howard
11.	Washington	8-2-0	Howard Odell
12.	Wyoming	9-0-0	Bowden Wyatt
13.	Illinois	7-2-0	Ray Eliot
14.	Ohio St	6-3-0	Wes Fesler
15.	Miami (FL)	9-0-1	Andy Gustafson
16.	Alabama	9-2-0	Red Drew
17.	Nebraska	6-2-1	Bill Glassford
18.	Washington & Lee	8-2-0	George Barclay
19.	Tulsa	9-1-1	J.O. Brothers
20.	Tulane	6-2-1	Henry Frnka

1951

		Record	Coach
1.	Tennessee	10-0-0	Bob Neyland
2.	Michigan St	9-0-0	Biggie Munn
3.	Maryland	9-0-0	Jim Tatum
4.	Illinois	8-0-1	Ray Eliot
5.	Georgia Tech	10-0-1	Bobby Dodd
6.	Princeton	9-0-0	Charlie Caldwell
7.	Stanford	9-1-0	Chuck Taylor
8.	Wisconsin	7-1-1	Ivy Williamson
9.	Baylor	8-1-1	George Sauer
10.	Oklahoma	8-2-0	Bud Wilkinson
11.	Texas Christian	6-4-0	Dutch Meyer
12.	California	8-2-0	Pappy Waldorf
13.	Virginia	8-1-0	Art Guepe
14.	San Francisco	9-0-0	Joe Kuharich
15.	Kentucky	7-4-0	Bear Bryant
16.	Boston University	6-4-0	Buff Donelli
17.	UCLA	5-3-1	Red Sanders
18.	Washington St	7-3-0	Forest Evashevski
19.	Holy Cross	8-2-0	Eddie Anderson
20.	Clemson	7-2-0	Frank Howard

1952

		Record	Coach
1.	Michigan St	9-0-0	Biggie Munn
2.	Georgia Tech	11-0-0	Bobby Dodd
3.	Notre Dame	7-2-1	Frank Leahy
4.	Oklahoma	8-1-1	Bud Wilkinson
5.	USC	9-1-0	Jess Hill
6.	UCLA	8-1-0	Red Sanders
7.	Mississippi	8-0-2	Johnny Vaught

1952 *(Cont.)*

		Record	Coach
8.	Tennessee	8-1-1	Bob Neyland
9.	Alabama	9-2-0	Red Drew
10.	Texas	8-2-0	Ed Price
11.	Wisconsin	6-2-1	Ivy Williamson
12.	Tulsa	8-1-1	J.O. Brothers
13.	Maryland	7-2-0	Jim Tatum
14.	Syracuse	7-2-0	Ben Schwartzwalder
15.	Florida	7-3-0	Bob Woodruff
16.	Duke	8-2-0	Bill Murray
17.	Ohio St	6-3-0	Woody Hayes
18.	Purdue	4-3-2	Stu Holcomb
19.	Princeton	8-1-0	Charlie Caldwell
20.	Kentucky	5-4-2	Bear Bryant

1953

		Record	Coach
1.	Maryland	10-0-0	Jim Tatum
2.	Notre Dame	9-0-1	Frank Leahy
3.	Michigan St	8-1-0	Biggie Munn
4.	Oklahoma	8-1-1	Bud Wilkinson
5.	UCLA	8-1-0	Red Sanders
6.	Rice	8-2-0	Jess Neely
7.	Illinois	7-1-1	Ray Eliot
8.	Georgia Tech	8-2-1	Bobby Dodd
9.	Iowa	5-3-1	Forest Evashevski
10.	W Virginia	8-1-0	Art Lewis
11.	Texas	7-3-0	Ed Price
12.	Texas Tech	10-1-0	DeWitt Weaver
13.	Alabama	6-2-3	Red Drew
14.	Army	7-1-1	Red Blaik
15.	Wisconsin	6-2-1	Ivy Williamson
16.	Kentucky	7-2-1	Bear Bryant
17.	Auburn	7-2-1	Shug Jordan
18.	Duke	7-2-1	Bill Murray
19.	Stanford	6-3-1	Chuck Taylor
20.	Michigan	6-3-0	Bennie Oosterbaan

1954

		Record	Coach
1.	Ohio St	9-0-0	Woody Hayes
2.	#UCLA	9-0-0	Red Sanders
3.	Oklahoma	10-0-0	Bud Wilkinson
4.	Notre Dame	9-1-0	Terry Brennan
5.	Navy	7-2-0	Eddie Erdelatz
6.	Mississippi	9-1-0	Johnny Vaught
7.	Army	7-2-0	Red Blaik
8.	Maryland	7-2-1	Jim Tatum
9.	Wisconsin	7-2-0	Ivy Williamson
10.	Arkansas	8-2-0	Bowden Wyatt
11.	Miami (FL)	8-1-0	Andy Gustafson
12.	W Virginia	8-1-0	Art Lewis
13.	Auburn	7-3-0	Shug Jordan
14.	Duke	7-2-1	Bill Murray
15.	Michigan	6-3-0	Bennie Oosterbaan
16.	Virginia Tech	8-0-1	Frank Moseley
17.	USC	8-3-0	Jess Hill
18.	Baylor	7-3-0	George Sauer
19.	Rice	7-3-0	Jess Neely
20.	Penn St	7-2-0	Rip Engle

#Selected No. 1 by UP.

1955

		Record	Coach
1.	Oklahoma	10-0-0	Bud Wilkinson
2.	Michigan St	8-1-0	Duffy Daugherty
3.	Maryland	10-0-0	Jim Tatum
4.	UCLA	9-1-0	Red Sanders
5.	Ohio St	7-2-0	Woody Hayes
6.	Texas Christian	9-1-0	Abe Martin
7.	Georgia Tech	8-1-1	Bobby Dodd
8.	Auburn	8-1-1	Shug Jordan
9.	Notre Dame	8-2-0	Terry Brennan
10.	Mississippi	9-1-0	Johnny Vaught
11.	Pittsburgh	7-3-0	John Michelosen
12.	Michigan	7-2-0	Bennie Oosterbaan
13.	USC	6-4-0	Jess Hill
14.	Miami (FL)	6-3-0	Andy Gustafson
15.	Miami (OH)	9-0-0	Ara Parseghian
16.	Stanford	6-3-1	Chuck Taylor
17.	Texas A&M	7-2-1	Bear Bryant
18.	Navy	6-2-1	Eddie Erdelatz
19.	W Virginia	8-2-0	Art Lewis
20.	Army	6-3-0	Red Blaik

1956

		Record	Coach
1.	Oklahoma	10-0-0	Bud Wilkinson
2.	Tennessee	10-0-0	Bowden Wyatt
3.	Iowa	8-1-0	Forest Evashevski
4.	Georgia Tech	9-1-0	Bobby Dodd
5.	Texas A&M	9-0-1	Bear Bryant
6.	Miami (FL)	8-1-1	Andy Gustafson
7.	Michigan	7-2-0	Bennie Oosterbaan
8.	Syracuse	7-1-0	Ben Schwartzwalder
9.	Michigan St	7-2-0	Duffy Daugherty
10.	Oregon St	7-2-1	Tommy Prothro
11.	Baylor	8-2-0	Sam Boyd
12.	Minnesota	6-1-2	Murray Warmath
13.	Pittsburgh	7-2-1	John Michelosen
14.	Texas Christian	7-3-0	Abe Martin
15.	Ohio St	6-3-0	Woody Hayes
16.	Navy	6-1-2	Eddie Erdelatz
17.	Geo Washington	7-1-1	Gene Sherman
18.	USC	8-2-0	Jess Hill
19.	Clemson	7-1-2	Frank Howard
20.	Colorado	7-2-1	Dallas Ward
	Penn St	6-2-1	Rip Engle

1957

		Record	Coach
1.	Auburn	10-0-0	Shug Jordan
2.	#Ohio St	8-1-0	Woody Hayes
3.	Michigan St	8-1-0	Duffy Daugherty
4.	Oklahoma	9-1-0	Bud Wilkinson
5.	Navy	8-1-1	Eddie Erdelatz
6.	Iowa	7-1-1	Forest Evashevski
7.	Mississippi	8-1-1	Johnny Vaught
8.	Rice	7-3-0	Jess Neely
9.	Texas A&M	8-2-0	Bear Bryant
10.	Notre Dame	7-3-0	Terry Brennan
11.	Texas	6-3-1	Darrell Royal
12.	Arizona St	10-0-0	Dan Devine
13.	Tennessee	7-3-0	Bowden Wyatt
14.	Mississippi St	6-2-1	Wade Walker
15.	N Carolina St	7-1-2	Earle Edwards
16.	Duke	6-2-2	Bill Murray

1957 *(Cont.)*

		Record	Coach
17.	Florida	6-2-1	Bob Woodruff
18.	Army	7-2-0	Red Blaik
19.	Wisconsin	6-3-0	Milt Brunt
20.	VMI	9-0-1	John McKenna

#Selected No. 1 by UP.

1958

		Record	Coach
1.	Louisiana St	10-0-0	Paul Dietzel
2.	Iowa	7-1-1	Forest Evashevski
3.	Army	8-0-1	Red Blaik
4.	Auburn	9-0-1	Shug Jordan
5.	Oklahoma	9-1-0	Bud Wilkinson
6.	Air Force	9-0-1	Ben Martin
7.	Wisconsin	7-1-1	Milt Bruhn
8.	Ohio St	6-1-2	Woody Hayes
9.	Syracuse	8-1-0	Ben Schwartzwalder
10.	Texas Christian	8-2-0	Abe Martin
11.	Mississippi	8-2-0	Johnny Vaught
12.	Clemson	8-2-0	Frank Howard
13.	Purdue	6-1-2	Jack Mollenkopf
14.	Florida	6-3-1	Bob Woodruff
15.	S Carolina	7-3-0	Warren Giese
16.	California	7-3-0	Pete Elliott
17.	Notre Dame	6-4-0	Terry Brennan
18.	SMU	6-4-0	Bill Meek
19.	Oklahoma St	7-3-0	Cliff Speegle
20.	Rutgers	8-1-0	John Stiegman

1959

		Record	Coach
1.	Syracuse	10-0-0	Ben Schwartzwalder
2.	Mississippi	9-1-0	Johnny Vaught
3.	Louisiana St	9-1-0	Paul Dietzel
4.	Texas	9-1-0	Darrell Royal
5.	Georgia	9-1-0	Wally Butts
6.	Wisconsin	7-2-0	Milt Bruhn
7.	Texas Christian	8-2-0	Abe Martin
8.	Washington	9-1-0	Jim Owens
9.	Arkansas	8-2-0	Frank Broyles
10.	Alabama	7-1-2	Bear Bryant
11.	Clemson	8-2-0	Frank Howard
12.	Penn St	8-2-0	Rip Engle
13.	Illinois	5-3-1	Ray Eliot
14.	USC	8-2-0	Don Clark
15.	Oklahoma	7-3-0	Bud Wilkinson
16.	Wyoming	9-1-0	Bob Devaney
17.	Notre Dame	5-5-0	Joe Kuharich
18.	Missouri	6-4-0	Dan Devine
19.	Florida	5-4-1	Bob Woodruff
20.	Pittsburgh	6-4-0	John Michelosen

1960

		Record	Coach
1.	Minnesota	8-1-0	Murray Warmath
2.	Mississippi	9-0-1	Johnny Vaught
3.	Iowa	8-1-0	Forest Evashevski
4.	Navy	9-1-0	Wayne Hardin
5.	Missouri	9-1-0	Dan Devine
6.	Washington	9-1-0	Jim Owens
7.	Arkansas	8-2-0	Frank Broyles
8.	Ohio St	7-2-0	Woody Hayes
9.	Alabama	8-1-1	Bear Bryant

1960 *(Cont.)*

		Record	Coach
10.	Duke	7-3-0	Bill Murray
11.	Kansas	7-2-1	Jack Mitchell
12.	Baylor	8-2-0	John Bridgers
13.	Auburn	8-2-0	Shug Jordan
14.	Yale	9-0-0	Jordan Oliver
15.	Michigan St	6-2-1	Duffy Daugherty
16.	Penn St	6-3-0	Rip Engle
17.	New Mexico St	10-0-0	Warren Woodson
18.	Florida	8-2-0	Ray Graves
19.	Syracuse	7-2-0	Ben Schwartzwalder
	Purdue	4-4-1	Jack Mollenkopf

1961

		Record	Coach
1.	Alabama	10-0-0	Bear Bryant
2.	Ohio St	8-0-1	Woody Hayes
3.	Texas	9-1-0	Darrell Royal
4.	Louisiana St	9-1-0	Paul Dietzel
5.	Mississippi	9-1-0	Johnny Vaught
6.	Minnesota	7-2-0	Murray Warmath
7.	Colorado	9-1-0	Sonny Grandelius
8.	Michigan St	7-2-0	Duffy Daugherty
9.	Arkansas	8-2-0	Frank Broyles
10.	Utah St	9-0-1	John Ralston
11.	Missouri	7-2-1	Dan Devine
12.	Purdue	6-3-0	Jack Mollenkopf
13.	Georgia Tech	7-3-0	Bobby Dodd
14.	Syracuse	7-3-0	Ben Schwartzwalder
15.	Rutgers	9-0-0	John Bateman
16.	UCLA	7-3-0	Bill Barnes
17.	Rice	7-3-0	Jess Neely
	Penn St	7-3-0	Rip Engle
	Arizona	8-1-1	Jim LaRue
20.	Duke	7-3-0	Bill Murray

1962

		Record	Coach
1.	USC	10-0-0	John McKay
2.	Wisconsin	8-1-0	Milt Bruhn
3.	Mississippi	9-0-0	Johnny Vaught
4.	Texas	9-0-1	Darrell Royal
5.	Alabama	9-1-0	Bear Bryant
6.	Arkansas	9-1-0	Frank Broyles
7.	Louisiana St	8-1-1	Charlie McClendon
8.	Oklahoma	8-2-0	Bud Wilkinson
9.	Penn St	9-1-0	Rip Engle
10.	Minnesota	6-2-1	Murray Warmath
11–20: UPI			
11.	Georgia Tech	7-2-1	Bobby Dodd
12.	Missouri	7-1-2	Dan Devine
13.	Ohio St	6-3-0	Woody Hayes
14.	Duke	8-2-0	Bill Murray
	Washington	7-1-2	Jim Owens
16.	Northwestern	7-2-0	Ara Parseghian
	Oregon St	8-2-0	Tommy Prothro
18.	Arizona St	7-2-1	Frank Kush
	Miami (FL)	7-3-0	Andy Gustafson
	Illinois	2-7-0	Pete Elliott

1963

		Record	Coach
1.	Texas	10-0-0	Darrell Royal
2.	Navy	9-1-0	Wayne Hardin
3.	Illinois	7-1-1	Pete Elliott

1963 *(Cont.)*

		Record	Coach
4.	Pittsburgh	9-1-0	John Michelosen
5.	Auburn	9-1-0	Shug Jordan
6.	Nebraska	9-1-0	Bob Devaney
7.	Mississippi	7-0-2	Johnny Vaught
8.	Alabama	8-2-0	Bear Bryant
9.	Oklahoma	8-2-0	Bud Wilkinson
10.	Michigan St	6-2-1	Duffy Daugherty

11–20: UPI

		Record	Coach
11.	Mississippi St	6-2-2	Paul Davis
12.	Syracuse	8-2-0	Ben Schwartzwalder
13.	Arizona St	8-1-0	Frank Kush
14.	Memphis St	9-0-1	Billy J. Murphy
15.	Washington	6-4-0	Jim Owens
16.	Penn St	7-3-0	Rip Engle
	USC	7-3-0	John McKay
	Missouri	7-3-0	Dan Devine
19.	N Carolina	8-2-0	Jim Hickey
20.	Baylor	7-3-0	John Bridgers

1964

		Record	Coach
1.	Alabama	10-0-0	Bear Bryant
2.	Arkansas	10-0-0	Frank Broyles
3.	Notre Dame	9-1-0	Ara Parseghian
4.	Michigan	8-1-0	Bump Elliott
5.	Texas	9-1-0	Darrell Royal
6.	Nebraska	9-1-0	Bob Devaney
7.	Louisiana St	7-2-1	Charlie McClendon
8.	Oregon St	8-2-0	Tommy Prothro
9.	Ohio St	7-2-0	Woody Hayes
10.	USC	7-3-0	John McKay

11–20: UPI

		Record	Coach
11.	Florida St	8-1-1	Bill Peterson
12.	Syracuse	7-3-0	Ben Schwartzwalder
13.	Princeton	9-0-0	Dick Colman
14.	Penn St	6-4-0	Rip Engle
	Utah	8-2-0	Ray Nagel
16.	Illinois	6-3-0	Pete Elliott
	New Mexico	9-2-0	Bill Weeks
18.	Tulsa	8-2-0	Glenn Dobbs
19.	Missouri	6-3-1	Dan Devine
20.	Mississippi	5-4-1	Johnny Vaught
	Michigan St	4-5-1	Duffy Daugherty

1965

		Record	Coach
1.	Alabama	9-1-1	Bear Bryant
2.	#Michigan St	10-1-0	Duffy Daugherty
3.	Arkansas	10-1-0	Frank Broyles
4.	UCLA	8-2-1	Tommy Prothro
5.	Nebraska	10-1-0	Bob Devaney
6.	Missouri	8-2-1	Dan Devine
7.	Tennessee	8-1-2	Doug Dickey
8.	Louisiana St	8-3-0	Charlie McClendon
9.	Notre Dame	7-2-1	Ara Parseghian
10.	USC	7-2-1	John McKay

11–20: UPI

		Record	Coach
11.	Texas Tech	8-2-0	J.T. King
12.	Ohio St	7-2-0	Woody Hayes
13.	Florida	7-3-0	Ray Graves
14.	Purdue	7-2-1	Jack Mollenkopf
15.	Georgia	6-4-0	Vince Dooley
16.	Tulsa	8-2-0	Glenn Dobbs
17.	Mississippi	6-4-0	Johnny Vaught

1965 *(Cont.)*

		Record	Coach
18.	Kentucky	6-4-0	Charlie Bradshaw
19	Syracuse	7-3-0	Ben Schwartzwalder
20.	Colorado	6-2-2	Eddie Crowder

#Selected No. 1 by UPI.

1966*

		Record	Coach
1.	Notre Dame	9-0-1	Ara Parseghian
2.	Michigan St	9-0-1	Duffy Daugherty
3.	Alabama	10-0-0	Bear Bryant
4.	Georgia	9-1-0	Vince Dooley
5.	UCLA	9-1-0	Tommy Prothro
6.	Nebraska	9-1-0	Bob Devaney
7.	Purdue	8-2-0	Jack Mollenkopf
8.	Georgia Tech	9-1-0	Bobby Dodd
9.	Miami (FL)	7-2-1	Charlie Tate
10.	SMU	8-2-0	Hayden Fry

11–20: UPI

		Record	Coach
11.	Florida	8-2-0	Ray Graves
12.	Mississippi	8-2-0	Johnny Vaught
13.	Arkansas	8-2-0	Frank Broyles
14.	Tennessee	7-3-0	Doug Dickey
15.	Wyoming	9-1-0	Lloyd Eaton
16.	Syracuse	8-2-0	Ben Schwartzwalder
17.	Houston	8-2-0	Bill Yeoman
18.	USC	7-3-0	John McKay
19.	Oregon St	7-3-0	Dee Andros
20.	Virginia Tech	8-1-1	Jerry Claiborne

1967*

		Record	Coach
1.	USC	9-1-0	John McKay
2.	Tennessee	9-1-0	Doug Dickey
3.	Oklahoma	9-1-0	Chuck Fairbanks
4.	Indiana	9-1-0	John Pont
5.	Notre Dame	8-2-0	Ara Parseghian
6.	Wyoming	10-0-0	Lloyd Eaton
7.	Oregon St	7-2-1	Dee Andros
8.	Alabama	8-1-1	Bear Bryant
9.	Purdue	8-2-0	Jack Mollenkopf
10.	Penn St	8-2-0	Joe Paterno

11–20: UPI†

		Record	Coach
11.	UCLA	7-2-1	Tommy Prothro
12.	Syracuse	8-2-0	Ben Schwartzwalder
13.	Colorado	8-2-0	Eddie Crowder
14.	Minnesota	8-2-0	Murray Warmath
15.	Florida St	7-2-1	Bill Peterson
16.	Miami (FL)	7-3-0	Charlie Tate
17.	N Carolina St	8-2-0	Earle Edwards
18.	Georgia	7-3-0	Vince Dooley
19.	Houston	9-2-0	Bill Yeoman
20.	Arizona St	8-2-0	Frank Kush

†UPI ranked Penn St 11th and did not rank Alabama, which was on probation.

1968

		Record	Coach
1.	Ohio St	10-0-0	Woody Hayes
2.	Penn St	11-0-0	Joe Paterno
3.	Texas	9-1-1	Darrell Royal
4.	USC	9-1-1	John McKay
5.	Notre Dame	7-2-1	Ara Parseghian

1968 *(Cont.)*

		Record	Coach
6.	Arkansas	10-1-0	Frank Broyles
7.	Kansas	9-2-0	Pepper Rodgers
8.	Georgia	8-1-2	Vince Dooley
9.	Missouri	8-3-0	Dan Devine
10.	Purdue	8-2-0	Jack Mollenkopf
11.	Oklahoma	7-4-0	Chuck Fairbanks
12.	Michigan	8-2-0	Bump Elliott
13.	Tennessee	8-2-1	Doug Dickey
14.	SMU	8-3-0	Hayden Fry
15.	Oregon St	7-3-0	Dee Andros
16.	Auburn	7-4-0	Shug Jordan
17.	Alabama	8-3-0	Bear Bryant
18.	Houston	6-2-2	Bill Yeoman
19.	Louisiana St	8-3-0	Charlie McClendon
20.	Ohio	10-1-0	Bill Hess

1969

		Record	Coach
1.	Texas	11-0-0	Darrell Royal
2.	Penn St	11-0-0	Joe Paterno
3.	USC	10-0-1	John McKay
4.	Ohio St	8-1-0	Woody Hayes
5.	Notre Dame	8-2-1	Ara Parseghian
6.	Missouri	9-2-0	Dan Devine
7.	Arkansas	9-2-0	Frank Broyles
8.	Mississippi	8-3-0	Johnny Vaught
9.	Michigan	8-3-0	Bo Schembechler
10.	Louisiana St	9-1-0	Charlie McClendon
11.	Nebraska	9-2-0	Bob Devaney
12.	Houston	9-2-0	Bill Yeoman
13.	UCLA	8-1-1	Tommy Prothro
14.	Florida	9-1-1	Ray Graves
15.	Tennessee	9-2-0	Doug Dickey
16.	Colorado	8-3-0	Eddie Crowder
17.	W Virginia	10-0-1	Jim Carlen
18.	Purdue	8-2-0	Jack Mollenkopf
19.	Stanford	7-2-1	John Ralston
20.	Auburn	8-3-0	Shug Jordan

1970

		Record	Coach
1.	Nebraska	11-0-1	Bob Devaney
2.	Notre Dame	10-1-0	Ara Parseghian
3.	#Texas	10-1-0	Darrell Royal
4.	Tennessee	11-0-1	Bill Battle
5.	Ohio St	9-1-0	Woody Hayes
6.	Arizona St	11-0-0	Frank Kush
7.	Louisiana St	9-3-0	Charlie McClendon
8.	Stanford	9-3-0	John Ralston
9.	Michigan	9-1-0	Bo Schembechler
10.	Auburn	9-2-0	Shug Jordan
11.	Arkansas	9-2-0	Frank Broyles
12.	Toledo	12-0-0	Frank Lauterbur
13.	Georgia Tech	9-3-0	Bud Carson
14.	Dartmouth	9-0-0	Bob Blackman
15.	USC	6-4-1	John McKay
16.	Air Force	9-3-0	Ben Martin
17.	Tulane	8-4-0	Jim Pittman
18.	Penn St	7-3-0	Joe Paterno
19.	Houston	8-3-0	Bill Yeoman
20.	Oklahoma	7-4-1	Chuck Fairbanks
	Mississippi	7-4-0	Johnny Vaught

#Selected No. 1 by UPI.

1971

		Record	Coach
1.	Nebraska	13-0-0	Bob Devaney
2.	Oklahoma	11-1-0	Chuck Fairbanks
3.	Colorado	10-2-0	Eddie Crowder
4.	Alabama	11-1-0	Bear Bryant
5.	Penn St	11-1-0	Joe Paterno
6.	Michigan	11-1-0	Bo Schembechler
7.	Georgia	11-1-0	Vince Dooley
8.	Arizona St	11-1-0	Frank Kush
9.	Tennessee	10-2-0	Bill Battle
10.	Stanford	9-3-0	John Ralston
11.	Louisiana St	9-3-0	Charlie McClendon
12.	Auburn	9-2-0	Shug Jordan
13.	Notre Dame	8-2-0	Ara Parseghian
14.	Toledo	12-0-0	John Murphy
15.	Mississippi	10-2-0	Billy Kinard
16.	Arkansas	8-3-1	Frank Broyles
17.	Houston	9-3-0	Bill Yeoman
18.	Texas	8-3-0	Darrell Royal
19.	Washington	8-3-0	Jim Owens
20.	USC	6-4-1	John McKay

1972

		Record	Coach
1.	USC	12-0-0	John McKay
2.	Oklahoma	11-1-0	Chuck Fairbanks
3.	Texas	10-1-0	Darrell Royal
4.	Nebraska	9-2-1	Bob Devaney
5.	Auburn	10-1-0	Shug Jordan
6.	Michigan	10-1-0	Bo Schembechler
7.	Alabama	10-2-0	Bear Bryant
8.	Tennessee	10-2-0	Bill Battle
9.	Ohio St	9-2-0	Woody Hayes
10.	Penn St	10-2-0	Joe Paterno
11.	Louisiana St	9-2-1	Charlie McClendon
12.	N Carolina	11-1-0	Bill Dooley
13.	Arizona St	10-2-0	Frank Kush
14.	Notre Dame	8-3-0	Ara Parseghian
15.	UCLA	8-3-0	Pepper Rodgers
16.	Colorado	8-4-0	Eddie Crowder
17.	N Carolina St	8-3-1	Lou Holtz
18.	Louisville	9-1-0	Lee Corso
19.	Washington St	7-4-0	Jim Sweeney
20.	Georgia Tech	7-4-1	Bill Fulch

1973

		Record	Coach
1.	Notre Dame	11-0-0	Ara Parseghian
2.	Ohio St	10-0-1	Woody Hayes
3.	Oklahoma	10-0-1	Barry Switzer
4.	#Alabama	11-1-0	Bear Bryant
5.	Penn St	12-0-0	Joe Paterno
6.	Michigan	10-0-1	Bo Schembechler
7.	Nebraska	9-2-1	Tom Osborne
8.	USC	9-2-1	John McKay
9.	Arizona St	11-1-0	Frank Kush
	Houston	11-1-0	Bill Yeoman
11.	Texas Tech	11-1-0	Jim Carlen
12.	UCLA	9-2-0	Pepper Rodgers
13.	Louisiana St	9-3-0	Charlie McClendon
14.	Texas	8-3-0	Darrell Royal
15.	Miami (OH)	11-0-0	Bill Mallory
16.	N Carolina St	9-3-0	Lou Holtz
17.	Missouri	8-4-0	Al Onofrio
18.	Kansas	7-4-1	Don Fambrough

1973 *(Cont.)*

		Record	Coach
19.	Tennessee	8-4-0	Bill Battle
20.	Maryland	8-4-0	Jerry Claiborne
	Tulane	9-3-0	Bennie Ellender

#Selected No. 1 by UPI.

1974

		Record	Coach
1.	Oklahoma	11-0-0	Barry Switzer
2.	#USC	10-1-1	John McKay
3.	Michigan	10-1-0	Bo Schembechler
4.	Ohio St	10-2-0	Woody Hayes
5.	Alabama	11-1-0	Bear Bryant
6.	Notre Dame	10-2-0	Ara Parseghian
7.	Penn St	10-2-0	Joe Paterno
8.	Auburn	10-2-0	Shug Jordan
9.	Nebraska	9-3-0	Tom Osborne
10.	Miami (Ohio)	10-0-1	Dick Crum
11.	N Carolina St	9-2-1	Lou Holtz
12.	Michigan St	7-3-1	Denny Stolz
13.	Maryland	8-4-0	Jerry Claiborne
14.	Baylor	8-4-0	Grant Teaff
15.	Florida	8-4-0	Doug Dickey
16.	Texas A&M	8-3-0	Emory Ballard
17.	Mississippi St	9-3-0	Bob Tyler
	Texas	8-4-0	Darrell Royal
18.	Houston	8-3-1	Bill Yeoman
20.	Tennessee	7-3-2	Bill Battle

#Selected No. 1 by UPI

1975

		Record	Coach
1.	Oklahoma	11-1-0	Barry Switzer
2.	Arizona St	12-0-0	Frank Kush
3.	Alabama	11-1-0	Bear Bryant
4.	Ohio St	11-1-0	Woody Hayes
5.	UCLA	9-2-1	Dick Vermeil
6.	Texas	10-2-0	Darrell Royal
7.	Arkansas	10-2-0	Frank Broyles
8.	Michigan	8-2-2	Bo Schembechler
9.	Nebraska	10-2-0	Tom Osborne
10.	Penn St	9-3-0	Joe Paterno
11.	Texas A&M	10-2-0	Emory Bellard
12.	Miami (OH)	11-1-0	Dick Crum
13.	Maryland	9-2-1	Jerry Claiborne
14.	California	8-3-0	Mike White
15.	Pittsburgh	8-4-0	Johnny Majors
16.	Colorado	9-3-0	Bill Mallory
17.	USC	8-4-0	John McKay
18.	Arizona	9-2-0	Jim Young
19.	Georgia	9-3-0	Vince Dooley
20.	W Virginia	9-3-0	Bobby Bowden

1976

		Record	Coach
1.	Pittsburgh	12-0-0	Johnny Majors
2.	USC	11-1-0	John Robinson
3.	Michigan	10-2-0	Bo Schembechler
4.	Houston	10-2-0	Bill Yeoman
5.	Oklahoma	9-2-1	Barry Switzer
6.	Ohio St	9-2-1	Woody Hayes
7.	Texas A&M	10-2-0	Emory Bellard
8.	Maryland	11-1-0	Jerry Claiborne

1976 *(Cont.)*

		Record	Coach
9.	Nebraska	9-3-1	Tom Osborne
10.	Georgia	10-2-0	Vince Dooley
11.	Alabama	9-3-0	Bear Bryant
12.	Notre Dame	9-3-0	Dan Devine
13.	Texas Tech	10-2-0	Steve Sloan
14.	Oklahoma St	9-3-0	Jim Stanley
15.	UCLA	9-2-1	Terry Donahue
16.	Colorado	8-4-0	Bill Mallory
17.	Rutgers	11-0-0	Frank Burns
18.	Kentucky	9-3-0	Fran Curci
19.	Iowa St	8-3-0	Earle Bruce
20.	Mississippi St	9-2-0	Bob Tyler

1977

		Record	Coach
1.	Notre Dame	11-1-0	Dan Devine
2.	Alabama	11-1-0	Bear Bryant
3.	Arkansas	11-1-0	Lou Holtz
4.	Texas	11-1-0	Fred Akers
5.	Penn St	11-1-0	Joe Paterno
6.	Kentucky	10-1-0	Fran Curci
7.	Oklahoma	10-2-0	Barry Switzer
8.	Pittsburgh	9-2-1	Jackie Sherrill
9.	Michigan	10-2-0	Bo Schembechler
10.	Washington	10-2-0	Don James
11.	Ohio St	9-3-0	Woody Hayes
12.	Nebraska	9-3-0	Tom Osborne
13.	USC	8-4-0	John Robinson
14.	Florida St	10-2-0	Bobby Bowden
15.	Stanford	9-3-0	Bill Walsh
16.	San Diego St	10-1-0	Claude Gilbert
17.	N Carolina	8-3-1	Bill Dooley
18.	Arizona St	9-3-0	Frank Kush
19.	Clemson	8-3-1	Charley Pell
20.	Brigham Young	9-2-0	LaVell Edwards

1978

		Record	Coach
1.	Alabama	11-1-0	Bear Bryant
2.	#USC	12-1-0	John Robinson
3.	Oklahoma	11-1-0	Barry Switzer
4.	Penn St	11-1-0	Joe Paterno
5.	Michigan	10-2-0	Bo Schembechler
6.	Clemson	11-1-0	Charley Pell
7.	Notre Dame	9-3-0	Dan Devine
8.	Nebraska	9-3-0	Tom Osborne
9.	Texas	9-3-0	Fred Akers
10.	Houston	9-3-0	Bill Yeoman
11.	Arkansas	9-2-1	Lou Holtz
12.	Michigan St	8-3-0	Darryl Rogers
13.	Purdue	9-2-1	Jim Young
14.	UCLA	8-3-1	Terry Donahue
15.	Missouri	8-4-0	Warren Powers
16.	Georgia	9-2-1	Vince Dooley
17.	Stanford	8-4-0	Bill Walsh
18.	N Carolina St	9-3-0	Bo Rein
19.	Texas A&M	8-4-0	Emory Bellard (4–2)
			Tom Wilson (4–2)
20.	Maryland	9-3-0	Jerry Claiborne

#Selected No. 1 by UPI.

1979

		Record	Coach
1.	Alabama	12-0-0	Bear Bryant
2.	USC	11-0-1	John Robinson
3.	Oklahoma	11-1-0	Barry Switzer
4.	Ohio St	11-1-0	Earle Bruce
5.	Houston	11-1-0	Bill Yeoman
6.	Florida St	11-1-0	Bobby Bowden
7.	Pittsburgh	11-1-0	Jackie Sherrill
8.	Arkansas	10-2-0	Lou Holtz
9.	Nebraska	10-2-0	Tom Osborne
10.	Purdue	10-2-0	Jim Young
11.	Washington	10-1-0	Don James
12.	Texas	9-3-0	Fred Akers
13.	Brigham Young	11-1-0	LaVell Edwards
14.	Baylor	8-4-0	Grant Teaff
15.	N Carolina	8-3-1	Dick Crum
16.	Auburn	8-3-0	Doug Barfield
17.	Temple	10-2-0	Wayne Hardin
18.	Michigan	8-4-0	Bo Schembechler
19.	Indiana	8-4-0	Lee Corso
20.	Penn St	8-4-0	Joe Paterno

1980

		Record	Coach
1.	Georgia	12-0-0	Vince Dooley
2.	Pittsburgh	11-1-0	Jackie Sherrill
3.	Oklahoma	10-2-0	Barry Switzer
4.	Michigan	10-2-0	Bo Schembechler
5.	Florida St	10-2-0	Bobby Bowden
6.	Alabama	10-2-0	Bear Bryant
7.	Nebraska	10-2-0	Tom Osborne
8.	Penn St	10-2-0	Joe Paterno
9.	Notre Dame	9-2-1	Dan Devine
10.	N Carolina	11-1-0	Dick Crum
11.	USC	8-2-1	John Robinson
12.	Brigham Young	12-1-0	LaVell Edwards
13.	UCLA	9-2-0	Terry Donahue
14.	Baylor	10-2-0	Grant Teaff
15.	Ohio St	9-3-0	Earle Bruce
16.	Washington	9-3-0	Don James
17.	Purdue	9-3-0	Jim Young
18.	Miami (FL)	9-3-0	H. Schnellenberger
19.	Mississippi St	9-3-0	Emory Bellard
20.	SMU	8-4-0	Ron Meyer

1981

		Record	Coach
1.	Clemson	12-0-0	Danny Ford
2.	Texas	10-1-1	Fred Akers
3.	Penn St	10-2-0	Joe Paterno
4.	Pittsburgh	11-1-0	Jackie Sherrill
5.	SMU	10-1-0	Ron Meyer
6.	Georgia	10-2-0	Vince Dooley
7.	Alabama	9-2-1	Bear Bryant
8.	Miami (FL)	9-2-0	H. Schnellenberger
9.	N Carolina	10-2-0	Dick Crum
10.	Washington	10-2-0	Don James
11.	Nebraska	9-3-0	Tom Osborne
12.	Michigan	9-3-0	Bo Schembechler
13.	Brigham Young	11-2-0	LaVell Edwards
14.	USC	9-3-0	John Robinson
15.	Ohio St	9-3-0	Earle Bruce
16.	Arizona St	9-2-0	Darryl Rogers
17.	W Virginia	9-3-0	Don Nehlen

1981 *(Cont.)*

		Record	Coach
18.	Iowa	8-4-0	Hayden Fry
19.	Missouri	8-4-0	Warren Powers
20.	Oklahoma	7-4-1	Barry Switzer

1982

		Record	Coach
1.	Penn St	11-1-0	Joe Paterno
2.	SMU	11-0-1	Bobby Collins
3.	Nebraska	12-1-0	Tom Osborne
4.	Georgia	11-1-0	Vince Dooley
5.	UCLA	10-1-1	Terry Donahue
6.	Arizona St	10-2-0	Darryl Rogers
7.	Washington	10-2-0	Don James
8.	Clemson	9-1-1	Danny Ford
9.	Arkansas	9-2-1	Lou Holtz
10.	Pittsburgh	9-3-0	Foge Fazio
11.	Louisiana St	8-3-1	Jerry Stovall
12.	Ohio St	9-3-0	Earle Bruce
13.	Florida St	9-3-0	Bobby Bowden
14.	Auburn	9-3-0	Pat Dye
15.	USC	8-3-0	John Robinson
16.	Oklahoma	8-4-0	Barry Switzer
17.	Texas	9-3-0	Fred Akers
18.	N Carolina	8-4-0	Dick Crum
19.	W Virginia	9-3-0	Don Nehlen
20.	Maryland	8-4-0	Bobby Ross

1983

		Record	Coach
1.	Miami (Fla.)	11-1-0	H. Schnellenberger
2.	Nebraska	12-1-0	Tom Osborne
3.	Auburn	11-1-0	Pat Dye
4.	Georgia	10-1-1	Vince Dooley
5.	Texas	11-1-0	Fred Akers
6.	Florida	9-2-1	Charlie Pell
7.	Brigham Young	11-1-0	LaVell Edwards
8.	Michigan	9-3-0	Bo Schembechler
9.	Ohio St	9-3-0	Earle Bruce
10.	Illinois	10-2-0	Mike White
11.	Clemson	9-1-1	Danny Ford
12.	SMU	10-2-0	Bobby Collins
13.	Air Force	10-2-0	Ken Hatfield
14.	Iowa	9-3-0	Hayden Fry
15.	Alabama	8-4-0	Ray Perkins
16.	W Virginia	9-3-0	Don Nehlen
17.	UCLA	7-4-1	Terry Donahue
18.	Pittsburgh	8-3-1	Foge Fazio
19.	Boston College	9-3-0	Jack Bicknell
20.	E Carolina	8-3-0	Ed Emory

1984

		Record	Coach
1.	Brigham Young	13-0-0	LaVell Edwards
2.	Washington	11-1-0	Don James
3.	Florida	9-1-1	Chas Pell (0-1-1) Galen Hall (9-0)
4.	Nebraska	10-2-0	Tom Osborne
5.	Boston College	10-2-0	Jack Bicknell
6.	Oklahoma	9-2-1	Barry Switzer
7.	Oklahoma St	10-2-0	Pat Jones
8.	SMU	10-2-0	Bobby Collins
9.	UCLA	9-3-0	Terry Donahue

1984 *(Cont.)*

		Record	Coach
10.	USC	10-3-0	Ted Tollner
11.	S Carolina	10-2-0	Joe Morrison
12.	Maryland	9-3-0	Bobby Ross
13.	Ohio St	9-3-0	Earle Bruce
14.	Auburn	9-4-0	Pat Dye
15.	Louisiana St	8-3-1	Bill Arnsparger
16.	Iowa	8-4-1	Hayden Fry
17.	Florida St	7-3-2	Bobby Bowden
18.	Miami (Fla.)	8-5-0	Jimmy Johnson
19.	Kentucky	9-3-0	Jerry Claiborne
20.	Virginia	8-2-2	George Welsh

1985

		Record	Coach
1.	Oklahoma	11-1-0	Barry Switzer
2.	Michigan	10-1-1	Bo Schembechler
3.	Penn St	11-1-0	Joe Paterno
4.	Tennessee	9-1-2	Johnny Majors
5.	Florida	9-1-1	Galen Hall
6.	Texas A&M	10-2-0	Jackie Sherrill
7.	UCLA	9-2-1	Terry Donahue
8.	Air Force	12-1-0	Fisher DeBerry
9.	Miami (Fla.)	10-2-0	Jimmy Johnson
10.	Iowa	10-2-0	Hayden Fry
11.	Nebraska	9-3-0	Tom Osborne
12.	Arkansas	10-2-0	Ken Hatfield
13.	Alabama	9-2-1	Ray Perkins
14.	Ohio St	9-3-0	Earle Bruce
15.	Florida St	9-3-0	Bobby Bowden
16.	Brigham Young	11-3-0	LaVell Edwards
17.	Baylor	9-3-0	Grant Teaff
18.	Maryland	9-3-0	Bobby Ross
19.	Georgia Tech.	9-2-1	Bill Curry
20.	Louisiana St	9-2-1	Bill Arnsparger

1986

		Record	Coach
1.	Penn St	12-0-0	Joe Paterno
2.	Miami (Fla.)	11-1-0	Jimmy Johnson
3.	Oklahoma	11-1-0	Barry Switzer
4.	Arizona St	10-1-1	John Cooper
5.	Nebraska	10-2-0	Tom Osborne
6.	Auburn	10-2-0	Pat Dye
7.	Ohio St	10-3-0	Earle Bruce
8.	Michigan	11-2-0	Bo Schembechler
9.	Alabama	10-3-0	Ray Perkins
10.	Louisiana St	9-3-0	Bill Arnsparger
11.	Arizona	9-3-0	Larry Smith
12.	Baylor	9-3-0	Grant Teaff
13.	Texas A&M	9-3-0	Jackie Sherrill
14.	UCLA	8-3-1	Terry Donahue
15.	Arkansas	9-3-0	Ken Hatfield
16.	Iowa	9-3-0	Hayden Fry
17.	Clemson	8-2-2	Danny Ford
18.	Washington	8-3-1	Don James
19.	Boston College	9-3-0	Jack Bicknell
20.	Virginia Tech.	9-2-1	Bill Dooley

1987

		Record	Coach
1.	Miami (Fla.)	12-0-0	Jimmy Johnson
2.	Florida St	11-1-0	Bobby Bowden
3.	Oklahoma	11-1-0	Barry Switzer
4.	Syracuse	11-0-1	Dick MacPherson
5.	Louisiana St	10-1-1	Mike Archer
6.	Nebraska	10-2-0	Tom Osborne
7.	Auburn	9-1-2	Pat Dye
8.	Michigan St	9-2-1	George Perles
9.	UCLA	10-2-0	Terry Donahue
10.	Texas A&M	10-2-0	Jackie Sherrill
11.	Oklahoma St	10-2-0	Pat Jones
12.	Clemson	10-2-0	Danny Ford
13.	Georgia	9-3-0	Vince Dooley
14.	Tennessee	10-2-1	Johnny Majors
15.	S Carolina	8-4-0	Joe Morrison
16.	Iowa	10-3-0	Hayden Fry
17.	Notre Dame	8-4-0	Lou Holtz
18.	USC	8-4-0	Larry Smith
19.	Michigan	8-4-0	Bo Schembechler
20.	Arizona St	7-4-1	John Cooper

1988

		Record	Coach
1.	Notre Dame	12-0-0	Lou Holtz
2.	Miami (Fla.)	11-1-0	Jimmy Johnson
3.	Florida St	11-1-0	Bobby Bowden
4.	Michigan	9-2-1	Bo Schembechler
5.	W Virginia	11-1-0	Don Nehlen
6.	UCLA	10-2-0	Terry Donahue
7.	USC	10-2-0	Larry Smith
8.	Auburn	10-2-0	Pat Dye
9.	Clemson	10-2-0	Danny Ford
10.	Nebraska	11-2-0	Tom Osborne
11.	Oklahoma St	10-2-0	Pat Jones
12.	Arkansas	10-2-0	Ken Hatfield
13.	Syracuse	10-2-0	Dick MacPherson
14.	Oklahoma	9-3-0	Barry Switzer
15.	Georgia	9-3-0	Vince Dooley
16.	Washington St	9-3-0	Dennis Erickson
17.	Alabama	9-3-0	Bill Curry
18.	Houston	9-3-0	Jack Pardee
19.	Louisiana St	8-4-0	Mike Archer
20.	Indiana	8-3-1	Bill Mallor

†1989

		Record	Coach
1.	Miami (Fla.)	11-1-0	Dennis Erickson
2.	Notre Dame	12-1-0	Lou Holtz
3.	Florida St	10-2-0	Bobby Bowden
4.	Colorado	11-1-0	Bill McCartney
5.	Tennessee	11-1-0	Johnny Majors
6.	Auburn	10-2-0	Pat Dye
7.	Michigan	10-2-0	Bo Schembechler
8.	USC	9-2-1	Larry Smith
9.	Alabama	10-2-0	Bill Curry
10.	Illinois	10-2-0	John Mackovic
11.	Nebraska	10-2-0	Tom Osborne
12.	Clemson	10-2-0	Danny Ford
13.	Arkansas	10-2-0	Ken Hatfield
14.	Houston	9-2-0	Jack Pardee
15.	Penn St	8-3-1	Joe Paterno
16.	Michigan St	8-4-0	George Perles
17.	Pittsburgh	8-3-1	Mike Gottfried
18.	Virginia	10-3-0	George Welsh

†1989 *(Cont.)*

		Record	Coach
19.	Texas Tech	9-3-0	Spike Dykes
20.	Texas A&M	8-4-0	R.C. Slocum
21.	W Virginia	8-3-1	Don Nehlen
22.	Brigham Young	10-3-0	LaVell Edwards
23.	Washington	8-4-0	Don James
24.	Ohio St	8-4-0	John Cooper
25.	Arizona	8-4-0	Dick Tomey

1990

		Record	Coach
1.	Colorado	11-1-1	Bill McCartney
2.	#Ga. Tech (UPI)	11-0-1	Bobby Ross
3.	Miami (Fla.)	10-2-0	Dennis Erickson
4.	Florida St	10-2-0	Bobby Bowden
5.	Washington	10-2-0	Don James
6.	Notre Dame	9-3-0	Lou Holtz
7.	Michigan	9-3-0	Gary Moeller
8.	Tennessee	9-2-2	Johnny Majors
9.	Clemson	10-2-0	Ken Hatfield
10.	Houston	10-1-0	John Jenkins
11.	Penn St	9-3-0	Joe Paterno
12.	Texas	10-2-0	David McWilliams
13.	Florida	9-2-0	Steve Spurrier
14.	Louisville	10-1-1	H. Schnellenberger
15.	Texas A&M	9-3-1	R.C. Slocum
16.	Michigan St	8-3-1	George Perles
17.	Oklahoma	8-3-0	Gary Gibbs
18.	Iowa	8-4-0	Hayden Fry
19.	Auburn	8-3-1	Pat Dye
20.	USC I.	8-4-1	Larry Smith
21.	Mississippi	9-3-0	Billy Brewer
22.	Brigham Young	10-3-0	LaVell Edwards
23.	Virginia	8-4-0	George Wells
24.	Nebraska	9-3-0	Tom Osborne
25.	Illinois	8-4-0	John Mackovic

1991

		Record	Coach
1.	Miami (Fla.)	12-0-0	Dennis Erickson
2.	#Washington	12-0-0	Don James
3.	Penn St	11-2-0	Joe Paterno
4.	Florida St	11-2-0	Bobby Bowden
5.	Alabama	11-1-0	Gene Stallings
6.	Michigan	10-2-0	Gary Moeller
7.	Florida	10-2-0	Steve Spurrier
8.	California	10-2-0	Bruce Snyder
9.	E Carolina	11-1-0	Bill Lewis
10.	Iowa	10-1-1	Hayden Fry
11.	Syracuse	10-2-0	Paul Pasqualoni
12.	Texas A&M	10-2-0	R.C. Slocum
13.	Notre Dame	10-3-0	Lou Holtz
14.	Tennessee	9-3-0	Johnny Majors
15.	Nebraska	9-2-1	Tom Osborne
16.	Oklahoma	9-3-0	Gary Gibbs
17.	Georgia	9-3-0	Ray Goff
18.	Clemson	9-2-1	Ken Hatfield
19.	UCLA	9-3-0	Terry Donahue
20.	Colorado	8-3-1	Bill McCartney
21.	Tulsa	10-2-0	David Rader
22.	Stanford	8-4-0	Dennis Green
23.	Brigham Young	8-3-2	LaVell Edwards
24.	N Carolina St.	9-3-0	Dick Sheridan
25.	Air Force	10-3-0	Fisher DeBerry

1992

		Record	Coach
1.	Alabama	13-0-0	Gene Stallings
2.	Florida St	11-1-0	Bobby Bowden
3.	Miami	11-1-0	Dennis Erickson
4.	Notre Dame	10-1-1	Lou Holtz
5.	Michigan	9-0-3	Gary Moeller
6.	Syracuse	10-2-0	Paul Pasqualoni
7.	Texas A&M	12-1-0	R.C. Slocum
8.	Georgia	10-2-0	Ray Goff
9.	Stanford	10-3-0	Bill Walsh
10.	Florida	9-4-0	Steve Spurrier
11.	Washington	9-3-0	Don James
12.	Tennessee	9-3-0	Johnny Majors
13.	Colorado	9-2-1	Bill McCartney
14.	Nebraska	9-3-0	Tom Osborne
15.	Washington St.	9-3-0	Mike Price
16.	Mississippi	9-3-0	Billy Brewer
17.	N Carolina St.	9-3-1	Dick Sheridan
18.	Ohio St	8-3-1	John Cooper
19.	N Carolina	9-3-0	Mack Brown
20.	Hawaii	11-2-0	Bob Wagner
21.	Boston College	8-3-1	Tom Coughlin
22.	Kansas	8-4-0	Glen Mason
23.	Mississippi St	7-5-0	Jackie Sherrill
24.	Fresno St	9-4-0	Jim Sweeney
25.	Wake Forest	8-4-0	Bill Dooley

1993

		Record	Coach
1.	Florida St	12-1-0	Bobby Bowden
2.	Notre Dame	11-1-0	Lou Holtz
3.	Nebraska	11-1-0	Tom Osborne
4.	Auburn	11-0-0	Terry Bowden
5.	Florida	11-2-0	Steve Spurrier
6.	Wisconsin	10-1-1	Barry Alvarez
7.	W Virginia	11-1-0	Don Nehlen
8.	Penn St	10-2-0	Joe Paterno
9.	Texas A&M	10-2-0	R.C. Slocum
10.	Arizona	10-2-0	Dick Tomey
11.	Ohio St	10-1-1	John Cooper
12.	Tennessee	9-2-1	Phil Fulmer
13.	Boston College	9-3-0	Tom Coughlin
14.	Alabama	9-3-1	Gene Stallings
15.	Miami	9-3-0	Dennis Erickson
16.	Colorado	8-3-1	Bill McCartney
17.	Oklahoma	9-3-0	Gary Gibbs
18.	UCLA	8-4-0	Terry Donahue
19.	N Carolina	10-3-0	Mack Brown
20.	Kansas St	9-2-1	Bill Snyder
21.	Michigan	8-4-0	Gary Moeller
22.	Virginia Tech	9-3-0	Frank Beamer
23.	Clemson	9-3-0	Ken Hatfield
24.	Louisville	9-3-0	H. Schnellenberger
25.	California	9-4-0	Keith Gilbertson

1994

		Record	Coach
1.	Nebraska	13-0-0	Tom Osborne
2.	Penn St	12-0-0	Joe Paterno
3.	Colorado	11-1-0	Bill McCartney
4.	Florida St	10-1-1	Bobby Bowden
5.	Alabama	12-1-0	Gene Stallings
6.	Miami (Fla.)	10-2-0	Dennis Erickson
7.	Florida	10-2-1	Steve Spurrier
8.	Texas A&M	10-0-1	R.C. Slocum

#Selected No. 1 by *USA Today*/CNN.

1994 *(Cont.)*

		Record	Coach
9.	Auburn	9-1-1	Terry Bowden
10.	Utah	10-2-0	Ron McBride
11.	Oregon	9-4-0	Rich Brooks
12.	Michigan	8-4-0	Gary Moeller
13.	USC	8-3-1	John Robinson
14.	Ohio St	9-4-0	John Cooper
15.	Virginia	9-3-0	George Welsh
16.	Colorado St	10-2-0	Sonny Lubick
17.	N Carolina St	9-3-0	Mike O'Cain
18.	Brigham Young	10-3-0	LaVell Edwards
19.	Kansas St	9-3-0	Bill Snyder
20.	Arizona	8-4-0	Dick Tomey
21.	Washington St	8-4-0	Mike Price
22.	Tennessee	8-4-0	Phillip Fulmer
23.	Boston College	7-4-1	Dan Henning
24.	Mississippi St	8-4-0	Jackie Sherrill
25.	Texas	8-4-0	John Mackovic

1995

		Record	Coach
1.	Nebraska	12-0-0	Tom Osborne
2.	Florida	12-1-0	Steve Spurrier
3.	Tennessee	11-1-0	Phillip Fulmer
4.	Florida St	10-2-0	Bobby Bowden
5.	Colorado	10-2-0	Rick Neuheisel
6.	Ohio St	11-2-0	John Cooper
7.	Kansas St	10-2-0	Bill Snyder
8.	Northwestern	10-2-0	Gary Barnett
9.	Kansas	10-2-0	Glen Mason
10.	Virginia Tech	10-2-0	Frank Beamer
11.	Notre Dame	9-3-0	Lou Holtz
12.	USC	9-2-1	John Robinson
13.	Penn St	9-3-0	Joe Paterno
14.	Texas	10-2-1	John Mackovic
15.	Texas A&M	9-3-0	S.C. Slocum
16.	Virginia	9-4-0	George Welsh
17.	Michigan	9-4-0	Lloyd Carr
18.	Oregon	9-3-0	Mike Bellotti
19.	Syracuse	9-3-0	Paul Pasqualoni
20.	Miami (Fla.)	8-3-0	Butch Davis
21.	Alabama	8-3-0	Gene Stallings
22.	Auburn	8-4-0	Terry Bowden
23.	Texas Tech	9-3-0	Spike Dykes
24.	Toledo	11-0-1	Gary Pinkel
25.	Iowa	8-4-0	Hayden Fry

1996

		Record*	Coach
1.	Florida	12-1	Steve Spurrier
2.	Ohio St	11-1	John Cooper
3.	Florida St	11-1	Bobby Bowden
4.	Arizona St	11-1	Bruce Snyder
5.	Brigham Young	14-1	LaVell Edwards
6.	Nebraska	11-2	Tom Osborne
7.	Penn St	11-2	Joe Paterno
8.	Colorado	10-2	Rick Neuheisel
9.	Tennessee	10-2	Phillip Fulmer
10.	N Carolina	10-2	Mack Brown
11.	Alabama	10-3	Gene Stallings
12.	Louisiana St	10-2	Gerry DiNardo
13.	Virginia Tech	10-2	Frank Beamer

1996 *(Cont.)*

		Record*	Coach
14.	Miami (Fla.)	9-3	Butch Davis
15.	Northwestern	9-3	Gary Barnett
16.	Washington	9-3	Jim Lambright
17.	Kansas St	9-3	Bill Snyder
18.	Iowa	9-3	Hayden Fry
19.	Notre Dame	8-3	Lou Holtz
20.	Michigan	8-4	Lloyd Carr
21.	Syracuse	9-3	Paul Pasqualoni
22.	Wyoming	10-2	Joe Tiller
23.	Texas	8-5	John Mackovic
24.	Auburn	8-4	Terry Bowden
25.	Army	10-2	Bob Sutton

1997

		Record	Coach
1.	Michigan	12-0	Lloyd Carr
2.	Nebraska	13-0	Tom Osborne
3.	Florida St	11-1	Bobby Bowden
4.	Florida	10-2	Steve Spurrier
5.	UCLA	10-2	Bob Toledo
6.	N Carolina	11-1	Mack Brown
7.	Tennessee	11-2	Phillip Fulmer
8.	Kansas St	11-1	Bill Snyder
9.	Washington St	10-2	Mike Price
10.	Georgia	10-2	Jim Donnan
11.	Auburn	10-3	Terry Bowden
12.	Ohio St	10-3	John Cooper
13.	Louisiana St	9-3	Gerry DiNardo
14.	Arizona St	8-3	Bruce Snyder
15.	Purdue	9-3	Joe Tiller
16.	Penn St	9-3	Joe Paterno
17.	Colorado St	11-2	Sonny Lubick
18.	Washington	8-4	Jim Lambright
19.	Southern Mississippi	9-3	Jeff Bower
20.	Texas A&M	9-4	R. C. Slocum
21.	Syracuse	9-4	Paul Pasqualoni
22.	Mississippi	8-4	Tommy Tuberville
23.	Missouri	7-5	Larry Smith
24.	Oklahoma St	8-4	Bob Simmons
25.	Georgia Tech	7-5	George O'Leary

1998

		Record	Coach
1.	Tennessee	13-0	Phillip Fulmer
2.	Ohio St	11-1	John Cooper
3.	Florida St	11-2	Bobby Bowden
4.	Arizona	12-1	Dick Tomey
5.	Florida	10-2	Steve Spurrier
6.	Wisconsin	11-1	Barry Alvarez
7.	Tulane	12-0	Tommy Bowden
8.	UCLA	10-2	Bob Toledo
9.	Georgia Tech	10-2	George O'Leary
10.	Kansas St	11-2	Bill Snyder
11.	Texas A&M	11-3	R.C. Slocum
12.	Michigan	10-3	Lloyd Carr
13.	Air Force	12-1	Fisher DeBerry
14.	Georgia	9-3	Jim Donnan
15.	Texas	9-3	Mack Brown
16.	Arkansas	9-3	Houston Nutt
17.	Penn St	9-3	Joe Paterno
18.	Virginia	9-3	George Welsh
19.	Nebraska	9-4	Frank Solich
20.	Miami (Fla.)	9-3	Butch Davis

†In 1989 the AP expanded its final poll to 25 teams.
*In 1996 the NCAA introduced overtime to break ties.

1998 *(Cont.)*

		Record	Coach
21.	Missouri	8–4	Larry Smith
22.	Notre Dame	9–3	Bob Davie
23.	Virginia Tech	9–3	Frank Beamer
24.	Purdue	9–4	Joe Tiller
25.	Syracuse	8–4	Paul Pasqualoni

1999

		Record	Coach
1.	Florida St	12–0	Bobby Bowden
2.	Virginia Tech	11–1	Frank Beamer
3.	Nebraska	12–1	Frank Solich
4.	Wisconsin	10–2	Barry Alvarez
5.	Michigan	10–2	Lloyd Carr
6.	Kansas St	11–1	Bill Snyder
7.	Michigan St	10–2	Nick Saban
8.	Alabama	10–3	Mike DuBose
9.	Tennessee	9–3	Phillip Fulmer
10.	Marshall	13–0	Bob Pruett
11.	Penn St	10–3	Joe Paterno
12.	Florida	9–4	Steve Spurrier
13.	Mississippi St	10–2	Jackie Sherrill
14.	Southern Miss	9–3	Jeff Bower
15.	Miami (Fla.)	9–4	Butch Davis
16.	Georgia	8–4	Jim Donnan
17.	Arkansas	8–4	Houston Nutt
18.	Minnesota	8–4	Glen Mason
19.	Oregon	9–3	Mike Bellotti
20.	Georgia Tech	8–4	Goerge O'Leary
21.	Texas	9–5	Mack Brown
22.	Mississippi	8–4	David Cutcliffe
23.	Texas A&M	8–4	R.C. Slocum
24.	Illinois	8–4	Ron Turner
25.	Purdue	7–5	Joe Tiller

2000

		Record	Coach
1.	Oklahoma	13–0	Bob Stoops
2.	Miami (Fla.)	11–1	Butch Davis
3.	Washington	11–1	Rick Neuheisel
4.	Oregon St	11–1	Dennis Erickson
5.	Florida St	11–2	Bobby Bowden
6.	Virginia Tech	11–1	Frank Beamer
7.	Oregon	10–2	Mike Belotti
8.	Nebraska	10–2	Frank Solich
9.	Kansas St	11–3	Bill Snyder
10.	Florida	10–3	Steve Spurrier
11.	Michigan	9–3	Lloyd Carr
12.	Texas	9–3	Mack Brown
13.	Purdue	8–4	Joe Tiller
14.	Colorado St	10–2	Sonny Lubeck
15.	Notre Dame	9–3	Bob Davie
16.	Clemson	9–3	Tommy Bowden
17.	Georgia Tech	9–3	George O'Leary
18.	Auburn	9–4	Tommy Tuberville
19.	S Carolina	8–4	Lou Holtz
20.	Georgia	8–4	Jim Donnan
21.	Texas Christian	10–2	Dennis Franchione
22.	Louisiana State	8–4	Nick Saban
23.	Wisconsin	9–4	Barry Alvarez
24.	Mississippi St	8–4	Jackie Sherrill
25.	Iowa St	9–3	Dan McCarney

2001

		Record	Coach
1.	Miami (Fla.)	12–0	Larry Coker
2.	Oregon	11–1	Mike Belotti
3.	Florida	10–2	Steve Spurrier
4.	Tennessee	11–2	Phillip Fulmer
5.	Texas	11–2	Mack Brown
6.	Oklahoma	11–2	Bob Stoops
7.	Louisiana St	10–3	Nick Saban
8.	Nebraska	11–2	Frank Solich
9.	Colorado	10–3	Gary Barnett
10.	Washington St	10–2	Mike Price
11.	Maryland	10–2	Ralph Friedgen
12.	Illinois	10–2	Ron Turner
13.	S Carolina	9–3	Lou Holtz
14.	Syracuse	10–3	Paul Pasqualoni
15.	Florida St	8–4	Bobby Bowden
16.	Stanford	9–3	Tyrone Willingham
17.	Louisville	11–2	John Smith
18.	Virginia Tech	8–4	Frank Beamer
19.	Washington	8–4	Rick Neuheisel
20.	Michigan	8–4	Lloyd Carr
21.	Boston College	8–4	Tom O'Brien
22.	Georgia	8–4	Mark Richt
23.	Toledo	10–2	Tom Amstutz
24.	Georgia Tech	8–5	George O'Leary
25.	Brigham Young	12–2	Gary Crowton

2002

		Record	Coach
1.	Ohio St	14–0	Jim Tressel
2.	Miami (Fla.)	12–1	Larry Coker
3.	Georgia	13–1	Mark Richt
4.	USC	11–2	Pete Carroll
5.	Oklahoma	12–2	Bob Stoops
6.	Texas	11–2	Mack Brown
7.	Kansas St	11–2	Bill Snyder
8.	Iowa	11–2	Kirk Ferentz
9.	Michigan	10–3	Lloyd Carr
10.	Washington St	10–3	Mike Price
11.	Alabama	10–3	Dennis Franchione
12.	N Carolina St	11–3	Chuck Amato
13.	Maryland	11–3	Ralph Friedgen
14.	Auburn	9–4	Tommy Tuberville
15.	Boise St	12–1	Dan Hawkins
16.	Penn St	9–4	Joe Paterno
17.	Notre Dame	10–3	Tyrone Willingham
18.	Virginia Tech	10–4	Frank Beamer
19.	Pittsburgh	9–4	Walt Harris
20.	Colorado	9–5	Gary Barnett
21.	Florida St	9–5	Bobby Bowden
22.	Viriginia	9–5	Al Groh
23.	Texas Christian	10–2	Gary Patterson
24.	Marshall	11–2	Bob Pruett
25.	W Virginia	9–4	Rich Rodriguez

2003

		Record	Coach
1.	USC	12–1	Pete Carroll
2.	LSU*	13–1	Nick Saban
3.	Oklahoma	12–2	Bob Stoops
4.	Ohio St	11–2	Jim Tressel
5.	Miami (Fla.)	11–2	Larry Coker
6.	Michigan	10–3	Lloyd Carr
7.	Georgia	11–3	Mark Richt
8.	Iowa	10–3	Kirk Ferentz
9.	Washington St	10–3	Bill Doba
10.	Miami (Ohio)	13–1	Terry Hoeppner
11.	Florida St	10–3	Bobby Bowden
12.	Texas	10–3	Mack Brown
13.	Kansas St	11–4	Bill Snyder
	Mississippi	10–3	David Cutcliffe
15.	Tennessee	10–3	Phillip Fulmer
16.	Boise St	13–1	Dan Hawkins
17.	Maryland	10–3	Ralph Friedgen
18.	Nebraska	10–3	Frank Solich/Bo Pelini
	Purdue	9–4	Joe Tiller
20.	Minnesota	10–3	Glen Mason
21.	Utah	10–2	Urban Meyer
22.	Clemson	9–4	Tommy Bowden
23.	Bowling Green	11–3	Gregg Brandon
24.	Florida	8–5	Ron Zook
25.	Texas Christian	11–2	Gary Patterson

*Ranked No. 1 in *USAToday*/ESPN Poll.

2004

		Record	Coach
1.	USC	13-0	Pete Carroll
2.	Auburn	13-0	Tommy Tuberville
3.	Oklahoma	12-1	Bob Stoops
4.	Utah	12-0	Kyle Whittingham
5.	Texas	11-1	Mack Brown
6.	Louisville	11-1	Bobby Petrino
7.	Georgia	10-2	Mark Richt
8.	Iowa	10-2	Kirk Ferentz
9.	California	10-2	Jeff Tedford
10.	Virginia Tech	10-3	Frank Beamer
11.	Miami	9-3	Larry Coker
12.	Tennessee	10-3	Phillip Fulmer
13.	Michigan	9-3	Lloyd Carr
14.	Florida	8-5	Ron Zook
15.	Michigan	9-3	Lloyd Carr
16.	LSU	9-3	Les Miles
17.	Wisconsin	9-3	Barry Alvarez
18.	Texas Tech	8-4	Mike Leach
19.	Arizona State	9-3	Dirk Koetter
20.	Ohio State	8-4	Jim Tressel
21.	Boston College	9-3	Tom O'Brien
22.	Fresno State	9-3	Pat Hill
23.	Virginia	8-4	Al Groh
24.	Navy	10-2	Paul Johnson
25.	Pittsburgh	8-4	Walt Harris

2005

		Record	Coach
1.	Texas	13-0	Mack Brown
2.	USC	12-1	Pete Carroll
3.	Penn St	11-1	Joe Paterno
4.	Ohio State	10-2	Jim Tressel
5.	Texas	11-1	Mack Brown
6.	LSU	11-2	Les Miles
7.	Virginia Tech	10-3	Frank Beamer
8.	Alabama	10-2	Mike Shula
9.	Notre Dame	9-3	Charlie Weis
10.	Georgia	10-3	Mark Richt
11.	TCU	11-1	Gary Patterson
12.	Florida	9-3	Urban Meyer
13.	Oregon	10-2	Mike Bellotti
14.	Auburn	9-3	Tommy Tuberville
15.	Wisconsin	9-3	Barry Alvarez
16.	Michigan	9-3	Lloyd Carr
17.	UCLA	10-2	Karl Dorrell
18.	Miami (Fla.)	9-3	Larry Coker
19.	Boston College	9-3	Tom O'Brien
20.	Louisville	9-3	Bobby Petrino
21.	Texas Tech	9-3	Mike Leach
22.	Clemson	8-4	Tommy Bowden
23.	Oklahoma	8-4	Bob Stoops
24.	Florida St	8-5	Bobby Bowden
25.	Nebraska	8-4	Bill Callahan
	California	8-4	Jeff Tedford

Division I-AA

Year	Winner	Runner-Up	Score
1978	Florida A&M	Massachusetts	35–28
1979	Eastern Kentucky	Lehigh	30–7
1980	Boise St	Eastern Kentucky	31–29
1981	Idaho St	Eastern Kentucky	34–23
1982	Eastern Kentucky	Delaware	17–14
1983	Southern Illinois	Western Carolina	43–7
1984	Montana St	Louisiana Tech	19–6
1985	Georgia Southern	Furman	44–42
1986	Georgia Southern	Arkansas St	48–21
1987	NE Louisiana	Marshall	43–42
1988	Furman	Georgia Southern	17–12
1989	Georgia Southern	Stephen F. Austin St	37–34
1990	Georgia Southern	NV-Reno	36–13
1991	Youngstown St	Marshall	25–17
1992	Marshall	Youngstown St	31–28
1993	Youngstown St	Marshall	17–5
1994	Youngstown St	Boise St	28–14
1995	Montana	Marshall	22–20
1996	Marshall	Montana	49–29
1997	Youngstown St	McNesse St	10–9
1998	Massachusetts	Georgia Southern	55–43
1999	Georgia Southern	Youngstown St	59–24
2000	Georgia Southern	Montana	27–25
2001	Montana	Furman	13–6
2002	Western Kentucky	McNeese St	34–14
2003	Delaware	Colgate	40–0
2004	James Madison	Montana	31–21
2005	Appalachian State	Northern Iowa	21–16

Division II

Year	Winner	Runner-Up	Score
1973	Louisiana Tech	Western Kentucky	34–0
1974	Central Michigan	Delaware	54–14
1975	Northern Michigan	Western Kentucky	16–14
1976	Montana St	Akron	24–13
1977	Lehigh	Jacksonville St	33–0
1978	Eastern Illinois	Delaware	10–9
1979	Delaware	Youngstown St	38–21
1980	Cal Poly SLO	Eastern Illinois	21–13
1981	SW Texas St	N Dakota St	42–13
1982	SW Texas St	UC–Davis	34–9
1983	N Dakota St	Central St (Ohio)	41–21
1984	Troy St	N Dakota St	18–17
1985	N Dakota St	N Alabama	35–7
1986	N Dakota St	S Dakota	27–7
1987	Troy St	Portland St	31–17
1988	N Dakota St	Portland St	35–21
1989	Mississippi College	Jacksonville St	3–0
1990	N Dakota St	Indiana (PA)	51–11
1991	Pittsburg St	Jacksonville St	23–6
1992	Jacksonville St	Pittsburg St	17–13
1993	N Alabama	Indiana (Pa.)	41–34
1994	N Alabama	Texas A&M–Kingsville	16–10
1995	N Alabama	Pittsburg St	27–7
1996	Northern Colorado	Carson-Newman	23–14
1997	Northern Colorado	New Haven	51–0
1998	NW Missouri St	Carson-Newman	24–6
1999	NW Missouri St	Carson-Newman	58–52 (OT)
2000	Delta St	Bloomsburg	63–34
2001	Grand Valley St	N Dakota	17–14
2002	Grand Valley St	Valdosta St	31–24
2003	Grand Valley St	N Dakota	10–3
2004	Valdosta State	Pittsburg State	36-31
2005	Grand Valley St	NW Missouri State	21–17

Division III

Year	Winner	Runner-Up	Score
1973	Wittenberg	Juniata	41–0
1974	Central (Iowa)	Ithaca	10–8
1975	Wittenberg	Ithaca	28–0
1976	St. John's (Minn.)	Towson St	31–28
1977	Widener	Wabash	39–36
1978	Baldwin-Wallace	Wittenberg	24–10
1979	Ithaca	Wittenberg	14–10
1980	Dayton	Ithaca	63–0
1981	Widener	Dayton	17–10
1982	W Georgia	Augustana (Ill.)	14–0
1983	Augustana (Ill.)	Union (N.Y.)	21–17
1984	Augustana (Ill.)	Central (Ia.)	21–12
1985	Augustana (Ill.)	Ithaca	20–7
1986	Augustana (Ill.)	Salisbury St	31–3
1987	Wagner	Dayton	19–3
1988	Ithaca	Central (Iowa)	39–24
1989	Dayton	Union (N.Y.)	17–7
1990	Allegheny	Lycoming	21–14 (OT)
1991	Ithaca	Dayton	34–20
1992	WI-LaCrosse	Washington & Jefferson	16–12
1993	Mount Union	Rowan	34–24
1994	Albion	Washington & Jefferson	38–15
1995	WI-LaCrosse	Rowan	36–7
1996	Mount Union	Rowan	56–24
1997	Mount Union	Lycoming	61–12
1998	Mount Union	Rowan	44–24
1999	Pacific Lutheran	Rowan	42–13
2000	Mount Union	St. John's (Minn.)	10–7
2001	Mount Union	Bridgewater	30–27
2002	Mount Union	Trinity (Tex.)	48–7
2003	St. John's (Minn.)	Mount Union	24–6
2004	Linfield	Mary Hardin-Baylor	28-21
2005	Mount Union	UW-Whitewater	35–28

NAIA Divisional Championships

Division I

Year	Winner	Runner-Up	Score
1956	St. Joseph's (Ind.)/Montana St		0–0
1957	Pittsburg St (Kan.)	Hillsdale	27–26
1958	NE Oklahoma	Northern Arizona	19–13
1959	Texas A&I	Lenoir-Rhyne	20–7
1960	Lenoir-Rhyne	Humboldt St	15–14
1961	Pittsburg St (Kan.)	Linfield	12–7
1962	Central St (Okla.)	Lenoir-Rhyne	28–13
1963	St. John's (Minn.)	Prairie View	33–27
1964	Concordia-Moorhead/ Sam Houston St		7–7
1965	St. John's (Minn.)	Linfield	33–0
1966	Waynesburg	UW-Whitewater	42–21
1967	Fairmont St	Eastern Washington	28–21
1968	Troy St (Mich.)	Texas A&I	43–35
1969	Texas A&I	Concordia-Moorhead (Minn.)	32–7
1970	Texas A&I	Wofford	48–7
1971	Livingston (Ala.)	Arkansas Tech	14–12
1972	E Texas St	Carson-Newman	21–18
1973	Abilene Christian	Elon	42–14
1974	Texas A&I	Henderson St	34–23
1975	Texas A&I	Salem (W.V.)	37–0
1976	Texas A&I	Central Arkansas	26–0
1977	Abilene Christian	SW Oklahoma	24–7
1978	Angelo St	Elon	34–14
1979	Texas A&I	Central St (Okla.)	20–14

Division I *(Cont.)*

Year	Winner	Runner-Up	Score
1980	Elon	NE Oklahoma	17–10
1981	Elon	Pittsburg St	3–0
1982	Central St (Okla.)	Mesa	14–11
1983	Carson-Newman	Mesa	36–28
1984	Carson-Newman/Central Arkansas		19–19
1985	Central Arkansas/Hillsdale		10–10
1986	Carson-Newman	Cameron	17–0
1987	Cameron	Carson-Newman	30–2
1988	Carson-Newman	Adams St (Colo.)	56–21
1989	Carson-Newman	Emporia St	34–20
1990	Central St (Ohio)	Mesa St	38–16
1991	Central Arkansas	Central St (Ohio)	19–16
1992	Central St (Ohio)	Gardner-Webb	19–16
1993	E Central (Okla.)	Glenville St	49–35
1994	Northeastern St (Okla.)	Arkansas–Pine Bluff	13–12
1995	Central St (Ohio)	Northeastern St (Okla.)	37–7
1996	SW Oklahoma St	Montana Tech	33–31
1997	Findlay	Willamette	14–7
1998	Azusa Pacific	Olivet Nazarene	17–14
1999	Northwestern Oklahoma St	Georgetown (Ken.)	34–26
2000	Georgetown (Ken.)	Northwestern Oklahoma St	20–0
2001	Georgetown (Ken.)	Sioux Falls	49–27
2002	Carroll (Minn.)	Georgetown (Ken.)	28–7
2003	Carroll (Minn.)	Northwestern Oklahoma St	41–28
2004	Carroll (Minn.)	St. Francis (Ind.)	15-13
2005	Carroll (Minn.)	St. Francis (Ind.)	27–10

Division II†

Year	Winner	Runner-Up	Score
1970	Westminster (Pa.)	Anderson	21–16
1971	California Lutheran	Westminster (Pa.)	30–14
1972	Missouri Southern	Northwestern (Iowa)	21–14
1973	Northwestern (Iowa)	Glenville St	10–3
1974	Texas Lutheran	Missouri Valley	42–0
1975	Texas Lutheran	California Lutheran	34–8
1976	Westminster (Pa.)	Redlands	20–13
1977	Westminster (Pa.0	California Lutheran	17–9
1978	Concordia-Moorhead (Minn.)	Findlay	7–0
1979	Findlay	Northwestern (Iowa)	51–6
1980	Pacific Lutheran	Wilmington (Ohio)	38–10
1981	Austin Coll./Conc.-Moorhead (Minn.)		24–24
1982	Linfield	William Jewell	33–15
1983	Northwestern (IA)	Pacific Lutheran	25–21
1984	Linfield	Northwestern (Iowa)	33–22
1985	WI-La Crosse	Pacific Lutheran	24–7
1986	Linfield	Baker	17–0
1987	Pacific Lutheran	UW-Stevens Point*	16–16
1988	Westminster (Pa.)	UW-La Crosse	21–14
1989	Westminster (Pa.)	UW-La Crosse	51–30
1990	Peru St	Westminster (Pa.)	17–7
1991	Georgetown (Ken.)	Pacific Lutheran	28–20
1992	Findlay	Linfield	26–13
1993	Pacific Lutheran	Westminster (Pa.)	50–20
1994	Westminster (Pa.)	Pacific Lutheran	27–7
1995	Findlay	Central Washington	21–21
1996	Sioux Falls	Western Washington	47–25

*Forfeited 1987 season due to use of an ineligible player.   †In 1997 the NAIA consolidated its two divisions into one.

Awards

Heisman Memorial Trophy

Awarded to the best college player by the Downtown Athletic Club of New York City. The trophy is named after John W. Heisman, who coached Georgia Tech to the national championship in 1917 and later served as DAC athletic director.

Year	Winner, College, Position	Winner's Season Statistics	Runner-Up, College
1935	Jay Berwanger, Chicago, HB	Rush: 119 Yds: 577 TD: 6	Monk Meyer, Army
1936	Larry Kelley, Yale, E	Rec: 17 Yds: 372 TD: 6	Sam Francis, Nebraska
1937	Clint Frank, Yale, HB	Rush: 157 Yds: 667 TD: 11	Byron White, Colorado
1938	†Davey O'Brien, Texas Christian, QB	Att/Comp: 194/110 Yds: 1733 TD: 19	Marshall Goldberg, Pittsburgh
1939	Nile Kinnick, Iowa, HB	Rush: 106 Yds: 374 TD: 5	Tom Harmon, Michigan
1940	Tom Harmon, Michigan, HB	Rush: 191 Yds: 852 TD: 16	John Kimbrough, Texas A&M
1941	†Bruce Smith, Minnesota, HB	Rush: 98 Yds: 480 TD: 6	Angelo Bertelli, Notre Dame
1942	Frank Sinkwich, Georgia, HB	Att/Comp: 166/84 Yds: 1392 TD: 10	Paul Governali, Columbia
1943	Angelo Bertelli, Notre Dame, QB	Att/Comp: 36/25 Yds: 511 TD: 10	Bob Odell, Pennsylvania
1944	Les Horvath, Ohio State, QB	Rush: 163 Yds: 924 TD: 12	Glenn Davis, Army
1945	*†Doc Blanchard, Army, FB	Rush: 101 Yds: 718 TD: 13	Glenn Davis, Army
1946	Glenn Davis, Army, HB	Rush: 123 Yds: 712 TD: 7	Charley Trippi, Georgia
1947	†John Lujack, Notre Dame, QB	Att/Comp: 109/61 Yds: 777 TD: 9	Bob Chappius, Michigan
1948	*Doak Walker, Southern Methodist, HB	Rush: 108 Yds: 532 TD: 8	Charlie Justice, N Carolina
1949	†Leon Hart, Notre Dame, E	Rec: 19 Yds: 257 TD: 5	Charlie Justice, N Carolina
1950	*Vic Janowicz, Ohio St, HB	Att/Comp: 77/32 Yds: 561 TD: 12	Kyle Rote, Southern Methodist
1951	Dick Kazmaier, Princeton, HB	Rush: 149 Yds: 861 TD: 9	Hank Lauricella, Tennessee
1952	Billy Vessels, Oklahoma, HB	Rush: 167 Yds: 1072 TD: 17	Jack Scarbath, Maryland
1953	John Lattner, Notre Dame, HB	Rush: 134 Yds: 651 TD: 6	Paul Giel, Minnesota
1954	Alan Ameche, Wisconsin, FB	Rush: 146 Yds: 641 TD: 9	Kurt Burris, Oklahoma
1955	Howard Cassady, Ohio St, HB	Rush: 161 Yds: 958 TD: 15	Jim Swink, Texas Christian
1956	Paul Hornung, Notre Dame, QB	Att/Comp: 111/59 Yds: 917 TD: 3	Johnny Majors, Tennessee
1957	John David Crow, Texas A&M, HB	Rush: 129 Yds: 562 TD: 10	Alex Karras, Iowa
1958	Pete Dawkins, Army, HB	Rush: 78 Yds: 428 TD: 6	Randy Duncan, Iowa
1959	Billy Cannon, Louisiana St, HB	Rush: 139 Yds: 598 TD: 6	Rich Lucas, Penn St
1960	Joe Bellino, Navy, HB	Rush: 168 Yds: 834 TD: 18	Tom Brown, Minnesota
1961	Ernie Davis, Syracuse, HB	Rush: 150 Yds: 823 TD: 15	Bob Ferguson, Ohio St
1962	Terry Baker, Oregon St, QB	Att/Comp: 203/112 Yds: 1738 TD: 15	Jerry Stovall, Louisiana St
1963	*Roger Staubach, Navy, QB	Att/Comp: 161/107 Yds: 1474 TD: 7	Billy Lothridge, Georgia Tech
1964	John Huarte, Notre Dame, QB	Att/Comp: 205/114 Yds: 2062 TD: 16	Jerry Rhome, Tulsa
1965	Mike Garrett, Southern Cal, HB	Rush: 267 Yds: 1440 TD: 16	Howard Twilley, Tulsa
1966	Steve Spurrier, Florida, QB	Att/Comp: 291/179 Yds: 2012 TD: 16	Bob Griese, Purdue
1967	Gary Beban, UCLA, QB	Att/Comp: 156/87 Yds: 1359 TD: 8	O.J. Simpson, Southern Cal
1968	O.J. Simpson, Southern Cal, HB	Rush: 383 Yds: 1880 TD: 23	Leroy Keyes, Purdue
1969	Steve Owens, Oklahoma, FB	Rush: 358 Yds: 1523 TD: 23	Mike Phipps, Purdue
1970	Jim Plunkett, Stanford, QB	Att/Comp: 358/191 Yds: 2715 TD: 18	Joe Theismann, Notre Dame
1971	Pat Sullivan, Auburn, QB	Att/Comp: 281/162 Yds: 2012; 20 TD	Ed Marinaro, Cornell
1972	Johnny Rodgers, Nebraska, FL	Rec: 55 Yds: 942 TD: 17	Greg Pruitt, Oklahoma
1973	John Cappelletti, Penn St, HB	Rush: 286 Yds: 1522 TD: 17	John Hicks, Ohio St
1974	*Archie Griffin, Ohio St, HB	Rush: 256 Yds: 1695 TD: 12	Anthony Davis, Southern Cal
1975	Archie Griffin, Ohio St, HB	Rush: 262 Yds: 1450 TD: 4	Chuck Muncie, California
1976	†Tony Dorsett, Pittsburgh, HB	Rush: 370 Yds: 2150 TD: 23	Ricky Bell, Southern Cal
1977	Earl Campbell, Texas, FB	Rush: 267 Yds: 1744 TD: 19	Terry Miller, Oklahoma St
1978	*Billy Sims, Oklahoma, HB	Rush: 231 Yds: 1762 TD: 20	Chuck Fusina, Penn St
1979	Charles White, Southern Cal, HB	Rush: 332 Yds: 1803 TD: 19	Billy Sims, Oklahoma
1980	George Rogers, S Carolina, HB	Rush: 324 Yds: 1894 TD: 14	Hugh Green, Pittsburgh
1981	Marcus Allen, Southern Cal, HB	Rush: 433 Yds: 2427 TD: 23	Herschel Walker, Georgia
1982	*Herschel Walker, Georgia, HB	Rush: 335 Yds: 1752 TD: 17	John Elway, Stanford
1983	Mike Rozier, Nebraska, HB	Rush: 275 Yds: 2148 TD: 29	Steve Young, Brigham Young
1984	Doug Flutie, Boston College, QB	Att/Comp: 396/233 Yds: 3454 TD: 27	Keith Byars, Ohio St
1985	Bo Jackson, Auburn, HB	Rush: 278 Yds: 1786 TD: 17	Chuck Long, Iowa
1986	Vinny Testaverde, Miami (FL), QB	Att/Comp: 276/175 Yds: 2557 TD: 26	Paul Palmer, Temple

Heisman Memorial Trophy (Cont.)

Year	Winner, College, Position	Winner's Season Statistics	Runner-Up, College
1987	...Tim Brown, Notre Dame, WR	Rec: 39 Yds: 846 TD: 7	Don McPherson, Syracuse
1988	...*Barry Sanders, Oklahoma St, RB	Rush: 344 Yds: 2628 TD: 39	Rodney Peete, Southern Cal
1989	...*Andre Ware, Houston, QB	Att/Comp: 578/365 Yds: 4699 TD: 46	Anthony Thompson, Indiana
1990	...*Ty Detmer, Brigham Young, QB	Att/Comp: 562/361 Yds: 5188 TD: 41	Raghib Ismail, Notre Dame
1991	...*Desmond Howard, Michigan, WR	Rec: 61 Yds: 950 TD: 23	Casey Weldon, Florida St
1992	...Gino Torretta, Miami (FL), QB	Att/Comp: 402/228 Yds: 3060 TD: 19	Marshall Faulk, San Diego St
1993	...†Charlie Ward, Florida St, QB	Att/Comp: 380/264 Yds: 3032 TD: 27	Heath Shuler, Tennessee
1994	...Rashaan Salaam, Colorado, RB	Rush: 298 Yds: 2055 TD: 24	Ki-Jana Carter, Penn St
1995	...Eddie George, Ohio State, RB	Rush: 303 Yds: 1826 TD: 23	Tommie Frazier, Nebraska
1996	...†Danny Wuerffel, Florida, QB	Att/Comp: 360/207 Yds: 3625 TD: 39	Troy Davis, Iowa St
1997	...†Charles Woodson, Michigan, CB/ WR	7 interceptions; Rec: 11 Yds: 231 TD: 4	Peyton Manning, Tennessee
1998	...Ricky Williams, Texas, RB	Rush: 361 Yds: 2124 TD: 28	Michael Bishop, Kansas St
1999	...Ron Dayne, Wisconsin, RB	Rush: 303 Yds: 1834 TD: 19	Joe Hamilton, Georgia Tech
2000	...Chris Weinke, Florida St, QB	Att/Comp: 431/266 Yds: 4167 TD: 33	Josh Heupel, Oklahoma
2001	...Eric Crouch, Nebraska, QB	Att/Comp: 189/105 Yds: 1510 TD: 7; Rush: 1115 Yds, 18 TD	Rex Grossman, Florida
2002	...Carson Palmer, Southern Cal, QB	Att/Comp: 450/228 Yds: 3639 TD: 32	Brad Banks, Iowa
2003	... Jason White, Oklahoma, QB	Pct. Comp: 64; 3744 Yds; TD: 40	Larry Fitzgerald, Pittsburgh
2004	...*†Matt Leinart, Southern Cal, QB	Att/Comp: 269/412 Yds: 2990 TD: 28	Adrian Peterson, Oklahoma
2005	...*Reggie Bush, USC, RB	Rush: 200 Yds:1,740 TD: 16	Vince Young, Texas

*Juniors (all others seniors). †Winners who played for national championship teams the same year.
Note: Former Heisman winners and national media cast votes, with ballots allowing for three names (3 points for first, 2 for second and 1 for third).

Maxwell Award

Given to the nation's outstanding college football player by the Maxwell Football Club of Philadelphia.

Year	Player, College, Position	Year	Player, College, Position
1937	Clint Frank, Yale, HB	1964	Glenn Ressler, Penn St, C
1938	Davey O'Brien, Texas Christian, QB	1965	Tommy Nobis, Texas, LB
1939	Nile Kinnick, Iowa, HB	1966	Jim Lynch, Notre Dame, LB
1940	Tom Harmon, Michigan, HB	1967	Gary Beban, UCLA, QB
1941	Bill Dudley, Virginia, HB	1968	O.J. Simpson, Southern Cal, RB
1942	Paul Governali, Columbia, QB	1969	Mike Reid, Penn St, DT
1943	Bob Odell, Pennsylvania, HB	1970	Jim Plunkett, Stanford, QB
1944	Glenn Davis, Army, HB	1971	Ed Marinaro, Cornell, RB
1945	Doc Blanchard, Army, FB	1972	Brad Van Pelt, Michigan St, DB
1946	Charley Trippi, Georgia, HB	1973	John Cappelletti, Penn St, RB
1947	Doak Walker, Southern Meth, HB	1974	Steve Joachim, Temple, QB
1948	Chuck Bednarik, Pennsylvania, C	1975	Archie Griffin, Ohio St, RB
1949	Leon Hart, Notre Dame, E	1976	Tony Dorsett, Pittsburgh, RB
1950	Reds Bagnell, Pennsylvania, HB	1977	Ross Browner, Notre Dame, DE
1951	Dick Kazmaier, Princeton, HB	1978	Chuck Fusina, Penn St, QB
1952	John Lattner, Notre Dame, HB	1979	Charles White, Southern Cal, RB
1953	John Lattner, Notre Dame, HB	1980	Hugh Green, Pittsburgh, DE
1954	Ron Beagle, Navy, E	1981	Marcus Allen, Southern Cal, RB
1955	Howard Cassady, Ohio St, HB	1982	Herschel Walker, Georgia, RB
1956	Tommy McDonald, Oklahoma, HB	1983	Mike Rozier, Nebraska, RB
1957	Bob Reifsnyder, Navy, T	1984	Doug Flutie, Boston College, QB
1958	Pete Dawkins, Army, HB	1985	Chuck Long, Iowa, QB
1959	Rich Lucas, Penn St, QB	1986	Vinny Testaverde, Miami (FL), QB
1960	Joe Bellino, Navy, HB	1987	Don McPherson, Syracuse, QB
1961	Bob Ferguson, Ohio St, FB	1988	Barry Sanders, Oklahoma St, RB
1962	Terry Baker, Oregon St, QB	1989	Anthony Thompson, Indiana, RB
1963	Roger Staubach, Navy, QB	1990	Ty Detmer, Brigham Young, QB

Maxwell Award (Cont.)

Year	Player, College, Position	Year	Player, College, Position
1991	Desmond Howard, Michigan, WR	1999	Ron Dayne, Wisconsin, RB
1992	Gino Torretta, Miami (FL), QB	2000	Drew Brees, Purdue, QB
1993	Charlie Ward, Florida St, QB	2001	Ken Dorsey, Miami (FL), QB
1994	Kerry Collins, Penn St, QB	2002	Larry Johnson, Penn St, RB
1995	Eddie George, Ohio St, RB	2003	Eli Manning, Mississippi, QB
1996	Danny Wuerffel, Florida, QB	2004	Jason White, Oklahoma, QB
1997	Peyton Manning, Tennessee, QB	2005	Vince Young, Texas, QB
1998	Ricky Williams, Texas, RB		

Davey O'Brien National Quarterback Award

Given to the top quarterback in the nation by the Davey O'Brien Educational and Charitable Trust of Fort Worth. Named for Texas Christian Hall of Fame quarterback Davey O'Brien (1936–38).

Year	Player, College	Year	Player, College
1981	Jim McMahon, Brigham Young	1994	Kerry Collins, Penn St
1982	Todd Blackledge, Penn St	1995	Danny Wuerffel, Florida
1983	Steve Young, Brigham Young	1996	Danny Wuerffel, Florida
1984	Doug Flutie, Boston College	1997	Peyton Manning, Tennessee
1985	Chuck Long, Iowa	1998	Michael Bishop, Kansas St
1986	Vinny Testaverde, Miami (FL)	1999	Joe Hamilton, Georgia Tech
1987	Don McPherson, Syracuse	2000	Chris Weinke, Florida St
1988	Troy Aikman, UCLA	2001	Eric Crouch, Nebraska
1989	Andre Ware, Houston	2002	Brad Banks, Iowa
1990	Ty Detmer, Brigham Young	2003	Jason White, Oklahoma
1991	Ty Detmer, Brigham Young	2004	Jason White, Oklahoma
1992	Gino Torretta, Miami (FL)	2005	Vince Young, Texas
1993	Charlie Ward, Florida St		

Note: Originally honored the outstanding football player in the Southwest as follows: 1977—Earl Campbell, Texas, RB; 1978—Billy Sims, Oklahoma, RB; 1979—Mike Singletary, Baylor, LB; 1980—Mike Singletary, Baylor, LB.

Vince Lombardi/Rotary Award

Given to the outstanding college lineman of the year, the award is sponsored by the Rotary Club of Houston.

Year	Player, College, Position	Year	Player, College, Position
1970	Jim Stillwagon, Ohio St, MG	1988	Tracy Rocker, Auburn, DT
1971	Walt Patulski, Notre Dame, DE	1989	Percy Snow, Michigan St, LB
1972	Rich Glover, Nebraska, MG	1990	Chris Zorich, Notre Dame, NG
1973	John Hicks, Ohio St, OT	1991	Steve Emtman, Washington, DT
1974	Randy White, Maryland, DT	1992	Marvin Jones, Florida St, LB
1975	Lee Roy Selmon, Oklahoma, DT	1993	Aaron Taylor, Notre Dame, OT
1976	Wilson Whitley, Houston, DT	1994	Warren Sapp, Miami (FL), DT
1977	Ross Browner, Notre Dame, DE	1995	Orlando Pace, Ohio St, OT
1978	Bruce Clark, Penn St, DT	1996	Orlando Pace, Ohio St, OT
1979	Brad Budde, Southern Cal, G	1997	Grant Wistrom, Nebraska, DE
1980	Hugh Green, Pittsburgh, DE	1998	Dat Nguyen, Texas A&M, LB
1981	Kenneth Sims, Texas, DT	1999	Corey Moore, Virginia Tech, DE
1982	Dave Rimington, Nebraska, C	2000	Jamal Reynolds, Florida St, DE
1983	Dean Steinkuhler, Nebraska, G	2001	Julius Peppers, N Carolina, DE
1984	Tony Degrate, Texas, DT	2002	Terrell Suggs, Arizona St, DL
1985	Tony Casillas, Oklahoma, NG	2003	Tommie Harris, Oklahoma, DT
1986	Cornelius Bennett, Alabama, LB	2004	David Pollack, Georgia
1987	Chris Spielman, Ohio St, LB	2005	A.J. Hawk, Ohio State

Outland Trophy

Given to the outstanding interior lineman, selected by the Football Writers Association of America.

Year	Player, College, Position	Year	Player, College, Position
1946	George Connor, Notre Dame, T	1954	Bill Brooks, Arkansas, G
1947	Joe Steffy, Army, G	1955	Calvin Jones, Iowa, G
1948	Bill Fischer, Notre Dame, G	1956	Jim Parker, Ohio St, G
1949	Ed Bagdon, Michigan St, G	1957	Alex Karras, Iowa, T
1950	Bob Gain, Kentucky, T	1958	Zeke Smith, Auburn, G
1951	Jim Weatherall, Oklahoma, T	1959	Mike McGee, Duke, T
1952	Dick Modzelewski, Maryland, T	1960	Tom Brown, Minnesota, G
1953	J.D. Roberts, Oklahoma, G	1961	Merlin Olsen, Utah St, T

Outland Trophy *(Cont.)*

Year	Player, College, Position	Year	Player, College, Position
1962	Bobby Bell, Minnesota, T	1984	Bruce Smith, Virginia Tech, DT
1963	Scott Appleton, Texas, T	1985	Mike Ruth, Boston College, NG
1964	Steve DeLong, Tennessee, T	1986	Jason Buck, Brigham Young, DT
1965	Tommy Nobis, Texas, G	1987	Chad Hennings, Air Force, DT
1966	Loyd Phillips, Arkansas, T	1988	Tracy Rocker, Auburn, DT
1967	Ron Yary, Southern Cal, T	1989	Mohammed Elewonibi, Brigham Young, G
1968	Bill Stanfill, Georgia, T	1990	Russell Maryland, Miami (FL), DT
1969	Mike Reid, Penn St, DT	1991	Steve Emtman, Washington, DT
1970	Jim Stillwagon, Ohio St, MG	1992	Will Shields, Nebraska, G
1971	Larry Jacobson, Nebraska, DT	1993	Rob Waldrop, Arizona, NG
1972	Rich Glover, Nebraska, MG	1994	Zach Wiegert, Nebraska, G
1973	John Hicks, Ohio St, OT	1995	Jonathan Ogden, UCLA, OT
1974	Randy White, Maryland, DE	1996	Orlando Pace, Ohio St, OT
1975	Lee Roy Selmon, Oklahoma, DT	1997	Aaron Taylor, Nebraska, G
1976	Ross Browner, Notre Dame, DE	1998	Kris Farris, UCLA, OL
1977	Brad Shearer, Texas, DT	1999	Chris Samuels, Alabama, OL
1978	Greg Roberts, Oklahoma, G	2000	John Henderson, Tennessee, DT
1979	Jim Ritcher, N Carolina St, C	2001	Bryant McKinnie, Miami (FL), OT
1980	Mark May, Pittsburgh, OT	2002	Rien Long, Washington St, DL
1981	Dave Rimington, Nebraska, C	2003	Robert Gallery, Iowa, OT
1982	Dave Rimington, Nebraska, C	2004	Jammal Brown, Oklahoma, OT
1983	Dean Steinkuhler, Nebraska, G	2005	Greg Eslinger, Minnesota, LB

Butkus Award

Given to the top collegiate linebacker, the award was established by the Downtown Athletic Club of Orlando and named for college Hall of Famer Dick Butkus of Illinois.

Year	Player, College	Year	Player, College
1985	Brian Bosworth, Oklahoma	1996	Matt Russell, Colorado
1986	Brian Bosworth, Oklahoma	1997	Andy Katzenmoyer, Ohio St
1987	Paul McGowan, Florida St	1998	Chris Claiborne, Southern Cal
1988	Derrick Thomas, Alabama	1999	LaVar Arrington, Penn St
1989	Percy Snow, Michigan St	2000	Dan Morgan, Miami (FL)
1990	Alfred Williams, Colorado	2001	Rocky Calmus, Oklahoma
1991	Erick Anderson, Michigan	2002	E.J. Henderson, Maryland
1992	Marvin Jones, Florida St	2003	Teddy Lehman, Oklahoma
1993	Trev Alberts, Nebraska	2004	Derrick Johnson, Texas
1994	Dana Howard, Illinois	2005	Paul Posluszny, Penn State
1995	Kevin Hardy, Illinois		

Jim Thorpe Award

Given to the best defensive back of the year, the award is presented by the Jim Thorpe Athletic Club of Oklahoma City.

Year	Player, College	Year	Player, College
1986	Thomas Everett, Baylor	1996	Lawrence Wright, Florida
1987	Bennie Blades, Miami (FL)	1997	Charles Woodson, Michigan
	Rickey Dixon, Oklahoma	1998	Antoine Winfield, Ohio St
1988	Deion Sanders, Florida St	1999	Tyrone Carter, Minnesota
1989	Mark Carrier, Southern Cal	2000	Jamar Fletcher, Wisconsin
1990	Darryl Lewis, Arizona	2001	Roy Williams, Oklahoma
1991	Terrell Buckley, Florida St	2002	Terence Newman, Kansas St
1992	Deon Figures, Colorado	2003	Derrick Strait, Oklahoma
1993	Antonio Langham, Alabama	2004	Carlos Rogers, Auburn
1994	Chris Hudson, Colorado	2005	Michael Huff, Texas
1995	Greg Myers, Colorado St		

Walter Payton Player of the Year Award

Given to the top Div. I-AA player, voted by Div. I-AA sports information directors. Sponsored by Sports Network.

Year	Player, College, Position	Year	Player, College, Position
1987	Kenny Gamble, Colgate, RB	1997	Brian Finneran, Villanova, WR
1988	Dave Meggett, Towson St, RB	1998	Jerry Azumah, New Hampshire, RB
1989	John Friesz, Idaho, QB	1999	Adrian Peterson, Georgia Southern, RB
1990	Walter Dean, Grambling, RB	2000	Louis Ivory, Furman, RB
1991	Jamie Martin, Weber St, QB	2001	Brian Westbrook, Villanova, RB
1992	Michael Payton, Marshall, QB	2002	Tony Romo, Eastern Ilinois, QB
1993	Doug Nussmeier, Idaho, QB	2003	Jamaal Branch, Colgate, RB
1994	Steve McNair, Alcorn St, QB	2004	Lang Campbell, William & Mary, QB
1995	Dave Dickenson, Montana, QB	2005	Erik Meyer, East Stroudsburg, QB
1996	Archie Amerson, Northern Arizona, RB		

NCAA Division I-A Individual Records

Career

SCORING

Most Points Scored: 468—Travis Prentice, Miami (OH), 1996–99
Most Points Scored per Game: 12.1—Marshall Faulk, San Diego St, 1991–93
Most Touchdowns Scored: 73—Travis Prentice, Miami (OH), 1996–99
Most Touchdowns Scored per Game: 2.0—Marshall Faulk, San Diego St, 1991–93
Most Touchdowns Scored, Rushing: 73—Travis Prentice, Miami (OH), 1996–99
Most Touchdowns Scored, Passing: 121—Ty Detmer, Brigham Young, 1988–91
Most Touchdowns Scored, Receiving: 50—Troy Edwards, Louisiana Tech, 1996–98
Most Touchdowns Scored, Interception Returns: 5—Ken Thomas, San Jose St, 1979–82; Jackie Walker, Tennessee, 1969–71; Deltha O'Neal, California, 1996–99; Darrent Williams, Okla St. 2001–04
Most Touchdowns Scored, Punt Returns: 8—Wes Walker, Texas Tech, 2000–03; Antonio Perkins, Oklahoma, 2001–04
Most Touchdowns Scored, Kickoff Returns: 6—Anthony Davis, Southern Cal, 1972–74; Ashlan Davis, Tulsa, 2002–05

TOTAL OFFENSE

Most Plays: 2,587—Timmy Chang, Hawaii, 2000–04
Most Plays per Game: 50.1—Kliff Kingsbury, Texas Tech, 1999–2002
Most Yards Gained: 16,910—Timmy Chang, Hawaii, 2000–04 (17,072 passing, -162 rushing)
Most Yards Gained per Game: 382.4—Tim Rattay, Louisiana Tech, 1997–99
Most 300+ Yard Games: 33 —Ty Detmer, Brigham Young, 1988–91

RUSHING

Most Rushes: 1,215—Steve Bartalo, Colorado St, 1983–86 (4813 yds)
Most Rushes per Game: 34.0—Ed Marinaro, Cornell, 1969–71
Most Yards Gained: 6,397—Ron Dayne, Wisconsin, 1996–99
Most Yards Gained per Game: 174.6—Ed Marinaro, Cornell, 1969–71
Most 100+ Yard Games: 34—DeAngelo Williams, Memphis, 2002–05
Most 200+ Yard Games: 11—Marcus Allen, Southern Cal, 1978–81; Ricky Williams, Texas, 1995–98; Ron Dayne, Wisconsin, 1996–99

PASSING

Highest Passing Efficiency Rating: 168.9—Ryan Dinwiddie, Boise St, 2000–03 (992 attempts, 622 completions, 82 touchdown passes, 21 interceptions, 9,819 yards)
Most Passes Attempted: 2,436—Timmy Chang, Hawaii, 2000–04
Most Passes Attempted per Game: 47.0—Tim Rattay, Louisiana Tech, 1997–99
Most Passes Completed: 1,388—Timmy Chang, Hawaii, 2000–04
Most Passes Completed per Game: 30.8—Tim Rattay, Louisiana Tech, 1997–99
***Highest Completion Percentage:** 68.2—Bruce Gadlowski, Toledo, 2002–05
Most Yards Gained: 17,072—Timmy Chang, Hawaii, 2000–04
Most Yards Gained per Game: 386.2—Tim Rattay, Louisiana Tech, 1997–99

RECEIVING

Most Passes Caught: 316—Taylor Stubblefield, Purdue, 2001–04
Most Passes Caught per Game: 10.5—Emmanuel Hazard, Houston, 1989–90
Most Yards Gained: 5,005—Trevor Insley, Nevada, 1996–99
Most Yards Gained per Game: 140.9—Alex Van Dyke, Nevada, 1994–95
Highest Average Gain per Reception: 25.7—Wesley Walker, California, 1973–75

ALL-PURPOSE RUNNING

Most Plays: 1,347—Steve Bartalo, Colorado St, 1983-86 (1,215 rushes, 132 receptions)
Most Yards Gained: 7,573—DeAngelo Williams, Memphis, 2002–05 (6,026 rushing, 723 receiving, 824 KO retrurns)
Most Yards Gained per Game: 237.8—Ryan Benjamin, Pacific, 1990–92
Highest Average Gain per Play: 17.4—Anthony Carter, Michigan, 1979–82

*Minimum 1,000 attempts.

Career *(Cont.)*

INTERCEPTIONS

Most Passes Intercepted: 29—Al Brosky, Illinois, 1950–52
Most Passes Intercepted per Game: 1.1—Al Brosky, Illinois, 1950–52
Most Yards on Interception Returns: 501—Terrell Buckley, Florida St, 1989–91
Highest Average Gain per Interception: 26.5—Tom Pridemore, W Virginia, 1975–77

SPECIAL TEAMS

Highest Punt Return Average: 23.6—Jack Mitchell, Oklahoma, 1946–48
Highest Kickoff Return Average: 36.2—Forrest Hall, San Francisco, 1946–47
Highest Average Yards per Punt: 46.3—Todd Sauerbrun, W Virginia, 1991–94
Note: 150–249 punts.

Single Season

SCORING

Most Points Scored: 234—Barry Sanders, Oklahoma St, 1988
Most Points Scored per Game: 21.3—Barry Sanders, Oklahoma St, 1988
Most Touchdowns Scored: 39—Barry Sanders, Oklahoma St, 1988
Most Touchdowns Scored, Rushing: 37—Barry Sanders, Oklahoma St, 1988
Most Touchdowns Scored, Passing: 54—David Klingler, Houston, 1990
Most Touchdowns Scored, Receiving: 27—Troy Edwards, Louisiana Tech, 1998
Most Touchdowns Scored, Interception Returns: 4—Deltha O'Neal, California, 1999
Most Touchdowns Scored, Punt Returns: 5—Chad Owens, Hawaii, 2004
Most Touchdowns Scored, Kickoff Returns: 5—Ashlan Davis, Tulsa, 2004

TOTAL OFFENSE

Most Plays: 814—Kliff Kingsbury, Texas Tech, 2002
Most Yards Gained: 5,976—B.J. Symons, Texas Tech, 2003
Most Yards Gained per Game: 474.6—David Klingler, Houston, 1990
Most 300+ Yard Games: 12—Ty Detmer, Brigham Young, 1990

RUSHING

Most Rushes: 403—Marcus Allen, Southern Cal, 1981
Most Rushes per Game: 39.6—Ed Marinaro, Cornell, 1971
Most Yards Gained: 2,628—Barry Sanders, Oklahoma St, 1988
Most Yards Gained per Game: 238.9—Barry Sanders, Oklahoma St, 1988
Most 100+ Yard Games: 12—Quentin Griffin, Oklahoma, 2002

PASSING

Highest Passing Efficiency Rating: 183.3—Shaun King, Tulane, 1998 (328 attempts, 223 completions, 6 interceptions, 3,232 yards, 36 TD passes)
Most Passes Attempted: 719—B.J. Symons, Texas Tech, 2003
Most Passes Attempted per Game: 58.5—David Klingler, Houston, 1990
Most Passes Completed: 479—Kliff Kingsbury, Texas Tech, 2002
Most Passes Completed per Game: 36.4—Tim Couch, Kentucky, 1998
Highest Completion Percentage: 73.6—Daunte Culpepper, Central Florida, 1998
*Minimum 1,000 attempts.

PASSING *(Cont.)*

Most Yards Gained: 5,833—B.J. Symons, Texas Tech, 2003
Most Yards Gained per Game: 467.3—David Klingler, Houston, 1990

RECEIVING

Most Passes Caught: 142—Emmanuel Hazard, Houston, 1989
Most Passes Caught per Game: 13.4—Howard Twilley, Tulsa, 1965
Most Yards Gained: 2,060—Trevor Insley, Nevada, 1999
Most Yards Gained per Game: 187.3—Trevor Insley, Nevada, 1999
Highest Average Gain per Reception: 27.9—Elmo Wright, Houston, 1968 (min. 30 receptions)

ALL-PURPOSE RUNNING

Most Plays: 432—Marcus Allen, Southern Cal, 1981
Most Yards Gained: 3,250—Barry Sanders, Oklahoma St, 1988
Most Yards Gained per Game: 295.5—Barry Sanders, Oklahoma St, 1988
Highest Average Gain per Play: 18.5—Henry Bailey, UNLV, 1992

INTERCEPTIONS

Most Passes Intercepted: 14 — Al Worley, Washington, 1968
Most Yards on Interception Returns: 302 — Charles Phillips, Southern Cal, 1974
Highest Average Gain per Interception: 50.6 — Norm Thompson, Utah, 1969

SPECIAL TEAMS

Highest Punt Return Average: 28.5—Maurice Drew, UCLA, 2005
Highest Kickoff Return Average: 40.1 — Paul Allen, Brigham Young, 1961
Highest Average Yards per Punt: 50.3 — Chad Kessler, Louisiana St, 1997

Single Game

SCORING

Most Points Scored: 48—Howard Griffith, Illinois, 1990 (vs Southern Illinois)
Most Field Goals: 7—Dale Klein, Nebraska, 1985 (vs Missouri); Mike Prindle, Western Michigan, 1984 (vs Marshall)
Most Extra Points (Kick): 13—Derek Mahoney, Fresno St, 1991 (vs New Mexico); Terry Leiweke, Houston, 1968 (vs Tulsa)
Most Extra Points (2-Pts): 6—Jim Pilot, New Mexico St, 1961 (vs Hardin-Simmons)

TOTAL OFFENSE

Most Yards Gained: 732—David Klingler, Houston, 1990 (vs Arizona St)

RUSHING

Most Yards Gained: 406—LaDainian Tomlinson, Texas Christian, 1999 (vs UTEP)
Most Touchdowns Rushed: 8—Howard Griffith, Illinois, 1990 (vs Southern Illinois)

PASSING

Most Passes Completed: 55—Rusty LaRue, Wake Forest, 1995 (vs Duke); Drew Brees, Purdue, 1998 (vs Wisconsin)
Most Yards Gained: 716—David Klingler, Houston, 1990 (vs Arizona St)
Most Touchdown Passes: 11—David Klingler, Houston, 1990 [vs Eastern Washington (I-AA)]

RECEIVING

Most Passes Caught: 23—Randy Gatewood, UNLV, 1994 (vs Idaho)
Most Yards Gained: 405—Troy Edwards, Louisiana Tech, 1998 (vs Nebraska)
Most Touchdown Catches: 7—Rashaun Woods, Oklahoma St, 2003 (vs Southern Methodist)

NCAA Division I-AA Individual Records

Career

SCORING

Most Points Scored: 544—Brian Westbrook, Villanova, 1998-01
Most Touchdowns Scored: 89—Brian Westbrook, Villanova, 1998-01
Most Touchdowns Scored, Rushing: 84—Adrian Peterson, Georgia Southern, 1998-01
Most Touchdowns Scored, Passing: 139—Willie Totten, Mississippi Valley, 1982-85
Most Touchdowns Scored, Receiving: 50—Jerry Rice, Mississippi Valley, 1981-84

RUSHING

Most Rushes: 1,124—Charles Roberts, Cal St-Sacramento, 1997-00
Most Rushes per Game: 38.2—Arnold Mickens, Butler, 1994-95
Most Yards Gained: 6,559—Adrian Peterson, Georgia Southern, 1998-01
Most Yards Gained per Game: 190.7—Arnold Mickens, Butler, 1994-95

PASSING

Highest Passing Efficiency Rating: 170.8—Shawn Knight, William & Mary, 1991-94
Most Passes Attempted: 1,680—Marcus Brady, Cal St—Northridge, 1998-01; Steve McNair, Alcorn St, 1991-94
Most Passes Completed: 1,039—Marcus Brady, Cal St—Northridge, 1998-01
Most Passes Completed per Game: 26.5—Chris Sanders, Chattanooga, 1999-00
Highest Completion Percentage: 67.3—Dave Dickenson, Montana, 1992-95
Most Yards Gained: 14,496—Steve McNair, Alcorn St, 1991-94
Most Yards Gained per Game: 350.0—Neil Lomax, Portland St, 1978-80

RECEIVING

Most Passes Caught: 317—Jacquay Nunnally, Florida A&M, 1997-00
Most Yards Gained: 4,693—Jerry Rice, Mississippi Valley, 1981-84
Most Yards Gained per Game: 119.1—Tramon Douglas, Grambling, 2002-03
Highest Average Gain per Reception: 24.3—John Taylor, Delaware St, 1982-85

Single Season

SCORING

Most Points Scored: 176—Brian Westbrook, Villanova, 2001
Most Touchdowns Scored: 29—Adrian Peterson, Georgia Southern, 1999; Brian Westbrook, Villanova, 2001
Most Touchdowns Scored, Rushing: 29—Jamaal Branch, Colgate, 2003
Most Touchdowns Scored, Passing: 56—Willie Totten, Mississippi Valley, 1984; Bruce Eugene, Grambling St, 2005
Most Touchdowns Scored, Receiving: 27—Jerry Rice, Mississippi Valley, 1984

RUSHING

Most Rushes: 450—Jamaal Branch, Colgate, 2003
Most Rushes per Game: 40.9—Arnold Mickens, Butler, 1994
Most Yards Gained: 2,326—Jamaal Branch, Colgate, 2003
Most Yards Gained per Game: 225.5—Arnold Mickens, Butler, 1994

Single Season *(Cont.)*

PASSING

Highest Passing Efficiency Rating: 204.6—
Shawn Knight, William & Mary, 1993
Most Passes Attempted: 592—Martin Hankins,
Southeastern La. 2003
Most Passes Completed: 405—Brett Gordon,
Villanova, 2002
Most Passes Completed per Game: 32.4—Willie
Totten, Mississippi Valley, 1984
Highest Completion Percentage: 70.6—Giovanni
Carmazzi, Hofstra, 1997
Most Yards Gained: 4,863—Steve McNair,
Alcorn St, 1994
Most Yards Gained per Game: 455.7—
Willie Totten, Mississippi Valley, 1984

RECEIVING

Most Passes Caught: 120—Stephen Campbell,
Brown, 2000
Most Yards Gained: 1,712—Eddie Conti,
Delaware, 1998
Most Yards Gained per Game: 168.2—
Jerry Rice, Mississippi Valley, 1984
Highest Average Gain per Reception: 28.9—
Mikhael Ricks, Stephen F. Austin, 1997; (min. 35
receptions)

Single Game

SCORING

Most Points Scored: 42—Jesse Burton, McNeese
St, 1998 (vs Southern Utah); Archie Amerson,
Northern Arizona, 1996 (vs Weber St)
Most Field Goals: 8—Goran Lingmerth,
Northern Arizona, 1986 (vs Idaho)

RUSHING

Most Yards Gained: 437—Maurice Hicks,
N Carolina A&T, 2001 (vs Morgan St)
Most Touchdowns Rushed: 7—Archie Amerson,
Northern Arizona, 1996 (vs Weber St)

PASSING

Most Passes Completed: 50—Martin Hankins,
Southeastern La., 2004, (vs. Jacksonville)
Most Yards Gained: 624—Jamie Martin, Weber St,
1991 (vs Idaho St)
Most Touchdown Passes: 9—Willie Totten,
Mississippi Valley, 1984 (vs Kentucky St)

RECEIVING

Most Passes Caught: 24—Chas Gessner, Brown,
2002, (vs Rhode Island); Jerry Rice, Mississippi
Valley, 1983 (vs Southern–BR)
Most Yards Gained: 376—Kassim Osgood,
Cal Poly, 2000 (vs Northern Iowa)
Most Touchdown Catches: 6—Cos DeMatteo,
Chattanooga, 2000 (vs Mississippi Valley)

NCAA Division II Individual Records

Career

SCORING

Most Points Scored: 570—Ian Smart,
C.W. Post, 1999–2002
Most Touchdowns Scored: 95—Ian Smart,
C.W. Post, 1999–2002
Most Touchdowns Scored, Rushing: 94—
Ian Smart, C.W. Post, 1999–2002
Most Touchdowns Scored, Passing: 121—Marc
Eddy, Bentley, 2001–04
Most Touchdowns Scored, Receiving: 78—
Dallas Mall, Bentley, 2001–04

RUSHING

Most Rushes: 1,131—Josh Ranek, S Dakota St,
1997–01
Most Rushes per Game: 29.8—Bernie Peeters,
Luther, 1968–71
Most Yards Gained: 6,958—Brian Shay,
Emporia St, 1995–98
Most Yards Gained per Game: 183.4—
Anthony Gray, Western NM, 1997–98

PASSING

Highest Passing Efficiency Rating: 190.8—
Dusty Bonner, Valdosta St, 2000–01
Most Passes Attempted: 1,898—Andrew Webb,
Fort Lewis, 2000–03

PASSING *(Cont.)*

Most Passes Completed: 1,007—Andrew Webb,
Fort Lewis, 2000–03
Most Passes Completed per Game: 25.7—Chris
Hatcher, Valdosta St, 1991–94
Highest Completion Percentage: 72.7—
Dusty Bonner, Valdosta St, 2000–01
Most Yards Gained: 11,742—Andrew Webb,
Fort Lewis, 2000–03
Most Yards Gained per Game: 323.7—
Dusty Bonner, Valdosta St, 2000–01

RECEIVING

Most Passes Caught: 323—Clarence Coleman,
Ferris St, 1998–01
Most Yards Gained: 4,983—Clarence Coleman,
Ferris St, 1998–01
Most Yards Gained per Game: 160.8—
Chris George, Glenville St, 1993–94
Highest Average Gain per Reception: 23.2—
Romar Crenshaw, Southeastern Okla., 2000–03

Single Season

SCORING

Most Points Scored: 212—David Kircus, Grand Valley St, 2002
Most Touchdowns Scored: 35—David Kircus, Grand Valley St, 2002
Most Touchdowns Scored, Rushing: 33—Ian Smart, C.W. Post, 2001; Germaine Race, Grambling St, 2005
Most Touchdowns Scored, Passing: 54—Dusty Bonner, Valdosta St, 2000
Most Touchdowns Scored, Receiving: 35—David Kircus, Grand Valley St, 2002

RUSHING

Most Rushes: 385—Joe Gough, Wayne St (Mich.), 1994
Most Rushes per Game: 38.6—Mark Perkins, Hobart, 1968
Most Yards Gained: 2,653—Kavin Gailliard, American International, 1999
Most Yards Gained per Game: 222.0—Anthony Gray, Western New Mexico, 1997

PASSING

Highest Passing Efficiency Rating: 221.63—Curt Anes, Grand Valley St, 2001
Most Passes Attempted: 559—Andrew Webb, Fort Lewis 2001
Most Passes Completed: 384—Chad Friehauf, Colorado Mines 2004
Most Passes Completed per Game: 32.4—Lance Funderburk, Valdosta St, 1995
Highest Completion Percentage: 74.7—Chris Hatcher, Valdosta St, 1994
Most Yards Gained: 4,646—Chad Friehauf, Colorado Mines 2004
Most Yards Gained per Game: 393.4—Grady Benton, W Texas A&M, 1994

RECEIVING

Most Passes Caught: 119—Brad Bailey, W Texas A&M, 1994
Most Yards Gained: 1,876—Chris George, Glenville St, 1993
Most Yards Gained per Game: 187.6—Chris George, Glenville St, 1993
Highest Average Gain per Reception: 32.5—Tyrone Johnson, Western St, 1991 (min. 30 receptions)

Single Game

SCORING

Most Points Scored: 48—Paul Zaeske, N Park, 1968 (vs N Central); Junior Wolf, Panhandle St, 1958 (vs St. Mary [Ks.])
Most Field Goals: 6—Steve Huff, Central Missouri St, 1985 (vs SE Missouri St); Austin Wellock, Ashland, 2002 (vs. Wayne St)

RUSHING

Most Yards Gained: 410—Andrew Terry, Ferris St, 2004 (vs Findlay)
Most Touchdowns Rushed: 8—Junior Wolf, Panhandle St, 1958 (vs St. Mary [Ks.])

PASSING

Most Passes Completed: 76—Jarrod DeGeorgia, Wayne St (NE),1996 (vs Drake)
Most Yards Gained: 645—Matt Kohn, Indianapolis, 2003 (vs Michigan Tech)
Most Touchdowns Passed: 10—Bruce Swanson, N Park, 1968 (vs N Central)

RECEIVING

Most Passes Caught: 23—Chris George, Glenville St, 1994 (vs WV Wesleyan); Barry Wagner, Alabama A&M, 1989 (vs Clark Atlanta)
Most Yards Gained: 401—Kevin Ingram, W Chester, 1998 (vs Clarion)
Most Touchdown Catches: 8—Paul Zaeske, N Park, 1968 (vs N Central)

NCAA Division III Individual Records

Career

SCORING

Most Points Scored: 562—R.J. Bowers, Grove City, 1997–00
Most Touchdowns Scored: 92—R.J. Bowers, Grove City, 1997–00
Most Touchdowns Scored, Rushing: 91—R.J. Bowers, Grove City, 1997–00
Most Touchdowns Scored, Passing: 148—Justin Peery, Westminster (Mo.), 1996–99
Most Touchdowns Scored, Receiving: 75—Scott Pingel, Westminster (Mo.), 1996–99

RUSHING

Most Rushes: 1,190—Steve Tardif, Maine Maritime, 1996–99
Most Rushes per Game: 32.7—Chris Sizemore, Bridgewater (VA), 1972–74

RUSHING *(Cont.)*

Most Yards Gained: 7,353—R.J. Bowers, Grove City, 1997–00
Most Yards Gained per Game: 187.1—Tony Sutton, Wooster, 2002–04

PASSING

Highest Passing Efficiency Rating: 194.2—Bill Borchert, Mount Union, 1994–97
Most Passes Attempted: 1,696—Kirk Baumgartner, UW–Stevens Point, 1986–89
Most Passes Completed: 1,012—Justin Peery, Westminster (Mo.), 1996–99
Most Passes Completed per Game: 25.9—Justin Peery, Westminster (Mo.), 1996–99
Highest Completion Percentage: 67.0—Gary Smeck, Mount Union, 1997–00

Career *(Cont.)*

PASSING *(Cont.)*

Most Yards Gained: 13,262—Justin Peery, Westminster (Mo.), 1996–99
Most Yards Gained per Game: 340.1—Justin Peery, Westminster (Mo.), 1996–99

RECEIVING

Most Passes Caught: 436—Scott Pingel, Westminster (Mo.), 1996–99
Most Yards Gained: 6,108—Scott Pingel, Westminster (Mo.), 1996–99
Most Yards Gained per Game: 156.6—Scott Pingel, Westminster (Mo.), 1996–99
Highest Average Gain per Reception: 23.4—Michael Coleman, Widener, 1998–2001

Single Season

SCORING

Most Points Scored: 248—Dan Pugh, Mount Union, 2002
Most Points Scored per Game: 20.8—James Regan, Pomona-Pitzer, 1997
Most Touchdowns Scored: 41—Dan Pugh Mount Union, 2002
Most Touchdowns Scored, Rushing: 35—Dan Pugh, Mount Union, 2002
Most Touchdowns Scored, Passing: 61—Brett Elliott, Linfield, 2004
Most Touchdowns Scored, Receiving: 26—Scott Pingel, Westminster (Mo.), 1998

RUSHING

Most Rushes: 463—Dante Washington, Carthage, 2004
Most Rushes per Game: 38.0—Mike Birosak, Dickinson, 1989
Most Yards Gained: 2,420—Justin Beaver, UW–Whitewater, 2005

PASSING

Highest Passing Efficiency Rating: 225.0—Mike Simpson, Eureka, 1994
Most Passes Attempted: 575—Brett Dietz, Hanover, 2003
Most Passes Completed: 360—Brett Dietz, Hanover, 2003
Most Passes Completed per Game: 32.9—Justin Peery, Westminster (Mo.), 1999
Highest Completion Percentage: 73.6—Mitch Tanney, Monmouth (Ill.), 2005
Most Yards Gained: 4,595—Brett Elliott, Linfield, 2004
Most Yards Gained per Game: 450.1—Justin Peery, Westminster (Mo.), 1998

RECEIVING

Most Passes Caught: 136—Scott Pingel, Westminster (Mo.), 1999
Most Yards Gained: 2,157—Scott Pingel, Westminster, (Mo.), 1998
Most Yards Gained per Game: 215.7—Scott Pingel, Westminster, (Mo.), 1998
Highest Average Gain per Reception: 26.9—Marty Redlawsk, Concordia (Ill.), 1985

Single Game

SCORING

Most Field Goals: 6—Jim Hever, Rhodes, 1984 (vs Millsaps)

PASSING

Most Passes Completed: 51—Scott Kello, Sul Ross St, 2002 (vs Howard Payne)
Most Yards Gained: 731—Zamir Amin, Menlo, 2000 (vs California Lutheran)
Most Touchdown Passes: 9—Joe Zarlinga, Ohio Northern, 1998 (vs Capital)

RUSHING

Most Yards Gained: 441—Dante Brown, Marietta, 1996 (vs Baldwin-Wallace)
Most Touchdowns Rushed: 8—Carey Bender, Coe, 1994 (vs Beloit)

RECEIVING

Most Passes Caught: 23—Sean Munroe, Mass-Boston, 1992 (vs Mass-Maritime)
Most Yards Gained: 418—Lewis Howes, Principia, 2002 (vs Martin Luther)
Most Touchdown Catches: 7—Matt Perceval, Wesleyan (Conn.), 1998 (vs Middlebury)

Career

Scoring

POINTS (KICKERS)

	Years	Pts
Roman Anderson, Houston	1988–91	423
Billy Bennett, Georgia	2000–03	409
Carlos Huerta, Miami (Fla.)	1988–91	397
Jason Elam, Hawaii	1988–92	395
Derek Schmidt, Florida St	1984–87	393
Nick Novak, Maryland	2001–04	393

POINTS (NON-KICKERS)

	Years	Pts
Travis Prentice, Miami (Ohio)	1996–99	468
Ricky Williams, Texas	1995–98	452
Taurean Henderson, Texas Tech	2002–05	414
Brock Forsey, Boise St	1999–02	408
Cedric Benson, Texas	2001–04	404

POINTS PER GAME (NON-KICKERS)

	Years	Pts/Game
Marshall Faulk, San Diego St	1991–93	12.1
Ed Marinaro, Cornell	1969–71	11.8
Bill Burnett, Arkansas	1968–70	11.3
Steve Owens, Oklahoma	1967–69	11.2
Eddie Talboom, Wyoming	1948–50	10.8

Total Offense

YARDS GAINED

	Years	Yds
Timmy Chang, Hawaii	2000–04	16,910
Ty Detmer, Brigham Young	1988–91	14,665
Philip Rivers, N Carolina St	2000–03	13,582
Brad Smith, Missouri	2002–05	13,088
Luke McCown, Louisiana Tech	2000–03	12,731

YARDS PER GAME

	Years	Yds/Game
Tim Rattay, Louisiana Tech	1997–99	382.4
Chris Vargas, Nevada	1992–93	320.9
Timmy Chang, Hawaii	2000–04	319.1
Ty Detmer, Brigham Young	1988–91	318.8
Daunte Culpepper, Central Florida	1996–98	313.5

Rushing

YARDS GAINED

	Years	Yds
Ron Dayne, Wisconsin	1996–99	6,397
Ricky Williams, Texas	1995–98	6,279
Tony Dorsett, Pittsburgh	1973–76	6,082
DeAngelo Williams, Memphis	2002–05	6,026
Charles White, USC	1976–79	5,598
Travis Prentice, Miami (Ohio)	1996–99	5,596

YARDS PER GAME

	Years	Yds/Game
Ed Marinaro, Cornell	1969–71	174.6
O.J. Simpson, USC	1967–68	164.4
Herschel Walker, Georgia	1980–82	159.4
LeShon Johnson, Northern Illinois	1992–93	150.6
Ron Dayne, Wisconsin	1996–99	148.8

TOUCHDOWNS RUSHING

	Years	TD
Travis Prentice, Miami (Ohio)	1996–99	73
Ricky Williams, Texas	1995–98	72
Anthony Thompson, Indiana	1986–89	64
Cedric Benson, Texas	2001–04	64
Ron Dayne, Wisconsin	1996–99	63
Eric Crouch, Nebraska	1998–01	59

Passing

PASSING EFFICIENCY

	Years	Rating
Ryan Dinwiddie, Boise St	2000–03	168.4
Danny Wuerffel, Florida	1993–96	163.6
Ty Detmer, Brigham Young	1988–91	162.7
Steve Sarkisian, Brigham Young	1995–96	162.0
Matt Leinart, USC	2002–05	159.5

Note: Minimum 500 completions.

YARDS GAINED

	Years	Yds
Timmy Chang, Hawaii	2000–04	17,072
Ty Detmer, Brigham Young	1988–91	15,031
Philip Rivers, N Carolina St	2000–03	13,484
Tim Rattay, Louisiana Tech	1997–99	12,746
Luke McCown, Louisiana Tech	2000–03	12,666

COMPLETIONS

	Years	Comp
Timmy Chang, Hawaii	2000–04	1,388
Kliff Kingsbury, Texas Tech	1999–02	1,231
Philip Rivers, N Carolina St	2000–03	1,147
Luke McCown, Louisiana Tech	2000–03	1,063
Chris Redman, Louisville	1996–99	1,031
Tim Rattay, Louisiana Tech	1997–99	1,015

TOUCHDOWNS PASSING

	Years	TD
Ty Detmer, Brigham Young	1988–91	121
Timmy Chang, Hawaii	2000–04	117
Tim Rattay, Louisiana Tech	1997–99	115
Danny Wuerffel, Florida	1993–96	114
Chad Pennington, Marshall	1997–99	100
Matt Leinart, USC	2002–05	99

Receiving

CATCHES

	Years	No.
Taylor Stubblefield, Purdue	2001–04	316
Josh Davis, Marshall	2001–04	306
Taurean Henderson, Texas Tech	2002–05	303
Arnold Jackson, Louisville	1997–00	300
Trevor Insley, Nevada	1996–99	298
Geoff Noisy, Nevada	1995–98	295

CATCHES PER GAME

	Years	No./Game
Emmanuel Hazard, Houston	1989–90	10.5
Alex Van Dyke, Nevada	1994–95	10.3
Howard Twilley, Tulsa	1963–65	10.0
Jason Phillips, Houston	1987–88	9.4
Troy Edwards, Louisiana Tech	1996–98	8.2
Bryan Reeves, Nevada	1992–93	8.2

YARDS GAINED

	Years	Yds
Trevor Insley, Nevada	1996–99	5,005
Marcus Harris, Wyoming	1993–96	4,518
Rashaun Woods, Oklahoma St	2000–03	4,412
Ryan Yarborough, Wyoming	1990–93	4,357
Troy Edwards, Louisiana Tech	1996–98	4,352

TOUCHDOWN CATCHES

	Years	TD
Troy Edwards, Louisiana Tech	1996–98	50
Darius Watts, Marshall	2000–03	47
Aaron Turner, Pacific	1989–92	43
Ryan Yarborough, Wyoming	1990–93	42
Rashaun Woods, Oklahoma St	2000–03	42
Braylon Edwards, Michigan	2001–04	39
Greg Jennings, West Michigan	2002–05	39

Career *(Cont.)*

All-Purpose Running

YARDS GAINED	Years	Yds
DeAngelo Williams, Memphis	2002–05	7,573
Ricky Williams, Texas	1996–98	7,206
Napoleon McCallum, Navy	1981–85	7,172
Darrin Nelson, Stanford	1977–78, 80–81	6,885
Kevin Faulk, Louisiana St	1995–98	6,833

YARDS PER GAME	Years	Yds/Game
Ryan Benjamin, Pacific	1990–92	237.8
Sheldon Canley, San Jose St	1988–90	205.8
Howard Stevens, Louisville	1971–72	193.7
O.J. Simpson, Southern Cal	1967–68	192.9
Alex Van Dyke, Nevada	1994–95	188.5

Interceptions

PLAYER/SCHOOL	Years	Int
Al Brosky, Illinois	1950–52	29
John Provost, Holy Cross	1972–74	27
Martin Bayless, Bowling Green	1980–83	27
Tom Curtis, Michigan	1967–69	25
Tony Thurman, Boston Col	1981–84	25
Tracy Saul, Texas Tech	1989–92	25

Punting Average

PLAYER/SCHOOL	Years	Avg
Todd Sauerbrun, W Virginia	1991–94	46.3
Reggie Roby, Iowa	1979–82	45.6
Greg Montgomery, Michigan St	1985–87	45.4
Ryan Plackemeier, Wake Forest	2002–05	45.3
Tom Tupa, Ohio St	1984–87	45.2

Note: 150–249 punts.

Punt Return Average

PLAYER/SCHOOL	Years	Avg
Jack Mitchell, Oklahoma	1946–48	23.6
Gene Gibson, Cincinnati	1949–50	20.5
Eddie Macon, Pacific	1949–51	18.9
Jackie Robinson, UCLA	1939–40	18.8
Dan Shelton, Illinois	2001–04	17.9
Bobby Dillon, Texas	1949–51	17.7
Mike Fuller, Auburn	1972–74	17.7

Note: At least 30 returns.

Kickoff Return Average

PLAYER/SCHOOL	Years	Avg
Anthony Davis, Southern Cal	1972–74	35.1
Eric Booth, Southern Miss	1994–97	32.4
Overton Curtis, Utah St	1957–58	31.0
Fred Montgomery, New Mexico St	1991–92	30.5
Altie Taylor, Utah St	1966–68	29.3

Note: At least 30 returns.

Single Season

Scoring

POINTS	Year	Pts
Barry Sanders, Oklahoma St	1988	234
Brock Forsey, Boise St	2002	192
Troy Edwards, Louisiana Tech	1998	186
Mike Rozier, Nebraska	1983	174
Lydell Mitchell, Penn St	1971	174

FIELD GOALS	Year	FG
Billy Bennett, Georgia	2003	31
John Lee, UCLA	1984	29
Paul Woodside, W Virginia	1982	28
Luis Zendejas, Arizona St	1983	28
Nick Browne, Texas Christian	2003	28

Three tied with 27.

All-Purpose Running

YARDS GAINED	Year	Yds
Barry Sanders, Oklahoma St	1988	3,250
Ryan Benjamin, Pacific	1991	2,995
Reggie Bush, USC	2005	2,890
Troy Edwards, Louisiana Tech	1998	2,784
Darren Sproles, Kansas St	2003	2,735

YARDS PER GAME	Year	Yds/Game
Barry Sanders, Oklahoma St	1988	295.5
Ryan Benjamin, Pacific	1991	249.6
Byron (Whizzer) White, Colorado	1937	246.3
Mike Pringle, Fullerton St	1989	244.6
Paul Palmer, Temple	1986	239.4

Total Offense

YARDS GAINED	Year	Yds
B.J. Symons, Texas Tech	2003	5,976
David Klingler, Houston	1990	5,221
Ty Detmer, Brigham Young	1990	5,022
Kliff Kingsbury, Texas Tech	2002	4,903
Tim Rattay, Louisiana Tech	1998	4,840

YARDS PER GAME	Year	Yds/Game
David Klingler, Houston	1990	474.6
B.J. Symons, Texas Tech	2003	459.7
Andre Ware, Houston	1989	423.7
Ty Detmer, Brigham Young	1990	418.5
Tim Rattay, Louisiana Tech	1998	403.3

Rushing

YARDS GAINED	Year	Yds
Barry Sanders, Oklahoma St	1988	2,628
Marcus Allen, Southern Cal	1981	2,342
Troy Davis, Iowa St	1996	2,185
LaDainian Tomlinson, Texas Christian	2000	2,158
Mike Rozier, Nebraska	1983	2,148

YARDS PER GAME	Year	Yds/Game
Barry Sanders, Oklahoma St	1988	238.9
Marcus Allen, Southern Cal	1981	212.9
Ed Marinaro, Cornell	1971	209.0
Troy Davis, Iowa St	1996	198.6
LaDainian Tomlinson, Texas Christian	2000	196.2

Single Season *(Cont.)*

Rushing *(Cont.)*

TOUCHDOWNS RUSHING

	Year	TD
Barry Sanders, Oklahoma St	1988	37
Mike Rozier, Nebraska	1983	29
Willis McGahee, Miami (FL)	2002	28
Ricky Williams, Texas	1998	27
Lee Suggs, Virginia Tech	2000	27
Brock Forsey, Boise St	2002	26
LenDale White, USC	2005	26

Passing

PASSING EFFICIENCY

	Year	Rating
Shaun King, Tulane	1998	183.3
Stefan Lefors, Louisville	2004	181.7
Michael Vick, Virginia Tech	1999	180.4
Danny Wuerffel, Florida	1995	178.4
Jim McMahon, Brigham Young	1980	176.9

YARDS GAINED

	Year	Yds
B.J. Symons, Texas Tech	2003	5,833
Ty Detmer, Brigham Young	1990	5,188
David Klingler, Houston	1990	5,140
Kliff Kingsbury, Texas Tech	2002	5,017
Tim Rattay, Louisiana Tech	1998	4,943

COMPLETIONS

	Year	Att	Comp
Kliff Kingsbury, Texas Tech	2002	712	479
B.J. Symons, Texas Tech	2003	719	470
Sonny Cumbie, Texas Tech	2004	642	421
Tim Couch, Kentucky	1998	553	400
Tim Rattay, Louisiana Tech	1998	559	380

TOUCHDOWNS PASSING

	Year	TD
David Klingler, Houston	1990	54
B.J. Symons, Texas Tech	2003	52
Jim McMahon, Brigham Young	1980	47
Andre Ware, Houston	1989	46
Tim Rattay, Louisiana Tech	1998	46

Receiving

CATCHES

	Year	GP	No.
Emmanuel Hazard, Houston	1989	11	142
Troy Edwards, Louisiana Tech	1998	12	140
Nate Burleson, Nevada	2002	12	138
Howard Twilley, Tulsa	1965	10	134
Trevor Insley, Nevada	1999	11	134

CATCHES PER GAME

	Year	No.	No./Game
Howard Twilley, Tulsa	1965	134	13.4
Emmanuel Hazard, Houston	1989	142	12.9
Trevor Insley, Nevada	1999	134	12.2
Troy Edwards, Louisiana Tech	1998	140	11.7
Alex Van Dyke, Nevada	1995	129	11.7

YARDS GAINED

	Year	Yds
Trevor Insley, Nevada	1999	2,060
Troy Edwards, Louisiana Tech	1998	1,996
Alex Van Dyke, Nevada	1995	1,854
J.R. Tolver, San Diego St	2002	1,785
Howard Twilley, Tulsa	1965	1,779

TOUCHDOWN CATCHES

	Year	TD
Troy Edwards, Louisiana Tech	1998	27
Randy Moss, Marshall	1997	25
Emmanuel Hazard, Houston	1989	22
Larry Fitzgerald, Pittsburgh	2003	22
Desmond Howard, Michigan	1991	19
Ashley Lelie, Hawaii	2001	19

Single Game

Scoring

POINTS

	Opponent	Year	Pts
Howard Griffith, Illinois	Southern Illinois	1990	48
Marshall Faulk, San Diego St	Pacific	1991	44
Jim Brown, Syracuse	Colgate	1956	43
Showboat Boykin, Mississippi	Mississippi St	1951	42
Fred Wendt, UTEP*	New Mexico St	1948	42
Rashaun Woods, Oklahoma St	SMU	2003	42

*UTEP was Texas Mines in 1948.

FIELD GOALS

	Opponent	Year	FG
Dale Klein, Nebraska	Missouri	1985	7
Mike Prindle, Western Michigan	Marshall	1984	7

Note: 17 tied with 6.

Klein's distances were 32-22-43-44-29-43-43.
Prindle's distances were 32-44-42-23-48-41-27.

Total Offense

YARDS GAINED

	Opponent	Year	Yds
David Klingler, Houston	Arizona St	1990	732
Matt Vogler, TCU	Houston	1990	696
B.J. Symons, Texas Tech	Mississippi	2003	681
Brian Lindgren, Idaho	Middle Tenn St	2001	657

Total Offense *(Cont.)*

YARDS GAINED

	Opponent	Year	Yds
David Klingler, Houston	Texas Christian	1990	625
Scott Mitchell, Utah	Air Force	1988	625

Passing

YARDS GAINED

	Opponent	Year	Yds
David Klingler, Houston	Arizona St	1990	716
Matt Vogler, TCU	Houston	1990	690
B.J. Symons, Texas Tech	Mississippi	2003	661
Cody Hodges, Texas Tech	Kansas St	2005	643
Brian Lindgren, Idaho	Middle Tenn St	2001	637

COMPLETIONS

	Opponent	Year	Comp
Drew Brees, Purdue	Wisconsin	1998	55
Rusty LaRue, Wake Forest	Duke	1995	55
Rusty LaRue, Wake Forest	NC St	1995	50
Brian Lindgren, Idaho	Middle Tenn St	2001	49
Kliff Kingsbury, Texas Tech	Missouri	2002	49
Kliff Kingsbury, Texas Tech	Texas A&M	2002	49
Bruce Gradkowski, Toledo	Pittsburgh	2003	49

TOUCHDOWNS PASSING

	Opponent	Year	TD
David Klingler, Houston	E Wash	1990	11

Note: Klingler's TD passes were 5-48-29-7-3-7-40-10-7-8-51.

Single Game (Cont.)

Rushing

YARDS GAINED	Opponent	Year	Yds
LaDainian Tomlinson ....UTEP		1999	406
Texas Christian			
Tony Sands, Kansas ....Missouri		1991	396
Marshall Faulk,			
San Diego St ....Pacific		1991	386
Troy Davis, Iowa St ....Missouri		1996	378
Anthony Thompson,			
Indiana..............................Wisconsin		1989	377
Robbie Mixon,			
Central Michigan ....Eastern Mich		2002	377

TOUCHDOWNS RUSHING	Opponent	Year	TD
Howard Griffith, Illinois .....Southern Illinois		1990	8

Note: Griffith's TD runs were 5-51-7-41-5-18-5-3.

Receiving

CATCHES	Opponent	Year	No.
Randy Gatewood, UNLV .....Idaho		1994	23
Jay Miller, Brigham Young ...New Mexico		1973	22
Troy Edwards, La. Tech ......Nebraska		1998	21
Chris Daniels, Purdue ....Michigan St		1999	21
Rick Eber, Tulsa ....Idaho St		1967	20
Kenny Christian,			
Eastern Michigan ....Temple		2000	20

YARDS GAINED	Opponent	Year	Yds
Troy Edwards,Louisiana Tech....Nebraska		1998	405
Randy Gatewood, UNLV ....Idaho		1994	363
Chuck Hughes, UTEP*............N Texas St		1965	349
Nate Burleson, Nevada...........San Jose St		2001	326
Rick Eber, Tulsa......................Idaho St		1967	322

*UTEP was Texas Western in 1965.

TOUCHDOWN CATCHES	Opponent	Year	TD
Rashaun Woods, Okla. St .....SMU		2003	7
Tim Delaney, San Diego St....New Mex. St		1969	6

Longest Plays (since 1941)

PASSING	Opponent	Year	Yds
Fred Owens to Jack Ford,			
Portland................................St. Mary's (Ca.)		1947	99
Bo Burris to Warren McVea,			
Houston.................................Washington St		1966	99
Colin Clapton to Eddie Jenkins,			
Holy Cross ....Boston U		1970	99
Terry Peel to Robert Ford,			
Houston.................................Syracuse		1970	99
Terry Peel to Robert Ford,			
Houston.................................San Diego St		1972	99
Cris Collinsworth to Derrick Gaffney,			
Florida...................................Rice		1977	99
Scott Ankrom to James Maness,			
Texas Christian......................Rice		1984	99
Gino Toretta to Horace Copeland,			
Miami (Fla.) ....Arkansas		1991	99
John Paci to Thomas Lewis,			
Indiana..................................Penn St		1993	99
Troy DeGar to Wes Caswell			
Tulsa.....................................Oklahoma		1996	99
Drew Brees to Vinny Sutherland,			
Purdue ....Northwestern		1999	99
Dan Urban to Justin McCariens,			
Northern Illinois.....................Ball St		2000	99
Jason Johnson to Brandon Marshall,			
Arizona..................................Idaho		2001	99
Dondrial Pinkins to Troy Williamson,			
S Carolina ....Virginia		2003	99
Jim Sorgi to Lee Evans,			
Wisconsin..............................Akron		2003	99

RUSHING	Opponent	Year	Yd
Gale Sayers, Kansas ....Nebraska		1963	99
Max Anderson, Arizona St....Wyoming		1967	99
Ralph Thompson,			
W Texas St ....Wichita St		1970	99
Kelsey Finch, Tennessee ......Florida		1977	99
Eric Vann, Kansas.................Oklahoma		1997	99

FIELD GOALS	Opponent	Year	Yds
Steve Little, Arkansas ....Texas		1977	67
Russell Erxleben, Texas ....Rice		1977	67
Joe Williams, Wichita St...Southern IL		1978	67
Martin Gramatica, Kansas St...Northern IL		1998	65
Tony Franklin, Texas A&M ......Baylor		1976	65

PUNTS	Opponent	Year	Yds
Pat Brady, Nevada*................Loyola (Ca.)		1950	99
George O'Brien, Wisconsin ...Iowa		1952	96
John Hadl, Kansas.................Oklahoma		1959	94
Carl Knox, Texas Christian.....Oklahoma St		1947	94
Preston Johnson, SMU...........Pittsburgh		1940	94

*Nevada was Nevada-Reno in 1950.

DIVISION I-A WINNINGEST TEAMS

Alltime Winning Percentage

	Yrs	W	L	T	Pct	GP	Bowl Record
Michigan	126	849	280	36	.7442	1,165	18-19-0
Notre Dame	117	811	266	42	.7435	1,119	13-14-0
Texas	113	800	310	33	.714	1,143	22-21-2
Oklahoma	111	757	289	53	.713	1,099	24-14-1
Alabama	111	774	301	43	.712	1,118	30-20-3
Ohio St.	116	774	300	53	.710	1,127	18-19-0
Nebraska	116	794	321	40	.705	1,155	22-21-0
USC	113	732	298	54	.700	1,084	28-16-0
Tennessee	109	752	312	53	.697	1,117	24-21-0
Penn St	119	771	39	41	.688	1,151	24-12-2
Boise St	38	304	140	2	.684	446	4-2-0
Florida St	59	436	205	17	.676	658	19-13-2
Georgia	112	693	375	54	.642	1,122	22-16-3
Miami (Fla.)	79	525	291	19	.640	835	17-13-0
Miami (Ohio)	117	639	352	44	.639	1,035	6-3-0
Louisiana St	112	669	374	47	.635	1,090	18-18-1
Washington	116	641	372	50	.627	1,063	14-14-1
Auburn	113	656	382	47	.626	1,085	17-13-2
Arizona St	93	523	318	24	.618	865	12-9-1
Florida	99	606	367	40	.618	1,013	15-18-0
Colorado	116	650	402	36	.614	1,088	12-15-0
South Florida	9	61	39	0	.610	100	0-1-0
Central Michigan	105	532	338	36	.607	906	0-2-0
UCLA	87	52	338	37	.602	896	13-13-1
Texas A&M	139	639	415	48	.602	1,102	13-15-0

Note: Includes bowl games.

Alltime Victories

Michigan	849	Georgia	693	Pittsburgh	633
Notre Dame	811	Louisiana St	669	Army	628
Texas	800	Syracuse	665	Arkansas	628
Nebraska	794	Auburn	656	Virginia Tech	626
Alabama	774	Colorado	650	N Carolina	624
Ohio St	774	W Virginia	642	Minnesota	623
Penn St.	771	Washington	641	Clemson	608
Oklahoma	757	Miami (Ohio)	639	Navy	607
Tennessee	752	Texas A&M	639	Florida	606
USC	732	Georgia Tech	637	Virginia	592

NUMBER ONE VS NUMBER TWO

The No. 1 and No. 2 teams, according to the Associated Press Poll, have met 33 times, including 13 bowl games, since the poll's inception in 1936. The No. 1 teams have a 20-11-2 record in these matchups. Notre Dame (4-3-2) has played in nine of the games.

Date	Results	Stadium
10-9-43	No. 1 Notre Dame 35, No. 2 Michigan 12	Michigan (Ann Arbor)
11-20-43	No. 1 Notre Dame 14, No. 2 Iowa Pre-Flight 13	Notre Dame (South Bend)
12-2-44	No. 1 Army 23, No. 2 Navy 7	Municipal (Baltimore)
11-10-45	No. 1 Army 48, No. 2 Notre Dame 0	Yankee (New York)
12-1-45	No. 1 Army 32, No. 2 Navy 13	Municipal (Philadelphia)
11-9-46	No. 1 Army 0, No. 2 Notre Dame 0	Yankee (New York)
1-1-63	No. 1 Southern Cal 42, No. 2 Wisconsin 37 (Rose Bowl)	Rose Bowl (Pasadena)
10-12-63	No. 2 Texas 28, No. 1 Oklahoma 7	Cotton Bowl (Dallas)
1-1-64	No. 1 Texas 28, No. 2 Navy 6 (Cotton Bowl)	Cotton Bowl (Dallas)
11-19-66	No. 1 Notre Dame 10, No. 2 Michigan St 10	Spartan (E Lansing)
9-28-68	No. 1 Purdue 37, No. 2 Notre Dame 22	Notre Dame (South Bend)
1-1-69	No. 1 Ohio St 27, No. 2 Southern Cal 16 (Rose Bowl)	Rose Bowl (Pasadena)
12-6-69	No. 1 Texas 15, No. 2 Arkansas 14	Razorback (Fayetteville)
11-25-71	No. 1 Nebraska 35, No. 2 Oklahoma 31	Owen Field (Norman)
1-1-72	No. 1 Nebraska 38, No. 2 Alabama 6 (Orange Bowl)	Orange Bowl (Miami)
1-1-79	No. 2 Alabama 14, No. 1 Penn St 7 (Sugar Bowl)	Sugar Bowl (New Orleans)
9-26-81	No. 1 Southern Cal 28, No. 2 Oklahoma 24	Coliseum (Los Angeles)
1-1-83	No. 2 Penn St 27, No. 1 Georgia 23 (Sugar Bowl)	Sugar Bowl (New Orleans)

NUMBER ONE VS NUMBER TWO *(Cont.)*

Date	Results	Stadium
10-19-85	No. 1 Iowa 12, No. 2 Michigan 10	Kinnick (Iowa City)
9-27-86	No. 2 Miami (Fla.) 28, No. 1 Oklahoma 16	Orange Bowl (Miami)
1-2-87	No. 2 Penn St 14, No. 1 Miami (FL) 10 (Fiesta Bowl)	Sun Devil (Tempe)
11-21-87	No. 2 Oklahoma 17, No. 1 Nebraska 7	Memorial (Lincoln)
1-1-88	No. 2 Miami (Fla.) 20, No. 1 Oklahoma 14 (Orange Bowl)	Orange Bowl (Miami)
11-26-88	No. 1 Notre Dame 27, No. 2 USC 10	Coliseum (Los Angeles)
9-16-89	No. 1 Notre Dame 24, No. 2 Michigan 19	Michigan (Ann Arbor)
11-16-91	No. 2 Miami (Fla.) 17, No. 1 Florida St 16	Campbell (Tallahassee)
1-1-93	No. 2 Alabama 34, No. 1 Miami (Fla.) 13 (Sugar Bowl)	Superdome (New Orleans)
11-13-93	No. 2 Notre Dame 31, No. 1 Florida St 24	Notre Dame (South Bend)
1-1-94	No. 1 Florida St 18, No. 2 Nebraska 16 (Orange Bowl)	Orange Bowl (Miami)
1-2-96	No. 1 Nebraska 62, No. 2 Florida 24 (Fiesta Bowl)	Sun Devil (Tempe)
11-30-96	No. 2 Florida St 24, No. 1 Florida 21	Campbell (Tallahassee)
1-4-99	No. 1 Tennessee 23, No. 2 Florida St 16 (Fiesta Bowl)	Sun Devil (Tempe)
1-4-00	No. 1 Florida St 46, No. 2 Virginia Tech 29 (Sugar Bowl)	Superdome (New Orleans)
1-3-03	No. 2 Ohio St 31, No. 1 Miami (Fla.) 24 [2OT] (Fiesta Bowl)	Sun Devil (Tempe)
1-4-05	No. 1 USC 55, No. 2 Oklahoma 19 (Orange Bowl)	Pro Player Stadium (Miami)
1-4-06	No. 2 Texas 41, No. 1 USC 38 (Rose Bowl)	Rose Bowl (Pasadena)

LONGEST DIVISION I-A WINNING STREAKS

Wins	Team	Yrs	Ended by	Score
47	Oklahoma	1953–57	Notre Dame	7–0
39	Washington	1908–14	Oregon St	0–0
37	Yale	1890–93	Princeton	6–0
37	Yale	1887–89	Princeton	10–0
35	Toledo	1969–71	Tampa	21–0
34	USC	2003–05	Texas	41–38
34	Miami	2000–03	Ohio St	31–24 (2ot)
34	Pennsylvania	1894–96	Lafayette	6–4
31	Oklahoma	1948–50	Kentucky	13–7
31	Pittsburgh	1914–18	Cleveland Naval Reserve	10–9
31	Pennsylvania	1896–98	Harvard	10–0

LONGEST DIVISION I-A UNBEATEN STREAKS

No.	W	T	Team	Yrs	Ended by	Score
63	59	4	Washington	1907–17	California	27–0
56	55	1	Michigan	1901–05	Chicago	2–0
50	46	4	California	1920–25	Olympic Club	15–0
48	47	1	Oklahoma	1953–57	Notre Dame	7–0
48	47	1	Yale	1885–89	Princeton	10–0
47	42	5	Yale	1879–85	Princeton	6–5
44	42	2	Yale	1894–96	Princeton	24–6
42	39	3	Yale	1904–08	Harvard	4–0
39	37	2	Notre Dame	1946–50	Purdue	28–14
37	36	1	Oklahoma	1972–75	Kansas	23–3
37	37	0	Yale	1890–93	Princeton	6–0
35	35	0	Toledo	1969–71	Tampa	21–0
35	34	1	Minnesota	1903–05	Wisconsin	16–12
34	34	0	USC	2003–05	Texas	41–38
34	34	0	Miami	2000–03	Ohio St	31–24 (2ot)
34	33	1	Nebraska	1912–16	Kansas	7–3
34	34	0	Pennsylvania	1894–96	Lafayette	6–4
34	32	2	Princeton	1884–87	Harvard	12–0
34	29	5	Princeton	1877–82	Harvard	1–0
33	30	3	Tennessee	1926–30	Alabama	18–6
33	31	2	Georgia Tech	1914–18	Pittsburgh	32–0
33	30	3	Harvard	1911–15	Cornell	10–0
32	31	1	Nebraska	1969–71	UCLA	20–17
32	30	2	Army	1944–47	Columbia	21–20
32	31	1	Harvard	1898–1900	Yale	28–0
31	30	1	Penn St	1967–70	Colorado	41–13
31	30	1	San Diego St	1967–70	Long Beach St	27–11
31	29	2	Georgia Tech	1950–53	Notre Dame	27–14
31	31	0	Oklahoma	1948–50	Kentucky	13–7
31	31	0	Pittsburgh	1914–18	Cleveland Naval	10–9
31	31	0	Pennsylvania	1896–98	Harvard	10–0

Note: Includes bowl games.

LONGEST DIVISION I-A LOSING STREAKS

Losses		Seasons	Ended Against	Score
34	Northwestern	1979–82	Northern Illinois	31–6
28	Virginia	1958–61	William & Mary	21–6
28	Kansas St	1945–48	Arkansas St	37–6
27	New Mexico St	1988–90	Cal St–Fullerton	43–9
27	Eastern Michigan	1980–82	Kent St	9–7

MOST-PLAYED DIVISION I-A RIVALRIES

GP	Opponents (Series Leader Listed First)	Record	First Game
115	Minnesota–Wisconsin	59-48-8	1890
114	Kansas–Missouri	53-52-9	1891
112	Nebraska–Kansas	87-22-3	1892
112	Texas–Texas A&M	73-34-5	1894
110	Miami (OH)–Cincinnati	59-44-7	1888
110	N Carolina–Virginia	†57-49-4	1892
109	Auburn–Georgia	53-48-8	1892
109	Oregon–Oregon St	55-44-10	1894
108	Purdue–Indiana	67-35-6	1891
108	Stanford–California	54-43-11	1892
106	Navy–Army	50-49-7	1890
104	Baylor–Texas Christian*	49-47-7	1899
104	Utah–Utah St	73-28-4	1892

GP	Opponents (Series Leader Listed First)	Record	First Game
103	Clemson–S Carolina	63-36-4	1896
103	Kansas–Kansas St	62-36-5	1902
102	Mississippi–Miss St	58-38-6	1901
101	N Carolina–Wake Forest	67-32-2	1897
101	Tennessee–Kentucky	69-23-9	1893
100	Georgia–Georgia Tech	57-38-5	1893
100	Nebraska–Iowa St	82-16-2	1896
100	Texas–Oklahoma	56-39-5	1900
100	Oklahoma–Oklahoma St	77-16-7	1904

*Have not met since 1995.
†Disputed series record: Virginia claims N Carolina leads series 55-51-4 based on a forfeited game in 1956.

NCAA Coaches' Records

ALLTIME WINNINGEST DIVISION I-A COACHES

Coach (Alma Mater)	Colleges Coached	Yrs	W	L	T	Pct
Knute Rockne (Notre Dame '14)†	Notre Dame 1918–30	13	105	12	5	.881
Frank W. Leahy (Notre Dame '31)†	Boston Col 1939–40; Notre Dame 1941–43, 1946–53	13	107	13	9	.864
George W. Woodruff (Yale 1889)†	Pennsylvania 1892–01; Illinois 1903; Carlisle 1905	12	142	25	2	.846
Barry Switzer (Arkansas '60)	Oklahoma 1973–88	16	157	29	4	.837
Tom Osborne (Hastings '59)†	Nebraska 1973–97	25	255	49	3	.836
Percy D. Haughton (Harvard 1899)†	Cornell 1899–1900; Harvard 1908–16; Columbia 1923–24	13	96	17	6	.832
Bob Neyland (Army '16)†	Tennessee 1926–34, 1936–40, 1946–52	21	173	31	12	.829
Fielding Yost (W Virginia 1895)†	Ohio Wesleyan 1897; Nebraska 1898; Kansas 1899; Stanford 1900; Michigan 1901–23, 1925–26	29	196	36	12	.828
Bud Wilkinson (Minnesota '37)†	Oklahoma 1947–63	17	145	29	4	.826
Jock Sutherland (Pittsburgh '18)†	Lafayette 1919–23; Pittsburgh 1924–38	20	144	28	14	.812
Bob Devaney (Alma, MI '39)†	Wyoming 1957–61; Nebraska 1962–72	16	136	30	7	.806
*Dan Hawkins (UC Davis, '84)	Wilmt.1996–2000; Boise St. 2001–05	10	93	22	1	.806
Frank W. Thomas (Notre Dame '23)†	Tenn.-Chattanooga 1925–28; Alabama 1931–42, 1944–46	19	141	33	9	.795
Henry L. Williams (Yale 1891)†	Army 1891; Minnesota 1900–21	23	141	34	12	.786
Gil Dobie (Minnesota '02)†	N Dakota St 1906–07; Washington 1908-16; Navy 1917–19; Cornell 1920–35; Boston College 1936–38	33	180	45	15	.781
Bear Bryant (Alabama '36)†	Maryland 1945, Kentucky 1946–53, Texas A&M 1954–57, Alabama 1958–82	38	323	85	17	.780
*Philip Fulmer (Tennessee '72)	Tennessee 1992–05	14	128	37	0	.776

*Active in 2005. †Hall of Fame member.
Note: Minimum 10 years as head coach at Division I institutions; record at four-year colleges only; bowl games included; ranked by percentage, ties computed as half won, half lost.

ALLTIME WINNINGEST DIVISION I-A COACHES *(Cont.)*
By Victories

	Yrs	W	L	T	Pct		Yrs	W	L	T	Pct
*Bobby Bowden	40	359	107	4	.768	Bo Schembechler	27	234	65	8	.775
*Joe Paterno	40	354	117	3	.750	Hayden Fry	37	232	178	10	.564
Paul (Bear) Bryant	38	323	85	17	.780	Jess Neely	40	207	176	19	.539
Glenn (Pop) Warner	44	319	106	32	.733	Warren Woodson	31	203	95	14	.673
Amos Alonzo Stagg	57	314	199	35	.605	Don Nehlen	30	202	128	8	.609
LaVell Edwards	29	257	100	3	.718	Vince Dooley	25	201	77	10	.715
Tom Osborne	25	255	49	3	.836	Eddie Anderson	39	201	128	15	.606
Lou Holtz	33	249	132	7	.651	Jim Sweeney	32	200	154	4	.564
Woody Hayes	33	238	72	10	.759						

*Active in 2005.

Most Bowl Victories

	W	L	T		W	L	T
*Joe Paterno	21	10	1	Jackie Sherrill	8	6	0
*Bobby Bowden	19	9	1	Darrell Royal	8	7	1
Paul (Bear) Bryant	15	12	2	Vince Dooley	8	10	2
Lou Holtz	12	8	2	Pat Dye	7	2	1
Tom Osborne	12	13	0	Bob Devaney	7	3	0
Don James	10	5	0	Dan Devine	7	3	0
John Vaught	10	8	0	Earle Bruce	7	5	0
Bobby Dodd	9	4	0	*Philip Fulmer	7	6	0
Johnny Majors	9	7	0	Charlie McClendon	7	6	0
John Robinson	8	1	0	Hayden Fry	7	9	1
Terry Donahue	8	4	1	LaVell Edwards	7	14	1
Barry Switzer	8	5	0				
*Mack Brown	8	6	0	*Active in 2005.			

WINNINGEST ACTIVE DIVISION I-A COACHES
By Percentage

Coach, College	Yrs	W	L	T	Pct.	Bowls W	L	T
Larry Coker, Miami (Fla.)	5	53	9	0	.855	3	2	0
Pete Carroll, USC	5	54	10	0	.844	3	2	0
Bob Stoops, Oklahoma	7	75	16	0	.824	4	3	0
Urban Meyer, Florida	5	48	11	0	.814	3	0	0
Dan Hawkins, Colorado	10	93	22	1	.806	2	2	0
Mark Richt, Georgia	5	52	13	0	.800	3	2	0
Phillip Fulmer, Tennessee	14	128	37	0	.776	7	6	0
Bobby Bowden, Florida St.	40	359	107	4	.768	19	9	1
Steve Spurrier, South Carolina	16	149	45	2	.765	6	7	0
Lloyd Carr, Michigan	11	102	34	0	.750	5	5	0
Joe Paterno, Penn St	40	354	117	3	.750	21	10	1
Jim Tressel, Ohio State	20	185	70	1	.724	4	1	0
Dennis Erickson, Idaho	17	144	57	1	.715	5	5	0
Tom Amstutz, Toledo	5	44	18	0	.710	2	2	0
Chris Ault, Nevada	21	177	73	1	.707	1	2	0
Gary Patterson, TCU	5	43	18	0	.705	2	3	0
Frank Solich, Ohio	7	62	26	0	.705	2	3	0
Ralph Friedgen, Maryland	5	41	18	0	.672	2	1	0
Tommy Bowden, Clemson	9	70	37	0	.654	4	2	0
Dennis Franchione, Texas A & M	23	171	92	2	.649	3	2	0

#Bowl games included. Ties computed as half win, half loss. Note: Min. five years as Div. I-A head coach at four-year collges only.

By Victories

Bobby Bowden, Florida St	359	Dick Tomey, San Jose St	161
Joe Paterno, Penn St	354	Steve Spurrier, South Carolina	149
Frank Beamer, Viginia Tech	188	Mike Price, UTEP	145
Jim Tressel, Ohio State	185	Dennis Erickson, Idaho	144
Chris Ault, Nevada	177	Phillip Fulmer, Tennessee	128
Dennis Franchione, Texas A&M	171	John L. Smith, Michigan St	128
Mack Brown, Texas	169	Howard Schellenberger, Fla. Atlantic	128
Fisher DeBerry, Air Force	165	Sonny Lubick, Colorado St	122

WINNINGEST ACTIVE DIVISION I-AA COACHES
By Percentage

Coach, College	Yrs	W	L	T	Pct*
Mike Kelly, Dayton	245	231	47	1	.830
Al Bagnoli, Pennsylvania	24	185	58	0	.761
Pete Lembo, Elon	5	44	14	0	.759
Pete Richardson, Southern	18	150	57	1	.724
Joe Taylor, Hampton	23	181	70	4	.718
Dick Biddle, Colgate	10	84	35	0	.706
Mark Farley, Northern Iowa	5	44	20	0	.688
Tommy Tate, McNeese St.	6	48	23	0	.676
Alvin Wyatt Sr., Bethune-Cookman	9	67	33	0	.670
Walt Hameline, Wagner	25	175	86	2	.669

*Playoff games included.
Note: Minimum five years as a Division I-A and/or Division I-AA head coach; record at four-year colleges only.

By Victories

Mike Kelly, Dayton	231	Jimmye Laycock, William & Mary	175
Bob Ford, Albany St.	210	Andy Talley, Villanova	169
Al Bagnoli, Pennsylvania	185	Rob Ash, Drake	167
Joe Taylor, Hampton	181	Jerry Moore, Appalachian St.	167
Walt Hameline, Wagner	175	Pete Richardson, Southern U.	150

WINNINGEST ACTIVE DIVISION II COACHES
By Percentage

Coach, College	Yrs	W	L	T	Pct*
Chris Hatcher, Valdosta St.	6	68	10	0	.872
Chuck Broyles, Pittsburg St (KS)	16	164	34	2	.825
Bryan Collins, C.W. Post	8	73	17	0	.811
Ken Sparks, Carson-Newman	26	250	59	2	.807
Peter Yetten, Bentley	17	133	46	1	.744
Dale Lennon, N Dakota	9	81	29	0	.736
Danny Hale, Bloomsburg	18	146	52	1	.736
Tom Sawyer, Winona St.	10	84	32	0	.724
Richard Cundiff, Tex. A&M-Kingsville	6	49	20	0	.710
Mel Tjeerdsma, Northwest Missouri St	22	177	74	4	.702

*Ties computed as half win, half loss. Playoff games included.
Note: Minimum five years as a college head coach; record at four-year colleges only.

By Victories

Ken Sparks, Carson-Newman	246	Monte Cater, Shepherd	158
Willard Bailey, St. Paul's	215	Danny Hale, Bloomsburg	146
Dennis Douds, E Stroudsburg	199	Peter Yetten, Bentley	133
Mel Tjeerdsma, NW Missouri St	177	Rocky Rees, Shippensburg	133
Chuck Broyles, Pittsburg St.	164	Pat Behms, Neb-Omaha	122

WINNINGEST ACTIVE DIVISION III
By Percentage

Coach, College	Yrs	W	L	T	Pct*
Larry Kehres, Mount Union	20	231	20	3	.915
Jim Purthill, St. Norbert	7	64	11	0	.853
Joe Fincham, Wittenberg	10	93	19	0	.830
Chris Creighton, Wabash	9	76	18	0	.809
John Gagliardi, St. John's (Minn.)	57	432	118	11	.780
Jimmie Keeling, Hardin-Simmons	16	135	39	0	.776
Dean Paul, Ohio Northern	6	48	14	0	.774
Mike Swider, Wheaton (III.)	10	78	25	0	.757
Jim Barnes, Augustana (III.)	11	85	28	0	.752
Pete Fredenberg, Mary Hardin-Baylor	8	65	22	0	.747

*Ties computed as half won, half lost. Playoff games included

Note: Minimum five years as a college head coach; record at four-year colleges only.

By Victories

John Gagliardi, St John's (Minn.)	432
Frank Girardi, Lycoming	250
Larry Kehres, Mount Union	231
Eric Hamilton, College of New Jersey	175
Wayne Perry, Hanover	168
Rick Giancola, Montclair St	157
Bob Berezowitz, UW-Whitewater	144
Rich Lockner, Carnegie Mellon	132
Dale Widolff, Occidental	137
Barry Streeter, Gettysburg	136
Larry Kindham, Wash U-St. Louis	136
Michael DeLong, Springfield	136

NAIA Coaches' Records

WINNINGEST ACTIVE NAIA COACHES
By Percentage

Coach, College	Yrs	W	L	T	Pct*
Bill Cronin, Georgetown (Ken.)	9	97	17	0	.851
Mike Van Diest, Carroll (Mont.)	8	78	16	0	.830
Mark Samson, Montana St-Northern	25	78	17	0	.821
Hank Biesiot, Dickinson St (N.D.)	30	219	74	1	.747
Carl Poelker, McKendree (III.)	24	165	68	1	.707
Orv Otten, Northwestern (Ia.)	11	79	38	0	.675
Phil Jones, Shorter (Ga.)	37	61	30	0	.670
Todd Sturdy, St. Ambrose (Ia.)	11	75	39	0	.658
Geno DeMarco, Geneva (Pa.)	13	91	48	0	.655
Larry Wilcox, Benedictine (Kan.)	27	187	100	0	.652
Kevin Donley, St. Francis (Ind.)	27	193	105	1	.647
Tommy Lee, Montana-Western	16	60	34	0	.638
Mike Feminis, St. Xavier (III.)	7	49	28	0	.636
Vic Wallace, Lambuth (Tenn.)	25	167	95	5	.635
Monty Lewis, Friends (Kan.)	12	75	45	0	.625

*Playoff games included.

Note: Minimum five years as a collegiate head coach and includes record against four-year institutions only.

By Victories

Hank Biesiot, Dickinson St (N.D.)	219
Kevin Donley, St. Francis (Ind.)	193
Larry Wilcox, Benedictine (Kan.)	187
David Bolstorff, Walfdorf (Ia.)	187
Vic Wallace, Lambuth (Tenn.)	167
Carl Poelker, McKendree (III.)	165
Jim Dennison, Walsh (Ohio)	159
Fran Schwenk, Doane (Neb.)	120
Bob Green, Montana Tech	115
Merle Masonholder, Central Methodist (Mo.)	102

Dwyane Wade (l.) of the NBA champion Miami Heat

Pro Basketball

Heat Rising

Although it wasn't exactly "Showtime II," Pat Riley
returned to coaching, guiding Shaq, D-Wade and
a group of veteran cast-offs to the NBA championship

BY STEPHEN CANNELLA

ADOPTING A BRUCE SPRING-steen song as an inspirational anthem is a tried and true motivational ploy, one familiar to politicians, high school coaches and any New Jerseyite who has ever blasted "the Boss" before walking down the aisle or into a job interview. Trite? Perhaps, but clichés become clichés for a reason—they often work. And if Pat Riley has proven anything in nearly three decades of NBA coaching and team building, it's that he knows what works.

The Miami Heat's team president also happens to be a major Springsteen fan—one of Riley's most treasured possessions is a harmonica Springsteen tossed to him during a concert. This season, though, Riley's devotion to the Boss was outdone in intensity by his craving for another NBA championship. Riley had won six rings—two as a player, four as a coach—but it had been 18 years since his last, won with the Los Angeles Lakers. For Riley, who joined the Heat in 1995 and spent eight seasons as coach before moving to the front office full-time, the years since had been a frustrating, fruitless quest for another shot at NBA glory.

So when the Armani-ed One stepped out of the Heat front office and resumed coaching after Stan Van Gundy resigned in December 2005, it was a given that he would pull out all the stops to motivate his team. Predictably, Miami's American Airlines Arena began to resemble Asbury Park South. Springsteen's "The Rising," one of Riley's favorite songs, blared after warmups at every home game. Clarence Clemons, the E Street Band saxophonist and Riley pal, wailed the national anthem before Game 5 of the NBA Finals. And when the Heat clinched that elusive championship the franchise's first—two days later, the 61-year-old coach boogied to Springsteen at a postgame party, forgetting for the moment about his achy hip, which would need to be replaced after the season.

For a future Hall of Fame coach desperate to prove that his skills hadn't eroded with age, it was a "rising" indeed. Riley had been widely criticized for building a flawed team during the offseason and surrounding the aging Shaquille O'Neal and rising superstar Dwyane Wade with four players—Gary Payton, Antoine Walker, Jason Williams and James Posey—thought of as clubhouse cancers. By his own admission, the Heat were "a mess" when he took over for Van Gundy. "No disrespect to anyone," center Alonzo Mourning said late in the season, "but we got better the minute Pat came back [to coach]. The man is all about championships."

Riley's mid-season return to the sidelines rejuvenated the Heat, who went on to win him his fifth NBA title as a head coach.

Indeed, the entire NBA seemed to be rising in 2005-06, or, at least, "born to run." The league enjoyed one of the most entertaining seasons of the A.J. (After Jordan) era. For starters, the basketball was more fluid and free-flowing than it had been in years, thanks mainly to rules changes enacted in 2004 that cracked down on overzealous defensive tactics. With referees on the lookout for illegal hand checks and defensive sets, the league's top players had newfound freedom to display their creativity and skills.

Suddenly, after years of miniscule point totals and domination by choking defenses, the NBA was a scorer's league again. Three players (Lakers guard Kobe Bryant, Philadelphia 76ers guard Allen Iverson and Cleveland Cavaliers guard LeBron James) averaged at least 30 points per game, the most 30-point scorers in a season in 24 years. Bryant led the league with a scoring average of 35.4 points per game, the NBA's highest since Michael Jordan averaged 37.1 in 1986-87, and on a January night in Los Angeles he turned in arguably the most electric performance the league has ever seen. Bryant scorched the Toronto Raptors, scoring 81 points (55 of them in the second half), the second-highest total in league history after Wilt Chamberlain's legendary 100-point performance. "Everybody called every player in the league," marveled Wade, who finished fifth in the scoring race (27.2 points per game), "because that's history right there."

Bryant continued his heroics in the playoffs, nearly leading the underdog Lakers to a

DAVID E. KLUTHO/SPORTS ILLUSTRATED

While his team didn't make it to the NBA Finals, LeBron James did lead Cleveland to its first playoff series win since 1993, returning respectability to the franchise.

first-round upset of the Phoenix Suns. (Phoenix prevailed in seven games, led by guard Steve Nash, the league's MVP for the second straight year.) Bryant was not the only one providing playoff highlights. The high-octane regular season turned out to be a fitting prelude to the postseason, which was one of the most intoxicating in memory; the early rounds even had the joyfully chaotic feel of the NCAA basketball tournament. Call

it May Madness: The games were close (24 games in the first two rounds were decided by five points or less), the series hard-fought (three of the four conference semifinals went the full seven games) and there were several near-upsets and career-defining performances by a new generation of stars.

Among them, no one was more scintillating than the 21-year-old James, who, in his third pro season, was making his postseason debut. In 13 playoff games, "King James" averaged 30.8 points, 8.1 rebounds and 5.8 assists per game, and he was downright Jordanesque in his ability to perform in the clutch. James hit a pair of buzzer beaters in Cleveland's first-round win over the Washington Wizards and, with little help from his overmatched supporting cast, nearly upset the defending champion Detroit Pistons in the Eastern Conference semis. (The Cavaliers lost in seven games.) "We did a great job of making the playoffs, but our goal is higher now," James said afterward. "We're going to try to get better and come back and win a championship."

In the Western Conference the rejuvenated Los Angeles Clippers, led by All-Star power forward Elton Brand, went 47-35 during the regular season (their highest win total in 31 years) and made the playoffs for the first time since 1997. They made the appearance count: The Clips' first-round victory over the Denver Nuggets was the first postseason series triumph in franchise history, and they took the powerhouse Suns to seven games before falling in the conference semifinals.

The Clippers may have been the feel-good story in the West, but it was the Mavericks who proved to be the class of the conference. Not that class is a word often associated with Dallas owner Mark Cuban. The league's most obnoxious—and, it must be admitted, effective—boss was his usual shy self during the postseason, berating refs from his courtside seats, bumping fists with his players and blogging to release any and every thought that popped into his head. But, though he comes across more as an adolescent superfan than a billionaire owner, there's no denying the substance behind the Cuban spectacle. He turned once-downtrodden Dallas into one of the NBA's premier franchises, and after the Mavs dispatched Phoenix in six games in the Western Conference finals, many observers considered them the favorite in the Finals matchup against Miami.

In fact, it was a minor miracle—and a testament to Riley's coaching savvy—the Heat even made it to the Finals. On Feb. 9, after a humiliating 112-76 road loss to the Mavs, the Heat's record was an unimpressive 30-20, and the team looked every bit the disaster that many around the league believed it would be. But Riley, whom conspiracy theorists believed had pushed out Van Gundy in December, rallied the team behind the slogan "15 strong," another tortured but effective motivational trick. The Heat finished the season on a 22-10 run to win the Southeast Division title, then breezed through the Eastern Conference playoffs with little difficulty, knocking off the Chicago Bulls, New Jersey Nets and Pistons in succession.

Miami's momentum suddenly went cold in the Finals. Dallas won Games 1 and 2 at home, each by a double-digit margin, thanks in large part to its ability to shut down Shaquille O'Neal. Forced to fight through the Mavericks' double- and triple-team defense, Shaq took only 16 shots and scored just 21 points in the two losses. He was as loquacious and funny as ever (he told reporters during the Finals that he is from another planet but can't prove it because "the files" were destroyed), but it was clear that, at age 34, the Diesel was slowing down.

It was also clear that the Heat could no longer be considered Shaq's Team: Any doubts that the 24-year-old Wade was now Miami's leader—and perhaps the league's best player this side of Bryant—were dispelled when the series shifted to South Florida. Wade exploded in Game 3, scoring 42 points (15 in the fourth quarter) and grabbing 13 rebounds, and helped the Heat rally from a 13-point fourth-quarter deficit to a 98-96 win. The victory was sealed when Payton, one of Riley's most criticized roster pickups, hit a go-ahead jumper with 9.3 seconds left. "The playoffs are about that," said Riley. "It comes down to one shot."

That game left Wade hobbling with a knee injury but, as the Mavs soon discovered, he's a quick healer. Behind 36 points from their superstar the Heat pulled off a 98-74 victory in Game 4 to tie the series. The story was the same in Game 5, when Wade poured in 43 points. Still, the game had almost gone the other way. With 9.1 seconds left in overtime, Dallas held a 100-99 advantage and was poised to take the series lead. During a timeout, Riley implored his team to get the ball to Wade and told O'Neal

to set a pick on the left side of the floor because that's the direction Wade wanted to take. "Besides Dwyane," Riley would say later, "we did not have a second option."

It was the kind of play call reserved for only the most elite stars—and Wade proved he was worthy of the respect. He dribbled through four Dallas defenders, drew a foul (Cuban threw a profanity-ridden fit at commissioner David Stern after the game) and calmly drained two free throws. The Heat won 101-100, and the reeling Mavericks found themselves in a 3-2 hole.

Miami clinched it with a 95-92 win in Dallas in Game 6, behind—you guessed it—a game-high 26 points from Wade, who was named the Finals MVP. The win made good the guarantee O'Neal had made when he joined the Heat in 2004 ("I will bring a

In January, Lakers guard Kobe Bryant scored an incredible 81 points, the second-highest single-game total in NBA history.

championship to Miami"), but the title may have tasted sweetest to Riley. The smile on his face after the victory was one of relief as much as joy, and he admitted that the season had been a particularly draining one. Riley would ponder his future during the offseason—he did not announce until late August that he would return—but first he treated himself to a little recreation. Before the heat's victory parade in Miami, Riley and his wife, Chris, jetted to New York to catch Springsteen in concert. "We'll be doing a lot of that over the next month or two," he said. For Riley and the Heat, the rising was complete.

FOR THE RECORD • 2005—2006

NBA Final Standings

Eastern Conference
ATLANTIC DIVISION

Team	W	L	Pct	GB
†New Jersey	49	33	.598	—
Philadelphia	38	44	.463	11
Boston	33	49	.402	16
Toronto	27	55	.329	22
New York	23	59	.280	26

CENTRAL DIVISION

Team	W	L	Pct	GB
†Detroit	64	18	.780	—
*Cleveland	50	32	.610	14
*Indiana	41	41	.500	23
*Chicago	41	41	.500	23
*Milwaukee	40	42	.488	24

SOUTHEAST DIVISION

Team	W	L	Pct	GB
†Miami	52	30	.634	—
*Washington	42	40	.512	10
Orlando	36	46	.439	16
Charlotte	26	56	.317	26
Atlanta	26	56	.317	26

Western Conference
NORTHWEST DIVISION

Team	W	L	Pct	GB
†Denver	44	38	.537	—
Utah	41	41	.500	3
Seattle	35	47	.427	9
Minnesota	33	49	.402	11
Portland	21	61	.256	23

PACIFIC DIVISION

Team	W	L	Pct	GB
†Phoenix	54	28	.659	—
*LA Clippers	47	35	.573	7
*LA Lakers	45	37	.549	9
*Sacramento	44	38	.537	10
Golden State	34	48	.415	20

SOUTHWEST DIVISION

Team	W	L	Pct	GB
†San Antonio	63	19	.768	—
*Dallas	60	22	.732	3
*Memphis	49	33	.598	14
NO/Oklahoma City	38	44	.463	25
Houston	34	48	.415	29

†Clinched division title.   *Clinched playoff berth.

2006 NBA Playoffs

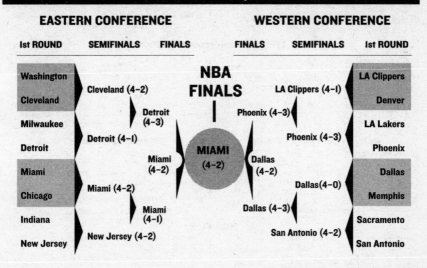

EASTERN CONFERENCE

1st ROUND — SEMIFINALS — FINALS

Washington
Cleveland — Cleveland (4-2)
Milwaukee
Detroit — Detroit (4-1) — Detroit (4-3)
Miami
Chicago — Miami (4-2) — Miami (4-2)
Indiana
New Jersey — New Jersey (4-2) — Miami (4-1)

NBA FINALS — MIAMI (4-2)

WESTERN CONFERENCE

FINALS — SEMIFINALS — 1st ROUND

LA Clippers
Denver — LA Clippers (4-1) — Phoenix (4-3)
LA Lakers
Phoenix — Phoenix (4-3) — Dallas (4-2)
Dallas
Memphis — Dallas (4-0) — Dallas (4-3)
Sacramento
San Antonio — San Antonio (4-2)

2006 NBA Playoff Results

Eastern Conference First Round

Game 1......Washington	86	at Cleveland	97
Game 2......Washington	89	at Cleveland	84
Game 3......Cleveland	97	at Washington	96
Game 4......Cleveland	96	at Washington	106
Game 5......Washington	120	at Cleveland	121*
Game 6......Cleveland	114	at Washington	113*

Cleveland won series 4–2.

Game 1......Milwaukee	74	at Detroit	92
Game 2......Milwaukee	98	at Detroit	109
Game 3......Detroit	104	at Milwaukee	124
Game 4......Detroit	109	at Milwaukee	99
Game 5......Milwaukee	93	at Detroit	122

Detroit won series 4–1.

Game 1......Chicago	106	at Miami	111
Game 2......Chicago	108	at Miami	115
Game 3......Miami	90	at Chicago	109
Game 4......Miami	87	at Chicago	93
Game 5......Chicago	78	at Miami	92
Game 6......Miami	113	at Chicago	96

Miami won series 4–2.

Game 1......Indiana	90	at New Jersey	88
Game 2......Indiana	75	at New Jersey	90
Game 3......New Jersey	95	at Indiana	107
Game 4......New Jersey	97	at Indiana	88
Game 5......Indiana	86	at New Jersey	92
Game 6......New Jersy	96	at Indiana	90

New Jersey won series 4–2.

Western Conference First Round

Game 1......Sacramento	88	at San Antonio	122
Game 2......Sacramento	119	at San Antonio	128*
Game 3......San Antonio	93	at Sacramento	94
Game 4......San Antonio	84	at Sacramento	102
Game 5......Sacramento	98	at San Antonio	109
Game 6......San Antonio	105	at Sacramento	83

San Antonio won series 4–2.

Game 1......Denver	87	at LA Clippers	89
Game 2......Denver	87	at LA Clippers	98
Game 3......LA Clippers	87	at Denver	94
Game 4......LA Clippers	100	at Denver	86
Game 5......Denver	83	at LA Clippers	101

LA Clippers won series 4–1.

Game 1......Memphis	93	at Dallas	103
Game 2......Memphis	79	at Dallas	94
Game 3......Dallas	94	at Memphis	89*
Game 4......Dallas	102	at Memphis	76

Dallas won series 4–0.

Game 1......LA Lakers	102	at Phoenix	107
Game 2......LA Lakers	99	at Phoenix	93
Game 3......Phoenix	92	at LA Lakers	99
Game 4......Phoenix	98	at LA Lakers	99*
Game 5......LA Lakers	97	at Phoenix	114
Game 6......Phoenix	126	at LA Lakers	118*
Game 7......LA Lakers	90	at Phoenix	121

Phoenix won series 4–3.

Eastern Conference Semifinals

Game 1......New Jersey	100	at Miami	88
Game 2......New Jersey	89	at Miami	111
Game 3......Miami	103	at New Jersey	92
Game 4......Miami	102	at New Jersey	92
Game 5......New Jersey	105	at Miami	106

Miami won series 4–1.

Game 1......Cleveland	86	at Detroit	113
Game 2......Cleveland	91	at Detroit	97
Game 3......Detroit	77	at Cleveland	86
Game 4......Detroit	72	at Cleveland	74
Game 5......Cleveland	86	at Detroit	84
Game 6......Detroit	84	at Cleveland	82
Game 7......Cleveland	61	at Detroit	79

Detroit won series 4–3.

Western Conference Semifinals

Game 1......LA Clippers	123	at Phoenix	130
Game 2......LA Clippers	122	at Phoenix	97
Game 3......Phoenix	94	at LA Clippers	91
Game 4......Phoenix	107	at LA Clippers	114
Game 5......LA Clippers	118	at Phoenix	125†
Game 6......Phoenix	106	at LA Clippers	118
Game 7......LA Clippers	107	at Phoenix	127

Phoenix won series 4–3

Game 1......Dallas	85	at San Antonio	87
Game 2......Dallas	113	at San Antonio	91
Game 3......San Antonio	103	at Dallas	104
Game 4......San Antonio	118	at Dallas	123*
Game 5......Dallas	97	at San Antonio	98
Game 6......San Antonio	91	at Dallas	86
Game 7......Dallas	119	at San Antonio	111*

Dallas won series 4–3.

Eastern Conference Finals

Game 1......Miami	91	at Detroit	86
Game 2......Miami	88	at Detroit	92
Game 3......Detroit	83	at Miami	98
Game 4......Detroit	78	at Miami	89
Game 5......Miami	78	at Detroit	91
Game 6......Detroit	78	at Miami	95

Miami won series 4–2.

Western Conference Finals

Game 1......Phoenix	121	at Dallas	118
Game 2......Phoenix	98	at Dallas	105
Game 3......Dallas	95	at Phoenix	88
Game 4......Dallas	86	at Phoenix	106
Game 5......Phoenix	101	at Dallas	117
Game 6......Dallas	102	at Phoenix	93

Dallas won series 4–2.

NBA Finals

Game 1......Miami	80	at Dallas	90
Game 2......Miami	85	at Dallas	99
Game 3......Dallas	96	at Miami	98
Game 4......Dallas	74	at Miami	98
Game 5......Dallas	100	at Miami	101*
Game 6......Miami	95	at Dallas	92

Miami won series 4–2.

* Overtime. †Double overtime.

NBA Finals Composite Box Score

MIAMI HEAT

Player	GP	Mpg	FG%	3FG%	FT%	Rebounds Off	Rebounds Total	Apg	Spg	Bpg	TO	Ppg
Dwyane Wade	6	43.5	.468	.273	.773	2.0	7.8	3.8	2.67	1.00	3.7	34.7
Antoine Walker	6	36.5	.391	.270	.556	0.7	5.5	2.2	0.67	0.50	2.0	13.8
Shaquille O'Neal	6	35.0	.607	.000	.292	2.5	10.2	2.8	0.50	0.83	3.2	13.7
Jason Williams	6	31.2	.360	.345	.636	0.0	1.8	4.7	0.50	0.00	1.3	8.8
James Posey	6	29.3	.419	.400	.769	1.0	6.0	0.3	1.00	0.00	1.2	7.3
Udonis Haslem	6	29.2	.500	.000	.300	2.8	6.2	0.3	1.17	0.00	2.3	6.5
Gary Payton	6	22.3	.368	.143	.333	0.5	2.0	2.0	1.00	0.00	1.0	2.7
Alonzo Mourning	6	11.0	.692	.000	.667	0.7	3.2	0.0	0.33	1.50	0.7	4.3
Shandon Anderson	4	7.8	.333	.000	.500	0.5	1.8	0.8	0.00	0.00	1.0	1.5
Jason Kapono	4	2.0	.000	.000	.000	0.0	0.0	0.0	0.00	0.00	0.0	0.0
Michael Doleac	1	1.0	.000	.000	.000	0.0	0.0	0.0	0.00	0.00	0.0	0.0
Avg/Total	6	248.8	.457	.305	.604	10.5	43.8	16.7	7.83	3.83	16.0	92.8

DALLAS MAVERICKS

Player	GP	Mpg	FG%	3FG%	FT%	Rebounds Off	Rebounds Total	Apg	Spg	Bpg	TO	Ppg
Dirk Nowitzki	6	43.7	.390	.250	.891	1.5	10.8	2.5	0.67	0.67	2.2	22.8
Jason Terry	6	40.0	.478	.317	.733	0.2	2.2	3.5	0.50	0.00	2.5	22.0
Josh Howard	6	38.5	.388	.263	.808	1.7	8.2	1.8	1.17	0.67	2.5	14.7
Jerry Stackhouse	5	29.8	.355	.368	.929	1.0	3.4	3.0	0.80	0.60	2.2	12.8
Devin Harris	6	24.5	.364	.000	.750	0.5	0.8	2.8	0.83	0.00	1.8	7.3
Erick Dampier	6	24.5	.722	.000	.500	2.7	8.2	0.3	1.00	0.67	1.3	5.7
DeSagana Diop	6	15.7	.500	.000	.500	0.8	3.3	0.2	0.33	0.83	0.5	1.7
Adrian Griffin	6	13.5	.563	.000	.000	1.9	3.2	0.8	0.83	0.00	0.5	3.0
Marquis Daniels	6	8.7	.545	.333	.800	0.3	0.5	1.3	0.00	0.00	0.7	2.8
Keith Van Horn	5	8.0	.273	.167	.000	0.2	1.2	0.0	0.00	0.00	0.6	1.4
Darrell Armstrong	1	6.0	.000	.000	.000	0.0	1.0	0.0	0.00	0.00	0.0	0.0
DJ Mbenga	2	4.5	.000	.000	.000	0.0	1.5	0.0	0.00	0.00	0.5	0.0
Josh Powell	1	4.0	.000	.000	.000	1.0	1.0	0.0	0.00	0.00	0.6	0.0
Avg/Total	6	261.4	.422	.284	.787	10.2	41.8	15.6	7.33	3.33	14.5	91.8

NBA Finals Box Scores

Game 1

MIAMI 80

Player	Min	FG M-A	FT M-A	Reb O-T	A	PF	S	TO	TP
A. Walker	42	7-19	0-0	0-6	4	3	1	6	17
U. Haslem	33	2-4	0-0	3-9	0	5	0	1	4
S. O'Neal	38	8-11	1-9	3-7	5	4	0	2	17
D. Wade	43	11-25	6-10	3-6	6	4	0	5	28
J. Williams	34	5-11	0-0	0-4	3	4	3	1	12
G. Payton	19	0-4	0-0	2-5	1	0	3	0	0
A. Mourning	5	0-1	0-0	0-1	0	1	0	0	0
J. Posey	25	1-3	0-0	1-7	0	5	1	0	2
Totals	239	34-78	7-19	12-45	20	25	10	15	80

Percentages: FG—.436, FT—.368. 3-pt goals: 5–20, .250 (Walker 3–9, Williams 2-5, Payton 0-3, Wade 0-2, Posey 0-1). Team rebounds: 10. Blocked shots: 1 (Wade).

DALLAS 90

Player	Min	FG M-A	FT M-A	Reb O-T	A	PF	S	TO	TP
J. Howard	44	3-14	4-6	0-12	4	4	1	5	10
D. Nowitzki	39	4-14	6-6	2-10	4	2	3	2	16
D. Diop	16	0-0	0-0	1-2	0	2	1	2	0
J. Terry	37	13-18	2-2	0-4	1	2	3	1	32
A. Griffin	13	4-6	0-0	1-1	1	1	1	0	8
E. Dampier	27	3-4	2-4	3-7	0	4	0	0	8
J. Stackhouse	29	4-11	5-6	0-5	4	0	0	3	13
D. Harris	18	0-3	1-2	0-0	2	1	0	1	1
K. Van Horn	11	0-0	0-0	0-2	0	0	0	0	0
M. Daniels	5	0-1	0-0	0-0	2	1	0	0	0
Totals	239	32-72	6-18	7-43	18	18	9	14	90

Percentages: FG—.444, FT—.769. 3-pt goals: 6–18, .333 (Terry 4-7, Nowitzki 2-4, Howard 0-4, Stackhouse 0-2, Harris 0-1). Team rebounds: 4. Blocked shots: 3 (Diop 2, Stackhouse).

A: 20,475. Officials: Salvatore, Crawford, Derosa.

NBA Finals Box Scores *(Cont.)*

Game 2

MIAMI 85

Player	Min	FG M-A	FT M-A	Reb O-T	A	PF	S	TO	TP
A. Walker	43	8-16	0-0	0-4	2	3	0	2	20
U. Haslem	20	3-6	0-0	0-1	0	2	0	2	6
S. O'Neal	28	2-5	1-7	1-6	2	1	0	2	5
D. Wade	40	6-19	11-14	4-8	3	4	2	4	23
J. Williams	31	3-10	4-5	0-2	4	2	1	0	11
J. Posey	28	2-6	1-1	2-5	1	6	0	1	7
G. Payton	28	1-4	0-0	0-1	4	2	2	0	2
A. Mourning	20	4-4	3-5	1-4	0	3	0	1	11
S. Anderson	2	0-0	0-0	0-1	0	0	0	1	0
Totals	240	29-70	20-32	8-32	16	23	5	13	85

Percentages: FG—.414, FT—.625. 3-pt goals: 7-17 .412 (Walker 4-7, Posey 2-4, Williams 1-4). Team rebounds: 12. Blocked shots: 3 (Walker, Wade, Mourning).

DALLAS 99

Player	Min	FG M-A	FT M-A	Reb O-T	A	PF	S	TO	TP
J. Howard	29	6-12	1-1	1-3	1	5	0	4	15
D. Nowitzki	41	8-16	10-11	1-16	4	2	0	1	26
D. Diop	12	0-0	1-2	1-4	0	5	1	1	5
J. Terry	41	6-15	3-5	0-1	9	2	2	3	16
A. Griffin	18	0-0	0-0	1-4	0	4	0	1	0
E. Dampier	29	2-3	2-3	4-13	1	2	1	2	6
J. Stackhouse	30	6-11	3-3	1-3	3	1	0	3	19
D. Harris	23	4-10	3-3	0-1	4	4	1	1	11
K. Van Horn	10	2-3	0-0	0-0	0	1	0	1	5
M. Daniels	6	0-0	0-0	0-0	1	1	0	1	0
Totals	239	34-70	23-28	9-46	23	27	5	18	99

Percentages: FG—.486, FT—.821. 3-pt goals: 8—19, .421 (Stackhouse 4-5, Howard 2-3, Terry 1-6, Van Horn 1-2, Nowitzki 0-2, Harris 0-1). Team rebounds: 4. Blocked shots: 5 (Howard 2, Nowitzki 2, Dampier).

A: 20,459. Officials: Delaney, Rush, Javie.

Game 3

DALLAS 96

Player	Min	FG M-A	FT M-A	Reb O-T	A	PF	S	TO	TP
J. Howard	42	8-13	2-2	0-5	1	4	0	1	21
D. Nowitzki	45	9-20	10-12	0-7	1	5	0	3	30
D. Diop	11	0-0	0-0	1-4	0	4	0	0	0
J. Terry	36	7-14	1-2	0-1	5	2	2	2	16
A. Griffin	14	1-3	0-0	1-5	3	3	2	1	2
E. Dampier	29	6-7	2-5	5-9	0	4	3	1	14
J. Stackhouse	31	1-9	2-2	0-1	1	2	7	2	4
D. Harris	18	4-7	1-3	0-0	4	3	1	2	9
K. Van Horn	9	0-2	0-0	0-2	0	2	0	2	0
M. Daniels	4	0-0	0-0	0-0	0	0	0	1	0
Totals	239	36-75	18-26	7-34	15	29	9	15	96

Percentages: FG—.480, FT—.692. 3-pt goals: 6-16, .375 (Howard 3-3, Nowitzki 2-7, Terry 1-3, Van Horn 0-2, Stackhouse 0-1). Team rebounds: 4. Blocked shots: 2 (Howard, Dampier).

MIAMI 98

Player	Min	FG M-A	FT M-A	Reb O-T	A	PF	S	TO	TP
A. Walker	35	6-17	0-2	1-7	1	3	0	2	12
U. Haslem	34	3-8	2-6	8-11	0	4	3	3	8
S. O'Neal	37	6-9	4-6	3-11	5	3	1	7	16
J. Williams	35	5-11	0-0	0-1	3	3	0	3	12
D. Wade	43	14-26	13-18	2-13	2	5	2	1	42
G. Payton	19	1-1	0-0	1-2	2	1	1	2	2
A. Mourning	9	1-2	0-0	1-1	0	3	2	1	2
J. Posey	28	1-2	0-0	1-5	0	1	0	1	2
Totals	240	37-76	20-34	16-49	13	23	9	20	98

Percentages: FG—.487, FT—.588. 3-pt goals: 4-14, .286 (Williams 2-5, Wade 1-2, Posey 1-2, Walker 0-5). Team rebounds: 13. Blocked shots: 2 (O'Neal).

A: 20,145. Officials: Crawford, Nies, Mauer.

Game 4

DALLAS 74

Player	Min	FG M-A	FT M-A	Reb O-T	A	PF	S	TO	TP
J. Howard	36	1-8	1-2	1-7	2	4	2	1	3
D. Nowitzki	41	2-14	11-13	1-9	1	2	1	4	16
D. Diop	18	1-1	3-5	1-2	0	3	0	0	5
J. Terry	33	8-18	0-1	0-1	0	2	1	3	17
D. Harris	28	4-8	3-3	0-0	2	3	0	3	11
J. Stackhouse	30	6-18	3-3	3-4	4	1	1	0	16
E. Dampier	18	0-1	0-0	1-4	1	5	1	1	0
A. Griffin	17	3-3	0-0	3-6	0	2	0	0	6
D. Armstrong	6	0-2	0-0	0-1	0	0	0	0	0
M. Daniels	5	0-2	0-0	0-0	0	0	0	1	0
K. Van Horn	5	0-3	0-0	1-2	0	2	0	0	0
J. Powell	4	0-1	0-0	1-2	0	2	0	0	0
Totals	241	25-79	21-27	11-36	10	24	6	13	74

Percentages: FG—.316, FT—.778. 3-pt goals: 3–22, .136 (Nowitzki 1-5, Terry 1-5, Stackhouse 1-5, Howard 0-4, Armstrong 0-1, Daniels 0-1, Van Horn 0-1). Team rebounds: 8. Blocked shots: 3 (Diop, Stackhouse, Dampier).

MIAMI 98

Player	Min	FG M-A	FT M-A	Reb O-T	A	PF	S	TO	TP
A. Walker	39	5-11	2-2	0-3	2	2	2	0	14
U. Haslem	18	1-2	0-0	0-2	1	5	2	4	2
S. O'Neal	30	6-8	5-10	3-13	3	4	0	3	17
J. Williams	31	1-5	3-5	0-2	6	0	1	1	6
D. Wade	40	13-23	8-9	0-6	3	4	1	4	36
A. Mourning	14	1-2	2-2	1-6	0	3	0	1	4
J. Posey	26	5-9	3-4	1-10	1	3	1	1	15
G. Payton	20	1-2	0-0	0-1	1	4	0	2	2
S. Anderson	19	1-4	0-2	1-5	2	1	0	2	2
J. Kapono	2	0-0	0-0	0-0	0	0	0	0	0
M. Doleac	1	0-0	0-0	0-0	0	0	0	0	0
Totals	240	34-66	23-36	6-48	19	26	7	18	98

Percentages: FG—.515, FT—.639. 3-pt goals: 7-19, .368 (Walker 2-6, Wade 2-5, Posey 2-4, Williams 1-3, Anderson 0-1). Team rebounds: 13. Blocked shots: 7 (Mourning 3, O'Neal 2, Walker, Wade).

A: 20.145. Officials: Fryer, Bavetta, Callahan.

Game 5

DALLAS 100

Player	Min	FG M-A	FT M-A	Reb O-T	A	PF	S	TO	TP
J. Howard	50	8-17	9-11	5-10	3	4	0	3	25
D. Nowitzki	49	8-19	4-5	2-8	3	4	0	2	20
D. Diop	21	1-2	0-0	1-4	0	6	0	0	2
Terry	50	13-23	5-5	1-5	1	2	1	4	35
D. Harris	34	2-12	2-2	0-1	1	5	1	0	6
E. Dampier	19	2-2	1-2	0-8	0	5	0	2	5
A. Griffin	15	1-2	0-0	1-2	1	3	1	1	2
K. Van Horn	5	0-1	0-0	1-1	0	2	0	0	0
M. Daniels	14	2-3	0-0	0-0	4	3	0	1	5
DJ Mbenga	8	0-0	0-0	0-3	0	4	0	1	0
Totals	265	37-81	21-25	11-42	13	38	3	14	100

Percentages: FG—.457, FT—.840. 3-pt goals: 5-19, .263 (Terry 4-9, Daniels 1-1, Nowitzki 0-4, Howard 0-3, Harris 0-1, Van Horn 0-1). Team rebounds: 12. Blocked shots: 0.

MIAMI 101 (OT)

Player	Min	FG M-A	FT M-A	Reb O-T	A	PF	S	TO	TP
A. Walker	26	2-7	1-2	0-2	2	4	0	2	6
U. Haslem	29	1-3	0-0	2-4	0	6	0	1	2
S. O'Neal	47	8-12	2-12	2-12	1	5	2	3	18
J. Williams	26	3-6	0-1	0-1	4	1	0	1	9
D. Wade	50	11-28	21-25	0-4	4	1	3	3	43
J. Posey	44	2-6	4-4	2-6	0	5	2	1	10
S. Anderson	7	1-2	2-2	1-1	1	0	0	0	4
G. Payton	30	3-5	1-1	0-2	2	4	0	0	8
A. Mourning	4	0-0	1-2	0-1	0	0	0	0	1
Totals	263	31-69	32-49	7-33	14	26	7	11	101

Percentages: FG—.449, FT—.653. 3-pt goals: 7–17, .412 (Williams 3-5, Posey 2-5, Walker 1-4, Wade 0-2). Team rebounds: 16. Blocked shots: 0

A: 20,145. Officials: Salvatore, Crawford, Derosa.

Game 6

MIAMI 95

Player	Min	FG M-A	FT M-A	Reb O-T	A	PF	S	TO	TP
A. Walker	34	6-17	2-3	3-11	2	2	1	0	14
U. Haslem	41	8-13	1-4	4-10	1	3	2	3	17
S. O'Neal	30	4-11	1-4	3-12	1	5	0	2	9
D. Wade	45	10-18	16-21	3-10	5	4	4	5	36
J. Williams	30	1-7	0-0	0-1	7	0	0	2	3
J. Posey	25	2-5	1-2	0-5	0	2	2	3	6
G. Payton	18	1-3	0-0	0-1	2	3	0	2	2
A. Mourning	14	3-4	2-3	1-6	0	4	0	1	8
S. Anderson	3	0-0	0-0	0-0	0	0	0	0	0
Totals	240	35-78	23-37	14-56	18	23	9	19	95

Percentages: FG—.449, FT—.622. 3-pt goals: 2–18, .111 (Williams 1-7, Posey 1-4, Walker 0-6, Payton 0-1). Team rebounds: 12. Blocked shots: 10 (Mourning 5, Wade 3, Walker, O'Neal).

DALLAS 92

Player	Min	FG M-A	FT M-A	Reb O-T	A	PF	S	TO	TP
J. Howard	30	5-16	4-4	3-12	0	5	4	1	14
D. Nowitzki	47	10-22	8-8	3-15	2	5	0	1	29
D. Diop	16	1-3	0-1	0-4	1	3	0	0	2
J. Terry	43	7-25	0-0	0-5	5	1	2	2	16
D. Harris	26	2-4	2-3	3-3	4	5	2	4	6
J. Stackhouse	29	5-13	0-0	1-4	3	5	2	3	12
E. Dampier	25	0-1	1-2	3-8	0	2	1	2	1
M. Daniels	18	4-6	4-5	2-2	1	2	0	0	12
DJ Mbenga	1	0-0	0-0	0-0	0	0	0	0	0
A. Griffin	4	0-2	0-0	1-1	0	1	0	0	0
Totals	240	34-92	19-23	16-50	16	28	12	13	92

Percentages: FG—.370, FT—.826. 3-pt goals: 5-22, .227 (Terry 2-11, Stackhouse 2-6, Nowitzki 1-2, Howard 0-2, Daniels 0-1). Team rebounds: 1. Blocked shots: 7 (Nowitzki 2, Diop 2, Howard, Stackhouse, Dampier).

A: 20,522. Officials: Crawford, Rush, Javie.

All-NBA Teams

FIRST TEAM	SECOND TEAM	THIRD TEAM
F LeBron James, Cleveland	F Elton Brand, LA Clippers	F Shawn Marion, Phoenix
F Dirk Nowitzki, Dallas	F Tim Duncan, San Antonio	F Carmelo Anthony, Denver
C Shaquille O'Neal, Miami	C Ben Wallance, Detroit	C Yao Ming, Houston
G Steve Nash, Phoenix	G Chauncey Billups, Detroit	G Allen Iverson, Philadelphia
G Kobe Bryant, LA Lakers	G Dwyane Wade, Miami	G Gilbert Arenas, Washington

All-Defensive Team

FIRST TEAM
C Ben Wallace, Detroit
F Andrei Kirilenko, Utah
F Ron Artest, Sacramento
G Kobe Bryant, LA Lakers
G Jason Kidd, New Jersey

SECOND TEAM
F Tim Duncan, San Antonio
G Chauncey Billups, Detroit
F Kevin Garnett, Minnesota
C Marcus Camby, Denver
F Tayshaun Prince, Detroit

All-Rookie Teams

FIRST TEAM
Chris Paul, New Orleans/Oklahoma City
Charlie Villanueva, Toronto
Andrew Bogut, Milwaukee
Deron Williams, Utah
Channing Frye, New York

SECOND TEAM
Danny Granger, Indiana
Raymond Felton, Charlotte
Luther Head, Houston
Marvin Williams, Atlanta
Ryan Gomes, Boston

NBA Individual Leaders

Scoring

	GP	Pts	Avg
Kobe Bryant LAL	80	2,832	35.4
Allen Iverson, Phi	72	2,478	33.0
LeBron James, Cle	79	2,377	31.4
Gilbert Arenas, Was	80	2,346	29.3
Dwyane Wade, Mia	75	2,151	27.2
Paul Pierce, Bos	79	2,122	26.8
Dirk Nowitzki, Dall	81	2,116	26.6
Carmelo Anthony, Denver	80	2,040	26.5
Michael Redd, Mil	80	2,028	25.5
Ray Allen, Sea	78	1,955	25.1

Assists

	GP	Assists	Avg
Steve Nash, Phoe	79	826	10.5
Baron Davis, GS	54	480	8.9
Brevin Knight, Char	69	610	8.8
Chauncey Billups, Det	81	699	8.6
Jason Kidd, NJ	80	672	8.4
Andre Miller, Den	82	674	8.2
Chris Paul, NOK	78	611	7.8
Allen Iverson, Phi	72	532	7.4
Luke Ridnour, Sea	79	550	7.0
Rafer Alston, Hou	63	425	6.7

Free-Throw Percentage

	FTA	FTM	Pct
Steve Nash, Phoe	279	257	.921
Peja Stojakovic, Ind	260	238	.915
Ray Allen, Sea	359	324	.903
Dirk Nowitzki, Dall	598	539	.901
Wally Szczerbiak, Bos	310	278	.897
Chauncey Billups, Det	520	465	.894
Jerry Stackhouse, Dall	221	195	.882
Michael Redd, Mil	571	501	.877
Luke Ridnour, Sea	227	199	.877
Earl Boykins, Den	174	152	.874

Steals

	GP	Steals	Avg
Gerald Wallace, Char	55	138	2.51
Brevin Knight, Char	69	157	2.28
Chris Paul, NOK	78	175	2.24
Gilbert Arenas, Was	80	161	2.01
Shawn Marion, Phoe	81	160	1.98
Dwyane Wade, Mia	75	146	1.95
Allen Iverson, Phi	72	140	1.94
Jason Kidd, NJ	80	150	1.88
Kobe Bryant, LAL	80	147	1.84
Ben Wallace, Det	82	146	1.78

Rebounds

	GP	Reb	Avg
Kevin Garnett, Minn	76	966	12.7
Dwight Howard, Orl	82	1,022	12.5
Shawn Marion, Phoe	81	959	11.8
Ben Wallace, Det	82	923	11.3
Tim Duncan, SA	80	881	11.0
Troy Murphy, GS	74	743	10.0
Elton Brand, LAC	79	790	10.0
Chris Webber, Phi	75	741	9.9
Chris Kaman, LAC	78	750	9.6
Jamaal Magloire, Mil	82	778	9.5

Field-Goal Percentage

	FGA	FGM	Pct
Shaquille O'Neal, Mia	800	480	.600
Eddy Curry, NY	597	336	.563
Tony Parker, SA	1,136	623	.548
Gerald Wallace, Char	589	317	.538
Andrew Bogut, Mil	606	323	.533
Dwight Howard, Orl	881	468	.531
Elton Brand, LAC	1,435	756	.527
Boris Diaw, Phoe	853	449	.526
Kevin Garnett, Minn	1,191	626	.526
Shareef Abdur-Rahim, Sac	632	332	.525

Three-Point Field-Goal Percentage

	3FGA	3FGM	Pct
Richard Hamilton, Det	120	55	.458
Tyronn Lue, Atl	127	58	.447
Leandro Barbosa, Phoe	196	87	.444
Mike James, Tor	382	169	.442
Raja Bell, Phoe	446	197	.442
Steve Nash, Phoe	342	150	.439
Ben Gordon, Chi	382	166	.435
Chauncey Billups, Det	425	184	.433
Bruce Bowen, SA	245	104	.424
Jameer Nelson, Orl	165	70	.424

Blocked Shots

	GP	BS	Avg
Marcus Camby, Den	56	184	3.29
Andrei Kirilenko, Utah	69	220	3.19
Alonzo Mourning, Mia	65	173	2.66
Josh Smith, Atl	80	208	2.60
Elton Brand, LAC	79	201	2.54
Samuel Dalembert, Phi	66	160	2.42
Joel Przybilla, Port	56	130	2.32
Jermaine O'Neal, Ind	51	117	2.29
Ben Wallace, Det	82	181	2.21
Eddie Griffin, Min	70	148	2.11

NBA Team Statistics

Offense

Team	FG Pct	3FG Pct	FT Pct	Rebound Avg Off	Total	A	TO	Stl	Scoring Avg
Phoenix	47.9	39.9	80.6	9.5	41.8	26.6	12.8	6.7	108.4
Seattle	45.9	37.1	78.5	12.4	39.6	20.7	14.0	7.6	102.6
Washington	44.7	35.7	75.7	12.6	41.2	18.6	13.4	8.0	101.7
Toronto	45.4	37.5	79.1	10.5	38.5	19.4	12.5	6.5	101.1
Denver	46.1	32.5	74.4	11.0	41.3	23.4	14.4	8.5	100.3
Miami	47.8	34.5	70.0	10.5	43.1	20.6	13.9	6.4	99.9
LA Lakers	45.3	34.9	74.5	11.8	42.2	21.1	13.4	7.7	99.4
Philadelphia	45.8	36.4	76.0	10.6	40.2	20.2	13.6	7.9	99.4
Dallas	46.2	37.4	78.3	12.6	42.2	18.0	12.9	7.2	99.1
Sacramento	45.4	35.1	78.4	10.4	40.5	22.3	14.0	7.4	98.9
Golden State	43.3	34.1	71.8	12.0	42.3	20.7	13.6	7.4	98.5
Boston	46.7	36.2	75.5	9.9	39.6	20.9	15.9	7.0	98.0
Milwaukee	45.3	38.0	73.8	11.3	41.2	21.6	14.0	7.3	97.8
Chicago	44.6	37.9	73.8	11.0	42.8	22.0	14.6	6.2	97.8
Cleveland	45.4	33.9	72.9	11.7	42.3	19.0	13.4	6.9	97.6
Atlanta	45.4	36.7	75.0	13.0	40.3	19.8	15.1	7.2	97.2
LA Clippers	46.5	34.4	79.1	10.1	43.1	20.8	13.8	6.5	97.2
Charlotte	43.3	33.9	72.9	12.1	39.8	20.9	13.6	10.0	96.9
Detroit	45.5	38.4	72.7	11.9	40.5	24.0	10.8	7.1	96.8
New York	45.5	36.2	72.6	12.6	41.4	17.9	17.0	6.8	95.6
San Antonio	47.2	38.5	70.2	10.4	41.5	20.9	13.3	6.6	95.6
Orlando	47.2	37.6	73.0	10.9	40.2	18.2	14.4	6.5	94.9
Indiana	44.4	34.9	73.7	11.0	42.2	19.9	14.7	7.3	93.9
New Jersey	44.0	33.0	75.8	10.0	41.0	23.0	13.0	6.8	93.8
New Orleans/Oklahoma City	44.0	33.9	75.8	11.2	40.1	18.5	12.5	7.5	92.8
Utah	44.2	33.6	71.9	13.1	42.1	21.6	14.8	6.4	92.4
Memphis	44.8	37.4	71.1	10.2	39.2	19.3	12.9	7.3	92.2
Minnesota	45.6	32.9	75.8	9.9	39.4	20.9	13.7	6.8	91.7
Houston	43.3	33.2	75.9	10.4	41.6	19.3	13.7	7.2	90.1
Portland	44.5	34.9	68.9	10.8	37.7	18.2	13.7	6.5	88.8

Defense (Opponents' Statistics)

Team	FG Pct	3FG Pct	FT Pct	Rebound Avg. Off	Total	A	TO	Stl	Scoring Avg
Memphis	43.6	33.4	75.4	11.3	40.6	19.6	14.0	7.3	88.5
San Antonio	43.3	33.9	74.0	10.8	40.3	16.3	13.3	7.3	88.8
Detroit	45.2	32.5	73.6	11.6	40.9	18.8	13.3	5.9	90.2
Houston	43.0	36.9	73.1	10.7	40.9	20.1	12.6	7.1	91.7
Indiana	43.5	34.3	73.4	11.8	41.3	18.5	13.0	8.1	92.0
New Jersey	43.9	34.8	74.1	9.6	41.3	20.0	13.6	7.2	92.4
Dallas	44.3	36.1	75.2	11.4	38.3	17.5	13.3	6.5	93.1
Minnesota	44.1	36.4	73.6	11.9	41.3	19.0	13.1	6.6	93.6
Utah	44.9	37.8	74.6	10.6	37.9	18.4	13.8	8.1	95.0
Cleveland	45.5	35.6	74.2	9.8	39.4	20.3	12.6	6.6	95.4
LA Clippers	43.5	34.7	73.2	10.5	40.1	21.5	12.1	7.0	95.6
New Orleans/Oklahoma City	45.9	36.7	76.0	10.5	41.0	19.3	14.1	6.4	95.6
Orlando	45.4	35.7	73.2	11.1	38.4	20.0	12.8	7.5	96.0
Miami	44.0	36.1	73.9	10.1	38.8	19.5	12.2	6.8	96.0
LA Lakers	45.0	35.3	74.7	10.9	40.1	21.1	13.4	6.5	96.9
Chicago	42.6	35.1	77.7	10.7	41.7	20.1	14.3	7.5	97.2
Sacramento	45.4	35.1	74.7	11.6	42.1	21.1	14.1	8.0	97.3
Portland	46.8	34.9	76.0	12.5	42.4	21.2	12.4	7.2	98.3
Milwaukee	46.6	35.4	74.7	10.1	40.3	22.5	14.0	7.4	98.8
Boston	45.6	35.3	74.3	11.1	40.0	21.5	13.9	8.4	99.5
Washington	46.5	36.3	74.5	11.8	42.0	21.5	15.6	6.5	99.8
Golden State	45.7	35.1	74.3	12.0	44.5	22.3	14.7	7.0	99.8
Denver	45.4	35.8	73.6	11.8	41.9	23.9	15.4	7.1	100.1
Charlotte	47.8	35.6	73.7	11.5	44.0	22.9	17.4	7.0	100.9
Philadelphia	46.3	35.1	76.2	11.9	42.8	23.0	14.6	7.7	101.3
Atlanta	47.8	36.8	74.5	12.0	40.4	20.6	14.2	7.3	102.0
New York	46.7	37.8	75.3	10.8	38.6	21.3	13.5	8.2	102.0
Phoenix	45.4	36.3	73.1	12.5	45.9	18.9	14.3	7.2	102.8
Toronto	49.1	37.3	74.8	10.2	41.1	23.6	13.6	6.3	104.0
Seattle	48.5	37.5	76.0	12.2	40.5	24.1	13.8	7.3	105.6

NBA Team-by-Team Statistical Leaders

Atlanta Hawks

Player	GP	MPG	FG%	3Pt%	FT%	OFF	DEF	Total	APG	SPG	BPG	TO	PF	PPG
Joe Johnson	82	40.7	45.3	35.6	79.1	1.2	2.9	4.1	6.5	1.3	0.4	3.3	2.3	20.2
Al Harrington	76	36.6	45.2	34.6	69.4	1.7	5.1	6.9	3.1	1.1	0.2	2.6	4.0	18.6
Zaza Pachulia	78	31.4	45.1	0.0	73.5	3.4	4.5	7.9	1.7	1.1	0.5	2.3	3.7	11.7
Josh Smith	80	31.8	42.5	30.9	71.9	2.2	4.4	6.6	2.4	0.8	2.6	2.0	3.3	11.3
Tyronn Lue	51	24.2	45.9	45.7	85.5	0.3	1.4	1.6	3.1	0.5	0.1	1.5	2.2	11.0
Josh Childress	74	30.4	55.2	49.2	76.6	1.8	3.4	5.2	1.8	1.2	0.5	1.4	2.5	10.0
Salim Stoudamire	61	20.3	41.5	38.0	90.0	0.2	1.7	1.9	1.2	0.4	0.1	1.3	1.9	9.7
Marvin Williams	79	24.7	44.3	24.5	74.7	1.5	3.3	4.9	0.8	0.6	0.3	1.1	2.9	8.5
Anthony Grundy	12	9.0	50.0	33.3	64.3	0.1	1.3	1.4	0.8	0.6	0.0	0.8	1.2	4.3
Royal Ivey	73	13.4	43.9	40.0	72.7	0.4	0.9	1.3	1.0	0.3	0.1	0.3	2.0	3.6
Esteban Batista	57	8.7	42.5	0.0	62.3	1.1	1.5	2.5	0.1	0.3	0.2	0.7	2.0	1.8
John Edwards	40	7.4	48.4	0.0	72.7	0.5	0.8	1.2	0.1	0.1	0.4	0.3	1.9	1.8
Donta Smith	23	5.5	55.6	50.0	50.0	0.1	0.5	0.6	0.4	0.4	0.0	0.2	0.9	1.7
John Thomas	11	6.0	0.0	0.0	75.0	0.3	0.6	0.9	0.1	0.2	0.0	0.4	0.9	0.8
Hawks	**82**	**242.4**	**45.4**	**36.7**	**75.0**	**13.0**	**27.2**	**40.3**	**19.8**	**7.2**	**4.8**	**15.1**	**25.1**	**97.2**
Opponents	**82**	**242.4**	**47.8**	**36.8**	**74.5**	**12.0**	**28.5**	**40.4**	**20.6**	**7.3**	**5.2**	**15.0**	**22.6**	**102.0**

Boston Celtics

Player	GP	MPG	FG%	3Pt%	FT%	OFF	DEF	Total	APG	SPG	BPG	TO	PF	PPG
Paul Pierce	79	39.0	47.1	35.4	77.2	1.0	5.7	6.7	4.8	1.4	0.4	3.5	2.8	26.8
Ricky Davis	42	41.6	46.4	32.0	78.7	1.0	3.5	4.5	5.3	1.2	0.2	2.7	2.2	19.7
Wally Szczerbiak	32	36.7	47.6	39.3	89.8	1.3	2.6	3.8	3.2	0.6	0.1	1.6	1.9	17.5
Mark Blount	39	27.8	51.1	0.0	76.4	0.9	3.2	4.2	1.7	0.4	0.9	3.1	2.7	12.4
Delonte West	71	34.0	48.7	38.5	85.2	0.8	3.3	4.1	4.6	1.2	0.7	1.9	2.8	11.8
Al Jefferson	59	18.0	49.9	0.0	64.2	1.6	3.4	5.1	0.5	0.5	0.8	1.1	2.8	7.9
Raef Lafrentz	82	24.8	43.1	39.2	68.0	1.0	4.0	5.0	1.4	0.4	0.9	0.8	3.3	7.8
Ryan Gomes	61	22.6	48.7	33.3	75.2	1.7	3.2	4.9	1.0	0.6	0.1	0.9	1.4	7.6
Tony Allen	51	19.2	47.1	32.4	74.6	0.6	1.6	2.2	1.3	1.0	0.4	1.3	2.5	7.2
Marcus Banks	18	14.9	41.3	31.6	90.0	0.2	0.8	1.1	1.8	0.4	0.0	1.3	2.1	5.5
Gerald Green	32	11.7	47.8	30.0	78.4	0.3	1.0	1.3	0.6	0.4	0.1	0.7	1.3	5.2
Kendrick Perkins	68	19.6	51.5	0.0	61.5	2.1	3.9	5.9	1.0	0.3	1.5	1.6	2.9	5.2
Dan Dickau	19	12.3	37.0	50.0	100.0	0.3	0.6	0.8	2.1	0.6	0.1	1.0	2.1	3.3
Orien Greene	80	15.4	39.5	22.5	66.2	0.5	1.4	1.8	1.6	1.0	0.1	1.4	2.3	3.2
Brian Scalabrine	71	13.2	38.3	35.6	72.2	0.4	1.2	1.6	0.7	0.3	0.3	0.7	1.8	2.9
Michael Olowokandi	16	10.4	44.4	0.0	62.5	0.3	2.3	2.6	0.4	0.2	0.4	0.9	1.4	2.8
Justin Reed	32	9.1	33.8	0.0	62.5	0.4	0.5	0.9	0.2	0.2	0.1	0.5	1.4	2.3
Dwayne Jones	14	6.2	40.0	0.0	46.2	0.7	1.5	2.2	0.1	0.1	0.2	0.2	1.1	1.9
Celtics	**82**	**242.4**	**46.7**	**36.2**	**75.5**	**9.9**	**29.7**	**39.6**	**20.9**	**7.1**	**5.2**	**15.9**	**24.8**	**98.0**
Opponents	**82**	**242.4**	**45.6**	**35.3**	**74.3**	**11.1**	**28.9**	**40.0**	**21.5**	**8.4**	**4.9**	**14.8**	**22.4**	**99.5**

Charlotte Bobcats

Player	GP	MPG	FG%	3Pt%	FT%	OFF	DEF	Total	APG	SPG	BPG	TO	PF	PPG
Gerald Wallace	55	34.5	53.8	28.0	61.4	2.2	5.3	7.5	1.8	2.5	2.1	1.8	2.7	15.2
Emeka Okafor	26	33.6	41.5	0.0	65.6	3.6	6.4	10.0	1.2	0.9	1.9	2.0	3.4	13.2
Brevin Knight	69	34.1	39.9	23.1	80.3	0.5	2.7	3.2	8.8	2.3	0.1	2.4	2.9	12.6
Primoz Brezec	79	27.4	51.7	0.0	73.2	2.3	3.3	5.6	0.4	0.2	0.4	1.1	2.9	12.4
Raymond Felton	80	30.1	39.1	35.8	72.5	1.0	2.4	3.3	5.6	1.3	0.1	2.3	2.3	11.9
Jumaine Jones	76	27.5	40.5	34.3	72.7	1.4	3.6	5.0	0.8	0.9	0.3	1.0	2.6	10.5
Kareem Rush	47	23.6	38.6	34.8	71.4	0.4	1.8	2.2	1.1	0.8	0.3	1.1	1.7	10.1
Melvin Ely	57	23.7	50.8	0.0	66.7	1.7	3.2	4.9	1.3	0.8	0.5	1.3	2.8	9.8
Keith Bogans	39	21.7	39.6	33.7	76.2	0.7	2.0	2.7	1.2	1.0	0.1	1.1	2.0	8.7
Sean May	23	17.3	40.9	0.0	76.6	1.8	2.9	4.7	1.0	0.7	0.5	1.4	2.5	8.2
Matt Carroll	78	16.3	40.3	38.9	82.1	0.4	1.6	2.0	0.5	06	0.1	0.6	1.5	7.6
Bernard Robinson	66	19.7	43.0	9.5	79.1	0.9	2.4	3.3	1.2	1.2	0.2	1.1	2.1	6.4
Alan Anderson	36	15.7	41.4	41.4	80.5	0.6	1.3	1.9	0.9	0.3	0.1	0.9	1.3	5.8
Jake Voskuhl	51	16.0	43.7	33.3	68.3	1.2	2.4	3.6	0.8	0.5	0.5	0.7	3.1	5.3
Lonny Baxter	18	6.6	37.5	0.0	75.0	0.4	1.4	1.4	0.1	0.1	0.1	0.4	0.4	20.
Kevin Burleson	39	8.7	25.0	18.5	94.1	0.1	0.6	0.7	1.2	0.7	0.1	0.6	1.6	1.8
Bobcats	**82**	**242.7**	**43.3**	**33.9**	**72.9**	**12.1**	**27.7**	**39.8**	**20.9**	**10.0**	**4.3**	**13.6**	**23.9**	**96.9**
Opponents	**82**	**242.7**	**47.8**	**35.6**	**73.7**	**11.5**	**32.5**	**44.0**	**22.9**	**7.0**	**5.4**	**17.8**	**23.5**	**100.9**

Chicago Bulls

Player	GP	MPG	FG%	3Pt%	FT%	OFF	DEF	Total	APG	SPG	BPG	TO	PF	PPG
Ben Gordon	80	31.0	42.2	43.5	78.7	0.5	2.2	2.7	3.0	0.9	0.1	2.3	3.0	16.9
Kirk Hinrich	81	36.5	41.8	37.0	81.5	0.4	3.2	3.6	6.4	1.2	0.3	2.3	3.1	15.9
Luol Deng	78	33.4	46.3	26.9	75.0	1.6	5.0	6.6	1.9	0.9	0.6	1.4	1.6	14.3
Andres Nocioni	82	27.3	46.1	39.1	84.3	1.1	5.0	6.1	1.4	0.5	0.6	1.5	3.1	13.0
Darius Songailia	62	21.4	48.1	40.00	81.7	1.2	2.7	4.0	1.4	0.6	0.3	1.4	2.5	9.2
Chris Duhon	74	29.1	40.0	36.0	81.8	0.4	2.6	3.0	5.0	1.0	0.0	1.6	2.1	8.7
Mike Sweetney	66	18.5	45.1	0.0	65.2	1.8	3.5	5.3	0.9	0.3	0.9	1.4	3.2	8.1
Tyson Chandler	79	26.8	56.5	0.0	50.3	3.4	5.7	9.0	1.0	0.5	1.3	1.6	3.8	5.3
Malik Allen	54	13.0	49.0	100.0	60.5	0.8	1.8	2.6	0.4	0.3	0.3	0.6	1.7	4.9
Othella Harrington	72	11.4	49.5	0.0	62.6	0.8	1.4	2.1	0.5	0.1	0.2	0.9	1.8	4.8
Jannero Pargo	57	11.3	37.3	37.9	81.0	0.1	0.9	1.1	1.7	0.4	0.0	1.1	1.0	4.8
Tim Thomas	3	10.5	37.5	16.7	0.0	0.0	1.3	1.3	0.7	0.0	0.3	0.3	0.3	4.3
Eddie Basden	19	7.4	40.5	14.3	80.0	1.4	1.1	1.5	0.4	0.5	0.1	0.5	0.9	2.1
Eric Piatkowski	29	7.9	39.3	27.3	40.0	0.1	0.7	0.8	0.5	0.2	0.0	0.4	0.7	2.0
Luke Schenscher	20	7.4	61.5	0.0	30.8	0.4	1.1	1.5	0.4	0.1	0.2	0.3	1.1	1.8
Stephen Graham	3	6.6	20.0	25.00	100.0	0.0	1.0	1.0	0.3	0.0	0.0	0.3	1.0	1.7
James Thomas	7	3.7	50.0	0.0	0.0	0.6	0.6	1.1	0.00	0.0	0.0	0.0	0.4	0.9
Randy Holcomb	4	2.6	100.0	0.0	0.0	0.3	0.0	0.3	0.00	0.0	0.0	0.0	0.5	0.5
Randy Livingston	5	4.5	0.0	0.0	0.0	0.0	0.8	0.8	0.2	0.2	0.0	0.2	1.2	0.04
Bulls	**82**	**242.7**	**44.6**	**37.9**	**73.8**	**11.1**	**31.7**	**42.8**	**22.0**	**6.2**	**4.2**	**14.6**	**24.9**	**97.8**
Opponents	**82**	**242.7**	**42.6**	**35.1**	**77.7**	**10.7**	**31.0**	**41.7**	**20.1**	**7.4**	**5.1**	**15.0**	**23.0**	**97.2**

Cleveland Cavaliers

Player	GP	MPG	FG%	3Pt%	FT%	OFF	DEF	Total	APG	SPG	BPG	TO	PF	PPG
LeBron James	79	42.5	48.0	33.5	73.8	1.0	6.1	7.0	6.6	1.6	0.8	3.6	2.3	31.4
Z. Ilgauskas	78	29.3	50.6	0.0	83.4	3.1	4.4	7.6	1.2	0.5	1.7	2.0	3.6	15.6
Larry Hughes	36	35.6	40.9	36.8	75.7	0.7	3.8	4.5	3.6	1.5	0.6	2.8	3.3	15.5
Ronald Murray	28	36.7	44.8	30.8	70.2	0.5	1.9	2.4	2.8	1.4	0.3	2.0	2.3	13.5
Drew Gooden	79	27.5	51.2	33.3	68.2	3.0	5.4	8.4	0.7	0.7	0.6	1.3	2.4	10.7
Donyell Marshall	81	25.6	39.5	32.4	74.8	1.3	4.8	6.1	0.7	0.5	0.5	1.1	2.0	9.3
Damon Jones	82	25.6	38.7	37.7	64.0	0.2	1.5	1.6	2.1	0.5	0.0	0.7	1.4	6.7
Eric Snow	82	28.7	40.9	10.0	68.8	0.5	2.0	2.4	4.2	0.9	0.2	1.4	2.7	4.8
Sasha Pavlovic	53	15.3	41.0	36.5	65.3	0.3	1.2	1.5	0.5	0.4	0.1	0.8	1.9	4.6
Anderson Varejao	48	15.9	52.7	0.0	51.3	1.6	3.3	4.9	0.4	0.7	0.4	0.6	2.5	4.6
Stephen Graham	13	9.0	42.4	0.0	88.9	0.3	1.0	1.3	0.2	0.2	0.2	0.5	1.8	2.8
Luke Jackson	36	8.8	34.1	33.3	78.8	0.4	0.7	1.1	0.7	0.3	0.1	0.9	0.8	2.7
Alan Henderson	51	10.4	51.7	0.0	67.4	1.2	1.5	2.7	0.2	0.2	0.2	0.4	1.1	2.5
Zendon Hamilton	11	4.1	53.9	0.0	68.8	0.3	0.7	1.0	0.0	0.3	0.0	0.6	0.4	2.3
Ira Newble	36	9.8	29.8	23.1	68.8	0.6	1.0	1.6	0.3	0.1	0.3	0.3	1.3	1.3
Mike Wilks	37	6.6	28.8	14.3	50.0	0.2	0.6	0.7	0.5	0.2	0.0	0.4	0.7	1.1
M. Andriuskevicius	5	1.6	0.0	0.0	0.0	0.2	0.5	0.7	0.0	0.3	0.0	0.0	0.2	0.0
Cavaliers	**82**	**241.8**	**45.4**	**33.9**	**72.9**	**11.7**	**30.6**	**42.3**	**19.0**	**6.9**	**4.8**	**13.4**	**21.1**	**97.6**
Opponents	**82**	**241.8**	**45.5**	**35.6**	**74.2**	**9.8**	**29.5**	**39.4**	**20.3**	**6.6**	**4.4**	**13.2**	**22.5**	**95.4**

Dallas Mavericks

Player	GP	MPG	FG%	3Pt%	FT%	OFF	DEF	Total	APG	SPG	BPG	TO	PF	PPG
Dirk Nowitzki	81	38.1	48.0	40.6	90.1	1.4	7.6	9.0	2.8	0.7	1.0	1.9	2.0	26.6
Jason Terry	80	35.0	47.0	41.1	80.0	0.4	1.6	2.0	3.8	1.3	0.3	1.7	2.5	17.1
Josh Howard	59	32.5	47.1	42.9	73.4	2.1	4.2	6.3	1.9	1.2	0.4	1.3	2.8	15.6
Jerry Stackhouse	55	27.7	40.1	27.7	88.2	0.6	2.2	2.8	2.9	0.7	0.2	2.2	1.8	13.0
Marquis Daniels	62	28.5	48.1	21.1	75.4	1.3	2.3	3.6	2.8	1.1	0.2	1.6	2.3	10.2
Devin Harris	56	22.8	46.9	23.8	71.6	0.5	1.8	2.2	3.2	1.0	0.3	1.5	2.2	9.9
Keith Van Horn	53	20.6	42.4	36.8	83.2	1.0	2.6	3.6	0.7	0.6	0.2	1.3	2.3	8.9
Erick Dampier	82	23.6	49.3	0.0	59.1	3.3	4.5	7.8	0.6	0.3	1.3	1.4	3.2	5.7
Adrian Griffin	52	24.0	48.0	0.0	77.4	1.4	2.9	4.4	1.7	1.0	0.2	0.8	2.2	4.6
Doug Christie	7	26.5	34.6	0.0	66.7	0.3	1.6	1.9	2.0	1.3	0.1	0.9	1.4	3.7
Rawle Marshall	23	10.5	40.0	33.3	75.9	0.4	1.0	1.4	0.4	0.4	0.3	0.7	0.7	3.1
Pavel Podkolzin	1	18.1	0.0	0.0	50.0	0.0	7.0	7.0	0.0	0.0	1.0	2.0	0.0	3.0
Josh Powell	37	11.6	45.7	0.0	80.0	0.8	1.4	2.2	0.2	0.2	0.1	0.6	1.4	3.0
DeSagana Diop	81	18.6	48.7	50.0	54.2	1.8	2.8	4.6	0.3	0.5	1.8	0.4	3.1	2.4
Darrell Armstrong	80	10.0	33.6	22.9	78.6	0.3	1.0	1.3	1.4	0.4	0.1	0.9	1.2	2.1
DJ Mbenga	43	5.5	53.3	0.0	50.0	0.4	0.9	1.3	0.1	0.1	0.6	0.4	1.1	1.7
Mavericks	**82**	**242.4**	**46.2**	**37.4**	**78.3**	**12.6**	**29.7**	**42.2**	**18.0**	**7.2**	**6.0**	**12.9**	**22.4**	**99.2**
Opponents	**82**	**242.4**	**44.3**	**36.1**	**75.2**	**11.4**	**26.9**	**38.3**	**17.5**	**6.5**	**4.9**	**14.0**	**23.9**	**93.1**

Denver Nuggets

Player	GP	MPG	FG%	3Pt%	FT%	OFF	DEF	Total	APG	SPG	BPG	TO	PF	PPG
			Field Goals				**Rebounds**							
Carmelo Anthony...80		36.8	48.1	24.3	80.8	1.5	3.4	4.9	2.7	1.1	0.5	2.7	2.9	26.5
Andre Milller........82		35.8	46.3	18.5	73.8	1.1	3.2	4.3	8.2	1.3	0.2	3.1	2.6	13.7
Ruben Patterson ..26		28.3	54.3	16.7	58.0	1.7	1.7	3.5	2.6	1.3	0.4	2.6	2.7	13.2
Kenyon Martin.....56		27.6	49.5	22.7	71.2	1.7	4.6	6.3	1.4	0.8	0.9	1.3	3.1	12.9
Marcus Camby 56		33.2	46.5	9.1	71.2	2.4	9.6	11.9	2.1	1.4	3.3	1.6	2.8	12.8
Earl Boykins 60		25.7	41.0	34.6	87.4	0.4	1.0	1.4	3.8	0.8	0.1	1.4	1.2	12.6
Voshon Lenard 12		19.8	40.8	28.6	38.5	0.2	2.2	2.3	1.5	0.7	0.2	0.9	1.8	8.3
Earl Watson 46		21.2	42.9	39.5	62.7	0.4	1.5	1.9	3.5	0.8	0.2	1.6	2.1	7.5
Greg Buckner.......73		24.1	43.4	35.4	78.2	0.4	2.4	2.9	1.7	1.2	0.3	0.7	2.5	6.7
DerMarr Johnson .58		15.9	43.1	35.0	81.0	0.3	1.3	1.7	1.0	0.4	0.5	0.8	1.5	6.1
Eduardo Najera....64		22.6	42.2	33.3	78.1	2.0	3.1	5.1	0.8	0.8	0.5	0.8	2.6	5.4
Reggie Evans.......26		23.3	45.3	0.0	50.5	2.2	6.5	8.7	0.6	0.6	0.2	1.7	2.7	5.2
Francisco Elson ...72		21.9	53.2	20.0	66.2	1.4	3.3	4.7	0.7	0.8	0.6	0.9	2.9	4.9
Howard Eisley 19		14.9	34.9	31.6	83.3	0.1	0.9	1.0	2.3	0.4	0.1	1.0	1.2	4.8
Linas Keliza.........61		8.5	44.5	15.4	70.4	0.6	1.3	1.9	0.3	0.2	0.2	0.3	1.4	3.5
Julius Hodge........14		2.4	38.5	0.0	37.5	0.4	0.1	0.5	0.4	0.1	0.0	0.6	0.5	0.9
Nuggets 82		243.0	46.I	32.5	74.4	II.0	30.3	4I.3	23.4	8.5	5.7	I4.4	22.7	100.3
Opponets 82		243.0	45.5	35.8	73.6	II.8	30.I	4I.9	23.9	7.2	5.3	I6.I	23.3	100.I

Detroit Pistons

Player	GP	MPG	FG%	3Pt%	FT%	OFF	DEF	Total	APG	SPG	BPG	TO	PF	PPG
			Field Goals				**Rebounds**							
Richard Hamilton..80		35.3	49.1	45.8	84.5	1.1	2.2	3.2	3.4	0.7	0.2	2.2	2.6	20.1
Chauncey Billups ..81		36.1	41.8	43.3	89.4	0.5	2.6	3.1	8.6	0.9	0.1	2.1	2.0	18.5
Rasheed Wallace..80		34.7	43.0	35.7	74.3	1.1	5.7	6.8	2.3	1.0	1.6	1.1	2.9	15.1
Tayshaun Prince..82		35.3	45.0	35.0	76.5	1.3	3.0	4.2	2.3	0.8	0.5	1.1	1.2	14.1
Tony Delk 23		16.4	44.4	42.6	72.0	0.6	1.7	2.2	1.4	0.6	0.0	0.8	1.2	7.8
Antonio McDyess.82		21.1	50.9	0.0	55.7	1.9	3.4	5.3	1.1	0.6	0.6	0.9	2.7	7.8
Ben Wallace 82		35.3	51.0	0.0	41.6	3.7	7.6	11.3	1.9	1.8	2.2	1.1	2.0	7.3
Amir Johnson 3		12.9	70.0	66.7	100.0	1.0	0.3	1.3	1.0	0.0	0.7	1.3	2.3	6.7
Maurice Evans 80		14.2	45.2	37.1	80.0	1.0	1.1	2.0	0.8	0.5	0.2	0.5	1.5	5.0
Carlos Delfino 68		10.7	40.3	33.3	67.2	0.4	1.3	1.7	0.7	0.3	0.2	0.5	1.3	3.6
Carlos Arroyo 50		12.0	36.3	33.3	72.4	0.5	0.9	1.4	3.1	0.4	0.1	0.9	1.5	3.2
Lindsey Hunter.....30		11.8	37.0	25.6	50.0	0.3	1.0	1.3	2.1	0.6	0.0	0.7	1.5	2.9
Kelvin Cato...........4		8.5	41.7	0.0	0.0	0.3	1.5	1.8	0.5	0.0	0.5	0.5	1.0	2.5
Jason Maxell 26		6.1	42.6	0.0	33.3	0.5	0.6	1.1	0.1	0.2	0.2	0.4	0.5	2.3
Alex Acher 5		7.0	25.0	20.0	0.0	0.2	0.8	1.0	0.8	0.2	0.0	0.8	0.8	1.8
Darko Milicic.......25		5.6	51.5	0.0	37.5	0.4	0.7	1.1	0.4	0.1	0.6	0.6	1.0	1.5
Dale Davis...........28		6.3	37.5	0.0	53.3	0.8	1.1	1.9	0.2	0.0	0.3	0.1	0.8	0.9
Pistons 82		241.8	45.5	38.4	72.7	II.9	28.6	40.5	24.0	7.I	6.0	I0.8	I8.5	96.8
Opponents.................82		241.8	45.2	32.5	73.6	II.6	29.3	40.9	I8.8	5.9	3.5	I4.0	2I.0	90.2

Golden State Warriors

Player	GP	MPG	FG%	3Pt%	FT%	OFF	DEF	Total	APG	SPG	BPG	TO	PF	PPG
			Field Goals				**Rebounds**							
J. Richardson 75		38.4	44.6	38.4	67.3	1.4	4.4	5.8	3.1	1.3	0.5	2.2	2.8	23.2
Baron Davis 54		36.5	38.9	31.5	67.5	0.8	3.5	4.4	8.9	1.7	0.3	2.9	3.1	17.9
Troy Murphy 74		34.0	43.3	32.0	78.7	2.6	7.4	10.0	1.4	0.6	0.4	1.5	2.6	14.0
Derek Fisher.........82		31.6	41.0	39.7	83.3	0.4	2.1	2.6	4.3	1.5	0.1	1.9	2.9	13.3
Mike Dunleavy 81		31.8	40.6	28.5	77.8	1.0	4.0	4.9	2.9	0.7	0.4	1.5	2.5	11.5
Mickael Pietrus....52		22.7	40.4	31.8	60.8	1.1	2.0	3.1	0.9	0.6	0.2	1.5	2.5	9.3
Ike Diogu............69		14.9	52.4	0.0	81.0	1.4	1.9	3.3	0.4	0.2	0.4	1.1	2.4	7.0
Monta Ellis..........49		18.1	41.5	34.2	71.2	0.5	1.7	2.1	1.6	0.7	0.2	1.2	1.4	6.8
Adonal Foyle.......77		23.7	50.7	0.0	61.2	1.9	3.7	5.5	0.4	0.6	1.6	1.0	2.8	4.5
Andris Biedrins 68		14.7	63.8	0.0	30.6	1.8	2.3	4.2	0.4	0.3	0.7	0.5	2.8	3.8
Will Bynum 15		10.8	40.4	22.2	62.5	0.2	0.6	0.8	1.3	0.5	0.0	0.9	0.7	3.6
Zarko Cabarkapa.61		8.3	38.5	25.0	71.4	0.6	1.2	1.8	0.3	0.2	0.1	0.6	1.4	3.3
Chris Taft............17		8.5	60.5	0.0	16.7	1.1	1.0	2.1	0.1	0.1	0.4	0.1	1.5	2.8
Calbert Cheaney..42		10.7	38.9	0.0	100.0	0.5	1.0	1.5	0.5	0.3	0.1	0.4	0.9	2.2
Aaron Miles 19		6.2	33.3	0.0	100.0	0.0	0.7	0.7	1.3	0.2	0.1	0.6	0.7	0.9
Warriors 82		241.8	43.3	34.I	7I.8	I2.0	30.3	42.3	20.7	7.4	4.4	I3.6	23.7	98.5
Opponents.................82		241.8	45.7	35.I	74.3	I2.0	32.5	44.5	22.3	7.0	5.0	I5.3	23.4	99.8

Houston Rockets

Player	GP	MPG	Field Goals FG%	3Pt%	FT%	Rebounds OFF	DEF	Total	APG	SPG	BPG	TO	PF	PPG
Tracy McGrady 47		37.1	40.6	31.2	74.7	1.0	5.6	6.5	4.8	1.3	0.9	2.6	1.9	24.4
Yao Ming 57		34.2	51.9	0.0	85.3	2.6	7.6	10.2	1.5	0.5	1.7	2.6	3.4	22.3
Rafer Alston 63		38.6	37.9	32.7	69.2	0.6	3.5	4.1	6.8	1.6	0.2	2.5	3.1	12.1
Juwan Howard 80		31.7	45.9	0.0	80.6	2.1	4.6	6.7	1.4	0.6	0.1	1.7	2.9	11.8
Derek Anderson ..20		29.1	39.3	28.4	83.6	0.6	3.6	4.2	2.7	0.8	0.2	1.9	2.5	10.8
David Wesley 71		33.4	40.3	36.5	80.8	0.3	2.2	2.5	2.9	0.8	0.1	1.7	3.0	9.9
Stromile Swift......66		20.4	49.1	0.0	65.1	1.6	2.9	4.4	0.4	0.6	0.8	1.4	3.0	8.9
Luther Head 80		28.9	40.3	36.1	69.9	0.4	2.9	3.3	2.7	1.1	0.1	1.5	2.1	8.8
Keith Bogans 33		32.3	39.5	31.4	58.0	0.8	3.7	4.5	2.5	1.0	0.2	1.5	2.7	8.5
Richie Frahm.........8		14.6	42.9	36.4	80.0	0.0	1.3	1.3	0.8	0.1	0.0	0.5	1.0	5.3
Jon Barry 20		17.1	38.5	37.5	82.8	0.1	1.5	1.6	1.3	0.7	0.1	1.1	1.3	4.3
Chuck Hayes 40		13.4	56.2	0.0	64.4	1.7	2.8	4.5	0.4	0.7	0.4	0.3	1.9	3.7
Lonny Baxter 23		12.5	45.8	0.0	84.2	1.7	2.0	3.7	0.1	0.4	0.3	0.6	2.1	3.6
Stephen Graham....6		6.3	37.5	20.0	100.0	0.2	1.0	1.2	0.5	0.3	0.0	0.8	0.8	2.8
Dikembe Mutombo64		14.9	52.6	0.0	75.8	1.6	3.2	4.8	0.1	0.3	0.9	0.6	2.0	2.6
John Lucas 13		8.2	38.9	22.2	0.0	0.2	0.2	0.4	0.9	0.4	0.0	0.5	0.5	2.3
Moochie Norris...29		8.3	40.0	0.0	76.5	0.3	0.9	1.2	1.0	0.5	0.0	0.6	1.1	2.2
Rick Brunson.......23		9.4	34.8	41.7	58.3	0.0	0.8	0.9	1.4	0.4	0.0	0.8	0.9	1.9
Ryan Bowen 68		9.6	29.8	13.6	78.6	0.5	0.8	1.3	0.4	0.3	0.1	0.2	1.3	1.3
Maciej Lampe 4		3.0	28.6	0.0	0.0	0.8	0.5	1.3	0.0	0.0	0.0	0.5	0.0	1.0
Rockets 82		**241.8**	**43.3**	**33.2**	**75.9**	**10.4**	**31.3**	**41.6**	**19.3**	**7.2**	**3.9**	**13.7**	**22.7**	**90.1**
Opponents..................82		**241.8**	**42.9**	**36.9**	**73.1**	**10.7**	**30.2**	**40.9**	**20.1**	**7.1**	**4.6**	**13.3**	**20.9**	**91.7**

Indiana Pacers

Player	GP	MPG	Field Goals FG%	3Pt%	FT%	Rebounds OFF	DEF	Total	APG	SPG	BPG	TO	PF	PPG
Jermaine O'Neal ..51		35.3	47.2	30.0	70.9	2.0	7.3	9.3	2.6	0.5	2.3	3.0	3.5	20.1
Peja Stojakovic....40		36.3	46.1	40.4	90.3	1.1	5.1	6.3	1.7	0.7	0.2	1.3	2.2	19.5
Ron Artest............16		37.7	46.0	33.3	61.2	1.6	3.3	4.9	2.2	2.6	0.7	2.7	2.8	19.4
Stephen Jackson 81		35.9	41.1	34.5	78.6	0.6	3.3	3.9	2.8	1.3	0.5	2.5	2.4	16.4
Fred Jones 68		27.0	41.7	33.7	76.3	0.3	2.2	2.5	2.3	0.8	0.3	1.6	2.1	9.6
Jamaal Tinsley 42		26.7	40.9	22.9	63.7	0.8	2.3	3.2	5.0	1.2	0.1	2.6	2.3	9.3
Anthony Johnson .75		26.4	44.3	32.9	75.2	0.4	1.8	2.2	4.3	0.8	0.3	1.5	1.8	9.2
Austin Croshere 50		23.0	46.3	38.6	88.2	1.2	4.1	5.3	1.2	0.4	0.1	1.0	2.1	8.2
Danny Granger 78		22.6	46.2	32.3	77.7	1.7	3.2	4.9	1.2	0.7	0.8	1.0	2.7	7.5
Sarunas Jasikevicius75		20.8	39.6	36.4	91.0	0.3	1.8	2.0	3.0	0.5	0.1	1.6	1.4	7.3
Jeff Foster 63		25.1	55.2	0.0	60.4	3.6	5.6	9.1	0.8	0.7	0.4	1.0	3.0	5.9
David Harrison 67		15.4	50.3	0.0	51.2	1.3	2.5	3.8	0.2	0.3	0.9	1.2	2.9	5.8
Jonathan Bender ...2		10.3	80.0	0.0	100.0	0.0	2.0	2.0	1.0	0.0	0.5	0.0	1.0	5.0
Scot Pollard.........45		17.1	45.5	0.0	76.3	1.6	3.2	4.8	0.5	0.8	0.4	0.6	2.6	3.8
Eddie Gill 41		3.0	22.2	30.4	78.3	0.0	0.4	0.4	0.3	0.3	0.0	0.2	0.3	1.1
Samaki Walker 7		3.1	0.0	0.0	100.0	0.0	0.4	0.4	0.0	0.0	0.1	0.3	1.0	0.3
Pacers.......................82		**240.6**	**44.4**	**34.9**	**73.7**	**11.0**	**31.2**	**42.2**	**19.9**	**7.3**	**5.0**	**14.7**	**22.2**	**93.9**
Opponents..................82		**240.6**	**43.5**	**34.3**	**73.3**	**11.8**	**29.5**	**41.3**	**18.5**	**8.1**	**4.9**	**13.6**	**22.0**	**92.0**

Los Angeles Clippers

Player	GP	MPG	Field Goals FG%	3Pt%	FT%	Rebounds OFF	DEF	Total	APG	SPG	BPG	TO	PF	PPG
Elton Brand 79		39.2	52.7	33.3	77.5	3.0	7.0	10.0	2.6	1.0	2.5	2.2	2.9	24.7
Corey Maggette ...32		29.5	44.5	33.8	82.8	0.9	4.4	5.3	2.1	0.6	0.1	2.4	3.0	17.8
Sam Cassell 78		34.0	44.3	36.8	86.3	0.5	3.2	3.7	6.3	1.0	0.1	2.2	2.9	17.2
Cuttino Mobley 79		37.7	42.6	33.9	83.9	0.6	3.7	4.3	3.0	1.2	0.5	1.8	2.6	14.8
Chris Kaman 78		32.8	52.3	0.0	77.0	2.4	7.2	9.6	1.0	0.6	1.4	2.3	3.5	12.0
V. Radmanovic ...30		29.5	41.7	41.8	73.1	0.8	4.9	5.7	2.1	1.0	0.5	1.3	2.7	10.7
Shawn Livingston ..61		25.0	42.7	12.5	68.8	0.7	2.3	3.0	4.5	0.8	0.5	1.8	2.6	5.8
Zeljko Rebraca.....29		14.2	54.2	0.0	75.6	0.5	1.8	2.2	0.3	0.2	0.7	0.8	2.5	4.7
Quinton Ross 67		22.6	42.2	0.0	76.0	0.6	2.0	2.5	1.2	0.8	0.2	0.7	2.3	4.7
Chris Wilcox 48		13.7	53.6	0.0	64.4	1.0	2.7	3.6	0.4	0.3	0.4	0.7	2.2	4.5
Daniel Ewing 66		14.7	38.0	28.2	78.3	0.4	0.9	1.3	1.3	0.6	0.1	0.9	1.3	3.8
Vin Baker..............8		10.6	46.7	0.0	72.2	0.3	2.1	2.4	0.5	0.5	0.5	1.1	1.6	3.4
James Singleton ..59		12.8	51.0	50.0	78.0	1.1	2.3	3.3	0.5	0.3	0.4	0.5	1.6	3.4
Walter McCarty 36		9.8	33.3	22.2	57.1	0.4	1.5	1.9	0.6	0.2	0.1	0.5	1.4	2.4
Boniface N'Dong..23		6.6	41.5	0.0	66.7	0.7	1.0	1.6	0.3	0.1	0.2	0.3	1.0	2.2
Yaroslav Koroley ..24		5.3	30.0	28.6	70.0	0.2	0.3	0.5	0.4	0.1	0.0	0.3	0.5	1.1
Howard Eisley 13		8.6	23.5	25.0	0.0	0.1	1.0	1.1	1.9	0.2	0.0	0.2	0.9	0.7
Clippers 82		**241.5**	**46.5**	**34.4**	**79.1**	**10.1**	**33.0**	**43.1**	**20.8**	**6.5**	**6.1**	**13.8**	**22.8**	**97.2**
Opponents..................82		**241.5**	**43.5**	**34.7**	**73.2**	**10.5**	**29.7**	**40.1**	**21.5**	**7.0**	**4.3**	**12.8**	**21.7**	**95.6**

Los Angeles Lakers

Player	GP	MPG	FG%	3Pt%	FT%	OFF	DEF	Total	APG	SPG	BPG	TO	PF	PPG
Kobe Bryant	80	41.0	45.0	34.8	85.0	0.9	4.4	5.3	4.5	1.8	0.4	3.1	2.9	35.4
Lamar Odom	80	40.3	48.1	37.2	69.0	2.3	7.0	9.2	5.5	0.9	0.8	2.7	3.2	14.8
Smush Parker	82	33.8	44.7	36.6	69.4	0.5	2.9	3.3	3.7	1.7	0.2	1.8	2.6	11.5
Chris Mihm	59	26.1	50.1	0.0	71.6	2.3	4.0	6.3	1.0	0.3	1.2	1.4	3.6	10.2
Brian Cook	81	19.0	51.1	42.9	83.2	1.1	2.3	3.4	0.9	0.5	0.4	0.8	2.5	7.9
Kwame Brown	72	27.5	52.6	0.0	54.5	2.5	4.0	6.6	1.0	0.4	0.6	1.4	2.7	7.4
Devean George	71	21.7	40.0	31.3	67.4	1.2	2.7	3.9	1.0	0.9	0.5	0.8	2.2	6.3
Luke Walton	69	19.3	41.2	32.7	75.0	1.3	2.3	3.6	2.3	0.6	0.2	1.1	1.7	5.0
Laron Profit	25	11.2	47.6	16.7	87.5	0.3	1.4	1.7	0.6	0.4	0.2	1.0	1.0	4.2
Sasha Vujacic	82	17.7	34.6	34.3	88.5	0.4	1.5	1.9	1.7	0.6	0.0	0.6	1.8	3.9
Ronny Turiaf	23	7.0	50.0	0.0	55.6	0.5	1.1	1.6	0.4	0.1	0.4	0.3	1.3	2.0
Jim Jackson	13	7.1	29.0	36.4	0.0	0.0	0.9	0.9	0.3	0.2	0.0	0.4	0.4	1.7
Andrew Bynum	46	7.4	40.2	0.0	29.6	0.7	1.0	1.7	0.2	0.1	0.5	0.4	1.2	1.6
Von Wafer	16	4.5	15.8	11.8	75.0	0.3	0.2	0.5	0.3	0.2	0.0	0.1	0.8	1.3
Devin Green	27	5.0	21.4	0.0	61.9	0.4	0.5	0.9	0.3	0.1	0.0	0.2	0.5	0.9
Aaron McKie	14	8.7	25.0	0.0	50.0	0.2	1.2	1.4	0.8	0.4	0.0	0.1	0.5	0.5
Lakers	82	242.1	45.3	34.9	74.5	11.8	30.3	42.2	21.2	7.7	4.3	13.4	23.1	99.4
Opponents	82	242.1	45.0	35.3	74.7	10.9	29.3	40.1	21.1	6.5	4.3	14.1	23.5	96.9

Memphis Grizzlies

Player	GP	MPG	FG%	3Pt%	FT%	OFF	DEF	Total	APG	SPG	BPG	TO	PF	PPG
Pau Gasol	80	39.2	50.3	25.0	68.9	2.4	6.5	8.9	4.6	0.6	1.9	2.9	2.3	20.4
Mike Miller	74	30.6	46.6	40.7	80.0	0.6	4.8	5.4	2.7	0.7	0.4	1.9	2.3	13.7
Eddie Jones	75	32.5	40.4	35.6	78.1	0.5	3.3	3.7	2.4	1.8	0.4	1.2	2.7	11.8
Damon Stoudamire	27	31.9	39.7	34.6	85.5	0.9	2.7	3.5	4.7	0.7	0.0	2.0	1.8	11.7
Chucky Atkins	43	27.0	40.1	35.2	81.1	0.3	1.5	1.7	3.0	0.7	0.1	1.3	2.2	11.4
Bobby Jackson	71	25.0	38.2	38.9	73.3	0.6	2.5	3.1	2.8	0.9	0.0	1.4	2.2	11.4
Shane Battier	81	35.1	48.8	39.4	70.7	2.0	3.3	5.3	1.7	1.1	1.4	1.1	2.8	10.1
Lorenzen Wright	78	21.7	47.8	0.0	56.4	1.8	3.2	5.1	0.6	0.7	0.6	0.9	2.6	5.8
Jake Tsakalidis	51	14.4	60.6	0.0	65.5	1.5	2.6	4.2	0.3	0.3	0.6	0.8	2.1	5.0
Hakim Warrick	68	10.6	44.3	0.0	66.1	0.6	1.5	2.1	0.4	0.2	0.3	0.8	1.7	4.1
Dahntay Jones	71	13.6	41.4	14.3	64.5	0.3	1.2	1.5	0.6	0.5	0.2	0.7	1.5	4.0
Brian Cardinal	36	11.2	41.4	44.8	70.4	0.3	1.2	1.5	0.9	0.6	0.0	0.8	1.8	3.4
Anthony Roberson	16	5.5	45.2	50.0	100.0	0.0	0.4	0.4	0.3	0.1	0.0	0.2	0.4	2.2
Antonio Burks	57	10.0	35.4	16.7	43.5	0.1	0.6	0.7	1.3	0.4	0.0	0.6	0.8	2.0
Lawrence Roberts	33	5.5	45.5	0.0	47.8	0.8	0.7	1.5	0.2	0.2	0.1	0.2	0.9	1.6
Grizzlies	82	242.1	44.8	37.4	71.1	10.2	29.0	39.2	19.3	12.9	5.4	12.9	21.4	92.2
Opponents	82	242.1	43.6	33.4	75.4	11.3	29.3	40.6	19.6	7.3	5.9	14.8	22.8	80.5

Miami Heat

Player	GP	MPG	FG%	3Pt%	FT%	OFF	DEF	Total	APG	SPG	BPG	TO	PF	PPG
Dwyane Wade	75	38.6	49.5	17.1	78.3	1.4	4.3	5.7	6.7	2.0	0.8	3.6	2.9	27.2
Shaquille O'Neal	59	30.6	60.0	0.0	46.9	2.9	6.3	9.2	1.9	0.4	1.8	2.9	3.9	20.0
Jason Williams	59	31.8	44.2	37.2	86.7	0.1	2.3	2.4	4.9	0.9	0.1	1.7	1.7	12.3
Antoine Walker	82	26.8	43.5	35.8	62.8	1.3	3.9	5.1	2.0	0.6	0.4	1.8	2.3	12.2
Udonis Haslem	81	30.8	50.8	0.0	78.9	2.1	5.8	7.8	1.2	0.6	0.2	1.2	2.7	9.4
Alonzo Mourning	65	20.0	59.7	0.0	59.4	1.9	3.6	5.5	0.2	0.2	2.7	1.2	2.7	7.8
Gary Payton	81	28.5	42.1	28.7	79.4	0.4	2.5	2.9	3.2	0.9	0.1	1.3	2.1	7.7
James Posey	67	28.6	40.3	40.3	78.7	0.5	4.3	4.8	1.3	0.8	0.3	0.9	2.9	7.2
Derek Anderson	23	20.2	30.8	31.3	84.2	0.4	2.2	2.6	2.1	0.4	0.1	0.7	2.1	5.8
Gerald Fitch	18	13.3	33.7	26.9	73.9	0.4	1.3	1.7	1.8	0.4	0.3	0.8	1.6	4.7
Jason Kapono	51	13.0	44.6	39.6	84.9	0.2	1.2	1.4	0.7	0.1	0.1	0.4	1.8	4.1
Wayne Simien	43	9.6	48.3	0.0	88.2	0.9	1.2	2.1	0.2	0.0	0.3	0.6	1.6	3.4
Michael Doleac	31	12.0	42.1	0.0	80.0	0.7	2.0	2.7	0.3	0.3	0.2	0.5	1.5	3.2
Dorell Wright	20	6.6	46.5	50.0	88.2	0.1	1.5	1.6	0.4	0.2	0.1	0.7	0.6	2.9
Shandon Anderson	48	13.3	42.9	26.3	72.2	0.4	1.3	1.7	0.6	0.4	0.1	0.5	1.6	2.6
Earl Barron	8	5.6	31.3	0.0	75.0	0.3	1.0	1.3	0.0	0.0	0.0	0.6	1.3	1.6
Heat	82	240.9	47.8	34.5	70.0	10.5	32.6	43.1	20.6	6.4	5.4	13.9	22.8	99.9
Opponents	82	240.9	44.0	36.1	73.9	10.1	28.8	38.8	19.5	6.8	3.6	13.0	23.6	96.0

Milwaukee Bucks

Player	GP	MPG	FG%	3Pt%	FT%	OFF	DEF	Total	APG	SPG	BPG	TO	PF	PPG
			Field Goals			**Rebounds**								
Michael Redd 80		39.1	45.0	39.5	87.7	1.0	3.3	4.3	2.9	1.2	0.1	2.1	2.0	25.4
Bobby Simmons...75		33.8	45.3	42.0	82.5	1.2	3.2	4.4	2.3	1.2	0.3	1.6	3.4	13.4
T.J. Ford 72		35.5	41.6	33.7	75.4	0.9	3.4	4.3	6.6	1.4	0.1	3.0	2.7	12.2
Maurice Williams...58		26.4	42.5	38.2	85.0	0.5	2.0	2.5	4.0	0.9	0.1	1.8	2.5	12.1
Andrew Bogut 82		28.6	53.3	0.0	62.9	2.3	4.7	7.0	2.3	0.6	0.8	1.5	3.2	9.4
Jamaal Magloire...82		30.1	46.7	0.0	53.5	2.7	6.8	9.5	0.7	0.4	1.0	2.0	3.4	9.2
Joe Smith 44		20.2	47.5	0.0	77.4	1.9	3.3	5.2	0.7	0.6	0.3	0.9	2.7	8.6
Charlie Bell..........59		21.7	43.9	42.3	70.8	0.7	1.7	2.0	2.2	1.0	0.1	0.7	2.1	8.4
Dan Gadzuric.......74		12.0	55.3	0.0	46.1	1.2	1.9	2.3	2.1	0.3	0.6	0.5	2.3	5.2
Toni Kukoc 65		15.7	38.9	30.6	71.4	0.4	1.9	2.3	2.1	0.5	0.3	1.0	1.3	4.9
Jiri Welsch...........58		14.9	38.7	28.6	74.7	0.4	1.5	1.9	1.1	0.6	0.0	0.7	1.1	4.3
Jermaine Jackson30		6.7	42.3	25.0	85.7	0.3	0.6	0.9	0.8	0.1	0.0	0.4	0.6	1.2
Reece Gaines 12		4.5	50.0	0.0	25.0	0.0	0.0	0.0	0.3	0.1	0.0	0.1	0.1	1.1
Ervin Johnson 18		4.5	41.2		50.0	0.3	1.1	1.3	0.1	0.1	0.1	0.3	1.3	0.8
Bucks.....................82		**242.1**	**45.3**	**38.0**	**73.8**	**11.3**	**29.9**	**41.2**	**21.6**	**7.3**	**3.3**	**14.0**	**23.2**	**97.8**
Opponents...............82		**242.1**	**46.6**	**35.4**	**74.7**	**10.1**	**30.2**	**40.3**	**22.5**	**7.4**	**5.0**	**14.4**	**23.8**	**98.8**

Minnesota Timberwolves

Player	GP	MPG	FG%	3Pt%	FT%	OFF	DEF	Total	APG	SPG	BPG	TO	PF	PPG
			Field Goals			**Rebounds**								
Kevin Garnett 76		38.9	52.6	26.7	81.0	2.8	9.9	12.7	4.1	1.4	1.4	2.4	2.7	21.8
Wally Szczerbiak ..40		38.9	49.5	40.6	89.6	0.9	3.9	4.8	2.8	0.5	0.4	2.2	2.3	20.1
Ricky Davis...........36		40.5	47.9	28.2	80.7	0.7	3.9	4.6	4.8	1.2	0.2	2.7	2.8	19.1
Marcus Banks 40		30.7	47.9	36.4	77.8	0.5	2.4	2.9	4.7	1.2	0.3	2.4	3.1	12.0
Mark Blount 42		27.5	50.6	0.0	74.7	1.4	3.4	4.8	0.8	0.6	1.0	1.8	3.5	10.2
Troy Hudson..........36		22.2	38.1	39.6	92.3	0.2	1.0	1.2	2.9	0.3	0.1	1.1	1.5	9.5
Trenton Hassell 77		32.7	46.4	30.4	74.4	1.1	1.7	2.8	2.6	0.6	0.4	1.6	2.6	9.2
Bracye Wright........7		19.3	41.2	35.3	87.5	0.4	2.1	2.6	0.7	0.1	0.0	1.1	1.1	8.9
Rashad McCants...79		17.2	45.1	37.2	73.6	0.4	1.4	1.8	0.8	0.6	0.3	1.1	2.2	7.9
Marko Jaric...........75		28.0	39.9	30.1	68.8	0.8	2.3	3.1	3.9	1.4	0.3	1.7	2.5	7.8
Justin Reed...........40		17.7	42.5	0.0	77.5	1.0	1.4	2.4	0.9	0.5	0.3	0.9	3.0	6.3
Michael Olowokandi32		23.5	44.6	0.0	48.7	1.4	4.2	5.6	0.5	0.6	0.8	1.3	3.1	6.0
Eddie Griffin..........70		19.4	35.1	19.5	59.5	1.5	4.0	5.6	0.6	0.2	2.1	0.6	1.8	4.6
Anthony Carter 45		13.1	38.7	26.7	72.7	0.2	1.2	1.4	2.2	0.5	0.2	0.9	1.6	3.3
Richie Frahm.........25		9.0	36.9	31.3	60.0	0.1	0.8	0.9	0.6	0.1	0.1	0.2	0.9	2.2
Ronald Dupree 36		7.4	52.4	0.0	34.2	0.6	0.8	1.4	0.4	0.3	0.0	0.4	1.2	2.2
Mark Madsen........62		10.9	40.9	0.0	42.6	0.8	1.5	2.3	0.2	0.4	0.3	0.4	1.8	1.2
Timberwolves............82		**242.1**	**45.6**	**32.9**	**75.8**	**9.9**	**29.5**	**39.4**	**20.9**	**6.8**	**5.7**	**13.7**	**23.0**	**91.7**
Opponents 82		**242.1**	**44.1**	**36.4**	**73.6**	**11.9**	**29.4**	**41.3**	**19.0**	**6.6**	**4.6**	**13.9**	**21.2**	**93.6**

New Jersey Nets

Player	GP	MPG	FG%	3Pt%	FT%	OFF	DEF	Total	APG	SPG	BPG	TO	PF	PPG
			Field Goals			**Rebounds**								
Vince Carter 79		36.8	43.0	34.1	79.9	1.7	4.1	5.9	4.3	1.2	0.7	2.7	3.0	24.2
R. Jefferson..........78		39.2	49.3	31.9	81.2	1.2	5.6	6.9	3.8	0.8	0.2	2.2	2.5	19.5
Nenad Krstic..........80		30.9	50.7	25.0	69.8	2.3	4.1	4.6	1.1	0.4	0.8	1.7	3.7	13.5
Jason Kidd............80		37.2	40.4	35.2	79.5	1.1	6.2	7.3	8.4	1.9	0.4	2.4	2.0	13.3
Clifford Robinson .80		23.3	42.7	34.3	65.8	0.7	2.7	3.3	1.1	0.6	0.5	0.8	2.6	6.9
Jeff McInnis..........28		17.4	44.1	18.8	69.0	0.4	1.4	1.8	1.9	0.4	0.1	1.0	1.3	5.3
Marc Jackson........37		11.7	44.6	0.0	79.2	0.8	1.6	2.4	0.6	0.1	0.2	0.8	1.9	4.6
Jason Collins........71		26.7	39.7	25.0	51.2	1.3	3.5	4.8	1.0	0.7	0.6	0.9	3.5	3.6
Zoran Planinic......50		16.0	36.1	23.2	69.7	0.3	1.1	1.3	1.0	0.4	0.1	0.8	1.6	3.4
Scott Padgett........62		11.6	35.3	34.7	79.4	0.9	1.8	2.7	0.7	0.5	0.2	0.3	1.5	3.4
Jacque Vaughn....80		15.4	43.7	16.7	72.8	0.2	0.9	1.1	1.5	0.5	0.0	0.7	1.8	3.4
Lamond Murray...57		10.1	39.8	34.6	62.5	0.5	1.8	2.3	0.2	0.3	0.1	0.4	1.2	3.4
Bostjan Nachbar...11		8.8	37.5	14.3	62.5	0.4	0.6	1.0	0.5	0.3	0.0	0.4	1.2	2.8
Antoine Wright......39		9.5	35.8	6.7	50.0	0.2	0.5	0.8	0.9	0.3	0.1	0.5	1.1	1.8
Linton Johnson 9		3.9	50.0	0.0	25.0	0.0	0.8	0.8	0.2	0.2	0.0	0.4	0.8	1.1
Nets.......................82		**241.2**	**44.0**	**33.0**	**75.8**	**10.0**	**31.0**	**41.0**	**23.0**	**6.8**	**3.4**	**13.0**	**23.2**	**93.8**
Opponents...............82		**241.2**	**43.9**	**34.8**	**74.1**	**9.6**	**31.7**	**41.3**	**20.0**	**7.2**	**4.0**	**14.4**	**23.0**	**92.4**

New Orleans Hornets

Player	GP	MPG	FG%	3Pt%	FT%	OFF	DEF	Total	APG	SPG	BPG	TO	PF	PPG
			Field Goals			**Rebounds**								
David West	74	34.1	51.2	27.3	84.3	2.3	5.1	7.4	1.2	0.8	0.9	1.4	2.9	17.1
Chris Paul	78	36.0	43.0	28.3	84.7	0.8	4.4	5.1	7.8	2.2	0.1	2.4	2.8	16.1
Speedy Claxton	71	28.4	41.3	27.0	76.9	0.6	2.2	2.7	4.8	1.5	0.1	2.2	2.5	12.3
Desmond Mason	70	30.0	39.9	16.7	68.2	0.9	3.3	4.3	0.9	0.6	0.2	1.6	1.9	10.8
Marc Jackson	27	22.0	48.9	50.0	82.4	2.1	2.7	4.7	0.8	0.3	0.1	1.4	2.1	9.1
P.J. Brown	75	31.7	46.1	0.0	82.7	2.4	4.9	7.3	1.2	0.6	0.7	1.2	2.9	9.0
Rasual Butler	79	23.7	40.6	38.0	69.3	0.7	2.3	2.9	0.5	0.4	0.6	0.8	1.8	8.7
Kirk Snyder	68	19.3	45.3	35.7	73.5	0.8	1.6	2.4	1.5	0.4	0.3	1.0	1.6	8.0
J.R. Smith	55	18.0	39.3	37.1	82.2	0.4	1.7	2.0	1.1	0.7	0.1	1.0	1.6	7.7
Marcus Fizer	3	13.0	52.9	100.0	50.0	0.3	2.0	2.3	0.3	0.0	0.0	0.7	1.7	6.7
Aaron Williams	34	20.4	51.6	0.0	67.3	1.7	3.2	4.9	0.5	0.4	0.5	0.7	3.2	5.8
Linton Johnson	27	18.1	40.3	36.1	73.9	1.5	2.8	4.3	0.4	0.4	0.4	0.9	1.7	5.3
Bostjan Nachbar	25	16.2	33.9	29.8	69.4	0.2	1.8	2.0	0.9	0.5	0.2	0.8	2.1	5.0
Chris Andersen	32	17.8	57.1	0.0	47.6	1.9	2.9	4.8	0.2	0.3	1.3	0.8	2.6	5.0
Moochie Norris	16	11.4	42.6	44.4	64.0	0.2	1.1	1.3	1.3	0.4	0.0	1.1	1.1	3.8
A. Macijauskas	19	7.1	34.2	25.0	86.7	0.2	0.4	0.5	0.3	0.4	0.0	0.4	0.5	2.3
Brandon Bass	29	9.3	40.0	0.0	63.2	0.6	1.7	2.3	0.1	0.1	0.2	0.4	0.6	2.3
Jackson Vroman	41	9.9	39.4	0.0	47.7	0.8	1.3	2.1	0.3	0.3	0.3	0.5	1.9	1.8
Hornets	**82**	**241.5**	**44.0**	**33.9**	**75.8**	**11.2**	**29.0**	**40.2**	**18.5**	**7.5**	**3.8**	**12.5**	**21.8**	**92.8**
Opponents	**82**	**241.5**	**45.9**	**36.7**	**76.0**	**10.5**	**30.5**	**41.0**	**19.3**	**6.4**	**5.3**	**14.6**	**23.3**	**95.6**

New York Knicks

Player	GP	MPG	FG%	3Pt%	FT%	OFF	DEF	Total	APG	SPG	BPG	TO	PF	PPG
			Field Goals			**Rebounds**								
Stephon Marbury	60	36.4	45.1	31.7	75.5	0.4	2.5	2.9	6.4	1.1	0.1	2.6	2.4	16.3
Jamal Crawford	79	32.3	41.6	34.5	82.6	0.5	2.7	3.1	3.8	1.1	0.2	2.2	1.9	14.3
Eddy Curry	72	25.9	56.3	0.0	63.2	2.0	4.0	6.0	0.3	0.4	0.8	2.5	3.3	13.6
Jalen Rose	26	28.7	46.0	49.1	81.2	0.5	2.7	3.2	2.6	0.4	0.1	1.9	2.1	12.7
Channing Frye	65	24.2	47.7	33.3	82.5	2.1	3.6	5.8	0.8	0.5	0.7	1.5	3.1	12.3
Steve Francis	24	27.5	44.2	53.9	76.2	0.6	2.4	3.0	3.5	1.1	0.3	2.4	2.6	10.8
Nate Robinson	74	21.4	40.7	39.7	75.3	0.8	1.5	2.3	2.0	0.8	0.0	1.6	2.8	9.3
Quentin Richardson	55	26.2	35.5	34.0	67.0	1.2	3.0	4.2	1.6	0.7	0.1	1.0	2.4	8.2
Qyntel Woods	49	20.7	50.8	36.7	64.5	0.9	3.0	3.9	1.0	0.7	0.3	1.2	2.0	6.7
Maurice Taylor	67	18.1	46.8	0.0	69.9	1.0	2.5	3.4	0.8	0.3	0.2	1.5	2.6	5.3
Jackie Butler	55	13.4	54.4	0.0	75.3	1.2	2.1	3.3	0.5	0.3	0.6	1.1	2.3	5.3
David Lee	67	16.8	59.6	0.0	57.7	1.6	2.9	4.5	0.6	0.5	0.3	0.8	1.9	5.2
Antonio Davis	36	20.8	42.8	0.0	73.8	2.1	2.7	4.8	0.4	0.6	0.3	1.2	2.8	5.0
Trevor Ariza	36	19.7	41.8	33.3	54.6	1.4	2.4	3.8	1.3	1.2	0.3	1.3	2.2	4.6
Malik Rose	72	15.5	37.4	100.0	78.1	1.2	2.4	3.6	0.9	0.6	0.2	1.0	1.3	4.3
Jerome James	44	9.2	46.3	0.0	62.5	0.9	1.2	2.1	0.3	0.1	0.5	1.2	2.4	3.1
Anfernee Hardaway	4	17.9	28.6	0.0	100.0	0.0	2.5	2.5	2.0	0.5	0.0	1.5	1.8	2.5
Knicks	**82**	**243.0**	**45.5**	**36.2**	**72.6**	**12.6**	**28.8**	**41.4**	**17.9**	**6.8**	**3.3**	**17.0**	**26.3**	**95.6**
Opponents	**82**	**243.0**	**46.7**	**37.8**	**75.3**	**10.8**	**27.8**	**38.6**	**21.3**	**8.2**	**5.3**	**14.1**	**25.4**	**102.0**

Orlando Magic

Player	GP	MPG	FG%	3Pt%	FT%	OFF	DEF	Total	APG	SPG	BPG	TO	PF	PPG
			Field Goals			**Rebounds**								
Steve Francis	46	37.7	43.3	25.7	79.7	1.3	3.5	4.8	5.7	1.1	0.2	3.4	3.1	16.2
Dwight Howard	82	36.8	53.1	0.0	59.5	3.5	9.0	12.5	1.5	0.8	1.4	2.7	3.4	15.8
Grant Hill	21	29.2	49.0	25.0	76.5	0.7	3.1	3.8	2.3	1.1	0.3	1.7	2.4	15.1
Hedo Turkoglu	78	33.5	45.4	40.3	86.2	0.9	3.4	4.3	2.8	0.9	0.3	1.7	3.0	14.9
Jameer Nelson	62	28.8	48.3	42.4	77.9	0.6	2.3	2.9	4.9	1.1	0.2	2.4	2.8	14.6
Deshawn Stevenson	82	32.3	46.0	13.3	74.4	0.7	2.2	2.9	2.0	0.7	0.2	1.5	2.2	11.0
Carlos Arroyo	27	22.0	50.2	35.7	81.0	0.3	1.9	2.2	2.9	0.7	0.0	1.4	1.6	10.8
Keyon Dooling	50	22.7	44.0	30.2	83.5	0.2	1.3	1.6	2.2	1.0	0.1	1.6	2.3	9.4
Tony Battie	82	27.0	50.7	0.0	66.4	1.8	3.8	5.6	0.6	0.6	0.8	1.1	3.1	7.9
Darko Milicic	30	20.9	50.8	0.0	59.5	1.1	3.0	4.1	1.1	0.4	2.1	1.2	2.2	7.6
Pat Garrity	57	16.5	41.7	38.8	81.1	0.5	1.4	1.9	0.7	0.2	0.2	0.7	1.9	5.0
Trevor Ariza	21	13.8	40.0	0.0	70.0	1.4	2.5	3.9	0.7	0.7	0.1	0.8	1.1	4.7
Kelvin Cato	23	13.0	43.1	0.0	74.3	0.8	1.9	2.7	0.1	0.3	0.4	0.7	2.1	3.8
Travis Diener	23	10.7	42.0	43.9	83.3	0.2	0.7	0.9	0.7	0.3	0.0	0.4	1.0	3.8
Mario Kasun	28	7.6	44.9	0.0	78.3	0.9	1.3	2.1	0.1	0.1	0.1	0.5	2.5	2.3
Bo Outlaw	32	11.1	60.3	0.0	62.5	1.0	1.4	2.4	0.4	0.3	0.4	0.5	1.6	2.3
Stacey Augmon	24	10.7	34.3	0.0	70.0	0.5	1.0	1.5	0.6	0.3	0.2	0.3	1.1	2.0
Terence Morris	22	8.7	32.7	0.0	100.0	0.3	1.5	1.7	0.2	0.3	0.2	0.3	0.9	1.6
Magic	**82**	**242.7**	**47.2**	**37.6**	**73.0**	**10.9**	**29.3**	**40.2**	**18.2**	**6.5**	**4.4**	**14.4**	**23.3**	**94.9**
Opponents	**82**	**242.7**	**45.4**	**35.7**	**73.2**	**11.1**	**27.3**	**38.4**	**20.0**	**7.5**	**4.7**	**13.4**	**23.2**	**96.0**

Philadelphia 76ers

Player	GP	MPG	FG%	3Pt%	FT%	OFF	DEF	Total	APG	SPG	BPG	TO	PF	PPG
			Field Goals			Rebounds								
Allen Iverson	72	43.1	44.7	32.3	81.4	0.6	2.6	3.2	7.4	1.9	1.0	3.4	1.7	33.0
Chris Webber	75	38.6	43.4	27.3	75.6	2.5	7.4	9.9	3.4	1.4	0.8	2.4	2.9	20.2
Andre Iguodala	82	37.6	50.0	35.4	75.4	1.4	4.4	5.9	3.1	1.7	0.3	1.9	2.4	12.3
Kyle Korver	82	31.3	43.0	42.0	84.9	0.3	3.0	3.3	2.0	0.8	0.3	1.2	2.7	11.5
John Salmons	82	25.1	42.0	29.9	77.5	0.6	2.1	2.7	2.7	0.9	0.2	1.5	2.2	7.6
S. Dalembert	66	26.7	53.1	0.0	70.5	2.4	5.8	8.2	0.4	0.5	2.4	1.6	3.7	7.4
Willie Green	10	15.3	42.4	52.6	80.0	0.1	1.4	1.5	0.5	0.2	0.0	1.2	1.3	7.0
Steven Hunter	69	19.0	60.1	0.0	51.5	1.6	2.3	3.9	0.3	0.2	1.1	0.9	1.7	6.1
Lee Nailon	22	10.8	50.0	0.0	86.7	1.1	0.9	1.9	0.3	0.4	0.2	0.5	1.5	4.2
Matt Barnes	50	10.8	53.6	18.2	67.4	0.8	1.1	1.9	0.4	0.3	0.1	0.5	1.8	3.0
Kevin Ollie	70	15.3	43.1	33.3	83.7	0.2	1.2	1.4	1.4	0.5	0.0	0.4	1.5	2.7
Shavlik Randolph	57	8.5	45.4	0.0	60.6	1.0	1.4	2.3	0.3	0.3	0.2	0.4	1.5	2.3
Louis Williams	30	4.8	44.2	22.2	61.5	0.1	0.5	0.6	0.3	0.2	0.0	0.4	0.4	1.9
James Thomas	15	8.3	53.9	0.0	57.1	0.5	1.5	2.1	0.1	0.0	0.2	0.5	2.1	1.5
Michael Bradley	46	8.0	40.5	20.0	66.7	0.9	1.5	2.3	0.4	0.1	0.2	0.4	0.9	1.5
76ers	**82**	**242.7**	**45.8**	**36.4**	**76.0**	**10.7**	**29.6**	**40.2**	**20.2**	**7.9**	**4.9**	**13.6**	**20.9**	**99.4**
Opponents	**82**	**242.7**	**46.3**	**35.1**	**76.2**	**11.9**	**30.9**	**42.8**	**23.0**	**7.7**	**4.7**	**15.5**	**23.1**	**101.3**

Phoenix Suns

Player	GP	MPG	FG%	3Pt%	FT%	OFF	DEF	Total	APG	SPG	BPG	TO	PF	PPG
			Field Goals			Rebounds								
Shawn Marion	81	40.3	52.5	33.1	80.9	3.1	8.8	11.8	1.8	2.0	1.7	1.5	2.8	21.8
Steve Nash	79	35.4	51.2	43.9	92.1	0.6	3.6	4.2	10.5	0.8	0.2	3.5	1.5	18.9
Raja Bell	79	37.5	45.7	44.2	78.8	0.6	2.7	3.2	2.6	1.0	0.3	1.1	3.1	14.7
Boris Diaw	81	35.5	52.6	26.7	73.1	2.0	4.9	6.9	6.2	0.7	1.1	2.3	3.2	13.3
Leandro Barbosa	57	27.9	48.2	44.4	75.5	0.5	2.1	2.6	2.8	0.8	0.1	1.6	2.5	13.1
Tim Thomas	26	24.4	43.5	42.9	66.7	0.9	4.0	4.9	0.7	0.6	0.2	1.2	3.0	11.0
Eddie House	81	17.5	42.2	38.9	80.5	0.2	1.4	1.6	1.8	0.5	0.2	0.9	1.2	9.8
James Jones	75	23.6	41.8	38.6	85.1	0.6	2.8	3.4	0.8	0.5	0.7	0.5	1.9	9.3
Kurt Thomas	53	26.6	48.6	0.0	81.5	1.9	5.9	7.8	1.1	0.4	1.0	1.1	3.6	8.6
Jim Jackson	27	15.6	29.5	22.2	69.2	0.2	2.0	2.0	1.2	0.4	0.2	1.1	1.7	3.7
Pat Burke	42	8.2	49.6	28.6	61.9	0.5	1.2	1.7	0.4	0.1	0.3	0.8	1.5	3.4
Brian Grant	21	11.8	41.5	0.0	87.5	0.5	2.2	2.7	0.3	0.2	0.1	0.3	2.1	2.8
Dijon Thompson	10	4.3	44.0	36.4	100.0	0.4	0.7	1.1	0.1	0.3	0.1	0.2	0.6	2.8
Nikoloz Tskitishvili	12	7.2	36.4	33.3	66.7	0.8	0.9	1.7	0.3	0.1	0.2	0.3	0.7	2.8
Suns	**82**	**243.4**	**47.9**	**39.9**	**80.6**	**9.5**	**32.3**	**41.8**	**26.6**	**6.7**	**5.0**	**12.8**	**20.5**	**108.4**
Opponents	**82**	**243.4**	**45.4**	**36.3**	**73.1**	**12.5**	**33.4**	**45.9**	**18.9**	**7.2**	**3.4**	**14.8**	**19.8**	**102.8**

Portland Trail Blazers

Player	GP	MPG	FG%	3Pt%	FT%	OFF	DEF	Total	APG	SPG	BPG	TO	PF	PPG
			Field Goals			Rebounds								
Zach Randolph	74	34.4	43.6	29.1	71.4	2.6	5.4	8.0	2.0	0.8	0.2	2.2	2.5	18.0
Darius Miles	40	32.1	46.1	20.0	53.4	0.6	4.0	4.6	1.8	1.1	1.0	2.5	2.5	14.0
Juan Dixon	76	25.3	43.5	38.2	80.4	0.4	1.9	2.3	2.0	0.8	0.1	1.5	2.1	12.3
Ruben Patterson	45	23.5	49.6	0.0	61.1	1.6	1.8	3.4	1.3	0.9	0.3	1.8	1.8	11.4
Sebastian Telfair	58	24.1	39.5	35.2	74.3	0.3	1.5	1.8	3.6	1.0	0.1	1.7	2.5	9.5
Steve Blake	68	26.2	43.8	41.3	79.1	0.4	1.8	2.2	4.5	0.6	0.1	1.2	1.6	8.2
Jarrett Jack	79	20.2	44.2	26.3	80.0	0.2	1.8	2.0	2.8	0.5	0.0	1.3	1.8	6.7
Voshon Lenard	14	15.7	37.5	34.9	61.1	0.2	1.1	1.4	1.6	0.9	0.1	1.4	1.3	6.6
Martell Webster	61	17.5	39.9	35.7	85.9	0.5	1.7	2.1	0.6	0.3	0.2	0.7	1.5	6.6
Joel Przybilla	56	24.9	54.8	0.0	53.3	2.6	4.4	7.0	0.8	0.4	2.3	1.4	2.7	6.1
Viktor Khryapa	69	21.6	46.2	33.3	69.4	1.7	2.8	4.5	1.3	0.7	0.4	1.2	3.0	5.8
Travis Outlaw	69	16.7	44.0	26.4	69.7	0.7	2.0	2.7	0.5	0.5	0.7	0.5	1.6	5.8
Theo Ratliff	55	23.7	57.1	0.0	65.1	1.6	3.5	5.1	0.5	0.3	1.6	0.9	2.6	4.9
Brian Skinner	27	19.1	48.4	0.0	51.7	1.7	3.0	4.7	0.5	0.5	0.9	1.0	2.4	3.8
Charles Smith	21	9.9	42.3	40.5	62.5	0.1	0.6	0.8	0.4	0.2	0.3	0.2	1.3	3.8
Sergei Monia	23	14.6	34.1	27.3	66.7	0.5	1.7	2.2	0.8	0.3	0.2	0.5	1.8	3.3
Ha Seung-Jin	27	7.8	58.1	0.0	47.1	0.5	1.3	1.8	0.0	0.1	0.3	0.5	1.5	1.6
Trail Blazers	**82**	**240.6**	**44.5**	**34.9**	**68.9**	**10.8**	**26.9**	**37.7**	**18.2**	**6.5**	**5.3**	**13.7**	**22.3**	**88.8**
Opponents	**82**	**240.6**	**46.8**	**38.1**	**76.0**	**12.5**	**29.8**	**42.4**	**21.2**	**7.2**	**4.9**	**12.9**	**20.8**	**98.3**

Sacramento Kings

Player	GP	MPG	FG%	3Pt%	FT%	OFF	DEF	Total	APG	SPG	BPG	TO	PF	PPG
			Field Goals			Rebounds								
Mike Bibby	82	38.6	43.2	38.6	84.9	0.4	2.6	2.9	5.4	1.0	0.1	2.4	2.1	21.1
Ron Artest	40	40.1	38.3	30.2	71.7	1.2	4.0	5.2	4.2	2.0	0.8	2.2	3.0	16.9
Peja Stojakovic	31	37.0	40.3	39.7	93.3	1.1	4.2	5.3	2.2	0.6	0.1	1.7	2.7	16.5
Brad Miller	79	37.0	49.5	38.6	82.8	1.5	6.2	7.8	4.7	0.8	0.8	2.3	3.0	15.0
Bonzi Wells	52	32.4	46.3	22.2	67.9	2.7	5.0	7.7	2.8	1.8	0.5	2.4	3.0	13.6
S. Abdur-Rahim	72	27.2	52.5	22.7	78.4	1.5	3.5	5.0	2.1	0.7	0.6	1.5	3.2	12.3
Kevin Martin	77	26.6	48.0	36.9	84.7	0.8	2.8	3.6	1.4	0.8	0.1	1.1	1.9	10.8
Kenny Thomas	82	28.0	50.5	0.0	67.7	2.4	1.5	7.5	2.1	0.9	0.5	1.7	2.4	9.1
Corliss Williamson	37	9.8	41.8	100.0	77.6	0.6	1.2	1.8	0.4	0.2	0.1	0.8	1.5	3.4
Jason Hart	66	12.4	38.9	29.0	66.1	0.2	0.9	1.1	1.0	0.5	0.1	0.7	1.3	3.3
Brian Skinner	38	11.3	55.1	0.0	44.4	0.8	1.9	2.7	0.5	0.3	0.5	0.5	1.4	2.3
Ronnie Price	29	5.2	36.2	22.2	100.00	0.2	0.3	0.5	0.4	0.2	0.0	0.3	0.3	2.1
Vitaly Potapenko	9	3.5	71.4	0.0	0.0	0.1	0.1	0.2	0.0	0.0	0.0	0.2	0.7	1.1
Jamal Sampson	12	3.2	71.4	0.0	0.0	0.4	1.1	1.5	0.4	0.0	0.3	0.0	0.4	0.8
Kings	82	241.8	45.5	35.1	78.4	10.4	30.2	40.6	22.3	7.4	3.7	14.0	20.4	98.9
Opponents	82	241.8	45.4	35.1	74.7	11.6	30.5	42.1	21.1	8.0	4.9	14.6	23.0	97.3

San Antonio Spurs

Player	GP	MPG	FG%	3Pt%	FT%	OFF	DEF	Total	APG	SPG	BPG	TO	PF	PPG
			Field Goals			Rebounds								
Tony Parker	80	33.9	54.8	30.6	70.7	0.5	2.8	3.3	5.8	1.0	0.1	3.1	2.0	18.9
Tim Duncan	80	34.8	48.4	40.0	62.9	2.9	8.1	11.0	3.2	0.9	2.0	2.5	2.7	18.6
Manu Ginobili	65	27.9	46.2	38.3	77.8	0.7	2.9	3.5	3.6	1.6	0.4	1.9	2.4	15.1
Michael Finley	77	26.5	41.2	39.4	85.2	0.4	2.8	3.2	1.5	0.5	0.1	0.8	2.3	7.6
Bruce Bowen	82	33.6	43.3	42.5	60.7	0.4	3.5	3.9	1.5	1.0	0.4	0.8	2.3	7.6
Nazr Mohammed	80	17.4	50.4	0.0	78.5	2.0	3.2	5.2	0.5	0.3	0.6	1.1	2.8	6.2
Brent Barry	74	17.0	45.2	39.6	66.1	0.4	1.8	2.2	1.7	0.5	0.4	0.7	1.3	5.8
Nick Van Exel	65	15.2	39.7	35.7	68.3	0.1	1.3	1.4	1.9	0.3	0.1	0.9	0.9	5.5
Robert Horry	63	18.8	38.4	36.8	64.7	1.1	2.7	3.8	1.3	0.7	0.8	0.7	1.8	5.1
Beno Udrih	54	10.9	48.5	34.3	78.0	0.3	0.6	1.0	1.7	0.3	0.0	1.0	1.0	5.1
Rasho Nesterovic	80	18.9	51.5	0.0	60.0	1.4	2.4	3.9	0.4	0.3	1.1	0.7	2.6	4.5
Sean Marks	25	7.2	52.1	0.0	58.3	0.5	1.2	1.7	0.3	0.2	0.3	0.3	0.8	3.2
Melvin Sanders	16	7.1	48.5	66.7	70.0	0.3	1.2	1.4	0.2	0.3	0.0	0.5	1.3	2.6
Fabricio Oberto	59	8.3	47.3	0.0	55.6	1.0	1.1	2.1	0.5	0.2	0.2	0.5	1.5	1.8
Spurs	82	241.5	47.2	38.5	70.2	10.4	31.1	41.5	20.9	6.6	5.7	13.3	20.9	95.6
Opponents	82	241.5	43.3	33.9	74.0	10.8	29.5	40.3	16.3	7.3	4.2	13.8	20.8	88.8

Seattle SuperSonics

Player	GP	MPG	FG%	3Pt%	FT%	OFF	DEF	Total	APG	SPG	BPG	TO	PF	PPG
			Field Goals			Rebounds								
Ray Allen	78	38.7	45.4	41.2	90.3	0.9	3.4	4.3	3.7	1.4	0.2	2.4	1.9	25.1
Rashard Lewis	78	36.9	46.7	38.4	81.8	1.4	3.6	5.0	2.3	1.3	0.6	1.8	2.5	20.1
Chris Wilcox	29	30.1	59.2	0.0	78.7	2.5	5.7	8.2	1.2	0.6	0.5	1.4	2.8	14.1
Luke Ridnour	79	33.2	41.8	28.9	87.7	0.6	2.4	3.0	7.0	1.6	0.3	2.1	2.3	11.5
Earl Watson	24	25.1	43.2	42.0	73.1	0.3	2.7	3.0	5.4	1.3	0.1	2.5	2.7	11.5
Ronald Murray	48	22.6	39.7	22.4	71.7	0.4	1.4	1.8	2.5	0.6	0.1	1.7	1.4	9.9
V Radmanovic	47	23.3	40.1	36.7	88.7	0.8	3.2	4.0	1.5	0.7	0.3	1.1	2.8	9.3
Nick Collison	66	21.9	52.5	0.0	69.9	2.2	3.4	5.6	1.1	0.3	0.5	1.2	3.2	7.5
Damien Wilkins	82	18.6	44.4	25.0	84.0	1.0	1.4	2.3	1.3	0.9	0.2	1.0	1.8	6.5
Robert Swift	47	21.0	51.5	0.0	58.2	2.0	3.6	5.6	0.2	0.3	1.2	1.0	3.0	6.4
Reggie Evans	41	19.2	50.9	0.0	55.0	2.8	4.0	6.7	0.6	0.6	0.1	1.0	2.3	5.9
Johan Petro	68	18.9	51.0	0.0	62.7	1.6	2.8	4.4	0.2	0.4	0.8	0.9	3.1	5.2
Mike Wilks	10	15.0	38.7	20.0	65.5	0.3	0.9	1.2	1.4	0.6	0.0	0.9	0.7	4.4
Danny Fortson	23	12.0	52.9	0.0	76.7	1.4	2.0	3.4	0.1	0.2	0.1	1.0	3.3	3.8
Mikki Moore	47	12.4	43.6	0.0	74.2	0.9	1.8	2.8	0.6	0.2	0.3	0.9	2.0	3.3
Vitaly Potapenko	24	13.4	50.0	0.0	58.8	1.1	1.5	2.6	0.3	0.1	0.1	0.6	1.8	3.0
Mateen Cleaves	27	8.5	35.2	25.0	79.2	0.1	0.4	0.5	1.6	0.1	0.1	0.5	1.1	2.7
Noel Felix	12	6.8	24.0	33.3	62.5	0.3	0.8	1.1	0.2	0.2	0.3	0.7	1.1	1.5
Sonics	82	241.8	45.9	37.1	78.5	12.4	27.2	39.6	20.7	7.6	3.7	14.0	23.6	102.6
Opponents	82	241.8	48.5	37.5	76.0	12.2	28.2	40.5	24.1	7.3	4.9	14.6	22.1	105.6

Toronto Raptors

Player	GP	MPG	FG%	3Pt%	FT%	OFF	DEF	Total	APG	SPG	BPG	TO	PF	PPG
			Field Goals			Rebounds								
Chris Bosh 70		39.3	50.5	0.0	81.6	2.9	6.3	9.2	2.6	0.7	1.1	2.2	3.0	22.5
Mike James 79		37.0	46.9	44.2	83.7	0.6	2.8	3.3	5.8	0.9	0.0	2.6	2.7	20.3
Morris Peterson.......82		38.3	43.6	39.5	82.0	0.8	3.9	4.7	2.3	1.3	0.2	15	2.7	16.8
Charlie Villanueva ...81		29.1	46.3	32.7	70.6	2.2	4.2	6.4	1.1	0.7	0.8	1.2	3.1	13.0
Jalen Rose 46		26.9	40.4	27.0	76.5	0.3	2.5	2.8	2.5	0.4	0.2	1.4	2.2	12.1
Matt Bonner 78		21.9	44.8	42.0	82.9	1.1	2.5	3.6	0.7	0.6	0.4	0.4	2.8	7.5
Joey Graham 80		19.8	47.8	33.3	81.2	0.7	2.3	3.1	0.8	0.5	0.2	1.2	2.9	6.7
Jose Calderon........64		23.2	42.3	16.3	84.8	0.5	1.7	2.2	4.5	0.7	0.1	1.6	1.5	5.5
Andre Barrett 17		15.5	36.1	15.4	66.7	0.5	0.8	1.3	2.9	0.6	0.0	0.8	0.7	4.6
Antonio Davis...........8		23.9	45.2	0.0	35.0	1.9	2.6	4.5	0.9	0.4	0.1	1.0	3.3	4.4
Pape Sow...............42		14.0	43.1	0.0	71.9	1.3	2.2	3.5	0.2	0.5	0.5	0.7	2.8	3.5
Eric Williams 28		12.6	38.7	27.8	73.7	0.4	1.4	1.8	0.5	0.3	0.1	0.5	2.0	3.3
Darrick Martin 40		8.5	35.1	40.0	75.0	0.1	0.5	0.5	1.4	0.4	0.0	0.4	1.1	2.6
Loren Woods...........27		12.0	47.5	0.0	42.9	1.6	2.4	4.1	0.2	0.3	0.9	0.6	1.8	2.3
Rafael Araujo 52		11.6	36.6	0.0	53.6	0.8	1.9	2.8	0.3	0.5	0.1	0.8	2.0	2.3
Alvin Williams............1		10.0	0.0	0.0	50.0	0.0	3.0	3.0	0.0	0.0	0.0	0.0	0.0	1.0
Raptors....................82		**243.4**	**45.4**	**37.5**	**79.1**	**10.5**	**27.9**	**38.5**	**19.4**	**6.5**	**3.3**	**12.5**	**24.0**	**101.1**
Opponets................82		**243.4**	**49.1**	**37.3**	**74.8**	**10.2**	**31.0**	**41.1**	**23.6**	**6.3**	**4.4**	**14.2**	**22.4**	**104.0**

Utah Jazz

Player	GP	MPG	FG%	3Pt%	FT%	OFF	DEF	Total	APG	SPG	BPG	TO	PF	PPG
			Field Goals			Rebounds								
Mehmet Okur 82		35.9	46.0	34.2	78.0	2.6	6.5	9.1	2.4	0.5	0.9	2.0	3.5	18.0
Carlos Boozer 33		31.1	54.9	0.0	72.3	2.2	6.4	8.6	2.7	0.9	0.2	2.1	3.2	16.3
Andrei Kirilenko....69		37.7	46.0	30.8	69.9	2.3	5.7	8.0	4.3	1.5	3.2	2.9	2.4	15.3
Matt Harpring.......71		27.4	47.5	35.9	72.5	2.2	3.0	5.2	1.4	0.8	0.2	1.5	2.9	12.5
Deron Williams 80		28.8	42.1	41.6	70.4	0.4	2.0	2.4	4.5	0.8	0.2	1.8	2.9	10.8
Gordan Giricek....37		25.8	43.3	30.5	75.4	0.4	1.5	1.9	1.7	0.4	0.1	1.7	2.4	10.6
Devin Brown........81		21.1	39.3	33.1	74.5	0.9	1.7	2.6	1.3	0.5	0.2	1.2	1.9	7.5
Milt Palacio.........71		19.4	42.4	6.3	65.3	0.2	1.7	1.9	2.7	0.7	0.2	1.6	1.8	6.2
Keith McLeod......66		18.7	35.3	29.3	79.7	0.2	1.0	1.2	2.3	0.6	0.1	1.2	2.0	5.6
Jarron Collins 79		21.9	46.1	0.0	71.7	1.7	2.5	4.2	1.2	0.5	0.3	0.8	3.2	5.3
C.J. Miles 23		8.8	36.8	25.0	75.0	0.8	0.9	1.7	0.7	0.3	0.1	0.4	0.9	3.4
Andre Owens 23		9.1	36.5	18.8	66.7	0.5	0.4	0.9	0.4	0.2	0.0	0.6	1.1	3.0
Kris Humphries 62		10.0	37.9	0.0	52.3	0.9	1.6	2.5	0.5	0.4	0.3	0.5	1.3	3.0
Greg Ostertag.....60		13.5	49.2	0.0	50.0	1.4	2.4	3.8	1.0	0.1	1.1	0.8	2.2	2.4
Robert Whaley 23		9.2	40.4	0.0	50.0	0.7	1.2	1.9	0.7	0.3	0.4	0.6	1.8	2.1
Jazz......................82		**242.4**	**44.2**	**33.6**	**71.9**	**13.1**	**29.0**	**42.1**	**21.6**	**6.4**	**6.0**	**14.8**	**24.8**	**92.4**
Opponents................82		**242.4**	**44.9**	**37.8**	**74.6**	**10.6**	**27.3**	**37.9**	**18.4**	**8.1**	**5.6**	**14.2**	**25.7**	**95.0**

Washington Wizards

Player	GP	MPG	FG%	3Pt%	FT%	OFF	DEF	Total	APG	SPG	BPG	TO	PF	PPG
			Field Goals			Rebounds								
Gilbert Arenas......80		42.3	44.7	36.9	82.0	0.7	2.8	3.5	6.1	2.0	0.3	3.7	3.6	29.3
Antawn Jamison....82		40.1	44.2	39.4	73.1	2.0	7.3	9.3	1.9	1.1	0.2	1.7	2.3	20.5
Caron Butler.........75		36.1	45.5	34.2	87.1	1.5	4.7	6.2	2.5	1.7	0.2	2.3	3.2	17.6
Antonio Daniels....80		28.5	41.8	22.8	84.5	0.2	1.9	2.2	3.6	0.7	0.1	1.1	1.2	9.6
Jarvis Hayes 21		24.6	42.1	36.2	83.3	0.9	2.7	3.6	1.3	0.8	0.1	1.1	1.8	9.3
Brendan Haywood.79		23.8	51.4	0.0	58.5	2.5	3.4	5.9	0.6	0.4	1.3	1.2	2.9	7.3
Chucky Atkins 28		19.7	37.9	35.9	71.0	0.4	1.2	1.6	2.5	0.5	0.0	1.1	2.1	6.7
Jared Jeffries 77		25.3	45.1	32.0	58.9	2.1	2.8	4.9	1.9	0.8	0.7	1.3	2.9	6.4
Etan Thomas..........71		15.8	53.3	0.0	60.0	1.4	2.5	3.9	0.2	0.3	1.0	0.7	2.1	4.8
Donell Taylor...........51		9.1	39.0	23.5	69.8	0.3	0.7	1.0	0.9	0.6	0.1	0.7	0.9	2.8
Andray Blatche......29		6.1	38.8	23.1	83.3	0.4	0.9	1.3	0.3	0.2	0.2	0.4	1.2	2.2
Billy Thomas.........17		7.7	32.5	33.3	100.0	0.3	0.5	0.8	0.5	0.6	0.1	0.4	1.1	2.2
Awvee Storey 25		4.7	39.0	42.9	57.1	0.3	0.6	0.9	0.2	0.1	0.0	0.2	0.9	1.7
Calvin Booth.........33		7.6	42.6	50.0	55.6	0.6	0.1	1.6	0.4	0.3	0.3	0.2	1.3	1.4
Michael Ruffin 76		13.3	44.2	0.0	50.0	1.6	2.0	3.6	0.4	0.4	0.4	0.5	2.4	1.4
Wizards 82		**241.8**	**44.7**	**35.7**	**75.7**	**12.6**	**28.6**	**41.2**	**18.6**	**8.0**	**4.1**	**13.4**	**22.6**	**101.7**
Opponents................82		**241.8**	**46.5**	**36.3**	**74.5**	**11.8**	**30.2**	**42.0**	**21.5**	**6.6**	**4.2**	**16.2**	**25.3**	**101.5**

2006 NBA Draft

The 2006 NBA Draft was held on June 28, 2006 in New York City.

First Round

1. Andrea Bargnani, Toronto
2. LaMarcus Aldridge, Chicago
3. Adam Morrison, Charlotte
4. Tyrus Thomas, Portland
5. Shelden Williams, Atlanta
6. Brandon Roy, Minnesota
7. Randy Foye, Boston
8. Rudy Gay, Houston
9. Patrick O'Bryant, Golden State
10. Mouhamed Saer Sene, Seattle
11. J.J. Redick, Orlando
12. Hilton Armstrong, NO/Oklahoma City
13. Thabo Sefolosha, Philadelphia
14. Ronnie Brewer, Utah
15. Cedric Simmons, NO/Oklahoma City (from Minnesota)
16. Rodney Carney, Chicago
17. Shawne Williams, Indiana
18. Olexsiy Pecherov, Washington
19. Quincy Douby, Sacramento
20. Renaldo Balkman, New York (from Denver)
21. Rajon Rondo, Phoenix
22. Marcus Williams, New Jersey (from LA Clippers)
23. Josh Boone, New Jersey
24. Kyle Lowry, Memphis
25. Shannon Brown, Cleveland
26. Jordan Farmar, LA Lakers (from Miami)
27. Sergio Rodriguez, Phoenix
28. Maurice Ager, Dallas
29. Mardy Collins, New York (from San Antonio)
30. Joel Freeland, Portland (from Detroit)

Second Round

31. James White, Portland
32. Steve Novak, Houston (from New York)
33. Solomon Jones, Atlanta
34. Paul Davis, LA Clippers (from Charlotte)
35. P.J. Tucker, Toronto
36. Craig Smith, Minnesota
37. Bobby Jones, Philadelphia
38. Kosta Perovic, Golden State (from Houston)
39. David Noel, Milwaukee
40. Denham Brown, Seattle
41. James Augustine, Orlando
42. Daniel Gibson, Cleveland (from Philadelphia)
43. Marcus Vinicius Vieira de Souza, NO/Oklahoma City
44. Lior Eliyahu, Orlando
45. Alexander Johnson, Indiana
46. Dee Brown, Utah (from Chicago)
47. Paul Millsap, Utah
48. Vladimir Veremeenko, Washington
49. Leon Powe, Denver
50. Ryan Hollins, Charlotte
51. Cheik Samb, LA Lakers
52. Guillermo Diaz, LA Clippers
53. Yotam Halperin, Seattle (from Memphis)
54. Hassan Adams, New Jersey
55. Ejike Ugboaja, Cleveland
56. Edin Bavcic, Toronto
57. Loukas Mavrokefalidis, Minnesota (from Phoenix)
58. Danilo Pinnock, Dallas
59. Damir Markota, San Antonio
60. Will Blalock, Detroit

Women's National Basketball Association

2006 Final Standings

EASTERN CONFERENCE

Team	W	L	Pct	GB
†Connecticut	26	8	.765	—
*Detroit	23	11	.676	3
*Indiana	21	13	.618	5
*Washington	18	16	.529	8
New York	11	23	.324	15
Charlotte	11	23	.324	15
Chicago	5	29	.147	21

WESTERN CONFERENCE

Team	W	L	Pct	GB
†Los Angeles	25	9	.735	—
*Sacramento	21	13	.618	4
*Houston	18	16	.529	7
*Seattle	18	16	.529	7
Phoenix	18	16	.529	7
San Antonio	13	21	.382	12
Minnesota	10	24	.294	15

†Clinched conference title. *Clinched playoff berth.

2006 Playoffs

FIRST ROUND

EASTERN CONFERENCE

Game 1......Detroit 68　　　at Indiana 56
Game 2......Indiana 83　　　at Detroit 98
　　　　Detroit won series 2–0.

Game 1......Washington 61　　at Connecticut 76
Game 2......Connecticut 68　　at Washington 65
　　　　Connecticut won series 2–0.

WESTERN CONFERENCE

Game 1......Los Angeles 72　　at Seattle 84
Game 2......Seattle 70　　　at Los Angeles 78
Game 3.....Seattle 63　　　at Los Angeles 68
　　　　Los Angeles won series 2–1.

Game 1......Sacramento 93　　at Houston 78
Game 2......Houston 64　　　at Sacramento 92
　　　　Sacramento won series 2–0.

EASTERN CONFERENCE FINALS

Game 1......Connecticut 59　　at Detroit 70
Game 2......Detroit 68　　　at Connecticut 77
Game 3......Detroit 79　　　at Connecticut 55
　　　　Detroit won series 2–1.

WESTERN CONFERENCE FINALS

Game 1......Los Angeles 61　　at Sacramento 64
Game 2......Sacramento 72　　at Los Angeles 58
　　　　Sacramento won series 2–0.

WNBA FINALS

Game 1 ....Sacramento 95　　at Detroit 71
Game 2 ....Sacramento 63　　at Detroit 73
Game 3 ....Detroit 69　　　at Sacramento 89
Game 4 ....Detroit 72　　　at Sacramento 52
Game 5 ....Sacramento 75　　at Detroit 80
　　　　Detroit won series 3–2.

NBA Champions

Season	Winner	Series	Runner-Up	Winning Coach	Finals MVP
1946–47	Philadelphia	4–1	Chicago	Eddie Gottlieb	—
1947–48	Baltimore	4–2	Philadelphia	Buddy Jeannette	—
1948–49	Minneapolis	4–2	Washington	John Kundla	—
1949–50	Minneapolis	4–2	Syracuse	John Kundla	—
1950–51	Rochester	4–3	New York	Les Harrison	—
1951–52	Minneapolis	4–3	New York	John Kundla	—
1952–53	Minneapolis	4–1	New York	John Kundla	—
1953–54	Minneapolis	4–3	Syracuse	John Kundla	—
1954–55	Syracuse	4–3	Ft Wayne	Al Cervi	—
1955–56	Philadelphia	4–1	Ft Wayne	George Senesky	—
1956–57	Boston	4–3	St Louis	Red Auerbach	—
1957–58	St Louis	4–2	Boston	Alex Hannum	—
1958–59	Boston	4–0	Minneapolis	Red Auerbach	—
1959–60	Boston	4–3	St Louis	Red Auerbach	—
1960–61	Boston	4–1	St Louis	Red Auerbach	—
1961–62	Boston	4–3	LA Lakers	Red Auerbach	—
1962–63	Boston	4–2	LA Lakers	Red Auerbach	—
1963–64	Boston	4–1	San Francisco	Red Auerbach	—
1964–65	Boston	4–1	LA Lakers	Red Auerbach	—
1965–66	Boston	4–3	LA Lakers	Red Auerbach	—
1966–67	Philadelphia	4–2	San Francisco	Alex Hannum	—
1967–68	Boston	4–2	LA Lakers	Bill Russell	—
1968–69	Boston	4–3	LA Lakers	Bill Russell	Jerry West, LA
1969–70	New York	4–3	LA Lakers	Red Holzman	Willis Reed, NY
1970–71	Milwaukee	4–0	Baltimore	Larry Costello	Kareem Abdul-Jabbar, Mil
1971–72	LA Lakers	4–1	New York	Bill Sharman	Wilt Chamberlain, LA
1972–73	New York	4–1	LA Lakers	Red Holzman	Willis Reed, NY
1973–74	Boston	4–3	Milwaukee	Tommy Heinsohn	John Havlicek, Bos
1974–75	Golden State	4–0	Washington	Al Attles	Rick Barry, GS
1975–76	Boston	4–2	Phoenix	Tommy Heinsohn	JoJo White, Bos
1976–77	Portland	4–2	Philadelphia	Jack Ramsay	Bill Walton, Port
1977–78	Washington	4–3	Seattle	Dick Motta	Wes Unseld, Wash
1978–79	Seattle	4–1	Washington	Lenny Wilkens	Dennis Johnson, Sea
1979–80	LA Lakers	4–2	Philadelphia	Paul Westhead	Magic Johnson, LA
1980–81	Boston	4–2	Houston	Bill Fitch	Cedric Maxwell, Bos
1981–82	LA Lakers	4–2	Philadelphia	Pat Riley	Magic Johnson, LA
1982–83	Philadelphia	4–0	LA Lakers	Billy Cunningham	Moses Malone, Phil
1983–84	Boston	4–3	LA Lakers	K.C. Jones	Larry Bird, Bos
1984–85	LA Lakers	4–2	Boston	Pat Riley	Kareem Abdul-Jabbar, LA
1985–86	Boston	4–2	Houston	K.C. Jones	Larry Bird, Bos
1986–87	LA Lakers	4–2	Boston	Pat Riley	Magic Johnson, LA
1987–88	LA Lakers	4–3	Detroit	Pat Riley	James Worthy, LA
1988–89	Detroit	4–0	LA Lakers	Chuck Daly	Joe Dumars, Det
1989–90	Detroit	4–1	Portland	Chuck Daly	Isiah Thomas, Det
1990–91	Chicago	4–1	LA Lakers	Phil Jackson	Michael Jordan, Chi
1991–92	Chicago	4–2	Portland	Phil Jackson	Michael Jordan, Chi
1992–93	Chicago	4–2	Phoenix	Phil Jackson	Michael Jordan, Chi
1993–94	Houston	4–3	New York	Rudy Tomjanovich	Hakeem Olajuwon, Hou
1994–95	Houston	4–0	Orlando	Rudy Tomjanovich	Hakeem Olajuwon, Hou
1995–96	Chicago	4–2	Seattle	Phil Jackson	Michael Jordan, Chi
1996–97	Chicago	4–2	Utah	Phil Jackson	Michael Jordan, Chi
1997–98	Chicago	4–2	Utah	Phil Jackson	Michael Jordan, Chi
1998–99	San Antonio	4–1	New York	Gregg Popovich	Tim Duncan, SA
1999–00	LA Lakers	4–2	Indiana	Phil Jackson	Shaquille O'Neal, LA
2000–01	LA Lakers	4–1	Philadelphia	Phil Jackson	Shaquille O'Neal, LA
2001–02	LA Lakers	4–0	New Jersey	Phil Jackson	Shaquille O'Neal, LA
2002–03	San Antonio	4–2	New Jersey	Gregg Popovich	Tim Duncan, SA
2003–04	Detroit	4–1	LA Lakers	Larry Brown	Chauncey Billups, Det
2004–05	San Antonio	4–3	Detroit	Gregg Popovich	Tim Duncan, SA
2005–06	Miami	4–2	Dallas	Pat Riley	Dwyane Wade, Mia

Most Valuable Player: Maurice Podoloff Trophy

Season	Player, Team	GP	Field Goals		3-Pt FG		Free Throws		Rebounds		A	Stl	BS	Avg
			FGM	Pct	FGM	Pct	FTM	Pct	Off	Total				
1955–56 ....Bob Pettit, StL		72	646	42.9	–	–	557	73.6	–	1,164	189	–	–	25.7
1956–57 ....Bob Cousy, Bos		64	478	37.8	–	–	363	82.1	–	309	478	–	–	20.6
1957–58 ....Bill Russell, Bos		69	456	44.2	–	–	230	51.9	–	1,564	202	–	–	16.6
1958–59 ....Bob Pettit, StL		72	719	43.8	–	–	667	75.9	–	1,182	221	–	–	29.2
1959–60 ....Wilt Chamberlain, Phil		72	1,065	46.1	–	–	577	58.2	–	1,941	168	–	–	37.6
1960–61 ....Bill Russell, Bos		78	532	42.6	–	–	258	55.0	–	1,868	264	–	–	16.9
1961–62 ....Bill Russell, Bos		76	575	45.7	–	–	286	59.5	–	1,891	341	–	–	18.9
1962–63 ....Bill Russell, Bos		78	511	43.2	–	–	287	55.5	–	1,843	348	–	–	16.8
1963–64 ....Oscar Robertson, Cin		79	840	48.3	–	–	800	85.3	–	783	868	–	–	31.4
1964–65 ....Bill Russell, Bos		78	429	43.8	–	–	244	57.3	–	1,878	410	–	–	14.1
1965–66 ....Wilt Chamberlain, Phil		79	1,074	54.0	–	–	501	51.3	–	1,943	414	–	–	33.5
1966–67 ....Wilt Chamberlain, Phil		81	785	68.3	–	–	386	44.1	–	1,957	630	–	–	24.1
1967–68 ....Wilt Chamberlain, Phil		82	819	59.5	–	–	354	38.0	–	1,952	702	–	–	24.3
1968–69 ....Wes Unseld, Balt		82	427	47.6	–	–	277	60.5	–	1,491	213	–	–	13.8
1969–70 ....Willis Reed, NY		81	702	50.7	–	–	351	75.6	–	1,126	161	–	–	21.7
1970–71 ....Kareem Abdul-Jabbar, Mil		82	1,063	57.7	–	–	470	69.0	–	1,311	272	–	–	31.7
1971–72 ....Kareem Abdul-Jabbar, Mil		81	1,159	57.4	–	–	504	68.9	–	1,346	370	–	–	34.8
1972–73 ....Dave Cowens, Bos		82	740	45.2	–	–	204	77.9	–	1,329	333	–	–	20.5
1973–74 ....Kareem Abdul-Jabbar, Mil		81	948	53.9	–	–	295	70.2	287	1,178	386	112	283	27.0
1974–75 ....Bob McAdoo, Buff		82	1,095	51.2	–	–	641	80.5	307	1,155	179	92	174	34.5
1975–76 ....Kareem Abdul-Jabbar, LA		82	914	52.9	–	–	447	70.3	272	1,383	413	119	338	37.7
1976–77 ....Kareem Abdul-Jabbar, LA		82	888	57.9	–	–	376	70.1	266	1,090	319	101	261	26.2
1977–78 ....Bill Walton, Port		58	460	52.2	–	–	177	72.0	118	766	291	60	146	18.9
1978–79 ....Moses Malone, Hou		82	716	54.0	–	–	599	73.9	587	1,444	147	79	119	24.8
1979–80 ....Kareem Abdul-Jabbar, LA		82	835	60.4	0	00.0	364	76.5	190	886	371	81	280	24.8
1980–81 ....Julius Erving, Phil		82	794	52.1	4	22.2	422	78.7	244	657	364	173	147	24.6
1981–82 ....Moses Malone, Hou		81	945	51.9	0	00.0	630	76.2	558	1,188	142	76	125	31.1
1982–83 ....Moses Malone, Phil		78	654	50.1	0	00.0	600	76.1	445	1,194	101	89	157	24.5
1983–84 ....Larry Bird, Bos		79	758	49.2	18	24.7	374	88.8	181	796	520	144	69	24.2
1984–85 ....Larry Bird, Bos		80	918	52.2	56	42.7	403	88.2	164	842	531	129	98	28.7
1985–86 ....Larry Bird, Bos		82	796	49.6	82	42.3	441	89.6	190	805	557	166	51	25.8
1986–87 ....Magic Johnson, LA Lakers		80	683	52.2	8	20.5	535	84.8	122	504	977	138	36	23.9
1987–88 ....Michael Jordan, Chi		82	1,069	53.5	7	13.2	723	84.1	139	449	485	259	131	35.0
1988–89 ....Magic Johnson, LA Lakers		77	579	50.9	59	31.4	513	91.1	111	607	988	138	22	22.5
1989–90 ....Magic Johnson, LA Lakers		79	546	48.0	106	38.4	567	89.0	128	522	907	132	34	22.3
1990–91 ....Michael Jordan, Chi		82	990	53.9	29	31.2	571	85.1	118	492	453	223	83	31.5
1991–92 ....Michael Jordan, Chi		80	943	51.9	27	27.0	491	83.2	91	511	489	182	75	30.1
1992–93 ....Charles Barkley, Phoe		76	716	52.0	67	30.5	445	76.5	237	928	385	119	74	25.6
1993–94 ....Hakeem Olajuwon, Hou		80	894	52.8	8	42.1	388	71.6	229	955	287	128	297	27.3
1994–95 ....David Robinson, SA		81	788	53.0	6	30.0	656	77.4	234	877	236	134	262	27.6
1995–96 ....Michael Jordan, Chi		82	916	49.5	111	42.7	548	83.4	148	543	352	180	42	30.4
1996–97 ....Karl Malone, Utah		82	864	55.0	0	00.0	521	75.5	193	809	368	113	48	27.4
1997–98 ....Michael Jordan, Chi		82	881	46.5	30	23.8	565	78.4	130	475	283	141	45	28.7
1998–99 ....Karl Malone, Utah		49	393	49.3	0	00.0	378	78.8	107	463	201	62	28	23.8
1999–00 ....Shaquille O'Neal, LA Lakers		79	956	57.4	0	00.0	432	52.4	336	1078	299	36	239	29.7
2000–01 ....Allen Iverson, Phil		71	762	42.0	98	32.0	585	81.4	50	273	325	78	20	31.1
2001–02 ....Tim Duncan, SA		82	764	50.8	1	10.0	560	79.9	268	1042	307	61	203	25.5
2002–03 ....Tim Duncan, SA		81	714	51.3	6	27.3	450	71.0	260	1045	316	55	237	23.3
2003–04 ....Kevin Garnett, Minn		82	804	49.9	11	25.6	368	79.1	245	1139	409	120	178	24.2
2004–05 ....Steve Nash, Phoe		75	430	50.2	94	43.1	211	88.7	80	330	861	74	6	26.0
2005–06 ....Steve Nash, Phoe		79	541	51.2	150	43.9	257	92.1	47	333	826	61	12	18.8

Coach of the Year: Arnold (Red) Auerbach Trophy

1962–63...Harry Gallatin, StL
1963–64...Alex Hannum, SF
1964–65...Red Auerbach, Bos
1965–66...Dolph Schayes, Phil
1966–67...Johnny Kerr, Chi
1967–68...Richie Guerin, StL
1968–69...Gene Shue, Balt
1969–70...Red Holzman, NY
1970–71...Dick Motta, Chi
1971–72...Bill Sharman, LA
1972–73...Tom Heinsohn, Bos
1973–74...Ray Scott, Det
1974–75...Phil Johnson, KC-Oma
1975–76...Bill Fitch, Clev
1976–77...Tom Nissalke, Hou

1977–78...Hubie Brown, Atl
1978–79...Cotton Fitzsimmons, KC
1979–80...Bill Fitch, Bos
1980–81...Jack McKinney, Ind
1981–82...Gene Shue, Wash
1982–83...Don Nelson, Mil
1983–84...Frank Layden, Utah
1984–85...Don Nelson, Mil
1985–86...Mike Fratello, Atl
1986–87...Mike Schuler, Port
1987–88...Doug Moe, Den
1988–89...Cotton Fitzsimmons, Phoe
1989–90...Pat Riley, LA Lakers
1990–91...Don Chaney, Hou
1991–92...Don Nelson, GS

1992–93...Pat Riley, NY
1993–94...Lenny Wilkens, Atl
1994–95...Del Harris, LA Lakers
1995–96...Phil Jackson, Chi
1996–97...Pat Riley, Mia
1997–98...Larry Bird, Ind
1998–99...Mike Dunleavy, Port
1999–00...Glenn (Doc) Rivers, Orl
2000–01...Larry Brown, Phil
2001–02...Rick Carlisle, Det
2002–03...Gregg Popovich, SA
2003–04...Hubie Brown, Mem
2004–05...Mike D'Antoni, Phoe
2005–06...Avery Johnson, Dall

Note: Award named after Auerbach in 1986.

Rookie of the Year: Eddie Gottlieb Trophy

1952–53...Don Meineke, FW
1953–54...Ray Felix, Balt
1954–55...Bob Pettit, Mil
1955–56...Maurice Stokes, Roch
1956–57...Tom Heinsohn, Bos
1957–58...Woody Sauldsberry, Phil
1958–59...Elgin Baylor, Minn
1959–60...Wilt Chamberlain, Phil
1960–61...Oscar Robertson, Cin
1961–62...Walt Bellamy, Chi
1962–63...Terry Dischinger, Chi
1963–64...Jerry Lucas, Cin
1964–65...Willis Reed, NY
1965–66...Rick Barry, SF
1966–67...Dave Bing, Det
1967–68...Earl Monroe, Balt
1968–69...Wes Unseld, Balt
1969–70...K. Abdul-Jabbar, Mil

1970–71...Dave Cowens, Bos
           Geoff Petrie, Port
1971–72...Sidney Wicks, Port
1972–73...Bob McAdoo, Buff
1973–74...Ernie DiGregorio, Buff
1974–75...Keith Wilkes, GS
1975–76...Alvan Adams, Phoe
1976–77...Adrian Dantley, Buff
1977–78...Walter Davis, Phoe
1978–79...Phil Ford, KC
1979–80...Larry Bird, Bos
1980–81...Darrell Griffith, Utah
1981–82...Buck Williams, NJ
1982–83...Terry Cummings, SD
1983–84...Ralph Sampson, Hou
1984–85...Michael Jordan, Chi
1985–86...Patrick Ewing, NY
1986–87...Chuck Person, Ind
1987–88...Mark Jackson, NY

1988–89...Mitch Richmond, GS
1989–90...David Robinson, SA
1990–91...Derrick Coleman, NJ
1991–92...Larry Johnson, Char
1992–93...Shaquille O'Neal, Orl
1993–94...Chris Webber, GS
1994–95...J. Kidd, Dall/G. Hill, Det
1995–96...Damon Stoudamire, Tor
1996–97...Allen Iverson, Phil
1997–98...Tim Duncan, SA
1998–99...Vince Carter, Tor
1999–00...Steve Francis, Hou
           Elton Brand, Chi
2000–01..Mike Miller, Orl
2001–02..Pau Gasol, Mem
2002–03..Amare Stoudemire, Phoe
2003–04..LeBron James, Clev
2004–05..Emeka Okafor, Char
2005–06..Chris Paul, NOK

Defensive Player of the Year

1982–83...Sidney Moncrief, Mil
1983–84...Sidney Moncrief, Mil
1984–85...Mark Eaton, Utah
1985–86...Alvin Robertson, SA
1986–87...Michael Cooper, Lakers
1987–88...Michael Jordan, Chi
1988–89...Mark Eaton, Utah
1989–90...Dennis Rodman, Det

1990–91...Dennis Rodman, Det
1991–92...David Robinson, SA
1992–93...Hakeem Olajuwon, Hou
1993–94...Hakeem Olajuwon, Hou
1994–95...Dikembe Mutombo, Den
1995–96...Gary Payton, Sea
1996–97...Dikembe Mutombo, Den
1997–98...Dikembe Mutombo, Atl

1998–99...Alonzo Mourning, Mia
1999–00...Alonzo Mourning, Mia
2000–01...Dikembe Mutombo, Phil
2001–02...Ben Wallace, Det
2002–03...Ben Wallace, Det
2003–04...Ron Artest, Ind
2004–05...Ben Wallace, Det
2005–06...Ben Wallace, Det

Sixth Man Award

1982–83...Bobby Jones, Phil
1983–84...Kevin McHale, Bos
1984–85...Kevin McHale, Bos
1985–86...Bill Walton, Bos
1986–87...Ricky Pierce, Mil
1987–88...Roy Tarpley, Dall
1988–89...Eddie Johnson, Phoe
1989–90...Ricky Pierce, Mil

1990–91...Detlef Schrempf, Ind
1991–92...Detlef Schrempf, Ind
1992–93...Cliff Robinson, Port
1993–94...Dell Curry, Char
1994–95...Anthony Mason, NY
1995–96...Tony Kukoc, Chi
1996–97...John Starks, NY
1997–98...Danny Manning, Phoe

1998–99...Darrell Armstrong, Orl
1999–00...Rodney Rogers, Phoe
2000–01...Aaron McKie, Phil
2001–02...Corliss Williamson, Det
2002–03...Bobby Jackson, Sac
2003–04...Antawn Jamison, Dall
2004–05...Ben Gordon, Chi
2005–06...Mike Miller, Mem

J. Walter Kennedy Citizenship Award

1974–75...Wes Unseld, Wash	1985–86...Michael Cooper, Lakers	1995–96...Chris Dudley, Port
1975–76...Slick Watts, Sea	Rory Sparrow, NY	1996–97...P.J. Brown, Mia
1976–77...Dave Bing, Wash	1986–87...Isiah Thomas, Det	1997–98...Steve Smith, Atl
1977–78...Bob Lanier, Det	1987–88...Alex English, Den	1998–99...Brian Grant, Port
1978–79...Calvin Murphy, Hou	1988–89...Thurl Bailey, Utah	1999–00...Vlade Divac, Sac
1979–80...Austin Carr, Clev	1989–90...Glenn Rivers, Atl	2000–01...Dikembe Mutombo, Phil
1980–81...Mike Glenn, NY	1990–91...Kevin Johnson, Phoe	2001–02...Alonzo Mourning, Mia
1981–82...Kent Benson, Det	1991–92...Magic Johnson, Lakers	2002–03...David Robinson, SA
1982–83...Julius Erving, Phil	1992–93...Terry Porter, Port	2003–04...Reggie Miller, Ind
1983–84...Frank Layden, Utah	1993–94...Joe Dumars, Det	2004–05...Eric Snow, Clev
1984–85...Dan Issel, Den	1994–95...Joe O'Toole, Atl	2005–06...Kevin Garnett, Minn

Most Improved Player

1985–86...Alvin Robertson, SA	1992–93...Chris Jackson, Den	1999–00...Jalen Rose, Ind
1986–87...Dale Ellis, Sea	1993–94...Don MacLean, Wash	2000–01...Tracy McGrady, Orl
1987–88...Kevin Duckworth, Port	1994–95...Dana Barros, Phil	2001–02...Jermaine O'Neal, Ind
1988–89...Kevin Johnson, Phoe	1995–96...Gheorghe Muresan, Wash	2002–03...Gilbert Arenas, GS
1989–90...Rony Seikaly, Mia	1996–97...Isaac Austin, Mia	2003–04...Zach Randolph, Port
1990–91...Scott Skiles, Orl	1997–98...Alan Henderson, Atl	2004–05...Bobby Simmons, LAC
1991–92...Pervis Ellison, Wash	1998–99...Darrell Armstrong, Orl	2005–06...Boris Diaw, Phoe

Executive of the Year

1972–73...Joe Axelson, KC-Oma	1984–85...Vince Boryla, Den	1996–97...Bob Bass, Char
1973–74...Eddie Donovan, Buff	1985–86...Stan Kasten, Atl	1997–98...Wayne Embry, Clev
1974–75...Dick Vertlieb, GS	1986–87...Stan Kasten, Atl	1998–99...Geoff Petrie, Sac
1975–76...Jerry Colangelo, Phoe	1987–88...Jerry Krause, Chi	1999–00...John Gabriel, Orl
1976–77...Ray Patterson, Hou	1988–89...Jerry Colangelo, Phoe	2000–01...Geoff Petrie, Sac
1977–78...Angelo Drossos, SA	1989–90...Bob Bass, SA	2001–02...Rod Thorn, NJ
1978–79...Bob Ferry, Wash	1990–91...Bucky Buckwalter, Port	2002–03...Joe Dumars, Det
1979–80...Red Auerbach, Bos	1991–92...Wayne Embry, Clev	2003–04...Jerry West, Mem
1980–81...Jerry Colangelo, Phoe	1992–93...Jerry Colangelo, Phoe	2004–05...Bryan Colangelo, Phoe
1981–82...Bob Ferry, Wash	1993–94...Bob Whitsitt, Sea	2005–06...Elgin Baylor, LAC
1982–83...Zollie Volchok, Sea	1994–95...Jerry West, LA Lakers	
1983–84...Frank Layden, Utah	1995–96...Jerry Krause, Chi	

NBA Alltime Individual Leaders

Scoring

MOST POINTS, CAREER

	Pts	Avg
Kareem Abdul-Jabbar	38,387	24.6
Karl Malone	36,928	25.0
Michael Jordan	32,292	30.1
Wilt Chamberlain	31,419	30.1
Moses Malone	27,409	20.6
Elvin Hayes	27,313	21.0
Hakeem Olajuwon	26,946	21.8
Oscar Robertson	26,710	25.7
Dominique Wilkins	26,669	24.8
John Havlicek	26,395	20.8

HIGHEST SCORING AVERAGE, CAREER

Michael Jordan	30.1	1,072 games
Wilt Chamberlain	30.1	1,045 games
Allen Iverson	27.4	610 games
Elgin Baylor	27.4	846 games
Jerry West	27.0	932 games
Shaquille O'Neal	26.7	882 games
Bob Pettit	26.4	792 games
George Gervin	26.2	791 games
Oscar Robertson	25.7	1,040 games

Note: Minimum 400 games.

MOST POINTS, SEASON

Wilt Chamberlain, Phil	4,029	1961–62
Wilt Chamberlain, SF	3,586	1962–63
Michael Jordan, Chi	3,041	1986–87
Wilt Chamberlain, Phil	3,033	1960–61
Wilt Chamberlain, SF	2,948	1963–64
Michael Jordan, Chi	2,868	1987–88
Kobe Bryant, LA	2,832	2005–06
Bob McAdoo, Buff	2,831	1974–75
Rick Barry, SF	2,775	1966–67
Michael Jordan, Chi	2,753	1989–90

HIGHEST SCORING AVERAGE, SEASON

Wilt Chamberlain, Phil	50.4	1961–62
Wilt Chamberlain, SF	44.8	1962–63
Wilt Chamberlain, Phil	38.4	1960–61
Wilt Chamberlain, Phil	37.6	1959–60
Michael Jordan, Chi	37.1	1986–87
Wilt Chamberlain, SF	36.9	1963–64
Rick Barry, SF	35.6	1966–67
Kobe Bryant, LA	35.4	2005–06
Michael Jordan, Chi	35.0	1987–88
Elgin Baylor, LA	34.8	1960–61

Note: Minimum 70 games.

Scoring *(Cont.)*

MOST POINTS, GAME

	Player, Team	Opp	Date
100	Wilt Chamberlain, Phil	NY	3/2/62
81	Kobe Bryant	Tor	1/30/06
78	Wilt Chamberlain, Phil	LA	12/8/61
73	Wilt Chamberlain, Phil	Chi	1/13/62
73	Wilt Chamberlain, SF	NY	11/16/62
73	David Thompson, Den	Det	4/9/78
72	Wilt Chamberlain, SF	LA	11/3/62
71	David Robinson, SA	LAC	4/24/94
71	Elgin Baylor, LA	NY	11/15/60
70	Wilt Chamberlain, SF	Syr	3/10/63

Field-Goal Percentage

Highest FG Percentage, Career: .599—Artis Gilmore

Highest FG Percentage, Season: .727—Wilt Chamberlain, LA Lakers, 1972–73 (426/586)

Free Throws

HIGHEST FREE-THROW PERCENTAGE, CAREER

Mark Price	.904
Rick Barry	.900
Steve Nash	.896
Peja Stojakovic	.894
Calvin Murphy	.892

Note: Minimum 1200 free throws made.

HIGHEST FREE-THROW PERCENTAGE, SEASON

Calvin Murphy, Hou	.958	1980–81
Mahmoud Abdul-Rauf, Den	.956	1993–94
Jeff Hornacek, Utah	.950	1999–00
Mark Price, Clev	.948	1992–93
Mark Price, Clev	.947	1991–92

MOST FREE THROWS MADE, CAREER

	No.	Yrs	Pct
Karl Malone	9,787	19	.742
Moses Malone	8,531	19	.769
Oscar Robertson	7,694	14	.838
Michael Jordan	7,327	15	.835
Jerry West	7,160	14	.814

Three-Point Field Goals

Most Three-Point Field-Goals, Career: 2,560—Reggie Miller

Highest Three-Point Field-Goal Percentage, Career: .454—Steve Kerr

Most Three-Point Field Goals, Season: 269—Ray Allen, Sea, 2005–06

Highest Three-Point Field-Goal Percentage, Season: .524—Steve Kerr, Chi, 1994–95

Most Three-Point Field Goals, Game: 12—Kobe Bryant, LA Lakers vs Seattle, 1/7/03; Donyell Marshall, Toronto vs. Philadelphia, 3/13/05

Note: First year of shot: 1979–80.

Steals

Most Steals, Career: 3,265—John Stockton

Most Steals, Season: 301—Alvin Robertson, San Antonio, 1985–86

Most Steals, Game: 11—Kendall Gill, New Jersey vs Miami, 4/3/99; Larry Kenon, San Antonio vs Kansas City, 12/26/76

Rebounds

MOST REBOUNDS, CAREER

	No.	Yrs	Avg
Wilt Chamberlain	23,924	14	22.9
Bill Russell	21,620	13	22.5
Kareem Abdul-Jabbar	17,440	20	11.4
Elvin Hayes	16,279	16	12.5
Moses Malone	16,212	19	12.2
Karl Malone	14,968	19	10.1
Robert Parish	14,715	21	9.1
Nate Thurmond	14,464	14	15.0
Walt Bellamy	14,241	14	13.7
Wes Unseld	13,769	13	14.0

MOST REBOUNDS, SEASON

	No.	
Wilt Chamberlain, Phil	2,149	1960–61
Wilt Chamberlain, Phil	2,052	1961–62
Wilt Chamberlain, Phil	1,957	1966–67
Wilt Chamberlain, Phil	1,952	1967–68
Wilt Chamberlain, SF	1,946	1962–63
Wilt Chamberlain, Phil	1,943	1965–66
Wilt Chamberlain, Phil	1,941	1959–60
Bill Russell, Bos	1,930	1963–64
Bill Russell, Bos	1,878	1964–65
Bill Russell, Bos	1,868	1960–61

MOST REBOUNDS, GAME

	Player, Team	Opp	Date
55	Wilt Chamberlain, Phil	Bos	11/24/60
51	Bill Russell, Bos	Syr	02/05/60
49	Bill Russell, Bos	Phil	11/16/57
49	Bill Russell, Bos	Det	03/11/65
45	Wilt Chamberlain, Phil	Syr	02/06/60
45	Wilt Chamberlain, Phil	LA	01/21/61

Assists

MOST ASSISTS, CAREER

John Stockton	15,806
Mark Jackson	10,334
Magic Johnson	10,141
Oscar Robertson	9,887
Isiah Thomas	9,061

MOST ASSISTS, SEASON

John Stockton, Utah	1,164	1990–91
John Stockton, Utah	1,134	1989–90
John Stockton, Utah	1,128	1987–88
John Stockton, Utah	1,126	1991–92
Isiah Thomas, Det	1,123	1984–85

MOST ASSISTS, GAME: 30—Scott Skiles, Orlando vs Denver, 12/30/90

Blocked Shots

MOST BLOCKED SHOTS, CAREER

Hakeem Olajuwon	3,830
Kareem Abdul-Jabbar	3,189
Dikembe Mutombo	3,089
Mark Eaton	3,064
David Robinson	2,954

MOST BLOCKED SHOTS, SEASON

Mark Eaton, Utah	456	1984–85
Manute Bol, Wash	397	1985–86
Elmore Smith, LA	393	1973–74

MOST BLOCKED SHOTS, GAME: 17—Elmore Smith, LA Lakers vs Portland, 10/28/73

Scoring

MOST POINTS, CAREER

	Pts	Yrs	Avg
Michael Jordan	5,987	13	33.4
Kareem Abdul-Jabbar	5,762	18	24.3
Shaquille O'Neal	4,970	14	25.6
Karl Malone	4,761	19	24.7
Jerry West	4,457	13	29.1
Larry Bird	3,897	12	23.8
John Havlicek	3,776	13	22.0
Hakeem Olajuwon	3,755	15	25.9
Magic Johnson	3,701	13	19.5
Scottie Pippen	3,642	15	17.7

*HIGHEST SCORING AVERAGE, CAREER

	Avg	Games
Michael Jordan	33.4	179
Allen Iverson	30.6	57
Tracy McGrady	29.8	25
Jerry West	29.1	153
Vince Carter	27.3	30
Elgin Baylor	27.0	134
George Gervin	27.0	59
Hakeem Olajuwon	25.9	145
Dirk Nowitzki	25.7	76
Shaquille O'Neal	25.6	194
Bob Pettit	25.5	88
Dominique Wilkins	25.4	55
Dwyane Wade	25.4	56

*Minimum of 25 games.

MOST POINTS, GAME

Player, Team	Opp	Date
†63.........Michael Jordan, Chi	Bos	4/20/86
61.........Elgin Baylor, LA	Bos	4/14/62
56.........Wilt Chamberlain, Phil	Syr	3/22/62
56.........Michael Jordan, Chi	Mia	4/29/92
56.........Charles Barkley, Phoe	GS	5/4/94
55.........Rick Barry, SF	Phil	4/18/67
55.........Michael Jordan, Chi	Clev	5/1/88
55.........Michael Jordan, Chi	Phoe	4/16/95
55.........Michael Jordan, Chi	Wash	4/27/97

†Double overtime game.

Rebounds

MOST REBOUNDS, CAREER

	No.	Yrs	Avg
Bill Russell	4,104	13	24.9
Wilt Chamberlain	3,913	13	24.5
Kareem Abdul-Jabbar	2,481	18	10.5
Shaquille O'Neal	2,367	14	12.2
Karl Malone	2,062	19	10.7

MOST REBOUNDS, GAME

Player, Team	Opp	Date
41.............Wilt Chamberlain, Phil	Bos	4/5/67
40.............Bill Russell, Bos	Phil	3/23/58
40.............Bill Russell, Bos	StL	3/29/60
*40.............Bill Russell, Bos	LA	4/18/62

Three tied at 39.
*Overtime game.

Assists

MOST ASSISTS, CAREER

	No.	Games
Magic Johnson	2,346	190
John Stockton	1,839	182
Larry Bird	1,062	164
Scottie Pippen	1,035	204
Michael Jordan	1,022	179

MOST ASSISTS, GAME

Player, Team	Opp	Date
24.............Magic Johnson, LAL	Pho	5/15/84
24.............John Stockton, Utah	LAL	5/17/88
23.............Magic Johnson, LAL	Port	5/3/85
22.............Doc Rivers, Atl	Bos	5/16/88

Four tied at 21.

Games played

Kareem Abdul-Jabbar	237
Robert Horry	211
Scottie Pippen	204
Shaquille O'Neal	194
Danny Ainge	193
Karl Malone	193

Appearances

John Stockton	19
Karl Malone	19
Kareem Abdul-Jabbar	18
Robert Parish	16
Dolph Schayes	15
Clyde Drexler	15
Tree Rollins	15
Jerome Kersey	15
Hakeem Olajuwon	15

Scoring

1946–47	Joe Fulks, Phil	1389	1978–79	George Gervin, SA	29.6	
1947–48	Max Zaslofsky, Chi	1007	1979–80	George Gervin, SA	33.1	
1948–49	George Mikan, Minn	1698	1980–81	Adrian Dantley, Utah	30.7	
1949–50	George Mikan, Minn	1865	1981–82	George Gervin, SA	32.3	
1950–51	George Mikan, Minn	1932	1982–83	Alex English, Den	28.4	
1951–52	Paul Arizin, Phil	1674	1983–84	Adrian Dantley, Utah	30.6	
1952–53	Neil Johnston, Phil	1564	1984–85	Bernard King, NY	32.9	
1953–54	Neil Johnston, Phil	1759	1985–86	Dominique Wilkins, Atl	30.3	
1954–55	Neil Johnston, Phil	1631	1986–87	Michael Jordan, Chi	37.1	
1955–56	Bob Pettit, StL	1849	1987–88	Michael Jordan, Chi	35.0	
1956–57	Paul Arizin, Phil	1817	1988–89	Michael Jordan, Chi	32.5	
1957–58	George Yardley, Det	2001	1989–90	Michael Jordan, Chi	33.6	
1958–59	Bob Pettit, StL	2105	1990–91	Michael Jordan, Chi	31.5	
1959–60	Wilt Chamberlain, Phil	2707	1991–92	Michael Jordan, Chi	30.1	
1960–61	Wilt Chamberlain, Phil	3033	1992–93	Michael Jordan, Chi	32.6	
1961–62	Wilt Chamberlain, Phil	4029	1993–94	David Robinson, SA	29.8	
1962–63	Wilt Chamberlain, SF	3586	1994–95	Shaquille O'Neal, Orl	29.3	
1963–64	Wilt Chamberlain, SF	2948	1995–96	Michael Jordan, Chi	30.4	
1964–65	Wilt Chamberlain, SF-Phil	2534	1996–97	Michael Jordan, Chi	29.6	
1965–66	Wilt Chamberlain, Phil	2649	1997–98	Michael Jordan, Chi	28.7	
1966–67	Rick Barry, SF	2775	1998–99	Allen Iverson, Phil	26.8	
1967–68	Dave Bing, Det	2142	1999–00	Shaquille O'Neal, LA Lakers	29.7	
1968–69	Elvin Hayes, SD	2327	2000–01	Allen Iverson, Phil	31.1	
1969–70	Jerry West, LA	*31.2	2001–02	Allen Iverson, Phil	31.4	
1970–71	Kareem Abdul-Jabbar, Mil	31.7	2002–03	Tracy McGrady, Orl	32.1	
1971–72	Kareem Abdul-Jabbar, Mil	34.8	2003–04	Tracy McGrady, Orl	28.0	
1972–73	Nate Archibald, KC-Oma	34.0	2004–05	Allen Iverson, Phil	30.7	
1973–74	Bob McAdoo, Buff	30.6	2005–06	Kobe Bryant, LA Lakers	35.4	
1974–75	Bob McAdoo, Buff	34.5				
1975–76	Bob McAdoo, Buff	31.1				
1976–77	Pete Maravich, NO	31.1				
1977–78	George Gervin, SA	27.2	*Based on per game average since 1969–70.			

Rebounding

1950–51	Dolph Schayes, Syr	1080	1981–82	Moses Malone, Hou	14.7	
1951–52	Larry Foust, FW	880	1982–83	Moses Malone, Phil	15.3	
	Mel Hutchins, Mil	880	1983–84	Moses Malone, Phil	13.4	
1952–53	George Mikan, Minn	1007	1984–85	Moses Malone, Phil	13.1	
1953–54	Harry Gallatin, NY	1098	1985–86	Bill Laimbeer, Det	13.1	
1954–55	Neil Johnston, Phil	1085	1986–87	Charles Barkley, Phil	14.6	
1955–56	Bob Pettit, StL	1164	1987–88	Michael Cage, LA Clippers	13.0	
1956–57	Maurice Stokes, Roch	1256	1988–89	Hakeem Olajuwon, Hou	13.5	
1957–58	Bill Russell, Bos	1564	1989–90	Hakeem Olajuwon, Hou	14.0	
1958–59	Bill Russell, Bos	1612	1990–91	David Robinson, SA	13.0	
1959–60	Wilt Chamberlain, Phil	1941	1991–92	Dennis Rodman, Det	18.7	
1960–61	Wilt Chamberlain, Phil	2149	1992–93	Dennis Rodman, Det	18.3	
1961–62	Wilt Chamberlain, Phil	2052	1993–94	Dennis Rodman, SA	17.3	
1962–63	Wilt Chamberlain, SF	1946	1994–95	Dennis Rodman, SA	16.8	
1963–64	Bill Russell, Bos	1930	1995–96	Dennis Rodman, Chi	14.9	
1964–65	Bill Russell, Bos	1878	1996–97	Dennis Rodman, Chi	16.1	
1965–66	Wilt Chamberlain, Phil	1943	1997–98	Dennis Rodman, Chi	15.0	
1966–67	Wilt Chamberlain, Phil	1957	1998–99	Chris Webber, Sac	13.0	
1967–68	Wilt Chamberlain, Phil	1952	1999–00	Dikembe Mutombo, Atl	14.1	
1968–69	Wilt Chamberlain, LA	1712	2000–01	Dikembe Mutombo, Atl	13.5	
1969–70	Elvin Hayes, SD	*16.9	2001–02	Ben Wallace, Det	13.0	
1970–71	Wilt Chamberlain, LA	18.2	2002–03	Ben Wallace, Det	15.4	
1971–72	Wilt Chamberlain, LA	19.2	2003–04	Kevin Garnett, Minn	13.9	
1972–73	Wilt Chamberlain, LA	18.6	2004–05	Kevin Garnett, Minn	13.5	
1973–74	Elvin Hayes, Capital	18.1	2005–06	Kevin Garnett, Minn	12.7	
1974–75	Wes Unseld, Wash	14.8				
1975–76	Kareem Abdul-Jabbar, LA	16.9				
1976–77	Bill Walton, Port	14.4				
1977–78	Len Robinson, NO	15.7				
1978–79	Moses Malone, Hou	17.6				
1979–80	Swen Nater, SD	15.0				
1980–81	Moses Malone, Hou	14.8	*Based on per game average since 1969–70.			

Assists

1946–47	Ernie Calverly, Prov	202
1947–48	Howie Dallmar, Phil	120
1948–49	Bob Davies, Roch	321
1949–50	Dick McGuire, NY	386
1950–51	Andy Phillip, Phil	414
1951–52	Andy Phillip, Phil	539
1952–53	Bob Cousy, Bos	547
1953–54	Bob Cousy, Bos	578
1954–55	Bob Cousy, Bos	557
1955–56	Bob Cousy, Bos	642
1956–57	Bob Cousy, Bos	478
1957–58	Bob Cousy, Bos	463
1958–59	Bob Cousy, Bos	557
1959–60	Bob Cousy, Bos	715
1960–61	Oscar Robertson, Cin	690
1961–62	Oscar Robertson, Cin	899
1962–63	Guy Rodgers, SF	825
1963–64	Oscar Robertson, Cin	868
1964–65	Oscar Robertson, Cin	861
1965–66	Oscar Robertson, Cin	847
1966–67	Guy Rodgers, Chi	908
1967–68	Wilt Chamberlain, Phil	702
1968–69	Oscar Robertson, Cin	772
1969–70	Lenny Wilkens, Sea	*9.1
1970–71	Norm Van Lier, Cin	10.1
1971–72	Jerry West, LA	9.7
1972–73	Nate Archibald, KC-Oma	11.4
1973–74	Ernie DiGregorio, Buff	8.2
1974–75	Kevin Porter, Wash	8.0
1975–76	Don Watts, Sea	8.1
1976–77	Don Buse, Ind	8.5
1977–78	Kevin Porter, NJ-Det	10.2
1978–79	Kevin Porter, Det	13.4
1979–80	Micheal Richardson, NY	10.1
1980–81	Kevin Porter, Wash	9.1
1981–82	Johnny Moore, SA	9.6
1982–83	Magic Johnson, LA	10.5
1983–84	Magic Johnson, LA	13.1
1984–85	Isiah Thomas, Det	13.9
1985–86	Magic Johnson, LA Lakers	12.6
1986–87	Magic Johnson, LA Lakers	12.2
1987–88	John Stockton, Utah	13.8
1988–89	John Stockton, Utah	13.6
1989–90	John Stockton, Utah	14.5
1990–91	John Stockton, Utah	14.2
1991–92	John Stockton, Utah	13.7
1992–93	John Stockton, Utah	12.0
1993–94	John Stockton, Utah	12.6
1994–95	John Stockton, Utah	12.3
1995–96	John Stockton, Utah	11.2
1996–97	Mark Jackson, Ind	11.4
1997–98	Rod Strickland, Wash	10.1
1998–99	Jason Kidd, Phoe	10.8
1999–00	Jason Kidd, Phoe	10.1
2000–01	Jason Kidd, Phoe	9.8
2001–02	Andre Miller, Clev	10.9
2002–03	Jason Kidd, NJ	8.9
2003–04	Jason Kidd, NJ	9.2
2004–05	Steve Nash, Phoe	11.5
2005–06	Steve Nash, Phoe	10.5

*Based on per game average since 1969–70.

Field-Goal Percentage

1946–47	Bob Feerick, Wash	40.1
1947–48	Bob Feerick, Wash	34.0
1948–49	Arnie Risen, Roch	42.3
1949–50	Alex Groza, Ind	47.8
1950–51	Alex Groza, Ind	47.0
1951–52	Paul Arizin, Phil	44.8
1952–53	Neil Johnston, Phil	45.2
1953–54	Ed Macauley, Bos	48.6
1954–55	Larry Foust, FW	48.7
1955–56	Neil Johnston, Phil	45.7
1956–57	Neil Johnston, Phil	44.7
1957–58	Jack Twyman, Cin	45.2
1958–59	Ken Sears, NY	49.0
1959–60	Ken Sears, NY	47.7
1960–61	Wilt Chamberlain, Phil	50.9
1961–62	Walt Bellamy, Chi	51.9
1962–63	Wilt Chamberlain, SF	52.8
1963–64	Jerry Lucas, Cin	52.7
1964–65	Wilt Chamberlain, SF-Phil	51.0
1965–66	Wilt Chamberlain, Phil	54.0
1966–67	Wilt Chamberlain, Phil	68.3
1967–68	Wilt Chamberlain, Phil	59.5
1968–69	Wilt Chamberlain, LA	58.3
1969–70	Johnny Green, Cin	55.9
1970–71	Johnny Green, Cin	58.7
1971–72	Wilt Chamberlain, LA	64.9
1972–73	Wilt Chamberlain, LA	72.7
1973–74	Bob McAdoo, Buff	54.7
1974–75	Don Nelson, Bos	53.9
1975–76	Wes Unseld, Wash	56.1
1976–77	Kareem Abdul-Jabbar, LA	57.9
1977–78	Bobby Jones, Den	57.8
1978–79	Cedric Maxwell, Bos	58.4
1979–80	Cedric Maxwell, Bos	60.9
1980–81	Artis Gilmore, Chi	67.0
1981–82	Artis Gilmore, Chi	65.2
1982–83	Artis Gilmore, SA	62.6
1983–84	Artis Gilmore, SA	63.1
1984–85	James Donaldson, LA Clippers	63.7
1985–86	Steve Johnson, SA	63.2
1986–87	Kevin McHale, Bos	60.4
1987–88	Kevin McHale, Bos	60.4
1988–89	Dennis Rodman, Det	59.5
1989–90	Mark West, Phoe	62.5
1990–91	Buck Williams, Port	60.2
1991–92	Buck Williams, Port	60.4
1992–93	Cedric Ceballos, Phoe	57.6
1993–94	Shaquille O'Neal, Orl	59.9
1994–95	Chris Gatling, GS	63.3
1995–96	Gheorghe Muresan, Wash	58.4
1996–97	Gheorghe Muresan, Wash	60.4
1997–98	Shaquille O'Neal, LA Lakers	58.4
1998–99	Shaquille O'Neal, LA Lakers	57.6
1999–00	Shaquille O'Neal, LA Lakers	57.4
2000–01	Shaquille O'Neal, LA Lakers	57.2
2001–02	Shaquille O'Neal, LA Lakers	57.9
2002–03	Eddy Curry, Chi	58.5
2003–04	Shaquille O'Neal, LA Lakers	58.4
2004–05	Shaquille O'Neal, Mia	60.1
2005–06	Shaquille O'Neal, Mia	60.0

Free-Throw Percentage

1946–47 ....Fred Scolari, Wash	81.1	
1947–48 ....Bob Feerick, Wash	78.8	
1948–49 ....Bob Feerick, Wash	85.9	
1949–50 ....Max Zaslofsky, Chi	84.3	
1950–51 ....Joe Fulks, Phil	85.5	
1951–52 ....Bob Wanzer, Roch	90.4	
1952–53 ....Bill Sharman, Bos	85.0	
1953–54 ....Bill Sharman, Bos	84.4	
1954–55 ....Bill Sharman, Bos	89.7	
1955–56 ....Bill Sharman, Bos	86.7	
1956–57 ....Bill Sharman, Bos	90.5	
1957–58 ....Dolph Schayes, Syr	90.4	
1958–59 ....Bill Sharman, Bos	93.2	
1959–60 ....Dolph Schayes, Syr	89.2	
1960–61 ....Bill Sharman, Bos	92.1	
1961–62 ....Dolph Schayes, Syr	89.6	
1962–63 ....Larry Costello, Syr	88.1	
1963–64 ....Oscar Robertson, Cin	85.3	
1964–65 ....Larry Costello, Phil	87.7	
1965–66 ....Larry Siegfried, Bos	88.1	
1966–67 ....Adrian Smith, Cin	90.3	
1967–68 ....Oscar Robertson, Cin	87.3	
1968–69 ....Larry Siegfried, Bos	86.4	
1969–70 ....Flynn Robinson, Mil	89.8	
1970–71 ....Chet Walker, Chi	85.9	
1971–72 ....Jack Marin, Balt	89.4	
1972–73 ....Rick Barry, GS	90.2	
1973–74 ....Ernie DiGregorio, Buff	90.2	
1974–75 ....Rick Barry, GS	90.4	
1975–76 ....Rick Barry, GS	92.3	
1976–77 ....Ernie DiGregorio, Buff	94.5	

1977–78 ....Rick Barry, GS	92.4
1978–79 ....Rick Barry, Hou	94.7
1979–80 ....Rick Barry, Hou	93.5
1980–81 ....Calvin Murphy, Hou	95.8
1981–82 ....Kyle Macy, Phoe	89.9
1982–83 ....Calvin Murphy, Hou	92.0
1983–84 ....Larry Bird, Bos	88.8
1984–85 ....Kyle Macy, Phoe	90.7
1985–86 ....Larry Bird, Bos	89.6
1986–87 ....Larry Bird, Bos	91.0
1987–88 ....Jack Sikma, Mil	92.2
1988–89 ....Magic Johnson, LA Lakers	91.1
1989–90 ....Larry Bird, Bos	93.0
1990–91 ....Reggie Miller, Ind	91.8
1991–92 ....Mark Price, Clev	94.7
1992–93 ....Mark Price, Clev	94.8
1993–94 ....Mahmoud Abdul-Rauf, Den	95.6
1994–95 ....Spud Webb, Sac	93.4
1995–96 ....Mahmoud Abdul-Rauf, Den	93.0
1996–97 ....Mark Price, GS	90.6
1997–98 ....Chris Mullin, Ind	93.9
1998–99 ....Reggie Miller, Ind	91.5
1999–00 ....Jeff Hornacek, Utah	95.0
2000–01 ....Reggie Miller, Ind	92.8
2001–02 ....Reggie Miller, Ind	91.1
2002–03 ....Allan Houston, NY	91.9
2003–04 ....Peja Stojakovic, Sac	92.7
2004–05 ....Reggie Miller, Ind	93.3
2005–06 ....Steve Nash, Phoe	92.1

Three-Point Field-Goal Percentage

1979–80 ....Fred Brown, Sea	44.3
1980–81 ....Brian Taylor, SD	38.3
1981–82 ....Campy Russell, NY	43.9
1982–83 ....Mike Dunleavy, SA	34.5
1983–84 ....Darrell Griffith, Utah	36.1
1984–85 ....Byron Scott, LA Lakers	43.3
1985–86 ....Craig Hodges, Mil	45.1
1986–87 ....Kiki Vandeweghe, Por	48.1
1987–88 ....Craig Hodges, Mil-Phoe	49.1
1988–89 ....Jon Sundvold, Mia	52.2
1989–90 ....Steve Kerr, Clev	50.7
1990–91 ....Jim Les, Sac	46.1
1991–92 ....Dana Barros, Sea	44.6
1992–93 .............B.J. Armstrong, Chi	45.3

1993–94 ....Tracy Murray, Por	45.9
1994–95 ....Steve Kerr, Chi	52.4
1995–96 ....Tim Legler, Wash	52.2
1996–97 ....Kevin Gamble, Sac	48.2
1997–98 ....Dale Ellis, Sea	46.0
1998–99 ....Dell Curry, Char	47.6
1999–00 ....Hubert Davis, Dall	49.1
2000–01 ....Brent Barry, Sea	47.6
2001–02 ....Steve Smith, SA	47.2
2002–03 ....Bruce Bowen, SA	44.1
2003–04 ....Anthony Peeler, Sac	48.2
2004–05 ....Fred Hoiberg, Minn	49.6
2005–06 ....Richard Hamilton, Det	45.8

Steals

1973–74 ....Larry Steele, Por	2.68
1974–75 ....Rick Barry, GS	2.85
1975–76 ....Don Watts, Sea	3.18
1976–77 ....Don Buse, Ind	3.47
1977–78 ....Ron Lee, Phoe	2.74
1978–79 .............M.L. Carr, Det	2.46
1979–80 ....Micheal Richardson, NY	3.23
1980–81 ....Magic Johnson, LA	3.43
1981–82 ....Magic Johnson, LA	2.67
1982–83 ....Micheal Richardson, GS-NJ	2.84
1983–84 ....Rickey Green, Utah	2.65
1984–85 ....Micheal Richardson, NJ	2.96
1985–86 ....Alvin Robertson, SA	3.67
1986–87 ....Alvin Robertson, SA	3.21
1987–88 ....Michael Jordan, Chi	3.16
1988–89 ....John Stockton, Utah	3.21
1989–90 ....Michael Jordan, Chi	2.77

1990–91 ....Alvin Robertson, Mil	3.04
1991–92 ....John Stockton, Utah	2.98
1992–93 ....Michael Jordan, Chi	2.83
1993–94 ....Nate McMillan, Sea	2.96
1994–95 ....Scottie Pippen, Chi	2.94
1995–96 ....Gary Payton, Sea	2.85
1996–97 ....Mookie Blaylock, Atl	2.72
1997–98 ....Mookie Blaylock, Atl	2.61
1998–99 ....Kendall Gill, NJ	2.68
1999–00 ....Eddie Jones, Char	2.67
2000–01 ....Allen Iverson, Phil	2.51
2001–02 ....Allen Iverson, Phil	2.80
2002–03 ....Allen Iverson, Phil	2.74
2003–04 ....Baron Davis, NO	2.36
2004–05 ....Larry Hughes, Wash	2.89
2005–06 ....Gerald Wallace, Char	2.51

Blocked Shots

1973–74	Elmore Smith, LA	4.85	1992–93	Hakeem Olajuwon, Hou	4.17
1974–75	Kareem Abdul-Jabbar, Mil	3.26	1993–94	Dikembe Mutombo, Den	4.10
1975–76	Kareem Abdul-Jabbar, LA	4.12	1994–95	Dikembe Mutombo, Den	3.91
1976–77	Bill Walton, Port	3.25	1995–96	Dikembe Mutombo, Den	4.49
1977–78	George Johnson, NJ	3.38	1996–97	Shawn Bradley, NJ	3.40
1978–79	Kareem Abdul-Jabbar, LA	3.95	1997–98	Marcus Camby, Tor	3.65
1979–80	Kareem Abdul-Jabbar, LA	3.41	1998–99	Alonzo Mourning, Mia	3.91
1980–81	George Johnson, SA	3.39	1999–00	Alonzo Mourning, Mia	3.72
1981–82	George Johnson, SA	3.12	2000–01	Theo Ratliff, Phil/Atl	3.74
1982–83	Wayne Rollins, Atl	4.29	2001–02	Ben Wallace, Det	3.48
1983–84	Mark Eaton, Utah	4.28	2002–03	Theo Ratliff, Atl	3.23
1984–85	Mark Eaton, Utah	5.56	2003–04	Theo Ratliff, Port	3.61
1985–86	Manute Bol, Wash	4.96	2004–05	Andrei Kirilenko, Utah	3.32
1986–87	Mark Eaton, Utah	4.06	2005–06	Marcus Camby, Den	3.29
1987–88	Mark Eaton, Utah	3.71			
1988–89	Manute Bol, GS	4.31			
1989–90	Hakeem Olajuwon, Hou	4.59			
1990–91	Hakeem Olajuwon, Hou	3.95			
1991–92	David Robinson, SA	4.49			

NBA All-Star Game Results

Year	Result	Site	Winning Coach	Most Valuable Player
1951	East 111, West 94	Boston	Joe Lapchick	Ed Macauley, Bos
1952	East 108, West 91	Boston	Al Cervi	Paul Arizin, Phil
1953	West 79, East 75	Ft Wayne	John Kundla	George Mikan, Minn
1954	East 98, West 93 (OT)	New York	Joe Lapchick	Bob Cousy, Bos
1955	East 100, West 91	New York	Al Cervi	Bill Sharman, Bos
1956	West 108, East 94	Rochester	Charley Eckman	Bob Pettit, StL
1957	East 109, West 97	Boston	Red Auerbach	Bob Cousy, Bos
1958	East 130, West 118	St Louis	Red Auerbach	Bob Pettit, StL
1959	West 124, East 108	Detroit	Ed Macauley	B. Pettit, StL/ E. Baylor, Minn
1960	East 125, West 115	Philadelphia	Red Auerbach	Wilt Chamberlain, Phil
1961	West 153, East 131	Syracuse	Paul Seymour	Oscar Robertson, Cin
1962	West 150, East 130	St Louis	Fred Schaus	Bob Pettit, StL
1963	East 115, West 108	Los Angeles	Red Auerbach	Bill Russell, Bos
1964	East 111, West 107	Boston	Red Auerbach	Oscar Robertson, Cin
1965	East 124, West 123	St Louis	Red Auerbach	Jerry Lucas, Cin
1966	East 137, West 94	Cincinnati	Red Auerbach	Adrian Smith, Cin
1967	West 135, East 120	San Francisco	Fred Schaus	Rick Barry, SF
1968	East 144, West 124	New York	Alex Hannum	Hal Greer, Phil
1969	East 123, West 112	Baltimore	Gene Shue	Oscar Robertson, Cin
1970	East 142, West 135	Philadelphia	Red Holzman	Willis Reed, NY
1971	West 108, East 107	San Diego	Larry Costello	Lenny Wilkens, Sea
1972	West 112, East 110	Los Angeles	Bill Sharman	Jerry West, LA
1973	East 104, West 84	Chicago	Tom Heinsohn	Dave Cowens, Bos
1974	West 134, East 123	Seattle	Larry Costello	Bob Lanier, Det
1975	East 108, West 102	Phoenix	K.C. Jones	Walt Frazier, NY
1976	East 123, West 109	Philadelphia	Tom Heinsohn	Dave Bing, Wash
1977	West 125, East 124	Milwaukee	Larry Brown	Julius Erving, Phil
1978	East 133, West 125	Atlanta	Billy Cunningham	Randy Smith, Buff
1979	West 134, East 129	Detroit	Lenny Wilkens	David Thompson, Den
1980	East 144, West 135 (OT)	Washington	Billy Cunningham	George Gervin, SA
1981	East 123, West 120	Cleveland	Billy Cunningham	Nate Archibald, Bos
1982	East 120, West 118	New Jersey	Bill Fitch	Larry Bird, Bos
1983	East 132, West 123	Los Angeles	Billy Cunningham	Julius Erving, Phil
1984	East 154, West 145 (OT)	Denver	K.C. Jones	Isiah Thomas, Det
1985	West 140, East 129	Indiana	Pat Riley	Ralph Sampson, Hou

Year	Result	Site	Winning Coach	Most Valuable Player
1986	East 139, West 132	Dallas	K.C. Jones	Isiah Thomas, Det
1987	West 154, East 149 (OT)	Seattle	Pat Riley	Tom Chambers, Sea
1988	East 138, West 133	Chicago	Mike Fratello	Michael Jordan, Chi
1989	West 143, East 134	Houston	Pat Riley	Karl Malone, Utah
1990	East 130, West 113	Miami	Chuck Daly	Magic Johnson, LA Lakers
1991	East 116, West 114	Charlotte	Chris Ford	Charles Barkley, Phil
1992	West 153, East 113	Orlando	Don Nelson	Magic Johnson, LA Lakers
1993	West 135, East 132	Salt Lake City	Paul Westphal	K. Malone/ J. Stockton, Utah
1994	East 127, West 118	Minneapolis	Lenny Wilkens	Scottie Pippen, Chi
1995	West 139, East 112	Phoenix	Paul Westphal	Mitch Richmond, Sac
1996	East 129, West 118	San Antonio	Phil Jackson	Michael Jordan, Chi
1997	East 132, West 120	Cleveland	Doug Collins	Glen Rice, Char
1998	East 135, West 114	New York	Larry Bird	Michael Jordan, Chi
1999	Cancelled due to lockout.			
2000	West 137, East 126	Oakland	Phil Jackson	O'Neal, Lakers/T. Duncan,SA
2001	East 111, West 110	Washington	Larry Brown	Allen Iverson, Phil
2002	West 135, East 120	Philadelphia	Don Nelson	Kobe Bryant, LA Lakers
2003	West 155, East 145 (2OT)	Atlanta	Rick Adelman	Kevin Garnett, Minn
2004	West 136, East 132	Los Angeles	Flip Saunders	Shaquille O'Neal, LA Lakers
2005	East 125, West 115	Denver	Stan Van Gundy	Allen Iverson, Phil
2006	East 122, West 120	Houston	Flip Saunders	LeBron James, Cle

Members of the Basketball Hall of Fame

Contributors

Senda Abbott (1984)
Forest C. (Phog) Allen (1959)
Clair F. Bee (1967)
Danny Biasone (2000)
Hubie Brown (2005)
Walter A. Brown (1965)
John W. Bunn (1964)
Jerry Colangelo (2004)
Bob Douglas (1971)
Al Duer (1981)
Wayne Embry (1999)
Clifford Fagan (1983)
Harry A. Fisher (1973)
Larry Fleisher (1991)
Edward Gottlieb (1971)
Luther H. Gulick (1959)
Lester Harrison (1979)
Chick Hearn (2003)
Ferenc Hepp (1980)
Edward J. Hickox (1959)
Paul D. (Tony) Hinkle (1965)
Ned Irish (1964)
R. William Jones (1964)

J. Walter Kennedy (1980)
Meadowlark Lemon (2003)
Emil S. Liston (1974)
Earl Lloyd (2003)
John B. McLendon (1978)
Bill Mokray (1965)
Ralph Morgan (1959)
Frank Morgenweck (1962)
James Naismith (1959)
Peter F. Newell (1978)
C.M. Newton (2000)
John J. O'Brien (1961)
Larry O'Brien (1991)
Harold G. Olsen (1959)
Maurice Podoloff (1973)
H. V. Porter (1960)
William A. Reid (1963)
Elmer Ripley (1972)
Lynn W. St. John (1962)
Abe Saperstein (1970)
Arthur A. Schabinger (1961)
Amos Alonzo Stagg (1959)

Boris Stankovic (1991)
Edward Steitz (1983)
Chuck Taylor (1968)
Oswald Tower (1959)
Arthur L. Trester (1961)
Clifford Wells (1971)
Lou Wilke (1982)
Fred Zollner (1999)

Players

Kareem Abdul-Jabbar (1995)
Nate (Tiny) Archibald (1991)
Paul J. Arizin (1977)
Thomas B. Barlow (1980)
Rick Barry (1987)
Elgin Baylor (1976)
John Beckman (1972)
Walt Bellamy (1993)
Sergei Belov (1992)
Dave Bing (1990)
Larry Bird (1998)
Carol Blazejowski (1994)
Bennie Borgmann (1961)
Bill Bradley (1982)
Joseph Brennan (1974)
Al Cervi (1984)
Wilt Chamberlain (1978)
Charles (Tarzan) Cooper (1976)
Kresimir Cosic (1996)
Bob Cousy (1970)
Dave Cowens (1991)
Joan Crawford (1997)
Billy Cunningham (1986)
Denise Curry (1997)
Drazen Dalipagic (2004)
Bob Davies (1969)
Forrest S. DeBernardi (1961)
Dave DeBusschere (1982)
H.G. (Dutch) Dehnert (1968)
Anne Donovan (1995)
Clyde Drexler (2004)
Paul Endacott (1971)
Alex English (1997)
Julius Erving (1993)
Harold (Bud) Foster (1964)
Walter (Clyde) Frazier (1987)
Max (Marty) Friedman (1971)
Joe Fulks (1977)
Lauren (Laddie) Gale (1976)
Harry (the Horse) Gallatin (1991)
William Gates (1989)
George Gervin (1996)
Tom Gola (1975)
Gail Goodrich (1996)

Hal Greer (1981)
Robert (Ace) Gruenig (1963)
Clifford O. Hagan (1977)
Victor Hanson (1960)
John Havlicek (1983)
Connie Hawkins (1992)
Elvin Hayes (1990)
Marques Haynes (1998)
Tom Heinsohn (1986)
Nat Holman (1964)
Robert J. Houbregs (1987)
Bailey Howell (1997)
Chuck Hyatt (1959)
Dan Issel (1993)
Harry (Buddy) Jeannette (1994)
Earvin (Magic) Johnson (2002)
William C. Johnson (1976)
D. Neil Johnston (1990)
K.C. Jones (1989)
Sam Jones (1983)
Edward (Moose) Krause (1975)
Bob Kurland (1961)
Bob Lanier (1992)
Joe Lapchick (1966)
Nancy Lieberman-Cline (1996)
Clyde Lovellette (1988)
Jerry Lucas (1979)
Angelo (Hank) Luisetti (1959)
C. Edward Macauley (1960)
Moses Malone (2001)
Peter P. Maravich (1987)
Hortencia Marcari (2005)
Slater Martin (1981)
Bob McAdoo (2000)
Branch McCracken (1960)
Jack McCracken (1962)
Bobby McDermott (1988)
Dick McGuire (1993)
Kevin McHale (1999)
Dino Meneghin (2003)
Ann Meyers (1993)
George L. Mikan (1959)
Vern Mikkelsen (1995)
Cheryl Miller (1995)

Earl Monroe (1990)
Calvin Murphy (1993)
Charles (Stretch) Murphy (1960)
H. O. (Pat) Page (1962)
Robert Parish (2003)
Drazen Petrovic (2002)
Bob Pettit (1970)
Andy Phillip (1961)
Jim Pollard (1977)
Frank Ramsey (1981)
Willis Reed (1981)
Arnie Risen (1998)
Oscar Robertson (1979)
John S. Roosma (1961)
Bill Russell (1974)
John (Honey) Russell (1964)
Adolph Schayes (1972)
Ernest J. Schmidt (1973)
John J. Schommer (1959)
Barney Sedran (1962)
Uljana Semjonova (1993)
Bill Sharman (1975)
Christian Steinmetz (1961)
Lusia Harris Stewart (1992)
Maurice Stokes (2004)
Isiah Thomas (2000)
David Thompson (1996)
John A. (Cat) Thompson (1962)
Nate Thurmond (1984)
Jack Twyman (1982)
Wes Unseld (1988)
Robert (Fuzzy) Vandivier (1974)
Edward A. Wachter (1961)
Bill Walton (1993)
Robert F. Wanzer (1987)
Jerry West (1979)
Nera White (1992)
Lenny Wilkens (1989)
Lynette Woodard (2004)
John R. Wooden (1960)
James Worthy (2003)
George (Bird) Yardley (1996)

Coaches

Harold Anderson (1984)
Red Auerbach (1968)
Leon Barmore (2003)
Sam Barry (1978)
Ernest A. Blood (1960)
Jim Boeheim (2005)
Larry Brown (2002)
Jim Calhoun (2005)
Howard G. Cann (1967)
H. Clifford Carlson (1959)
Lou Carnesecca (1992)
Ben Carnevale (1969)
Pete Carril (1997)
Everett Case (1981)
John Chaney (2001)
Jody Conradt (1998)
Denny Crum (1994)
Chuck Daly (1994)
Everett S. Dean (1966)

Antonio Diaz-Miguel (1997)
Edgar A. Diddle (1971)
Bruce Drake (1972)
Clarence Gaines (1981)
Jack Gardner (1983)
Amory T. (Slats) Gill (1967)
Aleksandr Gomelsky (1995)
Sue Gunter (2005)
Alex Hannum (1998)
Marv Harshman (1984)
Don Haskins (1997)
Edgar S. Hickey (1978)
Howard A. Hobson (1965)
Red Holzman (1986)
Hank Iba (1968)
Alvin F. (Doggie) Julian (1967)
Frank W. Keaney (1960)
George E. Keogan (1961)
Bob Knight (1991)

Mike Krzyzewski (2001)
John Kundla (1995)
Ward L. Lambert (1960)
Harry Litwack (1975)
Kenneth D. Loeffler (1964)
A.C. (Dutch) Lonborg (1972)
Arad A. McCutchan (1980)
Al McGuire (1992)
Frank McGuire (1976)
Walter E. Meanwell (1959)
Raymond J. Meyer (1978)
Ralph Miller (1988)
Billie Moore (1999)
Aleksandar Nikolic (1998)
Lute Olson (2002)
Jack Ramsay (1992)
Cesare Rubini (1994)
Adolph F. Rupp (1968)
Leonard D. Sachs (1961)

Note: Year of election in parentheses.

Coaches *(Cont.)*

Bill Sharman (2004)
Everett F. Shelton (1979)
Dean Smith (1982)
Pat Summitt (2000)
Fred R. Taylor (1985)

Bertha Teague (1984)
John Thompson (1999)
Margaret Wade (1984)
Stanley H. Watts (1985)
Lenny Wilkens (1998)

John R. Wooden (1972)
Morgan Wooten (2000)
Phil Woolpert (1992)
Kay Yow (2002)

Referees

James E. Enright (1978)
George T. Hepbron (1960)
George Hoyt (1961)
Matthew P. Kennedy (1959)
Lloyd Leith (1982)
Zigmund J. Mihalik (1985)

John P. Nucatola (1977)
Ernest C. Quigley (1961)
J. Dallas Shirley (1979)
Earl Strom (1995)
David Tobey (1961)
David H. Walsh (1961)

Teams

Buffalo Germans (1961)
First Team (1959)
Harlem Globetrotters (2002)
Original Celtics (1959)
Renaissance (1963)

ABA Champions

Year	Champion	Series	Runner-up	Winning Coach
1968	Pittsburgh Pipers	4–3	New Orleans Bucs	Vince Cazetta
1969	Oakland Oaks	4–1	Indiana Pacers	Alex Hannum
1970	Indiana Pacers	4–2	Los Angeles Stars	Bob Leonard
1971	Utah Stars	4–3	Kentucky Colonels	Bill Sharman
1972	Indiana Pacers	4–2	New York Nets	Bob Leonard
1973	Indiana Pacers	4–3	Kentucky Colonels	Bob Leonard
1974	New York Nets	4–1	Utah Stars	Kevin Loughery
1975	Kentucky Colonels	4–1	Indiana Pacers	Hubie Brown
1976	New York Nets	4–2	Denver Nuggets	Kevin Loughery

ABA Postseason Awards

Most Valuable Player

1967–68	Connie Hawkins, Pitt
1968–69	Mel Daniels, Ind
1969–70	Spencer Haywood, Den
1970–71	Mel Daniels, Ind
1971–72	Artis Gilmore, Ken
1972–73	Billy Cunningham, Car
1973–74	Julius Erving, NY
1974–75	Julius Erving, NY
	George McGinnis, Ind
1975–76	Julius Erving, NY

Rookie of the Year

1967–68	Mel Daniels, Minn
1968–69	Warren Armstrong, Oak
1969–70	Spencer Haywood, Den
1970–71	Charlie Scott, Vir
	Dan Issel, Ken
1971–72	Artis Gilmore, Ken
1972–73	Brian Taylor, NY
1973–74	Swen Nater, SA
1974–75	Marvin Barnes, StL
1975–76	David Thompson, Den

Coach of the Year

1967–68	Vince Cazetta, Pitt
1968–69	Alex Hannum, Oak
1969–70	Bill Sharman, LA
	Joe Belmont, Den
1970–71	Al Bianchi, Vir
1971–72	Tom Nissalke, Dall
1972–73	Larry Brown, Car
1973–74	Babe McCarthy, Ken
	Joe Mullaney, Utah
1974–75	Larry Brown, Den
1975–76	Larry Brown, Den

ABA Season Leaders

Scoring

	GP	Pts	Avg
1967–68...Connie Hawkins, Pitt	70	1875	26.8
1968–69...Rick Barry, Oak	35	1190	34.0
1969–70...Spencer Haywood, Den	84	2519	30.0
1970–71...Dan Issel, Ken	83	2480	29.4
1971–72...Charlie Scott, Vir	73	2524	34.6
1972–73...Julius Erving, Vir	71	2268	31.9
1973–74...Julius Erving, NY	84	2299	27.4
1974–75...George McGinnis, Ind	79	2353	29.8
1975–76...Julius Erving, NY	84	2462	29.3

Rebounds

1967–68................Mel Daniels, Minn	15.6
1968–69................Mel Daniels, Ind	16.5
1969–70................Spencer Haywood, Den	19.5
1970–71................Mel Daniels, Ind	18.0
1971–72................Artis Gilmore, Ken	17.8
1972–73................Artis Gilmore, Ken	17.5
1973–74................Artis Gilmore, Ken	18.3
1974–75................Swen Nater, SA	16.4
1975–76................Artis Gilmore, Ken	15.5

Assists

1967–68................Larry Brown, NO	6.5
1968–69................Larry Brown, Oak	7.1
1969–70................Larry Brown, Wash	7.1
1970–71................Bill Melchionni, NY	8.3
1971–72................Bill Melchionni, NY	8.4
1972–73................Bill Melchionni, NY	7.5
1973–74................Al Smith, Den	8.2
1974–75................Mack Calvin, Den	7.7
1975–76................Don Buse, Ind	8.2

Steals

1973–74................Ted McClain, Car	2.98
1974–75................Brian Taylor, NY	2.80
1975–76................Don Buse, Ind	4.12

Blocked Shots

1973–74................Caldwell Jones, SD	4.00
1974–75................Caldwell Jones, SD	3.24
1975–76................Billy Paultz, SA	3.05

World Championship of Basketball

Year	Winner	Runner-Up	Score	Site
1950	Argentina	United States	†	Rio de Janeiro
1954	United States	Brazil	†	Rio de Janeiro
1959	Brazil	United States	†	Santiago, Chile
1963	Brazil	Yugoslavia	†	Rio de Janeiro
1967	Soviet Union	Yugoslavia	†	Montevideo, Uruguay
1970	Yugoslavia	Brazil	†	Ljubljana, Yugoslavia
1974	Soviet Union	Yugoslavia	†	San Juan
1978	Yugoslavia	Soviet Union	82–81 (OT)	Manila
1982	Soviet Union	United States	95–94	Cali, Colombia
1986	United States	Soviet Union	87–85	Madrid
1990	Yugoslavia	Soviet Union	92–75	Buenos Aires
1994*	United States	Russia	137–91	Toronto
1998	Yugoslavia	Russia	64–62	Athens
2002	Yugoslavia	Argentina	84–77 (OT)	Indianapolis
2006	Spain	Greece	70–47	Saitama, Japan

*U.S. professionals began competing in 1994. In 1998, a labor dispute resulted in a boycott of the World Championship by NBA stars; the U.S. roster was filled by members of the CBA and European professional leagues and college players.
†Result determined by overall record in final round of competition.

College Basketball

Joakim Noah (l.) led
Florida to the
national championship

RICH CLARKSON/SPORTS ILLUSTRATED

Gator Bait

While familiar powerhouses dominated the regular season, unheralded Florida stole the show at a Big Dance that saw more than its share of Cinderella stories

BY B.J. SCHECTER

The beauty of the NCAA men's basketball tournament is that theoretically any of the 65 entrants has an equal shot at winning it. Sure, seeding, matchups and location play a pivotal role, but whether you're Duke or Davidson you need to win four games to reach the Final Four and six to take home the title. Historically, this has been a pipe dream for the lower-seeded teams and the schools in the mid-major conferences, but in recent years the gap has closed significantly. While it's true that a No. 16-seed has never beaten a No. 1, those games are no longer blowouts and the names on the front of the jerseys mean far less than what's underneath them.

Heart, desire and passion were on display in the 2006 NCAA tournament and if there was ever an event that validated the old axiom, "You're only as good as your last game," this was it. How else do you explain No. 16-seeds pushing No. 1s to the limit (see Albany, which led UConn by 12 points with 11 minutes remaining), mid-majors beating teams from the power conferences with regularity, Florida's fantastic under-the-radar run to the title, and George Mason?

While the Big Dance was filled with shining moments, in the end Florida stole the spotlight, first by upsetting No. 1 seed Vil-lanova in the Minneapolis regional final to earn a trip to Indianapolis, then bursting George Mason's bubble in the national semifinal and, finally, overwhelming UCLA to capture its first national basketball title. The Gators may have been unranked entering the season, but coach Billy Donovan's young team peaked at just the right time and proved that you don't necessarily need the best players to cut down the nets.

Donovan knows this all too well. When he first came to Gainesville as an up-and-coming young coach known as Billy The Kid, Donovan's philosophy was to go after every top prospect and stockpile McDonald's All-Americans. Doing so brought mixed results, and although the Gators made it to the national title game in 2000 (also played in Indianapolis), Florida was hurt by players who had one foot in college and the other in the NBA. Mike Miller and Donnell Harvey left early for the NBA and Kwame Brown (a No. 1 pick—and a bust) never made it on campus. What's more, coming into the 2005-06 season Donovan had lost his top three players—David Lee, Anthony Roberson and Matt Walsh—and just making the NCAA tournament was a lofty goal, let alone winning it.

But the more Donovan looked at his young team (the starting lineup was made up of four sophomores and a junior) the more he liked what he saw. The Gators'

chemistry—a problem the previous season—was terrific and they showed that team play is much more important than individual talent by winning their first 17 games. "The more I do this, the more I believe if you're building a successful company or program, so much of it comes down to the makeup of the people, from your coaches to your players," said Donovan. "What sets these kids apart isn't their talent. They all complement each other so well."

The Gators continued to complement one another and grow as a team throughout the season, but even after winning the SEC tournament and entering the NCAAs as a No. 3 seed, Florida was far from a favorite. However, Donovan's crew, led by breakout big men Joakim Noah, the son of former French tennis star Yannick Noah, and Al Horford, dangerous swingman Corey Brewer, sharp-

After falling one win short in 2000, Florida head coach Billy Donovan got to cut down the nets in 2006, winning his first national title.

shooter Lee Humphrey and steady point guard Taurean Green were as capable—and unflappable—as any team Donovan had ever coached. "I remember meeting these guys," says Horford, "and the first thing they said was, 'Let's go to the gym.' I was like, Damn, they're already thinking about playing. When you hear that you know you're with guys who want to win."

With its singular focus and unselfish play, Florida proved to be the ultimate team in the NCAA tournament and the matchup from hell for opponents. The catalyst was Noah, who went from a role player the previous year, to a sure NBA lottery pick. His post skills improving by the day, Noah dominated inside, showcasing his athleticism and blocking shots with reckless abandon. Horford was the perfect complement in the paint, while the silky smooth Brewer emerged as the Gators' best all-around player. In the backcourt, Green was the consummate floor leader and could impact the game without scoring a point while Humphrey could bury teams in an instant with his deadly three-point shooting.

That's exactly what Humphrey did to gritty George Mason. Fresh off a stunning run to the Final Four, Mason hung with Florida for 20 minutes, but at the start of the second half Humphrey and the Gators took off. In the locker room at intermission, Donovan stressed what kind of quality shots he wanted: layups, dunks and Lee Humphrey. Running a perfect inside-out game, Humphrey scored 16 of his game-high 19 points in the second half as the Gators sent Cinderella home with a 73–58 defeat.

"I was feeling as good as I've ever felt shooting the ball," said Humphrey. "They were collapsing on our big guys and coach told them to post up deeper so they could kick it out. That's what they did and all I had to do was knock them down."

Added Brewer, "Humphrey is a silent assassin. He doesn't get much hype, but he wins games for the Gators."

A few hours after Florida made its second national title game in six years, Gators fans were partying in the lobby of the Omni Severin Hotel in downtown Indianapolis. One floor below in a windowless bunker, Donovan and his staff gathered in the wee hours to break down film and formulate a game plan for UCLA, which steamrolled LSU in the other semifinal. Well-coached and not afraid to play ugly, the Florida coaches had reason to worry about UCLA and crafty point guard Jordan Farmar. "We've never guarded screen action like this," said Gators assistant Donnie Jones. "They're so spaced and they like to go wide. They run some real good stuff."

Standing before a massive dry-erase board, Donovan summed up how the Gators had to defend Farmar, for which

UCLA ran a plethora of screens and pick-and-rolls.

"You can't have two guys go out and play him," said Donovan. "That will leave one of their bigs wide open and that's exactly what they want. You want to make him turn the corner and take it to our bigs and throw it out. Don't go out on him. Don't run two guys at the ball."

Florida employed that strategy two nights later and it worked to perfection. The Gators took the Bruins out of their rhythm and rode Noah (16 points, nine rebounds and six blocks) to a 73–57 victory. Noah was brilliant throughout, altering far more shots than he blocked and exhibiting enthusiasm that was infectious. Florida's defense, which held UCLA to 36.1% shooting, was fantastic as was Humphrey, who buried the Bruins with three quick three-pointers to start the second half. Exclaimed Noah as he clutched the championship trophy: "This is better than sex!"

In the aftermath of the celebration, Donovan put the Gators' victory in perspective. Florida, a football school, was the king of college basketball because it was able to put everything together at the right time. But if the tournament were played all over again, Donovan knows the result probably would have been different. "We're sitting up here today as the national champions," the coach said. "But I still don't necessarily believe that we may be the best team in the country because when you're playing in an event that's a one-shot deal, anything can happen."

If anyone can relate to that statement it's George Mason. The Patriots weren't even supposed to make the NCAAs after losing to Hofstra in the semifinals of the Colonial Athletic Association tournament. But Mason made the field as a No. 11 seed, immediately drawing the ire of CBS commentators Jim Nantz and Billy Packer, and then took the Cinderella slipper and smashed it over the heads of Michigan State, North Carolina, Wichita State and Connecticut.

After beating the Spartans and the defending champion Tar Heels to get to the

Scrappy underdog George Mason embarassed pundits and opponents alike during its run to the Final Four.

WIN McNAMEE/GETTY IMAGES

Sweet 16, the Patriots were featured on the cover of *Sports Illustrated*, something that the team initially thought was a joke. "We thought Lamar [Butler's] dad might have put it together or something," said reserve swingman Gabe Norwood.

It wasn't, and with each game, coach Jim Larranaga's team proved it was for real. Still, Mason was a heavy underdog in its Elite Eight game against UConn, whom most experts had pegged as the pre-tournament favorite. But the sage Larranaga kept his troops loose with innovative motivational tactics. Before the upset of North Carolina, Larranaga told his players if the Tar Heels were Supermen, "we're going to be their kryptonite." And prior to the UConn game he told his troops that George Mason's conference, the CAA, stood for the "Connecticut Assassin Association."

The Patriots took Larranaga's words to heart and pulled off arguably the biggest upset in NCAA tournament history by defeating the No. 1-seeded Huskies, 86–84, in overtime. When it was over, Mason danced on the floor of the Verizon Center in Washington, D.C. and an entire nation cheered with them. The most improbable sports underdog story became a reality: George Mason was going to the Final Four!

A few hours later, when the team returned to their Fairfax, Va., campus, 6,000 fans cheered as they walked inside the Patriots Center. There, Larranaga greeted the boisterous crowd with a message: "From the bottom of my heart and on behalf of this basketball team, thank you for coming," he said. "Drive home safely and we'll see you in Indy!"

Two players whom many expected to be in Indy were Duke's J.J. Redick and Gonzaga's Adam Morrison, who engaged in a season-long battle for the scoring title and Player of the Year honors. The race was on ever since Dec. 10 when Redick exploded for 41 points in a rout of Texas and Morrison answered a few hours later day by banking in a ridiculous three-pointer at the buzzer to beat Oklahoma State in Seattle. Back and

BASEBALL POURS IT ON
<<< TOM VERDUCCI PREVIEWS THE WORLD CLASSIC
COCO CRISP GETS HIS RED SOX BAPTISM >>>

Sports Illustrated

WHO'S THE
BEST?
MORRISON vs. REDICK

PLUS

EXCLUSIVE PLAYERS POLL
THE MOST: Feared Shooters, Respected Coaches,
Frightening Fans and More . . .

Final Olympic Highs and Lows
Rick Reilly on Shani's Mom

MARCH 6, 2006 www.SI.com
JML Kersserk: Sports Illustrated

For much of the year, Redick and Morrison seemed to to be playing a game of "anything you can do, I can do better."

On the women's side, it was all about the ACC as the conference sent three teams—Duke, North Carolina and upstart Maryland—to the Final Four in Boston. There, they were joined by LSU and superstar Seimone Augustus. The top-ranked Tar Heels came in as the favorites, but they were soundly defeated by the young Terps, 81–70. Duke knocked off LSU in the other semifinal, settling up a Duke-Maryland clash for the fourth time of the season.

Prior to the ACC semifinals, Duke had won 14 straight over Maryland, but the up-and-coming Terps (their starting lineup consisted of two freshmen, two sophomores and a junior) had snapped that streak in the ACC tournament and so they entered the championship game playing with confidence and moxie. And Maryland never wavered, even after falling behind by 13 points, and battled back to send the game into overtime on Kristi Toliver's devastating step-back three-pointer.

Duke was deflated and like the Florida men, Maryland came out of nowhere to win the national title with an improbable 78–75 victory. "We've raised the bar high," said Toliver. I think we gained the respect we rightfully earned. Hop on the bandwagon, we're happy to have you."

And just like that another season was in the books with a pair of improbable and precocious champions, who showed heart and desire. Florida and Maryland may have finished on top of the college basketball world, but there were many winners. That's the beauty of the game. Even those who don't cut down the nets can leave you with a warm feeling in your gut after paying no attention to the prognosticators and proving that anything is possible.

forth they went, the respective scoring averages separated by just tenths of a point.

Redick and Morrison had met at a summer camp in 2004 and began text messaging one another and throughout this season they dueled in Xbox Halo 2 games over the Internet. "We've talked about how this whole thing between us has been created," said Redick. "I'll be watching Adam's game and Dick Vitale is calling me out and the fans are chanting, 'J.J. who?' Before we were just two buddies playing Halo together, and now we're like, 'Do you think our calls are being monitored?' But it's cool. Anytime you have story lines, it's good for the sport."

The tête-à-tête was great for college basketball and many hoops fans hoped that the battle would be decided at the Final Four. But both Redick and Morrison fell short in the Sweet 16—Duke lost to LSU, while UCLA eliminated Gonzaga—and Morrison won the scoring race, while Redick took home most of the Player of the Year awards.

NCAA Men's Championship Game Box Score

Florida 73

	Min	FG M-A	FT M-A	Reb O-T	A	PF	TP
C. Brewer	37	4-12	1-3	3-7	4	3	11
J. Noah	33	7-9	2-2	2-9	3	2	16
A. Horford	24	5-8	4-5	2-7	3	2	14
T. Green	36	1-9	0-1	0-4	8	1	2
L. Humphrey	36	4-8	3-3	0-1	2	1	15
A. Moss	10	3-6	3-4	2-6	0	0	9
W. Hodge	12	0-3	0-0	0-1	1	1	0
C. Richards	12	2-3	2-2	0-0	0	3	6
Totals		26-58	15-20	9-35	21	13	73

Percentages: FG-.448, FT-.750. 3-Point Goals: 6-19, .316 (C. Brewer 2-3, T. Green 0-7, L. Humphrey 4-8, W. Hodge 0-1). Team Rebounds: 35. Blocked Shots: 10 (C. Brewer 1, J. Noah 6, A. Horford 2, C. Richards 1). Turnovers: 6 (C. Brewers 2, J. Noah 2, A. Horford 1, T. Green 1,). Steals: 7 (C. Brewer 3, J. Noah 1, T Green 1, W. Hodge 2).
Halftime: Florida 36, UCLA 25.

A: 43,168.

UCLA 57

	Min	FG M-A	FT M-A	Reb O-T	A	PF	TP
C. Bozeman	25	2-3	5-6	0-3	3	2	9
L. Moute	32	3-9		3-10	1	4	6
R. Hollins	26	4-10	2-2	5-10	0	2	10
J. Farmar	34	8-21	1-2	0-2	4	2	18
A. Afflalo	32	3-10	2-2	0-2	1	2	10
D. Collison	21	0-3	0-0	1-3	1	3	0
A. Aboya	14	1-1	0-2	2-3	1	2	2
L. Mata	9	1-4	0-0	2-5	0	3	2
M. Roll	7	0-0	0-0	0-0	0	2	0
Totals		22-61	10-14	13-38	11	22	57

Percentages: FG-.361, FT-.714. 3-Point Goals:3-17, .176 (L. Moute 0-2, J. Farmar 1-8, A. Afflalo 2-7). Team Rebounds: 38. Blocked Shots: 1 (L. Mata 1). Turnovers: 12 (C. Bozeman 2, R. Hollins 1, J Farmar 2, A. Afflalo 3, D. Collison 3, L. Mata 1). Steals: 3 (J. Farmar 2, A. Afflalo 1).
Officials: James Burr, John Cahill, Tony Greene

Final Regular Season AP Top 25 Poll

1. Duke (59)	32-4
2. Connecticut (11)	30-4
3. Villanova (1)	28-5
4. Memphis	33-4
5. Gonzaga (1)	29-4
6. Ohio St.	26-6
7. Boston College	28-8
8. UCLA	32-7
9. Texas	30-7
10. North Carolina	23-8
11. Florida	33-6
12. Kansas	25-8
13. Illinois	26-7
14. George Washington	27-3
15. Iowa	25-9
16. Pittsburgh	25-8
17. Washington	26-7
18. Tennessee	22-8
19. LSU	27-9
20. Nevada	27-6
21. Syracuse	23-12
22. West Virginia	22-11
23. Georgetown	23-10
24. Oklahoma	20-9
25. UAB	24-7

National Invitation Tournament Scores

Opening round: Manhattan 80, Fairleigh Dickinson 77; Penn St 71, Rutgers 76; UTEP 85, Lipscomb 66; Temple 73, Akron 80 (OT); Northern Arizona 53, Delaware 54; Stanford 65, Virginia 49; Charlotte 77, Georgia Southern 61; Miami (Ohio) 52, Butler 53
First round: Maryland 84, Manhattan 87; Colorado 61, Old Dominion 79; St. Joseph's 71, Rutgers 62; Hofstra 73, Nebraska 62; Michigan 82, UTEP 67; Vanderbilt 69, Notre Dame 79; Creighton 71, Akron 60; Miami (Fla.) 62, Oklahoma St. 62; Louisville 71, Delaware 54; Clemson 69, La. Tech 53; Missouri St. 76, Stanford 67; Houston 77, Brigham Young 67; Cincinnati 86, Charlotte 80; Minnesota 73, Wake Forest 58; Florida St 67, Butler 63; South Carolina 74, W. Kentucky 55
Second round: Manhattan 66, Old Dominion 70; St. Joseph's 75, Hofstra 77 (OT); Michigan 87, Notre Dame 84 (2OT); Creighton 52, Miami (Fla.) 53; Louisville 74, Clemson 68; Missouri St. 60, Houston 59; Cincinnati 76, Minnesota 62; Florida St 68, South Carolina 69 (OT)
Quarterfinals: Old Dominion 61, Hofstra 51; Michigan 71, Miami (Fla.) 65; Louisville 74, Missouri St. 60; Cincinnati 62, South Carolina 65
Semifinals: Old Dominion 43, Michigan 66; Louisville 63, South Carolina 78
Championship Game: South Carolina 76, Michigan 64

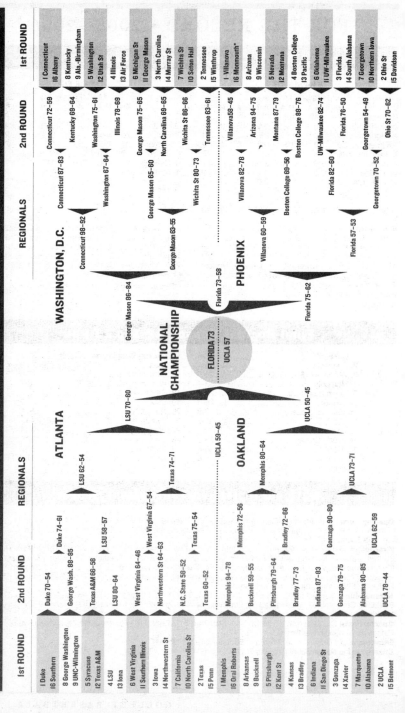

2006 NCAA Basketball Men's Division I Tournament

1st ROUND — **2nd ROUND** — **REGIONALS** — **REGIONALS** — **2nd ROUND** — **1st ROUND**

WASHINGTON, D.C.

1 Connecticut — Connecticut 72–59
16 Albany
8 Kentucky — Kentucky 69–64
9 Ala.-Birmingham
5 Washington — Washington 75–61
12 Utah St
4 Illinois — Illinois 78–69
13 Air Force
6 Michigan St — George Mason 75–65
11 George Mason
3 North Carolina — North Carolina 69–65
14 Murray St
7 Wichita St — Wichita St 86–66
10 Seton Hall
2 Tennessee — Tennessee 63–61
15 Winthrop

Connecticut 87–83
Washington 67–64
George Mason 65–60
Wichita St 80–73

Connecticut 98–92
George Mason 63–55

George Mason 86–84

PHOENIX

1 Villanova — Villanova58–45
16 Monmouth*
8 Arizona — Arizona 94–75
9 Wisconsin
5 Nevada — Montana 87–79
12 Montana
4 Boston College — Boston College 88–76
13 Pacific
6 Oklahoma — UW-Milwaukee 82–74
11 UW-Milwaukee
3 Florida — Florida 76–50
14 South Alabama
7 Georgetown — Georgetown 54–49
10 Northern Iowa
2 Ohio St — Ohio St 70–62
15 Davidson

Villanova 82–78
Boston College 69–56
Florida 82–60
Georgetown 70–52

Villanova 60–59
Florida 57–53

Florida 75–62

Florida 73–58

NATIONAL CHAMPIONSHIP

FLORIDA 73
UCLA 57

ATLANTA

1 Duke — Duke 70–54
16 Southern
8 George Washington — George Wash. 88–85
9 UNC-Wilmington
5 Syracuse — Texas A&M 66–58
12 Texas A&M
4 LSU — LSU 80–64
13 Iona
6 West Virginia — West Virginia 64–46
11 Southern Illinois
3 Iowa — Northwestern St 64–63
14 Northwestern St
7 California — N.C. State 58–52
10 North Carolina St
2 Texas — Texas 60–52
15 Penn

Duke 74–61
LSU 58–57
West Virginia 67–54
Texas 75–54

LSU 62–54
Texas 74–71

LSU 70–60

OAKLAND

1 Memphis — Memphis 94–78
16 Oral Roberts
8 Arkansas — Bucknell 59–55
9 Bucknell
5 Pittsburgh — Pittsburgh 79–64
12 Kent St
4 Kansas — Bradley 77–73
13 Bradley
6 Indiana — Indiana 87–83
11 San Diego St
3 Gonzaga — Gonzaga 79–75
14 Xavier
7 Marquette — Alabama 90–85
10 Alabama
2 UCLA — UCLA 78–44
15 Belmont

Memphis 72–56
Bradley 72–66
Gonzaga 90–80
UCLA 62–59

Memphis 80–64
UCLA 73–71

UCLA 50–45

UCLA 59–45

LSU 70–60

America East

	Conference			All Games		
	W	L	Pct	W	L	Pct
Albany	13	3	.813	21	11	.636
Binghamtom	12	4	.750	16	13	.464
Hartford	9	7	.562	13	15	.464
Boston Univ.	9	7	.562	11	16	.407
New Hampshire	8	8	.500	12	17	.414
Vermont	7	9	.438	13	17	.433
Maine	7	9	.438	12	16	.428
UMBC	5	11	.313	10	19	.344
Stony Brook	2	14	.125	4	24	.142
Hartford	4	14	.222	8	20	.286

Atlantic Coast

	Conference			All Games		
	W	L	Pct	W	L	Pct
Duke	14	2	.875	32	4	.888
North Carolina	12	4	.750	23	8	.742
Boston College	11	5	.688	28	8	.777
North Carolina St	10	6	.625	22	10	.687
Florida St	9	7	.562	19	9	.678
Maryland	8	8	.500	19	13	.608
Clemson	7	9	.438	18	12	.600
Miami (Fla.)	7	9	.438	16	15	.516
Virginia	7	9	438	16	15	.516
Virginia Tech	4	12	.250	14	16	.466
Georgia Tech	4	12	.250	11	17	.392
Wake Forest	3	13	.188	17	17	.500

Atlantic Sun

	Conference			All Games		
	W	L	Pct	W	L	Pct
Lipscomb	15	5	.750	21	11	.656
Belmont	15	5	.750	20	11	.645
Florida Atlantic	14	6	.700	15	13	.582
Gardner-Webb	13	7	.650	17	12	.586
East Tenn. St.	12	8	.600	15	13	.582
Stetson	11	9	.550	14	18	.437
Kennesaw St.	10	10	.500	12	16	.428
Campbell	9	11	.450	10	18	.357
Mercer	7	13	.350	9	19	.321
North Florida	3	17	.150	6	22	.214
Jacksonville	1	19	.050	1	26	.037

Atlantic 10

	Conference			All Games		
	W	L	Pct	W	L	Pct
George Washington	16	0	1.000	27	3	.900
Charlotte	11	5	.688	19	13	.593
La Salle	10	6	.625	18	10	.642
St. Louis	10	6	.625	16	13	.034
St. Joseph's	9	7	.562	18	13	.580
Fordham	9	7	.562	16	16	.500
Xavier	8	8	.500	21	11	.375
Temple	8	8	.500	17	15	.531
Rhode Island	8	8	.500	14	14	.500
Massachusetts	8	8	.500	13	15	.464
Dayton	6	10	.375	14	17	.451
Richmond	6	10	.375	13	17	.433
St. Bonaventure	2	14	.125	8	19	.296
Duquesne	1	15	.065	3	24	.111

Big East

	Conference			All Games		
	W	L	Pct	W	L	Pct
Connecticut	14	2	.875	30	4	.882
Villanova	14	2	.875	28	5	.848
West Virginia	11	5	.688	22	11	.666
Pittsburgh	10	6	.625	25	8	.757
Georgetown	10	6	.625	23	10	.696
Marquette	10	6	.625	20	11	.645
Seton Hall	9	7	.562	18	12	.600
Cincinnati	8	8	.500	21	13	.617
Syracuse	7	9	.438	23	12	.657
Rutgers	7	9	.438	19	14	.575
Louisville	6	10	.375	21	13	.617
Notre Dame	5	11	.312	12	15	.444
DePaul	5	11	.312	12	15	.444
Providence	5	11	.312	12	15	.444
St. John's	5	11	.312	12	15	.444
South Florida	1	15	.062	7	22	.241

Big Sky

	Conference			All Games		
	W	L	Pct	W	L	Pct
Northern Arizona	12	2	.857	20	11	.645
Montana	10	4	.714	24	7	.774
Eastern Washington	9	5	.642	15	15	.500
Montana St	7	7	.500	14	15	.482
Sacramento St	5	9	.357	14	15	.482
Portland St	5	9	.357	12	16	.428
Idaho St	4	10	.286	13	13	.500
Weber St	4	10	.214	10	17	.037

Big South

	Conference			All Games		
	W	L	Pct	W	L	Pct
Winthrop	13	3	.812	23	8	.741
Birmingham Southern	12	4	.750	18	9	.666
Coastal Carolina	12	4	.750	20	10	.666
Radford	9	7	.562	15	13	.535
High Point	8	8	.500	16	13	.551
Charleston Southern	7	9	.438	13	16	.448
UNC-Asheville	6	10	.375	9	19	.321
Liberty	3	13	.188	5	23	.178
VMI	2	14	.125	7	20	.259

Big 10

	Conference			All Games		
	W	L	Pct	W	L	Pct
Ohio St	12	4	.750	26	6	.812
Illinois	11	5	.688	26	7	.787
Iowa	11	5	.688	25	9	.735
Indiana	9	7	.562	19	12	.703
Wisconsin	9	7	.562	19	12	.703
Michigan	8	8	.500	22	11	.726
Michigan St	8	8	.500	22	12	.647
Penn St	6	10	.375	15	15	.500
Northwestern	6	10	.375	15	14	.517
Minnesota	5	11	.312	9	19	.321
Purdue	3	13	.187	9	19	.321

Note: Standings based on regular-season conference play only; overall records include all tournament play.

Big 12

	Conference			All Games		
	W	L	Pct	W	L	Pct
Texas	13	3	.812	30	7	.810
Kansas	13	3	.812	25	8	.825
Oklahoma	11	5	.687	20	9	.689
Texas A&M	10	6	.625	22	9	.709
Colorado	9	7	.562	20	10	.666
Nebraska	9	7	.562	19	14	.575
Kansas St	7	9	.437	15	13	.535
Iowa St	6	10	.375	16	14	.533
Oklahoma St	6	10	.375	17	16	.515
Texas Tech	6	10	.375	15	17	.468
Missouri	5	11	.312	12	16	.428
Baylor	4	12	.250	4	13	.235

Big West

	Conference			All Games		
	W	L	Pct	W	L	Pct
Pacific	12	2	.857	24	8	.750
UC-Irvine	10	4	.714	16	12	.571
Long Beach St	9	5	.642	18	12	.600
Cal Poly	7	7	.500	9	19	.321
UC-Santa Barb.	7	8	.466	14	14	.500
CSU-Fullerton	6	9	.400	15	13	.535
CSU-Northridge	4	11	.266	11	17	.392
UC-Riverside	3	12	.200	5	22	.185

Colonial

	Conference			All Games		
	W	L	Pct	W	L	Pct
George Mason	15	3	.833	27	8	.771
UNC-Wilmington	15	3	.833	25	8	.757
Hofstra	14	4	.777	24	6	.800
Old Dominion	13	5	.722	24	10	.705
Northeastern	12	6	.666	18	11	.620
VCU	11	7	.611	19	10	.655
Drexel	8	10	.444	15	16	.483
Towson	8	10	.444	12	16	.037
Delaware	4	14	.222	9	22	.290
William & Mary	3	15	.166	8	20	.285
Georgia St	3	15	.166	7	22	.241
James Madison	2	16	.111	5	22	.185

Conference USA

	Conference			All Games		
	W	L	Pct	W	L	Pct
Memphis	13	1	.928	33	4	.891
UAB	12	2	.857	24	7	.774
UTEP	11	3	.785	21	10	.677
Houston	9	5	.642	20	9	.689
Central Florida	8	7	.533	14	15	.482
Tulane	7	8	.466	12	16	.428
Rice	6	9	.400	11	16	.407
Tulsa	6	9	.400	11	17	.392
SMU	5	10	.333	13	16	.448
Marshall	5	10	.333	12	16	.428
Southern Miss	4	11	.266	10	21	.476
East Caro	2	13	.133	8	20	.285

Horizon League

	Conference			All Games		
	W	L	Pct	W	L	Pct
UW-Milwaukee	14	4	.777	22	9	.709
Butler	12	6	.666	20	13	.606
Loyola (Ill.)	9	9	.563	19	11	.633
Ill.-Chicago	9	9	.500	16	15	.516
Detroit	9	9	.500	16	16	.500
UW-Green Bay	9	9	.500	15	16	.483
Wright St	8	9	.470	13	15	.464
Cleveland St	5	12	.294	10	18	.357
Youngstown St	4	13	.235	7	21	.250

Ivy League

	Conference			All Games		
	W	L	Pct	W	L	Pct
Penn	12	2	.859	20	9	.689
Princeton	10	4	.714	12	15	.444
Cornell	8	6	.571	13	15	.464
Yale	7	7	.500	15	14	.517
Brown	6	8	.428	10	17	.370
Harvard	5	9	.357	13	14	.481
Columbia	4	10	.285	11	16	.407
Dartmouth	4	10	.285	6	20	.230

Metro Atlantic

	Conference			All Games		
	W	L	Pct	W	L	Pct
Manhattan	14	4	.777	18	10	.642
Iona	13	5	.722	23	8	.741
Marist	12	6	.666	19	10	.655
Siena	10	8	.555	15	13	.535
St. Peters	9	9	.500	17	15	.531
Loyola (Md.)	8	10	.444	15	13	.535
Fairfield	7	10	.411	9	19	.321
Niagara	7	11	.388	11	18	.379
Canisius	6	12	.333	9	20	.310
Rider	4	14	.222	8	19	.296

Mid-American

	Conference			All Games		
EAST	W	L	Pct	W	L	Pct
Kent St	15	3	.833	25	9	.735
Akron	14	4	.777	22	10	.687
Miami (Ohio)	14	4	.777	18	11	.620
Ohio	10	8	.555	18	11	.620
Buffalo	8	10	.444	18	13	.580
Bowling Green	5	13	.277	8	21	.275
WEST						
Northern Illinois	12	6	.666	17	11	.607
Toledo	10	8	.555	20	11	.645
Western Michigan	10	8	.555	14	17	.451
Ball St	6	12	.333	10	18	.357
Eastern Michigan	3	15	.166	7	21	.250
Central Michigan	1	17	.055	4	24	.142

Mid-Continent

	Conference			All Games		
	W	L	Pct	W	L	Pct
Oral Roberts	14	3	.823	21	12	.636
IUPUI	14	3	.823	17	10	.629
UMKC	11	5	.687	14	14	.500
Valparaiso	8	8	.500	17	12	.586
Chicago St.	8	8	.500	11	19	.366
Southern Utah	8	8	.500	10	20	.333
Oakland	6	11	.353	11	18	.379
Western Ill.	3	14	.176	6	21	.222
Centenary	2	14	.125	4	23	.148

Mid-Eastern Athletic

	Conference			All Games		
	W	L	Pct	W	L	Pct
Delaware St	16	2	.888	21	14	.600
Coppin St	12	6	.666	12	18	.400
Bethune-Cookman	11	6	.647	15	14	.517
South Carolina St	11	7	.611	14	15	.482
Hampton	10	8	.555	16	16	.500
Florida A&M	10	8	.555	14	17	.451
Norfolk St.	10	8	.555	13	18	.419
North Carolina A&T	6	12	.333	6	23	.206
Howard	5	13	.277	7	21	.250
Md.-Eastern Shore	4	14	.222	7	22	.241
Morgan St.	3	14	.176	3	26	.103

Missouri Valley

	Conference			All Games		
	W	L	Pct	W	L	Pct
Wichita St	14	4	.777	26	9	.742
Missouri St	12	6	.666	20	8	.714
Creighton	12	6	.666	19	9	.678
Southern Illinois	12	6	.666	22	11	.666
Northern Iowa	11	7	.611	23	10	.696
Bradley	11	7	.611	22	11	.666
Drake	5	13	.277	12	19	.387
Evansville	5	13	.277	10	19	.344
Indiana St	4	14	.222	13	16	.448
Illinois St	4	14	.222	9	19	.321

Mountain West

	Conference			All Games		
	W	L	Pct	W	L	Pct
San Diego St	13	3	.812	24	9	.727
Air Force	12	4	.750	24	7	.774
Brigham Young	12	4	.750	20	9	.689
UNLV	10	6	.625	17	13	.566
New Mexico	8	8	.500	17	13	.566
Utah	6	10	.375	14	15	.482
Wyoming	5	11	.312	14	18	.437
Colorado St	4	12	.250	16	15	.516
TCU	2	14	.125	6	25	.193

Northeast

	Conference			All Games		
	W	L	Pct	W	L	Pct
Fairleigh Dickinson	14	4	.777	20	12	.625
Cent. Connecticut St	13	5	.722	18	11	.620
Monmouth	12	6	.666	19	15	.558
Mt. St. Mary's	11	7	.611	13	17	.433
Robert Morris	10	8	.555	15	14	.517
Long Island	9	9	.500	12	16	.428
Sacred Heart	8	10	.444	11	17	.392
Quinnipac	7	11	.388	12	16	.428
St. Francis (N.Y.)	7	11	.388	10	17	.370
Wagner	6	12	.333	13	14	.481
St. Francis (Pa.)	2	16	.250	4	24	.142
Murray St.	17	3	.850	24	7	.705

Ohio Valley

	Conference			All Games		
	W	L	Pct	W	L	Pct
Samford	14	6	.700	20	11	.645
Tennessee Tech	13	7	.650	19	12	.612
Jacksonville	12	8	.600	16	13	.551
Austin Peay	11	9	.550	17	14	.548
Tennessee St	11	9	.550	13	15	.464
Eastern Kentucky	11	9	.550	13	16	.448
Tenn.-Martin	9	11	.450	13	15	.464
Eastern Illinois	5	15	.250	6	21	.222
SE Missouri St	4	16	.200	7	20	.259
Morehead St	3	17	.150	4	23	.148

Pac 10

	Conference			All Games		
	W	L	Pct	W	L	Pct
UCLA	14	4	.778	32	7	.821
Washington	13	5	.722	26	7	.788
California	12	6	.667	20	11	.646
Arizona	11	7	.611	20	13	.606
Stanford	11	7	.611	16	14	.533
USC	8	10	.444	17	13	.567
Oregon	7	11	.389	15	18	.455
Oregon St	5	13	.278	13	18	.419
Arizona St	5	13	.278	11	17	.393
Washington St	4	14	.222	11	17	.393

Patriot League

	Conference			All Games		
	W	L	Pct	W	L	Pct
Bucknell	14	0	1.00	27	5	.844
Holy Cross	11	3	.786	20	12	.625
Lehigh	11	3	.786	19	12	.613
American	7	7	.500	12	17	.414
Lafayette	5	9	.357	10	17	.370
Colgate	4	10	.286	10	19	.345
Navy	3	11	.214	9	18	.333
Army	1	13	.071	3	22	.120

Southeastern

EAST	Conference			All Games		
	W	L	Pct	W	L	Pct
Tennessee	12	4	.750	22	8	.733
Florida	10	6	.625	33	6	.846
Kentucky	9	7	.563	22	13	.629
Vanderbilt	7	9	.438	17	13	.567
South Carolina	6	10	.375	23	15	.605
Georgia	5	11	.313	15	15	.500
WEST						
LSU	14	2	.875	27	9	.750
Arkansas	10	6	.625	22	10	.686
Alabama	10	6	.625	18	13	.581
Mississippi St	5	11	.313	15	15	.500
Mississippi	4	12	.250	14	16	.467
Auburn	4	12	.250	12	16	.429

Southern

NORTH	Conference			All Games		
	W	L	Pct	W	L	Pct
Elon	10	4	.714	15	14	.517
Chattanooga	8	6	.571	18	13	.581
Western Carolina	7	7	.500	13	17	.433
Appalachian St	6	8	.429	14	16	.033
UNC-Greensboro	4	10	.285	12	19	.387
SOUTH						
Georgia Southern	11	4	.733	20	10	.667
Davidson	10	5	.667	18	11	.621
Col. of Charleston	9	6	.600	15	11	.577
Furman	8	7	.533	14	13	.519
Wofford	6	9	.400	11	18	.379
The Citadel	1	14	.067	8	21	.034

Southland

	Conference			All Games		
	W	L	Pct	W	L	Pct
Northwestern St	15	1	.938	26	8	.765
Sam Houston St	11	5	.688	22	9	.710
SE Louisiana	10	6	.625	15	12	.556
Stephen F. Austin	9	7	.563	16	12	.571
Lamar	9	7	.563	17	14	.548
McNeese St	9	7	.563	14	14	.500
Tex.-Arlington	7	9	.438	13	16	.034
Tex.-San Antonio	6	10	.375	10	17	.370
La.-Monroe	6	10	.375	9	18	.321
Nicholls St	5	11	.313	9	18	.321
Texas St	1	15	.063	3	24	.111

Southwestern Athletic

	Conference			All Games		
	W	L	Pct	W	L	Pct
Southern Univ.	18	3	.857	19	13	.594
Grambling	12	8	.600	14	13	.519
Alabama A&M	11	8	.579	13	13	.500
Jackson St.	11	9	.550	15	17	.469
Alabama St.	10	9	.526	12	18	.400
Ark.-Pine Bluff	10	11	.476	13	16	.448
Mississippi Valley St	9	10	.474	9	19	.321
Alcorn St.	8	11	.421	8	20	.286
Texas Southern	6	12	.333	8	22	.267
Prairie View	2	16	.111	5	24	.172

Sun Belt

EAST	Conference			All Games		
	W	L	Pct	W	L	Pct
Western Kentucky	12	2	.857	23	8	.742
Mid. Tennessee St	8	6	.571	15	12	.556
Arkansas St	7	7	.500	12	18	.400
Ark.-Little Rock	5	9	.357	12	15	.444
Florida Int'l	4	10	.286	8	20	.286
WEST						
South Alabama	12	3	.800	24	7	.745
Denver	7	8	.467	16	15	.516
La.-Lafayette	7	8	.467	13	16	.448
North Texas	6	9	.400	14	14	.500
Troy	6	9	.400	14	15	.483
New Orleans	6	9	.400	9	19	.321

West Coast

	Conference			All Games		
	W	L	Pct	W	L	Pct
Gonzaga	14	0	1.000	29	4	.878
St. Mary's (Ca.)	8	6	.571	17	12	.586
Loyola-Marymount	8	6	.571	12	18	.400
San Francisco	7	7	.500	11	17	.393
San Diego	6	8	.429	18	12	.600
Santa Clara	5	9	.357	13	16	.448
Portland	5	9	.357	11	18	.379
Pepperdine	3	11	.214	7	20	.259

Western Athletic

	Conference			All Games		
	W	L	Pct	W	L	Pct
Nevada	13	3	.812	27	6	.818
Utah St	11	5	.688	23	9	.742
Louisiana Tech	11	5	.688	20	13	.606
Hawaii	10	6	.625	17	11	.607
New Mexico St	10	6	.625	16	14	.533
Fresno St	8	8	.500	15	13	.536
Boise St	6	10	.375	14	15	.483
San Jose St	2	14	.125	6	25	.194
Idaho	1	15	.062	3	25	.107

Independents

	Conference			All Games		
	W	L	Pct	W	L	Pct
Tex. A&M-Corp. Chrs.	10	1	.909	19	8	.703
Utah Valley St	8	3	.727	16	13	.552
IPFW	6	5	.545	9	18	.333
South Dakota St	5	4	.556	9	20	.310
North Dakota St	3	3	.500	15	12	.556
UC-Davis	1	1	.500	7	20	.259
Savannah St	1	2	.333	2	27	.069
Longwood	2	4	.333	10	20	.333
Northern Colorado	2	7	.222	5	24	.172
Tex.-Pan American	1	9	.100	6	24	.200

Scoring

	Class	GP	FG	3FG	FT	Pts	Avg
Adam Morrison, Gonzaga	Jr.	33	306	74	240	926	28.1
J.J. Redick, Duke	Sr.	36	302	139	221	964	26.8
Keydren Clark, St. Peter's	Sr.	32	273	105	189	840	26.3
Andre Collins, Loyola (Md.)	Sr.	28	256	118	101	731	26.1
Brion Rush, Grambling	Sr.	21	189	54	109	541	25.8
Quincy Douby, Rutgers	Jr.	33	287	116	149	839	25.4
Steve Burtt, Iona	Sr.	31	258	96	168	780	25.2
Rodney Stuckey, Eastern Washington	Fr.	30	250	55	171	726	24.2
Alan Daniels, Lamar	Sr.	31	250	75	155	730	23.5
Trey Johnson, Jackson St.	Jr.	32	255	67	174	751	23.5
Whit Holcomb-Faye, Radford	Sr.	29	202	83	182	669	23.1
Larry Blair, Liberty	Jr.	30	234	64	147	679	22.6
Tim Smith, East Tennessee St.	Sr.	28	238	41	100	617	22.0
Roy Booker, SE Missouri St	Sr.	27	178	73	165	594	22.0
Morris Almond, Rice	Jr.	28	224	48	116	612	21.9
Nick Fazekas, Nevada	Jr.	33	268	31	154	721	21.8
Elton Nesbitt, Georgia Southern	Sr.	30	211	103	126	651	21.7
Jose Juan Barea, Northeastern	Sr.	29	209	66	126	610	21.0
Caleb Green, Oral Roberts	Jr.	33	224	3	235	686	20.8
Kenny Adeleke, Hartford	Sr.	28	223	0	133	579	20.7
Jarrius Jackson, Texas Tech	Jr.	32	216	73	152	657	20.5
Randy Foye, Villanova	Sr.	33	226	89	136	677	20.5
Leon Powe, California	So.	27	178	3	194	553	20.5
Quinton Day, UMKC	Jr.	27	186	73	103	548	20.3
Brandon Roy, Washington	Sr.	33	228	39	171	666	20.2

FIELD-GOAL PERCENTAGE

	Class	GP	FG	FGA	Pct
Randall Hanke, Providence	So.	27	149	220	67.7
Cedric Smith, Tex. A&M-CC	Jr.	27	139	210	66.2
Joakim Noah, Florida	So.	39	202	322	62.7
James Augustine, Illinois	Sr.	33	174	279	62.4
Michael Harrison, Colorado St.	Jr.	31	160	257	62.3
Kyle Hines, UNC-Greensboro	So.	30	239	384	62.2
Nate Harris, Utah St.	Sr.	32	215	346	62.1
Eric Williams, Wake Forest	Sr.	34	223	360	61.9
Kibwe Trim, Sacred Heart	Sr.	28	194	314	61.8
Michael So.uthall, La.-Lafayette	Sr.	28	164	266	61.7

Note: Minimum 5 made per game.

FREE-THROW PERCENTAGE

	Class	GP	FT	FTA	Pct
Blake Ahearn, Missouri St.	Jr.	31	117	125	93.6
J. Anderson, New Hampshire	Jr.	26	68	74	91.9
Shawan Robison, Clemson	Sr.	32	84	92	91.3
Derek Raivio, Gonzaga	Jr.	31	83	91	91.2
A. Vogelsberg, Middle Tenn. St.	Jr.	28	108	119	90.8
Gerry McNamara, Syracuse	Sr.	35	111	123	90.2
Andre Collins, Loyola (Md.)	Sr.	28	101	112	90.2
Chris Hernandez, Stanford	Sr.	30	109	121	90.1
Daniel Horton, Michigan	Sr.	33	136	151	90.1
Walker Russell, Jacksonville St.	Sr.	29	112	125	89.6

Note: Minimum 2.5 made per game.

REBOUNDS

	Class	GP	Reb	Avg
Paul Millsap, Louisiana Tech	Jr.	33	438	13.3
Kenny Adeleke, Hartford	Sr.	29	366	13.1
R. Jones-Jenning, Ark.-Little Rock	Jr.	29	329	11.3
Curtis Withers, Charlotte	Sr.	32	362	11.3
Ivan Almonte, Florida Int'l	Sr.	25	281	11.2
Marcus Slaughter, San Diego St.	Jr.	30	329	11.0
Justin Williams, Wyoming	Sr.	30	329	10.9
Yemi Nicholas, Denver	Sr.	31	339	10.9
Harding Nana, Delaware	Sr.	30	326	10.9
Ricky Woods, SE Louisiana	Sr.	28	304	10.9

ASSISTS

	Class	GP	A	Avg
Jared Jordan, Marist	Jr.	29	247	8.5
Jose Juan Barea, Northeastern	Sr.	29	244	8.4
Terrell Everett, Oklahoma	Sr.	29	199	6.8
Walker Russell, Jacksonville St.	Sr.	29	197	6.8
Kenny Grant, Davidson	Sr.	31	208	6.7
Bobby Dixon, Troy	Sr.	29	192	6.6
Aaron Fitzgerald, UC-Irvine	Sr.	29	190	6.6
Chris Quinn, Notre Dame	Sr.	29	187	6.4
Carldell Johnson, UAB	Sr.	31	194	6.3
Will Blalock, Iowa St.	Jr.	30	184	6.1

*Includes games played in tournaments.

THREE-POINT FIELD-GOAL PERCENTAGE

	Class	GP	FG	FGA	Avg
Stephen Sir, N. Arizona.	Sr.	32	93	190	48.9
J. Alexander, Stephen F. Austin ..	Fr.	29	73	153	47.7
J. Robert Merritt, Samford	Sr.	31	120	252	47.6
Ross Schraeder, UC-Irvine	Sr.	29	74	156	47.4
Chris-Hernandez, Stanford........	Sr.	30	75	159	47.2
Steve Novak, Marquette	Sr.	31	121	259	46.7
James Collins, Birmingham So...	Sr.	27	70	246	45.9
Lee Humphrey, Florida..............	Jr.	38	113	246	45.9
B.J. Spencer, Jacksonville St. ...	Sr.	27	82	179	45.8
M. Samarco, Bowling Green.......	Jr.	29	100	219	45.7

Note: Minimum 2.5 made per game.

BLOCKED SHOTS

	Class	GP	BSAvg
Shawn James, Northeastern	So.	30	196	6.5
Justin Williams, Wyoming..............	Sr.	30	163	5.4
Stephane Lasme, Massachusetts ...	Jr.	28	108	3.9
Sheldon Williams, Duke...................	Sr.	36	137	3.8
Slim Millien, Idaho St.	Sr.	27	93	3.4
Eric Hicks, Cincinnati	Sr.	34	113	3.3
Michael Southall, La.-Lafayette	Sr.	28	93	3.3
Hilton Armstrong, Connecticut	Sr.	34	107	3.1
Tyrus Thomas, LSU........................	Fr.	32	99	3.1
Soloman Jones, South Florida.........	Sr.	29	89	3.1

THREE-POINT FIELD GOALS MADE PER GAME

	Class	G	3FG	Avg
Andre Collins, Loyola (Md.)	Sr.	28	118	4.2
Jack Leqsure, Costal Carolina	So.	30	125	4.2
Steve Novak, Marquette	Sr.	31	121	3.9
J. Robert Merritt, Samford	Sr.	31	120	3.9
J.J. Redick, Duke............................	Sr..	36	139	3.9
Eric Smith, Campbell.......................	Jr.	28	107	3.8
Chris Lofton, Tennessee	So.	30	114	3.8
Will Whittington, Marist...................	Jr.	29	103	3.5
Quincy Douby, Rutgers	Jr.	33	116	3.5
Martin Samarco, Bowling Green	Jr.	29	100	3.4

STEALS

	Class	GP	S	Avg
Tim Smith, East Tennessee St........	Sr.	28	95	3.4
Oliver Lafayette, Houston	Jr.	31	105	3.4
Obie Trotter, Alabama A&M.............	Sr.	26	87	3.3
Ibrahim Jaaber, Penn......................	Jr.	29	96	3.3
Kevin Hamilton, Holy Cross.............	Sr.	31	102	3.3
Bobby Dixon, Troy	Sr.	29	88	3.0
Bryan Mullins, Southern Illinois.	Fr.	33	94	2.8
Quinton Day, UMKC........................	Jr.	27	76	2.8
Mardy Collins, Temple.....................	Sr.	32	89	2.8
Ricky Hickman, UNC-Greensboro...	Jr.	28	77	2.8

Single-Game Highs

POINTS

53.........Brion Rush, Grambling, February 4, 2006 (vs Southern U.)
45.........Rodney Stuckey, Eastern Wash., January 5, 2006 (vs N. Arizona)
44.........Adam Morrison, Gonzaga, February 18, 2006 (vs Loyola Marymount)

REBOUNDS

30..........R. Jones-Jennings, Ark. Little Rock , December 13, 2005 (vs Ark.-Pine Bluff)
24.........Paul Millsap, Louisiana Tech, February 15, 2006 (vs San Jose St)
23.........Paul Millsap, Louisiana Tech, March 4, 2006 (vs Hawaii)

ASSISTS

16.........Bobby Dixon, Troy, January 19, 2006 (vs Western Kentucky)
16.........Jared Jordan, Marist, January 15, 2006 (vs Rider)
Five tied with15

THREE POINT FIELD GOALS

11......Josh Goodwin, Belmont, December 1, 2005 (vs East Tenn. St)
10.........Chris Riouse, Oral Roberts, February 9, 2006 (vs Oakland)
10.........Jaycee Carroll, Utah St., February 2, 2006 (vs New Mexico St)

STEALS

12 ....Carldell Johnson, UAB, November 27, 2005 (vs South Carolina St)
10.........Ricky Woods, SE Louisiana, March 3, 2006 (vs Lamar)
10.........Obie Trotter, Alabama A&M, November 26, 2005 (vs Jarvis Christian)
10.........Ricky So.liver, Iona, November 25, 2005 (vs Portland St)

BLOCKED SHOTS

12.........Justin Williams, Wyoming, March 10, 2006 (vs Utah)
11.........Justin Williams, Wyoming, February 18, 2006 (vs Brigham Young)
11.........Shawn James, Northeastern, February 15, 2006 (vs James Madison)
11.........Michael So.uthall, La.-Lafayette, January 5, 2006 (vs North Texas)

SCORING OFFENSE

	GP	W	L	Pts	Avg
Long Beach St	30	18	12	2498	83.3
Campbell	28	10	18	2319	82.8
Tex. A&M-Corpus Christi	28	20	8	2307	82.4
Washington	33	26	7	27.6	82.0
Connecticut	34	30	4	2781	81.8
East Tennessee St.	28	15	13	2284	81.6
Duke	36	32	4	2921	81.1
Belmont	31	20	11	2499	80.6
Tennessee	30	22	8	2413	80.4
Lamar	31	17	14	2487	80.2

SCORING DEFENSE

	GP	W	L	Pts	Avg
Air Force	31	24	7	1695	54.7
Princeton	27	12	15	1500	55.6
Bucknell	32	27	5	1785	55.8
Southern Illinois	33	22	11	1864	56.5
Delaware St.	35	21	14	2011	57.5
Washington St.	28	11	17	1616	57.7
Northern Iowa	33	23	10	1907	57.8
Richmond	30	13	17	1735	57.8
Northwestern	29	14	15	1697	58.5
UCLA	39	32	7	2288	58.7

SCORING MARGIN

	Off	Def	Mar
Tex. A&M-Corpus Christi	82.4	67.4	15.0
Texas	75.2	60.3	14.9
Florida	78.3	63.5	14.7
Connecticut	81.8	67.1	14.6
Memphis	80.0	65.5	14.6
Kansas	75.2	61.3	13.8
Duke	81.1	68.1	13.0
Winthrop	73.4	61.2	12.2
Washington	82.0	69.9	12.1
Illinois	70.0	58.7	11.3

FIELD-GOAL PERCENTAGE

	FG	FGA	Pct
Tex. A&M-Corpus Christi	837	1671	50.1
Florida	1061	2120	50.0
Utah St.	853	1714	49.8
Belmont	897	1781	49.2
Montana	876	1781	49.2
Colorado St.	801	1630	49.1
Marist	790	1613	49.0
Northern Arizona	856	1754	48.8
Duke	979	2011	48.7
Pacific	858	1763	48.7

FIELD-GOAL PERCENTAGE DEFENSE

	FG	FGA	Pct
Kansas	702	1896	37.0
Memphis	795	2094	38.0
Iowa	732	1924	38.0
Connecticut	842	2200	38.3
Texas	805	2097	38.4
Lehigh	643	1672	38.5
Bucknell	596	1548	38.5
La.-Lafayette	659	1707	38.6
Tex. A&M-Corpus Christi	617	1596	38.7
George Mason	760	1958	38.8

FREE-THROW PERCENTAGE

	FT	FTA	Pct
St. Joseph's	525	657	79.9
New Hampshire	357	455	78.5
Gonzaga	667	853	78.2
Princeton	266	344	77.3
Michigan St.	524	681	76.9
Stanford	500	655	76.3
Duke	689	905	76.1
Gardner-Webb	340	447	76.1
Davidson	416	547	76.1
Siena	476	627	75.9

THREE-POINT FIELD GOALS MADE PER GAME

	GP	FG	Avg
Troy	29	344	11.9
West Virginia	33	337	10.2
Campbell	28	276	9.9
Samford	31	298	9.6
Notre Dame	30	288	9.6
Fresno St.	28	265	9.5
Houston	31	286	9.2
Butler	33	300	9.1
North Carolina St.	32	288	9.0
Robert Morris	29	260	9.0

REBOUNDING MARGIN

	GP	REB	Opp REB	Margin Avg
Texas	37	1498	1105	10.6
Connecticut	34	1488	1165	9.5
Col. of Charleston	28	1172	919	9.5
Oklahoma	29	1060	803	8.9
North Carolina	31	1237	986	8.1
LSU	36	1447	1167	7.8
Pittsburgh	33	1281	1030	7.6
St. John's (N.Y.)	27	1029	842	6.9
Memphis	34	1528	1281	6.7
Wake Forest	34	1338	1122	6.4

2006 NCAA Basketball Women's Division I Tournament

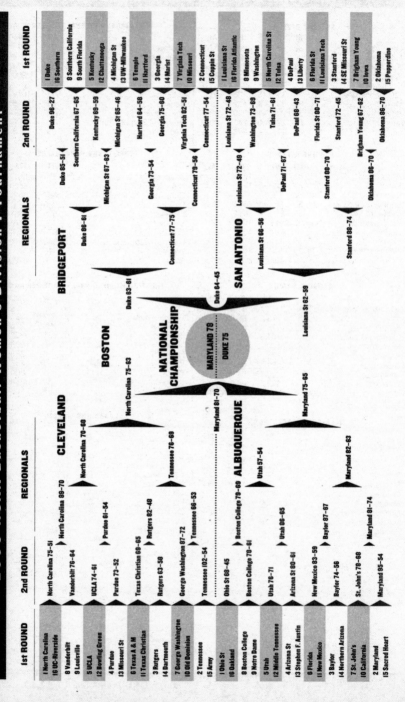

NCAA Women's Championship Game Box Score

Maryland 78

	Min	FG M-A	FT M-A	Reb O-T	A	PF	TP
L. Harper	37	6-14	4-6	4-7	0	4	16
M. Coleman	36	4-12	2-2	1-14	2	2	10
C. Langhorne	38	4-6	4-6	2-7	4	4	12
K. Toliver	43	6-18	2-2	1-3	4	2	16
S. Doron	36	4-9	6-6	0-3	1	4	16
A. Newman	17	1-3	1-2	0-0	0	3	4
C. Carr	3	0-0	0-0	1-1	0	0	0
J. Perry	15	2-3	0-0	0-2	0	1	4
Totals		27-65	19-24	9-37	11	20	78

Percentages: FG—.41.5, FT—.79.2, 3-pt goals: 5-14, .357 (S. Doron 2-4, A. Newman 1-2, M. Coleman 0-2, K. Toliver 2-6). Team rebounds: 37. Blocked shots: 0. Turnovers: 16 (S. Doron 4, L. Harper 2, A. Newman 2, J. Perry 2, M. Coleman 3, K. Toliver 3). Steals: 10 (S. Doron 4, C. Langhorne 2, A. Newman 1, M. Coleman 1, K. Toliver 2)
Halftime: Maryland 28, Duke 38

A: 18,642.

Duke 75

	Min	FG M-A	FT M-A	Reb O-T	A	PF	TP
M. Williams	36	1-8	1-3	0-3	3	3	3
W. Smith	8	0-2	0-0	1-4	0	1	0
A. Bales	41	7-11	5-6	3-12	1	4	19
L. Harding	38	6-14	4-5	0-3	1	5	16
M. Currie	37	7-16	8-9	3-6	4	4	22
A. Waner	37	1-6	2-3	3-4	4	1	5
C. Black	13	0-2	0-0	0-3	1	3	0
J. Foley	15	3-6	2-2	1-1	0	0	10
Totals		25-65	22-28	11-36	14	21	75

Percentages: FG—38.5, FT—78.6 3-pt goals: 3-11, .273 (M. Currie 0-1, L. Harding 0-1, J. Foley 2-5, W. Smith 0-1, A. Waner 1-3). Team rebounds: 36. Blocked shots: 5 (A. Bales 3, M. Williams 2). Turnovers: 16 (M. Currie 0-1, L. Harding 4, J. Foley 1, W. Smith 2, M. Williams 1, A. Waner 3). Steals: 11 (M. Currie 2, L. Harding 4, A. Bales 1, W. Smith 1, M. Williams 1, A. Waner 2)

Officials: Bob Trammell, Lisa Mattingly, Tina Napier

NCAA Women's Division I Individual Leaders

SCORING

Player and Team	Class	GP	TFG	3FG	FT	Pts	Avg
Seimone Augustus, LSU	Sr.	35	334	18	109	795	22.7
Sophia Young, Baylor	Sr.	33	301	0	134	736	22.3
Jessica Dickson, South Florida	Jr.	31	243	68	128	682	22.0
Courtney Paris, Oklahoma	Fr.	36	331	0	126	788	21.9
Candice Wiggins, Stanford	So.	34	248	90	154	740	21.8
Cappie Pondexter, Rutgers	Sr.	32	246	62	136	690	21.6
Mefertiti Walker, Stetson	Sr.	27	192	80	117	581	21.5
Chrissy Givens Middle Tennessee St	Jr.	31	246	46	129	667	21.5
Tamara James, Miami (Fla.)	Sr.	30	218	53	156	645	21.5
Tara Boothe, Xavier	Sr.	30	250	23	121	644	21.5
Emily Christian, Tennessee Tech	Sr.	32	259	24	144	686	21.4
Lindsay Shearer, Kent St	Sr.	30	204	31	184	623	20.8
Crystal Kelly, Western Kentucky	So.	34	235	0	217	687	20.2
Kari Kock, Missouri St.	Sr.	32	211	83	141	646	20.2
Tasha Humphrey, Georgia	So.	31	223	30	148	624	20.1
Alysha Clark, Belmont	Fr.	30	208	5	178	599	20.0
Tatiana Conceicao, SE Missouri St	Sr.	31	199	32	171	601	19.4
Kim Smith, Utah	Sr.	34	247	47	114	655	19.3
B.J. Banjo, East Tennessee St	Sr.	27	158	80	120	516	19.1
Terra Wallace, Tex.-Arlington	Jr.	29	176	65	136	553	19.1
LaToya Davis, Texas Tech	Sr.	29	218	0	113	549	18.9
Sherill Baker, Georgia	Sr.	32	242	4	110	598	18.7
Jessica Davenport, Ohio St	Jr.	32	241	7	109	598	18.7
Kyra Kaylor, William & Mary	So.	28	181	31	126	522	18.6
Kim Butler, Oregon St	Sr.	31	215	3	143	576	18.6

FIELD-GOAL PERCENTAGE

Player and Team	Class	GP	FG	FGA	Pct
Crystal Langhorne, Maryland	So.	38	248	370	67.0
Liz Sherwood, Vanderbilt	So.	32	172	268	64.2
Rebecca Brown, Princeton	Sr.	28	178	281	63.3
Jessica Davenport, Ohio St	Jr.	32	241	390	61.8
Courtney Paris, Oklahoma	Fr.	36	331	539	61.4
Heather Turner, Buffalo	So.	28	157	257	61.1
Sylvia Fowlers, LSU	So.	35	215	354	60.7
Crystal Kelly, W. Kentucky.	So.	34	235	391	60.1
Kristen Kovesdy, Arizona St	Sr.	32	165	275	60.0
Traci Edwards, UW-Milwaukee	Fr.	31	182	304	59.9

Note: Minimum 5 FG per game.

REBOUNDS

Player and Team	Class	GP	Reb	Avg
Courtney Paris, Oklahoma	Fr.	36	539	15.0
Ashley Haynes, Austin Peay	Sr.	28	374	13.4
Jillian Robbins, Tulsa.	Jr.	32	409	12.8
Kyra Kaylor, William & Mary	So.	28	334	11.9
LaKrisha Brown, Morehead St	Sr.	29	336	11.6
Sylvia Fowles, LSU	So.	32	358	11.2
Quanitra Hollingsworth, VCU	Fr.	28	311	11.1
Khara Smith, DePaul	Sr.	33	365	11.1
Meredith Alexis, James Madison.	Jr.	31	339	10.9
Jenny Callan, Lehigh	Sr.	28	306	10.9

FREE-THROW PERCENTAGE

Player and Team	Class	GP	FT	FTA	Pct
Adrienne Squire, Penn St.	So.	29	80	83	96.4
Chelsi Welch, Oklahoma	Jr.	36	92	99	92.9
Tommi Paris, Fuman	Sr.	30	102	110	92.7
Nefertiti Walker, Stetson	Sr.	27	117	128	91.4
Cyndi Valentin, Indiana	Sr.	33	147	163	90.2
Laura Shelton, E. Kentucky	Sr.	27	126	140	90.0
Jami Montagnino, Tulane	Jr.	27	80	89	89.9
Julie Briody, New Mexico	Jr.	29	77	86	89.5
Sara Ellis, Lehigh	Jr.	28	94	105	89.5
Megan Duffy, Notre Dame	Sr.	30	135	152	88.8

Note: Minimum 2.5 made per game.

ASSISTS

Player and Team	Class	GP	A	Avg
Lyndsey Medders, Iowa St	Jr.	28	215	7.7
Shona Thornburn, Utah	Sr.	34	242	7.1
Sally Skeldon, Mercer	Jr.	26	179	6.9
Dee Davis, Vanderbilt	Jr.	31	212	6.8
Ashley Langford, Tulane	Fr.	26	171	6.6
Melanie Boeglin, Indiana St	Sr.	33	217	6.6
Claire Sullivan, Lehigh.	So.	28	180	6.4
Erin Grant, Texas Tech	Sr.	29	183	6.3
Sharneé Zoll, Virginia	So.	32	201	6.3
Iva Milevoj, Winthrop	Sr.	29	179	6.2

THREE-POINT FIELD-GOAL PERCENTAGE

Player and Team	Class	GP	FG	FGA	Pct
Julie Larsen, Utah.	Sr.	34	69	137	50.4
Katie Montgomery, New Mexico.	Jr.	32	75	157	47.8
Amanda Cavo, Canisius	Fr.	29	62	131	47.3
Ellen Hamilton, Butler	Sr.	29	69	148	46.6
Marscilla Packer, Ohio St.	So.	32	79	171	46.2
Jenna Graber, La Salle	Jr.	28	74	164	45.1
Lisa Verhoff, Indiana St.	Sr.	33	78	174	44.8
Carolina Williams, Vanderbilt	Sr.	32	95	214	44.4
Carrie Mason, Virginia Tech	Sr.	31	62	140	44.3
Kara Pongonis, Tulsa	Sr.	32	69	156	44.2

Note: Minimum 2.0 made per game.

BLOCKED SHOTS

Player and Team	Class	GP	BS	Avg
Brook McAfee, IUPUI	Sr.	28	137	4.9
Cassie Hager, UNI.	Sr.	30	128	4.3
Zane Teilane, Western Ill.	Sr.	30	125	4.2
Marita Payne, Auburn	Sr.	29	107	3.7
Sara Beato, Columbia	Sr.	27	96	3.6
Allison Bales, Duke	Jr.	35	120	3.4
Courtney Paris, Oklahoma	Fr.	36	119	3.3
Hope Foster, Bucknell.	So.	29	95	3.3
Katie Beth Pate, Lipscomb	Sr.	21	66	3.1
Jessica Davenport, Ohio St	Jr.	32	98	3.1

NCAA Men's Division II Individual Leaders

SCORING

Player and Team	Class	GP	TFG	3FG	FT	Pts	Avg
Tayron Thomas, Philadephia U.	Sr.	31	298	42	260	898	29.0
Walt Baxley, Mars Hill	Sr.	28	234	81	233	782	27.9
Michael Ford, West Georgia	Sr.	23	180	71	135	566	24.6
Bradd Wierzbicki, Queens (N.Y.)	Jr.	28	234	59	162	689	24.6
Tyrone Anderson, Concord	Jr.	27	238	45	118	639	23.7
Armand Ivory, West Virginia Tech	Jr.	27	216	23	163	618	22.9
Taurean Temple, Wilimington (Del.)	So.	26	205	25	151	586	22.5
Raymond McKeithan, Glenville St.	Sr.	29	209	62	167	647	22.3
Austin Smylie BYU-Hawaii	Sr.	25	198	28	131	555	22.2
Antonio Fitzgerald, St. Augustine's	Jr.	22	158	58	114	488	22.2

REBOUNDS

Player and Team	Class	GP	Reb	Avg
Raheim Lowery, Dowling	Jr.	24	342	12.7
John Sullivan, New Haven	Sr.	28	329	11.8
Aurimas Truskauskas, Gannon	Jr.	27	314	11.6
Steve Raquet, CSU-Pueblo	Sr.	27	313	11.6
Vincent Falzone, Molloy	So.	25	269	10.8
Samario Clancy, Alderson-Broaddus	So.	31	319	10.3
John Smith, Winona St	So.	36	366	10.2
Sheldon Edwards, Lynn	Sr.	28	278	9.9
Justin Brown, Ashland	Sr.	29	286	9.9
Darren Stackhouse, Shepherd	Sr.	28	276	9.9

ASSISTS

Player and Team	Class	GP	A	Avg
Raymond Nelson, Grand Canyon	Sr.	27	263	9.7
Carlin Hughes, MSU-Billings	So.	28	269	9.6
Mark Borders, Tampa	Sr.	28	250	8.9
Sheldon Pace, Southwest Baptist	Sr.	32	265	8.3
Zack Whiting, Chaminade	Jr.	27	220	8.1
Ronnie Means, West Virginia Tech	So.	26	200	7.7
Christopher Dunn, West Virginia St	Sr.	34	241	7.1
Tyler Ryerson, Missouri Southern St	So.	28	182	6.5
Luke Cooper, AK-Anchorage	So.	31	199	6.4
Karim Telfer, Augusta St	Sr.	28	177	6.3

FIELD-GOAL PERCENTAGE

Player and Team	Class	GP	FG	FGA	Pct
Chris Gilliam, Pitt-Johnstown	So.	27	199	290	68.6
Rone Smith, Arkansas Tech	Sr.	27	155	230	67.4
Anthony Brown, Central Okla.	Jr.	30	220	330	66.7
Tyler MacMullen, Western Wash	Sr.	28	169	261	64.8
Shaun Bertin, Queens (N.Y.)	Sr.	29	203	322	63.0
Austin Smylie, BYU-Hawaii	Sr.	25	198	317	62.5
Corey Love, Bluefield St.	Jr.	28	246	394	62.4
Charles Clark, Johnson C. Smith	Sr.	31	220	353	62.3
B.Elisabeth-Mesnager, Cal. (Pa.)	Sr.	27	167	268	62.3
Rahiem Lowery, Dowling	Jr.	27	175	282	62.1

Note: Minimum 5 made per game.

FREE-THROW PERCENTAGE

Player and Team	Class	GP	FT	FTA	Pct
M. Martinez, CSU-Stanislaus	Jr.	27	75	80	93.8
Lance Den Boer, Central Wash.	Jr.	28	155	167	92.8
Cory Coe, Hillsdale	Sr.	28	104	114	91.2
Justin Griffin, Hawaii-Hilo	Sr.	25	133	147	90.5
E.J. Murray, Florida Tech	So.	28	74	82	90.2
Zach Green, Alderson-Broaddus	So.	30	108	120	90.0
Bernard Seals, Seattle	Sr.	23	88	99	88.9
Joey Ryan, Augustana (S.D.)	Jr.	28	70	79	88.6
David Dreas, St. Cloud St.	So.	31	113	128	88.3
Adrian Comer, Lane	So.	28	120	136	88.2

Note: Minimum 2.5 made per game.

NCAA Women's Division II Individual Leaders

SCORING

Player and Team	Class	GP	TFG	3FG	FT	Pts	Avg
Jennifer Harris, Washburn	Sr.	33	295	57	150	797	24.2
Nicole Woods, Belmont Abbey	Sr.	28	194	46	242	676	24.1
Lashonda Chiles, Anderson (S.C.)	Jr.	32	271	88	132	762	23.8
Michelle Stueve, Emporia St.	So.	33	259	98	161	777	23.5
Lindsey Dietz, Minn.-Duluth	Sr.	22	180	16	133	509	23.1
Erika Quigley, St. Cloud St.	Jr.	34	309	2	136	756	22.2
Leora Juster, UC-San Diego	Jr.	28	210	31	165	616	22.0
Tai Ellis, West Georgia	Sr.	29	223	68	111	625	21.6
Emily Brister, West Tex. A&M	Fr	32	205	70	196	676	21.1
Caronica Randle, Central Arkansas	Jr.	28	189	31	179	588	21.0

REBOUNDS

Player and Team	Class	GP	Reb	Avg
Celeste Trahan, Elizabeth City St.	So.	25	365	14.6
Keauna Vinson, Barton	Sr.	31	413	13.3
Denae Dobbins, Glenville St.	So.	33	427	12.9
Erika Quigley, St. Cloud St.	Jr.	34	430	12.6
Allyson Swailes, Bowie St.	So.	29	345	11.9
Christy Yusuf, Benedict	Jr.	29	328	11.3
Alisha Ferguson, Philadelphia U.	Jr.	25	280	11.2
Yakeeshia Ross, S.C. Upstate	Sr.	30	316	10.5
Megan Bauer, Holy Family	Jr.	32	337	10.5
Bianca Burton, Stillman	So.	29	305	10.5

ASSISTS

Player and Team	Class	GP	A	Avg
Brook Underwood, Tusculum	Jr.	28	246	8.8
Callie Iorfido, Edinboro	Sr.	30	249	8.3
Melissa Woods, Erskine	Sr.	28	198	7.1
Jennifer Brock, West Tex. A&M	Sr.	32	222	6.9
Meghan Woster, South Dakota	Sr.	28	194	6.9
Tiffany Davis, Missouri Western St.	Jr.	28	190	6.8
Deanna Price, Elizabeth City St.	Jr.	28	176	6.3
Jenna Eckleberry, Fairmont St.	Jr.	29	180	6.2
Krista Arase, CSU-Bakersfield	Fr.	28	172	6.1
Amber McFeely, Slippery Rock	Sr.	28	169	6.0

NCAA Women's Division II Individual Leaders (Cont.)

FIELD-GOAL PERCENTAGE

Player and Team	Class	GP	FG	FGA	Pct
B. Marquardt-King, Lk. Sup.St.	Sr.	29	202	284	71.1
Michelle Lieber, MSU-Billings	Jr.	27	163	243	67.1
Lindsey Dietz, Minn.-Duluth	Sr.	22	180	271	66.4
Sharie Hopkins, Presbyterian	Fr.	24	123	193	63.7
Ashley Langen, North Dakota	So.	34	219	354	61.9
Inga Buzoka, Missouri West. St.	Jr.	28	176	286	61.5
Ashlee Gustin, Fort Hays St.	Jr.	28	172	283	60.8
Catherine Portyrata, Ashland	Jr.	32	168	278	60.4
Tannesia Manley, Western N.M.	Jr.	24	138	230	60.0
Mary Moskal, Lewis	Jr.	30	156	273	57.1

Note: Minimum 5 FG per game.

FREE-THROW PERCENTAGE

Player and Team	Class	GP	FT	FTA	Pct
Kinsey Tucker, Harding	So.	27	74	82	90.2
Shannon Fr.ancis, St. Cloud St.	Jr.	32	81	91	89.0
Amber Rutherford, N. Alabama	Fr.	27	128	144	88.9
Katie Crawford, Tarleton St.	Jr.	29	79	89	88.8
L. Dooley, Ouachita Baptist	So.	27	102	115	88.7
Ashley Reed, Fairmont St.	Sr.	29	92	104	88.5
Amanda Norris, Indianapolis	Jr.	26	69	78	88.5
Lindsey Maple, Cent. Missouri St.	So.	32	103	117	88.0
Veronica Lee, West Alabama	Sr.	29	95	108	88.0
Kelly Calderone, Edinboro	Jr.	31	145	165	87.9

Note: Minimum 2.5 made per game.

NCAA Men's Division III Individual Leaders

SCORING

Player and Team	Class	GP	TFG	3FG	FT	Pts	Avg
Kyle Myrick, Lincoln (Pa.)	Sr.	30	387	59	177	1010	33.7
John Grotberg, Grinnell	Fr.	23	238	120	127	723	31.4
Mike Hoyt, Mt. St. Mary's	Jr.	28	234	112	179	759	27.1
Gian Paul Gonzalez, Montclair St.	Sr.	23	189	9	233	620	27.0
James Mooney, Mt. St. Vincent	Sr.	23	210	101	96	617	26.8
Matt Byrnes, Rowan	So.	25	218	96	124	656	26.2
James McNeil, Medaille	So.	24	206	63	131	606	25.3
Amir Mazarei, Redlands	Jr.	24	199	138	58	594	24.8
Tori Davis, Baldwin-Wallace	Jr.	30	250	0	203	703	23.4
Derek Yvon, Springfield	Sr.	26	198	78	123	597	23.0

REBOUNDS

Player and Team	Class	GP	Reb	Avg
Anthony Fitzgerald, Villa Julie	Sr.	29	416	14.3
Douglas Hammond, S. Vermont	Jr.	26	372	14.3
Jeff Kotkowski, Becker	Sr.	24	325	13.5
Sekani Francis, Lehman	Sr.	22	283	12.9
Chris Braier, Lawrence	Sr.	26	318	12.2
Josh Hinz, Beloit	Sr.	23	271	11.8
Kenny McMillan, Farmingdale	Sr.	29	329	11.3
Jeremiah Lawrence, Shenandoah	So.	25	283	11.3
Brandon Crawford, Albion	Sr.	26	293	11.3
Steve Georgouilis, Emerson	Sr.	26	289	11.1

FIELD-GOAL PERCENTAGE

Player and Team	Class	GP	FG	FGA	Pct
Brian Schmitting, Ripon	Jr.	21	122	160	76.3
Jason Boone, NYU	Jr.	22	128	186	68.8
Brandon Crawford, Albion	Sr.	26	210	307	68.4
R. Cates, Southwestern (Tex)	Sr.	26	155	230	67.4
Franklyn Beckford, Lake Forest	Sr.	23	130	193	67.4
Joe Terwelp, Monmouth (Ill.)	So.	21	133	201	66.2
Tim Vandervaart, Wooster	Jr.	30	178	271	65.7
Tim Williams, Stevens Tech	Jr.	27	156	238	65.5
Tori Davis, Baldwin-Wallace	Jr.	30	250	388	64.4
Zach McVey, Puget Sound	Sr.	28	164	257	63.8

Note: Minimum 5 made per game.

ASSISTS

Player and Team	Class	GP	A	Avg
David Arseneault, Grinnell	Fr.	23	198	8.6
Travis Magnusson, Me.-Farmington	Sr.	28	219	7.8
Kyle Myrick, Lincoln (Pa.)	Sr.	30	231	7.7
Mike McGarvey, Ursinus	Sr.	28	213	7.6
Jared Kildare, NYU	Sr.	25	185	7.4
Davon Barton, Chris. Newport	Fr.	28	190	6.8
David McMullen, Ripon	Jr.	22	142	6.5
Sean O'Brien, St. John Fisher	Sr.	30	192	6.4
Adam Dauksas, Illinois Wesleyan	Sr.	32	204	6.4
Sean Kelly, Wheaton (Mass.)	Sr.	29	183	6.3

FREE-THROW PERCENTAGE

Player and Team	Class	GP	FT	FTA	Pct
Tony Bollier, Wheaton (Ill.)	Sr.	25	104	112	92.9
Matt Secrease, Hendrix	Jr.	24	65	70	92.9
A. Schmitz, St. Scholastica	Jr.	27	86	93	92.5
Casey Meador, Louisiana Col.	Sr.	25	66	72	91.7
Ryan Cain, WPI	Jr.	27	139	152	91.4
Sean O'Brien, St. John Fisher	Sr.	30	104	113	91.2
Patrick Satalin, Catholic	Sr.	28	103	113	91.0
Steven Hicklin, UW-Stevens Pt	So.	26	71	78	91.0
Matt Fredrickson, Bethel (Minn.)	Jr.	26	75	83	90.4
Geoff Hensley, Norwich	Sr.	27	79	88	89.8

Note: Minimum 2.5 made per game.

NCAA Women's Division III Individual Leaders

SCORING

Player and Team	Class	GP	TFG	3FG	FT	Pts	Avg
Megan Silva, Randolph-Macon	Sr.	31	267	40	140	714	23.0
Leigh Sulkowski, Washington & Jefferson	Sr.	27	217	47	135	616	22.8
Staci Humphrey, Greensboro	Jr.	30	235	96	116	682	22.7
T'Neisha Turner, Wesley	Sr.	28	198	58	177	631	22.5
Lauren Stroot, Cal. Lutheran	Sr.	26	228	1	122	579	22.3
Christina Speer, Principia	Fr.	23	194	1	119	508	22.1
Jennifer King, Guilford	Sr.	27	199	46	150	594	22.0
Tori Huggins, Hendrix	Jr.	26	167	62	161	557	21.4
Rebekah Forsyth, Rose-Hulman	Jr.	23	180	3	129	492	21.4
Chelsea Luhta, Widener	Sr.	25	155	21	203	534	21.4

REBOUNDS

Player and Team	Class	GP	Reb	Avg
Taraja Laws, Newbury	Jr.	24	334	13.9
Mary Rotimi, Lincoln (Pa.)	Jr.	27	369	13.7
Chari Cooper, Kean	So.	29	357	12.3
Lashannen Hogue, John Jay	Fr.	23	279	12.0
Ashley Yeast, Monmouth (Ill.)	So.	23	275	12.0
Cheyenne Noble, Wentworth Inst.	Jr.	25	298	11.9
J. Calandrielle, Polytechnic (N.Y.)	So.	26	307	11.8
Christine Halter, D'Youville	Fr.	28	325	11.6
Lauren Byrne, Rowan	Jr.	25	289	11.6
Rebekah Forsyth, Rose-Hulman	Jr.	23	263	11.4

ASSISTS

Player and Team	Class	GP	A	Avg
Symbri Tuttle, McMurray	Jr.	29	235	8.1
Lindsay Wilson, Hartwick	Jr.	25	179	7.2
Sarah Barton, Bates	So.	28	199	7.0
Marylynn Skarzenski, Nichols	Fr.	28	195	7.0
Katie Maguire, Buena Vista	Sr.	27	179	6.6
Mallory Mann, Pacific Lutheran	Sr.	26	171	6.6
Brittany Beehler, Franklin	Jr.	28	184	6.6
Jessica Kunisaki, Chapman	So.	27	172	6.4
Staci Humphrey, Greensboro	Jr.	30	190	6.3
Marissa Coop, LeTourneau	Sr.	25	153	6.1

FIELD-GOAL PERCENTAGE

Player and Team	Class	GP	FG	FGA	Pct
Karalyn Dehn, Ripon	Sr.	24	161	247	65.2
Christine Halter, D'Youville	Fr.	28	161	249	64.7
Christina Speer, Principia	Fr.	23	194	307	63.2
Kelsey Duoss, UW-Stout	Jr.	29	211	338	62.4
Kayla Duncan, Piedmont	Fr.	27	136	218	62.4
Michelle Orton, Randolph-Macon	Sr.	31	194	315	61.6
Darcie Philp, Alma	So.	25	160	261	61.3
Kelly Peters, Wilmington (Ohio)	Jr.	27	171	284	60.2
Tarra Richardson, McMurray	So.	29	233	387	60.2
Lisa Winkle, Calvin	Jr.	28	179	300	59.7

Note: Minimum 5 made per game.

FREE-THROW PERCENTAGE

Player and Team	Class	GP	FT	FTA	Pct
Suzy Carlson, Rose-Hulman	Jr.	25	123	129	95.3
Lacey Baldviez, Redlands	Sr.	25	76	83	91.6
Katey Peacock, Alma	Sr.	25	69	77	89.6
Debbie Bruen, Mary Washington	Jr.	31	108	121	89.3
Kelly Turner, Pacific Lutheran	Sr.	28	96	108	88.9
Sara Franz, McDaniel	Sr.	28	79	89	88.8
Whitney Frament, Utica	Fr.	27	71	80	88.8
Annie McMahon, Albright	Fr.	25	88	100	88.0
Alicia Sanders, Shenandoah	Jr.	27	88	100	88.0
Elizabeth Fox, Wheaton (Ill.)	Jr.	30	108	123	87.8

Note: Minimum 2.5 made per game.

NCAA Men's Division I Championship Results

NCAA Final Four Results

Year	Winner	Score	Runner-up	Third Place	Fourth Place	Winning Coach
1939	Oregon	46–33	Ohio St	*Oklahoma	*Villanova	Howard Hobson
1940	Indiana	60–42	Kansas	*Duquesne	*USC	Branch McCracken
1941	Wisconsin	39–34	Washington St	*Pittsburgh	*Arkansas	Harold Foster
1942	Stanford	53–38	Dartmouth	*Colorado	*Kentucky	Everett Dean
1943	Wyoming	46–34	Georgetown	*Texas	*DePaul	Everett Shelton
1944	Utah	42–40 (OT)	Dartmouth	*Iowa St	*Ohio St	Vadal Peterson
1945	Oklahoma St	49–45	NYU	*Arkansas	*Ohio St	Hank Iba
1946	Oklahoma St	43–40	North Carolina	Ohio St	California	Hank Iba
1947	Holy Cross	58–47	Oklahoma	Texas	CCNY	Alvin Julian
1948	Kentucky	58–42	Baylor	Holy Cross	Kansas St	Adolph Rupp
1949	Kentucky	46–36	Oklahoma St	Illinois	Oregon St	Adolph Rupp
1950	CCNY	71–68	Bradley	North Carolina St	Baylor	Nat Holman
1951	Kentucky	68–58	Kansas St	Illinois	Oklahoma St	Adolph Rupp
1952	Kansas	80–63	St. John's (N.Y.)	Illinois	Santa Clara	Forrest Allen
1953	Indiana	69–68	Kansas	Washington	LSU	Branch McCracken
1954	La Salle	92–76	Bradley	Penn St	USC	Kenneth Loeffler
1955	San Francisco	77–63	La Salle	Colorado	Iowa	Phil Woolpert
1956	San Francisco	83–71	Iowa	Temple	SMU	Phil Woolpert
1957	North Carolina	54–53 (3OT)	Kansas	San Francisco	Michigan St	Frank McGuire
1958	Kentucky	84–72	Seattle	Temple	Kansas St	Adolph Rupp
1959	California	71–70	West Virginia	Cincinnati	Louisville	Pete Newell
1960	Ohio St	75–55	California	Cincinnati	NYU	Fred Taylor
1961	Cincinnati	70–65 (OT)	Ohio St	Vacated‡	Utah	Edwin Jucker
1962	Cincinnati	71–59	Ohio St	Wake Forest	UCLA	Edwin Jucker
1963	Loyola (Ill.)	60–58 (OT)	Cincinnati	Duke	Oregon St	George Ireland
1964	UCLA	98–83	Duke	Michigan	Kansas St	John Wooden
1965	UCLA	91–80	Michigan	Princeton	Wichita St	John Wooden
1966	UTEP	72–65	Kentucky	Duke	Utah	Don Haskins
1967	UCLA	79–64	Dayton	Houston	North Carolina	John Wooden
1968	UCLA	78–55	North Carolina	Ohio St	Houston	John Wooden
1969	UCLA	92–72	Purdue	Drake	North Carolina	John Wooden
1970	UCLA	80–69	Jacksonville	New Mexico St	St. Bonaventure	John Wooden
1971	UCLA	68–62	Vacated‡	Vacated‡	Kansas	John Wooden
1972	UCLA	81–76	Florida St	North Carolina	Louisville	John Wooden
1973	UCLA	87–66	Memphis St	Indiana	Providence	John Wooden
1974	North Carolina St	76–64	Marquette	UCLA	Kansas	Norm Sloan
1975	UCLA	92–85	Kentucky	Louisville	Syracuse	John Wooden
1976	Indiana	86–68	Michigan	UCLA	Rutgers	Bob Knight
1977	Marquette	67–59	North Carolina	UNLV	UNC-Charlotte	Al McGuire
1978	Kentucky	94–88	Duke	Arkansas	Notre Dame	Joe Hall
1979	Michigan St	75–64	Indiana St	DePaul	Penn	Jud Heathcote
1980	Louisville	59–54	Vacated‡	Purdue	Iowa	Denny Crum
1981	Indiana	63–50	North Carolina	Virginia	LSU	Bob Knight
1982	North Carolina	63–62	Georgetown	*Houston	*Louisville	Dean Smith
1983	North Carolina St	54–52	Houston	*Georgia	*Louisville	Jim Valvano
1984	Georgetown	84–75	Houston	*Kentucky	*Virginia	John Thompson
1985	Villanova	66–64	Georgetown	St. John's (N.Y.)	Vacated‡	Rollie Massimino
1986	Louisville	72–69	Duke	*Kansas	*LSU	Denny Crum
1987	Indiana	74–73	Syracuse	*UNLV	*Providence	Bob Knight
1988	Kansas	83–79	Oklahoma	*Arizona	*Duke	Larry Brown
1989	Michigan	80–79 (OT)	Seton Hall	*Duke	*Illinois	Steve Fisher
1990	UNLV	103–73	Duke	*Arkansas	*Georgia Tech	Jerry Tarkanian
1991	Duke	72–65	Kansas	*UNLV	*North Carolina	Mike Krzyzewski
1992	Duke	71–51	Michigan	*Cincinnati	*Indiana	Mike Krzyzewski
1993	North Carolina	77–71	Michigan	*Kansas	*Kentucky	Dean Smith
1994	Arkansas	76–72	Duke	*Arizona	*Florida	Nolan Richardson
1995	UCLA	89–78	Arkansas	*North Carolina	*Oklahoma St	Jim Harrick
1996	Kentucky	76–67	Syracuse	Vacated‡	Mississippi St	Rick Pitino
1997	Arizona	84–79 (OT)	Kentucky	*Minnesota	*North Carolina	Lute Olson
1998	Kentucky	78–69	Utah	*Stanford	*North Carolina	Tubby Smith
1999	Connecticut	77–74	Duke	*Michigan St	*Ohio St	Jim Calhoun
2000	Michigan St	89–76	Florida	*Wisconsin	*North Carolina	Tom Izzo
2001	Duke	82–72	Arizona	*Maryland	*Michigan St	Mike Krzyzewski

NCAA Final Four Results (Cont.)

Year	Winner	Score	Runner-up	Third Place	Fourth Place	Winning Coach
2002	Maryland	64–52	Indiana	*Kansas	*Oklahoma	Gary Williams
2003	Syracuse	81–78	Kansas	*Marquette	*Texas	Jim Boeheim
2004	Connecticut	82–73	Georgia Tech	*Oklahoma St	*Duke	Jim Calhoun
2005	North Carolina	75–70	Illinois	*Louisville	*Michigan St	Roy Williams
2006	Florida	73–57	UCLA	*George Mason	*LSU	Billy Donovan

*Tied for third place. ‡Student-athletes representing St. Joseph's (Pa.) in 1961, Villanova in 1971, Western Kentucky in 1971, UCLA in 1980, Memphis State in 1985 and Massachusetts in 1996 were declared ineligible subsequent to the tournament. Under NCAA rules, the teams' and ineligible student-athletes' records were deleted, and the teams' places in the standings were vacated.

NCAA Final Four Most Outstanding Players

Year	Winner, School	GP	Field Goals		3-Pt FG		Free Throws		Reb	Asst	Stl	BS	Avg
			FGM	Pct	FGA	FGM	FTM	Pct					
1939	None selected												
1940	Marv Huffman, Indiana	2	7	—	—	—	4	—	—	—	—	—	9.0
1941	John Kotz, Wisconsin	2	8	—	—	—	6	—	—	—	—	—	11.0
1942	Howard Dallmar, Stanford	2	8	—	—	—	4	66.7	—	—	—	—	10.0
1943	Ken Sailors, Wyoming	2	10	—	—	—	8	72.7	—	—	—	—	14.0
1944	Arnie Ferrin, Utah	2	11	—	—	—	6	—	—	—	—	—	14.0
1945	Bob Kurland, Oklahoma St	2	16	—	—	—	5	—	—	—	—	—	18.5
1946	Bob Kurland, Oklahoma St	2	21	—	—	—	10	66.7	—	—	—	—	26.0
1947	George Kaftan, Holy Cross	2	18	—	—	—	12	70.6	—	—	—	—	24.0
1948	Alex Groza, Kentucky	2	16	—	—	—	5	—	—	—	—	—	18.5
1949	Alex Groza, Kentucky	2	19	—	—	—	14	—	—	—	—	—	26.0
1950	Irwin Dambrot, CCNY	2	12	42.9	—	—	4	50.0	—	—	—	—	14.0
1951	None selected												
1952	Clyde Lovellette, Kansas	2	24	—	—	—	18	—	—	—	—	—	33.0
1953	*B.H. Horn, Kansas	2	17	—	—	—	17	—	—	—	—	—	25.5
1954	Tom Gola, La Salle	2	12	—	—	—	14	—	—	—	—	—	19.0
1955	Bill Russell, San Francisco	2	19	—	—	—	9	—	—	—	—	—	23.5
1956	*Hal Lear, Temple	2	32	—	—	—	16	—	—	—	—	—	40.0
1957	*Wilt Chamberlain, Kansas	2	18	51.4	—	—	19	70.4	25	—	—	—	32.5
1958	*Elgin Baylor, Seattle	2	18	34.0	—	—	12	75.0	41	—	—	—	24.0
1959	*Jerry West, West Virginia	2	22	66.7	—	—	22	68.8	25	—	—	—	33.0
1960	Jerry Lucas, Ohio St	2	16	66.7	—	—	3	100.0	23	—	—	—	17.5
1961	*Jerry Lucas, Ohio St	2	20	71.4	—	—	16	94.1	25	—	—	—	28.0
1962	Paul Hogue, Cincinnati	2	23	63.9	—	—	12	63.2	38	—	—	—	29.0
1963	Art Heyman, Duke	2	18	41.0	—	—	15	68.2	19	—	—	—	25.5
1964	Walt Hazzard, UCLA	2	11	55.0	—	—	8	66.7	10	—	—	—	15.0
1965	*Bill Bradley, Princeton	2	34	63.0	—	—	19	95.0	24	—	—	—	43.5
1966	*Jerry Chambers, Utah	2	25	53.2	—	—	20	83.3	35	—	—	—	35.0
1967	Lew Alcindor, UCLA	2	14	60.9	—	—	11	45.8	38	—	—	—	19.5
1968	Lew Alcindor, UCLA	2	22	62.9	—	—	9	90.0	34	—	—	—	26.5
1969	Lew Alcindor, UCLA	2	23	67.7	—	—	16	64.0	41	—	—	—	31.0
1970	Sidney Wicks, UCLA	2	15	71.4	—	—	9	60.0	34	—	—	—	19.5
1971	†Howard Porter, Villanova	2	20	48.8	—	—	7	77.8	24	—	—	—	23.5
1972	Bill Walton, UCLA	2	20	69.0	—	—	17	73.9	41	—	—	—	28.5
1973	Bill Walton, UCLA	2	28	82.4	—	—	2	40.0	30	—	—	—	29.0
1974	David Thompson, N.C. St	2	19	51.4	—	—	11	78.6	17	—	—	—	24.5
1975	Richard Washington, UCLA	2	23	54.8	—	—	8	72.7	20	—	—	—	27.0
1976	Kent Benson, Indiana	2	17	50.0	—	—	7	63.6	18	—	—	—	20.5
1977	Butch Lee, Marquette	2	11	34.4	—	—	8	100.0	6	2	1	1	15.0
1978	Jack Givens, Kentucky	2	28	65.1	—	—	8	66.7	17	4	1	3	32.0
1979	Earvin Johnson, Michigan St	2	17	68.0	—	—	19	86.4	17	3	0	2	26.5
1980	Darrell Griffith, Louisville	2	23	62.2	—	—	11	68.8	7	15	0	2	28.5
1981	Isiah Thomas, Indiana	2	14	56.0	—	—	9	81.8	4	9	3	4	18.5
1982	James Worthy, North Carolina	2	20	74.1	—	—	2	28.6	8	9	0	4	21.0
1983	*Akeem Olajuwon, Houston	2	16	55.2	—	—	9	64.3	40	3	2	5	20.5
1984	Patrick Ewing, Georgetown	2	8	57.1	—	—	2	100.0	18	1	1	15	9.0
1985	Ed Pinckney, Villanova	2	8	57.1	—	—	12	75.0	15	6	3	0	14.0
1986	Pervis Ellison, Louisville	2	15	60.0	—	—	6	75.0	24	2	3	1	18.0
1987	Keith Smart, Indiana	2	14	63.6	1	0	7	77.8	7	7	0	2	17.5
1988	Danny Manning, Kansas	2	25	55.6	1	0	6	66.7	17	4	8	9	28.0

*Not a member of the championship-winning team. †Record later vacated.

NCAA Final Four MOPs (Cont.)

			Field Goals		3-Pt FG		Free Throws						
Year	Winner, School	GP	FGM	Pct	FGA	FGM	FTM	Pct	Reb	Asst	Stl	BS	Avg
1989 ....Glen Rice, Michigan		2	24	49.0	16	7	4	100.0	16	1	0	3	29.5
1990 ....Anderson Hunt, UNLV		2	19	61.3	16	9	2	50.0	4	9	1	1	24.5
1991 ....Christian Laettner, Duke		2	12	54.5	1	1	21	91.3	17	2	1	2	23.0
1992 ....Bobby Hurley, Duke		2	10	41.7	12	7	8	80.0	3	11	0	3	17.5
1993 ....Donald Williams, North Carolina		2	15	65.2	14	10	10	100.0	4	2	2	0	25.0
1994 ....Corliss Williamson, Arkansas		2	21	50.0	0	0	10	71.4	21	8	4	3	26.0
1995 ....Ed O'Bannon, UCLA		2	16	45.7	8	3	10	76.9	25	3	7	1	22.5
1996 ....Tony Delk, Kentucky		2	15	41.7	16	8	6	54.6	9	2	3	2	22.0
1997 ....Miles Simon, Arizona		2	17	45.9	10	3	17	77.3	8	6	0	1	27.0
1998 ....Jeff Sheppard, Kentucky		2	16	55.2	10	4	7	77.8	10	7	4	0	21.5
1999 ....Richard Hamilton, Connecticut		2	20	51.3	7	3	8	72.7	12	4	2	1	25.5
2000 ....Mateen Cleaves, Michigan St		2	8	44.4	4	3	10	83.3	6	5	2	0	14.5
2001 ....Shane Battier, Duke		2	13	50.0	12	5	12	70.6	19	8	2	6	21.5
2002 ....Juan Dixon, Maryland		2	16	59.3	15	7	12	80.0	8	5	7	0	25.5
2003 ....Carmelo Anthony, Syracuse		2	19	54.3	6	9	9	81.1	24	8	4	0	26.5
2004 ....Emeka Okafor, Connecticut		2	17	65.4	0	0	8	53.3	22	2	1	4	21.0
2005 ....Sean May, North Carolina		2	19	65.5	0	0	10	71.4	17	5	1	2	24.0
2006 ....Joakim Noah, Florida		2	12	60.0	1	0	4	100.0	17	5	2	10	14.0

Best NCAA Tournament Single-Game Scoring Performances

Player and Team	Year	Round	FG	3FG	FT	TP
Austin Carr, Notre Dame vs Ohio	1970	1st	25	—	11	61
Bill Bradley, Princeton vs Wichita St	1965	C*	22	—	14	58
Oscar Robertson, Cincinnati vs Arkansas	1958	C	21	—	14	56
Austin Carr, Notre Dame vs Kentucky	1970	2nd	22	—	8	52
Austin Carr, Notre Dame vs TCU	1971	1st	20	—	12	52
David Robinson, Navy vs Michigan	1987	1st	22	0	6	50
Elvin Hayes, Houston vs Loyola (Ill.)	1968	1st	20	—	9	49
Hal Lear, Temple vs SMU	1956	C*	17	—	14	48
Austin Carr, Notre Dame vs Houston	1971	C	17	—	13	47
Dave Corzine, DePaul vs Louisville	1978	2nd	18	—	10	46

C=regional third place; C*=third-place game.

NIT Championship Results

Year	Winner	Score	Runner-up	Year	Winner	Score	Runner-up
1938 ....Temple	60–36	Colorado		1965 ....St. John's (N.Y.)	55–51	Villanova
1939 ....Long Island U.	44–32	Loyola (Ill.)		1966 ....BYU	97–84	NYU
1940 ....Colorado	51–40	Duquesne		1967 ....Southern Illinois	71–56	Marquette
1941 ....Long Island U.	56–42	Ohio U		1968 ....Dayton	61–48	Kansas
1942 ....West Virginia	47–45	W. Kentucky		1969 ....Temple	89–76	Boston College
1943 ....St. John's (N.Y.)	48–27	Toledo		1970 ....Marquette	65–53	St. John's (N.Y.)
1944 ....St. John's (N.Y.)	47–39	DePaul		1971 ....North Carolina	84–66	Georgia Tech
1945 ....DePaul	71–54	Bowling Green		1972 ....Maryland	100–69	Niagara
1946 ....Kentucky	46–45	Rhode Island		1973 ....Virginia Tech	92–91 (OT)	Notre Dame
1947 ....Utah	49–45	Kentucky		1974 ....Purdue	97–81	Utah
1948 ....St. Louis	65–52	NYU		1975 ....Princeton	80–69	Providence
1949 ....San Francisco	48–47	Loyola (Ill.)		1976 ....Kentucky	71–67	UNC-Charlotte
1950 ....CCNY	69–61	Bradley		1977 ....St. Bonaventure	94–91	Houston
1951 ....BYU	62–43	Dayton		1978 ....Texas	101–93	North Carolina St
1952 ....La Salle	75–64	Dayton		1979 ....Indiana	53–52	Purdue
1953 ....Seton Hall	58–46	St. John's (N.Y.)		1980 ....Virginia	58–55	Minnesota
1954 ....Holy Cross	71–62	Duquesne		1981 ....Tulsa	86–84 (OT)	Syracuse
1955 ....Duquesne	70–58	Dayton		1982 ....Bradley	67–58	Purdue
1956 ....Louisville	93–80	Dayton		1983 ....Fresno St	69–60	DePaul
1957 ....Bradley	84–83	Memphis St		1984 ....Michigan	83–63	Notre Dame
1958 ....Xavier (Ohio)	78–74 (OT)	Dayton		1985 ....UCLA	65–62	Indiana
1959 ....St. John's (N.Y.)	76–71 (OT)	Bradley		1986 ....Ohio St	73–63	Wyoming
1960 ....Bradley	88–72	Providence		1987 ....Southern Miss	84–80	La Salle
1961 ....Providence	62–59	St. Louis		1988 ....Connecticut	72–67	Ohio St
1962 ....Dayton	73–67	St. John's (N.Y.)		1989 ....St. John's (N.Y.)	73–65	St. Louis
1963 ....Providence	81–66	Canisius		1990 ....Vanderbilt	74–72	St. Louis
1964 ....Bradley	86–54	New Mexico		1991 ....Stanford	78–72	Oklahoma

NIT Championship Results (Cont.)

Year	Winner	Score	Runner-up	Year	Winner	Score	Runner-up
1992	Virginia	81–76	Notre Dame	2000	Wake Forest	71–61	Notre Dame
1993	Minnesota	62–61	Georgetown	2001	Tulsa	79–60	Alabama
1994	Villanova	80–73	Vanderbilt	2002	Memphis	72–62	South Carolina
1995	Virginia Tech	65–64 (OT)	Marquette	2003	St. John's	70–67	Georgetown
1996	Nebraska	60–56	St. Joseph's	2004	Michigan	62–55	Rutgers
1997	Michigan	82–73	Florida St	2005	South Carolina	60–57	Saint Joseph's
1998	Minnesota	79–72	Penn St	2006	South Carolina	76–64	Michigan
1999	California	61–60	Clemson				

NCAA Men's Division I Season Leaders

Scoring Average

Year	Player and Team	Ht	Class	GP	FG	3FG	FT	Pts	Avg
1948	Murray Wier, Iowa	5-9	Sr.	19	152	—	95	399	21.0
1949	Tony Lavelli, Yale	6-3	Sr.	30	228	—	215	671	22.4
1950	Paul Arizin, Villanova	6-3	Sr.	29	260	—	215	735	25.3
1951	Bill Mlkvy, Temple	6-4	Sr.	25	303	—	125	731	29.2
1952	Clyde Lovellette, Kansas	6-9	Sr.	28	315	—	165	795	28.4
1953	Frank Selvy, Furman	6-3	Jr.	25	272	—	194	738	29.5
1954	Frank Selvy, Furman	6-3	Sr.	29	427	—	355	1209	41.7
1955	Darrell Floyd, Furman	6-1	Jr.	25	344	—	209	897	35.9
1956	Darrell Floyd, Furman	6-1	Sr.	28	339	—	268	946	33.8
1957	Grady Wallace, South Carolina	6-4	Sr.	29	336	—	234	906	31.2
1958	Oscar Robertson, Cincinnati	6-5	So.	28	352	—	280	984	35.1
1959	Oscar Robertson, Cincinnati	6-5	Jr.	30	331	—	316	978	32.6
1960	Oscar Robertson, Cincinnati	6-5	Sr.	30	369	—	273	1011	33.7
1961	Frank Burgess, Gonzaga	6-1	Sr.	26	304	—	234	842	32.4
1962	Billy McGill, Utah	6-9	Sr.	26	394	—	221	1009	38.8
1963	Nick Werkman, Seton Hall	6-3	Jr.	22	221	—	208	650	29.5
1964	Howard Komives, Bowling Green	6-1	Sr.	23	292	—	260	844	36.7
1965	Rick Barry, Miami (Fla.)	6-7	Sr.	26	340	—	293	973	37.4
1966	Dave Schellhase, Purdue	6-4	Sr.	24	284	—	213	781	32.5
1967	Jim Walker, Providence	6-3	Sr.	28	323	—	205	851	30.4
1968	Pete Maravich, LSU	6-5	So.	26	432	—	274	1138	43.8
1969	Pete Maravich, LSU	6-5	Jr.	26	433	—	282	1148	44.2
1970	Pete Maravich, LSU	6-5	Sr.	31	522	—	337	1381	44.5
1971	Johnny Neumann, Mississippi	6-6	So.	23	366	—	191	923	40.1
1972	Dwight Lamar, SW Louisiana	6-1	Jr.	29	429	—	196	1054	36.3
1973	William Averitt, Pepperdine	6-1	Sr.	25	352	—	144	848	33.9
1974	Larry Fogle, Canisius	6-5	So.	25	326	—	183	835	33.4
1975	Bob McCurdy, Richmond	6-7	Sr.	26	321	—	213	855	32.9
1976	Marshall Rodgers, Tex.-Pan American	6-2	Sr.	25	361	—	197	919	36.8
1977	Freeman Williams, Portland St	6-4	Jr.	26	417	—	176	1010	38.8
1978	Freeman Williams, Portland St	6-4	Sr.	27	410	—	149	969	35.9
1979	Lawrence Butler, Idaho St	6-3	Sr.	27	310	—	192	812	30.1
1980	Tony Murphy, Southern-Birmingham	6-3	Sr.	29	377	—	178	932	32.1
1981	Zam Fredrick, South Carolina	6-2	Sr.	27	300	—	181	781	28.9
1982	Harry Kelly, Texas Southern	6-7	Jr.	29	336	—	190	862	29.7
1983	Harry Kelly, Texas Southern	6-7	Sr.	29	333	—	169	835	28.8
1984	Joe Jakubick, Akron	6-5	Sr.	27	304	—	206	814	30.1
1985	Xavier McDaniel, Wichita St	6-8	Sr.	31	351	—	142	844	27.2
1986	Terrance Bailey, Wagner	6-2	Jr.	29	321	—	212	854	29.4
1987	Kevin Houston, Army	5-11	Sr.	29	311	63	268	953	32.9
1988	Hersey Hawkins, Bradley	6-3	Sr.	31	377	87	284	1125	36.3
1989	Hank Gathers, Loyola Marymount	6-7	Jr.	31	419	0	177	1015	32.7
1990	Bo Kimble, Loyola Marymount	6-5	Sr.	32	404	92	231	1131	35.3
1991	Kevin Bradshaw, U.S. Int'l	6-6	Sr.	28	358	60	278	1054	37.6
1992	Brett Roberts, Morehead St	6-8	Sr.	29	278	66	193	815	28.1
1993	Greg Guy, Tex.-Pan American	6-1	Jr.	19	189	67	111	556	29.3
1994	Glenn Robinson, Purdue	6-8	Jr.	34	368	79	215	1030	30.3
1995	Kurt Thomas, TCU	6-9	Sr.	27	288	3	202	781	28.9
1996	Kevin Granger, Texas Southern	6-3	Sr.	24	194	30	230	648	27.0
1997	Charles Jones, LIU-Brooklyn	6-3	Jr.	30	338	109	118	903	30.1
1998	Charles Jones, LIU-Brooklyn	6-3	Sr.	30	326	116	101	869	29.0
1999	Alvin Young, Niagara	6-3	Sr.	29	253	65	157	728	25.1

Scoring Average (Cont.)

Year	Player and Team	Ht	Class	GP	FG	3FG	FT	Pts	Avg
2000....	Courtney Alexander, Fresno St	6-6	Sr.	27	252	58	107	669	24.8
2001....	Ronnie McCollum, Centenary	6-4	Sr.	27	244	85	214	787	29.1
2002....	Jason Conley, Virginia Military	6-5	Fr.	28	285	79	171	820	29.3
2003....	Ruben Douglas, New Mexico	6-5	Sr.	28	218	94	253	783	28.0
2004....	Keydren Clark, St. Peter's	5-8	So.	29	233	112	197	775	26.7
2005....	Keydren Clark, St. Peter's	5-9	Jr.	28	230	109	152	721	25.8
2006....	Adam Morrison, Gonzaga	6-8	Jr.	33	306	74	240	926	28.1

Rebounds

Year	Player and Team	Ht	Class	GP	Reb	Avg
1951...............	Ernie Beck, Pennsylvania	6-4	So.	27	556	20.6
1952...............	Bill Hannon, Army	6-3	So.	17	355	20.9
1953...............	Ed Conlin, Fordham	6-5	So.	26	612	23.5
1954...............	Art Quimby, Connecticut	6-5	Jr.	26	588	22.6
1955...............	Charlie Slack, Marshall	6-5	Jr.	21	538	25.6
1956...............	Joe Holup, George Washington	6-6	Sr.	26	604	†.256
1957...............	Elgin Baylor, Seattle	6-6	Jr.	25	508	†.235
1958...............	Alex Ellis, Niagara	6-5	Sr.	25	536	†.262
1959...............	Leroy Wright, Pacific	6-8	Jr.	26	652	†.238
1960...............	Leroy Wright, Pacific	6-8	Sr.	17	380	†.234
1961...............	Jerry Lucas, Ohio St	6-8	Jr.	27	470	†.198
1962...............	Jerry Lucas, Ohio St	6-8	Sr.	28	499	†.211
1963...............	Paul Silas, Creighton	6-7	Sr.	27	557	20.6
1964...............	Bob Pelkington, Xavier (Ohio)	6-7	Sr.	26	567	21.8
1965...............	Toby Kimball, Connecticut	6-8	Sr.	23	483	21.0
1966...............	Jim Ware, Oklahoma City	6-8	Sr.	29	607	20.9
1967...............	Dick Cunningham, Murray St	6-10	Jr.	22	479	21.8
1968...............	Neal Walk, Florida	6-10	Jr.	25	494	19.8
1969...............	Spencer Haywood, Detroit	6-8	So.	22	472	21.5
1970...............	Artis Gilmore, Jacksonville	7-2	Jr.	28	621	22.2
1971...............	Artis Gilmore, Jacksonville	7-2	Sr.	26	603	23.2
1972...............	Kermit Washington, American	6-8	Jr.	23	455	19.8
1973...............	Kermit Washington, American	6-8	Sr.	22	439	20.0
1974...............	Marvin Barnes, Providence	6-9	Sr.	32	597	18.7
1975...............	John Irving, Hofstra	6-9	So.	21	323	15.4
1976...............	Sam Pellom, Buffalo	6-8	So.	26	420	16.2
1977...............	Glenn Mosley, Seton Hall	6-8	Sr.	29	473	16.3
1978...............	Ken Williams, North Texas St	6-7	Sr.	28	411	14.7
1979...............	Monti Davis, Tennessee St	6-7	Jr.	26	421	16.2
1980...............	Larry Smith, Alcorn St	6-8	Sr.	26	392	15.1
1981...............	Darryl Watson, Miss. Valley St	6-7	Sr.	27	379	14.0
1982...............	LaSalle Thompson, Texas	6-10	Jr.	27	365	13.5
1983...............	Xavier McDaniel, Wichita St	6-7	So.	28	403	14.4
1984...............	Akeem Olajuwon, Houston	7-0	Jr.	37	500	13.5
1985...............	Xavier McDaniel, Wichita St	6-8	Sr	31	460	14.8
1986...............	David Robinson, Navy	6-11	Jr.	35	455	13.0
1987...............	Jerome Lane, Pittsburgh	6-6	So.	33	444	13.5
1988...............	Kenny Miller, Loyola (Ill.)	6-9	Fr.	29	395	13.6
1989...............	Hank Gathers, Loyola (Calif.)	6-7	Jr.	31	426	13.7
1990...............	Anthony Bonner, St. Louis	6-8	Sr.	33	456	13.8
1991...............	Shaquille O'Neal, LSU	7-1	So.	28	411	14.7
1992...............	Popeye Jones, Murray St	6-8	Sr.	30	431	14.4
1993...............	Warren Kidd, Middle Tenn. St	6-9	Sr.	26	386	14.8
1994...............	Jerome Lambert, Baylor	6-8	Jr.	24	355	14.8
1995...............	Kurt Thomas, TCU	6-9	Sr.	27	393	14.6
1996...............	Marcus Mann, Miss. Valley St	6-8	Sr.	29	394	13.6
1997...............	Tim Duncan, Wake Forest	6-11	Sr.	31	457	14.7
1998...............	Ryan Perryman, Dayton	6-7	Sr.	33	412	12.5
1999...............	Ian McGinnis, Dartmouth	6-8	So.	26	317	12.2
2000...............	Darren Phillips, Fairfield	6-7	Sr.	29	405	14.0
2001...............	Chris Marcus, Western Kentucky	7-1	Jr.	31	374	12.1
2002...............	Jeremy Bishop, Quinnipiac	6-6	J..	29	347	12.0
2003	Brandon Hunter, Ohio	6-7	Sr.	30	378	12.6
2004	Paul Millsap, Louisiana Tech	6-7	Fr.	30	374	12.5
2005	Paul Millsap, Louisiana Tech	6-8	So.	29	360	12.4
2006	Paul Millsap, Louisiana Tech	6-8	Jr.	33	438	13.3

†From 1956–1962, title was based on highest individual recoveries out of total by both teams in all games.

Assists

Year	Player and Team	Class	GP	Ast	Avg
1984	Craig Lathen, Ill.-Chicago	Jr.	29	274	9.45
1985	Rob Weingard, Hofstra	Sr.	24	228	9.50
1986	Mark Jackson, St. John's (N.Y.)	Jr.	36	328	9.11
1987	Avery Johnson, Southern-Birm.	Jr.	31	333	10.74
1988	Avery Johnson, Southern-Birm.	Sr.	30	399	13.30
1989	Glenn Williams, Holy Cross	Sr.	28	278	9.93
1990	Todd Lehmann, Drexel	Sr.	28	260	9.29
1991	Chris Corchiani, North Carolina St	Sr.	31	299	9.65
1992	Van Usher, Tennessee Tech	Sr.	29	254	8.76
1993	Sam Crawford, New Mex. St	Sr.	34	310	9.12
1994	Jason Kidd, California	So.	30	272	9.06
1995	Nelson Haggerty, Baylor	Sr.	28	284	10.10
1996	Raimonds Miglinieks, UC-Irvine	Sr.	27	230	8.52
1997	Kenny Mitchell, Dartmouth	Sr.	26	203	7.81
1998	Ahlon Lewis, Arizona St	Sr.	32	294	9.19
1999	Doug Gottlieb, Oklahoma St	Jr.	34	299	8.79
2000	Mark Dickel, UNLV	Sr.	31	280	9.03
2001	Markus Carr, CSU–Northridge	Jr.	32	286	8.94
2002	T.J. Ford, Texas	Fr.	33	273	8.27
2003	Martell Bailey, Ill.-Chicago	Jr.	30	244	8.13
2004	Greg Davis, Troy St	Sr.	31	256	8.26
2005	Damitrius Coleman, Mercer	Jr.	28	224	8.00
	Will Funn, Portland St	Sr.	28	224	8.00
2006	Jared Jordan, Marist	Jr.	29	247	8.52

Blocked Shots

Year	Player and Team	Class	GP	BS	Avg
1986	David Robinson, Navy	Jr.	35	207	5.91
1987	David Robinson, Navy	Sr.	32	144	4.50
1988	Rodney Blake, St. Joseph's (Pa.)	Sr.	29	116	4.00
1989	Alonzo Mourning, Georgetown	Fr.	34	169	4.97
1990	Kenny Green, Rhode Island	Sr.	26	124	4.77
1991	Shawn Bradley, BYU	Fr.	34	177	5.21
1992	Shaquille O'Neal, LSU	Jr.	30	157	5.23
1993	Theo Ratliff, Wyoming	Jr.	28	124	4.43
1994	Grady Livingston, Howard	Jr.	26	115	4.42
1995	Keith Closs, Central Conn. St	Fr.	26	139	5.35
1996	Keith Closs, Central Conn. St	So.	28	178	6.36
1997	Adonal Foyle, Colgate	Jr.	28	180	6.43
1998	Jerome James, Florida A&M	Sr.	27	125	4.63
1999	Tarvis Williams, Hampton	Jr.	27	135	5.00
2000	Ken Johnson, Ohio St	Sr.	30	161	5.37
2001	Tarvis Williams, Hampton	Sr	32	147	4.59
2002	Wojciech Myrda, La.-Monroe	Sr.	32	172	5.38
2003	Emeka Okafor, Connecticut	So.	33	156	4.73
2004	Anwar Ferguson, Houston	Sr.	27	111	4.11
2005	Deng Gai, Fairfield	Sr.	30	165	5.50
2006	Shawn James, Northeastern	So.	30	196	6.53

Steals

Year	Player and Team	Class	GP	Stl	Avg
1986	Darron Brittman, Chicago St	Sr.	28	139	4.96
1987	Tony Fairley, Charleston South.	Sr.	28	114	4.07
1988	Aldwin Ware, Florida A&M	Sr.	29	142	4.90
1989	Kenny Robertson, Cleveland St	Jr.	28	111	3.96
1990	Ronn McMahon, E. Washington	Sr.	29	130	4.48
1991	Van Usher, Tennessee Tech	Jr.	28	104	3.71
1992	Victor Snipes, NE Illinois	So.	25	86	3.44
1993	Jason Kidd, California	Fr.	29	110	3.80
1994	Shawn Griggs, SW Louisiana	Sr.	30	120	4.00
1995	Roderick Anderson, Texas	Sr.	30	101	3.37
1996	Pointer Williams, McNeese St	Sr.	27	118	4.37
1997	Joel Hoover, Md.-Eastern Shore	Fr.	28	90	3.21
1998	Bonzi Wells, Ball St	Sr.	29	103	3.55

Steals (Cont.)

Year	Player and Team	Class	GP	Stl	Avg
1999	Shawnta Rogers, George Wash.	Sr.	29	103	3.55
2000	Carl Williams, Liberty	Sr.	28	107	3.82
2001	Greedy Daniels, TCU	Jr.	25	108	4.32
2002	Desmond Cambridge, Ala. A&M	Sr.	29	160	5.52
2003	Alexis McMillan, Stetson	Sr.	22	87	3.95
2004	Marques Green, St. Bonaventure	Sr.	27	107	3.96
2005	Obie Trotter, Alabama A&M	Jr.	32	125	3.91
2006	Tim Smith, East Tennessee St	Sr.	28	95	3.39

NCAA Men's Division I Alltime Individual Leaders

Single Game Records

SCORING HIGHS VS DIVISION I OPPONENT

Pts	Player and Team vs Opponent	Date
72	Kevin Bradshaw, U.S. Int'l vs Loyola Marymount	1-5-91
69	Pete Maravich, LSU vs Alabama	2-7-70
68	Calvin Murphy, Niagara vs Syracuse	12-7-68
66	Jay Handlan, Washington & Lee vs Furman	2-17-51
66	Pete Maravich, LSU vs Tulane	2-10-69
66	Anthony Roberts, Oral Roberts vs North Carolina A&T	2-19-77
65	Anthony Roberts, Oral Roberts vs Oregon	3-9-77
65	Scott Haffner, Evansville vs Dayton	2-18-89
64	Pete Maravich, LSU vs Kentucky	2-21-70
63	Johnny Neumann, Mississippi vs LSU	1-30-71
63	Hersey Hawkins, Bradley vs Detroit	2-22-88

SCORING HIGHS VS NON-DIVISION I OPPONENT

Pts	Player and Team vs Opponent	Date
100	Frank Selvy, Furman vs Newberry	2-13-54
85	Paul Arizin, Villanova vs Philadelphia NAMC	2-12-49
81	Freeman Williams, Portland St vs Rocky Mountain	2-3-78
73	Bill Mlkvy, Temple vs Wilkes	3-3-51
71	Freeman Williams, Portland St vs S. Oregon	2-9-77

REBOUNDING HIGHS ALL-TIME

Reb	Player and Team vs Opponent	Date
51	Bill Chambers, William & Mary vs Virginia	2-14-53
43	Charlie Slack, Marshall vs Morris Harvey	1-12-54
42	Tom Heinsohn, Holy Cross vs Boston College	3-1-55
40	Art Quimby, Connecticut vs Boston University	1-11-55
39	Maurice Stokes, St. Francis (Pa.) vs John Carroll	1-28-55
39	Dave DeBusschere, Detroit vs C. Michigan	1-30-60
39	Keith Swagerty, Pacific vs UC-Santa Barbara	3-5-65

REBOUNDING HIGHS SINCE 1973*

Reb	Player and Team vs Opponent	Date
35	Larry Abney, Fresno St vs SMU	2-17-00
34	David Vaughn, Oral Roberts vs Brandeis	1-8-73
32	Jervaughn Scales, Southern-Birm. vs Grambling	2-7-94
32	Durand Macklin, LSU vs Tulane	11-26-76
31	Jim Bradley, Northern Illinois vs UW-Milwaukee	2-19-73
31	Calvin Natt, NE Louisiana vs Georgia Southern	12-29-76

ASSISTS

Asst	Player and Team vs Opponent	Date
22	Tony Fairley, Baptist vs Armstrong St	2-9-87
22	Avery Johnson, Southern-Birm. vs Texas Southern	1-25-88
22	Sherman Douglas, Syracuse vs Providence	1-28-89
21	Kelvin Scarborough, New Mexico vs Hawaii	2-13-87
21	Anthony Manuel, Bradley vs UC-Irvine	12-19-87
21	Avery Johnson, Southern-Birm. vs Alabama St	1-16-88

*Freshmen became eligible for varsity play in 1973.

Single Game Records (Cont.)

STEALS

Stl	Player and Team vs Opponent	Date
13	Mookie Blaylock, Oklahoma vs Centenary	12-12-87
13	Mookie Blaylock, Oklahoma vs Loyola Marymount	12-17-88
12	Kenny Robertson, Cleveland St vs Wagner	12-3-88
12	Terry Evans, Oklahoma vs Florida A&M	1-27-93
12	Richard Duncan, Middle Tenn. St vs Eastern Kentucky	2-20-99
12	Greedy Daniels, Texas Christian vs Ark.–Pine Bluff	12-30-00
12	Jehiel Lewis, Navy vs Bucknell	1-12-02
12	Carldell Johnson, Ala.-Birmingham vs. South Carolina St	11-27-05

BLOCKED SHOTS

BS	Player and Team vs Opponent	Date
14	David Robinson, Navy vs UNC–Wilmington	1-4-86
14	Shawn Bradley, BYU vs Eastern Kentucky	12-7-90
14	Roy Rogers, Alabama vs Georgia	2-10-96
14	Loren Woods, Arizona vs Oregon	2-3-00

Eight tied with 13

Single Season Records

POINTS

Player and Team	Year	GP	FG	3FG	FT	Pts
Pete Maravich, LSU	1970	31	522	—	337	1381
Elvin Hayes, Houston	1968	33	519	—	176	1214
Frank Selvy, Furman	1954	29	427	—	355	1209
Pete Maravich, LSU	1969	26	433	—	282	1148
Pete Maravich, LSU	1968	26	432	—	274	1138
Bo Kimble, Loyola Marymount	1990	32	404	92	231	1131
Hersey Hawkins, Bradley	1988	31	377	87	284	1125
Austin Carr, Notre Dame	1970	29	444	—	218	1106
Austin Carr, Notre Dame	1971	29	430	—	241	1101
Otis Birdsong, Houston	1977	36	452	—	186	1090

SCORING AVERAGE

Player and Team	Year	GP	FG	3FG	FT	Pts	Avg
Pete Maravich, LSU	1970	31	522		337	1381	44.5
Pete Maravich, LSU	1969	26	433		282	1148	44.2
Pete Maravich, LSU	1968	26	432		274	1138	43.8
Frank Selvy, Furman	1954	29	427		355	1209	41.7
Johnny Neumann, Mississippi	1971	23	366		191	923	40.1
Freeman Williams, Portland St	1977	26	417		176	1010	38.8
Billy McGill, Utah	1962	26	394		221	1009	38.8
Calvin Murphy, Niagara	1968	24	337		242	916	38.2
Austin Carr, Notre Dame	1970	29	444		218	1106	38.1
Austin Carr, Notre Dame	1971	29	430		241	1101	38.0

REBOUNDS

Player and Team	Year	GP	Reb	Player and Team	Year	GP	Reb
Walt Dukes, Seton Hall	1953	33	734	Artis Gilmore, Jacksonville	1970	28	621
Leroy Wright, Pacific	1959	26	652	Tom Gola, La Salle	1955	31	618
Tom Gola, La Salle	1954	30	652	Ed Conlin, Fordham	1953	26	612
Charlie Tyra, Louisville	1956	29	645	Art Quimby, Connecticut	1955	25	611
Paul Silas, Creighton	1964	29	631	Bill Russell, San Francisco	1956	29	609
Elvin Hayes, Houston	1968	33	624	Jim Ware, Oklahoma City	1966	29	607

REBOUND AVERAGE ALL-TIME

Player and Team	Year	GP	Reb	Avg
Charlie Slack, Marshall	1955	21	538	25.6
Leroy Wright, Pacific	1959	26	652	25.1
Art Quimby, Connecticut	1955	25	611	24.4
Charlie Slack, Marshall	1956	22	520	23.6
Ed Conlin, Fordham	1953	26	612	23.5

REBOUND AVERAGE SINCE 1973*

Player and Team	Year	GP	Reb	Avg
Kermit Washington, American	1973	22	439	20.0
Marvin Barnes, Providence	1973	30	571	19.0
Marvin Barnes, Providence	1974	32	597	18.7
Pete Padgett, Nev.-Reno	1973	26	462	17.8
Jim Bradley, Northern Illinois	1973	24	426	17.8

Single Season Records (Cont.)

ASSISTS

Player and Team	Year	GP	Asst	Player and Team	Year	GP	Asst
Mark Wade, UNLV	1987	38	406	Sherman Douglas, Syracuse	1989	38	326
Avery Johnson, Southern-Birm.	1988	30	399	Sam Crawford, New Mex. St	1993	34	310
Anthony Manuel, Bradley	1988	31	373	Greg Anthony, UNLV	1991	35	310
Avery Johnson, Southern-Birm.	1987	31	333	Reid Gettys, Houston	1984	37	309
Mark Jackson, St. John's (N.Y.)	1986	32	328	Carl Golston, Loyola (Ill.)	1985	33	305

ASSIST AVERAGE

Player and Team	Year	GP	Asst	Avg	Player and Team	Year	GP	Asst	Avg
Avery Johnson, Southern-Birm.	1988	30	399	13.3	Chris Corchiani, North Carolina St	1991	31	299	9.6
Anthony Manuel, Bradley	1988	31	373	12.0	Tony Fairley, Charleston South.*	1987	28	270	9.6
Avery Johnson, Southern-Birm.	1987	31	333	10.7	Tyrone Bogues, Wake Forest	1987	29	276	9.5
Mark Wade, UNLV	1987	38	406	10.7	Ron Weingard, Hofstra	1985	24	228	9.5
Nelson Haggerty, Baylor	1995	28	284	10.1	Craig Neal, Georgia Tech	1988	32	303	9.5
Glenn Williams, Holy Cross	1989	28	278	9.9					

FIELD-GOAL PERCENTAGE

Player and Team	Year	GP	FG	FGA	Pct
Steve Johnson, Oregon St	1981	28	235	315	74.6
Dwayne Davis, Florida	1989	33	179	248	72.2
Keith Walker, Utica	1985	27	154	216	71.3
Steve Johnson, Oregon St	1980	30	211	297	71.0
Adam Mark, Belmont	2002	26	150	212	70.8
Oliver Miller, Arkansas	1991	38	254	361	70.4
Alan Williams, Princeton	1987	25	163	232	70.3
Mark McNamara, California	1982	27	231	329	70.2
Warren Kidd, Middle Tennessee St	1991	30	173	247	70.0
Pete Freeman, Akron	1991	28	175	250	70.0

Based on qualifiers for annual championship.

FREE-THROW PERCENTAGE

Player and Team	Year	GP	FT	FTA	Pct
Blake Ahearn SW Missouri St†	2004	33	117	120	97.5
Craig Collins, Penn St	1985	27	94	98	95.9
J.J. Redick, Duke	2004	37	143	150	95.3
Steve Drabyn, Belmont	2003	29	78	82	95.1
Rod Foster, UCLA	1982	27	95	100	95.0
Clay McKnight, Pacific	2000	24	74	78	94.9
Matt Logie, Lehigh	2003	28	91	96	94.8
Blake Ahearn, Missouri State	2005	32	90	95	94.7
Danny Basile, Marist	1994	27	84	89	94.4
Carlos Gibson, Marshall	1978	28	84	89	94.4
Jim Barton, Dartmouth	1986	26	65	69	94.2

THREE-POINT FIELD-GOAL PERCENTAGE

Player and Team	Year	GP	3FG	3FGA	Pct
Glenn Tropf, Holy Cross	1988	29	52	82	63.4
Sean Wightman, Western Michigan	1992	30	48	76	63.2
Keith Jennings, East Tennessee St	1991	33	84	142	59.2
Dave Calloway, Monmouth (N.J.)	1989	28	48	82	58.5
Steve Kerr, Arizona	1988	38	114	199	57.3
Reginald Jones, Prairie View	1987	28	64	112	57.1
Jim Cantamessa, Siena	1998	29	66	117	56.4
Joel Tribelhorn, Colorado St	1989	33	76	135	56.3
Mike Joseph, Bucknell	1988	28	65	116	56.0
Brian Jackson, Evansville	1995	27	53	95	55.8

Based on qualifiers for annual championship.

*Formerly Baptist
†Southwest Missouri State changed name to Missouri State after 2004–05 season
Based on qualifiers for annual championship.

Single Season Records (Cont.)

STEALS

Player and Team	Year	GP	Stl
Desmond Cambridge, Alabama A&M	2002	29	160
Mookie Blaylock, Oklahoma	1988	39	150
Aldwin Ware, Florida A&M	1988	29	142
Darron Brittman, Chicago St.	1986	28	139
John Linehan, Providence	2002	31	139

BLOCKED SHOTS

Player and Team	Year	GP	BS
David Robinson, Navy	1986	35	207
Shawn James, Northeastern	2005	30	196
Adonal Foyle, Colgate	1997	28	180
Keith Closs, Central Conn. St.	1996	28	178
Shawn Bradley, BYU	1991	34	177

STEAL AVERAGE

Player and Team	Year	GP	Stl	Avg
D. Cambridge, Alabama A&M	2002	29	160	5.52
Darron Brittman, Chicago St.	1986	28	139	4.96
Aldwin Ware, Florida A&M	1988	29	142	4.90
John Linehan, Providence	2002	31	139	4.48
Ronn McMahon, E. Washington	1990	29	130	4.48

BLOCKED-SHOT AVERAGE

Player and Team	Year	GP	BS	Avg
Shawn James, Northeastern	2005	30	196	6.53
Adonal Foyle, Colgate	1997	28	180	6.43
Keith Closs, Central Conn. St.	1996	28	178	6.36
David Robinson, Navy	1986	35	207	5.91
Adonal Foyle, Colgate	1996	29	165	5.69

Career Records

POINTS

Player and Team	Ht	Final Year	GP	FG	3FG*	FT	Pts
Pete Maravich, LSU	6-5	1970	83	1387	—	893	3667
Freeman Williams, Portland St.	6-4	1978	106	1369	—	511	3249
Lionel Simmons, La Salle	6-7	1990	131	1244	56	673	3217
Alphonso Ford, Mississippi Valley St.	6-2	1993	109	1121	333	590	3165
Harry Kelly, Texas Southern	6-7	1983	110	1234	—	598	3066
Keydren Clark, St. Peter's	5-9	2006	118	967	435	689	3058
Hersey Hawkins, Bradley	6-3	1988	125	1100	118	690	3008
Oscar Robertson, Cincinnati	6-5	1960	88	1052	—	869	2973
Danny Manning, Kansas	6-10	1988	147	1216	10	509	2951
Alfredrick Hughes, Loyola (Ill.)	6-5	1985	120	1226	—	462	2914
Elvin Hayes, Houston	6-8	1968	93	1215	—	454	2884
Larry Bird, Indiana St.	6-9	1979	94	1154	—	542	2850
Otis Birdsong, Houston	6-4	1977	116	1176	—	480	2832
Kevin Bradshaw, Bethune-Cookman, U.S. Int'l	6-6	1991	111	1027	132	618	2804
Allan Houston, Tennessee	6-6	1993	128	902	346	651	2801
J.J. Redick, Duke	6-4	2006	139	825	457	662	2769
Hank Gathers, USC, Loyola Marymount	6-7	1990	117	1127	0	469	2723
Reggie Lewis, Northeastern	6-7	1987	122	1043	30 (1)	592	2708
Daren Queenan, Lehigh	6-5	1988	118	1024	29	626	2703
Byron Larkin, Xavier (Ohio)	6-3	1988	121	1022	51	601	2696
David Robinson, Navy	7-1	1987	127	1032	1	604	2669

*Listed is the number of three-pointers scored since it became the national rule in 1987; the number in the parentheses is number scored prior to 1987—these counted as three points in the game but counted as two-pointers in the national rankings. The three-pointers in the parentheses are not included in total points.

SCORING AVERAGE

Player and Team	Final Year	GP	FG	FT	Pts	Avg
Pete Maravich, LSU	1968	83	1387	893	3667	44.2
Austin Carr, Notre Dame	1971	74	1017	526	2560	34.6
Oscar Robertson, Cincinnati	1960	88	1052	869	2973	33.8
Calvin Murphy, Niagara	1970	77	947	654	2548	33.1
Dwight Lamar, SW Louisiana	1973	57	768	326	1862	32.7
Frank Selvy, Furman	1954	78	922	694	2538	32.5
Rick Mount, Purdue	1970	72	910	503	2323	32.3
Darrell Floyd, Furman	1956	71	868	545	2281	32.1
Nick Werkman, Seton Hall	1964	71	812	649	2273	32.0
Willie Humes, Idaho St.	1971	48	565	380	1510	31.5
William Averitt, Pepperdine	1973	49	615	311	1541	31.4
Elgin Baylor, Coll. of Idaho, Seattle	1958	80	956	588	2500	31.3
Elvin Hayes, Houston	1968	93	1215	454	2884	31.0
Freeman Williams, Portland St.	1978	106	1369	511	3249	30.7
Larry Bird, Indiana St.	1979	94	1154	542	2850	30.3

Career Records (Cont.)
REBOUNDS ALL-TIME

Player and Team	Final Year	GP	Reb
Tom Gola, La Salle	1955	118	2201
Joe Holup, George Washington	1956	104	2030
Charlie Slack, Marshall	1956	88	1916
Ed Conlin, Fordham	1955	102	1884
Dickie Hemric, Wake Forest	1955	104	1802

REBOUNDS SINCE 1973*

Player and Team	Final Year	GP	Reb
Tim Duncan, Wake Forest	1997	128	1570
Derrick Coleman, Syracuse	1990	143	1537
Malik Rose, Drexel	1996	120	1514
Ralph Sampson, Virginia	1983	132	1511
Pete Padgett, Nev.-Reno	1976	104	1464

ASSISTS

Player and Team	Final Year	GP	Asst
Bobby Hurley, Duke	1993	140	1076
Chris Corchiani, North Carolina St.	1991	124	1038
Ed Cota, North Carolina	2000	138	1030
Keith Jennings, East Tennessee St.	1991	127	983
Steve Blake, Maryland	2003	138	972

FIELD-GOAL PERCENTAGE

Player and Team	Final Year	FG	FGA	Pct
Steve Johnson, Oregon St.	1981	828	1222	67.8
Michael Bradley, Kentucky/Villanova	2001	441	651	67.7
Murray Brown, Florida St.	1980	566	847	66.8
Lee Campbell, SW Missouri St.	1990	411	618	66.5
Warren Kidd, Middle Tennessee St.	1993	496	747	66.4

Note: Minimum 400 field goals and 4 FG made per game.

FREE-THROW PERCENTAGE

Player and Team	Final Year	FT	FTA	Pct
Gary Buchanan, Villanova	2003	324	355	91.3
J.J. Redick, Duke	2006	662	726	91.2
Greg Starrick, Kentucky/Southern Illinois	1972	341	375	90.9
Jack Moore, Nebraska	1982	446	495	90.1
Steve Henson, Kansas St.	1990	361	401	90.0

Note: Minimum 300 free throws made.
*Freshmen became eligible for varsity play in 1973.

THREE-POINT FIELD GOALS MADE

Player and Team	Final Year	GP	3FG
J.J. Redick, Duke	2006	139	457
Keydren Clark, St. Peter's	2006	118	435
Curtis Staples, Virginia	1998	122	413
Keith Veney, Lamar/Marshall	1997	111	409
Doug Day, Radford	1993	117	401

THREE-POINT FIELD-GOAL PERCENTAGE

Player and Team	Final Year	3FG	3FGA	Pct
Tony Bennett, UW–Green Bay	1992	290	584	49.7
David Olson, Eastern Illinois	1992	262	562	46.6
Ross Land, Northern Arizona	2000	308	664	46.4
Dan Dickau, Washington/Gonzaga	2002	215	465	46.2
Steve Novak, Marquette	2006	354	768	46.1

Note: Minimum 200 3-point field goals and 2.0 3FG/G.

Career Records (Cont.)

STEALS

Player and Team	Final Year	GP	Stl
John Linehan, Providence	2002	122	385
Eric Murdock, Providence	1991	117	376
Pepe Sanchez, Temple	2000	116	365
Cookie Belcher, Nebraska	2001	131	353
Kevin Braswell, Georgetown	2002	128	349

BLOCKED SHOTS

Player and Team	Final Year	GP	BS
Wojciech Myrda, La.-Monroe	2002	115	535
Adonal Foyle, Colgate	1997	87	492
Tim Duncan, Wake Forest	1997	128	481
Alonzo Mourning, Georgetown	1992	120	453
Tarvis Williams, Hampton	2001	114	452

NCAA Men's Division I Team Leaders

Division I Team Alltime Wins

Team	First Year	Yrs	W	L	T
Kentucky	1903	103	1926	596	1
North Carolina	1911	96	1883	689	0
Kansas	1899	108	1873	777	0
Duke	1906	101	1796	791	0
Syracuse	1901	105	1680	771	0
Temple	1895	110	1656	917	0
St. John's (N.Y.)	1908	99	1643	816	0
Pennsylvania	1897	106	1612	904	2
Indiana	1901	106	1589	865	0
Utah	1909	98	1584	814	0
UCLA	1920	87	1581	707	0
Notre Dame	1898	101	1581	877	1
Oregon St	1902	105	1559	1116	0
Illinois	1906	101	1546	812	
Washington	1896	104	1529	1008	0

Division I Alltime Winning Percentage

Team	First Year	Yrs	W	L	T	Pct
Kentucky	1903	103	1926	596	1	.764
North Carolina	1911	96	1883	689	0	.732
UNLV	1959	48	980	403	0	.709
Kansas	1899	108	1873	777	0	.707
Duke	1906	101	1796	791	0	.694
UCLA	1920	87	1581	707	0	.691
Syracuse	1901	105	1680	771	0	.685
Western Kentucky	1915	87	1526	753	0	.670
St. John's (N.Y.)	1908	99	1643	816	0	.668
Utah	1909	98	1584	814	0	.661
Illinois	1906	101	1546	812	0	.656
Louisville	1912	92	1505	806	0	.651
Arizona	1905	101	1508	818	1	.648
Indiana	1901	106	1589	865	0	.648
Arkansas	1924	83	1429	780	0	.647

Note: Minimum of 25 years in Division I.

NCAA Men's Division I Winning Streaks

Longest—Full Season

Team	Games	Years	Ended by
UCLA	88	1971–74	Notre Dame (71–70)
San Francisco	60	1955–57	Illinois (62–33)
UCLA	47	1966–68	Houston (71–69)
UNLV	45	1990–91	Duke (79–77)
Texas	44	1913–17	Rice (24–18)
Seton Hall	43	1939–41	LIU-Brooklyn (49–26)
LIU-Brooklyn	43	1935–37	Stanford (45–31)
UCLA	41	1968–69	USC (46–44)
Marquette	39	1970–71	Ohio St (60–59)
Cincinnati	37	1962–63	Wichita St (65–64)
North Carolina	37	1957–58	W Virginia (75–64)

Longest—Regular Season

Team	Games	Years	Ended by
UCLA	76	1971–74	Notre Dame (71–70)
Indiana	57	1975–77	Toledo (59–57)
Marquette	56	1970–72	Detroit (70–49)
Kentucky	54	1952–55	Georgia Tech (59–58)
San Francisco	51	1955–57	Illinois (62–33)
Pennsylvania	48	1970–72	Temple (57–52)
Ohio State	47	1960–62	Wisconsin (86–67)
Texas	44	1913–17	Rice (24–18)
UCLA	43	1966–68	Houston (71–69)
LIU-Brooklyn	43	1935–37	Stanford (45–31)
Seton Hall	42	1939–41	LIU-Brooklyn (49–26)

Longest—Home Court

Team	Games	Years	Team	Games	Years
Kentucky	129	1943–55	Lamar	80	1978–84
St. Bonaventure	99	1948–61	Long Beach St	75	1968–74
UCLA	98	1970–76	UNLV	72	1974–78
Cincinnati	86	1957–64	Arizona	71	1987–92
Marquette	81	1967–73	Cincinnati	68	1972–78
Arizona	81	1945–51	Western Kentucky	67	1949–55

NCAA Men's Division I Winningest Coaches

Active Coaches*

WINS

Coach and Team	W
Bob Knight, Texas Tech	869
Eddie Sutton, Oklahoma St	798
Lute Olson, Arizona	760
Mike Krzyzewski, Duke	753
John Chaney, Temple	741
Jim Calhoun, Connecticut	733
Jim Boeheim, Syracuse	726
Billy Tubbs, Lamar	641
Tom Davis, Drake	581
Bob Huggins, Kansas St	567

Note: Minimum 5 years as a Division I head coach; includes record at 4-year colleges only.

WINNING PERCENTAGE

Coach and Team	Yrs	W	L	Pct
Mark Few, Gonzaga	7	188	41	.821
Roy Williams, North Carolina	18	493	124	.799
Bruce Pearl, Tennessee	14	339	92	.787
Bo Ryan, Wisconsin	22	495	152	.765
Thad Matta, Ohio St	6	148	49	.751
Mike Krzyzewski, Duke	31	753	250	.751
Jim Boeheim, Syracuse	30	726	253	.742
Bob Huggins, Kansas St	24	567	199	.740
Lute Olson, Arizona	33	760	269	.739
Tubby Smith, Kentucky	15	365	133	.733
Bruce Weber, Illinois	8	192	70	.733

Note: Minimum 5 years as a Division I head coach; includes record at 4-year colleges only.

Alltime Winningest Men's Division I Coaches

	W
Dean Smith (North Carolina)	879
Adolph Rupp (Kentucky)	876
*Bob Knight (Army, Indiana, Texas Tech)	869
Jim Phelan (Mt. St. Mary's)	830
*Eddie Sutton (Creighton, Arkansas, Kentucky, Oklahoma St)	798
Lefty Driesell (Davidson, Maryland, James Madison, Georgia St)	786
Lou Henson (Hardin-Simmons, New Mexico St, Illinois, New Mexico St)	779
Henry Iba (NW Missouri St, Colorado, Oklahoma St)	764
*Lute Olson (Long Beach St, Iowa, Arizona)	760
Ed Diddle (Western Kentucky)	759
*Mike Krzyzewski (Army, Duke)	753
Phog Allen (Baker, Kansas, Haskell, Central Missouri St, Kansas)	746
*John Chaney (Cheyney St, Temple)	741
*Jim Calhoun (Northeastern, Connecticut)	733
Jerry Tarkanian (Long Beach St, UNLV, Fresno St)	729
Norm Stewart (Northern Iowa, Missouri)	728
*Jim Boeheim (Syracuse)	726
Ray Meyer (DePaul)	724
Don Haskins (Oklahoma St, UTEP)	719
Denny Crum (UCLA, Louisville)	675
John Wooden (Purdue, Indiana St, UCLA)	664
Ralph Miller (Wichita St, Iowa, Oregon St)	657
Gene Bartow (C. Missouri St, Valparaiso, Memphis, Illinois, UCLA, UAB)	647
Billy Tubbs (Lamar, Southwestern [Tex.], Oklahoma, TCU)	641
Marv Harshman (Pacific Lutheran, Washington St, Washington)	637

Note: Minimum 10 head coaching seasons in Division I.
*Active in 2005–06.

Alltime Winningest Men's Division I Coaches (Cont.)

WINNING PERCENTAGE

Coach (Team, Years)	Yrs	W	L	Pct
Clair Bee (Rider 1929–31, LIU-Brooklyn 1932–45, 1946–51)...	21	412	87	.826
Adolph Rupp (Kentucky 1931–72)	41	876	190	.822
John Wooden (Indiana St 1947–48, UCLA 1949–75)...	29	664	162	.804
*Roy Williams (Kansas 1989–2003, North Carolina 2003–)	18	493	124	.799
John Kresse (College of Charleston 1980–2002)...	23	560	143	.797
Jerry Tarkanian (Long Beach St 1969–73, UNLV 1974–92, Fresno St 1995–2002)............	31	729	201	.784
Francis Schmidt (Tulsa 1916–17, Arkansas 1924–29, TCU 1930–34)	17	258	72	.782
Dean Smith (North Carolina 1962–97)..	36	879	254	.776
Jack Ramsay (St. Joseph's [Pa.] 1956–66)...	11	231	71	.765
Frank Keaney (Rhode Island 1921–48)...	28	401	124	.764
George Keogan (St. Louis 1916, Allegheny 1919, Valparaiso 1920–21, Notre Dame 1924–43).......	27	414	127	.764
Vic Bubas (Duke 1960–69)...	10	213	67	.761
Harry Fisher (Columbia 1907–16, Army 1922–23, 1925)..	16	189	60	.759
*Mike Krzyzewski (Army 1976–80, Duke 1981–)	31	753	250	.751
Fred Bennion (Brigham Young 1909–10, Utah 1911-14, Montana St 1915-19)...................	11	95	32	.748
Charles (Chick) Davies (Duquesne 1925–43, 1947–48)...	21	314	106	.748
Ray Mears (Wittenberg 1957–62, Tennessee 1963–77)...	21	399	135	.747
Edward McNichol (Penn 1921-30)	10	186	63	.747
Rick Majerus (Marquette 1984–86, Ball St 1988–89, Utah 1990–2004)............................	20	422	147	.742
*Jim Boeheim (Syracuse 1977–)	30	726	253	.742
Al McGuire (Belmont Abbey 1958–64, Marquette 1965–77)	20	406	142	.741
Bob Huggins (Walsh 1980–83, Akron 1984–89, Cincinnati 1989–2005)	24	567	199	.740
Phog Allen (Baker 1906–08, Haskell 1909, C. Mo. St 1913–19, Kansas 1908–09, 1920–56)	50	746	264	.739
*Lute Olson (Long Beach St 1973–74, Iowa 1974–83, Arizona 1983–)	33	760	269	.739
Everett Case (North Carolina St 1947–65)	19	377	134	.738

Note: Minimum 10 head coaching seasons in Division I.

*Active in 2005–06.

NCAA Women's Division I Championship Results

Year	Winner	Score	Runner-up	Winning Coach
1982	Louisiana Tech	76–62	Cheyney	Sonja Hogg
1983	USC	69–67	Louisiana Tech	Linda Sharp
1984	USC	72–61	Tennessee	Linda Sharp
1985	Old Dominion	70–65	Georgia	Marianne Stanley
1986	Texas	97–81	USC	Jody Conradt
1987	Tennessee	67–44	Louisiana Tech	Pat Summitt
1988	Louisiana Tech	56–54	Auburn	Leon Barmore
1989	Tennessee	76–60	Auburn	Pat Summitt
1990	Stanford	88–81	Auburn	Tara VanDerveer
1991	Tennessee	70–67 (OT)	Virginia	Pat Summitt
1992	Stanford	78–62	Western Kentucky	Tara VanDerveer
1993	Texas Tech	84–82	Ohio State	Marsha Sharp
1994	North Carolina	60–59	Louisiana Tech	Sylvia Hatchell
1995	Connecticut	70–64	Tennessee	Geno Auriemma
1996	Tennessee	83–65	Georgia	Pat Summitt
1997	Tennessee	68–59	Old Dominion	Pat Summitt
1998	Tennessee	93–75	Louisiana Tech	Pat Summitt
1999	Purdue	62–45	Duke	Carolyn Peck
2000	Connecticut	71–52	Tennessee	Geno Auriemma
2001	Notre Dame	68–66	Purdue	Muffet McGraw
2002	Connecticut	82–70	Oklahoma	Geno Auriemma
2003	Connecticut	73–68	Tennessee	Geno Auriemma
2004	Connecticut	70–61	Tennessee	Geno Auriemma
2005	Baylor	84–62	Michigan St	Kim Mulkey-Robinson
2006	Maryland	78–75	Duke	Brenda Frese

NCAA Women's Division I Alltime Individual Leaders

Single-Game Records

SCORING HIGHS

Pts	Player and Team vs Opponent	Year
60	Cindy Brown, Long Beach St vs San Jose St	1987
58	Kim Perrot, SW Louisiana vs SE Louisiana	1990
58	Lorri Bauman, Drake vs SW Missouri St	1984
56	Jackie Stiles, SW Missouri St vs Evansville	2000
55	Patricia Hoskins, Mississippi Valley St vs Southern-Birm.	1989
55	Patricia Hoskins, Mississippi Valley St vs Alabama St	1989
54	Anjinea Hopson, Grambling vs Jackson St	1994
54	Mary Lowry, Baylor vs Texas	1994
54	Wanda Ford, Drake vs SW Missouri St	1986

Three tied with 53.

REBOUNDS

Reb	Player and Team vs Opponent	Year
40	Deborah Temple, Delta St vs Ala.-Birmingham	1983
37	Rosina Pearson, Bethune-Cookman vs Florida Memorial	1985
33	Maureen Formico, Pepperdine vs Loyola (Calif.)	1985
31	Darlene Beale, Howard vs South Carolina St	1987
30	Cindy Bonforte, Wagner vs Queens (N.Y.)	1983
30	Kayone Hankins, New Orleans vs. Nicholls St	1994
30	Wanda Ford, Drake vs Eastern Illinois	1985
30	Jennifer Butler, Massachusetts vs Florida	2003

Three tied with 29.

ASSISTS

Asst	Player and Team vs Opponent	Year
23	Michelle Burden, Kent St vs Ball St	1991
22	Shawn Monday, Tennessee Tech vs Morehead St	1988
22	Veronica Pettry, Loyola (Ill.) vs Detroit	1989
22	Tine Freil, Pacific vs Wichita St	1991
21	Tine Freil, Pacific vs Fresno St	1992
21	Amy Bauer, Wisconsin vs Detroit	1989
21	Neacole Hall, Alabama St vs Southern-Birm.	1989

Six tied with 20.

Single Season Records

POINTS

Player and Team	Year	GP	FG	3FG	FT	Pts
Jackie Stiles, SW Missouri St*	2001	35	365	65	267	1062
Cindy Brown, Long Beach St	1987	35	362	—	250	974
Genia Miller, CSU-Fullerton	1991	33	376	0	217	969
Sheryl Swoopes, Texas Tech	1993	34	356	32	211	955
Andrea Congreaves, Mercer	1992	28	353	77	142	925
Wanda Ford, Drake	1986	30	390	—	139	919
Chamique Holdsclaw, Tennessee	1998	39	370	9	166	915
Barbara Kennedy, Clemson	1982	31	392	—	124	908
Patricia Hoskins, Mississippi Valley	1989	27	345	13	205	908
LaTaunya Pollard, Long Beach St	1983	31	376	—	155	907

SEASON SCORING AVERAGE

Player and Team	Year	GP	FG	3FG	FT	Pts	Avg
Patricia Hoskins, Mississippi Valley	1989	27	345	13	205	908	33.6
Andrea Congreaves, Mercer	1992	28	353	77	142	925	33.0
Deborah Temple, Delta St	1984	28	373	—	127	873	31.2
Andrea Congreaves, Mercer	1993	26	302	51	150	805	31.0
Wanda Ford, Drake	1986	30	390	—	139	919	30.6
Anucha Browne, Northwestern	1985	28	341	—	173	855	30.5
LeChandra LeDay, Grambling	1988	28	334	36	146	850	30.4
Jackie Stiles, SW MIssouri St*	2001	35	365	65	267	1062	30.3
Kim Perrot, SW Louisiana	1990	28	308	95	128	839	30.0
Tina Hutchinson, San Diego St	1984	30	383	—	132	898	29.9
Jan Jensen, Drake	1991	30	358	6	166	888	29.6
Genia Miller, CSU-Fullerton	1991	33	376	0	217	969	29.4
Barbara Kennedy, Clemson	1982	31	392	—	124	908	29.3
LaTaunya Pollard, Long Beach St	1983	31	376	—	155	907	29.3
Lisa McMullen, Alabama St	1991	28	285	126	119	815	29.1

REBOUNDS

Player and Team	Year	GP	Reb	Player and Team	Year	GP	Reb
Courtney Paris, Oklahoma	2006	36	539	Melanie Simpson, Okla. City	1982	37	481
Wanda Ford, Drake	1985	30	534	R. Pearson, Beth.-Cookman	1985	26	480
Wanda Ford, Drake	1986	30	506	Patricia Hoskins, Miss. Valley St	1987	28	476
Anne Donovan, Old Dominion	1983	35	504	Cheryl Miller, USC	1985	30	474
Darlene Jones, Miss Valley	1983	31	487	Darlene Beale, Howard	1987	29	459

REBOUND AVERAGE

Player and Team	Year	GP	Reb	Avg
Rosina Pearson, Bethune-Cookman	1985	26	480	18.5
Wanda Ford, Drake	1985	30	534	17.8
Katie Beck, East Tennessee St	1988	25	441	17.6
DeShawne Blocker, East Tennessee St	1994	26	450	17.3
Patricia Hoskins, Mississippi Valley St	1987	28	476	17.0
Wanda Ford, Drake	1986	30	506	16.9
Patricia Hoskins, Mississippi Valley St	1989	27	440	16.3
Joy Kellogg, Oklahoma City	1984	23	373	16.2
Deborah Mitchell, Mississippi Coll.	1983	28	447	16.0
Cheryl Miller, USC	1985	30	474	15.8

*school changed name to Missouri State after 2004–05 season

Single Season Records (Cont.)

FIELD-GOAL PERCENTAGE

Player and Team	Year	GP	FG	FGA	Pct
Myndee Larsen, Southern Utah	1998	28	249	344	72.4
Chantelle Anderson, Vanderbilt	2001	34	292	404	72.3
Deneka Knowles, SE Louisiana	1996	26	199	276	72.1
Barbara Farris, Tulane	1998	27	151	210	71.9
Renay Adams, Tennessee Tech	1991	30	185	258	71.7
Regina Days, Georgia Southern	1986	27	234	332	70.5
Kim Wood, UW-Green Bay	1994	27	188	271	69.4
Kelly Lyons, Old Dominion	1990	31	308	444	69.4
Alisha Hill, Howard	1995	28	194	281	69.0
Ruth Riley, Notre Dame	1999	31	198	290	68.3

Based on qualifiers for annual championship.

FREE-THROW PERCENTAGE

Player and Team	Year	GP	FT	FTA	Pct
Adrienne Squire, Penn St	2006	29	80	83	96.4
Shanna Zolman, Tennessee	2004	35	88	92	95.7
Ginny Doyle, Richmond	1992	29	96	101	95.0
Jill Marano, La Salle	2003	29	88	93	94.6
Sue Bird, Connecticut	2002	39	98	104	94.2
Paula Corder-King, SE Missouri St	1999	28	111	118	94.1
Kandi Brown, Morehead St	2003	28	104	111	93.7
Linda Cyborski, Delaware	1991	29	74	79	93.7
Kandi Brown, Morehead St	2002	29	74	79	93.7
Kristin Iwanaga, California	2005	29	85	91	93.4

Based on qualifiers for annual championship.

Career Records

POINTS

Player and Team	Yrs	GP	Pts
Jackie Stiles, SW Missouri St*	1997–01	129	3393
Patricia Hoskins, Mississippi Valley ST	1985–89	110	3122
Lorri Bauman, Drake	1981–84	120	3115
Chamique Holdsclaw, Tennessee	1995–99	148	3025
Cheryl Miller, USC	1983–86	128	3018
Cindy Blodgett, Maine	1994–98	118	3005
LaToya Thomas, Mississippi St	1999–2003	125	2981
Valorie Whiteside, Appalachian St	1984–88	116	2944
Kelly Mazzante, Penn St	2000–04	133	2919
Joyce Walker, LSU	1981–84	117	2906

SCORING AVERAGE

Player and Team	Yrs	GP	FG	3FG	FT	Pts	Avg
Patricia Hoskins, Mississippi Valley St	1985–89	110	1196	24	706	3122	28.4
Sandra Hodge, New Orleans	1981–84	107	1194	—	472	2860	26.7
Jackie Stiles, SW Missouri St*	1997–01	129	1160	221	852	3393	26.3
Lorri Bauman, Drake	1981–84	120	1104	—	907	3115	26.0
Andrea Congreaves, Mercer	1989–93	108	1107	153	429	2796	25.9
Cindy Blodgett, Maine	1994–98	118	1055	219	676	3005	25.5
Valorie Whiteside, Appalachian St	1984–88	116	1153	0	638	2944	25.4
Joyce Walker, LSU	1981–84	117	1259	—	388	2906	24.8
Tarcha Hollis, Grambling	1988–91	85	904	3	247	2058	24.2
Korie Hlede, Duquesne	1994–98	109	1045	162	379	2631	24.1

*school changed name to Missouri State after 2004–05 season

NCAA Men's Division II Championship Results

Year	Winner	Score	Runner-up	Third Place	Fourth Place
1957	Wheaton (Ill.)	89–65	Kentucky Wesleyan	Mt. St. Mary's (Md.)	CSU-Los Angeles
1958	South Dakota	75–53	St. Michael's	Evansville	Wheaton (Ill.)
1959	Evansville	83–67	SW Missouri St	North Carolina A&T	CSU-Los Angeles
1960	Evansville	90–69	Chapman	Kentucky Wesleyan	Cornell College
1961	Wittenberg	42–38	SE Missouri St	South Dakota St	Mt. St. Mary's (Md.)
1962	Mt. St. Mary's (Md.)	58–57 (OT)	CSU-Sacramento	Southern Illinois	Nebraska Wesleyan
1963	South Dakota St	44–42	Wittenberg	Oglethorpe	Southern Illinois
1964	Evansville	72–59	Akron	North Carolina A&T	Northern Iowa
1965	Evansville	85–82 (OT)	Southern Illinois	North Dakota	St. Michael's
1966	Kentucky Wesleyan	54–51	Southern Illinois	Akron	North Dakota
1967	Winston-Salem	77–74	SW Missouri St	Kentucky Wesleyan	Illinois St
1968	Kentucky Wesleyan	63–52	Indiana St	Trinity (Tex.)	Ashland
1969	Kentucky Wesleyan	75–71	SW Missouri St	†Vacated	Ashland
1970	Philadelphia Textile	76–65	Tennessee St	UC-Riverside	Buffalo St
1971	Evansville	97–82	Old Dominion	†Vacated	Kentucky Wesleyan
1972	Roanoke	84–72	Akron	Tennessee St	Eastern Mich
1973	Kentucky Wesleyan	78–76 (OT)	Tennessee St	Assumption	Brockport St
1974	Morgan St	67–52	SW Missouri St	Assumption	New Orleans
1975	Old Dominion	76–74	New Orleans	Assumption	Tenn.-Chattanooga
1976	Puget Sound	83–74	Tenn.-Chattanooga	Eastern Illinois	Old Dominion
1977	Tenn.-Chattanooga	71–62	Randolph-Macon	North Alabama	Sacred Heart
1978	Cheyney	47–40	UW-Green Bay	Eastern Illinois	Central Florida
1979	North Alabama	64–50	UW-Green Bay	Cheyney	Bridgeport
1980	Virginia Union	80–74	New York Tech	Florida Southern	North Alabama
1981	Florida Southern	73–68	Mt. St. Mary's (Md.)	Cal Poly-SLO	UW-Green Bay
1982	District of Columbia	73–63	Florida Southern	Kentucky Wesleyan	CSU-Bakersfield
1983	Wright St	92–73	District of Columbia	*CSU-Bakersfield	*Morningside
1984	Central Missouri St	81–77	St. Augustine's	*Kentucky Wesleyan	*N Alabama
1985	Jacksonville St	74–73	S Dakota St	*Kentucky Wesleyan	*Mt. St. Mary's (Md.)
1986	Sacred Heart	93–87	SE Missouri St	*Cheyney	*Florida Southern
1987	Kentucky Wesleyan	92–74	Gannon	*Delta St	*Eastern Montana
1988	Lowell	75–72	AK-Anchorage	Florida Southern	Troy St
1989	North Carolina Central	73–46	SE Missouri St	UC-Riverside	Jacksonville St
1990	Kentucky Wesleyan	93–79	CSU-Bakersfield	North Dakota	Morehouse
1991	North Alabama	79–72	Bridgeport (Conn.)	*CSU-Bakersfield	*Virginia Union
1992	Virginia Union	100–75	Bridgeport (Conn.)	*CSU-Bakersfield	*California (Pa.)
1993	CSU-Bakersfield	85–72	Troy St (Ala.)	*New Hampshire Coll	*Wayne St (MI)
1994	CSU-Bakersfield	92–86	Southern Indiana	*New Hampshire Coll	*Washburn
1995	Southern Indiana	71–63	UC-Riverside	*Norfolk St	*Indiana (Pa.)
1996	Fort Hays St	70–63	Northern Kentucky	*California (Pa.)	*Virginia Union
1997	CSU-Bakersfield	57–56	Northern Kentucky	*Lynn	*Salem-Teikyo
1998	UC-Davis	83–77	Kentucky Wesleyan	*St. Rose	*Virginia Union
1999	Kentucky Wesleyan	75–60	Metropolitan St	*Truman St	*Florida Southern
2000	Metropolitan St	97–79	Kentucky Wesleyan	*Missouri Southern	*Seattle Pacific
2001	Kentucky Wesleyan	72–63	Washburn	*Western Washington	*Tampa
2002	Metropolitan St	80–72	Kentucky Wesleyan	*Shaw	*Indiana (Pa.)
2003	Northeastern St (Okla.)	75–64	†Vacated	*Bowie St	*Queens (N.Y.)
2004	Kennesaw St	84–59	Southern Indiana	*Humboldt St	*Metropolitan St
2005	Virginia Union	63–58	Bryant	*Lynn	*Tarleton St
2006	Winona St (Minn.)	73–61	Virginia Union	*Seattle Pacific	*Stonehill

*tied for third place

*Indicates tied for third. †Student-athletes representing American International in 1969, Southwestern Louisiana in 1971, and Kentucky Wesleyan in 2003 were declared ineligible subsequent to the tournament. Under NCAA rules, the teams' and ineligible student-athletes' records were deleted, and the teams' places in the final standings were vacated.

SINGLE-GAME SCORING HIGHS

Pts	Player and Team vs Opponent	Date
113	Bevo Francis, Rio Grande vs Hillsdale	1954
84	Bevo Francis, Rio Grande vs Alliance	1954
82	Bevo Francis, Rio Grande vs Bluffton	1954
80	Paul Crissman, USC vs Pacific Christian	1966
77	William English, Winston-Salem vs Fayetteville St	1968

Single Season Records

SCORING AVERAGE

Player and Team	Year	GP	FG	FT	Pts	Avg
Bevo Francis, Rio Grande	1954	27	444	367	1255	46.5
Earl Glass, Mississippi Industrial	1963	19	322	171	815	42.9
Earl Monroe, Winston-Salem	1967	32	509	311	1329	41.5
John Rinka, Kenyon	1970	23	354	234	942	41.0
Willie Shaw, Lane	1964	18	303	121	727	40.4

REBOUND AVERAGE

Player and Team	Year	GP	Reb	Avg
Tom Hart, Middlebury	1956	21	620	29.5
Tom Hart, Middlebury	1955	22	649	29.5
Frank Stronczek, American Int'l	1966	26	717	27.6
R.C. Owens, College of Idaho	1954	25	677	27.1
Maurice Stokes, St. Francis (Pa.)	1954	26	689	26.5

ASSISTS

Player and Team	Year	GP	Asst
Steve Ray, Bridgeport	1989	32	400
Steve Ray, Bridgeport	1990	33	385
Tony Smith, Pfeiffer	1992	35	349
Jim Ferrer, Bentley	1989	31	309
Rob Paternostro, New Hamp. Coll.	1995	33	309

ASSIST AVERAGE

Player and Team	Year	GP	Asst	Avg
Steve Ray, Bridgeport	1989	32	400	12.5
Steve Ray, Bridgeport	1990	33	385	11.7
Demetri Beekman, Assumption	1993	23	264	11.5
Ernest Jenkins, N.M.-Highlands	1995	27	291	10.8
Brian Gregory, Oakland	1989	28	300	10.7

FIELD-GOAL PERCENTAGE

Player and Team	Year	Pct
Todd Linder, Tampa	1987	75.2
Maurice Stafford, North Alabama	1984	75.0
Matthew Cornegay, Tuskegee	1982	74.8
Callistus Eziukwu, Grand Valley St.	2005	73.7
Brian Moten, W. Georgia	1992	73.4

FREE-THROW PERCENTAGE

Player and Team	Year	Pct
Paul Cluxton, Northern Kentucky	1997	100.0
Tomas Rimkus, Pace	1997	95.6
C.J. Cowgill, Chaminade	2001	95.0
Billy Newton, Morgan St	1976	94.4
Kent Andrews, McNeese St	1968	94.4

Career Records

POINTS

Player and Team	Yrs	Pts
Travis Grant, Kentucky St	1969–72	4045
Bob Hopkins, Grambling	1953–56	3759
Tony Smith, Pfeiffer	1989–92	3350
Earnest Lee, Clark Atlanta	1984–87	3298
Joe Miller, Alderson-Broaddus	1954–57	3294

CAREER SCORING AVERAGE

Player and Team	Yrs	GP	Pts	Avg
Travis Grant, Kentucky St	1969–72	121	4045	33.4
John Rinka, Kenyon	1967–70	99	3251	32.8
Florindo Vieira, Quinnipiac	1954–57	69	2263	32.8
Willie Shaw, Lane	1961–64	76	2379	31.3
Mike Davis, Virginia Union	1966–69	89	2758	31.0

REBOUND AVERAGE

Player and Team	Yrs	GP	Reb	Avg
Tom Hart, Middlebury	1953, 55–56	63	1738	27.6
Maurice Stokes, St. Francis (Pa.)	1953–55	72	1812	25.2
Frank Stronczek, American Int'l	1965–67	62	1549	25.0
Bill Thieben, Hofstra	1954–56	76	1837	24.2
Hank Brown, Lowell Tech	1965–67	49	1129	23.0

Career Records (Cont.)

ASSISTS

Player and Team	Yrs	Asst
Demetri Beekman, Assumption	1990–93	1044
Adam Kaufman, Edinboro	1998–01	936
Rob Paternostro, New Hamp. Coll.	1992–95	919
Tony Smith, Pfeiffer	1989–92	828
Jamie Stevens, MSU-Billings	1996–99	805

ASSIST AVERAGE

Player and Team	Yrs	GP	Asst	Avg
Steve Ray, Bridgeport	1989–90	65	785	12.1
Demetri Beekman, Assumption	1990–93	119	1044	8.8
Ernest Jenkins, N.M.-Highlands	1992–95	84	699	8.3
Adam Kaufman, Edinboro	1998–01	116	936	8.1
Mark Benson, Texas A&I	1989–91	86	674	7.8

Note: Minimum 550 Assists.

FIELD-GOAL PERCENTAGE

Player and Team	Yrs	Pct
Todd Linder, Tampa	1984–87	70.8
Tom Schurfranz, Bellarmine	1989–92	70.2
Chad Scott, California (Pa.)	1991–94	70.0
Ed Phillips, Alabama A&M	1968–71	68.9
Ulysses Hackett, SC-Spartanburg	1990–92	67.9

Note: Minimum 400 FGM.

FREE-THROW PERCENTAGE

Player and Team	Yrs	Pct
Paul Cluxton, Northern Kentucky	1994–97	93.5
Kent Andrews, McNeese St	1967–69	91.6
Jon Hagen, Minnesota St–Mankato	1963–65	90.0
Dave Reynolds, Davis & Elkins	1986–89	89.3
Michael Shue, Lock Haven	1994–97	88.5

Note: Minimum 250 FTM.

NCAA Men's Division III Championship Results

Year	Winner	Score	Runner-up	Third Place	Fourth Place
1975	LeMoyne-Owen	57–54	Glassboro St	Augustana (Ill.)	Brockport St
1976	Scranton	60–57	Wittenberg	Augustana (Ill.)	Plattsburgh St
1977	Wittenberg	79–66	Oneonta St	Scranton	Hamline
1978	North Park	69–57	Widener	Albion	Stony Brook
1979	North Park	66–62	Potsdam St	Franklin & Marshall	Centre
1980	North Park	83–76	Upsala	Wittenberg	Longwood
1981	Potsdam St	67–65 (OT)	Augustana (Ill.)	Ursinus	Otterbein
1982	Wabash	83–62	Potsdam St	Brooklyn	CSU-Stanislaus
1983	Scranton	64–63	Wittenberg	Roanoke	UW–Whitewater
1984	UW–Whitewater	103–86	Clark (Mass.)	DePauw	Upsala
1985	North Park	72–71	Potsdam St	Nebraska Wesleyan	Widener
1986	Potsdam St	76–73	LeMoyne-Owen	Nebraska Wesleyan	Jersey City St
1987	North Park	106–100	Clark (Mass.)	Wittenberg	Stockton St
1988	Ohio Wesleyan	92–70	Scranton	Nebraska Wesleyan	Hartwick
1989	UW–Whitewater	94–86	Trenton St	Southern Maine	Centre
1990	Rochester	43–42	DePauw	Washington (Md.)	Calvin
1991	UW–Platteville	81–74	Franklin & Marshall	Otterbein	Ramapo (N.J.)
1992	Calvin	62–49	Rochester	UW–Platteville	Jersey City St
1993	Ohio Northern	71–68	Augustana	UMass–Dartmouth	Rowan
1994	Lebanon Valley Coll	66–59 (OT)	NYU	Wittenberg	St Thomas (Minn.)
1995	UW–Platteville	69–55	Manchester	Rowan	Trinity (Conn.)
1996	Rowan	100–93	Hope (Mich.)	Illinois Wesleyan	Franklin & Marshall
1997	Illinois Wesleyan	89–86	Nebraska Wesleyan	Williams	Alvernia
1998	UW–Platteville	69–56	Hope (Mich.)	Williams	Wilkes
1999	UW–Platteville	76–75 (2 OT)	Hampden-Sydney	William Paterson	Connecticut Coll.
2000	Calvin	79–74	UW–Eau Claire	Salem St	Franklin & Marshall
2001	Catholic	76–62	William Paterson	Illinois Wesleyan	Ohio Northern
2002	Otterbein	102–83	Elizabethtown	Carthage	Rochester
2003	Williams	67–65	Gustavus Adolphus	Wooster	Hampden Sydney
2004	UW–Stevens Point	84–82	Williams	John Carroll	Amherst
2005	UW–Stevens Point	73–49	Rochester	Calvin	York
2006	Virginia Wesleyan	59–56	Wittenberg	Illinois Wesleyan	Amherst

SINGLE-GAME SCORING HIGHS

Pts	Player and Team vs Opponent	Year
77	Jeff Clement, Grinnell vs Illinois College	1998
69	Steve Diekmann, Grinnell vs Simpson	1995
64	Tim Russell, Albertus Magnus	2005
63	Ryan Hodges, Cal-Lutheran	2005
63	Joe DeRoche, Thomas vs St. Joseph's (Me.)	1988
62	Kyle Myrick, Lincoln (Pa.) vs. Penn St.-Abington	2006
62	Nick Pelotte, Plymouth St	2005
62	Shannon Lilly, Bishop vs Southwest Assembly of God	1983
61	Steve Honderd, Calvin vs Kalamazoo	1993
61	Dana Wilson, Husson vs Ricker	1974

Single Season Records

SCORING AVERAGE

Player and Team	Year	GP	FG	FT	Pts	Avg
Steve Diekmann, Grinnell	1995	20	223	162	745	37.3
Rickey Sutton, Lyndon St	1976	14	207	93	507	36.2
Shannon Lilly, Bishop	1983	26	345	218	908	34.9
Dana Wilson, Husson	1974	20	288	122	698	34.9
Rickey Sutton, Lyndon St	1977	16	223	112	558	34.9

REBOUND AVERAGE

Player and Team	Year	GP	Reb	Avg
Joe Manley, Bowie St	1976	29	579	20.0
Fred Petty, New Hampshire Coll.	1974	22	436	19.8
Larry Williams, Pratt	1977	24	457	19.0
Charles Greer, Thomas	1977	17	318	18.7
Larry Parker, Plattsburgh St	1975	23	430	18.7

ASSISTS

Player and Team	Year	GP	Asst
Robert James, Kean	1989	29	391
Tennyson Whitted, Ramapo	2002	29	319
Ricky Spicer, UW-Whitewater	1989	31	295
Joe Marcotte, New Jersey Tech	1995	30	292
Andre Bolton, Chris. Newport	1996	30	289

ASSIST AVERAGE

Player and Team	Year	GP	Asst	Avg
Robert James, Kean	1989	29	391	13.5
Albert Kirchner, Mt. St. Vincent	1990	24	267	11.1
Tennyson Whitted, Ramapo	2002	29	319	11.0
Ron Torgalski, Hamilton	1989	26	275	10.6
Louis Adams, Rust	1989	22	227	10.3

FIELD-GOAL PERCENTAGE

Player and Team	Year	Pct
Travis Weiss, St. John's (Minn.)	1994	76.6
Brian Schmitting, Ripon	2006	76.3
Pete Metzelaars, Wabash	1982	75.3
Tony Rychlec, Mass. Maritime	1981	74.9
Tony Rychlec, Mass. Maritime	1982	73.1

FREE-THROW PERCENTAGE

Player and Team	Year	Pct
Korey Coon, Illinois Wesleyan	2000	96.3
Chanse Young, Manchester	1998	95.6
Andy Enfield, Johns Hopkins	1991	95.3
Nick Wilkins, Coe	2003	95.7
Chris Carideo, Widener	1992	95.2

Career Records

POINTS

Player and Team	Yrs	Pts
Andre Foreman, Salisbury St	1989–92	2940
Willie Chandler, Misericordia	2000–03	2898
Lamont Strothers, Chris. Newport	1988–91	2709
Matt Hancock, Colby	1987–90	2678
Scott Fitch, Geneseo St	1990–94	2634

SCORING AVERAGE

Player and Team	Yrs	GP	Avg
Dwain Govan, Bishop	1974–75	55	32.8
Dave Russell, Shepherd	1974–75	60	30.6
Kyle Myrick, Lincoln (Pa.)	2005–06	57	30.2
Rickey Sutton, Lyndon St	1976–79	80	29.7
John Atkins, Knoxville	1976–78	70	28.7

REBOUND AVERAGE

Player and Team	Yrs	GP	Reb	Avg
Larry Parker, Plattsburgh St	1975–78	85	1482	17.4
Charles Greer, Thomas	1975–77	58	926	16.0
Willie Parr, LeMoyne-Owen	1974–76	76	1182	15.6
Michael Smith, Hamilton	1989–92	107	1632	15.2
Dave Kufeld, Yeshiva	1977–80	81	1222	15.1

ASSIST AVERAGE

Player and Team	Yrs	Avg
Phil Dixon, Shenandoah	1993–96	8.6
Tennyson Whitted, Ramapo	2000–03	8.5
Steve Artis, Chris. Newport	1990–93	8.1
David Genovese, Mt. St. Vincent	1992–95	7.5
Kevin Root, Eureka	1989–91	7.1

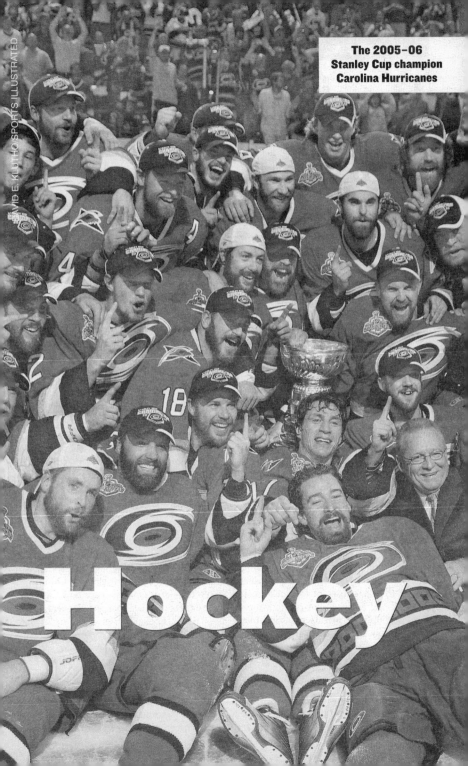

The 2005–06
Stanley Cup champion
Carolina Hurricanes

Hockey

Back From the Brink

The first season of post-lockout hockey was crisper, cleaner and more competitive, and the Carolina Hurricanes took advantage, rising up to capture the Stanley Cup

BY B.J. SCHECTER

THE SEASON-LONG LOCKOUT had become a sad part of the NHL's history, and as the fans' already-dwindling enthusiasm for the game continued to cool, one had to wonder if hockey would ever recover. Every major U.S. professional sports league has endured a work stoppage of some sort over the last 20 years, and each faced an uphill battle with the fans upon its return. Making matters worse, few in the United States seemed to miss hockey in the year that it was gone, and the lack of marketable stars appeared to spell doom for the so-called Not Happening League.

But NHL Commissioner Gary Bettman dug in his heels and vowed to resuscitate the game by fixing its faltering economic structure and improving the quality of play on the ice. It all seemed like a pipe dream during the dark days of the lockout, but Bettman had a vision and refused to back down to public or private pressure. In the end, Bettman got the Collective Bargaining Agreement he wanted, withstood numerous calls for his resignation and emerged as the winner of the sad ordeal—albeit with plenty of bruises.

When the puck finally dropped in October, the NHL was unquestionably better.

New rule changes were instituted to open up the game and get rid of the dirty play, in particular, clutching and grabbing, that made the sport unwatchable at times. The red line was taken out, allowing for longer passes, which created more scoring opportunities. Referees were instructed to strictly call penalties against slow play. And, most importantly, tie games would now be decided by shootouts.

The players were reluctant to embrace the changes, but by season's end nearly everyone had been converted to the new and improved NHL. The Players' Association conducted a poll that showed 95 percent of the players were happier with the game than they were before the lockout. Scoring immediately increased—there were seven 100-point scorers compared to none in 2003-04, five 50-goal scorers (none in '03-'04) and 79 hat tricks (up from 46 in '03-'04)—suspensions were down and the game was much crisper and cleaner.

"The hockey's entertaining," said Phoenix Coyotes coach Wayne Gretzky. "It's much faster than it was two years ago. The good players, who drive to the net and compete, either get a scoring opportunity or draw a penalty."

Most importantly for the NHL, fans started to come back. League-wide atten-

dance was up 2.4 percent to an average of 16,955 fans per game and 13 of the 30 teams played to 98 percent capacity or higher. Revenue reached $2.1 billion, the same point it was at before the lockout, and at season's end the league announced it would increase the salary cap from $39 million to $44 million for the 2006-07 season.

So, the real reason the league made it back seamlessly was that the ice had been symbolically leveled by the new salary cap. The Red Wings and Rangers were no longer allowed to stockpile talent and take on payroll simply because they could, putting smaller market teams very much in the game. The result was that by the end of the season, small market teams ruled the league. The Carolina Hurricanes and Edmonton Oilers didn't make the playoffs in 2004, but when all was said and done in '06 they were the last two teams standing. No lead—in a game or a series—was safe, and the Stanley Cup Finals took on the feel and attitude of a street fight. Carolina, playing with several

Hurricanes goalie Cam Ward's brilliant play during the Stanley Cup finals earned him the Conn Smythe Trophy.

seasoned veterans, quickly took control by jumping out to a 3-1 series lead. But the ultimate underdog Oilers battled back to win the next two games and force a Game 7.

Yes, hockey had come a long way. And so had the Hurricanes. The franchise began as the New England Whalers in the WHA and when the league went defunct in 1979 they entered the NHL as the Hartford Whalers. Never much more than the team that played in a mall (where Hartford Civic Center is located), the team moved to Carolina in 1997 and changed its name to the Hurricanes.

How would hockey play in the heart of college basketball country? Not surprisingly, it got off to a slow start, but the fan base built up quickly. Soon the Southern fans were embracing the sport and the small market team played fiercely. The fans were loyal, loud and a big spark to the home team. And when it came time for Game 7 of the Stanley Cup Finals, they stood the entire time—just as they would for any ACC game on Tobacco Road. Charged up by the raucous crowd and powered by captain Rod Brind'Amour and rookie goalie Cam Ward, the Hurricanes jumped out to a quick start and withstood a furious Oilers charge to come away with a 3-1 victory and capture Lord Stanley's Cup.

"Carolina, your new Stanley Cup Champion," doesn't flow off the tongue the way it would in, say, Detroit, New York or Montreal. But it's a sign of the times and an example of something the other three major pro leagues have been striving for—parity. True, the "P" word may not capture the nation's attention—ratings on both OLN and NBC were low, and the NHL was even outdrawn by the College World Series—but what better way to grow the sport than to install a system that enables any of the 30 teams to be competitive right away?

Take the Hurricanes. At the beginning of the season—or even at the beginning of the playoffs—few would have predicted that Carolina would win the Stanley Cup. But the NHL is no longer just about obvious favorites. This year, the league's new structure allowed unsung players on unheralded teams to flourish. Carolina's Ward didn't even start the first two games of the playoffs, but the 22-year-old rookie came on strong, grew more confident with every game and eventually won the Conn Smythe Trophy given to the Finals MVP. Said Brind'Amour, "We got to raise the Cup because of that kid."

And also because of winger Erik Cole, who fractured a vertebra in his neck on March 4, but was determined to come back in the Finals, even though the injury hadn't completely healed. On the flight back to Edmonton after Carolina's Game 5 loss, Cole made his pitch to get back into the lineup. Carolina coaches decided that if doctors cleared Cole he could play, and the forward flew to Denver to have a CT scan. Cole was told the injury was 90 percent healed and that there would essentially be no difference between playing now and three months later in training camp. "The healing has been maximized," Cole said, "and the risk is going to be with me the rest of my life."

So Cole came back, and after a 4-0 loss in Game 6, made his presence felt in the Cup-deciding game. Early in the second period on a Carolina power play, he barreled into the Edmonton zone, drew two defenders and set up Frantisek Kaberle's goal, which would turn out to be the game-winner.

"Long after I hold the Cup and have my time with it in the summer," said Carolina coach Peter Laviolette, "I will remember where this team came from, how hard they fought for each other."

And no one in Edmonton will soon forget how their beloved Oilers defied the odds and made it back to the Finals for the first time since 1990, when Mark Messier ruled the ice. Playing in the NHL's smallest market, the Oilers are a team of the people in every sense of the phrase. For one thing, the fans know their hockey and follow it with a passion that rivals the Red Sox Nation in baseball. For another, like the NFL's Green Bay Packers, the people of Edmonton, actually *own* the Oilers. The team is divided among 35 local businesses and it seems like everybody in the city knows someone who owns a piece of the team. And nearly 70 percent of the 15,000 season tickets are purchased by individuals.

"This is about hockey 24 hours a day," said Oilers defenseman Steve Staios. "There's nowhere you can go in this city and not be an Edmonton Oiler. Some people have trouble dealing with that, but some guys thrive."

Buoyed by their fans, the Oilers thrived in the playoffs. Though an underdog in every series, Edmonton found a way to win. And after knocking off the Mighty Ducks in five games to win the Western Conference and make it back to the Finals, it felt like the glory days all over again, back when the Oilers won five Stanley Cups between 1984 and 1990.

Edmonton still plays in an old, crumbling arena that's short on amenities but high on charm. One of the arena's most unique fea-

A bumper crop of rookies like Pittsburgh's Sidney Crosby and Washington's Alexander Ovechkin (above) enlivened the league.

tures is something called the Green Mile, which is what Edmontonians call the 29 steps from the Oilers' dressing room to the ice. Fans line the Mile and are vocal about their opinions of the team's play.

"When you talk to people in the street here, it's 'Jeez, we didn't play last night' or 'We had a great game,'" said Oilers coach Craig MacTavish, who played for three Edmonton Cup-winning teams. "In other cities it's, 'You guys weren't that sharp' or 'You guys gotta get it going.' Here it's 'we.' Everybody shares a piece."

Buffalo fans have felt the same way about the Sabres for several years, though there hasn't been much to own lately. In 2003, the team filed for bankruptcy and the Sabres'

fortunes on the ice similarly went down the tubes. But the team kept coach Lindy Ruff and the stability behind the bench paid off as the Sabres took the Hurricanes to seven games in the Eastern Conference Finals and woke up a hungry fan base along the way.

Sure, the game was alive and well in North Carolina, Edmonton and Buffalo, but what about in the major cities and at the league's grassroots level? Hockey will always be strong in Canada—fans north of the border welcomed the game back with open arms and Canadian TV ratings were up—but the game also bounced back in its most important outpost: New York City. Indeed, when the Rangers are competitive it's good for the league and thanks to a resurgent Jaromir Jagr, who finished with 123 points (54 goals, 69 assists), the Blueshirts played well on Broadway.

And the future of the NHL seemed to be

Gary Bettman proclaimed a hockey resurgence in 2005–06, but the NHL's TV ratings remained stubbornly low.

in good hands with a bevy of young stars who skate fast and score often. Pittsburgh Penguins phenom Sidney Crosby came to the league with much fanfare and didn't disappoint, becoming the youngest player ever to reach 100 points in a single season. But he was outdone by the Capitals' Alexander Ovechkin, who broke the 50-goal barrier (106 points) en route to winning the Calder Trophy for the league's top rookie. Sharks center Joe Thornton, who led the NHL with 125 points, won the Hart Trophy as league MVP, while Calgary defenseman Dion Phaneuf and Rangers goalie Henrik Lunqvist also left hockey fans with plenty to look forward to in the future.

"With speed and skill being a big factor, guys coming in have a good chance to use the things that have helped them in the past," said Crosby. "It's pretty unbelievable when you look at it, how many rookies had great seasons."

Not all the NHL news was positive, however. In February, a gambling scandal threatened to shake the league to its core. Wayne Gretzky's wife, Janet Jones, and his assistant coach, Rick Tocchet, were linked to a ring that took in $1.7 million in bets in a five-week period before the 2006 Super Bowl. Jones was alleged, among others, to have placed larged bets—totaling about $100,000. Could the Great One be involved as well? Gretzky denied he was ever involved, and neither he nor his wife ultimately faced criminal charges, but it became clear that gambling is a big problem the league must face.

Bettman will also have to get NHL broadcasts into more homes. No matter how he tried to spin it, OLN just wasn't reaching enough viewers and NBC didn't seem interested in trying to make the NHL "Must-See TV." But television ratings aside, it's apparent that hockey in the post-lockout era is a making great strides. Both sides seem to agree that the game is better and more fan-friendly now that players and owners seem to be skating along together. "We have the best fans in sports and they understood why we had to go through this process," said Bettman.

Understandably, statements like that may still be greeted with skepticism from fans, but what can't be argued is that Bettman came out of the '05–'06 season looking like a winner. The Cup was hoisted in Hurricane country—what the league hopes will be a new hockey hotbed—the game was flourishing and the league was financially stable again. And to hockey fans, that's just about as sweet a victory in Game 7 of the Stanley Cup Finals.

2006 NHL Final Standings

Eastern Conference

NORTHEAST DIVISION

	GP	W	L	OTL	Pts	GF	GA
Ottawa	82	52	21	9	113	314	211
Buffalo	82	52	24	6	110	281	239
Montreal	82	42	31	9	93	243	247
Toronto	82	41	33	8	90	257	270
Boston	82	29	37	16	74	230	266

ATLANTIC DIVISION

	GP	W	L	OTL	Pts	GF	GA
New Jersey	82	46	27	9	101	242	229
Philadelphia	82	45	26	11	101	267	259
NY Rangers	82	44	26	12	100	257	215
NY Islanders	82	36	40	6	78	230	278
Pittsburgh	82	22	46	14	58	244	316

SOUTHEAST DIVISION

	GP	W	L	OTL	Pts	GF	GA
Carolina	82	52	22	8	112	294	260
Tampa Bay	82	43	33	6	92	252	260
Atlanta	82	41	33	8	90	281	275
Florida	82	37	34	11	85	240	257
Washington	82	29	41	12	70	237	306

Western Conference

CENTRAL DIVISION

	GP	W	L	OTL	Pts	GF	GA
Detroit	82	58	16	8	124	305	209
Nashville	82	49	25	8	106	259	227
Columbus	82	35	43	4	74	223	279
Chicago	82	26	43	13	65	211	285
St. Louis	82	21	46	15	57	197	292

NORTHWEST DIVISION

	GP	W	L	OTL	Pts	GF	GA
Calgary	82	46	25	11	103	218	200
Colorado	82	43	30	9	95	283	257
Edmonton	82	41	28	13	95	256	251
Vancouver	82	42	32	8	92	256	255
Minnesota	82	38	36	8	84	231	215

PACIFIC DIVISION

	GP	W	L	OTL	Pts	GF	GA
Dallas	82	53	23	6	112	265	218
San Jose	82	44	27	11	99	266	242
Anaheim	82	43	27	12	98	254	229
Los Angeles	82	42	35	5	89	249	270
Phoenix	82	38	39	5	81	246	271

OTL=overtime loss; worth 1 pt.

2006 Stanley Cup Playoffs

EASTERN CONFERENCE

QUARTERFINALS   SEMIFINALS   CONFERENCE FINAL

WESTERN CONFERENCE

CONFERENCE FINAL   SEMIFINALS   QUARTERFINALS

STANLEY CUP

Eastern Conference bracket:
- Buffalo
- Philadelphia → Buffalo (4-2)
- Ottawa
- Tampa Bay → Ottawa (4-1) → Buffalo (4-1)
- New Jersey
- NY Rangers → New Jersey (4-0) → Carolina (4-3)
- Carolina
- Montreal → Carolina (4-2) → Carolina (4-1)

Champion: Carolina (4-3)

Western Conference bracket:
- Detroit
- Edmonton → Edmonton (4-2)
- Nashville
- San Jose → San Jose (4-1) → Edmonton (4-2)
- Calgary
- Anaheim → Anaheim (4-3) → Edmonton (4-1)
- Dallas
- Colorado → Colorado (4-1) → Anaheim (4-0)

Stanley Cup Playoff Results

Conference Quarterfinals

EASTERN CONFERENCE

April 22	NY Rangers	1	at New Jersey	6
April 24	NY Rangers	1	at New Jersey	4
April 26	New Jersey	3	at NY Rangers	0
April 29	New Jersey	4	at NY Rangers	2

New Jersey won series 4-0.

Conference Quarterfinals *(Cont.)*

EASTERN CONFERENCE *(CONT.)*

April 22	Philadelphia	2	at Buffalo	3†
April 24	Philadelphia	2	at Buffalo	8
April 26	Buffalo	2	at Philadelphia	4
April 28	Buffalo	4	at Philadelphia	5
April 30	Philadelphia	0	at Buffalo	3
May 2	Buffalo	7	at Philadelphia	1

Buffalo won series 4–2.

April 21	Tampa Bay	1	at Ottawa	4
April 23	Tampa Bay	4	at Ottawa	3
April 25	Ottawa	8	at Tampa Bay	4

April 27	Ottawa	5	at Tampa Bay	2
April 29	Tampa Bay	2	at Ottawa	3

Ottawa won series 4–1.

April 22	Montreal	6	at Carolina	1
April 24	Montreal	6	at Carolina	5†
April 26	Carolina	2	at Montreal	1*
April 28	Carolina	3	at Montreal	2
April 30	Montreal	1	at Carolina	2
May 2	Carolina	2	at Montreal	1*

Carolina won series 4–2.

WESTERN CONFERENCE

April 21	Edmonton	2	at Detroit	3†
April 23	Edmonton	4	at Detroit	2
April 25	Detroit	3	at Edmonton	4†
April 27	Detroit	4	at Edmonton	2
April 29	Edmonton	3	at Detroit	2
May 1	Detroit	3	at Edmonton	4

Edmonton won series 4–2.

April 21	Anaheim	1	at Calgary	2*
April 23	Anaheim	4	at Calgary	3
April 25	Calgary	5	at Anaheim	2
April 27	Calgary	2	at Anaheim	3*
April 29	Anaheim	2	at Calgary	3
May 1	Calgary	1	at Anaheim	2
May 3	Anaheim	3	at Calgary	0

Anaheim won series 4–3.

April 22	Colorado	5	at Dallas	2
April 24	Colorado	5	at Dallas	4*
April 26	Dallas	3	at Colorado	4*
April 28	Dallas	4	at Colorado	1
April 30	Colorado	3	at Dallas	2*

Colorado won series 4–1.

April 21	San Jose	3	at Nashville	4
April 23	San Jose	3	at Nashville	0
April 25	Nashville	1	at San Jose	4
April 27	Nashville	4	at San Jose	5
April 30	San Jose	2	at Nashville	1

San Jose won series 4–1.

Conference Semifinals

EASTERN CONFERENCE

May 6	New Jersey	0	at Carolina	6
May 8	New Jersey	2	at Carolina	3*
May 10	Carolina	3	at New Jersey	2
May 13	Carolina	1	at New Jersey	5
May 14	New Jersey	1	at Carolina	4

Carolina won series 4–1.

May 5	Buffalo	7	at Ottawa	6*
May 8	Buffalo	2	at Ottawa	1
May 10	Ottawa	2	at Buffalo	3*
May 11	Ottawa	2	at Buffalo	1
May 13	Buffalo	3	at Ottawa	2*

Buffalo won series 4–1.

WESTERN CONFERENCE

May 7	Edmonton	1	at San Jose	2
May 8	Edmonton	1	at San Jose	2
May 10	San Jose	2	at Edmonton	3**
May 12	San Jose	3	at Edmonton	6
May 14	Edmonton	6	at San Jose	3
May 17	San Jose	0	at Edmonton	2

Edmonton won series 4–2.

May 5	Colorado	0	at Anaheim	5
May 7	Colorado	0	at Anaheim	3
May 9	Anaheim	4	at Colorado	3*
May 11	Anaheim	4	at Colorado	1

Anaheim won series 4–0.

Eastern Finals

May 20	Buffalo	3	at Carolina	2
May 22	Buffalo	3	at Carolina	4
May 24	Carolina	3	at Buffalo	4
May 26	Carolina	4	at Buffalo	0
May 28	Buffalo	3	at Carolina	4*
May 30	Carolina	1	at Buffalo	2*
June 1	Buffalo	2	at Carolina	4

Carolina won series 4–3.

Western Finals

May 19	Edmonton	3	at Anaheim	1*
May 21	Edmonton	3	at Anaheim	1
May 23	Anaheim	4	at Edmonton	5
May 25	Anaheim	6	at Edmonton	3
May 27	Edmonton	2	at Anaheim	1

Edmonton won series 4–1.

Stanley Cup Finals

June 5	Edmonton	4	at Carolina	5
June 7	Edmonton	0	at Carolina	5
June 10	Carolina	1	at Edmonton	2
June 12	Carolina	2	at Edmonton	1

June 14	Edmonton	4	at Carolina	3*
June 17	Carolina	0	at Edmonton	4
June 19	Edmonton	1	at Carolina	3

Carolina won series 4–3.

*Overtime game. †Double overtime game. **Triple overtime game.

Game 1

| Edmonton | ....1 | 2 | 1——4 |
| Carolina | ....0 | 1 | 4——5 |

FIRST PERIOD

Scoring: 1, Edmonton, F Pisani 10 (R Torres, J Spacek), 8:18. Penalties: M Commodore, Car (roughing), 2:12; S Staios, Car (tripping), 11:45; M Bergeron, Edm (interference), 14:12; B Hedican, Car (tripping), 14:46; N Wallin, Car (tripping) 14:55; R Brind'Amour, Car (hooking), 16:33.

SECOND PERIOD

Scoring: 2, Edmonton, C Pronger 5 (penalty shot) (Unassisted), 10:36. 3, Edmonton, E Moreau 2 (M Greene), 16:23. 4, Carolina, R Brind'Amour 10 (J Williams, C Stillman), 17:17. Penalties: M Peca, Edm (elbowing), 5:59; R Dvorak, Edm (hooking) 18:33.

THIRD PERIOD

Scoring: 5, Carolina, R Whitney 7 (D Weight,

THIRD PERIOD *(CONT.)*

A Ladd), 1:40. 6, Carolina, R Whitney 8 (power play) (M Recchi, E Staal), 5:09. 7, Carolina, J Williams 6 (shorthanded) (C LaRose, A Ward), 10:02. 8, Edmonton, A Hemsky 5 (power play) (J Stoll, C Pronger), 13:31. 9, R Brind'Amour 11 (Unassisted), 19:28. Penalties: F Kaberle, Car (hooking), 2:11; E Moreau, Edm (cross checking); 4:28; B Hedican, Car (hooking), 8:11; E Staal, Car (high sticking), 12:53.

Shots on goal: EDM 8-12-18—38; CAR 8-7-11—26

Power-play opportunities: EDM 1-7, CAR 1-5.

Goalies: Edm, D Roloson (23 shots, 19 saves); Ty Conklin (3 shots, 2 saves). Car, C Ward (38 shots, 34 saves).

Referees: Devorski, McGeough. Linesmen: Morin, Racicot. A: 18,797.

Game 2

| Edmonton | ....0 | 0 | 0——0 |
| Carolina | ....1 | 2 | 2——5 |

FIRST PERIOD

Scoring: 1, Carolina, A Ladd 2 (E Staal, F Kaberle), 6:21. Penalties: C Adams, Car (interference), 3:26; C Pronger, Edm (hooking) 11:13; C Stillman, Car (goaltender interference), 12:47; R Whitney, Car (hooking), 18:46.

SECOND PERIOD

Scoring: 2, Carolina, F Kaberle 3 (power play) (R Whitney, M Cullen), 10:28. 3, Carolina, C Stillman 8 (N Wallin, Justin Williams), 19:57. Penalties: M Greene, Edm (cross checking), 5:34; J Smith, Edm (roughing), 6:20; R Torres, Edm (interference), 8:52; A Ward, Car (holding), 11:23; S Horcoff, Edm (interference), 14:20.

THIRD PERIOD

Scoring: 4, Carolina, D Weight 3 (power play) (M Recchi, M Cullen), 2:21. 5, Carolina, M Recchi 6 (power play) (F Kaberle, M Cullen), 4:12. Penalties: S Samsonov, Edm (goaltender interference), 1:31; E Moreau, Edm (roughing), 2:47; R Smyth, Edm (high sticking), 5:01; C Adams, Car (cross checking), 8:33; G Laraque, Edm (tripping), 11:14; G Wesley, Car (holding), 14:12; G Laraque, Edm (boarding), 16:44; G Laraque, Edm (misconduct), 16:44; G Wesley, Car (holding), 19:19.

Shots on goal: EDM 6-10-9—25; CAR 8-10-8—26

Power-play opportunities: EDM 0-6, CAR 3-10.

Goalies: Edm, J Markkanen (26 shots, 21 saves). Car, C Ward (25 shots, 25 saves).

Referees: McCreary, Watson. Linesmen: Devorski, Sharrers. A: 18,928.

Game 3

| Carolina | ....0 | 0 | 1——1 |
| Edmonton | ....1 | 0 | 1——2 |

FIRST PERIOD

Scoring: 1, Edmonton, S Horcoff 6 (J Spacek, A Hemsky), 2:31. Penalties: D Weight, Car (interference), 6:03; C Pronger, Edm (tripping), 10:02; C Adams, Car (tripping), 12:30; K Adams, Car (hooking), 13:03; M Recchi, Car (hooking), 15:53; R Dvorak, Edm (high sticking), 17:57.

SECOND PERIOD

Scoring: None. Penalties: M Cullen, Edm (holding), 1:37; S Horcoff, Edm (broken stick), 6:04; R Brind'Amour, Car (cross checking), 6:48; M Greene, Edm (interference),

SECOND PERIOD *(CONT.)*

10:25; D Tarnstrom, Edm (hooking), 16:04.

THIRD PERIOD

Scoring: 2, Carolina, R Brind'Amour 12 (Cory Stillman), 9:09. 3, Edmonton, R Smyth 6 (A Hemsky, J Spacek), 17:45. Penalties: B Hedican, Car (interference), 2:42.

Shots on goal: CAR 6-8-11—25; EDM 9-11-10—30

Power-play opportunities: CAR 0-5, EDM 0-7.

Goalies: Car, C Ward (30 shots, 28 saves). Edm, J Markkanen (25 shots, 24 saves).

Referees: Devorski, McGeough. Linesmen: Morin, Racicot. A: 16,839.

Game 4

| Carolina | ....1 | 1 | 0——2 |
| Edmonton | ....1 | 0 | 0——1 |

FIRST PERIOD

Scoring: 1, Edmonton, S Samsonov 4 (R Dvorak, J Stoll), 8:40. 2, Carolina, C Stillman 9 (power play) (F Kaberle, E Staal), 9:09. Penalties: R Torres, Edm (tripping), 8:57; A Ladd, Car (tripping), 10:04; R Whitney, Car (hooking), 13:98; R Whitney, Car (hooking), 15:35; A Ward, Car (high sticking), 16:23; J Stoll, Edm (interference), 19:20.

SECOND PERIOD

Scoring: 1, Carolina, M Recchi 7 (E Staal, C Stillman). Penalties: C Pronger, Edm (holding), 3:24; B

SECOND PERIOD *(CONT.)*

Hedican, Car (roughing), 8:54; M Greene, Edm (holding), 18:05; J Williams, Car (holding), 18:35; C Pronger, Edm (cross checking), 19:27.

THIRD PERIOD

Scoring: None. Penalties: J Smith, Edm (hooking), 15:22.

Shots on goal: CAR 4-11-5—20; EDM 8-8-5—21.

Power-play opportunities: CAR 1-6, EDM 0-5.

Goalies: Car, C Ward (21 shots, 20 saves). Edm, J Markkanen (20 shots, 18 saves).

Referees: McCreary, Watson. Linesmen: Devorski, Sharrers. A: 16,839.

Game 5

| Edmonton | 3 | 0 | 0 | 1——4 |
| Carolina | 2 | 1 | 0 | 0——3 |

FIRST PERIOD

Scoring: 1, Edmonton, F Pisani 11 (C Pronger, R Torres), 0:16. 2, Carolina, E Staal 8 (power play) (D Weight, B Hedican), 5:54. 3, Carolina, R Whitney 9 (power play) (E Staal, M Recchi), 10:16. 4, Edmonton, A Hemsky 6 (power play) (D Tarnstrom, S Staios), 13:25. 5, Edmonton, M Peca 6 (A Hemsky, C Pronger), 19:42. Penalties: A Hemsky, Edm (tripping), 2:27; M Greene, Edm (hooking), 5:03; M Greene, Edm (holding), 9:06; M Cullen, Car (hooking), 11:40; J Spacek, Edm (high sticking), 14:42; C Adams, Car (hooking), 17:17; D Tarnstrom, Edm (interference), 18:46; M Commodore, Car (goaltender interference), 19:13.

SECOND PERIOD

Scoring: 6, Carolina, E Staal 9 (power play) (R Whitney, C Stillman), 9:56. Penalties: B Hedican, Car

SECOND PERIOD (CONT.)

(interference), 2:43; J Stoll, Edm (hooking), 4:11; S Staios, Edm (hooking), 8:20; R Brind'Amour, Car (high sticking), 15:32.

THIRD PERIOD

Scoring: None. Penalties: M Commodore, Car (holding), 4:23; J Vasicek, Car (hooking), 7:53.

OVERTIME

Scoring: 7, Edmonton, F Pisani 12 (shorthanded) (Unassisted), 3:31. Penalties: S Staios, Edm (tripping), 3:03.

Shots on goal: EDM 10-7-5-7—29; CAR 14-8-2-0—24

Power-play Opportunities: EDM 1-7, CAR 3-7.

Goalies : Edm, JMarkkanen (24 shots, 21 saves). Car, C Ward (29 shots, 25 saves).

Referees: Devorksi, McGeough. Linesmen: Morin, Racicot. A: 18,974.

Game 6

| Carolina | 0 | 0 | 0——0 |
| Edmonton | 0 | 2 | 2——4 |

FIRST PERIOD

Scoring: None. Penalties: S Staios, Edm (interference), 1:09; B Hedican, Car (roughing), 6:02; B Hedican, Car (roughing), 11:41; F Pisani, Edm (hooking), 19:25.

SECOND PERIOD

Scoring: 1, Edmonton, F Pisani 13 (power play) (A Hemsky, J Spacek) 1:45. 2, Edmonton, R Torres 4 (S Staios, F Pisani), 9:54. Penalties: Bench, Car, served by A Ladd (too many men), 1:08; G Wesley, Car (roughing), 3:14; J Spacek, Edm (diving), 5:48; C Stillman, Car (hooking), 5:48; B Hedican, Car (tripping), 10:22; D Tarnstrom, Edm (interference), 15:59; J Smith, Edm (interference), 18:22.

THIRD PERIOD

Scoring: 3, Edmonton, R Smyth 7 (power play) (M Peca, J Spacek), 3:04. 4, Edmonton, S Horcoff 7 (power play) (R Dvorak, D Tarnstrom), 13:05. Penalties: R Whitney, Car (holding), 2:46; Bench, Car, served by A Ladd (too many men), 4:11; M Greene, Edm (interference), 9:29; M Cullen, Car (roughing), 15:04; Bench, Edm, served by R Torres (too many men), 15:41.

Shots on goal: CAR 3-4-9—16; EDM 10-11-13—34

Power-play opportunities: CAR 0-6, EDM 3-9.

Goalies: Car, C Ward (34 shots, 30 saves). Edm, J Markkanen (16 shots, 16 saves).

Referees: McCreary, Watson. Linesmen: Devorski, Sharrers. A: 16,839.

Game 7

| Edmonton | 0 | 0 | 1——1 |
| Carolina | 1 | 1 | 1——3 |

FIRST PERIOD

Scoring: 1, Carolina, A Ward 2 (M Recchi, M Cullen), 1:26. Penalties: E Staal, Car (goaltender interference), 3:17; J Spacek, Edm (holding), 11:03; M Greene, Edm (interference), 17:33; E Moreau, Edm (high sticking), 19:55.

SECOND PERIOD

Scoring: 2, Carolina, F Kaberle 4 (power play) (C Stillman, M Cullen), 4:18. Penalties: J Spacek, Edm (holding), 4:10; N Wallin, Car (hooking), 16:16; A Ward, Car (hooking), 16:21; R Smyth, Edm (hooking), 17:21.

THIRD PERIOD

Scoring: 3, Edmonton, F Pisani 14 (R Murray, R Torres), 1:03. 4, Carolina, J Williams 7 (empty net) (E Staal, B Hedican), 18:59. Penalties: B Hedican, Car (roughing), 12:38; J Williams, Car (roughing), 19:39; R Smyth, Edm (roughing), 19:39.

Shots on goal: EDM 5-8-10—23; CAR 10-11-6—27

Power-play opportunities: EDM 0-4, CAR 1-5.

Goalies: Edm, J Markkanen (26 shots, 24 saves). Car, C Ward, (23 shots, 22 saves).

Referees: McCreary, Watson. Linesmen: Devorski, Sharrers. A: 18,978.

Individual Playoff Leaders

Scoring

POINTS

Player and Team	GP	G	A	Pts	+/-	PM	Player and Team	GP	G	A	Pts	+/-	PM
Eric Staal, Car	25	9	29	28	0	8	Ryan Smyth, Edm	24	7	9	16	-2	22
Cory Stillman, Car	25	9	17	26	12	14	Patrik Elias, NJ	9	6	10	16	5	4
Chris Pronger, Edm	24	5	16	21	10	26	Doug Weight, Car	23	3	13	16	-3	14
Daniel Briere, Buf	18	8	11	19	0	12	Ray Whitney, Car	24	9	6	15	-1	14
Shawn Horcoff, Edm	24	7	12	19	4	12	Derek Roy, Buf	18	5	10	15	7	16
Fernando Pisani, Edm	24	14	4	18	4	10	Sergei Samsonov, Edm	24	4	11	15	2	14
Rod Brind'Amour, Car	25	12	6	18	9	16	Patrick Marleau, SJ	11	9	5	14	2	8
Chris Drury, Buf	18	9	9	18	5	10	J.P. Dumont, Buf	18	7	7	14	1	14
Justin Williams, Car	25	7	11	18	12	34	Teemu Selanne, Ana	16	6	8	14	0	6
Matt Cullen, Car	25	4	14	18	2	12	Jason Spezza, Ott	10	5	9	14	-1	2
Ales Hemsky, Edm	24	6	11	17	-3	14	Jaroslav Spacek, Edm	24	3	11	14	-3	24
Mark Recchi, Car	25	7	9	16	-5	18							

GOALS

Player and Team	GP	G
Fernando Pisani, Edm	24	14
Rod Brind'Amour, Car	25	12
Eric Staal, Car	25	9
Cory Stillman, Car	25	9
Chris Drury, Buf	18	9
Ray Whitney, Car	24	9
Patrick Marleau, SJ	11	9
Joffrey Lupul, Ana	16	9

SHORT-HANDED GOALS

Player and Team	GP	SH
John Madden, NJ	9	2

POWER PLAY GOALS

Player and Team	GP	PP
Eric Staal, Car	25	7
Rod Brind'Amour, Car	25	6
Chris Drury, Buf	18	5
Ray Whitney, Car	24	5

ASSISTS

Player and Team	GP	A
Eric Staal, Car	25	19
Cory Stillman, Car	25	17
Chris Pronger, Edm	24	16
Matt Cullen, Car	25	14
Doug Weight, Car	23	13

PLUS/MINUS

Player and Team	GP	+/-
Todd Marchant, Ana	16	14
Henrik Tallinder, Buf	14	14
Toni Lyndman, Buf	18	14
Cory Stillman, Car	25	12
Justin Williams, Car	25	12
Chris Pronger, Edm	25	10
Dustin Penner, Ana	25	10
Ruslan Salei, Ana	25	10
Rod Brind'Amour, Car	25	9
Joffrey Lupul, Ana	25	9
Sean O'Donnell, Ana	25	8

Goaltending (Minimum 420 minutes)

GOALS AGAINST AVERAGE

Player and Team	GP	W-L	Avg
Ilya Bryzgalov, Ana	11	6-4	1.46
Cam Ward, Car	23	15-8	2.14
Miikka Kiprusoff, Cgy	7	3-4	2.24
Martin Brodeur, NJ	9	5-4	2.25
Dwayne Roloson, Edm	18	12-5	2.33
Cristobal Huet, Mtl	6	2-4	2.33

SAVE PERCENTAGE

Player and Team	GP	W-L	GAA	GA	SV	SV%	SA
Ilya Bryzgalov, Ana	11	6-4	1.46	16	269	.944	285
Cristobal Huet, Mtl	6	2-4	2.33	15	197	.929	212
D. Roloson, Edm	18	12-5	2.33	45	573	.927	618
Martin Brodeur, NJ	9	5-4	2.25	20	241	.923	261
M. Kiprusoff, Cgy	7	3-4	2.24	16	186	.921	202
Cam Ward, Car	23	15-8	2.14	27	537	.920	584

NHL Awards

Award	Player and Team
Hart Trophy (MVP)	Joe Thornton, Bos/SJ
Calder Trophy (top rookie)	Alexander Ovechkin, Was
Vezina Trophy (top goaltender)	Miikka Kiprusoff, Cgy
Norris Trophy (top defenseman)	Nicklas Lidstrom, Det
Lady Byng Trophy (for gentlemanly play)	Pavel Datsyuk, Det
Adams Award (top coach)	Lindy Ruff, Buf
Selke Trophy (top defensive forward)	Rod Brind'Amour, Car
Jennings Trophy (goaltender on club allowing fewest goals)	Miikka Kiprusoff, Cgy
Conn Smythe Trophy (playoff MVP)	Cam Ward, Car

Individual Regular Season Leaders

Scoring

POINTS

Player and Team	GP	G	A	Pts	+/-	PM	Player and Team	GP	G	A	Pts	+/-	PM
Joe Thornton, SJ	81	29	96	125	31	61	J. Cheechoo, SJ	82	56	37	93	23	58
Jaromir Jagr, NYR	82	54	69	123	34	72	Marian Hossa, Atl	80	39	53	92	17	67
Alex. Ovechkin, Was	81	52	54	106	2	52	Brad Richards, TB	82	23	68	91	0	32
Dany Heatley, Ott	82	50	53	103	29	86	Teemu Selanne, Ana	80	40	50	90	28	44
Daniel Alfredsson, Ott	77	43	60	103	29	50	Jason Spezza, Ott	68	19	71	90	23	33
Sidney Crosby, Pit	81	39	63	102	-1	110	Brian Gionta, NJ	82	48	41	89	18	46
Eric Staal, Car	82	45	55	100	-8	81	Olli Jokinen, Fla	82	38	51	89	14	88
Ilya Kovalchuk, Atl	78	52	46	98	-6	68	Joe Sakic, Col	82	32	55	87	10	60
Marc Savard, Atl	82	28	69	97	7	100	Pavel Datsyuk, Det	75	28	59	87	26	22
							Scott Gomez, NJ	80	14	56	70	18	70

Scoring (Cont.)

GOALS

Player and Team	GP	G
J. Cheechoo, SJ	82	56
Jaromir Jagr, NYR	82	54
A. Ovechkin, Was	81	52
Ilya Kovalchuk, Atl	78	52
Dany Heatley, Ott	82	50
Brian Gionta, NJ	82	48
Simon Gagne, Phi	72	47
Eric Staal, Car	82	45
Daniel Alfredsson, Ott	77	43
Teemu Selanne, Anh	80	40
Brendan Shanahan, Det	82	40

POWER PLAY GOALS

Player and Team	GP	PP
Ilya Kovalchuk, Atl	78	27
J. Cheechoo, SJ	82	24
Jaromir Jagr, NYR	82	24
Brian Gionta, NJ	82	24
Dany Heatley, Ott	82	23

ASSISTS

Player and Team	GP	A
Joe Thornton,SJ	81	96
Jason Spezza, Ott	68	71
Jaromir Jagr, NYR	82	69
Marc Savard, Atl	82	69
Brad Richards, TB	82	68
Nicklas Lidstrom, Det	80	64
Sidney Crosby, Pitt	81	63
Daniel Alfredsson, Ott	77	60
Pavel Datsyuk, Det	85	59

SHORT-HANDED GOALS

Player and Team	GP	SHG
Marian Hossa, Atl	82	7
Antoine Vermette, Ott	67	6
Daniel Alfredsson, Ott	73	5
Brian Rolston, Minn	73	5
Pavol Demitra, LA	73	5
Ryan Malone, Pit	73	5
Matt Pettinger, Was	73	5

GAME-WINNING GOALS

Player and Team	GP	GW
J. Cheechoo, SJ	82	11
Brian Gionta, NJ	82	10
Marek Svatos, Col	61	9
Olli Jokinen, Fla	82	9
Henrik Zetterberg, Det	77	9
Jaromir Jagr, NYR	82	9

PLUS/MINUS

Player and Team	GP	+/-
Wade Redden, Ott	65	35
Michal Rozsival, NYR	82	35
Jaromir Jagr, NYR	82	34
Andrej Meszaros, Ott	82	34
Mathieu Schneider, Det	72	33
Joe Thornton, SJ	81	31
Simon Gagne, Phi	72	31
Michael Nylander, NYR	81	31
Brenden Morrow, Dal	81	30

Goaltending
(Minimum 25 games)

GOALS AGAINST AVERAGE

Player and Team	GP	W-L	GAA	GA
Miikka Kiprusoff, Cgy	74	42-20	2.07	151
Dominik Hasek, Ott	43	28-10	2.09	90
Manny Legace, Det	51	37-8	2.19	106
Cristobal Huet, Mtl	36	18-11	2.20	77
Henrik Lundqvist, NYR	53	30-12	2.24	116
M. Fernandez, Minn	58	30-18	2.29	130
Ilya Bryzgalov, Anh	31	13-12	2.51	66

SAVE PERCENTAGE

Player and Team	GP	W-L	GA	SA	Pct
Crisotbal Huet, Mtl	36	18-11	77	1085	.929
Dominik Hasek, Ott	43	28-10	90	1202	.925
Miikka Kiprusoff, Cgy	74	42-20	151	1951	.923
H. Lundqvist, NYR	53	30-12	116	1485	.922
Tomas Vokoun, Nash	61	36-18	160	1984	.919
M. Fernandez, Minn	58	30-18	130	1612	.919
Tim Thomas, Bos	38	12-13	101	1213	.917

WINS

Player and Team	GP	GAA	W	L
Martin Brodeur, NJ	73	2.03	43	23
Miikka Kiprusoff, Cgy	74	1.98	42	20
Marty Turco, Dal	68	2.53	41	19
Martin Gerber, Car	60	2.13	38	14
Manny Legace, Det	51	2.27	37	8
Tomas Vokoun, Nash	60	2.27	36	18

SHUTOUTS

Player and Team	GP	W	L	SO
Miikka Kiprusoff, Cgy	74	42	20	10
Manny Legace, Det	51	36	18	7
Cristobal Huet, Mtl	56	18	11	7
Martin Brodeur, NJ	73	43	23	5
John Grahame, TB	57	29	22	5
Dominik Hasek, Ott	43	28	10	5

NHL Team-by-Team Statistical Leaders

Mighty Ducks of Anaheim

SCORING

Player	GP	G	A	Pts	+/-	PM
Teemu Selanne, RW	80	40	50	90	28	44
Andy McDonald, C	82	34	51	85	24	32
Scott Niedermayer, D	82	13	50	63	8	96
Joffrey Lupul, C	81	28	25	53	-13	48
Chris Kunitz, LW	67	19	22	41	16	71
Andy McDonald, LW	79	9	21	30	-13	24
Rob Niedermayer, C	76	15	24	39	-5	89
Ryan Getzlaf, C	57	14	25	39	6	22
F. Beauchemin, D	72	8	28	36	2	52
Todd Marchant, C	79	9	25	34	2	66
Jonathan Hedstrom,RW	79	13	14	27	2	48
Corey Perrry, RW	56	13	12	25	1	50
Todd Fedoruk, LW	76	4	19	23	6	174
Samuel Pahlsson, c	82	11	10	21	-1	34
Ruslan Salei,D	78	1	18	19	17	114
Jeff Friesen, LW	51	4	7	11	-15	32

SCORING (CONT.)

Player	GP	G	A	Pts	+/-	PM
Sean O'Donnell,D	78	2	9	11	6	147
Tyler Wright, RW	43	2	6	8	-1	51
Joe Dipenta, D	72	2	6	8	8	46
Vitaly Vishnevsk, D	82	1	7	8	8	91
Dustin Penner, RW	19	4	3	7	3	14
Zenon Konopka, C	23	4	3	7	-4	48
Travis Moen, LW	39	4	1	5	-3	72
Jason Marshall, D	23	0	4	4	2	34
Bruno St. Jacques, D	1	1	0	1	1	0
Kip Brennan, LW	12	0	1	1	-2	35
AAron Gavey, C	5	0	0	0	0	2
Trevor Gillies, LW	1	0	0	0	0	21

GOALTENDING

Player	GP	Mins	W	L	TGA	GAA	SO
J. Giguere	60	3381	30	15	150	2.66	2
Ilya Bryzgalov	31	1575	13	12	66	2.51	1

Atlanta Thrashers

SCORING

Player	GP	G	A	Pts	+/-	PM
Ilya Kovalchuk, LW	78	52	46	98	-6	68
Marc Savard, C	82	28	69	97	7	100
Marian Hossa, RW	80	39	53	92	17	67
Vyacheslav Kozlov, LW	82	25	46	71	14	33
Peter Bondra, RW	60	21	18	39	-3	40
Jaroslav Modry, D	79	7	31	38	-9	76
Greg De Vries, D	82	7	28	35	1	76
Scott Mellanby, RW	71	12	22	34	5	55
Bobby Holik, C	64	15	18	33	-6	79
Niclas Havelid, D	82	4	28	32	9	48
Andy Sutton, D	76	8	17	25	13	144
Patrik Stefan, C	64	10	14	24	3	36
Serge Aubin, LW	74	7	17	24	-4	79
Jim Slater, C	71	10	10	20	1	46
Ronald Petrovicky, RW	60	8	12	20	-8	62
Steve McCarthy, D	67	9	7	16	3	51
Brad Larsen, LW	62	7	8	15	-3	21
Jean-Pierre Vigier, RW	41	4	6	10	-4	40
Garnet Exelby, D	75	1	9	10	11	75
Eric Boulton, LW	51	4	5	9	-4	87
Shane Hindy, D	66	0	3	3	1	33
Ramzi Abid, LW	6	0	2	2	1	6
Derek Mackenzie, C	11	0	1	1	0	8
Braydon Coburn, D	9	0	1	1	-2	4
Karl Stewart, LW	8	0	0	0	-3	15
Francis Lessard, RW	6	0	0	0	-2	0
Mark Popvich, D	7	0	0	0	-5	0
Scott Barney, RW	3	0	0	0	-1	0
Tomas Kloucek, D	1	0	0	0	00	2

GOALTENDING

Player	GP	Mins	W	L	TGA	GAA	SO
Kari Lehtonen	38	2165	20	15	106	2.94	2
Michael Garnett	24	1271	10	7	73	3.45	2
Mike Dunham	17	779	8	5	36	2.77	1
Adam Berkhoel	9	473	2	4	30	3.81	0

Boston Bruins

SCORING

Player	GP	G	A	Pts	+/-	PM
Patrice Bergeron, C	81	31	42	73	3	22
Brad Boyes, C	82	26	43	69	11	30
Marco Strum, LW	74	29	30	59	6	48
Glen Murray, RW	64	24	29	53	-8	52
Brad Stuart, D	78	12	31	43	-8	52
Matry Reasoner, C	77	11	23	34	-14	28
Brian Leetch, D	61	5	27	32	-10	36
P.J. Alexsson, LW	59	10	18	28	-3	4
Brad Isbister, LW	58	6	17	23	-2	46
Wayne Primeau, C	71	11	11	22	-16	57
Travis Grren, C	82	10	12	22	-2	79
David Tanabe, D	75	4	16	20	-6	56
Jiri Slegr, D	32	5	11	16	-2	56
Nick Boynton, D	54	5	7	12	-7	93
Josh Langfeld, LW	57	2	10	12	-2	26
Milan Jurcina, D	51	6	5	11	3	54
Mariusz Czerkawski, RW	35	8	2	10	-6	10
Tom Fitzgerald, RW	71	4	6	10	-10	40
Hal Gill, D	80	1	9	10	-4	124
Alexei Zhamnov, C	24	1	9	10	-4	30
Patrick Leahy, RW	43	4	4	8	-2	19
Shawn McEachern, LW	28	2	6	8	-12	22
Andrew Alberts, D	73	1	6	7	3	68
Eric Nickulas, RW	16	2	4	6	2	8
Dan Lacouture, LW	55	2	2	4	-6	53
Yan Stastny, C	20	1	3	4	-4	10
Mark Stuart, D	17	1	1	2	-1	10
Ian Moran, D	12	1	1	2	0	10

GOALTENDING

Player	GP	Mins	W	L	TGA	GAA	SO
Tim Thomas	38	2186	12	13	101	2.77	1
Hannu Toivonen	20	1162	9	5	51	2.63	1
Andrew Raycroft	30	1618	8	19	100	3.71	0
Jordan Sigalet	1	0.43	0	0	0	0.0	0

Buffalo Sabres

SCORING

Player	GP	G	A	Pts	+/-	PM
Maxim Afinogenov, RW	77	22	51	73	6	84
Chris Drury, C	81	30	37	67	-11	32
Ales Kotalik, RW	82	25	37	62	-3	62
Daniel Briere, C	48	25	33	58	3	48
Tim Connolly, C	63	16	39	55	5	28
Thomas Vanek, LW	81	25	23	48	-11	72
Derek Roy, C	70	18	28	46	1	57
Drian Campbell, D	79	12	32	44	-15	16
Jochien Hecht, LW	64	18	24	42	10	34
Jean-Pierre Dumont, RW	54	20	20	40	-1	38
Teppo Numminen, D	75	2	38	40	6	36
Jason Pominville, RW	57	18	12	30	-4	22
Paul Gaustad, C	78	9	15	24	4	65
Mike Grier, RW	81	7	16	23	-7	28
Henrik Tallinder, D	82	6	15	21	10	74
Dimitri Kalinin, D	55	2	16	18	14	54

SCORING (CONT.)

Player	GP	G	A	Pts	+/-	PM
Toni Lydman, D	75	1	16	17	9	82
Jay Mckee, D	75	5	11	16	0	57
Taylor Pyatt, LW	41	6	6	12	-1	33
Rory Fitzpatrick, D	56	4	5	9	-18	50
Adam Mair, C	40	2	5	7	-2	47
Jiri Novotny, C	14	2	1	3	-5	0
Daniel Paille, LW	14	1	2	3	5	2
Nathan Paetsch, D	1	0	1	1	-1	0
Chris Thorburn, C	2	0	1	1	-1	7
Andrew Paeters, LW	28	0	0	0	-2	100
Jeff Jillson, D	2	0	0	0	0	4

GOALTENDING

Player	GP	Mins	W	L	TGA	GAA	SO
Ryan Miller	48	2861	30	14	124	2.60	1
Martin Biron	35	1934	21	8	93	2.89	1

Calgary Flames

SCORING

Player	GP	G	A	Pts	+/–	PM
Jarome Iginla, RW	82	35	32	67	5	86
Daymond Langkow, C	82	25	34	59	2	46
Dion Phaneuf, D	82	20	29	49	5	93
Kristian Huselius, RW	78	20	27	47	-9	40
Tony Amonte, RW	80	14	28	42	3	43
Chuck Kobasew, RW	72	20	11	31	-10	64
Andrew Ference, D	82	4	27	31	-12	85
Jamie Lundmark, C	53	10	19	29	-1	62
Mike Leclerc, LW	50	10	16	26	0	37
Roman Hamrlik, D	51	7	19	26	8	56
Robyn Regehr, D	68	6	20	26	6	67
Matthew Lombardi, C	55	6	20	26	-1	48
Chris Simon, LW	72	8	14	22	0	94
Shean Donovan, RW	80	9	11	20	9	82
Jordan Leopold, D	74	2	18	20	6	68
Stephane Yelle, C	74	4	14	18	10	48
Marcus Nilson, LW	70	6	11	17	13	32
Darren McCarty, RW	67	7	6	13	-1	117
Byron Ritchie, C	45	4	2	6	-2	69
Rhette Warrener, D	61	3	3	6	7	54
Craig MacDonald, C	25	3	2	5	5	8
CaleHulse, D	39	0	4	4	-8	63
Bryan Marchment, D	37	1	2	3	8	75
Richie Refehr, C	14	0	2	2	0	6
Mark Giordano, D	7	0	1	1	2	8
Carsen German, RW	2	0	0	0	-1	0
Eric Nystrom, LW	2	0	0	0	-1	0

GOALTENDING

Player	GP	Mins	W	L	TGA	GAA	SO
Miikka Kiprusoff	72	4379	42	20	151	2.07	10
Brian Boucher	14	693	4	8	48	4.15	0

Carolina Hurricanes

SCORING

Player	GP	G	A	Pts	+/–	PM
Eric Staal, C	82	45	55	100	-8	81
Justin Williams, RW	82	31	45	76	1	60
Cory Stillman, LW	72	21	55	76	-9	32
Rod Brind'Amour, C	78	31	39	70	8	68
Mark Recchi, RW	83	28	36	64	-36	68
Erik Cole, LW	60	30	29	59	19	54
Doug Weight, C	70	15	42	57	-17	75
Ray Whitney, LW	63	17	38	55	0	42
Matt Cullen, C	78	25	24	49	4	40
Frantisek Kaberle, D	77	6	38	44	8	46
Bret Hedican, D	74	5	22	27	11	58
Aaron Ward, D	71	6	19	25	2	62
Kevyn Adams, C	82	15	8	23	0	36
Oleg Tverdovsky, D	72	3	20	23	-1	37
Craig Adams, RW	67	10	11	21	1	51
Mike Commodore, D	72	3	10	13	12	138
Chad Larose, RW	49	1	12	13	7	35
Andrew Ladd, LW	29	6	5	11	0	4
Andrew Hutchinson, D	36	3	8	11	-2	18
Anton Babchuk, D	39	5	5	10	-7	22
Glen Wesley, D	64	2	8	10	10	46
Josef Vasicek, C	23	4	5	9	3	8
Niclas Wallin, D	50	4	4	8	2	42
Keith Aucoin, C	7	0	1	1	-4	4
David Gove, LR	1	0	1	1	2	0

GOALTENDING

Player	GP	Mins	W	L	TGA	GAA	SO
Martin Gerber	60	3492	38	6	162	2.78	3
Cam Ward	28	1484	14	9	91	3.66	0

Chicago Blackhawks

SCORING

Player	GP	G	A	Pts	+/–	PM
Kyle Calder, LW	79	26	33	59	-4	52
Mark Bell, LW	82	25	23	48	-14	107
Radim Vrbata, RW	61	15	24	39	4	22
Rene Bourque, LR	77	16	18	34	3	56
Brent Seabrook, D	68	5	27	32	5	60
Martin Lapointe, RW	82	14	17	31	-30	106
Patrick Sharp, RW	72	14	17	31	5	46
Matthew Barnaby, RW	82	8	20	28	-11	178
Jim Vandermeer, D	76	6	18	24	-2	116
Pavel Vorobiev, RW	39	9	12	21	-2	34
Duncan Keith, D	81	9	12	21	-11	79
Mikael Homqvist, C	72	10	10	20	-14	16
B. Bochenski, RW	40	8	9	17	-2	22
Mark Cullen, C	29	7	9	16	7	2
Curtis Brown, C	71	5	10	15	-9	38

SCORING (CONT.)

Player	GP	G	A	Pts	+/–	PM
James Wisniewski, D	19	2	5	7	0	36
Jassen Cullimore, D	54	1	6	7	-24	53
Milan Bartovic, RW	24	1	6	7	0	8
Adrian Aucoin, D	33	1	5	6	-13	38
Dustin Byfuglien, D	25	3	2	5	-6	24
Tuomo Ruutu, C	15	2	3	5	-7	15
Danny Richmond, D	20	0	1	1	-6	25
Michal Barinka, D	25	0	1	1	-7	20
Shawn Thornton, LW	10	0	0	0	-5	46

GOALTENDING

Player	GP	Mins	W	L	TGA	GAA	SO
Nikolai Khabibulin	50	2814	17	26	157	3.35	0
Craig Anderson	29	1553	6	12	86	3.32	1
Adam Munro	10	500	3	5	25	2.99	1
Corey Crawford	2	86	0	0	5	3.49	0

Colorado Avalanche

SCORING

Player	GP	G	A	Pts	+/-	PM
Joe Sakic, C	82	32	55	87	10	60
Alex Tanguay, LW	71	29	49	78	8	46
Andrew Brunette, LR	82	24	39	63	9	48
Milan Hejduk, RW	74	24	34	58	13	24
Rob Blake, D	81	14	37	51	2	94
Marek Svatos, RW	61	32	18	50	0	60
John-Michael Liles, D	82	14	35	49	5	44
Pierre Turgeon, C	62	16	30	46	1	32
Ian Laperrier, RW	82	21	24	45	3	116
Brett McLean, C	82	9	31	40	-7	51
Patrice Brisebois, D	80	10	28	38	1	55
Brett Clark, D	80	9	27	36	3	56
Antti Laaksonen, LW	81	16	18	34	-2	40
Jim Dowd, C	78	5	13	18	-11	40
Steve Konowalchuk, LW	21	6	9	15	5	14
Karlis Skrastins, D	82	3	11	14	-7	65
Dan Hinote, R	73	5	8	13	-5	48
Brad Richardson, C	41	3	10	13	0	12
Cody Mccormick, C	45	4	4	8	1	29
Bob Boughner, D	41	1	6	7	2	54
Brad May, LW	54	3	3	6	-14	82
Kurt Sauer, D	37	1	4	5	5	24
Ossi Vaananen, D	53	0	4	4	10	56

GOALTENDING

Player	GP	Mins	W	L	TGA	GAA	SO
Jose Theodore	43	2410	18	18	137	3.41	0
Peter Budaj	34	1802	14	10	86	2.86	2
Vitaly Kolesnik	8	370	3	3	20	3.24	0

Dallas Stars

SCORING

Player	GP	G	A	Pts	+/-	PM
Mike Modano, C	78	27	50	77	23	58
Jason Arnott, C	81	32	44	76	13	102
Sergei Zubov, D	78	13	58	71	20	46
Brenden Morrow, LW	81	23	42	65	30	183
Jussi Jokinen, LW	81	17	38	55	9	30
Jere, Lehtinen, RW	80	33	19	52	9	30
Philippe Boucher, D	66	16	27	43	28	77
Bill Guerin, RW	70	13	27	40	0	115
Stu Barnes, C	78	15	21	36	9	44
Niko Kapanen, C	81	14	21	35	-10	36
Antti Miettinen, RW	79	11	20	31	0	46
Steve Ott, C	82	5	17	22	1	178
Niklas Hagman, LW	84	8	13	21	-10	18
Stephane Robidas, D	75	5	15	20	15	67
Janne Ninimaa, D	63	3	13	16	-12	86
Trevor Daley, D	81	3	11	14	-2	87
Jon Klemm,D	76	4	7	11	-3	60
Willie Mitchell, D	80	2	8	10	19	118
Jeremy Stevenson, LW	51	5	3	8	-3	95
Jaroslav Svoboda, LW	43	4	3	7	-3	22
Mathias Tjarnqvist, LW	33	2	4	6	4	18
Nathan Perrott, RW	26	2	1	3	-3	56
Junior Lessard, RW	5	1	0	1	0	12

GOALTENDING

Player	GP	Mins	W	L	TGA	GAA	SO
Marty Turco	68	3910	41	19	166	2.55	3
Johan Hedberg	19	1078	12	4	48	2.67	0

Columbus Blue Jackets

SCORING

Player	GP	G	A	Pts	+/-	PM
David Vyborny, RW	80	22	43	65	-9	50
Rick Nash, LW	54	31	23	54	5	51
Nikolai Zherdev, RW	73	27	27	54	-13	50
Sergei Fedorov, C	67	12	32	44	-2	66
Jan Hrdina, C	75	10	23	33	-8	78
Bryan Berard, D	44	12	20	32	-29	32
Manny Malhotra, C	58	10	21	31	1	41
Jason Chimera, LW	80	17	13	30	-10	95
Trevor Letowski, RW	81	10	18	28	-2	36
Duvie Westscott, D	78	6	22	28	1	133
Jaroslav Balastik, LW	66	12	10	22	-1	26
Adam Foote, D	65	6	16	22	-16	89
Rostislav Klesla, D	51	6	13	19	-4	75
Ron Hainsey, D	55	2	15	17	13	43
Dan Fritsche, C	59	6	7	13	-14	22
Mark Hartigan, C	33	9	3	12	-1	22
Jody Shelley, LW	80	3	7	10	-4	163
Aaron Johnson, D	26	2	6	8	9	23
Radoslav Suchy, D	79	1	7	8	-8	30
Michael Rupp, RW	40	4	2	6	-3	58
Geoff Platt, C	15	0	5	5	-4	16
Ben Simon, C	13	0	0	0	-4	4
Steven Goertzen, RW	39	0	0	0	-17	44

GOALTENDING

Player	GP	Mins	W	L	TGA	GAA	SO
Marc Denis	49	2786	21	25	151	3.25	1
Pascal Leclaire	33	1803	11	15	97	3.23	0
Martin Prusek	9	373	3	3	20	3.22	0

Detroit Red Wings

SCORING

Player	GP	G	A	Pts	+/-	PM
Pavel Datsyuk, C	75	28	59	87	26	22
Henrik Zetterberg, LW	77	39	46	85	29	30
B Shanahan, LW	82	40	41	81	29	105
Niklas Lidstrom, D	80	16	64	80	21	50
Robert Lang, C	72	20	42	62	17	72
Tomas Holmstrom, LW	81	29	30	59	14	66
Mathieu Schneider, D	72	21	38	59	33	86
Jason Williams, C	80	21	37	58	4	26
Mikael Samuelson, RW	71	23	22	45	27	45
Steve Yzerman, C	61	14	20	34	8	18
Kris Draper, C	80	10	22	32	3	56
Jason Wooley, D	53	1	18	19	3	28
Johan Franzen, C	80	12	4	16	4	36
Mark, Mowers, RW	46	4	11	15	13	16
Daniel Cleary, RW	77	3	12	15	5	40
Andreas Lilja, D	82	2	13	15	18	98
Brett Ledba, D	46	3	9	12	9	20
Kirk Maltby, D	82	5	6	11	-9	80
Chris Chelios, D	81	4	7	11	22	108
Niklas Kronwall. D	27	1	8	9	11	28
Jiri Fischer, D	22	3	5	8	8	33
Cory Cross, D	56	3	5	8	-3	59
Don MacLean, C	3	1	1	2	2	0
Valtteri Filppula, C	4	0	1	1	1	2
Jiri Hudler, C	4	0	0	0	2	0

GOALTENDING

Player	GP	Mins	W	L	TGA	GAA	SO
Manny Legace	51	2905	37	8	106	2.19	7
Chris Osgood	32	1846	20	6	85	2.76	2
James Howard	4	200	1	2	10	2.99	0

Edmonton Oilers

SCORING

Player	GP	G	A	Pts	+/-	PM
Ales Hemsky, RW	81	19	58	77	-5	64
Shawn Horcoff, C	79	22	51	73	0	85
Jarret Stoll, C	82	22	46	68	4	74
Ryan Smyth, LW	75	36	30	66	-5	58
Chris Progner, D	80	12	44	56	2	74
Sergei Samsonov, LW	74	23	30	53	-3	28
Jaroslav Spacek, D	76	12	31	43	11	96
Raffi Torres, LW	82	27	14	41	4	50
Fernando Pisani, RW	80	18	19	37	5	42
Marc-Andre Bergeron, D	75	15	20	35	3	38
Steve Staios, D	82	8	20	28	10	84
Radek Dvorak, RW	64	8	20	28	-2	26
Ethan Moreau, LW	74	11	16	27	6	87
Michael Peca, C	71	9	14	23	-4	56
Jason Smith, D	76	4	13	17	1	84
Dick Tarnstrom, D	55	6	8	14	-15	76
Georges Larque, RW	72	2	10	12	-5	73
Igor Ulanov, D	37	3	6	9	-11	29
Todd Harvey, LW	15	2	1	3	1	4
Krys Kolanos, C	15	2	1	3	1	4
Rem Murray, C	9	1	1	2	1	2
Matt Greene, D	27	0	2	2	-6	43
Marc-Antoine Pouliot, C	8	1	0	1	1	0
Brad Winchester, LW	19	0	1	1	-2	21
Jean-Francois Jacques, LW	7	0	0	0	-3	0
Danny Syvret, D	10	0	0	0	-1	6
Dan Smith, D	7	0	0	0	1	7
Kyle Brodziak, C	10	0	0	0	-4	4

GOALTENDING

Player	GP	Mins	W	L	TGA	GAA	SO
Jussi Markkanen	37	2015	15	12	105	3.13	0
Dwayne Roloson	43	2523	14	24	115	2.73	2
Ty Conklin	18	922	8	5	43	2.80	1

Florida Panthers

SCORING

Player	GP	G	A	Pts	+/-	PM
Olli Jokinen, C	82	38	51	89	14	88
Joe Nieuwendyk, C	65	26	30	56	-2	46
Jozef Stumpel, C	74	15	37	52	11	26
Nathan Horton, RW	71	28	19	47	8	89
Jay Bouwmeester, D	82	5	41	46	1	79
Martin Gelinas, LW	82	17	24	41	27	80
Gary Roberts, LW	58	14	26	40	4	51
Chris Gratton, C	76	17	22	39	6	104
Mike Van Ryn, D	80	8	29	37	15	90
Juraj Kolnik, RW	77	15	20	35	1	40
Jonathan Sim, RW	72	17	15	32	-7	54
Ric Jackman, D	64	7	23	30	-20	52
Stephen Weiss, C	41	9	12	21	-2	22
Rostislav Olesz, LW	58	8	13	21	-4	24
Sean Hill, D	78	2	18	20	3	80
Lukas Krajicek, D	67	2	14	16	1	50
Joel Kwiatkowski, D	73	4	8	12	3	86
Gregory Campbell, C	64	3	6	9	-11	40
Steve Montador, D	58	2	5	7	4	79
Serge Payer, LW	71	2	4	6	-7	26
Alexi Semenov, D	27	2	2	4	-4	38
Mikhail Yakubov, C	23	1	3	4	-1	12
Anthony Stewart, C	10	2	1	3	2	2
Rob Globke, C	18	1	0	1	0	6
Branislav Mezei, D	16	0	1	1	3	37
Greg Jacina, C	11	0	1	1	-1	4
Jamie Allison, D	27	0	1	1	-6	56

GOALTENDING

Player	GP	Mins	W	L	TGA	GAA	SO
Roberto Luongo	75	4304	35	30	213	2.97	4
Jamie McLennan	17	677	2	4	34	3.01	0

Los Angeles Kings

SCORING

Player	GP	G	A	Pts	+/-	PM
Lubomir Visnovsky, D	80	17	50	67	7	50
Craig Conroy, C	78	22	44	66	13	78
Pavol Demitra, C	58	25	37	62	21	42
Michael Cammalleri, C	80	26	29	55	-14	50
Alexander, Frolov, LW	69	21	33	54	17	40
Mark Parrish, RW	76	29	20	49	-23	20
Derek Armstrong, C	62	13	28	41	-2	46
Joseph Corvo, D	81	14	26	40	16	38
Sean Avery, LW	75	15	24	39	-5	257
Eric Belanger, C	65	17	20	37	-5	62
Dustin Brown, RW	79	14	14	28	-10	80
Brent Sopel, D	77	4	23	27	-3	58
Luc Robitaillie, LW	65	15	9	24	-6	52
Jeremy Roenick, C	58	9	13	22	-5	36

SCORING *(CONT.)*

Player	GP	G	A	Pts	+/-	PM
Tom Kostopoulos, RW	76	8	14	22	-8	100
Tim Gleason, D	78	2	19	21	0	77
Jeff Cowan, LW	46	8	1	9	-8	73
Mike Weaver, D	53	0	9	9	-3	14
Aaron Miller, D	56	0	8	8	-6	27
Jeff Giuliano, LW	48	3	4	7	0	26
George Parros, RW	55	2	3	5	1	138
Peter Kanko, RW	10	1	0	1	1	0
Matt Ryan, C	12	0	1	1	-4	2

GOALTENDING

Player	GP	Mins	W	L	TGA	GAA	SO
Mathieu Garon	63	3446	31	26	185	3.22	4
Jason LaBarbera	29	1432	11	9	69	2.89	1
Adam Hauser	1	50	0	0	6	7.06	0

Minnesota Wild

SCORING

Player	GP	G	A	Pts	+/-	PM
Brian Rolston, C	82	34	45	79	14	50
Marian Gaborik, RW	65	38	28	66	6	64
Pierre-Marc Bouchard, RW	80	17	42	59	3	28
Todd White, C	61	19	21	40	-1	18
Randy Robitaille, C	67	12	28	40	-5	54
Wes Walz, C	82	19	18	37	7	61
Marc Chouinard, C	74	14	16	30	1	34
Kurtis Foster, D	58	10	18	28	-3	60
Alexzander Daigle, RW	46	5	23	28	-6	12
Pascal Dupus, LW	67	10	16	26	-10	40
Flip Kuba, D	65	6	19	25	0	44
Mikko Koivo, C	64	6	15	21	-9	40
Martin Skoula, D	78	5	16	21	6	40
Andrei Zyuzin, D	57	7	11	18	-12	50
Daniel Tjarnqvist, D	60	3	15	18	-11	32
Stephane Veilleux, LW	71	7	9	16	-13	63
Brent Burns, D	72	4	12	16	-7	32
Nick Schultz, D	79	2	12	14	2	43
Kyle Wanvig, RW	51	4	8	12	-8	64
Mattias Weinhandl, RW	68	4	7	11	-4	24
Derek Boogaard, LW	65	2	4	6	2	158
Matt Foy, RW	19	2	3	5	-4	16
Alex Henry, D	10	0	1	1	-1	2
Scott Ferguson, D	15	0	0	0	-3	22

GOALTENDING

Player	GP	Mins	W	L	TGA	GAA	SO
Manny Fernandez	58	3411	30	18	130	2.29	1
Dwayne Roloson	24	1361	6	17	68	3.00	1
Josh Harding	3	185	2	1	8	2.59	1

Nashville Predators

SCORING

Player	GP	G	A	Pts	+/-	PM
Paul Kariya, LW	82	31	54	85	-6	40
Steve Sullivan, RW	69	31	37	68	2	50
Mike Sillinger, C	79	32	31	63	-17	63
Yanic Perreault, C	69	22	35	57	-3	30
Kimmo Timonen, D	79	11	39	50	-3	74
Martin Erat, LW	80	20	29	49	0	76
Marek Zidlicky, D	67	12	37	49	8	82
Scott Hartnell, LW	81	25	23	48	8	101
Dan Hamhuis, D	82	7	31	38	11	70
Adam Hall, RW	75	14	15	29	0	40
David Legwand, C	44	7	19	26	3	34
Scottie Upshall, RW	48	8	16	24	14	34
Greg Johnson, C	68	11	8	19	5	10
Scott Walker, RW	33	5	11	16	2	38
Ryan Suter, D	71	1	15	16	7	66
Jerred Smithson, C	65	5	9	14	9	54
Brendan Witt, D	75	1	13	14	0	209
Darcy Hordichuk, LW	74	7	6	13	9	163
Vernon Fiddler, C	40	8	4	12	-2	42
Danny Marko, D	58	0	11	11	9	62
Jordin Tootoo, RW	34	4	6	10	9	55
Shea Weber, D	28	2	8	10	8	42
Scott Nichol, C	34	3	3	6	3	79
Mark Eaton, D	69	3	1	4	-2	44

GOALTENDING

Player	GP	Mins	W	L	TGA	GAA	SO
Tomas Vokoun	61	3600	36	18	160	2.67	4
Chris Mason	23	1226	12	5	52	2.54	2
Pekka Rinne	2	63	1	1	4	3.81	0
Brian Finley	1	60	0	1	7	7.00	0

Montreal Canadiens

SCORING

Player	GP	G	A	Pts	+/-	PM
Alex Kovalev, RW	69	23	42	65	-1	76
Saku Koivu, C	72	17	45	62	1	70
Michael Ryder, RW	81	30	25	55	-5	40
Mike Ribeiro, C	79	16	35	51	-6	36
Andrei Markov, D	67	10	36	46	13	74
Jan Bulis, C	73	20	20	40	2	50
Sheldon Souray, D	75	12	27	39	-11	116
Chris Higgins, C	80	23	15	38	-1	26
Craig Rivet, D	82	7	27	34	-5	109
Richard Zednik, LW	67	16	14	30	-2	48
Thomas Plekanec, LW	67	9	20	29	4	32
Steve Begin, C	76	11	12	23	9	113
Francis Bouillon, D	67	3	19	22	-6	34
Radek Bonk, C	61	6	15	21	-3	52
Mathieu Dandenault, D	82	5	15	20	8	83
A. Perezhogin, RW	67	9	10	19	5	38
Niklas Sundstrom, RW	55	6	9	15	-6	30
Pierre Dagenais, LW	32	5	7	12	-5	16
Mark Streit, D	48	2	9	11	-6	28
Aaron Downey, RW	42	3	4	7	2	95
Garth Murray, C	36	5	1	6	-2	44
Michael Komisarek, D	71	2	4	6	-1	116
Andrei Kostitsyn, RW	12	2	1	3	1	2
Todd Simpson, D	51	0	3	3	-2	130
Jean-Philippe Cote, D	8	0	0	0	2	4

GOALTENDING

Player	GP	Mins	W	L	TGA	GAA	SO
Jose Theodore	38	2114	17	15	122	3.46	0
Cristobal Huet	36	2102	18	11	77	2.20	7
David Aebischer	7	418	4	3	26	3.73	0

New Jersey Devils

SCORING

Player	GP	G	A	Pts	+/-	PM
Brian Gionta, RW	82	48	41	89	18	46
Scott Gomez, C	82	33	51	84	8	42
J. Langenbrunner, RW	80	19	34	53	-1	74
Brian Rafalski, D	82	6	43	49	0	36
Patrik Elias, C	38	16	29	45	11	20
Sergei Brylin, LW	82	15	22	37	-4	46
Paul Martin, D	80	5	32	37	1	32
John Madden, C	82	16	20	36	-7	36
Zach Parise, C	81	14	18	32	-1	28
Viktor Kozlov, RW	69	12	13	25	0	16
Alexander Mogilny, R	34	12	13	25	-7	6
Grant Marshall, R	76	8	17	25	-18	70
Brad Lukowich, D	75	2	19	21	0	40
Jay Pandolfo, LW	82	10	10	20	2	16
Colin White, D	73	3	14	17	-2	91
Ken Klee, D	74	3	12	15	-4	80
Richard Matvichuk, D	62	1	10	11	2	40
Erik Rasmussen, C	67	5	5	10	-4	32
Vladimir Malakhov, D	29	4	5	9	-9	40
Dan McGillis, D	27	0	6	6	-5	38
Tommy Albelin, D	36	0	6	6	4	2
Jason Weimer, C	49	2	2	4	-4	103
David Hale, D	38	0	4	4	5	21
Thomas Philman, LW	11	1	1	2	-1	10
Darren Langdon, LW	14	0	1	1	-3	22
Cam Janssen, RW	47	0	0	0	-3	91

GOALTENDING

Player	GP	Mins	W	L	TGA	GAA	SO
Martin Brodeur	73	4364	43	23	187	2.57	5
S. Clemmensen	13	626	3	4	35	3.35	0

New York Islanders

SCORING

Player	GP	G	A	Pts	+/-	PM
Miroslav Satan, RW	82	35	31	66	-8	54
Alexei Yashin, C	82	28	38	66	-14	68
Jason Blake, LW	76	28	29	57	0	60
Mike York, C	75	13	39	52	-9	30
Trent Hunter, RW	82	16	19	35	-9	34
Shawn Bates, C	66	15	19	34	-11	60
Chris Campoli, D	80	9	25	34	-16	46
Alexei Zhitnik, D	59	5	24	29	4	88
Arron Asham, RW	63	9	15	24	-5	103
Robert Nilsson, RW	53	6	14	20	-6	26
Radek Martinek, D	74	1	16	17	-9	32
Sean Bergenheim, LW	28	4	5	9	-11	20
Joel Bouchard, D	25	1	8	9	5	23
Jeff Hamilton, LW	13	2	6	8	0	8
Wyatt Smith, C	42	0	8	8	-7	26
Bruno Gervais, D	27	3	4	7	-1	8
Denis Grebeshkov, D	29	0	5	5	-12	20
Eric Godard, RW	57	2	2	4	-2	115
Jeff Tambellini, LW	25	1	3	4	1	10
Rob Collins, C	8	1	1	2	1	0
Jeremy Colliton, C	19	1	1	2	2	6
Petteri Nokelainen, C	15	1	1	2	-1	4
John Erskine, D	60	1	0	1	-15	161
Steve Regier, LW	9	0	0	0	-1	0
Kevin Colley, C	16	0	0	0	-2	52

GOALTENDING

Player	GP	Mins	W	L	TGA	GAA	SO
Rick DiPietro	63	3571	30	24	180	3.02	1
Garth Snow	20	1096	4	13	68	3.72	0
Wade Dubielewicz	7	310	2	3	15	2.90	0

Ottawa Senators

SCORING

Player	GP	G	A	Pts	+/-	PM
Dany Heatley, LW	82	50	53	103	29	86
Daniel Alfredsson, RW	77	43	60	103	29	50
Jason Spezza, C	68	19	71	90	23	33
Peter Schaffer, LW	82	20	30	50	16	40
Wade Reddon, D	65	10	40	50	35	63
Bryan Smolinsky, C	81	17	31	48	8	46
Tyler Arnason, C	79	13	32	45	1	44
Mike Fisher, C	68	22	22	44	23	64
Zdeno Chara, D	71	16	27	43	17	135
Andrej Meszaros, D	82	10	29	39	34	61
Brian Pothier, D	77	5	30	35	29	59
Antoine Vermette, C	82	21	12	33	17	44
Chris Neil, RW	79	16	17	33	9	204
Chris Kelly, C	82	10	20	30	21	76
Patrick Eaves, RW	58	20	9	29	7	22
Vaclav Varada, LW	76	5	16	21	2	50
Chris Phillips, D	69	1	18	19	19	90
Anton Volchenkov, D	75	4	13	17	21	53
Martin Havlat, RW	18	9	7	16	6	4
Christopher Schubert, D	56	4	6	10	4	48
Brian McGrattan, RW	60	2	3	5	0	141
Flip Novak, D	11	0	0	0	-2	4

GOALTENDING

Player	GP	Mins	W	L	TGA	GAA	SO
Dominik Hasek	43	2583	28	10	90	2.09	5
Ray Emery	39	2167	23	11	102	2.82	3
Michael Morrison	4	207	1	0	12	3.47	0

New York Rangers

SCORING

Player	GP	G	A	Pts	+/-	PM
Jaromir Jagr, RW	82	54	69	123	34	72
Michael Nylander, C	81	23	56	79	31	76
Martin Straka, LW	82	22	54	76	17	42
Martin Rucinsky, LW	52	16	39	55	10	56
Peter Sykora, RW	74	23	28	51	6	50
Peter Prucha, RW	68	30	17	47	3	32
Steve Rucchin, C	72	13	23	36	6	10
Michal Rozsival, D	82	5	25	30	35	90
Jason Ward, RW	81	10	18	28	-4	44
Fedor Tyutin, D	77	6	19	25	-1	58
Tom Poti, D	73	3	20	23	16	70
Sandis Ozolinsh, D	36	6	14	20	-2	28
Dominic Moore, C	82	9	9	18	4	28
Marek Malik, D	74	2	16	18	28	78
Marcel Hossa, LW	64	10	6	16	-6	28
Blair Betts, C	66	8	2	10	-10	24
Jed Ortmeyer, RW	78	5	2	7	2	38
Jason Strudwick, D	65	3	4	7	-10	66
Darius Kasparaitis, D	67	0	6	6	7	97
Ryan Hollweg, LW	52	2	3	5	-3	84
Maxim Konderatiev, D	29	1	2	3	-2	22
Thomas Pock, D	8	1	1	2	-3	4
Colton Orr, RW	35	0	1	1	1	71

GOALTENDING

Player	GP	Mins	W	L	TGA	GAA	SO
Henrik Lundqvist	53	3111	30	12	116	2.24	2
Kevin Weekes	32	1850	14	14	91	2.95	0
Chris Holt	1	10	0	0	0	0.00	0

Philadelphia Flyers

SCORING

Player	GP	G	A	Pts	+/-	PM
Simon Gagne, LW	72	47	32	79	31	38
Peter Forsberg, C	60	19	56	75	21	46
Mike Knuble, RW	82	34	31	65	25	80
Joni Pitkanen, D	58	13	33	46	22	78
Michael Handzus, C	73	11	33	44	-2	38
Jeff Carter, C	81	23	19	42	10	40
R.J. Umberger, C	73	20	18	38	9	18
Sami Kapanen, RW	58	12	22	34	-9	12
Mike Richards, C	79	11	23	34	6	65
Frederick Meyer, D	57	6	21	27	10	33
Nicholas Dimitrakos, RW	64	9	16	25	4	32
Petr Nedved, C	53	7	18	25	-14	70
Kim Johnsson, D	47	5	20	25	5	34
Eric Desjardins, D	45	4	20	24	3	56
Mike Rathje, D	79	3	21	24	22	46
Derian Hatcher, D	77	4	13	17	2	93
Brian Savage, LW	66	9	5	14	-18	28
Branko Radivojevic, RW	64	8	6	14	-6	44
Matt Ellison, RW	31	3	10	13	-2	19
Denis Gauthier, D	62	2	9	11	2	98
Donald Brashear, LW	76	4	5	9	-2	166
Ben Eager, LW	25	3	5	8	0	18
Keith Primeau, C	9	1	6	7	0	6
Turner Stevenson, RW	31	1	3	4	-2	45
Chris Therien, D	47	0	4	4	-7	34

GOALTENDING

Player	GP	Mins	W	L	TGA	GAA	SO
Antero Niittymaki	46	2690	23	15	133	2.97	2
Robert Esche	40	2286	22	11	113	2.97	1

Pittsburgh Penguins

SCORING

Player	GP	G	A	Pts	+/-	PM
Sidney Crosby, C	81	39	63	102	-1	110
Sergei Gonchar, D	75	12	46	58	-13	100
John Leclair, LW	73	22	29	51	-24	61
Ryan Malone, LW	77	22	22	44	-22	63
Zigmund Palffy, RW	42	11	31	42	5	12
Colby Armstrong, RW	47	16	24	40	15	58
Ryan Whitney, D	68	6	32	38	-7	85
Michael Ouellet, RW	50	16	16	32	-13	16
Andy Hilbert, C	47	12	15	27	4	38
Tomas Surovy, LW	53	12	13	25	-13	45
Mario Lemieux, C	26	7	15	22	-16	16
Eric Boguniecki, RW	47	6	10	16	-3	33
Josef Melichar, D	72	3	12	15	-2	66
Erik Christensen, C	33	6	7	13	-3	34
Jani Rita, RW	51	6	4	10	-6	10
Konstantin Koltsov, RW	60	3	6	9	-10	20
Brooks Orpik, D	64	2	7	9	-3	124
Maxime Talbot, C	48	5	3	8	-12	59
Lasse Pirjeta, C	25	4	3	7	4	18
Niklas Nordgren, RW	58	4	2	6	-8	34
Matt Murley, LW	41	1	5	6	-9	24
Robert Scuderi, D	57	0	4	4	-18	36
Andre Rot, LW	42	2	1	3	-3	116
Shane Endicott, C	41	1	1	2	9	43
Eric Cairns, D	50	1	1	2	1	134
R.Vandenbussche, RW	20	1	0	1	0	42
Lyle Odelein, D	27	0	1	1	-10	50
Matt Hussey, C	13	0	1	1	-5	0

GOALTENDING

Player	GP	Mins	W	L	TGA	GAA	SO
Marc-Andre Fleury	50	2809	13	27	152	3.25	1
Sebastien Caron	26	1312	8	9	87	3.98	1
Jocelyn Thibault	16	806	1	9	60	4.46	0
Dany Sabourin	1	20	0	1	4	11.43	0

Phoenix Coyotes

SCORING

Player	GP	G	A	Pts	+/-	PM
Shane Doan, LW	82	30	36	66	-9	123
Mike Comrie, C	80	30	30	60	2	55
Ladislav Nagy, LW	51	15	41	56	8	74
Mike Johnson, RW	80	16	38	54	7	50
Steven Reinprecht, C	80	22	30	52	11	32
Paul Mara, D	78	15	32	47	-12	70
Geoff Sanderson, LW	77	25	21	46	-15	58
Keith Ballard, D	82	8	31	39	-18	99
Dave Scatchard, C	63	15	18	33	-13	112
Oleg Kvasha, LW	64	13	19	32	3	38
Derek Morris, D	53	6	21	27	-7	54
Oleg Saprykin, LW	67	11	14	25	-16	50
Zbynek Michalek, D	82	9	15	24	4	62
Fredrik Sjostrom, RW	75	6	17	23	1	42
Boyd Devereaux, C	78	8	14	22	-13	4
Dennis Seidenberg, D	63	3	15	18	-13	18
Mike Ricci, C	78	10	6	16	-22	69
Jamie Rivers, D	33	0	6	6	2	38
Tyson Nash, LW	50	0	6	6	-7	84
Bill Thomas, RW	9	1	2	3	-2	8
Matt Jones, D	16	0	2	2	-2	14
Josh Gratton, LW	14	1	0	1	-3	44
Steve Gainey, LW	20	0	1	1	-3	20
Pascal Rheaume, C	13	0	0	0	-7	4

GOALTENDING

Player	GP	Mins	W	L	TGA	GAA	SO
Curtis Joseph	60	3424	32	21	166	2.91	1
Philippe Sauve	13	589	7	39	3.97	0
David LeNeveu	15	814	3	8	44	3.24	0

San Jose Sharks

SCORING

Player	GP	G	A	Pts	+/-	PM
Joe Thornton, C	81	29	96	125	31	61
Jonathan Cheechoo, RW	82	56	37	93	23	58
Patrick Marleau, C	82	34	52	86	-12	26
Nils Ekman, LW	77	21	36	57	20	54
Tom Preissing, D	74	11	32	43	17	26
Milan Michalek, RW	81	17	18	35	1	45
Steve Bernier, RW	39	14	13	27	4	35
Alyn McCauley, C	76	12	14	26	-3	30
Mark Smith, C	80	9	15	24	3	97
Ville Nieminen, LW	70	8	16	24	7	63
Scott Hannan,	81	6	18	24	7	58
Christian Rhrhoff, D	64	5	18	23	10	32
Kyle Mclaren, D	77	2	21	23	6	66
Grant Stevenson, C	47	10	12	22	-7	14
Marcel Goc, C	81	8	14	22	-7	22

SCORING (CONT.)

Player	GP	G	A	Pts	+/-	PM
Scott Thornton, LW	71	10	11	21	-8	84
Patrick Rissmiller, C	18	3	3	6	1	8
Matthew Carle, D	12	3	3	6	-2	14
Rob Davison, D	69	1	5	6	6	76
Josh Gorges, D	49	0	6	6	5	31
Ryane Clowe, LW	18	0	2	2	-2	9
Jim Fahey, D	21	0	2	2	-11	14
Scott Parker, RW	10	1	0	1	3	38
Doug Murray, D	34	0	1	1	3	27

GOALTENDING

Player	GP	Mins	W	L	TGA	GAA	SO
Vesa Toskala	37	2039	23	7	87	2.56	2
Evgeni Nabokov	45	2574	16	19	133	3.10	1
Nolan Schaefer	7	352	5	1	11	1.88	1

St. Louis Blues

SCORING

Player	GP	G	A	Pts	+/-	PM
Scott Young, RW	79	18	31	49	-32	52
Peter Cajanek, C	71	10	31	41	-22	54
Dean McAmmond, C	78	15	22	37	-25	32
Keith Tkachuk, LW	41	15	21	36	-15	46
Lee Stempniak, RW	57	14	13	27	-10	22
Jay McClement, C	67	6	21	27	-23	30
Jamal Mayers, RW	67	15	11	26	-22	129
Dallas Drake, RW	62	2	24	26	-13	59
Dennis Wideman, D	67	8	16	24	-31	83
Christian Backman, D	52	6	12	18	-15	48
Kevin Dallman, D	67	4	10	14	-14	29
Mike Glumac, RW	35	7	5	12	-8	33
Mark Rycroft, RW	80	6	4	10	-14	46
Barret Jackman, D	63	4	6	10	-6	156
Eric Brewer, D	32	6	3	9	-17	45
Vladimir Orszagh, RW	16	4	5	9	-2	14
Ryan Johnson, C	65	3	6	9	-21	33
Jeff Hoggan, RW	52	2	6	8	-16	34
Simon Gamache, LW	26	3	4	7	-5	10
Trent Whitfield, C	30	2	5	7	-3	14
Timofei Shishkanov, RW	22	3	2	5	-1	6
Bryce Salvador, D	46	1	4	5	-24	26
Steve Popst, D	62	0	5	5	-26	47
Andy Roach, D	5	1	2	3	0	10
Peter Sejna, LW	6	1	1	2	1	4
Matt Walker, D	54	0	2	2	-7	79
Jeff Woywitka, D	26	0	2	2	-12	25
Micheal Zigomanis, C	23	1	0	1	1	4

GOALTENDING

Player	Mins	W	L	TGA	GAA	SO
Curtis Sanford	34	1830	13	13	81	2.66	3
Jason Bacashihua	19	966	4	10	52	3.23	0
Patrick Lalime	31	1699	4	18	103	3.64	0
Reinhard Divis	12	475	0	5	37	4.67	0

Tampa Bay Lightning

SCORING

Player	GP	G	A	Pts	+/-	PM
Brad Richards, C	82	23	68	91	0	32
Vaclav Prospal, LW	81	25	55	80	-3	50
Vincent Lecavalier, C	80	35	40	75	0	90
Martin St. Louis, RW	80	31	30	61	-3	38
Fredrik Modin, LW	77	31	23	54	5	56
Dan Boyle, D	79	15	38	53	-8	38
Ruslan Fedotenko, RW	80	26	15	41	-4	44
Pavel Kubina, D	76	5	33	38	-12	96
Ryan Craig, C	48	15	13	28	-4	6
Darryl Sydor, D	80	4	19	23	-18	30
Dave Andreychuk, LW	42	6	12	18	-13	16
Paul Ranger, D	76	1	17	18	5	58
Evgeny Artyukhin, RW	72	4	13	17	-4	90
Rob Dimaio, RW	61	4	13	17	-7	30
Dimitry Afanasenkov, LW	68	9	6	15	-7	16
Cory Sarich, D	82	1	14	15	-2	79
Tim Taylor, C	81	7	6	13	-12	22
Nolan Pratt, D	82	0	9	9	-7	60
Martin Cibak, C	65	2	6	8	-9	22
Norman Milley, RW	14	2	1	3	-2	4
Darren Reid, RW	7	0	1	1	-2	0
Timo Helbling, D	9	0	1	1	-3	6
Chris Dingman, LW	34	0	1	1	-10	22
Nick Tarnasky, C	12	0	1	1	-3	4
Doug O'Brien, D	5	0	0	0	0	2

GOALTENDING

Player	Mins	W	L	TGA	GAA	SO
John Grahame	57	3152	29	22	161	3.06	5
Sean Burke	35	1713	14	10	80	2.80	2
Gerald Coleman	2	43	0	0	2	2.79	0
Brian Eklund	1	58	0	1	3	3.10	0

Toronto Maple Leafs

SCORING

Player	GP	G	A	Pts	+/-	PM
Mats Sundin, C	70	31	47	78	7	58
Bryan McCabe, D	73	19	49	68	-1	116
Tomas Kaberle, D	82	9	58	67	-1	46
Darcy Tucker, RW	74	28	33	61	-12	100
Jason Allison, C	66	17	43	60	-18	76
Alex Steen, C	75	18	27	45	-9	42
Kyle Wellwood, C	81	11	34	45	0	14
Alexei Ponikarovsky, LW	81	21	17	38	15	68
Jeff O'Neill, RW	74	19	19	38	-19	64
Nik Antropov, C	57	12	19	31	13	56
Chad Kilger, LW	79	17	11	28	-6	63
Matt Stajan, C	80	15	12	27	-5	50
Eric Lindros, C	33	11	11	22	-3	43
Tie Domi, RW	77	5	11	16	-10	109
Alexander Khavanov, D	64	6	6	12	-11	60
Luke Richardson, D	65	1	9	10	-19	71

SCORING *(CONT.)*

Player	GP	G	A	Pts	+/-	PM
Clarke Wilm, C	60	1	7	8	-15	43
Aki Berg, D	75	0	8	8	-5	56
Carlo Colaiacovo, D	21	2	5	7	0	17
Ian White, D	12	1	5	6	2	10
John Pohl, C	7	3	1	4	2	4
Wade Belak, D	55	0	3	3	-13	109
Jay Harrison, D	8	0	1	1	5	2
Staffan Kronwall, D	34	0	1	1	-3	14
Andrew Wozniewski, D	13	0	1	1	-8	13
Ben Ondrus, RW	22	0	0	0	-10	18

GOALTENDING

Player	GP	Mins	W	L	TGA	GAA	SO
Ed Belfour	49	2.896	22	22	159	3.29	0
Mikael Tellqvist	25	1398	10	11	73	3.13	2
J. Aubin	11	677	9	0	25	2.22	1

Vancouver Canucks

SCORING

Player	GP	G	A	Pts	+/-	PM
Markus Naslund, LW	81	32	47	79	-19	66
Henrik Sedin, C	82	18	57	75	11	56
Todd Bertuzzi, RW	82	25	46	71	-17	120
Daniel Sedin, LW	82	22	49	71	7	34
Brendon Morrison, C	82	19	37	56	-1	84
Anson Carter, RW	81	33	22	55	-1	41
Nolan Baumgartner, D	70	5	29	34	11	30
Mattias Ohlund, D	78	13	20	33	-6	92
Sami Salo, D	59	10	23	33	9	38
Ed Jovanovski, D	44	8	25	33	-8	58
Ryan Kessler, C	82	10	13	23	1	79
Keith Carney, D	79	2	18	20	8	62
Matt Cooke, C	45	8	10	18	-8	71
Richard Park, RW	60	8	10	18	-2	29
Jarkko Ruutu, LW	82	10	7	17	1	142
Bryan Allen, D	77	7	10	17	4	115
Eric Weinrich, D	75	1	16	17	-23	52

SCORING

Player	GP	G	A	Pts	+/-	PM
Trevor Linden, C	82	7	9	16	3	15
Alexandre Burrows, LW	43	7	5	12	5	61
Sean Brown, D	47	1	11	12	-17	35
Josh Green, LW	33	4	2	6	2	14
Kevin Bieska, D	39	0	6	6	-1	77
Lee Goren, RW	28	1	2	3	-6	30
Wade Brookbank, D	32	1	2	3	3	81
Tyler Bouck, RW	12	1	1	2	0	21
Rick Rypien, RW	5	1	0	1	1	4
Tomas Mojzis, D	7	0	1	1	2	12

GOALTENDING

Player	GP	Mins	W	L	TGA	GAA	SO
Alexander Auld	67	3858	33	26	189	2.94	0
Dan Cloutier	13	680	8	3	36	3.17	0
Mika Noronen	8	338	2	3	22	3.89	0
Rob McVicar	1	2	0	0	0	0.0	0
Maxime Ouellet	4	221	0	2	12	3.24	0

Washington Capitals

SCORING

Player	GP	G	A	Pts	+/-	PM
Alexander Ovechkin, LW	81	52	54	106	2	52
Dainius Zubrus, RW	71	23	34	57	3	84
Jeff Halpren, C	70	11	33	44	-8	79
Brian Willsie, RW	82	19	22	41	-19	77
Chris Clark, RW	78	20	19	39	9	110
Matt Pettinger, LW	71	20	18	38	-2	39
Ben Clymer, LW	77	16	17	33	-7	72
Brain Sutherby, C	76	14	16	30	-17	73
Jamie Heward, D	71	7	21	28	-5	54
Bryan Muir, D	72	8	18	26	-9	72
Brooks Laich, C	73	7	14	21	-9	26
Matt Bradley, RW	74	7	12	19	-8	72
Steve Eminger, D	66	5	13	18	-12	81
Shaone Morrison, D	80	1	13	14	7	91
Mathieu Biron, D	52	4	9	13	-11	50
Andrew Cassels, C	31	4	8	12	-3	14

SCORING

Player	GP	G	A	Pts	+/-	PM
Ivan Majesky, D	57	1	8	9	-2	66
Rico Fata, C	47	3	4	7	-4	22
Nolan Yonkman, D	38	0	7	7	1	86
Peter Sykora, C	10	2	2	4	0	6
Jakub Klepis, C	25	1	3	4	-11	8
Kris Bleech, C	10	1	2	3	1	4
Mike Green, D	22	1	2	3	-8	18
Tomas Fleischmann, LW	14	0	2	2	-7	0
Boyd Kane, LW	5	0	1	1	1	2
Boyd Gordon, RW	25	0	1	1	-4	4

GOALTENDING

Player	GP	Mins	W	L	TGA	GAA	SO
Olaf Kolzig	59	3506	20	28	206	3.53	0
Brent Johnson	26	1412	9	12	81	3.44	1
Frederic Cassivi	1	58	0	1	4	4.07	0

2006 NHL Draft

First Round

The opening round of the 2006 NHL draft was held on June 24 in Vancouver, British Columbia, Canada.

	Team	Selection	Position		Team	Selection	Position
1.	St. Louis	Erik Johnson	D	16.	San Jose	Ty Wishart	D
2.	Pittsburgh	Jordan Staal	C	17.	Los Angeles	Trevor Lewis	C
3.	Chicago	Jonathan Toews	C	18.	Colorado	Chris Stewart	F
4.	Washington	Nicklas Backstrom	C	19.	Anaheim	Mark Mitera	D
5.	Boston	Phil Kessel	C	20.	Montreal	David Fischer	D
6.	Columbus	Derick Brassard	C	21.	NY Rangers	Bobby Sanguinetti	D
7.	NY Islanders	Kyle Okposo	F	22.	Philadelphia	Claude Giroux	F
8.	Phoenix	Peter Mueller	C	23.	Washington	Semen Varlamov	G
9.	Minnesota	James Sheppard	C	24.	Buffalo	Dennis Persson	D
10.	Florida	Michael Frolik	C	25.	St. Louis	Patrik Berglund	C
11.	Los Angeles	Jonathan Bernier	G	26.	Calgary	Leland Irving	G
12.	Atlanta	Bryan Little	C	27.	Dallas	Ivan Visknevskiy	D
13.	Toronto	Jiri Tlusty	F	28.	Ottawa	Nick Foligno	F
14.	Vancouver	Michael Grabner	F	29.	Phoenix	Chris Summers	D
15.	Tampa Bay	Riku Helenius	G	30.	New Jersey	Matthew Corrente	D

The Stanley Cup

Awarded annually to the team that wins the NHL's best-of-seven final-round playoffs. The Stanley Cup is the oldest trophy competed for by professional athletes in North America. It was donated in 1893 by Frederick Arthur, Lord Stanley of Preston.

Results

1892–93	Montreal A.A.A.
1893–94	Montreal A.A.A.
1894–95	Montreal Victorias
1895–96	Winnipeg Victorias (Feb)
1895–96	Montreal Victorias (Dec)
1896–97	Montreal Victorias
1897–98	Montreal Victorias
1898–99	Montreal Victorias (Feb)
1898–99	Montreal Shamrocks (Mar)
1899–1900	Montreal Shamrocks
1900–01	Winnipeg Victorias
1901–02	Winnipeg Victorias (Jan)
1901–02	Montreal A.A.A. (Mar)
1902–03	Montreal A.A.A. (Feb)
1902–03	Ottawa Silver Seven (Mar)
1903–04	Ottawa Silver Seven
1904–05	Ottawa Silver Seven
1905–06	Ottawa Silver Seven (Feb)
1905–06	Montreal Wanderers (Mar)
1906–07	Kenora Thistles (Jan)
1906–07	Montreal Wanderers (Mar)
1907–08	Montreal Wanderers
1908–09	Ottawa Senators
1909–10	Montreal Wanderers
1910–11	Ottawa Senators
1911–12	Quebec Bulldogs
1912–13	Quebec Bulldogs
1913–14	Toronto Blueshirts
1914–15	Vancouver Millionaires
1915–16	Montreal Canadiens
1916–17	Seattle Metropolitans

NHL WINNERS AND FINALISTS

Season	Champion	Finalist	GP in Final
1917–18	Toronto Arenas	Vancouver Millionaires	5
1918–19	No decision*	No decision*	5
1919–20	Ottawa Senators	Seattle Metropolitans	5
1920–21	Ottawa Senators	Vancouver Millionaires	5
1921–22	Toronto St. Pats	Vancouver Millionaires	5
1922–23	Ottawa Senators	Vancouver Maroons, Edmonton Eskimos	2, 4
1923–24	Montreal Canadiens	Vancouver Maroons, Calgary Tigers	2, 2
1924–25	Victoria Cougars	Montreal Canadiens	4
1925–26	Montreal Maroons	Victoria Cougars	4
1926–27	Ottawa Senators	Boston Bruins	4
1927–28	New York Rangers	Montreal Maroons	5
1928–29	Boston Bruins	New York Rangers	2
1929–30	Montreal Canadiens	Boston Bruins	2
1930–31	Montreal Canadiens	Chicago Blackhawks	5
1931–32	Toronto Maple Leafs	New York Rangers	3
1932–33	New York Rangers	Toronto Maple Leafs	4
1933–34	Chicago Blackhawks	Detroit Red Wings	4
1934–35	Montreal Maroons	Toronto Maple Leafs	3
1935–36	Detroit Red Wings	Toronto Maple Leafs	4
1936–37	Detroit Red Wings	New York Rangers	5
1937–38	Chicago Blackhawks	Toronto Maple Leafs	4
1938–39	Boston Bruins	Toronto Maple Leafs	5
1939–40	New York Rangers	Toronto Maple Leafs	6
1940–41	Boston Bruins	Detroit Red Wings	4
1941–42	Toronto Maple Leafs	Detroit Red Wings	7
1942–43	Detroit Red Wings	Boston Bruins	4
1943–44	Montreal Canadiens	Chicago Blackhawks	4
1944–45	Toronto Maple Leafs	Detroit Red Wings	7
1945–46	Montreal Canadiens	Boston Bruins	5
1946–47	Toronto Maple Leafs	Montreal Canadiens	6
1947–48	Toronto Maple Leafs	Detroit Red Wings	4
1948–49	Toronto Maple Leafs	Detroit Red Wings	4
1949–50	Detroit Red Wings	New York Rangers	7
1950–51	Toronto Maple Leafs	Montreal Canadiens	5
1951–52	Detroit Red Wings	Montreal Canadiens	4
1952–53	Montreal Canadiens	Boston Bruins	5
1953–54	Detroit Red Wings	Montreal Canadiens	7
1954–55	Detroit Red Wings	Montreal Canadiens	7

NHL WINNERS AND FINALISTS

Season	Champion	Finalist	GP in Final
1955–56	Montreal Canadiens	Detroit Red Wings	5
1956–57	Montreal Canadiens	Boston Bruins	5
1957–58	Montreal Canadiens	Boston Bruins	6
1958–59	Montreal Canadiens	Toronto Maple Leafs	5
1959–60	Montreal Canadiens	Toronto Maple Leafs	4
1960–61	Chicago Blackhawks	Detroit Red Wings	6
1961–62	Toronto Maple Leafs	Chicago Blackhawks	6
1962–63	Toronto Maple Leafs	Detroit Red Wings	5
1963–64	Toronto Maple Leafs	Detroit Red Wings	7
1964–65	Montreal Canadiens	Chicago Blackhawks	7
1965–66	Montreal Canadiens	Detroit Red Wings	6
1966–67	Toronto Maple Leafs	Montreal Canadiens	6
1967–68	Montreal Canadiens	St. Louis Blues	4
1968–69	Montreal Canadiens	St. Louis Blues	4
1969–70	Boston Bruins	St. Louis Blues	4
1970–71	Montreal Canadiens	Chicago Blackhawks	7
1971–72	Boston Bruins	New York Rangers	6
1972–73	Montreal Canadiens	Chicago Blackhawks	6
1973–74	Philadelphia Flyers	Boston Bruins	6
1974–75	Philadelphia Flyers	Buffalo Sabres	6
1975–76	Montreal Canadiens	Philadelphia Flyers	4
1976–77	Montreal Canadiens	Boston Bruins	4
1977–78	Montreal Canadiens	Boston Bruins	6
1978–79	Montreal Canadiens	New York Rangers	5
1979–80	New York Islanders	Philadelphia Flyers	6
1980–81	New York Islanders	Minnesota North Stars	5
1981–82	New York Islanders	Vancouver Canucks	4
1982–83	New York Islanders	Edmonton Oilers	4
1983–84	Edmonton Oilers	New York Islanders	5
1984–85	Edmonton Oilers	Philadelphia Flyers	5
1985–86	Montreal Canadiens	Calgary Flames	6
1986–87	Edmonton Oilers	Philadelphia Flyers	7
1987–88	Edmonton Oilers	Boston Bruins	4
1988–89	Calgary Flames	Montreal Canadiens	6
1989–90	Edmonton Oilers	Boston Bruins	5
1990–91	Pittsburgh Penguins	Minnesota North Stars	6
1991–92	Pittsburgh Penguins	Chicago Blackhawks	4
1992–93	Montreal Canadiens	Los Angeles Kings	5
1993–94	New York Rangers	Vancouver Canucks	7
1994–95	New Jersey Devils	Detroit Red Wings	4
1995–96	Colorado Avalanche	Florida Panthers	4
1996–97	Detroit Red Wings	Philadelphia Flyers	4
1997–98	Detroit Red Wings	Washington Capitals	4
1998–99	Dallas Stars	Buffalo Sabres	6
1999–2000	New Jersey Devils	Dallas Stars	6
2000–01	Colorado Avalanche	New Jersey Devils	7
2001–02	Detroit Red Wings	Carolina Hurricanes	5
2002–03	New Jersey Devils	Anaheim Mighty Ducks	7
2003–04	Tampa Bay Lightning	Calgary Flames	7
2004-05	No Stanley Cup due to season lockout		
2005–06	Carolina Hurricanes	Edmonton Oilers	7

*In 1919 the Montreal Canadiens traveled to meet Seattle, the PCHL champions. After 5 games had been played—the teams were tied at 2 wins and 1 tie—the series was called off by the local Department of Health because of the influenza epidemic and the death of Canadiens defenseman Joe Hall from influenza.

Conn Smythe Trophy

Awarded to the Most Valuable Player of the Stanley Cup playoffs, as selected by the Professional Hockey Writers Association. The trophy is named after the former coach, general manager, president and owner of the Toronto Maple Leafs.

1965	Jean Beliveau, Mtl
1966	Roger Crozier, Det
1967	Dave Keon, Tor
1968	Glenn Hall, StL
1969	Serge Savard, Mtl
1970	Bobby Orr, Bos
1971	Ken Dryden, Mtl
1972	Bobby Orr, Bos
1973	Yvan Cournoyer, Mtl
1974	Bernie Parent, Phil
1975	Bernie Parent, Phil
1976	Reggie Leach, Phil
1977	Guy Lafleur, Mtl
1978	Larry Robinson, Mtl
1979	Bob Gainey, Mtl
1980	Bryan Trottier, NYI
1981	Butch Goring, NYI
1982	Mike Bossy, NYI
1983	Bill Smith, NYI
1984	Mark Messier, Edm
1985	Wayne Gretzky, Edm
1986	Patrick Roy, Mtl
1987	Ron Hextall, Phil
1988	Wayne Gretzky, Edm
1989	Al MacInnis, Cgy
1990	Bill Ranford, Edm
1991	Mario Lemieux, Pitt
1992	Mario Lemieux, Pitt
1993	Patrick Roy, Mtl
1994	Brian Leetch, NYR
1995	Claude Lemieux, NJ
1996	Joe Sakic, Col
1997	Mike Vernon, Det
1998	Steve Yzerman, Det
1999	Joe Nieuwendyk, Dall
2000	Scott Stevens, NJ
2001	Patrick Roy, Col
2002	Nicklas Lidstrom, Det
2003	J.-S. Giguere, Ana
2004	Brad Richards, TB
2005	No Award–No Season
2006	Cam Ward, Car

Alltime Stanley Cup Playoff Leaders

Points

	Yrs	GP	G	A	Pts		Yrs	GP	G	A	Pts
Wayne Gretzky, four teams	16	208	122	260	382	Jean Beliveau, Mtl	17	162	79	97	176
Mark Messier, Edm, Van, NYR	18	236	109	186	295	Denis Savard, Chi, Mtl	16	169	66	109	175
Jari Kurri, four teams	15	200	106	127	233	*Mario Lemieux, Pitt	8	107	76	96	172
Glenn Anderson, four teams	15	225	93	121	214	Denis Potvin, NYI	14	185	56	108	164
Paul Coffey, six teams	16	198	59	137	196	*Sergei Fedorov, Det, Ana	13	162	50	113	163
*Brett Hull, four teams	19	202	103	87	190	*Peter Forsberg, Que, Col, Phi	11	139	61	101	162
Doug Gilmour, seven teams	18	182	60	128	188	Mike Bossy, NYI	10	129	85	75	160
Bryan Trottier, NYI, Pitt	17	221	71	113	184	Gordie Howe, Det, Hart	20	157	68	92	160
*Steve Yzerman, Det	20	196	70	115	185	Bobby Smith, Minn, Mtl	13	184	64	96	160
Ray Bourque, Bos, Col	21	214	41	139	180	Al MacInnis, Cgy, StL	19	177	39	121	160
*Joe Sakic, Que, Col	12	162	82	96	178						

*Active in 2005–06 season.

Goals

	Yrs	GP	G			Yrs	GP	G
Wayne Gretzky, four teams	17	208	122	Claude Lemieux, six teams	17	233	80
Mark Messier, Edm, NYR	18	236	109	Jean Beliveau, Mtl	17	162	79
Jari Kurri, five teams	15	200	106	*Mario Lemieux, Pitt	8	107	76
*Brett Hull, Cgy, StL, Dall, Det	19	202	103				
Glenn Anderson, four teams	15	225	93				
Mike Bossy, NYI	10	129	85				
*Joe Sakic, Que, Col	12	162	82				
Maurice Richard, Mtl	15	133	82				

*Active in 2005–06.

Assists

	Yrs	GP	A			Yrs	GP	A
Wayne Gretzky, four teams	17	208	260	Al MacInnis, Cgy, StL	19	177	121
Mark Messier, Edm, NYR	18	236	186	Larry Robinson, Mtl, LA	20	227	116
Ray Bourque, Bos, Col	21	214	139	Larry Murphy, six teams	15	215	115
Paul Coffey, six teams	16	198	137	Steve Yzerman, Det	20	196	115
Doug Gilmour, seven teams	18	182	128				
Jari Kurri, five teams	15	196	127				
Glenn Anderson, four teams	15	225	121				

*Active in 2005–06.

Alltime Stanley Cup Playoff Goaltending Leaders

WINS	W	L	Pct
Patrick Roy, Mtl, Col	151	94	.616
Grant Fuhr, five teams	92	50	.648
*Martin Brodeur, NJ	89	64	.582
Billy Smith, LA, NYI	88	36	.710
*Ed Belfour, four teams	88	68	.564
Ken Dryden, Mtl	80	32	.714
Mike Vernon, four teams	77	56	.579
Jacques Plante, five teams	71	37	.657
Andy Moog, four teams	68	57	.544
*Curtis Joseph, four teams	62	66	.484

*Active in 2005–06.

SHUTOUTS	GP	W	SO
Patrick Roy, Mtl, Col	247	151	23
*Martin Brodeur, NJ	153	89	21
*Curtis Joseph, four teams	133	62	16
Clint Benedict, Ott, Mtl M	48	25	15
*Ed Belfour, four teams	161	88	14
Jacques Plante, five teams	112	71	14

GOALS AGAINST AVG			Avg
*Martin Brodeur, NJ			1.89
George Hainsworth, Mtl, Tor			1.93
Turk Broda, Tor			1.98
*Dominik Hasek, Chi, Buff, Det			2.03
*Ed Belfour, four teams			2.17

Note: At least 50 games played.
*Active in 2005–06.

Alltime Stanley Cup Playoff Wins

TEAM	W	L	Pct
Montreal	393	266	.596
Detroit	259	240	.519
Toronto	251	269	.483
Boston	242	264	.478
Chicago	188	218	.463
NY Rangers	183	199	.479
Philadelphia	180	165	.522
Edmonton	150	99	.602
Dallas#	138	141	.495
St. Louis	138	165	.455
NY Islanders	131	102	.562
Colorado**	126	107	.541
New Jersey†	112	90	.554
Pittsburgh	109	99	.524

TEAM	W	L	Pct
Buffalo	103	117	.468
Calgary*	87	102	.460
Washington	69	85	.448
Vancouver	66	89	.426
Los Angeles	65	101	.392
Carolina§	51	58	.468
San Jose	45	50	.474
Ottawa	35	43	.449
Anaheim	28	24	.538
Phoenix††	28	63	.308
Tampa Bay	23	18	.551
Florida	13	18	.419
Minnesota	8	10	.444
Nashville	3	8	.273

*Atlanta Flames 1972–80. †Colorado Rockies 1976–82. #Minnesota North Stars 1967–93. **Quebec Nordiques 1979–95. ††Winnipeg Jets 1979–96. §Hartford Whalers 1979–97. Note: Teams ranked by playoff victories.

Stanley Cup Playoff Coaching Records

Coach	Team	Yrs	Series W	Series L	Games	Games W	Games L	T	Cups	Pct
Glen Sather	Edm	10	27	21	6	*126	89	37	0	4	.706
Toe Blake	Mtl	13	23	18	5	119	82	37	0	8	.689
Scott Bowman	Five teams	28	68	49	19	353	223	130	0	9	.632
†Bob Hartley	Col	4	13	10	3	80	49	31	0	1	.613
Hap Day	Tor	9	14	10	4	80	49	31	0	5	.613
Al Arbour	StL, NYI	16	42	30	12	209	123	86	0	4	.589
Mike Keenan	five teams	11	28	18	10	160	91	69	0	1	.569
Fred Shero	Phil, NYR	8	21	15	6	108	61	47	0	2	.565
†Jacques Lemaire	Mtl, NJ, Minn	7	18	12	6	101	57	44	0	1	.564
†Ken Hitchcock	Dall, Phil	8	20	13	7	117	66	51	0	1	.564

*Does not include suspended game, May 24, 1988. †Active in 2005–06.
Note: Coaches ranked by winning percentage. Minimum: 65 games.

The 10 Longest Overtime Games

Date	Result	OT	Scorer	Series	Series Winner
3-24-36	Det 1 vs Mtl M 0	116:30	Mud Bruneteau	SF	Det
4-3-33	Tor 1 vs Bos 0	104:46	Ken Doraty	SF	Tor
5-4-00	Phil 2 vs Pitt 1	92:01	Keith Primeau	CSF	Phil
4-24-03	Ana 4 vs Dall 3	80:48	Petr Sykora	CSF	Ana
4-24-96	Pitt 3 vs Wash 2	79:15	Petr Nedved	CQF	Pitt
3-23-43	Tor 3 vs Det 2	70:18	Jack McLean	SF	Det
3-28-30	Mtl 2 vs NYR 1	68:52	Gus Rivers	SF	Mtl
4-18-87	NYI 3 vs Wash 2	68:47	Pat LaFontaine	DSF	NYI
4-27-94	Buff 1 vs NJ 0	65:43	Dave Hannan	CQF	NJ
3-27-51	Mtl 3 vs Det 2	61:09	Maurice Richard	SF	Mtl

Hart Memorial Trophy

Awarded annually "to the player adjudged to be the most valuable to his team." The original trophy was donated by Dr. David A. Hart, father of Cecil Hart, former manager-coach of the Montreal Canadiens. In the 1980s Wayne Gretzky won the award nine times.

Year	Winner	Key Statistics	Runner-Up
1924	Frank Nighbor, Ott	10 goals, 3 assists in 20 games	Sprague Cleghorn, Mtl
1925	Billy Burch, Ham	20 goals, 4 assists in 27 games	Howie Morenz, Mtl
1926	Nels Stewart, Mtl M	42 points in 36 games	Sprague Cleghorn, Mtl
1927	Herb Gardiner, Mtl	12 points in 44 games as defenseman	Bill Cook, NYR
1928	Howie Morenz, Mtl	33 goals, 18 assists	Roy Worters, Pitt
1929	Roy Worters, NYA	1.21 goals against, 13 shutouts	Ace Bailey, Tor
1930	Nels Stewart, Mtl M	39 goals, 16 assists	Lionel Hitchman, Bos
1931	Howie Morenz, Mtl	28 goals, 23 assists	Eddie Shore, Bos
1932	Howie Morenz, Mtl	24 goals, 25 assists	Ching Johnson, NYR
1933	Eddie Shore, Bos	27 assists in 48 games as defenseman	Bill Cook, NYR
1934	Aurel Joliat, Mtl	27 points	Lionel Conacher, Chi
1935	Eddie Shore, Bos	26 assists in 48 games as defenseman	Charlie Conacher, Tor
1936	Eddie Shore, Bos	16 assists in 46 games as defenseman	Hooley Smith, Mtl M
1937	Babe Siebert, Mtl	28 points	Lionel Conacher, Mtl M
1938	Eddie Shore, Bos	17 points in 47 games as defenseman	Paul Thompson, Chi
1939	Toe Blake, Mtl	led NHL in points (47)	Syl Apps, Tor
1940	Ebbie Goodfellow, Det	28 points	Syl Apps, Tor
1941	Bill Cowley, Bos	led NHL in assists (45) and points (62)	Dit Clapper, Bos
1942	Tom Anderson, Bos	41 points	Syl Apps, Tor
1943	Bill Cowley, Bos	led NHL in assists (45)	Doug Bentley, Chi
1944	Babe Pratt, Tor	57 points in 50 games	Bill Cowley, Bos
1945	Elmer Lach, Mtl	led NHL in assists (54) and points (80)	Maurice Richard, Mtl
1946	Max Bentley, Chi	61 points in 47 games	Gaye Stewart, Tor
1947	Maurice Richard, Mtl	led NHL in goals (45); 26 assists	Milt Schmidt, Bos
1948	Buddy O'Connor, NYR	60 points in 60 games	Frank Brimsek, Bos
1949	Sid Abel, Det	28 goals, 26 assists	Bill Durnan, Mtl
1950	Charlie Rayner, NYR	6 shutouts	Ted Kennedy, Tor
1951	Milt Schmidt, Bos	61 points in 62 games	Maurice Richard, Mtl
1952	Gordie Howe, Det	led NHL in goals (47) and points (86)	Elmer Lach, Mtl
1953	Gordie Howe, Det	led NHL in goals (49) and points (95)	Al Rollins, Chi
1954	Al Rollins, Chi	5 shutouts	Red Kelly, Det
1955	Ted Kennedy, Tor	52 points	Harry Lumley, Tor
1956	Jean Beliveau, Mtl	led NHL in goals (47) and points (88)	Tod Sloan, Tor
1957	Gordie Howe, Det	led NHL in goals (44) and points (89)	Jean Beliveau, Mtl
1959	Andy Bathgate, NYR	74 points in 70 games	Gordie Howe, Det
1960	Gordie Howe, Det	45 assists, 73 points	Bobby Hull, Chi
1961	Bernie Geoffrion, Mtl	50 goals, 95 points	Johnny Bower, Tor
1962	Jacques Plante, Mtl	42 wins, 2.37 goals against avg.	Doug Harvey, NYR
1963	Gordie Howe, Det	47 assists, 73 points	Stan Mikita, Chi
1964	Jean Beliveau, Mtl	50 assists, 78 points	Bobby Hull, Chi
1965	Bobby Hull, Chi	39 goals, 32 assists	Norm Ullman, Det
1966	Bobby Hull, Chi	led NHL in goals (54) and points (97)	Jean Beliveau, Mtl
1967	Stan Mikita, Chi	led NHL in assists (62) and points (97)	Ed Giacomin, NYR
1968	Stan Mikita, Chi	40 goals, 47 assists	Jean Beliveau, Mtl
1969	Phil Esposito, Bos	led NHL in assists (77) and points (126)	Jean Beliveau, Mtl
1970	Bobby Orr, Bos	led NHL in assists (87) and points (120)	Tony Esposito, Chi
1971	Bobby Orr, Bos	102 assists, 139 points	Tony Esposito, Chi
1972	Bobby Orr, Bos	80 assists, 117 points	Ken Dryden, Mtl
1973	Bobby Clarke, Phil	67 assists, 104 points	Phil Esposito, Bos
1974	Phil Esposito, Bos	led NHL in goals (68) and points (145)	Bernie Parent, Phil
1975	Bobby Clarke, Phil	89 assists, 116 points	Rogatien Vachon, LA
1976	Bobby Clarke, Phil	89 assists, 119 points	Denis Potvin, NYI
1977	Guy Lafleur, Mtl	led NHL in assists (80) and points (136)	Bobby Clarke, Phil
1978	Guy Lafleur, Mtl	led NHL in goals (60) and points (132)	Bryan Trottier, NYI
1979	Bryan Trottier, NYI	led NHL in assists (87) and points (134)	Guy Lafleur, Mtl
1980	Wayne Gretzky, Edm	51 goals, 86 assists	Marcel Dionne, LA
1981	Wayne Gretzky, Edm	led NHL in assists (109) and points (164)	Mike Liut, StL
1982	Wayne Gretzky, Edm	NHL-record 92 goals and 212 points	Bryan Trottier, NYI
1983	Wayne Gretzky, Edm	led NHL in goals (71) and points (196)	Pete Peeters, Phil
1984	Wayne Gretzky, Edm	led NHL in goals (87) and points (205)	Rod Langway, Wash
1985	Wayne Gretzky, Edm	led NHL in goals (73) and points (208)	Dale Hawerchuk, Winn
1986	Wayne Gretzky, Edm	NHL-record 163 assists and 215 points	Mario Lemieux, Pitt
1987	Wayne Gretzky, Edm	led NHL in assists (121) and points (183)	Ray Bourque, Bos

Hart Memorial Trophy *(Cont.)*

Year	Winner	Key Statistics	Runner-Up
1988	Mario Lemieux, Pitt	led NHL in goals (70) and points (168)	Grant Fuhr, Edm
1989	Wayne Gretzky, LA	114 assists, 168 points	Mario Lemieux, Pitt
1990	Mark Messier, Edm	84 assists, 129 points	Ray Bourque, Bos
1991	Brett Hull, StL	led NHL in goals (86); 131 points	Wayne Gretzky, LA
1992	Mark Messier, NYR	72 assists, 107 points	Patrick Roy, Mtl
1993	Mario Lemieux, Pitt	69 goals, 91 assists in 60 games	Doug Gilmour, Tor
1994	Sergei Fedorov, Det	56 goals, 64 assists	Dominik Hasek, Buff
1995	Eric Lindros, Phil	29 goals, 41 assists in 46 games	Jaromir Jagr, Pitt
1996	Mario Lemieux, Pitt	led NHL in goals (69) and points (161)	Mark Messier, NYR
1997	Dominik Hasek, Buff	5 shutouts, 2.27 goals against avg.	Paul Kariya, Ana
1998	Dominik Hasek, Buff	13 shutouts, 2.09 goals against avg.	Jaromir Jagr, Pitt
1999	Jaromir Jagr, Pitt	44 goals, 127 points	Alexei Yashin, Ott
2000	Chris Pronger, StL	62 points, +52 plus/minus rating	Jaromir Jagr, Pitt
2001	Joe Sakic, Col	118 points, +45 plus/minus rating	Mario Lemieux, Pitt
2002	Jose Theodore, Mtl	2.11 goals against avg./7 shutouts	Jarome Iginla, Cal
2003	Peter Forsberg, Col	77 assists, +52 plus/minus rating	Markus Naslund, Van
2004	Martin St. Louis, TB	94 points, +35 plus/minus rating	Jarome Iginla, Cal
2005	No Award		
2006	Joe Thornton, Bos/SJ	29 goals, 96 assists; 125 points	Jaromir Jagr, NYR

Art Ross Trophy

Awarded annually "to the player who leads the league in scoring points at the end of the regular season." The trophy was presented to the NHL in 1947 by Arthur Howie Ross, former manager-coach of the Boston Bruins. The tie-breakers, in order, are as follows: (1) player with most goals, (2) player with fewer games played, (3) player scoring first goal of the season. Bobby Orr is the only defenseman in NHL history to win this trophy, and he won it twice (1970 and 1975).

Year	Winner	Pts	Year	Winner	Pts
1919	Newsy Lalonde, Mtl	44	1958	Dickie Moore, Mtl	84
1920	Joe Malone, Que	30	1959	Dickie Moore, Mtl	96
1921	Newsy Lalonde, Mtl	48	1960	Bobby Hull, Chi	81
1922	Punch Broadbent, Ott	41	1961	Bernie Geoffrion, Mtl	95
1923	Babe Dye, Tor	46	1962	Bobby Hull, Chi	84
1924	Cy Denneny, Ott	37	1963	Gordie Howe, Det	86
1925	Babe Dye, Tor	23	1964	Stan Mikita, Chi	89
1926	Nels Stewart, Mtl M	44	1965	Stan Mikita, Chi	87
1927	Bill Cook, NYR	42	1966	Bobby Hull, Chi	97
1928	Howie Morenz, Mtl	37	1967	Stan Mikita, Chi	97
1929	Ace Bailey, Tor	51	1968	Stan Mikita, Chi	87
1930	Cooney Weiland, Bos	32	1969	Phil Esposito, Bos	126
1931	Howie Morenz, Mtl	73	1970	Bobby Orr, Bos	120
1932	Harvey Jackson, Tor	51	1971	Phil Esposito, Bos	152
1933	Bill Cook, NYR	53	1972	Phil Esposito, Bos	133
1934	Charlie Conacher, Tor	50	1973	Phil Esposito, Bos	130
1935	Charlie Conacher, Tor	57	1974	Phil Esposito, Bos	145
1936	Sweeney Schriner, NYA	45	1975	Bobby Orr, Bos	135
1937	Sweeney Schriner, NYA	46	1976	Guy Lafleur, Mtl	125
1938	Gordie Drillon, Tor	52	1977	Guy Lafleur, Mtl	136
1939	Toe Blake, Mtl	47	1978	Guy Lafleur, Mtl	132
1940	Milt Schmidt, Bos	52	1979	Bryan Trottier, NYI	134
1941	Bill Cowley, Bos	62	1980	Marcel Dionne, LA	137
1942	Bryan Hextall, NYR	56	1981	Wayne Gretzky, Edm	164
1943	Doug Bentley, Chi	73	1982	Wayne Gretzky, Edm	212
1944	Herb Cain, Bos	82	1983	Wayne Gretzky, Edm	196
1945	Elmer Lach, Mtl	80	1984	Wayne Gretzky, Edm	205
1946	Max Bentley, Chi	61	1985	Wayne Gretzky, Edm	208
1947	*Max Bentley, Chi	72	1986	Wayne Gretzky, Edm	215
1948	Elmer Lach, Mtl	61	1987	Wayne Gretzky, Edm	183
1949	Roy Conacher, Chi	68	1988	Mario Lemieux, Pitt	168
1950	Ted Lindsay, Det	78	1989	Mario Lemieux, Pitt	199
1951	Gordie Howe, Det	86	1990	Wayne Gretzky, LA	142
1952	Gordie Howe, Det	86	1991	Wayne Gretzky, LA	163
1953	Gordie Howe, Det	95	1992	Mario Lemieux, Pitt	131
1954	Gordie Howe, Det	81	1993	Mario Lemieux, Pitt	160
1955	Bernie Geoffrion, Mtl	75	1994	Wayne Gretzky, LA	130
1956	Jean Beliveau, Mtl	88	1995	Jaromir Jagr, Pitt	70
1957	Gordie Howe, Det	89	1996	Mario Lemieux, Pitt	161

Art Ross Trophy *(Cont.)*

Year	Winner	Pts	Year	Winner	Pts
1997	Mario Lemieux, Pitt	122	2002	Jarome Iginla, Cgy	96
1998	Jaromir Jagr, Pitt	102	2003	Peter Forsberg, Col	106
1999	Jaromir Jagr, Pitt	127	2004	Martin St. Louis, TB	94
2000	Jaromir Jagr, Pitt	96	2005	No Award	
2001	Jaromir Jagr, Pitt	121	2006	Joe Thornton, Bos/SJ	125

Note: Listing includes scoring leaders prior to inception of Art Ross Trophy in 1947–48.

Lady Byng Memorial Trophy

Awarded annually "to the player adjudged to have exhibited the best type of sportsmanship and gentlemanly conduct combined with a high standard of playing ability." Lady Byng, who first presented the trophy in 1925, was the wife of Canada's Governor-General. She donated a second trophy in 1936 after the first was given permanently to Frank Boucher of the New York Rangers, who won it seven times in eight seasons. Stan Mikita, one of the league's most penalized players during his early years in the NHL, won the trophy twice late in his career (1967 and 1968).

1925.........Frank Nighbor, Ott	1953.........Red Kelly, Det	1981.........Rick Kehoe, Pitt
1926.........Frank Nighbor, Ott	1954.........Red Kelly, Det	1982.........Rick Middleton, Bos
1927.........Billy Burch, NYA	1955.........Sid Smith, Tor	1983.........Mike Bossy, NYI
1928.........Frank Boucher, NYR	1956.........Earl Reibel, Det	1984.........Mike Bossy, NYI
1929.........Frank Boucher, NYR	1957.........Andy Hebenton, NYR	1985.........Jari Kurri, Edm
1930.........Frank Boucher, NYR	1958.........Camille Henry, NYR	1986.........Mike Bossy, NYI
1931.........Frank Boucher, NYR	1959.........Alex Delvecchio, Det	1987.........Joe Mullen, Cgy
1932.........Joe Primeau, Tor	1960.........Don McKenney, Bos	1988.........Mats Naslund, Mtl
1933.........Frank Boucher, NYR	1961.........Red Kelly, Tor	1989.........Joe Mullen, Cgy
1934.........Frank Boucher, NYR	1962.........Dave Keon, Tor	1990.........Brett Hull, StL
1935.........Frank Boucher, NYR	1963.........Dave Keon, Tor	1991.........Wayne Gretzky, LA
1936.........Doc Romnes, Chi	1964.........Ken Wharram, Chi	1992.........Wayne Gretzky, LA
1937.........Marty Barry, Det	1965.........Bobby Hull, Chi	1993.........Pierre Turgeon, NYI
1938.........Gordie Drillon, Tor	1966.........Alex Delvecchio, Det	1994.........Wayne Gretzky, LA
1939.........Clint Smith, NYR	1967.........Stan Mikita, Chi	1995.........Ron Francis, Pitt
1940.........Bobby Bauer, Bos	1968.........Stan Mikita, Chi	1996.........Paul Kariya, Ana
1941.........Bobby Bauer, Bos	1969.........Alex Delvecchio, Det	1997.........Paul Kariya, Ana
1942.........Syl Apps, Tor	1970.........Phil Goyette, StL	1998.........Ron Francis, Pitt
1943.........Max Bentley, Chi	1971.........John Bucyk, Bos	1999.........Wayne Gretzky, NYR
1944.........Clint Smith, Chi	1972.........Jean Ratelle, NYR	2000.........Pavol Demitra, StL
1945.........Billy Mosienko, Chi	1973.........Gilbert Perreault, Buff	2001.........Joe Sakic, Col
1946.........Toe Blake, Mtl	1974.........John Bucyk, Bos	2002.........Ron Francis, Car
1947.........Bobby Bauer, Bos	1975.........Marcel Dionne, Det	2003.........Alexander Mogilny, Det
1948.........Buddy O'Connor, NYR	1976.........Jean Ratelle, NYR-Bos	2004.........Brad Richards, TB
1949.........Bill Quackenbush, Det	1977.........Marcel Dionne, LA	2005.........No Award
1950.........Edgar Laprade, NYR	1978.........Butch Goring, LA	2006.........Pavel Datsyuk, Det
1951.........Red Kelly, Det	1979.........Bob MacMillan, Atl	
1952.........Sid Smith, Tor	1980.........Wayne Gretzky, Edm	

James Norris Memorial Trophy

Awarded annually "to the defense player who demonstrates throughout the season the greatest all-around ability in the position." James Norris was the former owner-president of the Detroit Red Wings. Bobby Orr holds the record for most consecutive times winning the award (eight, 1968–1975).

1954......Red Kelly, Det	1972......Bobby Orr, Bos	1990......Ray Bourque, Bos
1955......Doug Harvey, Mtl	1973......Bobby Orr, Bos	1991......Ray Bourque, Bos
1956......Doug Harvey, Mtl	1974......Bobby Orr, Bos	1992......Brian Leetch, NYR
1957......Doug Harvey, Mtl	1975......Bobby Orr, Bos	1993......Chris Chelios, Chi
1958......Doug Harvey, Mtl	1976......Denis Potvin, NYI	1994......Ray Bourque, Bos
1959......Tom Johnson, Mtl	1977......Larry Robinson, Mtl	1995......Paul Coffey, Det
1960......Doug Harvey, Mtl	1978......Denis Potvin, NYI	1996......Chris Chelios, Chi
1961......Doug Harvey, Mtl	1979......Denis Potvin, NYI	1997......Brian Leetch, NYR
1962......Doug Harvey, NYR	1980......Larry Robinson, Mtl	1998......Rob Blake, LA
1963......Pierre Pilote, Chi	1981......Randy Carlyle, Pitt	1999......Al MacInnis, StL
1964......Pierre Pilote, Chi	1982......Doug Wilson, Chi	2000......Chris Pronger, StL
1965......Pierre Pilote, Chi	1983......Rod Langway, Wash	2001......Nicklas Lidstrom, Det
1966......Jacques Laperriere, Mtl	1984......Rod Langway, Wash	2002......Nicklas Lidstrom, Det
1967......Harry Howell, NYR	1985......Paul Coffey, Edm	2003......Nicklas Lidstrom, Det
1968......Bobby Orr, Bos	1986......Paul Coffey, Edm	2004......Scott Niedermayer, NJ
1969......Bobby Orr, Bos	1987......Ray Bourque, Bos	2005......No Award
1970......Bobby Orr, Bos	1988......Ray Bourque, Bos	2006......Nicklas Lidstrom, Det
1971......Bobby Orr, Bos	1989......Chris Chelios, Mtl	

Calder Memorial Trophy

Awarded annually "to the player selected as the most proficient in his first year of competition in the National Hockey League." Frank Calder was a former NHL president. Sergei Makarov, who won the award in 1989–90, was the oldest recipient of the trophy, at 31. Players are no longer eligible for the award if they are 26 or older as of September 15th of the season in question.

1933 ......Carl Voss, Det	1958 ......Frank Mahovlich, Tor	1983 ......Steve Larmer, Chi
1934 ......Russ Blinko, Mtl M	1959 ......Ralph Backstrom, Mtl	1984 ......Tom Barrasso, Buff
1935 ......Dave Schriner, NYA	1960 ......Bill Hay, Chi	1985 ......Mario Lemieux, Pitt
1936 ......Mike Karakas, Chi	1961 ......Dave Keon, Tor	1986 ......Gary Suter, Cgy
1937 ......Syl Apps, Tor	1962 ......Bobby Rousseau, Mtl	1987 ......Luc Robitaille, LA
1938 ......Cully Dahlstrom, Chi	1963 ......Kent Douglas, Tor	1988 ......Joe Nieuwendyk, Cgy
1939 ......Frank Brimsek, Bos	1964 ......Jacques Laperriere, Mtl	1989 ......Brian Leetch, NYR
1940 ......Kilby MacDonald, NYR	1965 ......Roger Crozier, Det	1990 ......Sergei Makarov, Cgy
1941 ......Johnny Quilty, Mtl	1966 ......Brit Selby, Tor	1991 ......Ed Belfour, Chi
1942 ......Grant Warwick, NYR	1967 ......Bobby Orr, Bos	1992 ......Pavel Bure, Van
1943 ......Gaye Stewart, Tor	1968 ......Derek Sanderson, Bos	1993 ......Teemu Selanne, Winn
1944 ......Gus Bodnar, Tor	1969 ......Danny Grant, Minn	1994 ......Martin Brodeur, NJ
1945 ......Frank McCool, Tor	1970 ......Tony Esposito, Chi	1995 ......Peter Forsberg, Que
1946 ......Edgar Laprade, NYR	1971 ......Gilbert Perreault, Buff	1996 ......Daniel Alfredsson, Ott
1947 ......Howie Meeker, Tor	1972 ......Ken Dryden, Mtl	1997 ......Bryan Berard, NYI
1948 ......Jim McFadden, Det	1973 ......Steve Vickers, NYR	1998 ......Sergei Samsonov, Bos
1949 ......Pentti Lund, NYR	1974 ......Denis Potvin, NYI	1999 ......Chris Drury, Col
1950 ......Jack Gelineau, Bos	1975 ......Eric Vail, Atl	2000 ......Scott Gomez, NJ
1951 ......Terry Sawchuk, Det	1976 ......Bryan Trottier, NYI	2001 ......Evgeni Nabakov, SJ
1952 ......Bernie Geoffrion, Mtl	1977 ......Willi Plett, Atl	2002 ......Dany Heatley, Atl
1953 ......Gump Worsley, NYR	1978 ......Mike Bossy, NYI	2003 ......Barret Jackman, StL
1954 ......Camille Henry, NYR	1979 ......Bobby Smith, Minn	2004 ......Andrew Raycroft, Bos
1955 ......Ed Litzenberger, Chi	1980 ......Ray Bourque, Bos	2005 ......No Award
1956 ......Glenn Hall, Det	1981 ......Peter Stastny, Que	2006.........Alexander Ovechkin, Was
1957 ......Larry Regan, Bos	1982 ......Dale Hawerchuk, Winn	

Vezina Trophy

Awarded annually "to the goalkeeper adjudged to be the best at his position." The trophy is named after Georges Vezina, an outstanding goalie for the Montreal Canadiens who collapsed during a game on November 28, 1925, and died four months later of tuberculosis. The general managers of the NHL teams vote on the award.

1927 ......George Hainsworth, Mtl	1958 ......Jacques Plante, Mtl	1980 ....Bob Sauve, Buff
1928 ......George Hainsworth, Mtl	1959 ......Jacques Plante, Mtl	Don Edwards, Buff
1929 ......George Hainsworth, Mtl	1960 ......Jacques Plante, Mtl	1981 ......Richard Sevigny, Mtl
1930 ......Tiny Thompson, Bos	1961 ......Johnny Bower, Tor	Denis Herron, Mtl
1931 ......Roy Worters, NYA	1962 ......Jacques Plante, Mtl	Michel Larocque, Mtl
1932 ......Charlie Gardiner, Chi	1963 ....Glenn Hall, Chi	1982 ....Billy Smith, NYI
1933 ......Tiny Thompson, Bos	1964 ....Charlie Hodge, Mtl	1983 ....Pete Peeters, Bos
1934 ......Charlie Gardiner, Chi	1965 ....Terry Sawchuk, Tor	1984 ....Tom Barrasso, Buff
1935 ......Lorne Chabot, Chi	Johnny Bower, Tor	1985 ....Pelle Lindbergh, Phil
1936 ......Tiny Thompson, Bos	1966 ....Gump Worsley, Mtl	1986 ....John Vanbiesbrouck,
1937 ......Normie Smith, Det	Charlie Hodge, Mtl	NYR
1938 ......Tiny Thompson, Bos	1967 ....Glenn Hall, Chi	1987 ....Ron Hextall, Phil
1939 ......Frank Brimsek, Bos	Rogie Vachon, Mtl	1988 ....Grant Fuhr, Edm
1940 ......Dave Kerr, NYR	1969 ....Jacques Plante, StL	1989 ....Patrick Roy, Mtl
1941 ......Turk Broda, Tor	Glenn Hall, StL	1990 ....Patrick Roy, Mtl
1942 ......Frank Brimsek, Bos	1970 ....Tony Esposito, Chi	1991 ....Ed Belfour, Chi
1943 ......Johnny Mowers, Det	1971 ....Ed Giacomin, NYR	1992 ....Patrick Roy, Mtl
1944 ......Bill Durnan, Mtl	Gilles Villemure, NYR	1993 ....Ed Belfour, Chi
1945 ......Bill Durnan, Mtl	1972 ....Tony Esposito, Chi	1994 ....Dominik Hasek, Buff
1946 ......Bill Durnan, Mtl	Gary Smith, Chi	1995 ....Dominik Hasek, Buff
1947 ......Bill Durnan, Mtl	1973 ....Ken Dryden, Mtl	1996 ....Jim Carey, Wash
1948 ......Turk Broda, Tor	1974 ....Bernie Parent, Phil	1997 ....Dominik Hasek, Buff
1949 ......Bill Durnan, Mtl	Tony Esposito, Chi	1998 ....Dominik Hasek, Buff
1950 ......Bill Durnan, Mtl	1975 ....Bernie Parent, Phil	1999 ....Dominik Hasek, Buff
1951 ....Al Rollins, Tor	1976 ....Ken Dryden, Mtl	2000 ....Olaf Kolzig, Wash
1952 ......Terry Sawchuk, Det	1977 ....Ken Dryden, Mtl	2001 ....Dominik Hasek, Buff
1953 ......Terry Sawchuk, Det	Michel Larocque, Mtl	2002 ....Jose Theodore, Mtl
1954 ......Harry Lumley, Tor	1978 ....Ken Dryden, Mtl	2003 ....Martin Brodeur, NJ
1955 ......Terry Sawchuk, Det	Michel Larocque, Mtl	2004 ....Martin Brodeur, NJ
1956 ......Jacques Plante, Mtl	1979 ....Ken Dryden, Mtl	2005 ....No Award
1957 ......Jacques Plante, Mtl	Michel Larocque, Mtl	2006 ....Miikka Kiprusoff, Cgy

Selke Trophy

Awarded annually "to the forward who best excels in the defensive aspects of the game." The trophy is named after Frank J. Selke, the architect of the Montreal Canadians dynasty that won five consecutive Stanley Cups in the late '50s. The winner is selected by a vote of the Professional Hockey Writers Association.

1978........Bob Gainey, Mtl	1988........Guy Carbonneau, Mtl	1998........Jere Lehtinen, Dall
1979........Bob Gainey, Mtl	1989........Guy Carbonneau, Mtl	1999........Jere Lehtinen, Dall
1980........Bob Gainey, Mtl	1990........Rick Meagher, StL	2000........Steve Yzerman, Det
1981........Bob Gainey, Mtl	1991........Dirk Graham, Chi	2001........John Madden, NJ
1982........Steve Kasper, Bos	1992........Guy Carbonneau, Mtl	2002........Michael Peca, NYI
1983........Bobby Clarke, Phil	1993........Doug Gilmour, Tor	2003........Jere Lehtinen, Dall
1984........Doug Jarvis, Wash	1994........Sergei Fedorov, Det	2004........Kris Draper, Det
1985........Craig Ramsay, Buff	1995........Ron Francis, Pitt	2005........No Award
1986........Troy Murray, Chi	1996........Sergei Fedorov, Det	2006........Rod Brind'Amour, Car
1987........Dave Poulin, Phil	1997........Michael Peca, Buff	

Adams Award

Awarded annually "to the NHL coach adjudged to have contributed the most to his team's success." The trophy is named in honor of Jack Adams, longtime coach and general manager of the Detroit Red Wings. The winner is selected by a vote of the National Hockey League Broadcasters' Association.

1974.....Fred Shero, Phil	1985.....Mike Keenan, Phil	1996.....Scotty Bowman, Det
1975.....Bob Pulford, LA	1986.....Glen Sather, Edm	1997.....Ted Nolan, Buff
1976.....Don Cherry, Bos	1987.....Jacques Demers, Det	1998.....Pat Burns, Bos
1977.....Scott Bowman, Mtl	1988.....Jacques Demers, Det	1999.....Jacques Martin, Ott
1978.....Bobby Kromm, Det	1989.....Pat Burns, Mtl	2000.....Joel Quenneville, StL
1979.....Al Arbour, NYI	1990.....Bob Murdoch, Winn	2001.....Bill Barber, Phil
1980.....Pat Quinn, Phil	1991.....Brian Sutter, StL	2002.....Bob Francis, Phoe
1981.....Red Berenson, StL	1992.....Pat Quinn, Van	2003.....Jacques Lemaire, Minn
1982.....Tom Watt, Winn	1993.....Pat Burns, Tor	2004.....John Tortorella, TB
1983.....Orval Tessier, Chi	1994.....Jacques Lemaire, NJ	2005.....No Award
1984.....Bryan Murray, Wash	1995.....Marc Crawford, Que	2006.....Lindy Ruff, Buff

Career Records

Alltime Point Leaders

	Player	Yrs	GP	G	A	Pts	Pts/game
1.	Wayne Gretzky, Edm, LA, StL, NYR...............20		1487	894	1963	2857	1.921
2.	Mark Messier, Edm, NYR, Van 25		1756	694	1193	1887	1.074
3.	Gordie Howe, Det, Hart 26		1767	801	1049	1850	1.047
4.	Ron Francis, four teams...............................23		1731	549	1249	1798	1.038
5.	Marcel Dionne, Det, LA, NYR 18		1348	731	1040	1771	1.314
6.	*Steve Yzerman, Det....................................22		1514	692	1065	1755	1.159
7.	*Mario Lemieux, Pitt.....................................17		915	690	1033	1723	1.883
8.	Phil Esposito, Chi, Bos, NYR 18		1282	717	873	1590	1.240
9.	Ray Bourque, Bos, Col 22		1612	410	1169	1579	.980
10.	Paul Coffey, eight teams 21		1409	396	1135	1531	1.087
11.	*Joe Sakic, Que, Col.....................................17		1237	574	915	1489	1.204
12.	Stan Mikita, Chi 22		1394	541	926	1467	1.052
13.	*Jaromir Jagr, Pitt, Was, NYR 15		1109	591	841	1432	1.291
14.	Bryan Trottier, NYI, Pitt 18		1279	524	901	1425	1.114
15.	Adam Oates, seven teams.............................19		1337	341	1079	1420	1.062

*Active in 2005–06.

Alltime Goal-Scoring Leaders

	Player	Yrs	GP	G	G/game
1.	Wayne Gretzky, Edm, LA, StL, NYR.................................20		1487	894	.601
2.	Gordie Howe, Det, Hart 26		1767	801	.453
3.	*Brett Hull, Cal, StL, Dall, Det 19		1264	741	.586
4.	Marcel Dionne, Det, LA, NYR 18		1348	731	.542
5.	Phil Esposito, Chi, Bos, NYR...18		1282	717	.559
6.	Mike Gartner, Wash, Minn, NYR, Tor, Phoe......................19		1432	708	.494
7.	Mark Messier, Edm, NYR, Van 25		1756	694	.395
8.	*Steve Yzerman, Det..22		1514	692	.457
9.	*Mario Lemieux, Pitt..17		915	690	.754
10.	Luc Robitaille, LA, Pitt, NYR, Det...................................19		1431	668	.469

*Active in 2005–06.

Alltime Assist Leaders

	Player	Yrs	GP	A	A/game
1.	Wayne Gretzky, Edm, LA, StL, NYR	20	1487	1963	1.320
2.	Ron Francis, Hart, Pitt, Car	23	1731	1249	.721
3.	Mark Messier, Edm, NYR, Van	25	1756	1193	.679
4.	Ray Bourque, Bos, Col	22	1612	1169	.725
5.	Paul Coffey, eight teams	21	1409	1135	.806
6.	Adam Oates, seven teams	22	1337	1079	.807
8.	*Steve Yzerman, Det	22	1514	1063	.702
7.	Gordie Howe, Det, Hart	26	1767	1049	.594
9.	Marcel Dionne, Det, LA, NYR	18	1348	1040	.771
10.	*Mario Lemieux, Pitt	17	915	1033	1.129

*Active player in 2005–06.

Alltime Penalty Minutes Leaders

	Player	Yrs	GP	PIM	Min/game
1.	Dave Williams, Tor, Van, Det, LA, Hart	14	962	3966	4.12
2.	Dale Hunter, Que, Wash, Col	19	1407	3565	2.53
3.	*Tie Domi, Tor, NYR, Winn	16	1020	3515	3.45
4.	Marty McSorley, Pitt, Edm, LA, NYR, SJ, Bos	17	961	3381	3.52
5.	Bob Probert, Det, Chi	16	935	3300	3.53
6.	Rob Ray, Buff, Ott	15	900	3207	3.56
7.	Craig Berube, Phil, Tor, Cgy, Wash, NYI	17	1054	3149	2.99
8.	Tim Hunter, Cgy, Que, Van, SJ	16	815	3142	3.86
9.	Chris Nilan, Mtl, NYR, Bos	13	688	3043	4.42
10.	Rick Tocchet, Phil, Pitt, LA, Bos, Wash, Phoe	18	1144	2974	2.60

*Active in 2005–06.

Goaltending Records

ALLTIME WIN LEADERS

Goaltender	W	L	T	Pct
Patrick Roy, Mtl, Col	551	315	131	.618
*Ed Belfour, Chi, SJ, Dall, Tor	457	303	111	.588
*Martin Brodeur, NJ	456	240	105	.638
Terry Sawchuk, five teams	447	330	173	.562
Jacques Plante, five teams	434	246	147	.614
*Curtis Joseph, StL, Edm, Tor, Det	428	310	90	.571
Tony Esposito, Mtl, Chi	423	306	152	.566
Glenn Hall, Det, Chi, StL	407	327	163	.545
Grant Fuhr, six teams	403	295	114	.567
Mike Vernon, Cgy, Det, SJ, Fla	385	273	92	.575

*Active in 2005–06.

ACTIVE GOALTENDING LEADERS

Goaltender	W	L	T	Pct
Marty Turco, Dall	137	62	26	.666
Martin Brodeur, NJ	446	240	105	.658
Chris Osgood, Det, NYI, StL	325	183	66	.624
Dominik Hasek, Chi, Buff, Det, Ott	324	202	82	.600
Ed Belfour, Chi, SJ, Dall, Tor	457	303	111	.588
Curtis Joseph, five teams	428	310	90	.571
Patrick Lalime, Pitt, Ott, StL	171	130	32	.562
Evgeni Nabokov, SJ	137	113	29	.543
Nikolai Khabibulin, Phoe, TB, Chi	226	213	58	.513
Olaf Kolzig, Wash	254	248	63	.505

Note: Ranked by winning percentage; minimum 250 games played. All players active in 2005–06.

ALLTIME SHUTOUT LEADERS

Goaltender	Team	Yrs	GP	SO
Terry Sawchuk	Det, Bos, Tor, LA, NYR	21	971	103
George Hainsworth	Mtl, Tor	11	465	94
Glenn Hall	Det, Chi, StL	18	906	84
Jacques Plante	Mtl, NYR, StL, Tor, Bos	18	837	82
Tiny Thompson	Bos, Det	12	553	81
Alex Connell	Ott, Det, NYA, Mtl M	12	417	81
*Martin Brodeur	NJ	13	813	80
Tony Esposito	Mtl, Chi	16	886	76
*Ed Belfour	Chi, SJ, Dall, Tor	16	905	75
Lorne Chabot	NYR, Tor, Mtl, Chi, Mtl M, NYA	11	411	73

*Active in 2005–06.

ALLTIME GOALS AGAINST AVERAGE LEADERS (PRE-1950)

Goaltender	Team	Yrs	GP	GA	GAA
George Hainsworth	Mtl, Tor	11	465	937	1.91
Alex Connell	Ott, Det, NYA, Mtl M	12	417	830	1.91
Chuck Gardiner	Chi	7	316	664	2.02
Lorne Chabot	NYR, Tor, Mtl, Chi, Mtl M, NYA	11	411	861	2.04
Tiny Thompson	Bos, Det	12	553	1183	2.08

ALLTIME GOALS AGAINST AVERAGE LEADERS (POST-1950)

Goaltender	Team	Yrs	GP	GA	GAA
*Martin Brodeur	NJ	13	813	1760	2.21
*Dominik Hasek	Chi, Buff, Det, Ott	14	638	1374	2.22
Ken Dryden	Mtl	8	397	870	2.24
Roman Turek	Dall, StL, Cgy	8	328	734	2.31
Jacques Plante	Mtl, NYR, StL, Tor, Bos	18	837	1965	2.38

*Active in 2005–06.
Note: Minimum 250 games played. Goals against average equals goals against per 60 minutes played.

Alltime Coaching Leaders

Coach	Team	Seasons	W	L	T/OTL	Pct
Scott Bowman	five teams	1967–87, 91–2002	1244	583	314	.654
Toe Blake	Mtl	1955–68	500	255	159	.634
Fred Shero	Phil, NYR	1971–81	390	225	119	.612
*Ken Hitchcock	Dall, Phil	1995–	407	243	99	.609
Glen Sather	Edm, NYR	1979-89, 93-94, 2003-04	497	310	125	.600
*Marc Crawford	Que, Col, Van, LA	1994–	411	285	111	.578
Emile Francis	NYR, StL	1965–77, 81–83	388	273	117	.574
Billy Reay	Tor, Chi	1957–59, 63–77	542	385	175	.571
Pat Burns	Mtl, Tor, Bos, NJ	1988–2001, 2002–05	501	359	153	.570
Al Arbour	StL, NYI	1970–94	781	577	248	.564
*Pat Quinn	Phil, LA, Van, Tor	1978–	657	493	165	.562

Note: Minimum 600 regular-season games. Ranked by percentage. *Active in 2005–06.

Single-Season Records

Goals

Player	Season	GP	G	Player	Season	GP	G
Wayne Gretzky, Edm	1981–82	80	92	Wayne Gretzky, Edm	1982–83	80	71
Wayne Gretzky, Edm	1983–84	74	87	Brett Hull, StL	1991–92	73	70
Brett Hull, StL	1990–91	78	86	Mario Lemieux, Pitt	1987–88	77	70
Mario Lemieux, Pitt	1988–89	76	85	Bernie Nicholls, LA	1988–89	79	70
Alexander Mogilny, Buff	1992–93	77	76	Mario Lemieux, Pitt	1992–93	60	69
Phil Esposito, Bos	1970–71	78	76	Mario Lemieux, Pitt	1995–96	70	69
Teemu Selanne, Winn	1992–93	84	76	Mike Bossy, NYI	1978–79	80	69
Wayne Gretzky, Edm	1984–85	80	73	Phil Esposito, Bos	1973–74	78	68
Brett Hull, StL	1989–90	80	72	Jari Kurri, Edm	1985–86	78	68
Jari Kurri, Edm	1984–85	73	71	Mike Bossy, NYI	1980–81	79	68

Assists

Player	Season	GP	Asst	Player	Season	GP	Asst
Wayne Gretzky, Edm	1985–86	80	163	Wayne Gretzky, LA	1989–90	73	102
Wayne Gretzky, Edm	1984–85	80	135	Bobby Orr, Bos	1970–71	78	102
Wayne Gretzky, Edm	1982–83	80	125	Mario Lemieux, Pitt	1987–88	77	98
Wayne Gretzky, LA	1990–91	78	122	Adam Oates, Bos	1992–93	84	97
Wayne Gretzky, Edm	1986–87	79	121	Joe Thornton, SJ	2005-06	81	96
Wayne Gretzky, Edm	1981–82	80	120	Doug Gilmour, Tor	1992–93	83	95
Wayne Gretzky, Edm	1983–84	74	118	Pat LaFontaine, Buff	1992–93	84	95
Mario Lemieux, Pitt	1988–89	76	114	Mario Lemieux, Pitt	1985–86	79	93
Wayne Gretzky, LA	1988–89	78	114	Peter Stastny, Que	1981–82	80	93
Wayne Gretzky, Edm	1987–88	64	109	Wayne Gretzky, LA	1993–94	81	92
Wayne Gretzky, Edm	1980–81	80	109	Mario Lemieux, Pitt	1995–96	70	92
				Ron Francis, Pitt	1995–96	77	92

Points

Player	Season	G	Asst	Pts	Player	Season	G	Asst	Pts
Wayne Gretzky, Edm	1985–86	52	163	215	Wayne Gretzky, LA	1990–91	41	122	163
Wayne Gretzky, Edm	1981–82	92	120	212	Mario Lemieux, Pitt	1995–96	69	92	161
Wayne Gretzky, Edm	1984–85	73	135	208	Mario Lemieux, Pitt	1992–93	69	91	160
Wayne Gretzky, Edm	1983–84	87	118	205	Steve Yzerman, Det	1988–89	65	90	155
Mario Lemieux, Pitt	1988–89	85	114	199	Phil Esposito, Bos	1970–71	76	76	152
Wayne Gretzky, Edm	1982–83	71	125	196	Bernie Nicholls, LA	1988–89	70	80	150
Wayne Gretzky, Edm	1986–87	62	121	183	Wayne Gretzky, Edm	1987–88	40	109	149
Mario Lemieux, Pitt	1987–88	70	98	168	Pat LaFontaine, Buff	1992–93	53	95	148
Wayne Gretzky, LA	1988–89	54	114	168	Mike Bossy, NYI	1981–82	64	83	147
Wayne Gretzky, Edm	1980–81	55	109	164	Phil Esposito, Bos	1973–74	68	77	145

Single-Season Records (Cont.)

Points per Game

Player	Season	GP	Pts	Avg
Wayne Gretzky, Edm	1983–84	74	205	2.77
Wayne Gretzky, Edm	1985–86	80	215	2.69
Mario Lemieux, Pitt	1992–93	60	160	2.67
Wayne Gretzky, Edm	1981–82	80	212	2.65
Mario Lemieux, Pitt	1988–89	76	199	2.62
Wayne Gretzky, Edm	1984–85	80	208	2.60
Wayne Gretzky, Edm	1982–83	80	196	2.45
Wayne Gretzky, Edm	1987–88	64	149	2.33
Wayne Gretzky, Edm	1986–87	79	183	2.32
Mario Lemieux, Pitt	1995–96	70	161	2.30
Mario Lemieux, Pitt	1987–88	77	168	2.18
Wayne Gretzky, LA	1988–89	78	168	2.15
Wayne Gretzky, LA	1990–91	78	163	2.09
Mario Lemieux, Pitt	1989–90	59	123	2.08
Wayne Gretzky, Edm	1980–81	80	164	2.05
Mario Lemieux, Pitt	1991–92	64	131	2.05
Bill Cowley, Bos	1943–44	36	71	1.97
Phil Esposito, Bos	1970–71	78	152	1.95
Wayne Gretzky, LA	1989–90	73	142	1.95
Steve Yzerman, Det	1988–89	80	155	1.94

Note: Minimum 50 points in one season.

Goals per Game

Player	Season	GP	G	Avg
Joe Malone, Mtl	1917–18	20	44	2.20
Cy Denneny, Ott	1917–18	22	36	1.64
Newsy Lalonde, Mtl	1917–18	14	23	1.64
Joe Malone, Que	1919–20	24	39	1.63
Newsy Lalonde, Mtl	1919–20	23	36	1.57
Joe Malone, Ham	1920–21	20	30	1.50
Babe Dye, Ham-Tor	1920–21	24	35	1.46
Cy Denneny, Ott	1920–21	24	34	1.42
Reg Noble, Tor	1917–18	20	28	1.40
Newsy Lalonde, Mtl	1920–21	24	33	1.38

Note: Minimum 20 goals in one season.

Assists per Game

Player	Season	GP	Asst	Avg
Wayne Gretzky, Edm	1985–86	80	163	2.04
Wayne Gretzky, Edm	1987–88	64	109	1.70
Wayne Gretzky, Edm	1984–85	80	135	1.69
Wayne Gretzky, Edm	1983–84	74	118	1.59
Wayne Gretzky, Edm	1982–83	80	125	1.56
Wayne Gretzky, LA	1990–91	78	122	1.56
Wayne Gretzky, Edm	1986–87	79	121	1.53
Mario Lemieux, Pitt	1992–93	60	91	1.52
Wayne Gretzky, Edm	1981–82	80	120	1.50
Mario Lemieux, Pitt	1988–89	76	114	1.50

Note: Minimum 35 assists in one season.

Shutout Leaders

	Season	SO	Length of Schedule
George Hainsworth, Mtl	1928–29	22	44
Alex Connell, Ott	1925–26	15	36
Alex Connell, Ott	1927–28	15	44
Hal Winkler, Bos	1927–28	15	44
Tony Esposito, Chi	1969–70	15	76
George Hainsworth, Mtl	1926–27	14	44
Clint Benedict, Mtl M	1926–27	13	44
Alex Connell, Ott	1926–27	13	44
George Hainsworth, Mtl	1927–28	13	44
John Roach, NYR	1928–29	13	44
Roy Worters, NYA	1928–29	13	44
Harry Lumley, Tor	1953–54	13	70
Dominik Hasek, Buff	1997–98	13	82
Tiny Thompson, Bos	1928–29	12	44
Lorne Chabot, Tor	1928–29	12	44
Chuck Gardiner, Chi	1930–31	12	44
Terry Sawchuk, Det	1951–52	12	70
Terry Sawchuk, Det	1953–54	12	70
Terry Sawchuk, Det	1954–55	12	70
Glenn Hall, Det	1955–56	12	70
Bernie Parent, Phil	1973–74	12	78
Bernie Parent, Phil	1974–75	12	80
Lorne Chabot, NYR	1927–28	11	44
Harry Holmes, Det	1927–28	11	44
Clint Benedict, Mtl M	1928–29	11	44
Joe Miller, Pitt Pirates	1928–29	11	44
Tiny Thompson, Bos	1932–33	11	48
Terry Sawchuck, Det	1950–51	11	70
Dominik Hasek, Buff	2000–01	11	82
Martin Brodeur, NJ	2003–04	11	82
Lorne Chabot, NYR	1926–27	10	44
Roy Worters, Pitt Pirates	1927–28	10	44
Clarence Dolson, Det	1928–29	10	44
John Roach, Det	1932–33	10	48
Chuck Gardiner, Chi	1933–34	10	48
Tiny Thompson, Bos	1935–36	10	48
Frank Brimsek, Bos	1938–39	10	48
Bill Durnan, Mtl	1948–49	10	60
Gerry McNeil, Mtl	1952–53	10	70
Harry Lumley, Tor	1952–53	10	70
Tony Esposito, Chi	1973–74	10	78
Ken Dryden, Mtl	1976–77	10	80
Martin Brodeur, NJ	1996–97	10	82
Martin Brodeur, NJ	1997–98	10	82
Roman Cechmanek, Phil	2000–01	10	82
Byron Dafoe, Bos	1998–99	10	82
Ed Belfour, Tor	2003–04	10	82
Miikka Kiprusoff, Cgy	2005–06	10	82

Wins

	Season	Record*
Bernie Parent, Phil	1973–74	47-13-12
Bernie Parent, Phil	1974–75	44-14-9
Terry Sawchuk, Det	1950–51	44-13-13
Terry Sawchuk, Det	1951–52	44-14-12
Tom Barasso, Pitt	1992–93	43-14-5
Ed Belfour, Chi	1990–91	43-19-7
Martin Brodeur, NJ	1997–98	43-17-8
Martin Brodeur, NJ	1999–00	43-20-8
Martin Brodeur, NJ	2005-06	43-23
Jacques Plante, Mtl	1955–56	42-12-10
Jacques Plante, Mtl	1961–62	42-14-14
Ken Dryden, Mtl	1975–76	42-10-8
Mike Richter, NYR	1993–94	42-12-6
Roman Turek, StL	1999–00	42-15-9
Martin Brodeur, NJ	2000–01	42-17-11
Miikka Kiprusoff, Cgy	2005–06	42-20

*Starting in the 2005-06 season, ties were eliminated.

Goals Against Average

(PRE-1950)	Season	GP	GAA
George Hainsworth, Mtl	1928–29	44	0.92
George Hainsworth, Mtl	1927–28	44	1.05
Alex Connell, Ott	1925–26	36	1.12
Tiny Thompson, Bos	1928–29	44	1.18
Roy Worters, NYA	1928–29	38	1.21

(POST-1950)	Season	GP	GAA
Miika Kiprusoff, Cal	2003–04	38	1.6949
Marty Turco, Dall	2002–03	55	1.7287
Tony Esposito, Chi	1971–72	48	1.7698
Al Rollins, Tor	1950–51	40	1.7744
Ron Tugnutt, Ott	1998–99	43	1.7943

Single-Game Records

Goals

	Date	G
Joe Malone, Que vs Tor	1-31-20	7
Newsy Lalonde, Mtl vs Tor	1-10-20	6
Joe Malone, Que vs Ott	3-10-20	6
Corb Denneny, Tor vs Ham	1-26-21	6
Cy Denneny, Ott vs Ham	3-7-21	6
Syd Howe, Det vs NYR	2-3-44	6
Red Berenson, StL vs Phil	11-7-68	6
Darryl Sittler, Tor vs Bos	2-7-76	6

Assists

	Date	A
Billy Taylor, Det vs Chi	3-16-47	7
Wayne Gretzky, Edm vs Wash	2-15-80	7
Wayne Gretzky, Edm vs Chi	12-11-85	7
Wayne Gretzky, Edm vs Que	2-14-86	7

Note: 24 tied with 6.

Points

	Date	G	A	Pts
Darryl Sittler, Tor vs Bos	2-7-76	6	4	10
Maurice Richard, Mtl vs Det	12-28-44	5	3	8
Bert Olmstead, Mtl vs Chi	1-9-54	4	4	8
Tom Bladon, Phil vs Clev	12-11-77	4	4	8
Bryan Trottier, NYI vs NYR	12-23-78	5	3	8
Peter Stastny, Que vs Wash	2-22-81	4	4	8
Anton Stastny, Que vs Wash	2-22-81	3	5	8
Wayne Gretzky, Edm vs NJ	11-19-83	3	5	8
Wayne Gretzky, Edm vs Minn	1-4-84	4	4	8
Paul Coffey, Edm vs Det	3-14-86	2	6	8
Mario Lemieux, Pitt vs StL	10-15-88	2	6	8
Bernie Nicholls, LA vs Tor	12-1-88	2	6	8
Mario Lemieux, Pitt vs NJ	12-31-88	5	3	8

NHL Season Leaders

Points

Season	Player and Club	Pts
1917–18	Joe Malone, Mtl	44
1918–19	Newsy Lalonde, Mtl	30
1919–20	Joe Malone, Que	48
1920–21	Newsy Lalonde, Mtl	41
1921–22	Punch Broadbent, Ott	46
1922–23	Babe Dye, Tor	37
1923–24	Cy Denneny, Ott	23
1924–25	Babe Dye, Tor	44
1925–26	Nels Stewart, Mtl M	42
1926–27	Bill Cook, NY	37
1927–28	Howie Morenz, Mtl	51
1928–29	Ace Bailey, Tor	32
1929–30	Cooney Weiland, Bos	73
1930–31	Howie Morenz, Mtl	51
1931–32	Harvey Jackson, Tor	53
1932–33	Bill Cook, NY	50
1933–34	Charlie Conacher, Tor	52
1934–35	Charlie Conacher, Tor	57
1935–36	Sweeney Schriner, NYA	45
1936–37	Sweeney Schriner, NYA	46
1937–38	Gord Drillon, Tor	52
1938–39	Hector Blake, Mtl	47
1939–40	Milt Schmidt, Bos	52
1940–41	Bill Cowley, Bos	62
1941–42	Bryan Hextall, NY	54
1942–43	Doug Bentley, Chi	73
1943–44	Herb Cain, Bos	82
1944–45	Elmer Lach, Mtl	80
1945–46	Max Bentley, Chi	61
1946–47	Max Bentley, Chi	72
1947–48	Elmer Lach, Mtl	61
1948–49	Roy Conacher, Chi	68
1949–50	Ted Lindsay, Det	78

Season	Player and Club	Pts
1950–51	Gordie Howe, Det	86
1951–52	Gordie Howe, Det	86
1952–53	Gordie Howe, Det	95
1953–54	Gordie Howe, Det	81
1954–55	Bernie Geoffrion, Mtl	75
1955–56	Jean Beliveau, Mtl	88
1956–57	Gordie Howe, Det	89
1957–58	Dickie Moore, Mtl	84
1958–59	Dickie Moore, Mtl	96
1959–60	Bobby Hull, Chi	81
1960–61	Bernie Geoffrion, Mtl	95
1961–62	Andy Bathgate, NY	84
	Bobby Hull, Chi	84
1962–63	Gordie Howe, Det	86
1963–64	Stan Mikita, Chi	89
1964–65	Stan Mikita, Chi	87
1965–66	Bobby Hull, Chi	97
1966–67	Stan Mikita, Chi	97
1967–68	Stan Mikita, Chi	87
1968–69	Phil Esposito, Bos	126
1969–70	Bobby Orr, Bos	120
1970–71	Phil Esposito, Bos	152
1971–72	Phil Esposito, Bos	133
1972–73	Phil Esposito, Bos	130
1973–74	Phil Esposito, Bos	145
1974–75	Bobby Orr, Bos	135
1975–76	Guy Lafleur, Mtl	125
1976–77	Guy Lafleur, Mtl	136
1977–78	Guy Lafleur, Mtl	132
1978–79	Bryan Trottier, NYI	134
1979–80	Marcel Dionne, LA	137
	Wayne Gretzky, Edm	137
1980–81	Wayne Gretzky, Edm	164

Points (Cont.)

Season	Player and Club	Pts	Season	Player and Club	Pts
1981–82	Wayne Gretzky, Edm	212	1994–95	Jaromir Jagr, Pitt	70
1982–83	Wayne Gretzky, Edm	196	1995–96	Mario Lemieux, Pitt	161
1983–84	Wayne Gretzky, Edm	205	1996–97	Mario Lemieux, Pitt	122
1984–85	Wayne Gretzky, Edm	208	1997–98	Jaromir Jagr, Pitt	102
1985–86	Wayne Gretzky, Edm	215	1998–99	Jaromir Jagr, Pitt	127
1986–87	Wayne Gretzky, Edm	183	1999–00	Jaromir Jagr, Pitt	96
1987–88	Mario Lemieux, Pitt	168	2000–01	Jaromir Jagr, Pitt	121
1988–89	Mario Lemieux, Pitt	199	2001–02	Jarome Iginla, Cgy	96
1989–90	Wayne Gretzky, LA	142	2002–03	Peter Forsberg, Col	106
1990–91	Wayne Gretzky, LA	163	2003–04	Martin St. Louis, TB	94
1991–92	Mario Lemieux, Pitt	131	2004–05	No season	
1992–93	Mario Lemieux, Pitt	160	2005–06	Joe Thornton, Bos/SJ	125
1993–94	Wayne Gretzky, LA	130			

Goals

Season	Player and Club	G	Season	Player and Club	G
1917–18	Joe Malone, Mtl	44	1962–63	Gordie Howe, Det	38
1918–19	Odie Cleghorn, Mtl	23	1963–64	Bobby Hull, Chi	43
1919–20	Joe Malone, Que	39	1964–65	Norm Ullman, Det	42
1920–21	Babe Dye, Ham-Tor	35	1965–66	Bobby Hull, Chi	54
1921–22	Punch Broadbent, Ott	32	1966–67	Bobby Hull, Chi	52
1922–23	Babe Dye, Tor	26	1967–68	Bobby Hull, Chi	44
1923–24	Cy Denneny, Ott	22	1968–69	Bobby Hull, Chi	58
1924–25	Babe Dye, Tor	38	1969–70	Phil Esposito, Bos	43
1925–26	Nels Stewart, Mtl	34	1970–71	Phil Esposito, Bos	76
1926–27	Bill Cook, NY	33	1971–72	Phil Esposito, Bos	66
1927–28	Howie Morenz, Mtl	33	1972–73	Phil Esposito, Bos	55
1928–29	Ace Bailey, Tor	22	1973–74	Phil Esposito, Bos	68
1929–30	Cooney Weiland, Bos	43	1974–75	Phil Esposito, Bos	61
1930–31	Bill Cook, NY	30	1975–76	Guy Lafleur, Mtl	56
1931–32	Charlie Conacher, Tor	34	1976–77	Steve Shutt, Mtl	60
	Bill Cook, NY	34	1977–78	Guy Lafleur, Mtl	60
1932–33	Bill Cook, NY	28	1978–79	Mike Bossy, NYI	69
1933–34	Charlie Conacher, Tor	32	1979–80	Charlie Simmer, LA	56
1934–35	Charlie Conacher, Tor	36		Blaine Stoughton, Hart	56
1935–36	Charlie Conacher, Tor	23	1980–81	Mike Bossy, NYI	68
	Bill Thoms, Tor	23	1981–82	Wayne Gretzky, Edm	92
1936–37	Larry Aurie, Det	23	1982–83	Wayne Gretzky, Edm	71
	Nels Stewart, Bos-NYA	23	1983–84	Wayne Gretzky, Edm	87
1937–38	Gord Drill, Tor	26	1984–85	Wayne Gretzky, Edm	73
1938–39	Roy Conacher, Bos	26	1985–86	Jari Kurri, Edm	68
1939–40	Bryan Hextall, NY	24	1986–87	Wayne Gretzky, Edm	62
1940–41	Bryan Hextall, NY	26	1987–88	Mario Lemieux, Pitt	70
1941–42	Lynn Patrick, NY	32	1988–89	Mario Lemieux, Pitt	85
1942–43	Doug Bentley, Chi	43	1989–90	Brett Hull, StL	72
1943–44	Doug Bentley, Chi	38	1990–91	Brett Hull, StL	78
1944–45	Maurice Richard, Mtl	50	1991–92	Brett Hull, StL	70
1945–46	Gaye Stewart, Tor	37	1992–93	Alexander Mogilny, Buff	76
1946–47	Maurice Richard, Mtl	50		Teemu Selanne, Winn	76
1947–48	Ted Lindsay, Det	33	1993–94	Pavel Bure, Van	60
1948–49	Sid Abel, Det	28	1994–95	Peter Bondra, Wash	34
1949–50	Maurice Richard, Mtl	43	1995–96	Mario Lemieux, Pitt	69
1950–51	Gordie Howe, Det	43	1996–97	Keith Tkachuk, Phoe	52
1951–52	Gordie Howe, Det	47	1997–98	Teemu Selanne, Ana	52
1952–53	Gordie Howe, Det	49		Peter Bondra, Wash	52
1953–54	Maurice Richard, Mtl	37	1998–99	Teemu Selanne, Ana	47
1954–55	Bernie Geoffrion, Mtl	38	1999–00	Pavel Bure, Fla	58
	Maurice Richard, Mtl	38	2000–01	Pavel Bure, Fla	59
1955–56	Jean Beliveau, Mtl	47	2001–02	Jarome Iginla, Cgy	52
1957–58	Dickie Moore, Mtl	36	2002–03	Milan Hejduk, Col	50
1956–57	Gordie Howe, Det	44	2003–04	Jarome Iginla, Cgy	41
1958–59	Jean Beliveau, Mtl	45		Rick Nash, Clb	41
1959–60	Bobby Hull, Chi	39		Ilya Kovalchuk, Atl	41
	Bronco Horvath, Bos	39	2004–05	No season	
1960–61	Bernie Geoffrion, Mtl	50	2005–06	Jonathan Cheechoo, SJ	56
1961–62	Bobby Hull, Chi	50			

Assists

Season	Player and Club	Asst	Season	Player and Club	Asst
1917–18	statistic not kept		1965–66	Stan Mikita, Chi	48
1918–19	Newsy Lalonde, Mtl	9		Bobby Rousseau, Mtl	48
1919–20	Corbett Denneny, Tor	12		Jean Beliveau, Mtl	48
1920–21	Louis Berlinquette, Mtl	9	1966–67	Stan Mikita, Chi	62
1921–22	Punch Broadbench, Ott	14	1967–68	Phil Esposito, Bos	49
1922–23	Babe Dye, Tor	11	1968–69	Phil Esposito, Bos	77
1923–24	Billy Boucher, Mtl	6	1969–70	Bobby Orr, Bos	87
1924–25	Cy Denneny, Ott	15	1970–71	Bobby Orr, Bos	102
1925–26	Cy Denneny, Ott	12	1971–72	Bobby Orr, Bos	80
1926–27	Dick Irvin, Chi	18	1972–73	Phil Esposito, Bos	75
1927–28	Howie Morenz, Mtl	18	1973–74	Bobby Orr, Bos	89
1928–29	Frank Boucher, NY	16	1974–75	Bobby Clarke, Phil	89
1929–30	Frank Boucher, NY	36		Bobby Orr, Bos	89
1930–31	Joe Primeau, Tor	36	1975–76	Bobby Clarke, Phil	89
1931–32	Joe Primeau, Tor	37	1976–77	Guy Lafleur, Mtl	80
1932–33	Frank Boucher, NY	28	1977–78	Bryan Trottier, NYI	77
1933–34	Joe Primeau, Tor	32	1978–79	Bryan Trottier, NYI	87
1934–35	Art Chapman, NYA	28	1979–80	Wayne Gretzky, Edm	86
1935–36	Art Chapman, NYA	28	1980–81	Wayne Gretzky, Edm	109
1936–37	Syl Apps, Tor	29	1981–82	Wayne Gretzky, Edm	120
1937–38	Syl Apps, Tor	29	1982–83	Wayne Gretzky, Edm	125
1938–39	Bill Cowley, Bos	34	1983–84	Wayne Gretzky, Edm	118
1939–40	Milt Schmidt, Bos	30	1984–85	Wayne Gretzky, Edm	135
1940–41	Bill Cowley, Bos	45	1985–86	Wayne Gretzky, Edm	163
1941–42	Phil Watson, NY	37	1986–87	Wayne Gretzky, Edm	121
1942–43	Bill Cowley, Bos	45	1987–88	Wayne Gretzky, Edm	109
1943–44	Clint Smith, Chi	49	1988–89	Wayne Gretzky, LA	114
1944–45	Elmer Lach, Mtl	54		Mario Lemieux, Pitt	114
1945–46	Elmer Lach, Mtl	34	1989–90	Wayne Gretzky, LA	102
1946–47	Billy Taylor, Det	46	1990–91	Wayne Gretzky, LA	122
1947–48	Doug Bentley, Chi	37	1991–92	Wayne Gretzky, LA	90
1948–49	Doug Bentley, Chi	43	1992–93	Adam Oates, Bos	97
1949–50	Ted Lindsay, Det	55	1993–94	Wayne Gretzky, LA	92
1950–51	Gordie Howe, Det	43	1994–95	Ron Francis, Pitt	48
	Ted Kennedy, Tor	43	1995–96	Mario Lemieux, Pitt	92
1951–52	Elmer Lach, Mtl	50		Ron Francis, Pitt	92
1952–53	Gordie Howe, Det	46	1996–97	Mario Lemieux, Pitt	72
1953–54	Gordie Howe, Det	48	1997–98	Jaromir Jagr, Pitt	67
1954–55	Bert Olmstead, Mtl	48		Wayne Gretzky, NYR	67
1955–56	Bert Olmstead, Mtl	56	1998–99	Jaromir Jagr, Pitt	83
1956–57	Ted Lindsay, Det	55	1999–00	Mark Recchi, Phil	63
1957–58	Henri Richard, Mtl	52	2000–01	Jaromir Jagr, Pitt	69
1958–59	Dickie Moore, Mtl	55		Adam Oates, Wash	69
1959–60	Bobby Hull, Chi	42	2001–02	Adam Oates, Wash	57
1960–61	Jean Beliveau, Mtl	58	2002–03	Peter Forsberg, Col	77
1961–62	Andy Bathgate, NY	56	2003–04	Scott Gomez, NJ	56
1962–63	Henri Richard, Mtl	50		Martin St. Louis, TB	56
1963–64	Andy Bathgate, NY-Tor	58	2004–05	No season	
1964–65	Stan Mikita, Chi	59	2005–06	Joe Thornton, Bos/SJ	96

Goals Against Average

Season	Goaltender and Club	GP	Min	GA	SO	Avg
1917–18	Georges Vezina, Mtl	21	1282	84	1	3.93
1918–19	Clint Benedict, Ott	18	1113	53	2	2.86
1919–20	Clint Benedict, Ott	24	1444	64	5	2.66
1920–21	Clint Benedict, Ott	24	1457	75	2	3.09
1921–22	Clint Benedict, Ott	24	1508	84	2	3.34
1922–23	Clint Benedict, Ott	24	1478	54	4	2.19
1923–24	Georges Vezina, Mtl	24	1459	48	3	1.97
1924–25	Georges Vezina, Mtl	30	1860	56	5	1.81
1925–26	Alex Connell, Ott	36	2251	42	15	1.12
1926–27	Clint Benedict, Mtl M	43	2748	65	13	1.42
1927–28	George Hainsworth, Mtl	44	2730	48	13	1.05
1928–29	George Hainsworth, Mtl	44	2800	43	22	0.92
1929–30	Tiny Thompson, Bos	44	2680	98	3	2.19

Goals Against Average *(Cont.)*

Season	Goaltender and Club	GP	Min	GA	SO	Avg
1930–31	Roy Worters, NYA	44	2760	74	8	1.61
1931–32	Chuck Gardiner, Chi	48	2989	92	4	1.85
1932–33	Tiny Thompson, Bos	48	3000	88	11	1.76
1933–34	Wilf Cude, Det-Mtl	30	1920	47	5	1.47
1934–35	Lorne Chabot, Chi	48	2940	88	8	1.80
1935–36	Tiny Thompson, Bos	48	2930	82	10	1.68
1936–37	Normie Smith, Det	48	2980	102	6	2.05
1937–38	Tiny Thompson, Bos	48	2970	89	7	1.80
1938–39	Frank Brimsek, Bos	43	2610	68	10	1.56
1939–40	Dave Kerr, NYR	48	3000	77	8	1.54
1940–41	Turk Broda, Tor	48	2970	99	5	2.00
1941–42	Frank Brimsek, Bos	47	2930	115	3	2.35
1942–43	Johnny Mowers, Det	50	3010	124	6	2.47
1943–44	Bill Durnan, Mtl	50	3000	109	2	2.18
1944–45	Bill Durnan, Mtl	50	3000	121	1	2.42
1945–46	Bill Durnan, Mtl	40	2400	104	4	2.60
1946–47	Bill Durnan, Mtl	60	3600	138	4	2.30
1947–48	Turk Broda, Tor	60	3600	143	5	2.38
1948–49	Bill Durnan, Mtl	60	3600	126	10	2.10
1949–50	Bill Durnan, Mtl	64	3840	141	8	2.20
1950–51	Al Rollins, Tor	40	2367	70	5	1.77
1951–52	Terry Sawchuk, Det	70	4200	133	12	1.90
1952–53	Terry Sawchuk, Det	63	3780	120	9	1.90
1953–54	Harry Lumley, Tor	69	4140	128	13	1.86
1954–55	Harry Lumley, Tor	69	4140	134	8	1.94
	Terry Sawchuk, Det	68	4060	132	12	1.94
1955–56	Jacques Plante, Mtl	64	3840	119	7	1.86
1956–57	Jacques Plante, Mtl	61	3660	123	9	2.02
1957–58	Jacques Plante, Mtl	57	3386	119	9	2.11
1958–59	Jacques Plante, Mtl	67	4000	144	9	2.16
1959–60	Jacques Plante, Mtl	69	4140	175	3	2.54
1960–61	Johnny Bower, Tor	58	3480	145	2	2.50
1961–62	Jacques Plante, Mtl	70	4200	166	4	2.37
1962–63	Jacques Plante, Mtl	56	3320	138	5	2.49
1963–64	Johnny Bower, Tor	51	3009	106	5	2.11
1964–65	Johnny Bower, Tor	34	2040	81	3	2.38
1965–66	Johnny Bower, Tor	35	1998	75	3	2.25
1966–67	Glenn Hall, Chi	32	1664	66	2	2.38
1967–68	Gump Worsley, Mtl	40	2213	73	6	1.98
1968–69	Jacques Plante, StL	37	2139	70	5	1.96
1969–70	Ernie Wakely, StL	30	1651	58	4	2.11
1970–71	Jacques Plante, Tor	40	2329	73	4	1.88
1971–72	Tony Esposito, Chi	48	2780	82	9	1.77
1972–73	Ken Dryden, Mtl	54	3165	119	6	2.26
1973–74	Bernie Parent, Phil	73	4314	136	12	1.89
1974–75	Bernie Parent, Phil	68	4041	137	12	2.03
1975–76	Ken Dryden, Mtl	62	3580	121	8	2.03
1976–77	Michael Larocque, Mtl	26	1525	53	4	2.09
1977–78	Ken Dryden, Mtl	52	3071	105	5	2.05
1978–79	Ken Dryden, Mtl	47	2814	108	5	2.30
1979–80	Bob Sauve, Buff	32	1880	74	4	2.36
1980–81	Richard Sevigny, Mtl	33	1777	71	2	2.40
1981–82	Denis Herron, Mtl	27	1547	68	3	2.64
1982–83	Pete Peeters, Bos	62	3611	142	8	2.36
1983–84	Pat Riggin, Wash	41	2299	102	4	2.66
1984–85	Tom Barrasso, Buff	54	3248	144	5	2.66
1985–86	Bob Froese, Phil	51	2728	116	5	2.55
1986–87	Brian Hayward, Mtl	37	2178	102	1	2.81
1987–88	Pete Peeters, Wash	35	1896	88	2	2.78
1988–89	Patrick Roy, Mtl	48	2744	113	4	2.47
1989–90	Patrick Roy, Mtl	54	3173	134	3	2.53
	Mike Liut, Hart-Wash	37	2161	91	4	2.53
1990–91	Ed Belfour, Chi	74	4127	170	4	2.47
1991–92	Patrick Roy, Mtl	67	3935	155	5	2.36
1992–93	Felix Potvin, Tor	48	2781	116	2	2.50
1993–94	Dominik Hasek, Buff	58	3358	109	7	1.95

Goals Against Average (Cont.)

Season	Goaltender and Club	GP	Min	GA	SO	Avg
1994–95	Dominik Hasek, Buff	41	2416	85	5	2.11
1995–96	Ron Hextall, Phil	53	3102	112	4	2.17
	Chris Osgood, Det	50	2933	106	5	2.17
1996–97	Martin Brodeur, NJ	67	3838	120	10	1.88
1997–98	Ed Belfour, Dall	61	3581	112	9	1.88
1998–99	Ron Tugnutt, Ott	43	2508	75	3	1.79
1999–00	Brian Boucher, Phil	35	2038	65	4	1.91
2000–01	Marty Turco, Dall	26	1266	40	3	1.90
2001–02	Patrick Roy, Col	63	3774	122	9	1.94
2002–03	Marty Turco, Dall	55	3193	92	7	1.72
2003–04	Miikka Kiprusoff, Cgy	38	2301	65	4	1.70
2004–05	No season					
2005–06	Miikka Kiprusoff, Cgy	74	4379	151	10	2.07

Penalty Minutes

Season	Player and Club	GP	PIM	Season	Player and Club	GP	PIM
1918–19	Joe Hall, Mtl	17	85	1962–63	Howie Young, Det	64	273
1919–20	Cully Wilson, Tor	23	79	1963–64	Vic Hadfield, NYR	69	151
1920–21	Bert Corbeau, Mtl	24	86	1964–65	Carl Brewer, Tor	70	177
1921–22	Sprague Cleghorn, Mtl	24	63	1965–66	Reggie Fleming, Bos-NYR	69	166
1922–23	Billy Boucher, Mtl	24	52	1966–67	John Ferguson, Mtl	67	177
1923–24	Bert Corbeau, Tor	24	55	1967–68	Barclay Plager, StL	49	153
1924–25	Billy Boucher, Mtl	30	92	1968–69	Forbes Kennedy, Phil-Tor	77	219
1925–26	Bert Corbeau, Tor	36	121	1969–70	Keith Magnuson, Chi	76	213
1926–27	Nels Stewart, Mtl M	44	133	1970–71	Keith Magnuson, Chi	76	291
1927–28	Eddie Shore, Bos	44	165	1971–72	Brian Watson, Pitt	75	212
1928–29	Red Dutton, Mtl M	44	139	1972–73	Dave Schultz, Phil	76	259
1929–30	Joe Lamb, Ott	44	119	1973–74	Dave Schultz, Phil	73	348
1930–31	Harvey Rockburn, Det	42	118	1974–75	Dave Schultz, Phil	76	472
1931–32	Red Dutton, NYA	47	107	1975–76	Steve Durbano, Pitt-KC	69	370
1932–33	Red Horner, Tor	48	144	1976–77	Dave Williams, Tor	77	338
1933–34	Red Horner, Tor	42	126	1977–78	Dave Schultz, LA-Pitt	74	405
1934–35	Red Horner, Tor	46	125	1978–79	Dave Williams, Tor	77	298
1935–36	Red Horner, Tor	43	167	1979–80	Jimmy Mann, Winn	72	287
1936–37	Red Horner, Tor	48	124	1980–81	Dave Williams, Van	77	343
1937–38	Red Horner, Tor	47	82	1981–82	Paul Baxter, Pitt	76	409
1938–39	Red Horner, Tor	48	85	1982–83	Randy Holt, Wash	70	275
1939–40	Red Horner, Tor	30	87	1983–84	Chris Nilan, Mtl	76	338
1940–41	Jimmy Orlando, Det	48	99	1984–85	Chris Nilan, Mtl	77	358
1941–42	Jimmy Orlando, Det	48	81	1985–86	Joey Kocur, Det	59	377
1942–43	Jimmy Orlando, Det	40	89	1986–87	Tim Hunter, Cgy	73	361
1943–44	Mike McMahon, Mtl	42	98	1987–88	Bob Probert, Det	74	398
1944–45	Pat Egan, Bos	48	86	1988–89	Tim Hunter, Cgy	75	375
1945–46	Jack Stewart, Det	47	73	1989–90	Basil McRae, Minn	66	351
1946–47	Gus Mortson, Tor	60	133	1990–91	Bob Ray, Buff	66	350
1947–48	Bill Barilko, Tor	57	147	1991–92	Mike Peluso, Chi	63	408
1948–49	Bill Ezinicki, Tor	52	145	1992–93	Marty McSorley, LA	81	399
1949–50	Bill Ezinicki, Tor	67	144	1993–94	Tie Domi, Winn	81	347
1950–51	Gus Mortson, Tor	60	142	1994–95	Enrico Ciccone, TB	41	225
1951–52	Gus Kyle, Bos	69	127	1995–96	Matthew Barnaby, Buff	73	335
1952–53	Maurice Richard, Mtl	70	112	1996–97	Gino Odjick, Van	70	371
1953–54	Gus Mortson, Chi	68	132	1997–98	Donald Brashear, Van	77	372
1954–55	Fern Flaman, Bos	70	150	1998–99	Rob Ray, Buff	76	261
1955–56	Lou Fontinato, NYR	70	202	1999–00	Denny Lambert, Atl	73	219
1956–57	Gus Mortson, Chi	70	147	2000–01	Matthew Barnaby, TB	76	265
1957–58	Lou Fontinato, NYR	70	152	2001–02	Peter Worrell, Fla	79	354
1958–59	Ted Lindsay, Chi	70	184	2002–03	Jody Shelley, Clb	68	249
1959–60	Carl Brewer, Tor	67	150	2003–04	Sean Avery, LA	76	261
1960–61	Pierre Pilote, Chi	70	165	2004–05	No season		
1961–62	Lou Fontinato, Mtl	54	167	2005–06	Sean Avery, LA	75	257

NHL All-Star Game

First played in 1947, this game was scheduled before the start of the regular season and used to match the defending Stanley Cup Champions against a squad made up of the league All-stars from other teams. In 1966 the games were moved to mid-season, although there was no game that year. The format changed to a conference versus conference showdown in 1969.

Results

Year	Site	Score	MVP	Attendance
1947	Toronto	All-Stars 4, Toronto 3	None named	14,169
1948	Chicago	All-Stars 3, Toronto 1	None named	12,794
1949	Toronto	All-Stars 3, Toronto 1	None named	13,541
1950	Detroit	Detroit 7, All-Stars 1	None named	9,166
1951	Toronto	1st team 2, 2nd team 2	None named	11,469
1952	Detroit	1st team 1, 2nd team 1	None named	10,680
1953	Montreal	All-Stars 3, Montreal 1	None named	14,153
1954	Detroit	All-Stars 2, Detroit 2	None named	10,689
1955	Detroit	Detroit 3, All-Stars 1	None named	10,111
1956	Montreal	All-Stars 1, Montreal 1	None named	13,095
1957	Montreal	All-Stars 5, Montreal 3	None named	13,003
1958	Montreal	Montreal 6, All-Stars 3	None named	13,989
1959	Montreal	Montreal 6, All-Stars 1	None named	13,818
1960	Montreal	All-Stars 2, Montreal 1	None named	13,949
1961	Chicago	All-Stars 3, Chicago 1	None named	14,534
1962	Toronto	Toronto 4, All-Stars 1	Eddie Shack, Tor	14,236
1963	Toronto	All-Stars 3, Toronto 3	Frank Mahovlich, Tor	14,034
1964	Toronto	All-Stars 3, Toronto 2	Jean Beliveau, Mtl	14,232
1965	Montreal	All-Stars 5, Montreal 2	Gordie Howe, Det	13,529
1967	Montreal	Montreal 3, All-Stars 0	Henri Richard, Mtl	14,284
1968	Toronto	Toronto 4, All-Stars 3	Bruce Gamble, Tor	15,753
1969	Montreal	East 3, West 3	Frank Mahovlich, Det	16,260
1970	St Louis	East 4, West 1	Bobby Hull, Chi	16,587
1971	Boston	West 2, East 1	Bobby Hull, Chi	14,790
1972	Minnesota	East 3, West 2	Bobby Orr, Bos	15,423
1973	NY Rangers	East 5, West 4	Greg Polis, Pitt	16,986
1974	Chicago	West 6, East 4	Garry Unger, StL	16,426
1975	Montreal	Wales 7, Campbell 1	Syl Apps Jr, Pitt	16,080
1976	Philadelphia	Wales 7, Campbell 5	Pete Mahovlich, Mtl	16,436
1977	Vancouver	Wales 4, Campbell 3	Rick Martin, Buff	15,607
1978	Buffalo	Wales 3, Campbell 2 (OT)	Billy Smith, NYI	16,433
1980	Detroit	Wales 6, Campbell 3	Reg Leach, Phil	21,002
1981	Los Angeles	Campbell 4, Wales 1	Mike Liut, StL	15,761
1982	Washington	Wales 4, Campbell 2	Mike Bossy, NYI	18,130
1983	NY Islanders	Campbell 9, Wales 3	Wayne Gretzky, Edm	15,230
1984	New Jersey	Wales 7, Campbell 6	Don Maloney, NYR	18,939
1985	Calgary	Wales 6, Campbell 4	Mario Lemieux, Pitt	16,825
1986	Hartford	Wales 4, Campbell 3 (OT)	Grant Fuhr, Edm	15,100
1988	St Louis	Wales 6, Campbell 5 (OT)	Mario Lemieux, Pitt	17,878
1989	Edmonton	Campbell 9, Wales 5	Wayne Gretzky, LA	17,503
1990	Pittsburgh	Wales 12, Campbell 7	Mario Lemieux, Pitt	16,236
1991	Chicago	Campbell 11, Wales 5	Vince Damphousse, Tor	18,472
1992	Philadelphia	Campbell 10, Wales 6	Brett Hull, StL	17,380
1993	Montreal	Wales 16, Campbell 6	Mike Gartner, NYR	17,137
1994	NY Rangers	East 9, West 8	Mike Richter, NYR	18,200
1996	Boston	East 5, West 4	Ray Bourque, Bos	17,565
1997	San Jose	East 11, West 7	Mark Recchi, Mtl	17,565
1998	Vancouver	N America 8, World 7	Teemu Selanne, Ana (World)	18,422
1999	Tampa Bay	N America 8, World 6	Wayne Gretzky, NYR (N America)	19,758
2000	Toronto	World 9, N America 4	Pavel Bure, Fla (World)	19,300
2001	Denver	N America 14, World 12	Bill Guerin, Bos (N America)	18,646
2002	Los Angeles	World 8, N America 5	Eric Daze, Chi (N America)	18,118
2003	Sunrise, Fla.	West 6, East 5 (shootout)	Dany Heatley, Atl (East)	19,250
2004	St. Paul, Minn.	East 6, West 4	Joe Sakic, Col (West)	19,434
2005	No game played			
2006	No game played due to Winter Olympics			

Note: The Challenge Cup, a series between the NHL All-Stars and the Soviet Union, was played instead of the All-Star Game in 1979. Eight years later, Rendez-Vous '87, a two-game series matching the Soviet Union and the NHL All-Stars, replaced the All-Star Game. The 1995 NHL All-Star game was cancelled due to a labor dispute. The 1998 NHL All-Star game, billed as a preview to the 1998 Winter Olympics in Nagano, Japan, matched North Amercian–born All-Stars and All-Stars born elsewhere. In 2005, no game was played due to season-long lockout.

Located in Toronto, the Hockey Hall of Fame was officially opened on August 26, 1961. The current chairman is William C. Hay. There are, at present, 306 members of the Hockey Hall of Fame—209 players, 84 "builders," and 14 on-ice officials. (One member, Alan Eagleson, resigned from the Hall 3-25-98.) To be eligible, player and referee/linesman candidates should have been out of the game for three years, but the Hall's Board of Directors can make exceptions.

Players

Sid Abel (1969)
Jack Adams (1959)
Charles (Syl) Apps (1961)
George Armstrong (1975)
Irvine (Ace) Bailey (1975)
Donald H. (Dan) Bain (1945)
Hobey Baker (1945)
Bill Barber (1990)
Marty Barry (1965)
Andy Bathgate (1978)
Bobby Bauer (1996)
Jean Beliveau (1972)
Clint Benedict (1965)
Douglas Bentley (1964)
Max Bentley (1966)
Hector (Toe) Blake (1966)
Leo Boivin (1986)
Dickie Boon (1952)
Mike Bossy (1991)
Emile (Butch) Bouchard (1966)
Frank Boucher (1958)
George (Buck) Boucher (1960)
Ray Bourque (2004)
Johnny Bower (1976)
Russell Bowie (1945)
Frank Brimsek (1966)
Harry L. (Punch) Broadbent (1962)
Walter (Turk) Broda (1967)
John Bucyk (1981)
Billy Burch (1974)
Harry Cameron (1962)
Gerry Cheevers (1985)
Francis (King) Clancy (1958)
Aubrey (Dit) Clapper (1947)
Bobby Clarke (1987)
Sprague Cleghorn (1958)
Paul Coffey (2004)
Neil Colville (1967)
Charlie Conacher (1961)
Lionel Conacher (1994)
Roy Conacher (1998)
Alex Connell (1958)
Bill Cook (1952)
Fred (Bun) Cook (1995)
Arthur Coulter (1974)
Yvan Cournoyer (1982)
Bill Cowley (1968)
Samuel (Rusty) Crawford (1962)
Jack Darragh (1962)
Allan M. (Scotty) Davidson (1950)
Clarence (Hap) Day (1961)
Alex Delvecchio (1977)
Cy Denneny (1959)
Marcel Dionne (1992)
Gordie Drillon (1975)
Charles Drinkwater (1950)
Ken Dryden (1983)
Terrance (Dick) Duff (2006)
Woody Dumart (1992)

Thomas Dunderdale (1974)
Bill Durnan (1964)
Mervyn A. (Red) Dutton (1958)
Cecil (Babe) Dye (1970)
Phil Esposito (1984)
Tony Esposito (1988)
Arthur F. Farrell (1965)
Bernie Federko (2002)
Viacheslav Fetisov (2001)
Ferdinand (Fern) Flaman (1990)
Frank Foyston (1958)
Frank Frederickson (1958)
Grant Fuhr (2003)
Bill Gadsby (1970)
Bob Gainey (1992)
Chuck Gardiner (1945)
Herb Gardiner (1958)
Jimmy Gardner (1962)
Mike Gartner (2001)
Bernie (Boom Boom) Geoffrion (1972)
Eddie Gerard (1945)
Ed Giacomin (1987)
Rod Gilbert (1982)
Clark Gilles (2002)
Hamilton (Billy) Gilmour (1962)
Frank (Moose) Goheen (1952)
Ebenezer R. (Ebbie) Goodfellow (1963)
Michel Goulet (1998)
Mike Grant (1950)
Wilfred (Shorty) Green (1962)
Wayne Gretzky (1999)
Si Griffis (1950)
George Hainsworth (1961)
Glenn Hall (1975)
Joe Hall (1961)
Doug Harvey (1973)
Dale Hawerchuk (2001)
George Hay (1958)
William (Riley) Hern (1962)
Bryan Hextall (1969)
Harry (Hap) Holmes (1972)
Tom Hooper (1962)
George (Red) Horner (1965)
Miles (Tim) Horton (1977)
Gordie Howe (1972)
Syd Howe (1965)
Harry Howell (1979)
Bobby Hull (1983)
John (Bouse) Hutton (1962)
Harry M. Hyland (1962)
James (Dick) Irvin (1958)
Harvey (Busher) Jackson (1971)
Ernest (Moose) Johnson (1952)
Ivan (Ching) Johnson (1958)
Tom Johnson (1970)
Aurel Joliat (1947)
Gordon (Duke) Keats (1958)

Players *(Cont.)*

Leonard (Red) Kelly (1969)
Ted (Teeder) Kennedy (1966)
Dave Keon (1986)
Valeri Kharmalov (2005)
Jari Kurri (2001)
Elmer Lach (1966)
Guy Lafleur (1988)
Pat LaFonaine (2003)
Edouard (Newsy) Lalonde (1950)
Rod Langway (2002)
Jacques Laperriere (1987)
Guy LaPointe (1993)
Edgar Laprade (1993)
Reed Larson (1996)
Jean (Jack) Laviolette (1962)
Hugh Lehman (1958)
Jacques Lemaire (1984)
Mario Lemieux (1997)
Percy LeSueur (1961)
Herbert A. Lewis (1989)
Ted Lindsay (1966)
Harry Lumley (1980)
Lanny McDonald (1992)
Frank McGee (1945)
Billy McGimsie (1962)
George McNamara (1958)
Duncan (Mickey) MacKay (1952)
Frank Mahovlich (1981)
Joe Malone (1950)
Sylvio Mantha (1960)
Jack Marshall (1965)
Fred G. (Steamer) Maxwell (1962)
Stan Mikita (1983)
Dicky Moore (1974)
Patrick (Paddy) Moran (1958)
Howie Morenz (1945)
Billy Mosienko (1965)
Joe Mullen (2000)
Larry Murphy (2004)
Cam Neely (2005)
Frank Nighbor (1947)
Reg Noble (1962)
Herbert (Buddy) O'Connor (1988)
Harry Oliver (1967)
Bert Olmstead (1985)
Bobby Orr (1979)
Bernie Parent (1984)
Brad Park (1988)
Lester Patrick (1947)
Lynn Patrick (1980)
Gilbert Perreault (1990)
Tommy Phillips (1945)
Pierre Pilote (1975)
Didier (Pit) Pitre (1962)
Jacques Plante (1978)
Denis Potvin (1991)
Walter (Babe) Pratt (1966)
Joe Primeau (1963)
Marcel Pronovost (1978)
Bob Pulford (1991)
Harvey Pulford (1945)

Hubert (Bill) Quackenbush (1976)
Frank Rankin (1961)
Jean Ratelle (1985)
Claude (Chuck) Rayner (1973)
Kenneth Reardon (1966)
Henri Richard (1979)
Maurice (Rocket) Richard (1961)
George Richardson (1950)
Gordon Roberts (1971)
Larry Robinson (1995)
Art Ross (1945)
Patrick Roy (2006)
Blair Russel (1965)
Ernest Russell (1965)
Jack Ruttan (1962)
Borje Salming (1996)
Denis Savard (2000)
Serge Savard (1986)
Terry Sawchuk (1971)
Fred Scanlan (1965)
Milt Schmidt (1961)
Dave (Sweeney) Schriner (1962)
Earl Seibert (1963)
Oliver Seibert (1961)
Eddie Shore (1947)
Steve Shutt (1993)
Albert C. (Babe) Siebert (1964)
Harold (Bullet Joe) Simpson (1962)
Daryl Sittler (1989)
Alfred E. Smith (1962)
Billy Smith (1993)
Clint Smith (1991)
Reginald (Hooley) Smith (1972)
Thomas Smith (1973)
Allan Stanley (1981)
Russell (Barney) Stanley (1962)
Peter Stastny (1998)
John (Black Jack) Stewart (1964)
Nels Stewart (1962)
Bruce Stuart (1961)
Hod Stuart (1945)
Frederic (Cyclone) (O.B.E.)
    Taylor (1947)
Cecil R. (Tiny) Thompson (1959)
Vladislav Tretiak (1989)
Harry J. Trihey (1950)
Bryan Trottier (1997)
Norm Ullman (1982)
Georges Vezina (1945)
Jack Walker (1960)
Marty Walsh (1962)
Harry Watson (1994)
Harry E. Watson (1962)
Ralph (Cooney) Weiland (1971)
Harry Westwick (1962)
Fred Whitcroft (1962)
Gordon (Phat) Wilson (1962)
Lorne (Gump) Worsley (1980)
Roy Worters (1969)

Note: Year of election to the Hall of Fame is in parentheses after the member's name.
*Eagleson resigned from Hall March 25, 1998.

Builders

Charles Adams (1960)
Weston W. Adams (1972)
Thomas (Frank) Ahearn (1962)
John (Bunny) Ahearne (1977)
Montagu Allan (C.V.O.) (1945)
Keith Allen (1992)
Al Arbour (1996)
Harold Ballard (1977)
David Bauer (1989)
John Bickell (1978)
Scott Bowman (1991)
Herb Brooks (2006)
George V. Brown (1961)
Walter A. Brown (1962)
Frank Buckland (1975)
Walter L. Bush (2000)
Jack Butterfield (1980)
Frank Calder (1947)
Angus D. Campbell (1964)
Clarence Campbell (1966)
Joe Cattarinich (1977)
Bob Cole (1996)
Murray Costello (2005)
Joseph (Leo) Dandurand (1963)
Francis Dilio (1964)
George S. Dudley (1958)
James A. Dunn (1968)
Robert Alan Eagleson (1989–98*)
Cliff Fletcher (2004)
Sergio Gambucci (1996)
Emile Francis (1982)
Jack Gibson (1976)
Tommy Gorman (1963)
Frank Griffiths (1993)
William Hanley (1986)
Charles Hay (1974)
James C. Hendy (1968)
Foster Hewitt (1965)
William Hewitt (1947)
Harley Hotchkiss (2006)
Fred J. Hume (1962)
Mike Ilitch (2003)
George (Punch) Imlach (1984)
Tommy Ivan (1974)
William M. Jennings (1975)
Bob Johnson (1992)
Gordon W. Juckes (1979)
John Kilpatrick (1960)
Brian Kilrea (2003)

Seymour Knox III (1993)
George Leader (1969)
Robert LeBel (1970)
Thomas F. Lockhart (1965)
Paul Loicq (1961)
Frederic McLaughlin (1963)
John Mariucci (1985)
Frank Mathers (1992)
John (Jake) Milford (1984)
Hartland Molson (1973)
Scotty Morrison (1999)
Mngr. Athol (Pere) Murray (1998)
Roger Neilson (2002)
Francis Nelson (1947)
Bruce A. Norris (1969)
James Norris, Sr. (1958)
James D. Norris (1962)
William M. Northey (1947)
John O'Brien (1962)
Brian O'Neill (1994)
Fred Page (1993)
Craig Patrick (1996)
Frank Patrick (1958)
Allan W. Pickard (1958)
Rudy Pilous (1985)
Norman (Bud) Poile (1990)
Samuel Pollock (1978)
Donat Raymond (1958)
John Robertson (1947)
Claude C. Robinson (1947)
Philip D. Ross (1976)
Gunther Sabetzki (1995)
Glen Sather (1997)
Frank J. Selke (1960)
Harry Sinden (1983)
Frank D. Smith (1962)
Conn Smythe (1958)
Edward M. Snider (1988)
Lord Stanley of Preston (1945)
James T. Sutherland (1947)
Anatoli V. Tarasov (1974)
Bill Torrey (1995)
Lloyd Turner (1958)
William Tutt (1978)
Carl Potter Voss (1974)
Fred C. Waghorn (1961)
Arthur Wirtz (1971)
Bill Wirtz (1976)
John A. Ziegler, Jr. (1987)

Referees/Linesmen

Neil Armstrong (1991)
John Ashley (1981)
William L. Chadwick (1964)
John D'Amico (1993)
Chaucer Elliott (1961)
George Hayes (1988)
Robert W. Hewitson (1963)

Fred J. (Mickey) Ion (1961)
Matt Pavelich (1987)
Mike Rodden (1962)
J. Cooper Smeaton (1961)
Roy (Red) Storey (1967)
Frank Udvari (1973)
Andy Van Hellemond (1999)

Tennis

Roger Federer won
three Grand Slam
events in 2006

Moving Out, Moving On Up

In 2006, tennis bid farewell to one legend, Andre Agassi,
while it watched another, Roger Federer, dominate the sport

BY MARK BECHTEL

HE LEFT THE COURT—AND the game—with a creaky old back and a lifetime of memories. As Andre Agassi exited Arthur Ashe Stadium for the final time after falling to Benjamin Becker 7-5, 6-7, 6-4, 7-5, in the third round of the U.S. Open, tears streamed down his cheeks and the fans stood saluting him and showing their appreciation.

There would be no fairy tale ending—the indomitable Roger Federer would go on to win his third consecutive Open and third Grand Slam of the year—but make no mistake Agassi was the people's champion of the 2006 U.S. Open. His 36-year-old body had finally failed him, but during his three matches Agassi showed flashes of the player who was once ranked No. 1 in the world. Three days earlier, he outlasted Marcos Baghdatis in an epic five-set match, but he couldn't handle the 25-year-old Becker (no relation to Boris), who had to win three qualifying matches just to make it to the Open.

Once the best returner of serve in the world, Agassi was a step slow against Becker, who landed 27 aces with his 140-mph serve. Entering the tournament, Agassi knew the end was near, and with his back requiring cortisone shots in between matches he wondered how long he could continue. When Agassi was asked why he didn't retire after the victory over Baghdatis, he turned serious and said he didn't come to the Open to quit. If he wanted to quit, he said, he would have done so years ago.

During his final match, the crowd tried to will Agassi to every point and booed his opponent when he started dinking in drop shots that Agassi couldn't run down. But Agassi just didn't have enough left and just like that it was over. After match point, he sat down in his chair by the net, looked up and saw the crowd cheering and chanting his name and just lost it. Crying uncontrollably, Agassi tried to compose himself but then enjoyed the moment.

Finally, he addressed the crowd, his voice cracking with emotion: "The scoreboard said I lost today, but what the scoreboard doesn't say is what it is I have found. And over the last 21 years, I have found loyalty. You have pulled for me on the court and also in life. I've found inspiration. You have willed me to succeed sometimes even in my lowest moments. And I've found generosity. You have given me your shoulders to stand on to reach for my dreams, dreams I could have never reached without you.

"Over the last 21 years, I have found you. And I will take you and the memory of you with me for the rest of my life. Thank you."

When he reached the locker room, Agassi's fellow players thanked him with a standing ovation. "That is the ultimate compliment," said Agassi.

Agassi went from a brash 16-year-old to a rebel early in his career (remember those "Image is Everything" commercials?) to one of the game's most thoughtful and well-respected players. Agassi won 60 tournaments, more than $30 million in prize money and was one of only five men in history to win all four major championships. And even though his last match as a professional ended in a loss, the experience—and outpouring of support—is something Agassi will cherish forever. "That was the greatest memory I've ever had," Agassi said after the Becker loss, "memories I'll keep with me forever."

Federer is quickly creating many memories—and nightmares—for opponents with his dominant play, unflappable demeanor and the ease with which he stands above his peers. Simply put, Federer is the most complete, most consistent player in history. To get past Federer, opponents have to play their very best because he simply does not make many mistakes. In 2006, Federer played in all four Grand Slam finals, winning three to give him nine career Slams—well within reach of Pete Sampras' record 14 titles.

The one chink in Federer's armor is dynamic Spaniard Rafael Nadal, who again

Agassi, winner of eight career Grand Slam tournaments, bid a tearful adieu to tennis fans in his final U.S. Open in 2006.

beat Federer to win the French Open, his fifth straight victory over Federer on clay. But Federer came right back to beat Nadal in the final at Wimbledon and made an emphatic statement that when he's on, everybody else is playing for second.

For years, golf fans have said the same thing about Tiger Woods, and Federer and Woods met for the first time just before the U.S. Open final. Woods was a guest in Federer's box for his match against resurgent American Andy Roddick and watched with awe as Federer did the very thing that Tiger does on Sundays during majors: turn it up and leave the competition in the dust.

After losing the first set Roddick clawed back to win the third, 6-4, and had the momentum going in the fourth. Roddick was taking chances, hitting winners, blasting serves. But then Federer gathered himself and was prepared to go five sets if need be.

"I was actually feeling quite calm," Federer said. "I knew if this match turns, I guess I'm going to go five. And I had no problem doing that. It's the feeling of belief: I'm ready. Years ago I would think, 'Oh, no: Five. That's a disaster.' But I was not nervous. He needed the set more than I did."

Credit: SIMON BRUTY/SPORTS ILLUSTRATED

met Henin-Hardenne. Mauresmo played brilliantly in the match and was looking forward to walking off triumphantly when just four games from defeat Henin-Hardenne walked off the court after complaining of an upset stomach, denying Mauresmo of her moment.

Known for her often unsportsmanlike gamesmanship, Henin-Hardenne was widely criticized for the move and it in effect ended her friendship with Mauresmo. Adding to the drama, Henin-Hardenne went on to win the French for the second straight time (her fifth major) before meeting Mauresmo in the final at Wimbledon. There was no love lost.

"I had a lot of respect for the champion she is and all that's she's achieved, but I don't feel [Henin-Hardenne's withdrawal at the Australian Open] is a champion's behavior."

At the All-England Club, Mauresmo proved she was a champion once and for all and this time she got to celebrate the victory in tennis' holiest cathedral. After winning match point, she dropped to her knees and began to cry. "That's why you play," she said. "That's why you practice: because you dream of that moment. It's tough to put into words the relief, the joy. Because when you think about it, when you look back, it's this you're going to remember: this moment. And this moment is amazing."

Blond bombshell Maria Sharapova had her own amazing moment in New York, winning the U.S. Open—her second Grand Slam—and proving again that she had the game to go along with her looks. But in the end, the year will be remembered for Agassi and Federer. As one champion rode off into retirement, another was enjoying the glory days of his prime, taking one step closer to becoming the best player in history.

Federer composed himself and wore Roddick down with precision strokes and sucked all the wind out of his opponent by winning the third set, 7-5, then breezing 6-1 in the fourth to close out the match. At one point when Federer was making his move, Woods turned and said, "He's just gone to another level."

After the match, Federer and Woods discussed the third set over a beer in the locker room. Federer talked to Tiger about, "how I felt I was not going to miss a shot anymore and everything Andy tried I knew I had an answer for. And Tiger knew exactly what I was talking about. He looked me in the eye and I thought, 'Okay, I know what you're talking about too.' It was a very strong moment for me."

Though lacking a dominant player like Federer, there were plenty of strong moments on the women's side thanks, in part, to a brewing rivalry between Amelie Mauresmo and Justine Henin-Hardenne. Good friends for many years, the two often hung out together on the road, but when they met in the Australian Open final the relationship quickly went south.

Eager to shed her reputation for tightening up in big matches, Mauresmo blazed to the final at the Australian Open, where she

FOR THE RECORD • 2006

Australian Open

Men's Singles

	Winner	Runner-up	Score
Quarterfinals	Roger Federer	Nikolay Davydenko	6-4, 3-6, 7-6 (9-7), 7-6 (7-5)
	Nicolas Kiefer	Sebastien Grosjean	6-3, 0-6, 6-4, 6-7 (1-7), 8-6
	David Nalbandian	Fabrice Santoro	7-5, 6-0, 6-0
	Marcos Baghdatis	Ivan Ljubicic	6-4, 6-2, 4-6, 3-6, 6-3
Semifinals	Roger Federer	Nathan Kiefer	6-3, 5-7, 6-0, 6-2
	Marcos Baghdatis	David Nalbandian	3-6, 5-7, 6-3, 6-4, 6-4
Final	Roger Federer	Marcos Baghdatis	5-7, 7-5, 6-0, 6-2

Women's Singles

	Winner	Runner-up	Score
Quarterfinals	Justine Henin-Hardenne	Lindsay Davenport	2-6, 6-2, 6-3
	Maria Sharapova	Nadia Petrova	7-6 (8-6), 6-4
	Amelie Mauresmo	Patty Schnyder	6-3, 6-0
	Kim Clijsters	Martina Hingis	6-3, 2-6, 6-4
Semifinals	Justine Henin-Hardenne	Maria Sharapova	4-6, 6-1, 6-4
	Amelie Mauresmo	Kim Clijsters	5-7, 6-2, 3-2, ret.
Final	Amelie Mauresmo	Justine Henin-Hardenne	6-1, 2-0, ret.

Doubles

	Winner	Runner-up	Score
Men's Final	Bob Bryan/ Mike Bryan	Leander Paes/ Martin Damm	4-6, 6-3, 6-4
Women's Final	Jie Zheng/ Zi Yan	Lisa Raymond/ Samantha Stosur	2-6, 7-6 (9-7), 6-3
Mixed Final	Mahesh Bhupathi/ Martina Hingis	Elena Likhovtseva/ Daniel Nestor	6-3, 6-3

French Open

Men's Singles

	Winner	Runner-up	Score
Quarterfinals	Roger Federer	Mario Ancic	6-4, 6-3, 6-4
	David Nalbandian	Nikolay Davydenko	6-3, 6-3, 2-6, 6-4
	Ivan Ljubici	Julien Benneteau	6-2, 6-2, 6-3
	Rafael Nadal	Novak Djokovic	6-4, 6-4, ret.
Semifinals	Roger Federer	David Nalbandian	3-6, 6-4, 5-2, ret.
	Rafael Nadal	Ivan Ljubici	6-4, 6-2, 7-6 (9-7)
Final	Rafael Nadal	Roger Federer	1-6, 6-1, 6-4, 7-6 (7-4)

Women's Singles

	Winner	Runner-up	Score
Quarterfinals	Nicole Vaidisova	Venus Williams	6-7 (5-7), 6-1, 6-3
	Svetlana Kuznetsova	Dinara Safina	7-6 (7-5),6-0
	Justine Henin-Hardenne	Anna-Lena Groenefeld	7-5, 6-2
	Kim Clijsters	Martina Hingis	7-6 (7-5), 6-1
Semifinals	Svetlana Kuznetsova	Nicole Vaidisova	5-7, 7-6 (7-5), 6-2
	Justine Henin-Hardenne	Kim Clijsters	6-3, 6-2
Final	Justine Henin-Hardenne	Svetlana Kuznetsova	6-4, 6-4

Doubles

	Winner	Runner-Up	Score
Men's Final	Max Mirnyi/ Jonas Bjorkman	Bob Bryan/ Mike Bryan	6-7 (5-7), 6-4, 7-5
Women's Final	Lisa Raymond/ Samantha Stosur	Daniela Hantuchova/ Ai Sugiyama	6-3, 6-2
Mixed Final	Katarina Srebotnik/ Nenad Zimonjic	Elena Likhovtseva/ Daniel Nestor	6-3, 6-4

Wimbledon

Men's Singles

	Winner	Runner-Up	Score
Quarterfinals	Roger Federer	Mario Ancic	6-4, 6-4, 6-4
	Jonas Bjorkman	Radek Stepanek	7-6 (7-3), 4-6, 6-7 (5-7), 7-6 (9-7), 6-4
	Lleyton Hewitt	Marcos Baghdatis	6-1, 5-7, 7-6(7-5), 6-2
	Rafael Nadal	Jarkko Nieminen	6-3, 6-4, 6-4
Semifinals	Roger Federer	Jonas Bjorkman	6-4, 6-0, 6-2
	Rafael Nadal	Marcos Baghdatis	6-1, 1-7-5, 6-3
Final	Roger Federer	Rafael Nadal	6-0, 7-6 (7-5), 6-7 (2-7), 6-3

Women's Singles

	Winner	Runner-Up	Score
Quarterfinals	Amelie Mauresmo	Anastasia Myskina	6-1, 3-6, 6-3
	Maria Sharapova	Elena Dementieva	6-1, 6-4
	Justine Henin-Hardenne	Severine Bremond	6-4, 6-4
	Kim Clijsters	Na Li	6-4, 7-5
Semifinals	Amelie Mauresmo	Maria Sharapova	6-3, 3-6, 6-2
	Justine Henin-Hardenne	Kim Clijsters	6-4, 7-6 (7-4)
Final	Amelie Mauresmo	Justine Henin-Hardenne	2-6, 6-3, 6-4

Doubles

	Winner	Runner-Up	Score
Men's Final	Bob Bryan/ Mike Bryan	Fabrice Santoro/ Nenad Zimonjic	6-3, 4-6, 6-4, 6-2
Women's Final	Virginia Ruano Pascual/ Paola Suarez	Zi Yan/ Jie Zheng	6-3, 3-6, 6-2
Mixed Final	Vera Zvonareva/ Andy Ram	Venus Williams/ Bob Bryan	6-3, 6-2

U.S. Open

Men's Singles

	Winner	Runner-Up	Score
Quarterfinals	Roger Federer	James Blake	7-6 (9-7), 6-0, 6-7 (9-11), 6-4
	Nikolay Davydenko	Tommy Haas	4-6, 6-7 (3-7), 6-3, 6-4, 6-4
	Andy Roddick	Lleyton Hewitt	6-3, 7-5, 6-4
	Rafael Nadal	Mikhail Youzhny	6-3, 5-7, 7-6 (7-5), 6-1
Semifinals	Roger Federer	Nikolay Davydenko	6-1, 7-5, 6-4
	Andy Roddick	Mikhail Youzhny	6-7 (5-7), 6-0, 7-6 (7-3), 6-3
Final	Roger Federer	Andy Roddick	6-2, 4-6, 7-5, 6-1

Women's Singles

	Winner	Runner-Up	Score
Quarterfinals	Amelie Mauresmo	Dinara Safina	6-2, 6-3
	Maria Sharapova	Tatiana Golovin	7-6 (7-4), 7-6
	Jelena Jankovic	Elena Dementieva	6-2, 6-1
	Justine Henin-Hardenne	Lindsay Davenport	6-4, 6-4
Semifinals	Maria Sharapova	Amelie Mauresmo	6-0, 6-6, 6-0
	Justine Henin-Hardenne	Jelena Jankovic	4-6, 6-4, 6-0
Final	Maria Sharapova	Justine Henin-Hardenne	6-4, 6-4

Doubles

	Winner	Runner-Up	Score
Men's Final	Martin Damm Leander Paes	Max Mirnyi/ Jonas Bjorkman	6-7 (5-7), 6-4, 6-3
Women's Final	Nathalie Dechy/ Vera Zvonareva	Dinara Safina/ Katarina Srebotnik	7-6, 7-5
Mixed Final	Martina Navratilova/ Bob Bryan	Kveta Peschke/ Martin Damm	6-2, 6-3

Major Tournament Results

Men's Tour (late 2005 through Sept. 20, 2006)

Date	Tournament	Site	Singles Winner	Surface	Prize Money ($)
Oct 10	Kremlin Cup	Moscow, Russia	Igor Andreev Soderling	Indoor Carpet	142,000
Oct 17	Madrid Masters	Madrid, Spain	Rafael Nadal	Outdoor Hard	450,000
Oct 24	Swiss Indoor	Basel, Switzerland	Fernando Gonzalez	Indoor Carpet	145,000
Oct 24	Lyon Grand Prix	Lyon, France	Andy Roddick	Indoor Carpet	115,000
Oct 24	St. Petersburg Open	St. Petersburg, Russia	Thomas Johansson	Indoor Carpet	142,000
Nov 13	Paris Masters	Paris, France	Tomas Berdych	Indoor Carpet	447,000
Nov 20	China Masters	Shanghai, China	David Nalbandian	Indoor Hard	1,400,000
Jan 3	Qatar Open	Doha, Qatar	Roger Federer	Outdoor Hard	142,000
Jan 16	Australian Open	Melbourne	Roger Federer	Outdoor Hard	922,560
Feb 13	Marseille Open	Marseille, France	Arnaud Clement	Indoor Hard	85,300
Feb 20	ABM/Amro	Rotterdam, Netherlands	Radek Stepanek	Indoor Hard	174,000
Feb 27	Dubai Open	Dubai, U.A.E.	Rafael Nadal	Outdoor Hard	187,500
Mar 6	Pacific Life Open	Indian Wells, California	Roger Federer	Outdoor Hard	455,000
Mar 20	Nasdaq 100 Open	Miami, Fla.	Roger Federer	Outdoor Hard	533,350
Apr 17	Monte Carlo Masters	Monte Carlo, Monaco	Rafael Nadal	Outdoor Clay	418,778
Apr 24	Open SEAT Godó	Barcelona, Spain	Rafael Nadal	Outdoor Clay	164,000
May 1	Estoril Open	Estoril, Portugal	David Nalbandian	Outdoor Clay	95,500
May 1	BMW Open	Munich, Germany	Olivier Rochus	Outdoor Clay	56,100
May 15	Hamburg Masters	Hamburg, Germany	Tommy Robredo	Outdoor Clay	340,000
May 28	French Open	Paris	Rafael Nadal	Outdoor Clay	1,180,000
June 12	Gerry Weber Open	Halle, Germany	Roger Federer	Outdoor Grass	120,000
June 19	Ordina Open	Hertog'bosch, Netherlands	Mario Ancic	Outdoor Grass	55,319
June 26	Wimbledon	Wimbledon, England	Roger Federer	Outdoor Grass	1,212,244
July 10	Allianz Suisse Open	Gstaad, Switzerland	Richard Gasquet	Outdoor Clay	74,200
July 17	Dutch Open	Amersfoort, Netherlands	Novak Djokovic	Outdoor Clay	56,000
July 17	Mercedes Cup	Stuttgart, Germany	David Ferrer	Outdoor Clay	127,000
July 17	RCA Championship	Indianapolis, Indiana	James Blake	Outdoor Hard	74,250
July 31	Generali Open	Kitzbuhel, Austria	Agustin Calleri	Outdoor Clay	110,000
Aug 7	Legg Mason Classic	Wash., D.C.	Arnaud Clement	Outdoor Hard	74,250
Aug 7	Rogers Cup	Toronto, Canada	Roger Federer	Outdoor Hard	95,500
Aug 14	Western & Southern	Cincinnati	Andy Roddick	Outdoor Hard	400,000
Aug 28	U.S. Open	New York City	Roger Federer	Outdoor Hard	1,200,000
Sept 11	China Open	Beijing, China	Marcos Baghdatis	Outdoor Hard	500,000

Women's Tour (Late 2005 through September 20, 2006)

Date	Tournament	Site	Winner	Runner-Up	Score
Sept 22	Sparkassen Cup	Leipzig, Germany	Anastasia Myskina	Justine Henin-Hardenne	3–6, 6–3, 6–3
Sept 29	Ladies Kremlin Cup	Moscow, Russia	Anastasia Myskina	Amelie Mauresmo	6–2, 6–4
Sept 29	Japan Open	Tokyo, Japan	Maria Sharapova	Aniko Kapros	2–6, 6–2, 7–6 (7-5)
Oct 13	Swisscom Challenge	Zurich, Switzerland	Justine Henin-Hardenne	Jelena Dokic	6–0, 6–4
Oct 20	Generali Ladies Open	Linz, Austria	Ai Sugiyama	Nadia Petrova	7–5, 6–4
Nov 3	Sanex Championships	Los Angeles	Kim Clijsters	Amelie Mauresmo	6–2, 6–0
Jan 8	Medibank Int'l	Sydney, Australia	Luci Safarova	Flavia Pennetta	6-3, 6-4
Jan 16	Australian Open	Melbourne	Marion Bartoli	Vera Zvonareva	6-2, 6-2
Jan 30	Pan Pacific Open	Tokyo, Japan	Elena Dementieva	Martina Hingis	6-2, 6-0
Feb 27	Qatar Open	Doha, Qatar	Nadia Petrova	Amelie Mauresmo	6-3, 7-5
Mar 6	Pacific Life Open	Indian Wells, California	Maria Sharapova	Elena Dementieva	6-1, 6-2
Mar 20	Nasdaq 100 Open	Key Biscayne, Florida	Svetlana Kuznetsova	Maria Sharapova	6-4, 6-3
Apr 3	Bausch & Lomb Championships	Amelia Island, Florida	Nadia Petrova	Francesca Schiavone	6-4, 6-4
Apr 10	Family Circle Cup	Charleston, South Carolina	Nadia Petrova	Patty Schnyder	6-3, 4-6, 6-1
May 1	J&S Cup	Warsaw, Poland	Kim Clijsters	Svetlana Kuznetsova	7-5, 6-2
May 8	German Open	Berlin	Nadia Petrova	Justine Henin-Hardenne	4-6, 6-4, 7-5
May 15	Italia Masters	Rome, Italy	Martina Hingis	Dinara Safina	6-2, 7-5
May 22	Int'l de Strasbourg	Strasbourg, France	Nicole Vaidisova	Shuai Peng	7-6 (9-7), 6-3
May 28	French Open	Paris	Justine Henin-Hardenne	Svetlana Kuznetsova	6-4, 6-4
June 19	Hastings Direct Int'l Championships	Eastbourne, England	Justine Henin-Hardenne	Anastasia Myskina	4-6, 6-1, 7-6 (7-5)
Jun 26	Wimbledon	Wimbledon, England	Amelie Mauresmo	Justine Henin-Hardenne	2-6, 6-3, 6-4
July 24	Bank of the West	Stanford, Calif.	Kim Clijsters	Patty Schnyder	6-4, 6-2
July 31	Acura Classic	San Diego, California	Maria Sharapova	Kim Clijsters	7-5, 7-5
Aug 7	JP Morgan Chase Open	Carson, California	Elena Dementieva	Jelena Jankovic	6-3, 4-6, 6-4
Aug 14	Rogers Cup	Toronto, Canada	Ana Ivanovic	Martina Hingis	6-2, 6-3
Aug 20	Pilot Pen Int'l	New Haven, Connecticut	Justine Henin-Hardenne	Lindsay Davenport	6-0, 6-1, ret.
Aug 28	U.S. Open	New York City	Maria Sharapova	Justine Henin-Hardenne	6-4, 6-4
Sept 11	Wismilak International	Bali, Indonesia	Svetlana Kuznetsova	Marion Bartoli	7-5, 6-2

2005 Singles Leaders

Men

Rank	Player	Country	Points	Events
1.	Roger Federer	SUI	6725	19
2.	Rafael Nadal	ESP	4765	24
3.	Andy Roddick	USA	3085	20
4.	Lleyton Hewitt	AUS	2490	17
5.	Nikolay Davydenko	RUS	2390	30
6.	David Nalbandian	ARG	2370	21
7.	Andre Agassi	USA	2275	17
8.	Guillermo Coria	ARG	2190	22
9.	Ivan Ljubicic	CRO	2180	25
10.	Gaston Gaudio	ARG	2150	25

Note: Compiled by the ATP Tour, through the 2005 season.

Women

Rank	Player	Country	Points
1.	Lindsay Davenport	USA	5169
2.	Maria Sharapova	RUS	4892
3.	Amelie Mauresmo	FRA	4808
4.	Serena Williams	USA	4174
5.	Elena Dementieva	RUS	3852
6.	Anastasia Myskina	RUS	3455
7.	Svetlana Kuznetsova	RUS	3128
8.	Alicia Molik	AUS	2585
9.	Venus Williams	USA	2369
10.	Vera Zvonareva	RUS	2179

Note: Compiled by the WTA, through the 2005 season.

National Team Competition

2005 Davis Cup World Group Final
Croatia def. Slovak Republic 3–2, Dec 2-4, 2005, in Bratislava, Slovak Republic
Ivan Ljubicic (CRO) def. Karol Kucera (SVK), 6-3, 6-4, 6-3
Dominik Hrbaty (SVK) def. Mario Ancic (CRO), 7-6 (7-4), 6-3, 6-7 (4-7), 6-4
Mario Ancic/Ivan Ljubicic (CRO) def. Dominik Hrbaty/Michal Mertinak (SVK), 7-6 (7-5), 6-3, 6-7 (7-5)
Dominik Hrbaty (SVK) def. Ivan Ljubicic (CRO), 4-6, 6-3, 6-4, 3-6, 6-4
Mario Ancic (CRO) def. Michal Mertinak (SVK), 7-6 (7-1), 6-3, 6-4

2006 Davis Cup World Group Tournament

FIRST ROUND
Croatia def. Austria 3-2
Argentina def. Sweden 5-0
Belarus def. Spain 4-1
Australia def. Switzerland 3-2
France def. Germany 3-2
Russia def. Netherlands 5-0
USA def. Romania 4-1
Chile def. Slovak Republic 4-1

QUARTERFINAL ROUND
Argentina def. Croatia 3-2
Australia def. Belarus 5-0
Russia def. France 4-1
USA def. Chile 3-2

SEMIFINALS

Argentina def. Australia 5-0
David Nalbandian (ARG) def. Mark Philippoussis (AUS) 6-4, 6-3, 6-3
Jose Acasuso (ARG) def. Lleyton Hewitt (AUS) 1-6, 6-4, 4-6, 6-2, 6-1
A. Calleri/D. Nalbandian (ARG) def. W. Arthurs/P. Hanley (AUS) 6-4, 6-4, 7-5
Agustin Calleri (ARG) def. Paul Hanley (AUS) 6-0, 6-3
Juan Ignacio Chela (ARG) def. Wayne Arthurs (AUS) 0-0 (retired)

Russia def. USA 3-2
Marat Safin (RUS) def. Andy Roddick (USA) 6-4, 6-3, 7-6 (7-5)
Mikhail Youzhny (RUS) def. James Blake (USA) 7-5, 1-6, 6-1, 7-5
B. Bryan/M. Bryan (USA) def. D. Tursunov/M. Youzhny (RUS) 6-3, 6-4, 6-2
Dmitry Tursunov (RUS) def. Andy Roddick (USA) 6-3, 6-4, 5-7, 3-6, 7-6 (17-15)
James Blake (USA) def. Marat Safin (RUS) 7-5, 7-6 (7-4)

FINAL: Russia versus Argentina to be held Dec. 1-3, 2006.

2006 Federation Cup World Group Tournament

QUARTERFINALS
Italy def. France 4-1
Spain def. Austria 5-0
United States def. Germany 3-2
Belgium def. Russia 3-2

SEMIFINALS
Italy def. Spain 3-1
Belgium def. United States 4-1

FINALS
Italy def. Belgium 3-2

Note: Finals were held Sept. 16-17, 2006, in Charleroi, Belgium.

FOR THE RECORD • Year by Year

MEN

Australian Championships

Year	Winner	Finalist	Score
1905	Rodney Heath	A. H. Curtis	4–6, 6–3, 6–4, 6–4
1906	Tony Wilding	H. A. Parker	6–0, 6–4, 6–4
1907	Horace M. Rice	H. A. Parker	6–3, 6–4, 6–4
1908	Fred Alexander	A. W. Dunlop	3–6, 3–6, 6–0, 6–2, 6–3
1909	Tony Wilding	E. F. Parker	6–1, 7–5, 6–2
1910	Rodney Heath	Horace M. Rice	6–4, 6–3, 6–2
1911	Norman Brookes	Horace M. Rice	6–1, 6–2, 6–3
1912	J. Cecil Parke	A. E. Beamish	3–6, 6–3, 1–6, 6–1, 7–5
1913	E. F. Parker	H. A. Parker	2–6, 6–1, 6–2, 6–3
1914	Pat O'Hara Wood	G. L. Patterson	6–4, 6–3, 5–7, 6–1
1915	Francis G. Lowe	Horace M. Rice	4–6, 6–1, 6–1, 6–4
1916–18	No tournament		
1919	A. R. F. Kingscote	E. O. Pockley	6–4, 6–0, 6–3
1920	Pat O'Hara Wood	Ron Thomas	6–3, 4–6, 6–8, 6–1, 6–3
1921	Rhys H. Gemmell	A. Hedeman	7–5, 6–1, 6–4
1922	Pat O'Hara Wood	Gerald Patterson	6–0, 3–6, 3–6, 6–3, 6–2
1923	Pat O'Hara Wood	C. B. St John	6–1, 6–1, 6–3
1924	James Anderson	R. E. Schlesinger	6–3, 6–4, 3–6, 5–7, 6–3
1925	James Anderson	Gerald Patterson	11–9, 2–6, 6–2, 6–3
1926	John Hawkes	J. Willard	6–1, 6–3, 6–1
1927	Gerald Patterson	John Hawkes	3–6, 6–4, 3–6, 18–16, 6–3
1928	Jean Borotra	R. O. Cummings	6–4, 6–1, 4–6, 5–7, 6–3
1929	John C. Gregory	R. E. Schlesinger	6–2, 6–2, 5–7, 7–5
1930	Gar Moon	Harry C. Hopman	6–3, 6–1, 6–3
1931	Jack Crawford	Harry C. Hopman	6–4, 6–2, 2–6, 6–1
1932	Jack Crawford	Harry C. Hopman	4–6, 6–3, 3–6, 6–3, 6–1
1933	Jack Crawford	Keith Gledhill	2–6, 7–5, 6–3, 6–2
1934	Fred Perry	Jack Crawford	6–3, 7–5, 6–1
1935	Jack Crawford	Fred Perry	2–6, 6–4, 6–4, 6–4
1936	Adrian Quist	Jack Crawford	6–2, 6–3, 4–6, 3–6, 9–7
1937	Vivian B. McGrath	John Bromwich	6–3, 1–6, 6–0, 2–6, 6–1
1938	Don Budge	John Bromwich	6–4, 6–2, 6–1
1939	John Bromwich	Adrian Quist	6–4, 6–1, 6–3
1940	Adrian Quist	Jack Crawford	6–3, 6–1, 6–2
1941–45	No tournament		
1946	John Bromwich	Dinny Pails	5–7, 6–3, 7–5, 3–6, 6–2
1947	Dinny Pails	John Bromwich	4–6, 6–4, 3–6, 7–5, 8–6
1948	Adrian Quist	John Bromwich	6–4, 3–6, 6–3, 2–6, 6–3
1949	Frank Sedgman	Ken McGregor	6–3, 6–3, 6–2
1950	Frank Sedgman	Ken McGregor	6–3, 6–4, 4–6, 6–1
1951	Richard Savitt	Ken McGregor	6–3, 2–6, 6–3, 6–1
1952	Ken McGregor	Frank Sedgman	7–5, 12–10, 2–6, 6–2
1953	Ken Rosewall	Mervyn Rose	6–0, 6–3, 6–4
1954	Mervyn Rose	Rex Hartwig	6–2, 0–6, 6–4, 6–2
1955	Ken Rosewall	Lew Hoad	9–7, 6–4, 6–4
1956	Lew Hoad	Ken Rosewall	6–4, 3–6, 6–4, 7–5
1957	Ashley Cooper	Neale Fraser	6–3, 9–11, 6–4, 6–2
1958	Ashley Cooper	Mal Anderson	7–5, 6–3, 6–4
1959	Alex Olmedo	Neale Fraser	6–1, 6–2, 3–6, 6–3
1960	Rod Laver	Neale Fraser	5–7, 3–6, 6–3, 8–6, 8–6
1961	Roy Emerson	Rod Laver	1–6, 6–3, 7–5, 6–4
1962	Rod Laver	Roy Emerson	8–6, 0–6, 6–4, 6–4
1963	Roy Emerson	Ken Fletcher	6–3, 6–3, 6–1
1964	Roy Emerson	Fred Stolle	6–3, 6–4, 6–2
1965	Roy Emerson	Fred Stolle	7–9, 2–6, 6–4, 7–5, 6–1
1966	Roy Emerson	Arthur Ashe	6–4, 6–8, 6–2, 6–3
1967	Roy Emerson	Arthur Ashe	6–4, 6–1, 6–1
1968	Bill Bowrey	Juan Gisbert	7–5, 2–6, 9–7, 6–4
1969*	Rod Laver	Andres Gimeno	6–3, 6–4, 7–5

*Became Open (amateur and professional) in 1969.

MEN *(Cont.)*
Australian Championships *(Cont.)*

Year	Winner	Finalist	Score
1970	Arthur Ashe	Dick Crealy	6–4, 9–7, 6–2
1971	Ken Rosewall	Arthur Ashe	6–1, 7–5, 6–3
1972	Ken Rosewall	Mal Anderson	7–6, 6–3, 7–5
1973	John Newcombe	Onny Parun	6–3, 6–7, 7–5, 6–1
1974	Jimmy Connors	Phil Dent	7–6, 6–4, 4–6, 6–3
1975	John Newcombe	Jimmy Connors	7–5, 3–6, 6–4, 7–5
1976	Mark Edmondson	John Newcombe	6–7, 6–3, 7–6, 6–1
1977 (Jan)	Roscoe Tanner	Guillermo Vilas	6–3, 6–3, 6–3
1977 (Dec)	Vitas Gerulaitis	John Lloyd	6–3, 7–6, 5–7, 3–6, 6–2
1978	Guillermo Vilas	John Marks	6–4, 6–4, 3–6, 6–3
1979	Guillermo Vilas	John Sadri	7–6, 6–3, 6–2
1980	Brian Teacher	Kim Warwick	7–5, 7–6, 6–3
1981	Johan Kriek	Steve Denton	6–2, 7–6, 6–7, 6–4
1982	Johan Kriek	Steve Denton	6–3, 6–3, 6–2
1983	Mats Wilander	Ivan Lendl	6–1, 6–4, 6–4
1984	Mats Wilander	Kevin Curren	6–7, 6–4, 7–6, 6–2
1985 (Dec)	Stefan Edberg	Mats Wilander	6–4, 6–3, 6–3
1987 (Jan)	Stefan Edberg	Pat Cash	6–3, 6–4, 3–6, 5–7, 6–3
1988	Mats Wilander	Pat Cash	6–3, 6–7, 3–6, 6–1, 8–6
1989	Ivan Lendl	Miloslav Mecir	6–2, 6–2, 6–2
1990	Ivan Lendl	Stefan Edberg	4–6, 7–6, 5–2, ret.
1991	Boris Becker	Ivan Lendl	1–6, 6–4, 6–4, 6–4
1992	Jim Courier	Stefan Edberg	6–3, 3–6, 6–4, 6–2
1993	Jim Courier	Stefan Edberg	6–2, 6–1, 2–6, 7–5
1994	Pete Sampras	Todd Martin	7–6, 6–4, 6–4
1995	Andre Agassi	Pete Sampras	4–6, 6–1, 7–6, 6–4
1996	Boris Becker	Michael Chang	6–2, 6–4, 2–6, 6–2
1997	Pete Sampras	Carlos Moya	6–2, 6–3, 6–3
1998	Petr Korda	Marcelo Ríos	6–2, 6–2, 6–2
1999	Yevgeny Kafelnikov	Thomas Enqvist	4–6, 6–0, 6–3, 7–6
2000	Andre Agassi	Yevgeny Kafelnikov	3–6, 6–3, 6–2, 6–4
2001	Andre Agassi	Arnaud Clement	6–4, 6–2, 6–2
2002	Thomas Johansson	Marat Safin	3–6, 6–4, 6–4, 7–6 (7-4)
2003	Andre Agassi	Rainer Schuettler	6–2, 6–2, 6–1
2004	Roger Federer	Marat Safin	7–6 (7-3), 6–4, 6–2
2005	Marat Safin	Lleyton Hewitt	1–6, 6–3, 6–4, 6–4
2006	Roger Federer	Marcos Baghdatis	5–7, 7–5, 6–0, 6–2

French Championships

Year	Winner	Finalist	Score
1925†	Rene Lacoste	Jean Borotra	7–5, 6–1, 6–4
1926	Henri Cochet	Rene Lacoste	6–2, 6–4, 6–3
1927	Rene Lacoste	Bill Tilden	6–4, 4–6, 5–7, 6–3, 11–9
1928	Henri Cochet	Rene Lacoste	5–7, 6–3, 6–1, 6–3
1929	Rene Lacoste	Jean Borotra	6–3, 2–6, 6–0, 2–6, 8–6
1930	Henri Cochet	Bill Tilden	3–6, 8–6, 6–3, 6–1
1931	Jean Borotra	Claude Boussus	2–6, 6–4, 7–5, 6–4
1932	Henri Cochet	Giorgio de Stefani	6–0, 6–4, 4–6, 6–3
1933	Jack Crawford	Henri Cochet	8–6, 6–1, 6–3
1934	Gottfried von Cramm	Jack Crawford	6–4, 7–9, 3–6, 7–5, 6–3
1935	Fred Perry	Gottfried von Cramm	6–3, 3–6, 6–1, 6–3
1936	Gottfried von Cramm	Fred Perry	6–0, 2–6, 6–2, 2–6, 6–0
1937	Henner Henkel	Henry Austin	6–1, 6–4, 6–3
1938	Don Budge	Roderick Menzel	6–3, 6–2, 6–4
1939	Don McNeill	Bobby Riggs	7–5, 6–0, 6–3
1940	No tournament		
1941‡	Bernard Destremau	n/a	n/a
1942‡	Bernard Destremau	n/a	n/a
1943‡	Yvon Petra	n/a	n/a
1944‡	Yvon Petra	n/a	n/a
1945‡	Yvon Petra	Bernard Destremau	7–5, 6–4, 6–2

†1925 was the first year that entries were accepted from all countries.
‡From 1941 to 1945 the event was called Tournoi de France and was closed to all foreigners.

MEN *(Cont.)*

French Championships *(Cont.)*

Year	Winner	Finalist	Score
1946	Marcel Bernard	Jaroslav Drobny	3–6, 2–6, 6–1, 6–4, 6–3
1947	Joseph Asboth	Eric Sturgess	8–6, 7–5, 6–4
1948	Frank Parker	Jaroslav Drobny	6–4, 7–5, 5–7, 8–6
1949	Frank Parker	Budge Patty	6–3, 1–6, 6–1, 6–4
1950	Budge Patty	Jaroslav Drobny	6–1, 6–2, 3–6, 5–7, 7–5
1951	Jaroslav Drobny	Eric Sturgess	6–3, 6–3, 6–3
1952	Jaroslav Drobny	Frank Sedgman	6–2, 6–0, 3–6, 6–4
1953	Ken Rosewall	Vic Seixas	6–3, 6–4, 1–6, 6–2
1954	Tony Trabert	Arthur Larsen	6–4, 7–5, 6–1
1955	Tony Trabert	Sven Davidson	2–6, 6–1, 6–4, 6–2
1956	Lew Hoad	Sven Davidson	6–4, 8–6, 6–3
1957	Sven Davidson	Herbie Flam	6–3, 6–4, 6–4
1958	Mervyn Rose	Luis Ayala	6–3, 6–4, 6–4
1959	Nicola Pietrangeli	Ian Vermaak	3–6, 6–3, 6–4, 6–1
1960	Nicola Pietrangeli	Luis Ayala	3–6, 6–3, 6–4, 4–6, 6–3
1961	Manuel Santana	Nicola Pietrangeli	4–6, 6–1, 3–6, 6–0, 6–2
1962	Rod Laver	Roy Emerson	3–6, 2–6, 6–3, 9–7, 6–2
1963	Roy Emerson	Pierre Darmon	3–6, 6–1, 6–4, 6–4
1964	Manuel Santana	Nicola Pietrangeli	6–3, 6–1, 4–6, 7–5
1965	Fred Stolle	Tony Roche	3–6, 6–0, 6–2, 6–3
1966	Tony Roche	Istvan Gulyas	6–1, 6–4, 7–5
1967	Roy Emerson	Tony Roche	6–1, 6–4, 2–6, 6–2
1968*	Ken Rosewall	Rod Laver	6–3, 6–1, 2–6, 6–2
1969	Rod Laver	Ken Rosewall	6–4, 6–3, 6–4
1970	Jan Kodes	Zeljko Franulovic	6–2, 6–4, 6–0
1971	Jan Kodes	Ilie Nastase	8–6, 6–2, 2–6, 7–5
1972	Andres Gimeno	Patrick Proisy	4–6, 6–3, 6–1, 6–1
1973	Ilie Nastase	Nikki Pilic	6–3, 6–3, 6–0
1974	Bjorn Borg	Manuel Orantes	6–7, 6–0, 6–1, 6–1
1975	Bjorn Borg	Guillermo Vilas	6–2, 6–3, 6–4
1976	Adriano Panatta	Harold Solomon	6–1, 6–4, 4–6, 7–6
1977	Guillermo Vilas	Brian Gottfried	6–0, 6–3, 6–0
1978	Bjorn Borg	Guillermo Vilas	6–1, 6–1, 6–3
1979	Bjorn Borg	Victor Pecci	6–3, 6–1, 6–7, 6–4
1980	Bjorn Borg	Vitas Gerulaitis	6–4, 6–1, 6–2
1981	Bjorn Borg	Ivan Lendl	6–1, 4–6, 6–2, 3–6, 6–1
1982	Mats Wilander	Guillermo Vilas	1–6, 7–6, 6–0, 6–4
1983	Yannick Noah	Mats Wilander	6–2, 7–5, 7–6
1984	Ivan Lendl	John McEnroe	3–6, 2–6, 6–4, 7–5, 7–5
1985	Mats Wilander	Ivan Lendl	3–6, 6–4, 6–2, 6–2
1986	Ivan Lendl	Mikael Pernfors	6–3, 6–2, 6–4
1987	Ivan Lendl	Mats Wilander	7–5, 6–2, 3–6, 7–6
1988	Mats Wilander	Henri Leconte	7–5, 6–2, 6–1
1989	Michael Chang	Stefan Edberg	6–1, 3–6, 4–6, 6–4, 6–2
1990	Andres Gomez	Andre Agassi	6–3, 2–6, 6–4, 6–4
1991	Jim Courier	Andre Agassi	3–6, 6–4, 2–6, 6–1, 6–4
1992	Jim Courier	Petr Korda	7–5, 6–2, 6–1
1993	Sergi Bruguera	Jim Courier	6–4, 2–6, 6–2, 3–6, 6–3
1994	Sergi Bruguera	Alberto Berasategui	6–3, 7–5, 2–6, 6–1
1995	Thomas Muster	Michael Chang	7–5, 6–2, 6–4
1996	Yevgeny Kafelnikov	Michael Stich	7–6, 7–5, 7–6
1997	Gustavo Kuerten	Sergi Bruguera	6–3, 6–4, 6–2
1998	Carlos Moya	Alex Corretja	6–3, 7–5, 6–3
1999	Andre Agassi	Andrei Medvedev	1–6, 2–6, 6–4, 6–3, 6–4
2000	Gustavo Kuerten	Magnus Norman	6–2, 6–3, 2–6, 7–6
2001	Gustavo Kuerten	Alex Corretja	6–7, 7–5, 6–2, 6–0
2002	Albert Costa	Juan Carlos Ferrero	6–1, 6–0, 4–6, 6–3
2003	Juan Carlos Ferrero	Martin Verkerk	6–1, 6–3, 6–2
2004	Gaston Gaudio	Guillermo Coria	8–6, 0–6, 3–6, 6–4, 6–1
2005	Rafael Nadal	Mariano Puerta	6–7, 6–3, 6–1, 7–5
2006	Rafael Nadal	Roger Federer	1–6, 6–1, 6–4, 7–6

*Became Open (amateur and professional) in 1968, but restricted to only contract professionals in 1972.

MEN *(Cont.)*

Wimbledon Championships

Year	Winner	Finalist	Score
1877	Spencer W. Gore	William C. Marshall	6–1, 6–2, 6–4
1878	P. Frank Hadow	Spencer W. Gore	7–5, 6–1, 9–7
1879	John T. Hartley	V. St Leger Gould	6–2, 6–4, 6–2
1880	John T. Hartley	Herbert F. Lawford	6–0, 6–2, 2–6, 6–3
1881	William Renshaw	John T. Hartley	6–0, 6–2, 6–1
1882	William Renshaw	Ernest Renshaw	6–1, 2–6, 4–6, 6–2, 6–2
1883	William Renshaw	Ernest Renshaw	2–6, 6–3, 6–3, 4–6, 6–3
1884	William Renshaw	Herbert F. Lawford	6–0, 6–4, 9–7
1885	William Renshaw	Herbert F. Lawford	7–5, 6–2, 4–6, 7–5
1886	William Renshaw	Herbert F. Lawford	6–0, 5–7, 6–3, 6–4
1887	Herbert F. Lawford	Ernest Renshaw	1–6, 6–3, 3–6, 6–4, 6–4
1888	Ernest Renshaw	Herbert F. Lawford	6–3, 7–5, 6–0
1889	William Renshaw	Ernest Renshaw	6–4, 6–1, 3–6, 6–0
1890	William J. Hamilton	William Renshaw	6–8, 6–2, 3–6, 6–1, 6–1
1891	Wilfred Baddeley	Joshua Pim	6–4, 1–6, 7–5, 6–0
1892	Wilfred Baddeley	Joshua Pim	4–6, 6–3, 6–3, 6–2
1893	Joshua Pim	Wilfred Baddeley	3–6, 6–1, 6–3, 6–2
1894	Joshua Pim	Wilfred Baddeley	10–8, 6–2, 8–6
1895	Wilfred Baddeley	Wilberforce V. Eaves	4–6, 2–6, 8–6, 6–2, 6–3
1896	Harold S. Mahoney	Wilfred Baddeley	6–2, 6–8, 5–7, 8–6, 6–3
1897	Reggie F. Doherty	Harold S. Mahoney	6–4, 6–4, 6–3
1898	Reggie F. Doherty	H. Laurie Doherty	6–3, 6–3, 2–6, 5–7, 6–1
1899	Reggie F. Doherty	Arthur W. Gore	1–6, 4–6, 6–2, 6–3, 6–3
1900	Reggie F. Doherty	Sidney H. Smith	6–8, 6–3, 6–1, 6–2
1901	Arthur W. Gore	Reggie F. Doherty	4–6, 7–5, 6–4, 6–4
1902	H. Laurie Doherty	Arthur W. Gore	6–4, 6–3, 3–6, 6–0
1903	H. Laurie Doherty	Frank L. Riseley	7–5, 6–3, 6–0
1904	H. Laurie Doherty	Frank L. Riseley	6–1, 7–5, 8–6
1905	H. Laurie Doherty	Norman E. Brookes	8–6, 6–2, 6–4
1906	H. Laurie Doherty	Frank L. Riseley	6–4, 4–6, 6–2, 6–3
1907	Norman E. Brookes	Arthur W. Gore	6–4, 6–2, 6–2
1908	Arthur W. Gore	H. Roper Barrett	6–3, 6–2, 4–6, 3–6, 6–4
1909	Arthur W. Gore	M. J. G. Ritchie	6–8, 1–6, 6–2, 6–2, 6–2
1910	Anthony F. Wilding	Arthur W. Gore	6–4, 7–5, 4–6, 6–2
1911	Anthony F. Wilding	H. Roper Barrett	6–4, 4–6, 2–6, 6–2, ret.
1912	Anthony F. Wilding	Arthur W. Gore	6–4, 6–4, 4–6, 6–4
1913	Anthony F. Wilding	Maurice E. McLoughlin	8–6, 6–3, 10–8
1914	Norman E. Brookes	Anthony F. Wilding	6–4, 6–4, 7–5
1915–18	No tournament		
1919	Gerald L. Patterson	Norman E. Brookes	6–3, 7–5, 6–2
1920	Bill Tilden	Gerald L. Patterson	2–6, 6–3, 6–2, 6–4
1921	Bill Tilden	Brian I. C. Norton	4–6, 2–6, 6–1, 6–0, 7–5
1922	Gerald L. Patterson	Randolph Lycett	6–3, 6–4, 6–2
1923	Bill Johnston	Francis T. Hunter	6–0, 6–3, 6–1
1924	Jean Borotra	Rene Lacoste	6–1, 3–6, 6–1, 3–6, 6–4
1925	Rene Lacoste	Jean Borotra	6–3, 6–3, 4–6, 8–6
1926	Jean Borotra	Howard Kinsey	8–6, 6–1, 6–3
1927	Henri Cochet	Jean Borotra	4–6, 4–6, 6–3, 6–4, 7–5
1928	Rene Lacoste	Henri Cochet	6–1, 4–6, 6–4, 6–2
1929	Henri Cochet	Jean Borotra	6–4, 6–3, 6–4
1930	Bill Tilden	Wilmer Allison	6–3, 9–7, 6–4
1931	Sidney B. Wood Jr	Francis X. Shields	walkover
1932	Ellsworth Vines	Henry Austin	6–4, 6–2, 6–0
1933	Jack Crawford	Ellsworth Vines	4–6, 11–9, 6–2, 2–6, 6–4
1934	Fred Perry	Jack Crawford	6–3, 6–0, 7–5
1935	Fred Perry	Gottfried von Cramm	6–2, 6–4, 6–4
1936	Fred Perry	Gottfried von Cramm	6–1, 6–1, 6–0
1937	Don Budge	Gottfried von Cramm	6–3, 6–4, 6–2
1938	Don Budge	Henry Austin	6–1, 6–0, 6–3
1939	Bobby Riggs	Elwood Cooke	2–6, 8–6, 3–6, 6–3, 6–2
1940–45	No tournament		
1946	Yvon Petra	Geoff E. Brown	6–2, 6–4, 6–7 (7–9), 5–7, 6–4
1947	Jack Kramer	Tom P. Brown	6–1, 6–3, 6–2
1948	Bob Falkenburg	John Bromwich	7–5, 0–6, 6–2, 3–6, 7–5
1949	Ted Schroeder	Jaroslav Drobny	3–6, 6–0, 6–3, 4–6, 6–4

Note: Prior to 1922 the tournament was run on a challenge-round system. The previous year's winner "stood out" of an All Comers event, which produced a challenger to play him for the title.

MEN *(Cont.)*

Wimbledon Championships *(Cont.)*

Year	Winner	Finalist	Score
1950	Budge Patty	Frank Sedgman	6–1, 6–7 (8–10), 6–2, 6–3
1951	Dick Savitt	Ken McGregor	6–4, 6–4, 6–4
1952	Frank Sedgman	Jaroslav Drobny	4–6, 6–3, 6–2, 6–3
1953	Vic Seixas	Kurt Nielsen	9–7, 6–3, 6–4
1954	Jaroslav Drobny	Ken Rosewall	13–11, 4–6, 6–2, 9–7
1955	Tony Trabert	Kurt Nielsen	6–3, 7–5, 6–1
1956	Lew Hoad	Ken Rosewall	6–2, 4–6, 7–5, 6–4
1957	Lew Hoad	Ashley Cooper	6–2, 6–1, 6–2
1958	Ashley Cooper	Neale Fraser	3–6, 6–3, 6–4, 13–11
1959	Alex Olmedo	Rod Laver	6–4, 6–3, 6–4
1960	Neale Fraser	Rod Laver	6–4, 3–6, 9–7, 7–5
1961	Rod Laver	Chuck McKinley	6–3, 6–1, 6–4
1962	Rod Laver	Martin Mulligan	6–2, 6–2, 6–1
1963	Chuck McKinley	Fred Stolle	9–7, 6–1, 6–4
1964	Roy Emerson	Fred Stolle	6–4, 12–10, 4–6, 6–3
1965	Roy Emerson	Fred Stolle	6–2, 6–4, 6–4
1966	Manuel Santana	Dennis Ralston	6–4, 11–9, 6–4
1967	John Newcombe	Wilhelm Bungert	6–3, 6–1, 6–1
1968*	Rod Laver	Tony Roche	6–3, 6–4, 6–2
1969	Rod Laver	John Newcombe	6–4, 5–7, 6–4, 6–4
1970	John Newcombe	Ken Rosewall	5–7, 6–3, 6–2, 3–6, 6–1
1971	John Newcombe	Stan Smith	6–3, 5–7, 2–6, 6–4, 6–4
1972	Stan Smith	Ilie Nastase	4–6, 6–3, 6–3, 4–6, 7–5
1973	Jan Kodes	Alex Metreveli	6–1, 9–8, 6–3
1974	Jimmy Connors	Ken Rosewall	6–1, 6–1, 6–4
1975	Arthur Ashe	Jimmy Connors	6–1, 6–1, 5–7, 6–4
1976	Bjorn Borg	Ilie Nastase	6–4, 6–2, 9–7
1977	Bjorn Borg	Jimmy Connors	3–6, 6–2, 6–1, 5–7, 6–4
1978	Bjorn Borg	Jimmy Connors	6–2, 6–2, 6–3
1979	Bjorn Borg	Roscoe Tanner	6–7, 6–1, 3–6, 6–3, 6–4
1980	Bjorn Borg	John McEnroe	1–6, 7–5, 6–3, 6–7, 8–6
1981	John McEnroe	Bjorn Borg	4–6, 7–6, 7–6, 6–4
1982	Jimmy Connors	John McEnroe	3–6, 6–3, 6–7, 7–6, 6–4
1983	John McEnroe	Chris Lewis	6–2, 6–2, 6–2
1984	John McEnroe	Jimmy Connors	6–1, 6–1, 6–2
1985	Boris Becker	Kevin Curren	6–3, 6–7, 7–6, 6–4
1986	Boris Becker	Ivan Lendl	6–4, 6–3, 7–5
1987	Pat Cash	Ivan Lendl	7–6, 6–2, 7–5
1988	Stefan Edberg	Boris Becker	4–6, 7–6, 6–4, 6–2
1989	Boris Becker	Stefan Edberg	6–0, 7–6, 6–4
1990	Stefan Edberg	Boris Becker	6–2, 6–2, 3–6, 3–6, 6–4
1991	Michael Stich	Boris Becker	6–4, 7–6, 6–4
1992	Andre Agassi	Goran Ivanisevic	6–7, 6–4, 6–4, 1–6, 6–4
1993	Pete Sampras	Jim Courier	7–6, 7–6, 3–6, 6–3
1994	Pete Sampras	Goran Ivanisevic	7–6, 7–6, 6–0
1995	Pete Sampras	Boris Becker	6–7, 6–2, 6–4, 6–2
1996	Richard Krajicek	MaliVai Washington	6–3, 6–4, 6–3
1997	Pete Sampras	Cedric Pioline	6–4, 6–2, 6–4
1998	Pete Sampras	Goran Ivanisevic	6–7, 7–6, 6–4, 3–6, 6–2
1999	Pete Sampras	Andre Agassi	6–3, 6–4, 7–5
2000	Pete Sampras	Patrick Rafter	6–7, 7–6, 6–4, 6–2
2001	Goran Ivanisevic	Patrick Rafter	6–3, 3–6, 6–3, 2–6, 7–6 (9–7)
2002	Lleyton Hewitt	David Nalbandian	6–1, 6–3, 6–2
2003	Roger Federer	Mark Philippoussis	7–6 (7-5), 6–2, 7–6 (7-3)
2004	Roger Federer	Andy Roddick	4–6, 7–5, 7–6 (7-3), 6–4
2005	Roger Federer	Andy Roddick	6-2, 7-6 (7-2), 6-4
2006	Roger Federer	Rafael Nadal	6-0, 7-6, (7-5), 6-7 (2-7), 6-3

*Became Open (amateur and professional) in 1968, but restricted to only contract professionals in 1972.

MEN *(Cont.)*

United States Championships

Year	Winner	Finalist	Score
1881	Richard D. Sears	W.E. Glyn	6–0, 6–3, 6–2
1882	Richard D. Sears	C.M. Clark	6–1, 6–4, 6–0
1883	Richard D. Sears	James Dwight	6–2, 6–0, 9–7
1884	Richard D. Sears	H.A. Taylor	6–0, 1–6, 6–0, 6–2
1885	Richard D. Sears	G.M. Brinley	6–3, 4–6, 6–0, 6–3
1886	Richard D. Sears	R.L. Beeckman	4–6, 6–1, 6–3, 6–4
1887	Richard D. Sears	H.W. Slocum Jr	6–1, 6–3, 6–2
1888†	H. W. Slocum Jr	H.A. Taylor	6–4, 6–1, 6–0
1889	H. W. Slocum Jr	Q.A. Shaw	6–3, 6–1, 4–6, 6–2
1890	Oliver S. Campbell	H.W. Slocum Jr	6–2, 4–6, 6–3, 6–1
1891	Oliver S. Campbell	Clarence Hobart	2–6, 7–5, 7–9, 6–1, 6–2
1892	Oliver S. Campbell	Frederick H. Hovey	7–5, 3–6, 6–3, 7–5
1893†	Robert D. Wrenn	Frederick H. Hovey	6–4, 3–6, 6–4, 6–4
1894	Robert D. Wrenn	M.F. Goodbody	6–8, 6–1, 6–4, 6–4
1895	Frederick H. Hovey	Robert D. Wrenn	6–3, 6–2, 6–4
1896	Robert D. Wrenn	Frederick H. Hovey	7–5, 3–6, 6–0, 1–6, 6–1
1897	Robert D. Wrenn	Wilberforce V. Eaves	4–6, 8–6, 6–3, 2–6, 6–2
1898†	Malcolm D. Whitman	Dwight F. Davis	3–6, 6–2, 6–2, 6–1
1899	Malcolm D. Whitman	J. Parmly Paret	6–1, 6–2, 3–6, 7–5
1900	Malcolm D. Whitman	William A. Larned	6–4, 1–6, 6–2, 6–2
1901†	William A. Larned	Beals C. Wright	6–2, 6–8, 6–4, 6–4
1902	William A. Larned	Reggie F. Doherty	4–6, 6–2, 6–4, 8–6
1903	H. Laurie Doherty	William A. Larned	6–0, 6–3, 10–8
1904†	Holcombe Ward	William J. Clothier	10–8, 6–4, 9–7
1905	Beals C. Wright	Holcombe Ward	6–2, 6–1, 11–9
1906	William J. Clothier	Beals C. Wright	6–3, 6–0, 6–4
1907†	William A. Larned	Robert LeRoy	6–2, 6–2, 6–4
1908	William A. Larned	Beals C. Wright	6–1, 6–2, 8–6
1909	William A. Larned	William J. Clothier	6–1, 6–2, 5–7, 1–6, 6–1
1910	William A. Larned	Thomas C. Bundy	6–1, 5–7, 6–0, 6–8, 6–1
1911	William A. Larned	Maurice E. McLoughlin	6–4, 6–4, 6–2
1912‡	Maurice E. McLoughlin	Bill Johnson	3–6, 2–6, 6–2, 6–4, 6–2
1913	Maurice E. McLoughlin	Richard N. Williams	6–4, 5–7, 6–3, 6–1
1914	Richard N. Williams	Maurice E. McLoughlin	6–3, 8–6, 10–8
1915	Bill Johnston	Maurice E. McLoughlin	1–6, 6–0, 7–5, 10–8
1916	Richard N. Williams	Bill Johnston	4–6, 6–4, 0–6, 6–2, 6–4
1917#	R.L. Murray	N. W. Niles	5–7, 8–6, 6–3, 6–3
1918	R.L. Murray	Bill Tilden	6–3, 6–1, 7–5
1919	Bill Johnston	Bill Tilden	6–4, 6–4, 6–3
1920	Bill Tilden	Bill Johnston	6–1, 1–6, 7–5, 5–7, 6–3
1921	Bill Tilden	Wallace F. Johnson	6–1, 6–3, 6–1
1922	Bill Tilden	Bill Johnston	4–6, 3–6, 6–2, 6–3, 6–4
1923	Bill Tilden	Bill Johnston	6–4, 6–1, 6–4
1924	Bill Tilden	Bill Johnston	6–1, 9–7, 6–2
1925	Bill Tilden	Bill Johnston	4–6, 11–9, 6–3, 4–6, 6–3
1926	Rene Lacoste	Jean Borotra	6–4, 6–0, 6–4
1927	Rene Lacoste	Bill Tilden	11–9, 6–3, 11–9
1928	Henri Cochet	Francis T. Hunter	4–6, 6–4, 3–6, 7–5, 6–3
1929	Bill Tilden	Francis T. Hunter	3–6, 6–3, 4–6, 6–2, 6–4
1930	John H. Doeg	Francis X. Shields	10–8, 1–6, 6–4, 16–14
1931	Ellsworth Vines	George M. Lott Jr	7–9, 6–3, 9–7, 7–5
1932	Ellsworth Vines	Henri Cochet	6–4, 6–4, 6–4
1933	Fred Perry	Jack Crawford	6–3, 11–13, 4–6, 6–0, 6–1
1934	Fred Perry	Wilmer L. Allison	6–4, 6–3, 1–6, 8–6
1935	Wilmer L. Allison	Sidney B. Wood Jr	6–2, 6–2, 6–3
1936	Fred Perry	Don Budge	2–6, 6–2, 8–6, 1–6, 10–8
1937	Don Budge	Gottfried von Cramm	6–1, 7–9, 6–1, 3–6, 6–1
1938	Don Budge	Gene Mako	6–3, 6–8, 6–2, 6–1
1939	Bobby Riggs	Welby Van Horn	6–4, 6–2, 6–4
1940	Don McNeill	Bobby Riggs	4–6, 6–8, 6–3, 6–3, 7–5
1941	Bobby Riggs	Francis Kovacs II	5–7, 6–1, 6–3, 6–3
1942	Ted Schroeder	Frank Parker	8–6, 7–5, 3–6, 4–6, 6–2
1943	Joseph R. Hunt	Jack Kramer	6–3, 6–8, 10–8, 6–0
1944	Frank Parker	William F. Talbert	6–4, 3–6, 6–3, 6–3

†No challenge round played. ‡Challenge round abolished. #National Patriotic Tournament.

MEN *(Cont.)*
United States Championships *(Cont.)*

Year	Winner	Finalist	Score
1945	Frank Parker	William F. Talbert	14–12, 6–1, 6–2
1946	Jack Kramer	Tom P. Brown	9–7, 6–3, 6–0
1947	Jack Kramer	Frank Parker	4–6, 2–6, 6–1, 6–0, 6–3
1948	Pancho Gonzales	Eric W. Sturgess	6–2, 6–3, 14–12
1949	Pancho Gonzales	Ted Schroeder	16–18, 2–6, 6–1, 6–2, 6–4
1950	Arthur Larsen	Herbie Flam	6–3, 4–6, 5–7, 6–4, 6–3
1951	Frank Sedgman	Vic Seixas	6–4, 6–1, 6–1
1952	Frank Sedgman	Gardnar Mulloy	6–1, 6–2, 6–3
1953	Tony Trabert	Vic Seixas	6–3, 6–2, 6–3
1954	Vic Seixas	Rex Hartwig	3–6, 6–2, 6–4, 6–4
1955	Tony Trabert	Ken Rosewall	9–7, 6–3, 6–3
1956	Ken Rosewall	Lew Hoad	4–6, 6–2, 6–3, 6–3
1957	Mal Anderson	Ashley J. Cooper	10–8, 7–5, 6–4
1958	Ashley J. Cooper	Mal Anderson	6–2, 3–6, 4–6, 10–8, 8–6
1959	Neale Fraser	Alex Olmedo	6–3, 5–7, 6–2, 6–4
1960	Neale Fraser	Rod Laver	6–4, 6–4, 9–7
1961	Roy Emerson	Rod Laver	7–5, 6–3, 6–2
1962	Rod Laver	Roy Emerson	6–2, 6–4, 5–7, 6–4
1963	Rafael Osuna	Frank Froehling III	7–5, 6–4, 6–2
1964	Roy Emerson	Fred Stolle	6–4, 6–2, 6–4
1965	Manuel Santana	Cliff Drysdale	6–2, 7–9, 7–5, 6–1
1966	Fred Stolle	John Newcombe	4–6, 12–10, 6–3, 6–4
1967	John Newcombe	Clark Graebner	6–4, 6–4, 8–6
1968*	Arthur Ashe	Tom Okker	14–12, 5–7, 6–3, 3–6, 6–3
1968**	Arthur Ashe	Bob Lutz	4–6, 6–3, 8–10, 6–0, 6–4
1969	Rod Laver	Tony Roche	7–9, 6–1, 6–3, 6–2
1969**	Stan Smith	Bob Lutz	9–7, 6–3, 6–1
1970	Ken Rosewall	Tony Roche	2–6, 6–4, 7–6, 6–3
1971	Stan Smith	Jan Kodes	3–6, 6–3, 6–2, 7–6
1972	Ilie Nastase	Arthur Ashe	3–6, 6–3, 6–7, 6–4, 6–3
1973	John Newcombe	Jan Kodes	6–4, 1–6, 4–6, 6–2, 6–3
1974	Jimmy Connors	Ken Rosewall	6–1, 6–0, 6–1
1975	Manuel Orantes	Jimmy Connors	6–4, 6–3, 6–3
1976	Jimmy Connors	Bjorn Borg	6–4, 3–6, 7–6, 6–4
1977	Guillermo Vilas	Jimmy Connors	2–6, 6–3, 7–6, 6–0
1978	Jimmy Connors	Bjorn Borg	6–4, 6–2, 6–2
1979	John McEnroe	Vitas Gerulaitis	7–5, 6–3, 6–3
1980	John McEnroe	Bjorn Borg	7–6, 6–1, 6–7, 5–7, 6–4
1981	John McEnroe	Bjorn Borg	4–6, 6–2, 6–4, 6–3
1982	Jimmy Connors	Ivan Lendl	6–3, 6–2, 4–6, 6–4
1983	Jimmy Connors	Ivan Lendl	6–3, 6–7, 7–5, 6–0
1984	John McEnroe	Ivan Lendl	6–3, 6–4, 6–1
1985	Ivan Lendl	John McEnroe	7–6, 6–3, 6–4
1986	Ivan Lendl	Miloslav Mecir	6–4, 6–2, 6–0
1987	Ivan Lendl	Mats Wilander	6–7, 6–0, 7–6, 6–4
1988	Mats Wilander	Ivan Lendl	6–4, 4–6, 6–3, 5–7, 6–4
1989	Boris Becker	Ivan Lendl	7–6, 1–6, 6–3, 7–6
1990	Pete Sampras	Andre Agassi	6–4, 6–3, 6–2
1991	Stefan Edberg	Jim Courier	6–2, 6–4, 6–0
1992	Stefan Edberg	Pete Sampras	3–6, 6–4, 7–6, 6–2
1993	Pete Sampras	Cedric Pioline	6–4, 6–4, 6–3
1994	Andre Agassi	Michael Stich	6–1, 7–6, 7–5
1995	Pete Sampras	Andre Agassi	6–4, 6–3, 4–6, 7–5
1996	Pete Sampras	Michael Chang	6–1, 6–4, 7–6
1997	Patrick Rafter	Greg Rusedski	6–3, 6–2, 4–6, 7–5
1998	Patrick Rafter	Mark Philippoussis	6–3, 3–6, 6–2, 6–0
1999	Andre Agassi	Todd Martin	6–4, 6–7, 6–7, 6–3, 6–2
2000	Marat Safin	Pete Sampras	6–4, 6–3, 6–3
2001	Lleyton Hewitt	Pete Sampras	7–6, 6–1, 6–1
2002	Pete Sampras	Andre Agassi	6–3, 6–4, 5–7, 6–4
2003	Andy Roddick	Juan Carlos Ferrero	6–3, 7–6 (7-2), 6–3
2004	Roger Federer	Lleyton Hewitt	6–0, 7–6 (7-3), 6–0
2005	Roger Federer	Andre Agassi	6–3, 7–6 (7-1), 6–1
2006	Roger Federer	Andy Roddick	6–2, 4–6, 7–5, 6–1

*Became Open (amateur and professional) in 1968. **Amateur event held.

WOMEN
Australian Championships

Year	Winner	Finalist	Score
1922	Margaret Molesworth	Esna Boyd	6–3, 10–8
1923	Margaret Molesworth	Esna Boyd	6–1, 7–5
1924	Sylvia Lance	Esna Boyd	6–3, 3–6, 6–4
1925	Daphne Akhurst	Esna Boyd	1–6, 8–6, 6–4
1926	Daphne Akhurst	Esna Boyd	6–1, 6–3
1927	Esna Boyd	Sylvia Harper	5–7, 6–1, 6–2
1928	Daphne Akhurst	Esna Boyd	7–5, 6–2
1929	Daphne Akhurst	Louise Bickerton	6–1, 5–7, 6–2
1930	Daphne Akhurst	Sylvia Harper	10–8, 2–6, 7–5
1931	Coral Buttsworth	Margorie Crawford	1–6, 6–3, 6–4
1932	Coral Buttsworth	Kathrine Le Messurier	9–7, 6–4
1933	Joan Hartigan	Coral Buttsworth	6–4, 6–3
1934	Joan Hartigan	Margaret Molesworth	6–1, 6–4
1935	Dorothy Round	Nancye Wynne Bolton	1–6, 6–1, 6–3
1936	Joan Hartigan	Nancye Wynne Bolton	6–4, 6–4
1937	Nancye Wynne Bolton	Emily Westacott	6–3, 5–7, 6–4
1938	Dorothy Bundy	D. Stevenson	6–3, 6–2
1939	Emily Westacott	Nell Hopman	6–1, 6–2
1940	Nancye Wynne Bolton	Thelma Coyne	5–7, 6–4, 6–0
1941–45	No tournament		
1946	Nancye Wynne Bolton	Joyce Fitch	6–4, 6–4
1947	Nancye Wynne Bolton	Nell Hopman	6–3, 6–2
1948	Nancye Wynne Bolton	Marie Toomey	6–3, 6–1
1949	Doris Hart	Nancye Wynne Bolton	6–3, 6–4
1950	Louise Brough	Doris Hart	6–4, 3–6, 6–4
1951	Nancye Wynne Bolton	Thelma Long	6–1, 7–5
1952	Thelma Long	H. Angwin	6–2, 6–3
1953	Maureen Connolly	Julia Sampson	6–3, 6–2
1954	Thelma Long	J. Staley	6–3, 6–4
1955	Beryl Penrose	Thelma Long	6–4, 6–3
1956	Mary Carter	Thelma Long	3–6, 6–2, 9–7
1957	Shirley Fry	Althea Gibson	6–3, 6–4
1958	Angela Mortimer	Lorraine Coghlan	6–3, 6–4
1959	Mary Carter-Reitano	Renee Schuurman	6–2, 6–3
1960	Margaret Smith	Jan Lehane	7–5, 6–2
1961	Margaret Smith	Jan Lehane	6–1, 6–4
1962	Margaret Smith	Jan Lehane	6–0, 6–2
1963	Margaret Smith	Jan Lehane	6–2, 6–2
1964	Margaret Smith	Lesley Turner	6–3, 6–2
1965	Margaret Smith	Maria Bueno	5–7, 6–4, 5–2, ret.
1966	Margaret Smith	Nancy Richey	Default
1967	Nancy Richey	Lesley Turner	6–1, 6–4
1968	Billie Jean King	Margaret Smith	6–1, 6–2
1969*	Margaret Smith Court	Billie Jean King	6–4, 6–1
1970	Margaret Smith Court	Kerry Melville Reid	6–3, 6–1
1971	Margaret Smith Court	Evonne Goolagong	2–6, 7–6, 7–5
1972	Virginia Wade	Evonne Goolagong	6–4, 6–4
1973	Margaret Smith Court	Evonne Goolagong	6–4, 7–5
1974	Evonne Goolagong	Chris Evert	7–6, 4–6, 6–0
1975	Evonne Goolagong	Martina Navratilova	6–3, 6–2
1976	Evonne Goolagong Cawley	Renata Tomanova	6–2, 6–2
1977 (Jan)	Kerry Melville Reid	Dianne Balestrat	7–5, 6–2
1977 (Dec)	Evonne Goolagong Cawley	Helen Gourlay	6–3, 6–0
1978	Chris O'Neil	Betsy Nagelsen	6–3, 7–6
1979	Barbara Jordan	Sharon Walsh	6–3, 6–3
1980	Hana Mandlikova	Wendy Turnbull	6–0, 7–5
1981	Martina Navratilova	Chris Evert Lloyd	6–7, 6–4, 7–5
1982	Chris Evert Lloyd	Martina Navratilova	6–3, 2–6, 6–3
1983	Martina Navratilova	Kathy Jordan	6–2, 7–6
1984	Chris Evert Lloyd	Helena Sukova	6–7, 6–1, 6–3
1985 (Dec)	Martina Navratilova	Chris Evert Lloyd	6–2, 4–6, 6–2
1987 (Jan)	Hana Mandlikova	Martina Navratilova	7–5, 7–6
1988	Steffi Graf	Chris Evert	6–1, 7–6
1989	Steffi Graf	Helena Sukova	6–4, 6–4
1990	Steffi Graf	Mary Joe Fernandez	6–3, 6–4
1991	Monica Seles	Jana Novotna	5–7, 6–3, 6–1

*Became Open (amateur and professional) in 1969.

WOMEN *(Cont.)*

Australian Championships *(Cont.)*

Year	Winner	Finalist	Score
1992	Monica Seles	Mary Joe Fernandez	6–2, 6–3
1993	Monica Seles	Steffi Graf	4–6, 6–3, 6–2
1994	Steffi Graf	Arantxa Sánchez Vicario	6–0, 6–2
1995	Mary Pierce	Arantxa Sánchez Vicario	6–3, 6–2
1996	Monica Seles	Anke Huber	6–4, 6–1
1997	Martina Hingis	Mary Pierce	6–2, 6–2
1998	Martina Hingis	Conchita Martinez	6–3, 6–3
1999	Martina Hingis	Amelie Mauresmo	6–2, 6–3
2000	Lindsay Davenport	Martina Hingis	6–1, 7–5
2001	Jennifer Capriati	Martina Hingis	6–4, 6–3
2002	Jennifer Capriati	Martina Hingis	4–6, 7–6 (9–7), 6–2
2003	Serena Williams	Venus Williams	7–6 (7-4), 3–6, 6–4
2004	Justine Henin-Hardenne	Kim Clijsters	6–3, 4–6, 6–3
2005	Serena Williams	Lindsay Davenport	2-6, 6-3, 6-0
2006	Amelie Mauresmo	Justine Henin-Hardenne	6-1, 2-0, ret.

French Championships

Year	Winner	Finalist	Score
1925†	Suzanne Lenglen	Kathleen McKane	6–1, 6–2
1926	Suzanne Lenglen	Mary K. Browne	6–1, 6–0
1927	Kea Bouman	Irene Peacock	6–2, 6–4
1928	Helen Wills	Eileen Bennett	6–1, 6–2
1929	Helen Wills	Simone Mathieu	6–3, 6–4
1930	Helen Wills Moody	Helen Jacobs	6–2, 6–1
1931	Cilly Aussem	Betty Nuthall	8–6, 6–1
1932	Helen Wills Moody	Simone Mathieu	7–5, 6–1
1933	Margaret Scriven	Simone Mathieu	6–2, 4–6, 6–4
1934	Margaret Scriven	Helen Jacobs	7–5, 4–6, 6–1
1935	Hilde Sperling	Simone Mathieu	6–2, 6–1
1936	Hilde Sperling	Simone Mathieu	6–3, 6–4
1937	Hilde Sperling	Simone Mathieu	6–2, 6–4
1938	Simone Mathieu	Nelly Landry	6–0, 6–3
1939	Simone Mathieu	Jadwiga Jedrzejowska	6–3, 8–6
1940–45	No tournament		
1946	Margaret Osborne	Pauline Betz	1–6, 8–6, 7–5
1947	Patricia Todd	Doris Hart	6–3, 3–6, 6–4
1948	Nelly Landry	Shirley Fry	6–2, 0–6, 6–0
1949	Margaret Osborne duPont	Nelly Adamson	7–5, 6–2
1950	Doris Hart	Patricia Todd	6–4, 4–6, 6–2
1951	Shirley Fry	Doris Hart	6–3, 3–6, 6–3
1952	Doris Hart	Shirley Fry	6–4, 6–4
1953	Maureen Connolly	Doris Hart	6–2, 6–4
1954	Maureen Connolly	Ginette Bucaille	6–4, 6–1
1955	Angela Mortimer	Dorothy Knode	2–6, 7–5, 10–8
1956	Althea Gibson	Angela Mortimer	6–0, 12–10
1957	Shirley Bloomer	Dorothy Knode	6–1, 6–3
1958	Zsuzsi Kormoczi	Shirley Bloomer	6–4, 1–6, 6–2
1959	Christine Truman	Zsuzsi Kormoczi	6–4, 7–5
1960	Darlene Hard	Yola Ramirez	6–3, 6–4
1961	Ann Haydon	Yola Ramirez	6–2, 6–1
1962	Margaret Smith	Lesley Turner	6–3, 3–6, 7–5
1963	Lesley Turner	Ann Haydon Jones	2–6, 6–3, 7–5
1964	Margaret Smith	Maria Bueno	5–7, 6–1, 6–2
1965	Lesley Turner	Margaret Smith	6–3, 6–4
1966	Ann Jones	Nancy Richey	6–3, 6–1
1967	Francoise Durr	Lesley Turner	4–6, 6–3, 6–4
1968*	Nancy Richey	Ann Jones	5–7, 6–4, 6–1
1969	Margaret Smith Court	Ann Jones	6–1, 4–6, 6–3
1970	Margaret Smith Court	Helga Niessen	6–2, 6–4

†1925 was the first year that entries were accepted from all countries. *Became Open (amateur and professional) in 1968, but restricted to only contract professionals in1972.

WOMEN *(Cont.)*

French Championships *(Cont.)*

Year	Winner	Finalist	Score
1971	Evonne Goolagong	Helen Gourlay	6–3, 7–5
1972	Billie Jean King	Evonne Goolagong	6–3, 6–3
1973	Margaret Smith Court	Chris Evert	6–7, 7–6, 6–4
1974	Chris Evert	Olga Morozova	6–1, 6–2
1975	Chris Evert	Martina Navratilova	2–6, 6–2, 6–1
1976	Sue Barker	Renata Tomanova	6–2, 0–6, 6–2
1977	Mima Jausovec	Florenza Mihai	6–2, 6–7, 6–1
1978	Virginia Ruzici	Mima Jausovec	6–2, 6–2
1979	Chris Evert Lloyd	Wendy Turnbull	6–2, 6–0
1980	Chris Evert Lloyd	Virginia Ruzici	6–0, 6–3
1981	Hana Mandlikova	Sylvia Hanika	6–2, 6–4
1982	Martina Navratilova	Andrea Jaeger	7–6, 6–1
1983	Chris Evert Lloyd	Mima Jausovec	6–1, 6–2
1984	Martina Navratilova	Chris Evert Lloyd	6–3, 6–1
1985	Chris Evert Lloyd	Martina Navratilova	6–3, 6–7, 7–5
1986	Chris Evert Lloyd	Martina Navratilova	2–6, 6–3, 6–3
1987	Steffi Graf	Martina Navratilova	6–4, 4–6, 8–6
1988	Steffi Graf	Natalia Zvereva	6–0, 6–0
1989	Arantxa Sánchez Vicario	Steffi Graf	7–6, 3–6, 7–5
1990	Monica Seles	Steffi Graf	7–6, 6–4
1991	Monica Seles	Arantxa Sánchez Vicario	6–3, 6–4
1992	Monica Seles	Steffi Graf	6–2, 3–6, 10–8
1993	Steffi Graf	Mary Joe Fernandez	4–6, 6–2, 6–4
1994	Arantxa Sánchez Vicario	Mary Pierce	6–4, 6–4
1995	Steffi Graf	Arantxa Sánchez Vicario	7–5, 4–6, 6–0
1996	Steffi Graf	Arantxa Sánchez Vicario	6–3, 6–7 (4–7), 10–8
1997	Iva Majoli	Martina Hingis	6–4, 6–2
1998	Arantxa Sánchez Vicario	Monica Seles	7–6 (7–5), 0–6, 6–2
1999	Steffi Graf	Martina Hingis	4–6, 7–5, 6–2
2000	Mary Pierce	Conchita Martinez	6–2, 7–5
2001	Jennifer Capriati	Kim Clijsters	1–6, 6–4, 12–10
2002	Serena Williams	Venus Williams	7–5, 6–3
2003	Justine Henin-Hardenne	Kim Clijsters	6–0, 6–4
2004	Anastasia Myskina	Elena Dementieva	6–1, 6–2
2005	Justine Henin-Hardenne	Mary Pierce	6–1, 6–1
2006	Justine Henin-Hardenne	Svetlana Kuznetsova	6–4, 6–4

Wimbledon Championships

Year	Winner	Finalist	Score
1884	Maud Watson	Lilian Watson	6–8, 6–3, 6–3
1885	Maud Watson	Blanche Bingley	6–1, 7–5
1886	Blanche Bingley	Maud Watson	6–3, 6–3
1887	Charlotte Dod	Blanche Bingley	6–2, 6–0
1888	Charlotte Dod	Blanche Bingley Hillyard	6–3, 6–3
1889	Blanche Bingley Hillyard	n/a	n/a
1890	Lena Rice	n/a	n/a
1891	Charlotte Dod	n/a	n/a
1892	Charlotte Dod	Blanche Bingley Hillyard	6–1, 6–1
1893	Charlotte Dod	Blanche Bingley Hillyard	6–8, 6–1, 6–4
1894	Blanche Bingley Hillyard	n/a	n/a
1895	Charlotte Cooper	n/a	
1896	Charlotte Cooper	Mrs. W. H. Pickering	6–2, 6–3
1897	Blanche Bingley Hillyard	Charlotte Cooper	5–7, 7–5, 6–2
1898	Charlotte Cooper	n/a	n/a
1899	Blanche Bingley Hillyard	Charlotte Cooper	6–2, 6–3
1900	Blanche Bingley Hillyard	Charlotte Cooper	4–6, 6–4, 6–4
1901	Charlotte Cooper Sterry	Blanche Bingley Hillyard	6–2, 6–2
1902	Muriel Robb	Charlotte Cooper Sterry	7–5, 6–1
1903	Dorothea Douglass	n/a	n/a
1904	Dorothea Douglass	Charlotte Cooper Sterry	6–0, 6–3
1905	May Sutton	Dorothea Douglass	6–3, 6–4
1906	Dorothea Douglass	May Sutton	6–3, 9–7

WOMEN *(Cont.)*

Wimbledon Championships *(Cont.)*

Year	Winner	Finalist	Score
1907	May Sutton	Dorothea Douglass Lambert Chambers	6–1, 6–4
1908	Charlotte Cooper Sterry	n/a	n/a
1909	Dora Boothby	n/a	n/a
1910	Dorothea Douglass Lambert Chambers	Dora Boothby	6–2, 6–2
1911	Dorothea Douglass Lambert Chambers	Dora Boothby	6–0, 6–0
1912	Ethel Larcombe	n/a	n/a
1913	Dorothea Douglass Lambert Chambers		
1914	Dorothea Douglass Lambert Chambers	Ethel Larcombe	7–5, 6–4
1915–18	No tournament		
1919	Suzanne Lenglen	Dorothea Douglass Lambert Chambers	10–8, 4–6, 9–7
1920	Suzanne Lenglen	Dorothea Douglass Lambert Chambers	6–3, 6–0
1921	Suzanne Lenglen	Elizabeth Ryan	6–2, 6–0
1922	Suzanne Lenglen	Molla Mallory	6–2, 6–0
1923	Suzanne Lenglen	Kathleen McKane	6–2, 6–2
1924	Kathleen McKane	Helen Wills	4–6, 6–4, 6–2
1925	Suzanne Lenglen	Joan Fry	6–2, 6–0
1926	Kathleen McKane Godfree	Lili de Alvarez	6–2, 4–6, 6–3
1927	Helen Wills	Lili de Alvarez	6–2, 6–4
1928	Helen Wills	Lili de Alvarez	6–2, 6–3
1929	Helen Wills	Helen Jacobs	6–1, 6–2
1930	Helen Wills Moody	Elizabeth Ryan	6–2, 6–2
1931	Cilly Aussem	Hilde Kranwinkel	7–5, 7–5
1932	Helen Wills Moody	Helen Jacobs	6–3, 6–1
1933	Helen Wills Moody	Dorothy Round	6–4, 6–8, 6–3
1934	Dorothy Round	Helen Jacobs	6–2, 5–7, 6–3
1935	Helen Wills Moody	Helen Jacobs	6–3, 3–6, 7–5
1936	Helen Jacobs	Hilde Kranwinkel Sperling	6–2, 4–6, 7–5
1937	Dorothy Round	Jadwiga Jedrzejowska	6–2, 2–6, 7–5
1938	Helen Wills Moody	Helen Jacobs	6–4, 6–0
1939	Alice Marble	Kay Stammers	6–2, 6–0
1940–45	No tournament		
1946	Pauline Betz	Louise Brough	6–2, 6–4
1947	Margaret Osborne	Doris Hart	6–2, 6–4
1948	Louise Brough	Doris Hart	6–3, 8–6
1949	Louise Brough	Margaret Osborne duPont	10–8, 1–6, 10–8
1950	Louise Brough	Margaret Osborne duPont	6–1, 3–6, 6–1
1951	Doris Hart	Shirley Fry	6–1, 6–0
1952	Maureen Connolly	Louise Brough	6–4, 6–3
1953	Maureen Connolly	Doris Hart	8–6, 7–5
1954	Maureen Connolly	Louise Brough	6–2, 7–5
1955	Louise Brough	Beverly Fleitz	7–5, 8–6
1956	Shirley Fry	Angela Buxton	6–3, 6–1
1957	Althea Gibson	Darlene Hard	6–3, 6–2
1958	Althea Gibson	Angela Mortimer	8–6, 6–2
1959	Maria Bueno	Darlene Hard	6–4, 6–3
1960	Maria Bueno	Sandra Reynolds	8–6, 6–0
1961	Angela Mortimer	Christine Truman	4–6, 6–4, 7–5
1962	Karen Hantze Susman	Vera Sukova	6–4, 6–4
1963	Margaret Smith	Billie Jean Moffitt	6–3, 6–4
1964	Maria Bueno	Margaret Smith	6–4, 7–9, 6–3
1965	Margaret Smith	Maria Bueno	6–4, 7–5
1966	Billie Jean King	Maria Bueno	6–3, 3–6, 6–1
1967	Billie Jean King	Ann Haydon Jones	6–3, 6–4
1968*	Billie Jean King	Judy Tegart	9–7, 7–5
1969	Ann Haydon Jones	Billie Jean King	3–6, 6–3, 6–2

Note: Prior to 1922 the tournament was run on a challenge-round system. The previous year's winner "stood out" of an All-Comers event, which produced a challenger to play her for the title.

*Became Open (amateur and professional) in 1968, but restricted to only contract professionals in 1972.

WOMEN (Cont.)

Wimbledon Championships (Cont.)

Year	Winner	Finalist	Score
1970	Margaret Smith Court	Billie Jean King	14–12, 11–9
1971	Evonne Goolagong	Margaret Smith Court	6–4, 6–1
1972	Billie Jean King	Evonne Goolagong	6–3, 6–3
1973	Billie Jean King	Chris Evert	6–0, 7–5
1974	Chris Evert	Olga Morozova	6–0, 6–4
1975	Billie Jean King	Evonne Goolagong Cawley	6–0, 6–1
1976	Chris Evert	Evonne Goolagong Cawley	6–3, 4–6, 8–6
1977	Virginia Wade	Betty Stove	4–6, 6–3, 6–1
1978	Martina Navratilova	Chris Evert	2–6, 6–4, 7–5
1979	Martina Navratilova	Chris Evert Lloyd	6–4, 6–4
1980	Evonne Goolagong Cawley	Chris Evert Lloyd	6–1, 7–6
1981	Chris Evert Lloyd	Hana Mandlikova	6–2, 6–2
1982	Martina Navratilova	Chris Evert Lloyd	6–1, 3–6, 6–2
1983	Martina Navratilova	Andrea Jaeger	6–0, 6–3
1984	Martina Navratilova	Chris Evert Lloyd	7–6, 6–2
1985	Martina Navratilova	Chris Evert Lloyd	4–6, 6–3, 6–2
1986	Martina Navratilova	Hana Mandlikova	7–6, 6–3
1987	Martina Navratilova	Steffi Graf	7–5, 6–3
1988	Steffi Graf	Martina Navratilova	5–7, 6–2, 6–1
1989	Steffi Graf	Martina Navratilova	6–2, 6–7, 6–1
1990	Martina Navratilova	Zina Garrison	6–4, 6–1
1991	Steffi Graf	Gabriela Sabatini	6–4, 3–6, 8–6
1992	Steffi Graf	Monica Seles	6–2, 6–1
1993	Steffi Graf	Jana Novotna	7–6, 1–6, 6–4
1994	Conchita Martinez	Martina Navratilova	6–4, 3–6, 6–3
1995	Steffi Graf	Arantxa Sánchez Vicario	4–6, 6–1, 7–5
1996	Steffi Graf	Arantxa Sánchez Vicario	6–3, 7–5
1997	Martina Hingis	Jana Novotna	2–6, 6–3, 6–3
1998	Jana Novotna	Nathalie Tauziat	6–4, 7–6
1999	Lindsay Davenport	Steffi Graf	6–4, 7–5
2000	Venus Williams	Lindsay Davenport	6–3, 7–6
2001	Venus Williams	Justine Henin	6–1, 3–6, 6–0
2002	Serena Williams	Venus Williams	7–6 (7–4), 6–3
2003	Serena Williams	Venus Williams	4–6, 6–4, 6–2
2004	Maria Sharapova	Serena Williams	6–1, 6–4
2005	Venus Williams	Lindsay Davenport	4–6, 7–6 (7–4), 7–6 (9–7)
2006	Amelie Mauresmo	Justine Henin-Hardenne	2–6, 6–3, 6–4

United States Championships

Year	Winner	Finalist	Score
1887	Ellen Hansell	Laura Knight	6–1, 6–0
1888	Bertha L. Townsend	Ellen Hansell	6–3, 6–5
1889	Bertha L. Townsend	Louise Voorhes	7–5, 6–2
1890	Ellen C. Roosevelt	Bertha L. Townsend	6–2, 6–2
1891	Mabel Cahill	Ellen C. Roosevelt	6–4, 6–1, 4–6, 6–3
1892	Mabel Cahill	Elisabeth Moore	5–7, 6–3, 6–4, 4–6, 6–2
1893	Aline Terry	Alice Schultze	6–1, 6–3
1894	Helen Hellwig	Aline Terry	7–5, 3–6, 6–0, 3–6, 6–3
1895	Juliette Atkinson	Helen Hellwig	6–4, 6–2, 6–1
1896	Elisabeth Moore	Juliette Atkinson	6–4, 4–6, 6–2, 6–2
1897	Juliette Atkinson	Elisabeth Moore	6–3, 6–3, 4–6, 3–6, 6–3
1898	Juliette Atkinson	Marion Jones	6–3, 5–7, 6–4, 2–6, 7–5
1899	Marion Jones	Maud Banks	6–1, 6–1, 7–5
1900	Myrtle McAteer	Edith Parker	6–2, 6–2, 6–0
1901	Elisabeth Moore	Myrtle McAteer	6–4, 3–6, 7–5, 2–6, 6–2
1902*	Marion Jones	Elisabeth Moore	6–1, 1–0, ret.
1903	Elisabeth Moore	Marion Jones	7–5, 8–6
1904	May Sutton	Elisabeth Moore	6–1, 6–2
1905	Elisabeth Moore	Helen Homans	6–4, 5–7, 6–1
1906	Helen Homans	Maud Barger-Wallach	6–4, 6–3
1907	Evelyn Sears	Carrie Neely	6–3, 6–2
1908	Maud Barger–Wallach	Evelyn Sears	6–3, 1–6, 6–3
1909	Hazel Hotchkiss	Maud Barger–Wallach	6–0, 6–1

*Five-set final abolished;

WOMEN (Cont.)

United States Championships (Cont.)

Year	Winner	Finalist	Score
1910	Hazel Hotchkiss	Louise Hammond	6–4, 6–2
1911	Hazel Hotchkiss	Florence Sutton	8–10, 6–1, 9–7
1912†	Mary K. Browne	Eleanora Sears	6–4, 6–2
1913	Mary K. Browne	Dorothy Green	6–2, 7–5
1914	Mary K. Browne	Marie Wagner	6–2, 1–6, 6–1
1915	Molla Bjurstedt	Hazel Hotchkiss Wightman	4–6, 6–2, 6–0
1916	Molla Bjurstedt	Louise Hammond Raymond	6–0, 6–1
1917‡	Molla Bjurstedt	Marion Vanderhoef	4–6, 6–0, 6–2
1918	Molla Bjurstedt	Eleanor Goss	6–4, 6–3
1919	Hazel Hotchkiss Wightman	Marion Zinderstein	6–1, 6–2
1920	Molla Bjurstedt Mallory	Marion Zinderstein	6–3, 6–1
1921	Molla Bjurstedt Mallory	Mary K. Browne	4–6, 6–4, 6–2
1922	Molla Bjurstedt Mallory	Helen Wills	6–3, 6–1
1923	Helen Wills	Molla Bjurstedt Mallory	6–2, 6–1
1924	Helen Wills	Molla Bjurstedt Mallory	6–1, 6–3
1925	Helen Wills	Kathleen McKane	3–6, 6–0, 6–2
1926	Molla Bjurstedt Mallory	Elizabeth Ryan	4–6, 6–4, 9–7
1927	Helen Wills	Betty Nuthall	6–1, 6–4
1928	Helen Wills	Helen Jacobs	6–2, 6–1
1929	Helen Wills	Phoebe Holcroft Watson	6–4, 6–2
1930	Betty Nuthall	Anna McCune Harper	6–1, 6–4
1931	Helen Wills Moody	Eileen Whitingstall	6–4, 6–1
1932	Helen Jacobs	Carolin Babcock	6–2, 6–2
1933	Helen Jacobs	Helen Wills Moody	8–6, 3–6, 3–0, ret.
1934	Helen Jacobs	Sarah Palfrey	6–1, 6–4
1935	Helen Jacobs	Sarah Palfrey Fabyan	6–2, 6–4
1936	Alice Marble	Helen Jacobs	4–6, 6–3, 6–2
1937	Anita Lizane	Jadwiga Jedrzejowska	6–4, 6–2
1938	Alice Marble	Nancye Wynne	6–0, 6–3
1939	Alice Marble	Helen Jacobs	6–0, 8–10, 6–4
1940	Alice Marble	Helen Jacobs	6–2, 6–3
1941	Sarah Palfrey Cooke	Pauline Betz	7–5, 6–2
1942	Pauline Betz	Louise Brough	4–6, 6–1, 6–4
1943	Pauline Betz	Louise Brough	6–3, 5–7, 6–3
1944	Pauline Betz	Margaret Osborne	6–3, 8–6
1945	Sarah Palfrey Cooke	Pauline Betz	3–6, 8–6, 6–4
1946	Pauline Betz	Patricia Canning	11–9, 6–3
1947	Louise Brough	Margaret Osborne	8–6, 4–6, 6–1
1948	Margaret Osborne duPont	Louise Brough	4–6, 6–4, 15–13
1949	Margaret Osborne duPont	Doris Hart	6–4, 6–1
1950	Margaret Osborne duPont	Doris Hart	6–4, 6–3
1951	Maureen Connolly	Shirley Fry	6–3, 1–6, 6–4
1952	Maureen Connolly	Doris Hart	6–3, 7–5
1953	Maureen Connolly	Doris Hart	6–2, 6–4
1954	Doris Hart	Louise Brough	6–8, 6–1, 8–6
1955	Doris Hart	Patricia Ward	6–4, 6–2
1956	Shirley Fry	Althea Gibson	6–3, 6–4
1957	Althea Gibson	Louise Brough	6–3, 6–2
1958	Althea Gibson	Darlene Hard	3–6, 6–1, 6–2
1959	Maria Bueno	Christine Truman	6–1, 6–4
1960	Darlene Hard	Maria Bueno	6–4, 10–12, 6–4
1961	Darlene Hard	Ann Haydon	6–3, 6–4
1962	Margaret Smith	Darlene Hard	9–7, 6–4
1963	Maria Bueno	Margaret Smith	7–5, 6–4
1964	Maria Bueno	Carole Graebner	6–1, 6–0
1965	Margaret Smith	Billie Jean Moffitt	8–6, 7–5
1966	Maria Bueno	Nancy Richey	6–3, 6–1
1967	Billie Jean King	Ann Haydon Jones	11–9, 6–4
1968**	Virginia Wade	Billie Jean King	6–4, 6–2
1968#	Margaret Smith Court	Maria Bueno	6–2, 6–2
1969	Margaret Smith Court	Nancy Richey	6–2, 6–2
1969#	Margaret Smith Court	Virginia Wade	4–6, 6–3, 6–0

†Challenge round abolished. ‡National Patriotic Tournament.
**Became Open (amateur and professional) in 1968. #Amateur event held.

WOMEN *(Cont.)*

United States Championships *(Cont.)*

Year	Winner	Finalist	Score
1970	Margaret Smith Court	Rosie Casals	6–2, 2–6, 6–1
1971	Billie Jean King	Rosie Casals	6–4, 7–6
1972	Billie Jean King	Kerry Melville	6–3, 7–5
1973	Margaret Smith Court	Evonne Goolagong	7–6, 5–7, 6–2
1974	Billie Jean King	Evonne Goolagong	3–6, 6–3, 7–5
1975	Chris Evert	Evonne Goolagong Cawley	5–7, 6–4, 6–2
1976	Chris Evert	Evonne Goolagong Cawley	6–3, 6–0
1977	Chris Evert	Wendy Turnbull	7–6, 6–2
1978	Chris Evert	Pam Shriver	7–6, 6–4
1979	Tracy Austin	Chris Evert Lloyd	6–4, 6–3
1980	Chris Evert Lloyd	Hana Mandlikova	5–7, 6–1, 6–1
1981	Tracy Austin	Martina Navratilova	1–6, 7–6, 7–6
1982	Chris Evert Lloyd	Hana Mandlikova	6–3, 6–1
1983	Martina Navratilova	Chris Evert Lloyd	6–1, 6–3
1984	Martina Navratilova	Chris Evert Lloyd	4–6, 6–4, 6–4
1985	Hana Mandlikova	Martina Navratilova	7–6, 1–6, 7–6
1986	Martina Navratilova	Helena Sukova	6–3, 6–2
1987	Martina Navratilova	Steffi Graf	7–6, 6–1
1988	Steffi Graf	Gabriela Sabatini	6–3, 3–6, 6–1
1989	Steffi Graf	Martina Navratilova	3–6, 6–4, 6–2
1990	Gabriela Sabatini	Steffi Graf	6–2, 7–6
1991	Monica Seles	Martina Navratilova	7–6, 6–1
1992	Monica Seles	Arantxa Sánchez Vicario	6–3, 6–2
1993	Steffi Graf	Helena Sukova	6–3, 6–3
1994	Arantxa Sánchez Vicario	Steffi Graf	1–6, 7–6, 6–4
1995	Steffi Graf	Monica Seles	7–6, 0–6, 6–3
1996	Steffi Graf	Monica Seles	7–5, 7–4
1997	Martina Hingis	Venus Williams	6–0, 6–4
1998	Lindsay Davenport	Martina Hingis	6–3, 7–5
1999	Serena Williams	Martina Hingis	6–3, 7–6
2000	Venus Williams	Lindsay Davenport	6–4, 7–5
2001	Venus Williams	Serena Williams	6–2, 6–4
2002	Serena Williams	Venus Williams	6–4, 6–3
2003	Justine Henin-Hardenne	Kim Clijsters	7–5, 6–1
2004	Svetlana Kuznetsova	Elena Dementieva	6–3, 7–5
2005	Kim Clijsters	Mary Pierce	6-3, 6-1
2006	Maria Sharapova	Justine Henin-Hardenne	6-4, 6-4

Single-Year Grand Slam Winners

Singles

Don Budge, 1938
Maureen Connolly, 1953
Rod Laver, 1962, 1969
Margaret Smith Court, 1970
Steffi Graf, 1988

Doubles

Frank Sedgman and Ken McGregor, 1951
Martina Navratilova and Pam Shriver, 1984
Maria Bueno and two partners, 1960
  Christine Truman (Australian),
  Darlene Hard (French, Wimbledon and U.S.)
Martina Hingis and two partners, 1998
  Mirjana Lucic (Australian),
  Jana Novotna (French, Wimbledon and U.S.)

Mixed Doubles

Margaret Smith and Ken Fletcher, 1963
Owen Davidson and two partners, 1967
  Lesley Turner (Australian),
  Billie Jean King (French, Wimbledon and U.S.)

Alltime Grand Slam Champions

Alltime Grand Slam Champions (Singles, Doubles, Mixed Doubles)

MEN

Player	Aus. S-D-M	French S-D-M	Wim. S-D-M	U.S. S-D-M	Total
Roy Emerson	6-3-0	2-6-0	2-3-0	2-4-0	28
John Newcombe	2-5-0	0-3-0	3-6-0	2-3-1	25
Frank Sedgman	2-2-2	0-3-2	1-2-2	2-2-2	22
Todd Woodbridge	0-3-1	0-1-1	0-9-1	0-3-3	22
Bill Tilden	†	0-0-1	3-1-0	7-5-4	21
Rod Laver	3-4-0	2-1-1	4-1-2	2-0-0	20
John Bromwich	2-8-1	0-0-0	0-2-2	0-3-1	19
Jean Borotra	1-1-1	1-5-2	2-3-1	0-0-1	18
Fred Stolle	0-3-1	1-2-0	0-2-3	1-3-2	18
Ken Rosewall	4-3-0	2-2-0	0-2-0	2-2-1	18
Neale Fraser	0-3-1	0-3-0	1-2-0	2-3-3	18
Adrian Quist	3-10-0	0-1-0	0-2-0	0-1-0	17
John McEnroe	0-0-0	0-0-1	3-4-0	4-5-0	17
Jack Crawford	4-4-3	1-1-1	1-1-1	0-0-0	17
Mark Woodforde	0-2-2	0-1-1	0-6-1	0-3-1	17

†Did not compete.

WOMEN

Player	Aus. S-D-M	French S-D-M	Wim. S-D-M	U.S. S-D-M	Total
Margaret Smith Court	11-8-2	5-4-4	3-2-5	5-5-8	62
*Martina Navratilova	3-8-1	2-7-2	9-7-4	4-9-3	59
Billie Jean King	1-0-1	1-1-2	6-10-4	4-5-4	39
Doris Hart	1-1-2	2-5-3	1-4-5	2-4-5	35
Helen Wills Moody	†	4-2-0	8-3-1	7-4-2	31
Louise Brough	1-1-0	0-3-0	4-5-4	1-8-3	30**
Margaret Osborne duPont	†	2-3-0	1-5-1	3-8-6	29**
Elizabeth Ryan	†	0-4-0	0-12-7	0-1-2	26
Steffi Graf	4-0-0	6-0-0	7-1-0	5-0-0	23
Pam Shriver	0-7-0	0-4-1	0-5-0	0-5-0	22
Chris Evert	2-0-0	7-2-0	3-1-0	6-0-0	21
Darlene Hard	†	1-3-2	0-4-3	2-6-0	21
Suzanne Lenglen	†	2-2-2#	6-6-3	0-0-0	21
Nancye Wynne Bolton	6-10-4	0-0-0	0-0-0	0-0-0	20
Maria Bueno	0-1-0	0-1-1	3-5-0	4-4-0	19
Thelma Coyne Long	2-12-4	0-0-1	0-0-0	0-0-0	19

*Active player in 2006. †Did not compete. #Suzanne Lenglen also won four singles titles at the French Championships before 1925, when competition was first opened to entries from all nations.**From 1940–45, with competition in the U.S. Championships thinned due to wartime constraints, Louise Brough Clapp also won four doubles titles (1942–45) and one mixed doubles title (1942); and Margaret Osborne duPont won five doubles titles (1941–45) and three mixed doubles titles (1943–45).

Alltime Grand Slam Singles Champions

MEN

Player	Aus.	French	Wim.	U.S.	Total
Pete Sampras	2	0	7	5	14
Roy Emerson	6	2	2	2	12
Bjorn Borg	0	6	5	0	11
Rod Laver	3	2	4	2	11
Bill Tilden	†	0	3	7	10
*Roger Federer	2	0	4	3	9
Jimmy Connors	1	0	2	5	8
Ivan Lendl	2	3	0	3	8
Fred Perry	1	1	3	3	8
Ken Rosewall	4	2	0	2	8
*Andre Agassi	4	1	1	2	8
Henri Cochet	†	4	2	1	7
Rene Lacoste	†	3	2	2	7
Bill Larned	†	†	0	7	7
John McEnroe	0	0	3	4	7
John Newcombe	2	0	3	2	7
Willie Renshaw	†	†	7	7	7
Dick Sears	†	†	0	7	7

WOMEN

Player	Aus.	French	Wim.	U.S.	Total
Margaret Smith Court	11	5	3	5	24
Steffi Graf	4	6	7	5	22
Helen Wills Moody	†	4	8	7	19
Chris Evert	2	7	3	6	18
Martina Navratilova	3	2	9	4	18
Billie Jean King	1	1	6	4	12
Maureen Connolly	1	2	3	3	9
*Monica Seles	4	3	0	2	9
Suzanne Lenglen	†	2#	6	0	8
Molla Bjurstedt Mallory	†	†	0	8	8
Maria Bueno	0	0	3	4	7
Evonne Goolagong	4	1	2	0	7
Dorothea D. Chambers	†	†	7	0	7
*Serena Williams	2	1	2	2	7
Nancye Wynne Bolton	6	0	0	0	6
Louise Brough	1	0	4	1	6
Margaret Osborne duPont	†	2	1	3	6
Doris Hart	1	2	1	2	6
Blanche Bingley Hillyard	†	†	6	†	6

*Active player in 2006. †Did not compete.
#Suzanne Lenglen also won four singles titles at the French Championships before 1925, when competition was first opened to entries from all nations.

Davis Cup

Started in 1900 as the International Lawn Tennis Challenge Trophy by America's Dwight Davis, the runner up in the 1898 U.S. Championships. A Davis Cup meeting between two countries is known as a tie and is a three-day event consisting of two singles matches, followed by one doubles match and then two more singles matches. The United States boasts the greatest number of wins (40), followed by Australia (22).

Year	Winner	Finalist	Site	Score
1900	United States	Great Britain	Boston	3–0
1901	No tournament			
1902	United States	Great Britain	New York	3–2
1903	Great Britain	United States	Boston	4–1
1904	Great Britain	Belgium	Wimbledon	5–0
1905	Great Britain	United States	Wimbledon	5–0
1906	Great Britain	United States	Wimbledon	5–0
1907	Australasia	Great Britain	Wimbledon	3–2
1908	Australasia	United States	Melbourne	3–2
1909	Australasia	United States	Sydney	5–0
1910	No tournament			
1911	Australasia	United States	Christchurch, NZ	5–0
1912	Great Britain	Australasia	Melbourne	3–2
1913	United States	Great Britain	Wimbledon	3–2
1914	Australasia	United States	New York	3–2
1915–18	No tournament			
1919	Australasia	Great Britain	Sydney	4–1
1920	United States	Australasia	Auckland, N.Z.	5–0
1921	United States	Japan	New York	5–0
1922	United States	Australasia	New York	4–1
1923	United States	Australasia	New York	4–1
1924	United States	Australia	Philadelphia	5–0
1925	United States	France	Philadelphia	5–0
1926	United States	France	Philadelphia	4–1
1927	France	United States	Philadelphia	3–2
1928	France	United States	Paris	4–1
1929	France	United States	Paris	3–2
1930	France	United States	Paris	4–1
1931	France	Great Britain	Paris	3–2
1932	France	United States	Paris	3–2
1933	Great Britain	France	Paris	3–2
1934	Great Britain	United States	Wimbledon	4–1
1935	Great Britain	United States	Wimbledon	5–0
1936	Great Britain	Australia	Wimbledon	3–2
1937	United States	Great Britain	Wimbledon	4–1
1938	United States	Australia	Philadelphia	3–2
1939	Australia	United States	Philadelphia	3–2
1940–45	No tournament			
1946	United States	Australia	Melbourne	5–0
1947	United States	Australia	New York	4–1
1948	United States	Australia	New York	5–0
1949	United States	Australia	New York	4–1
1950	Australia	United States	New York	4–1
1951	Australia	United States	Sydney	3–2
1952	Australia	United States	Adelaide	4–1
1953	Australia	United States	Melbourne	3–2
1954	United States	Australia	Sydney	3–2
1955	Australia	United States	New York	5–0
1956	Australia	United States	Adelaide	5–0
1957	Australia	United States	Melbourne	3–2
1958	United States	Australia	Brisbane	3–2
1959	Australia	United States	New York	3–2
1960	Australia	Italy	Sydney	4–1
1961	Australia	Italy	Melbourne	5–0
1962	Australia	Mexico	Brisbane	5–0
1963	United States	Australia	Adelaide	3–2
1964	Australia	United States	Cleveland	3–2
1965	Australia	Spain	Sydney	4–1
1966	Australia	India	Melbourne	4–1
1967	Australia	Spain	Brisbane	4–1
1968	United States	Australia	Adelaide	4–1
1969	United States	Romania	Cleveland	5–0
1970	United States	West Germany	Cleveland	5–0

Davis Cup *(Cont.)*

Year	Winner	Finalist	Site	Score
1971	United States	Romania	Charlotte, N.C.	3–2
1972	United States	Romania	Bucharest, Rom.	3–2
1973	Australia	United States	Cleveland	5–0
1974	South Africa	India	*	walkover
1975	Sweden	Czechoslovakia	Stockholm	3–2
1976	Italy	Chile	Santiago	4–1
1977	Australia	Italy	Sydney	3–1
1978	United States	Great Britain	Palm Springs	4–1
1979	United States	Italy	San Francisco	5–0
1980	Czechoslovakia	Italy	Prague	4–1
1981	United States	Argentina	Cincinnati	3–1
1982	United States	France	Grenoble, France	4–1
1983	Australia	Sweden	Melbourne	3–2
1984	Sweden	United States	Goteborg, Sweden	4–1
1985	Sweden	West Germany	Munich	3–2
1986	Australia	Sweden	Melbourne	3–2
1987	Sweden	India	Goteborg, Sweden	5–0
1988	West Germany	Sweden	Goteborg, Sweden	4–1
1989	West Germany	Sweden	Stuttgart	3–2
1990	United States	Australia	St. Petersburg	3–2
1991	France	United States	Lyon	3–1
1992	United States	Switzerland	Fort Worth, Tex.	3–1
1993	Germany	Australia	Dusseldorf	4–1
1994	Sweden	Russia	Moscow	4–1
1995	United States	Russia	Moscow	3–2
1996	France	Sweden	Malmo, Sweden	3–2
1997	Sweden	United States	Goteborg, Sweden	5–0
1998	Sweden	Italy	Milan	4–1
1999	Australia	France	Nice, France	3–2
2000	Spain	Australia	Barcelona	3–1
2001	France	Australia	Melbourne	3–2
2002	Russia	France	Paris	3–2
2003	Australia	Spain	Melbourne	3–1
2004	Spain	United States	Seville, Spain	3–2
2005	Croatia	Slovakia	Bratislava, Slovakia	3–2

*India refused to play the final in protest over South Africa's governmental policy of apartheid.
Note: Prior to 1972 the challenge-round system was in effect, with the previous year's winner "standing out" of the competition until the finals. A straight 16-nation tournament has been held since 1981.

Federation Cup

The Federation Cup was started in 1963 by the International Lawn Tennis Federation (now the ITF). Until 1991 all entrants gathered at one site at one time for a tournament that was concluded within one week. Since 1995 the Fed Cup, as it is now called, has been contested in three rounds by a World Group of eight nations. A meeting between two countries now consists of five matches: four singles and one doubles. The United States has the most wins (17), followed by Australia (7).

Year	Winner	Finalist	Site	Score
1963	United States	Australia	London	2–1
1964	Australia	United States	Philadelphia	2–1
1965	Australia	United States	Melbourne	2–1
1966	United States	West Germany	Turin	3–0
1967	United States	Great Britain	W Berlin	3–0
1968	Australia	Netherlands	Paris	3–0
1969	United States	Australia	Athens	2–1
1970	Australia	Great Britain	Freiburg	3–0
1971	Australia	Great Britain	Perth	3–0
1972	South Africa	Great Britain	Johannesburg	2–1
1973	Australia	South Africa	Bad Homburg	3–0
1974	Australia	United States	Naples	2–1
1975	Czechoslovakia	Australia	Aix-en-Provence	3–0

Federation Cup *(Cont.)*

Year	Winner	Finalist	Site	Score
1976	United States	Australia	Philadelphia	2–1
1977	United States	Australia	Eastbourne, Eng.	2–1
1978	United States	Australia	Melbourne	2–1
1979	United States	Australia	Madrid	3–0
1980	United States	Australia	West Berlin	3–0
1981	United States	Great Britain	Nagoya	3–0
1982	United States	West Germany	Santa Clara, Calif.	3–0
1983	Czechoslovakia	West Germany	Zurich	2–1
1984	Czechoslovakia	Australia	Sao Paulo	2–1
1985	Czechoslovakia	United States	Tokyo	2–1
1986	United States	Czechoslovakia	Prague	3–0
1987	West Germany	United States	Vancouver	2–1
1988	Czechoslovakia	USSR	Melbourne	2–1
1989	United States	Spain	Tokyo	3–0
1990	United States	USSR	Atlanta	2–1
1991	Spain	United States	Nottingham	2–1
1992	Germany	Spain	Frankfurt	2–1
1993	Spain	Australia	Frankfurt	3–0
1994	Spain	United States	Frankfurt	3–0
1995	Spain	United States	Valencia, Spain	3–2
1996	United States	Spain	Atlantic City	5–0
1997	France	Netherlands	Hertogenbosch, Neth.	4–1
1998	Spain	Switzerland	Geneva	3–2
1999	United States	Russia	Palo Alto, Calif.	4–1
2000	United States	Spain	Las Vegas	5–0
2001	Belgium	Russia	Barcelona	2–1
2002	Slovak Republic	Spain	Maspalomas, Canary Isl.	3–1
2003	France	United States	Moscow	4–1
2004	Russia	France	Moscow	3–2
2005	Russia	France	Paris	3–2
2006	Italy	Belgium	Charleroi, Belgium	3–2

Rankings

ATP Computer Year-End Top 10 — Men

1973
1 Ilie Nastase
2 John Newcombe
3 Jimmy Connors
4 Tom Okker
5 Stan Smith
6 Ken Rosewall
7 Manuel Orantes
8 Rod Laver
9 Jan Kodes
10 Arthur Ashe

1974
1 Jimmy Connors
2 John Newcombe
3 Bjorn Borg
4 Rod Laver
5 Guillermo Vilas
6 Tom Okker
7 Arthur Ashe
8 Ken Rosewall
9 Stan Smith
10 Ilie Nastase

1975
1 Jimmy Connors
2 Guillermo Vilas
3 Bjorn Borg
4 Arthur Ashe
5 Manuel Orantes
6 Ken Rosewall
7 Ilie Nastase
8 John Alexander
9 Roscoe Tanner
10 Rod Laver

1976
1 Jimmy Connors
2 Bjorn Borg
3 Ilie Nastase
4 Manuel Orantes
5 Raul Ramirez
6 Guillermo Vilas
7 Adriano Panatta
8 Harold Solomon
9 Eddie Dibbs
10 Brian Gottfried

1977
1 Jimmy Connors
2 Guillermo Vilas
3 Bjorn Borg
4 Vitas Gerulaitis
5 Brian Gottfried
6 Eddie Dibbs
7 Manuel Orantes
8 Raul Ramirez
9 Ilie Nastase
10 Dick Stockton

1978
1 Jimmy Connors
2 Bjorn Borg
3 Guillermo Vilas
4 John McEnroe
5 Vitas Gerulaitis
6 Eddie Dibbs
7 Brian Gottfried
8 Raul Ramirez
9 Harold Solomon
10 Corrado Barazzutti

1979
1 Bjorn Borg
2 Jimmy Connors
3 John McEnroe
4 Vitas Gerulaitis
5 Roscoe Tanner
6 Guillermo Vilas
7 Arthur Ashe
8 Harold Solomon
9 Jose Higueras
10 Eddie Dibbs

1980
1 Bjorn Borg
2 John McEnroe
3 Jimmy Connors
4 Gene Mayer
5 Guillermo Vilas
6 Ivan Lendl
7 Harold Solomon
8 Jose–Luis Clerc
9 Vitas Gerulaitis
10 Eliot Teltscher

1981
1 John McEnroe
2 Ivan Lendl
3 Jimmy Connors
4 Bjorn Borg
5 Jose–Luis Clerc
6 Guillermo Vilas
7 Gene Mayer
8 Eliot Teltscher
9 Vitas Gerulaitis
10 Peter McNamara

1982
1 John McEnroe
2 Jimmy Connors
3 Ivan Lendl
4 Guillermo Vilas
5 Vitas Gerulaitis
6 Jose–Luis Clerc
7 Mats Wilander
8 Gene Mayer
9 Yannick Noah
10 Peter McNamara

ATP Computer Year-End Top 10 — Men *(Cont.)*

1983
1. John McEnroe
2. Ivan Lendl
3. Jimmy Connors
4. Mats Wilander
5. Yannick Noah
6. Jimmy Arias
7. Jose Higueras
8. Jose–Luis Clerc
9. Kevin Curren
10. Gene Mayer

1984
1. John McEnroe
2. Jimmy Connors
3. Ivan Lendl
4. Mats Wilander
5. Andres Gomez
6. Anders Jarryd
7. Henrik Sundstrom
8. Pat Cash
9. Eliot Teltscher
10. Yannick Noah

1985
1. Ivan Lendl
2. John McEnroe
3. Mats Wilander
4. Jimmy Connors
5. Stefan Edberg
6. Boris Becker
7. Yannick Noah
8. Anders Jarryd
9. Miloslav Mecir
10. Kevin Curren

1986
1. Ivan Lendl
2. Boris Becker
3. Mats Wilander
4. Yannick Noah
5. Stefan Edberg
6. Henri Leconte
7. Joakim Nystrom
8. Jimmy Connors
9. Miloslav Mecir
10. Andres Gomez

1987
1. Ivan Lendl
2. Stefan Edberg
3. Mats Wilander
4. Jimmy Connors
5. Boris Becker
6. Miloslav Mecir
7. Pat Cash
8. Yannick Noah
9. Tim Mayotte
10. John McEnroe

1988
1. Mats Wilander
2. Ivan Lendl
3. Andre Agassi
4. Boris Becker
5. Stefan Edberg
6. Kent Carlsson
7. Jimmy Connors
8. Jakob Hlasek
9. Henri Leconte
10. Tim Mayotte

1989
1. Ivan Lendl
2. Boris Becker
3. Stefan Edberg
4. John McEnroe
5. Michael Chang
6. Brad Gilbert
7. Andre Agassi
8. Aaron Krickstein
9. Alberto Mancini
10. Jay Berger

1990
1. Stefan Edberg
2. Boris Becker
3. Ivan Lendl
4. Andre Agassi
5. Pete Sampras
6. Andres Gomez
7. Thomas Muster
8. Emilio Sanchez
9. Goran Ivanisevic
10. Brad Gilbert

1991
1. Stefan Edberg
2. Jim Courier
3. Boris Becker
4. Michael Stich
5. Ivan Lendl
6. Pete Sampras
7. Guy Forget
8. Karel Novacek
9. Petr Korda
10. Andre Agassi

1992
1. Jim Courier
2. Stefan Edberg
3. Pete Sampras
4. Goran Ivanisevic
5. Boris Becker
6. Michael Chang
7. Petr Korda
8. Ivan Lendl
9. Andre Agassi
10. Richard Krajicek

1993
1. Pete Sampras
2. Michael Stich
3. Jim Courier
4. Sergi Bruguera
5. Stefan Edberg
6. Andrei Medvedev
7. Goran Ivanisevic
8. Michael Chang
9. Thomas Muster
10. Cedric Pioline

1994
1. Pete Sampras
2. Andre Agassi
3. Boris Becker
4. Sergi Bruguera
5. Goran Ivanisevic
6. Michael Chang
7. Stefan Edberg
8. Alberto Berasategui
9. Michael Stich
10. Todd Martin

1995
1. Pete Sampras
2. Andre Agassi
3. Thomas Muster
4. Boris Becker
5. Michael Chang
6. Yevgeny Kafelnikov
7. Thomas Enqvist
8. Jim Courier
9. Wayne Ferreira
10. Goran Ivanisevic

1996
1. Pete Sampras
2. Michael Chang
3. Yevgeny Kafelnikov
4. Goran Ivanisevic
5. Thomas Muster
6. Boris Becker
7. Richard Krajicek
8. Andre Agassi
9. Thomas Enqvist
10. Wayne Ferreira

1997
1. Pete Sampras
2. Patrick Rafter
3. Michael Chang
4. Jonas Bjorkman
5. Yevgeny Kafelnikov
6. Greg Rusedski
7. Carlos Moya
8. Sergi Bruguera
9. Thomas Muster
10. Marcelo Ríos

1998
1. Pete Sampras
2. Marcelo Rios
3. Alex Corretja
4. Patrick Rafter
5. Carlos Moya
6. Andre Agassi
7. Tim Henman
8. Karol Kucera
9. Greg Rusedski
10. Richard Krajicek

1999
1. Andre Agassi
2. Yevgeny Kafelnikov
3. Pete Sampras
4. Thomas Enqvist
5. Gustavo Kuerten
6. Nicolas Kiefer
7. Todd Martin
8. Nicolas Lapentti
9. Marcelo Rios
10. Richard Krajicek

2000
1. Gustavo Kuerten
2. Marat Safin
3. Pete Sampras
4. Magnus Norman
5. Yevgeny Kafelnikov
6. Andre Agassi
7. Lleyton Hewitt
8. Alex Corretja
9. Thomas Enqvist
10. Tim Henman

2001
1. Lleyton Hewitt
2. Gustavo Kuerten
3. Andre Agassi
4. Yevgeny Kafelnikov
5. Juan Carlos Ferrero
6. Sebastien Grosjean
7. Patrick Rafter
8. Tommy Haas
9. Tim Henman
10. Pete Sampras

2002
1. Lleyton Hewitt
2. Andre Agassi
3. Marat Safin
4. Juan Carlos Ferrero
5. Carlos Moya
6. Roger Federer
7. Jiri Novak
8. Tim Henman
9. Albert Costa
10. Andy Roddick

2003
1. Andy Roddick
2. Roger Federer
3. Juan Carlos Ferrero
4. Andre Agassi
5. Guillermo Coria
6. Rainer Schuettler
7. Carlos Moya
8. David Nalbandian
9. Mark Philippoussis
10. Sebastien Grosjean

2004
1. Roger Federer
2. Andy Roddick
3. Lleyton Hewitt
4. Marat Safin
5. Carlos Moya
6. Tim Henman
7. Guillermo Coria
8. Andre Agassi
9. David Nalbandian
10. Gaston Gaudio

2005
1. Roger Federer
2. Rafael Nadal
3. Andy Roddick
4. Lleyton Hewitt
5. Nikolay Davydenko
6. David Nalbandian
7. Andre Agassi
8. Guillermo Coria
9. Ivan Ljubicic
10. Gaston Gaudio

WTA Computer Year-End Top 10 — Women

1973
1 Margaret Smith Court
2 Billie Jean King
3 Evonne Goolagong
4 Chris Evert
5 Rosie Casals
6 Virginia Wade
7 Kerry Reid
8 Nancy Gunter
9 Julie Heldman
10 Helga Masthoff

1974
1 Billie Jean King
2 Evonne Goolagong
3 Chris Evert
4 Virginia Wade
5 Julie Heldman
6 Rosie Casals
7 Kerry Reid
8 Olga Morozova
9 Lesley Hunt
10 Francoise Durr

1975
1 Chris Evert
2 Billie Jean King
3 Evonne Goolagong Cawley
4 Martina Navratilova
5 Virginia Wade
6 Margaret Smith Court
7 Olga Morozova
8 Nancy Gunter
9 Francoise Durr
10 Rosie Casals

1976
1 Chris Evert
2 Evonne Goolagong Cawley
3 Virginia Wade
4 Martina Navratilova
5 Sue Barker
6 Betty Stove
7 Dianne Balestrat
8 Mima Jausovec
9 Rosie Casals
10 Francoise Durr

1977
1 Chris Evert
2 Billie Jean King
3 Martina Navratilova
4 Virginia Wade
5 Sue Barker
6 Rosie Casals
7 Betty Stove
8 Dianne Balestrat
9 Wendy Turnbull
10 Kerry Reid

1978
1 Martina Navratilova
2 Chris Evert
3 Evonne Goolagong Cawley
4 Virginia Wade
5 Billie Jean King
6 Tracy Austin
7 Wendy Turnbull
8 Kerry Reid
9 Betty Stove
10 Dianne Balestrat

1979
1 Martina Navratilova
2 Chris Evert Lloyd
3 Tracy Austin
4 Evonne Goolagong Cawley
5 Billie Jean King
6 Dianne Balestrat
7 Wendy Turnbull
8 Virginia Wade
9 Kerry Reid
10 Sue Barker

1980
1 Chris Evert Lloyd
2 Tracy Austin
3 Martina Navratilova
4 Hana Mandlikova
5 Evonne Goolagong Cawley
6 Billie Jean King
7 Andrea Jaeger
8 Wendy Turnbull
9 Pam Shriver
10 Greer Stevens

1981
1 Chris Evert Lloyd
2 Tracy Austin
3 Martina Navratilova
4 Andrea Jaeger
5 Hana Mandlikova
6 Sylvia Hanika
7 Pam Shriver
8 Wendy Turnbull
9 Bettina Bunge
10 Barbara Potter

1982
1 Martina Navratilova
2 Chris Evert Lloyd
3 Andrea Jaeger
4 Tracy Austin
5 Wendy Turnbull
6 Pam Shriver
7 Hana Mandlikova
8 Barbara Potter
9 Bettina Bunge
10 Sylvia Hanika

1983
1 Martina Navratilova
2 Chris Evert Lloyd
3 Andrea Jaeger
4 Pam Shriver
5 Sylvia Hanika
6 Jo Durie
7 Bettina Bunge
8 Wendy Turnbull
9 Tracy Austin
10 Zina Garrison

1984
1 Martina Navratilova
2 Chris Evert Lloyd
3 Hana Mandlikova
4 Pam Shriver
5 Wendy Turnbull
6 Manuela Maleeva
7 Helena Sukova
8 Claudia Kohde-Kilsch
9 Zina Garrison
10 Kathy Jordan

1985
1 Martina Navratilova
2 Chris Evert Lloyd
3 Hana Mandlikova
4 Pam Shriver
5 Claudia Kohde-Kilsch
6 Steffi Graf
7 Manuela Maleeva
8 Zina Garrison
9 Helena Sukova
10 Bonnie Gadusek

1986
1 Martina Navratilova
2 Chris Evert Lloyd
3 Pam Shriver
4 Hana Mandlikova
5 Helena Sukova
6 Pam Shriver
7 Claudia Kohde-Kilsch
8 Manuela Maleeva
9 Kathy Rinaldi
10 Gabriela Sabatini

1987
1 Steffi Graf
2 Martina Navratilova
3 Chris Evert
4 Pam Shriver
5 Hana Mandlikova
6 Gabriela Sabatini
7 Helena Sukova
8 Manuela Maleeva
9 Zina Garrison
10 Claudia Kohde-Kilsch

1988
1 Steffi Graf
2 Martina Navratilova
3 Chris Evert
4 Gabriela Sabatini
5 Pam Shriver
6 Manuela Maleeva-Fragniere
7 Natalia Zvereva
8 Helena Sukova
9 Zina Garrison
10 Barbara Potter

1989
1 Steffi Graf
2 Martina Navratilova
3 Gabriela Sabatini
4 Zina Garrison
5 Arantxa Sánchez Vicario
6 Monica Seles
7 Conchita Martinez
8 Helena Sukova
9 Manuela Maleeva-Fragniere
10 Chris Evert*

1990
1 Steffi Graf
2 Monica Seles
3 Martina Navratilova
4 Mary Joe Fernandez
5 Gabriela Sabatini
6 Katerina Maleeva
7 Arantxa Sánchez Vicario
8 Jennifer Capriati
9 Manuela Maleeva-Fragniere
10 Zina Garrison

1991
1 Monica Seles
2 Steffi Graf
3 Gabriela Sabatini
4 Martina Navratilova
5 Arantxa Sánchez Vicario
6 Jennifer Capriati
7 Jana Novotna
8 Mary Joe Fernandez
9 Conchita Martinez
10 Manuela Maleeva-Fragniere

1992
1 Monica Seles
2 Steffi Graf
3 Gabriela Sabatini
4 Arantxa Sánchez Vicario
5 Martina Navratilova
6 Mary Joe Fernandez
7 Jennifer Capriati
8 Conchita Martinez
9 M. Maleeva-Fragniere
10 Jana Novotna

1993
1 Steffi Graf
2 Arantxa Sánchez Vicario
3 Martina Navratilova
4 Conchita Martinez
5 Gabriela Sabatini
6 Jana Novotna
7 Mary Joe Fernandez
8 Monica Seles
9 Jennifer Capriati
10 Anke Huber

1994
1 Steffi Graf
2 Arantxa Sánchez Vicario
3 Conchita Martinez
4 Jana Novotna
5 Mary Pierce
6 Lindsay Davenport
7 Gabriela Sabatini
8 Martina Navratilova
9 Kimiko Date
10 Natasha Zvereva

1995
1 Steffi Graf (co-No.1)
1 Monica Seles(co-No.1)
2 Conchita Martinez
3 A. S.Vicario
4 Kimiko Date
5 Mary Pierce
6 Magdalena Maleeva
7 Gabriela Sabatini
8 Mary Joe Fernandez
9 Iva Majoli
10 Anke Huber

1996
1 Steffi Graf
2 Monica Seles
3 Jana Novotna
4 Lindsay Davenport
5 Martina Hingis
6 Stephanie de Ville
7 Tamarine Tanasugarn
8 Anke Huber
9 Conchita Martinez
10 Julie Halard-Decugis

*When Chris Evert announced her retirement at the 1989 United States Open, she was ranked fourth in the world. That was her last official series tournament.

WTA Computer Year-End Top 10 — Women *(Cont.)*

1997
1 Martina Hingis
2 Jana Novotna
3 Lindsay Davenport
4 Amanda Coetzer
5 Monica Seles
6 Iva Majoli
7 Mary Pierce
8 Irina Spirlea
9 Arantxa Sánchez Vicario
10 Mary Joe Fernandez

1998
1 Lindsay Davenport
2 Martina Hingis
2 Jana Novotna
4 A.S. Vicario
5 Venus Williams
6 Monica Seles
7 Mary Pierce
8 Conchita Martinez
9 Steffi Graf
10 Nathalie Tauziat

1999
1 Martina Hingis
2 Lindsay Davenport
3 Venus Williams
4 Serena Williams
5 Mary Pierce
6 Monica Seles
7 Nathalie Tauziat
8 Barbara Schett
9 J. Halard-Decugis
10 Amelie Mauresmo

2000
1 Martina Hingis
2 Lindsay Davenport
3 Venus Williams
4 Monica Seles
5 Conchita Martinez
6 Serena Williams
7 Mary Pierce
8 Anna Kournikova
9 Arantxa Sánchez Vicario
10 Nathalie Tauziat

2001
1 Lindsay Davenport
2 Jennifer Capriati
3 Venus Williams
4 Martina Hingis
5 Kim Clijsters
6 Serena Williams
7 Justine Henin
8 Jelena Dokic
9 Amelie Mauresmo
10 Monica Seles

2002
1 Serena Williams
2 Venus Williams
3 Jennifer Capriati
4 Kim Clijsters
5 Justine Henin
6 Amelie Mauresmo
7 Monica Seles
8 Daniela Hantuchova
9 Jelena Dokic
10 Martina Hingis

2003
1 Justine Henin-Hardenne
2 Kim Clijsters
3 Serena Williams
4 Amelie Mauresmo
5 Lindsay Davenport
6 Jennifer Capriati
7 Anastasia Myskina
8 Elena Dementieva
9 Chandra Rubin
10 Ai Sugiyama

2004
1 Lindsay Davenport
2 Amelie Mauresmo
3 Anastasia Myskina
4 Maria Sharapova
5 Svetlana Kuznetsova
6 Elena Dementieva
7 Serena Williams
8 Justine Henin-Hardenne
9 Venus Williams
10 Jennifer Capriati

2005
1. Lindsay Davenport
2. Maria Sharapova
3. Amelie Mauresmo
4. Serena Williams
5. Elena Dementieva
6. Anastasia Myskina
7. Svetlana Kuznetsova
8. Alicia Molik
9. Venus Williams
10. Vera Zvonareva

Prize Money

Top 25 Men's Career Prize Money Leaders

Note: From arrival of Open tennis in 1968 through September 26, 2006.

	Earnings ($)
Pete Sampras	43,280,489
Andre Agassi	30,664,925
Boris Becker	25,080,956
Yevgeny Kafelnikov	23,883,797
Roger Federer	23,783,223
Ivan Lendl	21,262,417
Stefan Edberg	20,630,941
Goran Ivanisevic	19,876,579
Michael Chang	19,145,632
Lleyton Hewitt	15,669,666
Gustavo Kuerten	14,609,954
Jim Courier	14,033,132
Michael Stich	12,592,483
John McEnroe	12,539,622
Thomas Muster	12,224,410
Carlos Moya	11,767,562
Sergi Bruguera	11,632,199
Jonas Bjorkman	11,564,748
Patrick Rafter	11,127,058
Tim Henman	11,030,519
Petr Korda	10,448,450
Alex Corretja	10,338,209
Thomas Enqvist	10,290,743
Richard Krajicek	10,077,425
Wayne Ferreira	9,969,617

Top 25 Women's Career Prize Money Leaders

Note: From arrival of Open tennis in 1968 through September 26, 2006.

	Earnings ($)
Steffi Graf	21,895,277
Lindsay Davenport	21,763,653
Martina Navratilova	21,626,089
Martina Hingis	19,342,952
Arantxa Sánchez Vicario	16,942,640
Venus Williams	16,287,774
Serena Williams	16,006,592
Monica Seles	14,891,762
Kim Clijsters	14,009,637
Justine Henin-Hardenne	12,573,319
Amelie Mauresmo	12,310,262
Conchita Martinez	11,527,977
Jana Novotna	11,249,284
Jennifer Capriati	10,206,639
Mary Pierce	9,765,484
Chris Evert	8,896,195
Gabriela Sabatini	8,785,850
Natasha Zvereva	7,792,503
Maria Sharapova	7,774,967
Elena Dementieva	7,394,746
Lisa Raymond	6,851,566
Nathalie Tauziat	6,650,093
Helena Sukova	6,391,245
Ai Sugiyama	6,140,101
Svetlana Kuznetsova	5,801,267

Men's Career Leaders—Singles Titles Won

The top tournament-winning men from the institution of Open tennis in 1968 through Sept 26, 2005.

	W		W
Jimmy Connors	109	Thomas Muster	44
Ivan Lendl	94	Roger Federer	41
John McEnroe	77	Stefan Edberg	41
Pete Sampras	64	Stan Smith	39
Bjorn Borg	62	Michael Chang	34
Guillermo Vilas	62	Arthur Ashe	33
Andre Agassi	60	Mats Wilander	33
Ilie Nastase	57	John Newcombe	32
Boris Becker	49	Manuel Orantes	32
Rod Laver	47	Ken Rosewall	32
		Tom Okker	31

Women's Career Leaders—Singles Titles Won

The top tournament-winning women from the institution of Open tennis in 1968 through Sept. 26, 2005.

	W		W
Martina Navratilova	167	Helga Masthoff	37
Chris Evert	157	Venus Williams	33
Steffi Graf	107	Conchita Martinez	33
Margaret Smith Court	92	Olga Morozova	31
Evonne Goolagong Cawley	88	Kim Clijsters	29
Billie Jean King	67	Tracy Austin	29
Maria Bueno	63	Arantxa Sánchez Vicario	29
Virginia Wade	55	Hana Mandlikova	27
Monica Seles	53	Gabriela Sabatini	27
Lindsay Davenport	49	Francoise Durr-Browning	26
Martina Hingis	40	Serena Williams	26

Men—Tennis Masters Cup*

Year	Player	Year	Player	Year	Player
1970	Stan Smith	1983	Ivan Lendl	1995	Boris Becker
1971	Ilie Nastase	1984	John McEnroe	1996	Pete Sampras
1972	Ilie Nastase	1985	John McEnroe	1997	Pete Sampras
1973	Ilie Nastase	1986 (Jan)	Ivan Lendl	1998	Alex Corretja
1974	Guillermo Vilas	1986 (Dec)	Ivan Lendl	1999	Pete Sampras
1975	Ilie Nastase	1987	Ivan Lendl	2000	Gustavo Kuerten
1976	Manuel Orantes	1988	Boris Becker	2001	Lleyton Hewitt
1977	Not held	1989	Stefan Edberg	2002	Lleyton Hewitt
1978	Jimmy Connors	1990	Andre Agassi	2003	Roger Federer
1979	John McEnroe	1991	Pete Sampras	2004	Roger Federer
1980	Bjorn Borg	1992	Boris Becker	2005	David Nalbandian
1981	Bjorn Borg	1993	Michael Stich		
1982	Ivan Lendl	1994	Pete Sampras		

Women—WTA Tour Championships

Year	Player	Year	Player	Year	Player
1972	Chris Evert	1983	Martina Navratilova	1994	Gabriela Sabatini
1973	Chris Evert	1984*	Martina Navratilova	1995	Steffi Graf
1974	Evonne Goolagong	1985	Martina Navratilova	1996	Steffi Graf
1975	Chris Evert	1986 (Mar)	Martina Navratilova	1997	Jana Novotna
1976	Evonne Goolagong Cawley	1986 (Nov)	Martina Navratilova	1998	Martina Hingis
1977	Chris Evert	1987	Steffi Graf	1999	Lindsay Davenport
1978	Martina Navratilova	1988	Gabriela Sabatini	2000	Martina Hingis
1979	Martina Navratilova	1989	Steffi Graf	2001	Serena Williams
1980	Tracy Austin	1990	Monica Seles	2002	Kim Clijsters
1981	Martina Navratilova	1991	Monica Seles	2003	Kim Clijsters
1982	Sylvia Hanika	1992	Monica Seles	2004	Maria Sharapova
		1993	Steffi Graf	2005	Amelie Mauresmo

*From 1970 to 1989, tournament was known as the The Masters, from1990 to 1999, tournament was known as the ATP Tour World Championship.

Pauline Betz Addie (1965)
George T. Adee (1964)
Fred B. Alexander (1961)
Wilmer L. Allison (1963)
Manuel Alonso (1977)
Malcolm Anderson (2000)
Arthur Ashe (1985)
Juliette Atkinson (1974)
H.W. Bunny Austin (1997)
Tracy Austin (1992)
Lawrence A. Baker Sr. (1975)
Maud Barger–Wallach (1958)
Angela Mortimer Barrett (1993)
Boris Becker (2003)
Karl Behr (1969)
Nancy Wynne Bolton (2006)
Bjorn Borg (1987)
Jean Borotra (1976)
Lesley Turner Bowrey (1997)
Maureen Connolly Brinker (1968)
John Bromwich (1984)
Norman Everard Brookes (1977)
Mary K. Browne (1957)
Jacques Brugnon (1976)
Butch Buchholz (2005)
J. Donald Budge (1964)
Maria E. Bueno (1978)
May Sutton Bundy (1956)
Mabel E. Cahill (1976)
Rosie Casals (1996)
Oliver S. Campbell (1955)
Malcolm Chace (1961)
Dorothy (Dodo) Cheney (2004)
Dorothea Douglass Chambers (1981)
Philippe Chatrier (1992)
Louise Brough Clapp (1967)
Clarence Clark (1983)
Joseph S. Clark (1955)
Gianni Clerici (2006)
William J. Clothier (1956)
Henri Cochet (1976)
Arthur W. (Bud) Collins Jr. (1994)
Jimmy Connors (1998)
Ashley Cooper (1991)
Jim Courier (2004)
Margaret Smith Court (1979)
Gottfried von Cramm (1977)
Jack Crawford (1979)
Joseph F. Cullman III (1990)
Allison Danzig (1968)
Sarah Palfrey Danzig (1963)
Herman David (1998)
Dwight F. Davis (1956)
Charlotte Dod (1983)
John H. Doeg (1962)
Lawrence Doherty (1980)
Reginald Doherty (1980)
Jaroslav Drobny (1983)
Margaret Osborne duPont (1967)
Francoise Durr (2003)
James Dwight (1955)
Stefan Edberg (2004)
Roy Emerson (1982)
Pierre Etchebaster (1978)
Chris Evert (1995)
Robert Falkenburg (1974)
Marion Jones Farquhar (2006)

Neale Fraser (1984)
Shirley Fry-Irvin (1970)
Charles S. Garland (1969)
Althea Gibson (1971)
Kathleen McKane Godfree (1978)
Richard A. Gonzales (1968)
Evonne Goolagong Cawley (1988)
Arthur Gore (2006)
Steffi Graf (2004)
Bryan M. Grant Jr. (1972)
David Gray (1985)
Clarence Griffin (1970)
King Gustaf V of Sweden (1980)
Harold H. Hackett (1961)
Ellen Forde Hansell (1965)
Darlene R. Hard (1973)
Doris J. Hart (1969)
Gladys M. Heldman (1979)
W.E. (Slew) Hester Jr. (1981)
Bob Hewitt (1992)
Lew Hoad (1980)
Harry Hopman (1978)
Fred Hovey (1974)
Joseph R. Hunt (1966)
Lamar Hunt (1993)
Francis T. Hunter (1961)
Helen Hull Jacobs (1962)
William Johnston (1958)
Ann Haydon Jones (1985)
Perry Jones (1970)
Robert Kelleher (2000)
Billie Jean King (1987)
Jan Kodes (1990)
Karel Kozeluh (2006)
John A. Kramer (1968)
Rene Lacoste (1976)
Al Laney (1979)
William A. Larned (1956)
Arthur D. Larsen (1969)
Rod G. Laver (1981)
Herbert Lawford (2006)
Ivan Lendl (2001)
Suzanne Lenglen (1978)
Dorothy Round Little (1986)
George M. Lott Jr. (1964)
Gene Mako (1973)
Molla Bjurstedt Mallory (1958)
Hana Mandlikova (1994)
Alice Marble (1964)
Alastair B. Martin (1973)
William McChesney Martin (1982)
Dan Maskell (1996)
Simonne Mathieu (2006)
John McEnroe (1999)
Ken McGregor (1999)
Chuck McKinley (1986)
Maurice McLoughlin (1957)
Frew McMillan (1992)
W. Donald McNeill (1965)
Elisabeth H. Moore (1971)
Gardnar Mulloy (1972)
R. Lindley Murray (1958)
Julian S. Myrick (1963)
Ilie Nastase (1991)
Martina Navratilova (2000)
John D. Newcombe (1986)
Arthur C. Nielsen Sr (1971)

Yannick Noah (2005)
Jana Novotna (2005)
Hans Nusslein (2006)
Alex Olmedo (1987)
Rafael Osuna (1979)
Mary Ewing Outerbridge (1981)
Frank A. Parker (1966)
Gerald Patterson (1989)
Budge Patty (1977)
Theodore R. Pell (1966)
Fred Perry (1975)
Tom Pettitt (1982)
Nicola Pietrangeli (1986)
Adrian Quist (1984)
Patrick Rafter (2006)
Dennis Ralston (1987)
Ernest Renshaw (1983)
William Renshaw (1983)
Vincent Richards (1961)
Nancy Richey (2003)
Bobby Riggs (1967)
Helen Wills Moody Roark (1959)
Anthony D. Roche (1986)
Ellen C. Roosevelt (1975)
Mervyn Rose (2001)
Ken Rosewall (1980)
Elizabeth Ryan (1972)
Gabriela Sabatini (2006)
Manuel Santana (1984)
Richard Savitt (1976)
Frederick R. Schroeder (1966)
Eleonora Sears (1968)
Richard D. Sears (1955)
Frank Sedgman (1979)
Pancho Segura (1984)
Vic Seixas Jr. (1971)
Francis X. Shields (1964)
Betty Nuthall Shoemaker (1977)
Pam Shriver (2002)
Henry W. Slocum Jr. (1955)
Stan Smith (1987)
Fred Stolle (1985)
William F. Talbert (1967)
Bill Tilden (1959)
Lance Tingay (1982)
Ted Tinling (1986)
Brian Tobin (2003)
Bertha Townsend Toulmin (1974)
Tony Trabert (1970)
James H. Van Alen (1965)
John Van Ryn (1963)
Guillermo Vilas (1991)
Ellsworth Vines (1962)
Virginia Wade (1989)
Marie Wagner (1969)
Holcombe Ward (1956)
Watson Washburn (1965)
Malcolm D. Whitman (1955)
Hazel Hotchkiss Wightman (1957)
Mats Wilander (2002)
Anthony Wilding (1978)
Richard Norris Williams II (1957)
Mjr Walter Clopton Wingfield (1997)
Sidney B. Wood (1964)
Robert D. Wrenn (1955)
Beals C. Wright (1956)

Note: Years in parentheses are dates of induction.

Golf

2006 British Open
and PGA champion
Tiger Woods

Roaring Back

After struggling with his father's illness and eventual death during the first half of 2006, Tiger turned the final few months of the PGA Tour into a dazzling, one-man show

BY STEPHEN CANNELLA

For Tiger Woods's many fans, choosing the most enduring image from a roller-coaster year for golf's greatest player is difficult. Is it the pain that was evident on his face as he muddled through the 2006 U.S. Open in June, barely a month after his father and closest friend, Earl Woods, passed away? Perhaps it's the emotional embrace he shared with his caddie, Steve Williams, on the 18th green after he clinched the British Open championship in July, a rare moment of public soul-baring for a fiercely private man? Or is it the glamorous snapshot of Woods and his wife, Elin Nordgeren, arriving arm-in-arm for the pretournament gala at the Ryder Cup, the one-time wunderkind now, at 30, a man in full?

Woods would likely choose another defining moment for 2006. It took place far from the flashbulbs and the peering eyes of the golf public, on a practice range at Cog Hill Country Club in Chicago, the site of the Western Open in July. Woods had shot a first-round 72 and was still struggling to find his form in a year turned upside down by the death of his father on May 3. Woods was determined to correct a flaw—a slight movement of his head on his backswing and downswing—that was upsetting his balance and timing and wreaking havoc with his game. So he and Hank Haney, his swing

instructor, hunkered down at Cog Hill, with Haney pressing his hand against Woods's face, the teacher keeping the student's head stable as Woods concentrated on rotating his body smoothly through his swing.

It was a long afternoon, the sort of drudgery that few fans think about when they're watching Woods raise a trophy on a Sunday afternoon. It was also the sort of moment Woods had undoubtedly shared countless time with his late father. Later Woods would say the session "turned it all around," meaning both his swing and his season. He went on to finish second at the Western, giving him a much-needed jolt of confidence before the British Open.

After an unsettled few months on and off the golf course, Tiger was back, and by the end of 2006 the best player in the world had distinguished himself even further in the pantheon of his sport. After his British Open victory, Woods tacked on another major title with a commanding win at the PGA Championship, giving him 12 major victories, six short of Jack Nicklaus's record. The PGA was the third in a string of six straight PGA Tour wins for Woods, the second-longest streak in history and more than halfway to what was once deemed golf's most unbreakable record: Byron Nelson's 11 straight wins in 1945. "He's dominating the game," Australia's Adam Scott said after the

Although she didn't dominate the LPGA Tour as in years past, Annika Sorenstam did win her 10th career major at the U.S. Open.

American Express Championship in October, where Scott tied for second, eight strokes behind Woods. "It's not the first time he's done it, either."

Woods's streak was all the more impressive considering the emotional turmoil he was in. When Earl Woods died, after a long battle with cancer, Tiger lost his best friend and role model as well as his most trusted golf confidant. "If you take into account what happened off the golf course, it's my worst year," Woods said after the Amex Championship. "People asked me...'How do you consider the year?' I consider it as a loss. In the grand scheme of things, golf doesn't even compare to losing a parent."

Early in the year, it appeared 2006 would belong not to Woods but to his closest rival, Phil Mickelson. The lefthander, who capped 2005 with a win at the PGA Championship, took his second straight major title and third overall by thrashing the field at the Masters in April. (Tim Scott finished second, two shots back, while Woods finished in a five-way tie for third.) Mickelson took a one-stroke lead into the final round and then drained all drama from Masters Sunday with a flawless 69. By the time he reached the 16th hole he had a four-shot lead and was all but guaranteed of winning his second green jacket. Said his longtime swing coach, Rick Smith, "This is the best round I've ever seen him play."

It was the kind of victory—methodical, disciplined and demoralizing to his opponents—that had the golf community comparing the 35-year-old Mickelson, once famous for an 0-for-42 streak in majors and a propensity for final-round meltdowns, to the alltime greats. There was no such talk after the U.S. Open at Winged Foot, where fans were treated to an unsettling look at the old Phil. After 69 holes, Mickelson was on the precipice of greatness. He held a two-shot lead and was on the verge of joining Woods, Nicklaus and Ben Hogan as the only players to win three straight majors in the modern era. Even after stumbles on the 16th and 17th holes, Mickelson led Australia's Geoff Ogilvy, 29, by a stroke with one to play. Victory, and history, were still within reach.

That all changed when Mickelson hit one of the worst tee shots of his life, a monstrous slice that bounced off a hospitality tent left of the fairway. A comedy of errors followed: a three-iron that bounced off a tree, another iron that landed in a greenside bunker, a bunker shot that trickled off the green. Mickelson ended up with a double bogey, and Ogilvy with a giftwrapped major title, his first. "I still am in shock that I did that," Mickelson said. "I am such an idiot."

It wasn't Mickelson's first collapse on a major stage. He three-putted away the lead at the 2004 U.S. Open on the 71st hole of the tournament and at the British Open that same year he coughed up the lead over the final seven holes. "This one hurts more than

SIMON BRUTY

any [other] tournament because I had it won," he said at Winged Foot. "I had it in my grasp and just let it go."

Woods, meanwhile, was enduring a different sort of misery, playing his first tournament since his father's death. His mind was clearly elsewhere. "Dad would still want me to grind it and give it my best, and that's what I always do," he said. "That's what I will certainly try to do this week."

Three holes and three bogey in, however, it was clear that this was not himself. He ended up missing the cut by three strokes. It was the first time since he turned pro in 1997 that Woods was a spectator for the final two rounds of a major, a streak of 39 consecutive cuts made that tied Jack Nicklaus's alltime record.

In April, Phil Mickelson breezed to his second Masters victory, but after he imploded on the last hole of the U.S. Open in June, he never seemed quite the same.

Woods was a different player at the British Open at Hoylake, England, where he shot a final-round 67 to defeat Chris DiMarco by two and claim his second straight claret jug. It was a masterful display of tactical golf: Woods hit his driver just once in 72 holes and didn't hit a single fairway bunker. When it was over, Woods and his caddie engaged in a long, tearful embrace on the 18th green, a cathartic moment in a trying year. "It just came pouring out of me, all the things my dad meant to me, and the game of golf," Woods said. "I just wish he could have seen it one more time."

The British win started Woods on perhaps the most impressive run of his storied career. He blitzed the field at the PGA Championship at Medinah in August, tying the tournament scoring record (18 under par) that he set in 2000. During his six-match win streak he was a combined 109 under par and won by the astounding total of 20 strokes. "Yes," was his answer when asked at the PGA if he was playing as well as he did during his magical 2000 run, when he won three majors. "I feel like things are pretty darned good right now."

Alas, even Woods was unable to save the U.S. in the Ryder Cup in Straffan, Ireland, where the European team romped to its third straight win and fifth in the last six Cups. The U.S. lost 18½ to 9½, tying its record deficit of 2004. "We're going to have to start giving the Americans handicap strokes," former European Ryder Cup team member Sandy Lyle joked at one point. "This is getting boring."

The same might be said of Woods's dominance of the PGA. But for Woods, 2006 was more than just another stellar year. It was a year of loss and growth off the course, and a year in which he inched closer to his holy grail, Nicklaus's majors record, on it. Now a man of 30, Woods had left his youth behind him. In more than one way, 2006 was the first year of the rest of his life.

FOR THE RECORD • 2005–2006

Men's Majors

The Masters
Augusta National GC (par 72; 7,445 yds);
Augusta, Ga., April 6-9, 2006

Player	Score	Earnings ($)
Phil Mickelson	70-72-70-69—281	1,260,000
Tim Clark	70-72-72-69—283	756,000
Jose Maria Olazabal	76-71-71-66—284	315,700
Retief Goosen	70-73-72-69—284	315,700
Tiger Woods	72-71-71-70—284	315,700
Chad Campbell	71-67-75-71—284	315,700
Fred Couples	71-70-72-71—284	315,700
Angel Cabrera	73-74-70-68—285	210,000
Vijay Singh	67-74-73-71—285	210,000
Stewart Cink	72-73-71-70—286	189,000
Mike Weir	71-73-73-70—287	161,000
Miguel Angel Jimenez	72-74-69-72—287	161,000
Stephen Aames	74-70-70-73—287	161,000
Arron Oberholser	69-75-73-72—288	129,500
Billy Mayfair	71-72-73-71—288	129,500
Geoff Ogilvy	70-75-73-71—289	112,000
Scott Verplank	74-70-74-71—289	112,000
Rod Pampling	72-73-72-72—289	112,000
Nick O'Hern	71-72-76-71—290	91,000
Stuart Appleby	71-75-73-71—290	91,000
David Howell	71-71-76-72—290	91,000

U.S. Open
Winged Foot GC (par 70; 7,264 yds);
Mamaroneck, N.Y., June 15-18, 2006

Player	Score	Earnings ($)
Geoff Ogilvy	71-70-72-72—285	1,225,000
Jim Furyk	70-72-74-70—286	501,249
Colin Montgomerie	69-71-75-71—286	501,249
Phil Mickelson	70-73-69-74—286	501,249
Padraig Harrington	73-69-74-71—287	255,642
Nick O'Hern	75-70-74-69—288	183,225
Jeff Sluman	74-73-72-69—288	183,225
Mike Weir	71-74-71-72—288	183,225
Steve Stricker	70-69-76-73—288	183,225
Vijay Singh	71-74-70-73—288	183,225
Kenneth Ferrie	71-70-71-76—288	183,225
Ryuji Imada	76-73-69-71—289	131,670
Luke Donald	78-69-70-72—289	131,670
Ian Poulter	74-71-70-74—289	131,670
Paul Casey	77-72-72-69—290	116,735
David Howell	70-78-74-69—291	99,417
David Duval	77-68-75-71—291	99,417
Miguel Angel Jimenez	70-75-74-72—291	99,417
Robert Allenby	73-74-72-72—291	99,417
Arron Oberholser	75-68-74-74—291	99,417
Jose Maria Olazabel	75-73-73-71—292	74,252
Tom Pernice, Jr.	79-70-72-71—292	74,252

British Open
Royal Liverpool (par 72; 6,609 yds);
Hoylake, England, July 20–23, 2006

Player	Score	Earnings ($)
Tiger Woods	67-65-71-67—270	1,338,480
Chris DiMarco	70-65-69-68—272	799,370
Ernie Els	68-65-71-71—275	511,225
Jim Furyk	68-71-66-71—276	390,390
Hideto Tanihara	72-68-66-71—277	296,511
Sergio Garcia	68-71-65-73—277	296,511
Angel Cabrera	71-68-66-73—278	237,952
Carl Pettersson	68-72-70-69—279	177,225
Andres Romero	70-70-68-71—279	177,225
Adam Scott	68-69-70-72—279	177,225
AnthonyWall	67-73-71-69—280	128,891
Ben Crane	68-71-71-70—280	128,891
S.K. Ho	68-73-69-70—280	128,891
Sean O'Hair	69-73-72-67—281	105,034
Retief Goosen	70-66-72-73—281	105,034
Robert Rock	69-69-73-71—282	83,655
Bret Rumford	68-71-72-71—282	83,655
Mikko Ilonen	68-69-73-72—282	83,655
Geoff Ogilvy	71-69-70-72—282	83,655
Robert Allenby	69-70-69-74—282	83,655
Peter Lonard	71-69-68-74—282	83,655
Mark Hensby	68-72-74-69—283	65,762

PGA Championship
Medinah CC (par 70; 7,392 yds)
Medinah, Ill., August 17-20, 2006

Player	Score	Earnings ($)
Tiger Woods	69-68-65-68—270	1,224,000
Shaun Micheel	69-70-67-69—275	734,400
Adam Scott	71-69-69-67—276	353,600
Sergio Garcia	69-70-67-70—276	353,600
Luke Donald	68-68-66-74—276	353,600
Mike Weir	72-67-65-73—277	244,800
Steve Stricker	72-67-70-69—278	207,788
K.J. Choi	73-67-67-71—278	207,788
Ryan Moore	71-72-67-69—279	165,000
Ian Poulter	70-70-68-71—279	165,000
Geoff Ogilvy	69-68-68-74—279	165,000
Sean O'Hair	72-70-70-68—280	134,500
Chris DiMarco	71-70-67-72—280	134,500
Henrik Stenson	68-68-73-72—281	115,000
Tim Herron	69-67-72-73—281	115,000
Ernie Els	71-70-72-69—282	94,000
David Toms	71-67-71-73—282	94,000
Woody Austin	71-69-69-73—282	94,000
Phil Mickelson	69-71-68-74—282	94,000
Jonathan Byrd	69-72-74-68—283	71,250
Robert Allenby	68-74-71-70—283	71,250
Fred Funk	69-69-74-71—283	71,250

Late 2005 PGA Tour Events

Tournament	Final Round	Winner	Score/ Under Par	Earnings ($)
Funai Classic at Walt Disney World	Oct 23	Lucas Glover	265/-23	792,000
Chrysler Championship	Oct 30	Carl Pettersson	275/-9	954,000
Southern Farm Bureau Classic	Nov 6	Heath Slocum	267/-21	540,000
The Tour Championship	Nov 6	Bart Bryant	263/-17	1,170,000

2006 PGA Tour Events

Tournament	Final Round	Winner	Score/ Under Par	Earnings ($)
Mercedes Championships	Jan 8	Stuart Appleby	284/-8	1,080,000
Sony Open in Hawaii	Jan 15	David Toms	261/-19	918,000
Bob Hope Chrysler Classic	Jan 22	Chad Campbell	335/-25†	900,000
Buick Invitational	Jan 29	Tiger Woods	278/-10	918,000
FBR Open	Feb 5	J.B. Holmes	263/-21	936,000
AT&T Pebble Beach National Pro-Am	Feb 12	Arron Oberholser	271/-17	972,000
Nissan Open	Feb 19	Rory Sabbatini	271/-13	918,000
WGC Match Play Championship	Feb 26	Geoff Ogilvy	6&5	1,300,000
Chrysler Classic of Tucson	Feb 26	Kirk Triplett	266/-22	540,000
Ford Championship	Mar 5	Tiger Woods	268/-20	990,000
Honda Classic	Mar 12	Luke Donald	276/-12	990,000
Bay Hill Invitational	Mar 19	Rod Pampling	274/-14	990,000
The Players Championship	Mar 26	Stephen Ames	274/-14	1,440,000
BellSouth Classic	Apr 2	Phil Mickelson	260/-28	954,000
The Masters	Apr 9	Phil Mickelson	281/-7	1,260,000
Verizon Heritage	Apr 16	Aaron Baddeley	269/-15	990,000
Shell Houston Open	Apr 23	Stuart Appleby	269/-19	990,000
Zurich Classic of New Orleans	Apr 30	Chris Couch	269/-19	1,080,000
Wachovia Championship	May 7	Jim Furyk	276/-12	1,134,000
EDS Byron Nelson Classic	May 14	Brett Wetterich	268/-12	1,116,000
Bank of America Colonial	May 21	Tim Herron	268/-12	1,080,000
FedEx St. Jude Classic	May 28	Jeff Maggert	271/-9	936,000
Memorial Tournament	June 4	Carl Pettersson	276/-12	1,035,000
Barclays Classic	June 11	Vijay Singh	274/-10	1,035,000
U.S. Open Championship	June 18	Geoff Ogilvy	285/+5	1,225,000
Booz Allen Classic	June 25	Ben Curtis	264/-20	900,000
Cialis Western Open	July 9	Trevor Immelman	271/-13	900,000
John Deere Classic	July 16	John Senden	265/-19	720,000
British Open	July 23	Tiger Woods	270/-18	1,338,000
B.C. Open	July 23	John Rollins	269/-20	540,000
U.S. Bank Championship	July 30	Corey Pavin	260/-20	720,000
Buick Open	Aug 6	Tiger Woods	264/-24	864,000
The International	Aug 13	Dean Wilson	34‡	900,000
PGA Championship	Aug 20	Tiger Woods	270/-18	1,224,000
WGC Bridgestone Invitational	Aug 27	Tiger Woods	270/-10	1,300,000
Reno-Tahoe Open	Aug 27	Will MacKenzie	268/-16	540,000
Deutsche Bank Championship	Sept 4	Tiger Woods	268/-16	990,000
Bell Canadian Open	Sept 10	Jim Furyk	266/-14	900,000
84 Lumber Classic of Pennsylvania	Sept 17	Ben Curtis	274/-14	828,000
Valero Texas Open	Sept 24	Eric Axley	265/-15	720,000
WGC American Express Championship	Oct 1	Tiger Woods	261/-23	1,300,000
Southern Farm Bureau Classic	Oct 1	D.J. Trahan	275/-13	540,000
Chrysler Classic of Greensboro	Oct 8	Davis Love III	272/-16	900,000
Frys.com Open	Oct 15	Troy Matteson	265/-22	720,000

† Five-round tournament.

‡ Modified Stableford scoring.

Kraft Nabisco Championship

Mission Hills CC; (par 72; 6,569 yds)
Rancho Mirage, Calif., March 30–April 2, 2006

Player	Score	Earnings ($)
*Karrie Webb	70-68-76-65—279	270,000
Lorena Ochoa	62-71-74-72—279	168,226
Natalie Gulbis	73-71-68-68—280	108,222
Michelle Wie	66-71-73-70—280	108,222
Juli Inkster	69-73-74-68—284	75,895
Annika Sorenstam	71-72-73-70—286	57,104
Hee-Won Han	75-72-68-71—286	57,104
Brittany Lang	70-74-72-71—287	41,293
Helen Alfredsson	70-72-72-73—287	41,293
Shi Hyun Ahn	70-71-71-75—287	41,293
Stacy Prammanasudh	67-73-76-72—288	33,388
Michele Redman	72-72-72-72—288	33,388
Beth Daniel	72-72-72-73—289	29,289
Morgan Pressel	69-76-70-74—289	29,289
Yuri Fudoh	75-73-69-73—290	26,710
†Angela Park	69-73-75-74—290	26,170
Pat Hurst	73-73-73-72—291	24,592
Karen Stupples	69-74-72-76—291	24,592
Veronica Zorzi	74-72-75-71—292	21,221
Jeong Jang	71-75-76-70—292	21,221
Tina Barrett	72-75-74-71—292	21,221

†Amateur.

*Won playoff.

McDonald's LPGA Championship

Bulle Rock GC; (par 72; 6,596 yds)
Havre de Grace, Md., June 8-11, 2006

Player	Score	Earnings ($)
*Se Ri Pak	71-69-71-69—280	270,000
Karrie Webb	70-70-72-68—280	163,998
Mi Hyun Kim	68-71-71-71—281	105,501
Ai Miyazato	68-72-69-72—281	105,501
Cristie Kerr	66-74-74-68—282	57,464
Michelle Wie	71-68-71-72—282	57,464
Shi Hyun Ahn	69-70-71-72—282	57,464
Pat Hurst	66-71-72-73—282	57,464
Annika Sorenstam	71-69-75-68—283	34,174
Reilly Rankin	68-73-74-68—283	34,174
Sung Ah Yim	72-68-74-69—283	34,174
Young Kim	69-72-73-69—283	34,174
Lorena Ochoa	68-72-71-72—283	34,174
Meena Lee	71-72-69-72—284	26,847
Jee Young Lee	70-71-70-73—284	26,847
Seon Hwa Lee	67-74-75-69—285	22,896
Wendy Ward	69-74-70-72—285	22,896
Silvia Cavalleri	69-71-72-73—285	22,896
Sherri Steinhauer	70-71-71-73—285	22,896
Natalie Gulbis	72-73-72-69—286	19,215
Suzann Pettersen	70-72-74-70—286	19,215
Yuri Fudoh	69-74-71-72—286	19,215

*Won playoff.

U.S. Women's Open

Newport CC; (par 71; 6,616 yds)
Newport, R.I., June 23-26, 2006

Player	Score	Earnings ($)
*Annika Sorenstam	69-71-73-71—284	560,000
Pat Hurst	69-71-75-69—284	335,000
Se Ri Pak	69-74-74-69—286	156,038
Stacy Prammanasudh	72-71-71-72—286	156,038
Michelle Wie	70-72-71-73—286	156,038
Juli Inkster	73-70-71-73—287	103,575
Brittany Lincicome	72-72-69-78—291	93,026
Rachel Hetherington	74-72-73-73—292	82,460
Shi Hyun Ahn	71-71-74-76—292	82,460
†Amanda Blumenherst	70-77-73-73—293	66,174
Young Kim	75-69-75-74—293	66,174
Patricia Meunier-Lebouc	72-73-73-75—293	66,174
†Jane Park	69-73-75-76—293	66,174
Jee Young Lee	71-75-70-77—293	66,174
Sophie Gustafson	72-72-71-78—293	66,174
Sherri Turner	72-74-76-72—294	53,577
Natalie Gulbis	76-71-74-73—294	53,577
Paula Creamer	71-72-76-75—294	53,577
Catriona Matthew	74-76-72-73—295	48,007

†Amateur

*Won playoff.

Weetabix Women's British Open

Royal Lytham & St. Annes; (par 72; 6,480 yds)
Lancashire, England, August 3-6, 2006

Player	Score	Earnings ($)
Sherri Steinhauer	73-70-66-72—281	305,440
Cristie Kerr	71-76-66-71—284	162,265
Sophie Gustafson	76-67-69-72—284	162,265
Juli Inkster	66-72-74-73—285	95,450
Lorena Ochoa	74-73-65-73—285	95,450
Lorie Kane	73-69-74-70—286	70,633
Beth Daniel	73-71-70-72—286	70,633
Julieta Granada	71-73-70-73—287	61,088
Ai Miyazato	71-75-75-67—288	55,361
Hee-Won Han	80-71-69-70—290	40,566
Joo Mi Kim	73-73-73-71—290	40,566
Karine Icher	72-73-71-74—290	40,566
Nina Reis	70-76-69-75—290	40,566
Candie Kung	72-70-71-77—290	40,566
Karen Stupples	73-69-70-78—290	40,566
Sakura Yokomine	72-73-75-71—291	26,806
Il Mi Chung	72-71-75-73—291	26,806
Laura Davies	72-72-73-74—291	26,806
Heather Young	72-74-70-75—291	26,806
Gwladys Nocera	70-73-71-77—291	26,806

Late 2005 LPGA Tour Events

Tournament	Final Round	Winner	Score/Under Par	Earnings ($)
CJ Nine Bridges Classic	Oct 30	Jee Young Lee	211/-5	202,500
Mizuno Classic	Nov 7	Annika Sorenstam	195/-21	150,000
LPGA Tournament of Champions	Nov 13	Christina Kim	273/-15	138,000
ADT Championship	Nov 21	Annika Sorenstam	282/-6	215,000

2006 LPGA Tour Events

Tournament	Final Round	Winner	Score/Under Par	Earnings ($)
SBS Open	Feb 18	Joo Mi Kim*	206/-10	150,000
Fields Open	Feb. 25	Meena Lee*	202/-14	165,000
MasterCard Classic	Mar 12	Annika Sorenstam	208/-8	180,000
Safeway International	Mar 20	Juli Inkster	273/-15	210,000
Kraft Nabisco Championship	Apr 2	Karrie Webb*	279/-9	270,000
Takefuji Classic	Apr 15	Lorena Ochoa	197/-20	165,000
Florida's Natural Championship	Apr 23	Sung Ah Yim	272/-16	210,000
Ginn Clubs & Resorts Open	Apr 30	Mi Hyun Kim	276/-12	193,477
Franklin American Mortgage Champ	May 7	Cristie Kerr	269/-19	165,000
Michelob Ultra Open	May 14	Karrie Webb	270/-14	330,000
Sybase Classic	May 21	Lorena Ochoa	208/-5	195,000
LPGA Corning Classic	May 28	Hee-Won Han*	273/-15	180,000
ShopRite LPGA Classic	June 4	Seon Hwa Lee	197/-16	225,000
McDonald's LPGA Championship	June 11	Se Ri Pak*	280/-8	270,000
Wegman's Rochester LPGA	June 25	Jeong Jang	275/-13	270,000
U.S. Women's Open	July 2	Annika Sorenstam*	284/E	560,000
HSBC Women's World Match Play	July 9	Brittany Lincicome	3&2	500,000
Jamie Farr Owens Corning	July 16	Mi Hyun Kim*	266/-18	180,000
Evian Masters	July 29	Karrie Webb	272/-16	450,000
Weetabix Women's British Open	Aug 6	Sherri Steinhauer	281/-7	305,440
Canadian Women's Open	Aug 13	Cristie Kerr	276/-12	255,000
Safeway Classic	Aug 20	Pat Hurst	206/-10	210,000
Wendy's Championship for Children	Aug 27	Lorena Ochoa	264/-24	165,000
State Farm Classic	Sept 3	Annika Sorenstam	269/-19	195,000
John Q. Hammons Hotel Classic	Sept 10	Cristie Kerr	199/-14	150,000
Longs Drug Challenge	Sept. 24	Karrie Webb	273/-15	165,000
Corona Morelia Championship	Oct. 8	Lorena Ochoa	272/-20	150,000
Samsung World Championship	Oct. 15	Lorena Ochoa	272/-16	218,750

* Won playoff.

Champions Tour Results

Late 2005 Champions Tour Events

Tournament	Final Round	Winner	Score/ Under Par	Earnings ($)
SBC Championship	Oct 17	Mark McNulty	195/-18	225,000
Charles Schwab Cup Championship	Oct 24	Mark McNulty	277/-11	440,000

2006 Champions Tour Events

Tournament	Final Round	Winner	Score/ Under Par	Earnings ($)
MasterCard Championship	Jan 22	Loren Roberts	191/-25	290,000
Turtle Bay Championship	Jan 29	Loren Roberts	204/-12	225,000
ACE Group Classic	Feb 19	Loren Roberts	216/-14	240,000
Outback Steakhouse Pro-Am	Feb 26	Jerry Pate	202/-10	240,000
AT&T Classic	Mar 12	Tom Kite	204/-12	225,000
Toshiba Senior Classic	Mar 19	Brad Bryant	213/-9	240,000
Puerto Vallarta Blue Classic	Apr 2	Morris Hatalsky	207/-9	240,000
Liberty Mutual Legends of Golf	April 23	Jay Haas	201/-15	350,000
FedEx Kinko's Classic	Apr 30	Jay Haas	205/-11	240,000
Regions Charity Classic	May 7	Brad Bryant	199/-17	225,000
The Boeing Championship	May 14	Bobby Watkins	203/-10	240,000
Senior PGA Championship	May 28	Jay Haas*	279/-5	360,000
Allianz Championship	June 4	Gil Morgan	197/-16	225,000
Commerce Bank Championship	June 25	John Harris*	202/-11	225,000
Greater Kansas City Classic	July 2	Dana Quigley	198/-18	247,500
U.S. Senior Open	July 9	Allen Doyle	272/-8	470,000
Ford Senior Players Championship	July 16	Bobby Watkins	274/-14	375,000
Senior British Open	July 30	Loren Roberts*	274/-6	293,981
3M Championship	Aug 6	David Edwards	204/-12	262,500
Boeing Greater Seattle Classic	Aug 20	Tom Kite*	201/-15	240,000
Jeld-Wen Tradition	Aug 27	Eduardo Romero*	275/-13	375,000
First Tee Open at Pebble Beach	Sep 3	Scott Simpson	204/-12	300,000
Constellation Energy Classic	Sep 17	Bob Gilder	202/-14	225,000
Greater Hickory Classic	Oct 1	Andy Bean*	201/-15	225,000
SAS Championship	Oct 8	Tom Jenkins	134/-10	300,000
Administaff Small Business Classic	Oct. 15	Jay Haas	128/-16	240,000

*Won playoff.

U.S. Amateur Results*

Tournament	Final Round	Winner	Score	Runner-Up
Women's Amateur Public Links	June 25	Tiffany Joh	6 & 5	Kimberly Kim
Men's Amateur Public Links	July 15	Casey Watabu	4 & 3	Anthony Kim
Girls' Junior Amateur	July 22	Jenny Shin	1 up	Vicky Hurst
Boys' Junior Amateur	July 22	Philip Francis	3 & 2	Richard Lee
Women's Amateur	Aug 13	Kimberly Kim	1 up	Katharina Schallenberg
Men's Amateur	Aug 27	Richie Ramsay	3 up	John Kelly
Men's Mid-Amateur	Sep 14	Dave Womack	1 up	Ryan Hybl

*Results through 10/15/06.

International Results

Tournament	Final Round	Winner	Score	Runner-Up
Curtis Cup	July 30	United States	11½- 6½	Great Britain/Ireland
Ryder Cup	Sept 24	Europe	18½- 9½	United States

PGA Tour Final 2005 Money Leaders

Name	Events	Best Finish	Scoring Average*	Money ($)
Tiger Woods	21	1 (6)	68.66	10,628,023
Vijay Singh	30	1 (4)	69.04	8,017,336
Phil Mickelson	21	1 (4)	69.39	5,699,605
Jim Furyk	26	1 (1)	69.27	4,255,369
David Toms	25	1 (1)	69.66	3,962,013
Kenny Perry	23	1 (2)	69.48	3,607,155
Chris DiMarco	24	2 (1)	70.41	3,562,548
Retief Goosen	18	1 (1)	70.06	3,494,105
Bart Bryant	26	1 (2)	70.19	3,249,135
Sergio Garcia	20	1 (1)	69.64	3,213,375

*Adjusted for average score of field in each tournament entered.

LPGA Tour Final 2005 Money Leaders

Name	Events	Best Finish	Scoring Average	Money ($)
Annika Sorenstam	20	1 (10)	69.33	2,588,240
Paula Creamer	25	1 (2)	70.98	1,531,780
Cristie Kerr	22	1 (2)	70.86	1,360,941
Lorena Ochoa	23	1 (1)	71.39	1,201,786
Jeong Jang	27	1 (1)	71.17	1,131,986
Natalie Gulbis	27	2 (1)	71.24	1,010,154
Meena Lee	28	1 (1)	72.32	870,182
Hee-Won Han	27	1 (1)	71.31	856,364
Gloria Park	28	2 (1)	71.43	842,349
Catronia Matthew	26	2 (1)	71.46	776,924

Champions Tour Final 2005 Money Leaders

Name	Events	Best Finish	Scoring Average	Money ($)
Dana Quigley	27	1 (2)	69.64	2,170,258
Hale Irwin	22	1 (4)	69.97	1,983,596
Mark McNulty	23	1 (2)	69.41	1,791,452
D.A. Weibring	26	1 (1)	69.84	1,550,030
Tom Watson	13	1 (2)	69.88	1,532,482
Tom Jenkins	27	1 (1)	70.08	1,484,315
Gil Morgan	25	3 (3)	69.92	1,364,170
Morris Hatalsky	25	2 (4)	69.68	1,355,336
Craig Stadler	21	2 (2)	69.65	1,274,719
Des Smyth	21	1 (2)	70.74	1,238,876

Men's Golf

THE MAJOR TOURNAMENTS
The Masters

Year	Winner	Score	Runner-Up	Year	Winner	Score	Runner-Up
1934	Horton Smith	284	Craig Wood	1975	Jack Nicklaus	276	Johnny Miller
1935	Gene Sarazen* (144)	282	Craig Wood (149)				Tom Weiskopf
	(only 36-hole playoff)			1976	Ray Floyd	271	Ben Crenshaw
1936	Horton Smith	285	Harry Cooper	1977	Tom Watson	276	Jack Nicklaus
1937	Byron Nelson	283	Ralph Guldahl	1978	Gary Player	277	Hubert Green
1938	Henry Picard	285	Ralph Guldahl				Rod Funseth
			Harry Cooper				Tom Watson
1939	Ralph Guldahl	279	Sam Snead	1979	Fuzzy Zoeller* (4–3)†	280	Ed Sneed (4–4)
1940	Jimmy Demaret	280	Lloyd Mangrum				Tom Watson (4–4)
1941	Craig Wood	280	Byron Nelson	1980	Seve Ballesteros	275	Gibby Gilbert
1942	Byron Nelson* (69)	280	Ben Hogan (70)				Jack Newton
1943–45	No tournament			1981	Tom Watson	280	Johnny Miller
1946	Herman Keiser	282	Ben Hogan				Jack Nicklaus
1947	Jimmy Demaret	281	Byron Nelson	1982	Craig Stadler* (4)	284	Dan Pohl (5)
			Frank Stranahan	1983	Seve Ballesteros	280	Ben Crenshaw
1948	Claude Harmon	279	Cary Middlecoff				Tom Kite
1949	Sam Snead	282	Johnny Bulla	1984	Ben Crenshaw	277	Tom Watson
			Lloyd Mangrum	1985	Bernhard Langer	282	Curtis Strange
1950	Jimmy Demaret	283	Jim Ferrier				Seve Ballesteros
1951	Ben Hogan	280	Skee Riegel				Ray Floyd
1952	Sam Snead	286	Jack Burke Jr.	1986	Jack Nicklaus	279	Greg Norman
1953	Ben Hogan	274	Ed Oliver Jr.				Tom Kite
1954	Sam Snead* (70)	289	Ben Hogan (71)	1987	Larry Mize* (4–3)	285	Seve Ballesteros (5)
1955	Cary Middlecoff	279	Ben Hogan				Greg Norman (4–4)
1956	Jack Burke Jr.	289	Ken Venturi	1988	Sandy Lyle	281	Mark Calcavecchia
1957	Doug Ford	282	Sam Snead	1989	Nick Faldo* (5–3)	283	Scott Hoch (5–4)
1958	Arnold Palmer	284	Doug Ford	1990	Nick Faldo* (4–4)	278	Ray Floyd (4–x)
			Fred Hawkins	1991	Ian Woosnam	277	José María
1959	Art Wall Jr.	284	Cary Middlecoff				Olazábal
1960	Arnold Palmer	282	Ken Venturi	1992	Fred Couples	275	Ray Floyd
1961	Gary Player	280	Charles R. Coe	1993	Bernhard Langer	277	Chip Beck
			Arnold Palmer	1994	José María Olazábal	279	Tom Lehman
1962	Arnold Palmer* (68)	280	Gary Player (71)	1995	Ben Crenshaw	274	Davis Love III
			D. Finsterwald (77)	1996	Nick Faldo	276	Greg Norman
1963	Jack Nicklaus	286	Tony Lema	1997	Tiger Woods	270	Tom Kite
1964	Arnold Palmer	276	Dave Marr	1998	Mark O'Meara	279	David Duval
			Jack Nicklaus				Fred Couples
1965	Jack Nicklaus	271	Arnold Palmer	1999	José María Olazábal	280	Davis Love III
			Gary Player	2000	Vijay Singh	278	Ernie Els
1966	Jack Nicklaus* (70)	288	Tommy Jacobs (72)	2001	Tiger Woods	272	David Duval
			Gay Brewer Jr. (78)	2002	Tiger Woods	276	Retief Goosen
1967	Gay Brewer Jr.	280	Bobby Nichols	2003	Mike Weir	281	Len Mattiace
1968	Bob Goalby	277	Roberto DeVicenzo	2004	Phil Mickelson	279	Ernie Els
1969	George Archer	281	Billy Casper	2005	Tiger Woods	276	Chris DiMarco
			George Knudson	2006	Phil Mickelson	281	Tim Clark
			Tom Weiskopf				
1970	Billy Casper* (69)	279	Gene Littler (74)				
1971	Charles Coody	279	Johnny Miller				
			Jack Nicklaus				
1972	Jack Nicklaus	286	Bruce Crampton				
			Bobby Mitchell				
			Tom Weiskopf				
1973	Tommy Aaron	283	J.C. Snead				
1974	Gary Player	278	Tom Weiskopf				
			Dave Stockton				

*Winner in playoff. Playoff scores are in parentheses. †Playoff cut from 18 holes to sudden death.
Note: Played at Augusta National Golf Club, Augusta, GA.

United States Open Championship

Year	Winner	Score	Runner-Up	Site
1895	Horace Rawlins	†173	Willie Dunn	Newport GC, Newport, RI
1896	James Foulis	†152	Horace Rawlins	Shinnecock Hills GC, Southampton, NY
1897	Joe Lloyd	†162	Willie Anderson	Chicago GC, Wheaton, IL
1898	Fred Herd	328	Alex Smith	Myopia Hunt Club, Hamilton, MA
1899	Willie Smith	315	George Low Val Fitzjohn W.H. Way	Baltimore CC, Baltimore
1900	Harry Vardon	313	John H. Taylor	Chicago GC, Wheaton, IL
1901	Willie Anderson* (85)	331	Alex Smith (86)	Myopia Hunt Club, Hamilton, MA
1902	Laurie Auchterlonie	307	Stewart Gardner	Garden City GC, Garden City, NY
1903	Willie Anderson* (82)	307	David Brown (84)	Baltusrol GC, Springfield, NJ
1904	Willie Anderson	303	Gil Nicholls	Glen View Club, Golf, IL
1905	Willie Anderson	314	Alex Smith	Myopia Hunt Club, Hamilton, MA
1906	Alex Smith	295	Willie Smith	Onwentsia Club, Lake Forest, IL
1907	Alex Ross	302	Gil Nicholls	Philadelphia Cricket Club, Chestnut Hill, PA
1908	Fred McLeod* (77)	322	Willie Smith (83)	Myopia Hunt Club, Hamilton, MA
1909	George Sargent	290	Tom McNamara	Englewood GC, Englewood, NJ
1910	Alex Smith* (71)	298	John McDermott (75) Macdonald Smith (77)	Philadelphia Cricket Club, Chestnut Hill, PA
1911	John McDermott* (80)	307	Mike Brady (82) George Simpson (85)	Chicago GC, Wheaton, IL
1912	John McDermott	294	Tom McNamara	CC of Buffalo, Buffalo
1913	Francis Ouimet* (72)	304	Harry Vardon (77) Edward Ray (78)	The Country Club, Brookline, MA
1914	Walter Hagen	290	Chick Evans	Midlothian CC, Blue Island, IL
1915	Jerry Travers	297	Tom McNamara	Baltusrol GC, Springfield, NJ
1916	Chick Evans	286	Jock Hutchison	Minikahda Club, Minneapolis
1917–18	No tournament			
1919	Walter Hagen* (77)	301	Mike Brady (78)	Brae Burn CC, West Newton, MA
1920	Edward Ray	295	Harry Vardon Jack Burke Leo Diegel Jock Hutchison	Inverness CC, Toledo
1921	Jim Barnes	289	Walter Hagen Fred McLeod	Columbia CC, Chevy Chase, MD
1922	Gene Sarazen	288	John L. Black Bobby Jones	Skokie CC, Glencoe, IL
1923	Bobby Jones* (76)	296	Bobby Cruickshank (78)	Inwood CC, Inwood, NY
1924	Cyril Walker	297	Bobby Jones	Oakland Hills CC, Birmingham, MI
1925	W. MacFarlane* (75–72)	291	Bobby Jones (75–73)	Worcester CC, Worcester, MA
1926	Bobby Jones	293	Joe Turnesa	Scioto CC, Columbus, OH
1927	Tommy Armour* (76)	301	Harry Cooper (79)	Oakmont CC, Oakmont, PA
1928	Johnny Farrell* (143)	294	Bobby Jones (144)	Olympia Fields CC, Matteson, IL
1929	Bobby Jones* (141)	294	Al Espinosa (164)	Winged Foot GC, Mamaroneck, NY
1930	Bobby Jones	287	Macdonald Smith	Interlachen CC, Hopkins, MN
1931	Billy Burke* (149–148)	292	George Von Elm (149–149)	Inverness Club, Toledo
1932	Gene Sarazen	286	Phil Perkins Bobby Cruickshank	Fresh Meadow CC, Flushing, NY
1933	Johnny Goodman	287	Ralph Guldahl	North Shore CC, Glenview, IL
1934	Olin Dutra	293	Gene Sarazen	Merion Cricket Club, Ardmore, PA
1935	Sam Parks Jr.	299	Jimmy Thompson	Oakmont CC, Oakmont, PA
1936	Tony Manero	282	Harry Cooper	Baltusrol GC (Upper Course), Springfield, NJ
1937	Ralph Guldahl	281	Sam Snead	Oakland Hills CC, Birmingham, MI
1938	Ralph Guldahl	284	Dick Metz	Cherry Hills CC, Denver
1939	Byron Nelson* (68–70)	284	Craig Wood (68–73) Denny Shute (76)	Philadelphia CC, Philadelphia
1940	Lawson Little* (70)	287	Gene Sarazen (73)	Canterbury GC, Cleveland
1941	Craig Wood	284	Denny Shute	Colonial Club, Fort Worth
1942–45	No tournament			
1946	Lloyd Mangrum* (72–72)	284	Vic Ghezzi (72–73) Byron Nelson (72–73)	Canterbury GC, Cleveland
1947	Lew Worsham* (69)	282	Sam Snead (70)	St. Louis CC, Clayton, MO
1948	Ben Hogan	276	Jimmy Demaret	Riviera CC, Los Angeles
1949	Cary Middlecoff	286	Sam Snead Clayton Heafner	Medinah CC, Medinah, IL

United States Open Championship *(Cont.)*

Year	Winner	Score	Runner-Up	Site
1950	Ben Hogan* (69)	287	Lloyd Mangrum (73) George Fazio (75)	Merion GC, Ardmore, PA
1951	Ben Hogan	287	Clayton Heafner	Oakland Hills CC, Birmingham, MI
1952	Julius Boros	281	Ed Oliver	Northwood CC, Dallas
1953	Ben Hogan	283	Sam Snead	Oakmont CC, Oakmont, PA
1954	Ed Furgol	284	Gene Littler	Baltusrol GC (Lower Course), Springfield, NJ
1955	Jack Fleck* (69)	287	Ben Hogan (72)	Olympic Club (Lake Course), San Francisco
1956	Cary Middlecoff	281	Ben Hogan Julius Boros	Oak Hill CC, Rochester, NY
1957	Dick Mayer* (72)	282	Cary Middlecoff (79)	Inverness Club, Toledo
1958	Tommy Bolt	283	Gary Player	Southern Hills CC, Tulsa
1959	Billy Casper	282	Bob Rosburg	Winged Foot GC, Mamaroneck, NY
1960	Arnold Palmer	280	Jack Nicklaus	Cherry Hills CC, Denver
1961	Gene Littler	281	Bob Goalby Doug Sanders	Oakland Hills CC, Birmingham, MI
1962	Jack Nicklaus* (71)	283	Arnold Palmer (74)	Oakmont CC, Oakmont, PA
1963	Julius Boros* (70)	293	Jacky Cupit (73) Arnold Palmer (76)	The Country Club, Brookline, MA
1964	Ken Venturi	278	Tommy Jacobs	Congressional CC, Bethesda, MD
1965	Gary Player* (71)	282	Kel Nagle (74)	Bellerive CC, St. Louis
1966	Billy Casper* (69)	278	Arnold Palmer (73)	Olympic Club (Lake Course), San Francisco
1967	Jack Nicklaus	275	Arnold Palmer	Baltusrol GC (Lower Course), Springfield, NJ
1968	Lee Trevino	275	Jack Nicklaus	Oak Hill CC, Rochester, NY
1969	Orville Moody	281	Deane Beman Al Geiberger Bob Rosburg	Champions GC (Cypress Creek Course), Houston
1970	Tony Jacklin	281	Dave Hill	Hazeltine GC, Chaska, MN
1971	Lee Trevino* (68)	280	Jack Nicklaus (71)	Merion GC (East Course), Ardmore, PA
1972	Jack Nicklaus	290	Bruce Crampton	Pebble Beach GL, Pebble Beach, CA
1973	Johnny Miller	279	John Schlee	Oakmont CC, Oakmont, PA
1974	Hale Irwin	287	Forrest Fezler	Winged Foot GC, Mamaroneck, NY
1975	Lou Graham* (71)	287	John Mahaffey (73)	Medinah CC, Medinah, IL
1976	Jerry Pate	277	Tom Weiskopf Al Geiberger	Atlanta Athletic Club, Duluth, GA
1977	Hubert Green	278	Lou Graham	Southern Hills CC, Tulsa
1978	Andy North	285	Dave Stockton J.C. Snead	Cherry Hills CC, Denver
1979	Hale Irwin	284	Gary Player Jerry Pate	Inverness Club, Toledo
1980	Jack Nicklaus	272	Isao Aoki	Baltusrol GC (Lower Course), Springfield, NJ
1981	David Graham	273	George Burns Bill Rogers	Merion GC, Ardmore, PA
1982	Tom Watson	282	Jack Nicklaus	Pebble Beach GL, Pebble Beach, CA
1983	Larry Nelson	280	Tom Watson	Oakmont CC, Oakmont, PA
1984	Fuzzy Zoeller* (67)	276	Greg Norman (75)	Winged Foot GC, Mamaroneck, NY
1985	Andy North	279	Dave Barr T.C. Chen Denis Watson	Oakland Hills CC, Birmingham, MI
1986	Ray Floyd	279	Lanny Wadkins Chip Beck	Shinnecock Hills GC, Southampton, NY
1987	Scott Simpson	277	Tom Watson	Olympic Club (Lake Course), San Francisco
1988	Curtis Strange* (71)	278	Nick Faldo (75)	The Country Club, Brookline, MA
1989	Curtis Strange	278	Chip Beck Mark McCumber Ian Woosnam	Oak Hill CC, Rochester, NY
1990	Hale Irwin* (74) (3)	280	Mike Donald (74) (4)	Medinah CC, Medinah, IL
1991	Payne Stewart* (75)	282	Scott Simpson (77)	Hazeltine GC, Chaska, MN
1992	Tom Kite	285	Jeff Sluman	Pebble Beach GL, Pebble Beach, CA
1993	Lee Janzen	272	Payne Stewart	Baltusrol GC, Springfield, NJ
1994	Ernie Els*	279	Loren Roberts Colin Montgomerie	Oakmont CC, Oakmont, PA
1995	Corey Pavin	280	Greg Norman	Shinnecock Hills GC, Southampton, NY
1996	Steve Jones	278	Davis Love III Tom Lehman	Oakland Hills CC, Birmingham, MI
1997	Ernie Els	276	Colin Montgomerie	Congressional CC, Bethesda, MD

United States Open Championship *(Cont.)*

Year	Winner	Score	Runner-Up	Site
1998	Lee Janzen	280	Payne Stewart	The Olympic Club, San Francisco
1999	Payne Stewart	279	Phil Mickelson	Pinehurst Resort and CC, Pinehurst, NC
2000	Tiger Woods	272	Miguel Angel Jiménez	Pebble Beach GL, Pebble Beach, CA
			Ernie Els	
2001	Retief Goosen* (70)	276	Mark Brooks (72)	Southern Hills CC, Tulsa
2002	Tiger Woods	277	Phil Mickelson	Bethpage Black Course, Bethpage, NY
2003	Jim Furyk	272	Stephen Leaney	Olympia Fields CC, Olympia Fields, IL
2004	Retief Goosen	276	Phil Mickelson	Shinnecock Hills GC, Southampton, NY
2005	Michael Campbell	280	Tiger Woods	Pinehurst Resort and CC, Pinehurst, NC
2006	Geoff Ogilvy	285	Jim Furyk	Winged Foot GC, Mamaroneck, NY
			Colin Montgomerie	
			Phil Mickelson	

*Winner in playoff. Playoff scores are in parentheses. The 1990 playoff went to one hole of sudden death after an 18-hole playoff. In the 1994 playoff, Montgomerie was eliminated after 18 playoff holes, and Els beat Roberts on the 20th.
†Before 1898, 36 holes. From 1898 on, 72 holes.

British Open

Year	Winner	Score	Runner-Up	Site
1860†	Willie Park	174	Tom Morris Sr.	Prestwick, Scotland
1861‡	Tom Morris Sr.	163	Willie Park	Prestwick, Scotland
1862	Tom Morris Sr.	163	Willie Park	Prestwick, Scotland
1863	Willie Park	168	Tom Morris Sr.	Prestwick, Scotland
1864	Tom Morris, Sr.	160	Andrew Strath	Prestwick, Scotland
1865	Andrew Strath	162	Willie Park	Prestwick, Scotland
1866	Willie Park	169	David Park	Prestwick, Scotland
1867	Tom Morris Sr.	170	Willie Park	Prestwick, Scotland
1868	Tom Morris Jr.	154	Tom Morris Sr.	Prestwick, Scotland
1869	Tom Morris Jr.	157	Tom Morris Sr.	Prestwick, Scotland
1870	Tom Morris Jr.	149	David Strath	Prestwick, Scotland
			Bob Kirk	
1871	No tournament			
1872	Tom Morris Jr.	166	David Strath	Prestwick, Scotland
1873	Tom Kidd	179	Jamie Anderson	St. Andrews, Scotland
1874	Mungo Park	159	No record	Musselburgh, Scotland
1875	Willie Park	166	Bob Martin	Prestwick, Scotland
1876	Bob Martin#	176	David Strath	St. Andrews, Scotland
1877	Jamie Anderson	160	Bob Pringle	Musselburgh, Scotland
1878	Jamie Anderson	157	Robert Kirk	Prestwick, Scotland
1879	Jamie Anderson	169	Andrew Kirkaldy	St. Andrews, Scotland
			James Allan	
1880	Robert Ferguson	162	No record	Musselburgh, Scotland
1881	Robert Ferguson	170	Jamie Anderson	Prestwick, Scotland
1882	Robert Ferguson	171	Willie Fernie	St. Andrews, Scotland
1883	Willie Fernie*	159	Robert Ferguson	Musselburgh, Scotland
1884	Jack Simpson	160	Douglas Rolland	Prestwick, Scotland
			Willie Fernie	
1885	Bob Martin	171	Archie Simpson	St. Andrews, Scotland
1886	David Brown	157	Willie Campbell	Musselburgh, Scotland
1887	Willie Park Jr.	161	Bob Martin	Prestwick, Scotland
1888	Jack Burns	171	Bernard Sayers	St. Andrews, Scotland
			David Anderson	
1889	Willie Park Jr.* (158)	155	Andrew Kirkaldy (163)	Musselburgh, Scotland
1890	John Ball	164	Willie Fernie	Prestwick, Scotland
1891	Hugh Kirkaldy	166	Andrew Kirkaldy	St. Andrews, Scotland
			Willie Fernie	
1892	Harold Hilton	**305	John Ball	Muirfield, Scotland
			Hugh Kirkaldy	
1893	William Auchterlonie	322	John E. Laidlay	Prestwick, Scotland
1894	John H. Taylor	326	Douglas Rolland	Royal St. George's, England
1895	John H. Taylor	322	Alexander Herd	St. Andrews, Scotland
1896	Harry Vardon* (157)	316	John H. Taylor (161)	Muirfield, Scotland
1897	Harold Hilton	314	James Braid	Hoylake, England
1898	Harry Vardon	307	Willie Park Jr.	Prestwick, Scotland
1899	Harry Vardon	310	Jack White	Royal St. George's, England
1900	John H. Taylor	309	Harry Vardon	St. Andrews, Scotland

British Open (Cont.)

Year	Winner	Score	Runner-Up	Site
1901	James Braid	309	Harry Vardon	Muirfield, Scotland
1902	Alexander Herd	307	Harry Vardon	Hoylake, England
1903	Harry Vardon	300	Tom Vardon	Prestwick, Scotland
1904	Jack White	296	John H. Taylor	Royal St. George's, England
1905	James Braid	318	John H. Taylor	St. Andrews, Scotland
			Rolland Jones	
1906	James Braid	300	John H. Taylor	Muirfield, Scotland
1907	Arnaud Massy	312	John H. Taylor	Hoylake, England
1908	James Braid	291	Tom Ball	Prestwick, Scotland
1909	John H. Taylor	295	James Braid	Deal, England
			Tom Ball	
1910	James Braid	299	Alexander Herd	St. Andrews, Scotland
1911	Harry Vardon	303	Arnaud Massy	Royal St. George's, England
1912	Ted Ray	295	Harry Vardon	Muirfield, Scotland
1913	John H. Taylor	304	Ted Ray	Hoylake, England
1914	Harry Vardon	306	John H. Taylor	Prestwick, Scotland
1915–19	No tournament			
1920	George Duncan	303	Alexander Herd	Deal, England
1921	Jock Hutchison* (150)	296	Roger Wethered (159)	St. Andrews, Scotland
1922	Walter Hagen	300	George Duncan	Royal St. George's, England
			Jim Barnes	
1923	Arthur G. Havers	295	Walter Hagen	Troon, Scotland
1924	Walter Hagen	301	Ernest Whitcombe	Hoylake, England
1925	Jim Barnes	300	Archie Compston	Prestwick, Scotland
			Ted Ray	
1926	Bobby Jones	291	Al Watrous	Royal Lytham & St. Annes, England
1927	Bobby Jones	285	Aubrey Boomer	St. Andrews, Scotland
1928	Walter Hagen	292	Gene Sarazen	Royal St. George's, England
1929	Walter Hagen	292	Johnny Farrell	Muirfield, Scotland
1930	Bobby Jones	291	Macdonald Smith	Hoylake, England
			Leo Diegel	
1931	Tommy Armour	296	Jose Jurado	Carnoustie, Scotland
1932	Gene Sarazen	283	Macdonald Smith	Prince's, England
1933	Denny Shute* (149)	292	Craig Wood (154)	St. Andrews, Scotland
1934	Henry Cotton	283	Sidney F. Brews	Royal St. George's, England
1935	Alfred Perry	283	Alfred Padgham	Muirfield, Scotland
1936	Alfred Padgham	287	James Adams	Hoylake, England
1937	Henry Cotton	290	Reginald A. Whitcombe	Carnoustie, Scotland
1938	Reginald A. Whitcombe	295	James Adams	Royal St. George's, England
1939	Richard Burton	290	Johnny Bulla	St. Andrews, Scotland
1940–45	No tournament			
1946	Sam Snead	290	Bobby Locke	St. Andrews, Scotland
			Johnny Bulla	
1947	Fred Daly	293	Reginald W. Horne	Hoylake, England
			Frank Stranahan	
1948	Henry Cotton	294	Fred Daly	Muirfield, Scotland
1949	Bobby Locke* (135)	283	Harry Bradshaw (147)	Royal St. George's, England
1950	Bobby Locke	279	Roberto DeVicenzo	Troon, Scotland
1951	Max Faulkner	285	Tony Cerda	Portrush, Ireland
1952	Bobby Locke	287	Peter Thomson	Royal Lytham & St. Annes, England
1953	Ben Hogan	282	Frank Stranahan	Carnoustie, Scotland
			Dai Rees	
			Peter Thomson	
			Tony Cerda	
1954	Peter Thomson	283	Sidney S. Scott	Royal Birkdale, England
			Dai Rees	
			Bobby Locke	
1955	Peter Thomson	281	John Fallon	St. Andrews, Scotland
1956	Peter Thomson	286	Flory Van Donck	Hoylake, England
1957	Bobby Locke	279	Peter Thomson	St. Andrews, Scotland
1958	Peter Thomson* (139)	278	Dave Thomas (143)	Royal Lytham & St. Annes, England
1959	Gary Player	284	Fred Bullock	Muirfield, Scotland
			Flory Van Donck	
1960	Kel Nagle	278	Arnold Palmer	St. Andrews, Scotland
1961	Arnold Palmer	284	Dai Rees	Royal Birkdale, England
1962	Arnold Palmer	276	Kel Nagle	Troon, Scotland

British Open *(Cont.)*

Year	Winner	Score	Runner-Up	Site
1963	Bob Charles* (140)	277	Phil Rodgers (148)	Royal Lytham & St. Annes, England
1964	Tony Lema	279	Jack Nicklaus	St. Andrews, Scotland
1965	Peter Thomson	285	Brian Huggett	Southport, England
			Christy O'Connor	
1966	Jack Nicklaus	282	Doug Sanders	Muirfield, Scotland
			Dave Thomas	
1967	Robert DeVicenzo	278	Jack Nicklaus	Hoylake, England
1968	Gary Player	289	Jack Nicklaus	Carnoustie, Scotland
			Bob Charles	
1969	Tony Jacklin	280	Bob Charles	Royal Lytham & St. Annes, England
1970	Jack Nicklaus* (72)	283	Doug Sanders (73)	St. Andrews, Scotland
1971	Lee Trevino	278	Lu Liang Huan	Royal Birkdale, England
1972	Lee Trevino	278	Jack Nicklaus	Muirfield, Scotland
1973	Tom Weiskopf	276	Johnny Miller	Troon, Scotland
1974	Gary Player	282	Peter Oosterhuis	Royal Lytham & St. Annes, England
1975	Tom Watson* (71)	279	Jack Newton (72)	Carnoustie, Scotland
1976	Johnny Miller	279	Jack Nicklaus	Royal Birkdale, England
			Seve Ballesteros	
1977	Tom Watson	268	Jack Nicklaus	Turnberry, Scotland
1978	Jack Nicklaus	281	Ben Crenshaw	St. Andrews, Scotland
			Tom Kite	
			Ray Floyd	
			Simon Owen	
1979	Seve Ballesteros	283	Ben Crenshaw	Royal Lytham & St. Annes, England
			Jack Nicklaus	
1980	Tom Watson	271	Lee Trevino	Muirfield, Scotland
1981	Bill Rogers	276	Bernhard Langer	Royal St. George's, England
1982	Tom Watson	284	Nick Price	Troon, Scotland
			Peter Oosterhuis	
1983	Tom Watson	275	Andy Bean	Royal Birkdale, England
1984	Seve Ballesteros	276	Tom Watson	St. Andrews, Scotland
			Bernhard Langer	
1985	Sandy Lyle	282	Payne Stewart	Royal St. George's, England
1986	Greg Norman	280	Gordon Brand	Turnberry, Scotland
1987	Nick Faldo	279	Paul Azinger	Muirfield, Scotland
			Rodger Davis	
1988	Seve Ballesteros	273	Nick Price	Royal Lytham & St. Annes, England
1989††	Mark Calcavecchia* (4-3-3-3)	275	Wayne Grady (4-4-4-4)	Troon, Scotland
			Greg Norman (3-3-4-x)	
1990	Nick Faldo	270	Payne Stewart	St. Andrews, Scotland
			Mark McNulty	
1991	Ian Baker-Finch	272	Mike Harwood	Royal Birkdale, England
1992	Nick Faldo	272	John Cook	Muirfield, Scotland
1993	Greg Norman	267	Nick Faldo	Royal St. George's, England
1994	Nick Price	268	Jesper Parnevik	Turnberry, Scotland
1995	John Daly* (4-3-4-4)	282	C. Rocca (5-4-7-3)	St. Andrews, Scotland
1996	Tom Lehman	271	Mark McCumber	Royal Lytham & St. Annes, England
			Ernie Els	
1997	Justin Leonard	272	Jesper Parnevik	Troon, Scotland
			Darren Clarke	
1998	Mark O'Meara* (4-4-5-4)	280	Brian Watts (5-4-5-5)	Southport, England
1999	Paul Lawrie* (5-4-3-3)	290	Jean Van de Velde (6-4-3-5)	Carnoustie GC, Carnoustie,
			Justin Leonard (5-4-4-5)	Scotland
2000	Tiger Woods	269	Thomas Bjorn	St. Andrews, Scotland
			Ernie Els	
2001	David Duval	274	Niclas Fasth	Royal Lytham & St. Annes, England
2002	Ernie Els*	278	Stuart Appleby	Muirfield, Scotland
2003	Ben Curtis	283	Vijay Singh	Royal St. George's, England
2004	Todd Hamilton*	274	Ernie Els	Troon, Scotland
2005	Tiger Woods	274	Colin Montgomerie	St. Andrews, Scotland
2006	Tiger Woods	270	Chris DiMarco	Hoylake, England

*Winner in playoff. †The first event was open only to professional golfers.
‡The second annual open was open to amateurs and pros. #Tied, but refused playoff.
**Championship extended from 36 to 72 holes. ††Playoff cut from 18 holes to 4 holes.

PGA Championship

Year	Winner	Score	Runner-Up	Site
1916	Jim Barnes	1 up	Jock Hutchison	Siwanoy CC, Bronxville, NY
1917–18	No tournament			
1919	Jim Barnes	6 & 5	Fred McLeod	Engineers CC, Roslyn, NY
1920	Jock Hutchison	1 up	J. Douglas Edgar	Flossmoor CC, Flossmoor, IL
1921	Walter Hagen	3 & 2	Jim Barnes	Inwood CC, Far Rockaway, NY
1922	Gene Sarazen	4 & 3	Emmet French	Oakmont CC, Oakmont, PA
1923	Gene Sarazen	1 up	Walter Hagen	Pelham CC, Pelham, NY
		38 holes		
1924	Walter Hagen	2 up	Jim Barnes	French Lick CC, French Lick, IN
1925	Walter Hagen	6 & 5	William Mehlhorn	Olympia Fields CC, Olympia Fields, IL
1926	Walter Hagen	5 & 3	Leo Diegel	Salisbury GC, Westbury, NY
1927	Walter Hagen	1 up	Joe Turnesa	Cedar Crest CC, Dallas
1928	Leo Diegel	6 & 5	Al Espinosa	Five Farms CC, Baltimore
1929	Leo Diegel	6 & 4	Johnny Farrell	Hillcrest CC, Los Angeles
1930	Tommy Armour	1 up	Gene Sarazen	Fresh Meadow CC, Flushing, NY
1931	Tom Creavy	2 & 1	Denny Shute	Wannamoisett CC, Rumford, RI
1932	Olin Dutra	4 & 3	Frank Walsh	Keller GC, St. Paul
1933	Gene Sarazen	5 & 4	Willie Goggin	Blue Mound CC, Milwaukee
1934	Paul Runyan	1 up	Craig Wood	Park CC, Williamsville, NY
1935	Johnny Revolta	5 & 4	Tommy Armour	Twin Hills CC, Oklahoma City
		38 holes		
1936	Denny Shute	3 & 2	Jimmy Thomson	Pinehurst CC, Pinehurst, NC
1937	Denny Shute	1 up	Harold McSpaden	Pittsburgh FC, Aspinwall, PA
		37 holes		
1938	Paul Runyan	8 & 7	Sam Snead	Shawnee CC, Shawnee-on-Delaware, PA
1939	Henry Picard	1 up	Byron Nelson	Pomonok CC, Flushing, NY
		37 holes		
1940	Byron Nelson	1 up	Sam Snead	Hershey CC, Hershey, PA
1941	Vic Ghezzi	1 up	Byron Nelson	Cherry Hills CC, Denver
		38 holes		
1942	Sam Snead	2 & 1	Jim Turnesa	Seaview CC, Atlantic City
1943	No tournament			
1944	Bob Hamilton	1 up	Byron Nelson	Manito G & CC, Spokane, WA
1945	Byron Nelson	4 & 3	Sam Byrd	Morraine CC, Dayton
1946	Ben Hogan	6 & 4	Ed Oliver	Portland GC, Portland, OR
1947	Jim Ferrier	2 & 1	Chick Harbert	Plum Hollow CC, Detroit
1948	Ben Hogan	7 & 6	Mike Turnesa	Norwood Hills CC, St. Louis
1949	Sam Snead	3 & 2	Johnny Palmer	Hermitage CC, Richmond
1950	Chandler Harper	4 & 3	Henry Williams Jr.	Scioto CC, Columbus, OH
1951	Sam Snead	7 & 6	Walter Burkemo	Oakmont CC, Oakmont, PA
1952	Jim Turnesa	1 up	Chick Harbert	Big Spring CC, Louisville
1953	Walter Burkemo	2 & 1	Felice Torza	Birmingham CC, Birmingham, MI
1954	Chick Harbert	4 & 3	Walter Burkemo	Keller GC, St. Paul
1955	Doug Ford	4 & 3	Cary Middlecoff	Meadowbrook CC, Detroit
1956	Jack Burke	3 & 2	Ted Kroll	Blue Hill CC, Boston
1957	Lionel Hebert	2 & 1	Dow Finsterwald	Miami Valley CC, Dayton
1958	Dow Finsterwald	276	Billy Casper	Llanerch CC, Havertown, PA
1959	Bob Rosburg	277	Jerry Barber	Minneapolis GC, St. Louis Park, MN
			Doug Sanders	
1960	Jay Hebert	281	Jim Ferrier	Firestone CC, Akron
1961	Jerry Barber* (67)	277	Don January (68)	Olympia Fields CC, Olympia Fields, IL
1962	Gary Player	278	Bob Goalby	Aronimink GC, Newton Square, PA
1963	Jack Nicklaus	279	Dave Ragan Jr.	Dallas Athletic Club, Dallas
1964	Bobby Nichols	271	Jack Nicklaus	Columbus CC, Columbus, OH
			Arnold Palmer	
1965	Dave Marr	280	Billy Casper	Laurel Valley CC, Ligonier, PA
			Jack Nicklaus	
1966	Al Geiberger	280	Dudley Wysong	Firestone CC, Akron
1967	Don January* (69)	281	Don Massengale (71)	Columbine CC, Littleton, CO
1968	Julius Boros	281	Bob Charles	Pecan Valley CC, San Antonio
			Arnold Palmer	
1969	Ray Floyd	276	Gary Player	NCR CC, Dayton
1970	Dave Stockton	279	Arnold Palmer	Southern Hills CC, Tulsa
			Bob Murphy	
1971	Jack Nicklaus	281	Billy Casper	PGA Nat'l GC, Palm Beach Gardens, FL

PGA Championship (Cont.)

Year	Winner	Score	Runner-Up	Site
1972	Gary Player	281	Tommy Aaron Jim Jamieson	Oakland Hills CC, Birmingham, MI
1973	Jack Nicklaus	277	Bruce Crampton	Canterbury GC, Cleveland
1974	Lee Trevino	276	Jack Nicklaus	Tanglewood GC, Winston-Salem, NC
1975	Jack Nicklaus	276	Bruce Crampton	Firestone CC, Akron
1976	Dave Stockton	281	Ray Floyd Don January	Congressional CC, Bethesda, MD
1977†	Lanny Wadkins* (4-4-4)	282	Gene Littler (4-4-5)	Pebble Beach GL, Pebble Beach, CA
1978	John Mahaffey* (4-3)	276	Jerry Pate (4-4) Tom Watson (4-5)	Oakmont CC, Oakmont, PA
1979	David Graham* (4-4-2)	272	Ben Crenshaw (4-4-4)	Oakland Hills CC, Birmingham, MI
1980	Jack Nicklaus	274	Andy Bean	Oak Hill CC, Rochester, NY
1981	Larry Nelson	273	Fuzzy Zoeller	Atlanta Athletic Club, Duluth, GA
1982	Raymond Floyd	272	Lanny Wadkins	Southern Hills CC, Tulsa
1983	Hal Sutton	274	Jack Nicklaus	Riviera CC, Pacific Palisades, CA
1984	Lee Trevino	273	Gary Player Lanny Wadkins	Shoal Creek, Birmingham, AL
1985	Hubert Green	278	Lee Trevino	Cherry Hills CC, Denver
1986	Bob Tway	276	Greg Norman	Inverness CC, Toledo
1987	Larry Nelson* (4)	287	Lanny Wadkins (5)	PGA Natl GC, Palm Beach Gardens, FL
1988	Jeff Sluman	272	Paul Azinger	Oak Tree GC, Edmond, OK
1989	Payne Stewart	276	Mike Reid	Kemper Lakes GC, Hawthorn Woods, IL
1990	Wayne Grady	282	Fred Couples	Shoal Creek, Birmingham, AL
1991	John Daly	276	Bruce Lietzke	Crooked Stick GC, Carmel, IN
1992	Nick Price	278	Jim Gallagher Jr.	Bellerive CC, St. Louis
1993	Paul Azinger* (4-4)	272	Greg Norman (4-5)	Inverness CC, Toledo
1994	Nick Price	269	Corey Pavin	Southern Hills CC, Tulsa
1995	Steve Elkington* (3)	267	Colin Montgomerie (4)	Riviera CC, Pacific Palisades, CA
1996	Mark Brooks* (3)	277	Kenny Perry (x)	Valhalla GC, Louisville
1997	Davis Love III	269	Justin Leonard	Winged Foot GC, Mamaroneck, NY
1998	Vijay Singh	271	Steve Stricker	Sahalee CC, Redmond, WA
1999	Tiger Woods	277	Sergio Garcia	Medinah CC, Medinah, IL
2000	Tiger Woods* (3-4-5)	270	Bob May (4-4-x)	Valhalla GC, Louisville
2001	David Toms	265	Phil Mickelson	Atlanta AC, Duluth, GA
2002	Rich Beem	278	Tiger Woods	Hazeltine National GC, Shaska, MN
2003	Shaun Micheel	276	Chad Campbell	Oak Hill CC, Rochester, NY
2004	Vijay Singh*	280	Chris DiMarco	Whistling Straits GC, Kohler, WI
2005	Phil Mickelson	276	Steve Elkington	Baltusrol GC, Springfield, NJ
2006	Tiger Woods	270	Shaun Micheel	Medinah CC, Medinah, IL

*Winner in playoff. †Playoff changed from 18 holes to sudden death.

Alltime Major Championship Winners

	Masters	U.S. Open	British Open	PGA Champ.	U.S. Amateur	British Amateur	Total
Jack Nicklaus	6	4	3	5	2	0	20
*Tiger Woods	4	2	3	3	3	0	15
Bobby Jones	0	4	3	0	5	1	13
Walter Hagen	0	2	4	5	0	0	11
Ben Hogan	2	4	1	2	0	0	9
Gary Player	3	1	3	2	0	0	9
John Ball	0	0	1	0	0	8	9
Arnold Palmer	4	1	2	0	1	0	8
Tom Watson	2	1	5	0	0	0	8
Harold Hilton	0	0	2	0	1	4	7
Gene Sarazen	1	2	1	3	0	0	7
Sam Snead	3	0	1	3	0	0	7
Harry Vardon	0	1	6	0	0	0	7

*Active PGA Tour player.

Alltime Multiple Professional Major Winners

MASTERS

Jack Nicklaus 6
Arnold Palmer 4
Tiger Woods 4
Jimmy Demaret 3
Nick Faldo 3
Gary Player 3
Sam Snead................3
Seve Ballesteros.........2
Ben Crenshaw 2
Ben Hogan 2
Bernhard Langer 2
Phil Mickelson 2
Byron Nelson.............2
José María Olazábal ...2
Horton Smith 2
Tom Watson 2

U.S. OPEN

Willie Anderson 4
Ben Hogan 4
Bobby Jones 4
Jack Nicklaus 4

U.S. OPEN (Cont.)

Hale Irwin 3
Julius Boros 2
Billy Casper 2
Ernie Els 2
Retief Goosen...........2
Ralph Guldahl 2
Walter Hagen 2
Lee Janzen 2
John McDermott.........2
Cary Middlecoff..........2
Andy North 2
Gene Sarazen 2
Alex Smith 2
Payne Stewart 2
Curtis Strange 2
Lee Trevino 2
Tiger Woods 2

BRITISH OPEN

Harry Vardon 6
James Braid 5
J.H. Taylor..................5

BRITISH OPEN (Cont.)

Peter Thomson 5
Tom Watson................5
Walter Hagen 4
Bobby Locke..............4
Tom Morris Sr.............4
Tom Morris Jr. 4
Willie Park...................4
Jamie Anderson 3
Seve Ballesteros.........3
Henry Cotton 3
Nick Faldo 3
Robert Ferguson 3
Bobby Jones 3
Jack Nicklaus 3
Gary Player 3
Tiger Woods 3
Harold Hilton 2
Bob Martin..................2
Greg Norman 2
Arnold Palmer 2
Willie Park Jr. 2
Lee Trevino 2

PGA CHAMPIONSHIP

Walter Hagen 5
Jack Nicklaus.............5
Gene Sarazen 3
Sam Snead................3
Tiger Woods 3
Jim Barnes 2
Leo Diegel 2
Raymond Floyd 2
Ben Hogan 2
Byron Nelson.............2
Larry Nelson..............2
Gary Player 2
Paul Runyan 2
Denny Shute 2
Dave Stockton 2
Lee Trevino 2
Vijay Singh.................2

THE PGA TOUR

Most Career Wins*

	Wins		Wins		Wins
Sam Snead	82	Byron Nelson	52	Tom Watson	39
Jack Nicklaus	73	Billy Casper	51	Lloyd Mangrum	36
Ben Hogan	64	Walter Hagen	44	Horton Smith	32
Arnold Palmer	62	Cary Middlecoff	40	Harry Cooper	31
Tiger Woods	54	Gene Sarazen	39	Jimmy Demaret	31

* Through 10/15/06

Season Money Leaders

		Earnings ($)			Earnings ($)			Earnings ($)
1934	Paul Runyan	6,767.00	1958	Arnold Palmer	42,607.50	1982	Craig Stadler	446,462.00
1935	Johnny Revolta	9,543.00	1959	Art Wall	53,167.60	1983	Hal Sutton	426,668.00
1936	Horton Smith	7,682.00	1960	Arnold Palmer	75,262.85	1984	Tom Watson	476,260.00
1937	Harry Cooper	14,138.69	1961	Gary Player	64,540.45	1985	Curtis Strange	542,321.00
1938	Sam Snead	19,534.49	1962	Arnold Palmer	81,448.33	1986	Greg Norman	653,296.00
1939	Henry Picard	10,303.00	1963	Arnold Palmer	128,230.00	1987	Curtis Strange	925,941.00
1940	Ben Hogan	10,655.00	1964	Jack Nicklaus	113,284.50	1988	Curtis Strange	1,147,644.00
1941	Ben Hogan	18,358.00	1965	Jack Nicklaus	140,752.14	1989	Tom Kite	1,395,278.00
1942	Ben Hogan	13,143.00	1966	Billy Casper	121,944.92	1990	Greg Norman	1,165,477.00
1943	No statistics compiled		1967	Jack Nicklaus	188,998.08	1991	Corey Pavin	979,430.00
1944	Byron Nelson*	37,967.69	1968	Billy Casper	205,168.67	1992	Fred Couples	1,344,188.00
1945	Byron Nelson*	63,335.66	1969	Frank Beard	164,707.11	1993	Nick Price	1,478,557.00
1946	Ben Hogan	42,556.16	1970	Lee Trevino	157,037.63	1994	Nick Price	1,499,927.00
1947	Jimmy Demaret	27,936.83	1971	Jack Nicklaus	244,490.50	1995	Greg Norman	1,654,959.00
1948	Ben Hogan	32,112.00	1972	Jack Nicklaus	320,542.26	1996	Tom Lehman	1,780,159.00
1949	Sam Snead	31,593.83	1973	Jack Nicklaus	308,362.10	1997	Tiger Woods	2,066,833.00
1950	Sam Snead	35,758.83	1974	Johnny Miller	353,021.59	1998	David Duval	2,591,031.00
1951	Lloyd Mangrum	26,088.83	1975	Jack Nicklaus	298,149.17	1999	Tiger Woods	6,616,585.00
1952	Julius Boros	37,032.97	1976	Jack Nicklaus	266,438.57	2000	Tiger Woods	9,188,321.00
1953	Lew Worsham	34,002.00	1977	Tom Watson	310,653.16	2001	Tiger Woods	5,687,777.00
1954	Bob Toski	65,819.81	1978	Tom Watson	362,428.93	2002	Tiger Woods	6,912,625.00
1955	Julius Boros	63,121.55	1979	Tom Watson	462,636.00	2003	Vijay Singh	7,573,907.00
1956	Ted Kroll	72,835.83	1980	Tom Watson	530,808.33	2004	Vijay Singh	10,905,166.00
1957	Dick Mayer	65,835.00	1981	Tom Kite	375,698.84	2005	Tiger Woods	10,628,024.00

* War bonds. Note: Total money listed from 1968 through 1974. Official money listed from 1975 on.

Career Money Leaders*

		Earnings ($)			Earnings ($)			Earnings ($)
1	Tiger Woods	$65,712,324	18	Scott Hoch	$18,487,114	35	Billy Mayfair	$14,088,197
2.	Vijay Singh	$48,941,256	19	Stewart Cink	$18,419,738	36	Mark O'Meara	$14,052,768
3	Phil Mickelson	$39,514,038	20	Scott Verplank	$17,916,494	37	Greg Norman	$13,963,611
4	Davis Love III	$34,344,348	21	Jeff Sluman	$17,829,033	38	Tim Herron	$13,569,182
5	Jim Furyk	$30,415,766	22	Brad Faxon	$17,571,909	39	Richard Allenby	$13,441,140
6	Ernie Els	$28,060,045	23	Retief Goosen	$16,886,017	40	Kirk Triplett	$13,215,254
7	David Toms	$25,699,215	24	David Duval	$16,682,256	41	Corey Pavin	$13,183,622
8	Justin Leonard	$21,038,732	25	Sergio Garcia	$15,819,592	42	Jesper Parnevik	$13,145,600
9	Nick Price	$20,551,208	26	Bob Estes	$14,304,734	43	Lee Janzen	$12,871,055
10	Kenny Perry	$20,335,031	27	Hal Sutton	$15,267,685	44	Steve Flesch	$12,753,338
11	Fred Funk	$19,400,149	28	Loren Roberts	$15,090,850	45	Steve Lowery	$12,539,041
12	Fred Couples	$19,129,114	29	Jeff Maggert	$14,455,224	46	John Cook	$12,313,843
13	Mark Calcavecchia	$19,126,077	30	Bob Tway	$14,454,024	47	Charles Howell III	$12,271,786
14	Tom Lehman	$18,810,332	31	Jay Haas	$14,440,317	48	Chad Campbell	$12,248,881
15	Mike Weir	$18,785,533	32	Jerry Kelly	$14,302,685	49	Rocco Mediate	$12,186,167
16	Chris DiMarco	$18,686,371	33	Paul Azinger	$14,169,478	50	Shigeki Maruyama	$12,165,654
17	Stuart Appleby	$18,666,310	34	John Huston	$14,094,975			

*Through 10/8/06.

Year by Year Statistical Leaders

SCORING AVERAGE

1980	Lee Trevino	69.73
1981	Tom Kite	69.80
1982	Tom Kite	70.21
1983	Raymond Floyd	70.61
1984	Calvin Peete	70.56
1985	Don Pooley	70.36
1986	Scott Hoch	70.08
1987	David Frost	70.09
1988	Greg Norman	69.38
1989	Payne Stewart	69.485†
1990	Greg Norman	69.10
1991	Fred Couples	69.59
1992	Fred Couples	69.38
1993	Greg Norman	68.90
1994	Greg Norman	68.81
1995	Greg Norman	69.06
1996	Tom Lehman	69.32
1997	Nick Price	68.98
1998	David Duval	69.13
1999	Tiger Woods	68.43
2000	Tiger Woods	67.79
2001	Tiger Woods	68.81
2002	Tiger Woods	68.13
2003	Tiger Woods	68.41
2004	Vijay Singh	69.19
2005	Tiger Woods	68.66

Note: Scoring average per round, with adjustments made at each round for the field's course scoring average.

DRIVING DISTANCE

		Yds
1980	Dan Pohl	274.3
1981	Dan Pohl	280.1
1982	Bill Calfee	275.3
1983	John McComish	277.4
1984	Bill Glasson	276.5
1985	Andy Bean	278.2
1986	Davis Love III	285.7
1987	John McComish	283.9
1988	Steve Thomas	284.6
1989	Ed Humenik	280.9
1990	Tom Purtzer	279.6
1991	John Daly	288.9

DRIVING DISTANCE *(Cont.)*

1992	John Daly	283.4
1993	John Daly	288.9
1994	Davis Love III	283.8
1995	John Daly	289.0
1996	John Daly	288.8
1997	John Daly	302.0
1998	John Daly	299.4
1999	John Daly	305.6
2000	John Daly	301.4
2001	John Daly	306.7
2002	John Daly	306.8
2003	Hank Kuehne	321.4
2004	Hank Kuehne	314.4
2005	Scott Hend	318.9

Note: Average computed by charting distance of two tee shots on a predetermined par-four or par-five hole (one on front nine, one on back nine).

DRIVING ACCURACY

1980	Mike Reid	79.5
1981	Calvin Peete	81.9
1982	Calvin Peete	84.6
1983	Calvin Peete	81.3
1984	Calvin Peete	77.5
1985	Calvin Peete	80.6
1986	Calvin Peete	81.7
1987	Calvin Peete	83.0
1988	Calvin Peete	82.5
1989	Calvin Peete	82.6
1990	Calvin Peete	83.7
1991	Hale Irwin	78.3
1992	Doug Tewell	82.3
1993	Doug Tewell	82.5
1994	David Edwards	81.6
1995	Fred Funk	81.3
1996	Fred Funk	78.7
1997	Allen Doyle	80.8
1998	Bruce Fleisher	81.4
1999	Fred Funk	80.2
2000	Fred Funk	79.7
2001	Joe Durant	81.1
2002	Fred Funk	81.2

DRIVING ACCURACY *(Cont.)*

2003	Fred Funk	77.9
2004	Fred Funk	77.2
2005	Jeff Hart	76.0

Note: Percentage of fairways hit on number of par-four and par-five holes played; par-three holes excluded.

GREENS IN REGULATION

1980	Jack Nicklaus	72.1
1981	Calvin Peete	73.1
1982	Calvin Peete	72.4
1983	Calvin Peete	71.4
1984	Andy Bean	72.1
1985	John Mahaffey	71.9
1986	John Mahaffey	72.0
1987	Gil Morgan	73.3
1988	John Adams	73.9
1989	Bruce Lietzke	72.6
1990	Doug Tewell	70.9
1991	Bruce Lietzke	73.3
1992	Tim Simpson	74.0
1993	Fuzzy Zoeller	73.6
1994	Bill Glasson	73.0
1995	Lenny Clements	72.3
1996	Fred Couples	71.8
	Mark O'Meara	71.8
1997	Tom Lehman	72.7
1998	Hal Sutton	71.3
1999	Tiger Woods	71.4
2000	Tiger Woods	75.2
2001	Tom Lehman	74.5
2002	Tiger Woods	74.0
2003	Joe Durant	72.9
2004	Joe Durant	73.3
2005	Sergio Garcia	71.8

Note: Average of greens reached in regulation out of total holes played; hole is considered hit in regulation if any part of the ball rests on the putting surface in two shots less than the hole's par—a par-5 hit in two shots is one green in regulation.

† Number had to be carried to extra decimal place to determine winner.

Year by Year Statistical Leaders *(Cont.)*

PUTTING

1980	Jerry Pate	28.81
1981	Alan Tapie	28.70
1982	Ben Crenshaw	28.65
1983	Morris Hatalsky	27.96
1984	Gary McCord	28.57
1985	Craig Stadler	28.627†
1986	Greg Norman	1.736
1987	Ben Crenshaw	1.743
1988	Don Pooley	1.729
1989	Steve Jones	1.734
1990	Larry Rinker	1.7467†
1991	Jay Don Blake	1.7326†
1992	Mark O'Meara	1.731
1993	David Frost	1.739
1994	Loren Roberts	1.737
1995	Jim Furyk	1.708
1996	Brad Faxon	1.709
1997	Don Pooley	1.718
1998	Rick Fehr	1.722
1999	Brad Faxon	1.723
2000	Brad Faxon	1.704
2001	David Frost	1.708
2002	Bob Heintz	1.682
2003	John Huston	1.713
2004	Stewart Cink	1.723
2005	Arjun Atwal	1.710

Note: Average number of putts taken on greens reached in regulation; prior to 1986, based on average number of putts per 18 holes.

SAND SAVES

1980	Bob Eastwood	65.4
1981	Tom Watson	60.1
1982	Isao Aoki	60.2
1983	Isao Aoki	62.3
1984	Peter Oosterhuis	64.7
1985	Tom Purtzer	60.8
1986	Paul Azinger	63.8
1987	Paul Azinger	63.2
1988	Greg Powers	63.5
1989	Mike Sullivan	66.0
1990	Paul Azinger	67.2
1991	Ben Crenshaw	64.9
1992	Mitch Adcock	66.9
1993	Ken Green	64.4
1994	Corey Pavin	65.4
1995	Billy Mayfair	68.6
1996	Gary Rusnak	64.0
1997	Bob Estes	70.3
1998	Keith Fergus	71.0
1999	Jeff Sluman	67.3
2000	Fred Couples	67.0
2001	Franklin Langham	68.9
2002	J. Olazabal	64.9
2003	Stuart Appleby	62.1
2004	Dan Forsman	62.3
2005	Pat Perez	63.0

Note: Percentage of up-and-down efforts from greenside sand traps only—fairway bunkers excluded.

PAR BREAKERS

1980	Tom Watson	.213
1981	Bruce Lietzke	.225
1982	Tom Kite	.2154†
1983	Tom Watson	.211
1984	Craig Stadler	.220
1985	Craig Stadler	.218
1986	Greg Norman	.248
1987	Mark Calcavecchia	.221
1988	Ken Green	.236
1989	Greg Norman	.224
1990	Greg Norman	.219

Note: Average based on total birdies and eagles scored out of total holes played. Discontinued as an official category after 1990.

EAGLES

1980	Dave Eichelberger	16
1981	Bruce Lietzke	12
1982	Tom Weiskopf	10
	J.C. Snead	10
	Andy Bean	10
1983	Chip Beck	15
1984	Gary Hallberg	15
1985	Larry Rinker	14
1986	Joey Sindelar	16
1987	Phil Blackmar	20
1988	Ken Green	21
1989	Lon Hinkle	14
	Duffy Waldorf	14
1990	Paul Azinger	14
1991	Andy Bean	15
1992	Dan Forsman	18
1993	Davis Love III	15
1994	Davis Love III	18
1995	Kelly Gibson	16
1996	Tom Watson	97.2
1997	Tiger Woods	104.1
1998	Davis Love III	83.3
1999	Vijay Singh	104.8
2000	Tiger Woods	72.0
2001	Phil Mickelson	73.8
2002	John Daly	78.4
2003	Tiger Woods	76.5
2004	Nick Price	90.0
2005	Brenden Pappas	70.6

Note: Total of eagles scored 1980–1995. Since 1996 winner determined by number of holes played per eagle.

BIRDIES

1980	Andy Bean	388
1981	Vance Heafner	388
1982	Andy Bean	392
1983	Hal Sutton	399
1984	Mark O'Meara	419
1985	Joey Sindelar	411
1986	Joey Sindelar	415
1987	Dan Forsman	409
1988	Dan Forsman	465
1989	Ted Schulz	415
1990	Mike Donald	401
1991	Scott Hoch	446
1992	Jeff Sluman	417
1993	John Huston	426

BIRDIES *(Cont.)*

1994	Brad Bryant	397
1995	Steve Lowery	410
1996	Fred Couples	4.20
1997	Tiger Woods	4.25
1998	David Duval	4.29
1999	Tiger Woods	4.46
2000	Tiger Woods	4.92
2001	Phil Mickelson	4.49
2002	Tiger Woods	4.47
2003	Vijay Singh	4.41
2004	Vijay Singh	4.40
2005	Tiger Woods	4.57

Note: Total of birdies scored 1980–95. Since 1996, winner determined by average number of birdies per round.

ALL-AROUND

1987	Dan Pohl	170
1988	Payne Stewart	170
1989	Paul Azinger	250
1990	Paul Azinger	162
1991	Scott Hoch	283
1992	Fred Couples	256
1993	Gil Morgan	252
1994	Bob Estes	227
1995	Justin Leonard	323
1996	Fred Couples	214
1997	Bill Glasson	282
1998	John Huston	151
1999	Tiger Woods	120
2000	Tiger Woods	113
2001	Phil Mickelson	174
2002	Phil Mickelson	259
2003	Tiger Woods	206
2004	Jeff Ogilvy	268
2005	Tiger Woods	265

Note: Sum of the places of standing from the other statistical categories; the player with the number closest to zero leads.

† Number had to be carried to extra decimal place to determine winner.

PGA Player of the Year Award

1948	Ben Hogan	1968	Not awarded	1988	Curtis Strange
1949	Sam Snead	1969	Orville Moody	1989	Tom Kite
1950	Ben Hogan	1970	Billy Casper	1990	Wayne Levi
1951	Ben Hogan	1971	Lee Trevino	1991	Fred Couples
1952	Julius Boros	1972	Jack Nicklaus	1992	Fred Couples
1953	Ben Hogan	1973	Jack Nicklaus	1993	Nick Price
1954	Ed Furgol	1974	Johnny Miller	1994	Nick Price
1955	Doug Ford	1975	Jack Nicklaus	1995	Greg Norman
1956	Jack Burke	1976	Jack Nicklaus	1996	Tom Lehman
1957	Dick Mayer	1977	Tom Watson	1997	Tiger Woods
1958	Dow Finsterwald	1978	Tom Watson	1998	David Duval
1959	Art Wall	1979	Tom Watson	1999	Tiger Woods
1960	Arnold Palmer	1980	Tom Watson	2000	Tiger Woods
1961	Jerry Barber	1981	Bill Rogers	2001	Tiger Woods
1962	Arnold Palmer	1982	Tom Watson	2002	Tiger Woods
1963	Julius Boros	1983	Hal Sutton	2003	Tiger Woods
1964	Ken Venturi	1984	Tom Watson	2004	Vijay Singh
1965	Dave Marr	1985	Lanny Wadkins	2005	Tiger Woods
1966	Billy Casper	1986	Bob Tway		
1967	Jack Nicklaus	1987	Paul Azinger		

Vardon Trophy: Scoring Average

Year	Winner	Avg	Year	Winner	Avg	Year	Winner	Avg
1937	Harry Cooper	*500	1963	Billy Casper	70.58	1985	Don Pooley	70.36
1938	Sam Snead	520	1964	Arnold Palmer	70.01	1986	Scott Hoch	70.08
1939	Byron Nelson	473	1965	Billy Casper	70.85	1987	Don Pohl	70.25
1940	Ben Hogan	423	1966	Billy Casper	70.27	1988	Chip Beck	69.46
1941	Ben Hogan	494	1967	Arnold Palmer	70.18	1989	Greg Norman	69.49
1942–46	No award		1968	Billy Casper	69.82	1990	Greg Norman	69.10
1947	Jimmy Demaret	69.90	1969	Dave Hill	70.34	1991	Fred Couples	69.59
1948	Ben Hogan	69.30	1970	Lee Trevino	70.64	1992	Fred Couples	69.38
1949	Sam Snead	69.37	1971	Lee Trevino	70.27	1993	Nick Price	69.11
1950	Sam Snead	69.23	1972	Lee Trevino	70.89	1994	Greg Norman	68.81
1951	Lloyd Mangrum	70.05	1973	Bruce Crampton	70.57	1995	Steve Elkington	69.62
1952	Jack Burke	70.54	1974	Bruce Crampton	70.53	1996	Tom Lehman	69.32
1953	Lloyd Mangrum	70.22	1975	Bruce Crampton	70.51	1997	Nick Price	68.98
1954	E.J. Harrison	70.41	1976	Don January	70.56	1998	David Duval	69.13
1955	Sam Snead	69.86	1977	Tom Watson	70.32	1999	Tiger Woods	68.43
1956	Cary Middlecoff	70.35	1978	Tom Watson	70.16	2000	Tiger Woods	67.79
1957	Dow Finsterwald	70.30	1979	Tom Watson	70.27	2001	Tiger Woods	68.81
1958	Bob Rosburg	70.11	1980	Lee Trevino	69.73	2002	Tiger Woods	68.13
1959	Art Wall	70.35	1981	Tom Kite	69.80	2003	Tiger Woods	68.41
1960	Billy Casper	69.95	1982	Tom Kite	70.21	2004	Vijay Singh	68.84
1961	Arnold Palmer	69.85	1983	Raymond Floyd	70.61	2005	Tiger Woods	68.66
1962	Arnold Palmer	70.27	1984	Calvin Peete	70.56			

*Point system used, 1937–41. NOTE: As of 1988, based on minimum of 60 rounds per year. Adjusted for average score of field in tournaments entered.

Alltime PGA Tour Records*
Scoring

90 HOLES

324—(65-61-67-66-65) by Joe Durant, at four courses, La Quinta, CA, to win the 2001 Bob Hope Classic (36 under par).

72 HOLES

254—(64-62-63-65) by Tommy Armour III, at LaCantera GC, San Antonio, TX, to win the 2003 Valero Texas Open (26 under par).

54 HOLES, OPENING ROUNDS

189—(64-62-63) by John Cook, at the TPC at Southwind, Memphis, en route to winning the 1996 St. Jude Classic.

189—(65-60-64) Mark Calcavecchia, at the TPC at Scottsdale, Scottsdale, AZ, en route to winning the 2001 Phoenix Open.

54 HOLES, OPENING ROUNDS *(Cont.)*

189—(64-62-63) by Tommy Armour III, at LaCantera GC, San Antonio, TX, en route to winning the 2003 Valero Texas Open.

54 HOLES, CONSECUTIVE ROUNDS

189—(63-63-63) by Chandler Harper in the last three rounds to win the 1954 Texas Open at Brackenridge Park GC, San Antonio.

189—(64-62-63) by John Cook, at the TPC at Southwind, Memphis, in the first three rounds en route to winning the 1996 St. Jude Classic.

189—(65-60-64) Mark Calcavecchia, at the TPC at Scottsdale, Scottsdale, AZ, in the first three rounds en route to winning the 2001 Phoenix Open.

Alltime PGA Tour Records *(Cont.)**

Scoring *(Cont.)*

54 HOLES, CONSECUTIVE ROUNDS *(Cont.)*

189—(64-62-63) by Tommy Armour III, at LaCantera GC, San Antonio, TX, in the first three rounds en route to winning the 2003 Valero Texas Open.

36 HOLES, OPENING ROUNDS

125—(64-61) by Tiger Woods, in the 2000 World Golf Championships/ NEC Invitational, which he won, at Firestone CC, Akron.

125—(65-60) by Mark Calcavecchia, in the 2001 Phoenix Open, which he won, at TPC at Scottsdale, Scottsdale, AZ.

36 HOLES, CONSECUTIVE ROUNDS

125—(64-61) by Gay Brewer, in the middle rounds of the 1967 Pensacola Open, which he won, at Pensacola CC, Pensacola, FL.

125—(63-62) by Ron Streck, in the last two rounds to win the 1978 Texas Open at Oak Hills CC, San Antonio.

125—(62-63) by Blaine McCallister, in the middle two rounds of the 1988 Hardee's Golf Classic, which he won at Oakwood CC, Coal Valley, IL.

125—(62-63) by John Cook, in the middle two rounds of the 1996 St. Jude Classic, which he won at the TPC at Southwind, Memphis.

125—(62-63) by John Cook, in the fourth and fifth rounds in winning the 1997 Bob Hope Chrysler Classic at Indian Wells CC, Indian Hills, CA.

125—(64-61) by Tiger Woods, in the first two rounds of the 2000 World Golf Championship/ NEC Invitational, which he won, at Firestone CC, Akron.

125—(65-60) by Mark Calcavecchia, in the first two rounds of the 2001 Phoenix Open, which he won, at TPC at Scottsdale, Scottsdale, AZ.

125—(62-63) by Tommy Armour III, in the middle two rounds of the 2003 Valero Texas Open, which he won at LaCantera GC, San Antonio, TX.

18 HOLES

59—by Al Geiberger, at Colonial Country Club, Memphis, in second round in winning the 1977 Memphis Classic.

59—by Chip Beck, at Sunrise Golf Club, Las Vegas, in third round of the 1991 Las Vegas Invitational.

59—by David Duval, on the Palmer Course at PGA West, La Quinta, CA, in the fifth round of the 1999 Bob Hope Chrysler Classic.

9 HOLES

26—by Corey Pavin, at Brown Deer Park GC, Milwaukee, WI, on par-34 front nine during the first round of the 2006 US Bank Championship.

MOST CONSECUTIVE ROUNDS UNDER 70

19—Byron Nelson in 1945.

MOST BIRDIES IN A ROW

8—Bob Goalby, at Pasadena GC, St. Petersburg, FL, during fourth round in winning the 1961 St Petersburg Open.

8—Fuzzy Zoeller, at Oakwood CC, Coal Valley, IL, during first round of 1976 Quad Cities Open.

8—Dewey Arnette, at Warwick Hills GC, Grand Blanc, MI, during first round of the 1987 Buick Open.

8—Edward Fryatt, at the Blue Course of the Doral Resort and Spa, Miami, during second round of the 2000 Doral-Ryder Open.

MOST BIRDIES IN A ROW TO WIN

5—Jack Nicklaus, to win 1978 Jackie Gleason Inverrary Classic (last 5 holes).

*Through 10/15/2006

Wins

MOST CONSECUTIVE YEARS WINNING AT LEAST ONE TOURNAMENT

17—Jack Nicklaus, 1962–78.

17—Arnold Palmer, 1955–71.

16—Billy Casper, 1956–71.

MOST CONSECUTIVE WINS

11—Byron Nelson, from Miami Four Ball, March 8–11, 1945, through Canadian Open, August 2–4, 1945.

MOST WINS IN A SINGLE EVENT

8—Sam Snead, Greater Greensboro Open, 1938, 1946, 1949, 1950, 1955, 1956, 1960, and 1965.

MOST CONSECUTIVE WINS IN A SINGLE EVENT

4—Walter Hagen, PGA Championships, 1924–27.

4—Gene Sarazen, Miami Open, 1926, (schedule change) 1928–30.

4—Tiger Woods, Bay Hill Invitational, 2000–03

MOST WINS IN A CALENDAR YEAR

18—Byron Nelson, 1945

MOST YEARS BETWEEN WINS

15 yrs, 5 mos—Butch Baird, 1961–76.

MOST YEARS FROM FIRST WIN TO LAST

28 yrs, 11 mos, 20 days—Raymond Floyd, 1963–92.

YOUNGEST WINNERS

19 yrs, 10 mos—John McDermott, 1911 U.S. Open.

OLDEST WINNER

52 yrs, 10 mos—Sam Snead, 1965 Greater Greensboro Open.

WIDEST WINNING MARGIN: STROKES

16—Bobby Locke, 1948 Chicago Victory National Championship.

THE MAJOR TOURNAMENTS

LPGA Championship

Year	Winner	Score	Runner-Up	Site
1955	Beverly Hanson† (4 & 3)	220	Louise Suggs	Orchard Ridge CC, Ft Wayne, IN
1956	Marlene Hagge*	291	Patty Berg	Forest Lake CC, Detroit
1957	Louise Suggs	285	Wiffi Smith	Churchill Valley CC, Pittsburgh
1958	Mickey Wright	288	Fay Crocker	Churchill Valley CC, Pittsburgh
1959	Betsy Rawls	288	Patty Berg	Sheraton Hotel CC, French Lick, IN
1960	Mickey Wright	292	Louise Suggs	Sheraton Hotel CC, French Lick, IN
1961	Mickey Wright	287	Louise Suggs	Stardust CC, Las Vegas
1962	Judy Kimball	282	Shirley Spork	Stardust CC, Las Vegas
1963	Mickey Wright	294	Mary Lena Faulk Mary Mills Louise Suggs	Stardust CC, Las Vegas
1964	Mary Mills	278	Mickey Wright	Stardust CC, Las Vegas
1965	Sandra Haynie	279	Clifford A. Creed	Stardust CC, Las Vegas
1966	Gloria Ehret	282	Mickey Wright	Stardust CC, Las Vegas
1967	Kathy Whitworth	284	Shirley Englehorn	Pleasant Valley CC, Sutton, MA
1968	Sandra Post*	294	Kathy Whitworth (75)	Pleasant Valley CC, Sutton, MA
1969	Betsy Rawls	293	Susie Berning Carol Mann	Concord GC, Kiamesha Lake, NY
1970	Shirley Englehorn*	285	Kathy Whitworth (78)	Pleasant Valley CC, Sutton, MA
1971	Kathy Whitworth	288	Kathy Ahern	Pleasant Valley CC, Sutton, MA
1972	Kathy Ahern	293	Jane Blalock	Pleasant Valley CC, Sutton, MA
1973	Mary Mills	288	Betty Burfeindt	Pleasant Valley CC, Sutton, MA
1974	Sandra Haynie	288	JoAnne Carner	Pleasant Valley CC, Sutton, MA
1975	Kathy Whitworth	288	Sandra Haynie	Pine Ridge GC, Baltimore
1976	Betty Burfeindt	287	Judy Rankin	Pine Ridge GC, Baltimore
1977	Chako Higuchi	279	Pat Bradley Sandra Post Judy Rankin	Bay Tree Golf Plantation, N Myrtle Beach, SC
1978	Nancy Lopez	275	Amy Alcott	Jack Nicklaus GC, Kings Island, OH
1979	Donna Caponi	279	Jerilyn Britz	Jack Nicklaus GC, Kings Island, OH
1980	Sally Little	285	Jane Blalock	Jack Nicklaus GC, Kings Island, OH
1981	Donna Caponi	280	Jerilyn Britz Pat Meyers	Jack Nicklaus GC, Kings Island, OH
1982	Jan Stephenson	279	JoAnne Carner	Jack Nicklaus GC, Kings Island, OH
1983	Patty Sheehan	279	Sandra Haynie	Jack Nicklaus GC, Kings Island, OH
1984	Patty Sheehan	272	Beth Daniel Pat Bradley	Jack Nicklaus GC, Kings Island, OH
1985	Nancy Lopez	273	Alice Miller	Jack Nicklaus GC, Kings Island, OH
1986	Pat Bradley	277	Patty Sheehan	Jack Nicklaus GC, Kings Island, OH
1987	Jane Geddes	275	Betsy King	Jack Nicklaus GC, Kings Island, OH
1988	Sherri Turner	281	Amy Alcott	Jack Nicklaus GC, Kings Island, OH
1989	Nancy Lopez	274	Ayako Okamoto	Jack Nicklaus GC, Kings Island, OH
1990	Beth Daniel	280	Rosie Jones	Bethesda CC, Bethesda, MD
1991	Meg Mallon	274	Pat Bradley Ayako Okamoto	Bethesda CC, Bethesda, MD
1992	Betsy King	267	Karen Noble	Bethesda CC, Bethesda, MD
1993	Patty Sheehan	275	Lauri Merten	Bethesda CC, Bethesda, MD
1994	Laura Davies	279	Alice Ritzman	DuPont CC, Wilmington, DE
1995	Kelly Robbins	274	Laura Davies	DuPont CC, Wilmington, DE
1996	Laura Davies	213†	Julie Piers	DuPont CC, Wilmington, DE
1997	Chris Johnson*	281	Leta Lindley	DuPont CC, Wilmington, DE
1998	Se Ri Pak	273	Donna Andrews	DuPont CC, Wilmington, DE
1999	Juli Inkster	268	Liselotte Neumann	DuPont CC, Wilmington, DE
2000	Juli Inkster*	281	Stefania Croce	DuPont CC, Wilmington, DE
2001	Karrie Webb	270	Laura Diaz	DuPont CC, Wilmington, DE
2002	Se Ri Pak	279	Beth Daniel	DuPont CC, Wilmington, DE
2003	Annika Sorenstam*	278	Grace Park	DuPont CC, Wilmington, DE
2004	Annika Sorenstam	271	Shi Hyun Ahn	DuPont CC, Wilmington, DE
2005	Annika Sorenstam	277	Michelle Wie	Bulle Rock GC, Havre de Grace, MD
2006	Se Ri Pak*	280	Karrie Webb	Bulle Rock GC, Havre de Grace, MD

*Won playoff. †Won match-play final. #Shortened due to rain.

U.S. Women's Open

Year	Winner	Score	Runner-Up	Site
1946	Patty Berg	5 & 4	Betty Jameson	Spokane CC, Spokane, WA
1947	Betty Jameson	295	Sally Sessions	Starmount Forest CC, Greensboro, NC
			Polly Riley	
1948	Babe Zaharias	300	Betty Hicks	Atlantic City CC, Northfield, NJ
1949	Louise Suggs	291	Babe Zaharias	Prince George's G & CC, Landover, MD
1950	Babe Zaharias	291	Betsy Rawls	Rolling Hills CC, Wichita, KS
1951	Betsy Rawls	293	Louise Suggs	Druid Hills GC, Atlanta
1952	Louise Suggs	284	Marlene Bauer	Bala GC, Philadelphia
			Betty Jameson	
1953	Betsy Rawls* (71)	302	Jackie Pung (77)	CC of Rochester, Rochester, NY
1954	Babe Zaharias	291	Betty Hicks	Salem CC, Peabody, MA
1955	Fay Crocker	299	Mary Lena Faulk	Wichita CC, Wichita, KS
			Louise Suggs	
1956	Kathy Cornelius* (75)	302	Barbara McIntire (82)	Northland CC, Duluth, MN
1957	Betsy Rawls	299	Patty Berg	Winged Foot GC, Mamaroneck, NY
1958	Mickey Wright	290	Louise Suggs	Forest Lake CC, Detroit
1959	Mickey Wright	287	Louise Suggs	Churchill Valley CC, Pittsburgh
1960	Betsy Rawls	292	Joyce Ziske	Worcester CC, Worcester, MA
1961	Mickey Wright	293	Betsy Rawls	Baltusrol GC (Lower Course), Springfield, NJ
1962	Murle Breer	301	Jo Ann Prentice	Dunes GC, Myrtle Beach, SC
			Ruth Jessen	
1963	Mary Mills	289	Sandra Haynie	Kenwood CC, Cincinnati
			Louise Suggs	
1964	Mickey Wright* (70)	290	Ruth Jessen (72)	San Diego CC, Chula Vista, CA
1965	Carol Mann	290	Kathy Cornelius	Atlantic City CC, Northfield, NJ
1966	Sandra Spuzich	297	Carol Mann	Hazeltine Natl GC, Chaska, MN
1967	Catherine LaCoste	294	Susie Berning	Hot Springs GC (Cascades Course),
			Beth Stone	Hot Springs, VA
1968	Susie Berning	289	Mickey Wright	Moslem Springs GC, Fleetwood, PA
1969	Donna Caponi	294	Peggy Wilson	Scenic Hills CC, Pensacola, FL
1970	Donna Caponi	287	Sandra Haynie	Muskogee CC, Muskogee, OK
			Sandra Spuzich	
1971	JoAnne Carner	288	Kathy Whitworth	Kahkwa CC, Erie, PA
1972	Susie Berning	299	Kathy Ahern	Winged Foot GC, Mamaroneck, NY
			Pam Barnett	
			Judy Rankin	
1973	Susie Berning	290	Gloria Ehret	CC of Rochester, Rochester, NY
			Shelley Hamlin	
1974	Sandra Haynie	295	Carol Mann	La Grange CC, La Grange, IL
			Beth Stone	
1975	Sandra Palmer	295	JoAnne Carner	Atlantic City CC, Northfield, NJ
			Sandra Post	
			Nancy Lopez	
1976	JoAnne Carner* (76)	292	Sandra Palmer (78)	Rolling Green CC, Springfield, PA
1977	Hollis Stacy	292	Nancy Lopez	Hazeltine Natl GC, Chaska, MN
1978	Hollis Stacy	289	JoAnne Carner	CC of Indianapolis, Indianapolis
			Sally Little	
1979	Jerilyn Britz	284	Debbie Massey	Brooklawn CC, Fairfield, CT
			Sandra Palmer	
1980	Amy Alcott	280	Hollis Stacy	Richland CC, Nashville
1981	Pat Bradley	279	Beth Daniel	La Grange CC, La Grange, IL
1982	Janet Anderson	283	Beth Daniel	Del Paso CC, Sacramento
			Sandra Haynie	
			Donna White	
			JoAnne Carner	
1983	Jan Stephenson	290	JoAnne Carner	Cedar Ridge CC, Tulsa
			Patty Sheehan	
1984	Hollis Stacy	290	Rosie Jones	Salem CC, Peabody, MA
1985	Kathy Baker	280	Judy Dickinson	Baltusrol GC (Upper Course), Springfield, NJ
1986	Jane Geddes* (71)	287	Sally Little (73)	NCR GC, Dayton
1987	Laura Davies* (71)	285	Ayako Okamoto (73)	Plainfield CC, Plainfield, NJ
			JoAnne Carner (74)	
1988	Liselotte Neumann	277	Patty Sheehan	Baltimore CC, Baltimore
1989	Betsy King	278	Nancy Lopez	Indianwood G & CC, Lake Orion, MI
1990	Betsy King	284	Patty Sheehan	Atlanta Athletic Club, Duluth, GA
1991	Meg Mallon	283	Pat Bradley	Colonial Club, Fort Worth

U.S. Women's Open (Cont.)

Year	Winner	Score	Runner-Up	Site
1992	Patty Sheehan* (72)	280	Juli Inkster	Oakmont CC, Oakmont, PA
1993	Lauri Merten	280	Donna Andrew	Crooked Stick, Carmel, IN
			Helen Alfredsson	
1994	Patty Sheehan	277	Tammie Green	Indianwood G & CC, Lake Orion, MI
1995	Annika Sorenstam	278	Meg Mallon	The Broadmoor GC, Colorado Springs, CO
1996	Annika Sorenstam	272	Kris Tschetter	Pine Needles GC, Southern Pines, NC
1997	Alison Nicholas	274	Nancy Lopez	Pumpkin Ridge CC, North Plains, OR
1998	Se Ri Pak†	290	Jenny Chuasiriporn	Blackwolf Run Golf Resort, Kohler, WI
1999	Juli Inkster	272	Sherri Turner	Old Waverly GC, West Point, MS
2000	Karrie Webb	282	Cristie Kerr/ Meg Mallon	Merit GC, Libertyville, IL
2001	Karrie Webb	273	Se Ri Pak	Pine Needles GC, Southern Pines, NC
2002	Juli Inkster	276	Annika Sorenstam	Prairie Dunes CC, Hutchinson, KS
2003	Hilary Lunke*	283	Kelly Robbins	Pumpkin Ridge GC, North Plains, OR
2004	Meg Mallon	274	Annika Sorenstam	The Orchards GC, South Hadley, MA
2005	Birdie Kim	287	Brittany Lang	Cherry Hills CC, Cherry Hills Village, CO
			Morgan Pressel	
2006	Annika Sorenstam*	284	Pat Hurst	Newport CC, Newport, RI

* Winner in playoff. † Winner on second hole of sudden death after 18-hole playoff ended in a tie.

Nabisco Championship

Year	Winner	Score	Runner-Up	Year	Winner	Score	Runner-Up
1972	Jane Blalock	213	Carol Mann				JoAnne Carner
			Judy Rankin	1990	Betsy King	283	Kathy Postlewait
1973	Mickey Wright	284	Joyce Kazmierski				Shirley Furlong
1974	Jo Ann Prentice*	289	Jane Blalock	1991	Amy Alcott	273	Dottie Mochrie
			Sandra Haynie	1992	Dottie Mochrie*	279	Juli Inkster
1975	Sandra Palmer	283	Kathy McMullen	1993	Helen Alfredsson	284	Amy Benz
1976	Judy Rankin	285	Betty Burfeindt				Tina Barrett
1977	Kathy Whitworth	289	JoAnne Carner				Betsy King
			Sally Little	1994	Donna Andrews	276	Laura Davies
1978	Sandra Post*	283	Penny Pulz	1995	Nanci Bowen	285	Susie Redman
1979	Sandra Post	276	Nancy Lopez	1996	Patti Sheehan	281	Kelly Robbins
1980	Donna Caponi	275	Amy Alcott				Meg Mallon
1981	Nancy Lopez	277	Carolyn Hill				Annika Sörenstam
1982	Sally Little	278	Hollis Stacy	1997	Betsy King	276	Kris Tschetter
			Sandra Haynie	1998	Pat Hurst	281	Helen Dobson
1983	Amy Alcott	282	Beth Daniel	1999	Dottie Pepper	269	Meg Mallon
			Kathy Whitworth	2000	Karrie Webb	274	Dottie Pepper
1984	Juli Inkster*	280	Pat Bradley	2001	Annika Sorenstam	281	five players
1985	Alice Miller	275	Jan Stephenson	2002	Annika Sorenstam	280	Liselotte Neumann
1986	Pat Bradley	280	Val Skinner	2003	P. Meunier-Lebouc	281	Annika Sorenstam
1987	Betsy King*	283	Patty Sheehan	2004	Grace Park	277	Aree Song
1988	Amy Alcott	274	Colleen Walker	2005	Anika Sorenstam	273	Rosie Jones
1989	Juli Inkster	279	Tammie Green	2006	Karrie Webb*	279	Lorena Ochoa

*Winner in sudden-death playoff. Note: Designated fourth major in 1983; played at Mission Hills CC, Rancho Mirage, CA.

du Maurier Classic

Year	Winner	Score	Runner-Up	Site
1973	Jocelyne Bourassa*	214	Sandra Haynie	Montreal GC, Montreal
			Judy Rankin	
1974	Carole Jo Callison	208	JoAnne Carner	Candiac GC, Montreal
1975	JoAnne Carner*	214	Carol Mann	St. George's CC, Toronto
1976	Donna Caponi*	212	Judy Rankin	Cedar Brae G & CC, Toronto
1977	Judy Rankin	214	Pat Meyers	Lachute G & CC, Montreal
			Sandra Palmer	
1978	JoAnne Carner	278	Hollis Stacy	St. George's CC, Toronto
1979	Amy Alcott	285	Nancy Lopez	Richelieu Valley CC, Montreal
1980	Pat Bradley	277	JoAnne Carner	St. George's CC, Toronto
1981	Jan Stephenson	278	Nancy Lopez	Summerlea CC, Dorion, Quebec
			Pat Bradley	
1982	Sandra Haynie	280	Beth Daniel	St. George's CC, Toronto
1983	Hollis Stacy	277	JoAnne Carner	Beaconsfield GC, Montreal
			Alice Miller	
1984	Juli Inkster	279	Ayako Okamoto	St. George's G & CC, Toronto
1985	Pat Bradley	278	Jane Geddes	Beaconsfield CC, Montreal
1986	Pat Bradley*	276	Ayako Okamoto	Board of Trade CC, Toronto
1987	Jody Rosenthal	272	Ayako Okamoto	Islesmere GC, Laval, Quebec

du Maurier Classic *(Cont.)*

Year	Winner	Score	Runner-Up	Site
1988	Sally Little	279	Laura Davies	Vancouver GC, Coquitlam, British Columbia
1989	Tammie Green	279	Pat Bradley Betsy King	Beaconsfield GC, Montreal
1990	Cathy Johnston	276	Patty Sheehan	Westmount G & CC, Kitchener, Ontario
1991	Nancy Scranton	279	Debbie Massey	Vancouver GC, Coquitlam, British Columbia
1992	Sherri Steinhauer	277	Judy Dickinson	St. Charles CC, Winnipeg, Manitoba
1993	Brandie Burton	277	Betsy King	London Hunt and CC, London, Ontario
1994	Martha Nause	279	Michelle McGann	Ottawa Hunt and GC, Ottawa, Ont.
1995	Jenny Lidback	280	Liselotte Neumann	Beaconsfield GC, Pointe-Claire, Quebec
1996	Laura Davies	277	Nancy Lopez Karrie Webb	Edmonton CC, Edmonton, Alberta
1997	Colleen Walker	278	Liselotte Neumann	Glen Abbey GC, Oakville, Ontario
1998	Brandie Burton	270	Annika Sorenstam	Essex G & CC, Windsor, Ontario
1999	Karrie Webb	277	Laura Davies	Priddis Greens G & CC, Calgary, Alberta
2000	Meg Mallon	282	Rosie Jones	Royal Ottawa GC, Aylmer, Quebec

*Winner in sudden-death playoff. Note: Designated third major in 1979; discontinued in 2001.

Women's British Open

Year	Winner	Score	Runner-Up	Site
2001	Se Ri Pak	277	Mi Hyun Kim	Sunningdale GC, Berkshire, England
2002	Karrie Webb	273	Michelle Ellis Paula Marti	Turnberry GC, Ailsa, Scotland
2003	Annika Sorenstam	278	Se Ri Pak	Royal Lytham & St. Annes, England
2004	Karen Stupples	269	Rachel Teske	Sunningdale GC, Berjshire, England
2005	Jeong Jang	272	Sophie Gustafson	Royal Birkdale CC, Merseyside, England
2006	Sherri Steinhauer	281	Cristie Kerr	Royal Lytham & St. Anne's, England

Note: Designated fourth major in 2001.

Alltime Major Championship Winners

	LPGA	U.S. Open	Nabisco	Brit. Open	‡du Maurier	#Titleholders	†Western	U.S. Am	Brit. Am	Total
Patty Berg	0	1	0	0	0	7	7	1	0	16
Mickey Wright	4	4	0	0	0	2	3	0	0	13
Louise Suggs	1	2	0	0	0	4	4	1	1	13
Babe Zaharias	0	3	0	0	0	3	4	1	1	12
*Juli Inkster	2	2	2	0	1	0	0	3	0	10
*Annika Sorenstam	3	3	1	0	0	0	0	0	0	10
Betsy Rawls	2	4	0	0	0	0	2	0	0	8
JoAnne Carner	0	2	0	0	0	0	0	5	0	7
*Karrie Webb	1	2	2	1	1	0	0	0	0	7
Kathy Whitworth	3	0	0	0	0	2	1	0	0	6
Pat Bradley	1	1	1	0	3	0	0	0	0	6
*Patty Sheehan	3	2	1	0	0	0	0	0	0	6
Glenna Vare	0	0	0	0	0	0	0	6	0	6
*Betsy King	1	2	3	0	0	0	0	0	0	6

*Active LPGA player.
#Major from 1937–1972. †Major from 1937–1967. ‡Major from 1979–2000.

Alltime Multiple Professional Major Winners

LPGA

Player	Wins
Mickey Wright	4
Nancy Lopez	3
Se Ri Pak	3
Patty Sheehan	3
Annika Sorenstam	3
Kathy Whitworth	3
Donna Caponi	2
Sandra Haynie	2
Mary Mills	2
Betsy Rawls	2
Laura Davies	2
Juli Inkster	2

U.S. OPEN

Player	Wins
Betsy Rawls	4
Mickey Wright	4
Susie Maxwell Berning	3

U.S. OPEN *(Cont.)*

Player	Wins
Hollis Stacy	3
Babe Zaharias	3
Annika Sorenstam	3
JoAnne Carner	2
Donna Caponi	2
Betsy King	2
Meg Mallon	2
Patty Sheehan	2
Louise Suggs	2
Karrie Webb	2
Juli Inkster	2

DU MAURIER

Player	Wins
Pat Bradley	3
Brandie Burton	2
JoAnne Carner	2

NABISCO/DINAH SHORE

Player	Wins
Amy Alcott	3
Betsy King	3
Annika Sorenstam	3
Juli Inkster	2
Karrie Webb	2

TITLEHOLDERS

Player	Wins
Patty Berg	7
Louise Suggs	4
Babe Zaharias	3
Dorothy Kirby	2
Marilynn Smith	2
Kathy Whitworth	2
Mickey Wright	2

WESTERN OPEN

Player	Wins
Patty Berg	7
Louise Suggs	4
Babe Zaharias	4
Mickey Wright	3
June Beebe	2
Opal Hill	2
Betty Jameson	2
Betsy Rawls	2

THE LPGA TOUR

Most Career Wins†

	Wins		Wins		Wins
Kathy Whitworth	88	JoAnne Carner	43	Beth Daniel*	33
Mickey Wright	82	Sandra Haynie	42	Pat Bradley	31
Annika Sorenstam*	69	Babe Zaharias	41	Juli Inkster*	31
Patty Berg	60	Carol Mann	38	Amy Alcott*	29
Louise Suggs	58	Patty Sheehan*	35	Jane Blalock	29
Betsy Rawls	55	Betsy King*	34	Judy Rankin	26
Nancy Lopez	48	Karrie Webb*	34	Marlene Hagge	26

*Active player.

Season Money Leaders

		Earnings ($)			Earnings ($)			Earnings ($)
1950	Babe Zaharias	14,800	1969	Carol Mann	49,152	1988	Sherri Turner	350,851
1951	Babe Zaharias	15,087	1970	Kathy Whitworth	30,235	1989	Betsy King	654,132
1952	Betsy Rawls	14,505	1971	Kathy Whitworth	41,181	1990	Beth Daniel	863,578
1953	Louise Suggs	19,816	1972	Kathy Whitworth	65,063	1991	Pat Bradley	763,118
1954	Patty Berg	16,011	1973	Kathy Whitworth	82,864	1992	Dottie Mochrie	693,335
1955	Patty Berg	16,492	1974	JoAnne Carner	87,094	1993	Betsy King	595,992
1956	Marlene Hagge	20,235	1975	Sandra Palmer	76,374	1994	Laura Davies	687,201
1957	Patty Berg	16,272	1976	Judy Rankin	150,734	1995	Annika Sorenstam	666,533
1958	Beverly Hanson	12,639	1977	Judy Rankin	122,890	1996	Karrie Webb	1,002,000
1959	Betsy Rawls	26,774	1978	Nancy Lopez	189,814	1997	Annika Sorenstam	1,236,789
1960	Louise Suggs	16,892	1979	Nancy Lopez	197,489	1998	Annika Sorenstam	1,092,748
1961	Mickey Wright	22,236	1980	Beth Daniel	231,000	1999	Karrie Webb	1,591,959
1962	Mickey Wright	21,641	1981	Beth Daniel	206,998	2000	Karrie Webb	1,876,853
1963	Mickey Wright	31,269	1982	JoAnne Carner	310,400	2001	Annika Sorenstam	2,105,868
1964	Mickey Wright	29,800	1983	JoAnne Carner	291,404	2002	Annika Sorenstam	2,863.904
1965	Kathy Whitworth	28,658	1984	Betsy King	266,771	2003	Annika Sorenstam	2,029,506
1966	Kathy Whitworth	33,517	1985	Nancy Lopez	416,472	2004	Annika Sorenstam	2,544,707
1967	Kathy Whitworth	32,937	1986	Pat Bradley	492,021	2005	Annika Sorenstam	2,588,240
1968	Kathy Whitworth	48,379	1987	Ayako Okamoto	466,034			

Career Money Leaders†

		Earnings ($)			Earnings ($)			Earnings ($)
1.	Annika Sorenstam	20,238,948	11.	Christie Kerr	6,654,958	21.	Sherri Steinhauer	5,236,343
2.	Karrie Webb	12,626,495	12.	Mi-Hyun Kim	6,533,372	22.	Grace Park	5,113,047
3.	Juli Inkster	11,149,492	13.	Lorie Kane	6,468,171	23.	Rachel Hetherington	4,950,554
4.	Se Ri Pak	8,853,194	14.	Lorena Ochoa	5,819,222	24.	Michelle Redman	4,830,069
5.	Meg Mallon	8,818,462	15.	Pat Bradley	5,750,965	25.	Catriona Matthew	4,542,457
6.	Beth Daniel	8,755,733	16.	Liselotte Neumann	5,659,857	26.	Hee-Won Han	4,469,256
7.	Rosie Jones	8,355,068	17.	Kelly Robbins	5,621,742	27.	Brandie Burton	4,280,964
8.	Laura Davies	7,689,035	18.	Patty Sheehan	5,513,409	28.	Tammie Green	4,099,696
9.	Betsy King	7,637,621	19.	Pat Hurst	5,504,314	29.	Carin Koch	3,829,730
10.	Dottie Pepper	6,827,284	20.	Nancy Lopez	5,320,877	30.	Jeong Jang	3,806,642

LPGA Player of the Year

1966	Kathy Whitworth	1980	Beth Daniel	1994	Beth Daniel
1967	Kathy Whitworth	1981	JoAnne Carner	1995	Annika Sörenstam
1968	Kathy Whitworth	1982	JoAnne Carner	1996	Laura Davies
1969	Kathy Whitworth	1983	Patty Sheehan	1997	Annika Sorenstam
1970	Sandra Haynie	1984	Betsy King	1998	Annika Sorenstam
1971	Kathy Whitworth	1985	Nancy Lopez	1999	Karrie Webb
1972	Kathy Whitworth	1986	Pat Bradley	2000	Karrie Webb
1973	Kathy Whitworth	1987	Ayako Okamoto	2001	Annika Sorenstam
1974	JoAnne Carner	1988	Nancy Lopez	2002	Annika Sorenstam
1975	Sandra Palmer	1989	Betsy King	2003	Annika Sorenstam
1976	Judy Rankin	1990	Beth Daniel	2004	Annika Sorenstam
1977	Judy Rankin	1991	Pat Bradley	2005	Annika Sorenstam
1978	Nancy Lopez	1992	Dottie Mochrie		
1979	Nancy Lopez	1993	Betsy King		

†Through 10/15/06.

Vare Trophy: Best Scoring Average*

		Avg			Avg			Avg
1953	Patty Berg	75.00	1971	Kathy Whitworth	72.88	1989	Beth Daniel	70.38
1954	Babe Zaharias	75.48	1972	Kathy Whitworth	72.38	1990	Beth Daniel	70.54
1955	Patty Berg	74.47	1973	Judy Rankin	73.08	1991	Pat Bradley	70.76
1956	Patty Berg	74.57	1974	JoAnne Carner	72.87	1992	Dottie Mochrie	70.80
1957	Louise Suggs	74.64	1975	JoAnne Carner	72.40	1993	Nancy Lopez	70.83
1958	Beverly Hanson	74.92	1976	Judy Rankin	72.25	1994	Beth Daniel	70.90
1959	Betsy Rawls	74.03	1977	Judy Rankin	72.16	1995	Annika Sorenstam	71.00
1960	Mickey Wright	73.25	1978	Nancy Lopez	71.76	1996	Annika Sorenstam	70.47
1961	Mickey Wright	73.55	1979	Nancy Lopez	71.20	1997	Karrie Webb	70.00
1962	Mickey Wright	73.67	1980	Amy Alcott	71.51	1998	Annika Sorenstam	69.99
1963	Mickey Wright	72.81	1981	JoAnne Carner	71.75	1999	Karrie Webb	69.43
1964	Mickey Wright	72.46	1982	JoAnne Carner	71.49	2000	Karrie Webb	70.05
1965	Kathy Whitworth	72.61	1983	JoAnne Carner	71.41	2001	Annika Sorenstam	69.42
1966	Kathy Whitworth	72.60	1984	Patty Sheehan	71.40	2002	Annika Sorenstam	68.70
1967	Kathy Whitworth	72.74	1985	Nancy Lopez	70.73	2003	Se Ri Pak	70.03
1968	Carol Mann	72.04	1986	Pat Bradley	71.10	2004	Grace Park	69.99
1969	Kathy Whitworth	72.38	1987	Betsy King	71.14	2005	Annika Sorenstam	69.33
1970	Kathy Whitworth	72.26	1988	Colleen Walker	71.26			

Alltime LPGA Tour Records†

Scoring

72 HOLES

259—(65-62-67-65) by Wendy Doolan to win at the Dell Urich GC, Tucson, AZ, in the 2003 Welch's/Fry's Champ. (21 under par).

261—(71-61-63-66) by Se Ri Pak to win at the Highland Meadows CC, Sylvania, OH, in the 1998 Jamie Farr Kroger Classic (23 under par).

261—(65-59-69-68) by Annika Sorenstam to win at the Moon Valley CC, Phoenix, in the 2001 Standard Register PING (27 under par).

54 HOLES

192—(63-63-66) by Annika Sorenstam to win at the Seta GC, Otsu-shi, Shiga, Japan in the 2003 Mizuno Classic (24 under par).

193—(66-61-66) by Karrie Webb to lead at the Walnut Hills CC, East Lansing, MI, in the 2000 Oldsmobile Classic (23 under par).

193—(65-59-69) by Annika Sorenstam to lead at the Moon Valley CC, Phoenix, in the 2001 Standard Register PING (23 under par)

36 HOLES

124—(65-59) by Annika Sorenstam to lead at the Moon Valley CC, Phoenix, in the 2001 Standard Register PING (20 under par).

18 HOLES

59—by Annika Sorenstam at the Moon Valley CC, Phoenix, in the second round in winning the 2001 Standard Register PING (13 under par).

9 HOLES

28—by Mary Beth Zimmerman at Rail GC, 1984 Rail Charity Golf Classic, Springfield, IL (par 36). Zimmerman shot 64.

28—by Pat Bradley at Green Gables CC, Denver, 1984 Columbia Savings Classic (par 35). Bradley shot 65.

28—by Muffin Spencer-Devlin at Knollwood CC, Elmsford, NY, in winning the 1985 MasterCard International Pro-Am (par 35). Spencer-Devlin shot 64.

Scoring (Cont.)

9 HOLES (Cont.)

28—by Peggy Kirsch at Squaw Creek CC, Vienna, OH, in the 1991 Phar-Mor (par 35).

28—by Renee Heiken at Highland Meadows CC, Sylvania, OH, in the 1996 Jamie Farr Kroger Classic (par 34).

28—by Annika Sorenstam at the Moon Valley CC, Phoenix, in the 2001 Standard Register PING (par 36).

28—by Danielle Ammaccapane at Highland Meadows GC, Sylvania, OH, in the 2002 Jamie Farr Kroger Classic (par 34)

28—by Young Kim at Dell Urich GC, Tucson, AZ, in the 2003 Welch's/Fry's Championship (par 35)

28—by Chris Johnson at Highland Meadows GC, Sylvania, OH, in the 2003 Jamie Farr Kroger Classic (par 34)

MOST CONSECUTIVE ROUNDS UNDER 70

11—Annika Sorenstam, in 2002.

MOST BIRDIES IN A ROW

9—Beth Daniel at Onion Creek Club in Austin, in the second round of the 1999 Philips Invitational. Daniel shot 62 (8 under par).

Wins

MOST CONSECUTIVE WINS IN SCHEDULED EVENTS

4—Mickey Wright, in 1962.

4—Mickey Wright, in 1963.

4—Kathy Whitworth, in 1969.

4—Annika Sorenstam in 2001.

MOST CONSECUTIVE WINS IN ENTERED TOURNAMENTS

5—Nancy Lopez, in 1978.

MOST WINS IN A CALENDAR YEAR

13—Mickey Wright, in 1963.

WIDEST WINNING MARGIN, STROKES

14—Louise Suggs, 1949 U.S. Women's Open.

14—Cindy Mackey, 1986 MasterCard Int'l Pro-Am.

†Through 10/1/06. *Must play 70 rounds in order to qualify; Annika Sorenstam compiled an average of 69.02 in 60 rounds in 2003.

U.S. Senior Open

Year	Winner	Score	Runner-Up	Site
1980	Roberto DeVicenzo	285	William C. Campbell	Winged Foot GC, Mamaroneck, NY
1981	Arnold Palmer* (70)	289	Bob Stone (74)	Oakland Hills CC, Birmingham, MI
			Billy Casper (77)	
1982	Miller Barber	282	Gene Littler, Dan Sikes, Jr.	Portland GC, Portland, OR
1983	Billy Casper* (75) (3)	288	Rod Funseth (75) (4)	Hazeltine GC, Chaska, MN
1984	Miller Barber	286	Arnold Palmer	Oak Hill CC, Rochester, NY
1985	Miller Barber	285	Roberto DeVicenzo	Edgewood Tahoe GC, Stateline, NV
1986	Dale Douglass	279	Gary Player	Scioto CC, Columbus, OH
1987	Gary Player	270	Doug Sanders	Brooklawn CC, Fairfield, CT
1988	Gary Player* (68)	288	Bob Charles (70)	Medinah CC, Medinah, IL
1989	Orville Moody	279	Frank Beard	Laurel Valley GC, Ligonier, PA
1990	Lee Trevino	275	Jack Nicklaus	Ridgewood CC, Paramus, NJ
1991	Jack Nicklaus* (65)	282	Chi Chi Rodriguez (69)	Oakland Hills CC, Birmingham, MI
1992	Larry Laoretti	275	Jim Colbert	Saucon Valley CC, Bethlehem, PA
1993	Jack Nicklaus	278	Tom Weiskopf	Cherry Hills CC, Englewood, CO
1994	Simon Hobday	274	Jim Albus	Pinehurst Resort & CC, Pinehurst, NC
1995	Tom Weiskopf	275	Jack Nicklaus	Congressional CC, Bethesda, MD
1996	Dave Stockton	277	Hale Irwin	Canterbury GC, Beachwood, OH
1997	Graham Marsh	280	Hale Irwin	Olympia Fields CC, Olympia Fields, IL
1998	Hale Irwin	285	Vicente Fernandez	Riviera CC, Pacific Palisades, CA
1999	Dave Eichelberger	281	Ed Dougherty	Des Moines G & CC, Des Moines, IA
2000	Hale Irwin	267	Bruce Fleisher	Saucon Valley CC, Bethlehem, PA
2001	Bruce Fleisher	280	Isao Aoki, Gil Morgan	Salem CC, Peabody, MA
2002	Don Pooley* (19) (5)	274	Tom Watson (18)	Caves Valley GC, Owings Mill, MD
2003	Bruce Lietzke	277	Tom Watson	Inverness GC, Toledo, OH
2004	Peter Jacobsen	272	Hale Irwin	Bellerive CC, St. Louis, MO
2005	Allen Doyle	274	D.A. Weibring	NCR GC, Kettering, OH
			Loren Roberts	
2006	Allen Doyle	272	Tom Watson	Prairie Dunes CC, Hutchinson, KS

*Winner in playoff. Playoff scores are in parentheses. The 1983 playoff went to one hole of sudden death after an 18-hole playoff.

CHAMPIONS TOUR
Season Money Leaders

		Earnings ($)			Earnings ($)			Earnings ($)
1980	Don January	44,100	1989	Bob Charles	725,887	1998	Hale Irwin	2,861,945
1981	Miller Barber	83,136	1990	Lee Trevino	1,190,518	1999	Bruce Fleisher	2,515,705
1982	Miller Barber	106,890	1991	Mike Hill	1,065,657	2000	Larry Nelson	2,708,005
1983	Don January	237,571	1992	Lee Trevino	1,027,002	2001	Allen Doyle	2,553,582
1984	Don January	328,597	1993	Dave Stockton	1,175,944	2002	Hale Irwin	3,028,304
1985	Peter Thomson	386,724	1994	Dave Stockton	1,402,519	2003	Tom Watson	1,853,108
1986	Bruce Crampton	454,299	1995	Jim Colbert	1,444,386	2004	Craig Stadler	2,306,066
1987	Chi Chi Rodriguez	509,145	1996	Jim Colbert	1,627,890	2005	Dana Quigley	2,170,258
1988	Bob Charles	533,929	1997	Hale Irwin	2,449,420			

Career Money Leaders†

		Earnings ($)			Earnings ($)			Earnings ($)
1.	Hale Irwin	23,314,065	11.	Tom Kite	9,860,746	21.	Mike Hill	8,366,615
2.	Gil Morgan	17,151,530	12.	Lee Trevino	9,823,329	22.	John Jacobs	8,040,829
3.	Bruce Fleischer	13,260,442	13.	Isao Aoki	9,237,068	23.	Bob Gilder	7,991,835
4.	Dana Quigley	13,115,657	14.	Raymond Floyd	9,235,659	24.	Vicente Fernandez	7,946,675
5.	Larry Nelson	12,890,296	15.	Jay Sigel	9,074,994	25.	Doug Tewell	7,701,615
6.	Allen Doyle	12,093,728	16.	Bob Charles	9,009,316	26.	Tom Wargo	7,540,924
7.	Jim Colbert	11,573,540	17.	Jim Dent	8,887,055	27.	John Bland	7,359,179
8.	Jim Thorpe	10,962,600	18.	Graham Marsh	8,879,453	28.	J.C. Snead	7,329,244
9.	Dave Stockton	10,833,191	19.	Bruce Summerhays	8,590,049	29.	Jose Maria Canizares	7,156,132
10.	Tom Jenkins	10,551,127	20.	Tom Watson	8,581,118	30.	Bob Murphy	7,155,718

Most Career Wins†

	Wins		Wins
Hale Irwin	44	Jim Colbert	20
Lee Trevino	29	Bruce Crampton	20
Miller Barber	24	George Archer	19
Gil Morgan	24	Gary Player	19
Bob Charles	23	Larry Nelson	19
Don January	22	Bruce Fleisher	18
Chi Chi Rodriguez	22	Mike Hill	18

†Through 10/15/06

MAJOR MEN'S AMATEUR CHAMPIONSHIPS

U.S. Amateur

Year	Winner	Score	Runner-Up	Site
1895	Charles B. Macdonald	12 & 11	Charles E. Sands	Newport GC, Newport, RI
1896	H.J. Whigham	8 & 7	J.G Thorp	Shinnecock Hills GC, Southampton, NY
1897	H.J. Whigham	8 & 6	W. Rossiter Betts	Chicago GC, Wheaton, IL
1898	Findlay S. Douglas	5 & 3	Walter B. Smith	Morris County GC, Morristown, NJ
1899	H.M. Harriman	3 & 2	Findlay S. Douglas	Onwentsia Club, Lake Forest, IL
1900	Walter Travis	2 up	Findlay S. Douglas	Garden City GC, Garden City, NY
1901	Walter Travis	5 & 4	Walter E. Egan	CC of Atlantic City, NJ
1902	Louis N. James	4 & 2	Eben M. Byers	Glen View Club, Golf, IL
1903	Walter Travis	5 & 4	Eben M. Byers	Nassau CC, Glen Cove, NY
1904	H. Chandler Egan	8 & 6	Fred Herreshoff	Baltusrol GC, Springfield, NJ
1905	H. Chandler Egan	6 & 5	D.E. Sawyer	Chicago GC, Wheaton, IL
1906	Eben M. Byers	2 up	George S. Lyon	Englewood GC, Englewood, NJ
1907	Jerry Travers	6 & 5	Archibald Graham	Euclid Club, Cleveland, OH
1908	Jerry Travers	8 & 7	Max H. Behr	Garden City GC, Garden City, NY
1909	Robert A. Gardner	4 & 3	H. Chandler Egan	Chicago GC, Wheaton, IL
1910	William C. Fownes Jr.	4 & 3	Warren K. Wood	The Country Club, Brookline, MA
1911	Harold Hilton	1 up	Fred Herreshoff	The Apawamis Club, Rye, NY
1912	Jerry Travers	7 & 6	Charles Evans Jr.	Chicago GC, Wheaton, IL
1913	Jerry Travers	5 & 4	John G. Anderson	Garden City GC, Garden City, NY
1914	Francis Ouimet	6 & 5	Jerry Travers	Ekwanok CC, Manchester, VT
1915	Robert A. Gardner	5 & 4	John G. Anderson	CC of Detroit, Grosse Pt. Farms, MI
1916	Chick Evans	4 & 3	Robert A. Gardner	Merion Cricket Club, Haverford, PA
1917–18	No tournament			
1919	S. Davidson Herron	5 & 4	Bobby Jones	Oakmont CC, Oakmont, PA
1920	Chick Evans	7 & 6	Francis Ouimet	Engineers' CC, Roslyn, NY
1921	Jesse P. Guilford	7 & 6	Robert A. Gardner	St. Louis CC, Clayton, MO
1922	Jess W. Sweetser	3 & 2	Chick Evans	The Country Club, Brookline, MA
1923	Max R. Marston	1 up	Jess W. Sweetser	Flossmoor CC, Flossmoor, IL
1924	Bobby Jones	9 & 8	George Von Elm	Merion Cricket Club, Ardmore, PA
1925	Bobby Jones	8 & 7	Watts Gunn	Oakmont CC, Oakmont, PA
1926	George Von Elm	2 & 1	Bobby Jones	Baltusrol GC, Springfield, NJ
1927	Bobby Jones	8 & 7	Chick Evans	Minikahda Club, Minneapolis
1928	Bobby Jones	10 & 9	T. Phillip Perkins	Brae Burn CC, West Newton, MA
1929	Harrison R. Johnston	4 & 3	Dr. O.F. Willing	Del Monte G & CC, Pebble Beach, CA
1930	Bobby Jones	8 & 7	Eugene V. Homans	Merion Cricket Club, Ardmore, PA
1931	Francis Ouimet	6 & 5	Jack Westland	Beverly CC, Chicago, IL
1932	C. Ross Somerville	2 & 1	John Goodman	Baltimore CC, Timonium, MD
1933	George T. Dunlap Jr.	6 & 5	Max R. Marston	Kenwood CC, Cincinnati, OH
1934	Lawson Little	8 & 7	David Goldman	The Country Club, Brookline, MA
1935	Lawson Little	4 & 2	Walter Emery	The Country Club, Cleveland, OH
1936	John W. Fischer	1 up	Jack McLean	Garden City GC, Garden City, NY
1937	John Goodman	2 up	Raymond E. Billows	Alderwood CC, Portland, OR
1938	William P. Turnesa	8 & 7	B. Patrick Abbott	Oakmont CC, Oakmont, PA
1939	Marvin H. Ward	7 & 5	Raymond E. Billows	North Shore CC, Glenview, IL
1940	Richard D. Chapman	11 & 9	W. McCullough Jr.	Winged Foot GC, Mamaroneck, NY
1941	Marvin H. Ward	4 & 3	B. Patrick Abbott	Omaha Field Club, Omaha, NE
1942–45	No tournament			
1946	Ted Bishop	1 up	Smiley L. Quick	Baltusrol GC, Springfield, NJ
1947	Skee Riegel	2 & 1	John W. Dawson	Del Monte G & CC, Pebble Beach, CA
1948	William P. Turnesa	2 & 1	Raymond E. Billows	Memphis CC, Memphis, TN
1949	Charles R. Coe	11 & 10	Rufus King	Oak Hill CC, Rochester, NY
1950	Sam Urzetta	1 up	Frank Stranahan	Minneapolis CC, Minneapolis, MN
1951	Billy Maxwell	4 & 3	Joseph F. Gagliardi	Saucon Valley CC, Bethlehem, PA
1952	Jack Westland	3 & 2	Al Mengert	Seattle GC, Seattle, WA
1953	Gene Littler	1 up	Dale Morey	Oklahoma City G & CC, Oklahoma City
1954	Arnold Palmer	1 up	Robert Sweeny	CC of Detroit, Grosse Pt. Farms, MI
1955	E. Harvie Ward Jr.	9 & 8	William Hyndman III	CC of Virginia, Richmond, VA
1956	E. Harvie Ward Jr.	5 & 4	Charles Kocsis	Knollwood Club, Lake Forest, IL
1957	Hillman Robbins Jr.	5 & 4	Dr. Frank M. Taylor	The Country Club, Brookline, MA
1958	Charles R. Coe	5 & 4	Tommy Aaron	Olympic Club, San Francisco, CA
1959	Jack Nicklaus	1 up	Charles R. Coe	Broadmoor CC, Colorado Springs, CO
1960	Deane Beman	6 & 4	Robert W. Gardner	St. Louis CC, Clayton, MO
1961	Jack Nicklaus	8 & 6	H. Dudley Wysong	Pebble Beach GL, Pebble Beach, CA
1962	Labron E. Harris Jr.	1 up	Downing Gray	Pinehurst CC, Pinehurst, NC

U.S. Amateur (Cont.)

Year	Winner	Score	Runner-Up	Site
1963	Deane Beman	2 & 1	Richard H. Sikes	Wakonda Club, Des Moines, IA
1964	William C. Campbell	1 up	Edgar M. Tutwiler	Canterbury GC, Cleveland, OH
1965	Robert J. Murphy Jr.	291	Robert B. Dickson	Southern Hills, CC, Tulsa
1966	Gary Cowan	285–75	Deane Beman	Merion GC, Ardmore, PA
1967	Robert B. Dickson	285	Marvin Giles III	Broadmoor GC, Colorado Springs
1968	Bruce Fleisher	284	Marvin Giles III	Scioto CC, Columbus, OH
1969	Steven N. Melnyk	286	Marvin Giles III	Oakmont CC, Oakmont, PA
1970	Lanny Wadkins	279	Tom Kite	Waverley CC, Portland, OR
1971	Gary Cowan	280	Eddie Pearce	Wilmington CC, Wilmington DE
1972	Marvin Giles III	285	two tied	Charlotte CC, Charlotte, NC
1973	Craig Stadler	6 & 5	David Strawn	Inverness Club, Toledo
1974	Jerry Pate	2 & 1	John P. Grace	Ridgewood CC, Ridgewood, NJ
1975	Fred Ridley	2 up	Keith Fergus	CC of Virginia, Richmond
1976	Bill Sander	8 & 6	C. Parker Moore Jr.	Bel Air CC, Los Angeles
1977	John Fought	9 & 8	Doug Fischesser	Aronimink GC, Newton Square, PA
1978	John Cook	5 & 4	Scott Hoch	Plainfield CC, Plainfield, NJ
1979	Mark O'Meara	8 & 7	John Cook	Canterbury GC, Cleveland
1980	Hal Sutton	9 & 8	Bob Lewis	CC of North Carolina, Pinehurst, NC
1981	Nathaniel Crosby	1 up	Brian Lindley	Olympic Club, San Francisco
1982	Jay Sigel	8 & 7	David Tolley	The Country Club, Brookline, MA
1983	Jay Sigel	8 & 7	Chris Perry	North Shore CC, Glenview, IL
1984	Scott Verplank	4 & 3	Sam Randolph	Oak Tree GC, Edmond, OK
1985	Sam Randolph	1 up	Peter Persons	Montclair GC, West Orange, NJ
1986	Buddy Alexander	5 & 3	Chris Kite	Shoal Creek, Shoal Creek, AL
1987	Bill Mayfair	4 & 3	Eric Rebmann	Jupiter Hills Club, Jupiter, FL
1988	Eric Meeks	7 & 6	Danny Yates	Va. Hot Springs G & CC, VA
1989	Chris Patton	3 & 1	Danny Green	Merion GC, Ardmore, PA
1990	Phil Mickelson	5 & 4	Manny Zerman	Cherry Hills CC, Englewood, CO
1991	Mitch Voges	7 & 6	Manny Zerman	The Honors Course, Ooltewah, TN
1992	Justin Leonard	8 & 7	Tom Scherrer	Muirfield Village GC, Dublin, OH
1993	John Harris	5 & 3	Danny Ellis	Champions GC, Houston
1994	Tiger Woods	2 up	Trip Kuehne	TPC-Sawgrass, Ponte Vedre, FL
1995	Tiger Woods	2 up	Buddy Marucci	Newport Country Club, Newport, RI
1996	Tiger Woods	38 holes	Steve Scott	Pumpkin Ridge GC, Cornelius, OR
1997	Matthew Kuchar	2 & 1	Joel Kribel	Cog Hill G & CC, Lemont, IL
1998	Hank Kuehne	2 & 1	Tom McKnight	Oak Hill CC, Rochester, NY
1999	David Gossett	9 & 8	Sung Yoon Kim	Pebble Beach GL, Pebble Beach, CA
2000	Jeff Quinney	39 holes	James Driscoll	Baltusrol GC, Upper Springfield, NJ
2001	Bubba Dickerson	1 up	Robert Hamilton	East Lake CC, Atlanta
2002	Ricky Barnes	2 & 1	Hunter Mahan	Oakland Hills CC, Bloomfield Hills, MI
2003	Nick Flanagan	37 holes	Frank Abbott	East Lake CC, Atlanta
2004	Ryan Moore	2 & 1	Luke List	Winged Foot GC, Mamaroneck, NY
2005	Edoardo Molinari	4 & 3	Dillon Dougherty	Merion GC, Ardmore, PA
2006	Richie Ramsay	3 & 2	John Kelly	Hazeltine National GC, Chaska, MN

Note: All stroke play from 1965 to 1972.

U.S. Junior Amateur

1948...Dean Lind	1963...Gregg McHatton	1978...Don Hurter	1993...Tiger Woods
1949...Gay Brewer	1964...Johnny Miller	1979...Jack Larkin	1994...Terry Noe
1950...Mason Rudolph	1965...James Masserio	1980...Eric Johnson	1995...D. Scott Hailes
1951...Tommy Jacobs	1966...Gary Sanders	1981...Scott Erickson	1996...Shane McMenamy
1952...Don Bisplinghoff	1967...John Crooks	1982...Rich Marik	1997...Jason Allred
1953...Rex Baxter	1968...Eddie Pearce	1983...Tim Straub	1998...James Oh
1954...Foster Bradley	1969...Aly Trompas	1984...Doug Martin	1999...Hunter Mahan
1955...William Dunn	1970...Gary Koch	1985...Charles Rymer	2000...Matthew Rosenfeld
1956...Harlan Stevenson	1971...Mike Brannan	1986...Brian Montgomery	2001...Henry Liaw
1957...Larry Beck	1972...Bob Byman	1987...Brett Quigley	2002...Charlie Beljan
1958...Buddy Baker	1973...Jack Renner	1988...Jason Widener	2003...Brian Harman
1959...Larry Lee	1974...David Nevatt	1989...David Duval	2004...Sihwan Kim
1960...Bill Tindall	1975...Brett Mullin	1990...Mathew Todd	2005...Kevin Tway
1961...Charles McDowell	1976...Madden Hatcher III	1991...Tiger Woods	2006...Phillip Francis
1962...Jim Wiechers	1977...Willie Wood Jr.	1992...Tiger Woods	

Mid-Amateur Championship

1981...Jim Holtgrieve	1988...David Eger	1995...Jerry Courville Jr.	2002...George Zahringer
1982...William Hoffer	1989...James Taylor	1996...John Miller	2003...Nathan Smith
1983...Jay Sigel	1990...Jim Stuart	1997...Ken Bakst	2004...Austin Eaton III
1984...Mike Podolak	1991...Jim Stuart	1998...John Miller	2005...Kevin Marsh
1985...Jay Sigel	1992...Danny Yates	1999...Danny Green	2006...Dave Womack
1986...Bill Loeffler	1993...Jeff Thomas	2000...Greg Puga	
1987...Jay Sigel	1994...Tim Jackson	2001...Tim Jackson	

WHATABOUT 1885 HOYLAKE 1886 ST.ANDREWS (handwritten annotation)

British Amateur

1887 ....H. G. Hutchinson	1928 ............T.P. Perkins	1970 ....M. Bonallack
1888 ....John Ball	1929 ............C.J.H. Tolley	1971 ....Steve Melnyk
1889 ............J.E. Laidlay	1930 ....Robert T. Jones Jr	1972 ....Trevor Homer
1890 ....John Ball	1931 ....E. Martin Smith	1973 ....R. Siderowf
1891 ............J.E. Laidlay	1932 ....J. DeForest	1974 ....Trevor Homer
1892 ....John Ball	1933 ....M. Scott	1975 ....M. Giles
1893 ....Peter Anderson	1934 ....W. Lawson Little	1976 ....R. Siderowf
1894 ....John Ball	1935 ....W. Lawson Little	1977 ....P. McEvoy
1895 ............L.M.B. Melville	1936 ....H. Thomson	1978 ....P. McEvoy
1896 ............F.G. Tait	1937 ....R. Sweeney Jr	1979 ....J. Sigel
1897 ............A.J.T. Allan	1938 ............C.R. Yates	1980 ....D. Evans
1898 ............F.G. Tait	1939 ............A.T. Kyle	1981 ....P. Ploujoux
1899 ....John Ball	1940–45 ....not held	1982 ....M. Thompson
1900 ............H.H. Hilton	1946 ....J. Bruen	1983 ....A. Parkin
1901 ............H.H. Hilton	1947 ....Willie D. Turnesa	1984 ............J.M. Olazabal
1902 ....C. Hutchings	1948 ....Frank R. Stranahan	1985 ....G. McGimpsey
1903 ....R. Maxwell	1949 ............S.M. McReady	1986 ....D. Curry
1904 ............W.J. Travis	1950 ....Frank R. Stranahan	1987 ....P. Mayo
1905 ............A.G. Barry	1951 ....Richard D. Chapman	1988 ....C. Hardin
1906 ....James Robb	1952 ............E.H. Ward	1989 ....S. Dodd
1907 ....John Ball	1953 ............J.B. Carr	1990 ....R. Muntz
1908 ............E.A. Lassen	1954 ............D.W. Bachli	1991 ....G. Wolstenholme
1909 ....R. Maxwell	1955 ............J.W. Conrad	1992 ....S. Dundas
1910 ....John Ball	1956 ............J.C. Beharrell	1993 ....I. Pyman
1911 ............H.H. Hilton	1957 ....R. Reid Jack	1994 ....L. James
1912 ....John Ball	1958 ............J.B. Carr	1995 ....G. Sherry
1913 ............H.H. Hilton	1959 ....Deane Beman	1996 ....W. Bladon
1914 ............J.L.C. Jenkins	1960 ............J.B. Carr	1997 ....C. Watson
1915–19 ....not held	1961 ....M. Bonallack	1998 ....Sergio Garcia
1920 ............C.J.H. Tolley	1962 ....R. Davies	1999 ....Graeme Storm
1921 ............W.I. Hunter	1963 ....M. Lunt	2000 ....Mikko Ilonen
1922 ............E.W.E. Holderness	1964 ....C. Clark	2001 ....Michael Hoey
1923 ............R.H. Wethered	1965 ....M. Bonallack	2002 ....Alejandro Larrazabal
1924 ............E.W.E. Holderness	1966 ............C.R. Cole	2003 ....Gary Wolstenholme
1925 ....R. Harris	1967 ....R. Dickson	2004 ....Stuart Wilson
1926 ....Jess Sweetser	1968 ....M. Bonallack	2005 ....Brian McElhinney
1927 ....Dr. W. Tweddell	1969 ....M. Bonallack	2006 ....Julien Guerrier

Amateur Public Links

1922 ....Edmund R. Held	1938 ....Al Leach	1959 ....William A. Wright
1923 ....Richard J. Walsh	1939 ....Andrew Szwedko	1960 ....Verne Callison
1924 ....Joseph Coble	1940 ....Robert C. Clark	1961 ....Richard H. Sikes
1925 ....Raymond J. McAuliffe	1941 ....William M. Welch Jr	1962 ....Richard H. Sikes
	1942–45 ....not held	1963 ....Robert Lunn
1926 ....Lester Bolstad	1946 ....Smiley L. Quick	1964 ....William McDonald
1927 ....Carl F. Kauffmann	1947 ....Wilfred Crossley	1965 ....Arne Dokka
1928 ....Carl F. Kauffmann	1948 ....Michael R. Ferentz	1966 ....Lamont Kaser
1929 ....Carl F. Kauffmann	1949 ....Kenneth J. Towns	1967 ....Verne Callison
1930 ....Robert E. Wingate	1950 ....Stanley Bielat	1968 ....Gene Towry
1931 ....Charles Ferrera	1951 ....Dave Stanley	1969 ....John M. Jackson Jr
1932 ............R.L. Miller	1952 ....Omer L. Bogan	1970 ....Robert Risch
1933 ....Charles Ferrera	1953 ....Ted Richards Jr	1971 ....Fred Haney
1934 ....David A. Mitchell	1954 ....Gene Andrews	1972 ....Bob Allard
1935 ....Frank Strafaci	1955 ....Sam D. Kocsis	1973 ....Stan Stopa
1936 ....B. Patrick Abbott	1956 ....James H. Buxbaum	1974 ....Charles Barenaba
1937 ....Bruce N. McCormick	1957 ....Don Essig III	1975 ....Randy Barenaba
	1958 ....Daniel D. Sikes Jr	1976 ....Eddie Mudd

Amateur Public Links (Cont.)

1977 ....Jerry Vidovic	1988 ....Ralph Howe III	1999 ....Hunter Haas
1978 ....Dean Prince	1989 ....Tim Hobby	2000 ............D.J. Trahan
1979 ....Dennis Walsh	1990 ....Michael Combs	2001 ....Chez Reavie
1980 ....Jodie Mudd	1991 ....David Berganio Jr	2002 ....Ryan Moore
1981 ....Jodie Mudd	1992 ....Warren Schulte	2003 ....Brandt Snedeker
1982 ....Billy Tuten	1993 ....David Berganio Jr	2004 ....Ryan Moore
1983 ....Billy Tuten	1994 ....Guy Yamamoto	2005 ....Clay Ogden
1984 ....Bill Malley	1995 ....Chris Wollmann	2006 ....Casey Watabu
1985 ....Jim Sorenson	1996 ....Tim Hogarth	
1986 ....Bill Mayfair	1997 ....Tim Clark	
1987 ....Kevin Johnson	1998 ....Trevor Immelman	

U.S. Senior Men's Amateur

1955 ....J. Wood Platt	1973 ....William Hyndman III	1991 ....Bill Bosshard
1956 ....Frederick J. Wright	1974 ....Dale Morey	1992 ....Clarence Moore
1957 ....J. Clark Espie	1975 ....William F. Colm	1993 ....Joe Ungvary
1958 ....Thomas C. Robbins	1976 ....Lewis W. Oehmig	1994 ....O. Gordon Brewer
1959 ....J. Clark Espie	1977 ....Dale Morey	1995 ....James Stahl Jr.
1960 ....Michael Cestone	1978 ............K.K. Compton	1996 ....O. Gordon Brewer
1961 ....Dexter H. Daniels	1979 ....William C. Campbell	1997 ....Cliff Cunningham
1962 ....Merrill L. Carlsmith	1980 ....William C. Campbell	1998 ....Bill Shean Jr.
1963 ....Merrill L. Carlsmith	1981 ....Ed Updegraff	1999 ....Bill Ploeger
1964 ....William D. Higgins	1982 ....Alton Duhon	2000 ....Bill Shean Jr.
1965 ....Robert B. Kiersky	1983 ....William Hyndman III	2001 ....Kemp Richardson
1966 ....Dexter H. Daniels	1984 ....Bob Rawlins	2002 ....Greg Reynolds
1967 ....Ray Palmer	1985 ....Lewis W. Oehmig	2003 ....Kemp Richardson
1968 ....Curtis Person Sr.	1986 ....Bo Williams	2004 ....Mark Bemowski
1969 ....Curtis Person Sr.	1987 ....John Richardson	2005 ....Mike Rice
1970 ....Gene Andrews	1988 ....Clarence Moore	2006 ....Mike Bell
1971 ....Tom Draper	1989 ....Bo Williams	
1972 ....Lewis W. Oehmig	1990 ....Jackie Cummings	

Note: Event is for amateur golfers at least 55 years of age.

MAJOR WOMEN'S AMATEUR CHAMPIONSHIPS

U.S. Women's Amateur

Year	Winner	Score	Runner-Up	Site
1895 ....Mrs. Charles S. Brown		132	Nellie Sargent	Meadow Brook Club, Hempstead, NY
1896 ....Beatrix Hoyt		2 & 1	Mrs. Arthur Turnure	Morris Couty GC, Morristown, NJ
1897 ....Beatrix Hoyt		5 & 4	Nellie Sargent	Essex County Club, Manchester, MA
1898 ....Beatrix Hoyt		5 &3	Maude Wetmore	Ardsley Club, Ardsley-on-Hudson, NY
1899 ....Ruth Underhill		2 & 1	Margaret Fox	Philadelphia CC, Philadelphia, PA
1900 ....Frances C. Griscom		6 & 5	Margaret Curtis	Shinnecock Hills GC, Shinnecock Hills, NY
1901 ....Genevieve Hecker		5 & 3	Lucy Herron	Baltusrol GC, Springfield, NJ
1902 ....Genevieve Hecker		4 & 3	Louisa A. Wells	The Country Club, Brookline, MA
1903 ....Bessie Anthony		7 & 6	J. Anna Carpenter	Chicago GC, Wheaton, IL
1904 ....Georgianna M. Bishop		5 & 3	Mrs. E.F. Sanford	Merion Cricket Club, Haverford, PA
1905 ....Pauline Mackay		1 up	Margaret Curtis	Morris County CC, Convent, NJ
1906 ....Harriot S. Curtis		2 & 1	Mary B. Adams	Brae Burn CC, West Newton, MA
1907 ....Margaret Curtis		7 & 6	Harriot S. Curtis	Midlothian CC, Blue Island, IL
1908 ....Katherine C. Harley		6 & 5	Mrs. T.H. Polhemus	Chevy Chase Club, Chevy Chase, MD
1909 ....Dorothy I. Campbell		3 & 2	Nonna Barlow	Merion Cricket Club, Haverford, PA
1910 ....Dorothy I. Campbell		2 & 1	Mrs. G.M. Martin	Homewood CC, Flossmoor, IL
1911 ....Margaret Curtis		5 & 3	Lillian B. Hyde	Baltusrol GC, Springfield, NJ
1912 ....Margaret Curtis		3 & 2	Nonna Barlow	Essex County Club, Manchester, MA
1913 ....Gladys Ravenscroft		2 up	Marion Hollins	Wilmington CC, Wilmington, DE
1914 ....Katherine Harley		1 up	Elaine V. Rosenthal	Nassau CC, Glen Cove, NY
1915 ....Florence Vanderbeck		3 & 2	Margaret Gavin	Onwentsia Club, Lake Forest, IL
1916 ....Alexa Stirling		2 & 1	Mildred Caverly	Belmont Springs CC, Waverley, MA
1917–18 ...No tournament				
1919 ....Alexa Stirling		6 & 5	Margaret Gavin	Shawnee CC, Shawnee-on-Delaware, PA
1920 ....Alexa Stirling		5 & 4	Dorothy Campbell	Mayfield CC, Cleveland
1921 ....Marion Hollins		5 & 4	Alexa Stirling	Hollywood GC, Deal, NJ
1922 ....Glenna Collett		5 & 4	Margaret Gavin	Greenbriar GC, White Sulphur Springs, WV
1923 ....Edith Cummings		3 & 2	Alexa Stirling	Westchester-Biltmore CC, Rye, NY
1924 ....Dorothy Campbell		7 & 6	Mary K. Browne	Rhode Island CC, Nyatt, RI

U.S. Women's Amateur *(Cont.)*

Year	Winner	Score	Runner-Up	Site
1925	Glenna Collett	9 & 8	Alexa Stirling	St. Louis CC, Clayton, MO
1926	Helen Stetson	3 & 1	Elizabeth Goss	Merion Cricket Club, Ardmore, PA
1927	Miiriam Burns Horn	5 & 4	Maureen Orcutt	Cherry Valley Club, Garden City, NY
1928	Glenna Collett	13 & 12	Virginia Van Wie	Va. Hot Springs G & TC, Hot Springs, VA
1929	Glenna Collett	4 & 3	Leona Pressler	Oakland Hills CC, Birmingham, MI
1930	Glenna Collett	6 & 5	Virginia Van Wie	Los Angeles CC, Beverly Hills, CA
1931	Helen Hicks	2 & 1	Glenna Collet Vare	CC of Buffalo, Williamsville, NY
1932	Virginia Van Wie	10 & 8	Glenna Collet Vare	Salem CC, Peabody, MA
1933	Virginia Van Wie	4 & 3	Helen Hicks	Exmoor CC, Highland Park, IL
1934	Virginia Van Wie	2 & 1	Dorothy Traung	Whitemarsh Valley CC, Chestnut Hill, PA
1935	Glenna Collett Vare	3 & 2	Patty Berg	Interlachen CC, Hopkins, MN
1936	Pamela Barton	4 & 3	Maureen Orcutt	Canoe Brook CC, Summit, NJ
1937	Estelle Lawson	7 & 6	Patty Berg	Memphis CC, Memphis, TN
1938	Patty Berg	6 & 5	Estelle Lawson	Westmoreland CC, Wilmette, IL
1939	Betty Jameson	3 & 2	Dorothy Kirby	Wee Burn Club, Darien, CT
1940	Betty Jameson	6 & 5	Jane S. Cothran	Del Monte G & CC, Pebble Beach, CA
1941	Elizabeth Hicks	5 & 3	Helen Sigel	The Country Club, Brookline, MA
1942–45	No tournament			
1946	Babe Zaharias	11 & 9	Clara Sherman	Southern Hills CC, Tulsa
1947	Louise Suggs	2 up	Dorothy Kirby	Franklin Hills CC, Franklin, MI
1948	Grace S. Lenczyk	4 & 3	Helen Sigel	Del Monte G & CC, Pebble Beach, CA
1949	Dorothy Porter	3 & 2	Dorothy Kielty	Merion GC, Ardmore, PA
1950	Beverly Hanson	6 & 4	Mae Murray	Atlanta AC, Atlanta
1951	Dorothy Kirby	2 & 1	Claire Doran	Town & CC, St. Paul
1952	Jacqueline Pung	2 & 1	Shirley McFedters	Waverley CC, Portland, OR
1953	Mary Lena Faulk	3 & 2	Polly Riley	Rhode Island CC, West Barrington, RI
1954	Barbara Romack	4 & 2	Mickey Wright	Allegheny CC, Sewickley, PA
1955	Patricia A. Lesser	7 & 6	Jane Nelson	Myers Park CC, Charlotte
1956	Marlene Stewart	2 & 1	JoAnne Gunderson	Meridian Hills CC, Indianapolis
1957	JoAnne Gunderson	8 & 6	Ann Casey Johnstone	Del Paso CC, SacramentoA
1958	Anne Quast	3 & 2	Barbara Romack	Wee Burn CC, Darien, CT
1959	Barbara McIntire	4 & 3	Joanne Goodwin	Congressional CC, Washington, D.C.
1960	JoAnne Gunderson	6 & 5	Jean Ashley	Tulsa CC, Tulsa
1961	Anne Quast Decker	14 & 13	Phyllis Preuss	Tacoma G & CC, Tacoma, WA
1962	JoAnne Gunderson	9 & 8	Anne Baker	CC of Rochester, Rochester, NY
1963	Anne Quast Decker	2 & 1	Peggy Conley	Taconic GC, Williamstown, MA
1964	Barbara McIntire	3 & 2	JoAnne Gunderson	Prairie Dunes CC, Hutchinson, KS
1965	Jean Ashley	5 & 4	Anne Quast Decker	Lakewood CC, Denver
1966	JoAnne Gunderson	1 up	Marlene Stewart Streit	Sewickley Heights GC, Sewickley, PA
1967	Mary Lou Dill	5 & 4	Jean Ashley	Annandale GC, Pasadena
1968	JoAnne Gunderson Carner	5 & 4	Anne Quast Decker	Birmingham CC, Birmingham, MI
1969	Catherine Lacoste	3 & 2	Shelley Hamling	Las Colinas CC, Irving, TX
1970	Martha Wilkinson	3 & 2	Cynthia Hall	Wee Burn CC, Darien, CT
1971	Laura Baugh	1 up	Beth Barry	Atlanta CC, Atlanta
1972	Mary Budke	5 & 4	Cynthia Hill	St. Louis CC, St. Louis
1973	Carol Semple	1 up	Anne Quast Decker	Montclair GC, Montclair, NJ
1974	Cynthia Hill	5 & 4	Carol Semple	Broadmoor GC, Seattle
1975	Beth Daniel	3 & 2	Donna Horton	Brae Burn CC, West Newton, MA
1976	Donna Horton	2 & 1	Marianne Bretton	Del Paso CC, Sacramento
1977	Beth Daniel	3 & 1	Cathy Sherk	Cincinnati CC, Cincinnati
1978	Cathy Sherk	4 & 3	Judith Oliver	Sunnybrook GC, Plymouth Meeting, PA
1979	Carolyn Hill	7 & 6	Patty Sheehan	Memphis CC, Memphis
1980	Juli Inkster	2 up	Patti Rizzo	Prairie Dunes CC, Hutchinson, KS
1981	Juli Inkster	1 up	Lindy Goggin	Waverley CC, Portland, OR
1982	Juli Inkster	4 & 3	Cathy Hanlon	Broadmoor GC, Colorado Springs, CO
1983	Joanne Pacillo	2 & 1	Sally Quinlan	Canoe Brook CC, Summit, NJ
1984	Deb Richard	1 up	Kimberly Williams	Broadmoor GC, Seattle
1985	Michiko Hattori	5 & 4	Cheryl Stacy	Fox Chapel CC, Pittsburgh
1986	Kay Cockerill	9 & 7	Kathleen McCarthy	Pasatiempo GC, Santa Cruz, CA
1987	Kay Cockerill	3 & 2	Tracy Kerdyk	Rhode Island CC, Barrington, RI
1988	Pearl Sinn	6 & 5	Karen Noble	Minikahda Club, Minneapolis
1989	Vicki Goetze	4 & 3	Brandie Burton	Pinehurst CC (No. 2), Pinehurst, NC
1990	Pat Hurst	37 holes	Stephanie Davis	Canoe Brook CC, Summit, NJ
1991	Amy Fruhwirth	5 & 4	Heidi Voorhees	Prairie Dunes CC, Hutchinson, KN
1992	Vicki Goetz	1 up	Annika Sorensteam	Kemper Lakes GC, Hawthorne Hills, IL
1993	Jill McGill	1 up	Sarah Ingram	San Diego CC, Chula Vista, CA

U.S. Women's Amateur *(Cont.)*

Year	Winner	Score	Runner-Up	Site
1994	Wendy Ward	2 & 1	Jill McGill	The Homestead, Hot Springs, WV
1995	Kelli Kuehne	4 & 3	Anne-Marie Knight	The Country Club, Brookline, MA
1996	Kelli Kuehne	2 & 1	Marisa Baena	Firethorn GC, Lincoln, NE
1997	Silvia Cavalleri	5 & 4	Robin Burke	Brae Burn CC, West Newton, MA
1998	Grace Park	7 & 6	Jenny Chuasiriporn	Barton Hills CC, Ann Arbor, MI
1999	Dorothy Delasin	4 & 3	Jimin Kang	Biltmore Forest CC, Asheville, NC
2000	Marcy Newton	8 & 7	Laura Myerscough	Waverley CC, Portland, OR
2001	Meredith Duncan	37 holes	Nicole Perrot	Flint Hills GC, Wichita, KA
2002	Becky Lucidi	3 & 2	Brandi Jackson	Sleepy Hollow CC, Scarborough, NY
2003	Virada Nirapathpongporn	2 & 1	Jane Park	Philadelphia CC, Gladwyne, PA
2004	Jane Park	1 up	Amanda McCurdy	Kahkwa Club, Erie, PA
2005	Morgan Pressel	9 & 8	Maru Martinez	Ansley GC, Roswell, GA
2006	Kimberly Kim	1 up	Katharina Schallenberg	Pumpkin Ridge, North Plains, OR

U.S. Girls' Junior Amateur

1949	Marlene Bauer	
1950	Patricia Lesser	
1951	Arlene Brooks	
1952	Mickey Wright	
1953	Millie Meyerson	
1954	Margaret Smith	
1955	Carole Jo Kabler	
1956	JoAnne Gunderson	
1957	Judy Eller	
1958	Judy Eller	
1959	Judy Rand	
1960	Carol Sorenson	
1961	Mary Lowell	
1962	Mary Lou Daniel	
1963	Janis Ferraris	
1964	Peggy Conley	
1965	Gail Sykes	
1966	Claudia Mayhew	
1967	Elizabeth Story	
1968	Peggy Harmon	
1969	Hollis Stacy	
1970	Hollis Stacy	
1971	Hollis Stacy	
1972	Nancy Lopez	
1973	Amy Alcott	
1974	Nancy Lopez	
1975	Dayna Benson	
1976	Pilar Dorado	
1977	Althea Tome	
1978	Lori Castillo	
1979	Penny Hammel	
1980	Laurie Rinker	
1981	Kay Cornelius	
1982	Heather Farr	
1983	Kim Saiki	
1984	Cathy Mockett	
1985	Dana Lofland	
1986	Pat Hurst	
1987	Michelle McGann	
1988	Jamille Jose	
1989	Brandie Burton	
1990	Sandrine Mendiburu	
1991	Emilee Klein	
1992	Jamie Koizumi	
1993	Kellee Booth	
1962	Maureen Orcutt	
1963	Sis Choate	
1994	Kelli Kuehne	
1995	Marcy Newton	
1996	Dorothy Delasin	
1997	Beth Bauer	
1998	Leigh Anne Hardin	
1999	Aree Wongluekiet	
2000	Lisa Ferrero	
2001	Nicole Perrot	
2002	In-Bee Park	
2003	Sukjin-Lee Wuesthoff	
2004	J. Granada	
2005	In-Kyung Kim	
2006	Jenny Shin	

Women's British Open Amateur

1893	Lady Margaret Scott	
1894	Lady Margaret Scott	
1895	Lady Margaret Scott	
1896	Miss Pascoe	
1897	Miss E.C. Orr	
1898	Miss L. Thomson	
1899	Miss M. Hezlet	
1900	Miss Adair	
1901	Miss Graham	
1902	Miss M. Hezlet	
1903	Miss Adair	
1904	Miss L. Dod	
1905	Miss B. Thompson	
1906	Mrs. Kennon	
1907	Miss M. Hezlet	
1908	Miss M. Titterton	
1909	Miss D. Campbell	
1910	Miss Grant Suttie	
1911	Miss D. Campbell	
1912	Miss G. Ravenscroft	
1913	Miss M. Dodd	
1914	Miss C. Leitch	
1915–19	not held	
1920	Miss C. Leitch	
1921	Miss C. Leitch	
1922	Miss J. Wethered	
1923	Miss D. Chambers	
1924	Miss J. Wethered	
1925	Miss J. Wethered	
1926	Miss C. Leitch	
1927	Miss Thion de la Chaume	
1928	Miss N. Le Blan	
1929	Miss J. Wethered	
1930	Miss D. Fishwick	
1931	Miss E. Wilson	
1932	Miss E. Wilson	
1933	Miss E. Wilson	
1934	Mrs. A.M. Holm	
1935	Miss W. Morgan	
1936	Miss P. Barton	
1937	Miss J. Anderson	
1938	Mrs. A.M. Holm	
1939	Miss P. Barton	
1940–45	not held	
1946	G.W. Hetherington	
1947	B. Zaharias	
1948	L. Suggs	
1949	F. Stephens	
1950	Vicomtesse de Saint Sauveur	
1951	P.J. MacCann	
1952	M. Paterson	
1953	M. Stewart	
1954	F. Stephens	
1955	J. Valentine	
1956	M. Smith	
1957	P. Garvey	
1958	J. Valentine	
1959	E. Price	
1960	B. McIntyre	
1961	M. Spearman	
1962	M. Spearman	
1963	B. Varangot	
1964	C. Sorenson	
1965	B. Varangot	
1966	E. Chadwick	
1967	E. Chadwick	
1968	B. Varangot	
1975	C. Lacoste	
1976	D. Oxley	
1977	A. Uzielli	

Women's British Open Amateur *(Cont.)*

1978 ....E. Kennedy	1989 ....H. Dobson	2000 ....Rebecca Hudson
1979 ....M. Madill	1990 ....J. Hall	2001 ....Rebecca Hudson
1980 ....A. Quast	1991 ....V. Michaud	2002 ....Rebecca Hudson
1981 .............I.C. Robertson	1992 ....P. Pedersen	2003 ....Elisa Serramia
1982 ....K. Douglas	1993 ....Catriona Lambert	2004 ....Louise Stahle
1983 ....J. Thornhill	1994 ....Emma Duggleby	2005 ....Heather MacRae
1984 ....J. Rosenthal	1995 ....Julie Hall	2006 ....Belen Mozo
1985 ....L. Beman	1996 ....Kelli Kuehne	
1986 ....M. McGuire	1997 ....Alison Rose	
1987 ....J. Collingham	1998 ....K. Rostron	
1988 ....J. Furby	1999 ....Marine Monnet	

Women's Amateur Public Links

1977 ....Kelly Fuiks	1987 ....Tracy Kerdyk	1998 ....Amy Spooner
1978 ....Kelly Fuiks	1988 ....Pearl Sinn	1999 ....Jody Niemann
1979 ....Lori Castillo	1989 ....Pearl Sinn	2000 ....Catherine Cartwright
1980 ....Lori Castillo	1990 ....Cathy Mockett	2001 ....Candie Kung
1981 ....Mary Enright	1991 ....Tracy Hanson	2002 ....Annie Thurman
1982 ....Nancy Taylor	1992 ....Amy Fruhwirth	2003 ....Michelle Wie
1983 ....Kelli Antolock	1993 ....Connie Masterson	2004 ....Ya-Ni Tseng
1984 ....Heather Farr	1994 ....Jill McGill	2005 ....Eun Jung Lee
1985 ....Danielle	1995 ....Jo Jo Robertson	2006 ....Tiffany Joh
Ammaccapane	1996 ....Heather Graff	
1986 ....Cindy Schreyer	1997 ....Jo Jo Robertson	

U.S. Senior Women's Amateur

1964 ....Loma Smith	1979 ....Alice Dye	1994 ....Marlene Streit
1965 ....Loma Smith	1980 ....Dorothy Porter	1995 ....Jean Smith
1966 ....Maureen Orcutt	1981 ....Dorothy Porter	1996 ....Gayle Borthwick
1967 ....Marge Mason	1982 ....Edean Ihlanfeldt	1997 ....Nancy Fitzgerald
1968 ....Carolyn Cudone	1983 ....Dorothy Porter	1998 ....Gayle Borthwick
1969 ....Carolyn Cudone	1984 ....Constance Guthrie	1999 ....C. Semple Thompson
1970 ....Carolyn Cudone	1985 ....Marlene Streit	2000 ....C. Semple Thompson
1971 ....Carolyn Cudone	1986 ....Connie Guthrie	2001 ....C. Semple Thompson
1972 ....Carolyn Cudone	1987 ....Anne Sander	2002 ....C. Semple Thompson
1973 ....Gwen Hibbs	1988 ....Lois Hodge	2003 ....Marlene Streit
1974 ....Justine Cushing	1989 ....Anne Sander	2004 ....Carolyn Creekmore
1975 ....Alberta Bower	1990 ....Anne Sander	2005 ....Diane Lang
1976 ....Cecile H. Maclaurin	1991 ....Phyllis Preuss	2006 ....Diane Lang
1977 ....Dorothy Porter	1992 ....Rosemary Thompson	
1978 ....Alice Dye	1993 ....Anne Sander	

Women's Mid-Amateur Championship

1987 ....Cindy Scholefield	1995 ....Ellen Port	2002 ....Kathy Hartwiger
1988 ....Martha Lang	1996 ....Ellen Port	2003 ....Amber Marsh
1989 ....Robin Weiss	1997 ....C. Semple Thompson	2004 ....Corey Weworski
1990 ....C. Semple Thompson	1998 ....Virginia Derby	2005 ....Mary Anne Lapointe
1991 ....Sarah LeBrun Ingram	Grimes	
1992 ....M. Mamey-McInerney	1999 ....Alissa Herron	
1993 ....Sarah Ingram	2000 ....Ellen Port	
1994 ....Sarah Ingram	2001 ....Laura Shanahan	

Ryder Cup Matches

Year	Results	Site
1927	United States 9½, Great Britain 2½	Worcester CC, Worcester, MA
1929	Great Britain 7, United States 5	Moortown GC, Leeds, England
1931	United States 9, Great Britain 3	Scioto CC, Columbus, OH
1933	Great Britain 6½, United States 5½	Southport and Ainsdale Courses, Southport, England
1935	United States 9, Great Britain 3	Ridgewood CC, Ridgewood, NJ
1937	United States 8, Great Britain 4	Southport and Ainsdale Courses, Southport, England
1939–1945	No tournament	
1947	United States 11, Great Britain 1	Portland GC, Portland, OR
1949	United States 7, Great Britain 5	Ganton GC, Scarborough, England
1951	United States 9½, Great Britain 2½	Pinehurst CC, Pinehurst, NC
1953	United States 6½, Great Britain 5½	Wentworth Club, Surrey, England
1955	United States 8, Great Britain 4	Thunderbird Ranch & CC, Palm Springs, CA
1957	Great Britain 7½, United States 4½	Lindrick GC, Yorkshire, England
1959	United States 8½, Great Britain 3½	Eldorado CC, Palm Desert, CA
1961	United States 14½, Great Britain 9½	Royal Lytham & St. Annes GC, St Anne's-on-the-Sea, England
1963	United States 23, Great Britain 9	East Lake CC, Atlanta
1965	United States 19½, Great Britain 12½	Royal Birkdale GC, Southport, England
1967	United States 23½, Great Britain 8½	Champions GC, Houston
1969	United States 16, Great Britain 16	Royal Birkdale GC, Southport, England
1971	United States 18½, Great Britain 13½	Old Warson CC, St. Louis
1973	United States 19, Great Britain 13	Hon Co of Edinburgh Golfers, Muirfield, Scotland
1975	United States 21, Great Britain 11	Laurel Valley GC, Ligonier, PA
1977	United States 12½, Great Britain 7½	Royal Lytham & St. Annes GC, St. Annes-on-the-Sea, Eng.
1979	United States 17, Europe 11	Greenbrier, White Sulphur Springs, WV
1981	United States 18½, Europe 9½	Walton Heath GC, Surrey, England
1983	United States 14½, Europe 13½	PGA National GC, Palm Beach Gardens, FL
1985	Europe 16½, United States 11½	Belfry GC, Sutton Coldfield, England
1987	Europe 15, United States 13	Muirfield GC, Dublin, OH
1989	Europe 14, United States 14	Belfry GC, Sutton Coldfield, England
1991	United States 14½, Europe 13½	Ocean Course, Kiawah Island, SC
1993	United States 15, Europe 13	Belfry GC, Sutton Coldfield, England
1995	Europe 14½, United States 13½	Oak Hill CC, Rochester, NY
1997	Europe 14½, United States 13½	Valderrama GC, Sotogrande, Spain
1999	United States 14½, Europe 13½	The Country Club, Brookline, MA
2002	Europe 15½, Unites States 12½	Belfry GC, Sutton Coldfield, England
2004	Europe 18½, United States 9½	Oakland Hills CC, Bloomfield Hills, MI
2006	Europe 18½, United States 9½	The K Club, County Kildare, Ireland

Team matches held every odd year between U.S. professionals and those of Great Britain/Europe. Team members selected on basis of finishes in PGA and European tour events. Match in 2001 canceled due to 9/11 terrorist attacks.

Walker Cup Matches

Year	Results	Site
1922	United States 8, Great Britain 4	Nat'l Golf Links of America, Southampton, NY
1923	United States 6, Great Britain 5	St. Andrews, Scotland
1924	United States 9, Great Britain 3	Garden City GC, Garden City, NY
1926	United States 6, Great Britain 5	St. Andrews, Scotland
1928	United States 11, Great Britain 1	Chicago GC, Wheaton, IL
1930	United States 10, Great Britain 2	Royal St. George GC, Sandwich, England
1932	United States 8, Great Britain 1	The Country Club, Brookline, MA
1934	United States 9, Great Britain 2	St. Andrews, Scotland
1936	United States 9, Great Britain 0	Pine Valley GC, Clementon, NJ
1938	Great Britain 7, United States 4	St. Andrews, Scotland
1940–46	No tournament	
1947	United States 8, Great Britain 4	St. Andrews, Scotland
1949	United States 10, Great Britain 2	Winged Foot GC, Mamaroneck, NY
1951	United States 6, Great Britain 3	Birkdale GC, Southport, England
1953	United States 9, Great Britain 3	The Kittansett Club, Marion, MA
1955	United States 10, Great Britain 2	St. Andrews, Scotland
1957	United States 8, Great Britain 3	Minikahda Club, Minneapolis
1959	United States 9, Great Britain 3	Muirfield, Scotland
1961	United States 11, Great Britain 1	Seattle GC, Seattle
1963	United States 12, Great Britain 8	Ailsa Course, Turnberry, Scotland
1965	Great Britain 11, United States 11	Baltimore CC, Five Farms, Baltimore, MD
1967	United States 13, Great Britain 7	Royal St. George's GC, Sandwich, England
1969	United States 10, Great Britain 8	Milwaukee CC, Milwaukee, WI
1971	Great Britain 13, United States 11	St. Andrews, Scotland
1973	United States 14, Great Britain 10	The Country Club, Brookline, MA
1975	United States 15½, Great Britain 8½	St. Andrews, Scotland
1977	United States 16, Great Britain 8	Shinnecock Hills GC, Southampton, NY
1979	United States 15½, Great Britain 8½	Muirfield, Scotland
1981	United States 15, Great Britain 9	Cypress Point Club, Pebble Beach, CA
1983	United States 13½, Great Britain 10½	Royal Liverpool GC, Hoylake, England
1985	United States 13, Great Britain 11	Pine Valley GC, Pine Valley, NJ
1987	United States 16½, Great Britain 7½	Sunningdale GC, Berkshire, England
1989	Great Britain 12½, United States 11½	Peachtree Golf Club, Atlanta
1991	United States 14, Great Britain 10	Portmarnock GC, Dublin, Ireland
1993	United States 19, Great Britain 5	Interlachen CC, Edina, MN
1995	Great Britain/Ireland 14, United States 10	Royal Porthcawl, Porthcawl, Wales
1997	United States 18, Great Britain/Ireland 6	Quaker Ridge GC, Scarsdale, NY
1999	Great Britain/Ireland 15, United States 9	Nairn GC, Nairn, Scotland
2001	Great Britain/Ireland 15, United States 9	Ocean Forest GC, Sea Island, GA
2003	Great Britain/Ireland 12½, United States 11½	Ganton GC, Ganton, England
2005	United States 12½, Great Britain/Ireland 11½	Chicago GC, Wheaton IL

Men's amateur team competition every other year between United States and Great Britain/Ireland. U.S. team members selected by USGA.

Solheim Cup Matches

Year	Results	Site
1990	United States 11½, Europe 4½	Lake Nona GC, Orlando, FL
1992	Europe 11½, United States 6½	Dalmahoy Hotel GC, Edinburgh
1994	United States 13, Europe 7	The Greenbriar, White Sulpher Springs, WV
1996	United States 17, Europe 11	Marriot St Pierre Hotel & CC, Chepstow, Wales
1998	United States 16, Europe 12	Muirfield Village GC, Dublin, OH
2000	Europe 14½, United States, 11 ½	Loch Lomond GC, Luss, Scotand
2002	United States 15½, Europe 12 ½	Interlachen CC, Minneapolis, MN
2003	Europe 17½, United States 10 ½	Barseback G&CC, Malmo, Sweden
2005	United States 15½, Europe 12 ½	Crooked Stick GC, Carmel IN

Women's team matches held every other year between U.S. professionals and those of Europe. Team members selected on the basis of finishes in LPGA and European tour events.

Curtis Cup Matches

Year	Results	Site
1932	United States 5½, British Isles 3½	Wentworth GC, Wentworth, England
1934	United States 6½, British Isles 2½	Chevy Chase Club, Chevy Chase, MD
1936	United States 4½ British Isles 4½	King's Course, Gleneagles, Scotland
1938	United States 5½, British Isles 3½	Essex CC, Manchester, MA
1940–46	No tournament	
1948	United States 6½, British Isles 2½	Birkdale GC, Southport, England
1950	United States 7½, British Isles 1½	CC of Buffalo, Williamsville, NY
1952	British Isles 5, United States 4	Muirfield, Scotland
1954	United States 6, British Isles 3	Merion GC, Ardmore, PA
1956	British Isles 5, United States 4	Prince's GC, Sandwich Bay, England
1958	British Isles 4½, United States 4½	Brae Burn CC, West Newton, Mass.
1960	United States 6½, British Isles 2½	Lindrick GC, Worksop, England
1962	United States 8, British Isles 1	Broadmoor CG, Colorado Springs,CO
1964	United States 10½, British Isles 7½	Royal Porthcawl GC, Porthcawl, South Wales
1966	United States 13, British Isles 5	Va. Hot Springs G & TC, Hot Springs, VA
1968	United States 10½, British Isles 7½	Royal County Down GC, Newcastle, N. Ire.
1970	United States 11½, British Isles 6½	Brae Burn CC, West Newton, MA
1972	United States 10, British Isles 8	Western Gailes, Ayrshire, Scotland
1974	United States 13, British Isles 5	San Francisco GC, San Francisco
1976	United States 11½, British Isles 6½	Royal Lytham & St. Annes GC, England
1978	United States 12, British Isles 6	Apawamis Club, Rye, NY
1980	United States 13, British Isles 5	St. Pierre G & CC, Chepstow, Wales
1982	United States 14½, British Isles 3½	Denver CC, Denver
1984	United States 9½ British Isles 8½	Muirfield, Scotland
1986	British Isles 13, United States 5	Prairie Dunes CC, Hutchinson, KS
1988	British Isles 11, United States 7	Royal St. George's GC, Sandwich, England
1990	United States 14, British Isles 4	Somerset Hills CC, Bernardsville, NJ
1992	Great Britain/Ireland 10, United States 8	Royal Liverpool GC, Hoylake, England
1994	Great Britain/Ireland 9, United States 9	The Honors Course, Ooltewah, TN
1996	Great Britain/Ireland 11½, United States 6½	Killarney Golf & Fishing Club, Killarney, Ireland
1998	United States 10, Great Britain/Ireland 8	The Minikahda Club, Minneapolis
2000	United States 10, Great Britain/Ireland 8	Ganton GC, North Yorkshire, England
2002	United States 11, Great Britain/Ireland 7	Fox Chapel GC, Pittsburgh, PA
2004	United States 10, Great Britain/Ireland 8	Formby GC, Merseyside, England
2006	United States 11½, Great Britain/Ireland 6½	Bandon Dunes GC, Bandon, OR

Women's amateur team competition every other year between the United States and Great Britain/Ireland. U.S. team members selected by USGA.

Presidents Cup Matches

Year	Results	Site
1994	United States 20, International 12	Robert Trent Jones GC, Lake Manassas, VA
1996	United States 16½, International 15½	Robert Trent Jones GC, Lake Manassas, VA
1998	International 20½ United States 11½	Royal Melbourne GC, Melbourne, Australia
2000	United States 21½, International 10½	Robert Trent Jones GC, Lake Manassas, VA
2003	International 17, United States 17	Fan Court Hotel CC, George, South Africa
2005	United States 18½. International 15½	Robert Trent Jones GC, Lake Manassas, VA

A biennial event played in non-Ryder Cup years designed to provide non-European players with international team and match play.

Boxing

American Jermain Taylor (r.) continued his reign as WBA and WBC middleweight champ

From Russia With Gloves

Boxing's Balkanization reached its peak in 2006, as three different fighters born in the former Soviet Union laid claim to the title "Heavyweight Champion of the World"

BY STEPHEN CANNELLA

CHRISTMAS COULDN'T COME fast enough for many boxing fans in 2006. In addition to the usual tidings of comfort and joy—novelties in the sport at any time of year—the holiday season would mark the return of one of the giants of the sweet science, a charismatic champion who once upon a time galvanized diehard fight fans and casual watchers alike. In an industry in which improbable comebacks by aging stars are commonplace, this career revival would be followed by more than most.

No, the anticipation wasn't for the return of Evander Holyfield, though the "Real Deal", at age 43, did launch a delusional comeback in 2006. (The former heavyweight champ knocked out someone named Jeremy Bates in August and was scheduled to face Fres Oquendo in San Antonio on November 10.) The fighter in question was Rocky Balboa, the fictional pug who, it was announced in late 2005, would return to the screen for a sixth installment of the *Rocky* series in a holiday-season release. Titled *Rocky Balboa*, the film would again star Sylvester Stallone. Never mind that Sly, at 60, would be

at an age when even George Foreman knows it's unwise to climb into the ring.

Fictional or not, Rocky's return qualified as a big moment for boxing, a sport that will take publicity anywhere it can get it these days. The heavyweight division again failed to produce a marquee champ in 2006, and its crown remained Balkanized into three different titles awarded by three different sanctioning bodies. Adding to the confusion, at least for fans unfamiliar with the Cyrillic alphabet, was a thorough Sovietification of the division in 2006. When Oleg Maskaev, a former Russian Army officer from Kazakhstan, won a TKO over Hasim Rahman to capture the WBC belt on August 12, all four heavyweight titles were held by fighters from former Soviet territories. It was the first time since 1960 that an American failed to hold at least a share of the heavyweight title.

Perhaps Ivan Drago, not Rocky, should have been the one returning to the ring. Boxing's Russian Revolution began in December 2005, when Nikolay Valuev won a controversial decision over John Ruiz to gain the WBA belt. Suddenly, the largely unknown Valuev, 32, was the first Russian heavyweight champion and the biggest name in boxing. Literally. At 7' and 330

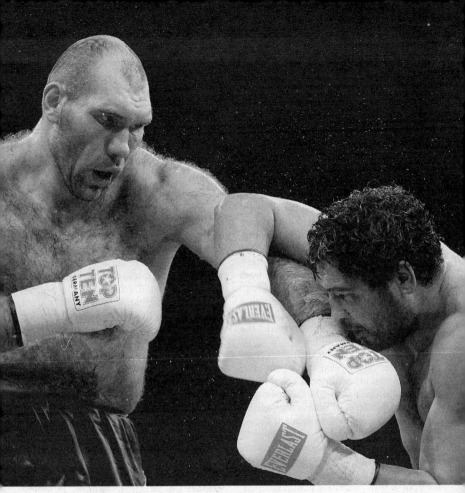

pounds, the Russian Giant (his nickname of choice, though many promoters still leaned toward The Beast from The East) was the tallest and heaviest champ ever.

Before the fight, Ruiz, who gave away 10 inches and 85 pounds to the challenger, declared that Valuev had "a head the size of a Volkswagen, I can't miss hitting him," and indeed Ruiz didn't. Many observers thought he won, and the split decision in Valuev's favor was booed by the crowd in Berlin. The victory did little to improve Valuev's reputation as a novelty act. Nor did the beating Valuev allegedly laid on a 61-year-old security guard in his hometown of St. Petersburg a few weeks later. The guard apparently had the temerity to ask Valuev's wife to move her car

After defeating Ruiz, seven-footer Valuev (l.) became boxing's tallest heavyweight champion in history.

while she dropped their three-year-old son off for skating lessons. Angered by the man's rudeness, Valuev allegedly put him in the hospital with a concussion and a bruised chest.

The incident seemed to be out of character for Valuev, known in his home country as a gentle giant who reads Tolstoy and writes poetry for his bride. He restored some luster to his title with a convincing defense of it in June, a third-round knockout of Jamaica's Owen Beck in Hanover, Germany, that ran the Russian Giant's record to 44–0 (32 KOs). (A stiffer test would come in October, when Valuev was scheduled to face the veteran Monte Barrett in Rosemont, Ill.) But by then, Valuev wasn't the only heavyweight celebrity in former Iron Curtain territories. On April 26, Ukraine's Wladimir Klitschko, the younger brother of former heavyweight champ Vitali Klitschko, beat Chris Byrd in Mannheim, Germany, winning the IBF belt with a TKO in the seventh round.

Though their aggregate Q ratings hovered in the single digits, the Soviet sluggers made for a colorful group. In the competition for the intellectual high ground Valuev had a worthy rival in Klitschko, who studied philosophy in college and earned a PhD in sports science in 2001. And Maskaev, who celebrated his title by moving from Staten Island to a Sacramento suburb shortly after winning, disclosed a rather idiosyncratic strategy for facing Rahman. "I hit him in the stomach," he explained. "The organs are in there."

They didn't exactly recall the Ali-Foreman-Frazier glory years, but the trio restored some entertainment value to the heavyweight division. Fight fans who preferred a higher level of skill in their champions needed only look to Jermain Taylor, who continued to dazzle the middleweight division or Floyd Mayweather Jr., the undisputed czar of the lower weight classes. In April, Mayweather, considered the sport's best pound-for-pound competitor, breezed to a unanimous decision victory over Zab Judah in Las Vegas to claim the IBF welterweight belt. It was Mayweather's fourth title, and the fourth weight class he had conquered

It also was evidence that the 29-year-old, usually one of the sport's most churlish figures, had matured. In the 10th round Judah, clearly heading for a loss, hit Mayweather below the belt and followed up that cheap shot with a rabbit punch. The tactics enraged Roger Mayweather, Floyd's uncle and trainer, who stormed into the ring mid-round. Both corners emptied and a brief free-for-all ensued—though, surprisingly, Mayweather stayed out of the fray. (He was lucky not to be disqualified for his trainer's misconduct.)

Afterward Mayweather displayed uncharacteristic poise when asked about Judah's dirty blows. "Things happen," he said.

The IBF wasn't so sanguine: A few weeks later it reprimanded Mayweather for his corner's actions, stripped him of the title and ordered a rematch between him and Judah. The undefeated Mayweather is good-looking and supremely talented, the kind of fighter who could carry a sport in dire need of a charismatic star. But a surly personality, several scrapes with the law and public feuds with both cable channel HBO and his father, Floyd Sr., have undermined his box-office appeal. Promoters were no doubt drooling at the notion that the Judah fight signified the emergence of a cuddlier Mayweather persona, one that might make him more like Oscar De La Hoya, the world's most popular fighter.

The Golden Boy himself returned to the ring in 2006, ending a 20-month layoff by knocking out Ricardo Mayorga in May to win the WBC super welterweight title, his ninth career title. De La Hoya immediately began campaigning for a shot at Mayweather, a dream matchup that De La Hoya said would be his last bout before retirement. There was a complication, however. De La Hoya is trained by Floyd Mayweather Sr., who said he would never prepare a fighter to take on his son.

Still, neither side ruled out a Mayweather-De La Hoya meeting in 2007. (Mayweather first faced welterweight champ Carlos Baldomir in Las Vegas on November 4.) It was a plot twist any screenwriter would be proud of—but then again, the line between Hollywood and professional boxing was a blurry one in 2006. Antonio Tarver, who lost his light heavyweight belt to Bernard Hopkins in June, played Mason (The Line) Dixon, Rocky's new archenemy, in *Rocky Balboa*. During filming Stallone told Tarver to throw real punches so the fight scenes would look authentic and, insiders reported, Sly held his own with the pro. Was that a testament to Stallone's fitness or the state of boxing in 2006? *Rocky* fans and fight fans will have to duke that one out.

Current Champions

Division	Weight Limit	WBA Champion	WBC Champion	IBF Champion
Heavyweight	None	Nikolay Valuev	Oleg Maskaev	Wladimir Klitschko
Cruiserweight	200	O'Neil Bell	O'Neil Bell	Vacant
Light Heavyweight	175	Fabrice Tiozzo	Tomasz Adamek	Clinton Woods
Super Middleweight	168	Mikel Kessler	Markus Beyer	Joe Calzaghe
Middleweight	160	Jermain Taylor	Jermain Taylor	Arthur Abraham
Super Welterweight	154	Jose Rivera	Oscar De La Hoya	Cory Spinks
Welterweight	147	Ricky Hatton	Carlos Baldomir	Vacant
Super Lightweight	140	Souleymane M'baye	Vacant	Juan Urango
Lightweight	135	Juan Diaz	Diego Corrales	Jesus Chavez
Super Featherweight	130	Edwin Valero	Marco Antonio Barrera	Gairy St. Clair
Featherweight	126	Chris John	Rodolfo Lopez	Robert Guerrero
Super Bantamweight	122	Somsak Sithchatawal	Israel Vazquez	Vacant
Bantamweight	118	Wladimir Sidorenko	Hozumi Hasegawa	Rafael Marquez
Super Flyweight	115	Nobuo Nashiro	Masamori Tokuyama	Luis Alberto Perez
Flyweight	112	Lorenzo Parra	Pongsaklek Wonjongkam	Vic Darchinyan
Light Flyweight	108	Koki Kameda	Omar Nino Romero	Ulises Solis
Strawweight	105	Yukata Niida	Eagle Kyowa	Muhammad Rachman

Note: WBC=World Boxing Council; WBA=World Boxing Association; IBF=International Boxing Federation. Champions as of October 1, 2006.

Championship and Major Fights of 2005 and 2006

Abbreviations: WBC=World Boxing Council; WBA= World Boxing Association; IBF=International Boxing Federation; KO=knockout; TKO=technical knockout; UD=unanimous decision; SD=split decision; DQ=disqualification; MD=majority decision; TD=technical decision. Bouts from Sept. 1, 2005 to Sept. 1, 2006.

Heavyweight

Date	Winner	Loser	Result	Title/Org.	Site
Dec 17	Nikolay Valuev	John Ruiz	MD	WBA	Berlin
Mar 18	Hasim Rahman	James Toney	MD	WBC	Atlantic City, N.J.
Apr 22	Wladimir Klitschko	Chris Byrd	TKO 7	IBF	Mannheim, Germany
Jun 3	Nikolay Valuev	Owen Beck	TKO 3	WBA	Hanover, Germany
Aug 12	Oleg Maskaev	Hasim Rahman	TKO 12	WBC	Las Vegas

Cruiserweight

Date	Winner	Loser	Result	Title/Org.	Site
Jan 7	O'Neil Bell	Jean-Marc Mormeck	KO 10	WBC/WBA	New York City
Jan 27	Virgil Hill	Valery Brudov	UD	Vacant WBA	Atlantic City, N.J.
*Apr 2	Jean-Marc Mormeck	Wayne Braithwaite	UD	WBC/WBA	Worcester, Mass.

Light Heavyweight

Date	Winner	Loser	Result	Title/Org.	Site
May 13	Clinton Woods	Jason DelLisle	TKO 6	IBF	Sheffield, England
Jul 27	Silvio Branco	Manny Siaca	TKO 10	Vacant Int. WBA	Milan, Italy

Super Middleweight

Date	Winner	Loser	Result	Title/Org.	Site
Nov 11	Jeff Lacy	Scott Pemberton	KO 2	IBF	Stateline, Nev.
Jan 14	Mikel Kessler	Eric Lucas	TKO 10	WBA	Copenhagen
Mar 4	Joe Calzaghe	Jeff Lacy	UD	IBF	Manchester, England
May 13	Markus Beyer	Sakio Bika	TD	WBC	Zwickau, Germany

*non-title bouts

Championship and Major Fights of 2005 and 2006 *(Cont.)*

Middleweight

Date	Winner	Loser	Result	Title/Org.	Site
Dec 3	Jermain Taylor	Bernard Hopkins	UD	WBC/WBA	Las Vegas
Mar 4	Arthur Abraham	Shannan Taylor	UD	IBF	Oldenberg, Germany
*Mar 11	Felix Sturm	Maselino Masoe	UD	WBA	Hamburg, Germany
May 13	Arthur Abraham	Kofi Jantuah	UD	IBF	Zwickau, Germany
Jun 7	Jermain Taylor	Ronald Wright	SD	WBC/WBA	Memphis, Tenn.
*Jul 15	Javier Castillejos	Felix Sturm	TKO 10	WBA	Hamburg, Germany

Junior Middleweight (Super Welterweight)

Date	Winner	Loser	Result	Title/Org.	Site
Jan 28	Markus Beyer	Alberto Colajanni	TKO 12	WBC	Berlin
May 6	Oscar De La Hoya	Ricardo Mayorga	TKO 6	WBC	Les Vegas
May 6	Jose A. Rivera	Alejandro Garcia	UD	WBA	Worcester, Mass.

Welterweight

Date	Winner	Loser	Result	Title/Org.	Site
Jan 7	Carlos Baldomir	Zab Judah	UD	WBC	New York City
Apr 8	Floyd Mayweather, Jr.	Zab Judah	UD	IBF	Las Vegas
May 13	Ricky Hatton	Luis Collazo	UD	WBA	Boston
Jul 22	Carlos Baldomir	Arturo Gatti	TKO 9	WBC	Atlantic City

Super Lightweight (Junior Welterweight)

Date	Winner	Loser	Result	Title/Org.	Site
*Oct 23	Vivian Harris	Oktay Urkal	TKO 11	WBA	Berlin
*Nov 26	Ricky Hatton	Carlos Maussa	KO 9	WBA/IBF	Sheffield, England

Lightweight

Date	Winner	Loser	Result	Title/Org.	Site
Apr 8	Juan Diaz	Jose Miguel Cotto	UD	WBA	Las Vegas
May 18	Julio Diaz	Ricky Quiles	UD	Interim IBF	Hollywood, Fla.
*May 20	Jose Santa Cruz	Chikashi Inada	TKO 6	WBC	Los Angeles
Jul 15	Juan Diaz	Randy Suico	TKO 9	WBA	Las Vegas
Aug 12	David Diaz	Jose Santa Cruz	TKO 10	Interim WBC	Las Vegas

Super Featherweight (Junior Lightweight)

Date	Winner	Loser	Result	Title/Org.	Site
*May 12	Vincente Mosquera	Jose Pablo Estrella	SD	WBA	Cordoba, Argentina
May 20	Marco Antonio Barrera	Ricardo Juarez	SD	WBC	Los Angeles
*May 31	Cassius Baloyi	Manuel Medina	TKO 11	IBF	Airway Heights, Wash.
Jul 29	Gairy St. Clair	Cassius Baloyi	UD	IBF	Kempton Park, S. Africa
Aug 5	Edwin Valero	Vincente Mosquera	TKO 10	WBA	Panama City, Panama

Featherweight

Date	Winner	Loser	Result	Title/Org.	Sit
Jan 20	Valdemir Pereira	Phafrakorb Rakkietgym	UD	Vacant IBF	Mashantucket, Conn.
Jan 29	Takashi Koshimoto	In-Jin Chi	SD	WBC	Fukuoka, Japan
Feb 17	Humberto Soto	Oscar Leon	TKO 9	Interim WBC	Los Mochis, Mexico
Mar 4	Chris John	Juan Manuel Marquez	UD	WBA	Borneo, Indonesia
*May 7	Juan Manuel Marquez	Victor Polo	UD	WBA/IBF	Las Vegas
May 13	Eric Aiken	Valdemir Pereira	DQ 8	IBF	Boston
Jul 30	Rodolfo Lopez	Takashi Koshimoto	TKO 7	WBC	Fukuoka, Japan

*non-title bouts

Super Bantamweight (Junior Featherweight)

Date	Winner	Loser	Result	Title/Org.	Site
Dec 3	Israel Vazquez	Oscar Larios	TKO 3	WBC/IBF	Las Vegas
Feb 14	Celestino Caballero	Roberto Bonilla	TKO 7	Interim WBA	Panama City, Panama
Mar 18	Somsak Sithchatchawal	Mahyar Monshipour	TKO 10	WBA	Levallois-Perret, France
Jun 10	Israel Vazquez	Ivan Hernandez	TKO 4	WBC	Atlantic City, N.J.

Bantamweight

Date	Winner	Loser	Result	Title/Org.	Site
Mar 11	Wladimir Sidorenko	Ricardo Cordoba	MD	WBA	Hamburg, Germany
Jul 15	Wladimir Sidorenko	P. Kratingdaenggym	UD	WBA	Hamburg, Germany
Aug 5	Rafael Marquez	Silence Mabuza	TKO 9	IBF	Stateline, Nev.

Super Flyweight (Junior Bantamweight)

Date	Winner	Loser	Result	Title/Org.	Site
Jan 14	Jose Martin Castillo	Alexander Munoz	SD	WBA	Las Vegas
Feb 27	Masamori Tokuyama	Jose Navarro	UD	WBC	Osaka, Japan
May 6	Luis Alberto Perez	Dimitri Kirilov	SD	IBF	Worcester, Mass.
Jul 22	Nobou Nashiro	Jose Martin Castillo	TKO 10	WBA	Osaka, Japan

Flyweight

Date	Winner	Loser	Result	Title/Org.	Site
Dec 6	Lorenzo Parra	Brahim Asloum	UD	WBA	Bercy, France
Dec 16	Jorge Arce	Adonis Rivas	TKO 10	Interim WBC	Monterrey, Mexico
Feb 16	Pongsaklek Wonjongkam	Gilberto Keb-Baas	UD	WBC	Chainart, Thailand
Mar 3	Vic Darchinyan	Diosdado Gabi	TKO 8	IBF	Santa Ynez, Calif.
May 1	Pongsakek Wonjongkam	Daigo Nakahiro	UD	WBC	Bangkok, Thailand
Jun 3	Vic Darchinyan	Luis Maldonado	TKO 8	IBF	Las Vegas

Light Flyweight

Date	Winner	Loser	Result	Title/Org.	Site
Jan 7	Ulises Solis	Will Grigsby	UD	IBF	New York City
Jan 28	Jorge Arce	Adonis Rivas	TKO 6	Interim WBC	Cancun, Mexico
Feb 18	Brian Viloria	Jose Aguirre	UD	WBC	Las Vegas
Mar 25	Ulises Solis	Erik Ortiz	TKO 9	IBF	Guadalajara, Mexico
July 18	Wandee Chor Chareon	Juanito Rubillar	UD	Vacant Int. WBC	Bangkok, Thailand
May 20	Roberto Vasquez	Noel Arambulet	UD	WBA	Panama City, Panama
*Jun 30	Pongsaklek Wonjongkam	Everardo Morales	TKO 4	WBC	Bangkok, Thailand
Aug 2	Koki Kameda	Juan Jose Landaeta	SD	Vacant WBA	Yokohama, Japan
Aug 4	Ulises Solis	Omar Salado	MD	IBF	Tijuana, Mexico
Aug 10	Omar Nino Romero	Brian Viloria	UD	WBC	Las Vegas

Strawweight (Mini Flyweight)

Date	Winner	Loser	Result	Title/Org.	Site
Jan 9	Eagle Kyowa	Ken Nakajima	TKO 7	WBC	Yokohama, Japan

*non-title bouts

World Champions

Sanctioning bodies: the National Boxing Association (NBA), the New York State Athletic Commission (NY), the World Boxing Association (WBA), the World Boxing Council (WBC), and the International Boxing Federation (IBF).

Heavyweights
(Weight: Unlimited)

Champion	Reign	Champion	Reign	Champion	Reign
John L. Sullivan*	1885–92	Jimmy Ellis WBA	1968–70	Riddick Bowe*	1992–93
James J. Corbett*	1892–97	Joe Frazier*	1970–73	Evander Holyfield*	1993–94
Bob Fitzsimmons*	1897–99	George Foreman*	1973–74	Michael Moorer*	1994
James J. Jeffries*	1899–05†	Muhammad Ali*	1974–78	George Foreman*	1994–95
Marvin Hart*	1905–06	Leon Spinks*	1978	Oliver McCall WBC	1995
Tommy Burns*	1906–08	Ken Norton WBC	1978	Frank Bruno WBC	1995–96
Jack Johnson*	1908–15	Larry Holmes WBC	1978–80	Bruce Seldon WBA	1995–96
Jess Willard*	1915–19	Muhammad Ali*	1978–79†	Mike Tyson WBA	1996
Jack Dempsey*	1919–26	John Tate WBA	1979–80	Michael Moorer IBF	1996–97
Gene Tunney*	1926–28†	Mike Weaver WBA	1980–82	Shannon Briggs*	1997–98
Max Schmeling*	1930–32	Larry Holmes*	1980–85	Lennox Lewis* WBC	1997–01
Jack Sharkey*	1932–33	Michael Dokes WBA	1982–83	E. Holyfield WBA, IBF	1996–99
Primo Carnera*	1933–34	Gerrie Coetzee WBA	1983–84	Lennox Lewis	1999–01
Max Baer*	1934–35	Tim Witherspoon WBC	1984	E. Holyfield WBA	2000–01
James J. Braddock*	1935–37	Pinklon Thomas WBC	1984–86	John Ruiz WBA	2001–03
Joe Louis*	1937–49†	Greg Page WBA	1984–85	Hasim Rahman* WBC, IBF	2001–05
Ezzard Charles*	1949–51	Michael Spinks*	1985–87	Chris Byrd IBF	2002–06
Jersey Joe Walcott*	1951–52	Tim Witherspoon WBA	1986	Roy Jones Jr. WBA	2003–05
Rocky Marciano*	1952–56†	Trevor Berbick WBC	1986	Lennox Lewis* WBC	2001–04
Floyd Patterson*	1956–59	Mike Tyson WBC	1986–87	John Ruiz WBA	2003–05
Ingemar Johansson*	1959–60	James Smith WBA	1986–87	Vitali Klitschko WBC	2004–05
Floyd Patterson*	1960–62	Tony Tucker IBF	1987	Hasim Rahman WBC	2005–06
Sonny Liston*	1962–64	Mike Tyson*	1987–90	Nikolay Valuev WBA	2005–
Muhammad Ali*	1964–70†	Buster Douglas*	1990	Oleg Maskaev WBC	2006–
Ernie Terrell WBA	1965–67	Evander Holyfield*	1990–92	Wladimir Klitschko IBF	2006–
Joe Frazier* NY	1968–70	Lennox Lewis WBC	1993–95		

Cruiserweights
(Weight Limit: 200 pounds)

Champion	Reign	Champion	Reign	Champion	Reign
Marvin Camel* WBC	1980	Evander Holyfield*	1988†	A. Washington IBF	1996–97
Carlos De Leon* WBC	1980–82	Toufik Belbouli WBA	1989	Uriah Grant IBF	1997
Ossie Ocasio WBA	1982–84	Robert Daniels WBA	1989–91	Imamu Mayfield IBF	1997–98
S.T. Gordon* WBC	1982–83	Carlos De Leon* WBC	1989–90	Fabrice Tiozzo WBA	1997–00
Carlos De Leon* WBC	1983–85	Glenn McCrory IBF	1989–90	J.C. Gomez* WBC	1998–02†
Marvin Camel IBF	1983–84	Jeff Lampkin IBF	1990	Arthur Williams IBF	1998–99
Lee Roy Murphy IBF	1984–86	M. Duran* WBC	1990–91	Vassiliy Girov* IBF	1999–03
Piet Crous WBA	1984–85	Bobby Czyz WBA	1991–92†	James Toney* IBF	2003
Alfonso Ratliff* WBC	1985	Anaclet Wamba* WBC	1991–95†	Virgil Hill WBA	2000–02
Dwight Braxton WBA	1985–86	James Pritchard WBA	1991	Wayne Braithwaite WBC	2002–05
Bernard Benton* WBC	1985–86	James Warring IBF	1991–92	J.M. Mormeck WBA	2002–06
Carlos De Leon* WBC	1986–88	Alfred Cole IBF	1992–96	J.M. Mormeck WBC	2005–06
Evander Holyfield* WBA	1986–88	Orlin Norris WBA	1993–95	Melvin Davis IBF	2004–05
Ricky Parkey IBF	1986–87	Nate Miller WBA	1995–97	O'Neil Bell IBF	2005
E. Holyfield* WBA, IBF	1987–88	M. Dominguez* WBC	1996–98	O'Neil Bell WBC/WBA	2006–

Light Heavyweights
(Weight Limit: 175 pounds)

Champion	Reign	Champion	Reign	Champion	Reign
Jack Root*	1903	Georges Carpentier*	1920–22	Tommy Loughran*	1927–29†
George Gardner*	1903	Battling Siki*	1922–23	Maxie Rosenbloom*	1930–34
Bob Fitzsimmons*	1903–05	Mike McTigue*	1923–25	George Nichols NBA	1932
Jack O'Brien*	1905–12†	Paul Berlenbach*	1925–26	Bob Godwin NBA	1933
Jack Dillon*	1914–16	Jack Delaney*	1926–27†	Bob Olin*	1934–35
Battling Levinsky*	1916–20	Jimmy Slattery NBA	1927	John Henry Lewis*	1935–38†

*Lineal champion.
†Champion relinquished title to retire or switch weight classes, or had title stripped by boxing organization.

Light Heavyweights *(Cont.)*

Champion	Reign
Melio Bettina	1939
Billy Conn*	1939–40†
Anton Christoforidis	1941
Gus Lesnevich*	1941–48
Freddie Mills*	1948–50
Joey Maxim*	1950–52
Archie Moore*	1952–62†
Harold Johnson NBA	1961
Harold Johnson*	1962–63
Willie Pastrano*	1963–65
Jose Torres*	1965–66
Dick Tiger*	1966–68
Bob Foster*	1968–74†
Vicente Rondon WBA	1971–72
John Conteh WBC	1974–77
Victor Galindez* WBA	1974–78
Miguel A. Cuello WBC	1977–78
Mate Parlov WBC	1978
Mike Rossman* WBA	1978–79
Victor Galindez* WBA	1979
Marvin Johnson* WBC	1978–79

Champion	Reign
M.S. Muhammad* WBC	1979–81
Marvin Johnson WBA	1979–80
E.M. Muhammad WBA	1980–81
Michael Spinks* WBA	1981–83
Dwight Qawi WBC	1981–83
Michael Spinks*	1983–85†
J. B. Williamson WBC	1985–86
Slobodan Kacar IBF	1985–86
Marvin Johnson* WBA	1986–87
Dennis Andries WBC	1986–87
Bobby Czyz IBF	1986–87
Leslie Stewart WBA	1987
Virgil Hill* WBA	1987–91
Pr Charles Williams IBF	1987–93
Thomas Hearns* WBC	1987†
Donny Lalonde WBC	1987–88
Sugar Ray Leonard WBC	1988
Dennis Andries WBC	1989
Jeff Harding WBC	1989–90
Dennis Andries WBC	1990–91
Thomas Hearns* WBA	1991–92

Champion	Reign
Jeff Harding WBC	1991–94
Iran Barkley* WBA	1992
Virgil Hill* WBA	1992–97
Henry Maske IBF	1993–96
Mike McCallum WBC	1994–95
Fabrice Tiozzo WBC	1995–96
D. Michalczewski* IBF	1997†
Roy Jones Jr. WBC, WBA	1997–03
William Guthrie IBF	1997–98
Reggie Johnson IBF	1998–99
Roy Jones Jr.*	1999–03
Bruno Girard WBA	2001–03
Mehdi Sahnoune WBA	2003
Silvio Branco WBA	2003–04
Antonio Tarver WBC, IBF	2003
Roy Jones Jr. WBC	2003
Glencoffe Johnson IBF	2004–05
Fabrice Tiozzo WBA	2004–
Antonio Tarver* WBC	2004–05
Clinton Woods IBF	2005–
Tomasz Adamek WBC	2005–

Super Middleweights
(Weight Limit: 168 pounds)

Champion	Reign
Murray Sutherland* IBF	1984
Chong-Pal Park* IBF	1984–87
Chong-Pal Park* WBA	1987–88
G. Rocchigiani IBF	1988–89
F. Obelmejias* WBA	1988–89
Sugar Ray Leonard WBC	1988–90†
In-Chul Baek* WBA	1989–90
Lindell Holmes IBF	1990–91
Chris Tiozzo* WBA	1990–91
Mauro Galvano WBC	1990–92
Victor Cordova* WBA	1991
Darrin Van Horn IBF	1991–92
Iran Barkley IBF	1992
Nigel Benn WBC	1992–96

Champion	Reign
James Toney IBF	1992–94
Michael Nunn* WBA	1992–94
Steve Little* WBA	1994
Frank Liles* WBA	1994–99
Roy Jones Jr. IBF	1994–96
Thulane Malinga WBC	1996
V. Nardiello WBC	1996
Robin Reid WBC	1996–97
Charles Brewer IBF	1997–98
Thulane Malinga WBC	1997–98
Richie Woodhall WBC	1998–99
Sven Ottke IBF	1998–03
Byron Mitchell* WBA	1999–00
Markus Beyer WBC	1999–00

Champion	Reign
Bruno Girard* WBA	2000–01†
Glenn Catley WBC	2000–01
Eric Lucas WBC	2000–03
Byron Mitchell WBA	2000–03
Sven Ottke IBF	2003†
Anthony Mundine WBA	2003
Markus Beyer WBC	2003–
Sven Ottke IBF	2003–05
Cristian Sanavia WBC	2004–05
Manny Siaca, WBA	2004–05
Mikel Kessler WBA	2005–
Markus Beyer WBC	2004–
Jeff Lacy IBF	2005
Joe Calzaghe IBF	2006–

Middleweights
(Weight Limit: 160 pounds)

Champion	Reign
Jack Dempsey*	1884–91
Bob Fitzsimmons*	1891–97†
Kid McCoy*	1897–98
Tommy Ryan*	1898–07†
Stanley Ketchel*	1908
Billy Papke*	1908
Stanley Ketchel*	1908–10†
Frank Klaus*	1913
George Chip*	1913–14
Al McCoy*	1914–17
Mike O'Dowd*	1917–20
Johnny Wilson*	1920–23
Harry Greb*	1923–26
Tiger Flowers*	1926
Mickey Walker*	1926–31†
Gorilla Jones*	1931–32
Marcel Thil*	1932–37
Fred Apostoli*	1937–39
Al Hostak NBA	1938

Champion	Reign
Solly Krieger NBA	1938–39
Al Hostak NBA	1939–40
Ceferino Garcia*	1939–40
Ken Overlin*	1940–41
Tony Zale NBA	1940–41
Billy Soose*	1941
Tony Zale*	1941–47
Rocky Graziano*	1947–48
Tony Zale*	1948
Marcel Cerdan*	1948–49
Jake La Motta*	1949–51
Sugar Ray Robinson*	1951
Randy Turpin*	1951
Sugar Ray Robinson*	1951–52†
Bobo Olson*	1953–55
Sugar Ray Robinson*	1955–57
Gene Fullmer*	1957
Sugar Ray Robinson*	1957
Carmen Basilio*	1957–58

Champion	Reign
Sugar Ray Robinson*	1958–60
Gene Fullmer NBA	1959–62
Paul Pender*	1960–61
Terry Downes*	1961–62
Paul Pender*	1962–63†
Dick Tiger WBA	1962–63
Dick Tiger*	1963
Joey Giardello*	1963–65
Dick Tiger*	1965–66
Emile Griffith*	1966–67
Nino Benvenuti*	1967
Emile Griffith*	1967–68
Nino Benvenuti*	1968–70
Carlos Monzon*	1970–77†
Rodrigo Valdez WBC	1974–76
Rodrigo Valdez*	1977–78
Hugo Corro*	1978–79
Vito Antuofermo*	1979–80
Alan Minter*	1980

*Lineal champion. †Champion retired or relinquished title.

Middleweights *(Cont.)*

Champion	Reign
Marvin Hagler*	1980–87
Sugar Ray Leonard*	1987†
Frank Tate IBF	1987–88
Sumbu Kalambay WBA	1987–89
Thomas Hearns* WBC	1987–88
Iran Barkley* WBC	1988–89
Michael Nunn IBF	1988–91
Roberto Duran* WBC	1989–90†
Michael Nunn* IBF	1991
Mike McCallum WBA	1989–91
Julian Jackson WBC	1990–93

Champion	Reign
James Toney* IBF	1991–93†
Reggie Johnson WBA	1992–94
Roy Jones Jr.* IBF	1993–95†
G. McClellan WBC	1993–95†
Jorge Castro WBA	1994–95
Shinji Takehara WBA	1995–96
Jullian Jackson WBC	1995
Quincy Taylor WBC	1995–96
Bernard Hopkins* IBF	1994–
Keith Holmes WBC	1996–98
William Joppy WBA	1996–97
J.C. Green WBA	1997

Champion	Reign
William Joppy WBA	1998–01
Hassine Cherifi WBC	1998–99
Keith Holmes WBC	1999–00
Felix Trinidad WBA	2001
William Joppy WBA	2001–03
Bernard Hopkins* WBC/IBF	2001–05
Bernard Hopkins WBA	2003–05
Jermain Taylor WBA/WBC	2005–
Jermain Taylor IBF	2005
Arthur Abraham IBF	2005–

Junior Middleweights
(Weight Limit: 154 pounds)

Champion	Reign
Emile Griffith (EBU)	1962–63
Dennis Moyer*	1962–63
Ralph Dupas*	1963
Sandro Mazzinghi*	1963–65
Nino Benvenuti*	1965–66
Ki-Soo Kim*	1966–68
Sandro Mazzinghi*	1968
Freddie Little*	1969–70
Carmelo Bossi*	1970–71
Koichi Wajima*	1971–74
Oscar Albarado*	1974–75
Koichi Wajima*	1975
Miguel de Oliveira WBC	1975–76
Jae-Do Yuh*	1975–76
Elisha Obed WBC	1975–76
Koichi Wajima*	1976
Jose Duran*	1976
Eckhard Dagge WBC	1976–77
Miguel Angel Castellini*	1976–77
Eddie Gazo*	1977–78
Rocky Mattioli WBC	1977–79
Masashi Kudo*	1978–79
Maurice Hope WBC	1979–81
Ayub Kalule*	1979–81
Wilfred Benitez WBC	1981–82
Sugar Ray Leonard*	1981–82†
Tadashi Mihara WBA	1981–82
Davey Moore WBA	1982–83

Champion	Reign
Thomas Hearns* WBC	1982–84
Roberto Duran WBA	1983–84
Mark Medal IBF	1984
Thomas Hearns*	1984–86†
Mike McCallum* WBA	1984–87†
Carlos Santos IBF	1984–86
Buster Drayton IBF	1986–87
Duane Thomas WBC	1986–87
Matthew Hilton IBF	1987–88
Lupe Aquino WBC	1987
Gianfranco Rosi WBC	1987–88
Julian Jackson WBA	1987–90
Donald Curry WBC	1988–89
Robert Hines IBF	1988–89
Darrin Van Horn IBF	1989
Rene Jacquot WBC	1989
John Mugabi* WBC	1989–90
Gianfranco Rosi IBF	1989–94
Terry Norris* WBC	1990–93
Gilbert Dele WBA	1991
Vinny Pazienza WBA	1991–92
Julio C. Vasquez WBA	1992–95
Simon Brown* WBC	1993–94
Terry Norris* WBC	1994
Luis Santana* WBC	1995–95
Vincent Pettway IBF	1994–95
Paul Vaden IBF	1995
Carl Daniels WBA	1995

Champion	Reign
Terry Norris* WBC	1995–97
Terry Norris* IBF	1995–96†
L. Boudouani WBA	1996–99
Raul Marquez IBF	1997
Keith Mullings* WBC	1997–99
Yori Boy Campas IBF	1997–98
Fernando Vargas IBF	1998–00
F. Javier Castillejo* WBC	1999–01
David Reid WBA	1999–00
Felix Trinidad WBA	2000–01
Felix Trinidad WBA, IBF	2001†
Oscar De La Hoya* WBC	2001–03
Fernando Vargas WBA	2001–02
Ronald Wright IBF†	2001–04
Oscar De La Hoya* WBC/WBA	2002–03
Shane Mosley* WBC	2003–04
Alejandro Garcia WBA	2003–05
Ronald Wright WBA, WBC	2004–05
Verno Phillips IBF	2004–05
Ricardo Mayora WBC	2005–06
Alex T. Garcia WBA	2005–06
Roman Karmazin IBF	2005–06
Jose A. Rivera WBA	2006–
Oscar De La Hoya WBC	2006–
Cory Spinks IBF	2006–

Welterweights
(Weight Limit: 147 pounds)

Champion	Reign
Paddy Duffy*	1888–90†
Mysterious Billy Smith*	1892–94
Tommy Ryan*	1894–98†
Mysterious Billy Smith*	1898–1900
Rube Ferns*	1900
Matty Matthews*	1900–01
Rube Ferns*	1901
Joe Walcott*	1901–04
The Dixie Kid*	1904–05†
Honey Mellody*	1906–07
Mike Sullivan*	1907–08†
Jimmy Gardner*	1908†
Jimmy Clabby*	1910–1†

Champion	Reign
Waldemar Holberg*	1914
Tom McCormick*	1914
Matt Wells*	1914–15
Mike Glover*	1915
Jack Britton*	1915
Ted "Kid" Lewis*	1915–16
Jack Britton*	1916–17
Ted "Kid" Lewis*	1917–19
Jack Britton*	1919–22
Mickey Walker*	1922–26
Pete Latzo*	1926–27
Joe Dundee*	1927–29
Jackie Fields*	1929–30

Champion	Reign
Young Jack Thompson*	1930
Tommy Freeman*	1930–31
Young Jack Thompson*	1931
Lou Brouillard*	1931–32
Jackie Fields*	1932–33
Young Corbett III*	1933
Jimmy McLarnin*	1933–34
Barney Ross*	1934
Jimmy McLarnin*	1934–35
Barney Ross*	1935–38
Henry Armstrong*	1938–40
Fritzie Zivic*	1940–41
Red Cochrane*	1941–46

*Lineal champion.
†Champion relinquished title to retire or switch weight classes, or had title stripped by boxing organization.

Welterweights *(Cont.)*

Champion	Reign
Marty Servo*	1946
Sugar Ray Robinson*	1946–51†
Johnny Bratton	1951
Kid Gavilan*	1951–54
Johnny Saxton*	1954–55
Tony DeMarco*	1955
Carmen Basilio*	1955–56
Johnny Saxton*	1956
Carmen Basilio*	1956–57†
Virgil Akins*	1958
Don Jordan*	1958–60
Kid Paret*	1960–61
Emile Griffith*	1961
Kid Paret*	1961–62
Emile Griffith*	1962–63
Luis Rodriguez*	1963
Emile Griffith*	1963–66†
Curtis Cokes*	1966–69
Jose Napoles*	1969–70
Billy Backus*	1970–71
Jose Napoles*	1971–75
Hedgemon Lewis NY	1972–73
Angel Espada WBA	1975–76
John H. Stracey*	1975–76

Champion	Reign
Carlos Palomino*	1976–79
Pipino Cuevas*	1976–80
Wilfredo Benitez*	1979
Sugar Ray Leonard*	1979–80
Roberto Duran*	1980
Thomas Hearns WBA	1980–81
Sugar Ray Leonard*	1980–82†
Donald Curry* WBA	1983–85
Milton McCrory WBC	1983–85
Donald Curry*	1985–86
Lloyd Honeyghan*	1986–87
Jorge Vaca* WBC	1987–88
Lloyd Honeyghan* WBC	1988–89
Mark Breland WBA	1987
Marlon Starling WBA	1987–88
Tomas Molinares WBA	1988–89
Simon Brown IBF	1988–91
Mark Breland WBA	1989–90
Marlon Starling* WBC	1989–90
Aaron Davis WBA	1990–91
Maurice Blocker* WBC	1990–91
Meldrick Taylor WBA	1991–92
Simon Brown* WBC	1991
Buddy McGirt* WBC	1991–93

Champion	Reign
Felix Trinidad IBF	1993–00
Pernell Whitaker* WBC	1993–97
Crisanto Espana WBA	1992–94
Ike Quartey WBA	1994–97†
Oscar De La Hoya* WBC	1997–99
James Page WBA	1998–01
Felix Trinidad* IBF, WBC	1999–00†
Shane Mosley* WBC	2000–02
Andrew Lewis WBA	2001–02
Vernon Forrest IBF	2001
Vernon Forrest* WBC	2001–03
Ricardo Mayorga WBA	2002
Ricardo Mayorga* WBC	2003–05
Michele Piccirillo IBF	2002–03
Jose Rivera WBA	2003
Cory Spinks IBF, WBC, WBA	2003–05
Zab Judah WBA/WBC/IBF	2005–06
Luis Collazo WBA	2006
Ricky Hatton WBA	2006–
Carlos Baldomir WBC	2006–
F. Mayweather, Jr. IBF	2006

Super Lightweights
(Weight Limit: 140 pounds)

Champion	Reign
Pinkey Mitchell*	1922–25
Red Herring	1925
Mushy Callahan*	1926–30
Jack (Kid) Berg*	1930–31
Tony Canzoneri*	1931–32
Johnny Jadick*	1932–33
Sammy Fuller	1932–33
Battling Shaw*	1933
Tony Canzoneri*	1933
Barney Ross*	1933–35†
Tippy Larkin*	1946
Carlos Ortiz*	1959–60
Duilio Loi*	1960–62
Eddie Perkins*	1962
Duilio Loi*	1962–63†
Roberto Cruz WBA	1963
Eddie Perkins*	1963–65
Carlos Hernandez*	1965–66
Sandro Lopopolo*	1966–67
Paul Fujii*	1967–68
Nicolino Loche*	1968–72
Pedro Adigue WBC	1968–70
Bruno Arcari WBC	1970–74
Alfonso Frazer*	1972
Antonio Cervantes*	1972–76
Perico Fernandez WBC	1974–75
S. Muangsurin WBC	1975–76
Wilfred Benitez*	1976–79†
M. Velasquez WBC	1976

Champion	Reign
S. Muangsurin WBC	1976–78
A. Cervantes WBA	1977–80
Sang-Hyun Kim WBC	1978–80
Saoul Mamby WBC	1980–82
Aaron Pryor* WBA	1980–83
Leroy Haley WBC	1982–83
Aaron Pryor* IBF	1983–85†
Bruce Curry WBC	1983–84
Johnny Bumphus WBA	1984
Bill Costello WBC	1984–85
Gene Hatcher WBA	1984–85
Ubaldo Sacco WBA	1985–86
Lonnie Smith* WBC	1985–86
Patrizio Oliva WBA	1986–87
Gary Hinton IBF	1986
Rene Arredondo* WBC	1986
Tsuyoshi Hamada WBC	1986–87
Joe Louis Manley IBF	1986–87
Terry Marsh IBF	1987
Juan Coggi WBA	1987–90
Rene Arredondo WBC	1987
R. Mayweather* WBC	1987–89
James McGirt IBF	1988
Meldrick Taylor IBF	1988–90
Julio César Chávez* WBC	1989–94
Julio César Chávez* IBF	1990–91
Loreto Garza WBA	1990–91
Juan Coggi WBA	1991
Edwin Rosario WBA	1991–92

Champion	Reign
Rafael Pineda IBF	1991–92
Akinobu Hiranaka WBA	1992
Pernell Whitaker IBF	1992–93†
Charles Murray IBF	1993–94
Jake Rodriguez IBF	1994–95
Juan Coggi WBA	1993–94
Frankie Randall* WBC	1994
Frankie Randall WBA	1994–96
Juan Coggi WBA	1996
Julio César Chávez* WBC	1994–96
Kostya Tszyu IBF	1995–97
Frankie Randall WBA	1996–97
Oscar De La Hoya* WBC	1996–97†
Khalid Rahilou WBA	1997–98
Vincent Phillips* IBF	1997–99
Sharmba Mitchell WBA	1998–01
Kostya Tszyu WBC	1998–
Terronn Millett* IBF	1999–00
Zab Judah* IBF	2000–01
Kostya Tszyu*† WBA/WBC	2001–05
Kostya Tszyu* IBF	2003–05
Vivian Harris WBA	2003–05
Arturo Gatti WBC	2004–05
F. Mayweather Jr. WBC	2005–06
Carlos Maussa WBA	2005–06
Ricky Hatton IBF	2005–06
Souleymane M'baye WBA	2006–
Juan Urango IBF	2006–

Lightweights
(Weight Limit: 135 pounds)

Champion	Reign
Jack McAuliffe*	1886–94†
Kid Lavigne*	1896–99
Frank Erne*	1899–1902
Joe Gans*	1902–04
Jimmy Britt*	1904–05
Battling Nelson*	1905–06

Champion	Reign
Joe Gans*	1906–08
Battling Nelson*	1908–10
Ad Wolgast*	1910–12
Willie Ritchie*	1912–14
Freddie Welsh*	1915–17
Benny Leonard*	1917–25†

Champion	Reign
Jimmy Goodrich*	1925
Rocky Kansas*	1925–26
Sammy Mandell*	1926–30
Al Singer*	1930
Tony Canzoneri*	1930–33
Barney Ross*	1933–35†

Lightweights *(Cont.)*

Champion	Reign
Tony Canzoneri*	1935–36
Lou Ambers*	1936–38
Henry Armstrong*	1938–39
Lou Ambers*	1939–40
Sammy Angott NBA	1940–41
Lew Jenkins*	1940–41
Sammy Angott*	1941–42†
Beau Jack* NY	1942–43
Bob Montgomery* NY	1943
Sammy Angott NBA	1943–44
Beau Jack* NY	1943–44
Bob Montgomery* NY	1944–47
Juan Zurita NBA	1944–45
Ike Williams*	1947–51
James Carter*	1951–52
Lauro Salas*	1952
James Carter*	1952–54
Paddy DeMarco*	1954
James Carter*	1954–55
Wallace Smith*	1955–56
Joe Brown*	1956–62
Carlos Ortiz	1962–65
Ismael Laguna*	1965
Carlos Ortiz*	1965–68
Carlos Teo Cruz*	1968–69
Mando Ramos*	1969–70
Ismael Laguna*	1970
Ken Buchanan*	1970–72
Roberto Duran*	1972–79†
Chango Carmona WBC	1972
Rodolfo Gonzalez WBC	1972–74
Ishimatsu Suzuki WBC	1974–76

Champion	Reign
Estaban DeJesus WBC	1976–78
Jim Watt WBC*	1979–81
Ernesto Espana WBA	1979–80
Hilmer Kenty WBA	1980–81
Sean O'Grady WBA	1981
Claude Noel WBA	1981
Alexis Arguello* WBC	1981–82†
Arturo Frias WBA	1981–82
Ray Mancini* WBA	1982–84
Alexis Arguello	1982–83
Edwin Rosario WBC	1983–84
Choo Choo Brown IBF	1984
L. Bramble* WBA	1984–86
Jose Luis Ramirez WBC	1984–85
Harry Arroyo IBF	1984–85
Jimmy Paul IBF	1985–86
Hector Camacho WBC	1985–86
Greg Haugen IBF	1986–87
Edwin Rosario* WBA	1986–87
Julio César Chávez WBA	1987–88
Jose Luis Ramirez WBC	1987–88
Julio César Chávez*	1988–89†
Vinny Pazienza IBF	1987–88
Greg Haugen IBF	1988–89
P. Whitaker* WBC, IBF	1989–90
Edwin Rosario WBA	1989–90
Juan Nazario WBA	1990
P. Whitaker* WBA, WBC	1990–92†
Pernell Whitaker* IBF	1991–92†
Julio César Chávez IBF	1990–91
Edwin Rosario WBA	1991–92
Julio César Chávez WBA	1990–92

Champion	Reign
Miguel Gonzalez WBC	1992–95
Joey Gamache WBA	1992–93
Dingaan Thobela WBA	1993
Fred Pendleton* IBF	1993–94
Orzubek Nazarov WBA	1993–98
Rafael Ruelas* IBF	1994–95
Oscar De La Hoya* IBF	1995†
Phillip Holiday IBF	1995–97
Jean B. Mendy* WBC	1996–97
Steve Johnston* WBC	1997–98
Shane Mosley IBF	1997–99†
Jean B. Mendy WBC	1998–99
Cesar Bazan* WBC	1998–99
Steve Johnston* WBC	1999–00
Julien Lorcy WBA	1999
Stefano Zoff WBA	1999
Paul Spadafora IBF	1999–03
Gilbert Serrano WBA	1999–00
T. Hatakeyama WBA	2000–01
Jose Luis Castillo* WBC	2000–02
Julien Lorcy WBA	2001
Raul Balbi WBA	2001
F. Mayweather* WBC	2002–03
Leonard Dorin WBA	2002–03
Javier Jauregui IBF	2003–04
Julio Diaz IBF	2004–05
Lakva Sim WBA	2004
Juan Diaz WBA	2004–
Jose Luis Castillo WBC	2004–05
Diego Corrales WBC	2005–
Jesus Chavez IBF	2005–

Super Featherweights
(Weight Limit: 130 pounds)

Champion	Reign
Johnny Dundee*	1921–23
Jack Bernstein*	1923
Johnny Dundee*	1923–24
Steve (Kid) Sullivan*	1924–25
Mike Ballerino*	1925
Tod Morgan*	1925–29
Benny Bass*	1929–31
Kid Chocolate*	1931–33
Frankie Klick*	1933–34†
Sandy Saddler*	1949–50†
Harold Gomes*	1959–60
Gabriel (Flash) Elorde*	1960–67
Yoshiaki Numata*	1967
Hiroshi Kobayashi*	1967–71
Rene Barrientos WBC	1969–70
Yoshiaki Numata WBC	1970–71
Alfredo Marcano*	1971–72
R. Arredondo WBC	1971–74
Ben Villaflor*	1972–73
Kuniaki Shibata*	1973
Ben Villaflor*	1973–76
Kuniaki Shibata WBC	1974–75
Alfredo Escalera WBC	1975–78
Samuel Serrano*	1976–80
Alexis Arguello WBC	1978–80
Yasutsune Uehara*	1980–81
Rafael Limon WBC	1980–81

Champion	Reign
C. Boza-Edwards WBC	1981
Samuel Serrano*	1981–83
R. Navarrete WBC	1981–82
Rafael Limon WBC	1982
Bobby Chacon WBC	1982–83
Roger Mayweather*	1983–84
Hector Camacho WBC	1983–84
Rocky Lockridge*	1984–85
Hwan-Kil Yuh IBF	1984–85
Julio César Chávez WBC	1984–87
Lester Ellis IBF	1985
Wilfredo Gomez*	1985–86
Barry Michael IBF	1985–87
Alfredo Layne* WBA	1986
Brian Mitchell* WBA	1986–91†
Rocky Lockridge IBF	1987–88
Azumah Nelson* WBC	1988–94
Tony Lopez IBF	1988–89
Juan Molina IBF	1989–90
Tony Lopez IBF	1990–91
Joey Gamache WBA	1991
Brian Mitchell IBF	1991
Genaro Hernandez WBA	1991–95
James Leija* WBC	1994
Juan Molina IBF	1991–95
Gabriel Ruelas* WBC	1994–95
Eddie Hopson IBF	1995

Champion	Reign
Tracy Patterson IBF	1995
Azumah Nelson* WBC	1995–97
Choi Yong-Soo WBA	1995–98
Arturo Gatti IBF	1995–98†
Genaro Hernandez* WBC	1997–98
Roberto Garcia IBF	1998–99
Floyd Mayweather* WBC	1998–01†
T. Hatakeyama WBA	1998–99
Lakva Sim WBA	1999
Diego Corrales IBF	1999–01
Jong Kwon Baek WBA	1999–00
Joel Casamayor WBA	2000–02
Steve Forbes IBF	2000–02†
Acelino Freitas* WBA	2002–04
Y. Nantachai WBA	2002–05
S. Singmanassak WBC	2002–03
Jesus Chavez WBC	2003–04
Carlos Hernandez IBF	2003–04
Erik Morales WBC/IBF	2004–05
Erik Morales IBF	2004–05
Marco A. Barrera WBC	2005–
Vicente Mosquera WBA	2005–06
Robbie Peden, IBF	2005
Marco A. Barrera, IBF	2005–06
Cassius Baloyi, IBF	2006
Edwin Valero, WBA	2006–
Gairy St. Clair IBF	2006–

Featherweights
(Weight Limit: 126 pounds)

Champion	Reign
Torpedo Billy Murphy*	1890
Young Griffo*	1890–92†
George Dixon*	1892–97
Solly Smith*	1897–98
Dave Sullivan*	1898
George Dixon*	1898–1900
Terry McGovern*	1900–01
Young Corbett II*	1901–03†
Abe Attell*	1903–04
Tommy Sullivan*	1904–05†
Abe Attell*	1906–12
Johnny Kilbane*	1912–23
Eugene Criqui*	1923
Johnny Dundee*	1923–24†
"Kid" Kaplan*	1925–26†
Tony Canzoneri*	1927–28
Andre Routis*	1928–29
Battling Battalino*	1929–32†
Tommy Paul NBA	1932–33
Kid Chocolate NY	1932–33†
Freddie Miller NBA	1933–36
Mike Beloise NY	1936–37
Petey Sarron NBA	1936–37
Maurice Holtzer	1937–38
Henry Armstrong*	1937–38†
Joey Archibald* NY	1938–39
Leo Rodak NBA	1938–39
Joey Archibald	1939–40
Petey Scalzo NBA	1940–41
Harry Jeffra*	1940–41
Joey Archibald*	1941
Richie Lamos NBA	1941
Chalky Wright*	1941–42
Jackie Wilson NBA	1941–43
Willie Pep*	1942–48
Jackie Callura NBA	1943
Phil Terranova NBA	1943–44
Sal Bartolo NBA	1944–46
Sandy Saddler*	1948–49
Willie Pep*	1949–50

Champion	Reign
Sandy Saddler*	1950–57†
Kid Bassey*	1957–59
Davey Moore*	1959–63
Sugar Ramos*	1963–64
Vicente Saldivar*	1964–67†
Paul Rojas WBA	1968
Jose Legra WBC	1968–69
Shozo Saijyo WBA	1968–71
J. Famechon* WBC	1969–70
Vicente Saldivar* WBC	1970
Kuniaki Shibata* WBC	1970–72
Antonio Gomez WBA	1971–72
C. Sanchez* WBC	1972
Ernesto Marcel WBA	1972–74
Jose Legra* WBC	1972–73
Eder Jofre* WBC	1973–74†
Ruben Olivares WBA	1974
Bobby Chacon WBC	1974–75
Alexis Arguello* WBA	1974–76†
Ruben Olivares WBA	1975
Poison Kotey WBC	1975–76
Danny Lopez* WBC	1976–80
Rafael Ortega WBA	1977
Cecilio Lastra WBA	1977–78
Eusebio Pedroza* WBA	1978–85
S. Sanchez* WBC	1980–82†
Juan LaPorte WBC	1982–84
Wilfredo Gomez WBC	1984
Min-Keun Oh IBF	1984–85
Azumah Nelson WBC	1984–88
Barry McGuigan* WBA	1985–86
Ki Young Chung IBF	1985–86
Steve Cruz* WBA	1986–87
Antonio Rivera IBF	1986–88
A. Esparragoza* WBA	1987–91
Calvin Grove IBF	1988
Jorge Paez IBF	1988–91
Jeff Fenech WBC	1988–90†
Marcos Villasana WBC	1990–91
Paul Hodkinson WBC	1991–93

Champion	Reign
Troy Dorsey IBF	1991
Manuel Medina IBF	1991–93
Yung Kyun Park* WBA	1991–93
Gregorio Vargas WBC	1993
Tom Johnson IBF	1993–97†
Eloy Rojas* WBA	1993–96
Kevin Kelley WBC	1993–95
A. Gonzalez WBC	1995
Manuel Medina WBC	1995–95
Luisito Espinosa WBC	1995–99
Wilfredo Vazquez* WBA	1996–98
Hector Lizarraga IBF	1997–98
Naseem Hamed* WBA	1998†
Naseem Hamed*	1998–01
Freddy Norwood WBA	1998
Manuel Medina IBF	1998–99
Antonio Cermeno WBA	1998–99
Cesar Soto WBC	1999
Freddy Norwood WBA	1999
Naseem Hamed* WBC	1999†
Paul Ingle IBF	1999–00
Guty Espadas WBC	2000–01
Erik Morales WBC	2000–02
Derrick Gainer WBA	2000–03
Mbulelo Botile IBF	2001
Frankie Toledo IBF	2001
Manuel Medina IBF	2001–02
Marco A. Barrera* WBA/WBC	2001–03
Johnny Tapia IBF	2002
Marco A. Barrera* WBC	2002†
Erik Morales WBC	2002–03
Juan Marquez IBF	2003–06
Chris John WBA	2005–
In Jin Chi WBC	2004–06
Valdemir Pereira, IBF	2006
Eric Aiken IBF	2006
T. Koshimoto, WBC	2006
Rudolfo Lopez WBC	2006–
Robert Guerrero IBF	2006–

Super Bantamweights
(Weight Limit: 122 pounds)

Champion	Reign
Jack (Kid) Wolfe*	1922–23
Carl Duane*	1923–24
Rigoberto Riasco* WBC	1976
R. Kobayashi* WBC	1976
Dong-Kyun Yum* WBC	1976–77
Wilfredo Gomez* WBC	1977–83†
Soo-Hwan Hong WBA	1977–78
Ricardo Cardona WBA	1978–80
Leo Randolph WBA	1980
Sergio Palma WBA	1980–82
Leonardo Cruz WBA	1982–84
Jaime Garza* WBC	1983
Bobby Berna IBF	1983–84
Loris Stecca WBA	1984
Seung-Il Suh IBF	1984–85
Victor Callejas WBA	1984–86
Juan Meza* WBC	1984–85
Ji-Won Kim IBF	1985–86
Lupe Pintor* WBC	1985–86
S. Payakaroon* WBC	1986–87
Seung-Hoon Lee IBF	1987–88

Champion	Reign
Louie Espinoza WBA	1987
Jeff Fenech* WBC	1987†
Julio Gervacio WBA	1987–88
Daniel Zaragoza* WBC	1988–90
Jose Sanabria IBF	1988–89
B. Pinango WBA	1988
J.J. Estrada WBA	1988–89
Fabrice Benichou IBF	1989–90
Jesus Salud WBA	1989–90
Welcome Ncita IBF	1990–92
Paul Banke* WBC	1990
Luis Mendoza WBA	1990–91
Raul Perez WBA	1992
Pedro Decima* WBC	1990–91
K. Hatanaka* WBC	1991
Daniel Zaragoza* WBC	1991–92
Thiery Jacob* WBC	1992
Tracy Patterson* WBC	1992–94
Kennedy McKinney IBF	1993–94
Wilfredo Vasquez WBA	1992–95
Vuyani Bungu IBF	1994–99†

Champion	Reign
H. Acero* Sanchez WBC	1994–95
Antonio Cermeno WBA	1995–98†
Daniel Zaragoza* WBC	1995–97
Erik Morales* WBC	1997–00†
Enrique Sanchez WBA	1998
Nestor Garza WBA	1998–00
Benedict Ledwaba IBF	1999–01
Clarence Adams WBA	2000–01†
Willie Jorrin WBC	2000–02
Manny Pacquiao IBF	2001–04
Yober Ortega WBA	2001–02
Y. Sithyodthong WBA	2002
Osamu Sato WBA	2002
Salim Medjkoune WBA	2002–03
Mahyar Monshipour WBA	2003–06
Oscar Larios WBC	2002–05
Israel Vazquez IBF	2004–05
S. Sithchatchawal WBA	2006–
Israel Vazquez WBC	2005–

*Lineal champion.
†Champion relinquished title to retire or switch weight classes, or had title stripped by boxing organization.

Bantamweights
(Weight Limit: 118 pounds)

Champion	Reign	Champion	Reign	Champion	Reign
Spider Kelly	1887	Lou Salica*	1940–42	W. Vasquez WBA	1987–88
Hughey Boyle	1887–88	Manuel Ortiz*	1942–47	Kevin Seabrooks* IBF	1987–88
Spider Kelly	1889	Harold Dade*	1947	Kaokor Galaxy WBA	1988
Chappie Moran	1889–90	Manuel Ortiz*	1947–50	Moon Sung-Kil WBA	1988–89
George Dixon	1890–91	Vic Toweel*	1950–52	Kaokor Galaxy WBA	1989
Pedlar Palmer	1895–99	Jimmy Carruthers*	1952–54†	Raul Perez WBC	1988–91
Terry McGovern*	1899–00†	Robert Cohen*	1954–56	O. Canizales* IBF	1988–95†
Harry Harris	1901	Paul Macias NBA	1955–57	Luisito Espinosa WBA	1989–91
Harry Forbes*	1901–03	Mario D'Agata*	1956–57	Israel Contreras WBA	1991–92
Frankie Neil*	1903–04	Alphonse Halimi*	1957–59	Eddie Cook WBA	1992–93
Joe Bowker*	1904–05†	Joe Becerra*	1959–60†	Greg Richardson WBC	1991
Jimmy Walsh*	1905–06†	Eder Jofre*	1961–65	J. Tatsuyoshi, WBC	1991–92
Owen Moran	1907–08	Fighting Harada*	1965–68	Victor Rabanales WBC	1992–93
Monte Attell	1909–10	Lionel Rose*	1968–69	Jung-Il Byun WBC	1993
Frankie Conley	1910–11	Ruben Olivares*	1969–70	Jorge Julio WBA	1993
Johnny Coulon*	1910–14	Chucho Castillo*	1970–71	Yasuei Yakushiji WBC	1993–95
Kid Williams*	1914–17	Ruben Olivares*	1971–72	Junior Jones WBA	1994
Kewpie Ertle	1915	Rafael Herrera*	1972	John M. Johnson WBA	1994
Pete Herman*	1917–20	Enrique Pinder*	1972–73	D. Chuvatana WBA	1994–95
Joe Lynch*	1920–21	Romeo Anaya*	1973	V. Sahaprom* WBA	1995–96
Pete Herman*	1921	Arnold Taylor*	1973–74	W. McCullough WBC	1995–96
Johnny Buff*	1921–22	Rafael Herrera WBC	1973–74	Harold Mestre IBF	1995
Joe Lynch*	1922–24	Soo-Hwan Hong*	1974–75	Mbulelo Botile IBF	1995–97
Abe Goldstein*	1924	Rodolfo Martinez WBC	1974–76	Nana Konadu* WBA	1996–98
Cannonball Martin*	1924–25	Alfonso Zamora*	1975–77	S. Singmanassak WBC	1996–97
Phil Rosenberg*	1925–27†	Carlos Zarate* WBC	1976–79	Tim Austin IBF	1997–03
Bud Taylor NBA	1927–28	Jorge Lujan	1977–80	J.Tatsuyoshi WBC	1997–98
Bushy Graham NY	1928–29	Lupe Pintor* WBC	1979–83†	Johnny Tapia* WBA	1998–99
Panama Al Brown*	1929–35	Julian Solis	1980	V. Sahaprom* WBC	1998–05
Sixto Escobar NBA	1934–35	Jeff Chandler*	1980–84	Paulie Ayala* WBA	1999–01†
Baltazar Sangchilli*	1935–36	Albert Davila WBC	1983–85	Eidy Moya WBA	2001–02
Lou Salica NBA	1935	Richard Sandoval*	1984–86	Johnny Bredahl WBA	2002–05
Sixto Escobar NBA	1935–36	Satoshi Shingaki IBF	1984–85	Rafael Marquez IBF	2003–
Tony Marino*	1936	Jeff Fenech IBF	1985	H. Hasegawa WBC	2005–
Sixto Escobar*	1936–37	Daniel Zaragoza WBC	1985	W. Sidorenko WBA	2005–
Harry Jeffra*	1937–38	Miguel Lora WBC	1985–88		
Sixto Escobar*	1938–39†	Gaby Canizales*	1986		
Georgie Pace NBA	1939–40	Bernardo Pinango*	1986–87†		

Super Flyweights
(Weight Limit: 115 pounds)

Champion	Reign	Champion	Reign	Champion	Reign
Rafael Orono* WBC	1980–81	Giberto Roman* WBC	1988–89	Satoshi Iida WBA	1997–98
Chul-Ho Kim* WBC	1981–82	Juan Polo Perez IBF	1989–90	In-Joo Cho* WBC	1998–00
Gustavo Ballas WBA	1981	Nana Konadu* WBC	1989–90	Jesus Rojas WBA	1998–99
Rafael Pedroza WBA	1981–82	Sung-Kil Moon* WBC	1990–93	Mark Johnson IBF	1999–00
Jiro Watanabe WBA	1982–84	Robert Quiroga IBF	1990–93	Hideki Todaka WBA	1999–00
Rafael Orono* WBC	1982–83	Julio Borboa IBF	1993–94	Felix Machado IBF	2000–03
Payao Poontarat* WBC	1983–84	Katsuya Onizuka WBA	1993–94	M. Tokuyama* WBC	2000–04
Joo-Do Chun IBF	1983–85	Lee Hyung-Chul WBA	1994–95	Leo Gamez WBA	2000–01
Jiro Watanabe*	1984–86	Jose Luis Bueno* WBC	1993–94	Celes Kobayashi WBA	2001–02
Kaosai Galaxy WBA	1984	H. Kawashima* WBC	1994–97	Alexander Munoz WBA	2002–05
Ellyas Pica IBF	1985–86	Harold Grey IBF	1994–95	Luis Alberto Perez IBF	2003–
Cesar Polanco IBF	1986	Alimi Goitia WBA	1995–96	Katsushige Kawashima	
Gilberto Roman* WBC	1986–87	Yokthai Sith-Oar WBA	1996–97	WBC	2004–05
Ellyas Pical IBF	1986	Carlos Salazar IBF	1995–96	M. Tokuyama* WBC	2005–
Santos Laciar* WBC	1987	Harold Grey IBF	1996	Jose M. Castillo WBA	2005–06
Tae-Il Chang IBF	1987	Danny Romero IBF	1996–97	Nobuo Nashiro WBA	2006–
Sugar Rojas* WBC	1987–88	Gerry Penalosa* WBC	1997–98		
Ellyas Pical IBF	1987–89	Johnny Tapia IBF	1997–99†		

*Lineal champion.
†Champion relinquished title to retire or switch weight classes, or had title stripped by boxing organization.

Flyweights
(Weight Limit: 112 pounds)

Champion	Reign	Champion	Reign	Champion	Reign
Sid Smith*	1913	Chartchai Chionoi*	1970	Bi-Won Chung IBF	1986
Bill Ladbury*	1913–14	B. Chartvanchai WBA	1970	Hi-Sup Shin IBF	1986–87
Percy Jones*	1914†	Masao Ohba WBA	1970–73	Dodie Penalosa IBF	1987
Joe Symonds*	1914–16	Erbito Salavarria*	1970–73†	Fidel Bassa WBA	1987–89
Jimmy Wilde*	1916–23	B. Gonzalez WBA	1972	Choi-Chang Ho IBF	1987–88
Pancho Villa*	1923–25†	V. Borkorsor WBC	1972–73†	Rolando Bohol IBF	1988
Fidel La Barba*	1925–27†	Venice Borkorsor*	1973†	Yong-Kang Kim* WBC	1988–89
Frenchy Belanger* NBA	1927–28	Chartchai Chionoi WBA	1973–74	Duke McKenzie IBF	1988–89
Izzy Schwartz NY	1927–29	B. Gonzalez* WBA	1973–74	Sot Chitalada* WBC	1989–91
Frankie Genaro* NBA	1928–29	Shoji Oguma* WBC	1974–75	Dave McAuley IBF	1989–92
Spider Pladner* NBA	1929	S. Hanagata WBA	1974–75	Jesus Rojas WBA	1989–90
Frankie Genaro* NBA	1929–31	Miguel Canto* WBC	1975–79	Yul-Woo Lee WBA	1990
Midget Wolgast NY	1930–35	Erbito Salavarria WBA	1975–76	L. Tamakuma WBA	1990–91
Young Perez* NBA	1931–32	Alfonso Lopez WBA	1976	M. Kittikasem* WBC	1991–92
Jackie Brown* NBA	1932–35	G. Espadas WBA	1976–78	Yuri Arbachakov* WBC	1992–97
Benny Lynch*	1935–38†	B. Gonzalez WBA	1978–79	Yong Kang Kim WBA	1991–92
Small Montana NY	1935–37	Chan-Hee Park* WBC	1979–80	Rodolfo Blanco IBF	1992–93
Peter Kane*	1938–43	Luis Ibarra WBA	1979–80	P. Sithbangprachan IBF	1993–95
Little Dado NY	1938–40	Tae-Shik Kim WBA	1980	David Griman WBA	1992–94
Jackie Paterson*	1943–48	Shoji Oguma* WBC	1980–81	S.S. Ploenchit WBA	1994–96
Rinty Monaghan*	1948–50†	Peter Mathebula WBA	1980–81	Francisco Tejedor IBF	1995
Terry Allen*	1950	Santos Laciar WBA	1981	Danny Romero IBF	1995–96
Dado Marino*	1950–52	Antonio Avelar* WBC	1981–82	Mark Johnson IBF	1996–99†
Yoshio Shirai*	1952–54	Luis Ibarra WBA	1981	Jose Bonilla WBA	1996–98
Pascual Perez*	1954–60	Juan Herrera WBA	1981–82	Chatchai Sasakul* WBC	1997–98
Pone Kingpetch*	1960–62	P. Cardona* WBC	1982	Hugo Soto WBA	1998–99
Masahiko Harada*	1962–63	Santos Laciar WBA	1982–85	Manny Pacquiao* WBC	1998–99
Pone Kingpetch*	1963	Freddie Castillo* WBC	1982	Leo Gamez WBA	1999
Hiroyuki Ebihara*	1963–64	E. Mercedes* WBC	1982–83	Irene Pacheco IBF	1999–05
Pone Kingpetch*	1964–65	Charlie Magri* WBC	1983	S. Pisnurachan WBA	1999–00
Salvatore Burrini*	1965–66	Frank Cedeno* WBC	1983–84	M. Sinsurat* WBC	1999–00
H. Accavallo WBA	1966–68	Soon-Chun Kwon IBF	1983–85	Malcolm Tunacao* WBC	2000–01
Walter McGowan*	1966	Koji Kobayashi* WBC	1984	Eric Morel WBA	2000–03
Chartchai Chionoi*	1966–69	Gabriel Bernal* WBC	1984	P. Wonjongkam* WBC	2001–
Efren Torres*	1969–70	Sot Chitalada* WBC	1984–88	Lorenzo Parra WBA	2003–
Hiroyuki Ebihara WBA	1969	Hilario Zapate WBA	1985–87	Vic Darchinyan IBF	2005–
B. Villacampo WBA	1969–70	Chong-Kwan Chung IBF	1985–86		

Light Flyweights
(Weight Limit: 108 pounds)

Champion	Reign	Champion	Reign	Champion	Reign
Franco Udella WBC	1975	Joey Olivo WBA	1985	Keiji Yamaguchi WBA	1996
Jaime Rios WBA	1975–76	Myung-Woo Yuh* WBA	1985–91	Michael Carbajal IBF	1996–97
Luis Estaba* WBC	1975–78	Jum-Hwan Choi IBF	1986–88	Saman Jaturong* WBC	1995–99
Juan Guzman WBA	1976	Tacy Macalos IBF	1988–89	Phichitchor Siriwat WBA	1996–00
Yoko Gushiken WBA	1976–81	German Torres WBC	1988–89	Mauricio Pastrana IBF	1997–98†
Freddy Castillo* WBC	1978	Yul-Woo Lee WBC	1989	Will Grigsby IBF	1998–99
Sor Vorasingh* WBC	1978	M. Kittikasem IBF	1989–90	Ricardo Lopez IBF	1999–02
Sung-Jun Kim* WBC	1978–80	H. Gonzalez WBC	1989–90	Yo-Sam Choi* WBC	1999–02
Shigeo Nakajima* WBC	1980	Michael Carbajal IBF	1990–94	Beibis Mendoza WBA	2000–01
Hilario Zapata* WBC	1980–82	R. Pascua WBC	1990	Rosendo Alvarez WBA	2001–05
Pedro Flores WBA	1981	M. C. Castro WBC	1991	Jorge Arce* WBC	2002–05
Hwan-Jin Kim WBA	1981	H. Gonzalez WBC	1991–93	Jose Burgos IBF	2003–05
Katsuo Tokashiki WBA	1981–83	Hirokia Ioka* WBA	1991–92	Brian Viloria WBC	2005–06
Amado Urzua* WBC	1982	Myung-Woo Yuh* WBA	1993†	R. Vasquez WBA	2005–06
Tadashi Tomori* WBC	1982	Michael Carbajal* WBC	1993–94	Will Grigsby IBF	2005–06
Hilario Zapata* WBC	1982–83	Leo Gamez WBA	1993–95	Koki Kameda WBA	2006–
Jung-Koo Chang* WBC	1983–88†	H. Gonzalez*, WBC, IBF	1994–95	Omar Nino Rivero WBC	2006–
Lupe Madera WBA	1983–84	Choi Hi-Yong WBA	1995–96	Ulises Solis IBF	2006–
Dodie Penalosa IBF	1983–86	S. Sor Jaturong WBC, IBF	1995–96		
Francisco Quiroz WBA	1984–85	Carlos Murillo WBA	1996		

*Lineal champion.

†Champion relinquished title to retire or switch weight classes, or had title stripped by boxing organization.

Strawweights
(Weight Limit: 105 pounds)

Champion	Reign	Champion	Reign	Champion	Reign
Kyung-Yun Lee* IBF	1987	Manny Melchor IBF	1992	Keitaro Hoshino WBA	2000–01
Hiroki Ioka* WBC	1987–88	Hideyuki Ohashi WBA	1992–93	Chana Porpaoin WBA	2001
Leo Gamez WBA	1988–89	R.S. Voraphin IBF	1992–96	Roberto Leyva IBF	2001–02
S. Sithnaruepol IBF	1988–89	Chana Porpaoin WBA	1993–95	Yutaka Niida WBA	2001†
N. Kiatwanchai* WBC	1988–89	Rosendo Alvarez WBA	1995–98	Miguel Barrera IBF	2002–03
Bong-Jun Kim WBA	1989–91	R. Sor Vorapin IBF	1996–97	Edgar Cardenas IBF	2003
Nico Thomas IBF	1989	Zolani Petelo* IBF	1997–00†	Noel Arambulet WBA	2002–04
Eric Chavez IBF	1989–90	W. Chor Charoen WBC	1998–00	Daniel Reyes IBF	2003–05
Jum-Hwan Choi* WBC	1989–90	R. Lopez* WBA, WBC	1998–99†	Eagle Kyowa WBC	2004–
Hideyuki Ohashi* WBC	1990	Songkram Popaoin WBA	1999	Yukata Niida WBA	2004–
F. Lookmingkwan IBF	1990–92	Noel Arambulet WBA	1999–00	M. Rachman IBF	2005–
Ricardo Lopez* WBC	1990–98†	Jose Aguirre* WBC	2000–04		
Hi-Yong Choi WBA	1991–92	Joma Gamboa WBA	2000		

*Lineal champion.
†Champion relinquished title to retire or switch weight classes, or had title stripped by boxing organization.

Alltime Career Leaders

Total Bouts

Name	Years Active	Bouts	Name	Years Active	Bouts
Len Wickwar	1928–47	463	Maxie Rosenbloom	1923–39	299
Jack Britton	1905–30	350	Harry Greb	1913–26	298
Johnny Dundee	1910–32	333	Young Stribling	1921–33	286
Billy Bird	1920–48	318	Battling Levinsky	1910–29	282
George Marsden	1928–46	311	Ted (Kid) Lewis	1909–29	279

Note: Based on records in *The Ring Record Book* and *Boxing Encyclopedia*.

Most Knockouts

Name	Years Active	KOs	Name	Years Active	KOs
Archie Moore	1936–63	130	Sandy Saddler	1944–56	103
Young Stribling	1921–33	126	Sam Langford	1902–26	102
Billy Bird	1920–48	125	Henry Armstrong	1931–45	100
George Odwell	1930–45	114	Jimmy Wilde	1911–23	98
Sugar Ray Robinson	1940–65	110	Len Wickwar	1928–47	93

Note: Based on records in *The Ring Record Book* and *Boxing Encyclopedia*.

World Heavyweight Championship Fights

Date	Winner	Wgt	Loser	Wgt	Result	Site
Sept 7, 1892	James J. Corbett*	178	John L. Sullivan	212	KO 21	New Orleans
Jan 25, 1894	James J. Corbett*	184	Charley Mitchell	158	KO 3	Jacksonville
Mar 17, 1897	Bob Fitzsimmons*	167	James J. Corbett	183	KO 14	Carson City, Nev.
June 9, 1899	James J. Jeffries*	206	Bob Fitzsimmons	167	KO 11	Coney Island, N.Y.
Nov 3, 1899	James J. Jeffries*	215	Tom Sharkey	183	Ref 25	Coney Island, N.Y.
Apr 6, 1900	James J. Jeffries*	n/a	Jack Finnegan	n/a	KO 1	Detroit
May 11, 1900	James J. Jeffries*	218	James J. Corbett	188	KO 23	Coney Island, N.Y.
Nov 15, 1901	James J. Jeffries*	211	Gus Ruhlin	194	TKO 6	San Francisco
July 25, 1902	James J. Jeffries*	219	Bob Fitzsimmons	172	KO 8	San Francisco
Aug 14, 1903	James J. Jeffries*	220	James J. Corbett	190	KO 10	San Francisco
Aug 25, 1904	James J. Jeffries*	219	Jack Munroe	186	TKO 2	San Francisco
July 3, 1905	Marvin Hart*	190	Jack Root	171	KO 12	Reno
Feb 23, 1906	Tommy Burns*	180	Marvin Hart	188	Ref 20	Los Angeles
Oct 2, 1906	Tommy Burns*	n/a	Jim Flynn	n/a	KO 15	Los Angeles
Nov 28, 1906	Tommy Burns*	172	Jack O'Brien	163½	Draw 20	Los Angeles
May 8, 1907	Tommy Burns*	180	Jack O'Brien	167	Ref 20	Los Angeles
Jul 4, 1907	Tommy Burns*	181	Bill Squires	180	KO 1	Colma, Calif.
Dec 2, 1907	Tommy Burns*	177	Gunner Moir	204	KO 10	London
Feb 10, 1908	Tommy Burns*	n/a	Jack Palmer	n/a	KO 4	London

Date	Winner	Wgt	Loser	Wgt	Result	Site
Mar 17, 1908	Tommy Burns*	n/a	Jem Roche	n/a	KO 1	Dublin
Apr 18, 1908	Tommy Burns*	n/a	Jewey Smith	n/a	KO 5	Paris
June 13, 1908	Tommy Burns*	184	Bill Squires	183	KO 8	Paris
Aug 24, 1908	Tommy Burns*	181	Bill Squires	184	KO 13	Sydney
Sept 2, 1908	Tommy Burns*	183	Bill Lang	187	KO 6	Melbourne
Dec 26, 1908	Jack Johnson*	192	Tommy Burns	168	TKO 14	Sydney
Mar 10, 1909	Jack Johnson*	n/a	Victor McLaglen	n/a	ND 6	Vancouver
May 19, 1909	Jack Johnson*	205	Jack O'Brien	161	ND 6	Philadelphia
June 30, 1909	Jack Johnson*	207	Tony Ross	214	ND 6	Pittsburgh
Sept 9, 1909	Jack Johnson*	209	Al Kaufman	191	ND 10	San Francisco
Oct 16, 1909	Jack Johnson*	205½	Stanley Ketchel	170¼	KO 12	Colma, Calif.
July 4, 1910	Jack Johnson*	208	James J. Jeffries	227	KO 15	Reno
July 4, 1912	Jack Johnson*	195½	Jim Flynn	175	TKO 9	Las Vegas
Dec 19, 1913	Jack Johnson*	n/a	Jim Johnson	n/a	Draw 10	Paris
June 27, 1914	Jack Johnson*	221	Frank Moran	203	Ref 20	Paris
Apr 5, 1915	Jess Willard*	230	Jack Johnson	205½	KO 26	Havana
Mar 25, 1916	Jess Willard*	225	Frank Moran	203	ND 10	New York City
July 4, 1919	Jack Dempsey*	187	Jess Willard	245	TKO 4	Toledo, Ohio
Sept 6, 1920	Jack Dempsey*	185	Billy Miske	187	KO 3	Benton Harbor, Mich.
Dec 14, 1920	Jack Dempsey*	188¼	Bill Brennan	197	KO 12	New York City
July 2, 1921	Jack Dempsey*	188	Georges Carpentier	172	KO 4	Jersey City
July 4, 1923	Jack Dempsey*	188	Tommy Givvons	175½	Ref 15	Shelby, Mont.
Sept 14, 1923	Jack Dempsey*	192½	Luis Firpo	216½	KO 2	New York City
Sept 23, 1926	Gene Tunney*	189½	Jack Dempsey	190	UD 10	Philadelphia
Sept 22, 1927	Gene Tunney*	189½	Jack Dempsey	192½	UD 10	Chicago
July 26, 1928	Gene Tunney*	192	Tom Heeney	203½	TKO 11	New York City
June 12, 1930	Max Schmeling*	188	Jack Sharkey	197	DQ 4	New York City
July 3, 1931	Max Schmeling*	189	Young Stribling	186½	TKO 15	Cleveland
June 21, 1932	Jack Sharkey*	205	Max Schmeling	188	Split 15	Long Island City
June 29, 1933	Primo Carnera*	260½	Jack Sharkey	201	KO 6	Long Island City
Oct 22, 1933	Primo Carnera*	259½	Paulino Uzcudun	229¼	UD 15	Rome
Mar 1, 1934	Primo Carnera*	270	Tommy Loughran	184	UD 15	Miami
June 14, 1934	Max Baer*	209½	Primo Carnera	263¼	TKO 11	Long Island City
June 13, 1935	James J. Braddock*	193¾	Max Baer	209½	UD 15	Long Island City
June 22, 1937	Joe Louis*	197¼	James J. Braddock	197	KO 8	Chicago
Aug 30, 1937	Joe Louis*	197	Tommy Farr	204¼	UD 15	New York City
Feb 23, 1938	Joe Louis*	200	Nathan Mann	193½	KO 3	New York City
Apr 1, 1938	Joe Louis*	202½	Harry Thomas	196	KO 5	Chicago
June 22, 1938	Joe Louis*	198¼	Max Schmeling	193	KO 1	New York City
Jan 25, 1939	Joe Louis*	200¼	John Henry Lewis	180¾	KO 1	New York City
Apr 17, 1939	Joe Louis*	201¼	Jack Roper	204¾	KO 1	Los Angeles
June 28, 1939	Joe Louis*	200¾	Tony Galento	233¾	TKO 4	New York City
Sept 20, 1939	Joe Louis*	200	Bob Pastor	183	KO 11	Detroit
Feb 9, 1940	Joe Louis*	203	Arturo Godoy	202	Split 15	New York City
Mar 29, 1940	Joe Louis*	201½	Johnny Paychek	187½	KO 2	New York City
June 20, 1940	Joe Louis*	199	Arturo Godoy	201¼	TKO 8	New York City
Dec 16, 1940	Joe Louis*	202¼	Al McCoy	180¾	TKO 6	Boston
Jan 31, 1941	Joe Louis*	202½	Red Burman	188	KO 5	New York City
Feb 17, 1941	Joe Louis*	203½	Gus Dorazio	193½	KO 2	Philadelphia
Mar 21, 1941	Joe Louis*	202	Abe Simon	254½	TKO 13	Detroit
Apr 8, 1941	Joe Louis*	203½	Tony Musto	199½	TKO 9	St Louis
May 23, 1941	Joe Louis*	201½	Buddy Baer	237½	DQ 7	Washington, D.C.
June 18, 1941	Joe Louis*	199½	Billy Conn	174	KO 13	New York City
Sept 29, 1941	Joe Louis*	202¼	Lou Nova	202½	TKO 6	New York City
Jan 9, 1942	Joe Louis*	206¾	Buddy Baer	250	KO 1	New York City
Mar 27, 1942	Joe Louis*	207½	Abe Simon	255½	KO 6	New York City
June 9, 1946	Joe Louis*	207	Billy Conn	187	KO 8	New York City
Sept 18, 1946	Joe Louis*	211	Tami Mauriello	198½	KO 1	New York City
Dec 5, 1947	Joe Louis*	211½	Jersey Joe Walcott	194½	Split 15	New York City
June 25, 1948	Joe Louis*	213½	Jersey Joe Walcott	194¾	KO 11	New York City
June 22, 1949	Ezzard Charles*	181¾	Jersey Joe Walcott	195½	UD 15	Chicago
Aug 10, 1949	Ezzard Charles*	180	Gus Lesnevich	182	TKO 8	New York City
Oct 14, 1949	Ezzard Charles*	182	Pat Valentino	188½	KO 8	San Francisco
Aug 15, 1950	Ezzard Charles*	183¼	Freddie Beshore	184½	TKO 14	Buffalo
Sept 27, 1950	Ezzard Charles*	184½	Joe Louis	218	UD 15	New York City
Dec 5, 1950	Ezzard Charles*	185	Nick Barone	178½	KO 11	Cincinnati
Jan 12, 1951	Ezzard Charles*	185	Lee Oma	193	TKO 10	New York City
Mar 7, 1951	Ezzard Charles*	186	Jersey Joe Walcott	193	UD 15	Detroit

World Heavyweight Championship Fights *(Cont.)*

Date	Winner	Wgt	Loser	Wgt	Result	Site
May 30, 1951	Ezzard Charles*	182	Joey Maxim	181½	UD 15	Chicago
July 18, 1951	Jersey Joe Walcott*	194	Ezzard Charles	182	KO 7	Pittsburgh
June 5, 1952	Jersey Joe Walcott*	196	Ezzard Charles	191½	UD 15	Philadelphia
Sept 23, 1952	Rocky Marciano*	184	Jersey Joe Walcott	196	KO 13	Philadelphia
May 15, 1953	Rocky Marciano*	184½	Jersey Joe Walcott	197¾	KO 1	Chicago
Sept 24, 1953	Rocky Marciano*	185	Roland LaStarza	184¾	TKO 11	New York City
June 17, 1954	Rocky Marciano*	187½	Ezzard Charles	185½	UD 15	New York City
Sept 17, 1954	Rocky Marciano*	187	Ezzard Charles	192½	KO 8	New York City
May 16, 1955	Rocky Marciano*	189	Don Cockell	205	TKO 9	San Francisco
Sept 21, 1955	Rocky Marciano*	188¼	Archie Moore	188	KO 9	New York City
Nov 30, 1956	Floyd Patterson*	182¼	Archie Moore	187¾	KO 5	Chicago
July 29, 1957	Floyd Patterson*	184	Tommy Jackson	192½	TKO 10	New York City
Aug 22, 1957	Floyd Patterson*	187¼	Pete Rademacher	202	KO 6	Seattle
Aug 18, 1958	Floyd Patterson*	184½	Roy Harris	194	TKO 13	Los Angeles
May 1, 1959	Floyd Patterson*	182½	Brian London	206	KO 11	Indianapolis
June 26, 1959	Ingemar Johansson*	196	Floyd Patterson	182	TKO 3	New York City
June 20, 1960	Floyd Patterson*	190	Ingemar Johansson	194¾	KO 5	New York City
Mar 13, 1961	Floyd Patterson*	194¾	Ingemar Johansson	206½	KO 6	Miami Beach
Dec 4, 1961	Floyd Patterson*	188½	Tom McNeeley	197	KO 4	Toronto
Sept 25, 1962	Sonny Liston*	214	Floyd Patterson	189	KO 1	Chicago
July 22, 1963	Sonny Liston*	215	Floyd Patterson	194½	KO 1	Las Vegas
Feb 25, 1964	Cassius Clay*	210½	Sonny Liston	218	TKO 7	Miami Beach
Mar 5, 1965	Ernie Terrell	199	Eddie Machen	192	UD 15	Chicago
May 25, 1965	Muhammad Ali*	206	Sonny Liston	215¼	KO 1	Lewiston, Me.
Nov 1, 1965	Ernie Terrell	206	George Chuvalo	209	UD 15	Toronto
Nov 22, 1965	Muhammad Ali*	210	Floyd Patterson	196¾	TKO 12	Las Vegas
Mar 29, 1966	Muhammad Ali*	214½	George Chuvalo	216	UD 15	Toronto
May 21, 1966	Muhammad Ali*	201½	Henry Cooper	188	TKO 6	London
June 28, 1966	Ernie Terrell	209½	Doug Jones	187½	UD 15	Houston
Aug 6, 1966	Muhammad Ali*	209½	Brian London	201½	KO 3	London
Sept 10, 1966	Muhammad Ali*	203½	Karl Mildenberger	194¼	TKO 12	Frankfurt
Nov 14, 1966	Muhammad Ali*	212¾	Cleveland Williams	210½	TKO 3	Houston
Feb 6, 1967	Muhammad Ali*	212¼	Ernie Terrell	212½	UD 15	Houston
Mar 22, 1967	Muhammad Ali*	211½	Zora Folley	202½	KO 7	New York City
Mar 4, 1968	Joe Frazier	204½	Buster Mathis	243½	TKO 11	New York City
Apr 27, 1968	Jimmy Ellis	197	Jerry Quarry	195	Maj 15	Oakland
June 24, 1968	Joe Frazier NY	203½	Manuel Ramos	208	TKO 2	New York City
Aug 14, 1968	Jimmy Ellis	198	Floyd Patterson	188	Ref 15	Stockholm
Dec 10, 1968	Joe Frazier NY	203	Oscar Bonavena	207	UD 15	Philadelphia
Apr 22, 1969	Joe Frazier NY	204½	Dave Zyglewicz	190½	KO 1	Houston
June 23, 1969	Joe Frazier NY	203½	Jerry Quarry	198½	TKO 8	New York City
Feb 16, 1970	Joe Frazier NY	205	Jimmy Ellis	201	TKO 5	New York City
Nov 18, 1970	Joe Frazier	209	Bob Foster	188	KO 2	Detroit
Mar 8, 1971	Joe Frazier*	205½	Muhammad Ali	215	UD 15	New York City
Jan 15, 1972	Joe Frazier*	215½	Terry Daniels	195	TKO 4	New Orleans
May 26, 1972	Joe Frazier*	217½	Ron Stander	218	TKO 5	Omaha
Jan 22, 1973	George Foreman*	217½	Joe Frazier	214	TKO 2	Kingston, Jam.
Sept 1, 1973	George Foreman*	219½	Jose Roman	196½	KO 1	Tokyo
Mar 26, 1974	George Foreman*	224¼	Ken Norton	212¼	TKO 2	Caracas
Oct 30, 1974	Muhammad Ali*	216½	George Foreman	220	KO 8	Kinshasa, Zaire
Mar 24, 1975	Muhammad Ali*	223½	Chuck Wepner	225	TKO 15	Cleveland
May 16, 1975	Muhammad Ali*	224½	Ron Lyle	219	TKO 11	Las Vegas
July 1, 1975	Muhammad Ali*	224½	Joe Bugner	230	UD 15	Kuala Lumpur, Malay.
Oct 1, 1975	Muhammad Ali*	224½	Joe Frazier	215	TKO 15	Manila
Feb 20, 1976	Muhammad Ali*	226	Jean Pierre Coopman	206	KO 5	San Juan
Apr 30, 1976	Muhammad Ali*	230	Jimmy Young	209	UD 15	Landover, Md.
May 24, 1976	Muhammad Ali*	230	Richard Dunn	206½	TKO 5	Munich
Sept 28, 1976	Muhammad Ali*	221	Ken Norton	217½	UD 15	New York City
May 16, 1977	Muhammad Ali*	221¼	Alfredo Evangelista	209¼	UD 15	Landover, Md.
Sept 29, 1977	Muhammad Ali*	225	Earnie Shavers	211¼	UD 15	New York City
Feb 15, 1978	Leon Spinks*	197¼	Muhammad Ali	224¼	Split 15	Las Vegas
June 9, 1978	Larry Holmes	209	Ken Norton	220	Split 15	Las Vegas
Sept 15, 1978	Muhammad Ali*	221	Leon Spinks	201	UD 15	New Orleans
Nov 10, 1978	Larry Holmes*	214	Alfredo Evangelista	208¼	KO 7	Las Vegas
Mar 23, 1979	Larry Holmes*	214	Osvaldo Ocasio	207	TKO 7	Las Vegas
June 22, 1979	Larry Holmes*	215	Mike Weaver	202	TKO 12	New York City
Sept 28, 1979	Larry Holmes*	210	Earnie Shavers	211	TKO 11	Las Vegas
Oct 20, 1979	John Tate	240	Gerrie Coetzee	222	UD 15	Pretoria
Feb 3, 1980	Larry Holmes *	213½	Lorenzo Zanon	215	TKO 6	Las Vegas

Date	Winner	Wgt	Loser	Wgt	Result	Site
Mar 31, 1980	Mike Weaver	232	John Tate	232	KO 15	Knoxville
Mar 31, 1980	Larry Holmes*	211	Leroy Jones	254½	TKO 8	Las Vegas
July 7, 1980	Larry Holmes*	214¼	Scott LeDoux	226	TKO 7	Minneapolis
Oct 2, 1980	Larry Holmes*	211¼	Muhammad Ali	217½	TKO 11	Las Vegas
Oct 25, 1980	Mike Weaver	210	Gerrie Coetzee	226½	KO 13	Sun City, S. Africa
Apr 11, 1981	Larry Holmes*	215	Trevor Berbick	215½	UD 15	Las Vegas
June 12, 1981	Larry Holmes*	212¼	Leon Spinks	200¼	TKO 3	Detroit
Oct 3, 1981	Mike Weaver	215	James Quick Tillis	209	UD 15	Rosemont, Ill.
Nov 6, 1981	Larry Holmes*	213¼	Renaldo Snipes	215¾	TKO 11	Pittsburgh
June 11, 1982	Larry Holmes*	212½	Gerry Cooney	225½	TKO 13	Las Vegas
Nov 26, 1982	Larry Holmes*	217½	Tex Cobb	234¼	UD 15	Houston
Dec 10, 1982	Michael Dokes	216	Mike Weaver	209¾	TKO 1	Las Vegas
Mar 27, 1983	Larry Holmes*	221	Lucien Rodriguez	209	UD 12	Scranton, Pa.
May 20, 1983	Michael Dokes	223	Mike Weaver	218½	Draw 15	Las Vegas
May 20, 1983	Larry Holmes*	213	Tim Witherspoon	219½	Split 12	Las Vegas
Sept 10, 1983	Larry Holmes*	223	Scott Frank	211¼	TKO 5	Atlantic City
Sept 23, 1983	Gerrie Coetzee	215	Michael Dokes	217	KO 10	Richfield, Ohio
Nov 25, 1983	Larry Holmes*	219	Marvis Frazier	200	TKO 1	Las Vegas
Mar 9, 1984	Tim Witherspoon	220¼	Greg Page	239½	Maj 12	Las Vegas
Aug 31, 1984	Pinklon Thomas	216	Tim Witherspoon	217	Maj 12	Las Vegas
Nov 9, 1984	Larry Holmes* IBF	221½	James Smith	227	TKO 12	Las Vegas
Dec 1, 1984	Greg Page	236½	Gerrie Coetzee	218	KO 8	Sun City, S. Africa
Mar 15, 1985	Larry Holmes*	223½	David Bey	233¼	TKO 10	Las Vegas
Apr 29, 1985	Tony Tubbs	229	Greg Page	239½	UD 15	Buffalo
May 20, 1985	Larry Holmes*	224¼	Carl Williams	215	UD 15	Las Vegas
June 15, 1985	Pinklon Thomas	220¼	Mike Weaver	221¼	KO 8	Las Vegas
Sept 21, 1985	Michael Spinks*	200	Larry Holmes	221½	UD 15	Las Vegas
Jan 17, 1986	Tim Witherspoon	227	Tony Tubbs	229	Maj 15	Atlanta
Mar 22, 1986	Trevor Berbick	218½	Pinklon Thomas	222¾	UD 15	Las Vegas
Apr 19, 1986	Michael Spinks*	205	Larry Holmes	223	Split 15	Las Vegas
July 19, 1986	Tim Witherspoon	234¾	Frank Bruno	228	TKO 11	Wembley, Eng.
Sept 6, 1986	Michael Spinks*	201	Steffen Tangstad	214¾	TKO 4	Las Vegas
Nov 22, 1986	Mike Tyson	221¼	Trevor Berbick	218½	TKO 2	Las Vegas
Dec 12, 1986	James Smith	228½	Tim Witherspoon	233½	TKO 1	New York City
Mar 7, 1987	Mike Tyson	219	James Smith	233	UD 12	Las Vegas
May 30, 1987	Mike Tyson	218¾	Pinklon Thomas	217¾	TKO 6	Las Vegas
May 30, 1987	Tony Tucker	222¼	Buster Douglas	227¼	TKO 10	Las Vegas
June 15, 1987	Michael Spinks*	208¾	Gerry Cooney	238	TKO 5	Atlantic City
Aug 1, 1987	Mike Tyson	221	Tony Tucker	221	UD 12	Las Vegas
Oct 16, 1987	Mike Tyson	216	Tyrell Biggs	228¾	TKO 7	Atlantic City
Jan 22, 1988	Mike Tyson	215¾	Larry Holmes	225¾	TKO 4	Atlantic City
Mar 20, 1988	Mike Tyson	216¼	Tony Tubbs	238¼	KO 2	Tokyo
June 27, 1988	Mike Tyson*	218¼	Michael Spinks	212¼	KO 1	Atlantic City
Feb 25, 1989	Mike Tyson*	218	Frank Bruno	228	TKO 5	Las Vegas
July 21, 1989	Mike Tyson*	219¼	Carl Williams	218	TKO 1	Atlantic City
Feb 10, 1990	Buster Douglas*	231½	Mike Tyson	220½	KO 10	Tokyo
Oct 25, 1990	Evander Holyfield*	208	Buster Douglas	246	KO 3	Las Vegas
Apr 19, 1991	Evander Holyfield*	212	George Foreman	257	UD 12	Atlantic City
Nov 23, 1991	Evander Holyfield*	210	Bert Cooper	215	TKO 7	Atlanta
June 19, 1992	Evander Holyfield*	210	Larry Holmes	233	UD 12	Las Vegas
Nov 13, 1992	Riddick Bowe*	235	Evander Holyfield	205	UD 12	Las Vegas
Feb 6, 1993	Riddick Bowe	243	Michael Dokes	244	KO 1	New York City
May 8, 1993	Lennox Lewis	235	Tony Tucker	235	UD 12	Las Vegas
May 22, 1993	Riddick Bowe*	244	Jesse Ferguson	224	KO 2	Washington, D.C.
Oct 2, 1993	Lennox Lewis	229	Frank Bruno	233	KO 7	London
Nov 6, 1993	Evander Holyfield*	217	Riddick Bowe	246	Split 12	Las Vegas
Apr 22, 1994	Michael Moorer*	214	Evander Holyfield	214	Split 12	Las Vegas
May 6, 1994	Lennox Lewis	235	Phil Jackson	218	TKO 8	Atlantic City
Nov 6, 1994	George Foreman*	250	Michael Moorer	222	KO 10	Las Vegas
Mar 11, 1995	Riddick Bowe	241	Herbie Hide	214	KO 6	Las Vegas
Apr 8, 1995	Oliver McCall	231	Larry Holmes	236	UD 12	Las Vegas
Apr 8, 1995	Bruce Seldon	236	Tony Tucker	243	TKO 7	Las Vegas
Apr 22, 1995	George Foreman*	256	Axel Schulz	221	Split 12	Las Vegas
Jun 17, 1995	Riddick Bowe	243	Jorge Luis Gonzalez	237	KO 6	Las Vegas
Aug 19, 1995	Bruce Seldon	234	Joe Hipp	233	TKO 10	Las Vegas
Sept 2, 1995	Frank Bruno	247¾	Oliver McCall	234¾	UD 12	London
Dec 9, 1995	Frans Botha	237	Axel Shulz	223	Split 12	Stuttgart
Mar 16, 1996	Mike Tyson	220	Frank Bruno	247	TKO 3	Las Vegas
June 22, 1996	Michael Moorer	222¼	Axel Shulz	222¾	Split 12	Dortmund, Germ.

Date	Winner	Wgt	Loser	Wgt	Result	Site
Sept 7, 1996	Mike Tyson	219	Bruce Seldon	229	TKO 1	Las Vegas
Nov 3, 1996	George Foreman*	253	Crawford Grimsley		UD 12	Tokyo
Nov 9, 1996	Evander Holyfied	215	Mike Tyson	222	TKO 11	Las Vegas
Feb 7, 1997	Lennox Lewis	251	Oliver McCall	237	TKO 5	Las Vegas
Apr 26, 1997	George Foreman*	253	Lou Savarese		Split 12	Atlantic City
June 28, 1997	Evander Holyfied	218	Mike Tyson	218	DQ 4	Las Vegas
Oct 4, 1997	Lennox Lewis	244	Andrew Golota	244	TKO 1	Atlantic City
Nov 8, 1997	Evander Holyfield	214	Michael Moorer	223	TKO 8	Las Vegas
Nov 22, 1997	Shannon Briggs*		George Foreman		MD 12	Atlantic City
Mar 28, 1998	Lennox Lewis*	243	Shannon Briggs	228	TKO 5	Atlantic City
Mar 13, 1999	Evander Holyfield	215	Lennox Lewis*	246	Draw 12	New York City
Nov 13, 1999	Lennox Lewis*	242	Evander Holyfield	217	UD 12	Las Vegas
Apr 29, 2000	Lennox Lewis*	247	Michael Grant	250	KO 2	New York
July 15, 2000	Lennox Lewis*	250	Frans Botha	236	TKO 2	London
Aug 12, 2000	Evander Holyfield	221	John Ruiz	224	UD 12	Las Vegas
Nov 11, 2000	Lennox Lewis*	249	David Tua	245	UD 12	Las Vegas
Mar 3, 2001	John Ruiz	227	Evander Holyfield	217	UD 12	Las Vegas
Apr 22, 2001	Hasim Rahman*	238	Lennox Lewis	253½	KO 5	Brakpan, S. Africa
Nov 17, 2001	Lennox Lewis*	246½	Hasim Rahman	236	KO 4	Las Vegas
Dec 15, 2001	John Ruiz	232	Evander Holyfield	219	Draw 12	Mashantucket, Conn.
June 8, 2002	Lennox Lewis*	249¼	Mike Tyson	234½	KO 8	Memphis, Tenn.
July 27, 2002	John Ruiz	233	Kirk Johnson	238	DQ 10	Las Vegas
Dec 14, 2002	Chris Byrd	214	Evander Holyfield	220	UD 12	Atlantic City
Mar 1, 2003	Roy Jones Jr.	193	John Ruiz	226	UD 12	Las Vegas
June 21, 2003	Lennox Lewis*	256½	Vitali Klitschko	248	TKO 6	Los Angeles
Sept 20, 2003	Chris Byrd	211½	Fres Oquendo	224	UD 12	Uncasville, Conn.
April 17, 2004	Chris Byrd	210½	Andrew Golota	237½	Draw 12	New York City
April 17, 2004	John Ruiz	240	Fres Oquendo	225	TKO 11	New York City
April 24, 2004	Vitali Klitschko	245	Corrie Sanders	235	TKO 8	Los Angeles
Nov 13, 2004	John Ruiz	239	Andrew Golota	238	UD	New York City
Nov 13, 2004	Chris Byrd	214	Jameel McCline	270	Split 12	New York City
Dec 11, 2004	Vitali Klitschko	250	Danny Williams	270	TKO 8	Las Vegas
April 30, 2005	James Toney	231	John Ruiz	244	ND	New York City
Aug 13, 2005	Hasim Rahman	236	Monte Barrett	224	UD	Chicago, Ill.
Dec 17, 2005	Nikolay Valuev	324	John Ruiz	237	MD	Berlin
Oct 1, 2005	Chris Byrd	213	DaVarryl Williamson	225	UD	Reno, Nev.
Mar 18, 2006	Hasim Rahman	238	James Toney	237	MD	Atlantic City
Apr 22, 2006	Wladimir Klitschko	241	Chris Byrd	213	TKO 7	Mannheim, Germ.
June 3, 2006	Nikolay Valuev	320	Owen Beck	242	TKO 3	Hanover, Germ.
Aug 12, 2006	Oleg Maskaev	238	Hasim Rahman	235	TKO 12	Las Vegas

*Lineal champion. KO=knockout; TKO=technical knockout; UD=unanimous decision; Split=split decision; Ref=referee's decision; MD=majority decision; DQ=disqualification; ND=no decision.

Ring Magazine Fighter and Fight of the Year

Year	Fighter	Year	Fighter	Year	Fighter
1928	Gene Tunney	1935	Barney Ross	1940	Billy Conn
1929	Tommy Loughran	1936	Joe Louis	1941	Joe Louis
1930	Max Schmeling	1937	Henry Armstrong	1942	Ray Robinson
1932	Jack Sharkey	1938	Joe Louis	1943	Fred Apostoli
1934	T. Canzoneri/B. Ross	1939	Joe Louis	1944	Beau Jack

Note: No award in 1933; no fight of the year named until 1945

Year	Fighter	Fight	Winner	Site
1945	Willie Pep	Rocky Graziano–Freddie Cochrane	Rocky Graziano	New York City
1946	Tony Zale	Tony Zale–Rocky Graziano	Tony Zale	New York City
1947	Gus Lesnevich	Rocky Graziano–Tony Zale	Rocky Graziano	Chicago
1948	Ike Williams	Marcel Cerdan–Tony Zale	Marcel Cerdan	Jersey City
1949	Ezzard Charles	Willie Pep–Sandy Saddler	Willie Pep	New York City
1950	Ezzard Charles	Jake LaMotta–Laurent Dauthuille	Jake LaMotta	Detroit
1951	Ray Robinson	Jersey Joe Walcott–Ezzard Charles	Jersey Joe Walcott	Pittsburgh
1952	Rocky Marciano	Rocky Marciano–Jersey Joe Walcott	Rocky Marciano	Philadelphia
1953	Carl Olson	Rocky Marciano–Roland LaStarza	Rocky Marciano	New York City
1954	Rocky Marciano	Rocky Marciano–Ezzard Charles	Rocky Marciano	New York City
1955	Rocky Marciano	Carmen Basilio–Tony DeMarco	Carmen Basilio	Boston
1956	Floyd Patterson	Carmen Basilio–Johnny Saxton	Carmen Basilio	Syracuse

Year	Fighter	Fight	Winner	Site
1957	Carmen Basilio	Carmen Basilio–Ray Robinson	Carmen Basilio	New York City
1958	Ingemar Johansson	Ray Robinson–Carmen Basilio	Ray Robinson	Chicago
1959	Ingemar Johansson	Gene Fullmer–Carmen Basilio	Gene Fullmer	San Francisco
1960	Floyd Patterson	Floyd Patterson–Ingemar Johansson	Floyd Patterson	New York City
1961	Joe Brown	Joe Brown–Dave Charnley	Joe Brown	London
1962	Dick Tiger	Joey Giardello–Henry Hank	Joey Giardello	Philadelphia
1963	Cassius Clay	Cassius Clay–Doug Jones	Cassius Clay	New York City
1964	Emile Griffith	Cassius Clay–Sonny Liston	Cassius Clay	Miami Beach
1965	Dick Tiger	Floyd Patterson–George Chuvalo	Floyd Patterson	New York City
1966	No award	Jose Torres–Eddie Cotton	Jose Torres	Las Vegas
1967	Joe Frazier	Nino Benvenuti–Emile Griffith	Nino Benvenuti	New York City
1968	Nino Benvenuti	Dick Tiger–Frank DePaula	Dick Tiger	New York City
1969	Jose Napoles	Joe Frazier–Jerry Quarry	Joe Frazier	New York City
1970	Joe Frazier	Carlos Monzon–Nino Benvenuti	Carlos Monzon	Rome
1971	Joe Frazier	Joe Frazier–Muhammad Ali	Joe Frazier	New York City
1972	Muhammad Ali Carlos Monzon	Bob Foster–Chris Finnegan	Bob Foster	London
1973	George Foreman	George Foreman–Joe Frazier	George Foreman	Kingston, Jam.
1974	Muhammad Ali	Muhammad Ali–George Foreman	Muhammad Ali	Kinshasa, Zaire
1975	Muhammad Ali	Muhammad Ali–Joe Frazier	Muhammad Ali	Manila
1976	George Foreman	George Foreman–Ron Lyle	George Foreman	Las Vegas
1977	Carlos Zarate	Joe Young–George Foreman	Joe Young	San Juan
1978	Muhammad Ali	Leon Spinks–Muhammad Ali	Leon Spinks	Las Vegas
1979	Ray Leonard	Danny Lopez–Mike Ayala	Danny Lopez	San Antonio
1980	Thomas Hearns	Saad Muhammad–Yaqui Lopez	Saad Muhammad	McAfee, N.J.
1981	Ray Leonard Salvador Sanchez	Ray Leonard–Tommy Hearns	Ray Leonard	Las Vegas
1982	Larry Holmes	Bobby Chacon–Rafael Limon	Bobby Chacon	Sacramento
1983	Marvin Hagler	Bobby Chacon–Cornelius Boza-Edwards	Bobby Chacon	Las Vegas
1984	Thomas Hearns	Jose Luis Ramirez–Edwin Rosario	Jose Luis Ramirez	San Juan
1985	Donald Curry Marvin Hagler	Marvin Hagler–Tommy Hearns	Marvin Hagler	Las Vegas
1986	Mike Tyson	Stevie Cruz–Barry McGuigan	Stevie Cruz	Las Vegas
1987	Evander Holyfield	Ray Leonard–Marvin Hagler	Ray Leonard	Las Vegas
1988	Mike Tyson	Tony Lopez–Rocky Lockridge	Tony Lopez	Inglewood, Calif.
1989	Pernell Whitaker	Roberto Duran–Iran Barkley	Roberto Duran	Atlantic City
1990	Julio César Chávez	Julio César Chávez–Meldrick Taylor	Julio César Chávez	Las Vegas
1991	James Toney	Robert Quiroga–Kid Akeem Anifowoshe	Robert Quiroga	San Antonio
1992	Riddick Bowe	Riddick Bowe–Evander Holyfield	Riddick Bowe	Las Vegas
1993	Michael Carbajal	Michael Carbajal–Humberto Gonzalez	Michael Carbajal	Las Vegas
1994	Roy Jones	Jorge Castro–John David Jackson	Jorge Castro	Monterrey, Mex.
1995	Oscar De La Hoya	Saman Sor Jaturong–Chiquita Gonzalez	Saman Sor Jaturong	Inglewood, Calif.
1996	Evander Holyfield	Evander Holyfield–Mike Tyson	Evander Holyfield	Las Vegas
1997	Evander Holyfield	Arturo Gatti–Gabriel Ruelas	Arturo Gatti	Atlantic City
1998	Floyd Mayweather	Ivan Robinson–Arturo Gatti	Ivan Robinson	Atlantic City
1999	Paulie Ayala	Paulie Ayala–Johnny Tapia	Paulie Ayala	Las Vegas
2000	Felix Trinidad	Erik Morales–Marco Antonio Barrera	Erik Morales	Las Vegas
2001	Bernard Hopkins	Micky Ward–Emanuel Burton	Micky Ward	Las Vegas
2002	Vernon Forrest	Micky Ward–Arturo Gatti	Micky Ward	Uncasville, Conn.
2003	James Toney	Micky Ward–Arturo Gatti	Arturo Gatti	Atlantic City
2004	Glen Johnson	Marco Antonio Barrera–Erik Morales	Marco Barrera	Las Vegas
2005	Ricky Hatton	Diego Corrales-Jose Luis Castillo	Diego Corrales	Las Vegas

U.S. Olympic Gold Medalists

LIGHT FLYWEIGHT
1984	Paul Gonzales

FLYWEIGHT
1904	George Finnegan
1920	Frank Di Gennara
1024	Fidel LaBarba
1952	Nathan Brooks
1976	Leo Randolph
1984	Steve McCrory

BANTAMWEIGHT
1904	Oliver Kirk
1988	Kennedy McKinney

FEATHERWEIGHT
1904	Oliver Kirk
1924	John Fields
1984	Meldrick Taylor

LIGHTWEIGHT
1904	Harry Spanger
1920	Samuel Mosberg
1968	Ronald W. Harris
1976	Howard Davis
1984	Pernell Whitaker
1992	Oscar De La Hoya

LIGHT WELTERWEIGHT
1952	Charles Adkins
1972	Ray Seales
1976	Ray Leonard
1984	Jerry Page

WELTERWEIGHT
1904	Albert Young
1932	Edward Flynn
1984	Mark Breland

LIGHT MIDDLEWEIGHT

1960	Wilbert McClure
1984	Frank Tate
1996	David Reid

MIDDLEWEIGHT

1904	Charles Mayer
1932	Carmen Bath
1952	Floyd Patterson
1960	Edward Crook
1976	Michael Spinks

LIGHT HEAVYWEIGHT

1920	Eddie Eagan
1952	Norvel Lee
1956	James Boyd
1960	Cassius Clay
1976	Leon Spinks
1988	Andrew Maynard
2004	Andre Ward

HEAVYWEIGHT

1984	Henry Tillman
1988	Ray Mercer

SUPER HEAVYWEIGHT

1904	Samuel Berger
1952	H. Edward Sanders
1956	T. Peter Rademacher
1964	Joe Frazier
1968	George Foreman
1984	Tyrell Biggs

Lineal Heavyweight Champions

Champion	Reign	Age*	Career	W-L-D (KO)	Successful Defenses
John L. Sullivan	1885–92	26	1878–92	38-1-3 (33)	0
James J. Corbett	1892–97	26	1884–03	11-4-2 (7)	1
Bob Fitzsimmons	1897–99	33	1880–16	74-8-3 (67)	0
James J. Jeffries†	1899–05	24	1896–10	18-1-2 (15)	7
Marvin Hart	1905–06	28	1899–10	28-7-4 (19)	0
Tommy Burns	1906–08	24	1900–20	46-5-8 (37)	11
Jack Johnson	1908–15	30	1894–28	77-13-14 (48)	9
Jess Willard	1915–19	33	1911–23	23-6-1 (20)	1
Jack Dempsey	1919–26	24	1914–27	60-6-8 (50)	5
Gene Tunney†	1926–28	29	1915–28	61-1-1 (45)	2
Max Schmeling	1930–32	24	1924–48	56-10-4 (39)	1
Jack Sharkey	1932–33	29	1924–36	38-13-3 (14)	0
Primo Carnera	1933–34	26	1928–37	88-14-0 (69)	2
Max Baer	1934–35	25	1929–41	72-12-0 (53)	0
James J. Braddock	1935–37	29	1926–38	51-26-7 (26)	0
Joe Louis†	1937–49	23	1934–51	68-3-0 (54)	25
Ezzard Charles	1949–51	27	1940–59	96-25-1 (59)	8
Jersey Joe Walcott	1951–52	37	1930–53	53-18-1 (33)	1
Rocky Marciano†	1952–56	29	1947–56	49-0-0 (43)	6
Floyd Patterson	1956–59	21	1952–72	55-8-1 (40)	4
Ingemar Johansson	1959–60	26	1952–63	26-2-0 (17)	0
Floyd Patterson	1960–62	25	1952–72	55-8-1 (40)	2
Sonny Liston	1962–64	30	1953–70	50-4-0 (39)	1
Muhammad Ali	1964–71	22	1960–81	56-5-0 (37)	9
Joe Frazier	1971–73	27	1965–81	32-4-1 (27)	2
George Foreman	1973–74	24	1969–97	76-5-0 (68)	2
Muhammad Ali	1974–78	32	1960–81	56-5-0 (37)	10
Leon Spinks	1978	24	1977–95	26-17-3 (14)	0
Muhammad Ali†	1978–79	36	1960–81	56-5-0 (37)	0
Larry Holmes	1980–85	29	1973–2002	69-6-0 (44)	20
Michael Spinks	1985–88	29	1977–88	32-1-0 (21)	3
Mike Tyson	1988–90	21	1985–2005	49-4-0 (43)	2
Buster Douglas	1990	29	1981–99	38-6-1 (25)	0
Evander Holyfield	1990–92	28	1984–	38-5-2 (26)	3
Riddick Bowe	1992–93	25	1989–96	40-1-0 (32)	2
Evander Holyfield	1993–94	31	1984–	38-5-2 (26)	0
Michael Moorer	1994	26	1988–97	39-2-0 (31)	0
George Foreman	1994–97	45	1969–97	76-5-0 (68)	3
Shannon Briggs	1997–98	25	1992–00	32-3-1 (25)	0
Lennox Lewis	1998–01	32	1989–2004	40-2-1 (31)	5
Hasim Rahman	2001	28	1994–	35-4-0 (29)	0
Lennox Lewis†	2001–04	36	1989–2004	41-2-1 (32)	2
Chris Byrd	2002–06	35	1993–	38-2-1 (20)	3
John Ruiz	2001–03	31	1992–	38-5-1 (28)	2
Roy Jones, Jr.	2003	34	1989–	49-3-0 (38)	0
John Ruiz	2003–05	33	1992–	41-6-1 (28)	2
Vitali Klitschko†	2004–05	34	1996–2005	34-2-0 (33)	1
Hasim Rahman	2005-06	33	1994–	41-5-2 (33)	1
Oleg Maskaev	2006–	37	1993–	32-5-0 (26)	0
Wladimir Klitschko	2006–	30	1996–	46-3-0 (41)	0
Nikolay Valuev	2005–	32	1993–	44-0-0 (32)	1

*Age when boxer won world championship. † Boxer retired or relinquished world title.

Horse
Racing

2006 Preakness
Stakes winner
Bernardini

Tragedy in the First Furlong

After an impressive victory at the Kentucky Derby,
Barbaro seemed poised for a run at the Triple Crown,
but a horrific accident instead left him fighting for his life

BY MARK BECHTEL

LESS THAN A WEEK BEFORE THE 2006 Preakness, Michael Matz sat in his office at the Fair Hill Training Center, a thoroughbred factory nestled in the rural hills of northern Maryland. Matz, 55, has been a horseman for four decades; before becoming a trainer in 1997, he was an accomplished equestrian rider, winning a silver medal at the '96 Olympics. So he knows well that keeping one's sanity in the horse game requires finding the delicate equilibrium between bountiful, irrational optimism and cold-blooded realism. "If we can just get past this weekend and have a chance at the Triple Crown," Matz said, his voice straining to mask the dreams of racing greatness that danced in his head. "I hate to get my hopes up so much, because in two minutes it could be out the window."

Matz was talking about Barbaro, his unbeaten, dark-bay colt who 10 days earlier had romped to the largest margin of victory in the Kentucky Derby in 60 years. Barbaro was a superstar in the making—and, it appeared, the horse that would finally end thoroughbred racing's Triple Crown drought. It had been 28 years since Affirmed swept the Derby, the Preakness

and the Belmont, and with each near-miss since then—in six of the last 10 years a horse has won two of the sport's three jewels—the Crown has taken on the aura of a winning lottery ticket, a goal that simultaneously seems both reachable and yet utterly improbable. Even before the sun set at Churchill Downs on the first Saturday in May, there was a buzz in the racing community. Thanks to Barbaro, this would finally be the year.

Matz was wrong: It took about 15 seconds, not two minutes, for the hopes and dreams of an entire sport to fizzle into tragedy. A few moments after breaking out of the gate at the Preakness, Barbaro pulled up with three fractures in his right hind leg, injuries that ended all Triple Crown talk as well as Barbaro's career as a racehorse. The stricken colt was rushed to the University of Pennsylvania's New Bolton Center in Kennett Square, Pa., where he underwent five hours of surgery the next day. The procedure, during which doctors inserted a plate and 23 screws into Barbaro's lower leg, very likely saved the horse's life—and even then, surgeon Dean Richardson said after the operation, Barbaro was "still a coin toss" for survival.

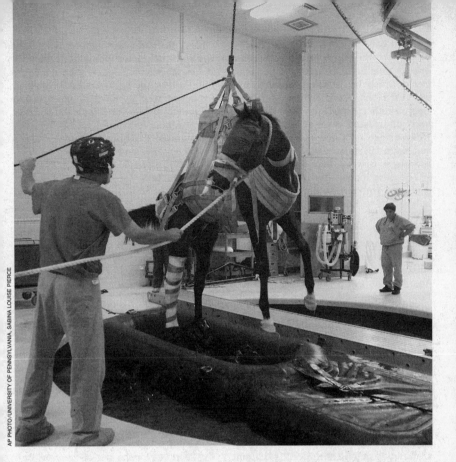

It was one of the most heart-wrenching episodes that could be witnessed on any track, court or field, and it left the sport shaken to its core. For the record, the Preakness champion was Bernardini, who, in his fourth career start, won by a commanding 5¼ lengths. But as he crossed the finish line, the thoughts of nearly everyone in the record crowd of 118,402 at Pimlico Race Course were with Barbaro. "No! No way!" Dan Hendricks, the trainer of fourth-place finisher Brother Derek shouted as he watched the race on TV beneath the grandstand. Hendricks buried his face in his hands and moaned, "S---, ah, God."

Barbaro had captured the racing public's imagination at the Derby, which began with no clear favorite among the field of 20. The pre-race parity was misleading. Matz, who

2006 Kentucky Derby winner Barbaro broke his leg in three places at the Preakness and required surgery to save his life.

was hailed as a hero when he helped pull fellow survivors from the wreckage of a plane crash in Sioux City, Iowa, hatched an unusual plan for Barbaro. The Derby was the horse's first race since the April 1 Florida Derby, and the long layoff didn't bode well for Barbaro's chances. It had been 50 years since a horse had won at Churchill Downs after a five-week layoff.

Matz's patience was rewarded, and Barbaro easily bucked the historical trend. Jockey Edgar Prado guided Barbaro into the lead on the far turn, past fading sprinters Keyed Entry and Sinister Minister, and the mammoth horse—at 17 hands high he towered over most of his competitors—breezed to the finish. He ran the final quarter mile in 24.34 seconds, the fastest Derby finish in 16 years. Barbaro, who went off as the second betting choice (6-1) after Sweetnorthernsaint, was only the second undefeated winner at Churchill Downs since 1977, and racing had a new superstar. "Every step of the way, he was running so easy," said Prado.

"Boy, he looked the part out there," said rival trainer Bob Baffert. "And now he's got the tough [race] out of the way, so look out."

The Triple Crown buzz grew to a roar over the ensuing fortnight. Barbaro was fresh; the Derby had been his sixth career start and only his second in 13 weeks, and he got better each time he ran. Prado, 39, was an experienced guide—he began his career in Maryland and knew the Pimlico course well, and he had twice won the Belmont. And in a quarter-mile workout two days before the Preakness, Barbaro wowed his trainer. "That was like turning on a switch," Matz said the morning of the race.

The Preakness began on a jarringly ominous note. Seconds after the horses were loaded into the starting gate, Barbaro bulled through the doors and took off down the track. Prado stopped him after 25 yards and, after a check by a veterinarian, the horse was reloaded. But when the gun went off and the gates opened, something was clearly wrong. Usually a fast and athletic starter, Barbaro looked slow over the first 200 yards. "I was right behind him," jockey Alex Solis, who was aboard Brother Derek, said. "I heard a crack. I knew [the leg] was broken." Prado stood in the saddle and, with the horse's right hind leg flopping grotesquely, eased him to a stop after another 100 yards. Barely an hour later, Barbaro was on his way, with a police escort, to the hospital.

With a Triple Crown no longer at stake and Barbaro's injury still haunting the sport, the Belmont went off with a decidedly anticlimactic feel. In addition to the Derby champ, the race was absent the Preakness champ; Bernardini's owners decided to rest the horse for competition late in the year. Before the Belmont, Baffert dubbed the race "the Test of the Leftovers." All of which explained why a crowd of only 61,000 showed up at Belmont Park on the first Saturday in June, and ratings for ABC's broadcast tumbled 38% from the previous year.

None of that made the day any less special, however, for Kiaran McLaughlin and Fernando Jara, the trainer and jockey, respectively, of Jazil. The three-year-old made the Belmont his coming-out party: Thanks to an expert ride by Jara, Jazil roared from last at the half-mile marker to victory. It was a scintillating performance, one that restored some luster to a sport in dire need of good news. It also suggested that the McLaughlin family, in addition to boasting a world-class trainer, has an elite handicapper in its hands. Before the race, the trainer's 12-year-old son, Ryan, gave his Dad the trifecta of Jazil, Bluegrass Cat and Sunriver. The boy was dead on, and his selection paid $436.

Bernardini returned to the track in August with a dominating 7½-length victory in the Travers Stakes at Saratoga. Clearly, his Preakness win had been no fluke, and Bernardini went into the Breeders Cup as a leading candidate for Horse of the Year. But for the rest of the year, Barbaro's condition was a point of national concern and the sport's most-watched story line. After stabilizing in the weeks after his operation, the horse took a turn for the worse in July: He developed laminitis, a potentially fatal condition in the injured limb that required surgery to remove most of his injured hoof. Despite the complication, Barbaro continued to cling to life. By late September, he was walking daily and grazing, though he was still in a cast and, according to Richardson, perhaps a year away from leaving the hospital and being able to stand on the shattered leg. Said Richardson, echoing the thoughts of an entire sport, "He feels so good, and he looks so much like a normal horse that you want to believe that there's no doubt that he's going to make it."

FOR THE RECORD • 2005—2006

THOROUGHBRED RACING

The Triple Crown

132nd Kentucky Derby

May 6, 2006. Grade I, 3-year-olds; 10th race, Churchill Downs, Louisville. All 126 lbs. Distance: 1¼ miles. Purse: $2,000,000 guaranteed. Track: Fast. Off: 6:15 p.m. Winner: Barbaro (By Dynaformer out of La Ville Rouge by Carson City); Times: 0:22.63, 0:46.07, 1:10.88, 1:37.02, 2:01.36. Won: Driving. Breeder: Mr & Mrs. M. Roy Jackson

Horse	Finish-PP	Margin	Jockey/Trainer
Barbaro	1–8	6½	Edgar Prado/Michael Matz
Bluegrass Cat	2–13	2	Ramon Dominguez/Todd Pletcher
Steppenwolfer	3–2	1	Robby Albarado/Daniel Peitz
*Jazil	4–1	½	Fernando Jara/Kiaran McLaughlin
*Brother Derek	4–18	½	Alex Solis /Dan Hendricks
Showing Up	5–6	3	Cornelio Velasquez/Barclay Tagg
Sweetnorthernsaint	6–11	1	Kent Desormeaux/Michael Trombetta
Deputy Glitters	7–14	1¼	Jose Lezcano/Thomas Albertrani
Point Determined	8–5	head	Rafael Bejarano/Bob Baffert
Seaside Retreat	9–15	4½	Patrick Husbands/Mark Casse
Storm Treasure	10–19	1¾	David Flores/Steven Asmussen
Lawyer Ron	11–17	nose	John McKee/Robert Holthus
Cause to Believe	12–16	3	Russell Baze/Jerry Hollendorfer
Flashy Bull	13–20	2½	Mike Smith/Kiaran McLaughlin
Private Vow	14–12	2¾	Shaun Bridgmohan/Steven Asmussen
Sinister Minister	15–4	1½	Victor Espinoza/Bob Baffert
Bob and John	16–7	neck	Garrett Gomez/Bob Baffert
A.P. Warrior	17–10	1½	Corey Nakatani/John Shirreffs
Sharp Humor	18–9	7½	Mark Guidry/Dale Romans
Keyed Entry	19–3		Pat Valenzuela/Todd Pletcher

* Dead heat

131st Preakness Stakes

May 20, 2006. Grade I, 3-year-olds; 12th race, Pimlico Race Course, Baltimore. All 126 lbs. Distance: 1³⁄₁₆ miles; Stakes value: $1,000,000. Off: 6:19 p.m. Winner: Bernardini (By A.P. Indy out of Cara Rafaela by Quiet American); Times: 0:23.21, 0:46.69, 1:10.24, 1:35.73, 1:54.65. Won: Driving. Breeder: Darley

Horse	Finish-PP	Margin	Jockey/Trainer
Bernardini	1-8	5¼	Javier Castellano/Thomas Albertrani
Sweetnorthernsaint	2-7	6	Kent Desormeaux/Michael Trombetta
Hemingway's Key	3-3	4	Jeremy Rose/Nicholas Zito
Brother Derek	4-5	7	Alex Solis /Dan Hendricks
Greeley's Legacy	5-4	1	Richard Migliore/George Weaver
Platinum Couple	6-2	3½	Jose Espinoza/Joseph Lostritto
Like Now	7-1	2¼	Garrett Gomez/Kiaran McLaughlin
Diabolical	8-9	—	Cornelio Velasquez/Kiaran McLaughlin
Barbaro	9-6	—	Edgar Prado/Michael Matz

138th Belmont Stakes

June 10, 2006. Grade I, 3-year-olds; 11th race, Belmont Park, Elmont, NY. All 126 lbs. Distance: 1½ miles. Stakes value: $1,000,000. Track: Fast. Off: 6:35 p.m. Winner: Jazil (By Seeking the Gold out of Better Than Honour by Deputy Minister); Times: 0:23.02, 47.36, 1:12.14, 1:37.53, 2:02.69, 2:27.86. Won: Driving. Breeder: Skara Glen Stables

Horse	Finish-PP	Margin	Jockey/Trainer
Jazil	1-8	1¼	Fernando Jara/Kiaran McLaughlin
Bluegrass Cat	2-9	2¼	John Velazquez/Todd Pletcher
Sunriver	3-2	1¼	Rafael Bejarano/Todd Pletcher
Steppenwolfer	4-11	5	Robby Albarado/Daniel Peitz
Oh So Awesome	5-6	2	Mike Smith/ James A. Jerkens
Hemingway's Key	6-3	4½	Jeremy Rose/ Nicholas Zito
Platinum Couple	7-1	2½	Jose Espinoza/Joseph Lostritto
Bob and John	8-4	4¼	Garrett Gomez/Bob Baffert
Sacred Light	9-12	6½	Victor Espinoza/David Hofmans
High Finance	10-5	11¼	Eibar Coa/Rick Violette Jr.
Deputy Glitters	11-7		Edgar Prado/Thomas Albertrani
Double Galore	12-10	—	Michael Luzzi/Myung Kwon Cho

Major Stakes Races

Late 2005

Date	Race	Track	Distance	Winner	Jockey/Trainer	Purse ($)
Sept 5	Pennsylvania Derby	Philadelphia	1⅛ miles	Sun King	R.Bejarano/ N. Zito	750,000
Sept 18	Atto Mile Stakes	Woodbine	1 mile	Leriodes-animaux	J. Velazquez/ R.Frankel	849,756
Sept 24	Hawthorne Gold Cup	Hawthorne	1¼ miles	Super-Frolic	Victor Espinoza/ V. Cerin	750,000
Oct 1	Super Derby XXV	Louisiana Downs	1⅛ miles	The Daddy	P. Morales/ S. Gonzalez	750,000
Oct 1	Jockey Club Gold Cup	Belmont	1¼ miles	Borrego	G. Gomez/ B. Greely	1,000,000
Oct 1	Hirsch Turf Classic Invitational	Belmont	1½ miles	Shakespeare	J. Bailey/ W. Mott	750,000
Oct 1	Vosburgh Stakes	Belmont	6 furlongs	Taste of Paradise	G. Gomez/ G. Mandella	500,000
Oct 1	Flower Bowl Invitational	Belmont	1¼ miles	Riskaverse	J. Santos/ P. Kelley	750,000
Oct 1	Yellow Ribbon Stakes	Santa Anita	1¼ miles	Megahertz	A. Solis/ R. Frankel	500,000
Oct 1	Goodwood B.C.	Santa Anita	1⅛ miles	Rock Hard Ten	G. Stevens/ R. Mandella	484,000
Oct 1	Indiana B.C. Oaks	Hoosier	1 1/16 miles	Flying Glitter	R. Albarado/ R. Werner	405,100
Oct 1	Beldame Stakes	Belmont	1⅛ miles	Ashado	J. Velazquez/ T. Pletcher	750,000
Oct 2	Indiana Derby	Hoosier	1 1/16 miles	Don't Get Mad	B. Blanc/ R. Ellis	511,300
Oct 7	Darley Alcibiades Stakes	Keeneland	1 1/16 miles	She says it Best	E.M. Martin/ V. Foley	400,000
Oct 7	Meadowlands B.C. Stakes	Meadowlands	1⅛ miles	Tap Day	E.Coa/ M. Hennig	500,000
Oct 8	Champagne Stakes	Belmont	1 miles	First Samurai	J. Bailey/ F. Brothers	500,000
Oct 8	Lane's End B. Futurity	Keeneland	1 1/16 miles	Dawn of War	J. Jacinto/ D. Romans	500,000
Oct 8	Frizette	Belmont	1 miles	Adieu	J. Velazquez/ T.Pletcher	500,000
Oct 8	Shadwell Turf Mile	Keeneland	1 mile	Host	R. Bejarano/ T.Pletcher	600,000
Oct 9	Juddmonte Spinster Stakes	Keeneland	1⅛ miles	Pampered Princess	E. Castro/ M. Wolfson	500,000
Oct 9	Winstar Galaxy Stakes	Keeneland	1 3/16 miles	Inter-continental	J. Bailey/ F. Frankel	400,000
Oct 15	Queen Elizabeth II Challenge Cup	Keeneland	1⅛ miles	Sweet Talker	R. Bejarano/ H. Pitts	500,000
Oct 23	Pattison Canadian International	Woodbine	1⅛ miles	Relaxed Gesture	C. Nakatani/ C. Clement	1,684,885
Oct 23	E.P. Taylor Stakes	Woodbine	1¼ miles	Honey Rider	J. Velasquez/ T. Pletcher	843,959
Oct 29	Breeders Cup Classic Stakes	Belmont	1¼ mile	Saint Liam	J. Bailey/ R. Dutrow Jr.	4,291,560
Oct 29	Breeders Cup Turf Stakes	Belmont	1½ miles	Shirocco	C. Soumillion/ A. Fabre	2,090,760
Oct 29	Breeders Cup Distaff	Belmont	1⅛ mile	Pleasant Home	C.H. Velazquez/ C. McGuaghey	1,834,000
Oct 29	Breeders Cup Mile Stakes	Belmont	1 mile	Artie Schiller	G. Gomez/ J. Jerkins	1,856,925
Oct 29	Breeders Cup Juvenile Stakes	Belmont	1 1/16 miles	Stevie Wonderboy	G. Gomez/ D. O'Neill	1,458,030
Oct 29	Breeders Cup Juvenile Fillies	Belmont	1 1/16 miles	Folklore	E. Prado/ D.W. Lukas	972,020
Oct 29	Breeders Cup Filly & Mare	Belmont	1⅜ miles	Intercon-tinental	R. Bejarano/ R. Frankel	972,020
Oct 29	Breeders Cup Sprint Stakes	Belmont	6 furlongs	Silver Train	E. Prado/ R. Dutrow Jr.	972,020
Nov 25	Clark Handicap	Churchill Downs	1⅛ miles	Magna Graduate	J. Velazquez/ T. Pletcher	573,500

2006 (through September 30)

Date	Race	Track	Distance	Winner	Jockey/Trainer	Purse ($)
Jan 28.....	Sunshine Millions Classic	Santa Anita	1⅛ miles	Lava Man	C. Nakatani/ D. O'Neill	1,000,000
Jan 28.....	Sunshine Millions Turf	Gulfstream	1⅛ miles	Miesque's Approval	E. Castro/ M. Wolfson	500,000
Jan 28.....	Sunshine Millions Distaff	Gulfstream	1¹⁄₁₆ miles	House of Fortune	P. Valenzuela/ R. McAnally	500,000
Jan 28.....	Sunshine Milions Sprint	Gulfstream	6 furlongs	Bordanaro	P. Valenzuela/ W. Spawr	300,000
Jan 28.....	Sunshine Millions F&M Turf	Santa Anita	1⅛ miles	Moscow Burning	D. Flores/ J. Cassidy	500,000
Feb 4......	Donn Handicap	Gulfstream	1⅛ miles	Brass Hat	W. Martinez/ W. Bradley	500,000
Mar 4......	Santa Anita Handicap	Santa Anita	1¼ miles	Lava Man	C. Nakatani/ D. O'Neill	1,000,000
Mar 25....	Dubai World Cup	Nad al Sheba	1½ miles	Electro-cutionist	L. Dettori/ S. bin Suroor	6,000,000
Mar 25....	Dubai Duty Free	Nad al Sheba	1⅛ miles	David Junior	J. Spencer/ B. Meehan	5,000,000
Mar 25....	Dubai Golden Shaheen	Nad al Sheba	6 furlongs	Proud Tower	D. Cohen/ S. Gonzalez	2,000,000
Mar 25....	UAE Derby	Nad al Sheba	1⅛ miles	Discreet Cat	L. Dettori/ S. bin Suroor/	2,000,000
Mar 25....	Lane's End Stakes	Turfway	1⅛ miles	With A City	B.Blanc/ M. Maker	500,000
Apr 1.......	Florida Derby	Gulfstream	1⅛ miles	Barbaro	E. Prado/ M. Matz	1,000,000
Apr 1.......	Winstar Derby	Sunland	1⅛ miles	Wanna Runner	V. Espinoza/ B. Baffert	600,000
Apr 8.......	Wood Memorial Stakes	Aqueduct	1⅛ miles	Bob and John	G. Gomez/ B. Baffert	750,000
Apr 8.......	Santa Anita Derby	Santa Anita	1⅛ miles	Buzzard's Bay	J. Mullins/ M. Guidry	750,000
Apr 8.......	Ashland Stakes	Keeneland	1¹⁄₁₆ miles	Bushfire	C. Velasqez/ E. Kenneally	500,000
Apr 8.......	Apple Blossom Handicap	Oaklawn	1¹⁄₁₆ miles	Spun Sugar	M. Luzzi/ T. Pletcher	500,000
Apr 8.......	Illinois Derby	Hawthorne	1⅛ miles	Sweetnorthernsaint	K. Desormeaux/ M. Trombetta	500,000
Apr 8.......	Oaklawn Handicap	Oaklawn	1⅛ miles	Buzzards Bay	J. Valdivia/ R. Ellis	500,000
Apr 15.....	Toyota Blue Grass	Keeneland	1⅛ miles	Sinister Minister	G. Gomez/ B. Baffert	750,000
Apr 15.....	Arkansas Derby	Belmont Park	1⅛ miles	Lawyer Ron	J. McKee/ R. Holthus	1,000,000
May 5......	Kentucky Oaks	Churchill Downs	1⅛ miles	Lemons Forever	M. Guidry/ D. Stewart	755,900
May 6......	Kentucky Derby	Churchill Downs	1¼ miles	Barbaro	E. Prado/ M. Matz	2,000,000
May 6......	Woodford Reserve Classic	Churchill Downs	1⅛ miles	English Channel	G. Gomez/ T. Pletcher	454,900
May 19....	Pimlico Special	Pimlico	1⅛ miles	Invasor	R. Dominguez/ K. McLaughlin	500,000
May 20....	Preakness Stakes	Pimlico	1³⁄₁₆ miles	Bernardini	J. Castellano/ T. Albertrani	1,000,000
May 29....	Metropolitan Handicap	Belmont Park	1 mile	Silver Train	R. Dutrow/ E. Prado	600,000
May 29....	Shoemaker B.C. Mile	Hollywood Park	1 mile	Aragon	C. Nakatani/ N. Drysdale	321,000
May 29....	Lone Star Park Stakes	Lone Star	1¹⁄₁₆ miles	Magnum	P. Valenzuela/ D. Vienna	400,000
June 10...	Belmont Stakes	Belmont	1½ miles	Jazil	F. Jara/ K. McLaughlin	1,000,000
June 10...	Manhattan Handicap	Belmont	1¼ miles	Cacique	E. Prado/ R. Frankel	400,000
June 17...	Stephen Foster Handicap	Churchill Downs	1⅛ miles	Seek Gold	C. Borel/ R. Moquett	844,500

Major Stakes Races (Cont.)

2006 (through September 30) *(Cont.)*

Date	Race	Track	Distance	Winner	Jockey/Trainer	Purse ($)
June 26	Queen's Plate Stakes	Woodbine	1¼ miles	Edenwold	E. Ramsammy/ J. Carroll	892,848
July 1	Suburban Handicap	Belmont	1¼ miles	Invasor	F. Jara/ K. McLaughlin	400,000
July 8	United Nations Stakes	Monmouth	1⅜ miles	English Channel	T. Pletcher J. Velazquez	750,000
July 8	Hollywood Gold Cup	Hollywood	1¼ miles	Lava Man	C. Nakatani/ D. O'Neill	750,000
July 15	Princess Rooney Handicap	Calder	6 furlongs	Malibu Mint	J. Acre/ J. Chapman	500,000
July 15	Smile Sprint Handicap	Calder	6 furlongs	Nightmare Affair	J. Sanchez/ M. Azpurua	500,000
July 15	Delaware Oaks	Delaware	1 1/16 miles	Adieu	J. Velazquez/ T. Pletcher	500,900
July 15	Virginia Derby	Colonial Downs	1 3/16 miles	Go Between	G. Gomez/ W. Mott	1,000,000
July 16	Delaware Handicap	Delaware	1¼ miles	Fleet Indian	J. Santos/ T. Pletcher	1,001,200
July 22	American Oaks	Belmont	1¼ miles	Wonder Lady Anne	E. Prado/ R. Dutrow Jr.	300,000
July 22	John C. Mabee Handicap	Del Mar	1⅛ miles	Dancing Edie	C. Nakatani/ C. Dollase	400,000
July 23	N. Dancer Handicap	Woodbine	1½ miles	Sky Conqueror	T. Kabel/ D. Banach	613,017
July 29	Diana Stakes	Saratoga	1⅛ miles	Angara	F. Jara/ W. Mott	500,000
July 29	Jim Dandy Stakes	Saratoga	1⅛ miles	Bernardini	J. Castellano/ T. Albertrani	500,000
Aug 6	Whitney Handicap	Saratoga	1⅛ miles	Invasor	F. Jara/ K. McLaughlin	750,000
Aug 6	Haskell Handicap	Monmouth	1⅛ miles	Bluegrass Cat	J. Velazquez/ T. Pletcher	1,030,000
Aug 6	West Virginia Derby	Mountaineer	1⅛ miles	Bright One	M. Guidry/ D. Romans	750,000
Aug 12	Arlington Million Stakes	Arlington	1¼ miles	The Tin Man	V. Espinoza/ R. Mandella	1,000,000
Aug 12	Beverly D. Stakes	Arlington	1 3/16 miles	Gorella	J. Laparoux/ P. Biancone	750,000
Aug 12	Secretariat Stakes	Arlington	1¼ miles	Showing up	C.H. Velasquez/ B. Tagg	400,000
Aug 12	Sword Dancer Invitational	Saratoga	1½ miles	Go Deputy	E. Coa/ T. Pletcher	500,000
Aug 19	Alabama Stakes	Saratoga	1¼ miles	Pine Island	J. Castellano/ C. McGaughey	600,000
Aug 20	Pacific Classic	Del Mar	1¼ miles	Lava Man	C. Nakatani/ D. O'Neill	1,000,000
Aug 26	Travers Stakes	Saratoga	1¼ miles	Bernardini	J. Castellano/ T. Albertrani	1,000,000
Sept 2	Woodward Stakes	Saratoga	1⅛ miles	Premium Tap	K. Desormeaux/ J. Kimmel	500,000
Sept 3	Del Mar Derby	Del Mar	1⅛ miles	Get Funky	J. Valdivia/ J. Sadler	400,000
Sept 9	Man O'War Stakes	Belmont	1⅜ miles	Cacique	E. Prado/ R. Frankel	500,000
Sept 17	Woodbine Mile	Woodbine	1 mile	Becrux	P. Valenzuela/ N. Drysdale	896,456
Sept 23	Super Derby	Louisiana Downs	1⅛ miles	Strong Contender	R. Albarado/ J. Ward	486,500
Sept 30	Yellow Ribbon Stakes	Santa Anita	1¼ miles	Wait A While	G. Gomez/ T. Pletcher	400,000
Sept 30	Hawthorne Gold Cup	Hawthorne	1¼ miles	It's No Joke	E. Razo Jr./ R. Maker	500,000

Horses

Horse	Starts	1st	2nd	3rd	Purses ($)	Horse	Starts	1st	2nd	3rd	Purses ($)
Saint Liam	6	4	1	0	3,696,960	Afleet Alex	6	4	0	1	2,085,000
Roses in May	2	1	1	0	3,695,000	Giacomo	6	1	1	2	1,846,876
Flower Alley	9	4	3	0	2,435,200	Borrego	8	3	1	2	1,536,600
Vengeance of Rain	2	2	0	0	2,349,545	Art Schiller	6	3	2	1	1,448,000
Alkaased	1	1	0	0	2,122,303	Makybe Diva	1	1	0	0	1,365,283

Jockeys

Jockey	Mounts	1st	2nd	3rd	Purses ($)	Win Pct	$ Pct*
John Velasquez	1148	251	177	146	24,459,923	.22	.50
Edgar Prado	1461	299	227	206	18,615,336	.20	.50
Jerry Bailey	654	169	103	91	18,297,384	.26	.56
Rafael Bejarano	1346	263	255	204	14,427,541	.20	.54
Garrett Gomez	1295	245	211	177	14,221,321	.19	.49
Javier Castellano	1158	206	188	177	12,507,012	.18	.49
Victor Espinoza	1107	192	182	161	12,054,776	.17	.48
Patrick Valenzuela	1012	202	196	144	11,794,244	.20	.54
Cornelio Velasquez	1456	216	217	200	11,430,591	.15	.43
Ramon Dominguez	1222	312	230	182	10,767,955	.26	.59

*Percentage in the Money (1st, 2nd, and 3rd).

Trainers

Trainer	Starts	1st	2nd	3rd	Purses ($)	Win Pct	$ Pct*
Todd Pletcher	1039	257	175	135	20,867,842	.25	.55
Robert Frankel	583	128	101	93	14,122,807	.22	.55
Steven Asmussen	2227	474	379	304	13,302,283	.21	.52
Richard Dutrow Jr	575	151	114	78	9,797,126	.26	.60
Doug O'Neill	893	158	149	121	9,476,801	.18	.48
William Mott	631	138	119	93	9,355,603	.22	.55
Scott Lake	1796	417	329	239	8,983,267	.23	.55
Nicholas Zito	462	86	70	64	8,199,368	.19	.48
Dale Romans	524	96	83	59	8,021,833	.18	.45
Jeff Mullins	497	118	88	64	6,279,989	.24	.54

*Percentage in the Money (1st, 2nd, and 3rd).

Owners

Owner	Starts	1st	2nd	3rd	Purses ($)
Kenneth & Sarah Ramsey	286	61	48	32	6,447,505
Michael Gill	1870	351	286	264	6,397,180
Melnyk Racing Stables, Inc	417	89	71	61	5,875,007
Live Oak Plantation	252	60	50	36	4,904,171
Robert Bone	589	156	116	89	4,513,264
Stronach Stables	466	113	81	53	4,383,153
Mr. & Mrs. William Warren Jr.	23	7	3	0	3,773,375
Mr. & Mrs. Jerome Moss	179	37	26	28	3,325,480
Phipps Stable	97	26	13	16	3,289,390
Robert and Beverly Lewis	264	46	43	40	3,250,422

HARNESS RACING

Major Stakes Races

Late 2005

Date	Race	Location	Winner	Driver/Trainer	Purse ($)
Oct 22	Goldsmith Maid	Woodbine	Passionate Glide	Ron Pierce/ Jim Takter	473,884
Oct 22	Governor's Cup	Woodbine	Jereme's Jet	Paul MacDonell/ Tom Harmer	593,032
Oct 22	Valley Victory	Meadowlands	RC Royalty	Dan Daley/ Dan Daley	472,162
Oct 22	Three Diamonds	Meadowlands	Darlin's Delight	Yannick Gingras/ Jeff Stafford	452,098
Nov 26	Breeders Crown Two-year-old Filly Trot	Meadowlands	Passionate Glide	Ron Pierce/ Jim Takter	516,800
Nov 26	Breeders Crown Two-year-old Filly Pace	Meadowlands	My Little Dragon	Ron Pierce/ Bob Johnson	500,000
Nov 26	Breeders Crown Two-year-old Colt Trot	Meadowlands	Chocolatier	D.R. Ackerman/ Doug Ackerman	507,600
Nov 26	Breeders Crown Two-year-old Colt Pace	Meadowlands	Jereme's Jet	Paul MacDonell/ Tom Harmer	575,400
Nov 26	Breeders Crown Three-year-old Filly Trot	Meadowlands	Blur	Brian Sears/ Trond Smedshammer	500,000
Nov 26	Breeders Crown Three-year-old Filly Pace	Meadowlands	Belovedangel	Ron Pierce/ Robert McIntosh	500,000
Nov 26	Breeders Crown Three-year-old Colt Trot	Meadowlands	Strong Yankee	Brian Sears/ Trond Smedshammer	610,000
Nov 26	Breeders Crown Three-year-old Colt Pace	Meadowlands	Rocknroll Hanover	Brian Sears/ Brett Pelling	555,000

2006 (through October 1)

Date	Race	Location	Winner	Driver/Trainer	Purse ($)
June 17	North America Cup	Woodbine	Total Truth	Brian Sears/ Brenda Teague	1,350,000
June 24	Canadian Pacing Derby	Mohawk	Lis Mara	Brian Sears/ Ervin Miller	830,370
July 15	Meadowlands Pace	Meadowlands	Artistic Fella	Catello Manzi/ Steve Elliott	1,000,000
July 15	Stanley Dancer Trot	Meadowlands	Mr. Pine Chip	Brian Sears/ Trond Smedshammer	375,000
July 29	Breeders Crown Open Trot	Meadowlands	Sand Vic	Brian Sears/ Trond Smedshammer	800,000
July 29	Breeders Crown Open Pace	Meadowlands	Lis Mara	Brian Sears/ Ervin Miller	500,000
July 29	Breeders Crown Mare Pace	Meadowlands	Burning Point	Ron Pierce/ Steve Elliott	331,500
July 29	Breeders Crown Mare Trot	Meadowlands	Mystical Sunshine	Ron Pierce/ Christopher Ryder	250,000
Aug 3	Peter Haughton	Meadowlands	Donato Hanover	Ron Pierce/ Steve Elliott	456,000
Aug 3	Merrie Annabelle	Meadowlands	Gerri's Joy	John Campbell/ Remi Jensen	537,000
Aug 4	Woodrow Wilson	Meadowlands	Fox Valley Barzgar	Anthony Morgan/ Tom Harmer	410,000
Aug 4	Sweetheart	Meadowlands	Isabella Blue Chip	David Miller/ George Teague	435,000
Aug 5	Hambletonian	Meadowlands	Glidemaster	John Campbell/ Blair Burgess	1,500,000
Aug 5	Hambletonian Oaks	Meadowlands	Passionate Glide	Ron Pierce/ Jim Takter	1,500,000
Aug 20	Confederation Cup	Flamboro	Ambro Deuce	George Brennan/ Blair Burgess	541,120
Sept 21	Little Brown Jug	Delaware, Ohio	Mr. Feelgood	Mark MacDonald/ Jim Takter	432,800
Sept 23	Canadian Trotting Classic	Mohawk	Majestic Son	Trevor Ritchie/ Mark Steacy	900,000

Major Stakes Races (*Cont.*)

The Hambletonian

Raced at The Meadowlands, East Rutherford, N.J., on August 5, 2006

Horse	Driver	PP	¼	½	¾	Stretch	Finish
Glidemaster	J. Campbell	8	8o	8o	6oo	5-1½	1-1¼
Chocolatier	D.R. Ackerman	10	10o	9o	9oo	6-3¼	2-1¼
Blue Mac Lad	G. Brennan	2	2	2	2	2-¾	3-1¾
Global Glide	R. Pierce	5	6	7	8	9-4¾	4-5½
Algiers Hall	J. Stark Jr.	1	4	5	7	7-3¼	5-7½
Here Comes Herbie	T. Smedshammer	4	1o	1	1	1-¾	6-7¾
Race Fan	S. Smith	9	9	10	10	10-5¾	7-9¼
Berto Primo	C. Manzi	7	5	4o	3o	3-1½	9P8-10½
Capetown Hall	D. Miller	3	3	3	4	8-3½	10P9-13½
Mr. Pine Chip	B. Sears	6	7o	6o	5oo	4x-1½	X8XP10-10

Times: 0:26.4, 0:54.3, 1:23.3, 1:51.1

The Little Brown Jug

Raced at the Delaware County Fairgrounds, in Delaware, Ohio, on September 21, 2006

Horse	Driver	PP	¼	½	¾	Stretch	Finish
Mr. Feelgood	M. MacDonald	1	2	2	2	1-¼	1-1¾
Cactus Creek	M. La Chance	2	3	3	3	3-1¼	2-1¾
Ambro Deuce	G. Brennan	5	1	1	1	2-¼	3-3½
Total Truth	R. Pierce	6	7	6IMo	X5	5-4¾	4-4½
Texas Shootout	D. Gingras	3	5	7IM	6	6-5¾	5-6
Ambro Dynamic	J. Campbell	4	6	54	4o	4-4¼	6-8
True North Hanover	D. Palone	7	8	8IMo	7	7-6¾	7-9¼
Western Ace	B. Sears	8	9	9	8	8-8¾	8-12
Doonbeg	J. Jamieson	9	4	5X	9	9-14¾	9-24

Times: 0:26.0, 0:54.3, 1:22.0, 1:50.3

2005 Statistical Leaders

2005 Leading Moneywinners by Age, Sex and Gait

Division	Horse	Starts	Ist	2nd	3rd	Earnings ($)
2-Year-Old Pacing Colts	Jereme's Jet	7	6	1	0	1,039,376
2-Year-Old Pacing Fillies	Darlin's Delight	14	9	5	0	560,404
3-Year-Old Pacing Colts	Rocknroll Hanover	18	12	4	2	2,223,257
3-Year-Old Pacing Fillies	Cabrini Hanover	18	8	5	5	917,440
Older Pacing Horses	Boulder Creek	25	6	6	3	978,645
Older Pacing Mares	Burning Point	27	8	7	3	687,142
2-Year-Old Trotting Colts	Chocolatier	10	8	0	0	508,250
2-Year-Old Trotting Fillies	Passionate Glide	11	5	5	0	638,947
3-Year-Old Trotting Colts	Vivid Photo	25	16	5	1	1,481,020
3-Year-Old Trotting Fillies	Blur	12	7	2	0	867,453
Older Trotting Horses	Mr. Muscleman	14	12	1	0	1,364,220
Older Trotting Mares	Peaceful Way	10	9	0	0	660,804

Drivers

Driver	Earnings ($)
Brian Sears	15,085,992
Ronald Pierce	13,538,851
David Miller	11,134,706
Catello Manzi	8,653,808
George Brennan	7,547,999
Mark MacDonald	7,199,600
Paul MacDonell	6,725,041
Luc Ouellette	6,309,393
Eric Ledford	5,526,285
Chris Christoforou	5,212,878

THOROUGHBRED RACING

Kentucky Derby

Run at Churchill Downs, Louisville, KY, on the first Saturday in May.

Year	Winner (Margin)	Jockey	Second	Third	Time
1875	Aristides (1)	Oliver Lewis	Volcano	Verdigris	2:37¾
1876	Vagrant (2)	Bobby Swim	Creedmoor	Harry Hill	2:38¼
1877	Baden-Baden (2)	William Walker	Leonard	King William	2:38
1878	Day Star (2)	Jimmie Carter	Himyar	Leveler	2:37¼
1879	Lord Murphy (1)	Charlie Shauer	Falsetto	Strathmore	2:37
1880	Fonso (1)	George Lewis	Kimball	Bancroft	2:37½
1881	Hindoo (4)	Jimmy McLaughin	Lelex	Alfambra	2:40
1882	Apollo (½)	Babe Hurd	Runnymede	Bengal	2:40¼
1883	Leonatus (3)	Billy Donohue	Drake Carter	Lord Raglan	2:43
1884	Buchanan (2)	Isaac Murphy	Loftin	Audrain	2:40¼
1885	Joe Cotton (Neck)	Erskine Henderson	Bersan	Ten Booker	2:37¼
1886	Ben Ali (½)	Paul Duffy	Blue Wing	Free Knight	2:36½
1887	Montrose (2)	Isaac Lewis	Jim Gore	Jacobin	2:39¼
1888	MacBeth II (1)	George Covington	Gallifet	White	2:38¼
1889	Spokane (Nose)	Thomas Kiley	Proctor Knott	Once Again	2:34½
1890	Riley (2)	Isaac Murphy	Bill Letcher	Robespierre	2:45
1891	Kingman (1)	Isaac Murphy	Balgowan	High Tariff	2:52¼
1892	Azra (Nose)	Alonzo Clayton	Huron	Phil Dwyer	2:41½
1893	Lookout (5)	Eddie Kunze	Plutus	Boundless	2:39¼
1894	Chant (2)	Frank Goodale	Pearl Song	Sigurd	2:41
1895	Halma (3)	Soup Perkins	Basso	Laureate	2:37½
1896	Ben Brush (Nose)	Willie Simms	Ben Eder	Semper Ego	2:07¼
1897	Typhoon II (Head)	Buttons Garner	Ornament	Dr. Catlett	2:12½
1898	Plaudit (Neck)	Willie Simms	Lieber Karl	Isabey	2:09
1899	Manuel (2)	Fred Taral	Corsini	Mazo	2:12
1900	Lieut. Gibson (4)	Jimmy Boland	Florizar	Thrive	2:06¼
1901	His Eminence (2)	Jimmy Winkfield	Sannazarro	Driscoll	2:07¾
1902	Alan-a-Dale (Nose)	Jimmy Winkfield	Inventor	The Rival	2:08¾
1903	Judge Himes (¾)	Hal Booker	Early	Bourbon	2:09
1904	Elwood (½)	Frankie Prior	Ed Tierney	Brancas	2:08½
1905	Agile (3)	Jack Martin	Ram's Horn	Layson	2:10¾
1906	Sir Huon (2)	Roscoe Troxler	Lady Navarre	James Reddick	2:08⅕
1907	Pink Star (2)	Andy Minder	Zal	Ovelando	2:12⅗
1908	Stone Street (1)	Arthur Pickens	Sir Cleges	Dunvegan	2:15⅕
1909	Wintergreen (4)	Vincent Powers	Miami	Dr. Barkley	2:08⅕
1910	Donau (½)	Fred Herbert	Joe Morris	Fighting Bob	2:06⅖
1911	Meridian (¾)	George Archibald	Governor Gray	Colston	2:05
1912	Worth (Neck)	Carroll H. Schilling	Duval	Flamma	2:09⅖
1913	Donerail (½)	Roscoe Goose	Ten Point	Gowell	2:04⅘
1914	Old Rosebud (8)	John McCabe	Hodge	Bronzewing	2:03⅖
1915	Regret (2)	Joe Notter	Pebbles	Sharpshooter	2:05⅖
1916	George Smith (Neck)	Johnny Loftus	Star Hawk	Franklin	2:04
1917	Omar Khayyam (2)	Charles Borel	Ticket	Midway	2:04⅗
1918	Exterminator (1)	William Knapp	Escoba	Viva America	2:10⅘
1919	Sir Barton (5)	Johnny Loftus	Billy Kelly	Under Fire	2:09⅘
1920	Paul Jones (Head)	Ted Rice	Upset	On Watch	2:09
1921	Behave Yourself (Head)	Charles Thompson	Black Servant	Prudery	2:04⅕
1922	Morvich (½)	Albert Johnson	Bet Mosie	John Finn	2:04⅗
1923	Zev (1½)	Earl Sande	Martingale	Vigil	2:05⅖
1924	Black Gold (½)	John Mooney	Chilhowee	Beau Butler	2:05⅕
1925	Flying Ebony (1½)	Earl Sande	Captain Hal	Son of John	2:07⅗
1926	Bubbling Over (5)	Albert Johnson	Bagenbaggage	Rock Man	2:03⅗
1927	Whiskery (Head)	Linus McAtee	Osmond	Jock	2:06
1928	Reigh Count (3)	Chick Lang	Misstep	Toro	2:10⅖
1929	Clyde Van Dusen (2)	Linus McAtee	Naishapur	Panchio	2:10⅘
1930	Gallant Fox (2)	Earl Sande	Gallant Knight	Ned O.	2:07⅗
1931	Twenty Grand (4)	Charles Kurtsinger	Sweep All	Mate	2:01⅘

Kentucky Derby *(Cont.)*

Year	Winner (Margin)	Jockey	Second	Third	Time
1932	Burgoo King (5)	Eugene James	Economic	Stepenfetchit	2:05⅕
1933	Brokers Tip (Nose)	Don Meade	Head Play	Charley O.	2:06⅘
1934	Cavalcade (2½)	Mack Garner	Discovery	Agrarian	2:04
1935	Omaha (1½)	Willie Saunders	Roman Soldier	Whiskolo	2:05
1936	Bold Venture (Head)	Ira Hanford	Brevity	Indian Broom	2:03⅗
1937	War Admiral (1¾)	Charles Kurtsinger	Pompoon	Reaping Reward	2:03⅕
1938	Lawrin (1)	Eddie Arcaro	Dauber	Can't Wait	2:04⅘
1939	Johnstown (8)	James Stout	Challedon	Heather Broom	2:03⅗
1940	Gallahadion (1½)	Carroll Bierman	Bimelech	Dit	2:05
1941	Whirlaway (8)	Eddie Arcaro	Staretor	Market Wise	2:01⅖
1942	Shut Out (2½)	Wayne Wright	Alsab	Valdina Orphan	2:04⅖
1943	Count Fleet (3)	John Longden	Blue Swords	Slide Rule	2:04
1944	Pensive (4½)	Conn McCreary	Broadcloth	Stir Up	2:04⅕
1945	Hoop Jr. (6)	Eddie Arcaro	Pot o' Luck	Darby Dieppe	2:07
1946	Assault (8)	Warren Mehrtens	Spy Song	Hampden	2:06⅗
1947	Jet Pilot (Head)	Eric Guerin	Phalanx	Faultless	2:06⅘
1948	Citation (3½)	Eddie Arcaro	Coaltown	My Request	2:05⅖
1949	Ponder (3)	Steve Brooks	Capot	Palestinian	2:04⅕
1950	Middleground (1¼)	William Boland	Hill Prince	Mr. Trouble	2:01⅗
1951	Count Turf (4)	Conn McCreary	Royal Mustang	Ruhe	2:02⅗
1952	Hill Gail (2)	Eddie Arcaro	Sub Fleet	Blue Man	2:01⅗
1953	Dark Star (Head)	Hank Moreno	Native Dancer	Invigorator	2:02
1954	Determine (1½)	Ray York	Hasty Road	Hasseyampa	2:03
1955	Swaps (1½)	Bill Shoemaker	Nashua	Summer Tan	2:01⅘
1956	Needles (¾)	Dave Erb	Fabius	Come On Red	2:03⅖
1957	Iron Liege (Nose)	Bill Hartack	Gallant Man	Round Table	2:02⅕
1958	Tim Tam (½)	Ismael Valenzuela	Lincoln Road	Noureddin	2:05
1959	Tomy Lee (Nose)	Bill Shoemaker	Sword Dancer	First Landing	2:02⅕
1960	Venetian Way (3½)	Bill Hartack	Bally Ache	Victoria Park	2:02⅖
1961	Carry Back (¾)	John Sellers	Crozier	Bass Clef	2:04
1962	Decidedly (2¼)	Bill Hartack	Roman Line	Ridan	2:00⅖
1963	Chateaugay (1¼)	Braulio Baeza	Never Bend	Candy Spots	2:01⅘
1964	Northern Dancer (Neck)	Bill Hartack	Hill Rise	The Scoundrel	2:00
1965	Lucky Debonair (Neck)	Bill Shoemaker	Dapper Dan	Tom Rolfe	2:01⅕
1966	Kauai King (½)	Don Brumfield	Advocator	Blue Skyer	2:02
1967	Proud Clarion (1)	Bobby Ussery	Barbs Delight	Damascus	2:00⅗
1968	Forward Pass (Disq.)	Ismael Valenzuela	Francie's Hat	T.V. Commercial	2:02⅕
1969	Majestic Prince (Neck)	Bill Hartack	Arts and Letters	Dike	2:01⅘
1970	Dust Commander (5)	Mike Manganello	My Dad George	High Echelon	2:03⅖
1971	Canonero II (3¾)	Gustavo Avila	Jim French	Bold Reason	2:03⅕
1972	Riva Ridge (3¼)	Ron Turcotte	No Le Hace	Hold Your Peace	2:01⅘
1973	Secretariat (2½)	Ron Turcotte	Sham	Our Native	1:59⅖
1974	Cannonade (2¼)	Angel Cordero Jr.	Hudson County	Agitate	2:04
1975	Foolish Pleasure (1¾)	Jacinto Vasquez	Avatar	Diabolo	2:02
1976	Bold Forbes (1)	Angel Cordero Jr.	Honest Pleasure	Elocutionist	2:01⅗
1977	Seattle Slew (1¾)	Jean Cruguet	Run Dusty Run	Sanhedrin	2:02⅕
1978	Affirmed (1½)	Steve Cauthen	Alydar	Believe It	2:01⅕
1979	Spectacular Bid (2¾)	Ronald J. Franklin	General Assembly	Golden Act	2:02⅖
1980	Genuine Risk (1)	Jacinto Vasquez	Rumbo	Jaklin Klugman	2:02
1981	Pleasant Colony (¾)	Jorge Velasquez	Woodchopper	Partez	2:02
1982	Gato Del Sol (2½)	Eddie Delahoussaye	Laser Light	Reinvested	2:02⅕
1983	Sunny's Halo (2)	Eddie Delahoussaye	Desert Wine	Caveat	2:02⅕
1984	Swale (3¼)	Laffit Pincay Jr.	Coax Me Chad	At the Threshold	2:02⅖
1985	Spend A Buck (5)	Angel Cordero Jr.	Stephan's Odyssey	Chief's Crown	2:00⅕
1986	Ferdinand (2¼)	Bill Shoemaker	Bold Arrangement	Broad Brush	2:02⅘
1987	Alysheba (¾)	Chris McCarron	Bet Twice	Avies Copy	2:03⅖
1988	Winning Colors (Neck)	Gary Stevens	Forty Niner	Risen Star	2:02⅕
1989	Sunday Silence (2½)	Pat Valenzuela	Easy Goer	Awe Inspiring	2:05
1990	Unbridled (3½)	Craig Perret	Summer Squall	Pleasant Tap	2:02
1991	Strike the Gold (1¾)	Chris Antley	Best Pal	Mane Minister	2:03
1992	Lil E. Tee (1)	Pat Day	Casual Lies	Dance Floor	2:03
1993	Sea Hero (2½)	Jerry Bailey	Prairie Bayou	Wild Gale	2:02⅖
1994	Go for Gin (2½)	Chris McCarron	Strodes Creek	Blumin Affair	2:03⅗
1995	Thunder Gulch (2¼)	Gary Stevens	Tejano Run	Timber Country	2:01⅕
1996	Grindstone (Nose)	Jerry Bailey	Cavonnier	Prince of Thieves	2:01
1997	Silver Charm (Head)	Gary Stevens	Captain Bodgit	Free House	2:02⅖

Kentucky Derby *(Cont.)*

Year	Winner (Margin)	Jockey	Second	Third	Time
1998	Real Quiet (½)	Kent Desormeaux	Victory Gallop	Indian Charlie	2:02⅒
1999	Charismatic (Neck)	Chris Antley	Menifee	Cat Thief	2:03⅕
2000	Fusaichi Pegasus (1½)	Kent Desormeaux	Aptitude	Impeachment	2:01.12
2001	Monarchos (4¾)	Jorge Chavez	Invisible Ink	Congaree	1:59.97
2002	War Emblem (4)	Victor Espinoza	Proud Citizen	Perfect Drift	2:01.13
2003	Funny Cide (1¾)	Jose Santos	Empire Maker	Peace Rules	2:01.19
2004	Smarty Jones (2¾)	Stewart Elliott	Lion Heart	Imperialism	2:04.06
2005	Giacomo (½)	Mike Smith	Closing Argument	Afleet Alex	2:02.75
2006	Barbaro (1½)	Edgar Prado	Bluegrass Cat	Steppenwolfer	2:01.36

Note: Distance: 1½ miles (1875–95), 1¼ miles (1896–present).

Preakness

Run at Pimlico Race Course, Baltimore, Md., two weeks after the Kentucky Derby.

Year	Winner (Margin)	Jockey	Second	Third	Time
1873	Survivor (10)	G. Barbee	John Boulger	Artist	2:43
1874	Culpepper (¾)	W. Donohue	King Amadeus	Scratch	2:56½
1875	Tom Ochiltree (2)	L. Hughes	Viator	Bay Final	2:43½
1876	Shirley (4)	G. Barbee	Rappahannock	Algerine	2:44¾
1877	Cloverbrook (4)	C. Holloway	Bombast	Lucifer	2:45½
1878	Duke of Magenta (6)	C. Holloway	Bayard	Albert	2:41¾
1879	Harold (3)	L. Hughes	Jericho	Rochester	2:40½
1880	Grenada (¾)	L. Hughes	Oden	Emily F.	2:40½
1881	Saunterer (½)	T. Costello	Compensation	Baltic	2:40½
1882	Vanguard (Neck)	T. Costello	Heck	Col Watson	2:44½
1883*	Jacobus (4)	G. Barbee	Parnell		2:42½
1884*	Knight of Ellerslie (2)	S. Fisher	Welcher		2:39½
1885	Tecumseh (2)	Jim McLaughlin	Wickham	John C.	2:49
1886	The Bard (3)	S. Fisher	Eurus	Elkwood	2:45
1887	Dunboyne (1)	W. Donohue	Mahoney	Raymond	2:39½
1888	Refund (3)	F. Littlefield	Judge Murray	Glendale	2:49
1889*	Buddhist (8)	W. Anderson	Japhet	*	2:17½
1890*	Montague (3)	W. Martin	Philosophy	Barrister	2:36¾
1894	Assignee (3)	Fred Taral	Potentate	Ed Kearney	1:49¼
1895	Belmar (1)	Fred Taral	April Fool	Sue Kittie	1:50½
1896	Margrave (1)	H. Griffin	Hamilton II	Intermission	1:51
1897	Paul Kauvar (1½)	C. Thorpe	Elkins	On Deck	1:51¼
1898	Sly Fox (2)	C. W. Simms	The Huguenot	Nuto	1:49⅗
1899	Half Time (1)	R. Clawson	Filigrane	Lackland	1:47
1900	Hindus (Head)	H. Spencer	Sarmation	Ten Candles	1:48⅖
1901	The Parader (2)	F. Landry	Sadie S.	Dr. Barlow	1:47⅕
1902	Old England (Nose)	L. Jackson	Major Daingerfield	Namtor	1:45⅘
1903	Flocarline (½)	W. Gannon	Mackey Dwyer	Rightful	1:44⅘
1904	Bryn Mawr (1)	E. Hildebrand	Wotan	Dolly Spanker	1:44⅕
1905	Cairngorm (Head)	W. Davis	Kiamesha	Coy Maid	1:45⅘
1906	Whimsical (4)	Walter Miller	Content	Larabie	1:45
1907	Don Enrique (1)	G. Mountain	Ethon	Zambesi	1:45⅖
1908	Royal Tourist (4)	E. Dugan	Live Wire	Robert Cooper	1:46⅖
1909	Effendi (1)	Willie Doyle	Fashion Plate	Hilltop	1:39⅘
1910	Layminster (½)	R. Estep	Dalhousie	Sager	1:40⅗
1911	Watervale (1)	E. Dugan	Zeus	The Nigger	1:51
1912	Colonel Holloway (5)	C. Turner	Bwana Tumbo	Tipsand	1:56⅗
1913	Buskin (Neck)	J. Butwell	Kleburne	Barnegat	1:53⅖
1914	Holiday (¾)	A. Schuttinger	Brave Cunarder	Defendum	1:53⅘
1915	Rhine Maiden (1½)	Douglas Hoffman	Half Rock	Runes	1:58
1916	Damrosch (1½)	Linus McAtee	Greenwood	Achievement	1:54⅘
1917	Kalitan (2)	E. Haynes	Al M. Dick	Kentucky Boy	1:54⅖
1918*	War Cloud (¾)	Johnny Loftus	Sunny Slope	Lanius	1:53⅗
1918*	Jack Hare, Jr (2)	C. Peak	The Porter	Kate Bright	1:53⅖
1919	Sir Barton (4)	Johnny Loftus	Eternal	Sweep On	1:53
1920	Man o' War (1½)	Clarence Kummer	Upset	Wildair	1:51⅗

Preakness *(Cont.)*

Year	Winner (Margin)	Jockey	Second	Third	Time
1921	Broomspun (¾)	F. Coltiletti	Polly Ann	Jeg	1:54⅕
1922	Pillory (Head)	L. Morris	Hea	June Grass	1:51⅗
1923	Vigil (1¼)	B. Marinelli	General Thatcher	Rialto	1:53⅗
1924	Nellie Morse (1½)	J. Merimee	Transmute	Mad Play	1:57⅕
1925	Coventry (4)	Clarence Kummer	Backbone	Almadel	1:59
1926	Display (Head)	J. Maiben	Blondin	Mars	1:59⅘
1927	Bostonian (½)	A. Abel	Sir Harry	Whiskery	2:01⅗
1928	Victorian (Nose)	Sonny Workman	Toro	Solace	2:00⅕
1929	Dr. Freeland (1)	Louis Schaefer	Minotaur	African	2:01⅗
1930	Gallant Fox (¾)	Earl Sande	Crack Brigade	Snowflake	2:00⅗
1931	Mate (1½)	G. Ellis	Twenty Grand	Ladder	1:59
1932	Burgoo King (Head)	E. James	Tick On	Boatswain	1:59⅘
1933	Head Play (4)	Charles Kurtsinger	Ladysman	Utopian	2:02
1934	High Quest (Nose)	R. Jones	Cavalcade	Discovery	1:58⅕
1935	Omaha (6)	Willie Saunders	Firethorn	Psychic Bid	1:58⅖
1936	Bold Venture (Nose)	George Woolf	Granville	Jean Bart	1:59
1937	War Admiral (Head)	Charles Kurtsinger	Pompoon	Flying Scot	1:58⅖
1938	Dauber (7)	M. Peters	Cravat	Menow	1:59⅘
1939	Challedon (1¼)	George Seabo	Gilded Knight	Volitant	1:59⅘
1940	Bimelech (3)	F. A. Smith	Mioland	Gallahadion	1:58⅗
1941	Whirlaway (5½)	Eddie Arcaro	King Cole	Our Boots	1:58⅘
1942	Alsab (1)	B. James	Requested Sun Again	(dead heat for second)	1:57
1943	Count Fleet (8)	Johnny Longden	Blue Swords	Vincentive	1:57⅖
1944	Pensive (¾)	Conn McCreary	Platter	Stir Up	1:59⅕
1945	Polynesian (2½)	W. D. Wright	Hoop Jr.	Darby Dieppe	1:58⅘
1946	Assault (Neck)	Warren Mehrtens	Lord Boswell	Hampden	2:01⅖
1947	Faultless (1¼)	Doug Dodson	On Trust	Phalanx	1:59
1948	Citation (5½)	Eddie Arcaro	Vulcan's Forge	Boyard	2:02⅖
1949	Capot (Head)	Ted Atkinson	Palestinian	Noble Impulse	1:56
1950	Hill Prince (5)	Eddie Arcaro	Middleground	Dooley	1:59⅕
1951	Bold (7)	Eddie Arcaro	Counterpoint	Alerted	1:56⅖
1952	Blue Man (3½)	Conn McCreary	Jampol	One Count	1:57⅖
1953	Native Dancer (Neck)	Eric Guerin	Jamie K.	Royal Bay Gem	1:57⅘
1954	Hasty Road (Neck)	Johnny Adams	Correlation	Hasseyampa	1:57⅖
1955	Nashua (1)	Eddie Arcaro	Saratoga	Traffic Judge	1:54⅗
1956	Fabius (¾)	Bill Hartack	Needles	No Regrets	1:58⅖
1957	Bold Ruler (2)	Eddie Arcaro	Iron Liege	Inside Tract	1:56⅕
1958	Tim Tam (1½)	I. Valenzuela	Lincoln Road	Gone Fishin'	1:57⅕
1959	Royal Orbit (4)	William Harmatz	Sword Dancer	Dunce	1:57
1960	Bally Ache (4)	Bobby Ussery	Victoria Park	Celtic Ash	1:57⅗
1961	Carry Back (¾)	Johnny Sellers	Globemaster	Crozier	1:57⅗
1962	Greek Money (Nose)	John Rotz	Ridan	Roman Line	1:56⅕
1963	Candy Spots (3½)	Bill Shoemaker	Chateaugay	Never Bend	1:56⅕
1964	Northern Dancer (2¼)	Bill Hartack	The Scoundrel	Hill Rise	1:56⅘
1965	Tom Rolfe (Neck)	Ron Turcotte	Dapper Dan	Hail to All	1:56⅕
1966	Kauai King (1¾)	Don Brumfield	Stupendous	Amberoid	1:55⅖
1967	Damascus (2¼)	Bill Shoemaker	In Reality	Proud Clarion	1:55⅕
1968	Forward Pass (6)	I. Valenzuela	Out of the Way	Nodouble	1:56⅘
1969	Majestic Prince (Head)	Bill Hartack	Arts and Letters	Jay Ray	1:55⅗
1970	Personality (Neck)	Eddie Belmonte	My Dad George	Silent Screen	1:56⅕
1971	Canonero II (1½)	Gustavo Avila	Eastern Fleet	Jim French	1:54
1972	Bee Bee Bee (1¼)	Eldon Nelson	No Le Hace	Key to the Mint	1:55⅗
1973	Secretariat (2½)	Ron Turcotte	Sham	Our Native	1:54⅖
1974	Little Current (7)	Miguel Rivera	Neapolitan Way	Cannonade	1:54⅗
1975	Master Derby (1)	Darrel McHargue	Foolish Pleasure	Diabolo	1:56⅖
1976	Elocutionist (3)	John Lively	Play the Red	Bold Forbes	1:55
1977	Seattle Slew (1½)	Jean Cruguet	Iron Constitution	Run Dusty Run	1:54⅖
1978	Affirmed (Neck)	Steve Cauthen	Alydar	Believe It	1:54⅖
1979	Spectacular Bid (5½)	Ron Franklin	Golden Act	Screen King	1:54⅕
1980	Codex (4¾)	Angel Cordero Jr.	Genuine Risk	Colonel Moran	1:54⅕
1981	Pleasant Colony (1)	Jorge Velasquez	Bold Ego	Paristo	1:54⅗
1982	Aloma's Ruler (½)	Jack Kaenel	Linkage	Cut Away	1:55⅖
1983	Deputed Testamony (2¾)	Donald Miller Jr.	Desert Wine	High Honors	1:55⅖
1984	Gate Dancer (1½)	Angel Cordero Jr.	Play On	Fight Over	1:53⅗
1985	Tank's Prospect (Head)	Pat Day	Chief's Crown	Eternal Prince	1:53⅖
1986	Snow Chief (4)	Alex Solis	Ferdinand	Broad Brush	1:54⅘
1987	Alysheba (½)	Chris McCarron	Bet Twice	Cryptoclearance	1:55⅘

Preakness (Cont.)

Year	Winner (Margin)	Jockey	Second	Third	Time
1988	Risen Star (1¼)	E. Delahoussaye	Brian's Time	Winning Colors	1:56⅕
1989	Sunday Silence (Nose)	Pat Valenzuela	Easy Goer	Rock Point	1:53⅘
1990	Summer Squall (2¼)	Pat Day	Unbridled	Mister Frisky	1:53⅗
1991	Hansel (Head)	Jerry Bailey	Corporate Report	Mane Minister	1:54
1992	Pine Bluff (¾)	Chris McCarron	Alydeed	Casual Lies	1:55⅗
1993	Prairie Bayou (½)	Mike Smith	Cherokee Run	El Bakan	1:56⅗
1994	Tabasco Cat (¾)	Pat Day	Go For Gin	Concern	1:56⅖
1995	Timber Country (½)	Pat Day	Oliver's Twist	Thunder Gulch	1:54⅖
1996	Louis Quatorze (3¼)	Pat Day	Skip Away	Editor's Note	1:53⅖
1997	Silver Charm (Head)	Gary Stevens	Free House	Captain Bodgit	1:54⅖
1998	Real Quiet (2¼)	Kent Desormeaux	Victory Gallop	Classic Cat	1:54⅗
1999	Charismatic (1½)	Chris Antley	Menifee	Badge	1:55⅕
2000	Red Bullet (3¾)	Jerry Bailey	Fusaichi Pegasus	Impeachment	1:56.04
2001	Point Given (2¼)	Gary Stevens	A P Valentine	Congaree	1:55.51
2002	War Emblem (¾)	Victor Espinoza	Magic Weisner	Proud Citizen	1:56.36
2003	Funny Cide (9¾)	Jose Santos	Midway Road	Scrimshaw	1:55.61
2004	Smarty Jones (11½)	Stewart Elliott	Rock Hard Ten	Eddington	1:55.59
2005	Afleet Alex (7)	Jeremy Rose	Scrappy T	Giacomo	1:55.04
2006	Bernardini (5¼)	Javier Castellano	Sweetnorthernsaint	Hemingway's Key	1:54.65

*Preakness was a two-horse race in 1883, '84 and '89. It was not run 1891–1893; and in 1918, it was run in two divisions.

Note: Distance: 1½ miles (1873–88), 1¼ miles (1889), 1½ miles (1890), 1 1/16 miles (1894–1900), 1 mile and 70 yards (1901–1907), 1 1/16 miles (1908), 1 mile (1909–10), 1⅛ miles (1911–24), 1 3/16 miles (1925–present).

Belmont

Run at Belmont Park, Elmont, NY, three weeks after the Preakness Stakes. Held previously at two locations in the Bronx (NY): Jerome Park (1867–1889) and Morris Park (1890–1904).

Year	Winner (Margin)	Jockey	Second	Third	Time
1867	Ruthless (Head)	J. Gilpatrick	De Courcy	Rivoli	3:05
1868	General Duke (2)	R. Swim	Northumberland	Fannie Ludlow	3:02
1869	Fenian (Unknown)	C. Miller	Glenelg	Invercauld	3:04¼
1870	Kingfisher (½)	E. Brown	Foster	Midday	2:59½
1871	Harry Bassett (3)	W. Miller	Stockwood	By-the-Sea	2:56
1872	Joe Daniels (¾)	James Rowe	Meteor	Shylock	2:58¼
1873	Springbok (4)	James Rowe	Count d'Orsay	Strachino	3:01¾
1874	Saxon (Neck)	G. Barbee	Grinstead	Aaron Pennington	2:39½
1875	Calvin (2)	R. Swim	Aristides	Milner	2:40¼
1876	Algerine (Head)	W. Donahue	Fiddlestick	Barricade	2:40½
1877	Cloverbrook (1)	C. Holloway	Loiterer	Baden-Baden	2:46
1878	Duke of Magenta (2)	L. Hughes	Bramble	Sparta	2:43½
1879	Spendthrift (5)	S. Evans	Monitor	Jericho	2:42¾
1880	Grenada (½)	L. Hughes	Ferncliffe	Turenne	2:47
1881	Saunterer (Neck)	T. Costello	Eole	Baltic	2:47
1882	Forester (5)	James McLaughlin	Babcock	Wyoming	2:43
1883	George Kinney (2)	James McLaughlin	Trombone	Renegade	2:42½
1884	Panique (½)	James McLaughlin	Knight of Ellerslie	Himalaya	2:42
1885	Tyrant (3½)	Paul Duffy	St. Augustine	Tecumseh	2:43
1886	Inspector B (1)	James McLaughlin	The Bard	Linden	2:41
1887*	Hanover (28-32)	James McLaughlin	Oneko		2:43½
1888*	Sir Dixon (12)	James McLaughlin	Prince Royal		2:40¼
1889	Eric (Head)	W. Hayward	Diable	Zephyrus	2:47
1890	Burlington (1)	S. Barnes	Devotee	Padishah	2:07¾
1891	Foxford (Neck)	E. Garrison	Montana	Laurestan	2:08¾
1892*	Patron (Unknown)	W. Hayward	Shellbark		2:17
1893	Comanche (Head)	Willie Simms	Dr. Rice	Rainbow	1:53¼
1894	Henry of Navarre (2-4)	Willie Simms	Prig	Assignee	1:56½
1895	Belmar (Head)	Fred Taral	Counter Tenor	Nanki Pooh	2:11½
1896	Hastings (Neck)	H. Griffin	Handspring	Hamilton II	2:24½
1897	Scottish Chieftain (1)	J. Scherrer	On Deck	Octagon	2:23¼
1898	Bowling Brook (8)	P. Littlefield	Previous	Hamburg	2:32
1899	Jean Bereaud (Head)	R. R. Clawson	Half Time	Glengar	2:23

Belmont *(Cont.)*

Year	Winner (Margin)	Jockey	Second	Third	Time
1900	Ildrim (Head)	N. Turner	Petrucio	Missionary	2:21½
1901	Commando (½)	H. Spencer	The Parader	All Green	2:21
1902	Masterman (2)	John Bullmann	Ranald	King Hanover	2:22½
1903	Africander (2)	John Bullmann	Whorler	Red Knight	2:23⅕
1904	Delhi (3½)	George Odom	Graziallo	Rapid Water	2:06⅗
1905	Tanya (1/2)	E. Hildebrand	Blandy	Hot Shot	2:08
1906	Burgomaster (4)	L. Lyne	The Quail	Accountant	2:20
1907	Peter Pan (1)	G. Mountain	Superman	Frank Gill	Unknown
1908	Colin (Head)	Joe Notter	Fair Play	King James	Unknown
1909	Joe Madden (8)	E. Dugan	Wise Mason	Donald MacDonald	2:21⅗
1910*	Sweep (6)	J. Butwell	Duke of Ormonde		2:22
1913	Prince Eugene (½)	Roscoe Troxler	Rock View	Flying Fairy	2:18
1914	Luke McLuke (8)	M. Buxton	Gainer	Charlestonian	2:20
1915	The Finn (4)	G. Byrne	Half Rock	Pebbles	2:18⅖
1916	Friar Rock (3)	E. Haynes	Spur	Churchill	2:22
1917	Hourless (10)	J. Butwell	Skeptic	Wonderful	2:17⅘
1918	Johren (2)	Frank Robinson	War Cloud	Cum Sah	2:20⅖
1919	Sir Barton (5)	Johnny Loftus	Sweep On	Natural Bridge	2:17⅖
1920*	Man o' War (20)	Clarence Kummer	Donnacona		2:14⅕
1921	Grey Lag (3)	Earl Sande	Sporting Blood	Leonardo II	2:16⅘
1922	Pillory (2)	C. H. Miller	Snob II	Hea	2:18⅘
1923	Zev (1½)	Earl Sande	Chickvale	Rialto	2:19
1924	Mad Play (2)	Earl Sande	Mr. Mutt	Modest	2:18⅘
1925	American Flag (8)	Albert Johnson	Dangerous	Swope	2:16⅘
1926	Crusader (1)	Albert Johnson	Espino	Haste	2:32⅕
1927	Chance Shot (1½)	Earl Sande	Bois de Rose	Flambino	2:32⅖
1928	Vito (3)	Clarence Kummer	Genie	Diavolo	2:33⅕
1929	Blue Larkspur (¾)	Mack Garner	African	Jack High	2:32⅘
1930	Gallant Fox (3)	Earl Sande	Whichone	Questionnaire	2:31⅗
1931	Twenty Grand (10)	Charles Kurtsinger	Sun Meadow	Jamestown	2:29⅗
1932	Faireno (1½)	T. Malley	Osculator	Flag Pole	2:32⅘
1933	Hurryoff (1½)	Mack Garner	Nimbus	Union	2:32⅗
1934	Peace Chance (6)	W. D. Wright	High Quest	Good Goods	2:29⅕
1935	Omaha (1½)	Willie Saunders	Firethorn	Rosemont	2:30⅗
1936	Granville (Nose)	James Stout	Mr. Bones	Hollyrood	2:30
1937	War Admiral (3)	Charles Kurtsinger	Sceneshifter	Vamoose	2:28⅗
1938	Pasteurized (Neck)	James Stout	Dauber	Cravat	2:29⅖
1939	Johnstown (5)	James Stout	Belay	Gilded Knight	2:29⅗
1940	Bimelech (¾)	F. A. Smith	Your Chance	Andy K	2:29⅗
1941	Whirlaway (2½)	Eddie Arcaro	Robert Morris	Yankee Chance	2:31
1942	Shut Out (2)	Eddie Arcaro	Alsab	Lochinvar	2:29⅕
1943	Count Fleet (25)	Johnny Longden	Fairy Manhurst	Deseronto	2:28⅕
1944	Bounding Home (½)	G. L. Smith	Pensive	Bull Dandy	2:32⅕
1945	Pavot (5)	Eddie Arcaro	Wildlife	Jeep	2:30⅕
1946	Assault (3)	Warren Mehrtens	Natchez	Cable	2:30⅘
1947	Phalanx (5)	R. Donoso	Tide Rips	Tailspin	2:29⅖
1948	Citation (8)	Eddie Arcaro	Better Self	Escadru	2:28⅕
1949	Capot (½)	Ted Atkinson	Ponder	Palestinian	2:30⅕
1950	Middleground (1)	William Boland	Lights Up	Mr. Trouble	2:28⅗
1951	Counterpoint (4)	D. Gorman	Battlefield	Battle Morn	2:29
1952	One Count (2½)	Eddie Arcaro	Blue Man	Armageddon	2:30⅕
1953	Native Dancer (Neck)	Eric Guerin	Jamie K.	Royal Bay Gem	2:38⅗
1954	High Gun (Neck)	Eric Guerin	Fisherman	Limelight	2:30⅘
1955	Nashua (9)	Eddie Arcaro	Blazing Count	Portersville	2:29
1956	Needles (Neck)	David Erb	Career Boy	Fabius	2:29⅘
1957	Gallant Man (8)	Bill Shoemaker	Inside Tract	Bold Ruler	2:26⅗
1958	Cavan (6)	Pete Anderson	Tim Tam	Flamingo	2:30⅕
1959	Sword Dancer (¾)	Bill Shoemaker	Bagdad	Royal Orbit	2:28⅖
1960	Celtic Ash (5½)	Bill Hartack	Venetian Way	Disperse	2:29⅗
1961	Sherluck (2¼)	Braulio Baeza	Globemaster	Guadalcanal	2:29⅕
1962	Jaipur (Nose)	Bill Shoemaker	Admiral's Voyage	Crimson Satan	2:28⅘
1963	Chateaugay (2½)	Braulio Baeza	Candy Spots	Choker	2:30⅕
1964	Quadrangle (2)	Manuel Ycaza	Roman Brother	Northern Dancer	2:28⅖
1965	Hail to All (Neck)	John Sellers	Tom Rolfe	First Family	2:28⅖
1966	Amberold (2½)	William Boland	Buffle	Advocator	2:29⅗
1967	Damascus (2½)	Bill Shoemaker	Cool Reception	Gentleman	2:28⅘

Belmont *(Cont.)*

Year	Winner (Margin)	Jockey	Second	Third	Time
1968	Stage Door Johnny (1¼)	Hellodoro Gustines	Forward Pass	James Call Me Prince	2:27⅕
1969	Arts and Letters (5½)	Braulio Baeza	Majestic Prince	Dike	2:28⅘
1970	High Echelon (¾)	John L. Rotz	Needles N Pins	Naskra	2:34
1971	Pass Catcher (¾)	Walter Blum	Jim French	Bold Reason	2:30⅖
1972	Riva Ridge (7)	Ron Turcotte	Ruritania	Cloudy Dawn	2:28
1973	Secretariat (31)	Ron Turcotte	Twice a Prince	My Gallant	2:24
1974	Little Current (7)	Miguel A. Rivera	Jolly Johu	Cannonade	2:29⅕
1975	Avatar (Neck)	Bill Shoemaker	Foolish Pleasure	Master Derby	2:28⅕
1976	Bold Forbes (Neck)	Angel Cordero Jr.	McKenzie Bridge	Great Contractor	2:29
1977	Seattle Slew (4)	Jean Cruguet	Run Dusty Run	Sanhedrin	2:29⅗
1978	Affirmed (Head)	Steve Cauthen	Alydar	Darby Creek Road	2:26⅘
1979	Coastal (3¼)	Ruben Hernandez	Golden Act	Spectacular Bid	2:28⅗
1980	Temperence Hill (2)	Eddie Maple	Genuine Risk	Rockhill Native	2:29⅘
1981	Summing (Neck)	George Martens	Highland Blade	Pleasant Colony	2:29
1982	Conquistador Cielo (14½)	Laffit Pincay, Jr.	Gato Del Sol	Illuminate	2:28⅕
1983	Caveat (3½)	Laffit Pincay Jr.	Slew o'Gold	Barberstown	2:27⅘
1984	Swale (4)	Laffit Pincay Jr.	Pine Circle	Morning Bob	2:27⅕
1985	Creme Fraiche (½)	Eddie Maple	Stephan's Odyssey	Chief's Crown	2:27
1986	Danzig Connection (1¼)	Chris McCarron	Johns Treasure	Ferdinand	2:29⅘
1987	Bet Twice (14)	Craig Perret	Cryptoclearance	Gulch	2:28⅕
1988	Risen Star (14¾)	Eddie Delahoussaye	Kingpost	Brian's Time	2:26⅖
1989	Easy Goer (8)	Pat Day	Sunday Silence	Le Voyageur	2:26
1990	Go and Go (8¼)	Michael Kinane	Thirty Six Red	Baron de Vaux	2:27⅕
1991	Hansel (Head)	Jerry Bailey	Strike the Gold	Mane Minister	2:28
1992	A.P. Indy (¾)	Eddie Delahoussaye	My Memoirs	Pine Bluff	2:26
1993	Colonial Affair (2¼)	Julie Krone	Kissin Kris	Wild Gale	2:29⅘
1994	Tabasco Cat (2)	Pat Day	Go For Gin	Strodes Creek	2:26⅘
1995	Thunder Gulch (2)	Gary Stevens	Star Standard	Citadeed	2:32
1996	Editor's Note (1)	Rene Douglas	Skip Away	My Flag	2:28⅘
1997	Touch Gold (¾)	Chris McCarron	Silver Charm	Free House	2:28⅘
1998	Victory Gallop (Nose)	Gary Stevens	Real Quiet	Thomas Jo	2:28⅘
1999	Lemon Drop Kid (Head)	Jose Santos	Vision and Verse	Charismatic	2:27⅘
2000	Commendable (1½)	Pat Day	Aptitude	Unshaded	2:31.19
2001	Point Given (12¼)	Gary Stevens	A P Valentine	Monarchos	2:26.56
2002	Sarava (½)	Edgar Prado	Medaglia d'Oro	Sunday Break	2:29.71
2003	Empire Maker (¾)	Jerry Bailey	Ten Most Wanted	Funny Cide	2:28.26
2004	Birdstone (1)	Edgar Prado	Smarty Jones	Royal Assault	2:27.59
2005	Afleet Alex(4¾)	Jeremy Rose	Andromeda's Hero	Nolan's Cat	2:28.75
2006	Jazil (1¼)	Fernando Jara	Bluegrass Cat	Sunriver	2:27.86

*Belmont was a two-horse race in 1887, '88, '92, 1910 and '20; and was not held in 1911–1912.
Note: Distance: 1 mile 5 furlongs (1867–89), 1¼ miles (1890–1905), 1⅜ miles (1906–25), 1½ miles (1926–present).

Triple Crown Winners

Year	Horse	Jockey	Owner	Trainer
1919	Sir Barton	John Loftus	J. K. L. Ross	H. G. Bedwell
1930	Gallant Fox	Earle Sande	Belair Stud	James Fitzsimmons
1935	Omaha	William Saunders	Belair Stud	James Fitzsimmons
1937	War Admiral	Charles Kurtsinger	Samuel D. Riddle	George Conway
1941	Whirlaway	Eddie Arcaro	Calumet Farm	Ben Jones
1943	Count Fleet	John Longden	Mrs J. D. Hertz	Don Cameron
1946	Assault	Warren Mehrtens	King Ranch	Max Hirsch
1948	Citation	Eddie Arcaro	Calumet Farm	Jimmy Jones
1973	Secretariat	Ron Turcotte	Meadow Stable	Lucien Laurin
1977	Seattle Slew	Jean Cruguet	Karen L. Taylor	William H. Turner Jr.
1978	Affirmed	Steve Cauthen	Harbor View Farm	Laz Barrera

Horse of the Year

Year	Horse	Owner	Trainer	Breeder
1936	Granville	Belair Stud	James Fitzsimmons	Belair Stud
1937	War Admiral	Samuel D. Riddle	George Conway	Mrs. Samuel D. Riddle
1938	Seabiscuit	Charles S. Howard	Tom Smith	Wheatley Stable
1939	Challedon	William L. Brann	Louis J. Schaefer	Branncastle Farm
1940	Challedon	William L. Brann	Louis J. Schaefer	Branncastle Farm
1941	Whirlaway	Calumet Farm	Ben Jones	Calumet Farm
1942	Whirlaway	Calumet Farm	Ben Jones	Calumet Farm
1943	Count Fleet	Mrs. John D. Hertz	Don Cameron	Mrs. John D. Hertz
1944	Twilight Tear	Calumet Farm	Ben Jones	Calumet Farm
1945	Busher	Louis B. Mayer	George Odom	Idle Hour Stock Farm
1946	Assault	King Ranch	Max Hirsch	King Ranch
1947	Armed	Calumet Farm	Jimmy Jones	Calumet Farm
1948	Citation	Calumet Farm	Jimmy Jones	Calumet Farm
1949	Capot	Greentree Stable	John M. Gaver Sr.	Greentree Stable
1950	Hill Prince	C.T. Chenery	Casey Hayes	C.T. Chenery
1951	Counterpoint	C.V. Whitney	Syl Veitch	C.V. Whitney
1952	One Count	Mrs. W. M. Jeffords	O. White	W M. Jeffords
1953	Tom Fool	Greentree Stable	John M. Gaver Sr.	D.A. Headley
1954	Native Dancer	A.G. Vanderbilt	Bill Winfrey	A.G. Vanderbilt
1955	Nashua	Belair Stud	James Fitzsimmons	Belair Stud
1956	Swaps	Ellsworth-Galbreath	Mesh Tenney	R. Ellsworth
1957	Bold Ruler	Wheatley Stable	James Fitzsimmons	Wheatley Stable
1958	Round Table	Kerr Stables	Willy Molter	Claiborne Farm
1959	Sword Dancer	Brookmeade Stable	Elliott Burch	Brookmeade Stable
1960	Kelso	Bohemia Stable	C. Hanford	Mrs. R.C. duPont
1961	Kelso	Bohemia Stable	C. Hanford	Mrs. R.C. duPont
1962	Kelso	Bohemia Stable	C. Hanford	Mrs. R.C. duPont
1963	Kelso	Bohemia Stable	C. Hanford	Mrs. R.C. duPont
1964	Kelso	Bohemia Stable	C. Hanford	Mrs. R.C. duPont
1965	Roman Brother	Harbor View Stable	Burley Parke	Ocala Stud
1966	Buckpasser	Ogden Phipps	Eddie Neloy	Ogden Phipps
1967	Damascus	Mrs. E. W. Bancroft	Frank Y. Whiteley Jr.	Mrs. E. W. Bancroft
1968	Dr. Fager	Tartan Stable	John A. Nerud	Tartan Farms
1969	Arts and Letters	Rokeby Stable	Elliott Burch	Paul Mellon
1970	Fort Marcy	Rokeby Stable	Elliott Burch	Paul Mellon
1971	Ack Ack	E.E. Fogelson	Charlie Whittingham	H.F. Guggenheim
1972	Secretariat	Meadow Stable	Lucien Laurin	Meadow Stud
1973	Secretariat	Meadow Stable	Lucien Laurin	Meadow Stud
1974	Forego	Lazy F Ranch	Sherrill W. Ward	Lazy F Ranch
1975	Forego	Lazy F Ranch	Sherrill W. Ward	Lazy F Ranch
1976	Forego	Lazy F Ranch	Frank Y. Whiteley Jr.	Lazy F Ranch
1977	Seattle Slew	Karen L. Taylor	Billy Turner Jr.	B.S. Castleman
1978	Affirmed	Harbor View Farm	Laz Barrera	Harbor View Farm
1979	Affirmed	Harbor View Farm	Laz Barrera	Harbor View Farm
1980	Spectacular Bid	Hawksworth Farm	Bud Delp	Mmes. Gilmore & Jason
1981	John Henry	Dotsam Stable	Ron McAnally and Lefty Nickerson	Golden Chance Farm
1982	Conquistador Cielo	H. de Kwiatkowski	Woody Stephens	L.E. Landoli
1983	All Along	Daniel Wildenstein	P.L. Biancone	Dayton
1984	John Henry	Dotsam Stable	Ron McAnally	Golden Chance Farm
1985	Spend a Buck	Hunter Farm	Cam Gambolati	Irish Hill & R.W. Harper
1986	Lady's Secret	Mr. & Mrs. Eugene Klein	D. Wayne Lukas	R.H. Spreen
1987	Ferdinand	Mrs. H.B. Keck	Charlie Whittingham	H.B. Keck
1988	Alysheba	D. & P. Scharbauer	Jack Van Berg	Preston Madden
1989	Sunday Silence	Gaillard, Hancock, & Whittingham	Charlie Whittingham	Oak Cliff Thoroughbreds
1990	Criminal Type	Calumet Farm	D. Wayne Lukas	Calumet Farm
1991	Black Tie Affair	Jeffrey Sullivan	Ernie Poulos	Stephen D. Peskoff
1992	A.P. Indy	Tomonori Tsurumaki	Neil Drysdale	W.S. Farish & W.S. Kilroy
1993	Kotashaan	La Presle Farm	Richard Mandella	La Presle Farm
1994	Holy Bull	Jimmy Croll	Jimmy Croll	Pelican Stable
1995	Cigar	Allen E. Paulson	William Mott	Allen E. Paulson
1996	Cigar	Allen E. Paulson	William Mott	Allen E. Paulson
1997	Favorite Trick	Joseph LaCombe	William Mott	Mr. & Mrs. M.L. Wood
1998	Skip Away	Carolyn Hine	Hubert Hine	Anna Marie Barnhart
1999	Charismatic	Robert & Beverly Lewis	D. Wayne Lukas	William Farish/Partners
2000	Tiznow	Michael Cooper and	Jay M. Robbins	Cecilia Straub-Rubens

Horse of the Year (Cont.)

Year	Horse	Owner	Trainer	Breeder
		Cecilia Straub-Rubens		
2001	Point Given	The Thoroughbred Corp.	Bob Baffert	The Thoroughbred Corp.
2002	Azeri	Allen Paulson Living Trust	Laura de Seroux	Allen Paulson
2003	Mineshaft	William Farish	Neil Howard	William Farish
2004	Ghostzapper	Frank Stronach	Bobby Frankel	Frank Stronach
2005	Saint Liam	William & Susan Warren Jr.	Richard Dutrow Jr.	Edward P. Evans

Note: From 1936 to 1970, the *Daily Racing Form* annually selected a "Horse of the Year." In 1971 the *Daily Racing Form*, with the Thoroughbred Racing Association and the National Turf Writers Association, jointly created the Eclipse Awards.

Eclipse Award Winners

2-YEAR-OLD COLT

1971	Riva Ridge
1972	Secretariat
1973	Protagonist
1974	Foolish Pleasure
1975	Honest Pleasure
1976	Seattle Slew
1977	Affirmed
1978	Spectacular Bid
1979	Rockhill Native
1980	Lord Avie
1981	Deputy Minister
1982	Roving Boy
1983	Devil's Bag
1984	Chief's Crown
1985	Tasso
1986	Capote
1987	Forty Niner
1988	Easy Goer
1989	Rhythm
1990	Fly So Free
1991	Arazi
1992	Gilded Time
1993	Dehere
1994	Timber Country
1995	Maria's Mon
1996	Boston Harbor
1997	Favorite Trick
1998	Answer Lively
1999	Anees
2000	Macho Uno
2001	Johannesburg
2002	Vindication
2003	Action This Day
2004	Declan's Moon
2005	Stevie Wonderboy

2-YEAR-OLD FILLY

1971	Numbered Account
1972	La Prevoyante
1973	Talking Picture
1974	Ruffian
1975	Dearly Precious
1976	Sensational
1977	Lakeville Miss
1978	Candy Eclair, It's in the Air
1979	Smart Angle
1980	Heavenly Cause
1981	Before Dawn
1982	Landaluce
1983	Althea
1984	Outstandingly
1985	Family Style
1986	Brave Raj
1987	Epitome
1988	Open Mind

2-YEAR-OLD FILLY (Cont.)

1989	Go for Wand
1990	Meadow Star
1991	Pleasant Stage
1992	Eliza
1993	Phone Chatter
1994	Flanders
1995	Golden Attraction
1996	Storm Song
1997	Countess Diana
1998	Silverbulletday
1999	Chilukki
2000	Caressing
2001	Tempera
2002	Storm Flag Flying
2003	Halfbridled
2004	Sweet Catomine
2005	Folklore

3-YEAR-OLD COLT

1971	Canonero II
1972	Key to the Mint
1973	Secretariat
1974	Little Current
1975	Wajima
1976	Bold Forbes
1977	Seattle Slew
1978	Affirmed
1979	Spectacular Bid
1980	Temperence Hill
1981	Pleasant Colony
1982	Conquistador Cielo
1983	Slew o' Gold
1984	Swale
1985	Spend A Buck
1986	Snow Chief
1987	Alysheba
1988	Risen Star
1989	Sunday Silence
1990	Unbridled
1991	Hansel
1992	A.P. Indy
1993	Prairie Bayou
1994	Holy Bull
1995	Thunder Gulch
1996	Skip Away
1997	Silver Charm
1998	Real Quiet
1999	Charismatic
2000	Tiznow
2001	Point Given
2002	War Emblem
2003	Funny Cide
2004	Smarty Jones
2005	Afleet Alex

CHAMPION TURF HORSE

1971	Run the Gantlet (3)
1972	Cougar II (6)
1973	Secretariat (3)
1974	Dahlia (4)
1975	Snow Knight (4)
1976	Youth (3)
1977	Johnny D (3)
1978	Mac Diarmida (3)

CHAMPION MALE TURF HORSE

1979	Bowl Game (5)
1980	John Henry (5)
1981	John Henry (6)
1982	Perrault (5)
1983	John Henry (8)
1984	John Henry (9)
1985	Cozzene (4)
1986	Manila (3)
1987	Theatrical (5)
1988	Sunshine Forever (3)
1989	Steinlen (6)
1990	Itsallgreektome (3)
1991	Tight Spot (4)
1992	Sky Classic (5)
1993	Kotashaan (5)
1994	Paradise Creek (5)
1995	Northern Spur (4)
1996	Singspiel (4)
1997	Chief Bearhart (4)
1998	Buck's Boy (5)
1999	Daylami (5)
2000	Kalanisi (4)
2001	Fantastic Light (5)
2002	High Chaparral (3)
2003	High Chaparral (4)
2004	Kitten's Joy
2005	Leroidesanimaux

CHAMPION FEMALE TURF HORSE

1979	Trillion (5)
1980	Just a Game II (4)
1981	De La Rose (3)
1982	April Run (4)
1983	All Along (4)
1984	Royal Heroine (4)
1985	Pebbles (4)
1986	Estrapade (6)
1987	Miesque (3)
1988	Miesque (4)
1989	Brown Bess (7)
1990	Laugh and Be Merry (5)
1991	Miss Alleged (4)
1992	Flawlessly (4)
1993	Flawlessly (5)

Eclipse Award Winners *(Cont.)*

CHAMPION FEMALE TURF HORSE *(Cont.)*

1994....Hatoof (5)
1995....Possibly Perfect (5)
1996....Wandesta (5)
1997....Ryafan (3)
1998....Fiji (4)
1999....Soaring Softly (4)
2000....Perfect Sting (4)
2001....Banks Hill (3)
2002....Golden Apples (4)
2003....Islington (4)
2004....Ouija Board
2005....Intercontinental

3-YEAR-OLD FILLY

1971........Turkish Trousers
1972........Susan's Girl
1973........Desert Vixen
1974........Chris Evert
1975........Ruffian
1976........Revidere
1977........Our Mims
1978........Tempest Queen
1979........Davona Dale
1980........Genuine Risk
1981........Wayward Lass
1982........Christmas Past
1983........Heartlight No. One
1984........Life's Magic
1985........Mom's Command
1986........Tiffany Lass
1987........Sacahuaista
1988........Winning Colors
1989........Open Mind
1990........Go for Wand
1991........Dance Smartly
1992........Saratoga Dew
1993........Hollywood Wildcat
1994........Heavenly Prize
1995........Serena's Song
1996........Yank's Music
1997........Ajina
1998........Banshee Breeze
1999........Silverbulletday
2000........Surfside
2001........Xtra Heat
2002........Farda Amiga
2003........Bird Town
2004........Ashado
2005........Smuggler

OLDER COLT, HORSE OR GELDING

1971........Ack Ack (5)
1972........Autobiography (4)
1973........Riva Ridge (4)
1974........Forego (4)
1975........Forego (5)
1976........Forego (6)
1977........Forego (7)
1978........Seattle Slew (4)
1979........Affirmed (4)
1980........Spectacular Bid (4)
1981........John Henry (6)
1982........Lemhi Gold (4)
1983........Bates Motel (4)

OLDER COLT, HORSE OR GELDING *(Cont.)*

1984........Slew o'Gold (4)
1985........Vanlandingham (4)
1986........Turkoman (4)
1987........Ferdinand (4)
1988........Alysheba (4)
1989........Blushing John (4)
1990........Criminal Type (5)
1991........Black Tie Affair (5)
1992........Pleasant Tap (5)
1993........Bertrando (4)
1994........The Wicked North (5)
1995........Cigar (5)
1996........Cigar (6)
1997........Skip Away (4)
1998........Skip Away (5)
1999........Victory Gallop (4)
2000........Lemon Drop Kid (4)
2001........Tiznow (4)
2002........Left Bank (5)
2003........Mineshaft (4)
2004........Ghostzapper (4)
2005........Saint Liam

OLDER FILLY OR MARE

1971........Shuvee (5)
1972........Typecast (4)
1973........Susan's Girl (4)
1974........Desert Vixen (4)
1975........Susan's Girl (6)
1976........Proud Delta (4)
1977........Cascapedia (4)
1978........Late Bloomer (4)
1979........Waya (5)
1980........Glorious Song (4)
1981........Relaxing (5)
1982........Track Robbery (6)
1983........Ambassador of Luck (4)
1984........Princess Rooney (4)
1985........Life's Magic (4)
1986........Lady's Secret (4)
1987........North Sider (5)
1988........Personal Ensign (4)
1989........Bayakoa (5)
1990........Bayakoa (6)
1991........Queena (5)
1992........Paseana (5)
1993........Paseana (6)
1994........Sky Beauty (4)
1995........Inside Information (4)
1996........Jewel Princess (4)
1997........Hidden Lake (4)
1998........Escena (5)
1999........Beautiful Pleasure (4)
2000........Riboletta (6)
2001........Gourmet Girl (6)
2002........Azeri (4)
2003........Azeri (5)
2004........Azeri (6)
2005........Ashado

STEEPLECHASE OR HURDLE HORSE

1971.....Shadow Brook (7)
1972.....Soothsayer (5)
1973.....Athenian Idol (5)
1974.....Gran Kan (8)

STEEPLECHASE OR HURDLE HORSE *(Cont.)*

1975....Life's Illusion (4)
1976....Straight & True (6)
1977....Cafe Prince (7)
1978....Cafe Prince (8)
1979....Martie's Anger (4)
1980....Zaccio (4)
1981....Zaccio (5)
1982....Zaccio (6)
1983....Flatterer (4)
1984....Flatterer (5)
1985....Flatterer (6)
1986....Flatterer (7)
1987....Inlander (6)
1988....Jimmy Lorenzo (6)
1989....Highland Bud (4)
1990....Morley Street (7)
1991....Morley Street (8)
1992....Lonesome Glory (4)
1993....Lonesome Glory (5)
1994....Warm Spell (6)
1995....Lonesome Glory (7)
1996....Corregio (5)
1997....Lonesome Glory (9)
1998....Flat Top (5)
1999....Lonesome Glory (11)
2000....All Gong (6)
2001....Pompeyo (7)
2002....Flat Top (9)
2003....McDynamo (6)
2004....Hirapour (8)
2005....McDynamo

SPRINTER

1971.....Ack Ack (5)
1972.....Chou Croute (4)
1973.....Shecky Greene (3)
1974.....Forego (4)
1975.....Gallant Bob (3)
1976.....My Juliet (4)
1977.....What a Summer (4)
1978.....Dr. Patches (4)
        J.O. Tobin (4)
1979.....Star de Naskra (4)
1980.....Plugged Nickel (3)
1981.....Guilty Conscience (5)
1982.....Gold Beauty (3)
1983.....Chinook Pass (4)
1984.....Eillo (4)
1985.....Precisionist (4)
1986.....Smile (4)
1987.....Groovy (4)
1988.....Gulch (4)
1989.....Safely Kept (3)
1990.....Housebuster (3)
1991.....Housebuster (4)
1992.....Rubiano (4)
1993.....Cardmania (7)
1994.....Cherokee Run (4)
1995.....Not Surprising (5)
1996.....Lit de Justice (6)
1997.....Smoke Glacken (3)
1998.....Reraise (3)
1999.....Artax (4)
2000.....Kone Gold (6)
2001.....Squirtle Squirt (3)
2002.....Orientate (4)

Note: Number in parentheses is horse's age.

Eclipse Award Winners *(Cont.)*

SPRINTER *(Cont.)*
2003.....Aldebaran (5)
2004.....Speightstown (6)
2005.....Lost in the Fog

OUTSTANDING OWNER
1971.....Mr. & Mrs. E. E. Fogleson
1974.....Dan Lasater
1975.....Dan Lasater
1976.....Dan Lasater
1977.....Maxwell Gluck
1978.....Harbor View Farm
1979.....Harbor View Farm
1980.....Mr. & Mrs. Bertram
1981.....Dotsam Stable
1982.....Viola Sommer
1983.....John Franks
1984.....John Franks
1985.....Mr. & Mrs. Eugene Klein
1986.....Mr. & Mrs. Eugene Klein
1987.....Mr. & Mrs. Eugene Klein
1988.....Ogden Phipps
1989.....Ogden Phipps
1990.....Frances Genter
1991.....Sam-Son Farm
1992.....Juddmonte Farms
1993.....John Franks
1994.....John Franks
1995.....Allen E. Paulson
1996.....Allen E. Paulson
1997.....Carolyn Hine
1998.....Frank Stronach
1999.....Frank Stronach
2000.....Frank Stronach
2001.....Richard Englander
2002.....Richard Englander
2003.....Juddmonte Farms
2004 .....Frank Stronach
2005.....Michael Gill

OUTSTANDING TRAINER
1971.....Charlie Whittingham
1972.....Lucien Laurin
1973.....H. Allen Jerkens
1974.....Sherrill Ward
1975.....Steve DiMauro
1976.....Lazaro Barrera
1977.....Lazaro Barrera
1978.....Lazaro Barrera
1979.....Lazaro Barrera
1980.....Bud Delp
1981.....Ron McAnally
1982.....Charlie Whittingham
1983.....Woody Stephens
1984.....Jack Van Berg
1985.....D. Wayne Lukas
1986.....D. Wayne Lukas
1987.....D. Wayne Lukas
1988.....Claude R. McGaughey III
1989.....Charlie Whittingham
1990.....Carl Nafzger
1991.....Ron McAnally
1992.....Ron McAnally
1993.....Bobby Frankel
1994.....D. Wayne Lukas
1995.....William Mott
1996.....William Mott

OUTSTANDING TRAINER *(Cont.)*
1997.....Bob Baffert
1998.....Bob Baffert
1999.....Bob Baffert
2000.....Robert Frankel
2001.....Robert Frankel
2002.....Robert Frankel
2003.....Robert Frankel
2004.....Todd Pletcher
2005.....Todd Pletcher

OUTSTANDING JOCKEY
1971.....Laffit Pincay Jr.
1972.....Braulio Baeza
1973.....Laffit Pincay Jr
1974.....Laffit Pincay Jr
1975.....Braulio Baeza
1976.....Sandy Hawley
1977.....Steve Cauthen
1978.....Darrel McHargue
1979.....Laffit Pincay Jr.
1980.....Chris McCarron
1981.....Bill Shoemaker
1982.....Angel Cordero Jr
1983.....Angel Cordero Jr
1984.....Pat Day
1985.....Laffit Pincay Jr
1986.....Pat Day
1987.....Pat Day
1988.....Jose Santos
1989.....Kent Desormeaux
1990.....Craig Perret
1991.....Pat Day
1992.....Kent Desormeaux
1993.....Mike Smith
1994.....Mike Smith
1995.....Jerry Bailey
1996.....Jerry Bailey
1997.....Jerry Bailey
1998.....Gary Stevens
1999.....Jorge Chavez
2000.....Jerry Bailey
2001.....Jerry Bailey
2002.....Jerry Bailey
2003.....Jerry Bailey
2004.....John Velasquez
2005.....John Velasquez

OUTSTANDING APPRENTICE JOCKEY
1971.....Gene St. Leon
1972.....Thomas Wallis
1973.....Steve Valdez
1974.....Chris McCarron
1975.....Jimmy Edwards
1976.....George Martens
1977.....Steve Cauthen
1978.....Ron Franklin
1979.....Cash Asmussen
1980.....Frank Lovato Jr.
1981.....Richard Migliore
1982.....Alberto Delgado
1983.....Declan Murphy
1984.....Wesley Ward
1985.....Art Madrid Jr.
1986.....Allen Stacy
1987.....Kent Desormeaux

OUTSTANDING APPRENTICE JOCKEY *(Cont.)*
1988.....Steve Capanas
1989.....Michael Luzzi
1990.....Mark Johnston
1991.....Mickey Walls
1992.....Jesus A. Bracho
1993.....Juan Umana
1994.....Dale Beckner
1995.....Ramon Perez
1996.....Neil Pozansky
1997.....Phil Teator
.........Roberto Rosado
1998.....Shaun Bridgmohan
1999.....Ariel Smith
2000.....Tyler Baze
2001.....Jeremy Rose
2002.....Ryan Fogelsonger
2003.....Eddie Castro
2004.....Brian Hernandez
2005.....Emma-Jayne Wilson

OUTSTANDING BREEDER
1974.....John W. Galbreath
1975.....Fred W. Hooper
1976.....Nelson Bunker Hunt
1977.....Edward Plunket Taylor
1978.....Harbor View Farm
1979.....Claiborne Farm
1980.....Mrs. Henry D. Paxson
1981.....Golden Chance Farm
1982.....Fred W. Hooper
1983.....Edward Plunket Taylor
1984.....Claiborne Farm
1985.....Nelson Bunker Hunt
1986.....Paul Mellon
1987.....Nelson Bunker Hunt
1988.....Ogden Phipps
1989.....North Ridge Farm
1990.....Calumet Farm
1991.....John and Betty Mabee
1992.....William S. Farish III
1993.....Allen Paulson
1994.....William T. Young
1995.....Juddmonte Farms
1996.....Fansworth Farms
1997.....Golden Eagle Farm
1998.....John and Betty Mabee
1999.....William Farish/Partners
2000.....Frank Stronach/Adena
.........Springs
2001.....Juddmonte Farms
2002.....Juddmonte Farms
2003.....Juddmonte Farms
2004.....Frank Stronach/Adena
.........Springs
2005.....Adena Springs Farms

Awards (*Cont.*)

Eclipse Award Winners (*Cont.*)

AWARD OF MERIT

1976.....Jack J. Dreyfus
1977.....Steve Cauthen
1978.....Ogden Phipps
1979.....Frank E. Kilroe
1980.....John D. Schapiro
1981.....Bill Shoemaker
1984.....John Gaines
1985.....Keene Daingerfield
1986.....Herman Cohen
1987.....J. B. Faulconer
1988.....John Forsythe
1989.....Michael P. Sandler
1991.....Fred W. Hooper
1994.....Alfred G. Vanderbilt
1996.....Allen E. Paulson
2002.....Howard Battle
Ogden Phipps

SPECIAL AWARD

1971.....Robert J. Kleberg
1974.....Charles Hatton
1976.....Bill Shoemaker
1980.....John T. Landry
Pierre E. Bellocq (Peb)
1984.....C. V. Whitney
1985.....Arlington Park
1987.....Anheuser-Busch
1988.....Edward J. DeBartolo Sr.
1989.....Richard Duchossois
1994.....John Longden
Edward Arcaro
1998.....Oak Tree Racing Association
2002.....Keeneland Library

Note: Special Award and Award of Merit, for long-term and/or outstanding service to the industry, not presented annually.

Breeders' Cup

Location: Hollywood 1984, '87, '97; Aqueduct 1985; Santa Anita 1986, '93, '03; Churchill Downs 1988, '91, '98,'00; Gulfstream (FL) 1989, '92, '99; Belmont 1990, '95, '01; Woodbine (Toronto) 1996; Arlington 2002.

Juveniles

Year	Winner (Margin)	Jockey	Second	Third	Time
1984	Chief's Crown (¾)	Don MacBeth	Tank's Prospect	Spend a Buck	1:36⅕
1985	Tasso (Nose)	Laffit Pincay Jr.	Storm Cat	Scat Dancer	1:36⅕
1986	Capote (1¼)	Laffit Pincay Jr.	Qualify	Alysheba	1:43⅘
1987	Success Express (1¾)	Jose Santos	Regal Classic	Tejano	1:35⅕
1988	Is It True (1¼)	Laffit Pincay Jr.	Easy Goer	Tagel	1:46⅗
1989	Rhythm (2)	Craig Perret	Grand Canyon	Slavic	1:43⅗
1990	Fly So Free (3)	Jose Santos	Take Me Out	Lost Mountain	1:43⅖
1991	Arazi (4¾)	Pat Valenzuela	Bertrando	Snappy Landing	1:44⅗
1992	Gilded Time (¾)	Chris McCarron	It'sali'lknownfact	River Special	1:43⅖
1993	Brocco (5)	Gary Stevens	Blumin Affair	Tabasco Cat	1:42⅘
1994	Timber Country (½)	Pat Day	Eltish	Tejano Run	1:44⅖
1995	Unbridled's Song (Neck)	Mike Smith	Hennessy	Editor's Note	1:41⅗
1996	Boston Harbor (Neck)	Jerry Bailey	Acceptable	Ordway	1:43⅖
1997	Favorite Trick (5½)	Pat Day	Dawson's Legacy	Nationalore	1:41⅗
1998	Answer Lively (Head)	Jerry Bailey	Aly's Alley	Cat Thief	1:44
1999	Anees (2½)	Gary Stevens	Chief Seattle	High Yield	1:42.29
2000	Macho Uno (Nose)	Jerry Bailey	Point Given	Street Cry	1:42.05
2001	Johannesburg (1¼)	Michael Kinane	Repent	Siphonic	1:42.27
2002	Vindication (2¾)	Mike Smith	Kafwain	Hold That Tiger	1:49.61
2003	Action This Day (2¼)	David Flores	Minister Eric	Chapel Royal	1:43.62
2004	Wilko (¾)	Frankie Dettori	Afleet Alex	Sun King	1:42.09
2005	Stevie Wonderboy(1¼)	Garrett Gomez	Henny Hughes	First Samuria	1:41.64

Note: One mile (1984–85, '87), 1$\frac{1}{16}$ miles (1986 and 1988–2001, '03), 1⅛ miles (2002).

Juvenile Fillies

Year	Winner (Margin)	Jockey	Second	Third	Time
1984	Outstandingly*	Walter Guerra	Dusty Heart	Fine Spirit	1:37⅘
1985	Twilight Ridge (1)	Jorge Velasquez	Family Style	Steal a Kiss	1:35⅘
1986	Brave Raj (5½)	Pat Valenzuela	Tappiano	Saros Brig	1:43⅕
1987	Epitome (Nose)	Pat Day	Jeanne Jones	Dream Team	1:36⅖
1988	Open Mind (1¾)	Angel Cordero Jr.	Darby Shuffle	Lea Lucinda	1:46⅗
1989	Go for Wand (2¾)	Randy Romero	Sweet Roberta	Stella Madrid	1:44⅕
1990	Meadow Star (5)	Jose Santos	Private Treasure	Dance Smartly	1:44
1991	Pleasant Stage (Neck)	Eddie Delahoussaye	La Spia	Cadillac Women	1:46⅖
1992	Eliza (1½)	Pat Valenzuela	Educated Risk	Boots 'n Jackie	1:42⅘
1993	Phone Chatter (Head)	Laffit Pincay	Sardula	Heavenly Prize	1:43
1994	Flanders (Head)	Pat Day	Serena's Song	Stormy Blues	1:45⅕
1995	My Flag (½)	Jerry Bailey	Cara Rafaela	Golden Attraction	1:42⅖
1996	Storm Song (4½)	Craig Perret	Love That Jazz	Critical Factor	1:43⅗
1997	Countess Diana (8½)	Shane Sellers	Career Collection	Primaly	1:42⅕

*In 1984, winner Fran's Valentine dq'd.

Juvenile Fillies *(Cont.)*

Year	Winner (Margin)	Jockey	Second	Third	Time
1998	Silverbulletday (½)	Gary Stevens	Excellent Meeting	Three Ring	1:43⅗
1999	Cash Run (1¼)	Jerry Bailey	Chilukki	Surfside	1:43.31
2000	Caressing (½)	John Velazquez	Platinum Tiara	Shes a Devil Due	1:42.72
2001	Tempera (1½)	David Flores	Imperial Gesture	Bella Bellucci	1:41.49
2002	Storm Flag Flying (½)	John Velazquez	Composure	Santa Catarina	1:49.60
2003	Halfbridled (2½)	Julie Krone	Ashado	Victory U.S.A.	1:42.75
2004	Sweet Catomine (3¾)	Corey Nakatani	Balleto	Runway Model	1:41.65
2005	Folklore (1¼)	Edgar Prado	Wild Fit	Original Spin	1:42.75

Note: One mile (1984-85, '87), 1 1/16 miles (1986 and 1988-01, '03), 1⅛ miles ('02).

Sprint

Year	Winner (Margin)	Jockey	Second	Third	Time
1984	Eillo (Nose)	Craig Perret	Commemorate	Fighting Fit	1:10⅕
1985	Precisionist (¾)	Chris McCarron	Smile	Mt. Livermore	1:08⅖
1986	Smile (1¼)	Jacinto Vasquez	Pine Tree Lane	Bedside Promise	1:08⅖
1987	Very Subtle (4)	Pat Valenzuela	Groovy	Exclusive Enough	1:08⅘
1988	Gulch (¾)	Angel Cordero Jr	Play the King	Afleet	1:10⅖
1989	Dancing Spree (Neck)	Angel Cordero Jr	Safely Kept	Dispersal	1:09
1990	Safely Kept (Neck)	Craig Perret	Dayjur	Black Tie Affair	1:09⅗
1991	Sheikh Albadou (Neck)	Pat Eddery	Pleasant Tap	Robyn Dancer	1:09⅕
1992	Thirty Slews (Neck)	Eddie Delahoussaye	Meafara	Rubiano	1:08⅕
1993	Cardmania (Neck)	Eddie Delahoussaye	Meafara	Gilded Time	1:08⅗
1994	Cherokee Run (Head)	Mike Smith	Soviet Problem	Cardmania	1:09⅖
1995	Desert Stormer (Neck)	Kent Desormeaux	Mr. Greeley	Lit de Justice	1:09
1996	Lit de Justice (1¼)	Corey Nakatani	Paying Dues	Honour and Glory	1:08⅗
1997	Elmhurst (½)	Corey Nakatani	Hesabull	Bet on Sunshine	1:08
1998	Reraise (2)	Corey Nakatani	Grand Slam	Kona Gold	1:09
1999	Artax (½)	Jorge Chavez	Kona Gold	Big Jag	1:07.89
2000	Kona Gold (½)	Alex Solis	Honest Lady	Bet on Sunshine	1:07.77
2001	Squirtle Squirt (½)	Jerry Bailey	Xtra Heat	Caller One	1:08.41
2002	Orientate (½)	Jerry Bailey	Thunderello	Crafty C.T.	1:08.89
2003	Cajun Beat (2¼)	Cornelio Velasquez	Bluesthestandard	Shake You Down	1:07.95
2004	Speightstown (1¼)	John Velasquez	Kela	My Cousin Matt	1:08.11
2005	Silver Train (Head)	Edgar Prado	Taste of Paradise	Lion Tamer	1:08.86

Note: Six furlongs (since 1984).

Mile

Year	Winner (Margin)	Jockey	Second	Third	Time
1984	Royal Heroine (1½)	Fernando Toro	Star Choice	Cozzene	1:32⅗
1985	Cozzene (2¼)	Walter Guerra	Al Mamoon*	Shadeed	1:35
1986	Last Tycoon (Head)	Yves St-Martin	Palace Music	Fred Astaire	1:35⅕
1987	Miesque (3½)	Freddie Head	Show Dancer	Sonic Lady	1:32⅘
1988	Miesque (4)	Freddie Head	Steinlen	Simply Majestic	1:38⅗
1989	Steinlen (¾)	Jose Santos	Sabona	Most Welcome	1:37⅕
1990	Royal Academy (Neck)	Lester Piggott	Itsallgreektome	Priolo	1:35⅕
1991	Opening Verse (2¼)	Pat Valenzuela	Val de Bois	Star of Cozzene	1:37⅖
1992	Lure (3)	Mike Smith	Paradise Creek	Brief Truce	1:32⅘
1993	Lure (2¼)	Mike Smith	Ski Paradise	Fourstars Allstar	1:33⅖
1994	Barathea (Head)	Frankie Dettori	Johann Quatz	Unfinished Symph	1:34⅖
1995	Ridgewood Pearl (2)	John Murtagh	Fastness	Sayyedati	1:43⅗
1996	Da Hoss (1½)	Gary Stevens	Spinning World	Same Old Wish	1:35⅘
1997	Spinning World (2)	Cash Asmussen	Geri	Decorated Hero	1:32⅘
1998	Da Hoss (Head)	John Velazquez	Hawksley Hill	Labeeb	1:35⅕
1999	Silic (Neck)	Corey Nakatani	Tuzla	Docksider	1:34.26
2000	War Chant (Neck)	Gary Stevens	North East Bound	Dansili	1:34.67
2001	Val Royal (1¾)	Jose Valdivia	Forbidden Apple	Bach	1:32.05
2002	Domedriver (¾)	Thierry Thulliez	Rock of Gibraltar	Good Journey	1:36.92
2003	Six Perfections (¾)	Jerry Bailey	Touch of the Blues	Century City	1:33.86
2004	Singletary (½)	David Flores	Antonius Pius	Six Perfections	1:36.90
2005	Artie Schiller (¾)	Garrett Gomez	Leroidesanimaux	Gorella	1:36:10

*2nd place finisher Palace Music was disqualified for interference and placed 9th.

Breeders' Cup *(Cont.)*

Distaff

Year	Winner (Margin)	Jockey	Second	Third	Time
1984	Princess Rooney (7)	Eddie Delahoussaye	Life's Magic	Adored	2:02⅖
1985	Life's Magic (6¼)	Angel Cordero Jr.	Lady's Secret	Dontstop themusic	2:02
1986	Lady's Secret (2½)	Pat Day	Fran's Valentine	Outstandingly	2:01⅕
1987	Sacahuista (2¼)	Randy Romero	Clabber Girl	Oueee Bebe	2:02⅘
1988	Personal Ensign (Nose)	Randy Romero	Winning Colors	Goodbye Halo	1:52
1989	Bayakoa (1½)	Laffit Pincay Jr.	Gorgeous	Open Mind	1:47⅖
1990	Bayakoa (6¾)	Laffit Pincay Jr.	Colonial Waters	Valay Maid	1:49⅕
1991	Dance Smarty (½)	Pat Day	Versailles Treaty	Brought to Mind	1:50⅘
1992	Paseana (4)	Chris McCarron	Versailles Treaty	Magical Maiden	1:48
1993	Hollywood Wildcat (Nose)	Eddie Delahoussaye	Paseana	Re Toss	1:48⅕
1994	One Dreamer (Neck)	Gary Stevens	Heavenly Prize	Miss Dominique	1:50⅗
1995	Inside Information (13½)	Mike Smith	Heavenly Prize	Lakeway	1:46
1996	Jewel Princess (1½)	Corey Nakatani	Serena's Song	Different	1:48⅖
1997	Ajina (2)	Mike Smith	Sharp Cat	Escena	1:47⅕
1998	Escena (Nose)	Gary Stevens	Banshee Breeze	Keeper Hill	1:49⅘
1999	Beautiful Pleasure (¾)	Jorge Chavez	Banshee Breeze	Heritage of Gold	1:47.56
2000	Spain (1½)	Victor Espinoza	Surfside	Heritage of Gold	1:47.66
2001	Unbridled Elaine (head)	Pat Day	Spain	Too Item Limit	1:49.21
2002	Azeri (5)	Mike Smith	Farda Amiga	Imperial Gesture	1:48.64
2003	Adoration (4½)	Pat Valenzuela	Elloluv	Got Koko	1:49.17
2004	Ashado (1¼)	J. Velasquez	Storm Flag Flying	Stellar Jane	1:48.26
2005	Pleasant Home (9¼)	Cornelio Velasquez	Society Selection	Ashado	1:48.34

Note: 1¼ miles (1984–87), 1⅛ miles (since 1988).

Turf

Year	Winner (Margin)	Jockey	Second	Third	Time
1984	Lashkari (Neck)	Yves St. Martin	All Along	Raami	2:25⅕
1985	Pebbles (Neck)	Pat Eddery	Strawberry Rd II	Mourjane	2:27
1986	Manila (Neck)	Jose Santos	Theatrical	Estrapade	2:25⅖
1987	Theatrical (½)	Pat Day	Trempolino	Village Star II	2:24⅖
1988	Great Communicator (½)	Ray Sibille	Sunshine Forever	Indian Skimmer	2:35⅕
1989	Prized (Head)	Eddie Delahoussaye	Sierra Roberta	Star Lift	2:28
1990	In the Wings (½)	Gary Stevens	With Approval	El Senor	2:29⅗
1991	Miss Alleged (2)	Eric Legrix	Itsallgreektome	Quest for Fame	2:30⅘
1992	Fraise (Nose)	Pat Valenzuela	Sky Classic	Quest For Fame	2:24
1993	Kotashaan (½)	Kent Desormeaux	Bien Bien	Luazar	2:25
1994	Tikkanen (1½)	Mike Smith	Hatoof	Paradise Creek	2:26⅖
1995	Northern Spur (Neck)	Chris McCarron	Freedom Cry	Carnegie	2:42
1996	Pilsudski (1¼)	Walter Swinburn	Singspiel	Swain	2:30⅕
1997	Chief Bearhart (¾)	Jose Santos	Borgia	Flag Down	2:23⅘
1998	Buck's Boy (1¼)	Shane Sellers	Yagli	Dushyantor	2:28⅗
1999	Daylami (2½)	Frankie Dettori	Royal Anthem	Buck's Boy	2:24.73
2000	Kalanisi (½)	John Murtagh	Quiet Resolve	John's Call	2:26.96
2001	Fantastic Light (¾)	Frankie Dettori	Milan	Timboroa	2:24.36
2002	High Chaparral (1¼)	Michael Kinane	With Anticipation	Falcon Flight	2:30.14
2003	High Chaparral/Johar	Michael Kinane/Alex Solis		Falbrav	2:24.24
2004	Better Talk Now (1¼)	R. Dominguez	Kitten's Joy	Powerscourt	2:29.15
2005	Intercontinental (1¼)	Rafael Bejarano	Ouija Board	Film Maker	2:02.34

Note: 1½ miles.

Classic

Year	Winner (Margin)	Jockey	Second	Third	Time
1984	Wild Again (Head)	Pat Day	Slew o' Gold*	Gate Dancer	2:03⅖
1985	Proud Truth (Head)	Jorge Velasquez	Gate Dancer	Turkoman	2:00⅘
1986	Skywalker (1¼)	Laffit Pincay Jr.	Turkoman	Precisionist	2:00⅖
1987	Ferdinand (Nose)	Bill Shoemaker	Alysheba	Judge Angelucci	2:01⅖
1988	Alysheba (Nose)	Chris McCarron	Seeking the Gold	Waquoit	2:04⅘
1989	Sunday Silence (½)	Chris McCarron	Easy Goer	Blushing John	2:00⅕
1990	Unbridled (1)	Pat Day	Ibn Bey	Thirty Six Red	2:02⅕
1991	Black Tie Affair (1¼)	Jerry Bailey	Twilight Agenda	Unbridled	2:02⅘
1992	A.P. Indy (2)	Eddie Delahoussaye	Pleasant Tap	Jolypha	2:00⅕
1993	Arcangues (2)	Jerry Bailey	Bertrando	Kissin Kris	2:00⅘
1994	Concern (Neck)	Jerry Bailey	Tabasco Cat	Dramatic Gold	2:02⅖
1995	Cigar (2½)	Jerry Bailey	L'Carriere	Unaccounted For	1:59⅖
1996	Alphabet Soup (Nose)	Chris McCarron	Louis Quatorze	Cigar	2:01

Classic (Cont.)

Year	Winner (Margin)	Jockey	Second	Third	Time
1997	Skip Away (6)	Mike Smith	Deputy Commander	Dowty	1:59½
1998	Awesome Again (¾)	Pat Day	Silver Charm	Swain	2:02
1999	Cat Thief (1¼)	Pat Day	Budroyale	Golden Missile	1:59.52
2000	Tiznow (Neck)	Chris McCarron	Giant's Causeway	Captain Steve	2:00.75
2001	Tiznow (Nose)	Chris McCarron	Sakhee	Albert the Great	2:00.62
2002	Volponi (6½)	Jose Santos	Medaglia d'Oro	Milwaukee Brew	2:01.39
2003	Pleasantly Perfect (1½)	Alex Solis	Medaglia d'Oro	Dynever	1:59.88
2004	Ghostzapper (3)	J. Castellano	Roses in May	Perfectly	1:59.02
2005	Saint Liam (1)	Jerry Bailey	Flower Alley	Perfect	2:01.49

*2nd place finisher Gate Dancer was disqualified for interference and placed 3rd. Note: 1¼ miles.

England's Triple Crown Winners

England's Triple Crown consists of the Two Thousand Guineas, held at Newmarket; the Epsom Derby, held at Epsom Downs; and the St. Leger Stakes, held at Doncaster.

Year	Horse	Owner	Year	Horse	Owner
1853	West Australian	Mr. Bowes	1900	Diamond Jubilee	Prince of Wales
1865	Gladiateur	F. DeLagrange	1903	*Rock Sand	J. Miller
1866	Lord Lyon	R. Sutton	1915	Pommern	S. Joel
1886	*Ormonde	Duke of Westminster	1917	Gay Crusader	Mr. Fairie
1891	Common	†F. Johnstone	1918	Gainsborough	Lady James
1893	Isinglass	H. McCalmont			Douglas
1897	Galtee More	J. Gubbins	1935	*Bahram	Aga Khan
1899	Flying Fox	Duke of Westminster	1970	‡Nijinsky II	C. W. Engelhard

*Imported into United States. †Raced in name of Lord Alington in Two Thousand Guineas. ‡Canadian-bred.

Annual Leaders

Horse—Money Won

Year	Horse	Age	Starts	1st	2nd	3rd	Winnings ($)
1919	Sir Barton	3	13	8	3	2	88,250
1920	Man o' War	3	11	11	0	0	166,140
1921	Morvich	2	11	11	0	0	115,234
1922	Pillory	3	7	4	1	1	95,654
1923	Zev	3	14	12	1	0	272,008
1924	Sarzen	3	12	8	1	1	95,640
1925	Pompey	2	10	7	2	0	121,630
1926	Crusader	3	15	9	4	0	166,033
1927	Anita Peabody	2	7	6	0	1	111,905
1928	High Strung	2	6	5	0	0	153,590
1929	Blue Larkspur	3	6	4	1	0	153,450
1930	Gallant Fox	3	10	9	1	0	308,275
1931	Gallant Flight	2	7	7	0	0	219,000
1932	Gusto	3	16	4	3	2	145,940
1933	Singing Wood	2	9	3	2	2	88,050
1934	Cavalcade	3	7	6	1	0	111,235
1935	Omaha	3	9	6	1	2	142,255
1936	Granville	3	11	7	3	0	110,295
1937	Seabiscuit	4	15	11	2	2	168,580
1938	Stagehand	3	15	8	2	3	189,710
1939	Challedon	3	15	9	2	3	184,535
1940	Bimelech	3	7	4	2	1	110,005
1941	Whirlaway	3	20	13	5	2	272,386
1942	Shut Out	3	12	8	2	0	238,872
1943	Count Fleet	3	6	6	0	0	174,055
1944	Pavot	2	8	8	0	0	179,040
1945	Busher	3	13	10	2	1	273,735

Horse—Money Won (Cont.)

Year	Horse	Age	Starts	1st	2nd	3rd	Winnings ($)
1946	Assault	3	15	8	2	3	424,195
1947	Armed	6	17	11	4	1	376,325
1948	Citation	3	20	19	1	0	709,470
1949	Ponder	3	21	9	5	2	321,825
1950	Noor	5	12	7	4	1	346,940
1951	Counterpoint	3	15	7	2	1	250,525
1952	Crafty Admiral	4	16	9	4	1	277,225
1953	Native Dancer	3	10	9	1	0	513,425
1954	Determine	3	15	10	3	2	328,700
1955	Nashua	3	12	10	1	1	752,550
1956	Needles	3	8	4	2	0	440,850
1957	Round Table	3	22	15	1	3	600,383
1958	Round Table	4	20	14	4	0	662,780
1959	Sword Dancer	3	13	8	4	0	537,004
1960	Bally Ache	3	15	10	3	1	445,045
1961	Carry Back	3	16	9	1	3	565,349
1962	Never Bend	2	10	7	1	2	402,969
1963	Candy Spots	3	12	7	2	1	604,481
1964	Gun Bow	4	16	8	4	2	580,100
1965	Buckpasser	2	11	9	1	0	568,096
1966	Buckpasser	3	14	13	1	0	669,078
1967	Damascus	3	16	12	3	1	817,941
1968	Forward Pass	3	13	7	2	0	546,674
1969	Arts and Letters	3	14	8	5	1	555,604
1970	Personality	3	18	8	2	1	444,049
1971	Riva Ridge	2	9	7	0	0	503,263
1972	Droll Role	4	19	7	3	4	471,633
1973	Secretariat	3	12	9	2	1	860,404
1974	Chris Evert	3	8	5	1	2	551,063
1975	Foolish Pleasure	3	11	5	4	1	716,278
1976	Forego	6	8	6	1	1	401,701
1977	Seattle Slew	3	7	6	0	1	641,370
1978	Affirmed	3	11	8	2	0	901,541
1979	Spectacular Bid	3	12	10	1	1	1,279,334
1980	Temperence Hill	3	17	8	3	1	1,130,452
1981	John Henry	6	10	8	0	0	1,798,030
1982	Perrault	5	8	4	1	2	1,197,400
1983	All Along	4	7	4	1	1	2,138,963
1984	Slew o'Gold	4	6	5	1	0	2,627,944
1985	Spend A Buck	3	7	5	1	1	3,552,704
1986	Snow Chief	3	9	6	1	1	1,875,200
1987	Alysheba	3	10	3	3	1	2,511,156
1988	Alysheba	4	9	7	1	0	3,808,600
1989	Sunday Silence	3	9	7	2	0	4,578,454
1990	Unbridled	3	11	4	3	2	3,718,149
1991	Dance Smartly	3	8	8	0	0	2,876,821
1992	A.P. Indy	3	7	5	0	1	2,622,560
1993	Kotashaan	3	10	6	3	0	2,619,014
1994	Paradise Creek	5	11	8	2	1	2,610,187
1995	Cigar	5	10	10	0	0	4,819,800
1996	Cigar	6	8	5	2	1	4,910,000
1997	Skip Away	4	11	4	5	2	4,089,000
1998	Silver Charm	4	9	6	2	0	4,696,506
1999	Almutawakel	4	4	1	1	1	3,290,000
2000	Dubai Millennium	4	1	1	0	0	3,600,000
2001	Captain Steve	4	6	2	1	1	4,201,200
2002	War Emblem	4	10	5	0	0	3,455,000
2003	Pleasantly Perfect	5	4	2	0	1	2,470,000
2004	Smarty Jones	3	7	6	1	0	7,563,535
2005	Saint Liam	5	6	4	1	0	3,696,960

Trainer—Money Won

Year	Trainer	Wins	Winnings ($)	Year	Trainer	Wins	Winnings ($)
1908	James Rowe, Sr.	50	284,335	1957	Jimmy Jones	70	1,150,910
1909	Sam Hildreth	73	123,942	1958	Willie Molter	69	1,116,544
1910	Sam Hildreth	84	148,010	1959	Willie Molter	71	847,290
1911	Sam Hildreth	67	49,418	1960	Hirsch Jacobs	97	748,349
1912	John F. Schorr	63	58,110	1961	Jimmy Jones	62	759,856
1913	James Rowe, Sr.	18	45,936	1962	Mesh Tenney	58	1,099,474
1914	R. C. Benson	45	59,315	1963	Mesh Tenney	40	860,703
1915	James Rowe, Sr.	19	75,596	1964	Bill Winfrey	61	1,350,534
1916	Sam Hildreth	39	70,950	1965	Hirsch Jacobs	91	1,331,628
1917	Sam Hildreth	23	61,698	1966	Eddie Neloy	93	2,456,250
1918	H. Guy Bedwell	53	80,296	1967	Eddie Neloy	72	1,776,089
1919	H. Guy Bedwell	63	208,728	1968	Eddie Neloy	52	1,233,101
1920	L. Feustal	22	186,087	1969	Elliott Burch	26	1,067,936
1921	Sam Hildreth	85	262,768	1970	Charlie Whittingham	82	1,302,354
1922	Sam Hildreth	74	247,014	1971	Charlie Whittingham	77	1,737,115
1923	Sam Hildreth	75	392,124	1972	Charlie Whittingham	79	1,734,020
1924	Sam Hildreth	77	255,608	1973	Charlie Whittingham	85	1,865,385
1925	G. R. Tompkins	30	199,245	1974	Pancho Martin	166	2,408,419
1926	Scott P. Harlan	21	205,681	1975	Charlie Whittingham	93	2,437,244
1927	W. H. Bringloe	63	216,563	1976	Jack Van Berg	496	2,976,196
1928	John F. Schorr	65	258,425	1977	Laz Barrera	127	2,715,848
1929	James Rowe, Jr.	25	314,881	1978	Laz Barrera	100	3,307,164
1930	Sunny Jim Fitzsimmons	47	397,355	1979	Laz Barrera	98	3,608,517
1931	Big Jim Healey	33	297,300	1980	Laz Barrera	99	2,969,151
1932	Sunny Jim Fitzsimmons	68	266,650	1981	Charlie Whittingham	74	3,993,300
1933	Humming Bob Smith	53	135,720	1982	Charlie Whittingham	63	4,587,457
1934	Humming Bob Smith	43	249,938	1983	D. Wayne Lukas	78	4,267,261
1935	Bud Stotler	87	303,005	1984	D. Wayne Lukas	131	5,835,921
1936	Sunny Jim Fitzsimmons	42	193,415	1985	D. Wayne Lukas	218	11,155,188
1937	Robert McGarvey	46	209,925	1986	D. Wayne Lukas	259	12,345,180
1938	Earl Sande	15	226,495	1987	D. Wayne Lukas	343	17,502,110
1939	Sunny Jim Fitzsimmons	45	266,205	1988	D. Wayne Lukas	318	17,842,358
1940	Silent Tom Smith	14	269,200	1989	D. Wayne Lukas	305	16,103,998
1941	Plain Ben Jones	70	475,318	1990	D. Wayne Lukas	267	14,508,871
1942	John M. Gaver Sr.	48	406,547	1991	D. Wayne Lukas	289	15,942,223
1943	Plain Ben Jones	73	267,915	1992	D. Wayne Lukas	230	9,806,436
1944	Plain Ben Jones	60	601,660	1993	Robert Frankel	79	8,883,252
1945	Silent Tom Smith	52	510,655	1994	D. Wayne Lukas	147	9,247,457
1946	Hirsch Jacobs	99	560,077	1995	D. Wayne Lukas	194	12,842,865
1947	Jimmy Jones	85	1,334,805	1996	D. Wayne Lukas	192	15,966,344
1948	Jimmy Jones	81	1,118,670	1997	D. Wayne Lukas	175	10,338,957
1949	Jimmy Jones	76	978,587	1998	Bob Baffert	139	15,000,870
1950	Preston Burch	96	637,754	1999	Bob Baffert	169	16,934,607
1951	John M. Gaver Sr.	42	616,392	2000	Bob Baffert	146	11,831,605
1952	Plain Ben Jones	29	662,137	2001	Bob Baffert	138	16,354,996
1953	Harry Trotsek	54	1,028,873	2002	Robert Frankel	117	17,748,340
1954	Willie Molter	136	1,107,860	2003	Robert Frankel	114	19,143,289
1955	Sunny Jim Fitzsimmons	66	1,270,055	2004	Todd A. Pletcher	240	17,511,923
1956	Willie Molter	142	1,227,402	2005	Todd A. Pletcher	257	20,867842

Jockey—Money Won

Year	Jockey	Mts	1st	2nd	3rd	Pct	Winnings ($)
1919	John Loftus	177	65	36	24	.37	252,707
1920	Clarence Kummer	353	87	79	48	.25	292,376
1921	Earl Sande	340	112	69	59	.33	263,043
1922	Albert Johnson	297	43	57	40	.14	345,054
1923	Earl Sande	430	122	89	79	.28	569,394
1924	Ivan Parke	844	205	175	121	.24	290,395
1925	Laverne Fator	315	81	54	44	.26	305,775
1926	Laverne Fator	511	143	90	86	.28	361,435
1927	Earl Sande	179	49	33	19	.27	277,877
1928	Pony McAtee	235	55	43	25	.23	301,295
1929	Mack Garner	274	57	39	33	.21	314,975
1930	Sonny Workman	571	152	88	79	.27	420,438
1931	Charles Kurtsinger	519	93	82	79	.18	392,095

Jockey—Money Won (Cont.)

Year	Jockey	Mts	1st	2nd	3rd	Pct	Winnings ($)
1932	Sonny Workman	378	87	48	55	.23	385,070
1933	Robert Jones	471	63	57	70	.13	226,285
1934	Wayne D. Wright	919	174	154	114	.19	287,185
1935	Silvio Coucci	749	141	125	103	.19	319,760
1936	Wayne D. Wright	670	100	102	73	.15	264,000
1937	Charles Kurtsinger	765	120	94	106	.16	384,202
1938	Nick Wall	658	97	94	82	.15	385,161
1939	Basil James	904	191	165	105	.21	353,333
1940	Eddie Arcaro	783	132	143	112	.17	343,661
1941	Don Meade	1,164	210	185	158	.18	398,627
1942	Eddie Arcaro	687	123	97	89	.18	481,949
1943	John Longden	871	173	140	121	.20	573,276
1944	Ted Atkinson	1,539	287	231	213	.19	899,101
1945	John Longden	778	180	112	100	.23	981,977
1946	Ted Atkinson	1,377	233	213	173	.17	1,036,825
1947	Douglas Dodson	646	141	100	75	.22	1,429,949
1948	Eddie Arcaro	726	188	108	98	.26	1,686,230
1949	Steve Brooks	906	209	172	110	.23	1,316,817
1950	Eddie Arcaro	888	195	153	144	.22	1,410,160
1951	Bill Shoemaker	1,161	257	197	161	.22	1,329,890
1952	Eddie Arcaro	807	188	122	109	.23	1,859,591
1953	Bill Shoemaker	1,683	485	302	210	.29	1,784,187
1954	Bill Shoemaker	1,251	380	221	142	.30	1,876,760
1955	Eddie Arcaro	820	158	126	108	.19	1,864,796
1956	Bill Hartack	1,387	347	252	184	.25	2,343,955
1957	Bill Hartack	1,238	341	208	178	.28	3,060,501
1958	Bill Shoemaker	1,133	300	185	137	.26	2,961,693
1959	Bill Shoemaker	1,285	347	230	159	.27	2,843,133
1960	Bill Shoemaker	1,227	274	196	158	.22	2,123,961
1961	Bill Shoemaker	1,256	304	186	175	.24	2,690,819
1962	Bill Shoemaker	1,126	311	156	128	.28	2,916,844
1963	Bill Shoemaker	1,203	271	193	137	.22	2,526,925
1964	Bill Shoemaker	1,056	246	147	133	.23	2,649,553
1965	Braulio Baeza	1,245	270	200	201	.22	2,582,702
1966	Braulio Baeza	1,341	298	222	190	.22	2,951,022
1967	Braulio Baeza	1,064	256	184	127	.24	3,088,888
1968	Braulio Baeza	1,089	201	184	145	.18	2,835,108
1969	Jorge Velasquez	1,442	258	230	204	.18	2,542,315
1970	Laffit Pincay Jr.	1,328	269	208	187	.20	2,626,526
1971	Laffit Pincay Jr.	1,627	380	288	214	.23	3,784,377
1972	Laffit Pincay Jr.	1,388	289	215	205	.21	3,225,827
1973	Laffit Pincay Jr.	1,444	350	254	209	.24	4,093,492
1974	Laffit Pincay Jr.	1,278	341	227	180	.27	4,251,060
1975	Braulio Baeza	1,190	196	208	180	.16	3,674,398
1976	Angel Cordero Jr.	1,534	274	273	235	.18	4,709,500
1977	Steve Cauthen	2,075	487	345	304	.23	6,151,750
1978	Darrel McHargue	1,762	375	294	263	.21	6,188,353
1979	Laffit Pincay Jr.	1,708	420	302	261	.25	8,183,535
1980	Chris McCarron	1,964	405	318	282	.20	7,666,100
1981	Chris McCarron	1,494	326	251	207	.22	8,397,604
1982	Angel Cordero Jr.	1,838	397	338	227	.22	9,702,520
1983	Angel Cordero Jr.	1,792	362	296	237	.20	10,116,807
1984	Chris McCarron	1,565	356	276	218	.23	12,038,213
1985	Laffit Pincay Jr.	1,409	289	246	183	.21	13,415,049
1986	Jose Santos	1,636	329	237	222	.20	11,329,297
1987	Jose Santos	1,639	305	268	208	.19	12,407,355
1988	Jose Santos	1,867	370	287	265	.20	14,877,298
1989	Jose Santos	1,459	285	238	220	.20	13,847,003
1990	Gary Stevens	1,504	283	245	202	.19	13,881,198
1991	Chris McCarron	1,440	265	228	206	.18	14,441,083
1992	Kent Desormeaux	1,568	361	260	208	.23	14,193,006
1993	Mike Smith	1,510	343	235	214	.23	14,008,148
1994	Mike Smith	1,484	317	250	196	.21	15,979,820
1995	Jerry Bailey	1,265	287	193	144	.23	16,308,230
1996	Jerry Bailey	1,187	298	189	165	.25	19,465,376
1997	Jerry Bailey	1,143	272	186	178	.26	18,260,553
1998	Gary Stevens	869	178	145	122	.20	19,358,840

Jockey—Money Won *(Cont.)*

Year	Jockey	Mts	Ist	2nd	3rd	Pct	Winnings ($)
1999	Pat Day	1,265	254	209	209	.20	18,092,845
2000	Pat Day	1,219	267	206	186	.22	17,479,838
2001	Jerry Bailey	912	227	194	137	.25	22,597,720
2002	Jerry Bailey	832	213	139	118	.26	19,271,814
2003	Jerry Bailey	776	206	149	97	.27	23,354,960
2004	John R. Velazquez	1,327	335	222	181	.25	22,248,661
2005	John R. Velazquez	1,148	251	177	146	.21	20,799,923

Jockey—Races Won

Year	Jockey	Mts	Ist	2nd	3rd	Pct
1895	J. Perkins	762	192	177	129	.25
1896	J. Scherrer	1,093	271	227	172	.24
1897	H. Martin	803	173	152	116	.21
1898	T. Burns	973	277	213	149	.28
1899	T. Burns	1,064	273	173	266	.26
1900	C. Mitchell	874	195	140	139	.23
1901	W. O'Connor	1,047	253	221	192	.24
1902	J. Ranch	1,069	276	205	181	.26
1903	G.C. Fuller	918	229	152	122	.25
1904	E. Hildebrand	1,169	297	230	171	.25
1905	D. Nicol	861	221	143	136	.26
1906	W. Miller	1,384	388	300	199	.28
1907	W. Miller	1,194	334	226	170	.28
1908	V. Powers	1,260	324	204	185	.26
1909	V. Powers	704	173	121	114	.25
1910	G. Garner	947	200	188	153	.20
1911	T. Koerner	813	162	133	112	.20
1912	P. Hill	967	168	141	129	.17
1913	M. Buxton	887	146	131	136	.16
1914	J. McTaggart	787	157	132	106	.20
1915	M. Garner	775	151	118	90	.19
1916	F. Robinson	791	178	131	124	.23
1917	W. Crump	803	151	140	101	.19
1918	F. Robinson	864	185	140	108	.21
1919	C. Robinson	896	190	140	126	.21
1920	J. Butwell	721	152	129	139	.21
1921	C. Lang	696	135	110	105	.19
1922	M. Fator	859	188	153	116	.22
1923	I. Parke	718	173	105	95	.24
1924	I. Parke	844	205	175	121	.24
1925	A. Mortensen	987	187	145	138	.19
1926	R. Jones	1,172	190	163	152	.16
1927	L. Hardy	1,130	207	192	151	.18
1928	J. Inzelone	1,052	155	152	135	.15
1929	M. Knight	871	149	132	133	.17
1930	H.R. Riley	861	177	145	123	.21
1931	H. Roble	1,174	173	173	155	.15
1932	J. Gilbert	1,050	212	144	160	.20
1933	J. Westrope	1,224	301	235	166	.25
1934	M. Peters	1,045	221	179	147	.21
1935	C. Stevenson	1,099	206	169	146	.19
1936	B. James	1,106	245	195	161	.22
1937	J. Adams	1,265	260	186	177	.21
1938	J. Longden	1,150	236	168	171	.21
1939	D. Meade	1,284	255	221	180	.20
1940	E. Dew	1,377	287	201	180	.21
1941	D. Meade	1,164	210	185	158	.18
1942	J. Adams	1,120	245	185	150	.22
1943	J. Adams	1,069	228	159	171	.21
1944	T. Atkinson	1,539	287	231	213	.19
1945	J.D. Jessop	1,085	290	182	168	.27
1946	T. Atkinson	1,377	233	213	173	.17

Jockey—Races Won *(Cont.)*

Year	Jockey	Mts	1st	2nd	3rd	Pct
1947	J. Longden	1,327	316	250	195	.24
1948	J. Longden	1,197	319	233	161	.27
1949	G. Glisson	1,347	270	217	181	.20
1950	W. Shoemaker	1,640	388	266	230	.24
1951	C. Burr	1,319	310	232	192	.24
1952	A. DeSpirito	1,482	390	247	212	.26
1953	W. Shoemaker	1,683	485	302	210	.29
1954	W. Shoemaker	1,251	380	221	142	.30
1955	W. Hartack	1,702	417	298	215	.25
1956	W. Hartack	1,387	347	252	184	.25
1957	W. Hartack	1,238	341	208	178	.28
1958	W. Shoemaker	1,133	300	185	137	.26
1959	W. Shoemaker	1,285	347	230	159	.27
1960	W. Hartack	1,402	307	247	190	.22
1961	J. Sellers	1,394	328	212	227	.24
1962	R. Ferraro	1,755	352	252	226	.20
1963	W. Blum	1,704	360	286	215	.21
1964	W. Blum	1,577	324	274	170	.21
1965	J. Davidson	1,582	319	228	190	.20
1966	A. Gomez	996	318	173	142	.32
1967	J. Velasquez	1,939	438	315	270	.23
1968	A. Cordero Jr.	1,662	345	278	219	.21
1969	L. Snyder	1,645	352	290	243	.21
1970	S. Hawley	1,908	452	313	265	.24
1971	L Pincay Jr.	1,627	380	288	214	.23
1972	S. Hawley	1,381	367	269	200	.27
1973	S. Hawley	1,925	515	336	292	.27
1974	C.J. McCarron	2,199	546	392	297	.25
1975	C.J. McCarron	2,194	458	389	305	.21
1976	S. Hawley	1,637	413	245	201	.25
1977	S. Cauthen	2,075	487	345	304	.23
1978	E. Delahoussaye	1,666	384	285	238	.23
1979	D. Gall	2,146	479	396	326	.22
1980	C.J. McCarron	1,964	405	318	282	.20
1981	D. Gall	1,917	376	305	297	.20
1982	Pat Day	1,870	399	326	255	.21
1983	Pat Day	1,725	454	321	251	.26
1984	Pat Day	1,694	399	296	259	.24
1985	C.W. Antley	2,335	469	371	288	.20
1986	Pat Day	1,417	429	246	202	.30
1987	Kent Desormeaux	2,207	450	370	294	.28
1988	Kent Desormeaux	1,897	474	295	276	.25
1989	Kent Desormeaux	2,312	598	385	309	.25
1990	Pat Day	1,421	364	265	222	.26
1991	Pat Day	1,405	430	256	213	.31
1992	Russell Baze	1,691	433	296	237	.25
1993	Russell Baze	1,579	410	297	225	.26
1994	Russell Baze	1,588	415	301	266	.26
1995	Russell Baze	1,531	445	310	232	.29
1996	Russell Baze	1,482	415	297	200	.28
1997	Edgar S. Prado	2,037	533	384	308	.26
1998	Edgar S. Prado	1,969	470	377	285	.23
1999	Edgar S. Prado	1,902	402	307	276	.21
2000	Ramon Dominguez	1,586	361	293	238	.23
2001	Ramon Dominguez	1,864	431	368	278	.23
2002	Russell Baze	1,508	431	302	219	.29
2003	Ramon Dominguez	1,627	453	316	252	.28
2004	Rafael Bejarano	1,922	455	355	280	.24
2005	Russell Baze	1,216	364	242	171	.29

Leading Jockeys—Career Records

Jockey	Years Riding	Mts	1st	2nd	3rd	Win Pct	Winnings ($)
Laffit Pincay Jr. (2003)	39	48,486	9,530	7,784	6,650	.197	237,120,625
*Russell Baze	33	42,385	9,484	7,274	6,044	.223	143,955,716
Bill Shoemaker (1990)	42	40,350	8,833	6,136	4,987	.219	123,375,524
Pat Day(2004)	33	40,298	8,803	6,860	5,687	.218	297,912,019
David Gall (1999)	41	41,775	7,396	6,525	6,131	.177	24,972,821
Chris McCarron (2002)	28	34,239	7,141	5,670	4,672	.209	263,985,505
Angel Cordero Jr. (1992)	31	38,657	7,057	6,136	5,359	.183	164,570,227
Jorge Velasquez (1998)	35	40,852	6,795	6,178	5,755	.166	125,544,379
Sandy Hawley (1998)	31	31,455	6,449	4,825	4,159	.205	88,681,292
*Earlie Fires	42	44,519	6,401	5,496	5,318	.144	84,360,966
Larry Snyder (1994)	35	35,681	6,388	5,030	3,440	.179	47,207,289
Eddie Delahoussaye (2002)	32	39,213	6,384	5,676	5,586	.163	195,884,940
Carl Gambardella (1994)	39	39,018	6,349	5,953	5,353	.163	29,389,041
John Longden (1966)	40	32,413	6,032	4,914	4,273	.186	24,665,800
*Jerry Bailey	32	30,855	5,893	4,553	3,925	.191	296,104,129
*Mario Pino	27	35,543	5,795	5,260	4,900	.163	96,580,264
*Edgar Prado	23	29,919	5,750	4,870	4,245	.192	182,973,310
Jacinto Vasquez (1998)	38	37,337	5,228	4,714	4,510	.140	85,754,115
Ron Ardoin (2003)	31	32,335	5,226	4,298	3,793	.162	58,908,059
*Anthony Black	30	32,747	5,042	4,342	4,211	.154	58,188,064

*Active jockeys. Note: Jockeys ranked by wins. Records go through September 2006, and include available statistics for races ridden in foreign countries. Figures in parentheses after jockey's name indicate last year in which they rode.

Leading jockeys courtesy of Equibase company and *National Thoroughbred Racing Association*.

HORSES

Ack Ack (1986, 1966)
Affectionately (1989, 1960)
Affirmed (1980, 1975)
All Along (1990, 1979)
Alsab (1976, 1939)
Alydar (1989, 1975)
Alysheba (1993, 1984)
American Eclipse (1970, 1814)
A.P. Indy (2000, 1989)
Armed (1963, 1941)
Artful (1956, 1902)
Arts and Letters (1994, 1966)
Assault (1964, 1943)
Battleship (1969, 1927)
Bayakoa (1998, 1984)
Bed o' Roses (1976, 1947)
Beldame (1956, 1901)
Ben Brush (1955, 1893)
Bewitch (1977, 1945)
Bimelech (1990, 1937)
Black Gold (1989, 1921)
Black Helen (1991, 1932)
Blue Larkspur (1957, 1926)
Bold 'n Determined (1997, 1977)
Bold Ruler (1973, 1954)
Bon Nouvel (1976, 1960)
Boston (1955, 1833)
Bowl of Flowers (2004, 1988)
Broomstick (1956, 1901)
Buckpasser (1970, 1963)
Busher (1964, 1942)
Bushranger (1967, 1930)
Cafe Prince (1985, 1970)
Carry Back (1975, 1958)
Cavalcade (1993, 1931)
Challedon (1977, 1936)
Chris Evert (1988, 1971)
Cicada (1967, 1959)
Cigar (2002, 1990)
Citation (1959, 1945)
Coaltown (1983, 1945)
Colin (1956, 1905)
Commando (1956, 1898)
Count Fleet (1961, 1940)
Crusader (1995, 1923)
Dahlia (1981, 1970)
Damascus (1974, 1964)
Dance Smartly (2003, 1988)
Dark Mirage (1974, 1965)
Davona Dale (1985, 1976)
Desert Vixen (1979, 1970)
Devil Diver (1980, 1939)
Discovery (1969, 1931)
Domino (1955, 1891)
Dr. Fager (1971, 1964)
Easy Goer (1997, 1986)
Eight Thirty (1994, 1936)

Elkridge (1966, 1938)
Emperor of Norfolk (1988, 1885)
Equipoise (1957, 1928)
Exceller (1999, 1973)
Exterminator (1957, 1915)
Fairmount (1985, 1921)
Fair Play (1956, 1905)
Fashion (1980, 1837)
Firenze (1981, 1884)
Flatterer (1994, 1979)
Flawlessly (2004, 1988)
Foolish Pleasure (1995, 1972)
Forego (1979, 1970)
Fort Marcy (1998, 1964)
Gallant Bloom (1977, 1966)
Gallant Fox (1957, 1927)
Gallant Man (1987, 1954)
Gallorette (1962, 1942)
Gamely (1980, 1964)
Genuine Risk (1986, 1977)
Go For Wand (1996, 1987)
Good and Plenty (1956, 1900)
Grandville (1997, 1933)
Grey Lag (1957, 1918)
Gun Bow (1999, 1960)
Hamburg (1986, 1895)
Hanover (1955, 1884)
Henry of Navarre (1985, 1891)
Hill Prince (1991, 1947)
Hindoo (1955, 1878)
Holy Bull (2001, 1991)
Imp (1965, 1894)
Jay Trump (1971, 1957)
John Henry (1990, 1975)
Johnstown (1992, 1936)
Jolly Roger (1965, 1922)
Kelso (1967, 1957)
Kentucky (1983, 1861)
Kingston (1955, 1884)
Lady's Secret (1992, 1982)
La Prevoyante (1995, 1970)
L'Escargot (1977, 1963)
Lexington (1955, 1850)
Lonesome Glory (2005, 1988)
Longfellow (1971, 1867)
Luke Blackburn (1956, 1877)
Majestic Prince (1988, 1966)
Man o' War (1957, 1917)
Maskette (2001, 1908)
Miesque (1999, 1984)
Miss Woodford (1967, 1880)
Myrtlewood (1979, 1932)
Nashua (1965, 1952)
Native Dancer (1963, 1950)
Native Diver (1978, 1959)
Needles (2000, 1953)
Neji (1966, 1950)

Noor (2002, 1945)
Northern Dancer (1976, 1961)
Oedipus (1978, 1946)
Old Rosebud (1968, 1911)
Omaha (1965, 1932)
Pan Zareta (1972, 1910)
Parole (1984, 1873)
Paseana (2001, 1987)
Personal Ensign (1993, 1984)
Peter Pan (1956, 1904)
Precisionist (2003, 1981)
Princess Doreen (1982, 1921)
Princess Rooney (1991, 1980)
Real Delight (1987, 1949)
Regret (1957, 1912)
Reigh Count (1978, 1923)
Riva Ridge (1998, 1969)
Roamer (1981, 1911)
Roseben (1956, 1901)
Round Table (1972, 1954)
Ruffian (1976, 1972)
Ruthless (1975, 1864)
Salvator (1955, 1886)
Sarazen (1957, 1921)
Seabiscuit (1958, 1933)
Searching (1978, 1952)
Seattle Slew (1981, 1974)
Secretariat (1974, 1970)
Serena's Song (2002, 1992)
Shuvee (1975, 1966)
Silver Spoon (1978, 1956)
Sir Archy (1955, 1805)
Sir Barton (1957, 1916)
Skip Away (2004, 1993)
Slew o' Gold (1992, 1980)
Spectacular Bid (1982, 1976)
Stymie (1975, 1941)
Sun Beau (1996, 1925)
Sunday Silence (1996, 1986)
Susan's Girl (1976, 1969)
Swaps (1966, 1952)
Sword Dancer (1977, 1956)
Sysonby (1956, 1902)
Ta Wee (1994, 1967)
Ten Broeck (1982, 1872)
Tim Tam (1985, 1955)
Tom Fool (1960, 1949)
Top Flight (1966, 1929)
Tosmah (1984, 1961)
Twenty Grand (1957, 1928)
Twilight Tear (1963, 1941)
Two Lea (1982, 1946)
War Admiral (1958, 1934)
Whirlaway (1959, 1938)
Whisk Broom II (1979, 1907)
Winning Colors (2000, 1985)
Zaccio (1990, 1976)
Zev (1983, 1920)

Note: Years of election and foaling in parentheses.

Major Races

Hambletonian

Year	Winner	Driver	Year	Winner	Driver
1926	Guy McKinney	Nat Ray	1967	Speedy Streak	Del Cameron
1927	Iosola's Worthy	Marvin Childs	1968	Nevele Pride	Stanley Dancer
1928	Spenser	W. H. Leese	1969	Lindy's Pride	H. Beissinger
1929	Walter Dear	Walter Cox	1970	Timothy T.	J. Simpson Jr.
1930	Hanover's Bertha	Tom Berry	1971	Speedy Crown	H. Beissinger
1931	Calumet Butler	R. D. McMahon	1972	Super Bowl	Stanley Dancer
1932	The Marchioness	William Caton	1973	Flirth	Ralph Baldwin
1933	Mary Reynolds	Ben White	1974	Christopher T.	Bill Haughton
1934	Lord Jim	Doc Parshall	1975	Bonefish	Stanley Dancer
1935	Greyhound	Sep Palin	1976	Steve Lobell	Bill Haughton
1936	Rosalind	Ben White	1977	Green Speed	Bill Haughton
1937	Shirley Hanover	Henry Thomas	1978	Speedy Somolli	H. Beissinger
1938	McLin Hanover	Henry Thomas	1979	Legend Hanover	George Sholty
1939	Peter Astra	Doc Parshall	1980	Burgomeister	Bill Haughton
1940	Spencer Scott	Fred Egan	1981	Shiaway St. Pat	Ray Remmen
1941	Bill Gallon	Lee Smith	1982	Speed Bowl	Tom Haughton
1942	The Ambassador	Ben White	1983	Duenna	Stanley Dancer
1943	Volo Song	Ben White	1984	Historic Freight	Ben Webster
1944	Yankee Maid	Henry Thomas	1985	Prakas	Bill O'Donnell
1945	Titan Hanover	H. Pownall Sr.	1986	Nuclear Kosmos	Ulf Thoresen
1946	Chestertown	Thomas Berry	1987	Mack Lobell	John Campbell
1947	Hoot Mon	Sep Palin	1988	Armbro Goal	John Campbell
1948	Demon Hanover	Harrison Hoyt	1989	Park Ave. Joe/Probe*	R. Waples/B. Fahy
1949	Miss Tilly	Fred Egan	1990	Harmonious	John Campbell
1950	Lusty Song	Del Miller	1991	Giant Victory	Jack Moiseyev
1951	Mainliner	Guy Crippen	1992	Alf Palema	Mickey McNichol
1952	Sharp Note	Bion Shively	1993	American Winner	Ron Pierce
1953	Helicopter	Harry Harvey	1994	Victory Dream	Michel Lachance
1954	Newport Dream	Del Cameron	1995	Tagliabue	John Campbell
1955	Scott Frost	Joe O'Brien	1996	Continentalvictory	Michel Lachance
1956	The Intruder	Ned Bower	1997	Malabar Man	Mal Burroughs
1957	Hickory Smoke	J. Simpson Sr.	1998	Muscles Yankee	John Campbell
1958	Emily's Pride	Flave Nipe	1999	Self Possessed	Michel Lachance
1959	Diller Hanover	Frank Ervin	2000	Yankee Paco	T.J. Ritchie
1960	Blaze Hanover	Joe O'Brien	2001	Scarlet Knight	Stefan Melander
1961	Harlan Dean	James Arthur	2002	Chip Chip Hooray	Eric Ledford
1962	A. C.'s Viking	Sanders Russell	2003	Amigo Hall	Mike Lachance
1963	Speedy Scot	Ralph Baldwin	2004	Windsong's Legacy	T. Smedshammer
1964	Ayres	J. Simpson Sr.	2005	P-Forty-Seven	Dave Palone
1965	Egyptian Candor	Del Cameron	2006	Glidemaster	John Campbell
1966	Kerry Way	Frank Ervin			

*Park Avenue Joe and Probe dead-heated for win. Park Avenue finished first in the summary 2-1-1 to Probe's 1-9-1 finish.
Note: Run at 1 mile since 1947.

Little Brown Jug

Year	Winner	Driver	Year	Winner	Driver
1946	Ensign Hanover	Wayne Smart	1977	Governor Skipper	John Chapman
1947	Forbes Chief	Del Cameron	1978	Happy Escort	William Popfinger
1948	Knight Dream	Frank Safford	1979	Hot Hitter	Herve Filion
1949	Good Time	Frank Ervin	1980	Niatross	Clint Galbraith
1950	Dudley Hanover	Del Miller	1981	Fan Hanover	Glen Garnsey
1951	Tar Heel	Del Cameron	1982	Merger	John Campbell
1952	Meadow Rice	Wayne Smart	1983	Ralph Hanover	Ron Waples
1953	Keystoner	Frank Ervin	1984	Colt Fortysix	Chris Boring
1954	Adios Harry	Morris MacDonald	1985	Nihilator	Bill O'Donnell
1955	Quick Chief	Bill Haughton	1986	Barberry Spur	Bill O'Donnell
1956	Noble Adios	John Simpson Sr.	1987	Jaguar Spur	Dick Stillings
1957	Torpid	John Simpso Sr.	1988	B. J. Scoot	Michel Lachance
1958	Shadow Wave	Joe O'Brien	1989	Goalie Jeff	Michel Lachance
1959	Adios Butler	Clint Hodgins	1990	Beach Towel	Ray Remmen
1960	Bullet Hanover	John Simpson Sr.	1991	Precious Bunny	Jack Moiseye
1961	Henry T. Adios	Stanley Dancer	1992	Fake Left	Ron Waples
1962	Lehigh Hanover	Stanley Dancer	1993	Life Sign	John Campbell
1963	Overtrick	John Patterson	1994	Magical Mike	Michel Lachance
1964	Vicar Hanover	Bill Haughton	1995	Nick's Fantasy	John Campbell
1965	Bret Hanover	Frank Ervin	1996	Armbro Operative	Jack Moiseyev
1966	Romeo Hanover	George Sholty	1997	Western Dreamer	Michel Lachance
1967	Best of All	James Hackett	1998	Shady Character	Ron Pierce
1968	Rum Customer	Bill Haughton	1999	Blissful Hall	Ron Pierce
1969	Laverne Hanover	Bill Haughton	2000	Astreos	Chris Christoforou
1970	Most Happy Fella	Stanley Dancer	2001	Bettor's Delight	Michel Lachance
1971	Nansemond	Herve Filion	2002	Million Dollar Cam	Luc Ouellette
1972	Strike Out	Keith Waples	2003	No Pan Intended	David S. Miller
1973	Melvin's Woe	Joe O'Brien	2004	Timesareachanging	Ron Pierce
1974	Armbro Omaha	Bill Haughton	2005	Vivid Photo	Roger Hammer
1975	Seatrain	Ben Webster	2006	Mr. Feelgood	Mark MacDonald
1976	Keystone Ore	Stanley Dancer			

Breeders' Crown

1984

Div	Winner	Driver
2PC	Dragon's Lair	Jeff Mallet
2PF	Amneris	John Campbell
3PC	Troublemaker	Bill O'Donnell
3PF	Naughty But Nice	Tommy Haughton
2TC	Workaholic	Berndt Lindstedt
2TF	Conifer	George Sholty
3TC	Baltic Speed	Jan Nordin
3TF	Fancy Crown	Bill O'Donnell

1985

Div	Winner	Driver
2PC	Robust Hanover	John Campbell
2PF	Caressable	Herve Filion
3PC	Nihilator	Bill O'Donnell
3PF	Stienam	Buddy Gilmour
2TC	Express Ride	John Campbell
2TF	JEF's Spice	Mickey McNichol
3TC	Prakas	John Campbell
3TF	Armbro Devona	Bill O'Donnell
AP	Division Street	Michel Lachance
AT	Sandy Bowl	John Campbell

1986

Div	Winner	Driver
2PC	Sunset Warrior	Bill Gale
2PF	Halcyon	Ray Remmen
3PC	Masquerade	Richard Silverman
3PF	Glow Softly	Ron Waples
2TC	Mack Lobell	John Campbell
2TF	Super Flora	Ron Waples
3TC	Sugarcane Hanover	Ron Waples
3TF	JEF's Spice	Bill O'Donnell
APM	Samshu Bluegrass	Michel Lachance
ATM	Grades Singing	Herve Filion
APH	Forrest Skipper	Lucien Fontaine
ATH	Nearly Perfect	Mickey McNichol

1987

Div	Winner	Driver
2PC	Camtastic	Bill O'Donnell
2PF	Leah Almahurst	Bill Fahy
3PC	Call For Rain	Clint Galbraith
3PF	Pacific	Tom Harmer
2TC	Defiant One	Howard Beissinger
2TF	Nan's Catch	Berndt Lindstedt
3TC	Mack Lobell	John Campbell
3TF	Armbro Fling	George Sholty
APM	Follow My Star	John Campbell
ATM	Grades Singing	Olle Goop
APH	Armbro Emerson	Walter Whelan
ATH	Sugarcane Hanover	Ron Waples

Breeders' Crown

1988

Div	Winner	Driver
2PC	Kentucky Spur	Dick Stillings
2PF	Central Park West	John Campbell
3PC	Camtastic	Bill O'Donnell
3PF	Sweet Reflection	Bill O'Donnell
2TC	Valley Victory	Bill O'Donnell
2TF	Peace Corps	John Campbell
3TC	Firm Tribute	Mark O'Mara
3TF	Nalda Hanover	Mickey McNichol
APM	Anniecrombie	Dave Magee
ATM	Armbro Flori	Larry Walker
APH	Call For Rain	Clint Galbraith
ATH	Mack Lobell	John Campbell

1989

Div	Winner	Driver
2PC	Till We Meet Again	Mickey McNichol
2PF	Town Pro	Doug Brown
3PC	Goalie Jeff	Michel Lachance
3PF	Cheery Hello	John Campbell
2TC	Royal Troubador	Carl Allen
2TF	Delphi's Lobell	Ron Waples
3TC	Esquire Spur	Dick Stillings
3TF	Pace Corps	John Campbell
APM	Armbro Feather	John Kopas
ATM	Grades Singing	Olle Goop
APH	Matt's Scooter	Michel Lachance
ATH	Delray Lobell	John Campbell

1990

Div	Winner	Driver
2PC	Artsplace	John Campbell
2PF	Miss Easy	John Campbell
3PC	Beach Towel	Ray Remmen
3PF	Town Pro	Doug Brown
2TC	Crysta's Best	Dick Richardson Jr.
2TF	Jean Bi	Jan Nordin
3TC	Embassy Lobell	Michel Lachance
3TF	Me Maggie	Berndt Lindstedt
APM	Caesar's Jackpot	Bill Fahy
ATM	Peace Corps	Stig Johansson
APH	Bay's Fella	Paul MacDonell
ATH	No Sex Please	Ron Waples

1991

Div	Winner	Driver
2PC	Digger Almahurst	Doug Brown
2PF	Hazleton Kay	John Campbell
3PC	Three Wizzards	Bill Gale
3PF	Miss Easy	John Campbell
2TC	King Conch	Bill Gale
2TF	Armbro Keepsake	John Campbell
3TC	Giant Victory	Ron Pierce
3TF	Twelve Speed	Ron Waples
APM	Delinquent Account	Bill O'Donnell
ATM	Me Maggie	Berndt Lindstedt
APH	Camluck	Michel Lachance
ATH	Billyjojimbob	Paul MacDonell

1992

Div	Winner	Driver
2PC	Village Jiffy	Ron Waples
2PF	Immortality	John Campbell
3PC	Kingsbridge	Roger Mayotte
3PF	So Fresh	John Campbell
2TC	Giant Chill	John Patterson Jr.
2TF	Winky's Goal	Cat Manzi
3TC	Baltic Striker	Michel Lachance
3TF	Imperfection	Michel Lachance
APM	Shady Daisy	Ron Pierce
ATM	Peace Corps	Torbjorn Jansson
APH	Artsplace	John Campbell
ATH	No Sex Please	Ron Waples

1993

Div	Winner	Driver
2PC	Expensive Scooter	Jack Moiseyev
2PF	Electric Scooter	Mike Lachance
3PC	Life Sign	John Campbell
3PF	Immortality	John Campbell
2TC	Westgate Crown	John Campbell
2TF	Gleam	Jimmy Takter
3TC	Pine Chip	John Campbell
3TF	Expressway Hanover	Per Henriksen
APM	Swing Back	Kelly Sheppard
ATM	Lifetime Dream	Paul MacDonell
APH	Staying Together	Bill O'Donnell
ATH	Earl	Chris Christoforou Jr.

1994

Div	Winner	Driver
2PC	Jenna's Beach Boy	Bill Fahy
2PF	Yankee Cashmere	Peter Wrenn
3PC	Magical Mike	Michel Lachance
3PF	Hardie Hanover	Tim Twaddle
2TC	Eager Seelster	Teddy Jacobs
2TF	Lookout Victory	John Patterson
3TC	Incredible Abe	Italo Tamborrino
3TF	Imageofa Clear Day	Bill O'Donnell
APM	Shady Daisy	Michel Lachance
ATM	Armbro Keepsake	Stig Johansson
APH	Village Jiffy	Paul MacDonell
ATH	Pine Chip	John Campbell

1995

Div	Winner	Driver
2PC	John Street North	Jack Moiseyev
2PF	Paige Nicole Q	John Campbell
3PC	Jenna's Beach Boy	Bill Fahy
3PF	Headline Hanover	Doug Brown
2TC	Armbro Officer	Steve Condren
2TF	Continentalvictory	Michel Lachance
3TC	Abundance	Bill O'Donnell
3TF	Lookout Victory	Sonny Patterson
APM	Ellamony	Mike Saftic
ATM	CR Kay Suzie	Rod Allen
APH	That'll Be Me	Roger Mayotte
ATH	Panifesto	Luc Ouellette

Note: 2=Two-year-old; T=Trotter; C=Colt; 3=Three-year-old; P=Pacer; F=Filly; A=Aged; H=Horse; M=Mare.

Breeders' Crown *(Cont.)*

1996

Div	Winner	Driver
2PC	His Mattjesty	Doug Brown
2PF	Before Sunrise	Steve Condren
3PC	Armbro Operative	Michel Lachance
3PF	Mystical Maddy	Michel Lachance
2TC	Malabar Man	Mal Burroughs
2TF	Armbro Prowess	Jimmy Takter
3TC	Running Sea	Wally Hennessey
3TF	Personal Banner	Peter Wrenn
APM	She's A Great Lady	John Campbell
APH	Jenna's Beach Boy	Bill Fahy
AT	CR Kay Suzie	Rod Allen

1997

Div	Winner	Driver
2PC	Artiscape	Michel Lachance
2PF	Take Flight	Luc Ouellette
3PC	Village Jasper	Paul McDonnell
3PF	Stienam's Place	Jack Moiseyev
2TC	Catch As Catch Can	Wally Hennessey
2TF	My Dolly	Wally Hennessey
3TC	Malabar Man	Malvern Burroughs
3TF	No Nonsense Woman	Jim Doherty
APM	Jay's Table	John Campbell
APH	Red Bow Tie	Luc Ouellette
AT	Moni Maker	Wally Hennessey

1998

Div	Winner	Driver
2PC	Badlands Hanover	Ron Pierce
2PF	Juliet's Fate	George Brennan
3PC	Artiscape	Michel Lachance
3PF	Galleria	George Brennan
2TC	CR Commando	Carl Allen
2TF	Musical Victory	Luc Ouellette
3TC	Muscles Yankee	John Campbell
3TF	Lassie's Goal	Mark O'Mara
APM	Shore By Five	Daniel Dube
APH	Red Bow Tie	Luc Ouellette
AT	Supergrit	Ron Pierce

1999

Div	Winner	Driver
2PC	Tyberwood	Richard Silverman
2PF	Eternal Camnation	Eric Ledford
3PC	Grinfromeartoear	Chris Christoforou
3PF	Odies Fame	David Wall
2TC	Master Lavec	Daniel Daley
2TF	Dream of Joy	James Meittinis
3TC	CR Renegade	Rodney Allen
3TF	Oolong	Ronald Pierce
APM	Shore By Five	Daniel Dube
APH	Red Bow Tie	Luc Ouellette
AT	Supergrit	Ronald Pierce

2000

Div	Winner	Driver
2PC	Bettor's Delight	Michel Lachance
2PF	Lady MacBeach	Luc Ouellette
3PC	Gallo Blue Chip	Daniel Dube
3PF	Popcorn Penny	Ryan Anderson
2TC	Banker Hall	Trevor Ritchie
2TF	Syrinx Hanover	Trevor Ritchie
3TC	Fast Photo	Michel Lachance
3TF	Aviano	Trevor Ritchie
APM	Ron's Girl	Michel Lachance
APH	Western Ideal	Michel Lachance
AT	Magician	David Miller

2001

Div	Winner	Driver
2PC	Western Shooter	John Campbell
2PF	Cam Swifty	Jim Meittinis
3PC	Real Desire	John Campbell
3PF	Bunny Lake	John Stark Jr.
2TC	Duke Of York	Paul MacDonnell
2TF	Cameron Hall	Michel Lachance
3TC	Liberty Balance	Randall Waples
3TF	Syrinx Hanover	John Campbell
APM	Eternal Camnation	Eric Ledford
APH	Goliath Bayama	Sylvain Filion
AT	Varenne	G. Minnucci

2002

Div	Winner	Driver
2PC	Totally Western	Mario Baillargeon
2PF	Armbro Amoretto	Luc Ouellette
3PC	Art Major	John Campbell
3PF	Allamerican Nadia	Chris Christoforou
2TC	Broadway Hall	John Campbell
2TF	Pick Me Up	Luc Ouellette
3TC	Kadabra	David S. Miller
3TF	Cameron Hall	Trevor Ritchie
APM	Molly Can Do It	Jack Moiseyev
APH	Real Desire	John Campbell
AT	Fool's Goal	Jack Moiseyev

2003

Div	Winner	Driver
2PC	I Am A Fool	Ron Pierce
2PF	Pans Culottes	Daniel Dube
3PC	No Pan Intended	David Miller
3PF	Burning Point	Kevin Wallis
2TC	Cantab Hall	Michel Lachance
2TF	Forever Starlet	David Miller
3TC	Mr. Muscleman	Ron Pierce
3TF	Stroke Play	Brian Sears
APM	Eternal Camnation	Eric Ledford
APH	Art Major	John Campbell
AT	Fool's Goal	Jack Moiseyev

Breeders' Crown *(Cont.)*

	2004			2005	
Div	**Winner**	**Driver**	**Div**	**Winner**	**Driver**
2PC	Village Jolt	Ron Pierce	2PC	Jereme's Jet	Paul MacDonell
2PH	Restive Hanover	Andy Miller	2PH	My Little Dragon	Ron Pierce
3PC	Western Terror	Brian Sears	3PC	Rocknroll Hanover	Brian Sears
3PF	Rainbow Blue	Ron Pierce	3PF	Belovedangel	Ron Pierce
2TC	Ken Warkentin	David Miller	2TC	Chocolatier	D.R. Ackerman
2TF	Flirtin Miss	John Campbell	2TF	Passionate Glide	Ron Pierce
3TC	Yankee Slide	Brian Sears	3TC	Strong Yankee	Brian Sears
3TF	Housethatruthbuilt	Brian Sears	3TF	Blur	Brian Sears
APM	Always Cam	David Miller	APM	Loyal Opposition	George Brennan
APH	Boulder Creek	Ron Pierce	APH	Boulder Creek	Brian Sears
AT	Ambro Affair	Ron Pierce	AT	Mr. Muscleman	Ron Pierce

Note: 2=Two-year-old; T=Trotter; C=Colt; 3=Three-year-old; P=Pacer; F=Filly; A=Aged; H=Horse; M=Mare.

Triple Crown Winners

Trotting

Trotting's Triple Crown consists of the Hambletonian (first run in 1926), the Kentucky Futurity (first run in 1893) and the Yonkers Trot (known as the Yonkers Futurity when it began in 1955).

Year	Horse	Owner	Breeder	Trainer & Driver
1955	Scott Frost	S.A. Camp Farms	Est of W.N. Reynolds	Joe O'Brien
1963	Speedy Scot	Castleton Farms	Castleton Farms	Ralph Baldwin
1964	Ayres	Charlotte Sheppard	Charlotte Sheppard	John Simpson Sr
1968	Nevele Pride	Nevele Acres & Lou Resnick	Mr & Mrs E.C. Quin	Stanley Dancer
1969	Lindy's Pride	Lindy Farm	Hanover Shoe Farms	Howard Beissinger
1972	Super Bowl	Rachel Dancer & Rose Hild Breeding Farm	Stoner Creek Stud	Stanley Dancer

Pacing

Pacing's Triple Crown consists of the Cane Pace (called the Cane Futurity when it began in 1955), the Little Brown Jug (first run in 1946) and the Messenger Stakes (first run in 1956).

Year	Horse	Owner	Breeder	Trainer/Driver
1959	Adios Butler	Paige West &	R.C. Carpenter	Paige West/Clint Hodgins Angelo Pellillo
1965	Bret Hanover	Richard Downing	Hanover Shoe Farms	Frank Ervin
1966	Romeo Hanover	Lucky Star Stables & Morton Finder	Hanover Shoe Farms	Jerry Silverman/ William Meyer (Cane) & George Sholty (Jug & Messenger)
1968	Rum Customer	Kennilworth Farms & L. C. Mancuso	Mr. & Mrs. R.C. Larkin	Bill Haughton
1970	Most Happy Fella	Egyptian Acres Stable	Stoner Creek Stud	Stanley Dancer
1980	Niatross	Niagara Acres, C. Galbraith & Niatross Stables	Niagara Acres	Clint Galbraith
1983	Ralph Hanover	Waples Stable, Pointsetta Stable, Grant's Direct Stable & P. J. Baugh	Hanover Shoe Farms	Stew Firlotte/Ron Waples
1997	Western Dreamer	Daniel and Matthew Daly and Patrick Daly Jr.	Kentuckiana Farms	Bill Robinson/Michel Lachance
1999	Blissful Hall	Daniel Plouffe	Walnut Hall Limited	Ben Wallace/Ron Pierce
2003	No Pan Intended	Peter Pan Stables, Inc.	Winbak Farm	Ivan Sugg/David Miller

Horse of the Year

Year	Horse	Gait	Owner
1947	Victory Song	T	Castleton Farm
1948	Rodney	T	R.H. Johnston
1949	Good Time	P	William Cane
1950	Proximity	T	Ralph and Gordon Verhurst
1951	Pronto Don	T	Hayes Fair Acres Stable
1952	Good Time	P	William Cane
1953	Hi Lo's Forbes	P	Mr. and Mrs. Earl Wagner
1954	Stenographer	T	Max Hempt
1955	Scott Frost	T	S.A. Camp Farms
1956	Scott Frost	T	S.A. Camp Farms
1957	Torpid	P	Sherwood Farm
1958	Emily's Pride	T	Walnut Hall and Castleton Farms
1959	Bye Bye Byrd	P	Mr. and Mrs. Rex Larkin
1960	Adios Butler	P	Adios Butler Syndicate
1961	Adios Butler	P	Adios Butler Syndicate
1962	Su Mac Lad	T	I.W. Berkemeyer
1963	Speedy Scot	T	Castleton Farm
1964	Bret Hanover	P	Richard Downing
1965	Bret Hanover	P	Richard Downing
1966	Bret Hanover	P	Richard Downing
1967	Nevele Pride	T	Nevele Acres
1968	Nevele Pride	T	Nevele Acres, Louis Resnick
1969	Nevele Pride	T	Nevele Acres, Louis Resnick
1970	Fresh Yankee	T	Duncan MacDonald
1971	Albatross	P	Albatross Stable
1972	Albatross	P	Amicable Stable
1973	Sir Dalrae	P	A La Carte Racing Stable
1974	Delmonica Hanover	T	Delvin Miller, W. Arnold Hanger
1975	Savoir	T	Allwood Stable
1976	Keystone Ore	P	Mr. and Mrs. Stanley Dancer, Rose Hild Farms, Robert Jones
1977	Green Speed	T	Beverly Lloyds
1978	Abercrombie	P	Shirley Mitchell, L. Keith Bulen
1979	Niatross	P	Niagara Acres, Clint Galbraith
1980	Niatross	P	Niatross Syndicate, Niagara Acres, Clint Galbraith
1981	Fan Hanover	P	Dr. J. Glen Brown
1982	Cam Fella	P	Norm Clements, Norm Faulkner
1983	Cam Fella	P	JEF's Standardbred, Norm Clements, Norm Faulkner
1984	Fancy Crown	T	Fancy Crown Stable
1985	Nihilator	P	Wall Street-Nihilator Syndicate
1986	Forrest Skipper	P	Forrest L. Bartlett
1987	Mack Lobell	T	One More Time Stable and Fair Wind Farm
1988	Mack Lobell	T	John Erik Magnusson
1989	Matt's Scooter	P	Gordon and Illa Rumpel, Charles Jurasvinski
1990	Beach Towel	P	Uptown Stables
1991	Precious Bunny	P	R. Peter Heffering
1992	Artsplace	P	George Segal
1993	Staying Together	P	Robert Hamather
1994	Cam's Card Shark	P	Jeffrey S. Snyder
1995	CR Kay Suzie	T	Carl & Rod Allen Stable, Inc.
1996	Continental-victory	T	Continentalvictory Stables
1997	Malabar Man	T	Malvern Burroughs
1998	Moni Maker	T	Moni Maker Stable
1999	Moni Maker	T	Moni Maker Stable
2000	Gallo Blue Chip	P	Dan Gernatt Farms
2001	Bunny Lake	P	W. Springtime Racing Stable
2002	Real Desire	P	Brittany Farms
2003	No Pan Intended	P	Peter Pan Stables, Inc.
2004	Rainbow Blue	P	George Teague Jr
2005	Rocknroll Hanover	P	Jeffrey Snyder, Lothlorien Equestrian Centre & Perretti Racing Stb LLC

Driver of the Year

Year	Driver	Year	Driver	Year	Driver
1968	Stanley Dancer	1981	Herve Filion	1995	Luc Ouellette
1969	Herve Filion	1982	Bill O'Donnell	1996	Tony Morgan
1970	Herve Filion	1983	John Campbell		Luc Ouellette
1971	Herve Filion	1984	Bill O'Donnell	1997	Tony Morgan
1972	Herve Filion	1985	Michel Lachance	1998	Walter Case Jr.
1973	Herve Filion	1986	Michel Lachance	1999	Dave Palone
1974	Herve Filion	1987	Michel Lachance	2000	Dave Palone
1975	Joe O'Brien	1988	John Campbell	2001	Stephane Bouchard
1976	Herve Filion	1989	Herve Filion	2002	Tony Morgan
1977	Donald Dancer	1990	John Campbell	2003	Dave Palone
1978	Carmine Abbatiello	1991	Walter Case Jr.	2004	Dave Palone
	Herve Filion	1992	Walter Case Jr.	2005	Catello Manzi
1979	Ron Waples	1993	Jack Moiseyev		
1980	Ron Waples	1994	Dave Magee		

Note: Balloting is conducted by the U.S Trotting Association for the U.S. Harness Writers Association.

Leading Drivers—Money Won

Year	Driver	Winnings ($)	Year	Driver	Winnings ($)
1946	Thomas Berry	121,933	1977	Herve Filion	2,551,058
1947	H.C. Fitzpatrick	133,675	1978	Carmine Abbatiello	3,344,457
1948	Ralph Baldwin	153,222	1979	John Campbell	3,308,984
1949	Clint Hodgins	184,108	1980	John Campbell	3,732,306
1950	Del Miller	306,813	1981	Bill O'Donnell	4,065,608
1951	John Simpson Sr.	333,316	1982	Bill O'Donnell	5,755,067
1952	Bill Haughton	311,728	1983	John Campbell	6,104,082
1953	Bill Haughton	374,527	1984	Bill O'Donnell	9,059,184
1954	Bill Haughton	415,577	1985	Bill O'Donnell	10,207,372
1955	Bill Haughton	599,455	1986	John Campbell	9,515,055
1956	Bill Haughton	572,945	1987	John Campbell	10,186,495
1957	Bill Haughton	586,950	1988	John Campbell	11,148,565
1958	Bill Haughton	816,659	1989	John Campbell	9,738,450
1959	Bill Haughton	771,435	1990	John Campbell	11,620,878
1960	Del Miller	567,282	1991	Jack Moiseyev	9,568,468
1961	Stanley Dancer	674,723	1992	John Campbell	8,202,108
1962	Stanley Dancer	760,343	1993	John Campbell	9,926,482
1963	Bill Haughton	790,086	1994	John Campbell	9,834,139
1964	Stanley Dancer	1,051,538	1995	John Campbell	9,469,797
1965	Bill Haughton	889,943	1996	Michel Lachance	8,408,231
1966	Stanley Dancer	1,218,403	1997	Michel Lachance	9,215,388
1967	Bill Haughton	1,305,773	1998	John Campbell	10,768,771
1968	Bill Haughton	1,654,463	1999	Luc Ouellette	10,841,495
1969	Del Insko	1,635,463	2000	John Campbell	11,160,462
1970	Herve Filion	1,647,837	2001	John Campbell	14,184,863
1971	Herve Filion	1,915,945	2002	John Campbell	11,967,597
1972	Herve Filion	2,473,265	2003	David Miller	11,490,590
1973	Herve Filion	2,233,303	2004	Ron Pierce	12,327,863
1974	Herve Filion	3,474,315	2005	Brian Sears	15,085,992
1975	Carmine Abbatiello	2,275,093			
1976	Herve Filion	2,278,634			

Motor Sports

**Racing legend
Michael Schumacher
retired in 2006**

Hard Corners, Harder Feelings

Both cars and drivers frequently got bent out of shape in 2006, as competition on the Formula One, Indy Car and NASCAR circuits proved to be very stiff indeed

BY MARK BECHTEL

It seemed like an odd time to ride off into the sunset. Michael Schumacher, the most successful Formula One driver ever, stuck it out through a miserable 2005 season (he finished a distant third to Fernando Alonso and had just one win) and a slow start early in 2006. But as the year wore on, things came together for the seven-time world champ, and by the time he won the Italian Grand Prix at Monza in September, he had pulled to within two points of series leader Fernando Alonso. But after the race, Schumacher told the delighted crowd of Ferrari fans that he was retiring at the end of the season. "It has been an exceptional time, what motorsports over 30 years has given me," he said. "I really loved every single moment, the good and the bad ones."

The 2006 season provided both for Schumacher. Engine and tire problems early in the year put him in a hole (he scored just 11 points in the first three races, while Alonso racked up 28 with two wins and a second). By the time the series rolled into Monaco, in late May, Schumacher had turned things around; in the three previous races he had two wins and a runner-up. He looked like a good bet to put up another strong performance in Monaco.

During pole position qualifying, Schumacher posted a time that appeared fast enough to get him the pole—until Alonso got off to a blazing start on a lap late in the session. Aware that his time was in danger, and that Alonso was behind him on the course, Schumacher "made a mistake" on a right-hander. He locked up and came to a stop with his car perpendicular to oncoming traffic and blocking half the track. No one was buying his assertion that it had been an accident, and Schumacher was stripped of his pole and sent to the back of the pack for the race. "You can't win seven world championships and behave like that," said Jacques Villeneuve—who had nearly been driven off the track by Schumacher in a crucial race in 1997. "You just can't. It's unacceptable, and it shows that every time he did something like that in the past, and people gave him the benefit of the doubt ... well, I think today just made it obvious."

Alonso also had some harsh words. "After dominating all weekend, to lose my best lap because of ... an accident is not really a good moment," he said while refusing to make eye contact with Schumacher. The Renault driver was less tactful after Monza. After Schumacher's retirement announcement, Alonso said, "Even (Zinedine) Zidane retired with more glory than Schumacher," a reference to the disgraced French soccer star whose last act as a player

was to headbutt an opponent in the World Cup final. "Michael is the man with the most sanctions and is the most unsporting driver in the history of Formula One."

The fighting words showed that even though Alonso eventually triumphed (he topped the final 2006 F1 points standings by 11 points over Schumacher) he was not immune from feeling the pressure that comes being the reigning champion. Entering July he had been 25 points ahead of Schumacher, who then reeled off consecutive wins in Indianapolis, France and Germany. And at Monza, it was the 25-year-old Alonso who was penalized for blocking during qualifying, though his infraction was far less severe than Schumacher's incident at Monaco. Alonso was dropped from the fifth starting spot to the tenth, which led him to rip into the stewards and the sport. "I love the sport, I love the fans coming here, a lot of them from Spain, but I don't consider F1 anymore a sport," said Alonso. He was no happier after the race, which he left early due to a mechanical failure, ensuring that he and Schumacher would duel down to the wire in one of the closest title races in F1 history.

As tight as the F1 race was, it had nothing on the IRL. Sam Hornish Jr. and Dan Wheldon finished the season in a flat-footed tie,

In 2006, Jimmie Johnson and his 48 car took the checkered flag at what was, coincidentally, the 48th Daytona 500.

with Hornish taking the title because he won four races to Wheldon's two. The second of those victories came at the final race of the season, the Peak Antifreeze Indy 300 at Chicagoland Speedway. But Hornish settled into third place late in the race, which he knew was enough to give him the title. So instead of making a run at Wheldon, he played it safe. His car owner, Roger Penske, told him, "Let's not get into a shoving match here. Finishing third, you've got the championship." Said Penske, "There was no reason to get into a battle. A win [in the race] wasn't what we came here for. We came here to win the championship."

It wasn't exactly the way Hornish envisioned wrapping up the title. "You don't want to tie and have it come down to race wins," Hornish said. "But sometimes you have to take it however you can get it."

And it's not as if Hornish didn't get to enjoy any trips to Victory Lane. He won the Indianapolis 500 in dramatic fashion, passing Marco Andretti—who improbably took the lead from his father, of all people, with four laps to go, a mere 250 yards from the finish line. For a while it looked as if Michael Andretti, who nearly won half a dozen Indy 500s but has came short each time, would get the win. He led the 426th lap of his Brickyard career on lap 196, but then his own kid blew by him on the frontstretch. Had Marco been able to hold on, it would have, if nothing else, made for some interesting dynamics at the Thanksgiving table: a brash 19-year-old winning the one race his old man couldn't—and in his first try, no less. Marco did his best to keep his lead, throwing an audacious block on Hornish two turns from home. But he couldn't hold off Hornish coming off of Turn 4. "I have a lot of shots left," Marco said afterward, "but [I learned] from my dad's career that you have to take advantage of every one of them."

The race—the second closest in Indy history (the margin of victory was .0635 of a second)—grabbed plenty of attention, but not nearly as much as last year, when Danica Patrick almost won. This year, Patrick finished eighth and was never much of a threat. But she made plenty of headlines later in the summer, when she mulled a move to NASCAR. Ultimately, she decided to stay in IndyCar. "Once you go away from open wheel, you can't come back and I'm not done here," she said. "I'm entering into the next phase of my career." But she did decide to switch teams, from Rahal-Letterman to Penske, effective in 2007. "For me, I need to go with who I feel is going to put every bit of effort into the program," she said.

Had Patrick jumped to NASCAR, she would have found the circuit as competitive as ever. Heading into the final race before the Chase for the Nextel Cup (the 10-race "playoff" instituted last year), only two drivers had locked up spots—Jimmie Johnson and Matt Kenseth. Nine drivers were alive for the remaining eight spots—with Kasey Kahne the one on the outside looking in. Kahne had been 90 points out of tenth place the week before, but he won at California to get within striking distance, then finished third at Richmond to secure a place in the Chase. The odd man out wound up being defending series champ Tony Stewart, who finished 18th in Richmond and ended up 16

points behind Kahne. "Tony Stewart—the greatest race car driver of this era, in my opinion—missed the Chase," said Mark Martin, who had locked up his own Cup berth at Richmond. "That's unbelievable."

The fiery driver took it well. "It's a big letdown, obviously," Stewart said. "This is proof of how tough this series is, and how tough it is to make the Chase."

Once the Chase began, the following week in New Hampshire, drivers were given a quick reminder of how fickle the racing gods are. Johnson, who coasted into the postseason, was taken out in a wreck that was not of his making. He finished 39th and plummeted to ninth in the standings—a far cry from where he was at the beginning of the season.

After a handful of close calls, Johnson finally got the Daytona 500 title that had eluded him—but it didn't come easily or without controversy. Like the Indy 500, it came down to a last lap move, but it wasn't Johnson making it. Ryan Newman, who was in third, swung out in Turn 3 and tried to get around Johnson, leaving Casey Mears, who was in second, with a choice: follow Newman around Johnson, or stick with the leader and push his longtime pal across the finish line. "Do I help my friend who I've known since I was 12 years old, or do I go with Newman?" said Mears, who was a groomsman when Johnson got married. "I help my friend. He deserves the win."

Johnson won despite racing without a crew chief after his was sent home for cheating during a qualifying race. (Johnson's rear window had been raised after the pre-race inspection.) Crew chief Chad Knaus had to keep in contact with the team via email, cellphone and fax. "Chad wanted me to stress that we all need to be patient and just do our jobs," said Johnson. "Maybe I wasn't patient enough in the past, and that's led to some of my problems. But tonight I was really, really relaxed. I let the race come to me. The championship is a long ways away, but we've got some great momentum going."

But as Johnson found out once the Chase started, in the racing game it doesn't take much for that mojo to vanish.

FOR THE RECORD • 2005–06

Indianapolis 500

Results of the 90th running of the Indianapolis 500 and fourth race of the 2006 Indy Racing League season. Held Sunday, May 28, 2006, at the 2.5-mile Indianapolis Motor Speedway in Indianapolis.

Distance, 500 miles; starters, 33; winning time of race, 3 hours, 10 mins., 58.759 seconds; average speed, 157.085 mph; margin of victory, 0.0635 seconds; caution flags, 5 for 44 laps; lead changes, 14 among seven drivers.

TOP 10 FINISHERS

Pos.	Driver (start pos.)	C/E/T	Qual. Speed	Laps	Status
1	Sam Hornish Jr.(1)	D/H/F	228.985	200	running
2	Marco Andretti (9)	D/H/F	224.918	200	running
3	Michael Andretti (13)	D/H/F	224.508	200	running
4	Dan Wheldon (3)	D/H/F	227.338	200	running
5	Tony Kanaan (5)	D/H/F	226.776	200	running
6	Scott Dixon (4)	D/H/F	226.921	200	running
7	Dario Franchitti (17)	D/H/F	223.345	200	running
8	Danica Patrick (10)	P/H/F	224.674	200	running
9	Scott Sharp (8)	D/H/F	225.321	200	running
10	Victor Meira (6)	D/H/F	226.156	200	running

2006 Indy Racing League Results

Date	Race	Winner (start pos.)	C/E/T	Qual. Speed
Mar 26	Miami 300	Dan Wheldon (6)	D/H/F	215.804
Apr 2	Grand Prix of St. Petersburg	Helio Castroneves (5)	D/H/F	103.270
Apr 22	Japan 300	Helio Castroneves (1)	D/H/F	0.000†
May 28	Indianapolis 500	Sam Hornish Jr.(1)	D/H/F	228.985
June 4	Grand Prix of Watkins Glen	Scott Dixon (4)	D/H/F	0.000†
June 10	Texas 500	Helio Castroneves (3)	D/H/F	213.182
June 24	Richmond 250*	Sam Hornish Jr. (3)	D/H/F	0.000†
July 2	Kansas 300	Sam Hornish Jr. (2)	D/H/F	213.372
July 15	Nashville 200	Scott Dixon (3)	D/H/F	202.194
July 23	Milwaukee 225	Tony Kanaan (4)	D/H/F	171.677
July 30	Michigan 400	Helio Castroneves (1)	D/H/F	216.777
Aug 13	Kentucky 300	Sam Hornish Jr. (2)	D/H/F	218.307
Aug 21	Sonoma Grand Prix	Marco Andretti (2)	D/H/F	107.417
Sept 11	Chicago 300	Dan Wheldon (3)	D/H/F	214.387

Note: Distances are in miles unless followed by * (laps). †Qualification round rained out.

2006 Final Championship Standings

Driver	Pts
Sam Hornish Jr.	475*
Dan Wheldon	475
Helio Castroneves	473
Scott Dixon	460
Victor Meira	411
Tony Kanaan	384
Marco Andretti	325
Dario Franchitti	311
Danica Patrick	302
Tomas Scheckter	298

*declared champion by tie-breaker based on number of race victories

Champ Car World Series

2006 Champ Car Series Results†

Date	Event	Winner (start pos.)	Car	Avg Speed
April 9	Grand Prix of Long Beach	Sebastian Bourdais (4)	Lola-Ford	87.268
May 21	Grand Prix of Monterrey	Sebastian Bourdais (1)	Lola-Ford	96.099
June 4	Milwaukee 250	Sebastian Bourdais (1)	Lola-Ford	116.101
June 18	Grand Prix of Portland	A.J. Allmendinger (2)	Lola-Ford	113.989
June 25	Grand Prix of Cleveland	A.J. Allmendinger (1)	Lola-Ford	99.722
July 9	Molson Indy Toronto	A.J. Allmendinger (2)	Lola-Ford	92.386
July 23	Grand Prix of Edmonton	Justin Wilson (3)	Lola-Ford	100.112
July 30	Grand Prix of San Jose	Sebastian Bourdais (1)	Lola-Ford	85.991
Aug 13	Grand Prix of Denver	A.J. Allmendinger (2)	Lola-Ford	91.852
Aug 28	Grand Prix of Montreal	Sebastian Bourdais (1)	Lola-Ford	101.868
Sept 24	Road America	A.J. Allmendinger (5)	Lola-Ford	79.026
Oct 22	Grand Prix of Australia	Nelson Philippe (5)	Lola-Ford	89.259

† Through October 22, 2006.

2005 Championship Standings

Driver	Overall	Road	Oval
Sebastian Bourdais	348	295	53
Oriol Servia	288	235	53
Justin Wilson	265	232	33
Paul Tracy	246	208	38
A.J. Allmendinger	227	192	35
Jimmy Vasser	217	169	48
Alex Tagliani	207	179	28
Timo Glock (R)	202	173	29
Mario Dominguez	198	157	41
Andrew Ranger (R)	140	128	12

National Association for Stock Car Auto Racing

Daytona 500

Results of the 48th Daytona 500, the opening round of the 2006 Nextel Cup series. Held Sunday, February 19, 2006, at the 2.5-mile high-banked Daytona International Speedway.

Distance, 500 miles; starters, 43; winning time of race, 3:33:26; average speed, 142.667 mph; margin of victory, under caution; caution flags, 10 for 38 laps; lead changes, 32.

TOP 10 FINISHERS

Pos.	Driver (start pos.)	Car	Laps	Winnings ($)
1	Jimmie Johnson (9)	Chevrolet	203	1,505,120
2	Casey Mears (14)	Dodge	203	1,095,770
3	Ryan Newman (18)	Dodge	203	796,116
4	Elliott Sadler (3)	Ford	203	684,076
5	Tony Stewart (15)	Chevrolet	203	537,944
6	Clint Bowyer† (37)	Chevrolet	203	411,683
7	Brian Vickers (35)	Chevrolet	203	347,583
8	Dale Earnhardt Jr. (7)	Chevrolet	203	377,694
9	Ken Schrader (23)	Ford	203	328,897
10	Dale Jarrett (25)	Ford	203	326,983

†-denotes rookie driver

2005 Nextel Cup* Final Standings

Driver	Pts	Starts	Wins	Top 5	Top 10
Tony Stewart	6533	36	5	17	25
Greg Biffle	6498	36	6	15	21
Carl Edwards	6498	36	4	13	18
Mark Martin	6428	36	1	12	19
Jimmie Johnson	6406	36	4	13	22
Ryan Newman	6359	36	1	8	16
Matt Kenseth	6352	36	1	12	17
Rusty Wallace	6140	36	0	8	17
Jeremy Mayfield	6073	36	1	4	9
Kurt Busch	5974	34	3	9	18

2005 Nextel Cup* Driver Winnings

Driver	Winnings ($)
Tony Stewart	6,987,530
Jeff Gordon	6,855,440
Jimmie Johnson	6,796,660
Kurt Busch	6,516,320
Mark Martin	5,994,350
Matt Kenseth	5,790,770
Dale Earnhardt Jr.	5,761,830
Greg Biffle	5,729,930
Ryan Newman	5,578,110
Elliott Sadler	5,024,120

*Series name changed from Winston Cup after 2003 season.

Late 2005 Nextel Cup Series Results

Date	Track/Distance	Winner (start pos.)	Car	Laps	Winnings ($)
Oct 2	Talladega 500	Dale Jarrett (2)	Ford	190	239,833
Oct 9	Kansas 400	Mark Martin(19)	Ford	267	339,725
Oct 15	Lowe's 500	Jimmie Johnson (3)	Chevrolet	336	264,991
Oct 23	Martinsville 500	Jeff Gordon (15)	Chevrolet	500	194,926
Oct 30	Southern 500	Carl Edwards (2)	Ford	325	314,700
Nov 13	Phoenix 500	Kyle Busch (15)	Chevrolet	312	199,225
Nov 20	Homestead 400	Greg Biffle (7)	Ford	267	308,675

2006 Nextel Cup Series Results†

Date	Track/Distance	Winner (start pos.)	Car	Laps	Winnings ($)
Feb 19	Daytona 500	Jimmie Johnson (9)	Chevrolet	203	1,505,120
Feb 27	Fontana 500	Greg Biffle (5)	Ford	250	288,650
Mar 12	Vegas 400	Jimmie Johnson (3)	Chevrolet	270	386,936
Mar 20	Atlanta 500	Kasey Kahne (1)	Dodge	325	197,664
Mar 26	Bristol 500	Kurt Busch (9)	Dodge	500	175,858
Apr 2	Martinsville 500	Tony Stewart (3)	Chevrolet	500	220,786
Apr 9	Texas 500	Kasey Kahne (1)	Dodge	334	530,164
Apr 22	Phoenix 500	Kevin Harvick (15)	Chevrolet	312	228,486
Apr 30	Lowe's 499	Jimmie Johnson (16)	Chevrolet	188	326,061
May 6	Richmond 400	Dale Earnhardt (10)	Chevrolet	400	239,166
May 13	Darlington 500	Greg Biffle(9)	Ford	367	290,175
May 28	Coca-Cola 600	Kasey Kahne (9)	Dodge	400	428,114
June 4	Dover 400	Matt Kenseth 19)	Ford	400	323,591
June 11	Pocono 500	Denny Hamlin (1)	Chevrolet	200	220,100
June 18	Michigan 400	Kasey Kahne (1)	Dodge	129	205,364
June 25	Infineon 350	Jeff Gordon (11)	Chevrolet	110	325,661
July 1	Daytona 400	Tony Stewart (2)	Chevrolet	160	369,586
July 9	Chicagoland 400	Jeff Gordon (13)	Chevrolet	270	327,761
July 16	New Hampshire 300	Kyle Busch (4)	Chevrolet	308	242,175
July 23	Pocono 500	Denny Hamlin (1)	Chevrolet	200	230,100
Aug 6	Brickyard 400	Jimmie Johnson (5)	Chevrolet	160	452,861
Aug 13	Watkins Glen	Kevin Harvick (7)	Chevrolet	90	223,161
Aug 20	Michigan 400	Matt Kenseth (3)	Ford	200	221,091
Aug 26	Bristol 500	Matt Kenseth (3)	Ford	200	336,516
Sept 3	California 500	Kasey Kahne (9)	Dodge	250	279,214
Sept 10	Richmond 400	Kevin Harvick (5)	Chevrolet	400	234,136
Sept 17	New Hampshire 300	Kevin Harvick (1)	Chevrolet	300	266,461
Sept 24	Dover 400	Jeff Burton (19)	Chevrolet	400	230,370
Oct 1	Kansas 400	Tony Stewart (21)	Chevrolet	267	346,361
Oct 8	Talladega 500	Brian Vickers (9)	Chevrolet	188	228,850
Oct 15	Charlotte 500	Kasey Kahne (2)	Dodge	334	305,889
Oct 22	Martinsville 500	Jimmie Johnson (9)	Chevrolet	500	191,886

† Through October 22, 2006.

Formula One Grand Prix Racing

2006 Formula One Results

Grand Prix	Date	Winner	Car	Laps	Time
Bahrain	Mar 12	Fernando Alonso	Renault	57	1:29:46.205
Malaysian	Mar 19	Giancarlo Fisichella	Renault	56	1:30:40.529
Australian	Apr 2	Fernando Alonso	Renault	57	1:34:27.870
San Marino	Apr 23	Michael Schumacher	Ferrari	62	1:31:06.486
European	May 7	Michael Schumacher	Ferrari	60	1:35:58.765
Spain	May 14	Fernando Alonso	Renault	66	1:26:21.759
Monaco	May 28	Fernando Alonso	Renault	78	1:43:43.116
Canadian	June 25	Fernando Alonso	Renault	70	1:34:37.308
United States	July 2	Michael Schumacher	Ferrari	73	1:34:35.199
British	July 10	Juan Pablo Montoya	McLaren-Mercedes	60	1:24:29.588
French	July 16	Michael Schumacher	Ferrari	70	1:32:07.803
German	July 30	Michael Schumacher	Ferrari	67	1:27:51.693
Hungarian	Aug 6	Jenson Button	Honda	70	1:52:20.941
Turkish	Aug 27	Felipe Massa	Ferrari	58	1:28:52.082
Italian	Sept 10	Michael Schumacher	Ferrari	53	1:15:51.975
China	Oct1	Michael Schumacher	Ferrari	57	1:29:46.205
Japan	Oct 8	Fernando Alonso	Renault	53	1:23:53.413
Brazil	Oct 22	Felipe Massa	Ferrari	71	1:33:53.751

2006 World Championship Final Standings

Drivers compete in Grand Prix races for the title of World Driving Champion. Below are the top 10 drivers from the 2005 season. Points are awarded for places 1–6 as follows: 10-6-4-3-2-1.

Driver	Country	Team	Pts
Fernando Alonso	Spain	Renault	134
Michael Schumacher	Germany	Ferrari	121
Felipe Massa	Brazil	Ferrari	80
Giancarlo Fisichella	Italy	Renault	72
Kimi Raikkonen	Finland	McLaren- Mercedes	65
Jenson Button	Great Britain	Honda	56
Rubens Barrichello	Brazil	Honda	30
Juan Pablo Montoya	Colombia	McLaren- Mercedes	26
Nick Heidfeld	Germany	BMW Sauber	23
Ralf Schumacher	Germany	Toyota	20

Professional Sports Car Racing

The 24 Hours of Daytona

Held at the Daytona International Speedway on Jan 28-29, 2006, the 24 Hours of Daytona serves as the opening round of the Grand American Road Racing Association's season.

Place	Drivers	Car (Class)	Distance
1	S. Dixon, D. Wheldon, C. Mears	Lexus Riley	734 laps (108.826 mph)
2	M. Patterson, O. Negri, A.J. Allmendinger, J. Wilson	Lexus Riley	733
3	M. Rockenfeller, P. Long, L. Luhr	Porsche Crawford	731
4	D. Donohue, D. Law, S. Maassen	Porsche Fabcar	730
5	T. Krohn, N. Jonsson, J. Bergmeister, C. Braun	Pontiac Riley	717

2006 American Le Mans Series—Prototype Class

Date	Race	Winners	Car
Mar 18	12 Hours of Sebring	R. Capello, T. Kristensen, A. McNish	Audi R10 TDI
May 12	Grand Prix of Houston	R. Capello, A. McNish	Audi R8
May 21	Mid Ohio	T. Benard, R. Dumas,	Porsche RS Spyder
July 1	Grand Prix of New England	R. Capello, A. McNish	Audi R8
July 15	Grand Prix of Utah	F. Biela, E. Pirro	Audi R10 TDI
July 22	Grand Prix of Portland	R. Capello, A. McNish,	Audi R10 TDI
Aug 20	Road America 500	F. Biela, E. Pirro	Audi R10 TDI
Sept 3	Grand Prix of Mosport	R. Capello, A. McNish	Audi R10 TDI
Sept 30	Petie Le Mans	R. Capello, A. McNish	Audi R10 TDI
Oct 21	Monterey Championships	R. Capello, A. McNish	Audi R10 TDI

2006 American Le Mans Series—GTS Class

Date	Race	Winners	Car
Mar 18	12 Hours at Sebring	O. Gavin, O. Beretta, J. Magnussen	Corvette C6-R
May 12	Grand Prix of Houston	O. Gavin, O. Beretta	Corvette C6-R

2006 American Le Mans Series—GTS Class *(Cont.)*

Date	Race	Winners	Car
May 21	Mid Ohio	O. Gavin, O. Beretta	Corvette C6-R
July 1	Grand Prix of New England	S. Sarrazin, P. Lamy	Aston Martin DB9
July 15	Grand Prix of Utah	D. Turner, T. Enge	Aston Martin DB9
July 22	Grand Prix of Portland	O. Beretta, O. Gavin	Corvette C6-R
Aug 20	Road America 500	R. Fellows, J. O'Connell	Corvette C6-R
Sept 3	Grand Prix of Mosport	S. Sarrazin, P. Lamy	Aston Martin DB9
Sept 30	Petit Le Mans	D. Turner, T. Enge	Aston Martin DB9
Oct 21	Monterey Championships	S. Sarrazin, P. Lamy	Aston Martin DB9

2006 American Le Mans Series—GT Class

Date	Race	Winners	Car
Mar 18	12 Hours at Sebring	D. Brabham, S. Maxwell, S. Bourdais	Panzo EsperanteGT
May 12	Grand Prix of Houston	M. Rockenfeller, K. Graf	Porsche 911 GT3
May 21	Mid Ohio	W. Henzler, J. Van Overbeek	Porsche 911 GT3
July 1	Grand Prix of New England	J. Bergmeister, P. Long	Porsche 911 GT3
July 15	Grand Prix of Utah	J. Melo, M. Salo	Ferrari 430 GT
July 22	Grand Prix of Portland	J. Melo, M. Salo	Ferrari 430 GT
Aug 20	Road America 500	J. Bergmeister, P. Long, M. Petersen	Porsche 911 GT3
Sept 3	Grand Prix of Mosport	J. Mowlem, S. Ortelli	Ferrari 430 GT
Sept 30	Petit Le Mans	J. Bergmeister, P. Long	Porsche 911 GT3
Oct 21	Monterey Championships	S. Ortelli, M. Salo	Ferrari 430 GT

2006 American Le Mans Series Championship Final Standings

PROTOTYPE CLASS	Pts	GTS CLASS	Pts	GT CLASS	Pts
Rinaldo Capiello	181	Oliver Gavin	157	Johannes Van Overbeek	132
Allan McNish	181	Oliver Beretta	157	Jorg Bergmeister	128
Bruce Leitzinger	106	Tomas Enge	146	Patrick Long	118
James Weaver	106	Stephane Sarrazin	140	Wolf Henzler	105
Frank Biela	80	Ron Fellows	136	Scott Maxwell	86
Emanuele Pirro	80	Johnny O'Connell	136	David Brabham	86

24 Hours of Le Mans

Held at Le Mans, France, on June 17-18, 2006, the 24 Hours of Le Mans is the most prestigious international event in endurance racing.

Place	Drivers	Car	Laps
1	F. Biela, E. Pirro, M. Werner	Audi R10	380
2	F. Montagny, E. Helary, S. Loeb,	Pescarolo Judd	376
3	R. Capello, T. Kristensen, A. McNish	Audi R10	367
4	O. Gavin, O. Beretta, J. Magnussen	Corvette C6-R	355
5	E. Collard, N. Minassian, E. Comas	Pescarolo Judd	352

National Hot Rod Association

2006 Results†

TOP FUEL

Date	Race, Site	Winner
Feb 9-12	Winter Nationals, Pomona, Calif.	Melanie Troxel
Feb 24-26	Kragen Nationals, Phoenix	Rod Fuller
Mar 16-19	Gatornationals, Gainesville, Fla.	David Grubnic
Mar 31-Apr 2	Spring Nationals, Houston	Brandon Bernstein
Apr 6-9	Las Vegas Nationals, Las Vegas	Melanie Troxel
Apr 28-30	Thunder Valley Nationals, Bristol, Tenn.	Doug Kalitta
May 4–7	Southern Nationals, Atlanta	Doug Kalitta
May 18-21	Pontiac Nationals, Columbus, Ohio	Brandon Bernstein
May 25–28	Summer Nationals, Topeka, Kan.	Doug Kalitta
June 8–11	Carquest Nationals, Joliet, Ill.	Doug Kalitta
June 15–18	Super Nationals, Englishtown, N.J.	Rod Fuller
June 23–25	Midwest Nationals, Madison, Ill.	Tony Schumacher
July 14-16	Mile High Nationals, Denver	J.R. Todd

† Through October 15, 2006.

2006 Results† *(Cont.)*

TOP FUEL *(CONT.)*

Date	Race, Site	Winner
July 21–23	Schuck's Nationals, Seattle	Tony Schumacher
July 28–30	Autolite Nationals, Sonoma, Calif.	J.R. Todd
Aug 10–13	Lucas Oil Nationals, Brainerd, Minn.	Brandon Bernstein
Aug 18–20	Mid-South Nationals, Memphis	Doug Kalitta
Aug 30–Sept 4	U.S. Nationals, Indianapolis	Tony Schumacher
Sept 21–24	Fall Nationals, Ennis, Tex.	Brandon Bernstein
Sept 29–Oct 1	Toyo Tires Nationals, Reading, Pa.	J.R. Todd
Oct 13–15	Torco Racing Fuels Nationals, Richmond, Va.	Cory McLenathan

FUNNY CAR

Date	Race, Site	Winner
Feb 9–12	Winter Nationals, Pomona, Calif.	Robert Hight
Feb 24-26	Kragen Nationals, Phoenix	Tommy Johnson Jr.
Mar 16-19	Gatornationals, Gainesville, Fla.	Ron Capps
Mar 31–Apr 2	Spring Nationals, Houston	Ron Capps
Apr 6-9	Las Vegas Nationals, Las Vegas	Cruz Pedregon
Apr 28–30	Thunder Valley Nationals, Bristol, Tenn.	Ron Capps
May 14–17	Southern Nationals, Atlanta	Tony Pedregon
May 18-21	Pontiac Nationals, Columbus, Ohio	Tony Pedregon
May 25-28	Summer Nationals, Topeka, Kan.	Ron Capps
June 8-11	Carquest Nationals, Joliet, Ill.	John Force
June 15–18	Super Nationals, Englishtown, N.J.	Ron Capps
June 23-25	Midwest Nationals, Madison, Ill.	Tony Pedregon
July 14-16	Mile High Nationals, Denver	Gary Scelzi
July 21–23	Schuck's Nationals, Seattle	Whit Bazemore
July 28– 30	Autolite Nationals, Sonoma, Calif.	Eric Medlen
Aug 10–13	Lucas Oil Nationals, Brainerd, Minn.	Tommy Johnson Jr.
Aug 18–20	Mid-South Nationals, Memphis	John Force
Aug 30–Sept 4	U.S. Nationals, Indianapolis	Robert Hight
Sept 21–24	Fall Nationals, Ennis, Tex.	Robert Hight
Sept 29–Oct 1	Toyo Tires Nationals Reading Pa.	Phil Burkart
Oct 13–15	Torco Racing Fuels Nationals, Richmond, Va.	Eric Medlen

PRO STOCK

Date	Race, Site	Winner
Feb 9-12	Winter Nationals, Pomona, Calif.	Greg Anderson
Feb 24-26	Kragen Nationals, Phoenix	Warren Johnson
Mar 16-19	Gatornationals, Gainesville, Fla.	Angelle Sampey
Mar 31-Apr 2	Spring Nationals, Houston	Mike Edwards
Apr 6–19	Las Vegas Nationals, Las Vegas	Kurt Johnson
May 28–30	Thunder Valley Nationals, Bristol, Tenn.	Jason Line
May 4–17	Southern Nationals, Atlanta	Dave Connolly
May 18-21	Pontiac Nationals, Columbus, Ohio	Jim Yates
May 25-28	Summer Nationals, Topeka, Kan.	Dave Connolly
June 8-11	Carquest Nationals, Joliet Ill.	Kurt Johnson
June 15-18	Super Nationals, Englishtown, N.J.	Jason Line
June 23-25	Midwest Nationals, Madison, Ill.	Mike Edwards
July 14-16	Mile High Nationals, Denver	Dave Connolly
July 21-23	Schuck's Nationals, Seattle	Allen Johnson
July 28–30	Autolite Nationals, Sonoma, Calif.	Jason Line
Aug 10-13	Lucas Oil Nationals, Brainerd, Minn.	Dave Connolly
Aug 18–20	Mid-South Nationals, Memphis	Kurt Johnson
Aug 30-Sept 4	U.S. Nationals, Indianapolis	Greg Anderson
Sept 21-24	Fall Nationals, Ennis, Tex.	Richie Stevens
Sept 29-Oct 1	Toyo Tires Nationals, Reading, Pa.	Greg Anderson
Oct 13–15	Torco Racing Fuels Nationals, Richmond, Va.	Jason Line

† Through October 15, 2006.

2005 NHRA Final Standings

TOP FUEL		FUNNY CAR		PRO STOCK	
Driver	Pts	Driver	Pts	Driver	Pts
Tony Schumacher	1981	Gary Scelzi	1516	Greg Anderson	1904
Larry Dixon	1566	Ron Capps	1508	Kurt Johnson	1700
Doug Kalitta	1538	John Force	1484	Jason Line	1599
David Grubnic	1407	Eric Medlen	1411	Warren Johnson	1488
Morgan Lucas	1357	Robert Hight	1379	Dave Connolly	1294

Indianapolis 500

First held in 1911, the Indianapolis 500—200 laps of the 2.5-mile Indianapolis Motor Speedway Track (called the Brickyard in honor of its original pavement)—grew to become the most famous auto race in the world. Though the Memorial Day weekend event lost participants and prestige in the mid-1990s due to feuding in the world of U.S. open-wheel racing, it annually attracts crowds of over 100,000.

Year	Winner (start pos.)	Chassis-Engine	Avg Speed	Pole Winner	Speed
1911	Ray Harroun (28)	Marmon-Marmon	74.590	Lewis Strang	First entered
1912	Joe Dawson (7)	National-National	78.720	Gil Anderson	First entered
1913	Jules Goux (7)	Peugeot-Peugeot	75.930	Caleb Bragg	Drew pole
1914	Rene Thomas (15)	Delage-Delage	82.470	Jean Chassagne	Drew pole
1915	Ralph DePalma (2)	Mercedes-Mercedes	89.840	Howard Wilcox	98.90
1916	Dario Resta (4)	Peugeot-Peugeot	84.000	John Aitken	96.69
1917–18	No race				
1919	Howard Wilcox (2)	Peugeot-Peugeot	88.050	Rene Thomas	104.78
1920	Gaston Chevrolet (6)	Frontenac-Frontenac	88.620	Ralph DePalma	99.15
1921	Tommy Milton (20)	Frontenac-Frontenac	89.620	Ralph DePalma	100.75
1922	Jimmy Murphy (1)	Duesenberg-Miller	94.480	Jimmy Murphy	100.50
1923	Tommy Milton (1)	Miller-Miller	90.950	Tommy Milton	108.17
1924	L.L. Corum Joe Boyer (21)	Duesenberg-Duesenberg	98.230	Jimmy Murphy	108.037
1925	Peter DePaolo (2)	Duesenberg-Duesenberg	101.130	Leon Duray	113.196
1926	Frank Lockhart (20)	Miller-Miller	95.904	Earl Cooper	111.735
1927	George Souders (22)	Duesenberg-Duesenberg	97.545	Frank Lockhart	120.100
1928	Louis Meyer (13)	Miller-Miller	99.482	Leon Duray	122.391
1929	Ray Keech (6)	Miller-Miller	97.585	Cliff Woodbury	120.599
1930	Billy Arnold (1)	Summers-Miller	100.448	Billy Arnold	113.268
1931	Louis Schneider (13)	Stevens-Miller	96.629	Russ Snowberger	112.796
1932	Fred Frame (27)	Wetteroth-Miller	104.144	Lou Moore	117.363
1933	Louis Meyer (6)	Miller-Miller	104.162	Bill Cummings	118.524
1934	Bill Cummings (10)	Miller-Miller	104.863	Kelly Petillo	119.329
1935	Kelly Petillo (22)	Wetteroth-Offy	106.240	Rex Mays	120.736
1936	Louis Meyer (28)	Stevens-Miller	109.069	Rex Mays	119.664
1937	Wilbur Shaw (2)	Shaw-Offy	113.580	Bill Cummings	123.343
1938	Floyd Roberts (1)	Wetteroth-Miller	117.200	Floyd Roberts	125.681
1939	Wilbur Shaw (3)	Maserati-Maserati	115.035	Jimmy Snyder	130.138
1940	Wilbur Shaw (2)	Maserati-Maserati	114.277	Rex Mays	127.850
1941	Floyd Davis Mauri Rose (17)	Wetteroth-Offy	115.117	Mauri Rose	128.691
1942–45	No race				
1946	George Robson (15)	Adams-Sparks	114.820	Cliff Bergere	126.471
1947	Mauri Rose (3)	Deidt-Offy	116.338	Ted Horn	126.564
1948	Mauri Rose (3)	Deidt-Offy	119.814	Rex Mays	130.577
1949	Bill Holland (4)	Deidt-Offy	121.327	Duke Nalon	132.939
1950	Johnnie Parsons (5)	Kurtis-Offy	124.002	Walt Faulkner	134.343
1951	Lee Wallard (2)	Kurtis-Offy	126.244	Duke Nalon	136.498
1952	Troy Ruttman (7)	Kuzma-Offy	128.922	Fred Agabashian	138.010
1953	Bill Vukovich (1)	KK500A-Offy	128.740	Bill Vukovich	138.392
1954	Bill Vukovich (19)	KK500A-Offy	130.840	Jack McGrath	141.033
1955	Bob Sweikert (14)	KK500C-Offy	128.209	Jerry Hoyt	140.045
1956	Pat Flaherty (1)	Watson-Offy	128.490	Pat Flaherty	145.596
1957	Sam Hanks (13)	Salih-Offy	135.601	Pat O'Connor	143.948
1958	Jim Bryan (7)	Salih-Offy	133.791	Dick Rathmann	145.974
1959	Rodger Ward (6)	Watson-Offy	135.857	Johnny Thomson	145.908
1960	Jim Rathmann (2)	Watson-Offy	138.767	Eddie Sachs	146.592
1961	A.J. Foyt (7)	Trevis-Offy	139.130	Eddie Sachs	147.481
1962	Rodger Ward (2)	Watson-Offy	140.293	Parnelli Jones	150.370
1963	Parnelli Jones (1)	Watson-Offy	143.137	Parnelli Jones	151.153
1964	A.J. Foyt (5)	Watson-Offy	147.350	Jim Clark	158.828
1965	Jim Clark (2)	Lotus-Ford	150.686	A.J. Foyt	161.233
1966	Graham Hill (15)	Lola-Ford	144.317	Mario Andretti	165.899
1967	A.J. Foyt (4)	Coyote-Ford	151.207	Mario Andretti	168.982
1968	Bobby Unser (3)	Eagle-Offy	152.882	Joe Leonard	171.559
1969	Mario Andretti (2)	Hawk-Ford	156.867	A.J. Foyt	170.568
1970	Al Unser (1)	PJ Colt-Ford	155.749	Al Unser	170.221
1971	Al Unser (5)	PJ Colt-Ford	157.735	Peter Revson	178.696
1972	Mark Donohue (3)	McLaren-Offy	162.962	Bobby Unser	195.940

Year	Winner (start pos.)	Chassis-Engine	Avg speed	Pole Winner	Speed
1973	Gordon Johncock (11)	Eagle-Offy	159.036	Johnny Rutherford	198.413
1974	Johnny Rutherford (25)	McLaren-Offy	158.589	A.J. Foyt	191.632
1975	Bobby Unser (3)	Racers Eagle-Offy	149.213	A.J. Foyt	193.976
1976	Johnny Rutherford (1)	McLaren-Offy	148.725	Johnny Rutherford	188.957
1977	A.J. Foyt (4)	Coyote-Ford	161.331	Tom Sneva	198.884
1978	Al Unser (5)	Lola-Cosworth	161.361	Tom Sneva	202.156
1979	Rick Mears (1)	Penske-Cosworth	158.899	Rick Mears	193.736
1980	Johnny Rutherford (1)	Chaparral-Cosworth	142.862	Johnny Rutherford	192.256
1981	Bobby Unser (1)	Penske-Cosworth	139.084	Bobby Unser	200.546
1982	Gordon Johncock (5)	Wildcat-Cosworth	162.026	Rick Mears	207.004
1983	Tom Sneva (4)	March-Cosworth	162.117	Teo Fabi	207.395
1984	Rick Mears (3)	March-Cosworth	163.612	Tom Sneva	210.029
1985	Danny Sullivan (8)	March-Cosworth	152.982	Pancho Carter	212.583
1986	Bobby Rahal (4)	March-Cosworth	170.722	Rick Mears	216.828
1987	Al Unser (20)	March-Cosworth	162.175	Mario Andretti	215.390
1988	Rick Mears (1)	Penske-Chevrolet	144.809	Rick Mears	219.198
1989	Emerson Fittipaldi (3)	Penske-Chevrolet	167.581	Rick Mears	223.885
1990	Arie Luyendyk (3)	Lola-Chevrolet	185.981*	Emerson Fittipaldi	225.301
1991	Rick Mears (1)	Penske-Chevrolet	176.457	Rick Mears	224.113
1992	Al Unser Jr. (12)	Galmer-Chevrolet	134.477	Roberto Guerrero	232.482
1993	Emerson Fittipaldi (9)	Penske-Chevrolet	157.207	Arie Luyendyk	223.967
1994	Al Unser Jr. (1)	Penske-Mercedes	160.872	Al Unser Jr.	228.011
1995	Jacques Villeneuve (5)	Reynard-Ford	153.616	Scott Brayton	231.616
1996	Buddy Lazier (5)	Reynard-Ford	147.956	Tony Stewart	233.100†
1997	Arie Luyendyk (1)	G Force-Oldsmobile	145.827	Arie Luyendyk	231.468
1998	Eddie Cheever (17)	Dallara-Oldsmobile	145.155	Billy Boat	223.503
1999	Kenny Brack (8)	Dallara-Oldsmobile	153.176	Arie Luyendyk	225.179
2000	Juan Montoya (2)	G Force-Oldsmobile	167.607	Greg Ray	223.471
2001	Helio Castroneves (11)	Dallara-Oldsmobile	153.601	Scott Sharp	226.037
2002	Helio Castroneves (13)	Dallara-Chevrolet	166.499	Bruno Junqueira	231.342
2003	Gil de Ferran	Panoz-Toyota	156.291	Helio Castroneves	231.725
2004	Buddy Rice (1)	G Force-Honda	138.518	Buddy Rice	222.024
2005	Dan Wheldon (1)	Dallara-Honda	157.603	Tony Kanaan	227.566
2006	Sam Hornish Jr.(1)	Dallara-Honda	157.085	Sam Hornish Jr.	228.985

*Track record, winning speed. †Track record, qualifying speed.

Indianapolis 500 Rookie of the Year Award

1952	Art Cross	1971	Denny Zimmerman	1989	Bernard Jourdain
1953	Jimmy Daywalt	1972	Mike Hiss		Scott Pruett
1954	Larry Crockett	1973	Graham McRae	1990	Eddie Cheever*
1955	Al Herman	1974	Pancho Carter	1991	Jeff Andretti
1956	Bob Veith	1975	Bill Puterbaugh	1992	Lyn St. James
1957	Don Edmunds	1976	Vern Schuppan	1993	Nigel Mansell
1958	George Amick	1977	Jerry Sneva	1994	Jacques Villeneuve*
1959	Bobby Grim	1978	Rick Mears*	1995	Gil de Ferran*
1960	Jim Hurtubise		Larry Rice	1996	Tony Stewart
1961	Parnelli Jones*	1979	Howdy Holmes	1997	Jeff Ward
	Bobby Marshman	1980	Tim Richmond	1998	Steve Knapp
1962	Jimmy McElreath	1981	Josele Garza	1999	Robby McGehee
1963	Jim Clark*	1982	Jim Hickman	2000	Juan Montoya*
1964	Johnny White	1983	Teo Fabi	2001	Helio Castroneves*
1965	Mario Andretti*	1984	Michael Andretti	2002	Alex Barron
1966	Jackie Stewart		Roberto Guerrero		Tomas Scheckter
1967	Denis Hulme	1985	Arie Luyendyk*	2003	Tora Tagaki
1968	Billy Vukovich	1986	Randy Lanier	2004	Kosuke Matsuura
1969	Mark Donohue*	1987	Fabrizio Barbazza	2005	Danica Patrick
1970	Donnie Allison	1988	Billy Vukovich III	2006	Marco Andretti

*Future winner of Indy 500.

Champ Car World Series Champions

From 1909 to 1955, this championship was awarded by the American Automobile Association (AAA), and from 1956 to 1979 by the United States Auto Club (USAC). Since 1979, Championship Auto Racing Teams (CART) has conducted the championship. Known as PPG CART World Series until 1998. Series name changed to Champ Car World Series for 2005 racing season.

1909 ....George Robertson	1942–45 ....No racing	1978 ....Tom Sneva
1910 ....Ray Harroun	1946 ....Ted Horn	1979 ............A.J. Foyt
1911 ....Ralph Mulford	1947 ....Ted Horn	1979 ....Rick Mears
1912 ....Ralph DePalma	1948 ....Ted Horn	1980 ....Johnny Rutherford
1913 ....Earl Cooper	1949 ....Johnnie Parsons	1981 ....Rick Mears
1914 ....Ralph DePalma	1950 ....Henry Banks	1982 ....Rick Mears
1915 ....Earl Cooper	1951 ....Tony Bettenhausen	1983 ....Al Unser
1916 ....Dario Resta	1952 ....Chuck Stevenson	1984 ....Mario Andretti
1917 ....Earl Cooper	1953 ....Sam Hanks	1985 ....Al Unser
1918 ....Ralph Mulford	1954 ....Jimmy Bryan	1986 ....Bobby Rahal
1919 ....Howard Wilcox	1955 ....Bob Sweikert	1987 ....Bobby Rahal
1920 ....Tommy Milton	1956 ....Jimmy Bryan	1988 ....Danny Sullivan
1921 ....Tommy Milton	1957 ....Jimmy Bryan	1989 ....Emerson Fittipaldi
1922 ....Jimmy Murphy	1958 ....Tony Bettenhausen	1990 ....Al Unser Jr.
1923 ....Eddie Hearne	1959 ....Rodger Ward	1991 ....Michael Andretti
1924 ....Jimmy Murphy	1960 ............A.J. Foyt	1992 ....Bobby Rahal
1925 ....Peter DePaolo	1961 ............A.J. Foyt	1993 ....Nigel Mansell
1926 ....Harry Hartz	1962 ....Rodger Ward	1994 ....Al Unser Jr.
1927 ....Peter DePaolo	1963 ............A.J. Foyt	1995 ....Jacques Villeneuve
1928 ....Louis Meyer	1964 ............A.J. Foyt	1996 ....Jimmy Vasser
1929 ....Louis Meyer	1965 ....Mario Andretti	1997 ....Alex Zanardi
1930 ....Billy Arnold	1966 ....Mario Andretti	1998 ....Alex Zanardi
1931 ....Louis Schneider	1967 ............A.J. Foyt	1999 ....Juan Montoya
1932 ....Bob Carey	1968 ....Bobby Unser	2000 ....Gil de Ferran
1933 ....Louis Meyer	1969 ....Mario Andretti	2001 ....Gil de Ferran
1934 ....Bill Cummings	1970 ....Al Unser	2002 ....Cristiano da Matta
1935 ....Kelly Petillo	1971 ....Joe Leonard	2003 ....Paul Tracy
1936 ....Mauri Rose	1972 ....Joe Leonard	2004 ....Sebastian Bourdais
1937 ....Wilbur Shaw	1973 ....Roger McCluskey	2005 ....Sebastian Bourdais
1938 ....Floyd Roberts	1974 ....Bobby Unser	
1939 ....Wilbur Shaw	1975 ............A.J. Foyt	
1940 ....Rex Mays	1976 ....Gordon Johncock	
1941 ....Rex Mays	1977 ....Tom Sneva	

Alltime Champ Car* Leaders

WINS		POLE POSITIONS	
A.J. Foyt	67	Mario Andretti	67
Mario Andretti	52	A.J. Foyt	53
†Michael Andretti	42	Bobby Unser	49
Al Unser	39	Rick Mears	40
Bobby Unser	35	Michael Andretti	32
Al Unser Jr	31	Al Unser	27
†Paul Tracy	30	†Paul Tracy	25
Rick Mears	29	†Sebastian Bourdais	23
Johnny Rutherford	27	Johnny Rutherford	23
Rodger Ward	26	Gordon Johncock	20
Gordon Johncock	25	Rex Mays	19
Bobby Rahal	24	Danny Sullivan	19
Ralph DePalma	24	Bobby Rahal	18
Tommy Milton	23	Emerson Fittipaldi	17
Tony Bettenhausen	22	Gil de Ferran	16
†Sebastian Bourdais	22	Tony Bettenhausen	14
Emerson Fittipaldi	22	Juan Montoya	14
Earl Cooper	20	Don Branson	14
Jimmy Bryan	19	Tom Sneva	14
Jimmy Murphy	19	Parnelli Jones	12
Danny Sullivan	17		
Ralph Mulford	17		

*Series known as CART prior to 2003 season
†Active driver. Note: Leaders through September 2006.

Stock Car Racing's Major Events

In 1985, Winston began offering a $1 million bonus to any driver to win three of the top four NASCAR events in the same season. A fifth event, the Brickyard 400 (in Indianapolis) was added in 1994. As of 1998 the Winston million was awarded to any driver who won three of the five events. The other four races are the richest (Daytona 500), the fastest (Talladega 500), the longest (Charlotte 600) and the oldest (Southern 500 at Darlington). Only five drivers, Lee Roy Yarbrough (1969), David Pearson (1976), Bill Elliott (1985), Dale Jarrett (1996) and Jeff Gordon (1997, '98) have scored the three-track hat trick.

Daytona 500

Year	Winner (start pos.)	Chassis-Engine	Avg speed	Pole Winner	Qual. speed
1959	Lee Petty	Oldsmobile	135.520	Cotton Owens	143.198
1960	Junior Johnson	Chevrolet	124.740	Fireball Roberts	151.556
1961	Marvin Panch	Pontiac	149.601	Fireball Roberts	155.709
1962	Fireball Roberts	Pontiac	152.529	Fireball Roberts	156.995
1963	Tiny Lund	Ford	151.566	Johnny Rutherford	165.183
1964	Richard Petty	Plymouth	154.345	Paul Goldsmith	174.910
1965	Fred Lorenzen	Ford	141.539	Darel Dieringer	171.151
1966	Richard Petty	Plymouth	160.627	Richard Petty	175.165
1967	Mario Andretti	Ford	149.926	Curtis Turner	180.831
1968	Cale Yarborough	Mercury	143.251	Cale Yarborough	189.222
1969	Lee Roy Yarbrough	Ford	157.950	David Pearson	190.029
1970	Pete Hamilton	Plymouth	149.601	Cale Yarborough	194.015
1971	Richard Petty	Plymouth	144.462	A.J. Foyt	182.744
1972	A.J. Foyt	Mercury	161.550	Bobby Isaac	186.632
1973	Richard Petty	Dodge	157.205	Buddy Baker	185.662
1974	Richard Petty	Dodge	140.894	David Pearson	185.017
1975	Benny Parsons	Chevrolet	153.649	Donnie Allison	185.827
1976	David Pearson	Mercury	152.181	A.J. Foyt	185.943
1977	Cale Yarborough	Chevrolet	153.218	Donnie Allison	188.048
1978	Bobby Allison	Ford	159.730	Cale Yarborough	187.536
1979	Richard Petty	Oldsmobile	143.977	Buddy Baker	196.049
1980	Buddy Baker	Oldsmobile	177.602*	A.J. Foyt	195.020
1981	Richard Petty	Buick	169.651	Bobby Allison	194.624
1982	Bobby Allison	Buick	153.991	Benny Parsons	196.317
1983	Cale Yarborough	Pontiac	155.979	Ricky Rudd	198.864
1984	Cale Yarborough	Chevrolet	150.994	Cale Yarborough	201.848
1985	Bill Elliott	Ford	172.265	Bill Elliott	205.114
1986	Geoff Bodine	Chevrolet	148.124	Bill Elliott	205.039
1987	Bill Elliott	Ford	176.263	Bill Elliott	210.364†
1988	Bobby Allison	Buick	137.531	Ken Schrader	193.823
1989	Darrell Waltrip	Chevrolet	148.466	Ken Schrader	196.996
1990	Derrike Cope	Chevrolet	165.761	Ken Schrader	196.515
1991	Ernie Irvan	Chevrolet	148.148	Davey Allison	195.955
1992	Davey Allison	Ford	160.256	Sterling Marlin	192.213
1993	Dale Jarrett	Chevrolet	154.972	Kyle Petty	189.426
1994	Sterling Marlin	Chevrolet	156.931	Loy Allen Jr	190.158
1995	Sterling Marlin	Chevrolet	141.710	Dale Jarrett	193.498
1996	Dale Jarrett	Ford	154.308	Dale Earnhardt	189.510
1997	Jeff Gordon	Chevrolet	148.295	Mike Skinner	189.813
1998	Dale Earnhardt	Chevrolet	172.712	Bobby Labonte	192.415
1999	Jeff Gordon	Chevrolet	161.551	Jeff Gordon	195.067
2000	Dale Jarrett	Ford	155.669	Dale Jarrett	191.091
2001	Michael Waltrip	Chevrolet	161.783	Bill Elliott	183.570
2002	Ward Burton	Dodge	142.971	Jimmie Johnson	185.831
2003	Michael Waltrip	Chevrolet	133.870	Jeff Green	186.606
2004	Dale Earnhardt Jr.	Chevrolet	156.345	Greg Biffle	188.387
2005	Jeff Gordon	Chevrolet	135.173	Dale Jarrett	188.312
2006	Jimmie Johnson	Chevrolet	142.667	Jeff Burton	188.887

Note: The Daytona 500, held annually in February, now opens the NASCAR season with 200 laps around the 2.5-mile high-banked Daytona International Speedway. Starting in 1988, cars racing at Daytona have used restrictor plates that lower power and acceleration.

*Track record, winning speed. †Track record, qualifying speed.

Brickyard 400

Year	Winner	Car	Avg Speed	Pole Winner	Speed
1994	Jeff Gordon	Chevrolet	131.977	Rick Mast	172.414
1995	Dale Earnhardt	Chevrolet	155.206	Jeff Gordon	172.536
1996	Dale Jarrett	Ford	139.508	Jeff Gordon	176.419
1997	Ricky Rudd	Ford	130.814	Ernie Irvan	177.736
1998	Jeff Gordon	Chevrolet	126.772	Ernie Irvan	179.394
1999	Dale Jarrett	Ford	148.194	Jeff Gordon	179.612
2000	Bobby Labonte	Pontiac	155.912*	Ricky Rudd	181.068
2001	Jeff Gordon	Chevrolet	130.790	Jimmy Spencer	179.666
2002	Bill Elliott	Dodge	125.033	Tony Stewart	182.960
2003	Kevin Harvick	Chevrolet	134.554	Kevin Harvick	184.343
2004	Jeff Gordon	Chevrolet	115.037	Casey Mears	186.293†
2005	Tony Stewart	Chevrolet	148.782	Elliott Sadler	184.117
2006	Jimmie Johnson	Chevrolet	137.182	Jeff Burton	182.778

Note: Held at the 2.5-mile Indianapolis Motor Speedway
*Track record, winning speed. †Track record, qualifying speed

Talladega 500

Year	Winner	Car	Avg Speed	Pole Winner	Speed
1970	Pete Hamilton	Plymouth	152.321	Bobby Isaac	199.658
1971	Donnie Allison	Mercury	147.419	Donnie Allison	185.869
1972	David Pearson	Mercury	134.400	Bobby Isaac	192.428
1973	David Pearson	Mercury	131.956	Buddy Baker	193.435
1974	David Pearson	Mercury	130.220	David Pearson	186.086
1975	Buddy Baker	Ford	144.94	Buddy Baker	189.947
1976	Buddy Baker	Ford	169.887	Dave Marcis	189.197
1977	Darrell Waltrip	Chevrolet	164.887	A.J. Foyt	192.424
1978	Cale Yarborough	Oldsmobile	155.699	Cale Yarborough	191.904
1979	Bobby Allison	Ford	154.770	Darrell Waltrip	195.644
1980	Buddy Baker	Oldsmobile	170.481	David Pearson	197.704
1981	Bobby Allison	Buick	149.376	Bobby Allison	195.864
1982	Darrell Waltrip	Buick	156.697	Benny Parsons	200.176
1983	Richard Petty	Pontiac	135.936	Cale Yarborough	202.650
1984	Cale Yarborough	Chevrolet	172.988	Cale Yarborough	202.692
1985	Bill Elliott	Ford	186.288	Bill Elliott	209.398
1986	Bobby Allison	Buick	157.698	Bill Elliott	212.229
1987	Davey Allison	Ford	154.228	Bill Elliott	221.809†
1988	Phil Parsons	Oldsmobile	156.547	Davey Allison	198.969
1989	Davey Allison	Ford	155.869	Mark Martin	193.061
1990	Dale Earnhardt	Chevrolet	159.571	Bill Elliott	199.388
1991	Harry Gant	Oldsmobile	165.620	Ernie Irvan	195.186
1992	Davey Allison	Ford	167.609	Ernie Irvan	192.831
1993	Ernie Irvan	Chevrolet	155.412	Dale Earnhardt	192.355
1994	Dale Earnhardt	Chevrolet	157.478	Ernie Irvan	193.298
1995	Mark Martin	Ford	178.902	Terry Labonte	196.532
1996	Sterling Marlin	Chevrolet	149.999	Ernie Irvan	192.855
1997	Mark Martin	Ford	188.354*	John Andretti	193.627
1998	Dale Jarrett	Ford	159.318	Ken Schrader	196.153
1999	Dale Earnhardt	Chevrolet	166.632	Joe Nemechek	198.331
2000	Dale Earnhardt	Chevrolet	165.681	Joe Nemechek	190.279
2001	Dale Earnhardt Jr.	Chevrolet	164.185	Stacy Compton	185.240
2002	Dale Earnhardt Jr.	Chevrolet	183.665	qualifying cancelled	—
2003	Michael Waltrip	Chevrolet	156.045	Elliott Sadler	189.943
2004	Jeff Gordon	Chevrolet	129.396	Ricky Rudd	191.180
2005	Dale Jarrett	Ford	143.818	Elliott Sadler	189.260
2006	Brian Vickers	Chevrolet	157.602	David Gilliland	191.712

Note: Formerly the Winston 500, held at the 2.66-mile Talladega Superspeedway. Starting in 1988, cars racing at Talladega have used restrictor plates that lower power and acceleration.
*Track record, winning speed. †Track record, qualifying speed.

Charlotte 600

Year	Winner	Car	Avg Speed	Pole Winner
1960	Joe Lee Johnson	Chevrolet	107.752	Joe Lee Johnson
1961	David Pearson	Pontiac	111.634	Richard Petty
1962	Nelson Stacy	Ford	125.552	Fireball Roberts
1963	Fred Lorenzen	Ford	132.418	Junior Johnson
1964	Jim Paschal	Plymouth	125.772	Junior Johnson
1965	Fred Lorenzen	Ford	121.772	Fred Lorenzon
1966	Marvin Panch	Plymouth	135.042	Paul Goldsmith
1967	Jim Paschal	Plymouth	135.832	Cale Yarborough
1968	Buddy Baker	Dodge	104.207	Donnie Allison
1969	Lee Roy Yarbrough	Mercury	134.631	Donnie Allison
1970	Donnie Allison	Ford	129.680	Bobby Isaac
1971	Bobby Allison	Mercury	140.442	Charlie Glotzbach
1972	Buddy Baker	Dodge	142.255	Bobby Allison
1973	Buddy Baker	Dodge	134.890	Buddy Baker
1974	David Pearson	Mercury	135.720	David Pearson
1975	Richard Petty	Dodge	145.327	David Pearson
1976	David Pearson	Mercury	137.352	David Pearson
1977	Richard Petty	Dodge	137.636	David Pearson
1978	Darrell Waltrip	Chevrolet	138.355	David Pearson
1979	Darrell Waltrip	Chevrolet	136.674	Neil Bonnet
1980	Benny Parsons	Chevrolet	119.265	Cale Yarborough
1981	Bobby Allison	Buick	129.326	Neil Bonnett
1982	Neil Bonnett	Ford	130.508	David Pearson
1983	Neil Bonnett	Chevrolet	140.406	Buddy Baker
1984	Bobby Allison	Buick	129.233	Harry Gant
1985	Darrell Waltrip	Chevrolet	141.807	Bill Elliott
1986	Dale Earnhardt	Chevrolet	140.406	Geoff Bodine
1987	Kyle Petty	Ford	131.483	Bill Elliott
1988	Darrell Waltrip	Chevrolet	124.460	Davey Allison
1989	Darrell Waltrip	Chevrolet	144.077	Alan Kulwicki
1990	Rusty Wallace	Pontiac	137.650	Ken Schrader
1991	Davey Allison	Ford	138.951	Mark Martin
1992	Dale Earnhardt	Chevrolet	132.980	Bill Elliott
1993	Dale Earnhardt	Chevrolet	145.504	Ken Schrader
1994	Jeff Gordon	Chevrolet	139.445	Jeff Gordon
1995	Bobby Labonte	Chevrolet	151.952*	Jeff Gordon
1996	Dale Jarrett	Ford	147.581	Jeff Gordon
1997	Jeff Gordon	Chevrolet	136.745	Jeff Gordon
1998	Jeff Gordon	Chevrolet	136.424	Jeff Gordon
1999	Jeff Burton	Ford	151.367	Bobby Labonte
2000	Matt Kenseth	Ford	142.640	Dale Earnhardt Jr
2001	Jeff Burton	Ford	138.107	Ryan Newman
2002	Mark Martin	Ford	137.729	Jimmie Johnson
2003	Jimmie Johnson	Chevrolet	126.198	Ryan Newman
2004	Jimmie Johnson	Chevrolet	142.763	Jimmie Johnson
2005	Jimmie Johnson	Chevrolet	114.698	Ryan Newman
2006	Kasey Kahne	Dodge	128.840	Scott Riggs

Note: Held at the 1.5 mile high-banked Lowe's Motor Speedway in Charlotte on Memorial Day weekend.

*Track record, winning speed.

Darlington 500

Year	Winner	Car	Avg Speed	Pole Winner
1950	Johnny Mantz	Plymouth	76.260	Wally Campbell
1951	Herb Thomas	Hudson	76.900	Marshall Teague
1952	Fonty Flock	Oldsmobile	74.510	Dick Rathman
1953	Buck Baker	Oldsmobile	92.780	Fonty Flock
1954	Herb Thomas	Hudson	94.930	Buck Baker
1955	Herb Thomas	Chevrolet	92.281	Tim Flock
1956	Curtis Turner	Ford	95.067	Buck Baker
1957	Speedy Thompson	Chevrolet	100.100	Paul Goldsmith
1958	Fireball Roberts	Chevrolet	102.590	Fireball Roberts
1959	Jim Reed	Chevrolet	111.836	Fireball Roberts
1960	Buck Baker	Pontiac	105.901	Cotton Owens
1961	Nelson Stacy	Ford	117.880	Fireball Roberts
1962	Larry Frank	Ford	117.965	Fireball Roberts
1963	Fireball Roberts	Ford	129.784	Fireball Roberts
1964	Buck Baker	Dodge	117.757	Richard Petty
1965	Ned Jarrett	Ford	115.924	Junior Johnson
1966	Darel Dieringer	Mercury	114.830	Lee Yarborough
1967	Richard Petty	Plymouth	131.933	David Pearson
1968	Cale Yarborough	Mercury	126.132	Charlie Glotzbach
1969	Lee Roy Yarbrough	Ford	105.612	Cale Yarborough
1970	Buddy Baker	Dodge	128.817	David Pearson
1971	Bobby Allison	Mercury	131.398	Bobby Allison
1972	Bobby Allison	Chevrolet	128.124	David Pearson
1973	Cale Yarborough	Chevrolet	134.033	David Pearson
1974	Cale Yarborough	Chevrolet	111.075	Richard Petty
1975	Bobby Allison	Matador	116.825	David Pearson
1976	David Pearson	Mercury	120.534	David Pearson
1977	David Pearson	Mercury	106.797	Darrell Waltrip
1978	Cale Yarborough	Oldsmobile	116.828	David Pearson
1979	David Pearson	Chevrolet	126.259	Bobby Allison
1980	Terry Labonte	Chevrolet	115.210	Darrell Waltrip
1981	Neil Bonnett	Ford	126.410	Harry Gant
1982	Cale Yarborough	Buick	126.703	David Pearson
1983	Bobby Allison	Buick	123.343	Neil Bonnett
1984	Harry Gant	Chevrolet	128.270	Harry Gant
1985	Bill Elliott	Ford	121.254	Bill Elliott
1986	Tim Richmond	Chevrolet	121.068	Tim Richmond
1987	Dale Earnhardt	Chevrolet	115.520	Davey Allison
1988	Bill Elliott	Ford	128.297	Bill Elliott
1989	Dale Earnhardt	Chevrolet	135.462	Alan Kulwicki
1990	Dale Earnhardt	Chevrolet	123.141	Dale Earnhardt
1991	Harry Gant	Oldsmobile	133.508	Davey Allison
1992	Darrell Waltrip	Chevrolet	129.114	Sterling Marlin
1993	Mark Martin	Ford	137.932	Ken Schrader
1994	Bill Elliott	Ford	127.915	Geoff Bodine
1995	Jeff Gordon	Chevrolet	121.231	John Andretti
1996	Jeff Gordon	Chevrolet	135.757	Dale Jarrett
1997	Jeff Gordon	Chevrolet	121.149	Bobby Labonte
1998	Jeff Gordon	Chevrolet	139.031*	Dale Jarrett
1999	Jeff Burton	Ford	100.816	Kenny Irwin
2000	Bobby Labonte	Pontiac	108.275	Jeremy Mayfield
2001	Ward Burton	Dodge	122.773	Kurt Busch
2002	Jeff Gordon	Chevrolet	118.617	Sterling Marlin
2003	Terry Labonte	Chevrolet	120.744	Ryan Newman
2004	Jimmie Johnson	Chevrolet	125.044	Kurt Busch
2005	Greg Biffle	Ford	135.127	Kasey Kahne
2006	Greg Biffle	Ford	123.031	Kasey Kahne

Through 2004, results listed were for the Southern 500, traditionally the second race of the year at the 1.366-mile Darlington (S.C.) Raceway. Starting in 2005, Darlington only hosted one race a year, in May.

*Track record, winning speed.

Nextel Cup* NASCAR Champions

Year	Driver	Car	Wins	Poles	Winnings ($)
1949	Red Byron	Oldsmobile	2	1	5,800
1950	Bill Rexford	Oldsmobile	1	0	6,175
1951	Herb Thomas	Hudson	7	4	18,200
1952	Tim Flock	Hudson	8	4	20,210
1953	Herb Thomas	Hudson	11	10	27,300
1954	Lee Petty	Dodge	7	3	26,706
1955	Tim Flock	Chrysler	18	19	33,750
1956	Buck Baker	Chrysler	14	12	29,790
1957	Buck Baker	Chevrolet	10	5	24,712
1958	Lee Petty	Oldsmobile	7	4	20,600
1959	Lee Petty	Plymouth	10	2	45,570
1960	Rex White	Chevrolet	6	3	45,260
1961	Ned Jarrett	Chevrolet	1	4	27,285
1962	Joe Weatherly	Pontiac	9	6	56,110
1963	Joe Weatherly	Mercury	3	6	58,110
1964	Richard Petty	Plymouth	9	8	98,810
1965	Ned Jarrett	Ford	13	9	77,966
1966	David Pearson	Dodge	14	7	59,205
1967	Richard Petty	Plymouth	27	18	130,275
1968	David Pearson	Ford	16	12	118,824
1969	David Pearson	Ford	11	14	183,700
1970	Bobby Isaac	Dodge	11	13	121,470
1971	Richard Petty	Plymouth	21	9	309,225
1972	Richard Petty	Plymouth	8	3	227,015
1973	Benny Parsons	Chevrolet	1	0	114,345
1974	Richard Petty	Dodge	10	7	299,175
1975	Richard Petty	Dodge	13	3	378,865
1976	Cale Yarborough	Chevrolet	9	2	387,173
1977	Cale Yarborough	Chevrolet	9	3	477,499
1978	Cale Yarborough	Oldsmobile	10	8	530,751
1979	Richard Petty	Chevrolet	5	1	531,292
1980	Dale Earnhardt	Chevrolet	5	0	588,926
1981	Darrell Waltrip	Buick	12	11	693,342
1982	Darrell Waltrip	Buick	12	7	873,118
1983	Bobby Allison	Buick	6	0	828,355
1984	Terry Labonte	Chevrolet	2	2	713,010
1985	Darrell Waltrip	Chevrolet	3	4	1,318,735
1986	Dale Earnhardt	Chevrolet	5	1	1,783,880
1987	Dale Earnhardt	Chevrolet	11	1	2,099,243
1988	Bill Elliott	Ford	6	6	1,574,639
1989	Rusty Wallace	Pontiac	6	4	2,247,950
1990	Dale Earnhardt	Chevrolet	9	4	3,083,056
1991	Dale Earnhardt	Chevrolet	4	0	2,396,685
1992	Alan Kulwicki	Ford	2	6	2,322,561
1993	Dale Earnhardt	Chevrolet	6	2	3,353,789
1994	Dale Earnhardt	Chevrolet	4	2	3,400,733
1995	Jeff Gordon	Chevrolet	7	9	4,347,343
1996	Terry Labonte	Chevrolet	2	4	4,030,648
1997	Jeff Gordon	Chevrolet	10	1	4,201,227
1998	Jeff Gordon	Chevrolet	13	7	6,175,867
1999	Dale Jarrett	Ford	4	0	3,608,829
2000	Bobby Labonte	Pontiac	4	2	4,041,750
2001	Jeff Gordon	Chevrolet	6	8	6,649,076
2002	Tony Stewart	Pontiac	3	4	4,695,150
2003	Matt Kenseth	Ford	1	2	4,038,120
2004	Kurt Busch	Ford	3	1	4,200,330
2005	Tony Stewart	Chevrolet	5	3	6,987,530

*Series name changed from Winston Cup after 2003 season.

Alltime NASCAR Leaders

WINS		POLE POSITIONS	
Richard Petty	200	Richard Petty	126
David Pearson	105	David Pearson	113
Bobby Allison	84	Cale Yarborough	70
Darrell Waltrip	84	Darrell Waltrip	59
Cale Yarborough	83	Bobby Allison	57
Dale Earnhardt	76	Bill Elliott	54
*Jeff Gordon	75	*Jeff Gordon	54
Rusty Wallace	55	Bobby Isaac	51
Lee Petty	54	Junior Johnson	47
Ned Jarrett	50	Buck Baker	44
Junior Johnson	50	*Mark Martin	41
Herb Thomas	48	Buddy Baker	40
Buck Baker	46	Tim Flock	39
Bill Elliott	44	Herb Thomas	39
Tim Flock	40	Geoff Bodine	37
		*Ryan Newman	37

*Active drivers. Note: NASCAR wins leaders and pole position leaders through Oct 22, 2006.

Formula One Grand Prix Racing

World Driving Champions

Year	Winner	Car	Year	Winner	Car
1950	Guiseppe Farina, Italy	Alfa Romeo	1976	James Hunt, Grt Britain	McLaren-Ford
1951	Juan-Manuel Fangio, Argentina	Alfa Romeo	1977	Niki Lauda, Austria	Ferrari
1952	Alberto Ascari, Italy	Ferrari	1978	Mario Andretti, U.S.	Lotus-Ford
1953	Alberto Ascari, Italy	Ferrari	1979	Jody Scheckter, S Africa	Ferrari
1954	Juan-Manuel Fangio, Argentina	Maserati-Mercedes	1980	Alan Jones, Australia	Williams-Ford
1955	Juan-Manuel Fangio, Argentina	Mercedes	1981	Nelson Piquet, Brazil	Brabham-Ford
1956	Juan-Manuel Fangio, Argentina	Ferrari	1982	Keke Rosberg, Finland	Williams-Ford
1957	Juan-Manuel Fangio, Argentina	Maserati	1983	Nelson Piquet, Brazil	Brabham-BMW
1958	Mike Hawthorn, Grt Britain	Ferrari	1984	Niki Lauda, Austria	McLaren-Porsche
1959	Jack Brabham, Australia	Cooper-Climax	1985	Alain Prost, France	McLaren-Porsche
1960	Jack Brabham, Australia	Cooper-Climax	1986	Alain Prost, France	McLaren-Porsche
1961	Phil Hill, U.S.	Ferrari	1987	Nelson Piquet, Brazil	Williams-Honda
1962	Graham Hill, Grt Britain	BRM	1988	Ayrton Senna, Brazil	McLaren-Honda
1963	Jim Clark, Scotland	Lotus-Climax	1989	Alain Prost, France	McLaren-Honda
1964	John Surtees, Grt Britain	Ferrari	1990	Ayrton Senna, Brazil	McLaren-Honda
1965	Jim Clark, Scotland	Lotus-Climax	1991	Ayrton Senna, Brazil	McLaren-Honda
1966	Jack Brabham, Australia	Brabham-Repco	1992	Nigel Mansell, Grt Britain	Williams-Renault
1967	Denny Hulme, New Zealand	Brabham-Repco	1993	Alain Prost, France	Williams-Renault
1968	Graham Hill, Grt Britain	Lotus-Ford	1994	Michael Schumacher, Ger	Benetton-Ford
1969	Jackie Stewart, Scotland	Matra-Ford	1995	Michael Schumacher, Ger	Benetton-Renault
1970	Jochen Rindt, Austria*	Lotus-Ford	1996	Damon Hill, Grt Britain	Williams-Renault
1971	Jackie Stewart, Scotland	Tyrell-Ford	1997	Jacques Villeneuve, Can	Williams-Renault
1972	Emerson Fittipaldi, Brazil	Lotus-Ford	1998	Mika Hakkinen, Finland	McLaren-Mercedes
1973	Jackie Stewart, Scotland	Tyrell-Ford	1999	Mika Hakkinen, Finland	McLaren-Mercedes
1974	Emerson Fittipaldi, Brazil	McLaren-Ford	2000	Michael Schumacher, Ger	Ferrari
1975	Niki Lauda, Austria	Ferrari	2001	Michael Schumacher, Ger	Ferrari
			2002	Michael Schumacher, Ger	Ferrari
			2003	Michael Schumacher, Ger	Ferrari
			2004	Michael Schumacher, Ger	Ferrari
			2005	Fernando Alonso, Spain	Renault
			2006	Fernando Alonso, Spain	Renault

*The championship was awarded posthumously, after Rindt was killed during practice for the Italian Grand Prix.

Alltime Grand Prix Winners

Driver	Wins	Driver	Wins
*Michael Schumacher, Germany	91	Jim Clark, Great Britain	25
Alain Prost, France	51	Niki Lauda, Austria	25
Ayrton Senna, Brazil	41	Juan Manuel Fangio, Argentina	24
Nigel Mansell, Great Britain	31	Nelson Piquet, Brazil	23
Jackie Stewart, Great Britain	27	Damon Hill, Great Britain	22

*Active driver in 2006. Note: Grand Prix winners through Oct 22, 2006.

Alltime Grand Prix Pole Winners

Driver	Poles	Driver	Poles
*Michael Schumacher, Germany	68	Juan Manuel Fangio, Argentina	29
Ayrton Senna, Brazil	65	Mika Hakkinen, Finland	26
Alain Prost, France	33	Niki Lauda, Austria	24
Jim Clark, Great Britain	33	Nelson Piquet, Brazil	24
Nigel Mansell, Great Britain	31	Damon Hill, Great Britain	20

*Active driver in 2006. Note: Grand Prix winners through Oct 22, 2006.

Professional Sports Car Racing

The 24 Hours of Daytona

Year	Winner	Car	Avg Speed	Distance
1962	Dan Gurney	Lotus 19-Class SP11	104.101 mph	3 hrs (312.42 mi)
1963	Pedro Rodriguez	Ferrari-Class 12	102.074 mph	3 hrs (308.61 mi)
1964	Pedro Rodriguez/Phil Hill	Ferrari 250 LM	98.230 mph	2,000 km
1965	Ken Miles/Lloyd Ruby	Ford	99.944 mph	2,000 km
1966	Ken Miles/Lloyd Ruby	Ford Mark II	108.020 mph	24 hrs (2,570.63 mi)
1967	Lorenzo Bandini/Chris Amon	Ferrari 330 P4	105.688 mph	24 hrs (2,537.46 mi)
1968	Vic Elford/Jochen Neerpasch	Porsche 907	106.697 mph	24 hrs (2,565.69 mi)
1969	Mark Donohue/Chuck Parsons	Chevy Lola	99.268 mph	24 hrs (2,383.75 mi)
1970	Pedro Rodriguez/Leo Kinnunen	Porsche 917	114.866 mph	24 hrs (2,758.44 mi)
1971	Pedro Rodriguez/Jackie Oliver	Porsche 917K	109.203 mph	24 hrs (2,621.28 mi)
1972*	Mario Andretti/Jacky Ickx	Ferrari 312/P	122.573 mph	6 hrs (738.24 mi)
1973	Peter Gregg/Hurley Haywood	Porsche Carrera	106.225 mph	24 hrs (2,552.7 mi)
1974	(No race)			
1975	Peter Gregg/Hurley Haywood	Porsche Carrera	108.531 mph	24 hrs (2,606.04 mi)
1976†	Peter Gregg/Brian Redman/ John Fitzpatrick	BMW CSL	104.040 mph	24 hrs (2,092.8 mi)
1977	John Graves/Hurley Haywood/ Dave Helmick	Porsche Carrera	108.801 mph	24 hrs (2,615 mi)
1978	Rolf Stommelen/ Antoine Hezemans/Peter Gregg	Porsche Turbo	108.743 mph	24 hrs (2,611.2 mi)
1979	Ted Field/Danny Ongais/ Hurley Haywood	Porsche Turbo	109.249 mph	24 hrs (2,626.56 mi)
1980	Volkert Meri/Rolf Stommelen/ Reinhold Joest	Porsche Turbo	114.303 mph	24 hrs
1981	Bob Garretson/Bobby Rahal/ Brian Redman	Porsche Turbo	113.153 mph	24 hrs
1982	John Paul Jr/John Paul Sr/ Rolf Stommelen	Porsche Turbo	114.794 mph	24 hrs
1983	Preston Henn/Bob Wollek/ Claude Ballot-Lena/A.J. Foyt	Porsche Turbo	98.781 mph	24 hrs
1984	Sarel van der Merwe/ Graham Duxbury/Tony Martin	Porsche March	103.119 mph	24 hrs (2,476.8 mi)
1985	A.J. Foyt/Bob Wollek/ Al Unser/Thierry Boutsen	Porsche 962	104.162 mph	24 hrs (2,502.68 mi)
1986	Al Holbert/Derek Bell/Al Unser Jr.	Porsche 962	105.484 mph	24 hrs (2,534.72 mi)
1987	Chip Robinson/Derek Bell/ Al Holbert/Al Unser Jr.	Porsche 962	111.599 mph	24 hrs (2,680.68 mi)
1988	Martin Brundle/John Nielsen/ Raul Boesel	Jaguar XJR-9	107.943 mph	24 hrs (2,591.68 mi)
1989	John Andretti/Derek Bell/ Bob Wollek	Porsche 962	92.009 mph	24 hrs (2,210.76 mi)
1990	Davy Jones/ Jan Lammers/ Andy Wallace	Jaguar XJR-12	112.857 mph	24 hrs (2,709.16 mi)

The 24 Hours of Daytona *(Cont.)*

Year	Winner	Car	Speed	Distance
1991	Hurley Haywood/ John Winter/ Frank Jelinski/ Henri Pescarolo/ Bob Wollek	Porsche 962C	106.633 mph	24 hrs (2,559.64 mi)
1992	Massahiro Hasemi/ Kazuoyshi Hoshino/ Toshio Suzuki/ Anders Olofsson	Nissan R91CP	112.987 mph	24 hrs (2,712.72 mi)
1993	P.J. Jones/Mark Dismore/ Rocky Moran	Toyota Eagle MK III	103.537 mph	24 hrs (2,484.88 mi)
1994	Paul Gentilozzi/ Scott Pruett/ Butch Leitzinger/ Steve Millen	Nissan 300 ZX	104.80 mph	24 hrs (2,693.67 mi)
1995	Jurgen Lassig/ Christophe Buochut/ Giovanni Lavaggi/ Marco Werner	Porsche Spyder K8	102.28 mph	690 laps (2,456.4 mi)
1996	Wayne Taylor/ Scott Sharp/ Jim Pace	Oldsmobile Mark III	103.32 mph	697 laps (2,481.32 mi)
1997	Elliot Forbes-Robinson/ John Schneider/Rob Dyson/ John Paul Jr/Butch Leitzinger/James Weaver/Andy Wallace	Ford R & S MK III	102.292 mph	690 laps (2,456.4 mi)
1998	Arie Luyendyk/Didier Theys/ Mauro Baldi	Ferrari 333 SP	105.565 mph	711 laps (2,531.16 mi)
1999	Elliott Forbes-Robinson/ Butch Leitzinger/ Andy Wallace	Ford R & S MK III	104.9 mph	708 laps (2,520.48 mi)
2000	Olivier Beretta/Karl Wendlinger/ Dominique Dupuy	Dodge Viper	107.207 mph	723 laps (2,573.88 m)
2001	Ron Fellows/Chris Kneifel/Franck Freon/Johnny O'Connell	Corvette	97.293 mph	656 laps (2,335.360 mi)
2002	Didier Theys/Fredy Lienhard/ Max Papis/Mauro Baldi	Dallara-Judd (SRP)	106.143 mph	716 laps (2,548.96 mi)
2003	Kevin Buckler/Michael Schrom Timo Bernhard/Jorg Bergmeister	Porsche GT3 RS	114.068† mph	694 laps (2,470.64 mi)
2004	Forest Barber/Terry Borcheller Andy Pilgrim/Christian Fittipaldi	Pontiac Doran	117.651 mph	526 laps (1,872.56 mi)
2005	Wayne Taylor, Max Angelelli, Emmanuel Collard	Pontiac Riley	119.397 mph	710 laps (2,527.60 mi)
2006	Scott Dixon/Dan Wheldon Casey Mears	Lexus Riley	108.826 mph	734 laps (2,613.04 mi)

*Race shortened due to fuel crisis. †Course lengthened from 3.81 miles to 3.84 miles. † Top speed.

World SportsCar Champions*

Year	Winner	Car	Year	Winner	Car
1978	Peter Gregg	Porsche 935	1989	Geoff Brabham	Nissan GTP
1979	Peter Gregg	Porsche 935	1990	Geoff Brabham	Nissan GTP
1980	John Fitzpatrick	Porsche 935	1991	Geoff Brabham	Nissan NPT
1981	Brian Redman	Chevy Lola	1992	Juan Fangio II	Toyota EGL MKIII
1982	John Paul Jr	Chevy Lola	1993	Juan Fangio II	Toyota EGL MKIII
1983	Al Holbert	Chevy March	1994	Wayne Taylor	Mazda Kudzu
1984	Randy Lanier	Chevy March	1995	Fermin Velez	Ferrari 333 SP
1985	Al Holbert	Porsche 962	1996	Wayne Taylor	Mazda Kudzu
1986	Al Holbert	Porsche 962	1997	Butch Leitzinger	Ford R&S MKIII
1987	Chip Robinson	Porsche 962	1998	Butch Leitzinger	Ford R&S MKIII
1988	Geoff Brabham	Nissan GTP			

Year	Prototype	GTS	GT
1999	Elliott Forbes-Robinson	Olivier Beretta	Cort Wagner
2000	Allan McNish	Olivier Beretta	Sascha Maassen
2001	Emanuele Pirro	Terry Borcheller	Jörg Müller
2002	Tom Kristensen	Ron Fellows	Lucas Luhr
2003	Frank Biela/Marco Werner	Ron Fellows/John O'Connell	Sascha Maassen/L. Luhr
2004	Frank Biela/Emanuele Pirro	Oliver Gavin/Olivier Beretta	Patrick Long/Jorg Bergmeister
2005	Frank Biela/Emanuele Pirro	Oliver Gavin/Olivier Beretta	Patrick Long/Jorg Bergmeister
2006	R. Capiello/A. McNish	Oliver Gavin/Olivier Beretta	Johannes Van Overbeek

*1978–93 champions raced in the GT series, which in 1994 was replaced by the World SportsCar series. Beginning in 1999, racing was reclassified according to the American Le Mans Series. The Series is comprised of two different types of race cars divided into two categories and five separate classes. The Prototype category features open-cockpit prototype as well as Grand Touring Prototype (GTP) class cars. The Grand Touring category features the Grand Touring S (GTS) class cars, formerly known as GT2, and Grand Touring (GT) cars, formerly known as GT3. Both classes feature purpose-built race cars with an emphasis on spectator car identification.

Alltime SportsCar Leaders

PROTOTYPE WINS (WSC/GTP ERA: 1994–2006)		GTS AND GT WINS (IMSA GT: 1971–1994)	
*Frank Biela	17	Al Holbert	49
*Rinaldo Capello	16	Peter Gregg	41
*James Weaver	16	Hurley Haywood	31
*Butch Leitzinger	15	Geoff Brabham	26
*Allan McNish	13	Parker Johnstone	25
J.J. Lehto	12	Jim Downing	23
*Emanuele Pirro	12	Irv Hoerr	23
Wayne Taylor	8	Jack Baldwin	22
David Brabham	8	Don Devendorf	22
Gianpiero Moretti	7	Bob Earl	22
		Tommy Riggins	22

* Active driver in 2006. Note: Leaders through Oct 22, 2006

24 Hours of Le Mans

Year	Winning Drivers	Car
1923	André Lagache/René Léonard	Chenard & Walker
1924	John Duff/Francis Clement	Bentley
1925	Gérard de Courcelles/André Rossignol	La Lorraine
1926	Robert Bloch/André Rossignol	La Lorraine
1927	J. Dudley Benjafield/Sammy Davis	Bentley
1928	Woolf Barnato/Bernard Rubin	Bentley
1929	Woolf Barnato/Sir Henry Birkin	Bentley Speed 6
1930	Woolf Barnato/Glen Kidston	Bentley Speed 6
1931	Earl Howe/Sir Henry Birkin	Alfa Romeo 8C-2300 sc
1932	Raymond Sommer/Luigi Chinetti	Alfa Romeo 8C-2300 sc
1933	Raymond Sommer/Tazio Nuvolari	Alfa Romeo 8C-2300 sc
1934	Luigi Chinetti/Philippe Etancelin	Alfa Romeo 8C-2300 sc
1935	John Hindmarsh/Louis Fontés	Lagonda M45R
1936	Race cancelled	
1937	Jean-Pierre Wimille/Robert Benoist	Bugatti 57G sc
1938	Eugene Chaboud/Jean Tremoulet	Delahaye 135M
1939	Jean-Pierre Wimille/Pierre Veyron	Bugatti 57G sc
1940–48	Races cancelled	
1949	Luigi Chinetti/Lord Selsdon	Ferrari 166MM
1950	Louis Rosier/Jean-Louis Rosier	Talbot-Lago
1951	Peter Walker/Peter Whitehead	Jaguar C
1952	Hermann Lang/Fritz Reiss	Mercedes-Benz 300 SL
1953	Tony Rolt/Duncan Hamilton	Jaguar C
1954	Froilan Gonzales/Maurice Trintignant	Ferrari 375
1955	Mike Hawthorn/Ivor Bueb	Jaguar D
1956	Ron Flockhart/Ninian Sanderson	Jaguar D
1957	Ron Flockhart/Ivor Bueb	Jaguar D
1958	Olivier Gendebien/Phil Hill	Ferrari 250 TR58
1959	Carroll Shelby/Roy Salvadori	Aston Martin DBR1
1960	Olivier Gendebien/Paul Frère	Ferrari 250 TR59/60
1961	Olivier Gendebien/Phil Hill	Ferrari 250 TR61

Year	Winning Drivers	Car
1962	Olivier Gendebien/Phil Hill	Ferrari 250P
1963	Lodovico Scarfiotti/Lorenzo Bandini	Ferrari 250P
1964	Jean Guichel/Nino Vaccarella	Ferrari 275P
1965	Jochen Rindt/Masten Gregory	Ferrari 250LM
1966	Chris Amon/Bruce McLaren	Ford Mk2
1967	Dan Gurney/A.J. Foyt	Ford Mk4
1968	Pedro Rodriguez/Lucien Bianchi	Ford GT40
1969	Jacky Ickx/Jackie Oliver	Ford GT40
1970	Hans Herrmann/Richard Attwood	Porsche 917
1971	Helmut Marko/Gijs van Lennep	Porsche 917
1972	Henri Pescarolo/Graham Hill	Matra-Simca MS670
1973	Henri Pescarolo/Gérard Larrousse	Matra-Simca MS670B
1974	Henri Pescarolo/Gérard Larrousse	Matra-Simca MS670B
1975	Jacky Ickx/Derek Bell	Mirage-Ford MB
1976	Jacky Ickx/Gijs van Lennep	Porsche 936
1977	Jacky Ickx/Jurgen Barth/Hurley Haywood	Porsche 936
1978	Jean-Pierre Jaussaud/Didier Pironi	Renault-Alpine A442
1979	Klaus Ludwig/Bill Whittington/Don Whittington	Porsche 935
1980	Jean-Pierre Jaussaud/Jean Rondeau	Rondeau-Ford M379B
1981	Jacky Ickx/Derek Bell	Porsche 936-81
1982	Jacky Ickx/Derek Bell	Porsche 956
1983	Vern Schuppan/Hurley Haywood/Al Holbert	Porsche 956-83
1984	Klaus Ludwig/Henri Pescarolo	Porsche 956B
1985	Klaus Ludwig/Paolo Barilla/John Winter	Porsche 956B
1986	Derek Bell/Hans-Joachim Stuck/Al Holbert	Porsche 962C
1987	Derek Bell/Hans-Joachim Stuck/Al Holbert	Porsche 962C
1988	Jan Lammers/Johnny Dumfries/Andy Wallace	Jaguar XJR9LM
1989	Jochen Mass/Manuel Reuter/Stanley Dickens	Sauber-Mercedes C9-88
1990	John Nielsen/Price Cobb/Martin Brundle	TWR Jaguar XJR-12
1991	Volker Weidler/Johnny Herbert/Bertrand Gachof	Mazda 787B
1992	Derek Warwick/Yannick Dalmas/Mark Blundell	Peugeot 905B
1993	Geoff Brabham/Christophe Bouchut/Eric Helary	Peugeot 905
1994	Yannick Dalmas/Hurley Haywood/Mauro Baldi	Porsche 962
1995	Yannick Dalmas/J.J. Lehto/Masanori Sekiya	McLaren BMW
1996	Manuel Reuter/Davy Jones/Alexander Wurz	TWR Porsche
1997	Michele Alboreto/Stefan Johansson/Tom Kristensen	TWR Porsche
1998	Allan McNish/Laurent Aiello/Stephane Ortelli	Porsche GT One
1999	Yannick Dalmas/Joachim Winkelhock/Pierluigi Martini	BMW V12 LMR
2000	Frank Biela/Tom Kristensen/Emanuele Pirro	Audi R8
2001	Frank Biela/Tom Kristensen/Emanuele Pirro	Audi R8
2002	Frank Biela/Tom Kristensen/Emanuele Pirro	Audi R8
2003	Rinaldo Capello/Tom Kristensen/Guy Smith	Bentley EXP Speed 8
2004	Rinaldo Capello/Seiji Ara/Tom Kristensen	Audi R8
2005	J.J. Lehto/Marco Werner/Tom Kristensen	Audi R8
2006	Frank Biela/Emanuele Pirro/Marco Werner	Audi R10

Drag Racing: Milestone Performances

Top Fuel
ELAPSED TIME

Time (Sec.)	Driver	Date	Site
9.00	Jack Chrisman	Feb 18, 1961	Pomona, Calif.
8.97	Jack Chrisman	May 20, 1961	Empona, Va.
7.96	Bobby Vodnick	May 16, 1964	Bayview, Md.
6.97	Don Johnson	May 7, 1967	Carlsbad, Calif.
5.97	Mike Snively	Nov 17, 1972	Ontario, Calif.
5.78	Don Garlits	Nov 18, 1973	Ontario, Calif.
5.698	Gary Beck	Oct 10, 1975	Ontario, Calif.
5.573	Gary Beck	Oct 18, 1981	Irvine, Calif.
5.484	Gary Beck	Sept 6, 1982	Clermont, Ind.
5.391	Gary Beck	Oct 1, 1983	Fremont, Calif.
5.280	Darrell Gwynn	Sept 25, 1986	Ennis, Tex.
5.176	Darrell Gwynn	April 4, 1987	Ennis, Tex.
5.090	Joe Amato	Oct 1, 1987	Ennis, Tex.
4.990	Eddie Hill	April 9, 1988	Ennis, Tex.
4.881	Gary Ormsby	Sept 28, 1990	Topeka, Kan.
4.799	Cory McClenathan	Sept 19, 1992	Mohnton, Pa.
4.762	Cory McClenathan	Oct 3, 1993	Topeka, Kan.
4.690	Michael Brotherton	May 20, 1994	Englishtown, N.J.
4.595	Joe Amato	July 5, 1996	Topeka, Kan.
4.539	Joe Amato	Mar 21, 1998	Baytown, Tex.
4.525	Gary Scelzi	Oct 23, 1998	Ennis, Tex.
4.503	Mike Dunn	Feb 5, 1999	Pomona, Calif.
4.486	Larry Dixon	Apr 9, 1999	Houston
4.480	Gary Scelzi	Oct 31, 1999	Houston
4.477	Kenny Bernstein	June 2, 2001	Joliet, Ill.
4.441	Tony Schumacher	Oct 4, 2003	Reading, Pa.
4.437	Tony Schumacher	Oct 1, 2005	Joliet, Ill.

SPEED

MPH	Driver	Date	Site
180.36	Connie Kalitta	Sept 3, 1962	Indianapolis
190.26	Don Garlits	Sept 21, 1963	East Haddam, Conn.
201.34	Don Garlits	Aug 1, 1964	Great Meadows, N.J.
211.26	Donny Milani	May 15, 1965	Sacramento, Calif.
223.32	Don Cook	Apr 24, 1965	Fremont, Calif.
230.17	James Warren	Apr 10, 1967	Fresno, Calif.
243.24	Don Garlits	Mar 18, 1973	Gainesville, Fla.
250.69	Don Garlits	Oct 11, 1975	Ontario, Calif.
260.11	Joe Amato	Mar 18, 1984	Gainesville, Fla.
272.56	Don Garlits	Mar 23, 1986	Gainesville, Fla.
282.13	Joe Amato	Sept 5, 1987	Clermont, Ind.
291.54	Connie Kalitta	Feb 11, 1989	Pomona, Calif.
301.70	Kenny Bernstein	Mar 20, 1992	Gainesville, Fla.
311.86	Kenny Bernstein	Oct 30, 1994	Pomona, Calif.
319.82	Joe Amato	Mar 21, 1998	Baytown, Tex.
323.50	Joe Amato	May 17, 1998	Englishtown, N.J.
326.44	Gary Scelzi	Nov 2, 1998	Houston
326.91	Tony Schumacher	Oct 22, 1999	Dallas
330.55	Mike Dunn	June 2, 2001	Joliet, Ill.
332.18	Kenny Bernstein	Oct. 7, 2001	Richardson, Tex.
332.75	Larry Dixon	Apr 3, 2003	Las Vegas
333.41	Brandon Bernstein	May 22, 2004	Joliet, Ill.
336.15	Tony Schumacher	May 25, 2005	Hebron, Ohio

Funny Car
ELAPSED TIME

Time (sec.)	Driver	Date	Site
6.92	Leroy Goldstein	Sept 3, 1970	Clermont, Ind.
5.987	Don Prudhomme	Oct 12, 1975	Ontario, Calif.
5.868	Raymond Beadle	July 16, 1981	Englishtown, N.J.
5.799	Tom Anderson	Sept 3, 1982	Clermont, Ind.
5.637	Don Prudhomme	Sept 4, 1982	Clermont, Ind.
5.588	Rick Johnson	Feb 3, 1985	Pomona, Calif.
5.425	Kenny Bernstein	Sept 26, 1986	Ennis, Tex.
5.397	Kenny Bernstein	April 5, 1987	Ennis, Tex.
5.255	Ed McCulloch	April 17, 1988	Ennis, Tex.
5.193	Don Prudhomme	Mar 2, 1989	Baytown, Tex.
5.077	Cruz Pedregon	Sept 20, 1992	Mohnton, Pa.
4.987	Chuck Etcholis	Oct 2, 1993	Topeka, Kan.
4.819	Cruz Pedregon	Mar 21, 1998	Baytown, Tex.
4.807	Cruz Pedregon	Nov 1, 1998	Houston
4.788	John Force	Apr 11, 1999	Houston
4.763	John Force	June 2, 2001	Joliet, Ill.
4.750	William Bazemore	Sept 28, 2001	Joliet, Ill.
4.731	John Force	Oct. 7, 2001	Yorba Linda, Calif.
4.713	Whit Bazemore	May 22, 2004	Joliet, Ill.
4.665	John Force	Oct 3, 2004	Joliet, Ill.

SPEED

MPH	Driver	Date	Site
200.44	Gene Snow	Aug, 1968	Houston
250.00	Don Prudhomme	May 23, 1982	Baton Rouge, La.
260.11	Kenny Bernstein	Mar 18, 1984	Gainesville, Fla.
271.41	Kenny Bernstein	Aug 30, 1986	Indianapolis
280.72	Mike Dunn	Oct 2, 1987	Ennis, Tex.
290.13	Jim White	Oct 11, 1991	Ennis, Tex.
291.82	Jim White	Oct 25, 1991	Pomona, Calif.
300.40	Jim Epler	Oct 3, 1993	Topeka, Kan.
303.64	John Force	Sept 2, 1995	Indianapolis
308.74	John Force	Sept 28, 1997	Topeka, Kan.
317.46	John Force	Mar 21, 1998	Baytown, Tex.
323.89	John Force	May 17, 1998	Englishtown, N.J.
324.05	John Force	Mar 19, 1999	Gainesville, Fla.
325.45	William Bazemore	Sept 28, 2001	Joliet, Ill.
326.87	Gary Densham	Feb. 9, 2002	Bellflower, Calif.
330.55	Gary Scelzi	May 22, 2004	Joliet, Ill.
333.58	John Force	Oct 3, 2004	Joliet, Ill.

Pro Stock
ELAPSED TIME

Time (sec.)	Driver	Date	Site
7.778	Lee Shepherd	Mar 12, 1982	Gainesville, Fla.
7.655	Lee Shepherd	Oct 1, 1982	Fremont, Calif.
7.557	Bob Glidden	Feb 2, 1985	Pomona, Calif.
7.497	Bob Glidden	Sep 13, 1985	Maple Grove, Pa.
7.377	Bob Glidden	Aug 28, 1986	Clermont, Ind.
7.294	Frank Sanchez	Oct 7, 1988	Baytown, Tex.
7.184	Darrell Alderman	Oct 12, 1990	Ennis, Tex.
7.099	Scott Geoffrion	Sept 19, 1992	Mohnton, Pa.
6.988	Kurt Johnson	May 20, 1994	Englishtown, N.J.
6.873	Warren Johnson	Mar 14, 1998	Gainesville, Fla.
6.867	Warren Johnson	Oct 23, 1998	Ennis, Tex.
6.866	Warren Johnson	Mar 19, 1999	Gainesville, Fla.
6.843	Warren Johnson	Apr 30, 1999	Dinwiddie, Va.
6.840	Kurt Johnson	May 1, 1999	Dinwiddie, Va.
6.822	Warren Johnson	Oct 23, 1999	Dallas
6.801	Kurt Johnson	Sept 29, 2001	Joliet, Ill.
6.750	Jeg Coughlin	Oct. 7, 2001	Delaware, Ohio
6.670	Greg Anderson	May 18, 2003	Englishtown, N.J.
6.633	Greg Anderson	March 19, 2005	Gainesville, Fla.
6.631	Greg Anderson	August 1, 2006	Sonoma, Calif.

Pro Stock *(Cont.)*

SPEED

Time (sec.)	Driver	Date	Site
181.08	Warren Johnson	Oct 1, 1982	Fremont, Calif.
190.07	Warren Johnson	Aug 29, 1986	Clermont, Ind.
191.32	Bob Glidden	Sept 4, 1987	Clermont, Ind.
192.18	Warren Johnson	Oct 13, 1990	Ennis, Tex.
193.21	Bob Glidden	July 28, 1991	Sonoma, Calif.
194.51	Warren Johnson	July 31, 1992	Sonoma, Calif.
195.99	Warren Johnson	May 21, 1993	Englishtown, N.J.
196.24	Warren Johnson	Mar 19, 1993	Gainesville, Fla.
197.15	Warren Johnson	Apr 23, 1994	Commerce, Ga.
199.15	Warren Johnson	Mar 10, 1995	Baytown, Tex.
201.20	Warren Johnson	Mar 14, 1998	Gainesville, Fla.
201.34	Warren Johnson	Oct 23, 1998	Ennis, Tex.
201.37	Warren Johnson	Mar 19, 1999	Gainesville, Fla.
202.24	Warren Johnson	Apr 30,1999	Dinwiddie, Va.
202.33	Warren Johnson	Oct 23, 1999	Dallas
202.36	Warren Johnson	Oct 31, 1999	Houston
202.70	Kurt Johnson	Sept 29, 2001	Joliet, Ill.
204.35	Mark Osborne	Oct. 6, 2001	Abdingdon, Va.
207.18	Greg Anderson	May 18, 2003	Englishtown, N.J.
208.23	Greg Anderson	March 19, 2005	Gainesville, Fla.

Alltime Drag Racing Leaders
NHRA CAREER WINS

*John Force	121
*Warren Johnson	96
Bob Glidden	85
*Pat Austin	75
Kenny Bernstein	69
*Frank Manzo	65
*David Rampy	62
Joe Amato	57
Don Prudhomme	49
*Bob Newberry	48

*Active driver in 2006. Note: Leaders through Oct 22, 2006.

Soccer

Zinedine Zidane's head butt of Italy's Marco Materazzi may have cost France the 2006 World Cup

Losing One's Head

The French succumbed to Italy after one of the most controversial moments in World Cup history, while the young U.S. team failed to live up to expectations

BY HANK HERSCH

A NATION'S HOPES RIDING ON his every decision, a global audience poised to celebrate his greatness, a chance to hoist the most coveted trophy in team sports. No athlete in the last appearance of his career could have even imagined a moment more ripe. On July 9, 2006, midfielder Zinedine Zidane—34 years old, bullet-headed, steely-eyed—marched into the Olympic Stadium in Berlin for the World Cup final. With equal parts genius and determination, he had improbably guided the France side to a match on the grandest stage in sports, after which he would make a confetti-strewn exit from his profession of 18 years.

At least 90 minutes of unscripted drama against Italy remained before Zidane's farewell, but already the parting lines were being written. Eight summers ago, he had announced his brilliance by leading *Les Bleus* to their first World Cup championship, a 3-0 rout of superpower Brazil in which Zidane scored twice on headers. As maestro of two of the planet's most glorious clubs, Juventus of Italy and Real Madrid, he had been a three-time FIFA world player of the year. Now, after

displaying his characteristic calm and prescient passing at Germany 2006, Zidane was on the verge of entering soccer's pantheon alongside such deities as Pelé, Maradona, Platini and Cruyff.

Through regulation play there was no reason to rewrite any of the paeans to Zidane, who is known to most football fans simply as "Zizou." In the seventh minute, he had become the first opponent to score against the Italian team in its seven World Cup matches, banging a penalty kick off the crossbar and past goalkeeper Gianlugi Buffon for a 1-0 lead. Marco "the Matrix" Materazzi drew the *Azzurri* even 12 minutes later, cashing in on an Andrew Pirlo corner kick with his head, but as the game ticked into the second 15-minute overtime, Zidane seemed a better-than-even bet to leave the Cup a champion.

Then, in a jaw-dropping turn, the man with the world at his most skilled feet kicked it away as a spoiled child would a broken toy. Or, more precisely, he head-butted it away. After being jostled by Materazzi in the Italian penalty box, Zidane and the hulking defender exchanged words; two months later "the Matrix" would reveal

that he had made a salubrious suggestion about Zizou's sister. Known for his sangfroid on the ball but prone to the occasional outburst, Zidane responded by lowering his noggin and driving it into the chest of Materazzi, who crumpled to the ground. Red-carded, Zidane left the field, his departure as detrimental to his legacy as it was to France's World Cup quest.

After hanging on through overtime, *Les Bleus* bowed 5-3 in penalty kicks, a forum in which the Italians' failures had been infamous. Zidane didn't speak to the media afterward, though he would apologize in a press conference after his return to France—sort of. "My act is not forgivable," he said. "But they must also punish the true guilty party, and the guilty party is the one who provokes."

Landon Donovan, 24, was named to his sixth MLS All-Star team in 2006, even though his team, the Los Angeles Galaxy, struggled.

Sadly, Zidane's meltdown obscured the glorious achievement of a deeply discounted Italian side, which entered the tournament under the cloud of a bribery scandal involving several of the nation's top clubs (Juventus included). Coach Marcello Lippi used all 20 of his field players and spread the goal-scoring among more players (10) than any champion in World Cup history. Led by 5'9" centerback Fabio Cannavaro, the defense was true to its longtime principles of *catenaccio*, or door-bolt, using superb discipline and communication to bar opponents' entry to their goal. Indeed, the Azzurri tied the record for the fewest goals allowed by a Cup winner: two.

The first of those scores came in group play against the U.S. in a match that turned out to be the highlight of the Americans' brief stay in Germany. Despite a daunting draw—the Czech Republic, Italy and Ghana—the Yanks entered with self-assurance built during their run to the quarterfinals in Japan and South Korea four years earlier. Much of their confidence stemmed from coach Bruce Arena, whose eight-year tenure was longer than any of his 31 peers at the tournament. How had he managed to stick around? "A bit of luck, some hard work, a good group of guys to work for," Arena, 54, told *Sports Illustrated*'s Grant Wahl. "The other part is, everyone likes a winner, and I am a winner. I know how to make a team."

Two of his more inspired choices to start in 2002 were midfielders Landon Donovan and DaMarcus Beasley, a couple of 20-somethings whose fearlessness and relentlessness were infusive. Arena turned to them again in Germany, but they struggled to flash their old form. The Americans dropped their opener to the Czechs 3-0 in Gelsenkirchen, mustering just one scoring chance—a Claudio Reyna blast that caromed off the left post. The drubbing extended the U.S.'s record in World Cup matches in Europe since 1990 to 0-7. "Landon showed no aggressiveness," lamented Arena, who had shifted Donovan to forward and moved his cohort from the left to the right side. "We got nothing out of Beasley."

Without at least a point against Italy in Kaiserslautern, the Yanks had no hope of advancing to the knockout stage. That they got a point was less significant than *how* they did. After surrendering a goal in the 22nd minute, the U.S. equalized in the 27th, when Italian defender Cristian Zaccardo registered an own-goal off a Bobby Convey free kick. A minute later, midfielder Daniele de Rossi's elbow opened a huge gash in U.S. striker Brian McBride's cheek, and the Italian was sent off. But midfielder Pablo Mastroeni squandered the man-advantage with a reckless challenge just before halftime. When veteran defender Eddie Pope was booked for a second yellow two minutes after intermission, the Yanks were fighting for their survival against a grizzled team while playing nine-on-ten.

But fight they did, and in holding on for the tie, they gained a measure of respect around the world. "An amazing result," Arena called it. Five days later in Nuremberg, though, the U.S. went down meekly to Ghana 2-0, and left the tournament having taken just four shots on goal, the fewest of any team. With a 71-30-29 record and .658 winning percentage—both the best in team history—Arena was relieved of his coaching duties.

The Americans' lackluster performance was one of several surprises. Australia, which had never scored a World Cup goal, reached the round of 16, where the Socceroos bowed 1-0 to Italy. German coach Jürgen Klinsmann, lambasted by the press at home for spending the runup to the Cup at his house in Southern California, had his young team playing attractive and attacking soccer—not usual qualities for *Die National-mannschaft*—until it fell 2-0 to Italy on a pair of last-minute goals. And Brazil, perhaps the deepest assemblage of talent in history, seldom summoned the flair for which it's known; even world player of the year Ronaldinho was less than his magical self before his team pulled a one-shot, 1-0 disappearing act against France in the quarterfinals.

But no development in Germany 2006 was as shocking as the great ZZ blowing his top. After Zidane was voted the World Cup's most outstanding player for the second time in his career, FIFA briefly considered stripping him of the award. But whatever ill will his cranial assault generated worldwide proved to be short-lived, especially back in his home country, where fans of his seemed eager to forgive him. Two months after his last match, a French publication did a poll to determine the nation's top celebrity. Replacing Yannick Noah, "Zizou" was No. 1.

World Cup 2006

Group Standings

GROUP A								GROUP E						
Country	GP	W	L	T	GF	GA	Pts	Country	GP	W	L	T	GF	GA	Pts
*Germany	3	3	0	0	8	2	9	*Italy	3	2	0	1	5	1	7
*Ecuador	3	2	1	0	5	3	6	*Ghana	3	2	1	0	4	3	6
Poland	3	1	2	0	2	4	3	Czech Rep.	3	1	2	0	3	4	3
Costa Rica	3	0	3	0	3	9	0	United States	3	0	2	1	2	6	1

GROUP B								GROUP F						
Country	GP	W	L	T	GF	GA	Pts	Country	GP	W	L	T	GF	GA	Pts
*England	3	2	0	1	5	2	7	*Brazil	3	3	0	0	7	1	9
*Sweden	3	1	0	2	3	2	5	*Australia	3	1	1	1	5	5	4
Paraguay	3	1	2	0	2	2	3	Croatia	3	0	1	2	2	3	2
Trin. & Tob.	3	0	2	1	0	4	1	Japan	3	0	2	1	2	7	1

GROUP C								GROUP G						
Country	GP	W	L	T	GF	GA	Pts	Country	GP	W	L	T	GF	GA	Pts
*Argentina	3	2	0	1	8	1	7	*Switzerland	3	2	0	1	4	0	7
*Netherlands	3	2	0	1	3	1	7	*France	3	1	0	2	3	1	5
Ivory Coast	3	1	2	0	5	6	3	South Korea	3	1	1	1	3	4	4
Serbia-Mont.	3	0	3	0	2	10	0	Togo	3	0	3	0	1	6	0

GROUP D								GROUP H						
Country	GP	W	L	T	GF	GA	Pts	Country	GP	W	L	T	GF	GA	Pts
*Portugal	3	3	0	0	5	1	9	*Spain	3	3	0	0	8	1	9
*Mexico	3	1	1	1	4	3	4	*Ukraine	3	2	1	0	5	4	6
Angola	3	0	1	2	1	2	2	Tunisia	3	0	2	1	3	6	1
Iran	3	0	2	1	2	6	1	Saudi Arabia	3	0	2	1	2	7	1

*Advanced to Round of 16.

Note: In group play, teams are awarded three points for a victory, one for a tie. The top two in each group advance to the Round of 16. First tiebreaker is head-to-head competition, second is goal differential, third goals scored.

First Round Scores

GROUP A

Germany 4, Costa Rica 2
Poland 0, Ecuador 2
Germany 1, Poland 0
Ecuador 3, Costa Rica 0
Costa Rica 1, Poland 2
Ecuador 0, Germany 3

GROUP B

England 1, Paraguay 0
Trin. & Tob. 0, Sweden 0
England 2, Trin. & Tob. 0
Sweden 1, Paraguay 0
Paraguay 2, Trin. & Tob. 0
Sweden 2, England 2

GROUP C

Argentina 2, Ivory Coast 1
Serbia-Mont. 0, N'lands 1
Argentina 6, Serbia-Mont. 0
N'lands 2, Ivory Coast 1
Ivory C. 3, Serbia-Mont. 2
N'lands 0, Argentina 0

GROUP D

Mexico 3, Iran 1
Angola 0, Portugal 1
Mexico 0, Angola 0
Portugal 2, Iran 0
Iran 1, Angola 1
Portugal 2, Mexico 1

GROUP E

U.S. 0, Czech Rep. 3
Italy 2, Ghana 0
Czech Rep. 0, Ghana 2
Italy 1, United States 1
Czech Rep. 0, Italy 2
Ghana 2, United States 1

GROUP F

Australia 3, Japan 1
Brazil 1, Croatia 0
Japan 0, Croatia 0
Brazil 2, Australia 0
Croatia 2, Australia 2
Brazil 4, Japan 1

GROUP G

South Korea 2, Togo 1
France 0, Switzerland 0
France 1, South Korea 1
Togo 0, Switzerland 2
Switzerland 2, S. Korea 0
Togo 0, France 2

GROUP H

Spain 4, Ukraine 0
Tunisia 2, Saudi Arabia 2
Saudi Arabia 0, Ukraine 4
Spain 3, Tunisia 1
Saudi Arabia 0, Spain 1
Ukraine 1, Tunisia 0

WORLD CUP FINAL

Germany | Germany (2-0)
Sweden | *Germany (1-1)
Argentina | Argentina (2-0)
Mexico
Italy | Italy (2-0) | *Italy (1-1) (5-3)
Australia | Italy (1-0) | Italy (3-0)
Switzerland
Ukraine | *Ukraine (0-0)

*Portugal (0-0) | England (1-0) | England
Portugal (1-0) | Ecuador
France (1-0) | Portugal
Brazil (3-0) | Netherlands
France (1-0) | Brazil
France (3-1) | Ghana
Spain
France

*Won tie-breaking shootout.

2005 Major League Soccer

2005 Final Standings

EASTERN CONFERENCE

Team	GP	W	L	T	Pts	GF	GA
†*New England	32	17	7	8	59	55	37
*D.C. United	32	16	10	6	54	58	37
*Chicago	32	15	13	4	49	49	50
*MetroStars	32	12	9	11	47	53	49
Kansas City	32	11	9	12	45	52	44
Columbus	32	11	16	5	38	34	45

WESTERN CONFERENCE

Team	GP	W	L	T	Pts	GF	GA
†*San Jose	32	18	4	10	64	53	31
*FC Dallas	32	13	10	9	48	52	44
*Colorado	32	13	13	6	45	40	37
*Los Angeles	32	13	13	6	45	44	45
Real Salt Lake	32	5	22	5	20	30	65
Chivas USA	32	4	22	6	18	31	67

Note: Three points for a win. One point for a tie. †Conference champion. *Qualified for playoffs

SCORING LEADERS

Player, Team	GP	G	A	Pts
Taylor Twellman, NE	25	17	7	41
Jaime Moreno, DC	29	16	7	39
Landon Donovan, LA	22	12	10	34
Amado Guevara, MetroStars	26	11	11	33
Christian Gomez, DC	31	11	9	31
Dwayne De Rosario, SJ	28	9	13	31
Clint Dempsey, NE	26	10	9	29
Josh Wolff, KC	22	10	9	29
Jeff Cunningham, Colo	26	12	3	27

GOALS LEADERS

Player, Team	GP	G
Taylor Twellman, NE	25	17
Jamie Moreno, DC	29	16
Jeff Cunningham, Colo	26	12
Landon Donovan, LA	22	12
Christian Gomez, DC	31	11
Herculez Gomez, LA	22	11
Amado Guevara, MetroStars	26	11
Carlos Ruiz, Dal	19	11

ASSISTS LEADERS

Player, Team	GP	A
Dwayne De Rosario, SJ	28	13
Ronnie O'Brien, Dal	28	12
Simon Elliott, Clmb	32	11
Amado Guevara, MetroStars	26	11
Landon Donovan, LA	22	10
Josh Wolff, KC	22	10
Ronald Cerritos, SJ	30	9
Clint Dempsey, NE	26	9
Christian Gomez, DC	31	9
Chris Klein, KC	31	9

GOALS-AGAINST-AVERAGE LEADERS

Player, Team	GAA
Pat Onstad, SJ	0.97
Jonny Walker, Clmb	1.13
Matt Reis, NE	1.13
Nick Rimando, DC	1.17
Joe Cannon, Colo	1.20
Zach Wells, MetroStars	1.24
Scott Garlick, Dal	1.36

2005 PLAYOFFS

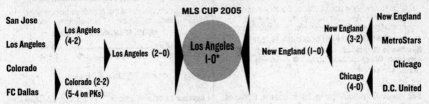

MLS CUP 2005

San Jose							New England
Los Angeles	Los Angeles (4-2)		Los Angeles 1-0*		New England (3-2)		MetroStars
		Los Angeles (2-0)		New England (1-0)			
Colorado							Chicago
FC Dallas	Colorado (2-2) (5-4 on PKs)				Chicago (4-0)		D.C. United

Note: Scores for conference semifinals are two-game aggregates, all others are single games. *Golden-goal overtime.

MLS Cup 2005
FRISCO, TEXAS, NOVEMBER 13, 2005

Los Angeles	0	0	1—1	
New England	0	0	0—0	

Goals: Ramirez 107

Los Angeles—Hartman, Albright, Ihemelu, Marshall, Dunivant, Jones (da Conceicao 11), Nagamura, Vagenas, Grabavoy (Ramirez 66), Donovan, Gomez (Gordan 12)

New England—Reis, Heaps, Pankhurst, Franchino, Riley (Latham 11), Dempsey, Hernandez (Dorman 91+), Joseph, Ralston, Twellman, Noonan, (Cancela 64)

Att: 21,193

International Competition

2006 U.S. Men's National Team Results

Date	Opponent	Result	U.S. Goals	Site
Jan. 22	Canada	0–0 T	—	San Diego, Calif.
Jan. 29	Norway	5-0 W	Twellman (3), Pope, Klein	Carson, Calif.
Feb. 10	Japan	3–2 W	Pope, Dempsey, Twellman	San Francisco, Calif.
Feb. 19	Guatemala	4-0 W	Olson, Ching, Johnson, Klein	Frisco, Tex.
March 1	Poland	1-0 W	Dempsey	Kaiserslautern, Germany
March 22	Germany	1–4 L	Cherundolo	Dortmund, Germany
April 11	Jamaica	1-1 T	Olsen	Cary, N.C.
May 23	Morocco	0–1 L	—	Nashville, Tenn.
May 26	Venezuela	2–0 W	Ching, Dempsey	Cleveland, Ohio
May 28	Latvia	1–0 W	McBride	East Hartford, Conn.
June 12	Czech Rep.†	0–3 L	—	Gelsenkirchen, Germany
June 17	Italy †	1-1 T	Zaccardo (own goal)	Kaiserslautern, Germany
June 22	Ghana †	1–2 L	Dempsey	Nuremberg, Germany

†-World Cup tournament play

2006 U.S. Women's National Team Results

Date	Opponent	Result	U.S. Goals	Site
Jan. 18	Norway #	3-1 W	Lilly, Boxx, Wambach	Guangzhou, China
Jan. 20	France #	0–0 T	—	Guangzhou, China
Jan. 22	China #	2-0 W	Lilly (2)	Guangzhou, China
March 9	China @	0–0 T	—	Faro, Portugal
March 11	Denmark @	5-0 W	Wambach, Lilly (2), Lilly, Kai	Quarteira, Portugal
March 13	France @	4–1 W	Lilly, Wagner, Tarpley, Kai	Faro, Portugal
March 15	Germany @	0-0 T (3-4 PKs)—		Faro, Portugal
May 7	Japan	3–1 W	Wambach (3)	Kumamoto, Japan
May 9	Japan	1–0 W	Kai	Osaka, Japan
July 15	Sweden	3-2 W	Wambach, Lilly, Kai	Blaine, Minn.
July 23	Ireland	5-0 W	Whitehill (2), Reilly, Wambach, Kai	San Diego, Calif.
July 30	Canada	2-0 W	Wambach, Kai	Cary, N.C.
Aug 27	China	4-1 W	Whitehill, Wagner, Lilly (2)	Bridgeview, Ill.
Sept. 13	Mexico	3–1 W	Wambach (2), Tarpley	Rochester, N.Y.

#Four Nations tournament play; @ Algarve Cup tournament play.

World Club Championship

Club champions from Europe, South America, Oceania, Asia, Africa and North America compete (was formerly Intercontinental Cup).

YOKOHAMA, JAPAN: DECEMBER 18, 2005

São Paulo (Braz) 0	1—1	
Liverpool (Eng) 0	0—0	

Goals: Mineiro 27

Att: 66,821

São Paulo: Rogerio, Cicinho, Fabio Santos, Edcarlos, Lugano, Junior, Mineiro, Josue, Danilo, Amoroso, Aloisio (Grafite 75).

Liverpool: Reina, Carragher, Warnock (Riise 79), Finnan, Hyypia, Kewell, Gerrard, Luis Garcia, Alonso, Morientes (Crouch 85), Sissoko (Sinama Pongolle 79).

UEFA Cup

Competition between teams other than league champions and cup-winners from UEFA.

EINDHOVEN, NETHERLANDS: MAY 10, 2006

FC Sevilla (Spain) 1	3—4	
Middlesbrough (Eng) 0	0—0	

Goals: Fabiano 27, Maresca 78, Maresca 84, Kanoute 89

Att: 36,500.

FC Sevilla: Palop, Daniel, David, Escude, Navarro, Maresca, Marti, Navas, Saviola (Kanoute 45), Fabiano (Renato 73), Adriano (Puerta 85).

Middlesbrough: Schwarzer, Parnaby, Queudrue , Riggott, Southgate, Boateng, Downing (Maccarone 45) Morrison, Rochemback, Viduka (Cattermole 85), Hasselbaink

European Cup (Champions League)

League champions of the countries belonging to UEFA (Union of European Football Associations).

PARIS, FRANCE: MAY 17, 2006

Arsenal (Eng) 1	0—1	
FC Barcelona (Spain) 0	2—2	

Goals: Campbell 37; Eto'o 76, Belletti 80.

Att: 79,500.

Arsenal: Lehmann, Eboue, Toure, Campbell, Cole, Pires (Almunia 20), Silva, Fabregas (Flamini 74), Hleb (Reyes 85), Ljungberg, Henry.

FC Barcelona: Valdes, Oleguer (Belletti 71), Marquez, Puyol, Van Bronckhorst, Deco, Edmilson (Iniesta 45), Van Bommel (Larsson 61), Giuly, Eto'o, Ronaldinho.

Libertadores Cup

Competition between champion clubs and runners-up of 10 South American National Associations.

(1ST LEG) SAO PAULO, BRAZIL: AUGUST 9, 2006

São Paulo (Braz) 0	1—1	
Internacional (Braz) 0	2—2	

(2ND LEG) PORTO ALEGRE, BRAZIL: AUGUST 16, 2006

São Paulo* (Braz) 0	2—2	
Internacional (Braz) 1	1—2	

Internacional wins, two-game aggregate score: 4—3;

(1ST LEG)

Goals: Sobis 53, Sobis 62, Edcarlos 75

Att: 71,456.

São Paulo: Rogerio Ceni, Fabao, Edcarlos (Aloisio 76), Lugano, Junior, Mineiro, Josué, Leandro (Richarlyson 86), Danilo (Lenilson 63), Ricardo Oliveira, Souza

Internacional: Clemer, Bolivar, Eller, Fabinho, Tinga, Fernandao, Sobis (Michel 78), Ceara (Monteiro 56), Edinho, Wagner, Alex (Indio 74)

(2ND LEG)

Goals: Fernando 29, Fabao 50, Tinga 66, Lenilson 85.

Att: 55,000.

São Paulo: Rogerio Ceni, Fabao, Richarlyson (Thiago 58), Edcarlos (Diaz 70), Lugano, Junior, Mineiro, Leandro, Danilo (Lenilson 58), Souza, Aloisio

Internacional: Clemer, Bolivar, Eller, Tinga, Fernandao, Sobis (Edigle 82), Indio, Ceara, Edinho, Wagner, Alex (Michel 78)

2005-2006 Club Champions—Europe

Country	League Champion	League Scoring Leader, Club	Cup Winner
Albania	SK Elbasani	Hamdi Salihi, SK Tirana	SK Tirana
Andorra	Ranger's FC	n/a	Santa Coloma
Armenia	Pyunik Yerevan*	Nshan Erzrumian, Kilikia Yerevan*	Mika Ashtarak
Austria	Austria Wien	Sanel Kuljic, Reid; Roland Linz, Austria Wien	Austria Wien
Azerbaijan	FK Baki	Yacouba Bamba, Karvan Yevlax	Qarabag Agdam
Belarus	Shakhtsyor Salihorsk*	Valery Stipeikis, Naftan Navapolatsk*	BATE Barysau
Belgium	Anderlecht	Tosin Dosunmu, Germinal Beerschot	Zulte-Waregem
Bosnia & Herz	Siroki Brijeg	n/a	Orasje
Bulgaria	Levski Sofia	Jose Furtado, Vihren/CSKA Sofia	CSKA Sofia
Channel Islands	Belgrave Wanderers	n/a	Northeners
Croatia	Dinamo Zagreb	n/a	Rijeka/Varteks Varazdin
Cyprus	Apollon Limasol	Lukasz Sosin, Apollon Limasol	APOEL Nicosia
Czech Republic	FC Slovan Liberec	Milan Ivana, Slovacko	AC Sparta Praha
Denmark	FC København	Steffen Højer, Viborg	Randers FC
England	Chelsea	Thierry Henry, Arsenal	Liverpool
Estonia	TVMK Tallinn*	Tarmo Neemelo, TVMK Tallinn*	TVMK Tallinn
Faroe Islands	B36*	Christian Hogni Jacbosen, NSI*	GI Gota*
Finland	MyPa Anjalankoski*	Juho Mäkela, HJK Helsinki*	Haka Valkeakoski*
France	Olympique Lyonnais	Pedro Pauleta, Paris Saint-Germain	Paris Saint-Germain FC
Georgia	Sioni Bolnisi	Jaba Dvali, Dinamo Tbilisi	Ameri Tblisi
Germany	Bayern München	Miroslav Klose, SV Werder Bremen	Bayern München
Greece	Olympiakos Piraeus	n/a	Olympiakos Piraeus
Hungary	Debreceni Vasutas	Peter Rajczi, Ujpest	Fehervar
Iceland	FH Hafnarfjörour	Marel Johann Baldvinsson, Breidablik	Valur*
Ireland	Cork City*	Jason Byrne, Shelbourne*	Drogheda United*
Israel	Maccabi Haifa	Shai Holtzman, Ashdod SC	Hapoel Tel Aviv
Italy	FC Internazionale †	Luca Toni, Fiorentina	FC Internazionale
Kazakhstan	Aktobe LenTo*	Murat Tleshev, Irtysh Pavlodar	Zhenis Astana
Latvia	Liepajas Metalurgs*	Viktor Dobrecovs, Metalurgs* Igors Slesarcuks, Venta/Ventspils*	FK Ventspils*
Lithuania	Ekranas Panevezys*	Mantas Savenas, Ekranas Panevezys*	FBK Kaunas*
Luxembourg	F 91 Dudelange	Fatih Sozen, Grevenmacher	F91 Dudelange
Macedonia	Rabotniki Kometal Skopje	Stevica Ristic, Sileks	Makedonija Skopje
Malta	Birkirkara	n/a	Hibernians
Moldova	Sheriff Tiraspol	Alexei Kuckiuk, Sheriff Tiraspol	Sheriff Tiraspol
Netherlands	PSV Eindhoven	Klass Jan Huntelaar, SC Heerenveen	Ajax Amsterdam
Northern Ireland	Linfield FC	Peter Thompson, Linfield FC	Linfield FC
Norway	Välerenga IF*	Ole Martin Årst, Tromsø*	Molde FK*
Poland	Legia Warszawa	n/a	Wisla Plock
Portugal	FC Porto	Albert Meyong Zé, CF "Os Belenenses"	FC Porto
Romania	Steaua Bucharesti	n/a	Rapid Bucharesti
Russia	CSKA Moskva*	Dmitriy Kirichenko, FK Moskva*	CSKA Moskva*
San Marino	SS Murata	n/a	Libertas
Scotland	Celtic	n/a	Heart of Midlothian
Serbia and Montenegro	Crvena zvevda Beograd	Srdjan Radonjic, Partizan	Crvena zvevda Beograd
Slovakia	MFK Ruzomberok	Robert Rak, FC Nitra Erik Jendrisek, Ruzomberok	MFK Ruzomberok
Slovenia	NK Rudar	Miran Burgic, HIT Gorica	Koper
Spain	FC Barcelona	Samuel Eto'o, FC Barcelona	RC Español
Sweden	Djurgårdens IF*	Gunnar Thorvaldsson, Halmstads BK*	Djurgårdens IF*
Switzerland	FC Zürich	Keita Alhassane, FC Zürich	FC Sion
Turkey	Galatasaray Istanbul	n/a	Besiktas Istanbul
Ukraine	Shakhtar Donetsk	Brandao, Shakhtar Donetsk Emmanuel Okoduwa, Arsenal Kiev	Dynamo Kiev
Wales	TNS Llansantffraid	Marc Lloyd-Williams, TNS Llant.	Rhyl FC

Note: Results are from 2006 unless followed by *.
†-Juventus had its title retroactively revoked for 2005–06 and 2004–05 due to player use of performance enhancing drugs.

The World Cup

Results

Year	Champion	Score	Runner-Up	Winning Coach
1930	Uruguay	4–2	Argentina	Alberto Supicci
1934	Italy	2–1	Czechoslovakia	Vittorio Pozzo
1938	Italy	4–2	Hungary	Vittorio Pozzo
1950	Uruguay	2–1	Brazil	Juan Lopez
1954	W Germany	3–2	Hungary	Sepp Herberger
1958	Brazil	5–2	Sweden	Vicente Feola
1962	Brazil	3–1	Czechoslovakia	Aymore Moreira
1966	England	4–2	W Germany	Alf Ramsey
1970	Brazil	4–1	Italy	Mario Zagalo
1974	W Germany	2–1	Netherlands	Helmut Schoen
1978	Argentina	3–1	Netherlands	César Menotti
1982	Italy	3–1	W Germany	Enzo Bearzot
1986	Argentina	3–2	W Germany	Carlos Bilardo
1990	W Germany	1–0	Argentina	Franz Beckenbauer
1994	Brazil	0–0 (3–2)	Italy	Carlos Alberto Parreira
1998	France	3–0	Brazil	Aime Jacquet
2002	Brazil	2–0	Germany	Luis Felipe Scolari
2006	Italy	1–1 (5–3)	France	Marcello Lippi

Alltime World Cup Participation

Nation	Matches	W	T	L	Goals For	Goals Against
Brazil	92	64	14	14	201	84
*Germany	92	55	19	18	190	112
Italy	77	44	19	14	122	69
Argentina	65	33	13	19	113	73
England	55	25	17	13	74	47
France	51	25	10	16	95	64
Spain	49	22	12	15	80	60
†Russia	37	17	6	14	64	44
Yugoslavia	37	17	6	14	60	46
Netherlands	35	16	10	9	58	36
Poland	31	15	5	11	44	40
Hungary	32	15	3	14	87	57
Uruguay	40	15	10	15	65	57
Sweden	45	15	11	19	70	69
Austria	29	12	4	13	42	48
Czech Republic	33	12	5	16	47	49
Portugal	19	11	1	7	32	21
Mexico	45	11	12	22	48	84
Belgium	36	10	9	17	46	63
Romania	21	8	5	8	30	32
Switzerland	26	8	5	13	37	51
Denmark	13	7	2	4	24	18
Chile	25	7	6	12	31	40
Paraguay	22	6	7	9	27	36
United States	25	6	3	16	27	51
Turkey	10	5	1	4	20	17
Croatia	12	5	2	5	13	10
Nigeria	11	4	1	6	14	16
Cameroon	17	4	7	6	16	28
Peru	15	4	3	8	19	31
Scotland	23	4	7	12	25	41
S. Korea	24	4	7	13	21	53
Ecuador	7	3	0	4	7	8
Northern Ireland	13	3	5	5	13	23
Costa Rica	10	3	1	6	12	21
Colombia	13	3	2	8	14	23
Bulgaria	25	3	8	14	22	49
Wales	5	2	6	1	10	7
Senegal	5	2	2	1	7	6
Ukraine	5	2	1	1	5	7
E Germany	6	2	2	2	5	5
Ghana	4	2	0	2	4	6
Norway	8	2	3	3	7	8
Algeria	6	2	1	3	6	10
Morocco	10	2	4	4	10	13
Japan	10	2	2	6	8	14
Saudi Arabia	13	2	2	9	9	32
Cuba	3	1	1	1	5	12
S Africa	6	1	3	2	8	11
N Korea	4	1	1	2	5	9
Ivory Coast	3	1	0	2	5	6
Jamaica	3	1	0	2	3	9
Israel	3	1	0	2	1	3
Republic of Ireland	13	2	7	4	10	10
Australia	7	1	2	4	5	11
Iran	9	1	2	6	6	18
Tunisia	12	1	4	7	8	17
Honduras	3	0	2	1	2	3
Angola	3	0	2	1	1	2
Dutch East Indies	1	0	0	1	0	6
Egypt	4	0	2	2	3	6
Kuwait	3	0	1	2	2	6
Trinidad and Tobago	3	0	1	2	0	4
Slovenia	3	0	0	3	2	7
Serbia & Montenegro	3	0	0	3	2	10
United Arab Emirates	3	0	0	3	2	11
New Zealand	3	0	0	3	2	12
Haiti	3	0	0	3	2	14
Iraq	3	0	0	3	1	4
Togo	3	0	0	3	1	6
Canada	3	0	0	3	0	5
Greece	3	0	0	3	0	8
China	3	0	0	3	0	9
Zaire	3	0	0	3	0	14
Bolivia	6	0	1	5	1	20
El Salvador	6	0	0	6	1	22

*Includes West Germany 1950–90. †Includes USSR 1930–1990.
Note: Matches decided by penalty kicks are shown as drawn games.

World Cup Final Box Scores

URUGUAY 1930

Uruguay	1	3	——4
Argentina	2	0	——2

FIRST HALF

Scoring: 1, Uruguay, Dorado (12); 2, Argentina, Peucelle (20); 3, Argentina, Stabile (37).

SECOND HALF

Scoring: 4, Uruguay, Cea (57); 5, Uruguay, Iriarte (68); 6, Uruguay, Castro (89).

Argentina: Botosso, Della Toree, Paternoster, J. Evaristo, Monti, Suarez, Peucelle, Varallo, Stabile, Ferreira, M. Evaristo.

Uruguay: Ballesteros, Nasazzi, Mascheroni, Andrade, Fernandez, Gestido, Dorado, Scarone, Castro, Cea, Iriarte.

Referee: Langenus (Belgium).

ITALY 1934

Italy	0	1	1——2
Czechoslovakia	0	1	0——1

SECOND HALF

Scoring: 1, Czech., Puc (70); 2, Italy, Orsi (80).

OVERTIME

Scoring: 3, Italy, Schiavio (95).

Italy: Combi, Monzeglio, Allemandi, Ferraris Monti, Monti, Bertolini, Guaita, Meazza, Schiavio, Ferrari, Orsi.

Czechoslovakia: Planicka, Zenisek, Ctyroky, Kostalek, Cambal, Cambal, Krcil, Junek, Svoboda, Sobotka, Nejedly, Puc.

Referee: Eklind (Sweden).

FRANCE 1938

Italy	3	1	——4
Hungary	1	1	——2

FIRST HALF

Scoring: 1, Italy, Colaussi (5); 2, Hungary, Titkos (7); 3, Italy, Piola (16); 4, Italy, Piola (35).

SECOND HALF

Scoring: 5, Hungary, Sarosi (70); 6, Italy, Colaussi (82).

Italy: Olivieri, Foni, Rava, Serantoni, Andreolo, Locatelli, Biavati, Meazza, Piola, Ferrari, Colaussi.

Hungary: Szabo, Polger, Biro, Szalay, Szucs, Lazar, Sas, Vincze, Sarosi, Zsengeller, Titkos.

Referee: Capdeville (France).

BRAZIL 1950

Uruguay	0	2	——2
Brazil	0	1	——1

SECOND HALF

Scoring: 1, Brazil, Friaca (47); 2, Uruguay, Schiaffino (66); 3, Uruguay, Ghiggia (79).

Uruguay: Maspoli, Gonzales, Tejera, Gambretta, Varela, Andrade, Ghiggia, Perez, Miguez, Schiffiano, Moran.

Brazil: Barbosa, Augusto, Juvenal, Bauer, Banilo, Bigode, Friaca, Zizinho, Ademir, Jair, Chico.

Referee: Reader (England).

SWITZERLAND 1954

W Germany	2	1	——3
Hungary	2	0	——2

FIRST HALF

Scoring: 1, Hungary, Puskas (6); 2, Hungary, Czibor (8); 3, W Germ., Morlock (10); 4, W Germ., Rahn (18).

SECOND HALF

Scoring: 5, W Germany, Rahn (84).

W Germany: Turek, Posipal, Kohlmeyer, Eckel, Liebrich, Mai, Rahn, Morlock, O.Walter, F. Walter, Schaefer.

Hungary: Grosics, Buzansky, Lantos, Bozsik, Lorant, Zakarias, Czibor, Kocsis, Hidegkuti, Puskas, Toth.

Referee: Ling (England).

SWEDEN 1958

Brazil	2	3	——5
Sweden	1	1	——2

FIRST HALF

Scoring:1, Sweden, Liedholm (3); 2, Brazil, Vava (9); 3, Brazil, Vava (32).

SECOND HALF

Scoring: 4, Brazil, Pelé (55); 5, Brazil, Zagalo (68); 6, Sweden Simonsson (80); 7, Brazil, Pelé (90).

Brazil: Glymar, D. Santos, N. Santos, Zito, Bellini, Orlando, Garrincha, Didi, Vava, Pelé, Zagalo.

Sweden: Svensson, Bergmark, Axbom, Boerjesson, Gustavsson, Parling, Hamrin, Gren, Simonsson, Liedholm, Skoglund.

Referee: Guigue (France).

CHILE 1962

Brazil	1	2	——3
Czechoslovakia	1	0	——1

FIRST HALF

Scoring: 1, Czech., Masopust (15); 2, Brazil, Amarildo (17).

SECOND HALF

Scoring: 3, Brazil, Zito (68); 4, Brazil, Vava (77).

Brazil: Glymar, D. Santos, N. Santos, Zito, Mauro, Zozimo, Garrincha, Didi, Vava, Amarildo, Zagalo.

Czechoslovakia: Schroiff, Tichy, Novak, Pluskal, Popluhar, Masopust, Pospichal, Scherer, Kvasnak, Kadraba, Jelinek.

Referee: Latychev (USSR).

World Cup Final Box Scores *(Cont.)*

ENGLAND 1966

England....................	l	l	2 ——4
W Germany.............	l	l	0 ——2

FIRST HALF

Scoring: 1, W Germany, Haller (12); 2, England, Hurst (18).

SECOND HALF

Scoring: 3, England, Peters (78); 4, W. Germany, Weber (90).

OVERTIME

Scoring: 5, England, Hurst (101); 6, England, Hurst (120).

England: Banks, Cohen, Wilson, Stiles, J. Charlton, Moore, Ball, Hurst, Hunt, R. Charlton, Peters.

W Germany: Tilkowski, Hottges, Schmellinger, Beckenbauer, Schulz, Weber, Held, Haller, Seeler, Overath, Emmerich.

Referee: Dienst (Switzerland).

MEXICO 1970

Brazil.....................	l	3 ——4
Italy	l	0 ——1

FIRST HALF

Scoring: 1, Brazil, Pelé (18); 2, Italy, Boninsegna (32).

SECOND HALF

Scoring: 3, Brazil, Gerson (65); 4, Brazil, Jairzinho (70); 5, Brazil, Alberto (86).

Brazil: Feliz, Alberto, Brito, Wilson, Piazza, Everaldo, Clodoaldo, Gerson, Jairzinho, Tostao, Pelé, Rivelino.

Italy: Albertosi, Burgnich, Cera, Rosato, Facchetti, Bertini (Juliano), Mazzola, De Sisti, Domenghini, Boninsegna (Rivera), Riva.

Referee: Glockner (E Germany).

W GERMANY 1974

W Germany 2	0 ——2
Netherlands.............l	0 ——1

FIRST HALF

Scoring: 1, Netherlands, Neeskens, PK (1); 2, W Germany, Breitner, PK (26); 3, W Germany, Müller (44).

W Germany: Maier, Vogts, Beckenbauer, Schwarzenbeck, Breitner, Hoeness, Bonhof, Overath, Grabowski, Müller, Holzenbein.

Netherlands: Jongbloed, Suurbier, Rijsbergen (de Jong), Haan, Krol, Jansen, Neeskens, van Hanagem, Cruyff, Rensenbrink (van der Kerkhof).

Referee: Taylor (England).

ARGENTINA 1978

Argentina l	0	2 ——3
Netherlands...........0	l	0 ——1

FIRST HALF

Scoring: 1, Argentina, Kempes (38).

SECOND HALF

Scoring: 2, Netherlands, Nanninga (81).

OVERTIME

Scoring: 3, Arg., Kempes (104); 4, Arg., Bertoni (114).

ARGENTINA 1978 *(Cont.)*

Argentina: Fillol, Olguin, Galvan, Passarella, Tarantini, Ardiles (Larrosa), Gallego, Kempes, Bertoni, Luque, Ortiz (Houseman).

Netherlands: Jongbloed, Jansen (Suurbier), Krol, Brandts, Poortvliet, Neeskens, Haan, W. van der Kerkhoff, R. van der Kerkhoff, Rep (Nanninga), Rensenbrink.

Referee: Gonella (Italy).

ITALY 1982

Italy 0	3 ——3
W Germany 0	l ——l

SECOND HALF

Scoring: 1, Italy, Rossi (57); 2, Italy, Tardelli (68); 3, Italy, Altobelli (81); 4, W Germany, Breitner (83).

Italy: Zoff, Bergomi, Scirea, Collovati, Cabrini, Oriali, Gentile, Tardelli, Conti, Rossi, Graziani (Altobelli, Causio).

W Germany: Schumacher, Kaltz, Stielike, K. Foerster, B. Foerster, Dremmler (Hrubesch), Breitner, Briegel, Rummenigge (Müller), Fishcher (Littbarski).

Referee: Coelho (Brazil).

MEXICO 1986

Argentina l	2 ——3
W Germany 0	2 ——2

FIRST HALF

Scoring: 1, Argentina, Brown (22).

SECOND HALF

Scoring: 2, Arg., Valdano (55); 3, W Germ., Rummenigge (73); 4, W Germ., Voller (81); 5, Arg., Burruchaga (83).

Argentina: Pumpido, Brown, Cuciuffo, Ruggeri, Olarticoecha, Bastista, Giusti, Burruchaga (Trobbiani 90), Enrique, Maradona, Valdona.

W Germany: Schumacher, Jakobs, Forster, Eder, Brehme, Matthaus, Berthold, Magath (Hoeness 62), Briegel, Rummenigge, Allofs (Voller 46).

Referee: Filho (Brazil).

ITALY 1990

W Germany 0	l —— l
Argentina 0	0 ——0

SECOND HALF

Scoring: 1, W Germany, Brehme, PK (84).

W Germany: Illgner, Brehme, Kohler, Augenthaler, Buchwald, Berthold (Reuter), Littbarski, Haessler, Mattaeus, Voeller, Klinsmann.

Argentina: Goychoechea, Lorenzo, Serrizuela, Sensini, Ruggeri (Monzon), Simon, Basualdo, Burruchag (Calderon), Maradona, Troglio, Dezottir.

Referee: Coelho (Brazil).

UNITED STATES 1994

Italy 0	0	0——0
Brazil........................0	0	0——0

Scoring: None. Shootout goals: Italy—2: Albertini, Evani; Brazil—3: Romario, Branco, Dunga.

Italy: Pagliuca, Benarrivo, Maldini, Baresi, Mussi

World Cup Final Box Scores *(Cont.)*

UNITED STATES 1994 *(Cont.)*

(Apolloni 35), Albertini, D. Baggio (Evani 95), Berti, Donadoni, Baggio, Massaro.

Brazil: Taffarel, Jorginho (Cafu 21), Branco, Aldair, Santos, Silva, Dunga, Zinho (Viola 106), Mazinho, Bebeto, Romario.

Referee: Puhl (Hungary).

FRANCE 1998

Brazil	0	0——0
France	2	1——3

FIRST HALF

Scoring: 1, France, Zidane (27); 2, France, Zidane (45).

SECOND HALF

Scoring: 3, France, Petit (90).

Brazil: Taffarel, Cafu, Aldair, Baiano, Carlos, Sampaio (Edmundo 74), Dunga, Rivaldo, Leonardo, (Denilson 46), Bebeto, Ronaldo.

France: Barthez, Lizarazu, Desailly, Thuram, Leboeuf, Djorkaeff (Vieira 75) Deschamps, Zidane, Petit, Karembeu (Boghossian 57), Guivarc'h (Dugarry 66).

Referee: Belqola (Morocco).

KOREA/JAPAN 2002

Brazil	0	2——2
Germany	0	0——0

SECOND HALF

Scoring: 1, Brazil, Ronaldo (67); 2, Brazil, Ronaldo (79).

Brazil: Marcos, Cafu, Lucio, Roque Junior, Edmilson, Carlos, Silva, Ronaldo (Denilson, 90), Rivaldo, Ronaldinho (Juninho, 85), Kleberson.

Germany: Kahn, Linke, Ramelow, Neuville, Hamann, Klose (Bierhoff, 74), Jeremies (Asamoah, 77), Bode (Ziege, 84), Schneider, Metzelder, Frings.

Referee: Collina (Italy).

GERMANY 2006

Italy	1	0	0 ——1
France	1	0	0 ——1

Italy won on penalty kicks, 5–3.

FIRST HALF

Scoring: 1, France, Zidane (7); 1, Italy, Materazzi (19).

Shootout Goals: Italy—Pirlo, Materazzi, De Rossi, Del Piero, Grosso; France—Wiltord, Abidal, Sagnol.

Italy: Buffon, Zambrotta, Cannavaro, Materazzi, Grosso, Camoranesi (Del Piero 86), Pirlo, Gattuso, Perrotta (Iaquinta 61), Totti (De Rossi 61), Toni.

France: Barthez, Sagnol, Thuram, Gallas, Abidal, Ribery (Trezeguet 100), Vieira (Diarra 56), Makelele, Zidane, Malouda, Henry (Wiltord 107).

Referee: Elizondo (Argentina).

Alltime Leaders

GOALS

Player, Nation	Tournaments	Goals	Player, Nation	Tournaments	Goals
Ronaldo, Brazil	1998, 2002, '04, '06	15	Miroslav Klose, Germany	2002, '04	10
Gerd Müller, W Germany	1970, '74	14	Ademir, Brazil	1950	9
Just Fontaine, France	1958	13	Eusebio, Portugal	1966	9
Pelé, Brazil	1958, '62, '66, '70	12	Jairzinho, Brazil	1970, '74	9
Sandor Kocsis, Hungary	1954	11	Paolo Rossi, Italy	1982, '86	9
Teofilo Cubillas, Peru	1970, '78	10	K.H. Rummenigge, W Ger	1978, '82, '86	9
Gregorz Lato, Poland	1974, '78, '82	10	Uwe Seeler, W Germany	1958, '62, '66, '70	9
Helmut Rahn, W Germany	1954, '58	10	Vava, Brazil	1958, '62	9
Gary Lineker, England	1986, '90	10			

LEADING SCORER, CUP BY CUP

Year	Player, Nation	Goals	Year	Player, Nation	Goals
1930	Guillermo Stabile, Argentina	8	1970	Gerd Müller, W Germany	10
1934	Oldrich Nejedly, Czechoslovakia	5	1974	Gregorz Lato, Poland	7
1938	Leonidas da Silva, Brazil	8	1978	Mario Kempes, Argentina	6
1950	Ademir de Menezes, Brazil	9	1982	Paolo Rossi, Italy	6
1954	Sandor Kocsis, Hungary	11	1986	Gary Lineker, England	6
1958	Just Fontaine, France	13	1990	Salvatore Schillaci, Italy	6
1962	Florian Albert, Hungary	4	1994	Hristo Stoichkov, Bulgaria	6
	Valentin Ivanov, USSR, Garrincha, Brazil,			Oleg Salenko, Russia	
	Vava, Brazil, Drazan Jerkovic, Yugoslavia,		1998	Davor Suker, Croatia	6
	Leonel Sanchez, Chile		2002	Ronaldo, Brazil	8
1966	Eusebio Ferreira, Portugal	9	2006	Miroslav Klose, Germany	5

Most Goals, Individual, One Game

Goals	Player, Nation	Score	Date
5	Oleg Salenko, Russia	Russia–Cameroon, 6–1	6-28-94
4	Leonidas, Brazil	Brazil–Poland, 6–5	6-5-38
4	Ernest Willimowski, Poland	Brazil–Poland, 6–5	6-5-38
4	Gustav Wetterstrîm, Sweden	Sweden–Cuba, 8–0	6-12-38
4	Juan Alberto Schiaffino, Uruguay	Uruguay–Bolivia, 8–0	7-2-50
4	Ademir, Brazil	Brazil–Sweden, 7–1	7-9-50

Most Goals, Individual, One Game *(Cont.)*

Goals	Player, Nation	Score	Date
4	Sandor Kocsis, Hungary	Hungary–W Germany, 8–3	6-20-54
4	Just Fontaine, France	France–W Germany, 6–3	6-28-58
4	Eusebio, Portugal	Portugal–N Korea, 5–3	7-23-66
4	Emilio Butragueño, Spain	Spain–Denmark, 5–1	6-18-86

Note: 31 players have scored 32 World Cup hat tricks. Gerd Müller of West Germany is the only man to have two World Cup hat tricks, both in 1970. The last hat tricks were 6-1-02, Miroslav Klose (Ger) vs. Saudi Arabia; 6-21-98, Gabriel Batistuta (Arg) vs. Jamaica; 6-23-90, Tomas Skuhravy (Czech) vs. Costa Rica; and 6-17-90, Michel (Spain) vs. S Korea.

Attendance and Goal Scoring, Year by Year

Year	Site	No. of Games	Goals	Goals/Game	Attendance	Avg Att
1930	Uruguay	18	70	3.89	434,500	24,139
1934	Italy	17	70	4.12	395,000	23,235
1938	France	18	84	4.67	483,000	26,833
1950	Brazil	22	88	4.00	1,337,000	60,773
1954	Switzerland	26	140	5.38	943,000	36,269
1958	Sweden	35	126	3.60	868,000	24,800
1962	Chile	32	89	2.78	776,000	24,250
1966	England	32	89	2.78	1,614,677	50,459
1970	Mexico	32	95	2.97	1,673,975	52,312
1974	W Germany	38	97	2.55	1,774,022	46,685
1978	Argentina	38	102	2.68	1,610,215	42,374
1982	Spain	52	146	2.80	1,856,277	35,698
1986	Mexico	52	132	2.54	2,441,731	46,956
1990	Italy	52	115	2.21	2,514,443	48,354
1994	United States	52	140	2.69	3,567,415	68,604
1998	France	64	171	2.67	2,775,400	43,366
2002	Korea/Japan	64	161	2.52	2,705,216	42,269
2006	Germany	64	147	2.23	3,353,655	52,401
Totals		644	1,901	2.95	28,418,310	44,128

The United States in the World Cup

Date	Opponent	Result	Scoring
URUGUAY 1930: FINAL COMPETITION			
7-13-30	Belgium	3–0 W	U.S.: McGhee 2, Patenaude
7-17-30	Paraguay	3–0 W	U.S.: Patenaude 2, Florie
7-26-30	Argentina	1–6 L	Arg.: Monti 2, Scopelli 2, Stabile 2; U.S.: Brown.
ITALY 1934: FINAL COMPETITION			
5-27-34	Italy	1–7 L	U.S.: Donelli; Italy: Schiavio 3, Orsi 2, Meazza, Ferrari
BRAZIL 1950: FINAL COMPETITION			
6-25-50	Spain	1–3 L	U.S.: Pariani; Spain: Igoa, Basora, Zarra
6-29-50	England	1–0 W	U.S.: Gaetjens.
7-2-50	Chile	2–5 L	U.S.: Wallace, Maca; Chile: Robledo, Cremaschi 3, Prieto
ITALY 1990: FINAL COMPETITION			
6-10-90	Czechoslovakia	1–5 L	U.S.: Caligiuri; Czech.: Skuhravy 2, Hasek, Bilek, Luhovy
6-14-90	Italy	0–1 L	Italy: Giannini
6-19-90	Austria	1–2 L	U.S.: Murray; Austria: Rodax, Ogris

Date	Opponent	Result	Scoring
UNITED STATES 1994: FINAL COMPETITION			
6-18-94	Switzerland	1–1 T	U.S.: Wynalda; Switz.: Bregy
6-22-94	Colombia	2–1 W	U.S.: Escobar (own goal), Stewart; Colombia: Valencia
6-26-94	Romania	1–0 L	Romania: Petrescu
7-4-94	Brazil	1–0 L	Brazil: Bebeto
FRANCE 1998: FINAL COMPETITION			
6-15-98	Germany	2–0 L	Germany: Möller, Klinsmann
6-21-98	Iran	2–1 L	U.S.: McBride; Iran: Estili, Mahdavikia
6-25-98	Yugoslavia	1–0 L	Yugoslavia: Komljenovic
KOREA/JAPAN 2002: FINAL COMPETITION			
6-5-02	Portugal	3–2 W	U.S.: O'Brien, Costa (own goal), McBride; Portugal: Beto, Agoos (own goal)
6-10-02	S Korea	1–1 T	U.S.: Mathis; S Korea: Ahn
6-14-02	Poland	3–1 L	Poland: Olisadebe, Kryszalowicz, Zewlakow; U.S.: Donovan
6-17-02	Mexico	2–0 W	U.S.: McBride, Donovan
6-21-02	Germany	1–0 L	Germany: Ballack

The United States in the World Cup *(Cont.)*

Date	Opponent	Result	Scoring
2006: FINAL COMPETITION			
6-12-06	Czech Rep.	0–3 L	Czech Rep: Koller, Rosicky (2)
6-17-06	Italy	1–1 T	U.S.: Zaccardo (own goal)
			Italy: Giardino
6-22-06	Ghana	1–2 L	U.S.: Dempsey
			Ghana: Draman, Appiah

European Championship

Official name: the European Football Championship. Held every four years since 1960.

Year	Champion	Score	Runner-up
1960	USSR	2–1	Yugoslavia
1964	Spain	2–1	USSR
1968	Italy	2–0	Yugoslavia
1972	W Germany	3–0	USSR
1976	Czechoslovakia*	2–2	W Germany
1980	W Germany	2–1	Belgium
1984	France	2–0	Spain
1988	Holland	2–0	USSR
1992	Denmark	2–0	Germany
1996	Germany†	2–1	Czech Republic
2000	France†	2–1	Italy
2004	Greece	1–0	Portugal

*Won on penalty kicks. †Won in sudden-death overtime.

Under-20 World Championship

Year	Host	Champion	Runner-Up
1977	Tunisia	USSR	Mexico
1979	Japan	Argentina	USSR
1981	Australia	W Germany	Qatar
1983	Mexico	Brazil	Argentina
1985	USSR	Brazil	Spain
1987	Chile	Yugoslavia	W Germany
1989	Saudi Arabia	Portugal	Nigeria
1991	Portugal	Portugal	Brazil
1993	Australia	Brazil	Ghana
1995	Qatar	Argentina	Brazil
1997	Malaysia	Argentina	Uruguay
1999	Nigeria	Spain	Japan
2001	Argentina	Argentina	Ghana
2003	UAE	Brazil	Spain
2005	Netherlands	Argentina	Nigeria

Under-17 World Championship

Year	Champion
1985	Nigeria
1987	USSR
1989	Saudi Arabia
1991	Ghana
1993	Nigeria
1995	Ghana
1997	Brazil
1999	Brazil
2001	France
2003	Brazil
2005	Mexico

Pan American Games

Year	Champion
1951	Argentina
1955	Argentina
1959	Argentina
1963	Brazil

Pan American Games

Year	Champion
1967	Mexico
1971	Argentina
1975	Brazil/Mexico (tie)
1979	Brazil
1983	Uruguay
1987	Brazil
1991	United States
1995	Argentina
1999	Mexico
2003	Argentina

South American Championship (Copa America)

Year	Champion	Host
1916	Uruguay	Argentina
1917	Uruguay	Uruguay
1919	Brazil	Brazil
1920	Uruguay	Chile
1921	Argentina	Argentina
1922	Brazil	Brazil
1923	Uruguay	Uruguay
1924	Uruguay	Uruguay
1925	Argentina	Argentina
1926	Uruguay	Chile
1927	Argentina	Peru
1929	Argentina	Argentina
1935	Uruguay	Peru
1937	Argentina	Argentina
1939	Peru	Peru
1941	Argentina	Chile
1942	Uruguay	Uruguay
1945	Argentina	Chile
1946	Argentina	Argentina
1947	Argentina	Ecuador
1949	Brazil	Brazil
1953	Paraguay	Peru
1955	Argentina	Chile
1956	Uruguay	Uruguay
1957	Argentina	Peru
1958	Argentina	Argentina
1959	Uruguay	Ecuador
1963	Bolivia	Bolivia
1967	Uruguay	Uruguay
1975	Peru	Various sites
1979	Paraguay	Various sites
1983	Uruguay	Various sites
1987	Uruguay	Argentina
1989	Brazil	Brazil
1990	Brazil	Argentina
1991	Argentina	Chile
1993	Argentina	Ecuador
1995	Uruguay	Uruguay
1997	Brazil	Bolivia
1999	Brazil	Paraguay
2001	Colombia	Colombia
2004	Brazil	Peru

Awards

European Footballer of the Year

Year	Player	Club	Year	Player	Club
1956	Stanley Matthews	Blackpool	1981	Karl-Heinz Rummenigge	Bayern Munich
1957	Alfredo Di Stefano	Real Madrid	1982	Paolo Rossi	Juventus
1958	Raymond Kopa	Real Madrid	1983	Michel Platini	Juventus
1959	Alfredo Di Stefano	Real Madrid	1984	Michel Platini	Juventus
1960	Luis Suarez	Barcelona	1985	Michel Platini	Juventus
1961	Omar Sivori	Juventus	1986	Igor Belanov	Dynamo Kiev
1962	Josef Masopust	Dukla Prague	1987	Ruud Gullit	AC Milan
1963	Lev Yashin	Moscow Dynamo	1988	Marco Van Basten	AC Milan
1964	Denis Law	Manchester United	1989	Marco Van Basten	AC Milan
1965	Eusebio	Benfica	1990	Lothar Matthaeus	Inter Milan
1966	Bobby Charlton	Manchester United	1991	Jean-Pierre Papin	Olympique Marseille
1967	Florian Albert	Ferencvaros	1992	Marco Van Basten	AC Milan
1968	George Best	Manchester United	1993	Roberto Baggio	Juventus
1969	Gianni Rivera	AC Milan	1994	Hristo Stoichkov	Barcelona
1970	Gerd Mueller	Bayern Munich	1995	George Weah	AC Milan
1971	Johan Cruyff	Ajax	1996	Matthias Sammer	Borussia Dortmund
1972	Franz Beckenbauer	Bayern Munich	1997	Ronaldo	Inter Milan
1973	Johan Cruyff	Barcelona	1998	Zinedine Zidane	Juventus
1974	Johan Cruyff	Barcelona	1999	Rivaldo	Barcelona
1975	Oleg Blokhin	Dynamo Kiev	2000	Luis Figo	Real Madrid
1976	Franz Beckenbauer	Bayern Munich	2001	Michael Owen	Liverpool
1977	Allan Simonsen	Borussia M'gladbach	2002	Ronaldo	Real Madrid
1978	Kevin Keegan	SV Hamburg	2003	Pavel Nedved	Juventus
1979	Kevin Keegan	SV Hamburg	2004	Andriy Shevchenko	AC Milan
1980	Karl-Heinz Rummenigge	Bayern Munich	2005	Ronaldinho	FC Barcelona

African Footballer of the Year

Year	Player	Club	Year	Player	Club
1970	Salif Keita	St. Etienne	1988	Kalusha Bwalya	Cercle Bruges
1971	Ibrahim Sunday	Asante Kotoko	1989	George Weah	Monaco
1972	Chérif Soueymane	Hafia	1990	Roger Milla	St. Denis
1973	Tshimen Bwanga	TP Mazembe	1991	Abedi Pele Ayew	Marseille
1974	Paul Moukila	CARA Brazzaville	1992	Abedi Pele Ayew	Marseille
1975	Ahmed Faras	Mohammedia	1993	Rashidi Yekini	FC Zurich
1976	Roger Milla	Canon Yaounde	1994	George Weah	Paris St. Germain
1977	Tarak Dhiab	Esperance	1995	George Weah	AC Milan
1978	Karim Abdul Razak	Asante Kotoko	1996	Nwankwo Kanu	Inter Milan
1979	Thomas Nkono	Canon Yaounde	1997	Victor Ikpeba	Monaco
1980	Jean Manga Onguene	Canon Yaounde	1998	Mustapha Hadji	Deportivo Coruna
1981	Lakhdar Belloumi	GCR Mascara	1999	Nwankwo Kanu	Arsenal
1982	Thomas Nkono	Espanol	2000	Patrick Mboma	Parma
1983	Mahmoud Al-Khatib	Al Ahli	2001	El Hadji Diouf	Lens
1984	Theophile Abega	Toulouse	2002	El Hadji Diouf	Lens
1985	Mohamed Timoumi	Royal Armed Forces	2003	Samuel Eto'o	Real Mallorca
1986	Badou Ezaki	Real Mallorca	2004	Samuel Eto'o	FC Barcelona
1987	Rabah Madjer	FC Porto	2005	Samuel Eto'o	FC Barcelona

South American Player of the Year

Year	Player	Club	Year	Player	Club
1971	Tostao	Cruzeiro	1989	Bebeto	Vasco da Gama
1972	Teofilo Cubillas	Alianza Lima	1990	Raul Amarilla	Olimpia
1973	Pelé	Santos	1991	Oscar Ruggeri	Velez Sarsfield
1974	Elias Figueroa	Internacional	1992	Rai	São Paulo
1975	Elias Figueroa	Internacional	1993	Carlos Valderrama	Junior Barranquilla
1976	Elias Figueroa	Internacional	1994	Cafu	São Paulo
1977	Zico	Flamengo	1995	Enzo Francescoli	River Plate
1978	Mario Kempes	Valencia	1996	Jose-Luis Chilavert	Velez Sarsfield
1979	Diego Maradona	Argentinos Juniors	1997	Marcelo Salas	River Plate
1980	Diego Maradona	Boca Juniors	1998	Martin Palermo	Boca Juniors
1981	Zico	Flamengo	1999	Javier Saviola	River Plate
1982	Zico	Flamengo	2000	Romario	Vasco da Gama
1983	Socrates	Corinthians	2001	Juan Riquelme	Boca Juniors
1984	Enzo Francescoli	River Plate	2002	Jose Cardozo	Toluca
1985	Julio Cesar Romero	Fluminense	2003	Carlos Tevez	Boca Juniors
1986	Antonio Alzamendi	River Plate	2004	Carlos Tevez	Boca Juniors
1987	Carlos Valderrama	Deportivo Cali	2005	Carlos Tevez	Corinthians
1988	Ruben Paz	Racing Buenos Aires			

International Club Competition

World Club Championship*

*Formerly the Intercontinental Cup. Competition between winners of European Cup and Libertadores Cup.

1960...Real Madrid, Spain
1961...Penarol, Uruguay
1962...Santos, Brazil
1963...Santos, Brazil
1964...Inter, Italy
1965...Inter, Italy
1966...Penarol, Uruguay
1967...Racing Club, Argentina
1968...Estudiantes, Argentina
1969...Milan, Italy
1970...Feyenoord, Netherlands
1971...Nacional, Uruguay
1972...Ajax Amsterdam,
        Netherlands
1973...Independiente, Argentina
1974...Atletico de Madrid, Spain
1975...No tournament
1976...Bayern Munich
1977...Boca Juniors, Argentina

1978...No tournament
1979...Olimpia, Paraguay
1980...Nacional, Uruguay
1981...Flamengo, Brazil
1982...Penarol, Uruguay
1983...Gremio, Brazil
1984...Independiente, Argentina
1985...Juventus, Italy
1986...River Plate, Argentina
1987...Porto, Portugal
1988...Nacional, Uruguay
1989...Milan, Italy
1990...Milan, Italy
1991...Red Star Belgrade, Yugos.
1992...São Paulo, Brazil
1993...São Paulo, Brazil
1994...Velez Sarsfield, Argentina
1995...Ajax Amsterdam,
        Netherlands

1996...Juventus, Italy
1997...Borussia Dortmund, Ger.
1998...Real Madrid, Spain
1999...Manchester United,
        England
2000...Boca Juniors, Argentina
2001...Bayern Munich, Germany
2002...Real Madrid, Spain
2003...Boca Juniors, Argentina
2004...FC Porto, Portugal
2005...São Paulo, Brazil

Note: Until 1968 a best-of-three-games format decided the winner. From 1968 to '79: two-game/total-goal format. One-game championship since 1980. The European Cup runner-up substituted for the winner in 1971, 1973, 1974, and 1979.

European Cup (Champions League)

1956...Real Madrid, Spain
1957...Real Madrid, Spain
1958...Real Madrid, Spain
1959...Real Madrid, Spain
1960...Real Madrid, Spain
1961...Benfica, Portugal
1962...Benfica, Portugal
1963...AC Milan, Italy
1964...Inter-Milan, Italy
1965...Inter-Milan, Italy
1966...Real Madrid, Spain
1967...Celtic, Scotland
1968...Manchester United,
        England
1969...AC Milan, Italy
1970...Feyenoord, Netherlands
1971...Ajax Amsterdam,
        Netherlands
1972...Ajax Amsterdam,
        Netherlands
1973...Ajax Amsterdam,
        Netherlands

1974...Bayern Munich,
        W Germany
1975...Bayern Munich,
        W Germany
1976...Bayern Munich,
        W Germany
1977...Liverpool, England
1978...Liverpool, England
1979...Nottingham Forest,
        England
1980...Nottingham Forest,
        England
1981...Liverpool, England
1982...Aston Villa, England
1983...SV Hamburg,
        W Germany
1984...Liverpool, England
1985...Juventus, Italy
1986...Steaua Bucharest,
        Romania
1987...Porto, Portugal
1988...PSV Eindhoven,
        Netherlands

1989...AC Milan, Italy
1990...AC Milan, Italy
1991....Red Star Belgrade, Yugoslav.
1992...Barcelona, Spain
1993...Olympique Marseille, France
1994...AC Milan, Italy
1995...Ajax Amsterdam,
        Netherlands
1996...Juventus, Italy
1997...Borussia Dortmund, Ger.
1998...Real Madrid, Spain
1999...Manchester United,
        England
2000...Real Madrid, Spain
2001...Bayern Munich, Germany
2002...Real Madrid, Spain
2003...AC Milan, Italy
2004...FC Porto, Portugal
2005...Liverpool, England
2006...FC Barcelona, Spain

Note: On four occasions the European Cup winner has refused to play in the Intercontinental Cup and has been replaced by the runner-up: Panathinaikos (Greece) in 1971, Juventus (Italy) in 1973, Atletico Madrid (Spain) in 1974, and Malmo (Sweden) in 1979.

Libertadores Cup

Competition between champion clubs and runners-up of 10 South American National Associations.

1960...Penarol, Uruguay
1961...Penarol, Uruguay
1962...Santos, Brazil
1963...Santos, Brazil
1964...Independiente, Argentina
1965...Independiente, Argentina
1966...Penarol, Uruguay
1967...Racing Club, Argentina

1968...Estudiantes, Argentina
1969...Estudiantes, Argentina
1970...Estudiantes, Argentina
1971...Nacional, Uruguay
1972...Independiente, Argentina
1973...Independiente, Argentina
1974...Independiente, Argentina
1975...Independiente, Argentina

1976...Cruzeiro, Brazil
1977...Boca Juniors, Argentina
1978...Boca Juniors, Argentina
1979...Olimpia, Paraguay
1980...Nacional, Uruguay
1981...Flamengo, Brazil
1982...Penarol, Uruguay
1983...Gremio, Brazil

Libertadores Cup *(Cont.)*

1984...Independiente, Argentina
1985...Argentinos Juniors, Arg
1986...River Plate, Argentina
1987...Penarol, Uruguay
1988...Nacional, Uruguay
1989...Atletico Nacional, Colombia
1990...Olimpia, Paraguay
1991...Colo Colo, Chile
1992...São Paulo, Brazil

1993...São Paulo, Brazil
1994...Velez Sarsfield, Argentina
1995...Gremio, Brazil
1996...River Plate, Argentina
1997...Cruzeiro, Brazil
1998...Vasco da Gama, Brazil
1999...Palmeiras, Brazil
2000...Boca Juniors, Argentina
2001...Boca Juniors, Argentina

2002...Olimpia, Paraguay
2003...Boca Juniors, Argentina
2004...Once Caldas, Colombia
2005...São Paulo, Brazil
2006...Internacional, Brazil

UEFA Cup

1958...Barcelona, Spain
1959...No tournament
1960...Barcelona, Spain
1961...AS Roma, Italy
1962...Valencia, Spain
1963...Valencia, Spain
1964...Real Zaragoza, Spain
1965...Ferencvaros, Hungary
1966...Barcelona, Spain
1967...Dynamo Zagreb, Yugoslav.
1968...Leeds United, England
1969...Newcastle United, England
1970...Arsenal, England
1971...Leeds United, England
1972...Tottenham Hotspur, England
1973...Liverpool, England
1974...Feyenoord, Netherlands
1975...Borussia Monchengladbach,
　　　W Germany

1976...Liverpool, England
1977...Juventus, Italy
1978...PSV Eindhoven, Netherl.
1979...Borussia Monchengladbach,
　　　W Germany
1980...Eintracht Frankfurt,
　　　W Germany
1981...Ipswich Town, England
1982...IFK Gothenburg, Sweden
1983...Anderlecht, Belgium
1984...Tottenham Hotspur, England
1985...Real Madrid, Spain
1986...Real Madrid, Spain
1987...IFK Gothenburg, Sweden
1988...Bayer Leverkusen,
　　　W Germany
1989...Naples, Italy
1990...Juventus, Italy
1991...Inter-Milan, Italy

1992...Torino, Italy
1993...Juventus, Italy
1994...Internazionale, Italy
1995...Parma, Italy
1996...Bayern Munich, Germany
1997...Schalke 04, Germany
1998...Inter Milan, Italy
1999...Parma, Italy
2000...Galatasaray, Turkey
2001...Liverpool, England
2002...Feyenoord, Netherlands
2003...FC Porto, Portugal
2004...Valencia, Spain
2005...CSKA Moskva, Russia
2006...FC Sevilla, Spain

European Cup-Winners' Cup

1961...AC Fiorentina, Italy
1962...Atletico Madrid, Spain
1963...Tottenham Hotspur, England
1964...Sporting Lisbon, Portugal
1965...West Ham United, England
1966...Borussia Dortmund, W Ger
1967...Bayern Munich, W Germ.
1968...AC Milan, Italy
1969...Slovan Bratislava, Czech.
1970...Manchester City, England
1971...Chelsea, England
1972...Glasgow Rangers, Scotland
1973...AC Milan, Italy

1974...Magdeburg, E Germany
1975...Dynamo Kiev, USSR
1976...Anderlecht, Belgium
1977...SV Hamburg, W Germ.
1978...Anderlecht, Belgium
1979...Barcelona, Spain
1980...Valencia, Spain
1981...Dynamo Tbilisi, USSR
1982...Barcelona, Spain
1983...Aberdeen, Scotland
1984...Juventus, Italy
1985...Everton, England
1986...Dynamo Kiev, USSR

1987...Ajax Amsterdam, Neth.
1988...Mechelen, Belgium
1989...Barcelona, Spain
1990...Sampdoria, Italy
1991...Manchester United, England
1992...Werder Bremen, Germany
1993...Parma, Italy
1994...Arsenal, England
1995...Real Zaragoza, Spain
1996...Paris St. Germain, France
1997...Barcelona, Spain
1998...Chelsea, England
1999...Lazio, Italy

Note: the Cup-Winners Cup was discontinued after 1999.

Major League Soccer

MLS Cup Results

Year	Champion	Score	Runner-up	Regular Season MVP
1996	D.C. United	3–2 (ot)	Los Angeles	Carlos Valderrama, TB
1997	D.C. United	2–1	Colorado	Preki, Kansas City
1998	Chicago	2–0	D.C. United	Marco Etcheverry, D.C.
1999	D.C. United	2–0	Los Angeles	Jason Kreis, Dallas
2000	Kansas City	1–0	Chicago	Tony Meola, Kansas City
2001	San Jose	2–1 (ot)	Los Angeles	Alex Pineda Chacon, Miami
2002	Los Angeles	1–0 (ot)	New England	Carlos Ruiz, Los Angeles
2003	San Jose	4–2	Chicago	Preki, Kansas City
2004	D.C. United	3–2	Kansas City	Amado Guevara, MetroStars
2005	Los Angeles	1-0 (ot)	New England	Taylor Twellman, NE

United Soccer Leagues

Year	Champion	Score	Runner-Up	Regular Season MVP
1991	San Francisco	1–3, 2–0 (1–0 on PKs)	Albany	Jean Harbor, Maryland
1992	Colorado	1–0	Tampa Bay	Taifour Diane, Colorado
1993	Colorado	3–1 (OT)	Los Angeles	Taifour Diane, Colorado
1994	Montreal	1–0	Colorado	Paulinho, Los Angeles
1995	Seattle	1–2 (SO), 3–0, 2–1 (SO)	Atlanta	Peter Hattrup, Seattle
1996	Seattle	2–0	Rochester	Wolde Harris, Colorado
1997	Milwaukee	2–1 (SO)	Carolina	Doug Miller, Rochester
1998	Rochester	3–1	Minnesota	Mark Baena, Seattle
1999	Minnesota	2–1	Rochester	John Swallen, Minnesota
2000	Rochester	3–1	Minnesota	Vitalis Takawira, Mil
2001	Rochester	2–0	Vancouver	Paul Conway, Charleston
2002	Milwaukee	2–1 (2 OT)	Richmond	Leighton O'Brien, Seattle
2003	Charleston	3–0	Minnesota	Thiago Martins, Pittsburgh
2004	Montreal	2–0	Seattle	Greg Sutton, Montreal
2005	Seattle	1–1 (4–3 on PKs)	Richmond	Jason Jordan, Vancouver
2006	Vancouver	3–0	Rochester	Joey Gjertsen, Vancouver

United Soccer Leagues includes several former U.S. professional soccer leagues, including the A-League.

Women's United Soccer Association

Founders Cup Results

Year	Champion	Score	Runner-up	Regular Season MVP
2001	Bay Area	3–3 (4–2 PKs)	Atlanta	Tiffeny Milbrett, New York
2002	Carolina	3–2	Washington	Marinette Pichon, Philadelphia
2003	Washington	2–1 (OT)	Atlanta	Maren Meinert, Boston

Note: WUSA suspended operations after the 2003 season.

U.S. Open Cup

Open to all amateur and professional teams in the United States, the annual U.S. Open Cup is the oldest cup competition in the country and among the oldest in the world. The tournament is a single-elimination event running concurrent to the MLS season. The winner advances to the CONCACAF Cup, a tournament of the top club teams from North and Central America and the Caribbean.

Year	Champion	Year	Champion
1914	Brooklyn Field Club (NYC)	1941	Pawtucket FC (RI)
1915	Bethlehem Steel FC (PA)	1942	Gallatin SC (PA)
1916	Bethlehem Steel FC (PA)	1943	Brooklyn Hispano SC (NYC)
1917	Fall River Rovers (MA)	1944	Brooklyn Hispano SC (NYC)
1918	Bethlehem Steel FC (PA)	1945	Brookhattan FC (NYC)
1919	Bethlehem Steel FC (PA)	1946	Chicago Viking FC (IL)
1920	Ben Miller FC (St. Louis)	1947	Ponta Delgada SC (Fall River, MA)
1921	Robbins Dry Dock FC (Brooklyn)		
1922	Scullin Steel FC (St. Louis)	1948	Simpkins-Ford SC (St. Louis)
1923	Paterson FC (NJ)	1949	Morgan SC (PA)
1924	Fall River FC (MA)	1950	Simpkins-Ford SC (St. Louis)
1925	Shawsheen FC (Andover, MA)	1951	German Hungarian SC (NYC)
1926	Bethlehem Steel FC (PA)	1952	Harmarville SC (PA)
1927	Fall River FC (MA)	1953	Falcons SC (Chicago)
1928	New York National FC (NYC)	1954	New York Americans (NYC)
1929	Hakoah All Star SC (NYC)	1955	Eintracht Sport Club (NYC)
1930	Fall River FC (MA)	1956	Harmarville SC (PA)
1931	Fall River FC (MA)	1957	Kutis SC (St. Louis)
1932	New Bedford FC (MA)	1958	Los Angeles Kickers (CA)
1933	Stix, Baer and Fuller FC (St. Louis)	1959	McIlvaine Canvasbacks (Los Angeles)
1934	Stix, Baer and Fuller FC (St. Louis)	1960	Ukrainian Nationals (Philadelphia)
1935	Central Breweries FC (Chicago)	1961	Ukrainian Nationals (Philadelphia)
1936	German-Americans (Philadelphia)	1962	New York Hungaria (NYC)
1937	New York American FC (NYC)	1963	Ukrainian Nationals (Philadelphia)
1938	Sparta A and BA (Chicago)		
1939	St. Mary's Celtic SC (Brooklyn)	1964	Los Angeles Kickers (CA)
1940	Baltimore SC/Sparta A and BA	1965	New York Hungaria (NYC)

Year	Champion
1966	Ukrainian Nationals (Philadelphia)
1967	Greek American AA (NYC)
1968	Greek American AA (NYC)
1969	Greek American AA (NYC)
1970	Elizabeth SC (Union, NJ)
1971	Hota SC (NYC)
1972	Elizabeth SC (Union, NJ)
1973	Maccabee SC (Los Angeles)
1974	Greek American AA (NYC)
1975	Maccabee SC (Los Angeles)
1976	San Francisco AC (CA)
1977	Maccabee SC (Los Angeles)
1978	Maccabee SC (Los Angeles)
1979	Brooklyn Dodgers SC (NYC)
1980	NY Pancyprian-Freedoms (NYC)
1981	Maccabee SC (Los Angeles)
1982	NY Pancyprian-Freedoms (NYC)
1983	NY Pancyprian-Freedoms (NYC)
1984	AO Krete (NYC)
1985	Greek American AC (San Francisco)
1986	Kutis SC (St. Louis)

Year	Champion
1987	Club Espana (Washington, D.C.)
1988	Busch SC (St. Louis)
1989	HRC Kickers (St. Petersburg, FL)
1990	AAC Eagles (Chicago)
1991	Brooklyn Italians SC (East NY)
1992	San Jose Oaks (CA)
1993	Club Deportivo Mexico (San Francisco)
1994	Greek American AC (San Francisco)
1995	Richmond Kickers (VA)
1996	D.C. United (MLS)
1997	Dallas Burn (MLS)
1998	Chicago Fire (MLS)
1999	Rochester Rhinos (A-League)
2000	Chicago Fire (MLS)
2001	Los Angeles Galaxy (MLS)
2002	Columbus Crew (MLS)
2003	Chicago Fire (MLS)
2004	Kansas City Wizards (MLS)
2005	Los Angeles Galaxy (MLS)
2006	Chicago Fire (MLS)

North American Soccer League

Formed in 1968 by the merger of the National Professional Soccer League and the USA League, both of which had begun operations a year earlier. The NPSL's lone champion was the Oakland Clippers. The USA League, which brought entire teams in from Europe, was won in 1967 by the L.A. Wolves, who were the English League's Wolverhampton Wanderers.

Year	Champion	Score	Runner-Up	Regular Season MVP
1968	Atlanta	0–0, 3–0	San Diego	John Kowalik, Chi
1969	Kansas City	No game	Atlanta	Cirilio Fernandez, KC
1970	Rochester	3–0,1–3	Washington	Carlos Metidieri, Roch
1971	Dallas	1–2, 4–1, 2–0	Atlanta	Carlos Metidieri, Roch
1972	New York	2–1	St. Louis	Randy Horton, NY
1973	Philadelphia	2–0	Dallas	Warren Archibald, Mia
1974	Los Angeles	4–3*	Miami	Peter Silvester, Balt
1975	Tampa Bay	2–0	Portland	Steve David, Mia
1976	Toronto	3–0	Minnesota	Pelé, NY
1977	New York	2–1	Seattle	Franz Beckenbauer, NY
1978	New York	3–1	Tampa Bay	Mike Flanagan, NE
1979	Vancouver	2–1	Tampa Bay	Johan Cruyff, LA
1980	New York	3–0	Ft. Lauderdale	Roger Davies, Sea
1981	Chicago	1–0*	New York	Giorgio Chinaglia, NY
1982	New York	1–0	Seattle	Peter Ward, Sea
1983	Tulsa	2–0	Toronto	Roberto Cabanas, NY
1984	Chicago	2–1, 3–2	Toronto	Steve Zungul, SJ

*Shootout.

Championship Format: 1968 and 1970: Two games/total goals. 1971 and 1984: Best-of-three series. 1972–1983: One-game championship. Title in 1969 went to the regular-season champion.

Statistical Leaders
SCORING

Year	Player/Team	Pts	Year	Player/Team	Pts
1968	John Kowalik, Chi	69	1977	Steven David, LA	58
1969	Kaiser Motaung, Atl	36	1978	Giorgio Chinaglia, NY	79
1970	Kirk Apostolidis, Dall	35	1979	Oscar Fabbiani, Tampa Bay	58
1971	Carlos Metidieri, Roch	46	1980	Giorgio Chinaglia, NY	77
1972	Randy Horton, NY	22	1981	Giorgio Chinaglia, NY	74
1973	Kyle Rote, Dall	30	1982	Giorgio Chinaglia, NY	55
1974	Paul Child, San Jose	36	1983	Roberto Cabanas, NY	66
1975	Steven David, Miami	52	1984	Slavisa Zungul, Golden Bay	50
1976	Giorgio Chinaglia, NY	49			

NCAA Sports

Men's NCAA Div. I
soccer champion
University of Maryland

AP PHOTO/GERRY BROOME

Margins of Victory

A few twists of fate led to bare-knuckle finishes at this year's NCAA championships in soccer, hockey, and baseball

BY HANK HERSCH

A DEFLECTED FREE KICK, A last-gasp slap shot, an errant infield throw: The thinnest of margins helped determine the NCAA winners and losers of 2005-06, when for three champions opportunity knocked—and, for three runners-up, inopportunity devastated.

MEN'S SOCCER

Three straight times Maryland had reached the semifinals of the College Cup; three straight times it had failed to advance to the championship match. Undaunted, the top-ranked Terrapins reached the final at last in 2005, defeating SMU 4-1 in the semis to draw No. 2 New Mexico at SAS Soccer Stadium in Cary, N.C., on Dec. 11.

In the 30th minute of a scoreless game, Lobos midfielder David Gualdarama fouled defender Chris Lancos seven yards to the right of New Mexico's penalty box, setting up a free kick for senior forward Marc Burch, who had spent the past three seasons playing at Evansville. "I was just trying to keep the ball in frame," Burch said. "Keep it in frame and get a lot of power behind it and hopefully get a rebound, a deflection — anything." His low, left-footed shot hit the Lobos' wall, nicked the boot of a defender, changed direction and rolled to the right of

goalkeeper Mike Graczyk, who had lunged to his left upon contact and could only watch the ball trickle into the goal. "Just one of those freak things," Graczyk said.

Shortly after halftime, the Terps' lead was in peril. A bicycle kick by Jeff Rowland, New Mexico's leading scorer, struck the hand of a Maryland player in the penalty area. As defender Andrew Boyens lined up to take the penalty kick, freshman goalkeeper Chris Seitz studied Boyens's posture, knowing that Boyens tended to push his PK's to the right; what the keeper saw confirmed that. "He opened up and from that point on I knew he was going to my left," Seitz said.

The shot bounced off Seitz's driving body back to Boyens, who blasted the rebound over the crossbar. "It's the most disappointing thing you can go through," said Boyens. You have the weight of the team on your shoulders when you're standing there by yourself. To miss it, it's horrible."

Maryland held on for the 1-0 victory, claiming its first title since 1968. Named the tournament's Most Outstanding Defensive Player, Seitz was the first freshman keeper to win a championship since 1990. "When the goalkeeper makes a save like that, the other team starts to feel, 'This is not our day,'" said Cirovski. "For our team, it was, 'This is it.'"

MEN'S HOCKEY

After a promising 18-2-2 start to the season, the Wisconsin Badgers went on a 3-7-1 tailspin, prompting one fan to send an e-mail to coach Mike Eaves (which he posted in the locker room) excoriating the team for letting slip away the home-state advantage it would have in the postseason: one NCAA regional was to be held in Green Bay, and the Frozen Four in Milwaukee. It also prompted a 20-minute closed-door meeting in late February, when the players rededicated themselves to getting hot.

The Badgers responded on all fronts—jumping on opponents early and holding on through the Green Bay regional and national semifinal to enter the April 8 championship game against Boston College on an 8-1 roll. At the 17,800-seat Bradley Center in downtown Milwaukee—a mere 78 miles east of Madison—college hockey's most vocal fans greeted the Badgers, who were 26-6-1 when they scored first and 3-4-2 when they didn't. "[The crowd] was clearly in their favor," said Eagles goalie Cory Schneider. "Our goal was to take them out of it early."

B.C. tried. Nine minutes into the game, Dan Bertram forced a turnover in Wisconsin's end and skipped the puck in front of the net, where Eagle forward Pat Gannon

Wisconsin goalie Elliott paced the Badgers to the national title thanks to an incredible 0.78 GAA during the postseason.

skillfully backhanded it past goalie Brian Elliott for a 1-0 lead. An injury to Elliott had precipitated the Badgers' midseason slump and now he was down in a duel against Schneider, the Team USA netminder in the world juniors. With Schneider making 37 saves in the game, good for Elliott wouldn't have been good enough. Instead, he was brilliant, shutting down the Eagles the rest of the game, lowering his goals-against average to 0.78 goals and lifting his save percentage to .962 for the postseason. Badgers forward Robbie Earl, the Frozen Four's Most Outstanding Player, tied the score early in the second period and then defenseman Tom Gilbert put Wisconsin up 2-1 midway through the third period on a power-play goal.

With 20 seconds left, BC pulled Schneider, and as the clock ticked down toward the Badgers' sixth title, Wisconsin fans held their breath. With only two seconds left, Peter Harrold blasted a shot past Elliott's outstretched leg pad. It hit the post flush and caromed away. "Posts are your best friend," Elliott said. "And I got one tonight."

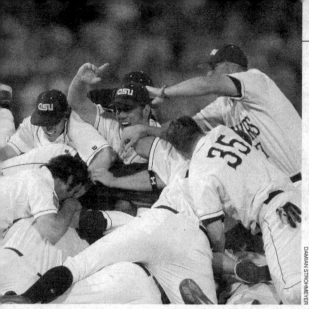

DAMIAN STROHMEYER

But the Tar Heels rallied to tie the score in the top of the fifth on RBIs by Seth Williams and Mike Cavasinni sandwiched around Oregon State's first error in 51⅓ innings. Except for those two unearned runs, North Carolina could muster nothing off junior Jonah Nickerson, who was making his third start in eight days. When the right-hander departed in the seventh inning after his 100th pitch of the night (and his 323rd in eight days) he earned a standing ovation. After the game, he was also named the series' Most Outstanding Player.

Time and again the Tar Heels were on the verge of breaking the tie (they would strand 10 base runners over the final five innings). After Johnson's whiff on a pitch out of the strike zone ended the top of the eighth, Bard got the first two outs in the bottom of the inning, but allowed two runners to reach, and Fox summoned lefty ace Andrew Miller. A No. 6 overall pick by the Detroit Tigers, Miller induced pinch-hitter Ryan Gipson to ground to second baseman Bryan Steed.

Steed, a defensive replacement, fielded the chest-high one-hopper cleanly, but threw wide of first baseman Tim Federowicz, allowing Bill Rowe to score and make it 3-2. "It was a pretty routine groundball," Steed said. "I probably just got rid of it a little too quick."

Gunderson relieved Buck in the ninth and stranded the tying run at third to give Oregon State just its second NCAA title in any sport (the men's cross country team had won in 1961). The Beavers also became the first team to lose twice in Omaha and come back to win the series. As their coach, Pat Casey, put it, "They bowed their neck, buried the thing in the dirt, and won the championship."

BASEBALL

It was, safe to say, a dramatic moment: With the bases loaded and the game tied, a batter swings at strike three to end the inning just before the potential winning run of the College World Series crosses the plate. Somewhat befuddled by it all was the hitter, North Carolina catcher Benji Johnson, who was facing a 1-2 count with two out in the eighth. As Oregon State reliever Dallas Buck delivered, Tar Heels shortstop Josh Horton broke from third and was nearly decapitated by Johnson's bat in the process. "It was just kind of crazy baseball, but we had two strikes," explained Tar Heels head coach Mike Fox. "I told Josh to duck his head and say a prayer."

You couldn't blame Fox for an act of desperation. As the favorite, UNC had won its first three CWS games, then beat Oregon State 4-3 to open the best-of-three championship series and held a 5-0 lead four innings into Game 2. But behind a heroic relief outing from 165-pound junior left-hander Kevin Gunderson, the Beavers rallied for an 11-7 victory to force a decisive Game 3 on June 26.

That game didn't begin well for the Tar Heels either: North Carolina starting pitcher Daniel Bard staked Oregon State to an early 2-0 lead when he committed two errors on the same play in the fourth.

NCAA Team Champions

Fall 2005

			Champion	Runner-Up
Cross-Country	MEN	Division I:	Wisconsin	Arkansas
		Division II:	Western	Adams
		Division III:	UW-La Crosse	Calvin College
	WOMEN	Division I:	Stanford	Colorado
		Division II:	Adams St	Grand Valley
		Division III:	Geneseo St	Williams College
Field Hockey	WOMEN	Division I:	Maryland	Duke
		Division II	UMass-Lowell	Bloomsburg
		Division III:	Messiah	Salisbury
Football	MEN	Division I-AA:	Appalachian	Northern Iowa
		Division II:	Grand Valley	NW Missouri St
		Division III:	Mount Union	UW-Whitewater
Soccer	MEN	Division I:	Maryland	New Mexico
		Division II:	Fort Lewis	Franklin-Pierce
		Division III:	Messiah	Gustavus Adolphus
	WOMEN	Division I:	Portland	UCLA
		Division II:	Nebraska-Omaha	Seattle Pacific
		Division III:	Messiah	College of New Jersey
Volleyball	WOMEN	Division I:	Washington	Nebraska
		Division II:	Grand Valley	Nebraska-Kearney
		Division III:	UW-Whitewater	Juniata
Water Polo	MEN		USC	Stanford

Winter 2005-2006

Basketball	MEN	Division I:	Florida	UCLA
		Division II:	Virginia Union	Winona
		Division III:	Virginia Wesleyan	Wittenberg
	WOMEN	Division I:	Maryland	Duke
		Division II:	Grand Valley	American Int'l
		Division III:	Hope College	Southern Maine
Fencing			Harvard	Penn St
Gymnastics	MEN		Oklahoma	Illinois
	WOMEN		Georgia	Utah
Ice Hockey	MEN	Division I:	Wisconsin	Boston College
		Division III:	Middlebury	St. Norbert
	WOMEN	Division I:	Wisconsin	Minnesota
		Division III:	Middlebury	Plattsburgh
Rifle			AK-Fairbanks	Nebraska
Skiing			Colorado	New Mexico
Swimming and Diving	MEN	Division I:	Auburn	Arizona
		Division II:	Drury	CSU–Bakersfield
		Division III:	Kenyon	Emory
	WOMEN	Division I:	Auburn	Georgia
		Division II:	Truman St	Drury
		Division III:	Emory	Kenyon
Wrestling	MEN	Division I:	Oklahoma St	Minnesota
		Division II:	Nebraska–Omaha	Nebraska-Kearney
		Division III:	Wartburg	UW-Lacrosse

Winter 2005-2006 *(Cont.)*

			Champion	Runner-Up
Indoor Track and Field	MEN	Division I:	Arkansas	LSU
		Division II:	St Augustine	Abilene Christian
		Division III:	UW-La Crosse	Lincoln Univ.
	WOMEN	Division I:	Texas	Stanford
		Division II:	Lincoln	Abilene Christian
		Division III:	UW-Oshkosh	Williams College

Spring 2006

Baseball		Division I:	Oregon St	North Carolina
		Division II:	Tampa	CSU-Chico
		Division III:	Marietta College	Wheaton College
Golf	MEN	Division I:	Oklahoma St	Florida
		Division II:	South Carolina-Aiken	Columbus
		Division III:	Nebraska-Wesleyan	Redlands
	WOMEN	Division I:	Duke	USC
		Division II:	Rollins College	Ferris
		Division III	Methodist	Gustavus Adolphus
Lacrosse	MEN	Division I:	Virginia	Massachusetts
		Division II:	Le Moyne	Dowling
		Division III:	Cortland St	Salisbury
	WOMEN	Division I:	Northwestern	Dartmouth
		Division II	Adelphi	West Chester
		Division III:	College of New Jersey	Gettysburg
Rowing	WOMEN	Division I:	California	Brown
		Division II	Western Washington	Barry
		Division III:	Williams	Ithaca
Softball		Division I:	Arizona	Northwestern
		Division II:	Lock Haven	Emporia St
		Division III:	Rutgers-Camden	St. Thomas
Tennis	MEN	Division I:	Pepperdine	Georgia
		Division II:	Valdosta	Lynn
		Division III:	Emory	Middlebury
	WOMEN	Division I:	Stanford	Miami (Fla.)
		Division II:	BYU-Hawaii	Armstrong Atlantic
		Division III:	Emory	Washington & Lee
Outdoor Track and Field	MEN	Division I:	Florida St	LSU
		Division II:	Abilene Christian	St. Augustine
		Division III:	UW-La Crosse	Lincoln Univ.
	WOMEN	Division I:	Auburn	USC
		Division II:	Lincoln	Abilene Christian
		Division III:	UW-Oshkosh	Williams College
Volleyball	MEN		UCLA	Penn St
Water Polo	WOMEN		UCLA	USC

Fall 2005
Cross Country

MEN

Champion	Runner-Up
Simon Bairu, Wisconsin	Richard Kiplagat, Iona

WOMEN

Champion	Runner-Up
Johanna Nilsson, Northern Arizona	Caroline Bierbaum, Columbia-Barnard

Winter 2005–2006
Fencing

MEN

	Champion	Runner-Up
Sabre	Adam Crompton, Ohio St	Patrick Ghattas, Notre Dame
Foil	Boaz Ellis, Ohio St	Andras Horanyi, Columbia
Épée	Benji Ungar, Harvard	Denis Tolkachev, Ohio St

WOMEN

	Champion	Runner-Up
Sabre	Mariel Zagunis, Notre Dame	Emily Jacobson, Columbia
Foil	Erzsebet Garay, St. John's	Jacqueline Leahy, Princeton
Épée	Katarzyna Trzopek, Penn	Anna Garina, Wayne St

Gymnastics

MEN

	Champion	Runner-Up
All-around	Jonathan Horton, Oklahoma	Justin Springs, Illinois
Vault	David Sender, Stanford	Jimmy Wickham, Ohio St
Parallel bars	Justin Springs, Illinois	Adam Pummer, Illinois
Horizontal bar	Justin Springs, Illinois	Willie Ito, Ohio St
	Dylan Carney, Stanford	
Floor exercise	Jonathan Horton, Oklahoma	Sho Nakamori, Stanford
Pommel horse	Timothy McNeill, California	Ted Brown, Illinois
Rings	Jonathan Horton, Oklahoma	Alex Schorsch, Stanford

WOMEN

	Champion	Runner-Up
All-around	Courtney Kupets, Georgia	Ashley Miles, Alabama
Balance beam	Courtney Kupets, Georgia	Tiffany Tolnay, Georgia
	April Burkholder, LSU	
Uneven bars	Courtney Kupets, Georgia	Ashley Kelly, Arizona St
	Kristina Baskett, Utah	
Floor exercise	Kate Richardson, UCLA	Courtney Kupets, Georgia
Vault	Ashley Miles, Alabama	Kristina Comforte, UCLA

Skiing

MEN

	Champion	Runner-Up
Slalom	Karl Johnson, Dartmouth	Timothee Theaux, AK-Anchorage
Giant slalom	Scott Veenis, Utah	Francesco Ghedina, Denver
10-kilometer classic	John Stene, Denver	Marius Korthauer, AK-Fairbanks
20-kilometer free	Kit Richmond, Colorado	Ben Sonntag, AK-Anchorage

WOMEN

	Champion	Runner-Up
Slalom	Lucie Zikova, Colorado	Jilyne McDonald, Vermont
Giant slalom	Abbi Lathrop, Colby	Florence Roujas, Denver
5-kilometer classic	Jana Rehemaa, Colorado	Maria Grevsgaard, Colorado
15-kilometer free	Jana Rehemaa, Colorado	Johanna Turunen, AK-Fairbanks

Wrestling

	Champion	Runner-Up
125 lb	Joe Dubuque, Indiana	Troy Nickerson, Cornell
133 lb	Matthew Valenti, Penn	Christopher Fleeger, Purdue
141 lb	Nate Gallick, Iowa	Teyon Ware, Oklahoma
149 lb	Dustin Schlatter, Minnesota	Tyler Eustice, Iowa
157 lb	Ben Cherrington, Boise St	Brian Smith, Arizona St
165 lb	Johny Hendricks, Oklahoma	Ryan Churella, Michigan
174 lb	Ben Askren, Missouri	Jake Herbert, Northwestern
184 lb	Shane Webster, Oregon	Roger Kish, Minnesota
197 lb	Jake Rosholt, Oklahoma	Phil Davis, Penn St
285 lb	Cole Konrad, Minnesota	Steve Mocco, Oklahoma

Swimming and Diving — Men

	Champion	Time	Runner-Up	Time
50-yd freestyle	Cullen Jones, N.Carolina St.	19:18	Ben Wildman-Tobriner, Stanford	19.22
100-yd freestyle	Garrett Weber-Gale, Texas	42:11	Ben Wildman-Tobriner, Stanford	42.17
200-yd freestyle	Simon Burnett, Arizona	1:31.20	Peter VanderKaay, Michigan	1:33.31
500-yd freestyle	Peter Vanderkaay, Michigan	4:08.60#*	Ousama Mellouli, USC	4:12.92
1650-yd freestyle	Sebastien Rouault, Georgia	14:29.43	PeterVanderkaay, Michigan	14:33.76
100-yd backstroke	Matt Grevers, Northwestern	45.93	Doug Van Wie, Auburn	46.22
200-yd backstroke	Ryan Lochete, Florida	1:37.68#*	Hongzhe Sun, Stanford	1:40.25

#American record. *NCAA record.

Winter 2005-2006 *(Cont.)*
Swimming and Diving — Men *(Cont.)*

	Champion	Time/Pts	Runner-Up	Time/Pts
100-yd breaststroke	Henrique Barbosa, California	52.52	Kevin Swander, Indiana	52.54
200-yd breaststroke	Henrique Barbosa, California	1:53.97	Vladislav Polyakovi, Alabama	1:54.08
100-yd butterfly	Lyndon Ferns, Arizona	45.89	Albert Subirats, Arizona	46.02
200-yd butterfly	Davis Tarwater, Michigan	1:41.84	Gil Sotvall, Georgia	1:42.10
200-yd IM	Ryan Lochte, Florida	1:40.55#*	Adam Ritter, Arizona	1:44.20
400-yd IM	Ryan Lochte, Florida	3:38.15*	Ousama Melloui, USC	3:39.47
1-meter diving	Chris Colwill, Georgia	407.10	Joona Puhakku, Arizona	398.20
3-meter diving	Chris Colwill, Georgia	460.95	Joona Puhakku, Arizona	413.05
Platform	Steven Segerlin, Auburn	469.30	Chris Colwill, Georgia	443.95

Swimming and Diving — Women

	Champion	Time/Pts	Runner-Up	Time/Pts
50-yd freestyle	Kara Lynn Joyce, Georgia	21.63*	Lacey Nymeyer, Arizona	22.10
100-yd freestyle	Kara Lynn Joyce, Georgia	47.41	Lacey Nymeyer, Arizona	48.43
200-yd freestyle	Kara Lynn Joyce, Georgia	1:43.96	Erin Reilly, California	1:44.63
500-yd freestyle	Laura Conway, Texas	4:40.01	Hayley Peirsol, Auburn	4:41.78
1650-yd freestyle	Hayley Peirsol, Auburn	15:49.48	Flavia Rigamonti, SMU	15:54.67
100-yd backstroke	Rachel Goh, Auburn	52.35	Jenna Gresdal, Arizona	52.74
200-yd backstroke	Helen Silver, California	1:53.01	Aleksandra Putra, Georgia	1:54.59
100-yd breaststroke	Jessica Hardy, California	1:00.02	Rebecca Soni, USC	1:00.07
200-yd breaststroke	Rebecca Soni, USC	2:09.37	Vipa Bernhardt, Florida	2:10.13
100-yd butterfly	Mary Descenza, Georgia	51.56	Caitlin Andrew, Arizona	52.23
200-yd butterfly	Mary Descenza, Georgia	1:53.78	Kimberly Vandenburg, UCLA	1:56.02
200-yd IM	Whitney Myers, Arizona	1:54.88	Tricia Ham, Georgia	1:57.28
400-yd IM	Whitney Myers, Arizona	4:06.32	Julie Stupp, Auburn	4:09.22
1-meter diving	Blythe Hartley, USC	353.50	Allison Brennen, USC	326.10
3-meter diving	Blythe Hartley, USC	373.15	Christina Loukas, Indiana	371.40
Platform	Taryn Ignacio, Kentucky	335.30	Rui Wang, Hawaii	320.00

Indoor Track and Field — Men

	Champion	Time/Mark	Runner-Up	Time/Mark
60-meter dash	Jacob Norman, Baylor	6.56	Walter Dix, Florida St	6.62
60-meter hurdles	Aries Merritt, Tennessee	7.51*	Jerome Miller, Baylor	7.66
200-meter dash	Willie Perry, Florida	20.62	Reggie Witherspoon, Baylor	20.71
400-meter dash	Xavier Carter, LSU	45.28	David Neville, Indiana	45.67
800-meter run	Jackson Langat, TCU	1:47.02	Prince Mumba, Oral Roberts	1:47.74
Mile run	Christian Smith, Kansas St	4:12.75	David Rotich, Iowa St	4:13.12
3,000-meter run	Chris Solinsky, Wisconsin	7:59.68	Robert Cheseret, Arizona	8:04.15
5,000-meter run	Josphat Boit, Arkansas	13:49.93	Richard Kiplagat, Iona	13:51.96
High jump	Jesse Williams, USC	2.29m	Kyle Lancaster, Kansas St	2.26m
Pole Vault	Thomas Skipper, Oregon	5.65m	John Russell, Akron	5.55m
	Robison Pratt, BYU	5.65m		
Long jump	Greig Cryer, South Carolina	7.92m	Cody Eichmeier, Northern Iowa	7.88m
Triple jump	Feranmi Okanlami, Stanford	15.33m	Mark Sturgis, Appalachian	15.25m
Shot put	Vikas Gowda, N. Carolina	19.10m	Karl Erickson, Minnesota	18.89m
35-pound wt throw	Spyridon Jullien, Virginia Tech	23.73m	Egor Agafonov, Kansas	23.19m

Indoor Track and Field — Women

	Champion	Time/Mark	Runner-Up	Time/Mark
60-meter dash	Marshevet Hooker, Texas	7.197	Ashley Owens, UNLV	7.20
60-meter hurdles	Virginia Powell, USC	7.84*	Priscilla Lopes, Nebraska	7.87
200-meter dash	Shalonda Solomon, South Carolina	22.57	Carol Rodriguez, USC	22.761
400-meter dash	Kineke Alexander, Iowa	52.16	Dominique Darden, Miami (Fla.)	52.17
800-meter run	Heather Dorniden, Minnesota	2:05.64	Rebekah Noble, Oregon	2:05.72
Mile run	Anne Shadle, Nebraska	4:38.23	Shannon Rowbury, Duke	4:39.02
3,000-meter run	Johanna Nilsson, Northern Arizona	9.06.61	Mary Cullen, Providence	9.10.22
5,000-meter run	Amy Hastings, Arizona St	15:51.63	Clara Horowitz, Duke	15:52.47
High jump	Sheena Gordon, North Carolina	1.86m	Jessica Stringer, Ohio St	1.83m
	Levern Spencer, Georgia	1.86m		
	Destinee Hooker, Texas	1.86m		
	Caroline Wolf, Texas A & M	1.86m		
Pole vault	Chelsea Johnson, UCLA	4.50m	Breanna Eveland, Kansas St	4.30m
	Lacy Janson, Florida St	4.50m		
Long jump	Marashevet Hooker, Texas	6.71m	Shameka Marshall, Rutgers	6.66m
Triple jump	Yvette Lewis, Hampton	13.75m	Patricia Sylvester, Georgia	13.33m
			Brenda Faludde, Miami (Fla.)	13.33m
Shot put	Michelle Carter, Texas	18.56m	Laura Gerraughty, North Carolina	18.25m
20-pound wt throw	Jenny Dahlgren, Georgia	24.04m	Amarachi Ukabam, Southern Illinois	22.65m

† World record. #American record. *NCAA record.

Winter 2005-2006 (Cont.)
Rifle

	Champion	Pts	Runner-Up	Pts
Smallbore	Jamie Beyerle, AK-Fairbanks	97.5	Shannon Wilson, Mississippi	101.5
Air rifle	Kristina Fehlings, Nebraska	100.0	Jamie Beyerle, AK-Fairbanks	102.4

Spring 2006
Golf

	Champion	Score	Runners-Up	Score
MEN	Jonathan Moore, Oklahoma St	276	Kyle Reifers, Wake Forest	280
			Chris Kirk, Georgia	280
WOMEN	Dewi Schreefel, USC	286	Jennie Lee, Duke	288

Outdoor Track and Field
MEN

	Champion	Mark	Runner-Up	Mark
100-meter dash	Xavier Carter, LSU	10.09	Walter Dix, Florida St	10.18
200-meter dash	Walter Dix, Florida St	20.30	Kelly Willie, LSU	20.48
400-meter dash	Xavier Carter, LSU	44.53	Ricardo Chambers, Florida St	44.71
800-meter run	Ryan Brown, Washington	1:46.29	Tim Bayley, Iona	1:46.64
1,500-meter run	Vincent Rono, South Alabama	3:44.07	Tom Lancashire, Florida St	3:44.20
5,000-meter run	Chris Solinsky, Wisconsin	14:11.71	Josphat Boit, Arkansas	14:13.81
10,000-meter run	Josphat Boit, Arkansas	28:37.64	Martin Fagan, Providence	28:41.41
110-meter hurdles	Aries Merritt, Tennessee	13.39	Dominic Berger, Maryland	13.49
400-meter hurdles	Michael Tinsley, Jackson St	48.25	Bryan Steele, Long Island	49.02
3,000-meter steeple	Josh McAdams, BYU	8:34.10	Mircea Bogdan, UTEP	8:35.35
High jump	Jesse Williams, USC	2.32m	Andra Manson, Texas	2.26m
Pole vault	Thomas Skipper, Oregon	5.70m	Robison Pratt, BYU	5.50m
Long jump	Arturs Abolins, Nebraska	8.00m	Fabrice Lapierre, Texas A&M	7.98m
Triple jump	Rafeeq Curr, Florida	16.07m	Michael Whitehead, Michigan	16.44m
Shot put	Garrett Johnson, Florida St	20.29m	Brian Robison, Texas	20.25m
Discus throw	Vikas Gowda, North Carolina	60.55m	Adam Kuehl, Arizona	59.64m
Hammer throw	Spyridon Jullien, Virginia Tech	72.29m	Mattias Jons, Boise St	71.31m
Javelin throw	Justin Ryncavage, North Carolina	74.18m	Eric Brown, Arkansas	72.63m
Decathlon	Jake Arnold, Arizona	7,870 pts	Chris Helwick, Tennessee	7,772 pts

WOMEN

	Champion	Mark	Runner-Up	Mark
100-meter dash	Amberly Nesbitt, South Carolina	11.34	Kerron Stewart, Auburn	11.36
200-meter dash	Shalonda Solomon, South Carolina	22.62	Kerron Stewart, Auburn	22.65
400-meter dash	Clora Williams, Texas A&M	51.11	Kineke Alexander, Iowa	51.35
800-meter run	Rebekah Noble, Oregon	2:02.07	Heather Dorniden, Minnesota	2:03.02
1,500-meter run	Amy Lia, Washington	4:14.63	Marina Muncan, Villanova	4:15.27
5,000-meter run	Mary Cullen, Providence	16:01.39	Molly Huddle, Notre Dame	16:05.93
10,000-meter run	Victoria Jackson, Arizona St	32:54.72	Clara Horowitz, Duke	33:00.85
100-meter hurdles	Virginia Powell, USC	12.48	Priscilla Lopes, Nebraska	12.6011
400-meter hurdles	Shauna Smith, Wyoming	54.32	Shevon Stoddart, South Carolina	54.47
3,000-meter steeple	Victoria Mitchell, Butler	9:54.32	Cassie Hunt, Illinois	9:59.82
High jump	Sharon Day, Cal Poly-SLO	1.93m	Chaunte Howard, Georgia Tech	1.86m
Pole vault	Kate Soma, Washington	4.30m	Shayla Balentine, San Diego	4.30m
Long jump	Tianna Madison, Tennessee	6.66m	Marshevet Hooker, Texas	6.60m
Triple jump	Candice Baucham, UCLA	14.07m	Gisele Oliveira, Clemson	13.73m
Shot put	Laura Gerraughty, North Carolina	18.32m	Becky Breisch, Nebraska	18.05m
Discus throw	Dace Ruskule, Nebraska	55.13m	Beth Mallory, Alabama	54.74m
Hammer throw	Jenny Dahlgren, Georgia	69.00m	Eva Orban, USC	67.35m
Javelin throw	Dana Pounds, Air Force	58.00m	Kayla Wilkinson, Nebraska	54.51m
Heptathlon	Jacquelyn Johnson, Arizona St	5,939 pts	Tracy Partain, Missouri St	5,827 pts

Tennis

		Champion	Score	Runner-Up
MEN	Singles	B. Dorsch, Baylor	6-2, 7-6 (6)	B. Kohloeffel, UCLA
	Doubles	Alberto Francis/Kris Kwinta, UCLA	7-6 (4), 7-5	Michael Kokta/Lars Poerschke, Baylor
WOMEN	Singles	Zuzana Zemenova, Georgia	7-5, 6-4	Audra Cohen, Northwestern
	Doubles	Alice Barnes/Erin Burdette, Stanford	6-3, 6-4	Amber Liu/Anne Yelsey, Stanford

*NCAA record.

FOR THE RECORD • Year by Year

CHAMPIONSHIP RESULTS

Baseball

DIVISION I

Year	Champion	Coach	Score	Runner-Up	Most Outstanding Player
1947	California*	Clint Evans	8–7	Yale	No award
1948	USC	Sam Barry	9–2	Yale	No award
1949	Texas*	Bibb Falk	10–3	Wake Forest	Charles Teague, Wake Forest, 2B
1950	Texas	Bibb Falk	3–0	Washington St	Ray VanCleef, Rutgers, CF
1951	Oklahoma*	Jack Baer	3–2	Tennnessee	Sidney Hatfield, Tennessee, P-1B
1952	Holy Cross	Jack Barry	8–4	Missouri	James O'Neill, Holy Cross, P
1953	Michigan	Ray Fisher	7–5	Texas	J.L. Smith, Texas, P
1954	Missouri	John (Hi) Simmons	4–1	Rollins	Tom Yewcic, Michigan St, C
1955	Wake Forest	Taylor Sanford	7–6	Western Michigan	Tom Borland, Oklahoma St, P
1956	Minnesota	Dick Siebert	12–1	Arizona	Jerry Thomas, Minnesota, P
1957	California*	George Wolfman	1–0	Penn St	Cal Emery, Penn St, P-1B
1958	USC	Rod Dedeaux	8–7†	Missouri	Bill Thom, USC, P
1959	Oklahoma St	Toby Greene	5–3	Arizona	Jim Dobson, Oklahoma St, 3B
1960	Minnesota	Dick Siebert	2–1‡	USC	John Erickson, Minnesota, 2B
1961	USC*	Rod Dedeaux	1–0	Oklahoma St	Littleton Fowler, Oklahoma St, P
1962	Michigan	Don Lund	5–4	Santa Clara	Bob Garibaldi, Santa Clara, P
1963	USC	Rod Dedeaux	5–2	Arizona	Bud Hollowell, USC, C
1964	Minnesota	Dick Siebert	5–1	Missouri	Joe Ferris, Maine, P
1965	Arizona St	Bobby Winkles	2–1#	Ohio St	Sal Bando, Arizona St, 3B
1966	Ohio St	Marty Karow	8–2	Oklahoma St	Steve Arlin, Ohio St, P
1967	Arizona St	Bobby Winkles	11–2	Houston	Ron Davini, Arizona St, C
1968	USC*	Rod Dedeaux	4–3	Southern Illinois	Bill Seinsoth, USC, 1B
1969	Arizona St	Bobby Winkles	10–1	Tulsa	John Dolinsek, Arizona St, LF
1970	USC	Rod Dedeaux	2–1	Florida St	Gene Ammann, Florida St, P
1971	USC	Rod Dedeaux	7–2	Southern Illinois	Jerry Tabb, Tulsa, 1B
1972	USC	Rod Dedeaux	1–0	Arizona St	Russ McQueen, USC, P
1973	USC*	Rod Dedeaux	4–3	Arizona St	Dave Winfield, Minnesota, P-OF
1974	USC	Rod Dedeaux	7–3	Miami (Fla.)	George Milke, USC, P
1975	Texas	Cliff Gustafson	5–1	S Carolina	Mickey Reichenbach, Texas, 1B
1976	Arizona	Jerry Kindall	7–1	Eastern Michigan	Steve Powers, Arizona, P-DH
1977	Arizona St	Jim Brock	2–1	S Carolina	Bob Horner, Arizona St, 3B
1978	USC*	Rod Dedeaux	10–3	Arizona St	Rod Boxberger, USC, P
1979	CSU–Fullerton	Augie Garrido	2–1	Arkansas	Tony Hudson, CSU–Fullerton, P
1980	Arizona	Jerry Kindall	5–3	Hawaii	Terry Francona, Arizona, LF
1981	Arizona St	Jim Brock	7–4	Oklahoma St	Stan Holmes, Arizona St, LF
1982	Miami (Fla.)*	Ron Fraser	9–3	Wichita St	Dan Smith, Miami (Fla.), P
1983	Texas*	Cliff Gustafson	4–3	Alabama	Calvin Schiraldi, Texas, P
1984	CSU–Fullerton	Augie Garrido	3–1	Texas	John Fishel, CSU–Fullerton, LF
1985	Miami (Fla.)	Ron Fraser	10–6	Texas	Greg Ellena, Miami (Fla.), DH
1986	Arizona	Jerry Kindall	10–2	Florida St	Mike Senne, Arizona, LF
1987	Stanford	Mark Marquess	9–5	Oklahoma St	Paul Carey, Stanford, RF
1988	Stanford	Mark Marquess	9–4	Arizona St	Lee Plemel, Stanford, P
1989	Wichita St	Gene Stephenson	5–3	Texas	Greg Brummett, Wichita St, P
1990	Georgia	Steve Webber	2–1	Oklahoma St	Mike Rebhan, Georgia, P
1991	LSU	Skip Bertman	6–3	Wichita St	Gary Hymel, LSU, C
1992	Pepperdine	Andy Lopez	3–2	CSU–Fullerton	Phil Nevin, CSU–Fullerton, 3B
1993	LSU	Skip Bertman	8–0	Wichita St	Todd Walker, LSU, 2B
1994	Oklahoma	Larry Cochell	13–5	Georgia Tech	Chip Glass, Oklahoma, CF
1995	CSU–Fullerton*	Augie Garrido	11–5	USC	Mark Kotsay, CSU–Fullerton, CF-P
1996	LSU*	Skip Bertman	9–8	Miami (Fla.)	Pat Burrell, Miami (Fla.), 3B
1997	LSU*	Skip Bertman	13–6	Alabama	Brandon Larson, LSU, SS
1998	USC	Mike Gillespie	21–14	Arizona St	Wes Rachels, USC, 2B
1999	Miami (Fla.)	Jim Morris	6–5	Florida St	Marshall McDougall, FSU 3B/2B
2000	LSU*	Skip Bertman	6–5	Stanford	Trey Hodges, LSU, P
2001	Miami (Fla.)*	Jim Morris	12–1	Stanford	Charlton Jimerson, Miami (Fla.), OF
2002	Texas	Augie Garrido	12–6	South Carolina	Huston Street, Texas, P
2003	Rice	Wayne Graham	14–2^	Stanford	John Hudgins, Stanford, P
2004	CSU–Fullerton	George Horton	3–2^	Texas	Jason Windsor, CSU–Fullerton
2005	Texas	Augie Garrido	6–2^	Florida	David Maroul, Texas
2006	Oregon St	Pat Casey	3–2^	North Carolina	Jonah Nickerson, Oregon, P

*Undefeated teams in College World Series play. †12 innings. ‡10 innings. #15 innings. ^Score of decisive game of best-of-three series.

DIVISION II

Year	Champion	Year	Champion	Year	Champion
1968	Chapman*	1982	UC–Riverside*	1996	Kennesaw St*
1969	Illinois St*	1983	Cal Poly–Pomona*	1997	CSU–Chico*
1970	CSU-Northridge	1984	CSU–Northridge	1998	Tampa*
1971	Florida Southern	1985	Florida Southern*	1999	CSU–Chico
1972	Florida Southern	1986	Troy St	2000	SE Oklahoma St
1973	UC–Irvine*	1987	Troy St*	2001	St. Mary's (Tex.)
1974	UC–Irvine	1988	Florida Southern*	2002	Columbus St
1975	Florida Southern	1989	Cal Poly–SLO	2003	Central Missouri St
1976	Cal Poly–Pomona	1990	Jacksonville St	2004	Kennesaw St
1977	UC–Riverside	1991	Jacksonville St	2005	Florida Southern
1978	Florida Southern	1992	Tampa*	2006	Tampa
1979	Valdosta St	1993	Tampa		
1980	Cal Poly–Pomona*	1994	Central Missouri St		
1981	Florida Southern*	1995	Florida Southern*		

DIVISION III

Year	Champion	Year	Champion	Year	Champion
1976	CSU-Stanislaus	1987	Montclair St	1998	Eastern Connecticut St
1977	CSU-Stanislaus	1988	Ithaca	1999	N.Carolina Wesleyan
1978	Glassboro St	1989	N. Carolina Wesleyan	2000	Montclair St
1979	Glassboro St	1990	Eastern Connecticut St	2001	St. Thomas (Minn.)
1980	Ithaca	1991	Southern Maine	2002	Eastern Connecticut St
1981	Marietta	1992	William Paterson	2003	Chapman
1982	Eastern Connecticut St	1993	Montclair St	2004	UW-Stevens Pt
1983	Marietta	1994	UW-Oshkosh	2005	Wisconsin
1984	Ramapo	1995	La Verne	2006	Marietta
1985	UW-Oshkosh	1996	William Paterson		
1986	Marietta	1997	Southern Maine		

*Undefeated teams in final series.

Cross-Country

Men
DIVISION I

Year	Champion	Coach	Pts	Runner-Up	Pts	Individual Champion	Time
1938	Indiana	Earle Hayes	51	Notre Dame	61	Greg Rice, Notre Dame	20:12.9
1939	Michigan St	Lauren Brown	54	Wisconsin	57	Walter Mehl, Wisconsin	20:30.9
1940	Indiana	Earle Hayes	65	Eastern Michigan	68	Gilbert Dodds, Ashland	20:30.2
1941	Rhode Island	Fred Tootell	83	Penn St	110	Fred Wilt, Indiana	20:30.1
1942	Indiana	Earle Hayes	57			Oliver Hunter, Notre Dame	20:18.0
	Penn St	Charles Werner	57				
1943	No meet						
1944	Drake	Bill Easton	25	Notre Dame	64	Fred Feiler, Drake	21:04.2
1945	Drake	Bill Easton	50	Notre Dame	65	Fred Feiler, Drake	21:14.2
1946	Drake	Bill Easton	42	NYU	98	Quentin Brelsford, Ohio Wesleyan	20:22.9
1947	Penn St	Charles Werner	60	Syracuse	72	Jack Milne, North Carolina	20:41.1
1948	Michigan St	Karl Schlademan	41	Wisconsin	69	Robert Black, Rhode Island	19:52.3
1949	Michigan St	Karl Schlademan	59	Syracuse	81	Robert Black, Rhode Island	20:25.7
1950	Penn St	Charles Werner	53	Michigan St	55	Herb Semper Jr, Kansas	20:31.7
1951	Syracuse	Robert Grieve	80	Kansas	118	Herb Semper Jr, Kansas	20:09.5
1952	Michigan St	Karl Schlademan	65	Indiana	68	Charles Capozzoli, Georgetown	19:36.7
1953	Kansas	Bill Easton	70	Indiana	82	Wes Santee, Kansas	19:43.5
1954	Oklahoma St	Ralph Higgins	61	Syracuse	118	Allen Frame, Kansas	19:54.2
1955	Michigan St	Karl Schlademan	46	Kansas	68	Charles Jones, Iowa	19:57.4
1956	Michigan St	Karl Schlademan	28	Kansas	88	Walter McNew, Texas	19:55.7
1957	Notre Dame	Alex Wilson	121	Michigan St	127	Max Truex, USC	19:12.3
1958	Michigan St	Francis Dittrich	79	Western Michigan	104	Crawford Kennedy, Michigan St	20:07.1
1959	Michigan St	Francis Dittrich	44	Houston	120	Al Lawrence, Houston	20:35.7
1960	Houston	John Morriss	54	Michigan St	80	Al Lawrence, Houston	19:28.2
1961	Oregon St	Sam Bell	68	San Jose St	82	Dale Story, Oregon St	19:46.6

Men *(Cont.)*

DIVISION I *(Cont.)*

Year	Champion	Coach	Pts	Runner-Up	Pts	Individual Champion	Time
1962	San Jose St	Dean Miller	58	Villanova	69	Tom O'Hara, Loyola (Ill.)	19:20.3
1963	San Jose St	Dean Miller	53	Oregon	68	Victor Zwolak, Villanova	19:35.0
1964	W. Michigan	George Dales	86	Oregon	116	Elmore Banton, Ohio	20:07.5
1965	W. Michigan	George Dales	81	Northwestern	114	John Lawson, Kansas	29:24.0
1966	Villanova	James Elliott	79	Kansas St	155	Gerry Lindgren, Wash. St	29:01.4
1967	Villanova	James Elliott	91	Air Force	96	Gerry Lindgren, Wash. St	30:45.6
1968	Villanova	James Elliott	78	Stanford	100	Michael Ryan, Air Force	29:16.8
1969	UTEP	Wayne Vandenburg	74	Villanova	88	Gerry Lindgren, Wash. St	28:59.2
1970	Villanova	James Elliott	85	Oregon	86	Steve Prefontaine, Oregon	28:00.2
1971	Oregon	Bill Dellinger	83	Washington St	122	Steve Prefontaine, Oregon	29:14.0
1972	Tennessee	Stan Huntsman	134	East Tennessee St	148	Neil Cusack, E Tenn St	28:23.0
1973	Oregon	Bill Dellinger	89	UTEP	157	Steve Prefontaine, Oregon	28:14.0
1974	Oregon	Bill Dellinger	77	Western Kentucky	110	Nick Rose, W. Kentucky	29:22.0
1975	UTEP	Ted Banks	88	Washington St	92	Craig Virgin, Illinois	28:23.3
1976	UTEP	Ted Banks	62	Oregon	117	Henry Rono, Washington St	28:06.6
1977	Oregon	Bill Dellinger	100	UTEP	105	Henry Rono, Washington St	28:33.5
1978	UTEP	Ted Banks	56	Oregon	72	Alberto Salazar, Oregon	29:29.7
1979	UTEP	Ted Banks	86	Oregon	93	Henry Rono, Washington St	28:19.6
1980	UTEP	Ted Banks	58	Arkansas	152	Suleiman Nyambui, UTEP	29:04.0
1981	UTEP	Ted Banks	17	Providence	109	Mathews Motshwarateu,UTEP	28:45.6
1982	Wisconsin	Dan McClimon	59	Providence	138	Mark Scrutton, Colorado	30:12.6
1983	Vacated			Wisconsin	164	Zakarie Barie,'JTEP	29:20.0
1984	Arkansas	John McDonnell	101	Arizona	111	Ed Eyestone, BYU	29:28.8
1985	Wisconsin	Martin Smith	67	Arkansas	104	Timothy Hacker, Wisconsin	29:17.88
1986	Arkansas	John McDonnell	69	Dartmouth	141	Aaron Ramirez, Arizona	30:27.53
1987	Arkansas	John McDonnell	87	Dartmouth	119	Joe Falcon, Arkansas	29:14.97
1988	Wisconsin	Martin Smith	105	Northern Arizona	160	Robert Kennedy, Indiana	29:20.0
1989	Iowa St	Bill Bergan	54	Oregon	72	John Nuttall, Iowa St	29:30.55
1990	Arkansas	John McDonnell	68	Iowa St	96	Jonah Koech, Iowa St	29:05.0
1991	Arkansas	John McDonnell	52	Iowa St	114	Sean Dollman, W. Kentucky	30:17.1
1992	Arkansas	John McDonnell	46	Wisconsin	87	Bob Kennedy, Indiana	30:15.3
1993	Arkansas	John McDonnell	31	BYU	153	Josephat Kapkory, Wash. St	29:32.4
1994	Iowa St	Bill Bergan	65	Colorado	88	Martin Keino, Arizona	30:08.7
1995	Arkansas	John McDonnell	100	Northern Arizona	142	Godfrey Siamusiye, Arkansas	30:09
1996	Stanford	Vin Lananna	46	Arkansas	74	Godfrey Siamusiye, Arkansas	29:49
1997	Stanford	Vin Lananna	53	Arkansas	56	Mebrahtom Keflezighi, UCLA	28:54
1998	Arkansas	John McDonnell	97	Stanford	114	Adam Goucher, Colorado	29:26
1999	Arkansas	John McDonnell	58	Wisconsin	185	David Kimani, S. Alabama	30:06.6
2000	Arkansas	John McDonnell	83	Colorado	94	Keith Kelly, Providence	30:14.5
2001	Colorado	Mark Wetmore	90	Stanford	91	Boaz Cheboiywo, E. Michigan	28:47
2002	Stanford	Andrew Gerard	47	Wisconsin	107	Jorge Torres, Colorado	29:04.7
2003	Stanford	Andrew Gerard	24	Wisconsin	124	Dathan Ritzenhein, Colorado	29:14.1
2004	Colorado	Mark Wetmore	90	Wisconsin	94	Simon Bairu, Wisconsin	30:37.7
2005	Wisconsin	Jerry Schumacher	37	Arkansas	105	Simon Bairu, Wisconsin	29:15.9

DIVISION II

Year	Champion	Year	Champion	Year	Champion
1958	Northern Illinois	1974	SW Missouri St	1990	Edinboro
1959	South Dakota St	1975	UC–Irvine	1991	UMass–Lowell
1960	Central St (Ohio)	1976	UC–Irvine	1992	Adams St
1961	South Illinois	1977	Eastern Illinois	1993	Adams St
1962	Central St (Ohio)	1978	Cal Poly–SLO	1994	Adams St
1963	Emporia St	1979	Cal Poly–SLO	1995	Western St
1964	Kentucky St	1980	Humbolt St	1996	South Dakota St
1965	San Diego St	1981	Millersville	1997	South Dakota
1966	San Diego St	1982	Eastern Washington	1998	Adams St
1967	San Diego St	1983	Cal Poly–Pomona	1999	Western St
1968	Eastern Illinois	1984	SE Missouri St	2000	Western St
1969	Eastern Illinois	1985	South Dakota St	2001	Western St
1970	Eastern Michigan	1986	Edinboro	2002	Western St
1971	CSU–Fullerton	1987	Edinboro	2003	Adams St
1972	North Dakota St	1988	Edinboro/ Mankato St	2004	Western St
1973	South Dakota St	1989	South Dakota St	2005	Western St

Men (Cont.)

DIVISION III

Year	Champion	Year	Champion	Year	Champion
1973	Ashland	1984	St. Thomas (Minn.)	1995	Williams
1974	Mount Union	1985	Luther	1996	UW–La Crosse
1975	North Central	1986	St. Thomas (Minn.)	1997	N. Central
1976	North Central	1987	N Central	1998	N. Central
1977	Occidental	1988	UW–Oshkosh	1999	N. Central
1978	N. Central	1989	UW–Oshkosh	2000	Calvin
1979	N. Central	1990	UW–Oshkosh	2001	UW–La Crosse
1980	Carleton	1991	Rochester	2002	UW-Oshkosh
1981	N. Central	1992	N. Central	2003	Calvin College
1982	N. Central	1993	N. Central	2004	Calvin College
1983	Brandeis	1994	Williams	2005	UW–La Crosse

Women

DIVISION I

Year	Champion	Coach	Pts	Runner-Up	Pts	Individual Champion	Time
1981	Virginia	John Vasvary	36	Oregon	83	Betty Springs, N.Carolina St	16:19.0
1982	Virginia	Martin Smith	48	Stanford	91	Lesley Welch, Virginia	16:39.7
1983	Oregon	Tom Heinonen	95	Stanford	98	Betty Springs, N.Carolina St	16:30.7
1984	Wisconsin	Peter Tegen	63	Stanford	89	Cathy Branta, Wisconsin	16:15.6
1985	Wisconsin	Peter Tegen	58	Iowa St	98	Suzie Tuffey, N.Carolina St	16:22.5
1986	Texas	Terry Crawford	62	Wisconsin	64	Angela Chalmers, N. Arizona	16:55.49
1987	Oregon	Tom Heinonen	97	North Carolina St	99	Kimberly Betz, Indiana	16:10.85
1988	Kentucky	Don Weber	75	Oregon	128	Michelle Dekkers, Indiana	16:30.0
1989	Villanova	Marty Stern	99	Kentucky	168	Vicki Huber, Villanova	15:59.86
1990	Villanova	Marty Stern	82	Providence	172	Sonia O'Sullivan, Villanova	16:06.0
1991	Villanova	Marty Stern	85	Arkansas	168	Sonia O'Sullivan, Villanova	16:30.3
1992	Villanova	Marty Stern	123	Arkansas	130	Carole Zajac, Villanova	17:01.9
1993	Villanova	Marty Stern	66	Arkansas	71	Carole Zajac, Villanova	16:40.3
1994	Villanova	John Marshall	75	Michigan	108	Jennifer Rhines, Villanova	16:31.2
1995	Providence	Ray Treacy	88	Colorado	123	Kathy Butler, Wisconsin	16:51
1996	Stanford	Beth Alford-Sullivan	101	Villanova	106	Amy Skieresz, Arizona	17:04
1997	BYU	Patrick Shane	100	Stanford	102	Carrie Tollefson, Villanova	16:58
1998	Villanova	Marcus O'Sullivan	106	BYU	110	Katie McGregor, Michigan	16:47.21
1999	BYU	Patrick Shane	72	Arkansas	125	Erica Palmer, Wisconsin	16:39.50
2000	Colorado	Mark Wetmore	117	BYU	167	Kara Grgas-Wheeler, Colorado	20:30.5
2001	BYU	Patrick Shane	62	North Carolina St	148	Tara Chaplin, Arizona	20:24
2002	BYU	Patrick Shane	85	Stanford	113	Shalane Flanagan	19:36.0
2003	Stanford	Dena Evans	120	BYU	128	Shalane Flanagan	19:30.4
2004	Colorado	Mark Wetmore	63	Duke	144	Kim Smith, Providence	20:08.5
2005	Stanford	Peter Tegen	146	Colorado	181	Johanna Nilsson, N. Arizona	19:33.9

DIVISION II

Year	Champion	Year	Champion	Year	Champion
1981	S Dakota St	1990	Cal Poly-SLO	1999	Adams St
1982	Cal Poly-SLO	1991	Cal Poly-SLO	2000	Western St
1983	Cal Poly-SLO	1992	Adams St	2001	Western St
1984	Cal Poly-SLO	1993	Adams St	2002	Western St
1985	Cal Poly-SLO	1994	Adams St	2003	Adams St
1986	Cal Poly-SLO	1995	Adams St	2004	Adams St
1987	Cal Poly-SLO	1996	Adams St	2005	Adams St
1988	Cal Poly-SLO	1997	Adams St		
1989	Cal Poly-SLO	1998	Adams St		

DIVISION III

Year	Champion	Year	Champion	Year	Champion
1981	Central (Iowa)	1989	Cortland St	1998	Calvin
1982	St. Thomas (Minn.)	1990	Cortland St	1999	Calvin
1983	UW–La Crosse	1991	UW–Oshkosh	2000	Middlebury
1984	St. Thomas (Minn.)	1992	Cortland St	2001	Middlebury
1985	Franklin & Marshall	1993	Cortland St	2002	Williams
1986	St. Thomas (Minn.)	1994	Cortland St	2003	Middlebury
1987	St. Thomas (Minn.)	1995	Cortland St	2004	Williams College
	UW–Oshkosh	1996	UW–Oshkosh	2005	Geneseo St
1988	UW–Oshkosh	1997	Cortland St		

Men's and Women's Combined
TEAM CHAMPIONS

Year	Champion	Coach	Pts	Runner-Up	Pts
1990	Penn St	Emmanuil Kaidanov	36	Columbia–Barnard	35
1991	Penn St	Emmanuil Kaidanov	4700	Columbia–Barnard	4200
1992	Columbia–Barnard	G. Kolombatovich/A. Kogler	4150	Penn St	3646
1993	Columbia–Barnard	G. Kolombatovich/A. Kogler	4525	Penn St	4500
1994	Notre Dame	Michael DeCicco	4350	Penn St	4075
1995	Penn St	Emmanuil Kaidanov	440	St. John's (N.Y.)	413
1996	Penn St	Emmanuil Kaidanov	1500	Notre Dame	1190
1997	Penn St	Emmanuil Kaidanov	1530	Notre Dame	1470
1998	Penn St	Emmanuil Kaidanov	149	Notre Dame	147
1999	Penn St	Emmanuil Kaidanov	171	Notre Dame	139
2000	Penn St	Emmanuil Kaidanov	175	Notre Dame	171
2001	St. John's (N.Y.)	Yuri Gelman	180	Penn St	172
2002	Penn St	Emmanuil Kaidanov	195	St. John's (N.Y.)	190
2003	Notre Dame	Janusz Bednarski	182	Penn St	179
2004	Ohio St	Vladimir Nazlymov	194	Penn St	160
2005	Notre Dame	Janusz Bednarski	173	Ohio St	171
2006	Harvard	Peter Brand	165	Penn St	159

Men
TEAM CHAMPIONS

Year	Champion	Coach	Pts	Runner-Up	Pts
1941	Northwestern	Henry Zettleman	28½	Illinois	27
1942	Ohio St	Frank Riebel	34	St. John's (N.Y.)	33½
1943–46	No tournament				
1947	NYU	Martinez Castello	72	Chicago	50½
1948	CCNY	James Montague	30	Navy	28
1949	Army/Rutgers	S. Velarde/D. Cetrulo	63		
1950	Navy	Joseph Fiems	67½	NYU/Rutgers	66½
1951	Columbia	Servando Velarde	69	Pennsylvania	64
1952	Columbia	Servando Velarde	71	NYU	69
1953	Pennsylvania	Lajos Csiszar	94	Navy	86
1954	Columbia	Irving DeKoff	61		
	NYU	Hugo Castello	61		
1955	Columbia	Irving DeKoff	62	Cornell	57
1956	Illinois	Maxwell Garret	90	Columbia	88
1957	NYU	Hugo Castello	65	Columbia	64
1958	Illinois	Maxwell Garret	47	Columbia	43
1959	Navy	Andre Deladrier	72	NYU	65
1960	NYU	Hugo Castello	65	Navy	57
1961	NYU	Hugo Castello	79	Princeton	68
1962	Navy	Andre Deladrier	76	NYU	74
1963	Columbia	Irving DeKoff	55	Navy	50
1964	Princeton	Stan Sieja	81	NYU	79
1965	Columbia	Irving DeKoff	76	NYU	74
1966	NYU	Hugo Castello	5–0	Army	5–2
1967	NYU	Hugo Castello	72	Pennsylvania	64
1968	Columbia	Louis Bankuti	92	NYU	87
1969	Pennsylvania	Lajos Csiszar	54	Harvard	43
1970	NYU	Hugo Castello	71	Columbia	63
1971	NYU/Columbia	Hugo Castello/Louis Bankuti	68		
1972	Detroit	Richard Perry	73	NYU	70
1973	NYU	Hugo Castello	76	Pennsylvania	71
1974	NYU	Hugo Castello	92	Wayne St	87
1975	Wayne St	Istvan Danosi	89	Cornell	83
1976	NYU	Herbert Cohen	79	Wayne St	77
1977	Notre Dame	Michael DeCicco	114*	NYU	114
1978	Notre Dame	Michael DeCicco	121	Pennsylvania	110
1979	Wayne St	Istvan Danosi	119	Notre Dame	108
1980	Wayne St	Istvan Danosi	111	Pennsylvania/MIT	106
1981	Pennsylvania	Dave Micahnik	113	Wayne St	111
1982	Wayne St	Istvan Danosi	85	Clemson	77
1983	Wayne St	Aladar Kogler	86	Notre Dame	80
1984	Wayne St	Gil Pezza	69	Penn St	50
1985	Wayne St	Gil Pezza	141	Notre Dame	140

Men

TEAM CHAMPIONS (CONT.)

Year	Champion	Coach	Pts	Runner-Up	Pts
1986	Notre Dame	Michael DeCicco	151	Columbia	141
1987	Columbia	George Kolombatovich	86	Pennsylvania	78
1988	Columbia	G. Kolombatovich/A. Kogler	90	Notre Dame	83
1989	Columbia	G. Kolombatovich/A. Kogler	88	Penn St	85

*Tie broken by a fence-off. Note: Beginning in 1990, men's and women's combined teams competed for the national championship. See p. 598.

INDIVIDUAL CHAMPIONS

	Foil	Sabre	Épée
1941	Edward McNamara, Northwestern	William Meyer, Dartmouth	G.H. Boland, Illinois
1942	Byron Kreiger, Wayne St	Andre Deladrier, St. John's (NY)	Ben Burtt, Ohio St
1943–46	No tournament		
1947	Abraham Balk, NYU	Oscar Parsons, Temple	Abraham Balk, NYU
1948	Albert Axelrod, CCNY	James Day, Navy	William Bryan, Navy
1949	Ralph Tedeschi, Rutgers	Alex Treves, Rutgers	Richard C. Bowman, Army
1950	Robert Nielsen, Columbia	Alex Treves, Rutgers	Thomas Stuart, Navy
1951	Robert Nielsen, Columbia	Chamberless Johnston, Princeton	Daniel Chafetz, Columbia
1952	Harold Goldsmith, CCNY	Frank Zimolzak, Navy	James Wallner, NYU
1953	Ed Nober, Brooklyn	Robert Parmacek, Penn	Jack Tori, Pennsylvania
1954	Robert Goldman, Pennsylvania	Steve Sobel, Columbia	Henry Kolowrat, Princeton
1955	Herman Velasco, Illinois	Barry Pariser, Columbia	Donald Tadrawski, Notre Dame
1956	Ralph DeMarco, Columbia	Gerald Kaufman, Columbia	Kinmont Hoitsma, Princeton
1957	Bruce Davis, Wayne St	Bernie Balaban, NYU	James Margolis, Columbia
1958	Bruce Davis, Wayne St	Art Schankin, Illinois	Roland Wommack, Navy
1959	Joe Paletta, Navy	Al Morales, Navy	Roland Wommack, Navy
1960	Gene Glazer, NYU	Mike Desaro, NYU	Gil Eisner, NYU
1961	Herbert Cohen, NYU	Israel Colon, NYU	Jerry Halpern, NYU
1962	Herbert Cohen, NYU	Barton Nisonson, Columbia	Thane Hawkins, Navy
1963	Jay Lustig, Columbia	Bela Szentivanyi, Wayne St	Larry Crum, Navy
1964	Bill Hicks, Princeton	Craig Bell, Illinois	Paul Pesthy, Rutgers
1965	Joe Nalven, Columbia	Howard Goodman, NYU	Paul Pesthy, Rutgers
1966	Al Davis, NYU	Paul Apostol, NYU	Bernhardt Hermann, Iowa
1967	Mike Gaylor, NYU	Todd Makler, Pennsylvania	George Masin, NYU
1968	Gerard Esponda, San Francisco	Todd Makler, Pennsylvania	Don Sieja, Cornell
1969	Anthony Kestler, Columbia	Norman Braslow, Penn	James Wetzler, Pennsylvania
1970	Walter Krause, NYU	Bruce Soriano, Columbia	John Nadas, Case Reserve
1971	Tyrone Simmons, Detroit	Bruce Soriano, Columbia	George Szunyogh, NYU
1972	Tyrone Simmons, Detroit	Bruce Soriano, Columbia	Ernesto Fernandez, Penn
1973	Brooke Makler, Pennsylvania	Peter Westbrock, NYU	Risto Hurme, NYU
1974	Greg Benko, Wayne St	Steve Danosi, Wayne St	Risto Hurme, NYU
1975	Greg Benko, Wayne St	Yuri Rabinovich, Wayne St	Risto Hurme, NYU
1976	Greg Benko, Wayne St	Brian Smith, Columbia	Randy Eggleton, Pennsylvania
1977	Pat Gerard, Notre Dame	Mike Sullivan, Notre Dame	Hans Wieselgren, NYU
1978	Ernest Simon, Wayne St	Mike Sullivan, Notre Dame	Bjorne Vaggo, Notre Dame
1979	Andrew Bonk, Notre Dame	Yuri Rabinovich, Wayne St	Carlos Songini, Cleveland St
1980	Ernest Simon, Wayne St	Paul Friedberg, Pennsylvania	Gil Pezza, Wayne St
1981	Ernest Simon, Wayne St	Paul Friedberg, Pennsylvania	Gil Pezza, Wayne St
1982	Alexander Flom, George Mason	Neil Hick, Wayne St	Peter Schifrin, San Jose St
1983	Demetrios Valsamis, NYU	John Friedberg, North Carolina	Ola Harstrom, Notre Dame
1984	Charles Higgs-Coulthard, Notre Dame	Michael Lofton, NYU	Ettore Bianchi, Wayne St
1985	Stephan Chauvel, Wayne St	Michael Lofton, NYU	Ettore Bianchi, Wayne St
1986	Adam Feldman, Penn St	Michael Lofton, NYU	Chris O'Loughlin, Pennsylvania
1987	William Mindel, Columbia	Michael Lofton, NYU	James O'Neill, Harvard
1988	Marc Kent, Columbia	Robert Cottingham, Columbia	Jon Normile, Columbia
1989	Edward Mufel, Penn St	Peter Cox, Penn	Jon Normile, Columbia
1990	Nick Bravin, Stanford	David Mandell, Columbia	Jubba Beshin, Notre Dame
1991	Ben Atkins, Columbia	Vitali Nazlimov, Penn St	Marc Oshima, Columbia
1992	Nick Bravin, Stanford	Tom Strzalkowski, Penn St	Harald Bauder, Wayne St
1993	Nick Bravin, Stanford	Tom Strzalkowski, Penn St	Ben Atkins, Columbia
1994	Kwame van Leeuwen, Harvard	Tom Strzalkowski, Penn St	Harald Winkman, Princeton
1995	Sean McClain, Stanford	Paul Palestis, NYU	Mike Gattner, Lawrence
1996	Thorstein Becker, Wayne St	Maxim Pekarev, Princeton	Jeremy Kahn, Duke
1997	Cliff Bayer, Pennsylvania	Keith Smart, St. John's (N.Y.)	Alden Clarke, Stanford
1998	Ayo Griffin, Yale	Luke LaValle, Notre Dame	George Hentea, St. John's (N.Y.)

Men *(Cont.)*
INDIVIDUAL CHAMPIONS *(Cont.)*

	Foil	Sabre	Épée
1999	Felix Reichling, Stanford	Keeth Smart, St. John's (N.Y.)	Alex Roytblat St. John's (N.Y.)
2000	Felix Reichling, Stanford	Gabor Szelle, Notre Dame	Daniel Landgren, Penn St
2001	William Jed Dupree, Columbia	Ivan Lee, St. John's (N.Y.)	Soren Thompson, Princeton
2002	Nontapat Panchan, Penn St	Ivan Lee, St. John's (N.Y.)	Arpád Horváth, St. John's (N.Y.)
2003	Nontapat Panchan, Penn St	Adam Crompton, Ohio St	Weston Kelsey, Air Force
2004	Boaz Ellis, Ohio St	Adam Crompton, Ohio St	Arpád Horváth, St. John's (N.Y.)
2005	Boaz Ellis, Ohio St	Sergey Isayenko, St. John's	Michal Sobieraj, Notre Dame
2006	Boaz Ellis, Ohio St	Adam Crompton, Ohio St	Benji Ungar, Harvard

Women
TEAM CHAMPIONS

Year	Champion	Coach	Rec	Runner-Up	Rec
1982	Wayne St	Istvan Danosi	7–0	San Jose St	6–1
1983	Penn St	Beth Alphin	5–0	Wayne St	3–2
1984	Yale	Henry Harutunian	3–0	Penn St	2–1
1985	Yale	Henry Harutunian	3–0	Pennsylvania	2–1
1986	Pennsylvania	David Micahnik	3–0	Notre Dame	2–1
1987	Notre Dame	Yves Auriol	3–0	Temple	2–1
1988	Wayne St	Gil Pezza	3–0	Notre Dame	2–1
1989	Wayne St	Gil Pezza	3–0	Columbia-Barnard	2–1

Note: Beginning in 1990, men's and women's combined teams competed for the national championship. See p. 598.

INDIVIDUAL CHAMPIONS

Foil	Foil *(Cont.)*	Épée
1982....Joy Ellingson, San Jose St	1998....F. Zimmermann, Stanford	1995....Tina Loven, St. John's (N.Y.)
1983....Jana Angelakis, Penn St	1999....Monique DeBruin, Stanford	1996....N. Dygert, St. John's (N.Y.)
1984....Mary Jane O'Neill, Penn	2000....Eva Petschnigg, Princeton	1997....Magda Krol, Notre Dame
1985....C. Bilodeaux, Columbia-Barn.	2001....Iris Zimmerman, Stanford	1998....Charlotte Walker, Penn St
1986....M. Sullivan, Notre Dame	2002....Alicja Kryczalo, Notre Dame	1999....F. Zimmermann, Stanford
1987....C. Bilodeaux, Columbia-Barn.	2003....Alicja Kryczalo, Notre Dame	2000....Jessica Burke, Penn St
1988....M. Sullivan, Notre Dame	2004....Alicja Kryczalo, Notre Dame	2001....E. Takács, St. John's (N.Y.)
1989....Yasemin Topcu, Wayne St	2005....Alicja Kryczalo, Notre Dame	2002....Stephanie Eim, Penn St
1990....Tzu Moy, Columbia-Barn.	2006....Ezsebet Garay, St John's (N.Y.)	2003....Katarzyna Trzopek, Penn St
1991....Heidi Piper, Notre Dame		2004....Anna Garina, Wayne St
1992....Olga Cheryak, Penn St	**Sabre**	2005....Anna Garina, Wayne St
1993....Olga Kalinovskaya, Penn St	2000....Caroline Purcell, MIT	2006....Katarzyna Trzopek, Penn St
1994....Olga Kalinovskaya, Penn St	2001....Sada Jacobson, Yale	
1995....Olga Kalinovskaya, Penn St	2002....Sada Jacobson, Yale	
1996....Olga Kalinovskaya, Penn St	2003....Alexis Jemal, Rutgers	
1997....Yelena Kalkina, Ohio St	2004....Valerie Providenza, Notre Dame	
	2005....Emily Jacobson, Barnard	
	2006....Mariel Zagunis, Notre Dame	

Field Hockey

DIVISION I

Year	Champion	Coach	Score	Runner-Up
1981	Connecticut	Diane Wright	4–1	Massachusetts
1982	Old Dominion	Beth Anders	3–2	Connecticut
1983	Old Dominion	Beth Anders	3–1 (3 OT)	Connecticut
1984	Old Dominion	Beth Anders	5–1	Iowa
1985	Connecticut	Diane Wright	3–2	Old Dominion
1986	Iowa	Judith Davidson	2–1 (2 OT)	New Hampshire
1987	Maryland	Sue Tyler	2–1 (OT)	North Carolina
1988	Old Dominion	Beth Anders	2–1	Iowa
1989	North Carolina	Karen Shelton	2–1 (3 OT)*	Old Dominion
1990	Old Dominion	Beth Anders	5–0	North Carolina
1991	Old Dominion	Beth Anders	2–0	North Carolina
1992	Old Dominion	Beth Anders	4–0	Iowa
1993	Maryland	Missy Meharg	2–1 (3 OT)*	North Carolina
1994	James Madison	Christy Morgan	2–1 (3 OT)*	North Carolina
1995	North Carolina	Karen Shelton-Scroggs	5–1	Maryland
1996	North Carolina	Karen Shelton-Scroggs	3–0	Princeton
1997	North Carolina	Karen Shelton	3–2	Old Dominion
1998	Old Dominion	Beth Anders	3–2	Princeton
1999	Maryland	Missy Meharg	2–1	Michigan
2000	Old Dominion	Beth Anders	3–1	North Carolina

DIVISION I (CONT.)

Year	Champion	Coach	Score	Runner-Up
2001	Michigan	Marcia Pankratz	2–0	Maryland
2002	Wake Forest	Jennifer Averill	2–0	Penn St
2003	Wake Forest	Jennifer Averill	3–1	Duke
2004	Wake Forest	Jennifer Averill	3–0	Duke
2005	Maryland	Missy Meharg	1–0	Duke

*Penalty strokes.

DIVISION II (Discontinued, then renewed)

Year	Champion	Coach	Score	Runner-Up
1981	Pfeiffer	Ellen Briggs	5–3	Bentley
1982	Lock Haven	Sharon E. Taylor	4–1	Bloomsburg
1983	Bloomsburg	Jan Hutchinson	1–0	Lock Haven
1992	Lock Haven	Sharon E. Taylor	3–1	Bloomsburg
1993	Bloomsburg	Jan Hutchinson	2–1 (2 OT)	Lock Haven
1994	Lock Haven	Sharon E. Taylor	2–1	Bloomsburg
1995	Lock Haven	Sharon E. Taylor	1–0	Bloomsburg
1996	Bloomsburg	Jan Hutchinson	1–0	Lock Haven
1997	Bloomsburg	Jan Hutchinson	2–0	Kutztown
1998	Bloomsburg	Jan Hutchinson	4–3 (OT)	Lock Haven
1999	Bloomsburg	Jan Hutchinson	2–0	Bentley
2000	Lock Haven	Pat Rudy	2–0	Bentley
2001	Bentley	Kell McGowan	4–2	E Stroudsburg
2002	Bloomsburg	Jan Hutchinson	5–0	Bentley
2003	Bloomsburg	Jan Hutchinson	4–1	UMass–Lowell
2004	Bloomsburg	Jan Hutchinson	3–2	Bentley
2005	UMass-Lowell	Shannon Hlebichuk	2–1	Bloomsburg

DIVISION III

Year	Champion	Year	Champion	Year	Champion
1981	Trenton St	1990	Trenton St	1999	College of New Jersey*
1982	Ithaca	1991	Trenton St	2000	William Smith
1983	Trenton St	1992	William Smith	2001	Cortland St
1984	Bloomsburg	1993	Cortland St	2002	Rowan
1985	Trenton St	1994	Cortland St	2003	Salisbury
1986	Salisbury St	1995	Trenton St	2004	Salisbury
1987	Bloomsburg	1996	College of New Jersey*	2005	Salisbury
1988	Trenton St	1997	William Smith		
1989	Lock Haven	1998	Middelbury		

*Formerly Trenton St

Golf

Men

DIVISION I — Results, 1897–1938

Year	Champion	Site	Individual Champion
1897	Yale	Ardsley Casino	Louis Bayard Jr, Princeton
1898	Harvard (spring)		John Reid Jr, Yale
1898	Yale (fall)		James Curtis, Harvard
1899	Harvard		Percy Pyne, Princeton
1900	No tournament		
1901	Harvard	Atlantic City	H. Lindsley, Harvard
1902	Yale (spring)	Garden City	Charles Hitchcock Jr, Yale
1902	Harvard (fall)	Morris County	Chandler Egan, Harvard
1903	Harvard	Garden City	F.O. Reinhart, Princeton
1904	Harvard	Myopia	A.L. White, Harvard
1905	Yale	Garden City	Robert Abbott, Yale
1906	Yale	Garden City	W.E. Clow Jr, Yale
1907	Yale	Nassau	Ellis Knowles, Yale
1908	Yale	Brae Burn	H.H. Wilder, Harvard
1909	Yale	Apawamis	Albert Seckel, Princeton
1910	Yale	Essex County	Robert Hunter, Yale
1911	Yale	Baltusrol	George Stanley, Yale
1912	Yale	Ekwanok	F.C. Davison, Harvard
1913	Yale	Huntingdon Valley	Nathaniel Wheeler, Yale
1914	Princeton	Garden City	Edward Allis, Harvard
1915	Yale	Greenwich	Francis Blossom, Yale
1916	Princeton	Oakmont	J.W. Hubbell, Harvard

Men

DIVISION I Results, 1897–1938 *(Cont.)*

Year	Champion	Site	Individual Champion
1917–18	No tournament		
1919	Princeton	Merion	A.L. Walker Jr, Columbia
1920	Princeton	Nassau	Jess Sweetster, Yale
1921	Dartmouth	Greenwich	Simpson Dean, Princeton
1922	Princeton	Garden City	Pollack Boyd, Dartmouth
1923	Princeton	Siwanoy	Dexter Cummings, Yale
1924	Yale	Greenwich	Dexter Cummings, Yale
1925	Yale	Montclair	Fred Lamprecht, Tulane
1926	Yale	Merion	Fred Lamprecht, Tulane
1927	Princeton	Garden City	Watts Gunn, Georgia Tech
1928	Princeton	Apawamis	Maurice McCarthy, Georgetown
1929	Princeton	Hollywood	Tom Aycock, Yale
1930	Princeton	Oakmont	G.T. Dunlap Jr, Princeton
1931	Yale	Olympia Fields	G.T. Dunlap Jr, Princeton
1932	Yale	Hot Springs	J.W. Fischer, Michigan
1933	Yale	Buffalo	Walter Emery, Oklahoma
1934	Michigan	Cleveland	Charles Yates, Georgia Tech
1935	Michigan	Congressional	Ed White, Texas
1936	Yale	North Shore	Charles Kocsis, Michigan
1937	Princeton	Oakmont	Fred Haas Jr, LSU
1938	Stanford	Louisville	John Burke, Georgetown

Results, 1939–2006

Year	Champion (Score)	Coach	Runner-Up (Score)	Host or Site	Individual Champion
1939	Stanford (612)	Eddie Twiggs	Northwestern (614) Princeton (614)	Wakonda	Vincent D'Antoni, Tulane
1940	Princeton (601) LSU (601)	Walter Bourne Mike Donahue		Ekwanok	Dixon Brooke, Virginia
1941	Stanford (580)	Eddie Twiggs	LSU (599)	Ohio St	Earl Stewart, LSU
1942	LSU (590) Stanford (590)	Mike Donahue Eddie Twiggs		Notre Dame	Frank Tatum Jr, Stanford
1943	Yale (614)	William Neale Jr	Michigan (618)	Olympia Fields	Wallace Ulrich, Carleton
1944	Notre Dame (311)	George Holderith	Minnesota (312)	Inverness	Louis Lick, Minnesota
1945	Ohio St (602)	Robert Kepler	Northwestern (621)	Ohio St	John Lorms, Ohio St
1946	Stanford (619)	Eddie Twiggs	Michigan (624)	Princeton	George Hamer, Georgia
1947	LSU (606)	T.P. Heard	Duke (614)	Michigan	Dave Barclay, Michigan
1948	San Jose St (579)	Wilbur Hubbard	LSU (588)	Stanford	Bob Harris, San Jose St
1949	North Texas (590)	Fred Cobb	Purdue (600) Texas (600)	Iowa St	Harvie Ward, North Carolina
1950	North Texas (573)	Fred Cobb	Purdue (577)	New Mexico	Fred Wampler, Purdue
1951	North Texas (588)	Fred Cobb	Ohio St (589)	Ohio St	Tom Nieporte, Ohio St
1952	North Texas (587)	Fred Cobb	Michigan (593)	Purdue	Jim Vickers, Oklahoma
1953	Stanford (578)	Charles Finger	North.Carolina (580)	Broadmoor	Earl Moeller, Oklahoma St
1954	SMU (572)	Graham Ross	North Texas (573)	Houston Hillman	Robbins, Memphis St
1955	LSU (574)	Mike Barbato	North Texas (583)	Tennessee	Joe Campbell, Purdue
1956	Houston (601)	Dave Williams	North Texas (602) Purdue (602)	Ohio St	Rick Jones, Ohio St
1957	Houston (602)	Dave Williams	Stanford (603)	Broadmoor	Rex Baxter Jr., Houston
1958	Houston (570)	Dave Williams	Oklahoma St (582)	Williams	Phil Rodgers, Houston
1959	Houston (561)	Dave Williams	Purdue (571)	Oregon	Dick Crawford, Houston
1960	Houston (603)	Dave Williams	Purdue (607) Oklahoma St (607)	Broadmoor	Dick Crawford, Houston
1961	Purdue (584)	Sam Voinoff	Arizona St (595)	Lafayette	Jack Nicklaus, Ohio St
1962	Houston (588)	Dave Williams	Oklahoma St (598)	Duke	Kermit Zarley, Houston
1963	Oklahoma St (581)	Labron Harris	Houston (582)	Wichita St	R.H. Sikes, Arkansas
1964	Houston (580)	Dave Williams	Oklahoma St (587)	Broadmoor	Terry Small, San Jose St
1965	Houston (577)	Dave Williams	CSU-L.A. (587)	Tennessee	Marty Fleckman, Houston
1966	Houston (582)	Dave Williams	San Jose St (586)	Stanford	Bob Murphy, Florida
1967	Houston (585)	Dave Williams	Florida (588)	Shawnee, Pa.	Hale Irwin, Colorado
1968	Florida (1154)	Buster Bishop	Houston (1156)	New Mexico St	Grier Jones, Oklahoma St
1969	Houston (1223)	Dave Williams	Wake Forest (1232)	Broadmoor	Bob Clark, CSU-LA
1970	Houston (1172)	Dave Williams	Wake Forest (1182)	Ohio St	John Mahaffey, Houston
1971	Texas (1144)	George Hannon	Houston (1151)	Arizona	Ben Crenshaw, Texas
1972	Texas (1146)	George Hannon	Houston (1159)	Cape Coral	Ben Crenshaw, Texas Tom Kite, Texas

Men - DIVISION I (Cont.)
Results, 1939-2006 (Cont.)

Year	Champion (Score)	Coach	Runner-Up (Score)	Host or Site	Individual Champion
1973	Florida (1149)	Buster Bishop	Oklahoma St (1159)	Oklahoma St	Ben Crenshaw, Texas
1974	Wake Forest (1158)	Jess Haddock	Florida (1160)	San Diego St	Curtis Strange, Wake Forest
1975	Wake Forest (1156)	Jess Haddock	Oklahoma St (1189)	Ohio St	Jay Haas, Wake Forest
1976	Oklahoma St (1166)	Mike Holder	BYU (1173)	New Mexico	Scott Simpson, USC
1977	Houston (1197)	Dave Williams	Oklahoma St (1205)	Colgate	Scott Simpson, USC
1978	Oklahoma St (1140)	Mike Holder	Georgia (1157)	Oregon	David Edwards, Oklahoma St
1979	Ohio St (1189)	James Brown	Oklahoma St (1191)	Wake Forest	Gary Hallberg, Wake Forest
1980	Oklahoma St (1173)	Mike Holder	BYU (1177)	Ohio St	Jay Don Blake, Utah St
1981	BYU (1161)	Karl Tucker	Oral Roberts (1163)	Stanford	Ron Commans, USC
1982	Houston (1141)	Dave Williams	Oklahoma St (1151)	Pinehurst	Billy Ray Brown, Houston
1983	Oklahoma St (1161)	Mike Holder	Texas (1168)	Fresno St	Jim Carter, Arizona St
1984	Houston (1145)	Dave Williams	Oklahoma St (1146)	Houston	John Inman, North Carolina
1985	Houston (1172)	Dave Williams	Oklahoma St (1175)	Florida	Clark Burroughs, Ohio St
1986	Wake Forest (1156)	Jess Haddock	Oklahoma St (1160)	Wake Forest	Scott Verplank, Oklahoma St
1987	Oklahoma St (1160)	Mike Holder	Wake Forest (1176)	Ohio St	Brian Watts, Oklahoma St
1988	UCLA (1176)	Eddie Merrins	UTEP (1179) Oklahoma (1179) Oklahoma St (1179)	USC	E.J. Pfister, Oklahoma St
1989	Oklahoma (1139)	Gregg Grost	Texas (1158)	Oklahoma Oklahoma St	Phil Mickelson, Arizona St
1990	Arizona St (1155)	Steve Loy	Florida (1157)	Florida	Phil Mickelson, Arizona St
1991	Oklahoma St (1161)	Mike Holder	North Carolina (1168)	San Jose St	Warren Schutte, UNLV
1992	Arizona St (1129)	Rick LaRose	Arizona St (1136)	New Mexico	Phil Mickelson, Arizona St
1993	Florida (1145)	Buddy Alexander	Georgia Tech (1146)	Kentucky	Todd Demsey, Arizona St
1994	Stanford (1129)	Wally Goodwin	Texas (1133)	McKinney, Tex.	Justin Leonard, Texas
1995	Oklahoma St* (1156)	Mike Holder	Stanford (1156)	Ohio St	Chip Spratlin, Auburn
1996	Arizona St (1186)	Randy Lein	UNLV (1189)	Chattanooga	Tiger Woods, Stanford
1997	Pepperdine (1148)	John Geiberger	Wake Forest (1151)	Evanston, Ill.	Charles Warren, Clemson
1998	UNLV (1118)	Dwaine Knight	Clemson (1121)	Albuquerque	James McLean, Minnesota
1999	Georgia (1180)	Chris Haack	Oklahoma (1183)	Chaska, Minn.	Donald Luke, Northwestern
2000	Oklahoma St* (1116)	Mike Holder	Georgia Tech (1116)	Opelika, Ala.	Charles Howell, Oklahoma St
2001	Florida (1126)	Buddy Alexander	Clemson (1144)	Durham, N.C.	Nick Gilliam, Florida
2002	Minnesota (1134)	Brad James	Georgia Tech	Ohio St	Troy Matteson, Georgia Tech
2003	Clemson (1191)	Larry Penley	Oklahoma St	Oklahoma St	A. Canizares, Arizona St
2004	California (1134)	Steve Desimone	UCLA (1140)	Hot Springs, Va.	Ryan Moore, UNLV
2005	Georgia, (1135)	Chris Haack	Georgia Tech (1145)	Owings Mills,Md.	James Lepp, Washington
2006	Oklahoma St (1143)	Mike McGraw	Florida (1146)	Sunriver, Ore.	Jonathan Moore, Okla. St

*Won sudden death playoff. Notes: Match play, 1897–1964; par-70 tournaments held in 1969, 1973 and 1989; par-71 tournaments held in 1968, 1981 and 1988; all other championships par-72 tournaments. Scores are based on 4 rounds instead of 2 after 1967.

DIVISION II

Year	Champion	Year	Champion	Year	Champion
1963	SW Missouri St	1978	Columbus St	1993	Abilene Christian
1964	Southern Illinois	1979	UC–Davis	1994	Columbus St
1965	Middle Tennessee St	1980	Columbus St	1995	Florida Southern
1966	CSU–Chico	1981	Florida Southern	1996	Florida Southern
1967	Lamar	1982	Florida Southern	1997	Columbus St
1968	Lamar	1983	SW Texas St	1998	Florida Southern
1969	CSU–Northridge	1984	Troy St	1999	Florida Southern
1970	Rollins	1985	Florida Southern	2000	Florida Southern
1971	New Orleans	1986	Florida Southern	2001	West Florida
1972	New Orleans	1987	Tampa	2002	Rollins
1973	CSU–Northridge	1988	Tampa	2003	Francis Marion
1974	CSU–Northridge	1989	Columbus St	2004	South Carolina–Aiken
1975	UC–Irvine	1990	Florida Southern	2005	West Florida
1976	Troy St	1991	Florida Southern	2006	South Carolina–Aiken
1977	Troy St	1992	Columbus St		

Note: Par-71 tournaments held in 1967, 1970, 1976–78, 1985, 1988 and 2001; par-70 tournament held in 1996; all other championships par-72 tournaments.

Men (Cont.)
DIVISION III

Year	Champion	Year	Champion	Year	Champion
1975	Wooster	1986	CSU-Stanislaus	1997	Methodist (N.C.)
1976	CSU-Stanislaus	1987	CSU-Stanislaus	1998	Methodist (N.C.)
1977	CSU-Stanislaus	1988	CSU-Stanislaus	1999	Methodist (N.C.)
1978	CSU-Stanislaus	1989	CSU-Stanislaus	2000	Greensboro
1979	CSU-Stanislaus	1990	Methodist (N.C.)	2001	UW-Eau Claire
1980	CSU-Stanislaus	1991	Methodist (N.C.)	2002	Guilford
1981	TCU	1992	Methodist (N.C.)	2003	Averett
1982	Ramapo	1993	UC-San Diego	2004	Gustavus Adolphus
1983	Allegheny	1994	Methodist (N.C.)	2005	Guilford
1984	CSU-Stanislaus	1995	Methodist (N.C.)	2006	Nebraska Wesleyan
1985	CSU-Stanislaus	1996	Methodist (N.C.)		

Note: All championships par-72 except for 1986, 1988 and 2001, which were par-71; fourth round of 1975 championships canceled as a result of bad weather; first round of 1988 championships canceled as a result of rain.

Women
DIVISION I

Year	Champion	Coach	Score	Runner-Up	Score	Individual Champion
1982	Tulsa	Dale McNamara	1191	TCU	1227	Kathy Baker, Tulsa
1983	TCU	Fred Warren	1193	Tulsa	1196	Penny Hammel, Miami (Fla.)
1984	Miami (Fla.)	Lela Cannon	1214	Arizona St	1221	Cindy Schreyer, Georgia
1985	Florida	Mimi Ryan	1218	Tulsa	1233	Danielle Ammaccapane, Arizona St
1986	Florida	Mimi Ryan	1180	Miami (Fla.)	1188	Page Dunlap, Florida
1987	San Jose St	Mark Gale	1187	Furman	1188	Caroline Keggi, New Mexico
1988	Tulsa	Dale McNamara	1175	Georgia/Arizona	1182	Melissa McNamara, Tulsa
1989	San Jose St	Mark Gale	1208	Tulsa	1209	Pat Hurst, San Jose St
1990	Arizona St	Linda Vollstedt	1206	UCLA	1222	Susan Slaughter, Arizona
1991	UCLA*	Jackie Steinmann	1197	San Jose St	1197	Annika Sorenstam, Arizona
1992	San Jose St	Mark Gale	1171	Arizona	1175	Vicki Goetze, Georgia
1993	Arizona St	Linda Vollstedt	1187	Texas	1189	Charlotta Sorenstam, Texas
1994	Arizona St	Linda Vollstedt	1189	USC	1205	Emilee Klein, Arizona St
1995	Arizona St	Linda Vollstedt	1155	San Jose St	1181	Kristel Mourgue d'Algue, Arizona St
1996	Arizona*	Rick LaRose	1240	San Jose St	1240	Marisa Baena, Arizona
1997	Arizona St	Linda Vollstedt	1178	San Jose St	1180	Heather Bowie, Texas
1998	Arizona St	Linda Vollstedt	1155	Florida	1173	Jennifer Rosales, USC
1999	Duke	Dan Brooks	895	Arizona St/Georgia	903	Grace Park, Arizona St
2000	Arizona	Todd McCorkle	1175	Stanford	1196	Jenna Daniels, Arizona
2001	Georgia	Todd McCorkle	1176	Duke	1179	Candy Hannemann, Duke
2002	Duke	Dan Brooks	1164	Arizona/Auburn/Texas	1160	Virada Nirapathpongporn, Duke
2003	USC	Andrea Gaston	1197	Pepperdine	1212	Mikaela Parmlid, USC
2004	UCLA	Carrie Forsyth	1148	Oklahoma St	1151	Sarah Huarte, California
2005	Duke	Dan Brooks	1170	UCLA	1175	Anna Grzebien, Duke
2006	Duke	Dan Brooks	1167	USC	1177	Dewi Schreefel, USC

*Won sudden death playoff. Note: Par-74 tournaments held in 1983 and 1988; par-72 tournament held in 1990, 2000 and 2001; all other championships par-73 tournaments.

DIVISIONS II AND III

Year	Champion	Year	Champion
1996	Methodist (N.C.)	1998	Methodist (N.C.)
1997	Lynn	1999	Methodist (N.C.)

DIVISION II

Year	Champion
2000	Florida Southern
2001	Florida Southern
2002	Florida Southern
2003	Rollins (Fla.)
2004	Rollins (Fla.)
2005	Rollins (Fla.)
2006	Rollins (Fla.)

DIVISION III

Year	Champion
2000	Methodist (N.C.)
2001	Methodist (N.C.)
2002	Methodist (N.C.)
2003	Methodist (N.C.)
2004	Methodist (N.C.)
2005	Methodist (N.C.)
2006	Methodist (N.C.)

Gymnastics

Men
TEAM CHAMPIONS

Year	Champion	Coach	Pts	Runner-Up	Pts
1938	Chicago	Dan Hoffer	22	Illinois	18
1939	Illinois	Hartley Price	21	Army	17
1940	Illinois	Hartley Price	20	Navy	17
1941	Illinois	Hartley Price	68.5	Minnesota	52.5
1942	Illinois	Hartley Price	39	Penn St	30
1943–47	No tournament				
1948	Penn St	Gene Wettstone	55	Temple	34.5
1949	Temple	Max Younger	28	Minnesota	18
1950	Illinois	Charley Pond	26	Temple	25
1951	Florida St	Hartley Price	26	Illinois/ USC	23.5
1952	Florida St	Hartley Price	89.5	USC	75
1953	Penn St	Gene Wettstone	91.5	Illinois	68
1954	Penn St	Gene Wettstone	137	Illinois	68
1955	Illinois	Charley Pond	82	Penn St	69
1956	Illinois	Charley Pond	123.5	Penn St	67.5
1957	Penn St	Gene Wettstone	88.5	Illinois	80
1958	Michigan St	George Szypula	79		
	Illinois	Charley Pond	79		
1959	Penn St	Gene Wettstone	152	Illinois	87.5
1960	Penn St	Gene Wettstone	112.5	USC	65.5
1961	Penn St	Gene Wettstone	88.5	Southern Illinois	80.5
1962	USC	Jack Beckner	95.5	Southern Illinois	75
1963	Michigan	Newton Loken	129	Southern Illinois	73
1964	Southern Illinois	Bill Meade	84.5	USC	69.5
1965	Penn St	Gene Wettstone	68.5	Washington	51.5
1966	Southern Illinois	Bill Meade	187.200	California	185.100
1967	Southern Illinois	Bill Meade	189.550	Michigan	187.400
1968	California	Hal Frey	188.250	Southern Illinois	188.150
1969	Iowa	Mike Jacobson	161.175	Penn St	160.450
	Michigan*	Newton Loken		Colorado St	
1970	Michigan	Newton Loken	164.150	Iowa St	164.050
				New Mexico St	
1971	Iowa St	Ed Gagnier	319.075	Southern Illinois	316.650
1972	Southern Illinois	Bill Meade	315.925	Iowa St	312.325
1973	Iowa St	Ed Gagnier	325.150	Penn St	323.025
1974	Iowa St	Ed Gagnier	326.100	Arizona St	322.050
1975	California	Hal Frey	437.325	LSU	433.700
1976	Penn St	Gene Wettstone	432.075	LSU	425.125
1977	Indiana St	Roger Counsil	434.475		
	Oklahoma	Paul Ziert	434.475		
1978	Oklahoma	Paul Ziert	439.350	Arizona St	437.075
1979	Nebraska	Francis Allen	448.275	Oklahoma	446.625
1980	Nebraska	Francis Allen	563.300	Iowa St	557.650
1981	Nebraska	Francis Allen	284.600	Oklahoma	281.950
1982	Nebraska	Francis Allen	285.500	UCLA	281.050
1983	Nebraska	Francis Allen	287.800	UCLA	283.900
1984	UCLA	Art Shurlock	287.300	Penn St	281.250
1985	Ohio St	Michael Willson	285.350	Nebraska	284.550
1986	Arizona St	Don Robinson	283.900	Nebraska	283.600
1987	UCLA	Art Shurlock	285.300	Nebraska	284.750
1988	Nebraska	Francis Allen	288.150	Illinois	287.150
1989	Illinois	Yoshi Hayasaki	283.400	Nebraska	282.300
1990	Nebraska	Francis Allen	287.400	Minnesota	287.300
1991	Oklahoma	Greg Buwick	288.025	Penn St	285.500
1992	Stanford	Sadao Hamada	289.575	Nebraska	288.950
1993	Stanford	Sadao Hamada	276.500	Nebraska	275.500
1994	Nebraska	Francis Allen	288.250	Stanford	285.925
1995	Stanford	Sadao Hamada	232.400	Nebraska	231.525
1996	Ohio St	Peter Kormann	232.150	California	231.775
1997	California	Barry Weiner	233.825	Oklahoma	232.725
1998	California	Barry Weiner	231.200	Iowa	229.675
1999	Michigan	Kurt Golder	232.550	Ohio St	230.850
2000	Penn St	Randy Jepson	231.975	Michigan	231.850
2001	Ohio St	Miles Avery	218.125	Oklahoma	217.775
2002	Oklahoma	Mark Williams	219.300	Ohio St	218.650
2003	Oklahoma	Mark Williams	222.600	Ohio St	220.700
2004	Penn St	Randy Jepson	223.350	Oklahoma	222.300

TEAM CHAMPIONS *(Cont.)*

Year	Champion	Coach	Pts	Runner-Up	Pts
2005	Oklahoma	Mark Williams	225.675	Ohio St	225.450
2006	Oklahoma	Mark Williams	221.400	Illinois	220.975

*Trampoline.

INDIVIDUAL CHAMPIONS

ALL-AROUND

1938.....Joe Giallombardo, Illinois
1939.....Joe Giallombardo, Illinois
1940.....Joe Giallombardo, Illinois
.........Paul Fina, Illinois
1941.....Courtney Shanken, Chicago
1942.....Newt Loken, Minnesota
1948.....Ray Sorenson, Penn St
1949.....Joe Kotys, Kent
1950.....Joe Kotys, Kent
1951.....Bill Roetzheim, Florida St
1952.....Jack Beckner, USC
1953.....Jean Cronstedt, Penn St
1954.....Jean Cronstedt, Penn St
1955.....Karl Schwenzfeier, Penn St
1956.....Don Tonry, Illlinois
1957.....Armando Vega, Penn St
1958.....Abie Grossfeld, Illinois
1959.....Armando Vega, Penn St
1960.....Jay Werner, Penn St
1961.....Gregor Weiss, Penn St
1962.....Robert Lynn, USC
1963.....Gil Larose, Michigan
1964.....Ron Barak, USC
1965.....Mike Jacobson, Penn St
1966.....Steve Cohen, Penn St
1967.....Steve Cohen, Penn St
1968.....Makoto Sakamoto, USC
1969.....Mauno Nissinen, Wash
1970.....Yoshi Hayasaki, Wash
1971.....Yoshi Hayasaki, Wash
1972.....Steve Hug, Stanford
1973.....Steve Hug, Stanford
.........Marshall Avener, Penn St
1974.....Steve Hug, Stanford
1975.....Wayne Young, BYU
1976.....Peter Kormann,
.........Southern Conn. St
1977.....Kurt Thomas, Indiana St
1978.....Bart Conner, Oklahoma
1979.....Kurt Thomas, Indiana St
1980.....Jim Hartung, Nebraska
1981.....Jim Hartung, Nebraska
1982.....Peter Vidmar, UCLA
1983.....Peter Vidmar, UCLA
1984.....Mitch Gaylord, UCLA
1985.....Wes Suter, Nebraska
1986.....Jon Louis, Stanford
1987.....Tom Schlesinger, Nebraska
1988.....Vacated†
1989.....Patrick Kirsey, Nebraska
1990.....Mike Racanelli, Ohio St
1991.....John Roethlisberger, Minn
1992.....John Roethlisberger, Minn
1993.....John Roethlisberger, Minn
1994.....Dennis Harrison, Nebraska
1995.....Richard Grace, Nebraska
1996.....Blaine Wilson, Ohio St
1997.....Blaine Wilson, Ohio St
1998.....Travis Romagnoli, Illinois
1999.....Justin Hardabura, Nebraska
2000.....Jamie Natalie, Ohio St
2001.....Jamie Natalie, Ohio St

ALL-AROUND *(Cont.)*

2002.....Raj Bhavsar, Ohio St
2003.....Daniel Furney, Oklahoma
2004.....Luis Vargas, Penn St
2005.....Luis Vargas, Penn St
2006.....Jonathan Horton, Oklahoma

HORIZONTAL BAR

1938.....Bob Sears, Army
1939.....Adam Walters, Temple
1940.....Norm Boardman, Temple
1941.....Newt Loken, Minnesota
1942.....Norm Boardman, Temple
1948.....Joe Calvetti, Illinois
1949.....Bob Stout, Temple
1950.....Joe Kotys, Kent
1951.....Bill Roetzheim, Florida St
1952.....Charles Simms, USC
1953.....Hal Lewis, Navy
1954.....Jean Cronstedt, Penn St
1955.....Carlton Rintz, Michigan St
1956.....Ronnie Amster, Florida St
1957.....Abie Grossfeld, Illinois
1958.....Abie Grossfeld, Illinois
1959.....Stanley Tarshis, Mich St
1960.....Stanley Tarshis, Mich St
1961.....Bruno Klaus, Southern Ill
1962.....Robert Lynn, USC
1963.....Gil Larose, Michigan
1964.....Ron Barak, USC
1965.....Jim Curzi, Michigan St
.........Mike Jacobsen, Penn St
1966.....Rusty Rock, CSU–
.........Northridge
1967.....Rich Grigsby, CSU–
.........Northridge
1968.....Makoto Sakamoto, USC
1969.....Bob Manna, New Mexico
1970.....Yoshi Hayasaki, Wash
1971.....Brent Simmons, Iowa St
1972.....Tom Lindner, Souhern Ill
1973.....Jon Aitken, New Mexico
1974.....Rick Banley, Indiana St
1975.....Rich Larsen, Iowa St
1976.....Tom Beach, California
1977.....John Hart, UCLA
1978.....Mel Cooley, Washington
1979.....Kurt Thomas, Indiana St
1980.....Philip Cahoy, Nebraska
1981.....Philip Cahoy, Nebraska
1982.....Peter Vidmar, UCLA
1983.....Scott Johnson, Nebraska
1984.....Charles Lakes, Illinois
1985.....Dan Hayden, Arizona St
.........Wes Suter, Nebraska
1986.....Dan Hayden, Arizona St
1987.....David Moriel, UCLA
1988.....Vacated†
1989.....Vacated†
1990.....Chris Waller, UCLA
1991.....Luis Lopez, New Mexico
1992.....Jair Lynch, Stanford
1993.....Steve McCain, UCLA

HORIZONTAL BAR *(Cont.)*

1994.....Jim Foody, UCLA
1995.....Rick Kieffer, Nebraska
1996.....Carl Imhauser, Temple
1997.....Marshall Nelson,Nebraska
1998.....Todd Bishop, Oklahoma
1999.....Todd Bishop, Oklahoma
2000.....Michael Ashe, California
2001.....Michael Ashe, California
2002.....Daniel Diaz-Luong, Mich.
2003.....Linas Gaveika, Iowa
2004.....Justin Spring, Illinois
2005.....Ronald Ferris, Ohio St
2006.....Justin Spring, Illinois

PARALLEL BARS

1938.....Erwin Beyer, Chicago
1939.....Bob Sears, Army
1940.....Bob Hanning, Minnesota
1941.....Caton Cobb, Illinois
1942.....Hal Zimmerman, Penn St
1948.....Ray Sorenson, Penn St
1949.....Joe Kotys, Kent
.........Mel Stout, Michigan St
1950.....Joe Kotys, Kent
1951.....Jack Beckner, USC
1952.....Jack Beckner, USC
1953.....Jean Cronstedt, Penn St
1954.....Jean Cronstedt, Penn St
1955.....Carlton Rintz, Michigan St
1956.....Armando Vega, Penn St
1957.....Armando Vega, Penn St
1958.....Tad Muzyczko, Mich St
1959.....Armando Vega, Penn St
1960.....Robert Lynn, USC
1961.....Fred Tijerina, Southern Ill
.........Jeff Cardinalli, Springfield
1962.....Robert Lynn, USC
1963.....Arno Lascari, Michigan
1964.....Ron Barak, USC
1965.....Jim Curzi, Michigan St
1966.....Jim Curzi, Michigan St
1967.....Makoto Sakamoto, USC
1968.....Makoto Sakamoto, USC
1969.....Ron Rapper, Michigan
1970.....Ron Rapper, Michigan
1971.....Brent Simmons, Iowa St
.........Tom Dunn, Penn St
1972.....Dennis Mazur, Iowa St
1973.....Steve Hug, Stanford
1974.....Steve Hug, Stanford
1975.....Yoichi Tomita,
.........Long Beach St
1976.....Gene Whelan, Penn St
1977.....Kurt Thomas, Indiana St
1978.....John Corritore, Michigan
1979.....Kurt Thomas, Indiana St
1980.....Philip Cahoy, Nebraska
1981.....Philip Cahoy, Nebraska
.........Peter Vidmar, UCLA
.........Jim Hartung, Nebraska
1982.....Jim Hartung, Nebraska
1983.....Scott Johnson, Nebraska

PARALLEL BARS *(Cont.)*

1984.....Tim Daggett, UCLA
1985.....Dan Hayden, Arizona St
      Noah Riskin, Ohio St
      Seth Riskin, Ohio St
1986.....Dan Hayden, Arizona St
1987.....Kevin Davis, Nebraska
      Tom Schlesinger, Nebraska
1988.....Kevin Davis, Nebraska
1989.....Vacated†
1990.....Patrick Kirksey, Nebraska
1991.....Scott Keswick, UCLA
      John Roethlisberger, Minn
1992.....Dom Minicucci, Temple
1993.....Jair Lynch, Stanford
1994.....Richard Grace, Nebraska
1995.....Richard Grace, Nebraska
1996.....Jamie Ellis, Stanford
      Blaine Wilson, Ohio St
1997.....Marshall Nelson, Nebraska
1998.....Marshall Nelson, Nebraska
1999.....Justin Toman, Michigan
2000.....Kris Zimmerman, Michigan
      Justin Toman, Michigan
2001 ...Raj Bhavsar, Ohio St
2002 ....Cody Moore, California
2003 ....Daniel Furney, Oklahoma
2004 ....Ramon Jackson, Wm & M
2005 ....Justin Springs, Illinois
2006 ....Justin Springs, Illinois

VAULT

1938.....Erwin Beyer, Chicago
1939.....Marv Forman, Illinois
1940.....Earl Shanken, Chicago
1941.....Earl Shanken, Chicago
1942.....Earl Shanken, Chicago
1948.....Jim Peterson, Minnesota
1962.....Bruno Klaus, S. Illinois
1963.....Gil Larose, Michigan
1964.....Sidney Oglesby, Syracuse
1965.....Dan Millman, California
1966.....Frank Schmitz, S. Illinois
1967.....Paul Mayer, S. Illinois
1968.....Bruce Colter, CSU–LA
1969.....Dan Bowles, California
      Jack McCarthy, Illinois
1970.....Doug Boger, Arizona
1971.....Pat Mahoney, CSU–N'ridge
1972.....Gary Morava, S. Illinois
1973.....John Crosby, S. Conn St
1974......Greg Goodhue, Oklahoma
1975.....Tom Beach, California
1976.....Sam Shaw, CSU-Fullerton
1977.....Steve Wejmar, Wash
1978.....Ron Galimore, LSU
1979.....Leslie Moore, Oklahoma
1980.....Ron Galimore, Iowa St
1981.....Ron Galimore, Iowa St
1982.....Randall Wickstrom, Cal
      Steve Elliott, Nebraska
1983.....Chris Riegel, Nebraska
      Mark Oates, Oklahoma
1984.....Chris Riegel, Nebraska
1985.....Derrick Cornelius, Cort. St
1986.....Chad Fox, New Mexico
1987.....Chad Fox, New Mexico

VAULT *(Cont.)*

1988.....Chad Fox, New Mexico
1989.....Chad Fox, New Mexico
1990.....Brad Hayashi, UCLA
1991.....Adam Carton, Penn St
1992.....Jason Hebert, Syracuse
1993.....Steve Wiegel, New Mexico
1994.....Steve McCain, UCLA
1995.....Ian Bachrach, Stanford
1996.....Jay Thornton, Iowa
1997.....Blaine Wilson, Ohio St
1998.....Travis Romagnoli, Illinois
1999.....Guard Young, BYU
2000.....Guard Young, BYU
2001.....Daren Lynch, Ohio St
2002.....Dan Gill, Stanford
2003.....Andrew DiGiore, Michigan
2004.....Graham Ackerman, Cal
2005.....Michael Reavis, Iowa
2006.....David Sender, Stanford

POMMEL HORSE

1938.....Erwin Beyer, Chicago
1939.....Erwin Beyer, Chicago
1940.....Harry Koehnemann, Illinois
1941.....Caton Cobb, Illinois
1942.....Caton Cobb, Illinois
1948.....Steve Greene, Penn St
1949.....Joe Berenato, Temple
1950.....Gene Rabbitt, Syracuse
1951.....Joe Kotys, Kent
1952.....Frank Bare, Illinois
1953.....Carlton Rintz, Michigan St
1954.....Robert Lawrence, Penn St
1955.....Carlton Rintz, Michigan St
1956.....James Brown, CSU–L.A.
1957.....John Davis, Illinois
1958.....Bill Buck, Iowa
1959.....Art Shurlock, California
1960.....James Fairchild, California
1961.....James Fairchild, California
1962.....Mike Aufrecht, Illinois
1963.....Russ Mills, Yale
1964.....Russ Mills, Yale
1965.....Bob Elsinger, Springfield
1966.....Gary Hoskins, CSU–L.A.
1967.....Keith McCanless, Iowa
1968.....Jack Ryan, Colorado
1969.....Keith McCanless, Iowa
1970.....Russ Hoffman, Iowa St
      John Russo, Wisconsin
1971.....Russ Hoffman, Iowa St
1972.....Russ Hoffman, Iowa St
1973.....Ed Slezak, Indiana St
1974.....Ted Marcy, Stanford
1975.....Ted Marcy, Stanford
1976.....Ted Marcy, Stanford
1977......Chuck Walter, New Mexico
1978.....Mike Burke, N. Illinois
1979.....Mike Burke, N. Illinois
1980.....David Stoldt, Illinois
1981 .....Mark Bergman, California
      Steve Jennings, New Mexico
1982.....Peter Vidmar, UCLA
      Steve Jennings, New Mexico
1983.....Doug Kieso, N. Illinois
1984.....Tim Daggett, UCLA

POMMEL HORSE *(Cont.)*

1985.....Tony Pineda, UCLA
1986.....Curtis Holdsworth, UCLA
1987.....Li Xiao Ping, CSU-Fullerton
1988.....Vacated†
      Mark Sohn, Penn St
1989.....Mark Sohn, Penn St
      Chris Waller, UCLA
1990.....Mark Sohn, Penn St
1991.....Mark Sohn, Penn St
1992.....Che Bowers, Nebraska
1993.....John Roethlisberger, Minn
1994.....Jason Bertram, California
1995.....Drew Durbin, Ohio St
1996.....Drew Durbin, Ohio St
1997.....Drew Durbin, Ohio St
1998.....Josh Birckelbaw, California
1999.....Brandon Stefaniak, Penn St
2000.....Brandon Stefaniak, Penn St
      Don Jackson, Iowa
2001......Clay Strother, Minnesota
2002......Clay Strother, Minnesota
2003.....Josh Landis, Oklahoma
2004.....Bob Rogers, Illinois
2005 ....Luis Vargas, Penn St
2006.....Timothy McNeill, California

FLOOR EXERCISE

1941.....Lou Fina, Illinois
1953.....Bob Sullivan, Illinois
1954.....Jean Cronsted, Penn St
1955.....Don Faber, UCLA
1956.....Jamile Ashmore, Florida St
1957.....Norman Marks, CSU–L.A.
1958.....Abie Grossfeld, Illinois
1959.....Don Tonry, Illinois
1960.....Ray Hadley, Illinois
1961.....Robert Lynn, USC
1962.....Robert Lynn, USC
1963.....Tom Seward, Penn St
      Mike Henderson, Michigan
1964.....Rusty Mitchell, S. Illinois
1965.....Frank Schmitz, S. Illinois
1966.....Frank Schmitz, S. Illinois
1967.....Dave Jacobs, Michigan
1968.....Toby Towson, Michigan St
1969.....Toby Towson, Michigan St
1970.....Tom Proulx, Colorado St
1971.....Stormy Eaton, New Mexico
1972.....Odessa Lovin, Oklahoma
1973.....Odessa Lovin, Oklahoma
1974.....Doug Fitzjarrell, Iowa St
1975.....Kent Brown, Arizona St
1976.....Bob Robbins, Colorado St
1977.....Ron Galimore, LSU
1978.....Curt Austin, Iowa St
1979.....Mike Wilson, Oklahoma
      Bart Conner, Oklahoma
1980.....Steve Elliott, Nebraska
1981.....James Yuhashi, Oregon
1982.....Steve Elliott, Nebraska
1983.....Scott Johnson, Nebraska
      David Branch, Arizona St
      Donnie Hinton, Arizona St
1984.....Kevin Ekburg, N. Illinois
1985.....Wes Suter, Nebraska
1986.....Jerry Burrell, Arizona St
      Brian Ginsberg, UCLA

Men *(Cont.)*
INDIVIDUAL CHAMPIONS *(Cont.)*

FLOOR EXERCISE *(CONT.)*

1987.....Chad Fox, New Mexico
1988....Chris Wyatt, Temple
1989....Jody Newman, Arizona St
1990.....Mike Racanelli, Ohio St
1991....Brad Hayashi, UCLA
1992....Brian Winkler, Michigan
1993....Richard Grace, Nebraska
1994....Mark Booth, Stanford
1995....Jay Thornton, Iowa
1996....Ian Bachrach, Stanford
1997....Jeremy Killen, Oklahoma
1998....Darin Gerlach, Temple
1999......Jason Hardabura, Nebraska
2000.....Jamie Natalie, Ohio St
2001....Clay Strother, Minnesota
2002....Clay Strother, Minnesota
2003....Josh Landis, Oklahoma
2004....Graham Ackerman, Cal
2005....Graham Ackerman, Cal
2006....Jonathan Horton, Okla

RINGS

1959.....Armando Vega, Penn St
1960.....Sam Garcia, USC
1961....Fred Orlofsky, S. Illinois
1962....Dale Cooper, Michigan St

RINGS *(CONT.)*

1963.....Dale Cooper, Michigan St
1964.....Chris Evans, Arizona St
1965.....Glenn Gailis, Iowa
1966.....Ed Gunny, Michigan St
1967.....Josh Robison, California
1968.....Pat Arnold, Arizona
1969.....Paul Vexler, Penn St
     Ward Maythaler, Iowa St
1970.....Dave Seal, Indiana St
1971.....Charles Ropiequet, S. Illinois
1972.....Dave Seal, Indiana St
1973.....Bob Mahorney, Indiana St
1974.....Keith Heaver, Iowa St
1975.....Keith Heaver, Iowa St
1976.....Doug Wood, Iowa St
1977.....Doug Wood, Iowa St
1978......Scott McEldowney, Oregon
1979.....Kirk Mango, N. Illinois
1980.....Jim Hartung, Nebraska
1981.....Jim Hartung, Nebraska
1982.....Jim Hartung, Nebraska
1983.....Alex Schwartz, UCLA
1984.....Tim Daggett, UCLA
1985.....Mark Diab, Iowa St
1986.....Mark Diab, Iowa St

RINGS *(CONT.)*

1987.....Paul O'Neill, Hou. Baptist
1988.....Paul O'Neill, New Mexico
1989.....Vacated†
     Paul O'Neill, New Mexico
1990.....Wayne Cowden, Penn St
1991.....Adam Carton, Penn St
1992....Scott Keswick, UCLA
1993....Chris LaMorte, New Mexico
1994....Chris LaMorte, New Mexico
1995....Dave Frank, Temple
1996....Scott McCall, Will. & Mary
     Blaine Wilson, Ohio St
1997.....Blaine Wilson, Ohio St
1998.....Dan Fink, Oklahoma
1999.....Cortney Bramwell, BYU
2000.....Cortney Bramwell, BYU
2001.....Chris Lakeman, Penn St
2002.....Marshall Erwin, Stanford
2003.....Kevin Tan, Penn St
2004.....Kevin Tan, Penn St
2005.....David Henderson, Okla.
2006.....Jonathan Horton, Okla.

†Championships won by Miguel Rubio (All Around, 1988; Horizontal Bar, 1988–89) and Alfonso Rodriguez (Pommel Horse, 1988; Rings, 1989; Parallel Bars, 1989) were vacated by action of the NCAA Committee on Infractions.

DIVISION II *(Discontinued after 1984)*

Year	Champion	Coach	Pts	Runner-Up	Pts
1968	CSU–Northridge	Bill Vincent	179.400	Springfield	178.050
1969	CSU–Northridge	Bill Vincent	151.800	Southern Connecticut St	145.075
1970	NW Louisiana	Armando Vega	160.250	Southern Connecticut St	159.300
1971	CSU–Fullerton	Dick Wolfe	158.150	Springfield	156.987
1972	CSU–Fullerton	Dick Wolfe	160.550	Southern Connecticut St	153.050
1973	Southern Conn. St	Abe Grossfeld	160.750	CSU–Northridge	158.700
1974	CSU–Fullerton	Dick Wolfe	309.800	Southern Connecticut St	309.400
1975	Southern Conn. St	Abe Grossfeld	411.650	Ill.–Chicago	398.800
1976	Southern Conn. St	Abe Grossfeld	419.200	Ill.–Chicago	388.850
1977	Springfield	Frank Wolcott	395.950	CSU–Northridge	381.250
1978	Ill.–Chicago	C. Johnson/A. Gentile	406.850	CSU–Northridge	400.400
1979	Ill.–Chicago	Clarence Johnson	418.550	UW–Oshkosh	385.650
1980	UW–Oshkosh	Ken Allen	260.550	CSU–Chico	256.050
1981	UW–Oshkosh	Ken Allen	209.500	Springfield	201.550
1982	UW–Oshkosh	Ken Allen	216.050	E Stroudsburg	211.200
1983	E. Stroudsburg	Bruno Klaus	258.650	UW–Oshkosh	257.850
1984	E. Stroudsburg	Bruno Klaus	270.800	Cortland St	246.350

Women
TEAM CHAMPIONS

Year	Champion	Coach	Pts	Runner-Up	Pts
1982	Utah	Greg Marsden	148.60	CSU–Fullerton	144.10
1983	Utah	Greg Marsden	184.65	Arizona St	183.30
1984	Utah	Greg Marsden	186.05	UCLA	185.55
1985	Utah	Greg Marsden	188.35	Arizona St	186.60
1986	Utah	Greg Marsden	186.95	Arizona St	186.70
1987	Georgia	Suzanne Yoculan	187.90	Utah	187.55
1988	Alabama	Sarah Patterson	190.05	Utah	189.50
1989	Georgia	Suzanne Yoculan	192.65	UCLA	192.60
1990	Utah	Greg Marsden	194.900	Alabama	194.575
1991	Alabama	Sarah Patterson	195.125	Utah	194.375
1992	Utah	Greg Marsden	195.650	Georgia	194.600
1993	Georgia	Suzanne Yoculan	198.000	Alabama	196.825
1994	Utah	Greg Marsden	196.400	Alabama	196.350
1995	Utah	Greg Marsden	196.650	Alabama	196.425
				Michigan	196.425

Women (Cont.)

TEAM CHAMPIONS

Year	Champion	Coach	Pts	Runner-Up	Pts
1996	Alabama	Sarah Patterson	198.025	UCLA	197.475
1997	UCLA	Valorie Kondos	197.150	Arizona St	196.850
1998	Georgia	Suzanne Yoculan	197.725	Florida	196.350
1999	Georgia	Suzanne Yoculan	196.850	Michigan	196.550
2000	UCLA	Valorie Kondos	197.300	Utah	196.875
2001	UCLA	Valorie Kondos	197.575	Georgia	197.400
2002	Alabama	Sarah Patterson	197.575	Georgia	197.250
2003	UCLA	Valorie Kondos Field	197.825	Alabama	197.275
2004	UCLA	Valorie Kondos Field	198.125	Georgia	197.200
2005	Georgia	Suzanne Yoculan	197.825	Alabama	197.400
2006	Georgia	Suzanne Yoculan	197.750	Utah	196.800

INDIVIDUAL CHAMPIONS

ALL-AROUND

1982.....Sue Stednitz, Utah
1983.....Megan McCunniff, Utah
1984......Megan McCunniff-Marsden, Utah
1985.......Penney Hauschild, Alabama
1986.......Penney Hauschild, Alabama
 Jackie Brummer, Arizona St
1987.....Kelly Garrison-Steves, Oklahoma
1988.....Kelly Garrison-Steves, Oklahoma
1989.....Corrinne Wright, Georgia
1990.....Dee Dee Foster, Alabama
1991.....Hope Spivey, Georgia
1992.....Missy Marlowe, Utah
1993.....Jenny Hansen, Kentucky
1994.....Jenny Hansen, Kentucky
1995.....Jenny Hansen, Kentucky
1996.....Meredith Willard, Alabama
1997.....Kim Arnold, Georgia
1998.....Kim Arnold, Georgia
1999.....Theresa Kulikowski, Utah
2000.....Mohini Bhardwaj, UCLA
 Heather Brink, Nebraska
2001 ....Onnis Willis, UCLA
 Elise Ray, Michigan
2002 ...Jamie Dantzscher, UCLA
2003 ....Richelle Simpson, Neb.
2004 ....Jeana Rice, Alabama
2005 ....Katie Heenan, Georgia
2006.....Courtney Kupets, Georgia

VAULT

1982.....Elaine Alfano, Utah
1983.....Elaine Alfano, Utah
1984.....Megan Marsden, Utah
1985.....Elaine Alfano, Utah
1986.....Kim Neal, Arizona St
 Pam Loree, Penn St
1987.....Yumi Mordre, Washington
1988.....Jill Andrews, UCLA
1989.....Kim Hamilton, UCLA
1990.....Michele Bryant, Nebraska
1991.....Anna Basaldva, Arizona
1992.....Tammy Marshall, Mass.
 Heather Stepp, Georgia
 Kristein Kenoyer, Utah
1993.....Heather Stepp, Georgia
1994.....Jenny Hansen, Kentucky
1995.....Jenny Hansen, Kentucky
1996.....Leah Brown, Georgia

VAULT (Cont.)

1997.....Susan Hines, Florida
1998.....Susan Hines, Florida
1999.....Heidi Moneymaker, UCLA
2000.....Heather Brink, Nebraska
2001 ....Cory Fritzinger, Georgia
2002.....Jamie Dantzscher, UCLA
2003.....Ashley Miles, Alabama
2004.....Ashley Miles, Alabama
2005.....Kristen Maloney, UCLA
2006.....Ashley Miles, Alabama

BALANCE BEAM

1982.....Sue Stednitz, Utah
1983.....Julie Goewey, CSU–Fullerton
1984.....Heidi Anderson, Oregon St
1985.....Lisa Zeis, Arizona St
1986.....Jackie Brummer, Arizona St
1987.....Yumi Mordre, Washington
1988.....Kelly Garrison-Steves, Oklahoma
1989.....Jill Andrews, UCLA
 Joy Selig, Oregon St
1990.....Joy Selig, Oregon St
1991.....Missy Marlowe, Utah
1992.....Missy Marlowe, Utah
1992 ....Dana Dobransky, Alabama
1993 ....Dana Dobransky, Alabama
1994.....Jenny Hansen, Kentucky
1995.....Jenny Hansen, Kentucky
1996.....Summer Reid, UUtah
1997.....Summer Reid, Utah
 Elizabeth Reid, Arizona St
1998 Larissa Fontaine, Stanford
 Susan Hines, Florida
1999.....Theresa Kulikowski, Utah
2000.....Lena Degteva, UCLA
2001.....Theresa Kulikowski, Utah
2002.....Elise Ray, Michigan
2003.....Kate Richardson, UCLA
2004.....Ashley Kelly, Arizona St
2005.....Kristen Maloney, UCLA
2006.....Courtney Kupets, Georgia

FLOOR EXERCISE

1982.....Mary Ayotte-Law, Oregon St
1983.....Kim Neal, Arizona St
1984.....Maria Anz, Florida
1985.....Lisa Mitzel, Utah

FLOOR EXERCISE (Cont.)

1986.....Lisa Zeis, Arizona St
 P. Hauschild, Alabama
1987.....Kim Hamilton, UCLA
1988.....Kim Hamilton, UCLA
1989.....Corrinne Wright, Georgia
 Kim Hamilton, UCLA
1990.....Joy Selig, Oregon St
1991.....Hope Spivey, Georgia
1992.....Missy Marlowe, Utah
1993.....Heather Stepp, Georgia
 Tammy Marshall, Mass.
 Amy Durham, Oregon St
1994.....Hope Spivey-Sheeley, Georgia
1995.....Jenny Hansen, Kentucky
 Stella Umeh, UCLA
 Leslie Angeles, Georgia
1996.....Heidi Hornbeek, Arizona
 Kim Kelly, Alabama
1997.....Leah Brown, Georgia
1998.....Kim Arnold, Georgia
 Jenni Beathard, Georgia
 Betsy Hamm, Florida
1999.....Marny Oestreng, Bowl. Green
2000.....Suzanne Sears, Georgia
2001.....Mohini Bhardwaj, UCLA
2002.....Jamie Dantzscher, UCLA
 Nicole Arnstad, LSU
2003.....Richelle Simpson, Neb.
2004.....Ashley Miles, Alabama
 Courtney Bumpers, N.Car.
2005.....Courtney Bumpers, N.Car.
2006.....Kate Richardson UCLA

UNEVEN BARS

1982.....Lisa Shirk, Pittsburgh
1983.....Jeri Cameron, Arizona St
1984.....Jackie Brummer, Arizona St
1985.....Penney Hauschild, Alabama
1986.....Lucy Wener, Georgia
1987.....Lucy Wener, Georgia
1988.....Kelly Garrison-Steves, Oklahoma
1989.....Lucy Wener, Georgia
1990.....Marie Roethlisberger, Minnesota
1991.....Kelly Macy, Georgia
1992.....Missy Marlowe, Utah
1993.....Agina Simpkins, Georgia
 Beth Wymer, Michigan

Women (Cont.)

INDIVIDUAL CHAMPIONS

UNEVEN BARS (CONT.)

1994.....Sandy Woolsey, Utah
     Beth Wymer, Michigan
     Lori Strong, Georgia
1995.....Beth Wymer, Michigan
1996.....Stephanie Woods, Alabama

1997.....Jenni Beathard, Georgia
1998.....Karin Lichey, Georgia
     Stella Umeh, UCLA
1999.....Angie Leionard, Utah
2000.....Mohini Bhardwaj, UCLA
2001.....Yvonne Tousek, UCLA

2002 .....Andree' Pickens, Alabama
2003 .....Jamie Dantzscher, UCLA
     Kate Richardson, UCLA
2004.....Elise Ray, Michigan
2005.....Terin Humphrey, Alabama
2006......Courtney Kupets, Georgia

Ice Hockey

Men

DIVISION I

Year	Champion	Coach	Score	Runner-Up	Most Outstanding Player
1948	Michigan	Vic Heyliger	8–4	Dartmouth	Joe Riley, Dartmouth, F
1949	Boston College	John Kelley	4–3	Dartmouth	Dick Desmond, Dartmouth, G
1950	Colorado College	Cheddy Thompson	13–4	Boston University	Ralph Bevins, Boston University, G
1951	Michigan	Vic Heyliger	7–1	Brown	Ed Whiston, Brown, G
1952	Michigan	Vic Heyliger	4–1	Colorado College	Kenneth Kinsley, Colorado Coll, G
1953	Michigan	Vic Heyliger	7–3	Minnesota	John Matchefts, Michigan, F
1954	Rensselaer	Ned Harkness	5–4 (OT)	Minnesota	Abbie Moore, Rensselaer, F
1955	Michigan	Vic Heyliger	5–3	Colorado College	Philip Hilton, Colorado College, D
1956	Michigan	Vic Heyliger	7–5	Michigan Tech	Lorne Howes, Michigan, G
1957	Colorado College	Thomas Bedecki	13–6	Michigan	Bob McCusker, Colorado Coll, F
1958	Denver	Murray Armstrong	6–2	North Dakota	Murray Massier, Denver, F
1959	North Dakota	Bob May	4–3 (OT)	Michigan St	Reg Morelli, North Dakota, F
1960	Denver	Murray Armstrong	5–3	Michigan Tech	Bob Marquis, Boston University, F
1961	Denver	Murray Armstrong	12–2	St. Lawrence	Barry Urbanski, Boston Univ, G
1962	Michigan Tech	John MacInnes	7–1	Clarkson	Louis Angotti, Michigan Tech, F
1963	North Dakota	Barney Thorndycraft	6–5	Denver	Al McLean, North Dakota, F
1964	Michigan	Allen Renfrew	6–3	Denver	Bob Gray, Michigan, G
1965	Michigan Tech	John MacInnes	8–2	Boston College	Gary Milroy, Michigan Tech, F
1966	Michigan St	Amo Bessone	6–1	Clarkson	Gaye Cooley, Michigan St, G
1967	Cornell	Ned Harkness	4–1	Boston University	Walt Stanowski, Cornell, D
1968	Denver	Murray Armstrong	4–0	North Dakota	Gerry Powers, Denver, G
1969	Denver	Murray Armstrong	4–3	Cornell	Keith Magnuson, Denver, D
1970	Cornell	Ned Harkness	6–4	Clarkson	Daniel Lodboa, Cornell, D
1971	Boston University	Jack Kelley	4–2	Minnesota	Dan Brady, Boston University, G
1972	Boston University	Jack Kelley	4–0	Cornell	Tim Regan, Boston University, G
1973	Wisconsin	Bob Johnson	4–2	Vacated	Dean Talafous, Wisconsin, F
1974	Minnesota	Herb Brooks	4–2	Michigan Tech	Brad Shelstad, Minnesota, G
1975	Michigan Tech	John MacInnes	6–1	Minnesota	Jim Warden, Michigan Tech, G
1976	Minnesota	Herb Brooks	6–4	Michigan Tech	Tom Vanelli, Minnesota, F
1977	Wisconsin	Bob Johnson	6–5 (OT)	Michigan	Julian Baretta, Wisconsin, G
1978	Boston University	Jack Parker	5–3	Boston College	Jack O'Callahan, Boston Univ, D
1979	Minnesota	Herb Brooks	4–3	North Dakota	Steve Janaszak, Minnesota, G
1980	North Dakota	John Gasparini	5–2	Northern Michigan	Doug Smail, North Dakota, F
1981	Wisconsin	Bob Johnson	6–3	Minnesota	Marc Behrend, Wisconsin, G
1982	North Dakota	John Gasparini	5–2	Wisconsin	Phil Sykes, North Dakota, F
1983	Wisconsin	Jeff Sauer	6–2	Harvard	Marc Behrend, Wisconsin, G
1984	Bowling Green	Jerry York	5–4 (OT)	Minn.–Duluth	Gary Kruzich, Bowling Green, G
1985	Rensselaer	Mike Addesa	2–1	Providence	Chris Terreri, Providence, G
1986	Michigan St	Ron Mason	6–5	Harvard	Mike Donnelly, Michigan St, F
1987	North Dakota	John Gasparini	5–3	Michigan St	Tony Hrkac, North Dakota, F
1988	Lake Superior St	Frank Anzalone	4–3 (OT)	St. Lawrence	Bruce Hoffort, Lake Superior St, G
1989	Harvard	Bill Cleary	4–3 (OT)	Minnesota	Ted Donato, Harvard, F
1990	Wisconsin	Jeff Sauer	7–3	Colgate	Chris Tancill, Wisconsin, F
1991	Northern Michigan	Rick Comley	8–7 (3OT)	Boston University	Scott Beattie, Northern Michigan, F
1992	Lake Superior St	Jeff Jackson	4–2	Wisconsin	Paul Constantin, Lake Superior St, F
1993	Maine	Shawn Walsh	5–4	Lake Superior St	Jim Montgomery, Maine, F
1994	Lake Superior St	Jeff Jackson	9–1	Boston University	Sean Tallaire, Lake Superior St, F
1995	Boston University	Jack Parker	6–2	Maine	Chris O'Sullivan, Boston Univ, F
1996	Michigan	Red Berenson	3–2 (OT)	Colorado College	Brendan Morrison, Michigan, F
1997	North Dakota	Dean Blais	6–4	Boston University	Matt Henderson, North Dakota, F
1998	Michigan	Red Berenson	3–2 (OT)	Boston College	Marty Turco, Michigan, G
1999	Maine	Shawn Walsh	3–2 (OT)	New Hampshire	Alfie Michaud, Maine, G
2000	North Dakota	Dean Blais	4–2	Boston College	Lee Goren, North Dakota, F

Men

DIVISION I *(Cont.)*

Year	Champion	Coach	Score	Runner-Up	Most Outstanding Player
2001	Boston College	Jerry York	3–2 (OT)	North Dakota	Chuck Kobasew, Boston Coll, F
2002	Minnesota	Don Lucia	4–3 (OT)	Maine	Grant Potulny, Minnesota, F
2003	Minnesota	Don Lucia	5–1	New Hampshire	Thomas Vanek, Minnesota, F
2004	Denver	George Gwozdecky	1–0	Maine	Adam Berkhoel, Denver, G
2005	Denver	George Gwozdecky	4–1	North Dakota	Peter Mannino, Denver
2006	Wisconsin	Mike Eaves	2–1	Boston College	Robbie Earl, Wisconsin, F

DIVISION II *(Discontinued)*

Year	Champion	Coach	Score	Runner-Up
1978	Merrimack	Thom Lawler	12–2	Lake Forest
1979	Lowell	Bill Riley Jr	6–4	Mankato St
1980	Mankato St	Don Brose	5–2	Elmira
1981	Lowell	Bill Riley Jr	5–4	Plattsburgh St
1982	Lowell	Bill Riley Jr	6–1	Plattsburgh St
1983	RIT	Brian Mason	4–2	Bemidji St
1984	Bemidji St	R.H. (Bob) Peters	14–4*	Merrimack
1993	Bemidji St	R.H. (Bob) Peters	15–6*	Mercyhurst
1994	Bemidji St	R.H. (Bob) Peters	7–6*	Ala.–Huntsville
1995	Bemidji St	R.H. (Bob) Peters	11–6*	Mercyhurst
1996	Ala.–Huntsville	Doug Ross	10–1*	Bemidji St
1997	Bemidji St	R.H. (Bob) Peters	7–4*	Ala.–Huntsville
1998	Ala.–Huntsville	Doug Ross	11–4*	Bemidji St
1999	St. Michael's (Vt.)	Lou DiMasi	12–9*	New Hamp. Coll

*Two-game, total-goal series.

DIVISION III

Year	Champion	Coach	Score	Runner-Up
1984	Babson	Bob Riley	8–0	Union (N.Y.)
1985	RIT	Bruce Delventhal	5–1	Bemidji St
1986	Bemidji St	R.H. (Bob) Peters	8–5	Vacated
1987	Vacated			Oswego St
1988	UW-River Falls	Rick Kozuback	7–1, 3–5, 3–0	Elmira
1989	UW-Stevens Point	Mark Mazzoleni	3–3, 3–2	RIT
1990	UW-Stevens Point	Mark Mazzoleni	10–1, 3–6, 1–0	Plattsburgh St
1991	UW-Stevens Point	Mark Mazzoleni	6–2	Mankato St
1992	Plattsburgh St	Bob Emery	7–3	UW-Stevens Point
1993	UW-Stevens Point	Joe Baldarotta	4–3	UW-River Falls
1994	UW-River Falls	Dean Talafous	6–4	UW-Superior
1995	Middlebury	Bill Beaney	1–0	Fredonia St
1996	Middlebury	Bill Beaney	3–2	RIT
1997	Middlebury	Bill Beaney	3–2	UW-Superior
1998	Middlebury	Bill Beaney	2–1	UW-Stevens Point
1999	Middlebury	Bill Beaney	5–0	UW-Superior
2000	Norwich	Michael McShane	2–1	St. Thomas (Minn.)
2001	Plattsburgh	Bob Emery	6–2	RIT
2002	UW-Superior	Dan Stauber	3–2	Norwich
2003	Norwich	Michael McShane	2–1	Oswego St
2004	Middlebury	Bill Beaney	1–0	St. Norbert
2005	Middlebury	Bill Beaney	5–0	St. Thomas (Minn.)
2006	Middlebury	Bill Beaney	3–0	St. Norbert

Women - DIVISION I

Year	Champion	Coach	Score	Runner-Up
2001	Minn.-Duluth	Shannon Miller	4–2	St. Lawrence
2002	Minn.-Duluth	Shannon Miller	3–2	Brown
2003	Minn.-Duluth	Shannon Miller	4–3 (2 OT)	Harvard
2004	Minnesota	Laura Holldorson	6–2	Harvard
2005	Minnesota	Laura Holldorson	4–3	Harvard
2006	Wisconsin	Mark Johnson	3–0	Minnesota

Men - DIVISION I

Year	Champion	Coach	Score	Runner-Up
1971	Cornell	Richie Moran	12–6	Maryland
1972	Virginia	Glenn Thiel	13–12	Johns Hopkins
1973	Maryland	Bud Beardmore	10–9 (2 OT)	Johns Hopkins
1974	Johns Hopkins	Bob Scott	17–12	Maryland
1975	Maryland	Bud Beardmore	20–13	Navy
1976	Cornell	Richie Moran	16–13 (OT)	Maryland
1977	Cornell	Richie Moran	16–8	Johns Hopkins
1978	Johns Hopkins	Henry Ciccarone	13–8	Cornell
1979	Johns Hopkins	Henry Ciccarone	15–9	Maryland
1980	Johns Hopkins	Henry Ciccarone	9–8 (2 OT)	Virginia
1981	North Carolina	Willie Scroggs	14–13	Johns Hopkins
1982	North Carolina	Willie Scroggs	7–5	Johns Hopkins
1983	Syracuse	Roy Simmons Jr	17–16	Johns Hopkins
1984	Johns Hopkins	Don Zimmerman	13–10	Syracuse
1985	Johns Hopkins	Don Zimmerman	11–4	Syracuse
1986	North Carolina	Willie Scroggs	10–9 (OT)	Virginia
1987	Johns Hopkins	Don Zimmerman	11–10	Cornell
1988	Syracuse	Roy Simmons Jr	13–8	Cornell
1989	Syracuse	Roy Simmons Jr	13–12	Johns Hopkins
1990	Syracuse	Roy Simmons Jr	21–9	Loyola (Md.)
1991	N.Carolina	Dave Klarmann	18–13	Towson St
1992	Princeton	Bill Tierney	10–9	Syracuse
1993	Syracuse	Roy Simmons Jr	13–12	N.Carolina
1994	Princeton	Bill Tierney	9–8 (OT)	Virginia
1995	Syracuse	Roy Simmons Jr	13–9	Maryland
1996	Princeton	Bill Tierney	13–12 (OT)	Virginia
1997	Princeton	Bill Tierney	19–7	Maryland
1998	Princeton	Bill Tierney	15–5	Maryland
1999	Virginia	Dom Starsia	12–10	Syracuse
2000	Syracuse	John Desko	13–7	Princeton
2001	Princeton	Bill Tierney	10–9 (OT)	Syracuse
2002	Syracuse	John Desko	13–12	Princeton
2003	Virginia	Dom Stargia	9–7	Johns Hopkins
2004	Syracuse	John Desko	14–13	Navy
2005	Johns Hopkins	Dave Pietramala	9–8	Duke
2006	Virgina	Dom Stargia	15–7	Massachusetts

DIVISION II *(Discontinued, then renewed)*

Year	Champion	Coach	Score	Runner-Up
1974	Towson St	Carl Runk	18–17 (OT)	Hobart
1975	Cortland St	Chuck Winters	12–11	Hobart
1976	Hobart	Jerry Schmidt	18–9	Adelphi
1977	Hobart	Jerry Schmidt	23–13	Washington (Md.)
1978	Roanoke	Paul Griffin	14–13	Hobart
1979	Adelphi	Paul Doherty	17–12	Md.–Baltimore County
1980	Md.–Baltimore County	Dick Watts	23–14	Adelphi
1981	Adelphi	Paul Doherty	17–14	Loyola (Md.)
1993	Adelphi	Kevin Sheehan	11–7	LIU–C.W. Post
1994	Springfield	Keith Bugbee	15–12	New York Tech
1995	Adelphi	Sandy Kapatos	12–10	Springfield
1996	LIU–C.W. Post	Tom Postel	15–10	Adelphi
1997	New York Tech	Jack Kaley	18–11	Adelphi
1998	Adelphi	Sandy Kapatos	18–6	LIU–C.W. Post
1999	Adelphi	Sandy Kapatos	11–8	LIU–C.W. Post
2000	Limestone	Mike Cerino	10–9	LIU–C.W. Post
2001	Adelphi	Sandy Kapatos	14–10	Limestone
2002	Limestone	T.W. Johnson	11–9	New York Tech
2003	New York Tech	Jack Kaley	9–4	Limestone
2004	Le Moyne	Dan Sheehan	11–10 (2OT)	Limestone
2005	NYIT	Jack Kaley	14–13	Limestone
2006	Le Moyne	Dan Sheehan	12–5	Dowling

DIVISION III

Year	Champion	Coach	Score	Runner-Up
1980	Hobart	Dave Urick	11–8	Cortland St
1981	Hobart	Dave Urick	10–8	Cortland St
1982	Hobart	Dave Urick	9–8 (OT)	Washington (Md.)
1983	Hobart	Dave Urick	13–9	Roanoke

Men *(Cont.)*

DIVISION III *(Cont.)*

Year	Champion	Coach	Score	Runner-Up
1984	Hobart	Dave Urick	12–5	Washington (Md.)
1985	Hobart	Dave Urick	15–8	Washington (Md.)
1986	Hobart	Dave Urick	13–10	Washington (Md.)
1987	Hobart	Dave Urick	9–5	Ohio Wesleyan
1988	Hobart	Dave Urick	18–9	Ohio Wesleyan
1989	Hobart	Dave Urick	11–8	Ohio Wesleyan
1990	Hobart	B.J. O'Hara	18–6	Washington (Md.)
1991	Hobart	B.J. O'Hara	12–11	Salisbury St
1992	Nazareth (NY)	Scott Nelson	13–12	Hobart
1993	Hobart	B.J. O'Hara	16–10	Ohio Wesleyan
1994	Salisbury St	Jim Berkman	15–9	Hobart
1995	Salisbury St	Jim Berkman	22–13	Nazareth
1996	Nazareth	Scott Nelson	11–10 (OT)	Washington (Md.)
1997	Nazareth	Scott Nelson	15–14 (OT)	Washington (Md.)
1998	Washington (Md.)	John Haus	16–10	Nazareth
1999	Salisbury St	Jim Berkman	13–6	Middlebury
2000	Middlebury	Erin Quinn	16–12	Salisbury St
2001	Middlebury	Erin Quinn	15–10	Gettysburg
2002	Middlebury	Erin Quinn	14–9	Gettysburg
2003	Salisbury	Jim Berkman	14–13	Middlebury
2004	Salisbury	Jim Berkman	13–9	Nazareth
2005	Salisbury	Jim Berkman	11–10	Middlebury
2006	Cortland	Rich Barnes	13–12 (OT)	Salisbury

Women

DIVISION I*

Year	Champion	Coach	Score	Runner-Up
2001	Maryland	Cindy Timchal	14–13 (OT)	Georgetown
2002	Princeton	Chris Sailer	12–7	Georgetown
2003	Princeton	Chris Sailer	8–7 (OT)	Virginia
2004	Virginia	Julie Myers	10–4	Princeton
2005	Northwestern	Kelly Amonte	13–10	Virginia
2006	Northwestern	Kelly Amonte Hiller	7–4	Dartmouth

DIVISION II

Year	Champion	Coach	Score	Runner-Up
2001	LIU–C.W. Post	Karen MacCrate	13–9	West Chester
2002	Westchester	Ginny Martino	11–6	Stonehill
2003	Stonehill	Michael Daly	9–8	Longwood
2004	Adelphi	Jill Lessne	12–11	West Chester
2005	Stonehill	Michael Daly	13–10	West Chester
2006	Adelphi	Jill Lessne-Solomon	16–8	West Chester

*Divisions I and II competed for a single championship until 2001.

DIVISIONS I AND II

Year	Champion	Coach	Score	Runner-Up
1982	Massachusetts	Pamela Hixon	9–6	Trenton St
1983	Delaware	Janet Smith	10–7	Temple
1984	Temple	Tina Sloan Green	6–4	Maryland
1985	New Hampshire	Marisa Didio	6–5	Maryland
1986	Maryland	Sue Tyler	11–10	Penn St
1987	Penn St	Susan Scheetz	7–6	Temple
1988	Temple	Tina Sloan Green	15–7	Penn St
1989	Penn St	Susan Scheetz	7–6	Harvard
1990	Harvard	Carole Kleinfelder	8–7	Maryland
1991	Virginia	Jane Miller	8–6	Maryland
1992	Maryland	Cindy Timchal	11–10	Harvard
1993	Virginia	Jane Miller	8–6 (OT)	Princeton
1994	Princeton	Chris Sailer	10–7	Virginia
1995	Maryland	Cindy Timchal	13–5	Princeton
1996	Maryland	Cindy Timchal	10–5	Virginia
1997	Maryland	Cindy Timchal	8–7	Loyola (Md.)
1998	Maryland	Cindy Timchal	11–5	Virginia
1999	Maryland	Cindy Timchal	16–6	Virginia
2000	Maryland	Cindy Timchal	16–8	Princeton

Women

DIVISION III

Year	Champion	Score	Runner-Up	Year	Champion	Score	Runner-Up
1985	Trenton St	7–4	Ursinus	1996	Trenton St	15–8	Middlebury
1986	Ursinus	12–10	Trenton St	1997	Middlebury	14–9	College of NJ*
1987	Trenton St	8–7 (ot)	Ursinus	1998	Coll of NJ	14–9	Williams
1988	Trenton St	14–11	William Smith	1999	Middlebury	10–9	Amherst
1989	Ursinus	8–6	Trenton St	2000	Coll of NJ	14–8	Williams
1990	Ursinus	7–6	St. Lawrence	2001	Middlebury	11–10	Amherst
1991	Trenton St	7–6	Ursinus	2002	Middlebury	12–6	College of NJ*
1992	Trenton St	5–3	William Smith	2003	Amherst	11–9	Middlebury
1993	Trenton St	10–9	William Smith	2004	Middlebury	13–11 (OT)	College of NJ*
1994	Trenton St	29–11	William Smith	2005	College of NJ*	10-4	Gettysburg
1995	Trenton St	14–13	William Smith	*Formerly Trenton St			

Rifle

Year	Champion	Coach	Score	Runner-Up	Score	Air Rifle	Smallbore
						INDIVIDUAL CHAMPIONS	
1980	Tennessee Tech	James Newkirk	6201	West Virginia	6150	Rod Fitz-Randolph, Tennessee Tech	Rod Fitz-Randolph, Tennessee Tech
1981	Tennessee Tech	James Newkirk	6139	West Virginia	6136	John Rost, West Virginia	Kurt Fitz-Randolph, Tennessee Tech
1982	Tennessee Tech	James Newkirk	6138	West Virginia	6136	John Rost, West Virginia	Kurt Fitz-Randolph, Tennessee Tech
1983	West Virginia	Edward Etzel	6166	Tennessee Tech	6148	Ray Slonena, Tennessee Tech	David Johnson, West Virginia
1984	West Virginia	Edward Etzel	6206	E Tennessee St	6142	Pat Spurgin, Murray St	Bob Broughton, West Virginia
1985	Murray St	Elvis Green	6150	West Virginia	6149	Christian Heller, West Virginia	Pat Spurgin, Murray St
1986	West Virginia	Edward Etzel	6229	Murray St	6163	Marianne Wallace, Murray St	Mike Anti, West Virginia
1987	Murray St	Elvis Green	6205	West Virginia	6203	Rob Harbison, Tenn.–Martin	Web Wright, West Virginia
1988	West Virginia	Greg Perrine	6192	Murray St	6183	Deena Wigger, Murray St	Web Wright, West Virginia
1989	West Virginia	Edward Etzel	6234	South Florida	6180	Michelle Scarborough, South Florida	Deb Sinclair, AK–Fairbanks
1990	West Virginia	Marsha Beasley	6205	Navy	6101	Gary Hardy, West Virginia	M. Scarborough, South Florida
1991	West Virginia	Marsha Beasley	6171	AK–Fairbanks	6110	Ann Pfiffner, West Virginia	Soma Dutta, UTEP
1992	West Virginia	Marsha Beasley	6214	AK–Fairbanks	6166	Ann Pfiffner, West Virginia	Tim Manges, West Virginia
1993	West Virginia	Marsha Beasley	6179	AK–Fairbanks	6169	Trevor Gathman, West Virginia	Eric Uptagrafft, West Virginia
1994	AK–Fairbanks	Randy Pitney	6194	West Virginia	6187	Nancy Napolski, Kentucky	Cory Brunetti, AK–Fairbanks
1995	West Virginia	Marsha Beasley	6241	Air Force	6187	Benji Belden, Murray St	Oleg Selezner, AK–Fairbanks
1996	West Virginia	Marsha Beasley	6179	Air Force	6168	T. Gathman, WVa	Joe Johnson, Navy
1997	West Virginia	Marsha Beasley	6223	Kentucky	6175	Marra Hastings, Murray St	Marcos Scrivner, West Virginia
1998	West Virginia	Marsha Beasley	6214	AK–Fairbanks	6175	Emily Caruso, Norwich	Karen Juzinuk, Xavier
1999	AK-Fairbanks	Randy Pitney	6276	Navy	6168	Kelly Mansfield, AK–Fairbanks	Kelly Mansfield, AK–Fairbanks
2000	AK-Fairbanks	Randy Pitney	6285	Xavier	6156	Kelly Mansfield, AK–Fairbanks	Nicole Allaire, Nebraska
2001	AK-Fairbanks	David Johnson	6283	Kentucky	6175	Matthew Emmons, AK–Fairbanks	Matthew Emmons, AK–Fairbanks
2002	AK-Fairbanks	Randy Pitney	6241	Kentucky	6209	Ryan Tanoue, Nevada	Matthew Emmons, AK–Fairbanks

Rifle (Cont.)

Year	Champion	Coach	Score	Runner-Up	Score	Air Rifle	Smallbore
2003	AK-Fairbanks	Glenn Dubis	6287	Xavier	6187	Jamie Beyerle, AK-Fairbanks	Matthew Emmons AK–Fairbanks
2004	AK-Fairbanks	Glenn Dubis	6273	Nevada	6185	Morgan Hicks, Murray St	Matthew Rawlings AK–Fairbanks
2005 ...Army		Ron Wigger	4659	Jacksonville	4658	Beth Tidmore, Murr St	Matthew Rawlings
2006 ...AK-Fairbanks		Dan Jordan	4682	Nebraska	4666	Kristina Fehlings, Nebraska	Jamie Beyerle, AK-Fairbanks

Skiing

Year	Champion	Coach	Pts	Runner-Up	Pts	Host or Site
1954	Denver	Willy Schaeffler	384.0	Seattle	349.6	Nev.–Reno
1955	Denver	Willy Schaeffler	567.05	Dartmouth	558.935	Norwich
1956	Denver	Willy Schaeffler	582.01	Dartmouth	541.77	Winter Park
1957	Denver	Willy Schaeffler	577.95	Colorado	545.29	Ogden Snow Basin
1958	Dartmouth	Al Merrill	561.2	Denver	550.6	Dartmouth
1959	Colorado	Bob Beattie	549.4	Denver	543.6	Winter Park
1960	Colorado	Bob Beattie	571.4	Denver	568.6	Bridger Bowl
1961	Denver	Willy Schaeffler	376.19	Middlebury	366.94	Middlebury
1962	Denver	Willy Schaeffler	390.08	Colorado	374.30	Squaw Valley
1963	Denver	Willy Schaeffler	384.6	Colorado	381.6	Solitude
1964	Denver	Willy Schaeffler	370.2	Dartmouth	368.8	Franconia Notch
1965	Denver	Willy Schaeffler	380.5	Utah	378.4	Crystal Mountain
1966	Denver	Willy Schaeffler	381.02	Western Colorado	365.92	Crested Butte
1967	Denver	Willy Schaeffler	376.7	Wyoming	375.9	Sugarloaf Mountain
1968	Wyoming	John Cress	383.9	Denver	376.2	Mount Werner
1969	Denver	Willy Schaeffler	388.6	Dartmouth	372.0	Mount Werner
1970	Denver	Willy Schaeffler	386.6	Dartmouth	378.8	Cannon Mountain
1971	Denver	Peder Pytte	394.7	Colorado	373.1	Terry Peak
1972	Colorado	Bill Marolt	385.3	Denver	380.1	Winter Park
1973	Colorado	Bill Marolt	381.89	Wyoming	377.83	Middlebury
1974	Colorado	Bill Marolt	176	Wyoming	162	Jackson Hole
1975	Colorado	Bill Marolt	183	Vermont	115	Fort Lewis
1976	Colo/Dart	Bill Marolt/Jim Page	112			Bates
1977	Colorado	Bill Marolt	179	Wyoming	154.5	Winter Park
1978	Colorado	Bill Marolt	152.5	Wyoming	121.5	Cannon Mountain
1979	Colorado	Tim Hinderman	153	Utah	130	Steamboat Springs
1980	Vermont	Chip LaCasse	171	Utah	151	Lake Placid and Stowe
1981	Utah	Pat Miller	183	Vermont	172	Park City
1982	Colorado	Tim Hinderman	461	Vermont	436.5	Lake Placid
1983	Utah	Pat Miller	696	Vermont	650	Bozeman
1984	Utah	Pat Miller	750.5	Vermont	684	New Hampshire
1985	Wyoming	Tim Ameel	764	Utah	744	Bozeman
1986	Utah	Pat Miller	612	Vermont	602	Vermont
1987	Utah	Pat Miller	710	Vermont	627	Anchorage
1988	Utah	Pat Miller	651	Vermont	614	Middlebury
1989	Vermont	Chip LaCasse	672	Utah	668	Jackson Hole
1990	Vermont	Chip LaCasse	671	Utah	571	Vermont
1991	Colorado	Richard Rokos	713	Vermont	682	Park City, Utah
1992	Vermont	Chip LaCasse	693.5	New Mexico	642.5	New Hampshire
1993	Utah	Pat Miller	783	Vermont	700.5	Steamboat Springs
1994	Vermont	Chip LaCasse	688	Utah	667	Sugarloaf, ME
1995	Colorado	Richard Rokos	720.5	Utah	711	New Hampshire
1996	Utah	Pat Miller	719	Denver	635.5	Montana St
1997	Utah	Pat Miller	686	Vermont	646.5	Vermont
1998	Colorado	Richard Rokos	654	Utah	651.5	Montana St
1999	Colorado	Richard Rokos	650	Denver	636	Bates College
2000	Denver	Kurt Smitz	720	Colorado	621	Park City, Utah
2001	Denver	Kurt Smitz	649	Vermont	605	Middlebury, Vt.
2002	Denver	Kurt Smitz	656	Colorado	612	Anchorage
2003	Utah	Kevin Sweeney	682	Vermont	551	Hanover, N.H.
2004	New Mexico	George Brooks	623	Utah	581	Donner Summit, Calif.
2005	Denver	Kurt Smitz	622.5	Vermont	575	Stowe, Vt.
2006	Colorodo	Richard Rokos	654	New Mexico	556	Steamboat Springs

Men
DIVISION I

Year	Champion	Coach	Score	Runner-Up
1959	St. Louis	Bob Guelker	5–2	Bridgeport
1960	St. Louis	Bob Guelker	3–2	Maryland
1961	West Chester	Mel Lorback	2–0	St. Louis
1962	St. Louis	Bob Guelker	4–3	Maryland
1963	St. Louis	Bob Guelker	3–0	Navy
1964	Navy	F.H. Warner	1–0	Michigan St
1965	St. Louis	Bob Guelker	1–0	Michigan St
1966	San Francisco	Steve Negoesco	5–2	LIU–Brooklyn
1967	Michigan St	Gene Kenney	0–0	Game called due to
	St. Louis	Harry Keough		inclement weather
1968	Maryland	Doyle Royal	2–2 (2 OT)	
	Michigan St	Gene Kenney		
1969	St. Louis	Harry Keough	4–0	San Francisco
1970	St. Louis	Harry Keough	1–0	UCLA
1971	Vacated		3–2	St. Louis
1972	St. Louis	Harry Keough	4–2	UCLA
1973	St. Louis	Harry Keough	2–1 (OT)	UCLA
1974	Howard	Lincoln Phillips	2–1 (4 OT)	St. Louis
1975	San Francisco	Steve Negoesco	4–0	SIU–Edwardsville
1976	San Francisco	Steve Negoesco	1–0	Indiana
1977	Hartwick	Jim Lennox	2–1	San Francisco
1978	Vacated		2–0	Indiana
1979	SIU–Edwardsville	Bob Guelker	3–2	Clemson
1980	San Francisco	Steve Negoesco	4–3 (OT)	Indiana
1981	Connecticut	Joe Morrone	2–1 (OT)	Alabama A&M
1982	Indiana	Jerry Yeagley	2–1 (8 OT)	Duke
1983	Indiana	Jerry Yeagley	1–0 (2 OT)	Columbia
1984	Clemson	I.M. Ibrahim	2–1	Indiana
1985	UCLA	Sigi Schmid	1–0 (8 OT)	American
1986	Duke	John Rennie	1–0	Akron
1987	Clemson	I.M. Ibrahim	2–0	San Diego St
1988	Indiana	Jerry Yeagley	1–0	Howard
1989	Santa Clara	Steve Sampson	1–1 (2 OT)	
	Virginia	Bruce Arena		
1990	UCLA	Sigi Schmid	1–0 (OT)	Rutgers
1991	Virginia	Bruce Arena	0–0*	Santa Clara
1992	Virginia	Bruce Arena	2–0	San Diego
1993	Virginia	Bruce Arena	2–0	South Carolina
1994	Virginia	Bruce Arena	1–0	Indiana
1995	Wisconsin	Jim Launder	2–0	Duke
1996	St. John's (N.Y.)	Dave Masur	4–1	Florida International
1997	UCLA	Sigi Schmid	2–1	Virginia
1998	Indiana	Jerry Yeagley	3–1	Stanford
1999	Indiana	Jerry Yeagley	1–0	Santa Clara
2000	Connecticut	Ray Reid	2–0	Creighton
2001	N.Carolina	Elmar Bolowich	2–0	Indiana
2002	UCLA	Tom Fitzgerald	1–0	Stanford
2003	Indiana	Jerry Yeagley	2–1	St. John's (N.Y.)
2004	Indiana	Jerry Yeagley	1–1 (2 OT 3-2)	UC–Santa Barbara
2005	Maryland	Sasho Cirovski	1–0	New Mexico

*Under a rule passed in 1991, the NCAA determined that when a score is tied after regulation and overtime, and the championship is determined by penalty kicks, the official score will be 0–0.

DIVISION II

Year	Champion	Year	Champion	Year	Champion
1972	SIU–Edwardsville	1982	Florida International	1992	Southern Connecticut St
1973	Missouri–St. Louis	1983	Seattle Pacific	1993	Seattle Pacific
1974	Adelphi	1984	Florida International	1994	Tampa
1975	Baltimore	1985	Seattle Pacific	1995	Southern Connecticut St
1976	Loyola (Md.)	1986	Seattle Pacific	1996	Grand Canyon
1977	Alabama A&M	1987	Southern Connecticut St	1997	CSU–Bakersfield
1978	Seattle Pacific	1988	Florida Tech	1998	Southern Connecticut St
1979	Alabama A&M	1989	New Hampshire College	1999	Southern Connecticut St
1980	Lock Haven	1990	Southern Connecticut St	2000	CSU–Dominguez Hills
1981	Tampa	1991	Florida Tech	2001	Tampa

Men — DIVISION II *(Cont.)*

Year	Champion	Year	Champion
2002	Sonoma St	2004	Seattle
2003	Lynn	2005	Fort Lewis

DIVISION III

Year	Champion	Year	Champion	Year	Champion
1974	Brockport St	1985	NC–Greensboro	1996	College of New Jersey*
1975	Babson	1986	NC–Greensboro	1997	Wheaton (Ill.)
1976	Brandeis	1987	NC–Greensboro	1998	Ohio Wesleyan
1977	Lock Haven	1988	UC–San Diego	1999	St. Lawrence
1978	Lock Haven	1989	Elizabethtown	2000	Messiah
1979	Babson	1990	Glassboro St	2001	Richard Stockton
1980	Babson	1991	UC–San Diego	2002	Messiah
1981	Glassboro St	1992	Kean	2003	Trinity (Tex.)
1982	NC–Greensboro	1993	UC–San Diego	2004	Messiah
1983	NC–Greensboro	1994	Bethany (W.V.)	2005	Messiah
1984	Wheaton (Ill.)	1995	Williams		

*Formerly Trenton St

Women — DIVISION I

Year	Champion	Coach	Score	Runner-Up
1982	North Carolina	Anson Dorrance	2–0	Central Florida
1983	North Carolina	Anson Dorrance	4–0	George Mason
1984	North Carolina	Anson Dorrance	2–0	Connecticut
1985	George Mason	Hank Leung	2–0	North Carolina
1986	North Carolina	Anson Dorrance	2–0	Colorado College
1987	North Carolina	Anson Dorrance	1–0	Massachusetts
1988	North Carolina	Anson Dorrance	4–1	North Carolina St
1989	North Carolina	Anson Dorrance	2–0	Colorado College
1990	North Carolina	Anson Dorrance	6–0	Connecticut
1991	North Carolina	Anson Dorrance	3–1	Wisconsin
1992	North Carolina	Anson Dorrance	9–1	Duke
1993	North Carolina	Anson Dorrance	6–0	George Mason
1994	North Carolina	Anson Dorrance	5–0	Notre Dame
1995	Notre Dame	Chris Petrucelli	1–0	Portland
1996	North Carolina	Anson Dorrance	1–0	Notre Dame
1997	North Carolina	Anson Dorrance	2–0	Connecticut
1998	Florida	Becky Burleigh	1–0	North Carolina
1999	North Carolina	Anson Dorrance	2–0	Notre Dame
2000	North Carolina	Anson Dorrance	2–1	UCLA
2001	Santa Clara	Jerry Smith	1–0	North Carolina
2002	Portland	Clive Charles	2–1	Santa Clara
2003	North Carolina	Anson Dorrance	6–0	Connecticut
2004	Norte Dame	Randy Waldrum	1–1(OT 4-3)	UCLA
2005	Portland	Garrett Smith	4–0	UCLA

DIVISION II

Year	Champion
1988	CSU–Hayward
1989	Barry
1990	Sonoma St
1991	CSU–Dominguez Hills
1992	Barry
1993	Barry
1994	Franklin Pierce
1995	Franklin Pierce
1996	Franklin Pierce
1997	Franklin Pierce
1998	Lynn
1999	Franklin Pierce
2000	UC-San Diego
2001	UC-San Diego
2002	Christian Brothers
2003	Kennesaw St
2004	Metro St
2005	Nebraska-Omaha

DIVISION III

Year	Champion
1986	Rochester
1987	Rochester
1988	William Smith
1989	UC–San Diego
1990	Ithaca
1991	Ithaca
1992	Cortland St
1993	Trenton St
1994	Trenton St
1995	UC–San Diego
1996	UC–San Diego
1997	UC–San Diego
1998	Macalester
1999	UC–San Diego
2000	College of New Jersey*
2001	Ohio Wesleyan
2002	Ohio Wesleyan
2003	Oneonta St
2004	Wheaton College
2005	Messiah

*Formerly Trenton St

DIVISION I

Year	Champion	Coach	Score	Runner-Up
1982	UCLA*	Sharron Backus	2–0†	Fresno St
1983	Texas A&M	Bob Brock	2–0‡	CSU–Fullerton
1984	UCLA	Sharron Backus	1–0#	Texas A&M
1985	UCLA	Sharron Backus	2–1**	Nebraska
1986	CSU–Fullerton*	Judi Garman	3–0	Texas A&M
1987	Texas A&M	Bob Brock	4–1	UCLA
1988	UCLA	Sharron Backus	3–0	Fresno St
1989	UCLA*	Sharron Backus	1–0	Fresno St
1990	UCLA	Sharron Backus	2–0	Fresno St
1991	Arizona	Mike Candrea	5–1	UCLA
1992	UCLA*	Sharron Backus	2–0	Arizona
1993	Arizona	Mike Candrea	1–0	UCLA
1994	Arizona	Mike Candrea	4–0	CSU–Northridge
1995	Vacated	—		Arizona
1996	Arizona*	Mike Candrea	6–4	Washington
1997	Arizona	Mike Candrea	10–2***	UCLA
1998	Fresno St	Margie Wright	1–0	Arizona
1999	UCLA	Sue Enquist	3–2	Washington
2000	Oklahoma	Patty Gasso	3–1	UCLA
2001	Arizona*	Mike Candrea	1–0	UCLA
2002	California	Diane Ninemire	6–0	Arizona
2003	UCLA	Sue Enquist	1–0**	California
2004	UCLA	Sue Enquist	3–1	California
2005	Michigan	Carol Hutchins	4–1	St. Thomas
2006	Arizona	Mike Candrea	5–0	Northwestern

*Undefeated teams in final series. †Eight innings. ‡12 innings. #13 innings. **Nine innings. ***Five innings.

DIVISION II

Year	Champion	Year	Champion	Year	Champion
1982	Sam Houston St	1991	Augustana (SD)	2000	N Dakota St
1983	CSU–Northridge	1992	Missouri Southern	2001	Nebraska–Omaha
1984	CSU–Northridge	1993	Florida Southern	2002	St. Mary's (Iowa)
1985	CSU–Northridge	1994	Merrimack	2003	UC Davis
1986	SF Austin St	1995	Kennesaw St	2004	Angelo St
1987	CSU–Northridge	1996	Kennesaw St	2005	Lynn University
1988	CSU–Bakersfield	1997	California (Pa.)*	2006	Lock Haven
1989	CSU–Bakersfield	1998	California (Pa.)		
1990	CSU–Bakersfield	1999	Humboldt St		

DIVISION III

Year	Champion	Year	Champion	Year	Champion
1982	Sam Houston St	1990	Eastern Connecticut St	1999	Simpson (Iowa)
1982	Eastern Connecticut St*	1991	Central (Iowa)	2000	St. Mary's
1983	Trenton St	1992	Trenton St	2001	Muskingum*
1984	Buena Vista*	1993	Central (Iowa)	2002	Williams
1985	Eastern Connecticut St	1994	Trenton St	2003	Central (Iowa)
1986	Eastern Connecticut St	1995	Chapman	2004	St. Thomas
1987	Trenton St*	1996	Trenton St*	2005	St. Thomas
1988	Central (Iowa)	1997	Simpson (Iowa)*	2006	Rutgers–Camden
1989	Trenton St*	1998	UW-Stevens Point		

*Undefeated teams in final series.

Swimming and Diving

Men
DIVISION I

Year	Champion	Coach	Pts	Runner-Up	Pts
1937	Michigan	Matt Mann	75	Ohio St	39
1938	Michigan	Matt Mann	46	Ohio St	45
1939	Michigan	Matt Mann	65	Ohio St	58
1940	Michigan	Matt Mann	45	Yale	42
1941	Michigan	Matt Mann	61	Yale	58
1942	Yale	Robert J.H. Kiphuth	71	Michigan	39
1943	Ohio St	Mike Peppe	81	Michigan	47
1944	Yale	Robert J.H. Kiphuth	39	Michigan	38

Men *(Cont.)*
DIVISION I *(Cont.)*

Year	Champion	Coach	Pts	Runner-Up	Pts
1945	Ohio St	Mike Peppe	56	Michigan	48
1946	Ohio St	Mike Peppe	61	Michigan	37
1947	Ohio St	Mike Peppe	66	Michigan	39
1948	Michigan	Matt Mann	44	Ohio St	41
1949	Ohio St	Mike Peppe	49	Iowa	35
1950	Ohio St	Mike Peppe	64	Yale	43
1951	Yale	Robert J.H. Kiphuth	81	Michigan St	60
1952	Ohio St	Mike Peppe	94	Yale	81
1953	Yale	Robert J.H. Kiphuth	96½	Ohio St	73½
1954	Ohio St	Mike Peppe	94	Michigan	67
1955	Ohio St	Mike Peppe	90	Yale/Michigan	51
1956	Ohio St	Mike Peppe	68	Yale	54
1957	Michigan	Gus Stager	69	Yale	61
1958	Michigan	Gus Stager	72	Yale	63
1959	Michigan	Gus Stager	137½	Ohio St	44
1960	USC	Peter Daland	87	Michigan	73
1961	Michigan	Gus Stager	85	USC	62
1962	Ohio St	Mike Peppe	92	USC	46
1963	USC	Peter Daland	81	Yale	77
1964	USC	Peter Daland	96	Indiana	91
1965	USC	Peter Daland	285	Indiana	278½
1966	USC	Peter Daland	302	Indiana	286
1967	Stanford	Jim Gaughran	275	USC	260
1968	Indiana	James Counsilman	346	Yale	253
1969	Indiana	James Counsilman	427	USC	306
1970	Indiana	James Counsilman	332	USC	235
1971	Indiana	James Counsilman	351	USC	260
1972	Indiana	James Counsilman	390	USC	371
1973	Indiana	James Counsilman	358	Tennessee	294
1974	USC	Peter Daland	339	Indiana	338
1975	USC	Peter Daland	344	Indiana	274
1976	USC	Peter Daland	398	Tennessee	237
1977	USC	Peter Daland	385	Alabama	204
1978	Tennessee	Ray Bussard	307	Auburn	185
1979	California	Nort Thornton	287	USC	227
1980	California	Nort Thornton	234	Texas	220
1981	Texas	Eddie Reese	259	UCLA	189
1982	UCLA	Ron Ballatore	219	Texas	210
1983	Florida	Randy Reese	238	SMU	227
1984	Florida	Randy Reese	287½	Texas	277
1985	Stanford	Skip Kenney	403½	Florida	302
1986	Stanford	Skip Kenney	404	California	335
1987	Stanford	Skip Kenney	374	USC	296
1988	Texas	Eddie Reese	424	USC	369½
1989	Texas	Eddie Reese	475	Stanford	396
1990	Texas	Eddie Reese	506	USC	423
1991	Texas	Eddie Reese	476	Stanford	420
1992	Stanford	Skip Kenney	632	Texas	356
1993	Stanford	Skip Kenney	520½	Michigan	396
1994	Stanford	Skip Kenney	566½	Texas	445
1995	Michigan	Jon Urbanchek	561	Stanford	475
1996	Texas	Eddie Reese	479	Auburn	443½
1997	Auburn	David Marsh	496½	Stanford	340
1998	Stanford	Skip Kenney	594	Auburn	394½
1999	Auburn	David Marsh	467½	Stanford	414½
2000	Texas	Eddie Reese	538	Auburn	385
2001	Texas	Eddie Reese	597½	Stanford	457½
2002	Texas	Eddie Reese	512	Stanford	5011
2003	Auburn	David Marsh	609½	Texas	413
2004	Auburn	David Marsh	634	Stanford	377½
2005	Auburn	David Marsh	491	Stanford	414
2006	Auburn	David Marsh	480.5	Arizona	440.5

Men *(Cont.)*

DIVISION II

Year	Champion	Year	Champion	Year	Champion
1963	SW Missouri St	1978	CSU–Northridge	1993	CSU–Bakersfield
1964	Bucknell	1979	CSU–Northridge	1994	Oakland (Mich.)
1965	San Diego St	1980	Oakland (Mich.)	1995	Oakland (Mich.)
1966	San Diego St	1981	CSU–Northridge	1996	Oakland (Mich.)
1967	UC–Santa Barbara	1982	CSU–Northridge	1997	Oakland (Mich.)
1968	Long Beach St	1983	CSU–Northridge	1998	CSU–Bakersfield
1969	UC–Irvine	1984	CSU–Northridge	1999	Drury
1970	UC–Irvine	1985	CSU–Northridge	2000	CSU–Bakersfield
1971	UC–Irvine	1986	CSU–Bakersfield	2001	CSU–Bakersfield
1972	Eastern Michigan	1987	CSU–Bakersfield	2002	CSU–Bakersfield
1973	CSU–Chico	1988	CSU–Bakersfield	2003	Drury
1974	CSU–Chico	1989	CSU–Bakersfield	2004	CSU–Bakersfield
1975	CSU–Northridge	1990	CSU–Bakersfield	2005	Drury
1976	CSU–Chico	1991	CSU–Bakersfield	2006	Drury
1977	CSU–Northridge	1992	CSU–Bakersfield		

DIVISION III

Year	Champion	Year	Champion	Year	Champion
1975	CSU–Chico	1986	Kenyon	1997	Kenyon
1976	St. Lawrence	1987	Kenyon	1998	Kenyon
1977	Johns Hopkins	1988	Kenyon	1999	Kenyon
1978	Johns Hopkins	1989	Kenyon	2000	Kenyon
1979	Johns Hopkins	1990	Kenyon	2001	Kenyon
1980	Kenyon	1991	Kenyon	2002	Kenyon
1981	Kenyon	1992	Kenyon	2003	Kenyon
1982	Kenyon	1993	Kenyon	2004	Kenyon
1983	Kenyon	1994	Kenyon	2005	Kenyon
1984	Kenyon	1995	Kenyon	2006	Kenyon
1985	Kenyon	1996	Kenyon		

Women

DIVISION I

Year	Champion	Coach	Pts	Runner-Up	Pts
1982	Florida	Randy Reese	505	Stanford	383
1983	Stanford	George Haines	418½	Florida	389½
1984	Texas	Richard Quick	392	Stanford	324
1985	Texas	Richard Quick	643	Florida	400
1986	Texas	Richard Quick	633	Florida	586
1987	Texas	Richard Quick	648½	Stanford	631½
1988	Texas	Richard Quick	661	Florida	542½
1989	Stanford	Richard Quick	610½	Texas	547
1990	Texas	Mark Schubert	632	Stanford	622½
1991	Texas	Mark Schubert	746	Stanford	653
1992	Stanford	Richard Quick	735½	Texas	651
1993	Stanford	Richard Quick	649½	Florida	421
1994	Stanford	Richard Quick	512	Texas	421
1995	Stanford	Richard Quick	497½	Michigan	478½
1996	Stanford	Richard Quick	478	SMU	397
1997	USC	Mark Schubert	406	Stanford	395
1998	Stanford	Richard Quick	422	Arizona	378
1999	Georgia	Jack Bauerle	504½	Stanford	441
2000	Georgia	Jack Bauerle	490½	Arizona	472
2001	Georgia	Jack Bauerle	389	Stanford	387½
2002	Auburn	David Marsh	474	Georgia	386
2003	Auburn	David Marsh	536	Georgia	373
2004	Auburn	David Marsh	569	Georgia	431
2005	Georgia	Jack Bauerle	609.5	Auburn	492
2006	Auburn	David Marsh	518.5	Georgia	515.5

Women
DIVISION II

Year	Champion	Year	Champion	Year	Champion
1982	CSU–Northridge	1991	Oakland (Mich.)	2000	Drury
1983	Clarion	1992	Oakland (Mich.)	2001	Truman St
1984	Clarion	1993	Oakland (Mich.)	2002	Truman St
1985	S Florida	1994	Oakland (Mich.)	2003	Truman St
1986	Clarion	1995	Air Force	2004	Truman St
1987	CSU–Northridge	1996	Air Force	2005	Truman St
1988	CSU–Northridge	1997	Drury	2006	Truman St
1989	CSU–Northridge	1998	Drury		
1990	Oakland (Mich.)	1999	Drury		

DIVISION III

Year	Champion	Year	Champion	Year	Champion
1982	Williams	1991	Kenyon	2000	Kenyon
1983	Williams	1992	Kenyon	2001	Denison
1984	Kenyon	1993	Kenyon	2002	Kenyon
1985	Kenyon	1994	Kenyon	2003	Kenyon
1986	Kenyon	1995	Kenyon	2004	Kenyon
1987	Kenyon	1996	Kenyon	2005	Emory
1988	Kenyon	1997	Kenyon	2006	Emory
1989	Kenyon	1998	Kenyon		
1990	Kenyon	1999	Kenyon		

Tennis

Men
INDIVIDUAL CHAMPIONS 1883–1945

Year	Champion	Year	Champion
1883	Joseph Clark, Harvard (spring)	1914	George Church, Princeton
1883	Howard Taylor, Harvard (fall)	1915	Richard Williams II, Harvard
1884	W.P. Knapp, Yale	1916	G. Colket Caner, Harvard
1885	W.P. Knapp, Yale	1917–18	No tournament
1886	G.M. Brinley, Trinity (Conn.)	1919	Charles Garland, Yale
1887	P.S. Sears, Harvard	1920	Lascelles Banks, Yale
1888	P.S. Sears, Harvard	1921	Philip Neer, Stanford
1889	R.P. Huntington Jr, Yale	1922	Lucien Williams, Yale
1890	Fred Hovey, Harvard	1923	Carl Fischer, Philadelphia Osteo
1891	Fred Hovey, Harvard	1924	Wallace Scott, Washington
1892	William Larned, Cornell	1925	Edward Chandler, California
1893	Malcolm Chace, Brown	1926	Edward Chandler, UC-Berkeley
1894	Malcolm Chace, Yale	1927	Wilmer Allison, Texas
1895	Malcolm Chace, Yale	1928	Julius Seligson, Lehigh
1896	Malcolm Whitman, Harvard	1929	Berkeley Bell, Texas
1897	S.G. Thompson, Princeton	1930	Clifford Sutter, Tulane
1898	Leo Ware, Harvard	1931	Keith Gledhill, Stanford
1899	Dwight Davis, Harvard	1932	Clifford Sutter, Tulane
1900	Raymond Little, Princeton	1933	Jack Tidball, UCLA
1901	Fred Alexander, Princeton	1934	Gene Mako, USC
1902	William Clothier, Harvard	1935	Wilbur Hess, Rice
1903	E.B. Dewhurst, Pennsylvania	1936	Ernest Sutter, Tulane
1904	Robert LeRoy, Columbia	1937	Ernest Sutter, Tulane
1905	E.B. Dewhurst, Pennsylvania	1938	Frank Guernsey, Rice
1906	Robert LeRoy, Columbia	1939	Frank Guernsey, Rice
1907	G. Peabody Gardner Jr, Harvard	1940	Donald McNeil, Kenyon
1908	Nat Niles, Harvard	1941	Joseph Hunt, Navy
1909	Wallace Johnson, Pennsylvania	1942	Frederick Schroeder Jr, Stanford
1910	R.A. Holden Jr, Yale	1943	Pancho Segura, Miami (Fla.)
1911	E.H. Whitney, Harvard	1944	Pancho Segura, Miami (Fla.)
1912	George Church, Princeton	1945	Pancho Segura, Miami (Fla.)
1913	Richard Williams II, Harvard		

Tennis

Men

DIVISION I

Year	Champion	Coach	Pts	Runner-Up	Pts	Individual Champion
1946 ....USC		William Moyle	9	William & Mary	6	Robert Falkenburg, USC
1947 ....William & Mary		Sharvey G. Umbeck	10	Rice	4	Gardner Larned, William & Mary
1948 ....William & Mary		Sharvey G. Umbeck	6	San Francisco	5	Harry Likas, San Francisco
1949 ....San Francisco		Norman Brooks	7	Rollins/Tulane/ Washington	4	Jack Tuero, Tulane
1950 ....UCLA		William Ackerman	11	California/ USC	5	Herbert Flam, UCLA
1951 ....USC		Louis Wheeler	9	Cincinnati	7	Tony Trabert, Cincinnati
1952 ....UCLA		J.D. Morgan	11	California/USC	5	Hugh Stewart, USC
1953 ....UCLA		J.D. Morgan	11	California	6	Hamilton Richardson, Tulane
1954 ....UCLA		J.D. Morgan	15	USC	10	Hamilton Richardson, Tulane
1955 ....USC		George Toley	12	Texas	7	Jose Aguero, Tulane
1956 ....UCLA		J.D. Morgan	15	USC	14	Alejandro Olmedo, USC
1957 ....Michigan		William Murphy	10	Tulane	9	Barry MacKay, Michigan
1958 ....USC		George Toley	13	Stanford	9	Alejandro Olmedo, USC
1959 ....Notre Dame		Thomas Fallon	8			Whitney Reed, San Jose St
Tulane		Emmet Pare	8			
1960 ....UCLA		J.D. Morgan	18	USC	8	Larry Nagler, UCLA
1961 ....UCLA		J.D. Morgan	17	USC	16	Allen Fox, UCLA
1962 ....USC		George Toley	22	UCLA	12	Rafael Osuna, USC
1963 ....USC		George Toley	27	UCLA	19	Dennis Ralston, USC
1964 ....USC		George Toley	26	UCLA	25	Dennis Ralston, USC
1965 ....UCLA		J.D. Morgan	31	Miami (Fla.)	13	Arthur Ashe, UCLA
1966 ....USC		George Toley	27	UCLA	23	Charles Pasarell, UCLA
1967 ....USC		George Toley	28	UCLA	23	Bob Lutz, USC
1968 ....USC		George Toley	31	Rice	23	Stan Smith, USC
1969 ....USC		George Toley	35	USC	23	Joaquin Loyo-Mayo, USC
1970 ....UCLA		Glenn Bassett	26	Trinity (Tex.)	22	Jeff Borowiak, UCLA
				Rice	22	
1971 ....UCLA		Glenn Bassett	35	Trinity (Tex.)	27	Jimmy Connors, UCLA
1972 ....Trinity (Tex.)		Clarence Mabry	36	Stanford	30	Dick Stockton, Trinity (Tex.)
1973 ....Stanford		Dick Gould	33	USC	28	Alex Mayer, Stanford
1974 ....Stanford		Dick Gould	30	USC	25	John Whitlinger, Stanford
1975 ....UCLA		Glenn Bassett	27	Miami (Fla.)	20	Bill Martin, UCLA
1976 ....USC		George Toley	21			Bill Scanlon, Trinity (Tex.)
UCLA		Glenn Bassett	21			
1977 ....Stanford		Dick Gould		Trinity (Tex.)		Matt Mitchell, Stanford
1978 ....Stanford		Dick Gould		UCLA		John McEnroe, Stanford
1979 ....UCLA		Glenn Bassett		Trinity (Tex.)		Kevin Curren, Texas
1980 ....Stanford		Dick Gould		California		Robert Van't Hof, USC
1981 ....Stanford		Dick Gould		UCLA		Tim Mayotte, Stanford
1982 ....UCLA		Glenn Bassett		Pepperdine		Mike Leach, Michigan
1983 ....Stanford		Dick Gould		SMU		Greg Holmes, Utah
1984 ....UCLA		Glenn Bassett		Stanford		Mikael Pernfors, Georgia
1985 ....Georgia		Dan Magill		UCLA		Mikael Pernfors, Georgia
1986 ....Stanford		Dick Gould		Pepperdine		Dan Goldie, Stanford
1987 ....Georgia		Dan Magill		UCLA		Andrew Burrow, Miami (Fla.)
1988 ....Stanford		Dick Gould		LSU		Robby Weiss, Pepperdine
1989 ....Stanford		Dick Gould		Georgia		Donni Leaycraft, LSU
1990 ....Stanford		Dick Gould		Tennessee		Steve Bryan, Texas
1991 ....USC		Dick Leach		Georgia		Jared Palmer, Stanford
1992 ....Stanford		Dick Gould		Notre Dame		Alex O'Brien, Stanford
1993 ....USC		Dick Leach		Georgia		Chris Woodruff, Tennessee
1994 ....USC		Dick Leach		Stanford		Mark Merklein, Florida
1995 ....Stanford		Dick Gould		Mississippi		Sargis Sargsian, Arizona St
1996 ....Stanford		Dick Gould		UCLA		Cecil Mamiit, USC
1997 ....Stanford		Dick Gould		Georgia		Luke Smith, UNLV
1998 ....Stanford		Dick Gould		Georgia		Bob Bryan, Stanford
1999 ....Georgia		Manuel Diaz		UCLA		Jeff Morrison, Florida
2000 ....Stanford		Dick Gould		Virginia Comm.		Alex Kim, Stanford
2001 ....Georgia		Manuel Diaz		Tennessee		Matias Boeker, Georgia
2002 ....USC		Dick Leach		Georgia		Matias Boeker, Georgia
2003 ....Illinois		Craig Tiley		Vanderbilt		Amer Delic, Illinois
2004 ....Baylor		Matt Knoll		UCLA		Benjamin Becker, Baylor
2005 ....UCLA		Billy Martin		Baylor		Benedikt Dorsch, Baylor
2006 ....Pepperdine		Adam Steinberg		Georgia		Benjamin Kohlleoffel, UCLA

Note: Prior to 1977, individual wins counted in the team's total points. In 1977, a dual-match single-elimination team championship was initiated, eliminating the point system.

Men

DIVISION II

Year	Champion
1963	CSU–L.A.
1964	CSU–L.A./Southern Illinois
1965	CSU–L.A.
1966	Rollins
1967	Long Beach St
1968	Fresno St
1969	CSU–Northridge
1970	UC–Irvine
1971	UC–Irvine
1972	UC–Irvine/ Rollins
1973	UC–Irvine
1974	San Diego
1975	UC–Irvine/San Diego
1976	Hampton
1977	UC–Irvine

Year	Champion
1978	SIU–Edwardsville
1979	SIU–Edwardsville
1980	SIU–Edwardsville
1981	SIU–Edwardsville
1982	SIU–Edwardsville
1983	SIU–Edwardsville
1984	SIU–Edwardsville
1985	Chapman
1986	Cal-Poly–SLO
1987	Chapman
1988	Chapman
1989	Hampton
1990	Cal-Poly–SLO
1991	Rollins
1992	UC–Davis

Year	Champion
1993	Lander
1994	Lander
1995	Lander
1996	Lander
1997	Lander
1998	Lander
1999	Lander
2000	Lander
2001	Rollins
2002	BYU-Hawaii
2003	BYU-Hawaii
2004	W Florida
2005	W Florida
2006	Valdosta

DIVISION III

Year	Champion
1976	Kalamazoo
1977	Swarthmore
1978	Kalamazoo
1979	Redlands
1980	Gustavus Adolphus
1981	Claremont-M-S/ Swarthmore
1982	Gustavus Adolphus
1983	Redlands
1984	Redlands
1985	Swarthmore

Year	Champion
1986	Kalamazoo
1987	Kalamazoo
1988	Washington & Lee
1989	UC–Santa Cruz
1990	Swarthmore
1991	Kalamazoo
1992	Kalamazoo
1993	Kalamazoo
1994	Washington (Md.)
1995	UC–Santa Cruz
1996	UC–Santa Cruz

Year	Champion
1997	Washington (Md.)
1998	UC–Santa Cruz
1999	Williams
2000	Trinity (Tex.)
2001	Williams
2002	Williams
2003	Emory
2004	Middlebury
2005	UC–Santa Cruz
2006	Emory

Women

DIVISION I

Year	Champion	Coach	Runner-Up	Individual Champion
1982	Stanford	Frank Brennan	UCLA	Alycia Moulton, Stanford
1983	USC	Dave Borelli	Trinity (Tex.)	Beth Herr, USC
1984	Stanford	Frank Brennan	USC	Lisa Spain, Georgia
1985	USC	Dave Borelli	Miami (Fla.)	Linda Gates, Stanford
1986	Stanford	Frank Brennan	USC	Patty Fendick, Stanford
1987	Stanford	Frank Brennan	Georgia	Patty Fendick, Stanford
1988	Stanford	Frank Brennan	Florida	Shaun Stafford, Florida
1989	Stanford	Frank Brennan	UCLA	Sandra Birch, Stanford
1990	Stanford	Frank Brennan	Florida	Debbie Graham, Stanford
1991	Stanford	Frank Brennan	UCLA	Sandra Birch, Stanford
1992	Florida	Andy Brandi	Texas	Lisa Raymond, Florida
1993	Texas	Jeff Moore	Stanford	Lisa Raymond, Florida
1994	Georgia	Jeff Wallace	Stanford	Angela Lettiere, Georgia
1995	Texas	Jeff Moore	Florida	Keri Phebus, UCLA
1996	Florida	Andy Brandi	Stanford	Jill Craybas, Florida
1997	Stanford	Frank Brennan	Florida	Lilia Osterloh, Stanford
1998	Florida	Andy Brandi	Duke	Vanessa Webb, Duke
1999	Stanford	Frank Brennan	Florida	Zuzana Lesenarova, UC–SD
2000	Georgia	Jeff Wallace	Stanford	Laura Granville, Stanford
2001	Stanford	Lele Forood	Vanderbilt	Laura Granville, Stanford
2002	Stanford	Lele Forood	Florida	Bea Bielek, Wake Forest
2003	Florida	Roland Thornqvist	Stanford	Amber Liu, Stanford
2004	Stanford	Lele Forood	UCLA	Amber Liu, Stanford
2005	Stanford	Lele Forood	Texas	Alice Barnes, Stanford
2006	Stanford	Lele Forood	Miami	Suzi Babos, California

Women (Cont.)
DIVISION II

Year	Champion	Year	Champion	Year	Champion
1982	CSU–Northridge	1991	Cal Poly–Pomona	2000	BYU–Hawaii
1983	Tenn.–Chattanooga	1992	Cal Poly–Pomona	2001	Lynn
1984	Tenn.–Chattanooga	1993	UC–Davis	2002	BYU–Hawaii
1985	Tenn.–Chattanooga	1994	North Florida	2003	BYU–Hawaii
1986	SIU–Edwardsville	1995	Armstrong St	2004	BYU–Hawaii
1987	SIU–Edwardsville	1996	Armstrong St	2005	Armstrong Atlantic
1988	SIU–Edwardsville	1997	Lynn	2006	BYU–Hawaii
1989	SIU–Edwardsville	1998	Lynn		
1990	UC–Davis	1999	BYU–Hawaii		

DIVISION III

Year	Champion	Year	Champion	Year	Champion
1982	Occidental	1991	Mary Washington	2000	Trinity (Tex.)
1983	Principia	1992	Pomona-Pitzer	2001	Williams
1984	Davidson	1993	Kenyon	2002	Williams
1985	UC–San Diego	1994	UC–San Diego	2003	Emory
1986	Trenton St	1995	Kenyon	2004	Emory
1987	UC–San Diego	1996	Emory	2005	Emory
1988	Mary Washington	1997	Kenyon	2006	Emory
1989	UC–San Diego	1998	Kenyon		
1990	Gustavus Adolphus	1999	Amherst		

Indoor Track and Field

Men
DIVISION I

Year	Champion	Coach	Pts	Runner-Up	Pts
1965	Missouri	Tom Botts	14	Oklahoma St	12
1966	Kansas	Bob Timmons	14	USC	13
1967	USC	Vern Wolfe	26	Oklahoma	17
1968	Villanova	Jim Elliott	35	USC	25
1969	Kansas	Bob Timmons	41½	Villanova	33
1970	Kansas	Bob Timmons	27½	Villanova	26
1971	Villanova	Jim Elliott	22	UTEP	19 ¼
1972	USC	Vern Wolfe	19	Bowling Green/Mich St	18
1973	Manhattan	Fred Dwyer	18	Kansas/Kent St/UTEP	12
1974	UTEP	Ted Banks	19	Colorado	18
1975	UTEP	Ted Banks	36	Kansas	17 ½
1976	UTEP	Ted Banks	23	Villanova	15
1977	Washington St	John Chaplin	25½	UTEP	25
1978	UTEP	Ted Banks	44	Auburn	38
1979	Villanova	Jim Elliott	52	UTEP	51
1980	UTEP	Ted Banks	76	Villanova	42
1981	UTEP	Ted Banks	76	SMU	51
1982	UTEP	John Wedel	67	Arkansas	30
1983	SMU	Ted McLaughlin	43	Villanova	32
1984	Arkansas	John McDonnell	38	Washington St	28
1985	Arkansas	John McDonnell	70	Tennessee	29
1986	Arkansas	John McDonnell	49	Villanova	22
1987	Arkansas	John McDonnell	39	SMU	31
1988	Arkansas	John McDonnell	34	Illinois	29
1989	Arkansas	John McDonnell	34	Florida	31
1990	Arkansas	John McDonnell	44	Texas A&M	36
1991	Arkansas	John McDonnell	34	Georgetown	27
1992	Arkansas	John McDonnell	53	Clemson	46
1993	Arkansas	John McDonnell	66	Clemson	30
1994	Arkansas	John McDonnell	83	UTEP	45
1995	Arkansas	John McDonnell	59	GMU/Tennessee	26
1996	George Mason	John Cook	39	Nebraska	31½
1997	Arkansas	John McDonnell	59	Auburn	27
1998	Arkansas	John McDonnell	56	Stanford	36½
1999	Arkansas	John McDonnell	65	Stanford	42½
2000	Arkansas	John McDonnell	69½	Stanford	52
2001	LSU	Pat Henry	34	TCU	33

Men *(Cont.)*
DIVISION I *(Cont.)*

Year	Champion	Coach	Pts	Runner-Up	Pts
2002	Tennessee	Bill Webb	62½	LSU	44
2003	Arkansas	John McDonnell	52	Auburn	28
2004	LSU	Pat Henry	45½	Florida	38
2005	Arkansas	John McDonnell	54	Wisconsin	43
2006	Arkansas	John McDonnell	53	LSU	45

DIVISION II

Year	Champion	Year	Champion	Year	Champion
1985	SE Missouri St	1993	Abilene Christian	2001	St. Augustine's
1986	Not held	1994	Abilene Christian	2002	Abilene Christian
1987	St. Augustine's	1995	St. Augustine's	2003	Abilene Christian
1988	Abil. Christian/St. August.	1996	Abilene Christian	2004	Abilene Christian
1989	St. Augustine's	1997	Abilene Christian	2005	Abilene Christian
1990	St. Augustine's	1998	Abilene Christian	2006	St. Augustine's
1991	St. Augustine's	1999	Abilene Christian		
1992	St. Augustine's	2000	Abilene Christian		

DIVISION III

Year	Champion	Year	Champion	Year	Champion
1985	St. Thomas (Minn.)	1993	UW-La Crosse	2001	UW-La Crosse
1986	Frostburg St	1994	UW-La Crosse	2002	UW-La Crosse
1987	UW-La Crosse	1995	Lincoln (Pa.)	2003	UW-La Crosse
1988	UW-La Crosse	1996	Lincoln (Pa.)	2004	UW-La Crosse
1989	N Central	1997	UW-La Crosse	2005	UW-La Crosse
1990	Lincoln (Pa.)	1998	Lincoln (Pa.)	2006	UW-La Crosse
1991	UW-La Crosse	1999	Lincoln (Pa.)		
1992	UW-La Crosse	2000	Lincoln (Pa.)		

Women
DIVISION I

Year	Champion	Coach	Pts	Runner-Up	Pts
1983	Nebraska	Gary Pepin	47	Tennessee	44
1984	Nebraska	Gary Pepin	59	Tennessee	48
1985	Florida St	Gary Winckler	34	Texas	32
1986	Texas	Terry Crawford	31	USC	26
1987	LSU	Loren Seagrave	49	Tennessee	30
1988	Texas	Terry Crawford	71	Villanova	52
1989	LSU	Pat Henry	61	Villanova	34
1990	Texas	Terry Crawford	50	Wisconsin	26
1991	LSU	Pat Henry	48	Texas	39
1992	Florida	Bev Kearney	50	Stanford	26
1993	LSU	Pat Henry	49	Wisconsin	44
1994	LSU	Pat Henry	48	Alabama	29
1995	LSU	Pat Henry	40	UCLA	37
1996	LSU	Pat Henry	52	Georgia	34
1997	LSU	Pat Henry	49	Texas/Wisconsin	39
1998	Texas	Bev Kearney	60	LSU	30
1999	Texas	Bev Kearney	61	LSU	57
2000	UCLA	Jeanette Bolden	51	South Carolina	41
2001	UCLA	Jeanette Bolden	53½	South Carolina	40
2002	LSU	Pat Henry	57	Florida	35
2003	LSU	Pat Henry	62	South Carolina/Florida	44
2004	Lousiana St	Pat Henry	52	Florida	51
2005	Tennessee	J.J. Clark	46	Florida	36
2006	Texas	Bev Kearney	51	Stanford	36

DIVISION II

Year	Champion	Year	Champion	Year	Champion
1985	St. Augustine's	1993	Abilene Christian	2001	St. Augustine's
1986	Not held	1994	Abilene Christian	2002	North Dakota St
1987	St. Augustine's	1995	Abilene Christian	2003	St. Augustine's
1988	Abilene Christian	1996	Abilene Christian	2004	Lincoln
1989	Abilene Christian	1997	Abilene Christian	2005	St.Augustine's
1990	Abilene Christian	1998	Abilene Christian	2006	Lincoln
1991	Abilene Christian	1999	Abilene Christian		
1992	Alabama A&M	2000	Abilene Christian		

Women (Cont.)
DIVISION III

Year	Champion	Year	Champion	Year	Champion
1985	UMass–Boston	1993	Lincoln (Pa.)	2001	Wheaton (Mass.)
1986	UMass–Boston	1994	UW-Oshkosh	2002	Wheaton (Mass.)
1987	UMass–Boston	1995	UW-Oshkosh	2003	Wheaton (Mass.)
1988	Christopher Newport	1996	UW-Oshkosh	2004	UW-Oshkosh
1989	Christopher Newport	1997	Christopher Newport	2005	UW-Oshkosh
1990	Christopher Newport	1998	Christopher Newport	2006	UW-Oshkosh
1991	Cortland St	1999	Wheaton (Mass.)		
1992	Christopher Newport	2000	Wheaton (Mass.)		

Outdoor Track and Field

Men

Year	Champion	Coach	Pts	Runner-Up	Pts
1921	Illinois	Harry Gill	20†	Notre Dame	16†
1922	California	Walter Christie	28†	Penn St	19†
1923	Michigan	Stephen Farrell	29†	Mississippi St	16
1924	No meet				
1925	Stanford*	R.L. Templeton	31†		
1926	USC*	Dean Cromwell	27†		
1927	Illinois*	Harry Gill	35†		
1928	Stanford	R.L. Templeton	72	Ohio St	31
1929	Ohio St	Frank Castleman	50	Washington	42
1930	USC	Dean Cromwell	55†	Washington	40
1931	USC	Dean Cromwell	77†	Ohio St	31†
1932	Indiana	Billy Hayes	56	Ohio St	49†
1933	LSU	Bernie Moore	58	USC	54
1934	Stanford	R.L. Templeton	63	USC	54†
1935	USC	Dean Cromwell	74†	Ohio St	40†
1936	USC	Dean Cromwell	103†	Ohio St	73
1937	USC	Dean Cromwell	62	Stanford	50
1938	USC	Dean Cromwell	67†	Stanford	38
1939	USC	Dean Cromwell	86	Stanford	44†
1940	USC	Dean Cromwell	47	Stanford	28†
1941	USC	Dean Cromwell	81†	Indiana	50
1942	USC	Dean Cromwell	85†	Ohio St	44†
1943	USC	Dean Cromwell	46	California	39
1944	Illinois	Leo Johnson	79	Notre Dame	43
1945	Navy	E.J. Thomson	62	Illinois	48†
1946	Illinois	Leo Johnson	78	USC	42†
1947	Illinois	Leo Johnson	59†	USC	34†
1948	Minnesota	James Kelly	46	USC	41†
1949	USC	Jess Hill	55†	UCLA	31
1950	USC	Jess Hill	49†	Stanford	28
1951	USC	Jess Mortenson	56	Cornell	40
1952	USC	Jess Mortenson	66†	San Jose St	24†
1953	USC	Jess Mortenson	80	Illinois	41
1954	USC	Jess Mortenson	66†	Illinois	31†
1955	USC	Jess Mortenson	42	UCLA	34
1956	UCLA	Elvin Drake	55†	Kansas	51
1957	Villanova	James Elliott	47	California	32
1958	USC	Jess Mortenson	48†	Kansas	40†
1959	Kansas	Bill Easton	73	San Jose St	48
1960	Kansas	Bill Easton	50	USC	37
1961	USC	Jess Mortenson	65	Oregon	47
1962	Oregon	William Bowerman	85	Villanova	40†
1963	USC	Vern Wolfe	61	Stanford	42
1964	Oregon	William Bowerman	70	San Jose St	40
1965	Oregon	William Bowerman	32		
	USC	Vern Wolfe	32		
1966	UCLA	Jim Bush	81	BYU	33
1967	USC	Vern Wolfe	86	Oregon	40
1968	USC	Vern Wolfe	58	Washington St	57
1969	San Jose St	Bud Winter	48	Kansas	45

Men — DIVISION I *(Cont.)*

Year	Champion	Coach	Pts	Runner-Up	Pts
1970	BYU	Clarence Robison	35		
	Kansas	Bob Timmons	35		
	Oregon	William Bowerman	35		
1971	UCLA	Jim Bush	52	USC	41
1972	UCLA	Jim Bush	82	USC	49
1973	UCLA	Jim Bush	56	Oregon	31
1974	Tennessee	Stan Huntsman	60	UCLA	56
1975	UTEP	Ted Banks	55	UCLA	42
1976	USC	Vern Wolfe	64	UTEP	44
1977	Arizona St	Senon Castillo	64	UTEP	50
1978	UCLA/UTEP	Jim Bush/Ted Banks	50		
1979	UTEP	Ted Banks	64	Villanova	48
1980	UTEP	Ted Banks	69	UCLA	46
1981	UTEP	Ted Banks	70	SMU	57
1982	UTEP	John Wedel	105	Tennessee	94
1983	SMU	Ted McLaughlin	104	Tennessee	102
1984	Oregon	Bill Dellinger	113	Washington St	94½
1985	Arkansas	John McDonnell	61	Washington St	46
1986	SMU	Ted McLaughlin	53	Washington St	52
1987	UCLA	Bob Larsen	81	Texas	28
1988	UCLA	Bob Larsen	82	Texas	41
1989	LSU	Pat Henry	53	Texas A&M	51
1990	LSU	Pat Henry	44	Arkansas	36
1991	Tennessee	Doug Brown	51	Washington St	42
1992	Arkansas	John McDonnell	60	Tennessee	46½
1993	Arkansas	John McDonnell	69	LSU/Ohio St	45
1994	Arkansas	John McDonnell	83	UTEP	45
1995	Arkansas	John McDonnell	61½	UCLA	55
1996	Arkansas	John McDonnell	55	George Mason	40
1997	Arkansas	John McDonnell	55	Texas	42½
1998	Arkansas	John McDonnell	58½	Stanford	51
1999	Arkansas	John McDonnell	59	Stanford	52
2000	Stanford	Vin Lananna	72	Arkansas	59
2001	Tennessee	Bill Webb	50	TCU	49
2002	LSU	Pat Henry	64	Tennessee	57
2003	Arkansas	John McDonnell	59	Auburn	50
2004	Arkansas	John McDonnell	65½	Florida	49
2005	Arkansa	John McDonnell	109	Adams St	84
2006	Florida St	Bob Bramen	67	LSU	51

*Unofficial championship. †Fraction of a point.

DIVISION II

Year	Champion	Year	Champion	Year	Champion
1963	Md.–Eastern Shore	1977	CSU–Hayward	1992	St. Augustine's
1964	Fresno St	1978	CSU–L.A.	1993	St. Augustine's
1965	San Diego St	1979	Cal Poly–SLO	1994	St. Augustine's
1966	San Diego St	1980	Cal Poly–SLO	1995	St. Augustine's
1967	Long Beach St	1981	Cal Poly–SLO	1996	Abilene Christian
1968	Cal Poly–SLO	1982	Abilene Christian	1997	Abilene Christian
1969	Cal Poly–SLO	1983	Abilene Christian	1998	St. Augustine's
1970	Cal Poly–SLO	1984	Abilene Christian	1999	Abilene Christian
1971	Kentucky St	1985	Abilene Christian	2000	Abilene Christian
1972	Eastern Michigan	1986	Abilene Christian	2001	St. Augustine's
1973	Norfolk St	1987	Abilene Christian	2002	Abilene Christian
1974	Eastern Illinois	1988	Abilene Christian	2003	Abilene Christian
	Norfolk St	1989	St. Augustine's	2004	Abilene Christian
1975	CSU–Northridge	1990	St. Augustine's	2005	Abilene Christian
1976	UC–Irvine	1991	St. Augustine's	2006	Abilene Christian

DIVISION III

Year	Champion	Year	Champion	Year	Champion
1974	Ashland	1979	Slippery Rock	1984	Glassboro St
1975	Southern–N. Orleans	1980	Glassboro St	1985	Lincoln (Pa.)
1976	Southern–N. Orleans	1981	Glassboro St	1986	Frostburg St
1977	Southern–N .Orleans	1982	Glassboro St	1987	Frostburg St
1978	Occidental	1983	Glassboro St	1988	UW-La Crosse

Men *(Cont.)*
DIVISION III *(CONT.)*

Year	Champion	Year	Champion	Year	Champion
1989	N. Central	1995	Lincoln (Pa.)	2001	UW-La Crosse
1990	Lincoln (Pa.)	1996	Lincoln (Pa.)	2002	UW-La Crosse
1991	UW-La Crosse	1997	UW-La Crosse	2003	UW-La Crosse
1992	UW-La Crosse	1998	N. Central	2004	UW-La Crosse
1993	UW-La Crosse	1999	Lincoln (Pa.)	2005	Lincoln (Pa.)
1994	N. Central	2000	Nebraska Wesleyan	2006	UW-La Crosse

Women
DIVISION I

Year	Champion	Coach	Pts	Runner-Up	Pts
1982	UCLA	Scott Chisam	153	Tennessee	126
1983	UCLA	Scott Chisam	116 ½	Florida St	108
1984	Florida St	Gary Winckler	145	Tennessee	124
1985	Oregon	Tom Heinonen	52	Florida St/LSU	46
1986	Texas	Terry Crawford	65	Alabama	55
1987	LSU	Loren Seagrave	62	Alabama	53
1988	LSU	Loren Seagrave	61	UCLA	58
1989	LSU	Pat Henry	86	UCLA	47
1990	LSU	Pat Henry	53	UCLA	46
1991	LSU	Pat Henry	78	Texas	67
1992	LSU	Pat Henry	87	Florida	81
1993	LSU	Pat Henry	93	Wisconsin	44
1994	LSU	Pat Henry	86	Texas	43
1995	LSU	Pat Henry	69	UCLA	58
1996	LSU	Pat Henry	81	Texas	52
1997	LSU	Pat Henry	63	Texas	62
1998	Texas	Bev Kearney	60	UCLA	55
1999	Texas	Bev Kearney	62	UCLA	60
2000	LSU	Pat Henry	59	USC	56
2001	USC	Ron Allice	64	UCLA	55
2002	South Carolina	Curtis Frye	82	UCLA	72
2003	LSU	Pat Henry	64	Texas	50
2004	UCLA	Jeanette Bolden	69	LSU	68
2005	Texas	Bev Kearney	55	CSU/South Carolina	48
2006	Auburn	Ralph Spry	57	USC	38.5

DIVISION II

Year	Champion	Year	Champion	Year	Champion
1982	Cal Poly–SLO	1991	Cal Poly–SLO	2000	St. Augustine's
1983	Cal Poly–SLO	1992	Alabama A&M	2001	St. Augustine's
1984	Cal Poly–SLO	1993	Alabama A&M	2002	St. Augustine's
1985	Abilene Christian	1994	Alabama A&M	2003	Lincoln (Pa.)
1986	Abilene Christian	1995	Abilene Christian	2004	Lincoln (Pa.)
1987	Abilene Christian	1996	Abilene Christian	2005	Lincoln (Pa.)
1988	Abilene Christian	1997	St. Augustine's	2006	Lincoln (Pa.)
1989	Cal Poly–SLO	1998	Abilene Christian		
1990	Cal Poly–SLO	1999	Abilene Christian		

DIVISION III

Year	Champion	Year	Champion	Year	Champion
1982	Central (Iowa)	1991	UW-Oshkosh	2000	Lincoln (Pa.)
1983	UW-La Crosse	1992	Chris. Newport	2001	Wheaton (Mass.)
1984	UW-La Crosse	1993	Lincoln (Pa.)	2002	Wheaton (Mass.)
1985	Cortland	1994	Chris. Newport	2003	Wheaton (Mass.)
1986	UMass–Boston	1995	UW-Oshkosh	2004	UW-Oshkosh
1987	Chris. Newport	1996	UW-Oshkosh	2005	Wartburg
1988	Chris. Newport	1997	UW-Oshkosh	2006	UW-Oshkosh
1989	Chris. Newport	1998	Chris. Newport		
1990	UW-Oshkosh	1999	Lincoln (Pa.)		

Volleyball

Men

Year	Champion	Coach	Score	Runner-Up	Most Outstanding Player
1970	UCLA	Al Scates	3–0	Long Beach St	Dane Holtzman, UCLA
1971	UCLA	Al Scates	3–0	UC–Santa Barbara	K. Kilgore, UCLA/T. Bonynge, UCSB
1972	UCLA	Al Scates	3–2	San Diego St	Dick Irvin, UCLA
1973	San Diego St	Jack Henn	3–1	Long Beach St	Duncan McFarland, San Diego St
1974	UCLA	Al Scates	3–2	UC–Santa Barbara	Bob Leonard, UCLA
1975	UCLA	Al Scates	3–1	UC–Santa Barbara	John Bekins, UCLA
1976	UCLA	Al Scates	3–0	Pepperdine	Joe Mika, UCLA
1977	USC	Ernie Hix	3–1	Ohio St	Celso Kalache, USC
1978	Pepperdine	Marv Dunphy	3–2	UCLA	Mike Blanchard, Pepperdine
1979	UCLA	Al Scates	3–1	USC	Sinjin Smith, UCLA
1980	USC	Ernie Hix	3–1	UCLA	Dusty Dvorak, USC
1981	UCLA	Al Scates	3–2	USC	Karch Kiraly, UCLA
1982	UCLA	Al Scates	3–0	Penn St	Karch Kiraly, UCLA
1983	UCLA	Al Scates	3–0	Pepperdine	Ricci Luyties, UCLA
1984	UCLA	Al Scates	3–1	Pepperdine	Ricci Luyties, UCLA
1985	Pepperdine	Marv Dunphy	3–1	USC	Bob Ctvrtlik, Pepperdine
1986	Pepperdine	Rod Wilde	3–2	USC	Steve Friedman, Pepperdine
1987	UCLA	Al Scates	3–0	USC	Ozzie Volstad, UCLA
1988	USC	Bob Yoder	3–2	UC–Santa Barbara	Jen-Kai Liu, USC
1989	UCLA	Al Scates	3–1	Stanford	Matt Sonnichsen, UCLA
1990	USC	Jim McLaughlin	3–1	Long Beach St	Bryan Ivie, USC
1991	Long Beach St	Ray Ratelle	3–1	USC	Brent Hilliard, Long Beach St
1992	Pepperdine	Marv Dunphy	3–0	Stanford	Alon Grinberg, Pepperdine
1993	UCLA	Al Scates	3–0	CSU–Northridge	Mike Sealy/Jeff Nygaard, UCLA
1994	Penn St	Tom Peterson	3–2	UCLA	Ramon Hernandez, Penn St
1995	UCLA	Al Scates	3–0	Penn St	Jeff Nygaard, UCLA
1996	UCLA	Al Scates	3–2	Hawaii	Yuval Katz, Hawaii
1997	Stanford	Ruben Nieves	3–2	UCLA	Mike Lambert, Stanford
1998	UCLA	Al Scates	3–2	Pepperdine	George Roumain, Pepperdine
1999	BYU	Carl McGown	3–0	Long Beach St	Ossie Antonetti, BYU
2000	UCLA	Al Scates	3–0	Ohio St	Brandon Taliaferro, UCLA
2001	BYU	Carl McGown	3–0	UCLA	Mike Wall, BYU
2002	Hawaii	Mike Wilton	3–1	Pepperdine	Costas Theochardis, Hawaii
2003	Lewis	Dave Deuser	3–2	BYU	Gustavo Meyer, Lewis
2004	BYU	Tom Peterson	3–2	Long Beach St	Carlos Moreno, BYU
2005	Pepperdine	Marv Dunphy	3–2	UCLA	Sean Rooney, Pepperdine
2006	UCLA	Al Scates	3–0	Penn	Steve Klosterman, UCLA

Women

DIVISION I

Year	Champion	Coach	Score	Runner-Up
1981	USC	Chuck Erbe	3–2	UCLA
1982	Hawaii	Dave Shoji	3–2	USC
1983	Hawaii	Dave Shoji	3–0	UCLA
1984	UCLA	Andy Banachowski	3–2	Stanford
1985	Pacific	John Dunning	3–1	Stanford
1986	Pacific	John Dunning	3–0	Nebraska
1987	Hawaii	Dave Shoji	3–1	Stanford
1988	Texas	Mick Haley	3–0	Hawaii
1989	Long Beach St	Brian Gimmillaro	3–0	Nebraska
1990	UCLA	Andy Banachowski	3–0	Pacific
1991	UCLA	Andy Banachowski	3–2	Long Beach St
1992	Stanford	Don Shaw	3–1	UCLA
1993	Long Beach St	Brian Gimmillaro	3–1	Penn St
1994	Stanford	Don Shaw	3–1	UCLA
1995	Nebraska	Terry Pettit	3–1	Texas
1996	Stanford	Don Shaw	3–0	Hawaii
1997	Stanford	Don Shaw	3–2	Penn St
1998	Long Beach St	Brian Gimmillaro	3–2	Penn St
1999	Penn St	Russ Rose	3–0	Stanford
2000	Nebraska	John Cook	3–2	Wisconsin
2001	Stanford	Don Shaw	3–0	Long Beach St
2002	USC	Mick Haley	3–1	Stanford
2003	USC	Mick Haley	3–1	Florida
2004	Stanford	Don Shaw	3–0	Minnesota
2005	Washington	Jim McLaughlin	3–0	Nebraska

Women *(Cont.)*

DIVISION II

Year	Champion	Year	Champion	Year	Champion
1981	CSU–Sacramento	1990	West Texas A&M	1999	BYU–Hawaii
1982	UC–Riverside	1991	West Texas A&M	2000	Hawaii Pacific
1983	CSU–Northridge	1992	Portland St	2001	Barry
1984	Portland St	1993	Northern Michigan	2002	BYU–Hawaii
1985	Portland St	1994	Northern Michigan	2003	N. Alabama
1986	UC–Riverside	1995	Barry	2004	Truman St
1987	CSU–Northridge	1996	Nebraska–Omaha	2005	Grand Valley
1988	Portland St	1997	West Texas A&M		
1989	CSU–Bakersfield	1998	Hawaii Pacific		

DIVISION III

Year	Champion	Year	Champion	Year	Champion	Year	Champion
1981	UC–San Diego	1988	UC–San Diego	1995	Washington (Mo.)	2002	UW-Whitewater
1982	La Verne	1989	Washington (Mo.)	1996	Washington (Mo.)	2003	Washington (Mo.)
1983	Elmhurst	1990	UC–San Diego	1997	UC–San Diego	2004	Juniata
1984	UC–San Diego	1991	Washington (Mo.)	1998	Central (Iowa)	2005	UW-Whitewater
1985	Elmhurst	1992	Washington (Mo.)	1999	Central (Iowa)		
1986	UC–San Diego	1993	Washington (Mo.)	2000	Central (Iowa)		
1987	UC–San Diego	1994	Washington (Mo.)	2001	La Verne		

Water Polo

Men

Year	Champion	Coach	Score	Runner-Up
1969	UCLA	Bob Horn	5–2	California
1970	UC–Irvine	Ed Newland	7–6 (3 OT)	UCLA
1971	UCLA	Bob Horn	5–3	San Jose St
1972	UCLA	Bob Horn	10–5	UC–Irvine
1973	California	Pete Cutino	8–4	UC–Irvine
1974	California	Pete Cutino	7–6	UC–Irvine
1975	California	Pete Cutino	9–8	UC–Irvine
1976	Stanford	Art Lambert	13–12	UCLA
1977	California	Pete Cutino	8–6	UC–Irvine
1978	Stanford	Dante Dettamanti	7–6 (3 OT)	California
1979	UC–Santa Barbara	Pete Snyder	11–3	UCLA
1980	Stanford	Dante Dettamanti	8–6	California
1981	Stanford	Dante Dettamanti	17–6	Long Beach St
1982	UC–Irvine	Ed Newland	7–4	Stanford
1983	California	Pete Cutino	10–7	USC
1984	California	Pete Cutino	9–8	Stanford
1985	Stanford	Dante Dettamanti	12–11 (2 OT)	UC–Irvine
1986	Stanford	Dante Dettamanti	9–6	California
1987	California	Pete Cutino	9–8 (OT)	USC
1988	California	Pete Cutino	14–11	UCLA
1989	UC–Irvine	Ed Newland	9–8	California
1990	California	Steve Heaston	8–7	Stanford
1991	California	Steve Heaston	7–6	UCLA
1992	California	Steve Heaston	12–11	Stanford
1993	Stanford	Dante Dettamanti	11–9	USC
1994	Stanford	Dante Dettamanti	14–10	USC
1995	UCLA	Guy Baker	10–8	California
1996	UCLA	Guy Baker	8–7	USC
1997	Pepperdine	Terry Schroeder	8–7 (OT)	USC
1998	USC	John Williams	9–8 (2 OT)	Stanford
1999	UCLA	Guy Baker	6–5	Stanford
2000	UCLA	Guy Baker/Adam Krikorian	11–2	UC–San Diego
2001	Stanford	Dante Dettamanti	8–5	UCLA
2002	Stanford	John Vargas	7–6	California
2003	USC	Jovan Vavic	9–7	Stanford
2004	UCLA	Adam Krikorian	10–9	Stanford
2005	USC	Jovan Vavic	3–2	Stanford

Women

Year	Champion	Coach	Score	Runner-Up
2001	UCLA	Adam Krikorian	5–4	Stanford
2002	Stanford	John Tanner	8–4	UCLA
2003	UCLA	Adam Krikorian	4–3	Stanford
2004	USC	Jovan Vavic	10–8	Loyola-Marymount
2005	UCLA	Adam Krikorian	3–2	Stanford
2006	UCLA	Adam Krikorian	9–8	USC

Wrestling

DIVISION I

Year	Champion	Coach	Pts	Runner-Up	Pts	Most Outstanding Wrestler
1928	Oklahoma St*	E.C. Gallagher				
1929	Oklahoma St	E.C. Gallagher	26	Michigan	18	
1930	Oklahoma St*	E.C. Gallagher	27	Illinois	14	
1931	Oklahoma St*	E.C. Gallagher		Michigan		
1932	Indiana*	W.H. Thom		Oklahoma St		Edwin Belshaw, Indiana
1933	OK St*/Iowa St*	E. Gallagher/H. Otopalik				A. Kelley, OK St/P. Johnson, Harv
1934	Oklahoma St	E.C. Gallagher	29	Indiana	19	Ben Bishop, Lehigh
1935	Oklahoma St	E.C. Gallagher	36	Oklahoma	18	Ross Flood, Oklahoma St
1936	Oklahoma	Paul Keen	14	Central St/ OK St	10	Wayne Martin, Oklahoma
1937	Oklahoma St	E.C. Gallagher	31	Oklahoma	13	Stanley Henson, Oklahoma St
1938	Oklahoma St	E.C. Gallagher	19	Illinois	15	Joe McDaniels, Oklahoma St
1939	Oklahoma St	E.C. Gallagher	33	Lehigh	12	Dale Hanson, Minnesota
1940	Oklahoma St	E.C. Gallagher	24	Indiana	14	Don Nichols, Michigan
1941	Oklahoma St	Art Griffith	37	Michigan St	26	Al Whitehurst, Oklahoma St
1942	Oklahoma St	Art Griffith	31	Michigan St	26	David Arndt, Oklahoma St
1946	Oklahoma St	Art Griffith	25	Northern Iowa	24	Gerald Leeman, Northern Iowa
1947	Cornell	Paul Scott	32	Northern Iowa	19	William Koll, Northern Iowa
1948	Oklahoma St	Art Griffith	33	Michigan St	28	William Koll, Northern Iowa
1949	Oklahoma St	Art Griffith	32	Northern Iowa	27	Charles Hetrick, Oklahoma St
1950	Northern Iowa	David McCuskey	30	Purdue	16	Anthony Gizoni, Waynesburg
1951	Oklahoma	Port Robertson	24	Oklahoma St	23	Walter Romanowski, Cornell
1952	Oklahoma	Port Robertson	22	Northern Iowa	21	Tommy Evans, Oklahoma
1953	Penn St	Charles Speidel	21	Oklahoma	15	Frank Bettucci, Cornell
1954	Oklahoma St	Art Griffith	32	Pittsburgh	17	Tommy Evans, Oklahoma
1955	Oklahoma St	Art Griffith	40	Penn St	31	Edward Eichelberger, Lehigh
1956	Oklahoma St	Art Griffith	65	Oklahoma	62	Dan Hodge, Oklahoma
1957	Oklahoma	Port Robertson	73	Pittsburgh	66	Dan Hodge, Oklahoma
1958	Oklahoma St	Myron Roderick	77	Iowa St	62	Dick Delgado, Oklahoma
1959	Oklahoma St	Myron Roderick	73	Iowa St	51	Ron Gray, Iowa St
1960	Oklahoma	Thomas Evans	59	Iowa St	40	Dave Auble, Cornell
1961	Oklahoma St	Myron Roderick	82	Oklahoma	63	E. Gray Simons, Lock Haven
1962	Oklahoma St	Myron Roderick	82	Oklahoma	45	E. Gray Simons, Lock Haven
1963	Oklahoma	Thomas Evans	48	Iowa St	45	Mickey Martin, Oklahoma
1964	Oklahoma St	Myron Roderick	87	Oklahoma	58	Dean Lahr, Colorado
1965	Iowa St	Harold Nichols	87	Oklahoma St	86	Yojiro Uetake, Oklahoma St
1966	Oklahoma St	Myron Roderick	79	Iowa St	70	Yojiro Uetake, Oklahoma St
1967	Michigan St	Grady Peninger	74	Michigan	63	Rich Sanders, Portland St
1968	Oklahoma St	Myron Roderick	81	Iowa St	78	Dwayne Keller, Oklahoma St
1969	Iowa St	Harold Nichols	104	Oklahoma	69	Dan Gable, Iowa St
1970	Iowa St	Harold Nichols	99	Michigan St	84	Larry Owings, Washington
1971	Oklahoma St	Tommy Chesbro	94	Iowa St	66	Darrell Keller, Oklahoma St
1972	Iowa St	Harold Nichols	103	Michigan St	72½	Wade Schalles, Clarion
1973	Iowa St	Harold Nichols	85	Oregon St	72½	Greg Strobel, Oregon St
1974	Oklahoma	Stan Abel	69½	Michigan	67	Floyd Hitchcock, Bloomsburg
1975	Iowa	Gary Kurdelmeier	102	Oklahoma	77	Mike Frick, Lehigh
1976	Iowa	Gary Kurdelmeier	123½	Iowa St	85¾	Chuch Yagla, Iowa
1977	Iowa St	Harold Nichols	95½	Oklahoma St	88¾	Nick Gallo, Hofstra
1978	Iowa	Dan Gable	94½	Iowa St	94	Mark Churella, Michigan
1979	Iowa	Dan Gable	122½	Iowa St	88	Bruce Kinseth, Iowa
1980	Iowa	Dan Gable	110¾	Oklahoma St	87	Howard Harris, Oregon St
1981	Iowa	Dan Gable	129¾	Oklahoma	100¼	Gene Mills, Syracuse

DIVISION I *(Cont.)*

Year	Champion	Coach	Pts	Runner-Up	Pts	Most Outstanding Wrestler
1982	Iowa	Dan Gable	131¾	Iowa St	111	Mark Schultz, Oklahoma
1983	Iowa	Dan Gable	155	Oklahoma St	102	Mike Sheets, Oklahoma St
1984	Iowa	Dan Gable	123¾	Oklahoma St	98	Jim Zalesky, Iowa
1985	Iowa	Dan Gable	145¼	Oklahoma	98½	Barry Davis, Iowa
1986	Iowa	Dan Gable	158	Oklahoma	84¼	Marty Kistler, Iowa
1987	Iowa St	Jim Gibbons	133	Iowa	108	John Smith, Oklahoma St
1988	Arizona St	Bobby Douglas	93	Iowa	85½	Scott Turner, N.Carolina St
1989	Oklahoma St	Joe Seay	91¼	Arizona St	70½	Tim Krieger, Iowa St
1990	Oklahoma St	Joe Seay	117¾	Arizona St	104¾	Chris Barnes, Oklahoma St
1991	Iowa	Dan Gable	157	Oklahoma St	108¾	Jeff Prescott, Penn St
1992	Iowa	Dan Gable	149	Oklahoma St	100½	Tom Brands, Iowa
1993	Iowa	Dan Gable	123¾	Penn St	87½	Terry Steiner, Iowa
1994	Oklahoma St	John Smith	94¾	Iowa	76½	Pat Smith, Oklahoma St
1995	Iowa	Dan Gable	134	Oregon St	77½	T.J. Jaworsky, North Carolina
1996	Iowa	Dan Gable	122½	Iowa St	78½	Les Gutches, Oregon St
1997	Iowa	Dan Gable	170	Oklahoma St	113½	Lincoln McIlravy, Iowa
1998	Iowa	Jim Zalesky	115	Minnesota	102	Joe Williams, Iowa
1999	Iowa	Jim Zalesky	100½	Minnesota	98½	Cael Sanderson, Iowa St
2000	Iowa	Jim Zalesky	116	Iowa St	109½	Cael Sanderson, Iowa St
2001	Minnesota	J Robinson	138½	Iowa	125½	Cael Sanderson, Iowa St
2002	Minnesota	J Robinson	126½	Iowa St	104	Cael Sanderson, Iowa St
2003	Oklahoma St	John Smith	143	Minnesota	104½	Eric Larkin, Arizona St
2004	Oklahoma St	John Smith	123½	Iowa	82	Jesse Jantzen, Harvard
2005	Oklahoma	John Smith	150	Michigan	83	Ryan Bertin, Michigan
2006	Oklahoma	John Smith	122½	Minnesota	84	Ben Askren, Missouri

*Unofficial champions.

DIVISION II

Year	Champion	Year	Champion	Year	Champion
1963	Western St (Colo.)	1979	CSU–Bakersfield	1995	Central Oklahoma
1964	Western St (Colo.)	1980	CSU–Bakersfield	1996	Pitt–Johnstown
1965	Mankato St	1981	CSU–Bakersfield	1997	San Francisco St
1966	Cal Poly–SLO	1982	CSU–Bakersfield	1998	North Dakota St
1967	Portland St	1983	CSU–Bakersfield	1999	Pittsburgh–Johnstown
1968	Cal Poly–SLO	1984	SIU–Edwardsville	2000	North Dakota St
1969	Cal Poly–SLO	1985	SIU–Edwardsville	2001	North Dakota St
1970	Cal Poly–SLO	1986	SIU–Edwardsville	2002	Central Oklahoma
1971	Cal Poly–SLO	1987	CSU–Bakersfield	2003	Central Oklahoma
1972	Cal Poly–SLO	1988	North Dakota St	2004	Nebraska–Omaha
1973	Cal Poly–SLO	1989	Portland St	2005	Omaha
1974	Cal Poly–SLO	1990	Portland St	2006	Nebraska–Omaha
1975	Northern Iowa	1991	Nebraska–Omaha		
1976	CSU–Bakersfield	1992	Central Oklahoma		
1977	CSU–Bakersfield	1993	Central Oklahoma		
1978	Northern Iowa	1994	Central Oklahoma		

DIVISION III

Year	Champion	Year	Champion	Year	Champion
1974	Wilkes	1986	Montclair St	1998	Augsburg
1975	John Carroll	1987	Trenton St	1999	Wartburg
1976	Montclair St	1988	St. Lawrence	2000	Augsburg
1977	Brockport St	1989	Ithaca	2001	Augsburg
1978	Buffalo	1990	Ithaca	2002	Augsburg
1979	Trenton St	1991	Augsburg	2003	Wartburg
1980	Brockport St	1992	Brockport	2004	Wartburg
1981	Trenton St	1993	Augsburg	2005	Augsburg
1982	Brockport St	1994	Ithaca	2006	Wartburg
1983	Brockport St	1995	Augsburg		
1984	Trenton St	1996	Wartburg		
1985	Trenton St	1997	Augsburg		

Individual Championship Records

SWIMMING

Men

Event	Time	Record Holder	Date
50-yard freestyle	18.90	Fred Bousquet, Auburn	3-24-05
100-yard freestyle	41.49	Duje Draganja, California	3-26-05
200-yard freestyle	1:33.03	Matt Biondi, California	4-3-87
500-yard freestyle	4:08.75	Tom Dolan, Michigan	3-23-95
1,650-yard freestyle	14:26.62	Chris Thompson, Michigan	3-24-01
100-yard backstroke	45.25	Neil Walker, Texas	3-28-97
200-yard backstroke	1:38.37	Ryan Lochete, Florida	3-26-05
100-yard breaststroke	52.32	Jeremy Linn, Tennessee	3-28-97
200-yard breaststroke	1:52.62	Brendan Hansen, Texas	3-29-03
100-yard butterfly	45.44	Ian Crocker, Texas	3-29-02
200-yard butterfly	1:41.78	Melvin Stewart, Tennessee	3-30-91
200-yard individual medley	1:41.71	Ryan Lochte, Florida	3-24-05
400-yard individual medley	3:38.18	Tom Dolan, Michigan	3-24-95

Women

Event	Time	Record Holder	Date
50-yard freestyle	21.69	Maritza Correia, Georgia	3-21-02
100-yard freestyle	47.29	Maritza Correia, Georgia	3-22-03
200-yard freestyle	1:43.08	Martina Moravcova, SMU	3-28-97
500-yard freestyle	4:34.39	Janet Evans, Stanford	3-15-90
1,650-yard freestyle	15:39.14	Janet Evans, Stanford	3-17-90
100-yard backstroke	49.97	Natalie Coughlin, California	3-22-02
200-yard backstroke	1:49.52	Natalie Coughlin, California	3-22-02
100-yard breaststroke	59.05	Kristy Kowal, Georgia	3-20-98
200-yard breaststroke	2:07.36	Tara Kirk, Stanford	3-22-02
100-yard butterfly	50.01	Natalie Coughlin, California	3-22-02
200-yard butterfly	1:53.36	Limin Liu, Nevada	3-20-99
200-yard individual medley	1:53.91	Maggie Bowen, Auburn	3-21-02
400-yard individual medley	4:02.28	Summer Sanders, Stanford	3-20-92

Individual Collegiate Records

INDOOR TRACK AND FIELD

Men

Event	Mark	Record Holder	Date
55-meter dash	6.00	Lee McRae, Pittsburgh	3-14-86
60-meter dash	6.45	Leonard Myles-Mills, BYU	2-20-99
55-meter hurdles	7.07	Allen Johnson, North Carolina	3-13-92
60-meter hurdles	7.47	Reggie Torian, Wsconsin	3-5-99
200-meter dash	20.10	Wallace Spearmon, Arkansas	3-12-05
400-meter dash	44.57	Kerron Clement, Florida	3-12-05
800-meter run	1:44.84	Paul Ereng, Virginia	3-4-89
Mile run	3:55.00	Tony Waldrop, North Carolina	2-17-74
3,000-meter run	7:46.03	Adam Goucher, Colorado	3-14-98
5,000-meter run	13:20.40	Suleiman Nyambui, UTEP	2-6-81
High jump	7 ft 9¼ in	Hollis Conway, SW Louisiana	3-11-89
Pole vault	19 ft 2¼ in	Jacob Davis, Texas	3-6-99
Long jump	28 ft 2¼ in	Miguel Pate, Alabama	3-1-02
Triple jump	57 ft 5 in	Charlie Simpkins, Baptist	1-17-86
Shot put	70 ft 6½ in	Terry Albritton, Stanford	2-4-77
35-pound weight throw	78 ft 6½ in	Tore Johnsen, UTEP	2-25-84

Women

Event	Mark	Record Holder	Date
55-meter dash	6.56	Gwen Torrence, Georgia	3-14-87
60-meter dash	7.09	Angela Williams, USC	3-11-01
55-meter hurdles	7.39	Tiffany Lott, BYU	3-7-97
60-meter hurdles	7.90	Perdita Felicien, Illinois	3-8-02
200-meter dash	22.49	Muna Lee, LSU	3-14-03
400-meter dash	51.05	Maicel Malone, Arizona St	3-9-91
800-meter run	2:01.65	Amy Wickus, Wisconsin	2-12-94

INDOOR TRACK AND FIELD (Cont.)

Women

Event	Mark	Record Holder	Date
Mile run	4:28.31	Vicki Huber, Villanova	2-5-88
3,000-meter run	8:53.54	PattiSue Plumer, Stanford	2-27-83
5,000-meter run	15:17.28	Sonia O'Sullivan, Villanova	1-26-91
High jump	6 ft 5½ in	Four recordholders	—
Pole vault	14 ft 10 ¼ in	Amy Linnen, Arizona	3-13-02
Long jump	22 ft 8 in	Elva Goulbourne, Auburn	2-23-02
Triple jump	46 ft 9 in	Suzette Lee, LSU	3-8-97
Shot put	61 ft 9½ in	Teri Tunks, SMU	2-28-98
20-pound weight throw	79 ft 3¼ in	Dawn Ellerbe, South Carolina	3-12-05

OUTDOOR TRACK AND FIELD

Men

Event	Mark	Record Holder	Date
100-meter dash	9.92	Ato Bolden, UCLA	6-1-96
200-meter dash	19.86	Justin Gatlin, Tennessee	5-12-02
400-meter dash	44.00	Quincy Watts, USC	6-6-92
800-meter run	1:44.74	Dmitrijs Milkevics, Nebraska	6-11-05
1,500-meter run	3:35.30	Sydney Maree, Villanova	6-6-81
3,000-meter steeplechase	8:05.40	Henry Rono, Washington St	4-8-78
5,000-meter run	13:08.40	Henry Rono, Washington St	4-8-78
10,000-meter run	27:36.20	Gabriel Kamau, UTEP	4-24-82
110-meter high hurdles	13.00	Renaldo Nehemiah, Maryland	5-6-79
400-meter intermediate hurdles	47.56	Kerron Clement, Florida	6-11-05
High jump	7 ft 9¾ in	Hollis Conway, SW Louisiana	6-3-89
Pole vault	19 ft 7½ in	Lawrence Johnson, Tennessee	5-25-96
Long jump	28 8¼ ft	Erick Walder, Arkansas	4-2-94
Triple jump	57 ft 7¾ in	Keith Connor, SMU	6-5-82
Shot put	72 ft 2¼ in	John Godina, UCLA	6-3-95
Discus throw	219 ft 6 in	Gábor Máté, Auburn	3-25-00
Hammer throw	268 ft 10 in	Balazs Kiss, USC	5-19-95
Javelin throw (new javelin)	268 ft 7 in	Esko Mikkola, Arizona	6-3-98
Decathlon	8463 pts	Tom Pappas, Tennessee	3-17/18-99

Women

Event	Mark	Record Holder	Date
100-meter dash	10.78	Dawn Sowell, LSU	6-3-89
200-meter dash	22.04	Dawn Sowell, LSU	6-2-89
400-meter dash	50.10	Monique Henderson, UCLA	6-11-05
800-meter run	1:59.11	Suzy Favor, Wisconsin	6-1-90
1,500-meter run	4:08.26	Suzy Favor, Wisconsin	6-2-90
3,000-meter run	8:47.35	Vicki Huber, Villanova	6-3-88
5,000-meter run	15:23.03	Kathy Hayes, Oregon	5-4-85
10,000-meter run	32:22.97	Carole Zajac, Villanova	4-23-92
100-meter hurdles	12.61	Gail Devers, UCLA	5-21-88
400-meter hurdles	54.54	Ryan Tolbert, Vanderbilt	6-6-97
High jump	6 ft 6 in	Amy Acuff, UCLA	5-19-95
		Kajsa Bergqvist, SMU	5-22-99
Pole vault	14 ft 10¼ in	Amy Linnen, Arizona	3-9-02
Long jump	22 ft 11¼ in	Jackie Joyner-Kersee, UCLA	5-4-85
Triple jump	46 ft 2in	Candice Bauchman, UCLA	6-11-05
Shot put	62 ft 3¼ in	Meg Ritchie, Arizona	5-7-83
Discus throw	222 ft 5 in	Meg Ritchie, Arizona	4-26-81
Hammer throw	220 ft 6 in	Jamine Moton, Clemson	5-29-02
Javelin throw (new javelin)	197 ft 8 in	Angeliki Tsiolakoudi, UTEP	6-3-00
Heptathlon	6527 pts	Diane Guthrie-Gresham, George Mason	6-2/3-95

Olympics

U.S. Olympic medalists
Hannah Teter (r.) and
Gretchen Bleiler

BOB MARTIN

Upstarts and Meltdowns

While numerous American underdogs struck gold, many of the heavy U.S. favorites stumbled in Turin and were more than happy to say, "*Arrivederci, Italia.*"

BY MERRELL NODEN

IF YOU WERE ASKED TO CHOOSE a poster child for U.S. fortunes at the XXth Winter Olympiad—someone whose performance was undeniably good, but who had seemed capable of so much more—you could do a whole lot worse than to nominate Lindsey Jacobellis. The 20-year-old from Stratton, Vermont, is widely considered to be the world's best in snowboardcross, or SBX, which, as the initials suggest, is one of those newfangled, X Games concoctions seemingly added to the Olympic program to boost either the Games' hipness quotient or the U.S. medal count. Take your pick: In Turin, they did both.

These were the first Olympics to include SBX, which sends four boarders hurtling down a tight, twisty, mile-long course, and as expected, Jacobellis quickly staked a strong claim to that historic, first-ever SBX gold. But late in the final, while leading by some 40 yards, she was seized by an irresistible urge to showboat. Flying off a jump in front of a packed grandstand, she reached down to grab the heel edge of her board, a stunt boarders call a "Method air." We, however, will call it a Reverse King Midas, since it had the effect of turning her sure-thing gold medal into silver. She wiped out, and before she could recover, a

disbelieving Tanja Frieden of Switzerland had swept past her for the win.

"I got caught up in the moment," Jacobellis explained glumly to Bob Costas of NBC. "I made a mistake."

It was an incomprehensible blunder, but it was hardly out of place for an American team that, despite some pleasant surprises, found creative new ways to under-perform. But despite these many lapses, the U.S. wound up second to Germany in the medal table, with 25 medals. Its nine golds—three of them in snowboard events—tied it for second with Austria, behind Germany's 11. This was impressive, considering that the last time the U.S. finished as high as second in an "away" Winter Olympics was 1952; never before had the U.S. won more than 13 medals outside its own borders. If the Turin performance didn't exactly feel like a new high watermark, it was because in so many marquee events—ice hockey, alpine skiing, and figure skating—the U.S. team had expected to do so much better.

It did not help that the U.S. Olympic team's best-known member, the much-beloved figure skater Michelle Kwan, who was seeking to win the gold that had eluded her in two previous Games, flew to Turin only to withdraw rather than compete with the injuries that had forced her

withdrawal from the U.S. nationals. She was replaced by Emily Hughes, the younger sister of the defending champion, Sarah Hughes (who did not try to qualify for the team). Though sad, Kwan's withdrawal was not deemed a complete disaster since her teammate, Sasha Cohen, was given a good shot at winning the gold.

Much was also expected from the U.S. skiers, and from superstar Bode Miller in particular, but they too proved to be major disappointments, straddling gates, taking tumbles, and—go figure—deciding at the last minute to race on unfamiliar skis. In race after race, U.S. skiers had a tough time just staying on their feet. During a practice run for the women's downhill, Lindsey Kildow suffered a horrific fall and had to spend a night in the hospital. She wasn't alone: U.S. sliders (competitors in luge, bobsled, and skeleton) made more trips to the hospital than to the medal stand. Luger Samantha Retrosi was lucky to suffer "only" a concussion after a crash that looked very serious. U.S. sliders had done well in 2002, winning

Shaun "Flying Tomato" White, 19, rode the half-pipe to Winter Olympic gold.

eight medals. But here, they took just one, the silver in the two-woman bobsled, which went to the team of Shauna Rohbock and Valerie Fleming.

For the longest time, these Winter Games felt muted or flat. Right up to and even beyond the Opening Ceremonies, on February 10th, ticket sales lagged, and NBC's nightly coverage, anchored by Costas, regularly lost the ratings war to *American Idol.* There was depressing news when Italian authorities raided houses rented to Austrian biathletes and cross-country skiers. The search turned up over 100 syringes, 30 packs of drugs, and equipment for blood transfusions, though the Austrians' in-competition drug tests came out negative. (The lone positive drug test in Turin belonged to a Russian biathlete, Olga Pyleva, who was stripped of her silver medal when her sample was found to contain a banned stimulant.)

Even the host Italians seemed uninter-

DAMIAN STROHMEYER

between Hedrick and teammate Shani Davis, ostensibly over Davis's decision not to compete in the inaugural Olympic team pursuit, a relay, in order to save himself for his best event, the 1,000 meters. "With Shani, we'd be the favorites for sure," grumbled Hedrick.

Controversy is nothing new to Davis, who has battled his sport's federation over sponsorship issues. A 23-year-old African American from Chicago, raised by a single mother, Davis was an Olympic alternate in 2002 in shorttrack. Against the advice of U.S. coaches, he has continued to pursue both disciplines, with the result that he brings to the big oval a daring on the turns that other skaters envy. Of course, no one will know how the U.S. pursuit team would have fared had Davis chosen to skate, but at least he backed up his talk by winning the 1,000, thus becoming the first African American to win gold in an individual event in the Winter Olympics.

If you were looking for positive vibes to go with fast times, you turned to Joey Cheek, 26, a North Carolinian who won the 500-meter gold by a comfortable margin and then announced that he was donating his $25,000 gold medal bonus from the USOC to Right to Play, a charity headed by Norwegian speedskater Johann Olav Koss, whose heroics at the 1994 Olympics had inspired Cheek to switch from inline skating to speedskating. Cheek earmarked his donation for refugees in Chad and then took on the thankless job of playing peace-

ested in the Games at first but once they were reminded that this was their party, they became giddy, passionate hosts. And by the time Enrico Fabris claimed his third speedskating medal (two golds and a bronze), his countrymen had passed from excitement to delirium. By the end of the Games, 900,000 tickets had been sold—90% of capacity—and a proud new chapter had been written in the sports history of the host country.

The first U.S. gold medal of the Games went to speedskater Chad Hedrick, in the 5,000 meters. Hedrick, a 28-year-old who grew up roller skating on the rink his dad owned in Spring, Texas, went to Turin with a slim chance of joining speedskating god Eric Heiden as a winner of four golds at a single Winter Olympics. But despite being cheered on by 30 family members, Hedrick did not come close, though he did go home with a complete set of medals, finishing second in the 10,000 and third in the 1,500.

Unfortunately, the biggest news from the speedskating oval was the bitter feud maker between his teammates.

There is no shortage of animosity in short track speedskating either, only not between teammates. The South Koreans who dominate short track are still bitter that Apolo Anton Ohno of the U.S. was awarded the gold in a controversial 1,500-meter final in Salt Lake City, and it would surely have given them great pleasure to deny him a gold four years later.

Led by three-time world champion Hyun-Soo Ahn, a veritable training machine who works out eight hours a day, the South Koreans went 1-2 in both the 1,000 and 1,500 and won the relay. Ohno's chances of winning a gold medal looked slim. But in the final individual event on the program, the 500, Ohno skated a tactically brilliant race and edged his rivals. Still, it was impossible not to be awed by the Koreans' dominance of this sport: In eight events they won six gold with three going to Ahn and another three to Sun-Yu Jin, the only woman to win three golds at these Games.

In alpine skiing, U.S. fortunes have been rising steadily of late, led by Miller and Daron Rahlves. For several years, the U.S. ski team has been using the slogan "Best in the World" to tout its aspirations. Certainly Miller, the 2005 World Cup overall champion, whom some consider to be the greatest talent in alpine skiing history, was widely expected to come home with a clutch of medals; no one would have been surprised if two or three of them were gold.

But Miller seemed distracted and beaten long before he got to Turin. Though he appeared on the covers of both *Time* and *Newsweek*, he generated far more bad publicity by joking on *60 Minutes* about skiing while still hung over from drinking. Once in Sestriere, he seemed almost bent on self-sabotage. He was out on the town on numerous nights, and on the morning of the downhill final he skipped the early-morning course inspection to sleep in. After finishing fifth in that race, he spoke of a "disconnect" between how he felt he'd performed and what the clock said. Rahlves, another

gold medal favorite skiing in his last big meet, also showed signs of uncertainty, choosing to switch from new skis back to familiar ones just minutes before his downhill run. He finished 10th. Then, in the second week Miller managed to sprain an ankle...playing basketball! It was hard not to get the feeling that for whatever reason, he just wasn't mentally ready, and the results showed it: A fifth, a sixth, and three flameouts.

Whereas the Austrians claimed 13 alpine medals, including four gold, the Americans won just two—Ted Ligety's unexpected gold in the alpine combined and Julia Mancuso's gold in the giant slalom. Those two are only 21 and have very bright futures, but there was genuine concern in the U.S. camp as to how the team's disappointing performance in Sestriere would effect the program's future.

For some time now, the excitement of women's ice hockey has been threatened by the lopsided dominance of North American teams over their European counterparts. That problem was partly solved in Turin—at the expense of the U.S. women, who had the misfortune of running up against a determined underdog in Sweden. To gird themselves against self-doubt, the Swedes had all but memorized *Miracle*, the 2004 film about the U.S. men's dramatic upset of the mighty Soviets in 1980. And darned if it didn't work a second miracle! Down 2–0 in the second period of their semifinal game, Sweden rallied to beat the U.S., 3–2. Swedish goalie Kim Martin had 37 stops. The U.S. women have now slipped from gold in 1998 to silver in 2002 and bronze here.

The U.S. men, however, did not even get to play for a medal. Winning just one of their six games—against lowly Kazhakstan—the U.S. men were eliminated in the quarterfinals, losing 4–3 to Finland. They surrendered one goal when defenseman Derian Hatcher lost a glove and went chasing after it, another when the puck bounced off goalie Rick DiPietro's back. But just as surprising was youthful Russia's 2–0 pounding of Canada in the quar-

Like much of the U.S. ski team, Bode Miller (seen here crashing during the Super G) disappointed fans at Turin.

falls, Tanith Belbin and Ben Agosto stayed on their feet to take the silver. The two had been skating together for eight years, but were only eligible to skate in the Olympics when Belbin, a Canadian by birth, was awarded U.S. citizenship on Dec. 31.

It was up to the snowboarders, those notorious free spirits, to boost U.S. spirits. "We kept it fun," was the way Jeremy Foster, director of the U.S. snowboarding program, described the team's approach. In the men's half-pipe Shaun White, an elfin 19-year-old Californian known as "Flying Tomato" for his long thick red hair, kept

ters. Wayne Gretzky, the executive director of Canada's Olympic team, could not bear to watch and left, in tears, before the end of the game. That left four European teams in the semis, and in a Scandinavian grudge match, Sweden beat Finland 3–2 to claim the gold medal.

There was more disappointment on ice for the U.S. figure skating team. Johnny Weir, who was considered a medal threat, finished fifth, far behind runaway winner Evgeni Plushenko of Russia. And just when it seemed that Sasha Cohen and Irina Slutskaya of Russia would have the two-woman duel everyone was expecting, Shizuka Arakawa of Japan outskated them both in the long program. Cohen won the silver, which was more than she had expected given the way she'd skated, while Slutskaya was a visibly disappointed third.

The bright spot for the U.S. came in the dance, where the U.S. had not medaled since 1976. Skating a lovely flamenco free dance in a competition marred by many

things interesting by sketching the landing on a backside 900 on his first run. That left him seventh with only six boarders going to the final. To right his head, White went free-riding on the nearby slopes, then returned to nail his second run. In the final, no one could touch White, whose teammate, Danny Kass, took second.

Hannah Teter, 19, from Belmont, VT, also took an unscheduled tour of the nearby slopes before her final and it too worked miracles. She and Gretchen Bleiler went 1-2 (with teammates Kelly Clark and Elena Hight fourth and sixth) and then headed home to serve as honorary starters for the Daytona 500. The final snowboarding gold went to Seth Westcott, an outdoor sports renaissance man who boards, kayaks, climbs, and does the halfpipe. A heavy favorite in the men's SBX, he used a nifty inside pass to claim the gold, and then offered a fair summary of what his sport had done for these Games: "Snowboarding is becoming the heart and soul of the Olympics."

2006 Winter Games

BIATHLON

Men		Women	
10 KILOMETERS		**7.5 KILOMETERS**	
1...........Sven Fisher, Germany	24:11.6	1...........Florence Baverel-Robert, France	22:31.4
2...........Halvard Hanevold, Norway	24:19.8	2...........Anna Carin Olofsson, Sweden	22:33.8
3...........Frode Andresen, Norway	24:31.3	3...........Lilia Efremova, Ukraine	22:38.0
12.5 KILOMETERS PURSUIT		**10 KILOMETERS PURSUIT**	
1...........Vincent Defrasne, France	35:20.2	1...........Kati Wilhelm, Germany	36:43.6
2...........Ole Einar Bjoerndalen, Norway	35:22.9	2...........Martina Glagow, Germany	37:57.2
3...........Sven Fisher, Germany	35:35.8	3...........Albina Akhatova, Russia	38:05.0
15 KILOMETERS		**12.5 KILOMETERS**	
1...........Michael Gries, Germany	47:20.0	1...........Anna Carin Olofsson, Sweden	40:36.5
2...........Tomasz Sikora, Poland	47:26.3	2...........Kati Wilhelm, Germany	40:55.3
3...........Ole Einar Bjoerndalen, Norway	47:32.3	3...........Uschi Disl, Germany	41:18.4
20 KILOMETERS		**15 KILOMETERS**	
1...........Michael Gries, Germany	54:23.0	1...........Svetlana Ishmouratova, Russia	49:24.1
2...........Ole Einar Bjoerndalen, Norway	54:39.0	2...........Martina Glagow, Germany	50:34.9
3...........Halvard Hanevold, Norway	55:31.9	3...........Albina Akhatova, Russia	50:55.0
4 X 7.5-KILOMETER RELAY		**4 X 6-KILOMETER RELAY**	
1...........Germany	1:21:51.5	1...........Russia	1:16:12.5
2...........Russia	1:22:12.4	2...........Germany	1:17:03.2
3...........France	1:22:35.1	3...........France	1:18:38.7

BOBSLED

Men		Women	
TWO-MAN		**TWO-PERSON**	
1......Andre Lange/ Kevin Kuske, Germany I	3:43.38	1......S. Kiriasis/ A. Schneiderheinze, Ger I	3:49.98
2......Pierre Lueders/ Lascelles Brown Canada I	3:43.59	2......Shauna Rohbock/Valerie Fleming, USA I	3:50.69
3......Martin Annen/ Beat Hefti, Switz I	3:43.73	3......G. Weissensteiner/J. Isacco, Italy I	3:51.01
FOUR-MAN			
1......Germany I	3:40.42		
2......Russia I	3:40.55		
3......Switzerland I	3:40.83		

CURLING

Men	Women
1...........Canada	1...........Sweden
2...........Finland	2...........Switzerland
3...........United States	3...........Canada

FIGURE SKATING

Men	Pts	Women	Pts
1. ....Evgeni Plushenko, Russia	258.33	1. .....Shizuka Arakawa, Japan	191.34
2. .....Stephane Lambiel, Switzerland	231.21	2. .....Sasha Cohen, United States	183.36
3. ......Jeffrey Buttle, Canada	227.59	3. ......Irina Slutskaya, Russia	181.44

Pairs	Pts	Ice Dancing	Pts
1......Tatiana Totmianina/Maxim Marinin, Russia	204.48	1......Tatiana Navka/Roman Kostomarov, Russia	200.64
2......Zhang Dan, Zhang Hao, China	189.73	2......Tanith Belbin, Ben Agosto, United States	196.06
3......Hongbo Zhao, Xue Shen, China	186.91	3......Elena Grushina, Ruslan Goncharov, Ukraine	195.85

ICE HOCKEY

Men	Women
1...........Sweden	1...........Canada
2...........Finland	2...........Sweden
3...........Czech Republic	3...........United States

LUGE

Men

SINGLES

1....Armin Zoeggeler, Italy	3:26.088
2....Albert Demtschenko, Russia	3:26.198
3....Martinus Rubenis, Latvia	3:26.445

DOUBLES

1....Andreas Linger/Wolfgang Linger, Austria	1:34.497
2....A. Florschuetz/T. Wustlich, Germany	1:34.807
3....G. Plankensteiner/O. Haselrieder, Italy	1:34.930

Women

SINGLES

1....Sylke Otto, Germany	3:07.979
2....Silke Kraushaar, Germany	3:08.115
3....Tatjana Huefner, Germany	3:08.460

SKELETON

Men

1.	Duff Gibson, Canada	1:55.88
2.	Jeff Pain, Canada	1:56.14
3.	Gregor Staehli, Switzerland	1:56.80

Women

1.	Maya Pedersen, Switzerland	1:59.83
2.	Shelley Rudman, United Kingdom	2:01.06
3.	Mellisa Hollingsworth-Richards, Canada	2:01.41

SPEED SKATING

Men

500 METERS

1....Joey Cheek, United States	1:09.76
2....Dmitry Dorofeyev, Russia	1:10.41
3....Lee Kang Seok, S Korea	1:10.43

1,000 METERS

1....Shani Davis, United States	1:08.89
2....Joey Cheek, United States	1:09.16
3....Erben Wennemars, Netherlands	1:09.32

1,500 METERS

1....Enrico Fabris, Italy	1:45.97
2....Shani Davis, United States	1:46.13
3....Chad Hedrick, United States	1:46.22

5,000 METERS

1....Chad Hedrick, United States	6:14.68
2....Sven Kramer, Netherlands	6:16.40
3....Enrico Fabris, Italy	6:18.25

10,000 METERS

1....Bob de Jong, Netherlands	13:01.57
2....Chad Hedrick, United States	13:05.40
3....Carl Verheijen, Netherlands	13:08.80

500 METERS SHORT TRACK

1....Apolo Anton Ohno, United States	41.935
2....Francois-Louis Tremblay, France	42.002
3....Hyun-Soo Ahn, S Korea	42.089

1,000 METERS SHORT TRACK

1....Hyun-Soo Ahn, S Korea	1:26.739 OR
2....Ho-Suk Lee, S Korea	1:26.764
3....Apolo Anton Ohno, United States	1:26.927

1,500 METERS SHORT TRACK

1....Hyun-Soo Ahn, S Korea	2:25.341
2....Ho-Suk Lee, S Korea	2:25.600
3....JiaJun Li, China	2:26.005

5,000-METER SHORT TRACK RELAY

1....S Korea	6:43.376 OR
2....Canada	6:43.707
3....United States	6:47.990

TEAM PURSUIT

1....Italy
2....Canada
3....Netherlands

Women

500 METERS

1....Svetlana Zhurova, Russia	1:16.57
2....Manli Wang, China	1:16.78
3....Hui Ren, China	1:16.87

1,000 METERS

1....Marianne Timmer, Netherlands	1:16.05
2....Cindy Klassen, Canada	1:16.09
3....Anni Friesinger,Germany	1:16.11

1,500 METERS

1....Cindy Klassen, Canada	1:55.27
2....Kristina Groves, Canada	1:56.74
3....Ireen Wust, Netherlands	1:56.90

3,000 METERS

1....Ireen Wust, Netherlands	4:02.43
2....Renate Groenewold, Netherlands	4:03.48
3....Cindy Klassen, Canada	4:04.37

5,000 METERS

1....Clara Hughes, Canada	6:59.07
2....Claudia Pechstein, Germany	7:00.08
3....Cindy Klassen, Canada	7:00.57

500 METERS SHORT TRACK

1....Meng Wang, China	44.345
2....Evgenia Radanova, Bulgaria	44.374
3....Anouk Leblanc-Boucher, Canada	44.759

1,000 METERS SHORT TRACK

1....Sun-Yu Jin, S Korea	1:32.859
2....Meng Wang, China	1:33.079
3....Yang A. Yang, China	1:33.937

1,500 METERS SHORT TRACK

1....Sun-Yu Jin, S Korea	2:23.494
2....Eun-Kyung Choi, Korea	2:24.069
3....Meng Wang, China	2:24.469

3,000-METER SHORT TRACK RELAY

1....S Korea	4:17.040
2....Canada	4:17.336
3....Italy	4:20.030

TEAM PURSUIT

1....Germany
2....Canada
3....Russia

Note: OR=Olympic Record. WR=World Record. EOR=Equals Olympic Record. EWR=Equals World Record. WB=World Best.

FREESTYLE SKIING

Men

MOGULS	Pts
1. ...Dale Begg-Smith, Australia	26.77
2. ...Mikko Ronkainen, Finland	26.62
3. ...Toby Dawson, United States	26.30

AERIALS	Pts
1. ...Han Xiaopeng, China	250.77
2. ...Dmitri Dashinski, Belarus	248.68
3. ...Vladimir Lebedev, Russia	246.76

Women

MOGULS	Pts
1. ...Jennifer Heil, Canada	26.50
2. ...Kari Traa, Norway	25.65
3. ...Sandra Laoura, France	25.37

AERIALS	Pts
1. ...Evelyne Leu, Switzerland	202.55
2. ...Nina Li, China	197.39
3. ...Alisa Camplin, Australia	191.39

ALPINE SKIING

Men

DOWNHILL
1. ...Antoine Deneriaz, France — 1:48.80
2. ...Michael Walchhofer, Austria — 1:49.52
3. ...Bruno Kernen, Switzerland — 1:49.82

SLALOM
1. ...Benjamin Raich, Austria — 1:43.14
2. ...Reinfried Herbst, Austria — 1:43.97
3. ...Rainer Schoenfelder, Austria — 1:44.15

GIANT SLALOM
1. ...Benjamin Raich, Austria — 2:35.00
2. ...Joel Chanel, France — 2:35.07
3. ...Hermann Maier, Germany — 2:35.16

SUPER GIANT SLALOM
1. ...Kjetil André Aamodt, Norway — 1:30.65
2. ...Hermann Maier, Germany — 1:30.78
3. ...Ambrosi Hoffman, Switzerland — 1:30.98

COMBINED
1. ...Ted Ligety, United States — 3:09.35
2. ...Ivica Kostelic, Croatia — 3:09.88
3. ...Rainer Schoenfelder, Austria — 3:10.67

Women

DOWNHILL
1. ...Michaela Dorfmeister, Austria — 1:56.49
2. ...Martina Schild, Switzerland — 1:56.86
3. ...Anja Paerson, Sweden — 1:57.13

SLALOM
1. ...Anja Paerson, Sweden — 1:29.04
2. ...Nicole Hosp, Austria — 1:29.33
3. ...Marlies Schild, Austria — 1:29.79

GIANT SLALOM
1. ...Julia Mancuso, United States — 2:09.19
2. ...Tanja Poutiainen, Finland — 2:09.86
3. ...Anna Ottosson, Sweden — 2:10.33

SUPER GIANT SLALOM
1. ...Michaela Dorfmeister, Austria — 1:32.47
2. ...Janica Kostelic, Croatia — 1:32.74
3. ...Alexandra Meissnitzer, Austria — 1:33.06

COMBINED
1. ...Janica Kostelic, Croatia — 2:51.08
2. ...Marlies Schild, Austria — 2:51.58
3. ...Anja Paerson, Sweden — 2:51.63

NORDIC SKIING

Men

1.3 KILOMETERS SPRINT
1. ...Bjoern Lind, Sweden — 2:26.5
2. ...Roddy Darragon, France — 2:27.1
3. ...Thobias Fredriksson, Sweden — 2:27.8

1.3 KILOMETERS TEAM SPRINT
1. ...Sweden — 17:02.9
2. ...Norway — 17:03.5
2. ...Russia — 17:05.2

15 KILOMETERS CLASSICAL
1. ...Andrus Veerpalu, Estonia — 38:01.3
2. ...Lukas Bauer, Czech Republic — 38:15.8
3. ...Tobias Angerer, Germany — 38:20.5

30 KILOMETERS PURSUIT
1. ...Eugeni Dementiev, Russia — 1:17:00.8
2. ...Frode Estil, Norway — 1:17:01.4
3. ...Pietro Piller Cottrer, Italy — 1:17:01.7

50 KILOMETERS CLASSICAL
1. ...Giorgio di Centa, Italy — 2:06:11.8
2. ...Eugeni Dementiev, Russia — 2:06:12.6
3. ...Mikhail Botwinov Austria — 2:08:12.7

4 X 10-KILOMETER RELAY MIXED
1. ...Italy — 1:43:45.7
2. ...Germany — 1:44:01.4
3. ...Sweden — 1:44:01.7

90-METER HILL SKI JUMPING	Pts
1. ...Lars Bystoel, Norway	266.5
2. ...Matti Hautamaeki, Finland	265.5
3. ...Roar Ljoekelsoey, Norway	264.5

120-METER HILL SKI JUMPING	Pts
1. ...Thomas Morgenstern, Austria	276.9
2. ...Andreas Kofler, Austria	276.8
3. ...Lars Bystoel, Norway	250.7

120-METER HILL TEAM SKI JUMPING	Pts
1. ...Austria	984.0
2. ...Finland	976.6
3. ...Norway	950.1

INDIVIDUAL COMBINED
1. ...Georg Hettich, Germany — 39:44.6
2. ...Felix Gottwald, Austria — 39:54.4
3. ...Magnus Moan, Norway — 40:00.8

INDIVIDUAL SPRINT COMBINED
1. ...Felix Gottwald, Austria — 17:35.0
2. ...Magnus Moan, Norway — 17:38.4
3. ...Georg Hettich, Germany — 18:38.6

TEAM COMBINED
1. ...Austria — 49:52.6
2. ...Germany — 50:07.9
3. ...Finland — 50:19.4

NORDIC SKIING
Women

1.1 KILOMETERS SPRINT
1. ...Chandra Crawford, Canada ... 2:12.3
2. ...Claudia Kuenzel, Germany ... 2:13.0
3. ...Alena Sidko, Russia ... 2:13.2

1.1 KILOMETERS TEAM SPRINT
1. ...Sweden ... 16:36.9
2. ...Canada ... 16:37.5
3. ...Finland ... 16:39.2

10 KILOMETERS CLASSICAL
1. ...Kristina Smigun, Estonia ... 27:51.4
2. ...Marit Bjorgen, Norway ... 28:12.7
3. ...Hilde G. Pedersen, Norway ... 28:14.0

15 KILOMETERS PURSUIT
1. ...Kristina Smigun, Estonia ... 42:48.7
2. ...Katerina Neumannova, Czech Rep. 42:50.6
3. ...Evgenia Medvedeva-Abruzova, Russia 43:03.2

30 KILOMETERS FREESTYLE
1. ...Katerina Neumannova, Czech Rep. 1:22:25.4
2. ...Julija Tchepalova, Russia ... 1:22:26.8
3. ...Justyna Kowalczyk, Poland ... 1:22:27.5

4 X 5-KILOMETER RELAY MIXED
1. ...Russia ... 54:47.7
2. ...Germany ... 54:57.7
3. ...Italy ... 54:58.7

SNOWBOARDING

Men

PARALLEL GIANT SLALOM
1. ...Philipp Schoch, Switzerland
2. ...Simon Schoch, Switzerland
3. ...Siegfried Grabner, Austria

HALF-PIPE	Pts
1. ...Shaun White, United States	46.8
2. ...Danny Kass, United States	44.0
3. ...Markku Koski, Finland	41.5

SNOWBOARD CROSS
1. ...Seth Wescott, United States
2. ...Radoslav Zidek, Slovakia
3. ...Paul-Henri Delerue, France

Women

PARALLEL GIANT SLALOM
1. ...Daniela Meuli, Switzerland
2. ...Amelie Kober, Germany
3. ...Rosey Fletcher, United States

HALF-PIPE	Pts
1. ...Hannah Teter, United States	46.4
2. ...Gretchen Bleiler, United States	43.4
3. ...Kjersti Buass, Norway	42.0

SNOWBOARD CROSS
1. ...Tanja Frieden, Switzerland
2. ...Lindsey Jacobellis, United States
3. ...Dominique Maltais, Canada

2004 Summer Games

TRACK AND FIELD
Men

100 METERS
1. ...Justin Gatlin, United States ... 9.85
2. ...Francis Obikwelu, Portugal ... 9.86
3. ...Maurice Greene, United States ... 9.87

200 METERS
1. ...Shawn Crawford, United States ... 19.79
2. ...Bernard Williams, United States ... 20.01
3. ...Justin Gatlin, United States ... 20.03

400 METERS
1. ...Jeremy Wariner, United States ... 44.00
2. ...Otis Harris, United States ... 44.16
3. ...Derrick Brew, United States ... 44.42

800 METERS
1. ...Yuriy Borzakovskiy, Russia ... 1:44.45
2. ...Mbulaeni Mulaudzi, S Africa ... 1:44.61
3. ...Wilson Kipketer, Denmark ... 1:44.65

1,500 METERS
1. ...Hicham El Guerrouj, Morocco ... 3:34.18
2. ...Bernard Lagat, Kenya ... 3:34.30
3. ...Rui Silva, Portugal ... 3:34.68

5,000 METERS
1. ...Hicham El Guerrouj, Morocco ... 13:14.39
2. ...Kenenisa Bekele, Ethiopia ... 13:14.59
3. ...Eliud Kipchoge, Kenya ... 13:15.10

10,000 METERS
1. ...Kenenisa Bekele, Ethiopia ... 27:05.10 OR
2. ...Sileshi Sihine, Ethiopia ... 27:09.39
3. ...Zersenay Tadesse, Eritrea ... 27:22.57

MARATHON
1. ...Stefano Baldini, Italy ... 2:10:55
2. ...Mebrahtom Keflezighi, United States 2:11:29
3. ...Vanderlei de Lima, Brazil ... 2:12:11

110-METER HURDLES
1. ...Xiang Liu, China ... 12.91 EWR
2. ...Terrence Trammell, United States ... 13.18
3. ...Anier García, Cuba ... 13.20

400-METER HURDLES
1. ...Felix Sanchez, Dominican Republic 47.63
2. ...Danny McFarlane, Jamaica ... 48.11
3. ...Naman Keita, France ... 48.26

3,000-METER STEEPLECHASE
1. ...Ezekiel Kemboi, Kenya ... 8:05.81
2. ...Brimin Kipruto, Kenya ... 8:06.11
3. ...Paul Kipsiele Koech, Kenya ... 8:06.64

4 X 100-METER RELAY
1. ...Great Britian: (Jason Gardener ... 38.07
   Darren Campbell, Marlon Devonish,
   Mark Lewis Francis)
2. ...United States ... 38.08
3. ...Nigeria ... 38.23

Note: OR=Olympic Record. WR=World Record. EOR=Equals Olympic Record. EWR=Equals World Record.

TRACK AND FIELD *(Cont.)*
Men

4 X 400-METER RELAY

1. ...United States: (Otis Harris, Derrick Brew, Jeremy Wariner, Darold Williamson)	2:55.91
2. ...Australia	3:00.60
3. ...Nigeria	3:00.90

20-KILOMETER WALK

1. ...Ivano Brugnetti, Italy	1:19:40
2. ...Francisco Javier Fernandez, Spain	1:19:45
3. ...Nathan Deakes, Australian	1:20:02

50-KILOMETER WALK

1. ...Robert Korzeniowski, Poland	3:38:46
2. ...Denis Nizhegorodov, Russia	3:42:50
3. ...Aleksey Voyevodin, Russia	3:43:34

HIGH JUMP

1. ...Stefan Holm, Sweden	7 ft 8¾ in
2. ...Matthew Hemingway, United States	7 ft 8 in
3. ...Yaroslav Baba, Czech Republic	7 ft 8 in

POLE VAULT

1. ...Timothy Mack, United States	19 ft 6¼ in
2. ...Toby Stevenson, United States	19 ft 4¼ in
3. ...Giuseppe Gibilisco, Italy	19 ft 2¼ in

LONG JUMP

1. ...Dwight Phillips, United States	28 ft 2¼ in
2. ...John Moffitt, United States	27 ft 9½ in
3. ...Joan Lino Martinez, Spain	27 ft 3¾ in

TRIPLE JUMP

1. ...Christian Olsson, Sweden	58 ft 4½ in
2. ...Marian Oprea, Romania	57 ft 7 in
3. ...Danila Burkenya, Russia	57 ft 4¼ in

SHOT PUT

1. ...Yuriy Bilonog, Ukraine	69 ft 5¼ in
2. ...Adam Nelson, United States	69 ft 5¼ in
3. ...Joachim Olsen, Denmark	69 ft 1½ in

DISCUS THROW

1. ...Virgilijus Alekna, Lithuania	229 ft 3 in
2. ...Zoltan Kovago, Hungary	219 ft 11 in
3. ...Aleksander Tammert, Estonia	218 ft 8 in

HAMMER THROW

1. ...Adrian Zsolt, Hungary	272 ft 11 in
2. ...Koji Murofushi, Japan	272 ft
3. ...Ivan Tikhon, Belarus	261 ft 10 in

JAVELIN

1. ...Andreas Thorkildsen, Norway	283 ft 9 in
2. ...Vadims Vasilevskis, Latvia	278 ft 8 in
3. ...Sergey Makarov, Russia	278 ft 4 in

DECATHLON

	Pts
1. ...Roman Seberle, Czech Republic	8893 OR
2. ...Bryan Clay, United States	8820
3. ...Dmitriy Karpov, Kazakhstan	8725

TRACK AND FIELD
Women

100 METERS

1. ...Yuliya Nesterenko, Belarus	10.93
2. ...Lauryn Williams, United States	10.96
3. ...Veronica Campbell, Jamaica	10.97

200 METERS

1. ...Veronica Campbell, Jamaica	22.05
2. ...Allyson Felix, United States	22.18
3. ...Debbie Ferguson, Bahamas	22.30

400 METERS

1. ...Tonique Williams-Darling, Bahamas	49.41
2. ...Ana Guevara, Mexico	49.56
3. ...Natalya Antyukh, Russia	49.89

800 METERS

1. ...Kelly Holmes, Great Britain	1:56.38
2. ...Hasna Benhassi, Morocco	1:56.43
3. ...Jolanda Ceplak, Slovenia	1:56.43

1,500 METERS

1. ...Kelly Holmes, Great Britain	3:57.90
2. ...Tatyana Tomashova, Russia	3:58.12
3. ...Maria Cioncan, Romania	3:58.39

5,000 METERS

1. ...Meseret Defar, Ethiopia	14:45.65
2. ...Isabella Ochichi, Kenya	14:48.19
3. ...Tirunesh Dibaba, Ethiopia	14:51.83

10,000 METERS

1. ...Huina Xing, China	30:24.36
2. ...Ejegayehu Dibaba, Ethiopia	30:24.98
3. ...Derartu Tulu, Ethiopia	30:26.42

MARATHON

1. ...Noguchi Mizuki, Japan	2:26:20
2. ...Nyambura Wincatherine, Kenya	2:26:32
3. ...Deena Kastor, United States	2:27:20

100-METER HURDLES

1. ...Joanna Hayes, United States	12.37 OR
2. ...Olena Krasovska, Ukraine	12.45
3. ...Melissa Morrison, United States	12.56

400-METER HURDLES

1. ...Faní Halkiá, Greece	52.82
2. ...Ionela Tirlea-Manolache, Romania	53.38
3. ...Tetiana Tereschuk-Antipova, Ukraine	53.44

4 X 100-METER RELAY

1. ...Jamaica (T. Lawrence, S. Simpson, Aleen Bailey, Veronica Campbell)	41.73
2. ...Russia	42.27
3. ...France	42.54

4 X 400-METER RELAY

1. ...United States (DeeDee Trotter, Monique Henderson, Sanya Richards, Monique Hennagan)	3:19.01
2. ...Russia	3:20.16
3. ...Jamaica	3:22.00

20-KILOMETER WALK

1. ...Athanasía Tsoumeléka, Greece	1:29:12
2. ...Olimpiada Ivanova, Russia	1:29:16
3. ...Jane Saville, Australia	1:29:25

HIGH JUMP

1. ...Yelena Slesarenko, Russia	6 ft 9 in
2. ...Hestrie Cloete, S Africa	6 ft 7½ in
3. ...Vita Styopina, Ukraine	6 ft 7½ in

TRACK AND FIELD *(Cont.)*

Women

POLE VAULT

1. ...Yelena Isinbayeva, Russia	16 ft 1¼ in WR
2. ...Svetlana Feofanova, Russia	15 ft 7 in
3. ...Anna Rogowska, Poland	15 ft 5 in

DISCUS THROW

1. ...Natalya Sadova, Russia	219 ft 10 in
2. ...Anastasia Kelesidou, Greece	218 ft 9 in
3. ...Iryna Yatchenko, Belarus	217 ft 1 in

LONG JUMP

1. ...Tatyana Lebedeva, Russia	23 ft 2½ in
2. ...Irina Simajina, Russia	23 ft 1¾ in
3. ...Tatyana Kotova, Russia	23 ft 1¾ in

JAVELIN

1. ...Osleidys Menendez, Cuba	234 ft 8 in OR
2. ...Steffi Nerius, Germany	215 ft 11 in
3. ...Mirela Manjani, Greece	210 ft 11 in

TRIPLE JUMP

1. ...Frangoise Mbango Etone, Cameroon	50 ft 2½ in
2. ...Chrysopigi Devetzi, Greece	50 ft ½ in
3. ...Tatyana Lebedeva, Russia	49 ft 8¼ in

HEPTATHLON

	Pts
1. ...Carolina Kluft, Sweden	6952
2. ...Austra Skujyte, Lithuania	6435
3. ...Kelly Sotherton, Great Britain	6424

SHOT PUT

1. ...Yumileidi Cumba Jay, Cuba	64 ft 3¼ in
2. ...Nadine Kleinert, Germany	64 ft 1¾ in
3. ...Svetlana Krivelyova, Russia	63 ft 11½ in

HAMMER THROW

1. ...Olga Kuzenkova, Russia	246 ft 1½ in OR
2. ...Yipsi Moreno, Cuba	240 ft 8¼ in
3. ...Yunaika Crawford, Cuba	240 ft ½ in

INDIVIDUAL ARCHERY

Men

1. ...Marco Galiazzo, Italy
2. ...Hiroshi Yamamoto, Japan
3. ...Tim Cuddihy, Australia

Women

1. ...Sung Hyun Park, S Korea
2. ...Sung Jin Lee, S Korea
3. ...Alison Williamson, Great Britain

TEAM ARCHERY

Men

1. ...S Korea
2. ...Taiwan
3. ...Ukraine

Women

1. ...S Korea
2. ...China
3. ...Taiwan

BADMINTON

Men

SINGLES

1. ...Taufik Hidayat, Indonesia
2. ...Seung Mo Shon, S Korea
3. ...Soni Dwi Kuncoro, Indonesia

Women

SINGLES

1. ...Ning Zhang, China
2. ...Mia Audina, Netherlands
3. ...Mi Zhou, China

DOUBLES

1. ...Ha Tae Kwon/ Dong Moon Kim, S Korea
2. ...Dong Soo Lee/ Yoo Yong Sung, S Korea
3. ...Eng Hian/ Limpele Flandy, Indonesia

DOUBLES

1. ...Yang Wei/ Jiewen Zhang, China
2. ...Gao Ling/ Sui Huang, China
3. ...Kyung Min Ra/ Lee Kyung Won, S Korea

MIXED DOUBLES

1. ...Jun Zhang/ Gao Ling, China
2. ...Nathan Robertson/ Gail Emms, Great Britain
3. ...Jens Eriksen/ Schjoldager Mette, Denmark

BASEBALL

1. ...Cuba
2. ...Australia
3. ...Japan

BASKETBALL

Men

Final: Argentina 84, Italy 69
United States (3rd)
Argentina: Juan Sanchez, Emanuel Ginobili, Alejandro Montecchia, Fabricio Oberto, Walter Herrmann, Gabriel Fernandez, Hugo Sconochini, Luis Scola, Leonardo Gutierrez, Andres Nocioni, Carlos Delfino, Ruben Wolkowyski.

Women

Final: United States 74, Australia 63
Russia (3rd)
United States: Shannon Johnson, Dawn Staley, Suzanne Bird, Sheryl Swoopes, Ruth Riley, Lisa Leslie, Tamika Catchings, Tina Thompson, Diana Taurasi, Yolanda Griffith, Katie Smith, Swintayla Cash.

Note: OR=Olympic Record. WR=World Record. EOR=Equals Olympic Record. EWR=Equals World Record.

BOXING

LIGHT FLYWEIGHT (106 LB)
1. ....Yan Bhartelemy Varela, Cuba
2. ....Atagun Yal Cinkaya, Turkey
3. ....Shiming Zou, China
3. ....Sergey Kazakov, Russia

FLYWEIGHT (112 LB)
1. ....Yuriokis Gamboa Toledano, Cuba
2. ....Jerome Thomas, France
3. ....Fuad Aslanov, Azerbaijan
3. ....Rustamhodza Rahimov, Germany

BANTAMWEIGHT (119 LB)
1. ....Guillermo Rigondeaux Ortiz, Cuba
2. ....Worapoj Petchkoom, Thailand
3. ....Aghasi Mammadov, Azerbaijan
3. ....Bahodirion Sooltonov, Uzbekistan

FEATHERWEIGHT (125 LB)
1. ....Alexei Tichtchenko, Russia
2. ....Song Guk Kim, N Korea
3. ....Vitali Tajbert, Germany
3. ....Seok Hwan Jo, S Korea

LIGHTWEIGHT (132 LB)
1. ....Mario Kindelan Mesa, Cuba
2. ....Amir Khan, Great Britain
3. ....Serik Yeleuov, Kazakhstan
3. ....Murat Khrachev, Russia

LIGHT WELTERWEIGHT (139 LB)
1. ....Manus Boonjumnong, Thailand
2. ....Yudel Johnson Cedeno, Cuba
3. ....Boris Georgive, Bulgaria
3. ....Ionut Gheorghe, Romania

WELTERWEIGHT (147 LB)
1. ....Bakhtiyar Artayev, Kazakhstan
2. ....Lorenzo Aragon Armenteros, Cuba
3. ....Oleg Saitov, Russia
3. ....Jung Joo Kim, S Korea

MIDDLEWEIGHT (165 LB)
1. ....Gaydarbek Gaydarbekov, Russia
2. ....Gennadiy Golovkin, Kazakhstan
3. ....Suriya Prasathinphimai, Thailand
3. ....Andre Dirrell, United States

LIGHT HEAVYWEIGHT (178 LB)
1. ....Andre Ward, United States
2. ....Magomed Aripgadjiev, Belarus
3. ....Utkirbek Haydarov, Uzbekistan
3. ....Ahmed Ismail, Egypt

HEAVYWEIGHT (201 LB)
1. ....Odlanier Solis Fonte, Cuba
2. ....Viktar Zuyev, Belarus
3. ....Mohamed Elsayed, Egypt
3. ....Naser Al Shami, Syria

SUPERHEAVYWEIGHT (201+ LB)
1. ....Alexander Povetkin, Russia
2. ....Mohamed Aly, Egypt
3. ....Roberto Cammarelle, Italy
3. ....Michel Lopez Nunez, Cuba

CANOE/KAYAK

Men

C-1 FLATWATER 500 METERS
1.	Andreas Dittmer, Germany	1:46.383
2.	David Cal, Spain	1:46.723
3.	Maxim Opalev, Russia	1:47.767

C-1 FLATWATER 1,000 METERS
1.	David Cal, Spain	3:46.201
2.	Andreas Dittmer, Germany	3:46.721
3.	Attila Vajda, Hungary	3:49.025

C-2 FLATWATER 500 METERS
1.	G. Meng/W. Yang, China	1:40.278
2.	I. Blanco/L. Pajon, Cuba	1:40.350
3.	A. Kostoglod/A. Kovalev, Russia	1:40.442

C-2 FLATWATER 1,000 METERS
1.	C. Gille/T. Wylenzek, Germany	3:41.802
2.	A. Kostoglod/A. Kovalev, Russia	3:42.990
3.	G. Kolonics/G. Kozmann, Hungary	3:43.106

C-1 WHITEWATER SLALOM
		Pts
1.	Tony Estanguet, France	189.16
2.	Michal Martikan, Slovakia	189.28
3.	Stefan Pfannmoeller, Germany	191.56

C-2 WHITEWATER SLALOM
		Pts
1.	Pavel/Peter Hochschorner, Slovakia	207.16
2.	M. Becker/S. Henze, Germany	210.98
3.	J. Volf/O. Stepanek, Czech Republic	212.86

Men *(Cont.)*

K-1 FLATWATER 500 METERS
1.	Adam Van Koeverden, Canada	1:37.919
2.	Nathan Baggaley, Australia	1:38.467
3.	Ian Wynne, Great Britain	1:38.547

K-1 FLATWATER 1,000 METERS
1.	Eirik Veraas Larsen, Norway	3:25.897
2.	Ben Fouhy, New Zealand	3:27.413
3.	Adam Van Koeverden, Canada	3:28.218

Women

K-1 FLATWATER 500 METERS
1.	Natasa Janics, Hungary	1:47.741
2.	Josefa Idem Guerrini, Italy	1:49.729
3.	Caroline Brunet, Canada	1:50.601

K-2 FLATWATER 500 METERS
1.	K. Kovacs/N. Janics, Hungary	1:38.101
2.	B. Fischer/C. Leonhardt, Germany	1:39.533
3.	A. Pastuszka/B. Sokoloska, Poland	1:40.077

K-4 FLATWATER 500 METERS
1.	Germany	1:34.340
2.	Hungary	1:34.536
3.	Ukraine	1:36.192

K-1 WHITEWATER SLALOM
		Pts
1.	Elena Kaliska, Slovakia	210.03
2.	Rebecca Giddens, United States	214.62
3.	Helen Reeves, Great Britain	218.77

CYCLING

Men

ROAD RACE

1. ...Paolo Bettini, Italy — 5:41:44
2. ...Sergio Paulinho, Portugal — 5:41:45
3. ...Axel Merckx, Belgium — 5:41:52

INDIVIDUAL TIME TRIAL

1. ...Tyler Hamilton, United States — 57:31.74
2. ...Vyatcheslav Ekimov, Russia — 57:50.58
3. ...Robert Julich, United States — 57:58.19

IKM TIME TRIAL

1. ...Chris Hoy, Great Britain — 1:00.711
2. ...Arnaud Tournant, France — 1:00.896
3. ...Stefan Nimke, Germany — 1:01.186

4,000-METER INDIVIDUAL PURSUIT

1. ...Bradley Wiggins, Great Britain — 4:16.304
2. ...Brad McGee, Australia — 4:20.436
3. ...Sergi Escobar, Spain — 4:17.947

4,000-METER TEAM PURSUIT

1. ...Australia (Graeme Brown, Brett Lancaster, Brad McGee, Luke Roberts) — 3:58.233
2. ...Great Britain — 4:01.760
3. ...Spain — 4:05.523

POINTS RACE

1. ...Olga Slyusareva, Russia — 20
2. ...Belem Guerrero Mendez, Mexico — 14
3. ...Erin Mirabella, United States — 9

INDIVIDUAL TIME TRIAL

1. ...L. Zijlaard-van Moorsel, Netherlands — 31:11.53
2. ...Deirdre Demet-Barry, United States — 31:35.62
3. ...Karin Thuerig, Switzerland — 31:54.89

3,000-METER INDIVIDUAL PURSUIT

1. ...Sarah Ulmer, New Zealand — 3:24.537 WR
2. ...Katie Mactier, Australia — 3:27.650
3. ...L. Zijlaard-van Moorsel, Netherlands — 3:27.037

SPRINT

1. ...Ryan Bayley, Australia — 10.743
2. ...Theo Bos, Netherlands — 10.710
3. ...Rene Wolff, German — 10.612

POINTS RACE

1. ...Mikhail Ignatyev, Russia — 93
2. ...Joan Llaneras, Spain — 82
3. ...Guido Fulst, Germany — 79

KIERIN

1. ...Ryan Bayley, Australia — 10.601
2. ...Jose Escuredo, Spain
3. ...Shane Kelly, Australia

MADISON

1. ...G. Brown/S. O'Grady, Australia — 22
2. ...F. Marvulli/B. Risi, Switzerland — 15
3. ...R. Hayles/B. Wiggins, Great Britain — 12

OLYMPIC SPRINT

1. ...Germany — 43.980
2. ...Japan — 44.246
3. ...France — 44.359

Women

SPRINT

1. ...Lori-Ann Muenzer, Canada — 12.140
2. ...Tamilla Abassova, Russia — —
3. ...Anna Meares, Australia — 11.822

ROAD RACE

1. ...Sara Carrigan, Australia — 3:24:24
2. ...Judith Arndt, Germany — 3:24:31
3. ...Olga Slyusareva, Russia — 3:25:03

500-M TIME TRIAL

1. ...Anna Meares, Australia — 33.952
2. ...Jiang Yonghua, China — 34.112
3. ...Natallia Tsylinskaya, Belarus — 34.167

DIVING

Men

SPRINGBOARD

	Pts
1.....Bo Peng, China	787.38
2.....Alexandre Despatie, Canada	755.97
3.....Dmitry Sautin, Russia	753.27

PLATFORM

	Pts
1.....Jia Hu, China	748.08
2.....Matthew Helm, Australia	730.56
3.....Liang Tian, China	729.66

Women

SPRINGBOARD

	Pts
1.....Jingjing Guo, China	633.15
2.....Minxia Wu, China	612.00
3.....Yulia Pakhalina, Russia	610.62

PLATFORM

	Pts
1.....Chantelle Newbery, Australia	590.31
2.....Lishi Lao, China	576.30
3....Loudy Tourky, Australia	561.66

EQUESTRIAN

TEAM EVENTING
1. France
2. Great Britain
3. United States

INDIVIDUAL EVENTING
		Pts
1.	Leslie Law, Great Britain	44.40
2.	Kim Severson, United States	45.20
3.	Philippa Funnell, Great Britain	46.60

TEAM DRESSAGE
1. Germany
2. Spain
3. United States

INDIVIDUAL DRESSAGE
		Pts
1.	Anky van Grunsven, Netherlands	85.825
2.	Ulla Salzgeber, Germany	83.450
3.	Beatriz Ferrer-Salat, Spain	79.575

TEAM JUMPING
1. Germany
2. United States
3. Sweden

INDIVIDUAL JUMPING
		Pts
1.	Cian O'Connor, Ireland	4.00
2.	Rodrigo Pessoa, Brazil	8.00
3.	Chris Kappler, United States	8.00

FENCING
Men

FOIL
1. Brice Guyart, France
2. Salvatore Sanzo, Italy
3. Andrea Cassara, Italy

SABRE
1. Aldo Montano, Italy
2. Zsolt Nemcsik, Hungary
3. Vladislav Tretiak, Ukraine

ÉPÉE
1. Marcel Fischer, Switzerland
2. Lei Wang, China
3. Pavel Kolobkov, Russia

TEAM FOIL
1. Italy
2. China
3. Russia

TEAM SABRE
1. France
2. Italy
3. Russia

TEAM ÉPÉE
1. France
2. Hungary
3. Germany

Women

FOIL
1. Valentina Vezzali, Italy
2. Giovanna Trillini, Italy
3. Sylwia Gruchala, Poland

ÉPÉE
1. Timea Nagy, Hungary
2. Laura Flessel-Colovic, France
3. Maureen Nisima, France

SABRE
1. Mariel Zagunis, United States
2. Xue Tan, China
3. Sada Jacobson, United States

TEAM ÉPÉE
1. Russia
2. Germany
3. France

FIELD HOCKEY

Men
1. Australia
2. Netherlands
3. Germany

Women
1. Germany
2. Netherlands
3. Argentina

GYMNASTICS
Men

ALL-AROUND
		Pts
1.	Paul Hamm, United States	57.823
2.	Dae Eun Kim, S Korea	57.811
3.	Tae Young Yang, S Korea	57.774

HORIZONTAL BAR
		Pts
1.	Igor Cassina, Italy	9.812
2.	Paul Hamm, United States	9.812
3.	Isao Yoneda, Japan	9.787

PARALLEL BARS
		Pts
1.	Valeri Goncharov, Ukraine	9.787
2.	Hiroyuki Tomita, Japan	9.775
3.	Xiaopeng Li, China	9.762

VAULT
		Pts
1.	Gervasio Deferr, Spain	9.737
2.	Evgeni Sapronenko, Latvia	9.706
3.	Marian Dragulescu, Romania	9.612

POMMEL HORSE
		Pts
1.	Haibin Teng, China	9.837
2.	Marius Urzica, Romania	9.825
3.	Takehiro Kashima, Japan	9.787

RINGS
		Pts
1.	Dimosthenis Tampakos, Greece	9.862
2.	Jordan Jovtchev, Bulgaria	9.850
3.	Yuri Chechi, Italy	9.812

GYMNASTICS *(Cont.)*

Men *(Cont.)*

FLOOR EXERCISE

	Pts
1. ....Kyle Shewfelt, Canada	9.787
2. ....Marian Dragulescu, Romania	9.787
3. ....Jordan Jovtchev, Bulgaria	9.775

TEAM COMBINED EXERCISES

1. ....Japan
2. ....United States
3. ....Romania

Women

ALL-AROUND

	Pts
1. ....Carly Patterson, United States	38.387
2. ....Svetlana Khorkina, Russia	38.211
3. ....Nan Zhang, China	38.049

VAULT

	Pts
1. ....Monica Rosu, Romania	9.656
2. ....Annia Hatch, United States	9.481
3. ....Anna Pavlova, Russia	9.475

UNEVEN BARS

	Pts
1. ....Emilie Lepennec, France	9.687
2. ....Terin Humphrey, United States	9.662
2. ....Courtney Kupets, United States	9.637

BALANCE BEAM

	Pts
1. ....Catalina Ponor, Romania	9.787
2. ....Carly Patterson, United States	9.775
3. ....Alexandra Eremia, Romania	9.700

FLOOR EXERCISE

	Pts
1. ....Catalina Ponor, Romania	9.750
2. ....Nicoleta Sofronie, Romania	9.562
3. ....Patricia Moreno, Spain	9.487

TEAM COMBINED EXERCISES

1. ....Romania
2. ....United States
3. ....Russia

JUDO

Men

EXTRA-LIGHTWEIGHT

1. ....Tadahiro Nomura, Japan
2. ....Nestor Khergiani, Georgia
3. ....Khashbaatar Tsagaanbaatar, Mongolia
3. ....Choi Min-ho, S Korea

HALF-LIGHTWEIGHT

1. ....Masato Uchishiba, Japan
2. ....Jozef Krnac, Slovakia
3. ....Georgi Georgiev, Bulgaria
3. ....Yordanis Arencibia, Cuba

LIGHTWEIGHT

1. ....Won Hee Lee, S Korea
2. ....Vitaliy Makarov, Russia
3. ....Leandro Guilheiro, Brazil
3. ....James Pedro, United States

HALF-MIDDLEWEIGHT

1. ....Ilias Iliadas, Greece
2. ....Roman Gontyuk, Ukraine
3. ....Flavio Canto, Brazil
3. ....Dmitri Nossov, Russia

MIDDLEWEIGHT

1. ....Zurab Zviadauri, Georgia
2. ....Hiroshi Izumi, Japan
3. ....Mark Huizinga, Netherlands
3. ....Khasanbi Taov, Russia

HALF-HEAVYWEIGHT

1. ....Ihar Makarau, Belarus
2. ....Sung Ho Jang, S Korea
3. ....Michael Jurack, Germany
3. ....Ariel Zeevi, Israel

HEAVYWEIGHT

1. ....Keiji Suzuki, Japan
2. ....Tamerlan Tmenov, Russia
3. ....Indrek Pertelson, Estonia
3. ....Dennis Van Der Geest, Netherlands

Women

EXTRA-LIGHTWEIGHT

1. ....Ryoko Tani, Japan
2. ....Frederique Jossinet, France
3. ....Feng Gao, China
3. ....Julia Matijass, Germany

HALF-LIGHTWEIGHT

1. ....Dongmei Xian, China
2. ....Yuki Yokosawa, Japan
3. ....Ilse Heylen, Belgium
3. ....Amarilis Savon, Cuba

LIGHTWEIGHT

1. ....Yvonne Boenisch, Germany
2. ....Sun-Hi Kye, N Korea
3. ....Deborah Gravenstijn, Netherlands
3. ....Yurisleidy Lupetey, Cuba

HALF-MIDDLEWEIGHT

1. ....Ayumi Tanimoto, Japan
2. ....Claudia Heill, Austria
3. ....Urska Zolnir, Slovenia
3. ....Driulys Gonzalez, Cuba

MIDDLEWEIGHT

1. ....Masae Ueno, Japan
2. ....Edith Bosch, Netherlands
3. ....Dongya Qin, China
3. ....Annett Boehm, Germany

HALF-HEAVYWEIGHT

1. ....Noriko Anno, Japan
2. ....Xia Liu, China
3. ....Lucia Morico, Italy
3. ....Yurisel Laborde, Cuba

HEAVYWEIGHT

1. ....Maki Tsukada, Japan
2. ....Daima Mayelis Beltran, Cuba
3. ....Fuming Sun, China
3. ....Tea Donguzashvili, Russia

MODERN PENTATHLON

Men	Women
1. ......Andrey Moiseev, Russia	1. ......Zsuzsanna Voros, Hungary
2. ......Andrejus Zadneprovskis, Lithuania	2. ......Jelena Rublevska, Latvia
3. ......Libor Capalini, Czech Republic	3. ......Georgina Harland, Great Britain

MOUNTAIN BIKING

Men		Women	
1. ......Julien Absalon, France	2:15.02	1. ......Gunn-Rita Dahle, Norway	1:56.51
2. ......Jose Antonio Hermida, Spain	2:16.02	2. ......Marie-Helene Premont, Canada	1:57.50
3. ......Bart Brentjens, Netherlands	2:17.05	3. ......Sabine Spitz, Germany	1:59.21

ROWING

Men

SINGLE SCULLS

1. ...Olaf Tufte, Norway	6:49.30
2. ...Jueri Jaanson, Estonia	6:51.42
3. ...Ivo Yanakiev, Bulgaria	6:52.80

COXLESS PAIR

1. ...D. Jinn/J. Tomkins, Australia	6:30.76
2. ...S. Skelin/N. Skelin, Croatia	6:32.64
3. ...D. Cech/R. di Clemente, S Africa	6:33.40

DOUBLE SCULLS

1. ...S. Vieilledent/A. Hardy, France	6:29.00
2. ...L. Spik/I. Cop, Slovenia	6:31.72
3. ...R. Galtarossa/A. Sartori, Italy	6:32.93

COXLESS FOUR

1. ...Great Britain	6:06.98
2. ...Canada	6:07.06
3. ...Italy	6:10.41

LIGHTWEIGHT DOUBLE SCULLS

1. ...T. Kucharski/R. Sycz, Poland	6:20.93
2. ...F. Dufour/P. Touron, France	6:21.46
3. ...V. Polymeros/N. Skiathitis, Greece	6:23.23

LIGHTWEIGHT COXLESS FOUR

1. ...Denmark	6:01.39
2. ...Australia	6:02.79
3. ...Italy	6:03.74

QUADRUPLE SCULLS

1. ...Russia	5:56.85
2. ...Czech Republic	5:57.43
3. ...Ukraine	5:58.87

EIGHT-OARS

1. ...United States	5:42.48
2. ...Netherlands	5:43.75
3. ...Australia	5:45.38

Women

SINGLE SCULLS

1. ...Katrin Rutschow-Stomporowski, Germany	7:18.12
2. ...Yekaterina Karsten, Belarus	7:22.04
3. ...Rumyana Neykova, Bulgaria	7:23.10

QUADRUPLE SCULLS

1. ...Germany	6:29.29
2. ...Great Britain	6:31.26
3. ...Australia	6:34.73

DOUBLE SCULLS

1. ...C. Evers-Swindell/G. Evers-Swindell, NZ	7:01.79
2. ...B. Oppelt/P. Waleska, Germany	7:02.78
3. ...E. Laverick/S. Winckless, Great Britain	7:07.58

COXLESS PAIR

1. ...G. Damian/V. Susanu, Romania	7:06.55
2. ...K. Grainger/C. Bishop, Great Britain	7:08.66
3. ...Y. Bichyk/N. Helakh, Bulgaria	7:09.86

LIGHTWEIGHT DOUBLE SCULLS

1. ...C. Burcica/A. Alupei, Romania	6:56.05
2. ...D. Reimer/C. Blasberg, Germany	6:57.33
3. ...K. van Der Kolk/M. van Eupen, Neth	6:58.54

EIGHT-OARS

1. ...Romania	6:17.70
2. ...United States	6:19.56
3. ...Netherlands	6:19.85

SHOOTING

Men

RAPID-FIRE PISTOL	Pts
1. ....Ralf Schumann, Germany	694.9
2. ....Sergei Poliakov, Russia	692.7
3. ....Serguie Alifirenko, Russia	692.3

RUNNING TARGET	Pts
1. ....Manfred Kurzer, Germany	682.4
2. ....Alexander Blinov, Russia	678.0
3. ....Dimitri Lykin, Russia	677.1

FREE PISTOL	Pts
1. ....Mikhail Nestruev, Russia	663.3
2. ....Jong Oh Jin, S Korea	661.5
3. ....Jong Su Kim, N Korea	657.7

SMALL-BORE RIFLE, THREE-POSITION	Pts
1. ....Zhanbo Gia, China	1264.5
2. ....Michael Anti, United States	1263.1
3. ....Christian Planer, Austria	1262.8

AIR PISTOL	Pts
1. ....Yifu Wang, China	690.0
2. ....Mikhail Nestruev, Russia	689.8
3. ....Vladimir Isakov, Russia	684.3

SMALL-BORE RIFLE, PRONE	Pts
1. ....Matt Emmons, United States	703.3
2. ....Christian Lusch, Germany	702.2
3. ....Serguei Martynov, Belarus	701.6

SHOOTING *(Cont.)*

Men *(Cont.)*

AIR RIFLE	Pts	DOUBLE TRAP	Pts
1. Qinan Zhu, China	702.7	1. Ahmed Al Maktoum, UAE	189.0
2. Jie Ling, China	701.3	2. Rajyavardhan Rathore, India	179.0
3. Jozef Gonci, Slovakia	697.4	3. Zheng Wang, China	178.0

TRAP	Pts	SKEET	Pts
1. Alexei Alipov, Russia	149.0	1. Andrea Benelli, Italy	149.0
2. Giovanni Pellielo, Italy	146.0	2. Marko Kemppainen, Finland	149.0
3. Adam Vella, Australia	145.0	3. Juan Miguel Rodriguez, Cuba	147.0

Women

SPORT PISTOL	Pts	DOUBLE TRAP	Pts
1. Mariya Grozdeva, Bulgaria	688.2	1. Kimberly Rhode, United States	146.0
2. Lenka Hykova, Czech Republic	687.8	2. Bo Na Lee, S Korea	145.0
3. Irada Ashumova, Azerbaijan	687.3	3. E Gao, China	142.0

AIR PISTOL	Pts	TRAP	Pts
1. Olena Kostevych, Ukraine	483.3	1. Suzanne Balogh, Australia	88.0
2. Jasna Sekaric, Serbia & Montenegro	483.3	2. Maria Quintanal, Spain	84.0
3. Mariya Grozdeva, Bulgaria	482.3	3. Bo Na Lee, S Korea	83.0

SMALL-BORE RIFLE, THREE-POSITION	Pts	SKEET	Pts
1. Lioubov Galkina, Russia	688.4	1. Diana Igaly, Hungary	97.0
2. Valentina Turisini, Italy	685.9	2. Ning Wei, China	93.0
3. Chengyi Wang, China	685.4	3. Zemfina Meftakhetdinova, Azerbaijan	93.0

AIR RIFLE	Pts
1. Li Du, China	502.0
2. Lioubov Galkina, Russia	501.5
3. Katerina Kurkova, Czech Republic	501.1

SOCCER

Men	Women
1. Argentina	1. United States
2. Paraguay	2. Brazil
3. Italy	3. Germany

SOFTBALL

1. United States
2. Australia
3. Japan

SWIMMING

Men

50-METER FREESTYLE		400-METER FREESTYLE	
1. Gary Hall Jr., United States	21.93	1. Ian Thorpe, Australia	3:43.10
2. Duje Draganja, Croatia	21.94	2. Grant Hackett, Australia	3:43.36
3. Roland Schoeman, S Africa	22.02	3. Klete Keller, United States	3:44.11

100-METER FREESTYLE		1,500-METER FREESTYLE	
1. Pieter van den Hoogenband, Netherlands	48.17	1. Grant Hackett, Australia	14:43.40 OR
2. Roland Schoeman, S Africa	48.23	2. Larsen Jensen, United States	14:45.29
3. Ian Thorpe, Australia	48.56	3. David Davies, Great Britain	14:45.95

200-METER FREESTYLE		100-METER BACKSTROKE	
1. Ian Thorpe, Australia	1:44.71 OR	1. Aaron Peirsol, United States	54.06
2. Pieter van den Hoogenband, Netherlands	1:45.23	2. Markus Rogan, Austria	54.35
3. Michael Phelps, United States	1:45.32	3. Tomomi Morita, Japan	54.36

		200-METER BACKSTROKE	
		1. Aaron Peirsol, United States	1:54.95 OR
		2. Markus Rogan, Austria	1:57.35
		3. Razvan Florea, Romania	1:57.56

Note: OR=Olympic record. WR=world record. EOR=equals Olympic record. EWR=equals world record.

SWIMMING *(Cont.)*

Men *(Cont.)*

100-METER BREASTSTROKE

1. ...Kosuke Kitajima, Japan — 1:00.08
2. ...Brendan Hansen, United States — 1:00.25
3. ...Hugues Duboscq, France — 1:00.88

200-METER BREASTSTROKE

1. ...Kosuke Kitajima, Japan — 2:09.44 OR
2. ...Daniel Gyurta, Hungary — 2:10.80
3. ...Brendan Hansen, United States — 2:10.87

100-METER BUTTERFLY

1. ...Michael Phelps, United States — 51.25 OR
2. ...Ian Crocker, United States — 51.29
3. ...Andriy Serdinov, Ukraine — 51.36

200-METER BUTTERFLY

1. ...Michael Phelps, United States — 1:54.04 OR
2. ...Takashi Yamamoto, Japan — 1:54.56
3. ...Stephen Parry, Great Britain — 1:55.52

200-METER INDIVIDUAL MEDLEY

1. ...Michael Phelps, United States — 1:57.14 OR
2. ...Ryan Lochte, United States — 1:58.78
3. ...George Bovell, Trinidad & Tobago — 1:58.80

400-METER INDIVIDUAL MEDLEY

1. ...Michael Phelps, United States — 4:08.26 WR
2. ...Eric Vendt, United States — 4:11.81
3. ...Laszlo Cseh, Hungary — 4:12.15

4 X 100-METER MEDLEY RELAY

1. ...United States (Aaron Peirsol, — 3:30.68 WR
   Brendan Hanson, Ian Crocker, Jason Lezak)
2. ...Germany — 3:33.62
3. ...Japan — 3:35.22

4 X 100-METER FREESTYLE RELAY

1. ...S Africa (Schoeman, Ferns, — 3:13.17 WR
   Townsend, Neethling)
2. ...Netherlands — 3:14.36
3. ...United States — 3:14.62

4 X 200-METER FREESTYLE RELAY

1. ...United States (Phelps, — 7:07.33
   Lochte, Vanderkaay, Keller)
2. ...Australia — 7:07.46
3. ...Italy — 7:11.83

Women

50-METER FREESTYLE

1. ...Inge de Bruijn, Netherlands — 24.58
2. ...Malia Metella, France — 24.89
3. ...Lisbeth Lenton, Australia — 24.91

100-METER FREESTYLE

1. ...Jodie Henry, Australia — 53.84
2. ...Inge de Bruijn, Netherlands — 54.16
3. ...Natalie Coughlin, United States — 54.40

200-METER FREESTYLE

1. ...Camelia Potec, Romania — 1:58.03
2. ...Federica Pellegrini, Italy — 1:58.22
3. ...Solenne Figues, France — 1:58.45

400-METER FREESTYLE

1. ...Laure Manaudou, France — 4:05.34
2. ...Otylia Jedrzejczak, Poland — 4:05.84
3. ...Kaitlin Sandeno, United States — 4:06.19

800-METER FREESTYLE

1. ...Ai Shibata, Japan — 8:24.54
2. ...Laure Manaudou, France — 8:24.96
3. ...Diana Munz, United States — 8:26.61

100-METER BACKSTROKE

1. ...Natalie Coughlin, United States — 1:00.37
2. ...Kirsty Coventry, Zimbabwe — 1:00.50
3. ...Laure Manaudou, France — 1:00.88

200-METER BACKSTROKE

1. ...Kirsty Coventry, Zimbabwe — 2:09.19
2. ...Stanislava Komarova, Russia — 2:09.72
3. ...Antie Buschschulte, Germany — 2:09.88

100-METER BREASTSTROKE

1. ...Xuejuan Luo, China — 1:06.64
2. ...Brooke Hanson, Australia — 1:07.15
3. ...Leisel Jones, Australia — 1:07.16

200-METER BREASTSTROKE

1. ...Amanda Beard, United States — 2:23.37 OR
2. ...Leisel Jones, Australia — 2:23.60
3. ...Anne Poleska, Germany — 2:25.82

100-METER BUTTERFLY

1. ...Petria Thomas, Australia — 57.72
2. ...Otylia Jedrzejczak, Poland — 57.84
3. ...Inge de Bruijn, Netherlands — 57.99

200-METER BUTTERFLY

1. ...Otylia Jedrzejczak, Poland — 2:06.05
2. ...Petria Thomas, Australia — 2:06.36
3. ...Yuko Nakanishi, Japan — 2:08.04

200-METER INDIVIDUAL MEDLEY

1. ...Yana Klochkova, Ukraine — 2:11.14
2. ...Amanda Beard, United States — 2:11.70
3. ...Kirsty Coventry, Zimbabwe — 2:12.72

400-METER INDIVIDUAL MEDLEY

1. ...Yana Klochkova, Ukraine — 4:34.83
2. ...Kaitlin Sandeno, United States — 4:34.95
3. ...Georgina Bardach, Argentina — 4:37.51

4 X 100-METER MEDLEY RELAY

1. ...Australia (Giaan Rooney, — 3:57.32 WR
   Leisel Jones, Petria Thomas,
   Jodie Henry)
2. ...United States — 3:59.12
3. ...Germany — 4:00.72

4 X 100-METER FREESTYLE RELAY

1. ...Australia (Alice Mills, — 3:35.94 WR
   Lisbeth Lenton, Petria Thomas,
   Jodie Henry)
2. ...United States — 3:36.39
3. ...Netherlands — 3:37.59

4 X 200-METER FREESTYLE RELAY

1. ...United States (Natalie Coughlin, — 7:53.42 WR
   Carly Piper, Dana Vollmer,
   Kaitlin Sandeno)
2. ...China — 7:55.97
3. ...Germany — 7:57.35

SYNCHRONIZED SWIMMING

DUET
1. ....Russia
2. ....Japan
3. ....United States

TEAM
1. ....Russia
2. ....Japan
3. ....United States

SYNCHRONIZED DIVING

Men

3M SPRINGBOARD
	Pts
1. ....N. Siranidis/T. Bimis, Greece	353.34
2. ....A. Wels/T. Schellenberg, Germany	350.01
3. ....R. Newbery/S. Barnett, Australia	349.59

10M PLATFORM
	Pts
1. ....L. Tian/J. Yang, China	383.88
2. ....P. Waterfield/L. Taylor, Great Britain	371.52
3. ....M. Helm/R. Newbery, Australia	366.84

Women

3M SPRINGBOARD
	Pts
1. ....J. Guo/M. Wu, China	336.90
2. ....V. Ilyina/Y. Pakhalina, Russia	330.84
3. ....I. Lashko/C. Newbery, Australia	309.30

10M PLATFORM
	Pts
1. ....L. Lao/T. Li, China	352.54
2. ....N. Goncharova/Y. Koltunova, Russia	340.92
3. ....B. Hartley/E. Heymans, Canada	327.78

TABLE TENNIS

Men

SINGLES
1. ....Seung Min Ryu, S Korea
2. ....Hao Wang, China
3. ....Ligin Wang, China

DOUBLES
1. ....M. Lin/Q. Chen, China
2. ....L. Chak Ko/L. Ching, Hong Kong
3. ....M. Maze/F. Tugwell, Denmark

Women

SINGLES
1. ....Zhang Yining, China
2. ....Hyang Mi Kim, N Korea
3. ....Kim Kyung Ah, S Korea

DOUBLES
1. ....N. Wang/Z. Yining, China
2. ....................E.-C. Lee/E. M. Seok, S Korea
3. ....N. Jianfeng/Y. Guo, China

TAEKWONDO

Men

FLYWEIGHT
1. ....Mu Yen Chu, Taiwan
2. ....Oscar Blanco, Mexico
3. ....Tamer Bayoumi, Egypt

FEATHERWEIGHT
1. ....Hadi Saeibonehkohal, Iran
2. ....Chih-Hsiung Huang, Taiwan
3. ....Myeong Seob Song, S Korea

WELTERWEIGHT
1. ....Steven Lopez, United States
2. ....Bahri Tanrikulu, Turkey
3. ....Yossef Karami, Iran

HEAVYWEIGHT
1. ....Dae Sung Moon, S Korea
2. ....Alexandros Nikolaidis, Greece
3. ....Pascal Gentil, France

Women

FLYWEIGHT
1. ....Shih Hsin Chen, Taiwan
2. ....Yanelis Diaz, Cuba
3. ....Yaowapa Boorapolchai, Thailand

FEATHERWEIGHT
1. ....Ji Won Jang, S Korea
2. ....Nia Abdallah, United States
3. ....Iridia Blanco, Mexico

WELTERWEIGHT
1. ....Wei Luo, China
2. ....Elisavet Mystakidou, Greece
3. ....Kyung Sun Hwang

HEAVYWEIGHT
1. ....Zhong Chen, China
2. ....Myriam Baverel, France
3. ....Adriana Carmona, Brazil

TEAM HANDBALL

Men
1. ....Croatia
2. ....Germany
3. ....Russia

Women
1. ....Denmark
2. ....S. Korea
3. ....Ukraine

TENNIS

Men

SINGLES
1..........Nicolas Massu, Chile
2..........Mardy Fish, United States
3..........Fernando Gonzalez, Chile

DOUBLES
1..........Fernando Gonzalez/Nicolas Massu, Chile
2..........Rainer Schuettler/Nicolas Kiefer, Germany
3..........Mario Ancic/Ljubicic Ivan, Croatia

Women

SINGLES
1..........Justine Henin-Hardenne, Belgium
2..........Amelie Mauresmo, France
3..........Alicia Molik, Australia

DOUBLES
1..........Ting Li/Tian Tian Sun, China
2..........Conchita Martinez/Virginia Ruano, Spain
3..........Paola Suares/Patricia Tarbabini, Argentina

TRAMPOLINE

Men
1..........Yuri Nikitin, Ukraine — 41.50
2..........Alexandre Moskalenko, Russia — 41.20
3..........Henrik Stehlik, Germany — 40.80

Women
1..........Anna Dogonadze, Germany — 39.60
2..........Karen Cockburn, Canada — 39.20
3..........Shaohua Huang, China — 39.00

TRIATHLON

Men
1..........Hamish Carter, New Zealand — 1:51:07
2..........Bevan Docherty, New Zealand — 1:51:15
3..........Sven Riederer, Switzerland — 1:51:33

Women
1..........Kate Allen, Austria — 2:04:43
2..........Loretta Harrop, Australia — 2:04:50
3..........Susan Williams, United States — 2:05:08

VOLLEYBALL

Men
1..........Brazil
2..........Italy
3..........Russia

Women
1..........China
2..........Russia
3..........Cuba

BEACH VOLLEYBALL

Men
1..........Emanuel Rigo/Ricardo Santos, Brazil
2..........Pablo Herrera/Javier Bosma, Spain
3..........Patrick Heuscher/Stefan Kobel, Switzerland

Women
1..........Misty May/Kerri Walsh, United States
2..........Shelda Bede/Adriana Behar, Brazil
3..........Holly McPeak/Elaine Youngs, United States

WATER POLO

Men
1..........Hungary
2..........Serbia & Montenegro
3..........Russia

Women
1..........Italy
2..........Greece
3..........United States

WEIGHTLIFTING

Men

123 POUNDS
1..........Halil Mutlu, Turkey — 649 lb
2..........Meijin Wu, China — 632.5 lb
3..........Sedat Artuc, Turkey — 616 lb

137 POUNDS
1..........Zhiyong Shi, China — 715 lb
2..........Maosheng Le, China — 687.5 lb
3..........Jose Israel Rubio, Venezuela — 649 lb

152 POUNDS
1..........Guozheng Zhang, China — 764.5 lb
2..........Bae Young Lee, S Korea — 753.5 lb
3..........Nikolay Pechalov, Croatia — 742.5 lb

170 POUNDS
1..........Taner Sagir, Turkey — 825 lb OR
2..........Sergei Filimonov, Kazakhstan — 819.5 lb
3..........Oleg Perepetchenov, Russia — 803 lb

187 POUNDS
1..........George Asanidze, Georgia — 841.5 lb
2..........Andrei Rybakou, Belarus — 836 lb
3..........Pyrros Dimas, Greece — 830.5 lb

207 POUNDS
1..........Milen Dobrev, Bulgaria — 896.5 lb
2..........Khadjimourad Akkaev, Russia — 891 lb
3..........Eduard Tjukin, Russia — 874.5

231 POUNDS
1..........Dmitry Berestov, Russia — 935 lb
2..........Igor Razoronov, Ukraine — 924 lb
3..........Gleb Pisarevskiy, Russia — 924 lb

231+ POUNDS
1..........Hossein Reza Zadeh, Iran — 1,039.5 lb
2..........Viktors Scerbatihs, Latvia — 1001 lb
3..........Velichko Cholakov, Bulgaria — 984.5 lb

WEIGHTLIFTING *(Cont.)*

Women

106 POUNDS
1. ....Taylan Nurcan, Turkey — 462 lb
2. ....Zhuo Li, China — 451 lb
3. ....Aree Wiratthaworn, Thailand — 440 lb

117 POUNDS
1. ....Udomporn Polsak, Thailand — 490 lb
2. ....Raema Lisa Rumbewas, Indonesia — 462 lb
3. ....Mabel Mosquera, Colombia — 434.4 lb

128 POUNDS
1. ....Yanging Chen, China — 523 lb
2. ....Song Hui Ri, N Korea — 512 lb
3. ....Wandee Kameajm, Thailand — 506 lb

139 POUNDS
1. ....Natalia Skakun, Ukraine — 535 lb
2. ....Hanna Batsiushka, Belarus — 535 lb
3. ....Tatsiana Stukalava, Belarus — 491 lb

152 POUNDS
1. ....Chunhong Liu, China — 606 lb WR
2. ....Eszter Krutzler, Hungary — 579 lb
3. ....Zarema Kasaeva, Russia — 579 lb

165 POUNDS
1. ....Pawina Thongsuk, Thailand — 601 lb
2. ....Natalia Zabolotnaia, Russia — 601 lb WR
3. ....Valentina Popova, Russia — 583 lb

165+ POUNDS
1. ....Gonghong Tang, China — 671 lb
2. ....Mi Ran Jang, S Korea — 666 lb
3. ....Agata Wrobel, Poland — 638

FREESTYLE WRESTLING

121 POUNDS
1. ....Mavlet Batirov, Russia
2. ....Stephen Abas, United States
3. ....Chikara Tanabe, Japan

132 POUNDS
1. ....Yandro Miguel Quintana, Cuba
2. ....Masuod Jokar, Iran
3. ....Kenji Inoue, Japan

145.5 POUNDS
1. ....Elbrus Tedeyev, Ukraine
2. ....Jamill Kelly, United States
3. ....Makhach Murtazaliev, Russia

163 POUNDS
1. ....Buvaysa Saytive, Russia
2. ....Gennadily Laliyev, Kazakhstan
3. ....Ivan Fundora, Cuba

185 POUNDS
1. ....Cael Sanderson, United States
2. ....Evi Jae Moon, S Korea
3. ....Sazhid Sazhidov, Russia

211.5 POUNDS
1. ....Khadjimourat Gatsalov, Russia
2. ....Magomed Ibragimov, Uzbekistan
3. ....Alireza Heidari, Iran

264.5 POUNDS
1. ....Artur Taymazov, Uzbekistan
2. ....Alireza Rezaei, Iran
3. ....Aydin Polatci, Turkey

GRECO-ROMAN WRESTLING

121 POUNDS
1. ....Istvan Majoros, Hungary
2. ....Gueidar Mamedaliev, Russia
3. ....Artiom Kjourejkian, Greece

132 POUNDS
1. ....Ji Hyun Jung, S Korea
2. ....Roberto Monzon, Cuba
3. ....Armen Nazarian, Bulgaria

145.5 POUNDS
1. ....Farid Monsurov, Azerbaijan
2. ....Seref Eroglu, Turkey
3. ....Mkkhitar Manukyan, Kazakhstan

163 POUNDS
1. ....Alexandr Dokturishivili, Uzbekistan
2. ....Marko Yli-Hannuksela, Finland
3. ....Varteres Samourgachev, Russia

185 POUNDS
1. ....Alexei Michine, Russia
2. ....Ara Abrahamian, Sweden
3. ....Viachaslau Makaranka, Belarus

211.5 POUNDS
1. ....Karam Ibrahim, Egypt
2. ....Ramaz Nozadze, Georgia
3. ....Mehmet Ozal, Turkey

264.5 POUNDS
1. ....Khasan Baroev, Russia
2. ....Georgiy Tsurtsumia, Kazakhstan
3. ....Rulon Gardner, United States

YACHTING

Men

470
1. ....United States
2. ....Great Britain
3. ....Japan

FINN
1. ....Great Britain
2. ....Spain
3. ....Poland

Note: OR=Olympic Record. WR=World Record. EOR=Equals Olympic Record. EWR=Equals World Record.

YACHTING *(Cont.)*
Men *(Cont.)*

MISTRAL
1. ....Israel
2. ....Greece
3. ....Great Britain

STAR
1. ....Brazil
2. ....Canada
3. ....France

TORNADO
1. ....Austria
2. ....United States
3. ....Argentina

MISTRAL
1. ....France
2. ....China
3. ....Italy

470
1. ....Greece
2. ....Spain
3. ....Sweden

LASER
1. ....Brazil
2. ....Austria
3. ....Slovenia

49ER
1. ....Spain
2. ....Ukraine
3. ....Great Britain

Women

EUROPE
1. ....Norway
2. ....Czech Republic
3. ....Denmark

KEEL
1. ....Great Britain
2. ....Ukraine
3. ....Denmark

FOR THE RECORD • Year by Year

Olympic Games Locations and Dates

Summary

	Year	Site	Dates	Men	Women	Nations	Most Medals	US Medals
I	1896	Athens, Greece	Apr 6–15	311	0	13	Greece (10-19-18—47)	11-6-2—19 (2nd)
II	1900	Paris, France	May 20–Oct 28	1319	11	22	France (29-41-32—102)	20-14-19—53 (2nd)
III	1904	St Louis, United States	July 1–Nov 23	681	6	12	United States (80-86-72—238)	
—	1906	Athens, Greece	Apr 22–May 28	77	7	20	France (15-9-16—40)	12-6-5—23 (4th)
IV	1908	London, Great Britain	Apr 27–Oct 31	1999	36	23	Britain (56-50-39—145)	23-12-12—47 (2nd)
V	1912	Stockholm, Sweden	May 5–July 22	2490	57	28	Sweden (24-24-17—65)	23-19-19—61 (2nd)
VI	1916	Berlin, Germany	Canceled because of war					
VII	1920	Antwerp, Belgium	Apr 20–Sep 12	2543	64	29	United States (41-27-28—96)	
VIII	1924	Paris, France	May 4–July 27	2956	136	44	United States (45-27-27—99)	
IX	1928	Amsterdam, Netherlands	May 17–Aug 12	2724	290	46	United States (22-18-16—56)	
X	1932	Los Angeles, United States	July 30–Aug 14	1281	127	37	United States (41-32-31—104)	
XI	1936	Berlin, Germany	Aug 1–16	3738	328	49	Germany (33-26-30—89)	24-20-12—56 (2nd)
XII	1940	Tokyo, Japan	Canceled because of war					
XIII	1944	London, Great Britain	Canceled because of war					
XIV	1948	London, Great Britain	July 29–Aug 14	3714	385	59	United States (38-27-19—84)	
XV	1952	Helsinki, Finland	July 19–Aug 3	4407	518	69	United States (40-19-17—76)	
XVI	1956	Melbourne, Australia*	Nov 22–Dec 8	2958	384	67	USSR (37-29-32—98)	32-25-17—74 (2nd)
XVII	1960	Rome, Italy	Aug 25–Sep 11	4738	610	83	USSR (43-29-31—103)	34-21-16—71 (2nd)
XVIII	1964	Tokyo, Japan	Oct 10–24	4457	683	93	United States (36-26-28—90)	
XIX	1968	Mexico City, Mexico	Oct 12–27	4750	781	112	United States (45-28-34—107)	
XX	1972	Munich, W Germany	Aug 26–Sep 10	5848	1299	122	USSR (50-27-22—99)	33-31-30—94 (2nd)
XXI	1976	Montreal, Canada	July 17–Aug 1	4834	1251	92†	USSR (49-41-35—125)	34-35-25—94 (3rd)
XXII	1980	Moscow, USSR	July 19–Aug 3	4265	1088	81‡	USSR (80-69-46—195)	Did not compete
XXIII	1984	Los Angeles, United States	July 28–Aug 12	5458	1620	141#	United States (83-61-30—174)	
XXIV	1988	Seoul, S Korea	Sep 17–Oct 2	7105	2476	160	USSR (55-31-46—132)	36-31-27—94 (3rd)
XXV	1992	Barcelona, Spain	July 25–Aug. 9	7555	3008	172	Unified Team (45-38-29—112)	37-34-37—108 (2nd)

Summer *(Cont.)*

	Year	Site	Dates	COMPETITORS Men	Women	Nations	Most Medals	US Medals
XXVI	1996	Atlanta, United States	July 19–Aug 4	6984	3766	197	United States (44-32-25—101)	
XXVII	2000	Sydney, Australia	Sept 15–Oct 1	6862	4254	199	United States (39-25-33—97)	
XXVIII	2004	Athens, Greece	Aug 11–Aug 29	11099 total		202	United States (35-39-29—103)	

*The equestrian events were held in Stockholm, Sweden, June 10–17, 1956.
†This figure includes Cameroon, Egypt, Morocco, and Tunisia, countries that boycotted the 1976 Olympics after some of their athletes had already competed.
‡The U.S. was among 65 countries that did not participate in the 1980 Summer Games in Moscow.
#The USSR, East Germany, and 14 other countries did not participate in the 1984 Summer Games in Los Angeles.

Winter

	Year	Site	Dates	Competitors Men	Women	Nations	Most Medals	US Medals
I	1924	Chamonix, France	Jan 25–Feb 4	281	13	16	Norway (4-7-6—17)	1-2-1—4 (3rd)
II	1928	St. Moritz, Switzerland	Feb 11–19	366	27	25	Norway (6-4-5—15)	2-2-2—6 (2nd)
III	1932	Lake Placid, United States	Feb 4–13	277	30	17	United States (6-4-2—12)	
IV	1936	Garmisch-Partenkirchen, Germany	Feb 6–16	680	76	28	Norway (7-5-3—15)	1-0-3—4 (T-5th)
—	1940	Garmisch-Partenkirchen, Germany	Canceled because of war					
—	1944	Cortina d'Ampezzo, Italy	Canceled because of war					
V	1948	St. Moritz, Switzerland	Jan 30–Feb 8	636	77	28	Norway (4-3-3—10) Sweden (4-3-3—10) Switzerland (3-4-3—10)	3-4-2—9 (4th)
VI	1952	Oslo, Norway	Feb 14–25	624	108	30	Norway (7-3-6—16)	4-6-1—11 (2nd)
VII	1956	Cortina d'Ampezzo, Italy	Jan 26–Feb 5	687	132	32	USSR (7-3-6—16)	2-3-2—7 (T-4th)
VIII	1960	Squaw Valley, United States	Feb 18–28	502	146	30	USSR (7-5-9—21)	3-4-3—10 (2nd)
IX	1964	Innsbruck, Austria	Jan 29–Feb 9	758	175	36	USSR (11-8-6—25)	1-2-3—6 (7th)
X	1968	Grenoble, France	Feb 6–18	1063	230	37	Norway (6-6-2—14)	1-5-1—7 (T-7th)
XI	1972	Sapporo, Japan	Feb 3–13	927	218	35	USSR (8-5-3—16)	3-2-3—8 (6th)
XII	1976	Innsbruck, Austria	Feb 4–15	1013	248	37	USSR (13-6-8—27)	3-3-4—10 (T-3rd)
XIII	1980	Lake Placid, United States	Feb 13–24	1012	271	37	East Germany (9-7-7—23)	6-4-2—12 (3rd)
XIV	1984	Sarajevo, Yugoslavia	Feb 8–19	1127	283	49	USSR (6-10-9—25)	4-4-0—8 (T-5th)
XV	1988	Calgary, Canada	Feb 13–28	1270	364	57	USSR (11-9-9—29)	2-1-3—6 (T-8th)
XVI	1992	Albertville, France	Feb 8–23	1313	488	65	Germany (10-10-6—26)	5-4-2—11 (6th)

Winter *(Cont.)*

	Year	Site	Dates	Men	Women	Nations	Most Medals	US Medals
				Competitors				
XVII	1994	Lillehammer, Norway	Feb 12–27	1302	542	67	Norway (10-11-5—26)	6-5-2—13 (T-5th)
XVIII	1998	Nagano, Japan Sweden	Feb 7–22	2302 (total)		72	Germany (12-9-8—29)	6-3-4—13 (6th)
XIX	2002	Salt Lake City, United States	Feb 8–24	1513	886	77	Germany (12-16-7—35)	10-13-11—34} (2nd)
XX	2006	Turin, Italy	Feb 10–26	1627	1006	80	Germany (11-12-6—29)	9-9-7—25} (2nd)

Alltime Olympic Medal Winners

Summary
NATIONS

Nation	Gold	Silver	Bronze	Total
United States	906	698	615	2219
USSR (1952–88)	395	319	296	1010
Great Britain	189	242	237	668
France	199	202	230	631
Italy	189	154	168	511
Germany (1896–1936, 1992–)	152	154	178	484
Sweden	140	157	179	476
Hungary	158	141	161	460
E. Germany (1956–88)	159	150	136	445
Australia	119	126	154	399
Japan	113	106	114	333
W. Germany (1952–88)	77	104	120	301
Finland	101	83	114	298
China	112	96	78	286
Romania	82	88	114	284
Poland	59	74	118	251
Russia	86	80	85	251
Canada	54	87	101	242
The Netherlands	65	76	94	235
Bulgaria	50	83	74	207
Switzerland	48	76	64	188
Denmark	42	63	64	169
Cuba	64	51	49	164

INDIVIDUALS – OVERALL
Men

Athlete, Nation	Sport	G	S	B	Tot
Nikolai Andrianov, USSR	Gym	7	5	3	15
Boris Shakhlin, USSR	Gym	7	4	2	13
Edoardo Mangiarotti, Italy	Fen	6	5	2	13
Takashi Ono, Japan	Gym	5	4	4	13
Paavo Nurmi, Finland	Track	9	3	0	12
Sawao Kato, Japan	Gym	8	3	1	12
Alexei Nemov, Russia	Gym	4	2	6	12
Mark Spitz, United States	Swim	9	1	1	11
Matt Biondi, United States	Swim	8	2	1	11
Viktor Chukarin, USSR	Gym	7	3	1	11
Carl Osburn, United States	Shoot	5	4	2	11
Ray Ewry, United States	Track	10	0	0	10
Carl Lewis, United States	Track	9	1	0	10
Aladár Gerevich, Hungary	Fen	7	1	2	10
Akinori Nakayama, Japan	Gym	6	2	2	10
Vitaly Scherbo, UT/Belarus	Gym	6	0	4	10
Aleksandr Dityatin, USSR	Gym	3	6	1	10

Women

Athlete, Nation	Sport	G	S	B	Tot
Larissa Latynina, USSR	Gym	9	5	4	18
Jenny Thompson, United States	Swim	8	3	1	12
Vera Cáslavská, Czech	Gym	7	4	0	11
Agnes Keleti, Hungary	Gym	5	3	2	10
Polina Astaknova, USSR	Gym	5	2	3	10
Dara Torres, United States	Swim	4	1	4	9
Nadia Comaneci, Romania	Gym	5	3	1	9
Lyudmila Tourischeva, USSR	Gym	4	3	2	9
Kornelia Ender, E Germany	Swim	4	4	0	8
Dawn Fraser, Australia	Swim	4	4	0	8
Shirley Babashoff, United States	Swim	2	6	0	8
Sofia Muratova, USSR	Gym	2	2	4	8
Inge de Bruijn, Netherlands	Swim	4	2	2	8
Eight tied with seven.					

Summer *(Cont.)*

INDIVIDUALS — GOLD

Men

Ray Ewry, United States 10
Paavo Nurmi, Finland 9
Carl Lewis, United States 9
Mark Spitz, United States 9

Sawao Kato, Japan 8
Matt Biondi, United States 8
Nikolai Andrianov, USSR 7
Boris Shakhlin, USSR 7

Viktor Chukarin, USSR...............7
Aladár Gerevich, Hungary 7

Women

Larissa Latynina, USSR.............9
Jenny Thompson, U.S. 8
Vera Cáslavská, Czech 7
Kristin Otto, E Germany 6
Agnes Keleti, Hungary..............5
Nadia Comaneci, Romania 5
Polina Astaknova, USSR 5

Krisztina Egerszegi, Hungary 5
Kornelia Ender, E Germany 4
Dawn Fraser, Australia..............4
Lyudmila Tourischeva, USSR.....4
Evelyn Ashford, United States...4
Janet Evans, United States 4
Fanny Blankers-Koen, Neth.......4

Betty Cuthbert, Australia............4
Pat McCormick, United States ..4
Bärbel Eckert Wöckel, E Ger.....4
Amy Van Dyken, United States...4
Inge de Bruijn, Netherlands.......4
Yana Klochkova, Ukraine...........4
Dana Torres................................4

Winter

NATIONS

Men					Women				
Nation	**Gold**	**Silver**	**Bronze**	**Total**	**Nation**	**Gold**	**Silver**	**Bronze**	**Total**
Norway..............96		101	82	279	Finland...............41		57	52	150
United States...................79		79	58	216	Canada 37		38	44	119
USSR (1956–88)..............78		56	59	193	Sweden 43		30	43	116
Austria 50		64	72	186	Switzerland 37		37	41	115
Germany 65		63	43	171	E Germany (1956-88) 39		37	35	111

INDIVIDUALS — OVERALL

Men						Women					
Athlete, Nation	**Sport**	**G**	**S**	**B**	**Tot**	**Athlete, Nation**	**Sport**	**G**	**S**	**B**	**Tot**
Bjørn Dæhlie, Norway.................N Ski		8	4	0	12	Raisa Smetanina, USSR/UT.......N Ski		4	5	1	10
Sixten Jernberg, Sweden ....N Ski		4	3	2	9	Lyubov Egorova, UT/Russia ......N Ski		6	3	0	9
Seven tied with 7.						Larissa Lazutina, UT/Russia ......N Ski		5	3	1	9
						Stefania Belmondo, Italy............N Ski		2	3	4	9
						Four tied with 8.					

INDIVIDUALS — GOLD

Men		Women	
Bjørn Dæhlie, Norway 8		Lyubov Egorova, UT/Russia...................6	
A. Clas Thunberg, Finland 5		Lydia Skoblikova, USSR............6	
O. Bjoerndalen, Norway.............5		Larissa Lazutina, UT/Russia 5	
Eric Heiden, United States.......5		Bonnie Blair, United States 5	
Nine tied with 4.		Four tied with 4.	

TRACK AND FIELD — Men

100 METERS

1896	Thomas Burke, United States	12.0
1900	Frank Jarvis, United States	11.0
1904	Archie Hahn, United States	11.0
1906	Archie Hahn, United States	11.2
1908	Reginald Walker, S Africa	10.8 OR
1912	Ralph Craig, United States	10.8
1920	Charles Paddock, United States	10.8
1924	Harold Abrahams, Great Britain	10.6 OR
1928	Percy Williams, Canada	10.8
1932	Eddie Tolan, United States	10.3 OR
1936	Jesse Owens, United States	10.3
1948	Harrison Dillard, United States	10.3
1952	Lindy Remigino, United States	10.4
1956	Bobby Morrow, United States	10.5
1960	Armin Hary, W Germany	10.2 OR
1964	Bob Hayes, United States	10.0 EWR
1968	Jim Hines, United States	9.95 WR
1972	Valery Borzov, USSR	10.14
1976	Hasely Crawford, Trinidad	10.06
1980	Allan Wells, Great Britain	10.25
1984	Carl Lewis, United States	9.99
1988	Carl Lewis, United States*	9.92 OR
1992	Linford Christie, Great Britain	9.96
1996	Donovan Bailey, Canada	9.84 WR
2000	Maurice Greene, United States	9.87
2004	Justin Gatlin, United States	9.85

*Ben Johnson, Canada, disqualified.

200 METERS

1900	John Walter Tewksbury, United States	22.2
1904	Archie Hahn, United States	21.6 OR
1906	Not held	
1908	Robert Kerr, Canada	22.6
1912	Ralph Craig, United States	21.7
1920	Allen Woodring, United States	22.0
1924	Jackson Scholz, United States	21.6
1928	Percy Williams, Canada	21.8
1932	Eddie Tolan, United States	21.2 OR
1936	Jesse Owens, United States	20.7 OR
1948	Mel Patton, United States	21.1
1952	Andrew Stanfield, United States	20.7
1956	Bobby Morrow, United States	20.6 OR
1960	Livio Berruti, Italy	20.5 EWR
1964	Henry Carr, United States	20.3 OR
1968	Tommie Smith, United States	19.83 WR
1972	Valery Borzov, USSR	20.00
1976	Donald Quarrie, Jamaica	20.23
1980	Pietro Mennea, Italy	20.19
1984	Carl Lewis, United States	19.80 OR
1988	Joe DeLoach, United States	19.75 OR
1992	Mike Marsh, United States	20.01
1996	Michael Johnson, United States	19.32 WR
2000	Konstadinos Kederis, Greece	20.09
2004	Shawn Crawford, United States	19.79

400 METERS

1896	Thomas Burke, United States	54.2
1900	Maxey Long, United States	49.4 OR
1904	Harry Hillman, United States	49.2 OR
1906	Paul Pilgrim, United States	53.2
1908	Wyndham Halswelle, Great Britain	50.0
1912	Charles Reidpath, United States	48.2 OR
1920	Bevil Rudd, South Africa	49.6
1924	Eric Liddell, Great Britain	47.6 OR
1928	Ray Barbuti, United States	47.8
1932	William Carr, United States	46.2 WR
1936	Archie Williams, United States	46.5
1948	Arthur Wint, Jamaica	46.2
1952	George Rhoden, Jamaica	45.9
1956	Charles Jenkins, United States	46.7

400 METERS (Cont.)

1960	Otis Davis, United States	44.9 WR
1964	Michael Larrabee, United States	45.1
1968	Lee Evans, United States	43.86 WR
1972	Vincent Matthews, United States	44.66
1976	Alberto Juantorena, Cuba	44.26
1980	Viktor Markin, USSR	44.60
1984	Alonzo Babers, United States	44.27
1988	Steve Lewis, United States	43.87
1992	Quincy Watts, United States	43.50 OR
1996	Michael Johnson, United States	43.49 OR
2000	Michael Johnson, United States	43.84
2004	Jeremy Wariner, United States	44.00

800 METERS

1896	Edwin Flack, Australia	2:11
1900	Alfred Tysoe, Great Britain	2:01.2
1904	James Lightbody, United States	1:56 OR
1906	Paul Pilgrim, United States	2:01.5
1908	Mel Sheppard, United States	1:52.8 WR
1912	James Meredith, United States	1:51.9 WR
1920	Albert Hill, Great Britain	1:53.4
1924	Douglas Lowe, Great Britain	1:52.4
1928	Douglas Lowe, Great Britain	1:51.8 OR
1932	Thomas Hampson, Great Britain	1:49.8 WR
1936	John Woodruff, United States	1:52.9
1948	Mal Whitfield, United States	1:49.2 OR
1952	Mal Whitfield, United States	1:49.2 EOR
1956	Thomas Courtney, United States	1:47.7 OR
1960	Peter Snell, New Zealand	1:46.3 OR
1964	Peter Snell, New Zealand	1:45.1 OR
1968	Ralph Doubell, Australia	1:44.3 EWR
1972	Dave Wottle, United States	1:45.9
1976	Alberto Juantorena, Cuba	1:43.50 WR
1980	Steve Ovett, Great Britain	1:45.40
1984	Joaquim Cruz, Brazil	1:43.00 OR
1988	Paul Ereng, Kenya	1:43.45
1992	William Tanui, Kenya	1:43.66
1996	Vebjoern Rodal, Norway	1:42.58 OR
2000	Nils Schumann, Germany	1:45.08
2004	Yuriy Borzakovskiy, Russia	1:44.45

1,500 METERS

1896	Edwin Flack, Australia	4:33.2
1900	Charles Bennett, Great Britain	4:06.2 WR
1904	James Lightbody, United States	4:05.4 WR
1906	James Lightbody, United States	4:12.0
1908	Mel Sheppard, United States	4:03.4 OR
1912	Arnold Jackson, Great Britain	3:56.8 OR
1920	Albert Hill, Great Britain	4:01.8
1924	Paavo Nurmi, Finland	3:53.6 OR
1928	Harry Larva, Finland	3:53.2 OR
1932	Luigi Beccali, Italy	3:51.2 OR
1936	Jack Lovelock, New Zealand	3:47.8 WR
1948	Henri Eriksson, Sweden	3:49.8
1952	Josef Barthel, Luxemburg	3:45.1 OR
1956	Ron Delany, Ireland	3:41.2 OR
1960	Herb Elliott, Australia	3:35.6 WR
1964	Peter Snell, New Zealand	3:38.1
1968	Kipchoge Keino, Kenya	3:34.9 OR
1972	Pekkha Vasala, Finland	3:36.3
1976	John Walker, New Zealand	3:39.17
1980	Sebastian Coe, Great Britain	3:38.4
1984	Sebastian Coe, Great Britain	3:32.53 OR
1988	Peter Rono, Kenya	3:35.96
1992	Fermin Cacho, Spain	3:40.12
1996	Noureddine Morceli, Algeria	3:35.78
2000	Noah Ngeni, Kenya	3:32.07 OR
2004	Hicham El Guerrouj, Morocco	3:34.18

5,000 METERS

1912	Hannes Kolehmainen, Finland	14:36.6 WR
1920	Joseph Guillemot, France	14:55.6

Note: OR=Olympic Record. WR=World Record. EOR=Equals Olympic Record. EWR=Equals World Record. WB=World Best.

TRACK AND FIELD — Men *(Cont.)*

5,000 METERS *(Cont.)*

1924	Paavo Nurmi, Finland	14:31.2 OR
1928	Villie Ritola, Finland	14:38
1932	Lauri Lehtinen, Finland	14:30 OR
1936	Gunnar Hickert, Finland	14:22.2 OR
1948	Gaston Reiff, Belgium	14:17.6 OR
1952	Emil Zatopek, Czechoslovakia	14:06.6 OR
1956	Vladimir Kuts, USSR	13:39.6 OR
1960	Murray Halberg, New Zealand	13:43.4
1964	Bob Schul, United States	13:48.8
1968	Mohamed Gammoudi, Tunisia	14:05.0
1972	Lasse Viren, Finland	13:26.4 OR
1976	Lasse Viren, Finland	13:24.76
1980	Miruts Yifter, Ethiopia	13:21.0
1984	Said Aouita, Morocco	13:05.59 OR
1988	John Ngugi, Kenya	13:11.70
1992	Dieter Baumann, Germany	13:12.52
1996	Venuste Niyongabo, Burundi	13:07.96
2000	Millon Wolde, Ethiopia	13:35.49
2004	Hicham El Guerrouj, Morocco	13:14.39

10,000 METERS

1912	Hannes Kolehmainen, Finland	31:20.8
1920	Paavo Nurmi, Finland	31:45.8
1924	Vilho (Ville) Ritola, Finland	30:23.2 WR
1928	Paavo Nurmi, Finland	30:18.8 OR
1932	Janusz Kusocinski, Poland	30:11.4 OR
1936	Ilmari Salminen, Finland	30:15.4
1948	Emil Zatopek, Czechoslovakia	29:59.6 OR
1952	Emil Zatopek, Czechoslovakia	29:17.0 OR
1956	Vladimir Kuts, USSR	28:45.6 OR
1960	Pyotr Bolotnikov, USSR	28:32.2 OR
1964	Billy Mills, United States	28:24.4 OR
1968	Naftali Temu, Kenya	29:27.4
1972	Lasse Viren, Finland	27:38.4 WR
1976	Lasse Viren, Finland	27:40.38
1980	Miruts Yifter, Ethiopia	27:42.7
1984	Alberto Cova, Italy	27:47.54
1988	Brahim Boutaib, Morocco	27:21.46 OR
1992	Khalid Skah, Morocco	27:46.70
1996	Haile Gebrselassie, Ethiopia	27:07.34 OR
2000	Haile Gebrselassie, Ethiopia	27:18.20
2004	Kenenisa Bekele, Ethiopia	27:05.10 OR

MARATHON

1896	Spiridon Louis, Greece	2:58:50
1900	Michel Theato, France	2:59:45
1904	Thomas Hicks, United States	3:28:53
1906	William Sherring, Canada	2:51:23.6
1908	John Hayes, United States	2:55:18.4 OR
1912	Kenneth McArthur, S Africa	2:36:54.8
1920	Hannes Kolehmainen, Finland	2:32:35.8 WB
1924	Albin Stenroos, Finland	2:41:22.6
1928	Boughera El Ouafi, France	2:32:57
1932	Juan Zabala, Argentina	2:31:36 OR
1936	Kijung Son, Japan (Korea)	2:29:19.2 OR
1948	Delfo Cabrera, Argentina	2:34:51.6
1952	Emil Zatopek, Czechoslovakia	2:23:03.2 OR
1956	Alain Mimoun O'Kacha, France	2:25:00.0
1960	Abebe Bikila, Ethiopia	2:15:16.2 WB
1964	Abebe Bikila, Ethiopia	2:12:11.2 WB
1968	Mamo Wolde, Ethiopia	2:20:26.4
1972	Frank Shorter, United States	2:12:19.8
1976	Waldemar Cierpinski, E Germ.	2:09:55 OR
1980	Waldemar Cierpinski, E Germ.	2:11:03.0
1984	Carlos Lopes, Portugal	2:09:21.0 OR
1988	Gelindo Bordin, Italy	2:10:32
1992	Hwang Young-Cho, S Korea	2:13:23
1996	Josia Thugwane, S Africa	2:12:36
2000	Gezahgne Abera, Ethiopia	2:10:11
2004	Stefano Baldini, Italy	2:10:55

110-METER HURDLES

1896	Thomas Curtis, United States	17.6
1900	Alvin Kraenzlein, United States	15.4 OR
1904	Frederick Schule, United States	16.0

110-METER HURDLES *(Cont.)*

1906	Robert Leavitt, United States	16.2
1908	Forrest Smithson, United States	15.0 WR
1912	Frederick Kelly, United States	15.1
1920	Earl Thomson, Canada	14.8 WR
1924	Daniel Kinsey, United States	15.0
1928	Sydney Atkinson, S Africa	14.8
1932	George Saling, United States	14.6
1936	Forrest Towns, United States	14.2
1948	William Porter, United States	13.9 OR
1952	Harrison Dillard, United States	13.7 OR
1956	Lee Calhoun, United States	13.5 OR
1960	Lee Calhoun, United States	13.8
1964	Hayes Jones, United States	13.6
1968	Willie Davenport, United States	13.3 OR
1972	Rod Milburn, United States	13.24 EWR
1976	Guy Drut, France	13.30
1980	Thomas Munkelt, E Germany	13.39
1984	Roger Kingdom, United States	13.20 OR
1988	Roger Kingdom, United States	12.98 OR
1992	Mark McKoy, Canada	13.12
1996	Allen Johnson, United States	12.95 OR
2000	Anier Garcia, Cuba	13.00
2004	Xiang Liu, China	12.91 EWR

400-METER HURDLES

1900	John Walter Tewksbury, U.S.	57.6
1904	Harry Hillman, United States	53.0
1906	Not held	
1908	Charles Bacon, United States	55.0 WR
1912	Not held	
1920	Frank Loomis, United States	54.0 WR
1924	F. Morgan Taylor, United States	52.6
1928	David Burghley, Great Britain	53.4 OR
1932	Robert Tisdall, Ireland	51.7
1936	Glenn Hardin, United States	52.4
1948	Roy Cochran, United States	51.1 OR
1952	Charles Moore, United States	50.8 OR
1956	Glenn Davis, United States	50.1 EOR
1960	Glenn Davis, United States	49.3 EOR
1964	Rex Cawley, United States	49.6
1968	Dave Hemery, Great Britain	48.12 WR
1972	John Akii-Bua, Uganda	47.82 WR
1976	Edwin Moses, United States	47.64 WR
1980	Volker Beck, E Germany	48.70
1984	Edwin Moses, United States	47.75
1988	Andre Phillips, United States	47.19 OR
1992	Kevin Young, United States	46.78 WR
1996	Derrick Adkins, United States	47.54
2000	Angelo Taylor, United States	47.50
2004	Felix Sanchez, Dominican Rep	47.63

3,000-METER STEEPLECHASE

1920	Percy Hodge, Great Britain	10:00.4 OR
1924	Vilho (Ville) Ritola, Finland	9:33.6 OR
1928	Toivo Loukola, Finland	9:21.8 WR
1932	Volmari Iso-Hollo, Finland	10:33.4*
1936	Volmari Iso-Hollo, Finland	9:03.8 WR
1948	Thore Sjöstrand, Sweden	9:04.6
1952	Horace Ashenfelter, U.S.	8:45.4 WR
1956	Chris Brasher, Great Britain	8:41.2 OR
1960	Zdzislaw Krzyszkowiak, Poland	8:34.2 OR
1964	Gaston Roelants, Belgium	8:30.8 OR
1968	Amos Biwott, Kenya	8:51
1972	Kipchoge Keino, Kenya	8:23.6 OR
1976	Anders Gärderud, Sweden	8:08.2 WR
1980	Bronislaw Malinowski, Poland	8:09.7
1984	Julius Korir, Kenya	8:11.8
1988	Julius Kariuki, Kenya	8:05.51 OR
1992	Matthew Birir, Kenya	8:08.84
1996	Joseph Keter, Kenya	8:07.12
2000	Reuben Kosgei, Kenya	8:21.43
2004	Ezekiel Kemboi, Kenya	8:05.81

*About 3,450 meters; extra lap by error.

TRACK AND FIELD — Men *(Cont.)*

4 X 100-METER RELAY

1912	Great Britain	42.4 OR
1920	United States	42.2 WR
1924	United States	41.0 EWR
1928	United States	41.0 EWR
1932	United States	40.0 EWR
1936	United States	39.8 WR
1948	United States	40.6
1952	United States	40.1
1956	United States	39.5 WR
1960	W Germany	39.5 EWR
1964	United States	39.0 WR
1968	United States	38.2 WR
1972	United States	38.19 EWR
1976	United States	38.33
1980	USSR	38.26
1984	United States	37.83 WR
1988	USSR	38.19
1992	United States	37.40 WR
1996	Canada	37.69
2000	United States	37.61
2004	Great Britain	38.07

4 X 400-METER RELAY

1908	United States	3:29.4
1912	United States	3:16.6 WR
1920	Great Britain	3:22.2
1924	United States	3:16.0 WR
1928	United States	3:14.2 WR
1932	United States	3:08.2 WR
1936	Great Britain	3:09.0
1948	United States	3:10.4 WR
1952	Jamaica	3:03.9 WR
1956	United States	3:04.8
1960	United States	3:02.2 WR
1964	United States	3:00.7 WR
1968	United States	2:56.16 WR
1972	Kenya	2:59.8
1976	United States	2:58.65
1980	USSR	3:01.1
1984	United States	2:57.91
1988	United States	2:56.16 EWR
1992	United States	2:55.74 WR
1996	United States	2:55.99
2000	United States	2:56.35
2004	United States	2:55.91

20-KILOMETER WALK

1956	Leonid Spirin, USSR	1:31:27.4
1960	Vladimir Golubnichiy, USSR	1:33:07.2
1964	Kenneth Mathews, Great Britain	1:29:34.0 OR
1968	Vladimir Golubnichiy, USSR	1:33:58.4
1972	Peter Frenkel, E Germany	1:26:42.4 OR
1976	Daniel Bautista, Mexico	1:24:40.6 OR
1980	Maurizio Damilano, Italy	1:23:35.5 OR
1984	Ernesto Canto, Mexico	1:23:13.0 OR
1988	Jozef Pribilinec, Czechoslovakia	1:19:57.0 OR
1992	Daniel Plaza, Spain	1:21:45.0
1996	Jefferson Pérez, Ecuador	1:20:07
2000	Robert Korzeniowski, Poland	1:18:59 OR
2004	Ivano Brugnetti, Italy	1:19:40

50-KILOMETER WALK

1932	Thomas Green, Great Britain	4:50:10
1936	Harold Whitlock, Great Britain	4:30:41.4 OR
1948	John Ljunggren, Sweden	4:41:52
1952	Giuseppe Dordoni, Italy	4:28:07.8 OR
1956	Norman Read, New Zealand	4:30:42.8
1960	Donald Thompson, Great Britain	4:25:30 OR
1964	Abdon Parnich, Italy	4:11:12.4 OR
1968	Christoph Höhne, E Germany	4:20:13.6
1972	Bernd Kannenberg, W Germany	3:56:11.6 OR

50-KILOMETER WALK *(CONT.)*

1980	Hartwig Gauder, E Germany	3:49:24.0 OR
1984	Raul Gonzalez, Mexico	3:47:26.0 OR
1988	Viacheslav Ivanenko, USSR	3:38:29.0 OR
1992	Andrey Perlov, Unified Team	3:50:13
1996	Robert Korzeniowski, Poland	3:43:30
2000	Robert Korzeniowski, Poland	3:42:22 OR
2004	Robert Korzeniowski, Poland	3:38:46

HIGH JUMP

1896	Ellery Clark, United States	5 ft 11¼ in
1900	Irving Baxter, United States	6 ft 2¾ in OR
1904	Samuel Jones, United States	5 ft 11 in
1906	Cornelius Leahy, Great Britain/Ireland	5 ft 10 in
1908	Harry Porter, United States	6 ft 3 in OR
1912	Alma Richards, United States	6 ft 4 in OR
1920	Richmond Landon, United States	6 ft 4 in OR
1924	Harold Osborn, United States	6 ft 6 in OR
1928	Robert W. King, United States	6 ft 4½ in
1932	Duncan McNaughton, Canada	6 ft 5½ in
1936	Cornelius Johnson, United States	6 ft 8 in OR
1948	John L. Winter, Australia	6 ft 6 in
1952	Walter Davis, United States	6 ft 8½ in OR
1956	Charles Dumas, United States	6 ft 11½ in OR
1960	Robert Shavlakadze, USSR	7 ft 1 in OR
1964	Valery Brumel, USSR	7 ft 1¾ in OR
1968	Dick Fosbury, United States	7 ft 4¼ in OR
1972	Yuri Tarmak, USSR	7 ft 3¾ in
1976	Jacek Wszola, Poland	7 ft 4½ in OR
1980	Gerd Wessig, E Germany	7 ft 8¾ in WR
1984	Dietmar Mögenburg, W Ger	7 ft 8½ in
1988	Gennadiy Avdeyenko, USSR	7 ft 9¾ in OR
1992	Javier Sotomayor, Cuba	7 ft 8 in.
1996	Charles Austin, United States	7 ft 10 in OR
2000	Sergey Kliugin, Russia	7 ft 8¼ in
2004	Stefan Holm, Sweden	7 ft 8¾ in

POLE VAULT

1896	William Hoyt, United States	10 ft 10 in
1900	Irving Baxter, United States	10 ft 10 in
1904	Charles Dvorak, United States	11 ft 5¾ in
1906	Fernand Gonder, France	11 ft 5¾ in
1908	Alfred Gilbert, United States Edward Cooke Jr., United States	12 ft 2 in OR
1912	Harry Babcock, United States	12 ft 11½ in OR
1920	Frank Foss, United States	13 ft 5 in WR
1924	Lee Barnes, United States	12 ft 11½ in
1928	Sabin Carr, United States	13 ft 9¼ in OR
1932	William Miller, United States	14 ft 1¾ in OR
1936	Earle Meadows, United States	14 ft 3¼ in OR
1948	Guinn Smith, United States	14 ft 1¼ in
1952	Robert Richards, United States	14 ft 11 in OR
1956	Robert Richards, United States	14 ft 11½ in OR
1960	Don Bragg, United States	15 ft 5 in OR
1964	Fred Hansen, United States	16 ft 8¾ in OR
1968	Bob Seagren, United States	17 ft 8½ in OR
1972	Wolfgang Nordwig, E Germany	18 ft ½ in OR
1976	Tadeusz Slusarski, Poland	18 ft ½ in EOR
1980	Wladyslaw Kozakiewicz, Pol	18 ft 11½ in WR
1984	Pierre Quinon, France	18 ft 10¼ in
1988	Sergei Bubka, USSR	19 ft 4¼ in OR
1992	Maksim Tarasov, Unified Team	19 ft ¼ in
1996	Jean Galfione, France	19 ft 5 ¼ in OR
2000	Nick Hysong, United States	19 ft 4¼ in
2004	Timothy Mack, United States	19 ft 6¼ in

Note: OR=Olympic Record. WR=World Record. EOR=Equals Olympic Record. EWR=Equals World Record. WB=World Best.

Summer Games Champions *(Cont.)*

TRACK AND FIELD — Men *(Cont.)*

LONG JUMP

1896...Ellery Clark, United States	20 ft 10 in
1900...Alvin Kraenzlein, United States	23 ft 6¾ in OR
1904...Meyer Prinstein, United States	24 ft 1 in OR
1906...Meyer Prinstein, United States	23 ft 7½ in
1908...Frank Irons, United States	24 ft 6½ in OR
1912...Albert Gutterson, United States	24 ft 11¼ in OR
1920...William Peterssen, Sweden	23 ft 5½ in
1924...DeHart Hubbard, United States	24 ft 5 in
1928...Edward B. Hamm, United States	25 ft 4½ in OR
1932...Edward Gordon, United States	25 ft ¾ in
1936...Jesse Owens, United States	26 ft 5½ in OR
1948...William Steele, United States	25 ft 8 in
1952...Jerome Biffle, United States	24 ft 10 in
1956...Gregory Bell, United States	25 ft 8¼ in
1960...Ralph Boston, United States	26 ft 7¾ in OR
1964...Lynn Davies, Great Britain	26 ft 5¾ in
1968...Bob Beamon, United States	29 ft 2½ in WR
1972...Randy Williams, United States	27 ft ½ in
1976...Arnie Robinson, United States	27 ft 4¾ in
1980...Lutz Dombrowski, E Germany	28 ft ¼ in
1984...Carl Lewis, United States	28 ft ¼ in
1988...Carl Lewis, United States	28 ft 7½ in
1992...Carl Lewis, United States	28 ft 5½ in
1996...Carl Lewis, United States	27 ft 10¾ in
2000...Ivan Pedrosa, Cuba	28 ft ¾ in
2004...Dwight Phillips, United States	28 ft 2¼ in

TRIPLE JUMP

1896...James Connolly, United States	44 ft 11¾ in
1900...Meyer Prinstein, United States	47 ft 5¾ in OR
1904...Meyer Prinstein, United States	47 ft 1 in
1906...Peter O'Connor, GB/ Ire	46 ft 2¼ in
1908...Timothy Ahearne, GB/ Ire	48 ft 11¼ in OR
1912...Gustaf Lindblom, Sweden	48 ft 5¼ in
1920...Vilho Tuulos, Finland	47 ft 7 in
1924...Anthony Winter, Australia	50 ft 11¼ in WR
1928...Mikio Oda, Japan	49 ft 11 in
1932...Chuhei Nambu, Japan	51 ft 7 in WR
1936...Naoto Tajima, Japan	52 ft 6 in WR
1948...Arne Ahman, Sweden	50 ft 6¼ in
1952...Adhemar da Silva, Brazil	53 ft 2¾ in WR
1956...Adhemar da Silva, Brazil	53 ft 7¾ in OR
1960...Jozef Schmidt, Poland	55 ft 2 in
1964...Jozef Schmidt, Poland	55 ft 3½ in OR
1968...Viktor Saneyev, USSR	57 ft ¾ in WR
1972...Viktor Saneyev, USSR	56 ft 11¾ in
1976...Viktor Saneyev, USSR	56 ft 8¾ in
1980...Jaak Uudmae, USSR	56 ft 11¼ in
1984...Al Joyner, United States	56 ft 7½ in
1988...Khristo Markov, Bulgaria	57 ft 9½ in OR
1992...Mike Conley, United States	59 ft 7½ in (w)
1996...Kenny Harrison, United States	59 ft 4¼ in OR
2000...Jonathon Edwards, G. Britain	58 ft 1¼ in
2004...Christian Olsson, Sweden	58 ft 4½ in

SHOT PUT

1896...Robert Garrett, United States	36 ft 9¾ in
1900...Richard Sheldon, United States	46 ft 3¼ in OR
1904...Ralph Rose, United States	48 ft 7 in WR
1906...Martin Sheridan, United States	40 ft 5¼ in
1908...Ralph Rose, United States	46 ft 7½ in
1912...Pat McDonald, United States	50 ft 4 in OR
1920...Ville Porhola, Finland	48 ft 7¼ in
1924...Clarence Houser, United States	49 ft 2¼ in
1928...John Kuck, United States	52 ft ¾ in WR
1932...Leo Sexton, United States	52 ft 6 in OR
1936...Hans Woellke, Germany	53 ft 1¾ in OR
1948...Wilbur Thompson, United States	56 ft 2 in OR

(w)-wind aided

SHOT PUT *(CONT.)*

1952...Parry O'Brien, United States	57 ft ½ in OR
1956...Parry O'Brien, United States	60 ft 11¼ in OR
1960...William Nieder, United States	64 ft 6¾ in OR
1964...Dallas Long, United States	66 ft 8½ in OR
1968...Randy Matson, United States	67 ft 4¾ in
1972...Wladyslaw Komar, Poland	69 ft 6 in OR
1976...Udo Beyer, E Germany	69 ft ¾ in
1980...Vladimir Kiselyov, USSR	70 ft ½ in OR
1984...Alessandro Andrei, Italy	69 ft 9 in
1988...Ulf Timmermann, E Germany	73 ft 8¾ in OR
1992...Mike Stulce, United States	71 ft 2½ in
1996...Randy Barnes, United States	70 ft 11 in
2000...Arsi Harju, Finland	69 ft 10¼ in
2004...Yuriy Bilonog, Ukraine	69 ft 5¼ in

DISCUS THROW

1896...Robert Garrett, United States	95 ft 7½ in
1900...Rudolf Bauer, Hungary	118 ft 3 in OR
1904...Martin Sheridan, United States	128 ft 10½ in OR
1906...Martin Sheridan, United States	136 ft
1908...Martin Sheridan, United States	134 ft 2 in OR
1912...Armas Taipele, Finland	148 ft 3 in OR
1920...Elmer Niklander, Finland	146 ft 7 in
1924...Clarence Houser, United States	151 ft 4 in OR
1928...Clarence Houser, United States	155 ft 3 in OR
1932...John Anderson, United States	162 ft 4 in OR
1936...Ken Carpenter, United States	165 ft 7 in OR
1948...Adolfo Consolini, Italy	173 ft 2 in OR
1952...Sim Iness, United States	180 ft 6 in OR
1956...Al Oerter, United States	184 ft 11 in OR
1960...Al Oerter, United States	194 ft 2 in OR
1964...Al Oerter, United States	200 ft 1 in OR
1968...Al Oerter, United States	212 ft 6 in OR
1972...Ludvik Danek, Czechoslovakia	211 ft 3 in
1976...Mac Wilkins, United States	221 ft 5 in OR
1980...Viktor Rashchupkin, USSR	218 ft 8 in
1984...Rolf Dannenberg, W Ger	218 ft 6 in
1988...Jürgen Schult, E Germany	225 ft 9 in OR
1992...Romas Ubartas, Lithuania	213 ft 8 in
1996...Lars Riedel, Germany	227 ft 8 in OR
2000...Virgilijus Alekna, Lithuania	227 ft 4 in
2004...Virgilijus Alekna, Lithuania	229 ft 3 in

HAMMER THROW

1900...John Flanagan, United States	163 ft 1 in
1904...John Flanagan, United States	168 ft 1 in OR
1906...Not held	
1908...John Flanagan, United States	170 ft 4 in OR
1912...Matt McGrath, United States	179 ft 7 in OR
1920...Pat Ryan, United States	173 ft 5 in
1924...Fred Tootell, United States	174 ft 10 in
1928...Patrick O'Callaghan, Ireland	168 ft 7 in
1932...Patrick O'Callaghan, Ireland	176 ft 11 in
1936...Karl Hein, Germany	185 ft 4 in OR
1948...Imre Nemeth, Hungary	183 ft 11 in
1952...Jozsef Csermak, Hungary	197 ft 11 in WR
1956...Harold Connolly, United States	207 ft 3 in OR
1960...Vasily Rudenkov, USSR	220 ft 2 in OR
1964...Romuald Klim, USSR	228 ft 10 in OR
1968...Gyula Zsivotsky, Hungary	240 ft 8 in OR
1972...Anatoli Bondarchuk, USSR	247 ft 8 in OR
1976...Yuri Sedykh, USSR	254 ft 4 in OR
1980...Yuri Sedykh, USSR	268 ft 4 in WR
1984...Juha Tiainen, Finland	256 ft 2 in
1988...Sergei Litvinov, USSR	278 ft 2 in OR
1992...Andrey Abduvaliyev, Unified T	270 ft 9 in
1996...Balazs Kiss, Hungary	266 ft 6 in
2000...Szymon Ziolkowski, Poland	262 ft 6 in
2004...Adrian Zsolt, Hungary	272 fr 11 in

TRACK AND FIELD — Men *(Cont.)*

JAVELIN

1908	Erik Lemming, Sweden	179 ft 10 in
1912	Erik Lemming, Sweden	198 ft 11 in WR
1920	Jonni Myyrä, Finland	215 ft 10 in OR
1924	Jonni Myyrä, Finland	206 ft 6 in
1928	Eric Lundkvist, Sweden	218 ft 6 in OR
1932	Matti Jarvinen, Finland	238 ft 6 in OR
1936	Gerhard Stöck, Germany	235 ft 8 in
1948	Kai Rautavaara, Finland	228 ft 10½ in
1952	Cy Young, United States	242 ft 1 in OR
1956	Egil Danielson, Norway	281 ft 2¼ in WR
1960	Viktor Tsibulenko, USSR	277 ft 8 in
1964	Pauli Nevala, Finland	271 ft 2 in
1968	Janis Lusis, USSR	295 ft 7 in OR
1972	Klaus Wolfermann, W Ger	296 ft 10 in OR
1976	Miklos Nemeth, Hungary	310 ft 4 in WR
1980	Dainis Kuta, USSR	299 ft 2⅔ in
1984	Arto Härkönen, Finland	284 ft 8 in
1988	Tapio Korjus, Finland	276 ft 6 in
1992	Jan Zelezny, Czechoslovakia	294 ft 2 in OR
1996	Jan Zelezny, Czech Republic	289 ft 3 in
2000	Jan Zelezny, Czech Republic	295 ft 9½ in OR
2004	Andrea Thorkildsen, Norway	283 ft 9 in

DECATHLON

		Pts
1904	Thomas Kiely, Ireland	6036
1912	Jim Thorpe, United States*	8412 WR
1920	Helge Lövland, Norway	6803
1924	Harold Osborn, United States	7711 WR
1928	Paavo Yrjölä, Finland	8053.29 WR
1932	James Bausch, United States	8462 WR
1936	Glenn Morris, United States	7900 WR
1948	Robert Mathias, United States	7139
1952	Robert Mathias, United States	7887 WR
1956	Milton Campbell, United States	7937 OR
1960	Rafer Johnson, United States	8392 OR
1964	Willi Holdorf, W Germany	7887
1968	Bill Toomey, United States	8193 OR
1972	Nikolai Avilov, USSR	8454 WR
1976	Bruce Jenner, United States	8617 WR
1980	Daley Thompson, Great Britain	8495
1984	Daley Thompson, Great Britain	8798 EWR
1988	Christian Schenk, E Germany	8488
1992	Robert Zmelik, Czechoslovakia	8611
1996	Dan O'Brien, United States	8824 OR
2000	Erki Nool, Estonia	8641
2004	Roman Seberle, Czech Rep	8893 OR

*In 1913, Thorpe was disqualified for having played professional baseball in 1910. His record was restored in 1982.

TRACK AND FIELD — Women

100 METERS

1928	Elizabeth Robinson, US	12.2 EWR
1932	Stella Walsh, Poland	11.9 EWR
1936	Helen Stephens, United States	11.5
1948	Francina Blankers-Koen, Neth	11.9
1952	Marjorie Jackson, Australia	11.5 EWR
1956	Betty Cuthbert, Australia	11.5 EWR
1960	Wilma Rudolph, United States	11.0
1964	Wyomia Tyus, United States	11.4
1968	Wyomia Tyus, United States	11.0 WR
1972	Renate Stecher, E Germany	11.07
1976	Annegret Richter, W Germany	11.08
1980	Lyudmila Kondratyeva, USSR	11.06
1984	Evelyn Ashford, United States	10.97 OR
1988	Florence Griffith Joyner, United States	10.54 WR
1992	Gail Devers, United States	10.82
1996	Gail Devers, United States	10.94
2000	Marion Jones, United States	10.75
2004	Yuliya Nesterenko, Belarus	10.93

200 METERS

1948	Francina Blankers-Koen, Neth	24.4
1952	Marjorie Jackson, Australia	23.7
1956	Betty Cuthbert, Australia	23.4 EOR
1960	Wilma Rudolph, United States	24.0
1964	Edith McGuire, United States	23.0 OR
1968	Irena Szewinska, Poland	22.5 WR
1972	Renate Stecher, E Germany	22.40 EWR
1976	Bärbel Eckert, E Germany	22.37 OR
1980	Bärbel Wöckel (Eckert), E Germ.	22.03 OR
1984	Valerie Brisco-Hooks, U.S.	21.81 OR
1988	Florence Griffith Joyner, U.S.	21.34 WR
1992	Gwen Torrence, United States	21.81
1996	Marie-José Pérec, France	22.12
2000	Marion Jones, United States	21.84
2004	Veronica Campbell, Jamaica	22.05

400 METERS

1964	Betty Cuthbert, Australia	52.0 OR
1968	Colette Besson, France	52.0 EOR
1972	Monika Zehrt, E Germany	51.08 OR
1976	Irena Szewinska, Poland	49.29 WR
1980	Marita Koch, E Germany	48.88 OR
1984	Valerie Brisco-Hooks, U.S.	48.83 OR
1988	Olga Bryzgina, USSR	48.65 OR
1992	Marie-José Pérec, France	48.83
1996	Marie-José Pérec, France	48.25 OR
2000	Cathy Freeman, Australia	49.11
2004	T. Williams-Darling, Bahamas	49.41

800 METERS

1928	Lina Radke, Germany	2:16.8 WR
1932-56	Not held	
1960	Lyudmila Shevtsova, USSR	2:04.3 EWR
1964	Ann Packer, Great Britain	2:01.1 OR
1968	Madeline Manning, United States	2:00.9 OR
1972	Hildegard Falck, W Germany	1:58.55 OR
1976	Tatyana Kazankina, USSR	1:54.94 WR
1980	Nadezhda Olizarenko, USSR	1:53.42 WR
1984	Doina Melinte, Romania	1:57.6
1988	Sigrun Wodars, E Germany	1:56.10
1992	Ellen Van Langen, Netherlands	1:55.54
1996	Svetlana Masterkova, Russia	1:57.73
2000	Maria Mutola, Mozambique	1:56.15
2004	Kelly Holmes, Great Britain	1:56.38

1,500 METERS

1972	Lyudmila Bragina, USSR	4:01.4 WR
1976	Tatyana Kazankina, USSR	4:05.48
1980	Tatyana Kazankina, USSR	3:56.6 OR
1984	Gabriella Dorio, Italy	4:03.25
1988	Paula Ivan, Romania	3:53.96 OR
1992	Hassiba Boulmerka, Algeria	3:55.30
1996	Svetlana Masterkova, Russia	4:00.83
2000	Nouria Merah-Benida, Algeria	4:05.10
2004	Kelly Holmes, Great Britain	3:57.90

Note: OR=Olympic Record. WR=World Record. EOR=Equals Olympic Record. EWR=Equals World Record. WB=World Best.

TRACK AND FIELD — Women (Cont.)

3,000 METERS

1984	Maricica Puica, Romania	8:35.96 OR
1988	Tatyana Samolenko, USSR	8:26.53 OR
1992	Elena Romanova, Unified Team	8:46.04

5,000 METERS

1996	Wang Junxia, China	14:57.88
2000	Gabriela Szabo, Romania	14:40.79 OR
2004	Meseret Defar, Ethiopia	14:45.65

10,000 METERS

1988	Olga Bondarenko, USSR	31:05.21 OR
1992	Derartu Tulu, Ethiopia	31:06.02
1996	Fernanda Ribeiro, Portugal	31:01.63 OR
2000	Derartu Tulu, Ethiopia	30:17.49 OR
2004	Huina Xing, China	30:24.36

MARATHON

1984	Joan Benoit, United States	2:24:52 OR
1988	Rosa Mota, Portugal	2:25:40
1992	Valentin Yegorova, Unified Team	2:32:41
1996	Fatuma Roba, Ethiopia	2:26:05
2000	Naoko Takahashi, Japan	2:23:14 OR
2004	Noguchi Mizuki, Japan	2:26:20

80-METER HURDLES

1932	Babe Didrikson, United States	11.7 WR
1936	Trebisonda Valla, Italy	11.7
1948	Francina Blankers-Koen, Neth	11.2 OR
1952	Shirley Strickland, Australia	10.9 WR
1956	Shirley Strickland, Australia	10.7 OR
1960	Irina Press, USSR	10.8
1964	Karin Balzer, E Germany	10.5
1968	Maureen Caird, Australia	10.3 OR

100-METER HURDLES

1972	Annelie Ehrhardt, E Germany	12.59 WR
1976	Johanna Schaller, E Germany	12.77
1980	Vera Komisova, USSR	12.56 OR
1984	Benita Fitzgerald-Brown, U.S.	12.84
1988	Yordanka Donkova, Bulgaria	12.38 OR
1992	Paraskevi Patoulidou, Greece	12.64
1996	Lyudmila Engqvist, Sweden	12.58
2000	Olga Shishigina, Kazakhstan	12.65
2004	Joanna Hayes, United States	12.37 OR

400-METER HURDLES

1984	Nawal el Moutawakel, Morocco	54.61 OR
1988	Debra Flintoff-King, Australia	53.17 OR
1992	Sally Gunnell, Great Britain	53.23
1996	Deon Hemmings, Jamaica	52.82 OR
2000	Irina Privalova, Russia	53.02
2004	Faní Halkiá, Greece	52.82

4 X 100-METER RELAY

1928	Canada	48.4 WR
1932	United States	46.9 WR
1936	United States	46.9
1948	Netherlands	47.5
1952	United States	45.9 WR
1956	Australia	44.5 WR
1960	United States	44.5
1964	Poland	43.6
1968	United States	42.8 WR
1972	W Germany	42.81 EWR
1976	E Germany	42.55 OR
1980	E Germany	41.60 WR
1984	United States	41.65
1988	United States	41.98
1992	United States	42.11
1996	United States	41.95

4 X 100-METER RELAY (Cont.)

2000	Bahamas	41.95
2004	Jamaica	41.73

4 X 400-METER RELAY

1972	E Germany	3:23 WR
1976	E Germany	3:19.23 WR
1980	USSR	3:20.02
1984	United States	3:18.29 OR
1988	USSR	3:15.18 WR
1992	Unified Team	3:20.20
1996	United States	3:20.91
2000	United States	3:22.62
2004	United States	3:19.01

10-KILOMETER WALK

1992	Chen Yueling, China	44:32
1996	Elena Nikolayeva, Russia	41:49 OR

20-KILOMETER WALK

2000	Liping Wang, China	1:29:05
2004	Athanasía Tsouméléka, Greece	1:29:12

HIGH JUMP

1928	Ethel Catherwood, Canada	5 ft 2½ in
1932	Jean Shiley, United States	5 ft 5¼ in WR
1936	Ibolya Csak, Hungary	5 ft 3 in
1948	Alice Coachman, United States	5 ft 6 in OR
1952	Esther Brand, South Africa	5 ft 5¾ in
1956	Mildred L. McDaniel, U.S.	5 ft 9¼ in WR
1960	Iolanda Balas, Romania	6 ft ¾ in OR
1964	Iolanda Balas, Romania	6 ft 2¾ in QR
1968	Miloslava Reskova, Czech.	5 ft 11½ in
1972	Ulrike Meyfarth, W. Germany	6 ft 3½ in EWR
1976	Rosemarie Ackermann, E Germ	6 ft 4 in OR
1980	Sara Simeoni, Italy	6 ft 5½ in OR
1984	Ulrike Meyfarth, W Germany	6 ft 7½ in OR
1988	Louise Ritter, United States	6 ft 8 in OR
1992	Heike Henkel, Germany	6 ft 7½ in
1996	Stefka Kostadinova, Bulgaria	6 ft 8¾ in OR
2000	Yelena Yelesina, Russia	6 ft 7 in
2004	Yelena Slesarenko, Russia	6 ft 9 in

POLE VAULT

2000	Stacy Dragila, United States	15 ft 1 in OR
2004	Yelena Isinbayeva, Russia	16 ft 1¼ in WR

LONG JUMP

1948	Olga Gyarmati, Hungary	18 ft 8¼ in
1952	Yvette Williams, New Zealand	20 ft 5¾ in OR
1956	Elzbieta Krzeskinska, Poland	20 ft 10 in EWR
1960	Vyera Krepkina, USSR	20 ft 10¾ in OR
1964	Mary Rand, Great Britain	22 ft 2¼ in WR
1968	Viorica Viscopoleanu, Rom	22 ft 4½ in WR
1972	Heidemarie Rosendahl, W Ger	22 ft 3 in
1976	Angela Voigt, E Germany	22 ft ¾ in
1980	Tatyana Kolpakova, USSR	23 ft 2 in OR
1984	Anisoara Stanciu, Romania	22 ft 10 in
1988	Jackie Joyner-Kersee, U.S.	24 ft 3½ in OR
1992	Heike Drechsler, Germany	23 ft 5¼ in
1996	Chioma Ajunwa, Nigeria	23 ft 4½ in
2000	Heike Drechsler, Germany	22 ft 11¼ in
2004	Tatyana Lebedeva, Russia	23 ft 2½ in

TRIPLE JUMP

1996	Inessa Kravets, Ukraine	50 ft 3½ in
2000	Tereza Marinova, Bulgaria	49 ft 10½ in
2004	Frangoise M. Etone, Cameroon	50 ft 2½ in

SHOT PUT

1948	Micheline Ostermeyer, France	45 ft 1½ in
1952	Galina Zybina, USSR	50 ft 1¾ in WR

Note: OR=Olympic Record; WR=World Record; EOR=Equals Olympic Record; EWR=Equals World Record; WB=World Best.
*In 1971, the 100-meter hurdles replaced the 80-meter hurdles, requiring a change in scoring tables.

TRACK AND FIELD — Women *(Cont.)*

SHOT PUT *(Cont.)*

1956...Tamara Tyshkevich, USSR	54 ft 5 in OR
1960...Tamara Press, USSR	56 ft 10 in OR
1964...Tamara Press, USSR	59 ft 6¼ in OR
1968...Margitta Gummel, E Germany	64 ft 4 in WR
1972...Nadezhda Chizhova, USSR	69 ft WR
1976...Ivanka Hristova, Bulgaria	69 ft 5¼ in OR
1980...Ilona Slupianek, E Germany	73 ft 6¼ in
1984...Claudia Losch, W Germany	67 ft 2¼ in
1988...Natalya Lisovskaya, USSR	72 ft 11¾ in
1992...Svetlana Kriveleva, Unified Team	69 ft 1¼ in
1996...Astrid Kumbernuss, Germany	67 ft 5½ in
2000...Yanina Korolchik, Belarus	67 ft 5½ in
2004...Yumileidi Cumba Jay, Cuba	64 ft 3¼ in

DISCUS THROW

1928...Helena Konopacka, Poland	129 ft 11¾ in WR
1932...Lillian Copeland, United States	133 ft 2 in OR
1936...Gisela Mauermayer, Germany	156 ft 3 in OR
1948...Micheline Ostermeyer, France	137 ft 6 in
1952...Nina Romaschkova, USSR	168 ft 8 in OR
1956...Olga Fikotova, Czechoslovakia	176 ft 1 in OR
1960...Nina Ponomaryeva, USSR	180 ft 9 in OR
1964...Tamara Press, USSR	187 ft 10 in OR
1968...Lia Manoliu, Romania	191 ft 2 in OR
1972...Faina Melnik, USSR	218 ft 7 in OR
1976...Evelin Schlaak, E Germany	226 ft 4 in OR
1980...Evelin Jahl (Schlaak), E Germ.	229 ft 6 in OR
1984...Ria Stalman, Netherlands	214 ft 5 in
1988...Martina Hellmann, E Germany	237 ft 2 in OR
1992...Maritza Martén, Cuba	229 ft 10 in
1996...Ilke Wyludda, Germany	228 ft 6 in
2000...Ellina Zvereva, Belarus	224 ft 5 in
2004...Natalya Sadova, Russia	219 ft 10 in

HAMMER THROW

2000...Kamila Skolimowska, Russia	233 ft 5 in OR
2004...Olga Kuzenkova, Russia	246 ft 1½ in OR

JAVELIN THROW

1932...Babe Didrikson, United States	143 ft 4 in OR
1936...Tilly Fleischer, Germany	148 ft 3 in OR
1948...Herma Bauma, Austria	149 ft 6 in
1952...Dana Zatopkova, Czechoslovakia	165 ft 7 in
1956...Inese Jaunzeme, USSR	176 ft 8 in
1960...Elvira Ozolina, USSR	183 ft 8 in OR
1964...Mihaela Penes, Romania	198 ft 7 in
1968...Angela Nemeth, Hungary	198 ft
1972...Ruth Fuchs, E Germany	209 ft 7 in OR
1976...Ruth Fuchs, E Germany	216 ft 4 in OR
1980...Maria Colon, Cuba	224 ft 5 in OR
1984...Tessa Sanderson, Great Britain	228 ft 2 in OR
1988...Petra Felke, E Germany	245 ft OR
1992...Silke Renk, Germany	224 ft 2 in
1996...Heli Rantanen, Finland	222 ft 11 in
2000...Trine Hattestad, Norway	226 ft ½ in OR
2004...Osleidys Menendez, Cuba	234 ft 8 in OR

PENTATHLON

	Pts
1964 ...Irina Press, USSR	5246 WR
1968 ...Ingrid Becker, W Germany	5098
1972 ...Mary Peters, Great Britain	4801 WR
1976 ...Siegrun Siegl, E Germany	4745
1980 ...Nadezhda Tkachenko, USSR	5083 WR

HEPTATHLON

	Pts
1984 ...Glynis Nunn, Australia	6390 OR
1988 ...Jackie Joyner-Kersee, U.S.	7291 WR
1992 ...Jackie Joyner-Kersee, U.S.	7044
1996 ...Ghada Shouaa, Syria	6780
2000 ...Denise Lewis, Great Britain	6584
2004 ...Carolina Kluft, Sweden	6952

BASKETBALL — Men

1936
Final: United States 19, Canada 8
United States: Ralph Bishop, Joe Fortenberry, Carl Knowles, Jack Ragland, Carl Shy, William Wheatley, Francis Johnson, Samuel Balter, John Gibbons, Frank Lubin, Arthur Mollner, Donald Piper, Duane Swanson, Willard Schmidt

1948
Final: United States 65, France 21
United States: Cliff Barker, Don Barksdale, Ralph Beard, Lewis Beck, Vince Boryla, Gordon Carpenter, Alex Groza, Wallace Jones, Bob Kurland, Ray Lumpp, Robert Pitts, Jesse Renick, Bob Robinson, Ken Rollins

1952
Final: United States 36, USSR 25
United States: Charles Hoag, Bill Hougland, Melvin Dean Kelley, Bob Kenney, Clyde Lovellette, Marcus Freiberger, Victor Wayne Glasgow, Frank McCabe, Daniel Pippen, Howard Williams, Ronald Bontemps, Bob Kurland, William Lienhard, John Keller

1956
Final: United States 89, USSR 55
United States: Carl Cain, Bill Hougland, K.C. Jones, Bill Russell, James Walsh, William Evans, Burdette Haldorson, Ron Tomsic, Dick Boushka, Gilbert Ford, Bob Jeangerard, Charles Darling

1960
Final: United States 90, Brazil 63
United States: Jay Arnette, Walt Bellamy, Bob Boozer, Terry Dischinger, Jerry Lucas, Oscar Robertson, Adrian Smith, Burdette Haldorson, Darrall Imhoff, Allen Kelley, Lester Lane, Jerry West

1964
Final: United States 73, USSR 59
United States: Jim Barnes, Bill Bradley, Larry Brown, Joe Caldwell, Mel Counts, Richard Davies, Walt Hazzard, Lucius Jackson, John McCaffrey, Jeff Mullins, Jerry Shipp, George Wilson

1968
Final: United States 65, Yugoslavia 50
United States: John Clawson, Ken Spain, Jo-Jo White, Michael Barrett, Spencer Haywood, Charles Scott, William Hosket, Calvin Fowler, Michael Silliman, Glynn Saulters, James King, Donald Dee

1972
Final: USSR 51, United States 50
United States: Kenneth Davis, Doug Collins, Thomas Henderson, Mike Bantom, Bobby Jones, Dwight Jones, James Forbes, James Brewer, Tom Burleson, Tom McMillen, Kevin Joyce, Ed Ratleff

BASKETBALL — Men *(Cont.)*

1976
Final: United States 95, Yugoslavia 74
United States: Phil Ford, Steve Sheppard, Adrian Dantley, Walter Davis, Quinn Buckner, Ernie Grunfield, Kenny Carr, Scott May, Michel Armstrong, Tom La Garde, Phil Hubbard, Mitch Kupchak

1980
Final: Yugoslavia 86, Italy 77
U.S. participated in boycott.

1984
Final: United States 96, Spain 65
United States: Steve Alford, Leon Wood, Patrick Ewing, Vern Fleming, Alvin Robertson, Michael Jordan, Joe Kleine, Jon Koncak, Wayman Tisdale, Chris Mullin, Sam Perkins, Jeff Turner

1988
Final: USSR 76, Yugoslavia 63
U.S. (3rd): Mitch Richmond, Charles E. Smith IV, Vernell Coles, Hersey Hawkins, Jeff Grayer, Charles D. Smith, Willie Anderson, Stacey Augmon, Dan Majerle, Danny Manning, J.R. Reid, David Robinson

1992
Final: United States 117, Croatia 85
  United States: David Robinson, Christian Laettner,

1992 *(Cont.)*
Patrick Ewing, Larry Bird, Scottie Pippen, Michael Jordan, Clyde Drexler, Karl Malone, John Stockton, Chris Mullin, Charles Barkley, Earvin Johnson

1996
Final: United States 95, Yugoslavia 69
United States: Charles Barkley, Anfernee Hardaway, Grant Hill, Karl Malone, Reggie Miller, Hakeem Olajuwon, Shaquille O'Neal, Scottie Pippen, Mitch Richmond, John Stockton, David Robinson, Gary Payton

2000
Final: United States 85, France 75
United States: Shareef Abdur-Rahim, Ray Allen, Vin Baker, Vince Carter, Kevin Garnett, Tim Hardaway, Allan Houston, Jason Kidd, Antonio McDyess, Alonzo Mourning, Gary Payton, Steve Smith

2004
Final: Argentina 84, Italy 69
U.S. (3rd): Allen Iverson, LeBron James, Tim Duncan, Carmelo Anthony, Dwyane Wade, Richard Jefferson, Lamar Odom, Stephon Marbury, Carlos Boozer, Emeka Okafor, Amare Stoudemire, Shawn Marion

BASKETBALL — Women

1976
Gold, USSR; Silver, United States*
United States: Cindy Brogdon, Susan Rojcewicz, Ann Meyers, Lusia Harris, Nancy Dunkle, Charlotte Lewis, Nancy Lieberman, Gail Marquis, Patricia Roberts, Mary Anne O'Connor, Patricia Head, Julienne Simpson

*In 1976 the women played a round-robin tournament, with the gold medal going to the team with the best record. The USSR won with a 5–0 record, and the USA, with a 3–2 record, was given the silver by virtue of a 95–79 victory over Bulgaria, which was also 3–2.

1980
Final: USSR 104, Bulgaria 73
U.S. participated in boycott.

1984
Final: United States 85, Korea 55
United States: Teresa Edwards, Lea Henry, Lynette Woodard, Anne Donovan, Cathy Boswell, Cheryl Miller, Janice Lawrence, Cindy Noble, Kim Mulkey, Denise Curry, Pamela McGee, Carol Menken-Schaudt

1988
Final: United States 77, Yugoslavia 70
United States: Teresa Edwards, Mary Ethridge, Cynthia Brown, Anne Donovan, Teresa Weatherspoon, Bridgette Gordon, Victoria Bullett, Andrea Lloyd, Katrina McClain, Jennifer Gillom, Cynthia Cooper, Suzanne McConnell

1992
Final: Unified Team 76, China 66
United States (3rd): Teresa Edwards, Teresa Weatherspoon, Victoria Bullett, Katrina McClain, Cynthia Cooper, Suzanne McConnell, Daedra Charles, Clarissa Davis, Tammy Jackson, Vickie Orr, Carolyn Jones, Medina Dixon

1996
Final: United States 111, Brazil 87
United States: Jennifer Azzi, Ruthie Bolton, Teresa Edwards, Lisa Leslie, Rebecca Lobo, Katrina McClain, Nikki McCray, Carla McGhee, Dawn Staley, Katy Steding, Sheryl Swoopes, Venus Lacey

2000
Final: United States 76, Australia 54
United States: Ruthie Bolton-Holifield, Teresa Edwards, Yolanda Griffith, Chamique Holdsclaw, Lisa Leslie, Nikki McCray, Delisha Milton, Katie Smith, Dawn Staley, Sheryl Swoopes, Natalie Williams, Kara Wolters

2004
Final: United States 74, Australia 63
United States: Dawn Staley, Diana Taurasi, Lisa Leslie, Sheryl Swoopes, Tamika Catchings, Sue Bird, Ruth Riley, Shannon Johnson, Katie Smith, Yolanda Griffith, Swintayla Cash, Tina Thompson

BOXING

LIGHT FLYWEIGHT (106 LB)

1968	Francisco Rodriguez,	Venezuela
1972	Gyorgy Gedo,	Hungary
1976	Jorge Hernandez,	Cuba
1980	Shamil Sabyrov,	USSR
1984	Paul Gonzalez,	United States

LIGHT FLYWEIGHT *(CONT.)*

1988	Ivailo Hristov,	Bulgaria
1992	Rogelio Marcelo,	Cuba
1996	Daniel Petrov,	Bulgaria
2000	Brahim Asloum,	France
2004	Yan Bhartelemy Varela,	Cuba

BOXING (Cont.)

FLYWEIGHT (112 LB)
1904 ....George Finnegan, United States
1920 ....Frank Di Gennara, United States
1924 ....Fidel LaBarba, United States
1928 ....Antal Kocsis, Hungary
1932 ....Istvan Enekes, Hungary
1936 ....Willi Kaiser, Germany
1948 ....Pascual Perez, Argentina
1952 ....Nathan Brooks, United States
1956 ....Terence Spinks, Great Britain
1960 ....Gyula Torok, Hungary
1964 ....Fernando Atzori, Italy
1968 ....Ricardo Delgado, Mexico
1972 ....Georgi Kostadinov, Bulgaria
1976 ....Leo Randolph, United States
1980 ....Peter Lessov, Bulgaria
1984 ....Steve McCrory, United States
1988 ....Kim Kwang Sun, S Korea
1992 ....Su Choi Chol, N Korea
1996 ....Maikro Romero, Cuba
2000 ....Wijan Ponlid, Thailand
2004 ....Yuriokis Toledano, Cuba

BANTAMWEIGHT (119 LB)
1904 ....Oliver Kirk, United States
1908 ....A. Henry Thomas, Great Britain
1920 ....Clarence Walker, S Africa
1924 ....William Smith, S Africa
1928 ....Vittorio Tamagnini, Italy
1932 ....Horace Gwynne, Canada
1936 ....Ulderico Sergo, Italy
1948 ....Tibor Csik, Hungary
1952 ....Pentti Hamalainen, Finland
1956 ....Wolfgang Behrendt, E Germany
1960 ....Oleg Grigoryev, USSR
1964 ....Takao Sakurai, Japan
1968 ....Valery Sokolov, USSR
1972 ....Orlando Martinez, Cuba
1976 ....Yong Jo Gu, N Korea
1980 ....Juan Hernandez, Cuba
1984 ....Maurizio Stecca, Italy
1988 ....Kennedy McKinney, United States
1992 ....Joel Casamayor, Cuba
1996 ....István Kovács, Hungary
2000 ....Guillermo Ortiz, Cuba
2004 ....Guillermo Ortiz, Cuba

FEATHERWEIGHT (125 LB)
1904 ....Oliver Kirk, United States
1908 ....Richard Gunn, Great Britain
1920 ....Paul Fritsch, France
1924 ....John Fields, United States
1928 ....Lambertus van Klaveren, Netherlands
1932 ....Carmelo Robledo, Argentina
1936 ....Oscar Casanovas, Argentina
1948 ....Ernesto Formenti, Italy
1952 ....Jan Zachara, Czechoslovakia
1956 ....Vladimir Safronov, USSR
1960 ....Francesco Musso, Italy
1964 ....Stanislav Stephashkin, USSR
1968 ....Antonio Roldan, Mexico
1972 ....Boris Kousnetsov, USSR
1976 ....Angel Herrera, Cuba
1980 ....Rudi Fink, E Germany
1984 ....Meldrick Taylor, United States
1988 ....Giovanni Parisi, Italy
1992 ....Andreas Tews, Germany
1996 ....Somluck Kamsing, Thailand
2000 ....Bekzat Sattarkhanox, Kazakhsta
2004 ....Alexei Tichtchenko, Russia

LIGHTWEIGHT (132 LB)
1904 ....Harry Spanger, United States
1908 ....Frederick Grace, Great Britain
1920 ....Samuel Mosberg, United States
1924 ....Hans Nielsen, Denmark
1928 ....Carlo Orlandi, Italy
1932 ....Lawrence Stevens, S Africa
1936 ....Imre Harangi, Hungary
1948 ....Gerald Dreyer, S Africa
1952 ....Aureliano Bolognesi, Italy
1956 ....Richard McTaggart, Great Britain
1960 ....Kazimierz Pazdzior, Poland
1964 ....Jozef Grudzien, Poland
1968 ....Ronald Harris, United States
1972 ....Jan Szczepanski, Poland
1976 ....Howard Davis, United States
1980 ....Angel Herrera, Cuba
1984 ....Pernell Whitaker, United States
1988 ....Andreas Zuelow, E Germany
1992 ....Oscar De La Hoya, United States
1996 ....Hocine Soltani, Algeria
2000 ....Mario Mesa, Cuba
2004 ....Mario Mesa, Cuba

LIGHT WELTERWEIGHT (139 LB)
1952 ....Charles Adkins, United States
1956 ....Vladimir Yengibaryan, USSR
1960 ....Bohumil Nemecek, Czechoslovakia
1964 ....Jerzy Kulej, Poland
1968 ....Jerzy Kulej, Poland
1972 ....Ray Seales, United States
1976 ....Ray Leonard, United States
1980 ....Patrizio Oliva, Italy
1984 ....Jerry Page, United States
1988 ....Viatcheslav Janovski, USSR
1992 ....Hector Vinent, Cuba
1996 ....Hector Vinent, Cuba
2000 ....Mahamadkadyz Abdullaev, Uzbekistan
2004 ....Manus Boonjumnong, Thailand

WELTERWEIGHT (147 LB)
1904 ....Albert Young, United States
1920 ....Albert Schneider, Canada
1924 ....Jean Delarge, Belgium
1928 ....Edward Morgan, New Zealand
1932 ....Edward Flynn, United States
1936 ....Sten Suvio, Finland
1948 ....Julius Torma, Czechoslovakia
1952 ....Zygmunt Chychla, Poland
1956 ....Nicolae Linca, Romania
1960 ....Giovanni Benvenuti, Italy
1964 ....Marian Kasprzyk, Poland
1968 ....Manfred Wolke, E Germany
1972 ....Emilio Correa, Cuba
1976 ....Jochen Bachfeld, E Germany
1980 ....Andres Aldama, Cuba
1984 ....Mark Breland, United States
1988 ....Robert Wangila, Kenya
1992 ....Michael Carruth, Ireland
1996 ....Oleg Saitov, Russia
2000 ....Oleg Saitov, Russia
2004 ....Bakhtiyar Artayev, Kazakhstan

LIGHT MIDDLEWEIGHT (156 LB)
1952 ....Laszlo Papp, Hungary
1956 ....Laszlo Papp, Hungary
1960 ....Wilbert McClure, United States
1964 ....Boris Lagutin, USSR
1968 ....Boris Lagutin, USSR
1972 ....Dieter Kottysch, W Germany
1976 ....Jerzy Rybicki, Poland
1980 ....Armando Martinez, Cuba
1984 ....Frank Tate, United States

BOXING (Cont.)

LIGHT MIDDLEWEIGHT (CONT.)

1988 ....Park Si-Hun, S Korea
1992 ....Juan Lemus, Cuba
1996 ....David Reid, United States
2000 ....Yermakhan Ibraimov, Kazakhstan

MIDDLEWEIGHT (165 LB)

1904 ....Charles Mayer, United States
1908 ....John Douglas, Great Britain
1920 ....Harry Mallin, Great Britain
1924 ....Harry Mallin, Great Britain
1928 ....Piero Toscani, Italy
1932 ....Carmen Barth, United States
1936 ....Jean Despeaux, France
1948 ....Laszlo Papp, Hungary
1952 ....Floyd Patterson, United States
1956 ....Gennady Schatkov, USSR
1960 ....Edward Crook, United States
1964 ....Valery Popenchenko, USSR
1968 ....Christopher Finnegan, Great Britain
1972 ....Vyacheslav Lemechev, USSR
1976 ....Michael Spinks, United States
1980 ....Jose Gomez, Cuba
1984 ....Shin Joon Sup, S Korea
1988 ....Henry Maske, E Germany
1992 ....Ariel Hernandez, Cuba
1996 ....Ariel Hernandez, Cuba
2000 ....Jorge Gutierrez, Cuba
2004 ....Gaydarbek Gaydarbekov, Russia

LIGHT HEAVYWEIGHT (178 LB)

1920 ....Edward Eagan, United States
1924 ....Harry Mitchell, Great Britain
1928 ....Victor Avendano, Argentina
1932 ....David Carstens, S Africa
1936 ....Roger Michelot, France
1948 ....George Hunter, S Africa
1952 ....Norvel Lee, United States
1956 ....James Boyd, United States
1960 ....Cassius Clay, United States
1964 ....Cosimo Pinto, Italy
1968 ....Dan Poznyak, USSR
1972 ....Mate Parlov, Yugoslavia
1976 ....Leon Spinks, United States

LIGHT HEAVYWEIGHT (CONT.)

1980 ....Slobodan Kacer, Yugoslavia
1984 ....Anton Josipovic, Yugoslavia
1988 ....Andrew Maynard, United States
1992 ....Torsten May, Germany
1996 ....Vassili Jirov, Kazakhstan
2000 ....Alexander Lebziak, Russia
2004 ....Andre Ward, United States

HEAVYWEIGHT (OVER 201 LB)

1904 ....Samuel Berger, United States
1908 ....Albert Oldham, Great Britain
1920 ....Ronald Rawson, Great Britain
1924 ....Otto von Porat, Norway
1928 ....Arturo Rodriguez Jurado, Argentina
1932 ....Santiago Lovell, Argentina
1936 ....Herbert Runge, Germany
1948 ....Rafael Inglesias, Argentina
1952 ....H. Edward Sanders, United States
1956 ....T. Peter Rademacher, United States
1960 ....Franco De Piccoli, Italy
1964 ....Joe Frazier, United States
1968 ....George Foreman, United States
1972 ....Teofilo Stevenson, Cuba
1976 ....Teofilo Stevenson, Cuba
1980 ....Teofilo Stevenson, Cuba

HEAVYWEIGHT (201* LB)

1984 ....Henry Tillman, United States
1988 ....Ray Mercer, United States
1992 ....Félix Sávon, Cuba
1996 ....Félix Sávon, Cuba
2000 ....Félix Sávon, Cuba
2004 ....Odlanier Fonte, Cuba

SUPERHEAVYWEIGHT (UNLIMITED)

1984 ....Tyrell Biggs, United States
1988 ....Lennox Lewis, Canada
1992 ....Roberto Balado, Cuba
1996 ....Vladimir Klitchko, Ukraine
2000 ....Audley Harrison, Great Britain
2004 ....Alexander Povetkin, Russia

*Until 1984 the heavyweight division was unlimited. With the addition of the super heavyweight division, a limit of 201 pounds was imposed.

SWIMMING— Men

50-METER FREESTYLE

1904	Zoltan Halmay, Hungary (50 yds)	28.0
1988	Matt Biondi, United States	22.14 WR
1992	Aleksandr Popov, Unified Team	22.30
1996	Aleksandr Popov, Russia	22.13
2000	Anthony Ervin, United States	21.98
	Gary Hall Jr, United States	21.98
2004	Gary Hall Jr, United States	21.93

100-METER FREESTLYE

1896	Alfred Hajos, Hungary	1:22.2 OR
1904	Zoltan Halmay, Hungary (100 yds)	1:02.8
1906	Charles Daniels, United States	1:13.4
1908	Charles Daniels, United States	1:05.6 WR
1912	Duke Kahanamoku, United States	1:03.4
1920	Duke Kahanamoku, United States	1:00.4 WR
1924	John Weissmuller, United States	59.0 OR
1928	John Weissmuller, United States	58.6 OR
1932	Yasuji Miyazaki, Japan	58.2
1936	Ferenc Csik, Hungary	57.6
1948	Wally Ris, United States	57.3 OR
1952	Clarke Scholes, United States	57.4
1956	Jon Henricks, Australia	55.4 OR

100-METER FREESTLYE (CONT.)

1960	John Devitt, Australia	55.2 OR
1964	Don Schollander, United States	53.4 OR
1968	Mike Wenden, Australia	52.2 WR
1972	Mark Spitz, United States	51.22 WR
1976	Jim Montgomery, United States	49.99 WR
1980	Jörg Woithe, E Germany	50.40
1984	Rowdy Gaines, United States	49.80 OR
1988	Matt Biondi, United States	48.63 OR
1992	Aleksandr Popov, Unified Team	49.02
1996	Aleksandr Popov, Russia	48.74
2000	P. van den Hoogenband, Neth	48.30
2004	P. van den Hoogenband, Neth	48.17

200-METER FREESTYLE

1900	Frederick Lane, Australia	2:25.2 OR
1904	Charles Daniels, United States	2:44.2
1968	Michael Wenden, Australia	1:55.2 OR
1972	Mark Spitz, United States	1:52.78 WR
1976	Bruce Furniss, United States	1:50.29 WR
1980	Sergei Kopliakov, USSR	1:49.81 OR
1984	Michael Gross, W Germany	1:47.44 WR

SWIMMING— Men *(Cont.)*

200-METER FREESTYLE *(CONT.)*

1988	Duncan Armstrong, Australia	1:47.25 WR
1992	Evgueni Sadovyi, Unified Team	1:46.70 OR
1996	Danyon Loader, New Zealand	1:47.63
2000	Pieter van den Hoogenband, Neth	1:45.35 EWR
2004	Ian Thorpe, Australia	1:44.71 OR

400-METER FREESTYLE

1896	Paul Neumann, Austria (500 yds)	8:12.6
1904	Charles Daniels, U.S. (440 yds)	6:16.2
1906	Otto Scheff, Austria (440 yds)	6:23.8
1908	Henry Taylor, Great Britain	5:36.8
1912	George Hodgson, Canada	5:24.4
1920	Norman Ross, United States	5:26.8
1924	John Weissmuller, United States	5:04.2 OR
1928	Albert Zorilla, Argentina	5:01.6 OR
1932	Buster Crabbe, United States	4:48.4 OR
1936	Jack Medica, United States	4:44.5 OR
1948	William Smith, United States	4:41.0 OR
1952	Jean Boiteux, France	4:30.7 OR
1956	Murray Rose, Australia	4:27.3 OR
1960	Murray Rose, Australia	4:18.3 OR
1964	Don Schollander, United States	4:12.2 WR
1968	Mike Burton, United States	4:09.0 OR
1972	Brad Cooper, Australia	4:00.27 OR
1976	Brian Goodell, United States	3:51.93 WR
1980	Vladimir Salnikov, USSR	3:51.31 OR
1984	George DiCarlo, United States	3:51.23 OR
1988	Uwe Dassler, E Germany	3:46.95 WR
1992	Evgueni Sadovyi, Unified Team	3:45.00 WR
1996	Danyon Loader, New Zealand	3:47.97
2000	Ian Thorpe, Australia	3:40.59 WR
2004	Ian Thorpe, Australia	3:43.10

1,500-METER FREESTYLE

1908	Henry Taylor, Great Britain	22:48.4 WR
1912	George Hodgson, Canada	22:00.0 WR
1920	Norman Ross, United States	22:23.2
1924	Andrew Charlton, Australia	20:06.6 WR
1928	Arne Borg, Sweden	19:51.8 OR
1932	Kusuo Kitamura, Japan	19:12.4 OR
1936	Noboru Terada, Japan	19:13.7
1948	James McLane, United States	19:18.5
1952	Ford Konno, United States	18:30.3 OR
1956	Murray Rose, Australia	17:58.9
1960	John Konrads, Australia	17:19.6 OR
1964	Robert Windle, Australia	17:01.7 OR
1968	Mike Burton, United States	16:38.9 OR
1972	Mike Burton, United States	15:52.58 OR
1976	Brian Goodell, United States	15:02.40 WR
1980	Vladimir Salnikov, USSR	14:58.27 WR
1984	Michael O'Brien, United States	15:05.20
1988	Vladimir Salnikov, USSR	15:00.40
1992	Kieren Perkins, Australia	14:43.48 WR
1996	Kieren Perkins, Australia	14:56.40
2000	Grant Hackett, Australia	14:48.33
2004	Grant Hackett, Australia	14:43.40 OR

100-METER BACKSTROKE

1904	Walter Brack, Germany (100 yds)	1:16.8
1908	Arno Bieberstein, Germany	1:24.6 WR
1912	Harry Hebner, United States	1:21.2
1920	Warren Kealoha, United States	1:15.2
1924	Warren Kealoha, United States	1:13.2 OR
1928	George Kojac, United States	1:08.2 WR
1932	Masaji Kiyokawa, Japan	1:08.6
1936	Adolph Kiefer, United States	1:05.9 OR
1948	Allen Stack, United States	1:06.4
1952	Yoshi Oyakawa, United States	1:05.4 OR

100-METER BACKSTROKE *(CONT.)*

1956	David Thiele, Australia	1:02.2 OR
1960	David Thiele, Australia	1:01.9 OR
1968	Roland Matthes, E Germany	58.7 OR
1972	Roland Matthes, E Germany	56.58 OR
1976	John Naber, United States	55.49 WR
1980	Bengt Baron, Sweden	56.33
1984	Rick Carey, United States	55.79
1988	Daichi Suzuki, Japan	55.05
1992	Mark Tewksbury, Canada	53.98 WR
1996	Jeff Rouse, United States	54.10
2000	Lenny Krayzelburg, United States	53.72 OR
2004	Aaron Peirsol, United States	54.06

200-METER BACKSTROKE

1900	Ernst Hoppenberg, Germany	2:47.0
1964	Jed Graef, United States	2:10.3 WR
1968	Roland Matthes, E Germany	2:09.6 OR
1972	Roland Matthes, E Germany	2:02.82 EWR
1976	John Naber, United States	1:59.19 WR
1980	Sandor Wladar, Hungary	2:01.93
1984	Rick Carey, United States	2:00.23
1988	Igor Polianski, USSR	1:59.37
1992	Martin Lopez-Zubero, Spain	1:58.47 OR
1996	Brad Bridgewater, United States	1:58.54
2000	Lenny Krayzelburg, United States	1:56.76 OR
2004	Aaron Peirsol, United States	1:54.95 OR

100-METER BREASTSTROKE

1968	Don McKenzie, United States	1:07.7 OR
1972	Nobutaka Taguchi, Japan	1:04.94 WR
1976	John Hencken, United States	1:03.11 WR
1980	Duncan Goodhew, Great Britain	1:03.44
1984	Steve Lundquist, United States	1:01.65 WR
1988	Adrian Moorhouse, Great Britain	1:02.04
1992	Nelson Diebel, United States	1:01.50 OR
1996	Fred DeBurghgraeve, Belgium	1:00.65
2000	Domenico Fioravanti, Italy	1:00.46 OR
2004	Kosuke Kitajima, Japan	1:00.08

200-METER BREASTSTROKE

1908	Frederick Holman, Great Britain	3:09.2 WR
1912	Walter Bathe, Germany	3:01.8 OR
1920	Haken Malmroth, Sweden	3:04.4
1924	Robert Skelton, United States	2:56.6
1928	Yoshiyuki Tsuruta, Japan	2:48.8 OR
1932	Yoshiyuki Tsuruta, Japan	2:45.4
1936	Tetsuo Hamuro, Japan	2:41.5 OR
1948	Joseph Verdeur, United States	2:39.3 OR
1952	John Davies, Australia	2:34.4 OR
1956	Masaru Furukawa, Japan	2:34.7 OR
1960	William Mulliken, United States	2:37.4
1964	Ian O'Brien, Australia	2:27.8 WR
1968	Felipe Munoz, Mexico	2:28.7
1972	John Hencken, United States	2:21.55 WR
1976	David Wilkie, Great Britain	2:15.11 WR
1980	Robertas Zhulpa, USSR	2:15.85
1984	Victor Davis, Canada	2:13.34 WR
1988	Jozsef Szabo, Hungary	2:13.52
1992	Mike Barrowman, United States	2:10.16 WR
1996	Norbert Rózsa, Hungary	2:12.57
2000	Domenico Fioravanti, Italy	2:10.87
2004	Kosuke Kitajima, Japan	2:09.44 OR

100-METER BUTTERFLY

1968	Doug Russell, United States	55.9 OR
1972	Mark Spitz, United States	54.27 WR
1976	Matt Vogel, United States	54.35
1980	Pär Arvidsson, Sweden	54.92

Note: OR=Olympic Record. WR=World Record. EOR=Equals Olympic Record. EWR=Equals World Record. WB=World Best.

SWIMMING — Men (Cont.)

100-METER BUTTERFLY (CONT.)

1984	Michael Gross, W Germany	53.08 WR
1988	Anthony Nesty, Suriname	53.00 OR
1992	Pablo Morales, United States	53.32
1996	Denis Pankratov, Russia	52.27 WR
2000	Lars Froelander, Sweden	52.00
2004	Michael Phelps, United States	51.25 OR

200-METER BUTTERFLY

1956	William Yorzyk, United States	2:19.3 OR
1960	Michael Troy, United States	2:12.8 WR
1964	Kevin Berry, Australia	2:06.6 WR
1968	Carl Robie, United States	2:08.7
1972	Mark Spitz, United States	2:00.70 WR
1976	Mike Bruner, United States	1:59.23 WR
1980	Sergei Fesenko, USSR	1:59.76
1984	Jon Sieben, Australia	1:57.04 WR
1988	Michael Gross, W Germany	1:56.94 OR
1992	Melvin Stewart, United States	1:56.26 OR
1996	Denis Pankratov, Russia	1:56.51
2000	Tom Malchow, United States	1:55.35 OR
2004	Michael Phelps, United States	1:54.04 OR

200-METER INDIVIDUAL MEDLEY

1968	Charles Hickcox, United States	2:12.0 OR
1972	Gunnar Larsson, Sweden	2:07.17 WR
1984	Alex Baumann, Canada	2:01.42 WR
1988	Tamas Darnyi, Hungary	2:00.17 WR
1992	Tamas Darnyi, Hungary	2:00.76
1996	Attila Czene, Hungary	1:59.91 OR
2000	Massimiliano Rosolino, Italy	1:58.98 OR
2004	Michael Phelps, United States	1:57.14 OR

400-METER INDIVIDUAL MEDLEY

1964	Richard Roth, United States	4:45.4 WR
1968	Charles Hickcox, United States	4:48.4
1972	Gunnar Larsson, Sweden	4:31.98 OR
1976	Rod Strachan, United States	4:23.68 WR
1980	Aleksandr Sidorenko, USSR	4:22.89 OR
1984	Alex Baumann, Canada	4:17.41 WR
1988	Tamas Darnyi, Hungary	4:14.75 WR
1992	Tamas Darnyi, Hungary	4:14.23 OR
1996	Tom Dolan United States	4:14.90
2000	Tom Dolan, United States	4:11.76 WR
2004	Michael Phelps, United States	4:08.26 WR

4 X 100-METER MEDLEY RELAY

1960	United States	4:05.4 WR
1964	United States	3:58.4 WR

4 X 100-METER MEDLEY RELAY (CONT.)

1968	United States	3:54.9 WR
1972	United States	3:48.16 WR
1976	United States	3:42.22 WR
1980	Australia	3:45.70
1984	United States	3:39.30 WR
1988	United States	3:36.93 WR
1992	United States	3:36.93 EWR
1996	United States	3:34.84 WR
2000	United States	3:33.73 WR
2004	United States	3:30.68 WR

4 X 100-METER FREESTYLE RELAY

1964	United States	3:32.2 WR
1968	United States	3:31.7 WR
1972	United States	3:26.42 WR
1984	United States	3:19.03 WR
1988	United States	3:16.53 WR
1992	United States	3:16.74
1996	United States	3:15.41 OR
2000	Australia	3:13.67 WR
2004	S Africa	3:13.17 WR

4 X 200-METER FREESTYLE RELAY

1906	Hungary (1,000 m)	16:52.4
1908	Great Britain	10:55.6
1912	Australia/New Zealand	10:11.6 WR
1920	United States	10:04.4 WR
1924	United States	9:53.4 WR
1928	United States	9:36.2 WR
1932	Japan	8:58.4 WR
1936	Japan	8:51.5 WR
1948	United States	8:46.0 WR
1952	United States	8:31.1 OR
1956	Australia	8:23.6 WR
1960	United States	8:10.2 WR
1964	United States	7:52.1 WR
1968	United States	7:52.33
1972	United States	7:35.78 WR
1976	United States	7:23.22 WR
1980	USSR	7:23.50
1984	United States	7:15.69 WR
1988	United States	7:12.51 WR
1992	Unified Team	7:11.95 WR
1996	United States	7:14.84
2000	Australia	7:07.05 WR
2004	United States	7:07.33

SWIMMING — Women

50-METER FREESTYLE

1988	Kristin Otto, E Germany	25.49 OR
1992	Yang Wenyi, China	24.79 WR
1996	Amy Van Dyken, United States	24.87
2000	Inge de Bruijn, Netherlands	24.32 WR
2004	Inge de Bruijn, Netherlands	24.58

100-METER FREESTYLE

1912	Fanny Durack, Australia	1:22.2
1920	Ethelda Bleibtrey, United States	1:13.6 WR
1924	Ethel Lackie, United States	1:12.4
1928	Albina Osipowich, United States	1:11.0 OR
1932	Helene Madison, United States	1:06.8 OR
1936	Hendrika Mastenbroek, Neth	1:05.9 OR
1948	Greta Andersen, Denmark	1:06.3
1952	Katalin Szöke, Hungary	1:06.8
1956	Dawn Fraser, Australia	1:02.0 WR
1960	Dawn Fraser, Australia	1:01.2 OR
1964	Dawn Fraser, Australia	59.5 OR

100-METER FREESTYLE (CONT.)

1968	Jan Henne, United States	1:00.0
1972	Sandra Neilson, United States	58.59 OR
1976	Kornelia Ender, E Germany	55.65 WR
1980	Barbara Krause, E Germany	54.79 WR
1984	Carrie Steinseifer, United States	55.92
	Nancy Hogshead, United States	55.92
1988	Kristin Otto, E Germany	54.93
1992	Zhuang Yong, China	54.64 OR
1996	Le Jingyi, China	54.50 OR
2000	Inge de Bruijn, Netherlands	53.83 OR
2004	Jodie Henry, Australia	53.84

200-METER FREESTYLE

1968	Debbie Meyer, United States	2:10.5 OR
1972	Shane Gould, Australia	2:03.56 WR
1976	Kornelia Ender, E Germany	1:59.26 WR
1980	Barbara Krause, E Germany	1:58.33 OR
1984	Mary Wayte, United States	1:59.23
1988	Heike Friedrich, E Germany	1:57.65 OR

Note: OR=Olympic Record. WR=World Record. EOR=Equals Olympic Record. EWR=Equals World Record. WB=World Best.

SWIMMING — Women *(Cont.)*

200-METER FREESTYLE *(CONT.)*

1992	Nicole Haislett, United States	1:57.90
1996	Claudia Poll, Costa Rica	1:58.16
2000	Susie O'Neill, Australia	1:58.24
2004	Camelia Potec, Romania	1:58.03

400-METER FREESTYLE

1924	Martha Norelius, United States	6:02.2 OR
1928	Martha Norelius, United States	5:42.8 WR
1932	Helene Madison, United States	5:28.5 WR
1936	Hendrika Mastenbroek, Neth	5:26.4 OR
1948	Ann Curtis, United States	5:17.8 OR
1952	Valeria Gyenge, Hungary	5:12.1 OR
1956	Lorraine Crapp, Australia	4:54.6 OR
1960	Chris von Saltza, United States	4:50.6 OR
1964	Virginia Duenkel, United States	4:43.3 OR
1968	Debbie Meyer, United States	4:31.8 OR
1972	Shane Gould, Australia	4:19.44 WR
1976	Petra Thümer, E Germany	4:09.89 WR
1980	Ines Diers, E Germany	4:08.76 WR
1984	Tiffany Cohen, United States	4:07.10 OR
1988	Janet Evans, United States	4:03.85 WR
1992	Dagmar Hase, Germany	4:07.18
1996	Michelle Smith, Ireland	4:07.25
2000	Brooke Bennett, United States	4:05.80
2004	Laure Manaudou, France	4:05.34

800-METER FREESTYLE

1968	Debbie Meyer, United States	9:24.0 OR
1972	Keena Rothhammer, United States	8:53.68 WR
1976	Petra Thümer, E Germany	8:37.14 WR
1980	Michelle Ford, Australia	8:28.90 OR
1984	Tiffany Cohen, United States	8:24.95 OR
1988	Janet Evans, United States	8:20.20 OR
1992	Janet Evans, United States	8:25.52
1996	Brooke Bennett, United States	8:27.89
2000	Brooke Bennett, United States	8:19.67 OR
2004	Ai Shibata, Japan	8:24.54

100-METER BACKSTROKE

1924	Sybil Bauer, United States	1:23.2 OR
1928	Marie Braun, Netherlands	1:22.0
1932	Eleanor Holm, United States	1:19.4
1936	Dina Senff, Netherlands	1:18.9
1948	Karen Harup, Denmark	1:14.4 OR
1952	Joan Harrison, South Africa	1:14.3
1956	Judy Grinham, Great Britain	1:12.9 OR
1960	Lynn Burke, United States	1:09.3 OR
1964	Cathy Ferguson, United States	1:07.7 WR
1968	Kaye Hall, United States	1:06.2 WR
1972	Melissa Belote, United States	1:05.78 OR
1976	Ulrike Richter, E Germany	1:01.83 OR
1980	Rica Reinisch, E Germany	1:00.86 WR
1984	Theresa Andrews, United States	1:02.55
1988	Kristin Otto, E Germany	1:00.89
1992	Krisztina Egerszegi, Hungary	1:00.68 OR
1996	Beth Botsford, United States	1:01.19
2000	Diana Iuliana Mocanu, Romania	1:00.21 OR
2004	Natalie Coughlin, United States	1:00.37

200-METER BACKSTROKE

1968	Pokey Watson, United States	2:24.8 OR
1972	Melissa Belote, United States	2:19.19 WR
1976	Ulrike Richter, E Germany	2:13.43 OR
1980	Rica Reinisch, E Germany	2:11.77 WR
1984	Jolanda De Rover, Netherlands	2:12.38
1988	Krisztina Egerszegi, Hungary	2:09.29 OR
1992	Krisztina Egerszegi, Hungary	2:07.06 OR
1996	Krisztina Egerszegi, Hungary	2:07.83
2000	Diana Iuliana Mocanu, Romania	2:08.16
2004	Kirsty Coventry, Zimbabwe	2:09.19

100-METER BREASTSTROKE

1968	Djurdjica Bjedov, Yugoslavia	1:15.8 OR
1972	Catherine Carr, United States	1:13.58 WR
1976	Hannelore Anke, E Germany	1:11.16
1980	Ute Geweniger, E Germany	1:10.22
1984	Petra Van Staveren, Netherlands	1:09.88 OR
1988	Tania Dangalakova, Bulgaria	1:07.95 OR
1992	Elena Roudkovskaia, Unified Team	1:08.00
1996	Penelope Heyns, S Africa	1:07.73
2000	Megan Quann, United States	1:07.05
2004	Xue Juan Luo, China	1:06.64

200-METER BREASTSTROKE

1924	Lucy Morton, Great Britain	3:33.2 OR
1928	Hilde Schrader, Germany	3:12.6
1932	Clare Dennis, Australia	3:06.3 OR
1936	Hideko Maehata, Japan	3:03.6
1948	Petronella Van Vliet, Netherlands	2:57.2
1952	Eva Szekely, Hungary	2:51.7 OR
1956	Ursula Happe, W Germany	2:53.1 OR
1960	Anita Lonsbrough, Great Britain	2:49.5 WR
1964	Galina Prozumenshikova, USSR	2:46.4 OR
1968	Sharon Wichman, United States	2:44.4 OR
1972	Beverly Whitfield, Australia	2:41.71 OR
1976	Marina Koshevaia, USSR	2:33.35 WR
1980	Lina Kaciusyte, USSR	2:29.54 OR
1984	Anne Ottenbrite, Canada	2:30.38
1988	Silke Hoerner, E Germany	2:26.71 WR
1992	Kyoko Iwasaki, Japan	2:26.65 OR
1996	Penelope Heyns, S Africa	2:25.41 OR
2000	Agnes Kovacs, Hungary	2:24.35 OR
2004	Amanda Beard, United States	2:23.37 OR

100-METER BUTTERFLY

1956	Shelley Mann, United States	1:11.0 OR
1960	Carolyn Schuler, United States	1:09.5 OR
1964	Sharon Stouder, United States	1:04.7 WR
1968	Lynn McClements, Australia	1:05.5
1972	Mayumi Aoki, Japan	1:03.34 WR
1976	Kornelia Ender, E Germany	1:00.13 EWR
1980	Caren Metschuck, E Germany	1:00.42
1984	Mary T. Meagher, United States	59.26
1988	Kristin Otto, E Germany	59.00 OR
1992	Qian Hong, China	58.62 OR
1996	Amy Van Dyken, United States	59.13
2000	Inge de Bruijn, Netherlands	56.61 WR
2004	Petria Thomas, Australia	57.72

200-METER BUTTERFLY

1968	Ada Kok, Netherlands	2:24.7 OR
1972	Karen Moe, United States	2:15.57 WR
1976	Andrea Pollack, E Germany	2:11.41 OR
1980	Ines Geissler, E Germany	2:10.44 OR
1984	Mary T. Meagher, United States	2:06.90 OR
1988	Kathleen Nord, E Germany	2:09.51
1992	Summer Sanders, United States	2:08.67
1996	Susan O'Neill, Australia	2:07.76
2000	Misty Hyman, United States	2:05.88 OR
2004	Otylia Jedrzegczak, Poland	2:06.05

200-METER INDIVIDUAL MEDLEY

1968	Claudia Kolb, United States	2:24.7 OR
1972	Shane Gould, Australia	2:23.07 WR
1984	Tracy Caulkins, United States	2:12.64 OR
1988	Daniela Hunger, E Germany	2:12.59 OR
1992	Lin Li, China	2:11.65 WR
1996	Michelle Smith, Ireland	2:13.93
2000	Yana Klochkova, Ukraine	2:10.68 OR
2004	Yana Klochkova, Ukraine	2:11.14

Note: OR=Olympic Record. WR=World Record. EOR=Equals Olympic Record. EWR=Equals World Record. WB=World Best.

SWIMMING — Women *(Cont.)*

400-METER INDIVIDUAL MEDLEY

1964	Donna de Varona, United States	5:18.7 OR
1968	Claudia Kolb, United States	5:08.5 OR
1972	Gail Neall, Australia	5:02.97 WR
1976	Ulrike Tauber, E Germany	4:42.77 WR
1980	Petra Schneider, E Germany	4:36.29 WR
1984	Tracy Caulkins, United States	4:39.24
1988	Janet Evans, United States	4:37.76
1992	Krisztina Egerszegi, Hungary	4:36.54
1996	Michelle Smith, Ireland	4:39.18
2000	Yana Klochkova, Ukraine	4:33.59 WR
2004	Yana Klochkova, Ukraine	4:34.83

4 X 100-METER MEDLEY RELAY

1960	United States	4:41.1 WR
1964	United States	4:33.9 WR
1968	United States	4:28.3 OR
1972	United States	4:20.75 WR
1976	E Germany	4:07.95 WR
1980	E Germany	4:06.67 WR
1984	United States	4:08.34
1988	E Germany	4:03.74 OR
1992	United States	4:02.54 WR
1996	United States	4:02.88
2000	United States	3:58.30 WR
2004	Australia	3:57.32 WR

4 X 100-METER FREESTYLE RELAY

1912	Great Britain	5:52.8 WR
1920	United States	5:11.6 WR
1924	United States	4:58.8 WR
1928	United States	4:47.6 WR
1932	United States	4:38.0 WR
1936	Netherlands	4:36.0 OR
1948	United States	4:29.2 OR
1952	Hungary	4:24.4 WR
1956	Australia	4:17.1 WR
1960	United States	4:08.9 WR
1964	United States	4:03.8 WR
1968	United States	4:02.5 OR
1972	United States	3:55.19 WR
1976	United States	3:44.82 WR
1980	E Germany	3:42.71 WR
1984	United States	3:43.43
1988	E Germany	3:40.63 OR
1992	United States	3:39.46 WR
1996	United States	3:39.29 OR
2000	United States	3:36.61 WR
2004	Australia	3:35.94 WR

4 X 200-METER FREESTYLE RELAY

1996	United States	7:59.87
2000	United States	7:57.80 OR
2004	United States	7:53.42 WR

DIVING — Men

SPRINGBOARD		Pts
1908	Albert Zürner, Germany	85.5
1912	Paul Günther, Germany	79.23
1920	Louis Kuehn, United States	675.40
1924	Albert White, United States	97.46
1928	Pete DesJardins, United States	185.04
1932	Michael Galitzen, United States	161.38
1936	Richard Degener, United States	163.57
1948	Bruce Harlan, United States	163.64
1952	David Browning, United States	205.29
1956	Robert Clotworthy, United States	159.56
1960	Gary Tobian, United States	170.00
1964	Kenneth Sitzberger, United States	159.90
1968	Bernie Wrightson, United States	170.15
1972	Vladimir Vasin, USSR	594.09
1976	Phil Boggs, United States	619.05
1980	Aleksandr Portnov, USSR	905.02
1984	Greg Louganis, United States	754.41
1988	Greg Louganis, United States	730.80
1992	Mark Lenzi, United States	676.53
1996	Xiong Ni, China	701.46
2000	Xiong Ni, China	708.72
2004	Bo Peng, China	787.38

PLATFORM		Pts
1904	George Sheldon, United States	12.66
1906	Gottlob Walz, Germany	156.0
1908	Hjalmar Johansson, Sweden	83.75
1912	Erik Adlerz, Sweden	73.94
1920	Clarence Pinkston, United States	100.67
1924	Albert White, United States	97.46
1928	Pete DesJardins, United States	98.74
1932	Harold Smith, United States	124.80
1936	Marshall Wayne, United States	113.58
1948	Sammy Lee, United States	130.05
1952	Sammy Lee, United States	156.28
1956	Joaquin Capilla, Mexico	152.44
1960	Robert Webster, United States	165.56
1964	Robert Webster, United States	148.58
1968	Klaus Dibiasi, Italy	164.18
1972	Klaus Dibiasi, Italy	504.12
1976	Klaus Dibiasi, Italy	600.51
1980	Falk Hoffmann, E Germany	835.65
1984	Greg Louganis, United States	710.91
1988	Greg Louganis, United States	638.61
1992	Sun Shuwei, China	677.31
1996	Dmitri Sautin, Russia	692.34
2000	Tian Liang, China	724.53
2004	Jia Hu, China	748.08

DIVING — Women

SPRINGBOARD		Pts
1920	Aileen Riggin, United States	539.90
1924	Elizabeth Becker, United States	474.50
1928	Helen Meany, United States	78.62
1932	Georgia Coleman, United States	87.52
1936	Marjorie Gestring, United States	89.27
1948	Victoria Draves, United States	108.74
1952	Patricia McCormick, United States	147.30
1956	Patricia McCormick, United States	142.36
1960	Ingrid Krämer, E Germany	155.81
1964	Ingrid Engel Krämer, E Germany	145.00

SPRINGBOARD *(CONT.)*		Pts
1968	Sue Gossick, United States	150.77
1972	Micki King, United States	450.03
1976	Jennifer Chandler, United States	506.19
1980	Irina Kalinina, USSR	725.91
1984	Sylvie Bernier, Canada	530.70
1988	Gao Min, China	580.23
1992	Gao Min, China	572.40
1996	Fu Mingxia, China	547.68
2000	Fu Mingxia, China	609.42
2004	Jingjing Guo, China	633.15

DIVING — Women (*Cont.*)

PLATFORM		Pts	PLATFORM		Pts
1912	Greta Johansson, Sweden	39.90	1968	Milena Duchkova, Czechoslovakia	109.59
1920	Stefani Fryland-Clausen, Denmark	34.60	1972	Ulrika Knape, Sweden	390.00
1924	Caroline Smith, United States	33.20	1976	Elena Vaytsekhovskaya, USSR	406.59
1928	Elizabeth B. Pinkston, United States	31.60	1980	Martina Jäschke, E Germany	596.25
1932	Dorothy Poynton, United States	40.26	1984	Zhou Jihong, China	435.51
1936	Dorothy Poynton Hill, United States	33.93	1988	Xu Yanmei, China	445.20
1948	Victoria Draves, United States	68.87	1992	Mingxia Fu, China	461.43
1952	Patricia McCormick, United States	79.37	1996	Mingxia Fu, China	521.58
1956	Patricia McCormick, United States	84.85	2000	Laura Wilkinson, United States	543.75
1960	Ingrid Krämer, E Germany	91.28	2004	Chantelle Newbery, Australia	590.31
1964	Lesley Bush, United States	99.80			

GYMNASTICS — Men

ALL-AROUND		Pts	PARALLEL BARS (*CONT*)		Pts
1900	Gustave Sandras, France	302	1924	August Güttinger, Switzerland	21.63
1904	Julius Lenhart, Austria	69.80	1928	Ladislav Vacha, Czechoslovakia	18.83
1906	Pierre Paysse, France	97	1932	Romeo Neri, Italy	18.97
1908	Alberto Braglia, Italy	317.0	1936	Konrad Frey, Germany	19.067
1912	Alberto Braglia, Italy	135.0	1948	Michael Reusch, Switzerland	19.75
1920	Giorgio Zampori, Italy	88.35	1952	Hans Eugster, Switzerland	19.65
1924	Leon Stukelj, Yugoslavia	110.340	1956	Viktor Chukarin, USSR	19.20
1928	Georges Miez, Switzerland	247.500	1960	Boris Shakhlin, USSR	19.40
1932	Romeo Neri, Italy	140.625	1964	Yukio Endo, Japan	19.675
1936	Alfred Schwarzmann, Germany	113.100	1968	Akinori Nakayama, Japan	19.475
1948	Veikko Huhtanen, Finland	229.70	1972	Sawao Kato, Japan	19.475
1952	Viktor Chukarin, USSR	115.70	1976	Sawao Kato, Japan	19.675
1956	Viktor Chukarin, USSR	114.25	1980	Aleksandr Tkachyov, USSR	19.775
1960	Boris Shakhlin, USSR	115.95	1984	Bart Conner, United States	19.95
1964	Yukio Endo, Japan	115.95	1988	Vladimir Artemov, USSR	19.925
1968	Sawao Kato, Japan	115.90	1992	Vitaly Scherbo, Unified Team	9.900
1972	Sawao Kato, Japan	114.65	1996	Rustan Sharipov, Ukraine	9.837
1976	Nikolai Andrianov, USSR	116.65	2000	Xiaopeng Li, China	9.825
1980	Aleksandr Dityatin, USSR	118.65	2004	Valeri Goncharov, Ukraine	9.787
1984	Koji Gushiken, Japan	118.70			
1988	Vladimir Artemov, USSR	119.125	VAULT		Pts
1992	Vitaly Scherbo, Unified Team	59.025	1896	Karl Schumann, Germany	—
1996	Li Xiaoshuang, China	58.423	1904	George Eyser, United States	36
2000	Alexei Nemov, Russia	58.474	1924	Frank Kriz, United States	9.98
2004	Paul Hamm, United States	57.823	1928	Eugen Mack, Switzerland	9.58
			1932	Savino Guglielmetti, Italy	18.03
HORIZONTAL BAR		Pts	1936	Alfred Schwarzmann, Germany	19.20
1896	Hermann Weingärtner, Germany	—	1948	Paavo Aaltonen, Finland	19.55
1904	Anton Heida, United States	40	1952	Viktor Chukarin, USSR	19.20
1924	Leon Stukelj, Yugoslavia	19.73	1956	Helmut Bantz, Germany	18.85
1928	Georges Miez, Switzerland	19.17	1960	Takashi Ono, Japan	19.35
1932	Dallas Bixler, United States	18.33	1964	Haruhiro Yamashita, Japan	19.60
1936	Aleksanteri Saarvala, Finland	19.367	1968	Mikhail Voronin, USSR	19.00
1948	Josef Stalder, Switzerland	19.85	1972	Klaus Köste, E Germany	18.85
1952	Jack Günthard, Switzerland	19.55	1976	Nikolai Andrianov, USSR	19.45
1956	Takashi Ono, Japan	19.60	1980	Nikolai Andrianov, USSR	19.825
1960	Takashi Ono, Japan	19.60	1984	Lou Yun, China	19.95
1964	Boris Shakhlin, USSR	19.625	1988	Lou Yun, China	19.875
1968	Akinori Nakayama, Japan	19.55	1992	Vitaly Scherbo, Unified Team	9.856
1972	Mitsuo Tsukahara, Japan	19.725	1996	Alexei Nemov, Russia	9.787
1976	Mitsuo Tsukahara, Japan	19.675	2000	Gervasio Deferr, Spain	9.712
1980	Stoyan Deltchev, Bulgaria	19.825	2004	Gervasio Deferr, Spain	9.737
1984	Shinji Morisue, Japan	20.00			
1988	Vladimir Artemov, USSR	19.90	POMMEL HORSE		Pts
1992	Trent Dimas, United States	9.875	1896	Louis Zutter, Switzerland	—
1996	Andreas Wecker, Germany	9.850	1904	Anton Heida, United States	42
2000	Alexei Nemov, Russia	9.787	1924	Josef Wilhelm, Switzerland	21.23
2004	Igor Cassina, Italy	9.812	1928	Hermann Hänggi, Switzerland	19.75
			1932	Istvan Pelle, Hungary	19.07
PARALLEL BARS		Pts	1936	Konrad Frey, Germany	19.333
1896	Alfred Flatow, Germany	—	1948	Paavo Aaltonen, Finland	19.35
1904	George Eyser, United States	44	1952	Viktor Chukarin, USSR	19.50

GYMNASTICS — Men (Cont.)

POMMEL HORSE (CONT.)	Pts
1956.....Boris Shakhlin, USSR	19.25
1960.....Eugen Ekman, Finland	19.375
1964.....Miroslav Cerar, Yugoslavia	19.525
1968.....Miroslav Cerar, Yugoslavia	19.325
1972.....Viktor Klimenko, USSR	19.125
1976.....Zoltan Magyar, Hungary	19.70
1980.....Zoltan Magyar, Hungary	19.925
1984.....Li Ning, China	19.95
1988.....Dmitri Bilozerchev, USSR	19.95
1992.....Vitaly Scherbo, Unified Team	9.925
1996.....Donghua Li, Switzerland	9.875
2000.....Marius Urzica, Romania	9.862
2004.....Haibin Teng, China	9.837

RINGS	Pts
1896.....Ioannis Mitropoulos, Greece	—
1904.....Hermann Glass, United States	45
1924.....Francesco Martino, Italy	21.553
1928.....Leon Stukelj, Yugoslavia	19.25
1932.....George Gulack, United States	18.97
1936.....Alois Hudec, Czechoslovakia	19.433
1948.....Karl Frei, Switzerland	19.80
1952.....Grant Shaginyan, USSR	19.75
1956.....Albert Azaryina, USSR	19.35
1960.....Albert Azaryan, USSR	19.725
1964.....Takuji Haytta, Japan	19.475
1968.....Akinori Nakayama, Japan	19.45
1972.....Akinori Nakayama, Japan	19.35
1976.....Nikolai Andrianov, USSR	19.65
1980.....Aleksandr Dityatin, USSR	19.875
1984.....Koji Gushiken, Japan	19.85
1988.....Holger Behrendt, E Germany	19.925
1992.....Vitaly Scherbo, Unified Team	9.937
1996.....Yuri Chechi, Italy	9.887
2000.....Szilveszter Csollany, Hungary	9.862
2004.....Dimosthenis Tampakos, Greece	9.862

FLOOR EXERCISE	Pts
1932.....Istvan Pelle, Hungary	9.60
1936.....Georges Miez, Switzerland	18.666
1948.....Ferenc Pataki, Hungary	19.35
1952.....K. William Thoresson, Sweden	19.25
1956.....Valentin Muratov, USSR	19.20

FLOOR EXERCISE (CONT.)	Pts
1960.....Nobuyuki Aihara, Japan	19.45
1964.....Franco Menichelli, Italy	19.45
1968.....Sawao Kato, Japan	19.475
1972.....Nikolai Andrianov, USSR	19.175
1976.....Nikolai Andrianov, USSR	19.45
1980.....Roland Brückner, E Germany	19.75
1984.....Li Ning, China	19.925
1988.....Sergei Kharkov, USSR	19.925
1992.....Li Xiaoshuang, China	9.925
1996.....Ioannis Melissanidis, Greece	9.850
2000.....Igors Vihrovs, Latvia	9.812
2004.....Kyle Shewfelt, Canada	9.787

TEAM COMBINED EXERCISES	Pts
1904.....Turngemeinde Philadelphia	374.43
1906.....Norway	19.00
1908.....Sweden	438
1912.....Italy	265.75
1920.....Italy	359.855
1924.....Italy	839.058
1928.....Switzerland	1718.625
1932.....Italy	541.850
1936.....Germany	657.430
1948.....Finland	1358.30
1952.....USSR	574.40
1956.....USSR	568.25
1960.....Japan	575.20
1964.....Japan	577.95
1968.....Japan	575.90
1972.....Japan	571.25
1976.....Japan	576.85
1980.....USSR	598.60
1984.....United States	591.40
1988.....USSR	593.35
1992.....Unified Team	585.45
1996.....Russia	576.778
2000.....China	231.919
2004.....Japan	173.821

GYMNASTICS — Women

ALL-AROUND	Pts
1952 .....Maria Gorokhovskaya, USSR	76.78
1956 .....Larissa Latynina, USSR	74.933
1960 .....Larissa Latynina, USSR	77.031
1964 .....Vera Caslavska, Czechoslovakia	77.564
1968 .....Vera Caslavska, Czechoslovakia	78.25
1972 .....Lyudmila Tousischeva, USSR	77.025
1976 .....Nadia Comaneci, Romania	79.275
1980 .....Yelena Davydova, USSR	79.15
1984 .....Mary Lou Retton, United States	79.175
1988 .....Yelena Shushunova, USSR	79.662
1992 .....Tatiana Gutsu, Unified Team	39.737
1996 .....Lilia Podkopayeva, Ukraine	39.255
2000 .....Simona Amanar, Romania	38.642
2004 .....Carly Patterson, United States	38.387

VAULT	Pts
1952 .....Yekaterina Kalinchuk, USSR	19.20
1956 .....Larissa Latynina, USSR	18.833
1960 .....Margarita Nikolayeva, USSR	19.316
1964 .....Vera Caslavska, Czechoslovakia	19.483
1968 .....Vera Caslavska, Czechoslovakia	19.775
1972 .....Karin Janz, E Germany	19.525

VAULT (CONT.)	Pts
1976 .....Nelli Kim, USSR	19.80
1980 .....Natalya Shaposhnikova, USSR	19.725
1984 .....Ecaterina Szabo, Romania	19.875
1988 .....Svetlana Boginskaya, USSR	19.905
1992 .....Henrietta Onodi, Hungary	9.925
.........Lavinia Milosovici, Romania	9.925
1996 .....Simona Amanar, Romania	9.825
2000 .....Yelena Zamolodtchikova, Russia	9.731
2004 .....Monica Rosu, Romania	9.656

UNEVEN BARS	Pts
1952 .....Margit Korondi, Hungary	19.40
1956 .....Agnes Keleti, Hungary	18.966
1960 .....Polina Astakhova, USSR	19.616
1964 .....Polina Astakhova, USSR	19.332
1968 .....Vera Caslavska, Czechoslovakia	19.65
1972 .....Karin Janz, E Germany	19.675
1976 .....Nadia Comaneci, Romania	20.00
1980 .....Maxi Gnauck, E Germany	19.875
1984 .....Ma Yanhong, China	19.95
1988 .....Daniela Silivas, Romania	20.00
1992 .....Lu Li, China	10.00

GYMNASTICS - Women *(Cont.)*

Women *(Cont.)*

UNEVEN BARS *(CONT.)*	Pts
1996 .....Svetlana Khorkina, Russia	9.850
2000 .....Svetlana Khorkina, Russia	9.862
2004 .....Emilie Lepennec, France	9.687

BALANCE BEAM	Pts
1952 .....Nina Bocharova, USSR	19.22
1956 .....Agnes Keleti, Hungary	18.80
1960 .....Eva Bosakova, Czechoslovakia	19.283
1964 .....Vera Caslavska, Czechoslovakia	19.449
1968 .....Natalya Kuchinskaya, USSR	19.65
1972 .....Olga Korbut, USSR	19.40
1976 .....Nadia Comaneci, Romania	19.95
1980 .....Nadia Comaneci, Romania	19.80
1984 .....Simona Pauca, Romania	19.80
1988 .....Daniela Silivas, Romania	19.924
1992 .....Tatiana Lisenko, Unified Team	9.975
1996 .....Shannon Miller, United States	9.862
2000 .....Xuan Li, China	9.825
2004 .....Catalina Ponor, Romania	9.787

FLOOR EXERCISE	Pts
1952 .....Agnes Keleti, Hungary	19.36
1956 .....Agnes Keleti, Hungary	18.733
1960 .....Larissa Latynina, USSR	19.583
1964 .....Larissa Latynina, USSR	19.599
1968 .....Vera Caslavska, Czechoslovakia	19.675
1972 .....Olga Korbut, USSR	19.575
1976 .....Nelli Kim, USSR	19.85
1980 .....Nadia Comaneci, Romania	19.875
1984 .....Ecaterina Szabo, Romania	19.975
1988 .....Daniela Silivas, Romania	19.937
1992 .....Lavinia Milosovici, Romania	10.00
1996 .....Lilia Podkopayeva, Ukraine	9.887
2000 .....Yelena Zamolodtchikova, Russia	9.850
2004 .....Catalina Ponor, Romania	9.750

TEAM COMBINED EXERCISES	Pts
1928 .....The Netherlands	316.75
1932 .....Not held	
1936 .....Germany	506.50
1948 .....Czechoslovakia	445.45
1952 .....USSR	527.03
1956 .....USSR	444.800
1960 .....USSR	382.320
1964 .....USSR	280.890
1968 .....USSR	382.85
1972 .....USSR	380.50
1976 .....USSR	466.00
1980 .....USSR	394.90
1984 .....Romania	392.02
1988 .....USSR	395.475
1992 .....Unified Team	395.666
1996 .....United States	389.225
2000 .....Romania	154.608
2004 .....Romania	114.283

RHYTHMIC ALL-AROUND	Pts
1984 .....Lori Fung, Canada	57.95
1988 .....Marina Lobach, USSR	60.00
1992 .....A. Timoshenko, Unified Team	59.037
1996 .....E. Serebrianskaya, Ukraine	39.683
2000 .....Yulia Barsukova, Russia	39.632
2004 .....Alina Kabaeva, Russia	108.400

RHYTHMIC TEAM COMBINED EXERCISES	Pts
1996 .....Spain	38.933
2000 .....Russia	39.500
2004 .....China	249.750

SOCCER

Men

1900 .....Great Britain	1928 .....Uruguay	1964 .....Hungary	1988 .....USSR
1904 .....Canada	1936 .....Italy	1968 .....Hungary	1992 .....Spain
1908 .....Great Britain	1948 .....Sweden	1972 .....Poland	1996 .....Nigeria
1912 .....Great Britain	1952 .....Hungary	1976 .....E Germany	2000 .....Cameroon
1920 .....Belgium	1956 .....USSR	1980 .....Czechoslovakia	2004 .....Argentina
1924 .....Uruguay	1960 .....Yugoslavia	1984 .....France	

Women

1996 ....United States	
2000 ....Norway	
2004 ....United States	

BIATHLON
Men

10 KILOMETERS

1980	Frank Ullrich, E Germany	32:10.69
1984	Eirik Kvalfoss, Norway	30:53.8
1988	Frank-Peter Rötsch, W Germany	25:08.1
1992	Mark Kirchner, Germany	26:02.3
1994	Sergei Tchepikov, Russia	28:07.0
1998	Ole Einar Bjorndalen, Norway	27:16.2
2002	Ole Einar Bjorndalen, Norway	24:51.3
2006	Sven Fischer, Germany	24:11.6

12.5 KILOMETERS PURSUIT

2002	Ole Einar Bjorndalen, Norway	24:51.3
2006	Vincent Defrasne, France	35:20.2

15 KILOMETERS

2006	Michael Greis, Germany	47:20.0

20 KILOMETERS

1960	Klas Lestander, Sweden	1:33:21.6
1964	Vladimir Melyanin, USSR	1:20:26.8
1968	Magnar Solberg, Norway	1:13:45.9
1972	Magnar Solberg, Norway	1:15:55.5
1976	Nikolay Kruglov, USSR	1:14:12.26

20 KILOMETERS (CONT.)

1980	Anatoliy Alyabiev, USSR	1:08:16.31
1984	Peter Angerer, W Germany	1:11:52.7
1988	Frank-Peter Rötsch, W Germany	56:33.3
1992	Evgueni Redkine, Unified Team	57:34.4
1994	Sergei Tarasov, Russia	57:25.3
1998	Halvard Hanevold, Norway	56:16.4
2002	Ole Einar Bjorndalen, Norway	51:03.3
2006	Michael Greis, Germany	54:23.0

4 X 7.5-KILOMETER RELAY

1968	USSR	2:13:02.4
1972	USSR	1:51:44.92
1976	USSR	1:57:55.64
1980	USSR	1:34:03.27
1984	USSR	1:38:51.7
1988	USSR	1:22:30.0
1992	Germany	1:24:43.5
1994	Germany	1:30:22.1
1998	Germany	1:19:43.3
2002	Norway	1:23:42.3
2006	Germany	1:21:51.5

Women

7.5 KILOMETERS

1992	Antissa Restzova, Unified Team	24:29.2
1994	Myriam Bedard, Canada	26:08.8
1998	Galina Koukleva, Russia	23:08.0
2002	Kati Wilhemn, Germany	20:41.4
2006	Florence Baverel-Robert, France	22:31.4

10 KILOMETERS PURSUIT

2002	Olga Pyleva, Russia	31:07.7
2006	Kati Wilhemn, Germany	36:43.6

12.5 KILOMETERS

2006	Anna Carin Olofsson, Sweden	40:36.5

15 KILOMETERS

1992	Antje Misersky, Germany	51:47.2
1994	Myriam Bedard, Canada	52:06.6
1998	Ekaterina Dofovska, Bulgaria	54:52.0
2002	Andrea Henkel, Germany	47:29.1
2006	Svetlana Ishmouratova, Russia	49:24.1

3 X 7.5-KILOMETER RELAY

1992	France	1:15:55.6
1994	Russia	1:47:19.5
1998	Germany	1:40:13.6
2002	Germany	1:27:55.0

4 X 6-KILOMETER RELAY

2006	Russia	1:16:12.5

BOBSLED

4-MAN

1924	Switzerland (Eduard Scherrer)	5:45.54
1928	United States (William Fiske) (5-man)	3:20.50
1932	United States (William Fiske)	7:53.68
1936	Switzerland (Pierre Musy)	5:19.85
1948	United States (Francis Tyler)	5:20.10
1952	Germany (Andreas Ostler)	5:07.84
1956	Switzerland (Franz Kapus)	5:10.44
1960	Not held	
1964	Canada (Victor Emery)	4:14.46
1968	Italy (Eugenio Monti) (2 runs)	2:17.39
1972	Switzerland (Jean Wicki)	4:43.07
1976	E Germany (Meinhard Nehmer)	3:40.43
1980	E Germany (Meinhard Nehmer)	3:59.92
1984	E Germany (Wolfgang Hoppe)	3:20.22
1988	Switzerland (Ekkehard Fasser)	3:47.51
1992	Austria (Ingo Appelt)	3:53.90
1994	Germany (Harold Czudaj)	3:27.78
1998	Germany (Christoph Langen)	2:39.41
2002	Germany (Andre Lange)	3:10.11
2006	Germany (Andre Lange)	3:40.42

Note: Driver in parentheses.

2-MAN

1932	United States (Hubert Stevens)	8:14.74
1936	United States (Ivan Brown)	5:29.29
1948	Switzerland (Felix Endrich)	5:29.20
1952	Germany (Andreas Ostler)	5:24.54
1956	Italy (Lamberto Dalla Costa)	5:30.14
1960	Not held	
1964	Great Britain (Anthony Nash)	4:21.90
1968	Italy (Eugenio Monti)	4:41.54
1972	W Germany (Wolfgang Zimmerer)	4:57.07
1976	E Germany (Meinhard Nehmer)	3:44.42
1980	Switzerland (Erich Schärer)	4:09.36
1984	E Germany (Wolfgang Hoppe)	3:25.56
1988	USSR (Janis Kipours)	3:53.48
1992	Switzerland (Gustav Weder)	4:03.26
1994	Switzerland (Gustav Weder)	3:30.81
1998	Canada (Pierre Lueders)	3:37.24
	Italy (Guenther Huber)	3:37.24
2002	Germany (Martin Annen)	3:10.11
2006	Germany (Andre Lange)	3:43.38

2-WOMAN

2002	United States (Jill Bakken)	1:37:76
2006	Germany (Sandra Kiriasis)	3:49.98

CURLING

Men

1998 .....Switzerland, Canada, Norway
2002 .....Norway, Canada, Switzerland
2006 .....Canada, Finland, United States
Note: Gold, silver, and bronze medals.

Women

1998 .....Canada, Denmark, Sweden
2002 .....Britain, Switzerland, Canada
2006 .....Sweden, Switzerland, Canada
Note: Gold, silver, and bronze medals.

ICE HOCKEY

Men

1920* ....Canada, United States, Czechoslovakia
1924 .....Canada, United States, Great Britain
1928 .....Canada, Sweden, Switzerland
1932 .....Canada, United States, Germany
1936 .....Great Britain, Canada, United States
1948 .....Canada, Czechoslovakia, Switzerland
1952 .....Canada, United States, Sweden
1956 .....USSR, United States, Canada
1960 .....United States, Canada, USSR
1964 .....USSR, Sweden, Czechoslovakia
1968 .....USSR, Czechoslovakia, Canada
1972 .....USSR, United States, Czechoslovakia

1976 .....USSR, Czechoslovakia, W Germany
1980 .....United States, USSR, Sweden
1984 .....USSR, Czechoslovakia, Sweden
1988 .....USSR, Finland, Sweden
1992 .....Unified Team, Canada, Czechoslovakia
1994 .....Sweden, Canada, Finland
1998 .....Czech Republic, Russia, Finland
2002 .....Canada, United States, Russia
2006 .....Sweden, Finland, Czech Republic
*Competition held at Summer Games in Antwerp.
Note: Gold, silver, and bronze medals.

Women

1998 .....United States, Canada, Finland
2002 .....Canada, United States, Sweden

2006 .....Canada, Sweden, United States
Note: Gold, silver, and bronze medals.

LUGE

Men

	SINGLES			DOUBLES	
1964	Thomas Köhler, East Germany	3:26.77	1964	Austria	1:41.62
1968	Manfred Schmid, Austria	2:52.48	1968	E Germany	1:35.85
1972	Wolfgang Scheidel, W Germany	3:27.58	1972	E Germany	1:28.35
1976	Detlef Guenther, W Germany	3:27.688	1976	E Germany	1:25.604
1980	Bernhard Glass, W Germany	2:54.796	1980	E Germany	1:19.331
1984	Paul Hildgartner, Italy	3:04.258	1984	W Germany	1:23.620
1988	Jens Müller, W Germany	3:05.548	1988	E Germany	1:31.940
1992	Georg Hackl, Germany	3:02.363	1992	Germany	1:32.053
1994	Georg Hackl, Germany	3:21.571	1994	Italy	1:36.720
1998	Georg Hackl, Germany	3:18.44	1998	Germany	1:41.105
2002	Armin Zoeggeler, Italy	2:57.941	2002	Germany	1:26.082
2006	Armin Zoeggeler, Italy	3:26.088	2006	Austria	1:34.497

Women

	SINGLES			SINGLES *(CONT.)*	
1964	Ortrun Enderlein, Germany	3:24.67	1988	Steffi Walter (Martin), E. Germany	3:03.973
1968	Erica Lechner, Italy	2:28.66	1992	Doris Neuner, Austria	3:06.696
1972	Anna-Maria Müller, E Germany	2:59.18	1994	Gerda Weissensteiner, Italy	3:15.517
1976	Margit Schumann, E Germany	2:50.621	1998	Silke Kraushaar, Germany	3:23.779
1980	Vera Zozulya, USSR	2:36.537	2002	Sylke Otto, Germany	2:52.464
1984	Steffi Martin, E Germany	2:46.570	2006	Sylke Otto, Germany	3:07.979

FIGURE SKATING

Men

1908* ....Ulrich Salchow, Sweden
1920† ....Gillis Grafström, Sweden
1924 ....Gillis Grafström, Sweden
1928 ....Gillis Grafström, Sweden
1932 ....Karl Schäfer, Austria
1936 ....Karl Schäfer, Austria
1948 ....Dick Button, United States
1952 ....Dick Button, United States
1956 ....Hayes Alan Jenkins, United States
1960 ....David Jenkins, United States
1964 ....Manfred Schnelldorfer, W Germany
1968 ....Wolfgang Schwarz, Austria
1972 ....Ondrej Nepela, Czechoslovakia
1976 ....John Curry, Great Britain
1980 ....Robin Cousins, Great Britain
1984 ....Scott Hamilton, United States

Women

1908* ....Madge Syers, Great Britain
1920† ....Magda Julin, Sweden
1924 ....Herma Szabo-Planck, Austria
1928 ....Sonja Henie, Norway
1932 ....Sonja Henie, Norway
1936 ....Sonja Henie, Norway
1948 ....Barbara Ann Scott, Canada
1952 ....Jeanette Altwegg, Great Britain
1956 ....Tenley Albright, United States
1960 ....Carol Heiss, United States
1964 ....Sjoukje Dijkstra, Netherlands
1968 ....Peggy Fleming, United States
1972 ....Beatrix Schuba, Austria
1976 ....Dorothy Hamill, United States
1980 ....Anett Pötzsch, E Germany
1984 ....Katarina Witt, E Germany

FIGURE SKATING (Cont.)

Men	Pts
1988 ....Brian Boitano, United States	
1992 ....Victor Petrenko, Unified Team	
1994 ....Alexei Urmanov, Russia	
1998 ....Ilia Kulik, Russia	
2002 ....Alexei Yagudin, Russia	
2006‡ ....Evgeni Plushenko, Russia	258.33

*Competition held at Summer Games in London.
†Competition held at Summer Games in Antwerp.
‡In 2004, the ISU adopted a new overall scoring system

Women	Pts
1988 ....Katarina Witt, E Germany	
1992 ....Kristi Yamaguchi, United States	
1994 ....Oksana Baiul, Ukraine	
1998 ....Tara Lipinski, United States	
2002 ....Sarah Hughes, United States	
2006‡ ....Shizuka Arakawa, Japan	191.34

*Competition held at Summer Games in London.
†Competition held at Summer Games in Antwerp.
‡In 2004, the ISU adopted a new overall scoring system

Mixed

PAIRS

1908* ....Anna Hübler, Heinrich Burger, Germany	
1920† ...Ludowika, Walter Jakobsson-Eilers, Finland	
1924 .....Helene Engelmann, Alfred Berger, Austria	
1928 .....Andree Joly, Pierre Brunet, France	
1932 .....Andree Brunet (Joly), Pierre Brunet, France	
1936 .....Maxi Herber, Ernst Baier, Germany	
1948 .....Micheline Lannoy, Pierre Baugniet, Belgium	
1952 .....Ria Falk and Paul Falk, W Germany	
1956 .....Elisabeth Schwartz, Kurt Oppelt, Austria	
1960 .....Barbara Wagner, Robert Paul, Canada	
1964 .....Lyudmila Beloussova, Oleg Protopopov, USSR	
1968 .....Lyudmila Beloussova, Oleg Protopopov, USSR	
1972 .....Irina Rodnina, Alexei Ulanov, USSR	
1976 .....Irina Rodnina, Aleksandr Zaitsev, USSR	
1980 .....Irina Rodnina, Aleksandr Zaitsev, USSR	
1984 .....Elena Valova, Oleg Vasiliev, USSR	
1988 .....Ekaterina Gordeeva, Sergei Grinkov, USSR	
1992 .....Natalia Michkouteniok, Artour Dmitriev, Unified Team	

PAIRS (CONT.)

	Pts
1994 .....Ekaterina Gordeeva, Sergei Grinkov, Russia	
1998 .....Oksana Kazakova, Artur Dmitriev, Russia	
2002 .....E. Berezhnaya, A. Sikharulidze, Russia J. Sales, D. Pelletier, Canada	
2006‡ ...T. Totmianina, M. Marinin, Russia	204.48

ICE DANCING

	Pts
1976 .....L. Pakhomova, A. Gorshkov, USSR	
1980 .....N. Linichuk, G. Karponosov, USSR	
1984 .....Jayne Torvill, Christopher Dean, UK	
1988 .....N. Bestemianova, A. Bukin, USSR	
1992 .....M. Klimova, S. Ponomarenko, Unified Team	
1994 .....Oksana Grishuk, Evgeny Platov, Russia	
1998 .....Pasha Grishuk, Evgeny Platov, Russia	
2002 .....Marina Anissina, Gwendal Peizeralt, France	
2006‡ ...T. Navka, R. Kostomarov, Russia	200.64

*Competition held at Summer Games in London.
†Competition held at Summer Games in Antwerp.
‡In 2004, the ISU adopted a new overall point-scoring system

SKELETON

Men	
1928 .....Jennison Heaton, United States	3:01.8
1948 .....Nino Bibbia, Italy	5:23.2
2002 .....Jim Shea Jr., United States	1:41.96
2006 .....Duff Gibson, Canada	1:55.88

Women	
2002 .....Tristan Gale, United States	1:45.11
2006 .....Maya Pedersen, Switzerland	1:59.83

SPEED SKATING
Men

500 METERS

1924 ....Charles Jewtraw, United States	44.0
1928 ....Clas Thunberg, Finland	43.4 OR
Bernt Evensen, Norway	43.4 OR
1932 ....John Shea, United States	43.4 EOR
1936 ....Ivar Ballangrud, Norway	43.4 EOR
1948 ....Finn Helgesen, Norway	43.1 OR
1952 ....Kenneth Henry, United States	43.2
1956 ....Yevgeny Grishin, USSR	40.2 EWR
1960 ....Yevgeny Grishin, USSR	40.2 EWR
1964 ....Terry McDermott, United States	40.1 OR
1968 ....Erhard Keller, W Germany	40.3
1972 ....Erhard Keller, W Germany	39.44 OR
1976 ....Yevgeny Kulikov, USSR	39.17 OR
1980 ....Eric Heiden, United States	38.03 OR
1984 ....Sergei Fokichev, USSR	38.19
1988 ....Uwe-Jens Mey, E Germany	36.45 WR
1992 ....Uwe-Jens Mey, E Germany	37.14

500 METERS (CONT.)

1994 ....Aleksandr Golubev, Russia	36.33
1998 ....Hiroyasu Shimizu, Japan (second run)	35.59 OR
2002 ....Casey FitzRandolph, United States	1:09.23*
2006 ....Joey Cheek, United States	1:09.76*

1,000 METERS

1976 ....Peter Mueller, United States	1:19.32
1980 ....Eric Heiden, United States	1:15.18 OR
1984 ....Gaetan Boucher, Canada	1:15.80
1988 ....Nikolai Gulyaev, USSR	1:13.03 OR
1992 ....Olaf Zinke, Germany	1:14.85
1994 ....Dan Jansen, United States	1:12.43 WR
1998 ....Ids Postma, Netherlands	1:10.64 OR
2002 ....Gerard van Velde, Netherlands	1:07.18
2006 ....Shani Davis, United States	1:08.89

SPEED SKATING *(Cont.)*
Men *(Cont.)*

1,500 METERS

1924	Clas Thunberg, Finland	2:20.8
1928	Clas Thunberg, Finland	2:21.1
1932	John Shea, United States	2:57.5
1936	Charles Mathisen, Norway	2:19.2 OR
1948	Sverre Farstad, Norway	2:17.6 OR
1952	Hjalmar Andersen, Norway	2:20.4
1956	Yevgeny Grishin, USSR	2:08.6 WR
	Yuri Mikhailov, USSR	2:08.6 WR
1960	Roald Aas, Norway	2:10.4
	Yevgeny Grishin, USSR	2:10.4
1964	Ants Anston, USSR	2:10.3
1968	Cornelis Verkerk, Netherlands	2:03.4 OR
1972	Ard Schenk, Netherlands	2:02.96 OR
1976	Jan Egil Storholt, Norway	1:59.38 OR
1980	Eric Heiden, United States	1:55.44 OR
1984	Gaetan Boucher, Canada	1:58.36
1988	Andre Hoffmann, E Germany	1:52.06 WR
1992	Johann Olav Koss, Norway	1:54.81
1994	Johann Olav Koss, Norway	1:51.29 WR
1998	Aadne Sondral, Norway	1:47.87 WR
2002	Derek Parra, United States	1:43.95
2006	Enrico Fabris, Italy	1:45.97

5,000 METERS

1924	Clas Thunberg, Finland	8:39.0
1928	Ivar Ballangrud, Norway	8:50.5
1932	Irving Jaffee, United States	9:40.8
1936	Ivar Ballangrud, Norway	8:19.6 OR
1948	Reidar Liaklev, Norway	8:29.4
1952	Hjalmar Andersen, Norway	8:10.6 OR
1956	Boris Shilkov, USSR	7:48.7 OR
1960	Viktor Kosichkin, USSR	7:51.3
1964	Knut Johannesen, Norway	7:38.4 OR

5,000 METERS *(CONT.)*

1968	Fred Anton Maier, Norway	7:22.4 WR
1972	Ard Schenk, Netherlands	7:23.61
1976	Sten Stensen, Norway	7:24.48
1980	Eric Heiden, United States	7:02.29 OR
1984	Sven Tomas Gustafson, Sweden	7:12.28
1988	Tomas Gustafson, Sweden	6:44.63 WR
1992	Geir Karlstad, Norway	6:59.97
1994	Johann Olav Koss, Norway	6:34.96 WR
1998	Gianni Romme, Netherlands	6:22.20 WR
2002	Jochem Uytdehaage, Neth.	6:41.66
2006	Chad Hedrick, United States	6:14.68

10,000 METERS

1924	Julius Skutnabb, Finland	18:04.8
1928	Not held due to thawing of ice	
1932	Irving Jaffee, United States	19:13.6
1936	Ivar Ballangrud, Norway	17:24.3 OR
1948	Ake Seyffarth, Sweden	17:26.3
1952	Hjalmar Andersen, Norway	16:45.8 OR
1956	Sigvard Ericsson, Sweden	16:35.9 OR
1960	Knut Johannesen, Norway	15:46.6 WR
1964	Jonny Nilsson, Sweden	15:50.1
1968	Johnny Höglin, Sweden	15:23.6 OR
1972	Ard Schenk, Netherlands	15:01.35 OR
1976	Piet Kleine, Netherlands	14:50.59 OR
1980	Eric Heiden, United States	14:28.13 WR
1984	Igor Malkov, USSR	14:39.90
1988	Tomas Gustafson, Sweden	13:48.20 WR
1992	Bart Veldkamp, Netherlands	14:12.12
1994	Johann Olav Koss, Norway	13:30.55 WR
1998	Gianni Romme, Netherlands	13:15.33 WR
2002	Jochem Uytdehaage, Netherlands	12:58.92 WR
2006	Bob de Jong, Netherlands	13:01.57

Women

500 METERS

1960	Helga Haase, E Germany	45.9
1964	Lydia Skoblikova, USSR	45.0 OR
1968	Lyudmila Titova, USSR	46.1
1972	Anne Henning, United States	43.33 OR
1976	Sheila Young, United States	42.76 OR
1980	Karin Enke, E Germany	41.78 OR
1984	Christa Rothenburger, E Germany	41.02 OR
1988	Bonnie Blair, United States	39.10 WR
1992	Bonnie Blair, United States	40.33
1994	Bonnie Blair, United States	39.25
1998	Catriona LeMay Doan, Canada (second run)	38.21 OR
2002	Catriona LeMay, Canada	1:14.75*
2006	Svetlana Zhurova, Russia	1:16.57*

1,000 METERS

1960	Klara Guseva, USSR	1:34.1
1964	Lydia Skoblikova, USSR	1:33.2 OR
1968	Carolina Geijssen, Netherlands	1:32.6 OR
1972	Monika Pflug, W Germany	1:31.40 OR
1976	Tatiana Averina, USSR	1:28.43 OR
1980	Natalya Petruseva, USSR	1:24.10 OR
1984	Karin Enke, E Germany	1:21.61 OR
1988	Christa Rothenburger, E Germany	1:17.65 WR
1992	Bonnie Blair, United States	1:21.90
1994	Bonnie Blair, United States	1:18.74

1,000 METERS *CONT.)*

1998	Marianne Timmer, Netherlands	1:16.51 OR
2002	Chris Witty, United States	1:13.83
2006	Marianne Timmer, Netherlands	1:16.05

1,500 METERS

1960	Lydia Skoblikova, USSR	2:25.2 WR
1964	Lydia Skoblikova, USSR	2:22.6 OR
1968	Kaija Mustonen, Finland	2:22.4 OR
1972	Dianne Holum, United States	2:20.85 OR
1976	Galina Stepanskaya, USSR	2:16.58 OR
1980	Anne Borckink, Netherlands	2:10.95 OR
1984	Karin Enke, E Germany	2:03.42 WR
1988	Yvonne van Gennip, Netherlands	2:00.68 OR
1992	Jacqueline Boerner, Germany	2:05.87
1994	Emese Hunyady, Austria	2:02.19
1998	Marianne Timmer, Netherlands	1:57.58 WR
2002	Anni Friesinger, Germany	1:54.02
2006	Cindy Klassen, Canada	1:55.27

3,000 METERS

1960	Lydia Skoblikova, USSR	5:14.3
1964	Lydia Skoblikova, USSR	5:14.9
1968	Johanna Schut, Netherlands	4:56.2 OR
1972	Christina Baas-Kaiser, Netherlands	4:52.14 OR
1976	Tatiana Averina, USSR	4:45.19 OR
1980	Bjorg Eva Jensen, Norway	4:32.13 OR
1984	Andrea Schöne, E Germany	4:24.79 OR
1988	Yvonne van Gennip, Netherlands	4:11.94 WR
1992	Gunda Niemann, Germany	4:19.90

Note: OR=Olympic Record; WR=World Record; EOR=Equals Olympic Record; EWR=Equals World Record; WB=World Best.
*Combined time.

SPEED SKATING — Women *(Cont.)*

3,000 METERS *(CONT.)*

1994	Svetlana Bazhanova, Russia	4:17.43
1998	Gunda Niemann-Stirnemann, Germany	4:07.29 OR
2002	Claudia Pechstein, Germany	3:57.70
2006	Ireen Wust, Netherlands	4:02.43

5,000 METERS

1988	Yvonne van Gennip, Netherlands	7:14.13 WR

5,000 METERS *(CONT.)*

1992	Gunda Niemann, Germany	7:31.57
1994	Claudia Pechstein, Germany	7:14.37
1998	Claudia Pechstein, Germany	6:59.61 WR
2002	Claudia Pechstein, Germany	6:46.91 WR
2006	Clara Hughes, Canada	6:59.07

TEAM PURSUIT

2006	Germany

SHORT TRACK SPEED SKATING

Men

500 METERS

1994	Chae Ji-Hoon, S Korea	43.54
1998	Takafumi Nishitani, Japan	42.862
2002	Marc Gagnon, Canada	41.802 OR
2006	Apolo Anton Ohno, United States	41.935

1,000 METERS

1992	Kim Ki-Hoon, S Korea	1:30.76
1994	Kim Ki-Hoon, S Korea	1:34.57
1998	Kim Dong Sung, S Korea	1:32.375
2002	Steve Bradbury, Austrailia	1:29.109
2006	Hyun-Soo Ahn, S Korea	1:26.739 OR

1,500 METERS

2002	Apolo Anton Ohno, United States	2:18.541
2006	Hyun-Soo Ahn, S Korea	2:25.341

5,000-METER RELAY

1992	S Korea	7:14.02
1994	Italy	7:11.74
1998	Canada	7:06.075
2002	Canada	6:51.579
2006	S Korea	6:43.376 OR

Women

500 METERS

1992	Cathy Turner, United States	47.04
1994	Cathy Turner, United States	45.98
1998	Annie Perreault, Canada	46.568
2002	Yang Yang, China	44.187
2006	Meng Wang, China	44.345

1,000 METERS

1994	Chun Lee Kyung, S Korea	1:36.87
1998	Chun Lee Kyung, S Korea	1:42.776
2002	Yang A. Yang, China	1:36.391
2006	Sun-Yu Jin, S Korea	1:32.859

1,500 METERS

2002	Ko Gi-Hyun, S Korea	2:31.581
2006	Sun-Yu Jin, China	2:23.494

3,000-METER RELAY

1992	Canada	4:36.62
1994	S Korea	4:26.64
1998	S Korea	4:16.260
2002	S Korea	4:12.793
2006	S Korea	4:17.040

ALPINE SKIING

Men

DOWNHILL

1948	Henri Oreiller, France	2:55.0
1952	Zeno Colo, Italy	2:30.8
1956	Anton Sailer, Austria	2:52.2
1960	Jean Vuarnet, France	2:06.0
1964	Egon Zimmermann, Austria	2:18.16
1968	Jean-Claude Killy, France	1:59.85
1972	Bernhard Russi, Switzerland	1:51.43
1976	Franz Klammer, Austria	1:45.73
1980	Leonhard Stock, Austria	1:45.50
1984	Bill Johnson, United States	1:45.59
1988	Pirmin Zurbriggen, Switzerland	1:59.63
1992	Patrick Ortlieb, Austria	1:50.37
1994	Tommy Moe, United States	1:45.75
1998	Jean-Luc Crétier, France	1:50.11
2002	Fritz Strobl, Austria	1:39.13
2006	Antoine Deneriaz, France	1:48.80

SLALOM

1948	Edi Reinalter, Switzerland	2:10.3
1952	Othmar Schneider, Austria	2:00.0
1956	Anton Sailer, Austria	3:14.7
1960	Ernst Hinterseer, Austria	2:08.9
1964	Josef Stiegler, Austria	2:11.13
1968	Jean-Claude Killy, France	1:39.73
1972	F. Fernandez Ochoa, Spain	1:49.27
1976	Piero Gros, Italy	2:03.29
1980	Ingemar Stenmark, Sweden	1:44.26
1984	Phil Mahre, United States	1:39.41
1988	Alberto Tomba, Italy	1:39.47
1992	Finn Christian Jagge, Norway	1:44.39
1994	Thomas Stangassinger, Austria	2:02.02

SLALOM *(CONT.)*

1998	Hans-Petter Buraas, Norway	1:49.31
2002	Jean-Pierre Vidal, France	1:41.06
2006	Benjamin Raich, Austria	1:43.14

GIANT SLALOM

1952	Stein Eriksen, Norway	2:25.0
1956	Anton Sailer, Austria	3:00.1
1960	Roger Staub, Switzerland	1:48.3
1964	Francois Bonlieu, France	1:46.71
1968	Jean-Claude Killy, France	3:29.28
1972	Gustav Thöni, Italy	3:09.62
1976	Heini Hemmi, Switzerland	3:26.97
1980	Ingemar Stenmark, Sweden	2:40.74
1984	Max Julen, Switzerland	2:41.18
1988	Alberto Tomba, Italy	2:06.37
1992	Alberto Tomba, Italy	2:06.98
1994	Markus Wasmeier, Germany	2:52.46
1998	Hermann Maier, Austria	2:38.51
2002	Stephan Eberharter, Austria	2:23.28
2006	Benjamin Raich, Austria	2:35.00

SUPER GIANT SLALOM

1988	Franck Piccard, France	1:39.66
1992	Kjetil André Aamodt, Norway	1:13.04
1994	Markus Wasmeier, Germany	1:32.53
1998	Hermann Maier, Austria	1:34.82
2002	Kjetil André Aamodt, Norway	1:21.58
2006	Kjetil André Aamodt, Norway	1:30.65

COMBINED

1936	Franz Pfnür, Germany	99.25
1948	Henri Oreiller, France	3.27

ALPINE SKIING — Men *(Cont.)*

COMBINED* *(cont'd.)*

1988	Hubert Strolz, Austria	36.55
1992	Josef Polig, Italy	14.58
1994	Lasse Kjus, Norway	3:17.53
1998	Mario Reiter, Austria	3:08.06

COMBINED* *(cont'd.)*

2002	Kjetil André Aamodt, Norway	3:17.56
2006	Ted Ligety, United States	3:09.35

*Beginning in 1994, scoring was based on time.

ALPINE SKIING — Women

DOWNHILL

1948	Hedy Schlunegger, Switzerland	2:28.3
1952	Trude Jochum-Beiser, Austria	1:47.1
1956	Madeleine Berthod, Switzerland	1:40.7
1960	Heidi Biebl, W Germany	1:37.6
1964	Christl Haas, Austria	1:55.39
1968	Olga Pall, Austria	1:40.87
1972	Marie-Theres Nadig, Switzerland	1:36.68
1976	Rosi Mittermaier, W Germany	1:46.16
1980	Annemarie Moser-Pröll, Austria	1:37.52
1984	Michela Figini, Switzerland	1:13.36
1988	Marina Kiehl, W Germany	1:25.86
1992	Kerrin Lee-Gartner, Canada	1:52.55
1994	Katja Seizinger, Germany	1:35.93
1998	Katja Seizinger, Germany	1:28.89
2002	Carole Montillet, France	1:39.56
2006	Michaela Dorfmeister, Austria	1:56.49

SLALOM

1948	Gretchen Fraser, United States	1:57.2
1952	Andrea Mead Lawrence, United States	2:10.6
1956	Renee Colliard, Switzerland	1:52.3
1960	Anne Heggtveigt, Canada	1:49.6
1964	Christine Goitschel, France	1:29.86
1968	Marielle Goitschel, France	1:25.86
1972	Barbara Cochran, United States	1:31.24
1976	Rosi Mittermaier, W Germany	1:30.54
1980	Hanni Wenzel, Liechtenstein	1:25.09
1984	Paoletta Magoni, Italy	1:36.47
1988	Vreni Schneider, Switzerland	1:36.69
1992	Petra Kronberger, Austria	1:32.68
1994	Vreni Schneider, Switzerland	1:56.01
1998	Hilde Gerg, Germany	1:32.40
2002	Janica Kostelic, Croatia	1:46.10
2006	Anja Paerson, Sweden	1:29.04

GIANT SLALOM

1952	Andrea Mead Lawrence, U.S.	2:06.8
1956	Ossi Reichert, W Germany	1:56.5
1960	Yvonne Rüegg, Switzerland	1:39.9
1964	Marielle Goitschel, France	1:52.24
1968	Nancy Greene, Canada	1:51.97
1972	Marie-Theres Nadig, Switzerland	1:29.90
1976	Kathy Kreiner, Canada	1:29.13
1980	Hanni Wenzel, Liechtenstein (2 runs)	2:41.66
1984	Debbie Armstrong, United States	2:20.98
1988	Vreni Schneider, Switzerland	2:06.49
1992	Pernilla Wiberg, Sweden	2:12.74
1994	Deborah Compagnoni, Italy	2:30.97
1998	Deborah Compagnoni, Italy	2:50.59
2002	Janica Kostelic, Croatia	2:30.01
2006	Julia Mancuso, United States	2:09.19

SUPER GIANT SLALOM

1988	Sigrid Wolf, Austria	1:19.03
1992	Deborah Compagnoni, Italy	1:21.22
1994	Diann Roffe-Steinrotter, U.S.	1:22.15
1998	Picabo Street, United States	1:18.02
2002	Daniela Ceccarelli, Italy	1:13.59
2006	Michaela Dorfmeister, Austria	1:32.47

COMBINED*

1988	Anita Wachter, Austria	29.25
1992	Petra Kronberger, Austria	2.55
1994	Pernilla Wiberg, Sweden	3:05.16
1998	Katja Seizinger, Germany	2:40.74
2002	Janica Kostelic, Croatia	2:43.28
2006	Janica Kostelic, Croatia	2:51.08

*Beginning in 1994, scoring was based on time.

FREESTYLE SKIING

Men
MOGULS

		Pts
1992	Edgar Grospiron, France	25.81
1994	Jean-Luc Brassard, Canada	27.24
1998	Jonny Moseley, United States	26.93
2002	Janne Lahtela, Finland	27.97
2006	Dale Begg-Smith, Australia	26.77

AERIALS

		Pts
1994	Andreas Schoenbaechler, Switz	234.67
1998	Eric Bergoust, United States	255.64
2002	Ales Valenta, Czech Republic	257.02
2006	Han Xiaopeng, China	250.77

Women
MOGULS

		Pts
1992	Donna Weinbrecht, United States	23.69
1994	Stine Lise Hattestad, Norway	25.97
1998	Tae Satoya, Japan	25.06
2002	Kari Traa, Norway	25.94
2006	Jennifer Heil, Canada	26.50

AERIALS

		Pts
1994	Lina Cherjazova, Uzbekistan	166.84
1998	Nikki Stone, United States	193.00
2002	Alisa Camplin, Australia	193.47
2006	Evelyne Leu, Switzerland	202.55

NORDIC SKIING — Men

10 KILOMETERS CLASSICAL

1992	Vegard Ulvang, Norway	27:36.0
1994	Bjørn Dæhlie, Norway	24:20.1
1998	Bjørn Dæhlie, Norway	27:24.5
1976	Nikolay Bajukov, Unified Team	43:58.47
1980	Thomas Wassberg, Sweden	41:57.63
1984	Gunde Swan, Sweden	41:25.6
1988	Michael Deviatyarov, USSR	41:18.9
2002	Andrus Veerpalu, Estonia	37:07.4
2006	Andrus Veerpalu, Estonia	38:01.3

15 KILOMETERS PURSUIT FREESTYLE

1992	Bjørn Dæhlie, Norway	1:05:37.9
1994	Bjørn Dæhlie, Norway	1:00:08.8
1998	Thomas Alsgaard, Norway	1:07:01.7

30 KILOMETERS CLASSICAL

1956	Veikko Hakulinen, Finland	1:44:06.0
1960	Sixten Jernberg, Sweden	1:51:03.9
1964	Eero Mantyränta, Finland	1:30:50.7
1968	Franco Nones, Italy	1:35:39.2
1972	Viaceslav Vedenine, USSR	1:36:31.2

NORDIC SKIING — Men *(Cont.)*

30 KILOMETERS CLASSICAL *(CONT.)*

1976	Sergei Savelyev, USSR	1:30:29.38
1980	Nikolai Simyatov, USSR	1:27:02.80
1984	Nikolai Simyatov, USSR	1:28:56.3
1988	Alexey Prokororov, USSR	1:24:26.3
1992	Vegard Ulvang, Norway	1:22:27.8
1994	Thomas Alsgaard, Norway	1:12:26.4
1998	Mika Myllylae, Finland	1:33:55.8

30 KILOMETERS PURSUIT

2006	Eugeni Dementiev, Russia	1:17:00.8

50 KILOMETERS FREESTYLE

1924	Thorleif Haug, Norway	3:44:32.0
1928	Per Erik Hedlund, Sweden	4:52:03.0
1932	Veli Saarinen, Finland	4:28:00.0
1936	Elis Wiklund, Sweden	3:30:11.0
1948	Nils Karlsson, Sweden	3:47:48.0
1952	Veikko Hakulinen, Finland	3:33:33.0
1956	Sixten Jernberg, Sweden	2:50:27.0
1960	Kalevi Hämäläinen, Finland	2:59:06.3
1964	Sixten Jernberg, Sweden	2:43:52.6
1968	Olle Ellefsaeter, Norway	2:28:45.8
1972	Paal Tyldrum, Norway	2:43:14.75
1976	Ivar Formo, Norway	2:37:30.50
1980	Nikolai Simyatov, USSR	2:27:24.60
1984	Thomas Wassberg, Sweden	2:15:55.8
1988	Gunde Svan, Sweden	2:04:30.9
1992	Bjørn Dæhlie, Norway	2:03:41.5
1994	Vladimir Smirnov, Kazakhstan	2:07:20.3
1998	Bjørn Dæhlie, Norway	2:05:08.2
2002	Mikhail Ivanov, Russia	2:06:20.8
2006	Giorgio di Centa, Italy	2:06:11.8

4 X 10-KILOMETER RELAY MIXED

1936	Finland	2:41:33.0
1948	Sweden	2:32:80.0
1952	Finland	2:20:16.0
1956	USSR	2:15:30.0
1960	Finland	2:18:45.6
1964	Sweden	2:18:34.6
1968	Norway	2:08:33.5
1972	USSR	2:04:47.94
1976	Finland	2:07:59.72
1980	USSR	1:57:03.46
1984	Sweden	1:55:06.3
1988	Sweden	1:43:58.6
1992	Norway	1:39:26.0
1994	Italy	1:41:15.0
1998	Norway	1:40:55.7
2002	Norway	1:32:45.5
2006	Italy	1:43:45.7

TEAM SPRINT

2006	Sweden	17:02.9

INDIVIDUAL SPRINT

2006	Bjoern Lind, Sweden	2:26.5

SKI JUMPING (90-M HILL)

		Pts
1964	Veikko Kankkonen, Finland	229.90
1968	Jiri Raska, Czechoslovakia	216.5
1972	Yukio Kasaya, Japan	244.2
1976	Hans-Georg Aschenbach, E Germany	252.0
1980	Toni Innauer, Austria	266.3
1984	Jens Weissflog, E Germany	215.2
1988	Matti Nykänen, Finland	229.1
1992	Ernst Vettori, Austria	222.8
1994	Espen Bredesen, Norway	282.0
1998	Jani Soininen, Finland	234.5

SKI JUMPING (90-M HILL) *(CONT.)*

		Pts
2002	Simon Ammann, Switzerland	269.0
2006	Lars Bystoel, Norway	266.5

SKI JUMPING (120-M HILL)

		Pts
1924	Jacob Tullin Thams, Norway	18.960
1928	Alf Andersen, Norway	19.208
1932	Birger Ruud, Norway	228.1
1936	Birger Ruud, Norway	232.0
1948	Petter Hugsted, Norway	228.1
1952	Arnfinn Bergmann, Norway	226.0
1956	Antti Hyvärinen, Finland	227.0
1960	Helmut Recknagel, E Germany	227.2
1964	Toralf Engan, Norway	230.70
1968	Vladimir Beloussov, USSR	231.3
1972	Wojciech Fortuna, Poland	219.9
1976	Karl Schnabl, Austria	234.8
1980	Jouko Tormanen, Finland	271.0
1984	Matti Nykänen, Finland	231.2
1988	Matti Nykänen, Finland	224.0
1992	Toni Nieminen, Finland	239.5
1994	Jens Weissflog, Germany	274.5
1998	Kazuyoshi Funaki, Japan	272.3
2002	Simon Amman, Switzerland	281.4
2006	Thomas Morgenstern, Austria	276.9

TEAM 120-M SKI JUMPING

		Pts
1988	Finland	634.4
1992	Finland	644.4
1994	Germany	970.1
1998	Japan	933.0
2002	Germany	974.1
2006	Austria	984.0

NORDIC COMBINED*

		Pts
1924	Thorleif Haug, Norway	18.906
1928	Johan Gröttumsbraaten, Norway	17.833
1932	Johan Gröttumsbraaten, Norway	446.0
1936	Oddbjörn Hagen, Norway	430.30
1948	Heikki Hasu, Finland	448.80
1952	Simon Slattvik, Norway	451.621
1956	Sverre Stenersen, Norway	455.0
1960	Georg Thoma, W Germany	457.952
1964	Tormod Knutsen, Norway	469.28
1968	Frantz Keller, W Germany	449.04
1972	Ulrich Wehling, E Germany	413.34
1976	Ulrich Wehling, E Germany	423.39
1980	Ulrich Wehling, E Germany	432.20
1984	Tom Sandberg, Norway	422.595
1988	Hippolyt Kempf, Switzerland	432.230
1992	Fabrice Guy, France	426.47
1994	Fred B. Lundberg, Norway	457.970
1998	Bjarte Engen Vik, Norway	41:21.1†
2002	Samppa Lajunen, Finland	38:18.7†
2006	Georg Hettich, Norway	39:44.6†

TEAM NORDIC COMBINED

1988	W Germany
1992	Japan
1994	Japan
1998	Norway
2002	Finland
2006	Austria

SPRINT NORDIC COMBINED

2002	Samppa Lajunen, Finland	123.8
2006	Felix Gottwald, Austria	17:35.0†

* Different scoring system; 1924–1952 distance was 18 km; 1952–present, 15 km.
† Times in the cross-country race were not converted into points. According to the Gundersen Method, used since 1988, starting times in the race are staggered in proportion to points earned in the ski jumping segment of the event.

NORDIC SKIING — Women

INDIVIDUAL SPRINT
2002	Julija Tchepalova, Russia	3:10.6
2006	Chandra Crawford, Canada	2:12.3

5 KILOMETERS PURSUIT
2002	Olga Danilova, Russia	24:52.1

5 KILOMETERS CLASSICAL
1964	Klaudia Boyarskikh, USSR	17:50.5
1968	Toini Gustafsson, Sweden	16:45.2
1972	Galina Kulakova, USSR	17:00.50
1976	Helena Takalo, Finland	15:48.69
1980	Raisa Smetanina, USSR	15:06.92
1984	Marja-Liisa Hamalainen, Finland	17:04.0
1988	Marjo Matikainen, Finland	15:04.0
1992	Marjut Lukkarinen, Finland	14:13.8
1994	Lyubova Egorova, Russia	14:08.8
1998	Larissa Lazhutina, Russia	17:37.9

10 KILOMETERS CLASSICAL
1952	Lydia Widemen, Finland	41:40.0
1956	Lyubov Kosyryeva, USSR	38:11.0
1960	Maria Gusakova, USSR	39:46.6
1964	Klaudia Boyarskikh, USSR	40:24.3
1968	Toini Gustafsson, Sweden	36:46.5
1972	Galina Kulakova, USSR	34:17.8
1976	Raisa Smetanina, USSR	30:13.41
1980	Barbara Petzold, E Germany	30:31.54
1984	Marja-Lissa Hamalainen, Finland	31:44.2
1988	Vida Ventsene, USSR	30:08.3
2002	Bante Skari, Norway	28:05.6
2006	Kristina Smigun, Estonia	27:51.4

10 KILOMETERS PURSUIT FREESTYLE
1992	Lyubov Egorova, Unified Team	40:07.7
1994	Lyubov Egorova, Russia	41:38.1
1998	Larissa Lazhutina, Russia	46:06.9

15 KILOMETERS CLASSICAL
1992	Lyubov Egorova, Unified Team	42:20.8
1994	Manuela Di Centa, Italy	39:44.5
1998	Olga Danilova, Russia	46:55.04

15 KILOMETERS FREESTYLE
2002	Stefania Belmondo, Italy	39:54.4

15 KILOMETERS PURSUIT
2006	Kristina Smigun, Estonia	42:48.7

20 KILOMETERS FREESTYLE
1984	Marja-Liisa Hamalainen, Finland	1:01:45.0
1988	Tamara Tikhonova, USSR	55:53.6

30 KILOMETERS FREESTYLE
1992	Stefania Belmondo, Italy	1:22:30.1
1994	Manuela Di Centa, Italy	1:25:41.6
1998	Julija Tchepalova, Russia	1:22:01.5
2002	Gabriela Paruzzi, Italy	1:30:57.1
2006	Katerina Neumannova, Czech Rep.	1:22:25.4

TEAM SPRINT
2006	Sweden	16:36.9

4 X 5-KILOMETER RELAY MIXED
1956	Finland	1:9:01.0
1960	Sweden	1:4:21.4
1964	USSR	59:20.0
1968	Norway	57:30.0
1972	USSR	48:46.15
1976	USSR	1:07:49.75
1980	E Germany	1:02:11.10
1984	Norway	1:06:49.7
1988	USSR	59:51.1
1992	Unified Team	59:34.8
1994	Russia	57:12.5
1998	Russia	55:13.5
2002	Germany	49:30.6
2006	Russia	54:47.7

SNOWBOARDING

Men

GIANT SLALOM
1998	Ross Rebagliati, Canada	2:03.96

PARALLEL GIANT SLALOM
2002	Philipp Schoch, Switzerland	
2006	Philipp Schoch, Switzerland	

HALF-PIPE
		Pts
1998	Gian Simmen, Switzerland	85.2
2002	Ross Powers, United States	46.1
2006	Shaun White, United States	46.8

SNOWBOARD CROSS
2006	Seth Wescott, United States	

Women

GIANT SLALOM
1998	Karine Ruby, France	2:17.34

PARALLEL GIANT SLALOM
2002	Isabella Blanc, France	
2006	Daniela Meuli, Switzerland	

HALF-PIPE
		Pts
1998	Nicola Thost, Germany	74.6
2002	Kelly Clark, United States	47.9
2006	Hannah Teter, United States	46.4

SNOWBOARD CROSS
2006	Tanja Frieden, Switzerland	

In 2006, Marion Jones' conflicting drug test results gave many track and field fans a reason to wonder.

Track & Field

The Needle and The Damage Done

America's top two sprinters found themselves mired in scandal in 2006 as doping allegations rocked the sport

BY MERRELL NODEN

T HIS WAS A PAINFUL, DEEPLY troubling year for track and field. As in the sports of cycling and baseball, the soul-deadening drumbeat of drug rumors and positive drug tests left even the sport's most ardent fans reeling, wondering not only when, but if it will ever be possible to believe beyond a doubt that we are watching clean athletes. The fact that the bad news involved the U.S.'s two most marketable stars—sprinting champions Justin Gatlin and Marion Jones—made things even worse. Even though Jones ultimately would be exonerated by her "B" sample, the three weeks she spent under a cloud of suspicion did her and the sport no favors.

Despite having been named by Victor Conte of the Bay Area Laboratory Co-Operative (BALCO) as a beneficiary of his pharmaceutical ministrations, Jones had always denied using drugs. And because she had been so good so young, fans were willing to suspend their disbelief even if select European meet directors took a harder line, refusing to invite her to their events. Still, Jones was off to her best season in years, in June winning her 14th national 100-meter title comfortably, in 11.10 seconds. She later ran a seasonal best of 10.91, a time eclipsed this year by only Sherone Simpson of Jamaica, who topped the list with a 10.82.

When, on August 18, it was announced that Jones's "A" sample from the U.S. Championships had come up positive, those hopes took a drastic tumble. What was perhaps most surprising was that Jones was accused of taking EPO, an endurance-boosting drug favored by cyclists and cross country skiers. Jones expressed her extreme shock at the result and on Sept. 7th she got the best news she could have hoped for: Her "B" sample was negative. "I have never, ever taken performance enhancing drugs, and I am pleased that a scientific process has now demonstrated that fact," she said.

If only it were that simple.

Gatlin's positive test was just as troubling. He has always gone out of his way to present himself as the anti-drug champion, even though in 2001 he had tested positive for an amphetamine. (He was judged to have taken it inadvertently). In late July, he acknowledged he had tested positive for testosterone at the Kansas Relays on April 22 and, at first, he blamed a vengeful massage therapist. Though a second infraction could have netted him a lifetime ban from the sport, Gatlin managed to strike a deal with the U.S. Anti-Doping Agency. He agreed not to contest the lab results and to help their investigation in exchange for a

Gatlin tested positive and was stripped of his share of the 100-meter world record.

ban of no more than eight years.

People wondered, quite reasonably, whether "cooperating" meant spilling the beans about Trevor Graham, who at one time had coached both Gatlin and Jones along with many other top sprinters. It was Graham who provided the USADA with the syringe of the designer steroid THG that originally triggered the whole BALCO episode. By August, when LaShinda Demus came up positive for the steroid nandrolone—the seventh Graham athlete to test positive for a banned substance—the sport had concluded it wanted no part of Mr. Graham, who in happier times had won an Olympic silver medal as part of Jamaica's 4 x 400 team in 1988. Nike terminated his contract and the U.S. Olympic Committee banned him from using its facilities.

With no Olympics or world championships being contested this year, the U.S. press seemed to run nothing but drug stories all summer. As usual, all this bad news seemed to call a slew of great performances into question. And there were many that were notable:

•Asafa Powell of Jamaica twice ran a world record 9.77 seconds in the 100 meters and will be both beneficiary and victim of Gatlin's suspension. With Gatlin gone, the 23-year-old Jamaican is clearly the world's top sprinter, but it's going to be hard to watch him run so fast without nagging doubts popping into one's head.

•Xavier Carter beat Tyson Gay in a fantastic 200 in Lausanne, clocking in at 19.63 to Gay's 19.70. Just 20, Carter is the first person in years to seem capable of challenging the Beamonesque 19.32 that Michael Johnson ran at the Atlanta Olympics in 1996.

•Jeremy Wariner dominated the 400 as thoroughly as Johnson, his agent, did 10

years ago. Not only did Johnson's fellow Baylor grad clock the fastest 400 since Johnson himself—a 43.62 in Rome—he went deep too, racking up the 10 fastest performances of the season.

•Xiang Liu of China set a world record in the 110-meter hurdles, clocking 12.88 in Lausanne, Switzerland, on July 11. Liu, who turned 23 two days later, would seem to be the early favorite to shoulder his country's high hopes for the Beijing Games in 2008.

But sadly, there is no doubt that the big story in 2006 was drugs, one top sprinter condemned by his "B" sample, the other cleared by hers. But as reassuring as it was to conclude that the system's checks and balances had actually worked, protecting an innocent athlete, it left doubts about the validity of the whole system: Why was Jones's "A" sample positive? If mistakes were made in her case, could they have been made in others as well, thus resulting in the Kafkaesque nightmare where innocent athletes are unfairly smeared for life? As we look ahead to the world championships scheduled for next summer in Osaka, one wonders if the sport can continue to absorb blows as hard as these and hope to inspire wonder rather than cynicism.

2006 USATF Outdoor Championships

Indianapolis June 21–25, 2006
Men

100 METERS
1. ....Tyson Gay, adidas — 10.07
2. ....Shawn Crawford, Nike — 10.26
3. ....Jordan Vaden, Nike — 10.27

200 METERS
1. ....Wallace Spearmon, Nike — 19.90
2. ....Jordan Vaden, Nike — 19.98
3. ....Rodney Martin, Nike — 20.14

400 METERS
1. ....Andrew Rock, adidas — 44.45
2. ....LaShawn Merritt, Nike — 44.50
3. ....David Neville, Indiana — 44.75

800 METERS
1. ....Khadevis Robinson, Nike — 1:44.13
2. ....Nicholas Symmonds, unattached — 1:45.83
3. ....Jebreh Harris, Reebok — 1:45.91

1,500 METERS
1. ....Bernard Lagat, Nike — 3:39.29
2. ....Gabriel Jennings, unattached — 3:39.42
3. ....Leonel Manzano, Texas — 3:39.49

3,000 M STEEPLECHASE
1. ....Daniel Lincoln, Nike — 8:22.78
2. ....Steve Slattery, Nike — 8:25.54
3. ....Daniel Huling, unattached — 8:27.41

5,000 METERS
1. ....Bernard Lagat, Nike — 13:14.32
2. ....Matt Tegenkamp, Nike — 13:15.00
3. ....Dathan Ritzenhein, Nike — 13:16.61

10,000 METERS
1. ....Jorge Torres, Reebok — 28:14.43
2. ....Meb Keflezighi, Nike — 28:18.74
3. ....Daniel Browne, Nike — 28:19.32

110-METER HURDLES
1. ....Dominique Arnold, Nike — 13.10
2. ....Terrence Trammell, Mizuno — 13.14
3. ....Ryan Wilson, unattached — 13.22

400-METER HURDLES
1. ....Kerron Clement, Nike — 47.39
2. ....Bershawn Jackson, Nike — 47.48
3. ....James Carter, Nike — 48.44

20-KILOMETER RACE WALK
1. ....Kevin Eastler, U.S. Air Force — 1:25:09.67
2. ....John Nunn, U.S. Army — 1:27:16.83
3. ....Tim Seaman, New York A.C. — 1:29:56.84

HIGH JUMP
1. ....Tora Harris, Shore A.C. — 2.33m
2. ....Keith Moffatt, Morehouse — 2.30m
3. ....Andra Manson, Texas — 2.24m

POLE VAULT
1. ....Russ Buller, Asics — 5.80m
2. ....Toby Stevenson, Nike — §5.80m
3. ....Thomas Skipper, Oregon — 5.60m
3 ....Jeff Hartwig, Nike — §5.60m

LONG JUMP
1. ....Brian Johnson, Nike — 8.10m
2. ....Dwight Phillips, Nike — 8.08m
3. ....Miguel Pate, Nike — 7.96m

TRIPLE JUMP
1. ....Walter Davis, Nike — 17.71m
2. ....Kenta Bell, Mizuno — 17.19m
3. ....Aarik Wilson, unattached — 16.91m

SHOT PUT
1. ....Adam Nelson, unattached — 22.04m
2. ....Reese Hoffa, New York A.C. — 21.96m
3. ....Christian Cantwell, Nike — 21.89m

DISCUS THROW
1. ....Ian Waltz, Nike — 64.52m
2. ....Casey Malone, Nike — 62.23m
3. ....Jarred Rome, Nike — 60.93m

HAMMER THROW
1. ............A.G. Kruger, Ashland Elite — 75.81m
2. ....James Parker, unattached — 72.33m
3. ....Thomas Freeman, New York A.C. — 71.87m

JAVELIN THROW
1. ....Breaux Greer, adidas — 85.40m
2. ....Robert Minnitti, unattached — 77.99m
3. ....Brian Chaput, New York A.C. — 76.44m

DECATHLON
1. ....Tom Poppas, Nike — 8319
2. ....Ryan Harlan, unattached — 7872
3. ....Robert Arnold, Arizona — 7827

MARATHON*
1. ....Mbarak Hussein — 2:13.52
2. ....Simon Sawe — 2:14.09
3. ....Ryan Shay — 2:14.58

*Held on Oct. 1 in Minneapolis, Minnesota.
§Final place in high jump decided by number of successful jumps at final height.

Women

100 METERS
1. ....Marion Jones, unattached — 11.100
2. ....Lauryn Williams, Nike — 11.161
3. ....Torri Edwards, Nike — 11.170

200 METERS
1. ....Rachelle Boone-Smith, Nike — 22.31
2. ....Shalonda Solomon, S. Carolina — 22.47
3. ....LaTasha Jenkins, Nike — 22.66

400 METERS
1. ....Sanya Richards, Nike — 49.27
2. ....De' Hashia Trotter, adidas — 50.40
3. ....Monique Henderson, Reebok — 50.71

800 METERS
1. ....Hazel Clark, Nike — 1:59.94
2. ....Alice Schmidt, adidas — 2:00.00
3. ....Frances Santin, S.M.T.C. — 2:01.15

1,500 METERS
1. ....Treniere Clement, Nike — 4:10.44
2. ....Lindsey Gallo, Reebok — 4:10.72
3. ....Sarah Schwald, Nike — 4:11.60

3,000 M STEEPLECHASE
1. ....Lisa Galaviz, Nike — 9:57.58
2. ....Kristin Anderson, unattached — 9:57.98
3. ....D DiCrescenzo, Westchester T.C. — 10:03.31

5,000 METERS
1. ....Lauren Fleshman, Nike — 15:12.37
2. ....Kara Goucher, Nike — 15:14.13
3. ....Blake Russell, Reebok — 15:19.07

10,000 METERS
1. ....Amy Rudolph, adidas — 32:25.56
2. ....Sara Slattery, adidas — 32:29.97
3. ....Samia Akbar, Reebok — 32:41.84

20-KILOMETER RACE WALK
1. ....Joanne Dow, adidas — 1:35:20.76
2. ....Teresa Vaill, Walk USA — 1:39:24.07
3. ....Sam Cohen, Parkside A.C. — 1:40:29.46

100-METER HURDLES
1. ....Virginia Powell, Nike — 12.63
2. ....Damu Cherry, Nike — 12.64
3. ....Michelle Perry, Nike — 12.67

400-METER HURDLES
1. ....LaShinda Demus, Nike — 53.07
2. ....Sheena Johnson, Nike — 53.90
3. ....Shauna Smith, Nike — 54.76

HIGH JUMP
1. ....Chaunte Howard, Nike — 2.01m
2. ....Amy Acuff, Asics — 1.92m
3. ....Destinee Hooker, unattached — 1.86m

POLE VAULT
1. ....Jennifer Stuczynski, adidas — 4.55m
2. ....Jillian Schwartz, Nike — 4.50m
3. ....Becky Holliday, New Balance — 4.45m

LONG JUMP
1. ....Rose Richmond, Nike — 6.93m
2. ....Tianna Madison, Nike — 6.77m
3. ....Grace Upshaw, Nike — 6.65m

TRIPLE JUMP
1. ....Shani Marks, unattached — 13.89m
2. ....Tiombe Hurd, Nike — 13.86m
3. ....Yvette Lewis, Hampton — 13.42m

SHOT PUT
1. ....Jillian Camarena, unattached — 18.92m
2. ....Laura Gerraughty, North Carolina — 18.24m
3. ....Elizabeth Wanless, New York A.C. — 18.11m

DISCUS THROW
1. ....Aretha Thurmond, Nike — 62.50m
2. ....Suzy Powell, Ascis — 58.68m
3. ....Rebecca Breisch, unattached — 57.97m

HAMMER THROW
1. ....Jessica Cosby, Nike — 70.78m
2. ....Erin Gilreath, New York A.C. — 69.39m
3. ....Amber Campbell, Mjolnir Throws — 67.52m

JAVELIN THROW
1. ....Kim Kreiner, Nike — 62.43m
2. ....Dana Pounds, Air Force Academy — 56.00m
3. ....Kayla Wilkinson, Nebraska — 52.30m

HEPTAHLON
1. ....GiGi Johnson, unattached — 6183
2. ....Hyleas Fountain, Nike — 6148
3. ....Fiona Asigbee, unattached — 6030

MARATHON*
1. ....Marla Runyan — 2:32.17
2. ....Mary Akor — 2:33.50
3. ....Zoila Gomez — 2:35.36

*Held on Oct. 1 in Minneapolis, Minnesota.

Boston, Feb 24–26, 2006

Men

60 METERS
1. ....Leonard Scott, Nike — 6.52
2. ....Terrence Trammell, Mizuno — 6.53
3. ....Jason Smoots, Nike — 6.55

400 METERS
1. ....Milton Campbell, unattached — 46.167
2. ....LaShawn Merritt, Nike — 46.169
3. ....Tyree Washington, Nike — 46.18

800 METERS
1. ....Khadevis Robinson, Nike — 1:46.98
2. ....David Krummenacker, adidas — 1:47.25
3. ....Samuel Burley, Asics — 1:48.54

1,500 METERS
1. ....Christoper Lukezic, Reebok — 3:41.84
2. ....Jason Lunn, Nike — 3:41.98
3. ....Sean O'Brien, The Farm Team, Inc. — 3:42.53

3,000 METERS
1. ....Adam Goucher, Nike — 7:49.78
2. ....Jonathon Riley, Nike — 7:51.88
3. ....Luke Watson, adidas — 7:55.29

5,000-METER RACE WALK
1. ....Tim Seaman, New York A.C. — 19:15.88
2. ....Kevin Eastler, U.S. Air Force — 19:43.41
3. ....Benjamin Shorey, unattached — 21:48.56

60-METER HURDLES
1. ....Terrence Trammell, Mizuno — 7.46
2. ....Dominique Arnold, Nike — 7.51
3. ....Anwar Moore, Nike — 7.52

HIGH JUMP
1. ....Adam Shunk, Nike — 2.25m
2 ....Tora Harris, Shore A.C. — J2.25m
3 ....Jesse Williams, USC — 2.22m

POLE VAULT
1. ....Brad Walker, Nike — 5.75m
2. ....Jeff Hartwig, Nike — 5.70m
3. ....Toby Stevenson, Nike — 5.60m

LONG JUMP
1. ....Brian Johnson, Nike — 7.95m
2. ....Joe Allen, unattached — 7.82m
3. ....Bashir Ramzy, unattached — 7.79m

TRIPLE JUMP
1. ....Walter Davis, Nike — 16.87m
2. ....Aarik Wilson, unattached — 16.60m
3. ....Joe Allen, unattached — 15.61m

SHOT PUT
1. ....Reese Hoffa, New York A.C. — 21.61m
1. ....Christian Cantwell, Nike — 21.10m
3. ....John Godina, adidas — 20.50m

WEIGHT THROW
1. .............A.G. Kruger, Ashland Elite — 23.74m
2. ....Kibwe Johnson, unattached — 23.72m
3. ....Thomas Freeman, New York A.C. — 23.48m

HEPTATHLON*
1. ....Ryan Harlan, unattached — 5949
2 ....Paul Terek, Asics — 5883
3. ....Chris Boyles, unattached — 5751

*Held on March 4–5 in Chapel Hill, North Carolina.
§Final place in high jump decided by number of successful jumps at final height.

Women

60 METERS
1. ....Me'Lisa Barber, adidas — 7.06
2. ....Lauryn Williams, Nike — 7.11
3. ....Torri Edwards, unattached — 7.12

200 METERS
1. ....Crystal Cox, unattached — 23.27
2. ....Rachelle Boone, Nike — 23.53
3. ....Debbie Dunn, unattached — 23.59

400 METERS
1. ....Sanya Richards, Nike — 51.28
2. ....Mary Danner, unattached — 52.69
3. ....Debbie Dunn, unattached — 53.17

800 METERS
1. ....Alice Schmidt, adidas — 2:01.93
2. ....Frances Santin, Santa Monica — 2:03.51
3. ....Krista Ferrara, The Farm Team, Inc — 2:04.51

1,500 METERS
1. ....Treniere Clement, Nike — 4:08.13
2. ....Tiffany McWilliams, adidas — 4:09.17
3. ....Jenelle Deatherage, Reebok — 4:11.75

3,000 METERS
1. ....Carrie Tollefson, adidas — 9:05.80
2. ....Sara Hall, Asics — 9:06.33
3. ....Sarah Schwald, NIke — 9:08.28

3,000-METER RACE WALK
1. ....Joanne Dow, adidas — 12:45.05
2. ....Jolene Moore, New York A.C. — 13:03.90
3. ....Amber Antonia, New York A.C. — 13:13.24

60-METER HURDLES
1. ....Danielle Carruthers, Nike — 7.93
2. ....Damu Cherry, unattached — 7.95
3. ....Lolo Jones, Nike — 7.98

HIGH JUMP
1. ....Chaunte Howard, Nike — 1.95m
2. ....Amy Acuff, Asics — 1.89m
3. ....Gwen Wentland, Nike — 1.86m

POLE VAULT
1. ....Kellie Suttle, Nike — 4.55m
2. ....Jillian Schwartz, Nike — §4.55m
3. ....Jennifer Stuczynski, adidas — 4.50m

LONG JUMP
1. ....Akiba McKinney, unattached — 6.62m
2. ....Tianna Madison, Nike — 6.59m
3. ....Grace Upshaw, Nike — 6.49m

TRIPLE JUMP
1. ....Tiombe Hurd, Nike — 13.89m
2. ....Shani Marks, unattached — 13.64m
3. ....Nicole Whitman, unattached — 13.42m

SHOT PUT
1. ....Jillian Camarena, unattached — 19.26m
2. ....Kristin Heaston, Nike — 18.24m
3. ....Jessica Cosby, Nike — 17.19m

WEIGHT THROW
1. ....Erin Gilreath, New York A.C. — 22.95m
2. ....Amber Campbell unattached — 22.66m
3. ....Loree Smith, New York A.C. — 21.82m

PENTATHLON*
1. ....Lela Nelson, Nike — 4123
2 ....Jackie Poulson, unattached — 4094
3. ....Danielle McNaney, unattached — 3886

*Held on March 4-5 in Chapel Hill, North Carolina.
§Final place in high jump decided by number of successful jumps at final height.

2006 IAAF World Cross-Country Championships

Fukuoka, Japan, April 1-2, 2006

MEN (12,000 METERS; 7.5 MILES)

1.	Kenenisa Bekele, Ethiopia	35:40
2.	Sileshi Sihine, Ethiopia	35:43
3.	Martin Mathathi, Kenya	35:44

WOMEN (8,000 METERS; 5 MILES)

1.	Tirunesh Dibaba, Ethiopia	25:21
2.	Lornah Kiplagat, Netherlands	25:26
3.	Meselech Melkamu, Ethiopia	25:38

Major Marathons

Chicago: October 09, 2005

MEN

1.	Felix Limo, Kenya	2:07:02
2.	Benjamin Maiyo Kenya	2:07:09
3.	Daniel Njenga, Kenya	2:07:14

WOMEN

1.	Deena Kastor, United States	2:21:25
2.	Constantina Tomescu-Dita, Romania	2:21:30
3.	Masako Chiba, Japan	2:26:00

New York City: November 6, 2005

MEN

1.	Paul Tergat, Kenya	2:09:30
2.	Hendrick Ramaala, South Africa	2:09:31
3.	Meb Keflezighi, United States	2:09:56

WOMEN

1.	Jelena Prokopcuka, Latvia	2:24:41
2.	Susan Chepkemei, Kenya	2:24:55
3.	Derartu Tulu, Ethiopia	2:25:21

Tokyo: November 20, 2005

WOMEN ONLY

1.	Naoko Takahashi, Japan	2:24:39
2.	Zivile Balciunaite, Lithuania	2:25:15
3.	Elfenesh Alemu, Ethopia	2:26:50

Tokyo: February 12, 2006

MEN ONLY

1.	Ambesse Tolossa, Ethiopia	2:08:58
2.	Toshinari Takaoka, Japan	2:09:31
3.	Sammy Korir, Kenya	2:10:07

Rome: March 26, 2006

MEN

1.	David Kipkorir, Kenya	2:08:38
2.	Daniele Caimmi, Italy	2:09:30
3.	Laban Kipngetich, Kenya	2:10:00

WOMEN

1.	Tatyana Hladyr, Ukraine	2:25:44
2.	Larissa Zousko, Russia	2:26:26
3.	Zekiros Adenech, Ethopia	2:27:38

Paris: April 09, 2006

MEN

1.	Gashaw Malese, Ethiopia	2:08:03
2.	Kiprotich Kenei, Kenya	2:08:51
3.	Bernard Barmasai, Kenya	2:08:52

WOMEN

1.	Irina Timofeyeva, Russia	2:27:22
2.	Natalya Volgina, Russia	2:27:32
3.	Pamela Chepchumba, Kenya	2:29:48

Boston: April 17, 2006

MEN

1.	Robert Cheruiyot, Kenya	2:07:14
2.	Benjamin Maiyo, Kenya	2:08:21
3.	Meb Keflezhigi, United States	2:09:56

WOMEN

1.	Rita Jeptoo, Kenya	2:23:38
2.	Jelena Prokopcuka, Latvia	2:23:48
3.	Rieka Tosa, Japan	2:24:11

Rotterdam: April 09, 2006

MEN

1.	Sammy Korir, Kenya	2:06:38
2.	Paul Kirui, Kenya	2:06:44
3.	Charles Kibiwott, Kenya	2:06:52

WOMEN

1.	Lornah Kiplagat, Netherlands	2:28:36
2.	Ana Dias, Portugal	2:31:27
3	Isabel Eizmendi, Spain	2:33:14

London: April 23, 2006

MEN

1.	Felix Limo, Kenya	2:06:39
2.	Martin Lel, Kenya	2:06:41
3.	Hendrick Ramaala, South Africa	2:06:55

WOMEN

1.	Deena Kastor, United States	2:19:36
2.	Lyudmila Petrova, Russia	2:21:29
3.	Susan Chepkemei, Kenya	2:21:46

TRACK AND FIELD

World Records

As of October 1, 2006. World outdoor records are recognized by the International Amateur Athletics Federation (IAAF).

Men

Event	Mark	Record Holder	Date	Site
100 meters	9.77†	Asafa Powell, Jamaica	8-18-06	Zurich, Switzerland
200 meters	19.32	Michael Johnson, United States	8-1-96	Atlanta
400 meters	43.18	Michael Johnson, United States	8-26-99	Seville, Spain
800 meters	1:41.11	Wilson Kipketer, Denmark	8-24-97	Cologne
1,000 meters	2:11.96	Noah Ngeny, Kenya	9-5-99	Rieti, Italy
1,500 meters	3:26.00	Hicham El Guerrouj, Morocco	7-14-98	Rome
Mile	3:43.13	Hicham El Guerrouj, Morocco	7-7-99	Rome
2,000 meters	4:44.79	Hicham El Guerrouj, Morocco	9-7-99	Berlin
3,000 meters	7:20.67	Daniel Komen, Kenya	9-1-96	Rieti, Italy
Steeplechase	7:53.63	Saif Saaeed Shaheen, Qatar	9-3-04	Brussels
5,000 meters	12:37.35	Kenenisa Bekele, Ethiopia	5-31-04	Hengelo, Netherlands
10,000 meters	26:17.53	Kenenisa Bekele, Ethiopia	8-26-05	Brussels
20,000 meters	56:55.6	Arturo Barrios, Mexico	3-30-91	La Flâche, France
Hour	21,101 meters	Arturo Barrios, Mexico	3-30-91	La Flâche, France
25,000 meters	1:13:55.8	Toshihiko Seko, Japan	3-22-81	Christchurch, New Zealand
30,000 meters	1:29:18.8	Toshihiko Seko, Japan	3-22-81	Christchurch, New Zealand
Marathon	2:04:55	Paul Tergat, Kenya	9-28-03	Berlin
110-meter hurdles	12.88	Xiang Liu, China	7-11-06	Lausanne, Switzerland
400-meter hurdles	46.78	Kevin Young, United States	8-6-92	Barcelona
20-kilometer walk	1:17:21	Jefferson Perez, Ecuador	8-23-03	Paris
30-kilometer walk	2:01:44.1	Maurizio Damilano, Italy	10-3-92	Cuneo, Italy
50-kilometer walk	3:36:03	Robert Korzeniowski, Poland	8-27-03	Paris
4 x 100-meter relay	37.40	United States (Mike Marsh, Leroy Burrell, Dennis Mitchell, Carl Lewis)	8-8-92	Barcelona
		United States (Jon Drummond, Andre Cason, Dennis Mitchell, Leroy Burrell)	8-21-93	Stuttgart, Germany
4 x 200-meter relay	1:18.68	Santa Monica TC (Mike Marsh, Leroy Burrell, Floyd Heard, Carl Lewis)	4-17-94	Walnut, Calif.
4 x 400-meter relay	2:54.20	United States (Jerome Young, Antonio Pettigrew, Tyree Washington, Michael Johnson)	7-22-98	New York City
4 x 800-meter relay	7:02.43†	Kenya (Wilfred Bungei, William Yiampoy, Joseph Mutua, Ismael Kombich)	8-25-06	Brussels
4 x 1,500-meter relay	14:38.8	W Germany (Thomas Wessinghage, Harald Hudak, Michael Lederer, Karl Fleschen)	8-17-77	Cologne, Germany
High jump	2.45m	Javier Sotomayor, Cuba	7-27-93	Salamanca, Spain
Pole vault	6.14m	Sergei Bubka, Ukraine	7-31-94	Sestriere, Italy
Long jump	8.95m	Mike Powell, United States	8-30-91	Tokyo
Triple jump	18.29m	Jonathan Edwards, Great Britain	8-7-95	Göteborg, Sweden
Shot put	23.12m	Randy Barnes, United States	5-20-90	Westwood, Calif.
Discus throw	74.08	Jürgen Schult, E Germany	6-6-86	Neubrandenburg, Germany
Hammer throw	86.74m	Yuri Syedykh, USSR	8-30-86	Stuttgart, Germany
Javelin throw	98.48m	Jan Zelezny, Czech Republic	5-25-96	Jena, Germany
Decathlon	9026 pts	Roman Sebrle, Czech Republic	5-27-01	Götzis, Austria

Note: The decathlon consists of 10 events: the 100 meters, long jump, shot put, high jump and 400 meters on the first day; the 110-meter hurdles, discus, pole vault, javelin and 1,500 meters on the second.

†Pending ratification.

Women

Event	Mark	Record Holder	Date	Site
100 meters	10.49	Florence Griffith Joyner, United States	7-16-88	Indianapolis
200 meters	21.34	Florence Griffith Joyner, United States	9-29-88	Seoul
400 meters	47.60	Marita Koch, E Germany	10-6-85	Canberra, Australia
800 meters	1:53.28	Jarmila Kratochvílová, Czechoslovakia	7-26-83	Munich
1,000 meters	2:28.98	Svetlana Masterkova, Russia	8-23-96	Brussels
1,500 meters	3:50.46	Yunxia Qu, China	9-11-93	Beijing
Mile	4:12.56	Svetlana Masterkova, Russia	8-14-96	Zurich
2,000 meters	5:25.36	Sonia O'Sullivan, Ireland	7-8-94	Edinburgh
3,000 meters	8:06.11	Junxia Wang, China	9-13-93	Beijing
Steeplechase	9:01.59	Gulnara Samitova, Russia	7-4-04	Iraklio, Greece
5,000 meters	14:24.53	Meseret Defar, Ethiopia	6-03-06	New York City
10,000 meters	29:31.78	Junxia Wang, China	9-8-93	Beijing
Hour	18,340 meters	Tegla Loroupe, Kenya	8-7-98	Borgholzhausen, Germany
20,000 meters	1:05:26.6	Tegla Loroupe, Kenya	9-3-00	Borgholzhausen, Germany
25,000 meters	1:27:05.9	Tegla Loroupe, Kenya	9-21-02	Mengerskirchen
30,000 meters	1:45:50	Tegla Loroupe, Kenya	6-6-03	Warstein, Germany
Marathon	2:15:25	Paula Radcliffe, Great Britain	4-13-03	London
100-meter hurdles	12.21	Yordanka Donkova, Bulgaria	8-20-88	Stara Zagora, Bulgaria
400-meter hurdles	52.34	Yuliya Nosova, Russia	8-8-03	Tula, Russia
5-kilometer walk	20:02.60	Gillian O'Sullivan, Ireland	7-13-02	Dublin
10-kilometer walk	41:56.23	Nadezhda Ryashkina, URS	7-24-90	Seattle
4 x 100-meter relay	41.37	East Germany (Silke Gladisch, Sabine Reiger, Ingrid Auerswald, Marlies Göhr)	10-6-85	Canberra, Australia
4 x 200-meter relay	1:27.46	United States (LaTasha Jenkins, LaTasha Colander-Richardson, Nanceen Perry, Marion Jones)	4-29-00	Philadelphia
4 x 400-meter relay	3:15.17	USSR (Tatyana Ledovskaya, Olga Nazarova, Maria Pinigina, Olga Bryzgina)	10-1-88	Seoul
4 x 800-meter relay	7:50.17	USSR (Nadezhda Olizarenko, Lyubov Gurina, Lyudmila Borisova, Irina Podyalovskaya)	8-5-84	Moscow
High jump	2.09m	Stefka Kostadinova, Bulgaria	8-30-87	Rome
Pole vault	5.01m	Yelena Isinbayeva, Russia	8-12-05	Brussels
Long jump	7.52m	Galina Chistyakova, USSR	6-11-88	Leningrad
Triple jump	15.50m	Inessa Kravets, Ukraine	8-10-95	Göteborg, Sweden
Shot put	22.63m	Natalya Lisovskaya, USSR	6-7-87	Moscow
Discus throw	76.80m	Gabriele Reinsch, E Germany	7-9-88	Neubrandenburg, Germany
Hammer throw	77.80m†	Tatyana Lysenko, Russia	8-15-06	Tallinn, Estonia
Javelin throw	71.70m	Osleidys Menéndez, Cuba	8-14-05	Helsinki
Heptathlon	7291 pts	Jackie Joyner-Kersee, United States	9-24-88	Seoul

Note: The heptathlon consists of 7 events: the 100-meter hurdles, high jump, shot put and 200 meters on the first day;
the long jump, javelin and 800 meters on the second.

†Pending ratification.

American Records

As of October 1, 2006. American outdoor records are recognized by USA Track and Field (USATF). WR=world record. EWR=equals world record.

Men

Event	Mark	Record Holder	Date	Site
100 meters	9.79	Maurice Greene	6-16-99	Athens Greece
200 meters	19.32 WR	Michael Johnson	8-1-96	Atlanta
400 meters	43.18 WR	Michael Johnson	8-26-99	Seville, Spain
800 meters	1:42.60	Johnny Gray	8-28-85	Koblenz, Germany
1,000 meters	2:13.9	Rick Wohlhuter	7-30-74	Oslo, Norway
1,500 meters	3:29.30	Bernard Lagat	8-28-05	Rieti, Italy
Mile	3:47.69	Steve Scott	7-7-82	Oslo, Norway

Men *(Cont.)*

Event	Mark	Record Holder	Date	Site
2,000 meters	4:52.44	Jim Spivey	9-15-87	Lausanne, Switz.
3,000 meters	7:30.84	Bob Kennedy	8-8-98	Monte Carlo
Steeplechase	8:08.82	Daniel Lincoln	7-14-06	Rome, Italy
5,000 meters	12:58.21	Bob Kennedy	8-14-96	Zurich
10,000 meters	27:13.98	Mebrahtom Keflezighi	5-4-01	Palo Alto, California
20,000 meters	58:25.0	Bill Rodgers	8-9-77	Boston
Hour	20,547 meters	Bill Rodgers	8-9-77	Boston
25,000 meters	1:14:11.8	Bill Rodgers	2-21-79	Saratoga, Calif.
30,000 meters	1:31:49	Bill Rodgers	2-21-79	Saratoga, Calif.
Marathon	2:05:38	Khalid Khannouchi	4-14-02	London
110-meter hurdles	12.90†	Dominique Arnold	7-11-06	Lausanne, Swtiz.
400-meter hurdles	46.78 WR	Kevin Young	8-6-92	Barcelona
20-kilometer walk	1:23:40	Tim Seaman	8-14-00	La Jolla, Calif.
30-kilometer walk	2:14:31	Allen James	10-31-93	Atlanta
50-kilometer walk	3:59:41.1	Herman Nelson	6-9-96	Seattle
4x100-meter relay	37.40 WR	United States (Mike Marsh, Leroy Burrell, Dennis Mitchell, Carl Lewis)	8-8-92	Barcelona
		United States (Jon Drummond, Andre Cason, Dennis Mitchell, Leroy Burrell)	8-21-93	Stuttgart, Germany
4x200-meter relay	1:18.68 WR	Santa Monica Track Club (Mike Marsh, Leroy Burrell, Floyd Heard, Carl Lewis)	4-17-94	Walnut, Calif.
4x400-meter relay	2:54.20 WR	United States (Jerome Young, Antonio Pettigrew, Tyree Washington, Michael Johnson)	7-22-98	New York City
4x800-meter relay	7:02.82	United States (Jebreh Harris, Khadevis Robinson, Sam Burley, David Krummenacker)	8-25-06	Brussels
4x1,500-meter relay	14:46.3	National Team (Dan Aldredge, Andy Clifford, Todd Harbour, Tom Duits)	6-24-79	Bourges, France
High jump	2.40m	Charles Austin	8-17-91	Zurich
Pole vault	6.03m	Jeff Hartwig	6-14-00	Jonesboro, Ark.
Long jump	8.95mWR	Mike Powell	8-30-91	Tokyo
Triple jump	18.09m	Kenny Harrison	7-27-96	Atlanta
Shot put	23.12mWR	Randy Barnes	5-20-90	Westwood, Calif.
Discus throw	72.34m	Ben Plucknett	7-7-81	Stockholm
Hammer throw	82.52m	Lance Deal	9-7-96	Milan
Javelin throw	87.68m	Breaux Greer	6-11-04	Bergen, Norway
Decathlon	8891 pts	Dan O'Brien	9-4/5-92	Talence, France

Women

Event	Mark	Record Holder	Date	Site
100 meters	10.49 WR	Florence Griffith Joyner	7-16-88	Indianapolis
200 meters	21.34 WR	Florence Griffith Joyner	9-29-88	Seoul
400 meters	48.70†	Sanya Richards	9-16-06	Athens, Greece
800 meters	1:56.40	Jearl Miles-Clark	8-11-99	Zurich
1,500 meters	3:57.12	Mary Slaney	7-26-83	Stockholm
Mile	4:16.71	Mary Slaney	8-21-85	Zurich
2,000 meters	5:32.7	Mary Slaney	8-3-84	Eugene, Ore.
3,000 meters	8:25.83	Mary Slaney	9-7-85	Rome
Steeplechase	9:29.32	Brianna Shook	7-31-04	Heusen-Zolder, Holland
5,000 meters	14:45.35	Regina Jacobs	7-21-00	Sacramento, Calif.
10,000 meters	30:50.32	Deena Drossin	5-3-02	Palo Alto, Calif.
Marathon	2:21:21	Joan Samuelson	10-20-85	Chicago
100-meter hurdles	12.33	Gail Devers	7-23-00	Sacramento, Calif.
400-meter hurdles	52.61	Kim Batten	8-11-95	Göteborg, Sweden
5,000-meter walk	20:56.88	Michelle Rohl	4-27-96	Philadelphia
10,000-meter walk	44:41.87	Michelle Rohl	7-26-94	St. Petersburg, Russia
4 x 100-meter relay	41.47	National Team (Chryste Gaines, Marion Jones, Inger Miller, Gail Devers)	8-9-97	Athens

†Pending ratification. WR-World record.

Women (Cont.)

Event	Mark	Record Holder	Date	Site
4 x 200-meter relay	1:27.46WR	USA Blue (LaTasha Jenkins, LaTasha Colander, Nanceen Perry, Marion Jones)	4-29-00	Philadelphia
4 x 400-meter relay	3:15.51	United States (Denean Howard, Diane Dixon, Valerie Brisco, Florence Griffith Joyner)	10-1-88	Seoul
4 x 800-meter relay	8:19.9	National Team(Robin Campbell, Joetta Clark, Chris Gregorek, Essie Kelley)	4-24-83	Walnut, Calif.
High jump	2.03m	Louise Ritter	7-9-88	Austin
		Louise Ritter	9-30-88	Seoul
Pole vault	4.83m	Stacy Dragila	6-9-01	Palo Alto, Calif.
Long jump	7.49m	Jackie Joyner-Kersee	5-22-94	New York City
			7-31-94	Sestriere, Italy
Triple jump	14.45m	Tiombe Hurd	7-11-04	Sacramento, Calif.
Shot put	20.18m	Ramona Pagel	6-25-88	San Diego
Discus throw	66.10m	Carol Grady	5-31-86	San Jose, Calif.
Hammer throw	73.87m	Erin Gilreath	6-25-05	Carson, Calif.
Javelin throw	62.44m†	Kim Kreiner	7-6-06	Arhus, Denmark
Heptathlon	7291 pts WR	Jackie Joyner-Kersee	9-23/24-88	Seoul

†Pending ratification. WR-World record.

World and American Indoor Records

As of September 15, 2004. American indoor records are recognized by USA Track and Field. World Indoor records are recognized by the International Amateur Athletics Federation (IAAF). (A) represents an American record, (W) represents a World record.

Men

Event	Mark	Record Holder	Date	Site
50 meters	5.56	Donovan Bailey, Canada (W)	2-9-96	Reno
	5.56	Maurice Greene (A)	2-13-99	Los Angeles
55 meters*	5.99	Obadele Thompson, Barbados (W)	2-22-97	Colorado Springs
	6.00	Lee McRae (A)	3-14-86	Oklahoma City
60 meters	6.39	Maurice Greene (W, A)	3-1-98	Madrid
	6.39	Maurice Greene (W, A)	3-3-01	Atlanta
200 meters	19.92	Frankie Fredericks, Namibia (W)	2-18-96	Liévin, France
	20.10	Wallace Spearmon(A)	3-11-05	Fayetteville, Ark.
400 meters	44.57	Kerron Clement (A, W)	3-12-05	Fayetteville, Ark.
800 meters	1:42.67	Wilson Kipketer, Denmark (W)	3-9-97	Paris
	1:45.00	Johnny Gray (A)	3-8-92	Sindelfingen, Germany
1,000 meters	2:14.96	Wilson Kipketer, Denmark (W)	2-20-00	Birmingham, England
	2:17.86	David Krummenacker (A)	1-27-02	Boston
1,500 meters	3:31.18	Hicham El Guerrouj, Morocco (W)	2-02-97	Stuttgart, Germany
	3:33.34	Bernard Lagat (A)	2-11-05	Fayetteville, Ark.
Mile	3:48.45	Hicham El Guerrouj, Morocco (W)	2-12-97	Ghent, Belgium
	3:49.89	Bernard Lagat (A)	2-11-05	Fayetteville, Ark.
3,000 meters	7:24.90	Daniel Komen, Kenya (W)	2-6-98	Budapest, Hungary
	7:39.23	Tim Broe (A)	1-27-02	Boston
5,000 meters	12:49.60	Kenenisa Bekele, Ethiopia (W)	2-20-04	Birmingham, England
	13:20.55	Doug Padilla (A)	2-12-82	New York City
50-meter hurdles	6.25	Mark McKoy, Canada (W)	3-5-86	Kobe, Japan
	6.35	Greg Foster (A)	1-27-85	Rosemont, Illinois
55-meter hurdles*	6.89	Renaldo Nehemiah (A)	1-20-79	New York City
60-meter hurdles	7.30	Colin Jackson, Great Britain (W)	3-6-94	Sindelfingen, Germany
	7.36	Greg Foster (A)	1-16-87	Los Angeles
	7.36	Allen Johnson (A)	3-6-04	Budapest, Hungary
5,000-meter walk	18:07.08	Mikhail Shchennikov, Russia (W)	2-14-95	Moscow
	19:18.40	Tim Lewis (A)	3-7-87	Indianapolis
4 x 200-meter relay	1:22.11	Great Britain (W) (Linford Christie, Darren Braithwaite, Ade Mafe, John Regis)	3-3-91	Glasgow
	1:22.71	National Team (A) (Thomas Jefferson, Raymond Pierre, Antonio McKay, Kevin Little)	3-3-91	Glasgow

*No recognized world record. †Pending ratification.

Men *(Cont.)*

Event	Mark	Record Holder	Date	Site
4 x 400-meter relay	3:01.96	United States (W, A) (Kerron Clement, Wallace Spearmon Darold Williamson, Jeremy Wariner)	2-11-06	Fayetteville, Arizona
4 x 800-meter relay	7:13.94	Global Athletics & Marketing (W, A) (Rich Kenah, Joel Woody, Karl Paranya, David Krummenacker)	2-6-00	Boston
High jump	2.43m	Javier Sotomayor, Cuba (W)	3-4-89	Budapest, Hungary
	2.40m	Hollis Conway (A)	3-10-91	Seville
Pole vault	6.15m	Sergei Bubka, Ukraine (W)	2-21-93	Donetsk, Ukraine
	6.02m	Jeff Hartwig (A)	3-10-02	Sindelfingen, Germany
Long jump	8.79m	Carl Lewis (W, A)	1-27-84	New York City
Triple jump	17.83m	Alicier Urrutia, Cuba (W)	3-1-97	Sindelfingen, Germany
	17.83m	Christian Olsson, Sweden (W)	3-7-04	Budapest, Hungary
	17.76m	Mike Conley (A)	2-27-87	New York City
Shot put	22.66m	Randy Barnes (W, A)	1-20-89	Los Angeles
Weight throw*	25.86m	Lance Deal (W, A)	3-4-95	Atlanta
Pentathlon*	4478 pts	Steve Fritz, (W, A)	1-14-95	Lawrence, Kan.
Heptathlon	6476 pts	Dan O'Brien (W, A)	3-13/14-93	Toronto

*No recognized world record.

Women

Event	Mark	Record Holder	Date	Site
50 meters	5.96	Irina Privolova, Russia (W)	2-9-95	Madrid
	6.02	Gail Devers (A)	2-21-99	Liévin, France
55 meters	6.56	Gwen Torrence (A)	3-14-87	Oklahoma City, OK
60 meters	6.92	Irina Privalova, Russia (W)	2-11-93	Madrid
	6.92	Irina Privalova, Russia (W)	2-9-95	Madrid
	6.95	Gail Devers (A)	3-12-93	Toronto
	6.95	Marion Jones (A)	3-7-98	Maebashi, Japan
200 meters	21.87	Merlene Ottey, Jamaica (W)	2-13-93	Liévin, France
	22.18	Michelle Collins (A)	3-15-03	Birmingham, England
400 meters	49.59	Jarmila Kratochvilová, Czech. (W)	3-7-82	Milan
	50.64	Diane Dixon (A)	3-10-91	Seville
800 meters	1:55.82	Jolanda Ceplak, Slovenia (W)	3-3-02	Vienna
	1:58.71	Nicole Teter (A)	3-2-02	New York
1,000 meters	2:30.94	Maria Mutola, Mozambique (W)	2-25-99	Stockholm
	2:34.19	Jennifer Toomey (A)	2-20-04	Birmingham, England
1,500 meters	3:58.28	Yelena Soboleva, Russia (W)	2-18-06	Moscow, Russia
	3:59.98	Regina Jacobs, United States (A)	2-1-03	Boston
Mile	4:17.14	Doina Melinte, Romania (W)	2-9-90	East Rutherford, N.J.
	4:20.5	Mary Slaney (A)	2-19-82	San Diego
3,000 meters	8:27.86	Liliy Shobukhova, Russia (W)	2-17-06	Moscow, Russia
	8:39.14	Regina Jacobs (A)	3-7-99	Maebashi, Japan
5,000 meters	13:32.93	Tirunesh Dibaba, Ethiopia (W)	1-29-05	Boston, MA
	15:07.44	Marla Runyan (A)	2-18-01	New York
50-meter hurdles	6.58	Cornelia Oschkenat, E Germany (W)	2-20-88	Berlin
	6.67	Jackie Joyner-Kersee (A)	2-10-95	Reno, NV
55-meter hurdles*	7.37	Jackie Joyner-Kersee (A)	2-3-89	New York
60-meter hurdles	7.69	Ludmila Narozhilenko, Russia (W)	2-4-90	Chelyabinsk, Russia
	7.74	Gail Devers (A)	3-1-03	Boston
3,000-meter walk	11:40.33	Claudia Stef, Romania	1-30-99	Bucharest, Romania
	12:20.79	Debbi Lawrence (A)	3-12-93	Toronto
4 x 200-meter relay	1:32.41	Russia (Y, Kondratyeva, I. Khabarova, Y.Pechonkina, Y. Gushchina) (W)	1-29-05	Glasgow, Scotand
	1:33.24	National Team (A) (Flirtisha Harris, Chryste Gaines, Terri Dendy, Michele Collins)	2-12-94	Glasgow
4 x 400-meter relay	3:23.37	Russia (W)	1-28-06	Glasgow, Scotand
	3:27.59	National Team (A) (Michelle Collins, Monique Hennagan, Zundra Feagin-Alexander, Shanelle Porter)	3-7-99	Maebashi, Japan

*No recognized world record.

Women (cont.)

Event	Mark	Record Holder	Date	Site
4 x 800-meter relay	8:18.71	Russia (W) (Natalya Zaytseva, Olga Kuvnetsova, Yelena Afanasyeva, Yekaterina Podkopayeva)	2-4-94	Moscow
	8:28.41	Univ of Wisconsin (A) (Sarah Renk, Kim Sherman, Sue Gentes, Amy Wickus)	3-14-92	Indianapolis, IN
High jump	2.08m	Kajsa Bergqvist, Sweden (W)	2-4-06	Arnstadt, Germany
	2.01m	Tisha Waller (A)	2-28-98	Atlanta
Pole vault	4.91m	Yelena Isinbayeva, Russia (W)	2-12-06	Donetsk, Ukraine
	4.81m	Stacy Dragila (A)	3-6-04	Budapest, Hungary
Long jump	7.37m	Heike Drechsler, E Germany (W)	2-13-88	Vienna
	7.13m	Jackie Joyner-Kersee (A)	3-5-94	Atlanta
Triple jump	15.36m	Tatyana Lebedeva, Russia (W)	3-6-04	Budapest, Hungary
	14.23m	Sheila Hudson-Strudwick (A)	3-4-95	Atlanta
Shot put	22.50m	Helena Fibingerová, Czech. (W)	2-19-77	Jablonec, Czech.
	19.83m	Ramona Pagel (A)	2-20-87	Inglewood, Calif.
Weight throw*	24.23m	Erin Gilreath (A)	1-25-04	Gainesville, Fla.
Pentathlon	4991 pts	Irina Byelova, CIS (W)	2-14/15-92	Berlin
	4753	De Dee Nathan (A)	3-4/5-99	Maebashi, Japan

*No recognized world record.

World Track and Field Championships

Men

100 METERS

1983	Carl Lewis, United States	10.07
1987*	Carl Lewis, United States	9.93 WR
1991	Carl Lewis, United States	9.86 WR
1993	Linford Christie, Great Britain	9.87
1995	Donovan Bailey, Canada	9.97
1997	Maurice Greene, United States	9.86
1999	Maurice Greene, United States	9.80
2001	Maurice Greene, United States	9.82
2003	Kim Collins, St. Kitts & Nevis	10.07
2005	Justin Gatlin, United States	9.88

200 METERS

1983	Calvin Smith, United States	20.14
1987	Calvin Smith, United States	20.16
1991	Michael Johnson, United States	20.01
1993	Frank Fredericks, Namibia	19.85
1995	Michael Johnson, United States	19.79
1997	Ato Boldon, Trinidad and Tobago	20.04
1999	Maurice Greene, United States	19.90
2001	Konstadínos Kedéris, Greece	20.04
2003	John Capel, United States	20.30
2005	Justin Gatlin, United States	20.04

400 METERS

1983	Bert Cameron, Jamaica	45.05
1987	Thomas Schoenlebe, E Germany	44.33
1991	Antonio Pettigrew, United States	44.57
1993	Michael Johnson, United States	43.65
1995	Michael Johnson, United States	43.39
1997	Michael Johnson, United States	44.12
1999	Michael Johnson, United States	43.18 WR
2001	Avard Moncur, Bahamas	44.64
2003	Jerome Young, United States	44.50
2005	Jeremy Wariner, United States	43.93

800 METERS

1983	Willi Wulbeck, W Germany	1:43.65
1987	Billy Konchellah, Kenya	1:43.06

800 METERS (CONT.)

1991	Billy Konchellah, Kenya	1:43.99
1993	Paul Ruto, Kenya	1:44.71
1995	Wilson Kipketer, Denmark	1:45.08
1997	Wilson Kipketer, Denmark	1:43.38
1999	Wilson Kipketer, Denmark	1:43.30
2001	André Bucher, Switzerland	1:43.70
2003	Djabir Saïd-Guerni, Algeria	1:44.81
2005	Rashid Ramzi, Brunei	1:44.24

1,500 METERS

1983	Steve Cram, Great Britain	3:41.59
1987	Abdi Bile, Somalia	3:36.80
1991	Noureddine Morceli, Algeria	3:32.84
1993	Noureddine Morceli, Algeria	3:34.24
1995	Noureddine Morceli, Algeria	3:33.73
1997	Hicham El Guerrouj, Morocco	3:35.83
1999	Hicham El Guerrouj, Morocco	3:27.65
2001	Hicham El Guerrouj, Morocco	3:30.68
2003	Hicham El Guerrouj, Morocco	3:31.77
2005	Rashid Ramzi, Brunei	3:37.88

STEEPLECHASE

1983	Patriz Ilg, W Germany	8:15.06
1987	Francesco Panetta, Italy	8:08.57
1991	Moses Kiptanui, Kenya	8:12.59
1993	Moses Kiptanui, Kenya	8:06.36
1995	Moses Kiptanui, Kenya	8:04.16
1997	Wilson Boit Kipketer, Kenya	8:05.84
1999	Christopher Koskei, Kenya	8:11.76
2001	Reuben Kosgei, Kenya	8:15.16
2003	Saif Saaeed Shaheen, Qatar	8:04.39
2005	Saif Saaeed Shaheen, Qatar	8:13.31

5,000 METERS

1983	Eamonn Coghlan, Ireland	13:28.53
1987	Said Aouita, Morocco	13:26.44
1991	Yobes Ondieki, Kenya	13:14.45
1993	Ismael Kirui, Kenya	13:02.75

WR=World record.   *Ben Johnson, Canada, disqualified.

Men *(Cont.)*

5,000 METERS *(CONT.)*

1995	Ismael Kirui, Kenya	13:16.77
1997	Daniel Komen, Kenya	13:07.38
1999	Salah Hissou, Morocco	12:58.13
2001	Richard Limo, Kenya	13:00.77
2003	Eliud Kipchoge, Kenya	12:52.79
2005	Benjamin Limo, Kenya	13:32.55

10,000 METERS

1983	Alberto Cova, Italy	28:01.04
1987	Paul Kipkoech, Kenya	27:38.63
1991	Moses Tanui, Kenya	27:38.74
1993	Haile Gebrselassie, Ethiopia	27:46.02
1995	Haile Gebrselassie, Ethiopia	27:12.95
1997	Haile Gebrselassie, Ethiopia	27:24.58
1999	Haile Gebrselassie, Ethiopia	27:57.27
2001	Charles Kamathi, Kenya	27:53.25
2003	Kenenisa Bekele, Ethiopia	26:49.57
2005	Kenenisa Bekele, Ethiopia	27:08.33

MARATHON

1983	Rob de Castella, Australia	2:10:03
1987	Douglas Wakiihuri, Kenya	2:11:48
1991	Hiromi Taniguchi, Japan	2:14:57
1993	Mark Plaatjes, United States	2:13:57
1995	Martín Fiz, Spain	2:11:41
1997	Abel Anton, Spain	2:13:16
1999	Abel Anton, Spain	2:13:36
2001	Gezahegne Abera, Ethiopia	2:12:42
2003	Jaouad Gharib, Morocco	2:08:31
2005	Jaouad Gharib, Morocco	2:10:10

110-METER HURDLES

1983	Greg Foster, United States	13.42
1987	Greg Foster, United States	13.21
1991	Greg Foster, United States	13.06
1993	Colin Jackson, Great Britain	12.91 WR
1995	Allen Johnson, United States	13.00
1997	Allen Johnson, United States	12.93
1999	Colin Jackson, Great Britain	13.04
2001	Allen Johnson, United States	13.04
2003	Allen Johnson, United States	13.12
2005	Ladji Doucoure, France	13:07

400-METER HURDLES

1983	Edwin Moses, United States	47.50
1987	Edwin Moses, United States	47.46
1991	Samuel Matete, Zambia	47.64
1993	Kevin Young, United States	47.18
1995	Derrick Adkins, United States	47.98
1997	Stéphane Diagana, France	47.70
1999	Fabrizio Mori, Italy	47.72
2001	Felix Sánchez, Dominican Rep.	47.49
2003	Felix Sánchez, Dominican Rep.	47.25
2005	Bershawn Jackson, United States	47.30

20-KILOMETER WALK

1983	Ernesto Canto, Mexico	1:20:49
1987	Maurizio Damilano, Italy	1:20:45
1991	Maurizio Damilano, Italy	1:19:37
1993	Valentin Massana, Spain	1:22:31
1995	Michele Didoni, Italy	1:19:59
1997	Daniel Garcia, Mexico	1:21:43
1999	Ilya Markov, Russia	1:23:34
2001	Roman Rasskazov, Russia	1:20:31
2003	Jefferson Pérez, Ecuador	1:17.21 WR
2005	Jefferson Pérez, Ecuador	1:18:35

50-KILOMETER WALK

1983	Ronald Weigel, East Germany	3:43:08
1987	Hartwig Gauder, East Germany	3:40:53
1991	Aleksandr Potashov, USSR	3:53:09

50-KILOMETER WALK *(CONT.)*

1993	Jesus Angel Garcia, Spain	3:41:41
1995	Valentin Kononen, Finland	3:43:42
1997	Robert Korzeniowski, Poland	3:44:46
1999	German Skurygin, Russia	3:44:23
2001	Robert Korzeniowski, Poland	3:42:08
2003	R. Korzeniowski, Poland	3:36:03 WR
2005	S. Kirdyapkin, Russia	3:38:08

4 X 100-METER RELAY

1983	United States (Emmit King, Willie Gault, Calvin Smith, Carl Lewis)	37.86
1987	United States (Lee McRae, Lee McNeil, Harvey Glance, Carl Lewis)	37.90
1991	United States (A. Cason L. Burrell, D. Mitchell, C. Lewis)	37.50 WR
1993	United States (J. Drummond, A. Cason, D. Mitchell, L. Burrell)	37.48
1995	Canada (Robert Esmie, Glenroy Gilbert, Bruny Surin, Donovan Bailey)	38.31
1997	Canada (Robert Esmie, Glenroy Gilbert, Bruny Surin, Donovan Bailey)	37.86
1999	United States (Jon Drummond, Tim Montgomery, Brian Lewis, Maurice Greene)	37.59
2001	United States (Mickey Grimes, Bernard Williams, Dennis Mitchell, Tim Montgomery)	37.96
2003	United States (J. Capel, B. Williams D.Patton, J. Johnson)	38.06
2005	Trinidad and Tobago (L. Doucoure, R. Pognon, E. De Lepine, Dovy Lueyi)	38.08

4 X 400-METER RELAY

1983	USSR (S. Lovachev, A. Troschilo, N. Chernyetski, V. Markin)	3:00.79
1987	United States (Danny Everett Rod Haley, Antonio McKay, Butch Reynolds)	2:57.29
1991	Great Britain (Roger Black Derek Redmond, John Regis, Kriss Akabusi)	2:57.53
1993	United States (Andrew Valmon, Quincy Watts, Butch Reynolds, Michael Johnson)	2:54.29 WR
1995	United States (Marlon Ramsey, Derek Mills, Butch Reynolds, Michael Johnson)	2:57.32
1997	United States (J. Young, A. Pettigrew, C. Jones, T. Washington)	2:56.47
1999	United States (Jerome Davis, Antonio Pettigrew, Angelo Taylor, Michael Johnson)	2:56.45
2001	United States (L. Byrd, A. Pettigrew, D. Brew, A. Taylor)	2:57.54
2003	United States (C. Harrison, T. Washington, D. Brew, J. Young)	2:58.88
2005	United States, (D. Brew, R. Andrew D. Williamson, B. Wariner)	2:56.91

HIGH JUMP

1983	Gennadi Avdeyenko, USSR	2.32m
1987	Patrik Sjoberg, Sweden	2.38m
1991	Charles Austin, United States	2.38m
1993	Javier Sotomayor, Cuba	2.40m WR
1995	Troy Kemp, Bahamas	2.37m
1997	Javier Sotomayor, Cuba	2.37m
1999	Vyacheslav Voronin, Russia	2.37m

Men (Cont.)

HIGH JUMP (CONT.)

2001	Martin Buss, Germany	2.36m
2003	Jacques Freitag, South Africa	2.35m
2005	Yuriy Krymarenko,Ukraine	2.32m

POLE VAULT

1983	Sergei Bubka, USSR	5.70m
1987	Sergei Bubka, USSR	5.85m
1991	Sergei Bubka, USSR	5.95m
1993	Sergei Bubka, Ukraine	6.00m
1995	Sergei Bubka, Ukraine	5.92m
1997	Sergei Bubka, Ukraine	6.01m
1999	Maksim Tarasov, Russia	6.02m
2001	Dmitri Markov, Australia	6.05mWR
2003	Guiseppe Gibilisco, Italy	5.90m
2005	Rens Blom, Netherlands	5.80m

LONG JUMP

1983	Carl Lewis, United States	8.55m
1987	Carl Lewis, United States	8.67m
1991	Mike Powell, United States	8.95mWR
1993	Mike Powell, United States	8.59m
1995	Iván Pedroso, Cuba	8.71m
1997	Iván Pedroso, Cuba	8.51m
1999	Iván Pedroso, Cuba	8.62m
2001	Iván Pedroso, Cuba	8.43m
2003	Dwight Phillips, United States	8.29m
2005	Dwight Phillips, United States	8.60m

TRIPLE JUMP

1983	Zdzislaw Hoffmann, Poland	17.42m
1987	Hristo Markov, Bulgaria	17.92m
1991	Kenny Harrison, United States	17.78m
1993	Mike Conley, United States	17.86m
1995	Jonathan Edwards, G.B.	18.29m WR
1997	Yoelvis Quesada, Cuba	17.85m
1999	Charles Friedek, Germany	17.59m
2001	Jonathan Edwards, G. Britain	17.92m
2003	Christian Olsson, Sweden	17.72m
2005	Walter Davis, United States	17.57m

SHOT PUT

1983	Edward Sarul, Poland	21.39m
1987	Werner Günthör, Switz.	22.23mWR
1991	Werner Günthör, Switz.	21.67m
1993	Werner Günthör, Switz.	21.97m
1995	John Godina, United States	21.47m
1997	John Godina, United States	21.44m
1999	C.J. Hunter, United States	21.79m
2001	John Godina, United States	21.87m
2003	Andrei Mikahnevic, Bulgaria	21.69m
2005	Adam Nelson, United States	21.73m

DISCUS THROW

1983	Imrich Bugar, Czechoslovakia	67.72m
1987	Juergen Schult, E Germany	68.74m
1991	Lars Riedel, Germany	66.20m
1993	Lars Riedel, Germany	67.72m
1995	Lars Riedel, Germany	68.76m
1997	Lars Riedel, Germany	68.54m
1999	Anthony Washington, U.S.	69.08m
2001	Lars Riedel, Germany	69.72m
2003	Virgilijus Alekna, Lithuania	69.69m
2005	Virgilijus Alekna, Lithuania	70.17mWR

HAMMER THROW

1983	Sergei Litvinov, USSR	82.68m
1987	Sergei Litvinov, USSR	83.06m
1991	Yuriy Sedykh, USSR	81.70m
1993	Andrey Abduvaliyev, Tajikistan	81.64m
1995	Andrey Abduvaliyev, Tajikistan	81.56m
1997	Heinz Weis, Germany	81.78m
1999	Karsten Kobs, Germany	80.24m
2001	Szymon Ziolkowski, Poland	83.38m
2003	Ivan Tikhon, Belarus	83.05m
2005	Ivan Tikhon, Belarus	83.89mWR

JAVELIN

1983	Detlef Michel, East Germany	89.48m
1987	Seppo Räty, Finland	83.54m
1991	Kimmo Kinnunen, Finland	90.82m
1993	Jan Zelezny, Czech Republic	85.98m
1995	Jan Zelezny, Czech Republic	89.58m
1997	Marius Corbett, South Africa	88.40m
1999	Aki Parviainen, Finland	89.52m
2001	Jan Zelezny, Czech Republic	92.80mWR
2003	Sergey Makarov, Russia	85.44m
2005	Andrus Varnik, Estonia	87.17m

DECATHLON

1983	Daley Thompson, Great Britain	8666 pts
1987	Torsten Voss, East Germany	8680 pts
1991	Dan O'Brien, United States	8812 pts
1993	Dan O'Brien, United States	8817 pts
1995	Dan O'Brien, United States	8695 pts
1997	Tomás Dvorák, Czech Rep.	8837 pts
1999	Tomás Dvorák, Czech Rep.	8744 pts
2001	Tomás Dvorák, Czech Rep.	8902 ptsWR
2003	Tom Pappas, United States	8750 pts
2005	Bryan Clay, United States	8732 pts

WR–World record.

Women

100 METERS

1983	Marlies Gohr, East Germany	10.97
1987	Silke Gladisch, East Germany	10.90
1991	Katrin Krabbe, Germany	10.99
1993	Gail Devers, United States	10.82
1995	Gwen Torrence, United States	10.85
1997	Marion Jones, United States	10.83
1999	Marion Jones, United States	10.70
2001	Zhanna Pintusevich-Block, Ukraine	10.82
2003	Kelli White, United States	10.85
2005	Lauryn Williams, United States	10.93

200 METERS

1983	Marita Koch, East Germany	22.13
1987	Silke Gladisch, East Germany	21.74
1991	Katrin Krabbe, Germany	22.09

200 METERS (CONT.)

1993	Merlene Ottey, Jamaica	21.98
1995	Merlene Ottey, Jamaica	22.12
1997	Zhanna Pintusevich, Ukraine	22.32
1999	Inger Miller, United States	21.77
2001	Marion Jones, United States	22.39
2003	Kelli White, United States	22.05
2005	Allyson Felix, United States	22.16

400 METERS

1983	Jarmila Kratochvilova, Czech.	47.99
1987	Olga Bryzgina, USSR	49.38
1991	Marie-José Pérec, France	49.13
1993	Jearl Miles, United States	49.82
1995	Marie-José Pérec, France	49.28
1997	Cathy Freeman, Australia	49.77

Women *(Cont.)*

400 METERS *(CONT.)*

1999	Cathy Freeman, Australia	49.67
2001	Amy Mbacke Thiam, Senegal	49.86
2003	Ana Guevara, Mexico	48.89
2005	Darling Williams, Bahamas	49.55

800 METERS

1983	Jarmila Kratochvilova, Czech.	1:54.68
1987	Sigrun Wodars, East Germany	1:55.26
1991	Lilia Nurutdinova, USSR	1:57.50
1993	Maria Mutola, Mozambique	1:55.43
1995	Ana Quirot, Cuba	1:56.11
1997	Ana Quirot, Cuba	1:57.14
1999	Ludmila Formanová, Czech Rep.	1:56.68
2001	Maria Mutola, Mozambique	1:57.17
2003	Maria Mutola, Mozambique	1:59.89
2005	Zulia Calatayud, Cuba	1:58.82

1,500 METERS

1983	Mary Slaney, United States	4:00.90
1987	Tatyana Samolenko, USSR	3:58.56
1991	Hassiba Boulmerka, Algeria	4:02.21
1993	Dong Liu, China	4:00.50
1995	Hassiba Boulmerka, Algeria	4:02.42
1997	Carla Sacramento, Portugal	4:04.24
1999	Svetlana Masterkova, Russia	3:59.53
2001	Gabriela Szabo, Romania	4:00.57
2003	Tatyana Tomashova, Russia	3:58.52
2005	Tatyana Tomashova, Russia	4:00.35

3,000 METERS

1983	Mary Slaney, United States	8:34.62
1987	Tatyana Samolenko, USSR	8:38.73
1991	Tatyana Dorovskikh, USSR	8:35.82
1993	Qu Yunxia, China	8:28.71

5,000 METERS

1995	Sonia O'Sullivan, Ireland	14:46.47
1997	Gabriela Szabo, Romania	14:57.68
1999	Gabriela Szabo, Romania	14:41.82
2001	Olga Yegorova, Russia	15:03.39
2003	Tirunesh Dibaba, Ethiopia	14:51.72
2005	Tirunesh Dibaba, Ethiopia	14:38.59

10,000 METERS

1987	Ingrid Kristiansen, Norway	31:05.85
1991	Liz McColgan, Great Britain	31:14.31
1993	Wang Junxia, China	30:49:30
1995	Fernanda Ribeiro, Portugal	31:04.99
1997	Sally Barsosio, Kenya	31:32.92
1999	Gete Wami, Ethiopia	30:24.56
2001	Derartu Tulu, Ethiopia	31:48.81
2003	Berhane Adere, Ethiopia	30:04.18
2005	Tirunesh Dibaba, Ethiopia	30:24.02

MARATHON

1983	Grete Waitz, Norway	2:28:09
1987	Rosa Mota, Portugal	2:25:17
1991	Wanda Panfil, Poland	2:29:53
1993	Junko Asari, Japan	2:30:03
1995	Manuela Machado, Portugal	2:25:39*
1997	Hiromi Suzuki, Japan	2:29:48
1999	Jong Song-Ok, North Korea	2:26:59
2001	Lidia Simon, Romania	2:26.01
2003	Catherine Ndereba, Kenya	2:23:55
2005	Paula Radcliffe, Great Britain	2:20:57

100-METER HURDLES

1983	Bettine Jahn, East Germany	12.35
1987	Ginka Zagorcheva, Bulgaria	12.34
1991	Lyudmila Narozhilenko, USSR	12.59

*400 meters short.

100-METER HURDLES *(CONT.)*

1993	Gail Devers, United States	12.46
1995	Gail Devers, United States	12.68
1997	Ludmila Engquist, Sweden	12.50
1999	Gail Devers, United States	12.37
2001	Anjanette Kirkland, United States	12.42
2003	Perdita Felicien, Canada	12.53
2005	Michelle Perry, United States	12:66

400-METER HURDLES

1983	Yekaterina Fesenko, USSR	54.14
1987	Sabine Busch, East Germany	53.62
1991	Tatyana Ledovskaya, USSR	53.11
1993	Sally Gunnell, Great Britain	52.74 WR
1995	Kim Batten, United States	52.61
1997	Nezha Bidouane, Morocco	52.97
1999	Daimi Pernia, Cuba	52.89
2001	Nezha Bidouane, Morocco	53.34
2003	Jana Pittman, Australia	53.22
2005	Yuliya Pechonkina, Russia	52.90

10-KILOMETER WALK

1987	Irina Strakhova, USSR	44:12
1991	Alina Ivanova, USSR	42:57
1993	Sari Essayah, Finland	42:59
1995	Irina Stankina, Russia	42:13
1997	Annarita Sidoti, Italy	42:56

20-KILOMETER WALK

1999	Hongyu Liu, China	1:30:50
2001	Olimpiada Ivanova, Russia	1:27:48
2003	Yelena Nikolayeva, Russia	1:26:52
2005	Olimpiada Ivanova, Russia	1:25:41

4 X 100-METER RELAY

1983	E Germany (S. Gladisch, M. Koch, I. Auerswald, M. Gohr)	41.76
1987	United States (A. Brown, D. Williams, F. Griffith, P. Marshall)	41.58
1991	Jamaica (Dalia Duhaney, Juliet Cuthbert, Beverley McDonald, Merlene Ottey)	41.94
1993	Russia (Olga Bogoslovskaya, Galina Malchugina, Natalya Voronova, Irina Privalova)	41.49
1995	United States (Celena Mondie-Milner, Carlette Guidry, Chryste Gaines, Gwen Torrence)	42.12
1997	United States (C. Gaines, M. Jones, I. Miller, G.Devers)	41.47
1999	Bahamas (S. Fynes, C. Sturrup, P. Davis-Thompson, D. Ferguson)	41.92
2001	United States (Kelli White, Chryste Gaines, Inger Miller, Marion Jones)	41.71
2003	France (P. Girard, M. Hurtis S. Félix, C. Arron)	41.78
2005	Jamaica, (A. Daigie, M. Lee, M. B.L. Williams)	41.78

4 X 400-METER RELAY

1983	East Germany (Kerstin Walther, Sabine Busch, Marita Koch, Dagmar Rubsam)	3:19.73
1987	East Germany (Dagmar Neubauer, Kirsten Emmelmann, Petra Müller, Sabine Busch)	3:18.63
1991	USSR (Tatyana Ledovskaya, Lyudmila Dzhigalova, Olga Nazarova, Olga Bryzgina)	3:18.43

Women (Cont.)

4 X 400-METER RELAY (CONT.)

1993	United States (Gwen Torrence, Maicel Malone, Natasha Kaiser-Brown, Jearl Miles)	3:16.71
1995	United States (Kim Graham, Rochelle Stevens, Camara Jones, Jearl Miles)	3:22.39
1997	Germany (A. Feller, U. Rohlander, A. Rucker, G. Breuer)	3:20.92
1999	Russia (Tatyana Chebykina, Svetlana Goncharenko, Olga Kotylarova, Natalya Nazarova)	3:21.98
2001	Jamaica (Sandie Richards, Catherine Scott, Debbie Ann Parris, Lorraine Fenton)	3:20.65
2003	United States (M. Barber, D. Washington, J. Miles-Clark, S. Richards)	3:22.63
2005	Russia, (Y. Pechonkina, O. Krasnomovets, N. Antyukh, S. Pospelova)	3:20.95

HIGH JUMP

1983	Tamara Bykova, USSR	2.01m
1987	Stefka Kostadinova, Bulgaria	2.09mWR
1991	Heike Henkel, Germany	2.05m
1993	Ioamnet Quintero, Cuba	1.99m
1995	Stefka Kostadinova, Bulgaria	2.01m
1997	Hanne Haugland, Norway	1.99m
1999	Inga Babakova, Ukraine	1.99m
2001	Hestrie Cloete, South Africa	2.00m
2003	Hestrie Cloete, South Africa	2.06m
2005	Kajsa Bergvist, Sweden	2.02m

POLE VAULT

1999	Stacy Dragila, United States	4.06m EWR
2001	Stacy Dragila, United States	4.75m
2003	Svetlana Feofanova, Russia	4.75m
2005	Yelena Isinbayeva, Russia	5.01mWR

LONG JUMP

1983	Heike Daute, E Germany	7.27m
1987	Jackie Joyner-Kersee, U.S.	7.36mWR
1991	Jackie Joyner-Kersee, United States	7.32m
1993	Heike Drechsler, Germany	7.11m
1995	Fiona May, Italy	6.98m
1997	Lyudmila Galkina, Russia	7.05m
1999	Niurka Montalvo, Spain	7.06m
2001	Fiona May, Italy	6.87m
2003	Eunice Barber, France	6.99m
2005	Tianna Madison, United States	6.89m

TRIPLE JUMP

1993	Ana Biryukova, Russia	15.09m
1995	Inessa Kravets, Ukraine	15.50m WR
1997	S. Kasparkova, Czech Rep.	15.20m
1999	Paraskevi Tsiamíta, Greece	14.88m
2001	Tatyana Lebedeva, Russia	15.25m
2003	Tatyana Lebedeva, Russia	15.18m
2005	Trecia Smith, Jamaica	15.11m

SHOT PUT

1983	Helena Fibingerova, Czech.	21.05m
1987	Natalya Lisovskaya, USSR	21.24mWR
1991	Zhihong Huang, China	20.83m
1993	Zhihong Huang, China	20.57m
1995	Astrid Kumbernuss, Germany	21.22m
1997	Astrid Kumbernuss, Germany	20.71m
1999	Astrid Kumbernuss, Germany	19.85m
2001	Yanina Korolchik, Belarus	20.61m
2003	Svetlana Krivelyova, Russia	20.63m
2005	Nadezhda Ostapchuk, Russia	20.51m

HAMMER THROW

1999	Mihaela Melinte, Romania	75.20mWR
2001	Yipsi Moreno, Cuba	70.65m
2003	Yipsi Moreno, Cuba	70.30m
2005	Olga Kuzenkova, Russia	75.10m

DISCUS THROW

1983	Martina Opitz, E Germany	68.94m
1987	Martina Hellmann, East Germ.	71.62mWR
1991	Tsvetanka Khristova, Bulgaria	71.02m
1993	Olga Burova, Russia	67.40m
1995	Ellina Zvereva, Belarus	68.64m
1997	Beatrice Faumuina, New Zeal.	66.82m
1999	Franka Dietzsch, Germany	68.14m
2001	Ellina Zvereva,, Belarus	67.10m
2003	Irina Yatchenko, Belarus	67.32m
2005	Franka Dietzsch, Germany	66.56m

JAVELIN

1983	Tiina Lillak, Finland	70.82m
1987	Fatima Whitbread, G. Britain	76.64m
1991	Xu Demei, China	68.78m
1993	Trine Hattestad, Finland	69.18m
1995	Natalya Shikolenko, Belarus	67.56m
1997	Trine Hattestad, Norway	68.78m
1999	Miréla Manjani-Tzelili, Greece	67.09m
2001	Osleidys Menéndez, Cuba	69.53m
2003	Miréla Manjani, Greece	66.52m
2005	Osleidys Menendez, Cuba	71.70mWR

HEPTATHLON

1983	Ramona Neubert, East Germany	6714 pts
1987	Jackie Joyner-Kersee, U.S.	7128 ptswR
1991	Sabine Braun, Germany	6672 pts
1993	Jackie Joyner-Kersee, U.S.	6837 pts
1995	Ghada Shouaa, Syria	6651 pts
1997	Sabine Braun, Germany	6739 pts
1999	Eunice Barber, France	6861 pts
2001	Yelena Prokhorova, Russia	6694 pts
2003	Carolina Klüft, Sweden	7001 pts
2005	Carolina Kluft, Sweden	6887 pts

WR-World record. EWR=equals world record.

Each year (since 1959 for men and 1974 for women) *Track and Field News* has chosen the outstanding athlete in the sport.

MEN

Year	Athlete	Event
1959	Martin Lauer, West Germany	110H/Decath
1960	Rafer Johnson, United States	Decathlon
1961	Ralph Boston, United States	Long jump
1962	Peter Snell, New Zealand	800/1,500
1963	C. K. Yang, Taiwan	Decath/PV
1964	Peter Snell, New Zealand	800/1,500
1965	Ron Clarke, Australia	5K/10K
1966	Jim Ryun, United States	800/1,500
1967	Jim Ryun, United States	1,500
1968	Bob Beamon, United States	Long jump
1969	Bill Toomey, United States	Decathlon
1970	Randy Matson, United States	Shot put
1971	Rod Milburn, United States	110H
1972	Lasse Viren, Finland	5K/10K
1973	Ben Jipcho, Kenya	1,500/5K/ST
1974	Rick Wohlhuter, United States	800/1,500
1975	John Walker, New Zealand	800/1,500
1976	Alberto Juantorena, Cuba	400/800
1977	Alberto Juantorena, Cuba	400/800
1978	Henry Rono, Kenya	5K/10K/ST
1979	Sebastian Coe, Great Britain	800/1,500
1980	Edwin Moses, United States	400H
1981	Sebastian Coe, Great Britain	800/1,500
1982	Carl Lewis, United States	100/200/LJ
1983	Carl Lewis, United States	100/200/LJ
1984	Carl Lewis, United States	100/200/LJ
1985	Said Aouita, Morocco	1,500/5000
1986	Yuri Syedikh, USSR	Hammer
1987	Ben Johnson, Canada	100
1988	Sergei Bubka, USSR	Pole vault
1989	Roger Kingdom, United States	110H
1990	Michael Johnson, United States	200/400
1991	Sergei Bubka, CIS	Pole vault
1992	Kevin Young, United States	400H
1993	Noureddine Morceli, Algeria	1,500/mile/3K
1994	Noureddine Morceli, Algeria	1,500/mile/3K
1995	Haile Gebrselassie, Ethiopia	5K/10K
1996	Michael Johnson, United States	200/400
1997	Wilson Kipketer, Denmark	800
1998	Haile Gebrselassie, Ethiopia	5K/10K
1999	Hicham El Guerrouj, Morocco	1,500/Mile
2000	Virgilijus Alekna, Lithuania	Discus
2001	Hicham El Guerrouj, Morocco	1,500/Mile
2002	Hicham El Guerrouj, Morocco	1,500/Mile
2003	Felix Sanchez, Dominican Rep.	400H
2004	Kenenisa Bekele, Ethiopia	5K/10K
2005	Kenenisa Bekele, Ethiopia	5K/10K

WOMEN

Year	Athlete	Event
1974	Irena Szewinska, Poland	100/200/400
1975	Faina Melnik, USSR	Shot/Discus
1976	Tatyana Kazankina, USSR	800/1,500
1977	R. Ackermann, East Germany	High jump
1978	Marita Koch, East Germany	100/200/400
1979	Marita Koch, East Germany	100/200/400
1980	Ilona Briesenick, East Germany	Shot put
1981	Evelyn Ashford, United States	100/200
1982	Marita Koch, East Germany	100/200/400
1983	J. Kratochvilova, Czechoslovakia	200/400/800
1984	Evelyn Ashford, United States	100
1985	Marita Koch, East Germany	100/200/400
1986	Jackie Joyner-Kersee, U.S.	LJ/Hept
1987	Jackie Joyner-Kersee, U.S	100H/LJ/Hept
1988	Florence Griffith Joyner, U.S.	100/200
1989	Ana Quirot, Cuba	400/800
1990	Merlene Ottey, Jamaica	100/200
1991	Heike Henkel, Germany	High jump
1992	Heike Drechsler, Germany	Long Jump
1993	Wang Junxia, China	1.5K/3K/10K
1994	Jackie Joyner-Kersee, U.S.	100H/LJ/Hept
1995	Sonia O'Sullivan, Ireland	1,500/3K/5K
1996	Svetlana Masterkova, Russia	800/1,500
1997	Marion Jones, United States	100/200/LJ
1998	Marion Jones, United States	100/200/LJ
1999	Gabriela Szabo, Romania	1,500/5,000
2000	Marion Jones, United States	100/200/LJ
2001	Stacy Dragila, United States	Pole vault
2002	Paula Radcliffe, Great Britain	Marathon
2003	Maria Mutola, Mozambique	800
2004	Yelena Isinbayeva, Russia	Pole vault
2005	Yelena Isinbayeva, Russia	Pole vault

Marathon World Record Progression

Men

Record Holder	Time	Date	Site
John Hayes, United States	2:55:18.4	7-24-08	Shepherd's Bush, London
Robert Fowler, United States	2:52:45.4	1-1-09	Yonkers, NY
James Clark, United States	2:46:52.6	2-12-09	New York City
Albert Raines, United States	2:46:04.6	5-8-09	New York City
Frederick Barrett, Great Britain	2:42:31	5-26-09	Shepherd's Bush, London
Harry Green, Great Britain	2:38:16.2	5-12-13	Shepherd's Bush, London
Alexis Ahlgren, Sweden	2:36:06.6	5-31-13	Shepherd's Bush, London
Johannes Kolehmainen, Finland	2:32:35.8	8-22-20	Antwerp, Belgium
Albert Michelsen, United States	2:29:01.8	10-12-25	Port Chester, NY
Fusashige Suzuki, Japan	2:27:49	3-31-35	Tokyo
Yasuo Ikenaka, Japan	2:26:44	4-3-35	Tokyo
Kitei Son, Japan	2:26:42	11-3-35	Tokyo
Yun Bok Suh, Korea	2:25:39	4-19-47	Boston
James Peters, Great Britain	2:20:42.2	6-14-52	Chiswick, England
James Peters, Great Britain	2:18:40.2	6-13-53	Chiswick, England
James Peters, Great Britain	2:18:34.8	10-4-53	Turku, Finland
James Peters, Great Britain	2:17:39.4	6-26-54	Chiswick, England
Sergei Popov, USSR	2:15:17	8-24-58	Stockholm
Abebe Bikila, Ethiopia	2:15:16.2	9-10-60	Rome
Toru Terasawa, Japan	2:15:15.8	2-17-63	Beppu, Japan
Leonard Edelen, United States	2:14:28	6-15-63	Chiswick, England
Basil Heatley, Great Britain	2:13:55	6-13-64	Chiswick, England
Abebe Bikila, Ethiopia	2:12:11.2	6-21-64	Tokyo
Morio Shigematsu, Japan	2:12:00	6-12-65	Chiswick, England
Derek Clayton, Australia	2:09:36.4	12-3-67	Fukuoka, Japan
Derek Clayton, Australia	2:08:33.6	5-30-69	Antwerp, Belgium
Rob de Castella, Australia	2:08:18	12-6-81	Fukuoka, Japan
Steve Jones, Great Britain	2:08:05	10-21-84	Chicago
Carlos Lopes, Portugal	2:07:12	4-20-85	Rotterdam, Netherlands
Belayneh Dinsamo, Ethiopia	2:06:50	4-17-88	Rotterdam, Netherlands
Ronaldo Da Costa, Brazil	2:06:05	9-20-98	Berlin, Germany
Khalid Khannouchi, Morocco	2:05:42	10-24-99	Chicago
Khalid Khannouchi, United States	2:05:38	4-14-02	London
Paul Tergat, Kenya	2:04:55	9-28-03	Berlin

Women

Record Holder	Time	Date	Site
Dale Greig, Great Britain	3:27:45	5-23-64	Ryde, England
Mildred Simpson, New Zealand	3:19:33	7-21-64	Auckland, New Zealand
Maureen Wilton, Canada	3:15:22	5-6-67	Toronto
Anni Pede-Erdkamp, West Germany	3:07:26	9-16-67	Waldniel, W Germany
Caroline Walker, United States	3:02:53	2-28-70	Seaside, Ore.
Elizabeth Bonner, United States	3:01:42	5-9-71	Philadelphia
Adrienne Beames, Australia	2:46:30	8-31-71	Werribee, Australia
Chantal Langlace, France	2:46:24	10-27-74	Neuf Brisach, France
Jacqueline Hansen, United States	2:43:54.5	12-1-74	Culver City, Calif.
Liane Winter, West Germany	2:42:24	4-21-75	Boston
Christa Vahlensieck, West Germany	2:40:15.8	5-3-75	Dülmen, W Germany
Jacqueline Hansen, United States	2:38:19	10-12-75	Eugene, Ore.
Chantal Langlace, France	2:35:15.4	5-1-77	Oyarzun, France
Christa Vahlensieck, West Germany	2:34:47.5	9-10-77	Berlin, W Germany
Grete Waitz, Norway	2:32:29.9	10-22-78	New York City
Grete Waitz, Norway	2:27:32.6	10-21-79	New York City
Grete Waitz, Norway	2:25:41.3	10-26-80	New York City
Grete Waitz, Norway	2:25:29	4-17-83	London
Joan Benoit Samuelson, United States	2:22:43	4-18-83	Boston
Ingrid Kristiansen, Norway	2:21:06	4-21-85	London
Tegla Loroupe, Kenya	2:20:47	4-19-98	Rotterdam, Netherlands
Tegla Loroupe, Kenya	2:20:43	9-26-99	Berlin
Naoko Takahashi, Japan	2:19:46	9-30-01	Berlin
Catherine Ndereba, Kenya	2:18:47	10-7-01	Chicago
Paula Radcliffe, Great Britain	2:17:18	10-13-02	Chicago
Paula Radcliffe, Great Britain	2:15:25	4-13-03	London

The Boston Marathon began in 1897 as a local Patriot's Day event. Run every year but 1918 since then, it has grown into one of the world's premier marathons.

Men

Year	Winner	Time	Year	Winner	Time
1897	John J. McDermott, United States	2:55:10	1955	Hideo Hamamura, Japan	2:18:22
1898	Ronald J. McDonald, United States	2:42:00	1956	Antti Viskari, Finland	2:14:14
1899	Lawrence J. Brignolia, United States	2:54:38	1957	John J. Kelley, United States	2:20:05
1900	James J. Caffrey, Canada	2:39:44	1958	Franjo Mihalic, Yugoslavia	2:25:54
1901	James J. Caffrey, Canada	2:29:23	1959	Eino Oksanen, Finland	2:22:42
1902	Sammy Mellor, United States	2:43:12	1960	Paavo Kotila, Finland	2:20:54
1903	John C. Lorden, United States	2:41:29	1961	Eino Oksanen, Finland	2:23:39
1904	Michael Spring, United States	2:38:04	1962	Eino Oksanen, Finland	2:23:48
1905	Fred Lorz, United States	2:38:25	1963	Aurele Vandendriessche, Belgium	2:18:58
1906	Timothy Ford, United States	2:45:45	1964	Aurele Vandendriessche, Belgium	2:19:59
1907	Tom Longboat, Canada	2:24:24	1965	Morio Shigematsu, Japan	2:16:33
1908	Thomas Morrissey, United States	2:25:43	1966	Kenji Kimihara, Japan	2:17:11
1909	Henri Renaud, United States	2:53:36	1967	David McKenzie, New Zealand	2:15:45
1910	Fred Cameron, Canada	2:28:52	1968	Amby Burfoot, United States	2:22:17
1911	Clarence H. DeMar, United States	2:21:39	1969	Yoshiaki Unetani, Japan	2:13:49
1912	Mike Ryan, United States	2:21:18	1970	Ron Hill, England	2:10:30
1913	Fritz Carlson, United States	2:25:14	1971	Alvaro Mejia, Colombia	2:18:45
1914	James Duffy, Canada	2:25:01	1972	Olavi Suomalainen, Finland	2:15:39
1915	Edouard Fabre, Canada	2:31:41	1973	Jon Anderson, United States	2:16:03
1916	Arthur Roth, United States	2:27:16	1974	Neil Cusack, Ireland	2:13:39
1917	Bill Kennedy, United States	2:28:37	1975	Bill Rodgers, United States	2:09:55
1919	Carl Linder, United States	2:29:13	1976	Jack Fultz, United States	2:20:19
1920	Peter Trivoulidas, Greece	2:29:31	1977	Jerome Drayton, Canada	2:14:46
1921	Frank Zuna, United States	2:18:57	1978	Bill Rodgers, United States	2:10:13
1922	Clarence H. DeMar, United States	2:18:10	1979	Bill Rodgers, United States	2:09:27
1923	Clarence H. DeMar, United States	2:23:37	1980	Bill Rodgers, United States	2:12:11
1924	Clarence H. DeMar, United States	2:29:40	1981	Toshihiko Seko, Japan	2:09:26
1925	Chuck Mellor, United States	2:33:00	1982	Alberto Salazar, United States	2:08:52
1926	John C. Miles, Canada	2:25:40	1983	Gregory A. Meyer, United States	2:09:00
1927	Clarence H. DeMar, United States	2:40:22	1984	Geoff Smith, England	2:10:34
1928	Clarence H. DeMar, United States	2:37:07	1985	Geoff Smith, England	2:14:05
1929	John C. Miles, Canada	2:33:08	1986	Rob de Castella, Australia	2:07:51
1930	Clarence H. DeMar, United States	2:34:48	1987	Toshihiko Seko, Japan	2:11:50
1931	James (Hinky) Henigan, United States	2:46:45	1988	Ibrahim Hussein, Kenya	2:08:43
1932	Paul de Bruyn, Germany	2:33:36	1989	Abebe Mekonnen, Ethiopia	2:09:06
1933	Leslie Pawson, United States	2:31:01	1990	Gelindo Bordin, Italy	2:08:19
1934	Dave Komonen, Canada	2:32:53	1991	Ibrahim Hussein, Kenya	2:11:06
1935	John A. Kelley, United States	2:32:07	1992	Ibrahim Hussein, Kenya	2:08:14
1936	Ellison M. (Tarzan) Brown, United States	2:33:40	1993	Cosmas N'Deti, Kenya	2:09:33
1937	Walter Young, Canada	2:33:20	1994	Cosmas N'Deti, Kenya	2:07:15
1938	Leslie Pawson, United States	2:35:34	1995	Cosmas N'Deti, Kenya	2:09:22
1939	Ellison M. (Tarzan) Brown, United States	2:28:51	1996	Moses Tanui, Kenya	2:09:16
1940	Gerard Cote, Canada	2:28:28	1997	Lameck Aguta, Kenya	2:10:34
1941	Leslie Pawson, United States	2:30:38	1998	Moses Tanui, Kenya	2:07:34
1942	Bernard Joseph Smith, United States	2:26:51	1999	Joseph Chebet, Kenya	2:09:52
1943	Gerard Cote, Canada	2:28:25	2000	Elijah Lagat, Kenya	2:09:47
1944	Gerard Cote, Canada	2:31:50	2001	Lee Bong-Ju, Korea	2:09:43
1945	John A. Kelley, United States	2:30:40	2002	Rodgers Rop, Kenya	2:09:02
1946	Stylianos Kyriakides, Greece	2:29:27	2003	Robert Cheruiyot, Kenya	2:10:11
1947	Yun Bok Suh, Korea	2:25:39	2004	Timothy Cherigat, Kenya	2:10:37
1948	Gerard Cote, Canada	2:31:02	2005	Hailu Negussie, Ethiopia	2:04.32
1949	Karl Gosta Leandersson, Sweden	2:31:50	2006	Robert Cheruiyot, Kenya	2:07:14
1950	Kee Yong Ham, Korea	2:32:39			
1951	Shigeki Tanaka, Japan	2:27:45			
1952	Doroteo Flores, Guatemala	2:31:53			
1953	Keizo Yamada, Japan	2:18:51			
1954	Veikko Karvonen, Finland	2:20:39			

Note: Over the years the Boston course has varied in length. The distances have been 24 miles, 1,232 yards (1897–1923); 26 miles, 209 yards (1924–1926); 26 miles, 385 yards (1927–1952); and 25 miles, 958 yards (1953–1956). Since 1957, the course has been certified to be the standard marathon distance of 26 miles, 385 yards. (*Unofficial.)

Boston Marathon (Cont.)

Women

Year	Winner	Time	Year	Winner	Time
1966	Roberta Gibb, United States	3:21:40*	1987	Rosa Mota, Portugal	2:25:21
1967	Roberta Gibb, United States	3:27:17*	1988	Rosa Mota, Portugal	2:24:30
1968	Roberta Gibb, United States	3:30:00*	1989	Ingrid Kristiansen, Norway	2:24:33
1969	Sara Mae Berman, United States	3:22:46*	1990	Rosa Mota, Portugal	2:25:24
1970	Sara Mae Berman, United States	3:05:07*	1991	Wanda Panfil, Poland	2:24:18
1971	Sara Mae Berman, United States	3:08:30*	1992	Olga Markova, Russia	2:23:43
1972	Nina Kuscsik, United States	3:10:36	1993	Olga Markova, Russia	2:25:27
1973	Jacqueline A. Hansen, United States	3:05:59	1994	Uta Pippig, Germany	2:21:45
1974	Miki Gorman, United States	2:47:11	1995	Uta Pippig, Germany	2:25:11
1975	Liane Winter, W Germany	2:42:24	1996	Uta Pippig, Germany	2:27:12
1976	Kim Merritt, United States	2:47:10	1997	Fatuma Roba, Ethiopia	2:26:23
1977	Miki Gorman, United States	2:48:33	1998	Fatuma Roba, Ethiopia	2:23:21
1978	Gayle Barron, United States	2:44:52	1999	Fatuma Roba, Ethiopia	2:23:25
1979	Joan Benoit, United States	2:35:15	2000	Catherine Ndereba, Kenya	2:26:11
1980	Jacqueline Gareau, Canada	2:34:28	2001	Catherine Ndereba, Kenya	2:23:53
1981	Allison Roe, New Zealand	2:26:46	2002	Margaret Okayo, Kenya	2:20:43
1982	Charlotte Teske, W Germany	2:29:33	2003	Svetlana Zakharova, Russia	2:25:20
1983	Joan Benoit, United States	2:22:43	2004	Catherine Ndereba, Kenya	2:24:27
1984	Lorraine Moller, New Zealand	2:29:28	2005	Catherine Ndereba, Kenya	2:17:38
1985	Lisa Larsen Weidenbach, United States	2:34:06	2006	Rita Jeptoo, Kenya	2:07:14
1986	Ingrid Kristiansen, Norway	2:24:55			

New York City Marathon

	MEN			WOMEN	
Year	Winner	Time	Year	Winner	Time
1970	Gary Muhrcke, United States	2:31:38	1970	No finisher	
1971	Norman Higgins, United States	2:22:54	1971	Beth Bonner, United States	2:55:22
1972	Sheldon Karlin, United States	2:27:52	1972	Nina Kuscsik, United States	3:08:41
1973	Tom Fleming, United States	2:21:54	1973	Nina Kuscsik, United States	2:57:07
1974	Norbert Sander, United States	2:26:30	1974	Katherine Switzer, United States	3:07:29
1975	Tom Fleming, United States	2:19:27	1975	Kim Merritt, United States	2:46:14
1976	Bill Rodgers, United States	2:10:10	1976	Miki Gorman, United States	2:39:11
1977	Bill Rodgers, United States	2:11:28	1977	Miki Gorman, United States	2:43:10
1978	Bill Rodgers, United States	2:12:12	1978	Grete Waitz, Norway	2:32:30
1979	Bill Rodgers, United States	2:11:42	1979	Grete Waitz, Norway	2:27:33
1980	Alberto Salazar, United States	2:09:41	1980	Grete Waitz, Norway	2:25:41
1981	Alberto Salazar, United States	2:08:13	1981	Allison Roe, New Zealand	2:25:29
1982	Alberto Salazar, United States	2:09:29	1982	Grete Waitz, Norway	2:27:14
1983	Rod Dixon, New Zealand	2:08:59	1983	Grete Waitz, Norway	2:27:00
1984	Orlando Pizzolato, Italy	2:14:53	1984	Grete Waitz, Norway	2:29:30
1985	Orlando Pizzolato, Italy	2:11:34	1985	Grete Waitz, Norway	2:28:34
1986	Gianni Poli, Italy	2:11:06	1986	Grete Waitz, Norway	2:28:06
1987	Ibrahim Hussein, Kenya	2:11:01	1987	Priscilla Welch, Great Britain	2:30:17
1988	Steve Jones, Great Britain	2:08:20	1988	Grete Waitz, Norway	2:28:07
1989	Juma Ikangaa, Tanzania	2:08:01	1989	Ingrid Kristiansen, Norway	2:25:30
1990	Douglas Wakiihuri, Kenya	2:12:39	1990	Wanda Panfiil, Poland	2:30:45
1991	Salvador Garcia, Mexico	2:09:28	1991	Liz McColgan, Scotland	2:27:23
1992	Willie Mtolo, S Africa	2:09:29	1992	Lisa Ondieki, Australia	2:24:40
1993	Andres Espinosa, Mexico	2:10:04	1993	Uta Pippig, Germany	2:26:24
1994	German Silva, Mexico	2:11:21	1994	Tegla Loroupe, Kenya	2:27:37
1995	German Silva, Mexico	2:11:00	1995	Tegla Loroupe, Kenya	2:28:06
1996	Giacomo Leone, Italy	2:09:54	1996	Anuta Catuna, Romania	2:28:18
1997	John Kagwe, Kenya	2:08:12	1997	Franziska Rochat-Moser, Switzerland	2:28:43
1998	John Kagwe, Kenya	2:08:45	1998	Franca Fiacconi, Italy	2:25:17
1999	Joseph Chebet, Kenya	2:09:14	1999	Adriana Fernandez, Mexico	2:25:06
2000	Abdelkhader El Mouaziz, Morocco	2:10:09	2000	Ludmila Petrova, Russia	2:25:45
2001	Tesfaye Jifar, Ethiopia	2:07:43	2001	Margaret Okayo, Kenya	2:24:21
2002	Rodgers Rop, Kenya	2:08:07	2002	Joyce Chepchumba, Kenya	2:25:56
2003	Martin Lel, Kenya	2:10:30	2003	Margaret Okayo, Kenya	2:22:31
2004	Hendrik Ramaala, South Africa	2:09:28	2004	Paula Radcliffe, England	2:23:10
2005	Paul Tergat, United States	2:09:30	2005	Jelena Prokopcuka, Latvia	2:24:41

World Cross-Country Championships

Men

Conducted by the International Amateur Athletic Federation (IAAF), this meet draws the best runners in the world at every distance from the mile to the marathon to compete in the same cross-country race.

Year	Winner	Winning Team	Year	Winner	Winning Team
1973	Pekka Paivarinta, Finland	Belgium	1991	Khalid Skah, Morocco	Kenya
1974	Eric DeBeck, Belgium	Belgium	1992	John Ngugi, Kenya	Kenya
1975	Ian Stewart, Scotland	New Zealand	1993	William Sigei, Kenya	Kenya
1976	Carlos Lopes, Portugal	England	1994	William Sigei, Kenya	Kenya
1977	Leon Schots, Belgium	Belgium	1995	Paul Tergat, Kenya	Kenya
1978	John Treacy, Ireland	France	1996	Paul Tergat, Kenya	Kenya
1979	John Treacy, Ireland	England	1997	Paul Tergat, Kenya	Kenya
1980	Craig Virgin, United States	England	1998	Paul Tergat, Kenya	Kenya
1981	Craig Virgin, United States	Ethiopia	1999	Paul Tergat, Kenya	Kenya
1982	Mohammed Kedir, Ethiopia	Ethiopia	2000	Mohammed Mourhit, Belgium	Kenya
1983	Bekele Debele, Ethiopia	Ethiopia	2001	Mohammed Mourhit, Belgium	Kenya
1984	Carlos Lopes, Portugal	Ethiopia	2002	Kenenisa Bekele , Ethiopia	Kenya
1985	Carlos Lopes, Portugal	Ethiopia	2003	Kenenisa Bekele, Ethiopia	Kenya
1987	John Ngugi, Kenya	Kenya	2004	Kenenisa Bekele, Ethiopia	Ethiopia
1988	John Ngugi, Kenya	Kenya	2005	Kenenisa Bekele, Ethiopia	Ethiopia
1989	John Ngugi, Kenya	Kenya	2006	Kenenisa Bekele, Ethiopia	Kenya
1990	Khalid Skah, Morocco	Kenya			

Women

Year	Winner	Winning Team	Year	Winner	Winning Team
1973	Paola Cacchi, Italy	England	1991	Lynn Jennings, United States	Kenya
1974	Paola Cacchi, Italy	England	1992	Lynn Jennings, United States	Kenya
1975	Julie Brown, United States	United States	1993	Albertina Dias, Portugal	Kenya
1976	Carmen Valero, Spain	USSR	1994	Helen Chepngeno, Kenya	Portugal
1977	Carmen Valero, Spain	USSR	1995	Derartu Tulu, Ethiopia	Kenya
1978	Grete Waitz, Norway	Romania	1996	Gete Wami, Ethiopia	Kenya
1979	Grete Waitz, Norway	United States	1997	Derartu Tulu, Ethiopia	Ethiopia
1980	Grete Waitz, Norway	USSR	1998	Sonia O'Sullivan, Ireland	Kenya
1981	Grete Waitz, Norway	USSR	1999	Gete Wami, Ethiopia	Ethiopia
1982	Maricica Puica, Romania	USSR	2000	Derartu Tulu, Ethiopia	Ethiopia
1983	Grete Waitz, Norway	United States	2001	Paula Radcliffe, Great Britain	Kenya
1984	Maricica Puica, Romania	United States	2002	Paula Radcliffe, Great Britain	Ethiopia
1985	Zola Budd, England	United States	2003	Werknesh Kidane, Ethiopia	Ethiopia
1986	Zola Budd, England	England	2004	Benita Johnson, Australia	Ethiopia
1987	Annette Sergent, France	United States	2005	Tirunesh Dibaba, Ethiopia	Ethiopia
1988	Ingrid Kristiansen, Norway	USSR	2006	Tirunesh Dibaba, Ethiopia	Ethiopia
1989	Annette Sergent, France	USSR			
1990	Lynn Jennings, United States	USSR			

Notable Achievements

Longest Winning Streaks

MEN

Event	Name and Nationality	Streak	Years
100 meters	Bob Hayes, United States	49	1962–64
200 meters	Manfred Gemar, Germany	41	1956–60
400 meters	Michael Johnson, United States	58	1989–97
800 meters	Mal Whitfield, United States	40	1951–54
1,500 meters	Hicham El Guerrouj, Morocco	23	1996–00
1,500 meters/mile	Steve Ovett, Great Britain	45	1977–80
Mile	Herb Elliott, Australia	35	1957–60
Steeplechase	Gaston Roelants, Belgium	45	1961–66
5,000 meters	Emil Zátopek, Czechoslovakia	48	1949–52
10,000 meters	Emil Zátopek, Czechoslovakia	38	1948–54
Marathon	Frank Shorter, United States	6	1971–73
110-meter hurdles	Jack Davis, United States	44	1952–55
400-meter hurdles	Edwin Moses, United States	107	1977–87
High jump	Ernie Shelton, United States	46	1953–55
Pole vault	Bob Richards, United States	50	1950–52
Long jump	Carl Lewis, United States	65	1981–91
Triple jump	Adhemar da Silva, Brazil	60	1950–56
Shot put	Parry O'Brien, United States	116	1952–56
Discus throw	Ricky Bruch, Sweden	54	1972–73

Longest Winning Streaks *(Cont.)*

MEN

Event	Name and Nationality	Streak	Years
Hammer throw	Imre Nemeth, Hungary	73	1946–50
Javelin throw	Janis Lusis, USSR	41	1967–70
Decathlon	Bob Mathias, United States	11	1948–56

WOMEN

Event	Name and Nationality	Streak	Years
100 meters	Merlene Ottey, Jamaica	56	1987–91
200 meters	Irena Szewinska, Poland	38	1973–75
400 meters	Irena Szewinska, Poland	36	1973–78
800 meters	Ana Fidelia Quirot, Cuba	36	1987–90
1,500 meters	Paula Ivan, Romania	15	1988–91
1,500 meters/mile	Paula Ivan, Romania	19	1988–90
3,000 meters	Mary Slaney, United States	10	1982–84
10,000 meters	Ingrid Kristiansen, Norway	5	1985–87
Marathon	Katrin Dörre, East Germany	10	1982–86
100-meter hurdles	Annelie Ernhardt, East Germany	44	1972–75
400-meter hurdles	Ann-Louise Skoglund, Sweden	18	1981–83
High jump	Iolanda Balas, Romania	140	1956–67
Long jump	Tatyana Shchelkanova, USSR	19	1964–66
Shot put	Nadezhda Chizhova, USSR	57	1969–73
Discus throw	Gisela Mauermeyer, Germany	65	1935–42
Javelin throw	Ruth Fuchs, East Germany	30	1972–73
Multi	Heide Rosendahl, West Germany	15	1969–72

Most Consecutive Years Ranked No. 1 in the World

MEN

No.	Name and Nationality	Event	Years
11	Sergei Bubka, Ukraine	Pole vault	1984–94
9	Viktor Saneyev, USSR	Triple jump	1968–76
8	Bob Richards, United States	Pole vault	1949–56
8	Ralph Boston, United States	Long jump	1960–67

WOMEN

No.	Name and Nationality	Event	Years
9	Iolanda Balas, Romania	High jump	1958–66
8	Ruth Fuchs, East Germany	Javelin	1972–79
7	Faina Melnick, USSR	Discus throw	1971–77

Major Barrier Breakers

MEN

Event	Mark	Name and Nationality	Date	Site
sub 10-second 100 meters	9.95	Jim Hines, United States	Oct. 14, 1968	Mexico City
sub 20-second 200 meters	19.83	Tommie Smith, United States	Oct. 16, 1968	Mexico City
sub 45-second 400 meters	44.9	Otis Davis, United States	Sept. 6, 1960	Rome
sub 1:45 800 meters	1:44.3	Peter Snell, New Zealand	Feb. 3, 1962	Christchurch, New Zealand
sub four minute mile	3:59.4	Roger Bannister, Great Britain	May 6, 1954	Oxford
sub 3:50 mile	3:49.4	John Walker, New Zealand	Aug. 12, 1975	Göteborg, Sweden
sub 13-minute 5,000 meters	12:58.39	Said Aouita, Morocco	July 22, 1986	Rome
sub 27:00 10,000 meters	26:58.38	Yobes Ondieki, Kenya	July 10, 1993	Oslo
sub 13-second 110-meter hurdles	12.93	Renaldo Nehemiah, United States	Aug. 19, 1981	Zurich
sub 50-second 400-meter hurdles	49.5	Glenn Davis, United States	June 29, 1956	Los Angeles
7 ft high jump	7 ft ⅝ in	Charles Dumas, United States	June 29, 1956	Los Angeles
8 ft high jump	8 ft	Javier Sotomayor, Cuba	July 29, 1989	San Juan
60 ft triple jump	60 ft ¼ in	Jonathan Edwards, Great Britain	Aug. 7, 1995	Göteborg, Sweden
20 ft pole vault	20 ft	Sergei Bubka, USSR	March 15, 1991	San Sebastian, Spain
70 ft shot put	70 ft 7¼ in	Randy Matson, United States	May 5, 1965	College Station, Texas
200 ft discus throw	200 ft 5 in	Al Oerter, United States	May 18, 1962	Los Angeles

Major Barrier Breakers *(Cont.)*

MEN *(CONT.)*

Event	Mark	Name and Nationality	Date	Site
300 ft (new) javelin	300 ft 1 in	Steve Backley, Great Britain	Jan. 25, 1992	Auckland, New Zealand
9,000-pt decathlon	9026	Roman Sebrle, Czech Republic	May 27, 2001	Gotzis, Austria

WOMEN

Event	Mark	Name and Nationality	Date	Site
sub 11-second 100 meters	10.88	Marlies Oelsner, East Germany	July 1, 1977	Dresden
sub 22-second 200 meters	21.71	Marita Koch, East Germany	June 10, 1979	Karl Marxstadt, E Germany
sub 50-second 400 meters	49.9	Irena Szewinska, Poland	June 22, 1974	Warsaw
sub 2:00 800 meters	1:59.1	Shin Geum Dan, North Korea	Nov. 12, 1963	Djakarta
sub 4:00 1,500 meters	3:56.0	Tatyana Kazankina, USSR	June 28, 1976	Podolsk, USSR
sub 4:20 mile	4:17.55	Mary Decker, United States	Feb. 16, 1980	Houston
sub 15:00 5,000 meters	14:58.89	Ingrid Kristiansen, Norway	June 28, 1984	Oslo
sub 30:00 10,000 meters	29:31.78	Wang Junxia, China	Sept. 8, 1993	Beijing
sub 2:30 marathon	2:27:33	Grete Waitz, Norway	Oct. 21, 1979	New York City
sub 2:20 marathon	2:19:46	Naoko Takahashi, Japan	Sept. 30, 2001	Berlin
sub 13-second 100-meter hurdles	12.9	Karin Balzer, East Germany	Sept. 5, 1969	Berlin
6 ft high jump	6 ft	Iolanda Balas, Romania	Oct. 18, 1958	Budapest
15 ft pole vault	15 ft ½ in	Emma George, Australia	March 14, 1998	Melbourne
70 ft shot put	70 ft 4½ in	Nadyezhda Chizhova, USSR	Sept. 29, 1973	Varna, Bulgaria
200 ft discus throw	201 ft	Liesel Westermann, W Germany	Nov. 5, 1967	Sao Paulo
200 ft javelin throw	201 ft 4 in	Elvira Ozolina, USSR	Aug. 27, 1964	Kiev
first 7,000-point heptathlon	7,148	Jackie Joyner-Kersee, U.S.	July 6–7, 1986	Moscow

Olympic Accomplishments

Oldest Olympic gold medalist—Patrick (Babe) McDonald, United States, 42 years, 26 days, 56-pound weight throw, 1920.

Oldest Olympic medalist—Tebbs Lloyd Johnson, Great Britain, 48 years, 115 days, 1948 (bronze), 50K walk.

Youngest Olympic gold medalist—Barbara Jones, United States, 15 years 123 days, 1952, 4 x 100 relay.

Youngest gold medalist in individual event—Ulrike Meyfarth, West Germany, 16 years, 123 days, 1972, high jump.

World Record Accomplishments*

Most world records equaled or set in a day—6, Jesse Owens, United States, 5-25-35, (9.4 100 yards; 26' 8¼" long jump; 20.3 200 meters and 220 yards; and 22.6 220-yard hurdles and 200-meter hurdles.

Most records in a year—10, Gunder Hägg, Sweden, 1941–42, 1,500 to 5,000 meters.

Most records in a career—35, Sergei Bubka, 1983–94, pole vault indoors and out.

Longest span of record setting—11 years, 20 days, Irena Szewinska, Poland, 1965–76, 200 meters.

Youngest person to set a set world record—Carolina Gisolf, Holland, 15 years, 5 days, 1928, high jump, 5 ft 3⅜ in.

Youngest man to set a world record—John Thomas, United States, 17 years, 355 days, 1959, high jump, 7 ft 1¼ in.

Oldest person to set world record—Carlos Lopes, Portugal, 38 years, 59 days, marathon, 2:07:12.

Greatest percentage improvement—6.59, Bob Beamon, United States, 1968, long jump.

Longest lasting record—long jump, 26 ft 8¼ in, Jesse Owens, United States, 25 years, 79 days (1935–60).

Highest clearance over head, men—23¼ in, Franklin Jacobs, United States (5' 8"), 1978.

Highest clearance over head, woman—12¾ in, Yolanda Henry, United States (5' 6"), 1990.

*Marks sanctioned by the IAAF.

Swimming

Brendan Hansen
of the United States

Smoke on the Water

In 2006, the US Swimming team got back on track, shaking off recent controversies and lackluster performances

BY MARK BECHTEL

THE U.S. TEAM LEFT THE 2004 Olympics in Athens with an impressive medal haul: 28 medals, nearly twice as many as the second-place Aussies. But not every swimmer went home happy. Katie Hoff, the youngest member of the U.S. team, had a disastrous showing, finishing seventh in one event and failing to qualify for the finals of her other. And Brendan Hansen lost both of his events—despite the fact that he entered the Games holding the world record in each.

The Pan Pacific Championships aren't quite the Olympic Games, but this year's competition, in Victoria, B.C., Canada, allowed Hoff and Hansen a measure of redemption—while sending the message that they'll be tough to beat in the 2008 Games in Beijing. Hansen walloped his rival, Japan's Kosuke Kitajima, in both the 100- and 200-meter breaststroke. In Athens, Kitajima controversially won both events. The U.S. protested that he used an illegal dolphin kick, but to no avail. And his post-race demeanor rubbed a few swimmers the wrong way. "At the finish he let out an unbelievable scream," said Hansen, who was in the lane next to Kitajima. "I told myself, 'Just soak it in.' I walked away from

Athens with a huge chip on my shoulder."

It showed in Victoria. Hansen won the 100, beating Kitajima by a full second, and then blew away the field in the 200, reclaiming the world record (he clipped a quarter of a second off the old mark) and finishing 2.37 seconds ahead of Kitajima. "I did it right, and everything clicked," Hansen said. "At the 150 I was like, 'See ya, I'm gone.'" The result appeared to set the stage for a rubber match at next year's worlds, but Hansen didn't see it that way. "I don't know how much of a rivalry it's going to be, because I don't plan on letting him get anywhere close to me again."

Hoff, meanwhile, won five medals in Victoria, leading a strong showing for the young women's team—and going a long way towards erasing the bad memories of Athens. At the Olympics, Hoff, then 15, was a bundle of nerves. To overcome them, she didn't rely on hypnosis or Buddhist chanting, instead she took a simpler route. "I've learned to relax and calm myself before races by taking deep breaths," she said. It doesn't sound like much, but it's tough to argue with the results. Hoff was so laid back at the nationals (two weeks before the Pan Pacs) that she was placing bets with a U.S. Swimming official on how much lactic acid

would show up in her post-race blood test. She won $6.50. (Not that she's hurting for cash. Speedo signed her to a 10-year endorsement deal.) In Victoria, she won three golds (the 200-meter freestyle, 400-meter individual medley and the 4 x 200 freestyle relay) and two silvers (400 freestyle and 200 IM). Said coach Mark Schubert, "She is on a trajectory to be one of the greatest swimmers in the history of our country." We'll find out just how great in Beijing—Hoff expects to swim in 13 events.

The Pan Pacs weren't bad for established stars either. Aaron Peirsol broke his own 200-meter backstroke world record, a feat made more impressive by the fact that he strained his right shoulder arm wrestling two months before the meet. And Michael Phelps used the meet to show that he's still got some competitive fire in him.

After his masterful performance in Athens catapulted him into the superstar stratosphere, Phelps predictably suffered a drop-off. He had a lackluster 2005 worlds, failing to break a single world record. At the

Hoff's impressive medal haul in 2006 made a bold statement and the 17-year-old looks to be a tough opponent come 2008.

Pan Pacs, though, he showed that he's got his head back where it needs to be. "It was a big thing for me to get re-excited to swim, re-excited to train," he said. He broke marks in the 200 butterfly and 200 IM, and was part of the record breaking 4 x 100 freestyle relay team. The records were especially sweet since he promised his grandmother, who died of cancer earlier in the year, that he'd break a record. "I was going to break a world record for her. To be able to come in and break two [individual marks] is unbelievable. She is definitely watching."

And so were a whole lot of swimmers with ideas about beating Phelps in Beijing. They couldn't have liked what they saw: the most talented swimmer in the world, back to doing what he does best—and making it look easy. Said a beaming Phelps, "It's pretty much the first meet where I have been happy after last summer."

2005–2006 Major Competitions

Men

U.S. OPEN
Auburn, Ala., December 1–3, 2005

50 free	Nicho Brunelli, Sun Devil Aqua.	22.13
100 free	Nicho Brunelli, Sun Devil Aqua.	48.98
200 free	Van De Hoogen, P S V	1:46.23
400 free	Mark Randell, Univ. of Ala.	3:52.14
1,500 free	Mark Randell, Univ. of Ala	15:03.62
100 back	Ryan Lochte, Univ. of Fla.	55.83
200 back	Ryan Lochte, Univ. of Fla.	2:00.88
100 breast	Vladislav Polyakov, Univ. of Ala	1:01.98
200 breast	Vladislav Polyakov, Univ. of Ala	2:14.10
100 fly	Todd Cooper, Scotland	53.66
200 fly	Daniel Madwed, Sharks	1:58.21
200 IM	Ryan Lochte, Univ. of Fla	2:01.98
400 IM	Robert Margalis, St. Petersburg	4:23.94
400 m relay	University of Ala.	3:49.26
400 f relay	Scotland A	3:25.34
800 f relay	University of Fla.	7:35.01

U.S. NATIONAL CHAMPIONSHIPS
Irvine, Calif., August 1–5, 2006

50 free	Cullen Jones, NC State Aqua.	21.94
100 free	Jason Lezak, Irvine Nova.	48.63
200 free	Michael Phelps, Club Wolverine	1:45.63
400 free	Klete Keller, Club Wolverine	3:44.27
1,500 free	Erik Vendt, Club Wolverine	15:05.41
100 back	Aaron Peirsol, Longhorn Aqua.	53.38
200 back	Aaron Peirsol, Longhorn Aqua.	1:56.36
100 breast	Brendan Hansen, Longhorn Aqua.	59.13
200 breast	Brendan Hansen, Longhorn Aqua.	2:08.74
100 fly	Michael Phelps, Club Wolverine	51.51
200 fly	Michael Phelps, Club Wolverine	1:54.32
200 IM	Michael Phelps, Club Wolverine	1:56.50
400 IM	Michael Phelps, Club Wolverine	4:10.16
400 m relay	Club Wolverine	3:41.96
400 f relay	Longhorn Aqua.	3:24.14
800 f relay	Club Wolverine	7:26:35

PAN PACIFIC CHAMPIONSHIPS
Victoria, B.C., Canada, August 17–20, 2006

50 free	Cullen Jones, United States	21.84
100 free	Brent Hayden, Canada	48.59
200 free	Klete Keller, United States	1:46.20

PAN PACIFIC CHAMPIONSHIPS (CONT.)

400 free	Tae Hwan Park, Korea	3:45.72
800 free	Andrew Hurd, Canada	7:55.88
1,500 free	Tae Hwan Park, Korea	15:06.11
100 back	Aaron Peirsol, United States	53.32
200 back	Aaron Peirsol, United States	1:54.44
100 breast	Brendan Hansen, U.S.	59.90
200 breast	Brendan Hansen, U.S.	2:08.50
100 fly	Ian Crocker, United States	51.47
200 fly	Michael Phelps, United States	1:53.80
200 IM	Michael Phelps, United States	1:55.84
400 IM	Michael Phelps, United States	4:10.47
400 f relay	United States	3:12.46
800 f relay	United States	7:05.28

FINA WORLD CHAMPIONSHIPS
Shanghai, China, April 5–9, 2006

50 free	Duje Draganja, Croatia	21.38
100 free	Filippo Magnini, Russia	47.24
200 free	Ryk Neethling, Russia	1:43.51
400 free	Yury Prilukov, Russia	3:38.08
1,500 free	Yury Prilukov, Russia	14:23.92
50 back	Matthew Welsh, Australia	23.53
100 back	Matthew Welsh, Australia	51.09
200 back	Ryan Lochte, United States	1:49.05
50 breast	Oleg Lisogor, Ukraine	26.39
100 breast	Oleg Lisogor, Ukraine	58.14
200 breast	Vladislav Polyakov, Kazahstan	2:06.95
50 fly	Matthew Welsh, Australia	23.05
100 fly	Kaio Almeida, Brazil	51.07
200 fly	Peng Wu, China	1:52.36
200 IM	Ryan Lochte, United States	1:53.31
400 IM	Ryan Lochte, United States	4:02.49
400 m relay	Australia	3:27.71
400 f relay	Italy	3:10.74
800 f relay	Italy	6:59.08

FINA WORLD DIVING CHAMPIONSHIPS
Montreal, Canada, July 17–24, 2005

1-m spgbd	Alexandre Despatie, Canada	489.69
3-m spgbd	Alexandre Despatie, Canada	813.60
Platform	Jia Hu, China	698.01
3-m sync	He/Wang, China	384.42
10-m sync	Dobrosok/Galperin, Russia	392.88

Women

U.S. OPEN
Auburn, Ala., December 1–3, 2005

50 free	Amanda Weir, Swim Atl-Ga.	25.40
100 free	Amanda Weir, Swim Atl-Ga.	55.22
200 free	Katie Hoff, North Baltimore	1:59.47
400 free	Hayley Peirsol, Auburn Univ.	4:15.24
800 free	Hayley Peirsol, Auburn Univ	8:34.34
100 back	Margaret Hoelzer, Auburn Aqua.	1:02.26
200 back	Margaret Hoelzer, Auburn Aqua.	2:13.65
100 breast	Tara Kirk, Unattached	1:07.36
200 breast	Megan Jendrick, King Aqua.	2:28.89
100 fly	Katie Hoff, North Baltimore	1:00.18
200 fly	Katie Hoff, North Baltimore	2:09.81
200 IM	Katie Hoff, North Baltimore	2:11.90
400 IM	Courtney Kalisz, North Baltimore	4:45.64

U.S. OPEN (CONT.)

400 m relay	King Aqua.	4:15.93
400 f relay	Auburn Univ.	3:50.06
800 f relay	Auburn Univ.	8:22.05

U.S. NATIONAL CHAMPIONSHIPS
Irvine, Calif., August 1–5, 2006

50 free	Kara Lynn Joyce, Athens Bulldogs	24.97
100 free	Amanda Weir, Swim Atl-Ga.	53.58
200 free	Natal Coughlin, California Aqua.	1:58.11
400 free	Kate Ziegler, The Fish	4:05.75
800 free	Haley Peirsol, Club Wolverine	8:26.45
100 back	Leyla Vaziri, Coral Springs	1:01.69
200 back	Margaret Hoelzer, Auburn Aqua.	2:10.71
100 breast	Megan Jendrick, King Aqua.	1:07.54
200 breast	Tara Kirk, Stanford Swim.	2:28.46

Women (Cont.)

U.S. NATIONAL CHAMPIONSHIPS (CONT.)

100 fly	Natalie Coughlin, Calif. Aqua.	57.78
200 fly	Kim Vandenberg, UCLA	2:08.51
200 IM	Katie Hoff, North Baltimore	2:10.05
400 IM	Katie Hoff, North Baltimore	4:35.82
400 m relay	California Aqua.	4:03.32
400 f relay	Tucson Ford-Ariz.	3:42.90
800 f relay	California Aqua.	8:08.16

PAN PACIFIC CHAMPIONSHIPS
Victoria, B.C., Canada, August 17-20, 2006

50 free	Kara Lynn Joyce, United States	25.10
100 free	Natalie Coughlin, United States	53.87
200 free	Katie Hoff, United States	1:58.02
400 free	Ai Shibata, Japan	4:07.61
800 free	Kate Ziegler, United States	8:24.56
1,500 free	Kate Ziegler, United States	15.55.01
100 back	Hanae Ito, Japan	1:00.63
200 back	Reiko Nakamura, Japan	2:08.86
100 breast	Tara Kirk, United States	1:07.56
200 breast	Suzaan Van Biljon, Russia	2:26.36
100 fly	Jessicah Schipper, Australia	57.30
200 fly	Jessicah Schipper, Australia	2:05.40
200 IM	Whitney Myers, United States	2:10.11
400 IM	Katie Hoff, United States	4:36.82
400 m relay	United States	3:58.38
400 f relay	United States	3:35.80
800 f relay	United States	7:54.62

FINA WORLD CHAMPIONSHIPS
Shanghai, China, April 5-9, 2006

50 free	Lisbeth Lenton, Australia	23.97
100 free	Lisbeth Lenton, Australia	52.33
200 free	Yu Yang, China	1:54.94
400 free	Kate Ziegler, United States	4:01.79
50 back	Janine Pietsch, Germany	27.00
100 back	Janine Pietsch, Germany	58.02
200 back	Margaret Hoelzer, United States	2:05.29
50 breast	Jade Edmiston, Australia	30:22
100 breast	Tara Kirk, United States	1:05.25
200 breast	Hui Qi, China	2:20.72
50 fly	Therese Alshammar, Sweden	25.76
100 fly	Lisbeth Lenton, Australia	56.61
200 fly	Jessicah Schipper, Australia	2:05.11
200 IM	Hui Qi, China	2:09.33
400 IM	Hui Qi, China	4:34.28
400 m relay	Australia	3:51.84
400 f relay	Netherlands	3:33.32
800 f relay	Australia	7:46.96

FINA WORLD DIVING CHAMPIONSHIPS
Montreal, Canada, July 17-24, 2005

1-m spgbd	Blythe Hartley, Canada	325.65
3-m spgbd	Jingjing Guo, China	645.54
Platform	Laura Ann Wilkinson, United States	564.87
3-m sync	Li/Guo, China	349.80
10-m sync	Jia/Yuan, China	351.60

World and American Records Set in 2006

Men

Event	Mark	Record Holder	Date	Site
100 breast	59.13	Brendan Hansen, United States (W,A)	8-01-06	Irvine, Calif.
200 breast	2:08.74	Brendan Hansen, United States (W,A)	8-05-06	Irvine, Calif.
200 fly	1:53.80	Michael Phelps, United States (W,A)	8-17-06	Victoria, Can.
200 breast	2:08.50	Brendan Hansen, United States (W,A)	8-20-06	Victoria, Can.
200 back	1:54.44	Aaron Peirsol, United States (W,A)	8-19-06	Victoria, Can.
200 IM	1:55.84	Michael Phelps, United States (W,A)	8-20-06	Victoria, Can.
400 free relay	3:12.46	United States (W,A)	8-19-06	Victoria, Can.
		(Phelps, Lochte, Vanderkaay and Keller)		

Women

Event	Mark	Record Holder	Date	Site
100 free	53.30	Britta Steffen, Germany (W)	8-02-06	Budapest, Hung.
100 free	53.58	Amanda Weir, United States (A)	8-05-06	Irvine, Calif.
400 free	4:02.13	Laure Manaudou, France (W)	8-08-06	Budapest, Hung.
50 back	28.19	Aleksandra Gerasimenia, Belguim (EW)	5-31-06	Minsk, Belarus
50 back	28.35	Natalie Coughlin, United States (A)	6-03-06	Zagreb, Croatia
50 breast	30.31	Jade Edmiston, Australia (W)	1-30-06	Melbourne, Aust.
100 breast	1:05.09	Leisel Jones, Australia (W)	3-20-06	Melbourne, Aust.
200 breast	2:20.54	Leisel Jones, Australia (W)	2-01-06	Melbourne, Aust.
200 fly	2:05.40	Jessicah Schipper, Australia (W)	8-17-06	Victoria, Can.
200 IM	2:10.05	Katie Hoff, United States (A)	8-01-06	Irvine, Calif.
400 m relay	3:56.30	Australia (W)	3-21-06	Budapest, Hung.
		(Edington, Jones, Schipper, Lenton)		
400 f relay	3:35.22	Germany (W)	7-31-06	Budapest, Hung.
		(Dallman, Goetz, Steffen, Liebs)		
400 f relay	3:35.80	United States (A)	8-19-06	Victoria, Can.
		(Weir, Coughlin, Joyce and Nymeyer)		
800 f relay	7:50.82	Germany (W)	8-03-06	Budapest, Hung.
		(Dallman, Samulski, Steffen, Liebs)		

W= World Record. A= American Record. EW=Equals World Record.

World and American Records

Men

Freestyle

Event	Time	Record Holder	Date	Site
50 meters	21.64	Alexander Popov, Russia (W)	6-16-00	Moscow
	21.76	Gary Hall Jr. (A)	8-15-00	Indianapolis
100 meters	47.84	Pieter van den Hoogenband, Netherlands (W)	9-19-00	Sydney
	48.17	Jason Lezak (A)	7-10-04	Long Beach, Calif.
200 meters	1:44.06	Ian Thorpe, Australia (W)	7-25-01	Fukuoka, Japan
	1:45.32	Michael Phelps (A)	8-16-04	Athens
400 meters	3:40.08	Ian Thorpe, Australia (W)	7-30-02	Manchester, Eng.
	3:44.11	Klete Keller (A)	8-14-04	Athens
800 meters	7:38.65	Grant Hackett, Australia (W)	7-27-05	Montreal
	7:45.63	Larsen Jensen (A)	7-25-03	Montreal
1,500 meters	14:34.56	Grant Hackett, Australia (W)	7-30-01	Fukuoka, Japan
	14:45.29	Larsen Jensen (A)	8-21-04	Athens

Backstroke

Event	Time	Record Holder	Date	Site
50 meters	24.80	Thomas Rupprath, Germany (W)	7-27-03	Barcelona
	24.99	Lenny Krayzelburg (A)	8-28-99	Sydney
100 meters	53.17	Aaron Peirsol (W,A)	4-2-05	Indianapolis
200 meters	1:54.44	Aaron Peirsol (W,A)	8-19-06	Victoria, Can.

Breaststroke

Event	Time	Record Holder	Date	Site
50 meters	27.18	Oleg Lisogor, Ukraine (W)	8-1-02	Berlin
	27.39	Ed Moses (A)	3-31-01	Austin, Texas
100 meters	59.13	Brendan Hansen (W,A)	8-01-06	Irvine, Calif.
200 meters	2:08.50	Brendan Hansen (W,A)	8-20-06	Victoria, Can.

Butterfly

Event	Time	Record Holder	Date	Site
50 meters	22.96	Roland Schoeman, Russia (W)	7-25-05	Montreal
50 meters	23.30	Ian Crocker (W,A)	2-29-04	Austin, Texas
100 meters	50.40	Ian Crocker (W,A)	7-30-05	Montreal
200 meters	1:53.80	Michael Phelps (W,A)	8-17-06	Victoria, Can.

Individual Medley

Event	Time	Record Holder	Date	Site
200 meters	1:55.84	Michael Phelps (W,A)	8-20-06	Victoria, Can.
400 meters	4:08.26	Michael Phelps (W,A)	8-14-04	Athens

Relays

Event	Time	Record Holder	Date	Site
400-meter medley	3:30.68	United States (W,A)	8-21-04	Athens
		(Aaron Peirsol, Brendan Hansen, Ian Crocker, Jason Lezak)		
400-meter freestyle	3:12.46	United States (W,A)	8-19-06	Victoria, Can.
		(Michael Phelps, Neil Walker, Cullen Jones and Jason Lezak)		
800-meter freestyle	7:04.66	Australia (W)	7-27-01	Fukuoka, Japan
		(Ian Thorpe, Michael Klim, Bill Kirby, Grant Hackett)		
	7:05.28	United States (A)	8-18-06	Victoria, Can.
		(Michael Phelps, Ryan Lochte, Peter Vanderkaay and Klete Keller)		

Note: Records through Oct 1, 2006.

Women

Freestyle

Event	Time	Record Holder	Date	Site
50 meters	24.13	Inge de Bruijn, Netherlands (W)	9-22-00	Sydney
	24.63	Dara Torres (A)	9-23-00	Sydney
100 meters	53.30	Britta Steffen, Germany (W)	8-02-06	Budapest, Hung.
	53.58	Amanda Weir (A)	8-05-06	Irvine, Calif.
200 meters	1:56.64	Franziska van Almsick, Germany (W)	8-3-02	Berlin
	1:57.41	Lindsay Benko (A)	7-24-03	Barcelona
400 meters	4:02.13	Laure Manaudou, France (W)	8-08-06	Budapest, Hung.
800 meters	8:16.22	Janet Evans (W,A)	8-20-89	Tokyo
1,500 meters	15:52.10	Janet Evans (W,A)	3-26-88	Orlando, Fla.

Backstroke

Event	Time	Record Holder	Date	Site
50 meters	28.19	Aleksandra Gerasimenia, Belguim (W)	5-31-06	Minsk, Belarus
		Janine Pietsch, Germany (W)	5-25-05	Melbourne, Aust.
	28.35	Natalie Coughlin (A)	6-03-06	Zagreb, Croatia
100 meters	59.58	Natalie Coughlin (W,A)	8-13-02	Fort Lauderdale, Fla.
200 meters	2:06.62	Krisztina Egerszegi, Hungary (W)	8-25-91	Athens
	2:08.53	Natalie Coughlin (A)	8-16-02	Fort Lauderdale, Fla.

Breaststroke

Event	Time	Record Holder	Date	Site
50 meters	30.31	Jade Edmistone, Australia (W)	1-30-06	Melbourne, Aust.
	30.85	Jessica Hardy (A)	7-25-05	Montreal
100 meters	1:05.09	Leisel Jones, Australia (W)	3-20-06	Melbourne, Aust.
	1:06.20	Jessica Hardy (A)	7-25-05	Montreal
200 meters	2:20.54	Leisel Jones, Australia (W)	2-01-06	Melbourne, Aust.
	2:22.44	Jessica Hardy (A)	7-12-04	Long Beach, Calif.

Butterfly

Event	Time	Record Holder	Date	Site
50 meters	25.57	Anna-Karin Kammerling, Sweden (W)	7-30-02	Berlin
	26.50	Dara Torres (A)	8-9-00	Indianapolis
100 meters	56.61	Inge de Bruijn, Netherlands (W)	9-17-00	Sydney
	57.58	Dara Torres (A)	8-9-00	Indianapolis
200 meters	2:05.40	Jessicah Schipper (W)	8-17-06	Victoria, Can.
	2:05.88	Misty Hyman (A)	9-20-00	Sydney

Individual Medley

Event	Time	Record Holder	Date	Site
200 meters	2:09.72	Yanyan Wu, China (W)	10-17-97	Shanghai
	2:10.05	Katie Hoff (A)	8-01-06	Irvine, Calif.
400 meters	4:33.59	Yana Klochkova, Ukraine (W)	9-16-00	Sydney
	4:34.95	Kaitlin Sandeno (A)	8-14-04	Athens

Relays

Event	Time	Record Holder	Date	Site
400-meter medley	3:56.30	Australia (W)	3-21-06	Melbourne, Aust.
		(Sophie Edington, Leisel Jones, Jessicah Schipper, Libby Lenton)		
	3:58.30	United States (A)	9-23-00	Sydney
		(BJ Bedford, Megan Quann, Jenny Thompson, Dana Torres)		
400-meter freestyle	3:35.22	Germany (W)	7-31-06	Budapest, Hung.
		(Petra Dallman, Daniela Goetz, Britta Steffen, Annika Liebs)		
	3:35.80	United States (A)	8-19-06	Victoria, Can.
		(Amanda Weir, Natalie Coughlin, Kara Lynn Joyce, Lacey Nymeyer)		
800-meter freestyle	7:50.82	Germany (W)	8-3-06	Budapest, Hung.
		(Petra Dallman, Daniela Samulski, Britta Steffen, Annika Liebs)		
	7:53.42	United States (A)	8-18-04	Athens
		(Natalie Coughlin, Carly Piper, Dana Vollmer, Kaitlin Sandeno)		

Men

50-meter Freestyle

1986	Tom Jager, United States	22.49‡
1991	Tom Jager, United States	22.16‡
1994	Alexander Popov, Russia	22.17
1998	Bill Pilczuk, United States	22.29
2001	Anthony Ervin, United States	22.09
2003	Alexander Popov, Russia	21.92‡
2005	Roland Schoeman, Russia	21.69

100-meter Freestyle

1973	Jim Montgomery, United States	51.70
1975	Andy Coan, United States	51.25
1978	David McCagg, United States	50.24
1982	Jorg Woithe, E. Germany	50.18
1986	Matt Biondi, United States	48.94
1991	Matt Biondi, United States	49.18
1994	Alexander Popov, Russia	49.12
1998	Alexander Popov, Russia	48.93‡
2001	Anthony Ervin, United States	48.33‡
2003	Alexander Popov, Russia	48.42
2005	Filippo Magnini, Italy	48:12

200-meter Freestyle

1973	Jim Montgomery, United States	1:53.02
1975	Tim Shaw, United States	1:52.04‡
1978	Billy Forrester, United States	1:51.02‡
1982	Michael Gross, W Germany	1:49.84
1986	Michael Gross, W Germany	1:47.92
1991	Giorgio Lamberti, Italy	1:47.27‡
1994	Antti Kasvio, Finland	1:47.32
1998	Michael Klim, Australia	1:47.41
2001	Ian Thorpe, Australia	1:44.06*
2003	Ian Thorpe, Australia	1:45.14
2005	Michael Phelps, United States	1:45.20

400-meter Freestyle

1973	Rick DeMont, United States	3:58.18‡
1975	Tim Shaw, United States	3:54.88‡
1978	Vladimir Salnikov, U.S.S.R.	3:51.94‡
1982	Vladimir Salnikov, U.S.S.R.	3:51.30‡
1986	Rainer Henkel, W Germany	3:50.05
1991	Joerg Hoffman, Germany	3:48.04‡
1994	Kieran Perkins, Australia	3:43.80*
1998	Ian Thorpe, Australia	3:46.29
2001	Ian Thorpe, Australia	3:40.17*
2003	Ian Thorpe, Australia	3:42.58
2005	Grant Hackett, Australia	3:42.91

1,500-meter Freestyle

1973	Stephen Holland, Australia	15:31.85
1975	Tim Shaw, United States	15:28.92‡
1978	Vladimir Salnikov, U.S.S.R.	15:03.99‡
1982	Vladimir Salnikov, U.S.S.R.	15:01.77‡
1986	Rainer Henkel, W Germany	15:05.31
1991	Joerg Hoffman, Germany	14:50.36*
1994	Kieran Perkins, Australia	14:50.52
1998	Grant Hackett, Australia	14:51.70
2001	Grant Hackett, Australia	14:34.56*
2003	Grant Hackett, Australia	14:43.14
2005	Grant Hackett, Australia	14:42.58

100-meter Backstroke

1973	Roland Matthes, E. Germany	57.47
1973	Roland Matthes, E. Germany	58.15

* World record; ‡Meet record

100-meter Backstroke (Cont.)

1978	Bob Jackson, United States	56.36‡
1982	Dirk Richter, E. Germany	55.95
1986	Igor Polianski, U.S.S.R.	55.58‡
1991	Jeff Rouse, United States	55.23‡
1994	Martin Lopez Zubero, Spain	55.17‡
1998	Lenny Krayzelburg, United States	55.00‡
2001	Matt Welsh, Australia	54.31‡
2003	Aaron Peirsol, United States	53.61‡
2005	Aaron Peirsol, United States	53:62

200-meter Backstroke

1973	Roland Matthes, E. Germany	2:01.87‡
1975	Zoltan Varraszto, Hungary	2:05.05
1978	Jesse Vassallo, United States	2:02.16
1982	Rick Carey, United States	2:00.82‡
1986	Igor Polianski, U.S.S.R.	1:58.78‡
1991	Martin Zubero, Spain	1:59.52
1994	Vladimir Selkov, Russia	1:57.42‡
1998	Lenny Krayzelburg, United States	1:58.84
2001	Aaron Peirsol, United States	1:57.13‡
2003	Aaron Peirsol, United States	1:55.92
2005	Aaron Peirsol, United States	1:54.66*

100-meter Breaststroke

1973	Roland Matthes, E. Germany	2:01.87‡
1973	John Hencken, United States	1:04.02‡
1975	David Wilkie, Great Britain	1:04.26‡
1978	Walter Kusch, W Germany	1:03.56‡
1982	Steve Lundquist, United States	1:02.75‡
1986	Victor Davis, Canada	1:02.71
1991	Norbert Rozsa, Hungary	1:01.45*
1994	Norbert Rozsa, Hungary	1:01.24‡
1998	Frederik Deburghgraeve, Belgium	1:01.34
2001	Roman Sloudnov, Russia	1:00.16
2003	Kosuke Kitajima, Japan	59.78*
2005	Brendan Hansen, United States	59:13*

200-meter Breaststroke

1973	David Wilkie, Great Britain	2:19.28‡
1975	David Wilkie, Great Britain	2:18.23‡
1978	Nick Nevid, United States	2:18.37
1982	Victor Davis, Canada	2:14.77*
1986	Jozsef Szabo, Hungary	2:14.27‡
1991	Mike Barrowman, United States	2:11.23*
1994	Norbert Rozsa, Hungary	2:12.81
1998	Kurt Grote, United States	2:13.40
2001	Brendan Hansen, United States	2:10.69‡
2003	Kosuke Kitajima, Japan	2:09.42*
2005	Brendan Hansen, United States	2:08.74*

100-meter Butterfly

1973	Bruce Robertson, Canada	55.69
1975	Greg Jagenburg, United States	55.63
1978	Joe Bottom, United States	54.30
1982	Matt Gribble, United States	53.88‡
1986	Pablo Morales, United States	53.54‡
1991	Anthony Nesty, Suriname	53.29‡
1994	Rafal Szukala, Poland	53.51
1998	Michael Klim, Australia	52.25‡
2001	Lars Frolander, Sweden	52.10‡
2003	Ian Crocker, United States	50.98*
2005	Ian Crocker, United States	50:40*

200-meter Butterfly

1973	Robin Backhaus, United States	2:03.32
1975	Bill Forrester, United States	2:01.95‡

Men (Cont.)

200-meter Butterfly (Cont.)

1978	Mike Bruner, United States	1:59.38‡
1982	Michael Gross, E. Germany	1:58.85‡
1986	Michael Gross, E. Germany	1:56.53‡
1991	Melvin Stewart, United States	1:55.69*
1994	Denis Pankratov, Russia	1:56.54
1998	Denys Sylantyev, Ukraine	1:56.61
2001	Michael Phelps, United States	1:54.58*
2003	Michael Phelps, United States	1:54.35
2005	Pawel Korzeniowski, Poland	1:55.02

200-meter Individual Medley

1973	Gunnar Larsson, Sweden	2:08.36
1975	Andras Hargitay, Hungary	2:07.72
1978	Graham Smith, Canada	2:03.65*
1982	Aleksandr Sidorenko, U.S.S.R.	2:03.30‡
1986	Tamás Darnyi, Hungary	2:01.57‡
1991	Tamás Darnyi, Hungary	1:59.36*
1994	Jani Sievin, Finland	1:58.16*
1998	Marcel Wouda, Netherlands	2:01.18
2001	Massimiliano Rosolino, Italy	1:59.71
2003	Michael Phelps, United States	1:56.04*
2005	Ryan Lochte, United States	1;58.06

400-meter Individual Medley

1975	Andras Hargitay, Hungary	4:32.57
1978	Jesse Vassallo, United States	4:20.05*
1982	Ricardo Prado, Brazil	4:19.78*
1986	Tamás Darnyi, Hungary	4:18.98‡
1991	Tamás Darnyi, Hungary	4:12.36*
1994	Tom Dolan, United States	4:12.30*
1998	Tom Dolan, United States	4:14.95
2001	Alessio Boggiatto, Italy	4:13.15
2003	Michael Phelps, United States	4:09.09*
2005	Laszlo Cseh, Hungary	4:09.63

400-meter Medley Relay

1973	United States (Mike Stamm, John Hencken, Joe Bottom, Jim Montgomery)	3:49.49
1975	United States (John Murphy, Rick Colella, Greg Jagenburg, Andy Coan)	3:49.00
1978	United States (Robert Jackson, Nick Nevid, Joe Bottom, David McCagg)	3:44.63
1982	United States (Rick Carey, Steve Lundquist, Matt Gribble, Rowdy Gaines)	3:40.84*
1986	United States (Dan Veatch, David Lundberg, Pablo Morales, Matt Biondi)	3:41.25
1991	United States (Jeff Rouse, Eric Wunderlich, Mark Henderson Matt Biondi)	3:39.66‡
1994	United States (Jeff Rouse, Eric Wunderlich, Mark Henderson, Gary Hall Jr.)	3:37.74‡
1998	Australia (Matt Welsh, Phil Rogers, Robin Backhaus, Rick Klatt, Jim Montgomery)	3:37.98
2001	Australia (Matt Welsh, Ian Thorpe, Geoff Huegill, Regan Harrison)	3:35.35
2003	United States (Aaron Peirsol Brendan Hansen, Ian Crocker, Jason Lezak)	3:31.54*
2005	United States (Aaron Peirsol Brendan Hansen, Ian Crocker, Jason Lezak)	3:31.85

400-meter Freestyle Relay

1973	United States (Mel Nash, Joe Bottom, Jim Montgomery, John Murphy)	3:27.18
1975	United States (Bruce Furniss, Jim Montgomery, Andy Coan, John Murphy)	3:24.85
1978	United States (Jack Babashoff, Rowdy Gaines, Jim Montgomery, David McCagg)	3:19.74
1982	United States (Chris Cavanaugh, Robin Leamy, David McCagg, Rowdy Gaines)	3:19.26*
1986	United States (Tom Jager, Mike Heath, Paul Wallace, Matt Biondi)	3:19.89
1991	United States (Tom Jager, Brent Lang, Doug Gjertsen, Matt Biondi)	3:17.15‡
1994	United States (Jon Olsen, Josh Davis, Ugur Taner, Gary Hall Jr.)	3:16.90‡
1998	United States (Bryan Jones, Jon Olsen, Bradley Schumacher, Gary Hall Jr.)	3:16.69‡
2001	Australia (Michael Klim, Ian Thorpe, Todd Pearson, Ashley Callus)	3:14.10‡
2003	Russia (Andrei Kapralov, Ivan Usov, Denis Pimankov Alexander Popov)	3:14.06‡
2005	United States (Michael Phelps, Neil Walker, Nate Dusing, Jason Lezak)	3:13.77

800-meter Freestyle Relay

1973	United States (Kurt Krumpholz, Robin Backhaus, Rick Klatt, Jim Montgomery)	7:33.22*
1975	W Germany (Klaus Steinbach, Werner Lampe, Hans Joachim Geisler, Peter Nocke)	7:39.44
1978	United States (Bruce Furniss, Billy Forrester, Bobby Hackett, Rowdy Gaines)	7:20.82
1982	United States (Rich Saeger, Jeff Float, Kyle Miller, Rowdy Gaines)	7:21.09
1986	E. Germany (Lars Hinneburg, Thomas Flemming, Dirk Richter, Sven Lodziewski)	7:15.91‡
1991	Germany (Peter Sitt, Steffan Zesner, Stefan Pfeiffer, Michael Gross)	7:13.50‡
1994	Sweden (Christer Waller, Tommy Werner, Lars Frolander, Anders Holmertz)	7:17.34
1998	Australia (Daniel Kowalski, Grant Hackett, Ian Thorpe, Anthony Rogis)	7:12.48‡
2001	Australia (Michael Klim, Ian Thorpe, William Kirby, Grant Hackett)	7:04.66*
2003	Australia (Grant Hackett, Craig Stevens, Nicholas Springer, Ian Thorpe)	7:08.58
2005	United States (Michael Phelps, Ryan Lochte, Peter Vanderkaay, Klete Keller)	7:06.58

Women

50-meter Freestyle

1986	Tamara Costache, Romania	25.28*
1991	Zhuang Yong, China	25.47
1994	Le Jingyi, China	24.51*
1998	Amy Van Dyken, United States	25.15
2001	Inge de Bruijn, Netherlands	24.47
2003	Inge de Bruijn, Netherlands	24.47
2005	Lisbeth Lenton, Australia	24.59

100-meter Freestyle

1973	Kornelia Ender, E. Germany	57.54
1975	Kornelia Ender, E. Germany	56.50
1978	Barbara Krause, E. Germany	55.68‡
1982	Birgit Meineke, E. Germany	55.79
1986	Kristin Otto, E. Germany	55.05‡
1991	Nicole Haislett, United States	55.17
1994	Le Jingyi, China	54.01*
1998	Jenny Thompson, United States	54.95
2001	Inge de Bruijn, Netherlands	54.18
2003	Hanna-Maria Seppälä, Finland	54.37
2005	Britta Steffen, Germany	53.30*

200-meter Freestyle

1973	Keena Rothhammer, United States	2:04.99
1975	Shirley Babashoff, United States	2:02.50
1978	Cynthia Woodhead, United States	1:58.53*
1982	Annemarie Verstappen, Netherlands	1:59.53‡
1986	Heike Friedrich, E. Germany	1:58.26‡
1991	Hayley Lewis, Australia	2:00.48
1994	Franziska Van Almsick, Germany	1:56.78*
1998	Claudia Poll, Costa Rica	1:58.90
2001	Giaan Rooney, Australia	1:58.57
2003	Alena Popchanka, Bulgaria	1:58.32
2005	Solenne Figues, France	1:58.60

400-meter Freestyle

1973	Heather Greenwood, United States	4:20.28
1975	Shirley Babashoff, United States	4:22.70
1978	Tracey Wickham, Australia	4:06.28*
1982	Carmela Schmidt, E. Germany	4:08.98
1986	Heike Friedrich, E. Germany	4:07.45
1991	Janet Evans, United States	4:08.63
1994	Yang Aihua, China	4:09.64
1998	Chen Yan, China	4:06.72
2001	Yana Klochkova, Ukraine	4:07.30
2003	Hannah Stockbauer, Germany	4:06.75
2005	Laure Manaudou, France	4:02.13*

800-meter Freestyle

1973	Novella Calligaris, Italy	8:52.97
1975	Jenny Turrall, Australia	8:44.75‡
1978	Tracey Wickham, Australia	8:24.94‡
1982	Kim Linehan, United States	8:27.48
1986	Astrid Strauss, E. Germany	8:28.24
1991	Janet Evans, United States	8:24.05‡
1994	Janet Evans, United States	8:29.85
1998	Brooke Bennett, United States	8:28.71
2001	Hannah Stockbauer, Germany	8:24.66
2003	Hannah Stockbauer, Germany	8:23.66‡
2005	Kate Ziegler, United States	8:25.31

100-meter Backstroke

1973	Ulrike Richter, E. Germany	1:05.42
1975	Ulrike Richter, E. Germany	1:03.30‡

100-meter Backstroke *(Cont.)*

1978	Linda Jezek, United States	1:02.55‡
1982	Kristin Otto, E. Germany	1:01.30‡
1986	Betsy Mitchell, United States	1:01.74
1991	Krisztina Egerszegi, Hungary	1:01.78
1994	He Cihong, China	1:00.57
1998	Lea Maurer, United States	1:01.16
2001	Natalie Coughlin, United States	1:00.37
2003	Antje Buschschulte, Germany	1:00.50
2005	Kirsty Coventry, Zimbabwe	1:00.24

200-meter Backstroke

1973	Melissa Belote, United States	2:20.52
1975	Birgit Treiber, E. Germany	2:15.46*
1978	Linda Jezek, United States	2:11.93*
1982	Cornelia Sirch, E. Germany	2:09.91*
1986	Cornelia Sirch, E. Germany	2:11.37
1991	Krisztina Egerszegi, Hungary	2:09.15‡
1994	He Cihong, China	2:07.40
1998	Roxanna Maracineanu, France	2:11.26
2001	Diana Mocanu, Romania	2:09.94
2003	Katy Sexton, Great Britain	2:08.74
2005	Kirsty Coventry, Zimbabwe	2:08.52

100-meter Breaststroke

1973	Renate Vogel, E. Germany	1:13.74
1975	Hannalore Anke, E. Germany	1:12.72
1978	Julia Bogdanova, U.S.S.R.	1:10.31*
1982	Ute Geweniger, E. Germany	1:09.14‡
1986	Sylvia Gerasch, E. Germany	1:08.11*
1991	Linley Frame, Australia	1:08.81
1994	Samantha Riley, Australia	1:07.96*
1998	Kristy Kowal, United States	1:08.42
2001	Xuejuan Luo, China	1:07.18‡
2003	Xuejuan Luo, China	1:06.80
2005	Leisel Jones, Australia	1:05.09*

200-meter Breaststroke

1973	Renate Vogel, E. Germany	2:40.01
1975	Hannalore Anke, E. Germany	2:37.25‡
1978	Lina Kachushite, U.S.S.R.	2:31.42*
1982	Svetlana Varganova, U.S.S.R.	2:28.82‡
1986	Silke Hoerner, E. Germany	2:27.40*
1991	Elena Volkova, U.S.S.R.	2:29.53
1994	Samantha Riley, Australia	2:26.87‡
1998	Agnes Kovacs, Hungary	2:25.45‡
2001	Agnes Kovacs, Hungary	2:24.90
2003	Amanda Beard, United States	2:22.99*
2005	Leisel Jones, Australia	2:20.54*

100-meter Butterfly

1973	Kornelia Ender, E. Germany	1:02.53
1975	Kornelia Ender, E. Germany	1:01.24*
1978	Joan Pennington, United States	1:00.20‡
1982	Mary T. Meagher, United States	59.41‡
1986	Kornelia Gressler, E. Germany	59.51
1991	Qian Hong, China	59.68
1994	Liu Limin, China	58.98‡
1998	Jenny Thompson, United States	58.46‡
2001	Petria Thomas, Australia	58:27
2003	Jenny Thompson, United States	57.96‡
2005	Jessicah Schipper, Australia	57.23‡

* World record; ‡Meet record.

Women *(Cont.)*

200-meter Butterfly

1973	Rosemarie Kother, E. Germany	2:13.76‡
1975	Rosemarie Kother, E. Germany	2:15.92
1978	Tracy Caulkins, United States	2:09.87*
1982	Ines Geissler, E. Germany	2:08.66‡
1986	Mary T. Meagher, United States	2:08.41‡
1991	Summer Sanders, United States	2:09.24
1994	Liu Limin, China	2:07.25‡
1998	Susie O'Neill, Australia	2:07.93‡
2001	Petria Thomas, Australia	2:06.73‡
2003	Otylia Jedrzejczak, Poland	2:07.56
2005	Otylia Jedrzejczak, Poland	2:05.61*

200-meter Individual Medley

1973	Andrea Huebner, E. Germany	2:20.51
1975	Kathy Heddy, United States	2:19.80
1978	Tracy Caulkins, United States	2:14.07*
1982	Petra Schneider, E. Germany	2:11.79
1986	Kristin Otto, E. Germany	2:15.56
1991	Li Lin, China	2:13.40
1994	Lu Bin, China	2:12.34‡
1998	Wu Yanyan, China	2:10.88
2001	Martha Bowen, United States	2:11.93
2003	Yana Klochkova, Ukraine	2:10.75‡
2005	Katie Hoff, United States	2:10.41‡

400-meter Individual Medley

1973	Gudrun Wegner, E. Germany	4:57.71
1975	Ulrike Tauber, E. Germany	4:52.76‡
1978	Tracy Caulkins, United States	4:40.83*
1982	Petra Schneider, E. Germany	4:36.10*
1986	Kathleen Nord, E. Germany	4:43.75
1991	Lin Li, China	4:41.45
1994	Dai Guohong, China	4:39.14
1998	Chen Yan, China	4:36.66
2001	Yana Klochkova, Ukraine	4:36.98
2003	Yana Klochkova, Ukraine	4:36.74
2005	Katie Hoff, United States	4:36.07‡

400-meter Medley Relay

1973	E. Germany (Ulrike Richter, Renate Vogel, Rosemarie Kother, Kornelia Ender)	4:16.84
1975	E. Germany (Ulrike Richter, Hannelore Anke, Rosemarie Kother, Kornelia Ender)	4:14.74
1978	United States (Linda Jezek, Tracy Caulkins, Joan Pennington, Cynthia Woodhead)	4:08.21‡
1982	E. Germany (Kristin Otto, Ute Gewinger, Ines Geissler, Birgit Meineke)	4:05.8*
1986	E. Germany (Kathrin Zimmermann, Sylvia Gerasch, Kornelia Gressler, Kristin Otto)	4:04.82
1991	United States (Janie Wagstaff, Tracey McFarlane, Crissy Ahmann-Leighton, Nicole Haislett)	4:06.51
1994	China (He Cihong, Dai Guohong, Liu Limin, Lu Bin)	4:01.67*
1998	United States (Kristy Kowal, Lea Maurer, Jenny Thompson, Amy Van Dyken)	4:01.93
2001	Australia (Dyana Calub, Sarah Ryan, Petria Thomas, Leisel Jones)	4:07.30

400-meter Medley Relay *(Cont.)*

2003	China (Shu Xhan, Xuejuan Luo Yafei Zhou, Yu Yang)	3:59.89‡
2005	Australia (Sophie Edington, Leisel Jones, J. Schipper Lisbeth Lenton)	3:56.30*

400-meter Freestyle Relay

1973	E. Germany (Kornelia Ender, Andrea Eife, Andrea Huebner, Sylvia Eichner)	3:52.45
1975	E. Germany (Kornelia Ender, Barbara Krause, Claudia Hempel, Ute Bruckner)	3:49.37
1978	United States (Tracy Caulkins, Stephanie Elkins, Joan Pennington, Cynthia Woodhead)	3:43.43*
1982	E. Germany (Birgit Meineke, Susanne Link, Kristin Otto, Caren Metschuk)	3:43.97
1986	E. Germany (Kristin Otto, Manuela Stellmach, Sabine Schulze, Heike Friedrich)	3:40.57*
1991	United States (Nicole Haislett, Julie Cooper, Whitney Hedgepeth, Jenny Thompson)	3:43.26
1994	China (Le Jingyi, Ying Shan, Le Ying, Lu Bin)	3:37.91*
1998	United States (Catherine Fox, Lindsey Farella, Melanie Valerio, B.J. Bedford)	3:42.11
2001	Germany (Petra Dallman, Antje Buschschulte, Katrin Meissner, Sandra Volkner)	3:39.58
2003	United States (Natalie Coughlin, Lindsay Benko, Rhiannon Jeffrey, Jenny Thompson)	3:38.09
2005	Germany (Petra Dallman, Daniela Goetz, Britta Steffen, Annika Liebs)	3:35.22*

800-meter Freestyle Relay

1986	E. Germany (Manuela Stellmach, Astrid Strauss, Nadja Bergknecht, Heike Friedrich)	7:59.33*
1991	Germany (Kerstin Kielgass, Manuela Stellmach, Dagmar Hase, Stephanie Ortwig)	8:02.56
1994	China (Le Ying, Yang Alhua, Zhou Guabin, Lu Bin)	7:57.96
1998	Germany (Silvia Szalai, Antje Buschschulte, Janina Goetz, Franziska Van Almsick)	8:02.56
2001	Great Britain (Nicola Jackson, Janine Belton, Karen Legg, Karen Pickering)	7:58.69
2003	United States (Lindsay Benko, Rachel Komisarz, Rhiannon Jeffrey, Diana Munz)	7:55.70‡
2005	Germany (Petra Dallman, Daniela Samulski, Britta Steffen, Annika Liebs)	7:50.82*

* World record; ‡Meet record.

World Diving Championships

Men

1-meter Springboard

		Pts
1991	Edwin Jongejans, Netherlands	588.51
1994	Evan Stewart, Zimbabwe	382.14
1998	Yu Zhuocheng, China	417.54
2001	Wang Feng, China	444.03
2003	Xiang Xu, China	431.94
2005	Alexandre Despatie, Canada	489.69

3-meter Springboard

		Pts
1973	Phil Boggs, United States	618.57
1975	Phil Boggs, United States	597.12
1978	Phil Boggs, United States	913.95
1982	Greg Louganis, United States	752.67
1986	Greg Louganis, United States	750.06
1991	Kent Ferguson, United States	650.25
1994	Wu Zhuocheng, China	655.44
1998	Dmitry Sautin, Russia	746.79
2001	Dmitry Sautin, Russia	725.82
2003	Alexander Dobrosok, Russia	788.37
2005	Alexandre Despatie, Canada	813.60

Platform

		Pts
1973	Klaus Dibiasi, Italy	559.53
1975	Klaus Dibiasi, Italy	547.98
1978	Greg Louganis, United States	844.11
1982	Greg Louganis, United States	634.26
1986	Greg Louganis, United States	668.58
1991	Sun Shuwei, China	626.79
1994	Dmitry Sautin, Russia	634.71
1998	Dmitry Sautin, Russia	750.90
2001	Tian Lang, China	688.77
2003	Alexandre Despatie, Canada	716.91
2005	Jia Hu, China	698.01

3-meter Synchronized

		Pts
1998	China (Sun Shuwei, Tian Liang)	313.50
2001	China (Bo Peng, Kenan Wang)	342.63
2003	Russia (A. Dobrosok, D. Sautin)	369.18
2005	China (Chong He, Feng Wang)	384.42

10-meter Synchronized

		Pts
1998	China (Xu Hao, Yu Zhuocheng)	326.34
2001	China (Jian Tian, Jia Bu)	361.41
2003	Australia (M. Helm, R. Newbery)	384.6
2005	Russia (D. Dobroskok, G. Galperin)	392.88

Women

1-meter Springboard

		Pts
1991	Gao Min, China	478.26
1994	Chen Lixia, China	279.30
1998	Irina Lashko, Russia	296.07
2001	Blythe Hartley, Canada	300.81
2003	Irina Lashko, Australia	299.97
2005	Blythe Hartley, Canada	325.65

3-meter Springboard

		Pts
1973	Christa Koehler, E. Germany	442.17
1975	Irina Kalinina, U.S.S.R.	489.81
1978	Irina Kalinina, U.S.S.R.	691.43
1982	Megan Neyer, United States	501.03
1986	Gao Min, China	582.90
1991	Gao Min, China	539.01
1994	Tan Shuping, China	548.49
1998	Yulia Pakhalina, Russia	544.62
2001	Jingjing Guo, China	596.67
2003	Jingjing Guo, China	617.94
2005	Jingjing Guo, China	645.54

Platform

		Pts
1973	Ulrike Knape, Sweden	406.77
1975	Janet Ely, United States	403.89
1978	Irina Kalinina, U.S.S.R.	412.71
1982	Wendy Wyland, United States	438.79
1986	Chen Lin, China	449.67
1991	Fu Mingxia, China	426.51
1994	Fu Mingxia, China	434.04
1998	Olena Zhupyna, Ukraine	550.41
2001	Mian Xu, China	532.65
2003	Emilie Heymans, Canada	597.45
2005	Laura Ann Wilkinson, United States	564.87

3-meter Synchronized

		Pts
1998	Russia (Irina Lashko, Yulia Pakhalina)	282.30
2001	China (Minxia Wu, Jingjing Guo)	347.31
2003	China (Minxia Wu, Jingjing Guo)	357.30
2005	China (Ting Li, Jingjing Guo)	349.80

10-meter Synchronized

		Pts
1998	Ukraine (O. Zhupyna, S. Serbina)	278.28
2001	China (Qing Duan, Xue Sang)	329.94
2003	China (Lishi Lao, Ting Li)	344.58
2005	China (Tong Jia, Pei Lin Yuan)	351.60

* World record; ‡Meet (Olympic) record.

Men

50-METER FREESTYLE

1988	Matt Biondi	22.14*
2000	Gary Hall Jr.	21.98
	Anthony Ervin	21.98
2004	Gary Hall Jr.	21.93

100-METER FREESTLYE

1906	Charles Daniels	1:13.4
1908	Charles Daniels	1:05.6*
1912	Duke Kahanamoku	1:03.4
1920	Duke Kahanamoku	1:00.4
1924	John Weissmuller	59.0‡
1928	John Weissmuller	58.6‡
1948	Wally Ris	57.3‡
1952	Clarke Scholes	57.4
1964	Don Schollander	53.4‡
1972	Mark Spitz	51.22*
1976	Jim Montgomery	49.99*
1984	Rowdy Gaines	49.80‡
1988	Matt Biondi	48.63‡

200-METER FREESTYLE

1904	Charles Daniels	2:44.2
1906–1964	Not held	
1972	Mark Spitz	1:52.78*
1976	Bruce Furniss	1:50.29*

400-METER FREESTYLE

1904	Charles Daniels (440 yds)	6:16.2
1920	Norman Ross	5:26.8
1924	John Weissmuller	5:04.2‡
1932	Buster Crabbe	4:48.4‡
1936	Jack Medica	4:44.5‡
1948	William Smith	4:41.0‡
1964	Don Schollander	4:12.2*
1968	Mike Burton	4:09.0‡
1976	Brian Goodell	3:51.93*
1984	George DiCarlo	3:51.23‡

1,500-METER FREESTYLE

1920	Norman Ross	22:23.2
1948	James McLane	19:18.5
1952	Ford Konno	18:30.3‡
1968	Mike Burton	16:38.9‡
1972	Mike Burton	15:52.58‡
1976	Brian Goodell	15:02.40*
1984	Michael O'Brien	15:05.20

100-METER BACKSTROKE

1912	Harry Hebner	1:21.2
1920	Warren Kealoha	1:15.2
1924	Warren Kealoha	1:13.2‡
1928	George Kojac	1:08.2*
1936	Adolph Kiefer	1:05.9‡
1948	Allen Stack	1:06.4
1952	Yoshi Oyakawa	1:05.4‡
1976	John Naber	55.49*
1984	Rick Carey	55.79
1996	Jeff Rouse	54.10
2000	Lenny Krayzelburg	53.60‡
2004	Aaron Peirsol	54.06

200-METER BACKSTROKE

1964	Jed Graef	2:10.3*
1976	John Naber	1:59.19*
1984	Rick Carey	2:00.23
1996	Brad Bridgewater	1:58.54
2000	Lenny Krayzelburg	1:56.76‡
2004	Aaron Peirsol	1:54.95‡

100-METER BREASTSTROKE

1968	Donald McKenzie	1:07.7‡
1976	John Hencken	1:03.11*
1984	Steve Lundquist	1:01.65 *
1992	Nelson Diebel	1:01.50‡

200-METER BREASTSTROKE

1924	Robert Skelton	2:56.6
1948	Joseph Verdeur	2:39.3‡
1960	William Mulliken	2:37.4
1972	John Hencken	2:21.55
1992	Mike Barrowman	2:10.16*

100-METER BUTTERFLY

1968	Douglas Russell	55.9‡
1972	Mark Spitz	54.27*
1976	Matt Vogel	54.35
1992	Pablo Morales	53.32
2004	Michael Phelps	51.24‡

200-METER BUTTERFLY

1956	William Yorzyk	2:19.3‡
1960	Michael Troy	2:12.8*
1968	Carl Robie	2:08.7
1972	Mark Spitz	2:00.70*
1976	Mike Bruner	1:59.23*
1992	Melvin Stewart	1:56.26
2000	Tom Malchow	1:55.35‡
2004	Michael Phelps	1:54.04‡

200-METER INDIVIDUAL MEDLEY

1968	Charles Hickcox	2:12.0‡
2004	Michael Phelps	1:57.14‡

400-METER INDIVIDUAL MEDLEY

1964	Richard Roth	4:45.4*
1968	Charles Hickcox	4:48.4
1976	Rod Strachan	4:23.68*
1996	Tom Dolan	4:14.90
2000	Tom Dolan	4:11.76‡
2004	Michael Phelps	4:08.26*

* World record; ‡Meet (Olympic) record.

Men (Cont.)

3-METER SPRINGBOARD DIVING

	Pts
1920.....Louis Kuehn	675.4
1924.....Albert White	696.4
1928.....Pete Desjardins	185.04
1932.....Michael Galitzen	161.38
1936.....Richard Degener	163.57
1948.....Bruce Harlan	163.64
1952.....David Browning	205.29
1956.....Robert Clotworthy	159.56
1960.....Gary Tobian	170.00
1964.....Kenneth Sitzberger	159.90
1968.....Bernard Wrightson	170.15
1976.....Philip Boggs	619.05
1984.....Greg Louganis	754.41
1988.....Greg Louganis	730.80

PLATFORM DIVING

	Pts
1904.....George Sheldon	12.66
1920.....Clarence Pinkston	100.67
1924.....Albert White	97.46
1928.....Pete Desjardins	98.74
1932.....Harold Smith	124.80
1936.....Marshall Wayne	113.58
1948.....Sammy Lee	130.05
1952.....Sammy Lee	156.28
1960.....Robert Webster	165.56
1964.....Robert Webster	148.58
1984.....Greg Louganis	576.99
1988.....Greg Louganis	638.61

Women

50-METER FREESTYLE

1996......Amy Van Dyken	24.87

100-METER FREESTLYE

1920.....Ethelda Bleibtrey	1:13.6*
1924.....Ethel Lackie	1:12.4
1928.....Albina Osipowich	1:11.0‡
1932.....Helene Madison	1:06.8‡
1968.....Jan Henne	1:00.0
1972.....Sandra Neilson	58.59‡
1984.....Carrie Steinseifer	55.92 (tie)
........Nancy Hogshead	55.92

200-METER FREESTYLE

1968.....Debbie Meyer	2:10.5‡
1984.....Mary Wayte	1:59.23
1992.....Nicole Haislett	1:57.90

400-METER FREESTYLE

1924.....Martha Norelius	6:02.2‡
1928.....Martha Norelius	5:42.8*
1932.....Helene Madison	5:28.5*
1948.....Ann Curtis	5:17.8‡
1960.....Chris von Saltza	4:50.6
1964.....Virginia Duenkel	4:43.3‡
1968.....Debbie Meyer	4:31.8‡
1984.....Tiffany Cohen	4:07.10‡
1988.....Janet Evans	4:03.85*

800-METER FREESTYLE

1968.....Debbie Meyer	9:24.0‡
1972.....Keena Rothhammer	8:53.86*
1984.....Tiffany Cohen	8:24.95‡
1988.....Janet Evans	8:20.20‡
1992.....Janet Evans	8:25.52
1996......Brooke Bennett	8:27.89
2000......Brooke Bennett	8:19.67

100-METER BACKSTROKE

1924.....Sybil Bauer	1:23.2‡
1932.....Eleanor Holm	1:19.4
1960.....Lynn Burke	1:09.3‡
1964.....Cathy Ferguson	1:07.7*
1968.....Kaye Hall	1:06.2*
1972.....Melissa Belote	1:05.78‡
1984.....Theresa Andrews	1:02.55
1996.....Beth Botsford	1:01.19
2004.....Natalie Coughlin	1:00.37

200-METER BACKSTROKE

1968.....Pokey Watson	2:24.8‡
1972.....Melissa Belote	2:19.19*

100-METER BREASTSTROKE

1972.....Catherine Carr	1:13.58*
2000.....Megan Quann	1:07.05

200-METER BREASTSTROKE

1968.....Sharon Wichman	2:44.4‡
2004.....Amanda Beard	2:23.37‡

100-METER BUTTERFLY

1956.....Shelley Mann	1:11.0‡
1960.....Carolyn Schuler	1:09.5‡
1964.....Sharon Stouder	1:04.7*
1984.....Mary T. Meagher	59.26
1996.....Amy Van Dyken	59.13

200-METER BUTTERFLY

1972.....Karen Moe	2:15.57*
1984.....Mary T. Meagher	2:06.90‡
1992.....Summer Sanders	2:08.67
2000.....Misty Hyman	2:05.88‡

200-METER INDIVIDUAL MEDLEY

1968.....Sharon Wichman	2:44.4‡
1984.....Tracy Caulkins	2:12.64‡

400-METER INDIVIDUAL MEDLEY

1964.....Donna De Varona	5:18.7‡
1968.....Claudia Kolb	5:08.5‡
1984.....Tracy Caulkins	4:39.24
1988.....Janet Evans	4:37.76

* World record; ‡Meet (Olympic) record.

Women (Cont.)

3-METER SPRINGBOARD DIVING			PLATFORM DIVING		
		Pts			Pts
1920	Aileen Riggin	539.9	1924	Caroline Smith	33.2
1924	Elizabeth Becker	474.5	1928	Elizabeth Becker Pinkston	31.6
1928	Helen Meany	78.62	1932	Dorothy Poynton	40.26
1932	Georgia Coleman	87.52	1936	Dorothy Poynton Hill	33.93
1936	Marjorie Gestring	89.27	1948	Victoria Draves	68.87
1948	Victoria Draves	108.74	1952	Patricia McCormick	79.37
1952	Patricia McCormick	147.30	1956	Patricia McCormick	84.85
1956	Patricia McCormick	142.36	1964	Lesley Bush	99.80
1968	Sue Gossick	150.77	2000	Laura Wilkinson	543.75
1972	Micki King	450.03			
1976	Jennifer Chandler	506.19			

* World record; ‡Meet (Olympic) record.

Notable Achievements

Barrier Breakers
MEN

Event	Barrier	Athlete and Nation	Time	Date
100 Freestyle	1:00	Johnny Weissmuller, United States	58.6	7-9-22
100 Freestyle	:50	James Montgomery, United States	49.99	7-25-76
200 Freestyle	2:00	Don Schollander, United States	1:58.8	7-27-63
200 Freestyle	1:50	Sergei Kopliakov, U.S.S.R.	1:49.83	4-7-79
200 Freestyle	1:45	Ian Thorpe, Australia	1:44.06	7-25-01
400 Freestyle	4:00	Rick DeMont, United States	3:58.18	9-6-73
400 Freestyle	3:50	Vladimir Salnikov, U.S.S.R.	3:49.57	3-12-82
800 Freestyle	8:00	Vladimir Salnikov, U.S.S.R.	7:56.49	3-23-79
800 Freestyle	7:40	Ian Thorpe, Australia	7:39.16	7-24-01
1500 Freestyle	15:00	Vladimir Salnikov, U.S.S.R.	14:58.27	7-22-80
1500 Freestyle	14:35	Grant Hackett, Australia	14:34.56	7-29-01
100 Backstroke	1:00	Thompson Mann, United States	59.6	10-16-64
200 Backstroke	2:00	John Naber, United States	1:59.19	7-24-76
100 Breaststroke	1:00	Roman Sloudnov, Russia	59.97	6-28-01
200 Breaststroke	2:30	Chester Jastremski, United States	2:29.6	8-19-61
200 Breaststroke	2:10	Kosuke Kitajima, Japan	2:09.42	7-24-03
100 Butterfly	1:00	Lance Larson, United States	59.0	6-29-60
200 Butterfly	2:00	Roger Pyttel, E. Germany	1:59.63	6-3-76

WOMEN

Event	Barrier	Athlete and Nation	Time	Date
100 Freestyle	1:00	Dawn Fraser, Australia	59.9	10-27-62
200 Freestyle	2:00	Kornelia Ender, E. Germany	1:59.78	6-2-76
400 Freestyle	4:30	Debbie Meyer, United States	4:29.0	8-18-67
800 Freestyle	10:00	Jane Cederqvist, Sweden	9:55.6	8-17-60
800 Freestyle	9:00	Ann Simmons, United States	8:59.4	9-10-71
1500 Freestyle	20:00	Ilsa Konrads, Australia	19:25.7	1-14-60
	16:00	Janet Evans, United States	15:52.10	3-26-88
100 Backstroke	1:00	Natalie Coughlin, United States	59.58	8-16-02
200 Backstroke	2:30	Satoko Tanaka, Japan	2:29.6	2-10-63
100 Butterfly	1:00	Christiane Knacke, E. Germany	59.78	8-28-77
400 Individual Medley	5:00	Gudrun Wegner, E. Germany	4:57.51	9-6-73

Olympic Achievements

MOST INDIVIDUAL GOLDS IN SINGLE OLYMPICS

MEN

No.	Athlete and Nation	Olympic Year	Events
4	Mark Spitz, United States	1972	100, 200 free; 100, 200 fly
4	Michael Phelps, United States	2004	100, 200 fly, 200 IM, 400 IM

WOMEN

No.	Athlete and Nation	Olympic Year	Events
4	Kristin Otto, E. Germany	1988	50, 100 free; 100 back; 100 fly
3	Debbie Meyer, United States	1968	200, 400, 800 free
3	Shane Gould, Australia	1972	200, 400 free; 200 IM
3	Kornelia Ender, E. Germany	1976	100, 200 free; 100 fly
3	Janet Evans, United States	1988	400, 800 free; 400 IM
3	Krisztina Egerszegi, Hungary	1992	100, 200 back; 400 IM
3	Michelle Smith, Ireland	1996	400 free; 200, 400 IM
3	Inge de Bruijn, Netherlands	2000	50, 100 free; 100 fly

MOST INDIVIDUAL OLYMPIC GOLD MEDALS, CAREER

MEN

No.	Athlete and Nation	Olympic Years and Events
4	Charles Meldrum Daniels, United States	1904 (220, 440 free); 1906 (100 free) 1908 (100 free)
4	Roland Matthes, E. Germany	1968 (100, 200 back); 1972 (100, 200 back)
4	Mark Spitz, United States	1972 (100, 200 free; 100, 200 fly)
4	Michael Phelps, United States	2004 (100, 200 fly; 200, 400 IM)

WOMEN

No.	Athlete and Nation	
4	Kristin Otto, E. Germany	1988 (50 free; 100 free, back and fly)
4	Janet Evans, United States	1988 (400, 800 free; 400 IM); 1992 (800 free)
4	Krisztina Egerszegi, Hungary	1992 (100, 200 back; 400 IM); 1996 (200 back)
4	Inge de Bruijn, Netherlands	2000 (50, 100 free; 100 fly); 2004 (50 free)
4	Yana Klochkova, Ukraine	2000 (200, 400 IM); 2004 (200, 400 IM)

Most Olympic Gold Medals in a Single Olympics, Men—7, Mark Spitz, United States, 1972: 100, 200 Free; 100, 200 Fly; 4 x 100, 4 x 200 Free Relays; 4 x 100 Medley Relay.

Most Olympic Gold Medals in a Single Olympics, Women—6, Kristin Otto, E. Germany, 1988: 50, 100 Free; 100 Back; 100 Fly; 4 x 100 Free Relay; 4 x 100 Medley Relay.

Most Olympic Medals in a Single Olympics, Men—8, Michael Phelps, United States, 2004: (six gold, two bronze).

Most Olympic Medals in a Single Olympics, Women—5, Natalie Coughlin, United States, 2004: (two gold, two silver, one bronze)

Most Olympic Medals in a Career, Men—11, Matt Biondi, United States: 1984 (one gold), 1988 (five gold, one silver, one bronze), 1992 (two gold, one silver); 11, Mark Spitz, United States: 1968 (two gold, one silver, one bronze), 1972 (seven gold); 10, Gary Hall Jr., United States 1996 (one gold, three silver), 2000 (three gold, one bronze), 2004 (two gold).

Most Olympic Medals in a Career, Women—12, Jenny Thompson, United States: 1992 (two gold, one silver), 1996 (three gold), 2000 (three gold, one bronze), 2004 (two silver); 8, Dawn Fraser, Australia: 1956 (two gold, one silver), 1960 (one gold, one silver), 1964 (one gold, one silver); 8, Kornelia Ender, E. Germany: 1972 (three silver), 1976 (four gold, one silver); 8, Shirley Babashoff, United States: 1972 (one gold, two silver), 1976 (one gold, four silver); 8, Inge de Bruijn, Netherlands: 2000 (three gold, one silver), 2004 (one gold, one silver, two bronze).

Winner, Same Event, Three Consecutive Olympics—Dawn Fraser, Australia, 100 Freestyle, 1956, 1960, 1964; Krisztina Egerszegi, Hungary, 200 backstroke, 1988, 1992, 1996.

Youngest Person to Win an Olympic Diving Gold—Marjorie Gestring, United States, 1936, 13 years, 9 months, springboard diving.

Youngest Person to Win an Olympic Swimming Gold—Krisztina Egerszegi, Hungary, 1988, 14 years, one month, 200 backstroke.

World Record Achievements

Most World Records, Career, Men—32, Arne Borg, Sweden, 1921–29.

Most World Records, Career, Women—42, Ragnhild Hveger, Denmark, 1936–42.

Most Freestyle Records Held Concurrently—5, Helene Madison, United States, 1931–33; 5, Shane Gould, Australia, 1972.

Most Consecutive Lowerings of a Record—10, Kornelia Ender, E. Germany, 100 Freestyle, 7-13-73 to 7-19-76.

Longest Duration of World Record—19 years, 359 days, 1:04.6 in 100 Free, (1936–56) Willy den Ouden, Netherlands.

Skiing

Olympic gold medalist
Julia Mancuso of the
United States

Bode-acious Problems

Bode Miller's disappointing 0-for-5 performance
and his controversial behavior off the slopes
helped derail the U.S. Ski Team in Turin

BY MARK BECHTEL

Perhaps the bluntest assessment of the U.S. ski team's performance at the Olympics came from Daron Rahlves: "This sucks." Tactful, no, but the man had a point. The U.S. Ski and Snowboard Association assumed the slogan "Best in the World" and set a goal of eight medals in Turin. The squad's actual haul: two—a dozen fewer than Austria, which eliminated any doubt as to which team deserved to be called the world's best.

The most disappointing U.S. performer was Bode Miller. The reigning World Cup champ failed to medal, going 0-for-5, and did so in the same manner in which he did most things in 2006: controversially. A month before the Games began, Miller went on *60 Minutes* and talked about his hard partying ways: "There's been times when I've been in really tough shape at the top of the course . . . If you ever tried to ski when you're wasted, it's not easy." Amid calls for him to be tossed from the team, Miller issued a public apology. Then a few weeks later, in an interview with *Rolling Stone*, he accused Lance Armstrong and Barry Bonds of taking performance-enhancing drugs.

Miller took a week off before the Games began—the first race he missed in four years—to rest up and lay low. But when he got to Italy he wasted little time attracting all the wrong kinds of attention. Miller slept through the course inspection the morning of his first event, the downhill, prompting speculation that he had been out late the night before. Coach Phil McNichol maintained that Miller—who'd been out for dinner and drinks with his cousin, his agent and his Nike rep—hadn't stayed out too late, but he was none too pleased that Miller missed inspection. "More of the same old thing," he said. The result wasn't the same old thing for Miller—he finished fifth. Rahlves, who had announced he would be retiring after the Olympics, was tenth. Antoine Deneriaz of France, the last of the top skiers to run, came out of nowhere to win the event by a whopping .72 seconds.

That was just the beginning of the disappointment for Miller and his teammates. Though he led after the downhill portion of the combined, Miller was disqualified from the event for straddling a gate on his first slalom run. (Miller saw a silver lining in missing out on another medal ceremony, which would have forced him to leave Sestriere, the village where skiing events were held. "At least now I don't have to go all the way to Torino," he said.) He straddled another gate in the Super G—a virtually unheard-of mistake in that race—and then, after a decent sixth-place showing in the giant slalom, went off the course during his last event, the slalom, after missing a gate 15

seconds into his run. Said former Olympian Chad Fleischer, who was on the national team from 1992 until 2002, "Bode has been mismanaged. The organization has let him get bigger than the sport. Would that happen with a quarterback in the NFL?"

Rahlves, meanwhile, was medal-less in his three events, and Lindsey Kildow, who was expected to contend in the downhill, injured her hip in a training run crash and finished tied for eighth. The only skiers who won medals were a pair of 21-year-olds, Ted Ligety and Julia Mancuso. Ligety took gold in the combined, while Mancuso won the giant slalom. Mancuso's was an especially popular victory. Occasionally criticized for not taking her skiing seriously enough—she often races in a plastic tiara and "Super Jules" underwear, which she designed—she left the tiara at home and roared down the mountain in Sestriere two-thirds of a second faster than silver medalist Tanja Poutiainen of Finland. When Mancuso crossed the line, the Italian crowd, which had adopted the Italian-American skier for the race, was chanting "Julia! Julia!"

Miller didn't medal at the Winter Olympics in Turin and slipped from first to third in the overall World Cup standings in 2006.

But those victories were overshadowed by the rest of the team's shortcomings—especially Miller's. The 28-year-old seemed indifferent to the fact that he was letting the Games get away from him. (He wasn't much better in this World Cup season; Miller finished third in the overall, well behind Austria's Benjamin Raich, who won two golds in Italy.) For many, the lingering image of Miller is of him sitting in a Sestriere bar with a former Playboy bunny while flipping off the camera. Though Miller left Turin with nothing to show for his time there, he said that he was pleased with his overall performance. "I just want to go out and rock, and, man, I rocked here," he said. He added, "I'm comfortable with what I accomplished."

Although he may have been shut out on the slopes, when it came to the nightlife in the Italian Alps, Miller apparently struck gold, saying, "I got to party and socialize at the Olympic level."

FOR THE RECORD • 2005–2006

World Cup Alpine Racing Season Results

Men

Date	Event	Site	Winner
10-23-05	Giant Slalom	Söelden, Austria	Herman Maier, Austria
11-26-05	Downhill	Lake Louise, Alberta	Fritz Strobl, Austria
11-27-05	Super G	Lake Louise, Alberta	Aksel Lund Svindal, Norway
12-1-05	Super G	Beaver Creek, Colorado	Hannes Reichelt, Austria
12-2-05	Downhill	Beaver Creek, Colorado	Daron Rahlves, United States
12-3-05	Giant Slalom	Beaver Creek, Colorado	Bode Miller, United States
12-4-05	Slalom	Beaver Creek, Colorado	Giorgio Rocca, Italy
12-10-05	Downhill	Val d'Isere, France	Michael Walchhofer, Austria
12-11-05	Combined	Val d'Isere, France	Michael Walchhofer, Austria
12-12-05	Slalom	Modonna Di Campiglio, Italy	Giorgio Rocca, Italy
12-16-05	Super G	Val Gardena, Italy	Hans Grugger, Austria
12-17-05	Downhill	Val Gardena, Italy	Marco Buechel, Liechtenstein
12-18-05	Giant Slalom	Alta Badia, Italy	Massimiliano Blardone, Italy
12-21-05	Giant Slalom	Kranjska Gora, Slovenia	Benjamin Raich, Austria
12-22-05	Slalom	Kranjska Gora, Slovenia	Giorgio Rocca, Italy
12-29-05	Downhill	Bormio, Italy	Daron Rahlves, United States
1-7-06	Giant Slalom	Adelboden, Switzerland	Benjamin Raich, Austria
1-8-06	Slalom	Adelboden, Switzerland	Giorgio Rocca, Italy
1-13-06	Combined	Wengen, Switzerland	Benjamin Raich, Austria
1-14-06	Downhill	Wengen, Switzerland	Daron Rahlves, United States
1-15-06	Slalom	Wengen, Switzerland	Giorgio Rocca Italy
1-20-06	Super G	Kitzbuhel, Austria	Hermann Maier, Austria
1-21-06	Downhill	Kitzbuhel, Austria	Michael Walchhofer, Austria
1-22-06	Slalom	Kitzbuhel, Austria	Jean-Pierre Vidal, France
1-22-06	Combined	Kitzbuhel, Austria	Benjamin Raich, Austria
1-24-06	Slalom	Schladming, Austria	Kalle Palander, Finland
1-28-06	Downhill	Garmisch, Germany	Herman Maier, Austria
1-29-06	Super G	Garmisch, Germany	Christopher Gruber, Austria
2-3-06	Combined	Chamonix, Frances	Benjamin Raich, Austria
3-4-06	Giant Slalom	Yongpyong, Korea	Davide Simoncelli, Italy
3-5-06	Giant Slalom	Yongpyong, Korea	Ted Ligety, United States
3-10-06	Slalom	Kogen, Japan	Benjamin Raich, Austria
3-11-06	Slalom	Kogen, Japan	Reinfried Herbst, Austria
3-15-06	Downhill	Aare, Sweden	Aksel Lund Svindal, Norway
3-16-06	Super G	Aare, Sweden	Bode Miller, United States
3-17-06	Giant Slalom	Aare, Sweden	Benjamin Raich, Austria
3-18-06	Slalom	Aare, Sweden	Markus Larsson, Sweden

Women

Date	Event	Site	Winner
10-22-05	Giant Slalom	Soelden, Austria	Tina Maze, Slovenia
12-2-05	Downhill	Aare, Sweden	Elena Franchini, Italy
12-3-05	Downhill	Lake Louise, Alberta	Lindsey Kildow, United States
12-4-05	Super G	Lake Louise, Alberta	Alexandra Meissnitzer, Austria
12-4-05	Slalom	Aspen, Colorado	Anja Paerson, Sweden
12-9-05	Super G	Aspen Colorado	Nadia Styger, Switzerland
12-10-05	Giant Slalom	Aspen, Colorado	M. J. Rienda Contreras, Spain
12-17-05	Downhill	Val D'Isere, France	Lindsey Kildow, United States
12-18-05	Super G	Val D'Isere, France	Michaela Dorfmeister, Austria
12-21-05	Giant Slalom	Spindleruv Mlyn, Czech Republic	Janica Kostelic, Croatia
12-22-05	Slalom	Spindleruv Mlyn, Czech Republic	Anja Paerson, Sweden
12-28-05	Giant Slalom	Lienz, Austria	Anja Paerson, Sweden
12-29-05	Slalom	Lienz, Austria	Marlies Schild, Austria
1-5-06	Slalom	Zagreb-Sljeme, Croatia	Marlies Schild, Austria
1-8-06	Slalom	Maribor, Slovenia	Marlies Schild, Austria
1-13-06	Downhill	Bad Kleinkirchheim, Austria	Anja Paerson, Sweden
1-14-06	Downhill	Bad Kleinkirchheim, Austria	Janica Kostelic, Croatia
1-15-06	Super G	Bad Kleinkirchheim, Austria	Janica Kostelic, Croatia
1-20-06	Super G	St. Moritz, Switzerland	Michaela Dorfmeister, Austria
1-21-06	Downhill	St. Moritz, Switzerland	Michaela Dorfmeister, Austria
1-22-06	Combined	St. Moritz, Switzerand	Janica Kostelic, Croatia

Women *(Cont.)*

Date	Event	Site	Winner
1-27-06	Super G	Cortina D'Amprezzo, Italy	Anja Paerson, Sweden
1-28-06	Downhill	Cortina D'Amprezzo, Italy	Renate Goetschl, Austria
1-29-06	Giant Slalom	Cortina D'Amprezzo, Italy	Nicole Hosp, Austria
2-3-06	Giant Slalom	Ofterschwang, Germany	Maria Jose Rienda, Spain
2-4-06	Giant Slalom	Ofterschwang, Germany	Maria Jose Rienda, Spain
2-5-06	Slalom	Ofterschwang, Germany	Janica Kostelic, Croatia
3-3-06	Super G	Hafjell-Kvitfjell, Norway	Michaela Dorfmeister, Austria
3-4-06	Combined	Hafjell-Kvitfjell, Norway	Janica Kostelic, Croatia
3-5-06	Giant Slalom	Hafjell-Kvitfjell, Norway	Maria Jose Rienda, Spain
3-10-06	Slalom	Levi, Finland	Janica Kostelic, Croatia
3-11-06	Slalom	Levi, Finland	Anja Paerson, Sweden
3-15-06	Downhill	Aare, Sweden	Anja Paerson, Sweden
3-16-06	Super G	Aare, Sweden	Nicole Hosp, Austria
3-17-06	Slalom	Aare, Sweden	Janica Kostelic, Croatia
3-18-06	Giant Slalom	Aare, Sweden	Janica Kostelic, Croatia

World Cup Alpine Racing Final Standings

Men

OVERALL	Pts	SLALOM	Pts	SUPER G	Pts
Benjamin Raich, Austria	1410	Giorgio Rocca, Italy	547	Aksel Lund Svindal, Norway	284
Aksel Lund Svindal, Norway	1006	Kalle Palander, Finland	495	Hermann Maier, Austria	282
Bode Miller, United States	928	Benjamin Raich, Austria	410	Daron Rahlves, United States	269
Daron Rahlves, United States	903	Ted Ligety, United States	396	Hannes Reichelt, Austria	250
Michael Walchhoffer, Austria	855	Thomas Grandi, Canada	360	Kjetil-André Aamodt, Norway	223
Hermann Maier, Austria	818	Stehpane Tissot, France	336	Erik Guay, Canada	204
Kalle Paander, Finland	801	Akira Sasaki, Japan	333	Ambrosi Hoffmann, Switzerland	165
Kjetil-André Aamodt, Norway	707	Reinfried Herbst, Austria	316	Peter Fill, Italy	162
Ted Ligety, United States	636	Markus Larsson, Sweden	291	Christoph Gruber, Austria	147
Marco Buechel, Liechtenstein	626	Jean-Pierre Vidal, France	253	Bode Miller, United States	145

DOWNHILL	Pts	GIANT SLALOM	Pts	COMBINED	Pts
Michael Walchhoffer, Austria	522	Benjamin Raich, Austria	481	Benjamin Raich, Austria	345
Fritz Strobl, Austria	491	Massimiliano Blardone, Italy	442	Bode Miller, United States	200
Daron Rahlves, United States	455	Frederick Nyberg, Sweden	414	Michael Walchhoffer, Austria	200
Marco Buechel, Liechtenstein	340	Davide Simoncelli, Italy	314	Rainer Schoenfelder, Austria	182
Bode Miller, United States	322	Kalle Palander, Finland	306	Kjetil-André Aamodt, Norway	162
Kjetil-André Aamodt, Norway	305	Thomas Grandi, Canada	259	Peter Fill, Italy	142
Hermann Maier, Austria	305	Francois Bourque, Canada	230	Aksel Lund Svindal, Norway	140
Bruno Kernen, Switzerland	268	Hermann Maier, Austria	223	Andrej Sporn, Slovenia	123
Didier Defago, Switzerland	246	Bode Miller, United States	198	Didier Defago, Switzerland	95
Kristian Ghedina, Italy	235	Aksel Lund Svindal, Norway	195	Silvan Zurbriggen, Switzerland	93

Women

OVERALL	Pts	SLALOM	Pts	SUPER G	Pts
Janica Kostelic, Croatia	1970	Janica Kostelic, Croatia	740	Michaela Dorfmeister, Austria	626
Anja Paerson, Sweden	1662	Marlies Schild, Austria	550	A. Meissnitzer, Austria	437
Michaela Dorfmeister, Austria	1364	Anja Paerson, Sweden	485	Nadia Styger, Switzerland	360
Nicole Hosp, Austria	1112	Kathrin Zettel, Austria	399	Lindsey Kildow, United States	326
Lindsey Kildow, United States	1067	Tanja Poutiainen, Finland	320	Janica Kostelic, Croatia	266
Marlies Schild, Austria	961	Nicole Hosp, Austria	307	Julia Mancuso, United States	239
Kathrin Zettel, Austria	872	Therese Borssen, Sweden	248	Andrea Fischbacher, Austria	231
Julia Mancuso, United States	755	Laure Pequegnot, France	227	Kirsten Clark, United States	201
A. Meissnitzer, Austria	753	Lindsey Kildow, United States	214	Anja Paerson, Sweden	182
Elisabeth Goergl, Austria	602	Sarka Zahrobska, Czech Rep.	206	Nicole Hosp, Austria	175

DOWNHILL	Pts	GIANT SLALOM	Pts	COMBINED	Pts
Michaela Dorfmeister, Austria	498	Anja Paerson, Sweden	586	Janica Kostelic, Croatia	200
Lindsey Kildow, United States	410	M. Rienda Contreras, Spain	537	Anja Paerson, Sweden	160
Renate Goetschl, Austria	315	Janica Kostelic, Croatia	464	Lindsey Kildow, United States	110
Janica Kostelic, Croatia	300	Nicole Hosp, Austria	461	Marlies Schild, Austria	105
F. Aufdenblatten, Swtizerland	272	Genevieve Simard, Canada	343	Nicole Hosp, Austria	90
A. Meissnitzer, Austria	267	Kathrin Zettel, Austria	314	Kathrin Zettel, Austria	85
Anja Paerson, Sweden	249	Tina Maze, Slovenia	309	Martina Ertl-Renz, Germany	58
Elisabeth Goergl, Austria	227	Tanja Poutiainen, Finland	260	Julia Mancuso, United States	53
Sylviane Berthod, Switzerland	223	Michaela Kirchgasser, Austria	227	J. Lindell-Virkarby, Sweden	44
Nike Bent, Sweden	187	Anna Ottosson, Sweden	224	Andrea Fischbacher, Austria	42

FOR THE RECORD • Year by Year

Event Descriptions

Downhill: A speed event entailing a single run on a course with a minimum vertical drop of 500 meters (800 for men's World Cup) and very few control gates.

Slalom: A technical event in which times for runs on two courses are totaled to determine the winner. Skiers must make many quick, short turns through a combination of gates (55–75 gates for men, 40–60 for women) over a short course (140–220-meter vertical drop for men, 120–180 for women).

Combined: An event in which scores from designated slalom and downhill races are combined to determine finish order.

Giant Slalom: A faster technical event with fewer, more broadly spaced gates than in the slalom. Times for runs on two courses with vertical drops of 250–400 meters for men and 250–300 meters for women are combined to determine the winner.

Super Giant Slalom: A speed event that is a cross between the downhill and the giant slalom.

Parallel Slalom: A technical event that combines slalom and giant slalom turns.

FIS World Championships

Sites

1931	Mürren, Switzerland	1936	Innsbruck, Austria
1932	Cortina d'Ampezzo, Italy	1937	Chamonix, France
1933	Innsbruck, Austria	1938	Engelberg, Switzerland
1934	St. Moritz, Switzerland	1939	Zakopane, Poland
1935	Mürren, Switzerland		

Results

Men

DOWNHILL

1931	Walter Prager, Switzerland
1932	Gustav Lantschner, Austria
1933	Walter Prager, Switzerland
1934	David Zogg, Switzerland
1935	Franz Zingerle, Austria
1936	Rudolf Rominger, Switzerland
1937	Émile Allais, France
1938	James Couttet, France
1939	Hans Lantschner, Germany

SLALOM

1931	David Zogg, Switzerland
1932	Friedrich Dauber, Germany
1933	Anton Seelos, Austria
1934	Franz Pfnuer, Germany
1935	Anton Seelos, Austria
1936	Rudi Matt, Austria
1937	Émile Allais, France
1938	Rudolf Rominger, Switzerland
1939	Rudolf Rominger, Switzerland

Women

DOWNHILL

1931	Esme Mackinnon, Great Britain
1932	Paola Wiesinger, Italy
1933	Inge Wersin-Lantschner, Austria
1934	Anni Ruegg, Switzerland
1935	Christel Cranz, Germany
1936	Evie Pinching, Great Britain
1937	Christel Cranz, Germany
1938	Lisa Resch, Germany
1939	Christel Cranz, Germany

SLALOM

1931	Esme Mackinnon, Great Britain
1932	Rösli Streiff, Switzerland
1933	Inge Wersin-Lantschner, Austria
1934	Christel Cranz, Germany
1935	Anni Rüegg, Switzerland
1936	Gerda Paumgarten, Austria
1937	Christel Cranz, Germany
1938	Christel Cranz, Germany
1939	Christel Cranz, Germany

FIS World Alpine Ski Championships

Sites

1950	Aspen, Colorado	1987	Crans-Montana, Switzerland
1954	Aare, Sweden	1989	Vail, Colorado
1958	Badgastein, Austria	1991	Saalbach-Hinterglemm, Austria
1962	Chamonix, France	1993	Morioka-Shizukuishi, Japan
1966	Portillo, Chile	1996	Sierra Nevada, Spain
1970	Val Gardena, Italy	1997	Sestriere, Italy
1974	St. Moritz, Switzerland	1999	Vail, Colorado
1978	Garmisch-Partenkirchen, W Germany	2001	St. Anton, Switzerland
1982	Schladming, Austria	2003	St. Moritz, Switzerland
1985	Bormio, Italy	2005	Bormio, Italy

Men's Results

DOWNHILL

1950............Zeno Colo, Italy	1989............Hansjörg Tauscher, W Germany
1954............Christian Pravda, Austria	1991............Franz Heinzer, Switzerland
1958............Toni Sailer, Austria	1993............Urs Lehmann, Switzerland
1962............Karl Schranz, Austria	1996............Patrick Ortlieb, Austria
1966............Jean-Claude Killy, France	1997............Bruno Kernen, Switzerland
1970............Bernard Russi, Switzerland	1999............Hermann Maier, Austria
1974............David Zwilling, Austria	2001............Hannes Trinkl, Austria
1978............Josef Walcher, Austria	2003............Michael Walchhofer, Austria
1982............Harti Weirather, Austria	2005............Bode Miller, United States
1985............Pirmin Zurbriggen, Switzerland	
1987............Peter Müller, Switzerland	

SLALOM

1950............Zeno Colo, Italy	1989............Hansjörg Tauscher, W Germany
1954............Christian Pravda, Austria	1991............Franz Heinzer, Switzerland
1958............Toni Sailer, Austria	1993............Urs Lehmann, Switzerland
1962............Karl Schranz, Austria	1996............Patrick Ortlieb, Austria
1966............Jean-Claude Killy, France	1997............Bruno Kernen, Switzerland
1970............Bernard Russi, Switzerland	1999............Hermann Maier, Austria
1974............David Zwilling, Austria	2001............Hannes Trinkl, Austria
1978............Josef Walcher, Austria	2003............Ivica Kostelic, Croatia
1982............Harti Weirather, Austria	2005............Benjamin Raich, Austria
1985............Pirmin Zurbriggen, Switzerland	
1987............Peter Müller, Switzerland	

GIANT SLALOM

1950............Zeno Colo, Italy	1989............Rudolf Nierlich, Austria
1954............Stein Eriksen, Norway	1991............Rudolf Nierlich, Austria
1958............Toni Sailer, Austria	1993............Kjetil André Aamodt, Norway
1962............Egon Zimmermann, Austria	1996............Alberto Tomba, Italy
1966............Guy Périllat, France	1997............Michael von Gruenigen, Switzerland
1970............Karl Schranz, Austria	1999............Marco Büchel, Liechtenstein
1974............Gustavo Thoeni, Italy	2001............Michael von Gruenigen, Switzerland
1978............Ingemar Stenmark, Sweden	2003............Bode Miller, United States
1982............Steve Mahre, United States	2005............Hermann Maier, Austria
1985............Markus Wasmaier, W Germany	
1987............Pirmin Zurbriggen, Switzerland	

COMBINED

1982............Michel Vion, France	1997............Kjetil André Aamodt, Norway
1985............Pirmin Zurbriggen, Switzerland	1999............Kjetil André Aamodt, Norway
1987............Marc Girardelli, Luxembourg	2001............Kjetil André Aamodt, Norway
1989............Marc Girardelli, Luxembourg	2003............Bode Miller, United States
1991............Stefan Eberharter, Austria	2005............Benjamin Raich, Austria
1993............Lasse Kjus, Norway	
1996............Marc Girardelli, Luxembourg	

SUPER G

1987............Pirmin Zurbriggen, Switzerland	1999............Hermann Maier, Austria
1989............Martin Hangl, Switzerland	Lasse Kjus, Norway
1991............Stefan Eberharter, Austria	2001............Daron Rahlves, United States
1993............Cancelled due to weather	2003............Stephan Eberharter, Austria
1996............Atle Skaardal, Norway	2005............Bode Miller, United States
1997............Atle Skaardal, Norway	

Women's Results

DOWNHILL

1950............Trude Beiser-Jochum, Austria	1989............Maria Walliser, Switzerland
1954............Ida Schopfer, Switzerland	1991............Petra Kronberger, Austria
1958............Lucile Wheeler, Canada	1993............Kate Pace, Canada
1962............Christl Haas, Austria	1996............Picabo Street, United States
1966............Erika Schinegger, Austria	1997............Hilary Lindh, United States
1970............Anneroesli Zryd, Switzerland	1999............Renate Goetschl, Austria
1974............Annemarie Moser-Proell, Austria	2001............Michaela Dorfmeister, Austria
1978............Annemarie Moser-Proell, Austria	2003............Melanie Turgeon, Canada
1982............Gerry Sorensen, Canada	2005............Janica Kostelic, Croatia
1985............Michela Figini, Switzerland	
1987............Maria Walliser, Switzerland	

Women (*Cont.*)

SLALOM

1950............Dagmar Rom, Austria	1989............Mateja Svet, Yugoslavia
1954............Trude Klecker, Austria	1991............Vreni Schneider, Switzerland
1958............Inger Bjornbakken, Norway	1993............Karin Buder, Austria
1962............Marianne Jahn, Austria	1996............Pernilla Wiberg, Sweden
1966............Annie Famose, France	1997............Deborah Compagnoni, Italy
1970............Ingrid Lafforgue, France	1999............Trine Bakke, Norway
1974............Hanni Wenzel, Liechtenstein	2001............Anja Paerson, Sweden
1978............Lea Soelkner, Austria	2003............Janica Kostelic, Croatia
1982............Erika Hess, Switzerland	2005............Janica Kostelic, Croatia
1985............Perrine Pelen, France	
1987............Erika Hess, Switzerland	

GIANT SLALOM

1950............Dagmar Rom, Austria	1989............Vreni Schneider, Switzerland
1954............Lucienne Schmith-Couttet, France	1991............Pernilla Wiberg, Sweden
1958............Lucile Wheeler, Canada	1993............Carole Merle, France
1962............Marianne Jahn, Austria	1996............Deborah Compagnoni, Italy
1966............Marielle Goitschel, France	1997............Deborah Compagnoni, Italy
1970............Betsy Clifford, Canada	1999............Anita Wachter, Austria
1974............Fabienne Serrat, France	2001............Sonja Nef, Switzerland
1978............Maria Epple, W Germany	2003............Anja Paerson, Sweden
1982............Erika Hess, Switzerland	2005............Anja Paerson, Sweden
1985............Diann Roffe, United States	
1987............Vreni Schneider, Switzerland	

COMBINED

1982............Erika Hess, Switzerland	1996............Pernilla Wiberg, Sweden
1985............Erika Hess, Switzerland	1997............Renate Goetschl, Austria
1987............Erika Hess, Switzerland	1999............Pernilla Wiberg, Sweden
1989............Tamara McKinney, United States	2001............Martina Ertl, Germany
1991............Chantal Bournissen, Switzerland	2003............Janica Kostelic, Croatia
1993............Miriam Vogt, Germany	2005............Janica Kostelic, Croatia

SUPER G

1987............Maria Walliser, Switzerland	1997............Isolde Kostner, Italy
1989............Ulrike Maier, Austria	1999............Alexandra Meissnitzer, Austria
1991............Ulrike Maier, Austria	2001............Regine Cavagnoud, France
1993............Katja Seizinger, Germany	2003............Michaela Dorfmeister, Austria
1996............Isolde Kostner, Italy	2005............Anja Paerson, Sweden

Note: The 1995 FIS World Alpine Ski Championships were postponed to 1996 due to lack of snow.

World Cup Season Title Holders

Men
OVERALL

1967 ....Jean-Claude Killy, France	1987 ....Pirmin Zurbriggen, Switzerland
1968 ....Jean-Claude Killy, France	1988 ....Pirmin Zurbriggen, Switzerland
1969 ....Karl Schranz, Austria	1989 ....Marc Girardelli, Luxembourg
1970 ....Karl Schranz, Austria	1990 ....Pirmin Zurbriggen, Switzerland
1971 ....Gustavo Thoeni, Italy	1991 ....Marc Girardelli, Luxembourg
1972 ....Gustavo Thoeni, Italy	1992 ....Paul Accola, Switzerland
1973 ....Gustavo Thoeni, Italy	1993 ....Marc Girardelli, Luxembourg
1974 ....Piero Gros, Italy	1994 ....Kjetil André Aamodt, Norway
1975 ....Gustavo Thoeni, Italy	1995 ....Alberto Tomba, Italy
1976 ....Ingemar Stenmark, Sweden	1996 ....Lasse Kjus, Norway
1977 ....Ingemar Stenmark, Sweden	1997 ....Luc Alphand, France
1978 ....Ingemar Stenmark, Sweden	1998 ....Hermann Maier, Austria
1979 ....Peter Lüscher, Switzerland	1999 ....Lasse Kjus, Norway
1980 ....Andreas Wenzel, Liechtenstein	2000 ....Hermann Maier, Austria
1981 ....Phil Mahre, United States	2001 ....Hermann Maier, Austria
1982 ....Phil Mahre, United States	2002 ....Stephan Eberharter, Austria
1983 ....Phil Mahre, United States	2003 ....Stephan Eberharter, Austria
1984 ....Pirmin Zurbriggen, Switzerland	2004 ....Hermann Maier, Austria
1985 ....Marc Girardelli, Luxembourg	2005 ....Bode Miller, United States
1986 ....Marc Girardelli, Luxembourg	2006 ....Benjamin Raich, Austria

Men *(Cont.)*
DOWNHILL

1967 ....Jean-Claude Killy, France	1986 ....Peter Wirnsberger, Austria
1968 ....Gerhard Nenning, Austria	1987 ....Pirmin Zurbriggen, Switzerland
1969 ....Karl Schranz, Austria	1988 ....Pirmin Zurbriggen, Switzerland
1970 ....Karl Schranz, Austria	1989 ....Marc Girardelli, Luxembourg
........................Karl Cordin, Austria	1990 ....Helmut Hoeflehner, Austria
1971 ....Bernhard Russi, Switzerland	1991 ....Franz Heinzer, Switzerland
1972 ....Bernhard Russi, Switzerland	1992 ....Franz Heinzer, Switzerland
1973 ....Roland Collumbin, Switzerland	1993 ....Franz Heinzer, Switzerland
1974 ....Roland Collumbin, Switzerland	1994 ....Marc Girardelli, Luxembourg
1975 ....Franz Klammer, Austria	1995 ....Luc Alphand, France
1976 ....Franz Klammer, Austria	1996 ....Luc Alphand, France
1977 ....Franz Klammer, Austria	1997 ....Luc Alphand, France
1978 ....Franz Klammer, Austria	1998 ....Andreas Schifferer, Austria
1979 ....Peter Müller, Switzerland	1999 ....Lasse Kjus, Norway
1980 ....Peter Müller, Switzerland	2000 ....Hermann Maier, Austria
1981 ....Harti Weirather, Austria	2001 ....Hermann Maier, Austria
1982 ....Steve Podborski, Canada	2002 ....Stephan Eberharter, Austria
........................Peter Mueller, Switzerland	2003 ....Stephan Eberharter, Austria
1983 ....Franz Klammer, Austria	2004 ....Stephan Eberharter, Austria
1984 ....Urs Raber, Switzerland	2005 ....Michael Walchhofer, Austria
1985 ....Helmut Hoeflehner, Austria	2006 ....Michael Walchhofer, Austria

SLALOM

1967 ....Jean-Claude Killy, France	1987 ....Bojan Krizaj, Yugoslavia
1968 ....Domeng Giovanoli, Switzerland	1988 ....Alberto Tomba, Italy
1969 ....Jean-Noel Augert, France	1989 ....Armin Bittner, W Germany
1970 ....Patrick Russel, France	1990 ....Armin Bittner, W Germany
........................Alain Penz, France	1991 ....Marc Girardelli, Luxembourg
1971 ....Jean-Noel Augert, France	1992 ....Alberto Tomba, Italy
1972 ....Jean-Noel Augert, France	1993 ....Tomas Fogdof, Sweden
1973 ....Gustavo Thoeni, Italy	1994 ....Alberto Tomba, Italy
1974 ....Gustavo Thoeni, Italy	1995 ....Alberto Tomba, Italy
1975 ....Ingemar Stenmark, Sweden	1996 ....Sebastien Amiez, France
1976 ....Ingemar Stenmark, Sweden	1997 ....Thomas Sykora, Austria
1977 ....Ingemar Stenmark, Sweden	1998 ....Thomas Sykora, Austria
1978 ....Ingemar Stenmark, Sweden	1999 ....Thomas Stangassinger, Austria
1979 ....Ingemar Stenmark, Sweden	2000 ....Kjetil André Aamodt, Norway
1980 ....Ingemar Stenmark, Sweden	2001 ....Benjamin Raich, Austria
1981 ....Ingemar Stenmark, Sweden	2002 ....Ivica Kostelic, Croatia
1982 ....Phil Mahre, United States	2003 ....Kalle Palander, Finland
1983 ....Ingemar Stenmark, Sweden	2004 ....Rainer Schoenfelder, Austria
1984 ....Marc Girardelli, Luxembourg	2005 ....Benjamin Raich, Austria
1985 ....Marc Girardelli, Luxembourg	2006 ....Giorgio Rocca, Italy
1986 ....Rok Petrovic, Yugoslavia	

GIANT SLALOM

1967 ....Jean-Claude Killy, France	1987 ....Joel Gaspoz, Switzerland
1968 ....Jean-Claude Killy, France	........................Pirmin Zurbriggen, Switzerland
1969 ....Karl Schranz, Austria	1988 ....Alberto Tomba, Italy
1970 ....Gustavo Thoeni, Italy	1989 ....Pirmin Zurbriggen, Switzerland
1971 ....Patrick Russel, France	1990 ....Ole-Cristian Furuseth, Norway
1972 ....Gustavo Thoeni, Italy	........................Günther Mader, Austria
1973 ....Hans Hinterseer, Austria	1991 ....Alberto Tomba, Italy
1974 ....Piero Gros, Italy	1992 ....Alberto Tomba, Italy
1975 ....Ingemar Stenmark, Sweden	1993 ....Kjetil André Aamodt, Norway
1976 ....Ingemar Stenmark, Sweden	1994 ....Christian Mayer, Austria
1977 ....Heini Hemmi, Switzerland	1995 ....Alberto Tomba, Italy
........................Ingemar Stenmark, Sweden	1996 ....Michael von Gruenigen, Switzerland
1978 ....Ingemar Stenmark, Sweden	1997 ....Michael von Gruenigen, Switzerland
1979 ....Ingemar Stenmark, Sweden	1998 ....Hermann Maier, Austria
1980 ....Ingemar Stenmark, Sweden	1999 ....Michael von Gruenigen, Switzerland
1981 ....Ingemar Stenmark, Sweden	2000 ....Hermann Maier, Austria
1982 ....Phil Mahre, United States	2001 ....Hermann Maier, Austria
1983 ....Phil Mahre, United States	2002 ....Frederic Covili, France
1984 ....Ingemar Stenmark, Sweden	2003 ....Michael von Gruenigen, Switzerland
........................Pirmin Zurbriggen, Switzerland	2004 ....Bode Miller, United States
1985 ....Marc Girardelli, Luxembourg	2005 ....Benjamin Raich, Austria
1986 ....Joel Gaspoz, Switzerland	2006 ....Benjamin Raich, Austria

Men *(Cont.)*

SUPER G

1986 ....Markus Wasmeier, W Germany	1997 ....Luc Alphand, France
1987 ....Pirmin Zurbriggen, Switzerland	1998 ....Hermann Maier, Austria
1988 ....Pirmin Zurbriggen, Switzerland	1999 ....Hermann Maier, Austria
1989 ....Pirmin Zurbriggen, Switzerland	2000 ....Hermann Maier, Austria
1990 ....Pirmin Zurbriggen, Switzerland	2001 ....Hermann Maier, Austria
1991 ....Franz Heinzer, Switzerland	2002 ....Stephan Eberharter, Austria
1992 ....Paul Accola, Switzerland	2003 ....Stephan Eberharter, Austria
1993 ....Kjetil André Aamodt, Norway	2004 ....Hermann Maier, Austria
1994 ....Jan Einar Thorsen, Norway	2005 ....Bode Miller, United States
1995 ....Peter Runggaldier, Italy	2006 ....Aksel Lund Svindal, Norway
1996 ....Atle Skaardal, Norway	

COMBINED

1979 ....Andreas Wenzel, Liechtenstein	1994 ....Kjetil André Aamodt, Norway
1980 ....Andreas Wenzel, Liechtenstein	1995 ....Marc Girardelli, Luxembourg
1981 ....Phil Mahre, United States	1996 ....Günther Mader, Austria
1982 ....Phil Mahre, United States	1997 ....Kjetil André Aamodt, Norway
1983 ....Phil Mahre, United States	1998 ....Werner Franz, Austria
1984 ....Andreas Wenzel, Liechtenstein	1999 ....Kjetil André Aamodt, Norway
1985 ....Andreas Wenzel, Liechtenstein	2000 ....Kjetil André Aamodt, Norway
1986 ....Markus Wasmeier, W Germany	Lasse Kjus, Norway
1987 ....Pirmin Zurbriggen, Switzerland	2001 ....Lasse Kjus, Norway
1988 ....Hubert Strolz, Austria	2002 ....Kjetil André Aamodt, Norway
1989 ....Marc Girardelli, Luxembourg	2003 ....Bode Miller, United States
1990 ....Pirmin Zurbriggen, Switzerland	2004 ....Bode Miller, United States
1991 ....Marc Girardelli, Luxembourg	2005 ....Benjamin Raich, Austria
1992 ....Paul Accola, Switzerland	2006 ....Benjamin Raich, Austria
1993 ....Marc Girardelli, Luxembourg	

Women

OVERALL

1967 ....Nancy Greene, Canada	1987 ....Maria Walliser, Switzerland
1968 ....Nancy Greene, Canada	1988 ....Michela Figini, Switzerland
1969 ....Gertrud Gabl, Austria	1989 ....Vreni Schneider, Switzerland
1970 ....Michèle Jacot, France	1990 ....Petra Kronberger, Austria
1971 ....Annemarie Pröll, Austria	1991 ....Petra Kronberger, Austria
1972 ....Annemarie Pröll, Austria	1992 ....Petra Kronberger, Austria
1973 ....Annemarie Pröll, Austria	1993 ....Anita Wachter, Austria
1974 ....Annemarie Moser-Proell, Austria	1994 ....Vreni Schneider, Switzerland
1975 ....Annemarie Moser-Proell, Austria	1995 ....Vreni Schneider, Switzerland
1976 ....Rosi Mitermaier, W Germany	1996 ....Katja Seizinger, Germany
1977 ....Lise-Marie Morerod, Switzerland	1997 ....Pernilla Wiberg, Sweden
1978 ....Hanni Wenzel, Liechtenstein	1998 ....Katja Seizinger, Germany
1979 ....Annemarie Moser-Proell, Austria	1999 ....Alexandra Meissnitzer, Austria
1980 ....Hanni Wenzel, Liechtenstein	2000 ....Renate Goetschl, Austria
1981 ....Marie-Thérèse Nadig, Switzerland	2001 ....Janica Kostelic, Croatia
1982 ....Erika Hess, Switzerland	2002 ....Michaela Dorfmeister, Austria
1983 ....Tamara McKinney, United States	2003 ....Janica Kostelic, Croatia
1984 ....Erika Hess, Switzerland	2004 ....Anja Paerson, Sweden
1985 ....Michela Figini, Switzerland	2005 ....Anja Paerson, Sweden
1986 ....Maria Walliser, Switzerland	2006 ....Janica Kostelic, Croatia

DOWNHILL

1967 ....Marielle Goitschel, France	1977 ....Brigitte Totschnig-Habersatter, Austria
1968 ....Isabelle Mir, France & Olga Pall, Austria	1978 ....Annemarie Moser-Proell, Austria
1969 ....Wiltrud Drexel, Austria	1979 ....Annemarie Moser-Proell, Austria
1970 ....Isabelle Mir, France	1980 ....Marie-Thérèse Nadig, Switzerland
1971 ....Annemarie Proell, Austria	1981 ....Marie-Thérèse Nadig, Switzerland
1972 ....Annemarie Proell, Austria	1982 ....Marie-Cecile Gros-Gaudenier, France
1973 ....Annemarie Proell, Austria	1983 ....Doris De Agostini, Switzerland
1974 ....Annemarie Moser-Proell, Austria	1984 ....Maria Walliser, Switzerland
1975 ....Annemarie Moser-Proell, Austria	1985 ....Michela Figini, Switzerland
1976 ....Brigitte Totschnig, Austria	1986 ....Maria Walliser, Switzerland

Women *(Cont.)*

DOWNHILL *(Cont.)*

1987	Michela Figini, Switzerland	1997	Renate Goetschl, Austria
1988	Michela Figini, Switzerland	1998	Katja Seizinger, Germany
1989	Michela Figini, Switzerland	1999	Renate Goetschl, Austria
1990	Katrin Gutensohn-Knopf, Germany	2000	Regina Haeusl, Germany
1991	Chantal Bournissen, Switzerland	2001	Isolde Kostner, Italy
1992	Katja Seizinger, Germany	2002	Isolde Kostner, Italy
1993	Katja Seizinger, Germany	2003	Michaela Dorfmeister, Austria
1994	Katja Seizinger, Germany	2004	Renate Goetschl, Austria
1995	Picabo Street, United States	2005	Anja Paerson, Sweden
1996	Picabo Street, United States	2006	Michaela Dorfmeister, Austria

SLALOM

1967	Nancy Greene, Canada	1987	Maria Walliser, Switzerland
1968	Nancy Greene, Canada	1988	Michela Figini, Switzerland
1969	Gertrud Gabl, Austria	1989	Vreni Schneider, Switzerland
1970	Michèle Jacot, France	1990	Petra Kronberger, Austria
1971	Annemarie Proell, Austria	1991	Petra Kronberger, Austria
1972	Annemarie Proell, Austria	1992	Petra Kronberger, Austria
1973	Annemarie Proell, Austria	1993	Anita Wachter, Austria
1974	Annemarie Moser-Proell, Austria	1994	Vreni Schneider, Switzerland
1975	Annemarie Moser-Proell, Austria	1995	Vreni Schneider, Switzerland
1976	Rosi Mitermaier, W Germany	1996	Katja Seizinger, Germany
1977	Lise-Marie Morerod, Switzerland	1997	Pernilla Wiberg, Sweden
1978	Hanni Wenzel, Liechtenstein	1998	Katja Seizinger, Germany
1979	Annemarie Moser-Proell, Austria	1999	Alexandra Meissnitzer, Austria
1980	Hanni Wenzel, Liechtenstein	2000	Renate Goetschl, Austria
1981	Marie-Thérèse Nadig, Switzerland	2001	Janica Kostelic, Croatia
1982	Erika Hess, Switzerland	2002	Laure Pequegnot, France
1983	Tamara McKinney, United States	2003	Janica Kostelic, Croatia
1984	Erika Hess, Switzerland	2004	Anja Paerson, Sweden
1985	Michela Figini, Switzerland	2005	Tanja Poutiainen, Finland
1986	Maria Walliser, Switzerland	2006	Janica Kostelic, Croatia

GIANT SLALOM

1967	Nancy Greene, Canada	1987	Vreni Schneider/ Maria Walliser, Switz
1968	Nancy Greene, Canada	1988	Mateja Svet, Yugoslavia
1969	Marilyn Cochran, United States	1989	Vreni Schneider, Switzerland
1970	Michèle Jacot/Françoise Macchi, France	1990	Anita Wachter, Austria
1971	Annemarie Proell, Austria	1991	Vreni Schneider, Switzerland
1972	Annemarie Proell, Austria	1992	Carole Merle, France
1973	Monika Kaserer, Austria	1993	Carole Merle, France
1974	Hanni Wenzel, Liechtenstein	1994	Anita Wachter, Austria
1975	Annemarie Moser-Proell, Austria	1995	Vreni Schneider, Switzerland
1976	Lise-Marie Morerod, Switzerland	1996	Martina Ertl, Germany
1977	Lise-Marie Morerod, Switzerland	1997	Deborah Compagnoni, Italy
1978	Lise-Marie Morerod, Switzerland	1998	Martina Ertl, Germany
1979	Christa Kinshofer, W Germany	1999	Alexandra Meissnitzer, Austria
1980	Hanni Wenzel, Liechtenstein	2000	Michaela Dorfmeister, Austria
1981	Marie-Thérèse Nadig, Switzerland	2001	Sonja Nef, Switzerland
1982	Irene Epple, W Germany	2002	Sonja Nef, Switzerland
1983	Tamara McKinney, United States	2003	Anja Paerson, Sweden
1984	Erika Hess, Switzerland	2004	Anja Paerson, Sweden
1985	Maria Keihl, W Germany	2005	Tanja Poutiainen, Finland
	Michela Figini, Switzerland	2006	Anja Paerson, Sweden
1986	Vreni Schneider, Switzerland		

SUPER G

1986	Maria Kiehl, W Germany	1993	Katja Seizinger, Germany
1987	Maria Walliser, Switzerland	1994	Katja Seizinger, Germany
1988	Michela Figini, Switzerland	1995	Katja Seizinger, Germany
1989	Carole Merle, France	1996	Katja Seizinger, Germany
1990	Carole Merle, France	1997	Hilde Gerg, Germany
1991	Carole Merle, France	1998	Katja Seizinger, Germany
1992	Carole Merle, France	1999	Alexandra Meissnitzer, Austria

Women *(Cont.)*

SUPER G *(CONT.)*

2000 ....Renate Goetschl, Austria	2004 ....Renate Goetschl, Austria
2001 ....Regine Cavagnoud, France	2005 ....Michaela Dorfmeister, Austria
2002 ....Hilde Gerg, Germany	2006 ....Michaela Dorfmesiter, Austria
2003 ....Carole Montillet, France	

COMBINED

1979 ....Annemarie Moser-Proell, Austria	1993 ....Anita Wachter, Austria
Hanni Wenzel, Liechtenstein	1994 ....Pernilla Wiberg, Sweden
1980 ....Hanni Wenzel, Liechtenstein	1995 ....Pernilla Wiberg, Sweden
1981 ....Marie-Thérèse Nadig, Switzerland	1996 ....Anita Wachter, Austria
1982 ....Irene Epple, W Germany	1997 ....Pernilla Wiberg, Sweden
1983 ....Hanni Wenzel, Liechtenstein	1998 ....Hilde Gerg, Germany
1984 ....Erika Hess, Switzerland	1999 ....Hilde Gerg, Germany
1985 ....Brigitte Oertli, Switzerland	2000 ....Renate Goetschl, Austria
1986 ....Maria Walliser, Switzerland	2001 ....Janica Kostelic, Croatia
1987 ....Brigitte Oertli, Switzerland	2002 ....Renate Goetschl, Austria
1988 ....Brigitte Oertli, Switzerland	2003 ....Janica Kostelic, Croatia
1989 ....Brigitte Oertli, Switzerland	2004 ....Anja Paerson, Sweden
1990 ....Anita Wachter, Austria	2005 ....Janica Kostelic, Croatia
1991 ....Sabine Ginther, Austria	2006 ....Janica Kostelic, Croatia
1992 ....Sabine Ginther, Austria	

World Cup Career Victories

Men

DOWNHILL

25 ....Franz Klammer, Austria
19 ....Peter Müller, Switzerland
18 ....Stephan Eberharter, Austria

SLALOM

40 ....Ingemar Stenmark, Sweden
35 ....Alberto Tomba, Italy
16 ....Marc Girardelli, Luxembourg

GIANT SLALOM

46 ....Ingemar Stenmark, Sweden
23 ....Michael Von Gruenigen, Switz
15 ....Alberto Tomba, Italy

SUPER G

22 ....*Hermann Maier, Austria
10 ....Pirmin Zurbriggen, Switzerland
7 ....Marc Girardelli, Luxembourg

COMBINED

11 ....Phil Mahre, United States
Pirmin Zurbriggen, Switzerland
Marc Girardelli, Luxembourg

*Active in 2005–06.

Women

DOWNHILL

36 ....Annemarie Moser-Proell, Austria
20 ....*Renate Goetschl, Austria
17 ....Michela Figini, Switzerland

SLALOM

34 ....Vreni Schneider, Switzerland
21 ....Erika Hess, Switzerland
20 ....*Janica Kostelic, Croatia

GIANT SLALOM

20 ....Vreni Schneider, Switzerland
16 ....Annemarie Moser-Pröell, Austria
14 ....Anita Wachter, Austria

SUPER G

16 ....Katja Seizinger, Germany
13 ....*Renate Goetschl, Austria
12 ....Carole Merle, France

COMBINED

8 ....Hanni Wenzel, Liechtenstein
7 ....Annemarie Moser-Proell, Austria
Brigitte Oertli, Switzerland

U.S. Olympic Gold Medalists

Men

Year	Winner	Event
1980 ....Phil Mahre		Combined
1984 ....Bill Johnson		Downhill
1984 ....Phil Mahre		Slalom
1994 ....Tommy Moe		Downhill
2006 ....Ted Ligety		Combined

Women

Year	Winner	Event
1948 ....Gretchen Fraser		Slalom
1952 ....Andrea Mead Lawrence		Slalom
1952 ....Andrea Mead Lawrence		Giant Slalom
1972 ....Barbara Ann Cochran		Slalom
1984 ....Debbie Armstrong		Giant Slalom
1994 ....Diann Roffe-Steinrotter		Super G
1998 ....Picabo Street		Super
2006 ....Julia Mancuso		Giant Slalom

Figure Skating

Olympic ice dancing
silver medalists
Tanith Belbin and Ben Agosto

Silver Sunrise

U.S. figure skating saw a changing of the guard in 2006 and the next generation proved American prospects are bright

BY MERRELL NODEN

For U.S. figure skating fans, it was a year of surprises, some good, some bad. It began with a question: Would this be the year that Michelle Kwan finally won an Olympic gold medal? After sitting out the Grand Prix season and missing the U.S. championships with a groin injury, she had successfully petitioned the U.S. federation for a medical waiver to make the Olympic team. All the federation required of her was that she prove her fitness, which she did, looking sharp during a monitoring session on January 27.

But in the end Kwan, surely the most beloved of all U.S. skaters—not to mention the winner of nine national titles, five world championships, and two Olympic medals, one silver, one bronze—did not even compete in Turin. The long flight and a cold march in the Opening Ceremonies made her tighten up, and after a dismal practice session on the first weekend of the Games, Kwan announced she was withdrawing from the team. She was replaced by Emily Hughes, younger sister of the defending champion, Sarah Hughes (who had not tried to make the team).

Kwan's withdrawal was a sad moment for U.S. Figure Skating and for a woman who has brought so much grace to the sport,

on and off the ice. "Michelle Kwan means more to the United States Olympic Committee than maybe any athlete that's ever competed [under its colors]," declared USOC chairman Peter Ueberroth, and she showed what he was talking about by turning down an offer to do commentary for NBC, explaining that she did not wish to be an ongoing distraction in Turin.

In a way, it was too bad Kwan said no. It would have been fascinating to hear her thoughts on competitions that were full of jarring falls, a glare fest between two partners, and two gold medal-winning performances, one as dominant as expected, the other a huge surprise. The ice dancing competition in particular was marred by a startling number of spills, some of them scary to behold. After Maurizio Margaglio dropped Barbara Fusar Poli, the Italian duo refused to speak to each other before their free dance. Indeed, they looked as ready to duel with pistols as to skate. They actually performed well in the free dance, but still finished out of the medals, far behind the winners, Russia's Tatiana Navka and Roman Kostomarov.

The nice surprise for U.S. skating fans was the performance of Tanith Belbin, 21, and Ben Agosto, 24, who, skating a smoldering flamenco dance, won the country's first medal in the discipline since 1976 and its first-ever silver. The two have been skating together for eight years, but seemed destined never to compete at the Olympics since he was American and she Canadian. That changed on December 31, thanks to a special act of Congress, signed into law by President Bush, which extended U.S. citizenship to about 100 people with special abilities.

There was no doubt as to who was the best male skater in Turin. Evgeni Plushenko, who'd finished second four years earlier in Salt Lake City, arrived as the strong favorite and left as the fifth straight male skater from either Russia or the Soviet Union to reign as Olympic champion. Skating to the theme from *The Godfather*, the 23-year-old from St. Petersburg never let anyone else into the competition, ultimately beating runnerup Stephane Lambiel of Switzerland by a whopping score of 258.33 to 231.21 points. Johnny Weir of the U.S., who had high expectations, got to the arena late, made numerous mistakes and finished fifth.

After Tatiana Totmianina and Maxim Marinin claimed the gold in pairs, the Russians needed just one more gold, in the ladies, for an unprecedented sweep. That seemed a real possibility, since veteran Irina Slutskaya was as much the favorite as anyone.

Even without Kwan, the ladies short program competition turned out to be the greatest in Olympic history, with Sasha Cohen of the U.S. skating an almost perfect routine to finish barely ahead of Slutskaya. No one paid all that much attention to 24-year-old veteran Shizuka Arakawa, who after making the Japanese Olympic team in Nagano eight years earlier had nearly quit the sport on several occasions.

All this seemed to open the door for Cohen, the 21-year-old Californian with the elfin smile and talent for perfect spins. But Cohen suffered a slight groin strain during a fall in practice, and during her warm-ups she was struggling. She fell twice in the first minute of her program before grittily landing five clean triples. She left the ice certain that her early stumbles had cost her any shot at a medal. "I definitely didn't think I

CARL YARBROUGH

Sasha Cohen led after the short program, but had to settle for a silver medal at Turin.

was going to get any medal," she said later.

But it turned out she was not the only skater suffering from nerves. Skating last, Slutskaya never looked confident. After falling on a triple loop midway through her program, she checked out mentally and wound up with the bronze.

Even Arakawa didn't really wow the audience. She did none of her triple jumps. In fact, no skater even attempted to do one. But Arakawa did skate with grace and power, and her gold was Japan's only medal of these Games. And there's no reason to think the Japanese won't be back. Plucky Emily Hughes will get better, as should Kimmie Meissner, a 16-year-old from Bel Air, MD, who, after finishing sixth in the Olympics, won the world championships in March. In April, Kwan too made it sound as if she might not retire. That can only be a good thing for the sport, though she is going to have a lot of competition.

FOR THE RECORD • 2006

World Champions

Calgary, Alberta, Canada; March 20-26, 2006

Women

1........Kimmie Meissner, United States
2........Fumie Suguri, Japan
3........Elena Soklova, Russia

Men

1.........Stephane Lambiel, Switzerland
2.........Brian Joubert, France
3.........Evan Lysacek, United States

Pairs

1........Oing Pang/Jian Tong, China
2........Maria Petrova/Alexei Tikhonov, Russia
3........Rena Inoue/John Baldwin, United States

Dance

1.........Albena Denkova/Maxim Staviski, Bulgaria
2.........Isabelle Delobel/Olivier Schoenfelder, France
3.........Marie-France Dubreuil/ Patrice Lauzon, Canada

2006 World Figure Skating Championships Medal Table

Country	Gold	Silver	Bronze	Total
United States	1	0	2	3
France	0	2	0	2
Russia	0	1	1	2
Bulgaria	1	0	0	1
China	1	0	0	1
Switzerland	1	0	0	1
Japan	0	1	0	1
Canada	0	0	1	1

Champions of the United States

St. Louis Missouri; January 7–15, 2006

Women

1.....................Sasha Cohen,Orange County FSC
2.....................Kimmie Meissner, University Of Delaware FSC
3.....................Emily Hughes, SC of New York

Men

1.....................Johnny Weir, SC of New York
2.....................Evan Lysacek, Dupage FSC
3.....................Matthew Savoie, Illinois Valley FSC

Pairs

1.....................Rena Inoue, John Baldwin, All Year FSC
2.....................Marcy Hinzmann, Aaron Parchem, Winterhurst/Detroit FSC
3.....................Kathryn Orscher, Garret Lucash, Charter Oak FSC

Dance

1....................Tanith Belbin, Ben Agosto, Arctic FSC
2.....................Melissa Gregory, Denis Petukhov, SC of New York
3.....................Jamie Silverstein, Ryan O'Meara, Arctic/Coyotes SC of Arizona

FOR THE RECORD • Year by Year

Skating Terminology*

Basic Skating Terms

Edges: The two sides of the skating blade, on either side of the grooved center. There is an inside edge, on the inner side of the leg; and an outside edge, on the outer side of the leg.

Free Foot, Hip, Knee, Side, etc.: The foot a skater is not skating on at any one time is the free foot; everything on that side of the body is then called "free." (See also "skating foot.")

Free Skating (Freestyle): A 4- or 5-minute competition program of free-skating components, choreographed to music, with no set elements. Skating moves include jumps, spins, steps and other linking movements.

Skating Foot, Hip, Knee, Side, etc.: Opposite of the free foot, hip, knee, side, etc. The foot a skater is skating on at any one time is the skating foot; everything on that side of the body is then called "skating."

Toe Picks (Toe Rakes): The teeth at the front of the skate blade, used primarily for certain jumps and spins.

Trace, Tracing: The line left on the ice by the skater's blade.

Jumps

Waltz: A beginner's jump, involving half a revolution in the air, taken from a forward outside edge and landed on the back outside edge of the other foot.

Toe Loop: A one-revolution jump taken off from and landed on the same back outside edge. This jump is similar to the loop jump except that the skater kicks the toe pick of the free leg into the ice upon takeoff, providing added power.

Toe Walley: A jump similar to the toe loop, except that the takeoff is from the inside edge.

Flip: A jump taken off with the toe pick of the free leg from a back inside edge and landed on a back outside edge, with one in-air revolution.

Lutz: A toe jump similar to the flip, taken off with the toe pick of the free leg from a backward outside edge. The skater enters the jump skating in one direction, and concludes the jump skating in the opposite direction. Usually performed in the corners of the rink. Named after inventor Alois Lutz, who first landed the jump in Vienna, 1918.

Salchow: A one-, two- or three-revolution jump. The skater takes off from the back inside edge of one foot and lands backwards on the outside edge of the free foot, the opposite foot from which the skater took off. Named for its originator and first Olympic champion (1908), Sweden's Ulrich Salchow.

Axel: A combination of the waltz and loop jumps, including one-and-a-half revolutions. The only jump begun from a forward outside edge, the Axel is landed on the back outside edge of the opposite foot. Named for its inventor, Norway's Axel Paulsen.

Spins

Spin: The rotation of the body in one place on the ice. Various spins are the back, fast or scratch, sit, camel, butterfly and layback.

Camel Spin: A spin with the skater in an arabesque position (the free leg at right angles to the leg on the ice).

Flying Camel Spin: A jump spin ending in the camel-spin position.

Flying Sit Spin: A jump spin in which the skater leaps off the ice, assumes a sitting position at the peak of the jump, lands and spins in a similar sitting position.

Pair Movements/Techniques

Death Spiral: One of the most dramatic moves in figure skating. The man, acting as the center of a circle, holds tightly to the hand of his partner and pulls her around him. The woman, gliding on one foot, achieves a position almost horizontal to the ice.

Lifts: The most spectacular moves in pairs skating. They involve any maneuver in which the man lifts the woman off the ice. The man often holds his partner above his head with one hand.

Throws: The man lifts the woman into the air and throws her away from him. She spins in the air and lands on one foot.

Twist: The man throws the woman into the air. She spins in the air (either a double- or triple-twist), and he catches her at the landing.

*Compiled by the United States Figure Skating Association.

World Champions

Women

1906	Madge Sayers-Cave, Great Britain
1907	Madge Sayers-Cave, Great Britain
1908	Lily Kronberger, Hungary
1909	Lily Kronberger, Hungary
1910	Lily Kronberger, Hungary
1911	Lily Kronberger, Hungary
1912	Opika von Meray Horvath, Hungary
1913	Opika von Meray Horvath, Hungary
1914	Opika von Meray Horvath, Hungary
1915–21	No competition
1922	Herma Plank-Szabo, Austria
1923	Herma Plank-Szabo, Austria
1924	Herma Plank-Szabo, Austria
1925	Herma Jaross-Szabo, Austria
1926	Herma Jaross-Szabo, Austria
1927	Sonja Henie, Norway
1928	Sonja Henie, Norway
1929	Sonja Henie, Norway
1930	Sonja Henie, Norway
1931	Sonja Henie, Norway
1932	Sonja Henie, Norway
1933	Sonja Henie, Norway
1934	Sonja Henie, Norway
1935	Sonja Henie, Norway
1936	Sonja Henie, Norway
1937	Cecilia Colledge, Great Britain
1938	Megan Taylor, Great Britain
1939	Megan Taylor, Great Britain
1940–46	No competition
1947	Barbara Ann Scott, Canada
1948	Barbara Ann Scott, Canada
1949	Alena Vrzanova, Czechoslovakia
1950	Alena Vrzanova, Czechoslovakia
1951	Jeannette Altwegg, Great Britain
1952	Jacqueline duBief, France
1953	Tenley Albright, United States
1954	Gundi Busch, W. Germany
1955	Tenley Albright, United States
1956	Carol Heiss, United States
1957	Carol Heiss, United States
1958	Carol Heiss, United States
1959	Carol Heiss, United States
1960	Carol Heiss, United States
1961	No competition
1962	Sjoukje Dijkstra, Netherlands
1963	Sjoukje Dijkstra, Netherlands
1964	Sjoukje Dijkstra, Netherlands
1965	Petra Burka, Canada
1966	Peggy Fleming, United States
1967	Peggy Fleming, United States
1968	Peggy Fleming, United States
1969	Gabriele Seyfert, E. Germany
1970	Gabriele Seyfert, E. Germany
1971	Beatrix Schuba, Austria
1972	Beatrix Schuba, Austria
1973	Karen Magnussen, Canada
1974	Christine Errath, E. Germany
1975	Dianne DeLeeuw, Netherlands

Women *(Cont.)*

1976	Dorothy Hamill, United States
1977	Linda Fratianne, United States
1978	Annett Poetzsch, E. Germany
1979	Linda Fratianne, United States
1980	Annett Poetzsch, E. Germany
1981	Denise Biellmann, Switzerland
1982	Elaine Zayak, United States
1983	Rosalynn Sumners, United States
1984	Katarina Witt, E. Germany
1985	Katarina Witt, E. Germany
1986	Debi Thomas, United States
1987	Katarina Witt, E. Germany
1988	Katarina Witt, E. Germany
1989	Midori Ito, Japan
1990	Jill Trenary, United States
1991	Kristi Yamaguchi, United States
1992	Kristi Yamaguchi, United States
1993	Oksana Baiul, Ukraine
1994	Yuka Sato, Japan
1995	Chen Lu, China
1996	Michelle Kwan, United States
1997	Tara Lipinski, United States
1998	Michelle Kwan, United States
1999	Maria Butyrskaya, Russia
2000	Michelle Kwan, United States
2001	Michelle Kwan, United States
2002	Irina Slutskaya, Russia
2003	Michelle Kwan, United States
2004	Shizuka Arakawa, Japan
2005	Irina Slutskaya, Russia
2006	Kimmie Meissner, United States

Men

1896	Gilbert Fuchs, Germany
1897	Gustav Hugel, Austria
1898	Henning Grenander, Sweden
1899	Gustav Hugel, Austria
1900	Gustav Hugel, Austria
1901	Ulrich Salchow, Sweden
1902	Ulrich Salchow, Sweden
1903	Ulrich Salchow, Sweden
1904	Ulrich Salchow, Sweden
1905	Ulrich Salchow, Sweden
1906	Gilbert Fuchs, Germany
1907	Ulrich Salchow, Sweden
1908	Ulrich Salchow, Sweden
1909	Ulrich Salchow, Sweden
1910	Ulrich Salchow, Sweden
1911	Ulrich Salchow, Sweden
1912	Fritz Kachler, Austria
1913	Fritz Kachler, Austria
1914	Gosta Sandhal, Sweden
1915–21	No competition
1922	Gillis Grafstrom, Sweden
1923	Fritz Kachler, Austria
1924	Gillis Grafstrom, Sweden
1925	Willy Bockl, Austria
1926	Willy Bockl, Austria
1927	Willy Bockl, Austria
1928	Willy Bockl, Austria
1929	Gillis Grafstrom, Sweden
1930	Karl Schafer, Austria
1931	Karl Schafer, Austria
1932	Karl Schafer, Austria
1933	Karl Schafer, Austria
1934	Karl Schafer, Austria
1935	Karl Schafer, Austria
1936	Karl Schafer, Austria
1937	Felix Kaspar, Austria
1938	Felix Kaspar, Austria
1939	Graham Sharp, Great Britain
1940–46	No competition
1947	Hans Gerschwiler, Switzerland
1948	Dick Button, United States
1949	Dick Button, United States
1950	Dick Button, United States
1951	Dick Button, United States
1952	Dick Button, United States
1953	Hayes Alan Jenkins, United States
1954	Hayes Alan Jenkins, United States
1955	Hayes Alan Jenkins, United States
1956	Hayes Alan Jenkins, United States
1957	David W. Jenkins, United States
1958	David W. Jenkins, United States
1959	David W. Jenkins, United States
1960	Alan Giletti, France
1961	No competition
1962	Donald Jackson, Canada
1963	Donald McPherson, Canada
1964	Manfred Schneldorfer, W. Germany
1965	Alain Calmat, France
1966	Emmerich Danzer, Austria
1967	Emmerich Danzer, Austria
1968	Emmerich Danzer, Austria
1969	Tim Wood, United States
1970	Tim Wood, United States
1971	Andrej Nepela, Czechoslovakia
1972	Andrej Nepela, Czechoslovakia
1973	Andrej Nepela, Czechoslovakia
1974	Jan Hoffmann, E. Germany
1975	Sergei Volkov, USSR
1976	John Curry, Great Britain
1977	Vladimir Kovalev, USSR
1978	Charles Tickner, United States
1979	Vladimir Kovalev, USSR
1980	Jan Hoffmann, E. Germany
1981	Scott Hamilton, United States
1982	Scott Hamilton, United States
1983	Scott Hamilton, United States
1984	Scott Hamilton, United States
1985	Aleksandr Fadeev, USSR
1986	Brian Boitano, United States
1987	Brian Orser, Canada
1988	Brian Boitano, United States
1989	Kurt Browning, Canada
1990	Kurt Browning, Canada
1991	Kurt Browning, Canada
1992	Viktor Petrenko, CIS
1993	Kurt Browning, Canada
1994	Elvis Stojko, Canada
1995	Elvis Stojko, Canada
1996	Todd Eldredge, United States
1997	Elvis Stojko, Canada
1998	Alexei Yagudin, Russia
1999	Alexei Yagudin, Russia
2000	Alexei Yagudin, Russia
2001	Evgeni Plushenko, Russia
2002	Alexei Yagudin, Russia
2003	Evgeni Plushenko, Russia
2004	Evgeni Plushenko, Russia
2005	Stephane Lambiel, Switzerland
2006	Stephane Lambiel, Switzerland

Pairs

1908 ....Anna Hubler, Heinrich Burger, Germany
1909 ....Phyllis Johnson, James H. Johnson, Great Britain
1910 ....Anna Hubler, Heinrich Burger, Germany
1911 ....Ludowika Eilers, Walter Jakobsson, Germany/Finland
1912 ....Phyllis Johnson, James H. Johnson, Great Britain
1913 ....Helene Engelmann, Karl Majstrik, Germany
1914 ....Ludowika Jakobsson-Eilers, Walter Jakobsson-Eilers, Finland
1915–21 .....No competition
1922 ....Helene Engelmann, Alfred Berger, Germany
1923 ....Ludowika Jakobsson-Eilers, Walter Jakobsson-Eilers, Finland
1924 ....Helene Engelmann, Alfred Berger, Germany
1925 ....Herma Jaross-Szabo, Ludwig Wrede, Austria
1926 ....Andree Joly, Pierre Brunet, France
1927 ....Herma Jaross-Szabo, Ludwig Wrede, Austria
1928 ....Andree Joly, Pierre Brunet, France
1929 ....Lilly Scholz, Otto Kaiser, Austria
1930 ....Andree Brunet-Joly, Pierre Brunet-Joly, France
1931 ....Emilie Rotter, Laszlo Szollas, Hungary
1932 ....Andree Brunet-Joly, Pierre Brunet-Joly, France
1933 ....Emilie Rotter, Laszlo Szollas, Hungary
1934 ....Emilie Rotter, Laszlo Szollas, Hungary
1935 ....Emilie Rotter, Laszlo Szollas, Hungary
1936 ....Maxi Herber, Ernst Bajer, Germany
1937 ....Maxi Herber, Ernst Bajer, Germany
1938 ....Maxi Herber, Ernst Bajer, Germany
1939 ....Maxi Herber, Ernst Bajer, Germany
1940–46 .....No competition
1947 ....Micheline Lannoy, Pierre Baugniet, Belgium
1948 ....Micheline Lannoy, Pierre Baugniet, Belgium
1949 ....Andrea Kekessy, Ede Kiraly, Hungary
1950 ....Karol Kennedy, Peter Kennedy, United States
1951 ....Ria Baran, Paul Falk, W. Germany
1952 ....Ria Baran Falk, Paul Falk, W. Germany
1953 ....Jennifer Nicks, John Nicks, Great Britain
1954 ....Frances Dafoe, Norris Bowden, Canada
1955 ....Frances Dafoe, Norris Bowden, Canada
1956 ....Sissy Schwarz, Kurt Oppelt, Austria
1957 ....Barbara Wagner, Robert Paul, Canada
1958 ....Barbara Wagner, Robert Paul, Canada
1959 ....Barbara Wagner, Robert Paul, Canada
1960 ....Barbara Wagner, Robert Paul, Canada
1961 ....No competition
1962 ....Maria Jelinek, Otto Jelinek, Canada
1963 ....Marika Kilius, Hans-Jurgen Baumler, W. Germany

1964 ....Marika Kilius, Hans-Jurgen Baumler, W. Germany
1965 ....Ljudmila Protopopov, Oleg Protopopov, USSR
1966 ....Ljudmila Protopopov, Oleg Protopopov, USSR
1967 ....Ljudmila Protopopov, Oleg Protopopov, USSR
1968 ....Ljudmila Protopopov, Oleg Protopopov, USSR
1969 ....Irina Rodnina, Aleksey Ulanov, USSR
1970 ....Irina Rodnina, Aleksey Ulanov, USSR
1971 ....Irina Rodnina, Aleksey Ulanov, USSR
1972 ....Irina Rodnina, Aleksey Ulanov, USSR
1973 ....Irina Rodnina, Aleksandr Zaytsev, USSR
1974 ....Irina Rodnina, Aleksandr Zaytsev, USSR
1975 ....Irina Rodnina, Aleksandr Zaytsev, USSR
1976 ....Irina Rodnina, Aleksandr Zaytsev, USSR
1977 ....Irina Rodnina, Aleksandr Zaytsev, USSR
1978 ....Irina Rodnina, Aleksandr Zaytsev, USSR
1979 ....Tai Babilonia, Randy Gardner, United States
1980 ....Maria Cherkasova, Sergei Shakhrai, USSR
1981 ....Irina Vorobieva, Igor Lisovsky, USSR
1982 ....Sabine Baess, Tassilio Thierbach, E. Germany
1983 ....Elena Valova, Oleg Vasiliev, USSR
1984 ....Barbara Underhill, Paul Martini, Canada
1985 ....Elena Valova, Oleg Vasiliev, USSR
1986 ....Ekaterina Gordeeva, Sergei Grinkov, USSR
1987 ....Ekaterina Gordeeva, Sergei Grinkov, USSR
1988 ....Elena Valova, Oleg Vasiliev, USSR
1989 ....Ekaterina Gordeeva, Sergei Grinkov, USSR
1990 ....Ekaterina Gordeeva, Sergei Grinkov, USSR
1991 ....Natalia Mishkutienok, Artur Dmitriev, USSR
1992 ....Natalia Mishkutienok, Artur Dmitriev, CIS
1993 ....Isabelle Brasseur, Lloyd Eisler, Canada
1994 ....Evgenia Shishkova, Vadim Naumov, Russia
1995 ....Radka Kovarikova, Rene Novotny, Czech Republic
1996 ....Marina Eltsova, Andrey Buskhov, Russia
1997 ....Mandy Wötzel, Ingo Steuer, Germany
1998 ....Jenni Meno, Todd Sand, United States
1999 ....Elena Berezhnaya, Anton Sikharulidze, Russia
2000 ....Maria Petrova, Aleksei Tikhonov, Russia
2001 ....Jamie Salé, David Pelletier, Canada
2002 ....Xue Shen, Hongbo Zhao, China
2003 ....Xue Shen, Hongbo Zhao, China
2004 ....Tatiana Totmianina, Maxim Marinin, Russia
2005 ....Tatiana Totmianina, Maxim Marinin, Russia
2006 ....Qing Pang, Jian Tong, China

Dance

1950 ....Lois Waring, Michael McGean, United States
1951 ....Jean Westwood, Lawrence Demmy, Great Britain
1952 ....Jean Westwood, Lawrence Demmy, Great Britain

1953 ....Jean Westwood, Lawrence Demmy, Great Britain
1954 ....Jean Westwood, Lawrence Demmy, Great Britain
1955 ....Jean Westwood, Lawrence Demmy, Great Britain

Dance *(Cont.)*

1956 ....Pamela Wieght, Paul Thomas, Great Britain	1977 ....Irina Moiseeva, Andreij Minenkov, USSR
1957 ....June Markham, Courtney Jones, Great Britain	1978 ....Natalia Linichuk, Gennadi Karponosov, USSR
1958 ....June Markham, Courtney Jones, Great Britain	1979 ....Natalia Linichuk, Gennadi Karponosov, USSR
1959 ....Doreen D. Denny, Courtney Jones, Great Britain	1980 ....Krisztina Regoeczy, Andras Sallai, Hungary
1960 ....Doreen D. Denny, Courtney Jones, Great Britain	1981..............Jayne Torvill, Christopher Dean, Great Britain
1961 ....No competition	1982 ....Jayne Torvill, Christopher Dean, Great Britain
1962 ....Eva Romanova, Pavel Roman, Czechoslovakia	1983 ....Jayne Torvill, Christopher Dean, Great Britain
1963 ....Eva Romanova, Pavel Roman, Czechoslovakia	1984 ....Jayne Torvill, Christopher Dean, Great Britain
1964 ....Eva Romanova, Pavel Roman, Czechoslovakia	1985............Natalia Bestemianova, Andrei Bukin, USSR
1965 ....Eva Romanova, Pavel Roman, Czechoslovakia	1986............Natalia Bestemianova, Andrei Bukin, USSR
1966 ....Diane Towler, Bernard Ford, Great Britain	1987............Natalia Bestemianova, Andrei Bukin, USSR
1967 ....Diane Towler, Bernard Ford, Great Britain	1988............Natalia Bestemianova, Andrei Bukin, USSR
1968 ....Diane Towler, Bernard Ford, Great Britain	1989..........Marina Klimova, Sergei Ponomarenko, USSR
1969 ....Diane Towler, Bernard Ford, Great Britain	1990 ....Marina Klimova, Sergei Ponomarenko, USSR
1970 ....Ljudmila Pakhomova, Aleksandr Gorshkov, USSR	1991..............Isabelle Duchesnay, Paul Duchesnay, France
1971 ....Ljudmila Pakhomova, Aleksandr Gorshkov, USSR	1992 ....Marina Klimova, Sergei Ponomarenko, CIS
1972 ....Ljudmila Pakhomova, Aleksandr Gorshkov, USSR	1993 ....Renee Roca, Gorsha Sur, United States
1973 ....Ljudmila Pakhomova, Aleksandr Gorshkov, USSR	1994 ....Oksana Grishuk, Evgeny Platov, Russia
1974 ....Ljudmila Pakhomova, Aleksandr Gorshkov, USSR	1995 ....Oksana Grishuk, Evgeny Platov, Russia
1975 ....Irina Moiseeva, Andreij Minenkov, USSR	1996 ....Oksana Grishuk, Evgeny Platov, Russia
1976 ....Ljudmila Pakhomova, Aleksandr Gorshkov, USSR	1997 ....Oksana Grishuk, Evgeny Platov, Russia
	1998 ....Anjelika Krylova, Oleg Ovsyannikov, Russia
	1999 ....Anjelika Krylova, Oleg Ovsyannikov, Russia
	2000..........Marina Anissina, Gwendal Peizerat, France
	2001..........Barbara Fusar Poli, Maurizio Margaglio, Italy
	2002 ....Irina Lobacheva, Ilia Averbukh, Russia
	2003............Shae-Lynn Bourne, Victor Kraatz, Canada
	2004 ....Tatiana Navka, Roman Kostomarov, Russia
	2005 ....Tatiana Navka, Roman Kostomarov, Russia
	2006 ....Albena Denkova, Maxim Staviski, Bulgaria

Champions of the United States

The championships held in 1914, 1918, 1920 and 1921 under the auspices of the International Skating Union of America were open to Canadians, although the competitions were considered to be United States championships. Beginning in 1922, the championships have been held under the auspices of the United States Figure Skating Association.

Women

1914 ....Theresa Weld, SC of Boston	1936 ....Maribel Y. Vinson, SC of Boston
1915–17 .....No competition	1937 ....Maribel Y. Vinson, SC of Boston
1918............Rosemary S. Beresford, New York SC	1938 ....Joan Tozzer, SC of Boston
1919 ....No competition	1939 ....Joan Tozzer, SC of Boston
1920 ....Theresa Weld, SC of Boston	1940 ....Joan Tozzer, SC of Boston
1921 ....Theresa Weld Blanchard, SC of Boston	1941 ....Jane Vaughn, Philadelphia SC & HS
1922 ....Theresa Weld Blanchard, SC of Boston	1942 ....Jane Vaughn Sullivan, Phila. SC & HS
1923 ....Theresa Weld Blanchard, SC of Boston	1943............Gretchen Van Zandt Merrill, SC of Boston
1924 ....Theresa Weld Blanchard, SC of Boston	1944............Gretchen Van Zandt Merrill, SC of Boston
1925 ....Beatrix Loughran, New York SC	1945............Gretchen Van Zandt Merrill, SC of Boston
1926 ....Beatrix Loughran, New York SC	1946............Gretchen Van Zandt Merrill, SC of Boston
1927 ....Beatrix Loughran, New York SC	1947............Gretchen Van Zandt Merrill, SC of Boston
1928 ....Maribel Y. Vinson, SC of Boston	1948............Gretchen Van Zandt Merrill, SC of Boston
1929 ....Maribel Y. Vinson, SC of Boston	1949 ....Yvonne Claire Sherman, SC of New York
1930 ....Maribel Y. Vinson, SC of Boston	1950 ....Yvonne Claire Sherman, SC of New York
1931 ....Maribel Y. Vinson, SC of Boston	1951 ....Sonya Klopfer, Junior SC of New York
1932 ....Maribel Y. Vinson, SC of Boston	1952 ....Tenley E. Albright, SC of Boston
1933 ....Maribel Y. Vinson, SC of Boston	1953 ....Tenley E. Albright, SC of Boston
1934 ....Suzanne Davis, SC of Boston	1954 ....Tenley E. Albright, SC of Boston
1935 ....Maribel Y. Vinson, SC of Boston	1955 ....Tenley E. Albright, SC of Boston

Women *(Cont.)*

1956 ....Tenley E. Albright, SC of Boston	1982 ....Rosalynn Sumners, Seattle SC
1957 ....Carol E. Heiss, SC of New York	1983 ....Rosalynn Sumners, Seattle SC
1958 ....Carol E. Heiss, SC of New York	1984 ....Rosalynn Sumners, Seattle SC
1959 ....Carol E. Heiss, SC of New York	1985 ....Tiffany Chin, San Diego FSC
1960 ....Carol E. Heiss, SC of New York	1986 ....Debi Thomas, Los Angeles FSC
1961 ....Laurence R. Owen, SC of Boston	1987 ....Jill Trenary, Broadmoor SC
1962 ....Barbara Roles Pursley, Arctic Blades FSC	1988 ....Debi Thomas, Los Angeles FSC
1963 ....Lorraine G. Hanlon, SC of Boston	1989 ....Jill Trenary, Broadmoor SC
1964 ....Peggy Fleming, Arctic Blades FSC	1990 ....Jill Trenary, Broadmoor SC
1965 ....Peggy Fleming, Arctic Blades FSC	1991 ....Tonya Harding, Carousel FSC
1966 ....Peggy Fleming, City of Colorado Springs	1992 ....Kristi Yamaguchi, St Moritz ISC
1967 ....Peggy Fleming, Broadmoor SC	1993 ....Nancy Kerrigan, Colonial FSC
1968 ....Peggy Fleming, Broadmoor SC	1994 ....Tonya Harding, Portland FSC
1969 ....Janet Lynn, Wagon Wheel FSC	1995 ....Nicole Bobek, Los Angeles FSC
1970 ....Janet Lynn, Wagon Wheel FSC	1996 ....Michelle Kwan, Los Angeles FSC
1971 ....Janet Lynn, Wagon Wheel FSC	1997 ....Tara Lipinski, Detroit SC
1972 ....Janet Lynn, Wagon Wheel FSC	1998 ....Michelle Kwan, Los Angeles FSC
1973 ....Janet Lynn, Wagon Wheel FSC	1999 ....Michelle Kwan, Los Angeles FSC
1974 ....Dorothy Hamill, SC of New York	2000 ....Michelle Kwan, Los Angeles FSC
1975 ....Dorothy Hamill, SC of New York	2001 ....Michelle Kwan, Los Angeles FSC
1976 ....Dorothy Hamill, SC of New York	2002 ....Michelle Kwan, Los Angeles FSC
1977 ....Linda Fratianne, Los Angeles FSC	2003 ....Michelle Kwan, Los Angeles FSC
1978 ....Linda Fratianne, Los Angeles FSC	2004 ....Michelle Kwan, Los Angeles FSC
1979 ....Linda Fratianne, Los Angeles FSC	2005 ....Michelle Kwan, Los Angeles FSC
1980 ....Linda Fratianne, Los Angeles FSC	2006 ....Sasha Cohen, Orange County FSC
1981 ....Elaine Zayak, SC of New York	

Men

1914 ....Norman M. Scott, WC of Montreal	1957 ....David Jenkins, Broadmoor SC
1915–17 .....No competition	1958 ....David Jenkins, Broadmoor SC
1918 ....Nathaniel W. Niles, SC of Boston	1959 ....David Jenkins, Broadmoor SC
1919 ....No competition	1960 ....David Jenkins, Broadmoor SC
1920 ....Sherwin C. Badger, SC of Boston	1961 ....Bradley R. Lord, SC of Boston
1921 ....Sherwin C. Badger, SC of Boston	1962 ....Monty Hoyt, Broadmoor SC
1922 ....Sherwin C. Badger, SC of Boston	1963 ....Thomas Litz, Hershey FSC
1923 ....Sherwin C. Badger, SC of Boston	1964 ....Scott Ethan Allen, SC of New York
1924 ....Sherwin C. Badger, SC of Boston	1965 ....Gary C. Visconti, Detroit SC
1925 ....Nathaniel W. Niles, SC of Boston	1966 ....Scott Ethan Allen, SC of New York
1926 ....Chris I. Christenson, Twin City FSC	1967 ....Gary C. Visconti, Detroit SC
1927 ....Nathaniel W. Niles, SC of Boston	1968 ....Tim Wood, Detroit SC
1928 ....Roger F. Turner, SC of Boston	1969 ....Tim Wood, Detroit SC
1929 ....Roger F. Turner, SC of Boston	1970 ....Tim Wood, City of Colorado Springs
1930 ....Roger F. Turner, SC of Boston	1971 ....John Misha Petkevich, Great Falls FSC
1931 ....Roger F. Turner, SC of Boston	1972 ....Kenneth Shelley, Arctic Blades FSC
1932 ....Roger F. Turner, SC of Boston	1973 ....Gordon McKellen Jr., SC of Lake Placid
1933 ....Roger F. Turner, SC of Boston	1974 ....Gordon McKellen Jr., SC of Lake Placid
1934 ....Roger F. Turner, SC of Boston	1975 ....Gordon McKellen Jr., SC of Lake Placid
1935 ....Robin H. Lee, SC of New York	1976 ....Terry Kubicka, Arctic Blades FSC
1936 ....Robin H. Lee, SC of New York	1977 ....Charles Tickner, Denver FSC
1937 ....Robin H. Lee, SC of New York	1978 ....Charles Tickner, Denver FSC
1938 ....Robin H. Lee, Chicago FSC	1979 ....Charles Tickner, Denver FSC
1939 ....Robin H. Lee, St Paul FSC	1980 ....Charles Tickner, Denver FSC
1940 ....Eugene Turner, Los Angeles FSC	1981 ....Scott Hamilton, Philadelphia SC & HS
1941 ....Eugene Turner, Los Angeles FSC	1982 ....Scott Hamilton, Philadelphia SC & HS
1942 ....Robert Specht, Chicago FSC	1983 ....Scott Hamilton, Philadelphia SC & HS
1943 ....Arthur R. Vaughn Jr., Phila. SC & HS	1984 ....Scott Hamilton, Philadelphia SC & HS
1944–45 .....No competition	1985 ....Brian Boitano, Peninsula FSC
1946 ....Dick Button, Philadelphia SC & HS	1986 ....Brian Boitano, Peninsula FSC
1947 ....Dick Button, Philadelphia SC & HS	1987 ....Brian Boitano, Peninsula FSC
1948 ....Dick Button, Philadelphia SC & HS	1988 ....Brian Boitano, Peninsula FSC
1949 ....Dick Button, Philadelphia SC & HS	1989 ....Christopher Bowman, Los Angeles FSC
1950 ....Dick Button, SC of Boston	1990 ....Todd Eldredge, Los Angeles FSC
1951 ....Dick Button, SC of Boston	1991 ....Todd Eldredge, Los Angeles FSC
1952 ....Dick Button, SC of Boston	1992 ....Christopher Bowman, Los Angeles FSC
1953 ....Hayes Alan Jenkins, Cleveland SC	1993 ....Scott Davis, Broadmoor SC
1954 ....Hayes Alan Jenkins, Broadmoor SC	1994 ....Scott Davis, Broadmoor SC
1955 ....Hayes Alan Jenkins, Broadmoor SC	1995 ....Todd Eldredge, Detroit SC
1956 ....Hayes Alan Jenkins, Broadmoor SC	1996 ....Rudy Galindo, St Moritz ISC

Men *(Cont.)*

1997 ....Todd Eldredge, Detroit SC	2002 ....Todd Eldredge, Los Angeles FSC
1998 ....Todd Eldredge, Detroit SC	2003 ....Michael Weiss, Washington FSC
1999 ....Michael Weiss, Washington FSC	2004 ....Johnny Weir, SC of New York
2000 ....Michael Weiss, Washington FSC	2005 ....Johnny Weir, SC of New York
2001 ....Timothy Goebel, Winterhurst FSC	2006 ....Johnny Weir, SC of New York

Pairs

1914 ......Jeanne Chevalier, Norman M. Scott, WC of Montreal	1950 ......Karol Kennedy, Peter Kennedy, Broadmoor SC
1915–17...No competition	1951 ......Karol Kennedy, Peter Kennedy, Broadmoor SC
1918 ......Theresa Weld, Nathaniel W. Niles, SC of Boston	1952 ......Karol Kennedy, Peter Kennedy, Broadmoor SC
1919 ......No competition	1953 ......Carole Ann Ormaca, Robin Greiner, SC of Fresno
1920 ......Theresa Weld, Nathaniel W. Niles, SC of Boston	1954 ......Carole Ann Ormaca, Robin Greiner, SC of Fresno
1921 ......Theresa Weld Blanchard, Nathaniel W. Niles, SC of Boston	1955 ......Carole Ann Ormaca, Robin Greiner, St Moritz ISC
1922 ......Theresa Weld Blanchard, Nathaniel W. Niles, SC of Boston	1956 ......Carole Ann Ormaca, Robin Greiner, St Moritz ISC
1923 ......Theresa Weld Blanchard, Nathaniel W. Niles, SC of Boston	1957 ......Nancy Rouillard Ludington, Ronald Ludington, Commonwealth FSC/ SC of Boston
1924 ......Theresa Weld Blanchard, Nathaniel W. Niles, SC of Boston	1958 ......Nancy Rouillard Ludington, Ronald Ludington, Commonwealth FSC/ SC of Boston
1925 ......Theresa Weld Blanchard, Nathaniel W. Niles, SC of Boston	1959 ......Nancy Rouillard Ludington, Ronald Ludington, Commonwealth FSC
1926 ......Theresa Weld Blanchard, Nathaniel W. Niles, SC of Boston	1960 ......Nancy Rouillard Ludington, Ronald Ludington, Commonwealth FSC
1927 ......Theresa Weld Blanchard, Nathaniel W. Niles, SC of Boston	1961 ......Maribel Y. Owen, Dudley S. Richards, SC of Boston
1928 ......Maribel Y. Vinson, Thornton L. Coolidge, SC of Boston	1962 ......Dorothyann Nelson, Pieter Kollen, Village of Lake Placid
1929 ......Maribel Y. Vinson, Thornton L. Coolidge, SC of Boston	1963 ......Judianne Fotheringill, Jerry J. Fotheringill, Broadmoor SC
1930 ......Beatrix Loughran, Sherwin C. Badger, SC of New York	1964 ......Judianne Fotheringill, Jerry J. Fotheringill, Broadmoor SC
1931 ......Beatrix Loughran, Sherwin C. Badger, SC of New York	1965 ......Vivian Joseph, Ronald Joseph, Chicago FSC
1932 ......Beatrix Loughran, Sherwin C. Badger, SC of New York	1966 ......Cynthia Kauffman, Ronald Kauffman, Seattle SC
1933 ......Maribel Y. Vinson, George E. B. Hill, SC of Boston	1967 ......Cynthia Kauffman, Ronald Kauffman, Seattle SC
1934 ......Grace E. Madden, James L. Madden, SC of Boston	1968 ......Cynthia Kauffman, Ronald Kauffman, Seattle SC
1935 ......Maribel Y. Vinson, George E. B. Hill, SC of Boston	1969 ......Cynthia Kauffman, Ronald Kauffman, Seattle SC
1936 ......Maribel Y. Vinson, George E. B. Hill, SC of Boston	1970 ......Jo Jo Starbuck, Kenneth Shelley, Arctic Blades FSC
1937 ......Maribel Y. Vinson, George E. B. Hill, SC of Boston	1971 ......Jo Jo Starbuck, Kenneth Shelley, Arctic Blades FSC
1938 ......Joan Tozzer, M. Bernard Fox, SC of Boston	1972 ......Jo Jo Starbuck, Kenneth Shelley, Arctic Blades FSC
1939 ......Joan Tozzer, M. Bernard Fox, SC of Boston	1973 ......Melissa Militano, Mark Militano, SC of New York
1940 ......Joan Tozzer, M. Bernard Fox, SC of Boston	1974 ......Melissa Militano, Johnny Johns, SC of New York/Detroit SC
1941 ......Donna Atwood, Eugene Turner, Mercury FSC/Los Angeles FSC	1975 ......Melissa Militano, Johnny Johns, SC of NY/ Detroit SC
1942 ......Doris Schubach, Walter Noffke, Springfield Ice Birds	1976 ......Tai Babilonia, Randy Gardner, LA FSC
1943 ......Doris Schubach, Walter Noffke, Springfield Ice Birds	1977 ......Tai Babilonia, Randy Gardner, LA FSC
1944 ......Doris Schubach, Walter Noffke, Springfield Ice Birds	1978 ......Tai Babilonia, Randy Gardner, Los Angeles FSC/Santa Monica FSC
1945 ......Donna Jeanne Pospisil, Jean-Pierre Brunet, SC of New York	1979 ......Tai Babilonia, Randy Gardner, Los Angeles FSC/Santa Monica FSC
1946 ......Donna Jeanne Pospisil, Jean-Pierre Brunet, SC of New York	1980 ......Tai Babilonia, Randy Gardner, Los Angeles FSC/Santa Monica FSC
1947 ......Yvonne Claire Sherman, Robert J. Swenning, SC of New York	
1948 ......Karol Kennedy, Peter Kennedy, Seattle SC	
1949 ......Karol Kennedy, Peter Kennedy, Seattle SC	

Pairs *(Cont.)*

1981 ......Caitlin Carruthers, Peter Carruthers,
SC of Wilmington
1982 ......Caitlin Carruthers, Peter Carruthers,
SC of Wilmington
1983 ......Caitlin Carruthers, Peter Carruthers,
SC of Wilmington
1984 ......Caitlin Carruthers, Peter Carruthers,
SC of Wilmington
1985 ......Jill Watson, Peter Oppegard, LA FSC
1986 ......Gillian Wachsman, Todd Waggoner,
SC of Wilmington
1987 ......Jill Watson, Peter Oppegard, LA FSC
1988 ......Jill Watson, Peter Oppegard,
Los Angeles FSC
1989 ......Kristi Yamaguchi, Rudy Galindo, St Mortiz ISC
1990 ......Kristi Yamaguchi, Rudy Galindo, St Mortiz ISC
1991 ......Natasha Kuchiki, Todd Sand, LA FSC
1992 ......Calla Urbanski, Rocky Marval,
U of Delaware FSC/SC of New York
1993 ......Calla Urbanski, Rocky Marval,
U of Delaware FSC/SC of New York

1994 ......Jenni Meno, Todd Sand,
Winterhurst FSC/Los Angeles FSC
1995 ......Jenni Meno, Todd Sand,
Winterhurst FSC/Los Angeles FSC
1996 ......Jenni Meno, Todd Sand,
Winterhurst FSC/Los Angeles FSC
1997 ......Kyoko Ina, Jason Dungjen, SC of New York
1998 ......Kyoko Ina, Jason Dungjen, SC of New York
1999 ......Danielle Hartsell, Steve Hartsell, Detroit SC
2000 ......Kyoko Ina, John Zimmerman, SC of New
York/Birmingham FSC
2001 ......Kyoko Ina, John Zimmerman, SC of New
York/Birmingham FSC
2002 ......Kyoko Ina, John Zimmerman, SC of New
York/Birmingham FSC
2003 ......Tiffany Scott, Philip Dulebohn, Colonial FSC/
Univ of Delaware FSC
2004 ......Rena Inoue, John Baldwin, All Year FSC
2005 ......Kathryn Orscher, Garrett Lucash,
Charter Oak FSC
2006 ......Rena Inoue, John Baldwin, All Year FSC

Dance

1914 ......Waltz: Theresa Weld, Nathaniel W. Niles,
SC of Boston
1915–19..No competition
1920 ......Waltz: Theresa Weld, Nathaniel W. Niles,
SC of Boston
Fourteenstep: Gertrude Cheever Porter,
Irving Brokaw, New York SC
1921 ......Waltz and Fourteenstep: Theresa Weld
Blanchard, Nathaniel W. Niles, SC of Boston
1922 ......Waltz: Beatrix Loughran, Edward M.
Howland, New York SC/SC of Boston
Fourteenstep: Theresa Weld Blanchard,
Nathaniel W. Niles, SC of Boston
1923 ......Waltz: Mr. & Mrs. Henry W. Howe,
New York SC
Fourteenstep: Sydney Goode, James B.
Greene, New York SC
1924 ......Waltz: Rosaline Dunn, Frederick Gabel,
New York SC
Fourteenstep: Sydney Goode, James B.
Greene, New York SC
1925 ......Waltz and Fourteenstep: Virginia Slattery,
Ferrier T. Martin, New York SC
1926 ......Waltz: Rosaline Dunn, Joseph K. Savage,
New York SC
Fourteenstep: Sydney Goode, James B.
Greene, New York SC
1927 ......Waltz and Fourteenstep: Rosaline Dunn,
Joseph K. Savage, New York SC
1928 ......Waltz: Rosaline Dunn, Joseph K. Savage,
New York SC
Fourteenstep: Ada Bauman Kelly, George T.
Braakman, New York SC
1929 ......Waltz and Original Dance combined:
Edith C. Secord, Joseph K. Savage,
SC of New York
1930 ......Waltz: Edith C. Secord, Joseph K. Savage,
SC of New York
Original: Clara Rotch Frothingham, George
E. B. Hill, SC of Boston
1931 ......Waltz: Edith C. Secord, Ferrier T. Martin,
SC of New York
Original: Theresa Weld Blanchard,
Nathaniel W. Niles, SC of Boston

1932 ......Waltz: Edith C. Secord, Joseph K. Savage,
SC of New York
Original: Clara Rotch Frothingham, George
E. B. Hill, SC of Boston
1933 ......Waltz: Ilse Twaroschk, Frederick F.
Fleishmann, Brooklyn FSC
Original: Suzanne Davis, Frederick
Goodridge, SC of Boston
1934 ......Waltz: Nettie C. Prantel, Roy Hunt, SC of
New York
Original: Suzanne Davis, Frederick
Goodridge, SC of Boston
1935 ......Waltz: Nettie C. Prantel, Roy Hunt,
SC of New York
1936 ......Marjorie Parker, Joseph K. Savage,
SC of New York
1937 ......Nettie C. Prantel, Harold Hartshorne,
SC of New York
1938 ......Nettie C. Prantel, Harold Hartshorne,
SC of New York
1939 ......Sandy Macdonald, Harold Hartshorne,
SC of New York
1940 ......Sandy Macdonald, Harold Hartshorne,
SC of New York
1941 ......Sandy Macdonald, Harold Hartshorne, SCNY
1942 ......Edith B. Whetstone, Alfred N. Richards, Jr,
Philadelphia SC & HS
1943 ......Marcella May, James Lochead Jr, Skate & Ski Club
1944 ......Marcella May, James Lochead Jr, Skate & Ski Club
1945 ......Kathe Mehl Williams, Robert J. Swenning,
SC of New York
1946 ......Anne Davies, Carleton C. Hoffner Jr.,
Washington FSC
1947 ......Lois Waring, Walter H. Bainbridge Jr.,
Baltimore FSC/Washigton FSC
1948 ......Lois Waring, Walter H. Bainbridge Jr.,
Baltimore FSC/Washington FSC
1949 ......Lois Waring, Walter H. Bainbridge Jr.,
Baltimore FSC/Washington FSC
1950 ......Lois Waring, Michael McGean, Baltimore FSC
1951 ......Carmel Bodel, Edward L. Bodel, St. Moritz ISC
1952 ......Lois Waring, Michael McGean,
Baltimore FSC

Dance *(Cont.)*

1953 ......Carol Ann Peters, Daniel C. Ryan,
Washington FSC
1954 ......Carmel Bodel, Edward L. Bodel, St Moritz ISC
1955 ......Carmel Bodel, Edward L. Bodel,
St Moritz ISC
1956 ......Joan Zamboni, Roland Junso,
Arctic Blades FSC
1957 ......Sharon McKenzie, Bert Wright,
Los Angeles FSC
1958 ......Andree Anderson, Donald Jacoby, Buffalo SC
1959 ......Andree Anderson Jacoby, Donald Jacoby,
Buffalo SC
1960 ......Margie Ackles, Charles W. Phillips Jr.,
Los Angeles FSC/Arctic Blades FSC
1961 ......Diane C. Sherbloom, Larry Pierce,
Los Angeles FSC/WC of Indianapolis
1962 ......Yvonne N. Littlefield, Peter F. Betts,
Arctic Blades FSC/ Paramount, CA
1963 ......Sally Schantz, Stanley Urban,
SC of Boston/Buffalo SC
1964 ......Darlene Streich, Charles D. Fetter Jr.,
WC of Indianapolis
1965 ......Kristin Fortune, Dennis Sveum, Los Angeles FSC
1966 ......Kristin Fortune, Dennis Sveum, Los Angeles FSC
1967 ......Lorna Dyer, John Carrell, Broadmoor SC
1968 ......Judy Schwomeyer, James Sladky,
WC of Indianapolis/Genesee FSC
1969 ......Judy Schwomeyer, James Sladky,
WC of Indianapolis/Genesee FSC
1970 ......Judy Schwomeyer, James Sladky,
WC of Indianapolis/Genesee FSC
1971 ......Judy Schwomeyer, James Sladky,
WC of Indianapolis/Genesee FSC
1972 ......Judy Schwomeyer, James Sladky,
WC of Indianapolis/Genesee FSC
1973 ......Mary Karen Campbell, Johnny Johns,
Lansing SC/Detroit SC
1974 ......Colleen O'Connor, Jim Millns, Broadmoor
SC/ City of Colorado Springs
1975 ......Colleen O'Connor, Jim Millns, Broadmoor SC
1976 ......Colleen O'Connor, Jim Millns, Broadmoor SC
1977 ......Judy Genovesi, Kent Weigle,
SC of Hartford/Charter Oak FSC
1978 ......Stacey Smith, John Summers,
SC of Wilmington

1979 ......Stacey Smith, John Summers,
SC of Wilmington
1980 ......Stacey Smith, John Summers,
SC of Wilmington
1981 ......Judy Blumberg, Michael Seibert,
Broadmoor SC/ISC of Indianapolis
1982 ......Judy Blumberg, Michael Seibert,
Broadmoor SC/ISC of Indianapolis
1983 ......Judy Blumberg, Michael Seibert,
Pittsburgh FSC
1984 ......Judy Blumberg, Michael Seibert,
Pittsburgh FSC
1985 ......Judy Blumberg, Michael Seibert,
Pittsburgh FSC
1986 ......Renee Roca, Donald Adair,
Genesee FSC/Academy FSC
1987 ......Suzanne Semanick, Scott Gregory,
U of Delaware SC
1988 ......Suzanne Semanick, Scott Gregory,
U of Delaware SC
1989 ......Susan Wynne, Joseph Druar,
Broadmoor SC/Seattle SC
1990 ......Susan Wynne, Joseph Druar,
Broadmoor SC/Seattle SC
1991 ....Elizabeth Punsalan, Jerod Swallow,
Broadmoor SC
1992 ......April Sargent, Russ Witherby,
Ogdensburg FSC/U of Delaware FSC
1993 ......Renee Roca, Gorsha Sur, Broadmoor SC
1994 ......Elizabeth Punsalan, Jerod Swallow,
Broadmoor SC/Detroit SC
1995 ......Renee Roca, Gorsha Sur, Broadmoor SC
1996 ......Elizabeth Punsalan, Jerod Swallow, Detroit SC
1997 ......Elizabeth Punsalan, Jerod Swallow, Detroit SC
1998 ......Elizabeth Punsalan, Jerod Swallow, Detroit SC
1999 ......Naomi Lang, Peter Tchernyshev, Detroit SC
2000 ......Naomi Lang, Peter Tchernyshev, Detroit SC
2001 ......Naomi Lang, Peter Tchernyshev, Detroit SC
2002 ......Naomi Lang, Peter Tchernyshev, American
Academy FSC
2003 ....Naomi Lang, Peter Tchernyshev, American
Academy FSC
2004 ......Tanith Belbin, Ben Agosto, Detroit SC
2005 ....Tanith Belbin, Ben Agosto, Detroit SC
2006 ......Tanith Belbin, Ben Agosto, Arctic FSC

U.S. Olympic Gold Medalists

Women

1956	Tenley Albright
1960	Carol Heiss
1968	Peggy Fleming
1976	Dorothy Hamill
1992	Kristi Yamaguchi
1998	Tara Lipinski
2002	Sarah Hughes

Men

1948	Dick Button
1952	Dick Button
1956	Hayes Alan Jenkins
1960	David W. Jenkins
1984	Scott Hamilton
1988	Brian Boitano

Special Achievements

Women successfully landing a triple Axel in competition:
  Midori Ito, Japan, 1988 free-skating competition at Aichi, Japan.
  Tonya Harding, United States, 1991 U.S. Figure Skating Championship, Minneapolis, Minn.
  Yukari Nakano, Japan, 2002 Skate America, Spokane, Wash.
  Ludmila Nelidina, Russia, 2002 Skate America, Spokane Wash.
  Kimmie Meissner, United States, 2005 U.S. Figure Skating Championship, Portland, Ore.
Men successfully landing three quadruple jumps in competition:
  Timothy Goebel, United States, 1999 Skate America, Colorado Springs, Colo. (two Salchows and one toe loop).

Miscellaneous Sports

Was Floyd Landis' historic
Tour de France comeback
too good to be true?

Going Downhill Fast

Cycling was rocked by one scandal after another in 2006, most notably Floyd Landis' precipitous rise and fall at the Tour de France, the sport's most prestigious event

BY MERRELL NODEN

IT WAS A LOUSY YEAR FOR cycling. No, let's not kid ourselves—it was far worse than that. It was a catastrophically awful year, one in which even diehard cycling fans spoke of temporarily dismantling the sport in hopes of finding a way to put it back together again without the plague of performance-enhancing drug use. The trouble is, no one seems to have any idea how to do that.

The sucker punch delivered by Floyd Landis in the form of a positive testosterone test was the year's worst news, for sure. It occasioned disgust and disbelief in the same people who just days before had been toasting this gutsy new Tour de France champion. The news was especially bitter coming in a year during which Lance Armstrong continued to fend off accusations of past drug use and 13 other cyclists, including 2006 Tour favorites Ivan Basso and Jan Ullrich, had been banned from the race for their association with a drug-dispensing doctor. Cycling fans felt tricked and teased into trusting one of those delightfully uplifting stories. This year's version was nearly as improbable as the one about the man who almost died of cancer and then came back to win the world's most grueling bike race.

Still, we shouldn't be too hard on ourselves. Landis, who not so long ago was a lowly spear-carrier for Armstrong's U.S. Postal Service team, was undeniably an inspiring and interesting figure. Raised in the Mennonite faith, which eschews such modern comforts as telephones, computers and televisions, he had begun his cycling career as a mountain biker, winning the U.S. junior title in 1992 and the senior title a year later. After switching to road racing in 1998, he had undergone the long apprenticeship riders must serve before a lucky few are chosen to lead a team. This year, as "The Man" for the Phonak team, Landis sought to improve upon on his previous best finish in the Tour, a ninth place in 2005—though he was still regarded as a long shot to win.

And there was one more incredible aspect of the Landis story: The great cyclist walks with a limp that's painful just to watch. Following a bad bike crash in January 2003, his right hip has been steadily crumbling—dying, in effect—because of a condition called osteonecrosis. He limped noticeably, Kirk Gibson-like, while climbing the stairs to the awards podium after the Tour, and had the hip replaced in late September.

Landis had first donned the Yellow Jersey on Stage 11, the final day in the Pyrenees. He lost it, regained it once more on

Stage 15, and then lost it again in dramatic fashion when, during Stage 16, with absolutely nothing in the tank, he seemingly stood still, as if his tires were sinking in sand. Cyclists call this "bonking," and Landis bonked terrifically. He fell from first place to 11th, 8:08 behind the new leader, Oscar Pereiro of Spain. It seemed as if this had utterly doomed his chances, but no—it had instead set up what many observers would describe as the greatest Tour stage ever cycled by anyone.

The 17th Stage covers 200 kilometers (roughly 125 miles) and crosses three mountains. Launching his attack 50 kilometers into the race, Landis caught up to a pack of breakaway riders and sailed past them, finishing the stage nearly 19 minutes clear of any other cyclist. "It was incredible," marveled Australian cyclist Stuart O'Grady. "I've done 10 Tours and I've never seen anything like it." Jean-Marie Blanc, who served as the Tour's race director for the 18 years, rated Landis's ride "the best performance in the modern history of the Tour."

Landis now stood third, just 30 seconds behind leader Pereiro. Two days later, he used the penultimate stage—a time trial, a discipline at which he excels—to grab the yellow jersey for good. He triumphantly rode the final miles into Paris as the third American winner of the Tour, after Armstrong and Greg LeMond. Pereiro was the runner-up, 30 seconds behind. It was an extraordinary finish to a wide-open Tour.

But of course, the story wasn't finished. Several days later, on July 27, it was revealed that Landis had produced a positive drug test. Because testosterone occurs naturally, the test for its use traces the ratio of testosterone to epitestosterone, with anything greater than 4:1 considered to be a positive test. Landis's ratio turned out to be 11 to 1, a level that would make a bull elephant blush during mating season.

Landis had a number of explanations for the positive test, suggesting that perhaps the beer and whiskey he'd drunk after his bonked day had caused a spike. He also wondered if he might have a naturally high testosterone ratio "produced by my own

AP PHOTO/PAUL WHITE

After his "B" sample tested positive for synthetic testosterone, Landis lost his team sponsorship and his Tour de France title was in jeopardy, as well.

organism." But his secondary sample showed the same result. What's more, it was determined to be synthetic testosterone, seemingly refuting Landis's claim that his ratio is naturally high.

Landis was quickly cut adrift by virtually the whole cycling world. "It goes without saying that, for us, Floyd Landis is no longer the winner of the 2006 Tour de France," announced Christian Prudhomme, the Tour's race director. Phonak wasted little time severing ties with Landis, dropping him from the team even as he was still vowing to clear his name.

There was a tone of overwhelming self-righteousness about the whole reaction. With 13 banned cyclists and all the other arrests and rumors over the years, shouldn't the sport's leaders have been a wee bit suspicious of Landis's incredible comeback? Consequently, hard as it is to imagine that Landis could find a way to clear his name, it's even harder to see how the whole sport of cycling can resurrect its terribly tarnished reputation.

Archery

National Men's Champions

1879...Will H. Thompson	1911...Dr. Robert Elmer	1949...Russ Reynolds	1981...Rick McKinney
1880...L.L. Pedinghaus	1912...George Bryant	1950...Stan Overby	1982...Rick McKinney
1881...F.H. Walworth	1913...George Bryant	1951...Russ Reynolds	1983...Rick McKinney
1882...D.H. Nash	1914...Dr. Robert Elmer	1952...Robert Larson	1984...Darrell Pace
1883...Col. Robert Williams	1915...Dr. Robert Elmer	1953...Bill Glackin	1985...Rick McKinney
1884...Col. Robert Williams	1916...Dr. Robert Elmer	1954...Robert Rhode	1986...Rick McKinney
1885...Col. Robert Williams	1919...Dr. Robert Elmer	1955...Joe Fries	1987...Rick McKinney
1886...W.A. Clark	1920...Dr. Robert Elmer	1956...Joe Fries	1988...Jay Barrs
1887...W.A. Clark	1921...James Jiles	1957...Joe Fries	1989...Ed Eliason
1888...Lewis Maxson	1922...Dr. Robert Elmer	1958...Robert Bitner	1990...Ed Eliason
1889...Lewis Maxson	1923...Bill Palmer	1959...Wilbert Vetrovsky	1991...Ed Eliason
1890...Lewis Maxson	1924...James Jiles	1960...Robert Kadlec	1992...Alan Rasor
1891...Lewis Maxson	1925...Dr. Paul Crouch	1961...Clayton Sherman	1993...Jay Barrs
1892...Lewis Maxson	1926...Stanley Spencer	1962...Charles Sandlin	1994...Jay Barrs
1893...Lewis Maxson	1927...Dr. Paul Crouch	1963...Dave Keaggy Jr.	1995...Justin Huish
1894...Lewis Maxson	1928...Bill Palmer	1964...Dave Keaggy Jr.	1996...Richard (Butch)
1895...W.B. Robinson	1929...Dr. E.K. Roberts	1965...George Slinzer	Johnson
1896...Lewis Maxson	1930...Russ Hoogerhyde	1966...Hardy Ward	1997...Richard (Butch)
1897...W.A. Clark	1931...Russ Hoogerhyde	1967...Ray Rogers	Johnson
1898...Lewis Maxson	1932...Russ Hoogerhyde	1968...Hardy Ward	1998...Victor Wunderle
1899...M.C. Howell	1933...Ralph Miller	1969...Ray Rogers	1999...Victor Wunderle
1900...A.R. Clark	1934...Russ Hoogerhyde	1970...Joe Thornton	2000...Richard (Butch)
1901...Will H. Thompson	1935...Gilman Keasey	1971...John Williams	Johnson
1902...Will H. Thompson	1936...Gilman Keasey	1972...Kevin Erlandson	2001...Richard (Butch)
1903...Will H. Thompson	1937...Russ Hoogerhyde	1973...Darrell Pace	Johnson
1904...George Bryant	1938...Pat Chambers	1974...Darrell Pace	2002...Victor Wunderle
1905...George Bryant	1939...Pat Chambers	1975...Darrell Pace	2003...Joseph Bailey
1906...Henry Richardson	1940...Russ Hoogerhyde	1976...Darrell Pace	2004...Sagar Mistry
1907...Henry Richardson	1941...Larry Hughes	1977...Rick McKinney	2005...Guy Krueger
1908...Will H. Thompson	1946...Wayne Thompson	1978...Darrell Pace	2006...Victor Wunderle
1909...George Bryant	1947...Jack Wilson	1979...Rick McKinney	
1910...Henry Richardson	1948...Larry Hughes	1980...Rick McKinney	

National Women's Champions

1879...Mrs. S. Brown	1910...J.V. Sullivan	1947...Ann Weber	1976...Luann Ryon
1880...Mrs. T. Davies	1911...Mrs. J.S. Taylor	1948...Jean Lee	1977...Luann Ryon
1881...Mrs. A.H. Gibbes	1912...Mrs. Witwer Tayler	1949...Jean Lee	1978...Luann Ryon
1882...Mrs. A.H. Gibbes	1913...Mrs. P. Fletcher	1950...Jean Lee	1979...Lynette Johnson
1883...Mrs. M.C. Howell	1914...Mrs. B.P. Gray	1951...Jean Lee	1980...Judi Adams
1884...Mrs. H. Hall	1915...Cynthia Wesson	1952...Ann Weber	1981...Debra Metzger
1885...Mrs. M.C. Howell	1916...Cynthia Wesson	1953...Ann Weber	1982...Luann Ryon
1886...Mrs. M.C. Howell	1919...Dorothy Smith	1954...Laurette Young	1983...Nancy Myrick
1887...Mrs. A.M. Phillips	1920...Cynthia Wesson	1955...Ann Clark	1984...Ruth Rowe
1888...Mrs. A.M. Phillips	1921...Mrs. L.C. Smith	1956...Carole Meinhart	1985...Terri Pesho
1889...Mrs. A.M. Phillips	1922...Dorothy Smith	1957...Carole Meinhart	1986...Debra Ochs
1890...Mrs. M.C. Howell	1923...Norma Pierce	1958...Carole Meinhart	1987...Terry Quinn
1891...Mrs. M.C. Howell	1924...Dorothy Smith	1959...Carole Meinhart	1988...Debra Ochs
1892...Mrs. M.C. Howell	1925...Dorothy Smith	1960...Ann Clark	1989...Debra Ochs
1893...Mrs. M.C. Howell	1926...Dorothy Smith	1961...Victoria Cook	1990...Denise Parker
1894...Mrs. Albert Kern	1927...Mrs. R. Johnson	1962...Nancy	1991...Denise Parker
1895...Mrs. M.C. Howell	1928...Beatrice Hodgson	Vonderheide	1992...Sherry Block
1896...Mrs. M.C. Howell	1929...Audrey Grubbs	1963...Nancy	1993...Denise Parker
1897...Mrs. J.S. Baker	1930...Audrey Grubbs	Vonderheide	1994...Judy Adams
1898...Mrs. M.C. Howell	1931...DorothyCummings	1964...Victoria Cook	1995...Jessica Carlson
1899...Mrs. M.C. Howell	1932...Ilda Hanchette	1965...Nancy Pfeiffer	1996...Janet Dykman
1900...Mrs. M.C. Howell	1933...Madelaine Taylor	1966...Helen Thornton	1997...Janet Dykman
1901...Mrs. C.E.Woodruff	1934...Desales Mudd	1967...Ardelle Mills	1998...Janet Dykman
1902...Mrs. M.C. Howell	1935...Ruth Hodgert	1968...Victoria Cook	1999...Denise Parker
1903...Mrs. M.C. Howell	1936...Gladys Hammer	1969...Doreen Wilber	2000...Karen Scavatto
1904...Mrs. M.C. Howell	1937...Gladys Hammer	1970...Nancy Myrick	2001...Kathie Loesch
1905...Mrs. M.C. Howell	1938...Jean Tenney	1971...Doreen Wilber	2002...Jessica Peterson
1906...Mrs. E.C. Cook	1939...Belvia Carter	1972...Ruth Rowe	2003...Samantha Marino
1907...Mrs. M.C. Howell	1940...Ann Weber	1973...Doreen Wilber	2004...Khatuna Lorig
1908...Harriet Case	1941...Ree Dillinger	1974...Doreen Wilber	2005...Khatuna Lorig
1909...Harriet Case	1946...Ann Weber	1975...Irene Lorensen	2006...Karen Scavatto

THE MAJORS

2006 Tournament of Champions

	Games	Total	Earnings ($)
Chris Barnes	2	489	100,000
Steve Jaros	2	474	30,000
Tommy Jones	1	233	10,000
Amleto Monacelli	1	191	10.000

Playoff Results: Barnes def. Jaros 234-227; Barnes def. Monacelli 255–191; Jaros def. Jones 247–233.

Held at the Mohegan Sun in Uncasville, Conn., April 5-9, 2006.

2006 U.S. Open

	Games	Total	Earnings ($)
Tommy Jones	2	468	100,000
Ryan Shafer	1	223	50,000
Michael Fagan	2	442	25,000
Robert Smith	1	214	15,000

Playoff Results: Jones def. Shafer 237-223; Fagan def Smith 216-214; Jones def Fagan 231-226

Held at Brunswick Zone Carolier in North Brunswick,New Jersey, February 12–19, 2006.

2005 USBC Masters
CHAMPIONSHIP ROUND

Bowler	Games	Total	Earnings ($)
Mike Scroggins	2	485	100,000
Norm Duke	1	238	50,000
Art Brown	2	403	25,000
Ken Muscato	1	180	15,000

Playoff Results: Scroggins def Duke 245-238, Brown def Muscato 201-180, Scroggins def Brown 240-202

Held at AMF Bowlero Lanes in Wauwatosa, Wisconsin, November 14-20, 2005.

2006 PBA World Championship
CHAMPIONSHIP ROUND

Bowler	Games	Total	Earnings ($)
Walter Ray Williams Jr	2	460	100,000
Pete Weber	2	440	50,000
Ryan Shafer	1	201	20,000
Brad Angelo	1	214	20,000

Playoff Results: Williams def Weber 236-213, Weber def Angelo 227-214, Williams def Shafer 224-201

Held at Woodland Bowl in Indianapolis, Indiana March 20-26, 2006

PBA TOUR RESULTS

2005–06 Tour

Date	Event	Winner	Earnings ($)	Runner-Up
Sept 15-20	Dydo Drinco Japan Cup	Tommy Jones	50,000	Norm Duke
Oct. 26-30	Tulsa Championship	Tommy Jones	40,000	Wes Malott
Nov. 2-6	Mile High Classic	Wes Malott	40,000	Mika LKoivuniemi
Nov 9-13	Greater Omaha Classic	Michael Machuga	40,000	Bill O'Neill
Nov 14-20	USBC Masters	Mike Scroggins	100,000	Norm Duke
Nov 23-27	Chicago Classic	Jason Couch	40,000	Joe Ciccone
Nov 30-Dec 4	BowlersParadise.com Classic	Pete Weber	40,000	Ryan Shafer
Dec 7-11	Keystone State Championship	Patrick Allen	40,000	Tom Baker
Dec 14-18	Empire State Classic	Mike Wolfe	40,100	Christopher Collins
Jan 4-8	Earl Anthony Medford Classic	Brian Himmler	40,000	Mika Loivuniemi
Jan 10-15	Dick Weber Open	Jason Couch	30,000	Parker Bohn III
Jan 18-22	Motel 6 Phoenix Classic	Ritchie Allen	40,000	Del Ballard Jr
Jan 25-29	Jackson Hewitt Tax Service Classic	Brian Voss	40,100	Steve Wilson

PBA TOUR RESULTS — *(Cont.)*

2005–06 Tour

Date	Event	Winner	Earnings ($)	Runner-Up
Feb 1-5	Bayer Atlantic Classic	Tommy Jones	40,000	Mike Scroggins
Feb 8-12	West Virginia Championship	Sean Rash	40,000	Mike DeVaney
Feb 12-19	63rd United States Open	Tommy Jones	100,000	Ryan Shafer
Feb. 22-26	Geico Classic	Doug Kent	40,000	Norm Duke
March 1-5	Pepsi Championship	Christopher Collins	40,000	Walter Ray Williams
March 15-19	Ace Hardware Championship	Norm Duke	40,000	Chris Loschetter
March 20-26	Denny's World Championship	Walter Ray Williams Jr	100,000	Pete Weber
March 29-April 2	Great Lakes Classic	Patrick Allen	40,000	Patrick Healey Jr
April 5-9	Dexter Tournament of Champions	Chris Barnes	100,000	Steve Jaros
April 13	Motel 6 Roll to Riches	Chris Barnes	200,000	Mike Scroggins

2006 Senior Tour

Date	Event	Winner	Earnings ($)	Runner-Up
April 22–25	Manassas Open	Henry Gonzalez	8,000	Tom Baker
April 29–May 5	Chillicothe Open	Tom Baker	8,000	Teata Semiz
June 10–14	Senior Tuscon Open	Tom Baker	8,000	Pete Couture
June 18–23	Senior U.S. Open	Tom Baker	20,000	Dick Baker
June 25–28	Epicenter Classic	James Brenner	8,000	Henry Gonzalez
July 2–5	Northern California Classic	Gary Dickerson	8,000	Ty Dawson
July 9-14	USBC Senior Masters	Tom Baker	18,000	Bob Kelly
Aug 7–10	Lake County Open	Jimmy Young	8,000	Ron Winger
Aug 12–15	Decatur Open	Charlie Tapp	8,000	David Ozio

TOUR LEADERS

PBA: 2005–06

MONEY LEADERS

Name (Titles)	Events	Earnings ($)
Tommy Jones	21	301,700
Norm Duke	22	211,800
Mike Scroggins	21	205,270
Walter Ray Williams Jr	22	183,500
Mika Koivuniemi	19	174,700

AVERAGE

Name	Events	Average
Norm Duke	22	224.29
Mike Scroggins	21	223.82
Walter Ray Williams Jr	22	223.65
Wes Malott	22	221.83
Tommy Jones	21	221.68

Seniors: 2006

MONEY LEADERS

Name	Events	Earnings ($)
Tom Baker	9	66,000
Henry Gonzalez	9	21,335
Roger Kossert.	9	15,900
David Ozio	4	15,600
Bob Kelly	9	15,352

AVERAGE

Name	Events	Average
Tom Baker	9	226.32
Gary Dickinson	5	214.13
Roger LeClair	9	213.35
Roger Kossert	9	213.04
Dale Eagle	8	213.02

MEN'S AWARDS

BWAA Bowler of the Year

1942	Johnny Crimmins	1975	Earl Anthony
1943	Ned Day	1976	Earl Anthony
1944	Ned Day	1977	Mark Roth
1945	Buddy Bomar	1978	Mark Roth
1946	Joe Wilman	1979	Mark Roth
1947	Buddy Bomar	1980	Wayne Webb
1948	Andy Varipapa	1981	Earl Anthony
1949	Connie Schwoegler	1982	Earl Anthony
1950	Junie McMahon	1983	Earl Anthony
1951	Lee Jouglard	1984	Mark Roth
1952	Steve Nagy	1985	Mike Aulby
1953	Don Carter	1986	Walter Ray Williams Jr.
1954	Don Carter	1987	Marshall Holman
1955	Steve Nagy	1988	Brian Voss
1956	Bill Lillard	1989	Mike Aulby / Amleto Monacelli*
1957	Don Carter	1990	Amleto Monacelli
1958	Don Carter	1991	David Ozio
1959	Ed Lubanski	1992	Dave Ferraro
1960	Don Carter	1993	Walter Ray Williams Jr.
1961	Dick Weber	1994	Norm Duke
1962	Don Carter	1995	Mike Aulby
1963	Dick Weber / Billy Hardwick*	1996	Walter Ray Williams Jr.
1964	Billy Hardwick / Bob Strampe*	1997	Walter Ray Williams Jr.
1965	Dick Weber	1998	Walter Ray Williams Jr.
1966	Wayne Zahn	1999	Parker Bohn III
1967	Dave Davis	2000	Norm Duke
1968	Jim Stefanich	2001	Parker Bohn III
1969	Billy Hardwick	2002	Walter Ray Williams Jr.
1970	Nelson Burton Jr.	2003	Walter Ray Williams Jr.
1971	Don Johnson	2004	Mika Koivuniemi
1972	Don Johnson	2005	Patrick Allen
1973	Don McCune	2006	Walter Ray Williams Jr.
1974	Earl Anthony		

PBA Bowler of the Year. The PBA began selecting a player of the year in 1963. Its selection has been the same as the BWAA's in all but three years.

CAREER LEADERS

Earnings

MEN		WOMEN	
Walter Ray Williams Jr.	$3,553,132	Wendy Macpherson	$1,194,535
Pete Weber	$2,805,818	Aleta Sill	$1,071,194
Parker Bohn III	$2,400,264	Tish Johnson	$1,063,062
Mike Aulby	$2,097,253	Leanne Barrette	$1,010,343
Brian Voss	$2,293,317	Anne Marie Duggan	$936,421

Titles

MEN		WOMEN	
Earl Anthony	41	Lisa Wagner	32
Walter Ray Williams Jr.	41	Aleta Sill	31
Mark Roth	34	Leanne Barrette	26
Pete Weber	32	Patty Costello	25
Parker Bohn III	30	Tish Johnson	25

Note: Leaders through Sept 1, 2006

Chess

World Champions

FIDE

1866–94	Wilhelm Steinitz, Austria
1894–1921	Emanuel Lasker, Germany
1921–27	Jose Capablanca, Cuba
1927–35	Alexander Alekhine, France
1935–37	Max Euwe, Holland
1937–47	Alexander Alekhine, France
1948–57	Mikhail Botvinnik, USSR
1957–58	Vassily Smyslov, USSR
1958–59	Mikhail Botvinnik, USSR
1960–61	Mikhail Tal, USSR
1961–63	Mikhail Botvinnik, USSR
1963–69	Tigran Petrosian, USSR
1969–72	Boris Spassky, USSR

FIDE (CONT.)

1972–75	Bobby Fischer, United States
1975–85	Anatoly Karpov, USSR
1985–93	*Garry Kasparov, USSR
1994–98	Anatoly Karpov, Russia
1999–2000	Alexander Khalifman, Russia
2000–01	Anand Viswanathan, India
2002–04	Ruslan Ponomariov, Ukraine
2004–05	Rustam Kasimdzhanov, Uzbekistan
2005–	Veselin Topalov, Bulgaria

Professional Chess Association

1993–95	Garry Kasparov

*Kasparov stripped of title by FIDE in 1993.

United States Champions

1857–71	Paul Morphy	1961–62	Larry Evans	1989	R. Dzindzichashvili
1871–76	George Mackenzie	1962–68	Bobby Fischer		Stuart Rachels
1876–80	James Mason	1968–69	Larry Evans		Yasser Seirawan
1880–89	George Mackenzie	1969–72	Samuel Reshevsky	1990	Lev Alburt
1889–90	Samuel Lipschutz	1972–73	Robert Byrne	1991	Gata Kamski
1890	Jackson Showalter	1973–74	Lubomir Kavale	1992	Patrick Wolff
1890–91	Max Judd		John Grefe	1993	Alex Yermolinsky
1891–92	Jackson Showalter	1974–77	Walter Browne		A. Shabalov
1892–94	Samuel Lipschutz	1978–80	Lubomir Kavalek	1994	Boris Gulko
1894	Jackson Showalter	1980–81	Larry Evans	1995	Patrick Wolff
1894–95	Albert Hodges		Larry Christiansen		Nick DeFirmian
1895–97	Jackson Showalter		Walter Browne		Alexander Ivanov
1897–1906	Harry Pillsbury	1981–83	Walter Browne	1996	Alex Yermolinsky
1906–09	Vacant		Yasser Seirawan	1997	Alex Yermolinsky
1909–36	Frank Marshall	1983	R. Dzindzichashvili	1998	Alex Yermolinsky
1936–44	Samuel Reshevsky	1983	Larry Christiansen	1999	Boris Gulko
1944–46	Arnold Denker		Walter Browne	2000	Joel Benjamin
1946–48	Samuel Reshevsky	1984–85	Lev Alburt	2001	Joel Benjamin
1948–51	Herman Steiner	1986	Yasser Seirawan	2002	Larry Christiansen
1951–54	Larry Evans	1987	Joel Benjamin	2003	Alexander Shabalov
1954–57	Arthur Bisguier		Nick DeFirmian	2004	Hikaru Nakamura
1957–61	Bobby Fischer	1988	Michael Wilder	2005	Hikaru Nakamura

Curling

World Men's Champions

Year	Country, Skip	Year	Country, Skip	Year	Country, Skip
1972	Canada, Crest Melesnuk	1984	Norway, Eigil Ramsfjell	1996	Canada, Jeff Stoughton
1973	Sweden, Kjell Oscarius	1985	Canada, Al Hackner	1997	Sweden, Peter Lindholm
1974	U.S., Bud Somerville	1986	Canada, Ed Luckowich	1998	Canada, Wayne Middaugh
1975	Switzerland, Otto Danieli	1987	Canada, Russ Howard	1999	Scotland, Hammy McMillan
1976	U.S., Bruce Roberts	1988	Norway, Eigil Ramsfjell	2000	Canada, Greg McAulay
1977	Sweden, Ragnar Kamp	1989	Canada, Pat Ryan	2001	Sweden, Peter Lindholm
1978	U.S., Bob Nichols	1990	Canada, Ed Werenich	2002	Canada, Randy Ferbey
1979	Norway, Kristian Soerum	1991	Scotland, David Smith	2003	Canada, Randy Ferbey
1980	Canada, Rich Folk	1992	Switz., Markus Eggler	2004	Sweden, Peja Lindholm
1981	Switzerland, Jurg Tanner	1993	Canada, Russ Howard	2005	Canada, David Nedohin
1982	Canada, Al Hackner	1994	Canada, Rick Folk	2006	Scotland, David Murdoch
1983	Canada, Ed Werenich	1995	Canada, Kerry Burtnyk		

World Women's Champions

Year	Country, Skip	Year	Country, Skip	Year	Country, Skip
1979	Switzerland, Gaby Casanova	1987	Canada, Pat Sanders	1998	Sweden, Elisabet Gustafson
1980	Canada, Marj Mitchell	1988	Germany, Andrea Schopp	1999	Sweden, Elisabet Gustafson
1981	Sweden, Elisabeth Hogstrom	1989	Canada, Heather Houston	2000	Canada, Kelley Law
1982	Denmark, Marianne Jorgenson	1990	Norway, Dordi Nordby	2001	Canada, Colleen Jones
1983	Switzerland, Erika Mueller	1991	Norway, Dordi Nordby	2002	Scotland, Jackie Lockhart
1984	Canada, Connie Lallberte	1992	Sweden, Elisabet Johanssen	2003	United States, Debbie McCormick
1985	Canada, Linda Moore	1993	Canada, Sandra Peterson	2004	Canada, Colleen Jones
1986	Canada, Marilyn Darte	1994	Canada, Sandra Peterson	2005	Sweden, Anette Norberg
		1995	Sweden, Elisabet Gustafson	2006	Sweden, Anette Norberg
		1996	Canada, Marilyn Bodogh		
		1997	Canada, Sandra Schmirler		

U.S. Men's Champions

Year	Site	Winning Club	Skip
1957	Chicago, Ill.	Hibbing, Minn.	Harold Lauber
1958	Milwaukee, Wisc.	Detroit, Mich.	Douglas Fisk
1959	Green Bay, Wisc.	Hibbing, Minn.	Fran Kleffman
1960	Chicago, Ill.	Grafton, N.D.	Orvil Gilleshammer
1961	Grand Forks, N.D.	Seattle, Wash.	Frank Crealock
1962	Detroit, Mich.	Hibbing, Minn.	Fran Kleffman
1963	Duluth, Minn.	Detroit, Mich.	Mike Slyziuk
1964	Utica, N.Y.	Duluth, Minn.	Robert Magle Jr.
1965	Seattle, Wash.	Superior, Wisc.	Bud Somerville
1966	Hibbing, Minn.	Fargo, N.D.	Joe Zbacnik
1967	Winchester, Mass.	Seattle, Wash.	Bruce Roberts
1968	Madison, Wisc.	Superior, Wisc.	Bud Somerville
1969	Grand Forks, N.D.	Superior, Wisc.	Bud Somerville
1970	Ardsley, N.Y.	Grafton, N.D.	Art Tallackson
1971	Duluth, Minn.	Edmore, N.D.	Dale Dalziel
1972	Wilmette, Ill.	Grafton, N.D.	Robert Labonte
1973	Colorado Springs, Colo.	Winchester, Mass.	Charles Reeves
1974	Schenectady, N.Y.	Superior, Wisc.	Bud Somerville
1975	Detroit, Mich.	Seattle, Wash.	Ed Risling
1976	Wausau, Wisc.	Hibbing, Minn.	Bruce Roberts
1977	Northbrook, Ill.	Hibbing, Minn.	Bruce Roberts
1978	Utica, N.Y.	Superior, Wisc.	Bob Nichols
1979	Superior, Wisc.	Bemidji, Minn.	Scott Baird
1980	Bemidji, Minn.	Hibbing, Minn.	Paul Pustovar
1981	Fairbanks, Ak.	Superior, Wisc.	Bob Nichols
1982	Brookline, Mass.	Madison, Wisc.	Steve Brown
1983	Colorado Springs, Colo.	Colorado Springs, Colo.	Don Cooper
1984	Hibbing, Minn.	Hibbing, Minn.	Bruce Roberts
1985	Mequon, Wisc.	Wilmette, Ill.	Tim Wright
1986	Seattle, Wash.	Madison, Wisc.	Steve Brown
1987	Lake Placid, N.Y.	Seattle, Wash.	Jim Vukich
1988	St. Paul, Minn.	Seattle, Wash.	Doug Jones
1989	Detroit, Mich.	Seattle, Wash.	Jim Vukich
1990	Superior, Wisc.	Seattle, Wash.	Doug Jones
1991	Utica, N.Y.	Madison, Wisc.	Steve Brown
1992	Grafton, N.D.	Seattle, Wash.	Doug Jones
1993	St. Paul, Minn.	Bemidji, Minn.	Scott Baird
1994	Duluth, Minn.	Bemidji, Minn.	Scott Baird
1995	Appleton, Wisc.	Superior, Wisc.	Tim Somerville
1996	Bemidji, Minn.	Superior, Wisc.	Tim Somerville
1997	Seattle, Wash.	Langdon, N.D.	Craig Disher
1998	Bismarck, N.D.	Stevens Pt., Wisc.	Paul Pustovar
1999	Duluth, Minn.	Superior, Wisc.	Tim Somerville
2000	Ogden, Utah	Madison, Wisc.	Craig Brown
2001	Madison, Wisc.	Washington	Jason Larway
2002	Virginia, Minn.	Madison, Wisc.	Paul Pustovar
2003	Utica, N.Y.	Bemidji, MInn.	Pete Fenson
2004	Grand Forks, N.D.	Seattle, Wash.	Jason Larway
2005	Chicago, Ill.	Illinois	Russ Armstrong
2006	Superior, Wisc.	Bemidji, Minn.	Pete Fenson

U.S. Women's Champions

Year	Site	Winning Club	Skip
1977	Wilmette, Ill.	Hastings, N.Y.	Margaret Smith
1978	Duluth, Minn.	Wausau, Wisc.	Sandy Robarge
1979	Winchester, Mass.	Seattle, Wash.	Nancy Langley
1980	Seattle, Wash.	Seattle, Wash.	Sharon Kozal
1981	Kettle Moraine, Wisc.	Seattle, Wash.	Nancy Langley
1982	Bowling Green, Ohio	Oak Park, Ill.	Ruth Schwenker
1983	Grafton, N.D.	Seattle, Wash.	Nancy Langley
1984	Wauwatosa, Wisc.	Duluth, Minn.	Amy Hatten
1985	Hershey, Pa.	Fairbanks, Ak.	Bev Birklid
1986	Chicago, Ill.	St Paul, Minn.	Gerri Tilden
1987	St Paul, Minn.	Seattle, Wash.	Sharon Good
1988	Darien, Conn.	Seattle, Wash.	Nancy Langley
1989	Detroit, Mich.	Rolla, N.D.	Jan Lagasse
1990	Superior, Wisc.	Denver, Colo.	Bev Behnke
1991	Utica, N.Y.	Houston, Tex.	Maymar Gemmell

U.S. Women's Champions (Cont.)

Year	Site	Winning Club	Skip
1992	Grafton, N.D.	Madison, Wisc.	Lisa Schoeneberg
1993	St Paul, Minn.	Denver, Colo.	Bev Behnke
1994	Duluth, Minn.	Denver, Colo.	Bev Behnke
1995	Appleton, Wisc.	Madison, Wisc.	Lisa Schoeneberg
1996	Bemidji, Minn.	Madison, Wisc.	Lisa Schoeneberg
1997	Seattle, Wash.	Arlington, Wisc.	Patti Lank
1998	Bismarck, N.D.	Wilmette, Ill.	Kari Erickson
1999	Duluth, Minn.	Madison, Wisc.	Patti Lank
2000	Ogden, Utah	Nebraska	Amy Wright
2001	Madison, Wisc.	Illinois	Kari Erickson
2002	Virginia, Minn.	Madison, Wisc.	Patti Lank
2003	Utica, N.Y.	Illinois	Debbie McCormick
2004	Grand Forks, N.D.	Madison, Wisc.	Patti Lank
2005	Chicago, Ill.	Massachusetts	Shelly Dropkin
2006	Superior, Wisc.	Madison, Wisc.	Debbie McCormick

Cycling

Professional Road Race World Champions

Year	Champion
1927	Alfred Binda, Italy
1928	George Ronsse, Belgium
1929	George Ronsse, Belgium
1930	Alfred Binda, Italy
1931	Learco Guerra, Italy
1932	Alfred Binda, Italy
1933	George Speicher, France
1934	Karel Kaers, Belgium
1935	Jean Aerts, Belgium
1936	Antonio Magne, France
1937	Elio Meulenberg, Belgium
1938	Marcel Kint, Belgium
1939–45	No competition
1946	Hans Knecht, Switzerland
1947	Theo. Middelkamp, Holland
1948	Alberic Schotte, Belgium
1949	Henri Van Steenbergen, Belgium
1950	Alberic Schotte, Belgium
1951	Ferdinand Kubler, Switzerland
1952	Heinz Mueller, Germany
1953	Fausto Coppi, Italy
1954	Louison Bobet, France
1955	Stan Ockers, Belgium
1956	Rik Van Steenbergen, Belg.
1957	Rik Van Steenbergen, Belgium
1958	Ercole Baldini, Italy
1959	Andre Darrigade, France
1960	Rik van Looy, Belgium
1961	Rik van Looy, Belgium
1962	Jean Stablenski, France
1963	Bennoni Beheyt, Belgium
1964	Jan Janssen, Holland
1965	Tommy Simpson, England
1966	Rudi Altig, West Germany
1967	Eddy Merckx, Belgium
1968	Vittorio Adorni, Italy
1969	Harm Ottenbros, Netherlands
1970	J.P. Monseré, Belgium
1971	Eddy Merckx, Belgium
1972	Marino Basso, Italy
1973	Felice Gimondi, Italy
1974	Eddy Merckx, Belgium
1975	Hennie Kuiper, Holland
1976	Freddy Maertens, Belgium
1977	Francesco Moser, Italy
1978	Gerri Knetemann, Holland
1979	Jan Raas, Holland
1980	Bernard Hinault, France
1981	Freddy Maertens, Belgium
1982	Giuseppe Saronni, Italy
1983	Greg LeMond, United States
1984	Claude Criquielion, Belgium
1985	Joop Zoetemelk, Holland
1986	Moreno Argentin, Italy
1987	Stephen Roche, Ireland
1988	Maurizio Fondriest, Italy
1989	Greg LeMond, United States
1990	Rudy Dhaenene, Belgium
1991	Gianni Bugno, Italy
1992	Gianni Bugno, Italy
1993	Lance Armstrong, United States
1994	Luc LeBlanc, France
1995	Abraham Olano, Spain
1996	Johan Museeuw, Belgium
1997	Laurent Brochard, France
1998	Oskar Camenzind, Switz
1999	Oscar Gomez Freire, Spain
2000	Romans Vainsteins, Latvia
2001	Oscar Gomez Freire, Spain
2002	Mario Cipollini, Italy
2003	Igor Astraloa, Spain
2004	Oscar Freire Gomez, Spain
2005	Tom Boonen, Belarus
2006	Paolo Bettini, Italy

Tour DuPont Winners

Year	Winner	Time
1989	Dag Otto Lauritzen, Norway	33 hrs, 28 min, 48 sec
1990	Raul Alcala, Mexico	45 hrs, 20 min, 9 sec
1991	Erik Breukink, Holland	48 hrs, 56 min, 53 sec
1992	Greg LeMond, United States	44 hrs, 27 min, 43 sec
1993	Raul Alcala, Mexico	46 hrs, 42 min, 52 sec
1994	Viatcheslav Ekimov, Russia	47 hrs, 14 min, 29 sec
1995	Lance Armstrong, United States	46 hrs, 31 min, 16 sec
1996	Lance Armstrong, United States	48 hrs, 20 min, 5 sec

Note: Race not held since 1996.

Tour de France Winners

Year	Winner	Time
1903	Maurice Garin, France	94 hrs, 33 min
1904	Henry Cornet, France	96 hrs, 5 min, 56 sec
1905	Louis Trousselier, France	110 hrs, 26 min, 58 sec
1906	Rene Pottier, France	Not available
1907	Lucien Petit-Breton, France	158 hrs, 54 min, 5 sec
1908	Lucien Petit-Breton, France	Not available
1909	Francois Faber, Luxembourg	157 hrs, 1 min, 22 sec
1910	Octave Lapize, France	162 hrs, 41 min, 30 sec
1911	Gustave Garrigou, France	195 hrs, 37 min
1912	Odile Defraye, Belgium	190 hrs, 30 min, 28 sec
1913	Philippe Thys, Belgium	197 hrs, 54 min
1914	Philippe Thys, Belgium	200 hrs, 28 min, 48 sec
1915–18	No race	
1919	Firmin Lambot, Belgium	231 hrs, 7 min, 15 sec
1920	Philippe Thys, Belgium	228 hrs, 36 min, 13 sec
1921	Leon Scieur, Belgium	221 hrs, 50 min, 26 sec
1922	Firmin Lambot, Belgium	222 hrs, 8 min, 6 sec
1923	Henri Pelissier, France	222 hrs, 15 min, 30 sec
1924	Ottavio Bottechia, Italy	226 hrs, 18 min, 21 sec
1925	Ottavio Bottechia, Italy	219 hrs, 10 min, 18 sec
1926	Lucien Buysse, Belgium	238 hrs, 44 min, 25 sec
1927	Nicolas Frantz, Luxembourg	198 hrs, 16 min, 42 sec
1928	Nicolas Frantz, Luxembourg	192 hrs, 48 min, 58 sec
1929	Maurice Dewaele, Belgium	186 hrs, 39 min, 16 sec
1930	Andre Leducq, France	172 hrs, 12 min, 16 sec
1931	Antonin Magne, France	177 hrs, 10 min, 3 sec
1932	Andre Leducq, France	154 hrs, 12 min, 49 sec
1933	Georges Speicher, France	147 hrs, 51 min, 37 sec
1934	Antonin Magne, France	147 hrs, 13 min, 58 sec
1935	Romain Maes, Belgium	141 hrs, 32 min
1936	Sylvere Maes, Belgium	142 hrs, 47 min, 32 sec
1937	Roger Lapebie, France	138 hrs, 58 min, 31 sec
1938	Gino Bartali, Italy	148 hrs, 29 min, 12 sec
1939	Sylvere Maes, Belgium	132 hrs, 3 min, 17 sec
1940–46	No race	
1947	Jean Robic, France	148 hrs, 11 min, 25 sec
1948	Gino Bartali, Italy	147 hrs, 10 min, 36 sec
1949	Fausto Coppi, Italy	149 hrs, 40 min, 49 sec
1950	Ferdi Kubler, Switzerland	145 hrs, 36 min, 56 sec
1951	Hugo Koblet, Switzerland	142 hrs, 20 min, 14 sec
1952	Fausto Coppi, Italy	151 hrs, 57 min, 20 sec
1953	Louison Bobet, France	129 hrs, 23 min, 25 sec
1954	Louison Bobet, France	140 hrs, 6 min, 5 sec
1955	Louison Bobet, France	130 hrs, 29 min, 26 sec
1956	Roger Walkowiak, France	124 hrs, 1 min, 16 sec
1957	Jacques Anquetil, France	129 hrs, 46 min, 11 sec
1958	Charly Gaul, Luxembourg	116 hrs, 59 min, 5 sec
1959	Federico Bahamontes, Spain	123 hrs, 46 min, 45 sec
1960	Gastone Nencini, Italy	112 hrs, 8 min, 42 sec
1961	Jacques Anquetil, France	122 hrs, 1 min, 33 sec
1962	Jacques Anquetil, France	114 hrs, 31 min, 54 sec
1963	Jacques Anquetil, France	113 hrs, 30 min, 5 sec
1964	Jacques Anquetil, France	127 hrs, 9 min, 44 sec
1965	Felice Gimondi, Italy	116 hrs, 42 min, 6 sec
1966	Lucien Aimar, France	117 hrs, 34 min, 21 sec
1967	Roger Pingeon, France	136 hrs, 53 min, 50 sec
1968	Jan Janssen, Netherlands	133 hrs, 49 min, 32 sec
1969	Eddy Merckx, Belgium	116 hrs, 16 min, 2 sec
1970	Eddy Merckx, Belgium	119 hrs, 31 min, 49 sec
1971	Eddy Merckx, Belgium	96 hrs, 45 min, 14 sec
1972	Eddy Merckx, Belgium	108 hrs, 17 min, 18 sec
1973	Luis Ocana, Spain	122 hrs, 25 min, 34 sec
1974	Eddy Merckx, Belgium	116 hrs, 16 min, 58 sec
1975	Bernard Thevenet, France	114 hrs, 35 min, 31 sec
1976	Lucien Van Impe, Belgium	116 hrs, 22 min, 23 sec
1977	Bernard Thevenet, France	115 hrs, 38 min, 30 sec
1978	Bernard Hinault, France	108 hrs, 18 min
1979	Bernard Hinault, France	103 hrs, 6 min, 50 sec

Tour de France Winners *(Cont.)*

Year	Winner	Time
1980	Joop Zoetemelk, Netherlands	109 hrs, 19 min, 14 sec
1981	Bernard Hinault, France	96 hrs, 19 min, 38 sec
1982	Bernard Hinault, France	92 hrs, 8 min, 46 sec
1983	Laurent Fignon, France	105 hrs, 7 min, 52 sec
1984	Laurent Fignon, France	112 hrs, 3 min, 40 sec
1985	Bernard Hinault, France	113 hrs, 24 min, 23 sec
1986	Greg LeMond, United States	110 hrs, 35 min, 19 sec
1987	Stephen Roche, Ireland	115 hrs, 27 min, 42 sec
1988	Pedro Delgado, Spain	84 hrs, 27 min, 53 sec
1989	Greg LeMond, United States	87 hrs, 38 min, 35 sec
1990	Greg LeMond, United States	90 hrs, 43 min, 20 sec
1991	Miguel Induráin, Spain	101 hrs, 1 min, 20 sec
1992	Miguel Induráin, Spain	100 hrs, 49 min, 30 sec
1993	Miguel Induráin, Spain	95 hrs, 57 min, 9 sec
1994	Miguel Induráin, Spain	103 hrs, 38 min, 38 sec
1995	Miguel Induráin, Spain	92 hrs, 44 min, 59 sec
1996	Bjarne Riis, Denmark	95 hrs, 57 min, 16 sec
1997	Jan Ullrich, Germany	100 hrs, 30 min, 35 sec
1998	Marco Pantani, Italy	92 hrs, 49 min, 46 sec
1999	Lance Armstrong, United States	91 hrs, 32 min, 16 sec
2000	Lance Armstrong, United States	92 hrs, 33 min, 8 sec
2001	Lance Armstrong, United States	86 hrs, 17 min, 28 sec
2002	Lance Armstrong, United States	82 hrs, 5 min, 12 sec
2003	Lance Armstrong, United States	83 hrs, 41 min, 12 sec
2004	Lance Armstrong, United States	83 hrs, 36 min, 2 sec
2005	Lance Armstrong, United States	82 hrs, 34 min, 5 sec
2006	Floyd Landis, United States†	89 hrs, 39 min, 30sec

†As of Oct. 12, 2006 (Landis tested positive for a banned substance after Stage 17 of the Tour and the ICU may strip him of title.)

Sled Dog Racing

Iditarod

Year	Winner	Time	Year	Winner	Time
1973	Dick Wilmarth	20 days, 00:49:41	1990	Susan Butcher	11 days, 01:53:23
1974	Carl Huntington	20 days, 15:02:07	1991	Rick Swenson	12 days, 16:34:39
1975	Emmitt Peters	14 days, 14:43:45	1992	Martin Buser	10 days, 19:17:15
1976	Gerald Riley	18 days, 22:58:17	1993	Jeff King	10 days, 15:38:15
1977	Rick Swenson	16 days, 16:27:13	1994	Martin Buser	10 days, 13:02:39
1978	Dick Mackey	14 days, 18:52:24	1995	Doug Swingley	9 days, 02:42:19
1979	Rick Swenson	15 days, 10:37:47	1996	Jeff King	9 days, 05:43:13
1980	Joe May	14 days, 07:11:51	1997	Martin Buser	9 days, 08:30:45
1981	Rick Swenson	12 days, 08:45:02	1998	Jeff King	9 days, 05:52:26
1982	Rick Swenson	16 days, 04:40:10	1999	Doug Swingley	9 days, 14:31:19
1983	Dick Mackey	12 days, 14:10:44	2000	Doug Swingley	9 days, 00:58:06
1984	Dean Osmar	12 days, 15:07:33	2001	Doug Swingley	9 days, 19:55:50
1985	Libby Riddles	18 days, 00:20:17	2002	Martin Buser	8 days, 22:46:02
1986	Susan Butcher	11 days, 15:06:00	2003	Robert Sorlie	9 days, 15:47:36
1987	Susan Butcher	11 days, 02:05:13	2004	Mitch Seavey	9 days, 12:20:22
1988	Susan Butcher	11 days, 11:41:40	2005	Robert Sorlie	9 days, 18:39:31
1989	Joe Runyan	11 days, 05:24:34	2006	Jeff King	9 days, 11:11:36

Saltwater Fishing Records

Species	Weight	Where Caught	Date	Angler
Albacore	88 lb 2 oz	Gran Canaria, Canary Islands	Nov 19, 1977	Siegfried Dickemann
Amberjack, greater	155 lb 12 oz	Bermuda	Aug 16, 1992	Larry Trott
Amberjack, Pacific	104 lb	Baja California, Mexico	July 4, 1984	Richard Cresswell
Angler	126 lb 12 oz	Sognefjorden Hoyanger, Norway	July 4, 1996	Gunnar Thorsteinsen
Barracuda, great	85 lb	Christmas Island, Kiribati	April 11, 1992	John W. Helfrich
Barracuda, Mexican	21 lb	Phantom Isle, Costa Rica	Mar 27, 1987	E. Greg Kent
Barracuda, pickhandle	29 lb 12 oz	Malindi, Kenya	Nov 7, 2002	Paul Gerritsen
Bass, barred sand	13 lb 3 oz	Huntington Beach, California	Aug 29, 1988	Robert Halal
Bass, black sea	10 lb 4 oz	Virginia Beach, Virginia	Jan 1, 2000	Allan P. Paschall
Bass, European	20 lb 14 oz	Cap d'Agde, France	Sept. 8, 1999	Robert Mari
Bass, giant sea	563 lb 8 oz	Anacapa Island, California	Aug 20, 1968	James D. McAdam Jr.
Bass, striped	78 lb 8 oz	Atlantic City, New Jersey	Sept 21, 1982	Albert R. McReynolds
Bluefish	31 lb 12 oz	Hatteras Inlet, North Carolina	Jan 30, 1972	James M. Hussey
Bonefish	19 lb	Zululand, South Africa	May 26, 1962	Brian W. Batchelor
Bonito, Atlantic	18 lb 4 oz	Faial Island, Azores	July 8, 1953	D.G. Higgs
Bonito, Pacific	21 lb 3 oz	Malibu, California	July 30, 1978	Gino M. Picciolo
Cabezon	23 lb	Juan De Fuca Strait, Washington	Aug 4, 1990	Wesley S. Hunter
Cobia	135 lb 9 oz	Shark Bay, Australia	July 9, 1985	Peter W. Goulding
Cod, Atlantic	98 lb 12 oz	Isle of Shoals, New Hampshire	June 8, 1969	Alphonse Bielevich
Cod, Pacific	35 lb	Unalaska Bay, Alaska	June 16, 1999	Jim Johnson
Conger	133 lb 4 oz	South Devon, England	June 5, 1995	Vic Evans
Dolphinfish	87 lb	Papagallo Gulf, Costa Rica	Sept 25, 1976	Manuel Salazar
Drum, black	113 lb 1 oz	Lewes, Delaware	Sept 15, 1975	Gerald M. Townsend
Drum, red	94 lb 2 oz	Avon, North Carolina	Nov 7, 1984	David Deuel
Eel, American	9 lb 4 oz	Cape May, New Jersey	Nov 9, 1995	Jeff Pennick
Eel, marbled	36 lb 1 oz	Durban, South Africa	June 10, 1984	Ferdie van Nooten
Flounder, southern	20 lb 9 oz	Nassau Sound, Florida	Dec 23, 1983	Larenza W. Mungin
Flounder, summer	22 lb 7 oz	Montauk, New York	Sept 15, 1975	Charles Nappi
Grouper, Warsaw	436 lb 12 oz	Destin, Florida	Dec 22, 1985	Steve Haeusler
Halibut, Atlantic	355 lb 6 oz	Valevag, Norway	Oct 20, 1997	Odd Arve Gunderstad
Halibut, California	58 lb 9 oz	Santa Rosa Island, California	June 26, 1999	Roger W. Borrell
Halibut, Pacific	459 lb	Dutch Harbor, Alaska	June 11, 1996	Jack Tragis
Herring, Red	7 lb 7 oz	Sargasso Sea, Bahamas	Apr 1, 1965	Ward Bolster
Jack, crevalle	58 lb 6 oz	Barro do Kwanza, Angola	Dec 10, 2000	Nuno A. P. da Silva
Jack, horse-eye	29 lb 8 oz	Ascencion Island, S. Atlantic Ocean	May 28, 1993	Mike Hanson
Jack, Pacific crevalle	39 lb	Playa Zancudo, Costa Rica	Mar 3, 1997	Ingrid Callaghan
Jewfish	680 lb	Fernandina Beach, Florida	May 20, 1961	Lynn Joyner
Kawakawa	29 lb	Isla Clarion, Mexico	Dec 17, 1986	Ronald Nakamura
Lingcod	76 lb 9 oz	Gulf of Alaska, Alaska	Aug 11, 2001	Antwan D. Tinsley
Mackerel, cero	17 lb 2 oz	Islamorada, Florida	Apr 5, 1986	G. Michael Mills
Mackerel, king	93 lb	San Juan, Puerto Rico	Apr 18, 1999	Steve Perez Graulau
Mackerel, narrowbarred	99 lb	Natal, South Africa	Mar 14, 1982	Michael J. Wilkinson
Mackerel, Spanish	13 lb	Ocracoke Inlet, North Carolina	Nov 4, 1987	Robert Cranton
Marlin, Atlantic blue	1,402 lb 2 oz	Vitoria, Brazil	Feb 29, 1992	Paulo R.A. Amorim
Marlin, black	1,560 lb	Cabo Blanco, Peru	Aug 4, 1953	Alfred C. Glassell Jr.
Marlin, Pacific blue	1,376 lb	Kaaiwi Point, Hawaii	May 31, 1982	J.W. de Beaubien
Marlin, striped	494 lb	Tutukaka, New Zealand	Jan 16, 1986	Bill Boniface
Marlin, white	181 lb 14 oz	Vitoria, Brazil	Dec 8, 1979	Evandro Luiz Coser
Permit	60 lb	Ilha do Mel Paranagua, Brazil	Dec 14, 2002	Renato P. Fiedler
Pollock	50 lb	Salstraumen, Norway	Nov 30, 1995	Thor Magnus-Lekang
Pompano, African	50 lb 8 oz	Daytona Beach, Florida	Apr 21, 1990	Tom Sargent
Roosterfish	114 lb	La Paz, Mexico	June 1, 1960	Abe Sackheim
Runner, blue	11 lb 2 oz	Dauphin Island, Alaska	June 28, 1997	Stacey M. Moiren
Runner, rainbow	37 lb 9 oz	Isla Clarion, Mexico	Nov 21, 1991	Tom Pfleger
Sailfish, Atlantic	141 lb 1 oz	Luanda, Angola	Feb 19, 1994	Alfredo de Sousa Neves
Sailfish, Pacific	221 lb	Santa Cruz Island, Ecuador	Feb 12, 1947	Carl W. Stewart
Seabass, white	83 lb 12 oz	San Felipe, Mexico	Mar 31, 1953	Lyal C. Baumgardner
Seatrout, spotted	17 lb 7 oz	Ft. Pierce, Florida	May 11, 1995	Craig F. Carson
Shark, bigeye thresher	802 lb	Tutukaka, New Zealand	Feb 8, 1981	Dianne North
Shark, blue	528 lb	Montauk Point, New York	Aug 9, 2001	Joe Seidel
Shark, grter hammrhd	1280 lb	Boca Grande, Florida	May 23, 2006	Bucky Dennis
Shark, Greenland	1,708 lb 9 oz	Trondheimsfjord, Norway	Oct 18, 1987	Terje Nordtvedt
Shark, porbeagle	507 lb	Caithness, Scotland	Mar 9, 1993	Christopher Bennet
Shark, shortfin mako	1,221 lb	Chatham, Massachusetts	July 21, 2001	Luke Sweeney
Shark, tiger	1,780 lb	Cherry Grove, South Carolina	June 14, 1964	Walter Maxwell
Shark, tope	72 lb 12 oz	Parengarenga Harbor, N.Z.	Dec 19, 1986	Melanie B. Feldman

Saltwater Fishing Records

Species	Weight	Where Caught	Date	Angler
Shark, white	2,664 lb	Ceduna, Australia	Apr 21, 1959	Alfred Dean
Skipjack, black	26 lb	Baja California, Mexico	Oct 23, 1991	Clifford K. Hamaishi
Snapper, cubera	121 lb 8 oz	Cameron, Louisiana	July 5, 1982	Mike Hebert
Snook, common	53 lb 10 oz	Parismina Ranch, Costa Rica	Oct 18, 1978	Gilbert Ponzi
Spearfish, Mediterr.	90 lb 13 oz	Madeira Island, Portugal	June 2, 1980	Joseph Larkin
Spearfish, longbill	127 lb 13 oz	Puerto Rico, Gran Canaria, Spain	May 20, 1999	Paul Cashmore
Spearfish, shortbill	81 lb 2 oz	White Island, New Zealand	Feb 2, 2006	Adrian Lewis
Swordfish	1,182 lb	Iquique, Chile	May 7, 1953	Louis Marron
Tarpon	286 lb 9 oz	Rubane, Guinea-Bissau	Mar 20, 2003	Max Domecq
Tautog	25 lb	Ocean City, New Jersey	Jan 20, 1998	Anthony Monica
Tilapia, Mozambique	6 lb 13 oz	Loskop Dam, S Africa	Apr 4, 2003	Eugene C. Kruger
Trevally, bigeye	31 lb 8 oz	Poivre Island, Seychelles	Apr 23, 1997	Les Sampson
Trevally, giant	160 lb 7 oz	Kagoshima, Japan	May 22, 2006	Keiki Hamasaiki
Tuna, Atlantic bigeye	392 lb 6 oz	Puerto Rico, Gran Caneria, Spain	July 25, 1996	Dieter Vogel
Tuna, blackfin	45 lb 8 oz	Key West, Florida	May 4, 1996	Sam J. Burnett
Tuna, bluefin	1,496 lb	Aulds Cove, Nova Scotia	Oct 26, 1979	Ken Fraser
Tuna, longtail	79 lb 2 oz	Montague Island, New South Wales, Australia	Apr 12, 1982	Tim Simpson
Tuna, Pacific bigeye	435 lb	Cabo Blanco, Peru	Apr 17, 1957	Russel Lee
Tuna, skipjack	45 lb 4 oz	Baja California, Mexico	Nov 16, 1996	Brian Evans
Tuna, southern bluefin	348 lb 5 oz	Whakatane, New Zealand	Jan 16, 1981	Rex Wood
Tuna, yellowfin	388 lb 12 oz	San Benedicto Is, Mexico	Apr 1, 1977	Curt Wiesenhutter
Tunny, little	35 lb 2 oz	Cape de Garde, Algeria	Dec 14, 1988	Jean Yves Chatard
Wahoo	158 lb 8 oz	Loreto, Baja California, Mexico	June 10, 1996	Keith Winter
Weakfish	19 lb 2 oz	Jones Beach Inlet, New York	Oct 11, 1984	Dennis Rooney
		Delaware Bay, Delaware	May 20, 1989	William E. Thomas
Yellowtail, California	88 lb 3 oz	Alijos Rocks, Baja Calif., Mexico	Jun 21, 2000	Ronald Fujii
Yellowtail, southern	114 lb 10 oz	Tauranga, New Zealand	Feb 5, 1984	Mike Godfrey

Freshwater Fishing Records

Species	Weight	Where Caught	Date	Angler
Barramundi	83 lb 7 oz	Lake Tinaroo, N Queensl'd, Aus.	Sept 23, 1999	David Powell
Bass, largemouth	22 lb 4 oz	Montgomery Lake, Georgia	June 2, 1932	George W. Perry
Bass, rock	3 lb	York River, Ontario	Aug 1, 1974	Peter Gulgin
Bass, shoal	8 lb 12 oz	Apalatchicola River, Florida	Jan 28, 1995	Carl W. Davis
Bass, smallmouth	10 lb 14 oz	Dale Hollow, Tennessee	April 24, 1969	John T. Gorman
Bass, Suwannee	3 lb 14 oz	Suwannee River, Florida	Mar 2, 1985	Ronnie Everett
Bass, white	6 lb 13 oz	Orange, Virginia	July 31, 1989	Ronald Sprouse
Bass, whiterock	27 lb 5 oz	Greers Ferry Lake, Arkansas	Apr 24, 1997	Jerald Shaum
Bass, yellow	2 lb 9 oz	Waverly, Tennessee	Feb 27, 1998	John Chappell
Bluegill	4 lb 12 oz	Ketona Lake, Alabama	Apr 9, 1950	T.S. Hudson
Bowfin	21 lb 8 oz	Florence, South Carolina	Jan 29, 1980	Robert Harmon
Buffalo, bigmouth	70 lb 5 oz	Bastrop, Louisiana	Apr 21, 1980	Delbert Sisk
Buffalo, black	63 lb 6 oz	Mississippi River, Iowa	Aug 14, 1999	Jim Winters
Buffalo, smallmouth	82 lb 3 oz	Athens Lake, Georgia	June 6, 1993	Randy Collins
Bullhead, brown	6 lb 5 oz	Lake Mahopac, New York	Sept 8, 2002	Ray Lawrence
Bullhead, yellow	4 lb 4 oz	Mormon Lake, Arizona	May 11, 1984	Emily Williams
Burbot	18 lb 11 oz	Angenmanalren, Sweden	Oct 22, 1996	Margit Agren
Carp, common	75 lb 11 oz	Lac de St. Cassien, France	May 21, 1987	Leo van der Gugten
Catfish, blue	116 lb 12 oz	Mississippi River, Arkansas	Aug 3, 2001	Charles Ashley Jr.
Catfish, channel	58 lb	Santee-Cooper Reservoir, SC	July 7, 1964	W.B. Whaley
Catfish, flathead	123 lb	Elk City Reservoir, Indep., KS	May 14, 1998	Ken Paulie
Catfish, white	21 lb 8 oz	Gorton Pond, East Lime, Conn.	Apr 22, 2001	Thomas Urquhart
Char, Arctic	32 lb 9 oz	Tree River, Canada	July 30, 1981	Jeffrey Ward
Crappie, white	5 lb 3 oz	Enid Dam, Mississippi	July 31, 1957	Fred L. Bright
Dolly Varden	20 lb 14 oz	Wulik River, Alaska	July 7, 2001	Raz Reid
Dorado	51 lb 5 oz	Corrientes, Argentina	Sep 27, 1984	Armando Giudice
Drum, freshwater	54 lb 8 oz	Nickajack Lake, Tennessee	Apr 20, 1972	Benny E. Hull
Gar, alligator	279 lb	Rio Grande River, Texas	Dec 2, 1951	Bill Valverde
Gar, Florida	10 lb	Florida Everglades, Florida	Jan 28, 2002	Herbert Ratner Jr.
Gar, longnose	50 lb 5 oz	Trinity River, Texas	July 30, 1954	Townsend Miller
Gar, shortnose	5 lb 12 oz	Rend Lake, Illinois	July 16, 1995	Donna K. Willmert
Gar, spotted	9 lb 12 oz	Lake Mexia, Texas	Apr 7, 1994	Rick Rivard
Grayling, Arctic	5 lb 15 oz	Katseyedie River, Northwest Territories	Aug 16, 1967	Jeanne P. Branson

Freshwater Fishing Records *(Cont.)*

Species	Weight	Where Caught	Date	Angler
Inconnu	53 lb	Pah River, Alaska	Aug 20, 1986	Lawrence Hudnall
Kokanee	9 lb 6 oz	Okanagan Lake, Vernon, B.C.	June 18, 1988	Norm Kuhn
Muskellunge	67 lb 8 oz	Hayward, Wisconsin	July 24, 1949	Cal Johnson
Muskellunge, tiger	51 lb 3 oz	Lac Vieux-Desert, Michigan	July 16, 1919	John Knobla
Peacock, speckled	27 lb	Rio Negro, Brazil	Dec 4, 1994	Gerald (Doc) Lawson
Perch, Nile	230 lb	Lake Nasser, Egypt	Dec 20, 2000	William Toth
Perch, white	3 lb 1 oz	Forest Hill Park, N.J.	May 6, 1989	Edward Tango
Perch, yellow	4 lb 3 oz	Bordentown, New Jersey	May 1865	C.C. Abbot
Pickerel, chain	9 lb 6 oz	Homerville, Georgia	Feb 17, 1961	Baxley McQuaig Jr.
Pike, northern	55 lb 1 oz	Lake of Grefeern, West Germany	Oct 16, 1986	Lothar Louis
Redhorse, greater	9 lb 3 oz	Salmon River, Pulaski, New York	May 11, 1985	Jason Wilson
Redhorse, silver	11 lb 7 oz	Plum Creek, Wisconsin	May 29, 1985	Neal Long
Salmon, Atlantic	79 lb 2 oz	Tana River, Norway	1928	Henrik Henriksen
Salmon, Chinook	97 lb 4 oz	Kenai River, Alaska	May 17, 1985	Les Anderson
Salmon, chum	35 lb	Edye Pass, Canada	July 11, 1995	Todd A. Johansson
Salmon, coho	33 lb 4 oz	Pulaski, New York	Sep 27, 1989	Jerry Lifton
Salmon, pink	14 lb 13 oz	Monroe, Washington	Sep 30, 2001	Alexander Minerich
Salmon, sockeye	15 lb 3 oz	Kenai River, Alaska	Aug 9, 1987	Stan Roach
Sauger	8 lb 12 oz	Lake Sakakawea, North Dakota	Oct 6, 1971	Mike Fischer
Shad, American	11 lb 4 oz	Connecticut River, Massachusetts	May 19, 1986	Bob Thibodo
Sturgeon, white	468 lb	Benicia, California	July 9, 1983	Joey Pallotta III
Sunfish, green	2 lb 2 oz	Stockton Lake, Missouri	June 18, 1971	Paul M. Dilley
Sunfish, redbreast	1 lb 12 oz	Suwannee River, Florida	May 29, 1984	Alvin Buchanan
Sunfish, redear	5 lb 7 oz	Diverson Canal, Georgia	Nov 6, 1998	Amos M. Gay
Tigerfish, giant	97 lb	Zaire River, Kinshasa, Zaire	July 9, 1988	Raymond Houtmans
Trout, Apache	5 lb 3 oz	Apache Reservation, Arizona	May 29, 1991	John Baldwin
Trout, brook	14 lb 8 oz	Nipigon River, Ontario	July 1916	W.J. Cook
Trout, brown	40 lb 4 oz	Heber Springs, Arkansas	May 9, 1992	Howard (Rip) Collins
Trout, bull	32 lb	Lake Pond Oreille, Idaho	Oct 27, 1949	N.L. Higgins
Trout, cutthroat	41 lb	Pyramid Lake, Nevada	Dec 1925	John Skimmerhorn
Trout, golden	11 lb	Cook's Lake, Wyoming	Aug 5, 1948	Charles S. Reed
Trout, lake	72 lb	Great Bear Lake, Northwest Territories, Canada	Aug 19, 1995	Lloyd Bull
Trout, rainbow	42 lb 2 oz	Bell Island, Alaska	June 22, 1970	David Robert White
Trout, tiger	20 lb 13 oz	Lake Michigan, Wisconsin	Aug 12, 1978	Pete M. Friedland
Walleye	25 lb	Old Hickory Lake, Tennessee	Aug 2, 1960	Mabry Harper
Warmouth	2 lb 7 oz	Yellow River, Holt, Florida	Oct 19, 1985	Tony D. Dempsey
Whitefish, lake	14 lb 6 oz	Meaford, Ontario	May 21, 1984	Dennis Laycock
Whitefish, mountain	5 lb 8 oz	Elbow River, Calgary, Alberta	Aug 1, 1995	Randy Woo
Whitefish, broad	9 lb	Tozitna River, Alaska	July 17, 1989	Al Mathews
Whitefish, round	6 lb	Putahow River, Manitoba	June 14, 1984	Allan J. Ristori
Zander	25 lb 2 oz	Trosa, Sweden	June 12, 1986	Harry Lee Tennison

Greyhound Racing

Annual Greyhound Race of Champions Winners*

Year	Winner (Sex)	Affiliation/Owner	Year	Winner (Sex)	Affiliation/Owner
1982	DD's Jackie (F)	Wonderland Park/ R.H. Walters Jr.	1988	BB's Old Yellow (M)	Supplemental (Southland)/ Margie Bonita Hyers
1983	Comin' Attraction (F)	Rocky Mt. Greyhound Park/ Bob Riggin	1989	Osh Kosh Juliet (F)	Tampa Greyhound Track/ William F. Pollard
1984	Fallon (F)	Tampa Greyhound Track/ E.J. Alderson	1990	Daring Don (M)	Interstate Kennel Club/ Perry Padrta
1985	Lady Delight (F)	Lincoln Greyhound Park/ Julian A. Gay	1991	Mo Kick (M)	Flagler Greyhound Track/ Eric M. Kennon
1986	Ben G Speedboat (M)	Multnomah Kennel Club/ Louis Bennett	1992	Dicky Vallie (M)	Dairyland Greyhound Track/ George Benjamin
1987	ET's Pesky (F)	Supplemental (Flagler)/ Emil Tanis	1993	Mega Morris (M)	Jacksonville Kennel Club/ Ferrell's Kennel

* The Greyhound Race of Champions has not been held since 1993.

World Champions — Men

All-Around

Year	Champion, Nation
1903	Joseph Martinez, France
1905	Marcel Lalue, France
1907	Joseph Czada, Czechoslovakia
1909	Marcos Torres, France
1911	Ferdinand Steiner, Czechoslovakia
1913	Marcos Torres, France
1922	Peter Sumi, Yugoslavia
	F. Pechacek, Czechoslovakia
1926	Peter Sumi, Yugoslavia
1930	Josip Primozic, Yugoslavia
1934	Eugene Mack, Switzerland
1938	Jan Gajdos, Czechoslovakia
1950	Walter Lehmann, Switzerland
1954	Valentin Mouratov, USSR
	Victor Chukarin, USSR
1958	Boris Shaklin, USSR
1962	Yuri Titov, USSR
1966	Mikhail Voronin, USSR
1970	Eizo Kenmotsu, Japan
1974	Shigeru Kasamatsu, Japan
1978	Nikolai Andrianov, USSR
1979	Alexander Ditiatin, USSR
1981	Yuri Korolev, USSR
1983	Dimitri Bilozertchev, USSR
1985	Yuri Korolev, USSR
1987	Dimitri Bilozertchev, USSR
1989	Igor Korobchinsky, USSR
1991	Grigori Misutin, CIS
1993	Vitaly Scherbo, Belarus
1994	Ivan Ivankov, Belarus
1995	Li Xiaoshuang, China
1997	Ivan Ivankov, Belarus
1999	Nicolae Krukov, Russia
2001	Feng Jing, China
2003	Paul Hamm, United States
2005	Hiroyuki Tomita, Japan

Pommel Horse

Year	Champion, Nation
1930	Josip Primozic, Yugoslavia
1934	Eugene Mack, Switzerland
1938	Michael Reusch, Switzerland
1950	Josef Stalder, Switzerland
1954	Grant Chaguinjan, USSR
1958	Boris Shaklin, USSR
1962	Miroslav Cerar, Yugoslavia
1966	Miroslav Cerar, Yugoslavia
1970	Miroslav Cerar, Yugoslavia
1974	Zoltan Magyar, Hungary
1978	Zoltan Magyar, Hungary
1979	Zoltan Magyar, Hungary
1981	Michael Mikolai, East Germany
1983	Dmitri Bilozertchev, USSR
1985	Valentin Moguilny, USSR
1987	Zsolt Borkai, Hungary
	Dmitri Bilozertchev, USSR
1989	Valentin Moguilny, USSR
1991	Valeri Belenki, USSR
1992	Pae Gil Su, North Korea
	Vitaly Scherbo, CIS
	Li Jing, China
1993	Pae Gil Su, North Korea

Pommel Horse (Cont.)

Year	Champion, Nation
1994	Marius Urzica, Romania
1995	Li Donghua, Switzerland
1996	Pae Gil Su, North Korea
1997	Valeri Belenki, Germany
1999	Alexei Nemov, Russia
2001	Marius Urzica, Romania
2003	Teng Haibin, China
	Takehiro Kashima, Japan
2005	Qin Xiao, China

Floor Exercise

Year	Champion, Nation
1930	Josip Primozic, Yugoslavia
1934	Georges Miesz, Switzerland
1938	Jan Gajdos, Czechoslovakia
1950	Josef Stalder, Switzerland
1954	Valentin Mouratov, USSR
	Masao Takemoto, Japan
1958	Masao Takemoto, Japan
1962	Nobuyuki Aihara, Japan
	Yukio Endo, Japan
1966	Akinori Nakayama, Japan
1970	Akinori Nakayama, Japan
1974	Shigeru Kasamatsu, Japan
1978	Kurt Thomas, United States
1979	Kurt Thomas, United States
	Roland Brucker, East Germ.
1981	Yuri Korolev, USSR
	Li Yuejui, China
1983	Tong Fei, China
1985	Tong Fei, China
1987	Lou Yun, China
1989	Igor Korobchinsky, USSR
1991	Igor Korobchinsky, USSR
1993	Grigori Misutin, Ukraine
1994	Vitaly Scherbo, Belarus
1995	Vitaly Scherbo, Belarus
1996	Vitaly Scherbo, Belarus
1997	Alexei Nemov, Russia
1999	Alexei Nemov, Russia
2001	Marian Dragulescu, Romania
2003	Paul Hamm, United States
	Jordan Jovtchev, Bulgaria
2005	Diego Hypolito, Brazil

Rings

Year	Champion, Nation
1930	Emanuel Loffler, Czechoslovakia
1934	Alois Hudec, Czechoslovakia
1938	Alois Hudec, Czechoslovakia
1950	Walter Lehmann, Switzerland
1954	Albert Azarian, USSR
1958	Albert Azarian, USSR
1962	Yuri Titov, USSR
1966	Mikhail Voronin, USSR
1970	Akinori Nakayama, Japan
1974	N. Andrianov, USSR
	D. Grecu, Rom.
1978	Nikolai Andrianov, USSR
1979	Alexander Ditiatin, USSR
1981	Alexander Ditiatin, USSR
1983	Dimitri Bilozertchev, USSR
1985	Li Ning, China
	Yuri Korolev, USSR

Rings (Cont.)

Year	Champion, Nation
1987	Yuri Korolev, USSR
1989	Andreas Aguilar, West Germ.
1991	Grigory Misutin, USSR
1992	Vitaly Scherbo, CIS
1993	Yuri Chechi, Italy
1994	Yuri Chechi, Italy
1995	Yuri Chechi, Italy
1996	Yuri Chechi, Italy
1997	Yuri Chechi, Italy
1999	Zhen Dong, China
2001	Jordan Jovtchev, Bulgaria
2003	Jordan Jovtchev, Bulgaria
	Dimosthenis Tampakos, Greece
2005	Yuri Van Gelder, Netherlands

Parallel Bars

Year	Champion, Nation
1930	Josip Primozic, Yugoslavia
1934	Eugene Mack, Switzerland
1938	Michael Reusch, Switzerland
1950	Hans Eugster, Switzerland
1954	Victor Chukarin, USSR
1958	Boris Shaklin, USSR
1962	Miroslav Cerar, Yugoslavia
1966	Sergei Diamidov, USSR
1970	Akinori Nakayama, Japan
1974	Eizo Kenmotsu, Japan
1978	Eizo Kenmotsu, Japan
1979	Bart Conner, United States
1981	Koji Gushiken, Japan
	Alexandr Ditiatin, USSR
1983	Vladimir Artemov, USSR
	Lou Yun, China
1985	Sylvio Kroll, East Germany
	Valentin Moguilny, USSR
1987	Vladimir Artemov, USSR
1989	Li Jing, China
	Vladimir Artemov, USSR
1991	Li Jing, China
1992	Li Jin, China
	Alexei Voropaev, CIS
1993	Vitaly Scherbo, Belarus
1994	Huang Liping, China
1995	Vitaly Scherbo, Belarus
1996	Rustam Sharipov, Ukraine
1997	Zhang Jinjing, China
1999	Joo-Hyung Lee, South Korea
2001	Sean Townsend, U.S.
2003	Li Xiao-Peng, China
2005	Mitja Petkovsek, Slovenia

High Bar

Year	Champion, Nation
1930	Istvan Pelle, Hungary
1934	Ernst Winter, Germany
1938	Michael Reusch, Switzerland
1950	Paavo Aaltonen, Finland
1954	Valentin Mouratov, USSR
1958	Boris Shaklin, USSR
1962	Takashi Ono, Japan
1966	Akinori Nakayama, Japan
1970	Eizo Kenmotsu, Japan
1974	Eberhard Gienger, West Germany
1978	Shigeru Kasamatsu, Japan
1979	Kurt Thomas, United States

World Champions — Men (Cont.)

High Bar (Cont.)

Year	Champion, Nation
1981	Alexander Takchev, USSR
1983	Dimitri Bilozertchev, USSR
1985	Tong Fei, China
1987	Dimitri Bilozertchev, USSR
1989	Li Chunyang, China
1991	Li Chunyang, China
	R. Buechner, Germ
1992	Grigori Misutin, CIS
1993	Sergei Kharkov, Russia
1994	Vitaly Scherbo, Belarus
1995	Andreas Wecker, Germany
1996	Jesús Carballo, Spain
1997	Jani Tanskanen, Finland
1999	Jesus Carballo, Spain
2001	Vlasios Maras, Greece
2003	Takehiro Kashima, Japan
2005	Vlasios Maras, Greece

Vault

Year	Champion, Nation
1934	Eugene Mack, Switzerland
1938	Eugene Mack, Switzerland
1950	Ernst Gebendinger, Switzerland
1954	Leo Sotornik, Czechoslovakia
1958	Yuri Titov, USSR
1962	Premysel Krbec, Czechoslovakia
1966	Haruhiro Yamashita, Japan
1970	Mitsuo Tsukahara, Japan
1974	Shigeru Kasamatsu, Japan
1978	Junichi Shimizu, Japan
1979	Alexander Ditiatin, USSR
1981	Ralf-Peter Hemmann, East Germany
1983	Arthur Akopian, USSR
1985	Yuri Korolev, USSR

Vault (Cont.)

Year	Champion, Nation
1987	Lou Yun, China
	Sylvio Kroll, East Germany
1989	Joreg Behrend, East Germany
1991	Yoo Ok Youl, South Korea
1992	Yoo Ok Youl, South Korea
1993	Vitaly Scherbo, Belarus
1994	Vitaly Scherbo, Belarus
1995	G. Misutin, Ukraine
	A. Nemov, Russia
1996	Alexei Nemov, Russia
1997	Sergei Fedorchenko, Kazakhstan
1999	Li Xiao-Peng, China
2001	Marian Dragulescu, Romania
2003	Li Xiao-Peng, China
2005	Eichi Sekiguchi, Japan

World Champions — Women

All-Around

Year	Champion, Nation
1934	Vlasta Dekanova, Czechoslovakia
1938	Vlasta Dekanova, Czechoslovakia
1950	Helena Rakoczy, Poland
1954	Galina Roudiko, USSR
1958	Larissa Latynina, USSR
1962	Larissa Latynina, USSR
1966	Vera Caslavska, Czechoslovakia
1970	Ludmilla Tourischeva, USSR
1974	Ludmilla Tourischeva, USSR
1978	Elena Mukhina, USSR
1979	Nelli Kim, USSR
1981	Olga Bicherova, USSR
1983	Natalia Yurchenko, USSR
1985	Elena Shoushounova, USSR
	Oksana Omeliantchik, USSR
1987	Aurelia Dobre, Romania
1989	Svetlana Bouguinskaia, USSR
1991	Kim Zmeskal, United States
1993	Shannon Miller, United States
1994	Shannon Miller, United States
1995	Lilia Podkopayeva, Ukraine
1997	Svetlana Khorkina, Russia
1999	Maria Olaru, Romania
2001	Svetlana Khorkina, Russia
2003	Svetlana Khorkina, Russia
2005	Chellsie Memmel, USA

Floor Exercise

Year	Champion, Nation
1950	Helena Rakoczy, Poland
1954	Tamara Manina, USSR
1958	Eva Bosakava, Czechoslovakia
1962	Larissa Latynina, USSR
1966	Natalia Kuchinskaya, USSR
1970	Ludmilla Tourischeva, USSR
1974	Ludmilla Tourischeva, USSR
1978	Nelli Kim, USSR
	Elena Mukhina, USSR

Floor Exercise (Cont.)

Year	Champion, Nation
1979	Emilia Eberle, Romania
1981	Natalia Ilenko, USSR
1983	Ecaterina Szabo, Romania
1985	Oksana Omeliantchik, USSR
1987	Elena Shoushounova, Romania
	Daniela Silivas, Romania
1989	Svetlana Bouguinskaia, USSR
	Daniela Silivas, Romania
1991	Cristina Bontas, Romania
	Oksana Tchusovitina, USSR
1992	Kim Zmeskal, United States
1993	Shannon Miller, United States
1994	Dina Kochetkova, Russia
1995	Gina Gogean, Romania
1996	Gina Gogean, Romania
1997	Gina Gogean, Romania
1999	Andreea Raducan, Romania
2001	Andreea Raducan, Romania
2003	Daiane Dos Santos, Brazil
2005	Anastasia Liukin, United States

Uneven Bars

Year	Champion, Nation
1950	Gertchen Kolar, Austria
	Anna Pettersson, Sweden
1954	Agnes Keleti, Hungary
1958	Larissa Latynina, USSR
1962	Irina Pervuschina, USSR
1966	Natalia Kuchinskaya, USSR
1970	Karin Janz, East Germany
1974	Annelore Zinke, East Germany
1978	Marcia Frederick, United States
1979	Ma Yanhong, China
	Maxi Gnauck, East Germany
1981	Maxi Gnauck, East Germany
1983	Maxi Gnauck, East Germany
1985	Gabriele Fahnrich, East Germany
1987	Daniela Silivas, Romania
	Doerte Thuemmler, East Germany

Uneven Bars (Cont.)

Year	Champion, Nation
1989	Fan Di, China
	Daniela Silivas, Romania
1991	Gwang Suk Kim, North Korea
1992	Lavinia Milosivici, Romania
1993	Shannon Miller, United States
1994	Luo Li, China
1995	Svetlana Khorkina, Russia
1996	Svetlana Khorkina, Russia
1997	Svetlana Khorkina, Russia
1999	Svetlana Khorkina, Russia
2001	Svetlana Khorkina, Russia
2003	Chellsie Memmel, U.S.
	Hollie Vise, United States
2005	Anastasia Liukin, United States

Balance Beam

Year	Champion, Nation
1950	Helena Rakoczy, Poland
1954	Keiko Tanaka, Japan
1958	Larissa Latynina, USSR
1962	Eva Bosakova, Czech.
1966	Natalia Kuchinskaya, USSR
1970	Erika Zuchold, East Germany
1974	Ludmilla Tourischeva, USSR
1978	Nadia Comaneci, Romania
1979	Vera Cerna, Czechoslovakia
1981	Maxi Gnauck, East Germany
1983	Olga Mostepanova, USSR
1985	Daniela Silivas, Romania
1987	Aurelia Dobre, Romania
1989	Daniela Silivas, Romania
1991	Svetlana Boguinskaia, USSR
1992	Kim Zmeskal, United States
1993	Lavinia Milosovici, Romania
1994	Shannon Miller, United States
1995	Mo Huilan, China
1996	Dina Kochetkova, Russia
1997	Gina Gogean, Romania
1999	E. Zamolodchikova, Russia
2001	Andreea Raducan, Romania
2003	Fan Ye, China
2005	Nan Zhang, China

World Champions — Women (Cont.)
Vault

Year	Champion, Nation	Year	Champion, Nation	Year	Champion, Nation
1950	Helena Rakoczy, Poland	1981	Maxi Gnauck, East Germany	1995	L. Podkopayeva, Ukraine
1954	T. Manina, USSR	1983	Boriana Stoyanova, Bulgaria		Simona Amanar, Rom.
	Anna Pettersson, Sweden	1985	Elena Shoushounova, USSR	1996	Gina Gogean, Romania
1958	Larissa Latynina, USSR	1987	Elena Shoushounova, USSR	1997	Simona Amanar, Romania
1962	Vera Caslavska, Czech.	1989	Olesia Durnik, USSR	1999	Jie Ling, China
1966	Vera Caslavska, Czech.	1991	Lavinia Milosovici, Romania	2001	Svetlana Khorkina, Russia
1970	Erika Zuchold, East Germany	1992	Henrietta Onodi, Hungary	2003	Oksana Chusovitina,
1974	Olga Korbut, USSR	1993	Elena Piskun, Belarus		Uzbekistan
1978	Nelli Kim, USSR	1994	Gina Gogean, Romania	2005	Fei Cheng, China
1979	Dumitrita Turner, Romania				

National Champions — Men

All-Around

Year	Champion
1963	Art Shurlock
1964	Rusty Mitchell
1965	Rusty Mitchell
1966	Rusty Mitchell
1967	Katsuzoki Kanzaki
1968	Yoshi Hayasaki
1969	Steve Hug
1970	Makoto Sakamoto
	Mas Watanabe
1971	Yoshi Takei
1972	Yoshi Takei
1973	Marshall Avener
1974	John Crosby
1975	Tom Beach
	Bart Conner
1976	Kurt Thomas
1977	Kurt Thomas
1978	Kurt Thomas
1979	Bart Conner
1980	Peter Vidmar
1981	Jim Hartung
1982	Peter Vidmar
1983	Mitch Gaylord
1984	Mitch Gaylord
1985	Brian Babcock
1986	Tim Daggett
1987	Scott Johnson
1988	Dan Hayden
1989	Tim Ryan
1990	John Roethlisberger
1991	Chris Waller
1992	John Roethlisberger
1993	John Roethlisberger
1994	Scott Keswick
1995	John Roethlisberger
1996	Blaine Wilson
1997	Blaine Wilson
1998	Blaine Wilson
1999	Blaine Wilson
2000	Blaine Wilson
2001	Sean Townsend
2002	Paul Hamm
2003	Paul Hamm
2004	Paul Hamm
2005	Todd Thornton
2006	Alexander Artemev

Floor Exercise

Year	Champion
1963	Tom Seward
1964	Rusty Mitchell

Floor Exercise (Cont.)

Year	Champion
1965	Rusty Mitchell
1966	Dan Millman
1967	Katsuzoki Kanzaki
	Ron Aure
1968	Katsuzoki Kanzaki
1969	Steve Hug
	Dave Thor
1970	Makoto Sakamoto
1971	John Crosby
1972	Yoshi Takei
1973	John Crosby
1974	John Crosby
1975	Peter Korman
1977	Ron Galimore
1978	Kurt Thomas
1979	Ron Galimore
1980	Ron Galimore
1981	Jim Hartung
1982	Jim Hartung
1983	Mitch Gaylord
1984	Peter Vidmar
1985	Mark Oates
1986	Robert Sundstrom
1987	John Sweeney
1988	Mark Oates
	Charles Lakes
1989	Mike Racanelli
1990	Bob Stelter
1991	Mike Racanelli
1992	Gregg Curtis
1993	Kerry Huston
1994	Jeremy Killen
1995	Daniel Stover
1996	Jay Thornton
1997	Jason Gatson
1998	Jason Gatson
1999	Jason Gatson
2000	Blaine Wilson
2001	Sean Townsend
2002	Morgan Hamm
2003	Morgan Hamm
2004	Paul Hamm
2005	Guillermo Alvarez
2006	Jonathan Horton

Pommel Horse

Year	Champion
1963	Larry Spiegel
1964	Sam Bailie
1965	Jack Ryan
1966	Jack Ryan

Pommel Horse (Cont.)

Year	Champion
1967	Paul Mayer/Dave Doty
1968	Katsuoki Kanzaki
1969	Dave Thor
1970	Mas Watanabe
1971	Leonard Caling
1972	Sadao Hamada
1973	Marshall Avener
1974	Marshall Avener
1975	Bart Conner
1977	Gene Whelan
1978	Jim Hartung
1979	Bart Conner
1980	Jim Hartung
1981	Jim Hartung
1982	Jim Hartung
1983	Bart Conner
1984	Tim Daggett
1985	Phil Cahoy
1986	Phil Cahoy
1987	Tim Daggett
1988	Kevin Davis
1989	Kevin Davis
1990	Patrick Kirksey
1991	Chris Waller
1992	Chris Waller
1993	Chris Waller
1994	Mihai Begiu
1995	Mark Sohn
1996	Josh Stein
1997	John Roethlisberger
1998	John Roethlisberger
1999	John Roethlisberger
2000	John Roethlisberger
2001	Brett McClure
2002	Paul Hamm
2003	Paul Hamm
2004	Brett McClure
2005	Yewki Tomita
2006	Alexander Artemev

Rings

Year	Champion
1963	Art Shurlock
1964	Glen Gailis
1965	Glen Gailis
1966	Glen Gailis
1967	Fred Dennis
	Don Hatch
1968	Yoshi Hayasaki
1969	Fred Dennis
	Bob Emery

Gymnastics *(Cont.)*

National Champions — Men *(Cont.)*

Rings *(Cont.)*

Year	Champion
1970	Makoto Sakamoto
1971	Yoshi Takei
1972	Yoshi Takei
1973	Jim Ivicek
1974	Tom Weeder
1975	Tom Beach
1977	Kurt Thomas
1978	Mike Silverstein
1979	Bart Conner
1980	Jim Hartung
1981	Jim Hartung
1982	Jim Hartung
	Peter Vidmar
1983	Mitch Gaylord
1984	Jim Hartung
1985	Dan Hayden
1986	Dan Hayden
1987	Scott Johnson
1988	Dan Hayden
1989	Scott Keswick
1990	Scott Keswick
1991	Scott Keswick
1992	Tim Ryan
1993	John Roethlisberger
1994	Scott Keswick
1995	Paul O'Neill
1996	Kip Simons
1997	Blaine Wilson
1998	Jeff Johnson
1999	Blaine Wilson
2000	Blaine Wilson
2001	Sean Townsend
2002	Blaine Wilson
2003	Blaine Wilson
2004	Raj Bhavsar
2005	Sean Golden
2006	Kevin Tan

Vault

Year	Champion
1963	Art Shurlock
1964	Gary Hery
1965	Brent Williams
1966	Dan Millman
1967	Jack Kenan
	Sid Jensen
1968	Rich Scorza
1969	Dave Butzman
1970	Makoto Sakamoto
1971	Gary Morava
1972	Mike Kelley
1973	Gary Morava
1974	John Crosby
1975	Tom Beach
1977	Ron Galimore
1978	Jim Hartung
1979	Ron Galimore
1980	Ron Galimore
1981	Ron Galimore
1982	Jim Hartung/Jim Mikus
1983	Chris Reigel
1984	Chris Reigel
1985	Scott Johnson
	Mark Oates

Vault *(Cont.)*

Year	Champion
1986	Scott Wilbanks
1987	John Sweeney
1988	John Sweeney/Bill Paul
1989	Bill Roth
1990	Lance Ringnald
1991	Scott Keswick
1992	Trent Dimas
1993	Bill Roth
1994	Keith Wiley
1995	David St. Pierre
1996	Blaine Wilson
1997	Blaine Wilson
1998	Brent Klaus
1999	Guard Young
2000	Blaine Wilson
2001	Jason Furr
2002	Paul Hamm
2003	Raj Bhavsar
2004	David Sender
2005	Sean Golden
2006	David Sender

Parallel Bars

Year	Champion
1963	Tom Seward
1964	Rusty Mitchell
1965	Glen Gailis
1966	Ray Hadley
1967	Katsuzoki Kanzaki
	Tom Goldsborough
1968	Yoshi Hayasaki
1969	Steve Hug
1970	Makoto Sakamoto
1971	Brent Simmons
1972	Yoshi Takei
1973	Marshall Avener
1974	Jim Ivicek
1975	Bart Conner
1977	Kurt Thomas
1978	Bart Conner
1979	Bart Conner
1980	Phil Cahoy/Larry Gerard
1981	Bart Conner
1982	Peter Vidmar
1983	Mitch Gaylord
1984	Peter Vidmar
	Mitch Gaylord
	Tim Daggett
1985	Tim Daggett
1986	Tim Daggett
1987	Scott Johnson
1988	D. Hayden/K. Davis
1989	Conrad Voorsanger
1990	Trent Dimas
1991	Scott Keswick
1992	Jair Lynch
1993	Chainey Umphrey
1994	Steve McCain
1995	John Roethlisberger
1996	Jair Lynch
1997	Blaine Wilson
1998	Blaine Wilson
1999	Jason Gatson
2000	Trent Wells
2001	Sean Townsend
2002	Sean Townsend

Parallel Bars *(Cont.)*

Year	Champion
2003	Jason Gatson
2004	Alexander Artemev
2005	D.J. Bucher
2006	Alexander Artemev

High Bars

Year	Champion
1963	Art Shurlock
1964	Glen Gailis
1965	Rusty Mitchell
1966	Katsuzoki Kanzaki
1967	Katsuzoki Kanzaki
	Jerry Fontana
1968	Yoshi Hayasaki
1969	Rich Grisby
1970	Makoto Sakamoto
1971	Yoshi Takei
1972	Tom Lindner
1973	John Crosby
1974	Brent Simmons
1975	Tom Beach
1977	Kurt Thomas
1978	Kurt Thomas
1979	Yoichi Tomita
1980	Jim Hartung
1981	Bart Conner
1982	Mitch Gaylord
1983	Mario McCutcheon
1984	Peter Vidmar
	Tim Daggett
	Mitch Gaylord
1985	Dan Hayden
1986	D. Hayden/D. Moriel
1987	David Moriel
1988	Dan Hayden
1989	Tim Ryan
1990	Trent Dimas
	Lance Ringnald
1991	Lance Ringnald
1992	Jair Lynch
1993	Steve McCain
1994	Scott Keswick
1995	John Roethlisberger
1996	Bill Roth
1997	Douglas Stibel
1998	Jason Gatson
1999	Jamie Natalie
2000	Trent Wells
	Jamie Natalie
2001	Daniel Diaz-Luong
2002	Blaine Wilson
2003	Paul Hamm
2004	Paul Hamm
2005	D.J. Bucher
2006	Chris Brooks

National Champions — Women

All-Around

Year	Champion
1963	Donna Schanezer
1965	Gail Daley
1966	Donna Schanezer
1968	Linda Scott
1969	Joyce Tanac Schroeder
1970	Cathy Rigby
1971	Joan Moore Gnat Linda Metheny Mulvihill
1972	Joan Moore Gnat Cathy Rigby
1973	Joan Moore Gnat
1974	Joan Moore Gnat
1975	Tammy Manville
1976	Denise Cheshire
1977	Donna Turnbow
1978	Kathy Johnson
1979	Leslie Pyfer
1980	Julianne McNamara
1981	Tracee Talavera
1982	Tracee Talavera
1983	Dianne Durham
1984	Mary Lou Retton
1985	Sabrina Mar
1986	Jennifer Sey
1987	Kristie Phillips
1988	Phoebe Mills
1989	Brandy Johnson
1990	Kim Zmeskal
1991	Kim Zmeskal
1992	Kim Zmeskal
1993	Shannon Miller
1994	Dominique Dawes
1995	Dominique Moceanu
1996	Shannon Miller
1997	V. Adler/ K. Powell
1998	Kristen Maloney
1999	Kristen Maloney
2000	Elise Ray
2001	Tasha Schwikert
2002	Tasha Schwikert
2003	Courtney Kupets
2004	Courtney Kupets/ Carly Patterson
2005	Anastasia Liukin
2006	Anastasia Liukin

Vault

Year	Champion
1963	Donna Schanezer
1965	Gail Daley
1966	Donna Schanezer
1968	Terry Spencer
1969	Joyce Tanac Schroeder Cleo Carver
1970	Cathy Rigby
1971	Joan Moore Gnat Adele Gleaves
1972	Cindy Eastwood
1973	Roxanne Pierce Mancha
1974	Dianne Dunbar

Vault *(Cont.)*

Year	Champion
1975	Kolleen Casey
1976	Debbie Wilcox
1977	Lisa Cawthron
1978	Rhonda Schwandt Sharon Shapiro
1979	Christa Canary
1980	J. McNamara/B. Kline
1981	Kim Neal
1982	Yumi Mordre
1983	Dianne Durham
1984	Mary Lou Retton
1985	Yolanda Mavity
1986	Joyce Wilborn
1987	Rhonda Faehn
1988	Rhonda Faehn
1989	Brandy Johnson
1990	Brandy Johnson
1991	Kerri Strug
1992	Kerri Strug
1993	Dominique Dawes
1994	Dominique Dawes
1995	Shannon Miller
1996	Dominique Dawes
1997	Vanessa Atler
1998	Dominique Moceanu
1999	Vanessa Atler
2000	Kristen Maloney
2001	Mohini Bhardwaj
2002	Elizabeth Tricase
2003	Annia Hatch
2004	Liz Tricase
2005	Alicia Sacramone
2006	Alicia Sacramone

Uneven Bars

Year	Champion
1963	Donna Schanezer
1965	Irene Haworth
1966	Donna Schanezer
1968	Linda Scott
1969	Joyce Tanac Schroeder Lisa Nelson
1970	Roxanne Pierce Mancha
1971	Joan Moore Gnat
1972	Cathy Rigby
1973	Roxanne Pierce Mancha
1974	Diane Dunbar
1975	Leslie Wolfsberger
1976	Leslie Wolfsberger
1977	Donna Turnbow
1978	Marcia Frederick
1979	Marcia Frederick
1980	Marcia Frederick
1981	Julianne McNamara
1982	Marie Roethlisberger
1983	Julianne McNamara
1984	Julianne McNamara
1985	Sabrina Mar
1986	Marie Roethlisberger
1987	Melissa Marlowe
1988	Chelle Stack

Uneven Bars *(Cont.)*

Year	Champion
1989	Chelle Stack
1990	Sandy Woolsey
1991	Elisabeth Crandall
1992	Dominique Dawes
1993	Shannon Miller
1994	Dominique Dawes
1995	Dominique Dawes
1996	Dominique Dawes
1997	Kristy Powell
1998	Elise Ray
1999	Jamie Dantzscher Jennie Thompson
2000	Elise Ray
2001	Katie Heenan
2002	Tasha Schwikert
2003	Katie Heenan
2004	Courtney Kupets
2005	Anastasia Liukin
2006	Anastasia Liukin

Balance Beam

Year	Champion
1963	Leissa Krol
1965	Gail Daley
1966	Irene Haworth Linda Scott
1968	Linda Scott
1969	Lonna Woodward
1970	Joyce Tanac Schroeder
1971	Linda Metheny Mulvihill
1972	Kim Chace
1973	Nancy Thies Marshall
1974	Joan Moore Gnat
1975	Kyle Gayner
1976	Carrie Englert
1977	Donna Turnbow
1978	Christa Canary
1979	Heidi Anderson
1980	Kelly Garrison-Steves
1981	Tracee Talavera
1982	Julianne McNamara
1983	Dianne Durham
1984	Pam Bileck Tracee Talavera
1986	Angie Denkins
1987	Kristie Phillips
1985	Kelly Garrison-Steves
1988	Kelly Garrison-Steves
1989	Brandy Johnson
1990	Betty Okino
1991	Shannon Miller
1992	Kerri Strug Kim Zmeskal
1993	Dominique Dawes
1994	Dominique Dawes
1995	Doni Thompson Monica Flammer
1996	Dominique Dawes
1997	Kendall Beck
1998	Dominique Moceanu
1999	Vanessa Atler
2000	Alyssa Beckerman Amy Chow
2001	Tasha Schwikert

National Champions — Women *(Cont.)*

Balance Beam *(Cont.)*

Year	Champion
2002	Tasha Schwikert
2003	Hollie Vise
2004	Courtney Kupets
2005	Anastasia Liukin
2006	Anastasia Liukin

Floor Exercise

Year	Champion
1963	Donna Schanezer
1965	Gail Daley
1966	Donna Schanezer
1968	Linda Scott
1970	Cathy Rigby
1971	Joan Moore Gnat
	Linda Metheny
	Mulvihill
1972	Joan Moore Gnat
1973	Joan Moore Gnat

Floor Exercise *(Cont.)*

Year	Champion
1974	Joan Moore Gnat
1975	Kathy Howard
1976	Carrie Englert
1977	Kathy Johnson
1978	Kathy Johnson
1979	Heidi Anderson
1980	Beth Kline
1981	Michelle Goodwin
1982	Amy Koopman
1983	Dianne Durham
1984	Mary Lou Retton
1985	Sabrina Mar
1986	Yolanda Mavity
1987	Kristie Phillips
1988	Phoebe Mills
1989	Brandy Johnson
1990	Brandy Johnson

Floor Exercise *(Cont.)*

Year	Champion
1991	Kim Zmeskal
	Dominique Dawes
1992	Kim Zmeskal
1993	Shannon Miller
1994	Dominique Dawes
1995	Dominique Dawes
1996	Dominique Dawes
1997	Lindsay Wing
1998	Vanessa Atler
1999	Elise Ray
2000	Kristen Maloney
2001	Tabitha Yim
2002	Tasha Schwikert
2003	Ashley Postell
2004	Carly Patterson
2005	Alicia Sacramone
2006	Alicia Sacramone
	Randi Stageberg

Handball

National Four-Wall Champions

MEN

Year	Champion	Year	Champion	Year	Champion	Year	Champion
1919	Bill Ranft	1941	Joe Platak	1963	Oscar Obert	1985	Naty Alvarado
1920	Max Gold	1942	Jack Clemente	1964	Jimmy Jacobs	1986	Naty Alvarado
1921	Carl Haedge	1943	Joe Platak	1965	Jimmy Jacobs	1987	Naty Alvarado
1922	Art Shinners	1944	Frank Coyle	1966	Paul Haber	1988	Naty Alvarado
1923	Joe Murray	1945	Joe Platak	1967	Paul Haber	1989	Poncho Monreal
1924	Maynard Laswe	1946	Angelo Trutio	1968	Stuffy Singer	1990	Naty Alvarado
1925	Maynard Laswe	1947	Gus Lewis	1969	Paul Haber	1991	John Bike
1926	Maynard Laswe	1948	Gus Lewis	1970	Paul Haber	1992	Octavio Silveyra
1927	George Nelson	1949	Vic Hershkowitz	1971	Paul Haber	1993	David Chapman
1928	Joe Griffin	1950	Ken Schneider	1972	Fred Lewis	1994	Octavio Silveyra
1929	Al Banuet	1951	Walter Plakan	1973	Terry Muck	1995	David Chapman
1930	Al Banuet	1952	Vic Hershkowitz	1974	Fred Lewis	1996	David Chapman
1931	Al Banuet	1953	Bob Brady	1975	Fred Lewis	1997	Octavio Silveyra
1932	Angelo Trutio	1954	Vic Hershkowitz	1976	Fred Lewis	1998	David Chapman
1933	Sam Atcheson	1955	Jimmy Jacobs	1977	Naty Alvarado	1999	David Chapman
1934	Sam Atcheson	1956	Jimmy Jacobs	1978	Fred Lewis	2000	David Chapman
1935	Joe Platak	1957	Jimmy Jacobs	1979	Naty Alvarado	2001	Vince Munoz
1936	Joe Platak	1958	John Sloan	1980	Naty Alvarado	2002	David Chapman
1937	Joe Platak	1959	John Sloan	1981	Fred Lewis	2003	John Bike
1938	Joe Platak	1960	Jimmy Jacobs	1982	Naty Alvarado	2004	David Chapman
1939	Joe Platak	1961	John Sloan	1983	Naty Alvarado	2005	Paul Brady
1940	Joe Platak	1962	Oscar Obert	1984	Naty Alvarado	2006	Paul Brady

WOMEN

Year	Champion	Year	Champion	Year	Champion	Year	Champion
1980	Rosemary Bellini	1987	Rosemary Bellini	1994	Anna Engele	2001	Anna Christoff
1981	Rosemary Bellini	1988	Rosemary Bellini	1995	Anna Engele	2002	Priscilla Shumate
1982	Rosemary Bellini	1989	Anna Engele	1996	Anna Engele	2003	Lisa Gilmore
1983	Diane Harmon	1990	Anna Engele	1997	Lisa Fraser	2004	Yvonne August
1984	Rosemary Bellini	1991	Anna Engele	1998	Lisa Fraser	2005	Jennifer Schmitt
1985	Peanut Motal	1992	Lisa Fraser	1999	Anna Christoff	2006	Jennifer Schmitt
1986	Peanut Motal	1993	Anna Engele	2000	Priscilla Shumate		

Handball

National Three-Wall Champions

MEN

1950 .....Vic Hershkowitz	1965 .....Carl Obert	1980 .....Lou Russo	1995 .....David Chapman
1951 .....Vic Hershkowitz	1966 .....Marty Decatur	1981 .....Naty Alvarado	1996 .....Vince Munoz
1952 .....Vic Hershkowitz	1967 .....Carl Obert	1982 .....Naty Alvarado	1997 .....Vince Munoz
1953 .....Vic Herskkowitz	1968 .....Marty Decatur	1983 .....Naty Alvarado	1998 .....Vince Munoz
1954 .....Vic Hershkowitz	1969 .....Marty Decatur	1984 .....Naty Alvarado	1999 .....Vince Munoz
1955 .....Vic Hershkowitz	1970 .....Steve August	1985 .....Vern Roberts	2000 .....Vince Munoz
1956 .....Vic Hershkowitz	1971 .....Lou Russo	1986 .....Vern Roberts	2001 .....Vince Munoz
1957 .....Vic Hershkowitz	1972 .....Lou Russo	1987 .....Vern Roberts	2002 .....Vince Munoz
1958 .....Vic Hershkowitz	1973 .....Paul Haber	1988 .....Jon Kendler	2003 .....Vince Munoz
1959 .....Jimmy Jacobs	1974 .....Fred Lewis	1989 .....John Bike	2004 .....Sean Lenning
1960 .....Jimmy Jacobs	1975 .....Lou Russo	1990 .....Vince Munoz	2005 .....Vince Munoz
1961 .....Jimmy Jacobs	1976 .....Lou Russo	1991 .....John Bike	2006 .....Emmett Peixoto
1962 .....Oscar Obert	1977 .....Fred Lewis	1992 .....John Bike	
1963 .....Marty Decatur	1978 .....Fred Lewis	1993 .....Eric Klarman	
1964 .....Marty Decatur	1979 .....Naty Alvarado	1994 .....David Chapman	

WOMEN

1981 .....Allison Roberts	1988 .....Rosemary Bellini	1995 .....Allison Roberts	2002 ......Priscilla Shumate
1982 .....Allison Roberts	1989 .....Rosemary Bellini	1996 .....Anna Engele	2003 .....Lisa Gilmore
1983 .....Allison Roberts	1990 .....Rosemary Bellini	1997 .....Allison Roberts	2004 .....Jennifer Schmitt
1984 .....Rosemary Bellini	1991 .....Rosemary Bellini	1998 .....Anna Christoff	2005 .....Megan Mehilos
1985 .....Rosemary Bellini	1992 .....Anna Engele	1999 .....Allison Roberts	2006 .....Megan Mehilos
1986 .....Rosemary Bellini	1993 .....Anna Engele	2000 ......Priscilla Shumate	
1987 .....Rosemary Bellini	1994 .....Anna Engele	2001 .....Anna Christoff	

World Four-Wall Champions

1984 ....Merv Deckert, Canada	1997 ....John Bike Jr., United States
1986 ....Vern Roberts, United States	2000 ....David Chapman, United States
1988 ....Naty Alvarado, United States	2003 ....Paul Brady, Ireland
1991 ....Pancho Monreal, United States	2006 ....Paul Brady, Ireland
1994 ....David Chapman, United States	

Lacrosse

United States Club Lacrosse Association Champions

1960 ......Mt. Washington Club	1976 ......Mt. Washington Club	1992 ......Maryland Lacrosse Club
1961 ......Baltimore Lacrosse Club	1977 ......Mt. Washington Club	1993 ......Mt. Washington Club
1962 ......Mt. Washington Club	1978 ......Long Island Athletic Club	1994 ......LI-Hofstra Lacrosse Club
1963 ......University Club	1979 ......Maryland Lacrosse Club	1995 ......Mt. Washington Club
1964 ......Mt. Washington Club	1980 ......Long Island Athletic Club	1996 ......LI-Hofstra Lacrosse Club
1965 ......Mt. Washington Club	1981 ......Long Island Athletic Club	1997 ......LI-Hofstra Lacrosse Club
1966 ......Mt. Washington Club	1982 ......Maryland Lacrosse Club	1998 ......LI-Hofstra Lacrosse Club
1967 ......Mt. Washington Club	1983 ......Maryland Lacrosse Club	1999 ......New York Athletic Club
1968 ......Long Island Athletic Club	1984 ......Maryland Lacrosse Club	2000 ......Team Toyota (Baltimore)
1969 ......Long Island Athletic Club	1985 ......LI-Hofstra Lacrosse Club	2001 ......LI Lacrosse Club
1970 ......Long Island Athletic Club	1986 ......LI-Hofstra Lacrosse Club	2002 ......Single Source Solutions
1971 ......Long Island Athletic Club	1987 ......LI-Hofstra Lacrosse Club	2003 ......Single Source Solutions
1972 ......Carling	1988 ......Maryland Lacrosse Club	2004 ......Single Source Solutions
1973 ......Long Island Athletic Club	1989 ......LI-Hofstra Lacrosse Club	2005 ......Team Source (Annapolis)
1974 ......Long Island Athletic Club	1990 ......Mt. Washington Club	2006 ....MAB Paints (Philadelphia)
1975 ......Mt. Washington Club	1991 ......Mt. Washington Club	

National Lacrosse League Champions*

1987 ......Baltimore Thunder	1994 ......Philadelphia Wings	2001 ......Philadelphia Wings
1988 ......New Jersey Saints	1995 ......Philadelphia Wings	2002 ......Toronto Rock
1989 ......Philadelphia Wings	1996 ......Buffalo Bandits	2003 ......Toronto Rock
1990 ......Philadelphia Wings	1997 ......Rochester Knighthawks	2004 ......Calgary Roughnecks
1991 ......Detroit Turbos	1998 ......Philadelphia Wings	2005 ......Toronto Rock
1992 ......Buffalo Bandits	1999 ......Toronto Rock	2006 ......Colorado Mammoth
1993 ......Buffalo Bandits	2000 ......Toronto Rock	

*Indoor league formerly known as the Eagle Pro Box Lacrosse League, and the Major Indoor Lacrosse League.

Major League Lacrosse

2001 .....Long Island Lizards	2003 .....Long Island Lizards	2005 .....Baltimore Bayhawks
2002 .....Baltimore Bayhawks	2004 .....Philadelphia Barrage	2006 .....Philadelphia Barrage

Little League Baseball

Little League World Series Champions

CYear	Champion	Runner-Up	Score	Year	Champion	Runner-Up	Score
1947	Williamsport, Pa.	Lock Haven, Pa.	16–7	1977	Kao-Hsiung, Taiwan	El Cajun, Calif.	7–2
1948	Lock Haven, Pa.	St. Petersburg, Fla.	6–5	1978	Pin-Tung, Taiwan	Danville, Calif.	11–1
1949	Hammonton, N.J.	Pensacola, Fla.	5–0	1979	Hsien, Taiwan	Campbell, Calif.	2–1
1950	Houston, Tex.	Bridgeport, Conn.	2–1	1980	Hua Lian, Taiwan	Tampa, Fla.	4–3
1951	Stamford, Conn.	Austin, Tex.	3–0	1981	Tai-Chung, Taiwan	Tampa, Fla.	4–2
1952	Norwalk, Conn.	Monongahela, Pa.	4–3	1982	Kirkland, Wash.	Hsien, Taiwan	6–0
1953	Birmingham, AL	Schenectady, N.Y.	1–0	1983	Marietta, Ga.	Barahona, D.Rep.	3–1
1954	Schenectady, N.Y.	Colton, Calif.	7–5	1984	Seoul, S. Korea	Altamonte Sgs, Fla.	6–2
1955	Morrisville, Pa.	Merchantville, N.J.	4–3	1985	Seoul, S. Korea	Mexicali, Mex.	7–1
1956	Roswell, NM	Merchantville, N.J.	3–1	1986	Tainan Park, Taiwan	Tucson, Ariz.	12–0
1957	Monterrey, Mex.	LaMesa, Calif.	4–0	1987	Hua Lian, Taiwan	Irvine, Calif.	21–1
1958	Monterrey, Mex.	Kankakee, Ill.	10–1	1988	Tai-Chung, Taiwan	Pearl City, Hawaii	10–0
1959	Hamtramck, Mich.	Auburn, Calif.	12–0	1989	Trumbull, Conn.	Kaohsiung, Taiwan	5–2
1960	Levittown, Pa.	Ft. Worth, Tex.	5–0	1990	Taipei, Taiwan	Shippensburg, Pa.	9–0
1961	El Cajon, Calif.	El Campo, Tex.	4–2	1991	Tai-Chung, Taiwan	San Ramon Vly, Calif.	
1962	San Jose, Calif.	Kankakee, Ill.	3–0				11–0
1963	Granada Hills, Calif.	Stratford, Conn.	2–1	1992*	Long Beach, Calif.	Zamboanga, Phil.	6–0
1964	Staten Island, N.Y.	Monterrey, Mex.	4–0	1993	Long Beach, Calif.	David Chiriqui, Pan.	3–2
1965	Windsor Locks, Conn.	Stoney Creek, Can.		1994	Maracaibo, Venez.	Northridge, Calif.	4–3
			3–1	1995	Tainan, Taiwan	Sprint, Tex.	17–3
1966	Houston, Tex.	W. New York, N.J.	8–2	1996	Kao-Hsiung, Taiwan	Cranston, RI	13–3
1967	West Tokyo, Japan	Chicago, Ill.	4–1	1997	Guadalupe, Mex.	Mission Viejo, Calif.	5–4
1968	Osaka, Japan	Richmond, VA	1–0	1998	Toms River, N.J.	Kashima, Japan	12–9
1969	Taipei, Taiwan	Santa Clara, Calif.	5–0	1999	Osaka, Japan	Phenix City, AL	5–0
1970	Wayne, N.J.	Campbell, Calif.	2–0	2000	Maracaibo, Venez.	Bellaire, Tex.	3–2
1971	Tainan, Taiwan	Gary, Ind.	12–3	2001	Tokyo, Japan	Apopka, Fla.	2–1
1972	Taipei, Taiwan	Hammond, Ind.	6–0	2002	Louisville, Ky.	Sendai, Japan	1–0
1973	Tainan City, Taiwan	Tucson, Ariz.	12–0	2003	Tokyo, Japan	Boynton Beach, Fla.	10–1
1974	Kao-Hsiung, Taiwan	El Cajun, Calif.	7–2	2004	Willemstad, Curacao	Thousand Oaks, Calif.	5–2
1975	Lakewood, N.J.	Tampa, Fla.	4–3	2005	West Oahu, Hawaii	Willemstad, Curacao	7–6
1976	Tokyo, Japan	Campbell, Calif.	10–3	2006	Columbus, Georgia	Kawaguchi, Japan	2–1

*Long Beach declared a 6–0 winner after the international tournament committee determined that Zamboanga City had used players that were not within its city limits.

Motor Boat Racing

American Boat Racing Association Gold Cup Champions

Year	Boat	Driver	Avg MPH	Year	Boat	Driver	Avg MPH
1904	Standard (June)	Carl Riotte	23.160	1927	Greenwich Folly	George Townsend	47.662
1904	Vingt-et-Un II (Sep)	W. Sharpe Kilmer	24.900	1928	No race		
1905	Chip I	J. Wainwright	15.000	1929	Imp	Richard Hoyt	48.662
1906	Chip II	J. Wainwright	25.000	1930	Hotsy Totsy	Vic Kliesrath	52.673
1907	Chip II	J. Wainwright	23.903	1931	Hotsy Totsy	Vic Kliesrath	53.602
1908	Dixie II	E.J. Schroeder	29.938	1932	Delphine IV	Bill Horn	57.775
1909	Dixie II	E.J. Schroeder	29.590	1933	El Lagarto	George Reis	56.260
1910	Dixie III	F.K. Burnham	32.473	1934	El Lagarto	George Reis	55.000
1911	MIT II	J.H. Hayden	37.000	1935	El Lagarto	George Reis	55.056
1912	P.D.Q. II	A.G. Miles	39.462	1936	Impshi	Kaye Don	45.735
1913	Ankle Deep	Cas Mankowski	42.779	1937	Notre Dame	Clell Perry	63.675
1914	Baby Speed Demon II	Jim Blackton & Bob Edgren	48.458	1938	Alagi	Theo Rossi	64.340
1915	Miss Detroit	Johnny Milot & Jack Beebe	37.656	1939	My Sin	Z.G. Simmons Jr.	66.133
				1940	Hotsy Totsy III	Sidney Allen	48.295
1916	Miss Minneapolis	Bernard Smith	48.860	1941	My Sin	Z.G. Simmons Jr.	52.509
1917	Miss Detroit II	Gar Wood	54.410	1942–45	No race	—	
1918	Miss Detroit II	Gar Wood	51.619	1946	Tempo VI	Guy Lombardo	68.132
1919	Miss Detroit III	Gar Wood	42.748	1947	Miss Peps V	Danny Foster	57.000
1920	Miss America I	Gar Wood	62.022	1948	Miss Great Lakes	Danny Foster	46.845
1921	Miss America I	Gar Wood	52.825	1949	My Sweetie	Bill Cantrell	73.612
1922	Packard Chriscraft	J.G. Vincent	40.253	1950	Slo-Mo-Shun IV	Ted Jones	78.216
1923	Packard Chriscraft	Caleb Bragg	43.867	1951	Slo-Mo-Shun V	Lou Fageol	90.871
1924	Baby Bootlegger	Caleb Bragg	45.302	1952	Slo-Mo-Shun IV	Stan Dollar	79.923
1925	Baby Bootlegger	Caleb Bragg	47.240	1953	Slo-Mo-Shun IV	Joe Taggart & Lou Fageol	99.108
1926	Greenwich Folly	George Townsend	47.984	1954	Slo-Mo-Shun IV	Joe Taggart & Lou Fageol	92.613

American Boat Racing Association Gold Cup Champions *(Cont.)*

Year	Boat	Driver	Avg MPH	Year	Boat	Driver	Avg MPH
1955	Gale V	Lee Schoenith	99.552	1982	Atlas Van Lines	Chip Hanauer	120.050
1956	Miss Thriftaway	Bill Muncey	96.552	1983	Atlas Van Lines	Chip Hanauer	118.507
1957	Miss Thriftaway	Bill Muncey	101.787	1984	Atlas Van Lines	Chip Hanauer	130.175
1958	Hawaii Kai III	Jack Regas	103.000	1985	Miller American	Chip Hanauer	120.643
1959	Maverick	Bill Stead	104.481	1986	Miller American	Chip Hanauer	116.523
1960	No race	—	—	1987	Miller American	Chip Hanauer	127.620
1961	Miss Century 21	Bill Muncey	99.678	1988	Miss Circus Circus	Chip Hanauer & Jim Prevost	123.756
1962	Miss Century 21	Bill Muncey	100.710				
1963	Miss Bardahl	Ron Musson	105.124	1989	Miss Budweiser	Tom D'Eath	131.209
1964	Miss Bardahl	Ron Musson	103.433	1990	Miss Budweiser	Tom D'Eath	143.176
1965	Miss Bardahl	Ron Musson	103.132	1991	Winston Eagle	Mark Tate	137.771
1966	Tahoe Miss	Mira Slovak	93.019	1992	Miss Budweiser	Chip Hanauer	136.282
1967	Miss Bardahl	Bill Shumacher	101.484	1993	Miss Budweiser	Chip Hanauer	141.195
1968	Miss Bardahl	Bill Shumacher	108.173	1994	Smokin' Joe Camel	Mark Tate	145.260
1969	Miss Budweiser	Bill Sterett	98.504	1995	Miss Budweiser	Chip Hanauer	149.160
1970	Miss Budweiser	Dean Chenoweth	99.562	1996	PICO American Dream	Dave Villwock	149.328
				1997	Miss Budweiser	Dave Villwock	129.366
1971	Miss Madison	Jim McCormick	98.043	1998	Miss Budweiser	Dave Villwock	140.309
1972	Atlas Van Lines	Bill Muncey	104.277	1999	Miss PICO	Chip Hanauer	152.591
1973	Miss Budweiser	Dean Chenoweth	99.043	2000	Miss Budweiser	Dave Villwock	162.850
				2001	Miss Tubby's Subs	Michael Hanson	140.519
1974	Pay 'n Pak	George Henley	104.428	2002	Miss Budweiser	Dave Villwock	143.093
1975	Pay 'n Pak	George Henley	108.921	2003	Miss Fox Hills	Mitch Evans	144.152
1976	Miss U.S.	Tom D'Eath	100.412	2004	Miss Detroit Yacht Club	Nate Brown	141.195
1977	Atlas Van Lines	Bill Muncey	111.822				
1978	Atlas Van Lines	Bill Muncey	111.412	2005	Miss Al Deeby Dodge	Terry Troxell	142.448
1979	Atlas Van Lines	Bill Muncey	100.765				
1980	Miss Budweiser	Dean Chenoweth	106.932	2006	Miss Beccon Plumbing	Jean Theoret	142.441
1981	Miss Budweiser	Dean Chenoweth	116.932				

Hydro-Prop* Annual Champion Drivers

Year	Driver	Boat	Wins	Year	Driver	Boat	Wins
1947	Danny Foster	Miss Peps V	6	1978	Bill Muncey	Atlas Van Lines	6
1948	Dan Arena	Such Crust	2	1979	Bill Muncey	Atlas Van Lines	7
1949	Bill Cantrell	My Sweetie	7	1980	Dean Chenoweth	Miss Budweiser	5
1950	Dan Foster	Such Crust/DaphneX	2	1981	Dean Chenoweth	Miss Budweiser	6
1951	Chuck Thompson	Miss Pepsi	5	1982	Chip Hanauer	Atlas Van Lines	5
1952	Chuck Thompson	Miss Pepsi	3	1983	Chip Hanauer	Atlas Van Lines	3
1953	Lee Schoenith	Gale II	1	1984	Jim Kropfeld	Miss Budweiser	6
1954	Lee Schoenith	Gale V	4	1985	Chip Hanauer	Miller American	5
1955	Lee Schoenith	Gale V/Wha Hoppen	1	1986	Jim Kropfeld	Miss Budweiser	3
1956	Russ Schleeh	Shanty I	3	1987	Jim Kropfeld	Miss Budweiser	5
1957	Jack Regas	Hawaii Kai III	5	1988	Tom D'Eath	Miss Budweiser	4
1958	Mira Slovak	Bardah/Miss Buren	3	1989	Chip Hanauer	Miss Circus Circus	3
1959	Bill Stead	Maverick	5	1990	Chip Hanauer	Miss Circus Circus	6
1960	Bill Muncey	Miss Thriftway	4	1991	Mark Tate	Winston/Oberto	3
1961	Bill Muncey	Miss Century 21	4	1992	Chip Hanauer	Miss Budweiser	7
1962	Bill Muncey	Miss Century 21	5	1993	Chip Hanauer	Miss Budweiser	7
1963	Bill Cantrell	Gale V	0	1994	Mark Tate	Smokin' Joe Camel	2
1964	Ron Musson	Miss Bardahl	4	1995	Mark Tate	Smokin' Joe Camel	4
1965	Ron Musson	Miss Bardahl	4	1996	Dave Villwock	PICO American Dream	6
1966	Mira Slovak	Tahoe Miss	4	1997	Mark Tate	Close Call	1
1967	Bill Schumacher	Miss Bardahl	6	1998	Dave Villwock	Miss Budweiser	8
1968	Bill Schumacher	Miss Bardahl	4	1999	Dave Villwock	Miss Budweiser	8
1969	Bill Sterett Sr.	Miss Budweiser	4	2000	Dave Villwock	Miss Budweiser	6
1970	Dean Chenoweth	Miss Budweiser	4	2001	Dave Villwock	Miss Budweiser	1
1971	Dean Chenoweth	Miss Budweiser	2	2002	Dave Villwock	Miss Budweiser	3
1972	Bill Muncey	Atlas Van Lines	6	2003	Dave Villwock	Miss Budweiser	2
1973	Mickey Remund	Pay 'n Pak	4	2004	Dave Villwock	Miss Budweiser	2
1974	George Henley	Pay 'n Pak	7	2005	Steve David	Miss Madison	0
1975	Billy Schumacher	Weisfield's	2	2006	Steve David	Miss Madison	1
1976	Bill Muncey	Atlas Van Lines	5				
1977	Mickey Remund	Miss Budweiser	3				

Hydro-Prop* Annual Champion Boats

Year	Boat	Owner	Wins	Year	Boat	Owner	Wins
1970	Miss Budweiser	Little-Friedkin	4	1989	Miss Budweiser	Bernie Little	4
1971	Miss Budweiser	Little-Friedkin	2	1990	Miss Circus Circus	Bill Bennett	6
1972	Atlas Van Lines	Joe Schoenith	6	1991	Miss Budweiser	Bernie Little	4
1973	Pay 'n Pak	Dave Heerensperger	4	1992	Miss Budweiser	Bernie Little	7
1974	Pay 'n Pak	Dave Heerensperger	7	1993	Miss Budweiser	Bernie Little	7
1975	Pay 'n Pak	Dave Heerensperger	5	1994	Miss Budweiser	Bernie Little	4
1976	Atlas Van Lines	Bill Muncey	5	1995	Miss Budweiser	Bernie Little	5
1977	Miss Budweiser	Bernie Little	3	1996	PICO Amer. Dream	Fred Leland	6
1978	Atlas Van Lines	Bill Muncey	6	1997	Miss Budweiser	Bernie Little	5
1979	Atlas Van Lines	Bill Muncey	7	1998	Miss Budweiser	Bernie Little	8
1980	Miss Budweiser	Bernie Little	5	1999	Miss Budweiser	Bernie Little	8
1981	Miss Budweiser	Bernie Little	6	2000	Miss Budweiser	Bernie Little	6
1982	Atlas Van Lines	Fran Muncey	5	2001	Miss Budweiser	Bernie Little	1
1983	Atlas Van Lines	Muncey-Lucero	3	2002	Miss Budweiser	Bernie Little	3
1984	Miss Budweiser	Bernie Little	6	2003	Miss Budweiser	Joe Little	2
1985	Miller American	Muncey-Lucero	5	2004	Miss Budweiser	Joe Little	2
1986	Miss Budweiser	Bernie Little	3	2005	Miss Elam	Erick Ellstrom	3
1987	Miss Budweiser	Bernie Little	5	2006	FormulaBoats.com II	Ted Porter	1
1988	Miss Budweiser	Bernie Little	4				

*Formerly known as Unlimited Hydroplane Racing Association.

Polo

United States Open Polo Champions

1904 ...Wanderers	1934 ...Templeton	1962 ...Santa Barbara	1985 ...Carter Ranch
1905–09 Not contested	1935 ...Greentree	1963 ...Tulsa	1986 ...Retama II
1910 ...Ranelagh	1936 ...Greentree	1964 ...Concar Oak Brook	1987 ...Aloha
1911 ...Not contested	1937 ...Old Westbury	1965 ...Oak Brook–	1988 ...Les Diables Bleus
1912 ...Cooperstown	1938 ...Old Westbury	Santa Barbara	1989 ...Les Diables Bleus
1913 ...Cooperstown	1939 ...Bostwick Field	1966 ...Tulsa	1990 ...Les Diables Bleus
1914 ...Meadow Brook	1940 ...Aknusti	1967 ...Bunntyco–	1991 ...Grant's Farm
Magpies	1941 ...Gulf Stream	Oak Brook	Manor
1915 ...Not contested	1942–45 Not contested	1968 ...Midland	1992 ...Hanalei Bay
1916 ...Meadow Brook	1946 ...Mexico	1969 ...Tulsa Greenhill	1993 ...Gehache
1917–18 Not contested	1947 ...Old Westbury	1970 ...Tulsa Greenhill	1994 ...Aspen
1919 ...Meadow Brook	1948 ...Hurricanes	1971 ...Oak Brook	1995 ...Outback
1920 ...Meadow Brook	1949 ...Hurricanes	1972 ...Milwaukee	1996 ...Outback
1921 ...Great Neck	1950 ...Bostwick	1973 ...Oak Brook	1997 ...Isla Carroll
1922 ...Argentine	1951 ...Milwaukee	1974 ...Milwaukee	1998 ...Esque
1923 ...Meadow Brook	1952 ...Beverly Hills	1975 ...Milwaukee	1999 ...Outback
1924 ...Midwick	1953 ...Meadow Brook	1976 ...Willow Bend	2000 ...Outback
1925 ...Orange County	1954 ...C.C.C.–Meadow	1977 ...Retama	2001 ...Outback
1926 ...Hurricanes	Brook	1978 ...Abercrombie &	2002 ...Team Coca Cola
1927 ...Sands Point	1955 ...C.C.C.	Kent	2003 ...C Spear
1928 ...Meadow Brook	1956 ...Brandywine	1979 ...Retama	2004 ...Isla Carroll
1929 ...Hurricanes	1957 ...Detroit	1980 ...Southern Hills	2005 ...White Birch
1930 ...Hurricanes	1958 ...Dallas	1981 ...Rolex A & K	2006 ...Las Monjitas
1931 ...Santa Paula	1959 ...Circle F	1982 ...Retama	
1932 ...Templeton	1960 ...Oak Brook–C.C.C.	1983 ...Ft. Lauderdale	
1933 ...Aurora	1961 ...Milwaukee	1984 ...Retama	

Top-Ranked Players

The United States Polo Association ranks its registered players from minus 2 to plus 10 goals, with 10-Goal players being the game's best. At present, the USPA recognizes eleven 10-Goal and twelve 9-Goal players:

10-GOAL		9-GOAL	
Mariano Aguerre	Juan Ignacio Merlos	Eduardo Novillo Astrada	Matias G. Magrini
Miguel Novillo Astrada	Sebastian Merlos	Francisco Bensadon	Agustin Merlos
Javier Novillo Astrada	Adam Snow	Lucas A. Criado	Pablo MacDonough
Michael Vincent Azzaro		Francisco de Narvaez	Facundo Pieres
Adolfo Cambiaso		Melo E. Fernandez-	Gonzalo Pieres Jr.
Carlos Gracida		Araujo	
Bautista Heguy		Guillermo M. Gracida Jr.	
Marcos Heguy		Eduardo Heguy	

Professional Rodeo Cowboys Association World Champions

All-Around

1929....Earl Thode	1950....Bill Linderman	1969....Larry Mahan	1988....Dave Appleton
1930....Clay Carr	1951....Casey Tibbs	1970....Larry Mahan	1989....Ty Murray
1931....John Schneider	1952....Harry Tompkins	1971....Phil Lyne	1990....Ty Murray
1932....Donald Nesbit	1953....Bill Linderman	1972....Phil Lyne	1991....Ty Murray
1933....Clay Carr	1954....Buck Rutherford	1973....Larry Mahan	1992....Ty Murray
1934....Leonard Ward	1955....Casey Tibbs	1974....Tom Ferguson	1993....Ty Murray
1935....Everett Bowman	1956....Jim Shoulders	1975....Tom Ferguson	1994....Ty Murray
1936....John Bowman	1957....Jim Shoulders	1976....Tom Ferguson	1995....Joe Beaver
1937....Everett Bowman	1958....Jim Shoulders	1977....Tom Ferguson	1996....Joe Beaver
1938....Burel Mulkey	1959....Jim Shoulders	1978....Tom Ferguson	1997....Dan Mortensen
1939....Paul Carney	1960....Harry Tompkins	1979....Tom Ferguson	1998....Ty Murray
1940....Fritz Truan	1961....Benny Reynolds	1980....Paul Tierney	1999....Fred Whitfield
1941....Homer Pettigrew	1962....Tom Nesmith	1981....Jimmie Cooper	2000....Joe Beaver
1942....Gerald Roberts	1963....Dean Oliver	1982....Chris Lybbert	2001....Cody Ohl
1943....Louis Brooks	1964....Dean Oliver	1983....Roy Cooper	2002....Trevor Brazile
1944....Louis Brooks	1965....Dean Oliver	1984....Dee Picket	2003....Trevor Brazile
1947....Todd Whatley	1966....Larry Mahan	1985....Lewis Feild	2004....Trevor Brazile
1948....Gerald Roberts	1967....Larry Mahan	1986....Lewis Feild	2005....Ryan Jarrett
1949....Jim Shoulders	1968....Larry Mahan	1987....Lewis Feild	

Saddle Bronc Riding

1929....Earl Thode	1950....Bill Linderman	1970....Dennis Reiners	1990....Robert Etbauer
1930....Clay Carr	1951....Casey Tibbs	1971....Bill Smith	1991....Robert Etbauer
1931....Earl Thode	1952....Casey Tibbs	1972....Mel Hyland	1992....Billy Etbauer
1932....Peter Knight	1953....Casey Tibbs	1973....Bill Smith	1993....Dan Mortensen
1933....Peter Knight	1954....Casey Tibbs	1974....John McBeth	1994....Dan Mortensen
1934....Leonard Ward	1955....Deb Copenhaver	1975....Monty Henson	1995....Dan Mortensen
1935....Peter Knight	1956....Deb Copenhaver	1976....Monty Henson	1996....Billy Etbauer
1936....Peter Knight	1957....Alvin Nelson	1977....Bobby Berger	1997....Dan Mortensen
1937....Burel Mulkey	1958....Marty Wood	1978....Joe Marvel	1998....Dan Mortensen
1938....Burel Mulkey	1959....Casey Tibbs	1979....Bobby Berger	1999....Billy Etbauer
1939....Fritz Truan	1960....Enoch Walker	1980....Clint Johnson	2000....Billy Etbauer
1940....Fritz Truan	1961....Winston Bruce	1981....B. Gjermundson	2001....Tom Reeves
1941....Doff Aber	1962....Kenny McLean	1982....Monty Henson	2002....Glen O'Neil
1942....Doff Aber	1963....Guy Weeks	1983....B. Gjermundson	2003....Dan Mortensen
1943....Louis Brooks	1964....Marty Wood	1984....B. Gjermundson	2004....Billy Etbauer
1944....Louis Brooks	1965....Shawn Davis	1985....B. Gjermundson	2005....Jeffery Willert
1947....Carl Olson	1966....Marty Wood	1986....Bud Munroe	
1948....Gene Pruett	1967....Shawn Davis	1987....Clint Johnson	
1949....Casey Tibbs	1968....Shawn Davis	1988....Clint Johnson	
	1969....Bill Smith	1989....Clint Johnson	

Bareback Riding

1932....Smoky Snyder	1954....Eddy Akridge	1974....Joe Alexander	1994....Marvin Garrett
1933....Nate Waldrum	1955....Eddy Akridge	1975....Joe Alexander	1995....Marvin Garrett
1934....Leonard Ward	1956....Jim Shoulders	1976....Joe Alexander	1996....Mark Garrett
1935....Frank Schneider	1957....Jim Shoulders	1977....Joe Alexander	1997....Eric Mouton
1936....Smoky Snyder	1958....Jim Shoulders	1978....Bruce Ford	1998....Mark Gomes
1937....Paul Carney	1959....Jack Buschbom	1979....Bruce Ford	1999....Lan LaJeunesse
1938....Pete Grubb	1960....Jack Buschbom	1980....Bruce Ford	2000....Jeffrey Collins
1939....Paul Carney	1961....Eddy Akridge	1981....J.C. Trujillo	2001....Lan LaJeunesse
1940....Carl Dossey	1962....Ralph Buell	1982....Bruce Ford	2002....Bobby Mote
1941....George Mills	1963....John Hawkins	1983....Bruce Ford	2003....Will Lowe
1942....Louis Brooks	1964....Jim Houston	1984....Larry Peabody	2004....Kelly Timberman
1943....Bill Linderman	1965....Jim Houston	1985....Lewis Feild	2005....Will Lowe
1944....Louis Brooks	1966....Paul Mayo	1986....Lewis Feild	
1947....Larry Finley	1967....Clyde Vamvoras	1987....Bruce Ford	
1948....Sonny Tureman	1968....Clyde Vamvoras	1988....Marvin Garrett	
1949....Jack Buschbom	1969....Gary Tucker	1989....Marvin Garrett	
1950....Jim Shoulders	1970....Paul Mayo	1990....Chuck Logue	
1951....Casey Tibbs	1971....Joe Alexander	1991....Clint Corey	
1952....Harry Tompkins	1972....Joe Alexander	1992....Wayne Herman	
1953....Eddy Akridge	1973....Joe Alexander	1993....Deb Greenough	

Professional Rodeo Cowboys Association World Champions (Cont.)

Bull Riding

1929....John Schneider	1949....Harry Tompkins	1969....Doug Brown	1989....Tuff Hedeman
1930....John Schneider	1950....Harry Tompkins	1970....Gary Leffew	1990....Jim Sharp
1931....Smokey Snyder	1951....Jim Shoulders	1971....Bill Nelson	1991....Tuff Hedeman
1932....John Schneider	1952....Harry Tompkins	1972....John Quintana	1992....Cody Custer
1932....Smokey Snyder	1953....Todd Whatley	1973....Bobby Steiner	1993....Ty Murray
John Schneider	1954....Jim Shoulders	1974....Don Gay	1994....Daryl Mills
1933....Frank Schneider	1955....Jim Shoulders	1975....Don Gay	1995....Jerome Davis
1934....Frank Schneider	1956....Jim Shoulders	1976....Don Gay	1996....Terry West
1935....Smokey Snyder	1957....Jim Shoulders	1977....Don Gay	1997....Scott Mendes
1936....Smokey Snyder	1958....Jim Shoulders	1978....Don Gay	1998....Ty Murray
1937....Smokey Snyder	1959....Jim Shoulders	1979....Don Gay	1999....Mike White
1938....Kid Fletcher	1960....Harry Tompkins	1980....Don Gay	2000....Cody Hancock
1939....Dick Griffith	1961....Ronnie Rossen	1981....Don Gay	2001....Blue Stone
1940....Dick Griffith	1962....Freckles Brown	1982....Charles Sampson	2002....Blue Stone
1941....Dick Griffith	1963....Bill Kornell	1983....Cody Snyder	2003....Terry West
1942....Dick Griffith	1964....Bob Wegner	1984....Don Gay	2004....Dustin Elliott
1943....Ken Roberts	1965....Larry Mahan	1985....Ted Nuce	2005....Matt Austin
1944....Ken Roberts	1966....Ronnie Rossen	1986....Tuff Hedeman	
1947....Wag Blessing	1967....Larry Mahan	1987....Lane Frost	
1948....Harry Tompkins	1968....George Paul	1988....Jim Sharp	

Calf Roping

1929:...Everett Bowman	1951....Don McLaughlin	1971....Phil Lyne	1991....Fred Whitfield
1930:...Jake McClure	1952....Don McLaughlin	1972....Phil Lyne	1992....Joe Beaver
1931....Herb Meyers	1953....Don McLaughlin	1973....Ernie Taylor	1993....Joe Beaver
1932....Richard Merchant	1954....Don McLaughlin	1974....Tom Ferguson	1994....Herbert Theriot
1933....Bill McFarlane	1955....Dean Oliver	1975....Jeff Copenhaver	1995....Fred Whitfield
1934....Irby Mundy	1956....Ray Wharton	1976....Roy Cooper	1996....Fred Whitfield
1935....Everett Bowman	1957....Don McLaughlin	1977....Roy Cooper	1997....Cody Ohl
1936....Clyde Burk	1958....Dean Oliver	1978....Roy Cooper	1998....Cody Ohl
1937....Everett Bowman	1959....Jim Bob Altizer	1979....Paul Tierney	1999....Fred Whitfield
1938....Burel Mulkey	1960....Dean Oliver	1980....Roy Cooper	2000....Fred Whitfield
1939....Toots Mansfield	1961....Dean Oliver	1981....Roy Cooper	2001....Cody Ohl
1940....Toots Mansfield	1962....Dean Oliver	1982....Roy Cooper	2002...Fred Whitfield
1941....Toots Mansfield	1963....Dean Oliver	1983....Roy Cooper	2003....Cody Ohl
1942....Clyde Burk	1964....Dean Oliver	1984....Roy Cooper	2004....Monty Lewis
1943....Toots Mansfield	1965....Glen Franklin	1985....Joe Beaver	2005....Fred Whitfield
1944....Clyde Burk	1966....Junior Garrison	1986....Chris Lybbert	
1947....Troy Fort	1967....Glen Franklin	1987....Joe Beaver	
1948....Toots Mansfield	1968....Glen Franklin	1988....Joe Beaver	
1949....Troy Fort	1969....Dean Oliver	1989....Rabe Rabon	
1950....Toots Mansfield	1970....Junior Garrison	1990....Troy Pruitt	

Steer Wrestling

1929....Gene Ross	1951....Dub Phillips	1971....Billy Hale	1991....Ote Berry
1930....Everett Bowman	1952....Harley May	1972....Roy Duvall	1992....Mark Roy
1931....Gene Ross	1953....Ross Dollarhide	1973....Bob Marshall	1993....Steve Duhon
1932....Hugh Bennett	1954....James Bynum	1974....Tommy Puryear	1994....Blaine Pederson
1933....Everett Bowman	1955....Benny Combs	1975....F. Shepperson	1995....Ote Berry
1934....Shorty Ricker	1956....Harley May	1976....Tom Ferguson	1996....Chad Bedell
1935....Everett Bowman	1957....Clark McEntire	1977....Larry Ferguson	1997....Brad Gleason
1936....Jack Kerschner	1958....James Bynum	1978....Byron Walker	1998....Mike Smith
1937....Gene Ross	1959....Harry Charters	1979....Stan Williamson	1999....Mickey Gee
1938....Everett Bowman	1960....Bob A. Robinson	1980....Butch Myers	2000....Frank Thompson
1939....Harry Hart	1961....Jim Bynum	1981....Byron Walker	2001....Rope Myers
1940....Homer Pettigrew	1962....Tom Nesmith	1982....Stan Williamson	2002....Sid Steiner
1941....Hub Whiteman	1963....Jim Bynum	1983....Joel Edmondson	2003....Teddy Johnson
1942....Homer Pettigrew	1964....C.R. Boucher	1984....John W. Jones	2004....Luke Branquinho
1943....Homer Pettigrew	1965....Harley May	1985....Ote Berry	2005....Lee Graves
1944....Homer Pettigrew	1966....Jack Roddy	1986....Steve Duhon	
1947....Todd Whatley	1967....Roy Duvall	1987....Steve Duhon	
1948....Homer Pettigrew	1968....Jack Roddy	1988....John W. Jones	
1949....Bill McGuire	1969....Roy Duvall	1989....John W. Jones	
1950....Bill Linderman	1970....John W. Jones	1990....Ote Berry	

Professional Rodeo Cowboys Association World Champions *(Cont.)*

Team Roping

1929....Charles Maggini	1952....Asbury Schell	1975....Leo Camarillo	1996....Steve Purcella
1930....Norman Cowan	1953....Ben Johnson	1976....Leo Camarillo	Steve Northcott
1931....Arthur Beloat	1954....Eddie Schell	1977....Jerold Camarillo	1997....Speed Williams
1932....Ace Gardner	1955....Vern Castro	1978....Doyle Gellerman	Rich Skelton
1933....Roy Adams	1956....Dale Smith	1979....Allen Bach	1998....Speed Williams
1934....Andy Jauregui	1957....Dale Smith	1980....Tee Woolman	Rich Skelton
1935....Lawrence Conltk	1958....Ted Ashworth	1981....Walt Woodard	1999....Speed Williams
1936....John Rhodes	1959....Jim Rodriguez Jr.	1982....Tee Woolman	Rich Skelton
1937....Asbury Schell	1960....Jim Rodriguez Jr.	1983....Leo Camarillo	2000....Speed Williams
1938....John Rhodes	1961....Al Hooper	1984....Dee Pickett	Rich Skelton
1939....Asbury Schell	1962....Jim Rodriguez Jr.	1985....Jake Barnes	2001....Speed Williams
1940....Pete Grubb	1963....Les Hirdes	1986....Clay O. Cooper	Rich Skelton
1941....Jim Hudson	1964....Bill Hamilton	1987....Clay O. Cooper	2002....Speed Williams
1942....Verne Castro	1965....Jim Rodriguez Jr.	1988....Jake Barnes	Rich Skelton
Vic Castro	1966....Ken Luman	1989....Jake Barnes	2003....Speed Williams
1943....Mark Hull	1967....Joe Glenn	1990....Allen Bach	Rich Skelton
Leonard Block	1968....Art Arnold	1991....Bob Harris	2004....Speed Williams
1944....Murphy Chaney	1969....Jerold Camarillo	1992....Clay O. Cooper	Rich Skelton
1947....Jim Brister	1970....John Miller	1993....Bobby Hurley	2005....Clay Tryan,
1948....Joe Glenn	1971....John Miller	1994....Jake Barnes	Patrick Smith
1949....Ed Yanez	1972....Leo Camarillo	Clay O. Cooper	
1950....Buck Sorrels	1973....Leo Camarillo	1995....Bobby Hurley	
1951....Olan Sims	1974....H.P. Evetts	Allen Bach	

Steer Roping

1929....Charles Maggini	1949....Shoat Webster	1969....Walter Arnold	1989....Guy Allen
1930....Clay Carr	1950....Shoat Webster	1970....Don McLaughlin	1990....Phil Lyne
1931....Andy Jauregui	1951....Everett Shaw	1971....Olin Young	1991....Guy Allen
1932....George Weir	1952....Buddy Neal	1972....Allen Keller	1992....Guy Allen
1933....John Bowman	1953....Ike Rude	1973....Roy Thompson	1993....Guy Allen
1934....John McEntire	1954....Shoat Webster	1974....Olin Young	1994....Guy Allen
1935....Richard Merchant	1955....Shoat Webster	1975....Roy Thompson	1995....Guy Allen
1936....John Bowman	1956....Jim Snively	1976....Marvin Cantrell	1996....Guy Allen
1937....Everett Bowman	1957....Clark McEntire	1977....Buddy Cockrell	1997....Guy Allen
1938....Hugh Bennett	1958....Clark McEntire	1978....Sonny Worrell	1998....Guy Allen
1939....Dick Truitt	1959....Everett Shaw	1979....Gary Good	1999....Guy Allen
1940....Clay Carr	1960....Don McLaughlin	1980....Guy Allen	2000....Guy Allen
1941....Ike Rude	1961....Clark McEntire	1981....Arnold Felts	2001....Guy Allen
1942....King Merritt	1962....Everett Shaw	1982....Guy Allen	2002....Buster Record
1943....Tom Rhodes	1963....Don McLaughlin	1983....Roy Cooper	2003....Guy Allen
1944....Tom Rhodes	1964....Sonny Davis	1984....Guy Allen	2004....Guy Allen
1945....Everett Shaw	1965....Sonney Wright	1985....Jim Davis	2005....Scott Snedecor
1946....Everett Shaw	1966....Sonny Davis	1986....Jim Davis	
1947....Ike Rude	1967....Jim Bob Altizer	1987....Shaun Burchett	
1948....Everett Shaw	1968....Sonny Davis	1988....Shaun Burchett	

Note: In 1945–46 champions were crowned only in Steer Roping.

Rowing

National Collegiate Rowing Champions

MEN

1985 ....Harvard	1994 ....Brown	2003 ....Harvard
1986 ....Wisconsin	1995 ....Brown	2004 ....Harvard
1987 ....Harvard	1996 ....Princeton	2005 ....Harvard
1988 ....Harvard	1997 ....Washington	2006 ....California
1989 ....Harvard	1998 ....Princeton	
1990 ....Wisconsin	1999 ....California	
1991 ....Pennsylvania	2000 ....California	
1992 ....Harvard	2001 ....California	
1993 ....Brown	2002 ....California	

National Collegiate Rowing Champions

WOMEN

1979 ....Yale	1989 ....Cornell	1999 ....Brown
1980 ....California	1990 ....Princeton	2000 ....Brown
1981 ....Washington	1991 ....Boston University	2001 ....Washington
1982 ....Washington	1992 ....Boston University	2002 ....Brown
1983 ....Washington	1993 ....Princeton	2003 ....Harvard
1984 ....Washington	1994 ....Princeton	2004 ....Brown
1985 ....Washington	1995 ....Princeton	2005 ....California
1986 ....Wisconsin	1996 ....Brown	2006 ....California
1987 ....Washington	1997 ....Washington	
1988 ....Washington	1998 ....Washington	

Rugby Union

National Men's Club Championship

Year	Winner	Runner-Up	Year	Winner	Runner-Up
1979	Old Blues (Calif.)	St. Louis Falcons	1994	Old Mission Beach A.C.	Life College (Ga.)
1980	Old Blues (Calif.)	St. Louis Falcons	1995	Potomac Athletic Club	Old Mission Beach
1981	Old Blues (Calif.)	Old Blue (N.Y.)			
1982	Old Blues (Calif.)	Denver Barbos	1996	Old Mission Beach A.C.	Old Blues (Calif.)
1983	Old Blues (Calif.)	Dallas Harlequins	1997	Gentlemen of Aspen	Old Blue (N.Y.)
1984	Dallas Harlequins	Los Angeles	1998	Gentlemen of Aspen	Old Blue (N.Y.)
1985	Milwaukee	Denver Barbos	1999	Gentlemen of Aspen	Golden Gate (Calif.)
1986	Old Blues (Calif.)	Old Blue (N.Y.)	2000	Gentlemen of Aspen	Hayward Griffins
1987	Old Blues (Calif.)	Pittsburgh	2001	San Mateo	New York A.C.
1988	Old Mission Beach A.C.	Milwaukee	2002	San Mateo	Austin
1989	Old Mission Beach A.C.	Philly/Whitemarsh	2003	Boston Irish Wolfhounds	San Mateo
1990	Denver Barbos	Old Blues (Calif.)	2004	Boston Irish Wolfhounds	Austin
1991	Old Mission Beach A.C.	Washington	2005	Santa Monica	Back Bay
1992	Old Blues (Calif.)	Mystic River (Mass.)	2006	Santa Monica	Boston Irish Wolfhounds
1993	Old Mission Beach A.C.	Milwaukee			

National Men's Collegiate Championship

Year	Winner	Runner-Up	Year	Winner	Runner-Up
1980	California	Air Force	1994	California	Navy
1981	California	Harvard	1995	California	Air Force
1982	California	Life College	1996	California	Penn St
1983	California	Air Force	1997	California	Penn St
1984	Harvard	Colorado	1998	California	Stanford
1985	California	Maryland	1999	California	Penn St
1986	California	Dartmouth	2000	California	Wyoming
1987	San Diego State	Air Force	2001	California	Penn St
1988	California	Dartmouth	2002	California	Utah
1989	Air Force	Long Beach	2003	Air Force	Harvard
1990	Air Force	Army	2004	California	Cal Poly SLO
1991	California	Army	2005	California	Utah
1992	California	Army	2006	California	BYU
1993	California	Air Force			

World Cup Championship

Year	Winner	Runner-Up	Year	Winner	Runner-Up
1987	New Zealand	France	1999	Australia	France
1991	Australia	England	2003	England	Australia
1995	South Africa	New Zealand			

Rugby League

American National Rugby League Champions

Year	Winner	Runner-Up
1998	Glen Mills Bulls	Philadelphia Bulldogs
1999	Glen Mills Bulls	New Jersey Sharks
2000	Glen Mills Bulls	Philadelphia Fight
2001	Glen Mills Bulls	Media Mantarays
2002	New York Knights	Glen Mills Bulls
2003	Connecticut Wildcats	Glen Mills Bulls
2004	Glen Mills Bulls	Connecticut Wildcats
2005	Glen Mills Bulls	Connecticut Wildcats

World Cup Championship

Year	Winner	Runner-Up	Host
1954	Great Britain	France	France
1957	Australia	International Team	Australia
1960	Great Britain	International Team	England
1968	Australia	France	Australia–New Zealand
1970	Great Britain	Australia	England
1972	Australia	Great Britain	France
1975	Australia	England	Worldwide
1977	Australia	Great Britain	Australia–New Zealand
1985–88	Australia	New Zealand	Worldwide
1989–92	Australia	Great Britain	Worldwide
1995	Australia	England	Great Britain
2000	Australia	New Zealand	G. Britain-Ireland-France

Sailing

America's Cup Champions

SCHOONERS AND J-CLASS BOATS

Year	Winner	Skipper	Series	Loser	Skipper
1851	America	Richard Brown			
1870	Magic	Andrew Comstock	1–0	Cambria, Great Britain	J. Tannock
1871	Columbia (2–1)	Nelson Comstock	4–1	Livonia, Great Britain	J.R. Woods
	Sappho (2–0)	Sam Greenwood			
1876	Madeleine	Josephus Williams	2–0	Countess of Dufferin, Canada	J.E. Ellsworth
1881	Mischief	Nathanael Clock	2–0	Atalanta, Canada	Alexander Cuthbert
1885	Puritan	Aubrey Crocker	2–0	Genesta, Great Britain	John Carter
1886	Mayflower	Martin Stone	2–0	Galatea, Great Britain	Dan Bradford
1887	Volunteer	Henry Haff	2–0	Thistle, Great Britain	John Barr
1893	Vigilant	William Hansen	3–0	Valkyrie II, Great Britain	William Granfield
1895	Defender	Henry Haff	3–0	Valkyrie III, Great Britain	William Granfield
1899	Columbia	Charles Barr	3–0	Shamrock I, Great Britain	Archie Hogarth
1901	Columbia	Charles Barr	3–0	Shamrock II, Great Britain	E.A. Sycamore
1903	Reliance	Charles Barr	3–0	Shamrock III, Great Britain	Bob Wringe
1920	Resolute	Charles F. Adams	3–2	Shamrock IV, Great Britain	William Burton
1930	Enterprise	Harold Vanderbilt	4–0	Shamrock V, Great Britain	Ned Heard
1934	Rainbow	Harold Vanderbilt	4–2	Endeavour, Great Britain	T.O.M. Sopwith
1937	Ranger	Harold Vanderbilt	4–0	Endeavour II, Great Britain	T.O.M. Sopwith

12-METER BOATS

Year	Winner	Skipper	Series	Loser	Skipper
1958	Columbia	Briggs Cunningham	4–0	Sceptre, Great Britain	Graham Mann
1962	Weatherly	Bus Mosbacher	4–1	Gretel, Australia	Jock Sturrock
1964	Constellation	Bob Bavier & Eric Ridder	4–0	Sovereign, Australia	Peter Scott
1967	Intrepid	Bus Mosbacher	4–0	Dame Pattie, Australia	Jock Sturrock
1970	Intrepid	Bill Ficker	4–1	Gretel II, Australia	Jim Hardy
1974	Courageous	Ted Hood	4–0	Southern Cross, Australia	John Cuneo
1977	Courageous	Ted Turner	4–0	Australia	Noel Robins
1980	Freedom	Dennis Conner	4–1	Australia	Jim Hardy
1983	Australia II	John Bertrand	4–3	Liberty, United States	Dennis Conner
1987	Stars & Stripes	Dennis Conner	4–0	Kookaburra III, Australia	Iain Murray

Sailing

America's Cup Champions (Cont.)

60-FOOT CATAMARAN vs 133-FOOT MONOHULL

Year	Winner	Skipper	Series	Loser	Skipper
1988	Stars & Stripes	Dennis Conner	2–0	New Zealand	David Barnes

75-FOOT MONOHULL (IACC)

Year	Winner	Skipper	Series	Loser	Skipper
1992	America3	Bill Koch	4–1	Il Moro di Venezia, Italy	Paul Cayard
1995	Black Magic I	Russell Coutts	5–0	Young America, United States	Dennis Conner
2000	New Zealand	Russell Coutts	5–0	Luna Rossa, Italy	Francesco de Angelis
2003	Swiss Alinghi	Russell Coutts	5–0	New Zealand	Dean Barker

Note: Winning entries have been from the United States every year but four: In 1983 an Australian vessel won, in 1995 and 2000 a vessel from New Zealand won and in 2003 a Swiss vessel won.

Shooting World Champions

Men

50M FREE RIFLE PRONE
1947 .....O. Sannes, Norway
1949 .....A.C. Jackson, U.S.
1952 .....A.C. Jackson, U.S.
1954 .....G. Boa, Canada
1958 .....M. Nordquist
1962 .....K. Wenk, W Germany
1966 .....D. Boyd, U.S.
1970 .....M. Fiess, S. Africa
1974 .....K. Bulan, Czechoslovakia
1978 .....A. Allan, Great Britain
1982 .....V. Danilschenko, USSR
1986 .....S. Bereczky, Hungary
1990 .....V. Bochkarev, USSR
1994 .....Venjie Li, China
1998 .....Thomas Tamas, U.S.
1999 .....Thomas Tamas, U.S.
2000 .....Siarhei Martynau, Belarus
2001 .....Matthew Emmons, U.S.
2002 .....Matthew Emmons, U.S.
2006 .....Sergei Martynov, Belarus

AIR RIFLE
1966 .....G. Kümmet, W Germany
1970 .....G. Kusterman, W Germ.
1974 .....E. Pedzisz, Poland
1978 .....O. Schlipf, W. Germany
1979 .....K. Hillenbrand
1981 .....F. Bessy, France
1982 .....F. Rettkowski, E Germ.
1983 .....P. Heberle, France
1985 .....P. Heberle, France
1986 .....H. Riederer, W Germany
1987 .....K. Ivanov, USSR
1989 .....J. P. Amet, France
1990 .....H. Riederer, W Germany
1994 .....Boris Polak, Israel
1998 .....Artem Khadjibekov, Russia
1999 .....Jozef Gonci, Slovakia
2000 .....Artem Khadjibekov, Russia
2001 .....Jason Parker, U.S.
2002 .....Jason Parker, U.S.
2006 .....Abhinav Bindra, India

MEN'S TRAP
1929 .....De Lumniczer, Hungary
1930 .....M. Arie, U.S.
1931 .....Kiszkurno, Poland
1933 .....De Lumniczer, Hungary

MEN'S TRAP (Cont.)
1934 .....A. Montagh, Hungary
1935 .....R. Sack, W Germany
1936 .....Kiszkurno, Poland
1937 .....K. Huber, Finland
1938 .....I. Strassburger, Hungary
1939 .....De Lumniczer, Hungary
1947 .....H. Liljedahl, Sweden
1949 .....F. Rocchi, Argentina
1950 .....C. Sala, Italy
1952 .....P.J. Grossi, Argentina
1954 .....C. Merlo, Italy
1958 .....F. Eisenlauer, U.S.
1959 .....H. Badravi, Egypt
1961 .....E. Mattarelli, Italy
1962 .....W. Zimenko, USSR
1965 .....J.E. Lire, Chile
1966 .....K. Jones, U.S.
1967 .....G. Rennard, Belgium
1969 .....E. Mattarelli, Italy
1970 .....M. Carrega, France
1971 .....M. Carrega, France
1973 .....A. Andrushkin, USSR
1974 .....M. Carrega, France
1975 .....J. Primrose, Canada
1977 .....E. Azkue, Spain
1978 .....E. Vallduvi, Spain
1979 .....M. Carrega, France
1981 .....A. Asanov, USSR
1982 .....L. Giovonnetti, Italy
1983 .....J. Primrose, Canada
1985 .....M. Bednarik, Czechoslovakia
1986 .....M. Bednarik, Czechoslovakia
1987 .....D. Monakov, USSR
1989 .....M. Venturini, Italy
1990 .....J. Damne, E Germany
1994 .....Dmitriy Monakov, Ukraine
1995 .....Giovanni Pellielo, Italy
1998 .....Giovanni Pellielo, Italy
1999 .....Joao Rebelo, Portugal
2000 .....Michael Diamond, Australia
2001 .....Michael Diamond, Australia
2002 .....Khaled Almudhaf, Kuwait
2005 .....Massimo Fabrizzi, Italy
2006 .....Manavjit Singh Sandu, India

THREE POSITION RIFLE
1929 .....O. Ericsson, Sweden
1930 .....Petersen, Denmark
1931 .....Amundson, Norway
1933 .....De Lisle, France
1935 .....Leskinnen, Finland
1937 .....Mazoyer, France
1939 .....Steigelmann, Germany
1947 .....I.H. Erben, Sweden
1949 .....P. Janhonen, Finland
1952 .....Kongshaug, Norway
1954 .....A. Bugdanov, USSR
1958 .....Itkis, USSR
1962 .....G. Anderson, U.S.
1966 .....G. Anderson, U.S.
1970 .....Parkhimovitch, USSR
1974 .....L. Wigger, U.S.
1978 .....E. Svensson, Sweden
1982 .....K. Ivanov, USSR
1986 .....P. Heinz, W Germany
1990 .....E. C. Lee, S Korea
1994 .....P. Kurka, Czech Republic
1998 .....Jozef Gonci, Slovakia
1999 .....Jozef Gonci, Slovakia
2000 .....Jozef Gonci, Slovakia
2001 .....Marcel Bürge, Switz
2002 .....Marcel Bürge, Switz
2006 .....Artem Khadjibekov, Russia

Women

THREE POSITION RIFLE

1966 .....M. Thompson, U.S.
1970 .....M. Thompson Murdock, U.S.
1974 .....A. Pelova, Bulgaria
1978 .....W. Oliver, U.S.
1982 .....M. Helbig, E Germany
1986 .....V. Letcheva, Bulgaria
1990 .....V. Letcheva, Bulgaria
1994 .....A. Maloukhina, Russia
1998 .....Sonja Pfeilschifter, Germany
1999 .....Sonja Pfeilschifter, Germany
2000 .....Hong Shan, China
2001 .....Petra Horneber, Germany
2002 .....Petra Horneber, Germany
2006 .....Charlotte Jakobsen, Denmark

AIR RIFLE

1970 .....V. Cherkasque, USSR
1974 .....T. Ratkinova, USSR
1978 .....W. Oliver, U.S.
1979 .....K. Monez, U.S.
1981 .....S. Romaristova, USSR
1982 .....S. Lang, W Germany
1983 .....M. Helbig, E Germany
1985 .....E. Forian, Hungary
1986 .....V. Letcheva, Bulgaria
1987 .....V. Letcheva, Bulgaria
1989 .....V. Letcheva, Bulgaria

AIR RIFLE *(Cont.)*

1990 .....E. Joc, Hungary
1994 .....Sonja Pfeilschifter, Germany
1998 .....Sonja Pfeilschifter, Germany
1999 .....Sonja Pfeilschifter, Germany
2000 .....Sonja Pfeilschifter, Germany
2001 .....Katerina Kurkova, Czech.
2002 .....Katerina Kurkova, Czech.
2006 .....Du Li, China

SPORT PISTOL

1966 .....N. Rasskazova, USSR
1970 .....N. Stoljarova, USSR
1974 .....N. Stoljarova, USSR
1978 .....K. Dyer, U.S.
1982 .....P. Balogh, Hungary
1986 .....M. Dobrantcheva, USSR
1990 .....M. Logvinenko, USSR
1994 .....Soon Hee Boo, S Korea
1998 .....Yieqing Cai, China
1999 .....Soon Hee Boo, S Korea
2000 .....Lalita Vauhleuskaya, Belarus
2001 .....Munkhbayar Dorjsuren, Germany
2002 .....Munkhbayar Dorjsuren, Germany
2006 .....Chen Ying, China

AIR PISTOL

1970 .....S. Carroll, U.S.
1974 .....Z. Simonian, USSR
1978 .....K. Hansson, Sweden
1979 .....R. Fox, U.S.
1981 .....N. Kalinina, USSR
1982 .....M. Dobrantcheva, USSR
1983 .....K. Bodin, Sweden
1985 .....M. Dobrantcheva, USSR
1986 .....A. Völker, E Germany
1987 .....J. Brajkovic, Yugoslavia
1989 .....N. Salukvadse, USSR
1990 .....Jasna Sekaric, Yugoslavia
1994 .....Jasna Sekaric, IOP
1998 .....Dorisuren Munkhbayar, Mongolia
1999 .....Nino Salukvadse, Georgia
2000 .....Luna Tao, China
2001 .....Olena Kostevych, Ukraine
2002 .....Olena Kostevych, Ukraine
2006 .....Natalia Paderina, Russia

Softball

U.S. Champions—Men

MAJOR FAST PITCH

1933 ..........J.L. Gill Boosters, Chicago
1934 ....Ke-Nash-A, Kenosha, Wisc.
1935 ....Crimson Coaches, Toledo, Ohio
1936 ....Kodak Park, Rochester, N.Y.
1937 ....Briggs Body Team, Detroit
1938 ....The Pohlers, Cincinnati
1939 ....Carr's Boosters, Covington, Ky.
1940 ....Kodak Park, Rochester, N.Y.
1941 ....Bendix Brakes, South Bend, Ind.
1942 ....Deep Rock Oilers, Tulsa
1943 ....Hammer Air Field, Fresno
1944 ....Hammer Air Field, Fresno
1945 ....Zollner Pistons, Fort Wayne, Ind.
1946 ....Zollner Pistons, Fort Wayne, Ind.
1947 ....Zollner Pistons, Fort Wayne, Ind.
1948 ....Briggs Beautyware, Detroit
1949 ....Tip Top Tailors, Toronto
1950 ....Clearwater (Fla.) Bombers
1951 ....Dow Chemical, Midland, Mich.
1952 ....Briggs Beautyware, Detroit
1953 ....Briggs Beautyware, Detroit
1954 ....Clearwater (Fla.) Bombers
1955 ....Raybestos Cardinals, Stratford, Conn.
1956 ....Clearwater (Fla.) Bombers
1957 ....Clearwater (Fla.) Bombers
1958 ....Raybestos Cardinals, Stratford, Conn.
1959 ....Sealmasters, Aurora, Ill.
1960 ....Clearwater (Fla.) Bombers
1961 ....Sealmasters, Aurora, Ill.
1962 ....Clearwater (Fla.) Bombers
1963 ....Clearwater (Fla.) Bombers
1964 ....Burch Tool, Detroit
1965 ....Sealmasters, Aurora, Ill.
1966 ....Clearwater (Fla.) Bombers
1967 ....Sealmasters, Aurora, Ill.
1968 ....Clearwater (Fla.) Bombers
1969 ....Raybestos Cardinals, Stratford, Conn.
1970 ....Raybestos Cardinals, Stratford, Conn.
1971 ....Welty Way, Cedar Rapids, Iowa
1972 ....Raybestos Cardinals, Stratford, Conn.
1973 ....Clearwater (Fla.) Bombers
1974 ....Gianella Bros, Santa Rosa, Calif.
1975 ....Rising Sun Hotel, Reading, Pa.
1976 ....Raybestos Cardinals, Stratford, Conn.
1977 ....Billard Barbell, Reading, Pa.
1978 ....Billard Barbell, Reading, Pa.
1979 ....McArdle Pontiac/Cadillac, Midland, Mich.
1980 ....Peterbilt Western, Seattle
1981 ....Archer Daniels Midland, Decatur, Ill.
1982 ....Peterbilt Western, Seattle
1983 ....Franklin Cardinals, Stratford, Conn.
1984 ....California Kings, Merced, Calif.
1985 ....Pay'n Pak, Seattle
1986 ....Pay'n Pak, Seattle
1987 ....Pay'n Pak, Seattle
1988 ....TransAire, Elkhart, Ind.
1989 ....Penn Corp, Sioux City, Iowa
1990 ....Penn Corp, Sioux City, Iowa
1991 ....Guanella Brothers, Rohnert Park, Calif.
1992 ....Natl Health Care Disc, Sioux City, Iowa
1993 ....Natl Health Care Disc, Sioux City, Iowa
1994 ....Decatur Pride, Decatur, Ill.
1995 ....Decatur Pride, Decatur, Ill.
1996 ....Green Bay All-Car, Green Bay, Wisc.
1997 ....Green Bay All-Car, Green Bay, Wisc.

U.S. Champions—Men *(Cont.)*

MAJOR FAST PITCH *(CONT.)*

1998..........Meierhoffer-Fleeman, St. Joseph, Mo.	2003..........Farm Tavern, Madison, Wisc.
1999..........Decatur Pride, Decatur, Ill.	2004..........Farm Tavern, Madison, Wisc.
2000..........Meierhoffer, St. Joseph, Mo.	2005..........Tampa Bay Smokers, Tampa Bay, Fla.
2001..........Frontier Players Casino, St. Joseph, Mo.	2006..........Circle Tap, Green Bay, Wisc.
2002..........Frontier Players Casino, St. Joseph, Mo.	

SUPER SLOW PITCH

1981..........Howard's/Western Steer, Denver, N.C.	1994..........Bell Corp, Tampa, Fla.
1982..........Jerry's Catering, Miami, Fla.	1995..........Lighthouse/Worth, Stone Mt., Ga.
1983..........Howard's/Western Steer, Denver, N.C.	1996..........Ritch's Superior, Windsor Locks, Conn.
1984..........Howard's/Western Steer, Denver, N.C.	1997..........Ritch's Superior, Windsor Locks, Conn.
1985..........Steele's Sports, Grafton, Ohio	1998..........Lighthouse/Worth, Stone Mt., Ga.
1986..........Steele's Sports, Grafton, Ohio	1999..........Team Easton, Wilmington, N.C.
1987..........Steele's Sports, Grafton, Ohio	2000..........Team TPS, Louisville, Ky.
1988..........Starpath, Monticello, Ky.	2002..........Long Haul/Taylor Bros./Shen Corp./TPS,
1989..........Ritch's Salvage, Harrisburg, N.C.	Albertville, Minn.
1990..........Steele's Silver Bullets, Grafton, Ohio	2003..........Resmondo/Hagae/Sunbelt/Taylor,
1991..........Sunbelt/Worth, Centerville, Ga.	Winchester, Ohio
1992..........Ritch's Superior, Windsor Locks, Conn.	Note: Beginning in 2004 the Super Slow Division was
1993..........Ritch's Superior, Windsor Locks, Conn.	disbanded

MAJOR SLOW PITCH

1953..........Shields Construction, Newport, Ky.	1981..........Elite Coating, Gordon, Calif.
1954..........Waldneck's Tavern, Cincinnati	1982..........Triangle Sports, Minneapolis
1955..........Lang Pet Shop, Covington, Ky.	1983..........No. 1 Electric & Heating, Gastonia, N.C.
1956..........Gatliff Auto Sales, Newport, Ky.	1984..........Lilly Air Systems, Chicago
1957..........Gatliff Auto Sales, Newport, Ky.	1985..........Blanton's, Fayetteville, N.C.
1958..........East Side Sports, Detroit	1986..........Non-Ferrous Metals, Cleveland
1959..........Yorkshire Restaurant, Newport, Ky.	1987..........Starpath, Monticello, Ky.
1960..........Hamilton Tailoring, Cincinnati	1988..........Bell Corp/FAF, Tampa, Fla.
1961..........Hamilton Tailoring, Cincinnati	1989..........Ritch's Salvage, Harrisburg, N.C.
1962..........Skip Hogan A.C., Pittsburgh	1990..........New Construction, Shelbyville, Ind.
1963..........Gatliff Auto Sales, Newport, Ky.	1991..........Riverside Paving, Louisville, Ky.
1964..........Skip Hogan A.C., Pittsburgh	1992..........Vernon's, Jacksonville, Fla.
1965..........Skip Hogan A.C., Pittsburgh	1993..........Back Porch/Destin Roofing, Destin, Fla.
1966..........Michael's Lounge, Detroit	1994..........Riverside RAM/Taylor Bros., Louisville, Ky.
1967..........Jim's Sport Shop, Pittsburgh	1995..........Riverside/RAM/Taylor/TPS, Louisville, Ky.
1968..........County Sports, Levittown, N.Y.	1996..........Bell 2/Robert's/Easton, Orlando, Fla.
1969..........Copper Hearth, Milwaukee	1997..........Long Haul/TPS, Albertville, Minn.
1970..........Little Caesar's, Southgate, Mich.	1998..........Chase Mortgage/Easton, Wilmington, N.C.
1971..........Pile Drivers, Virginia Beach, Va.	1999..........Gasoline Heaven/Worth, Commack, N.Y.
1972..........Jiffy Club, Louisville, Ky.	2000..........Long Haul/TPS, Albertville, Minn.
1973..........Howard's Furniture, Denver, N.C.	2001..........New Construction, Shelbyville, Ind.
1974..........Howard's Furniture, Denver, N.C.	2002..........Twin States/Worth, Montgomery, Ala.
1975..........Pyramid Cafe, Lakewood, Ohio	2003..........New Construction/B&J/Snap-On,
1976..........Warren Motors, Jacksonville, Fla.	Metamora, Ill.
1977..........Nelson Painting, Oklahoma City	2004..........U.S. Vinyl/ZWear, Lafayette, Ga.
1978..........Campbell Carpets, Concord, Calif.	2005..........Vegas/Benfield/Easton, Manassas, Va.
1979..........Nelco Mfg Co., Oklahoma City	2006..........Northwest Pipe/Bud Light/3N2/Easton,
1980..........Campbell Carpets, Concord, Calif.	Westland, Mich.

U.S. Champions—Women
MAJOR FAST PITCH

1933	Great Northerns, Chicago
1934	Hart Motors, Chicago
1935	Bloomer Girls, Cleveland
1936	Nat'l Screw & Mfg., Cleveland
1937	Nat'l Screw & Mfg., Cleveland
1938	J.J. Krieg's, Alameda, Calif.
1939	J.J. Krieg's, Alameda, Calif.
1940	Arizona Ramblers, Phoenix
1941	Higgins Midgets, Tulsa
1942	Jax Maids, New Orleans
1943	Jax Maids, New Orleans
1944	Lind & Pomeroy, Portland, Ore.
1945	Jax Maids, New Orleans
1946	Jax Maids, New Orleans
1947	Jax Maids, New Orleans
1948	Arizona Ramblers, Phoenix
1949	Arizona Ramblers, Phoenix
1950	Orange (Calif.) Lionettes
1951	Orange (Calif.) Lionettes
1952	Orange (Calif.) Lionettes
1953	Betsy Ross Rockets, Fresno
1954	Leach Motor Rockets, Fresno
1955	Orange (Calif.) Lionettes
1956	Orange (Calif.) Lionettes
1957	Hacienda Rockets, Fresno
1958	Raybestos Brakettes, Stratford, Conn.
1959	Raybestos Brakettes, Stratford, Conn.
1960	Raybestos Brakettes, Stratford, Conn.
1961	Gold Sox, Whittier, Calif.
1962	Orange (Calif.) Lionettes
1963	Raybestos Brakettes, Stratford, Conn.
1964	Erv Lind Florists, Portland, Ore.
1965	Orange (Calif.) Lionettes
1966	Raybestos Brakettes, Stratford, Conn.
1967	Raybestos Brakettes, Stratford, Conn.
1968	Raybestos Brakettes, Stratford, Conn.
1969	Orange (Calif.) Lionettes
1970	Orange (Calif.) Lionettes
1971	Raybestos Brakettes, Stratford, Conn.
1972	Raybestos Brakettes, Stratford, Conn.
1973	Raybestos Brakettes, Stratford, Conn.
1974	Raybestos Brakettes, Stratford, Conn.
1975	Raybestos Brakettes, Stratford, Conn.
1976	Raybestos Brakettes, Stratford, Conn.
1977	Raybestos Brakettes, Stratford, Conn.
1978	Raybestos Brakettes, Stratford, Conn.
1979	Sun City (Ariz.) Saints
1980	Raybestos Brakettes, Stratford, Conn.
1981	Orlando (Fla.) Rebels
1982	Raybestos Brakettes, Stratford, Conn.
1983	Raybestos Brakettes, Stratford, Conn.
1984	Los Angeles Diamonds
1985	Hi-Ho Brakettes, Stratford, Conn.
1986	Southern California Invasion, Los Angeles
1987	Orange County Majestics, Anaheim, Calif.
1988	Hi-Ho Brakettes, Stratford, Conn.
1989	Whittier (Calif.) Raiders
1990	Raybestos Brakettes, Stratford, Conn.
1991	Raybestos Brakettes, Stratford, Conn.
1992	Raybestos Brakettes, Stratford, Conn.
1993	Redding Rebels, Redding, Calif.
1994	Redding Rebels, Redding, Calif.
1995	Redding Rebels, Redding, Calif.
1996	California Commotion, Woodland Hills, Calif.
1997	California Commotion, Woodland Hills, Calif.
1998	California Commotion, Woodland Hills, Calif.
1999	California Commotion, Woodland Hills, Calif.
2000	Phoenix Storm, Phoenix
2001	Phoenix Storm, Phoenix
2002	Stratford Brakettes, Stratford, Conn.
2003	Stratford Brakettes, Stratford, Conn.
2004	Stratford Brakettes, Stratford, Conn.
2005	Schutt Hurricanes, Burbank, Calif.
2006	Stratford Brakettes, Stratford, Conn.

MAJOR SLOW PITCH

1959	Pearl Laundry, Richmond, Va.
1960	Carolina Rockets, High Pt, N.C.
1961	Dairy Cottage, Covington, Ky.
1962	Dana Gardens, Cincinnati
1963	Dana Gardens, Cincinnati
1964	Dana Gardens, Cincinnati
1965	Art's Acres, Omaha, Neb.
1966	Dana Gardens, Cincinnati
1967	Ridge Maintenance, Cleveland
1968	Escue Pontiac, Cincinnati
1969	Converse Dots, Hialeah, Fla.
1970	Rutenschruder Floral, Cincinnati
1971	Gators, Ft. Lauderdale, Fla.
1972	Riverside Ford, Cincinnati
1973	Sweeney Chevrolet, Cincinnati
1974	Marks Brothers Dots, Miami, Fla.
1975	Marks Brothers Dots, Miami, Fla.
1976	Sorrento's Pizza, Cincinnati
1977	Fox Valley Lassies, St. Charles, Ill.
1978	Bob Hoffman's Dots, Miami, Fl.a
1979	Bob Hoffman's Dots, Miami, Fla.
1980	Howard's Rubi-Otts, Graham, N.C.
1981	Tifton (Ga.) Tomboys
1982	Richmond (Va.) Stompers
1983	Spooks, Anoka, Minn.
1984	Spooks, Anoka, Minn.
1985	Key Ford Mustangs, Pensacola, Fla.
1986	Sur-Way Tomboys, Tifton, Ga.
1987	Key Ford Mustangs, Pensacola, Fla.
1988	Spooks, Anoka, Minn.
1989	Canaan's Illusions, Houston
1990	Spooks, Anoka, Minn.
1991	Kannan's Illusions, San Antonio, Tex.
1992	Universal Plastics, Cookeville, Tenn.
1993	Universal Plastics, Cookeville, Tenn.
1994	Universal Plastics, Cookeville, Tenn.
1995	Armed Forces, Sacramento, Calif.
1996	Spooks, Anoka, Minn.
1997	Taylor's Major Slow Pitch, Glendale, Md.
1998	Lakerettes, Conneaut Lake, Pa.
1999	Lakerettes, Conneaut Lake, Pa.
2000	Premier Motor Sports, Pittsboro, N.C.
2001	Shooters/Nike, Orlando, Fla.
2002	Diamond Queens, Nashville, Tenn.
2003	Shooters/Worth, Orlando, Fla.
2004	Enough Said/Easton, Tallahassee, Fla.
2005	Armed Forces, San Antonio, Tex.
2006	Long Haul/Enough Said/Easton, Tallahassee, Fla.

Beginning in 2003, the ASA combined the Women's Class Major, Class-A and Class-B into 1 'open' class.

All-Around World Champions

MEN

1891.....Joseph F. Donoghue, U.S.	1936.....Ivar Ballangrud, Norway	1976.....Piet Kleine, Netherlands
1893.....Jaap Eden, Netherlands	1937.....Michael Staksrud, Nor.	1977.....Eric Heiden, U.S.
1895.....Jaap Eden, Netherlands	1938.....Ivar Ballangrud, Norway	1978.....Eric Heiden, U.S.
1896.....Jaap Eden, Netherlands	1939.....Birger Wasenius, Finland	1979.....Eric Heiden, U.S.
1897.....Jack K. McCulloch, Can.	1947.....Lassi Parkkinen, Finland	1980.....Hilbert van der Duin, Neth.
1898.....Peder Ostlund, Norway	1948.....Odd Lundberg, Norway	1981.....Amund Sjobrand, Norway
1899.....Peder Ostlund, Norway	1949.....Kornel Pajor, Hungary	1982.....Hilbert van der Duin, Neth.
1900.....Edvard Engelsaas, Norw.	1950.....Hjalmar Andersen, Norw.	1983.....Rolf Falk-Larssen, Norw.
1901.....Franz F. Wathan, Finland	1951.....Hjalmar Andersen, Norw.	1984.....Oleg Bozhev, USSR
1904.....Sigurd Mathisen, Norway	1952.....Hjalmar Andersen, Norw.	1985.....Hein Vergeer, Netherlands
1905.....C. Coen de Koning, Neth.	1953.....Oleg Goncharenko, USSR	1986.....Hein Vergeer, Netherlands
1908.....Oscar Mathisen, Norway	1954.....Boris Shilkov, USSR	1987.....Nikolai Guliaev, USSR
1909.....Oscar Mathisen, Norway	1955.....Sigvard Ericsson, Swe.	1988.....Eric Flaim, U.S.
1910.....Nikolai Strunnikov, Russia	1956.....Oleg Goncharenko, USSR	1989.....Leo Visser, Netherlands
1911.....Nikolai Strunnikov, Russia	1957.....Knut Johannesen, Norw.	1990.....Johann Olav Koss, Norw.
1912.....Oscar Mathisen, Norway	1958.....Oleg Goncharenko, USSR	1991.....Johann Olav Koss, Norw.
1913.....Oscar Mathisen, Norway	1959.....Juhani Järvinen, Finland	1992.....Roberto Sighel, Italy
1914.....Oscar Mathisen, Norway	1960.....Boris Stenin, USSR	1993.....Falko Zandstra, Neth.
1922.....Harald Strom, Norway	1961.....Henk van der Grift, Neth.	1994.....Johann Olav Koss, Norw.
1923.....Klas Thunberg, Finland	1962.....Viktor Kosichkin, USSR	1995.....Rintje Ritsma, Netherlands
1924.....Roald Larsen, Norway	1963.....Jonny Nilsson, Sweden	1996.....Rintje Ritsma, Netherlands
1925.....Klas Thunberg, Finland	1964.....Knut Johannesen, Norw.	1997.....Ids Postma, Netherlands
1926.....Ivar Ballangrud, Norway	1965.....Per Ivar Moe, Norway	1998.....Ids Postma, Netherlands
1927.....Bernt Evensen, Norway	1966.....Kees Verkerk, Neth.	1999.....Rintje Ritsma, Neth.
1928.....Klas Thunberg, Finland	1967.....Kees Verkerk, Neth.	2000.....Gianni Romme, Neth.
1929.....Klas Thunberg, Finland	1968.....Fred Anton Maier, Norw.	2001.....Rintje Ritsma, Neth.
1930.....Michael Staksrud, Norw.	1969.....Dag Fornaes, Norway	2002.....Jochem Uytdehaage, Neth.
1931.....Klas Thunberg, Finland	1970.....Ard Schenk, Netherlands	2003.....Gianni Romme, Neth.
1932.....Ivar Ballangrud, Norway	1971.....Ard Schenk, Netherlands	2004.....Chad Hedrick, United States
1933.....Hans Engnestangen, Norw.	1972.....Ard Schenk, Netherlands	2005.....Shani Davis, United States
1934.....Bernt Evensen, Norway	1973.....Göran Claeson, Sweden	2006.....Shani Davis, United States
1935.....Michael Staksrud, Norw.	1974.....Sten Stensen, Norway	
	1975.....Harm Kuipers, Netherlands	

WOMEN

1936.....Kit Klein, United States	1965.....Inga Artamonova, USSR	1987.....Karin Kania, East Gemr.
1937.....Laila Schou Nilsen, Norw.	1966.....Valentina Stenina, USSR	1988.....Karin Kania, East Germ.
1938.....Laila Schou Nilsen, Norw.	1967.....Stien Kaiser, Netherlands	1989.....Constanze Moser, East Germ.
1939.....Verné Lesche, Finland	1968.....Stien Kaiser, Netherlands	1990.....Jacqueline Börner, East Germ.
1947.....Verné Lesche, Finland	1969.....Lasma Kauniste, USSR	1991.....Gunda Kleemann, Germ.
1948.....Maria Isakova, USSR	1970.....Atje Keulen-Deelstra, Neth.	1992.....Gunda Niemann-Kleemann, Germany
1949.....Maria Isakova, USSR	1971.....Nina Statkevich, USSR	1993.....Gunda Niemann, Germany
1950.....Maria Isakova, USSR	1972.....Atje Keulen-Deelstra, Neth.	1994.....Emese Hunyady, Austria
1951.....Eevi Huttunen, Finland	1973.....Atje Keulen-Deelstra, Neth.	1995.....Gunda Niemann, Germany
1952.....Lidia Selikhova, USSR	1974.....Atje Keulen-Deelstra, Neth.	1996.....Gunda Niemann, Germany
1953.......Khalida Shchegoleeva, USSR	1975.....Karin Kessow, East Ger.	1997.......Gunda Niemann, Germany
1954.....Lidia Selikhova, USSR	1976.....Sylvia Burka, Canada	1997.....Gunda Niemann, Germany
1955.....Rimma Zhukova, USSR	1977.....Vera Bryndzej, USSR	1998.....Gunda Niemann, Germany
1956.....Sofia Kondakova, USSR	1978.....Tatiana Averina, USSR	1999.....Gunda Niemann, Germany
1957.....Inga Artamonova, USSR	1979.....Beth Heiden, United States	2000.....Claudia Pechstein, Germ.
1958.....Inga Artamonova, USSR	1980.....Natalia Petruseva, USSR	2001.....Anni Friesinger, Germany
1959.....Tamara Rylova, USSR	1981.....Natalia Petruseva, USSR	2002.....Anni Friesinger, Germany
1960.....Valentina Stenina, USSR	1982.....Karin Busch, East Ger.	2003.....Cindy Klassen, Canada
1961.....Valentina Stenina, USSR	1983.....Andrea Schöne, East Germ.	2004.....Renate Groenewold, Neth.
1962.....Inga Artamonova, USSR	1984.....Karin Enke-Busch, East Germ.	2005.....Anni Friesinger, Germany
1963.....Lidia Skoblikova, USSR	1985.....Andrea Schöne, East Germ.	2006.....Cindy Klassen, Canada
1964.....Lidia Skoblikova, USSR	1986.....Karin Enke-Busch, East Germ.	

National Men's Champions

HARD BALL

Year	Champion	Year	Champion	Year	Champion
1907	John A. Miskey	1941	Charles M.P. Britton	1975	Victor Niederhoffer
1908	John A. Miskey	1942	Charles M.P. Britton	1976	Peter Briggs
1909	William L. Freeland	1943–45	No tournament	1977	Thomas E. Page
1910	John A. Miskey	1946	Charles M.P. Britton	1978	Michael Desaulniers
1911	Francis S. White	1947	Charles M.P. Britton	1979	Mario Sanchez
1912	Constantine Hutchins	1948	Stanley W. Pearson Jr.	1980	Michael Desaulniers
1913	Morton L. Newhall	1949	H. Hunter Lott Jr.	1981	Mark Alger
1914	Constantine Hutchins	1950	Edward J. Hahn	1982	John Nimick
1915	Stanley W. Pearson	1951	Edward J. Hahn	1983	Kenton Jernigan
1916	Stanley W. Pearson	1952	Harry B. Conlon	1984	Kenton Jernigan
1917	Stanley W. Pearson	1953	Ernest Howard	1987	Frank J. Stanley IV
1918–19	No tournament	1954	G. Diehl Mateer Jr.	1988	Scott Dulmage
1920	Charles C. Peabody	1955	Henri R. Salaun	1989	Rodolfo Rodriquez
1921	Stanley W. Pearson	1956	G. Diehl Mateer Jr.	1990	Hector Barragan
1922	Stanley W. Pearson	1957	Henri R. Salaun	1991	Hector Barragan
1923	Stanley W. Pearson	1958	Henri R. Salaun	1992	Hector Barragan
1924	Gerald Roberts	1959	Benjamin H. Heckscher	1985	Kenton Jernigan
1925	W. Palmer Dixon	1960	G. Diehl Mateer Jr.	1986	Hugh LaBossier
1926	W. Palmer Dixon	1961	Henri R. Salaun	1993	Hector Barragan
1927	Myles Baker	1962	Samuel P. Howe III	1994	Hector Barragan
1928	Herbert N. Rawlins Jr.	1963	Benjamin H. Heckscher	1995	W. Keen Butcher
1929	J. Lawrence Pool			1996	W. Keen Butcher
1930	Herbert N. Rawlins Jr.	1964	Ralph E. Howe	1997	Rob Hill
1931	J. Lawrence Pool	1965	Stephen T. Vehslage	1998	Rob Hill
1932	Beckman H. Pool	1966	Victor Niederhoffer	1999	Rob Hill
1933	Beckman H. Pool	1967	Samuel P. Howe III	2000	Thomas Harrity
1934	Neil J. Sullivan II	1968	Colin Adair	2001	Rob Hill
1935	Donald Strachan	1969	Anil Nayar	2002	Gary Waite
1936	Germain G. Glidden	1970	Anil Nayar	2003	Thomas Harrity
1937	Germain G. Glidden	1971	Colin Adair	2004	Thomas Harrity
1938	Germain G. Glidden	1972	Victor Niederhoffer	2005	Thomas Harrity
1939	Donald Strachan	1973	Victor Niederhoffer		
1940	A. Willing Patterson	1974	Victor Niederhoffer		

SOFT BALL

Year	Champion	Year	Champion	Year	Champion
1983	Kenton Jernigan	1992	Phil Yarrow	2001	Damian Walker
1984	Kenton Jernigan	1993	Phil Yarrow	2002	Damian Walker
1985	Kenton Jernigan	1994	Roberto Rosales	2003	Preston Quick
1986	Darius Pandole	1995	A. Martin Clark	2004	Preston Quick
1987	Richard Hashim	1996	Mohsen Mir	2005	Jullian Illingworth
1988	John Phelan	1997	A. Martin Clark		
1989	Will Carlin	1998	A. Martin Clark		
1990	Syed Jafry	1999	David McNeely		
1991	Hector Barragan	2000	A. Martin Clark		

National Women's Champions

HARD BALL

Year	Champion	Year	Champion	Year	Champion
1928	Eleanora Sears	1954	Lois Dilks	1976	Gretchen Spruance
1929	Margaret Howe	1955	Janet Morgan	1977	Gretchen Spruance
1930	Hazel Wightman	1956	Betty Howe Constable	1978	Gretchen Spruance
1931	Ruth Banks	1957	Betty Howe Constable	1979	Heather McKay
1932	Margaret Howe	1958	Betty Howe Constable	1980	Barbara Maltby
1933	Susan Noel	1959	Betty Howe Constable	1981	Barbara Maltby
1934	Margaret Howe	1960	Margaret Varner	1982	Alicia McConnell
1935	Margot Lumb	1961	Margaret Varner	1983	Alicia McConnell
1936	Anne Page	1962	Margaret Varner	1984	Alicia McConnell
1937	Anne Page	1963	Margaret Varner	1985	Alicia McConnell
1938	Cecile Bowes	1964	Ann Wetzel	1986	Alicia McConnell
1939	Anne Page	1965	Joyce Davenport	1987	Alicia McConnell
1940	Cecile Bowes	1966	Betty Meade	1988	Alicia McConnell
1941	Cecile Bowes	1967	Betty Meade	1986	Alicia McConnell
1942–46	No tournament	1968	Betty Meade	1987	Alicia McConnell
1947	Anne Page Homer	1969	Joyce Davenport	1988	Alicia McConnell
1948	Cecile Bowes	1970	Nina Moyer	1989	Demer Holleran
1949	Janet Morgan	1971	Carol Thesieres	1990	Demer Holleran
1950	Betty Howe	1972	Nina Moyer	1991	Demer Holleran
1951	Jane Austin	1973	Gretchen Spruance	1992	Demer Holleran
1952	Margaret Howe	1974	Gretchen Spruance	1993	Demer Holleran
1953	Margaret Howe	1975	Ginny Akabane	1994	Demer Holleran

Note: Tournament not held since 1994.

SOFT BALL

Year	Champion	Year	Champion	Year	Champion
1983	Alicia McConnell	1991	Ellie Pierce	1999	Demer Holleran
1984	Julie Harris	1992	Demer Holleran	2000	Latasha Khan
1985	Sue Clinch	1993	Demer Holleran	2001	Shabana Khan
1986	Julie Harris	1994	Demer Holleran	2002	Latasha Khan
1987	Diana Staley	1995	Ellie Pierce	2003	Latasha Khan
1988	Sara Luther	1996	Demer Holleran	2004	Latasha Khan
1989	Nancy Gengler	1997	Demer Holleran	2005	Latasha Khan
1990	Joyce Maycock	1998	Latasha Khan		

Triathlon

Ironman World Championship

MEN			WOMEN		
Year	Winner	Time	Year	Winner	Time
1978	Gordon Haller	11:46	1978	No finishers	
1979	Tom Warren	11:15:56	1979	Lyn Lemaire	12:55
1980	Dave Scott	9:24:33	1980	Robin Beck	11:21:24
1981	John Howard	9:38:29	1981	Linda Sweeney	12:00:32
1982	Scott Tinley	9:19:41	1982	Kathleen McCartney	11:09:40
1982	Dave Scott	9:08:23	1982	Julie Leach	10:54:08
1983	Dave Scott	9:05:57	1983	Sylviane Puntous	10:43:36
1984	Dave Scott	8:54:20	1984	Sylviane Puntous	10:25:13
1985	Scott Tinley	8:50:54	1985	Joanne Ernst	10:25:22
1986	Dave Scott	8:28:37	1986	Paula Newby-Fraser	9:49:14
1987	Dave Scott	8:34:13	1987	Erin Baker	9:35:25
1988	Scott Molina	8:31:00	1988	Paula Newby-Fraser	9:01:01
1989	Mark Allen	8:09:15	1989	Paula Newby-Fraser	9:00:56
1990	Mark Allen	8:28:17	1990	Erin Baker	9:13:42
1991	Mark Allen	8:18:32	1991	Paula Newby-Fraser	9:07:52
1992	Mark Allen	8:09:09	1992	Paula Newby-Fraser	8:55:29
1993	Mark Allen	8:07:46	1993	Paula Newby-Fraser	8:58:23
1994	Greg Welch	8:20:27	1994	Paula Newby-Fraser	9:20:14
1995	Mark Allen	8:20:34	1995	Karen Smyers	9:16:46
1996	Luc Van Lierde	8:04:08	1996	Paula Newby-Fraser	9:06:49
1997	Thomas Hellriegel	8:33:01	1997	Heather Fuhr	9:31:43
1998	Peter Reid	8:24:20	1998	Natascha Badmann	9:24:16
1999	Luc Van Lierde	8:17:17	1999	Lori Bowden	9:13:02
2000	Peter Reid	8:21:01	2000	Natascha Badmann	9:26:17
2001	Tim DeBoom	8:31:18	2001	Natascha Badmann	9:28:37
2002	Tim DeBoom	8:29:56	2002	Natascha Badmann	9:07:54
2003	Peter Reid	8:22:35	2003	Lori Bowden	9:11:55
2004	Normann Stadler	8:33:20	2004	Natascha Badmann	9:50:04
2005	Faris Al-Sutan	8:14:17	2005	Natascha Badmann	9:09:30

Note: The Ironman Championship was contested twice in 1982.

Sites: Waikiki Beach (1978–79); Ala Moana Park (1980); Kailua-Kona (since 1981).

U.S. Triathlon National Champions*

MEN		MEN (CONT.)		WOMEN		WOMEN (CONT.)	
Year	Winner	Year	Winner	Year	Winner	Year	Winner
1984	Scott Molina	1996	Jeff Devlin	1984	Beth Mitchell	1996	Susan Latshaw
1985	Scott Molina	1997	C. Wydoff	1985	L. Buchanan	1997	Sian Welch
1986	Scott Molina	1998	Hunter Kemper	1986	K. Hanssen	1998	Siri Lindley
1987	Mike Pigg	1999	Hunter Kemper	1987	K. Hanssen	1999	Barb Lindquist
1988	Mike Pigg	2000	Marcel Viffian	1988	C. Kaushansky	2000	Joanna Zeiger
1989	Ken Glah	2001	Hunter Kemper	1989	Jan Ripple	2001	Karen Smyers
1990	Scott Molina	2002	Seth Wealing	1990	Karen Smyers	2002	Barb Lindquist
1991	Mike Pigg	2003	Hunter Kemper	1991	Karen Smyers	2003	Laura Reback
1992	Mike Pigg	2004	Matt Reed	1992	Karen Smyers	2004	Courtney Bennigson
1993	Bill Braun	2005	Hunter Kemper	1993	Karen Smyers		
1994	Scott Molina	2006	M.Bonnet-Eymard	1994	Karen Smyers	2005	Becky Lavelle
1995	Jeff Devlin			1995	Karen Smyers	2006	Jennifer Garrison

*Olympic distances: 1.5 km swim, 40km bike, 10km run.

Volleyball

World Champions — Men

Year	Winner	Runner-up	Site
1949	Soviet Union	Czechoslovakia	Prague
1952	Soviet Union	Czechoslovakia	Moscow
1956	Czechoslovakia	Soviet Union	Paris
1960	Soviet Union	Czechoslovakia	Rio de Janeiro
1962	Soviet Union	Czechoslovakia	Moscow
1966	Czechoslovakia	Romania	Prague
1970	East Germany	Bulgaria	Sofia, Bulgaria
1974	Poland	Soviet Union	Mexico City
1978	Soviet Union	Italy	Rome
1982	Soviet Union	Brazil	Buenos Aires
1986	United States	Soviet Union	Paris
1990	Italy	Cuba	Rio de Janeiro
1994	Italy	Netherlands	Athens
1998	Italy	Yugoslavia	Tokyo
2002	Brazil	Russia	Buenos Aires

World Champions — Women

Year	Winner	Runner-up	Site
1952	Soviet Union	Poland	Moscow
1956	Soviet Union	Romania	Paris
1960	Soviet Union	Japan	Rio de Janeiro
1962	Japan	Soviet Union	Moscow
1966	Japan	United States	Prague
1970	Soviet Union	Japan	Sofia, Bulgaria
1974	Japan	Soviet Union	Mexico City
1978	Cuba	Japan	Rome
1982	China	Peru	Lima, Peru
1986	China	Cuba	Prague
1990	Soviet Union	China	Beijing
1994	Cuba	Brazil	Sao Paulo, Brazil
1998	Cuba	China	Osaka, Japan
2002	Italy	United States	Berlin

U.S. Men's Open Champions—Gold Division

Year	Champion
1928	Germantown, Pa. YMCA
1929	Hyde Park YMCA, Ill.
1930	Hyde Park YMCA, Ill.
1931	San Antonio, Tex. YMCA
1932	San Antonio, Tex. YMCA
1933	Houston, Tex. YMCA
1934	Houston, Tex. YMCA
1935	Houston, Tex. YMCA
1936	Houston, Tex. YMCA
1937	Duncan YMCA, Ill.
1938	Houston, Tex. YMCA
1939	Houston, Tex. YMCA
1940	Los Angeles A.C., CA
1941	North Ave. YMCA, Ill.
1942	North Ave. YMCA, Ill.
1943–44	No championships
1945	North Ave. YMCA, Ill.
1946	Pasadena, Calif. YMCA
1947	North Ave. YMCA, Ill.
1948	Hollywood, Calif. YMCA
1949	Downtown YMCA, Calif.
1950	Long Beach, Calif. YMCA
1951	Hollywood, Calif. YMCA
1952	Hollywood, Calif. YMCA
1953	Hollywood, Calif. YMCA
1954	Stockton, Calif. YMCA
1955	Stockton, Calif. YMCA
1956	Hollywood, Calif. YMCA Stars
1957	Hollywood, Calif. YMCA Stars
1958	Hollywood, Calif. YMCA Stars
1959	Hollywood, Calif. YMCA Stars
1960	Westside JCC, Calif.
1961	Hollywood, Calif. YMCA
1962	Hollywood, Calif. YMCA
1963	Hollywood, Calif. YMCA
1964	Hollywood, Calif. YMCA Stars
1965	Westside JCC, Calif.
1966	Sand & Sea Club, Calif.
1967	Fresno, Calif. VBC
1968	Westside JCC, Los Angeles, Calif.
1969	Los Angeles, Calif. YMCA
1970	Chart House, San Diego
1971	Santa Monica, Calif. YMCA
1972	Chart House, San Diego
1973	Chuck's Steak, Los Angeles
1974	UC Santa Barbara, Calif.
1975	Chart House, San Diego
1976	Malibu, Los Angeles
1977	Chuck's, Santa Barbara
1978	Chuck's, Los Angeles
1979	Nautilus, Long Beach Calif.
1980	Olympic Club, San Francisco
1981	Nautilus, Long Beach Calif.
1982	Chuck's, Los Angeles
1983	Nautilus Pacifica, Calif.
1984	Nautilus Pacifica, Calif.
1985	Molten/SSI Torrance, Calif.
1986	Molten, Torrance, Calif.
1987	Molten, Torrance, Calif.
1988	Molten, Torrance, Calif.
1989	Not held
1990	Nike, Carson, Calif.

U.S. Men's Open Champions—Gold Division *(Cont.)*

1991	Offshore, Woodland Hills, Calif.
1992	Creole Six Pack, Elmhurst, N.Y.
1993	Asics, Huntington Beach, Calif.
1994	Asics/Paul Mitchell, Hunt. Beach, Calif.
1995	Shakter, Belagarad, Ukraine
1996	POL-AM-VBC, Brooklyn, N.Y.
1997	Canuck Stuff VBC, Calgary
1998	T-Town, Tulsa, OK
1999	Los Angeles Athletic Club,
2000	Paul Mitchell, Huntington Beach, Calif.
2001	Los Angeles Athletic Club,
2002	Paul Mitchell, Huntington Beach, Calif.
2003	Paul Mitchell, Huntington Beach, Calif.
2004	Bameso-I Dig, Dominican Republic
2005	Bameso-USA, Columbia, S.C.
2006	Paul Mitchell, Los Angeles, Calif.

U.S. Women's Open Champions—Gold Division

1949	Eagles, Houston
1950	Voit #1, Santa Monica, Calif.
1951	Eagles, Houston
1952	Voit #1, Santa Monica, Calif.
1953	Voit #1, Los Angeles
1954	Houstonettes, Houston, Tex.
1955	Mariners, Santa Monica, Calif.
1956	Mariners, Santa Monica, Calif.
1957	Mariners, Santa Monica, Calif.
1958	Mariners, Santa Monica, Calif.
1959	Mariners, Santa Monica, Calif.
1960	Mariners, Santa Monica, Calif.
1961	Breakers, Long Beach, Calif.
1962	Shamrocks, Long Beach, Calif.
1963	Shamrocks, Long Beach, Calif.
1964	Shamrocks, Long Beach, Calif.
1965	Shamrocks, Long Beach, Calif.
1966	Renegades, Los Angeles
1967	Shamrocks, Long Beach, Calif.
1968	Shamrocks, Long Beach, Calif.
1969	Shamrocks, Long Beach, Calif.
1970	Shamrocks, Long Beach, Calif.
1971	Renegades, Los Angeles
1972	E Pluribus Unum, Houston
1973	E Pluribus Unum, Houston
1974	Renegades, Los Angeles
1975	Adidas, Norwalk, Calif.
1976	Pasadena, Tex.
1977	Spoilers, Hermosa, Calif.
1978	Nick's, Los Angeles
1979	Mavericks, Los Angeles
1980	NAVA, Fountain Valley, Calif.
1981	Utah State, Logan, Utah
1982	Monarchs, Hilo, Hawaii
1983	Syntex, Stockton, Calif.
1984	Chrysler, Palo Alto, Calif.
1985	Merrill Lynch, Ariz.
1986	Merrill Lynch, Ariz.
1987	Chrysler, Pleasanton, Calif.
1988	Chrysler, Hayward, Calif.
1989	Plymouth, Hayward, Calif.
1990	Plymouth, Hayward, Calif.
1991	Fitness, Champaign, Ill.
1992	Nick's Kronies, Chicago
1993	Nick's Fishmarket, Chicago
1994	Nick's Fishmarket, Chicago
1995	Kittleman/Branfield's/Nick's, Chic., Ill.
1996	Pure Texas Nuts, Austin, Tex.
1997	Kittleman/Branfield's/Nick's, Chi.
1998	The Exterminators, Barrington, Ill.
1999	Dominican Dream Team, Santo Domingo, D.R.
2000	Dominican Dream Team II, Santo Domingo, D.R.
2001	Dominican Dream Team III, Santo Domingo, D.R.
2002	Team Trim, Long Beach, Calif.
2003	The Exterminators, Barrington, Ill.
2004	U.S.A.-A2, Barrington, Ill.
2005	Bameso-USA, Columbia, S.C.
2006	The Exterminators, Barrington, Ill.

Wrestling

United States National Champions

1983

FREESTYLE

105.5	Rich Salamone
114.5	Joe Gonzales
125.5	Joe Corso
136.5	Rich Dellagatta*
149.5	Bill Hugent
163	Lee Kemp
180.5	Chris Campbell
198	Pete Bush
220	Greg Gibson
Hvy	Bruce Baumgartner
Team	Sunkist Kids

GRECO-ROMAN

105.5	T.J. Jones
114.5	Mark Fuller
125.5	Rob Hermann
136.5	Dan Mello
149.5	Jim Martinez
163	James Andre
180.5	Steve Goss
198	Steve Fraser*
220	Dennis Koslowski
Hvy	No champion
Team	Minn. Wrestling Club

1984

FREESTYLE

105.5	Rich Salamone
114.5	Charlie Heard
125.5	Joe Corso
136.5	Rich Dellagatta*
149.5	Andre Metzger
163	Dave Schultz*
180.5	Mark Schultz
198	Steve Fraser
220	Harold Smith
Hvy	Bruce Baumgartner
Team	Sunkist Kids

GRECO-ROMAN

105.5	T.J. Jones
114.5	Mark Fuller
136.5	Dan Mello
149.5	Jim Martinez*
163	John Matthews
180.5	Tom Press
198	Mike Houck
220	No champion
Hvy	No champion
Team	Adirondack 3-Style, Wash.

*Outstanding wrestler.

1985

FREESTYLE

105.5	Tim Vanni
114.5	Jim Martin
125.5	Charlie Heard
136.5	Darryl Burley
149.5	Bill Nugent*
163	Kenny Monday
180.5	Mike Sheets
198	Mark Schultz
220	Greg Gibson
286	Bruce Baumgartner
Team	Sunkist Kids

GRECO-ROMAN

105.5	T.J. Jones
114.5	Mark Fuller
125.5	Eric Seward*
136.5	Buddy Lee
149.5	Jim Martinez
163	David Butler
180.5	Chris Catallo
198	Mike Houck
220	Greg Gibson
286	Dennis Koslowski
Team	U.S. Marine Corps

1986

FREESTYLE

105.5	Rich Salamone
114.5	Joe Gonzales
125.5	Kevin Darkus
136.5	John Smith
149.5	Andre Metzger*
163	Dave Schultz
180.5	Mark Schultz
198	Jim Scherr
220	Dan Severn
286	Bruce Baumgartner
Team	Sunkist Kids (Div. I)
	Hawkeye Wrestling Club (Div. II)

GRECO-ROMAN

105.5	Eric Wetzel
114.5	Shawn Sheldon
125.5	Anthony Amado
136.5	Frank Famiano
149.5	Jim Martinez
163	David Butler*
180.5	Darryl Gholar
198	Derrick Waldroup
220	Dennis Koslowski
286	Duane Koslowski
Team	U.S. Marine Corps (Div. I)
	U.S. Navy (Div. II)

1987

FREESTYLE

105.5	Takashi Irie
114.5	Mitsuru Sato
125.5	Barry Davis
136.5	Takumi Adachi
149.5	Andre Metzger
163	Dave Schultz*
180.5	Mark Schultz
198	Jim Scherr
220	Bill Scherr
286	Bruce Baumgartner
Team	Sunkist Kids (Div. I)
	Team Foxcatcher (Div. II)

GRECO-ROMAN

105.5	Eric Wetzel
114.5	Shawn Sheldon
125.5	Eric Seward
136.5	Frank Famiano
149.5	Jim Martinez
163	David Butler
180.5	Chris Catallo
198	Derrick Waldroup*
220	Dennis Koslowski
286	Duane Koslowski
Team	U.S. Marine Corp (Div. I)
	U.S. Army (Div. II)

1988

FREESTYLE

105.5	Tim Vanni
114.5	Joe Gonzales
125.5	Kevin Darkus
136.5	John Smith*
149.5	Nate Carr
163	Kenny Monday
180.5	Dave Schultz
198	Melvin Douglas III
220	Bill Scherr
286	Bruce Baumgartner
Team	Sunkist Kids (Div. I)
	Team Foxcatcher (Div. II)

GRECO-ROMAN

105.5	T.J. Jones
114.5	Shawn Sheldon
125.5	Gogi Parseghian*
136.5	Dalen Wasmund
149.5	Craig Pollard
163	Tony Thomas
180.5	Darryl Gholar
198	Mike Carolan
220	Dennis Koslowski
286	Duane Koslowski
Team	U.S. Marine Corps (Div. I)
	Sunkist Kids (Div. II)

United States National Champions *(Cont.)*

1989

FREESTYLE
105.5	Tim Vanni
114.5	Zeke Jones
125.5	Brad Penrith
136.5	John Smith
149.5	Nate Carr
163	Rob Koll
180.5	Rico Chiapparelli
198	Jim Scherr*
220	Bill Scherr
286	Bruce Baumgartner
Team	Sunkist Kids (Div. I)
	Team Foxcatcher (Div. II)

GRECO-ROMAN
105.5	Lew Dorrance
114.5	Mark Fuller
125.5	Gogi Parseghian
136.5	Isaac Anderson
149.5	Andy Seras*
163	David Butler
180.5	John Morgan
198	Michial Foy
220	Steve Lawson
286	Craig Pittman
Team	U.S. Marine Corps (Div. I)
	Jets USA (Div. II)

1990

FREESTYLE
105.5	Rob Eiter
114.5	Zeke Jones
125.5	Joe Melchiore
136.5	John Smith
149.5	Nate Carr
163	Rob Koll
180.5	Royce Alger
198	Chris Campbell*
220	Bill Scherr
286	Bruce Baumgartner
Team	Sunkist Kids (Div. I)
	Team Foxcatcher (Div. II)

GRECO-ROMAN
105.5	Lew Dorrance
114.5	Sam Henson
125.5	Mark Pustelnik
136.5	Isaac Anderson
149.5	Andy Seras
163	David Butler
180.5	Derrick Waldroup
198	Randy Couture*
220	Chris Tironi
286	Matt Ghaffari
Team	Jets USA (Div. I)
	California Jets (Div. II)

1991

FREESTYLE
105.5	Tim Vanni
114.5	Zeke Jones
125.5	Brad Penrith
136.5	John Smith*
149.5	Townsend Saunders
163	Kenny Monday
180.5	Kevin Jackson
198	Chris Campbell
220	Mark Coleman
286	Bruce Baumgartner
Team	Sunkist Kids (Div. I)
	Jets USA (Div. II)

GRECO-ROMAN
105.5	Eric Wetzel
114.5	Shawn Sheldon
125.5	Frank Famiano
136.5	Buddy Lee
149.5	Andy Seras
163	Gordy Morgan
180.5	John Morgan*
198	Michial Foy
220	Dennis Koslowski
286	Craig Pittman
Team	Jets USA (Div. I)
	Sunkist Kids (Div. II)

1992

FREESTYLE
105.5	Rob Eiter
114.5	Jack Griffin
125.5	Kendall Cross*
136.5	John Fisher
149.5	Matt Demaray
163	Greg Elinsky
180.5	Royce Alger
198	Dan Chaid
220	Bill Scherr
286	Bruce Baumgartner
Team	Sunkist Kids (Div. I)
	Team Foxcatcher (Div. II)

GRECO-ROMAN
105.5	Eric Wetzel
114.5	Mark Fuller
125.5	Dennis Hall
136.5	Buddy Lee*
149.5	Rodney Smith
163	Travis West
180.5	John Morgan
198	Michial Foy
220	Dennis Koslowski
286	Matt Ghaffari
Team	N.Y. Athletic Club (Div. I)
	Sunkist Kids (Div. II)

1993

FREESTYLE
105.5	Rob Eiter
114.5	Zeke Jones
125.5	Brad Penrith
136.5	Tom Brands
149.5	Matt Demaray
163	Dave Schultz*
180.5	Kevin Jackson
198	Melvin Douglas
220	Kirk Trost
286	Bruce Baumgartner
Team	Sunkist Kids (Div. I)
	Team Foxcatcher (Div. II)

GRECO-ROMAN
105.5	Eric Wetzel
114.5	Shawn Sheldon
125.5	Dennis Hall*
136.5	Shon Lewis
149.5	Andy Seras
163	Gordy Morgan
180.5	Dan Henderson
198	Randy Couture
220	James Johnson
286	Matt Ghaffari
Team	N.Y. Athletic Club (Div. I)
	Sunkist Kids (Div. II)

1994

FREESTYLE
105.5	Tim Vanni
114.5	Zeke Jones
125.5	Terry Brands
136.5	Tom Brands
149.5	Matt Demaray
163	Dave Schultz
180.5	Royce Alger
198	Melvin Douglas
220	Mark Kerr
286	Bruce Baumgartner*
Team	Sunkist Kids (Div. I)
	Team Foxcatcher (Div. II)

GRECO-ROMAN
105.5	Isaac Ramaswamy
114.5	Shawn Sheldon
125.5	Dennis Hall
136.5	Shon Lewis
149.5	Andy Seras*
163	Gordy Morgan
180.5	Dan Henderson
198	Derrick Waldroup
220	James Johnson
286	Matt Ghaffari
Team	Armed Forces (Div. I)
	N.Y. Athletic Club (Div. II)

*Outstanding wrestler.

United States National Champions (Cont.)

1995
FREESTYLE

105.5 ......Tim Vanni
114.5 ......Zeke Jones
125.5 ......Terry Brands
136.5 ......Tom Brands
149.5 ......Matt Demaray
163 ....Dave Schultz
180.5 ......Royce Alger
198 ....Melvin Douglas
220 ....Mark Kerr
286 ....Bruce Baumgartner*
Team.......Sunkist Kids (Div. I)
Team Foxcatcher (Div. II)

GRECO-ROMAN

105.5 ......Isaac Ramaswamy
114.5 ......Shawn Sheldon
125.5 ......Dennis Hall
136.5 ......Shon Lewis
149.5 ......Andy Seras*
163 ....Gordy Morgan
180.5 ......Dan Henderson
198 ....Derrick Waldroup
220 ....James Johnson
286 ....Matt Ghaffari
Team.......Armed Forces (Div. I)
N.Y. Athletic Club (Div. II)

1996
FREESTYLE

105.5 ......Rob Eiter
114.5 ......Lou Rosselli
125.5 ......Kendall Cross*
136.5 ......Tom Brands
149.5 ......Matt Demaray
163 ....Dave Schultz
180.5 ......Kevin Jackson
198 ....Melvin Douglas
220 ....Kurt Angle
286 ....Bruce Baumgartner
Team.......Sunkist Kids (Div. I)
Team Foxcatcher (Div. II)

GRECO-ROMAN

105.5 ......Isaac Ramaswamy
114.5 ......Shawn Sheldon
125.5 ......Dennis Hall*
136.5 ......Van Fronhofer
149.5 ......Heath Sims
163 ....Matt Lindland
180.5 ......Marty Morgan
198 ....Michial Foy
220 ....James Johnson
286 ....Rulon Gardner
Team.......Armed Forces (Div. I)
Sunkist Kids (Div. II)

1997
FREESTYLE

110 ....Kanamti Soloman
119 ....Zeke Jones
127.75 .....Terry Brands
138.75 .....Carl Kolat
152 ....Lincoln McIlravy*
167.5 ......Dan St. John
187.25 .....Les Gutches
213.75 .....Melvin Douglas
275.5 ......Tom Erikson
Team.......Sunkist Kids (Div. I)
N.Y. Athletic Club (Div. II)

GRECO-ROMAN

110 ....Mark Yanagihara
119 ....Broderick Lee
127.75 .....Dennis Hall
138.75 .....Kevin Bracken
152 ....Chris Saba
167.5 ......Miguel Spencer
187.25 .....Dan Henderson
213.75 .....Randy Couture*
275.5 ......Rulon Gardner
Team.......Armed Forces (Div. I)
N.Y. Athletic Club (Div. II)

1998
FREESTYLE

119 ....Sam Henson
127.75 .....Tony Purler
138.75 .....Shawn Charles
152 ....Lincoln McIlravy
167.5 ......Steve Marianetti
187.25 .....Les Gutches*
213.75 .....Melvin Douglas
286 ....Tolly Thompson
Team.......Sunkist Kids (Div. I)
N.Y. Athletic Club (Div. II)

GRECO-ROMAN

119 ....Shawn Sheldon
127.75 .....Dennis Hall
138.75 .....Shon Lewis
152 ....Chris Saba
167.5 ......Matt Lindland
187.25 .....Dan Niebuhr*
213.75 .....Jason Klohs
286 ....Matt Ghaffari
Team.......Armed Forces (Div. I)
Sunkist Kids (Div. II)

1999
FREESTYLE

119 ....Lou Rosselli
127.75 .....Terry Brands
138.75 .....Cary Kolat
152 ....Lincoln McIlravy
167.5 ......Joe Williams
187.25 .....Les Gutches
213.75 .....Dominic Black
286 ....Stephen Neal*
Team.......Sunkist Kids (Div. I)
N.Y. Athletic Club (Div. II)

GRECO-ROMAN

119 ....Steven Mays
127.75 .....Dennis Hall
138.75 .....Glen Nieradka
152 ....David Zuniga
167.5 ......Matt Lindland
187.25 .....Quincey Clark
213.75 .....Randy Couture
286 ....Dremiel Byers*
Team.......Minnesota Storm (Div. I)
Sunkist Kids (Div. II)

2000
FREESTYLE

119 ....Sammie Henson
127.75 .....Keyy Boumans
138.75 .....Cary Kolat
152 ....Lincoln McIlravy
167.5 ......Brandon Slay*
187.25 .....Les Gutches
213.75 .....Melvin Douglas
286 ....Kerry McCoy
Team.......Sunkist Kids (Div. I)
N.Y. Athletic Club (Div. II)

GRECO-ROMAN

119 ....Brandon Paulson
127.75 .....Dennis Hall
138.75 .....Kevin Bracken
152 ....Heath Sims
167.5 ......Matt Lindland
187.25 .....Quincey Clark*
213.75 .....Jason Gleasman
286 ....Rulon Gardner
Team.......Armed Forces (Div. I)
Sunkist Kids (Div. II)

*Outstanding wrestler.

United States National Champions (Cont.)

2001

FREESTYLE
119 ....Eric Akin
127.75 .....Eric Guerrero
138.75 ....Bill Zadick
152 ....Ramico Blackmon
167.5 ....Joe Williams
187.25 ....Cael Sanderson*
213.75 .....Dominic Black
286 ....Kerry McCoy
Team........Sunkist Kids (Div. I)
       New York A.C. (Div. II)

GRECO-ROMAN
119 ....Jeff Cervone
127.75 ....Dennis Hall
138.75 ....Kevin Bracken
152 ....Marcel Cooper
167.5 ....Keith Sieracki
187.25 ....Matt Lindland*
213.75 .....Garrett Lowney
286 ....Rulon Gardner
Team........Army (Div. I)
       Sunkist Kids (Div. II)

2002

FREESTYLE
121 ....Teague Moore
132 ....Eric Guerrero
145.5 ....Bill Zadick
163 ....Joe Williams*
185 ....Cael Sanderson
211.5 ....Tim Hartung
264.5 ....Kerry McCoy
Team........Sunkist Kids (Div. I)
       New York A.C. (Div. II)

GRECO-ROMAN
121 ....Brandon Paulson
132 ....Glenn Nieradka*
145.5 ....Kevin Bracken
163 ....Keith Sieracki
185 ....Ethan Bosch
211.75 .....Garrett Lowney
264.5 ....Dremiel Byers
Team........Army (Div. I)
       New York A.C. (Div. II)

2003

FREESTYLE
121 ....Stephen Abas
132 ....Eric Guerrero*
145.5 ....Chris Bono
163 ....Joe Williams
185 ....Cael Sanderson
211.5 ....Daniel Cormier
264.5 ....Kerry McCoy
Team........Sunkist Kids (Div. I)
       Gator WC (Div. II)

GRECO-ROMAN
121 ....Brandon Paulson
132 ....James Gruenwald*
145.5 ....Kevin Bracken
163 ....Keith Sieracki
185 ....Brad Vering
211.5 ....Garrett Lowney
264.5 ....Dremiel Byers
Team........Army (Div. I)
       Air Force (Div. II)

2004

FREESTYLE
121 ....Stephen Abbas
132 ....Eric Guerrero
145.5 ....Jamill Kelly
163 ....Joe Williams
185 ....Lee Fullhart*
211.5 ....Daniel Cormier
264.5 ....Kerry McCoy
Team........Sunkist Kids (Div. I)
       Gator WC (Div. II)

GRECO-ROMAN
121 ....Brandon Paulson
132 ....James Gruenwald
145.5 ....Faruk Sahin
163 ....Darryl Christian
185 ....Brad Vering
211.5 ....Justin Ruiz
264.5 ....Dremiel Byers*
Team........New York A.C. (Div. I)
       Air Force (Div. II)

2005

FREESTYLE
121 ....Sam Henson
132 ....Michael Lightner*
145.5 ....Chris Bono
163 ....Joe Williams
185 ....Mo Lawal
211.5 ....Daniel Cormier
264.5 ....Tolly Thompson
Team........Sunkist Kids (Div. I)
       Gator WC (Div. II)

GRECO-ROMAN
121 ....Sam Hazewinkel
132 ....Joseph Warren
145.5 ....Harry Lester
163 ....Darryl Christian
185 ....Brad Vering
211.5 ....Justin Ruiz
264.5 ....Dremiel Byers*
Team........New York A.C. (Div.I)
       Air Force (Div. II)

2006

FREESTYLE
121 ....Henry Cejudo
132 ....Zach Roberson
145.5 ....Chris Bono
163 ....Donny Pritzlaff*
185 ....Mo Lawal
211.5 ....Daniel Cormier
264.5 ....Tolly Thompson
Team........Sunkist Kids (Div. I)
       Gator WC (Div. II)

GRECO-ROMAN
121 ....Lindsey Durlacher
132 ....Joseph Warren
145.5 ....Marcel Cooper
163 .........T.C. Dantzler
185 ....Jacob Clark*
211.5 ....Justin Ruiz
264.5 ....Dremiel Byers
Team........Army (Div. I)
       New York A.C. (Div. II)

*Outstanding wrestler.

The Sports Market

LOST OUR HOME
BUT NOT OUR FAITH

LOST OUR HOME
BUT NOT OUR FAITH

New Orleans' sports teams found 2006 anything but easy

SAIN

Old Faces, New Places

From sidelines to broadcast booths to executive boardrooms, 2006 saw a number of shake-ups in the world of sports

BY MERRELL NODEN

SPORTS FANS FEELING A BIT DISoriented this year needn't be alarmed. What they were experiencing was a perfectly natural response to all of the dislocation going on in the world of sports. Everywhere one looked one saw not strange faces, but familiar ones in strange surroundings: After 35 years on ABC, *Monday Night Football* moved to ESPN, sending the venerable *MNF* broadcast team of John Madden and Al Michaels to NBC on Sunday nights. And taking over from Paul Tagliabue as commissioner of the NFL was Roger Goodell, who in 25 years had worked his way up from a league intern to chief operating officer. He now assumes perhaps the most important job in all of professional sports. And yes, those were the New Orleans Hornets playing almost all of their "home" games in Oklahoma City, while the New Orleans Saints went marching out, away from the swath of destruction left by Hurricane Katrina, to play their "home" games in San Antonio and Baton Rouge.

All this dislocation was probably inevitable in a football season that began with the deadliest, costliest natural disaster the U.S. has suffered in decades. When Hurricane Katrina came roaring out of the Gulf of Mexico and made land just east of New Orleans on the morning of August 29, it killed at least 1,723 people and sent survivors fleeing all over the country in search of safe harbor. The Louisiana Superdome, which in happier times has hosted six Super Bowls, was designated an evacuation center and almost immediately became a heartbreaking symbol of government neglect and incompetence, as thousands of thirsty and desperate people, most of them poor and black, huddled outside, waiting for someone to come and rescue them.

The Dome took a terrible beating. It needed $185 million in repairs, $116 million of which came from the Federal Emergency Management Agency (FEMA). It took three months to remove 5,000 tons of waterlogged carpeting, ceiling tiles, and sheetrock, and to pump 3.8 million gallons of water from the Dome and its garages. And the facility's 9.7-acre roof needed $32.5 million in repairs.

But the overhaul seems to have worked. "The world is going to come back and see a rebuilt Superdome," vowed Paul Griesemer, the architectural director of Kansas City-based Ellerbe Becket, the firm hired to perform the largest stadium overhaul ever undertaken. "It's been a Herculean effort, just like this whole city and whole community has gone through a Herculean effort,

and it's going to be a symbol of these people [getting] something done."

After all that, the omens for the Saints' 2006 season were good. Buoyed partly by the acquisition of Heisman Trophy-winning running back Reggie Bush and partly by a shrewd ticket plan that reduced the price of 20,000 seats to no more than $35—with many as little as $14—the Saints had sold out nearly their entire season before Labor Day. They returned to the Dome on September 25, blasting the Atlanta Falcons 23–3 before a sellout crowd of 70,003.

Still, the question of whether the 31-year-old Superdome will continue to serve as the Saints' home or will be just a stop on the way to a more lucrative market is unresolved. "It's still an open question," allowed outgoing NFL commissioner Tagliabue, noting that the prospects of the Saints staying in New Orleans depended on how well the local economy rebounded. New Orleans has always been one of the NFL's smallest markets, and after the mass exodus prompted by Katrina, it got even smaller, ranking just 54th in the U.S., down from

New NFL Commissioner Roger Goodell (left) takes over a thriving league, but questions about the future of the Saints remain.

43rd last year. The desire to rally around a city so sadly abandoned by all levels of government seems to be strong for now. But one wonders how long that empathy will last. "We're finding there's a lot of disposable income in the hands of the people living here," said Doug Thornton, regional vice president of SMG, which manages both the Superdome and the New Orleans Arena for the state. "What we don't yet see is the depth of the corporate market here. That will probably be slower to recover."

It's the corporate market that fuels an NBA franchise, which must sell tickets for not just eight, but 41 games per season. The New Orleans Arena, home to the NBA Hornets, sustained much less damage than the Superdome, but the Hornets also had mixed feelings about their home city and its future. In 2004–05 the Hornets had the league's worst attendance. After playing just three "home" games in New Orleans last season—with the vast majority in Oklahoma City—the Hornets will double that number to six in 2006–07. After that, the team insists that it plans to return full-time for the 2007-08 season.

The future of New Orleans is just one of many dilemmas now facing new NFL commissioner Goodell, who is only the third person to hold that office in 46 years, after Pete Rozelle (1960-89) and Tagliabue (1989-2006). Tagliabue departs with a long list of achievements. On his watch, the league expanded from 28 to 32 teams and 17 new stadiums were built. In his first season, the TV revenues were $16.7 million per team, a figure that has now grown to $87.5 million. Most importantly, the NFL is the only one of the major pro sports leagues not to have suffered a work stoppage during Tagliabue's 17-year tenure, a testament to his skill at fine-tuning the balance of power and revenue-sharing between players and owners. One of Tagliabue's final acts was to oversee the adoption of a new collective bargaining agreement, which runs six more years.

Even in his absence, Tagliabue's influence will extend into the future through the owners' unanimous choice of Goodell on the fifth ballot. As chief operating officer for the past four seasons, Goodell had been instrumental in virtually every aspect of the league's growth, charting its global expansion and helping create the NFL Network, the league's television outlet. One good omen for Goodell was that in early September, just as he was assuming his new job, the NFL-themed feature film, *Invincible*, starring Mark Wahlberg as Vince Papale, a substitute teacher who makes the Philadelphia Eagles team during an open tryout, surprised everyone by spending two straight weeks at the top of the box office.

Taking over a league that is now earning a whopping $5 billion a year, Goodell immediately cited some areas he plans to explore, including the possibility of installing transmitters in linemen's helmets in order to cut back on false starts caused by crowd noise and the interruptions to game flow they inevitably create. A bigger challenge will be in framing an effective drug testing policy that the Players Association will agree to.

Far from resting on its laurels, the league has also been exploring new ways to expand its reach. In April, after signing a five-year, $600 million deal with Sprint to serve as the league's official wireless telecommunication service, the league streamed live coverage of the NFL draft to 20 million cellphone users. EA Sports timed the release of Madden NFL 07, the top selling video football game in history (51 million units sold since its debut in 1989), to the already frenzied beginning of the season. And, hoping to appeal to the 40% of NFL fans who are female, the league was offering a new line of purses and handbags adorned with the logos of all 32 teams.

Most important of all, the NFL Network, now in its third season, will broadcast eight late-season games during primetime on Thursdays and Saturdays. The league hopes to expand Network access beyond the 41 million households it currently reaches and to increase the amount each cable user pays from as low as 25 cents to as much as 90 cents per month. The Network also began airing a Sunday night highlight show that will compete with ESPN's *SportsCenter*.

Beyond that, the NFL signed a welter of lucrative new broadcast deals with established networks. When ABC, which had been losing at least $150 million per year despite the ratings dominance of *Monday Night Football*, decided to pull out, its Disney partner, ESPN, stepped in to buy *MNF* for $1.1 billion a year. ESPN is going to have to work hard and imaginatively to capitalize on its investment. The show's ratings have been declining steadily for the past decade, bottoming out at an alltime low of 10.8 last season; at the same time, the average age of its viewers has increased, to 45 last season.

Among the changes ESPN instituted in hopes of reversing that trend was a much-ballyhooed Monday night doubleheader to kick off the season and a regular 8:40 kick-off time, 25 minutes earlier than ABC had used. It also put three men back in the booth: Mike Tirico, Joe Theismann, and Tony Kornheiser, the *Washington Post* writer

Monday Night Football's **broadcast team of John Madden (l.) and Al Michaels switched networks and nights in 2006.**

who lately has been a ubiquitous presence on radio and, as co-host, with Michael Wilbon, of ESPN's popular afternoon yak-fest, *Pardon the Interruption.*

Meanwhile, NBC, which had severed its relationship with the league in 1998, decided to step back in, paying $600 million for the right to broadcast a Sunday night game. It hired *MNF*'s former duo of Al Michaels and John Madden to work the booth. Part of NBC's deal is the right to choose which game it will broadcast in seven of the final eight weeks of the season, giving it the power to choose the most meaningful game for its broadcast.

In all, there was so much shifting and changing and experimenting going on early in the NFL season that no one could pretend to have a clue which of these many ventures will thrive and which will disappoint.

Other sports market news included:

•Michael Jordan returned to the NBA in an official capacity as a minority owner of the Charlotte Bobcats.

•Both the New York Yankees and their crosstown rival Mets broke ground on new stadiums this year. The Yankees' new home, which will replace the most famous stadium in America, the "House That Ruth Built," which opened in 1923, is to stand just north of the current stadium, in Macombs Dam Park. It will seat 51,000 and is scheduled to open in 2009. Also expected to be completed in time for the 2009 season was the new Mets Ballpark, which will seat 45,000

and have an exterior façade inspired by old Ebbets Field in Brooklyn. And on the eastern shore of the Passaic River, in Harrison, N.J., the New York Red Bulls of the MLS broke ground on Red Bull Park, the team's $220 million, 25,000-seat soccer-specific stadium. It will feature a roof over all the seats but not the playing field.

•NBC, which had been splitting NASCAR's 36-race season with Fox as part of a six-year, $2.8 billion deal, decided not to renew its contract when it expires at the end of the 2006 season. ABC/ESPN picked up NBC's half for $4 billion over five or six years. Mind-boggling numbers when you consider that before inking the deal with Fox and NBC in 1999, NASCAR had received just $3 million for the broadcast rights to 28 races.

•In July, U.S. authorities signaled their seriousness about fighting internet gambling by arresting Peter Carruthers, chief executive of BetOnSports, a leading internet gambling company that is publicly traded in England. Carruthers was en route to Costa Rica, where the company has its headquarters, when he was arrested at Dallas-Fort Worth Airport and charged with racketeering conspiracy. In September, authorities arrested the chairman of another online gambling concern, Peter Dicks, at Kennedy Airport in New York.

Major League Baseball

Address: 245 Park Avenue, 31st Floor
             New York, NY 10167 USA
Telephone: (212) 931-7800
Commissioner: Allan H. (Bud) Selig
Chief Operating Officer: Robert DuPuy
Senior VP, Public Relations: Richard Levin
www.majorleaguebaseball.com

Major League Baseball Players Association

Address: 12 East 49th Street, 24th Floor
             New York, NY 10017
Telephone: (212) 826-0808
Executive Director: Donald Fehr
Director of Communications: Greg Bouris
Director of Business Affairs & Licensing: Judy Heeter
www.mlbplayers.com

Los Angeles Angels of Anaheim

Address: 2000 Gene Autry Way
             Anaheim, CA 92806
Telephone: (714) 940-2000
Stadium (Capacity): Angel Stadium
 of Anaheim (45,050)
Owner: Arturo Moreno
Vice President & General Manager: Bill Stoneman
Manager, Baseball Operations: Abe Flores
Vice President of Communications: Tim Mead
www.angelsbaseball.com

Arizona Diamondbacks

Address: 401 East Jefferson Street
             Phoenix, AZ 85001
Telephone: (602) 462-6500
Stadium (Capacity): Chase Field (49,033)
General Partner: Jeff Moorad
Senior V.P. & General Manager: Josh Byrnes
Manager: Bob Melvin
Senior Director of Public Relations: Mike Swanson
www.diamondbacks.com

Atlanta Braves

Address: 755 Hank Aaron Drive
             Atlanta, GA 30315
Telephone: (404) 522-7630
Stadium (Capacity): Turner Field (50,091)
Vice Chrmn./Sr. Advisor of Time Warner/AOL: Ted Turner
Executive VP & General Manager: John Schuerholz
Manager: Bobby Cox
Director of Media Relations: Brad Hainje
www.atlantabraves.com

Baltimore Orioles

Address: Oriole Park at Camden Yards
             333 W Camden Street
             Baltimore, MD 21201
Telephone: (410) 685-9800
Stadium (Capacity): Oriole Park at Camden Yards
 (48,876)
Chairman of the Board/CEO: Peter G. Angelos
Vice Chairman/COO: Joseph E. Foss
Manager: Sam Perlozzo
Director of Public Relations: Bill Stetka
www.orioles.com

Boston Red Sox

Address: 4 Yawkey Way
             Fenway Park
             Boston, MA 02215
Telephone: (617) 267-9440
Stadium (Capacity): Fenway Park (33,993)
Principal Owner: John W. Henry
Executive VP and General Manager: Theo Epstein
Manager: Terry Francona
VP of Communications: Glenn Geffner
www.redsox.com

Chicago Cubs

Address: Wrigley Field
             1060 West Addison
             Chicago, IL 60613
Telephone: (773) 404-2827
Stadium (Capacity): Wrigley Field (39,538)
President and CEO: Andrew B. MacPhail
Vice President/GM: Jim Hendry
Manager: Lou Piniella
Director of Media Relations: Sharon Pannozzo
www.cubs.com

Chicago White Sox

Address: U.S. Cellular Field
             333 West 35th Street
             Chicago, IL 60616
Telephone: (312) 674-1000
Stadium (Capacity): U.S. Cellular Field (40,615)
Chairman: Jerry Reinsdorf
General Manager: Kenny Williams
Manager: Ozzie Guillen
VP of Communications: Scott Reifert
www.whitesox.com

Cincinnati Reds

Address: 100 Main Street
             Cincinnati, OH 45202
Telephone: (513) 765-7000
Stadium (Capacity): Great American Ball Park
(42,059)
CEO/General Partner: Carl Lindner
COO: John L. Allen
General Manager: Wayne Krivsky
Manager: Jerry Narron
Director of Media Relations: Rob Butcher
www.reds.com

Cleveland Indians

Address: Jacobs Field
             2401 Ontario Street
             Cleveland, OH 44115-4003
Telephone: (216) 420-4200
Stadium (Capacity): Jacobs Field (43,368)
Owner and CEO: Lawrence J. Dolan
Executive VP and General Manager: Mark Shapiro
Manager: Eric Wedge
Director of Media Relations: Bart Swain
www.indians.com

Colorado Rockies

Address: 2001 Blake Street
             Denver, CO 80205
Telephone: (303) 292-0200
Stadium (Capacity): Coors Field (50,445)
Chairman and CEO: Charles K. Monfort
President: Keli McGregor
General Manager and Executive VP: Dan O'Dowd
Manager: Clint Hurdle
Vice President of Communications/PR: Jay Alves
www.coloradorockies.com

Detroit Tigers

Address: Comerica Park
             2100 Woodward Avenue
             Detroit, MI 48201
Telephone: (313) 471-2000
Stadium (Capacity): Comerica Park (40,120)
Owner: Mike Ilitch
President CEO & GM: Dave Dombrowski
Manager: Jim Leyland
Manager of Baseball Media Relations: Brian Britten
www.tigers.com

Florida Marlins
Address: 2267 Dan Marino Boulevard
Miami, FL 33056
Telephone: (305) 626-6100
Stadium (Capacity): Dolphin Stadium (47,662)
Owner: Jeffrey H. Loria
President: David Samson
Executive VP and General Manager: Larry Beinfest
Manager: Fredi Gonzalez
Sr. VP of Communications/Broadcasting:P.J. Loyello
www.floridamarlins.com

Houston Astros
Address: 501 Crawford Street
Houston, TX 77002
Telephone: (713) 259-8000
Stadium (Capacity): Minute Maid Park (40,950)
Chairman: Drayton McLane
President of Baseball Operations: Tal Smith
Manager: Phil Garner
Director of Media Relations: Jimmy Stanton
www.astros.com

Kansas City Royals
Address: 1 Royal Way
Kansas City, MO 64141
Telephone: (816) 921-8000
Stadium (Capacity): Kauffman Stadium (40,785)
Owner and Chairman of the Board: David D. Glass
VP & General Manager: Dayton Moore
Manager: Buddy Bell
VP of Communications & Marketing: David Witty
www.royals.com

Los Angeles Dodgers
Address: 1000 Elysian Park Avenue
Los Angeles, CA 90012-1199
Telephone: (323) 224-1500
Stadium (Capacity): Dodger Stadium (56,000)
Chairman: Frank McCourt
COO: Martin Greenspun
GM: Ned Colletti
Manager: Grady Little
Director Public Relations: Josh Rawitch
www.dodgers.com

Milwaukee Brewers
Address: 1 Brewers Way
Milwaukee, WI 53214
Telephone: (414) 902-4400
Stadium (Capacity): Miller Park (41,900)
Owner and Chairman: Mark Attanasio
Executive VP & General Manager: Doug Melvin
Manager: Ned Yost
Vice President of Communications: Tyler Barnes
www.milwaukeebrewers.com

Minnesota Twins
Address: 34 Kirby Puckett Place
Minneapolis, MN 55415
Telephone: (612) 375-1366
Stadium (Capacity): Hubert H. Humphrey
Metrodome (56,000)
Owner: Carl Pohlad
Vice President, General Manager: Terry Ryan
Manager: Ron Gardenhire
Manager of Baseball Communications: Mike Herman
www.twinsbaseball.com

Washington Nationals
Address: 2400 East Capitol Street SE
Washington, D.C. 20003
Telephone: (202) 675-5100
Stadium (Capacity): RFK Stadium (56,000)
President & CEO: Stan Kasten

Washington Nationals *(Cont.)*
Vice President and General Manager: Jim Bowden
Manager: TBA
Vice President of Communications: Chartese Burnett
www.nationals.com

New York Mets
Address: Shea Stadium
123-01 Roosevelt Ave.
Flushing, NY 11368
Telephone: (718) 507-6387
Stadium (Capacity): Shea Stadium (56,749)
Chairman of the Board & CEO: Fred Wilpon
Executive VP/General Manager: Omar Minaya
Manager: Willie Randolph
VP of Media Relations: Jay Horwitz
www.mets.com

New York Yankees
Address: 161st Street and River Avenue
Bronx, NY 10451
Telephone: (718) 293-4300
Stadium (Capacity): Yankee Stadium (57,746)
Principal Owner: George Steinbrenner
Chief Operating Officer: Lonn Trost
VP/General Manager: Brian Cashman
Manager: Joe Torre
Sr. Director Media Relations & Publicity: Rick Cerrone
www.yankees.com

Oakland Athletics
Address: 7000 Coliseum Way
Oakland, CA 94621
Telephone: (510) 638-4900
Stadium (Capacity): Network Associates Coliseum
(50,000)
Co-Owner/Managing Partner: Lewis Wolff
President: Michael Crowley
VP & General Manager: Billy Beane
Manager: TBA
Director of Public Relations: Jim Young
www.oaklandathletics.com

Philadelphia Phillies
Address: One Citizens Bank Way
Philadelphia, PA 19101-7575
Telephone: (215) 463-6000
Stadium (Capacity): Citizens Bank Park (43,500)
Chairman: Bill Giles
President: David P. Montgomery
General Manager: TBA
Manager: Charlie Manuel
Vice President, Public Relations: Larry Shenk
www.phillies.com

Pittsburgh Pirates
Address: 115 Federal Street
Pittsburgh, PA 15212
Telephone: (412) 323-5000
Stadium (Capacity): PNC Park (37,496)
CEO and Managing General Partner: Kevin McClatchy
Senior VP and General Manager: Dave Littlefield
Manager: Jim Tracy
Director of Media Relations: Jim Trdinich
www.pirates.com

St. Louis Cardinals
Address: 100 S. 4th Street
St. Louis, MO 63102
Telephone: (314) 345-9600
Stadium (Capacity): Busch Stadium (50,345)
President: Mark Lamping
Senior Vice President and GM: Walt Jocketty
Manager: Tony La Russa
Director of Media Relations: Brian Bartow
www.stlcardinals.com

San Diego Padres
Address: 100 Park Boulevard
San Diego, CA 92101
Telephone: (619) 795-5000
Stadium (Capacity): PETCO Park (42,445)
Chairman: John Moores
Executive VP/General Manager: Kevin Towers
Manager: TBA
Director of Media Relations: Luis Garcia
www.padres.com

San Francisco Giants
Address: 24 Willie Mays Plaza
San Francisco, CA 94107
Telephone: (415) 972-2000
Stadium (Capacity): AT&T Park (41,503)
President/Managing General Partner: Peter Magowan
Senior VP & General Manager: Brian Sabean
Manager: Bruce Bochy
Director of Media Relations: Blake Rhodes
www.sfgiants.com

Seattle Mariners
Address: P.O Box 4100
Seattle, WA 98104
Telephone: (206) 346-4000
Stadium (Capacity): SAFECO Field (47,116)
Chairman and CEO: Howard Lincoln
Executive VP of Baseball Operations/GM: Bill Bavasi
Manager: Mike Hargrove
Director of Baseball Information: Tim Hevly
www.seattlemariners.com

Tampa Bay Devil Rays
Address: One Tropicana Drive
St. Petersburg, FL 33705
Telephone: (727) 825-3137
Stadium (Capacity): Tropicana Field (43,761)
President: Matthew Silverman
Executive VP Baseball Operations: Andrew Friedman
Manager: Joe Maddon
Vice President of Communications: Rick Vaughn
www.devilrays.com

Texas Rangers
Address: 1000 Ballpark Way
Arlington, TX 76011
Telephone: (817) 273-5222
Stadium (Capacity): Ameriquest Field (49,115)
Chairman of the Board: Thomas O. Hicks
General Manager: Jon Daniels
Manager: TBA
Manager of Media Relations: Jeff Evans
www.texasrangers.com

Toronto Blue Jays
Address: Rogers Centre
1 Blue Jays Way, Suite 3200
Toronto, Ontario M5V 1J1 Canada
Telephone: (416) 341-1000
Stadium (Capacity): Rogers Centre (50,516)
President/CEO: Paul Godfrey
Senior Vice President/GM: J.P. Ricciardi
Manager: John Gibbons
VP of Communications: Jay Stenhouse
www.bluejays.com

Pro Football Directory

National Football League
Address: 280 Park Avenue
New York, NY 10017
Telephone: (212) 450-2000
Commissioner: Roger Goodell
VP of Public Relations: Greg Aiello
www.nfl.com

NFL Players Association
Address: 2021 L Street, N.W.
Washington, D.C. 20036
Telephone: (202) 463-2200
Executive Director: Gene Upshaw
Director of Communications: Carl Francis
www.nflpa.org

Arizona Cardinals
Address: P.O. Box 888
Phoenix, AZ 85001
Telephone: (602) 379-0101
Stadium (Capacity): Cardinals Stadium (73,000)
Chairman & President: Bill Bidwill
VP of Football Operations: Rod Graves
Coach: Dennis Green
Sr. Director Media Relations: Mark Dalton
www.azcardinals.com

Atlanta Falcons
Address: 4400 Falcon Park Way
Flowery Branch, GA 30542
Telephone: (770) 965-3115
Stadium (Capacity): Georgia Dome (71,149)
Owner and CEO: Arthur Blank
President and GM: Rich McKay
Coach: Jim Mora Jr.
Senior Director of Media Relations: Frank Kleha
www.atlantafalcons.com

Baltimore Ravens
Address: 1 Winning Drive.
Owings Mills, MD 21117
Telephone: (410) 701-4000
Stadium (Capacity): M & T Bank Stadium (69,084)
Owner: Steve Bisciottill
President: Dick Cassl
Coach: Brian Billick
Sr. VP of Public & Community Relations: Kevin Byrne
www.baltimoreravens.com

Buffalo Bills
Address: One Bills Drive
Orchard Park, NY 14127
Telephone: (716) 648-1800
Stadium (Capacity): Ralph Wilson Stadium (73,967)
Owner & President: Ralph C. Wilson Jr.
GM/Football Operations: Marv Levy
Coach: Dick Jauron
Vice President of Communications: Scott Berchtold
www.buffalobills.com

Carolina Panthers
Address: Ericsson Stadium
800 South Mint St.
Charlotte, NC 28202
Telephone: (704) 358-7000
Stadium (Capacity): Bank of America Stadium (73,298)
Founder and Owner: Jerry Richardson
President: Mark Richardson
General Manager: Marty Hurney
Coach: John Fox
Director of Communications: Charlie Dayton
www.panthers.com

Chicago Bears
Address: 1000 Football Drive
             Lake Forest, IL 60045
Telephone: (847) 295-6600
Stadium (Capacity): Soldier Field (61,500)
President/CEO: Ted Phillips
General Manager: Jerry Angelo
Coach: Lovie Smith
Director of Public Relations: Scott Hagel
www.chicagobears.com

Cincinnati Bengals
Address: One Paul Brown Stadium
             Cincinnati, OH 45202
Telephone: (513) 621-3550
Stadium (Capacity): Paul Brown Stadium (65,327)
President: Mike Brown
Executive Vice President: Katherine Blackburn
Coach: Marvin Lewis
Director of Public Relations: Jack Brennan
www.bengals.com

Cleveland Browns
Address: 76 Lou Groza Boulevard
             Berea, OH 44017
Telephone: (440) 891-5000
Stadium (Capacity): Cleveland Browns Stadium
(73,200)
Owner: Randy Lerner
Senior VP and General Manager: Phil Savage
Coach: Romeo Crennel
VP of Communications: Bill Bonsiewicz
www.clevelandbrowns.com

Dallas Cowboys
Address: One Cowboys Parkway
             Irving, TX 75063
Telephone: (972) 556-9900
Stadium (Capacity): Texas Stadium (65,639)
Owner, President and General Manager: Jerry Jones
Coach: Bill Parcells
Public Relations Director: Rich Dalrymple
www.dallascowboys.com

Denver Broncos
Address: 13655 Broncos Parkway
             Englewood, CO 80112
Telephone: (303) 649-9000
Stadium (Capacity): INVESCO Field at Mile High
(76,125)
President and Chief Executive Officer: Pat Bowlen
General Manager: Ted Sundquist
Executive VP of Football Ops/Coach: Mike Shanahan
VP of Public Relations: Jim Saccomano
www.denverbroncos.com

Detroit Lions
Address: 222 Republic Drive
             Allen Park, MI 48101
Telephone: (313) 216-4000
Stadium (Capacity): Ford Field (65,000)
Owner/Chairman: William Clay Ford
President/CEO: Matt Millen
Coach: Rod Marinellii
Director of Media Relations: Matt Barnhart
www.detroitlions.com

Green Bay Packers
Address: 1265 Lombardi Avenue
             Green Bay, WI 54304
Telephone: (920) 569-7500
Stadium (Capacity): Lambeau Field (72,515)
Chairman of the Board & CEO: Bob Harlan
Exec VP/GM/Director Football Ops: Ted Thompson
Coach: Mike McCarthy
Executive Director of Public Relations: Jeff Blumb
www.packers.com

Houston Texans
Address: Two Reliant Park
             Houston, TX 77054
Telephone: (832) 667-2000
Stadium (Capacity): Reliant Stadium (71,054)
Chairman and CEO: Robert C. McNair
General Manager: Rick Smith
Coach: Gary Kublak
Director of Media Realtions: Kevin Cooper
www.houstontexans.com

Indianapolis Colts
Address: 7001 West 56th Street
             Indianapolis, IN 46254
Telephone: (317) 297-2658
Stadium (Capacity): RCA Dome (56,127)
Owner and Chief Executive Officer: Jim Irsay
President: Bill Polian
Senior Executive Vice President: Pete Ward
Coach:Tony Dungy
Vice President of Public Relations: Craig Kelley
www.colts.com

Jacksonville Jaguars
Address: One Alltel Stadium Place
             Jacksonville, FL 32202
Telephone: (904) 633-6000
Stadium (Capacity): Alltel Stadium (73,000)
Chairman & CEO: J. Wayne Weaver
Vice President and CFO: Bill Prescott
Senior VP of Football Operations: Paul Vance
Coach: Jack Del Rio
VP of Communications and Media: Dan Edwards
www.jaguars.com

Kansas City Chiefs
Address: One Arrowhead Drive
             Kansas City, MO 64129
Telephone: (816) 920-9300
Stadium (Capacity): Arrowhead Stadium (79,451)
Founder: Lamar Hunt
CEO, President and General Manager: Carl Peterson
Coach: Herm Edwards
Public Relations Director: Bob Moore
www.kcchiefs.com

Miami Dolphins
Address: 2269 Dan Marino Blvd.
             Miami Gardens, Florida 33056
Telephone: (305) 623-6100
Stadium (Capacity): Dolphin Stadium (75,000)
Chairman of the Board/Owner: H. Wayne Huizenga
General Manager: Randy Mueller
Head Coach: Nick Saban
Senior VP Media Relations: Harvey Greene
www.miamidolphins.com

Minnesota Vikings
Address: 9520 Viking Drive
             Eden Prairie, MN 55344
Telephone: (952) 828-6500
Stadium (Capacity): HHH Metrodome (64,121)
Owner/Chairman: Zygi Wilf
Owner/President: Mark Wilf
Coach: Brad Childress
Public Relations Director: Bob Hagan
www.vikings.com

New England Patriots
Address: Gillette Stadium
             1 Patriot Place, Foxboro, MA 02035
Telephone: (508) 543-8200
Stadium (Capacity): Gillette Stadium (68,436)
Owner and Chairman: Robert K. Kraft
President: Jonathan Kraft
Coach: Bill Belichick
Director of Media Relations: Stacey James
www.patriots.com

New Orleans Saints
Address: 5800 Airline Drive
Metairie, LA 70003
Telephone: (504) 733-0255
Stadium (Capacity): Louisiana Superdome (68,390)
Owner: Tom Benson
Executive VP/GM: Mickey Loomis
Coach: Sean Payton
VP of Communications: Greg Bensel
www.neworleanssaints.com

New York Giants
Address: Giants Stadium
East Rutherford, NJ 07073
Telephone: (201) 935-8111
Stadium (Capacity): Giants Stadium (80,242)
President and co-CEO: John K. Mara
Chairman and Executive VP: Steven Tisch
Senior VP and General Manager: Ernie Accorsi
Coach: Tom Coughlin
Vice President of Communications: Pat Hanlon
www.giants.com

New York Jets
Address: 1000 Fulton Avenue
Hempstead, NY 11550
Telephone: (516) 560-8100
Stadium (Capacity): Giants Stadium (80,062)
Owner: Robert Wood Johnson IV
General Manager: Mike Tannenbaum
Coach: Eric Mangini
VP of Public Relations: Ron Colangelo
www.newyorkjets.com

Oakland Raiders
Address: 1220 Harbor Bay Parkway
Alameda, CA 94502
Telephone: (510) 864-5000
Stadium (Capacity): McAfee Coliseum (63,132)
Owner: Al Davis
Coach: Art Shell
Director of Public Relations: Mike Taylor
www.raiders.com

Philadelphia Eagles
Address: NovaCare Complex
1 NovaCare Way
Philadelphia, PA 19145
Telephone: (215) 463-2500
Stadium (Capacity): Lincoln Financial Field (68,532)
Chairman: Jeffrey Lurie
Coach/Exec. VP of Football Operations: Andy Reid
Director of Football Media Services: Derek Boyko
www.philadelphiaeagles.com

Pittsburgh Steelers
Address: 3400 South Water Street
Pittsburgh, PA 15203
Telephone: (412) 432-7800
Stadium (Capacity): Heinz Field (64,350)
Chairman: Dan Rooney
Director of Football Operations: Kevin Colbert
Coach: Bill Cowher
Manager of Public Relations: Burt Lauten
www.steelers.com

St. Louis Rams
Address: One Rams Way
St. Louis, MO 63045
Telephone: (314) 982-7267
Stadium (Capacity): Edward Jones Dome (66,000)
Owner and Chairman: Georgia Frontiere
President: John Shaw
Coach: Scott Linehan
Director of Corporate Communications: Allison Collinger
www.stlouisrams.com

San Diego Chargers
Address: Qualcomm Stadium
4020 Murphy Canyon Road
San Diego, CA 92123
Telephone: (858) 874-4500
Stadium (Capacity): Qualcomm Stadium (71,500)
Chairman: Alex G. Spanos
President and CEO: Dean A. Spanos
Executive VP and General Manager: A.J. Smith
Coach: Marty Schottenheimer
Director of Public Relations: Bill Johnston
www.chargers.com

San Francisco 49ers
Address: 4949 Centennial Boulevard
Santa Clara, CA 95054
Telephone: (408) 562-4949
Stadium (Capacity): Monster Park (69,734)
Owner: Denise DeBartolo York
Owner: John York
VP of Player Personnel: Scot McCloughan
Coach: Mike Nolan
Public Relations Director: Aaron Salkin
www.sf49ers.com

Seattle Seahawks
Address: 11220 N.E. 53rd Street
Kirkland, WA 98033
Telephone: (425) 827-9777
Stadium (Capacity): Qwest Field (67,000)
Owner: Paul Allen
President & CEO: Jody Patton
President of Football Operations: Tim Ruskell
Coach: Mike Holmgren
Director Communications/Broadcasting: Dave Pearson
www.seahawks.com

Tampa Bay Buccaneers
Address: One Buccaneer Place
Tampa, FL 33607
Telephone: (813) 870-2700
Stadium (Capacity): Raymond James Stadium (66,321)
Owner: Malcolm Glazer
General Manager: Bruce Allen
Coach: Jon Gruden
Director of Communications: Jeff Kamis
www.buccaneers.com

Tennessee Titans
Address: 460 Great Circle Road
Nashville, TN 37228
Telephone: (615) 565-4000
Stadium (Capacity): The Coliseum (68,798)
Owner: K.S. Adams Jr.
General Manager: Floyd Reese
Coach: Jeff Fisher
Director of Media Relations: Robbie Bohren
www.titansonline.com

Washington Redskins
Address: 21300 Redskins Park Drive
Ashburn, VA 20147
Telephone: (703) 726-7000
Stadium (Capacity): Fedex Field (86,484)
Owner: Daniel M. Snyder
VP of Football Operations: Vinny Cerrato
Coach: Joe Gibbs
VP of Public Relations: Chris Helein
www.redskins.com

Other Leagues

Canadian Football League
Address: 50 Wellington Street East - 3rd Floor
               Toronto, Ontario M5E1C8 Canada
Telephone: (416) 322-9650
Commissioner:Tom E.S. Wright
COO: Michael Copeland
Director of Communications: Perry Lefko
www.cfl.ca

NFL EUROPE
Address: 280 Park Avenue
            New York, NY 10017
Telephone: (212) 450-2000
Managing Directrors: John Beake and Jim Connelly
Director of Public Relations: David Tossell
www.nfleurope.com

Pro Basketball Directory

National Basketball Association

National Basketball Association
Address: 645 Fifth Avenue
            New York, NY 10022
Telephone: (212) 826-7000
Commissioner: David Stern
Deputy Commissioner & COO: Adam Silver
Sr. VP Marketing/Communications: Greg Economou
www.nba.com

National Basketball Association Players Association
Address: 2 Penn Plaza
            Suite 2430
            New York, NY 10121
Telephone: (212) 655-0880
Executive Director: William Hunter
www.nbpa.com

Atlanta Hawks
Address: 101 Marietta St NW, Suite 1900
            Atlanta, GA 30303
Telephone: (404) 827-3800
Arena (Capacity): Philips Arena (19,445)
Owner: Atlanta Spirit, LLC
President and CEO: Bernie Mullin
General Manager: Billy Knight
Coach: Mike Woodson
VP of Public Relations: Arthur Triche
www.nba.com/hawks/

Boston Celtics
Address: 226 Causeway Street, 4th Floor
            Boston, MA 02114
Telephone: (617) 854-8000
Arena (Capacity): FleetCenter (18,624)
CEO and Managing Partner: Wyc Grousbeck
Executive Dir. of Basketball Operations: Danny Ainge
Coach: Doc Rivers
VP of Media Relations Jeffrey Twiss
www.nba.com/celtics/

Charlotte Bobcats
Address: 333 East Trade Street
            Charlotte, NC 28202
Telephone: (704) 688-8600
Arena (Capacity): Charlotte Bobcats Arena (19,026)
Owner: Robert L. Johnson
General Manager and Coach: Bernie Bickerstaff
Director of Public Relations: Scott Leightman
www.nba.com/bobcats/

Chicago Bulls
Address: 1901 W. Madison Street
            Chicago, IL 60612
Telephone: (312) 455-4000
Arena (Capacity): United Center (21,711)
Chairman: Jerry Reinsdorf
Executive VP of Basketball Operations: John Paxson
Coach: Scott Skiles
Sr. Director of Public/Media Relations: Tim Hallam
www.nba.com/bulls/

Cleveland Cavaliers
Address: One Center Court
            Cleveland, OH 44115
Telephone: (216) 420-2000
Arena (Capacity): Quicken Loans Arena (20,562)
Chairman & Owner: Dan Gilbert
GM: Danny Ferry
Coach: Mike Brown
Director of Public Relations: Amanda Mercado
www.nba.com/cavaliers/

Dallas Mavericks
Address: 2909 Taylor Street
            Dallas, TX 75226
Telephone: (214) 747-6287
Arena (Capacity): American Airlines Center (19,200)
Owner: Mark Cuban
General Manager: Don Nelson
Head Coach: Avery Johnson
Sr. VP of Marketing/Communications: Matt Fitzgerald
www.nba.com/mavericks/

Denver Nuggets
Address: Pepsi Center
            1000 Chopper Circle
            Denver, CO 80204
Telephone: (303) 405-1100
Arena (Capacity): Pepsi Center (19,099)
Owner: E. Stanley Kroenke
VP of Basketball Operations:Mark Warkentein
Coach: George Karl
Director of Media Relations: Eric Sebastian
www.nba.com/nuggets/

Detroit Pistons
Address: The Palace of Auburn Hills
            Four Championship Drive
            Auburn Hills, MI 48326
Telephone: (248) 377-0100
Arena (Capacity): The Palace of Auburn Hills (22,076)
Owner: William M. Davidson
President of Basketball Operations: Joe Dumars
Coach: Flip Saunders
VP of Public Relations: Matt Dobek
www.nba.com/pistons/

National Basketball Association *(Cont.)*

Golden State Warriors
Address: 1011 Broadway
Oakland, CA 94607-4019
Telephone: (510) 986-2200
Arena (Capacity): The Arena in Oakland (19,596)
Owner and CEO: Christopher Cohan
Executive VP of Basketball Operations: Chris Mullin
Coach: Don Nelson
Director of Public Relations: Raymond Ridder
www.nba.com/warriors/

Houston Rockets
Address: 1510 Polk Street
Houston, TX 77002
Telephone: (713) 758-7200
Arena (Capacity): Toyota Center (18,300)
Owner: Leslie Alexander
President and CEO: George Postolos
General Manager: Carroll Dawson
Coach: Jeff Van Gundy
Director of Team Communications: Nelson Luis
www.nba.com/rockets/

Indiana Pacers
Address: 125 S. Pennsylvania Street
Indianapolis, IN 46204
Telephone: (317) 917-2500
Arena (Capacity): Conseco Fieldhouse (18,345)
Owners: Melvin Simon and Herbert Simon
CEO/President: Donnie Walsh
President of Basketball Operations: Larry Bird
Head Coach: Rick Carlisle
Media Relations Director: David Benner
www.nba.com/pacers/

Los Angeles Clippers
Address: The Staples Center
1111 S. Figueroa Street - St. 1100
Los Angeles, CA 90015
Telephone: (213) 742-7500
Arena (Capacity): The Staples Center (19,060)
Owner: Donald T. Sterling
Vice President of Basketball Operations: Elgin Baylor
Coach: Mike Dunleavy
Vice President of Communications: Joe Safety
www.nba.com/clippers/

Los Angeles Lakers
Address: 555 North Nash Street
El Segundo, CA 90245
Telephone: (310) 426-6000
Arena (Capacity): The Staples Center (18,997)
Owner: Dr. Jerry Buss
General Manager: Mitch Kupchak
Coach: Phil Jackson
Director of Public Relations: John Black
www.nba.com/lakers/

Memphis Grizzlies
Address: 191 Beale Street
Memphis TN 38103
Telephone: (901) 888-4667
Arena (Capacity): FedEx Forum (18,500)
Majority Owner: Michael E. Heisley
General Manager: Jerry West
Coach: Mike Fratello
Director of Media Relations: Kirk Clayborn
www.nba.com/grizzlies/

Miami Heat
Address: American Airlines Arena
601 Biscayne Boulevard
Miami, FL 33132
Telephone: (786) 777-1000
Arena (Capacity): American Airlines Arena (16,500)
Managing General Partner: Micky Arison
President & GM: Pat Riley
General Manager: Randy Pfund
Coach: Pat Riley
VP of Sports Media Relations: Tim Donovan
www.nba.com/heat/

Milwaukee Bucks
Address: The Bradley Center
1001 N. Fourth Street
Milwaukee, WI 53203
Telephone: (414) 227-0500
Arena (Capacity): The Bradley Center (18,717)
Owner: Herb Kohl
General Manager: Larry Harris
Coach: Terry Stotts
Public Relations Director: Cheri Hanson
www.nba.com/bucks/

Minnesota Timberwolves
Address: 600 First Avenue North
Minneapolis, MN 55403
Telephone: (612) 673-1600
Arena (Capacity): Target Center (19,006)
Owner: Glen Taylor
VP of Basketball Operations: Kevin McHale
Coach: Dwane Casey
Director of Communications: Ted Johnson
www.nba.com/timberwolves/

New Jersey Nets
Address: 390 Murray Hill Parkway
East Rutherford, NJ 07073
Telephone: (800) 765-6387
Arena (Capacity): Continental Airlines Arena (20,049)
Owner: Bruce Ratner
General Manager: Ed Stefanski
Coach: Lawrence Frank
Director of Public Relations: Aaron Harris
www.nba.com/nets/

New Orleans/Oklahoma City Hornets
Address: 1615 Poydras Street, Floor 20
New Orleans, LA70112
Telephone: (504) 525-4667
Arena (Capacity): New Orleans Arena (18,500)
Majority Owner: George Shinn
General Manager: Jeff Bower
Coach: Byron Scott
Director of Basketball Communications: Scott Hall
www.nba.com/hornets/

New York Knicks
Address: Madison Square Garden
Two Pennsylvania Plaza
New York, NY 10121
Telephone: (212) 465-6471
Arena (Capacity): Madison Square Garden (19,763)
Owner: ITT/Sheraton and Cablevision
Chairman: James Dolan
President of Basketball Operations: Isiah Thomas
Coach: Isiah Thomas
Vice President of Public Relations: Jon Supranowitz
www.nba.com/knicks/

National Basketball Association (Cont.)

Orlando Magic
Address: Two Magic Place
           8701 Maitland Summit Blvd.
           Orlando, FL 32810
Telephone: (407) 916-2400
Arena (Capacity): TD Waterhouse Centre (17,248)
Owner: Rich DeVos
Senior Executive Vice President: Pat Williams
Coach: Brian Hill
Director of Communication: Joel Glass
www.nba.com/magic/

Philadelphia 76ers
Address: First Union Center
           3601 South Broad Street
           Philadelphia, PA 19148
Telephone: (215) 339-7600
Arena (Capacity): Wachovia Center (20,444)
Chairman: Ed Snider
General Manager: Billy King
Coach: Maurice Cheeks
Director of Public Relations: Michael Preston
www.nba.com/sixers/

Phoenix Suns
Address: 201 East Jefferson Street
           Phoenix, AZ 85004
Telephone: (602) 379-7900
Arena (Capacity): US Airways Center (19,000)
Chairman/CEO: Jerry Colangelo
President and COO: Rick Welts
Coach/Vp of Basketball Ops/GM: Mike D'Antoni
VP of Basketball Communications: Julie Fie
www.nba.com/suns/

Portland Trail Blazers
Address: One Center Court
           Suite 200
           Portland, OR 97227
Telephone: (503) 234-9291
Arena (Capacity): Rose Garden Arena (19,980)
Chairman of the Board: Paul Allen
President: Steve Patterson
General Manager: John Nash
Coach: Nate McMillan
Executive Director of Communications: Mike Hanson
www.nba.com/blazers/

Sacramento Kings
Address: One Sports Parkway
           Sacramento, CA 95834
Telephone: (916) 928-0000
Arena (Capacity): ARCO Arena (17,317)
Owners: Joe and Gavin Maloof
President of Basketball Operations: Geoff Petrie
Coach: Eric Musselman
VP of Media Relations/Basketball Ops: Troy Hanson
www.nba.com/kings/

San Antonio Spurs
Address: AT&T Center
           San Antonio, TX 78219
Telephone: (210) 444-5000
Arena (Capacity): AT&T Center (18,797)
Chairman: Peter Holt
General Manager: R.C. Buford
Head Coach : Gregg Popovich
Director of Media Services: Tom James
www.nba.com/spurs/

Seattle SuperSonics
Address: 351 Elliott Avenue West
           Suite 500
           Seattle, WA 98119
Telephone: (206) 281-5800
Arena (Capacity): KeyArena (17,072)
Owner: The Basketball Club of Seattle, LLC
Chairman: Howard Schultz
President/CEO: Wally Walker
General Manager: Rick Sund
Coach: Bob Hill
Sr. VP of Communications: Karen Bryant
www.nba.com/sonics/

Toronto Raptors
Address: 40 Bay Street, Suite 400
           Toronto, Ontario M5J 2X2 Canada
Telephone: (416) 815-5600
Arena (Capacity): Air Canada Centre (19,800)
Owner: Maple Leaf Sports and Entertainment, Ltd.
President & GM: Bryan Colangelo
Coach: Sam Mitchell
Director of Media Relations: Jim Labumbard
www.nba.com/raptors/

Utah Jazz
Address: 301 West So. Temple
           Salt Lake City, UT 84101
Telephone: (801) 325-2500
Arena (Capacity): Delta Center (19,911)
Owner: Larry H. Miller
President: Dennis Haslam
VP of Basketball Operations: Kevin O'Connor
Coach: Jerry Sloan
Sr. Director of Media Relations: Kim Turner
www.nba.com/jazz/

Washington Wizards
Address: 601 F Street NW
           Washington D.C. 20004
Telephone: (202) 661-5000
Arena (Capacity): Verizon Center (20,674
Owner: Abe Pollin
President of Basketball Operations: Ernie Grunfeld
Coach: Eddie Jordan
Director of Public Relations: Zack Bolno
www.nba.com/wizards/

Women's National Basketball Association

Women's National Basketball Association
Address: 645 Fifth Avenue
             New York, NY 10022
Telephone: (212) 688-9622
President: Donna Orender
Director of WNBA Communications: Ron Howard
www.wnba.com

Charlotte Sting
Address: 333 East Trade Street
             Charlotte, NC 28202
Telephone: (704) 688-8860
Arena (Capacity): Charlotte Bobcats Arena (19,026)
Owner Robert Johnson
Coach: Muggsy Bogues
Director of Public Relations: Scott Leightman
www.wnba.com/sting/

Connecticut Sun
Address: One Mohegan Sun Blvd.
             Uncasville, CT 06382
Telephone: (877) 786-8499
Arena (Capacity): Mohegan Sun Arena (9,341)
CEO: Mitchell Etess
General Manager: Chris Sienko
Coach: Mike Thibault
Media Relations Manager: Bill Tavares
www.wnba.com/sun/

Detroit Shock
Address: 2 Championship Drive
             Auburn Hills, MI 48326
Telephone: (248) 377-0100
Arena (Capacity): The Palace of Auburn Hills (19,000)
Managing Partner: William Davidson
President: Tom Wilson
Coach: Bill Laimbeer
Director of Media Relations: Paul Hickey
www.wnba.com/shock/

Houston Comets
Address: Two Greenway Plaza, Suite 400
             Houston, TX 77046-3865
Telephone: (713) 627-9622
Arena (Capacity): Toyota Center (18,500)
Owner: Leslie L. Alexander
Coach and General Manager: Van Chancellor
Director of Media Relations: John Maxwell
www.wnba.com/comets/

Indiana Fever
Address: 125 S. Pennsylvania Street
             Indianapolis, IN 46204
Telephone: (317) 917-2500
Arena (Capacity): Conseco Field House (18,345)
CEO & President: Donnie Walsh
Pres. of Basketball Operatons: Larry Bird
Coach: Rick Carlisle
VP of Communications: Quinn Buckner
www.wnba.com/fever/

Los Angeles Sparks
Address: 2151 E. Grand Ave
             El Segundo, CA 90245
Telephone: (310) 341-1000
Arena (Capacity): Staples Center (19,282)
Chairman: Dr. Jerry Buss
General Manager: Virginia (Penny) Toler
Coach: Joe Bryant
Public Relations Coordinator: Ashley King
www.wnba.com/sparks/

Minnesota Lynx
Address: Target Center
             600 First Avenue North
             Minneapolis, MN 55403
Telephone: (612) 673-8400
Arena (Capacity): Target Center (19,006)
Owner: Glen Taylor
Coach: Carolyn Jenkins
Public Relations Manager: Mike Cristaldi
www.wnba.com/lynx/

New York Liberty
Address: Two Penn Plaza
             New York, NY 10121
Telephone: (212) 564-9622
Arena (Capacity): Madison Square Garden (19,763)
GM and Vice President: Carol Blazejowski
Coach: Pat Coyle
VP of Marketing and Communications: Amy Scheer
www.wnba.com/liberty/

Phoenix Mercury
Address: 201 East Jefferson Street
             Phoenix, AZ 85004
Telephone: (602) 514-8333
Arena (Capacity): US Airways Center (10,746)
Chairman and CEO: Jerry Colangelo
General Manager & VP of Operations: Seth Sulka
Coach: Paul Westhead
Communications Manager: Vince Kozar
www.wnba.com/mercury/

Sacramento Monarchs
Address: One Sports Parkway
             Sacramento, CA 95834
Telephone: (916) 928-0000
Arena (Capacity): ARCO Arena (17,317)
Owners: Joe and Gavin Maloof
President: John Thomas
GM and Coach: John Whisenant
Manager of Media Relations: Rebecca Brutlag
www.wnba.co/monarchs/

San Antonio Silver Stars
Address: One AT&T Center
             San Antonio, TX 78219
Telephone: (210) 444-5050
Arena (Capacity): AT&T Center (18,500)
Owner: Peter Holt
COO: Clarissa Davis-Wrightsil
GM/Coach: Dan Hughes
Media Services Manager: Kris Davis
www.wnba.com/silverstars/

Women's National Basketball Association *(Cont.)*

Seattle Storm
Address: 351 Elliott Avenue West
               Suite 500
               Seattle, WA 98119
Telephone: (206) 281-5800
Arena (Capacity): Key Arena (12,000)
Owners: The Basketball Club of Seattle LLC
Chairman: Howard Schultz
Coach: Anne Donovan
Director, Public Relations: Tom Savage
www.wnba.com/storm/

Washington Mystics
Address: Verizonl Center
               401 9ᵗʰ Street NW
               Washington, DC 20004
Telephone: (202) 266-2200
Arena (Capacity): Verizon Center (20,173)
President: Sheila Jackson
General Manager: Linda Hargrove
Coach: Richie Adubato
Director, Public Relations: Ketsia Colimon
www.wnba.com/mystics/

Hockey Directory

National Hockey League
Address: 1251 Avenue of the Americas
               47th floor
               New York, NY 10020-1198
Telephone: (212) 789-2000
Commissioner: Gary Bettman
President of NHL Enterprises: Ed Horne
Executive VP and Dir. of Hockey Operations: Colin Campbell
Sr. VP of Communications: Bernadette Mansur
www.nhl.com

National Hockey League Players Association
Address: 777 Bay Street, Suite 2400
               Toronto, Ontario M5G 2C8 Canada
Telephone: (416) 313-2300
Executive Director: Ted Saskin
Manager, Media Relations: Jonathan Weatherdon
www.nhlpa.com

Anaheim Ducks
Address: Arrowhead Pond of Anaheim
               2695 Katella Avenue
               Anaheim, CA 92806
Telephone: (877) 945-9464
Arena (Capacity): Arrowhead Pond of Anaheim (17,174)
CEO: Michael Schulman
Executive VP and General Manager: Brian Burke
Coach: Randy Carlyle
Director of Communications: Alex Gilchrist
www.anaheimducks.com

Atlanta Thrashers
Address: Centennial Tower
               101 Marietta Street
               Atlanta, GA 30303
Telephone: (404) 878-3300
Arena (Capacity): Philips Arena (18,545)
Owner: Atlanta Spirit, LLC
Governor: Bruce Levenson
VP and General Manager: Don Waddell
Coach: Bob Hartley
Senior VP Communications: Tom Hughes
www.atlantathrashers.com

Boston Bruins
Address: TD Banknorth Garden,
               100 Legends Way
               Boston, MA 02114
Telephone: (617) 624-1900
Arena (Capacity): TD Banknorth Garden (17,565)
Chairman & CEO: Jeremy M. Jacobs
Alternative Governor and President: Harry Sinden
GM: Peter Chiarelli
Coach: Dave Lewis
Director of Media Relations: Heidi Holland
www.bostonbruins.com

Buffalo Sabres
Address: HSBC Arena
               One Seymour H. Knox III Plaza
               Buffalo, NY 14203
Telephone: (716) 855-4100
Arena (Capacity): HSBC Arena (18,690)
Owner: B. Thomas Golisano
General Manager: Darcy Regier
Coach: Lindy Ruff
Director of Public Relations: Michael Gilbert
www.sabres.com

Calgary Flames
Address: Pengrowth Saddledome
               P.O.Box 1540 Stn. M.
               Calgary, Alberta Canada T2P3B9
Telephone: (403) 777-2177
Arena (Capacity): Pengrowth Saddledome (17,409)
Owners: Harley N. Hotchkiss, N. Murray Edwards, Alvin G. Libin, Allan P. Markin, J.R. "Bud" McCaig, Byron J.Seaman, Daryl K. Seaman, Clayton H. Riddell
President and CEO: Ken King
General Manager : Darryl Sutter
Coach: Jim Playfair
Director of Communications: Peter Hanlon
www.calgaryflames.com

Carolina Hurricanes
Address: 1400 Edwards Mill Road
               Raleigh, NC 27607
Telephone: (919) 467-7825
Arena (Capacity): RBC Center (18,730)
Owner: Peter Karmanos Jr.
President and General Manager: Jim Rutherford
VP/Assistant General Manager: Jason Karmanos
Coach: Peter Laviolette
Director of Media Relations: Mike Sundheim
www.carolinahurricanes.com

Chicago Blackhawks

Address: United Center
             1901 W. Madison Street
             Chicago, IL 60612
Telephone: (312) 455-7000
Arena (Capacity): United Center (20,500)
President: William W. Wirtz
General Manager: Dave Tallon
Coach: Trent Yawney
Executive Director of Communications: Jim DeMaria
www.chicagoblackhawks.com

Colorado Avalanche

Address: Pepsi Center
             1000 Chopper Circle
             Denver, CO 80204
Telephone: (303) 405-1100
Arena (Capacity): Pepsi Center (18,007)
Owner and Governor: E. Stanley Kroenke
Executive VP & GM: Francois Giguere
Coach: Joel Quenneville
Sr. VP of Communications and Business Operations:
Jean Martineau
www.coloradoavalanche.com

Columbus Blue Jackets

Address: 200 West Nationwide Boulevard
             Columbus, OH 43215
Telephone: (614) 246-4625
Arena (Capacity): Nationwide Arena (18,136)
Owner/Governor: John H. McConnell
President, GM and Coach: Doug MacLean
Coach: Gerard Gallant
Manager of Communications: Ryan Holtmann
www.bluejackets.com

Dallas Stars

Address: 2601 Avenue of the Stars
             Frisco, TX 75034
Telephone: (218) 387-5500
Arena (Capacity): American Airlines Center (18,532)
Owner: Thomas O. Hicks
General Manager: Doug Armstrong
Coach: Dave Tippett
Director of Public Relations: Mark Janko
www.dallasstars.com

Detroit Red Wings

Address: Joe Louis Arena
             600 Civic Center Drive
             Detroit, MI 48226
Telephone: (313) 983-6606
Arena (Capacity): Joe Louis Arena (20,056)
Owner and Governor: Mike Ilitch
Owner, Secretary and Treasurer: Marian Ilitch
Senior Vice President/Alt. Governor: Jim Devellano
General Manager: Ken Holland
Coach: Mike Babcock
Senior Director of Communications: John Hahn
www.detroitredwings.com

Edmonton Oilers

Address: 11230 110th Street
             Edmonton, Alberta T5G 3H7
Telephone: (780) 414-4000
Arena (Capacity): Rexall Place (16,839)
Owner: Edmonton Investors Group
President and CEO: Patrick LaForge
General Manager: Kevin Lowe
Coach: Craig MacTavish
Manager, Media Relations: J.J.Herbert
www.edmontonoilers.com

Florida Panthers

Address: 1 Panther Parkway
              Sunrise, FL 33323
Telephone: (954) 835-7000
Arena (Capacity): Bank Atlantic Center (19,250)
Chairman of the Board/CEO: Alan Cohen
Alternate Governor: William A. Torrey
GM/Coach: Jacques Martin
Manager of Communications: Justin Copertino
www.floridapanthers.com

Los Angeles Kings

Address: The Staples Center
              1111 South Figueroa Street
              Los Angeles, CA 90015
Telephone: (213) 742-7100
Arena (Capacity): The Staples Center (18,118)
Owners: Philip Anschutz and Edward P. Roske Jr.
President/GM: Dean Lombardi
Coach: Marc Crawford
Director of Communications: Jeff Moeller
www.lakings.com

Minnesota Wild

Address: 317 Washington Street
              St. Paul, MN, 55102
Telephone: (651) 602-6000
Arena (Capacity): Xcel Energy Center (18,064)
Chairman: Bob Naegele Jr.
President & GM: Doug Risebrough
Coach: Jacques Lemaire
VP of Communications/Broadcasting: Bill Robertson
www.wild.com

Montreal Canadiens

Address: Bell Centre
              1275 St. Antoine Street West
              Montreal, Quebec H3C 5L2 Canada
Telephone: (514) 932-2582
Arena (Capacity): Bell Centre (21,273)
Owner: George N. Gillett Jr.
President and Governor: Pierre Boivin
Executive VP and General Manager: Bob Gainey
Coach: Guy Carbonneau
VP, Communications/Community Relations: Donald
Beauchamp
www.canadiens.com

Nashville Predators

Address: Gaylord Entertainment Center
              501 Broadway
              Nashville, TN 37203
Telephone: (615) 770-2300
Arena (Capacity): Gaylord Entertainment Center
(17,113)
Owner, Chairman and Governor: Craig Leipold
Executive VP of Hockey Operations/GM: David Poile
Coach: Barry Trotz
Director of Communications: Ken Anderson
www.nashvillepredators.com

New Jersey Devils

Address: Continental Airlines Arena, PO Box 504
              East Rutherford, NJ 07073
Telephone: (201) 935-6050
Arena (Capacity): Continental Airlines Arena (19,040)
Chairman and Managing Partner: Jeff Vanderbeek
CEO, President and GM: Lou Lamoriello
Coach:Claude Julien
Director of Public Relations: Jeff Altstadter
www.newjerseydevils.com

New York Islanders

Address: 1535 Old Country Road
Plainview, NY 11803
Telephone: (516) 501-6700
Arena (Capacity): Nassau Coliseum (16,234)
Owners: Charles Wang and Sanjay Kumar
Senior VP of Operations and Alt. Governor: Michael J Picker
General Manager: Garth Snow
Coach: Ted Nolan
VP of Communications: Chris Botta
www.newyorkislanders.com

New York Rangers

Address: Madison Square Garden
2 Pennsylvania Plaza
New York, NY 10121
Telephone: (212) 465-6000
Arena (Capacity): Madison Square Garden (18,200)
Owner: Cablevision
President and General Manager: Glen Sather
Coach: Tom Renney
VP of Public Relations: John Rosasco
www.newyorkrangers.com

Ottawa Senators

Address: Scotiabank Place
1000 Palladium Drive
Ottawa, Ontario K2V 1A5 Canada
Telephone: (613) 599-0250
Arena (Capacity): Scotiabank Place (20,500)
Owner, Governor and Chairman: Eugene Melnyk
President and Chief Executive Officer: Roy Mlakar
General Manager: John Muckler
Coach: Bryan Murray
VP of Communications: Phil Legault
www.ottawasenators.com

Philadelphia Flyers

Address: Wachovia Complex
3601 South Broad Street
Philadelphia, PA 19148
Telephone: (215) 465-4500
Arena (Capacity): Wachovia Center (19,523)
Majority Owner: Comcast Spectacor
Chairman: Ed Snider
President: Peter Luukko
General Manager: Paul Holmgren
Coach: John Stevens
Sr.. Director of Communications: Zack Hill
www.philadelphiaflyers.com

Phoenix Coyotes

Address: Glendale Arena
5800 W. Glen Drive, Suite 350
Glendale, AZ 85301
Telephone: (623) 463-8800
Arena (Capacity): Glendale Arena (17,653)
Chairman and Governor: Steve Ellman
Managing Partner and Alt. Governor: Wayne Gretzky
VP and General Manager: Michael Barnett
Coach: Wayne Gretzky
VP of Media and Player Relations: Richard Nairn
www.phoenixcoyotes.com

Pittsburgh Penguins

Address: Mellon Arena
One Chatham center, suite 400
Pittsburgh, PA 15219
Telephone: (412) 642-1300
Arena (Capacity): Mellon Arena (16,958)
Owner: Mario Lemieux (Lemieux Ownership Group)
Executive VP & GM: Ray Shero
Coach: Michael Therrien
Director of Media Relations: Keith Wehner
www.pittsburghpenguins.com

St. Louis Blues

Address: Savvis Center
1401 Clark Avenue
St. Louis, MO 63103
Telephone: (314) 622-2500
Arena (Capacity): Savvis Center (19,022)
CEO: Peter Mc Loughlin
Senior VP and General Manager: Larry Pleau
Coach: Mike Kitchen
Sr. Director of Media Relations/Team Services:
Michael Caruso
www.stlouisblues.com

San Jose Sharks

Address: HP Pavilion at San Jose
525 West Santa Clara Street
San Jose, CA 95113
Telephone: (408) 287-7070
Arena (Capacity): HP Pavilion at San Jose (17,496)
Owner: San Jose Sports And Entertainment Enterprises
President and CEO: Greg Jamison
Executive VP and General Manager: Doug Wilson
Coach: Ron Wilson
Director of Media Relations: Scott Emmert
www.sjsharks.com

Tampa Bay Lightning

Address: 401 Channelside Drive
Tampa, FL 33602
Telephone: (813) 301-6600
Arena (Capacity): St. Pete Times Forum (19,758)
Owner: Palace Sports & Entertainment/Bill Davidson and David Hermelin
CEO and Governor: Tom Wilson
GM/Exec VP/Alt Governor: Jay Feaster
Coach: John Tortorella
Sr. VP of Communications: Bill Wickett
www.tampabaylightning.com

Toronto Maple Leafs

Address: Air Canada Centre
40 Bay Street - St. 400
Toronto, Ontario M5J 2X2 Canada
Telephone: (416) 815-5500
Arena (Capacity): Air Canada Centre (18,819)
Chairman: Lawrence M. Tanenbaum
President and CEO: Richard Peddie
Vice President and GM: John Ferguson
Coach: Paul Maurice
Director of Media Relations: Pat Park
www.mapleleafs.com

Vancouver Canucks

Address: General Motors Place/800 Griffiths Way
Vancouver, B.C. V6B 6G1
Telephone: (604) 899-4600
Arena (Capacity): General Motors Place (18,422)
Chairman and Governor: John E. McCaw Jr.
Deputy Chairman: Francesco Aquilini
Executive Vice President: Jon Festinger
Senior VP/GM: David Nonis
Coach: Alain Vigneault
Manager of Media Relations: Chris Brumwell
www.canucks.com

Washington Capitals

Address: 401 Ninth Street, NW
Suite 750
Washington, DC 20004
Telephone: (202) 266-2200
Arena (Capacity): Verizon Center (20,674)
Majority Owner and Chairman: Ted Leonsis
Owner and President: Richard M. Patrick
VP and General Manager: George McPhee
Coach: Glen Hanlon
Director of Media Relations: Nate Ewell
www.washingtoncaps.com

Olympic Sports Directory

United States Olympic Committee

Address: Olympic House
1 Olympic Plaza
Colorado Springs, CO 80909
Telephone: (719) 632-5551
CEO: Jim Scherr
Chief Communications Officer: Darryl Seibel
www.usolympicteam.com

U.S. Olympic Training Centers

Address: 1 Olympic Plaza
Colorado Springs, CO 80909
Telephone: (719) 866-4500
Managing Director: Mike English

Address: 421 Old Military Road
Lake Placid, NY 12946
Telephone: (518) 523-2600
Director: Jack Favro

Address: 2800 Olympic Parkway
Chula Vista, CA 91915
Telephone: (619) 656-1500
Director: Patrice Milkovich
www.olympic.org

International Olympic Committee

Address: Chateau de Vidy
Case Postale 356
CH-1007 Lausanne, Switzerland
Telephone: 41-21-621-6111
President: Jacques Rogge
Director General: Urs Lacotte
www.olympic.org

Vancouver 2010 Olympic Organizing Committee (VANOC)

Address: 3835 Graveley Street
Vancouver, BC, V5K 5J5
Telephone: 1.778.328.2010
CEO: John Furlong
Exec VP of Marketing/Communications: Dave Cobb
(XX Winter Games; Feb 12–28, 2010)
www.vancouver2010.com

Beijing 2008 Olympic Organizing Committee (BOCOG)

Address: 24 Dongsi Shitao Street
Beijing, China 100007
Telephone: (8610) 65282009
(XXVIII Summer Games; Aug 8–24, 2008)
www.beijing-olympic.org.cn

U.S. Olympic Organizations

National Archery Association (NAA)

Address: 1 Olympic Plaza
Colorado Springs, CO 80909
Telephone: (719) 866-4576
President: Darrell Pace
Executive Director: Brad Camp
Media Relations: Mary Beth Vorwerk
www.usarchery.org

USA Badminton (USAB)

Address: 1 Olympic Plaza
Colorado Springs, CO 80909
Telephone: (719) 866-4808
President: Cliff Peters
Executive Director: Dan Cloppas
USOC NGB Media Services Manager: Cecil Bleiker
www.usabadminton.org

USA Baseball

Address: P.O. Box 1131
Durham, NC 27702
Telephone: (919) 474-8721
President: Mike Gaski
Executive Director/CEO: Paul V. Seiler
Director of Communications: TBD
www.usabaseball.com

USA Basketball

Address: 5465 Mark Dabling Blvd.
Colorado Springs, CO 80918
Telephone: (719) 590-4800
President: Val Ackerman
Executive Director: Jim Tooley
Director of Communications: Caroline Williams
www.usabasketball.com

U.S. Biathlon Association (USBA)

Address: New Gloucester Hall, suite 301A
49 Pinelind Drive
New Gloucester, ME 04260
Telephone: (207) 688-6500
President: Bob Lilly
Executive Director: Maxx Cobb
Media Coordinator: Jerry Kokesh
www.usbiathlon.org

U.S. Bobsled and Skeleton Federation

Address: P.O. Box 828
Lake Placid, NY 12946
Telephone: (518) 523-1842
President: James Shea Sr.
Interim Executive Director: Terry Kent
Public Relations & Media Director: Tom LaDue
www.usabsf.com

U.S. Olympic Organizations (Cont.)

USA Boxing, Inc.
Address: 1 Olympic Plaza
            Colorado Springs, CO 80909
Telephone: (719) 866-4506
President: Bill Meartz
Executive Director: Ed Weichers
Director of PR and Media: Julie Goldsticker
www.usaboxing.org

U.S. Canoe and Kayak Team
Address: 230 South Tryon Street - Suite 220
            Charlotte, NC 28202
Telephone: (704) 348-4330
Chair: Mike Sloan
Executive Director: David Yarborough
Media/Communications: Luke Dieker
www.usacanoekayak.org

USA Cycling
Address: 1 Olympic Plaza
            Colorado Springs, CO 80909
Telephone: (719) 866-4581
President: Jim Ochowicz
Chief Executive Officer: Steve Johnson
Communications Coordinators: Andy Lee, Jessica
De Los Reyes
www.usacycling.org

United States Diving, Inc. (USD)
Address: Pan American Plaza, Suite 430
            201 South Capitol Avenue
            Indianapolis, IN 46225
Telephone: (317) 237-5252
President: Dave Burgering
Executive Director: Todd Smith
Communication Coordinator: Jennifer Lowery
www.usdiving.org

U.S. Equestrian Team (USET)
Address: Pottersville Rd.
            Gladstone, NJ 07934
Telephone: (908) 234-1251
Executive Director: Bonnie Jenkins
Commuications Coordinator: Maureen Pethick
www.uset.org

U.S. Fencing Association (USFA)
Address: 711 North Tejon
            Colorado Springs, CO 80903
Telephone: (719) 866-4511
President: Nancy Anderson
Executive Director: Michael Massik
Media Relations Director: Cynthia Bent
www.usfencing.org

U.S. Field Hockey Association (USFHA)
Address: 711 North Tejon
            Colorado Springs, CO 80903
Telephone: (719) 866-4567
President: Sharon Taylor
Executive Director: Sheila Walker
Sport and Public Information Director:
    Howard Thomas
www.usfieldhockey.com

U.S. Figure Skating Association
Address: 20 First Street
            Colorado Springs, CO 80906
Telephone: (719) 635-5200
President: Ron Hershberger
Director of Media Relations: Lindsay DeWall
www.usfsa.org

USA Gymnastics
Address: Pan American Plaza, Suite 300
            201 South Capitol Avenue
            Indianapolis, IN 46225
Telephone: (317) 237-5050
Chairman of the Board: Ron Froehlich
President/CEO: Steve Penny
Managing Director of Communications: Leslie King
www.usa-gymnastics.org

USA Hockey
Address: 1775 Bob Johnson Drive
            Colorado Springs, CO 80906
Telephone: (719) 576-8724
President: Ron DeGregorio
Executive Director: Dave Ogrean
Director of Media & Public Relations: Dave Fischer
www.usahockey.com

United States Judo, Inc. (USJ)
Address: 1 Olympic Plaza Suite 202
            Colorado Springs, CO 80909
Telephone: (719) 866-4730
President: Dr. Ronald Tripp
Executive Director: Jose Rodriguez
www.usjudo.org

U.S. Luge Association (USLA)
Address: 57 Church Street
            Lake Placid, NY 12946
Telephone: (518) 523-2071
President: Doug Bateman
Executive Director: Ron Rossi
Public Relations Manager: Jon Lundin
www.usaluge.org

U.S. Modern Pentathlon Association
Address: 1 Olympic Plaza
            Colorado Springs, CO 80909
Telephone: (719)866-4234
USOC NGB Media Services Manager: Cecil Bleiker

U.S. Racquetball Association
Address: 1685 West Uintah
            Colorado Springs, CO 80904
Telephone: (719) 635-5396
President: Randy Stafford
Executive Director: Jim Hiser
Media & Public Relations Manager:TBD
www.usra.org

USA Roller Sports
Address: 4730 South Street
            P.O. Box 6579
            Lincoln, NE 68506
Telephone: (402) 483-7551
President: George Kolibaba
Communications Director: Bill Wolf
www.usarollersports.org

U.S. Rowing
Address: 2 Wall Street
            Princeton, NJ 08540
Telephone: (800) 314-4769/ 1 (609) 751-0700
Executive Director: Glenn Merry
Communications Director: Brett Johnson
www.usrowing.org

U.S. Olympic Organizations *(Cont.)*

U.S. Sailing Association
Address: 15 Maritime Drive
             P.O. Box 1260
             Portsmouth, RI 02871
Telephone: (401) 683-0800
President: Janet C. Baxter
Executive Director: Charlie Leighton
Communications Manager: Marlieke de Lange Eaton
Olympic Yachting Director: Katie Kelly
www.ussailing.org

USA Shooting
Address: 1 Olympic Plaza
             Colorado Springs, CO 80909
Telephone: (719) 866-4670
Chairman of the Board: Dr. James Lally
CEO: Robert K. Mitchell
Media Relations Manager: Najasila Campbell
www.usashooting.com

U.S. Ski and Snowboard Association
Address: P.O. Box 100
             Park City, UT 84060
Telephone: (435) 649-9090
Chairman: Dexter Paine
President and CEO: Bill Marolt
V.P. of Communications and Media: Tom Kelly
www.usskiteam.com

U.S. Soccer Federation (USSF)
Address: 1801-1811 South Prairie Avenue
             Chicago, IL 60616
Telephone: (312) 808-1300
President: Sunil Gulati
Secretary General: Dan Flynn
Director of Communications: Jim Moorhouse
www.ussoccer.com

Amateur Softball Association (ASA)
Address: 2801 N.E. 50th Street
             Oklahoma City, OK 73111
Telephone: (405) 424-5266
President: D Stephen Monson
Executive Director: Ron Radigonda
Director of Communications: Brian McCall
www.softball.org

U.S. Speed Skating
Address: P.O. Box 450639
             Westlake, OH 44145
Telephone: (440) 899-0128
President: Brad Goskowicz
Executive Director: Bob Crowley
Public Relations Director: Melissa Scott
www.usspeedskating.org

U.S. Swimming, Inc. (USS)
Address: 1 Olympic Plaza
             Colorado Springs, CO 80909
Telephone: (719) 866-4578
President: Ron Van Pool
Executive Director: Chuck Wielgus
Media Coordinator: Sara Hunninghake
www.usa-swimming.org

U.S. Synchronized Swimming, Inc. (USSS)
Address: Pan American Plaza, Suite 901
             201 South Capitol Avenue
             Indianapolis, IN 46225
Telephone: (317) 237-5700
President: Virginia Jasontek
Executive Director: Terry Harper
Media Relations Director: Mandy Harlan
www.usasynchro.org

U.S. Table Tennis Association (USTTA)
Address: 1 Olympic Plaza
             Colorado Springs, CO 80909
Telephone: (719) 866-4583
Executive Director: Doru Gheorghe
President: Sheri Pittman
Progam Coordinator: Dana Schnell
www.usatt.org

U.S. Taekwondo
Address: 1 Olympic Plaza, Suite 405
             Colorado Springs, CO 80909
Telephone: (719) 866-4632
CEO: David Askinas
Executive Director: R. Jay Warwick
Media Contact: Bill Kellick
www.usa-taekwondo.us

USA Team Handball
Address: 1 Olympic Plaza
             Colrado Springs, CO 80909
Telephone: (719) 866-4565
President: Bob Djokovich
Manager of High Performance: Mike Cavanaugh
www.usateamhandball.org

U.S. Tennis Association
Address: 70 West Red Oak Lane
             White Plains, NY 10604-3602
Telephone: (914) 696-7000
President: Franklin R. Johnson
Executive Director: D. Lee Hamilton
Director Marketing/Communications: David Newman
www.usta.com

USA Track & Field (formerly TAC)
Address: 1 RCA Dome, Suite 140
             Indianapolis, IN 46225
Telephone: (317) 261-0500
President: Bill Roe
Chief Executive Officer: Craig A. Masback
Director of Communications: Jill Geer
www.usatf.org

USA Volleyball
Address: 715 South Circle Drive
             Colorado Springs, CO 80910
Telephone: (719) 228-6800
President: Albert M. Monaco Jr.
CEO: Doug Beal
Manager of Media Relations & Publications: Bill Kaufman
www.usavolleyball.org

U.S. Olympic Organizations *(Cont.)*

United States Water Polo (USWP)
Address: 1631 Mesa Avenue - Suite 1A
             Colorado Springs, CO 80906
Telephone: (719) 634-0699
President: Rich Foster
Executive Director care of Marti Torres, Director of
Finance and Business Administration
Director of Media Relations: Kelly Foster
www.usawaterpolo.com

USA Weightlifting
Address: 1 Olympic Plaza
             Colorado Springs, CO 80909
Telephone: (719) 866-4508
President: Dennis Snethen
Executive Director and Media Contact: Wesley
  Barnett
www.usaweightlifting.org

USA Wrestling
Address: 6155 Lehman Drive
             Colorado Springs, CO 80918
Telephone: (719) 598-8181
President: Stan Dziedzic
Executive Director: Rich Bender
Director of Communications: Gary Abbott
www.usawrestling.org

Affiliated Sports Organizations

Amateur Athletic Union (AAU)
Address: Walt Disney World Resort; P.O. Box 22409
             Lake Buena Vista, FL 32830-1000
Telephone: (407) 934-7200
President & CEO: Bobby Dodd
Director, Marketing/PublicRelations/Communications:
John D. Hodges
www.aausports.org

U.S. Curling Association (USCA)
Address: 1100 Center Point Drive
             P.O. Box 866
             Stevens Point, WI 54481
Telephone: (715) 344-1199
President: Mark Swandby
Chief Operating Officer: Rick Patzke
Communications Manager: Terry Luder
www.usacurl.org

USA Karate Federation
Address: 1300 Kenmore Boulevard
             Akron, OH 44314
Telephone: (330) 753-3114
President: George Anderson
www.usakarate.org

U.S. Orienteering Federation
Address: P.O. Box 1444
             Forest Park, GA 30298
Telephone: (404) 363-2110
President: Chuck Ferguson
Executive Director: Robin Shannonhouse
Marketing and Public Relations VP: Jerry Rhodes,
Donna Fluegel

Publicity telephone: (203) 798-9231
www.us.orienteering.org

U.S. Squash Racquets Association
Address: 23 Cynwyd Road
             P.O. Box 1216
             Bala Cynwyd, PA 19004
Telephone: (610) 667-4006
Chief Executive Officer: Kevin D. Klipstein
Director/Junior Development/National Teams/Events:
Vijay Chitnis
www.us-squash.org

USA Triathlon
Address: 1365 Graden of the Gods Road
             Colorado Springs, CO 80907
Telephone: (719) 597-9090
President: Brad Davison
Executive Director: Skip Gilbert
Communications Director: Jason Mucher
www.usatriathlon.org

USA Waterski
Address: 1251 Holy Cow Road
             Polk City, FL 33868
Telephone: (863) 324-4341
President: Sherm Schraft
Executive Director: Andy Jugan
Communications Director & Editor Scott Atkinson
www.usawaterski.org

Championship Auto Racing Teams (CART)
Address: 5350 Lakeview Parkway South Drive
Building 36 - Inner Park/Park 100
Indianapolis, IN 46268
Telephone: (317) 715-4100
President & COO: Brian Barnhart
Sr. Director of Media Relations: Tom Savage
www.champcarworldseries.com

Indy Racing League
Address: 4565 West 16th Street
Indianapolis, IN 46222
Telephone: (317) 484-6526
President and Founder: Tony George
Sr. Director of Media Relations: Tom Savage
www.indyracing.com

International Motor Sports Association
Address: 1394 Broadway Avenue
Braselton, GA 30517
Telephone: (706) 658-2120
COO: Tim Mayer
Executive Director: Doug Robinson
www.imsaracing.net

National Association for Stock Car Auto Racing (NASCAR)
Address: 1801 W International Speedway Blvd.
Daytona Beach, FL 32114-1243
Telephone: (386) 253-0611
CEO/Chairman: Brian France
President: Mike Helton
VP of Corporate Communications: Jim Hunter
www.nascar.com

National Hot Rod Association
Address: 2035 East Financial Way
Glendora, CA 91741
Telephone: (626) 914-4761
President: Tom Compton
VP of PR and Communications: Jerry Archambeault
www.nhra.com

Professional Bowlers Association LLC
Address: 719 Second Avenue - Suite 701
Seattle, WA 98104
Telephone: (206) 332-9688
Commissioner: Fred Schreyer
Director of Public Relations: Mitch Germann
www.pba.com

U.S. Chess Federation
Address: 65 East Street
Crossville, TN 38557
Telephone: (931) 787-1234
President: Bill Goichberg
Executive Director: Bill Hall
Director of Communications: Joan DuBois
www.uschess.org

International Game Fish Association
Address: 300 Gulf Stream Way
Dania Beach, FL 33004
Telephone: (954) 927-2628
President: Rob Kramer
www.igfa.org

Ladies Professional Golf Association
Address: 100 International Golf Drive
Daytona Beach, FL 32124
Telephone: (386) 274-6200
Commissioner: Carolyn Bivens
Sr. Director of Media Relations: Connie Wilson
www.lpga.com

PGA Tour
Address: 112 PGA Tour Boulevard
Ponte Vedra Beach, FL 32082
Telephone: (904) 285-3700
Commissioner: Tim Finchem
Senior VP of Communications: Bob Combs
www.pgatour.com

Professional Golfers' Association of America
Address: 100 Avenue of the Champions
Box 109601
Palm Beach Gardens, FL 33410-9601
Telephone: (561) 624-8400
President: Roger Warren
Sr. Director, Communication/Media Relations: Julius Mason
www.pgaonline.com

United States Golf Association
Address: P.O. Box 708, Golf House
Liberty Corner Road
Far Hills, NJ 07931-0708
Telephone: (908) 234-9687
President: Walter W. Driver Jr.
Director of Media Relations: Craig Smith
www.usga.org

U.S. Handball Association
Address: 2333 North Tucson Boulevard
Tucson, AZ 85716
Telephone: (520) 795-0434
President: Mike Steele
Executive Director: Vern Roberts
Director of Public Relations: Mark Carpenter
www.ushandball.org

Breeders' Cup Limited
Address: 2525 Harrodsburg Road
PO Box 4230
Lexington, KY 40504
Telephone: (859) 223-5444
Chief Executive Officer: Greg C. Avioli
Sr. VP, Marketing/Industry Relations:' Keith Chamblin
www.breederscup.com

The Jockeys' Guild, Inc.
Address: P.O. Box 150
Monrovia, CA 91017
Telephone: (866) 465-6257
Chairman of the Board: Dave Shepherd
www.jockeysguild.com

Thoroughbred Racing Associations of America
Address: 420 Fair Hill Drive, Suite 1
Elkton, MD 21921
Telephone: (410) 392-9200
Executive Vice President: Chris Scherf
www.tra-online.com

National Thoroughbred Racing Association
Address: 800 Third Avenue - Suite 901
             New York, NY 10022
Telephone: (212) 230-9500
Senior VP/Mrkting & Industry Rels: Keith Chamblin
www.ntra.com

United States Trotting Association
Address: 750 Michigan Avenue
             Columbus, OH 43215
Telephone: (614) 228-1385
President: F. Phillip Langley
Director of Public Relations: John Pawlak
www.ustrotting.com

Iditarod Trail Committee
Address: P.O. Box 870800; Wasilla, AK 99687
Telephone: (907) 376-5155
Executive Director: Stan Hooley
Race Director: Joanne Potts
www.iditarod.com

U.S. Lacrosse
Address: 113 W University Parkway
             Baltimore, MD 21210
Telephone: (410) 235-6882
Executive Director: Steven B. Stenersen
www.lacrosse.org

Little League Baseball, Inc.
Address: P.O. Box 3485
             Williamsport, PA 17701
Telephone: (570) 326-1921
President & CEO: Stephen D. Keener
Senior Communications Executive: Lance Van Auken
www.littleleague.org

U.S. Polo Association
Address: 771 Corporate Drive, Suite 505
             Lexington, KY 40503
Telephone: (859) 219-1000
Chairman: Jack Shelton
www.uspolo.org

American Powerboating Association
Address: 17640 Nine Mile Road
             Eastpointe, MI 48021
Telephone: (586) 773-9700
Executive Administrator: Gloria Urbin
www.apba-racing.com

Professional Rodeo Cowboys Association
Address: 101 Pro Rodeo Drive
             Colorado Springs, CO 80919
Telephone: (719) 593-8840
Commissioner: Troy Ellerman
Director of Communications: Leslie King
www.prorodeo.org

USA Rugby Football Union
Address: 1033 Walnut Street
             Suite 200
             Boulder, CO 80302
Telephone: (303) 539-0300
Chairman: Neal Brendel
CEO: Steve Griffiths
Communications: Sara John
www.usarugby.org

The United Soccer Leagues
Address: 14497 North Dale Mabry Highway, Ste 201
             Tampa, FL 33618
Telephone: (813) 963-3909
President and A-League Commissioner: Francisco
  Marcos
Director of Public Relations:Gerald Barnhart
www.uslsoccer.com

Major League Soccer
Address: 110 East 42nd Street, Suite 1000
             New York, NY 10017
Telephone: (212) 687-1400
Commissioner: Don Garber
Director of Communications: Will Kuhns
www.mlsnet.com

Major Indoor Soccer League
Address: 1175 Post Road East
             Westport, CT 06880
Telephone: (203) 222-4900
Commissioner: Steve Ryan
VP Marketing & Communications: Jay Cavallo
www.misl.net

Women's United Soccer Association
Address: P.O. Box 8338
             Charlotteville VA 22906
Telephone: (678) 645-0800
CEO: Tanya Antonucci
Public Relations Consultant: Dan Courtemanche
League Operations suspended since 2003.
Expected re-launch 2008. (www.wusa.com)

Association of Tennis Professionals Tour
Address: 201 ATP Tour Boulevard
             Ponte Vedra Beach, FL 32082
Telephone: (904) 285-8000
Chief Executive Officer: Flip Galloway
VP of Comm. and Media Relations: Graeme Agars
www.atptennis.com

Sony Ericsson WTA Tour (Women's Tennis)
Address: One Progress Plaza - Suite 1500
             St. Petersburg, FL 33701
Telephone: (727) 895-5000
Chief Executive Officer: Larry Scott
Director of Corporate Communications: Darrell Fry
www.sonyericssonwtatour.com

Association of Volleyball Professionals
Address: 6100 Center Drive - 9th Floor
             Los Angeles, CA 90045
Telephone: (310) 426-8000
Commissioner: Leonard Armato
www.avp.com

MINOR LEAGUES

Baseball (AAA)

Minor League Baseball
Address: 201 Bayshore Drive S.E. - P.O. Box A
             St. Petersburg, FL 33731
Telephone: (727) 822-6937
President: Mike Moore
Director of Media Relations: Jim Ferguson
www.milb.com

MINOR LEAGUES *(Cont.)*

Baseball (AAA) *(Cont.)*

International League
Address: 55 South High Street, Suite 202
             Dublin, OH 43017
Telephone: (614) 791-9300
President: Randy Mobley
www.ilbaseball.com

Pacific Coast League
Address: 1631 Mesa Avenue, Suite A
             Colorado Springs, CO 80906
Telephone: (719) 636-3399
President: Ken Young
www.pclbaseball.com

Hockey

American Hockey League
Address: 1 Monarch Place Suite 2400
             Springfield, MA 01144
Telephone: (413) 781-2030
President, CEO & Treasurer: David A. Andrews
VP of Hockey Operations: Jim Mill
VP of Communications: Jason Chaimovitch
www.theahl.com

Halls of Fame Directory

National Baseball Hall of Fame and Museum
Address: P.O. Box 590/25 Main Street
             Cooperstown, NY 13326
Telephone: (607) 547-7200
President: Dale Petroskey
Senior Vice President: Bill Haase
V.P. of Communications and Education: Jeff Idelson
www.baseballhalloffame.org

**Naismith Memorial Basketball Hall
of Fame**
Address: 1000 West Columbus Avenue
             Springfield, MA 01105
Telephone: (413) 781-6500
President and CEO: John L. Doleva
VP of Marketing and Sales: Dan O'Keefe
www.hoophall.com

**International Bowling Museum and Hall of
Fame**
Address: 111 Stadium Plaza
             St. Louis, MO 63102
Telephone: (314) 231-6340
Executive Director: Gerald Baltz
Marketing Director: Jim Baer
www.bowlingmuseum.com

International Boxing Hall of Fame
Address: 1 Hall of Fame Drive
             Canastota, NY 13032
Telephone: (315) 697-7095
President: Donald Ackerman
Executive Director: Edward Brophy
www.ibhof.com

Professional Football Hall of Fame
Address: 2121 George Halas Drive NW
             Canton, OH 44708
Telephone: (330) 456-8207
President/Executive Director: Stephen A. Perry
VP of Communications: Joe Horrigan
www.profootballhof.com

LPGA Hall of Fame
Address: 100 International Golf Drive
             Daytona Beach, FL 32124
Telephone: (386) 274-6200
Commissioner: Carolyn Bivens
Director of Public Relations: Laura Neal
www.lpga.com

Hockey Hall of Fame
Address: 30 Yonge Street BCE Place
             Toronto, Ontario Canada M5E 1X8
Telephone: (416) 360-7735
Chairman: William Hay
President & COO: Jeff Denomme
VP of Marketing: Perter Jagla
www.hhof.com

National Museum of Racing and Hall of Fame
Address: 191 Union Avenue
             Saratoga Springs, NY 12866
Telephone: (518) 584-0400
Executive Director: Peter Hammell
Assistant Director: Catherine Maguire
Communications Officer: Mike Kane
www.racingmuseum.org

National Soccer Hall of Fame
Address: Wright Soccer Campus
             18 Stadium Circle
             Oneonta, NY 13820
Telephone: (607) 432-3351
President: Will Lunn
www.soccerhall.org

International Swimming Hall of Fame
Address: 1 Hall of Fame Drive
             Fort Lauderdale, FL 33316
Telephone: (954) 462-6536
President: Bruce Wigo
Director of Operations: Laurie Marchwinski
www.ishof.org

International Tennis Hall of Fame
Address: 194 Bellevue Avenue
             Newport, RI 02840
Telephone: (401) 849-3990
CEO: Mark Stenning
Marketing Manager: Kat Anderson
www.tennisfame.com

National Track & Field Hall of Fame
Address: 216 Ft. Washington Avenue
             The Armory Foundation
             New York, NY 10032
Telephone: (317) 261-0500
Chief Executive Officer: Criag Masback
Director of Communications: Jill Geer
www.usatf.org

Negro League legend Josh Gibson hit as many as 962 home runs during his career

Sports Illustrated Trivia Quiz

Weeeer'e baaaack. But don't make the mistake of thinking that our second-annual *Sports Illustrated Almanac* Trivia Quiz is going to suffer from some kind of sophomore slump. Far from it. In fact, we've once again meticulously combed over the many record-setting and jaw-dropping events from the past year—like Kobe Byrant's 81-point, single-game explosion (above)—to provide you, our fans, with some of the most obscure, most difficult, most up-to-date trivia questions around. Of course, we know you're no rookie when it comes to sports knowledge, you may even be a grizzled pro. And you're probably someone who knows that Bill Veeck's last name rhymes with Georgia Tech's nickname rather than Isiah Thomas' and that the list of alltime home run leaders really starts with Gibson and Oh. So, if you think you're really ready, pull on your thinking cap, helmet, headband, visor and goggles and get right to it.

NFL

1. In 2006, at 23 years, 340 days old, Ben Roethlisberger became the youngest starting QB in NFL history to win a Super Bowl. Which player was the youngest starting QB to lose a Super Bowl?
HINT: Pittsburgh connection, too.

2. Who is the only player in NFL history to gain more than 2,000 career yards apiece in kickoff returns, punt returns, rushing and receiving?

3. Whose alltime NFL record did San Diego Chargers RB LaDainian Tomlinson tie when he scored a TD in 18 consecutive games from 2004 to 2005?

4. What is the combined alltime Super Bowl record of teams from California?

5. From 1977 to 1983, seven straight running backs were chosen as NFL Rookie of the Year, five of them former Heisman Trophy winners. Name three of the five.
PAT: Name one of the two RoY RBs from that period who *didn't* have a Heisman in his trophy case.

6. Which player was the very first number-one overall pick in USFL draft history?

7. (See previous question) What position was this same player chosen in that year's NFL draft?

8. Before the start of the 2006–07 season, linebacker Junior Seau retired (and then un-retired). Seau is one of only four players to make 12 consecutive Pro Bowl appearances since the 1970 NFL-AFL merger. Name the other three.
HINT: Think *DE*fensively.

9. What legendary football figure did Babe Ruth replace in right field for the 1920 New York Yankees?

10. In NFL history, only three sets of RBs from the same team have reached 1,000 rushing yards in the same season. Name these three prodigious pairs, their teams, and the seasons that they did it.

NFL

Eric Metcalf, seen here playing for the Atlanta Falcons in a 1995 NFC Wild Card game, gained 17,230 all-purpose yards during his 13 seasons.

AP PHOTO/MORRY GASH

5. 1977—Tony Dorsett (1976 Heisman), 1978—Earl Campbell (1977 Heisman), 1980—Billy Sims (1978 Heisman), 1981—George Rogers (1980 Heisman), 1982—Marcus Allen (1981 Heisman)
5 PAT. 1979—Ottis Anderson, 1983—Eric Dickerson

6. Dan Marino, chosen first by the Los Angeles Express in Jan. 1983.

7. Marino was chosen by the Miami Dolphins as the 27th pick of the 1983 NFL draft.

1. Miami Dolphins QB (and former Pitt Panther QB) Dan Marino was 23 years, 127 days old when he started Super Bowl XIX on Jan. 20, 1985 (Miami lost to San Francisco 38–16)

2. Eric Metcalf (5,813 KO return yards, 3,453 punt return yards, 2,392 rushing yards and 5,572 receiving yards)

3. Lenny Moore, RB, Baltimore Colts, whose 18 consecutive games with a TD ran from 1963–65.

4. 8–4 (San Francisco 49ers, 5–0; L.A./Oakland Raiders, 3–2; San Diego Chargers, 0–1; L.A. Rams, 0–1)

8. Bruce Matthews (14, 1988–2001); Reggie White (13, 1986–1998); Randall McDaniel (12, 1989–2000)

9. George Halas, who played 12 games in RF for the Yankees between May and July of 1919, batting .091 with 2 hits, 0 runs, 0 RBIs, 0 HRs, and 8 strikeouts.

10. Larry Csonka and Mercury Morris, 1972 Miami Dolphins; Franco Harris and Rocky Bleier, 1976 Pittsburgh Steelers; Earnest Byner and Kevin Mack, 1985 Cleveland Browns

NFL

11. In what year was the first NFL championship game played indoors?

12. The Indianapolis Colts started the 2005–06 season with 13 straight wins—only the fourth team in NFL history to reach this mark—but they failed to reach the Super Bowl. Of the other three teams to start 13–0, how many never reached that same season's Super Bowl/title game?
2-PT. CONVERSION: Name the leading rushers on three of these four teams.

13. Which player holds the NFL record for most career rushing TDs by a quarterback?

14. Which three-time All-Pro punter famously wore a wristwatch during NFL games so he could better time his punts?

15. Which player first set the current NFL record—since tied by three other players—for most receptions in a playoff game, with 13?
HINT: He also famously blocked a field goal in the same game.

16. Which AFL franchise drafted, but did not sign, LB Dick Butkus?
BONUS: What jersey number did Butkus wear while playing in college?

17. A forward pass hits the crossbar in the back of the end zone, bounces up and through the uprights, and is then caught on its way back down by a receiver who has both feet inbounds. What is the ruling on the field?
a) Touchdown!
b) Field goal!
c) Incomplete pass.
d) 5-yard illegal touching penalty.
e) Do over?!

18. Which running back was the fastest in NFL history to reach 10,000 career rushing yards?
HINT: In college, he was part of the famed "Pony Express" backfield.

19. Which RB, as a rookie, led the NFL in TDs scored in 1980?
a) Billy Sims   b) Earl Campbell
c) Curtis Dickey   d) Charles White
e) George Rogers   f) Joe Cribbs

PETER READ MILLER

Steve Young and fellow NFL Hall of Famer Sammy Baugh are the only QBs in NFL history to have won six passing titles during their careers.

13. Steve Young—43 career rushing TDs (4,239 career rushing yards)

14. Reggie Roby—Roby's 16-year career net punting average of 43.3 yards is ninth-best in NFL history.

11. 1932—Originally scheduled for December 18th at Wrigley Field, the 1932 NFL Championship Game between the Chicago Bears and the Portsmouth Spartans was moved indoors to nearby Chicago Stadium due to snow and extremely cold weather. The Bears won 9–0.

12. Zero—The 1972 Miami Dolphins and 1998 Denver Broncos both went on to win the Super Bowl, while the 1934 Chicago Bears lost the NFL Championship Game to the N.Y. Giants.

12 2-PC. '34 Bears—Beattie Feathers (1,004 yards); '72 Dolphins—Larry Csonka (1,117 yards); '98 Broncos—Terrell Davis (2,008 yards); '05 Colts—Edgerrin James (1,506 yards)

15. Chargers TE Kellen Winslow—Winslow had 13 receptions for 166 yards and 1 TD (and a blocked FG) in San Diego's legendary 41–38 overtime win against Miami in the 1982 AFC Divisional playoffs.

16. Denver Broncos
16 BONUS. Butkus wore #50 while playing for the University of Illinois.

17. c)—Incomplete pass

18. Eric Dickerson—The former SMU Mustang RB reached 10,000 career yards in his 91st NFL game.

19. Billy Sims—Sims scored 96 points (16 TDs–13 rushing, 3 receiving) for the Lions in 1980.

NFL

20. Name the only three QBs in NFL history who have thrown 40 or more TDs during a single season.

21. During the 2005–06 NFL season, there were two sets of brothers listed as quarterbacks on team rosters. Name these two pairs of brothers.
HINT: One NFC team had one from each set of brothers on their roster.

22. Name the most recent year that an NFL Championship Game or Super Bowl went into overtime.

23. The 2003 AFC Wild Card game between the Colts and the Jets featured, for the first time in NFL history, two teams with African-American head coaches. Name these two head coaches.
EXTRA POINT: One of these two coaches had moved to a new team for the start of the 2006–07 NFL season. Name his new team.

24. Other than the Oakland Raiders, name the only other NFL franchise, in existence at the time of the 1970 AFL-NFL merger, that has yet to retire a single jersey number.

25. Which two active NFL wide receivers, on opposite sidelines at the 2006 Pro Bowl, once ran routes side-by-side for the Santa Monica College Corsairs?
HINT: They combined for 2,995 total receiving yards during the 2005–06 season.

26. Through the 2005–06 season, which NFL player has an active streak of scoring in each of the past 17 consecutive playoff games he's played in, the second-longest streak in NFL history?

27. Which two active NFL running backs currently share the league's single-season rushing touchdowns record, with 27?

Eli (l.) and Peyton Manning are among seven pairs of brothers (Bradshaws, McCowns, Hasselbecks, Detmers, Huards, and Sternamans) who have both played QB in the NFL.

23. Tony Dungy (Indianapolis Colts) and Herm Edwards (New York Jets) **23 XP.** Herm Edwards' new team for the 2006–07 season was the Kansas City Chiefs.

24. Dallas Cowboys

25. Steve Smith and Chad Johnson. Smith played two years and Johnson played three seasons at Santa Monica before they transferred and finished their college careers at Utah and Oregon State, respectively.

AL TIELEMANS (LEFT); DAMIAN STROHMEYER (RIGHT)

20. Dan Marino (twice: 48—1984 Miami Dolphins, 44—1986 Miami Dolphins) Kurt Warner (41—1999 St. Louis Rams) Peyton Manning (49—2004 Indianapolis Colts)

21. Mannings (Peyton—Indianapolis Colts, Eli—N.Y. Giants) and Hasselbecks (Matt—Seattle Seahawks, Tim—N.Y. Giants)

22. 1958 NFL Championship Game. The Baltimore Colts beat the N.Y. Giants 23–17 on a one-yard TD run by RB Alan Ameche.

26. Adam Vinatieri—The NFL's longest consecutive playoff-game scoring streak was 19 games by George Blanda.

27. Priest Holmes (first set the record in 2003 with Kansas City) and Shaun Alexander (tied record in 2005 with Seattle)

COLLEGE FOOTBALL

28. Which Division I head football coach had the highest winning percentage in the 1960s and 1970s?

29. In 2005, Division I national champion Texas set a NCAA single-season record by scoring 652 points. Which college team had previously held the record with 624 points?
HINT: Its roster included the 1983 Heisman Trophy winner.

30. Only four colleges have ever had back-to-back Heisman Trophy winners. The first was Yale (Larry Kelley in 1936 and Clint Frank in 1937). Name two of the other three schools.

31. In 1996, this college football head coach became the first former Heisman Trophy winner to also coach a Heisman Trophy winner. Name him.
HINT: Both coach and player won their Heisman Trophies while at the same school.

32. Among head coaches with at least five career bowl victories, which one has the highest alltime winning percentage in bowl games?

33. Which college football rivalry rewards the winner with the "Old Oaken Bucket?"

34. What is the maximum number of full athletic scholarships NCAA Division III football teams are allowed to award?

35. The epic 2006 Rose Bowl featured No. 1 USC versus No. 2 Texas. When was the last time No. 1 and No. 2-ranked teams played in the Rose Bowl for the national title?

36. Which player became the first three-time, consensus All-American in NCAA football history?
BONUS: He later "enlisted" to play for which USFL team?

37. Reggie Bush set a Pac-10 single-game record in 2005 with 513 all-purpose yards against Fresno State. Whose 33-year old record did he break?
a) O.J. Simpson   b) Mike Garrett
c) Marcus Allen   d) Anthony Davis

COLLEGE FOOTBALL

WALTER IOOSS/SPORTS ILLUSTRATED

Before Bear Bryant began his tenure as head coach at Alabama in 1958, he turned around woeful football programs at Maryland, Kentucky and Texas A&M.

(Archie Griffin in 1974 & 1975); USC (Matt Leinart in 2004 & Reggie Bush in 2005)

31. Steve Spurrier (Spurrier won the 1966 Heisman Trophy while attending Florida and then, 30 years later, while coaching Florida, his quarterback, Danny Wuerffel, won the 1996 Heisman Trophy.)

32. John Robinson (.889, 8–1 at USC and UNLV)

33. Purdue vs. Indiana (Purdue leads the series 53–25–3.)

34. Zero (No Div. III athletic program can offer athletic scholarships.)

35. Jan. 1, 1969 (1969 Rose Bowl—No. 1 Ohio St. beat No. 2 USC 27–16)

36. Herschel Walker, Georgia (1980-82)
36 BONUS. New Jersey Generals

37. d) Anthony Davis—Davis set the previous record by amassing 368 all-purpose yards against Notre Dame in the last game of the 1972 season.

28. Alabama's Paul "Bear" Bryant—1960s—.822 win percentage (98–20–3 record, national championships in 1961, 1964, & 1965); 1970s—.892 win percentage (107–13 record, national championships in 1973, 1978, & 1979)

29. 1983 Nebraska Cornhuskers (Husker RB Mike Rozier won the 1983 Heisman Trophy.)

30. Army (Doc Blanchard in 1945 & Glenn Davis in 1946); Ohio State

NBA

38. Prior to the 2005–06 Dallas Mavericks, 28 teams had taken a 2–0 series lead in NBA Finals history. How many of those teams went on to lose the series, as Dallas did?

39. Which team won an NBA-record 12 straight playoff games on its way to that franchise's first-ever NBA title?

DOUBLE BONUS: Name the NBA Finals MVP from that team AND the ACC college that he played for.

40. In 2005–06, Ray Allen set an NBA single-season record, making 269 three-point field goals. Whose ten-year-old record did he break?

41. Over the past three full NBA seasons, one player has made more than 90% of his free throw attempts and at least 40% of his three-point field goal attempts, a first in league history. Name him.

HINT: Sacto to Indy

42. In Game Three of the 2006 NBA Finals, Mavericks forward Jerry Stackhouse made three three-point field goals in a span of only 77 seconds, the second-fastest run of its kind in NBA Finals history. Who holds the record, with three three-pointers in only 52 seconds?

HINT: He blazed the Blazers.

43. Among active NBA players, who is the alltime leader in triple doubles?

44. Who was the only player to have won MVP awards in both the ABA and NBA during his career?

AND I: Name the comical 1979 basketball movie this player starred in.

45. Name the three head coaches who, since 1980, have won only one NBA championship.

NBA

From 1999 to 2001, Jason Kidd led the NBA in assists, making him one of only four players in league history to accomplish this feat for three or more consecutive years (Bob Cousy 1953–60, Oscar Robertson 1964–66, John Stockton 1988–96).

MANNY MILLAN/SPORTS ILLUSTRATED

while his 3FG% during those three years was .433, .402, and .401.

42. Isiah Thomas (Detroit Pistons against Portland in Game 3 of the 1990 NBA Finals)

43. Jason Kidd—His 76 career triple doubles, place him fourth on the alltime list, behind only Oscar Robertson (181), Magic Johnson (138) and Wilt Chamberlain (78).

44. Julius Erving—1973–74 & 1975–76 ABA MVP (New York Nets), 1980–81 NBA MVP (Philadelphia 76ers); **44 AND I.** *The Fish That Saved Pittsburgh*

45. Bill Fitch—1980–81 Boston Celtics; Billy Cunningham—1982–83 Philadelphia 76ers; Larry Brown—2003–04 Detroit Pistons. The other 23 NBA Finals victories since 1980 are split among Phil Jackson (9), Pat Riley (5), Gregg Popovich (3), K.C. Jones (2), Chuck Daly (2) and Rudy Tomjanovich (2).

38. 2—1968–69 L.A. Lakers, up 2–0, were defeated by the Boston Celtics 4–3; 1976–77 Philadelphia 76ers, up 2–0, lost to the Portland Trail Blazers, who reeled off four straight to win 4–2.

39. 1998–99 San Antonio Spurs; **39DB.** Tim Duncan, who played his college ball for Wake Forest.

40. Dennis Scott—Scott had a record-setting 267 3FGs during the 1995–96 season for the Orlando Magic.

41. Peja Stojakovic—For the 2003–04 through 2005–06 seasons, his FT% was .927, .920, and .915, respectively,

NBA

46. 2006 NBA Finals MVP Dwyane Wade scored 208 points in six games against the Mavericks, the second-highest total in NBA Finals history. Which player still holds the Finals record for total points?

47. Of the following six NBA players, which one was the shortest?
a) Calvin Murphy   b) Spud Webb
c) Nate Robinson   d) Earl Boykins
e) Muggsy Bogues   f) Charlie Criss

48. When Kobe Bryant scored 81 points against Toronto in January 2006, he became only the fifth player in NBA history to score more than 70 points in a single game. One is obviously Wilt Chamberlain, can you name two of the other three players?
HINT: A Laker, a Spur, and a Nugget.

49. Name the NBA players that are attached to the following colorful nicknames: "The Human Eraser," "The Microwave," "The Truth," "The Answer," "The Glide," "The Glove," and "The Owl without a Vowel."

50. Which NBA head coach, active during the 2005–06 season, holds the current league record for most alltime playoff losses?
HINT: He's 2nd in career playoff wins and tied for 2nd in career titles won.

51. Put the following NBA players, active during the 2005–06 season, in ascending order based on their total career rebounds.
a) Tim Duncan
b) Kevin Garnett
c) Dikembe Mutumbo
d) Shaquille O'Neal

52. Wilt Chamberlain played in 1,205 games during his NBA career. In how many of those games did he foul out (within five games)?

53. In which season was the NBA's three-point line first instituted?

54. During the 2005–06 season, Cavs guard LeBron James became only the fourth player in NBA history to average more than 30 points, 7 rebounds and 6 assists in a season. Name the other three.

55. Name the last player from an Eastern Conference team to win the NBA's regular season MVP award?

ANSWERS
NBA

In 2006, Dwyane Wade set NBA records for most playoff points scored during a player's first three years in the league (1,272) and youngest player to score 1,000 career playoff points.

46. Lakers guard Jerry West scored 265 total points in the 1969 NBA Finals against the Boston Celtics. (Though the Celtics took the series 4–3, West was named Finals MVP, the only time in NBA history that a player from a losing team has won the award.)

47. e)—Muggsy Bogues (5'3") (Boykins—5'5"; Webb—5'7"; Criss—5'8"; Murphy and Robinson—5'9")

48. David Robinson (71 points—San Antonio vs. L.A. Clippers, 4/24/94); David Thompson (78 points—Denver vs. Detroit, 4/9/78); Elgin Baylor (71 points—L.A. Lakers vs. N.Y. Knicks, 11/15/60). [Note: Wilt Chamberlain scored over 70 points in a game *six* different times in his career.]

49. Marvin Webster, Vinnie Johnson, Paul Pierce, Allen Iverson, Clyde Drexler, Gary Payton, and Bill Mlkvy

50. Pat Riley—171-107 career playoff coaching record. (Riley has more career playoff losses than Lenny Wilkens and seven fewer career playoff wins than Phil Jackson. Riley's five titles tie him with John Kundla for second alltime. Jackson and Auerbach are tied for first with nine NBA titles.)

JOHN McDONOUGH/SPORTS ILLUSTRATED

51. 4. Tim Duncan (8,020);
3. Kevin Garnett (9,567);
2. Shaquille O'Neal (11,082);
1. Dikembe Mutumbo (11,639)

52. Zero

53. 1979–80 season

54. Oscar Robertson (1960-61, 1961-62, 1963-64, 1964-65, 1965-66), Jerry West (1965-66) and Michael Jordan (1988-89)

55. Allen Iverson, Phila. 76ers (2000-01)

COLLEGE BASKETBALL

56. George Mason's incredible run in the 2006 NCAA tournament marked the first time that a team from a mid-major conference reached the Final Four since 1979, when two teams did it. Name them.
HINT: Sycamores and Quakers.

57. Of the record four Missouri Valley Conference teams selected to play in the 2006 NCAA tournament, how many won at least one game?

58. By the second weekend of the 2006 NCAA tournament, not one of the previous year's Final Four teams was still alive. When was the last time that this happened?

59. I've won one NCAA title as a head coach, spent my entire career coaching at the same school and, among head coaches active during the 2005–06 season, I was ranked fifth in career victories. Who am I?
a) Lute Olson   b) Jim Boeheim
c) Jim Calhoun   d) Eddie Sutton
e) Mike Krzyzewski f) John Chaney

60. What college has hosted the NCAA tournament's "play-in game" every year since it began in 2001?

61. Charles Barkley, Dominique Wilkins and Joe Dumars—three members of the Basketball Hall of Fame's Class of 2006—played college ball for teams from three different Southern states. Name two of the states and colleges they attended.

62. A No. 16 seed has never beaten a No. 1 seed in men's NCAA tournament history. But how many times has a No. 15 seed beaten a No. 2 seed in the first round?

63. Through the 2005–06 season, which school has lost the most title games in NCAA history?

64. Coming into the 2006–07 NCAA basketball season, which Div. I head coach had an active streak of 19 straight 20-plus win seasons, the second-longest streak of its kind in NCAA history?

COLLEGE BASKETBALL

Since the 1986–87 season, Arizona Wildcats' head coach Lute Olson has the nation's second-best winning percentage and his teams have made it to four Final Fours and won one national championship (1997).

ROBERT BECK

56. Indiana State and Penn (Indiana State, led by Larry Bird, made it to the title game, but lost to Michigan State and Magic Johnson.)

57. Two—Wichita State and Bradley both went 2–1, reaching the Sweet Sixteen. (N. Iowa and S. Illinois lost in the first round.)

58. 1988—Defending champion Indiana lost in the first round, UNLV and Syracuse lost in the second round and Providence was not selected for the tournament.

59. Jim Boeheim—(Syracuse, 726 career victories from 1977–2006; 2003 NCAA national champion)

60. University of Dayton (Ohio)

61. Alabama (Charles Barkley, Auburn), Georgia (Dominique Wilkins, Univ. of Georgia), Louisiana (Joe Dumars, McNeese State)

62. four times (Richmond def. Syracuse, 1991; UC-Santa Clara def. Arizona, 1993; Coppin State def. South Carolina, 1997; Hampton def. Iowa State, 2001)

63. Duke—6 NCAA title games lost (1964, vs. UCLA; 1978, vs. Kentucky; 1986, vs. Louisville, 1990, vs. UNLV; 1994, vs. Arkansas; 1999, vs. UConn)

64. Lute Olson, Arizona (1988–2006). Former North Carolina head coach Dean Smith holds the record with 27 consecutive 20-plus win seasons.

BASEBALL

65. In 2006, Twins rookie catcher Joe Mauer reached base four times in five straight games, breaking the old major-league record of four straight games shared by three players. Name two of these other three players.

66. Which player holds the record for the highest season-long pinch-hitting batting average?

67. This past season, Jamie Moyer gave up his 400th career home run, making him only the ninth pitcher in major-league history to allow this many homers. Which pitcher has given up the most HRs? **HINT:** A little alliteration in his name and the team he's most associated with.

68. The Chicago Cubs have had seven relief pitchers with 300-plus saves play for them at some point in their careers, the most in the majors. Name five of the seven. **HINT:** All of them are retired and two are enshrined in Cooperstown.

69. Other than being major-league pitchers whose fathers had also been major-league pitchers, what other notable connection do Jim Bagby Jr. and Ed Walsh Jr. share?

70. In July 2006, Alex Rodriguez, at 30 years, 359 days old, homered to collect his 2,000th hit. Name five of the other seven players in major-league history to reach this milestone before age 31. **EXTRA BASES:** With that same homer, A-Rod set a major-league record as the youngest player to reach 450 home runs. Whose record did he break?

71. On July 1, 2006, Garret Anderson and Manny Ramirez both collected their 2,000th career hit. The last time two players reached this same milestone on the same day was June 19, 1973. Name these two players, both outfielders. **HINT:** One had a famous Davey as a teammate, the other a famous Dave.

ANSWERS
BASEBALL

CHUCK SOLOMON

65. Babe Ruth (New York Yankees, June 12–15, 1930); Barry Bonds (San Francisco Giants, October 2–5, 2001); and Mike Stock (Brooklyn Dodgers, June 30–July 3, 1925)

66. Ed Kranepool—He went 17-for-35 pinch-hitting for the 1974 New York Mets, a .468 batting average.

67. Robin Roberts—505 career HRs allowed in 20 seasons (with Philadelphia Phillies—14 seasons, Baltimore Orioles, Houston Astros and Chicago Cubs)

68. Lee Smith, Randy Myers, Rick Aguilera, Goose Gossage, Doug Jones, Dennis Eckersley (HOF), and Bruce Sutter (HOF)

Ken Griffey, Jr. has 563 career HRs, tying Reggie Jackson for 10th alltime.

69. They both stopped one of Joe DiMaggio's hitting streaks. (Jim Bagby Jr.—DiMaggio's major-league record 56-game streak, Ed Walsh Jr.—DiMaggio's minor-league-record 61-game streak)

70. Ty Cobb (29), Rogers Hornsby (29), Jimmie Foxx (30), Joe Medwick (30), Mel Ott (30), Hank Aaron (30), Robin Yount (30)
70EB. Ken Griffey, Jr., who collected his 450th HR at age 31 years, 261 days old

71. Willie Davis (L.A. Dodgers—Davey Lopes) and Pete Rose (Cincinnati Reds—Dave Concepcion)

BASEBALL

72. In my 23-year career, I won 245 games and recorded 2,199 strikeouts as a starting pitcher for the Orioles, Indians, Expos, Mariners and Braves, but I never won more than 16 games in any one season. Who am I?

73. Which active pitcher is the alltime leader in postseason wins?
HINT: For all his efforts, he only has one World Series ring to show for it.

74. Which managers led the AL and NL teams in the 1995 All-Star Game?

75. The DiMaggio brothers (Joe, Vince and Dom) are third on the alltime list of major league hits collected by brothers, with 4,853. Name the only two sets of siblings in baseball history to have more.

76. Which two players are the only ones in major-league history to win a league MVP award while playing on a last-place team?
HINT: Roger Clemens earned his first Cy Young award the year before the first player did it and he won his most recent Cy Young award the year after the second player did it.

77. Of Roger Clemens' 348 career victories, how many were outings in which he lasted only the minimum five innings required of a starting pitcher to qualify for a major-league win?

78. Of the 18 players who started in the very first All-Star Game in 1933, only one did not make it into Cooperstown. Name him.
HINT: Hank Aaron, Dale Murphy and Andruw Jones have all followed in his footsteps during their careers.

79. Prior to the 2006 All-Star break, both 23-year old Devil Rays pitcher Scott Kazmir and 22-year old Tigers pitcher Justin Verlander had won 10 games. Name the only two other pitchers in major-league history, who, not yet 24, had both won 10 or more victories before the All-Star Break in the same year and league.
HINT: NL, 1988.

BASEBALL

JONATHAN DANIEL/GETTY IMAGES

Andre "The Hawk" Dawson won eight Gold Gloves during his career and was also named to eight All-Star teams.

72. Dennis Martinez

73. John Smoltz—Career postseason statistics: 15–4 with a 2.66 ERA and 194 strikeouts.

74. Montreal Expos' manager Felipe Alou (NL) and New York Yankees' manager Buck Showalter (AL) were selected because their teams had the best league records on the last day of the 1994 season before the strike began.

75. Waners (Paul and Lloyd) 5,611; Alous (Felipe, Matty and Jesus) 5,094

76. Andre Dawson (1987 NL MVP—Chicago Cubs; Clemens won his first Cy Young in 1986); Alex Rodriguez (2003 AL MVP—Texas Rangers; Clemens won his 7th Cy Young in 2004)

77. 7 (He has pitched 118 career CGs.)

78. Wally Berger, centerfielder for the 1933 Boston Braves.

79. Greg Maddux (22 years old, 15 wins—Chicago Cubs); Dwight Gooden (23 years old, 11 wins—N.Y. Mets).

BASEBALL

80. In 2006, Baltimore Orioles rookie pitcher Adam Loewen faced a former Cy Young winner in each of his first four career starts, a first in major-league history. (He lost all four games.) Name the opposing pitchers.
HINT: All from the East, he faced one twice.

81. In 2006, I became the oldest player in 97 years to steal a base in major league baseball. Unfortunately, I'm also the active leader in hitting into double plays. What's my name?

82. Since 1945, five MLB teams have, at one point, simultaneously shared their nicknames with an NFL or NHL team. Name all five teams.

83. In 2006, two players joined Barry and Bobby Bonds, Willie Mays, and Andre Dawson as the only major leaguers with at least 300 career home runs and 300 career stolen bases club. Name them both.

84. Of the 18 grand slams in World Series history, eight have been hit by New York Yankees. But of the following five Yankees, which one has *not* hit a World Series grand slam?
a) Yogi Berra
b) Reggie Jackson
c) Joe Pepitone
d) Tino Martinez

85. The Boston Red Sox went 17 consecutive games without an error in 2006, a major-league record. Which team had previously held the record?

86. When Yankees reliever Mariano Rivera recorded his 400th career save this past year, it was only the 11th time in his career he had earned a save by pitching two or more innings. In how many of Rollie Fingers' 341 career saves did he pitch at least two innings?

87. White Sox pitcher Jose Contreras won 19 consecutive decisions from August 2005 to July 2006. Only two other active pitchers have won 17 or more straight decisions. Name these two pitchers.

HINT: They both won Cy Young awards in 2004.

In 2003, Roy Halladay won the AL Cy Young award thanks to a 22–7 record that included two shutouts, 204 strikeouts and an ERA of 3.25.

AL BELLO/GETTY IMAGES

82. Washington Senators (NHL—same name); St. Louis Browns (NFL—Cleveland Browns); N.Y./S.F. Giants (NFL—N.Y. Giants); St. Louis Cardinals (NFL—St. Louis/Phoenix/Arizona Cardinals); Texas Rangers (NHL—N.Y. Rangers)

83. Reggie Sanders (303 HRs/304 SBs) and Steve Finley (303 HRs/320 SBs)

84. b)—Reggie Jackson

85. St. Louis Cardinals, who played 16 straight error-free games from July 30-August 16, 1992.

80. Roy Halladay (twice), Randy Johnson and Tom Glavine

81. Julio Franco, who at 47 years, 246 days old stole second base against the S.F. Giants on April 22, 2006. Through the 2006 regular season, Franco has hit into 310 DPs during his career.

86. 135—Nearly 40% of his successful save outings

87. Johan Santana and Roger Clemens (Santana—17 straight from July 2004 to April 2005; Clemens—20 straight from 1998 to 1999).

WILD CARD

88. Which player is now the alltime goal-scoring leader in World Cup history?

89. Through the 2005–06 season, which pro athlete has made more three-point field goals during their career, Peja Stojakovic or Pete Stoyanovich?

90. What is the oldest continuously-awarded trophy in sport?

91. Which distance is greater: from the hoop to the NBA three-point line at the top of the key or the current Olympic long-jump record?

92. Steve Yzerman, who retired in 2006, played all 22 of his NHL seasons with the Detroit Red Wings. No NBA or NFL player can match this, but six MLB players have had 22 or more seasons with one team. Name four of them. **HINT:** No Ripken.

93. What is the sum total of the jersey numbers worn by Jim Kelly, Hakeem Olajuwon, Bob Gibson, Julius Erving, Babe Ruth and Jim Otto. **HINT:** It's one more than the number worn by Lakers legend George Mikan.

94. Soccer star Landon Donovan, who turned 24 in March 2006, was chosen for his sixth MLS All-Star Game that same year. Of the four major professional sports, only two players have been six-time All-Stars before age 25 and they both played in the NHL. Name them. **HINT:** Their jersey numbers added together equalled 103. **BONUS:** The youngest six-time All-Stars in NBA and MLB history were both 25 years old. Name them.

95. Name the only person to have won both an Olympic gold medal as well as a Super Bowl ring during his athletic career?

WILD CARD

AP PHOTO / JACK DEMPSEY

Landon Donovan has won three MLS championships during his six-year career and is the MLS' alltime leading scorer in the postseason with 14 career playoff goals.

90. America's Cup—First created after America's yachting victory over Britain in 1851, it has been continuously awarded since 1857.

91. Olympic long-jump record (Bob Beamon, 1968—29'2½" vs. NBA three-point line at the top of the key—23'9")

92. Brooks Robinson (23—Baltimore Orioles); Carl Yastrzemski (23—Boston Red Sox); Cap Anson (22—Chicago Cubs); Al Kaline (22—Detroit Tigers); Stan Musial (22—St. Louis Cardinals); Mel Ott (22—N.Y. Giants)

93.
100=12+34+45+6+3+00

94. Bobby Orr (4) & Wayne Gretzky (99)
94B. Kobe Bryant (NBA); Al Kaline (MLB)

88. Brazil's Ronaldo, who passed Germany's Gerd Muller in 2006 with his 15th career World Cup goal.

89. Peja Stojakovic (1,161 3FGs in eight NBA seasons vs. Pete Stoyanovich's 272 FGs in 13 NFL seasons)

95 . Bob Hayes—Hayes won golds in the 100-meter sprint and 4x100-meter relay at the 1964 Olympics and was a wide receiver for the victorious Dallas Cowboys in Super Bowl VI.

HOCKEY

96.

Steve Yzerman scored 692 goals in his 22-year career with Detroit, the most goals in NHL history by a player who spent his whole career with one team. Name the 2nd, 3rd, and 4th-highest alltime goal-scorers to play for only one franchise throughout their career.

97. Who set an NHL record in 2006 by scoring his seventh career playoff game-winning overtime goal?

98. Mario Lemieux, Wayne Gretzky and Bobby Orr all won the Conn Smythe Trophy (playoff MVP) twice during their careers. Who's the only player to have won it three times?
HINT: He won one trophy during each of the past three decades.

99. Ducks goalie Ilja Bryzgalov recorded the second-longest shutout streak in NHL playoff history in 2006. Who stills owns the record?

100. Capitals left-winger Alexander Ovechkin scored 52 goals during the 2005–06 season, making him one of only four players in NHL history to score over 50 goals as a rookie. Name two of the other three.
HINT: Two were active in '05-'06.

101. Which "Original Six" team has more of its former players represented in the Hockey Hall of Fame than any other franchise?

102. Name the last NHL player to score 50 or more goals within a span of 50 of his team's games?

103. Who is the only player in NHL history to score a goal in all five game situations—even strength, power play, short-handed, penalty shot and empty net—all in the same game?

104. Which player set an NHL single-season record in 2006 for the most points scored—125–by someone who spent time with two different NHL teams during the same season?

HOCKEY

JOHN BIEVER / SPORTS ILLUSTRATED

Steve Yzerman scored 185 points in 196 career playoff games, which ranks him eighth alltime in NHL postseason history.

96. 2. Mario Lemieux (690—Pittsburgh Penguins); 3. Joe Sakic (574—Quebec Nordiques/Colorado Avalanche); 4. Mike Bossy (573—N.Y. Islanders)

97. Joe Sakic—Game 2 (Colo. vs. Dal.)

98. Patrick Roy (1986, Montreal; 1993, Montreal; 2001, Colorado)

99. George Hainsworth, 1930 Montreal Canadiens (270 minutes, 8 seconds); Bryzgalov's 2006 playoff shutout streak was 249 minutes, 15 seconds.

100. Teemu Selanne (76 goals, 1992–93 Winnipeg Jets); Mike Bossy (53 goals, 1977–78 New York Islanders); Joe Nieuwendyk (51 goals, 1987–88 Calgary Flames)

101. Montreal Canadiens—50 (Boston and Toronto are tied for 2nd with 46.)

102. Brett Hull, St. Louis Blues (the first 50 games of the 1991-92 season)

103. Mario Lemieux, Dec. 31, 1988 vs. New Jersey Devils

104. Joe Thornton played 23 games of the 2005–06 season with Boston, scoring 33 points, but was then traded to San Jose, where he played 58 games and scored 92 points.

TENNIS

105. Before retiring in 2006, Martina Navratilova, collected her 59th Grand Slam victory, winning the mixed doubles title at the U.S. Open. What year did she make her first appearance in a Grand Slam final?

106. When was the last time a women's U.S. Open singles final wasn't decided in straight sets?

107. In 2006, for the first time in modern tennis history, the same women's player appeared in all four Grand Slam finals. Name her.

108. In 2006, Roger Federer won the 7th, 8th, and 9th Grand Slam singles titles of his career, but he has yet to win a French Open. Name one of only two tennis players with more singles titles than Federer who have also won at least one of each of the four Grand Slams.

BOXING

109. As of September 1, 2006, all three heavyweight champions of the world (WBA, WBC and IBF) had been born in which foreign country?

110. Name the two most recent heavyweight champions who have also won an Olympic gold medal in boxing (any weight class).

111. In what year were both the 10-point must system and the mandatory eight-second count after a knockdown instituted by the World Boxing Council?

112. In total, how many boxers who used either "Rocky" or "Sugar" in their professional names are enshrined in the International Boxing Hall of Fame in Canastota, New York?

TENNIS

105. 1975—The 18-year old Navratilova lost the 1975 Australian Open final to Evonne Goolagong. In Grand Slam events, Navratilova went on to win 18 singles titles, 31 doubles titles, and 10 mixed doubles titles during her 34-year career.

106. 1995—Steffi Graf outdueled Monica Seles 7–6, 0–6, 6–3.

107. Justine Henin-Hardenne—She won the French Open, lost the U.S. Open and Wimbledon and retired at the Australian Open.

108. Roy Emerson—12 (6 Aust., 2 U.S. 2 French, 2 Wimb.); Rod Laver —11 (3 Aust., 2 French, 4 Wimb., 2 U.S.). Pete Sampras (14) and Bill Tilden (10) never won a French Open and Bjorn Borg (11) never won Wimbledon.

BOXING

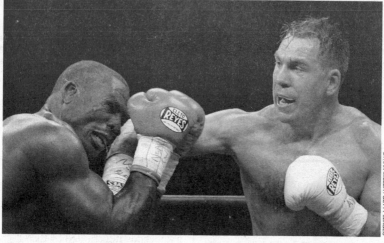

ETHAN MILLER / GETTY IMAGES

109. Soviet Union (WBA—Nikolai Valuev, WBC—Oleg Maskaev, and IBF—Wladimir Klitschko)

110. Wladimir Klitschko (1996 Superheavyweight—Ukraine); Lennox Lewis (1988 Superheavyweight—Canada)

WBC heavyweight champion Oleg Maskaev (r.), was born in Kazakhstan, but immigrated to the U.S. in 1995.

111. 1963

112. Five (Rocky Graziano, Rocky Marciano, Sugar Ray Leonard, Sugar Ramos, Sugar Ray Robinson)

THE DRAFT

113. When DE Mario Williams was chosen first in the 2006 NFL draft, it extended to 11 years the drought for running backs as the No. 1 overall pick. Name the last true RB who was the NFL's top pick. **HINT:** Lion to a Tiger.

114. Name the three players from the then-reigning NCAA national champion UNLV Running Rebels who were chosen in the first round of the 1991 NBA draft.
AND I: What jersey number did all three of them choose to wear in their rookie NBA season and why?

115. Name the two most recent members of the Pro Football Hall of Fame who were also picked consecutively in the NFL draft.

116. In the 2006 NBA draft, five different colleges had more than one player chosen in the first round. What year was the last (and only other) time this happened?

117. Prior to Erik Johnson in 2006, when was the last time a defenseman was the number-one pick in the NHL entry draft?

118. Who was the first player ever chosen in a NBA lottery draft?

119. This year, for the first time in the 40-year history of the NBA draft, one team chose players from the same school with consecutive first-round picks. Name the NBA team and the school.

HINT: Big East country

120. Only one player from each of the 1954 and 1955 NFL draft classes—drafted 232nd overall and 102nd overall, respectively—made it into the Pro Football Hall of Fame. Name these two players.

HINT: They teamed up to become one of the greatest QB-receiver tandems in NFL history, linking up for 63 career touchdowns.

ANSWERS
THE DRAFT

Shelden Williams (l.), taken fifth, and J.J. Redick, chosen 11th, were among five sets of college teammates taken during the first round of the 2006 NBA draft.

BOB ROSATO

113. Ki-Jana Carter (Penn State Nittany Lions) was chosen by the Cincinnati Bengals as the first overall pick in 1995.

114. Larry Johnson (1st overall–Charlotte Hornets); Stacey Augmon (9th–Atlanta Hawks) and Greg Anthony (12th–New York Knicks); **114 AND I.** #2, in honor of UNLV head coach Jerry Tarkanian, who wore the same number when he was a player.

115. John Elway and Eric Dickerson (drafted 1st and 2nd overall, respectively, in the 1983 NFL draft).

116. 1989–Illinois (Nick Anderson, Kenny Battle); Louisville (Pervis Ellison, Kenny Payne); Arizona (Sean Elliott, Anthony Cook); Iowa (B.J. Armstrong, Roy Marble); and Oklahoma (Stacey King, Mookie Blaylock)

117. 1996–Defenseman Chris Phillips was chosen by the Ottawa Senators as the No. 1 overall pick.

118. Patrick Ewing, taken by the New York Knicks, was the No. 1 overall pick of the 1985 NBA Draft.

119. The New Jersey Nets chose UConn's Marcus Williams and Josh Boone as the 22nd and 23rd overall picks.

120. Raymond Berry (1954, chosen in the 20th round by the Baltimore Colts) and Johnny Unitas (1955, chosen in the 9th round by the Pittsburgh Steelers)

GOLF

121.

Name the two players in PGA Tour history who have lost each of golf's four modern majors in a playoff?

HINT: One is infamous for his 1996 disaster at The Masters.

122.
How many different golf courses are currently in the British Open rota?

TAP-IN: Name all of the English golf courses in the British Open rota.

123.
Which golfer holds the career record for most points scored (23.5) by an American in Ryder Cup history?

124.
Which two of the following six legendary golfers never captained a U.S. Ryder Cup team?
a) Walter Hagen
b) Gene Sarazen
c) Byron Nelson
d) Sam Snead
e) Bobby Jones
f) Ben Hogan

125.
Prior to Australian Geoff Ogilvy's U.S. Open victory at Winged Foot in 2006, name the last Aussie to win a major on the PGA Tour.

126.
In 2006, for the first time in women's professional golf, three of the four majors were decided by playoffs, and one player, Karrie Webb, both won and lost one of these playoffs. Name the only other player in professional golf history that both won and lost major golf tournament playoffs in the same calendar year.

127.
When was the last year that Annika Sorenstam didn't win a women's golf major?

TAP-IN: When was the last year that neither Annika Sorenstam nor Tiger Woods won one of golf's majors?

GOLF

Through 2006, Steve Elkington, 43, has 10 career PGA Tour victories and over $12 million in career earnings, ranking him 51st on the alltime money list.

AP PHOTO / ERIC RISBERG

Scottish courses are St. Andrews, Muirfield, Royal Troon, Carnoustie and Turnberry.

123. Billy Casper (20–10–7 career record on eight straight Ryder Cup teams from 1961–75)

124. b) Gene Sarazen, e) Bobby Jones

125. Steve Elkington—1995 PGA Championship at Riviera Country Club

121. Craig Wood and Greg Norman —Wood's playoff losses include 1933 British Open, to Denny Shute; 1934 PGA Championship, to Paul Runyan; 1935 Masters, to Gene Sarazen; 1939 U.S. Open, to Byron Nelson.) —Norman's playoff losses include the 1984 U.S. Open, to Fuzzy Zoeller; 1987 Masters, to Larry Mize; 1989 British Open, to Mark Calcavecchia; 1993 PGA Championship, to Paul Azinger)

122. 9—Four English courses (Royal St. George's, Hoylake–Royal Liverpool, Royal Lytham and St. Anne's, and Royal Birkdale) The five

126. Arnold Palmer (won 1962 Masters playoff against Gary Player and Dow Finsterwald; lost 1962 U.S. Open playoff against Jack Nicklaus)

127. 2000—Sorenstam's top finish in a major that year was a third place finish at the duMaurier Classic.

127 TAP IN. 1998—Sorenstam's top finish in a major that year was runner-up at the duMaurier Classic, while Tiger's best major finish was third at the British Open.

Awards

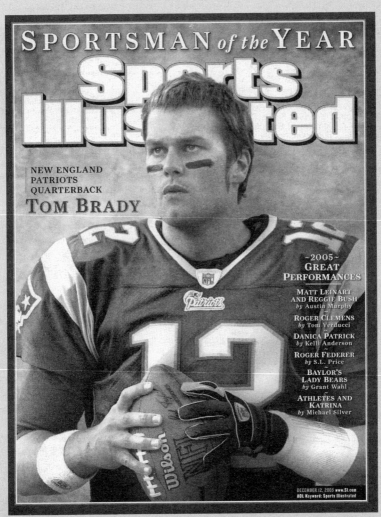

SPORTSMAN *of the* YEAR

Sports Illustrated

NEW ENGLAND
PATRIOTS
QUARTERBACK

TOM BRADY

~2005~
GREAT
PERFORMANCES

MATT LEINART
AND REGGIE BUSH
by Austin Murphy
~
ROGER CLEMENS
by Tom Verducci
~
DANICA PATRICK
by Kelli Anderson
~
ROGER FEDERER
by S.L. Price
~
BAYLOR'S
LADY BEARS
by Grant Wahl
~
ATHLETES AND
KATRINA
by Michael Silver

DECEMBER 12, 2005 www.SI.com
AOL Keyword: Sports Illustrated

SPORTS ILLUSTRATED'S
2005 Sportsman of the Year
Tom Brady

Athlete Awards

Sports Illustrated Sportsman of the Year

1954	Roger Bannister, Track and Field	1986	Joe Paterno, Football
1955	Johnny Podres, Baseball	1987	Athletes Who Care:
1956	Bobby Morrow, Track and Field		Bob Bourne, Hockey
1957	Stan Musial, Baseball		Kip Keino, Track and Field
1958	Rafer Johnson, Track and Field		Judi Brown King, Track and Field
1959	Ingemar Johansson, Boxing		Dale Murphy, Baseball
1960	Arnold Palmer, Golf		Chip Rives, Football
1961	Jerry Lucas, Basketball		Patty Sheehan, Golf
1962	Terry Baker, Football		Rory Sparrow, Pro Basketball
1963	Pete Rozelle, Pro Football		Reggie Williams, Pro Football
1964	Ken Venturi, Golf	1988	Orel Hershiser, Baseball
1965	Sandy Koufax, Baseball	1989	Greg LeMond, Cycling
1966	Jim Ryun, Track and Field	1990	Joe Montana, Pro Football
1967	Carl Yastrzemski, Baseball	1991	Michael Jordan, Pro Basketball
1968	Bill Russell, Pro Basketball	1992	Arthur Ashe, Tennis
1969	Tom Seaver, Baseball	1993	Don Shula, Pro Football
1970	Bobby Orr, Hockey	1994	Bonnie Blair, Speed Skating
1971	Lee Trevino, Golf		Johann Olav Koss, Speed Skating
1972	B.J. King, Tennis/ J. Wooden, Bask	1995	Cal Ripken Jr, Baseball
1973	Jackie Stewart, Auto Racing	1996	Tiger Woods, Golf
1974	Muhammad Ali, Boxing	1997	Dean Smith, College Basketball
1975	Pete Rose, Baseball	1998	Mark McGwire, Sammy Sosa,
1976	Chris Evert, Tennis		Baseball
1977	Steve Cauthen, Horse Racing	1999	U.S. Women's Soccer Team
1978	Jack Nicklaus, Golf	2000	Tiger Woods, Golf
1979	Terry Bradshaw, Pro Football	2001	C. Schilling/ R. Johnson, Baseball
	Willie Stargell, Baseball	2002	Lance Armstrong, Cycling
1980	U.S. Olympic Hockey Team	2003	Tim Duncan/David Robinson,
1981	Sugar Ray Leonard, Boxing		Basketball
1982	Wayne Gretzky, Hockey	2004	Boston Red Sox, Baseball
1983	Mary Decker, Track and Field	2005	Tom Brady, Pro Football
1984	Mary Lou Retton, Gymnastics		
	Edwin Moses, Track and Field		
1985	Kareem Abdul-Jabbar, Pro Basketball		

Associated Press Athletes of the Year

	MEN	WOMEN
1931	Pepper Martin, Baseball	Helene Madison, Swimming
1932	Gene Sarazen, Golf	Babe Didrikson, Track and Field
1933	Carl Hubbell, Baseball	Helen Jacobs, Tennis
1934	Dizzy Dean, Baseball	Virginia Van Wie, Golf
1935	Joe Louis, Boxing	Helen Wills Moody, Tennis
1936	Jesse Owens, Track and Field	Helen Stephens, Track and Field
1937	Don Budge, Tennis	Katherine Rawls, Swimming
1938	Don Budge, Tennis	Patty Berg, Golf
1939	Nile Kinnick, Football	Alice Marble, Tennis
1940	Tom Harmon, Football	Alice Marble, Tennis
1941	Joe DiMaggio, Baseball	Betty Hicks Newell, Golf
1942	Frank Sinkwich, Football	Gloria Callen, Swimming
1943	Gunder Haegg, Track and Field	Patty Berg, Golf
1944	Byron Nelson, Golf	Ann Curtis, Swimming
1945	Bryon Nelson, Golf	Babe Didrikson Zaharias, Golf
1946	Glenn Davis, Football	Babe Didrikson Zaharias, Golf
1947	Johnny Lujack, Football	Babe Didrikson Zaharias, Golf
1948	Lou Boudreau, Baseball	Fanny Blankers-Koen, Track and Field
1949	Leon Hart, Football	Marlene Bauer, Golf
1950	Jim Konstanty, Baseball	Babe Didrikson Zaharias, Golf
1951	Dick Kazmaier, Football	Maureen Connolly, Tennis
1952	Bob Mathias, Track and Field	Maureen Connolly, Tennis
1953	Ben Hogan, Golf	Maureen Connolly, Tennis
1954	Willie Mays, Baseball	Babe Didrikson Zaharias, Golf
1955	Hopalong Cassidy, Football	Patty Berg, Golf

Associated Press Athletes of the Year *(Cont.)*

	MEN	WOMEN
1956	Mickey Mantle, Baseball	Pat McCormick, Diving
1957	Ted Williams, Baseball	Althea Gibson, Tennis
1958	Herb Elliott, Track and Field	Althea Gibson, Tennis
1959	Ingemar Johansson, Boxing	Maria Bueno, Tennis
1960	Rafer Johnson, Track and Field	Wilma Rudolph, Track and Field
1961	Roger Maris, Baseball	Wilma Rudolph, Track and Field
1962	Maury Wills, Baseball	Dawn Fraser, Swimming
1963	Sandy Koufax, Baseball	Mickey Wright, Golf
1964	Don Schollander, Swimming	Mickey Wright, Golf
1965	Sandy Koufax, Baseball	Kathy Whitworth, Golf
1966	Frank Robinson, Baseball	Kathy Whitworth, Golf
1967	Carl Yastrzemski, Baseball	Billie Jean King, Tennis
1968	Denny McLain, Baseball	Peggy Fleming, Skating
1969	Tom Seaver, Baseball	Debbie Meyer, Swimming
1970	George Blanda, Pro Football	Chi Cheng, Track and Field
1971	Lee Trevino, Golf	Evonne Goolagong, Tennis
1972	Mark Spitz, Swimming	Olga Korbut, Gymnastics
1973	O.J. Simpson, Pro Football	Billie Jean King, Tennis
1974	Muhammad Ali, Boxing	Chris Evert, Tennis
1975	Fred Lynn, Baseball	Chris Evert, Tennis
1976	Bruce Jenner, Track and Field	Nadia Comaneci, Gymnastics
1977	Steve Cauthen, Horse Racing	Chris Evert, Tennis
1978	Ron Guidry, Baseball	Nancy Lopez, Golf
1979	Willie Stargell, Baseball	Tracy Austin, Tennis
1980	U.S. Olympic Hockey Team	Chris Evert Lloyd, Tennis
1981	John McEnroe, Tennis	Tracy Austin, Tennis
1982	Wayne Gretzky, Hockey	Mary Decker, Track and Field
1983	Carl Lewis, Track and Field	Martina Navratilova, Tennis
1984	Carl Lewis, Track and Field	Mary Lou Retton, Gymnastics
1985	Dwight Gooden, Baseball	Nancy Lopez, Golf
1986	Larry Bird, Pro Basketball	Martina Navratilova, Tennis
1987	Ben Johnson, Track and Field	Jackie Joyner-Kersee, Track and Field
1988	Orel Hershiser, Baseball	Florence Griffith Joyner, Track and Field
1989	Joe Montana, Pro Football	Steffi Graf, Tennis
1990	Joe Montana, Pro Football	Beth Daniel, Golf
1991	Michael Jordan, Pro Basketball	Monica Seles, Tennis
1992	Michael Jordan, Pro Basketball	Monica Seles, Tennis
1993	Michael Jordan, Pro Basketball	Sheryl Swoopes, Basketball
1994	George Foreman, Boxing	Bonnie Blair, Speed Skating
1995	Cal Ripken Jr, Baseball	Rebecca Lobo, Basketball
1996	Michael Johnson, Track and Field	Amy Van Dyken, Swimming
1997	Tiger Woods, Golf	Martina Hingis, Tennis
1998	Mark McGwire, Baseball	Se Ri Pak, Golf
1999	Tiger Woods, Golf	U.S. Women's Soccer Team
2000	Tiger Woods, Golf	Marion Jones, Track and Field
2001	Barry Bonds, Baseball	Jennifer Capriati, Tennis
2002	Lance Armstrong, Cycling	Serena Williams, Tennis
2003	Lance Armstrong, Cycling	Annika Sorenstam, Golf
2004	Lance Armstrong, Cycling	Annika Sorenstam, Golf
2005	Lance Armstrong, Cycling	Annika Sorenstam, Golf

James E. Sullivan Award

Presented annually by the AAU to the athlete who "by his or her performance, example and influence as an amateur, has done the most during the year to advance the cause of sportsmanship."

1930	Bobby Jones, Golf
1931	Barney Berlinger, Track and Field
1932	Jim Bausch, Track and Field
1933	Glenn Cunningham, Track and Field
1934	Bill Bonthron, Track and Field
1935	Lawson Little, Golf
1936	Glenn Morris, Track and Field
1937	Don Budge, Tennis
1938	Don Lash, Track and Field
1939	Joe Burk, Rowing
1940	Greg Rice, Track and Field
1941	Leslie MacMitchell, Track and Field
1942	Cornelius Warmerdam, Track
1943	Gilbert Dodds, Track and Field
1944	Ann Curtis, Swimming
1945	Doc Blanchard, Football
1946	Arnold Tucker, Football
1947	John B. Kelly Jr, Rowing
1948	Bob Mathias, Track and Field
1949	Dick Button, Skating
1950	Fred Wilt, Track and Field
1951	Bob Richards, Track and Field
1952	Horace Ashenfelter, Track and Field
1953	Sammy Lee, Diving
1954	Mal Whitfield, Track and Field
1955	Harrison Dillard, Track and Field
1956	Pat McCormick, Diving
1957	Bobby Morrow, Track and Field
1958	Glenn Davis, Track and Field
1959	Parry O'Brien, Track and Field
1960	Rafer Johnson, Track and Field
1961	Wilma Rudolph, Track and Field
1962	Jim Beatty, Track and Field
1963	John Pennel, Track and Field
1964	Don Schollander, Swimming
1965	Bill Bradley, Basketball
1966	Jim Ryun, Track and Field
1967	Randy Matson, Track and Field
1968	Debbie Meyer, Swimming
1969	Bill Toomey, Track and Field
1970	John Kinsella, Swimming
1971	Mark Spitz, Swimming
1972	Frank Shorter, Track and Field
1973	Bill Walton, Basketball
1974	Rich Wohlhuter, Track and Field
1975	Tim Shaw, Swimming
1976	Bruce Jenner, Track and Field
1977	John Naber, Swimming
1978	Tracy Caulkins, Swimming
1979	Kurt Thomas, Gymnastics
1980	Eric Heiden, Speed Skating
1981	Carl Lewis, Track and Field
1982	Mary Decker, Track and Field
1983	Edwin Moses, Track and Field
1984	Greg Louganis, Diving
1985	Joan B.-Samuelson, T & F
1986	Jackie Joyner-Kersee, T & F
1987	Jim Abbott, Baseball
1988	Florence Griffith Joyner, Track
1989	Janet Evans, Swimming
1990	John Smith, Wrestling

James E. Sullivan Award (Cont.)

1991	Mike Powell, Track and Field
1992	Bonnie Blair, Speed Skating
1993	Charlie Ward, Football, Basketball
1994	Dan Jansen, Speed Skating
1995	Bruce Baumgartner, Wrestling
1996	Michael Johnson, Track and Field
1997	Peyton Manning, Football
1998	Chamique Holdsclaw, Basketball
1999	Kelly and Coco Miller, Basketball
2000	Rulon Gardner, Wrestling
2001	Michelle Kwan, Figure Skating
2002	Sarah Hughes, Figure Skating
2003	Michael Phelps, Swimming
2004	Paul Hamm, Gymnastics
2005	J. J. Redick, College Basketball

The Sporting News Sportsman of the Year

1968	Denny McLain, Baseball
1969	Tom Seaver, Baseball
1970	John Wooden, Basketball
1971	Lee Trevino, Golf
1972	Charles O. Finley, Baseball
1973	O.J. Simpson, Pro Football
1974	Lou Brock, Baseball
1975	Archie Griffin, Football
1976	Larry O'Brien, Pro Basketball
1977	Steve Cauthen, Horse Racing
1978	Ron Guidry, Baseball
1979	Willie Stargell, Baseball
1980	George Brett, Baseball
1981	Wayne Gretzky, Hockey
1982	Whitey Herzog, Baseball
1983	Bowie Kuhn, Baseball
1984	Peter Ueberroth, LA Olympics
1985	Pete Rose, Baseball
1986	Larry Bird, Pro Basketball
1987	No award
1988	Jackie Joyner-Kersee, T & F
1989	Joe Montana, Pro Football
1990	Nolan Ryan, Baseball
1991	Michael Jordan, Pro Basketball
1992	Mike Krzyzewski, Basketball
1993	Pat Gillick/Cito Gaston, Baseball
1994	Emmitt Smith, Pro Football
1995	Cal Ripken Jr, Baseball
1996	Joe Torre, Baseball
1997	Michael Jordan, Basketball
1998	Mark McGwire, Baseball
1999	New York Yankees, Baseball
2000	Kurt Warner/ Marshall Faulk, Pro Football
2001	Curt Schilling, Baseball
2002	Tyrone Willingham, Football
2003	Jack McKeon, Baseball Dick Vermeil, Pro Football
2004	Tom Brady, Pro Football
2005	Matt Leinart, College Football

United Press International Male and Female Athlete of the Year

MEN	WOMEN
1974.............................Muhammad Ali, Boxing	Irena Szewinska, Track and Field
1975.............................Joao Oliveira, Track and Field	Nadia Comaneci, Gymnastics
1976.............................Alberto Juantorena, Track and Field	Nadia Comaneci, Gymnastics
1977.............................Alberto Juantorena, Track and Field	Rosie Ackermann, Track and Field
1978.............................Henry Rono, Track and Field	Tracy Caulkins, Swimming
1979.............................Sebastian Coe, Track and Field	Marita Koch, Track and Field
1980.............................Eric Heiden, Speed Skating	Hanni Wenzel, Alpine Skiing
1981.............................Sebastian Coe, Track and Field	Chris Evert Lloyd, Tennis
1982.............................Daley Thompson, Track and Field	Marita Koch, Track and Field
1983.............................Carl Lewis, Track and Field	Jarmila Kratochvilova, Track and Field
1984.............................Carl Lewis, Track and Field	Martina Navratilova, Tennis
1985.............................Steve Cram, Track and Field	Mary Decker Slaney, Track and Field
1986.............................Diego Maradona, Soccer	Heike Drechsler, Track and Field
1987.............................Ben Johnson, Track and Field	Steffi Graf, Tennis
1988.............................Matt Biondi, Swimming	Florence Griffith Joyner, Track and Field
1989.............................Boris Becker, Tennis	Steffi Graf, Tennis
1990.............................Stefan Edberg, Tennis	Merlene Ottey, Track and Field
1991.............................Michael Jordan, Pro Basketball	Monica Seles,. Tennis
1992.............................Mario Lemieux, Hockey	Monica Seles, Tennis
1993.............................Michael Jordan, Pro Basketball	Steffi Graf, Tennis
1994.............................Nick Price, Golf	Bonnie Blair, Speed Skating
1995.............................Cal Ripken Jr, Baseball	Steffi Graf, Tennis

Note: Award not given since 1995.

Dial Award

Presented by the Dial Corporation to the male and female national high school athlete/scholar of the year.

BOYS	GIRLS
1979.............................Herschel Walker, Football	No award
1980.............................Bill Fralic, Football	Carol Lewis, Track and Field
1981.............................Kevin Willhite, Football	Cheryl Miller, Basketball
1982.............................Mike Smith, Basketball	Elaine Zayak, Skating
1983.............................Chris Spielman, Football	Melanie Buddemeyer, Swimming
1984.............................Hart Lee Dykes, Football	Nora Lewis, Basketball
1985.............................Jeff George, Football	Gea Johnson, Track and Field
1986.............................Scott Schaffner, Football	Mya Johnson, Track and Field
1987.............................Todd Marinovich, Football	Kristi Overton, Water Skiing
1988.............................Carlton Gray, Football	Courtney Cox, Basketball
1989.............................Robert Smith, Football	Lisa Leslie, Basketball
1990.............................Derrick Brooks, Football	Vicki Goetze, Golf
1991.............................Jeff Buckey, Football, Track and Field	Katie Smith, Basketball, Volleyball, Track
1992 ....Jacque Vaughn, Basketball	Amanda White, Track and Field, Swimming
1993.............................Tiger Woods, Golf	Kristin Folkl, Basketball
1994 ....Taymon Domzalski, Basketball	Shannon Miller, Gymnastics
1995 ....Brent Abernathy, Baseball	Shea Ralph, Basketball
1996.............................Grant Irons, Football	Grace Park, Golf
1997.............................Ronald Curry, Football	Michelle Kwan, Figure Skating

Note: Award not given since 1997.

Obituaries

Byron Nelson
1912–2006

Leavander Johnson, 35, boxer. *Former lightweight champ who died after sustaining head injuries in a fight.*

Shortly after referee Tony Weeks stopped his Las Vegas bout with Jesus Chavez in the 11th round, Johnson, who had taken a severe beating from Chavez, began having trouble walking. He was rushed to the hospital for brain surgery and was put into a medically induced coma. He never regained consciousness and died after being removed from life support. "There'll be a lot of people who'll take pokes at boxing for this," said Lou DiBella, Johnson's promoter. "But this is not a situation where anyone failed Leavander Johnson. It was just God's will. It's a sport that's inherently dangerous."

In Las Vegas, of brain injuries, on Sept. 22, 2005.

Wellington Mara, 89, NFL team co-owner.

Becoming a ballboy for the Giants the day his father, Tim Mara, purchased the team in 1925, Mara remained involved with the team's operations for the next eight decades. He became the team's co-owner, along with older brother Jack, in 1930.

Mara's unselfish support, in the early 1960's, for the equal distribution of revenue allowed the league to flourish while preserving its competitive balance. "Without Wellington's influence, the Packers would either have been out of business today or totally uncompetitive," said Green Bay Packers president Bob Harlan, whose team received the same $84.2 million in 2004 broadcast revenue as Mara's Giants. He was elected to the Pro Football Hall of Fame in 1997.

In Rye, N.Y., of lymphoma, on Oct. 25, 2005.

Al Lopez, 97, baseball manager. *The only manager to finish ahead of the Yankees from 1949 through '64. SI writes:*

"In 1954, as his Cleveland Indians were en route to a then AL-record 111 wins, Al Lopez was asked if he was having fun. "Fun?" said Lopez. "How can you have any fun managing?" It might not have been the most enjoyable profession for Lopez, but it suited him well. Besides winning the '54 pennant, he led the White Sox to the AL flag in 1959.

In '54 *Life* called Lopez "a quiet, anxious man who undergoes agonies during games but seldom leaves the dugout." That self-control was his greatest asset on the bench. He rarely yelled at his players. ("They're old enough to know what's good for them," he said.) In return, they bought into whatever style he was preaching. In Cleveland he won with great pitching and home runs; in Chicago it was defense and speed.

Lopez was a fair-hitting catcher, so good at handling pitchers that his 1,918 games stood as a record for 40 years. But it was primarily for his managerial skills that he was inducted into the Hall of Fame in 1977. In 1998, Al Rosen, who played third base for Lopez in Cleveland said, "He was the consumate gentleman, and you knew he was always in your corner."

In Tampa, Fla., of complications of a heart attack on Oct. 30, 2005.

Jerry Wachter, 61, sports photographer. *SI writes:*

"When a fellow photographer once asked Jerry Wachter what the key to shooting a good football picture was, Wachter replied, "Always have someone to throw your 600mm [lens] to." Of course, photography isn't that simple, even if Wachter made it

seem so. Over his 35-year career, Wachter, was a versatile master, adept at shooting all sports, and he produced some of *SI*'s most iconic images of the 1980's and '90s. The longtime Baltimore Orioles team photographer shot his first SI cover in 1979, and over the next two decades hundreds of his photographs appeared in the magazine, including 35 more on the cover."

In Baltimore. Md., of Merkel cell carcinoma, on Nov. 10, 2005.

Steve Courson, 50, football player. *Courson won two Super Bowl rings as an offensive lineman for the Steelers. SI writes:*

"Courson was long-haired, wild-eyed, hyper-aggressive and, as it turned out, 'roided up. Though he felt his outspokenness hurt his relationship with his former team, he was open about his steroid use; he frequently talked about the dangers of steroids, and in April 2005, he testified before Congress. ("The only reason I talk about it," he said after his testimony, "is because of those kids.") He was cutting down a dead oak on the property outside his two story log cabin when it suddenly fell, crushing him and pinning one of his two black labs, Rufus, who survived. E.J. Sherry, the neighbor who helped remove Courson's body from beneath the tree, said he suspected Courson was trying to get his dog out of the way when the tree brought him down.

In Farmington, Pa., of injuries sustained from a falling tree, on Nov. 10, 2005.

Robert Tisch, 79, NFL team co-owner. *SI writes:*

"Tisch a former postmaster general and the longtime chairman of Loews Corp., bought 50% of the Giants in 1991, and he and fellow owner Wellington Mara were regulars at team practices and games. (Mara died of cancer on October 25.) A few days before he died, Tisch was visited at his Manhattan home by Giants coach Tom Coughlin, G.M. Ernie Accorsi and players Tiki Barber and Michael Strahan, and on November 12 his sons Jonathan, the Giants' treasurer, and Steve, the executive vice president, addressed the team. "My father loved the players," Jonathan said. "He loved the organization. Every Sunday he was so looking forward to being in the football world."

In New York City, of inoperable brain cancer, on Nov. 15, 2005.

Vic Power, 78, baseball player. *One of the first Hispanic players in the majors, the native of Puerto Rico was signed by the Yankees in 1952 and broke into the big leagues with the Philadelphia A's in 1954. SI writes:*

"Over the next 12 seasons, mostly with the A's, Indians and Twins, Power won seven Gold Gloves and was known for a flamboyant, one-handed fielding style and for countering racism with a sense of humor. Once, while playing in the south as a minor leaguer, he was refused service by a waitress that said the restaurant did not serve Negroes. "That's O.K.," he replied. "I don't eat Negroes."

In San Juan, Puerto Rico, of cancer, on Nov. 29, 2005.

Malik Joyeux, 25, surfer.

A native of the Tahitian island of Moorea, Joyeux made a name for himself as a big wave surfer, but also captured the 2003 Billabong XXL Tube of the Year championship and set a world-first record in tow-kiting at Teahupoo, getting him on the cover of *Surfer* magazine.

Joyeux wiped out violently while surfing at the notoriously dangerous Banzai Pipeline in Hawaii. When his body was pulled from the water—about 15 minutes later—one of surfing's most popular competitors was dead. "[Joyeux] was a very positive and happy person, always stoked," Laird Hamilton told the *Los Angeles Times*.

In Pupukea Beach, Hi., of injuries sustained in a surfing accident, on December 2, 2005.

Rod Dedeaux, 91, college baseball coach.
SI writes:

A backslapper who called everyone "Tiger" and was fond of making his freshmen wear a red wig on road trips, Dedeaux led USC baseball for 45 years. He was also quick with a quip. Describing his major league career—two games with the Brooklyn Dodgers in 1935—the former shortstop said, "I had a cup of coffee with no sugar in it." As laid-back as he was, Dedeaux got the most out of his players One of them, former big leaguer Roy Smalley, said Dedeaux had "the ability to be a disciplinarian without you knowing he was." Dedeaux's 45 Trojan teams won a record 11 NCAA titles, and he sent nearly 60 players to the majors, including Mark McGwire, Randy Johnson and Tom Seaver.

Until 2005, he continued to work at the multimillion dollar transportation company he started in 1935 when he bought a truck with $500 of the $1,500 signing bonus he got from Casey Stengel. When asked for his formula for success, Dedeaux said, "First, you have to play smart, in baseball and in business ... Secondly, stay loose. When we work, we work hard. But we have fun too. A little clowning around always helps."

In Glendale, Ca., of complications from a stroke, on January 5.

Dave Brown, 52, football player.
A three time selection to the All-Big Ten team while at the University of Michigan, Brown joined the Steelers in 1975. The next year, he was chosen by the Seattle Seahawks as part of their expansion draft. He remained with the Seahawks for 10 seasons, and was selected to the 1984 Pro Bowl. He was signed by the Packers in 1986 and retired in 1990 with 62 career interceptions. In '92, he became the defensive backs coach for the Seahawks, a position he held until '98.

In Lubbock, Tex., of a heart attack, on January 10.

Jack Fiske, 88, boxing writer.
For more than 40 years, Fiske covered boxing for the San Francisco Chronicle. SI writes:

He'd chew on a toothpick as he watched a fight, then dictate his stories into a pay phone from the notes scribbled onto a single sheet of paper. Fiske also wrote a column called "Punching the Bag", in which his phrases jabbed and hooked. "If he had to hurt someone's feelings, he didn't mind doing that," former trainer Emanuel Steward told the *Chronicle*. "He told it like it was."

Fiske was inducted into the International Boxing Hall of Fame in 2003.

In Redwood City. Calif., of Parkinson's disease, on January 24.

Curt Gowdy, 86, sportscaster.
After starting out in Oklahoma City, broadcasting the play-by-play results of baseball and basketball games, in 1949 Gowdy was paired with Mel Allen as sportscasters for the New York Yankees. Three years later, he was named lead announcer for the Boston Red Sox. Moving into television, Gowdy became well known for broadcasting a wide variety of sporting events, including Super Bowl III; the '76 Olympics, 16 All-Star baseball games and 13 World Series.

The first sportscaster to receive the Peabody award, he hosted *American Sportsman* a fishing and hunting-oriented TV show that ran on ABC from the '60s through the '80s and featured guests including George H. W. Bush and Jimmy Carter, among with many prominent athletes. After the series cancellation in '85, Gowdy retired. He was inducted into the Baseball Hall of Fame in 1984.

In Palm Beach, Fla., of leukemia, on February 20.

Kirby Puckett, 45, baseball player.
Puckett played centerfield for the Minnesota Twins for his 10-season major league career, helping lead the team to two World Series titles in 1987 and '91. He remains the Twins' all time leader in hits, runs, doubles and total bases. In 1995, he was forced to retire from baseball due to glaucoma-induced vision loss in one eye. He was elected to the Baseball Hall of Fame in 2001.

In Phoenix, Ariz., of complications resulting from a stroke, on March 6.

Bernie Geoffrion, 75, hockey player. *SI writes:*
"At first Bernie (Boom Boom) Geoffrion's nickname was not an entirely complimentary reference to his slap shot, a novelty he helped popularize in the NHL. Bestowed on him by a sportswriter when young Bernard played junior hockey in the 1940's, the moniker described the sounds heard when Geoffrion unleashed his notoriously inaccurate slapper—one boom when his stick hit the puck, another when the rubber flew past the goal and crashed into the boards.

Not that Geoffrion minded. The Hall of Famer eventually found the net with regularity: He scored 393 goals in 16 NHL seasons in the 1950s and '60s, all but two with the Canadiens, and played on six Stanley Cup winners. And no one enjoyed a good joke more than Boom Boom, one of the Original Six's most charismatic stars. He starred in popular Miller Lite ads, and the Atlanta Flames hired him as their coach in 1972—more for the power of his personality than for his bench acumen. (He once told a friend, 'There are three things to hockey—skating and shooting.'")

Geoffrion died hours before his number 5 was to be retired by the Canadiens; his sweater now hangs from the rafters of the Bell Centre next to that of his father-in-law, Montreal legend Howie Morenz."

In Atlanta, Ga., of stomach cancer, on March 11.

Ann Calvello, 76, roller derbyist. *SI writes:*
"She was, simply, the best villain there ever was in sport. She was the Meanest Mama on Skates and the Queen of the Penalty Box—and proud of it. She was also a terrific athlete, but she knew far better how to entertain that any of the jerks today who prance around in the end zone. Nobody in any sport knew how to wear a uniform so well as she did, topping off her rakish ensemble with garishly dyed hair (green for St. Paddy's Day, pink, purple, maybe some polka dots or stars). Whatever. Ann Calvello was the whole package.

She started in roller derby in 1948. For several years she was the star of the Bay Bombers, but then she "went red shirt," over to whoever the Bombers' main opposition was on a given night, and there she thrived as a baddie. Her classic duels with the winsome Blond Bomber, Joanie Weston, were the best Good vs. Evil confrontations this side of Snow White and the Wicked Stepmother. Off the track, though, Ann was sweet and thoughtful and full of fun. The license plate on her '74 Lincoln was LOVER. A 2001 documentary on Calvello helped spark renewed interest in women's derby and remade her as a cult figure for young women. In Texas, rollergirls now play for the Calvello Cup. If she'd played an uptown sport, Ann Calvello would be in the company of Babe Didrikson, Chris Evert and Peggy Fleming. As it is, she'll just have to be remembered as an absolute original."

San Bruno, Calif., of liver cancer, on March 14.

Paul Dana, 30, race car driver
A graduate of Northwestern University, Dana won his first race at 21 while working at the Bridgestone Racing School in Ontario, Canada. In 2004, he placed second at the Infiniti Pro Series championship. A spinal fracture kept him out of the 2005 Indianapolis 500. During a practice race at Homestead-Miami Speedway, he collided with a disabled car on the track at approximately 176 mph.

In Miami, Fla., from a racing accident, on March 26.

Margaret Dixon, 28, college basketball coach
After four years as an assistant coach at DePaul University, in 2005, Dixon became the women's basketball coach at the United States Military Academy. She led the Army women to a 20-11 season and victory in the Patriot League conference tournament. The Army women became the first Army basketball team to appear in a NCAA tournament when they lost to Tennessee 102-54 in 2006.

Dixon's brother Jamie is the University of Pittsburgh's head men's basketball coach.

In Valhalla, N.Y., of heart failure, on April 6.

Steve Howe, 48, baseball player. *1980 National League Rookie of the Year.*
During his rookie season with the Dodgers, Howe saved 17 games, a record at the time. His 12-season major league career was marred by substance abuse issues—Howe was suspended seven times for substance abuse, including for the entire 1984 season. In 1992, while playing for the Yankees, he became the second player to be banned for life from major league baseball, but succeeded in overturning the ban after an appeal. He was released from the Yankees in 1996.

In Coachella, Calif., of injuries sustained after his pickup truck rolled over, on April 28.

Harold (Bunny) Levitt, 96, basketball player. *Former Harlem Globetrotter. SI writes:*
"In 1935, Levitt, who was white, sank a record 499 consecutive foul shots during a contest in Chicago. He was quickly recruited by Harlem Globetrotters G.M. Abe Saperstein and toured with the all-black team from 1935 to 1940. Between quarters the 5 foot 4 inch Levitt—nicknamed Bunny by his mother because of his small size and speed—would challenge fans to outshoot him from the foul line, offering a $1,000 prize. The Globetrotters never had to pay the prize."

In Ocala, Fla., of natural causes, on April 30.

Floyd Patterson, 71, boxer. *Former heavyweight boxing champion.*
A boxer from the age of 14, Patterson competed at the Helsinki Olympics at the age of 17, winning a gold medal as a middleweight. Although considered a natural middleweight, Patterson fought Archie Moore for the heavyweight title (left vacant by Rocky Marciano) in 1956. Patterson knocked Moore out in the fifth round, becoming the youngest heavyweight champion in history at the time, and the first Olympic medalist to hold the title. He lost the title to Sweden's Ingemar Johansson in '59, but recaptured it in a '60 rematch with Johansson. He lost the title in '62 to Sonny Liston.

In New Paltz, N.Y., of prostate cancer, on May 11.

Jim Lemon, 78, baseball player.
After a number of trips to the minor leagues, Lemon got his chance at the majors when he was signed to the Washington Senators in 1956. He hit 27 home runs in '56, 33 in '59, and 38 in '60. He moved with the team to St. Paul in 1960, where it became the Minnesota Twins, but retired three years later. Lemon later served as a coach for the Twins and briefly as manager of the expansion Washington Senators.

In Brandon, Miss., of cancer, on May 14.

Hans Horrevoets, 32, sailor. *The Dutch sailor was swept overboard in stormy Atlantic seas during the Volvo Ocean Race. It was the first fatality in the 32,700-mile around-the-world yacht race since 1989. SI writes:*
"Horrevoets was trimming the spinnaker on the ABN AMRO TWO when a wave crashed over the vessel. He was found after a 60-minute search and was pulled aboard unconscious; attempts to revive him were unsuccessful. The ABN AMRO TWO eventually finished the seventh leg of the race in Portsmouth, England in fifth place."

In the North Atlantic, of drowning, on May 18.

Ted Schroeder, 84, tennis player. *Winner of the Wimbledon singles title in 1949. SI writes:*
"He also won singles and mixed doubles titles at the U.S. National Championships, a precursor to the Open. Schroeder never turned pro, but he continued to follow tennis, and regularly attended Wimbledon. He was often a critic of the sport and, occasionally, of its players, whom he thought were greedy and undisciplined. Schroeder was inducted into the International Tennis Hall of Fame in 1966.

In La Jolla, Ca., of cancer, on May 26.

Craig Heyward, 39, football player. *SI writes:*
"After dropping nearly 100 pounds, Heyward—who had a size-8¾ head—went from being a Chicago Bears cast off in 1994 to a 1,000-yard rusher for the Atlanta Falcons the next season. He lost his job to Jamal Anderson in 1996 though, and signed with the Rams. He was with the Colts in 1998 when he was diagnosed with a brain tumor. Heyward, a hard partyer (nicknamed Ironhead by teammates) early in his career, underwent a transformation when he began treatment. 'I wish I could take all of today's athletes and have them go see those kids in the hospital,' Heyward said in 1999. 'It would allow them to appreciate life so much more. Their whole attitude would change. Mine has.'"

In Atlanta, Ga., of brain cancer, on May 27.

Gert Fredriksson, 86, Olympic canoeist. *SI writes:*
"The Swede won his first gold medal in the 1,000- and 10,000-meter kayak singles at the London Games of 1948—he won the 10,000 by 30.5 seconds, a record margin that still stands—and in three more Olympiads he added four more golds, a silver and a bronze. Frederiksson's total of eight canoeing medals is surpassed only by that of Birgit Fischer, who won eight gold and four silver medals."

In Nykoping, Sweden, of cancer, on June 5.

Moe Drabowsky, 70, baseball player.
Drabowsky pitched for eight teams in a 17-year big league career that ended in 1972. SI writes:
"Used mostly as a reliever, Drabowsky was hardly a star—he was 88-105 with a career ERA of 3.71—but his antics off the field made him one of his generation's most memorable players. He was a master in the art of clubhouse tomfoolery: hiding pythons in teammates' shoes and lockers, contaminating opposing teams' air-

conditioning systems with sneezing powder, slipping goldfish into their watercoolers and making crank calls to their bullpens. 'Players seem more serious now,' he said in 1987. 'I would tend to believe they don't have as much fun.'"

In Little Rock, Ark., of multiple myeloma, on June 10.

Steve Mizerak, 61, pool player. *SI writes:*
"It took appearing alongside Rodney Dangerfield for Steve Mizerak to finally get some respect. Mizerak was a masterly pool player who controlled the cue ball as if it had attended obedience school. For four straight years (1970-73) he won the U.S. Open in pocket billiards, all the while moonlighting as a New Jersey middle school teacher—so meager were the wages conferred on even the most skilled pool practitioners at the time. In the late 1970's, "The Miz", as he was affectionately known, successfully auditioned to play alongside Dangerfield, Bubba Smith and other self-deprecating B-listers in a memorable series of Miller Lite beer ads. After nearly 200 takes, Mizerak potted a you-gotta-be-kidding-me trick shot and intoned, "It's easy to work up a thirst even when you're just showing off."

Mizerak often remarked that those 29 seconds accorded him more notoriety than any tournament victory. In the Republic of Pool, however, Mizerak is recognized as one of the great ones, his reputation for shotmaking only rivaled by his reputation for honor. In the sport's rich compendium of bawdy stories, Mizerak's name is notably absent. "He was a responsible guy, a family man, who wasn't interested in gambling or road playing," says Toupee Jay Helfert, a Mizerak contemporary. "But the truth is, no hustlers would have messed with him anyway. That's how good he was."

In Palm Beach, Fla., of complications from gall bladder surgery, on June 29.

Andrew Sudduth, 44, Olympic rower. *At the 1984 Los Angeles games, Sudduth won a silver as a member of the eight-man U.S. team. SI writes:*
"One of the best rowers the U.S. has produced, Sudduth won four World Rowing Championship medals and singles sculling events at five Head of the Charles regattas in Boston.

After retiring from rowing, he worked as a computer programmer at Cisco Systems at which he helped develop servers that became the foundation of the Internet."

In Marion, Mass., of pancreatic cancer, on July 15.

Galen Fiss, 75, football player. *A linebacker and captain of the last Cleveland Browns NFL championship team, Fiss made a touchdown-saving tackle of Lenny Moore in the 1964 NFL title game, in which the Browns upset the Colts 27-0. SI writes:*
"Before his football career, Fiss played minor league baseball in the Indians' system with Roger Maris and was Dean Smith's roommate when they played basketball at Kansas. 'He was a born leader,' Browns teammate Vince Costello said. 'He got along with everybody, and everybody listened to him.'"

In Kansas City, Mo., of undisclosed causes, on July 17.

Kevin Brophy, 21, college basketball player.
Brophy, a junior guard with the Georgia Bulldogs, was driving from Athens to Savannah after working at a basketball camp when he collided with another car. Originally from Melbourne, Australia, Brophy started as a walk-on for the Bulldogs, but ended up playing 28 games in his freshman season and was awarded an athletic scholarship before the 2006 season. "Things were really, really coming together for Kevin in every way," said Bulldogs coach Dennis Felton. "He was going to have a tremendous life."

In Greensboro, Ga., of injuries resulting from an automobile accident, on July 20.

Elden Auker, 95, baseball player. *The last living pitcher to have faced Babe Ruth. SI writes:*
"The Bambino was the first hitter Auker faced as a Tigers rookie in 1933. Auker, a submariner, struck him out on four pitches, then got the next hitter, Lou Gehrig, to pop out. Auker was 130-101 in his ten year career. He was the losing pitcher—to Dizzy Dean of the Cardinals—in Game 7 of the 1934 World Series. The next year, after the Tigers beat the Cubs in the Series, Auker was interviewed by Ronald Reagan, then an up-and-coming young broadcaster. According to Auker, Reagan later told him that interview was his "first big break."

In Vero Beach, Fla., of heart failure, on August 4.

Susan Butcher, 51, dogsled racer.
A former veterinary technician, Butcher was forced to withdraw from the 1985 Iditarod after a moose killed two of her dogs. She came back to win the race in 1986, becoming only the second woman to do so (after Libby Riddles in '85). She repeated the feat in 1987, 1988, and 1990, becoming one of dogsledding's most dominant competitors. Butcher married fellow dogsled racer David Monson.

In Seattle, Wash., of complications from a bone marrow transplant, on August 5.

Al Hostak, 90, boxer. *SI writes:*
"Hostak won the world middleweight title in 1938 in what was, at the time, the biggest sporting event ever held in Seattle. Fighting in his hometown, Hostak floored champ Freddie Steele of Tacoma four times in the first round before the referee, former heavyweight champ Jack Dempsey, counted him out. (A sellout crowd of 35,000—including Bob Hope and Jack Benny—was on hand to watch.) Dempsey later said he was glad the fight lasted only one round because he was afraid Steele was going to be hurt by Hostak, whom Dempsey called 'the fastest puncher I have ever seen.'"

In Kirkland, Wash., of a complications from a stroke, on August 13.

Bob Mathias, 75, olympic decathlete. *Two time Olympic gold medalist, college football player, actor and congressman. SI writes:*
"Shortly after 17-year-old Bob Mathias won the 1948 Olympic decathlon in London, most of the 14,000 citizens of his hometown of Tulare, Calif., joined a spontaneous victory parade led by someone carrying a sign that read BOB MATHIAS FOR PRESIDENT. That notion was no joke; Mathias went on to represent the area in the House for four terms.

"Before Tulareans sent Mathias to the Hill, they sent him to the Olympics. After he won the first decathlon he entered, at the 1948 Southern Pacific AAU Games in Pasadena, the local Elks Club passed the hat and collected $2,500 to send Mathias to the Olympic trials in New Jersey. He won there too, and made it look easy in London. (While other competitors were stressing out between events, Mathias took catnaps under the stands at Wembley.) Four years later he became the first Olympic decathlon champ to repeat.

"In between his high school and college wins Mathias played football at Stanford. The Redskins drafted him, but he spurned Washington for Hollywood, playing himself in 1954's *The Bob Mathias Story*. He finally made it to D.C.—as a Republican—in 1967. 'He is absolutely the greatest athlete I have ever seen,' Ray Dean, who coached Mathias in track at Stanford, said in 1952.

'He's the dream competitor—the one in 10,000 who has the temperament to match the talent.'"

In Fresno, Calif., of cancer, on September 2.

Erskine "Erk" Russell, 80, college football coach. *Head football coach of the Georgia Southern Eagles from 1981 to '89. SI writes:*

"[Russell] left his job as defensive coordinator at Georgia to build Georgia Southern into a Division I-AA powerhouse. Russell, who dubbed his Georgia defenses Junkyard Dawgs, would fire his players up before games by butting them in the chest with his bald head—occasionally drawing blood (his own). After Georgia won the 1980 NCAA title, Russell left for Georgia Southern, which had dropped football in '41. Within four years, Russell had led the school to a national championship. By the time he retired in '89, the Eagles had won two more. 'If I was picking a top list of 10 coaches that I have ever met and wanted to play for, Erk Russell would be on that list,' Florida State coach Bobby Bowden once said. 'He is unsurpassed as a motivator.'"

In Statesboro, Ga., of a stroke, on September 8.

Patty Berg, 88, golfer. *Founding member of the LPGA. SI writes:*

"Sometime in the early 1950's, just before Bud Wilkinson's Oklahoma team embarked on its NCAA-record 47-game winning streak, the coach brought a 5'2" thirtysomething woman to practice. Pointing to Patty Berg, Wilkinson told his players, 'This is the kind old lady who taught me how to play football.' Berg grew up on the same Minneapolis block as Wilkinson, and she quarterbacked his sandlot team, the 50th Street Tigers. (Wilkinson, two years younger, played right tackle.) Berg, who had no future as a football player, turned to golf in her early teens, and it was on the links that she made a name for herself.

"In 1940, after a successful amateur career, she turned pro—though the decision barely affected her income. Her prize for winning the '41 Western Open: a $100 war bond. A few years later she helped the war effort more directly, serving in the Marine Corps Women's Reserve. After the war, she and 12 other women formed the LPGA; Berg was its first president. She stopped playng full time in '62 after she had won 83 tournaments, including a record 15 majors. But even in retirement, Berg was never far from the game or its players. (When pro Heath Farr underwent cancer treatment in '91, Berg wrote her a letter a day for months, many scathingly funny.) 'She was quite hysterical, with a great sense of humor, and a pioneer,' said Annika Sorenstam. 'We're all going to miss her.'"

In Fort Myers, Fla., of complications from Alzheimer's disease, on September 10.

Byron Nelson, 94, golfer. *In a relatively brief career as a professional golfer, Byron won 52 tournaments, including 11 in a row in 1945. He won the Vardon Trophy in 1939. SI writes:*

"Lord Byron, to use his most unfitting nickname, was a deeply religious man who in retirement led a simple life on a working ranch in Texas. But unlike Ben Hogan, his former caddie-yard rival, he made himself available to golfers and taught what he knew, mostly to Ken Venturi and Tom Watson, who learned from Nelson how to slow down and breathe deeply while walking to the ball. Generations of teachers have been fixated on Hogan's odd, flat, handsy swing, but Nelson was the true progenitor of the modern golf swing; upright, simple, beautifully balanced, with few moving parts. You see echoes of Nelson's action every time Tiger Woods makes a swing.

"He had been an honored ancient for decades, but remained relevant all the while. At the Masters each April, Woods would always make it a point to spend time with Nelson. Tom Lehman, the U.S. Ryder Cup captain this year, sought advice and Biblical inspiration from Nelson. Lehman pulled out of a tournament in England to attend Nelson's funeral, where he was joined by dozens of other players, active and retired.

"When a player received a handwritten note, adorned with that elegant signature, asking him to come play in the Byron Nelson Classic, it was almost impossible to say no. In 1996 Nelson requested the presence of Phil Mickelson, who was supposed to go on a vacation with his then-fiancee, Amy. Mickelson played—and won. The Mickelsons were among the 2,220 mourners at Nelson's funeral. 'Amy and I are so sorry for [Nelson's widow] Peggy, but so happy for the great life of Byron Nelson,' Mickelson said. 'It should be an example for all golfers and for us all.'"

In Roanoke, Tex., of natural causes, on September 26.

Buck O'Neil, 94, baseball player and coach. From 1937 to '48, O'Neil was a first baseman for the Monarchs of the Negro American League, leading the league in batting in '40 and again in '46, after returning from Navy service during the war. In 1948, he became the Monarchs' manager, as well as a player. In 1955, he was hired by the Chicago Cubs as a scout. Seven years later, the Cubs elevated him to coach, making him the first African-American coach in the major leagues. After his days with the Cubs, O'Neil slid into obscurity until Ken Burns's 1994 documentary *Baseball* rekindled interest in the Negro Leagues. "Thanks to Ken Burns, I became an overnight star in my 80's," O'Neil wrote in his autobiography, *I Was Right on Time.*

In 2006, O'Neil evoked both tears and laughter at the National Baseball Hall of Fame as he introduced the largest-ever class of inductees—17 in all—to have played in the Negro Leagues, a storied group that he reportedly fell just one vote short of joining himself. After getting the crowd in Cooperstown to join him in a sing-a-long, O'Neil wound up his speech, as he often did whenever he spoke, by saying, "I could talk to you 10 minutes longer, but I've got to go to the bathroom."

In Kansas City, of undisclosed causes, on October 6.

Cory Lidle, 34, baseball player. *In a nine-season career in the major leagues, Lidle played for seven teams, including the Yankees, to which he was traded in July 2006. Just four days after the Yankees were shut out of the post season, Lidle and his flight instructor were killed when the Cirrus CR20 they were flying crashed into a 50-story residential tower on New York's Upper East Side. SI writes:*

"Everywhere he went, and Lidle bounced among 10 organizations in 17 years, Lidle made an impression on people with his down-to-earth, convivial manner. He liked action, be it pool, cards, golf or, especially, flying. He was not the kind to sit still. There's a saying in baseball that you can take the measure of a player by how he treats the little people around him—the clubhouse attendants, ushers, public relations people and, yes, media people. Too many players take no note of those considered 'beneath' them. Lidle, though, was quick with a smile, a hello or a conversation starter for all.

That kind of damn-glad-to-be-here feeling never left Lidle. The guy was signed out of high school as an undrafted free agent, was released less than three years into pro ball, and somehow went on to win 82 games in the big leagues, help carry Oakland to an AL record 20-straight wins in 2002, and earn almost $18 million, a largesse that made his dream of airplane ownership possible. Can such a journey happen with no work ethic?"

In New York City, in an airplane crash, on October 11.

2007 MAJOR EVENTS

JANUARY

Major College Bowl Games	Jan 1–7
NFL Wild-Card Playoffs	Jan 6 & 7
U.S. Figure Skating Championships	Jan 21–28
BCS Championship Game	Jan 8
NFL Divisional Playoffs	Jan 13 & 14
Australian Open Tennis	Jan 15-28
NFL Conference Championships	Jan 21
NHL All-Star Game	Jan 24

FEBRUARY

Millrose Games	Feb 3
Super Bowl XLI	Feb 4
AFC-NFC Pro Bowl	Feb 10
NBA All-Star Game	Feb 19
Daytona 500	Feb 18

MARCH

March Madness Begins	*March 15*
PBA World Championship	March 19–25

APRIL

NCAA Men's Basketball Final Four	March 31 & April 2
Major League Soccer Season Begins	*April 1**
NCAA Women's Basketball Final Four	April 1 & 3
Baseball Opening Day	*April 2**
NCAA Men's Hockey Frozen Four	April 5–7
Masters Tournament	April 5–8
NHL Playoffs Begin	*April 11**
Boston Marathon	April 16
NBA Playoffs Begin	*April 21*
NFL Draft	April 28-29

MAY

Kentucky Derby	May 5
The Players Championship	May 10–13
Preakness Stakes	May 19
NASCAR All-Star Challenge	May 19
Stanley Cup Finals Begin	*May 23**
Indianapolis 500	May 27

JUNE

French Open Tennis	May 27–June 10
NBA Finals Begin	*June 8**
Belmont Stakes	June 9
U.S. Open Golf	June 14–17
College World Series	June 15–25
NBA Draft	June 23

JULY

Wimbledon Tennis	June 25–July 8
Baseball All-Star Game	July 10
British Open Golf	July 19–22
Tour de France	July 7–29

AUGUST

Brickyard 400	Aug 5
PGA Championship	Aug 9–12
College Football Season Begins	*Aug 25**

SEPTEMBER

U.S. Open Tennis	Aug 27–Sept 9
FIFA Women's World Cup	Sept 10–30
NFL Season Begins	*Sept 6*
NASCAR Chase for the Cup Begins	*Sept 16*
Presidents Cup	Sept 27–30

OCTOBER

NHL Season Begins	*Oct 2**
World Series Begins	*Oct 23**
NBA Regular Season Begins	*Oct 30**

NOVEMBER

Women's Tennis Tour Championships	Nov 6–11*
Breeders' Cup	Nov 3*
New York Marathon	Nov 4
MLS Cup 2007	Nov 11*
Tennis Masters Cup	Nov 8–18
NASCAR Chase for the Cup Ends	*Nov 18*

DECEMBER

Heisman Trophy Presentation	Dec 8
Major College Bowl Games Begin	*Dec 18**

* Approximate date.

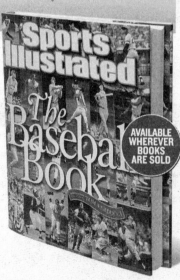